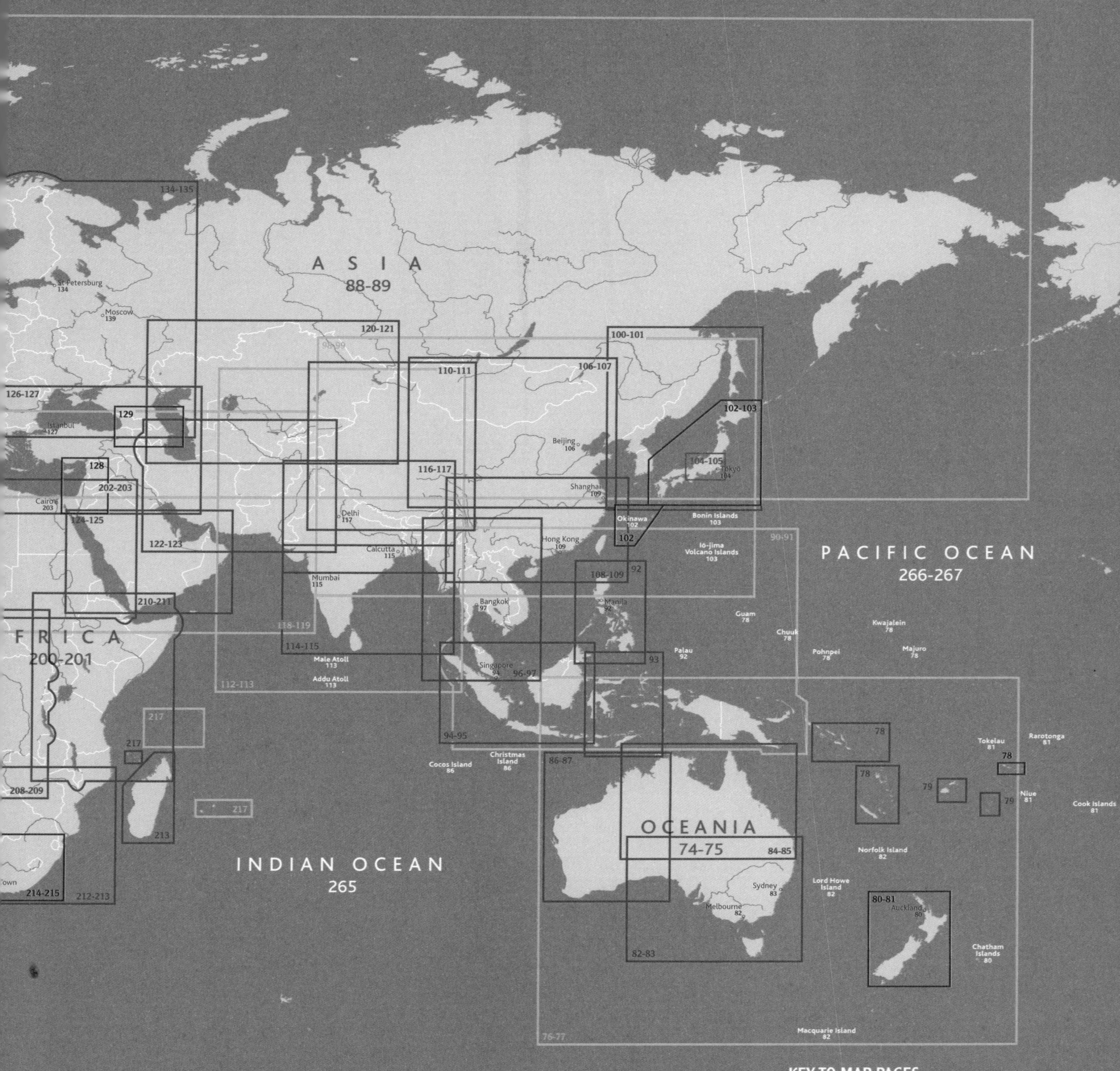

ARCTIC OCEAN
268

KT-873-373

ASIA
88-89

St Petersburg
134

Moscow
139

134-135

120-121

110-111

100-101

106-107

102-103

126-127

129

Istanbul
127

128

202-203

Cairo
203

124-125

122-123

116-117

Beijing
106

Shanghai
109

Delhi
117

Calcutta
115

Mumbai
115

Okinawa
102

Bonin Islands
103

Iō-jima
Volcano Islands
103

102

PACIFIC OCEAN
266-267

210-211

FRICA
200-201

Bangkok
97

Hong Kong
109

Manila
92

108-109

92

Guam
78

Chuuk
78

Kwajalein
78

Pohnpei
78

Majuro
78

118-119

114-115

Male Atoll
113

Addu Atoll
113

Singapore
94

96-97

93

Palau
92

112-113

217

217

217

208-209

213

INDIAN OCEAN
265

94-95

Cocos Island
86

Christmas
Island
86

86-87

78

78

79

Tokelau
81

Rarotonga
81

78

79

Niue
81

Cook Islands
81

OCEANIA
74-75

84-85

Norfolk Island
82

Lord Howe
Island
82

80-81

Auckland
80

Chatham
Islands
80

Sydney
83

Melbourne
82

82-83

76-77

Macquarie Island
82

ANTARCTICA
262-263

Town

214-215

212-213

KEY TO MAP PAGES

112-113

1:9 000 000 and smaller

86-87

1:5 000 000 - 1:8 000 000

214-215

1:2 000 000 - 1:4 000 000

104-105

1:1 000 000 - 1:2 000 000

Inset maps of islands and cities are named.
See back endpapers for detailed keys to North America and Europe.

THE TIMES

CONCISE

ATLAS
OF THE
WORLD

TED SMART

CONTENTS

THE WORLD TODAY

GEOGRAPHICAL INFORMATION

ATLAS OF THE WORLD

WORLD

OCEANIA

ASIA

This image shows the continent of
Asia from the Mediterranean Sea
and the distinctive shape of
The Gulf in the west, to Japan in
the east, and from snow-covered
Siberia in the north to the tropical
islands of Indonesia in the south.
The shapes of the Caspian and Aral Seas
appear in the northwest.

The image illustrates a wide range of land cover –
particularly in China, with great variation
between the intricate patterns of vegetation in
the southeast and the large, relatively featureless
areas of the Tarim Pendi basin in the northwest,
in the centre of the image. The snow covered
Himalaya form a dominating feature of the
image, stretching in a gentle white arc between
the Indian sub-continent and China.

See pages 88–89 for a map of Asia.

Data from the 1km AVHRR Global Land dataset project by ESA, CEOS,
IGBP, NASA, NOAA, USGS, IONIA processed by ESA/ESRIN distributed
by Eurimage S.p.A

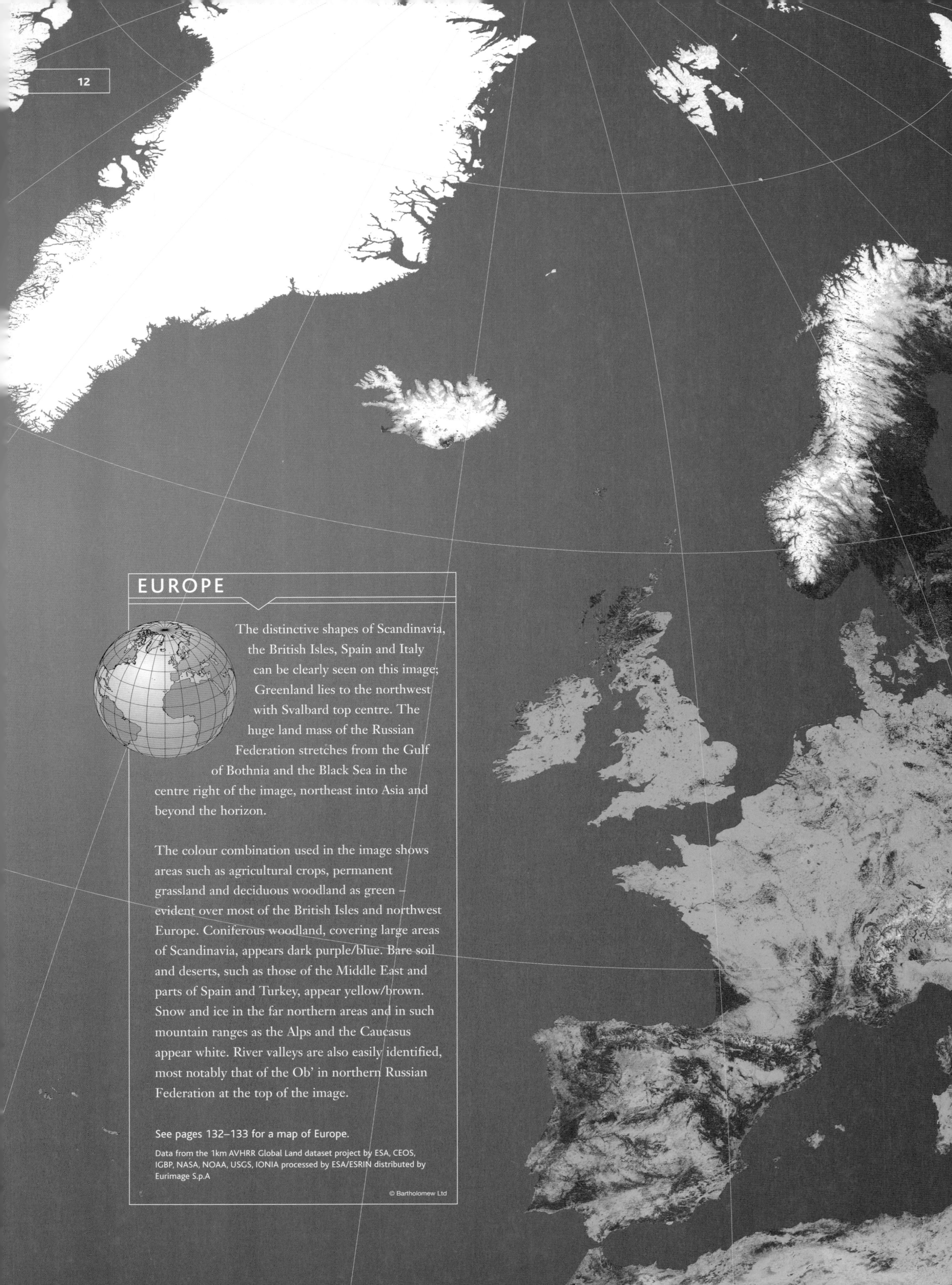

EUROPE

The distinctive shapes of Scandinavia, the British Isles, Spain and Italy can be clearly seen on this image; Greenland lies to the northwest with Svalbard top centre. The huge land mass of the Russian Federation stretches from the Gulf of Bothnia and the Black Sea in the centre right of the image, northeast into Asia and beyond the horizon.

The colour combination used in the image shows areas such as agricultural crops, permanent grassland and deciduous woodland as green – evident over most of the British Isles and northwest Europe. Coniferous woodland, covering large areas of Scandinavia, appears dark purple/blue. Bare soil and deserts, such as those of the Middle East and parts of Spain and Turkey, appear yellow/brown. Snow and ice in the far northern areas and in such mountain ranges as the Alps and the Caucasus appear white. River valleys are also easily identified, most notably that of the Ob' in northern Russian Federation at the top of the image.

See pages 132–133 for a map of Europe.

Data from the 1km AVHRR Global Land dataset project by ESA, CEOS, IGBP, NASA, NOAA, USGS, IONIA processed by ESA/ESRIN distributed by Eurimage S.p.A

AFRICA

This view of Africa looks north, with South America just appearing in the southwest, the island of Madagascar to the southeast and Arabia and Asia to the northeast.

Subtle variations in vegetation are evident, particularly across the north of the continent and in the Sahara – an area of desert that could be expected to be more uniform in appearance. Also clearly shown are the variations in basic land cover with latitude. The gradations in colour southwards from the Sahara indicate a steady change in vegetation type through the equatorial regions. Sharp contrasts in land use are also clear along the northern coast of Africa with the cultivated area of the Nile valley and delta particularly impressive.

See pages 200–201 for a map of Africa.

Data from the 1km AVHRR Global Land dataset project by ESA, CEOS, IGBP, NASA, NOAA, USGS, IONIA processed by ESA/ESRIN distributed by Eurimage S.p.A

© Bartholomew Ltd

NORTH AMERICA

This image views North America from above the centre of the continent and includes most of the Arctic Ocean. The Aleutian Islands in the northwest stretch in an arc toward the Kamchatka Peninsula in eastern Asia, and western Europe and northwest Africa appear to the northeast. The islands of the Caribbean lie east and south of Florida in the bottom right of the image.

The contrast between land and water areas is very clear, with the complex drainage patterns and coastlines of Alaska, northern Canada and Greenland shown in great detail. In northwest Canada the Great Slave Lake, Great Bear Lake and thousands of others in the far north are clearly visible, as is the Mackenzie river in northwest Canada. The outlines of the Great Lakes are also impressively clear. The easy identification of specific variations in vegetation and land cover is also illustrated by the prominence of such features as the Mississippi river valley, and the San Joaquin and Sacramento valleys of California. The dominance of coniferous forest (dark purple/blue) across large areas of Canada, stretching in a wide band virtually across the whole continent, is also clearly seen.

See pages 218–219 for a map of North America.

Data from the 1km AVHRR Global Land dataset project by ESA, CEOS, IGBP, NASA, NOAA, USGS, IONIA processed by ESA/ESRIN distributed by Eurimage S.p.A

SOUTH AMERICA

South and Central America appear in the centre of this image with the Pacific Ocean to the west and the Atlantic Ocean to the east, and Africa appearing on the northeast and southeast horizons. The Galapagos Islands lie off the coast of Ecuador and the Falkland Islands, South Georgia and the Antarctic Peninsula off the southern tip of the continent.

The great range of green and blue tones represent different types and conditions of vegetation across the Amazon basin. Although the data contains no indication of surface height, it can indicate the underlying structure of the land. Here, the mountain ranges of the northern Andes and western Colombia are clearly evident. The small red areas on the east coast of Brazil, representing the major urban areas of São Paulo and Rio de Janeiro, illustrate the impressive level of detail available from this type of imagery.

See pages 248–249 for a map of South America.

Data from the 1km AVHRR Global Land dataset project by ESA, CEOS, IGBP, NASA, NOAA, USGS, IONIA processed by ESA/ESRIN distributed by Eurimage S.p.A

ANTARCTICA

This image positions the Antarctic
continent with the Greenwich
meridian to the top centre. The
distinctive shape of the Antarctic
Peninsula lies to the top left and
the prominent Ross Ice Shelf can
be identified to the bottom of the
image, below the Transantarctic
Mountains range.

Although not completely cloud-free – there is some
cloud cover in the eastern area to the right of the
image – the image is impressive in its depiction of
the physical features of the continent. The Ronne
Ice Shelf, including Berkner Island, and the
Transantarctic Mountains are particularly
spectacular. Floating ice is excluded from the image,
resulting in a clear definition of the extent of the
continental ice sheet in an austral summer.

See pages 262–263 for a continental map of Antarctica.

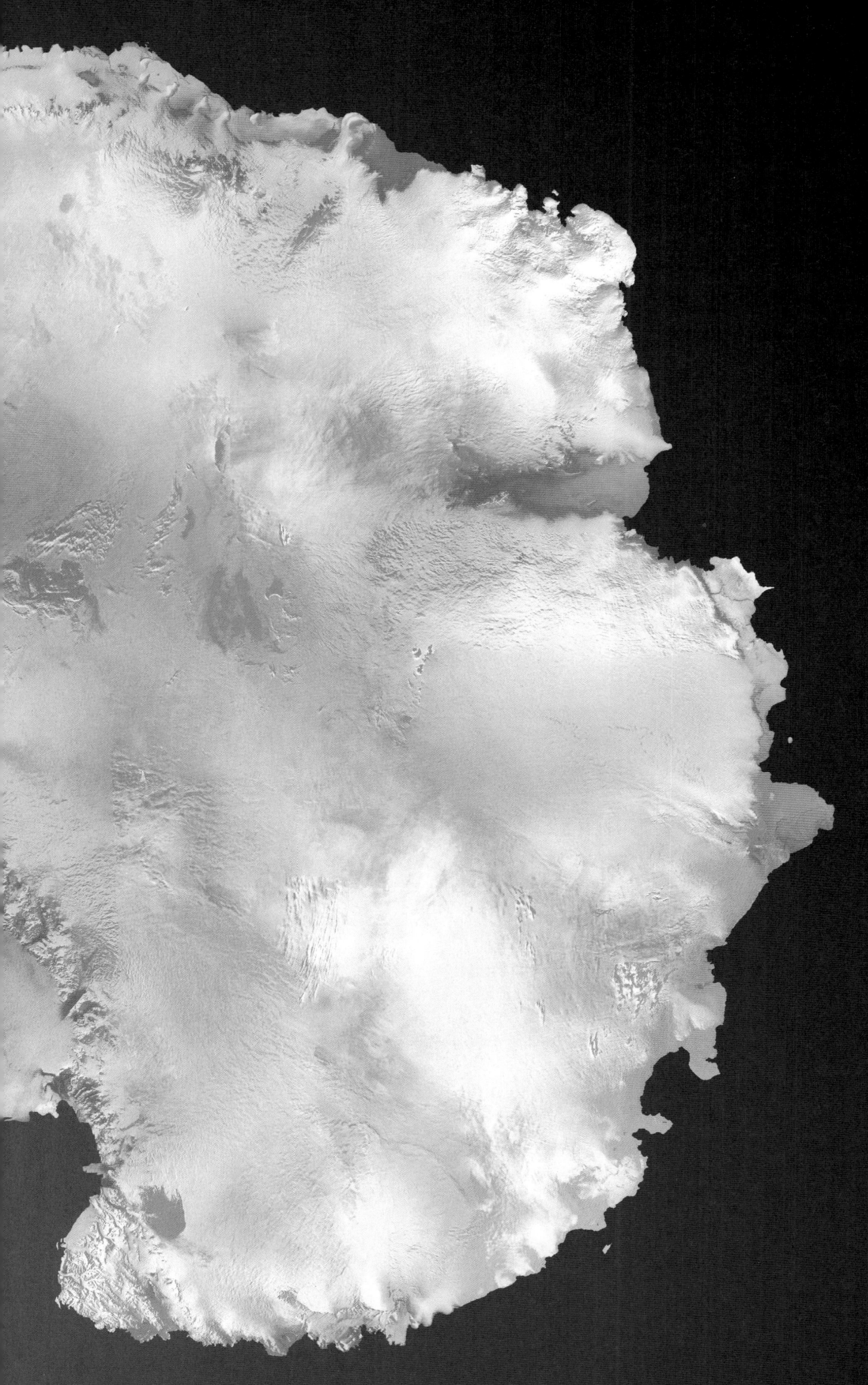

NEPTUNE

ORIGINS OF THE SOLAR SYSTEM

The nature and origin of our Solar System has been a subject of much debate. Early ideas of an Earth-centred system took many hundreds of years to be discarded in favour of Copernicus' heliocentric, or sun-centred model. More refined theories followed with Kepler's laws of orbital motion, and Newton's laws of gravity. The question of origin remained unanswered, and was regarded more as a philosophical matter.

The fact that the Sun and the planets rotate in a similar direction suggests a common formation mechanism - that of a large collapsing cloud or nebula. It is now believed that this did happen, about 4 600 million years ago. The nebula consisted of predominantly hydrogen and helium, but with a small amount of heavier elements. Over time, the cloud collapsed to form a rotating disk around a dense core. As core collapse continued and pressure in the core increased, material was heated enough to allow the nuclear fusion of hydrogen. Meanwhile as the disk cooled, the heavier elements began to condense and agglomerate. Larger bodies grew rapidly by sweeping up much of the remaining smaller material. As the core began to shine, its radiation pushed back much of the nearby volatile disk material into the outer Solar System, where it condensed and accumulated on the more distant planetary cores. This left the Inner Planets as small rocky bodies, and produced the Gas Giants of the outer system. Bombardment of the planets by a decreasing number of small bodies continued for several hundred million years, causing the craters now seen on many of the planets and moons.

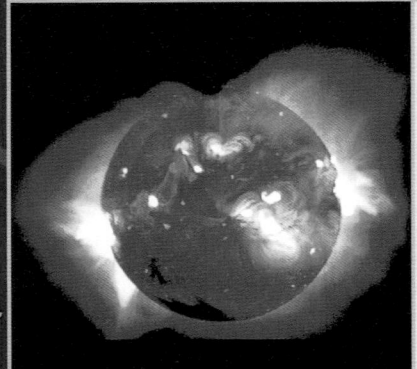

The Sun

The Sun is a typical star. It accounts for 99.85 per cent of the total mass contained within the Solar System, ensuring that it provides a dominating gravitational hold on its orbiting planets. The tremendous amount of heat and light produced by the Sun is the result of nuclear fusion reactions which occur in its core. In this process, hydrogen is converted into helium to produce a core temperature of roughly 15 million°C. Intense magnetic fields can induce cooling zones seen as dark sun spots on the Sun's surface. The Sun constantly emits a stream of charged particles which form the solar wind and cause auroral activity which can be seen on Earth.

	Sun	Mercury	Venus	Earth	Mars	Jupiter	Saturn	Uranus	Neptune	Pluto
Mass (Earth=1)	332 830	0.055	0.815	1(6 x 10²⁴)	0.107	317.9	95.2	14.5	17.1	0.002
Volume (Earth=1)	1 306 000	0.06	0.89	1	0.157	1 323	752	64	54	0.006
Density (Water=1)	1.41	5.43	5.25	5.52	3.95	1.33	0.69	1.29	1.64	2.03
Equatorial diameter (km)	1 392 000	4 879	12 104	12 756	6 794	142 984	120 536	51 118	49 492	2 320
Polar flattening	0	0	0	0.003	0.005	0.065	0.108	0.03	0.021	0
Surface gravity (Earth=1)	27.5	0.38	0.902	1	0.382	0.248	1.02	0.9	1.13	0.4
Number of satellites > 100 km	-	0	0	1	0	7	13	8	6	1
Total number of satellites	-	0	0	1	2	16	20	17	8	1
Rotation period (Earth days)	25 - 36	58.65	-243	23hr 56m 4s	1.03	0.414	0.444	-0.71	0.67	-6.39
Year (Earth days/years)	-	88 days	224.7 days	365.26 days	687 days	11.86 years	29.46 years	84.01 years	164.8 years	248.6 years
Mean orbital distance (million km)	-	57.9	108.2	149.6	227.9	778.3	1 249	2 871	4 504	5 914
Orbital eccentricity	-	0.2056	0.0068	0.0167	0.0934	0.0483	0.056	0.0461	0.0097	0.2482
Mean orbital velocity (km/s)	-	47.88	35.02	29.79	24.13	13.06	9.65	6.81	5.44	4.74
Inclination of equator to orbit	7.25	0	177.3	23.45	25.19	3.12	26.73	97.86	29.56	122.46
Orbital inclination (w.r.t. ecliptic)	-	7.01	3.4	0	1.85	1.31	2.49	0.77	1.77	17.13
Mean surface temperature (°C)	700	427(d), -173(n)	482	15	63	153	185	215	225	235
Atmospheric pressure (bars)				1.013	0.007					3 x 10⁻⁶
Atmospheric composition	H_2 92.1% He 7.8% O_2 0.061%	He 42% Na 42% O_2 15%	CO_2 96% N_2 3%	N_2 77% O_2 21% Ar 1.6%	CO_2 95.3% N_2 2.7%	H_2 90% He 10%	H_2 97% He 3%	H_2 83% He 15% CH_4 2%	H_2 85% He 13% CH_4 2%	N_2 CO CH_4

PLUTO

SATURN

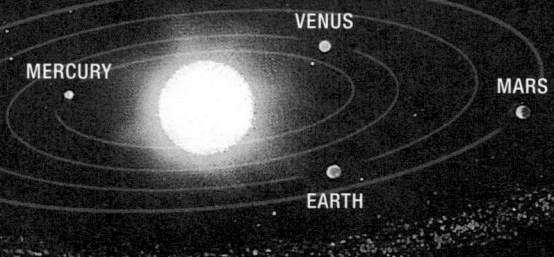

VENUS

MERCURY

MARS

EARTH

URANUS

JUPITER

Mercury

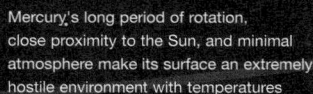

Mercury's long period of rotation, close proximity to the Sun, and minimal atmosphere make its surface an extremely hostile environment with temperatures ranging from 427 to minus 173°C between its day and night side. Mercury is similar to Earth's Moon in size and appearance; its cratered surface was first photographed in detail in the mid-1970s by the Mariner 10 space probe. However the internal structure differs from the Moon; analysis of its magnetic field suggests that the core consists of molten iron, believed to be 40 per cent of the planet's volume. Mercury has a very eccentric orbit with its orbital distance varying from 46 to 70 million km.

Venus

Venus' thick atmosphere of carbon dioxide and nitrogen creates not only a huge surface pressure of over ninety times that on Earth but also a greenhouse effect producing temperatures in excess of 480°C. Traces of sulphur dioxide and water vapour form clouds of dilute sulphuric acid, making the atmosphere extremely corrosive. This atmosphere reflects almost all incident visible radiation and prevents direct observation of surface features. In 1990 use of radar imaging enabled the Magellan space probe to see through the cloud. Magellan mapped 98 per cent of the planet during three years to find a surface covered in craters, volcanoes, mountains and solidified lava flows. Venus is the brightest object in the sky after the Sun and Moon and is unusual in that its year is less than its rotation period.

Earth

Earth is the largest and densest of the Inner Planets. Created some 4 500 million years ago, the core, rocky mantle and crust are similar in structure to Venus. The Earth's core is composed almost entirely of iron and oxygen compounds which exist in a molten state at temperatures of around 5 000°C. Earth is the only planet with vast quantities of life-sustaining water, with the oceans covering 70.8 per cent of its surface. The action of plate tectonics has created vast mountain ranges and is responsible for volcanic activity. The Moon is Earth's only natural satellite and with a diameter of over one quarter that of the Earth's, makes the Earth-Moon system a near double-planet.

Mars

Named after the Roman god of war because of its blood-red appearance, Mars is the last of the Inner Planets. The red colour comes from the high concentration of iron-oxides on its surface. Mars has impressive surface features, including the highest known peak in the Solar System, Olympus Mons, an inactive volcano reaching a height of 23 km above the surrounding plains, and Marineris, a 2 500 km long canyon four times as deep as the Grand Canyon. The Pathfinder mission in 1997 has shown that much of the Martian surface is shaped by intense dust storms which often engulf the entire planet. Mars has polar caps composed of water and carbon dioxide ice which partially evaporate during its summer.

Jupiter

Jupiter is by far the most massive of all the planets and is the dominant body in the Solar System after the Sun. It is the innermost of the Gas Giants. The dense surface atmosphere is predominantly hydrogen, with helium, water vapour, and methane. Below this is a layer of liquid hydrogen, then an even deeper layer of metallic hydrogen. Unlike solid bodies, Jupiter's rotation period is somewhat ill-defined, with equatorial regions rotating faster than the polar caps; this, combined with convection currents in lower layers, cause intense magnetic fields and rapidly varying surface features. Most notable of these is the Great Red Spot, a giant circular storm visible since the first observations of Jupiter's surface, which shows no signs of abating.

Saturn

Although only slightly smaller that Jupiter, Saturn is a mere one third of Jupiter's mass, and is the least dense of all the planets - less dense than water. The low mass, combined with a fast rotation rate, leads to the planet's significant polar flattening. Saturn exhibits a striking ring system, more than twice the diameter of the planet; the rings consist of countless small rock and ice clumps which vary in size from a grain of sand to tens of metres in diameter. It is believed that the rings were formed from a stray moon coming too close to, and being ripped apart by Saturn. Distinct bands and gaps in the rings are the result of complex interactions between Saturn and its closer moons. Recent rare opportunities to view Saturn's rings edge ways have yielded the discovery of at least two other moons.

Uranus

Uranus has many surprising features; the most prominent of these is the tilt of its rotation axis by over 90 degrees caused by a series of large collisions in its early history. Like the other Gas Giants, Uranus is predominantly hydrogen and helium with a small proportion of methane and other gases. However, because Uranus is colder than Jupiter and Saturn, the methane forms ice crystals which give Uranus a featureless blue-green colour. The interior is also different from that expected. Instead of having a gaseous atmosphere above liquid and metallic hydrogen layers, Uranus has a super dense gaseous atmosphere extending down to its core. Uranus' magnetic field is inclined at 60 degrees to the rotation axis, and is off centre by one third of the planet's radius, which suggests that it is not generated by the core. The system of eleven narrow rings around Uranus is prevented from spreading by the interaction of nearby 'shepherd' moons. Two new moons, Caliban and Sycorax, were discovered in 1997 although their large orbits indicate they are probably captured asteroids.

Neptune

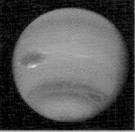

Neptune has always been associated with Uranus because of its similar size, composition and appearance, but, unexpectedly, Neptune's atmosphere is more active than that of Uranus. This was shown by Voyager 2 in 1989 with the observation of the Great Dark Spot, Neptune's equivalent to Jupiter's Great Red Spot. Voyager 2 recorded the fastest winds ever seen in the Solar System, 2 000 km per hour, around the Dark Spot. This feature disappeared in 1994, but has been replaced by a similar storm in the northern polar cap. Like Uranus, Neptune has a magnetic field highly inclined to the planet's axis of rotation and off-centre by more than half of the planet's radius. The cause of this magnetic field is convection currents in conducting fluid layers outside the core. Neptune's largest moon, Triton, is in an inclined retrograde orbit, indicating that it was captured by Neptune rather than formed alongside it. The slowly decaying orbit will one day bring Triton too close to Neptune, and it will be torn apart forming a spectacular ring.

Pluto

Pluto's existence was predicted before its discovery in 1930, from perturbations in Neptune's orbital motion. Pluto's orbit is highly eccentric and tilted with respect to the solar plane, unusually so for a planet. Its only moon, Charon, is abnormally large, and orbits Pluto at 90 degrees to the solar plane. Both Pluto and Charon have an uncharacteristically high proportion of rock, 70 per cent, with only 30 per cent water ice. All these anomalies bring Pluto's planetary status into question. It is likely that Pluto is a large planetesimal formed farther out of the Solar System, and is now in a stable orbit. Pluto, unlike Charon, possesses a methane ice surface layer, which forms a tenuous yet deep atmosphere when close to the Sun.

THE EARTH'S STRUCTURE

The interior of the Earth can be divided into three principal regions (*see 1*). The outermost region is known as the crust, which is extremely thin compared to the Earth as a whole. Under the continents the crust is about 33 km thick on average, only 0.5 per cent of the total radius of the Earth (6 370 km). Under the oceans the crust is even thinner: perhaps a third of its continental thickness. Over the course of geological time the Earth's crust has broken up into large fragments, which are known as lithospheric plates. These plates are slowly moving relative to one another at rates of a few centimetres per year – a process know as continental drift.

The next layer down is known as the mantle which is about 2 850 km thick. The distinction between the mantle and crust is made on the basis of composition and strength. There is a zone of the upper mantle, at depths between about 100 and 700 km, which behaves like a fluid when under stress. This weak zone is called the asthenosphere. The outermost 70 km or so of the mantle, together with the crust, is known as the lithosphere and is much stronger. The transition between the lithosphere and asthenosphere is due to variation in temperature, and is therefore gradual rather than being a distinct boundary.

Below the mantle is the Earth's core, which is about 3 470 km in radius, and is mainly made up of iron. The greater part of the core is completely liquid; however, there is a solid inner core, about 1 220 km in radius.

It is the dynamic processes operating in the upper parts of the Earth's interior which give rise to very dramatic and violent expressions of the huge energies involved: earthquakes and volcanoes. Both of these can be very destructive, even disastrous, in terms of both loss of life and economic impact. Consequently, study of these phenomena is very important if the natural disasters arising from them are to be mitigated.

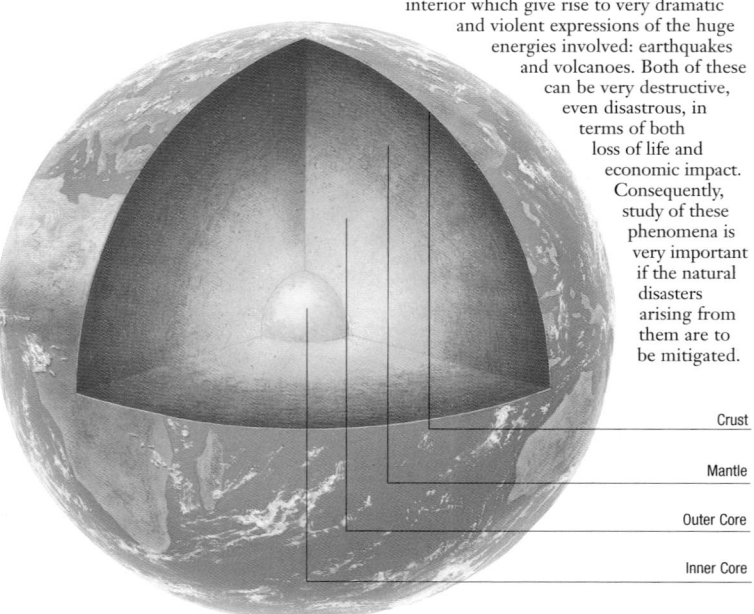

Crust

Mantle

Outer Core

Inner Core

1. THE EARTH'S INTERIOR

DISTRIBUTION OF EARTHQUAKES AND VOLCANOES

Any map showing the distribution of earthquakes and volcanoes (*see 2*) will inevitably look very similar to a map showing the boundaries of the tectonic plates (*see 3*). This is because both phenomena are largely controlled by the processes of plate tectonics. The vast majority of the world's earthquakes occur at plate boundaries as a result of one plate pushing past another along what is known as a constructive boundary, or under another at a destructive boundary, creating a subduction zone. Even those earthquakes which occur away from

plate margins (intraplate earthquakes) are still mostly due to stresses in the rocks that result indirectly from plate movements.

Most major volcanoes occur along lines parallel to subduction zones, as for example, in the Andes. Other volcanoes can form along mid-ocean ridges where the asthenosphere is close to the surface; such volcanoes can produce what are known as fissure eruptions, where vast amounts of basaltic lava suddenly erupt on the surface, inundating huge areas.

3. PLATE BOUNDARIES

scale 1:270 000 000

Constructive - mid ocean ridge	Destructive	Conservative

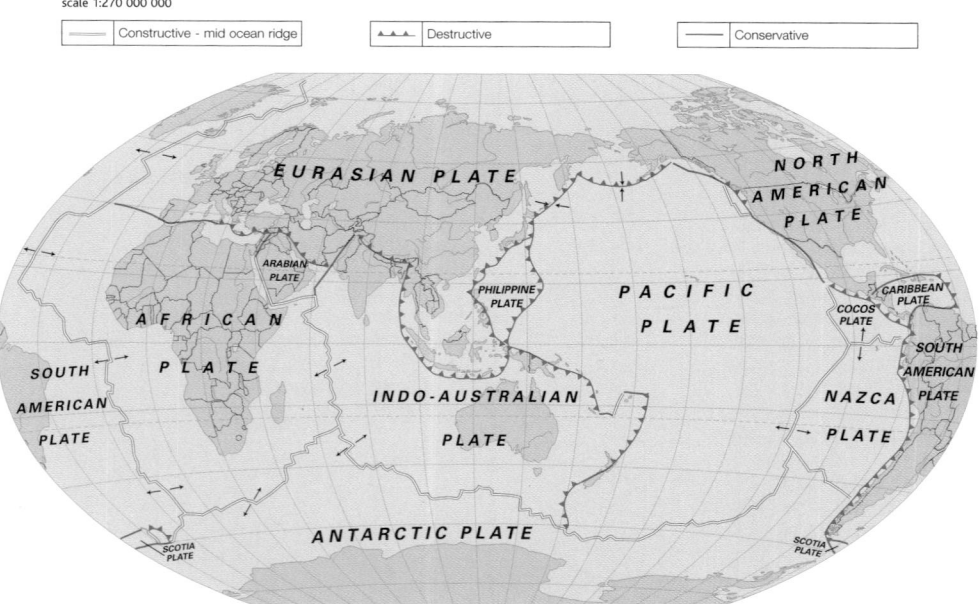

2. DISTRIBUTION OF MAJOR EARTHQUAKES AND VOLCANOES

Winkel Tripel Projection
scale 1:90 000 000

Key

▲ Volcanoes active between 1900 and 2000

● Earthquakes between 1900 and 2000 causing over 10 000 deaths.

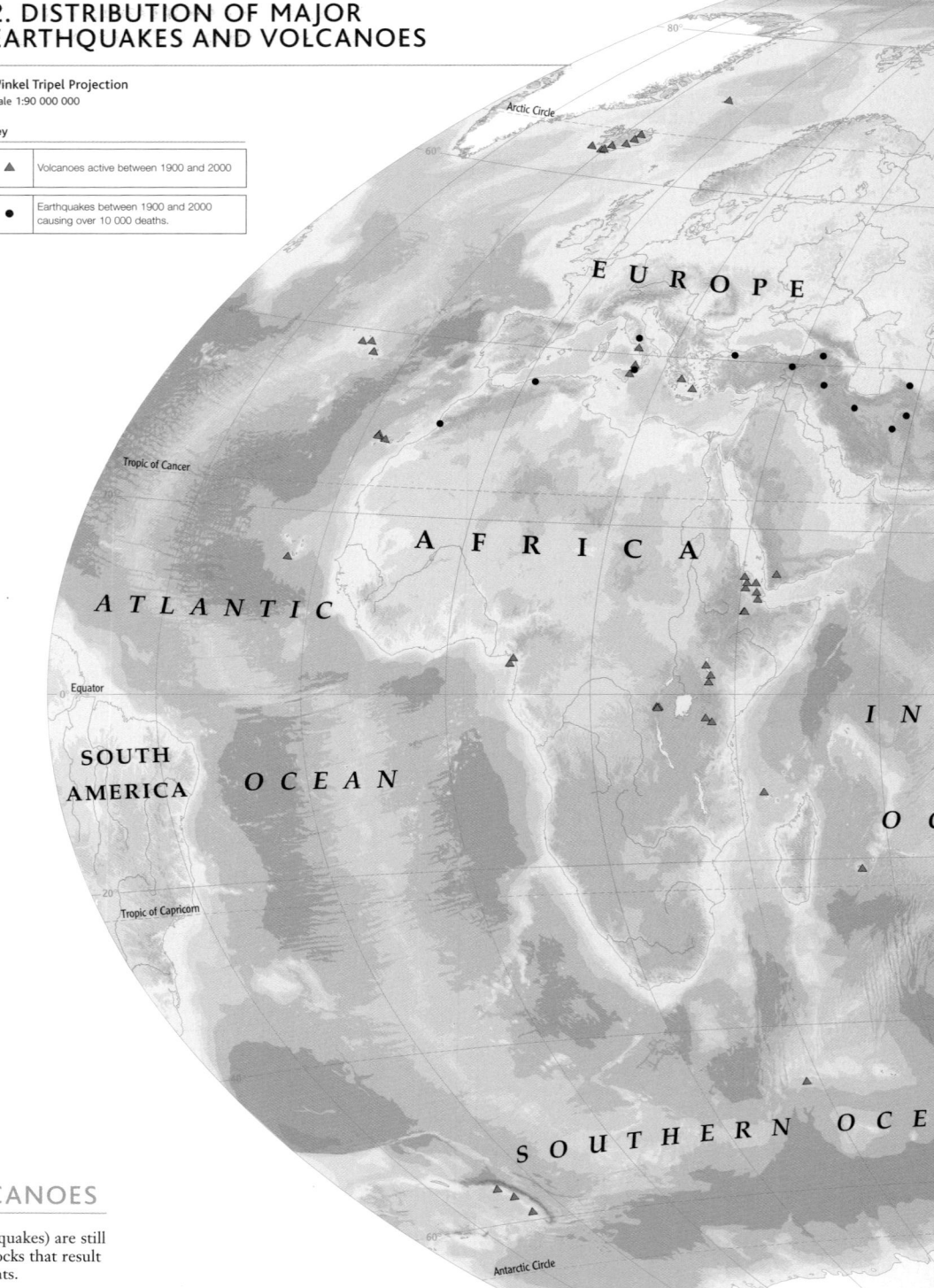

EARTHQUAKES

An earthquake is produced by a sudden breaking of rock in the Earth's crust as the stresses become too great for the strength of the rock to withstand. Naturally, this is most likely to happen where the rock is weakest. Where the rock breaks, a fracture line, known as a fault is left, and because there is now a break, future movements are likely to happen along the same weakness. The forces involved derive mostly from the movements of the tectonic plates; for example, between the upper surface of a subducting plate and the lower surface of the plate under which it is sliding – conditions which have caused some of the world's largest earthquakes.

The force with which the rock breaks releases a large amount of energy in the form of waves that travel through the Earth. These radiate outwards from where the fault has ruptured. The point on the fault at which the rupture begins is known as the hypocentre; this is usually at a depth of 10 to 30 km for shallow earthquakes; earthquakes in subduction zones can be as deep as 600 km below the Earth's surface. The point on the Earth's surface directly above the hypocentre is called the epicentre; this is what can be shown on a map. The magnitude of an earthquake, the so-call Richter scale, is a logarithmic approximation of the total amount of energy released. A large earthquake which may be severely damaging at the epicentre, is less strongly felt by people at greater distances. The strength of shaking at any point is known as the intensity, and this decreases with distance from the epicentre.

The earthquake off the southern coast of Honshū, Japan in January 1995 caused over 5 500 deaths and extensive damage in the Kōbe area and on Awaji-shima; the photo shows damage in Kōbe.

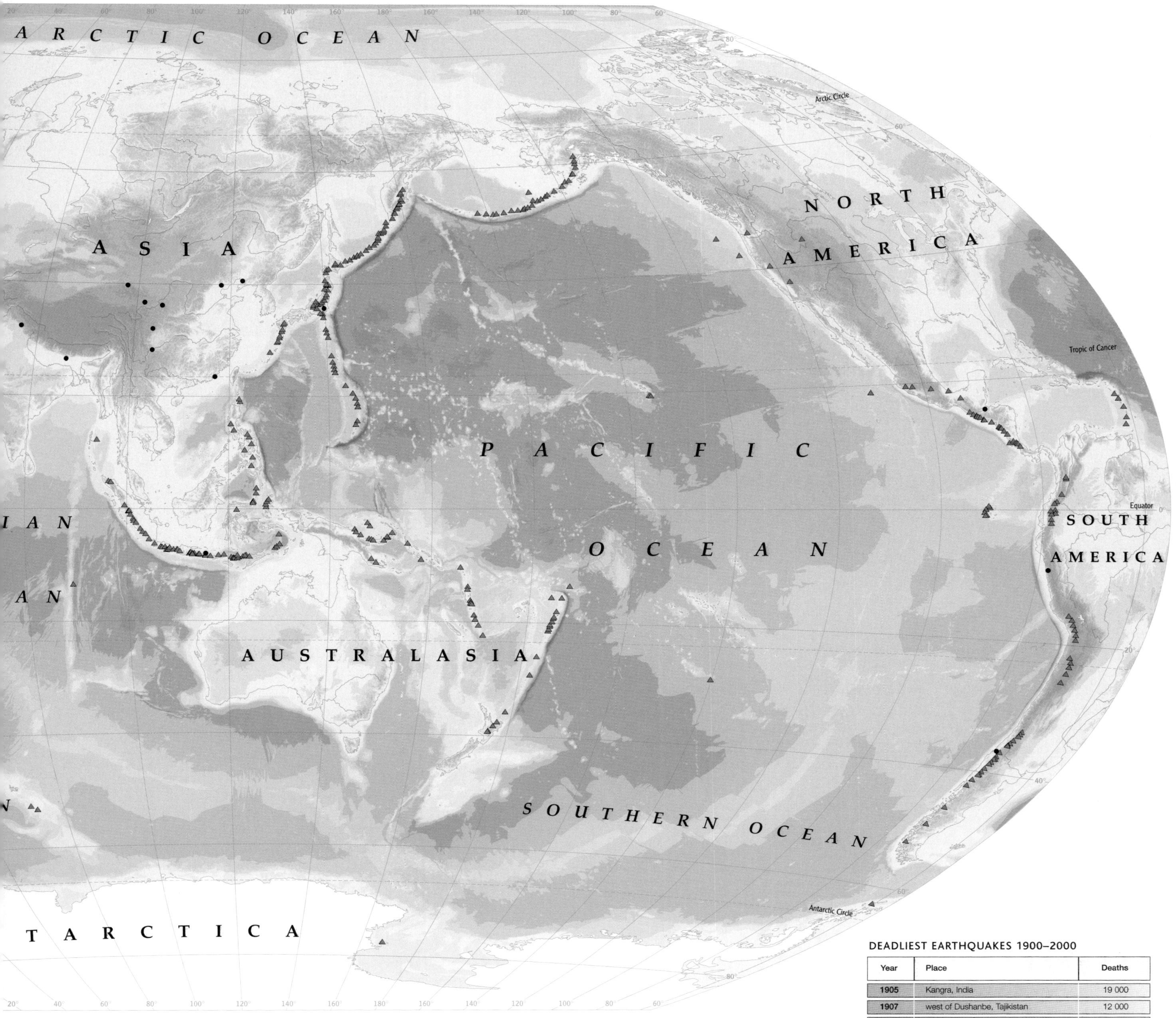

ARCTIC OCEAN

Arctic Circle

NORTH AMERICA

ASIA

Tropic of Cancer

PACIFIC OCEAN

SOUTH AMERICA

Equator

AUSTRALASIA

SOUTHERN OCEAN

Antarctic Circle

ANTARCTICA

VOLCANOES

In the simplest terms, a volcano is a vent at the surface of the Earth where molten rock (magma) from the interior can reach the surface. The magma originates ultimately in the Earth's mantle. It then erupts either as a stream of liquid rock (called lava when it appears at the surface) or as fine particles of ash or cinder. The erupted material builds up over time into a mountain, typically conical in shape. The exact shape of the volcano is controlled by the type of material erupted. Volcanoes in oceanic locations (such as Hawaii) tend to erupt very basic (non-acidic) lava which flows relatively easily. Because it can run quite far before cooling, this produces a very flat volcano with gentle slopes, known as a shield volcano. Continental volcanoes produce more acidic lava which flows more slowly, and they produce more ash, and therefore have steeper-sided cones. Such volcanoes also tend to erupt more explosively, because of the greater amount of steam or gas in the lava, and are generally more dangerous. They can produce what is know as a pyroclastic flow, a fast-moving cloud of super-heated ash and gases, which is what destroyed Pompeii in AD79.

Volcanoes can also be classified according to their eruptive history. Active volcanoes are those that are currently erupting; an eruption can go on intermittently for years, and some volcanoes, such as Stromboli in Italy, are almost permanently active. However, most volcanoes erupt much less frequently, and those that have not erupted for tens or hundreds of years, but may be expected to erupt again, are said to be dormant. Volcanoes which were once active in response to the tectonic situation as it was millions of years ago, and which cannot possibly erupt again today are said to be extinct.

Kilauea volcano, Hawaii, showing lava flows

DEADLIEST EARTHQUAKES 1900–2000

Year	Place	Deaths
1905	Kangra, India	19 000
1907	west of Dushanbe, Tajikistan	12 000
1908	Messina, Italy	110 000
1915	Abruzzo, Italy	35 000
1917	Bali, Indonesia	15 000
1918	Guangdong Province, China	10 000
1920	Ningxia Province, China	200 000
1923	Tokyo, Japan	142 807
1927	Qinghai Province, China	200 000
1932	Gansu Province, China	70 000
1933	Sichuan Province, China	10 000
1934	Nepal/India	10 700
1935	Quetta, Pakistan	30 000
1939	Chillán, Chile	28 000
1939	Erzincan, Turkey	32 700
1948	Ashgabat, Turkmenistan	19 800
1960	Agadir, Morocco	12 000
1962	northwest Iran	12 225
1968	Dasht-e-Bayaz, Iran	12 100
1970	Huánuco Province, Peru	66 794
1974	Yunnan and Sichuan Provinces, China	20 000
1975	Liaoning Province, China	10 000
1976	central Guatemala	22 778
1976	Hebei Province, China	242 000
1978	Khorāsan Province, Iran	20 000
1980	Ech Chélif, Algeria	11 000
1988	Spitak, Armenia	25 000
1990	Manjil, Iran	50 000
1999	Kocaeli (Izmit), Turkey	17 000

OBSERVING THE OCEANS

The oceans cover 70.8 per cent of the surface of the Earth and exert an extraordinary influence on the physical processes of the Earth and its atmosphere. The circulation of water throughout the oceans is critical to world climate and climate change. Any study of these relationships relies upon a clear understanding of the role of the oceans and of the complex processes within them. Methods of direct and indirect observation of the oceans, particularly by sampling and through the application of satellite remote sensing, have developed enormously over the last forty years and continue to provide the data required to develop this understanding.

Until the advent of Earth-observation satellites in the late 1970s all ocean observations were made from ships. The first global survey of the oceans, their bathymetry and their physical and biological characteristics, was made by HMS Challenger between 1872 and 1876. Throughout the 20th century, comprehensive descriptions of the distributions of temperature and salinity were made through numerous regional and global expeditions. Analysis of the temperature and salinity characteristics of a water sample allowed its origins to be determined, and enabled overall patterns of water circulation to be deduced.

Until the 1960s there was no means of directly measuring currents below the ocean surface. Parallel developments produced two solutions to this problem. In the USA, current-recording meters were designed which returned records of current speed and direction, and water temperature. In the UK, devices were produced which could be made to drift with the currents at a predetermined depth and which could be tracked from an attendant ship. Such floats can now be used globally, independent of ships.

Earth observation satellites have become increasingly important in observing the oceans. Radiometers allow sea surface temperatures to be monitored and radar altimeters permit ocean surface currents to be inferred from measurements of sea surface height. Such developments meant that by the early 1990s routine monitoring of ocean surface currents was possible. The combination of satellite altimetry and other observation methods has also allowed a detailed picture of the ocean floor to be established (*see 1*).

1. GLOBAL SEAFLOOR TOPOGRAPHY

This image has been produced from a combination of shipboard depth soundings and gravity data derived from satellite altimetry from the ERS-1 and Geosat satellites. The range of colours represents different depths of the ocean – from orange and yellow on the shallow continental shelves to dark blues in the deepest ocean trenches. The heavily fractured mid-ocean ridges (ranging from green to yellow) are particularly prominent.

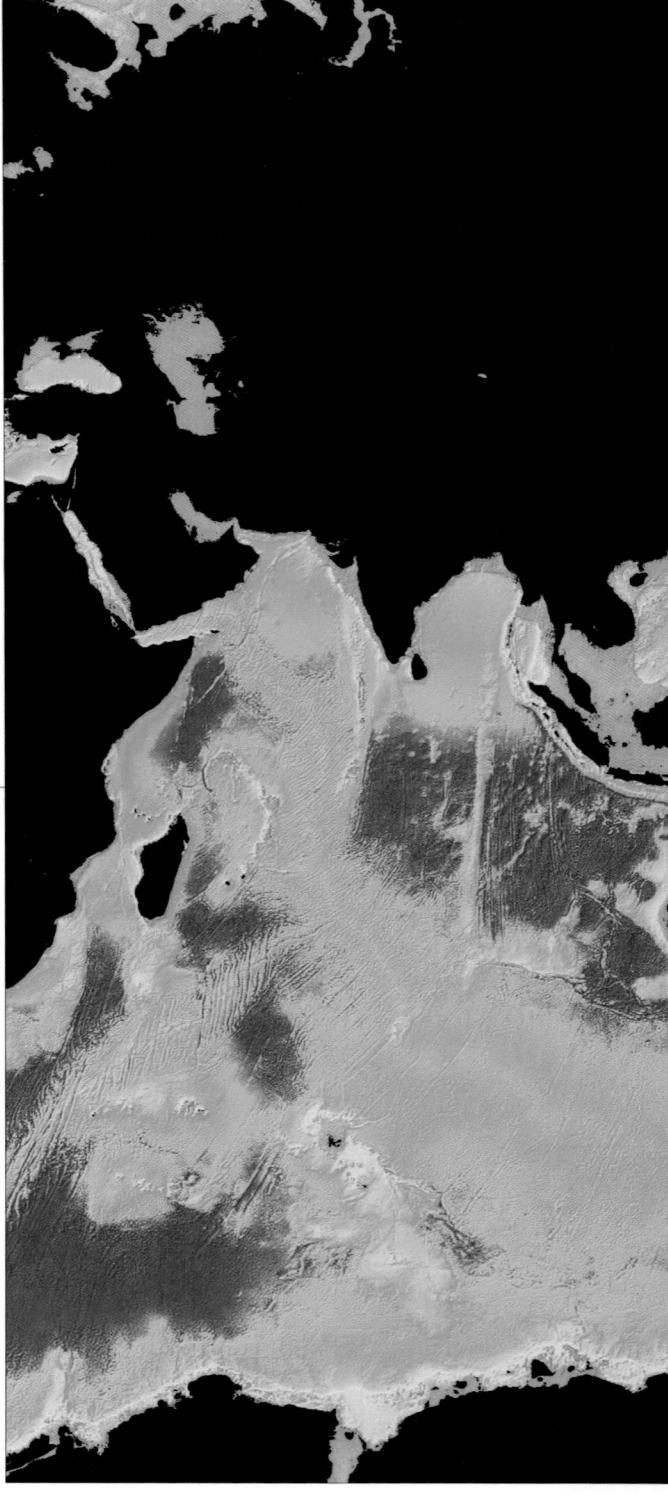

OCEAN CIRCULATION

Most of the Earth's incoming solar radiation is absorbed in the top few tens of metres of the ocean. Thus the upper ocean is warmed, the warming being greatest around the equator. Sea water has a high thermal capacity in comparison with the atmosphere or lithosphere and as a consequence, the ocean is an extremely effective store of thermal energy. Slow ocean currents play a major role in redistributing this heat around the globe and the oceans and their circulation are thus key elements in the climate system.

Estimates of the global transport of heat by the oceans (*see 2*) show a pattern of heat flow in the Indian and North Pacific Oceans away from the equator and towards the poles. However, the Atlantic Ocean has a clear northward flow throughout, decreasing from a maximum value of 1.4 petawatts (PW) at 24°N to effectively zero in the Arctic Ocean. This decrease is indicative of the heat loss to the atmosphere which is responsible for the temperate climate of western Europe.

Ocean currents are influenced by winds, by density gradients and by the Earth's rotation. They are also constrained by the topography of the seafloor. Surface currents are usually strong, narrow, western-boundary currents flowing towards the poles. Some of these are well known, for example the Gulf Stream in the North Atlantic Ocean, the Kuroshio Current in the northwest Pacific, and the Brazil Current (*see 3*). These poleward flows are returned towards the equator in broad, slow, interior flows which complete a gyre in each hemisphere basin. Sea surface circulation is reflected in variations in sea surface height which can vary greatly across currents (*see 4*). For example, differences in sea surface height of over 1m are evident across the Kuroshio Current. At high latitudes, winter cooling produces high density water which sinks towards the ocean floor and flows towards the equator, being constrained by the sea floor topography (*see 5*). This fills the deep ocean basins with water at temperatures close to 0°C.

2. OCEAN TRANSPORT OF HEAT

In petawatts (PW) (10^{15} watts). 1 PW is about sixty times the global consumption of energy.

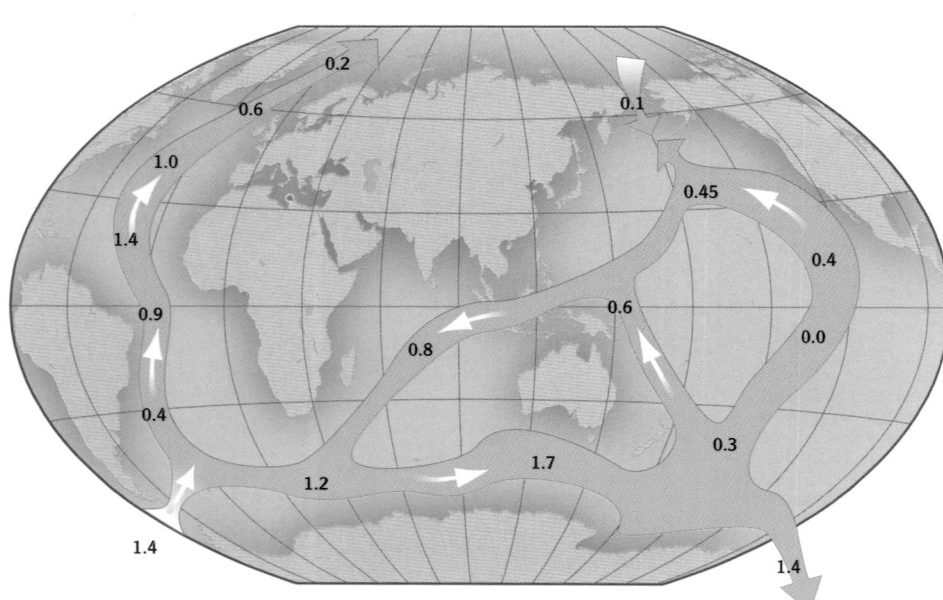

3. OCEAN SURFACE CURRENTS

scale 1 : 200 000 000

→	Warm current
→	Cold current
→	Seasonal drift during northern winter

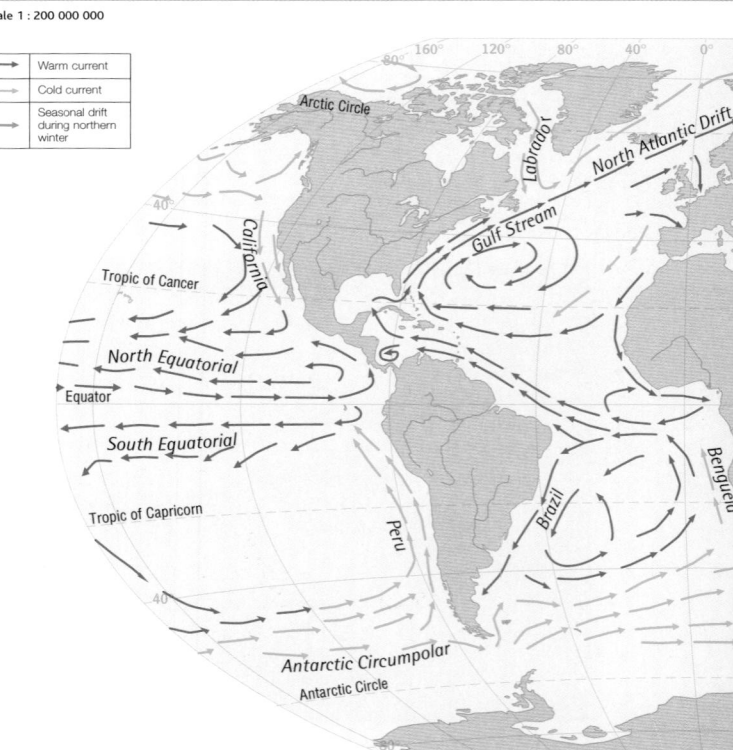

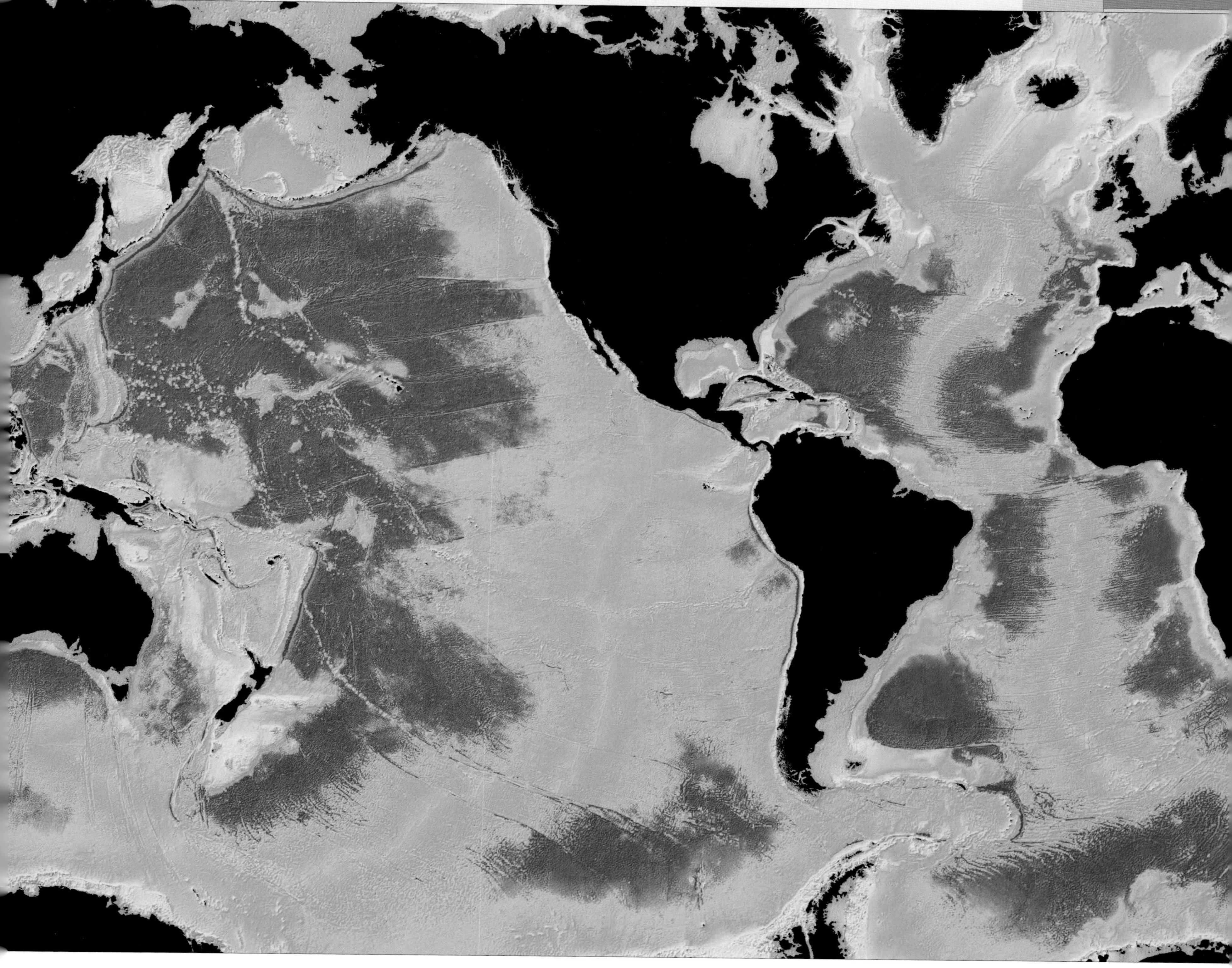

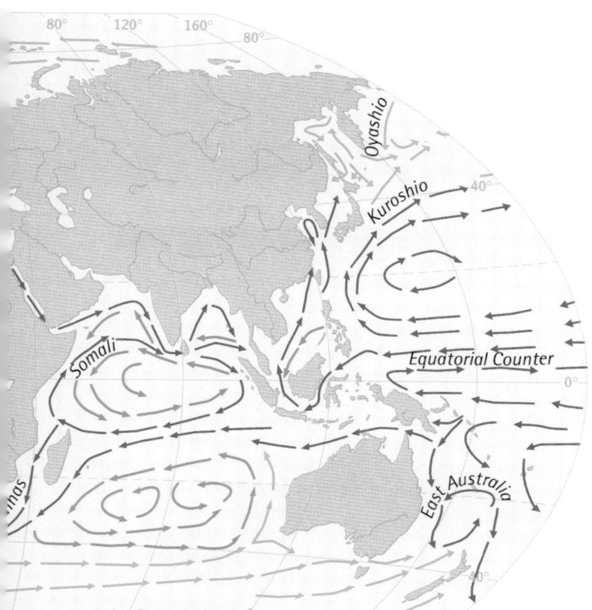

4. SEA SURFACE HEIGHT

From the TOPEX/POSEIDON satellite. Currents flow along the slopes and are strongest where the slopes are greatest.

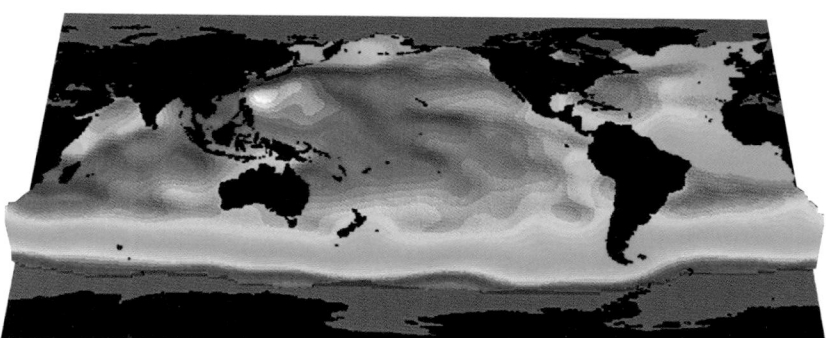

5. CROSS-SECTION OF SALINITY AND THE OCEAN FLOOR

Stretching 12 000 km across the Pacific Ocean from Antarctica (left) to Alaska (right) approximately along longitude 150°W. It shows water modified in the Antarctic descending to the ocean floor and into the ocean interior.

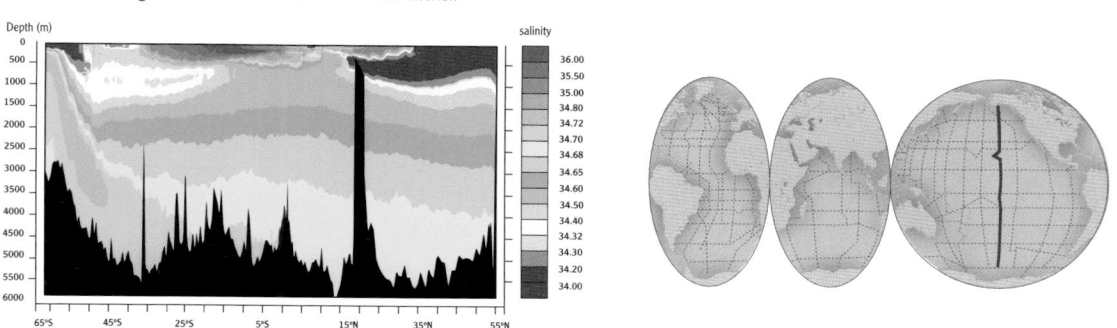

THE CLIMATE SYSTEM

The Earth's climate system is a highly complex interactive system involving the atmosphere, hydrosphere (oceans, lakes and rivers), biosphere (the Earth's living resources), cryosphere (particularly sea ice and polar ice caps) and lithosphere (the Earth's crust and upper mantle). This results in a great variety of climate types (*see 1*). Man's activities are affecting this system, and the monitoring of climate change, and of human influences upon it, is now a major issue.

Greenhouse gases such as carbon dioxide, methane and chlorofluorocarbons (CFCs) act to trap outgoing long-wave radiation, keeping the Earth's surface and lower atmosphere warmer than it would be otherwise. This is the phenomenon usually referred to as the greenhouse effect. Human activity has increased the atmospheric concentration of some of these gases and has therefore contributed to the effect. As a result of this, the world is about 0.6°C warmer than it was a hundred years ago with the three warmest years globally (in decreasing order) being 1998, 1997 and 1995 (*see 2*).

CLIMATE GRAPHS

These graphs relate by number, name and colour to the selected stations on the map and present mean temperature and precipitation values for each month. Red bars show average daily maximum and minimum temperatures for each month in degrees centigrade and fahrenheit. Vertical blue columns depict precipitation in millimetres and inches, with the total mean annual precipitation shown under the graph. The altitude of each station above sea level is given in metres and feet.

- Precipitation (average monthly total)
- Temperature (average daily maximum and minimum)

1. MAJOR CLIMATIC REGIONS AND SUB-TYPES

Köppen classification system
Winkel Tripel Projection
scale 1:110 000 000

• Climate graph location   ○ Weather extreme location

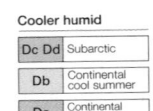
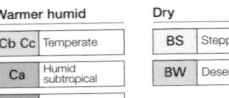

Polar
| EF | Ice cap |
| ET | Tundra |

Cooler humid
Dc Dd	Subarctic
Db	Continental cool summer
Da	Continental warm summer

Warmer humid
Cb Cc	Temperate
Ca	Humid subtropical
Cs	Mediterranean

Dry
| BS | Steppe |
| BW | Desert |

Tropical humid
| Aw As | Savanna |
| Af Am | Rain forest |

A   Rainy climate with no winter:
coolest month above 18°C (64.4°F).

B   Dry climates; limits are defined by formulae based on rainfall effectiveness:
BS Steppe or semi-arid climate.
BW Desert or arid climate.

*C Rainy climates with mild winters:
coolest month above 0°C (32°F), but below 18°C (64.4°F); warmest month above 10°C (50°F).

*D Rainy climates with severe winters:
coldest month below 0°C (32°F);
warmest month above 10°C (50°F).

E   Polar climates with no warm season:
warmest month below 10°C (50°F).
ET Tundra climate: warmest month below 10°C (50°F) but above 0°C (32°F).
EF Perpetual frost: all months below 0°C (32°F).

* Modification of Köppen definition

a   Warmest month above 22°C (71.6°F).

b   Warmest month below 22°C (71.6°F).

c   Less than four months over 10°C (50°F).

d   As 'c', but with severe cold: coldest month below -38°C (-36.4°F).

f   Constantly moist rainfall throughout the year.

*h Warmer dry: all months above 0°C (32°F).

*k Cooler dry: at least one month below 0°C (32°F).

m   Monsoon rain: short dry season, but is compensated by heavy rains during rest of the year.

s   Frequent fog.

s   Dry season in summer.

w   Dry season in winter.

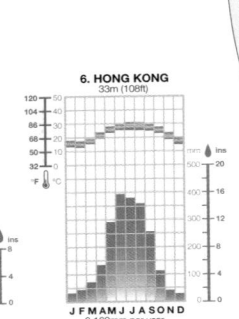
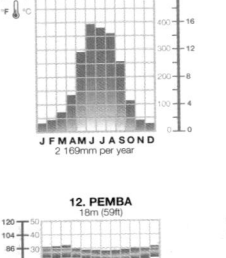
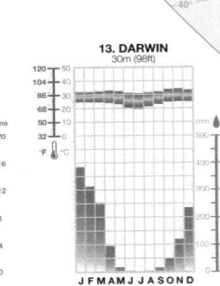
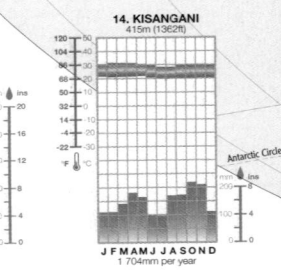

1. NOME 7m (23ft) — 454mm per year

2. ARKHANGEL'SK 3m (10ft) — 530mm per year

3. MOSKVA 167m (548ft) — 624mm per year

4. KĀBUL 1799m (5902ft) — 339mm per year

5. VICTORIA 26m (85ft) — 696mm per year

6. HONG KONG 33m (108ft) — 2 169mm per year

7. SYDNEY 42m (138ft) — 1 181mm per year

8. ATHINA 107m (351ft) — 402mm (16ins)

9. CAPE TOWN 12m (39ft) — 509mm per year

10. ULAANBAATAR 1309m (4295ft) — 209mm per year

11. LIMA 128m (420ft) — 43mm per year

12. PEMBA 18m (59ft) — 1 819mm per year

13. DARWIN 30m (98ft) — 1 492mm per year

14. KISANGANI 415m (1362ft) — 1 704mm per year

CLIMATE CHANGE

Future climate change depends on how quickly and to what extent the concentration of greenhouse gases and aerosols in the atmosphere increases. If we assume that no action is taken to limit future greenhouse gas emissions, then a warming during the 21st century of 0.2 to 0.3°C per decade is likely. Such a rate of warming would be greater than anything that has occurred over the last 10 000 years.

The detailed climatic response to the increase in carbon dioxide and other greenhouse gases is predicted using complex mathematical models of the climate. One of the most advanced climate models in the world is that produced by the Hadley Centre of the UK Meteorological Office. This model has produced predictions of climatic change, including changes in temperature and precipitation (*see 3 and 4*). According to this model, some regions of the world will warm more quickly than others and precipitation will increase in some areas and decrease in others. Such changes are likely to have significant impacts on sea-level which could rise by as much as 50 cm over the next century. Human impacts would also be through the effects on water resources, food production and health.

2. COMBINED GLOBAL LAND, AIR AND SEA SURFACE TEMPERATURES 1860-1999

Relative to 1961-1990 average. The black line is a smoothing of the annual values to suppress sub-decadal time-scale variations.

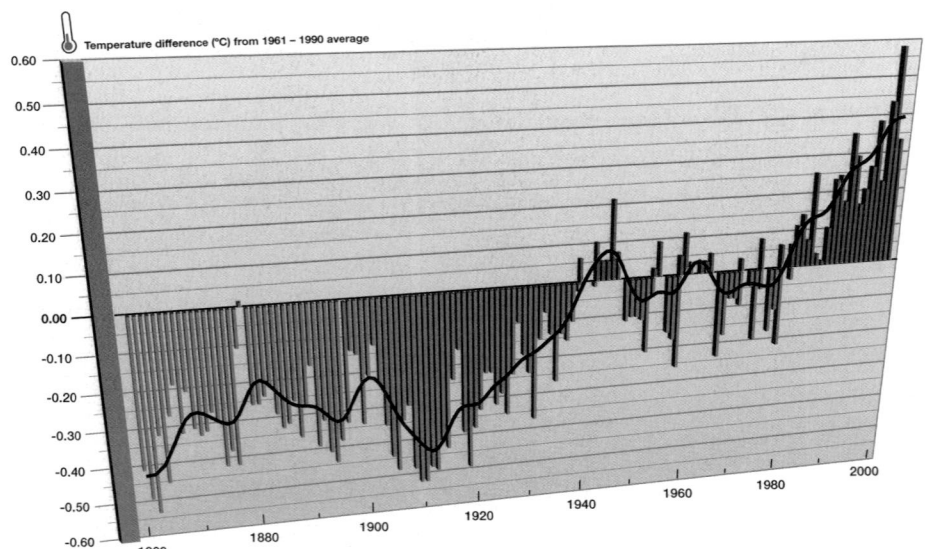

3. TEMPERATURE IN THE 2050s

Predicted annual mean temperature change

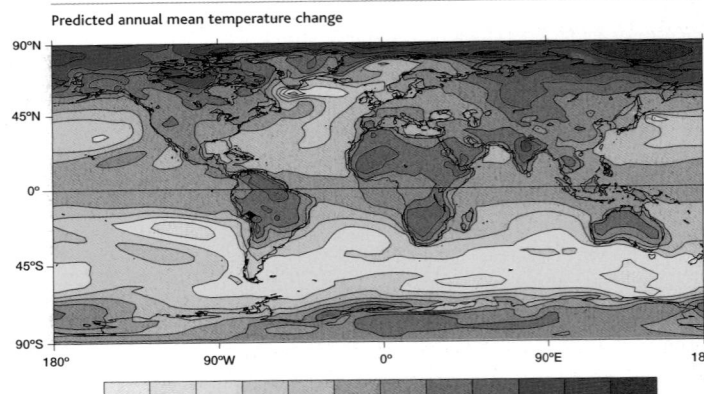

Annual mean temperature change (°C)

4. PRECIPITATION IN THE 2050s

Predicted average precipitation change

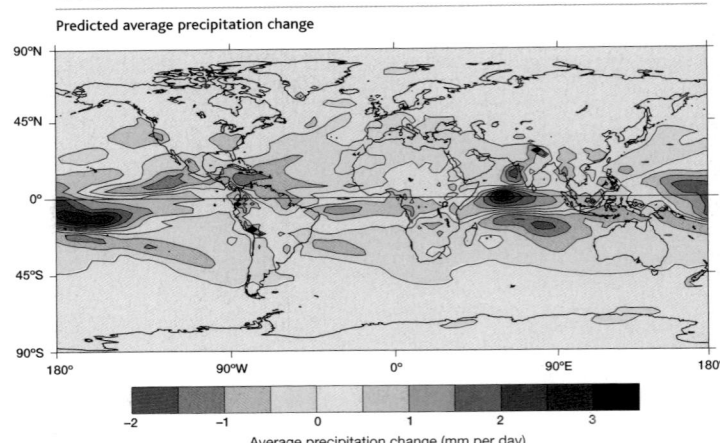

Average precipitation change (mm per day)

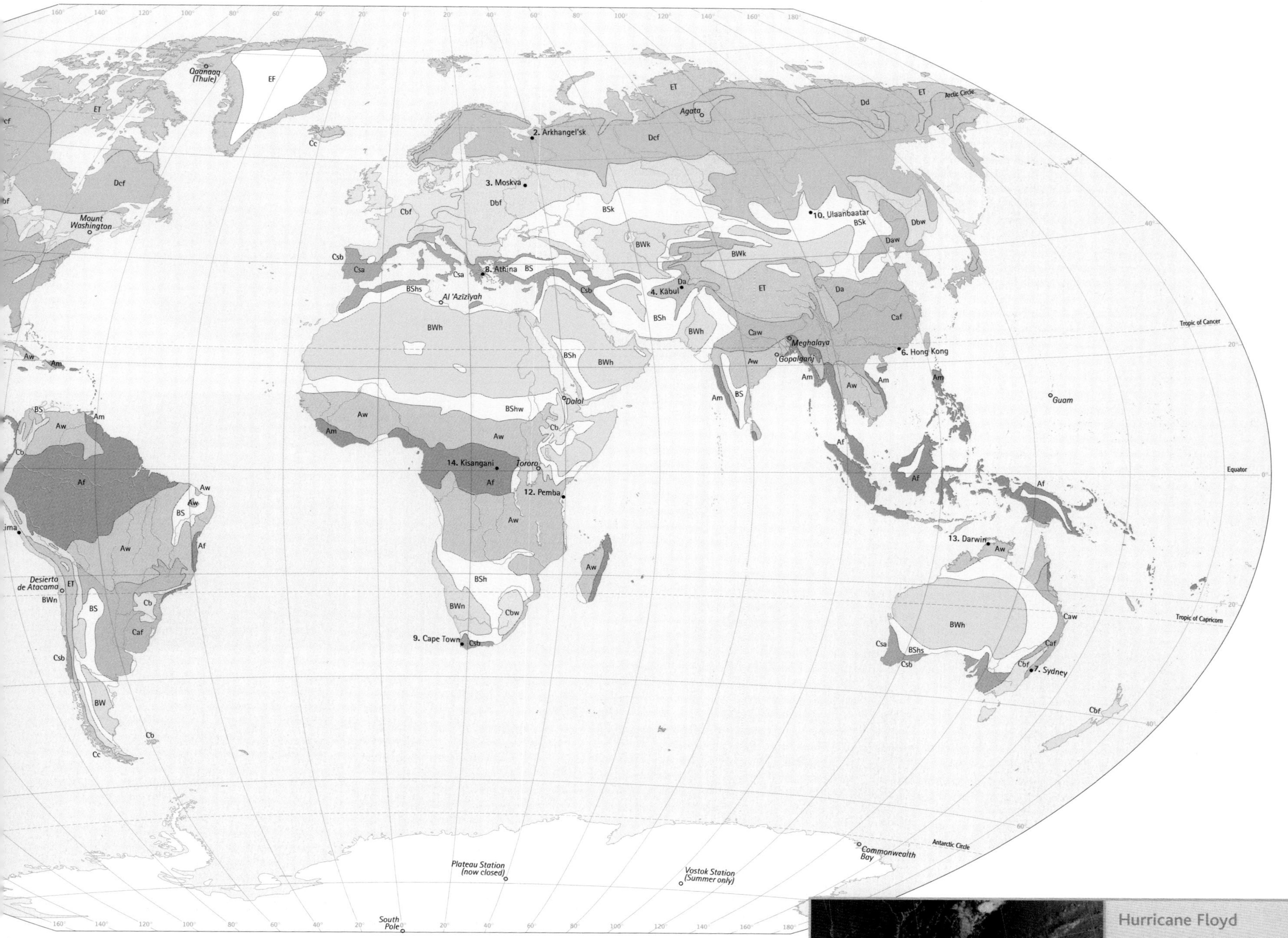

TROPICAL STORMS

Tropical storms develop, and have different names, in different parts of the world: hurricanes in the north Atlantic and east Pacific; typhoons in the northwest Pacific; and cyclones in the Indian Ocean region. There are also many local names for these events – those affecting the northern coast of Australia are known colloquially as the 'Willy-willies' (see 5).

Tropical storms are among the most powerful and destructive weather systems on Earth. Of the eighty to one hundred which develop annually over the tropical oceans, many make landfall and cause considerable damage to property and loss of life as a result of high winds and heavy rain.

The majority of tropical storms originate in the northwest Pacific, where as typhoons they commonly affect areas from

the Philippines through to China and Japan. They are also found as cyclones in the Bay of Bengal, either developing locally or on occasion being the remnants of typhoons which have moved westwards across Thailand. These storms bring heavy rains to eastern India or to the Ganges Delta in Bangladesh. In these places the land is so close to sea level that the rise in water levels has great potential for heavy loss of life.

The conditions required for the development of tropical storms – warm (over 26.5°C) ocean waters to a depth of at least 50 m; pre-existing cyclonic (low pressure) systems; thunderstorm activity; and moist layers of air in the mid-troposphere (around 5 km above the Earth's surface) – mean that most occur in mid- to late-summer in the areas concerned.

Hurricane Floyd

Hurricane Floyd developed in the northern Atlantic during early September 1999. It increased in intensity to maximum sustained wind speeds of 249 km per hour – a high category 4 hurricane – on 13 September just west of The Bahamas. From here, it turned to the north and made landfall near Cape Fear, North Carolina, USA early on the 16th. Although wind speeds had dropped to around 166 km per hour, it had a devastating effect. Serious flooding affected several states, in particular North Carolina. 57 deaths were directly attributed to the hurricane, making it the deadliest US hurricane since Hurricane Agnes in 1972.

Image from the National Climatic Data Center, NOAA.

5. TRACKS OF TROPICAL STORMS

Wind speeds often over 160 km per hour
scale 1:295 000 000

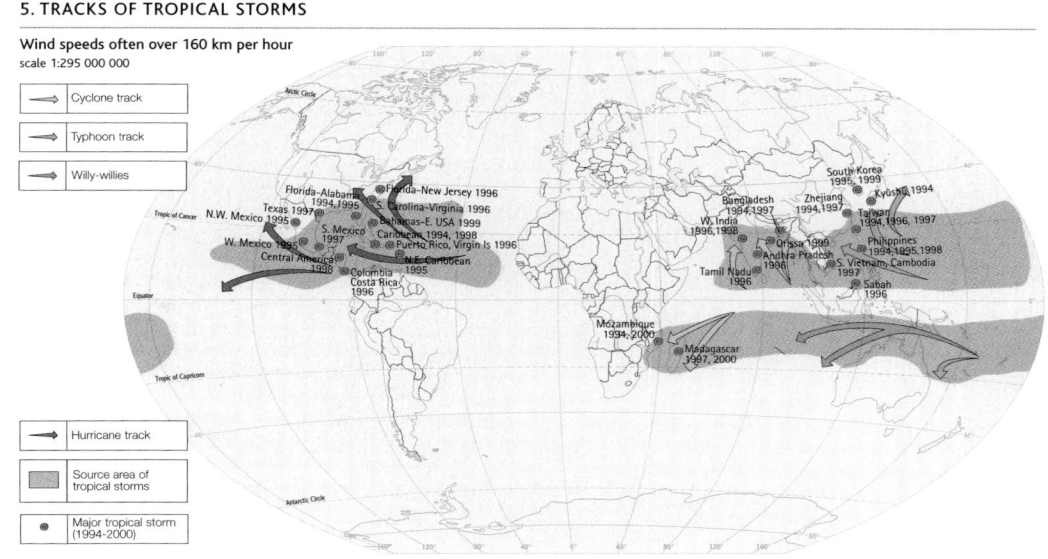

WORLD WEATHER EXTREMES

Highest shade temperature	57.8°C/136°F Al 'Azizīyah, Libya (13th September 1922)
Hottest place — Annual mean	34.4°C/93.9°F Dalol, Ethiopia
Driest place — Annual mean	0.1 mm/0.004 inches Desierto de Atacama, Chile
Most sunshine — Annual mean	90% Yuma, Arizona, USA (over 4 000 hours)
Least sunshine	Nil for 182 days each year, South Pole
Lowest screen temperature	-89.2°C/-128.6°F Vostok Station, Antarctica (21st July 1983)
Coldest place — Annual mean	-56.6°C/-69.9°F Plateau Station, Antarctica
Wettest place — Annual mean	11 873 mm/467.4 inches Meghalaya, India
Most rainy days	Up to 350 per year Mount Waialeale, Hawaii, USA
Windiest place	322 km per hour/200 miles per hour in gales, Commonwealth Bay, Antarctica
Highest surface wind speed High altitude	372 km per hour/231 miles per hour Mount Washington, New Hampshire, USA, (12th April 1934)
Low altitude	333 km per hour/207 miles per hour Qaanaaq (Thule), Greenland 8th March 1972)
Tornado	512 km per hour/318 miles per hour Oklahoma City, Oklahoma, USA (3rd May 1999)
Greatest snowfall	31 102 mm/1 224.5 inches Mount Rainier, Washington, USA (19th February 1971 — 18th February 1972)
Heaviest hailstones	1 kg/2.21 lb Gopalganj, Bangladesh (14th April 1986)
Thunder-days Average	251 days per year Tororo, Uganda
Highest barometric pressure	1 083.8 mb Agata, Siberia, Russian Federation (31st December 1968)
Lowest barometric pressure	870 mb 483 km/300 miles west of Guam, Pacific Ocean (12th October 1979)

© Bartholomew Ltd

THE DISCover PROJECT

Most existing global land cover maps show only a general idea of the actual conditions on the Earth's surface. They tend to be fairly coarse, of unknown accuracy, and are derived from a variety of primary data sources. Most also contain a climate element in the class definitions which leads to a mixture of potential versus actual land cover. Since 1992 the International Geosphere Biosphere Programme's (IGBP) Data and Information System (DIS) has been working towards the completion of a new global land cover data set without these shortcomings. The resulting land cover map as shown here – known as DISCover – was completed in June 1997 and shows the Earth's land cover as it was in 1992/1993 at a ground resolution of 1 km (*see 1*).

The final data set has been created from over 4.4 terabytes of data from the Advanced Very High Resolution Radiometer (AVHRR) sensor on board the polar orbiting satellites of the US National Oceanic and Atmospheric Administration (NOAA). These satellites provide images of the entire Earth's surface every day at a ground resolution of 1 km (see also the continental satellite images on pages 8-21). Development of the data set used to create DISCover was endorsed by the G7 Committee on Earth Observation Satellites, and implemented by the United States Geological Survey (USGS), the National Aeronautics and Space Administration (NASA), NOAA, and the European Space Agency (ESA).

Collecting the data involved the collaborative efforts of twenty-three satellite receiving stations around the world.

The subsequent classification of the data was performed at the USGS Earth Resources Observation Systems (EROS) Data Center in Sioux Falls, South Dakota, at the University of Nebraska–Lincoln, USA and at the European Commission's Joint Research Centre (JRC) in Italy. The accuracy of the map classification is currently being assessed by specialists in the USA, comparing it with a sample of more than 400 high resolution satellite images from the US Landsat (*see 2*) and French SPOT (*see 3*) satellites.

The land cover classes shown on the map are not the typical vegetation classes often found in world vegetation maps. For example, there are no tundra or tropical rainforest classes. This is because the philosophy for DISCover was to describe land cover in terms of structure – in particular the three components of above-ground biomass, leaf longevity and leaf type – mainly for the science community interested in global change, and not in terms of traditional climate/vegetation distinctions.

4. GLOBAL LAND COVER COMPOSITION

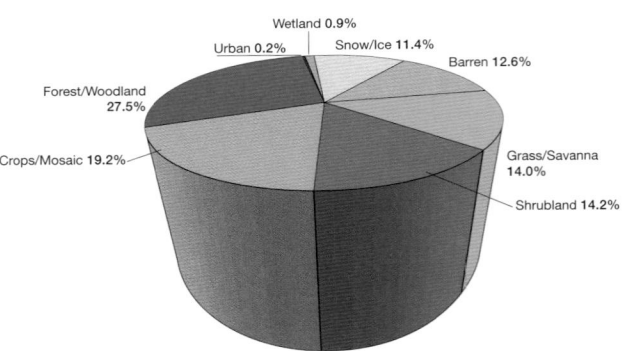

Wetland 0.9%
Urban 0.2%
Snow/Ice 11.4%
Barren 12.6%
Forest/Woodland 27.5%
Crops/Mosaic 19.2%
Grass/Savanna 14.0%
Shrubland 14.2%

2. Agricultural land use in Florida, USA

This example of high resolution Landsat satellite imagery illustrates the level of land cover detail available from such images. It shows part of Florida, USA with Lake Okeechobee to the top left and the city of West Palm Beach to the far right. The regular field pattern shows crops at different stages of growth and the dark green, mottled areas (top centre and bottom centre) are parts of the Everglades swamp.

1. WORLD LAND COVER

Goode Interrupted Homolosine Projection
scale approximately 1:75 000 000
Map courtesy of IGBP, JRC and USGS

1. Evergreen needleleaf forest
2. Evergreen broadleaf forest
3. Deciduous needleleaf forest
4. Deciduous broadleaf forest
5. Mixed forest
6. Closed shrublands
7. Open shrublands
8. Woody savannas
9. Savannas
10. Grasslands
11. Permanent wetlands
12. Croplands
13. Urban and built-up
14. Cropland/Natural vegetation mosaic
15. Snow and Ice
16. Barren or sparsely vegetated
17. Water bodies

LANDCOVER GRAPHS - CLASSIFICATION

Class description	IGBP/DISCover classes
Forest/Woodland	1 Evergreen needleleaf forest 2 Evergreen broadleaf forest 3 Deciduous needleleaf forest 4 Deciduous broadleaf forest 5 Mixed forest
Shrubland	6 Closed shrublands 7 Open shrublands
Grass/Savanna	8 Woody savannas 9 Savannas 10 Grasslands
Wetland	11 Permanent wetlands
Crops/Mosaic	12 Croplands 14 Cropland/Natural vegetation mosaic
Urban	13 Urban and built-up
Snow/Ice	15 Snow and Ice
Barren	16 Barren or sparsely vegetated

5. CONTINENTAL LAND COVER COMPOSITION

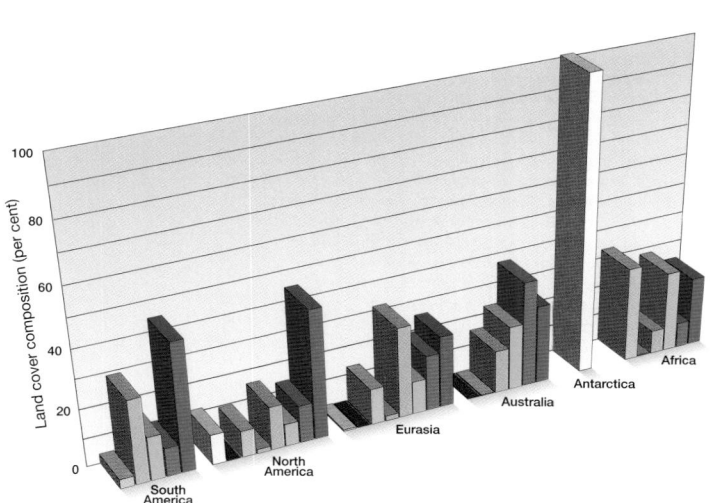

Land cover composition (per cent)

South America · North America · Eurasia · Australia · Antarctica · Africa

INTERPRETATION AND USES

The high resolution of the imagery used to compile the data set and map allows detailed interpretation of land cover patterns across the world. An additional benefit of holding the data in digital form is the ease with which land cover on global and continental scales can be extracted and analysed (*see 4 and 5*).

The small areas of permanent wetlands show just how rare these fragile ecosystems are. Apart from those in Sudan and the Okavango Delta in Botswana, only the swamp areas of Siberia are really evident on the global scale. In contrast, the concentration the world's extensive croplands in the northern hemisphere is obvious with the cereal belt in North America clearly visible. This contrasts with western Europe where the smaller field sizes and more common mixed farming lead to much of this region being classified as cropland/natural vegetation mosaics. The cereal belts of eastern Europe show the transition once again to extensive agriculture.

One of the most striking agricultural features on the Earth's surface is the heavily cultivated Nile valley and delta. In fact, humankind's influence on the Earth's vegetation is apparent throughout the map. Tropical forest cover is far from the uniform, unbroken swath so often depicted on world vegetation maps. In all areas of the world the tropical forest margins show encroachment of cropland or savanna in the wake of human activity (*see 3*), although parts of their interiors still remain largely untouched. In the light of such patterns, the global figures for tropical deforestation rates (typically around 0.5–1 per cent per year) become even more alarming. Deforestation is not uniform, so such figures hide far more rapid rates of loss in the forest margins.

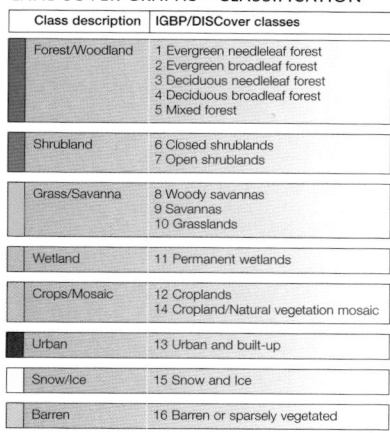

3. Deforestation in Brazil

This SPOT satellite image shows part of the tropical rain forest near Aldeia Velha in northern Brazil. The indigenous forest is bright green and areas cleared and planted with crops show as yellow-green and brown.

POPULATION DISTRIBUTION AND GROWTH

People are distributed very unevenly over the Earth. As shown on the population distribution map (see 1), over a quarter of the land area is uninhabited or has extremely low population density. Barely a quarter of the land area is occupied at densities of 10 or more persons per square km, with the three largest concentrations in east Asia, the Indian subcontinent and Europe accounting for over half the world total. China and India dominate the scene, together accounting for nearly two-fifths of world population (see 2).

Over the past half century world population has been growing faster than it has ever done before. Whereas world population did not pass the one billion mark until 1804 and took another 123 years to reach two billion in 1927, it then added the third billion in 33 years, the fourth in 14 years and the fifth in 13 years, with the 6 billion mark being passed only 12 years after this in 1999. It is expected that another three billion people will have been added to the world population by 2050 (see 3).

Population growth since 1950 has been spread very unevenly between the continents. While overall numbers have been growing extremely rapidly since 1950, a massive 89 per cent increase has taken place in the less developed regions, especially southern and eastern Asia, while Europe's population is now almost stationary and ageing rapidly. India and China alone are responsible for over one-third of current growth, but most of the highest percentage rates of growth are to be found in Sub-Saharan Africa. The latest trends in population growth at country level (see 4) emphasize the continuing contrast between the more and less developed regions. Annual growth rates of 1.5 per cent or more are very common in Latin America, Africa and the southern half of Asia. A number of countries have rates in excess of 3.0 per cent, which if continued would lead to the doubling of their populations in 23 years or less.

2. TOP TEN COUNTRIES BY POPULATION AND POPULATION DENSITY

TOTAL POPULATION 1998	COUNTRY	RANK	COUNTRY	POPULATION DENSITY 1998 (countries with populations over 10 million)	
				per sq mile	per sq km
1 262 817 000	China	1	Bangladesh	2 244	866
982 223 000	India	2	Taiwan	1 568	606
274 028 000	USA	3	South Korea	1 203	465
206 338 000	Indonesia	4	Netherlands	978	378
165 851 000	Brazil	5	Japan	866	334
148 166 000	Pakistan	6	Belgium	861	332
147 434 000	Russian Federation	7	India	830	320
126 281 000	Japan	8	Sri Lanka	729	281
124 774 000	Bangladesh	9	Philippines	630	243
106 409 000	Nigeria	10	UK	622	240

3. WORLD POPULATION GROWTH BY CONTINENT 1750–2050

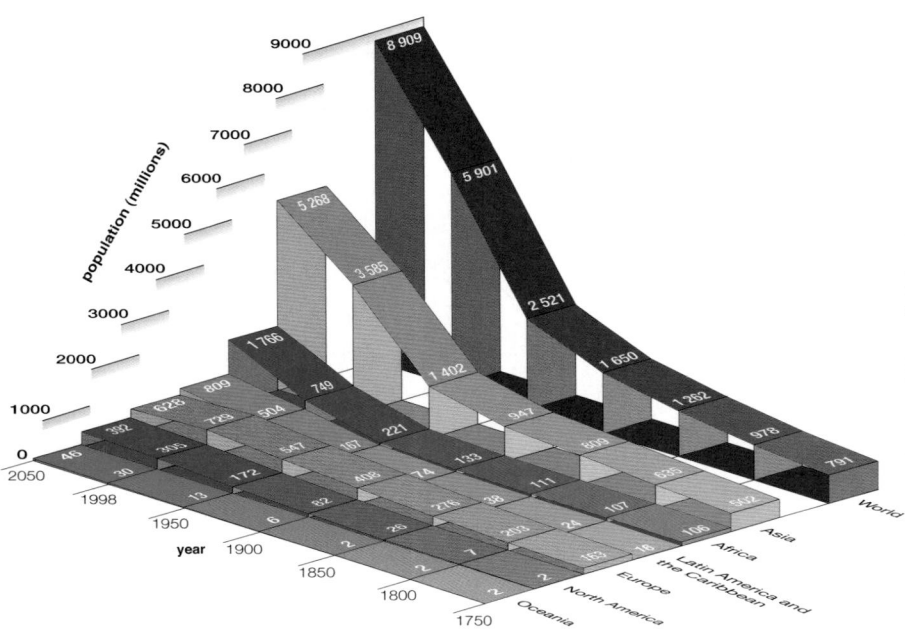

4. POPULATION CHANGE 1995–2000

Average annual rate of population change (per cent) and the top ten contributors to world population growth (net annual addition)
scale 1:255 000 000

increase	>5.6
	2.9 – 5.6
	1.5 – 2.8
	0.8 – 1.4
	0.0 – 0.7
decrease	-0.7 – -0.1
	<-0.7
	no data

1. WORLD POPULATION DISTRIBUTION

Winkel Tripel Projection
scale 1:93 000 000

Population density

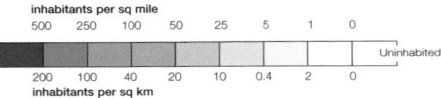

inhabitants per sq mile
500 250 100 50 25 5 1 0   Uninhabited
200 100 40 20 10 0.4 2 0
inhabitants per sq km

5. KEY POPULATION STATISTICS FOR MAJOR REGIONS

	Population 1998 (millions)	Growth (per cent)	Infant mortality rate	Total fertility rate	Life expectancy (years)
World	5 901	1.33	57	2.7	65
More developed regions[1]	1 182	0.28	9	1.6	75
Less developed regions[2]	4 719	1.59	63	3.0	63
Africa	749	2.37	87	5.1	51
Asia	3 585	1.38	57	2.6	66
Europe[3]	729	0.03	12	1.4	73
Latin America and the Caribbean[4]	504	1.57	36	2.7	69
North America	305	0.85	7	1.9	77
Oceania	30	1.30	24	2.4	74

Except for population (1998), the data are annual averages projected for the period 1995-2000.

1. Europe, North America, Australia, New Zealand and Japan.

2. Africa, Asia (excluding Japan), Latin America and the Caribbean, and Oceania (excluding Australia and New Zealand).

3. Includes Russian Federation.

4. South America, Central America (including Mexico) and all Carribean Islands.

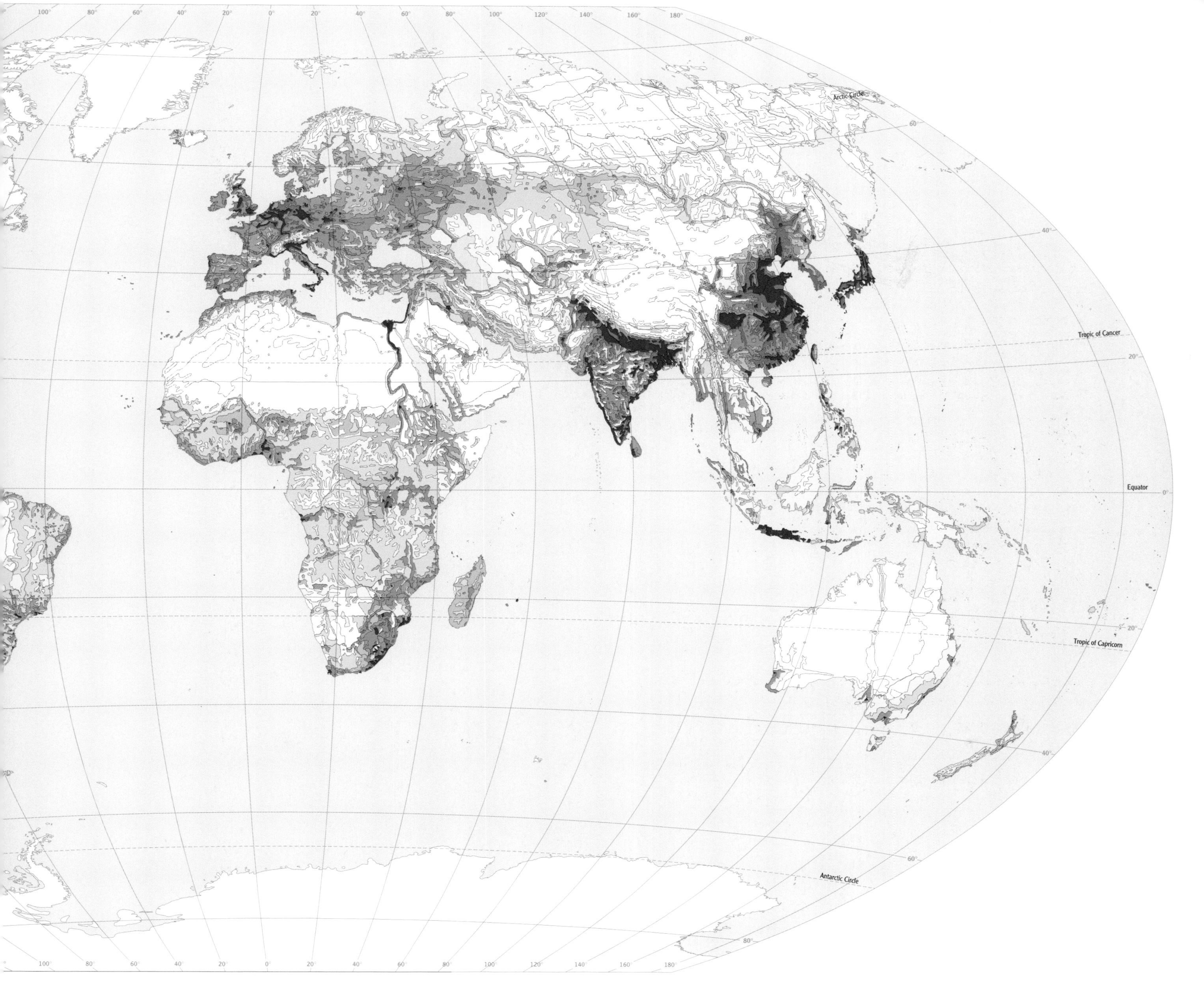

DEMOGRAPHIC TRANSITION

Behind patterns of population growth lies the 'demographic transition' process, where countries pass through a phase of falling death rates and then a phase of falling fertility. Most parts of the world have passed through the first phase, with the average life expectancy of 63 years in the less developed world now not far behind that of 75 years in the more developed regions (see 5). Even so, infant mortality – a very

good indicator of human development levels – remains a major challenge in the less developed regions (see 6). Here, an average of sixty-three out of every one thousand babies die before their first birthday, compared to only nine out of every one thousand in the more developed regions. Sub-Saharan Africa started this transitional phase later than most other parts of the world and has so far seen life expectancy rise

to only 48 years, with progress being hampered by continuing high levels of infant mortality and by rising numbers of AIDS-related deaths.

Reductions in fertility rate (see 7) hold the key to the successful completion of the transition and the future stabilization of population growth. Much of the more developed world is well advanced in this process. In particular,

Europe's total fertility rate (broadly the average number of babies born to each woman) is now down to 1.4 – well below the 'replacement rate' of 2.1 needed to give a constant population in the long term. By contrast, the average for less developed regions, excluding China, is 3.8 and it is as high as 6.5 in Sub-Saharan Africa.

6. INFANT MORTALITY RATE 1995–2000

Deaths of infants less than one year old per 1000 live births
scale 1:315 000 000

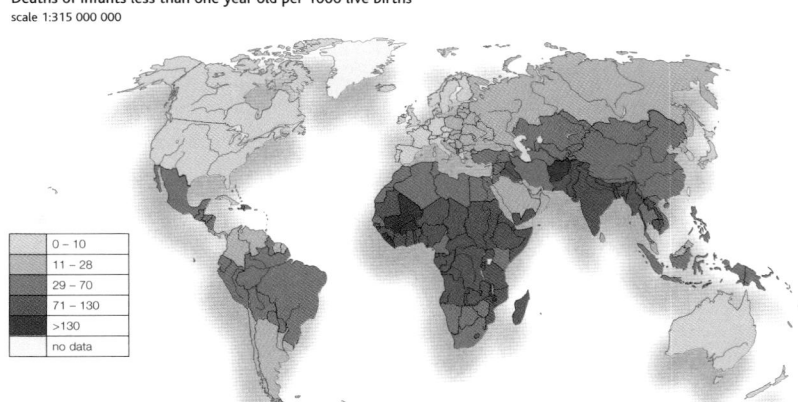

	0 – 10
	11 – 28
	29 – 70
	71 – 130
	>130
	no data

7. TOTAL FERTILITY RATE 1995–2000

Estimate of the number of children a woman will bear during her child-bearing years.
scale 1:315 000 000

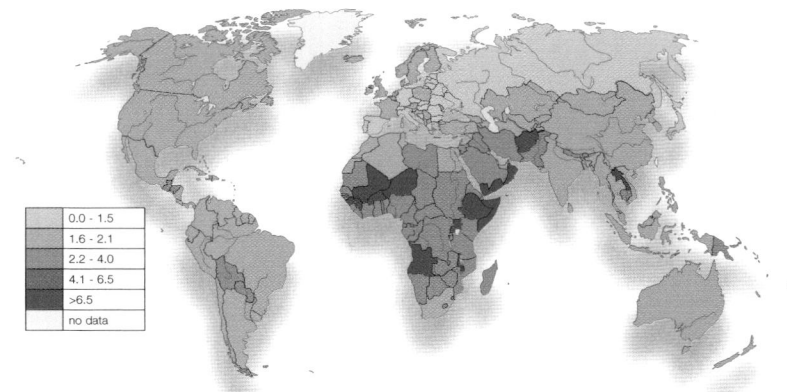

	0.0 – 1.5
	1.6 – 2.1
	2.2 – 4.0
	4.1 – 6.5
	>6.5
	no data

© Bartholomew Ltd

TOWARDS AN URBANIZED WORLD

World population is urbanizing rapidly but the current level of urbanization – the proportion of the population living in urban conditions – varies greatly across the world, as does its rate of increase. In the hundred years up to 1950 the greatest changes in urban population patterns took place in Europe and North America. Relatively few large cities developed elsewhere and most of these were in coastal locations with good trading connections with the imperial and industrial nations. This legacy is still highly visible on the world map of major cities (*see 1*). The main feature of the past half century has been the massive growth in the numbers of urban dwellers in the less developed regions. This process is still accelerating, posing an even greater logistical challenge during the next few decades than it did in the closing decades of the twentieth century.

The year 2006 is likely to be a momentous point in world history, when for the first time urban dwellers will outnumber those living in traditionally rural areas, according to UN projections. The annual rise in the percentage of the world's population living in cities has been accelerating steadily since the 1970s and will be running at unprecedentedly high levels for the next three decades. As a result, by 2030, 61.1 per cent of the world's population will be urbanites compared to 36.7 per cent in 1970 and 47.4 per cent in 2000 (*see 2*). In absolute terms, the global urban population more than doubled between 1970 and 2000 and is expected to grow by a further 2.2 billion by 2030 (*see 3*).

2. LEVEL OF URBANIZATION BY MAJOR REGION 1970–2030

Urban population as a percentage of total population

	1970	2000	2030
World	36.7	47.4	61.1
More developed regions[1]	67.7	76.1	83.7
Less developed regions[2]	25.1	40.5	57.3
Africa	23.0	37.8	54.4
Asia	23.4	37.6	55.2
Europe[3]	64.5	74.9	82.9
Latin America and the Caribbean[4]	57.4	75.4	83.2
North America	73.8	77.2	84.4
Oceania	70.8	70.0	74.5

1. Europe, North America, Australia, New Zealand and Japan.
2. Africa, Asia (excluding Japan), Latin America and the Caribbean, and Oceania (excluding Australia and New Zealand).
3. Includes Russian Federation.
4. South America, Central America (including Mexico) and all Caribbean Islands.

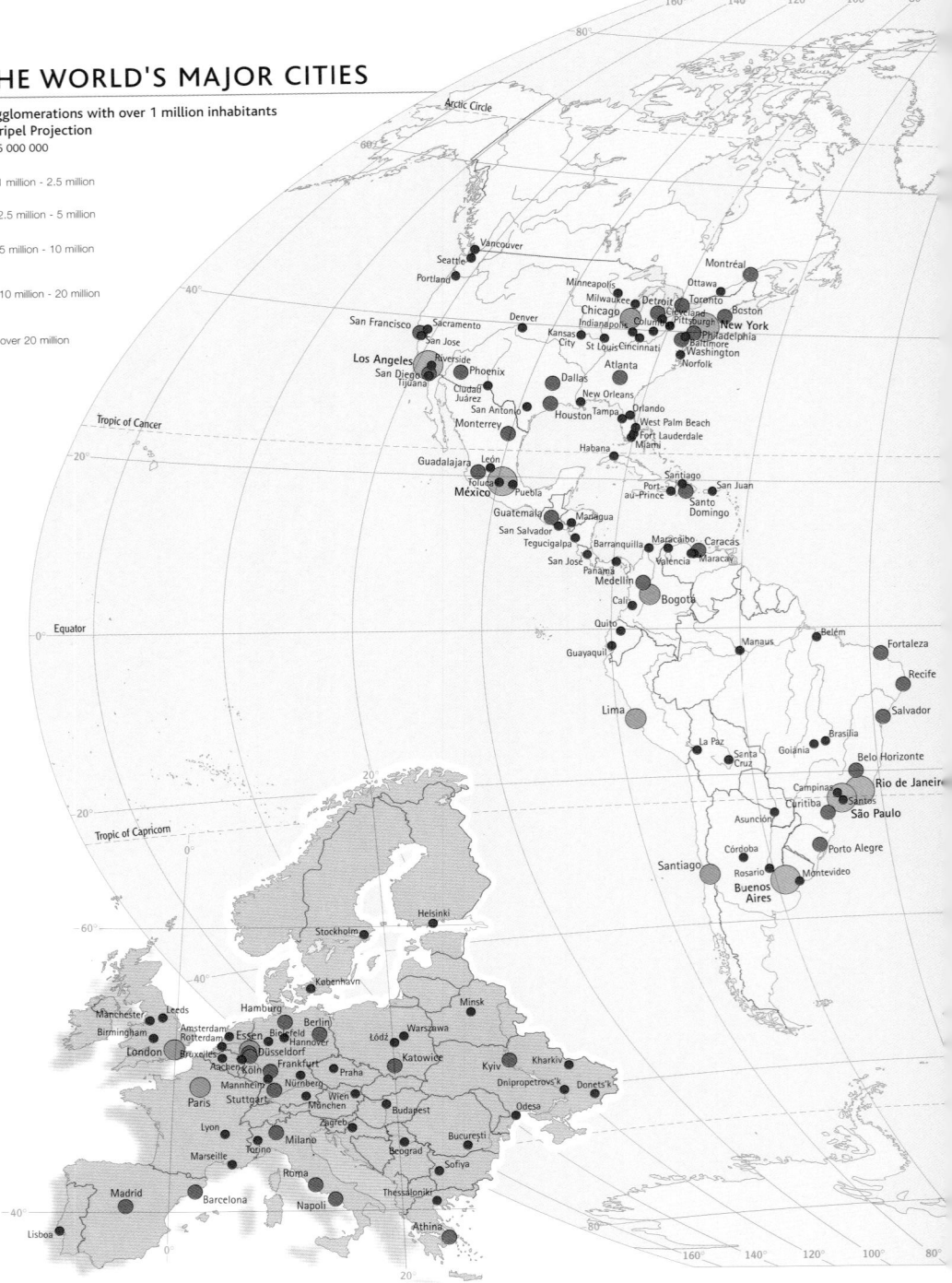

1. THE WORLD'S MAJOR CITIES

Urban agglomerations with over 1 million inhabitants
Winkel Tripel Projection
scale 1:106 000 000

- 1 million – 2.5 million
- 2.5 million – 5 million
- 5 million – 10 million
- 10 million – 20 million
- over 20 million

3. TOTAL URBAN POPULATION OF MAJOR REGIONS 1950–2030

4. LEVEL OF URBANIZATION

Percentage of total population living in urban areas 2000 and growth in urbanization 1950-2025 (selected countries)
scale 1:250 000 000

Map Key – per cent

- 81 – 100
- 61 – 80
- 41 – 60
- 21 – 40
- 0 – 20

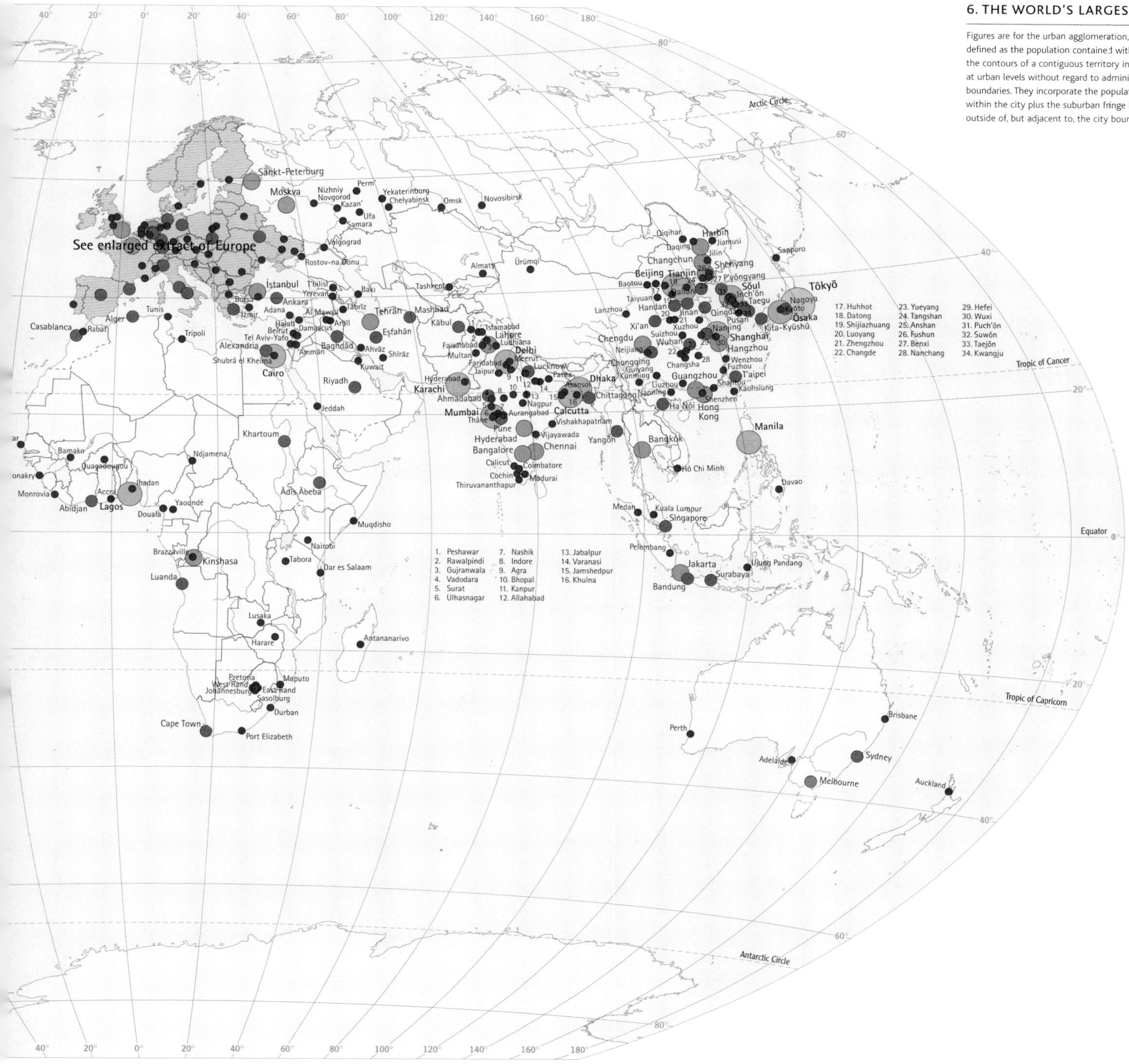

6. THE WORLD'S LARGEST CITIES 2000

Figures are for the urban agglomeration, defined as the population contained within the contours of a contiguous territory inhabited at urban levels without regard to administrative boundaries. They incorporate the population within the city plus the suburban fringe lying outside of, but adjacent to, the city boundaries.

City	Population
Tōkyō Japan	28 025 000
México Mexico	18 131 000
Mumbai India	18 042 000
São Paulo Brazil	17 711 000
New York USA	16 626 000
Shanghai China	14 173 000
Lagos Nigeria	13 488 000
Los Angeles USA	13 129 000
Calcutta India	12 900 000
Buenos Aires Argentina	12 431 000
Sŏul South Korea	12 215 000
Beijing China	12 033 000
Karachi Pakistan	11 774 000
Delhi India	11 680 000
Dhaka Bangladesh	10 979 000
Manila Philippines	10 818 000
Cairo Egypt	10 772 000
Ōsaka Japan	10 609 000
Rio de Janeiro Brazil	10 556 000
Tianjin China	10 239 000
Jakarta Indonesia	9 815 000
Paris France	9 638 000
İstanbul Turkey	9 413 000
Moskva Russian Federation	9 299 000
London United Kingdom	7 640 000
Lima Peru	7 443 000
Tehrān Iran	7 380 000
Bangkok Thailand	7 221 000
Chicago USA	6 945 000
Bogotá Colombia	6 834 000
Hyderabad India	6 833 000
Chennai India	6 639 000
Essen Germany	6 559 000
Hangzhou China	6 389 000
Hong Kong China	6 097 000
Lahore Pakistan	6 030 000
Shenyang China	5 681 000
Changchun China	5 566 000
Bangalore India	5 544 000
Harbin China	5 475 000
Chengdu China	5 293 000
Santiago Chile	5 261 000
Guangzhou China	5 162 000
Sankt-Peterburg Russian Federation	5 132 000
Kinshasa Dem. Rep. Congo	5 068 000
Baghdād Iraq	4 796 000
Jinan China	4 789 000
Wuhan China	4 750 000
Toronto Canada	4 657 000
Yangôn Myanmar	4 458 000
Alger Algeria	4 447 000
Philadelphia USA	4 398 000
Qingdao China	4 376 000
Milano Italy	4 251 000
Pusan South Korea	4 239 000
Belo Horizonte Brazil	4 160 000
Ahmadabad India	4 154 000
Madrid Spain	4 072 000
San Francisco USA	4 051 000
Alexandria Egypt	3 995 000
Washington USA	3 927 000
Dallas USA	3 912 000
Guadalajara Mexico	3 908 000
Chongqing China	3 896 000
Medellín Colombia	3 831 000
Detroit USA	3 785 000
Handan China	3 763 000
Frankfurt Germany	3 700 000
Porto Alegre Brazil	3 699 000
Ha Nôi Vietnam	3 678 000
Sydney Australia	3 665 000
Santo Domingo Dominican Republic	3 601 000
Singapore Singapore	3 587 000
Casablanca Morocco	3 535 000
Katowice Poland	3 488 000
Pune India	3 485 000
Bandung Indonesia	3 420 000
Monterrey Mexico	3 416 000
Montréal Canada	3 401 000
Nagoya Japan	3 377 000
Nanjing China	3 375 000
Houston USA	3 365 000
Abidjan Côte d'Ivoire	3 359 000
Xi'an China	3 352 000
Berlin Germany	3 337 000
Riyadh Saudi Arabia	3 328 000
Recife Brazil	3 307 000
Düsseldorf Germany	3 251 000
Ankara Turkey	3 190 000
Melbourne Australia	3 188 000
Salvador Brazil	3 180 000
Dalian China	3 153 000
Caracas Venezuela	3 153 000
Ādīs Ābeba Ethiopia	3 112 000
Athina Greece	3 103 000
Cape Town South Africa	3 092 000
Köln Germany	3 067 000
Maputo Mozambique	3 017 000
Napoli Italy	3 012 000
Fortaleza Brazil	3 007 000
San Diego USA	2 983 000
Boston USA	2 915 000
Chittagong Bangladesh	2 906 000
Kita-Kyūshū Japan	2 898 000
Kyiv Ukraine	2 897 000
T'aipei Taiwan	2 880 000
Inch'ŏn South Korea	2 837 000
Barcelona Spain	2 819 000
Khartoum Sudan	2 748 000
P'yŏngyang North Korea	2 726 000
Kābul Afghanistan	2 716 000
Guatemala Guatemala	2 697 000
Atlanta USA	2 689 000
Stuttgart Germany	2 688 000
Roma Italy	2 688 000
Hamburg Germany	2 680 000
Luanda Angola	2 665 000
Esfahān Iran	2 644 000
Phoenix USA	2 607 000
Lucknow India	2 565 000
Taegu South Korea	2 559 000
Curitiba Brazil	2 519 000
Surabaya Indonesia	2 507 000
Tashkent Uzbekistan	2 495 000
Kanpur India	2 447 000
Johannesburg South Africa	2 412 000
İzmir Turkey	2 399 000
Mashhad Iran	2 378 000
Arbil Iraq	2 368 000
Minneapolis USA	2 363 000
Surat India	2 341 000
Damascus Syria	2 335 000
Nairobi Kenya	2 320 000
München Germany	2 306 000
Habana Cuba	2 302 000
Taiyuan China	2 280 000
Zhengzhou China	2 275 000
Birmingham United Kingdom	2 271 000
Warszawa Poland	2 269 000
Manchester United Kingdom	2 252 000
Guiyang China	2 230 000
Faisalabad Pakistan	2 228 000
Miami USA	2 210 000
Halab Syria	2 173 000
Tel Aviv-Yafo Israel	2 170 000
Jaipur India	2 143 000
Bucureşti Romania	2 130 000
Guayaquil Ecuador	2 127 000
Peshawar Pakistan	2 094 000
Seattle USA	2 084 000
Cali Colombia	2 082 000
Dakar Senegal	2 077 000
Wien Austria	2 072 000
St Louis USA	2 071 000
Nagpur India	2 060 000

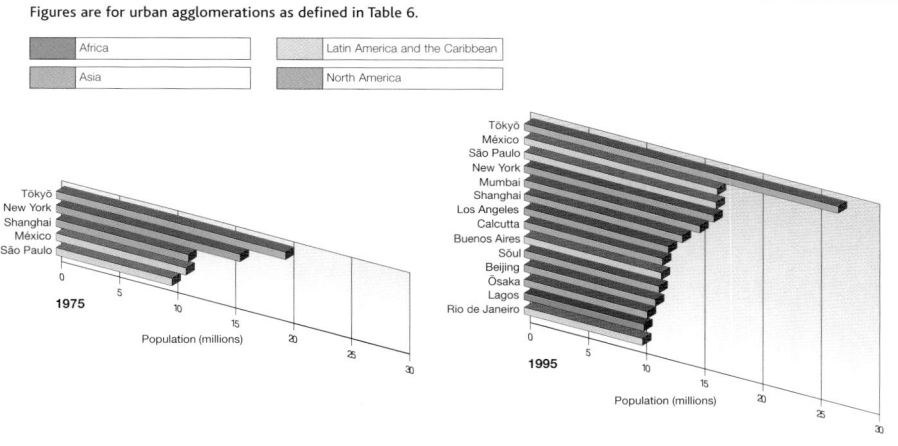

REGIONAL PATTERNS OF URBANIZATION

There is a broad contrast in the levels of urbanization between the more and less developed regions (see 4). In the more developed regions as a whole, three-quarters of the population now live in urban places. Excluding city states, levels range from 97 per cent for Belgium to under 40 per cent for Albania, Bosnia-Herzegovina and Portugal. Many countries have seen very little increase in their level of urbanization over the last few decades, with some reporting renewed population growth in rural areas. Only 40.5 per cent of the population in the less developed regions are urbanites, but this represents a big jump from the 25.1 per cent figure for 1970. Africa and Asia both currently average less than this, but will be seeing the greatest changes in the future, with their urban proportions likely to pass the 50 per cent mark by 2025. Between 2000 and 2030, Africa and Asia are expected to account for 86 per cent of the world's new urbanites – around 550 and 1 350 million people in absolute terms.

Alongside the rise in the world's urban population has occurred a massive increase in the number and size of cities. In 1950, New York was the only urban agglomeration with over 10 million inhabitants, but the number of cities of this size had grown to five by 1975 and to fourteen by 1995. There are expected to be twenty-six such cities by 2015, according to UN figures (see 5). This increase is principally an Asian phenomenon. Asia's total of cities of this size has grown from two to seven between 1975 and 1995, and today Asia dominates any list of the world's largest cities (see 6). Even more impressively, eleven of the additional twelve megacities that are expected to emerge by 2015 are in Asian countries, nine of them in south and east Asia. This massive growth is due to a combination of in-migration and natural increase, together with the physical outward expansion of their built-up areas and the incorporation of nearby settlements.

5. CITIES OF OVER 10 MILLION INHABITANTS 1975–2015

Figures are for urban agglomerations as defined in Table 6.

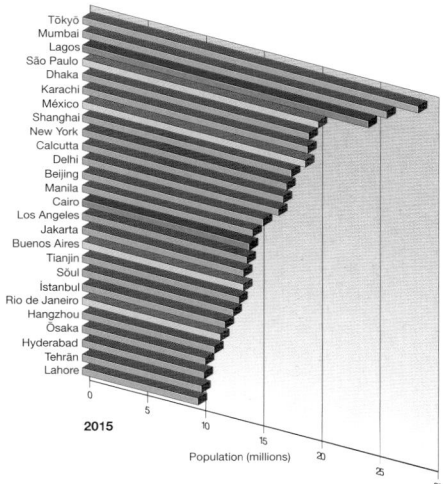

© Bartholomew Ltd

THE DISTRIBUTION OF MINERALS

Geological processes have determined the distribution of mineral resources but the location of productive mines is the result of geological, economic and political factors. The map (see 1) shows the locations of the most important mines producing industrial and metallic minerals. The bulk of world reserves – those resources which can be extracted economically at a particular time – are located at the mines shown.

Many aspects of the distribution of mineral resources are related to the Earth's tectonic structure. For example, the numerous large copper mines around parts of the Pacific rim are related to the destructive plate margins in these areas (see pages 24-25). Most iron ore now comes from giant sedimentary deposits which have been naturally enriched by near-surface processes. These occur in ancient 'cratons' which are areas of the crust which have been internally stable for more than half a billion years and are typified by western Australia, eastern Brazil and the Canadian and Eurasian 'shields'. Output from the main iron ore producers has varied over time, with China becoming the leading world producer in the 1990s (see 2).

Another striking relationship of mineral resources to geography and climate is provided by the distribution of bauxite, the main ore of aluminium. With few exceptions, major bauxite deposits are situated in the tropics, because bauxite is formed by the weathering of rocks at the Earth's surface under tropical climatic conditions (see 3).

TYPES OF MINERAL

Minerals are usually grouped into four classes defined chiefly by their use:

Industrial minerals are minerals such as salt, fluorspar, barytes and sulphur, which are used in their natural state in industrial processes, and phosphate rock and potash which are vital constituents of fertilizers in addition to other uses. Gemstones are a special case in that, with the exception of industrial diamonds which are used as an abrasive, they are valued only for their aesthetic appearance.

Metallic minerals are mined to extract the metals they contain. Deposits of metallic minerals are evaluated chiefly on the costs of mining the ore and of extracting the metal from it.

Construction minerals such as sand, gravel, clay and gypsum, are used to make building materials. Their production costs are relatively low, but because their transport costs are high, they are normally used close to where they are produced. They are produced in most countries and are not shown on the map.

Energy minerals comprise coal, oil and natural gas, collectively known as 'fossil fuels', and uranium, the raw material for nuclear power. In terms of mass they are the most important traded minerals. Uranium is shown on the map; the others are shown on pages 38-39.

MINERAL PRODUCTION

Economies of scale have always been a strong influence on the geographic patterns of mineral production: a very large orebody is able to supply a significant proportion of world demand and can often be worked at a lower unit cost than a smaller deposit. Thus, for example, only a handful of giant mines in the Americas dominate the world supply of copper (see 4). Similar geographical concentration of supply are marked also in other minerals, including chromium and nickel (see 5 and 6). Production of gold (see 7) and diamonds was until fairly recently dominated by southern African countries but advances in exploration and processing technology have led to many new discoveries of both of these commodities in other continents, notably Australia and North America. China is the dominant producer of tungsten, antimony and fluorspar (see 8), having a large number of small to medium sized mines. The absence of mines of these materials elsewhere indicates not a lack of resources, but a lack of economic reserves.

1. LOCATION OF SIGNIFICANT MINES

Producing mines or major deposits in active development, 1999
See table below for index to sites
Winkel Tripel Projection
scale 1:100 000 000

	>5% of world production
	1-5% of world production
	Other selected deposits (<1% of world production)

METALLIC MINERALS

- Iron **Fe**
- Copper **Cu**
- Gold **Au**
- Uranium **U**
- Aluminium **Al**
- Manganese **Mn**
- Lead **Pb**, Zinc **Zn**, Cadmium **Cd**, Silver **Ag**
- Tin **Sn**, Tantalum **Ta**, Beryllium **Be**, Antimony **Sb**, Mercury **Hg**, Bismuth **Bi**, Caesium **Cs**, Rubidium **Rb**
- Nickel **Ni**, Molybdenum **Mo**, Niobium **Nb**, Cobalt **Co**, Chromium **Cr**, Platinum **Pt**, Palladium **Pd**, Vanadium **V**, Tungsten **W**

INDUSTRIAL (NON METALLIC) MINERALS

- Potash **K**, Phosphate **P**, Borates **B**, Sulphur **S**, Lithium **Li**
- Baryte **Ba**, Fluorspar **F**, Asbestos **Asb**
- Titanium minerals (ilmenite, rutile) **Ti**, Zircon **Zr**
- Diamonds **Diam.**

2. IRON ORE PRODUCERS 1972-1998

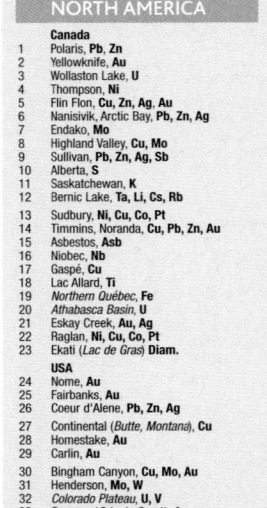

China
Former Soviet Union[1]
Brazil
Australia
India
USA
Canada
South Africa
France
Liberia

[1]Ukraine: 111.8
Russian Federation: 72.3
Kazakhstan: 18.0

(y-axis: Tonnes (millions), 0–300; x-axis: Year 1972, 1977, 1982, 1987, 1992, 1997, 1998)

3. ALUMINIUM ORE PRODUCTION 1998

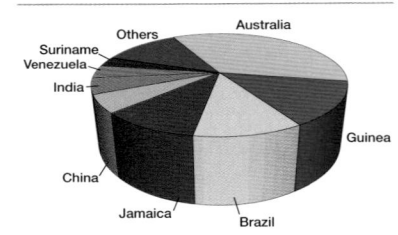

Others, Suriname, Venezuela, India, China, Jamaica, Brazil, Guinea, Australia

4. COPPER PRODUCTION 1998

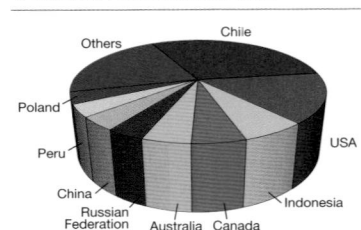

Others, Chile, USA, Indonesia, Canada, Australia, Russian Federation, China, Peru, Poland

INDEX TO SITES ON THE MAP

KEY: SITE NUMBER, MINE/*PROVINCE*/*DISTRICT*/*AREA*, **MINERALS**

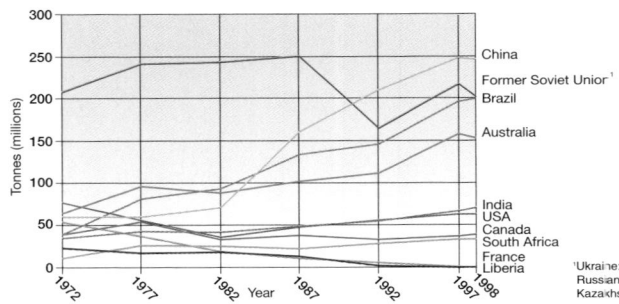

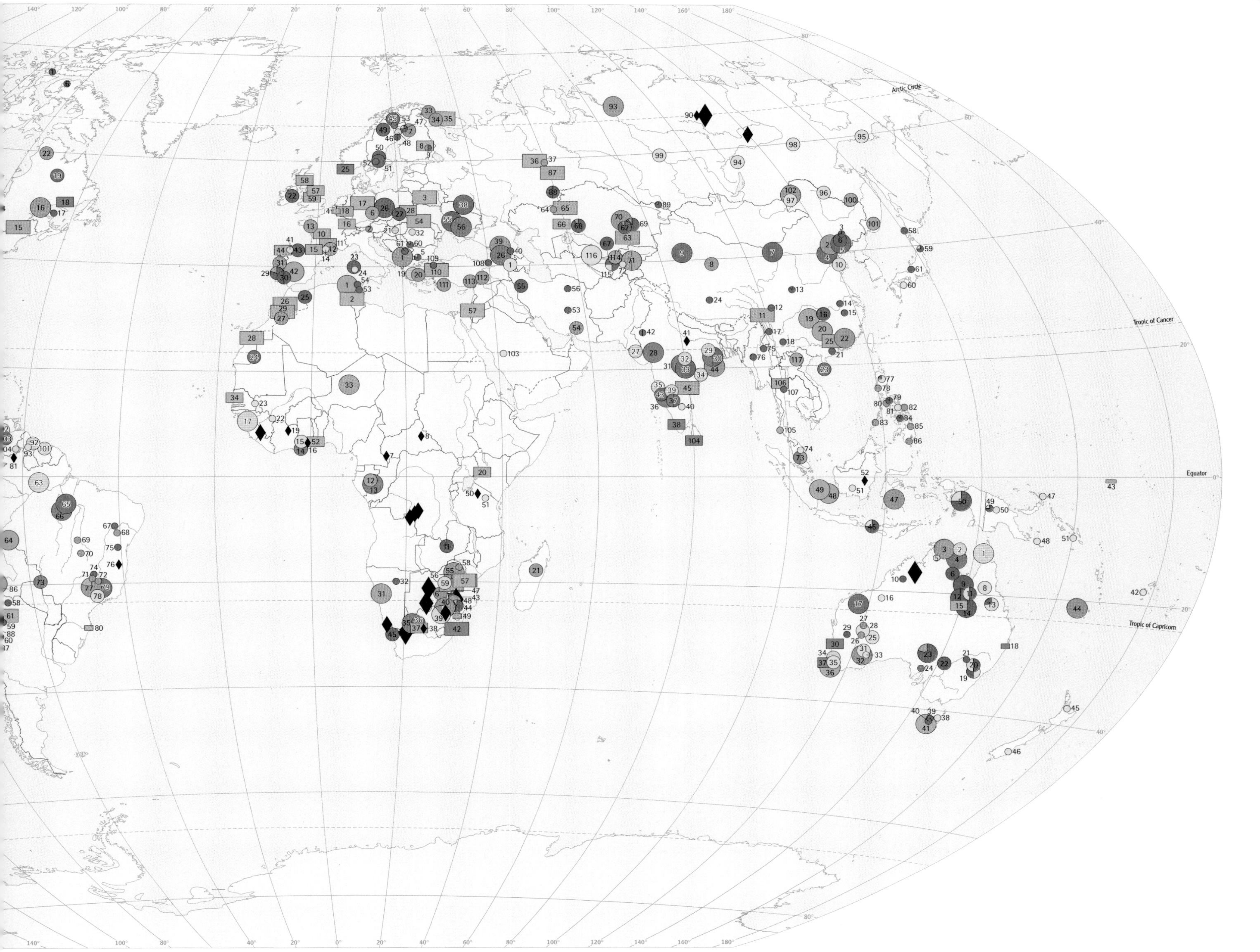

Equator

Tropic of Cancer

Tropic of Capricorn

Arctic Circle

---

5. CHROMIUM ORE PRODUCTION 1998

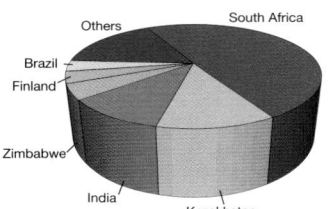

Others · South Africa · Brazil · Finland · Zimbabwe · India · Kazakhstan

6. NICKEL PRODUCTION 1998

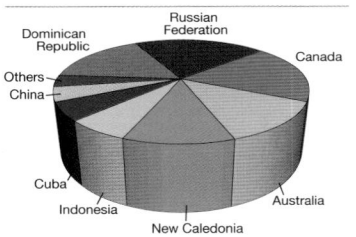

Russian Federation · Dominican Republic · Canada · Others · China · Australia · Cuba · Indonesia · New Caledonia

7. GOLD PRODUCTION 1972–1998

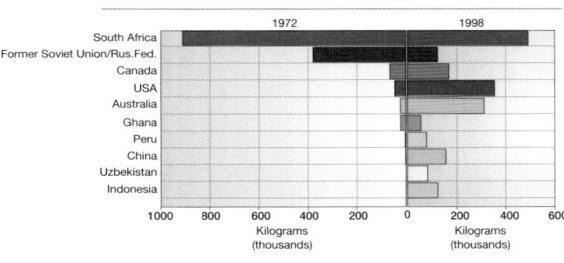

	1972	1998
South Africa		
Former Soviet Union/Rus.Fed.		
Canada		
USA		
Australia		
Ghana		
Peru		
China		
Uzbekistan		
Indonesia		

1000 800 600 400 200 0 200 400 600
Kilograms (thousands)   Kilograms (thousands)

8. FLUORSPAR PRODUCTION 1998

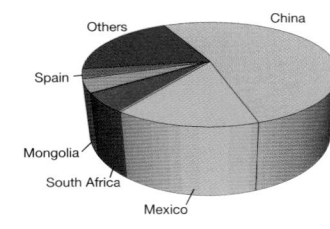

Others · China · Spain · Mongolia · South Africa · Mexico

Liberia
18 Kono, Sanniquellie, Macenta, **Diam.**

Madagascar
21 Andriamena, **Cr**

Mali
22 Syama, **Au**
23 Sadiola, **Au**

Mauritania
24 Fdérik, **Fe**

Morocco
25 Touissit, Boubeker, **Pb, Zn, Ag**
26 Central Morocco, **P**
27 Bou Azzer, **Co**
28 Boukra, **P**
29 Jebel Irhoud, Jebel Zelmou, **Ba, F**

Namibia
30 Oranjemund, **Diam.**
31 Rossing, **U**
32 Kombat, **Pb, Zn, Ag**

Niger
33 Agadez, **U**

Senegal
34 Taiba, **P**

Sierra Leone
35 Kono, Sanniquellie, Macenta, **Diam.**

South Africa, Republic of
35 Northern Cape, **Mn**
36 Sishen, **Fe**
37 Griqualand, **Asb**
38 Kimberley, **Diam.**
39 Witwatersrand, **Au, U**
40 Bushveld, **Cr, Pt, Ni, V, F**
41 Premier Mine, **Diam.**
42 Richards Bay, **Ti, Zr**
43 Murchison Range, **Sb**
44 Phalaborwa, **Cu, P**

45 Black Mountain, **Pb, Zn, Ag**
46 Finsch, **Diam.**
47 Messina, **Cu**
48 Venetia, **Diam.**

Swaziland
49 Swaziland, **Asb**

Tanzania
50 Northern Tanzania, **Diam.**
51 Golden Pride, **Au**

Togo
52 Hahotoé, Akoumapé, **P**

Tunisia
2 Djebel Onk and Gafsa Region, **P**
53 Northern Tunisia, **Pb, F**
54 Bou Grine, **Zn, Pb**

Zambia
11 Copperbelt, **Cu, Co**

Zimbabwe
55 Great Dyke, **Cr, Pt, Pd**
56 Zvishavane, **Asb**
57 Bikita, **Li, Be**
58 Bindura, **Ni, Cu**
59 Bulawayo, **Au**

ASIA

Armenia
1 Armenia, **Cu, Mo, Au**

China
2 Jinzhou, **Mo**
3 Hongtoushan, **Cu, Zn**
4 Shijiaying, Shuicheng, **Fe**
5 Nanfen, **Fe**
6 Chengchengtsu, **Pb, Zn**
7 Bayan Obo, **Fe**
8 Jinchuan, **Ni, Cu**
9 Xinjiang Uygur Zizhiqu (Sinkiang), **Fe**

10 Penglai, **Au**
11 Sichuan, **Asb**
12 Cheng Xian, **Pb, Zn**
13 Changduicheng, **Cu, Mo**
14 Shinchao, **Cu**
15 Tongshankou, **Cu**
16 Dexing, **Cu, Ag, Au**
17 Lanping, **Pb, Zn**
18 Zhehai, **Sn**
19 Hunan-Sichuan, **Hg, Sb**
20 Hunan-Guangxi, **Sn, W**
21 Fankou, **Pb, Zn**
22 South Jiangxi, Guangdong, **W**
23 Hainan, **Fe**
24 Xitieshan, **Pb, Zn**
25 South China, **Ba, F**

Georgia
26 Chiatura, **Mn**

India
27 Bhuj, **Al**
28 Panch Mahals, **Mn**
29 Ranchi, **Al**
30 Bihar, Orissa, **Fe, Mn**
31 Nagpur, Balaghat, **Mn**
32 Madhya Pradesh, **Al**
33 Rowghat, Bailadila, **Fe**
34 Koraput, **Al**
35 Maharashtra, **Al**
36 Karnataka, **Fe**
37 Southeast Kerala (Travancore), **Ti, Zr**
38 Hutti, **Al**
39 Kolar, **Au**
40 Majhgawan, **Diam.**
41 Rajasthan, **Cu, Zn, Pb, Ag**
42 Goa, **Fe**
43 Cuttack, **Cr**
44 Mangampet, **Ba**

Indonesia
46 Batu Hijau, **Cu, Au**
47 Pomalaa, **Ni**
48 Belitung, **Sn**
49 Bangka, **Sn**
50 Grasberg, **Cu, Au**
51 Kelian, **Au**
52 Kalimantan, **Diam.**

Iran
53 Sar Cheshmeh, **Cu, Ag, Au, Mo**
54 Faryab Area, **Cr**
55 Angorhan, **Pb, Zn**
56 Nakhlak, **Pb, Zn, Ag**

Israel
57 Dead Sea Region, **K, P**

Japan
58 Toyoha, **Pb, Zn, Ag**
59 Hokuroko District, **Pb, Zn, Ag, Cu**
60 Hishikari, **Au**
61 Kamioka, **Pb, Zn, Ag**

Jordan
Dead Sea Region, **K, P**

Kazakhstan
62 Balkhash, **Cu, Mo**
63 Chiganak, Baikanour, **Ba**
64 Khrom Tau, **Cr**
65 Kiembay, **Asb**
66 Kara Tau, **P**
67 Achisay, **Pb, Zn, Ag**
68 Dzhezkazgan, **Cu, Ag**
69 Kounrad, **Cu, Mo**
70 Akchatau, **W, Mo**

Kyrgystan
71 Kyrgyzstan, **Hg, Sb, U**
72 Kumtor, **Au**

Malaysia
73 Malaya, **Sn, Ti**
74 Penjom, **Au**

Myanmar
75 Bawdwin, **Zn, Pb, Ag**
76 Monywa, **Cu**

Philippines
77 Luzon, **Au, Cu**
78 Zambales Mountains, **Cr**
79 Marinduque, **Cu, Mo, Au**
80 Mindoro, **Ni, Co**
81 Masbate, **Au**
82 Samar, **Cr**
83 Palawan, **Ni, Co**
84 Cebu, **Cu, Mo, Au**
85 Northern Mindanao, **Ni, Co**
86 Southern Mindanao, **Ni, Co**

Russian Federation (in Asia)
87 Bazhenovskoye, **Asb**
88 Central Urals, **Cu, Zn, Au**
89 Altay, **Pb, Zn, Ag, Cu**
90 Alakit, **Diam.**
91 Daldyn, **Diam.**
92 Malaya Botuobiya, **Diam.**
93 Noril'sk, **Ni, Cu, Pt, Co**
94 Lena, Vitim, **Au**
95 Magadan Region, **Au**
96 Amur, **Au**
97 Zabaykal'sk, **Au**
98 Yakutsk, **Au**
99 Yenisey, **Au**
100 Birobidzhan, **Sn**
101 Primorskiy Kray, **Sn, W**
102 Chitinskaya, **W, Sn**

Saudi Arabia
103 Madh adh Dhahab, **Au, Ag, Cu, Zn**

Sri Lanka
104 Southern Sri Lanka, **Ti, Zr**

Thailand
105 Southern Thailand, Phuket, **Sn, W**
106 Northern Thailand, **Ba, F**

107 Mae Sod, **Zn, Cd**

Turkey
108 Murgul, **Cu**
109 Biga Region, **Pb, Zn, Ag, Ba**
110 Balikesir, Emet, **B**
111 Fethiye, **Cr**
112 Malatya, Guleman, **Cr, Fe**
113 Karsanti, **Cr**

Uzbekistan/Tajikistan
114 Almalyk, **U, F**
115 Southeast Uzbekistan/Tajikistan, **Cu, Au,**
116 Muruntau, Zarafshan, **Au**

Vietnam
117 Vietnam, **Sn**

OCEANIA

Australia
1 Weipa, **Al**
2 Gove, **Al**
3 Ranger, **U**
4 Groote Eylandt, **Mn**
5 Mount Todd, **Au**
6 McArthur River, **Pb, Zn, Ag**
7 Argyll, **Diam.**
8 Kidston, **Au, Ag**
9 Century, **Zn, Pb, Ag**
10 Lennard Shelf, **Zn, Pb, Ag**
11 Ernest Henry, **Cu, Au**
12 Mount Isa Region, **Cu, Pb, Zn, Ag**
13 Mount Leyshon, **Au, Ag**
14 Cannington, **Ag, Pb**
15 Phosphate Hill, **P**
16 Telfer, **Au**
17 Hamersley Range, **Fe**
18 Sydney, Brisbane, **Ti, Zr**
19 Cadia, **Au, Cu**
20 North Parkes, **Cu, Au, Ag**

21 Elura, **Zn, Pb**
22 Broken Hill, **Pb, Zn, Ag**
23 Olympic Dam, **Cu, U**
24 Middleback Ranges, **Fe**
25 Granny Smith, **Au**
26 Leinster, **Ni, Cu**
27 Mount Keith, **Ni, Cu**
28 Agnew, **Au**
29 Golden Grove, **Zn, Ag, Au, Cu**
30 Eneabba, **Ti, Zr**
31 Kalgoorlie Region, **Au, Ag**
32 Kambalda, **Ni, Cu, Co, Pt**
33 St Ives, **Au**
34 Darling Ranges, **Al**
35 Boddington, **Au, Cu**
36 Greenbushes, **Ta, Li**
37 Capel, **Ti, Zr**
38 Beaconsfield, **Au**
39 Hellyer, **Zn, Pb, Ag**
40 Rosebery, **Zn, Pb, Ag**
41 Renison Bell, **Sn**

Fiji
42 Viti Levu, Emperor, **Au**

Nauru
43 Nauru, **P**

New Caledonia
44 New Caledonia, **Ni, Co**

New Zealand
45 Martha Hill, **Au, Ag**
46 Macraes, **Au, Ag**

Papua New Guinea
47 Lihir, **Au**
48 Misima, **Au, Ag**
49 Ok Tedi, **Cu, Au**
50 Porgera, **Au**

Solomon Islands
51 Gold Ridge, **Au**

© Bartholomew Ltd

ENERGY PRODUCTION AND CONSUMPTION

The world's energy resources are unevenly distributed (*see 1*). Similarly, the geography of energy production and consumption is highly uneven, with three countries, the USA, Russian Federation and China, dominating both the production and consumption of energy (*see 2*). Some countries – typically the oil-exporting states, such as Saudi Arabia, Nigeria, Venezuela, Mexico and Indonesia – produce much more than they consume, but many of the most advanced industrial economies, such as the USA and Japan, consume vastly more energy than they produce. The USA is the largest single energy consumer, using over a quarter of the world's energy despite having only 5 per cent of its population.

As a result of the uneven geography of production and consumption, energy sources are the largest single item in international trade (*see 3*). Taking the example of oil, some regions are net exporters, such as the Middle East and West Africa. Others rely heavily upon imported oil and so have to generate wealth by other means to be able to pay for their imports. These include the USA, Central and Western Europe and Japan (*see 4*).

2. WORLD'S TOP 10 ENERGY PRODUCERS AND CONSUMERS 1998

Million tonnes of oil equivalent

Producers		Consumers	
USA	1 835	USA	2 389
Russian Federation	1 034	China	855
China	835	Russian Federation	655
Saudi Arabia	529	Japan	536
Canada	433	Germany	349
UK	293	India	315
India	251	Canada	299
Iran	249	France	252
Mexico	234	UK	246
Australia	209	Brazil	204
World total	9 631	World total	9 519

3. THE ENERGY TRADE

Major trade flows between trading regions 1999
scale 1:217 000 000

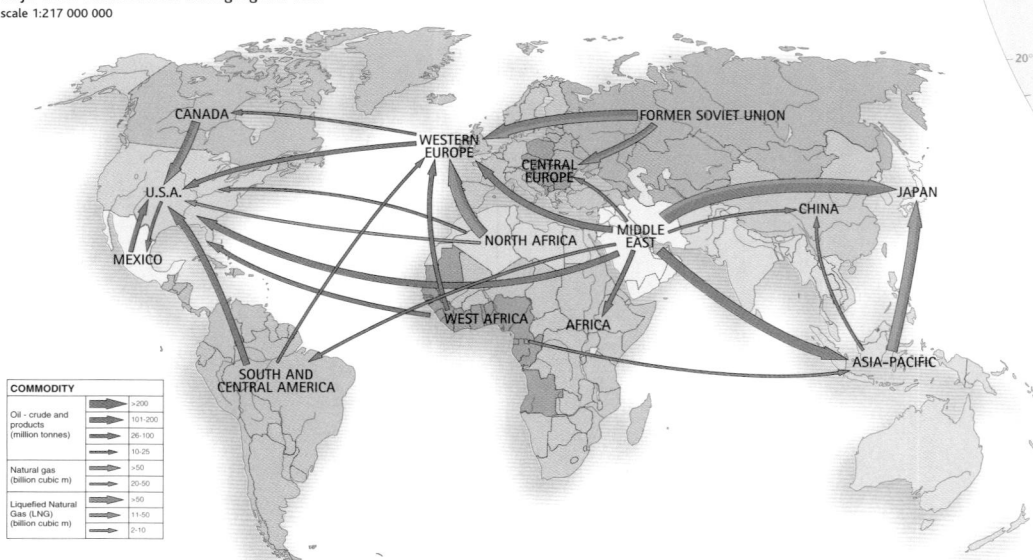

1. DISTRIBUTION OF RESOURCES

Winkel Tripel Projection
scale 1:94 000 000

- ▲ Major oil fields
- ▲ Major gas fields
- ■ Major coal deposits
- ■ Major lignite deposits
- ▽ Major nuclear reactors
- ● Major hydro plants

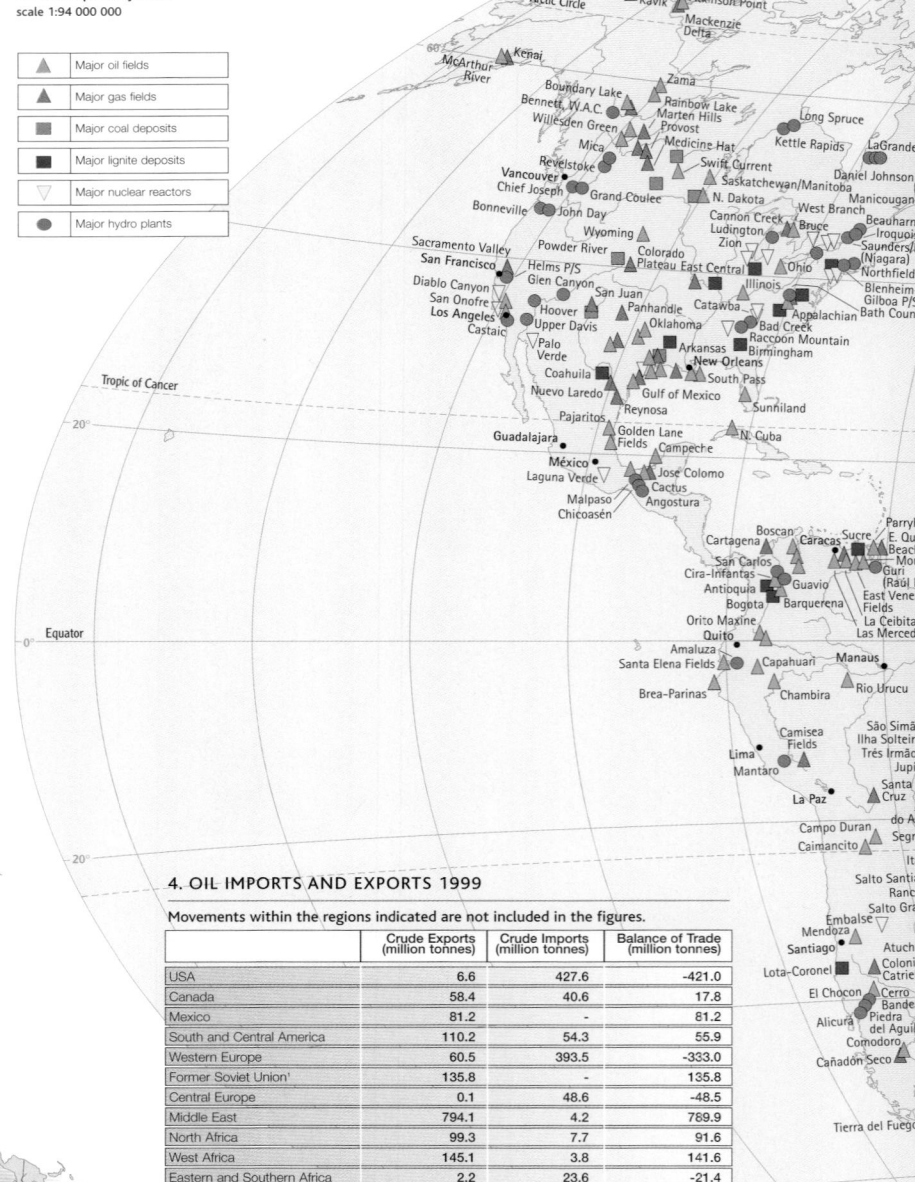

4. OIL IMPORTS AND EXPORTS 1999

Movements within the regions indicated are not included in the figures.

	Crude Exports (million tonnes)	Crude Imports (million tonnes)	Balance of Trade (million tonnes)
USA	6.6	427.6	-421.0
Canada	58.4	40.6	17.8
Mexico	81.2	-	81.2
South and Central America	110.2	54.3	55.9
Western Europe	60.5	393.5	-333.0
Former Soviet Union[1]	135.8	-	135.8
Central Europe	0.1	48.6	-48.5
Middle East	794.1	4.2	789.9
North Africa	99.3	7.7	91.6
West Africa	145.1	3.8	141.6
Eastern and Southern Africa	2.2	23.6	-21.4
Australasia	10.4	28.6	-18.2
China	7.9	36.6	-28.7
Japan	0.2	214.9	-214.7
Other Asia-Pacific	53.6	294.1	-240.5
Unidentified	12.2	-	12.2
Total World	1578.1	1578.1	0.0

1. Comprises: Russian Federation, Estonia, Latvia, Lithuania, Belarus, Ukraine, Moldova, Georgia, Armenia, Azerbaijan, Kazakhstan, Uzbekistan, Turkmenistan, Tajikistan and Kyrgyzstan.

ENERGY RESERVES AND RATES OF CONSUMPTION

Proven energy reserves are also unevenly distributed (*see 5*). Nearly two-thirds of proven oil reserves are concentrated in the Middle East. Reserves in the USA and Russian Federation have declined and Europe's reserves are expected to dry up early this century. Central America and Africa are expected to cease oil exports around 2025. Proven reserves of natural gas are dominated by the Former Soviet Union and the Middle East while coal reserves are more evenly distributed between the Asia-Pacific region, North America and the Former Soviet Union.

Between 1989 and 1999 the world level of primary energy consumption increased by 11 per cent (*see 6*). This change was led by the Middle East with a 52 per cent increase, followed by South and Central America with a 38 per cent rise. Relatively costly energy in Europe depressed consumption to the comparatively low growth level of 2 per cent, while the dissolution of the Soviet Union led to the collapse in consumption there by over a third. If rates of energy consumption were to remain constant, then it has been estimated that proven oil reserves would last forty years, natural gas sixty years and coal three hundred years. However, because energy consumption rates are increasing these estimates may need revision.

6. PRIMARY ENERGY CONSUMPTION

Million tonnes of oil equivalent

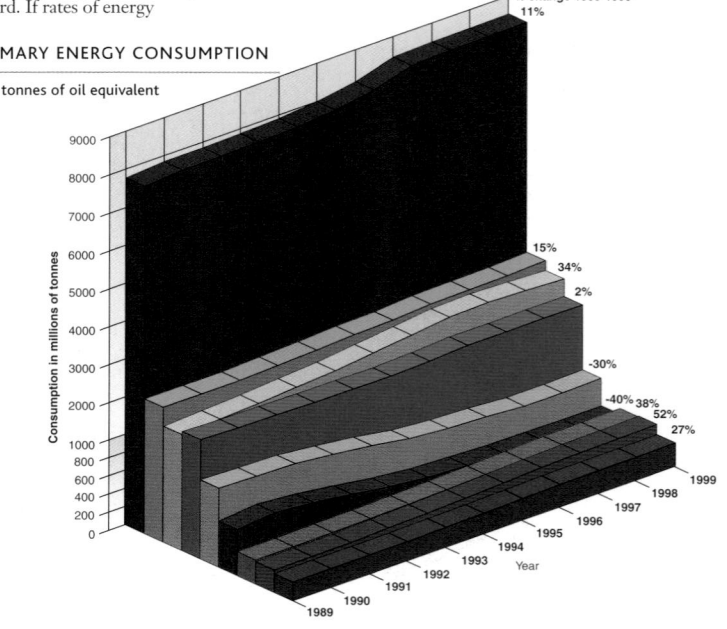

5. PROVEN ENERGY RESERVES 1999

	💧	%	🔥	%	⬛	%
North America[1]	8.4	6.0	7.31	5.0	256 477	26.1
South & Central America	12.9	9.2	6.31	4.3	21 574	2.2
Europe	2.7	1.9	5.15	3.5	122 032	12.4
Former Soviet Union[2]	9.0	6.4	56.70	38.7	230 178	23.4
Middle East	91.5	65.2	49.52	33.8	193	-
Africa	10.0	7.1	11.16	7.7	61 412	6.2
Asia-Pacific	5.9	4.2	10.28	7.0	292 345	29.7
World	140.4	100	146.43	100	984.211	100

1. Canada, USA and Mexico 2. See footnote for table 4

💧 Oil (thousand million barrels) 🔥 Natural Gas (trillion cubic metres) ⬛ Coal (million tonnes)

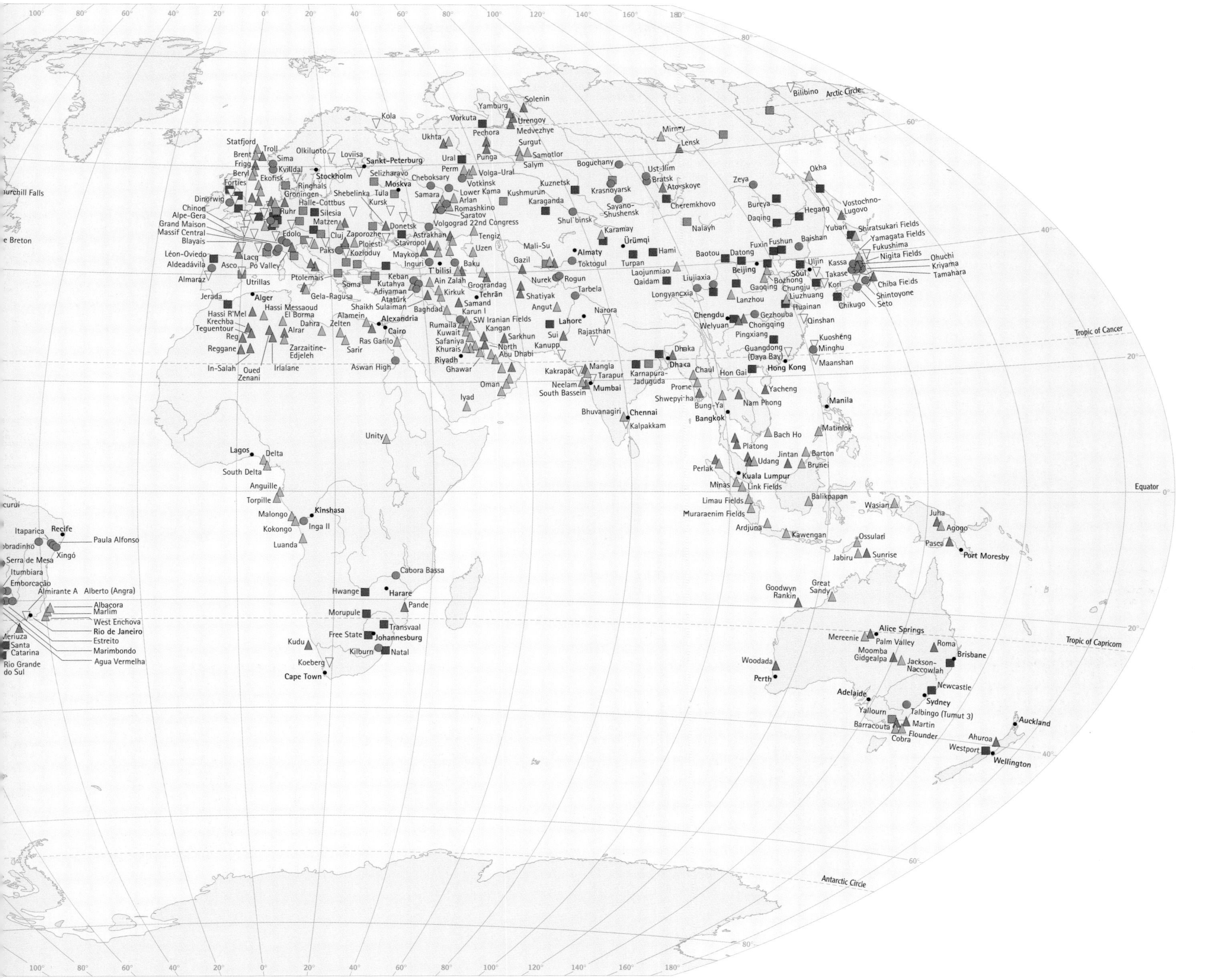

Churchill Falls
e Breton

Statfjord
Brent Troll Sima Olkiluoto
Frigg Ekofisk Kvilldal Loviisa
Beryl Forties Stockholm
Dinorwig Ringhals Selizharovo Cheboksary
Chinon Halle-Cottbus Moskva Votkinsk
Alpe-Gera Groningen Tula Kursk Lower Kama Kushmurun
Grand Maison Ruhr Silesia Samara Romashkino
Massif Central Matzen Donetsk Volgograd 22nd Congress
Blayais Edolo Zaporozhe Saratov Karaganda
Léon-Oviedo Lacq Paks Kozloduy Astrakhan Tengiz
Aldeadávila Asco Po Valley Maykop Uzen
Almaraz Utrillas T'bilisi Baku
Jerada Alger Keban Inguri Gazli
Hassi R'Mel Gela-Ragusa Kutahya Soma Adiyaman Grograndag
Krechba El Borma Alameim Ataturk Kirkuk Tehrān
Teguentour Reg Dahra Zelten Alexandria Baghdad SW Iranian Fields
Reggane Alrar Cairo Rumaila Kangan
In-Salah Zarzaitine- Ras Garlio Kuwait Safaniya Sarkhun
Zenani Edjeleh Sarir Riyadh North Abu Dhabi Kanupp
Irlalane Aswan High Khurais Sui
Ghawar Oman

Lagos Delta Unity
South Delta
Anguille
Torpille Bhuvanagiri Chennai
Malongo Kokongo Inga II Kalpakkam
Luanda

Itaparica Recife
obradinho Paula Alfonso
Serra de Mesa Xingó
Itumbiara
Emborcação
Almirante A Alberto (Angra)
Albacora
Marlim Hwange Harare
West Erichova Morupule Pande
Rio de Janeiro
Estreito Free State Transvaal
Marimbondo Kudu Johannesburg
Agua Vermelha Kilburn Natal
Santa Catarina Koeberg
Rio Grande do Sul Cape Town

Kola
Vorkuta Yamburg Solenin Bilibino Arctic Circle
Urengoy Mirny
Pechora Medvezhye Lensk
Ukhta Punga Surgut Samotlor
Ural Volga-Ural Salym Boguchany Ust-Ilim
Perm Kuznetsk Krasnoyarsk Bratsk Atosskoye Zeya Okha
Shebelinka Kushmurun Sayano- Bureya Hegang Vostochno-
Mali-Su Almaty Shushensk Cheremkhovo Daqing Lugovo
Nalayh Ürümqi Karamay Fuxin Fushun Baishan Yubari Shiratsukari Fields
Baotou Datong Yamagata Fields
Turpan Beijing Fukushima
Laojunmiao Qaidam Bozhong Sŏul Nigita Fields
Longyangxia Liujiaxia Chongqing Gaoqing Uljin Kassa Ohuchi
Chengdu Lanzhou Liuzhuang Kori Chiba Fields Kriyama
Welyuan Gezhouba Takase Shintoyone Tamahara
Pingxiang Chongqing Chikugo Seto
Guangdong Qinshan
(Daya Bay) Kuosheng
Hong Kong Minghu
Prome Maanshan
Dhaka Chaul Hon Gai Yacheng
Kakrapar Mangla Karnapura- Hon Dha
Neelam Tarapur Jaduguda Bung-Ya Manila
South Bassein Mumbai Shwepyi-ha Nam Phong
Bangkok Bach Ho Matinlok
Platong Jintan Barton
Perlak Udang Brunei
Kuala Lumpur Link Fields
Minas Balikpapan Wasian Juha
Limau Fields Agogo
Murraenim Fields Pasca
Ardjuna Kawengan Ossulari Port Moresby
Jabiru Sunrise
Goodwyn Great
Rankin Sandy
Alice Springs
Mereenie Palm Valley Roma
Moomba Jackson- Brisbane
Woodada Gidgealpa Naccowlah
Perth Newcastle
Adelaide Sydney
Yallourn Talbingo (Tumut 3) Auckland
Barracouta Martin Ahuroa
Cobra Flounder Westport Wellington

Tropic of Cancer
Equator
Tropic of Capricorn
Antarctic Circle

ALTERNATIVE ENERGY SOURCES

Alternatives to traditional energy sources are nuclear power and renewable resources. Consumption of nuclear power (*see 7*) has been at relatively low levels and has grown more slowly than traditional energy sources. Asia-Pacific and South and Central America have experienced the highest growth in the past decade, led by Japan, which generates two-thirds of its electricity from nuclear sources. The question of sustainability has underpinned the search for new sources of energy which are less detrimental to the environment than traditional sources and nuclear power. One proposed solution is conservation through increased energy efficiency, i.e. increasing the ratio of useful energy input to output. Other solutions lie in energy resources which are renewable, such as geothermal, wind, solar, biomass and hydropower. Around 5 per cent of total primary energy requirements in Australia, Austria, Canada, Denmark, Sweden and Switzerland are currently met by renewables. The most successful form of renewable energy has been hydroelectric power, consumption of which has risen over 20 per cent in world terms between 1989 and 1999 (*see 8*), with South and Central America showing the largest rise (52 per cent), followed by Asia-Pacific (31 per cent).

7. NUCLEAR ENERGY CONSUMPTION

Million tonnes of oil equivalent

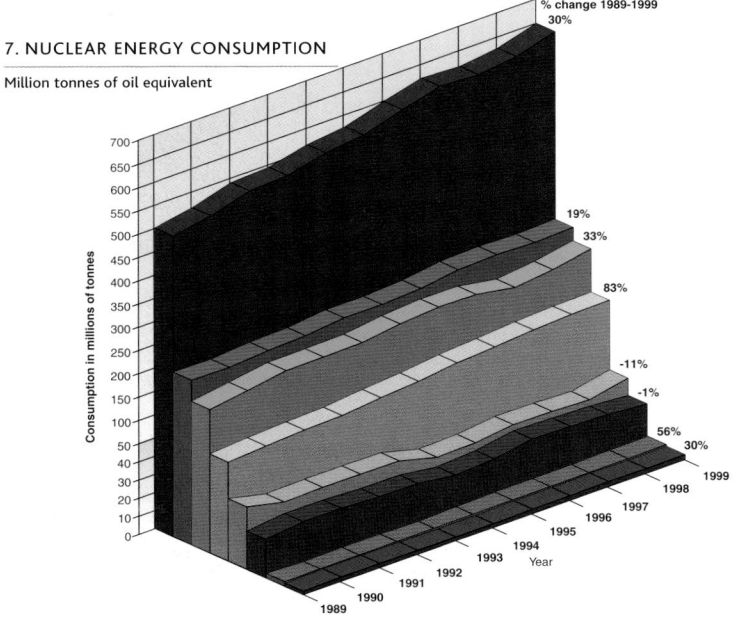

8. HYDROELECRICITY CONSUMPTION

Million tonnes of oil equivalent

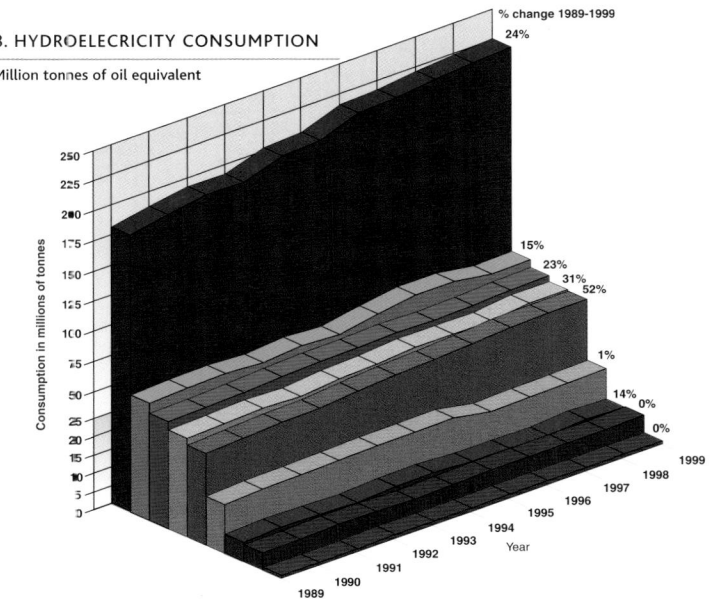

© Bartholomew Ltd

GLOBAL TOURISM AND AIR TRAVEL

The globalization of the world's social, economic and financial markets, whereby physical and political boundaries are no longer obstacles to movement between countries, has been made possible by improved transport and telecommunications networks. The growth of international air travel has meant that more people can move between countries with greater frequency and more cheaply.

International tourism grew throughout the world in the latter part of the 20th century. Between 1989-1999 the average annual growth rate for international tourist arrivals worldwide was nearly 5 per cent (over 230 million people – see 1). This global figure masks wide regional variations, however (see 2). Europe contributes the most to worldwide figures in terms of volume, but the rate of growth there has slowed, due mainly to the growing accessibility of East Asian and Pacific destinations. The regional share of tourist arrivals in this region has grown significantly in the last thirty years.

Improvements in air transport technology, an increasing number of air carriers and favourable economic conditions have combined to produce large increases in worldwide air travel. Passenger and freight traffic grew steadily in the latter half of the 20th century and this pattern is expected to continue. The largest proportion of international travel today occurs between the USA and Europe, and within the East Asia and Pacific region (see 3). Routes between the Middle East and both Africa and Europe – carrying high numbers of passengers in the 1980s – have been overtaken by routes within the East Asia and Pacific region and by long haul flights from Europe to East Asia and western USA. The pattern is reinforced by airport statistics (see 4). Airports in the USA – where air travel is used as much for internal as for international travel – and Europe dominate. However, as Far Eastern economies have developed, these countries have become more popular destinations for both business and leisure travellers.

1. INTERNATIONAL TOURIST ARRIVALS 1989 – 1999

'Tourist' refers to a visitor (visiting for either leisure or business) who stays for at least one night in the country visited

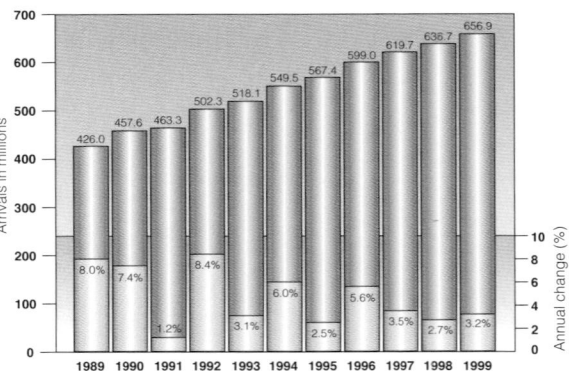

2. REGIONAL SHARE OF INTERNATIONAL TOURIST ARRIVALS 1970–1999

Height of each chart relates to total worldwide tourist arrivals

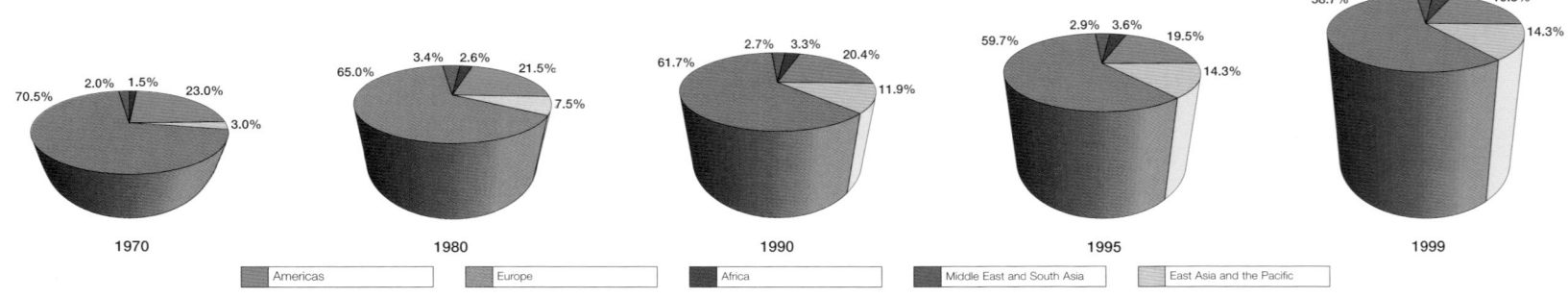

| Americas | Europe | Africa | Middle East and South Asia | East Asia and the Pacific |

3. BUSIEST SCHEDULED INTERNATIONAL AIR PASSENGER ROUTES 1999

Figures are for scheduled international passenger traffic in both directions. Land colours represent World Tourism Organization regions
Briesemeister Projection
scale 1:129 500 000

thickness of line symbolizes volume of international passenger traffic
• World's busiest airports

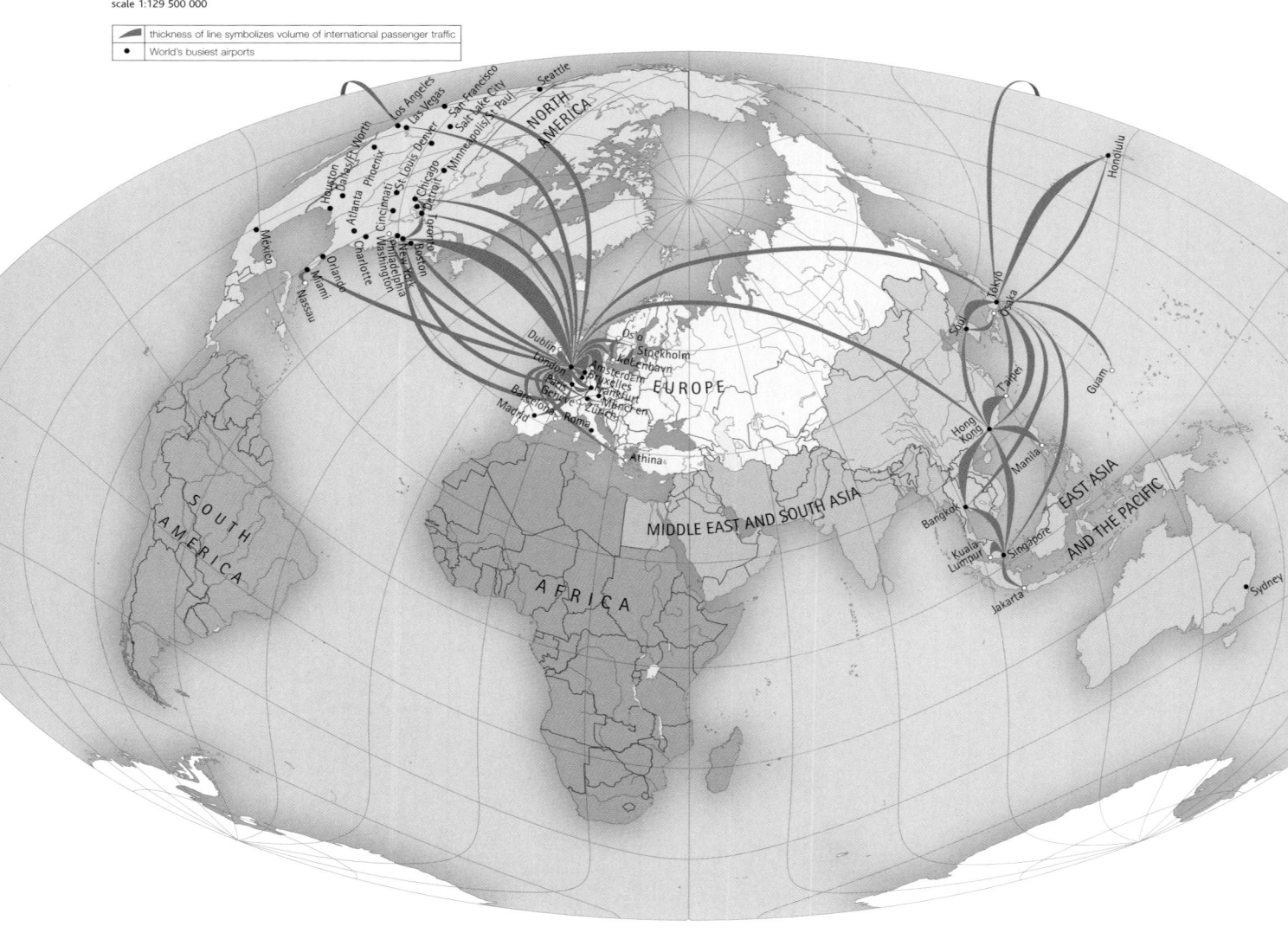

Route	Number of passengers
London–New York	3 793 405
Amsterdam–London	2 992 447
London–Paris	2 449 049
Hong Kong–T'aipei	2 381 710
Sŏul–Tōkyō	2 154 211
Kuala Lumpur–Singapore	2 073 874
Bangkok–Hong Kong	1 975 228
Frankfurt–London	1 928 209
Honolulu–Tōkyō	1 890 343
Bangkok–Singapore	1 798 607
Hong Kong–Tōkyō	1 678 542
Hong Kong–Manila	1 463 014
Hong Kong–Singapore	1 456 021
Dublin–London	1 387 477
Bangkok–Tōkyō	1 286 850
London–Madrid	1 264 659
New York–Toronto	1 262 157
New York–Paris	1 253 899
Los Angeles–London	1 244 180
Bruxelles–London	1 223 334
Jakarta–Singapore	1 181 580
Ōsaka–Sŏul	1 157 984
Hong Kong–Sŏul	1 146 669
Los Angeles–Tōkyō	1 142 747
Chicago–London	1 110 305
London–Zürich	1 083 403
Singapore–Tōkyō	1 071 597
Boston–London	1 055 978
London–Stockholm	1 055 828
Barcelona–London	1 028 320
Madrid–Paris	1 021 285
London–San Francisco	1 016 824
Chicago–Toronto	991 529
T'aipei–Tōkyō	986 424
London–München	975 606
Frankfurt–New York	965 365
Frankfurt–Paris	965 231
London–Toronto	945 283
Genève–London	945 223
London–Washington	925 487
London–Tōkyō	924 232
København–London	884 971
London–Miami	882 245
Hong Kong–London	881 924
Honolulu–Ōsaka	871 907
København–Oslo	870 994
Guam–Tōkyō	867 245
Miami–Nassau	858 866
Athina–London	850 610

4. THE WORLD'S BUSIEST AIRPORTS 1999

Figures given are total passenger arrivals and departures.
See map 3 for airport locations

| Atlanta Hartsfield USA 77 939 536 | Chicago O'Hare USA 72 568 076 | Los Angeles USA 63 876 561 | London Heathrow UK 62 263 710 | Dallas/Ft Worth USA 60 000 125 | Tōkyō Haneda Japan 54 338 212 | Frankfurt Germany 45 858 315 | Paris Charles de Gaulle France 43 596 943 | San Francisco USA 40 387 422 | Denver USA 38 034 231 | Amsterdam Netherlands 36 781 015 | Minneapolis/St Paul USA 34 216 331 | Detroit Wayne County USA 34 038 381 | Miami USA 33 899 246 | New York Newark USA 33 814 000 | Las Vegas McCarran USA 33 669 185 | Phoenix Sky Harbor USA 33 533 353 | Sŏul Kimpo South Korea 33 371 074 | Houston USA 33 089 333 | New York JFK USA 32 003 000 | London Gatwick UK 30 559 461 | St Louis Lambert USA 30 188 973 |

INTERNATIONAL TELECOMMUNICATIONS

Increased availability and ownership of telecommunications equipment over the last thirty years (*see 5*) has aided the globalization of the world economy. Over half of the world's fixed telephone lines have been installed since 1987, and the majority of the world's Internet hosts have come on-line since 1997. Network access is uneven, however. Over half of existing telephone lines and cellular phones are in North America and Europe, and over

70 per cent of Internet host computers are located in North America (*see 6*).

One measure of the perceived 'death of distance' is the steady rise in international telephone calls, which has increased nearly 400 per cent since 1988. The map (*see 8*) shows telephone and fax traffic between countries in different continents for routes using at least 100 million minutes of

telecommunications time in 1998. In that year, these streams totalled 27.3 billion minutes, which accounted for approximately 29 per cent of global international traffic.

Growing volumes of data traffic, particularly from the Internet, have boosted demand for international transmission capacity. Most traffic is routed over fibre-optic cables which encode electronic signals into beams of laser

light, which are sent down fine fibres of coated glass. In 1999, the world's trans-oceanic cables could carry approximately 250 gigabits per second (Gbps), which is equivalent to 17.5 million simultaneous phone calls. By 2001, international cable capacity will have grown by close to 400 per cent, although the largest cable systems will still only link a relative handful of countries (*see 7*).

5. WORLD COMMUNICATIONS EQUIPMENT 1970–2000

Source: TeleGeography, Inc and International Telecommunications Union

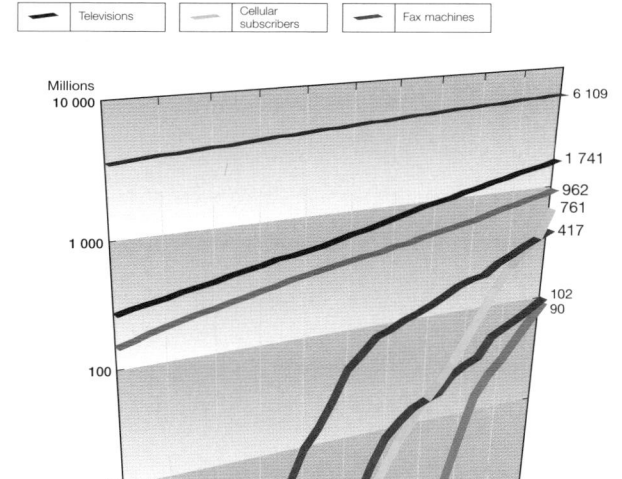

© TeleGeography, Inc.

6. INTERNATIONAL TELECOMMUNICATIONS INDICATORS BY REGION 1998

Source: TeleGeography, Inc and International Telecommunications Union

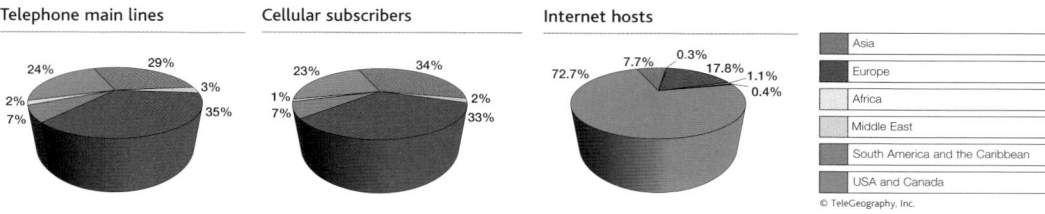

© TeleGeography, Inc.

7. CAPACITY OF MAJOR INTERNATIONAL SUBMARINE CABLES 1999 AND 2001

Each 10 Gbps of cable capacity can carry approximately 700 000 simultaneous calls

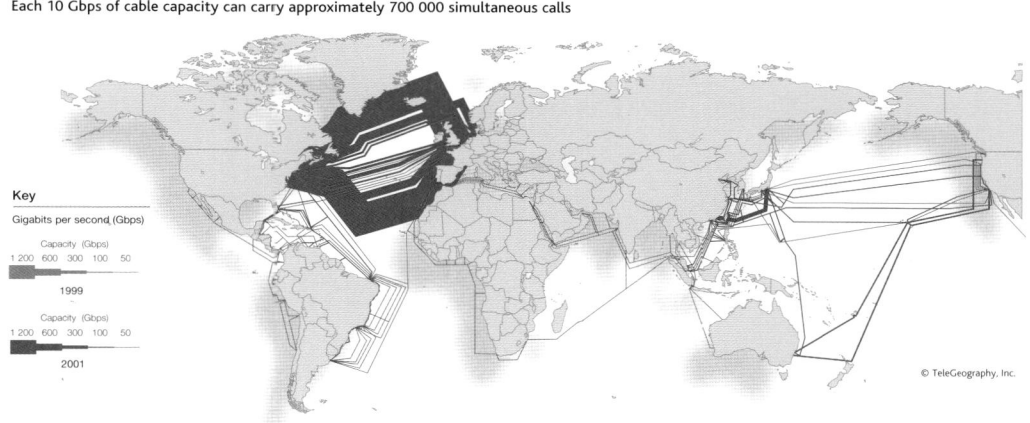

© TeleGeography, Inc.

8. INTERNATIONAL TELECOMMUNICATIONS TRAFFIC 1998

Each band is proportional to the total annual traffic on the public telephone network in both directions between each pair of countries
Robinson Projection
scale 1:144 000 000

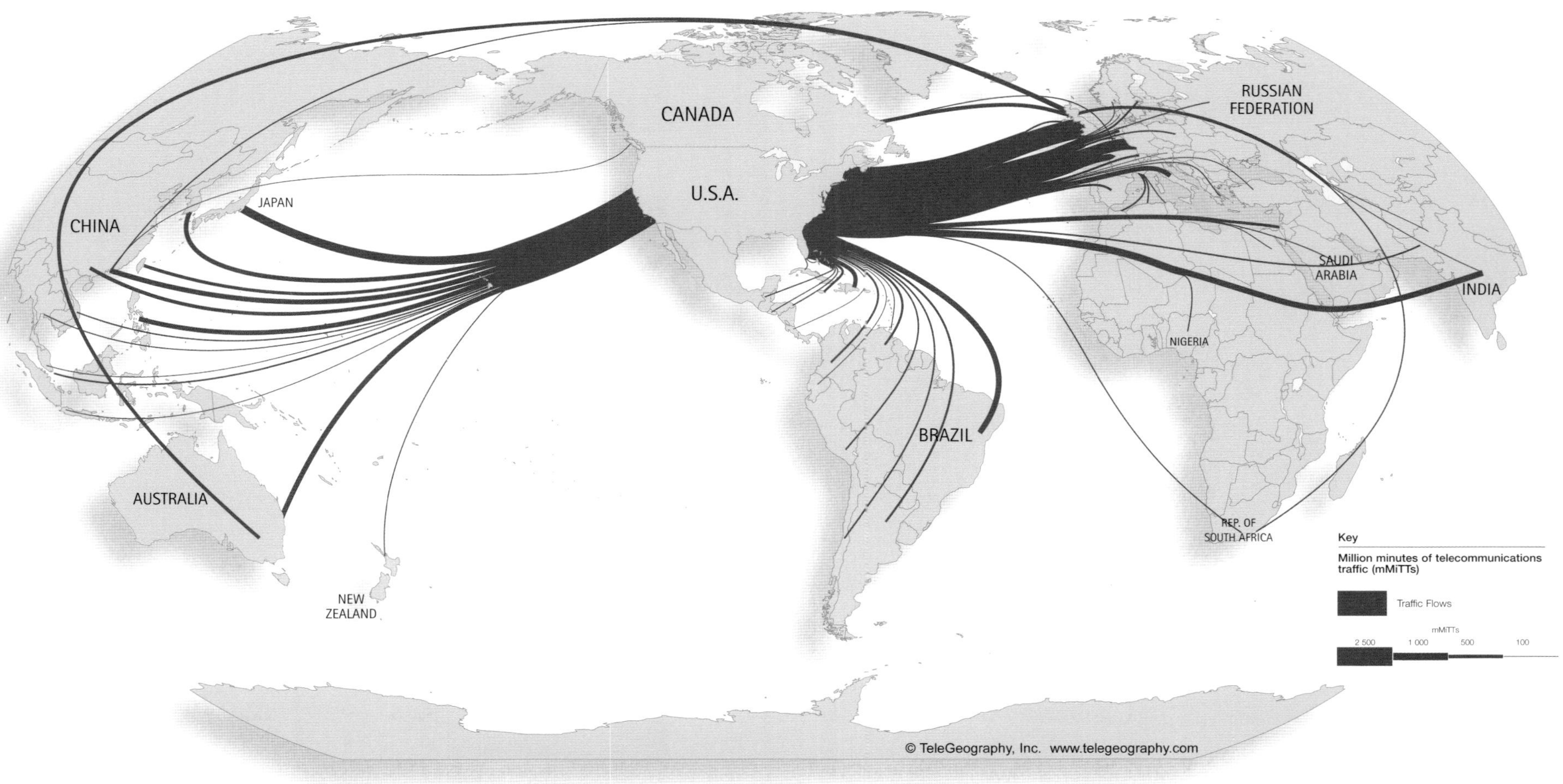

© TeleGeography, Inc. www.telegeography.com

Key

Million minutes of telecommunications traffic (mMiTTs)

Traffic Flows

mMiTTs
2 500   1 000   500   100

Hong Kong
China
29 733 470

Orlando
USA
29 173 491

Toronto Lester B. Pearson
Canada
27 771 473

Seattle/Tacoma
USA
27 699 733

Madrid
Spain
27 532 237

Bangkok
Thailand
27 289 863

Boston
USA
26 964 864

Singapore Changi
Singapore
26 064 645

Tōkyō Narita
Japan
25 667 634

Paris Orly
France
25 349 270

Roma Leonardo da Vinci
Italy
24 023 952

Philadelphia
USA
23 786 285

New York La Guardia
USA
23 796 000

Honolulu
USA
22 640 670

Cincinnati
USA
21 771 689

Sydney Kingsford Smith
Australia
21 542 000

Charlotte
USA
21 449 392

München Franz Josef Strauss
Germany
21 202 906

Zürich
Switzerland
20 900 179

Mexico
Mexico
20 453 568

Salt Lake City
USA
20 033 241

Bruxelles
Belgium
20 025 014

© Bartholomew Ltd

PREHISTORIC AND CLASSICAL CARTOGRAPHY (500 BC – AD 500)

The evolution of mapping has been inextricably linked to people's knowledge of the world and to related scientific and technological developments. Mapping skills have been influenced by factors such as way of life and the nature of the physical environment, and maps can therefore provide an excellent insight into cultures and civilizations. Surviving examples of ancient maps are rare. Their limits of coverage tended to be the extent of the producers' accurate geographical knowledge. Beyond the local area, maps appeared to reflect a speculative or cosmological approach (see 1).

The most significant contribution of the Greeks to cartography was theoretical rather than practical. It is primarily the work of Claudius Ptolemy, a Greek mathematician, astronomer and geographer living in the 2nd century AD, which provides us with information about the level of geographical knowledge at this time. Ptolemy's work *Geographia* included theoretical principles of cartography, lists of place names and computed co-ordinates. Later maps, based on this work, show how he believed the world to look at that time (see 2).

1. MAP OF THE WORLD

Carved on a Babylonian clay tablet, c. 600 BC. Babylon is shown as a rectangle intersected by vertical lines representing the Euphrates river. Small circles show other cities and countries, and the world is encircled by an ocean – the 'Bitter River'. British Museum, Department of Western Asiatic Antiquities, London, UK.

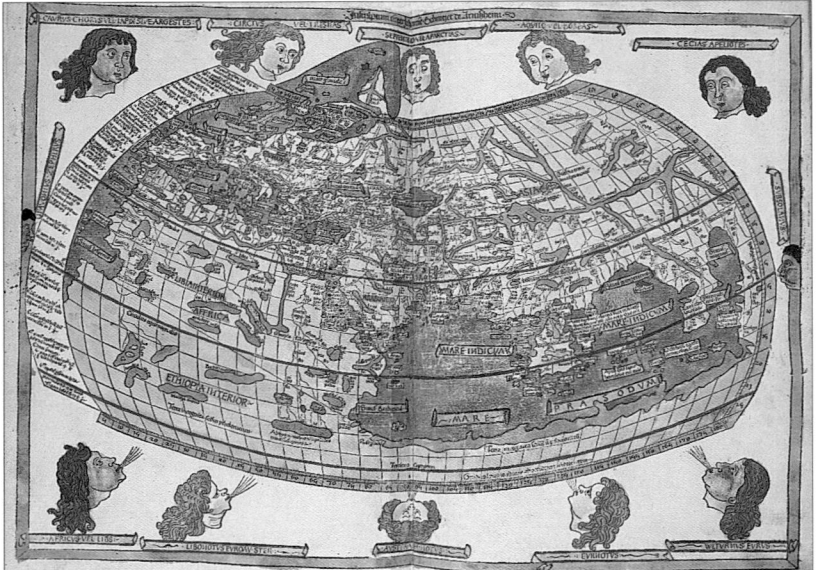

2. PTOLEMAIC WORLD MAP

Based on the work of Claudius Ptolemy, produced by Donis Nicolaus in Ulm, Germany, 1630. The map includes lines of latitude and longitude which give a sense of accuracy. The figures represent different wind directions.
British Library, London, UK.

AD 500–1600

During this period, maps originating in the classical tradition were overlain with later Christian elements. Such maps were usually oval or circular in shape, schematic in content, and centred on Jerusalem. These world maps (*mappæmundi*) conveyed a Christian perspective of the world, and their detail ranged from the virtually diagrammatic to the highly complex (see 3).

Maps from the later medieval period include sea charts, town plans and local, district and route maps. Of these, portolan charts – sea charts designed primarily for navigation – were by far the most significant (see 4). Providing impressively detailed and accurate information on coastlines, harbours and related navigational matters, the charts appear to have been regularly updated. Route maps, for the use of pilgrims and merchants travelling overland, also developed over this period, as exemplified by Matthew Paris's map of the route from London to Otranto, Italy produced around AD 1250 (see 5).

The 15th and 16th centuries were essentially the age of exploration and discovery, a period which witnessed an explosion of global knowledge and a veritable renaissance in cartography. The period saw a great development of world maps, many of which began to include the coastal detail of the earlier portolan charts and to show the latest geographical information resulting from the voyages of discovery. Rome and Venice dominated European map production from 1550 to 1570, but later in the period dominance in mapmaking passed to the Low Countries. This 'Golden Age' of Dutch cartography is exemplified by the first printed 'atlas' of map sheets by Abraham Ortelius in 1570 – the *Theatrum Orbis Terrarum*. The term 'atlas' was coined by Gerard Mercator the Flemish cartographer – perhaps the most widely known figure in the history of cartography. His work, in particular his map projection published in 1569, make him the geographical colossus of the period.

3. THE HEREFORD MAPPAMUNDI

Produced on vellum, and attributed to Richard of Haldingham and Lafford, c. 1290. The map follows the form of a T-O map, centred on Jerusalem, with east to the top. The continents of Asia (top), Africa (lower right) and Europe (lower left) are separated by the Mediterranean Sea and the Nile and Don rivers.
Hereford Cathedral, Hereford, UK.

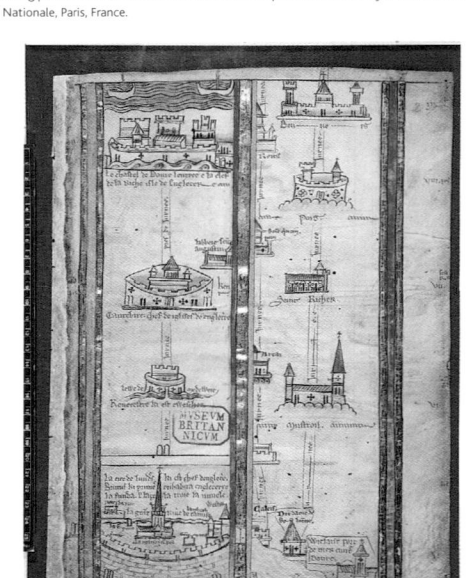

4. THE CARTE PISANE

The oldest surviving portolan chart, c. 1290. It shows most of Europe, with a remarkably detailed coastline of the Mediterranean Sea with Italy and Sicily in the centre.
Bibliothèque Nationale, Paris, France.

5. ITINERARY MAP OF A ROUTE FROM LONDON TO ITALY

Produced by Matthew Paris, c. 1250. This is a fine, early example of a road map in strip form. This extract includes Rochester, Canterbury and Dover.
British Library, London, UK.

1600–1900

Cartography in the earlier years of the 17th century was dominated by the Low Countries, epitomized by the Blaeu publishing house (*see 6*) but, by the late 17th century, the world centre for cartographic production had shifted from Amsterdam to Paris. France was one of the first countries to recognize the importance of establishing a national survey and mapping programme. There, the Cassini family established the national survey of France well ahead of other such surveys in western Europe (*see 7*).

The colonial scramble for North America, and the American War of Independence (1775–1783), drove the development of cartography in North America, and it was an age, too, when the exploration of Australia, Tasmania and New Zealand resulted in their appearance on world maps. Such exploration was aided by great developments in navigation and particularly the ability to establish longitude more precisely.

During the 19th century special maps appeared in greater numbers reflecting scientific and social observation and analysis. One significant example of this development of thematic mapping was the *Physikalischer Atlas* of Heinrich Berghaus, published in two volumes in 1845 and 1848 (*see 8*). Lithographic printing of maps was developed in the early years of the century allowing the production of multiple copies of maps very much more cheaply, stimulating a proliferation of maps for mass consumption and for educational purposes.

As the 19th century progressed, factors such as exploration and emigration were reflected in extended world coverage of maps and charts. Work on national surveys proceeded, one particularly notable national cartographic achievement being the Great Trigonometrical Survey (GTS) of India which facilitated the creation of extensive and detailed topographic maps of the sub-continent.

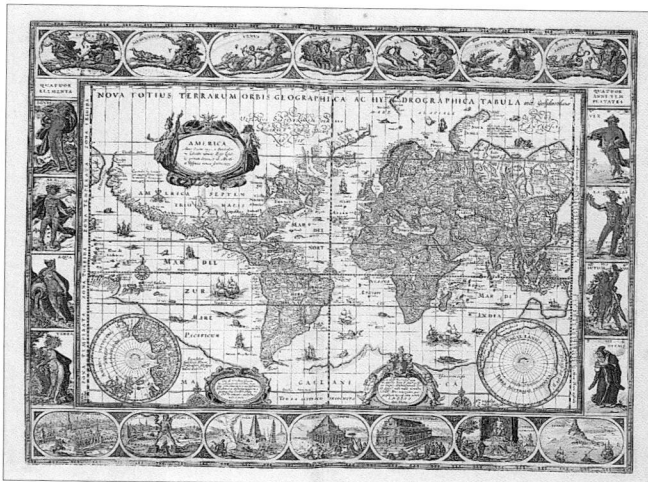

6. WORLD MAP

Produced in Amsterdam by Willem Blaeu, 1630. This is one of the finest examples of early maps on Mercator's projection. British Library, London, UK.

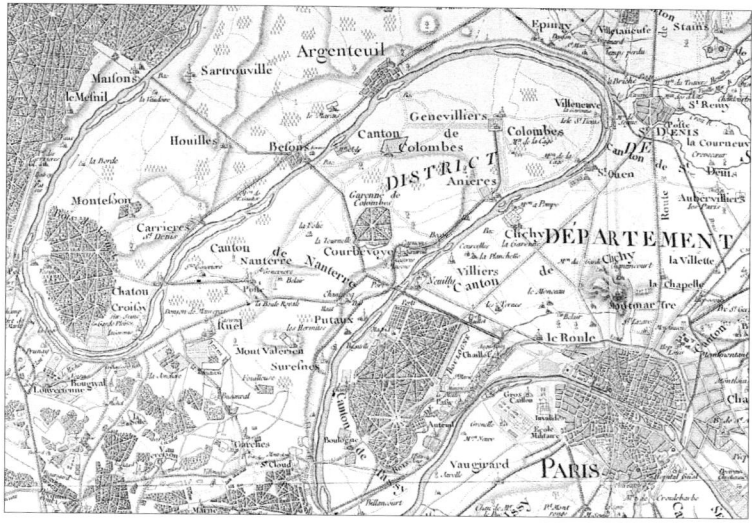

7. CARTE DE FRANCE

Detail from the first sheet – Sheet No. 1 Paris – by Cassini de Thury, 1736. Original scale 1:86 400. National Library of Scotland, Edinburgh, UK.

20TH CENTURY

War, politics and technological development were instrumental in prompting the expansion of map and chart coverage throughout the 20th century. The development of aviation and, in turn, space exploration, and photography and imagery possible through them, have been particularly significant in recent developments in cartography and have spawned a new age in cartography. The development of the computer has led to the production of digital maps and the consequent development of Geographical Information Systems (GIS) which allow users to combine and manipulate geographical data sets of many kinds.

There has been a significant increase in map coverage throughout the world, and yet the fact that comprehensive national topographic mapping has been produced, does not mean that it is readily available (*see 9*). Many countries, particularly in Africa and Asia, impose strict restrictions on the release of their mapping. The question of national map coverage and availability is complicated by the activities of external mapping organizations. The former USSR had extensive programmes producing topographic mapping of countries throughout the world (*see 10*). Easy access to this previously classified military mapping has recently served to extend map availability.

8. THEMATIC ATLAS MAP

Extract from a map of the *Survey of the geographical distribution and cultivation of the most important plants which are used as food for man: with indications of the isotheres and isokhimenes*, 1842. Published in the *Physikalischer Atlas* by Heinrich Berghaus, 1845 and 1848. This English language version appeared as Plate 44 in W & A K Johnston's *National Atlas of Historical, Commercial and Political Geography*, 1847. National Library of Scotland, Edinburgh, UK.

10. GROZNYY, RUSSIAN FEDERATION

Extract from a Russian military topographic map 1:500 000, 1988.

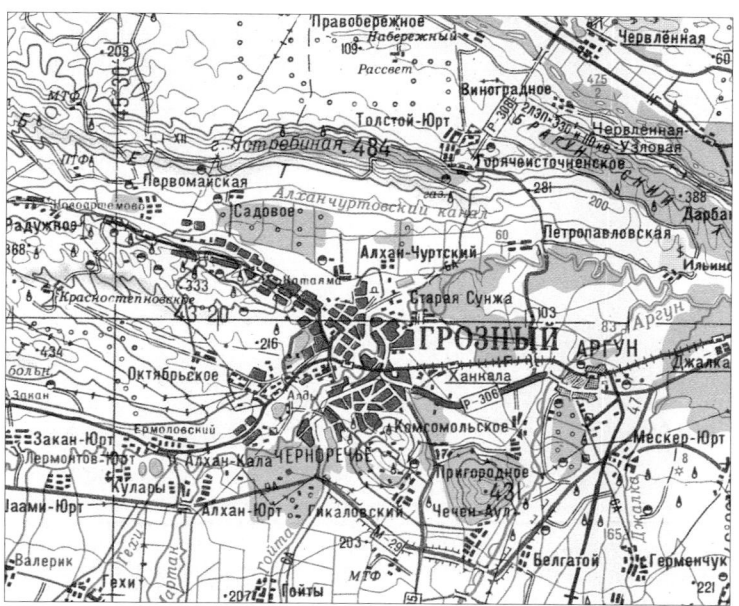

9. AVAILABILITY OF TOPOGRAPHIC MAPPING

Degree of access to topographic mapping of scales 1:100 000 or larger

Readily available		Not available locally for public distribution
Some restrictions on availability		no data

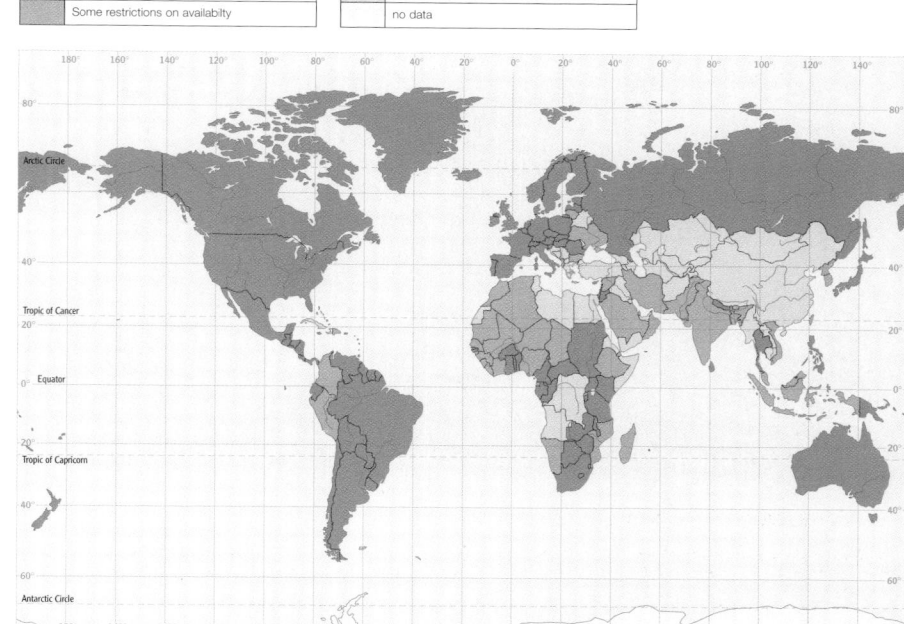

MEASURING THE EARTH

Speculation on the form of the universe and the place of the known world in it, and the attempts to express these graphically, constituted an important influence on mapmakers from earliest times. The Greeks inherited from the Babylonians such beliefs that the Earth was stationary, flat, the centre of the universe, and surrounded by water. Pythagoras in the 6th century BC and Aristotle in the 4th century BC proposed that the Earth was a sphere, revolving on its own axis. In Alexandria, Egypt, Eratosthenes (c. 276–194 BC) measured the circumference of the Earth using elementary geometric techniques. His value proved to be only 320 kilometres less than the true value, an error of less than 1 per cent.

One of the principal challenges of cartography is how to depict the spherical world on a flat map surface. It is essentially an impossible task without distorting the map in terms of either shape, azimuth (angles or bearings), area or distance. The problem assumed greater importance with the development of sea charts and the need to navigate in safety, preferably in straight lines (to reflect constant compass bearing) over considerable distances while simultaneously compensating for the curvature of the Earth. Mercator achieved this in the 16th century with his map projection in which the distance between the lines of latitude increases away from the equator. This projection, in modified form, still serves navigators well but has also resulted in distorted perceptions of the relative sizes of land areas, as those in high latitudes (eg Greenland) appear relatively too large, and those in low latitudes (eg India) appear relatively too small.

As far as establishing position on the Earth in terms of latitude and longitude is concerned, the concept of the tropics and the equator was established in early times through astronomical observation of the sun, moon and planets. The concept was later refined by Hipparchus and incorporated by Ptolemy into his *Geographia* (see page 42). The development of navigational instruments allowed latitude to be determined relatively easily. However, the establishment of longitude proved more problematic. In the 17th century Galileo established a method of determining longitude based on observations of the movement of Jupiter's moons, which served reasonably well on land. But the ability to establish longitude correctly at sea was believed to be so crucial that a Board of Longitude was established by the UK government in 1714 offering a prize of £20 000 for any method of defining longitude to within half a degree. In the search for a mechanical means of establishing longitude which could be used both on land and at sea, the principal difficulty was the lack of an accurate timepiece: the longitudinal value of a position being the distance reflected by the difference between local time and the time of a known position, with 15° of longitude equivalent to a time difference of one hour. The prize was eventually awarded to the Englishman John Harrison (*see 1*) whose marine chronometers, culminating in the one known as H4 which won the prize (*see 2*), were remarkably accurate and also highly reliable at sea.

Any longitudinal position needs to be defined with reference to a standard position. Such a line of zero longitude, usually referred to as the prime meridian, could, in theory, be placed anywhere. Separate prime meridians were established in, for example, Paris, Cadiz, Naples, Pulkova and Stockholm, as well as London. The universal acceptance, in 1884, of a single prime meridian – the Greenwich Meridian – was an early example of international standardization in cartography.

1. JOHN HARRISON (1693–1776)

2. JOHN HARRISON'S FOURTH MARINE CHRONOMETER, H4.

Made c. 1760. This was the first truly accurate chronometer and won Harrison the Board of Longitude prize in 1772.

SURVEYING

Surveying is the initial data collection stage in the mapmaking process and it was the Greeks who established the first systematic approach. Astronomy underpinned its development and instruments such as the gnomon, a sundial device, and the astrolabe, a navigational instrument, were adopted by land surveyors to establish position. Major advances took place during the 16th, 17th and 18th centuries with the development of increasingly accurate surveying instruments which improved the precision of measurements and allowed the introduction of greater topographical detail into maps. The systematic surveying of entire countries, and the subsequent production of detailed, large scale maps, began in earnest in the 18th century, notably in France (see page 43). It was James Cook (1728–1779) who combined the traditional approach to marine surveying with newer land surveying techniques and laid the foundations of modern nautical charting (*see 3*).

In the 20th century, technological developments have been reflected in related advances in surveying. The availability of aerial photography and satellite imagery allowed cartography to extend to formerly inaccessible parts of the world and have provided a vast amount of data for numerous mapping applications. Aerial photography and high resolution satellite imagery (*see 4*, and also pages 8-21) are important for the production of large-scale topographic mapping, while lower resolution imagery from a variety of sensors provides data on a global scale. The accurate coverage provided by the Global Positioning System (GPS), a satellite navigation system designed in the USA primarily for military use, is now widely used by surveyors for position fixing and also for navigation.

4. SPOT satellite image.

Showing Bandar Seri Begawan, Brunei. A high level of detail is visible within the built-up area and also along the coast within Brunei Bay. Variations in sediments and currents produce the variety of colours within the bay itself.

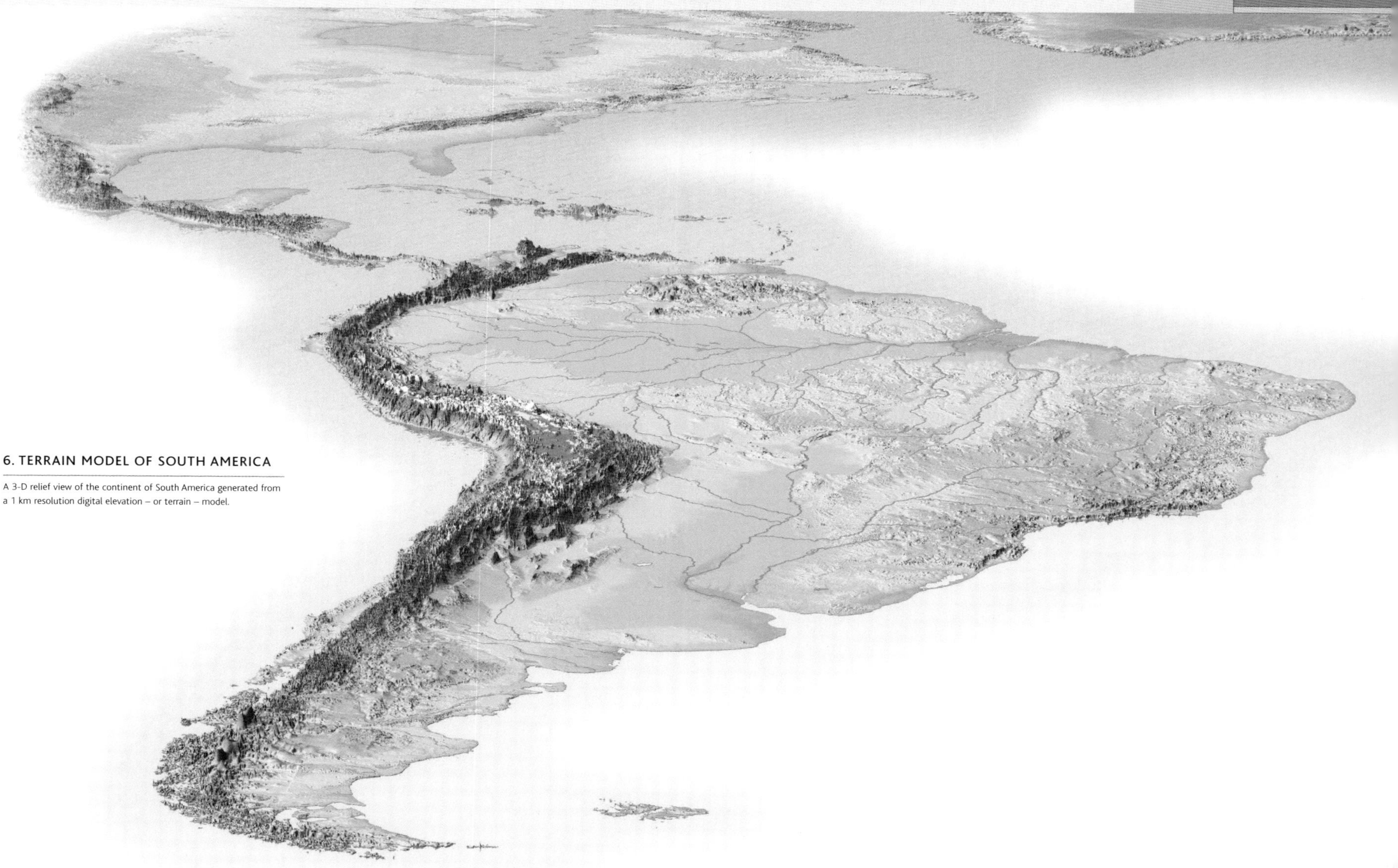

6. TERRAIN MODEL OF SOUTH AMERICA

A 3-D relief view of the continent of South America generated from
a 1 km resolution digital elevation – or terrain – model.

3. CAPTAIN COOK'S CHART OF NEW ZEALAND 1772

This chart was published following Cook's explorations in 1769 and 1770. The chart is remarkably accurate in terms of the shape of the islands
and in terms of latitude. However, the coloured overlays representing the coastline from a later survey in 1788 (green) and from British
Admiralty charts up to 1968 (red), illustrate well the problems of establishing longitude at the time of Cook's voyages.

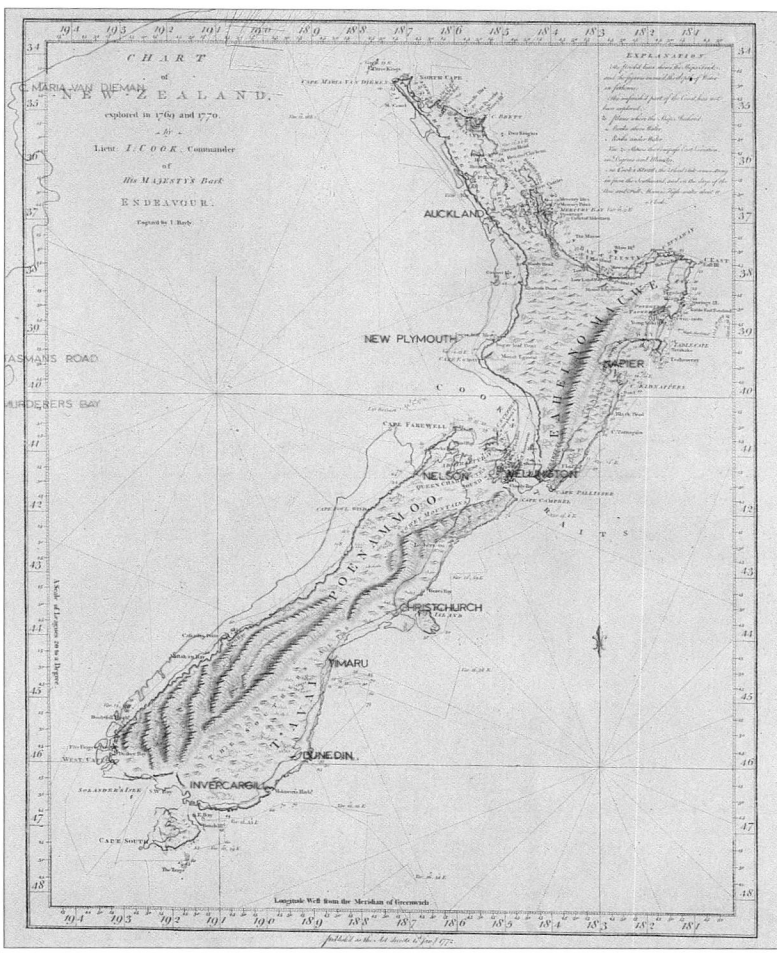

MAP PRODUCTION TECHNIQUES

For centuries, the only method of producing maps was to draw and copy them by hand.
Production was, therefore, time-consuming and labour-intensive. As a result, few maps
were produced and even fewer survived. In the 15th century, the invention of printing
prompted a veritable revolution in mapmaking. It allowed the production of repeat copies
and in a form consistent with the original, thus eliminating human error likely in hand
copying. Early relief woodcut prints gave way during the 16th century to printing from
engraved copper plates (*see 5*). This allowed greater versatility and continued to be the
principal method of map reproduction until the introduction of the much faster process
of lithographic printing in the early 19th century. Later in the 19th century the
development of photographic techniques was applied to mapmaking, eventually
becoming an integral part of the process and facilitating the greater use of colour.

The most significant revolution in cartographic production, since the introduction of
printing, dates from the late 1950s with the increasing use of the computer. This accelerated
map production processes and allowed the generation of digital data, the manipulation
of which supports new forms of output and visualization (*see 6*). Maps can now be produced
from scale-free and seamless databases, allowing individual customization of the output,
and the ability to produce digital images of early maps by scanning allows their increased
copying and wider dissemination. Digital maps are also now widely available on the
Internet and the World Wide Web.

5. Copper Engraving

The highly skilled task of engraving a map on a copper plate. The image had to be drawn in reverse,
for the map to appear correct when printed.

EUROPE total land area: 9 908 599 sq km / 3 825 731 sq miles

Elbrus	5 642m	18 510ft	Russian Federation
Gora Dykh-Tau	5 204m	17 073ft	Russian Federation
Shkhara	5 201m	17 063ft	Georgia/ Russian Federation
Kazbek	5 047m	16 558ft	Georgia/ Russian Federation
Mont Blanc	4 808m	15 774ft	France/Italy
Dufourspitze	4 634m	15 203ft	Italy/Switzerland

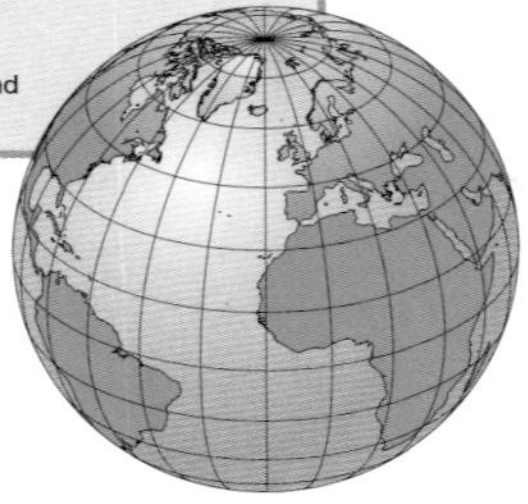

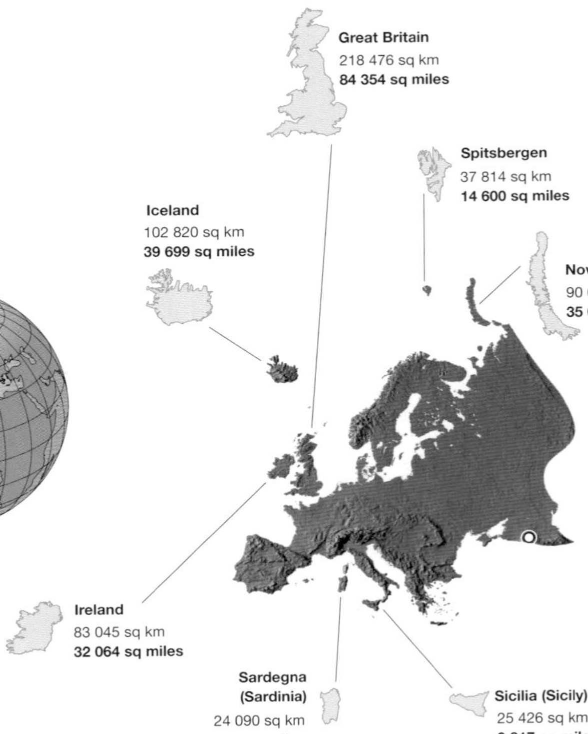

Great Britain
218 476 sq km
84 354 sq miles

Spitsbergen
37 814 sq km
14 600 sq miles

Iceland
102 820 sq km
39 699 sq miles

Novaya Zemlya
90 650 sq km
35 000 sq miles

Ireland
83 045 sq km
32 064 sq miles

**Sardegna
(Sardinia)**
24 090 sq km
9 301 sq miles

Sicilia (Sicily)
25 426 sq km
9 817 sq miles

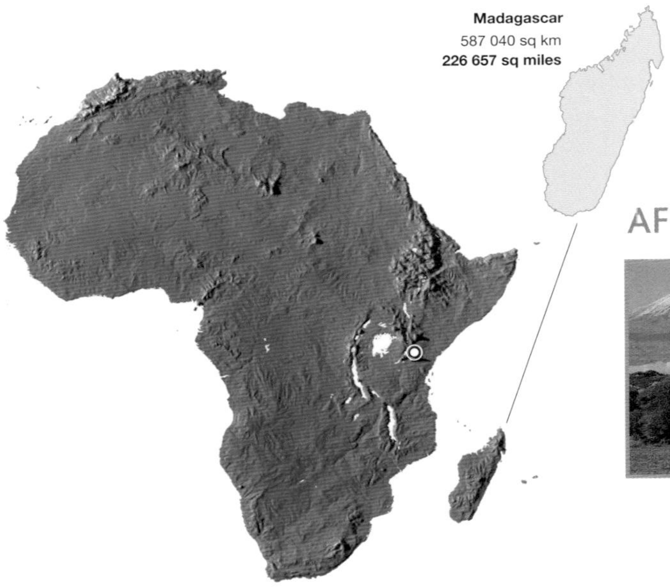

Madagascar
587 040 sq km
226 657 sq miles

AFRICA total land area: 30 343 578 sq km / 11 715 721 sq miles

Kilimanjaro	5 892m	19 331ft	Tanzania
Kirinyaga (Mt Kenya)	5 199m	17 057ft	Kenya
Margherita Peak (Mt Stanley)	5 110m	16 765ft	Democratic Republic of Congo/Uganda
Meru	4 565m	14 977ft	Tanzania
Ras Dashen	4 533m	14 872ft	Ethiopia
Mt Karisimbi	4 510m	14 796ft	Rwanda

New Guinea
808 510 sq km
312 167 sq miles

North Island (New Zealand)
115 777 sq km
44 702 sq miles

South Island (New Zealand)
151 215 sq km
58 384 sq miles

AUSTRALASIA total land area: 8 820 962 sq km / 3 405 792 sq miles

Puncak Jaya	5 030m	16 502ft	Indonesia
Puncak Trikora	4 730m	15 518ft	Indonesia
Puncak Mandala	4 700m	15 420ft	Indonesia
Puncak Yamin	4 595m	15 075ft	Indonesia
Mt Wilhelm	4 509m	14 793ft	Papua New Guinea
Mt Kubor	4 359m	14 301ft	Papua New Guinea

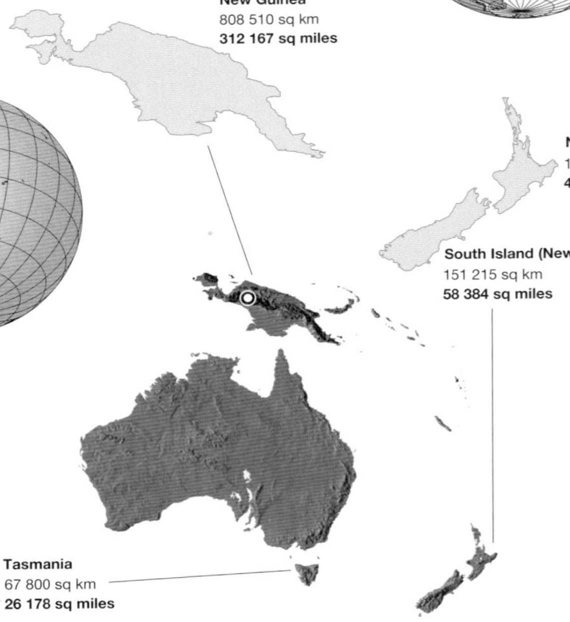

Tasmania
67 800 sq km
26 178 sq miles

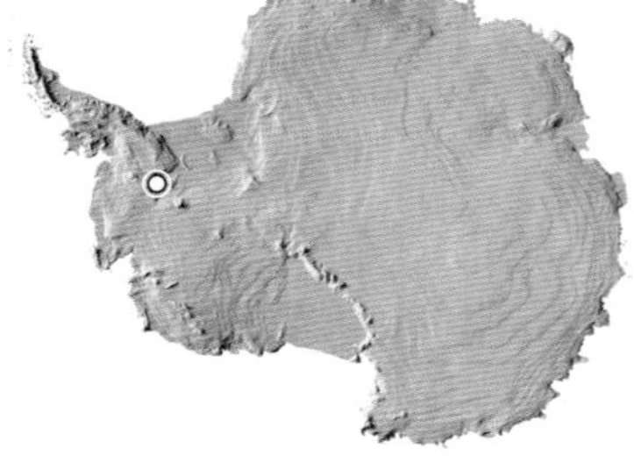

ANTARCTICA total land area: 12 093 000 sq km * / 4 669 133 sq miles *
*excluding ice shelves

Vinson Massif	4 897m	16 066ft	
Mt Tyree	4 852m	15 918ft	
Mt Kirkpatrick	4 528m	14 855ft	
Mt Markham	4 351m	14 275ft	
Mt Jackson	4 190m	13 747ft	
Mt Sidley	4 181m	13 717ft	

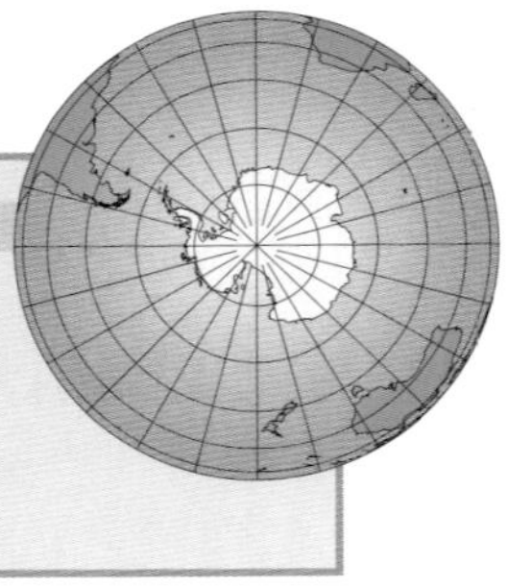

Mt Everest China/Nepal 8 848m / 29 028ft
K2 China/Jammu and Kashmir 8 611m / 28 251ft
Kangchenjunga India/Nepal 8 586m / 28 169ft
Lhotse China/Nepal 8 516m / 27 939ft
Makalu China/Nepal 8 463m / 27 765ft
Cho Oyu China/Nepal 8 201m / 26 906ft
Dhaulagiri Nepal 8 167m / 26 794ft
Manaslu Nepal 8 163m / 26 781ft
Nanga Parbat Jammu and Kashmir 8 126m / 26 660ft
Annapurna I Nepal 8 091m / 26 545ft
Gasherbrum I China/Jammu and Kashmir 8 068m / 26 469ft
Broad Peak China/Jammu and Kashmir 8 047m / 26 401ft
Gasherbrum II China/Jammu and Kashmir 8 035m / 26 361ft
Xixabangma Feng China 8 012m / 26 286ft
Annapurna II Nepal 7 937m / 26 040ft
Nuptse Nepal 7 885m / 25 869ft
Himalchul Nepal 7 864m / 25 800ft
Masherbrum Jammu and Kashmir 7 821m / 25 659ft
Nanda Devi India 7 816m / 25 643ft
Rakaposhi Jammu and Kashmir 7 788m / 25 551ft
Namjagbarwa Feng China 7 756m / 25 446ft
Kamet China 7 756m / 25 446ft

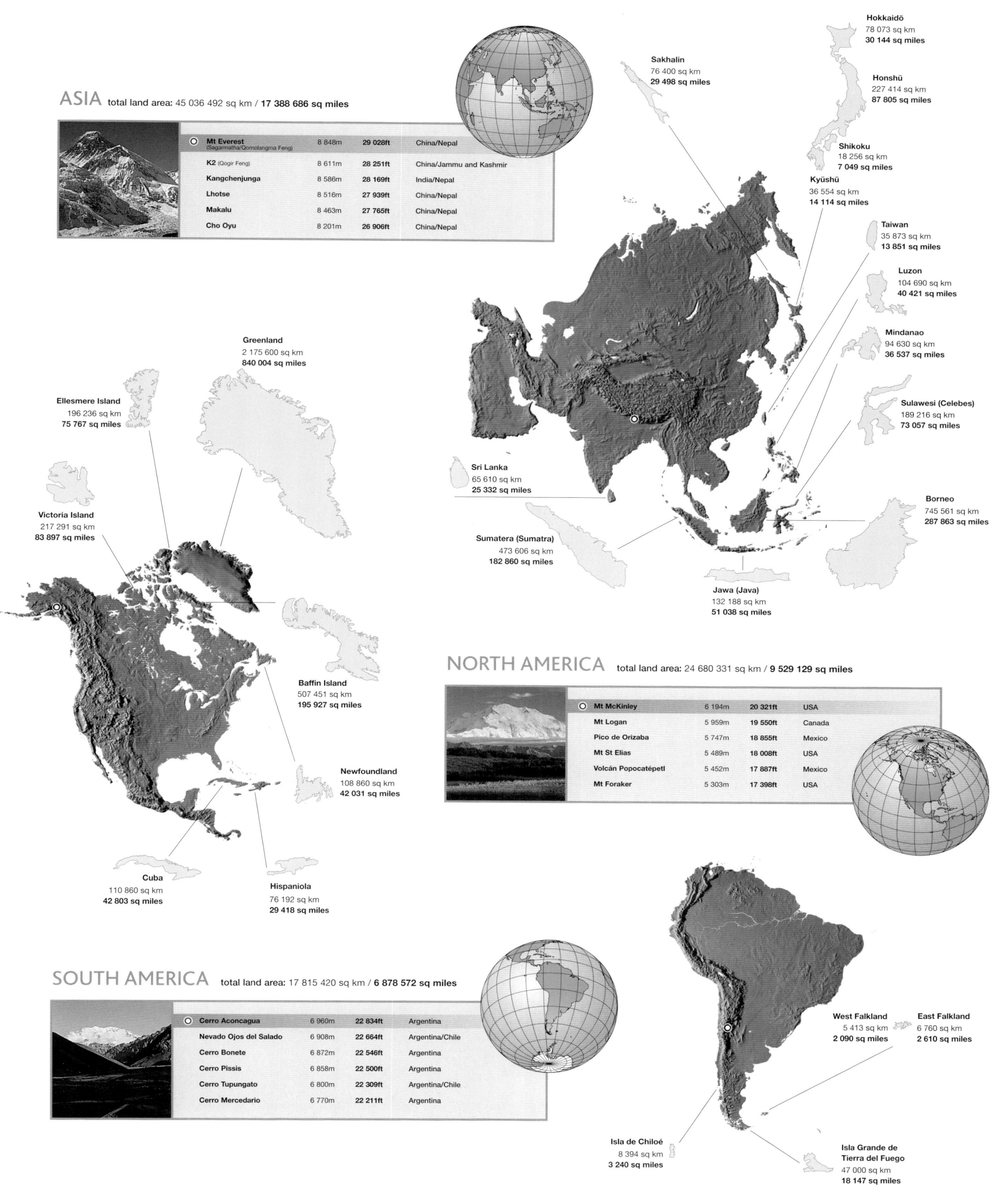

ASIA total land area: 45 036 492 sq km / **17 388 686 sq miles**

⊙	**Mt Everest** (Sagarmatha/Qomolangma Feng)	8 848m	**29 028ft**	China/Nepal
	K2 (Qogir Feng)	8 611m	**28 251ft**	China/Jammu and Kashmir
	Kangchenjunga	8 586m	**28 169ft**	India/Nepal
	Lhotse	8 516m	**27 939ft**	China/Nepal
	Makalu	8 463m	**27 765ft**	China/Nepal
	Cho Oyu	8 201m	**26 906ft**	China/Nepal

Hokkaidō
78 073 sq km
30 144 sq miles

Honshū
227 414 sq km
87 805 sq miles

Shikoku
18 256 sq km
7 049 sq miles

Sakhalin
76 400 sq km
29 498 sq miles

Kyūshū
36 554 sq km
14 114 sq miles

Taiwan
35 873 sq km
13 851 sq miles

Luzon
104 690 sq km
40 421 sq miles

Mindanao
94 630 sq km
36 537 sq miles

Sulawesi (Celebes)
189 216 sq km
73 057 sq miles

Borneo
745 561 sq km
287 863 sq miles

Greenland
2 175 600 sq km
840 004 sq miles

Ellesmere Island
196 236 sq km
75 767 sq miles

Victoria Island
217 291 sq km
83 897 sq miles

Sri Lanka
65 610 sq km
25 332 sq miles

Sumatera (Sumatra)
473 606 sq km
182 860 sq miles

Jawa (Java)
132 188 sq km
51 038 sq miles

Baffin Island
507 451 sq km
195 927 sq miles

Newfoundland
108 860 sq km
42 031 sq miles

Cuba
110 860 sq km
42 803 sq miles

Hispaniola
76 192 sq km
29 418 sq miles

NORTH AMERICA total land area: 24 680 331 sq km / **9 529 129 sq miles**

⊙	**Mt McKinley**	6 194m	**20 321ft**	USA
	Mt Logan	5 959m	**19 550ft**	Canada
	Pico de Orizaba	5 747m	**18 855ft**	Mexico
	Mt St Elias	5 489m	**18 008ft**	USA
	Volcán Popocatépetl	5 452m	**17 887ft**	Mexico
	Mt Foraker	5 303m	**17 398ft**	USA

SOUTH AMERICA total land area: 17 815 420 sq km / **6 878 572 sq miles**

⊙	**Cerro Aconcagua**	6 960m	**22 834ft**	Argentina
	Nevado Ojos del Salado	6 908m	**22 664ft**	Argentina/Chile
	Cerro Bonete	6 872m	**22 546ft**	Argentina
	Cerro Pissis	6 858m	**22 500ft**	Argentina
	Cerro Tupungato	6 800m	**22 309ft**	Argentina/Chile
	Cerro Mercedario	6 770m	**22 211ft**	Argentina

West Falkland
5 413 sq km
2 090 sq miles

East Falkland
6 760 sq km
2 610 sq miles

Isla de Chiloé
8 394 sq km
3 240 sq miles

Isla Grande de Tierra del Fuego
47 000 sq km
18 147 sq miles

Gurla Mandhata
China
7 728m / 25 390ft

Muztag
China
7 723m / 25 338ft

Kongur Shan
China
7 719m / 25 324ft

Tirich Mir
Pakistan
7 690m / 25 229ft

Kula Kangri
Bhutan
7 554m / 24 783ft

Muztagata
China
7 546m / 24 757ft

Gongga Shan
China
7 514m / 24 652ft

Qullai Garmo
Tajikistan
7 495m / 24 590ft

Jongsong
India/Nepal
7 483m / 24 550ft

Teram Kangri
China/Jammu and Kashmir
7 470m / 24 508ft

Pik Pobedy
China/Kyrgyzstan
7 439m / 24 406ft

Ganesh I
India/Nepal
7 415m / 24 327ft

Churen Himal
Nepal
7 371m / 24 183ft

Sad Istragh
Afghanistan/Pakistan
7 367m / 24 170ft

Kabru
India/Nepal
7 353m / 24 124ft

Chamlang
Nepal
7 319m / 24 012ft

Choksiam
China
7 316m / 24 002ft

Chomo Lhari
Bhutan
7 313m / 23 992ft

Muztag
China
7 282m / 23 891ft

Langtang Lirung
Nepal
7 234m / 23 799ft

Gankar Punsum
Bhutan
7 239m / 23 750ft

Nagarzê
China
7 223m / 23 697ft

© Bartholomew Ltd

OCEANS AND SEAS

Area
sq km
sq miles

Maximum Depth
metres
feet

Red Sea
453 000
175 000
3 040
9 973

The Gulf
238 000
92 000
73
239

Bay of Bengal
2 172 000
839 000
4 500
14 763

Sea of Japan
1 013 000
391 000
3 743
12 280

Yellow Sea (Huang Hai)
91
298

East China Sea (Dong Hai)
and Yellow Sea (Huang Hai)
1 202 000
464 000

East China Sea (Dong Hai)
2 717
8 913

South China Sea
2 590 000
1 000 000
5 514
18 090

Sea of Okhotsk (Okhotskoye More)
1 392 000
537 000
3 363
11 033

Bering Sea
2 261 000
873 000
4 150
13 615

Hudson Bay
1 233 000
476 000
259
849

Gulf of Mexico
1 544 000
596 000
3 504
11 495

Caribbean Sea
2 512 000
970 000
7 680
25 196

Arctic Ocean
9 485 000
3 662 000
5 450
17 880

Baltic Sea
382 000
147 000
460
1 509

North Sea
575 000
222 000
661
2 168

Black Sea
508 000
196 000
2 245
7 365

Mediterranean Sea
2 510 000
969 000
5 121
16 800

INDIAN OCEAN
73 427 000
28 350 000
7 288
23 910

PACIFIC OCEAN
166 241 000
64 186 000
10 920
35 826

ATLANTIC OCEAN
86 557 000
33 420 000
8 605
28 231

EUROPE

Volga	3 688 km	2 291 miles
Danube	2 850 km	1 770 miles
Dnieper	2 285 km	1 419 miles
Kama	2 028 km	1 260 miles
Don	1 931 km	1 199 miles
Pechora	1 802 km	1 119 miles

Rybinskoye Vodokhranilishche
Nyalka
Kama
Oka
Volga
Volga
Caspian Sea

Volga drainage basin
1 380 000 sq km
533 000 sq miles

Vänern
5 585 sq km
2 156 sq miles

Ladozhskoye Ozero (Lake Ladoga)
18 390 sq km
7 100 sq miles

Onezhskoye Ozero (Lake Onega)
9 600 sq km
3 706 sq miles

Rybinskoye Vodokhranilishche
5 180 sq km
2 000 sq miles

AFRICA

Lake Chad
10 000 - 26 000 sq km
3 861 - 10 039 sq miles

Lake Turkana
6 475 sq km
2 500 sq miles

Lake Victoria
68 800 sq km
26 563 sq miles

Lake Volta
8 485 sq km
3 276 sq miles

Lake Tanganyika
32 900 sq km
12 702 sq miles

Lake Nyasa (Lake Malawi)
30 044 sq km
11 600 sq miles

Nile	6 695 km	4 160 miles
Congo	4 667 km	2 900 miles
Niger	4 184 km	2 599 miles
Zambezi (Zambeze)	2 736 km	1 700 miles
Webi Shabeelle	2 490 km	1 547 miles
Ubangi	2 250 km	1 398 miles

Mediterranean Sea
Nile
Atbara
Bahr el Azraq (Blue Nile)
Bahr el Abiad (White Nile)
Bahr el Jebel
Lake Albert
Lake Kyoga
Lake Victoria

Nile drainage basin
3 349 000 sq km
1 293 000 sq miles

Lungwebungo
Luampa
Kafue
Cuando
Zambezi
Zambezi
Lake Kariba
Lake Nyasa (Lake Malawi)
Indian Ocean

Zambezi (Zambeze) drainage basin
1 330 000 sq km
514 000 sq miles

Uele
Congo
Ubangi
Congo
Kasai
Kwango
Oubangui
Lualaba
Lake Tanganyika
Lake Mweru
Atlantic Ocean

Congo drainage basin
3 700 000 sq km
1 429 000 sq miles

Niger
Bani
Kaduna
Benue
Gulf of Guinea

Niger drainage basin
1 890 000 sq km
730 000 sq miles

AUSTRALASIA

Murray-Darling	3 750 km	2 330 miles
Darling	2 739 km	1 702 miles
Murray	2 589 km	1 608 miles
Murrumbidgee	1 690 km	1 050 miles
Lachlan	1 480 km	919 miles
Macquarie	950 km	590 miles

Lake Eyre
0 - 8 900 sq km
0 - 3 436 sq miles

Lake Torrens
0 - 5 780 sq km
0 - 2 232 sq miles

Darling
Warrego
Lachlan
Murray
Encounter Bay
Murrumbidgee

Murray-Darling drainage basin
1 058 000 sq km
408 000 sq miles

Nile
Africa
6 695 km / 4 160 miles

Amazonas (Amazon)
South America
6 516 km / 4 049 miles

Chang Jiang (Yangtze)
Asia
6 380 km / 3 964 miles

Mississippi-Missouri
North America
5 969 km / 3 709 miles

Ob'-Irtysh
Asia
5 568 km / 3 459 miles

Yenisey-Angara-Selenga
Asia
5 550 km / 3 448 miles

Huang He (Yellow River)
Asia
5 464 km / 3 395 miles

Congo
Africa
4 667 km / 2 900 miles

Rio de la Plata-Paraná
South America
4 500 km / 2 796 miles

Irtysh
Asia
4 440 km / 2 759 miles

Mekong
Asia
4 425 km / 2 749 miles

Heilong Jiang (Amur)-Argun'
Asia
4 416 km / 2 744 miles

Lena-Kirenga
Asia
4 400 km / 2 734 miles

Mackenzie-Peace-Finlay
North America
4 241 km / 2 635 miles

Niger
Africa
4 184 km / 2 599 miles

Yenisey
Asia
4 090 km / 2 541 miles

Missouri
North America
4 086 km / 2 539 miles

Mississippi
North America
3 765 km / 2 339 miles

Murray-Darling
Australasia
3 750 km / 2 330 miles

Ob'
Asia
3 701 km / 2 300 miles

Volga
Europe
3 688 km / 2 291 miles

Purus
South America
3 218 km / 2 000 miles

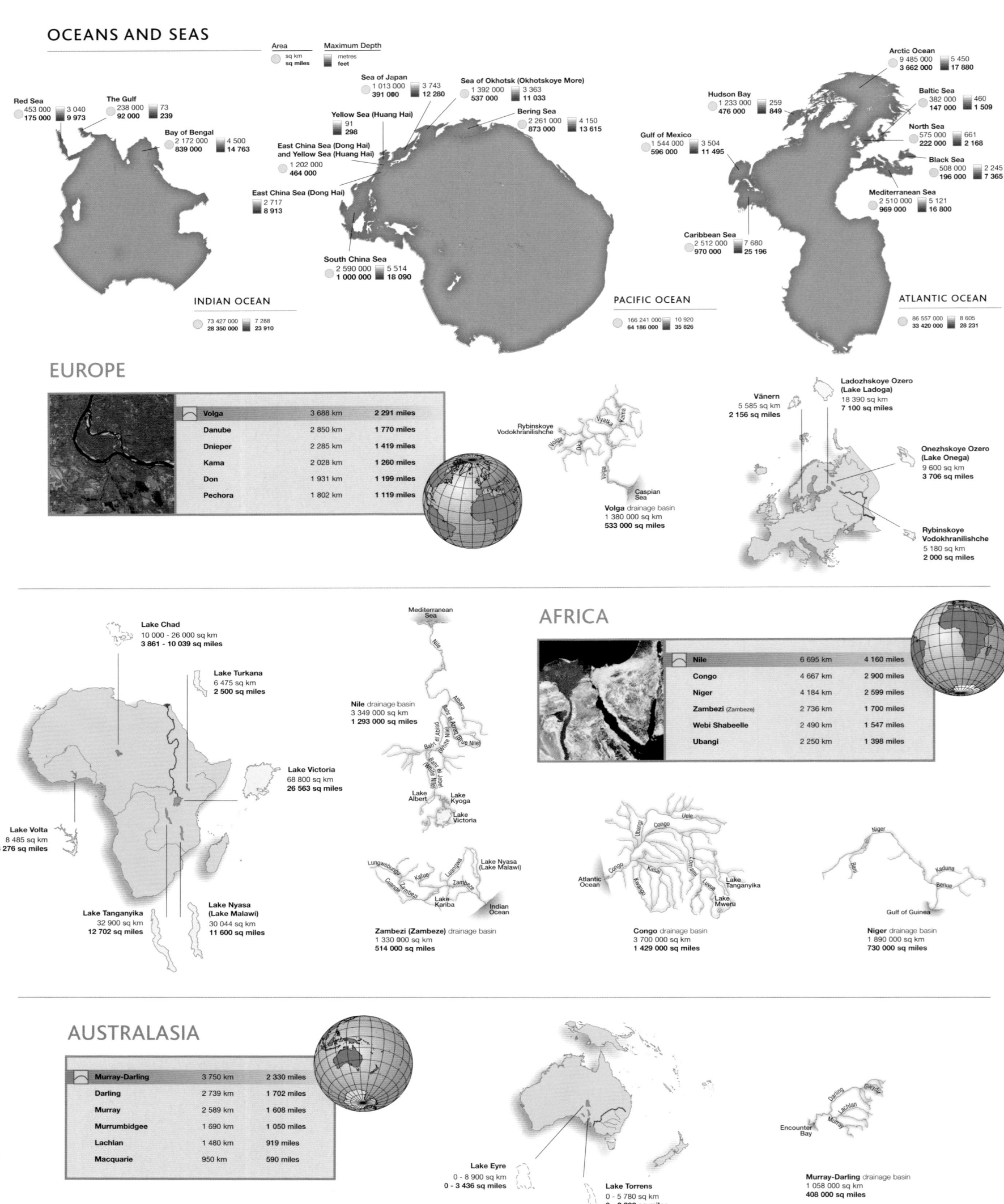

ASIA

	Chang Jiang (Yangtze)	6 380 km	3 964 miles
	Ob'-Irtysh	5 568 km	3 459 miles
	Yenisey-Angara-Selenga	5 550 km	3 448 miles
	Huang He (Yellow River)	5 464 km	3 395 miles
	Mekong	4 425 km	2 749 miles
	Heilong Jiang (Amur)-**Argun'**	4 416 km	2 744 miles

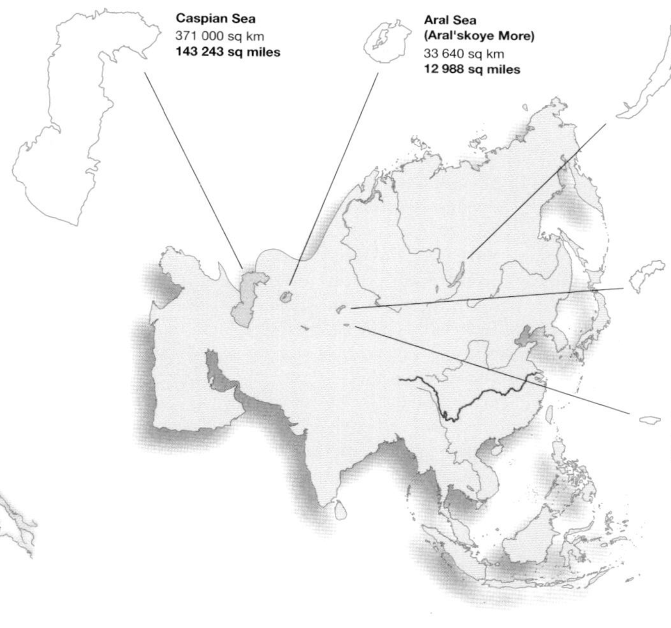

Caspian Sea
371 000 sq km
143 243 sq miles

Aral Sea
(Aral'skoye More)
33 640 sq km
12 988 sq miles

Ozero Baykal
(Lake Baikal)
30 500 sq km
11 776 sq miles

Ozero Balkhash
17 400 sq km
6 718 sq miles

Ysyk-Köl
6 200 sq km
2 393 sq miles

Chang Jiang (Yangtze) drainage basin
1 959 000 sq km
756 000 sq miles

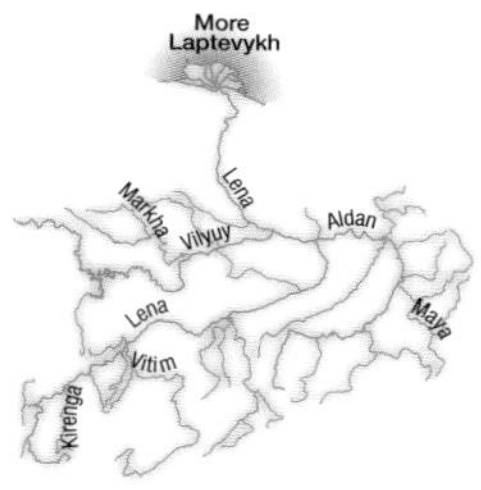

Lena-Kirenga drainage basin
2 490 000 sq km
961 000 sq miles

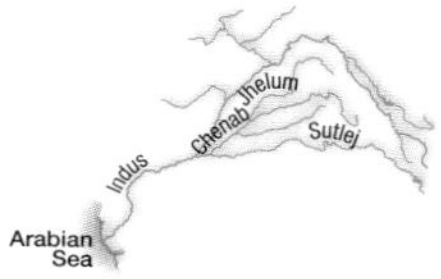

Indus drainage basin
1 166 000 sq km
450 000 sq miles

Ganga (Ganges)-Brahmaputra drainage basin
1 621 000 sq km
626 000 sq miles

Shatt al'Arab drainage basin
1 114 000 sq km
430 000 sq miles

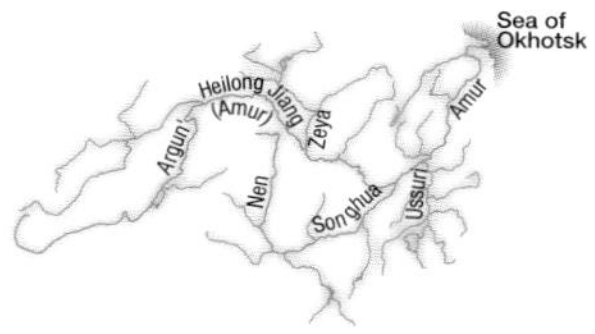

Heilong Jiang (Amur)-Argun' drainage basin
1 855 000 sq km
716 000 sq miles

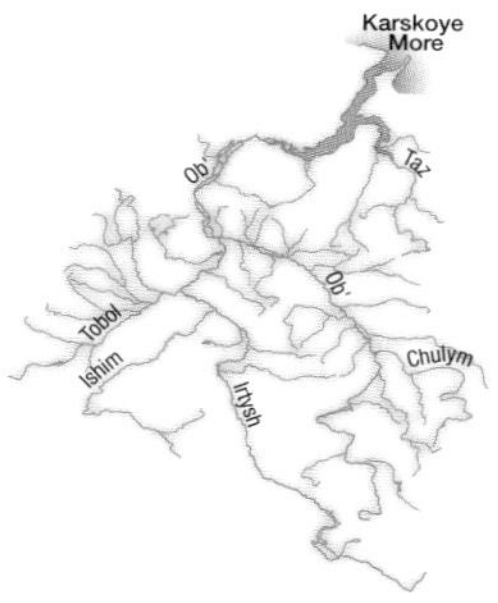

Ob'-Irtysh drainage basin
2 990 000 sq km
1 154 000 sq miles

Yenisey-Angara-Selenga drainage basin
2 580 000 sq km
996 000 sq miles

NORTH AMERICA

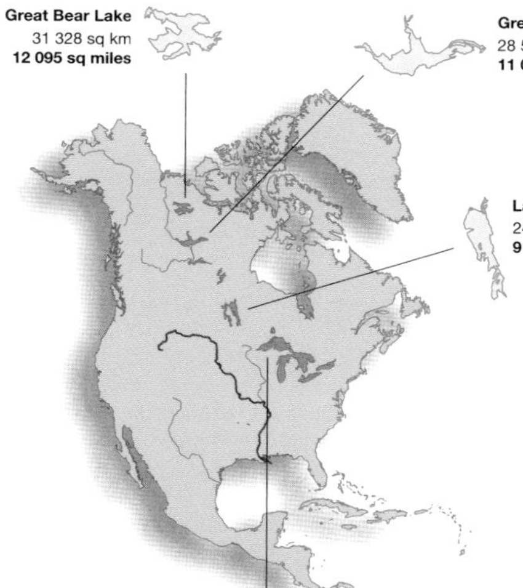

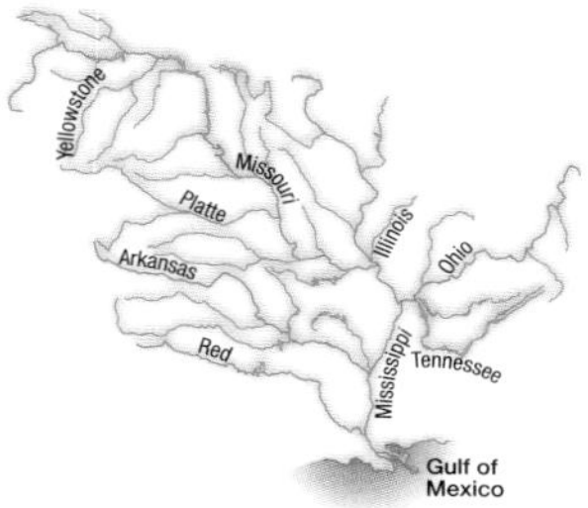

Great Bear Lake
31 328 sq km
12 095 sq miles

Great Slave Lake
28 568 sq km
11 030 sq miles

Lake Winnipeg
24 387 sq km
9 415 sq miles

	Mississippi-Missouri	5 969 km	3 709 miles
	Mackenzie-Peace-Finlay	4 241 km	2 635 miles
	Missouri	4 086 km	2 539 miles
	Mississippi	3 765 km	2 339 miles
	Yukon	3 185 km	1 979 miles
	Rio Grande (Rio Bravo del Norte)	3 057 km	1 899 miles

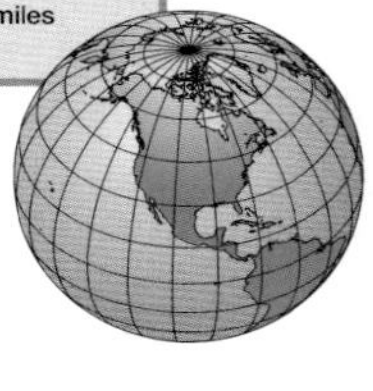

Mississippi-Missouri drainage basin
3 250 000 sq km
1 255 000 sq miles

Lake Superior
82 100 sq km
31 698 sq miles

Lake Huron
59 600 sq km
23 011 sq miles

Lake Ontario
18 960 sq km
7 320 sq miles

Lake Michigan
57 800 sq km
22 316 sq miles

Lake Erie
25 700 sq km
9 922 sq miles

Nelson-Saskatchewan drainage basin
1 150 000 sq km
444 000 sq miles

Mackenzie-Peace-Finlay drainage basin
1 805 000 sq km
697 000 sq miles

St Lawrence-St Louis drainage basin
1 463 000 sq km
565 000 sq miles

SOUTH AMERICA

	Amazonas (Amazon)	6 516 km	4 049 miles
	Río de la Plata-Paraná	4 500 km	2 796 miles
	Purus	3 218 km	1 999 miles
	Madeira	3 200 km	1 988 miles
	São Francisco	2 900 km	1 802 miles
	Tocantins	2 750 km	1 708 miles

Amazonas (Amazon) drainage basin
7 050 000 sq km
2 722 000 sq miles

Río de la Plata-Paraná drainage basin
3 100 000 sq km
1 197 000 sq miles

Lago Titicaca
8 340 sq km
3 220 sq miles

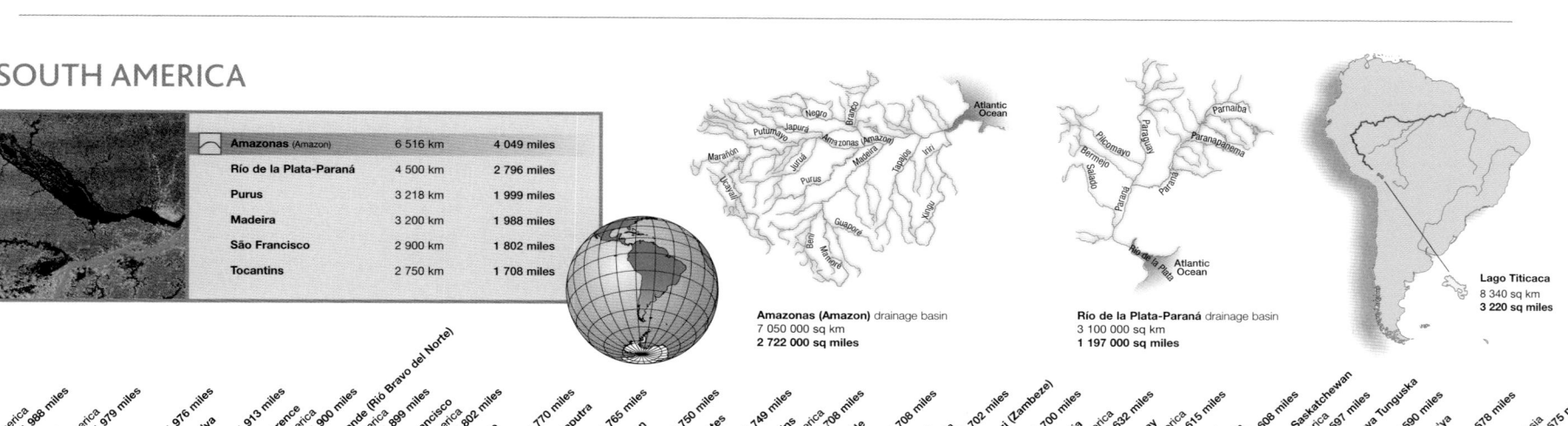

Madeira
South America
3 200 km / 1 988 miles

Yukon
North America
3 185 km / 1 979 miles

Indus
Asia
3 180 km / 1 976 miles

Syrdar'ya
Asia
3 078 km / 1 913 miles

St Lawrence
North America
3 058 km / 1 900 miles

Rio Grande (Rio Bravo del Norte)
North America
3 057 km / 1 899 miles

São Francisco
South America
2 900 km / 1 802 miles

Danube
Europe
2 850 km / 1 770 miles

Brahmaputra
Asia
2 840 km / 1 765 miles

Salween
Asia
2 816 km / 1 750 miles

Euphrates
Asia
2 815 km / 1 749 miles

Tocantins
South America
2 750 km / 1 708 miles

Tarim He
Asia
2 750 km / 1 708 miles

Darling
Australasia
2 739 km / 1 702 miles

Zambezi (Zambeze)
Africa
2 736 km / 1 700 miles

Araguaia
South America
2 627 km / 1 632 miles

Paraguay
South America
2 600 km / 1 615 miles

Murray
Australasia
2 589 km / 1 608 miles

Nelson-Saskatchewan
North America
2 570 km / 1 597 miles

Nizhnyaya Tunguska
Asia
2 559 km / 1 590 miles

Amudar'ya
Asia
2 540 km / 1 578 miles

Ural
Europe / Asia
2 534 km / 1 575 miles

© Bartholomew Ltd

All independent countries and populated dependent and disputed territories are included in this list of the states and territories of the world; the list is arranged in alphabetical order by the conventional name form. For independent states, the full name is given below the conventional name, if this is different; for territories, the status is given. The capital city name is given in the local form as shown on the reference maps.

The statistics used for the area and population are the latest available and include estimates. The information on languages and religions is based on the latest information on 'de facto' speakers of the language or 'de facto' adherents of the religion. The information available on languages and religions varies greatly from country to country, some countries include questions in census others do not, in which case best estimates are used. The order of the languages and religions reflect their relative importance within the country; generally, languages or religions are included when more than one per cent of the population are estimated to be speakers or adherents.

Membership of the following international organizations is shown by the abbreviations below; territories are not shown as having separate memberships of these organizations.

APEC	Asia-Pacific Economic Cooperation
ASEAN	Association of Southeast Asian Nations
CARICOM	Caribbean Community
CIS	Commonwealth of Independent States
Comm.	The Commonwealth
EU	European Union
OECD	Organization of Economic Cooperation and Development
OPEC	Organization of Petroleum Exporting Countries
SADC	Southern African Development Community
UN	United Nations

AFGHANISTAN
Islamic Emirate of Afghanistan

Area Sq Km	652 225	Currency	Afghani
Area Sq Miles	251 825	Languages	Dari, Pushtu, Uzbek, Turkmen
Population	21 354 000	Religions	Sunni Muslim, Shi'a Muslim
Capital	Kābul	Organizations	UN

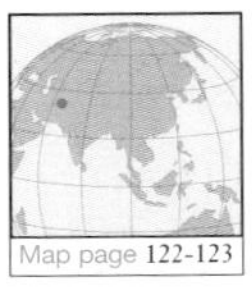
Map page 122-123

A landlocked country in central Asia, Afghanistan borders Pakistan, Iran, Turkmenistan, Uzbekistan, Tajikistan and China. The central highlands are bordered by plains in the north and southwest, and by the Hindu Kush to the northeast. The climate is dry with cold winters and hot summers. Over the last twenty years war has disrupted the economy which was highly dependent on farming and livestock rearing.

ALBANIA
Republic of Albania

Area Sq Km	28 748	Currency	Lek
Area Sq Miles	11 100	Languages	Albanian, Greek
Population	3 119 000	Religions	Sunni Muslim, Orthodox, Roman Catholic
Capital	Tiranë	Organizations	UN

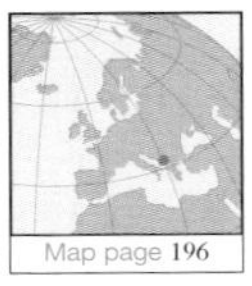
Map page 196

Albania lies in the western Balkans in southeast Europe, on the Adriatic Sea. It is mountainous, with coastal plains where half the population lives. The economy is based on agriculture and mining, mainly chromium. The fall of communism brought foreign aid for the ailing economy, but Albania remains one of the poorest countries in Europe.

ALGERIA
Democratic and Popular Republic of Algeria

Area Sq Km	2 381 741	Currency	Dinar
Area Sq Miles	919 595	Languages	Arabic, French, Berber
Population	30 081 000	Religions	Sunni Muslim
Capital	Alger	Organizations	OPEC, UN

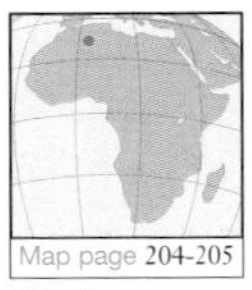
Map page 204-205

Algeria is on the Mediterranean coast of northwest Africa. The second largest country in Africa, it extends southwards from the coastal plain to the Atlas Mountains and to the Sahara which is dry sandstone plateau and desert, cut by valleys and rocky mountains, including the Hoggar in the southeast. The climate is Mediterranean on the coast, but dry inland. Most people live on the coastal plain and on the fertile northern slopes of the Atlas Mountains. Oil, natural gas and related products are the mainstay of the economy and account for over ninety five per cent of export earnings. Agriculture employs about a quarter of the workforce, producing mainly food crops; attempts are being made to diversify the economy, but unemployment remains high, as do social tensions.

American Samoa
United States Unincorporated Territory

Area Sq Km	197	Currency	US dollar
Area Sq Miles	76	Languages	Samoan, English
Population	63 000	Religions	Protestant, Roman Catholic
Capital	Fagatogo		

Lying in the south Pacific Ocean, American Samoa consists of five main islands and two coral atolls. The main island is Tutuila. The economy is strongly linked to the USA, tuna and tuna products are the main export.

Map page 78

ANDORRA
Principality of Andorra

Area Sq Km	465	Currency	French franc, Spanish peseta
Area Sq Miles	180	Languages	Spanish, Catalan, French
Population	72 000	Religions	Roman Catholic
Capital	Andorra la Vella	Organizations	UN

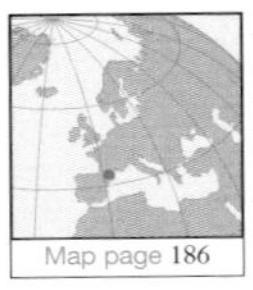
Map page 186

A landlocked state in southwest Europe, Andorra nestles in the Pyrenees between France and Spain. It consists of deep valleys and gorges, surrounded by mountains. Tourism (there are about ten million visitors a year) is the mainstay of the economy, banking is also important.

ANGOLA
Republic of Angola

Area Sq Km	1 246 700	Currency	Kwanza
Area Sq Miles	481 354	Languages	Portuguese, Bantu, local languages
Population	12 092 000	Religions	Roman Catholic, Protestant, traditional beliefs
Capital	Luanda	Organizations	SADC, UN

Angola lies on the Atlantic coast of southern central Africa. Its small northern province, Cabinda, is separated from the rest of the country by part of Democratic Republic of Congo. Much of Angola is high plateau, with a narrow coastal plain where most people live. The climate is equatorial in the north but desert in the south. Over eighty per cent of the population rely on subsistence agriculture. Angola is rich in minerals, and oil accounts for around seventy five per cent of exports earnings. Continued civil war for the last twenty years has restricted economic development.

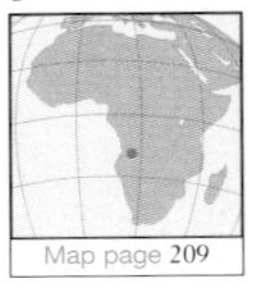
Map page 209

Anguilla
United Kingdom Overseas Territory

Area Sq Km	155	Currency	E. Carib. dollar
Area Sq Miles	60	Languages	English
Population	8 000	Religions	Protestant, Roman Catholic
Capital	The Valley		

Anguilla lies at the northern end of the Leeward Islands in the Caribbean. Tourism and fishing are the basis of the economy

Map page 247

ANTIGUA AND BARBUDA

Area Sq Km	442	Currency	E. Carib. dollar
Area Sq Miles	171	Languages	English, creole
Population	67 000	Religions	Protestant, Roman Catholic
Capital	St John's	Organizations	CARICOM, Comm., UN

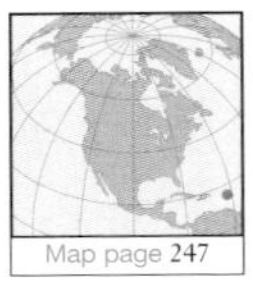
Map page 247

The state comprises Antigua, Barbuda and the tiny island of Redonda, in the Leeward Islands in the eastern Caribbean. Antigua, the largest and most populous, is mainly hilly scrubland, with many beaches and a warm, dry climate. The economy relies heavily on tourism with about half the tourists coming from the USA.

ARGENTINA
Argentine Republic

Area Sq Km	2 766 889	Currency	Peso
Area Sq Miles	1 068 302	Languages	Spanish, Italian, Amerindian languages
Population	36 123 000	Religions	Roman Catholic, Protestant
Capital	Buenos Aires	Organizations	UN

Argentina occupies almost the whole of the southern part of South America, from Bolivia to Cape Horn and from the Andes to the Atlantic Ocean. The second largest South American state has four geographical regions: the subtropical forests and swampland in the northeast; the temperate fertile plains or Pampas in the centre, which support most of the farming and the bulk of the population; the wooded foothills and valleys of the Andes in the west; and the cold, semi-arid plateaus of Patagonia, in the south. The highest mountain in South America, Cerro Aconcagua is in Argentina. Nearly ninety per cent of the population live in towns and cities. Though declining as a percentage of the GDP, agricultural products still dominate exports, which include motor vehicles and crude oil. Most trade is with Brazil and the USA.

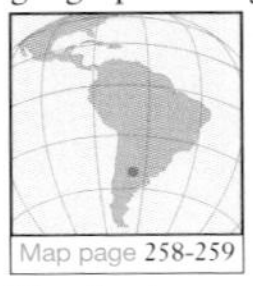
Map page 258-259

ARMENIA
Republic of Armenia

Area Sq Km	29 800	Currency	Dram
Area Sq Miles	11 506	Languages	Armenian, Azeri
Population	3 536 000	Religions	Armenian Orthodox
Capital	Yerevan	Organizations	CIS, UN

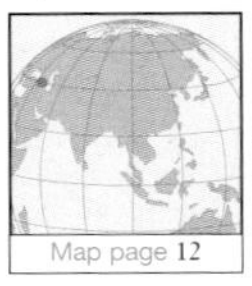
Map page 12

A landlocked state in southwest Asia, Armenia is in the south of the Lesser Caucasus and borders Georgia, Azerbaijan, Iran and Turkey. It is mountainous, with a central plateau-basin, and dry, with warm summers and cold winters. One third of the population lives in Yerevan. Armenia supports the ethnic Armenians in Nagorno-Karabkh in their separatist dispute with Azerbaijan. Economic growth has been slow; gold, jewellery and precious stones are important exports; many Armenians depend on remittances from abroad.

Aruba
Self-governing Netherlands Territory

Area Sq Km	193	Currency	Florin
Area Sq Miles	75	Languages	Papiamento, Dutch, English
Population	94 000	Religions	Roman Catholic, Protestant
Capital	Oranjestad		

The most southwesterly of the islands in the Lesser Antilles in the Caribbean, Aruba lies just off the coast of Venezuela. Tourism and offshore finance are the most important sectors of the economy.

Map page 247

Ascension Dependency of St Helena

Area Sq Km (Miles) 88 (34) Population 1 100 Capital Georgetown

A volcanic island in the south Atlantic Ocean about 1300 kilometres (800 miles) northwest of St Helena.

Map page 216

AUSTRALIA
Commonwealth of Australia

Area Sq Km	7 682 395	Currency	Dollar
Area Sq Miles	2 966 189	Languages	English, Italian, Greek
Population	18 520 000	Religions	Protestant, Roman Catholic, Orthodox
Capital	Canberra	Organizations	APEC, Comm., OECD, UN

Australia, the world's sixth largest country, occupies the smallest, flattest and driest continent. The western half of the continent is mostly arid plateaus, ridges and vast deserts. The central-eastern area comprises the lowlands of river systems draining into Lake Eyre, while to the east is the Great Dividing Range, a belt of ridges and plateaus running from Queensland to Tasmania. Climatically more than two-thirds of the country is arid or semi-arid. The north is tropical monsoon, the east subtropical, and the southwest and southeast temperate. A majority of Australia's highly urbanized population lives in cities along on the east, southeast and southwest coasts. Australia is rich in natural resources. It has vast mineral deposits and various sources of energy. It is among the world's leading producers of iron ore, bauxite, nickel, copper and uranium, and other minerals include lead, gold, silver, zinc, manganese, tungsten and gems. It is a major producer of coal; oil and natural gas are also being exploited. Although accounting for only five per cent of the workforce, agriculture continues to be an important sector of the economy with food and agricultural raw materials making up around one third of exports by value; fuel, ores and metals, and manufactures account for the remainder of exports. Japan and the USA are Australia's main trading partners.

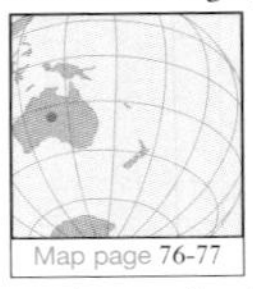
Map page 76-77

Australian Capital Territory (Federal territory)
Area Sq Km (Miles) 2 400 (927) Population 299 243 Capital Canberra

New South Wales (State)
Area Sq Km (Miles) 801 600 (309 499) Population 6 038 696 Capital Sydney

Northern Territory (Territory)
Area Sq Km (Miles) 1 346 200 (519 771) Population 195 101 Capital Darwin

Queensland (State)
Area Sq Km (Miles) 1 727 200 (666 876) Population 3 368 850 Capital Brisbane

South Australia (State)
Area Sq Km (Miles) 984 000 (379 925) Population 1 427 936 Capital Adelaide

Tasmania (State)
Area Sq Km (Miles) 67 800 (26 178) Population 459 659 Capital Hobart

Victoria (State)
Area Sq Km (Miles) 227 600 (87 877) Population 4 373 520 Capital Melbourne

Western Australia (State)
Area Sq Km (Miles) 2 525 500 (975 101) Population 1 726 095 Capital Perth

AUSTRIA
Republic of Austria

Area Sq Km	83 855	Currency	Schilling, Euro
Area Sq Miles	32 377	Languages	German, Croatian, Turkish
Population	8 140 000	Religions	Roman Catholic, Protestant
Capital	Wien (Vienna)	Organizations	EU, OECD, UN

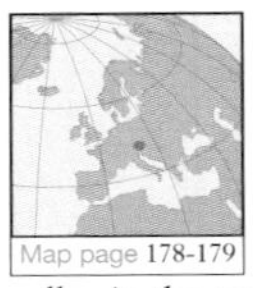
Map page 178-179

A landlocked state in central Europe, Austria borders the Czech Republic, Hungary, Slovenia, Switzerland, Italy, Germany and Liechtenstein. Two-thirds of the country, from the Swiss border to eastern Austria, lies within the Alps, with low mountains to the north. The only lowlands are in the east. The Danube river valley in the northeast contains almost all the agricultural land and most of the population. Though the climate varies with altitude, in general summers are warm and winters cold with heavy snowfalls. Manufacturing industry and tourism are the most important sectors of the economy. Exports are dominated by manufactured goods of which machinery and transport equipment make up over one third; Germany is Austria's main trading partner.

AZERBAIJAN
Azerbaijani Republic

Area Sq Km	86 600	Currency	Manat
Area Sq Miles	33 436	Languages	Azeri, Armenian, Russian, Lezgian
Population	7 669 000	Religions	Shi'a Muslim, Sunni Muslim, Orthodox
Capital	Bakı	Organizations	CIS, UN

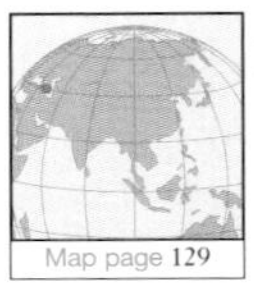
Map page 129

Azerbaijan lies to the southeast of the Caucasus, on the Caspian Sea. Its region of Naxçivan is separated from the rest of the country by part of Armenia. It has mountains in the northeast and west, valleys in the centre and a low coastal plain. The climate is continental. It is rich in energy and mineral resources. Oil production, onshore and offshore, is the main industry and the basis of heavy industries. Agriculture is still important, with cotton and tobacco the main cash crops. War with Armenia has reduced output.

THE BAHAMAS
Commonwealth of The Bahamas

Area Sq Km	13 939	Currency	Dollar
Area Sq Miles	5 382	Languages	English, creole
Population	296 000	Religions	Protestant, Roman Catholic
Capital	Nassau	Organizations	CARICOM, Comm., UN

The Bahamas is an archipelago of about seven hundred islands and over two thousand cays, to the northeast of Cuba and east of the Florida coast of the USA. Twenty-two islands are inhabited, and two

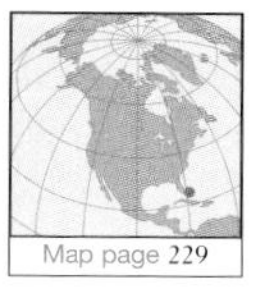
Map page 229

thirds of the population live on the main island of New Providence. The climate is warm for much of the year, with heavy rainfall in the summer. Tourism is the islands' main industry. Offshore banking, insurance and ship registration are also major foreign exchange earners.

BAHRAIN
State of Bahrain

Area Sq Km	691	Currency	Dinar
Area Sq Miles	267	Languages	Arabic, English
Population	595 000	Religions	Shi'a Muslim, Sunni Muslim, Christian
Capital	Manama	Organizations	UN

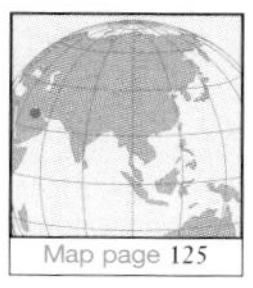
Map page 125

Bahrain consists of more than thirty islands lying in a bay in The Gulf, off the coasts of Saudi Arabia and Qatar. Bahrain Island, the largest island is connected to Muharraq and Sitrah islands by causeways. Oil production and processing are the main sectors of the economy.

BANGLADESH
People's Republic of Bangladesh

Area Sq Km	143 998	Currency	Taka
Area Sq Miles	55 598	Languages	Bengali, English
Population	124 774 000	Religions	Sunni Muslim, Hindu
Capital	Dhaka	Organizations	Comm., UN

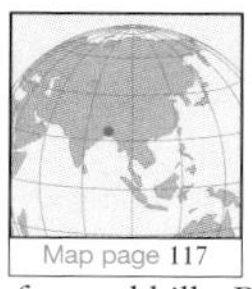
Map page 117

The south Asian state of Bangladesh is in the northeast of the Indian subcontinent, on the Bay of Bengal. It consists almost entirely of the low-lying alluvial plains and deltas of the Ganges and Brahmaputra rivers. The southwest is swampy, with mangrove forests in the delta area. The north, northeast and southeast have low forested hills. Bangladesh is one of the world's most densely populated and least developed countries. The economy is agriculture based, though the garment industry is the main export sector. Floods and cyclones during the summer monsoon season often cause devastating flooding and destroy crops. The country relies on large scale foreign aid and remittances from workers abroad.

BARBADOS

Area Sq Km	430	Currency	Dollar
Area Sq Miles	166	Languages	English, creole
Population	268 000	Religions	Protestant, Roman Catholic
Capital	Bridgetown	Organizations	CARICOM, Comm, UN

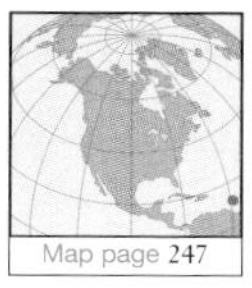
Map page 247

The most easterly of the Caribbean islands, Barbados is small and densely populated, with white-sand beaches and a tropical climate. The economy is based on tourism, financial services, light industries and sugar production.

BELARUS
Republic of Belarus

Area Sq Km	207 600	Currency	Rouble
Area Sq Miles	80 155	Languages	Belorussian, Russian
Population	10 315 000	Religions	Belorussian Orthodox, Roman Catholic
Capital	Minsk	Organizations	CIS, UN

Belarus is a landlocked state in east Europe, bounded by Lithuania, Latvia, Russia, Ukraine and Poland. Belarus consists of low hills and plains, with many lakes, rivers and, in the south, extensive marshes; forests cover around a third of the country. It has a continental climate. Agriculture contributes a third of national income, with beef cattle and grains as the major products. Manufacturing industries produce a range of items, from construction equipment to textiles. Belarus remains closely tied economically to Russia.

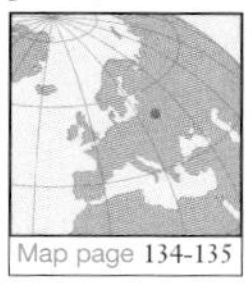
Map page 134-135

BELGIUM
Kingdom of Belgium

Area Sq Km	30 520	Currency	Franc, Euro
Area Sq Miles	11 784	Languages	Dutch (Flemish), French (Walloon), German
Population	10 141 000	Religions	Roman Catholic, Protestant
Capital	Bruxelles	Organizations	EU, OECD, UN

Belgium lies on the North Sea coast of western Europe. Beyond low sand dunes and a narrow belt of reclaimed land are fertile plains which extend to the Sambre-Meuse river valley from where the land rises to the forested Ardennes plateau in the southeast. Belgium has mild winters and cool summers. It is densely populated and has a highly urbanized population. The economy is based on trade, industry and services. With few mineral resources, Belgium imports raw materials for processing and manufacture. The agricultural sector is small, but provides for most food needs and a tenth of exports. A large services sector reflects Belgium's position as the home base for over eight hundred international institutions. The headquarters of the EU are in Bruxelles.

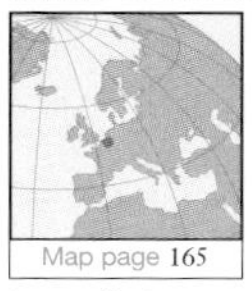
Map page 165

BELIZE

Area Sq Km	22 965	Currency	Dollar
Area Sq Miles	8 867	Languages	English, Spanish, Mayan, creole
Population	230 000	Religions	Roman Catholic, Protestant
Capital	Belmopan	Organizations	CARICOM, Comm., UN

Belize is on the Caribbean coast of central America and includes cays and a large barrier reef offshore. Belize's coastal areas are flat and swampy; the north and west are hilly, to the southwest are the Maya Mountains. Forests cover about half of the country. The climate is humid tropical, but tempered by sea breezes. A third of the population lives in the capital. The economy is based primarily on agriculture, forestry and fishing. Exports include raw sugar, orange concentrate and bananas.

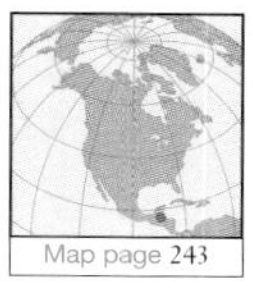
Map page 243

BENIN
Republic of Benin

Area Sq Km	112 620	Currency	CFA franc
Area Sq Miles	43 483	Languages	French, Fon, Yoruba, Adja, local languages
Population	5 781 000	Religions	Traditional beliefs, Roman Catholic, Sunni Muslim
Capital	Porto-Novo	Organizations	UN

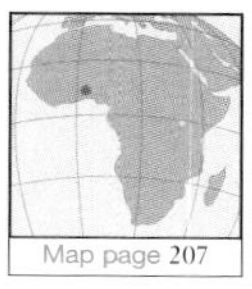
Map page 207

Benin is in west Africa, on the Gulf of Guinea. The climate is tropical in the north, but equatorial in the south. The economy is based mainly on agriculture and transit trade. Agricultural products account for two thirds of export earnings. Oil, produced offshore, is also a major export.

Bermuda
United Kingdom Overseas Territory

Area Sq Km	54	Currency	Dollar
Area Sq Miles	21	Languages	English
Population	64 000	Religions	Protestant, Roman Catholic
Capital	Hamilton		

In the Atlantic Ocean to the east of the USA, Bermuda is a group of small islands. The climate is warm and humid. The economy is based on tourism, insurance and shipping.

Map page 231

BHUTAN
Kingdom of Bhutan

Area Sq Km	46 620	Currency	Ngultrum
Area Sq Miles	18 000	Languages	Dzongkha, Nepali, Assamese
Population	2 004 000	Religions	Buddhist, Hindu
Capital	Thimphu	Organizations	UN

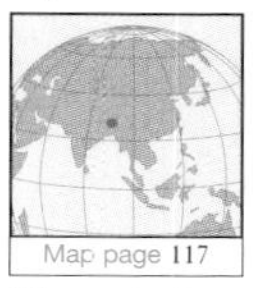
Map page 117

Bhutan is in the eastern Himalaya, between China and India. It is mountainous in the north, with fertile valleys where most people live. The climate ranges between permanently cold in the far north and subtropical in the south. Most of the population is involved in livestock raising and subsistence farming. Bhutan is the world's largest producer of cardamom. Tourism is an increasingly important foreign currency earner.

BOLIVIA
Republic of Bolivia

Area Sq Km	1 098 581	Currency	Boliviano
Area Sq Miles	424 164	Languages	Spanish, Quechua, Aymara
Population	7 957 000	Religions	Roman Catholic, Protestant, Baha'i
Capital	La Paz/Sucre	Organizations	UN

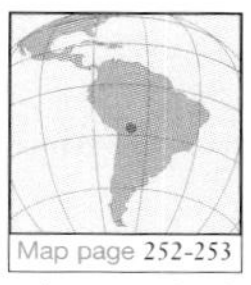
Map page 252-253

A landlocked state in central South America, Bolivia borders Brazil, Paraguay, Argentina, Chile and Peru. Most Bolivians live in the high plateau within the Andes ranges. The lowlands range between dense rainforest in the northeast and semi-arid grasslands in the southeast. Bolivia is rich in minerals (zinc, tin and silver) and sales generate around half of export income. Natural gas and timber are also exported. Subsistence farming predominates, though soya beans and, unofficially, coca are exported. USA is the main trading partner.

Bonaire part of Netherlands Antilles

Area Sq Km (Miles) 288 (111) Population 14 218

An island in the Caribbean Sea off the north coast of Venezuela; known for its fine beaches; tourism is the mainstay of the economy.

Map page 247

BOSNIA-HERZEGOVINA
Republic of Bosnia and Herzegovina

Area Sq Km	51 130	Currency	Marka
Area Sq Miles	19 741	Languages	Bosnian, Serbian, Croatian
Population	3 675 000	Religions	Sunni Muslim, Orthodox, Roman Catholic, Protestant
Capital	Sarajevo	Organizations	UN

Bosnia-Herzegovina lies in the western Balkans of southern Europe, on the Adriatic Sea. It is mountainous, with ridges running northwest-southeast. The main lowlands are around the Sava valley in the north. Summers are warm, but winters can be very cold. The Dayton Accord split the country into Republika Srpska and Federacija Bosna i Hercegovina. Much of the population relies on UN aid.

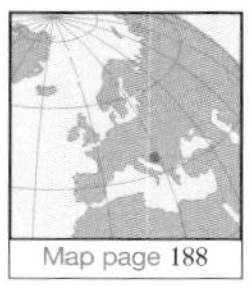
Map page 188

BOTSWANA
Republic of Botswana

Area Sq Km	581 370	Currency	Pula
Area Sq Miles	224 468	Languages	English, Setswana, Shona, local languages
Population	1 570 000	Religions	Traditional beliefs, Protestant, Roman Catholic
Capital	Gaborone	Organizations	Comm., SADC, UN

Botswana, a landlocked state in southern Africa, borders South Africa, Namibia, and Zimbabwe. Over half of the country lies within the Kalahari Desert, with swamps to the north and salt-pans to the northeast. Most people live near the eastern border. As a result of the AIDS epidemic, life expectancy has fallen by fourteen per cent since 1975. The climate is subtropical, but drought-prone. The economy was founded on cattle rearing, and though beef remains an important export, the economy is now based on mining. Diamonds account for eighty per cent of export earnings. Copper-nickel matte is also exported.

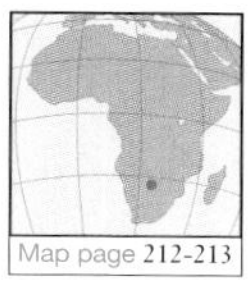
Map page 212-213

BRAZIL
Federative Republic of Brazil

Area Sq Km	8 547 379	Currency	Real
Area Sq Miles	3 300 161	Languages	Portuguese
Population	165 851 000	Religions	Roman Catholic, Protestant
Capital	Brasília	Organizations	UN

Brazil, in eastern South America, covers almost half of the continent - making it the world's fifth largest country - and borders ten countries and the Atlantic Ocean. The northwest contains the vast basin of the Amazon. The centre west is largely a vast plateau of savanna and rock escarpments. The northeast is mostly semi-arid plateaus, while to the east and south are rugged mountains, fertile valleys and narrow, fertile coastal plains. The Amazon basin is hot, humid and wet; the rest of Brazil is cooler and drier, with seasonal variations. The northeast is drought-prone. Most Brazilians live in urban areas along the coast and on the central plateau. Brazil has large and well developed agricultural, mining, and service sectors and the economy is larger than that of all other South American countries combined. Brazil is the world's largest producer of coffee, other agricultural crops include grains and sugar cane; mineral production includes iron, aluminium, and gold. Manufactured goods include food products, transport equipment, machinery and industrial chemicals. The main trading partners are USA and Argentina. Despite its natural wealth and being one of the largest economies in the world, Brazil has a large external debt and growing poverty gap.

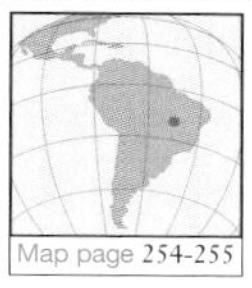
Map page 254-255

British Indian Ocean Territory
United Kingdom Overseas Territory

Area Sq Km (Miles) 60 (23) Population *uninhabited*

The territory consists of the Chagos Archipelago in central Indian Ocean. The islands are uninhabited apart from the joint British-US military base on Diego Garcia.

Map page 88

BRUNEI
State of Brunei Darussalam

Area Sq Km	5 765	Currency	Dollar
Area Sq Miles	2 226	Languages	Malay, English, Chinese
Population	315 000	Religions	Sunni Muslim, Buddhist, Christian
Capital	Bandar Seri Begawan	Organizations	APEC, ASEAN, Comm., UN

The southeast Asian state of Brunei lies on the northwest coast of the island of Borneo, on the South China Sea. Its two enclaves are surrounded inland by the Malaysian state of Sarawak. Tropical rainforest covers over two thirds of Brunei. The narrow coastal plain supports some crops and most of the population. The economy is dominated by the oil and gas industries.

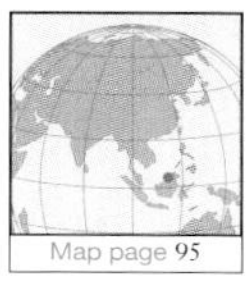
Map page 95

BULGARIA
Republic of Bulgaria

Area Sq Km	110 994	Currency	Lev
Area Sq Miles	42 855	Languages	Bulgarian, Turkish, Romany, Macedonian
Population	8 336 000	Religions	Bulgarian Orthodox, Sunni Muslim
Capital	Sofiya	Organizations	UN

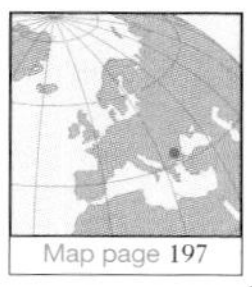
Map page 197

Bulgaria, in south Europe, borders Romania, Yugoslavia, Macedonia, Greece, Turkey and the Black Sea. The Balkan Mountains separate the Danube plains in the north from the Rhodope Mountains and the lowlands in the south. The economy is based on agriculture and manufacturing, chiefly machinery, consumer goods, chemicals and metals. Recent fiscal reforms have reduced inflation and helped economic recovery. Bulgaria is negotiating to join the EU.

BURKINA
Democratic Republic of Burkina Faso

Area Sq Km	274 200	Currency	CFA franc
Area Sq Miles	105 869	Languages	French, Moore (Mossi), Fulani, local languages
Population	11 305 000	Religions	Sunni Muslim, traditional beliefs, Roman Catholic
Capital	Ouagadougou	Organizations	UN

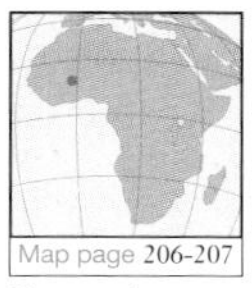
Map page 206-207

Burkina, a landlocked country in west Africa, borders Mali, Niger, Benin, Togo, Ghana and Côte d'Ivoire. The north of Burkina lies within the Sahara and is arid. The south is mainly semi-arid savanna. Rainfall is erratic and droughts are common. Livestock rearing and farming are the main activities. Cotton, livestock, groundnuts and some minerals are exported. Burkina relies heavily on aid, and is amongst the poorest and least developed countries in the world.

BURUNDI
Republic of Burundi

Area Sq Km	27 835	Currency	Franc
Area Sq Miles	10 747	Languages	Kirundi (Hutu, Tutsi), French
Population	6 457 000	Religions	Roman Catholic, traditional beliefs, Protestant
Capital	Bujumbura	Organizations	UN

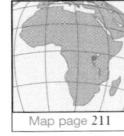

The densely populated east African state of Burundi borders Rwanda, Democratic Republic of Congo, Tanzania and Lake Tanganyika. It is hilly with high plateaus and a tropical climate. Burundi depends upon subsistence farming, coffee exports; ethnic violence in the mid 1990s increased dependence on foreign aid.

Map page 211

CAMBODIA
Kingdom of Cambodia

Area Sq Km	181 000	Currency	Riel
Area Sq Miles	69 884	Languages	Khmer, Vietnamese
Population	10 716 000	Religions	Buddhist, Roman Catholic, Sunni Muslim
Capital	Phnum Pénh	Organizations	ASEAN, UN

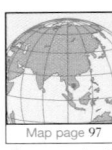

Cambodia lies in southeast Asia, on the Gulf of Thailand and occupies the Mekong river basin, with the Tônlé Sap at its centre; there are mountains in the southwest and north. The climate is tropical monsoon, forests cover half the land. Most people live on the plains and are engaged in farming (chiefly rice growing), fishing and forestry. Devastated by decades of civil war, continued political instability hampers development.

Map page 97

CAMEROON
Republic of Cameroon

Area Sq Km	475 442	Currency	CFA franc
Area Sq Miles	183 569	Languages	French, English, Fang, Bamileke, local languages
Population	14 305 000	Religions	Roman Catholic, Sunni Muslim, Protestant
Capital	Yaoundé	Organizations	Comm., UN

Cameroon is in west Africa, on the Gulf of Guinea. The coastal plains, southern and central plateaus are covered with tropical forest. Despite oil resources and favourable agricultural conditions Cameroon still faces problems of underdevelopment. Oil, timber and cocoa are the main exports. France is the main trading partner.

Map page 207

CANADA

Area Sq Km	9 970 610	Currency	Dollar
Area Sq Miles	3 849 674	Languages	English, French
Population	30 563 000	Religions	Roman Catholic, Protestant, Orthodox, Jewish
Capital	Ottawa	Organizations	APEC, Comm., OECD, UN

The world's second largest country, Canada covers the northern two-fifths of North America and has coastlines on the Atlantic, Arctic and Pacific Oceans. On the west coast, the mountain ranges include the Coast Mountains, interior plateaus and the Rocky Mountains. In the centre lie the fertile prairies. Further east, covering about half the total land area, is the Canadian Shield, fairly flat lowlands around the Hudson Bay extending to Labrador. The Shield is bordered to the south by the fertile Great Lakes-St Lawrence lowlands. In the far north

climatic conditions are polar, the rest of Canada has a continental climate. Winters are long and cold with heavy snowfalls, while summers are hot with light to moderate rainfall. Most Canadians live in the south, chiefly in the southeast, in the urban areas of the Great Lakes-St Lawrence basin. Canada is rich in mineral and energy resources. Only five per cent of land is as arable, but that is still a large area. Canada is among the world's leading producers of wheat, a leading exporter of wood from its vast coniferous forests, and fish and seafood from its rich Atlantic and Pacific fishing grounds. It is a top producer of nickel, uranium, copper, iron ore, zinc and other minerals, as well as oil and natural gas. Its abundant raw materials are the basis for manufacturing industries. Main exports are machinery, motor vehicles, oil, timber, newsprint and paper, wood pulp and wheat. Since the 1989 free trade agreement with USA and the 1994 North America Free Trade Agreement (which includes Mexico), trade with the USA has grown and now accounts for around eighty per cent of imports and around seventy five per cent of exports.

Map page 220-221

Alberta (Province)		
Area Sq Km (Miles) 661 190 (255 287)	Population 2 914 900	Capital Edmonton

British Columbia (Province)		
Area Sq Km (Miles) 947 800 (365 948)	Population 4 009 900	Capital Victoria

Manitoba (Province)		
Area Sq Km (Miles) 649 950 (250 947)	Population 1 138 000	Capital Winnipeg

New Brunswick (Province)		
Area Sq Km (Miles) 73 440 (28 355)	Population 753 000	Capital Fredericton

Newfoundland (Province)		
Area Sq Km (Miles) 405 720 (156 649)	Population 544 400	Capital St John's

Northwest Territories (Territory)		
Area Sq Km (Miles) 1 432 320 (553 022)	Population 45 500	Capital Yellowknife

Nova Scotia (Province)		
Area Sq Km (Miles) 55 490 (21 425)	Population 934 600	Capital Halifax

Nunavut (Territory)		
Area Sq Km (Miles) 1 994 000 (769 888)	Population 22 000	Capital Iqaluit

Ontario (Province)		
Area Sq Km (Miles) 1 068 580 (412 581)	Population 11 411 500	Capital Toronto

Prince Edward Island (Province)		
Area Sq Km (Miles) 5 660 (2 185)	Population 136 400	Capital Charlottetown

Québec (Province)		
Area Sq Km (Miles) 1 540 680 (594 860)	Population 7 333 300	Capital Québec

Saskatchewan (Province)		
Area Sq Km (Miles) 652 330 (251 866)	Population 1 024 400	Capital Regina

Yukon Territory (Territory)		
Area Sq Km (Miles) 483 450 (186 661)	Population 31 700	Capital Whitehorse

CAPE VERDE
Republic of Cape Verde

Area Sq Km	4 033	Currency	Escudo
Area Sq Miles	1 557	Languages	Portuguese, creole
Population	408 000	Religions	Roman Catholic, Protestant
Capital	Praia	Organizations	UN

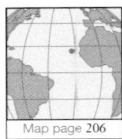

Cape Verde is a group of ten semi-arid volcanic islands off the coast of west Africa. The economy is based on fishing and subsistence farming, but relies on emigrant workers' remittances and foreign aid.

Map page 206

Cayman Islands
United Kingdom Overseas Territory

Area Sq Km	259	Currency	Dollar
Area Sq Miles	100	Languages	English
Population	36 000	Religions	Roman Catholic, Protestant
Capital	George Town	Organizations	UN

A group of islands in the Caribbean, northwest of Jamaica; there are three main islands: Grand Cayman, Little Cayman and Cayman Brac. They form one of the world's major offshore financial centres, tourism is also important and is aimed at the luxury market.

Map page 246

CENTRAL AFRICAN REPUBLIC

Area Sq Km	622 436	Currency	CFA franc
Area Sq Miles	240 324	Languages	French, Sango, Banda, Baya, local languages
Population	3 485 000	Religions	Protestant, Roman Catholic, trad. beliefs, Muslim
Capital	Bangui	Organizations	UN

The landlocked Central African Republic borders Chad, Sudan, Democratic Republic of Congo, Congo and Cameroon. Most of the country is savanna plateau, drained by the Ubangi and Chari river systems, with mountains to the east and west. The climate is tropical with high rainfall. Most of the population live in the south and west, and a majority of the workforce is involved in subsistence farming. Some cotton, coffee, tobacco and timber are exported, but diamonds account for around half of export earnings.

Map page 208

CHAD
Republic of Chad

Area Sq Km	1 284 000	Currency	CFA franc
Area Sq Miles	495 755	Languages	Arabic, French, Sara, local languages
Population	7 270 000	Religions	Sunni Muslim, Roman Catholic, Protestant
Capital	Ndjamena	Organizations	UN

Chad is a landlocked state of central Africa, bordered by Libya, Sudan, Central African Republic, Niger, Nigeria and Cameroon. It consists of plateaus, the Tibesti mountains in the north and Lake Chad basin in the west. Climatic conditions range between desert in the north and tropical forest in the southwest. The largely rural population live in the south and near Lake Chad. Farming, cattle herding and fishing are the main activities; raw cotton is the main export. Chad relies heavily on foreign aid.

Map page 202

CHILE
Republic of Chile

Area Sq Km	756 945	Currency	Peso
Area Sq Miles	292 258	Languages	Spanish, Amerindian languages
Population	14 824 000	Religions	Roman Catholic, Protestant
Capital	Santiago	Organizations	APEC, UN

Chile lies along the Pacific coast of the southern half of South America. Between the Andes in the east and the lower coastal ranges, is a central valley, with a mild climate, where most Chileans live. To the north is the arid Atacama Desert, to the south is cold, wet forested grassland. Chile is the world's leading exporter of copper; nitrates, molybdenum, gold, iron are also important. Agriculture, forestry and fishing are important activities. Copper accounts for a third of the value of exports, other minerals, timber and fish production are also important.

Map page 258-259

CHINA
People's Republic of China

Area Sq Km	9 584 492	Currency	Yuan
Area Sq Miles	3 700 593	Languages	Mandarin, Wu, Cantonese, Hsiang, regional languages
Population	1 262 817 000		
Capital	Beijing	Religions	Confucian, Taoist, Buddhist, Christian, Muslim
		Organizations	APEC, UN

China, the world's most populous and third largest country, occupies almost the whole of east Asia, borders fourteen states and has coastlines on the Yellow, East China and South China Seas. It has an amazing variety of landscapes. The southwest contains the high Plateau of Tibet, flanked by the Himalaya and Kunlun Shan. The north is mountainous with arid basins and extends from the Tien Shan and Altai Mountains and vast Taklimakan Shamo in the west to the plateau and Gobi desert in the centre-east. Eastern China is predominantly lowland and is divided broadly into the basins of the Huang He (Yellow River) in the north, Chang Jiang (Yangtze) in the centre and Xi Jiang (Pearl River) in the southeast. Climatic conditions and vegetation are as diverse as the topography: much of the country experiences temperate conditions, while southwest China has an extreme mountain climate, and the southeast enjoys a moist, warm subtropical climate. Nearly seventy per cent of China's huge population live in rural areas, chiefly in the northern part of the eastern lowlands, in the Red Basin and along the coast. Agriculture employs around half of the working

population. The main crops are rice, wheat, soya beans, peanuts, cotton, tobacco and hemp. China is rich in coal, oil and natural gas and has the world's largest potential in hydroelectric power; it is a major world producer of iron ore, molybdenum, copper, asbestos and gold. Economic reforms from the early 1980's onward led to an explosion in manufacturing development concentrated on the 'coastal economic open region'. The main exports are machinery, textiles, footwear, toy and sports goods. Japan and the USA are the main trading partners.

Map page 98

Anhui (Province)		
Area Sq Km (Miles) 139 000 (53 668)	Population 60 130 000	Capital Hefei

Beijing (Municipality)		
Area Sq Km (Miles) 16 800 (6 487)	Population 12 510 000	Capital Beijing

Chongqing (Municipality)		
Area Sq Km (Miles) 23 000 (8 880)	Population 14 600 000	Capital Chongqing

Fujian (Province)		
Area Sq Km (Miles) 121 400 (46 873)	Population 32 370 000	Capital Fuzhou

Gansu (Province)		
Area Sq Km (Miles) 453 700 (175 175)	Population 24 380 000	Capital Lanzhou

Guangdong (Province)		
Area Sq Km (Miles) 178 000 (68 726)	Population 68 680 000	Capital Guangzhou

Guangxi Zhuangzu Zizhiqu (Autonomous Region)		
Area Sq Km (Miles) 236 000 (91 120)	Population 45 430 000	Capital Nanning

Guizhou (Province)		
Area Sq Km (Miles) 176 000 (67 954)	Population 35 080 000	Capital Guiyang

Hainan (Province)		
Area Sq Km (Miles) 34 000 (13 127)	Population 7 240 000	Capital Haikou

Hebei (Province)		
Area Sq Km (Miles) 187 700 (72 471)	Population 64 370 000	Capital Shijiazhuang

Heilongjiang (Province)		
Area Sq Km (Miles) 454 600 (175 522)	Population 37 010 000	Capital Harbin

Henan (Province)		
Area Sq Km (Miles) 167 000 (64 479)	Population 91 000 000	Capital Zhengzhou

Hong Kong (Special Administrative Region)		
Area Sq Km (Miles) 1 075 (415)	Population 6 706 965	Capital Hong Kong

Hubei (Province)		
Area Sq Km (Miles) 185 900 (71 776)	Population 57 720 000	Capital Wuhan

Hunan (Province)		
Area Sq Km (Miles) 210 000 (81 081)	Population 63 920 000	Capital Changsha

Jiangsu (Province)		
Area Sq Km (Miles) 102 600 (39 614)	Population 70 660 000	Capital Nanjing

Jiangxi (Province)		
Area Sq Km (Miles) 166 900 (64 440)	Population 40 630 000	Capital Nanchang

Jilin (Province)		
Area Sq Km (Miles) 187 000 (72 201)	Population 25 920 000	Capital Changchun

Liaoning (Province)		
Area Sq Km (Miles) 147 400 (56 911)	Population 40 920 000	Capital Shenyang

Macau (Special Administrative Region)		
Area Sq Km (Miles) 17 (7)	Population 459 000	Capital Macau

Nei Mongol Zizhiqu (Inner Mongolia) (Autonomous Region)		
Area Sq Km (Miles) 1 183 000 (456 759)	Population 22 840 000	Capital Huhhot

Ningxia Huizu Zizhiqu (Autonomous Region)		
Area Sq Km (Miles) 66 400 (25 637)	Population 5 130 000	Capital Yinchuan

Qinghai (Province)		
Area Sq Km (Miles) 721 000 (278 380)	Population 4 810 000	Capital Xining

Shaanxi (Province)		
Area Sq Km (Miles) 205 600 (79 383)	Population 35 140 000	Capital Xi'an

Shandong (Province)		
Area Sq Km (Miles) 153 300 (59 189)	Population 87 050 000	Capital Jinan

Shanghai (Municipality)		
Area Sq Km (Miles) 6 300 (2 432)	Population 14 150 000	Capital Shanghai

Shanxi (Province)		
Area Sq Km (Miles)156 300 (60 348)	Population 30 770 000	Capital Taiyuan

Sichaun (Province)		
Area Sq Km (Miles) 569 000 (219 692)	Population 98 650 000	Capital Chengdu

Tianjin (Municipality)		
Area Sq Km (Miles) 11 300 (4 363)	Population 9 420 000	Capital Tianjin

Xinjiang Uygur Zizhiqu (Sinkiang) (Autonomous Region)		
Area Sq Km (Miles) 1 600 000 (617 763)	Population 16 610 000	Capital Ürümqi

Xizang Zizhiqu (Tibet) (Autonomous Region)		
Area Sq Km (Miles) 1 228 400 (474 288)	Population 2 400 000	Capital Lhasa

Yunnan (Province)		
Area Sq Km (Miles) 394 000 (152 124)	Population 39 900 000	Capital Kunming

Zhejiang (Province)		
Area Sq Km (Miles) 101 800 (39 305)	Population 43 190 000	Capital Hangzhou

Christmas Island
Australian External Territory

Area Sq Km	135	Currency	Austr. dollar
Area Sq Miles	52	Languages	English
Population	2 195	Religions	Buddhist, Sunni Muslim, Protestant, Roman Catholic
Capital	The Settlement		

The island is situated in the east of the Indian Ocean, to the south of Indonesia. The economy is based on phosphate extraction, though reserves are nearing depletion; tourism is developing and is the major employer.

Map page 86

Cocos Islands (Keeling Islands)
Australian External Territory

Area Sq Km	14	Currency	Austr. dollar
Area Sq Miles	5	Languages	English
Population	637	Religions	Sunni Muslim, Christian
Capital	West Island		

The Cocos Islands are two separate coral atolls in the east of the Indian Ocean between Sri Lanka and Australia. Most of the population live on West Island and Home Island. Coconuts are the only cash crop and the economy is based on these and on tourism.

Map page 86

COLOMBIA
Republic of Colombia

Area Sq Km	1 141 748	Currency	Peso
Area Sq Miles	440 831	Languages	Spanish, Amerindian languages
Population	40 803 000	Religions	Roman Catholic, Protestant
Capital	Bogotá	Organizations	APEC, UN

A state in northwest South America, Colombia has coastlines on the Pacific Ocean and the Caribbean Sea. Behind coastal plains lie three ranges of the Andes, separated by high valleys and plateaus where most Colombians live. To the southeast are grasslands and then the forests of the Amazon. Colombia has a tropical climate, though temperatures vary with altitude. Only five per cent of land can be cultivated, but a range of crops are grown. Coffee (Colombia is the world's second largest producer), sugar, bananas, cotton and flowers are exported. Coal, nickel, gold, silver, platinum and emeralds (Colombia is the world's largest producer) are mined. Oil and its products are the main export. Industry involves processing minerals and agricultural produce. The main trade partner is the USA. In spite of government efforts to stop the drugs trade, coca growing and cocaine smuggling are rife.

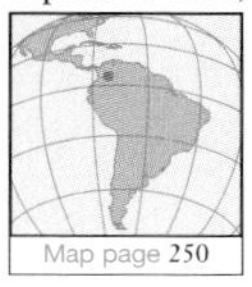
Map page 250

COMOROS
Federal Islamic Republic of the Comoros

Area Sq Km	1 862	Currency	Franc
Area Sq Miles	719	Languages	Comorian, French, Arabic
Population	658 000	Religions	Sunni Muslim, Roman Catholic
Capital	Moroni	Organizations	UN

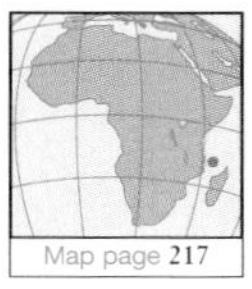
Map page 217

The state comprises three volcanic islands: Grande Comore, Anjouan and Mohéil, and some coral atolls in the Indian Ocean, off the east African coast. The tropical islands are mountainous, with poor soil. Subsistence farming predominates, but vanilla, cloves and ylang-ylang (an essential oil) are exported.

CONGO
Republic of the Congo

Area Sq Km	342 000	Currency	CFA franc
Area Sq Miles	132 047	Languages	French, Kongo, Monokutuba, local languages
Population	2 785 000	Religions	Roman Catholic, Protestant, trad. beliefs, Muslim
Capital	Brazzaville	Organizations	UN

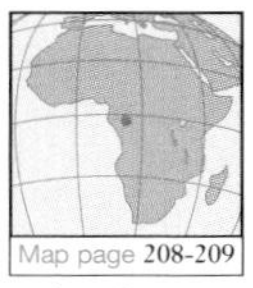
Map page 208-209

Congo, in central Africa, is mostly forest or savanna-covered plateaus drained by the Ubangi-Congo river systems. Sand dunes and lagoons line the short Atlantic coast. The climate is hot and tropical. Most Congolese live in the southern third of the country. Half of the workforce are farmers, growing food crops and cash crops including sugar, coffee, cocoa and oil palms. Oil makes up over three quarters of export revenues, hardwoods are the second biggest export earner.

CONGO, DEMOCRATIC REPUBLIC OF

Area Sq Km	2 345 410	Currency	Franc
Area Sq Miles	905 568	Languages	French, Lingala, Swahili, Kongo, local languages
Population	49 139 000	Religions	Christian, Sunni Muslim
Capital	Kinshasa	Organizations	SADC, UN

The central African state consists of the basin of the Congo river flanked by plateaus, with high mountain ranges to the east and a short Atlantic coastline to the west. The climate is tropical with rainforest close to the Equator and savannas to the north and south. Congo has fertile land that grows a range of food crops and cash crops, chiefly coffee. It has vast mineral resources, copper, cobalt and diamonds being the most important. Continued political instability inhibits development.

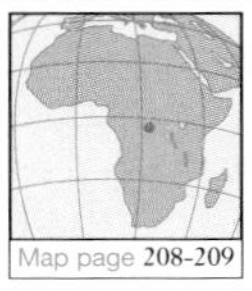
Map page 208-209

Cook Islands
Self-governing New Zealand Territory

Area Sq Km	293	Currency	Dollar
Area Sq Miles	113	Languages	English, Maori
Population	19 000	Religions	Protestant, Roman Catholic
Capital	Avarua		

Groups of coral atolls and volcanic islands in the southwest Pacific Ocean. The main island is Rarotonga. Distance from foreign markets and few natural resources hinder development and there were severe economic problems in the late 1990s.

Map page 81

COSTA RICA
Republic of Costa Rica

Area Sq Km	51 100	Currency	Colón
Area Sq Miles	19 730	Languages	Spanish
Population	3 841 000	Religions	Roman Catholic, Protestant
Capital	San José	Organizations	UN

Costa Rica has coastlines on the Caribbean Sea and Pacific Ocean. From the tropical coastal plains, the land rises to mountains and a temperate central plateau where most people live. The economy depends on tourism, with ecotourism becoming increasingly important, and agriculture; main exports are textiles, coffee and bananas; almost half of all trade is with USA.

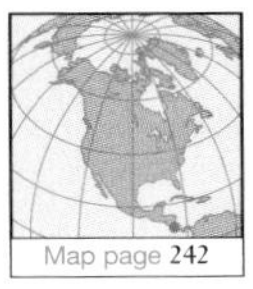
Map page 242

CÔTE D'IVOIRE
Republic of Côte d'Ivoire

Area Sq Km	322 463	Currency	CFA franc
Area Sq Miles	124 504	Languages	French, creole, Akan, local languages
Population	14 292 000	Religions	Muslim, Roman Catholic, trad. beliefs, Protestant
Capital	Yamoussoukro	Organizations	UN

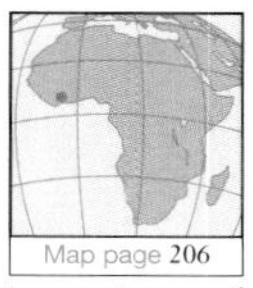
Map page 206

Côte d'Ivoire is in west Africa, on the Gulf of Guinea. In the north are plateaus and savanna, in the south are low undulating plains and rainforest, with sand-bars and lagoons on the coast. Temperatures are warm, and rainfall is heavier in the south. Most of the workforce is engaged in farming. Côte d'Ivoire is a major producer of cocoa and coffee, and agricultural products (including cotton and timber) are the main export. Oil and gas have begun to be exploited.

CROATIA
Republic of Croatia

Area Sq Km	56 538	Currency	Kuna
Area Sq Miles	21 829	Languages	Croatian, Serbian
Population	4 481 000	Religions	Roman Catholic, Serbian Orthodox, Sunni Muslim
Capital	Zagreb	Organizations	UN

The south European state of Croatia has a long coastline on the Adriatic Sea and many offshore islands. Coastal areas have a Mediterranean climate, inland is colder and wetter. Croatia was strong agriculturally and industrially, but conflict in 1991-1992, the loss of markets and tourist revenue have caused economic difficulties; recovery has been slow.

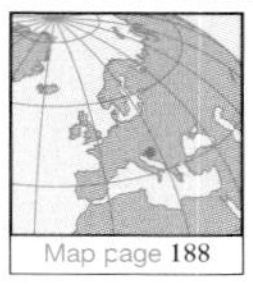
Map page 188

CUBA
Republic of Cuba

Area Sq Km	110 860	Currency	Peso
Area Sq Miles	42 803	Languages	Spanish
Population	110 860	Religions	Roman Catholic, Protestant
Capital	La Habana	Organizations	UN

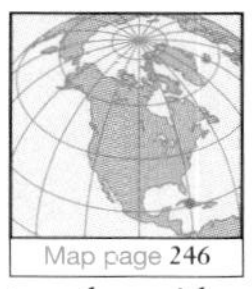
Map page 246

Cuba comprises the island of Cuba, the largest island in the Caribbean, and many islets and cays. A fifth of Cubans live in and around La Habana. Cuba is slowly recovering from the withdrawal of aid and subsidies from the former USSR. Sugar remains the basis of the economy, though tourism is developing and is, together with remittances from workers abroad, an important source of foreign currency.

Curaçao part of Netherlands Antilles

Area Sq Km (Miles)	444 (171)	Population	151 448	Capital	Willemstad

An island in the Caribbean Sea off the north coast of Venezuela, it is the largest and most populous island of the Netherlands Antilles. Oil refining and tourism form the basis of the economy.

Map page 247

CYPRUS
Republic of Cyprus

Area Sq Km	9 251	Currency	Pound
Area Sq Miles	3 572	Languages	Greek, Turkish, English
Population	771 000	Religions	Greek Orthodox, Sunni Muslim
Capital	Lefkosia	Organizations	Comm., UN

The eastern Mediterranean island of Cyprus has hot dry summers and mild winters. The economy of the Greek south is based mainly on specialist agriculture and tourism, though shipping and offshore banking are also major sources of income. The Turkish north depends upon agriculture, tourism and aid from Turkey. Cyprus is negotiating to join the EU.

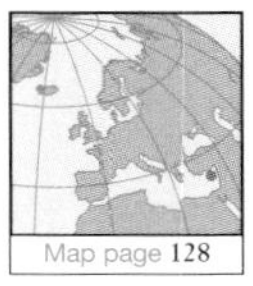
Map page 128

CZECH REPUBLIC

Area Sq Km	78 864	Currency	Koruna
Area Sq Miles	30 450	Languages	Czech, Moravian, Slovak
Population	10 282 000	Religions	Roman Catholic, Protestant
Capital	Praha	Organizations	UN

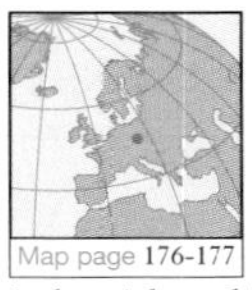
Map page 176-177

The landlocked Czech Republic in central Europe consists of rolling countryside, wooded hills and fertile valleys. The climate is temperate, but winters are fairly cold. The country has substantial reserves of coal and lignite, timber and some minerals, chiefly iron ore. It is highly industrialized and major manufactures include industrial machinery, consumer goods, cars, iron and steel, chemicals and glass. Germany is the main trading partner. The Czech Republic began formal talks on EU accession in 1998.

DENMARK
Kingdom of Denmark

Area Sq Km	43 075	Currency	Krone
Area Sq Miles	16 631	Languages	Danish
Population	5 270 000	Religions	Protestant
Capital	København	Organizations	EU, OECD, UN

In north Europe, Denmark occupies the Jylland (Jutland) peninsula and nearly five hundred islands in and between the North and Baltic Seas. The country is low-lying, with long, indented coastlines. The climate is cool and temperate, with rainfall throughout the year. A fifth of the population lives around København on the largest of the islands, Sjaelland (Zealand). Denmark's main natural resource is its agricultural potential; two thirds of the total area is fertile farmland or pasture. But agriculture is now high-tech and with forestry and fishing employs only around six per cent of the workforce. Denmark is self-sufficient in oil and natural gas, produced from fields in the North Sea. Manufacturing, largely based on imported raw materials, now accounts for over half of exports which include machinery, food, furniture, and pharmaceuticals. The main trading partners are Germany and Sweden.

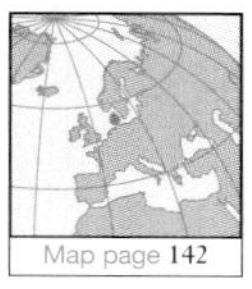
Map page 142

DJIBOUTI
Republic of Djibouti

Area Sq Km	23 200	Currency	Franc
Area Sq Miles	8 958	Languages	Somali, Afar, French, Arabic
Population	623 000	Religions	Sunni Muslim, Christian
Capital	Djibouti	Organizations	UN

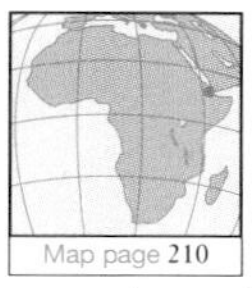
Map page 210

Djibouti lies in northeast Africa, on the Gulf of Aden at the entrance to the Red Sea. Most of the country is semi-arid desert with high temperatures and low rainfall. More than half of the population live in the capital. There is some camel, sheep and goat herding but with few natural resources, the economy is based on services and trade. The deep-water port and the railway line to Ādīs Ābeba in Ethiopia account for about two thirds of national income.

DOMINICA
Commonwealth of Dominica

Area Sq Km	750	Currency	E. Carib.dollar
Area Sq Miles	290	Languages	English, creole
Population	71 000	Religions	Roman Catholic, Protestant
Capital	Roseau	Organizations	CARICOM, Comm., UN

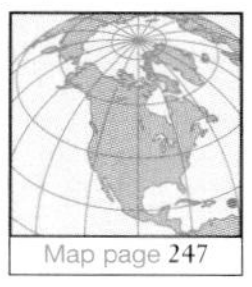
Map page 247

Dominica is the most northerly of the Windward Islands in the eastern Caribbean. It is very mountainous and forested, with a coastline of steep cliffs. The climate is tropical and rainfall abundant. Around a quarter of Dominicans live in the capital. The economy is based on agriculture, with bananas (the major export), coconuts and citrus fruits the most important crops. Tourism is developing, but is hindered by the rugged coastline and lack of sandy beaches.

DOMINICAN REPUBLIC

Area Sq Km	48 442	Currency	Peso
Area Sq Miles	18 704	Languages	Spanish, creole
Population	8 232 000	Religions	Roman Catholic, Protestant
Capital	Santo Domingo	Organizations	UN

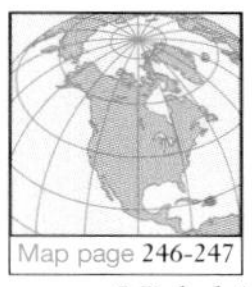
Map page 246-247

The state occupies the eastern two thirds of the Caribbean island of Hispaniola (the western third is Haiti). The frontier with Haiti is closed. It has a series of mountain ranges, fertile valleys and a large coastal plain in the east. The climate is hot tropical, with heavy rainfall. Sugar, coffee and cocoa are the main cash crops. Nickel (the main export), and gold are mined, and there is some light industry. USA is the main trading partner. Tourism is the main foreign exchange earner.

East Timor
under UN Transitional Administration

Area Sq Km	14 874	Languages	Portuguese, Tetun, English
Area Sq Miles	5 743	Religions	Roman Catholic
Population	857 000		
Capital	Dili		

The eastern part, and a small coastal enclave to the west, of the island Timor, which is part of Indonesian archipelago to the north of Western Australia. A referendum in 1999 officially ended Indonesia's occupation; East Timor is under a UN transitional administration.

Map page 93

ECUADOR
Republic of Ecuador

Area Sq Km	272 045	Currency	Sucre
Area Sq Miles	105 037	Languages	Spanish, Quechua, and other Amerindian languages
Population	12 175 000	Religions	Roman Catholic
Capital	Quito	Organizations	APEC, UN

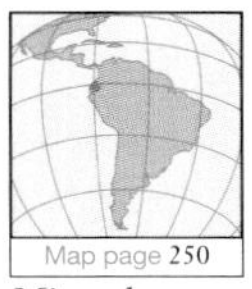
Map page 250

Ecuador is in northwest South America, on the Pacific coast. It consists of a broad coastal plain, the high ranges of the Andes and the forested upper Amazon basin to the east. The climate is tropical, moderated by altitude. Most people live on the coast or in the mountain valleys. Ecuador is one of South America's main oil producers. Mineral reserves include gold. Most of the workforce depends on agriculture; bananas, shrimps, coffee and cocoa are exported; USA is the main trading partner.

EGYPT
Arab Republic of Egypt

Area Sq Km	1 000 250	Currency	Pound
Area Sq Miles	386 199	Languages	Arabic
Population	65 978 000	Religions	Sunni Muslim, Coptic Christian
Capital	Cairo	Organizations	UN

Egypt, on the eastern Mediterranean coast of North Africa, is low-lying, with areas below sea level in the Qattâra depression, and mountain ranges along the Red Sea coast and in the Sinai peninsula. It is a land of desert and semi-desert, except for the Nile valley, where ninety nine per cent of Egyptians live, nearly half of them in towns and cities. A project for the development of Sinai aims to resettle over three million people in the area by 2017. The summers are hot, the winters mild and rainfall is negligible. Less than four per cent of land (chiefly around the Nile floodplain and delta) is cultivated, but farming employs about one third of the workforce; cotton is the main cash crop, rice, fruit and vegetables are exported, but Egypt imports

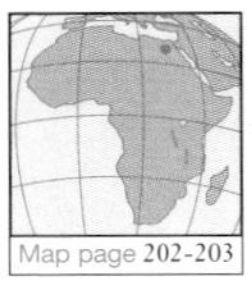
Map page 202-203

over half its food needs. There are oil and natural gas reserves, though nearly a quarter of electricity comes from hydro-electric power. Main exports are oil and oil products, cotton, textiles and clothing.

EL SALVADOR
Republic of El Salvador

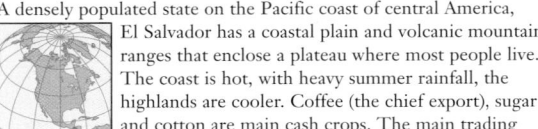

Area Sq Km	21 041	Currency	Colón
Area Sq Miles	8 124	Languages	Spanish
Population	6 032 000	Religions	Roman Catholic, Protestant
Capital	San Salvador	Organizations	UN

A densely populated state on the Pacific coast of central America, El Salvador has a coastal plain and volcanic mountain ranges that enclose a plateau where most people live. The coast is hot, with heavy summer rainfall, the highlands are cooler. Coffee (the chief export), sugar and cotton are main cash crops. The main trading partners are USA and Guatemala.

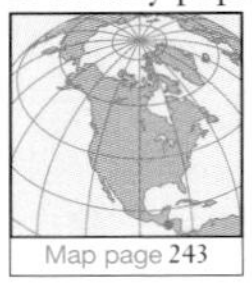
Map page 243

EQUATORIAL GUINEA
Republic of Equatorial Guinea

Area Sq Km	28 051	Currency	CFA franc
Area Sq Miles	10 831	Languages	Spanish, French, Fang
Population	431 000	Religions	Roman Catholic, traditional beliefs
Capital	Malabo	Organizations	UN

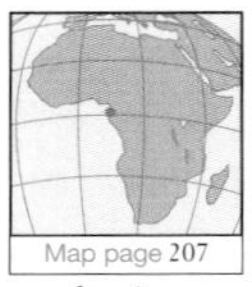
Map page 207

The state consists of Rio Muni, an enclave on the Atlantic coast of central Africa, and the islands of Bioco, Annobón and the Corisco group. Most people live on the coastal plain and upland plateau of Rio Muni; the capital is on the fertile volcanic island of Bioco. The climate is hot, humid and wet. Oil production started in 1992 and oil is now the main export along with timber, but the economy depends heavily upon foreign aid.

ERITREA
State of Eritrea

Area Sq Km	117 400	Currency	Nakfa
Area Sq Miles	45 328	Languages	Tigrinya, Tigre
Population	3 577 000	Religions	Sunni Muslim, Coptic Christian
Capital	Asmara	Organizations	UN

Eritrea, on the Red Sea coast of northeast Africa, consists of high plateau in the north and a coastal plain that widens to the south. The coast is hot, inland is cooler. Rainfall is unreliable. The agricultural-based economy has suffered from over thirty years of war and occasional poor rains. Eritrea is one of the least developed countries in the world.

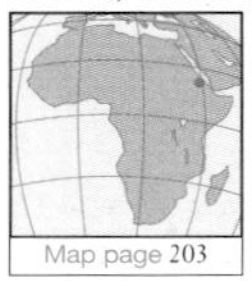
Map page 203

ESTONIA
Republic of Estonia

Area Sq Km	45 200	Currency	Kroon
Area Sq Miles	17 452	Languages	Estonian, Russian
Population	1 429 000	Religions	Protestant, Estonian and Russian Orthodox
Capital	Tallinn	Organizations	UN

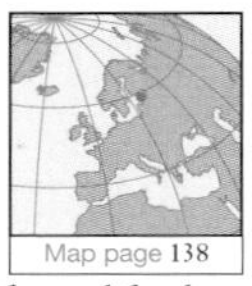
Map page 138

Estonia is in north Europe, on the Gulf of Finland and Baltic Sea. The land, over one third of which is forested, is generally low-lying, with many lakes. The climate is temperate. About one third of Estonians live in Tallinn. Industries and exported goods include timber, furniture production, shipbuilding, leather, fur and food processing. The main trading partners are Russia, Finland and Sweden. Estonia is negotiating to join the EU.

ETHIOPIA
Federal Democratic Republic of Ethiopia

Area Sq Km	1 133 880	Currency	Birr
Area Sq Miles	437 794	Languages	Oromo, Amharic, Tigrinya, local languages
Population	59 649 000	Religions	Ethiopian Orthodox, Muslim, trad. beliefs
Capital	Ādīs Ābeba	Organizations	UN

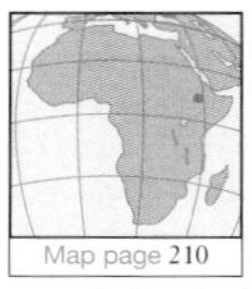
Map page 210

A landlocked country in northeast Africa, Ethiopia borders Eritrea, Djibouti, Somalia, Kenya and Sudan. The western half is a mountainous region traversed by the Great Rift Valley. To the east is mostly arid plateaus. The highlands are warm with summer rainfall, though droughts occur; the east is hot and dry. Most people live in the centre-north. Civil war, continued conflict with Eritrea and poor infrastructure hamper economic development. Subsistence farming is the main activity, though droughts have led to famine. Coffee is the main export and there is some light industry; Ethiopia remains one of the least developed countries in the world.

Falkland Islands
United Kingdom Overseas Territory

Area Sq Km	12 170	Currency	Pound
Area Sq Miles	4 699	Languages	English
Population	2 000	Religions	Protestant, Roman Catholic
Capital	Stanley		

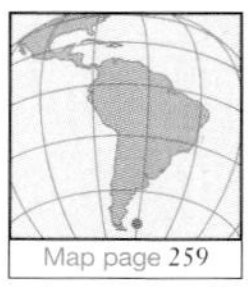
Map page 259

Lying in the southwest Atlantic Ocean, northeast of Cape Horn, there are two main islands, West Falkland and East Falkland, where most of the population live, and many smaller islands. The economy is based on sheep farming and the sale of fishing licences, though oil has been discovered off-shore.

Faroe Islands
Self-governing Danish Territory

Area Sq Km	1 399	Currency	Danish krone
Area Sq Miles	540	Languages	Faroese, Danish
Population	43 000	Religions	Protestant
Capital	Tórshavn	Organizations	UN

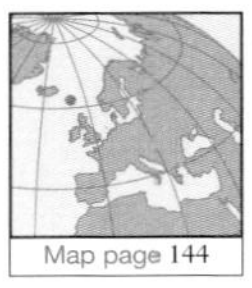
Map page 144

A self governing territory, lying in the north Atlantic Ocean between the UK and Iceland. The islands benefit from the North Atlantic Drift which has a moderating effect on the climate. The economy is based on deep-sea fishing.

FIJI
Sovereign Democratic Republic of Fiji

Area Sq Km	18 330	Currency	Dollar
Area Sq Miles	7 077	Languages	English, Fijian, Hindi
Population	796 000	Religions	Christian, Hindu, Sunni Muslim
Capital	Suva	Organizations	Comm., UN

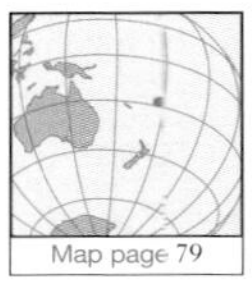
Map page 79

Fiji comprises two main islands, Vanua Levu and Viti Levu of volcanic origin and mountainous, and over three hundred smaller islands in the south Pacific Ocean. The climate is tropical and the economy is based on agriculture (chiefly sugar, the main export), fishing, forestry, gold mining and tourism.

FINLAND
Republic of Finland

Area Sq Km	338 145	Currency	Markka, Euro
Area Sq Miles	130 559	Languages	Finnish, Swedish
Population	5 154 000	Religions	Protestant, Greek Orthodox
Capital	Helsinki	Organizations	EU, OECD, UN

Finland is in north Europe, on the Gulf of Bothnia and the Gulf of Finland. It is low-lying, forests cover over seventy per cent of the land area, only about eight per cent is cultivated, though Finland is self-sufficient in cereals and dairy products. Summers are short and warm, and winters are long and severe, particularly in the north. Most people live in the southern third of the country, along the coast or near the many lakes. Timber is a major resource and there are important mineral resources, chiefly chromium. Main industries include metal working, electronics, paper and paper products, and chemicals; these account for most of the exports. The main trading partners are Germany, Sweden and the UK.

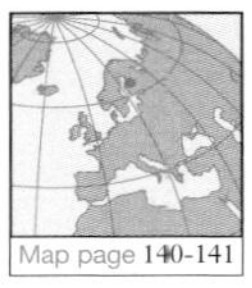
Map page 140-141

FRANCE
French Republic

Area Sq Km	543 965	Currency	Franc, Euro
Area Sq Miles	210 026	Languages	French, Arabic
Population	58 683 000	Religions	Roman Catholic, Protestant, Sunni Muslim
Capital	Paris	Organizations	EU, OECD, UN

France lies in southwest Europe, with coastlines on the Atlantic Ocean and Mediterranean Sea; it includes the Mediterranean island of Corsica. Northern and western regions consist mostly of flat or rolling countryside, and include the major lowlands of the Paris basin, the Loire valley and the Aquitaine basin, drained by the Seine, Loire and Garonne river systems respectively. The centre-south is dominated by the Massif Central. Eastwards, are the Vosges and Jura mountains and the Alps. In the southwest, the Pyrenees form a natural border with Spain. The climate is temperate with warm summers and cool winters, apart from the Mediterranean coast which has hot, dry summers and mild winters with some rainfall. Over seventy per cent of the population live in towns, but Greater Paris is the only major conurbation, with almost a sixth of the French population. Rich soil, a large cultivable area and contrasts in temperature and relief have given France a substantial and varied agricultural base; it is a major producer of both fresh and processed food. Major agricultural exports include cereals (chiefly wheat), dairy products, wines and sugar. France has relatively few mineral resources; it has coal reserves, some oil and natural gas but it relies heavily on nuclear and hydroelectric power and imported fuels. France is one of the world's major industrial countries. Main industries include food processing, iron, steel and aluminium production, chemicals, cars, electronics and oil refining. The main exports are machinery, agricultural products, cars and other transport equipment. France has a strong services sector and tourism is a major source of revenue and employment. Trade is predominantly with other EU countries.

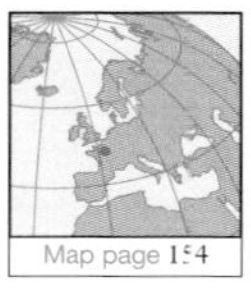
Map page 154

French Guiana
French Overseas Department

Area Sq Km	90 000	Currency	French franc
Area Sq Miles	34 749	Languages	French, creole
Population	167 000	Religions	Roman Catholic
Capital	Cayenne		

French Guiana, on the northeast coast of South America, is densely forested. The climate is tropical with high rainfall. Most people live in the coastal strip; agriculture is mostly subsistence farming; forestry and fishing are important, though timber and mineral resources are largely unexploited and industry is limited. French Guiana depends upon French aid. The European Space Agency (ESA) base is near Kourou.

Map page 251

FRENCH POLYNESIA
French Overseas Territory

Area Sq Km	3 265	Currency	Pacific franc
Area Sq Miles	1 261	Languages	French, Tahitian, Polynesian languages
Population	227 000	Religions	Protestant, Roman Catholic
Capital	Papeete		

Extending over a vast area of the southeast Pacific Ocean, French Polynesia comprises more than one hundred and thirty islands and coral atolls. The main island groups are the Marquesas Islands, the Tuamotu Archipelago and the Society Islands. The capital, Papeete, is on Tahiti in the Society Islands. The climate is subtropical and the economy is based on tourism.

Map page 79

French Southern and Antarctic Lands
French Overseas Territory

Area Sq Km (Miles) 439 580 (169 723)   Population *uninhabited*

This territory includes Crozet Island, Kerguelen, Amsterdam Island and St Paul Island. All are uninhabited apart from scientific research staff. In accordance with the Antarctic Treaty, French territorial claims in Antarctica have been suspended.

Map page 73

GABON
Gabonese Republic

Area Sq Km	267 667	Currency	CFA franc
Area Sq Miles	103 347	Languages	French, Fang, local languages
Population	1 167 000	Religions	Roman Catholic, Protestant, traditional beliefs
Capital	Libreville	Organizations	UN

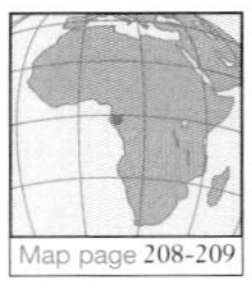
Map page 208-209

Gabon, on the Atlantic coast of central Africa consists of low plateaus, with a coastal plain lined by lagoons and mangrove swamps. The climate is tropical and rainforests cover over three quarters of the land area. Over seventy per cent of the population lives in towns. The economy is heavily dependent on oil, which accounts for around eighty per cent of exports; manganese, uranium and timber are the other exports. Agriculture is mainly at subsistence level.

THE GAMBIA
Republic of The Gambia

Area Sq Km	11 295	Currency	Dalasi
Area Sq Miles	4 361	Languages	English, Malinke, Fulani, Wolof
Population	1 229 000	Religions	Sunni Muslim, Protestant
Capital	Banjul	Organizations	Comm., UN

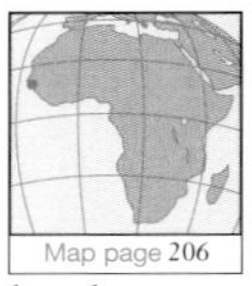
Map page 206

The Gambia, on the coast of west Africa, occupies a strip of land along the lower Gambia river. Sandy beaches are backed by mangrove swamps, beyond which is savanna. The climate is tropical, with rainfall in the summer. Over seventy per cent of Gambians are farmers, growing chiefly groundnuts (the main export) but also cotton, oil palms and food crops. Livestock rearing and fishing are important, while manufacturing is limited. Re-exports, mainly from Senegal, and tourism are major sources of income.

Gaza semi-autonomous region

Area Sq Km	363	Currency	Israeli shekel
Area Sq Miles	140	Languages	Arabic
Population	1 036 000	Religions	Sunni Muslim, Shi'a Muslim
Capital	Gaza		

Gaza is a narrow strip of land on the southeast corner of the Mediterranean Sea, between Egypt and Israel. The Palestinian territory has limited autonomy from Israel.

Map page 128

GEORGIA
Republic of Georgia

Area Sq Km	69 700	Currency	Lari
Area Sq Miles	26 911	Languages	Georgian, Russian, Armenian, Azeri, Ossetian, Abkhaz
Population	5 059 000	Religions	Georgian Orthodox, Russian Orthodox, Sunni Muslim
Capital	T'bilisi	Organizations	CIS, UN

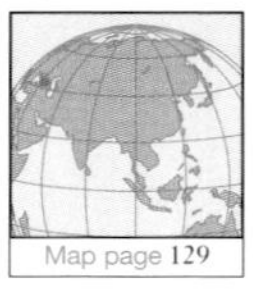
Map page 129

Georgia is in the northwest Caucasus, in southwest Asia, on the Black Sea. Mountain ranges in the north and south flank the Kura and Rioni valleys. The climate is generally mild, but subtropical along the coast. Agriculture is important, with tea, grapes, and citrus fruits the main crops. Mineral resources include manganese, coal and oil, and the main industries are steel, oil refining and machine building. Economic development remains slow.

GERMANY
Federal Republic of Germany

Area Sq Km	357 028	Currency	Mark, Euro
Area Sq Miles	137 849	Languages	German, Turkish
Population	82 133 000	Religions	Protestant, Roman Catholic
Capital	Berlin	Organizations	EU, OECD, UN

The west European state of Germany borders nine countries and has coastlines on the North and Baltic Seas. Behind the indented coastline, and covering about one third of the country, is the north German plain, a region of fertile farmland and sandy heaths drained by the country's major rivers. The central highlands are a belt of forested hills and plateaus which stretches from the Eifel region in the west to the Erzgebirge along the border with the Czech Republic. Farther south the land rises to the Schwäbische Alb, with the high rugged and forested Schwarzald (Black Forest) in the southwest and the Alps in the far south. The climate is temperate, with continental conditions in eastern areas where

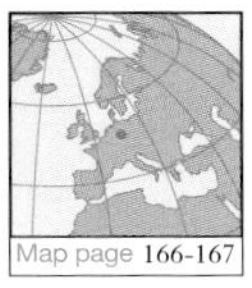
Map page 166-167

winters are colder. The population is highly urbanized with over eighty-five per cent living in cities and towns. With the exception of coal, lignite, potash and baryte, Germany lacks minerals and other industrial raw materials. It has a small agricultural base, though a few products (chiefly wines and beers) enjoy an international reputation. Germany is the world's third ranking economy after that of USA and Japan. It's industries are amongst the world's most technologically advanced, producing machinery, motor vehicles, electrical equipment, chemicals and pharmaceuticals. The majority of trade is with other countries in the EU.

Baden-Württemberg (State)
Area Sq Km (Miles) 35 751 (13 804) Population 10 374 505 Capital Stuttgart

Bayern (State)
Area Sq Km (Miles) 70 552 (27 240) Population 12 043 869 Capital München

Berlin(State)
Area Sq Km (Miles) 891 (344) Population 3 467 322 Capital Berlin

Brandenburg(State)
Area Sq Km (Miles) 29 476 (11 381) Population 2 554 441 Capital Potsdam

Bremen(State)
Area Sq Km (Miles) 404 (156) Population 678 731 Capital Bremen

Hamburg(State)
Area Sq Km (Miles) 755 (292) Population 1 708 528 Capital Hamburg

Hessen(State)
Area Sq Km (Miles) 21 114 (8 152) Population 6 027 284 Capital Wiesbaden

Mecklenburg-Vorpommern(State)
Area Sq Km (Miles) 23 170 (8 946) Population 1 817 196 Capital Schwerin

Niedersachsen(State)
Area Sq Km (Miles) 47 612 (18 383) Population 7 795 149 Capital Hannover

Nordrhein-Westfalen(State)
Area Sq Km (Miles) 34 079 (13 158) Population 17 947 715 Capital Düsseldorf

Rheinland-Pfalz(State)
Area Sq Km (Miles) 19 853 (7 665) Population 4 009 753 Capital Mainz

Saarland(State)
Area Sq Km (Miles) 2 570 (992) Population 1 084 184 Capital Saarbrücken

Sachsen(State)
Area Sq Km (Miles) 18 413 (7 109) Population 4 545 702 Capital Dresden

Sachsen-Anhalt(State)
Area Sq Km (Miles) 20 446 (7 894) Population 2 731 463 Capital Magdeburg

Schleswig-Holstein(State)
Area Sq Km (Miles) 15 771 (6 089) Population 2 742 293 Capital Kiel

Thüringen(State)
Area Sq Km (Miles) 16 171 (6 244) Population 2 491 119 Capital Erfurt

GHANA
Republic of Ghana

Area Sq Km	238 537	Currency	Cedi
Area Sq Miles	92 100	Languages	English, Hausa, Akan, local languages
Population	19 162 000	Religions	Christian, Sunni Muslim, traditional beliefs
Capital	Accra	Organizations	Comm., UN

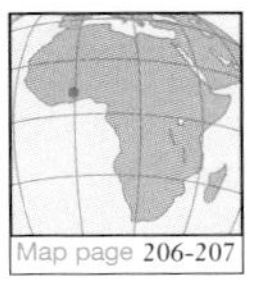
Map page 206-207

A west African state on the Gulf of Guinea, Ghana is a land of plains and low plateaus covered with savanna and rainforest. In the east is the Volta basin. The climate is tropical, with high rainfall in the south, where most people live. Agriculture employs around sixty per-cent of the workforce, main exports are gold, timber, cocoa and manganese ore.

Gibraltar
United Kingdom Overseas Territory

Area Sq Km	7	Currency	Pound
Area Sq Miles	3	Languages	English, Spanish
Population	25 000	Religions	Roman Catholic, Protestant, Sunni Muslim
Capital	Gibraltar		

Gibraltar lies on the south coast of Spain at the western entrance to the Mediterranean Sea. The economy depends on tourism, offshore banking and shipping services.

Map page 185

GREECE
Hellenic Republic

Area Sq Km	131 957	Currency	Drachma
Area Sq Miles	50 949	Languages	Greek
Population	10 600 000	Religions	Greek Orthodox, Sunni Muslim
Capital	Athina	Organizations	EU, OECD, UN

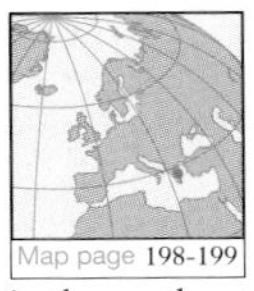
Map page 198-199

Greece occupies the southern Balkans in south Europe and many islands in the Ionian, Aegean and Mediterranean Seas. The islands make up over one fifth of its area. Mountains and hills cover much of the country. The most important lowlands are the plains of Thessalia in the centre-east and around Thessalonika in the northeast. Summers are hot and dry. Winters are mild and wet, but colder in the north with heavy snowfalls in the mountains. One third of Greeks live in the Athina area. Employment in agriculture is decreasing, but still accounts for around twenty per cent of the workforce and exports include citrus fruits, raisins, wine, olives and olive oil. Aluminium and nickel are mined and a wide range of manufactures are produced including food and tobacco, textiles, clothing, and chemicals. Tourism is an important industry and there is a large services sector. Most trade is with other EU countries.

GREENLAND
Self-governing Danish Territory

Area Sq Km	2 175 600	Currency	Danish krone
Area Sq Miles	840 004	Languages	Greenlandic, Danish
Population	56 000	Religions	Protestant
Capital	Nuuk		

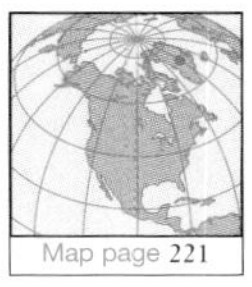
Map page 221

Situated to the northeast of North America between the Atlantic and Arctic Oceans, Greenland is the largest island in the world. It has a polar climate and over eighty per cent of the land area is permanent ice cap. The economy is based on fishing and fish processing.

GRENADA

Area Sq Km	378	Currency	E. Carib. dollar
Area Sq Miles	146	Languages	English, creole
Population	93 000	Religions	Roman Catholic, Protestant
Capital	St George's	Organizations	CARICOM, Comm., UN

The Caribbean state comprises Grenada, the most southerly of the Windward Islands, and the southern islands of The Grenadines. Grenada has wooded hills, beaches in the southwest, a warm climate and good rainfall. Agriculture is the main activity, with bananas, nutmeg and cocoa the main exports. Tourism is the main foreign exchange earner.

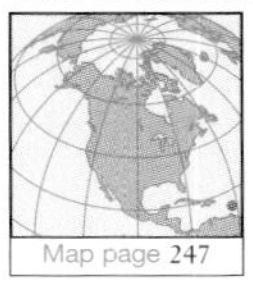
Map page 247

Guadeloupe
French Overseas Department

Area Sq Km	1 780	Currency	French franc
Area Sq Miles	687	Languages	French, creole
Population	443 000	Religions	Roman Catholic
Capital	Basse-Terre		

Guadeloupe, in the Leeward Islands in the Caribbean, consists of two main islands, Basse-Terre and Grande Terre, connected by a bridge, Marie Galante and a few outer islands. The climate is tropical, but moderated by trade winds. Bananas, sugar and rum, tourism and French aid are the main sources of foreign exchange.

Map page 247

Guam
United States Unincorporated Territory

Area Sq Km	541	Currency	US dollar
Area Sq Miles	209	Languages	Chamorro, English, Tagalog
Population	161 000	Religions	Roman Catholic
Capital	Agana		

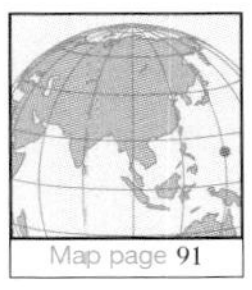
Map page 91

Lying at the south end of the North Mariana Islands in the western Pacific Ocean, Guam has a humid tropical climate. The island has a large US military base and the economy relies on that and on tourism, which has grown rapidly.

GUATEMALA
Republic of Guatemala

Area Sq Km	108 890	Currency	Quetzal
Area Sq Miles	42 043	Languages	Spanish, Mayan languages
Population	10 801 000	Religions	Roman Catholic, Protestant
Capital	Guatemala	Organizations	UN

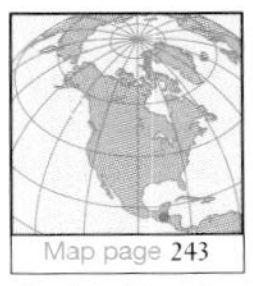
Map page 243

The most populous country in Central America after Mexico, Guatemala has a long Pacific and a short Caribbean coastline. Northern areas are lowland tropical forests. To the south lie mountain ranges with some active volcanoes, then the Pacific coastal plain. The climate is hot tropical in the lowlands, cooler in the highlands, where most people live. Farming is the main activity, coffee, sugar and bananas are the main exports. There is some manufacturing (chiefly clothing and textiles). Most trade is with USA.

GUERNSEY
United Kingdom Crown Dependency

Area Sq Km	78	Currency	Pound
Area Sq Miles	30	Languages	English, French
Population	64 555	Religions	Protestant, Roman Catholic
Capital	St Peter Port		

One of the Channel Islands lying off the west coast of the Cherbourg peninsula in northern France.

Map page 158

GUINEA
Republic of Guinea

Area Sq Km	245 857	Currency	Franc
Area Sq Miles	94 926	Languages	French, Fulani, Malinke, local languages
Population	7 337 000	Religions	Sunni Muslim, traditional beliefs, Christian
Capital	Conakry	Organizations	UN

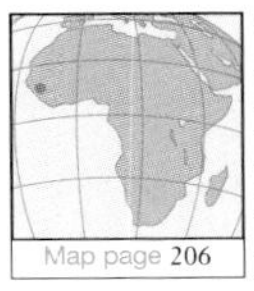
Map page 206

Guinea is in west Africa, on the Atlantic Ocean. There are mangrove swamps along the coast, inland are lowlands and then the Fouta Djallon mountains and plateaus. To the east are savanna plains drained by the upper Niger river system, while to the southeast are mountains. The climate is tropical, with high coastal rainfall. Agriculture is the main activity employing nearly eighty per cent of the workforce, with coffee, bananas and pineapples the chief cash crops. There are huge reserves of bauxite; bauxite, alumina, gold, coffee and diamonds are the main exports.

GUINEA-BISSAU
Republic of Guinea-Bissau

Area Sq Km	36 125	Currency	CFA franc
Area Sq Miles	13 948	Languages	Portuguese, crioulo, local languages
Population	1 161 000	Religions	Traditional beliefs, Sunni Muslim, Christian
Capital	Bissau	Organizations	UN

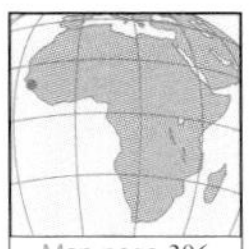
Map page 206

Guinea-Bissau, on the Atlantic coast of west Africa, includes the Bijagos Archipelago. The mainland coast is swampy and contains many estuaries. Inland are forested plains and to the east are savanna plateaus. The climate is tropical. The economy is based mainly on subsistence farming, there is little industry and timber and mineral resources are largely unexploited. Cashews make up over eighty per cent of exports. Guinea-Bissau is one of the least developed countries in the world.

GUYANA
Co-operative Republic of Guyana

Area Sq Km	214 969	Currency	Dollar
Area Sq Miles	83 000	Languages	English, creole, Amerindian languages
Population	850 000	Religions	Protestant, Hindu, Roman Catholic, Sunni Muslim
Capital	Georgetown	Organizations	CARICOM, Comm., UN

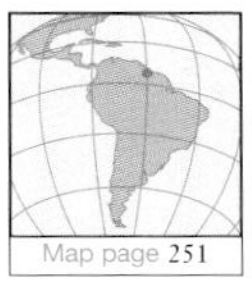
Map page 251

Guyana, on the northeast coast of South America, consists of the highlands in the west, and the savanna uplands of the southwest. Most of the country is densely forested; a lowland coastal belt supports crops and most of the population. The generally hot, humid and wet conditions are modified along the coast by sea breezes. The economy is based on agriculture, mining and forestry. Sugar, bauxite, gold, rice and timber are the main exports.

HAITI
Republic of Haiti

Area Sq Km	27 750	Currency	Gourde
Area Sq Miles	10 714	Languages	French, creole
Population	7 952 000	Religions	Roman Catholic, Protestant, Voodoo
Capital	Port-au-Prince	Organizations	CARICOM, UN

Haiti, occupying the western third of the Caribbean island of Hispaniola, is a mountainous state, with small coastal plains and a central valley. The Dominican Republic occupies the rest of the island. The climate is tropical, hottest in coastal areas. Haiti has few natural resources, is overpopulated and relies on exports of local crafts and coffee, and remittances from workers abroad.

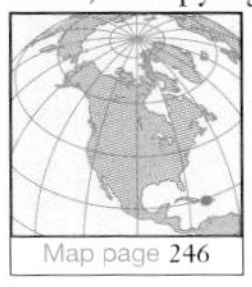
Map page 246

HONDURAS
Republic of Honduras

Area Sq Km	112 088	Currency	Lempira
Area Sq Miles	43 277	Languages	Spanish, Amerindian languages
Population	6 147 000	Religions	Roman Catholic, Protestant
Capital	Tegucigalpa	Organizations	UN

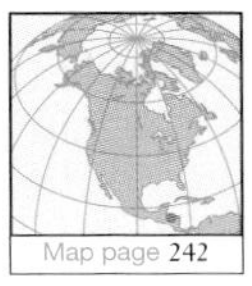
Map page 242

Honduras, in central America, is a mountainous and forested country with lowland areas along its long Caribbean and short Pacific coasts. Coastal areas are hot and humid with heavy summer rainfall, inland is cooler and drier. Most people live in the central valleys. Coffee and bananas are the main exports, along with shrimps and zinc. Industry involves mainly agricultural processing. Honduras was the country hardest hit by hurricane Mitch in 1998 but has received significant aid for reconstruction.

HUNGARY
Republic of Hungary

Area Sq Km	93 030	Currency	Forint
Area Sq Miles	35 919	Languages	Hungarian
Population	10 116 000	Religions	Roman Catholic, Protestant
Capital	Budapest	Organizations	OECD, UN

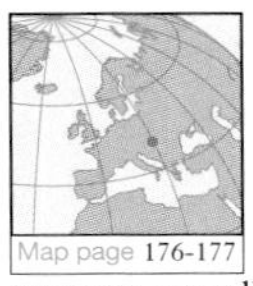
Map page 176-177

A landlocked country in central Europe, Hungary borders Austria, Slovakia, Ukraine, Romania, Yugoslavia, Croatia and Slovenia. The Danube river flows north-south through central Hungary. To the east lies a great plain, flanked by highlands in the north. To the west low mountains and Lake Balaton separate a small plain and southern uplands. The climate is continental, with warm summers and cold winters. Sixty per cent of the population live in urban areas, and one fifth lives in Budapest. Some minerals and energy resources are exploited, chiefly bauxite, coal and natural gas. Hungary has an industrial economy. The main industries produce metals, machinery, transport equipment, chemicals and food products. The main trading partners are Germany and Austria. Hungary is negotiating to join the EU.

ICELAND
Republic of Iceland

Area Sq Km	102 820	Currency	Króna
Area Sq Miles	39 699	Languages	Icelandic
Population	276 000	Religions	Protestant
Capital	Reykjavik	Organizations	OECD, UN

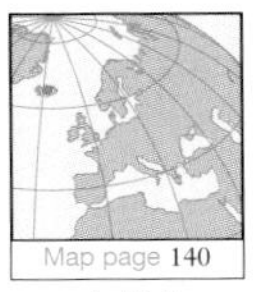
Map page 140

Iceland lies in the Atlantic Ocean, near the Arctic Circle to the northwest of Scandinavia. It consists mainly of a plateau of basalt lava flows. Some of its two hundred volcanoes are active, and there are geysers and hot springs; one tenth of the country is covered by ice caps. Only coastal lowlands can be cultivated and settled, and over half the population lives in the Reykjavik area. The climate is mild, moderated by the North Atlantic Drift and southwesterly winds. The mainstay of the economy is fishing and fish processing, which account for seventy per cent of exports. Agriculture involves mainly sheep and dairy farming. Hydro-electric and geothermal energy resources are considerable. The main industries produce aluminium, ferro-silicon and fertilizers. Tourism, including ecotourism, is growing in importance.

© Bartholomew Ltd

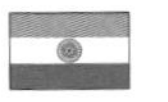

INDIA
Republic of India

Area Sq Km	3 065 027	Currency	Rupee
Area Sq Miles	1 183 414	Languages	Hindi, English, many regional languages
Population	982 223 000	Religions	Hindu, Sunni Muslim, Shi'a Muslim, Sikh, Christian
Capital	New Delhi	Organizations	Comm., UN

The south Asian state of India occupies a peninsula that juts out into the Indian Ocean between the Arabian Sea and Bay of Bengal. The heart of the peninsula is the Deccan plateau, bordered on either side by ranges of hills, the Western Ghats and the lower Eastern Ghats, which fall away to narrow coastal plains. To the north is a broad plain, drained by the Indus, Ganges and Brahmaputra rivers and their tributaries. The plain is intensively farmed and is the most populous region. In the west is the Thar Desert. The Himalaya form India's northern border, together with parts of the Karakoram and Hindu Kush ranges in the northwest. The climate shows marked seasonal variation: the hot season from March to June; the monsoon season from June to October; and the cold season from November to

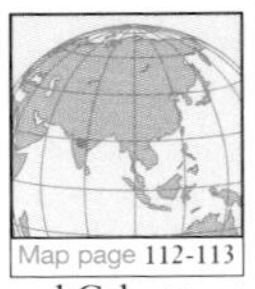
Map page 112-113

February. Rainfall ranges between very high in the northeast Assam region to negligible in the Thar Desert, while temperatures range from very cold in the Himayalas to tropical heat over much of the south. Over seventy per cent of the huge population – the second largest in the world – is rural, though Mumbai and Calcutta rank among the ten largest cities in the world. Agriculture, forestry and fishing account for a quarter of national output and two thirds of employment. Much of the farming is on a subsistence basis and involves mainly rice and wheat growing. India is a major world producer of tea, sugar, jute, cotton and tobacco. Livestock is raised mainly for dairy products and hides. India has major reserves of coal, reserves of oil and natural gas and many minerals, including iron, manganese, bauxite, diamonds and gold. The manufacturing sector is large and diverse. The main manufactures are chemicals and chemical products, textiles, iron and steel, food products, electrical goods and transport equipment; software and pharmaceuticals are also important. All the main manufactured products are exported, together with diamonds and jewellery. The USA, Germany, Japan and the UK are the main trading partners.

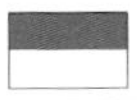

INDONESIA
Republic of Indonesia

Area Sq Km	1 919 445	Currency	Rupiah
Area Sq Miles	741 102	Languages	Indonesian, local languages
Population	206 338 000	Religions	Sunni Muslim, Protestant, Roman Catholic
Capital	Jakarta	Organizations	APEC, ASEAN, OPEC, UN

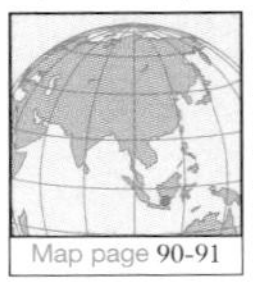
Map page 90-91

Indonesia, the largest and most populous country in southeast Asia, consists of over thirteen thousand islands extending along the equator between the Pacific and Indian Oceans. Sumatera, Jawa, Sulawesi, Kalimantan (two thirds of Borneo) and Irian Jaya (western New Guinea) make up ninety per cent of the land area. Most of Indonesia is mountainous and covered with rainforest or mangrove swamps, and there are over three hundred volcanoes, many active. Two thirds of the population live in the lowland areas of Jawa and Madura. The climate is tropical monsoon. Agriculture is the largest sector of the economy and Indonesia is among the world's top producers of rice, palm oil, tea, coffee, rubber and tobacco. It is the world's leading exporter of natural gas, a major exporter of oil and timber, and a major producer of tin. A range of goods are produced including textiles, clothing, cement, fertilizer and vehicles. Main exports are oil, natural gas, timber products and clothing. The main trading partner is Japan. However, Indonesia remains a relatively poor country, and ethnic tensions and civil unrest are hindering economic development.

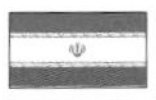

IRAN
Islamic Republic of Iran

Area Sq Km	1 648 000	Currency	Rial
Area Sq Miles	636 296	Languages	Farsi, Azeri, Kurdish, regional languages
Population	65 758 000	Religions	Shi'a Muslim, Sunni Muslim
Capital	Tehrān	Organizations	OPEC, UN

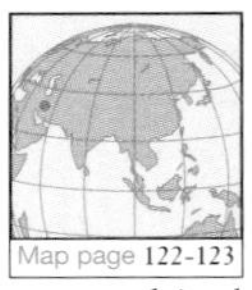
Map page 122-123

Iran is in southwest Asia, on The Gulf, the Gulf of Oman and Caspian Sea. Eastern Iran is high plateau, with large salt pans and a vast sand desert. In the west the Zagros Mountains form a series of ridges, while to the north lie the Elburz Mountains. Most farming and settlement is on the narrow plain along the Caspian Sea and the foothills of the north and west. The climate is one of extremes, with hot summers and very cold winters. Most of the light rainfall is in the winter months. Agriculture involves about a third of the workforce. Wheat is the main crop but fruit (chiefly dates) and pistachio nuts are grown for export. Petroleum (the main export) and natural gas are Iran's leading natural resources. Manufactures include carpets, clothing, food products and construction materials.

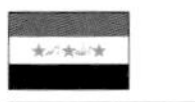

IRAQ
Republic of Iraq

Area Sq Km	438 317	Currency	Dinar
Area Sq Miles	169 235	Languages	Arabic, Kurdish, Turkmen
Population	21 800 000	Religions	Shi'a Muslim, Sunni Muslim, Christian
Capital	Baghdād	Organizations	OPEC, UN

Iraq, which lies on the northwest shores of The Gulf in southwest Asia, has at its heart the lowland valley of the Tigris and Euphrates rivers. In the southeast where the two rivers join are marshes and the Shatt al Arab waterway. Northern Iraq is hilly, while western Iraq is desert. Summers are hot and dry, while winters are mild with light, unreliable

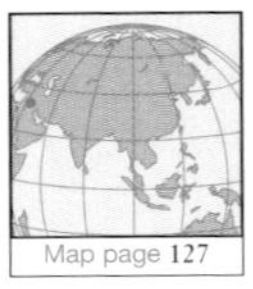
Map page 127

rainfall. The Tigris-Euphrates valley contains most of the arable land and population, including one in five who live in Baghdād. Defeat in the 1991 Gulf war and continued international sanctions have ruined the economy and caused considerable hardship. Oil is exported, almost all to Japan.

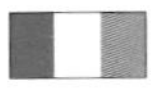

IRELAND, REPUBLIC OF

Area Sq Km	70 282	Currency	Punt, Euro
Area Sq Miles	27 136	Languages	English, Irish
Population	3 681 000	Religions	Roman Catholic, Protestant
Capital	Dublin	Organizations	EU, OECD, UN

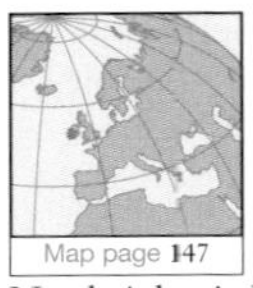
Map page 147

A state in northwest Europe, the Irish Republic occupies some eighty per cent of the island of Ireland. It is a lowland country of wide valleys, lakes and peat bogs, with isolated mountain ranges around the coast. The west coast is rugged and indented with many bays. The climate is mild due to the North Atlantic Drift and rainfall is plentiful, though highest in the west. Nearly sixty per cent of people live in urban areas, Dublin and Cork being the main cities. Resources include natural gas, peat, lead and zinc. Agriculture, the traditional mainstay, now employs less than ten per cent of the workforce, while industry employs nearly thirty per cent. The main industries are electronics, pharmaceuticals and engineering as well as food processing, brewing and textiles. Service industries are expanding, with tourism a major foreign exchange earner. The UK is the main trading partner.

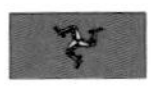

Isle of Man
United Kingdom Crown Dependency

Area Sq Km	572	Currency	Pound
Area Sq Miles	221	Languages	English
Population	77 000	Religions	Protestant, Roman Catholic
Capital	Douglas		

In the Irish Sea, the island is self governing while the UK is responsible for defense and foreign affairs. The island is not part of the EU, but has a special relationship with the EU which allows for free trade.

Map page 145

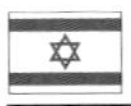

ISRAEL
State of Israel

Area Sq Km	20 770	Currency	Shekel
Area Sq Miles	8 019	Languages	Hebrew, Arabic
Population	5 984 000	Religions	Jewish, Sunni Muslim, Christian, Druze
Capital	Jerusalem	Organizations	UN

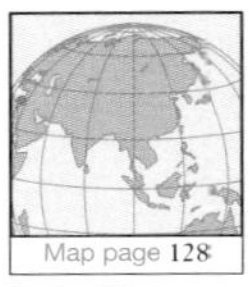
Map page 128

Israel lies on the Mediterranean coast of southwest Asia. Beyond the coastal Plain of Sharon are the hills and valleys of Samaria with the Galilee highlands to the north. In the east is the rift valley, which extends from Lake Tiberias to the Gulf of Aqaba and contains the Jordan river and Dead Sea. In the south is the Negev, a triangular semi-desert plateau. Most people live on the coastal plain or in northern and central areas. Much of Israel has warm summers and mild, wet winters. Southern Israel is hot and dry. Agricultural production was boosted by the inclusion of the West Bank in 1967. Mineral resources are few, and manufacturing makes the largest contribution to the economy. Israel exports machinery and transport equipment, diamonds, clothing, fruit and vegetables. Tourism and foreign aid are important to the economy.

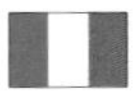

ITALY
Italian Republic

Area Sq Km	301 245	Currency	Lira, Euro
Area Sq Miles	116 311	Languages	Italian
Population	57 369 000	Religions	Roman Catholic
Capital	Roma	Organizations	EU, OECD, UN

Most of the south European state of Italy occupies a peninsula that juts out into the Mediterranean Sea. It includes the islands of Sicily and Sardinia and about seventy much smaller islands in the surrounding seas. Italy is mountainous and dominated by two high ranges: the Alps, which form its northern border; and the various ranges of the Apennines, which run almost the full length of the peninsula. Many of Italy's mountains are of volcanic origin and its active volcanoes are

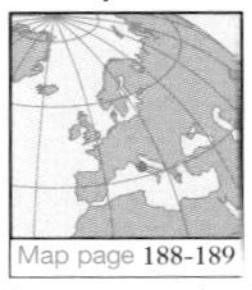
Map page 188-189

Vesuvio, near Naples, Etna and Stromboli. The main lowland area, the Po river valley in the northeast, is the main agricultural and industrial area and is the most populous region. Italy has a Mediterranean climate with warm, dry summers and mild winters. Northern Italy experiences colder, wetter winters, with heavy snow in the Alps. Italy's natural resources are limited. Only about twenty per cent of the land is suitable for cultivation. Some oil, natural gas and coal are produced, but most fuels and minerals used by industry must be imported. Italy has a fairly diversified economy. Agriculture is important, with cereals, vines, fruit and vegetables the main crops; Italy is the world's largest wine producer. The north is the centre of Italian industry, especially around Turin, Milan and Genoa. Italy's leading manufactures include industrial and office equipment, domestic appliances, cars, textiles, clothing, leather goods, chemicals and metal products. Italy has a strong service sector. With over twenty-five million visitors a year, tourism is a major employer and accounts for five per cent of the national income. Finance and banking are also important. Most trade is with other EU countries.

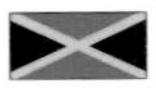

JAMAICA

Area Sq Km	10 991	Currency	Dollar
Area Sq Miles	4 244	Languages	English, creole
Population	2 538 000	Religions	Protestant, Roman Catholic
Capital	Kingston	Organizations	CARICOM, Comm., UN

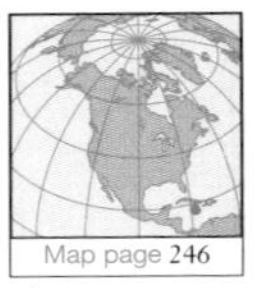
Map page 246

Jamaica, the third largest Caribbean island, has beaches and densely populated coastal plains traversed by hills and plateaus rising to the forested Blue Mountains in the east. The climate is tropical, but cooler and wetter on high ground. The economy is based on tourism, agriculture, mining and light manufacturing. Bauxite, alumina, sugar and bananas are the main exports. The USA is the main trading partner. Jamaica receives foreign aid.

Jammu and Kashmir Disputed territory (India,Pakistan)

Area Sq Km (Miles) 222 236 (85 806) Population 13 000 000 Capital Srinagar

A region in the north of Pakistan and India to the west of the Karakoram and Himalaya. The 'Line of control' separates the northern, Pakistani controlled area and the southern, Indian controlled area.

Map page 116

JAPAN

Area Sq Km	377 727	Currency	Yen
Area Sq Miles	145 841	Languages	Japanese
Population	126 281 000	Religions	Shintoist, Buddhist, Christian
Capital	Tōkyō	Organizations	APEC, OECD, UN

Japan, lies in the Pacific Ocean off the coast of east Asia and consists of four main islands - Hokkaidō, Honshū, Shikoku and Kyūshū - and more than three thousand smaller islands in the surrounding Sea of

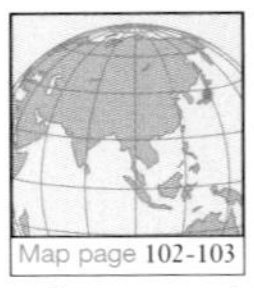
Map page 102-103

Japan, East China Sea and Pacific Ocean. The central island of Honshū accounts for sixty per cent of the total land area and contains eighty per cent of the population. Behind the long and deeply indented coastline, nearly three quarters of Japan is mountainous and heavily forested. Japan has over sixty active volcanoes, and is subject to frequent earthquakes, typhoons and tidal waves. The climate is generally temperate maritime, with warm summers and mild winters, except in western Hokkaidō and northwest Honshū, where the winters are very cold with heavy snow. Japan has few natural resources. It has a limited land area of which only fourteen per cent is suitable for cultivation, and production of its few industrial raw materials: coal, oil, natural gas, lead, zinc and copper is insufficient for its industry. Most raw materials must be imported, including about ninety per cent of energy requirements. Yet Japan is the world's second largest industrial economy, with a range of modern heavy and light industries centred mainly around the major ports of Yokohama, Ōsaka and Tōkyō. It is the world's largest manufacturer of cars, motorcycles and merchant ships, and a major producer of steel, textiles, chemicals and cement. It is a leading producer of many consumer durables, such as washing machines, and electronic equipment, chiefly office equipment and computers. Japan has a strong service sector, banking and finance are particularly important and Tōkyō is one of the world's major stock exchanges. Owing to intensive agricultural production, Japan is seventy per cent self-sufficient in food. The main food crops are rice, barley, fruit, wheat and soya beans. Livestock raising (chiefly cattle, pigs and chickens) and fishing are also important. Japan has one of the largest fishing fleets in the world. A major trading nation, Japan has trade links with many countries in southeast Asia and in Europe, though the main trading partner is USA.

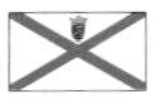

Jersey
United Kingdom Crown Dependency

Area Sq Km	116	Currency	Pound
Area Sq Miles	45	Languages	English, French
Population	89 136	Religions	Protestant, Roman Catholic
Capital	St Helier		

One of the Channel Islands lying off the west coast of the Cherbourg peninsula in northern France.

Map page 148

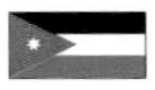

JORDAN
Hashemite Kingdom of Jordan

Area Sq Km	89 206	Currency	Dinar
Area Sq Miles	34 443	Languages	Arabic
Population	6 304 000	Religions	Sunni Muslim, Christian
Capital	'Ammān	Organizations	UN

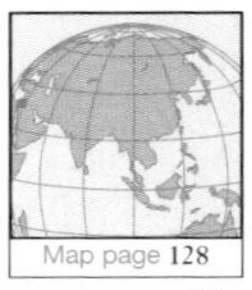
Map page 128

Jordan, in southwest Asia, is landlocked apart from a short coastline on the Gulf of Aqaba. Much of Jordan is rocky desert plateaus. To the west of the mountains, the land falls below sea level to the Dead Sea and Jordan river. Much of Jordan is hot and dry, the west is cooler and wetter; most people live in the northwest. Phosphates, potash, pharmaceuticals, fruit and vegetables are the main exports. Jordan's economy relies upon tourism, workers' remittances and foreign aid.

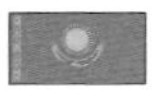

KAZAKHSTAN
Republic of Kazakhstan

Area Sq Km	2 717 300	Currency	Tenge
Area Sq Miles	1 049 155	Languages	Kazakh, Russian, Ukrainian, German, Uzbek, Tatar
Population	16 319 000	Religions	Sunni Muslim, Russian Orthodox, Protestant
Capital	Astana	Organizations	CIS, UN

Stretching across central Asia, Kazakhstan covers a vast area of steppe land and semi-desert. The land is flat in the west rising to mountains in

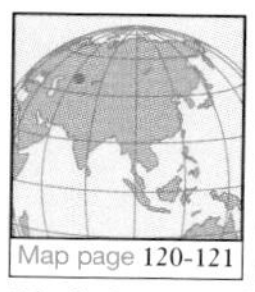
Map page 120-121

the southeast. The climate is continental and mainly dry. Agriculture and livestock rearing are important, with cotton and tobacco the main cash crops. Kazakhstan is very rich in minerals, including coal, chromium, gold, molybdenum, lead and zinc and has substantial reserves of oil and gas; oil pipelines to the Black Sea are planned. Mining, metallurgy, machine building and food processing are major industries. Oil and gas, and minerals are the main exports and Russia is the dominant trading partner.

KENYA
Republic of Kenya

Area Sq Km	582 646	Currency	Shilling
Area Sq Miles	224 961	Languages	Swahili, English, local languages
Population	29 008 000	Religions	Christian, traditional beliefs
Capital	Nairobi	Organizations	Comm., UN

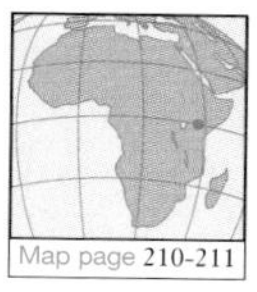
Map page 210-211

Kenya is in east Africa, on the Indian Ocean. Inland beyond the coastal plains the land rises to plateaus interrupted by volcanic mountains. The Great Rift Valley runs north-south to the west of Nairobi. Most people live in central Kenya. Conditions are tropical on the coast, semi-desert in the north and savanna in the south. Hydro-electric power from the Upper Tana river provides most of the electricity requirement. Agricultural products, mainly tea, coffee, fruit and vegetables are the main exports. Light industry is important. Tourism is the main foreign exchange earner; oil refining and re-exports for landlocked neighbours are others.

KIRIBATI
Republic of Kiribati

Area Sq Km	717	Currency	Australian dollar
Area Sq Miles	277	Languages	Gilbertese, English
Population	81 000	Religions	Roman Catholic, Protestant
Capital	Bairiki	Organizations	Comm., UN

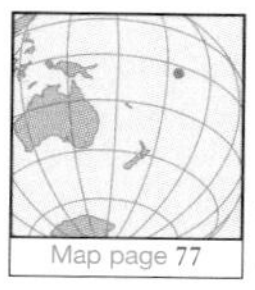
Map page 77

Kiribati comprises coral islands in the Gilbert, Phoenix and Line groups and the volcanic island of Banaba, straddling the equator in the Pacific Ocean. Most people live on the Gilbert Islands, and the capital, Bairiki, is on Tarawa, one of the Gilbert Islands. The climate is hot, wetter in the north. Copra and fish are exported, but Kiribati relies on remittances from workers abroad and foreign aid.

KUWAIT
State of Kuwait

Area Sq Km	17 818	Currency	Dinar
Area Sq Miles	6 880	Languages	Arabic
Population	1 811 000	Religions	Sunni Muslim, Shi'a Muslim, Christian, Hindu
Capital	Kuwait	Organizations	OPEC, UN

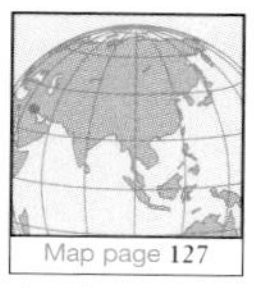
Map page 127

Kuwait lies on the northwest shores of The Gulf in southwest Asia. It is mainly low-lying desert, with irrigated areas along the bay, Kuwait Jun, where most people live. Summers are hot and dry, winters are cool with some rainfall. The oil industry, which accounts for eighty per cent of exports, has largely recovered from the damage caused by Iraq in 1991. Income is also derived from extensive overseas investments.

KYRGYZSTAN
Kyrgyz Republic

Area Sq Km	198 500	Currency	Som
Area Sq Miles	76 641	Languages	Kyrgyz, Russian, Uzbek
Population	4 643 000	Religions	Sunni Muslim, Russian Orthodox
Capital	Bishkek	Organizations	CIS, UN

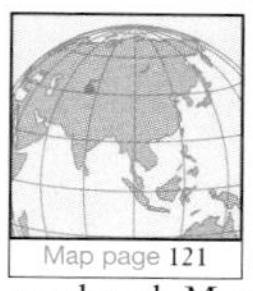
Map page 121

A landlocked central Asian state, Kyrgyzstan is rugged and mountainous, lying to the west of the Tien Shan range. Most people live in the valleys of the north and west. Summers are hot and winters cold. Agriculture (chiefly livestock farming) is the main activity. Some oil and gas, coal, gold, antimony and mercury are produced. Manufactures include machinery, metals and products, which are the main exports. Most trade is with the Russian Federation, Kazakhstan and Uzbekistan.

LAOS
Lao People's Democratic Republic

Area Sq Km	236 800	Currency	Kip
Area Sq Miles	91 429	Languages	Lao, local languages
Population	5 163 000	Religions	Buddhist, traditional beliefs
Capital	Viangchan	Organizations	ASEAN, UN

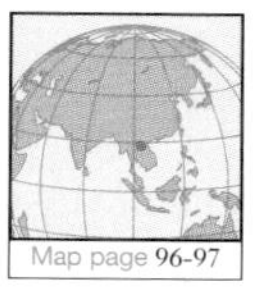
Map page 96-97

A landlocked country in southeast Asia, Laos borders Vietnam, Cambodia, Thailand, Myanmar and China. The land is mostly forested mountains and plateaus. The climate is tropical monsoon. Most people live in the Mekong valley and the low plateau in the south, and grow food crops, chiefly rice. Hydro-electricity from a plant on the Mekong, timber, coffee and tin are exported, but Laos depends on aid.

LATVIA
Republic of Latvia

Area Sq Km	63 700	Currency	Lat
Area Sq Miles	24 595	Languages	Latvian, Russian
Population	2 424 000	Religions	Protestant, Roman Catholic, Russian Orthodox
Capital	Riga	Organizations	UN

Latvia is in north Europe, on the Baltic Sea and Gulf of Riga. The land is flat near the coast but hilly with woods and lakes inland. Latvia has a modified continental climate. One third of the people live in Riga.

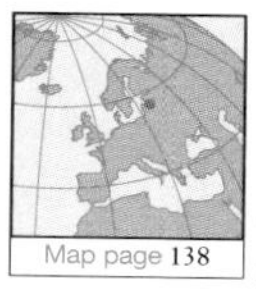
Map page 138

Crop and livestock farming are important. Latvia has few natural resources. Industries include food products, transport equipment, wood and wood products and textiles; these form most of the exports. The main trading partners are Russia and Germany. Latvia is negotiating to join the EU.

LEBANON
Republic of Lebanon

Area Sq Km	10 452	Currency	Pound
Area Sq Miles	4 036	Languages	Arabic, Armenian, French
Population	3 191 000	Religions	Shi'a Muslim, Sunni Muslim, Christian
Capital	Beirut	Organizations	UN

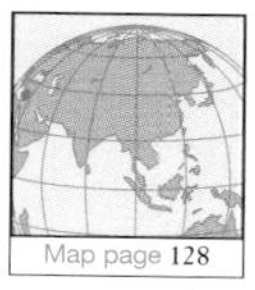
Map page 128

Lebanon lies on the Mediterranean coast of southwest Asia. Beyond the coastal strip, where most people live, are two parallel mountain ranges, separated by the El Beq'a valley. The 1975-1991 civil war crippled the traditional sectors of banking, commerce and tourism; some fruit production and light industry survived; reconstruction of the infrastructure is under way, and financial service companies are beginning to return.

LESOTHO
Kingdom of Lesotho

Area Sq Km	30 355	Currency	Loti
Area Sq Miles	11 720	Languages	Sesotho, English, Zulu
Population	2 062 000	Religions	Christian, traditional beliefs
Capital	Maseru	Organizations	Comm., SADC, UN

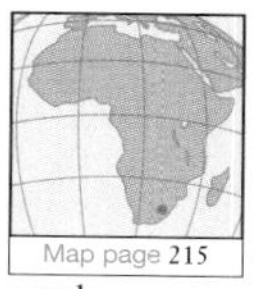
Map page 215

Lesotho is a landlocked state surrounded by the Republic of South Africa. It is a mountainous country lying within the Drakensberg range. Farming and herding are the main activities. Exports include livestock, vegetables, wool and mohair. The economy depends heavily on South Africa for transport links and employment; a major hydro-electric plant completed in 1998 will allow the sale of water to South Africa.

LIBERIA
Republic of Liberia

Area Sq Km	111 369	Currency	Dollar
Area Sq Miles	43 000	Languages	English, creole, local languages
Population	2 666 000	Religions	Traditional beliefs, Christian, Sunni Muslim
Capital	Monrovia	Organizations	UN

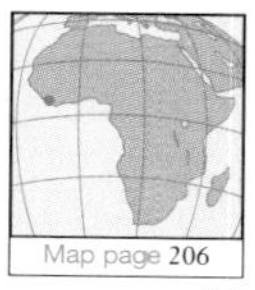
Map page 206

Liberia is on the Atlantic coast of west Africa. Beyond the coastal belt of sandy beaches and mangrove swamps the land rises to a forested plateau, with highlands along the Guinea border. A quarter of the population lives along the coast. The climate is hot with heavy rainfall. Sporadic civil war throughout the 1990's has ruined the economy and destroyed much of the infrastructure especially around Monrovia; Liberia relies on foreign aid.

LIBYA
Socialist People's Libyan Arab Jamahiriya

Area Sq Km	1 759 540	Currency	Dinar
Area Sq Miles	679 362	Languages	Arabic, Berber
Population	5 339 000	Religions	Sunni Muslim
Capital	Tripoli	Organizations	OPEC, UN

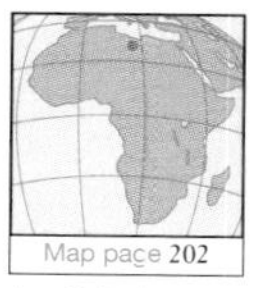
Map page 202

Libya lies on the Mediterranean coast of north Africa. The desert plains and hills of the Sahara dominate the landscape and the climate is hot and dry. Most people live in cities near the coast, where the climate is cooler with moderate rainfall. Farming and herding, chiefly in the northwest, are important but the main industry is oil. Libya is a major oil producer and oil accounts for virtually all of export earnings. Italy and Germany are the main trading partners.

LIECHTENSTEIN
Principality of Liechtenstein

Area Sq Km	160	Currency	Swiss franc
Area Sq Miles	62	Languages	German
Population	32 000	Religions	Roman Catholic, Protestant
Capital	Vaduz	Organizations	UN

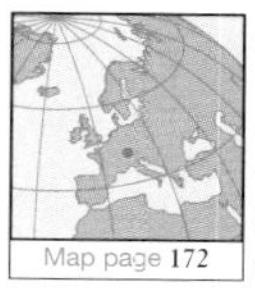
Map page 172

A landlocked state between Switzerland and Austria Liechtenstein has an industrialized, free-enterprize economy. Low business taxes have attracted companies to establish nominal offices providing about a third of state revenues. Banking is also important. Major products include precision instruments, ceramics and textiles.

LITHUANIA
Republic of Lithuania

Area Sq Km	65 200	Currency	Litas
Area Sq Miles	25 174	Languages	Lithuanian, Russian, Polish
Population	3 694 000	Religions	Roman Catholic, Protestant, Russian Orthodox
Capital	Vilnius	Organizations	UN

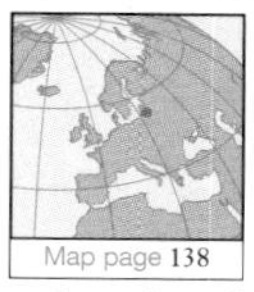
Map page 138

Lithuania is in north Europe, on the eastern shores of the Baltic Sea. It is mainly lowland with many lakes, rivers and marshes. The climate is generally temperate. Agriculture, fishing and forestry are important, but manufacturing dominates the economy. The main products are processed foods, textiles, chemicals and wood and wood products. Russia and Germany are the main trading partners. Lithuania is negotiating to join the EU.

LUXEMBOURG
Grand Duchy of Luxembourg

Area Sq Km	2 586	Currency	Franc, Euro
Area Sq Miles	998	Languages	Letzeburgish, German, French
Population	422 000	Religions	Roman Catholic
Capital	Luxembourg	Organizations	EU, OECD, UN

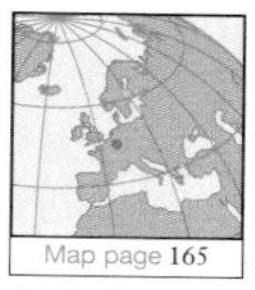
Map page 165

Luxembourg, a small landlocked country in west Europe, borders Belgium, France and Germany. The hills and forests of the Ardennes dominate the north, with rolling pasture to the south, where the main towns, farms and industries are found. The iron and steel industry is still important, but light industries (including textiles, chemicals and food products) are growing. Luxembourg is a major banking centre and the home base of key European Union institutions.

MACEDONIA (F.Y.R.O.M.)
Republic of Macedonia

Area Sq Km	25 713	Currency	Denar
Area Sq Miles	9 928	Languages	Macedonian, Albanian, Turkish
Population	1 999 000	Religions	Macedonian Orthodox, Sunni Muslim
Capital	Skopje	Organizations	UN

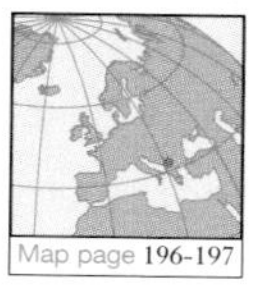
Map page 196-197

The Former Yugoslav Republic of Macedonia, is a landlocked state in southern Europe, bordered by Yugoslavia, Bulgaria, Greece and Albania. Lying within the south Balkans, it is a mountainous country, traversed northwest-southeast by the Vardar valley. It has hot summers, but very cold winters. The economy is based on industry, mining and agriculture. But the conflicts in the region have reduced trade and caused economic difficulties. Aid and loans are now assisting in modernization and development.

MADAGASCAR
Republic of Madagascar

Area Sq Km	587 041	Currency	Franc
Area Sq Miles	226 658	Languages	Malagasy, French
Population	15 057 000	Religions	Traditional beliefs, Christian, Sunni Muslim
Capital	Antananarivo	Organizations	UN

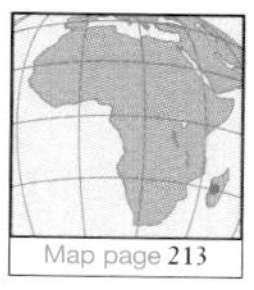
Map page 213

Madagascar lies off the east coast of southern Africa. The world's fourth largest island, it is mainly a high plateau with a coastal strip to the east and scrubby plain to the west. The climate is tropical with heavy rainfall in the north and east. Most people live on the plateau. Though the amount of arable land is limited the economy is based on agriculture. The main industries are agricultural processing, textile manufacturing and oil refining, foreign aid is important. Exports include coffee, vanilla, cloves, cloth, sugar and shrimps. France is the main trading partner.

MALAWI
Republic of Malawi

Area Sq Km	118 484	Currency	Kwacha
Area Sq Miles	45 747	Languages	Chichewa, English, local languages
Population	10 346 000	Religions	Christian, traditional beliefs, Sunni Muslim
Capital	Lilongwe	Organizations	Comm., SADC, UN

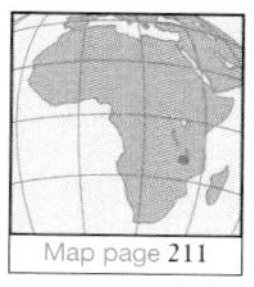
Map page 211

Landlocked Malawi in central Africa is a narrow hilly country at the southern end of the Great Rift Valley. One fifth of the country is covered by Lake Malawi, which lies above sea level. Most people live in the southern regions. The climate is mainly subtropical with varying rainfall. The economy is predominantly agricultural. Tobacco, tea and sugar are the main exports. The small manufacturing sector involves mainly chemicals, textiles and agricultural products. Malawi relies heavily on foreign aid.

MALAYSIA
Federation of Malaysia

Area Sq Km	332 965	Currency	Ringgit
Area Sq Miles	128 559	Languages	Malay, English, Chinese, Tamil, local languages
Population	21 410 000	Religions	Sunni Muslim, Buddhist, Hindu, Christian
Capital	Kuala Lumpur	Organizations	APEC, ASEAN, Comm., UN

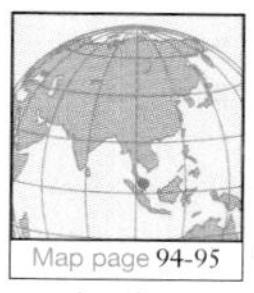
Map page 94-95

The Federation of Malaysia, in southeast Asia, comprises two regions, separated by the South China Sea. The western region occupies the southern Malay Peninsula, which has a chain of mountains dividing the eastern coastal strip from the wider plains to the west. To the east, the states of Sabah and Sarawak in the north of the island of Borneo are mainly rainforest-covered hills and mountains with mangrove swamps along the coast. Both regions have a tropical climate with heavy rainfall. About eighty per cent of the population live in the western part of the country, Peninsular Malaysia, mainly on the coasts. The country is rich in natural resources and has reserves of minerals and fuels. It is an important producer of tin, oil, natural gas and tropical hardwoods. Agriculture remains a substantial part of the economy, but industry has become the most important sector. The main exports are transport and electronic equipment, oil, palm oil, wood and rubber. The main trading partners are Japan, USA and Singapore.

MALDIVES
Republic of the Maldives

Area Sq Km	298	Currency	Rufiyaa
Area Sq Miles	115	Languages	Divehi (Maldivian)
Population	271 000	Religions	Sunni Muslim
Capital	Male	Organizations	Comm., UN

The Maldive archipelago comprises over a thousand coral atolls (around two hundred of which are inhabited), in the Indian Ocean, southwest of India. Over eighty per cent of the land area is less than one metre above sea level. The main atolls are North and South Male

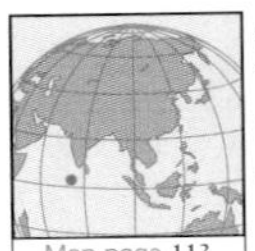
Map page 113

and Addu. The climate is hot, humid and monsoonal. There is little cultivation and almost all food is imported. Tourism has expanded rapidly and is the most important sector of the economy.

MALI
Republic of Mali

Area Sq Km	1 240 140	Currency	CFA franc
Area Sq Miles	478 821	Languages	French, Bambara, local languages
Population	10 694 000	Religions	Sunni Muslim, traditional beliefs, Christian
Capital	Bamako	Organizations	UN

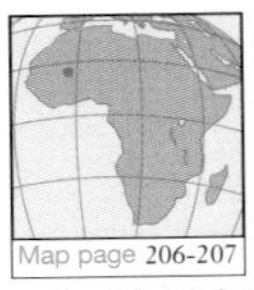
Map page 206-207

A landlocked state in west Africa, Mali is low-lying, rising to mountains in the northeast. Northern regions lie within the Sahara desert. To the south, around the Niger river, are marshes and savanna grassland. Rainfall is unreliable. Most people live along the Niger and Sénégal rivers. Exports include cotton, livestock and gold. Mali is one of the least developed countries in the world and relies heavily on foreign aid.

MALTA
Republic of Malta

Area Sq Km	316	Currency	Lira
Area Sq Miles	122	Languages	Maltese, English
Population	384 000	Religions	Roman Catholic
Capital	Valletta	Organizations	Comm., UN

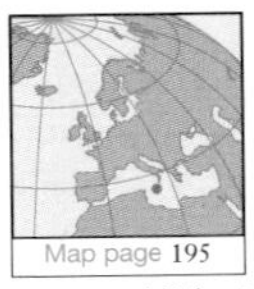
Map page 195

The islands of Malta and Gozo lie in the Mediterranean Sea, off the coast of south Italy. Malta, the main island, has low hills and an indented coastline. The islands have hot, dry summers and mild winters. The main industries are tourism, ship building and repair, electronics and textiles, which are the main exports. Malta is negotiating to join the EU.

MARSHALL ISLANDS
Republic of the Marshall Islands

Area Sq Km	181	Currency	US dollar
Area Sq Miles	70	Languages	English, Marshallese
Population	60 000	Religions	Protestant, Roman Catholic
Capital	Dalap-Uliga-Darrit	Organizations	UN

The Marshall Islands consist of over a thousand atolls, islands and islets, within two chains, in the north of the Pacific Ocean. The main atolls are Majuro (home to half the population), Kwajalein, Jaluit, Enewetak and Bikini. The climate is tropical with heavy autumn rainfall. About half the workforce are employed in farming or fishing but the islands depend heavily on US aid.

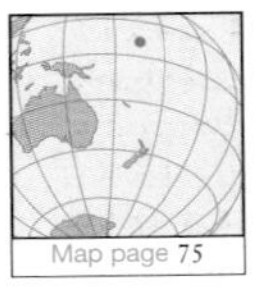
Map page 75

Martinique
French Overseas Department

Area Sq Km	1 079	Currency	French franc
Area Sq Miles	417	Languages	French, creole
Population	389 000	Religions	Roman Catholic, traditional beliefs
Capital	Fort-de-France		

Martinique, one of the Caribbean Windward Islands, has volcanic peaks in the north, a populous central plain, and hills and beaches in the south. The economy is based on sugar cane, bananas, oil refining, rum distilling, tourism and French aid.

Map page 247

MAURITANIA
Islamic Arab and African Republic of Mauritania

Area Sq Km	1 030 700	Currency	Ouguiya
Area Sq Miles	397 955	Languages	Arabic, French, local languages
Population	2 529 000	Religions	Sunni Muslim
Capital	Nouakchott	Organizations	UN

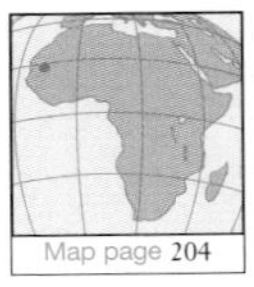
Map page 204

Mauritania is on the Atlantic coast of northwest Africa and lies almost entirely within the Sahara desert. Oases and a fertile strip along the Sénégal river to the south are the only areas suitable for cultivation. The climate is generally hot and dry. About a quarter of Mauritanians live in Nouakchott. Though most of the workforce depend on livestock rearing and subsistence farming, the economy is heavily dependent on iron ore mining and fishing, which together account for ninety per cent of export earnings, and foreign aid.

MAURITIUS
Republic of Mauritius

Area Sq Km	2 040	Currency	Rupee
Area Sq Miles	788	Languages	English, creole, Hindi, Bhojpuri, French
Population	1 141 000	Religions	Hindu, Roman Catholic, Sunni Muslim
Capital	Port Louis	Organizations	Comm., SADC, UN

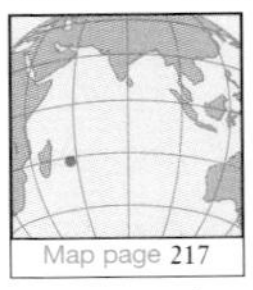
Map page 217

The state comprises Mauritius, Rodrigues and some twenty small islands in the Indian Ocean, east of Madagascar. The main island of Mauritius is volcanic in origin and has a coral coast rising to a central plateau. Most people live in the north and west side of the island. The climate is warm and humid. The economy is based on sugar production, light manufacturing (chiefly clothing) and tourism.

Mayotte
French Territorial Collectivity

Area Sq Km	373	Currency	French franc
Area Sq Miles	144	Languages	French, Mahorian
Population	144 944	Religions	Sunni Muslim, Christian
Capital	Dzaoudzi		

Lying in the Indian Ocean off the east coast of central Africa, Mayotte is geographically part of the Comoros archipelago. The economy is based on agriculture, but Mayotte depends heavily on aid from France.

Map page 217

MEXICO
United Mexican States

Area Sq Km	1 972 545	Currency	Peso
Area Sq Miles	761 604	Languages	Spanish, Amerindian languages
Population	95 831 000	Religions	Roman Catholic, Protestant
Capital	México	Organizations	APEC, OECD, UN

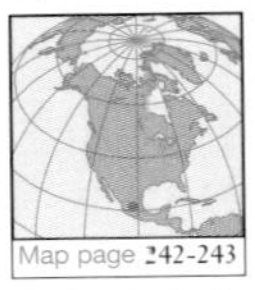
Map page 242-243

The largest country in Central America, Mexico extends south from the USA to Guatemala and Belize, and from the Pacific Ocean to the Gulf of Mexico. The greater part of the country is high plateau flanked by the western and eastern ranges of the Sierra Madre mountains. The principal lowland is the Yucatán peninsula in the southeast. The climate varies with latitude and altitude: hot and humid in the lowlands, warm on the plateau and cool with cold winters in the mountains. The north is arid, while the far south has heavy rainfall. México is one of the world's largest conurbations and the centre of trade and industry. Agriculture involves a quarter of the workforce, crops include grains, sugar cane, coffee, cotton and vegetables. Mexico is rich in minerals, including copper, zinc, lead, tin, sulphur, and silver. It is one of the world's largest producers of oil, from vast oil and gas reserves in the Gulf of Mexico. The oil and petrochemical industries still dominate, but a variety of manufactures are now produced including iron and steel, motor vehicles, textiles, chemicals and food and tobacco products. Tourism is growing in importance. Around three-quarters of all trade is with USA.

MICRONESIA, FEDERATED STATES OF

Area Sq Km	701	Currency	US dollar
Area Sq Miles	271	Languages	English, Chuukese, Pohnpeian, local languages
Population	114 000	Religions	Roman Catholic, Protestant
Capital	Palikir	Organizations	UN

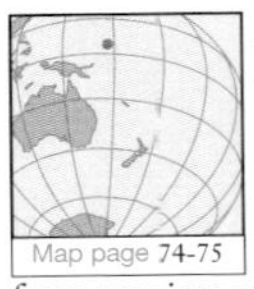
Map page 74-75

Micronesia comprises over six hundred atolls and islands of the Caroline Islands in the north Pacific Ocean. A third of the population lives on Pohnpei. The climate is tropical with heavy rainfall. Fishing and subsistence farming are the main activities. Copra and fish are the main exports. Income also derives from tourism and the licensing of foreign fishing fleets. The islands depend heavily on US aid.

MOLDOVA
Republic of Moldova

Area Sq Km	33 700	Currency	Leu
Area Sq Miles	13 012	Languages	Romanian, Ukrainian, Gagauz, Russian
Population	4 378 000	Religions	Romanian Orthodox, Russian Orthodox
Capital	Chişinău	Organizations	CIS, UN

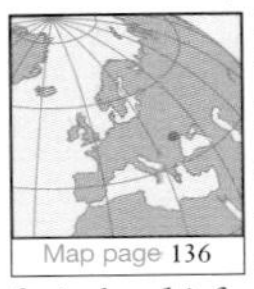
Map page 136

Moldova is in east Europe, between Romania and Ukraine. It consists of hilly steppe land, drained by the Prut and Nistru (Dniester) rivers; the latter provides access to the Black Sea through Ukrainian territory. Moldova has no mineral resources and the economy is mainly agricultural, with sugar beet, tobacco, wine and fruit the chief products. Food processing and textiles are the main industries Russia is the main trading partner.

MONACO
Principality of Monaco

Area Sq Km	2	Currency	French franc
Area Sq Miles	1	Languages	French, Monegasque, Italian
Population	33 000	Religions	Roman Catholic
Capital	Monaco-Ville	Organizations	UN

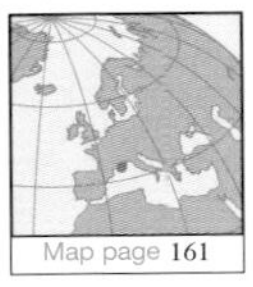
Map page 161

The principality occupies a rocky peninsula and a strip of land on France's Mediterranean coast. It depends on service industries (chiefly tourism, banking and finance) and light industry.

MONGOLIA

Area Sq Km	1 565 000	Currency	Tugrik
Area Sq Miles	604 250	Languages	Khalka (Mongolian), Kazakh, local languages
Population	2 579 000	Religions	Buddhist, Sunni Muslim
Capital	Ulaanbaatar	Organizations	UN

Mongolia is a landlocked country in east Asia between Russia and China. Much of it is high steppe land, with mountains and lakes in the west and north. In the south is the Gobi desert. Mongolia has long, cold winters and short, mild summers. A quarter of the population lives in the capital. Livestock breeding and agricultural processing are important; there are some mineral resources. Copper and textiles are the main exports.

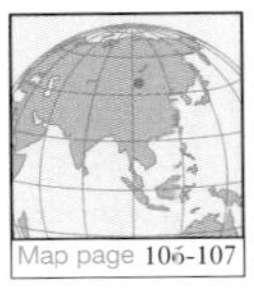
Map page 106-107

Montserrat
United Kingdom Overseas Territory

Area Sq Km	100	Currency	E. Carib. dollar
Area Sq Miles	39	Languages	English
Population	11 000	Religions	Protestant, Roman Catholic
Capital	Plymouth	Organizations	CARICOM

An island in the Leeward Island group in the Lesser Antilles in the Caribbean. From 1995 to 1997 the volcanoes in the Soufrière Hills erupted for the first time since 1630, over sixty per cent of the island was covered in volcanic ash, the capital town was destroyed, many people emigrated and the remaining population moved to the north of the island. Reconstruction, funded by aid from the UK has begun.

Map page 247

MOROCCO
Kingdom of Morocco

Area Sq Km	446 550	Currency	Dirham
Area Sq Miles	172 414	Languages	Arabic, Berber, French
Population	27 377 000	Religions	Sunni Muslim
Capital	Rabat	Organizations	UN

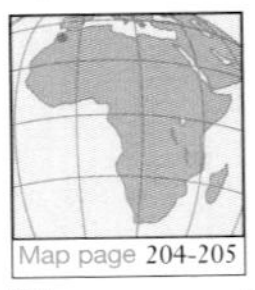
Map page 204-205

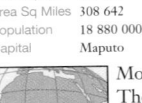

Lying in the northwest corner of Africa, Morocco has both Atlantic and Mediterranean coasts. The Atlas Mountains separate the arid south and disputed region of Western Sahara from the fertile regions of the west and north, which have a milder climate. Most Moroccans live on the Atlantic coastal plain. The economy is based mainly on agriculture, phosphate mining and tourism, the main industries are food processing, textiles and chemicals. France is the main trading partner.

MOZAMBIQUE
Republic of Mozambique

Area Sq Km	799 380	Currency	Metical
Area Sq Miles	308 642	Languages	Portuguese, Makua, Tsonga, local languages
Population	18 880 000	Religions	Traditional beliefs, Roman Catholic, Sunni Muslim
Capital	Maputo	Organizations	Comm., SADC, UN

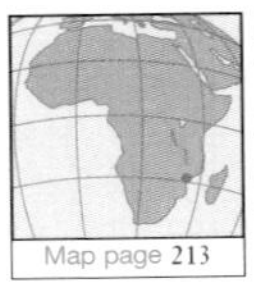
Map page 213

Mozambique lies on the east coast of southern Africa. The land is mainly a savanna plateau drained by the Zambezi and Limpopo rivers, with highlands to the north. Most people live on the coast or in the river valleys. In general the climate is tropical with winter rainfall, but droughts occur. Reconstruction began in 1992 after sixteen years of civil war. The economy is based on subsistence agriculture. Exports include shrimps, cashews, cotton and sugar, but Mozambique relies heavily on aid, and remains one of the least developed countries in the world.

MYANMAR
Union of Myanmar

Area Sq Km	676 577	Currency	Kyat
Area Sq Miles	261 228	Languages	Burmese, Shan, Karen, local languages
Population	44 497 000	Religions	Buddhist, Christian, Sunni Muslim
Capital	Yangôn	Organizations	ASEAN, UN

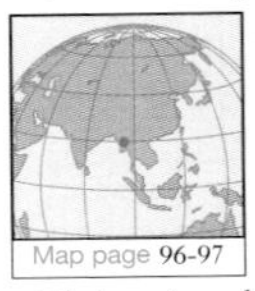
Map page 96-97

Myanmar is in southeast Asia, on the Bay of Bengal and Andaman Sea. Most people live in the valley and delta of the Irrawaddy river, which is flanked on three sides by mountains and high plateaus. The climate is hot and monsoonal, and rainforest covers much of the land. Most people are employed in agriculture. Myanmar is rich in minerals, including zinc, lead, copper and silver. Political and social unrest and lack of foreign investment have affected economic development.

NAMIBIA
Republic of Namibia

Area Sq Km	824 292	Currency	Dollar
Area Sq Miles	318 261	Languages	English, Afrikaans, German, Ovambo, local languages
Population	1 660 000	Religions	Protestant, Roman Catholic
Capital	Windhoek	Organizations	Comm., SADC, UN

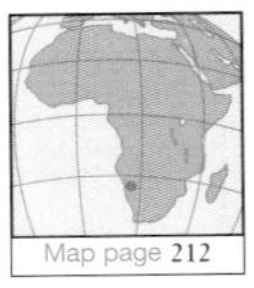
Map page 212

Namibia lies on the Atlantic coast of southern Africa. Mountain ranges separate the coastal Namib Desert from the interior plateau, bordered to the south and east by the Kalahari Desert. Namibia is hot and dry, but some summer rain falls in the north which supports crops and livestock; most of the population live in this area. Most of the workforce are employed in farming though the economy is based on mineral extraction, predominantly diamonds, but also uranium, lead, zinc and silver. Fishing is increasingly important. The economy is closely linked to that of South Africa.

NAURU
Republic of Nauru

Area Sq Km	21	Currency	Australian dollar
Area Sq Miles	8	Languages	Nauruan, English
Population	11 000	Religions	Protestant, Roman Catholic
Capital	Yaren	Organizations	Comm., UN

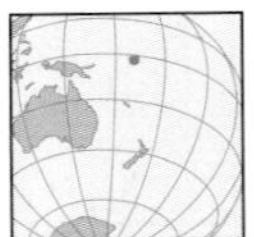
Map page 77

Nauru is a coral island near the equator in the Pacific Ocean, it has a fertile coastal strip, a barren central plateau and a tropical climate. The economy is based on phosphate mining, but reserves are near exhaustion and replacement of this income is a serious long-term problem.

NEPAL
Kingdom of Nepal

Area Sq Km	147 181	Currency	Rupee
Area Sq Miles	56 827	Languages	Nepali, Maithili, Bhojpuri, English, local languages
Population	22 847 000	Religions	Hindu, Buddhist, Sunni Muslim
Capital	Kathmandu	Organizations	UN

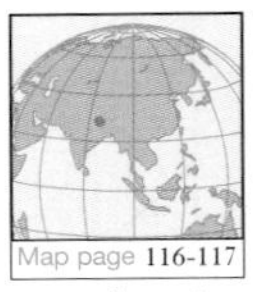
Map page 116-117

The south Asian country of Nepal lies in the eastern Himalaya between India and China. High mountains (including Everest) dominate northern Nepal. Most people live in the temperate central valleys and subtropical southern plains. The economy is based largely on agriculture and forestry; there is some manufacturing, chiefly textiles and carpets, and tourism is important. Nepal relies heavily on foreign aid.

NETHERLANDS
Kingdom of the Netherlands

Area Sq Km	41 526	Currency	Guilder, Euro
Area Sq Miles	16 033	Languages	Dutch, Frisian
Population	15 678 000	Religions	Roman Catholic, Protestant, Sunni Muslim
Capital	Amsterdam/'s-Gravenhage	Organizations	EU, OECD, UN

The Netherlands lie on the North Sea coast of western Europe. Apart from low hills in the far southeast, the land is flat and low-lying, much of it below sea level. The coastal region includes the delta of five rivers and polders (reclaimed land), protected by sand dunes, dikes and canals. The climate is temperate, with cool summers and mild winters. Rainfall is spread evenly throughout the year. The Netherlands is a

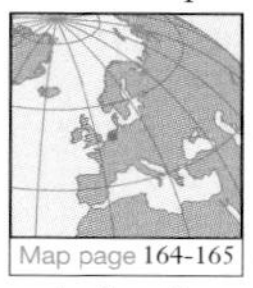

Map page 164-165

densely populated and highly urbanized country, with the majority of people living in the western Amsterdam-Rotterdam-s'Gravenhage area. Horticulture and dairy farming are important activities, though they employ less than four per cent of the workforce. The Netherlands rank as the world's third agricultural exporter, and is a leading producer and exporter of natural gas from reserves in the North Sea, but otherwise lacks raw materials. The economy is based mainly on international trade and manufacturing industry. The main industries produce food products, chemicals, machinery, electric and electronic goods and transport equipment. Germany is the main trading partner followed by other EU countries.

Netherlands Antilles
Self-governing Netherlands Territory

Area Sq Km	800	Currency	NA guilder
Area Sq Miles	309	Languages	Dutch, Papiamento, English
Population	213 000	Religions	Roman Catholic, Protestant
Capital	Willemstad		

The territory comprises two separate island groups: Curaçao and Bonaire off the northern coast of Venezuela, and Saba, Sint Eustatius and the southern part of Sint Maarten in the northern Lesser Antilles.

Map page 247

New Caledonia
French Overseas Territory

Area Sq Km	19 058	Currency	Pacific franc
Area Sq Miles	7 358	Languages	French, local languages
Population	206 000	Religions	Roman Catholic, Protestant, Sunni Muslim
Capital	Nouméa		

An island group, lying in the southwest Pacific, with a sub-tropical climate. The economy is based on nickel mining and tourism, and aid from France.

Map page 78

NEW ZEALAND

Area Sq Km	270 534	Currency	Dollar
Area Sq Miles	104 454	Languages	English, Maori
Population	3 796 000	Religions	Protestant, Roman Catholic
Capital	Wellington	Organizations	APEC, Comm., OECD, UN

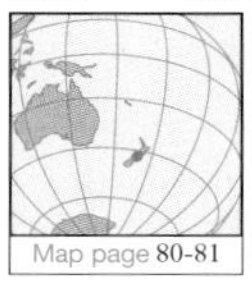

Map page 80-81

New Zealand comprises two main islands separated by the narrow Cook Strait, and a number of smaller islands. North Island, where three quarters of the population live, has mountain ranges, broad fertile valleys and a central plateau with hot springs and active volcanoes. South Island is also mountainous with the Southern Alps running its entire length. The only major lowland area is the Canterbury Plains in the centre east. The climate is generally temperate, though South Island has colder winters. Farming is the mainstay of the economy. New Zealand is one of the world's leading producers of meat (beef, lamb and mutton), wool and dairy products; fruit and fish are also important. Coal, oil and natural gas are produced, but hydroelectric and geothermal power provide much of the country's energy needs. Other industries produce timber, wood pulp, iron, aluminium, machinery and chemicals. Tourism is the fastest growing sector of the economy. The main trading partners are Australia, USA and Japan.

NICARAGUA
Republic of Nicaragua

Area Sq Km	130 000	Currency	Córdoba
Area Sq Miles	50 193	Languages	Spanish, Amerindian languages
Population	4 807 000	Religions	Roman Catholic, Protestant
Capital	Managua	Organizations	UN

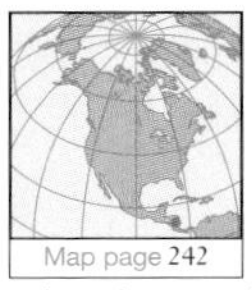

Map page 242

Nicaragua lies at the heart of Central America, with both Pacific and Caribbean coasts. Mountain ranges separate the east, which is largely rainforest, from the more developed western regions, which include Lake Nicaragua and some active volcanoes. The highest land is in the north. The climate is tropical. The economy is largely agricultural. Exports include coffee, seafood and bananas. Nicaragua relies heavily on aid and was one of the countries worse hit by hurricane Mitch in 1998; though it has received significant relief to help reconstruction, development has been seriously affected.

NIGER
Republic of Niger

Area Sq Km	1 267 000	Currency	CFA franc
Area Sq Miles	489 191	Languages	French, Hausa, Fulani, local languages
Population	10 078 000	Religions	Sunni Muslim, traditional beliefs
Capital	Niamey	Organizations	UN

A landlocked state of west Africa, Niger lies mostly within the Sahara desert, but with savanna in the south and Niger valley. The mountains of the Air massif dominate central regions. Much of the country is hot

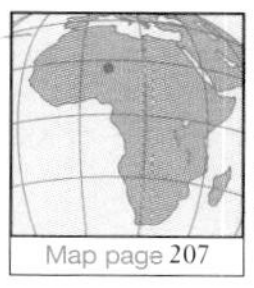

Map page 207

and dry. The south has some summer rainfall, though droughts occur. The economy depends on subsistence farming and herding, and uranium exports, but Niger is one of the world's least developed countries and relies heavily on foreign aid.

NIGERIA
Federal Republic of Nigeria

Area Sq Km	923 768	Currency	Naira
Area Sq Miles	356 669	Languages	English, Hausa, Yoruba, Ibo, Fulani, local languages
Population	106 409 000	Religions	Sunni Muslim, Christian, traditional beliefs
Capital	Abuja	Organizations	Comm., OPEC, UN

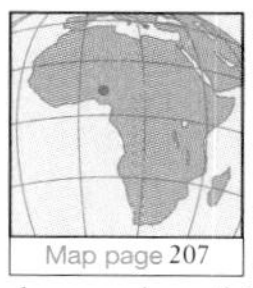

Map page 207

Nigeria is in west Africa, on the Gulf of Guinea, and is the most populous country in Africa. The Niger delta dominates coastal areas, fringed with sandy beaches, mangrove swamps and lagoons. Inland is a belt of rainforest that gives way to woodland or savanna on high plateaus. The far north is the semi-desert edge of the Sahara. The climate is tropical with heavy summer rainfall in the south but low rainfall in the north. Most people live in the coastal lowlands or in western Nigeria. About half the workforce is involved in agriculture, mainly growing subsistence crops, but agricultural production has failed to keep up with the rapid population growth and Nigeria is now a net importer of food. Cocoa and rubber are the only significant export crops. The economy is heavily dependent on vast oil resources in the Niger delta and shallow offshore waters, which account for over ninety per cent of export earnings. Nigeria also has natural gas reserves and some mineral deposits, but these are largely undeveloped. Industry involves mainly oil refining, chemicals (chiefly fertilizer), agricultural processing, textiles, steel manufacture and vehicle assembly. Political instability has left Nigeria with heavy debts, poverty and unemployment.

Niue
Self-governing New Zealand Overseas Territory

Area Sq Km	258	Currency	NZ dollar
Area Sq Miles	100	Languages	English, Polynesian
Population	2 000	Religions	Christian
Capital	Alofi		

One of the largest coral islands in the world, in the south Pacific Ocean about 500 kilometres (300 miles) east of Tonga. The economy depends on aid and remittances from New Zealand. The population is declining because of migration to New Zealand.

Map page 81

Norfolk Island
Australian External Territory

Area Sq Km	35	Currency	Australian dolla
Area Sq Miles	14	Languages	English
Population	2 000	Religions	Protestant, Roman Catholic
Capital	Kingston		

In the south Pacific Ocean, between Vanuatu and New Zealand; tourism has increased steadily and is the mainstay of the economy, providing revenues for agricultural development.

Map page 82

Northern Mariana Islands
United States Commonwealth

Area Sq Km	477	Currency	US dollar
Area Sq Miles	184	Languages	English, Chamorro, local languages
Population	70 000	Religions	Roman Catholic
Capital	Saipan		

A chain of islands in the northwest Pacific Ocean, extending over 550 kilometres (350 miles) north to south; the main island is Saipan; tourism is a major industry employing around half the workforce, the majority of tourists are from Japan.

Map page 74

NORTH KOREA
People's Democratic Republic of Korea

Area Sq Km	120 538	Currency	Won
Area Sq Miles	46 540	Languages	Korean
Population	23 348 000	Religions	Traditional beliefs, Chondoist, Buddhist
Capital	P'yŏngyang	Organizations	UN

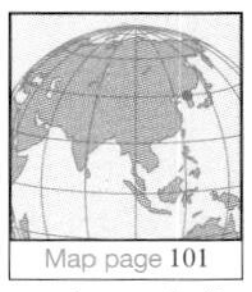

Map page 101

Occupying the northern half of the Korean peninsula in east Asia, North Korea is a rugged and mountainous country. The principal lowlands and the main agricultural areas are the plains in the southwest. More than half the population lives in urban areas, mainly on the coastal plains. North Korea has a continental climate, with cold, dry winters and hot, wet summers. About a third of the workforce is involved in agriculture, mainly growing food crops on cooperative farms. A variety of minerals and ores, chiefly iron ore, are mined and are the basis of the country's heavy industry. Exports include minerals (lead, magnesite and zinc) and metal products (chiefly iron and steel). The economy has declined since 1991 when ties to the former USSR and eastern bloc collapsed, and there were serious food shortages between 1994 and 1998. North Korea receives some foreign aid.

NORWAY
Kingdom of Norway

Area Sq Km	323 878	Currency	Krone
Area Sq Miles	125 050	Languages	Norwegian
Population	4 419 000	Religions	Protestant, Roman Catholic
Capital	Oslo	Organizations	OECD, UN

Norway stretches along the north and west coasts of Scandinavia, from the Arctic Ocean to the southern North Sea. Its extensive coastline is

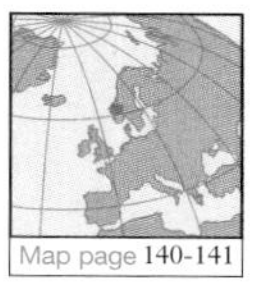

Map page 140-141

indented with fjords and fringed with many islands. Inland, the terrain is mountainous, with coniferous forests and lakes in the south. The only major lowland areas are along the southern North Sea and Skagerrak coasts, where most people live. The climate is modified by the North Atlantic Drift. Norway has vast petroleum and natural gas resources in the North Sea. It is west one of Europe's leading producers of oil and gas, which account for around half of export earnings. Related industries include engineering (oil and gas platforms) and petrochemicals. More traditional industries process local raw materials: fish, timber and minerals. Agriculture is limited, but fishing and fish farming are important. Norway is the world's leading exporter of farmed salmon. Merchant shipping and tourism are major sources of foreign exchange.

OMAN
Sultanate of Oman

Area Sq Km	309 500	Currency	Rial
Area Sq Miles	119 499	Languages	Arabic, Baluchi, Indian languages
Population	2 382 000	Religions	Ibadhi Muslim, Sunni Muslim
Capital	Muscat	Organizations	UN

In southwest Asia, Oman occupies the east and southeast coasts of the Arabian Peninsula and an enclave north of the United Arab Emirates.

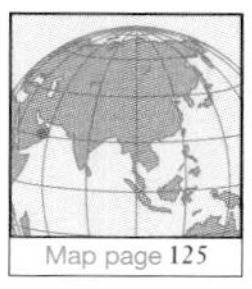

Map page 125

Most of the land is desert, with mountains in the north and south. The climate is hot and mainly dry. Most people live on the coastal strip on the Gulf of Oman. The majority depend on farming and fishing, but the oil and gas industries dominate the economy, with around eighty per cent of export revenues from oil.

PAKISTAN
Islamic Republic of Pakistan

Area Sq Km	803 940	Currency	Rupee
Area Sq Miles	310 403	Languages	Urdu, Punjabi, Sindhi, Pushtu, English
Population	148 166 000	Religions	Sunni Muslim, Shi'a Muslim, Christian, Hindu
Capital	Islamabad	Organizations	Comm., UN

Pakistan is in the northwest part of the Indian subcontinent in south Asia, on the Arabian Sea. Eastern and southern Pakistan are dominated by the great basin drained by the Indus river system. It is the main

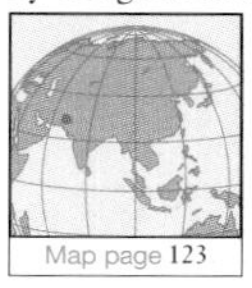

Map page 123

agricultural area and contains most of the predominantly rural population. To the north the land rises to the mountains of the Karakoram, Hindu Kush and Himalaya. The west is semi-desert plateaus and mountain ranges. The climate ranges between dry desert and tundra on the mountain tops. However, temperatures are generally warm and rainfall is monsoonal. Agriculture is the main sector of the economy, employing about half the workforce; cultivation is based on extensive irrigation schemes. Pakistan is one of the world's leading producers of cotton and an important exporter of rice. However, much of the country's food needs must be imported. Pakistan produces natural gas and has a variety of mineral deposits including coal and gold, but they are little developed. The main industries are textiles and clothing manufacture and food processing, with fabrics and ready-made clothing the leading exports. Pakistan also produces leather goods, fertilizers, chemicals, paper and precision instruments. The country depends heavily upon foreign aid and remittances from Pakistanis working abroad.

PALAU
Republic of Palau

Area Sq Km	497	Currency	US dollar
Area Sq Miles	192	Languages	Palauan, English
Population	19 000	Religions	Roman Catholic, Protestant, traditional beliefs
Capital	Koror	Organizations	UN

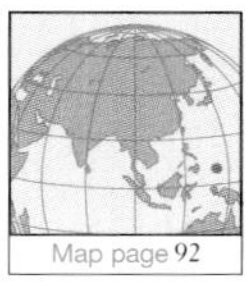

Map page 92

Palau comprises over three hundred islands in the western Caroline Islands in the west Pacific Ocean. The climate is tropical. The economy is based on farming, fishing and tourism; Palau is heavily dependent on US aid.

PANAMA
Republic of Panama

Area Sq Km	77 082	Currency	Balboa
Area Sq Miles	29 762	Languages	Spanish, English, Amerindian languages
Population	2 767 000	Religions	Roman Catholic, Protestant, Sunni Muslim
Capital	Panamá	Organizations	UN

Panama is the most southerly state in central America and has Pacific and Caribbean coasts. It is hilly, with mountains in the west and jungle

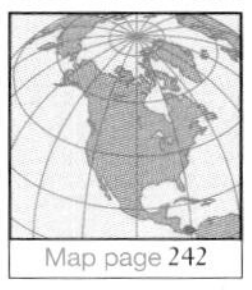

Map page 242

near the Colombian border. The climate is tropical. Most people live on the drier Pacific side. The economy is based mainly on services related to the canal: shipping, banking and tourism. Exports include bananas, shrimps, coffee, clothing and fish products. USA is the main trading partner.

PAPUA NEW GUINEA
Independent State of Papua New Guinea

Area Sq Km	462 840	Currency	Kina
Area Sq Miles	178 704	Languages	English, Tok Pisin (creole), local languages
Population	4 600 000	Religions	Protestant, Roman Catholic, traditional beliefs
Capital	Port Moresby	Organizations	Comm., UN

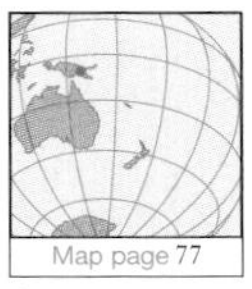

Map page 77

Papua New Guinea, in Australasia, occupies the eastern half of the island of New Guinea and includes many island groups. Papua New Guinea has a forested and mountainous interior, bordered by swampy plains, and a tropical monsoon climate. Most of the workforce are farmers. Timber, copra, coffee and cocoa are important, but exports are dominated by minerals, chiefly gold and copper. The country depends on foreign aid. Australia and Japan are the main trading partners.

PARAGUAY
Republic of Paraguay

Area Sq Km	406 752	Currency	Guaraní
Area Sq Miles	157 048	Languages	Spanish, Guaraní
Population	5 222 000	Religions	Roman Catholic, Protestant
Capital	Asunción	Organizations	UN

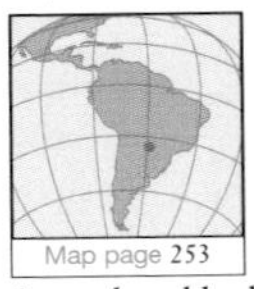
Map page 253

Paraguay is a landlocked country in central South America, bordering Bolivia, Brazil and Argentina. The river Paraguay separates a sparsely populated western zone of marsh and flat alluvial plains from a more developed, hilly and forested region to the east and south. The climate is subtropical. Virtually all electricity is produced by hydro plants and surplus power is exported to Brazil and Argentina. The hydroelectric dam at Itaipu is the largest in the world. The mainstay of the economy is agriculture and agricultural industries. Exports include cotton, soya bean and edible oil products, timber and meat. Brazil and Argentina are the main trading partners.

PERU
Republic of Peru

Area Sq Km	1 285 216	Currency	Sol
Area Sq Miles	496 225	Languages	Spanish, Quechua, Aymara
Population	24 797 000	Religions	Roman Catholic, Protestant
Capital	Lima	Organizations	APEC, UN

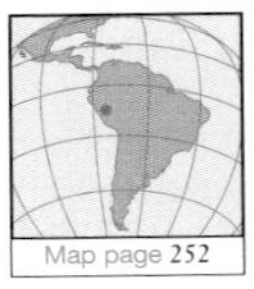
Map page 252

Peru lies on the Pacific coast of South America. Most people live on the coastal strip and the plateaus of the high Andes. East of the Andes is the Amazon rainforest. The coast is temperate with low rainfall, while the east is hot, humid and wet. Agriculture involves one third of the workforce, fishing is also important; agriculture and fishing were both disrupted by the El Nino effect in the 1990s. Sugar, cotton, coffee and, illegally, coca are the main cash crops. Copper and copper products, fishmeal, zinc products, coffee, petroleum and its products, and textiles are the main exports. America is the main trading partner.

PHILIPPINES
Republic of the Philippines

Area Sq Km	300 000	Currency	Peso
Area Sq Miles	115 831	Languages	English, Pilipino, Cebuano, local languages
Population	72 944 000	Religions	Roman Catholic, Protestant, Sunni Muslim
Capital	Manila	Organizations	APEC, ASEAN, UN

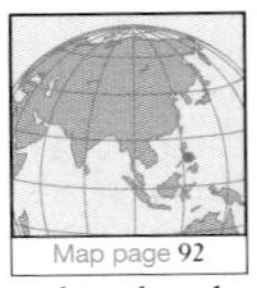
Map page 92

The Philippines, in southeast Asia, consists of over seven thousand islands and atolls lying between the South China Sea and the Pacific Ocean. The islands of Luzon and Mindanao account for two thirds of the land area. They and nine other fairly large islands are mountainous and forested. There are active volcanoes, and earthquakes are common. Most people live in the plains on the larger islands or on the coastal strips. The climate is hot and humid with heavy monsoonal rainfall. Coconuts, sugar, pineapples and bananas are the main agricultural crops; fish and timber are also important. The Philippines produces copper, gold, chromium, cobalt and nickel as well as oil, though geothermal power is also used. The main industries process raw materials and produce electrical and electronic equipment and components, footwear and clothing, textiles and furniture. These manufactured goods are the main exports. Foreign aid and remittances from workers abroad are important to the economy, which faces problems of high population growth rate and high unemployment. USA is the main trading partner.

Pitcairn Islands
United Kingdom Overseas Territory

Area Sq Km	45	Currency	NZ dollar
Area Sq Miles	17	Languages	English
Population	46	Religions	Protestant
Capital	Adamstown		

An island group in the southeast Pacific Ocean consisting of Pitcairn Island and three uninhabited islands. It was originally settled by mutineers from HMS Bounty.

Map page 75

POLAND
Polish Republic

Area Sq Km	312 683	Currency	Złoty
Area Sq Miles	120 728	Languages	Polish, German
Population	38 718 000	Religions	Roman Catholic, Polish Orthodox
Capital	Warszawa	Organizations	OECD, UN

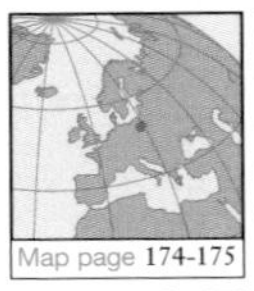
Map page 174-175

Poland lies on the Baltic coast of central Europe. The Odra (Oder) and Wisla (Vistula) deltas dominate the coast. Inland, much of Poland is low-lying with woods and lakes. In the south the land rises to the Sudety and western part of the Carpathian Mountains which form the borders with the Czech Republic and Slovakia respectively. The climate is continental, with warm summers and cold winters. Around a quarter of the workforce is involved in agriculture, and exports include livestock products and sugar. The economy is heavily industrialized, with mining and manufacturing accounting for forty per cent of national income. Poland is one of the world's major producers of coal, and also produces copper, zinc, lead, sulphur and natural gas. The main industries are machinery and transport equipment, ship building, metal and chemical production. Germany is the main trading partner. Poland is negotiating to join the EU.

PORTUGAL
Portuguese Republic

Area Sq Km	88 940	Currency	Escudo, Euro
Area Sq Miles	34 340	Languages	Portuguese
Population	9 869 000	Religions	Roman Catholic, Protestant
Capital	Lisboa	Organizations	EU, OECD, UN

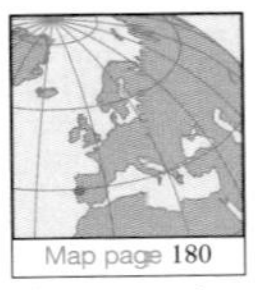
Map page 180

Portugal lies in the western part of the Iberian peninsula in southwest Europe, has an Atlantic coastline and is bordered by Spain to the north and east. The land north of the river Tejo (Tagus) is mostly highland with extensive forests of pine and cork. South of the river is undulating lowland. The climate in the north is cool and moist, the south is warmer, with dry, mild winters. Most Portuguese live near the coast, with one third of the total population in Lisbon (Lisboa) and Oporto. Agriculture, fishing and forestry involve about twelve per cent of the workforce. Mining and manufacturing are the main sectors of the economy. Portugal produces kaolin, copper, tin, zinc, tungsten and salt. Export manufactures include textiles, clothing and footwear, electrical machinery and transport equipment, cork and wood products, and chemicals. Service industries, chiefly tourism and banking, are important to the economy as are remittances from workers abroad. Most trade is with other EU countries.

PUERTO RICO
United States Commonwealth

Area Sq Km	9 104	Currency	US dollar
Area Sq Miles	3 515	Languages	Spanish, English
Population	3 810 000	Religions	Roman Catholic, Protestant
Capital	San Juan		

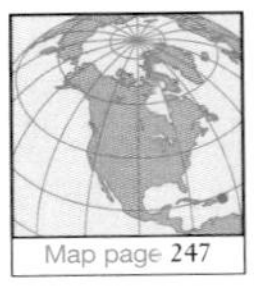
Map page 247

The Caribbean island of Puerto Rico has a forested, hilly interior, coastal plains and a tropical climate. Half the population lives in the San Juan area. The economy is based on manufacturing (chiefly chemicals, electronics and food), tourism and agriculture. USA is the predominant trading partner.

QATAR
State of Qatar

Area Sq Km	11 437	Currency	Riyal
Area Sq Miles	4 416	Languages	Arabic
Population	579 000	Religions	Sunni Muslim
Capital	Doha	Organizations	OPEC, UN

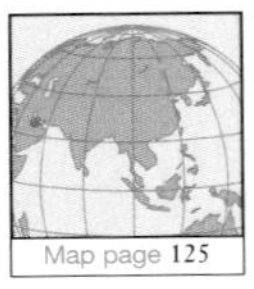
Map page 125

The emirate occupies a peninsula that extends northwards from east-central Saudi Arabia into The Gulf in southwest Asia. The land is flat and barren with sand dunes and salt pans. The climate is hot and mainly dry. Most people live in the Doha area. The economy is heavily dependent on oil and natural gas production and the oil-refining industry. Income also comes from overseas investment. Japan is the largest trading partner.

Réunion
French Overseas Department

Area Sq Km	2 551	Currency	French franc
Area Sq Miles	985	Languages	French, creole
Population	682 000	Religions	Roman Catholic
Capital	St-Denis		

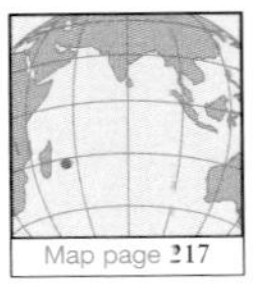
Map page 217

The Indian Ocean island of Réunion is mountainous, with coastal lowlands and a warm climate. It depends heavily on sugar, tourism and French aid. Some uninhabited islets to the east are administered from Réunion.

ROMANIA

Area Sq Km	237 500	Currency	Leu
Area Sq Miles	91 699	Languages	Romanian, Hungarian
Population	22 474 000	Religions	Romanian Orthodox, Protestant, Roman Catholic
Capital	București	Organizations	UN

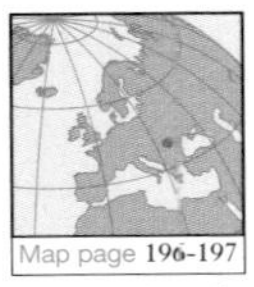
Map page 196-197

Romania lies on the Black Sea coast of east Europe. Mountains separate the Transylvanian Basin at the centre of the country from the populous plains of the east and south and the Danube delta. The climate is continental. Romania has mineral resources (zinc, lead, silver and gold), and oil and natural gas reserves. Economic reform has been slow and sporadic, but measures to accelerate change were introduced in 1999. Agriculture still employs over a quarter of the workforce. The main exports are textiles, mineral products, chemicals, machinery and footwear. The most important trading partners are Germany and Italy. Negotiations to join the EU have been started.

RUSSIAN FEDERATION

Area Sq Km	17 075 400	Currency	Rouble
Area Sq Miles	6 592 849	Languages	Russian, Tatar, Ukrainian, local languages
Population	147 434 000	Religions	Russian Orthodox, Sunni Muslim, Protestant
Capital	Moskva	Organizations	APEC, CIS, UN

Russia occupies much of east Europe and all of north Asia, and is the world's largest state, nearly twice the size of the USA. It borders thirteen countries to the west and south and has long coastlines on the Arctic and Pacific Oceans to the north and east. European Russia lies west of the Ural mountains. To the south the land rises to uplands and the Caucasus on the border with Georgia and Azerbaijan. East of the Urals lies the flat West Siberian Plain; much of central Siberia is plateau. In the south is Lake Baikal, the world's deepest lake, and the Sayan ranges on the border with Kazakhstan and Mongolia. Eastern Siberia is rugged and mountainous with many active volcanoes in the Kamchatka Peninsula. Russia's major rivers are the Volga in the west and the Ob', Yenisey, Lena and Amur in Siberia. The climate and vegetation range between arctic tundra in the north and semi-arid steppe towards the Black and Caspian Sea coasts in the south. In general, the climate is continental

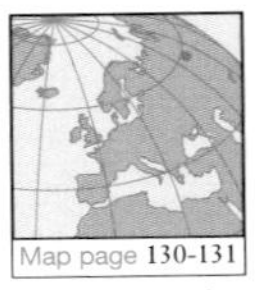
Map page 130-131

with extreme temperatures. The majority of the population (the seventh largest in the world), and industry and agriculture are concentrated in European Russia, but there has been increased migration to Siberia to exploit its vast natural resources. The economy is heavily dependent on exploitation of raw materials and on heavy industry. Russia has a wealth of mineral resources, though they are often difficult to exploit because of the climate and remote locations. It is one of the world's leading producers of petroleum, natural gas and coal as well as iron ore, nickel, copper and bauxite, and many precious and rare metals. Forests cover over forty per cent of the land area and supply an important timber, paper and pulp industry; around eight per cent of land is suitable for cultivation, but farming is generally inefficient and food, especially grains, must be imported. Fishing is important and Russia has a large fleet operating around the world. The transition to a market economy has been slow and difficult, with high unemployment and considerable underemployment. As well as mining and extractive industries there is a wide range of manufacturing industry from steel mills to aircraft and space vehicles, shipbuilding, synthetic fabrics, plastics, cotton fabrics, consumer durable, chemicals and fertilizers. Exports include fuels, metals, machinery, chemicals and forest products. The most important trading partners include Germany, Italy, USA, China and Switzerland.

RWANDA
Republic of Rwanda

Area Sq Km	26 338	Currency	Franc
Area Sq Miles	10 169	Languages	Kinyarwanda, French, English
Population	6 604 000	Religions	Roman Catholic, traditional beliefs, Protestant
Capital	Kigali	Organizations	UN

A densely populated and landlocked state in east Africa, Rwanda is situated in the mountains and plateaus to the east of the Great Rift Valley. The climate is warm with a summer dry season. Rwanda depends upon subsistence farming, coffee and tea exports, light industry and foreign aid, but in the 1990s civil war and ethnic conflict devastated the country.

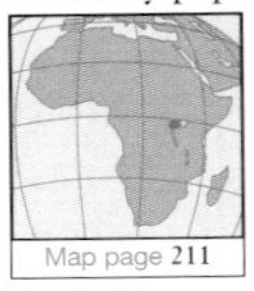
Map page 211

Saba part of Netherlands Antilles

Area Sq Km (Miles) 13 (5) | Population 1 200 | Capital Bottom

An island in the Leeward Islands in the Lesser Antilles in the Caribbean, to the south of Sint Maarten.

Map page 247

St-Barthélémy Dependency of Guadeloupe

Area Sq Km (Miles) 21 (8) | Population 5 038 | Capital Gustavia

An island in the Leeward Islands in the Lesser Antilles in the Caribbean south of Sint Maarten. Tourism is the main economic activity.

Map page 247

St Helena
United Kingdom Overseas Territory

Area Sq Km	121	Currency	Pound sterling
Area Sq Miles	47	Languages	English
Population	5 644	Religions	Protestant, Roman Catholic
Capital	Jamestown		

St Helena and its dependencies, Ascension and Tristan da Cunha are isolated island groups lying in the south Atlantic Ocean. St Helena is a rugged island of volcanic origin; the main activity is fishing but the island depends on financial aid from the UK.

Map page 216

ST KITTS AND NEVIS
Federation of St Kitts and Nevis

Area Sq Km	261	Currency	E. Carib. dollar
Area Sq Miles	101	Languages	English, creole
Population	39 000	Religions	Protestant, Roman Catholic
Capital	Basseterre	Organizations	CARICOM, Comm., UN

St Kitts and Nevis are in the Leeward Islands in the Caribbean Sea. Both volcanic islands are mountainous and forested with sandy beaches and a warm, wet climate. About three-quarters of the population live on St Kitts. Agriculture is the main activity, with sugar the main product. Tourism and manufacturing (chiefly garments and electronic components) are important.

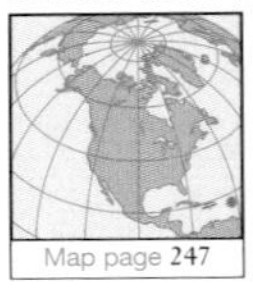
Map page 247

ST LUCIA

Area Sq Km	616	Currency	E. Carib. dollar
Area Sq Miles	238	Languages	English, creole
Population	150 000	Religions	Roman Catholic, Protestant
Capital	Castries	Organizations	CARICOM, Comm., UN

St Lucia, one of the Windward Islands in the Caribbean Sea, is a volcanic island with forested mountains, hot springs, sandy beaches and a wet tropical climate. Agriculture is the main activity, with bananas accounting for about forty per cent of export earnings. Tourism, agricultural processing and light manufacturing are increasingly important.

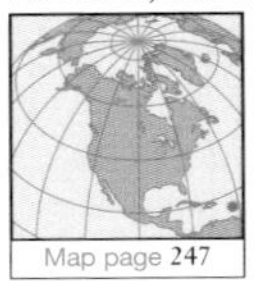
Map page 247

St Martin Dependency of Guadeloupe

Area Sq Km (Miles) 54 (21) | Population 28 518 | Capital Marigot

The northern part of one of the Leeward Islands is in the Caribbean, the other part of the island is part of the Netherlands Antilles. Tourism is the main source of income.

Map page 247

St Pierre and Miquelon
French Territorial Collectivity

Area Sq Km	242	Currency	French franc
Area Sq Miles	93	Languages	French
Population	7 000	Religions	Roman Catholic
Capital	St-Pierre		

A group of islands off the south coast of Newfoundland in eastern Canada. The islands are unsuitable for agriculture; fishing and fish processing are still important, though the islands rely heavily on assistance from France.

Map page 225

ST VINCENT AND THE GRENADINES

Area Sq Km	389	Currency	E. Carib. dollar
Area Sq Miles	150	Languages	English, creole
Population	112 000	Religions	Protestant, Roman Catholic
Capital	Kingstown	Organizations	CARICOM, Comm., UN

St Vincent, whose territory includes islets and cays in The Grenadines, is in the Windward Islands in the Caribbean Sea. St Vincent is forested and mountainous, with an active volcano, Soufrière. The climate is tropical and wet. The economy is based mainly on agriculture and tourism. Bananas account for around a third of export earnings, arrowroot is also important.

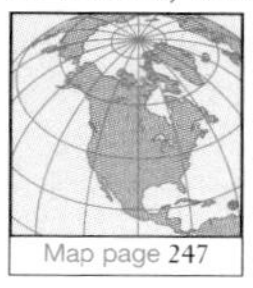
Map page 247

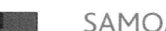

SAMOA
Independent State of Samoa

Area Sq Km	2 831	Currency	Tala
Area Sq Miles	1 093	Languages	Samoan, English
Population	174 000	Religions	Protestant, Roman Catholic
Capital	Apia	Organizations	Comm., UN

Samoa consists of two larger mountainous and forested islands, Savai'i and Upolu, and seven smaller islands in the south Pacific Ocean. Over half the population live on Upolu. The climate is tropical. The economy is based on agriculture, with some fishing and light manufacturing. Traditional exports are coconut products, timber, taro, cocoa and fruit. Tourism is increasing, but the islands depend upon workers' remittances and foreign aid.

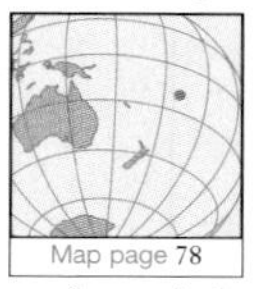
Map page 78

SAN MARINO
Republic of San Marino

Area Sq Km	61	Currency	Ital. lira
Area Sq Miles	24	Languages	Italian
Population	26 000	Religions	Roman Catholic
Capital	San Marino	Organizations	UN

Landlocked San Marino lies in northeast Italy. A third of the people live in the capital. There is some agriculture and light industry, but most income comes from tourism. Most trade is with Italy.

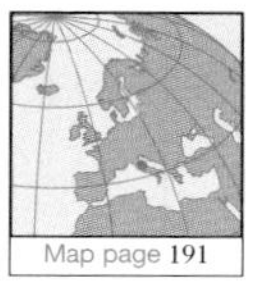
Map page 191

SÃO TOMÉ AND PRÍNCIPE
Democratic Republic of São Tomé and Príncipe

Area Sq Km	964	Currency	Dobra
Area Sq Miles	372	Languages	Portuguese, creole
Population	141 000	Religions	Roman Catholic, Protestant
Capital	São Tomé	Organizations	UN

The two main islands and adjacent islets lie off the coast of west Africa in the Gulf of Guinea. São Tomé is the larger island with over ninety per cent of the population. Both São Tomé and Príncipe are mountainous and tree-covered, and have a hot and humid climate. The economy is heavily dependent on cocoa, which accounts for around ninety per cent of export earnings.

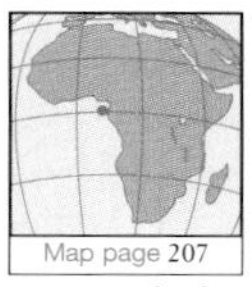
Map page 207

SAUDI ARABIA
Kingdom of Saudi Arabia

Area Sq Km	2 200 000	Currency	Riyal
Area Sq Miles	849 425	Languages	Arabic
Population	20 181 000	Religions	Sunni Muslim, Shi'a Muslim
Capital	Riyadh	Organizations	OPEC, UN

Saudi Arabia occupies most of the Arabian Peninsula in southwest Asia. The terrain is desert or semi-desert plateaus, which rise to mountains running parallel to the Red Sea in the west and slope down to plains in the southeast and along The Gulf in the east. Over eighty per cent of the population live in urban areas. There are around four million foreign workers in Saudi Arabia employed mainly in the oil and service industries. Summers are hot, winters are warm and rainfall is low. Saudi Arabia has the world's largest reserves of oil and significant natural gas reserves, located in the northeast, both onshore and in The Gulf. Crude oil and refined products account for over ninety per cent of export earnings. Other industries and irrigated agriculture are being encouraged, but most food and raw materials are imported. Saudi Arabia has important banking and commercial interests. Each year around two million pilgrims visit Islam's holiest cities, Mecca and Medina, in the west. Japan, USA, South Korea and Singapore are the main export trading partners.

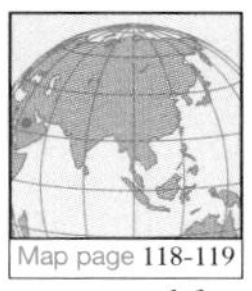
Map page 118-119

SENEGAL
Republic of Senegal

Area Sq Km	196 720	Currency	CFA franc
Area Sq Miles	75 954	Languages	French, Wolof, Fulani, local languages
Population	9 003 000	Religions	Sunni Muslim, Roman Catholic, traditional beliefs
Capital	Dakar	Organizations	UN

Senegal lies on the Atlantic coast of west Africa. The north is arid semi-desert, while the south is mainly fertile savanna bushland. The climate is tropical with summer rains, though droughts occur. One fifth of the population lives in and around Dakar. Fish, chemical products, groundnuts and phosphates are the main exports. Dakar is a major port and tourism is developing. France is the main trading partner.

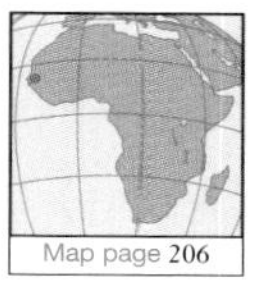
Map page 206

SEYCHELLES
Republic of the Seychelles

Area Sq Km	455	Currency	Rupee
Area Sq Miles	176	Languages	English, French, creole
Population	76 000	Religions	Roman Catholic, Protestant
Capital	Victoria	Organizations	Comm., SADC, UN

The Seychelles comprises an archipelago of over one hundred granitic and coral islands in the western Indian Ocean. Over ninety per cent of the population live on the main island, Mahé. The climate is hot and humid with heavy rainfall. The economy is based mainly on tourism, fishing and light manufacturing.

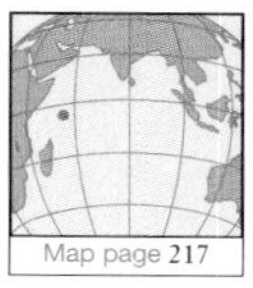
Map page 217

SIERRA LEONE
Republic of Sierra Leone

Area Sq Km	71 740	Currency	Leone
Area Sq Miles	27 699	Languages	English, creole, Mende, Temne, local languages
Population	4 568 000	Religions	Sunni Muslim, traditional beliefs
Capital	Freetown	Organizations	Comm., UN

Sierra Leone lies on the Atlantic coast of west Africa. Its coast is heavily indented and lined with mangrove swamps. Inland is a forested area rising to savanna plateaus, with the mountains to the northeast. The climate is tropical and rainfall is heavy. Most of the workforce is involved in subsistence farming. Cocoa and coffee are the main cash crops, but diamonds and rutile (titanium ore) are the main exports, though a substantial amount of diamonds are smuggled out of the country. Civil war and economic decline have caused serious difficulties.

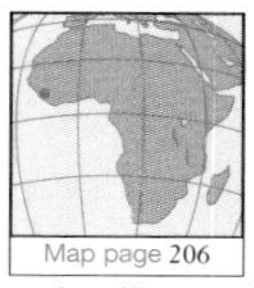
Map page 206

SINGAPORE
Republic of Singapore

Area Sq Km	639	Currency	Dollar
Area Sq Miles	247	Languages	Chinese, English, Malay, Tamil
Population	3 476 000	Religions	Buddhist, Taoist, Sunni Muslim, Christian, Hindu
Capital	Singapore	Organizations	APEC, ASEAN, Comm., UN

The state comprises the main island of Singapore and over fifty other islands, lying off the southern tip of the Malay Peninsula in southeast Asia. Singapore is generally low-lying and includes land reclaimed from swamps and the sea. It is hot and humid, with heavy rainfall throughout the year. There are fish farms and vegetable gardens in the north and east of the island, but most food needs must be imported. Singapore also lacks mineral and energy resources. Manufacturing industries and services are the main sectors of the economy. Their rapid development has fuelled the nation's impressive economic growth over the last three decades. The main industries include electronics, oil refining, chemicals, pharmaceuticals, ship repair, food processing and textiles. Singapore is a major financial centre. Its port is one of the world's largest and busiest and acts as an entrepôt for neighbouring states. Tourism is also important. Japan, USA and Malaysia are the main trading partners.

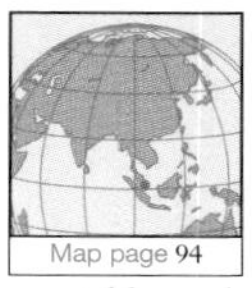
Map page 94

Sint Eustatius part of Netherlands Antilles

Area Sq Km (Miles) 21 (8)	Population 1 900	Capital Oranjestad

An island in the Leeward Islands in the Lesser Antilles in the Caribbean south of Sint Maarten; there is a developing tourism industry.

Map page 247

Sint Maarten part of Netherlands Antilles

Area Sq Km (Miles) 34 (13)	Population 38 567	Capital Philipsburg

The southern part of one of the Leeward Islands is in the Caribbean, the other part of the island is a dependency of Guadeloupe. Tourism and fishing are the most important industries.

Map page 247

SLOVAKIA
Slovak Republic

Area Sq Km	49 035	Currency	Koruna
Area Sq Miles	18 933	Languages	Slovak, Hungarian, Czech
Population	5 377 000	Religions	Roman Catholic, Protestant, Orthodox
Capital	Bratislava	Organizations	UN

A landlocked country in central Europe, Slovakia borders the Czech Republic, Poland, Ukraine, Hungary and Austria. Slovakia is mountainous along the border with Poland in the north, but low-lying in the southwest. The climate is continental. There are a range of manufacturing industries and the main exports are machinery and transport equipment, but during the 1990s there were continued economic difficulties and economic growth has been slow. Most trade is with EU countries and the Czech Republic and negotiations to join the EU have begun.

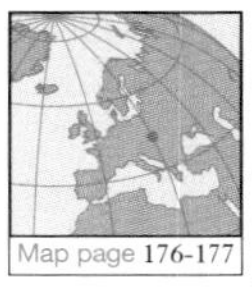
Map page 176-177

SLOVENIA
Republic of Slovenia

Area Sq Km	20 251	Currency	Tólar
Area Sq Miles	7 819	Languages	Slovene, Croatian, Serbian
Population	1 993 000	Religions	Roman Catholic, Protestant
Capital	Ljubljana	Organizations	UN

Slovenia lies in the northwest Balkans of south Europe and has a short coastline on the Adriatic Sea. It is mountainous and hilly, with lowlands on the coast and in the Sava and Drava river valleys. The climate is generally continental, but Mediterranean nearer the coast. The main agricultural products are potatoes, grains and sugar beet; the main industries include metal processing, electronics and consumer goods. Trade has been re-orientated towards western markets, the main trading partners are Germany and Italy. Negotiations to join the EU have begun.

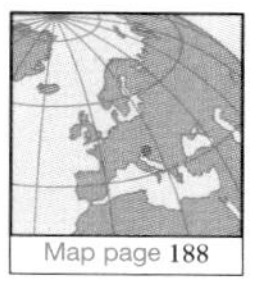
Map page 188

SOLOMON ISLANDS

Area Sq Km	28 370	Currency	Dollar
Area Sq Miles	10 954	Languages	English, creole, local languages
Population	417 000	Religions	Protestant, Roman Catholic
Capital	Honiara	Organizations	Comm., UN

The state consists of the Solomon, Santa Cruz and Shortland Islands in the southwest Pacific Ocean. The six main islands are volcanic, mountainous and forested, though Guadalcanal, the most populous, has a large lowland area. The climate is generally hot and humid. Subsistence farming, forestry and fishing predominate. Exports include timber products, fish, copra and palm oil. The islands depend on foreign aid.

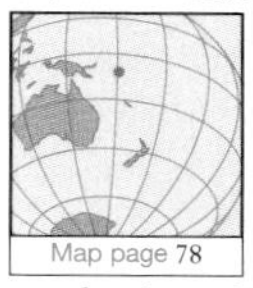
Map page 78

SOMALIA
Somali Democratic Republic

Area Sq Km	637 657	Currency	Shilling
Area Sq Miles	246 201	Languages	Somali, Arabic
Population	9 237 000	Religions	Sunni Muslim
Capital	Muqdisho	Organizations	UN

Somalia is in the northeast Africa, on the Gulf of Aden and Indian Ocean. It consists of a dry scrubby plateau, rising to highlands in the north. The climate is hot and dry, but coastal areas and the Jubba and Webi Shabeelle river valleys support crops and most of the population. Subsistence farming and livestock rearing are the main activities. Exports include livestock and bananas. Frequent drought and civil war have prevented economic development. Somalia is one of the poorest and least developed countries in the world.

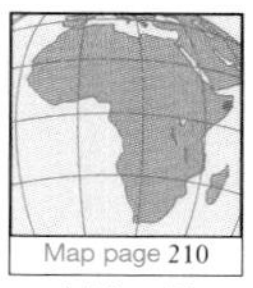
Map page 210

SOUTH AFRICA, REPUBLIC OF

Area Sq Km	1 219 090	Currency	Rand
Area Sq Miles	470 693	Languages	Afrikaans, English, nine official local languages
Population	39 357 000	Religions	Protestant, Roman Catholic, Sunni Muslim, Hindu
Capital	Pretoria/ Cape Town	Organizations	Comm., SADC, UN

South Africa occupies most of the southern part of Africa. It borders five states, surrounds Lesotho and has a long coastline stretching from the Atlantic to the Indian Ocean. Much of the land is a vast plateau, covered with grassland or bush and drained by the Orange and Limpopo river systems. A fertile coastal plain rises to mountain ridges in the south and east, including Table Mountain near Cape Town and the Drakensberg range in the east. Gauteng is the most populous province, with Johannesburg and Pretoria its main cities. South Africa has warm summers and mild winters. Most of the country has rainfall in summer, but the coast around Cape Town has winter rains. South Africa is the largest and most developed economy in Africa, though wealth and economic control is unevenly distributed and unemployment is very high. Agriculture employs about a third of the workforce, crops include fruit, wine, wool and maize. South Africa is rich in minerals. It is the world's leading producer of gold and chromium and an important producer of diamonds; many other minerals are also mined. The main industries process minerals and agricultural produce, manufacture chemical products, electrical equipment and textiles, and assemble motor vehicles. Financial services are also important.

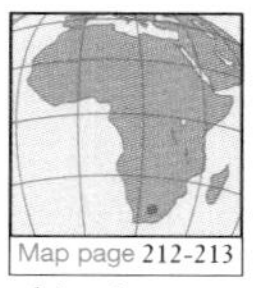
Map page 212-213

SOUTH KOREA
Republic of Korea

Area Sq Km	99 274	Currency	Won
Area Sq Miles	38 330	Languages	Korean
Population	46 109 000	Religions	Buddhist, Protestant, Roman Catholic
Capital	Sŏul	Organizations	APEC, UN

The state consists of the southern half of the Korean Peninsula in east Asia and many islands lying off the western and southern coasts in the Yellow Sea. The terrain is mountainous, though less rugged than that of North Korea. Population density is high and highly urbanized; most people live on the western coastal plains and in the basins of the Han-gang in the northwest and the Naktong-gang in the southeast. South Korea has a continental climate, with hot, wet summers and dry, cold winters. Arable land is limited by the mountainous terrain, but because of intensive farming South Korea is nearly self-sufficient in food. Sericulture is important as is fishing, which contributes to exports. South Korea has few mineral resources, except for coal and tungsten. It has achieved high economic growth based mainly on export manufacturing. The main manufactures are cars, electronic and electrical goods, ships, steel, chemicals, and toys as well as textiles, clothing, footwear and food products. USA and Japan are the main trading partners.

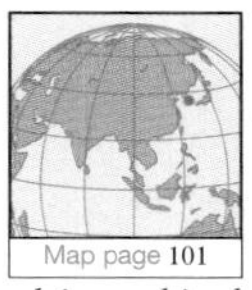
Map page 101

SPAIN
Kingdom of Spain

Area Sq Km	504 782	Currency	Peseta, Euro
Area Sq Miles	194 897	Languages	Castilian, Catalan, Galician, Basque
Population	39 628 000	Religions	Roman Catholic
Capital	Madrid	Organizations	EU, OECD, UN

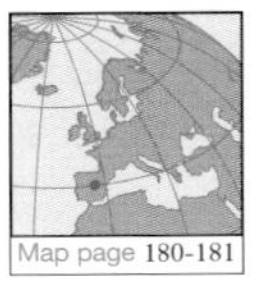
Map page 180-181

Spain occupies the greater part of the Iberian peninsula in southwest Europe, with coastlines on the Atlantic Ocean and Mediterranean Sea. It includes the Balearic and Canary Islands in the Mediterranean and Atlantic, and two enclaves in north Africa, Ceuta and Melilla. Much of the mainland is a high plateau drained by the Duero, Tagus and Guadiana rivers. The plateau is interrupted by a low mountain range and bounded to the east and north also by mountains, including the Pyrenees which form the border with France and Andorra. The main lowland areas are the Ebro basin in the northeast, the eastern coastal plains and the Guadalquivir basin in the southwest. Over three quarters of the population live in urban areas. The plateau experiences hot summers and cold winters. Conditions are cooler and wetter to the north, though warmer and drier to the south. Agriculture involves about ten per cent of the workforce and fruit, vegetables and wine are exported. Fishing is an important industry and Spain has a large fishing fleet. Mineral resources include lead, copper, mercury and fluorspar. Some oil is produced, but Spain has to import most energy needs. The economy is based on manufacturing and services. The principal products are machinery, transport equipment, and motor vehicles; other manufactures are agricultural products, chemicals, steel and other metals, paper products, wood and cork products, clothing and footwear, and textiles. With around fifty million visitors a year, tourism is a major industry, banking and commerce are also important. Around seventy per cent of trade is with other EU countries.

SRI LANKA
Democratic Socialist Republic of Sri Lanka

Area Sq Km	65 610	Currency	Rupee
Area Sq Miles	25 332	Languages	Sinhalese, Tamil, English
Population	18 455 000	Religions	Buddhist, Hindu, Sunni Muslim, Roman Catholic
Capital	Sri Jayewardenepura Kotte	Organizations	Comm., UN

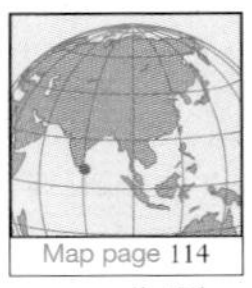
Map page 114

Sri Lanka lies in the Indian Ocean off the southeast coast of India in south Asia. It has rolling coastal plains with mountains in the centre-south. The climate is hot and monsoonal and most people live on the west coast. Manufactures (chiefly textiles and clothing), tea, rubber, copra and gems are exported. The economy relies on aid and workers' remittances. Tourism has been damaged by separatist activities.

SUDAN
Republic of the Sudan

Area Sq Km	2 505 813	Currency	Dinar
Area Sq Miles	967 500	Languages	Arabic, Dinka, Nubian, Beja, Nuer, local languages
Population	28 292 000	Religions	Sunni Muslim, traditional beliefs, Christian
Capital	Khartoum	Organizations	UN

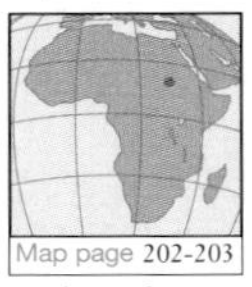
Map page 202-203

Africa's largest country, Sudan is in the northeast, on the Red Sea. It lies within the upper Nile basin, much of which is arid plain but with swamps to the south. Mountains lie to the northeast, west and south. The climate is hot and arid with light summer rainfall, though droughts occur. Most people live along the Nile and are farmers and herders. Cotton, gum arabic, livestock and other agricultural products are exported. The government is working with foreign investors to develop oil resources; but civil war in the south of Sudan continues to restrict growth of the economy.

SURINAME
Republic of Suriname

Area Sq Km	163 820	Currency	Guilder
Area Sq Miles	63 251	Languages	Dutch, Surinamese, English, Hindi
Population	414 000	Religions	Hindu, Roman Catholic, Protestant, Sunni Muslim
Capital	Paramaribo	Organizations	CARICOM, UN

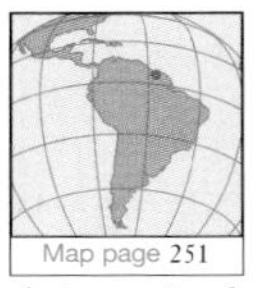
Map page 251

Suriname, on the Atlantic coast of northern South America, consists of a swampy coastal plain (where most people live), central plateaus and highlands in the south. The climate is tropical and rainforest covers much of the land. Bauxite mining is the main industry, and alumina and aluminium are the chief exports, with shrimps, rice, bananas and timber also exported. The main trading partners are The Netherlands, Norway and USA.

SWAZILAND
Kingdom of Swaziland

Area Sq Km	17 364	Currency	Lilangeni
Area Sq Miles	6 704	Languages	Swazi, English
Population	952 000	Religions	Christian, traditional beliefs
Capital	Mbabane	Organizations	Comm., SADC, UN

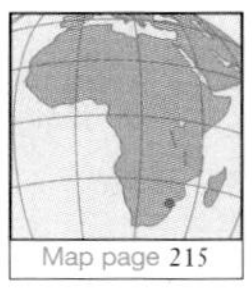
Map page 215

Landlocked Swaziland in southern Africa lies between Mozambique and South Africa. Savanna plateaus descend from mountains in the west towards hill country in the east. The climate is subtropical, but temperate in the mountains. Subsistence farming predominates. Asbestos and some diamonds are mined. Exports include sugar, fruit and wood pulp. Tourism and workers' remittances are important to the economy. Most trade is with South Africa.

SWEDEN
Kingdom of Sweden

Area Sq Km	449 964	Currency	Krona
Area Sq Miles	173 732	Languages	Swedish
Population	8 875 000	Religions	Protestant, Roman Catholic
Capital	Stockholm	Organizations	EU, OECD, UN

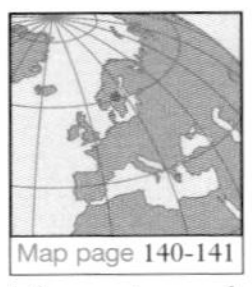
Map page 140-141

Sweden, the largest and most populous of the Scandinavian countries, occupies the eastern part of the peninsula in north Europe and borders the North and Baltic Seas and Gulf of Bothnia. Forested mountains cover the northern half of the country, part of which lies within the Arctic Circle. Southwards is a lowland lake region, where most of the population lives. Farther south is an upland region, and then a fertile plain at the tip of the peninsula. Sweden has warm summers and cold winters, though the latter are longer and more severe in the north. Natural resources include coniferous forests, mineral deposits and water resources. There is little agriculture, though some dairy products, meat, cereals and vegetables are produced in the south. The forests supply timber for export and for the important pulp, paper and furniture industries. Sweden is an important producer of iron ore and copper; zinc, lead, silver and gold are also mined. Machinery and transport equipment, chemicals, electrical goods and telecommunications equipment are the main industries. The majority of trade is with other EU countries.

SWITZERLAND
Swiss Confederation

Area Sq Km	41 293	Currency	Franc
Area Sq Miles	15 943	Languages	German, French, Italian, Romansch
Population	7 299 000	Religions	Roman Catholic, Protestant
Capital	Bern	Organizations	OECD

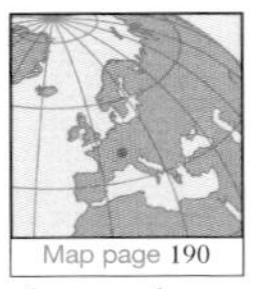
Map page 190

Switzerland is a landlocked country of west central Europe that is surrounded by France, Germany, Austria, Liechtenstein and Italy. It is also Europe's most mountainous country. The southern half lies within the Alps, while the northwest is dominated by the Jura mountains. The rest of the land is a high plateau where most people live. The climate varies greatly, depending on altitude and relief, but in general summers are mild and winters are cold with heavy snowfalls. Switzerland has one of the highest standards of living in the world. Yet it has few mineral resources and most food and industrial raw materials have to be imported. Manufacturing makes the largest contribution to the economy and though varied is specialist in certain products. Engineering is the most important industry, producing precision instruments and heavy machinery, other important industries are chemicals and pharmaceuticals. Banking and financial services are very important and Zurich is one of the world's leading banking cities. Tourism, and international organizations based in Switzerland are also major foreign currency earners. Germany is the main trading partner.

SYRIA
Syrian Arab Republic

Area Sq Km	185 180	Currency	Pound
Area Sq Miles	71 498	Languages	Arabic, Kurdish, Armenian
Population	15 333 000	Religions	Sunni Muslim, Shi'a Muslim, Christian
Capital	Damascus	Organizations	UN

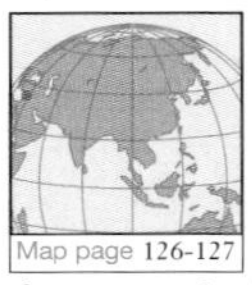
Map page 126-127

Syria is in southwest Asia, on the Mediterranean Sea. Behind the coastal plain lies a range of hills and then a plateau cut by the Euphrates river. Mountains flank the southwest borders with Lebanon and Israel, east of which is desert. The climate is Mediterranean in coastal regions, hotter and drier inland. Most Syrians live on the coast or in the river valleys. Cotton, cereals and fruit are important, but the main exports are petroleum and its products, and textiles.

TAIWAN

Area Sq Km	36 179	Currency	Dollar
Area Sq Miles	13 969	Languages	Mandarin, Min, Hakka, local languages
Population	21 908 135	Religions	Buddhist, Taoist, Confucian, Christian
Capital	T'aipei	Organizations	APEC

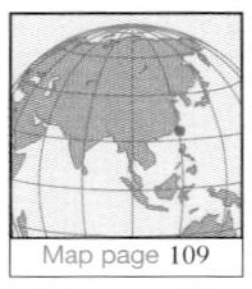
Map page 109

The east Asian state consists of the island of Taiwan, separated from mainland China by the Taiwan Strait, and several much smaller islands. Much of Taiwan is mountainous and forested. Densely populated coastal plains in the west contain the bulk of the population and most economic activity. Taiwan has a tropical monsoon climate, with warm, wet summers and mild winters. Agriculture is highly productive. Taiwan is virtually self-sufficient in food and exports some products. Coal, oil and natural gas are produced and a few minerals are mined but none of them are of great significance to the economy. Taiwan depends heavily on imports of raw materials and exports of manufactured goods. The main manufactures are electrical and electronic goods, including television sets, personal computers and calculators, textiles, fertilizers, clothing, footwear and toys. The main trading partners are USA, Japan and Germany.

TAJIKISTAN
Republic of Tajikistan

Area Sq Km	143 100	Currency	Rouble
Area Sq Miles	55 251	Languages	Tajik, Uzbek, Russian
Population	6 015 000	Religions	Sunni Muslim
Capital	Dushanbe	Organizations	CIS, UN

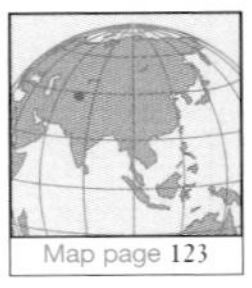
Map page 123

Landlocked Tajikistan in central Asia is a mountainous country, occupying the Alai Range and the Pamir. In less mountainous western areas summers are warm though winters are cold. Agriculture is the main sector of the economy, chiefly cotton growing and cattle breeding. Mineral deposits include lead, zinc, and uranium. Metal processing, textiles and clothing are the main manufactures; the main exports are aluminium and cotton. Russia, Kazakhstan and Uzbekistan are the main trading partners.

TANZANIA
United Republic of Tanzania

Area Sq Km	945 087	Currency	Shilling
Area Sq Miles	364 900	Languages	Swahili, English, Nyamwezi, local languages
Population	32 102 000	Religions	Muslim, traditional beliefs, Christian
Capital	Dodoma	Organizations	Comm., SADC, UN

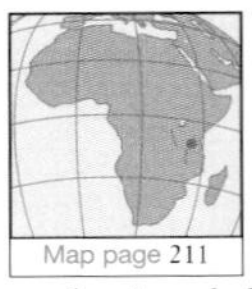
Map page 211

Tanzania lies on the coast of east Africa and includes the island of Zanzibar in the Indian Ocean. Most of the mainland is a savanna plateau lying east of the Great Rift Valley. In the north are Kilimanjaro, the highest mountain in Africa, and the Serangeti National Park. The climate is tropical. The economy is predominantly based on agriculture which employs an estimated ninety per cent of the workforce. Coffee, cotton, cashew nuts and tobacco are the main exports, with cloves from Zanzibar. Agricultural processing and gold and diamond mining are the main industries, though tourism is growing. Tanzania is one of the least developed countries in the world and depends heavily on aid.

THAILAND
Kingdom of Thailand

Area Sq Km	513 115	Currency	Baht
Area Sq Miles	198 115	Languages	Thai, Lao, Chinese, Malay, Mon-Khmer languages
Population	60 300 000	Religions	Buddhist, Sunni Muslim
Capital	Bangkok	Organizations	APEC, ASEAN, UN

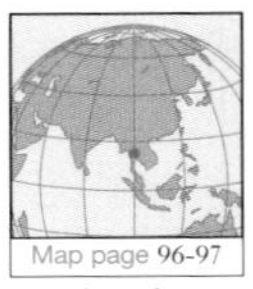
Map page 96-97

A country in southeast Asia, Thailand borders Myanmar, Laos, Cambodia and Malaysia and has coastlines on the Gulf of Thailand and Andaman Sea. Central Thailand is dominated by the Chao Phraya river basin, which contains Bangkok, the only major urban centre, and most economic activity. To the east is a dry plateau drained by tributaries of the Mekong river, while to the north, west and south, extending halfway down the Malay peninsula, are forested hills and mountains. Many small islands line the coast. The climate is hot, humid and monsoonal. About half the workforce is involved in agriculture. Thailand is one of the world's leading exporters of rice and rubber, and a major exporter of maize and tapioca. Fish and fish processing are important. Thailand produces natural gas, some oil and lignite, minerals (chiefly tin, tungsten and baryte) and gemstones. Manufacturing is the largest contributor to national income, with electronics, textiles, clothing and footwear, and food processing the main industries. With around seven million visitors a year, tourism is the major source of foreign exchange. Japan and USA are the main trading partners.

TOGO
Republic of Togo

Area Sq Km	56 785	Currency	CFA franc
Area Sq Miles	21 925	Languages	French, Ewe, Kabre, local languages
Population	4 397 000	Religions	Traditional beliefs, Christian, Sunni Muslim
Capital	Lomé	Organizations	UN

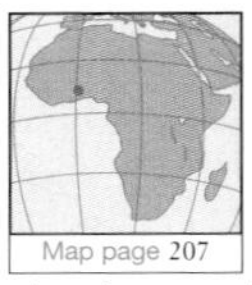
Map page 207

Togo is a long narrow country in west Africa with a short coastline on the Gulf of Guinea. The interior consists of plateaus rising to mountainous areas. The climate is tropical, drier inland. Agriculture is the mainstay of the economy. Phosphate mining and food processing are the main industries. Cotton, phosphates, coffee and cocoa are the main exports. Lomé is an entrepôt trade centre.

Tokelau New Zealand Overseas Territory

Area Sq Km (Miles)	10 (4)	Population	1 000

Tokelau consists of three atolls, Atafu, Nukunonu and Fakaofa, in the Pacific Ocean north of Samoa. Subsistence agriculture is the main activity, and the islands rely on aid and remittances from New Zealand.

Map page 81

TONGA
Kingdom of Tonga

Area Sq Km	748	Currency	Pa'anga
Area Sq Miles	289	Languages	Tongan, English
Population	98 000	Religions	Protestant, Roman Catholic
Capital	Nuku'alofa	Organizations	Comm., UN

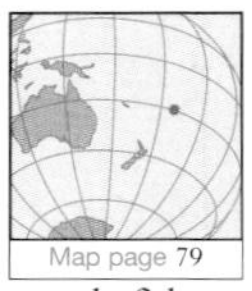
Map page 79

Tonga comprises some one hundred and seventy islands in the south Pacific Ocean, northeast of New Zealand. The three main groups are Tongatapu (where sixty per cent of Tongans live), Ha'apai and Vava'u. The climate is warm with good rainfall and the economy relies heavily on agriculture. Exports include squash, fish, vanilla beans and root crops. Tourism and light industry are increasingly important.

TRINIDAD AND TOBAGO
Republic of Trinidad and Tobago

Area Sq Km	5 130	Currency	Dollar
Area Sq Miles	1 981	Languages	English, creole, Hindi
Population	1 283 000	Religions	Roman Catholic, Hindu, Protestant, Sunni Muslim
Capital	Port of Spain	Organizations	CARICOM, Comm., UN

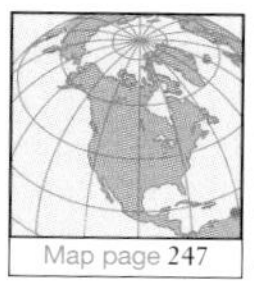

Map page 247

Trinidad, the most southerly Caribbean island, lies off the Venezuelan coast. It is hilly in the north, with a central plain. Tobago, to the northeast, is smaller, more mountainous and less developed. The climate is tropical. Oil and petrochemicals industries dominate the economy. The main crops are cocoa, sugar cane, coffee and fruit and vegetables. Tourism is also important.USA is the main trading partner.

Tristan da Cunha Dependency of St Helena

Area Sq Km (Miles) 98 (38) Population 300 Capital Settlement of Edinburgh

A group of volcanic islands in the south Atlantic Ocean, the other main islands in the group are Nightingale Island and Inaccessible Island; the group is over 2000 kilometres (1250 miles) south of St Helena. The economy is based on fishing, fish processing and agriculture, and ecotourism is increasing.

Map page 216

TUNISIA
Republic of Tunisia

Area Sq Km	164 150	Currency	Dinar
Area Sq Miles	63 379	Languages	Arabic, French
Population	9 335 000	Religions	Sunni Muslim
Capital	Tunis	Organizations	UN

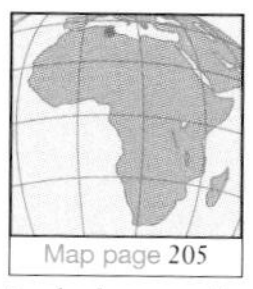

Map page 205

Tunisia is on the Mediterranean coast of north Africa. The north is mountainous with valleys and coastal plains, where most people live. The north has a Mediterranean climate, the south is hot and arid. Oil and phosphates are the main resources. The main crops are olives and citrus fruit. Exports include petroleum products, textiles, fruit and phosphorus; tourism is important with around five million visitors a year. Most trade is with EU countries; Tunisia has an agreement with the EU to create a free trade zone.

TURKEY
Republic of Turkey

Area Sq Km	779 452	Currency	Lira
Area Sq Miles	300 948	Languages	Turkish, Kurdish
Population	64 479 000	Religions	Sunni Muslim, Shi'a Muslim
Capital	Ankara	Organizations	OECD, UN

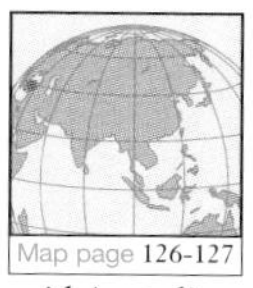

Map page 126-127

Turkey occupies the Asia Minor peninsula of southwest Asia and has coastlines on the Black, Mediterranean and Aegean Seas. It includes eastern Thrace, which is in south Europe and separated from the rest of the country by the Bosporus, Sea of Marmara and Dardanelles. The Asian mainland consists of the semi-arid Anatolian plateau, flanked to the north, south and east by mountains. Over forty per cent of Turks live in central Anatolia and the Marmara and Aegean coastal plains. The coast has a Mediterranean climate, but inland conditions are more extreme with hot, dry summers and cold, snowy winters. Agriculture involves about forty per cent of the workforce and products include cotton, grain, tobacco, fruit, nuts and livestock. Turkey is a leading producer of chrome, iron ore, lead, tin, borates, and baryte; coal is also mined. The main manufactures are textiles (the chief export), food processing, steel, vehicles and chemicals; tourism is a major industry with nine million visitors a year. Germany and USA are the main trading partners. Remittances by workers aboard are important.

TURKMENISTAN
Republic of Turkmenistan

Area Sq Km	488 100	Currency	Manat
Area Sq Miles	188 456	Languages	Turkmen, Uzbek, Russian
Population	4 309 000	Religions	Sunni Muslim, Russian Orthodox
Capital	Ashgabat	Organizations	CIS, UN

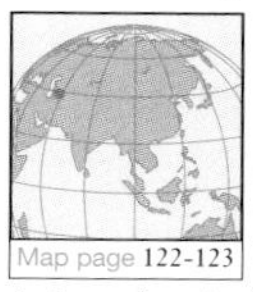

Map page 122-123

Turkmenistan, in central Asia, lies mainly within the plains of the Karakum Desert; most people live on the desert fringes: the foothills of the Kopet Dag in the south, Amudar'ya valley in the north and Caspian Sea plains in the west. The climate is dry with extreme temperatures. The economy is based mainly on irrigated agriculture, chiefly cotton growing, and the production of natural gas; there are also reserves of oil. Development of the natural gas and oil resources depend on building further pipelines. Russia is the main trading partner.

Turks and Caicos Islands
United Kingdom Overseas Territory

Area Sq Km (Miles) 430 (166) Population 16 000 Capital Grand Turk

The state consists of forty or so low-lying islands and cays in the northern Caribbean. Only eight islands are inhabited; two fifths of the people live on Grand Turk and Salt Cay. The climate is tropical. The economy is based on tourism, fishing and offshore banking.

Map page 246

TUVALU

Area Sq Km	25	Currency	Dollar
Area Sq Miles	10	Languages	Tuvaluan, English
Population	11 000	Religions	Protestant
Capital	Vaiaku	Organizations	Comm.

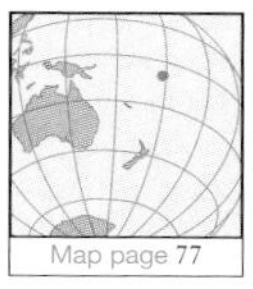

Map page 77

Tuvalu comprises nine low lying coral atolls in the south Pacific Ocean. One third of the population lives on Funafuti and most people depend on subsistence farming and fishing. The islands export copra, stamps and clothing, but rely heavily on foreign aid. Tuvalu is a special member of the Commonwealth.

UGANDA
Republic of Uganda

Area Sq Km	241 038	Currency	Shilling
Area Sq Miles	93 065	Languages	English, Swahili, Luganda, local languages
Population	20 554 000	Religions	Roman Catholic, Protestant, Muslim, trad. beliefs
Capital	Kampala	Organizations	Comm., UN

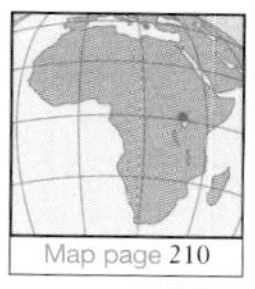

Map page 210

A landlocked country in east Africa, Uganda consists of a savanna plateau with mountains and lakes. The climate is warm and wet. Most people live in the southern half of the country; life expectancy in Uganda has fallen by fifteen per cent since 1975 because of AIDS. Agriculture employs around eighty per cent of the workforce and dominates the economy. Coffee, cotton and tea are the main exports. Uganda relies heavily on aid.

UKRAINE

Area Sq Km	603 700	Currency	Hryvnia
Area Sq Miles	233 090	Languages	Ukrainian, Russian
Population	50 861 000	Religions	Orthodox, Ukrainian Catholic, Roman Catholic
Capital	Kyiv	Organizations	CIS, UN

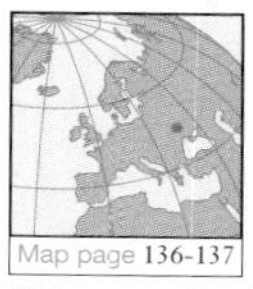

Map page 136-137

Ukraine lies on the Black Sea coast of east Europe. Much of the land is steppe, generally flat and treeless, but with rich black soil and drained by the river Dnieper. Along the border with Belarus are forested, marshy plains. The only uplands are the Carpathian Mountains in the west and smaller ranges on the Crimea peninsula. Summers are warm and winters are cold, with milder conditions in the Crimea. About a quarter of the population lives in the mainly industrial areas around Donets'k, Kyiv and Dnipropetrovs'k. The Ukraine is rich in natural resources: fertile soil, substantial mineral and natural gas deposits, and forests. Agriculture and livestock raising are important, but mining and manufacturing are the most important sectors of the economy. Coal, iron and manganese mining, steel and metal production, machinery, chemicals and food processing are the main industries. Russia is the main trading partner.

UNITED ARAB EMIRATES
Federation of Emirates

Area Sq Km	83 600	Currency	Dirham
Area Sq Miles	32 278	Languages	Arabic,English
Population	2 377 453	Religions	Sunni Muslim, Shi'a Muslim
Capital	Abu Dhabi	Organizations	OPEC, UN

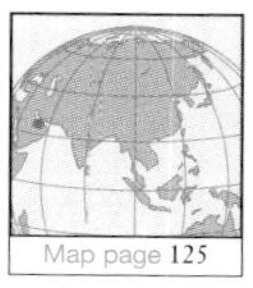

Map page 125

The UAE lies on the northeast of the Arabian Peninsula, in southwest Asia. Six emirates lie on The Gulf while the seventh, Fujairah, lies on the Gulf of Oman. Most of the land is flat desert with sand dunes and salt pans. The only hilly area is in the northeast. Over eighty per cent of the population live in three emirates - Abu Dhabi, Dubai and Sharjah. Summers are hot and winters are mild with occasional rainfall in coastal areas. Fruit and vegetables are grown in oases and irrigated areas, but the Emirates wealth is based on hydrocarbons, mainly within Abu Dhabi, but with smaller supplies in Dubai, Sharjah and Ras al Khaimah. The UAE is the third largest oil producer in the Middle East after Saudi Arabia and Iran. Dubai is an important entrepôt trade centre; tourism is increasing in importance.

Abu Dhabi (Emirate)
Area Sq Km (Miles) 73 060 (28 209) Population 928 360 Capital Abu Dhabi

Ajman (Emirate)
Area Sq Km (Miles) 260 (100) Population 118 812 Capital Ajman

Dubai (Emirate)
Area Sq Km (Miles) 3 900 (1 506) Population 674 101 Capital Dubai

Fujairah (Emirate)
Area Sq Km (Miles) 1 300 (502) Population 76 254 Capital Fujairah

Ras al Khaimah (Emirate)
Area Sq Km (Miles) 1 700 (656) Population 144 430 Capital Ras al Khaimah

Sharjah (Emirate)
Area Sq Km (Miles) 2 600 (1 004) Population 400 339 Capital Sharjah

Umm al Qaiwain (Emirate)
Area Sq Km (Miles) 780 (301) Population 35 157 Capital Umm al Qaiwain

UNITED KINGDOM
United Kingdom of Great Britain and Northern Ireland

Area Sq Km	244 082	Currency	Pound
Area Sq Miles	94 241	Languages	English, Welsh, Gaelic
Population	58 649 000	Religions	Protestant, Roman Catholic, Muslim
Capital	London	Organizations	Comm., EU, OECD, UN

A country in northwest Europe, the United Kingdom occupies the island of Great Britain, part of Ireland and many small adjacent islands. Great Britain comprises the countries of England, Scotland and Wales. England covers over half the land area and supports over four-fifths of the population, chiefly in the southeast region. The landscape is flat or rolling with some uplands, notably the Cheviot Hills on the Scottish border, the Pennines in the centre-north and the hills of the Lake District in the northwest. Scotland consists of southern uplands, central lowlands, highlands (which include the UK's highest peak) and islands. Wales is a land of mountains and river valleys. Northern Ireland contains uplands, plains and the UK's largest lake, Lough Neagh. The climate is mild, wet and variable. The UK has few mineral deposits, but has important energy resources. Over forty per cent of land is suitable for grazing, about twenty five per cent is cultivated, and ten per cent is forested. Agriculture involves mainly sheep and cattle raising and dairy farming, with crop and fruit growing in the east and southeast. Productivity is high, but about one third of food needs must be imported. The UK produces petroleum and natural gas from reserves in the North Sea and is self-sufficient in energy in net terms. It also has

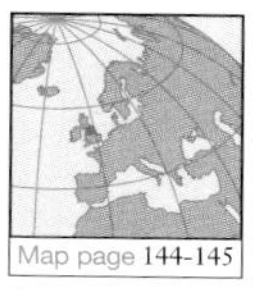

Map page 144-145

reserves of coal, though the coal industry has contracted. Major manufactures are food and drinks, motor vehicles and parts, aerospace equipment, machinery, electronic and electrical equipment, and chemicals and chemical products. However, the economy is dominated by service industries, including banking, insurance, finance and business services. London is one of the world's major financial centres. Tourism is a major industry, with around twenty five million visitors a year. International trade is also important, equivalent to a third of national income; over half of trade is with other EU countries.

England (Constituent country)
Area Sq Km (Miles) 130 423 (50 357) Population 49 284 200 Capital London

Northern Ireland (Province)
Area Sq Km (Miles) 14 121 (5 452) Population 1 675 000 Capital Belfast

Scotland (Constituent country)
Area Sq Km (Miles) 78 772 (30 414) Population 5 122 500 Capital Edinburgh

Wales (Principality)
Area Sq Km (Miles) 20 766 (8 018) Population 2 926 900 Capital Cardiff

UNITED STATES OF AMERICA
Federal Republic

Area Sq Km	9 809 378	Currency	Dollar
Area Sq Miles	3 787 422	Languages	English, Spanish
Population	274 028 000	Religions	Protestant, Roman Catholic, Sunni Muslim, Jewish
Capital	Washington	Organizations	APEC, OECD, UN

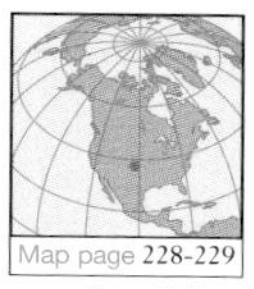

Map page 228-229

The USA comprises forty eight contiguous states in North America, bounded by Canada and Mexico, and the states of Alaska, to the northwest of Canada, and Hawaii, in the Pacific Ocean. The populous eastern states consist of the Atlantic coastal plain (which includes the Florida peninsula and the Gulf of Mexico coast) and the Appalachian Mountains. The central states form a vast interior plain drained by the Mississippi-Missouri river system. To the west lie the Rocky Mountains, separated from the Pacific coastal ranges by the intermontane plateaus. The coastal ranges are prone to earthquakes. Hawaii is a group of some twenty volcanic islands. Climatic conditions range between arctic in Alaska to desert in the intermontane plateaus. Most of the USA is temperate, though the interior has continental conditions. The USA has abundant natural resources. It has major reserves minerals and energy resources. About twenty per cent of the land can be used for crops, over twenty five per cent is suitable for livestock rearing and over thirty per cent is forested. The USA has the largest and most technologically advanced economy in the world, based on manufacturing and services. Though agriculture accounts for only about two per cent national income, productivity is high and the USA is a net exporter of food, chiefly grains and fruit. Cotton is the major industrial crop; livestock rearing, forestry and fishing are also important. The USA produces iron ore, copper, lead, zinc, and many other minerals. It is a major producer of coal, petroleum and natural gas, though being the world's biggest energy user it imports significant quantities of petroleum and its products. Manufacturing is well diversified. The main industries are: petroleum, steel, motor vehicles, aerospace, telecommunications, electrics, food processing, chemicals and consumer goods. Tourism is a major foreign currency earner with around forty-five million visitors a year. Other important service industries are banking and finance, and Wall Street in New York is a major stock exchange.

Alabama (State)
Area Sq Km (Miles) 135 775 (52 423) Population 4 351 999 Capital Montgomery

Alaska (State)
Area Sq Km (Miles) 1 700 130 (656 424) Population 614 010 Capital Juneau

Arizona (State)
Area Sq Km (Miles) 295 274 (114 006) Population 4 668 631 Capital Phoenix

Arkansas (State)
Area Sq Km (Miles) 137 741 (53 182) Population 2 538 303 Capital Little Rock

California (State)
Area Sq Km (Miles) 423 999 (163 707) Population 32 666 550 Capital Sacramento

Colorado (State)
Area Sq Km (Miles) 269 618 (104 100) Population 3 970 971 Capital Denver

Connecticut (State)
Area Sq Km (Miles) 14 359 (5 544) Population 3 274 069 Capital Hartford

Delaware (State)
Area Sq Km (Miles) 6 446 (2 489) Population 743 603 Capital Dover

District of Columbia (District)
Area Sq Km (Miles) 176 (68) Population 523 124 Capital Washington

Florida (State)
Area Sq Km (Miles) 170 312 (65 758) Population 14 915 980 Capital Tallahassee

Georgia (State)
Area Sq Km (Miles) 153 951 (59 441) Population 7 642 207 Capital Atlanta

Hawaii (State)
Area Sq Km (Miles) 28 314 (10 932) Population 1 193 001 Capital Honolulu

Idaho (State)
Area Sq Km (Miles) 216 456 (83 574) Population 1 228 684 Capital Boise

Illinois (State)
Area Sq Km (Miles) 150 007 (57 918) Population 13 045 326 Capital Springfield

Indiana (State)
Area Sq Km (Miles) 94 327 (36 420) Population 5 899 195 Capital Indianapolis

Iowa (State)
Area Sq Km (Miles) 145 754 (56 276) Population 2 862 447 Capital Des Moines

Kansas (State)
Area Sq Km (Miles) 213 109 (82 282) Population 2 629 067 Capital Topeka

Kentucky (State)
Area Sq Km (Miles) 104 664 (40 411) Population 3 936 499 Capital Frankfort

Louisiana (State)
Area Sq Km (Miles) 134 273(51 843) Population 4 368 967 Capital Baton Rouge

Maine (State)
Area Sq Km (Miles) 91 652(35 387) Population 1 244 250 Capital Augusta

Maryland (State)
Area Sq Km (Miles) 32 134(12 407) Population 5 134 808 Capital Annapolis

Massachusetts (State)
Area Sq Km (Miles) 27 337 (10 555) Population 6 147 132 Capital Boston

Michigan (State)
Area Sq Km (Miles) 250 737 (96 810) Population 9 817 242 Capital Lansing

Minnesota (State)
Area Sq Km (Miles) 225 181 (86 943) Population 4 725 419 Capital St Paul

Mississippi (State)
Area Sq Km (Miles) 125 443 (48 434) Population 2 752 092 Capital Jackson

Missouri (State)
Area Sq Km (Miles) 180 545 (69 709) Population 5 438 559 Capital Jefferson City

Montana (State)
Area Sq Km (Miles) 380 847 (147 046) Population 880 453 Capital Helena

Nebraska (State)
Area Sq Km (Miles) 200 356 (77 358) Population 1 662 719 Capital Lincoln

Nevada (State)
Area Sq Km (Miles) 286 367 (110 567) Population 1 746 898 Capital Carson City

New Hampshire (State)
Area Sq Km (Miles) 24 219 (9 351) Population 1 185 048 Capital Concord

New Jersey (State)
Area Sq Km (Miles) 22 590 (8 722) Population 8 115 011 Capital Trenton

New Mexico (State)
Area Sq Km (Miles) 314 937(121 598) Population 1 736 931 Capital Santa Fe

New York (State)
Area Sq Km (Miles) 141 090 (54 475) Population 18 175 301 Capital Albany

North Carolina (State)
Area Sq Km (Miles) 139 396 (53 821) Population 7 546 493 Capital Raleigh

North Dakota (State)
Area Sq Km (Miles) 183 123 (70 704) Population 638 244 Capital Bismarck

Ohio (State)
Area Sq Km (Miles) 116 104 (44 828) Population 11 209 493 Capital Columbus

Oklahoma (State)
Area Sq Km (Miles) 181 048 (69 903) Population 3 346 713 Capital Oklahoma City

Oregon (State)
Area Sq Km (Miles) 254 819 (98 386) Population 3 281 974 Capital Salem

Pennsylvania (State)
Area Sq Km (Miles) 119 290 (46 058) Population 12 001 451 Capital Harrisburg

Rhode Island (State)
Area Sq Km (Miles) 4 002 (1 545) Population 988 480 Capital Providence

South Carolina (State)
Area Sq Km (Miles) 82 898 (32 007) Population 3 835 962 Capital Columbia

South Dakota (State)
Area Sq Km (Miles) 199 742 (77 121) Population 738 171 Capital Pierre

Tennessee (State)
Area Sq Km (Miles) 109 158 (42 146) Population 5 430 621 Capital Nashville

Texas (State)
Area Sq Km (Miles) 695 673 (268 601) Population 19 759 614 Capital Austin

Utah (State)
Area Sq Km (Miles) 219 900 (84 904) Population 2 099 758 Capital Salt Lake City

Vermont (State)
Area Sq Km (Miles) 24 903 (9 615) Population 590 883 Capital Montpelier

Virginia (State)
Area Sq Km (Miles) 110 771 (42 769) Population 6 791 345 Capital Richmond

Washington (State)
Area Sq Km (Miles) 184 674 (71 303) Population 5 689 263 Capital Olympia

West Virginia (State)
Area Sq Km (Miles) 62 758 (24 231) Population 1 811 156 Capital Charleston

Wisconsin (State)
Area Sq Km (Miles) 169 652 (65 503) Population 5 223 500 Capital Madison

Wyoming (State)
Area Sq Km (Miles) 253 347 (97 818) Population 480 907 Capital Cheyenne

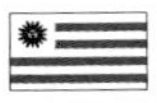

URUGUAY
Oriental Republic of Uruguay

Area Sq Km	176 215	Currency	Peso
Area Sq Miles	68 037	Languages	Spanish
Population	3 289 000	Religions	Roman Catholic, Protestant, Jewish
Capital	Montevideo	Organizations	UN

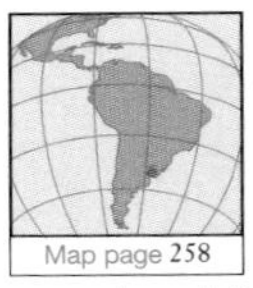

Map page 258

Uruguay, on the Atlantic coast of central South America, is a low-lying land of prairies. The coast and the River Plate estuary in the south are fringed with lagoons and sand dunes. Almost half the population lives in Montevideo. Uruguay has warm summers and mild winters. The economy is based on cattle and sheep ranching, and the main industries produce food products, textiles, and petroleum products. Meat, wool, hides, textiles and agricultural products are the main exports. Brazil and Argentina are the main trading partners.

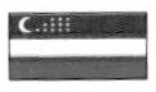

UZBEKISTAN
Republic of Uzbekistan

Area Sq Km	447 400	Currency	Sum
Area Sq Miles	172 742	Languages	Uzbek, Russian, Tajik, Kazakh
Population	23 574 000	Religions	Sunni Muslim, Russian Orthodox
Capital	Tashkent	Organizations	CIS, UN

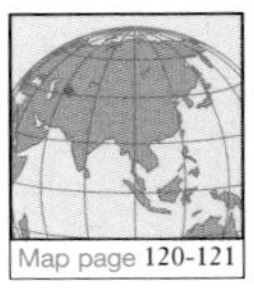

Map page 120-121

A landlocked country of central Asia, Uzbekistan borders the Aral Sea and five countries. It consists mainly of the flat Kyzylkum Desert, which rises eastwards towards the mountains. Most settlement is in the basin around Fergana. The climate is dry and arid. The economy is based mainly on irrigated agriculture, chiefly cotton production. Uzbekistan is rich in minerals including gold, copper, lead, zinc and uranium and has the largest gold mine in the world. Industry specializes in fertilizers and machinery for cotton harvesting and textile manufacture. Russia is the main trading partner.

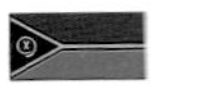

VANUATU
Republic of Vanuatu

Area Sq Km	12 190	Currency	Vatu
Area Sq Miles	4 707	Languages	English, Bislama (creole), French
Population	182 000	Religions	Protestant, Roman Catholic, traditional beliefs
Capital	Port Vila	Organizations	Comm., UN

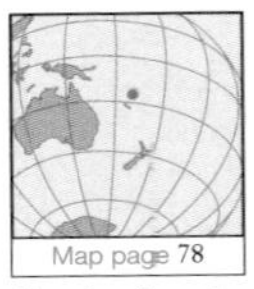

Map page 78

Vanuatu occupies an archipelago of some eighty islands in the southwest Pacific. Many of the islands are mountainous, of volcanic origin and densely forested. The climate is tropical with heavy rainfall. Half the population lives on the main islands of Éfaté and Espíritu Santo, and the majority of people live by farming. Copra, beef, timber, vegetables, and cocoa are the main exports; tourism is growing. Australia and Japan are the main trading partners.

VATICAN CITY
Vatican City State

Area Sq Km	0.5	Currency	Italian lira
Area Sq Miles	0.2	Languages	Italian
Population	480	Religions	Roman Catholic
Capital	Vatican City		

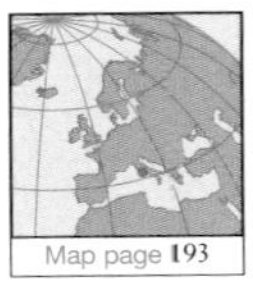

Map page 193

The world's smallest sovereign state, the Vatican City occupies a hill to the west of the river Tiber in the Italian capital, Rome. It is the headquarters of the Roman Catholic church and income comes from investments, voluntary contributions and tourism.

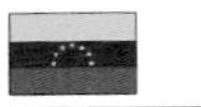

VENEZUELA
Republic of Venezuela

Area Sq Km	912 050	Currency	Bolívar
Area Sq Miles	352 144	Languages	Spanish, Amerindian languages
Population	23 242 000	Religions	Roman Catholic, Protestant
Capital	Caracas	Organizations	OPEC, UN

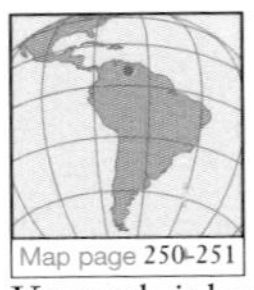

Map page 250-251

Venezuela is in northern South America, on the Caribbean Sea. Its coast is much indented, with the oil-rich area of Lago de Maracaibo at the western end and the swampy Orinoco Delta in the east. Mountain ranges run parallel to the coast then turn southwestwards to form the northern extension of the Andes. Central Venezuela is lowland grasslands drained by the Orinoco river system, while to the south are the Guiana Highlands which contain the Angel Falls, the world's highest waterfall. Over eighty per cent of the population live in towns, mostly in the coastal mountain areas. The climate is tropical, with summer rainfall. Temperatures are lower in the mountains. Farming is important, particularly cattle ranching and dairy farming; coffee, maize, rice and sugar cane are the main crops. Venezuela is a major oil producer, and sales account for about seventy five per cent of export earnings. Aluminium, iron ore, copper and gold are also mined and manufactures include petrochemicals, aluminium, steel, textiles and food products. USA is the dominant trading partner.

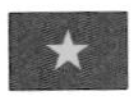

VIETNAM
Socialist Republic of Vietnam

Area Sq Km	329 565	Currency	Dong
Area Sq Miles	127 246	Languages	Vietnamese, Thai, Khmer, Chinese, local languages
Population	77 562 000	Religions	Buddhist, Taoist, Roman Catholic
Capital	Ha Nôi	Organizations	APEC, ASEAN, UN

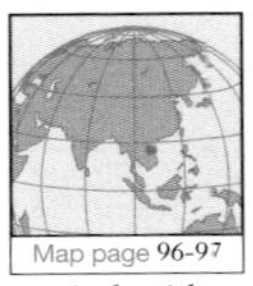

Map page 96-97

Vietnam is in southeast Asia, with the South China Sea to the east and south. The Red River delta lowlands in the north are separated from the huge Mekong delta in the south by long, narrow coastal plains backed by the mountainous and forested terrain of the Annam Plateau. Most people live in the river deltas. The climate is tropical, with summer monsoon rains. Over three quarters of the workforce is involved in agriculture, forestry and fishing. Rice is the main crop; coffee, tea and rubber are important cash crops. Vietnam is the world's third largest rice exporter, after the USA and Thailand. Oil, coal and copper are produced; the main industries are food processing, clothing and footwear, cement and fertilizers. Exports include oil, coffee, rice, clothing, fish and fish products. Japan and Singapore are the main trading partners.

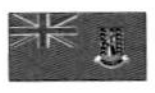

Virgin Islands (U.K.)
United Kingdom Overseas Territory

Area Sq Km	153	Currency	US dollar
Area Sq Miles	59	Languages	English
Population	20 000	Religions	Protestant, Roman Catholic
Capital	Road Town		

The Caribbean territory comprises four main islands and over thirty islets at the eastern end of the Virgin Islands group. Apart from the flat coral atoll of Anegada, the islands are volcanic in origin and hilly. The climate is subtropical and tourism is the main industry.

Map page 247

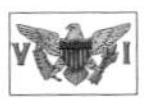

Virgin Islands (U.S.A.)
United States Unincorporated Territory

Area Sq Km	352	Currency	US dollar
Area Sq Miles	136	Languages	English, Spanish
Population	94 000	Religions	Protestant, Roman Catholic
Capital	Charlotte Amalie		

The territory consists of three main islands and over fifty islets in the Caribbean's western Virgin Islands. The islands are mostly hilly and of volcanic origin and the climate is subtropical. The economy is based on tourism, with some manufacturing, including a major oil refinery, on St Croix.

Map page 247

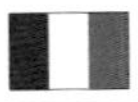

Wallis and Futuna Islands
French Overseas Territory

Area Sq Km	274	Currency	Pacific franc
Area Sq Miles	106	Languages	French, Wallisian, Futunian
Population	14 000	Religions	Roman Catholic
Capital	Matā'utu		

The south Pacific territory comprises the volcanic islands of the Wallis archipelago and Hoorn Islands. The climate is tropical. The islands depend upon subsistence farming, the sale of licences to foreign fishing fleets, workers' remittances and French aid.

Map page 75

West Bank
Territory Occupied by Israel

Area Sq Km	5 860	Languages	Arabic, Hebrew
Area Sq Miles	2 263	Religions	Sunni Muslim, Jewish, Shi'a Muslim, Christian

The territory consists of the west bank of the river Jordan and parts of Judea and Samaria. The land was annexed by Israel in 1967, but the Jericho area was granted self-government under an agreement between Israel and the PLO in 1993.

Map page 128

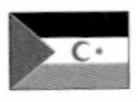

WESTERN SAHARA
Disputed territory (Morocco)

Area Sq Km	266 000	Currency	Moroccan dirham
Area Sq Miles	102 703	Languages	Arabic
Population	275 000	Religions	Sunni Muslim
Capital	Laâyoune		

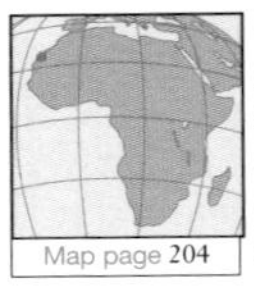

Map page 204

Situated on the northwest coast of Africa, the territory of Western Sahara is controlled by Morocco. The land is low, flat desert with higher land in the northeast. There is little cultivation and only about twenty per cent of the land is pasture. Livestock herding, fishing and phosphate mining are the main activities. All trade is controlled by Morocco.

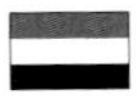

YEMEN
Republic of Yemen

Area Sq Km	527 968	Currency	Rial
Area Sq Miles	203 850	Languages	Arabic
Population	16 887 000	Religions	Sunni Muslim, Shi'a Muslim
Capital	Şan'ā'	Organizations	UN

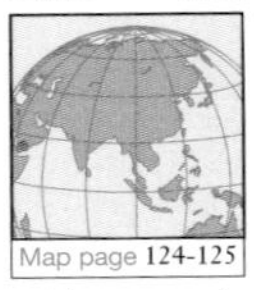

Map page 124-125

Yemen occupies the southwestern Arabian Peninsula, on the Red Sea and Gulf of Aden. Beyond the Red Sea coastal plain the land rises to a mountain range then descends to desert plateaus. Much of Yemen is hot and arid, but rainfall in the west supports crops and most settlement. Farming and fishing are the main activities, with cotton the main cash crop. The main exports are crude oil, cotton, coffee and dried fruit. Despite its oil resources Yemen is one of the poorest countries in the Arab World.

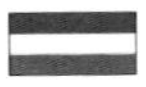

YUGOSLAVIA
Federal Republic of Yugoslavia

Area Sq Km	102 173	Currency	Dinar
Area Sq Miles	39 449	Languages	Serbian, Albanian, Hungarian
Population	10 635 000	Religions	Serbian and Montenegrin Orthodox, Muslim
Capital	Beograd	Organizations	UN

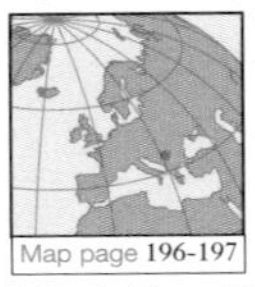

Map page 196-197

The south European state comprises two of the former Yugoslav republics: Serbia and the much smaller Montenegro. The landscape is for the most part rugged, mountainous and forested. Northern Serbia is low-lying, drained by the Danube river system. The climate is Mediterranean on the coast, continental inland. Since 1991 the economy has been seriously affected by war, trade embargoes and economic sanctions.

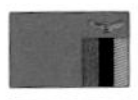

ZAMBIA
Republic of Zambia

Area Sq Km	752 614	Currency	Kwacha
Area Sq Miles	290 586	Languages	English, Bemba, Nyanja, Tonga, local languages
Population	8 781 000	Religions	Christian, traditional beliefs
Capital	Lusaka	Organizations	Comm., SADC, UN

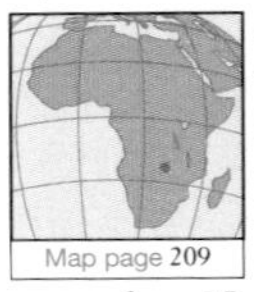

Map page 209

A landlocked state in central Africa, Zambia borders seven countries. It is dominated by high savanna plateaus and bordered by the Zambezi river in the south. Most people live in the Copperbelt area. Life expectancy has dropped by seventeen per cent because of AIDS, compared to 1975. The climate is tropical with a rainy season from November to May. Agriculture employs around eighty per cent of the workforce, but is mainly at subsistence level. Copper mining is the mainstay of the economy, though reserves are declining. Copper and cobalt are the main exports.

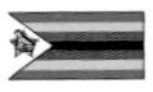

ZIMBABWE
Republic of Zimbabwe

Area Sq Km	390 759	Currency	Dollar
Area Sq Miles	150 873	Languages	English, Shona, Ndebele
Population	11 377 000	Religions	Christian, traditional beliefs
Capital	Harare	Organizations	Comm., SADC, UN

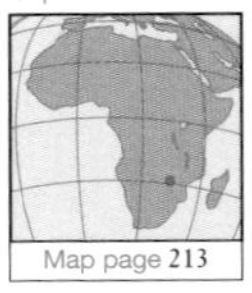

Map page 213

Zimbabwe, a landlocked state in southern central Africa, consists of high plateaus flanked by the Zambezi river valley and Lake Kariba in the north and the Limpopo in the south. Most people live in central Zimbabwe. The effect of AIDS has reduced life expectancy by seventeen per cent compared to 1975. There are significant mineral resources including gold, nickel, copper, asbestos, platinum and chromium. Agriculture is a major sector of the economy, crops include tobacco, maize, sugar cane, and cotton, and beef cattle are important. Exports include tobacco, gold, ferroalloys, nickel and cotton. South Africa is the main trading partner.

ATLAS OF THE WORLD

ATLAS MAPPING

The Atlas of the World includes a variety of styles and scales of mapping which together provide comprehensive coverage of all parts of the world; the map styles and editorial policies followed are introduced here. The area covered by each map is shown on the front and back endpapers.

Each continent is introduced by a politically coloured map followed by reference maps of sub-continental regions and then more detailed reference mapping of regions and individual countries. Scales for continental maps (see 1) range between 1:15 000 000 and 1:27 000 000 and regional maps (see 2) are in the range 1:11 000 000 to 1:13 000 000. Mapping for most countries is at scales between 1:3 000 000 and 1:7 500 000 (see 3) although selected, more densely populated areas of Europe, North America

and Asia are mapped at larger scales, up to 1:1 000 000 (see 4). Large-scale city plans of a selection of the world's major cities (see 5), are included on the appropriate map pages. A suite of maps covering the world's oceans and poles (see 6) at a variety of scales, concludes the main reference map section.

The symbols and place name abbreviations used on the maps are fully explained on pages 68–69 and a glossary of geographical terms is included at the back of the atlas on pages 269–272. The alphanumeric reference system used in the index is based on latitude and longitude, and the number and letter for each graticule square are shown within each map frame, in red. The numbers of adjoining or overlapping pages are shown by arrows in the page frame and accompanying numbers in the margin.

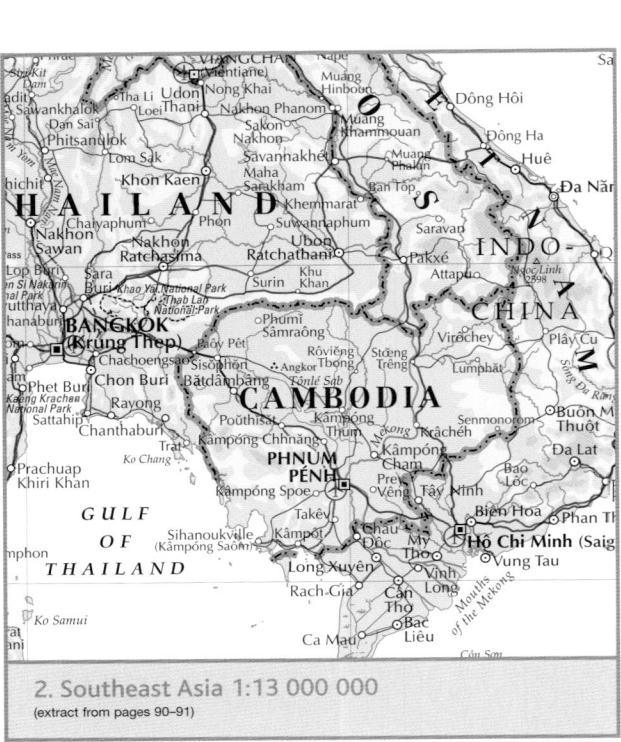

1. Continental map of Asia
(extract from pages 88–89)

BOUNDARIES

The status, names and boundaries of nations are shown in this atlas as they are at the time of going to press, as far as can be ascertained. Where an international boundary symbol appears in the sea or ocean it does not necessarily infer a legal maritime boundary, but shows which off-shore islands belong to which country.

Where international boundaries are the subject of dispute it may be that no portrayal of them will meet with the approval of any of the countries involved, but it is not seen as the function of this atlas to try to adjudicate between the rights and wrongs of political issues. The atlas aims to take a neutral viewpoint of all such cases. Although reference mapping at atlas scales is not the ideal medium for indicating territorial claims, every reasonable attempt is made to show where an active territorial dispute exists, and where there is an important difference between 'de facto' (existing in fact, on the ground) and 'de jure' (according to law) boundaries. This is done by the use of a different symbol where international boundaries are disputed, or where the alignment is unconfirmed, to that used for settled international boundaries. Cease-fire lines are also shown by a separate symbol. For clarity, disputed boundaries and areas are annotated where this is considered necessary.

The latest internal administrative division boundaries are shown on the maps for selected countries where the combination of map scale and the number of divisions permits, with recent changes to local government systems being taken into account as far as possible. Towns which are first-order and second-order administrative centres are also symbolized where scale permits.

2. Southeast Asia 1:13 000 000
(extract from pages 90–91)

3. Africa East Central 1:7 500 000
(extract from pages 210–211)

PLACE NAMES

The spelling of place names on maps has always been a matter of great complexity, because of the variety of the world's languages and the systems used to write them down. Continuing changes in official languages, and in writing systems, also have to be taken into account. In many countries different languages are in use in different regions, or side-by-side in the same region. Sometimes the problem is dealt with by the use of a 'lingua franca' such as English to provide a mutually intelligible standard. In many cases the most spoken language takes precedence, but there is still the potential for widely varying name forms even within a single country. A worldwide trend towards national, regional and ethnic self-determination is operating at the same time as pressure towards increased international standardization of name forms.

There is no standard way of spelling names or of converting them from one alphabet, or symbol set, to another. Instead, conventional ways of spelling have evolved in each of the world's major languages, and the results often differ significantly from the name as it is spelled in the original language. Familiar examples of English conventional names include Munich (München), Florence (Firenze) and Moscow (from the transliterated form, Moskva).

In this atlas, local name forms are used where these are in the Roman alphabet. Such a policy results in mapping which

is internally consistent and which closely reflects name forms found in the country itself. These local forms are those which are officially recognized by the government of the country concerned, usually as represented by its official mapping agency. This is a basic principle laid down by the United Kingdom government's Permanent Committee on Geographical Names (PCGN) and the equivalent United States Board on Geographic Names (BGN).

For languages in non-Roman alphabets and syllabaries, the atlas generally follows BGN/PCGN romanization principles. For example, Russian-language names are spelled using the standard BGN/PCGN system, which gives names such as Lipetsk and Yoshkar-Ola as opposed to a system used in eastern Europe which gives Lipeck and Joškar-Ola.

Although local forms are preferred, prominent English-language conventional names and historic names are not neglected. Together with significant superseded names and other alternate spellings, they are included in brackets on the maps where space permits, and are cross-referenced in the index. The names of continents, oceans, seas and under-water features in international waters appear in English throughout the atlas, as do those of other international features – features crossing one or more

international boundary – where such an English form exists and is in common use.

Country names are shown in conventional English form, and include changes promulgated by national governments and adopted by the United Nations – Myanmar (replacing Burma), Belarus (replacing Belorussia and a variety of other versions including the traditional White Russia), Kyrgyzstan (for Kirghizia or Kirgizia), Moldova (Moldavia), and Côte d'Ivoire (Ivory Coast). In the adoption of these name forms for country names, and for certain city names, such as Beijing (replacing Peking), the gradual incorporation of local forms into common English usage can be seen at work. This atlas reflects that process.

CHANGES IN NAME FORMS

Place names are, to an extent, a mirror for the changes that continue to transform the political world. Predictably, changes of territorial control have an effect on name forms. Yet even in countries where name forms could be expected to have been standardized, there are continuing issues for the cartographer to address. In the UK, for example, the increased prominence given to the use of Gaelic and Welsh has meant that more consideration has been given to the use of Gaelic and Welsh name forms in relation to the English form. Name spelling

PROJECTIONS

The creation of computer-generated maps presents the opportunity to select projections specifically for the area and scale of each map. As the only way to show the Earth with absolute accuracy is on a globe, all map projections are compromises. Some projections seek to maintain correct area relationships (equal area projections), true distances and bearings from a point (equidistant projections) or correct angles and shapes (conformal projections); others attempt to achieve a balance between these properties. The choice of projections used in this atlas has been made on an individual continental and regional basis. Projections used, and their individual parameters, have been defined to minimize distortion and to reduce scale errors as much as possible.

For world maps, the Bartholomew version of the Winkel Tripel Projection is used. This projection combines elements of conformality with that of equal area, and shows, over the world as a whole, relatively true shapes and reasonably equal areas. The Mercator Projection (see 7) has been selected for the regional maps of southeast Asia along the Equator , while in higher latitudes, particularly in Europe and to some extent in North America, the Conic Equidistant Projection (see 8) has been used extensively for regional mapping. The Lambert Azimuthal Equal Area Projection (see 9) has been employed in both South America and Australia.

7. MERCATOR PROJECTION

This rectangular or cylindrical projection is constructed on the basis of a cylinder in contact with the globe, in this case around the Equator. Scale is correct along the Equator and distortion increases away from it in both directions.

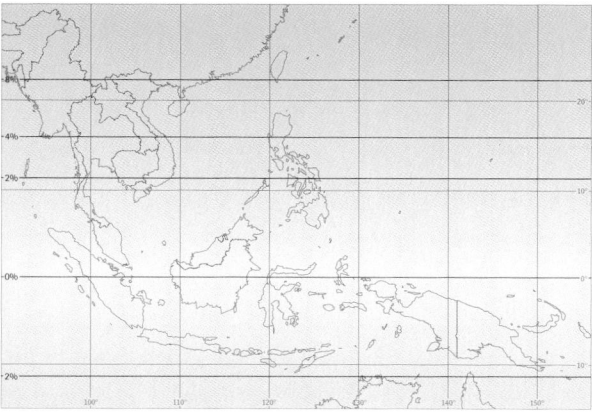

8. CONIC EQUIDISTANT PROJECTION

Constructed on the basis of a cone intersecting the globe along two standard parallels (55°N and 75°N in this illustration), along both of which scale is correct. Lines of equal scale error are parallel to the standard lines, with distortion increasing away from each.

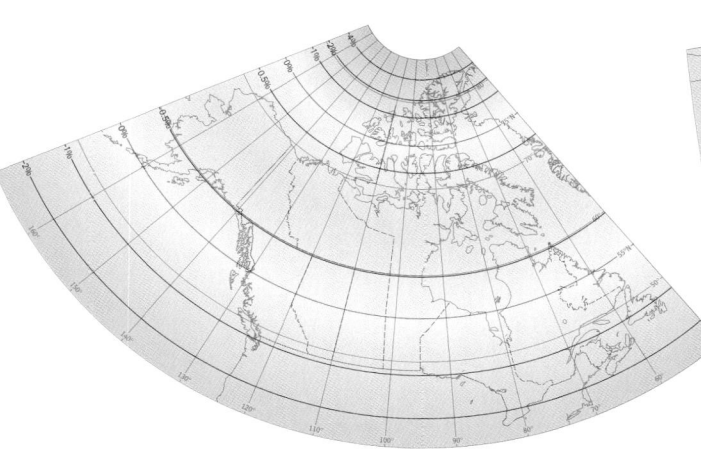

9. LAMBERT AZIMUTHAL EQUAL AREA PROJECTION

Points are projected onto a plane in contact with the globe at the centre point (25°S, 135°E in this illustration). Scale is correct at the centre, and scale errors increase in concentric circles away from it. Areas are true in relation to the corresponding areas on the globe.

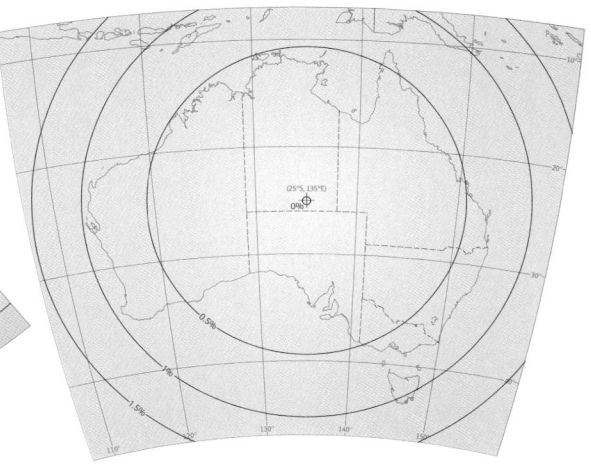

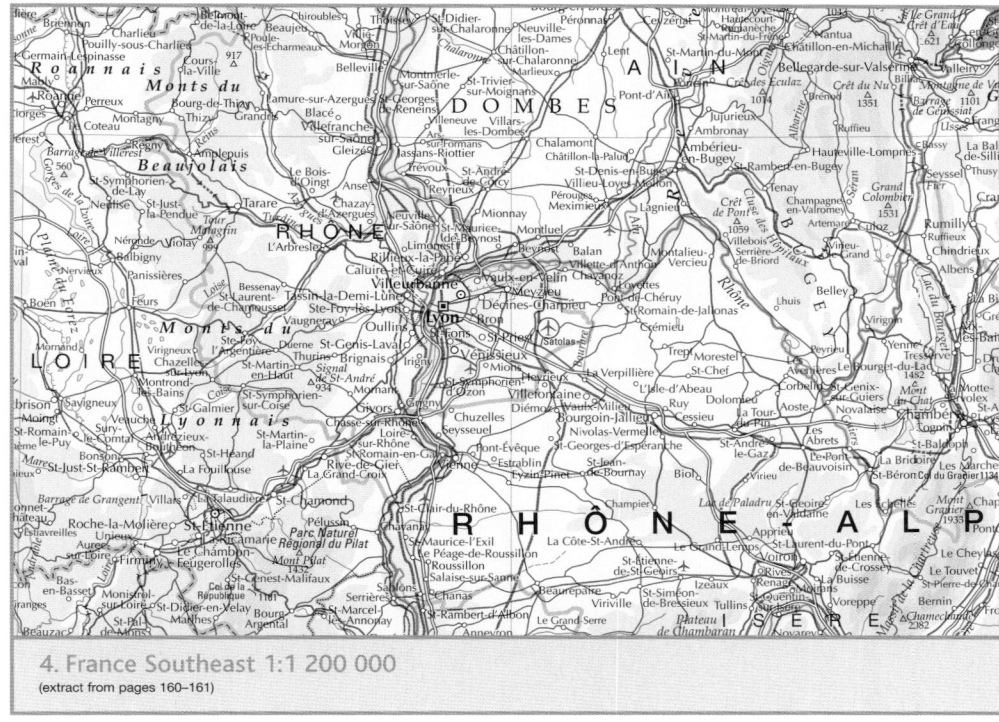

4. France Southeast 1:1 200 000
(extract from pages 160–161)

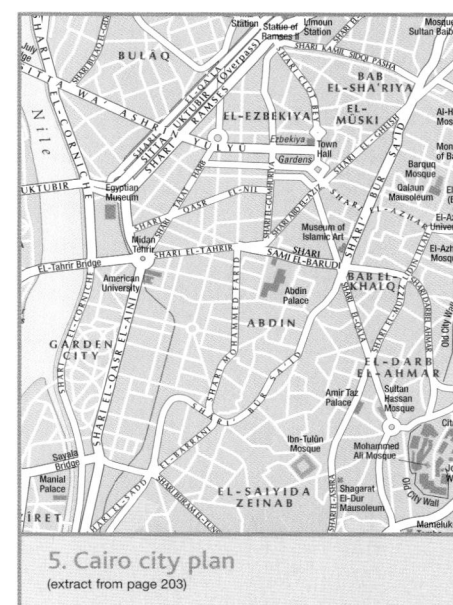

5. Cairo city plan
(extract from page 203)

issues are, in fact, likely to emerge in any part of the world. A close watch is kept on areas where changes might be expected, although sometimes they crop up in unexpected places.

The dissolution of the former USSR gave rise to many changes in name forms. Names were converted from Russian to the main national language in Belarus, Ukraine, Moldova, Armenia, Georgia, Azerbaijan, Kyrgyzstan and Tajikistan. On the maps, where space permits, the main Russian-language forms for significant places are shown as alternatives in such cases. Russian naturally continues to be used as the main form in the Russian Federation, although in Chechnia main Chechen alternative forms have been included in the index as cross-references. Russian also continues to be used as the prime language on maps of Kazakhstan, Turkmenistan and Uzbekistan. In Kazakhstan, both Russian and Kazakh are recognized as joint official languages, and Russian is maintained as the first form, while Kazakh alternatives (derived from Kazakh cyrillic), are included for main place names where space permits on the maps, with additional alternatives in the index.

In Spain, account is taken of the official prominence now given to Catalan, Galician and some Basque names, which results in name forms such as Eivissa for Ibiza; A Coruña for La Coruña; and San Sebastián amended to Donostia-San Sebastián.

Chinese name forms, which use the official Pinyin romanization system continue to change. Name forms have been brought into line with the latest official sources resulting in a more rigorous and updated use of the principle whereby numerous towns, which are the centres of administrative units such as the county or 'xian', officially take the name of the county itself. The alternative place name in common local use is shown in brackets where possible.

CHANGES IN NAME FORMS

As well as the above-mentioned systematic changes in name forms, which mostly involve official modifications in the way all names in a country are rendered in the Roman alphabet, the atlas also aims to account for entirely new names being adopted. Such name changes can happen for a variety of reasons – one example is the move away from communist-inspired names in the former Soviet Union. Changes can be a result of official policy changes, such as those in India when Bombay was changed to Mumbai, and Madras to Chennai. Although particularly prominent, these in fact represent the continuation of a long process of name amendments in India since independence.

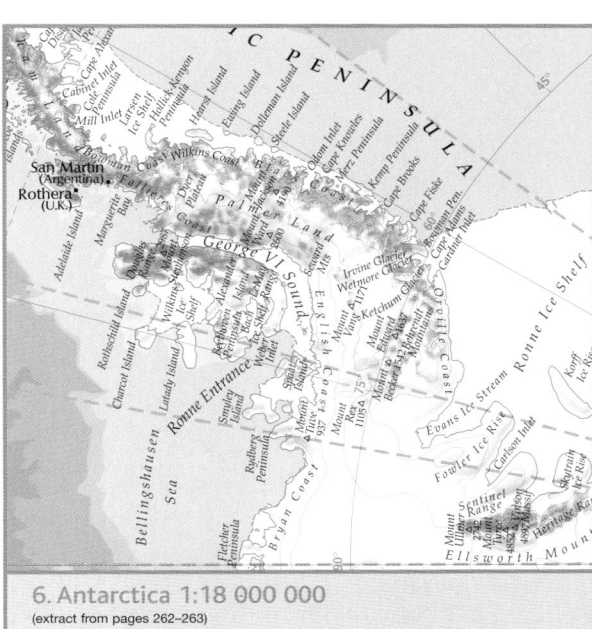

6. Antarctica 1:18 000 000
(extract from pages 262–263)

REFERENCE MAPS

CITIES AND TOWNS

Population	National Capital	Administrative Capital (Shown for selected countries only)		Other City or Town
		First order	Second order (Scales larger than 1:9 000 000.)	
over 5 million	**BEIJING** ■	**Tianjin** ■	**Los Angeles** ◉	**New York** ◉
1 million to 5 million	**KĀBUL** ■	**Sydney** ■	**Tangshan** ◉	**Kaohsiung** ◉
500 000 to 1 million	BANGUI ▣	Trujillo ▣	Agra ◎	Jeddah ◎
100 000 to 500 000	WELLINGTON ▣	Mansa ▣	Naogaon ◎	Apucarana ◎
50 000 to 100 000	PORT OF SPAIN □	Potenza □	Trier ○	Arecibo ○
10 000 to 50 000	MALABO □	Chinhoyi □	Willimantic ○	Ceres ○
1 000 to 10 000	VALLETTA ▫	Ati ▫	Nepalganj ○	Abla ○
under 1000 (Scales 1: 4 000 000 and larger)		Chhukha ▫	Carmel ○	Lopigna ○

⬭ Built-up area

MISCELLANEOUS FEATURES

---------- National park   ·················· Regional park   ·················· Reserve or special land area   ∴ Site of specific interest   ∿∿∿∿∿ Wall

RELIEF

Contour intervals used in layer-colouring for land height and sea depth

Scales 1:4 000 000 and larger	Scales 1:4 000 000 and larger (Europe only)	Scales smaller than 1:4 000 000	Oceans and Antarctica (Pages 262-268)
METRES FEET	**METRES** FEET	**METRES** FEET	**METRES** FEET
6000 / 19686	6000 / 19686	6000 / 19686	4000 / 13124
5000 / 16404	5000 / 16404	5000 / 16404	2000 / 6562
4000 / 13124	4000 / 13124	4000 / 13124	1000 / 3281
3000 / 9843	3000 / 9843	3000 / 9843	500 / 1640
2000 / 6562	2000 / 6562	2000 / 6562	200 / 656
1500 / 4921	1500 / 4921	1000 / 3281	0 / 0
1000 / 3281	1000 / 3281	500 / 1640	LAND BELOW SEA LEVEL
500 / 1640	500 / 1640	200 / 656	200 / 656
200 / 656	200 / 656	0 / 0	2000 / 6562
100 / 328	100 / 328	LAND BELOW SEA LEVEL	3000 / 9843
0 / 0	0 / 0	200 / 656	4000 / 13124
LAND BELOW SEA LEVEL	LAND BELOW SEA LEVEL	2000 / 6562	5000 / 16409
200 / 656	50 / 164	4000 / 13124	6000 / 19686
1000 / 3281	200 / 656	6000 / 19686	7000 / 22967
2000 / 6562	1000 / 3281		9000 / 29529
	2000 / 6562		

1234 △ Summit Height in metres

-123 • Spot height Surface height in metres for depressions and areas below sea level.

5678 • Ocean deep In metres. Ocean pages only.

STYLES OF LETTERING

Cities and towns are explained separately

		Physical features	
Country	**FRANCE**		
Overseas Territory/Dependency	**Guadeloupe**	Island	*Gran Canaria*
Disputed Territory	AKSAI CHIN	Lake	*LAKE ERIE*
Administrative name, first order internal division (Shown for selected countries only.)	SCOTLAND	Mountain	*Mt Blanc*
Administrative name, second order internal division (Scales 1:4 000 000 and larger. Shown for selected countries only.)	MANCHE	River	*Thames*
Area name	ARTOIS	Region	*PAMPAS*

BOUNDARIES

▭▬▭ International boundary

▰▰▰ Disputed international boundary or alignment unconfirmed

⬦ Undefined international boundary in the sea. All land within this boundary is part of state or territory named.

▭▭▭ Administrative boundary, first order internal division. Scales 1:4 000 000 and larger. Shown for selected countries only.

▬▬▬ Administrative boundary, first order internal division. Scales smaller than 1:4 000 000. Shown for selected countries only.

▬▬▬ Administrative boundary, second order internal division. Scales 1:4 000 000 and larger. Shown for selected countries only.

▰▰▰ Disputed administrative boundary Scales 1:4 000 000 and larger. Shown for selected countries only.

●●●●● Ceasefire line or other boundary described on the map

LAND AND SEA FEATURES

⦂⦂ Rock desert

⦂⦂ Sand desert / Dunes

˅ Oasis

⦂⦂ Lava field

1234 ▲ Volcano height in metres

⦂⦂ Marsh

⬭ Ice cap / Glacier

⬭ Nunatak

····· Coral reef

·············· Escarpment

············· Flood dyke

][123 Pass height in metres

········ Ice shelf

LAKES AND RIVERS

⬭ Lake

⬭ Impermanent lake

⬭ Salt lake or lagoon

⬭ Impermanent salt lake

⬭ Dry salt lake or salt pan

123 Lake height surface height above sea level, in metres

——— River

------ Impermanent river

-- -- Wadi or watercourse

‖ Waterfall

— Dam

| Barrage

TRANSPORT

══════ Motorway Scales 1:4 000 000 and larger.

——— Main road

——— Secondary road

⚎⚎⚎ Motorway tunnel

—⊢— Road tunnel

----- Track

——— Main railway

——— Secondary railway

➤⋯⊢ Railway tunnel

·············· Canal

——— Minor canal

⊕ Main airport

✈ Regional airport

CITY PLANS

- Built-up area
- Cemetery
- Park
- Place of worship
- General place of interest
- Transport location
- Academic / municipal building

CONTINENTAL MAPS

BOUNDARIES

——————	International boundary
- - - - - - -	Disputed international boundary or alignment unconfirmed
/	Undefined international boundary in the sea. All land within this boundary is part of state or territory named.
••••••••	Ceasefire line
- - - - -	Administrative boundary Shown for selected countries only.

CITIES AND TOWNS

Population	National Capital	Other City or Town
over 5 million	**Beijing** ■	New York ◉
1 million to 5 million	**Kabul** ■	Kaohsiung ◉
500 000 to 1 million	**Bangui** ⊡	Khulna ◎
100 000 to 500 000	**Wellington** ⊡	Iquitos ⊙
50 000 to 100 000	**Port of Spain** ▢	Naga ○
10 000 to 50 000	**Malabo** ▫	Ushuaia ○
under 10 000	**Valletta** ▫	Arviat ○

ABBREVIATIONS

A.C.T.	Australian Capital Territory		
Arch.	Archipelago		
	Archipiélago	Spanish	archipelago
B.	Bay		
	Bahia, Baía	Portuguese	bay
	Bahía	Spanish	bay
	Baie	French	bay
Bol.	Bol'shaya, Bol'shoy, Bol'shoye	Russian	big
C.	Cape		
	Cabo	Portuguese, Spanish	cape, headland
	Cap	Catalan, French	cape, headland
Cach.	Cachoeira	Portuguese	waterfall, rapids
Can.	Canal	French, Portuguese, Spanish	canal, channel
Cd	Ciudad	Spanish	city, town
Chan.	Channel		
Co	Cerro	Spanish	hill, mountain, peak
Cord.	Cordillera	Spanish	mountain range
Cr.	Creek		
Cuch.	Cuchilla	Spanish	hills, mountain range
D.	Dağ, Dağı	Turkish	mountain
	Dāgh	Farsi	mountain, mountains
	Dağları	Turkish	mountain range
	Danau	Indonesian, Malay	lake
Div.	Division		
Dr	Doctor		
E.	East, Eastern		
Emb.	Embalse	Spanish	reservoir
Est.	Estero	Spanish	estuary, inlet
	Estrecho	Spanish	strait
Fj.	Fjörður	Icelandic	fjord, inlet
Ft	Fort		
G.	Gebel	Arabic	hill, mountain
	Golfo	Italian, Spanish	gulf, bay
	Gora	Russian	mountain
	Gunung	Indonesian, Malay	hill, mountain
Gd	Grand	French	big
Gde	Grande	French, Italian, Portuguese, Spanish	big
Geb.	Gebergte	Afrikaans, Dutch	mountain range
Gen.	General		
Gl.	Glacier		
Gp	Group		
Gt	Great		
Harb.	Harbour		
Hd	Head		
I.	Island, Isle		
	Ilha	Portuguese	island
	Isla	Spanish	island
Î.	Île	French	island
im.	imeni	Russian	'in the name of'
Ind. Res.	Indian Reservation		
Ing.	Ingeniero	Spanish	engineer
Is	Islands, Isles		
	Islas	Spanish	islands
Îs	Îles	French	islands
J.	Jabal, Jebel	Arabic	mountain, mountains
Kep.	Kepulauan	Indonesian, Malay	archipelago, islands
Khr.	Khrebet	Russian	mountain range
L.	Lake		
	Loch	(Scotland)	lake
	Lough	(Ireland)	lake
	Lac	French	lake
	Lago	Portuguese, Spanish	lake
Lag.	Laguna	Spanish	lagoon
M.	Mys	Russian	cape, point
Mt	Mount		
	Mont	French	hill, mountain
Mt.	Mountain		
Mte	Monte	Portuguese, Spanish	hill, mountain

Mts	Mountains		
	Monts	French	hills, mountains
N.	North, Northern		
Nev.	Nevado	Spanish	peak
Nat.	National		
Nat. Park	National Park		
Nat. Res.	Nature Reserve		
Nizh.	Nizhniy, Nizhnyaya	Russian	lower
N.E.	Northeast, Northeastern		
N.H.S.	National Heritage Site		
N.W.	Northwest, Northwestern		
O.	Ostrov	Russian	island
O-va	Ostrova	Russian	islands
Oz.	Ozero	Russian, Ukrainian	lake
P.	Paso	Spanish	pass
	Pulau	Indonesian, Malay	island
Pass.	Passage		
Peg.	Pegunungan	Indonesian, Malay	mountain range
Pen.	Peninsula		
	Península	Spanish	peninsula
Pk	Peak		
	Puncak	Indonesian	mountain, peak
P-ov	Poluostrov	Russian	peninsula
P. P.	Pulau-pulau	Indonesian	islands
Psa	Presa	Spanish	reservoir
Pt	Point		
Pta	Punta	Italian, Spanish	cape, point
Pte	Pointe	French	cape, point
Pto	Porto	Portuguese	harbour, port
	Puerto	Spanish	harbour, port
R.	River		
	Rio	Portuguese	river
	Río	Spanish	river
	Rivière	French	river
	Rūd	Farsi	river
Ra.	Range		
Rec.	Recreation		
Res.	Reservation, Reserve		
Resr	Reservoir		
S.	South, Southern		
	Salar, Salina, Salinas	Spanish	salt pan, salt pans
Sa	Serra	Portuguese	mountain range
	Sierra	Spanish	mountain range
Sd	Sound		
S.E.	Southeast, Southeastern		
Serr.	Serranía	Spanish	mountain range
Sk.	Shuiku	Chinese	reservoir
Sr.	Sredniy, Srednyaya	Russian	middle, central
St	Saint		
	Sankt	German, Russian	saint
	Sint	Dutch	saint
Sta	Santa	Italian, Portuguese, Spanish	saint
Ste	Sainte	French	saint
Sto	Santo	Italian, Portuguese, Spanish	saint
Str.	Strait		
S.W.	Southwest, Southwestern		
Tg	Tanjong, Tanjung	Indonesian, Malay	cape, point
Tk	Teluk, Telukan	Indonesian, Malay	bay, gulf
Tte	Teniente	Spanish	lieutenant
Va	Villa	Spanish	town
Vdkhr.	Vodokhranilishche	Russian	reservoir
Verkh.	Verkhniy, Verkhnyaya	Russian	upper
Vol.	Volcano		
	Volcan	French	volcano
	Volcán	Spanish	volcano
Vozv.	Vozvyshennost'	Russian	hills, upland
W.	West, Western		
	Wadi, Wâdi, Wādī	Arabic	watercourse

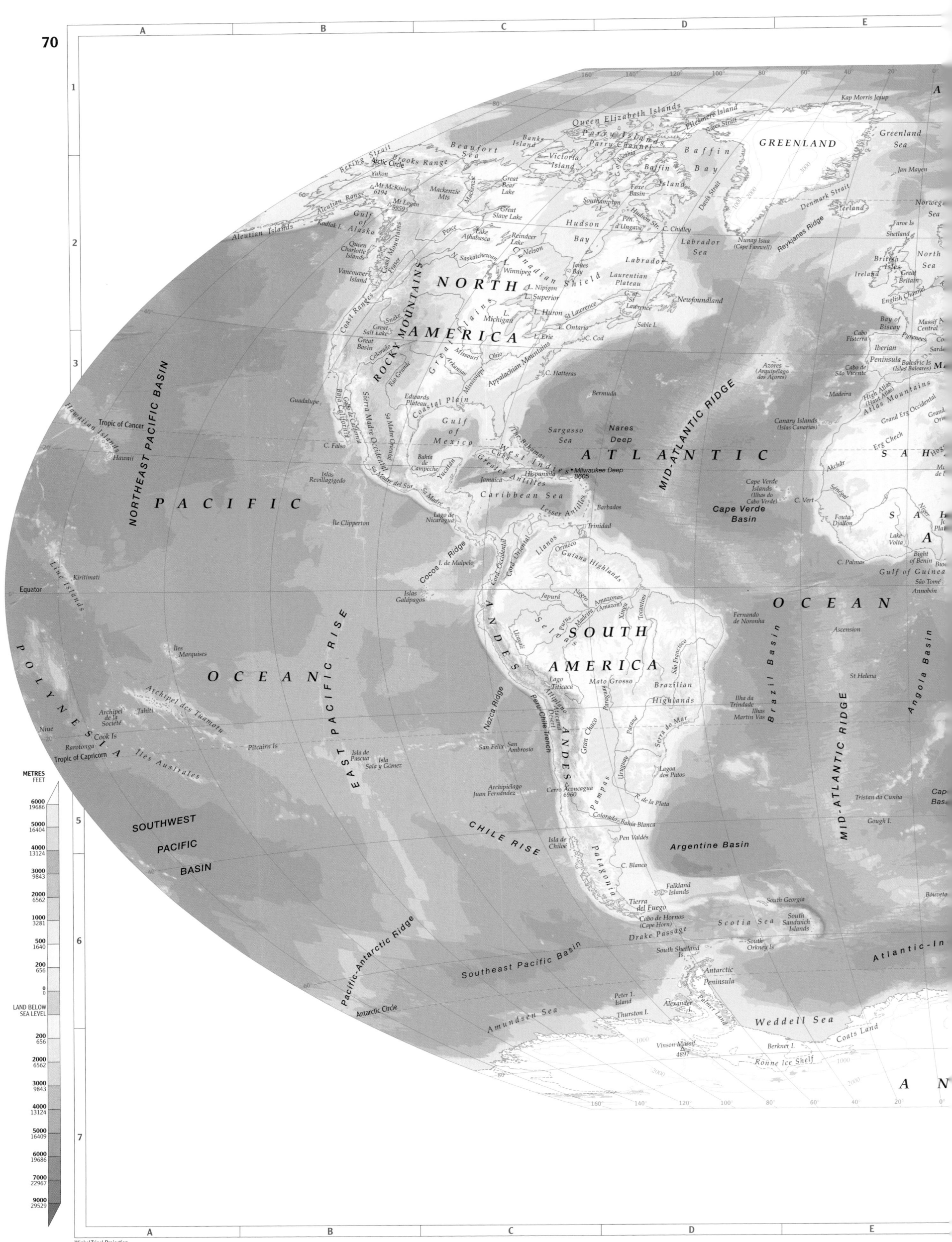

A B C D E

1

80°

160° 140° 120° 100° 80° 60° 40° 20°

Kap Morris Jesup

A

Queen Elizabeth Islands
Parry Islands   Ellesmere Island   Nares Strait
Banks   Parry Channel   GREENLAND   Greenland
Beaufort   Island   Baffin   Sea
Brooks Range   Sea   Victoria   Baffin   Bay   Jan Mayen
Bering Strait   Island   Bay   2000
Arctic Circle   Island   Foxe   Denmark Strait
Yukon   Great   Basin   Iceland   Norweg
60°   Mt McKinley   Bear   Southampton   Davis Strait   Sea
Aleutian Range   6194   Mackenzie   Lake   Hudson Str.   Nunap Isua   Reykjanes Ridge
Mt Logan   Mts   d'Ungava   C. Chidley   (Cape Farewell)   Faroe Is
Aleutian Islands   5959   Reindeer   Hudson   Labrador   Shetland   North
Kodiak I.   Gulf   Lake   Nelson   Bay   Sea   British   Sea
of   Lake   James   Labrador   Ireland   Isles
Queen   Alaska   N. Saskatchewan   Athabasca   Bay   Sea   Great
Charlotte   Winnipeg   Canadian   Laurentian   Britain
Islands   Great   L. Nipigon   Shield   Plateau   English Channel
Vancouver   NORTH   L. Superior   G. of   Newfoundland   Bay of
Island   Plains   L. Huron   St Lawrence   Biscay   Massif N
Coast Ranges   Michigan   L. Ontario   Sable I.   Pyrenees   Central
Coast Mountains   Snake   L. Erie   C. Cod   Iberian   Sarde
40°   Salt   AMERICA   Missouri   Ohio   Peninsula   Balearic Is   M
Great   Lake   Colorado   Appalachian Mountains   Cabo   (Islas Baleares)
Great   Basin   Arkansas   C. Hatteras   Fisterra
Basin   Sierra   Mississippi   Azores   Cabo de   Madeira   High Atlas
Guadalupe   Rio Grande   Bermuda   (Arquipélago   São Vicente   (Haut Atlas)
Edwards   dos Açores)   Atlas Mountains
Plateau   Coastal Plain   Canary Islands   Grand Erg Occidental
Tropic of Cancer   Sierra Madre Occidental   Gulf   (Islas Canarias)   S A H
C. Falso   of   Nares   Akchâr   Erg Chech   Hog
Hawaiian Islands   Mexico   Sargasso   Deep   C. Vert   of
Hawaii   Bahia   Yucatán   Sea   Cape Verde   Senegal   M
de   West Indies   Milwaukee Deep   Islands   Fouta   de I
Islas   Campeche   Greater   8605   (Ilhas do   Djallon   S A
Revillagigedo   Cuba   Antilles   Hispaniola   Cabo Verde)   Lake   J
Jamaica   ATLANTIC   C. Palmas   Volta   Pla
Ile Clipperton   Caribbean Sea   Lesser Antilles   Barbados   Cape Verde   Bight
Lago de   Basin   of Benin   Bioc
Equator   Nicaragua   Trinidad   São Tomé   A
PACIFIC   I. de Malpelo   Llanos   Orinoco   Gulf of Guinea   Annobón
Cord. Occidental   Guiana Highlands
Kiritimati   Cocos   Cord. Oriental   OCEAN
Line Islands   Ridge   Negro   Amazonas
Islas   Japurá   (Amazon)   Fernando
Galápagos   Selvas   Madeira   Xingu   de Noronha   Ascension
Andes   Ucayali   Amazonas   Tocantins
OCEAN   (Amazon)   Brazil Basin   St Helena
Iles   SOUTH   São Francisco
Marquises   Purus   AMERICA   Ilha da
Lago   Mato Grosso   Trindade
Archipel des Tuamotu   Titicaca   Brazilian   Ilhas
Altiplano   Highlands   Martín Vas
Archipel   Nazca Ridge   Andes   Gran Chaco   Paraná   Serra do Mar
de la   Tahiti   Peru-Chile Trench   Uruguay   Lagoa
Société   dos Patos   MID-ATLANTIC RIDGE   Angola Basin
Niue   EAST PACIFIC RISE   Pampas   R. de la Plata   Tristan da Cunha
Cook Is   Cerro Aconcagua   Colorado   Bahia Blanca   Cap
Rarotonga   6960   Pen. Valdés   Gough I.   Base
Tropic of Capricorn   Iles Australes   Isla de   Argentine Basin
Archipiélago   Pascua   Patagonia
Juan Fernández   Isla   C. Blanco
Sala y Gómez   Falkland   Bouveto
San Felix   San   Islands
Ambrosio   Tierra   South Georgia
SOUTHWEST   del Fuego   CHILE RISE   South
PACIFIC   Isla de   Cabo de Hornos   Scotia Sea   Sandwich
BASIN   Chiloé   (Cape Horn)   Islands
Drake Passage   South
Pacific-Antarctic Ridge   Orkney Is   Atlantic-In
South Shetland
Antarctic Circle   Southeast Pacific Basin   Is.   Antarctic
Antarctic Ridge   Peninsula
Peter 1.   Alexander   Palmer Land   Weddell Sea
Island   I.   Thurston I.
Amundsen Sea   Coats Land
1000
Vinson Massif   Berkner I.
4897   Ronne Ice Shelf   A   N
80°   2500   1000
160° 140° 120° 100° 80° 60° 40° 20°

5

6

7

A B C D E

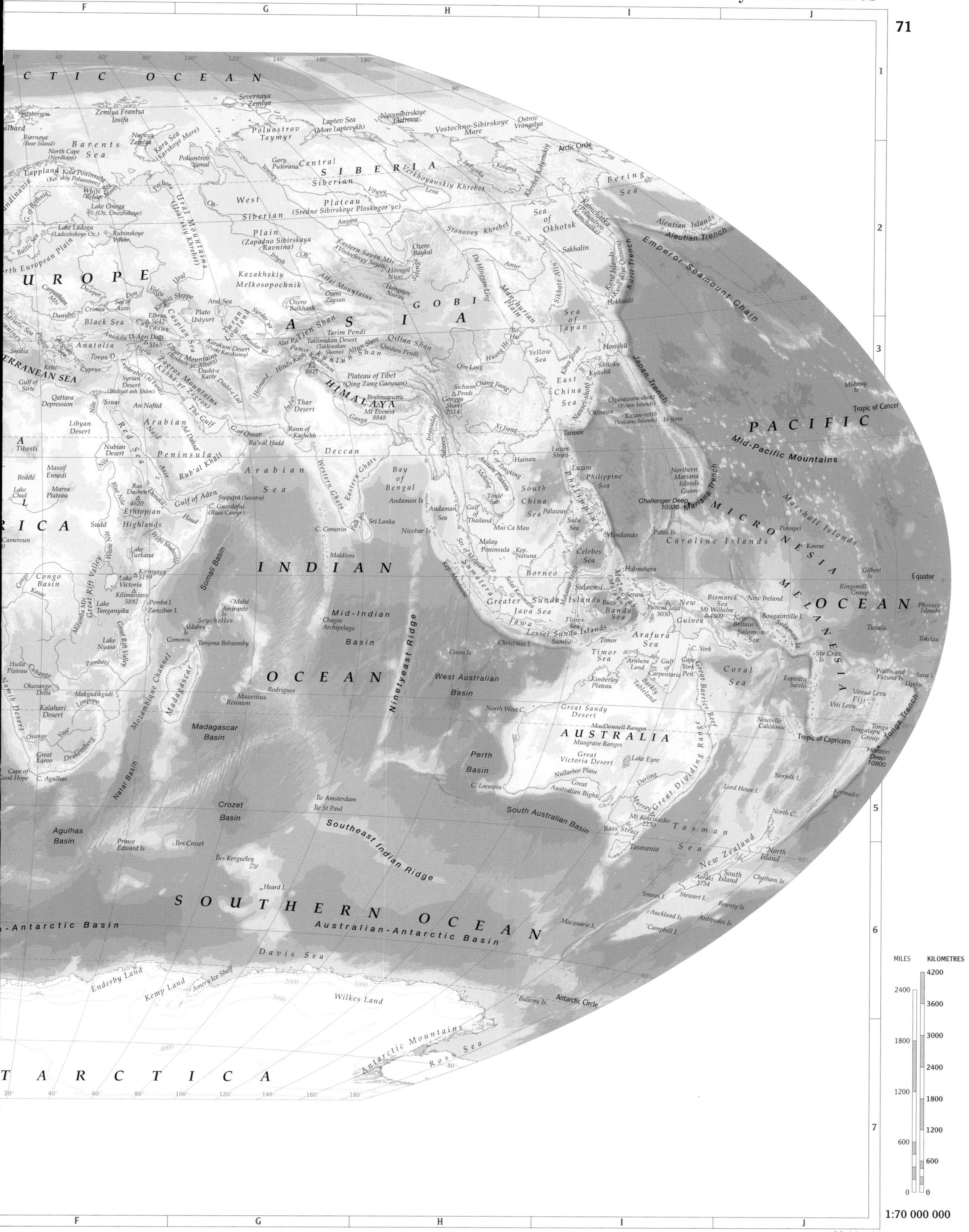

ARCTIC OCEAN

Spitsbergen
Svalbard
Bjørnøya (Bear Island)
North Cape (Nordkapp)
Barents Sea
Zemlya Frantsa Iosifa
Novaya Zemlya
Kara Sea (Karskoye More)
Severnaya Zemlya
Poluostrov Taymyr
Laptev Sea (More Laptevykh)
Novosibirskiye Ostrova
Vostochno-Sibirskoye More
Ostrov Vrangelya
Arctic Circle
Bering Sea

Lappland
Kola Peninsula (Kol'skiy Poluostrov)
White Sea (Beloye More)
Lake Onega (Oz. Onezhskoye)
Lake Ladoga (Ladozhskoye Oz.)
Rubinskoye Vdkhr.
Pechora
Poluostrov Yamal
Gory Putorana
Yenisey
Central Siberian Plateau (Sredne Sibirskoye Ploskogor'ye)
Verkhoyanskiy Khrebet
Lena
Indigirka
Kolyma
Khrebet Kolymskiy
Aleutian Islands
Aleutian Trench
Emperor Seamount Chain

G. of Bothnia
Scandinavia
Baltic Sea
North European Plain
Ural Mountains (Ural'skiy Khrebet)
Ob'
West Siberian Plain (Zapadno Sibirskaya Ravnina)
Irtysh
Ob'
Angara
Eastern Sayan Mts (Vostochnyy Sayan)
Ozero Baykal
Stanovoy Khrebet
Amur
Da Hinggan Ling
Manchurian Plain
Sikhote Alin'
Sakhalin
Sea of Okhotsk
Kamchatka (Poluostrov Kamchatka)
Kuril Islands (Kuril'skiye Ostrova)
Kuril Trench
Hokkaidō

EUROPE
Carpathian Mts
Dnieper
Don
Sea of Azov
Crimea
Volga
Ural
Kirgiz Steppe
Kazakhskiy Melkosopochnik
Aral Sea
Syrdar'ya
Ozero Balkhash
Altai Mountains
Hangayn Nuruu
Hövsgöl Nuur
Ozero Zaysan
GOBI
ASIA
Bo Hai
Sea of Japan
Honshū
Korea Strait
Kyūshū

Adriatic Sea
Apennines
Danube
Black Sea
Caucasus
Elbrus 5642
Caspian Sea
Plato Ustyurt
Turan Lowland (Turanskaya)
Karakum Desert (Peski Karakumy)
Tien Shan
Tarim Pendi
Taklimakan Desert (Taklimakan Shamo)
Altun Shan
Qilian Shan
Qaidam Pendi
Huang He
Qin Ling
Chang Jiang
Sichuan Pendi
Sea of Japan
East China Sea
Ogasawara-shotō (Bonin Islands)
Kazan-rettō (Volcano Islands)
Iō-jima

Sicilia
Kriti
MEDITERRANEAN SEA
Gulf of Sirte
Anatolia
Anadolu D. Agri Dagi 5165
Toros D.
Cyprus
Tigris
Euphrates (Al Furat)
Zagros Mountains (Reshteh-ye Kühha-ye Alborz)
Elburz Mountains
Dasht-e Kavir
Dasht-e Lut
Hindu Kush
Pamir
K2 8611
Plateau of Tibet (Qing Zang Gaoyuan)
HIMALAYA
Mt Everest 8848
Brahmaputra
Ganga
Thar Desert
Irrawaddy
Chang Jiang
Qönggai Shan 7514
Xi Jiang
Hwang He
Yellow Sea
Taiwan
Luzon Strait
PACIFIC
Tropic of Cancer
Mid-Pacific Mountains
Midway Is

Qattara Depression
Sinai
An Nafud
Red Sea
Nile
Libyan Desert
Tibesti
Nubian Desert
Arabian Peninsula
Najd
Ad Dahna
The Gulf
G. of Oman
Ra's al Hadd
G. of Tonking
Hainan
Luzon
Northern Mariana Islands
Guam
Philippine Sea
Marshall Islands
MICRONESIA
Kosrae
Pohnpei
Palau Is
Caroline Islands
Gilbert Is
Kingsmill Group
Equator
Phoenix Islands

Massif Ennedi
Bodélé
Lake Chad
Marra Plateau
Blue Nile
Ras Dashen 4620
Denakil
C. Guardafui (Raas Caseyr)
Suqutrā (Socotra)
Gulf of Aden
Haud
Ethiopian Highlands
Asir
Rub' al Khali
Arabian Sea
Western Ghats
Eastern Ghats
Deccan
Bay of Bengal
Andaman Is
Andaman Sea
Gulf of Thailand
Tônlé Sab
Mekong
Mui Ca Mau
South China Sea
Palawan
Sulu Sea
Mindanao
Celebes Sea
Halmahera

AFRICA
Cameroun
Sudd
White Nile
Wabi Shabeelle
Lake Turkana
Kirinyaga 5199
Lake Victoria
Kilimanjaro 5892
Pemba I.
Zanzibar I.
Mahé
Amirante
Seychelles
Aldabra
Comoros
C. Comorin
Sri Lanka
Nicobar Is
Maldives
Chagos Archipelago
INDIAN OCEAN
Malay Peninsula
Kep. Natuna
Str. of Malacca
Sumatera
Kep. Mentawai
Borneo
Sulawesi
Greater Sunda Islands
Jawa
Java Sea
Lesser Sunda Islands
Flores Sea
Sumba
Timor
Banda Sea
Buru
Seram
Puncak Jaya 5030
New Guinea
Mt Wilhelm 4509
Bismarck Sea
New Ireland
New Britain
Solomon Is
Bougainville I.
MELANESIA
Sta Cruz Is
Tuvalu
Tokelau

Congo Basin
Kasaï
Mitumba Mts
Great Rift Valley
Lake Tanganyika
Lake Nyasa
Mid-Indian Basin
Ninetyeast Ridge
West Australian Basin
Arafura Sea
Gulf of Carpentaria
C. York
Cape York Pen.
Great Barrier Reef
Coral Sea
Espiritu Santo
Vanua Levu
Viti Levu
Fiji
Wallis and Futuna Is
Savai'i
Upolu

Hulla Plateau
Cubango
Zambezi
Lake Nyasa
Madagascar
Mozambique Channel
Mahé
Tanjona Bobaomby
Mauritius
Réunion
Rodrigues
Cocos Is
Christmas I.
Timor Sea
Arnhem Land
Kimberley Plateau
North West C.
Great Sandy Desert
MacDonnell Ranges
Barkly Tableland
Great Dividing Range
Nouvelle Calédonie
Norfolk I.
Tropic of Capricorn
Horizon Deep 10800
Kermadec Tr.

Namib Desert
Okavango Delta
Makgadikgadi
Limpopo
Kalahari Desert
Orange
Vaal
Drakensberg
Great Karoo
Cape of Good Hope
C. Agulhas
Madagascar Basin
Ile Amsterdam
Ile St Paul
Perth Basin
Great Victoria Desert
Nullarbor Plain
Great Australian Bight
C. Leeuwin
AUSTRALIA
Musgrave Ranges
Lake Eyre
Darling
Murray
Mt Kosciuszko 2230
Lord Howe I.
Bass Strait
Tasman Sea
Tasmania
New Zealand
South Island
North Island
Aoraki 3754
Snares Is
Stewart I.
Chatham Is
Auckland Is
Antipodes Is
Bounty Is
Campbell I.
North C.

Agulhas Basin
Prince Edward Is
Iles Crozet
Crozet Basin
Iles Kerguélen
Heard I.
Southeast Indian Ridge
South Australian Basin
Macquarie I.

SOUTHERN OCEAN
-Antarctic Basin
Australian-Antarctic Basin
Davis Sea
Enderby Land
Kemp Land
Amery Ice Shelf
Wilkes Land
Ballery Is
Antarctic Circle
Ross Sea
Antarctic Mountains
ANTARCTICA

1:70 000 000

MILES   KILOMETRES
2400   4200
              3600
1800   3000
              2400
1200   1800
              1200
600   600
0   0

© Bartholomew Ltd

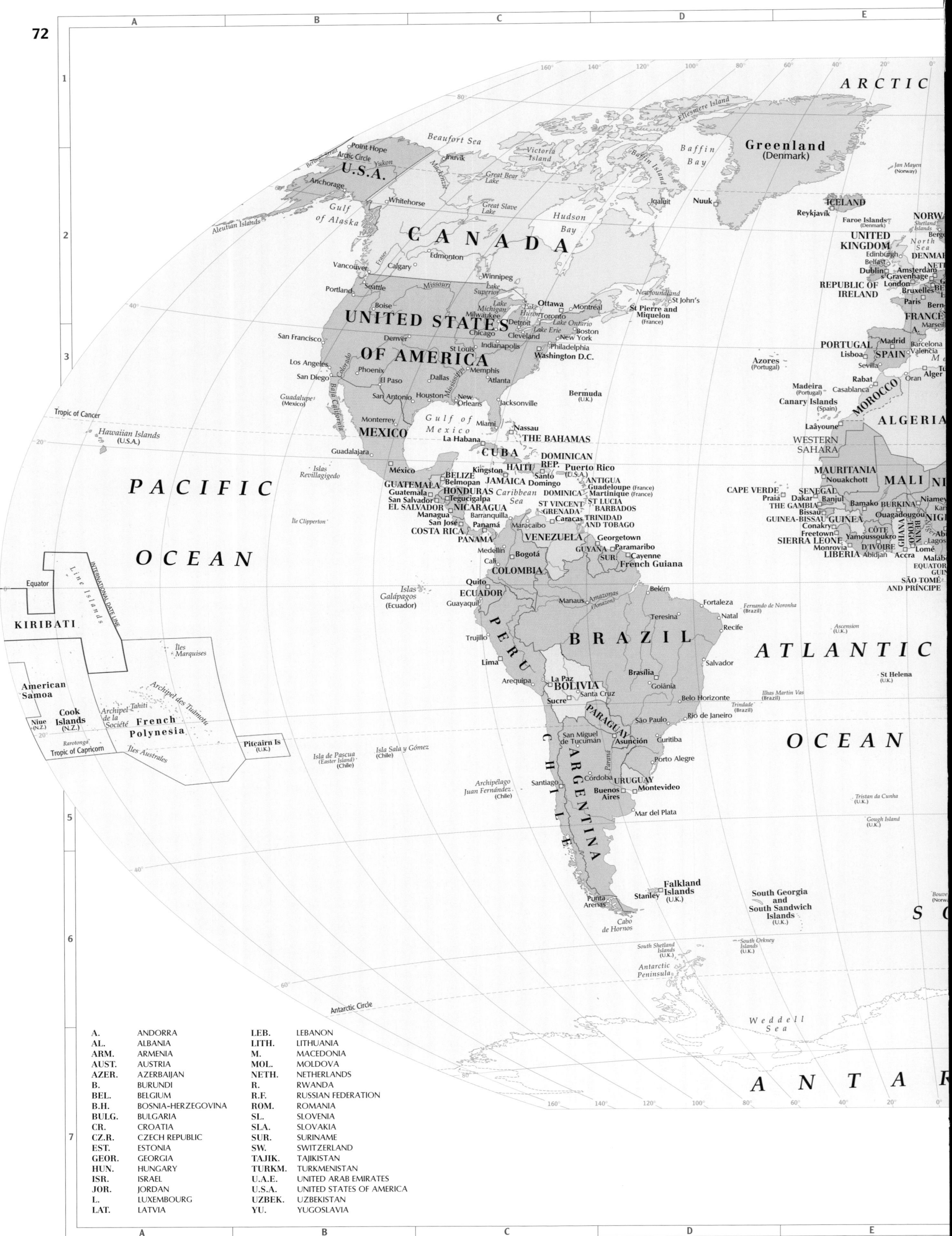

Winkel Tripel Projection

OCEAN

Zemlya Frantsa-Iosifa

Svalbard (Norway)

Barents Sea

Novaya Zemlya

Severnaya Zemlya

Arctic Circle

SWEDEN

FINLAND

Stockholm Helsinki

EST. Tallinn

Nizhniy Novgorod

Perm'

Yekaterinburg

Novosibirsk

Krasnoyarsk

Yakutsk

Bering Sea

Sea of Okhotsk

Aleutian Islands

RUSSIAN FEDERATION

Murmansk Arkhangel'sk

Yenisey

Ob'

Lena

Komsomol'sk-na-Amure

Riga LAT. Vilnius

LITH.

BELARUS Minsk

Moskva

Kazan'

Samara

Chelyabinsk

Omsk

Novokuznetsk

Irkutsk

Ozero Baykal

Khabarovsk

Vladivostok

Sapporo

Berlin POL. Warszawa

UKRAINE Kyiv

Kharkiv

Volgograd

KAZAKHSTAN

Astana

Karaganda

Ulaanbaatar

MONGOLIA

Yichun

Qiqihar

Harbin

Changchun

Shenyang

N. KOREA P'yŏngyang

Sendai

JAPAN

Praha SLK.

AUD. HUN. ROM.

SLN. Budapest

Bucureşti

MOL. Chişinău

Rostov-na-Donu

Krasnodar

Aral Sea

Bishkek

KYRGYZSTAN

Almaty

Ürümqi

Lanzhou

Beijing

Tianjin

Dalian

Jinan

S. KOREA Sŏul

Pusan

Tōkyō Yokohama

Kōbe Nagoya

Kyōto Ōsaka

Fukuoka

ITALY Roma

BUL.

GREECE Athina

Tirane

Skopje

Beograd

YUG.

Sofiya

İzmir

Istanbul

TURKEY

Ankara

Black Sea

GEOR. T'bilisi

ARM. AZER. Baki

Yerevan

Caspian Sea

Tashkent

UZBEK.

TURKM. Ashgabat

TAJIK. Dushanbe

Huang He

Xi'an

Nanjing

Chengdu

Chongqing

Wuhan

Shanghai

East China Sea

Ogasawara-shotō (Bonin Islands) (Japan)

PACIFIC

Kazan-rettō (Volcano Islands) (Japan)

Midway Islands (U.S.A.)

Tropic of Cancer

NISIA

CYPRUS

Lefkosia

SYRIA

LEB. Damascus

Beirut

Jerusalem

ISR.

JOR. Amman

Baghdad

IRAQ

Al Başrah

IRAN

Tehrān

Mashhad

Kābul

AFGHANISTAN

Islamabad

Lahore

CHINA

Lhasa

Chang Jiang

Kunming

Nanning

Guangzhou

Fuzhou

Macau Hong Kong

Zhanjiang

T'aipei

TAIWAN

Kaohsiung

OCEAN

Palermo

Tripoli

LIBYA

EGYPT

Alexandria

El Giza Cairo

Al Mawşil

Tabrīz

Eşfahān

Shīrāz

KUWAIT

BAHRAIN

QATAR

Riyadh

U.A.E.

Abu Dhabi

Muscat

OMAN

PAKISTAN

Karachi

Delhi

New Delhi

Jaipur

NEPAL Kathmandu

BHUTAN

Lucknow

Patna

BANGLADESH

Dhaka

Chittagong

Khulna

MYANMAR

Mandalay

LAOS

Ha Nôi

Hainan

South China Sea

Luzon

Quezon City

Manila

PHILIPPINES

Mindanao

Northern Mariana Islands (U.S.A.)

Guam (U.S.A.)

MARSHALL ISLANDS

Delap-Uliga-Djarrit

SAUDI ARABIA

Jeddah

Mecca

Red Sea

Nile

Khartoum

Asmara

San'ā'

Aden

YEMEN

Suquṭrā (Yemen)

Arabian Sea

Ahmadabad

Indore

Bhopal

Nagpur

Calcutta

INDIA

Mumbai

Pune

Faisalabad

Hyderabad

Bangalore

Chennai

Vijayawada

Andaman Islands (India)

Yangon

THAILAND

Bangkok

CAMBODIA

Phnum Pénh

VIETNAM

Hô Chi Minh

Viangchan

BRUNEI

Bandar Seri Begawan

Caroline Islands

Koror

PALAU

FEDERATED STATES OF MICRONESIA

Palikir

Bairiki Gilbert Islands

Equator

Yaren

NAURU

Kingsmill Group

KIRIBATI

Phoenix Islands

CHAD

Ndjamena

SUDAN

ERITREA

DJIBOUTI

Djibouti

ETHIOPIA

Ādīs Ābeba

SOMALIA

Muqdisho

Trivandrum

Sri Jayewardenepura Kotte

SRI LANKA

MALDIVES

Male

Medan

Kuala Lumpur

MALAYSIA

SINGAPORE

Padang

Sumatera

Borneo

Sulawesi

INDONESIA

Irian Jaya

New Guinea

PAPUA NEW GUINEA

Port Moresby

SOLOMON ISLANDS

Honiara

TUVALU

Vaiaku

Tokelau (N.Z.)

CENTRAL AFRICAN REPUBLIC

Yaoundé

Bangui

CONGO

DEM. REP. OF CONGO

Kinshasa

Brazzaville

UGANDA

Kampala

RWANDA Kigali

BURUNDI Bujumbura

KENYA

Nairobi

Lake Victoria

TANZANIA

Dodoma

Dar es Salaam

Victoria

SEYCHELLES

British Indian Ocean Territory

Cocos Islands (Australia)

Christmas Island (Australia)

Jakarta

Jawa

Palembang

Surabaya

Darwin

Wallis and Futuna Islands (France)

SAMOA

Apia

Luanda

ANGOLA

ZAMBIA

Lusaka

Lilongwe

MALAWI

MOZAMBIQUE

Harare

ZIMBABWE

Bulawayo

COMOROS

Moroni

Mayotte (France)

Antananarivo

MADAGASCAR

Port Louis

Réunion (France)

MAURITIUS

INDIAN

EAST TIMOR

Timor

Coral Sea

VANUATU

Port Vila

FIJI

Suva

TONGA

NEW Caledonia (France)

Nouméa

NAMIBIA

Windhoek

BOTSWANA

Gaborone

Pretoria

Johannesburg

Maputo

SWAZILAND Mbabane

Maseru LESOTHO

REPUBLIC OF SOUTH AFRICA

Durban

Cape Town

Cape Agulhas

OCEAN

Alice Springs

AUSTRALIA

Perth

Brisbane

Darling

Norfolk Island (Australia)

Lord Howe Island (Australia)

Kermadec Islands (N.Z.)

Tropic of Capricorn

Prince Edward Island (South Africa)

Îles Crozet

French Southern and Antarctic Lands

Îles Kerguélen

Heard Island (Australia)

Île Amsterdam

Île St Paul

Adelaide

Murray

Sydney

Canberra

Melbourne

Tasman Sea

Tasmania

Hobart

Auckland

North Island

NEW ZEALAND

Wellington

Christchurch

South Island

Dunedin

Chatham Islands (N.Z.)

SOUTHERN OCEAN

Snares Islands (N.Z.)

Bounty Islands (N.Z.)

Auckland Islands (N.Z.)

Antipodes Islands (N.Z.)

Macquarie Island (Australia)

Campbell Island (N.Z.)

Antarctic Circle

Ross Sea

ANTARCTICA

INTERNATIONAL DATE LINE

MILES KILOMETRES

2400 4200

3600

1800 3000

2400

1200 1800

1200

600 600

0 0

1:70 000 000

© Bartholomew Ltd

A B C D E

A S I A

Kuril'skiye Ostro

Hokkaidō

Sea of
Japan

Honshū

East
China
Sea

Ogasawara-shotō

Kyūshū

Shikoku

Nansei-shotō

Kazan-rettō

Pagan

Luzon Strait

Tinian *Saipan*

**Northern Mariana
Islands**
(U.S.A.)

Guam
(U.S.A.) **Hagåtña**

Rota

Luzon

Hainan

Luzon Strait

South China Sea

Ulithi *Fais*

Yap *Sorol* *Faraulep*

Ngulu *Eauripik*

C a r o l i n e   I s l a n d s

Pikelot *Hall Islands*

Chuuk

*Mortlo
Island*

Palawan

Sulu
Sea

Panay

Negros

Mindanao

Samar

Celebes
Sea

Palau Islands

FEDERATED STATE

Admiralty Islands *Mussau Island* *New Hanover*

New Irela

Bay
of Bengal

Gulf of
Thailand

Molucca
Sea

Halmahera

Vanimo
Wewak

Madang

Mt Wilhelm

Goroka

Bougain
Isla

Borneo

Makassar Strait

Sulawesi

New
Guinea

Lae

Kerema
PAPUA

So l o

Banda Sea

Balimo

Gulf
of Papua

Daru

NEW GUINEA

*Woodlar
Island*

*D'Entrecasteaux
Islands*

Strait of Malacca

Arafura Sea

Port
Moresby

Torres Strait

Louisiade Archipel

Sumatera

Flores Sea

Timor

Melville
Island

Wessel Islands

Cape Arnhem

Cape York

Great Barrier Reef

Coral Sea
Islands
Territory
(Australia)

Kepulauan Mentawai

Java
Sea

Sumbawa

Sumba

Flores

Gulf
of Carpentaria

Cape
York
Peninsula

Cora
Sea

Bali

Java (Jawa)

Timor Sea

Bathurst Island

Darwin

*Arnhem
Land*

*Groote
Eylandt*

Wellesley
Islands

Mitchell

Cooktown

Equator

Cape
Londonderry

Ashmore and Cartier
Islands
(Australia)

Cairns

Gilbert

Normanton

Christmas Island
(Australia)

Wyndham

Cape Lévêque

Broome

Halls
Creek

NORTHERN

TERRITORY

Mount Isa

Cloncurry

Townsville

Mackay

Rockhampton

Gladstone

I N D I A N

O C E A N

Port
Hedland

Great Sandy
Desert

Lake
Mackay

Mount Liebig
1524

Alice
Springs

QUEENSLAND

Longreach

Great Dividing

Fra
Isle

Cocos Islands
(Australia)

Karratha

Barrow Island

Newman

Lake
Disappointment

A U S T R A L I A

Charleville

Maryborou

Balonne

Darling

Brisban

North West Cape

Paraburdoo

WESTERN

Lake
Amadeus

Oodnadatta

Lake Eyre
(North)

Toowoomba
Gold Co

Meekatharra

AUSTRALIA

SOUTH

Grafton

Mount
Magnet

Leonora

Great Victoria

Desert

AUSTRALIA

NEW SOUTH

Tamworth

Woomera

Port Augusta

Broken Hill

Newcas

Geraldton

Lake
Moore

Kalgoorlie

Ceduna

Whyalla

Port Pirie

Orange

WALES

Lithgow

Lachlan

Wagga Wagga

A.C.T.

Sydney

Wollongon

Great

Australian

Bight

Port Lincoln

Adelaide

Murray

Albury
Bendigo

Canberra

Esperance

Cape Carnot

Kangaroo
Island

VICTORIA

Melbourne

Perth

Geelong

Fremantle

Bunbury

Mount Gambier

Bass Strait

Flinders Island

Albany

Cape Leeuwin

King Island

Devonport

Launceston

S O U T H E R N   O C E A N

TASMANIA

Hobart

*South East
Cape*

Tropic of Capricorn

A B C D E

60° 30° 75° 90° 45° 105° 120° 135° 150°

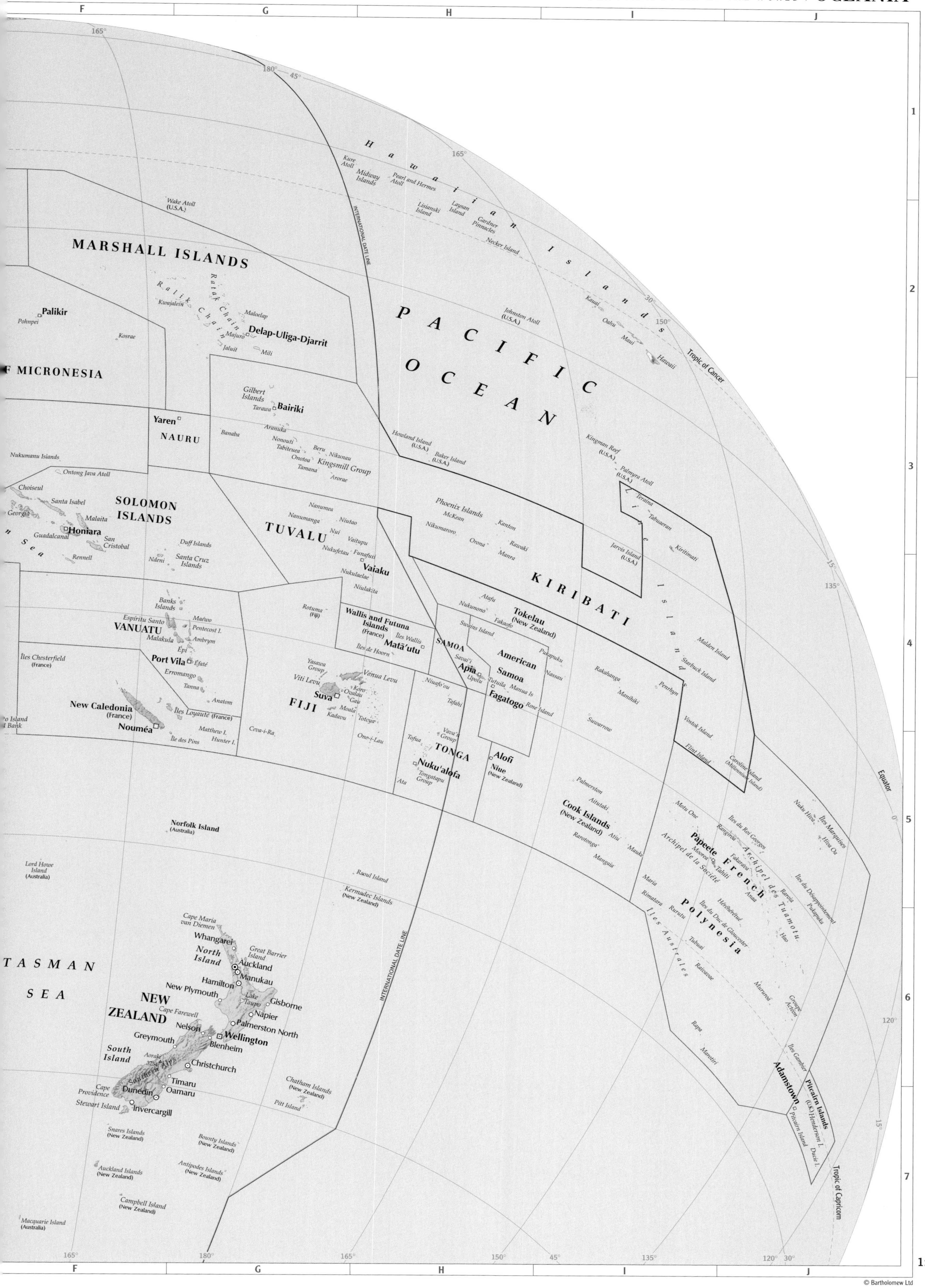

F   G   H   I   J

165°   180°   45°   165°   150°

H a w a i i a n   I s l a n d s

Kure Atoll   Midway Islands   Pearl and Hermes Atoll
Lisianski Island   Laysan Island   Gardner Pinnacles   Necker Island

MARSHALL ISLANDS

Wake Atoll (U.S.A.)

Ralik Chain   *Ratak Chain*
Kwajalein   Maloelap
Delap-Uliga-Djarrit
Majuro
Jaluit   Mili

Palikir
Pohnpei
Kosrae

PACIFIC

Johnston Atoll (U.S.A.)

Kauai   Oahu
Maui   Hawaii

Tropic of Cancer

F MICRONESIA

OCEAN

Gilbert Islands
Tarawa   **Bairiki**

Yaren
NAURU
Banaba   Aranuka
Nonouti   Howland Island (U.S.A.)
Tabiteuea   Beru   Nikunau   Baker Island (U.S.A.)
Onotoa   Kingsmill Group
Tamana   Arorae

Kingman Reef (U.S.A.)
Palmyra Atoll (U.S.A.)

Nukumanu Islands
Ontong Java Atoll

Choiseul   Santa Isabel
Georgia
Guadalcanal   **SOLOMON**
Malaita   **ISLANDS**
San Cristobal
Rennell

n Sea

P a c i f i c   I s l a n d s

Nanumea
Nanumanga   Niutao
Nui   Vaitupu   **TUVALU**
Nukufetau   Funafuti
Vaiaku
Nukulaelae
Niulakita

Duff Islands
Ndeni
Santa Cruz Islands

Phoenix Islands
McKean   Kanton
Nikumaroro   Rawaki
Orona   Manra

Teraina
Tabuaeran

Jarvis Island (U.S.A.)

Kiritimati

15°   135°

Banks Islands
Espíritu Santo   Maéwo
VANUATU   Pentecost I.
Malakula   Ambrym
Epi   Efaté
Port Vila
Erromango
Tanna   Anatom

Rotuma (Fiji)

Wallis and Futuna Islands (France)
Îles Wallis
Matā'utu
Îles de Hoorn

Atafu
Nukunono   **Tokelau**
Fakaofo   (New Zealand)

Swains Island

SAMOA
Savai'i
Apia
Upolu

American Samoa
Tutuila   Manua Is
Fagatogo   Rose Island

Pukapuka
Nassau

Suwarrow

Malden Island

Starbuck Island

Vostok Island

Flint Island

Caroline Island (Millennium Island)

KIRIBATI

Îles Chesterfield (France)

Yasawa Group
Viti Levu   Vanua Levu
Vanua Levu
Suva   Koro   Ovalau
Gau
Moala
Kadavu   Totoya

New Caledonia (France)
Nouméa
Îles Loyauté (France)
Matthew I.   Hunter I.
Île des Pins

Niuafo'ou
Tafahi
Niuatoputapu
Vava'u
Tofua   **TONGA**
Ata   **Nuku'alofa**
Tongatapu Group

Alofi
Niue (New Zealand)

Palmerston
Aitutaki

Cook Islands (New Zealand)
Atiu   Manuae
Rarotonga   Mauke
Mangaia

Maria

Mora One
Rangiroa   **Papeete   French**
Moorea   Tahiti
Archipel des Tuamotu
Faaiteva
Mehetia   **Archipel de la Société**
Hereheretue
Polynesia

Rimatara
Rurutu   Îles du Duc de Gloucester

Tubuai   Îles Australes
Raivavae

Îles Marquises
Nuku Hiva
Hiva Oa

Îles du Désappointement
Pukapuka   Hao

Rangahua
Actéon

Equator

120°

'o Island
d Bank

Ceva-i-Ra
Ono-i-Lau

FIJI

Île des Pins

Marutea

Gambier
Îles Gambier

TASMAN

SEA

Norfolk Island (Australia)

Lord Howe Island (Australia)

Raoul Island

Kermadec Islands (New Zealand)

INTERNATIONAL DATE LINE

Raga

Manoriri

15°

Cape Maria van Diemen
Whangarei
North Island
Great Barrier Island
Auckland
Hamilton   **Manukau**
New Plymouth
Cape Farewell   Lake Taupo   Gisborne
NEW   Napier
ZEALAND   Palmerston North
Nelson   **Wellington**
Greymouth   Blenheim
South Island
Aoraki
3724 ALPS
Southern Alps   Christchurch
Cape   Timaru
Providence   Oamaru
Dunedin
Stewart Island   Invercargill

Chatham Islands (New Zealand)

Pitt Island

Adamstown
Pitcairn Islands (U.K.) Henderson I.
Pitcairn Island   Ducie I.

Tropic of Capricorn

Snares Islands (New Zealand)

Bounty Islands (New Zealand)

Auckland Islands (New Zealand)

Antipodes Islands (New Zealand)

Macquarie Island (Australia)

Campbell Island (New Zealand)

165°   180°   165°   150°   45°   135°   120°   30°

F   G   H   I   J

MILES   KILOMETRES
1000

1500

750   1250

1000

500   750

250   500

250

0   0

1:27 000 000

© Bartholomew Ltd

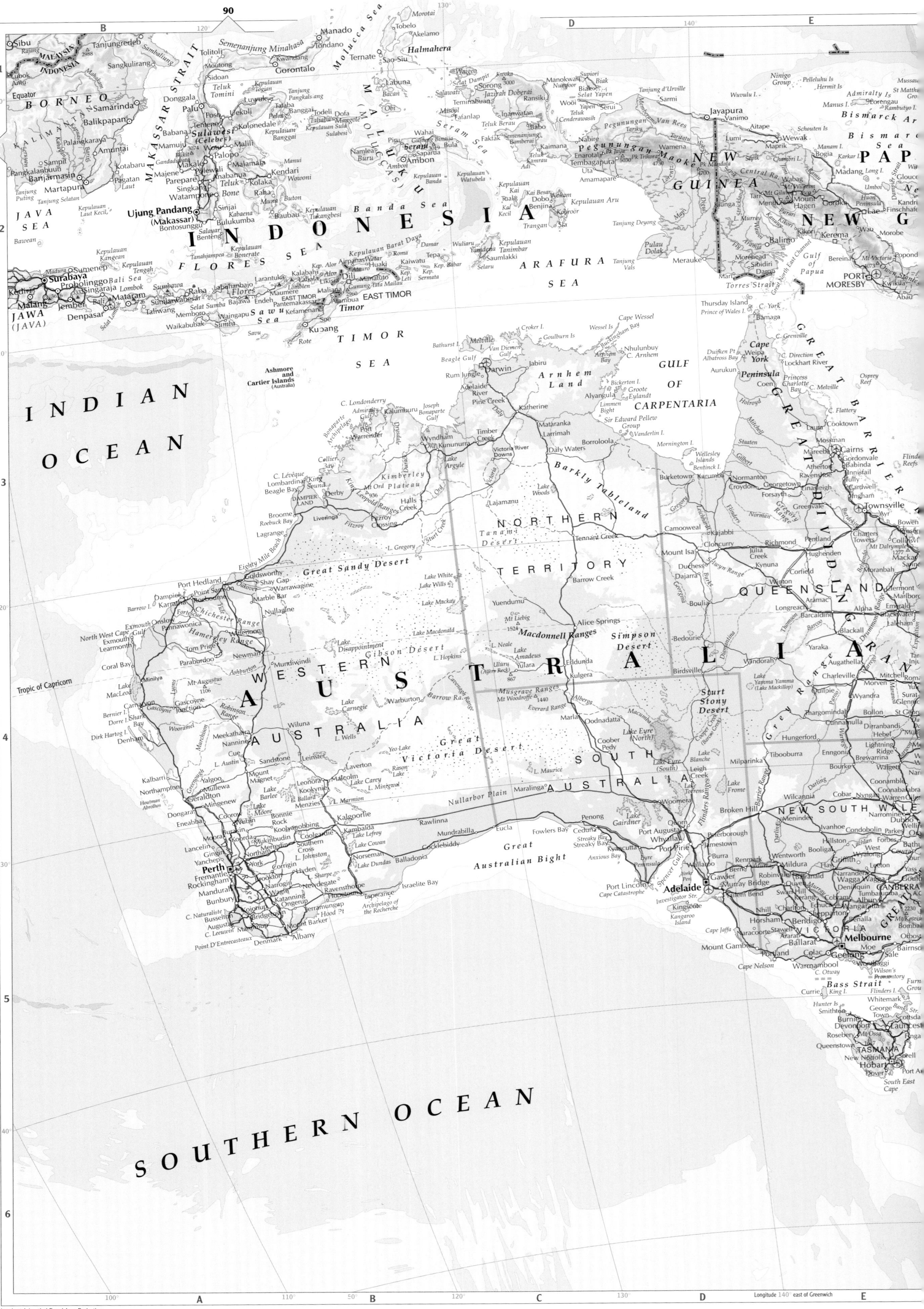

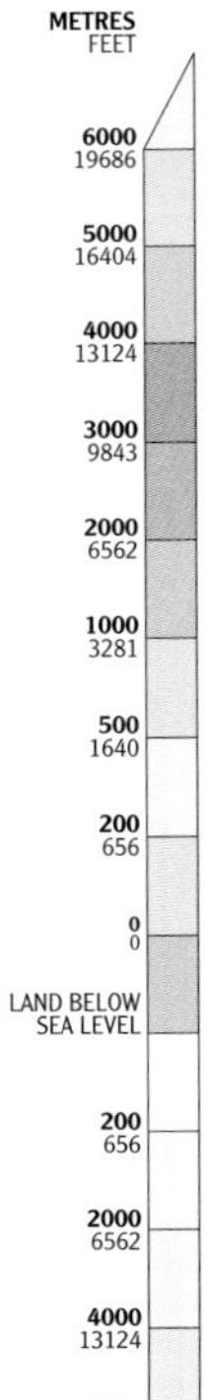

90

B 120° D 140° E

BORNEO

KALIMANTAN

MALAYSIA
INDONESIA

Equator

MAKASSAR STRAIT

MOLUCCA SEA

Halmahera

INDONESIA

SULAWESI
(Celebes)

Ujung Pandang
(Makassar)

JAVA SEA

Surabaya

JAWA
(JAVA)

BANDA SEA

FLORES SEA

Flores

EAST TIMOR

Timor

Kupang

SERAM SEA

NEW GUINEA

Jayapura

PEGUNUNGAN MAOKE

ARAFURA SEA

Merauke

PAPUA NEW G

BISMARCK SEA

PORT MORESBY

Gulf of Papua

Torres Strait

INDIAN OCEAN

TIMOR SEA

Ashmore and Cartier Islands
(Australia)

Darwin

Arnhem Land

GULF OF CARPENTARIA

Kimberley

Broome

NORTHERN TERRITORY

Tanami Desert

Great Sandy Desert

Gibson Desert

Tennant Creek

Alice Springs

Macdonnell Ranges

Simpson Desert

Tropic of Capricorn

WESTERN AUSTRALIA

AUSTRALIA

Great Victoria Desert

Musgrave Ranges

SOUTH AUSTRALIA

Lake Eyre

Sturt Stony Desert

GREAT DIVIDING RANGE

QUEENSLAND

Townsville

Cairns

Cape York Peninsula

GREAT BARRIER REEF

Mount Isa

Nullarbor Plain

Great Australian Bight

Kalgoorlie

Perth

Fremantle

Albany

Esperance

NEW SOUTH WALES

Broken Hill

Port Augusta

Adelaide

VICTORIA

Melbourne

Geelong

CANBERRA

Murray

BASS STRAIT

TASMANIA

Hobart

SOUTHERN OCEAN

METRES / FEET

6000 / 19686
5000 / 16404
4000 / 13124
3000 / 9843
2000 / 6562
1000 / 3281
500 / 1640
200 / 656
0
LAND BELOW SEA LEVEL
200 / 656
2000 / 6562
4000 / 13124
6000 / 19686

Lambert Azimuthal Equal Area Projection

100° A 110° B 120° C 130° D Longitude 140° east of Greenwich E

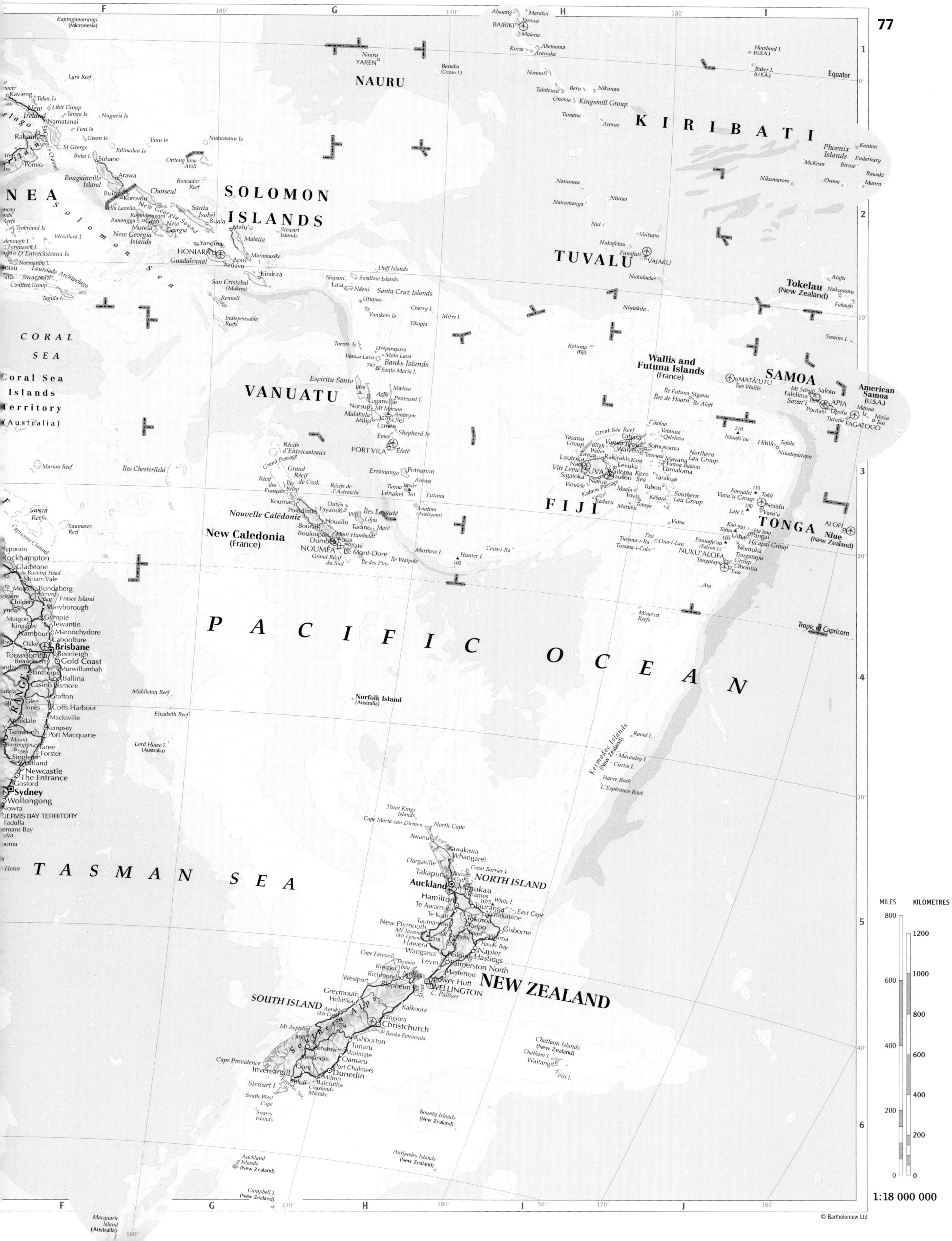

Kapingamarangi (Micronesia)

Abaiang Marakei
BAIRIKI Tarawa
Maiana

Howland I. (U.S.A.)

Lyra Reef

Nauru YAREN

Banaba (Ocean I.)

Kuria Abemama
Aranuka

Baker I. (U.S.A.)

Equator

NAURU

Nonouti

Tabiteuea Beru Nikunau
Onotoa Kingsmill Group
Tamana

Kaping

New Ireland
Tabar Is.
Lihir Group
Tanga Is.
Namatanai
Feni Is.
Green Is.
C. St George
Rabaul
Pomio

Buka I.
Sohano
Korovou Arawa
Bougainville Island
Buin
Choiseul

Nuguria Is.

Tauu Is.

Nukumanu Is.

Ontong Java Atoll

Roncador Reef

Arorae

K I R I B A T I

Phoenix Islands

Kanton
Enderbury
McKean Birnie Rawaki
Orona Manra

Nikumaroro

NEA

Trobriand Is.
Woodlark I.
Fergusson I.
D'Entrecasteaux Is
Normanby I.
Louisiade Archipelago
Conflict Group
Tagula I.

Kavieng

Vella Lavella
New Georgia
Kolombangara Gizo
Ranongga Munda
New Georgia Islands
Yandina

Bella Lavella
Santa Isabel
Buala

Malu'u
Stewart Islands
Malaita

HONIARA
Guadalcanal
Apio
Avuavu

Kirakira
San Cristobal (Makira)

Rennell

Maramasike

SOLOMON ISLANDS

Nupani
Lata Ndeni
Utupua

Swallow Islands
Santa Cruz Islands

Cherry I.
Mitre I.

Duff Islands

Nanumea

Nanumanga

Niutao

Nui

Nukufetau
Vaitupu

Atafu

Nukunonu

T U V A L U

Funafuti
VAIAKU

Nukulaelae

Niulakita

Tokelau (New Zealand)

Fakaofo

Swains I.

C O R A L
S E A

Coral Sea Islands Territory (Australia)

Marion Reef

Îles Chesterfield

Vanikoro Is.
Tikopia

Torres Is.
Vanua Lava
Santa María I.
Banks Islands
797

Uréparapara
Mota Lava

Espíritu Santo

Aoba
Luganville Pentecost I.
1879 Mt Murum
Maéwo

V A N U A T U

Norsup Ambrym
Malakula Ulei
Milip Lamen
Shepherd Is.

Rotuma (Fiji)

Emaé
FORT VILA Efaté

Wallis and Futuna Islands (France)

MATÁ'UTU
Îles Wallis

Île Futuna Sigave
Îles de Hoorn Île Alofi

S A M O A

Mt Silisili Safotu
Falelima Safata
Savai'i Apia
Poutasi Upolu

American Samoa (U.S.A.)

Manua
Tutuila FAGATOGO
Maia
Tau

Récifs d'Entrecasteaux

Grand Passage
Grand Récif de Cook
Récifs de Belep
Récifs de l'Astrolabe

Koumac
Poindimié Fayaoué
Ouvéa Lifou
Bourail Houailou
Bouloupari Tadine Maré
Dumbéa Mont Dore
NOUMÉA Yaté
Grand Récif du Sud
Île des Pins

Erromango

Potnarvin

Anatom (Aneityum)

Tanna Yasur
Lénakel 361 Futuna

Nouvelle Calédonie

New Caledonia (France)

Amiva

Matthew I.

Île Walpole

Ceva-i-Ra

Hunter I.
100

Great Sea Reef

Yasawa Group
Lautoka Ba Rakiraki Koro
Viti Levu Nadi Levuka
Sigatoka SUVA Nausori
Vatulele
Kadavu
Kadavu Passage

Vanua Levu
Water
Somosomo
Taveuni
Mavana
Vanua Balavu
Tomaloma

Cikobia
Vetaua
Qelelevu

Northern Lau Group

210

Fulaga

Southern Lau Group

Moala
Totoya
Matuku

Tubou
Kabara

Tuvana-i-Ra
Tuvana-i-Colo

Ono-i-Lau

Niuafo'ou Tafahi
Hihifo Niuatoputapu

F I J I

Vatoa

Vava'u Group
Fonualei Tokú
Neiafu
Late 150

Kao 500 Tofua
Nomuka
NUKU'ALOFA Ha'apai Group
Tongatapu Nomuka
Ohonua
Eua

T O N G A

ALOFI
Niue (New Zealand)

Fonuafo'ou (Falcon I.)

Ata

Minerva Reefs

Tropic of Capricorn

P A C I F I C   O C E A N

Yeppoon
Rockhampton
Gladstone
Bustard Head
Miriam Vale
Bundaberg
Hervey Bay Fraser Island
Childers
Maryborough
Murgon Gympie
Kingaroy Tewantin
Nambour Maroochydore
Oakey Caboolture
Toowoomba Beenleigh
Brisbane
Gold Coast
Beaudesert Murwillumbah
Stanthorpe Ballina
Warialda Casino Lismore
Glen Innes Grafton
Inverell Coffs Harbour
Armidale Macksville
Tamworth Kempsey
Mount Port Macquarie
Barrington Taree
1585 Forster
Singleton Maitland
Newcastle
The Entrance
Gosford
Sydney
Wollongong
Nowra
JERVIS BAY TERRITORY
Ulladulla
Batemans Bay
Bega

Middleton Reef

Elizabeth Reef

Norfolk Island (Australia)

Lord Howe I. (Australia)

Kermadec Islands (New Zealand)
Raoul I.
Macauley I.
Curtis I.
Havre Rock
L'Espérance Rock

T A S M A N   S E A

Howe

Three Kings Islands

Cape Maria van Diemen
North Cape
Awanui
Kaitaia
Kaikohe Kawakawa
Dargaville Whangarei
Takapuna Warkworth
Auckland Great Barrier I.
Manukau Hauraki Gulf
Thames
Hamilton 1075 White I.
Te Awamutu Tauranga East Cape
Te Kuiti Rotorua Whakatane
Taumarunui Tokoroa Gisborne
New Plymouth Taupo
Mt Taranaki Wairoa
(Mt Egmont) Hawke Bay
2518 Napier
Hawera Hastings
Wanganui Palmerston North
Levin Masterton
Feilding
Lower Hutt
WELLINGTON
C. Palliser

NORTH ISLAND

Cape Farewell
Tasman Bay
Riwaka
Westport Nelson Blenheim
Greymouth Picton
Hokitika

Mt Aspiring

Cape Providence
Invercargill
Stewart I.
South West Cape

Kangiora
Christchurch
Banks Peninsula

Ashburton
Timaru
Waimate
Oamaru
Port Chalmers
Dunedin
Balclutha
Milton

Queenstown
Alexandra
Gore
Bluff

SOUTH ISLAND

Mt Cook
Aoraki

Kaikoura

N E W   Z E A L A N D

Chatham Islands (New Zealand)
Chatham I.
Waitangi
Pitt I.

Bounty Islands (New Zealand)

Snares Islands

Auckland Islands (New Zealand)

Antipodes Islands (New Zealand)

Campbell I. (New Zealand)

Macquarie Island (Australia)

MILES KILOMETRES

800
1200
600
1000
800
400
600
200
400
200
0

1:18 000 000

© Bartholomew Ltd

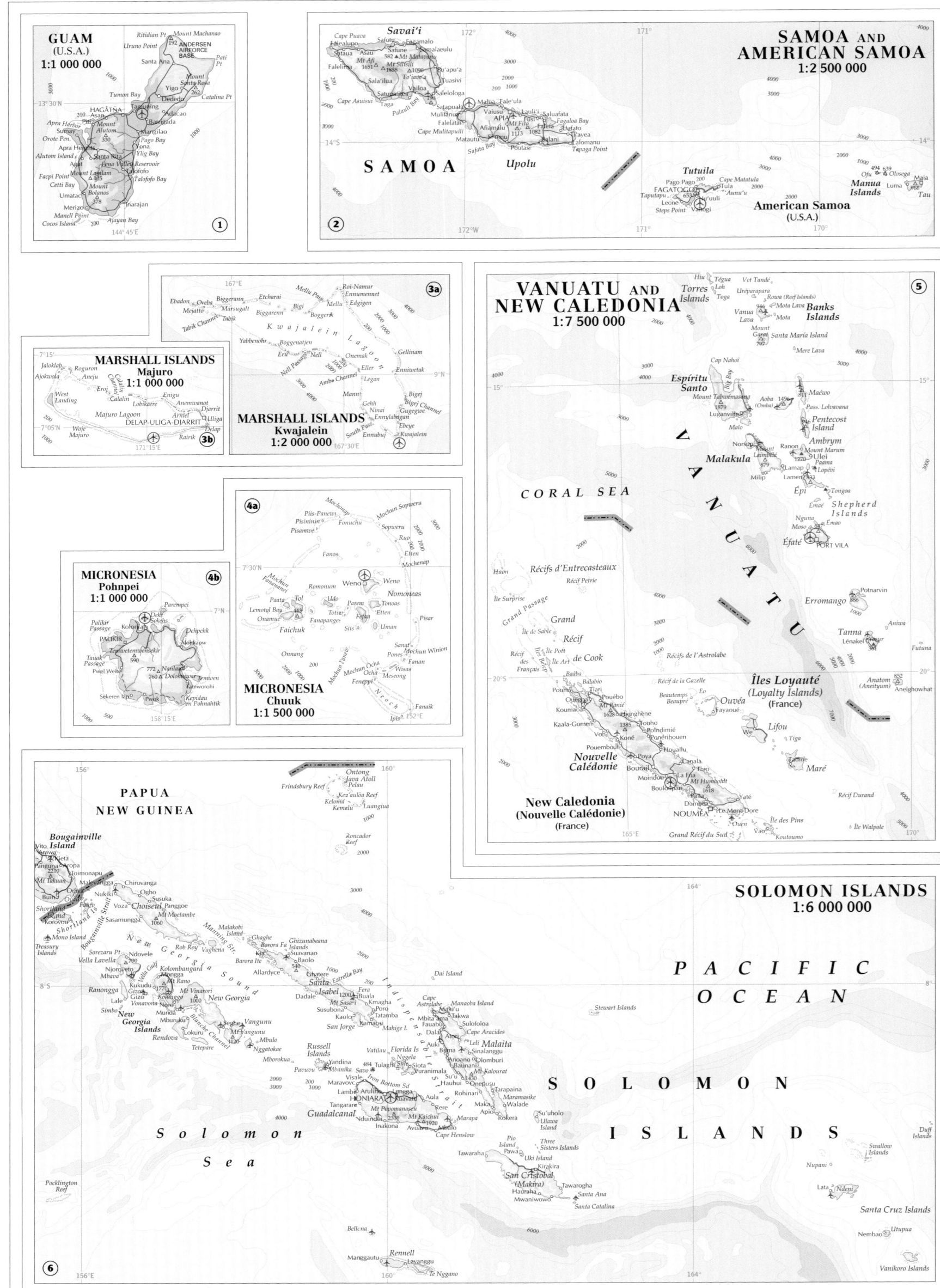

GUAM
(U.S.A.)
1:1 000 000

Ritidian Pt   Mount Machanao
Uruno Point   192   Mount
ANDERSEN
AIR FORCE
BASE
Santa Ana   Pati
Pt
Mount
Santa Rosa
HAGÅTÑA   Yigo   262   Catalina Pt
Dededo
Barrigada
Mangilao
Apra Harbor   Asan   Mount   Yona   Pago Bay
Sumay   Alutom   330   Yona
Orote Pen.   Santa Rita
Apra Heights   Fena Valley
Alutom Island   Agat   Reservoir
Facpi Point   Mount Lamlam   Talofofo   Talofofo Bay
Cetti Bay   405   Mount
Umatac   Bolanos   Inarajan
Merizo   378   Ajayan Bay
Manell Point
Cocos Island

① ②

SAMOA AND
AMERICAN SAMOA
1:2 500 000

Savai'i
Cape Puava   Safotu   Fanamalo
Asau   Safune   Samalaeulu
Sataua   582 ▲ Mt Mafane
Falelima   1651   1858   Mt Silisili   1090
Sala'ilua   Satupa'itea   Salelologa   Fa'apu'a'a
Cape Asuisui   Taga   Palauli Bay   Mulifanua   Vaiusu   Laulii   Saluafata
Cape Multapuili   Apia   Falelatai   Mt Fito   Fagaloa Bay
Mataatu   Afiamalu   1103   Foleta   Lalomanu
Safata Bay   Poutasi   Lufilufi   Lalomanu
Upolu   Tiapaga Point

SAMOA

Tutuila
Pago Pago   200   Cape Matatula
FAGATOGO   Tula   Aunu'u
Taputapu   653   Aunu'u
Leone   Nu'uuli
Steps Point   Vailogi

American Samoa
(U.S.A.)

Ofu   494 639   Olosega
Manua   Maia
Islands   Luma ♦ Tau

③a

167°E
Ebadon   Oreba   Etcharai   Mellu Pass
Mejatto   Marsugalt   Bigi   Roi-Namur
Tabik Channel   Biggarenn   Boggenen   Ennumennet
Tabik   Biggarenn   Edgigen
Kwajalein   Lagoon
Yabbonohr   Boggenatjen
Eniwetak
Erid   Nell   Gellinam
Nell Passage   Nell   Onemak   Eller   Ennwetak
Amba Channel   Legan
Mann
Gehh   Bigej
Bigej Channel
Guegegwe
Ninai   Ennylabegan   Ebeye
South Pass   Ebeye
Ennubuj   ✈ Kwajalein

MARSHALL ISLANDS
Majuro
1:1 000 000

7°15'   Jaloklab   Roguron   Aneju
Ajokwola   Eroj   Calalin
Lobikaere   Enigu
Majuro Lagoon   Arniel   Anemwanot   Djarrit
Uliga   Uliga
200   DELAP-ULIGA-DJARRIT
7°05'N   Woje   Delap
Majuro   Rairik   ✈

171°15'E   ③b

MARSHALL ISLANDS
Kwajalein
1:2 000 000

167°30'E

④a
Mochonap
Piis-Panewu   Mochun Sopweru
Pisininin   Fonuchu
Pisamwe   Sopweru   200
Fanos   Ruo   300   500
Etten   100
Mochenap
7°30'N   Mochun
Fonuabu   Romanum   Weno   Weno
Paata   Udo   ✈   Nomoneas
Lemotol Bay   Tol   443   Parem   Tonoas
Onamue   Totiw   Fefan   'Etten
Faichuk   Fanapanges   Siis   Uman
Onnang   Sanat   Mochun Winion
Neoch   Ponés   Fanan
Wisas   Meseong
3000   1000   Fenéppi
1000   200
Mochun Ocha   Ocha
Ipis   152°E   Fanaik

MICRONESIA
Pohnpei
1:1 000 000

Parempei
Palikir   Dekt
Passage   Sokehs
Kolonia   ✈
PALIKIR   Delpelk
Tauak   Temwetemwensekir   Alohkapw
Passage   590
772   Nanlaud
Pwel Weite   760 ▲ Dolohmwar   Temtem
Sekeren Iapi   Tamworohi
Kepidau   en Pohnahtik
Pwok

158°15'E

MICRONESIA
Chuuk
1:1 500 000

④b

VANUATU AND
NEW CALEDONIA
1:7 500 000

Hiu Tégua   Vot Tandé
Torres   Loh   Uréparapara
Islands   Toga   Rowa (Reef Islands)
Vanua   Mota Lava   Banks
Lava   Mota   Islands
Mount   Santa María Island
Gaua   745
Mere Lava

Cap Nahoi
Espíritu
Santo   Maéwo
Mount Tabwémasana   Aoba   1496
1879   Luganville   (Ombi)
Malo   Pentecost
Island
Norsup   Ambrym
Lakatoro   Ranon
Laïmbele   Mount Marum
Malakula   Ilei   1270   Paama
Lamap ♦   Lopévi
Milip   Lamen   Épi
Tongoa
Émaé   Shepherd
Islands
Nguna   Emao
Moso   Éfaté
Récifs d'Entrecasteaux   ✈   PORT VILA
Récif Petrie

CORAL SEA

VANUATU

Huon   Ile Surprise   Erromango   Potnarvin
Grand Passage   Grand   Récif   Aniwa
Ile de Sable   Récif   Tanna
Ile Pott   Récifs de l'Astrolabe   Lénakel
Récif   Ile Art   de Cook   Futuna
des   Français   Baaba
Poum   Balabio   Récif de la Gazelle   Anatom
Pouébo   (Aneityum)   852
Ouégoa   Mt Panié   Beautemps   Eo   Anelghowhat
Koumac   1628   Beaupré   Ouvéa
Kaala-Gomen   Hienghène   Fayaoué
Voh   1385   Touho   We   Lifou   Îles Loyauté
Koné   Poindimié   Tiga   (Loyalty Islands)
Ponérihouen   Maré   (France)
Pouembout   Poya   Houaïlou
Bourail   Thio   Lifou
Moindou   Canala
Boulouparis   Mt Humboldt   Yaté   Récif Durand
Païta   1618   Île Ouen
NOUMÉA   Dumbéa   Île Mont-Dore
Île des Pins
Grand Récif du Sud   Vao   Île Walpole
Koutoumo

Nouvelle
Calédonie

New Caledonia
(Nouvelle Calédonie)
(France)

⑤

PAPUA
NEW GUINEA

156°   Ontong   160°
Java Atoll
Frindsbury Reef   Pelau   Kea'auloa Reef
Kelonia
Kemelu   Luangiua

Bougainville   Zoncador
Island   Reef
Vito   Arawa
Panguna   Kieta
2210   Toimonapu   Chirovanga
Buin   Ogho   Ogho   Malenggaua
Shortland   Panggoe   Susuka
Island   Voza   Sasamungga   Mt Maetambe
Korovou   1060
Mono Island   Choiseul
Bougainville   Strait
Treasury   Malakobi
Islands   Island
Sorezaru Pt   Ghaghe   Ghizunabeana
Vella Lavella   Ndovele   Barora Fa   Islands
Njoroveto   200   Barora Ite   Suavanao
Mbava   Allardyce   Baolo
Ranongga   Vonavona   510   Estrella Bay   Dai Island
Kukudu   Mt Vinakuri   Fera   Buala   Cape   Manaoba Island
Gizo   Knungguru   1000   Dadale   Kmagha   Takwa
Simbo   New   Munda   Santa   Poro
Vonavona   Mt Sasari   Isabel   Tatamba   Auki
Rendova   Seghe   Vangunu   1230   San Jorge   Kaolo   Mahige I.   Dala   Sulufoloa
New   Lokuru   Mt Vangunu   Kamosti   Cape Aracides
Georgia   Tetepare   1120   Mbulo   Su'u   Kalourat
Islands   Ngatokae   Russell   Vatilau   Florida Is   Borna   Sinalanggu
Mborokua   Islands   Negela   Tulaghi   Siota   Su'u   Leli
484   Olomburi   Malaita
Yandina   Mbanika   Savo   Siota   Olombuti
Visale   Iron   Bottom Sd   Maravovo   Maravovo   Vuranimala   Hauhui   Onepusu
Lambi   Arulinga   485   Lunga   HONIARA   Ngavana   Rohinari   Marapa   Aola   Walade
Tangarare   250   ✈   Maka   Tarapaina   Maramasike   Su'uholo
Guadalcanal   Mt Kaichui   Ataa   Rokera   Ulawa
Nduindui   1920   Avuavu   Island
Inakona   Cape Henslow   Pio   Three
Sisters Islands
Tawaraha   Pawa   Uki Island
San Cristóbal   Tawarogha
(Makira)   Santa Ana
Haūraha   Santa Catalina
Mwaniwowo

Solomon
Sea

Pocklington
Reef

Bellona

Rennell
Kanggautu   Lavangu
Te Nggano

156°E   ⑥   160°

SOLOMON ISLANDS
1:6 000 000

164°

PACIFIC

OCEAN

Stewart Islands

SOLOMON

ISLANDS

Duff
Islands
Swallow
Islands

Nupani

Lata ♦ Ndeni

Santa Cruz Islands

Nerabao   Utupua

Vanikoro Islands

164°

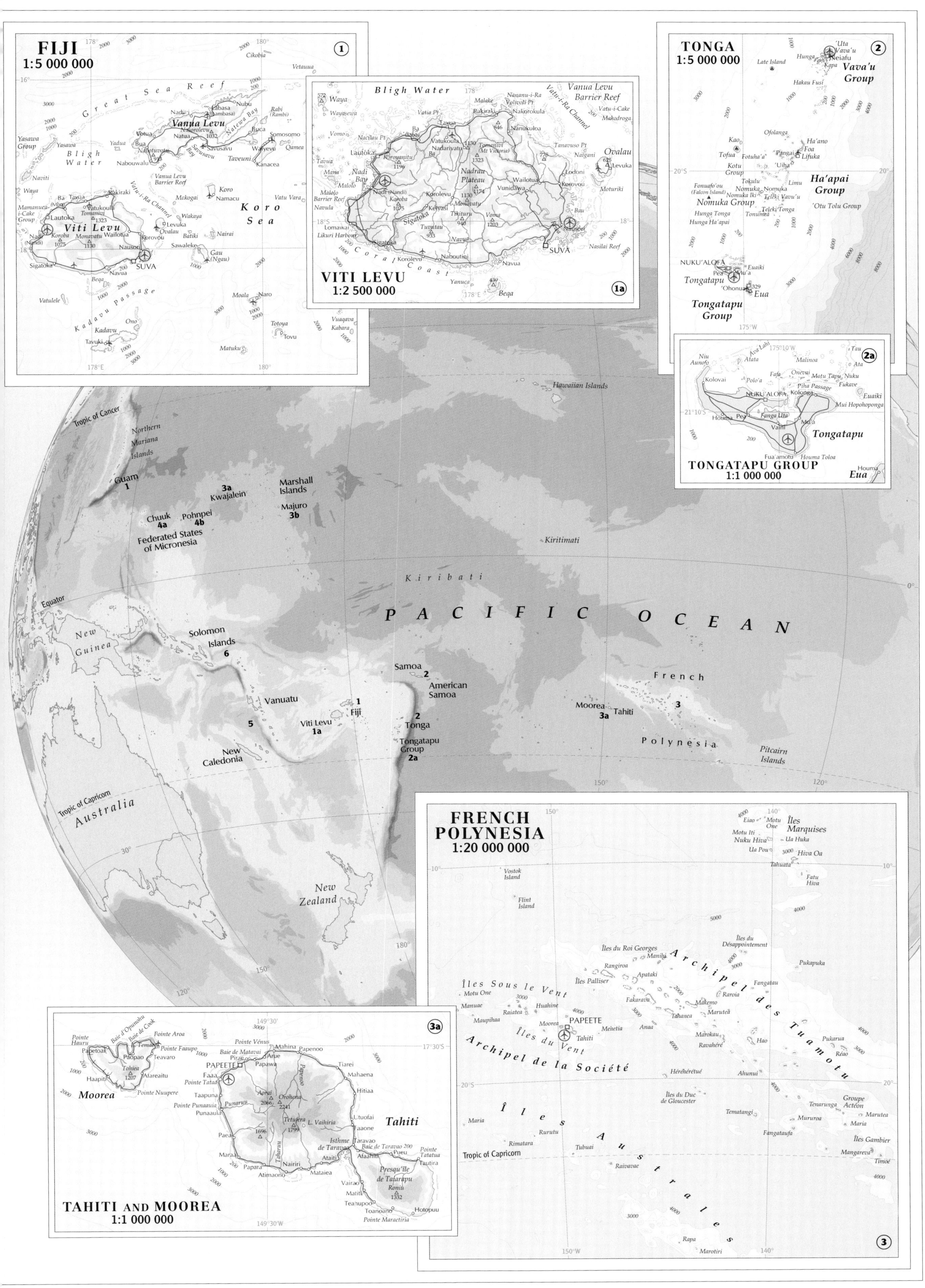

FIJI
1:5 000 000 ①

Great Sea Reef
Cikobia
Vetauua
Nubu
Nadi
Labasa (Lambasa)
Rabi (Rambi)
Vanua Levu
1032
Buca
Somosomo
Natewa Bay
Yasawa Group
Yasawa
Yadua
Votua
Bua
Nabouwalu
Savusavu
Taveuni
Kanacea
Bligh Water
Naviti
Waya
Wayasewa
Vanua Levu Barrier Reef
Mekogai
Koro
Namacu
Koro Sea
Vatu Vara
Mamanuca-i-Cake Group
Ba Tavua
Rakiraki
Tomanivi 1323
Wakaya
Ovalau
Levuka
Batiki
Nairai
Waya
Nadi Nandi 1075
Koroba
Monavatu Wailotua 1130
Korovou
Sawaleke
Gau (Ngau)
Vatulele
Sigatoka
Navua
SUVA
Beqa
1000
2000
Kadavu Passage
Vuaqava
Totoya
Tovu
Ono
Kadavu
Tavuki
Moala
Naro
Matuku
Kabara

Bligh Water
Waya
Wayasewa
Vomo
Malake
Nananu-i-Ra
Volivoli Pt
Vatu-i-Ra Channel
Vanua Levu Barrier Reef
Vatu-i-Cake
Nakorokula
Nacilau Pt
Tavua
Nadarivatu 1196
Tomaniivi (Mt Victoria) 1323
Nananu-i-Ra
Nakurokula
Tavanuso Pt
Naigani
Ovalau
625
Levuka
Lautoka
Koroyanitu Bd
Nadrau Plateau
Vunidawa
Lodoni
Korovou
Moturiki
Mana
Malolo
Nadi (Nandi)
Korolevu
1124
Naitasiri
Nausori
Bau
Malolo Barrier Reef
Navula
Keiyasi
1075
Monasavu
Thuturu
Tokituri
Vona 1203
SUVA
Lomawai
Sigatoka
Tuvatau 933
Nabouti
Lukuri Harbour
Korolevu
Coral Coast
Navua
Nasilai Reef
Yanuca
430
Moala
VITI LEVU
1:2 500 000 ①a

Coral Coast
Beqa

TONGA
1:5 000 000 ②

Late Island
Hunga
'Uta Vava'u
Neiafu
Kapa
Vava'u Group
Hakau Fusi
Kao
Ofolanga
Ha'ano
Tofua
Fotuha'a
Fangai
Foa
Lifuka
Kotu Group
'Uiha
Ha'apai Group
Fonuafo'ou (Falcon Island)
Nomuka
Tokulu
Limu
Nomuka Group
Nomuka Iki
Telekitonga
Telekivava'u
'Otu Tolu Group
Hunga Tonga
Tonumea
Hunga Ha'apai
NUKU'ALOFA
Euaiki
Pea Mu'a
Tongatapu
'Ohonua 329
'Eua
Tongatapu Group

TONGATAPU GROUP
1:1 000 000 ②a

Niu Auro'o
Ata Lahi
175°10'W
Tau
Ata
Kolovai
Polo'a
Fafa
Onevai
Malinoa
Motu Tapu
Nuku
Fukave
Piha Passage
NUKU'ALOFA
Kolonga
Euaiki
Houma
Pea
Fanga Uta
Mui Hopohoponga
Hoisina
Vaini
Ma'a
Tongatapu
Fua'amotu
Houma Toloa
Houma
'Eua

FRENCH POLYNESIA
1:20 000 000 ③

Eiao
Motu One
Îles Marquises
Motu Iti
Nuku Hiva
Ua Huka
Ua Pou
Hiva Oa
Tahuata
Fatu Hiva
Vostok Island
Flint Island
Îles du Roi Georges
Manihi
Archipel des Tuamotu
Rangiroa
Apataki
Pukapuka
Îles Sous le Vent
Îles Palliser
Fangatau
Motu One
Huahine
Fakarava
Raroia
Manuae
Raiatea
Makemo
Maupihaa
Moorea
Tahanea
Marutea
Anaa
PAPEETE
Meheetia
Tahiti
Marokau
Hao
Îles du Vent
Ravahere
Pukarua
Réao
Archipel de la Société
Hérehérétué
Ahunui
Îles du Duc de Gloucester
Groupe Actéon
Maria
Tenururunga
Marutea
Rimatara
Rurutu
Tubuai
Tematangi
Mururoa
Maria
Fangataufa
Îles Gambier
Mangareva
Timoe
Îles Australes
Raivavae
Rapa
Marotiri
Tropic of Capricorn

TAHITI AND MOOREA
1:1 000 000 ③a

Baie d'Opunohu
Pointe Aroa
Pointe Hauru
Baie de Cook
Pointe Vénus
Mahina
Papenoo
Papetoai
Temae
Pointe Faaupo
Baie de Matavai
Arue
Tiarei
Paopao
Teavaro
PAPEETE
Papawa
Pirae
Mahaena
Tohiea 1207
Mareaitu
Faaa
Haapiti
Moorea
Pointe Nuupere
Pointe Tataa
Punaauia
Orohena 2066
Aorai 2041
Hitiaa
Pointe Punanuia
Punaauia
Tetuera
L. Vaihiria
Utuofai
Tahiti
Paea
1696
1799
Maraa
Isthme de Taravao
Baie de Taravao
Taravao
Pointe Tatutira
Nairiri
Afaahiti
Pueu
Atimaono
Papara
Ataiti
Tautira
Mataiea
Presqu'île de Tafarapu
Ronui 1332
Matiti
Vairao
Teanupoo
Toahotu
Hotopuu
Pointe Maraetiria

(Main ocean map labels:)
Hawaiian Islands
Tropic of Cancer
Northern Mariana Islands
Guam 1
Marshall Islands
3a Kwajalein
Majuro 3b
Chuuk 4a
Pohnpei 4b
Federated States of Micronesia
Kiritimati
Kiribati
PACIFIC OCEAN
Equator
New Guinea
Solomon Islands 6
Samoa 2
American Samoa
French
Vanuatu
Viti Levu 1
Fiji
1a
Moorea Tahiti
3a 3
Polynesia
5
New Caledonia
Tonga 2
Tongatapu Group 2a
Pitcairn Islands
Tropic of Capricorn
Australia
New Zealand

© Bartholomew Ltd

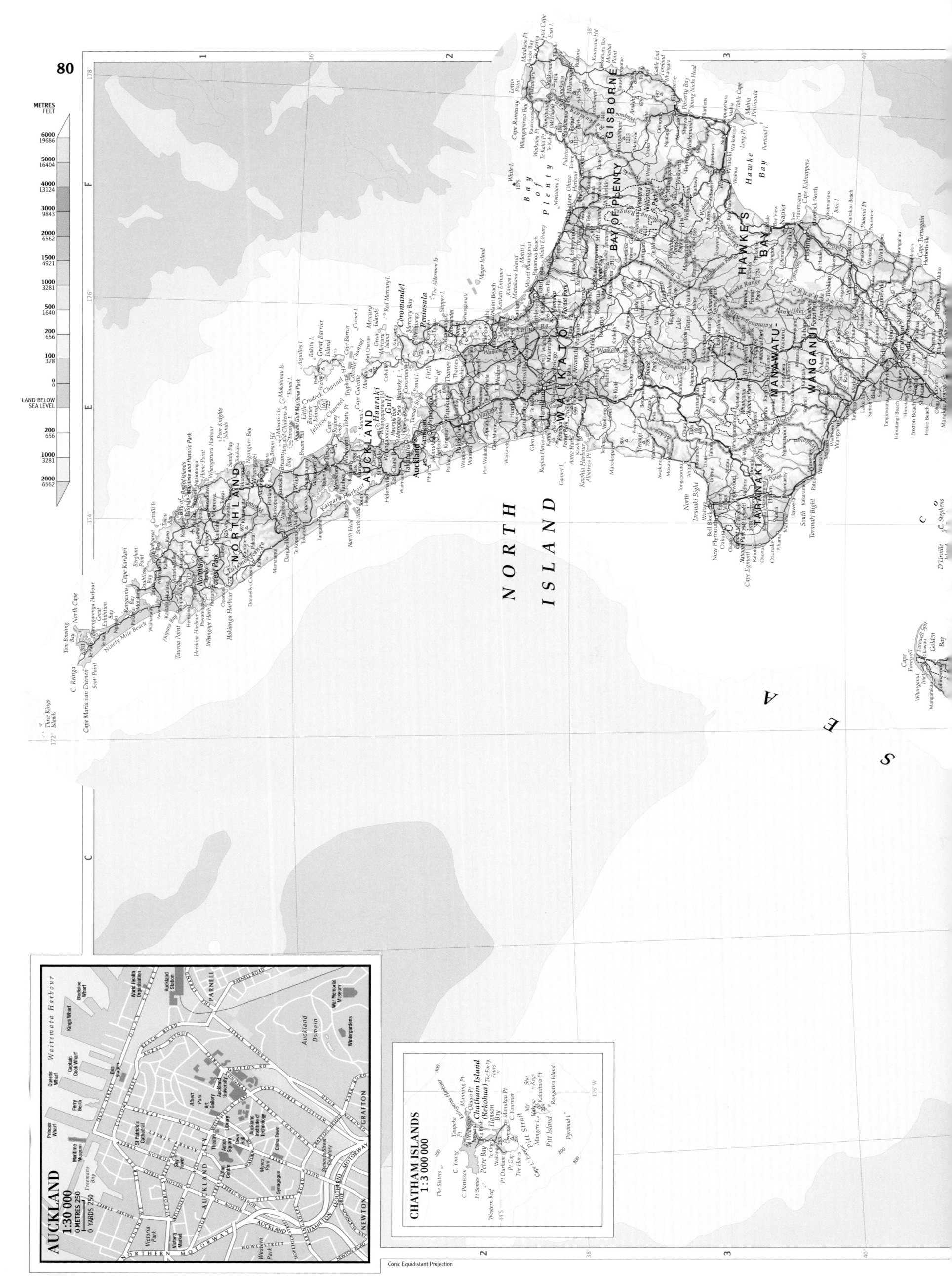

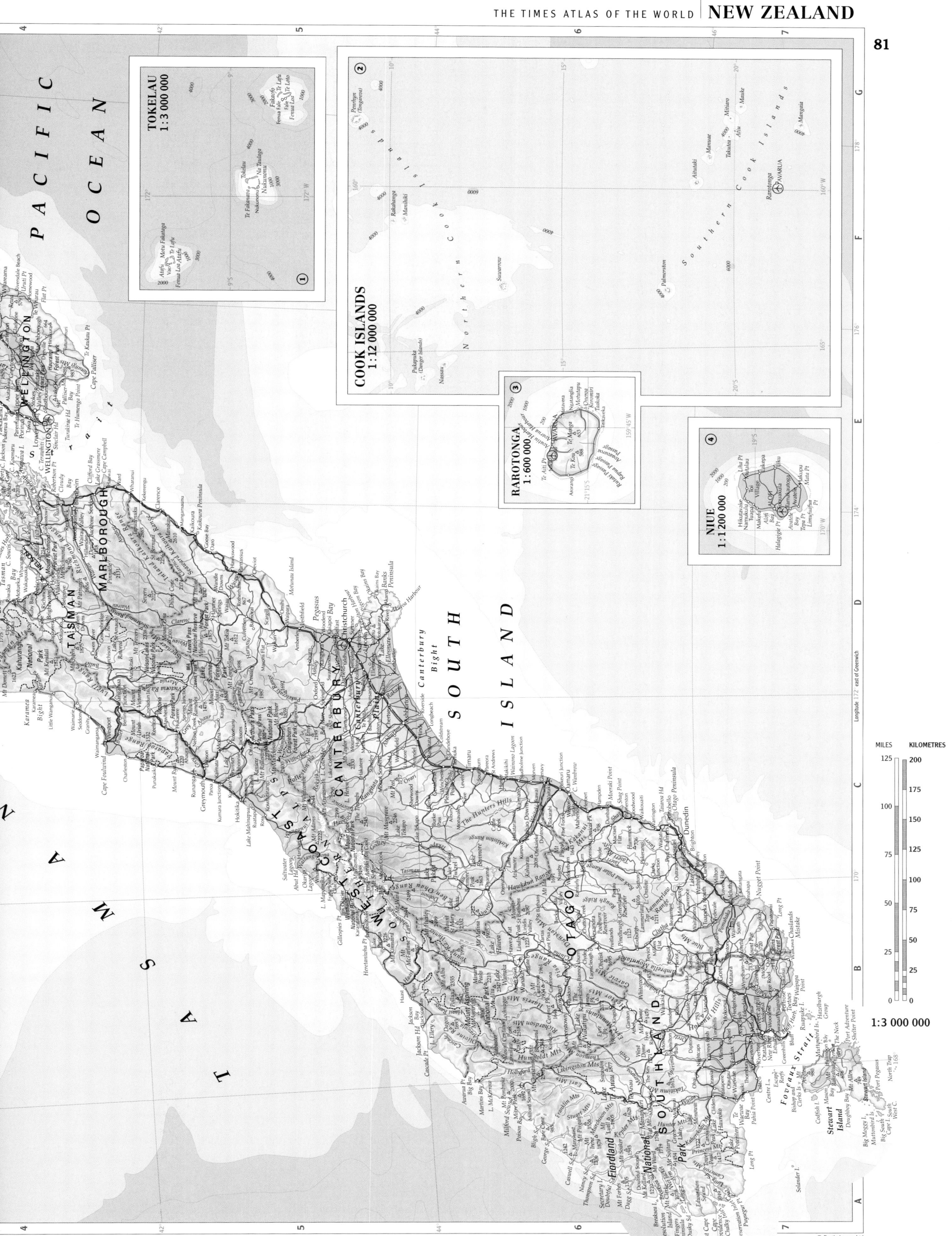

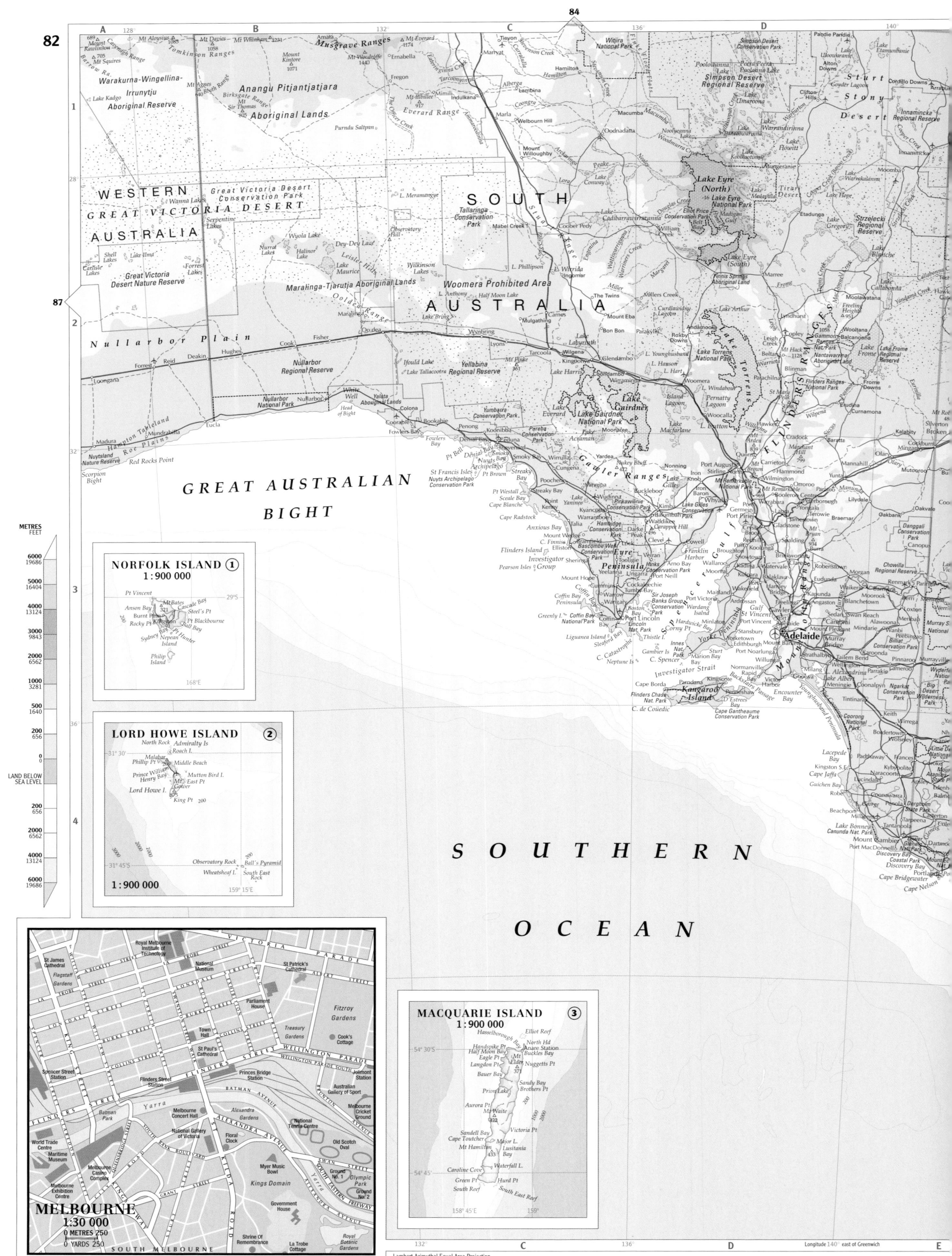

QUEENSLAND

NEW SOUTH WALES

VICTORIA

TASMANIA

Brisbane

Gold Coast

Tweed Heads

Melbourne

Geelong

Frankston

CANBERRA

AUSTRALIAN CAPITAL TERRITORY

Sydney

Parramatta

Campbelltown

Liverpool

Penrith

Hornsby

Newcastle

Wollongong

Port Kembla

Shellharbour

Kiama

The Entrance

Wyong

Gosford

Darling Downs

GREAT DIVIDING RANGE

GREY RANGE

NEW ENGLAND RANGE

KOSCIUSZKO NAT. PARK

T A S M A N   S E A

Bass Strait

King Island

Flinders Island

Furneaux Group

Kent Group

Banks Strait

Hobart

Launceston

Devonport

Burnie

MILES   KILOMETRES

250   400

200   350

300

150   250

200

100   150

100

50

50

0   0

1:6 000 000

SYDNEY
1:45 000

0 METRES 500

0 YARDS 500

Sydney Harbour

THE ROCKS

MILLERS POINT

Sydney Opera House

Government House

Royal Botanic Gardens

The Domain

Mrs Macquarie's Point

Farm Cove

Elizabeth Bay

WOOLLOOMOOLOO

DARLINGHURST

KINGS CROSS

PADDINGTON

SURRY HILLS

ULTIMO

Central Station

Sydney Football Stadium

CAHILL EXPRESSWAY

© Bartholomew Ltd

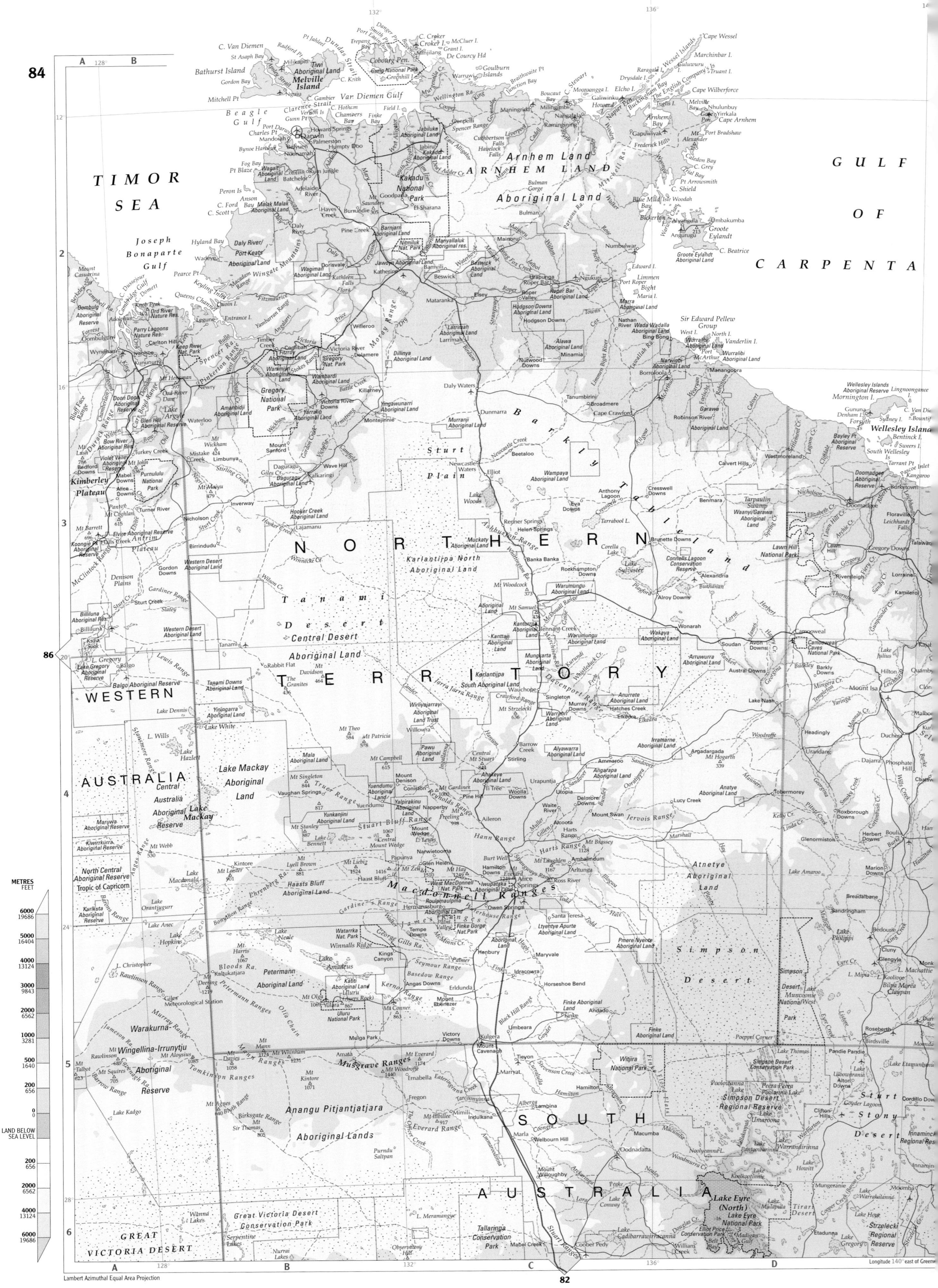

TIMOR SEA

GULF OF CARPENTARIA

Joseph Bonaparte Gulf

Arnhem Land
ARNHEM LAND
Aboriginal Land

Kakadu National Park

Tiwi Aboriginal Land
Melville Island
Bathurst Island

Darwin

Van Diemen Gulf

Groote Eylandt
Groote Eylandt Aboriginal Land

Sir Edward Pellew Group

Wessel Islands

Cape Arnhem

NORTHERN TERRITORY

WESTERN AUSTRALIA

Kimberley Plateau

Tanami Desert
Central Desert Aboriginal Land

Lake Mackay
Lake Mackay Aboriginal Land

Lake Amadeus

Macdonnell Ranges

Alice Springs

Simpson Desert

Tropic of Capricorn

Gregory National Park

Barkly Tableland

SOUTH AUSTRALIA

Musgrave Ranges

Anangu Pitjantjatjara Aboriginal Lands

Great Victoria Desert

Great Victoria Desert Conservation Park

Lake Eyre (North)

Sturt Stony Desert

Simpson Desert Regional Reserve

Lambert Azimuthal Equal Area Projection

Longitude 140° east of Greenwich

METRES / FEET
6000 / 19686
5000 / 16404
4000 / 13124
3000 / 9843
2000 / 6562
1000 / 3281
500 / 1640
200 / 656
0
LAND BELOW SEA LEVEL
200 / 656
2000 / 6562
4000 / 13124
6000 / 19686

CORAL SEA

PAPUA NEW GUINEA

Coral Sea Islands

Territory

CAPE YORK PENINSULA

GREAT DIVIDING RANGE

QUEENSLAND

GREAT BARRIER REEF

Great Barrier Reef Marine Park (Far North Section)

Great Barrier Reef Marine Park (Cairns Section)

Great Barrier Reef Marine Park (Central Section)

Great Barrier Reef Marine Park (Capricorn Section)

Cairns

Townsville

Mackay

Rockhampton

Gladstone

Bundaberg

Maryborough

Brisbane

Fraser Island

Tropic of Capricorn

Darling Downs

GREAT RANGE

MILES	KILOMETRES
250	400
200	350
	300
150	250
	200
100	150
50	100
	50
0	0

1:6 000 000

© Bartholomew Ltd

84

93

TIMOR SEA
INDIAN OCEAN
INDONESIA
NORTHERN TERRITORY
GREAT SANDY DESERT
Tanami Desert
Joseph Bonaparte Gulf
Kimberley Plateau
Melville Island
Bathurst Island
Darwin
Kakadu National Park
Van Diemen Gulf
Beagle Gulf
Ashmore and Cartier Islands (Australia)
Eighty Mile Beach
Port Hedland
Broome
Derby
Wyndham
Kununurra
Halls Creek
Fitzroy Crossing
Katherine
Dampier Archipelago
Hamersley Range
Lake Mackay
Lake Argyle
Rowley Shoals
Dampier Land
King Leopold Ranges
Gregory National Park
Bonaparte Archipelago
Buccaneer Archipelago
CHRISTMAS ISLAND 1
1:1 200 000
COCOS ISLANDS 2
1:1 200 000
METRES
FEET
6000 19686
5000 16404
4000 13124
3000 9843
2000 6562
1000 3281
500 1640
200 656
0 0
LAND BELOW SEA LEVEL
200 656
2000 6562
4000 13124
6000 19686
Lambert Azimuthal Equal Area Projection

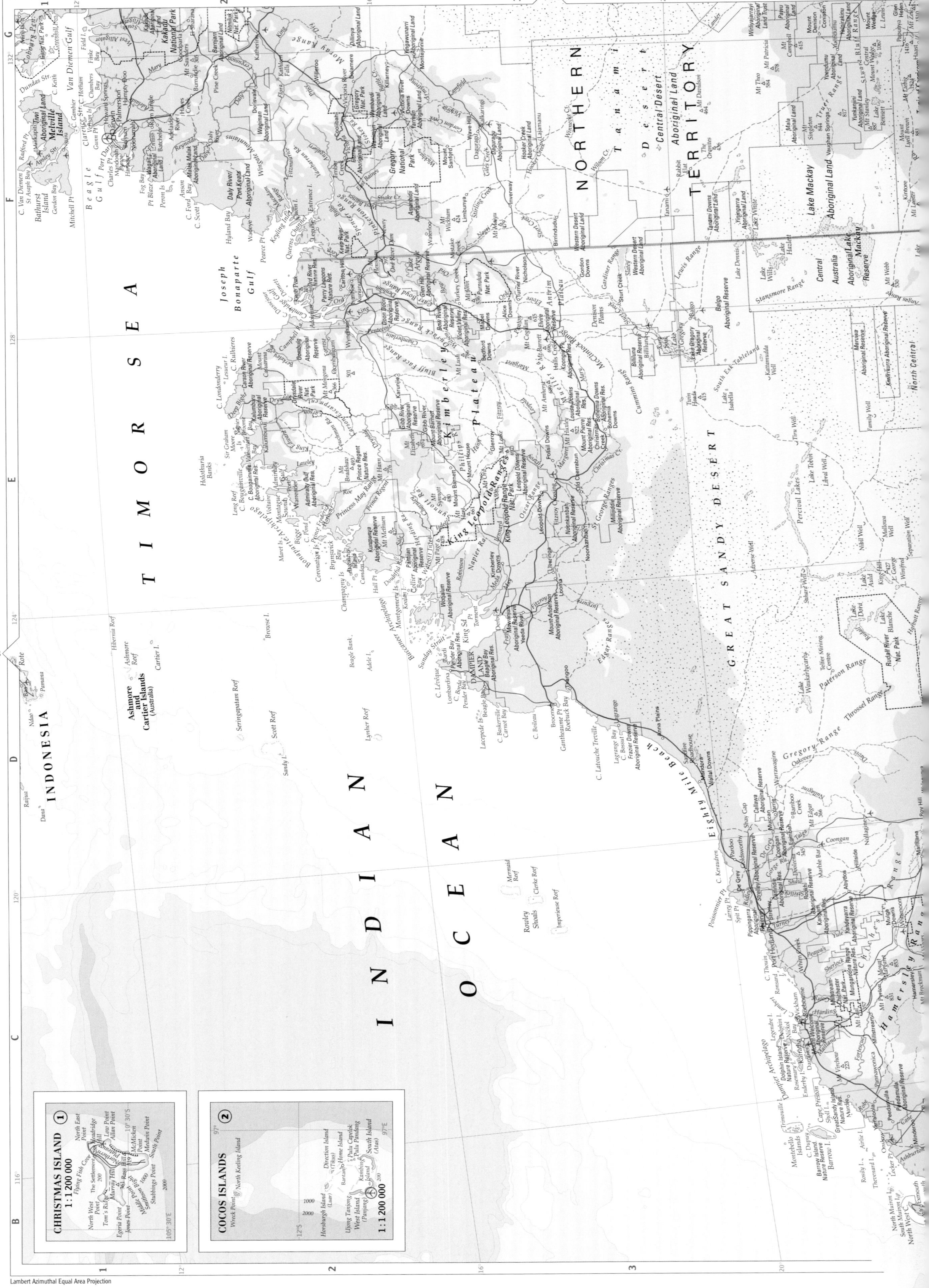

SOUTH AUSTRALIA

WESTERN AUSTRALIA

GIBSON DESERT

GREAT VICTORIA DESERT

GREAT AUSTRALIAN BIGHT

Nullarbor Plain

Musgrave Ranges

Anangu Pitjantjatjara Aboriginal Lands

Great Victoria Desert Conservation Park

Maralinga-Tjarutja Aboriginal Lands

Great Victoria Desert Nature Reserve

Nullarbor Regional Reserve

Nullarbor National Park

Warburton

Perth

Tropic of Capricorn

Shark Bay

Ningaloo Marine Park

Houtman Abrolhos

MILES | KILOMETRES

250 | 400
| 350
200 |
| 300
150 | 250
| 200
100 | 150
| 100
50 |
| 50
0 | 0

1:6 000 000

© Bartholomew Ltd

A B C D E

ARCTIC

15° 30° 45°

Nordvik

Karskoye More 75°

Gulf of Bothnia

Beloye More Arctic Circle

E U R O P E

Baltic Sea

R U S S I A N

Ozero
Onezhskoye

Ural'skiy Khrebet
(Ural Mountains)

Noril'sk

1

Alps

Adriatic Sea

Carpathian Mountains

Rybinskoye
Vodokhranilishche

Volga

Irtysh

Surgut

Yekaterinburg
Tobol'sk
Chelyabinsk

Omsk Tomsk Krasnoyarsk

Novosibirsk
Novokuznetsk

Ural'sk ◻ **Astana** Pavlodar Barnaul

Sea of
Azov Aktyubinsk

Atyrau K A Z A K H S T A N Karaganda Semipalatinsk Ust'-
Kamenogorsk Ulaangom

Black Sea *Volga*

2

Bursa Samsun Aral'sk Balkhash Tacheng *Altai Mountains* Altay

Izmir Ankara T'bilisi GEORGIA Aktau *Aral*
Sea *Ozero*
Zaysan

ARMENIA Yerevan AZERBAIJAN *Ozero*
Balkhash

Konya Erzurum Bakı *Caspian Sea* Shymkent Almaty Yining Ürümqi

Antalya T U R K E Y Sivas Kayseri *Zaliv Kara*
Bogaz-Gol Bishkek KYRGYZSTAN *Tien Shan* Turpan

Gaziantep Malatya Tabriz Turkmenbashi U Z B E K I S T A N Tashkent Andizhan Korla XINJIANG UYGUR ZIZHIQU

Adana Halab Al Mawṣil Ardabil T U R K M E N I S T A N Samarkand Khujand Kokand Aksu (SINKIANG)

Lefkosia CYPRUS Arbil *Tigris* Gorgān ◻ Ashgabat Kashi *Tarim Pendi* Lop Nur *Qaidam Pe*

LEBANON Beirut SYRIA Kirkūk ◻ **Tehrān** Mashhad T A J I K I S T A N Dushanbe Hotan *Kunlun Shan* Golmud

30° *Mediterranean Sea* Kermānshāh Qom Kūh-e Zagros Borūjerd Esfahān *Dasht-e Kavir* Birjand *Hindu Kush* Kābul Peshawar Islāmābād AKSAI
CHIN *Himalaya* XIZANG ZIZHIQU Lhasa *Siling Co* *Nam Co*

3

Damascus Baghdad I R A Q An Najaf Herāt A F G H A N I S T A N Rawalpindi Gujranwala (TIBET) C

ISRAEL Amman Ahvāz Abādān Kandahar Lahore Amritsar *Yarlung Zangbo (Brahmaputra)* Xigazê Mount
Everest Mount

Tel Aviv-Yafo Gaza Jerusalem JORDAN Al Baṣrah Kermān I R A N Zāhedān Quetta Faisalabad Multan Ludhiana Thimphu Dibrugarh

An Najaf An Nafūd Kuwait KUWAIT Shīrāz P A K I S T A N Ganganagar Chandigarh New Delhi Meerut Kathmandu NEPAL BHUTAN Guwahati

Libyan Desert *Tropic of Cancer* Būshehr Bandar-
e Abbās Jodhpur Delhi Faridabad Ghaziabad Darjiling Patna Shillong

Nile Ad Dammām BAHRAIN *The Gulf* *Thar Desert* Jaipur Agra Gorakhpur *Ghaghara* *Ganga (Ganges)*

4 Al Manāmah QATAR Dubai *Gulf of Oman* Pasni Hyderabad *Indus* Lucknow Kanpur Allahabad Varanasi Asansol Dhaka

Al Hufūf Doha **Abu Dhabi** Muscat Karachi Kota Beawar Gwalior Jabalpur Ranchi Jamshedpur Calcutta
(Kolkata) Khulna BANGLADESH Chittagong

Al Madīnah Riyadh UNITED ARAB
EMIRATES Ibrā' Ṣūr Ahmadabad Bhopal *Ganges* Cuttack MYA

Jeddah Mecca S A U D I Vadodara Indore *Mouths of the Ganges* Mandala

Red Sea A R A B I A *Maṣīrah* Surat Nagpur Meiktila

15° *Baiyuda*
Desert *Rub' al Khālī* O M A N Nashik I N D I A Sittwe

Al Hudaydah Ṣan'ā' Thane Ulhasnagar Aurangabad *Deccan* Vishakhapatnam *Andaman*
Islands
(India)

Ta'izz YEMEN Ṣalālah *Arabian*
Sea Mumbai Pune Solapur Hyderabad B A Y *Andam*
Sea

5 Aden Al Mukallā *Krishna* Dharwad Kurnool Vijayawada O F B E N G A L Yango

Gulf of Aden *Suquṭra* Nellore Bassein

Mangalore Bangalore Chennai *Andaman Sea*

A F R I C A *Laccadive Islands*
(India) Mysore Salem *Nicobar*
Islands
(India)

Calicut Coimbatore Tiruchchirappalli

Cochin Madurai

30° Trivandrum *Gulf*
of Mannar Jaffna Trincomalee

Lake
Victoria Kandy SRI LANKA

Colombo Sri Jayewardenepura
Kotte

6 *Equator* *Lake*
Nyasa Male Banda
Aceh

MALDIVES

5° *Simeuluë*

Njazidja

7 *Seychelles* *Mahé* I N D I A N O C E A N

Comoros *Coëtivy* British
Indian Ocean
Territory *Chagos*
Archipelago

Mayotte *Aldabra Islands*
(Seychelles) *Farquhar Islands*
(Seychelles) *Diego Garcia*

Agalega Islands
(Mauritius)

30° 45° 60° 75° 90°

A B C D E

OCEAN

180°

165°

150°

135°

120°

105°

Bering Strait

Arctic Circle

Khrebet Kolymskiy

Ugol'nyye Kopi

60°

SREDNE - SIBIRSKOYE

PLOSKOGOR'YE

Tiksi

Verkhoyanskiy Khrebet

Lena

BERING

SEA

Pribilof
Islands

Nizhnyaya Tunguska

Vilyuy

Yakutsk

Aldan

Susuman

Poluostrov Kamchatka

Aleutian
Islands

Podkamennaya Tunguska

Mirnyy

Magadan

Angara

Kansk

Bratsk

Bodaybo

Ust'-Kut

F E D E R A T I O N

Aldan

Stanovoy Khrebet

Sea
of Okhotsk

Petropavlovsk-
Kamchatskiy

45°

Irkutsk

Ozero
Baykal

Tynda

Amur

Komsomol'sk-
na-Amure

Sakhalin

Kamchatskiye Ostrova

Ulan-Ude

Chita

Heilong Jiang

Blagoveshchensk

Khabarovsk

Yuzhno-
Sakhalinsk

Korsakov

2

Höysgöl
Nuur

Darhan

Hulun
Nur

Hailar

Da Hinggan Ling

Qiqihar

Suihua

Jiamusi

Wakkanai

180°

Uliastay

Ulaanbaatar

Jargalant

Buir
Nur

Daqing

Harbin

Hokkaidō

M O N G O L I A

G O B I

Changchun

Jilin

Vladivostok

Sapporo

Hakodate

Dalandzadgad

NEI MONGOL ZIZHIQU
(INNER MONGOLIA)

Shenyang

Fushun

NORTH
KOREA

Sea

Akita

Yumen

Jining

Zhangjiakou

Anshan

Benxi

of Japan

Honshū

Niigata

Sendai

ilian Shan

Baotou

Huhhot

Datong

Beijing

Tangshan

Dalian

P'yŏngyang

Sŏul

Kanazawa

Tōkyō

Wuhai

Huang He
(Yellow River)

Korea
Bay

Puch'ŏn

Inch'ŏn

Suwŏn

Kyōto

Nagoya

Yokohama

J A P A N

Yinchuan

Shijiazhuang

Tianjin

Bo Hai

Yantai

SOUTH
KOREA

Taejŏn

Pusan

Kōbe
Osaka

Hiroshima

Qinghai Hu

Xining

Taiyuan

Jinan

Zibo

Qingdao

Kwangju

Taegu

Kita-Kyūshū

Shikoku

Lanzhou

Handan

Xinxiang

Jining

Yellow

Mokp'o

Fukuoka

Nagasaki

Kumamoto

Kyūshū

aring Hu

Weinan

Luoyang

Zhengzhou

Xuzhou

Sea

Kagoshima

Xi'an

Pingdingshan

Huainan

Nanjing

Changzhou

Shanghai

East China

C H I N A

Chengdu

Nanchong

Huang He
(Yellow River)

Hefei

Wuhu

Wuxi

Jiaxing

Hangzhou

Sea

Chongqing

Yueyang

Wuhan

Jingdezhen

Ningbo

Chang Jiang (Yangtze)

Neijiang

Changde

Nanchang

Quzhou

Wenzhou

Ogasawara-shotō
(Japan)

P A C I F I C

Yibin

Zhaotong

Guiyang

Changsha

Hengyang

Fuzhou

Okinawa

Nansei-shotō

Kazan-rettō
(Japan)

Tropic of Cancer

Panzhihua

Qujing

Liuzhou

Meizhou

Xiamen

T'aipei

Myitkyina

Kunming

Xun Jiang

Guangzhou

Shenzhen

Shantou

TAIWAN

T'aitung

O C E A N

Nanning

Macau

Hong Kong

Kaohsiung

Taiwan Strait

165°

AR

Ha Nôi

Haï Phong

Zhanjiang

Batan Islands

Pagan

Chiang
Mai

Louangphrabang

Gulf
of Tongking

Haikou

Hainan

Luzon Strait

Northern
Mariana
Islands

Viangchan

L A O S

Huế

Đa Nẵng

Paracel Islands

Aparri

Saipan

15°

Moulmein

V I E T N A M

SOUTH

Luzon

PHILIPPINES

Tinian
Rota

THAILAND

Nakhon
Ratchasima

CHINA

Quezon
City

Guam

Bangkok

Tônlé
Sab

SEA

Manila

Naga

ergui

CAMBODIA

Nha Trang

Mindoro

Masbate

Samar

Yap

Caroline Islands

Chuuk

Phnum
Penh

Hồ Chí Minh

Sihanoukville

Spratly Islands

Palawan

Iloilo

Panay

Cebu

Surigao

PALAU

Mortlock
Islands

Nakhon Si
Thammarat

Negros

Dipolog

Koror

Sulu
Sea

Mindanao

Davao

Kota Bharu

Kota Kinabalu

Sandakan

Zamboanga

George
Town

SABAH

Sulu
Archipelago

Kepulauan
Talaud

6

Ipoh

M A L A Y S I A

BRUNEI

Bandar Seri
Begawan

Kepulauan
Sangir

Equator

edan

Strait of Malacca

Kuala
Lumpur

Putrajaya

SARAWAK

Kuching

Sibu

Sri Aman

Celebes
Sea

Manado

Molucca Sea

Halmahera

Manokwari

Nias

Singapore

Borneo

Pontianak

Kepulauan
Maluku

Jazirah
Doberai

Bismarck Archipelago

Sumatera

Kepulauan
Lingga

Ketapang

Balikpapan

Sulawesi

Seram Sea

Pegunungan Van Rees

Jayapura

Bismarck
Sea

Siberut

Padang

Kepulauan
Mentawai

Bangka

Banjarmasin

Palu

Seram

New Britain

Kepulauan
Sula

Puncak Jaya

Central Range

Digul

NEW

Enggano

Palembang

Java Sea

Barito

Macassar Strait

Parepare

Buru

Buton

Banda Sea

Kepulauan
Aru

GUINEA

Solomon
Sea

Bougainville
Island

Bengkulu

Tanjungkarang-
Telukbetung

I N D O N E S I A

Ujung Pandang

Flores Sea

Wetar

Kepulauan
Tanimbar

Owen Stanley Range

Gulf
of Papua

7

Jakarta

Bandung

Jawa
(Java)

Semarang

Surabaya

Madura

Bali

Bali
Sea

Sumbawa

Flores

Sumba

Sawu
Sea

Dili

EAST
TIMOR

Arafura Sea

Torres Strait

Cape
York
Peninsula

CORAL
SEA

Yogyakarta

Surakarta

Lombok

Raba

Timor

Kupang

Rote

Melville Island

O C E A N I A

F

G

H

I

J

© Bartholomew Ltd

MILES

KILOMETRES

1000

1500

1250

750

1000

500

750

500

250

250

0

0

1:24 000 000

98 112

CHINA

YUNNAN · GUIZHOU · GUANGXI ZHUANGZU ZIZHIQU · GUANGDONG · HUNAN · JIANGXI · FUJIAN

Kunming · Guiyang · Duyun · Anshun · Quijing · Panxian · Guilin · Liuzhou · Nanning · Guangzhou (Canton) · Shenzhen · Kowloon · Hong Kong · Macau · Shantou · Fuzhou · Xiamen (Amoy) · Quanzhou · Zhangzhou · Shaoguan · Meizhou · Zhanjiang · Maoming

TAIWAN · **T'AIPEI** · T'aichung · Kaohsiung · T'ainan · Hualien

MYANMAR

HA NỘI · Hai Phong · Hòng Gai · Nam Định · Thanh Hoa · Vinh · Hà Tĩnh · Đồng Hới · Huê · Đà Nẵng · Quảng Ngãi · Qui Nhơn · Nha Trang · Đà Lat · **Hồ Chí Minh (Saigon)** · Biên Hoa · Phan Thiết · Vũng Tàu · Cần Thơ · Bạc Liêu · Cà Mau

LAOS · **VIANGCHAN** · Louangphrabang · Savannakhét · Pakxé

THAILAND · **BANGKOK (Krung Thep)** · Nakhon Ratchasima · Chiang Mai · Phuket · Hat Yai · Songkhla

INDO-CHINA

CAMBODIA · **PHNUM PENH** · Battambang · Sihanoukville (Kâmpóng Saôm)

Gulf of Tongking · HAINAN · Haikou · Sanya

GULF OF THAILAND

SOUTH CHINA SEA

Paracel Islands (Xisha Qundao) · Macclesfield Bank · Scarborough Shoal · Spratly Islands

PHILIPPINE Sea · Luzon · **MANILA** · Quezon City · LUZON · San Fernando · Mindoro · Panay · Cebu · Negros · Palawan · Puerto Princesa

SULU SEA · Zamboanga · Sandakan · SABAH · Kota Kinabalu · BRUNEI · **BANDAR SERI BEGAWAN**

CELEBES SEA

MALAYSIA · **KUALA LUMPUR** · George Town · Ipoh · Johor Bahru · Melaka · SARAWAK · Kuching · Sibu · Miri

SINGAPORE

SUMATERA · Medan · Padang · Palembang · Bengkulu · Banda Aceh · Pekanbaru · Jambi

BORNEO · KALIMANTAN · Pontianak · Banjarmasin · Balikpapan · Samarinda

SULAWESI (CELEBES) · Palu · Ujung Pandang (Makassar) · Palopo

MAKASSAR STRAIT

JAVA SEA

INDONESIA

JAKARTA · Bandung · Semarang · Surabaya · Surakarta · Yogyakarta · Malang · JAWA (JAVA) · Bali · Denpasar · Sumbawa · Lombok · Mataram · FLORES · Flores

INDIAN OCEAN

BALI SEA · FLORES SEA · SAWU SEA

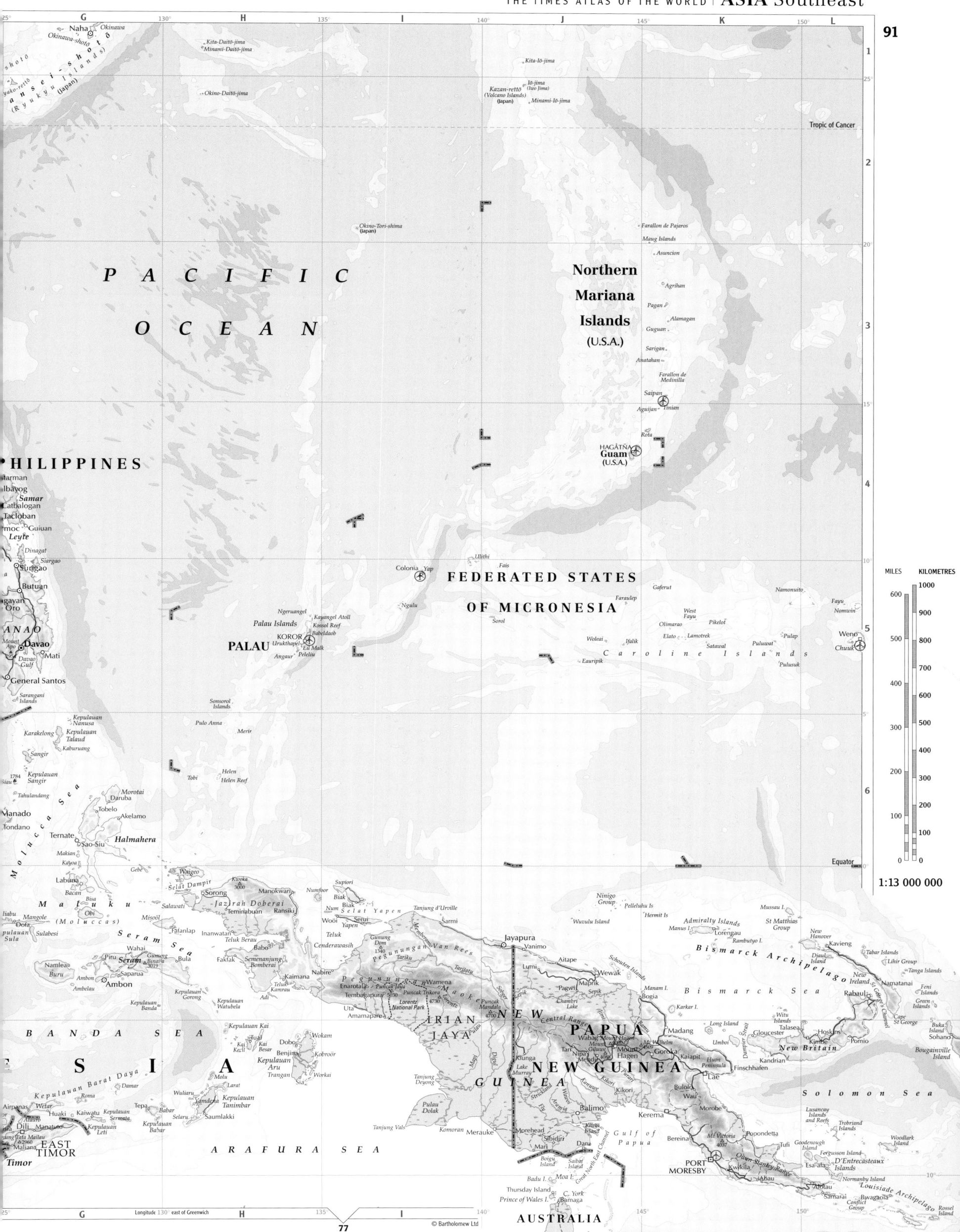

PACIFIC

OCEAN

Northern
Mariana
Islands
(U.S.A.)

Tropic of Cancer

Naha Okinawa

Okinawa-shotō

Kita-Daitō-jima
Minami-Daitō-jima

Okino-Daitō-jima

nsei-shotō
(Ryukyu Islands) (Japan)

Kita-Iō-jima

Iō-jima
(Iwo Jima)
Kazan-rettō
(Volcano Islands)
(Japan) Minami-Iō-jima

Okino-Tori-shima
(Japan)

Farallon de Pajaros
Maug Islands
Asuncion

Agrihan

Pagan

Alamagan
Guguan

Sarigan
Anatahan

Farallon de
Medinilla

Saipan

Aguijan Tinian

Rota

HAGÅTÑA
Guam
(U.S.A.)

PHILIPPINES

Starman
Ibayog
Catbalogan Samar
Tacloban
moc Guiuan
Leyte

Dinagat
Surigao Siargao
Butuan

ANAO
Monet Apo Davao
Davao
Gulf
General Santos Mati

Sarangani
Islands

FEDERATED STATES

OF MICRONESIA

Ulithi Fais
Colonia Yap

Ngulu

Ngeruangel
Palau Islands Kayangel Atoll
KOROR Kossol Reef
Urukthapel Babeldaob
Eil Malk
Angaur Peleliu

PALAU

Sorol

Gaferut

Faraulep

Olimarao West
Fayu
Woleai Pikelot
Ifalik Elato Lamotrek
Eauripik Satawal Puluwat
Pulusuk

Namonuito

Fayu
Nomwin

Puluwat Pulap Weno
Chuuk

Caroline Islands

Sonsorol
Islands

Pulo Anna

Merir

Helen
Tobi Helen Reef

MILES KILOMETRES
1000
600 900
800
500 700
600
400 500
300 400
300
200 200
100
100 100
0 0

1:13 000 000

Kepulauan
Nanusa
Karakelong Kepulauan
Talaud
Sangir Kaburuang

1784
Kepulauan
Sangir
Tahulandang Siau

Manado
Tondano
Ternate

Morotai
Daruba
Tobelo
Akelamo
Sao-Siu Halmahera
Makian
Kayoa

labung
Bacan
Bisa
Obi
Mangole
(Moluccas)
Dofa
Sula Sulabesi

Gebe
Waigeo
Selat Dampir Kuwoka
Sorong 3000
Jazirah Doberai
Salawati Manokwari
Misool Teminabuan Ransiki
Batanlap
Inanwatan Teluk Berau Babo
Fakfak Semenanjung
Bomberai
Kaimana

Numfoor
Supiori
Biak
Num Selat Yapen
Wooi Serui
Yapen
Cenderawasih

Tanjung d'Urville
Sarmi

Pegunungan Van Rees
Gunung
Dom Tariku

Ninigo
Group
Pelleluhu Is
Wuvulu Island

Mussau I.

Admiralty Islands
Manus I. Lorengau
Rambutyo I.

St Matthias
Group

New
Hanover

Bismarck Archipelago
Djaul
Island

Lihir Group

Matuku

Seram Sea
Wahai
Piru Gunung
Namlea Seram Binaie 3019
Buru Ambon Saparua
Ambalau Ambon

Kepulauan
Gorong
Kepulauan
Banda

Kamrau
Adi

Region
Enarotali Puncak Jaya
Tembagapura Puncak Trikora
Uta 4730
Amamapare

Wamena
1340
Lorentz
National Park

Jayapura
Vanimo

Lumi Aitape

Maoke

IRIAN
JAYA

Central
Digul Klunga

NEW
GUINEA

Wabag Mount Hagen
Mount
Nipa Medina
Hagen

Wewak
Pagwi Maprik
Sepik
Chambri
Lake

Mount Wilhelm
Tari Goroka
Kaiapit

Manam I.
Bogia
Karkar I.

Schouten Islands

Bismarck Sea

Long Island
Madang

Umboi
Gloucester

Witu
Islands Talasea
Long Island
Kandrian
Finschhafen

Kavieng

New
Ireland

Tanga Islands

Namatanai
Feni
Islands

Rabaul Green
Islands

New Britain
Kimbe
Hoskins
Pomio

Buka Island
Sohano
Bougainville
Island

BANDA SEA

SIA

Kepulauan Kai
Dobo Kai
Benjina Besar
Kepulauan Kai
Watubela Kecil
Kepulauan
Aru
Wokam
Kobroör
Trangan Workai

PAPUA

NEW GUINEA

Lae
Bulolo
Wau

Morobe

Solomon Sea

Lusancay
Islands
and Reefs

Trobriand
Islands

Cape
St George

Kepulauan Barat Daya
Molu
Wuliaru Kepulauan
Damar Tanimbar
Tepa Selaru
Babar Saumlaki
Selaru Kepulauan
Leti Babar

Roma
Romang

Tanjung
Deyong

Pulau
Dolak

Tanjung Vals

Komoran
Merauke

Morehead

Kawa

Balimo

Strickland Kikori
Fly

Kerema

Kikori

Gulf of
Papua

Goodenough
Island

Fergusson Island

D'Entrecasteaux
Islands

Normanby
Island

Samarai

Airpanas Welar Welar
Huaki Kepulauan
Dili Manatuto Sermata
Maliana Kepulauan
Leti

EAST
TIMOR
Timor

ARAFURA SEA

Sibidiri
Mari
Boigu
Island
Saibai
Island
Daru
North East Channel
Kiwai
Island

Morehead

Bereina
PORT
MORESBY

Owen Stanley Range

Mt Victoria
4037

Popondetta
Tufi

Kwikila
Abau

Esa'ala

D'Entrecasteaux
Islands

Conflict
Group

Louisiade Archipelago

Rossel Island

Equator

Thursday Island
Prince of Wales I. Bamaga
C. York

PALAU
1:1 200 000

MANILA
1:75 000
0 METRES 750
0 YARDS 750

LUZON STRAIT

PHILIPPINE SEA

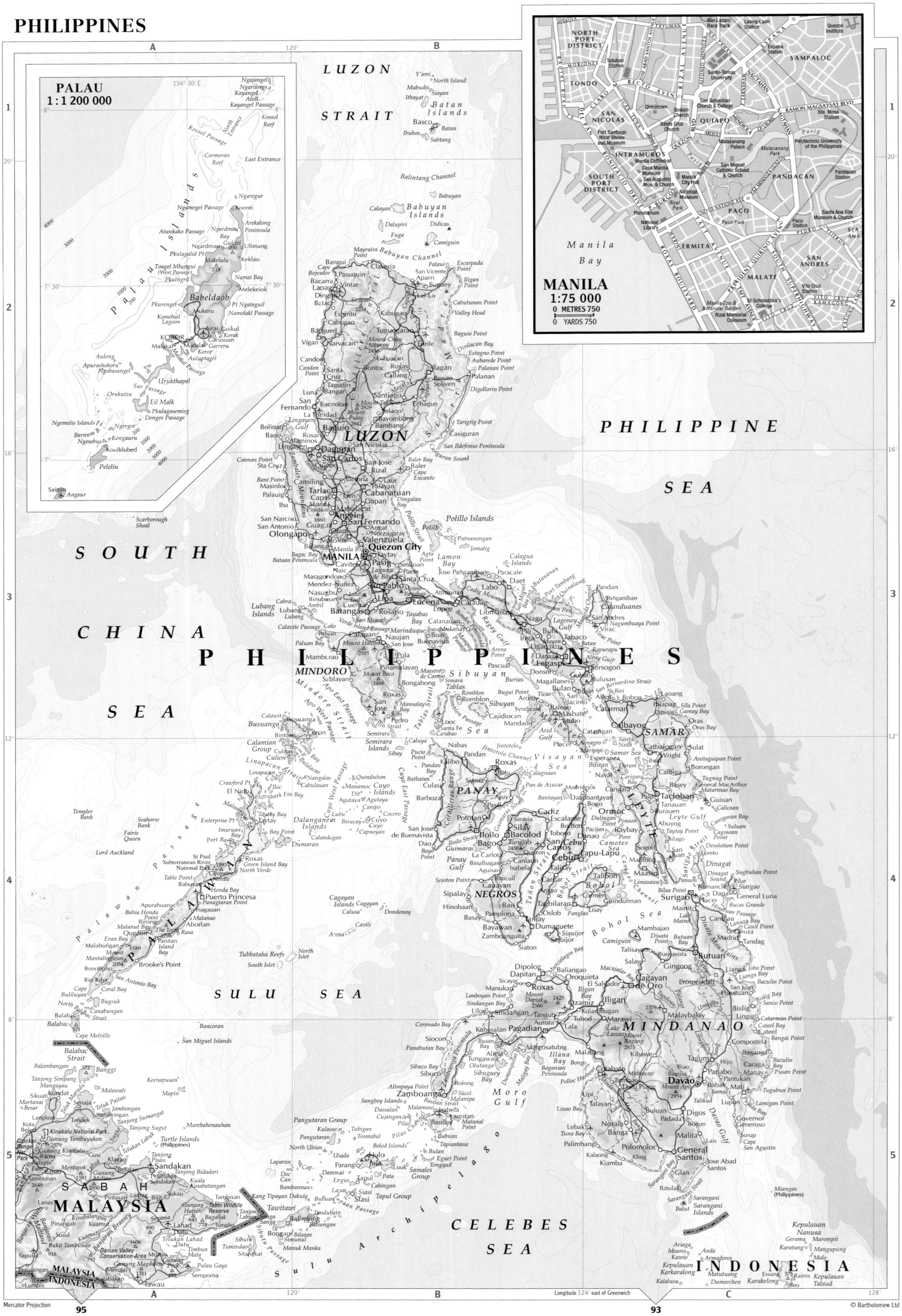

SOUTH CHINA SEA

PHILIPPINES

LUZON

MANILA
Quezon City

MINDORO

PANAY

SAMAR

LEYTE

NEGROS

CEBU

BOHOL

PALAWAN

SULU SEA

Bohol Sea

MINDANAO

Davao

Zamboanga

Moro Gulf

CELEBES SEA

MALAYSIA

SABAH

INDONESIA

METRES FEET
6000 19686
5000 16404
4000 13124
3000 9843
2000 6562
1000 3281
500 1640
200 656
0 0
LAND BELOW SEA LEVEL
200 656
2000 6562
4000 13124
6000 19686

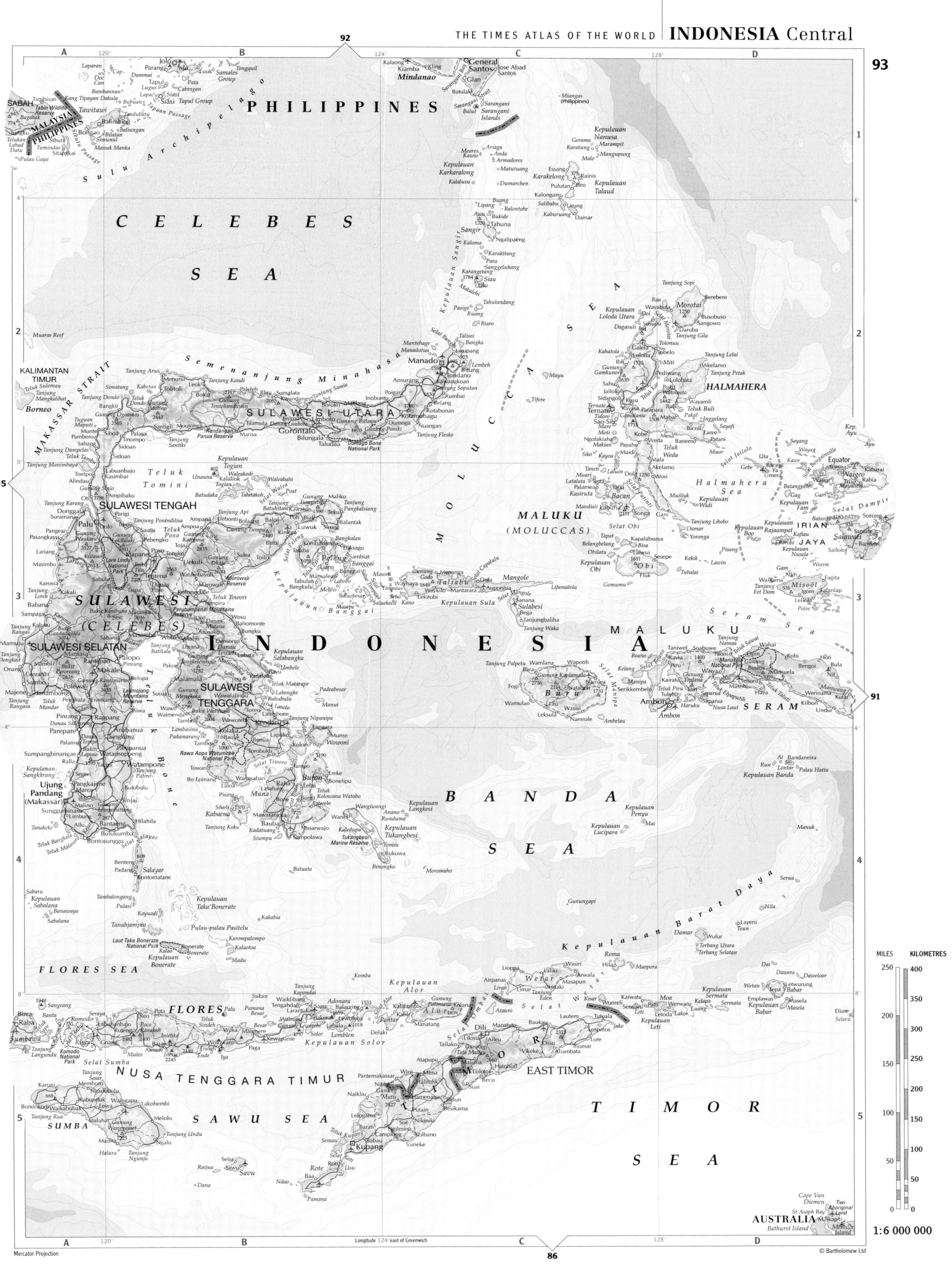

1:6 000 000

97

A   96°   B   100°   C   104°   D

THAILAND

Ko Racha Yai
Ko Racha Noi
Hai
Muk
Ko Libong
Ko Lanta
Ko Lanta
Kantang
Trang
Phatthalung
Thale Luang
Khao Pu-Khao
Ya National Park
Pak Phayun
Songkhla
Khao Banthat
Wildlife Reserve
Hat Yai
Ban
Thepha
Chana
Terutao
National Park
Butang
Group
Ko Racha Noi
Satun
Kangar
Sadao
Yala
Pattani
Sai
Buri
Narathiwat
Tak Bai
Langkawi
Kuah
Perlis
Kubang Pasu
Bukit Kayu Hitam
Kota Bharu
Pasir Mas
Perhentian
Besar
Kedah

1

Sabang
Pulau We
Pulau Breueh
Pulau Rondo
Banda
Aceh
Silawaih Agam
Sigli
Alor Setar
George
Town
PINANG
Butterworth
Pinang

Meureudu
ACEH
Tangse
Bireun
Lhokseumawe
Panton Labu
Langsa
Perak
KELANTAN
Sungei Petani
Baling
Gerik
Kuala Nerang
PERAK
TERENGGANU
Kuala Terengganu
Marang

SOUTH

4°

Medan
SELANGOR
KUALA LUMPUR
MALAYSIA
PAHANG
Kuantan

2°

SUMATERA
UTARA
Pekanbaru
JOHOR
Johor Bahru
SINGAPORE
SINGAPORE

Nias

RIAU
Kepulauan Riau

0° Equator

SUMATERA
BARAT
Padang
JAMBI
Jambi
INDO

3°

INDIAN
Kepulauan Mentawai
BENGKULU
SUMATERA
SELATAN
Palembang
Bangka

OCEAN
Bengkulu
LAMPUNG
Tanjungkarang-Telukbetung

4°

METRES
FEET
6000 19686
5000 16404
4000 13124
3000 9843
2000 6562
1000 3281
500 1640
200 656
0 0
LAND BELOW
SEA LEVEL
200 656
2000 6562
4000 13124
6000 19686

JAKART
Bekasi
Serang
Bogor
JAWA

Krakatau Volcano
National Park

SINGAPORE
1:360 000

Johor Bahru
MALAYSIA
SEMBAWANG
WOODLANDS
YISHUN
Selat Johor
Pasir Gudang
Sungai Johor
MANDAI
JALAN KAYU
PUNGGOL
Pulau Ubin
Pulau Tekong
Lim Chu Kang
Murai Reservoir
Kranji
Reservoir
Seletar Reservoir
SELETAR
ANG MO KIO
HOUGANG
Serangoon
Harbour
CHANGI
Choa Chu Kang
BUKIT PANJANG
Upper Peirce
Reservoir
Lower Peirce
Reservoir
BEDOK
TAMPINES
BUKIT BATOK
BUKIT TIMAH
TOA PAYOH
BEDOK
JURONG
CLEMENTI
QUEENSTOWN
GEYLANG
KATONG
SIGLAP
SINGAPORE
PASIR PANJANG
Jurong Island
Sentosa
Strait of Singapore

Mercator Projection

Longitude 104° east of Greenwich

Christmas Island
(Australia)

95

92

93

CHINA SEA

SULU SEA
PHILIPPINES

BRUNEI

MALAYSIA

SABAH

SARAWAK

CELEBES SEA

KALIMANTAN TIMUR

B O R N E O

KALIMANTAN BARAT

KALIMANTAN TENGAH

KALIMANTAN SELATAN

K A L I M A N T A N

SULAWESI TENGAH

SULAWESI (CELEBES)

SULAWESI SELATAN

M A K A S S A R   S T R A I T

N E S I A

Selat Karimata

J A V A   S E A

J A V A   S E A

JAWA TENGAH

JAWA TIMUR

Semarang **Surabaya**
Surakarta
YOGYAKARTA

J A W A   (J A V A)

BALI SEA

Bali **Denpasar** **Mataram**

Lombok **SUMBAWA**

NUSA TENGGARA BARAT

FLORES SEA

Ujung Pandang (Makassar)

Balikpapan

Samarinda

Banjarmasin

Pontianak

Kuching

Sibu

Bintulu

Miri

Singkawang

Kota Kinabalu

Sandakan

Tawau

Tarakan

Palu

Pare pare

Makale

MILES   KILOMETRES

1:6 000 000

© Bartholomew Ltd

Mercator Projection

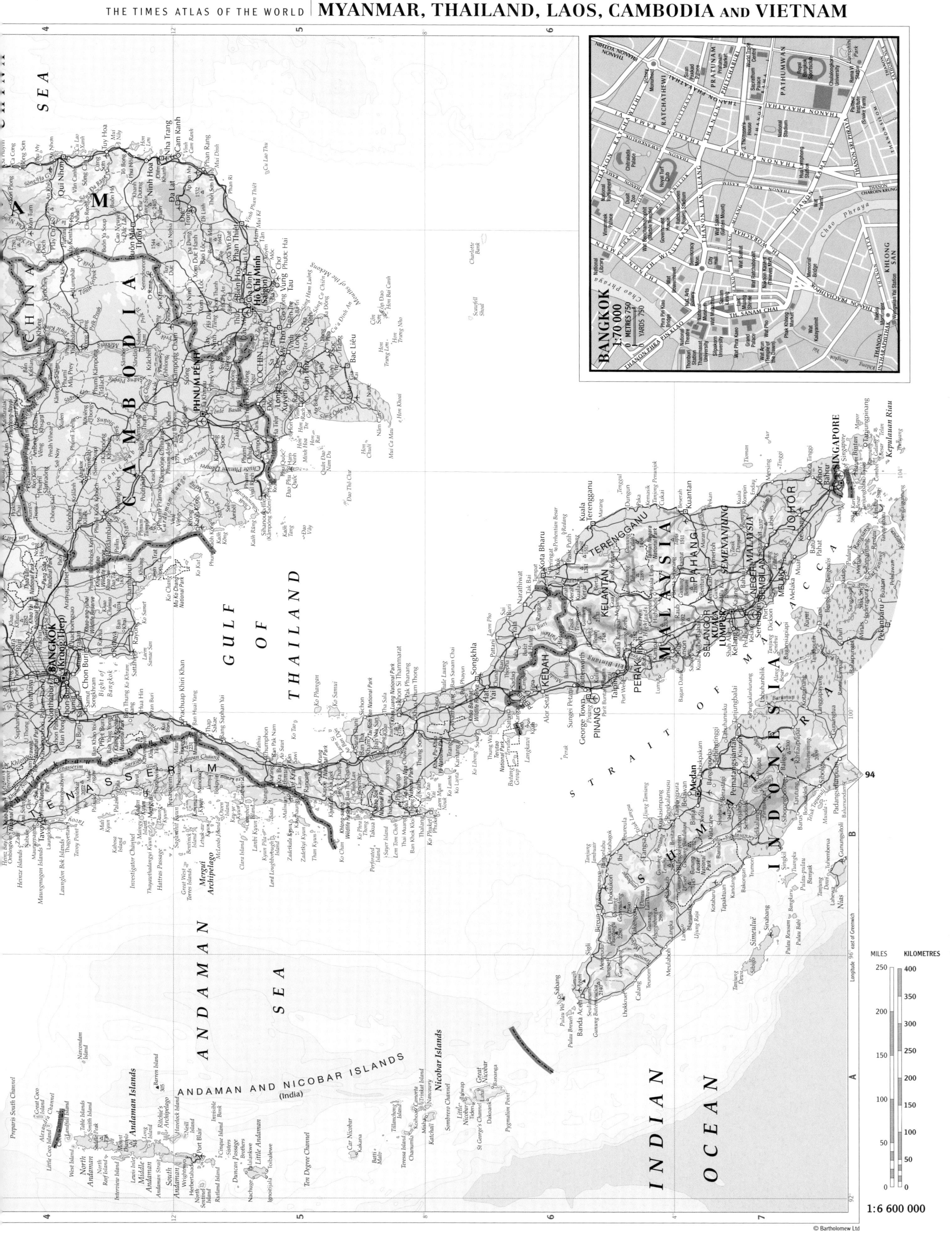

© Bartholomew Ltd

1:6 600 000

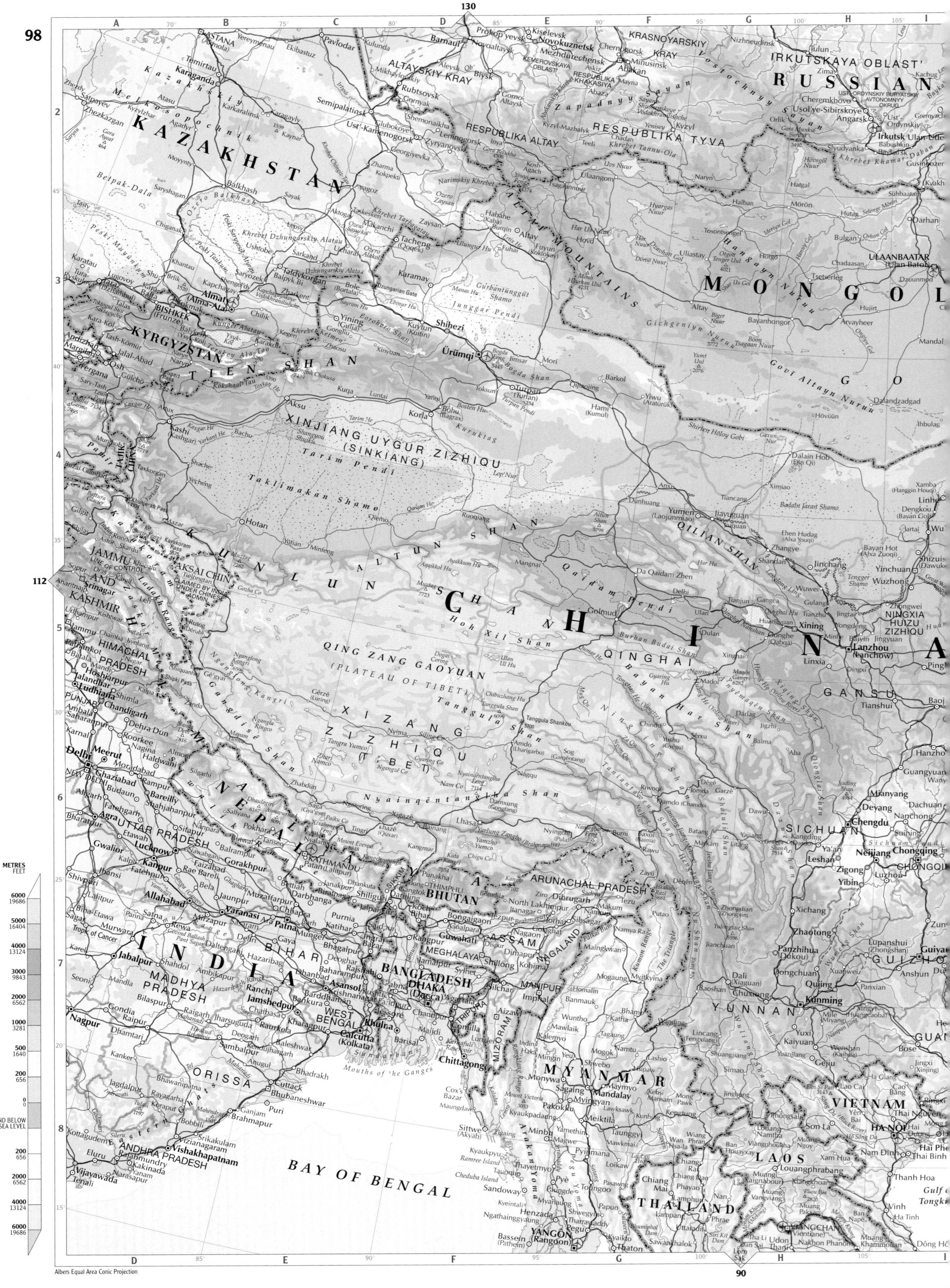

KAZAKHSTAN

RUSSIAN

MONGOLIA

KYRGYZSTAN

TIEN SHAN

XINJIANG UYGUR ZIZHIQU
(SINKIANG)

Taklimakan Shamo

Tarim Pendi

KUNLUN SHAN

C H I N A

QINGHAI

QING ZANG GAOYUAN
(PLATEAU OF TIBET)

XIZANG
ZIZHIQU
(TIBET)

JAMMU
AND
KASHMIR

HIMACHAL
PRADESH

PUNJAB

NEPAL

BHUTAN

ARUNACHAL PRADESH

UTTAR PRADESH

I N D I A

MADHYA
PRADESH

BIHAR

BANGLADESH
DHAKA
(Dacca)

WEST
BENGAL

ORISSA

ANDHRA
PRADESH

ASSAM

MEGHALAYA

NAGALAND

MANIPUR

MIZORAM

TRIPURA

MYANMAR

YANGON
(Rangoon)

BAY OF BENGAL

THAILAND

LAOS

VIETNAM
HANOI

YUNNAN

SICHUAN

GANSU

GUIZHOU

Lanzhou

Chengdu

Kunming

NINGXIA
HUIZU
ZIZHIQU

Albers Equal Area Conic Projection

FEDERATION

RESPUBLIKA
BURYATIYA

CHITINSKAYA OBLAST'

AMURSKAYA
OBLAST'

KHABAROVSKIY KRAY

SAKHALINSKAYA
OBLAST'

SEA OF OKHOTSK
(OKHOTSKOYE MORE)

Sakhalin

Yuzhno-Sakhalinsk

YEVREYSKAYA
AVTONOMNAYA
OBLAST'

Khabarovsk

PRIMORSKIY KRAY

Vladivostok

Hokkaidō

Sapporo

HEILONGJIANG

Qiqihar
Daqing
(Anda)
Suihua
Jiamusi
Shuangyashan
Harbin
Mudanjiang

JILIN

Changchun
Jilin
(Kirin)

LIAONING

Shenyang
Fushun
Benxi
Anshan
Jinzhou

NEI MONGOL ZIZHIQU
(INNER MONGOLIA)

Baotou
Huhhot

Beijing
(Peking)

TIANJIN
Tianjin
(Tientsin)
Tangshan

HEBEI

Baoding

Shijiazhuang
Taiyuan

SHANXI

Dalian
(Lüda)

Bo Hai

NORTH
KOREA

P'YONGYANG

SOUTH
KOREA

SŎUL
(Seoul)
Inch'ŏn
Suwŏn
Taejŏn
Taegu
Pusan
Kwangju

SEA
OF
JAPAN

JAPAN

Sendai

TŌKYŌ
Yokohama
Nagoya
Kyōto
Ōsaka
Kōbe
Hiroshima
Fukuoka
Kita-Kyūshū
Nagasaki
Kagoshima

Kyūshū

Shikoku

SHANDONG

Jinan
Qingdao
(Tsingtao)
Zibo
Weifang
Yantai
Weihai

Yellow Sea
(Huang Hai)

HENAN

Zhengzhou
Luoyang
(Loyang)
Xuzhou

Xi'an

SHAANXI

HUBEI

Wuhan

JIANGSU

Nanjing
Hefei

ANHUI

Changzhou (Wujin)
Wuxi
Shanghai
Suzhou
Hangzhou

ZHEJIANG

Ningbo
Wenzhou

EAST CHINA SEA
(DONG HAI)

HUNAN

Changsha
Zhuzhou

JIANGXI

Nanchang

FUJIAN

Fuzhou
Xiamen
(Amoy)

TAIWAN
T'AIPEI
T'aichung
T'ainan
Kaohsiung

GUANGDONG

Guangzhou
(Canton)
Shenzhen
Kowloon
Hong Kong
Macau
Shantou

Tropic of Cancer

HAINAN

Haikou

SOUTH CHINA SEA

PACIFIC

OCEAN

PHILIPPINES

LUZON

MILES KILOMETRES

600 1000
500 900
     800
400 700
     600
300 500
     400
200 300
100 200
     100
0   0

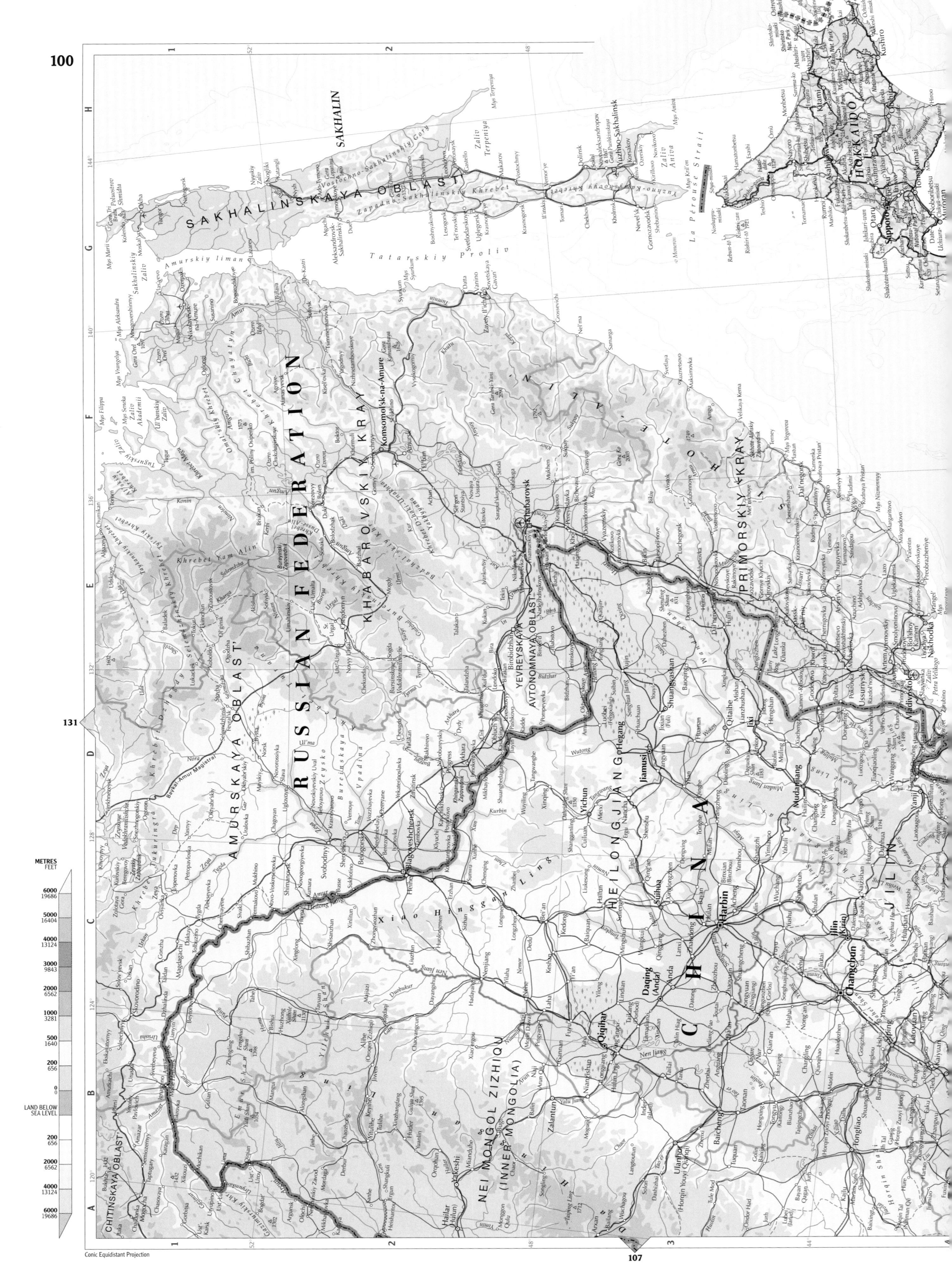

131

Conic Equidistant Projection

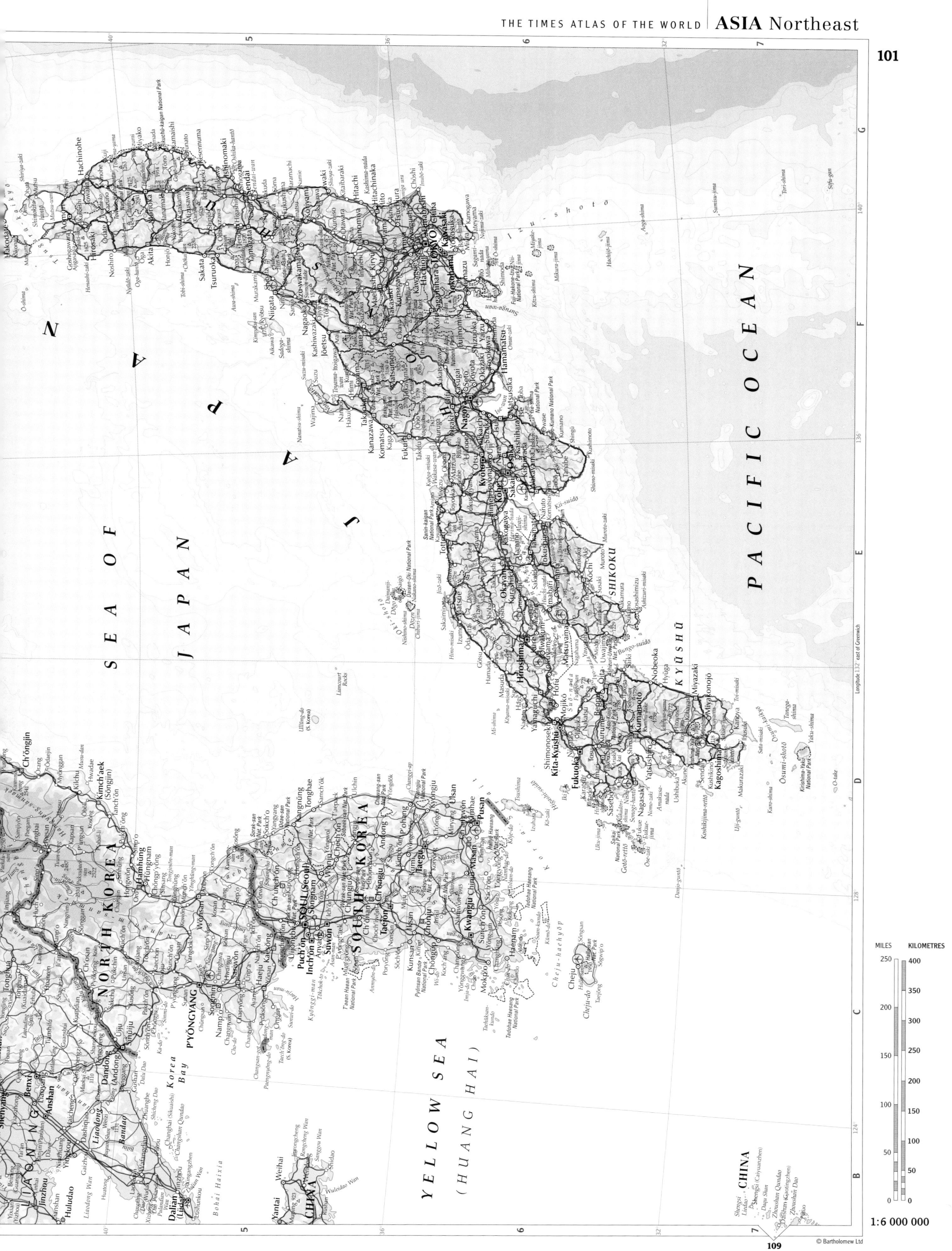

1:6 000 000

© Bartholomew Ltd

Administrative divisions
numbered on the map:
1. CHIBA (J6)
2. KANAGAWA (I6)
3. ŌSAKA (G6)
4. SAITAMA (I6)
5. TŌKYŌ (I6)
6. YAMANASHI (I6)

PACIFIC OCEAN

I n u - s h o t ō

① BONIN ISLANDS AND VOLCANO ISLANDS 1 : 3 600 000

② Iō-jima (Iōo jima) 1 : 300 000

Ogasawara-shotō (Bonin Islands)

Kazan-rettō (Volcano Islands)

PACIFIC OCEAN

PACIFIC OCEAN

FUKUSHIMA

TOCHIGI

NAGANO

GIFU

AICHI

MIE

NARA

WAKAYAMA

HYOGO

KYOTO

FUKUI

ISHIKAWA

TOTTORI

OKAYAMA

HIROSHIMA

SHIMANE

YAMAGUCHI

SHIKOKU

TOKUSHIMA

KAGAWA

EHIME

KOCHI

S E A   O F   J A P A N

KYŪSHŪ

FUKUOKA

SAGA

NAGASAKI

KUMAMOTO

OITA

MIYAZAKI

KAGOSHIMA

SOUTH KOREA

Korea Strait

Pusan

MILES   KILOMETRES

1 : 3 600 000

Longitude 134 east of Greenwich

© Bartholomew Ltd

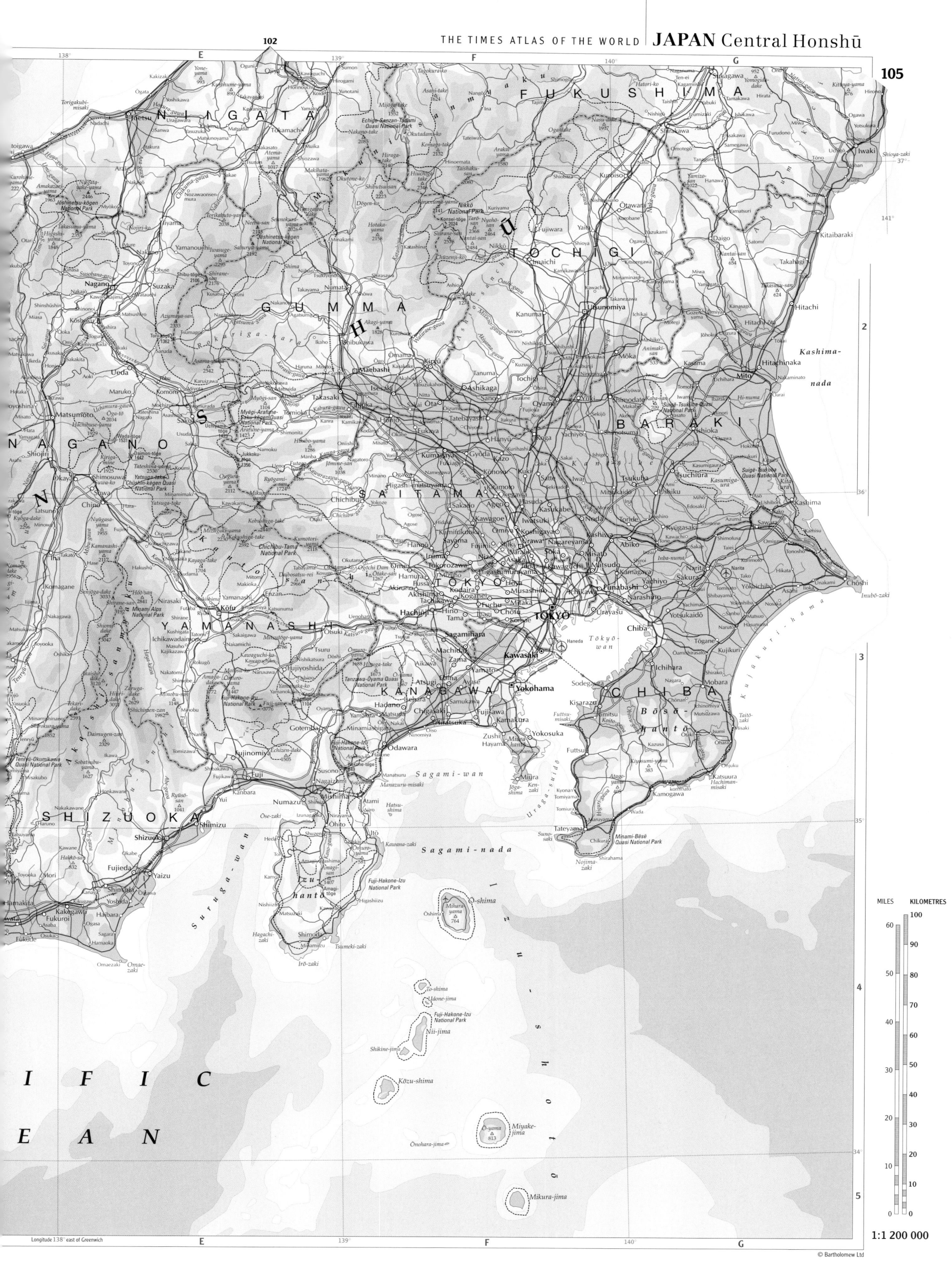

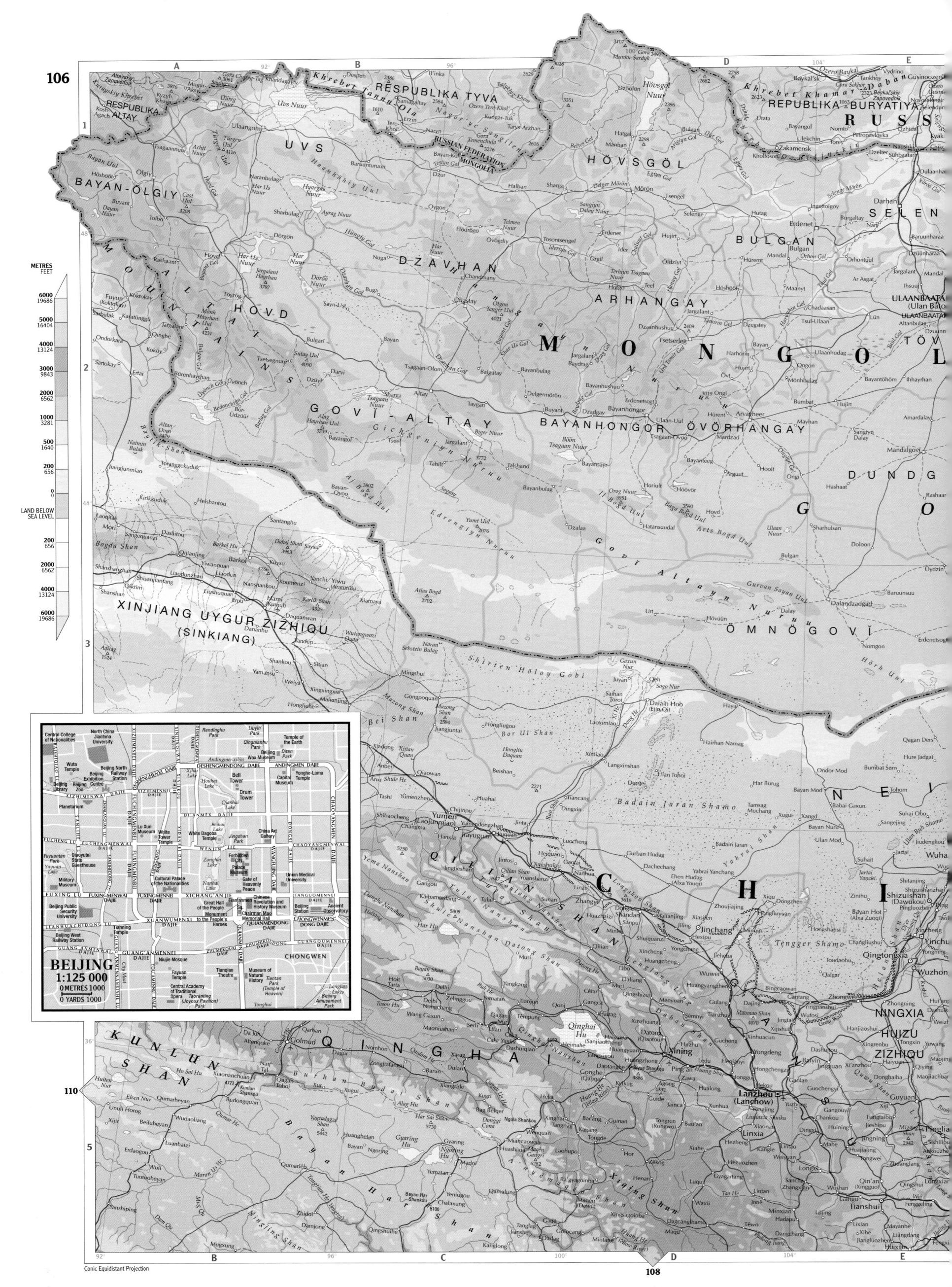

106

Conic Equidistant Projection

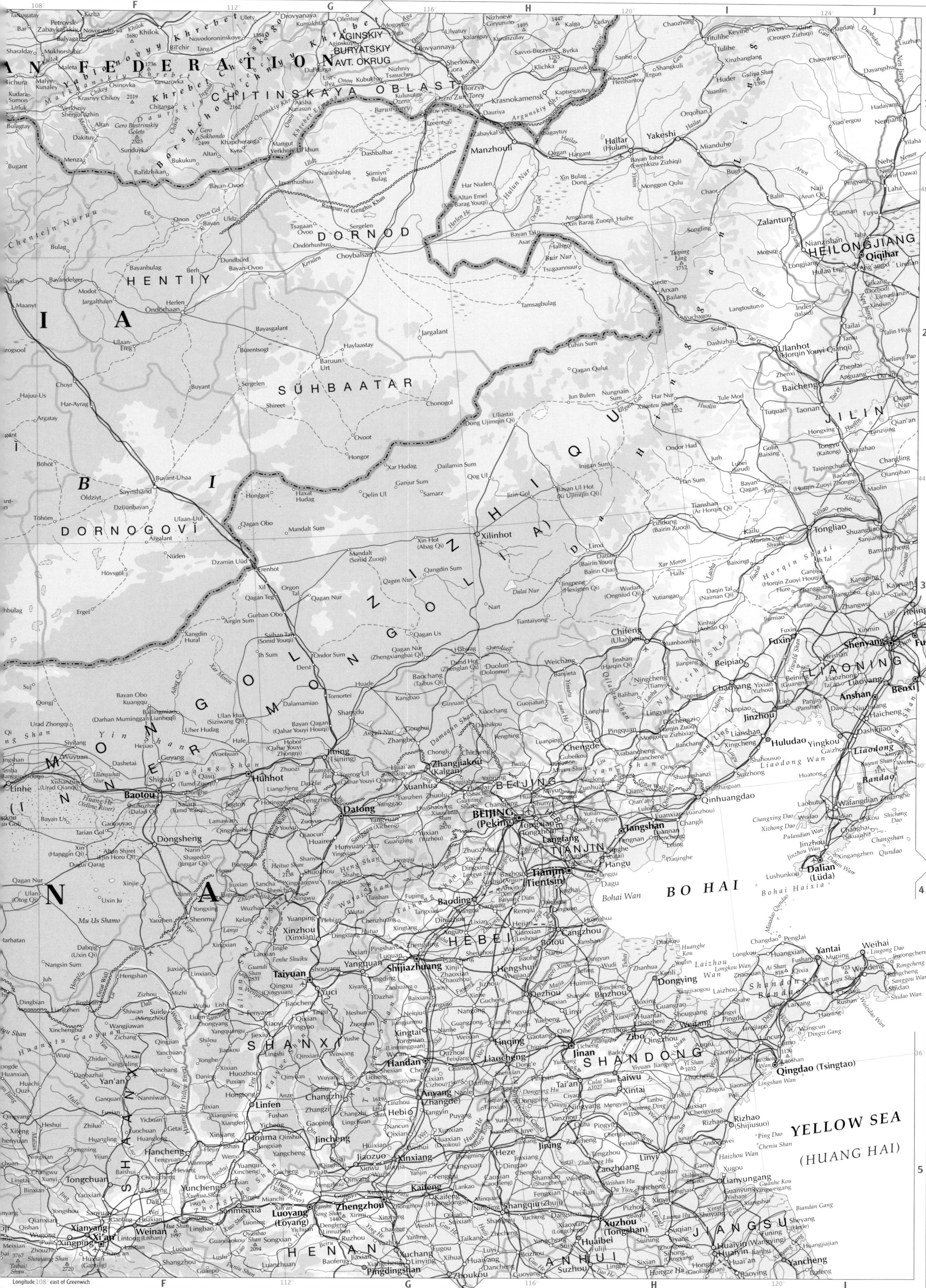

107

100

CONFEDERATION

CHITINSKAYA OBLAST

AGINSKIY BURYATSKIY AVT. OKRUG

HENTIY

DORNOD

SÜHBAATAR

HEILONGJIANG
Qiqihar

JILIN

Manzhouli

Hailar (Hulun)
Yakeshi

DORNOGOVI

Choybalsan

Buir Nur

Hulun Nur

MONGOL ZIZHIQU

Ulanhot

Baicheng

Xilinhot

Tongliao

Shenyang
Fushun
Benxi

LIAONING

Fuxin

Anshan

Liaodong

Chifeng (Ulanhad)

NEI MONGOL ZIZHIQU

Chengde

Beipiao
Jinzhou

Huludao
Yingkou

Zhangjiakou
Kalgan

Huhhot

Baotou

Qinhuangdao

Dongsheng

Datong

BEIJING

BEIJING (Peking)

Tangshan

Langfang

TIANJIN
Tianjin (Tientsin)

Dalian (Lüda)

BO HAI

Bohai Wan

HEBEI

Baoding

Cangzhou

Botou

Yantai
Weihai

Taiyuan

Shijiazhuang

Hengshui

Dongying

SHANDONG

Xinzhou (Xinxian)

Yangquan

Yuci

Qingdao (Tsingtao)

Jinan

SHANXI

Handan

Zibo

Weifang

Anyang
Zhangde

Linfen

Hebi

Jincheng

Xinxiang

Rizhao (Shijiusuo)

YELLOW SEA
(HUANG HAI)

Yan'an

Zhengzhou

Kaifeng

Xuzhou (Tongshan)

Luoyang (Loyang)

HENAN

Xi'an

Weinan

JIANGSU

ANHUI

Pingdingshan

Huaibei

MILES	KILOMETRES
250	400
	350
200	300
150	250
	200
100	150
50	100
	50
0	0

1:6 000 000

101

Longitude 108° east of Greenwich

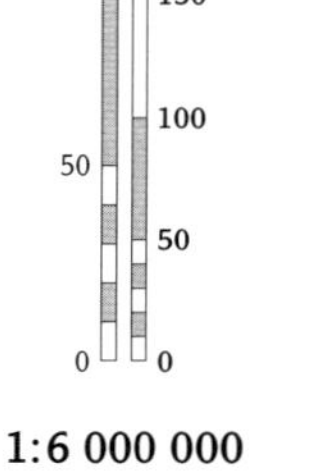

© Bartholomew Ltd

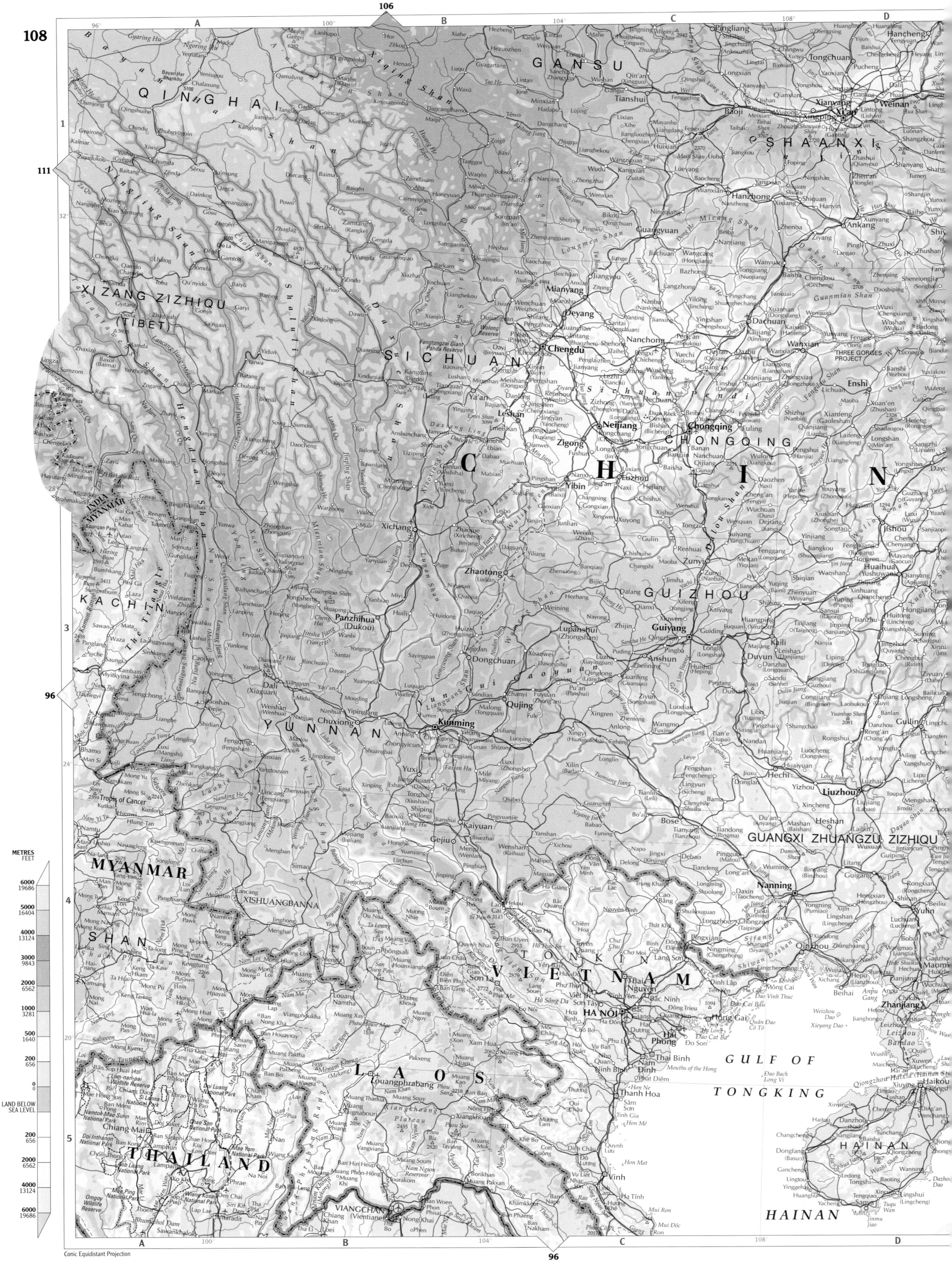

CHINA

QINGHAI
GANSU
SHAANXI
XIZANG ZIZHIQU
(TIBET)
SICHUAN
CHONGQING
GUIZHOU
YUNNAN
GUANGXI ZHUANGZU ZIZHIQU
KACHIN
MYANMAR
SHAN
THAILAND
LAOS
VIETNAM
TONKIN
HAINAN
INDIA
MYANMAR

THREE GORGES PROJECT

Tropic of Cancer

GULF OF TONGKING

METRES / FEET
6000 / 19686
5000 / 16404
4000 / 13124
3000 / 9843
2000 / 6562
1000 / 3281
500 / 1640
200 / 656
0 / 0
LAND BELOW SEA LEVEL
200 / 656
2000 / 6562
4000 / 13124
6000 / 19686

Conic Equidistant Projection

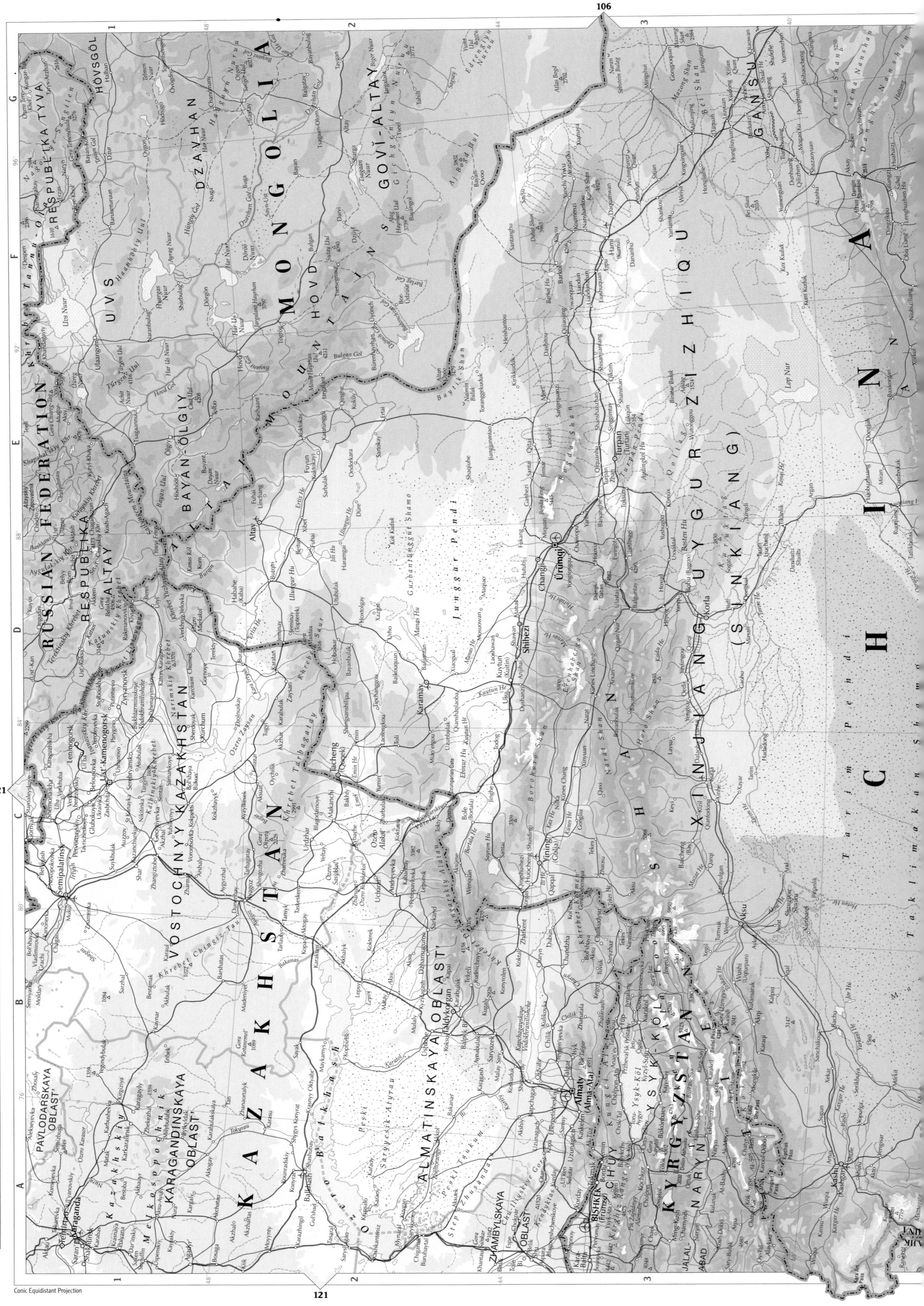

106

121

RUSSIAN FEDERATION

RESPUBLIKA TYVA

HÖVSGÖL

MONGOLIA

DZAVHAN

UVS

BAYAN-ÖLGIY

HOVD

GOVĬ-ALTAY

A l t a y   M o u n t a i n s

KAZAKHSTAN

VOSTOCHNYY KAZAKHSTAN

KARAGANDINSKAYA OBLAST'

PAVLODARSKAYA OBLAST'

ALMATINSKAYA OBLAST'

ZHAMBYLSKAYA OBLAST'

KYRGYZSTAN

NARYN

JALAL-ABAD

CHÜY

XINJIANG UYGUR ZIZHIQU (SINKIANG)

GANSU

CHINA

Jŭnggar Pendi

Tarim Pendi

Taklimakan Shamo

Ürümqi

Almaty (Alma-Ata)

Semipalatinsk

Ust'-Kamenogorsk

Leninogorsk

Karagandy

BISHKEK (Frunze)

Turpan

Kashi (Kashgar)

Aksu

Korla

Shihezi

Changji

Karamay

Tacheng (Qoqek)

Altay

Yining (Gulja)

Bole (Bortala)

Ozero Balkhash

Ozero Zaysan

ISSYK-KÖL

METRES FEET
6000 19686
5000 16404
4000 13124
3000 9843
2000 6562
1000 3281
500 1640
200 656
0
LAND BELOW SEA LEVEL
200 656
2000 6562
4000 13124
6000 19686

Conic Equidistant Projection

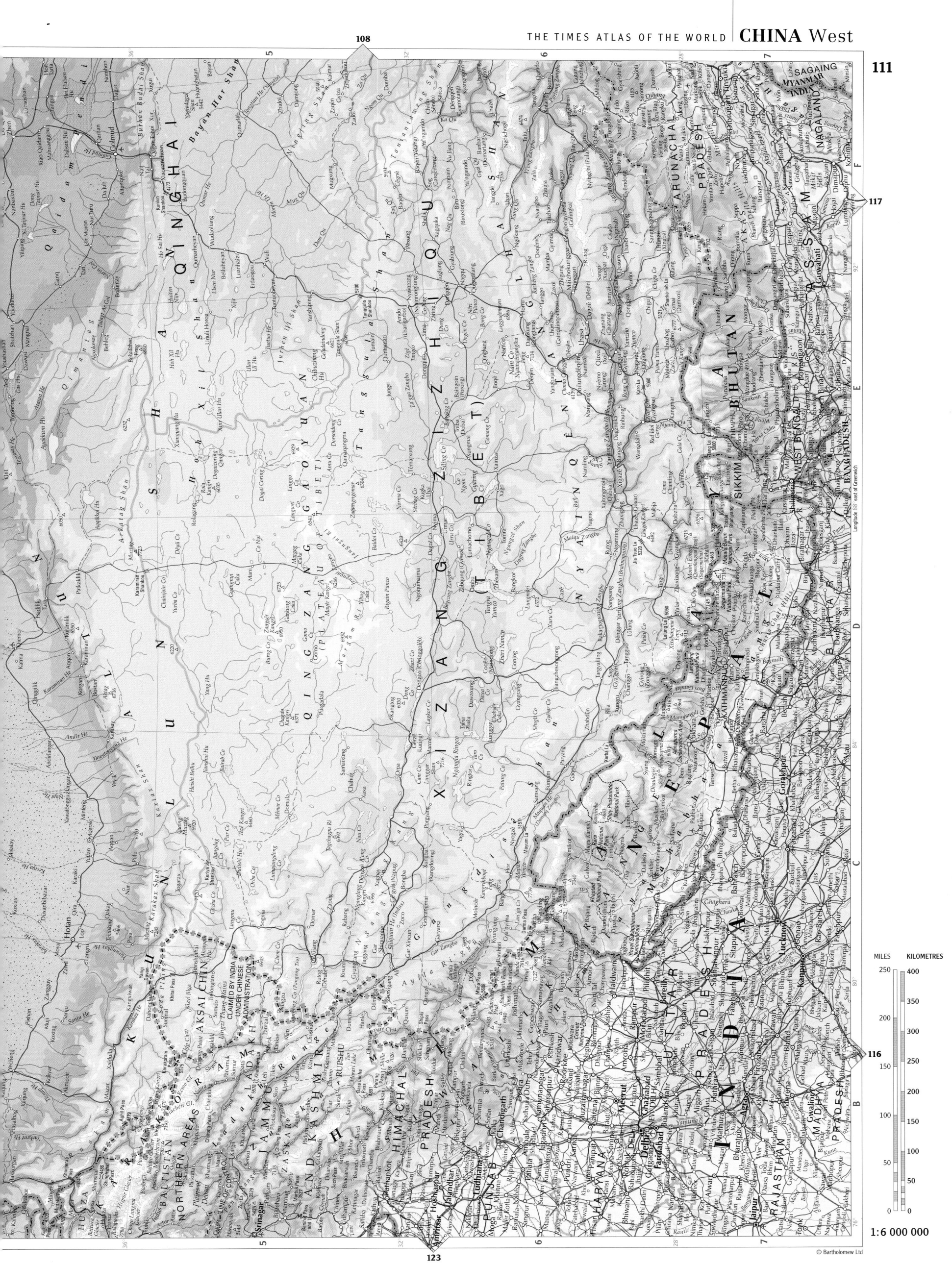

108

117

116

123

1:6 000 000

MILES   KILOMETRES

© Bartholomew Ltd

METRES
FEET

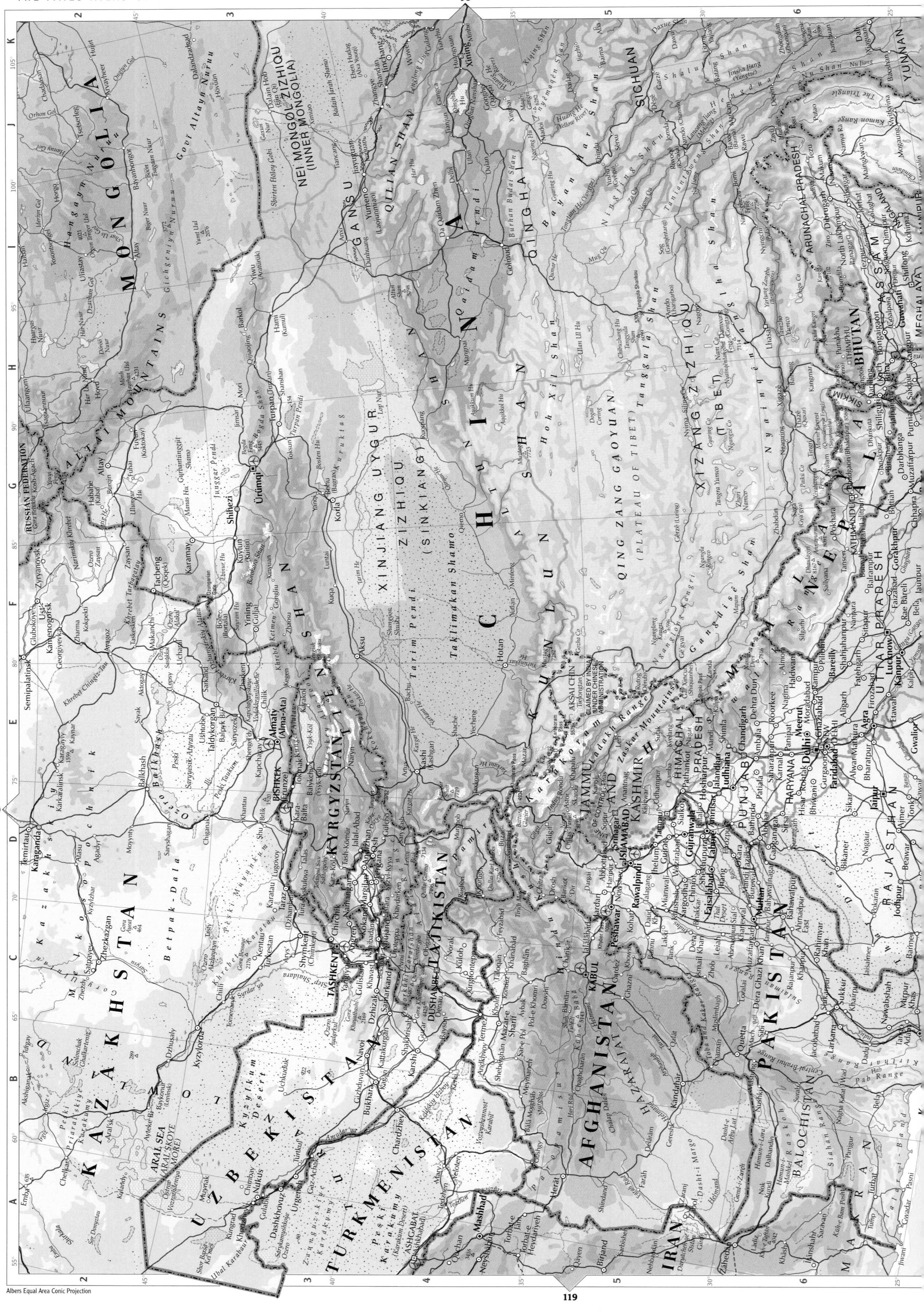

6000 / 19686
5000 / 16404
4000 / 13124
3000 / 9843
2000 / 6562
1000 / 3281
500 / 1640
200 / 656
0

LAND BELOW
SEA LEVEL

200 / 656
2000 / 6562
4000 / 13124
6000 / 19686

130

Albers Equal Area Conic Projection

MONGOLIA
RUSSIAN FEDERATION
KAZAKHSTAN
UZBEKISTAN
TURKMENISTAN
KYRGYZSTAN
TAJIKISTAN
AFGHANISTAN
PAKISTAN
IRAN
NEPAL
BHUTAN
QINGHAI
GANSU
XINJIANG UYGUR (SINKIANG)
XIZANG ZIZHIQU (TIBET)
SICHUAN
YUNNAN
NEI MONGOL ZIZHIQU (INNER MONGOLIA)
C H I N A

ALTAI MOUNTAINS
TIEN SHAN
KUNLUN
QILIAN SHAN
QING ZANG GAOYUAN (PLATEAU OF TIBET)
HIMALAYA
Taklimakan Shamo
Tarim Pendi
ARAL SEA
ARAL'SKOYE MORE
Kyzylkum Desert
Karakum
Betpak-Dala

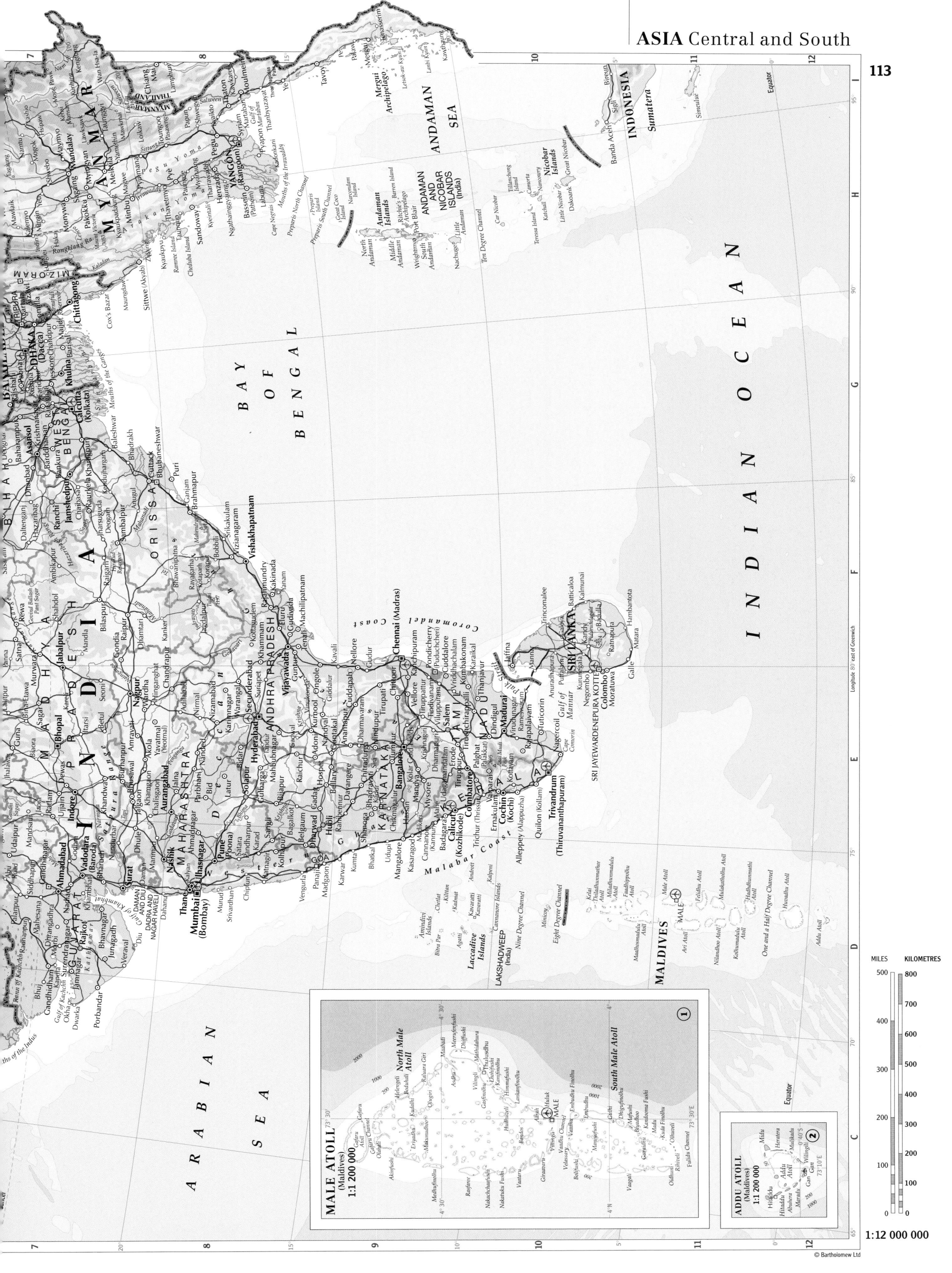

MYANMAR

THAILAND

ANDAMAN
SEA

Mergui
Archipelago

INDONESIA
Sumatera

ANDAMAN
AND
NICOBAR
ISLANDS
(India)

Andaman
Islands

Nicobar
Islands

BANGLADESH

DHAKA
(Dacca)

Chittagong

Khulna

Calcutta
(Kolkata)

WEST
BENGAL

BIHAR

ORISSA

Asansol

Jamshedpur

Ranchi

Cuttack

Bhubaneshwar

Puri

B A Y

O F

B E N G A L

I N D I A N   O C E A N

M A D H Y A   P R A D E S H

Bhopal

Jabalpur

Nagpur

MAHARASHTRA

ANDHRA PRADESH

Vishakhapatnam

Hyderabad

Vijayawada

Secunderabad

I N D I A

Coromandel Coast

Chennai (Madras)

Nellore

Pondicherry
(Puducherri)

Cuddalore

TAMIL
NADU

Bangalore

KARNATAKA

Madurai

GOA

Mangalore

Calicut
(Kozhikode)

Cochin
(Kochi)

Trivandrum
(Thiruvananthapuram)

Coimbatore

SRI LANKA

Colombo

SRI JAYEWARDENEPURA KOTTE

Jaffna

Gulf of
Mannar

Palk
Strait

Cape Comorin

Malabar Coast

LAKSHADWEEP
(India)

Laccadive
Islands

Amindivi
Islands

Cannanore Islands

Nine Degree Channel

Eight Degree Channel

Minicoy

Male Atoll

MALE

MALDIVES

A R A B I A N

S E A

Mumbai
(Bombay)

Thane

Pune
(Poona)

Nashik

Surat

Ahmadabad

Vadodara
(Baroda)

GUJARAT

Rajkot

Jamnagar

Bhavnagar

DAMAN AND DIU

DADRA AND
NAGAR HAVELI

Gulf of Khambhat

Gulf of Kachchh

Rann of Kachchh (Kutch)

Porbandar

Dwarka

MYANMAR

YANGON
(Rangon)

Mandalay

© Bartholomew Ltd

MALE ATOLL
(Maldives)
1:1 200 000

North Male
Atoll

South Male Atoll

MALE

ADDU ATOLL
(Maldives)
1:1 200 000

Addu
Atoll

Gan

MILES	KILOMETRES
500	800
400	700
	600
300	500
	400
200	300
100	200
	100
0	0

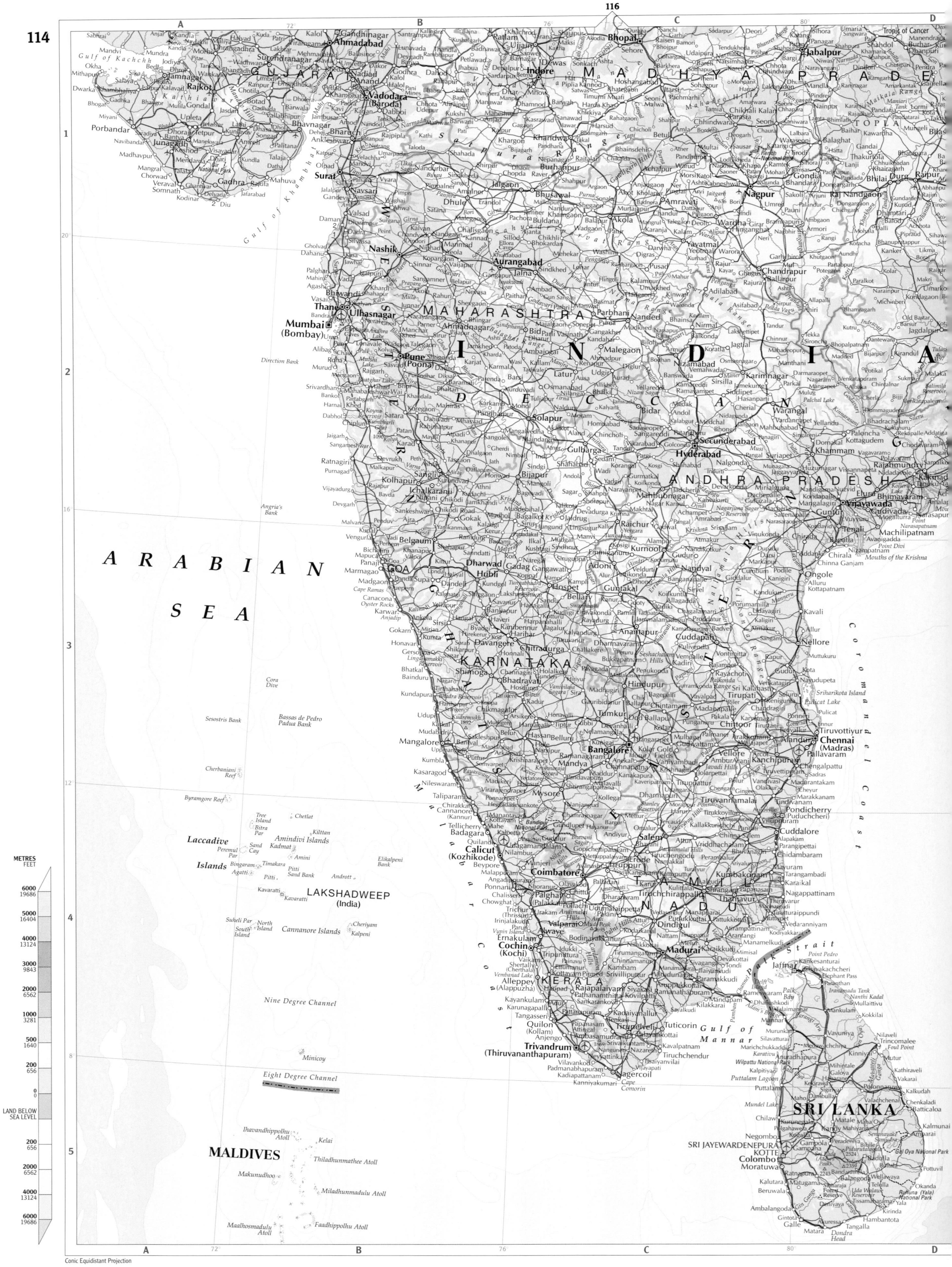

A B C D

MADHYA PRADESH

GUJARAT

MAHARASHTRA

INDIA

DECCAN

ANDHRA PRADESH

KARNATAKA

GOA

KERALA

TAMIL NADU

ARABIAN SEA

LAKSHADWEEP (India)

Laccadive Islands

Aminidivi Islands

Cannanore Islands

MALDIVES

SRI LANKA

Gulf of Mannar

Coromandel Coast

Tropic of Cancer

Major cities and towns

Gandhinagar, Ahmadabad, Vadodara (Baroda), Bhavnagar, Rajkot, Jamnagar, Porbandar, Junagadh, Surat, Surendranagar, Nadiad, Anand

Bhopal, Jabalpur, Indore, Dewas, Ujjain, Nagpur, Bhilai, Durg, Gondia

Nashik, Aurangabad, Mumbai (Bombay), Thane, Ulhasnagar, Pune (Poona), Solapur, Kolhapur, Sangli, Satara, Ratnagiri, Nanded, Parbhani, Latur, Osmanabad, Bidar, Gulbarga, Nizamabad, Karimnagar, Warangal, Amravati, Akola, Jalgaon, Dhule, Bhusawal, Nizamabad

Hyderabad, Secunderabad, Vijayawada, Guntur, Machilipatnam, Tenali, Nellore, Ongole, Kurnool, Nandyal, Anantapur, Cuddapah, Tirupati, Chittoor, Rajahmundry, Khammam

Belgaum, Dharwad, Hubli, Gadag, Bijapur, Raichur, Bellary, Hospet, Davangere, Chitradurga, Shimoga, Bhadravati, Mangalore, Hassan, Mysore, Mandya, Bangalore, Tumkur, Kolar

Panaji, Marmagao, Madgaon

Calicut (Kozhikode), Coimbatore, Cochin (Kochi), Ernakulam, Alleppey (Alappuzha), Quilon (Kollam), Trivandrum (Thiruvananthapuram), Nagercoil, Palghat, Trichur (Thrissur)

Chennai (Madras), Pallavaram, Kanchipuram, Vellore, Salem, Erode, Tiruppur, Tiruchirappalli, Thanjavur, Dindigul, Madurai, Tuticorin, Tirunelveli, Pondicherry (Puducherry), Cuddalore, Chidambaram, Kumbakonam, Nagapattinam

Jaffna, Colombo, Moratuwa, Sri Jayewardenepura Kotte, Negombo, Kandy, Trincomalee, Anuradhapura, Galle, Matara, Batticaloa

Kanniyakumari, Cape Comorin

Palk Strait, Palk Bay, Gulf of Khambhat, Gulf of Kachchh

Nine Degree Channel, Eight Degree Channel

Minicoy, Kavaratti, Kadmat, Andrott, Agatti

Cora Divh, Sesostris Bank, Bassas de Pedro, Padua Bank, Cherbaniani Reef, Byramgore Reef

Scale / Elevation key

METRES	FEET
6000	19686
5000	16404
4000	13124
3000	9843
2000	6562
1000	3281
500	1640
200	656
0	0

LAND BELOW SEA LEVEL

200	656
2000	6562
4000	13124
6000	19686

Conic Equidistant Projection

BAY

OF

BENGAL

Administrative areas not named on the map:
INDIA
1. DADRA AND NAGAR HAVELI (B1)
2. DAMAN AND DIU (A1,B1)
3. PONDICHERRY (D2,C4)

INDIAN

OCEAN

CALCUTTA 1:70 000

0 METRES 750
0 YARDS 750

MUMBAI 1:90 000

0 METRES 1000
0 YARDS 1000

ANDAMAN
AND
NICOBAR
ISLANDS
(India)

Andaman Islands

Nicobar Islands

MILES   KILOMETRES

250   400
        350
200   300
        250
150   200
100   150
        100
50   50
0   0

1:6 000 000

© Bartholomew Ltd

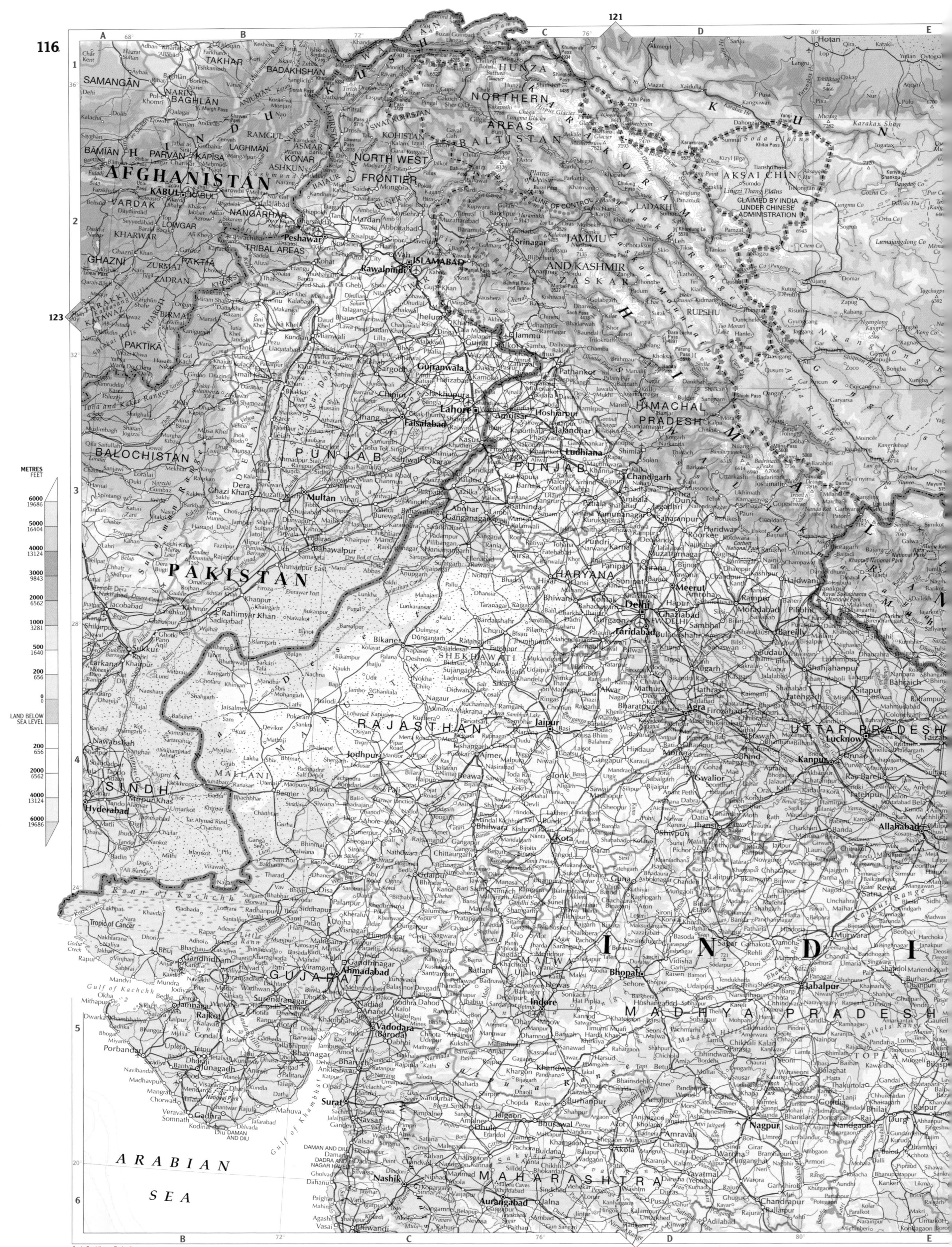

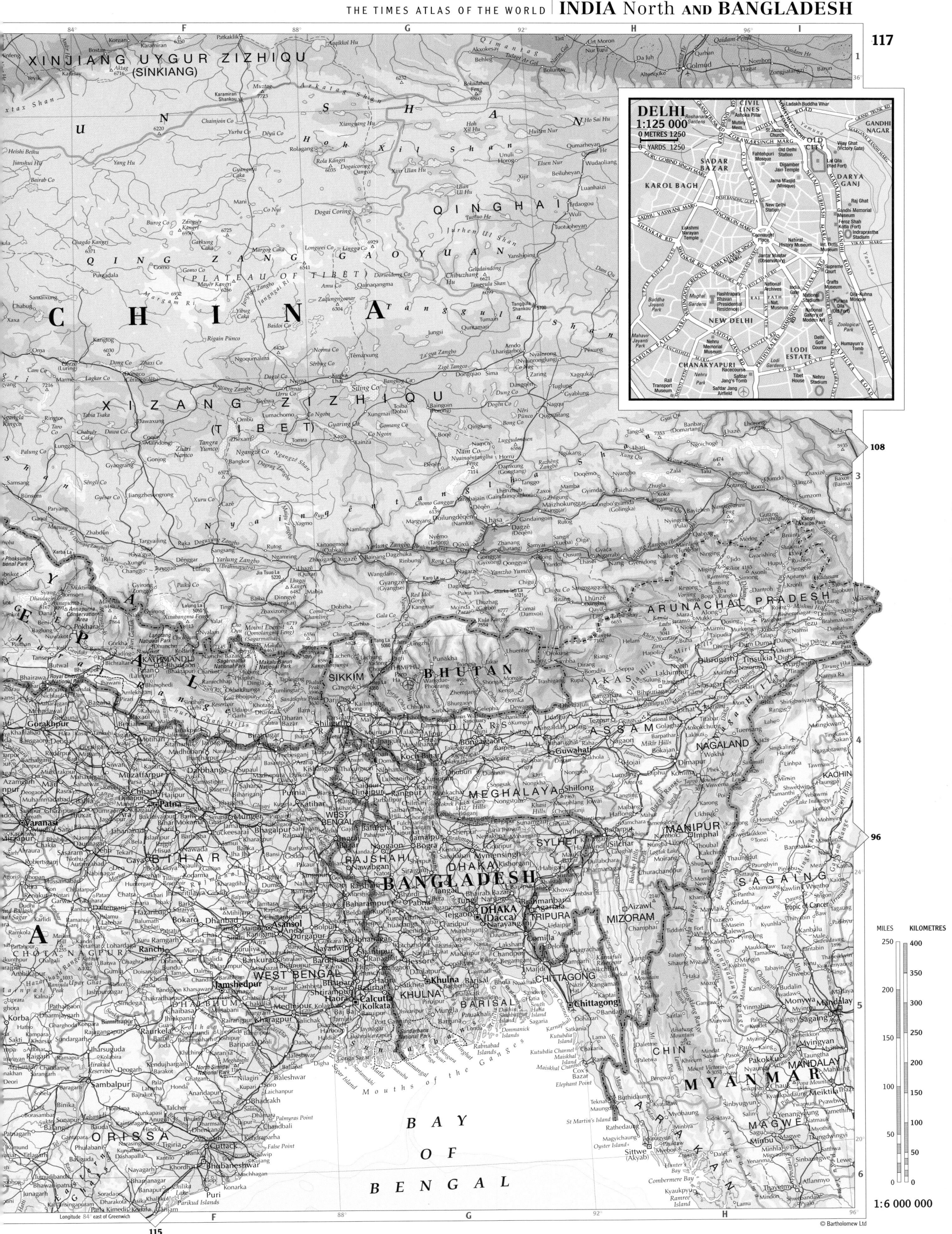

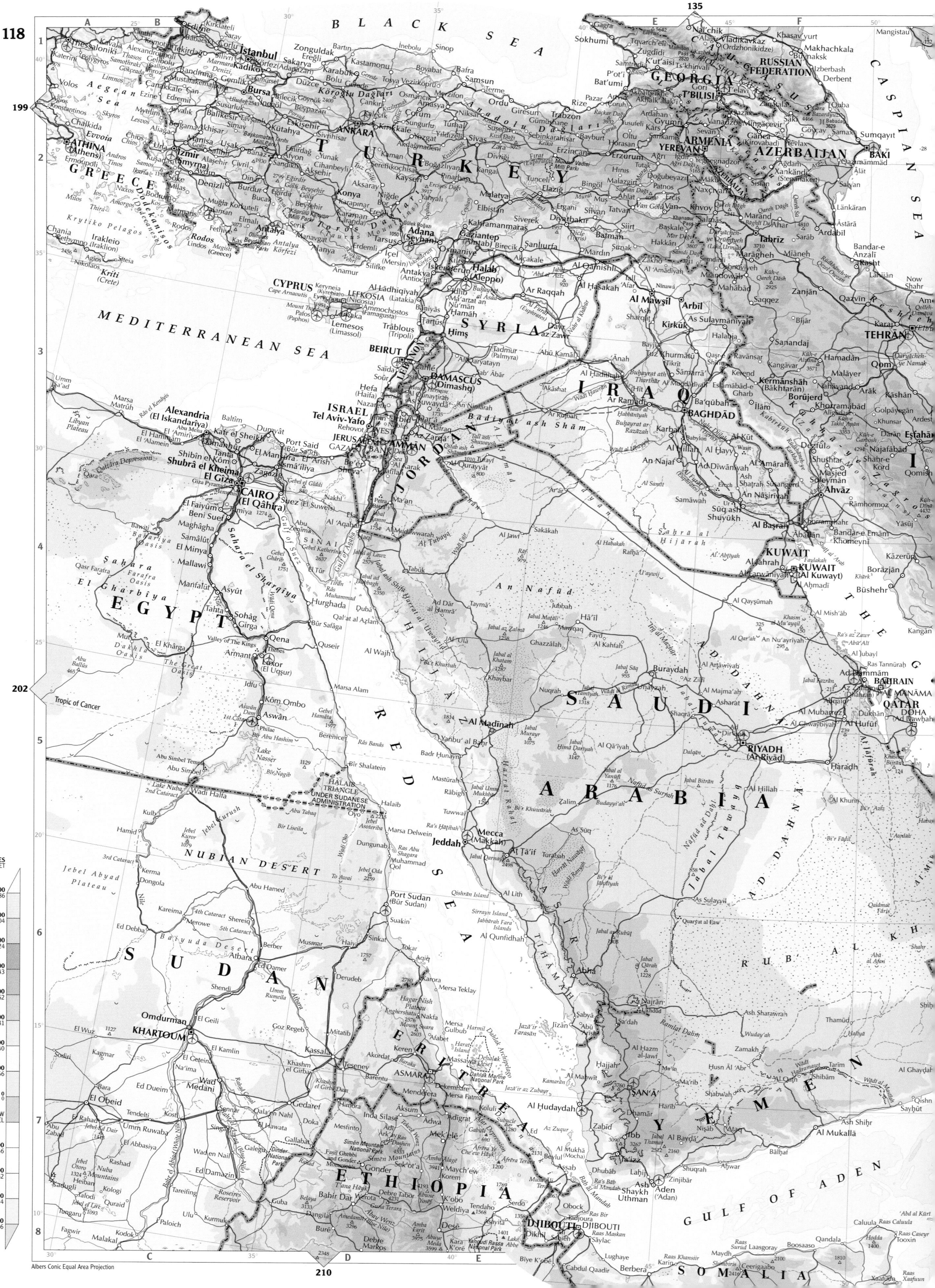

199

202

210

BLACK SEA

CASPIAN SEA

MEDITERRANEAN SEA

RED SEA

GULF OF ADEN

GREECE

TURKEY

GEORGIA

RUSSIAN FEDERATION

ARMENIA

AZERBAIJAN

CYPRUS

SYRIA

IRAQ

LEBANON

ISRAEL

JORDAN

EGYPT

SAUDI ARABIA

KUWAIT

BAHRAIN

QATAR

SUDAN

ERITREA

ETHIOPIA

DJIBOUTI

SOMALIA

YEMEN

Istanbul
ANKARA
ATHINA (Athens)
İzmir (Smyrna)
Bursa
T'BILISI
YEREVAN
BAKI
TEHRĀN
Tabrīz
BEIRUT
DAMASCUS (Dimashq)
Ḩalab (Aleppo)
Al Mawşil
Arbīl
BAGHDĀD
JERUSALEM
AMMAN
Tel Aviv-Yafo
CAIRO (El Qâhira)
Alexandria (El Iskandarîya)
El Giza
KUWAIT (Al Kuwayt)
RIYADH (Ar Riyāḑ)
Mecca (Makkah)
Jeddah
Al Madīnah
DOHA
Al Manāmā
KHARTOUM
Omdurman
ASMARA
ŞAN'Ā'
DJIBOUTI

MÉTRES / FEET
6000 / 19686
5000 / 16404
4000 / 13124
3000 / 9843
2000 / 6562
1000 / 3281
500 / 1640
200 / 656
0 / 0
LAND BELOW SEA LEVEL
200 / 656
2000 / 6562
4000 / 13124
6000 / 19686

Tropic of Cancer

Albers Conic Equal Area Projection

135

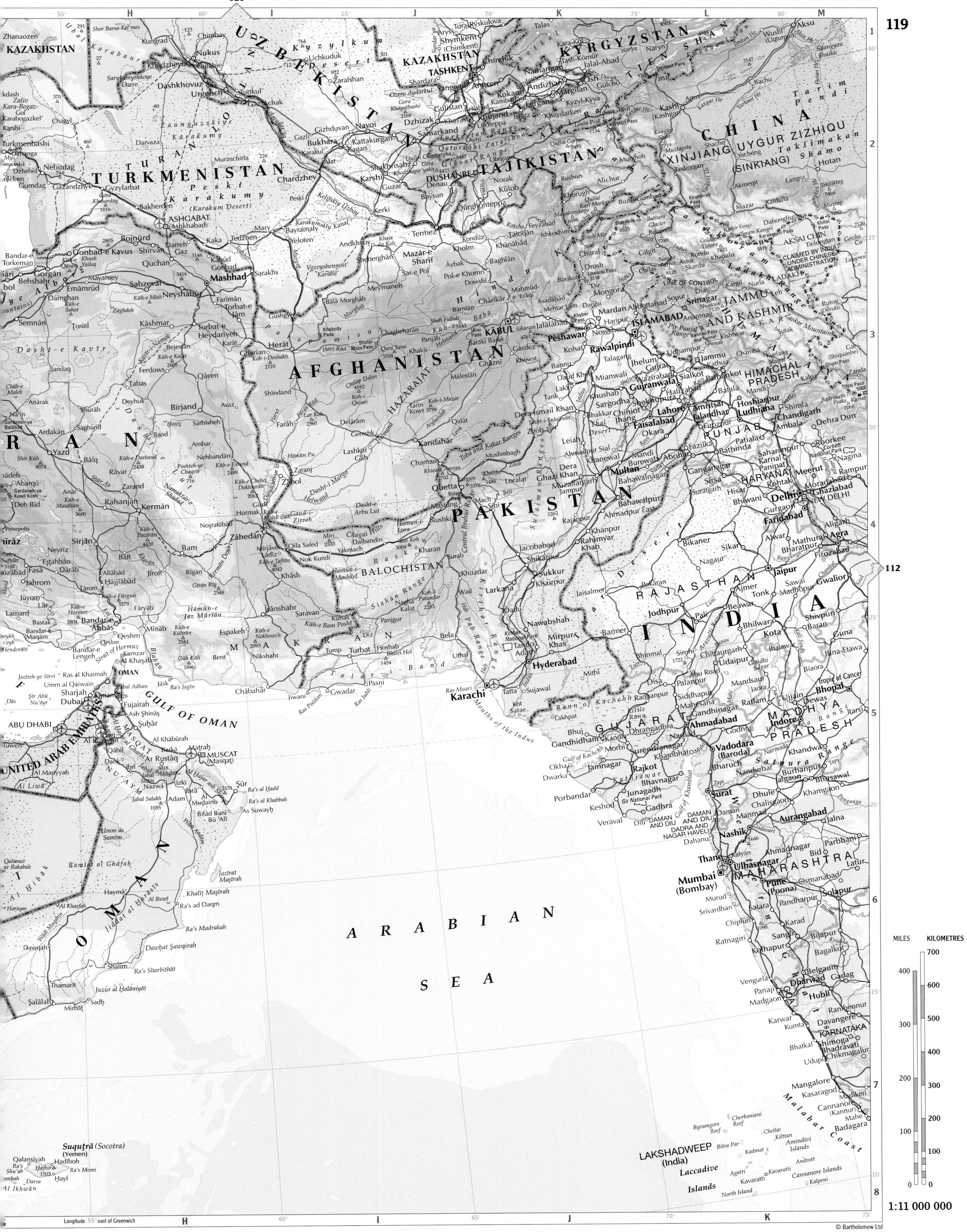

KAZAKHSTAN

TURKMENISTAN

UZBEKISTAN

TASHKENT

KYRGYZSTAN

TAJIKISTAN

DUSHANBE

CHINA

XINJIANG UYGUR ZIZHIQU
(SINKIANG) Taklimakan
Shamo

Tarim
Pendi

ASHGABAT
(Ashkhabad)

Mashhad

AFGHANISTAN

HAZARAJAT

KABUL

HINDU KUSH

JAMMU
AND KASHMIR

Srinagar

ISLAMABAD

Peshawar
Rawalpindi

HIMACHAL
PRADESH

PUNJAB

Lahore
Faisalabad
Multan

Amritsar
Jalandhar Ludhiana
Chandigarh

HARYANA

Delhi
NEW DELHI
Faridabad

I R A N

PAKISTAN

BALOCHISTAN

MAKRAN

Quetta

Kandahar

RAJASTHAN

Jaipur Gwalior
Agra
Aligarh

INDIA

Bandar-e
Abbas

OMAN

UNITED ARAB EMIRATES

ABU DHABI
Dubai

MUSCAT
(Masqat)

GULF OF OMAN

Karachi

Hyderabad

GUJARAT

Ahmadabad

Vadodara
(Baroda)

Rajkot
Surat

MADHYA
PRADESH

Indore
Bhopal

Tropic of Cancer

MAHARASHTRA

Nashik
Thane
Ulhasnagar
Mumbai
(Bombay)
Pune
(Poona)
Solapur

Aurangabad

A R A B I A N

S E A

Suquṭrā (Socotra)
(Yemen)

KARNATAKA

Hubli
Dharwad

Mangalore

Malabar Coast

LAKSHADWEEP
(India)

Laccadive
Islands

MILES KILOMETRES
700
600
400
500
300 400
300
200
200
100
100
0 0

A · B · C · D · E

134

RESPUBLIKA
BASHKORTOSTAN

RUSSIAN FEDERATION

CHELYABINSKAYA
OBLAST'

SAMARSKAYA
OBLAST'

SARATOVSKAYA
OBLAST'

ORENBURGSKAYA OBLAST'

KUSTANAYSKAYA OBLAST'

Orenburg

ZAPADNYY

KAZAKHSTAN

AKTYUBINSKAYA

Aktyubinsk

OBLAST'

K A Z A K

Astrakhan'

ASTRAKHANSKAYA
OBLAST'

PRIKASPIYSKAYA NIZMENNOST'
(Caspian Lowland)
Ryn-
Peski

ATYRAUSKAYA OBLAST'

Atyrau
(Gur'yev)

KZYL-ORDINSKAYA OBLAST'

ARAL SEA

Peski
Priaral'skiye
Karakumy

RESPUBLIKA
DAGESTAN

Makhachkala

C A S P I A N   S E A

MANGISTAUSKAYA
OBLAST'

Aktau
(Shevchenko)

Ustyurt
Plateau

RESPUBLIKA KARAKALPAKISTAN

(ARAL'SKOYE MORE)

K Y Z Y L K U M

D E S E R T

U Z B E K I S T A N

AZERBAIJAN

BAKI

Sumqayıt

Kara-Bogaz-
Gol

Nukus

NAVOIYSKAYA OBLAST'

DASHKHOVUZSKAYA
OBLAST'

Dashkhovuz

KHOREZMSKAYA
OBLAST'

BALKANSKAYA OBLAST'

Turkmenbashi

Nebitdag

OBLAST'
Zaunguzskiye
Karakumy

BUKHARSKAYA

OBLAST'
Bukhara

T U R K M E N I S T A N

T u r k m e n

PESKI KARAKUMY
(KARAKUM DESERT)

LEBAPSKAYA OBLAST'

Chardzhev

AKHAL'SKAYA OBLAST'

ASHGABAT (Ashkhabad)

MARYYSKAYA

OBLAST'

MĀZANDARĀN

I R A N

KHORĀSAN

GOLESTĀN

SEMNĀN

Gorgān

FĀRYĀB

Administrative regions numbered on the map:

UZBEKISTAN

1. ANDIZHANSKAYA OBLAST' (H4)
2. DZHIZAKSKAYA OBLAST' (F5)
3. FERGANSKAYA OBLAST' (G4)
4. KASHKADAR'INSKAYA OBLAST' (F5)
5. NAMANGANSKAYA OBLAST' (G4)
6. SAMARKANDSKAYA OBLAST' (F5)
7. SYRDAR'INSKAYA OBLAST' (G4)
8. TASHKENTSKAYA OBLAST' (G4)

METRES
FEET

6000
19686

5000
16404

4000
13124

3000
9843

2000
6562

1000
3281

500
1640

200
656

0
0

LAND BELOW
SEA LEVEL

200
656

2000
6562

4000
13124

6000
19686

Conic Equidistant Projection

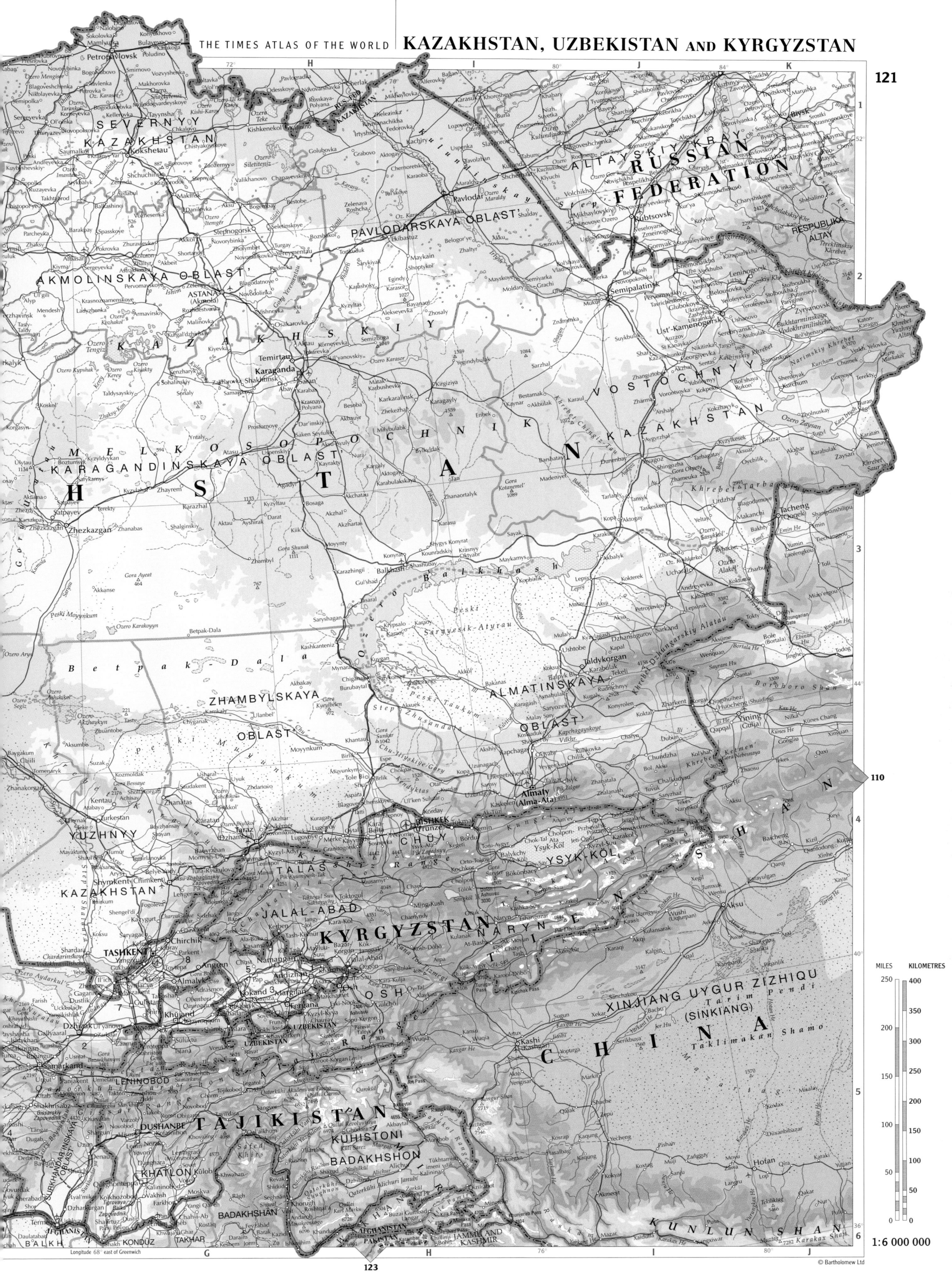

RUSSIAN FEDERATION

RESPUBLIKA ALTAY

SEVERNYY KAZAKHSTAN

AKMOLINSKAYA OBLAST'

KARAGANDINSKAYA OBLAST'

K A Z A K H S T A N

VOSTOCHNYY KAZAKHSTAN

MELKOSOPOCHNIK

ZHAMBYLSKAYA OBLAST'

ALMATINSKAYA OBLAST'

YUZHNYY KAZAKHSTAN

XINJIANG UYGUR ZIZHIQU (SINKIANG)

C H I N A

KYRGYZSTAN

JALAL-ABAD

NARYN

OSH

YSYK-KÖL

CHÜY

TALAS

UZBEKISTAN

TASHKENT

TAJIKISTAN

KUHISTONI BADAKHSHON

KHATLON

BADAKHSHAN

AFGHANISTAN

PAKISTAN

JAMMU AND KASHMIR

MILES   KILOMETRES

1:6 000 000

© Bartholomew Ltd

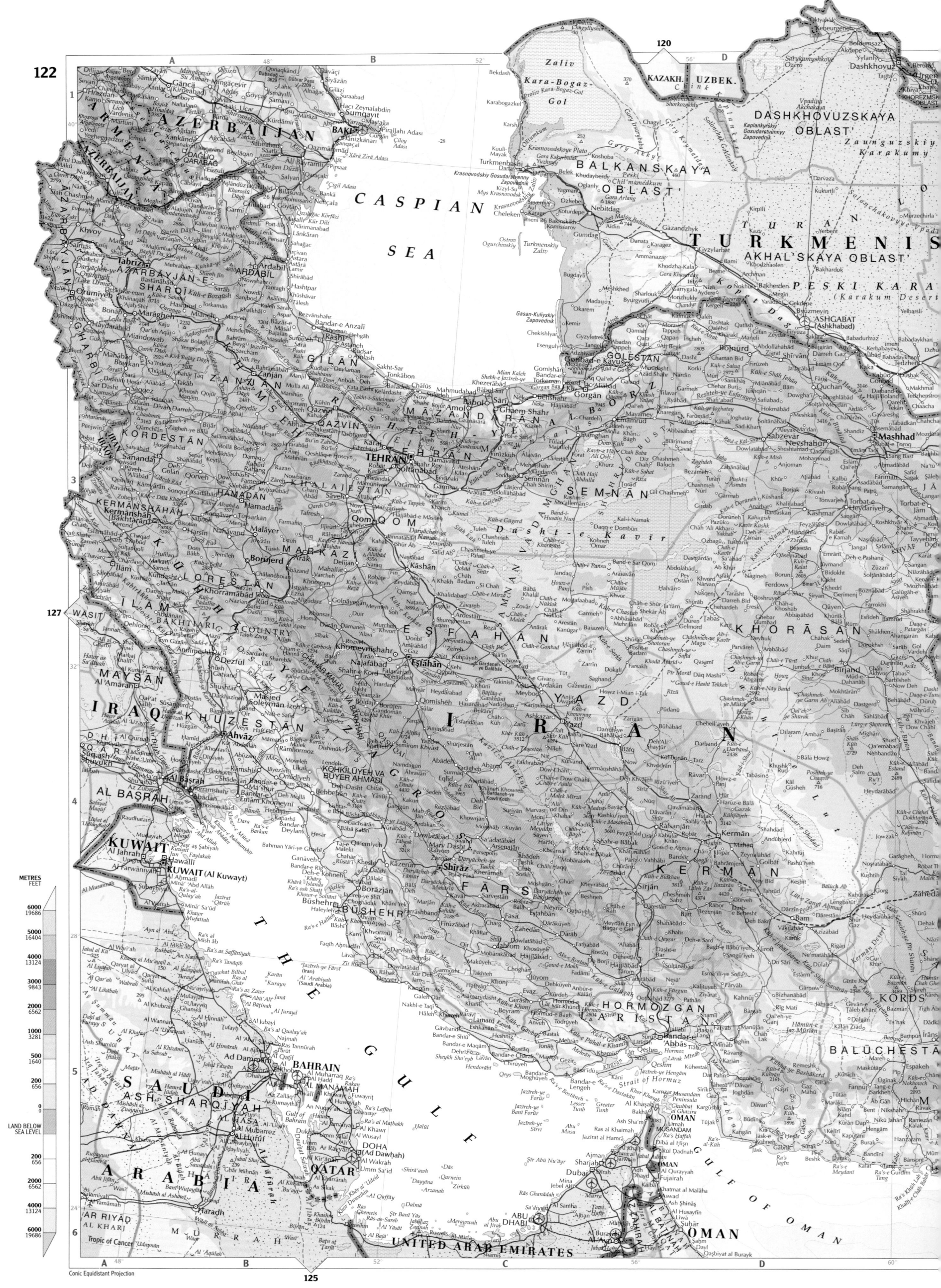

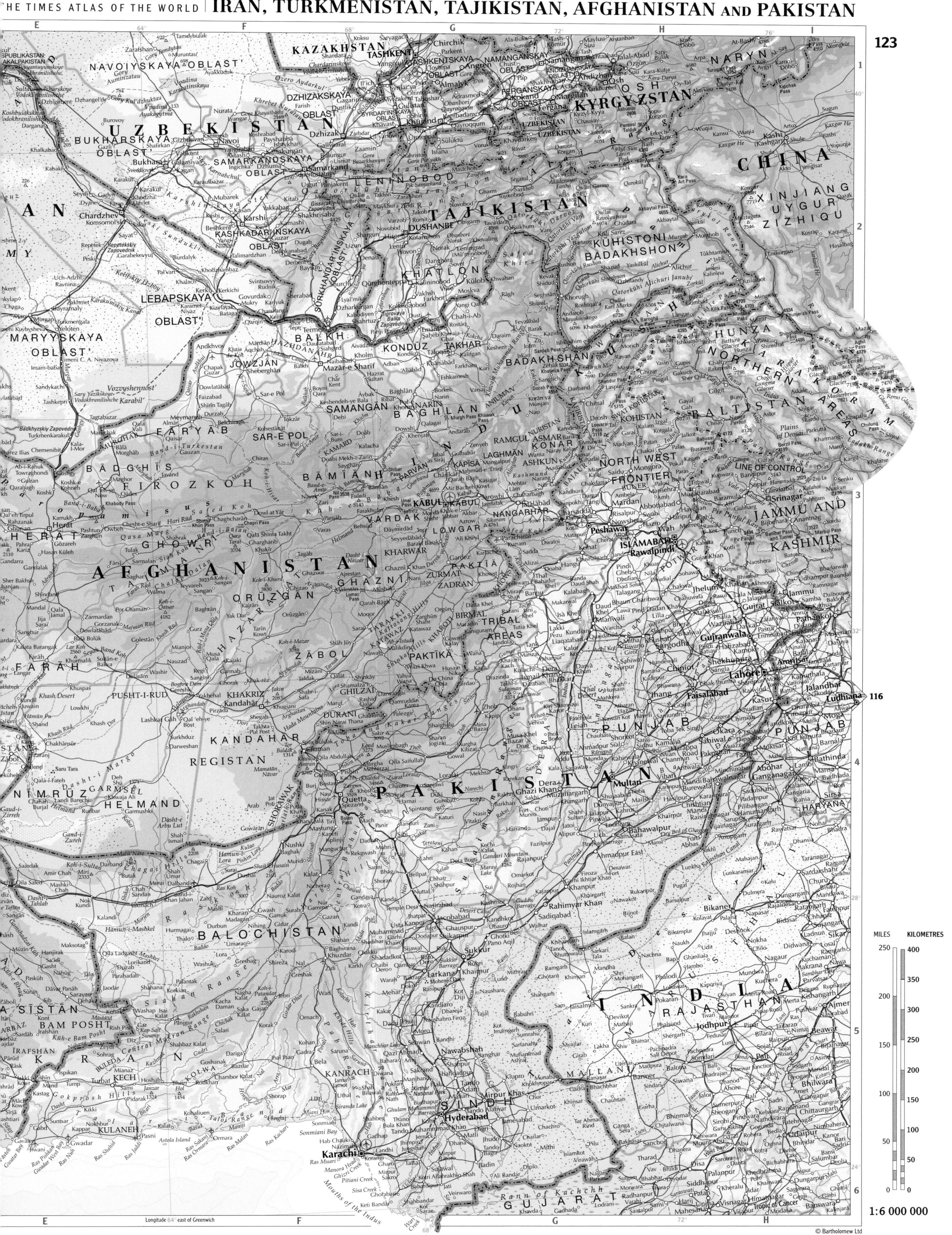

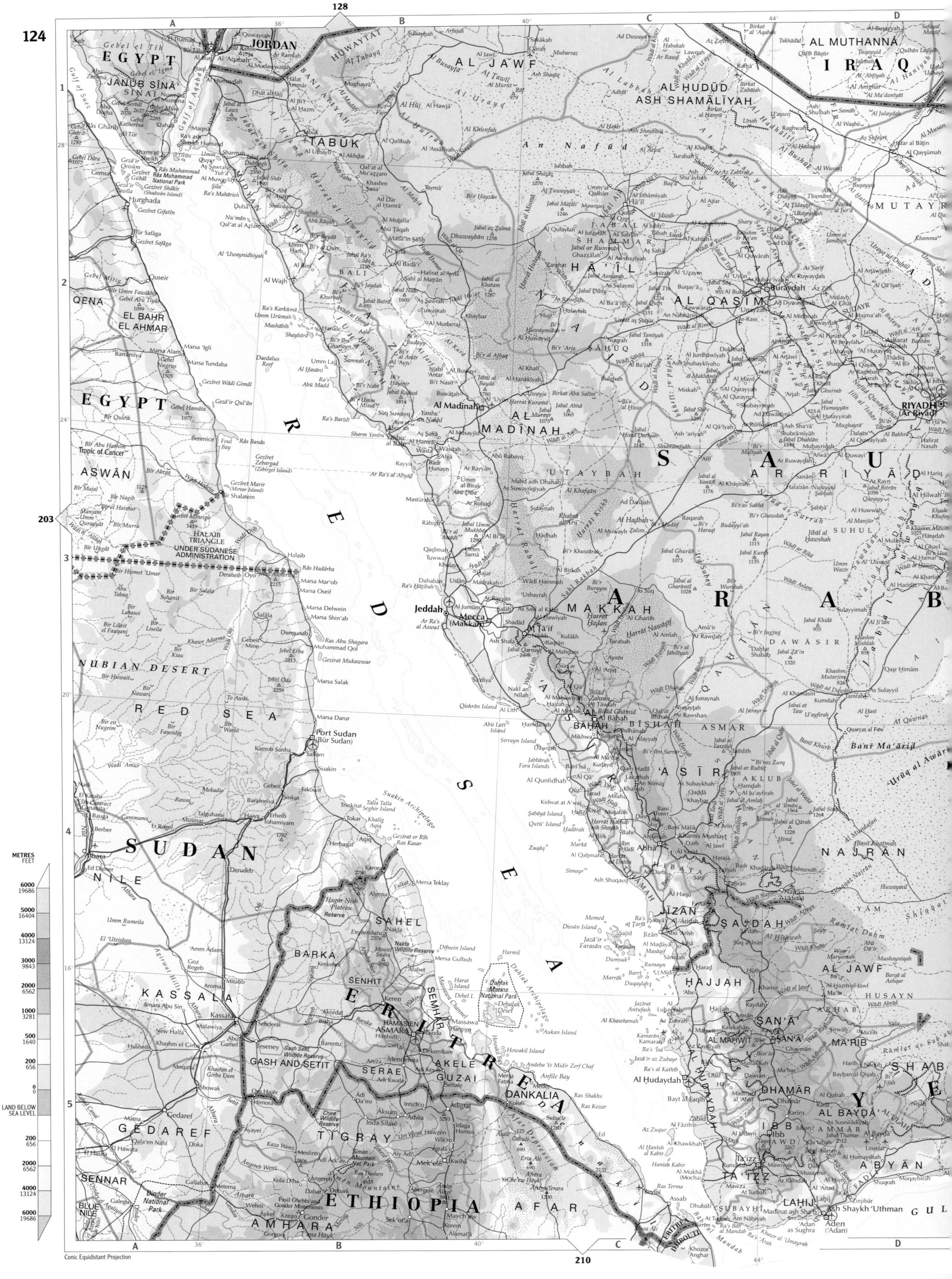

128

EGYPT

JORDAN

JANÛB SÍNÂ'
SINAI

IRAQ

AL MUTHANNÁ

AL HUDÛD
ASH SHAMÁLIYAH

AL JAWF

TABUK

MUTAYR

An Nafûd

QENA

EL BAHR
EL AHMAR

HÁ'IL

AL QASIM

RIYÁD
Ar Riyad

EGYPT

S   A   U

ASWÂN

Tropic of Cancer

HALAIB
TRIANGLE
UNDER SUDANESE
ADMINISTRATION

203

R   E   D

AL MADÎNAH

DI   A   R   I   Y   Á   D

Al Madinah

Jeddah

Mecca
(Makkah)

MAKKAH

A   R   A   B   I   A

NUBIAN DESERT

S   E   A

RED SEA

Port Sudan
(Bûr Sudan)

DAWÁSIR

Banî Ma'árid

BÁHAH

BÎSHAH

ASMAR

SUDAN

'ASÎR

AL JAWF

NILE

NAJRÁN

SAHEL

JIZÁN

SA'DAH

BARKA

KASSALA

ERITREA

HAJJAH

AL JAWF

HUSAYN

SENHIT

SEMHAR

ASMARA

HAMASEN

Dahlak
Marine
National Park
Dehalak
Deset

SAN'Á'

MA'RIB

GASH AND SETIT

AKELE
GUZAI

SERAE

AL HUDAYDAH

DHAMÁR

SHAB

DANKALIA

IBB

AL BAYDÁ'

GEDARF

TIGRAY

AFAR

TA'IZZ

LAHIJ

ABYAN

SENNAR

BLUE
NILE

Binder
National Park

ETHIOPIA

AMHARA

Aden
('Adan)

GUL

METRES
FEET

6000
19686

5000
16404

4000
13124

3000
9843

2000
6562

1000
3281

500
1640

200
656

0

LAND BELOW
SEA LEVEL

200
656

2000
6562

4000
13124

6000
19686

Conic Equidistant Projection

IRAN

KHUZESTĀN

KUWAIT

AL BAŞRAH

KUWAIT (Al Kuwayt)

BAHRAIN

AL MANĀMAH

QATAR

DOHA (Ad Dawḩah)

AL HASA

Ad Dammām

KERMAN

HORMOZGAN

FĀRS

LĀRISTĀN

BALŪCHESTĀN VA SISTĀN

KORDŚ

SARḨAD

THE GULF

Strait of Hormuz

GULF OF OMAN

ABU DHABI

Dubai

UNITED ARAB EMIRATES

AL DHAFRAH

MANĀŞĪR

Tropic of Cancer

MUSCAT (Masqat)

MASQAṬ

AL BĀṬINAH

AZ ZĀHIRAH

AD DĀKHILIYAH

ASH SHARQIYAH

O M A N

RUB' AL KHĀLĪ

ASH SHARQIYAH

AL WUSṬÁ

AL GHUBR

Arabian Oryx Sanctuary

ḨAḌRAMAWT

ZUFĀR

AL MAHRAH

AL MAHRAH

Y E M E N

A R A B I A N   S E A

Suquṭrā (Socotra) (Yemen)

MILES   KILOMETRES

250   400

200   350

     300

150   250

     200

100   150

     100

50

     50

0   0

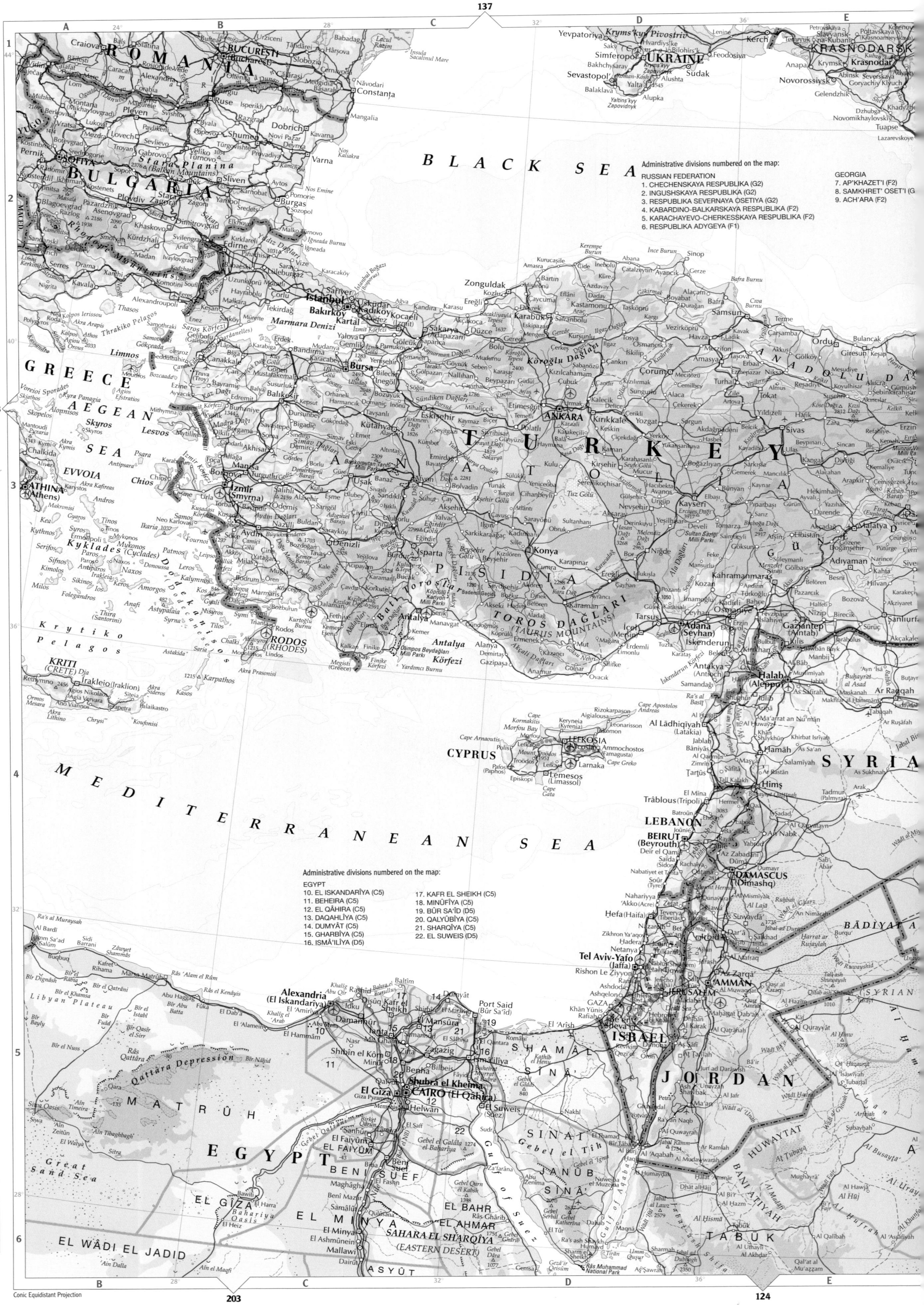

Major features

BLACK SEA

ROMANIA
BUCUREŞTI (Bucharest)

BULGARIA
SOFIYA

GREECE
ATHINA (Athens)

AEGEAN SEA

UKRAINE

KRASNODARSK
Krasnodar

GEORGIA

TURKEY
ANKARA

ANATOLIA

CYPRUS
LEFKOSIA (Nicosia)

SYRIA
Halab (Aleppo)
Hamah
Himş
DAMASCUS (Dimashq)

LEBANON
BEIRUT (Beyrouth)

ISRAEL
JERUSALEM
Tel Aviv-Yafo (Jaffa)

JORDAN
AMMAN

MEDITERRANEAN SEA

EGYPT
Alexandria (El Iskandarîya)
CAIRO (El Qâhira)
El Gîza
Shubra el Kheima

Administrative divisions numbered on the map:

RUSSIAN FEDERATION
1. CHECHENSKAYA RESPUBLIKA (G2)
2. INGUSHSKAYA RESPUBLIKA (G2)
3. RESPUBLIKA SEVERNAYA OSETIYA (G2)
4. KABARDINO-BALKARSKAYA RESPUBLIKA (F2)
5. KARACHAYEVO-CHERKESSKAYA RESPUBLIKA (F2)
6. RESPUBLIKA ADYGEYA (F1)

GEORGIA
7. AP'KHAZET'I (F2)
8. SAMKHRET' OSET'I (G
9. ACH'ARA (F2)

Administrative divisions numbered on the map:

EGYPT
10. EL ISKANDARÎYA (C5)
11. BEHEIRA (C5)
12. EL QÂHIRA (C5)
13. DAQAHLÎYA (C5)
14. DUMYÂT (C5)
15. GHARBÎYA (C5)
16. ISMÂ'ILÎYA (D5)
17. KAFR EL SHEIKH (C5)
18. MINÛFÎYA (C5)
19. BÛR SA'ÎD (D5)
20. QALYÛBÎYA (C5)
21. SHARQÎYA (C5)
22. EL SUWEIS (D5)

METRES / FEET
6000 / 19686
5000 / 16404
4000 / 13124
3000 / 9843
2000 / 6562
1000 / 3281
500 / 1640
200 / 656
0 / 0
LAND BELOW SEA LEVEL
200 / 656
2000 / 6562
4000 / 13124
6000 / 19686

Conic Equidistant Projection

TURKEY, IRAQ, SYRIA, JORDAN and TRANS-CAUCASIAN REPUBLICS

RUSSIAN FEDERATION

STAVROPOL'SKIY KRAY

GEORGIA

T'BILISI

ARMENIA

YEREVAN

AZERBAIJAN

BAKI

RESPUBLIKA DAGESTAN

KAZAKHSTAN

MANGISTAUSKAYA OBLAST'

UZBEKISTAN

TURKMENISTAN

BALKANSKAYA OBLAST

GOLESTAN

MAZANDARAN

SEMNAN

C A S P I A N   S E A

Kara-Bogaz-Gol

Zaliv

AZER.

AZARBAYJAN-E SHARQI

AZARBAYJAN-E GHARB

Tabriz

Maragheh

Orumiyeh

Van Gölü (Lake Van)

Van

Erzurum

Diyarbakir

GILAN

Rasht

QAZVIN

TEHRAN

ZANJAN

KORDESTAN

HAMADAN

KERMANSHAH

LORESTAN

ILAM

I R A N

DAHUK

Al Mawsil

NINAWA

AL HASAKAH

Al Qamishli

ARBIL

Kirkuk

AS SULAYMANIYAH

AT TA'MIM

SALAH AD DIN

DIYALA

BAGHDAD

I R A Q

AL ANBAR

WASIT

BABIL

KARBALA

AN NAJAF

AL QADISIYAH

AL MUTHANNA

DHI QAR

MAYSAN

Al Basrah

KHUZESTAN

Ahvaz

FARS

Shiraz

BUSHEHR

Büshehr

KUWAIT

KUWAIT (Al Kuwayt)

SAUDI ARABIA

AL HUDUD ASH SHAMALIYAH

ASH SHARQIYAH

An Nafud

T H E   G U L F

MILES   KILOMETRES

250   400
350
200   300
250
150   200
100   150
100
50   50
0   0

1:6 000 000

ISTANBUL

1:60 000

KULAKSIZ

KURTULUS

DOLMABAHCE

TAKSIM

BEYOGLU

Galata Tower

KARAKÖY

ÜSKÜDAR

Haliç (Golden Horn)

İstanbul Boğazı (Bosporus)

Süleymaniye Mosque

Istanbul University

Kapalı Çarşı (Grand Bazaar)

Beyazıt Tower

SULTANAHMET

Ayasofya Museum (Hagia Sophia)

Sultan Ahmet Mosque (Blue Mosque)

Topkapı Palace

Dolmabahçe Palace

KUMKAPI

UNKAPANI

EMINÖNÜ

Town Hall

Kız Kulesi (Maiden's Tower)

0 METRES   750
0 YARDS   750

Longitude 44° east of Greenwich

© Bartholomew Ltd

MEDITERRANEAN SEA

CYPRUS
LEFKOSIA (Nicosia)
Larnaka
Lemesos (Limassol)
Akrotiri Sovereign Base Area (U.K.)
Dhekelia Sovereign Base Area (U.K.)

ANTALYA
İCEL
KARAMAN
TOROS MOUNTAINS
ADANA (Seyhan)
TURKEY
OSMANIYE
GAZIANTEP
ŞANLIURFA
KİLİS
HATAY
İskenderun
Antakya (Antioch)

SYRIA
HALAB
Halab (Aleppo)
IDLIB
AR RAQQAH
NUZAYZAH
Al Lādhiqīyah (Latakia)
AL LĀDHIQĪYAH
HAMĀH
Ḥamāh
HIMS
Ḥimş
TARTUS
Ṭarṭūs
DIMASHQ

LEBANON
Trâblous (Tripoli)
BEIRUT (Beyrouth)
DAMASCUS (Dimashq)

ISRAEL
Hefa (Haifa)
Mount Carmel
Tel Aviv-Yafo (Jaffa)
Holon
Rishon Le Ziyyon
Ashdod
Ashqelon
JERUSALEM (El Quds) (Yerushalayim)
Bethlehem
Hebron (El Khalîl)
WEST BANK
GAZA

AL QUNAYTIRAH
CEASE-FIRE LINES 1974
DAR'Ā
AS SUWAYDĀ'
Irbid
AMMAN
JORDAN
Az Zarqā'

BADIYAT ASH SHĀM
(SYRIAN DESERT)
IRAQ

EL SUWEIS
Port Said (Bûr Sa'îd)
ISMA'ILIYA
EGYPT
SHAMÂL SÎNÂ
JANÛB SÎNÂ
EL BAHR EL AHMAR
Gulf of Suez

Khān Yūnis
Rafaḥ
El 'Arîsh
Be'er Sheva'
Dimona

'Aqaba
Gulf of Aqaba

SAUDI ARABIA
AL JAWF
TABŪK
AL HUDŪD ASH SHAMĀLIYAH

© Bartholomew Ltd

METRES / FEET
6000 / 19686
5000 / 16404
4000 / 13124
3000 / 9843
2000 / 6562
1500 / 4921
1000 / 3281
500 / 1640
200 / 656
100 / 328
0
LAND BELOW SEA LEVEL
200 / 164
1000 / 656
2000 / 3281

1:3 000 000
Conic Equidistant Projection
Longitude 36° east of Greenwich

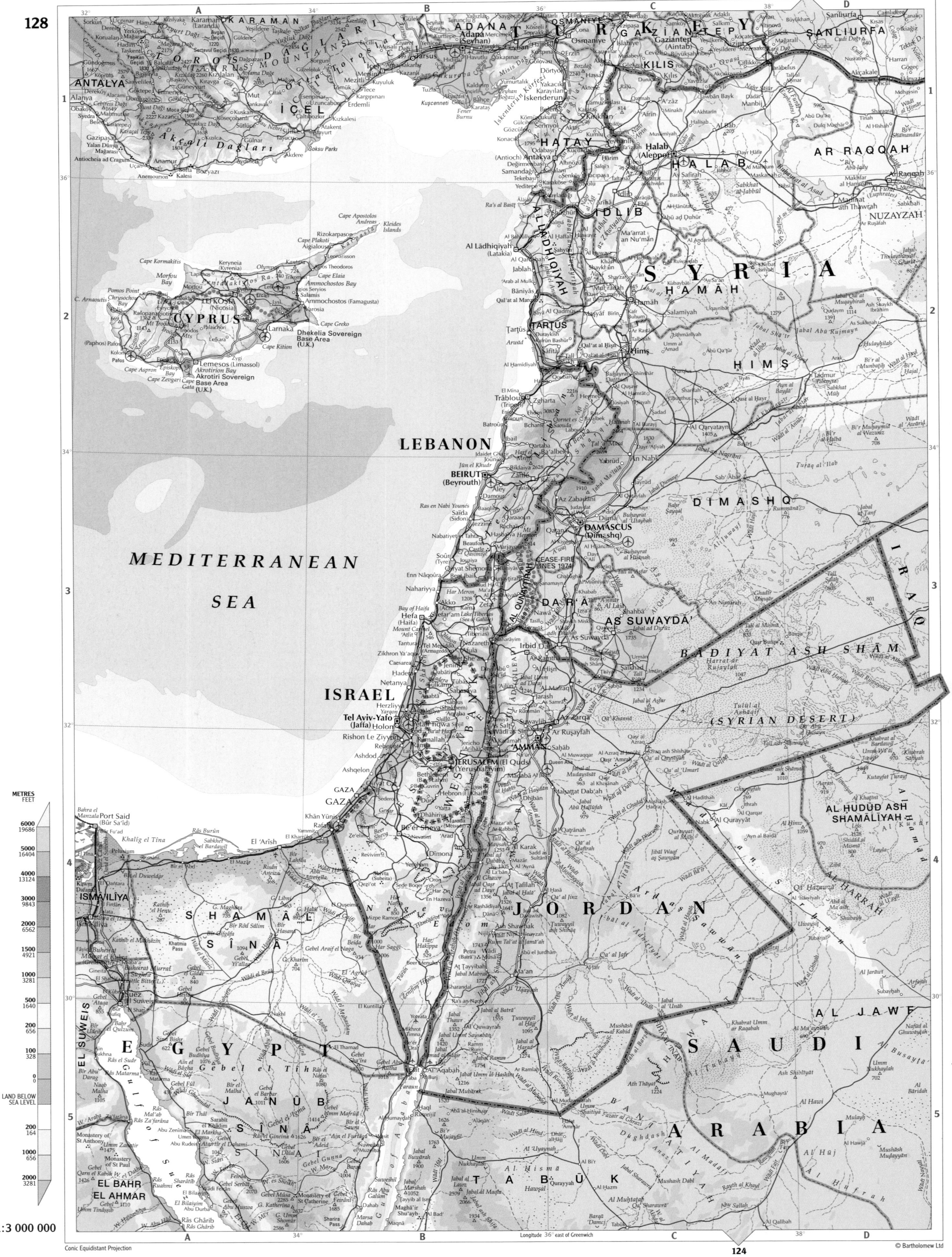

127

C A S P I A N   S E A

KAZAKHSTAN

R U S S I A N   F E D E R A T I O N

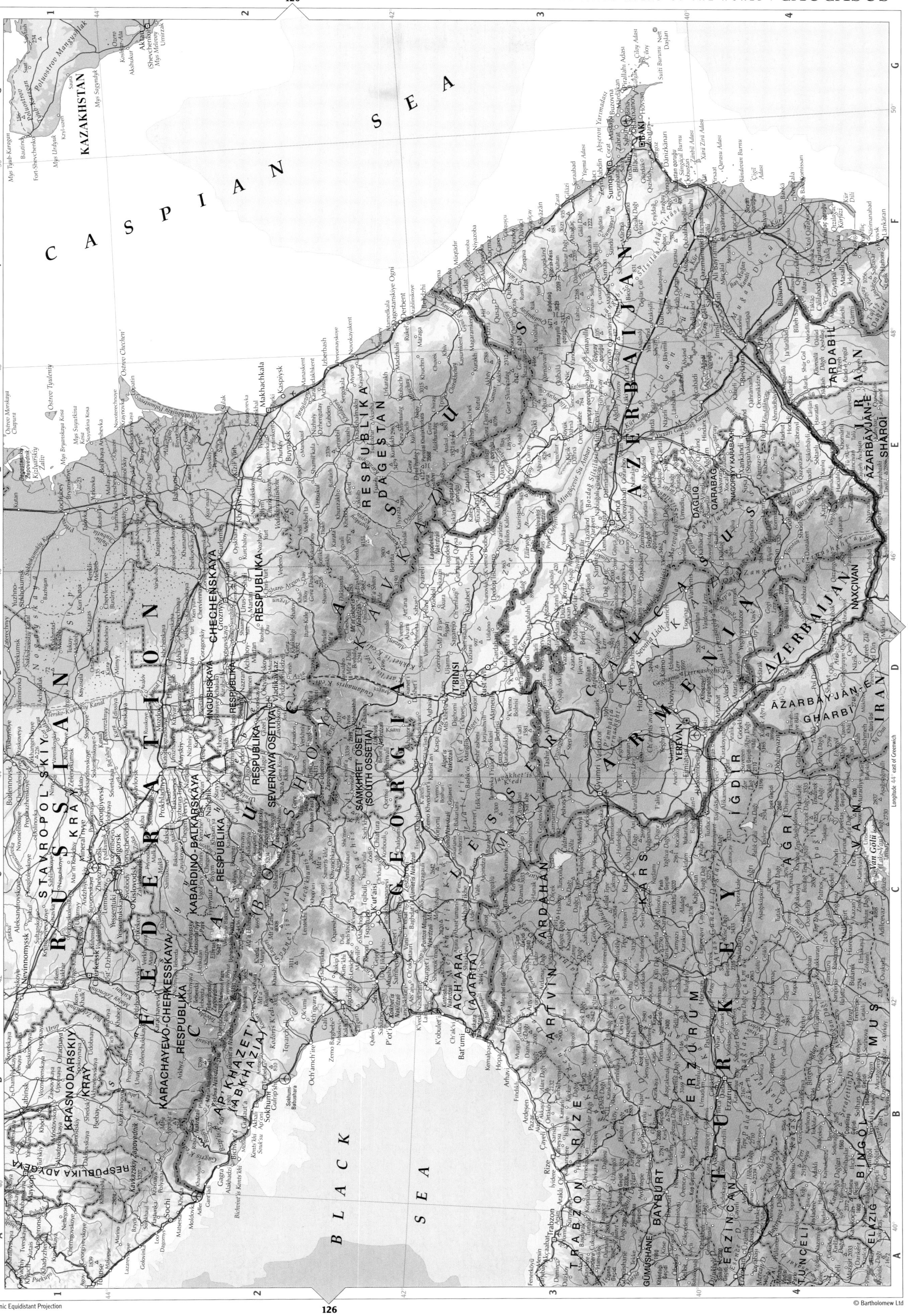

KRASNODARSKIY KRAY

STAVROPOL'SKIY KRAY

RESPUBLIKA ADYGEYA

KARACHAYEVO-CHERKESSKAYA RESPUBLIKA

KABARDINO-BALKARSKAYA RESPUBLIKA

RESPUBLIKA SEVERNAYA OSETIYA

RESPUBLIKA INGUSHSKAYA

CHECHENSKAYA RESPUBLIKA

RESPUBLIKA DAGESTAN

Makhachkala

Derbent

B O L ' S H O Y   K A V K A Z

AP'KHAZETI (ABKHAZIA)

SAMKHRET OSET'I (SOUTH OSSETIA)

G E O R G I A

TBILISI

ACH'ARA (AJARIA)

K'UT'AISI

Sokhumi

Bat'umi

A R M E N I A

YEREVAN

A Z E R B A I J A N

BAKI

Sumqayıt

Gäncä

DAGLIQ QARABAĞ (NAGORNY KARABAKH)

NAXÇIVAN

I R A N

ÄRDABĪL

ĀZARBĀYJĀN-E SHARQĪ

ĀZARBĀYJĀN-E GHARBĪ

T U R K E Y

TRABZON

RIZE

ARTVIN

ARDAHAN

KARS

IĞDIR

AĞRI

ERZURUM

ERZINCAN

BAYBURT

GÜMÜŞHANE

BINGÖL

MUŞ

VAN

TUNCELI

ELAZIĞ

Van Gölü

B L A C K   S E A

K'EDI

L E S S E R   C A U C A S U S

	MILES	KILOMETRES
	125	200
	100	175
		150
	75	125
		100
	50	75
	25	50
		25
	0	0

1 : 3 000 000

Conic Equidistant Projection

© Bartholomew Ltd

Conic Equidistant Projection

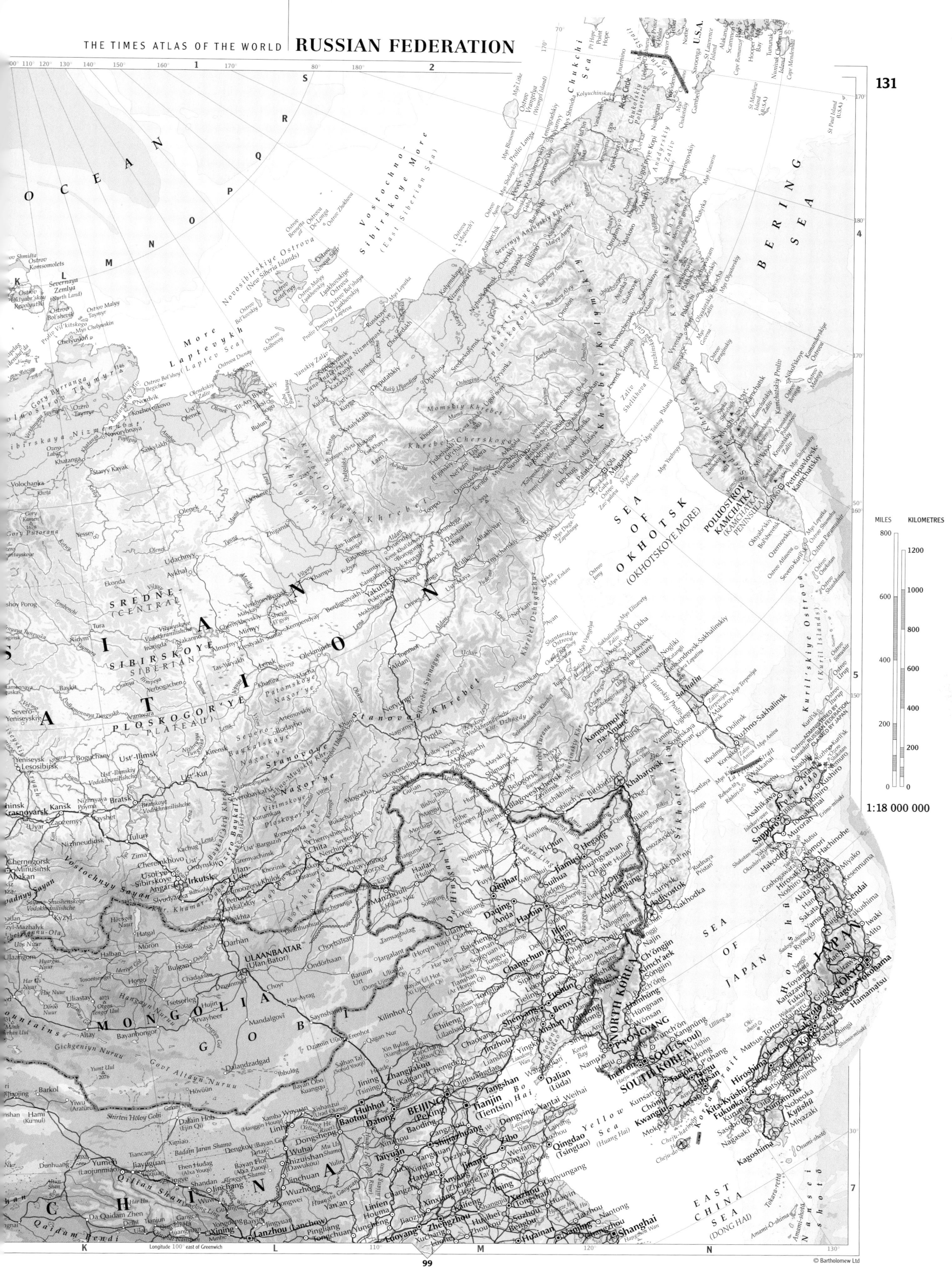

© Bartholomew Ltd

N O R T H   A M E R I C A

Baffin Bay

Greenland

Arctic Circle

75°

60°

Nordaustlandet

Spitsbergen

Longyearbyen

Svalbard
(Norway)

Zemlya Frantsa-Iosifa

Greenland Sea

B A R E N T S   S E A

Bjørnøya
(Norway)

Jan Mayen
(Norway)

Denmark Strait

60°

45°

I C E L A N D

Reykjavík

N O R W E G I A N

S E A

N O R W A Y

Nordkapp

Gulf of Bot

Trondheim

S W E D E N

Faroe Islands
(Denmark)

Tórshavn

Shetland Islands

Bergen

Oslo

Stockho

Vänern

Vättern

Göteborg

Skagerrak

Kattegat

Ålborg

D E N M A R K

København

Malmö

Orkney Islands

Outer Hebrides

SCOTLAND

Glasgow

Edinburgh

Bornho

Odense

N O R T H

S E A

NORTHERN
IRELAND

Belfast

Dublin

REPUBLIC
OF IRELAND

UNITED
KINGDOM

Leeds

Manchester

Liverpool

Birmingham

WALES

Cardiff

ENGLAND

London

Hamburg

Bremen

Berli

NETHERLANDS

Amsterdam

's-Gravenhage

Rotterdam

Hannover

Bielefeld

G E R M A N

Essen

Düsseldorf

Köln

Aachen

Bonn

Frankfurt am Main

Leipzig

A T L A N T I C

O C E A N

45°

English Channel

Bruxelles

BELGIUM

Lille

LUXEMBOURG

Luxembourg

Mannheim

Nürnbe

Stuttgart

München

Channel Islands

Brest

Rennes

Paris

Orléans

Strasbourg

Loire

LIECHTEN-
STEIN

Zürich

Bern

SWITZERLAND

Innsbru

Dijon

Nantes

F R A N C E

Genève

Lyon

Bay of Biscay

Bordeaux

Toulouse

Marseille

Milano

Torino

Geno

MONACO
Nice

Corvo

Flores

Arquipélago dos Açores

São Jorge

Faial

Terceira

Pico

Azores
(Portugal)

São Miguel

Ponta Delgada

Santa Maria

A Coruña

Bilbao

Pyrenees

Andorra la Vella

ANDORRA

Zaragoza

Ebro

Barcelona

Corse

Porto

P O R T U G A L

Salamanca

Madrid

Tajo

S P A I N

Valencia

Islas Baleares

Menorca

Mallorca

Eivissa

Sardegna

30°

Lisboa

Córdoba

Cartagena

M E D

Sevilla

Cádiz

Málaga

Gibraltar (U.K.)

Ceuta (Spain)

Melilla
(Spain)

Arquipélago da Madeira

Madeira
(Portugal)

Ilha de Porto Santo

Funchal

15°

0°

A

F

Karskoye More

Novaya Zemlya

F   G   H   I   J

Ostrov Kolgueyev

Yenisey

Arctic Circle

Vorkuta

Pechora

RUSSIAN FEDERATION

Ob'

Irtysh

ASIA

Altai Mountains

Murmansk

Beloye More

Arkhangel'sk

Severnaya Dvina

Petrozavodsk

Onezhskoye Ozero

Perm'

Kirov

Izhevsk

Naberezhnyye Chelny

Ufa

Ozero Balkhash

FINLAND

Tampere

Turku

Helsinki

Ladozhskoye Ozero

Sankt-Peterburg

Rybinskoye Vodokhranilishche

Vologda

Yaroslavl'

Nizhniy Novgorod

Volga

Kazan'

Ul'yanovsk

Samara

Orenburg

Tallinn

ESTONIA

Lake Peipus

Moskva

Tula

Penza

Saratov

Tyan'-Shan'

LATVIA

Riga

Gotland

Vitsyebsk

Smolensk

Voronezh

Aral Sea

LITHUANIA

Vilnius

Minsk

Mahilyow

Baltic Sea

Kaliningrad

RUS. FED.

Gdańsk

Hrodna

BELARUS

Homyel'

Chernihiv

Belgorod

Don

Volgograd

Astrakhan

Caspian Sea

Bydgoszcz

Białystok

Brest

Sumy

Kharkiv

POLAND

Poznań

Warszawa

Łódź

Wisła

Rivne

Kyiv

UKRAINE

Dnipropetrovs'k

Donets'k

Rostov-na-Donu

Volga

Oder

Wrocław

Katowice

Kraków

L'viv

Dnister (Dniester)

Kirovohrad

Mykolayiv

Dnipro

Sea of Azov

Krasnodar

Stavropol'

Groznyy

Zaliv Kara-Bogaz-Gol

Praha

CZECH REPUBLIC

Brno

SLOVAKIA

Košice

Carpathian Mountains

MOLDOVA

Iaşi

Chişinău

Odesa

Simferopol'

Novorossiysk

Caucasus

Wien

Bratislava

Debrecen

Salzburg

AUSTRIA

Budapest

HUNGARY

Szeged

Oradea

ROMANIA

Timişoara

Brašov

Black Sea

TURKEY

Kühhā-ye Zagros

ASIA

SLOVENIA

Ljubljana

Trieste

Zagreb

CROATIA

Beograd

Bucureşti

Craiova

Varna

Venezia

BOSNIA-HERZEGOVINA

Sarajevo

YUGOSLAVIA

Niš

Pleven

BULGARIA

Burgas

Bologna

SAN MARINO

Firenze

Split

Adriatic Sea

Podgorica

Sofiya

Edirne

İstanbul

Marmara Denizi

ITALY

VATICAN CITY

Roma

Napoli

Bari

ALBANIA

Tiranë

Skopje

MACEDONIA

Thessaloniki

Larisa

GREECE

Aegean Sea

Al Furāt (Euphrates)

Salt Desert

Zāgros Mountains

Tyrrhenian Sea

Cosenza

Ionian Sea

Athina

Dodekanisos

Rodos

Cyprus

The Gulf

Palermo

Messina

Sicilia

Siracusa

Kriti

MALTA

Valletta

MEDITERRANEAN SEA

AFRICA

F   G   H   I   J

75°   90°   105°

60°

45°

30°

15°

30°   45°

1:15 000 000

MILES   KILOMETRES

600   1000

800

400   600

400

200   200

0   0

© Bartholomew Ltd

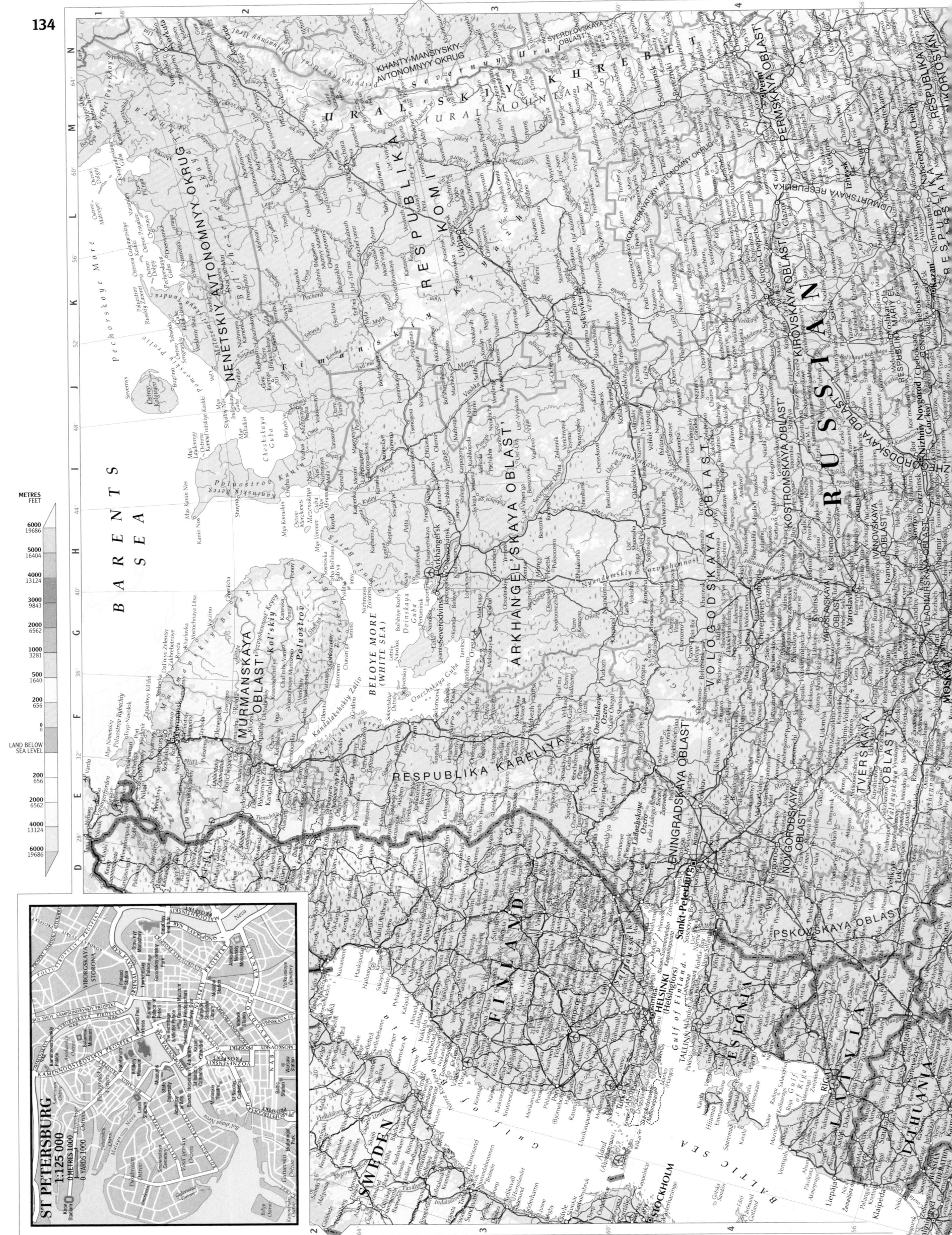

Conic Equidistant Projection

KHANTY-MANSIYSKIY-
AVTONOMNYY OKRUG

URAL'SKIY KHREBET
(URAL MOUNTAINS)

SVERDLOVSKAYA
OBLAST'

RESPUBLIKA KOMI

KOMI-PERMYATSKIY AVTONOMNY OKRUG

PERMSKAYA OBLAST'

UDMURTSKAYA RESPUBLIKA

R U S S I A N
RESPUBLIKA

NENETSKIY AVTONOMNYY OKRUG

KIROVSKAYA OBLAST'

RESPUBLIKA MARIY EL

B A R E N T S
S E A

ARKHANGEL'SKAYA OBLAST'

KOSTROMSKAYA OBLAST'

NIZHEGORODSKAYA OBLAST'

IVANOVSKAYA
OBLAST'

VLADIMIRSKAYA

MURMANSKAYA
OBLAST'

Kol'skiy

Poluostrov

BELOYE MORE
(WHITE SEA)

VOLOGODSKAYA OBLAST'

YAROSLAVSKAYA
OBLAST'

MOSKVA

RESPUBLIKA KARELIYA

TVERSKAYA OBLAST'

LENINGRADSKAYA OBLAST'

Sankt-Peterburg

NOVGORODSKAYA
OBLAST'

PSKOVSKAYA OBLAST

F I N L A N D

HELSINKI
(Helsingfors)

Gulf of Finland

TALLINN

ESTONIA

LATVIA

Riga

S W E D E N

STOCKHOLM

Gulf of Riga

B A L T I C
S E A

LITHUANIA

ST PETERSBURG
1:125 000

0 METRES 1000
0 YARDS 1000

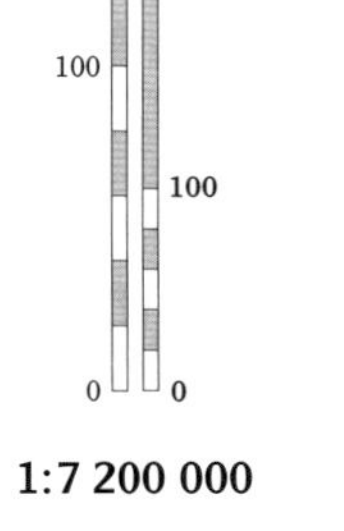

120

135

RUSSIAN FEDERATION

KAZAKHSTAN

ZAPADNYY KAZAKHSTAN

ORENBURGSKAYA OBLAST'

SAMARSKAYA OBLAST'

ULYANOVSKAYA OBLAST'

PENZENSKAYA OBLAST'

SARATOVSKAYA OBLAST'

VOLGOGRADSKAYA OBLAST'

Volgograd (Stalingrad)

ASTRAKHANSKAYA OBLAST'

Astrakhan'

RESPUBLIKA KALMYKIYA - KHALMG-TANGCH

Chernyye Zemli

RESPUBLIKA DAGESTAN

Makhachkala

CASPIAN SEA

MANGISTAUSKAYA OBLAST'

ATYRAUSKAYA OBLAST'

TURKMENISTAN

AZERBAIJAN

BAKI

Sumqayıt

TAMBOVSKAYA OBLAST'

VORONEZHSKAYA OBLAST'

ROSTOVSKAYA OBLAST'

Rostov-na-Donu

STAVROPOL'SKIY KRAY

Stavropol'

KRASNODARSKIY KRAY

Krasnodar

CHECHENSKAYA RESPUBLIKA

KARACHAY-CHERKESS

KABARDINO-BALKARSKAYA

Nal'chik

RESPUBLIKA SEVERNAYA OSETIYA

GEORGIA

T'BILISI

ARMENIA

TURKEY

Trabzon

Samsun

RYAZANSKAYA OBLAST'

TUL'SKAYA OBLAST'

KALUZHSKAYA OBLAST'

SMOLENSKAYA OBLAST'

BRYANSKAYA OBLAST'

KURSKAYA OBLAST'

BELGORODSKAYA OBLAST'

RESPUBLIKA MORDOVIYA

Saransk

BELARUS

MINSK

POLAND

Lublin

UKRAINE

KYIV (Kiev)

Kharkiv

Donets'k

Dnipropetrovs'k

Zaporizhzhya

Mariupol'

Sea of Azov

Simferopol'

Sevastopol'

Yalta

Odesa

MOLDOVA

CHIŞINĂU (Kishinev)

ROMANIA

BUCUREŞTI (Bucharest)

BULGARIA

Sochi

Novorossiysk

Tuapse

BLACK SEA

İstanbul

Bursa

Administrative divisions in Russian Federation numbered on the map:
1. INGUSHSKAYA RESPUBLIKA (18)
2. RESPUBLIKA SEVERNAYA OSETIYA (18)

122

126

175

MILES | KILOMETRES

300 | 500
     | 400
200 | 300
     | 200
100 | 100
0 | 0

1:7 200 000

© Bartholomew Ltd

Longitude 40 east of Greenwich

167

197

POLAND

BELARUS

BRESTSKAYA VOBLASTS'

HRODZYENSKAYA VOBLASTS'

MINSKAYA VOBLASTS'

MAHILYOVSKAYA VOBLASTS'

HOMYEL'SKAYA VOBLASTS'

PRYPYATS' MARSHES

VOLYNS'KA OBLAST'

RIVNENS'KA OBLAST'

ZHYTOMYRS'KA OBLAST'

L'VIVS'KA OBLAST'

TERNOPIL'S'KA OBLAST'

KHMEL'NYTS'KA OBLAST'

KYIVS'KA

UKRAINE

IVANO-FRANKIVS'KA OBLAST'

ZAKARPATS'KA OBLAST'

VINNYTS'KA OBLAST'

CHERKA

CHERNIVTS'KA OBLAST'

SLOVAKIA

HUNGARY

CARPATHIAN MOUNTAINS

ROMANIA

MOLDOVA

ODES'KA OBLAST'

CHISINAU (Kishinev)

WARSZAWA (Warsaw)

Brest

KYIV (KIEV)

CARPAȚII MERIDIONALI

TRANSYLVANIAN ALPS

Podișul Transilvaniei (Transylvanian Basin)

BUCUREȘTI (Bucharest)

METRES / FEET

6000 / 19686
5000 / 16404
4000 / 13124
3000 / 9843
2000 / 6562
1500 / 4921
1000 / 3281
500 / 1640
200 / 656
100 / 328
0
LAND BELOW SEA LEVEL
50 / 164
200 / 656
1000 / 3281
2000 / 6562

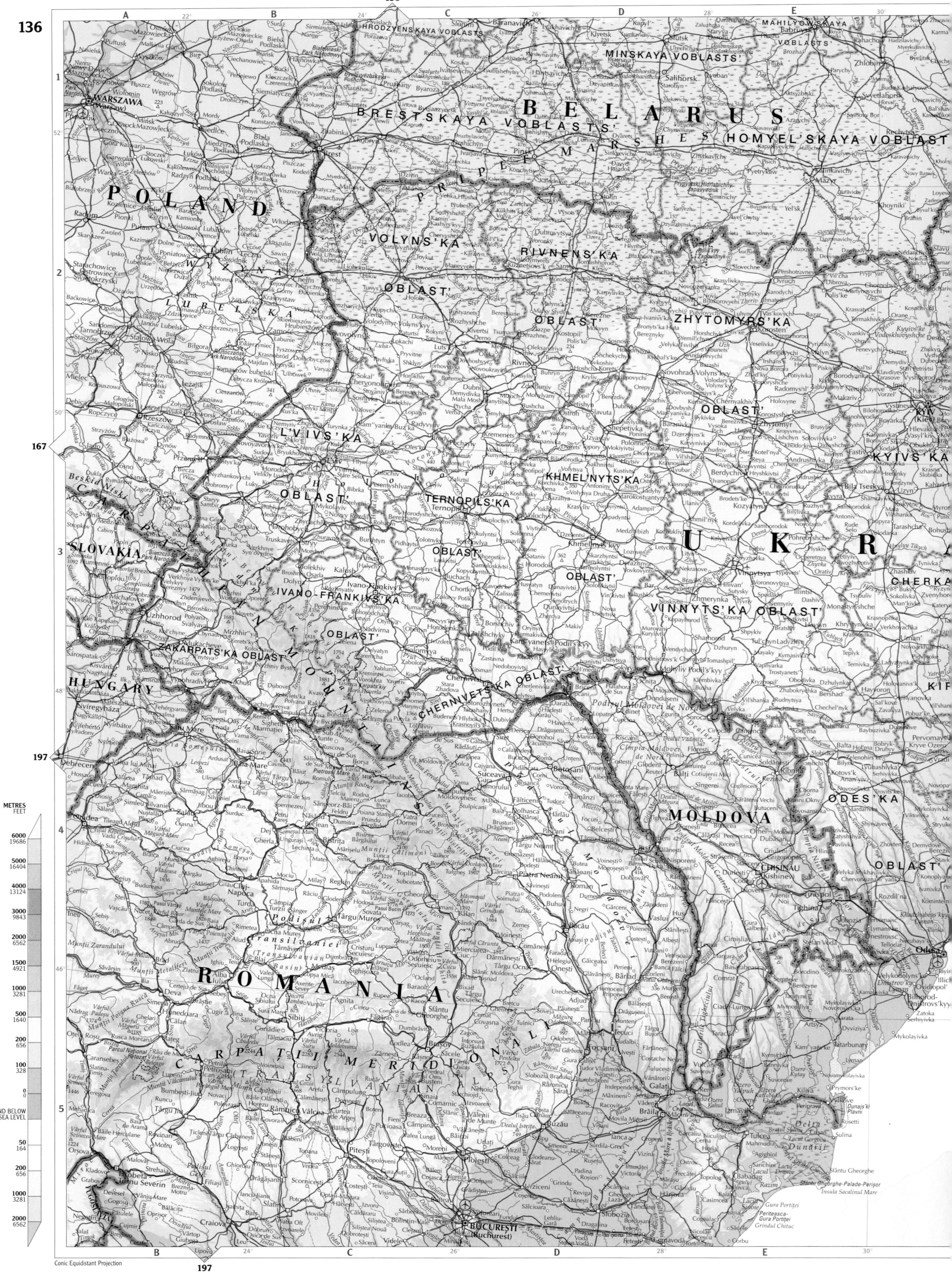

Conic Equidistant Projection

139

RUSSIAN

FEDERATION

BRYANSKAYA OBLAST'

ORLOVSKAYA OBLAST'

LIPETSKAYA OBLAST'

TAMBOVSKAYA OBLAST'

KURSKAYA OBLAST'

VORONEZHSKAYA OBLAST'

BELGORODSKAYA OBLAST'

CHERNIHIVS'KA OBLAST'

SUMS'KA OBLAST'

KHARKIVS'KA OBLAST'

LUHANS'KA OBLAST'

POLTAVS'KA OBLAST'

UKRAINE

DNIPROPETROVS'KA OBLAST'

DONETS'KA OBLAST'

ROSTOVSKAYA OBLAST'

KIROVOHRADS'KA OBLAST'

ZAPORIZ'KA OBLAST'

MYKOLAYIVS'KA OBLAST'

KHERSONS'KA OBLAST'

Kharkiv

Poltava

Dnipropetrovs'k

Dnipradzerzhyns'k

Zaporizhzhya

Kryvyy Rih

Donets'k

Mariupol'

Berdyans'k

Melitopol'

Mykolayiv

Kherson

Rakhova

Voronezh

Oryol

Rostov-na-Donu

Taganrog

Yeysk

Sea

of Azov

Gulf of Taganrog

KRASNODARSKIY KRAY

Krasnodar

Novorossiysk

Anapa

RESPUBLIKA KRYM

Simferopol'

Sevastopol'

Yevpatoriya

Yalta

Krym'skyy Pivostriv

Kerch

B L A C K   S E A

MILES / KILOMETRES

125 / 200

100 / 150

75 / 125

50 / 75

25 / 25

141

A 18 B 20 C 22 D E 24 F 26 G 28

GULF OF BOTHNIA

Åland (Ahvenanmaa)

VARSINAIS-SUOMI

LÄNSI-SUOMI

FINLAND

ETELÄ-SUOMI

UPPSALA

SWEDEN

STOCKHOLM

STOCKHOLM

HELSINKI (Helsingfors)

143

GULF OF FINLAND

Narva Bay

TALLINN Tallinna

ESTONIA

Lake Peipus

Hiiumaa

Saaremaa

GULF OF RIGA

Lake Pskov

Irbe Strait

GOTLAND

Gotland (Sweden)

Ruhnu (Estonia)

B A L T I C   S E A

Ventspils

LATVIA

PSKOVSKAYA OBLAST'

Vidzemes Centrala Augstiene

RĪGA

Liepāja

3

Jelgava

Daugavpils

56

VITSYEBSKAYA VOBLASTS'

Klaipėda

LITHUANIA

4

Gulf of Gdańsk

RUSSIAN FEDERATION

KALININGRADSKAYA OBLAST'

Kaliningrad

VILNIUS

Kaunas

MINSKAYA VOBLASTS'

MINSK

54

POJEZIERZE MAZURSKIE

BELARUS

HRODZYENSKAYA VOBLASTS'

POLAND

5

NIZINA MAZOWIECKA

WARSZAWA

BRESTSKAYA VOBLASTS'

167

52

20 C 22 D 24 E 26 F 28 G

Conic Equidistant Projection

136

METRES / FEET
6000 / 19686
5000 / 16404
4000 / 13124
3000 / 9843
2000 / 6562
1500 / 4921
1000 / 3281
500 / 1640
200 / 656
100 / 328
0 / 0
LAND BELOW SEA LEVEL
50 / 164
200 / 656
1000 / 3281
2000 / 6562

MOSCOW 1:80 000

1:3 000 000

© Bartholomew Ltd

ICELAND
AT THE SAME SCALE

SVALBARD
(Norway)
1:6 000 000

© Bartholomew Ltd

140

E

1

A 6° B 8° C 10° D 12° E

Blomøy Dale Vangsnatnet Stramdavatnet Skjelbreide Hov Lena Mjøsa Våler Finnskogen Letten Ramba
Askvoll Telakrsmten Hol Ål Hallingdal 860 Brumunddal Skasberget Orrekloppen Ha
Bergen Vaksdal Granvin 1933 Hulderset Hønefoss Vassfaret og Vidalen Finnmarka Oppskardkampen Rödfjället
HORDALAND Inne Sound Søvarnitem Haugastøl Geilo Redungen Nesbyen Bremnen Hakalagd Bandhu Hagalland Maura Bidvoll Kongsvinger Gräsmarken
Store Sotra Øystese Hardangerjøkulen Tunnhovd HEDMARK Skarnes
Vaksdal Hamlagørudnd Nasjonalpark Tunnhovd BUSKERUD Nittedal Oppkamjen Maura Matrand Kymmen Charlottenberg
Hufardn Indre Sound Samlen 1640 Graffjell AKERSHUS Bjørkelangen Gra Glasskogens naturreservat
Bjørnafjorden Hardmanhslagen Möar Hallingby Jevnaker Nitelva OSLO Askim VÄRML
Rosendal 1649 Bjørnefjorden Krøderen 1045 Honefoss OSLO Oyern Löken ØSTFOLD Smolmark
Rolvsøy Ulvenøen Möar Tyrifjorden Drammen Askerby Tokstera Stora Gla
NORWAY Masvain Austfjell Tinn Rjukan TELEMARK Notodden Kongsberg Lampeland Sandel Mysen Fredrikstad Glaskogens naturreservat
RO GALAND Hvitingtossee Skien Moss Askim Aremark Töcksfors
Stavanger Nisser AUST-AGDER Arendal Risør Kosterøarna naturreservat Strømstad SW
VEST-AGDER Kristiansand VÄST GÖTAL

SKAGERRAK Skagen Grenen
Hirtshals Tannis Bugt Skagen
Lønstrup Hirsholmene HALLAND
Løkken Frederikshavn
Hanstholm Vra Sæby Læsø Falkenberg
NORDJYLLAND Ålborg Ålborg Bugt KATTEGAT
VIBORG Randers ÅRHUS Grenå Halmstad
RINGKØBING Herning Århus Ebeltoft Helsingborg
DENMARK Silkeborg Skanderborg
Ringkøbing Fjord Vejle FREDERIKSBORG
VEJLE Odense KØBENHAVN
RIBE Kolding Fredericia ROSKILDE København
Esbjerg FYN VESTSJÆLLAND SJÆLLAND
SØNDERJYLLAND Svendborg STORSTRØM Møn
Sylt Falster
Lolland Nykøbing
GERMANY Kieler Bucht Mecklenburger Bucht

A 6° B 8° C 10° D 12° E
Conic Equidistant Projection 168 170

1:2 250 000

Longitude 14° east of Greenwich

© Bartholomew Ltd

MILES   KILOMETRES

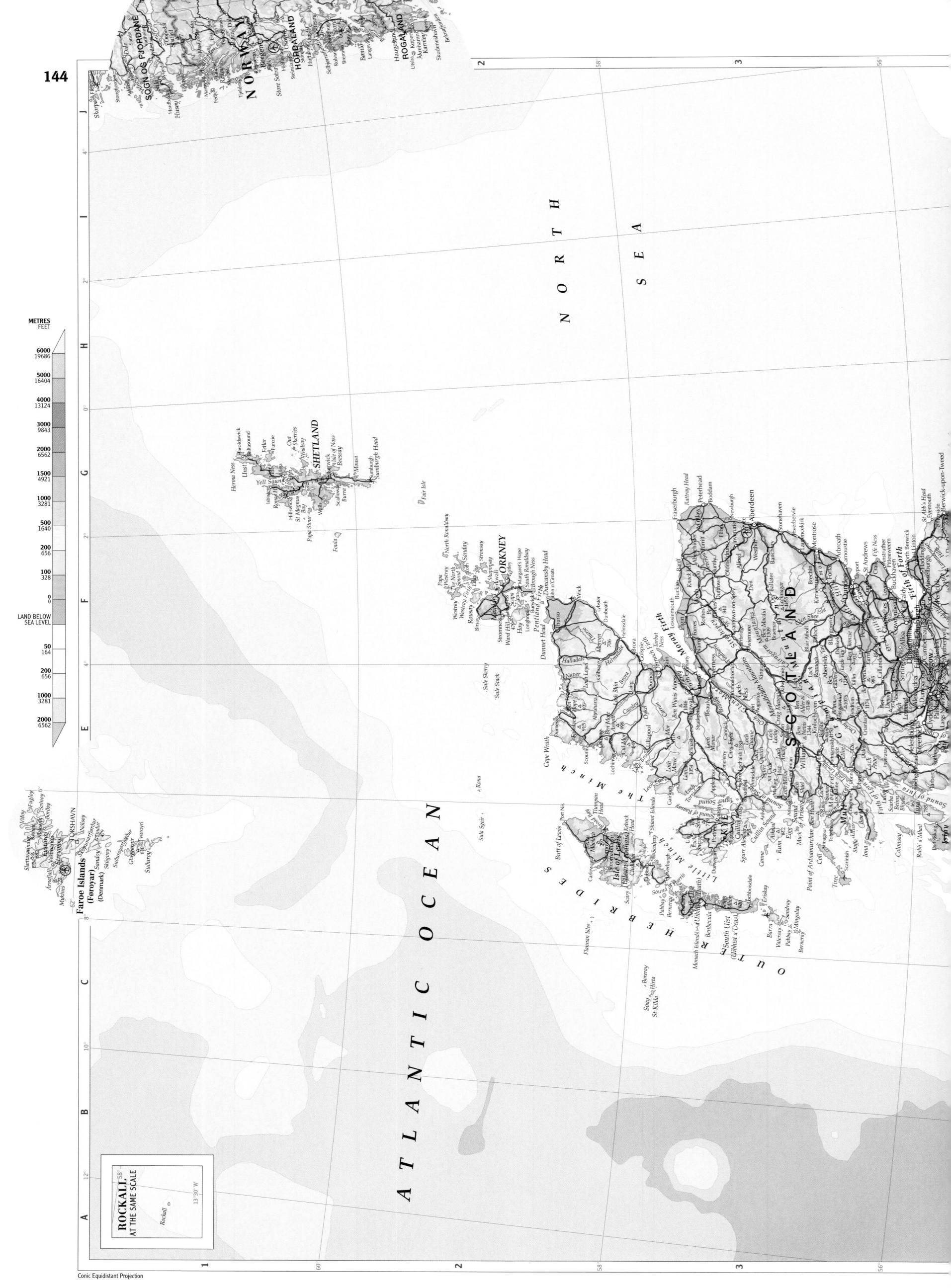

NORWAY

SOGN OG FJORDANE

HORDALAND

ROGALAND

Bergen

NORTH

SEA

METRES
FEET

6000
19686

5000
16404

4000
13124

3000
9843

2000
6562

1500
4921

1000
3281

500
1640

200
656

100
328

0

LAND BELOW
SEA LEVEL

50
164

200
656

1000
3281

2000
6562

SHETLAND

Herma Ness
Unst
Fetlar
Out Skerries
Whalsay
Yell Sound
Isle of Noss
Bressay
Mousa
Scalloway
Burra
Sumburgh Head

Foula

Fair Isle

Papa Stour

ORKNEY

Papa Westray
North Ronaldsay
Westray
Sanday
The North Sound
Stronsay
Rousay
Eday
Stromness
Scapa Flow
Kirkwall
Hoy
Longhope
South Ronaldsay
Burwick
Duncansby Head
John o'Groats

Ward Hill

Dunnet Head
Pentland Firth
Thurso
Wick

Cape Wrath

ATLANTIC OCEAN

Faroe Islands
(Føroyar)
(Denmark)

TÓRSHAVN

Rona

Sula Sgeir

Sule Skerry

Sule Stack

SCOTLAND

Fraserburgh
Peterhead
Aberdeen
Stonehaven
Montrose
St Andrews
Firth of Forth
Berwick-upon-Tweed

Moray Firth

HEBRIDES

THE MINCH

Butt of Lewis
Port Nis
Tiumpan Head

Isle of Lewis

Shiant Islands

Little Minch

Flannan Isles

OUTER

SKYE

Cuillin Sound

Sound of Rum

Rum

Eigg

Muck

Coll

Point of Ardnamurchan

Tiree

Staffa

Iona

Colonsay

Sound of Jura

OUTER HEBRIDES

South Uist
(Uibhist a Deas)

Benbecula

Barra

Vatersay

Pabbay

Mingulay

Berneray

Monach Islands
(Uibhist a Tuath)

Soay
Hirta
St Kilda

Boreray

NORTH

SEA

ROCKALL
AT THE SAME SCALE

Rockall

13°30' W

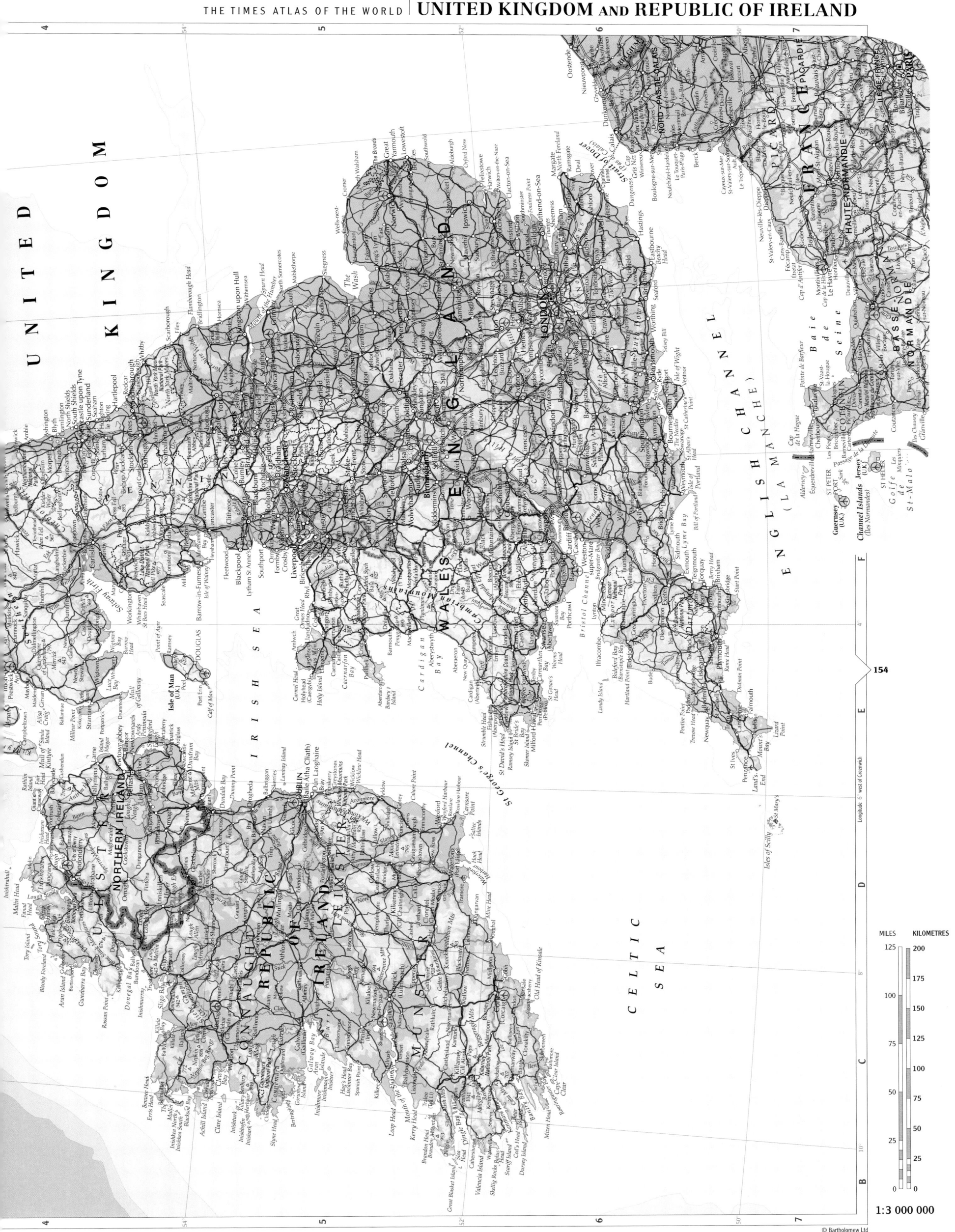

1:3 000 000

© Bartholomew Ltd

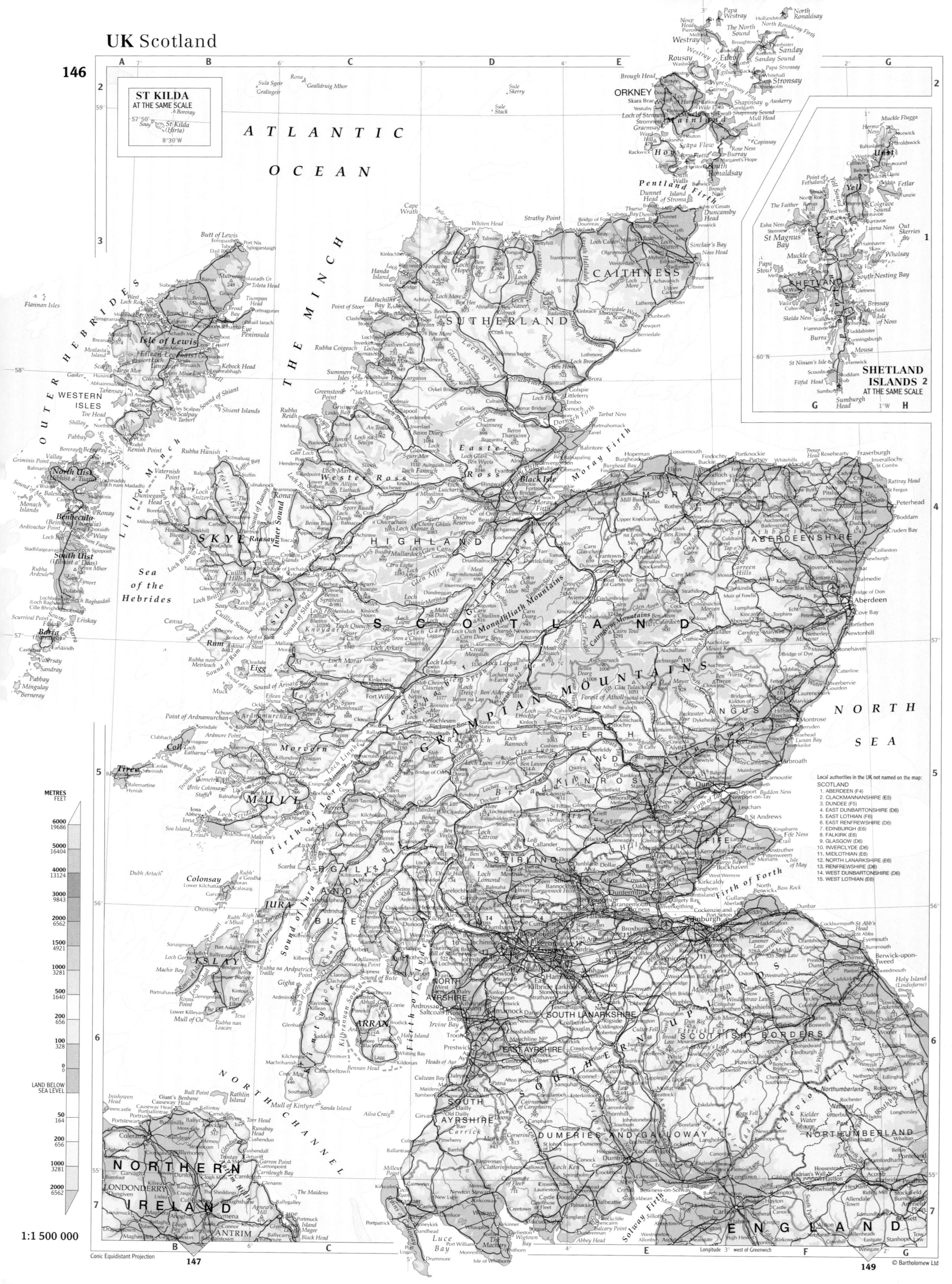

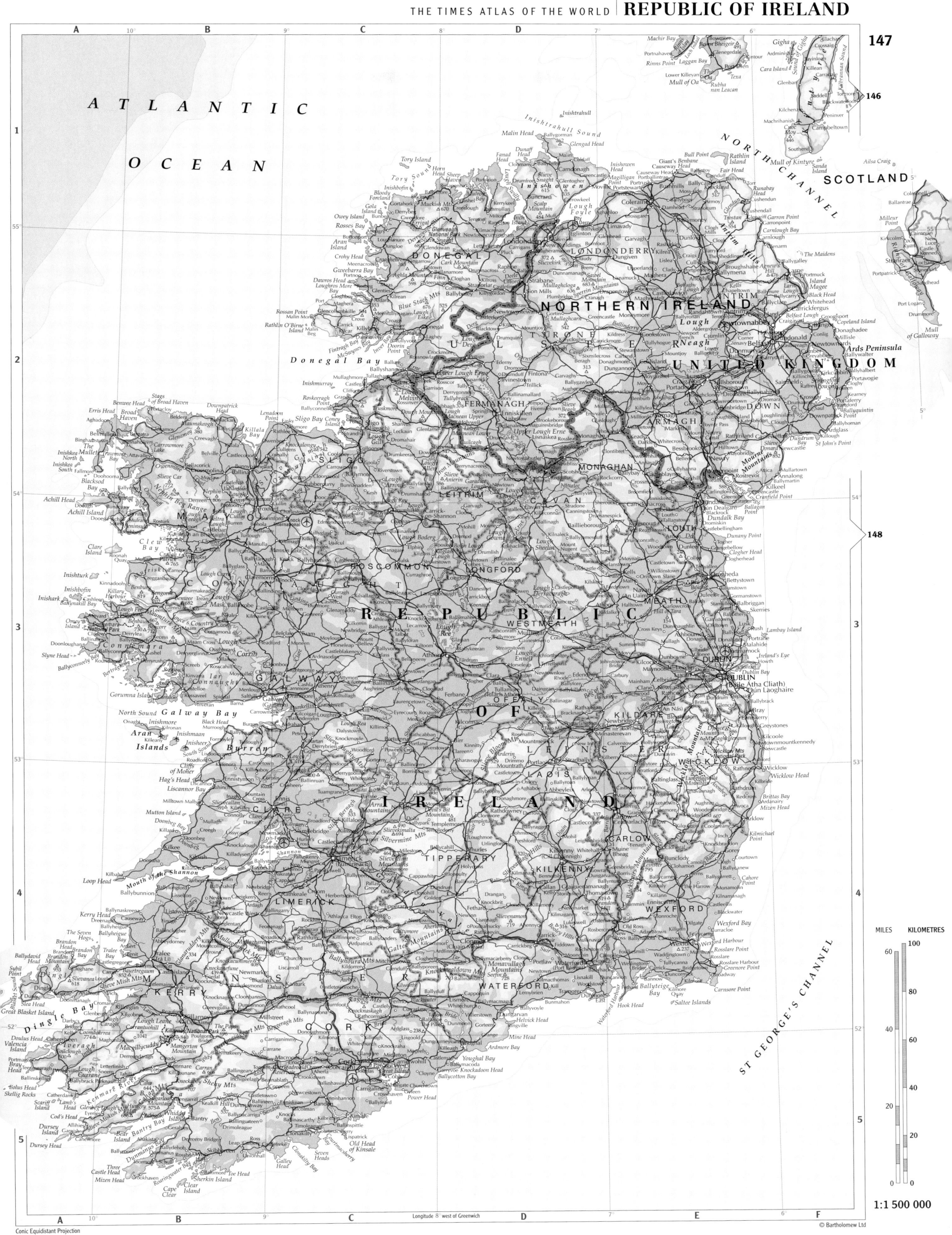

146

147

A B C D E

Legend

Conic Equidistant Projection

Major regions and features

REPUBLIC OF IRELAND

NORTHERN IRELAND

UNITED KINGDOM

ULSTER

LEINSTER

DONEGAL

LONDONDERRY

ANTRIM

TYRONE

FERMANAGH

ARMAGH

DOWN

MONAGHAN

CAVAN

LEITRIM

LONGFORD

WESTMEATH

MEATH

LOUTH

OFFALY

KILDARE

DUBLIN

WICKLOW

LAOIS

CARLOW

KILKENNY

TIPPERARY

WEXFORD

STIRLING

ARGYLL AND BUTE

NORTH AYRSHIRE

EAST AYRSHIRE

SOUTH AYRSHIRE

SOUTH LANARKSHIRE

DUMFRIES AND GALLOWAY

GWYNEDD

ISLE OF ANGLESEY

SNOWDONIA NATIONAL PARK

Isle of Man (U.K.)

DOUGLAS

DUBLIN (Baile Átha Cliath)

Seas and water features

NORTH CHANNEL

IRISH SEA

Firth of Clyde

Loch Fyne

Lough Neagh

Lough Foyle

Upper Lough Erne

Lower Lough Erne

Dundalk Bay

Dublin Bay

Caernarfon Bay

Luce Bay

Wigtown Bay

Islands and points

Colonsay

JURA

ISLAY

ARRAN

Rathlin Island

Lambay Island

Ireland's Eye

Holyhead

Anglesey (Ynys Môn)

Malin Head

Mull of Galloway

Mull of Kintyre

Mourne Mountains

Sperrin Mountains

Wicklow Mountains

Giant's Causeway

Ards Peninsula

Local authorities in the UK not named on the map:

SCOTLAND
1. CLACKMANNANSHIRE (F1)
2. EAST DUNBARTONSHIRE (E2)
3. EAST LOTHIAN (G2)
4. EAST RENFREWSHIRE (E2)
5. EDINBURGH (F2)
6. FALKIRK (F2)
7. GLASGOW (E2)
8. INVERCLYDE (E2)
9. MIDLOTHIAN (F2)
10. NORTH LANARKSHIRE (F2)
11. PERTH AND KINROSS (F1)
12. RENFREWSHIRE (E2)
13. WEST DUNBARTONSHIRE (E2)
14. WEST LOTHIAN (F2)

ENGLAND
15. BLACKPOOL (F4)
16. DARLINGTON (H3)
17. HARTLEPOOL (H3)
18. KINGSTON UPON HULL (I4)
19. MIDDLESBROUGH (H3)
20. NORTH EAST LINCOLNSHIRE (I4)
21. STOCKTON-ON-TEES (H3)
22. STOKE-ON-TRENT (G4)

NORTH

SEA

1:1 200 000

MILES   KILOMETRES

© Bartholomew Ltd

REPUBLIC
OF IRELAND

IRISH

SEA

CARDIGAN

BAY

St George's Channel

Local authorities in the UK not named on the map:

ENGLAND
1. BATH AND N.E. SOMERSET (E3)
2. BRACKNELL FOREST (G3)
3. BRIGHTON AND HOVE (G4)
4. BRISTOL (E3)
5. BOURNEMOUTH (F4)
6. GREATER MANCHESTER (E1)
7. LUTON (G3)
8. MILTON KEYNES (G2)
9. NOTTINGHAM (F2)
10. PLYMOUTH (C4)
11. POOLE (F4)
12. PORTSMOUTH (F4)
13. READING (G3)
14. SLOUGH (G3)
15. SOUTHAMPTON (F4)
16. SOUTHEND (H3)
17. STOKE-ON-TRENT (E1)
18. SWINDON (F3)
19. THURROCK (H3)
20. TORBAY (D4)
21. WEST MIDLANDS (F2)
22. WINDSOR AND MAIDENHEAD (G3)
23. WOKINGHAM (G3)

WALES
24. BLAENAU GWENT (D3)
25. BRIDGEND (D3)
26. CAERPHILLY (D3)
27. CARDIFF (D3)
28. MERTHYR TYDFIL (D3)
29. NEWPORT (E3)
30. RHONDDA CYNON TAFF (D3)
31. TORFAEN (D3)

WALES

UNITED

POWYS

PEMBROKESHIRE

CARMARTHENSHIRE

SWANSEA

NEATH
PORT TALBOT

VALE OF
GLAMORGAN

Bristol Channel

CORNWALL

DEVON

SOMERSET

DORSET

METRES
FEET

6000
19686
5000
16404
4000
13124
3000
9843
2000
6562
1500
4921
1000
3281
500
1640
200
656
100
328
0
0

LAND BELOW
SEA LEVEL

50
164
200
656
1000
3281
2000
6562

ISLE OF
ANGLESEY

CONWY

DENBIGHSHIRE

WREXHAM

GWYNEDD

Snowdonia
National
Park

SHROPSHIRE

CEREDIGION

HEREFORDSHIRE

GLOUCESTE

Pembrokeshire Coast
National Park

Brecon Beacons
National Park

MONMOUTHSHIRE

SOUTH
GLOUCESTERSHIRE

NORTH

MERSEYSIDE

CHESHIRE

STAFFO

Exmoor
National
Park

Dartmoor
National
Park

ISLES OF SCILLY
CONTINUATION AT THE SAME SCALE

Isles
of Scilly

St Mary's

St Martin's

Land's
End

Conic Equidistant Projection

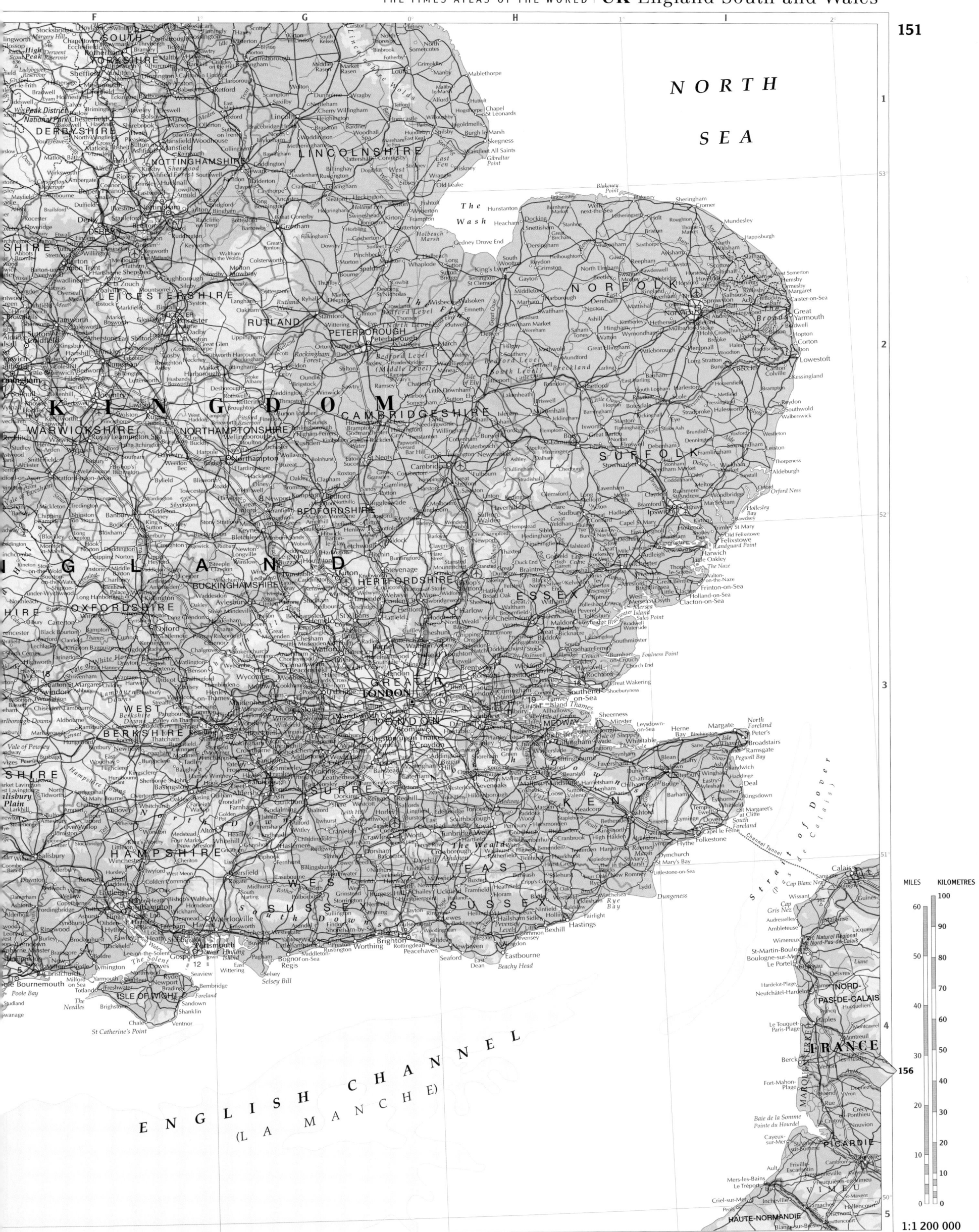

1:1 200 000

© Bartholomew Ltd

© Bartholomew Ltd

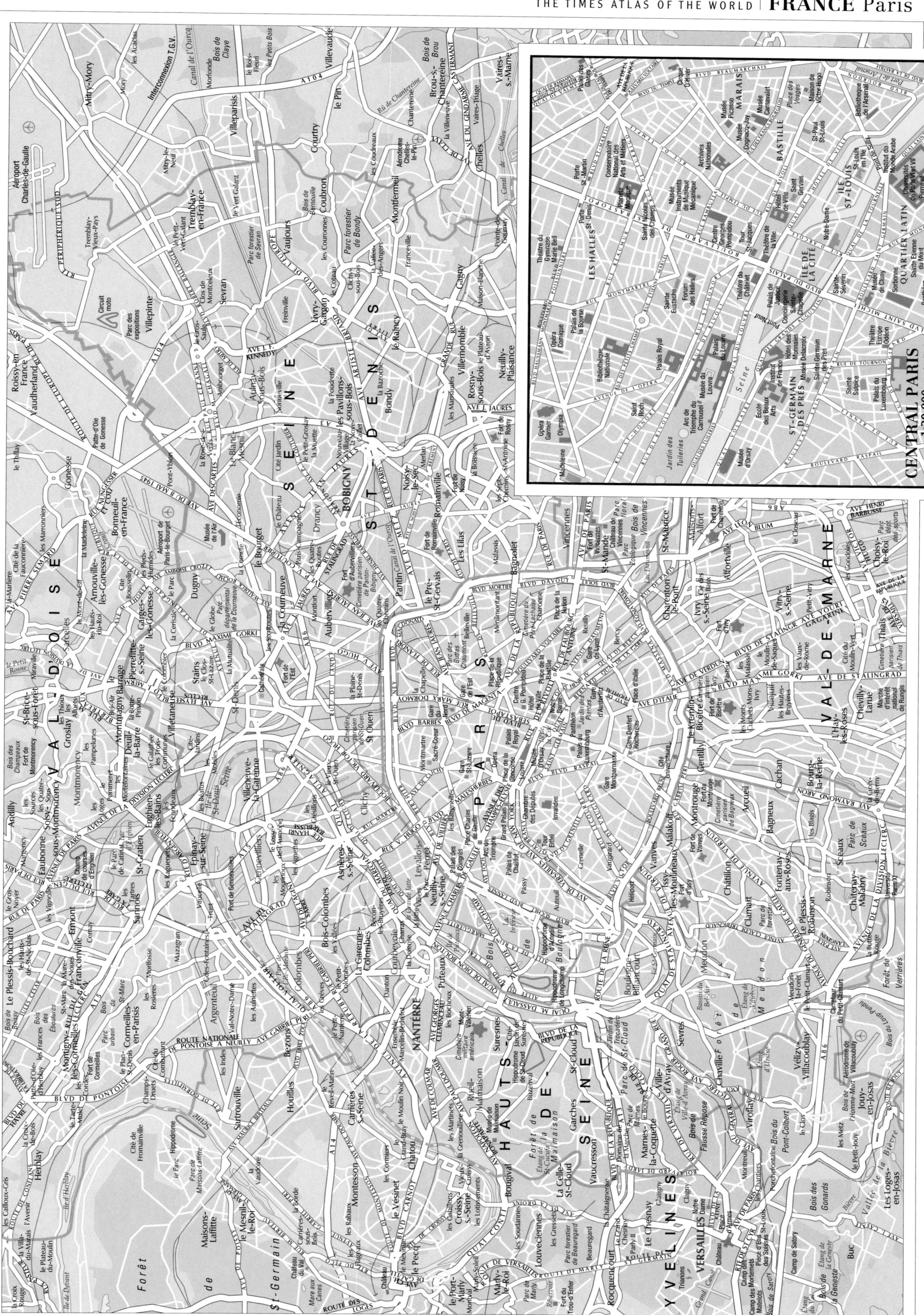

CENTRAL PARIS 1:30 000

1:125 000

© Bartholomew Ltd

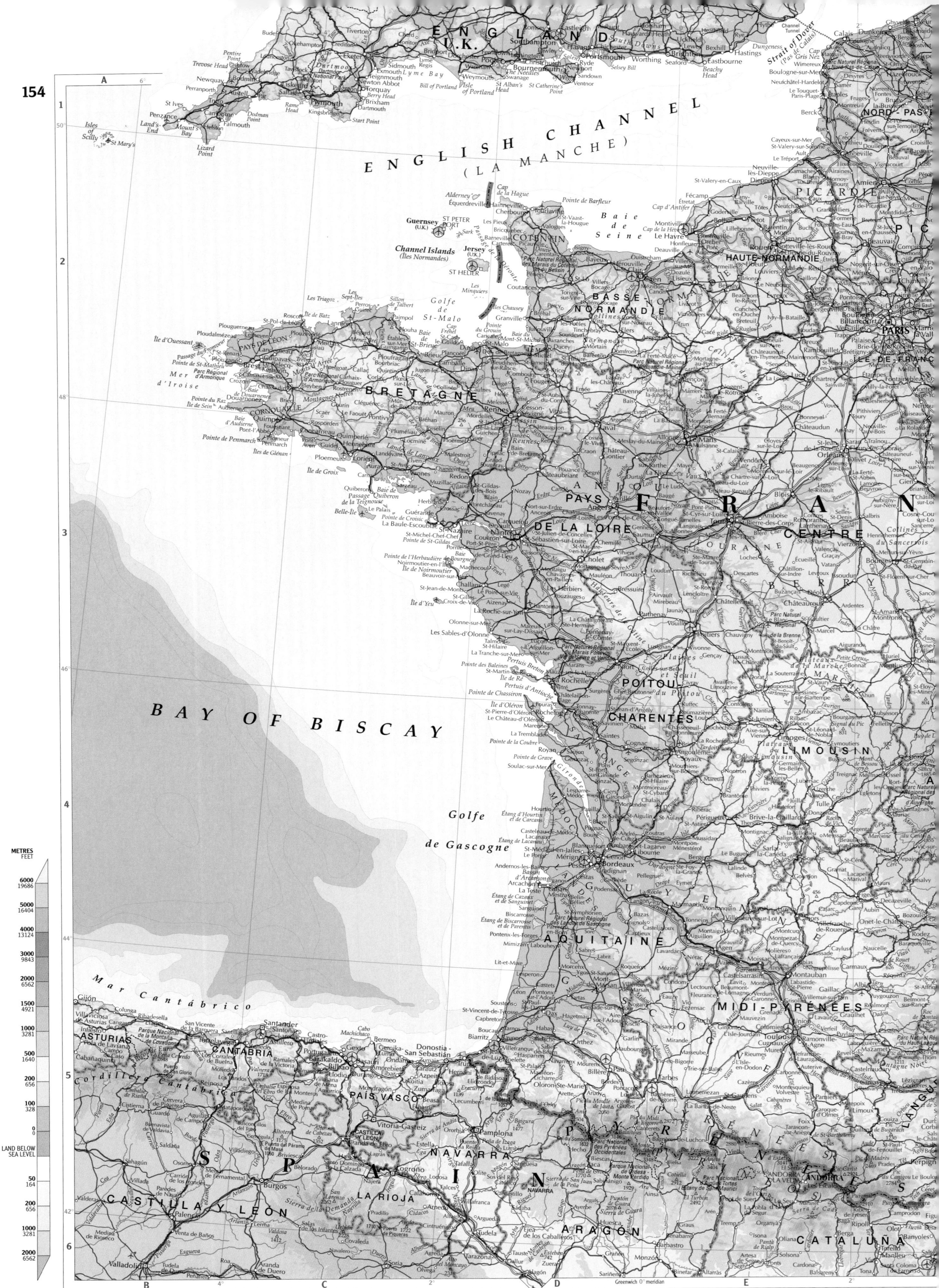

154

ENGLAND (U.K.)

ENGLISH CHANNEL
(LA MANCHE)

Channel Islands
(Îles Normandes)

PICARDIE

HAUTE-NORMANDIE

PARIS

ÎLE-DE-FRANCE

BASSE-NORMANDIE

BRETAGNE

PAYS DE LA LOIRE

FRANCE

CENTRE

BAY OF BISCAY

Golfe de Gascogne

POITOU

CHARENTES

LIMOUSIN

AQUITAINE

MIDI-PYRÉNÉES

Mar Cantábrico

ASTURIAS

CANTABRIA

PAÍS VASCO

NAVARRA

LA RIOJA

ARAGÓN

CATALUÑA

SPAIN

CASTILLA Y LEÓN

Cordillera Cantábrica

PYRÉNÉES

ANDORRA

1:3 000 000

© Bartholomew Ltd

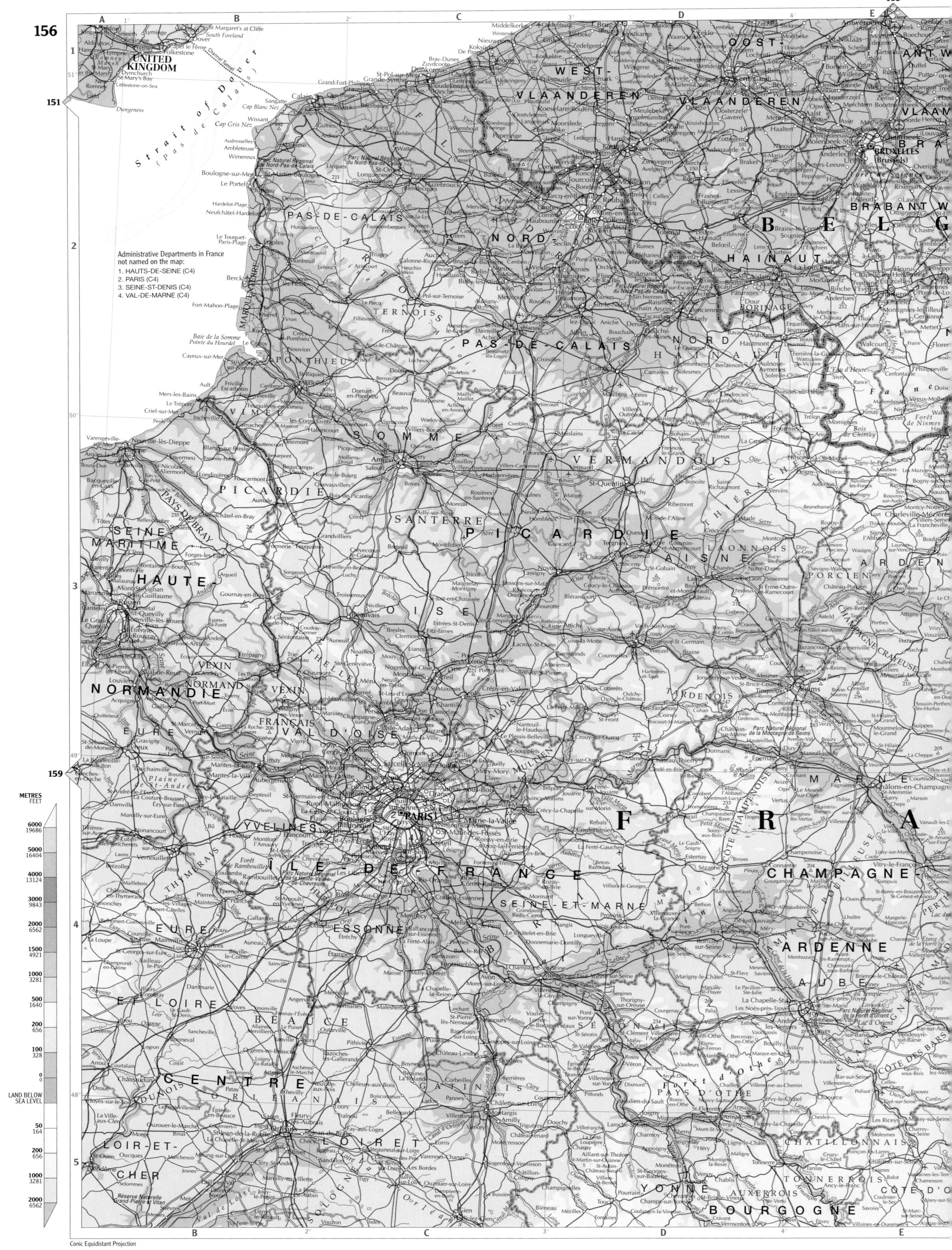

A   B   C   D   E

165

151

159

UNITED KINGDOM

Strait of Dover
(Pas de Calais)

Administrative Departments in France
not named on the map:
1. HAUTS-DE-SEINE (C4)
2. PARIS (C4)
3. SEINE-ST-DENIS (C4)
4. VAL-DE-MARNE (C4)

WEST-VLAANDEREN

OOST-VLAANDEREN

VLAAM

BRABANT W

BELG

BRUXELLES (Brussels)

HAINAUT

NORD

NORD

HAINAUT

PAS-DE-CALAIS

PAS-DE-CALAIS

TERNOIS

PONTHIEU

VIMEU

SOMME

SANTERRE

VERMANDOIS

PICARDIE

PICARDIE

AISNE

LAONNOIS

ARDEN

PORCIEN

PICARDIE

OISE

SEINE-MARITIME

HAUTE-NORMANDIE

PAYS DE BRAY

NORMANDIE

VEXIN

NORMAND

VEXIN

FRANÇAIS

VAL D'OISE

ÎLE-DE-FRANCE

EURE

YVELINES

PARIS

SEINE-ET-MARNE

ESSONNE

CHAMPAGNE-ARDENNE

MARNE

ARDENNE

AUBE

REIMS

EURE-ET-LOIRE

BEAUCE

GATINAIS

CENTRE

ORLEANAIS

LOIRET

YONNE

AUXERROIS

BOURGOGNE

PAYS D'OTHE

LOIR-ET-CHER

FRA

Conic Equidistant Projection

METRES FEET
6000 19686
5000 16404
4000 13124
3000 9843
2000 6562
1500 4921
1000 3281
500   1640
200   656
100   328
0   0
LAND BELOW
SEA LEVEL
50   164
200   656
1000 3281
2000 6562

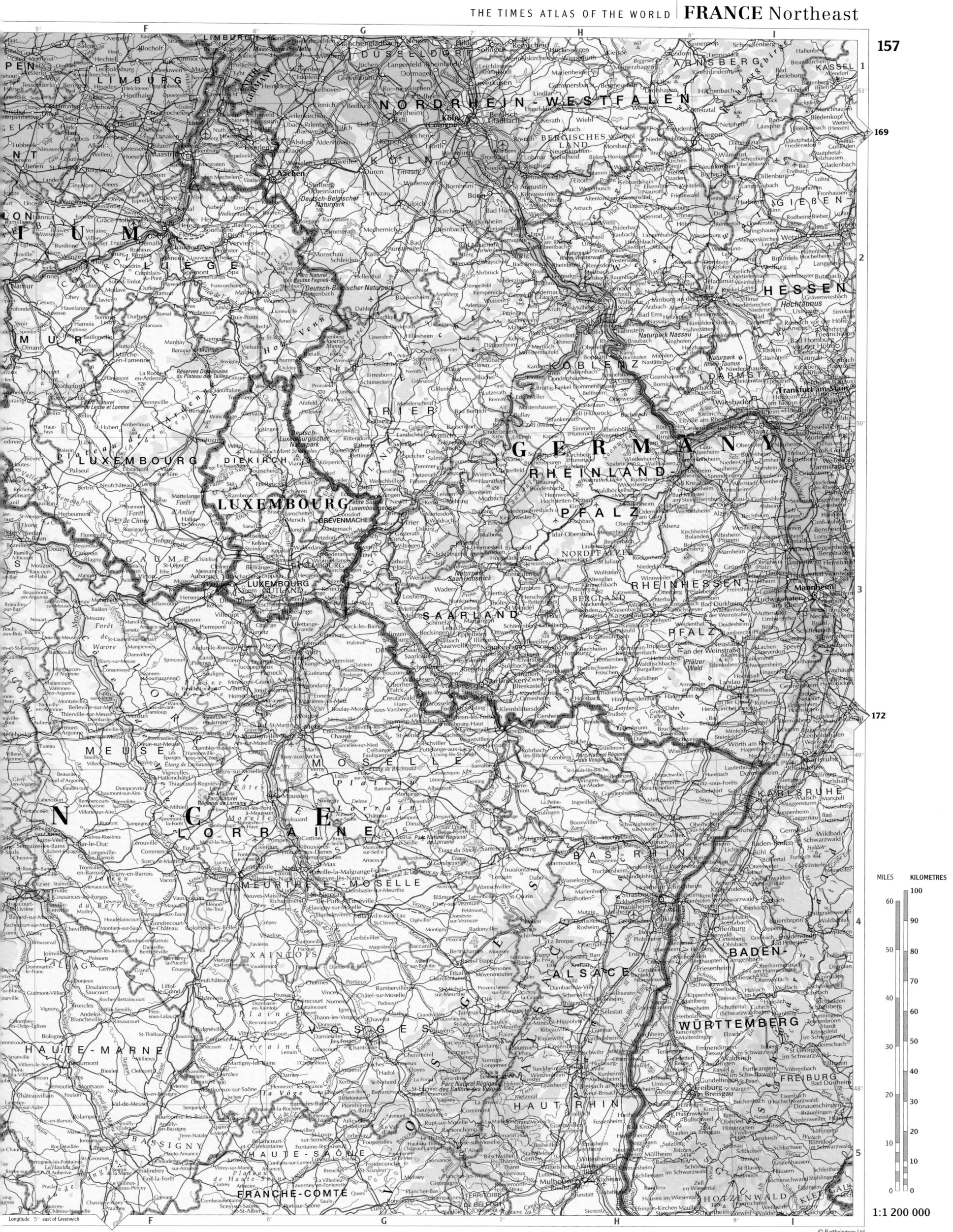

169

172

MILES   KILOMETRES

1:1 200 000

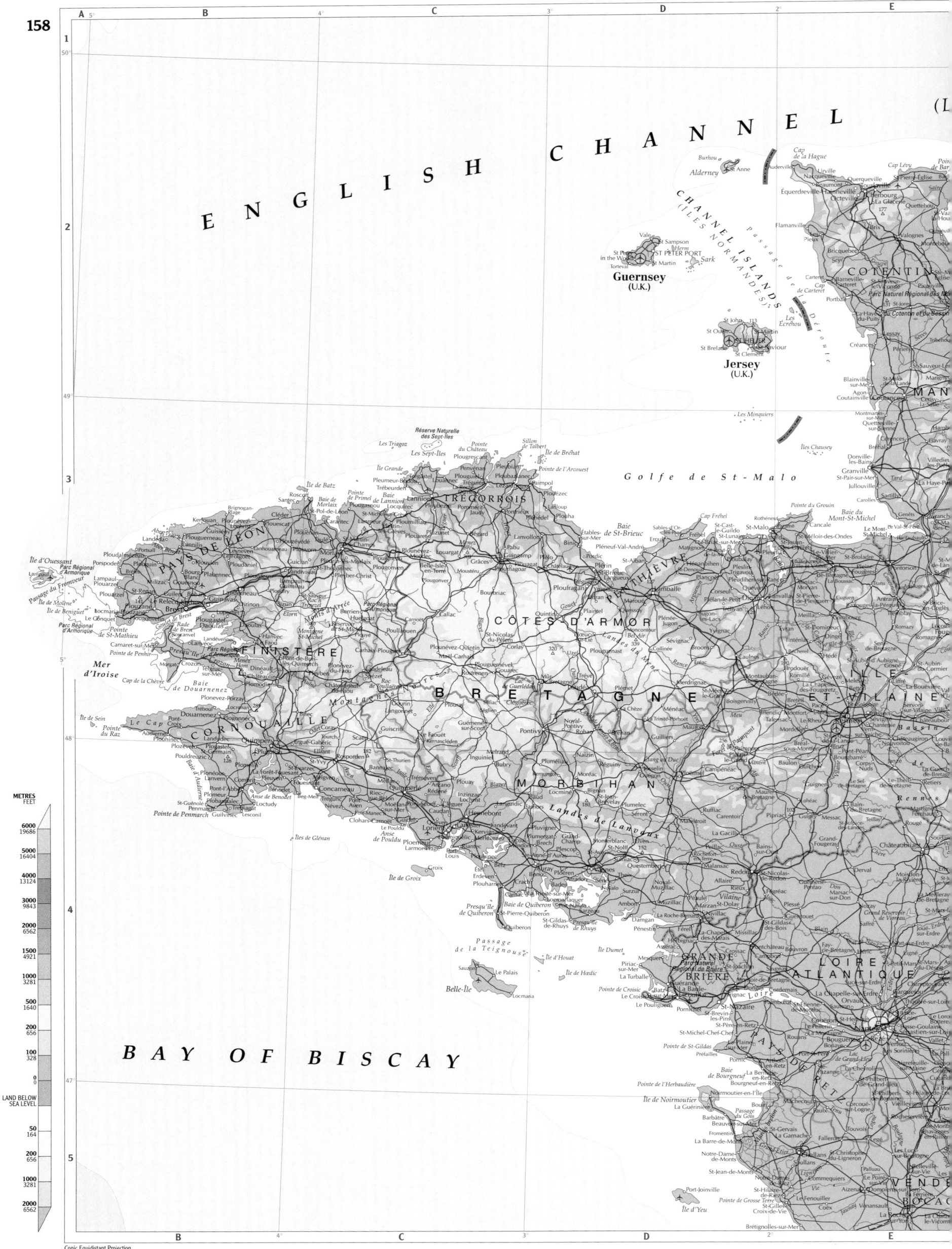

A B 4° C 3° D 2° E

50°

1

E N G L I S H   C H A N N E L (L

Cap
de la Hague
Burhou
Alderney St Anne
Auderville Urville Querqueville St Pierre-Église
Nacqueville Beaumont Tourlaville Cherbourg La Glacerie Quettehou
177
Équerdreville Octeville
Flamanville Pieux Briquebec Valognes
COTENTIN

2

CHANNEL ISLANDS
(ÎLES NORMANDES)
Passage de la Déroute

Vale St Sampson
Herm St Martin
St Peter ST PETER PORT
in the Wood Sark
Torteval St Martin
Guernsey
(U.K.)

St John 113
St Ouen St Martin
St Brelade St Saviour St Clement
Jersey
(U.K.)

Carteret
Cap de Carteret
Portbail
Parc Naturel Régional du
St-Lô-d'Ourville
Les Écréhou
Créances
Périers

Barneville-
Carteret
Le Havre-de-Portbail
Le Puits
St-Sauveur-le-
Lessay

Blainville-
sur-Mer
Agon-
Coutainville
MANCHE

49°

Les Minquiers
Îles Chausey

Golfe de St-Malo

St-Malo
St-Aubin-d'Aubigné
Îles Chausey

Montmartin-
sur-Mer
Quettreville-
sur-Sienne
Villedieu-
les-Poêles
Granville Bréha
Donville-
les-Bains
St-Pair-sur-Mer
Jullouville

3

Réserve Naturelle
des Sept-Îles
Les Triagoz
Les Sept-Îles
Pointe
du Château Sillon
de Talbert Île de Bréhat
Plougrescant Pointe de l'Arcouest

Île Grande Penvénan Plouézec
Pleubian Tréguier

Île de Batz Pointe de
Roscoff Santec Primel Plougasnou Lannion TRÉGORROIS Paimpol Plouha
St-Pol-de-Léon Trébeurden Pabu
Cléder Carantec Plouigneau Mousterlin Lanvollon
Brignogan- Guissény Locquirec Morlaix Plougonver Plouagat Binic
Plage Kerlouan Plouescat Plouvien Plouzélambre Guingamp Plérin St-Brieuc
Cancale
Cap Fréhel St-Cast- Matignon Hillion Baie
Rothéneuf le-Guildo Pléneuf-Val-André de St-Brieuc
Fréhel St-Lunaire Dinard Pleurtuit Dinan Pléhérel
Sables-d'Or St-Briac-sur-Mer Ploubalay
Pointe du Grouin

Baie du
Mont-St-Michel
Le Mont-St-Michel
Pontorson

PAYS DE LÉON
Kerfouan Plouguerneau Lesneven
Île d'Ouessant Landéda Ploudaniel Plabennec Guiclan Le Ponthou Plouaret
Parc Régional Porspoder Bourg- Blanc Landivisiau St-Thégonnec
d'Armorique Lampaul- Ploudalmézeau Gouesnou Landerneau Plounéour-Ménez Callac
Plouarzel Guipavas Sizun Huelgoat Bourbriac Quintin
Île de Molène St-Renan Brest Plougastel- Le Drennec Maël-Carhaix Plaintel
Île de Béniguet Le Conquet Landévennec Daoulas Commana St-Nicolas- Corlay COTES D'ARMOR Broons Bécherel
Parc Régional Plougonvelin Rade Le Faou Brasparts du-Pélem Plouguenast La Chèze Montauban-
d'Armorique de Brest Bodilis Parc Régional Rostrenen Loudéac de-Bretagne
Pointe de St-Mathieu Camaret-sur-Mer Bourg- d'Armorique Carhaix-Plouguer Collinée
Ménez-Hom Pleyben Gouarec

5° Pointe de Penhir Crozon Châteaulin Landeleau Guémené- Merdrignac BRETAGNE La Chapelle-
Mer Cap de la Chèvre Châteauneuf- sur-Scorff Pontivy Josselin des-Fougeretz
d'Iroise Morgat Telgruc- du-Faou 320 Pontivy Guilliers Boisgervilly Bédée ILLE-ET-VILAINE
sur-Mer Plomodiern Le Guerlédan Rohan Plémet Ploërmel
Baie de Pont-de-Buis Plévin St-Gérand La Trinité-Porhoët Montfort- Rennes
Douarnenez Montagnes Locunolé Guéméné- Plumelec Mauron sur-Meu
Douarnenez Plonévez-Porzay Noires Langonnet sur-Scorff Naizin Plumelin Guer Messac
Île de Sein Montagnes Le Faouët Guiscriff Réguiny 256

48° Pointe du Raz Le Cap Pont- Kernascléden Plumelec Bain-de-Bretagne
Plogoff Croix Quimper Melrand Elven Plaudren Baulon Le Theil-
Audierne Pluguffan Scaër Inguiniel Questembert de-Bretagne
Plouhinec Pont- Rosporden Bubry MORBIHAN Vannes Malestroit Pipriac Grand-
St-Yvi Banalec Plouay Moréac Carentoir Fougeray Châteaubriant
Plozévet Germain 182 St-Thurien Bignan Grand- Sérent Ruffiac
Pouldreuzic Plonéour- Rédéné Arzano Locmine Champ St-Nolff La Gacilly
Plobannalec Lanvern Quimperlé Moëlan- Inzinzac- Landévant St-Jean- Redon
Pointe de Penmarch St-Guénolé Pont-l'Abbé La Forêt-Fouesnant sur-Mer Lochrist Brévelay St-Nicolas- Derval
Penmarch Loctudy Fouesnant Clohars-Carnoët Hennebont Pluvigner Grand- de-Redon
Guilvinec Lesconil Beg-Meil Trégunc Le Pouldu Languidic Auray Plescop 152 Rochefort- Allaire Pipriac
Névez Anse Lorient Brech en-Terre Questembert Malansac
Concarneau de Pouldu Port- Ploemeur Pluméliau St-Avé Rieux
Îles de Glénan Larmor-Plage Louis Lanester Ste-Anne-d'Auray Elven Pénestin St-Nicolas-
Vilaine de-Redon

4

Île de Groix Étel Auray Ploeren Vannes Surzur Muzillac Nivillac
Plouharnel Locoal- Baden Le Bono Sarzeau Marzan St-Dolay
Carnac-Plage Mendon Île aux Moines Ambon La Roche-Bernard Plessé
Presqu'île Carnac Presqu'île Damgan
de Quiberon St-Pierre-Quiberon de Rhuys St-Gildas- La Gacilly
St-Gildas- Pénestin des-Bois
Quiberon de-Rhuys Férel La Chapelle- Missillac Guenrouet
Passage des-Marais Fégréac
de la Baie de Quiberon Herbignac
Teignouse Île d'Houat Île Dumet Assérac GRANDE Montoir-de-Bretagne
Piriac- BRIÈRE Pontchâteau Bouvron
sur-Mer Parc Naturel St-Joachim
Belle-Île Île Hœdic Mesquer Régional de Brière Savenay
La Turballe St-Lyphard Crossac
Sauzon Guérande Trignac St-Étienne- Blain
Le Palais Pointe de Croisic St-Nazaire de-Montluc La Chapelle-sur-Erdre
Locmaria Le Croisic La Baule Nantes
Batz- Pornichet Loire Orvault
Belle-Île sur-Mer Loire St-Herblain
Le Pouliguen Montoir-de-Bretagne LOIRE Couëron
St-Brévin- St-Père-en-Retz Paimbœuf St-Herblain ATLANTIQUE
les-Pins St-Michel-Chef-Chef Bouguenais

BAY   OF   BISCAY
Pointe de St-Gildas PAYS DE RETZ
Préfailles Pornic Rezé Basse-Goulaine
Bouaye St-Sébastien-sur-Loire
Machecoul Le Pellerin
Bourg Corcoué-sur-Logne
Pointe de l'Herbaudière Beauvoir-sur-Mer Sornin
Noirmoutier-en-l'Île Challans
47° Baie La Guérinière Bois-de-Céné
de Bourgneuf La Bernerie-en-Retz Legé
Île de Noirmoutier Bouin
Barbâtre Passage St-Jean-de-Monts
Beauvoir-sur-Mer du Gois
Fromentine St-Gervais La Garnache
La Barre-de-Monts St-Christophe- Falleron
Touvois du-Ligneron
Notre-Dame- St-Hilaire- VENDÉE
de-Monts Palluau Aizenay BOCAGE
St-Jean-de-Monts Vie Le Poiré-sur-Vie La Roche-
Port-Joinville St-Hilaire- Commequiers Apremont
de-Riez Le Fenouiller Coëx
Île d'Yeu Pointe de Grosse Terre St-Gilles- La Chaize-
Croix-de-Vie Vanneau
Brétignolles-sur-Mer

5

B 4° C 3° D 2° E

METRES
FEET

6000
19686
5000
16404
4000
13124
3000
9843
2000
6562
1500
4921
1000
3281
500
1640
200
656
100
328
0
0
LAND BELOW
SEA LEVEL
50
164
200
656
1000
3281
2000
6562

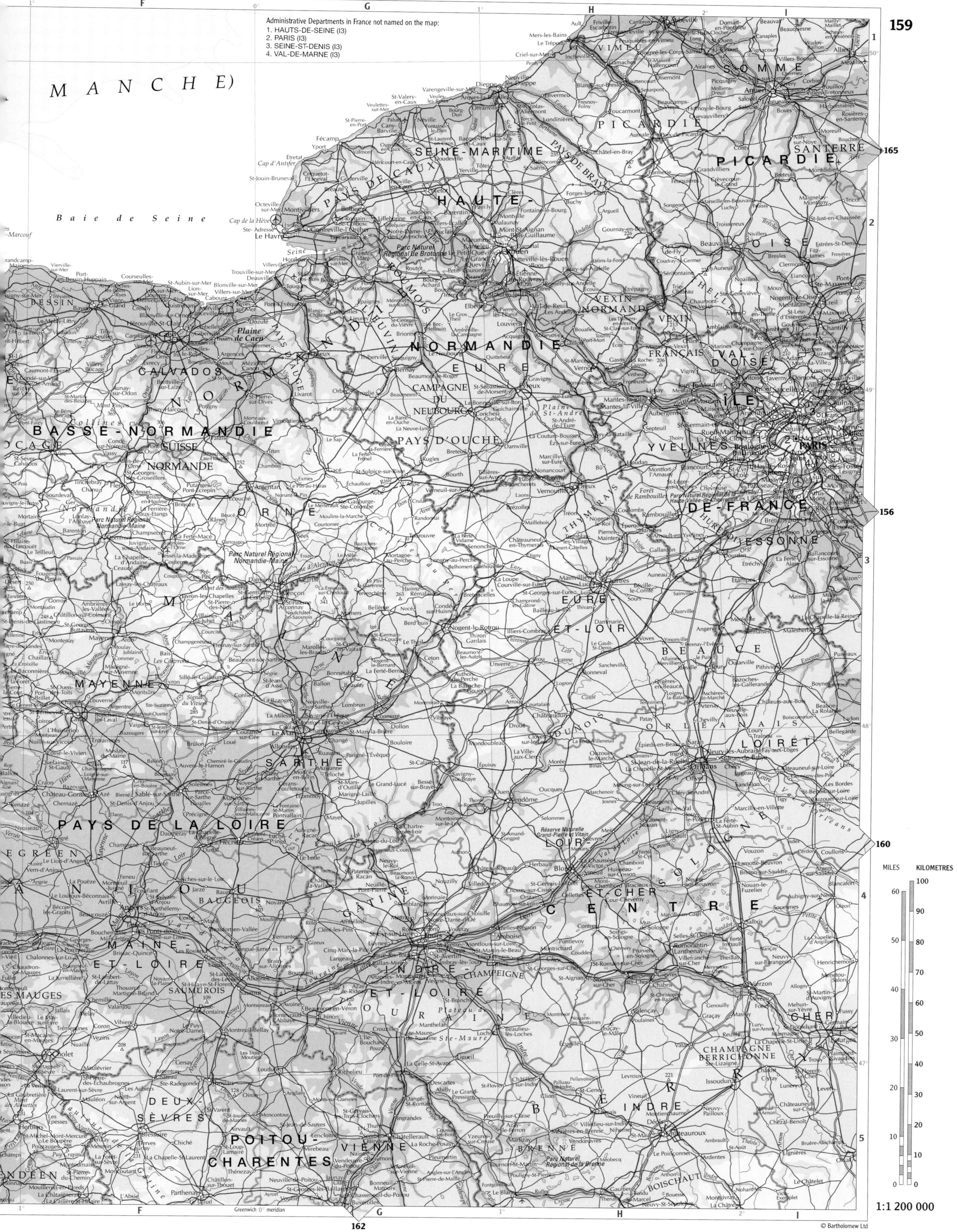

Administrative Departments in France not named on the map:
1. HAUTS-DE-SEINE (I3)
2. PARIS (I3)
3. SEINE-ST-DENIS (I3)
4. VAL-DE-MARNE (I3)

M A N C H E (LA)

Baie de Seine

MANCHE

SEINE-MARITIME

HAUTE-NORMANDIE

PAYS DE CAUX

PAYS DE BRAY

PICARDIE

SOMME

OISE

VAL-D'OISE

VEXIN NORMAND

VEXIN FRANÇAIS

BESSIN

CALVADOS

BASSE-NORMANDIE

SUISSE NORMANDE

BOCAGE

NORMANDIE

ORNE

EURE

PAYS D'OUCHE

CAMPAGNE DU NEUBOURG

ÎLE-DE-FRANCE

YVELINES

PARIS

ESSONNE

EURE-ET-LOIR

BEAUCE

MAINE

MAYENNE

SARTHE

PERCHE

ORLÉANAIS

LOIRET

PAYS DE LA LOIRE

SEGRÉEN

ANJOU

BAUGEOIS

MAINE-ET-LOIRE

SAUMUROIS

LES MAUGES

TOURAINE

INDRE-ET-LOIRE

CHAMPEIGNE

LOIR-ET-CHER

SOLOGNE

CENTRE

CHER

CHAMPAGNE BERRICHONNE

DEUX-SÈVRES

POITOU-CHARENTES

VIENNE

INDRE

BRENNE

BOISCHAUT

VENDÉEN

MILES | KILOMETRES
60 | 100
| 90
50 | 80
| 70
40 | 60
| 50
30 | 40
20 | 30
10 | 20
| 10
0 | 0

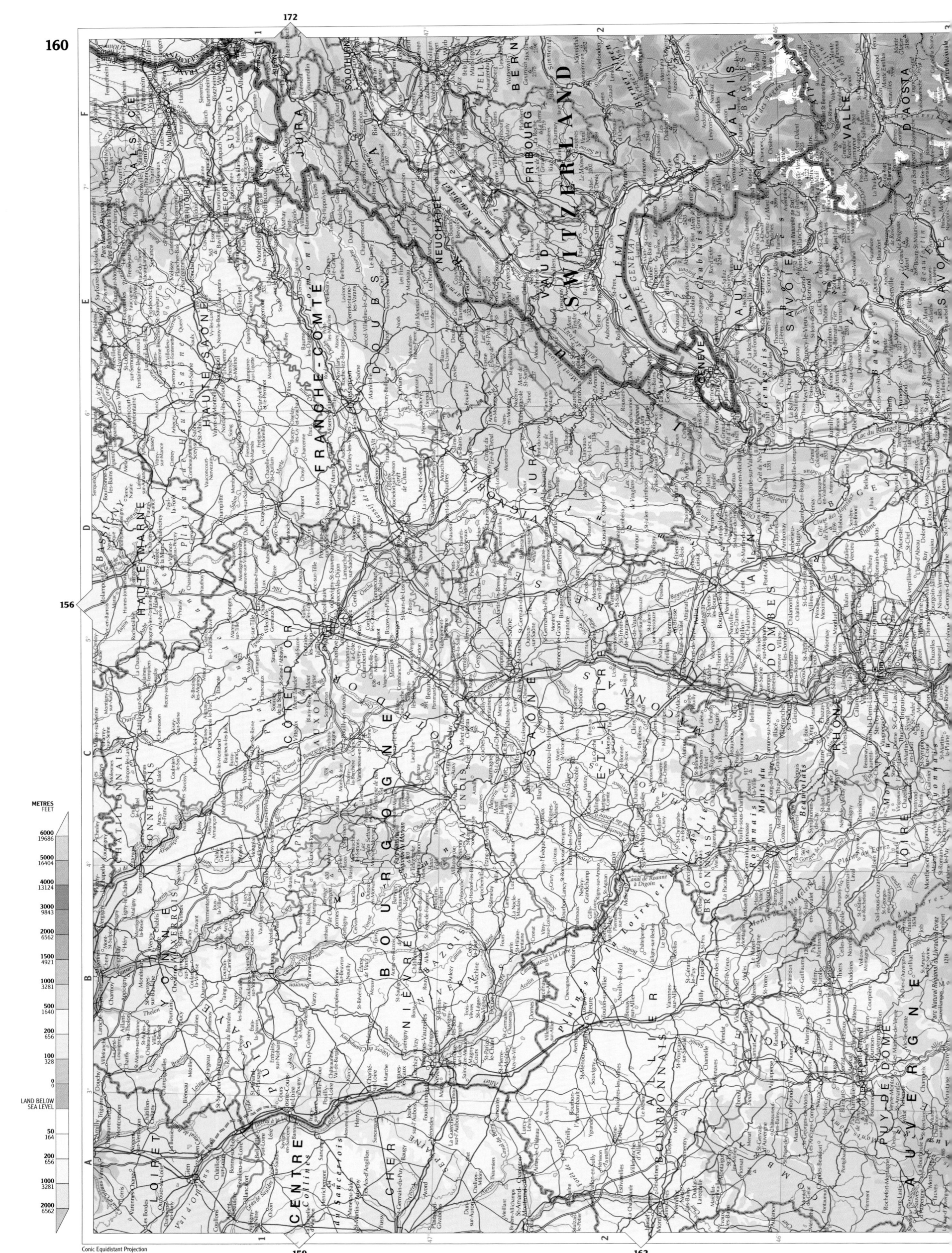

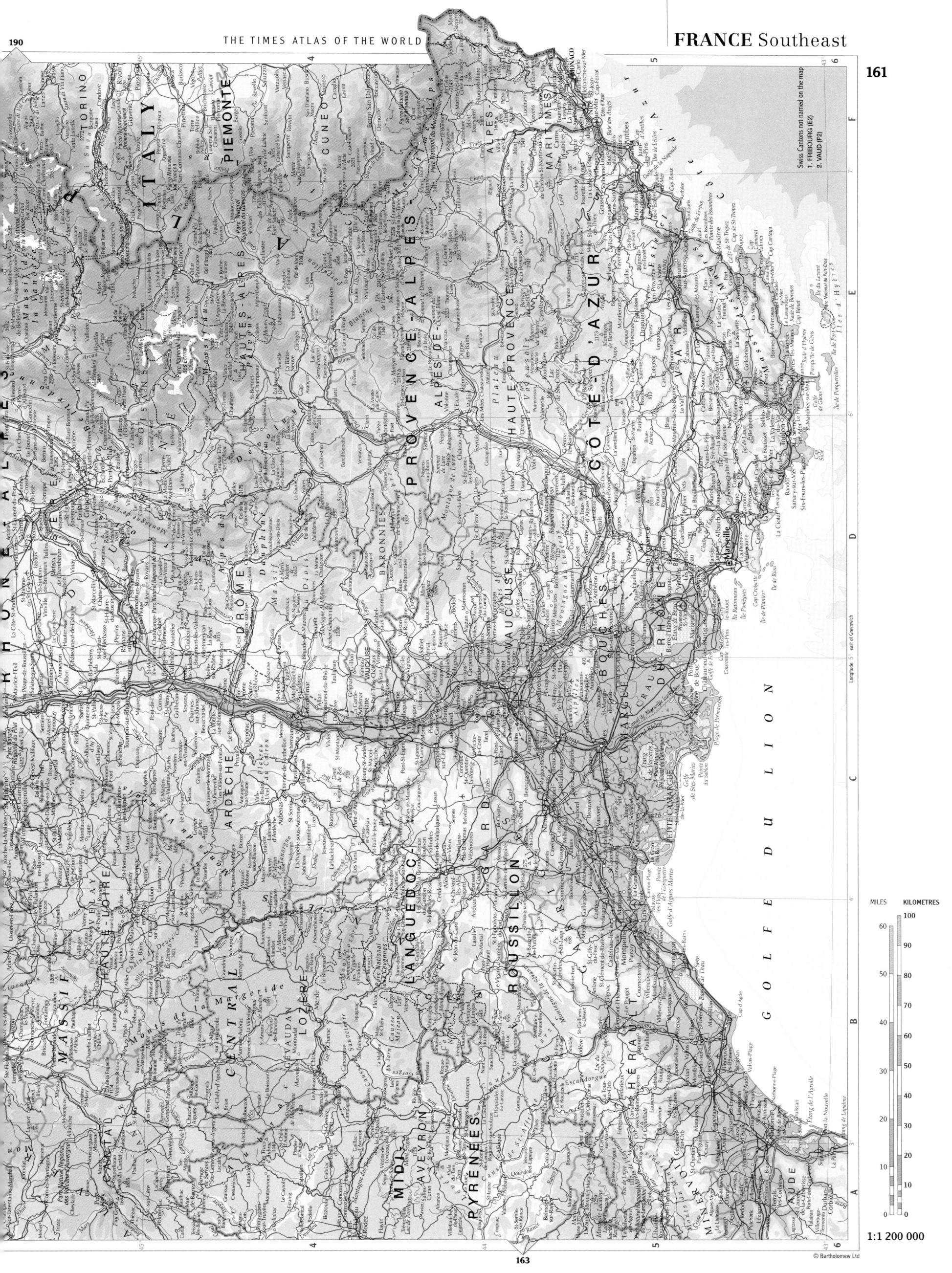

Swiss Cantons not named on the map
1. FRIBOURG (E2)
2. VAUD (F2)

MILES   KILOMETRES

1:1 200 000

© Bartholomew Ltd

160

159

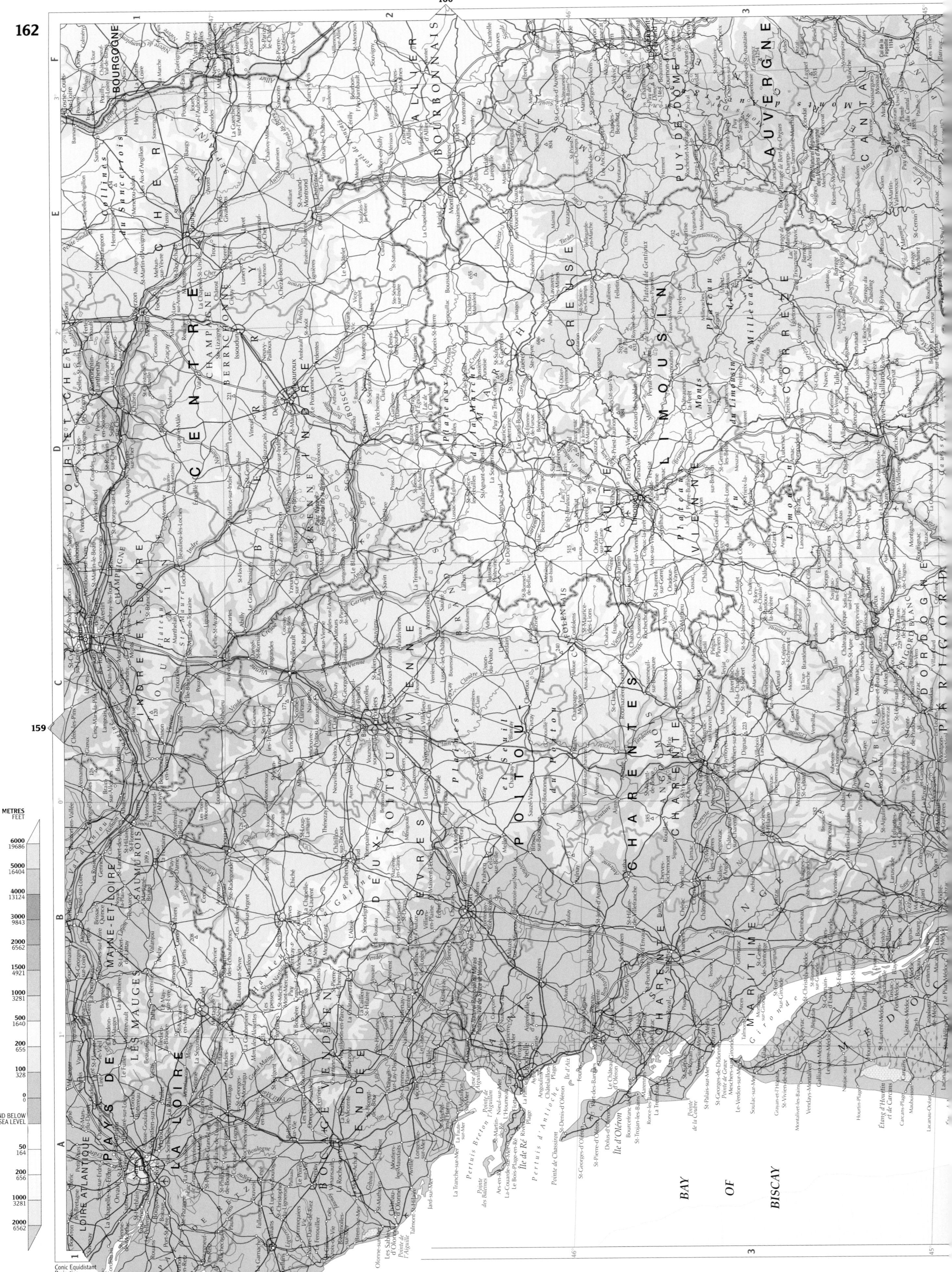

BOURGOGNE

CHER

LOIR-ET-CHER

CENTRE

INDRE-ET-LOIRE

INDRE

BERRICHONNE

CHAMPAGNE

BRENNE

ALLIER

BOURBONNAIS

AUVERGNE

PUY-DE-DÔME

CANTAL

CREUSE

MARCHE

LIMOUSIN

HAUTE-VIENNE

Plateau de Millevaches

CORRÈZE

Monts du Limousin

Plateau de Gentioux

MAINE-ET-LOIRE

LES MAUGES

PAYS DE LA LOIRE

SAUMUROIS

CHAMPAGNE

VENDÉE

BOCAGE VENDÉEN

DEUX-SÈVRES

HAUT-POITOU

VIENNE

POITOU

BRANDE

MONTMORILLONNAIS

CONFOLENTAIS

ANGOUMOIS

CHARENTE

CHARENTE-MARITIME

LOIRE-ATLANTIQUE

Île de Ré

Île d'Oléron

Île d'Aix

PÉRIGORD BLANC

DORDOGNE

MÉDOC

Gironde

Étang d'Hourtin et de Carcans

BAY OF BISCAY

Conic Equidistant Projection

METRES FEET

METRES	FEET
6000	19686
5000	16404
4000	13124
3000	9843
2000	6562
1500	4921
1000	3281
500	1640
200	655
100	328
0	0

LAND BELOW SEA LEVEL

50	164
200	656
1000	3281
2000	6562

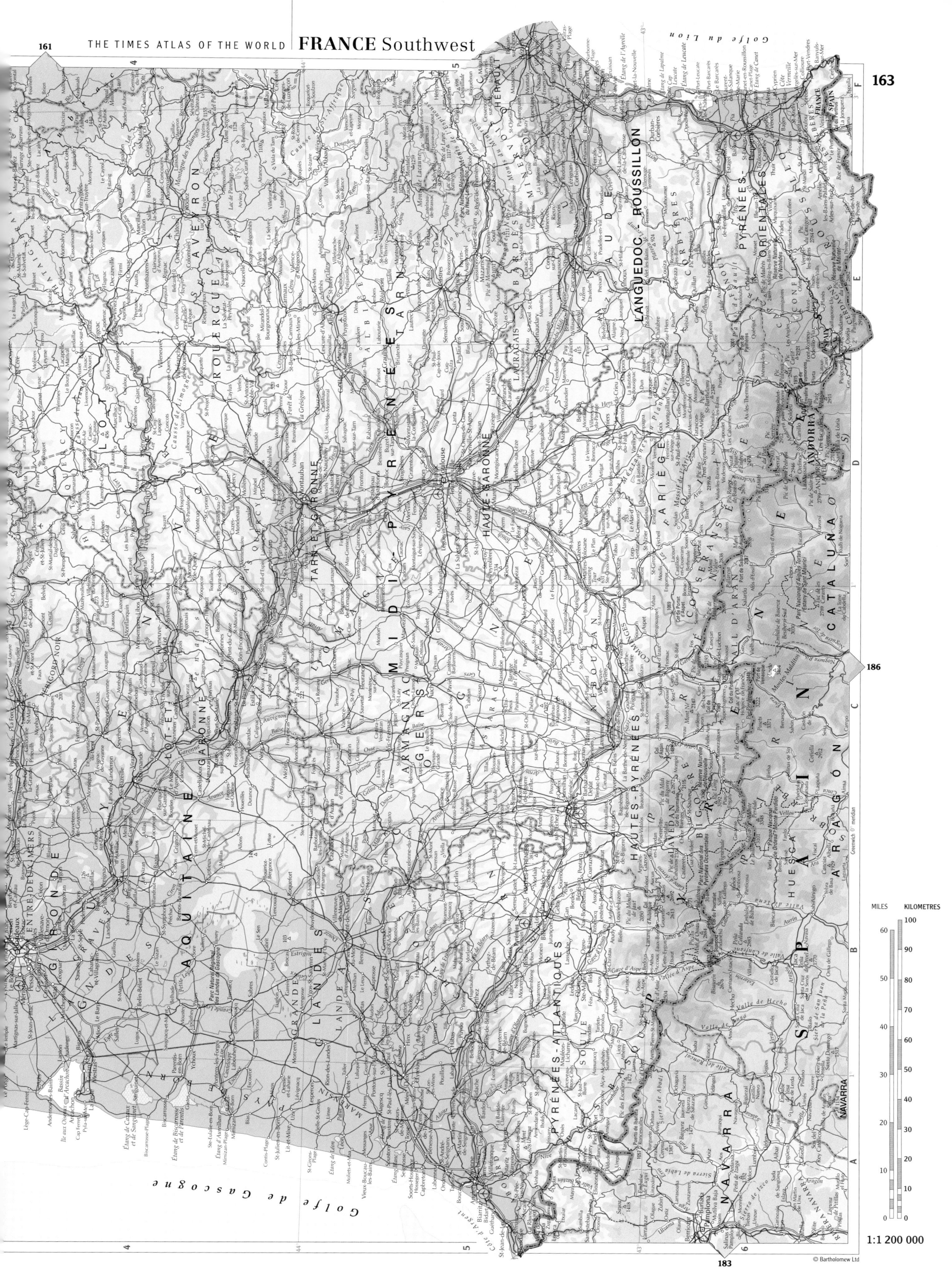

186

183

MILES   KILOMETRES

60   100

50   90

      80

40   70

     60

30   50

     40

20   30

10   20

     10

0   0

1:1 200 000

© Bartholomew Ltd

168

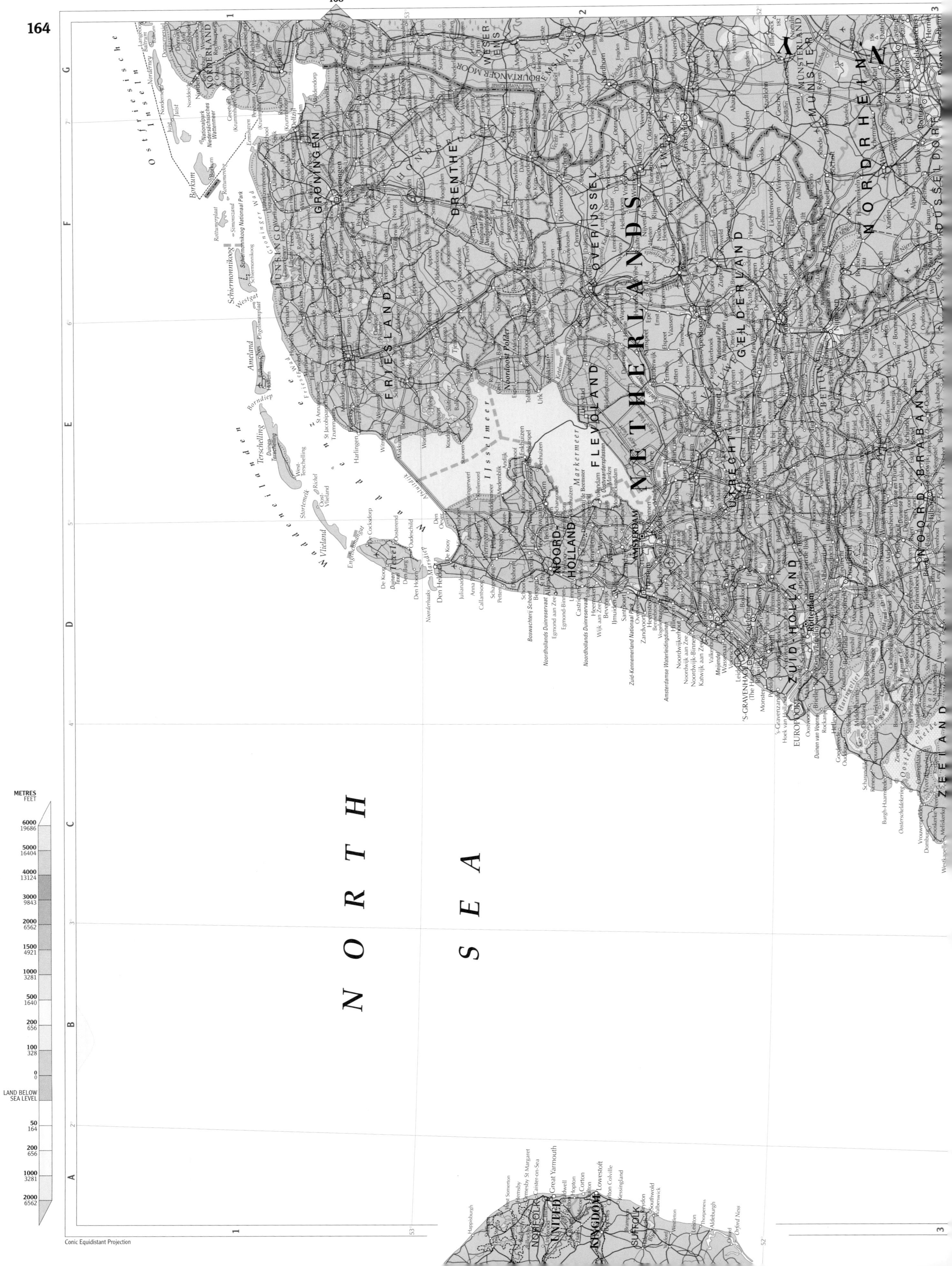

NORTH SEA

NETHERLANDS

NORDRHEIN

MÜNSTER

WESER-EMS

GRONINGEN

FRIESLAND

DRENTHE

OVERIJSSEL

FLEVOLAND

GELDERLAND

UTRECHT

NOORD-HOLLAND

ZUID-HOLLAND

NOORD-BRABANT

ZEELAND

NORDERLAND

EMSLAND

Ostfriesische Inseln

Waddeneilanden

IJsselmeer

Markermeer

Noordoost Polder

UNITED KINGDOM

NORFOLK

SUFFOLK

'S-GRAVENHAGE (The Hague)

Rotterdam

METRES / FEET

6000	19686
5000	16404
4000	13124
3000	9843
2000	6562
1500	4921
1000	3281
500	1640
200	656
100	328
0	0

LAND BELOW SEA LEVEL

50	164
200	656
1000	3281
2000	6562

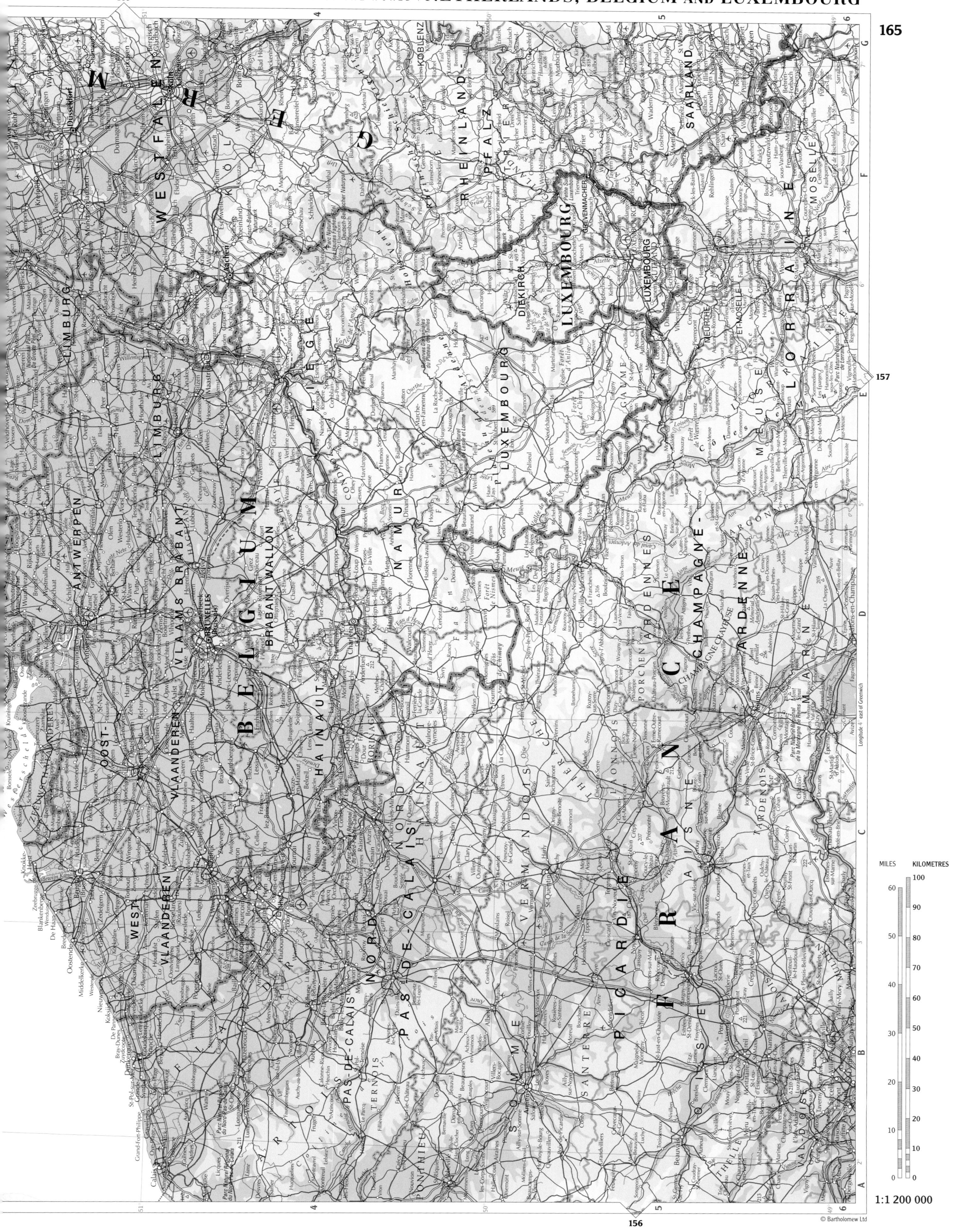

NETHERLANDS, BELGIUM AND LUXEMBOURG

WESTFALEN

LIMBURG

ANTWERPEN

OOST-VLAANDEREN

WEST-VLAANDEREN

VLAAMS-BRABANT

BRABANT WALLON

BELGIUM

HAINAUT

NAMUR

LIÈGE

LUXEMBOURG

LUXEMBOURG

DIEKIRCH

GREVENMACHER

RHEINLAND-PFALZ

SAARLAND

LORRAINE

MEUSE

MEURTHE-ET-MOSELLE

MOSELLE

ARDENNE

CHAMPAGNE-ARDENNE

PORCIEN

MARNE

AISNE

VERMANDOIS

PICARDIE

FRANCE

PAS-DE-CALAIS

NORD

BORINAGE

Longitude 4 east of Greenwich

MILES KILOMETRES

60 100
    90
50 80
    70
40 60
    50
30 40
20 30
    20
10
    10
0   0

1:1 200 000

© Bartholomew Ltd

NORTH SEA

DENMARK

SCHLESWIG-
HOLSTEIN

MECKLENBURG-
VORPOMMERN

NETHERLANDS

NIEDERSACHSEN

AMSTERDAM

'S-GRAVENHAGE
(The Hague)

Rotterdam

IJsselmeer

Den Helder

Haarlem

Hamburg

Bremen

Bremerhaven

Hannover

Ostfriesland

SACHSEN-
ANHALT

BELGIUM

NORDRHEIN-WESTFALEN

Essen

Düsseldorf

Köln
(Cologne)

Aachen

BRUXELLES
Brussel

GERMANY

HESSEN

THÜRINGEN

Frankfurt am Main

Wiesbaden

RHEINLAND-PFALZ

NORD-
PAS-DE-
CALAIS

PICARDIE

CHAMPAGNE-
ARDENNE

LORRAINE

SAARLAND

Mannheim

Ludwigshafen am Rhein

BADEN-
WÜRTTEMBERG

BAYERN

Nürnberg

Stuttgart

Karlsruhe

ALSACE

München
(Munich)

FRANCE

BOURGOGNE

FRANCHE-
COMTÉ

Lyon

SWITZERLAND

BERN

LIECHTENSTEIN
VADUZ

AUSTRIA

ALPS

RHÔNE-ALPES

TRENTINO-
ALTO-ADIGE

LOMBARDIA

PIEMONTE

ITALY

VENETO

VENEZIA GIULIA
FRIULI

155

METRES
FEET

6000	19686
5000	16404
4000	13124
3000	9843
2000	6562
1500	4921
1000	3281
500	1640
200	656
100	328
0	0

LAND BELOW
SEA LEVEL

50	164
200	656
1000	3281
2000	6562

Conic Equidistant Projection

1:3 000 000

© Bartholomew Ltd

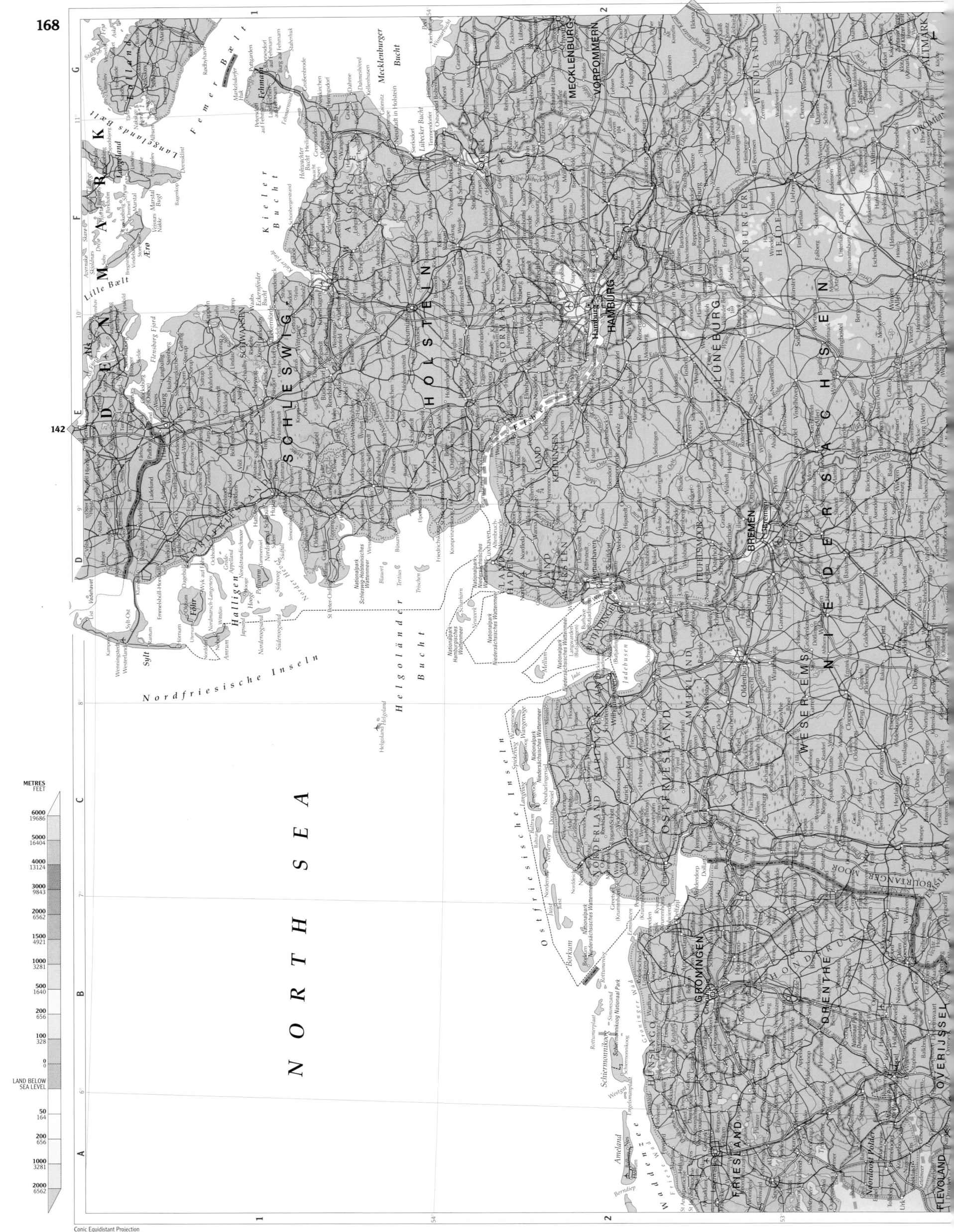

METRES
FEET

6000
19686

5000
16404

4000
13124

3000
9843

2000
6562

1500
4921

1000
3281

500
1640

200
656

100
328

0

LAND BELOW
SEA LEVEL

50
164

200
656

1000
3281

2000
6562

Conic Equidistant Projection

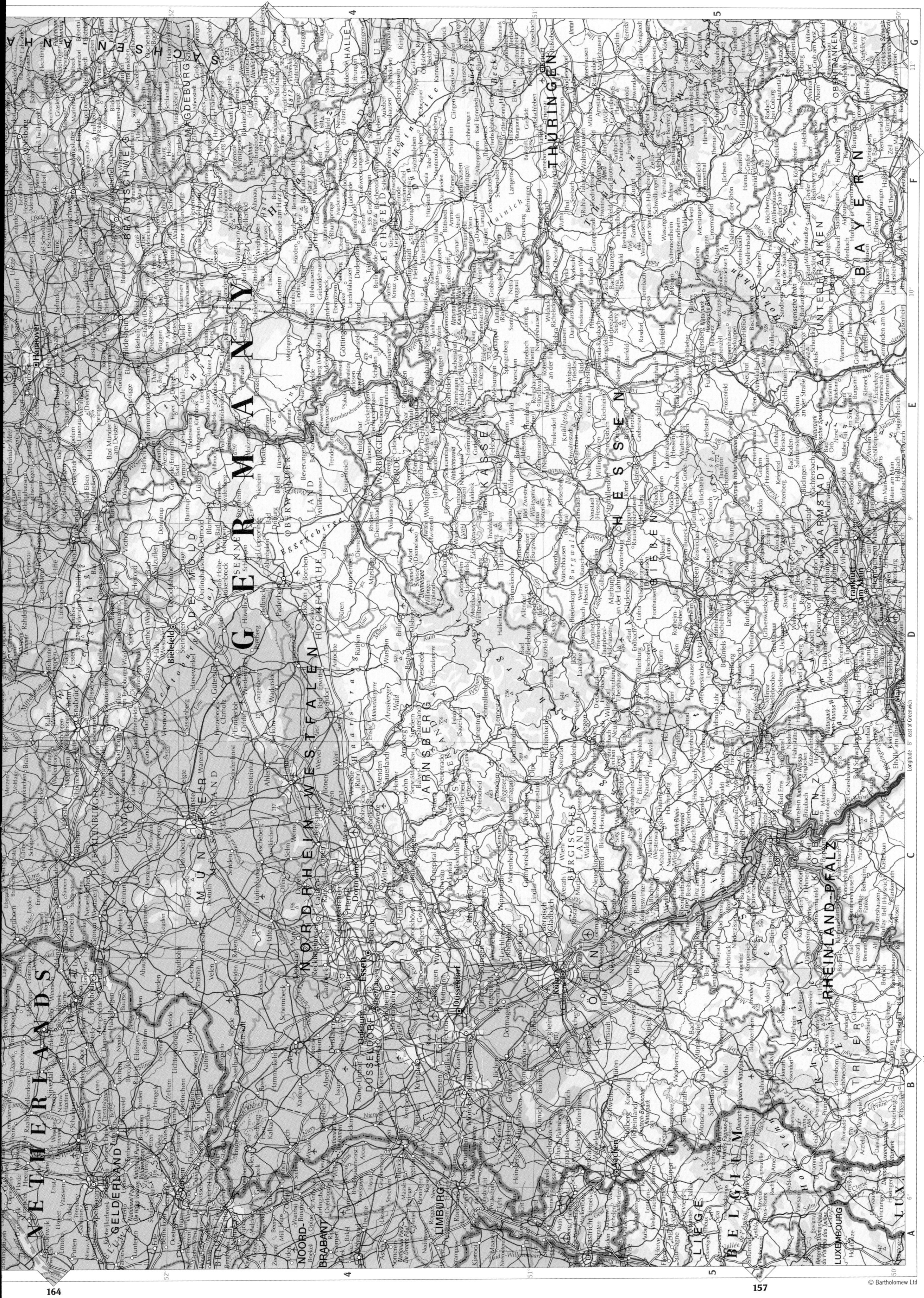

173

172

164

GERMANY

NETHERLANDS

BELGIË

THÜRINGEN

BAYERN

HESSEN

NORDRHEIN-WESTFALEN

RHEINLAND-PFALZ

Longitude 8° east of Greenwich

MILES	KILOMETRES
60	100
50	90
40	80
	70
30	60
20	50
	40
10	30
	20
	10
0	0

1:1 200 000

© Bartholomew Ltd

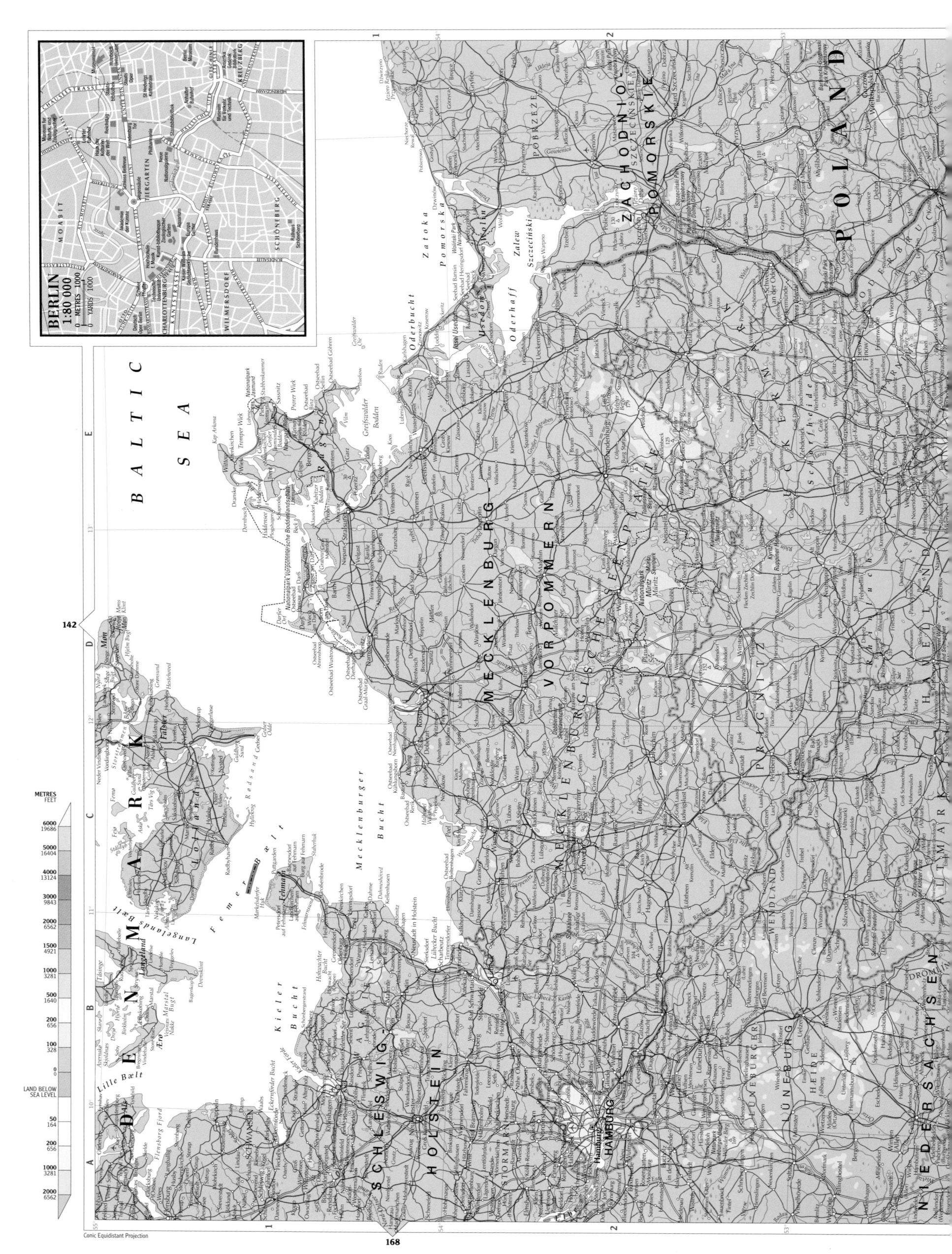

Conic Equidistant Projection

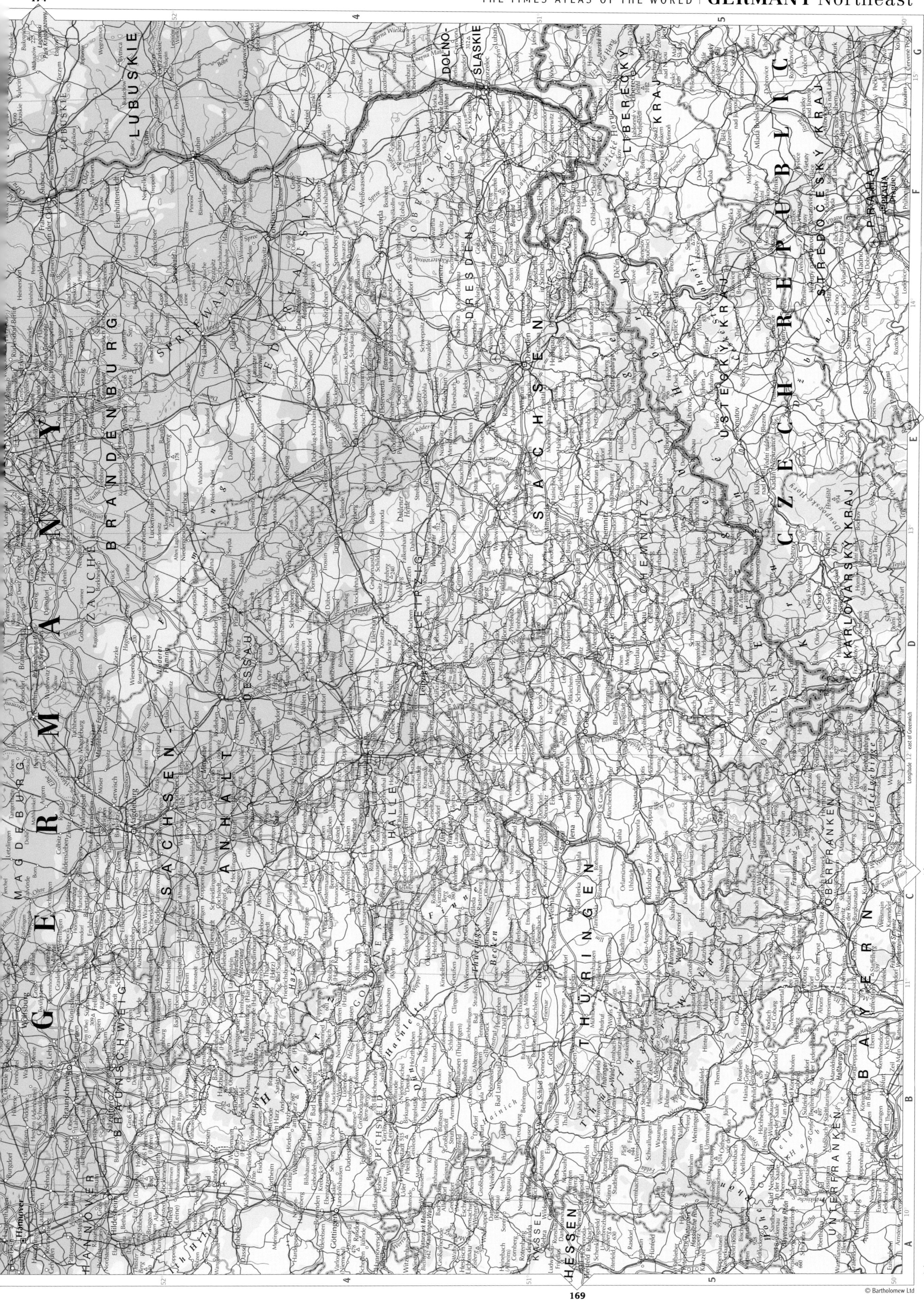

174

176

173

169

GERMANY

LUBUSKIE

BRANDENBURG

ZAUCHE

SPREEWALD

NIEDERLAUSITZ

OBERLAUSITZ

DOLNO-ŚLĄSKIE

DRESDEN

SACHSEN

SACHSEN-ANHALT

MAGDEBURG

BRAUNSCHWEIG

HALLE

ERZGEBIRGE

CHEMNITZ

VOGTLAND

THÜRINGEN

GOLDENE AUE

EICHSFELD

HARZ

HANNOVER

KASSEL

HESSEN

BAYERN

UNTERFRANKEN

OBERFRANKEN

CZECH REPUBLIC

LIBERECKÝ KRAJ

ÚSTECKÝ KRAJ

KARLOVARSKÝ KRAJ

STŘEDOČESKÝ KRAJ

PRAHA / PRAGUE

Leipzig

Jena

Longitude 12 east of Greenwich

MILES | KILOMETRES

60 | 100
50 | 90
40 | 80
30 | 70
20 | 60
10 | 50
0 | 40

1:1 200 000

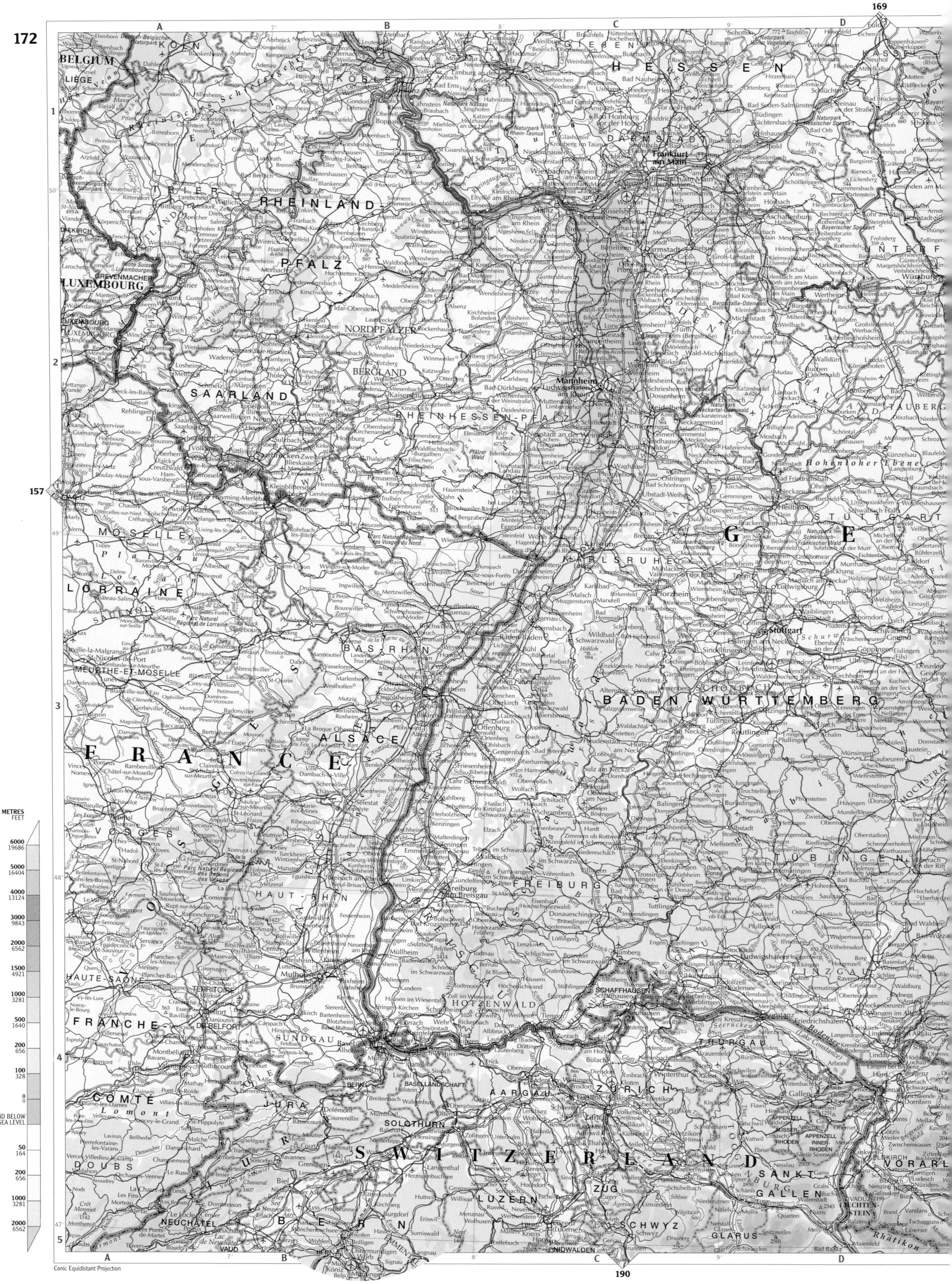

A 7 B 8 C 9 D

BELGIUM
LIEGE
DIEKIRCH
LUXEMBOURG
LUXEMBOURG

RHEINLAND
PFALZ
NORDPFÄLZER
BERGLAND
SAARLAND
RHEINHESSEN-PFALZ

HESSEN
DARMSTADT
Frankfurt am Main
Wiesbaden
Mainz
Mannheim
Ludwigshafen am Rhein
Heidelberg

MOSELLE
LORRAINE
MEURTHE-ET-MOSELLE

BAS-RHIN
ALSACE
Strasbourg

KARLSRUHE
Karlsruhe
Baden-Baden
Pforzheim
Stuttgart

FRANCE
VOSGES
HAUT-RHIN
Mulhouse
HAUTE-SAÔNE
FRANCHE-
COMTÉ
TERRITOIRE
DE BELFORT
JURA
DOUBS

BADEN-WÜRTTEMBERG
TÜBINGEN
FREIBURG
Freiburg im Breisgau
SCHAFFHAUSEN
HOTZENWALD

SWITZERLAND
SUNDGAU
Basel
BASELLANDSCHAFT
SOLOTHURN
AARGAU
ZÜRICH
THURGAU
ZUG
LUZERN
BERN
NEUCHÂTEL
VAUD
SCHWYZ
GLARUS
SANKT GALLEN
APPENZELL
VORARLBERG
LIECHTENSTEIN

METRES	FEET
6000	19686
5000	16404
4000	13124
3000	9843
2000	6562
1500	4921
1000	3281
500	1640
200	656
100	328
0	0

LAND BELOW SEA LEVEL

50	164
200	656
1000	3281
2000	6562

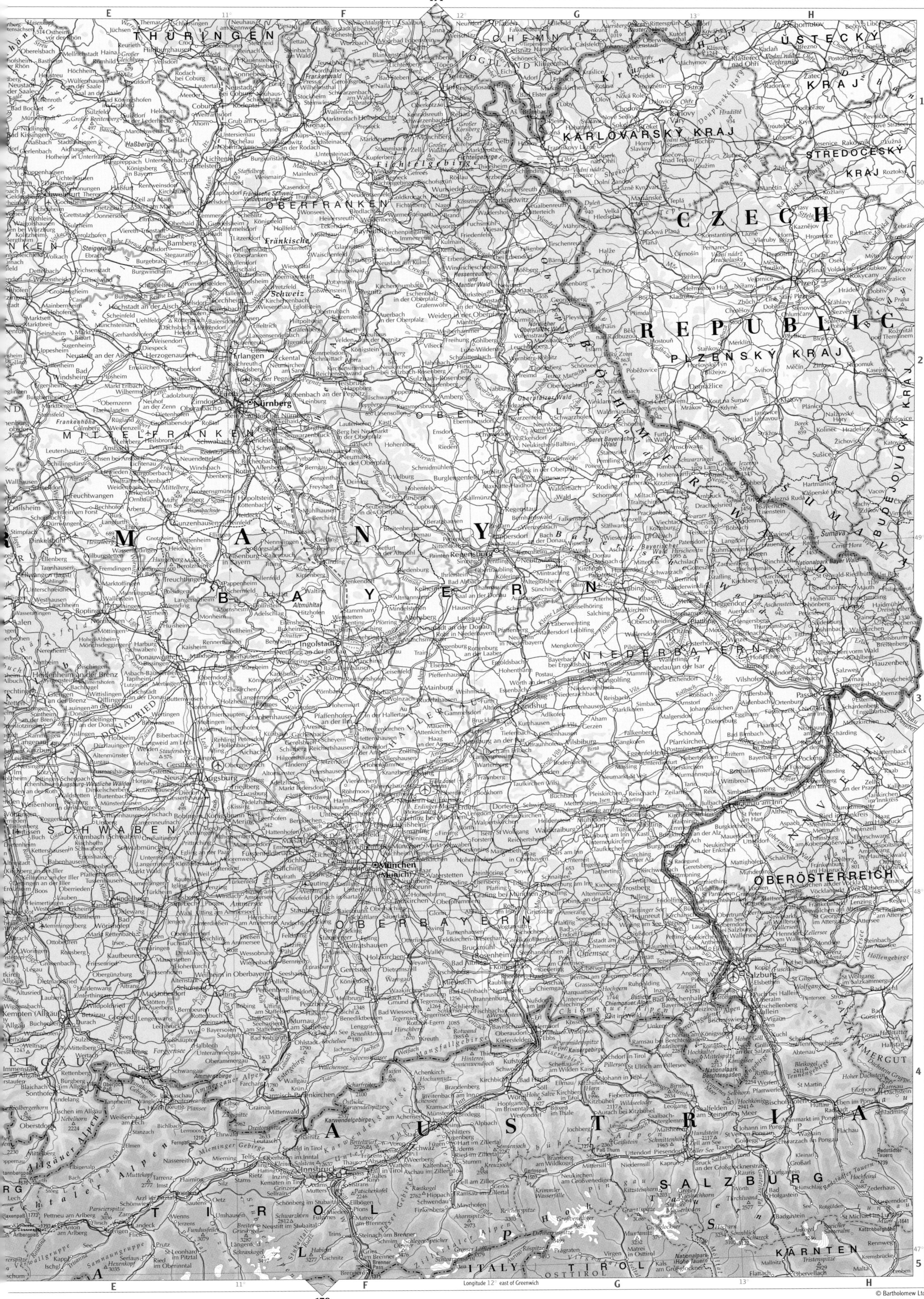

171

THÜRINGEN

KARLOVARSKÝ KRAJ

ÚSTECKÝ KRAJ

STŘEDOČESKÝ KRAJ

174

C Z E C H

R E P U B L I C

PLZEŇSKÝ KRAJ

OBERFRANKEN

Fichtelgebirge

BUDĚJOVICKÝ KRAJ

Bamberg

Fränkische Schweiz

MITTELFRANKEN

Nürnberg

OBERPFALZ

Erlangen

G E R M A N Y

B A Y E R N

Regensburg

NIEDERBAYERN

176

Ingolstadt

DONAU

SCHWABEN

Augsburg

OBERBAYERN

München
Munich

OBERÖSTERREICH

Ammersee

Chiemsee

Salzburg

SALZBURG

A U S T R I A

Allgäuer Alpen

T I R O L

KÄRNTEN

ITALY   TIROL
OSTTIROL

MILES	KILOMETRES
60	100
	90
50	80
	70
40	60
30	50
	40
20	30
	20
10	10
0	0

1:1 200 000

Longitude 12° east of Greenwich

© Bartholomew Ltd

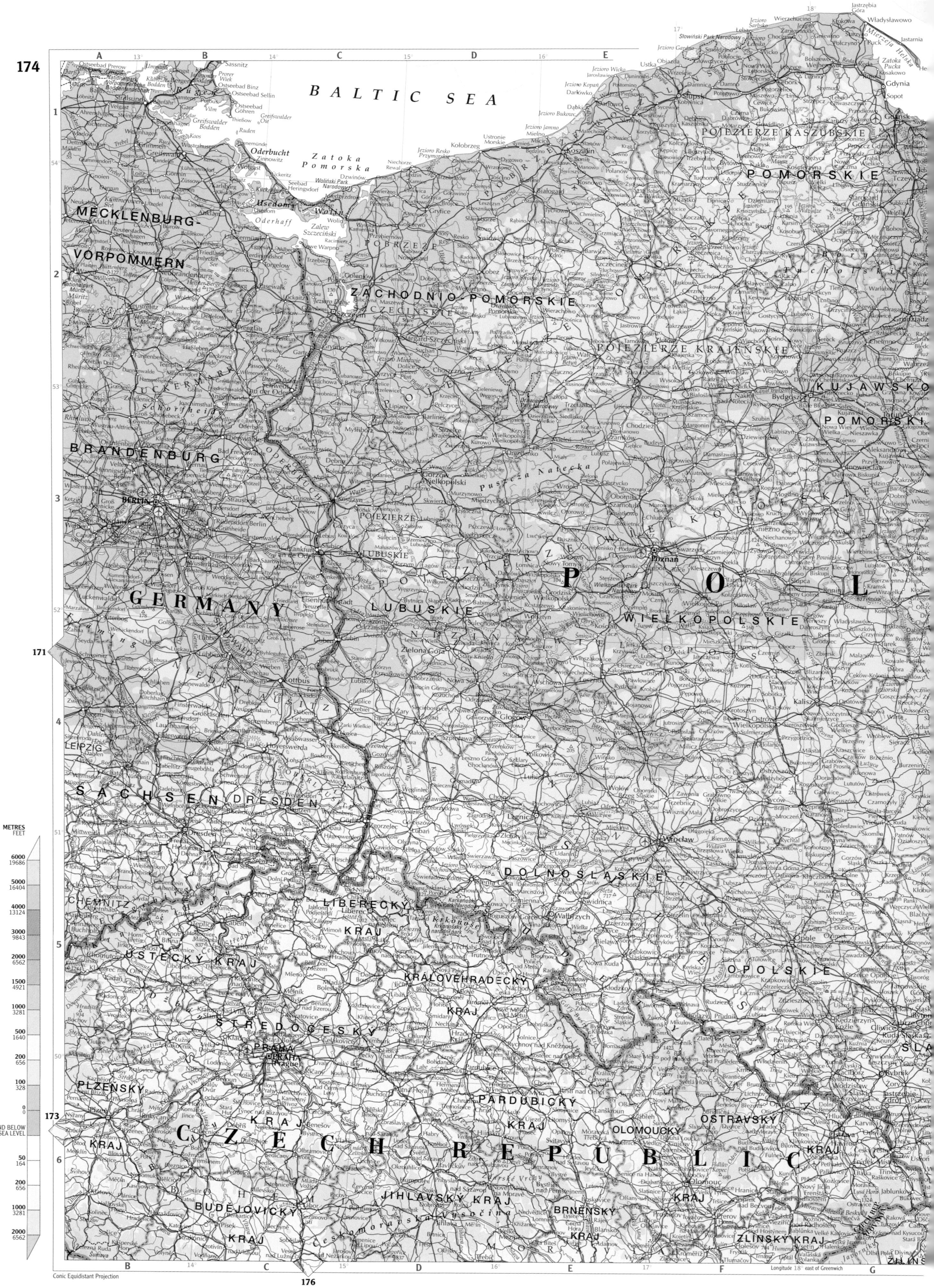

BALTIC SEA

Zatoka
Pomorska

Oderbucht

MECKLENBURG-
VORPOMMERN

ZACHODNIO-POMORSKIE

POMORSKIE

POJEZIERZE KASZUBSKIE

Gdynia
Sopot

POJEZIERZE KRAJEŃSKIE

KUJAWSKO-
POMORSKI

BRANDENBURG

BERLIN

GERMANY

LUBUSKIE

WIELKOPOLSKIE

P O L

Poznań

171

LEIPZIG

SACHSEN DRESDEN

CHEMNITZ

LIBERECKÝ
KRAJ

DOLNOŚLĄSKIE

Wrocław

OPOLSKIE

ÚSTECKÝ KRAJ

KRÁLOVEHRADECKÝ
KRAJ

STŘEDOČESKÝ

PRAHA
PRAHA
Prague

PLZEŇSKÝ
KRAJ

PARDUBICKÝ
KRAJ

OLOMOUCKÝ
KRAJ

OSTRAVSKÝ
KRAJ

173

C Z E C H   R E P U B L I C

BUDĚJOVICKÝ
KRAJ

JIHLAVSKÝ KRAJ

BRNĚNSKÝ
KRAJ

ZLÍNSKÝ KRAJ

ZLÍN

Conic Equidistant Projection

Longitude 18 east of Greenwich

METRES
FEET
6000
19686
5000
16404
4000
13124
3000
9843
2000
6562
1500
4921
1000
3281
500
1640
200
656
100
328
0
0
LAND BELOW
SEA LEVEL
50
164
200
656
1000
3281
2000
6562

136

1:1 800 000

© Bartholomew Ltd

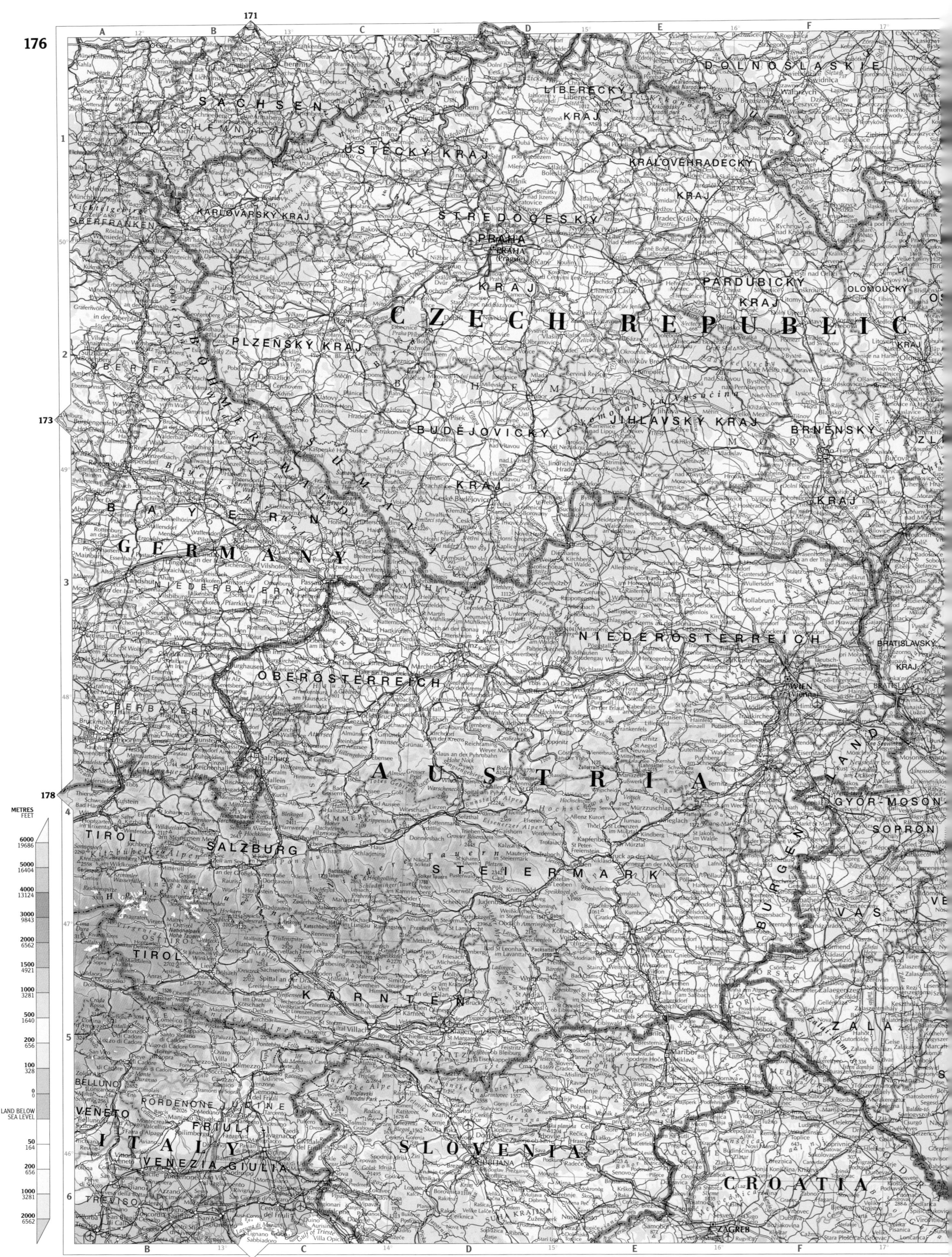

SACHSEN

CHEMNITZ

OBERFRANKEN

KARLOVARSKÝ KRAJ

ÚSTECKÝ KRAJ

LIBERECKÝ KRAJ

LIBEREC

DOLNOŚLĄSKIE

KRÁLOVÉHRADECKÝ KRAJ

STŘEDOČESKÝ KRAJ

PRAHA
Prague

PARDUBICKÝ KRAJ

OLOMOUCKÝ KRAJ

PLZEŇSKÝ KRAJ

CZECH REPUBLIC

KRAJ

OBERPFALZ

B O H E M I A

VYSOČINA KRAJ

IHLAVSKÝ KRAJ

BRNĚNSKÝ KRAJ

Š U M A V A

BUDĚJOVICKÝ

KRAJ

M O R A V I A

BAYERN

GERMANY

B Ö H M E R W A L D

NIEDERBAYERN

N I E D E R Ö S T E R R E I C H

BRATISLAVSKÝ KRAJ

WIEN
Vienna

OBERÖSTERREICH

OBERBAYERN

A U S T R I A

BRATISLAVA

BURGENLAND

GYÖR-MOSON

SOPRON

TIROL

SALZBURG

S T E I E R M A R K

VAS

TIROL

K Ä R N T E N

ZALA

BELLUNO

VENETO

FRIULI

SLOVENIA

I T A L Y

VENEZIA GIULIA

CROATIA

TREVISO

ZAGREB

METRES
FEET

6000
19686

5000
16404

4000
13124

3000
9843

2000
6562

1500
4921

1000
3281

500
1640

200
656

100
328

0

LAND BELOW
SEA LEVEL

50
164

200
656

1000
3281

2000
6562

Conic Equidistant Projection

POLSKIE

P O L A N D

ŚLĄSKIE

MAŁOPOLSKIE

PODKARPACKIE

AVSKY

KRAJ

KÝ KRAJ

C A R P A T H I A N   M O U N T A I N S

ŽILINSKÝ KRAJ

TRENČIANSKY KRAJ

S L O V A K I A

PREŠOVSKÝ KRAJ

KOŠICKÝ KRAJ

BANSKOBYSTRICKÝ KRAJ

SLOVENSKÉ RUDOHORIE

NITRIANSKY

KRAJ

INAVSKÝ

KRAJ

U K R A I N E

BORSOD-ABAÚJ-

ZEMPLÉN

SZABOLCS

SZATMÁR-BEREG

NÓGRÁD

HEVES

SATU MARE

KOMÁROM-

ESZTERGOM

HAJDÚ-BIHAR

BUDAPEST

PEST

JÁSZ-NAGYKUN-

SZOLNOK

SÁLAJ

PRÉM

H U N G A R Y

FEJÉR

BIHOR

Oradea

Debrecen

ARAD

BÉKÉS

TOLNA

CSONGRÁD

BÁCS

KISKUN

R O M A N I A

BARANYA

VOJVODINA

Y U G O S L A V I A

TIMIŞ

Longitude 18° east of Greenwich

MILES   KILOMETRES

1:1 800 000

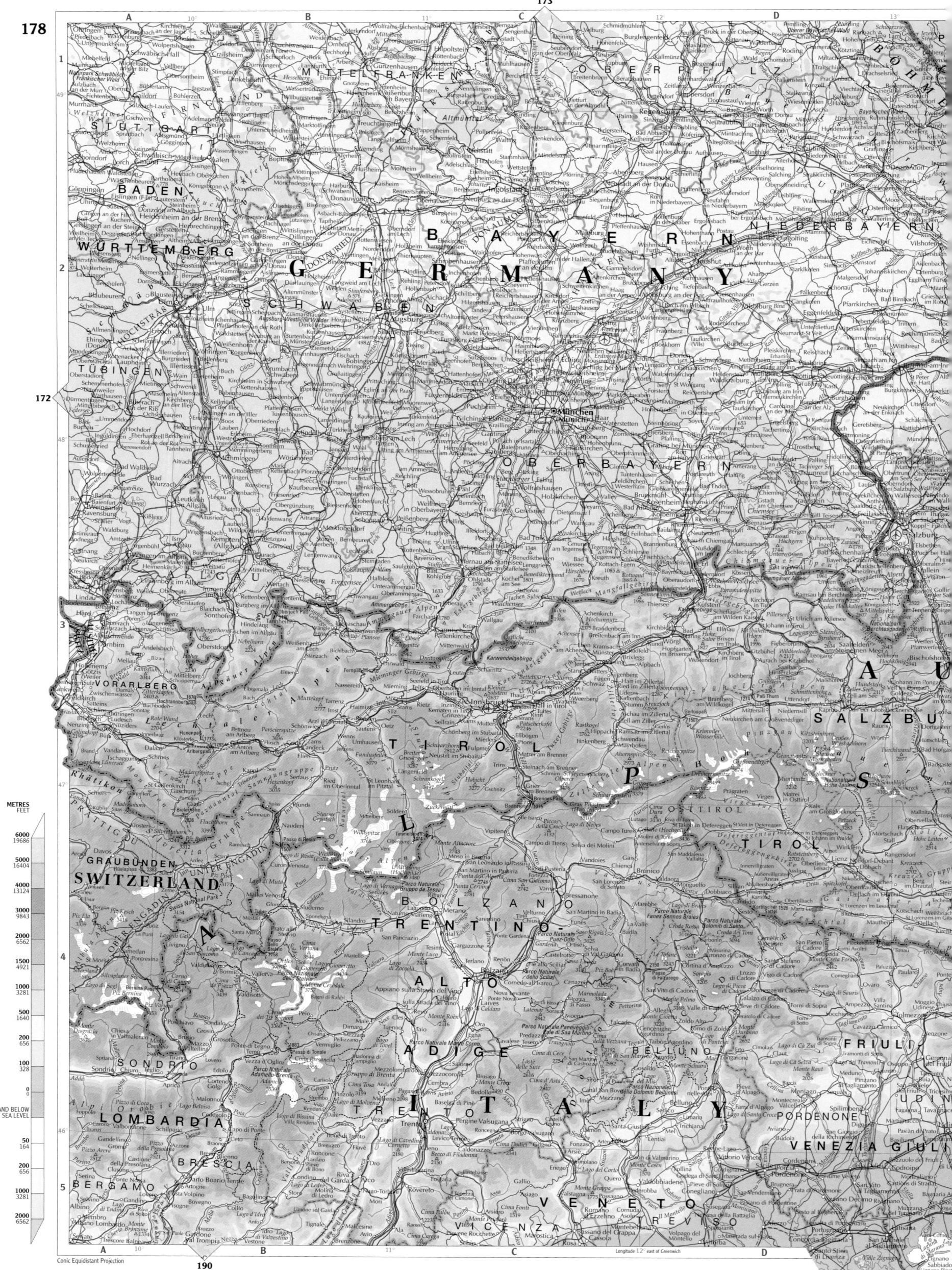

Conic Equidistant Projection

Longitude 12° east of Greenwich

CZECH REPUBLIC

BUDĚJOVICKÝ KRAJ

JIHLAVSKÝ KRAJ

BRNĚNSKÝ KRAJ

MÜHLVIERTEL

NIEDERÖSTERREICH

WIEN
WIEN
Vienna

OBERÖSTERREICH

STIRIA
STEIERMARK

BURGENLAND

VAS

HUNGARY

KÄRNTEN

ZALA

SLOVENIA

CROATIA

ZAGREB

177

MILES   KILOMETRES

1:1 200 000

© Bartholomew Ltd

Map: Portugal and western Spain

Oceans / seas:
- ATLANTIC OCEAN
- Mar Cantábrico
- BAY OF (BISCAY)
- GOLFO DE CÁDIZ
- MEDITERRANEAN (MEDITERRÁNEO)

Countries / regions:
- PORTUGAL
- GALICIA
- ASTURIAS
- CANTABRIA
- CASTILLA Y LEÓN
- EXTREMADURA
- CASTILLA–LA MANCHA
- ANDALUCÍA
- MINHO
- TRÁS-OS-MONTES
- BEIRA ALTA
- MORROCO / MOROCCO

Portuguese districts / cities:
- VIANA DO CASTELO
- BRAGA
- VILA REAL
- BRAGANÇA
- PORTO (Oporto)
- VISEU
- GUARDA
- AVEIRO
- COIMBRA
- CASTELO BRANCO
- LEIRIA
- SANTARÉM
- PORTALEGRE
- LISBOA (Lisbon)
- ÉVORA
- SETÚBAL
- BEJA
- FARO
- ALGARVE

Spanish cities:
- A Coruña
- Ferrol
- Santiago de Compostela
- Lugo
- Ourense
- Pontevedra
- Vigo
- León
- Oviedo
- Santander
- Burgos
- Valladolid
- Zamora
- Salamanca
- Ávila
- MADRID
- Segovia
- Toledo
- Cáceres
- Badajoz
- Mérida
- Ciudad Real
- Córdoba
- Sevilla
- Huelva
- Jaén
- Granada
- Málaga
- Cádiz
- Gibraltar (U.K.)
- Jerez de la Frontera
- Algeciras
- Tarifa

Morocco:
- Tanger / TANGER
- Ceuta (Spain)
- TETOUAN / TÉTOUAN
- LARACHE
- CHAOUEN / CHAOUÉN
- AL HOCEIMA
- NADOR

Capes / coastal features:
- Cabo Ortegal
- Punta da Estaca de Bares
- Cabo Fisterra
- Cabo de São Vicente
- Ponta de Sagres
- Cabo de Santa Maria
- Cabo Espichel
- Cabo Carvoeiro
- Cabo Mondego
- Strait of Gibraltar
- Costa del Sol
- Costa de la Luz
- Cabo Trafalgar

Elevation key (METRES / FEET):

METRES	FEET
6000	19686
5000	16404
4000	13124
3000	9843
2000	6562
1500	4921
1000	3281
500	1640
200	656
100	328
0	0

LAND BELOW SEA LEVEL

METRES	FEET
50	164
200	656
1000	3281
2000	6562

154

BISCAY

FRANCE

AQUITAINE

MIDI-PYRÉNÉES

LANGUEDOC

ROUSSILLON

GOLFE DU LION

Marseille

CÔTE-D'AZUR

PROVENCE-ALPES

PAYS VASCO

NAVARRA

LA RIOJA

CASTILLA Y LEÓN

Pamplona

Zaragoza

ARAGÓN

CATALUÑA

Barcelona

Lleida

Tarragona

Costa Dorada

Costa Brava

Girona

Perpignan

ANDORRA

ANDORRA LA VELLA

PYRÉNÉES

Costa del Azahar

Castelló de la Plana

VALENCIA

VALENCIA

CASTILLA-LA MANCHA

Cuenca

Albacete

Alicante

Costa Blanca

MURCIA

Murcia

Cartagena

Almería

MEDITERRANEAN SEA

Mallorca (Majorca)

Menorca (Minorca)

Palma de Mallorca

Eivissa (Ibiza)

Formentera

Cabrera

ISLAS BALEARES
(BALEARIC ISLANDS)

ALGERIA

Melilla

Nador

CANARY ISLANDS
(Spain)
AT THE SAME SCALE

ATLANTIC OCEAN

ISLAS CANARIAS

Lanzarote

Fuerteventura

Gran Canaria

Las Palmas de Gran Canaria

Tenerife

Santa Cruz de Tenerife

San Cristóbal de la Laguna

La Palma

Santa Cruz de la Palma

La Gomera

El Hierro

Arrecife

Puerto del Rosario

MILES   KILOMETRES

125   200

175

100   150

125

75   100

50   75

50

25   25

1:3 000 000

© Bartholomew Ltd

ATLANTIC OCEAN

GALICIA

A CORUÑA

LUGO

PONTEVEDRA

OURENSE

PORTUGAL

VIANA DO CASTELO

BRAGA

BRAGANÇA

VILA REAL

MINHO

PORTO

DOURO

AVEIRO

VISEU

BEIRA ALTA

GUARDA

COIMBRA

CASTELO BRANCO

BEIRA BAIXA

LEIRIA

ASTURIAS

CORDILLERA CANTÁBRICA

MARAGATERÍA

ZAMORA

SALAMANCA

CÁCERES

EXTREMADURA

Mar Cantábrico

METRES / FEET
6000 / 19686
5000 / 16404
4000 / 13124
3000 / 9843
2000 / 6562
1500 / 4921
1000 / 3281
500 / 1640
200 / 656
100 / 328
0 / 0
LAND BELOW SEA LEVEL
50 / 164
200 / 656
1000 / 3281
2000 / 6562

Conic Equidistant Projection

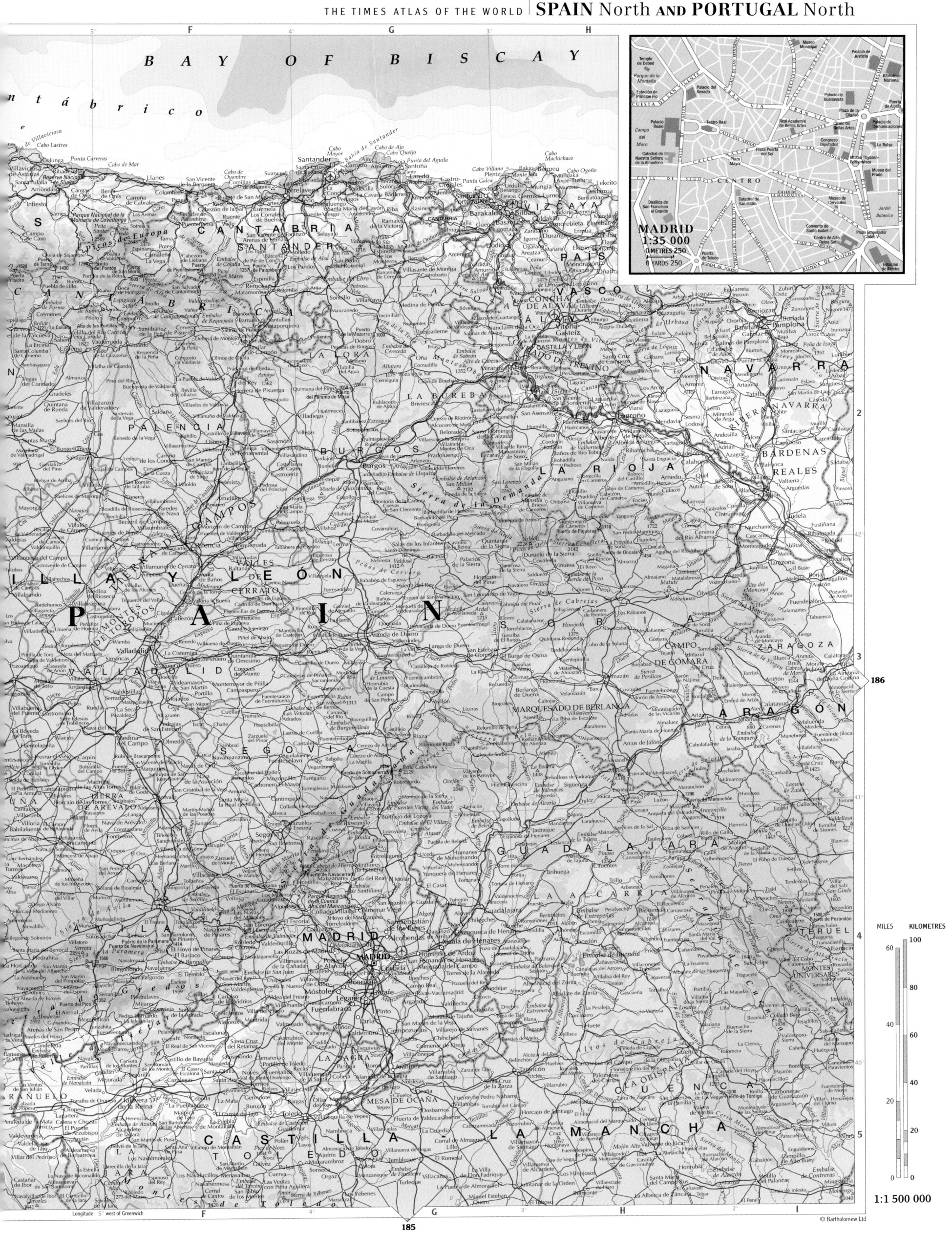

A   B   C   D

PORTUGAL

LEIRIA
CASTELO BRANCO
BAIXA
CÁCERES
SANTARÉM
PORTALEGRE
EXTREMADUR
CÁM
RIBATEJO
LISBOA
LISBOA (Lisbon)
ÉVORA
BADAJOZ
TIERRA DE BARROS
LLANOS DE OLIVENZA
Badajoz
Mérida
SETÚBAL
Baía de Setúbal
Costa da Caparica
BEJA
SIE
HUELVA
Sierra de Aracena
CONDADO DE NIEBLA
EL ANDÉVALO
EL ALJARAFE
SEV
ALGARVE
FARO
Cabo de São Vicente
Ponta de Sagres
Costa de la Luz
GOLFO DE CÁDIZ
CÁDIZ
Bahía de Cádiz
Las Marismas
Parque Nacional de Doñana
Playa de Castilla
MORO
TANGER
Strait
Cap Spartel

MADEIRA
(Portugal)
1:1 250 000

Arquipélago da Madeira
Ilha de Porto Santo
Ilha da Madeira
FUNCHAL
Ilhas Desertas
Deserta Grande
Bugio
Ponta do Pargo
Porto Moniz
São Vicente
Santana
Câmara de Lobos

METRES / FEET
6000 / 19686
5000 / 16404
4000 / 13124
3000 / 9843
2000 / 6562
1500 / 4921
1000 / 3281
500 / 1640
200 / 656
100 / 328
0 / 0
LAND BELOW SEA LEVEL
50 / 164
200 / 656
1000 / 3281
2000 / 6562

Conic Equidistant Projection

1   2   3   4   5

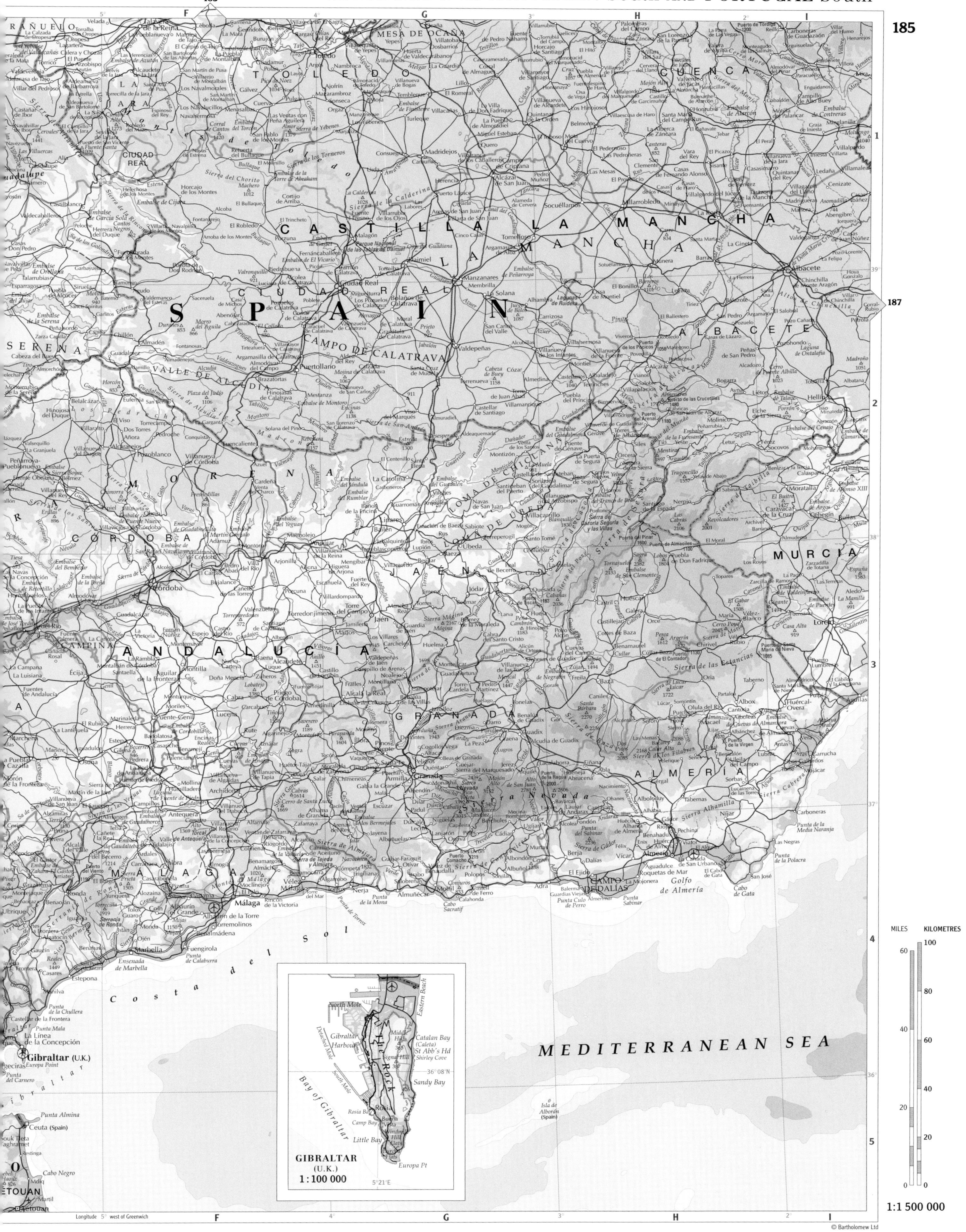

CASTILLA LA MANCHA

SPAIN

TOLEDO

CUENCA

ALBACETE

CIUDAD REAL

CAMPO DE CALATRAVA

SERENA

CÓRDOBA

SIERRA MORENA

JAÉN

ANDALUCÍA

GRANADA

MURCIA

ALMERÍA

MÁLAGA

Costa del Sol

MEDITERRANEAN SEA

Golfo de Almería

Cabo de Gata

Gibraltar (U.K.)
Europa Point

Ceuta (Spain)

Longitude 5° west of Greenwich

GIBRALTAR
(U.K.)
1:100 000

North Mole
Eastern Beach
Gibraltar Harbour
Detached Mole
Catalan Bay
(Caleta)
St Abb's Hd
Shirley Cove
THE ROCK
Middle Hill
Signal Hill
Sandy Bay
South Mole
Rosia Bay
Camp Bay
Little Bay
Europa Pt
Bay of Gibraltar
Isla de Alborán (Spain)
36° 08'N
5° 21'E

MILES KILOMETRES
100
80
60
60
40
40
20
20
0 0

1:1 500 000

© Bartholomew Ltd

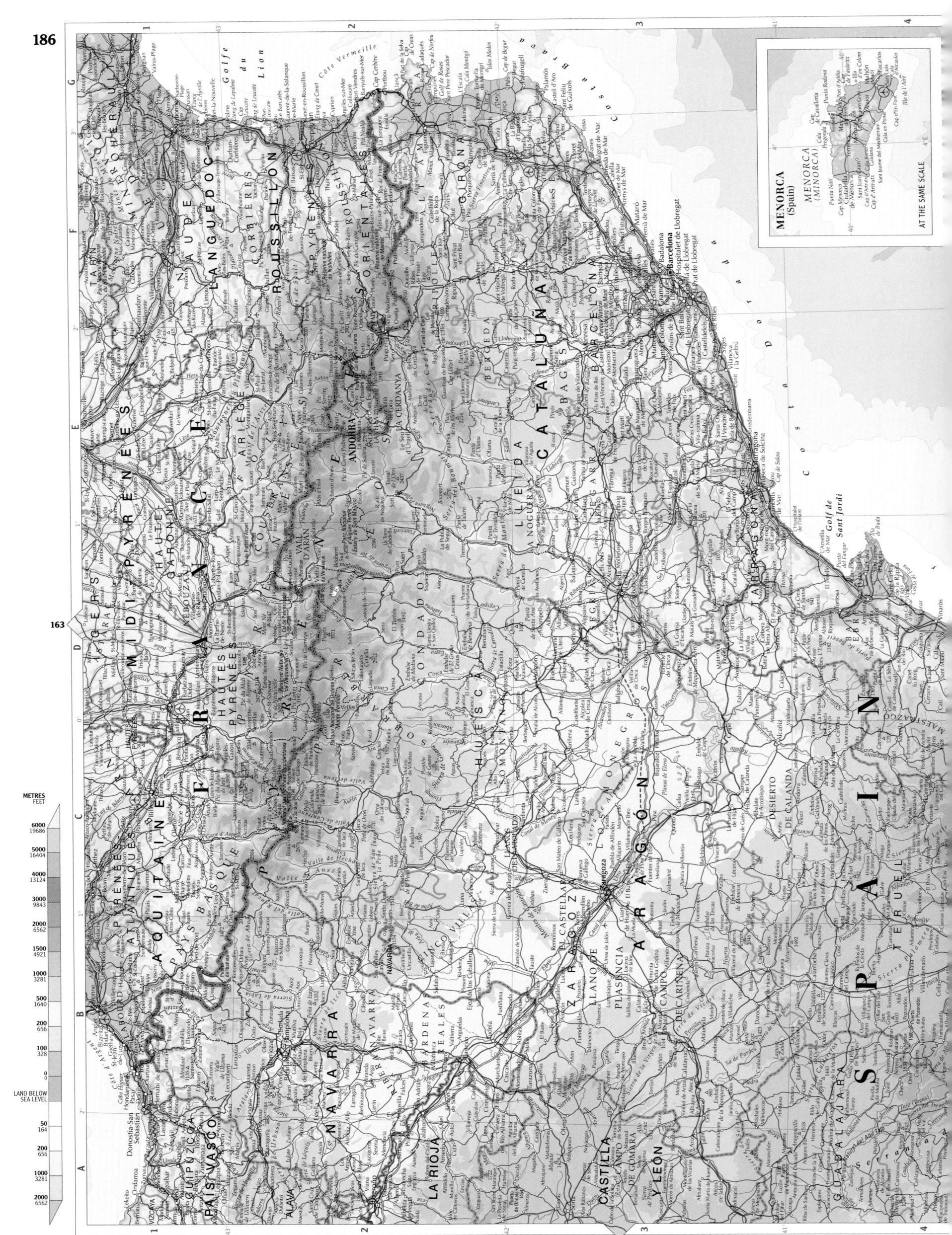

MENORCA
(Spain)

MENORCA
(MINORCA)

AT THE SAME SCALE

METRES
FEET

6000
19686

5000
16404

4000
13124

3000
9843

2000
6562

1500
4921

1000
3281

500
1640

200
656

100
328

0

LAND BELOW
SEA LEVEL

50
164

200
656

1000
3281

2000
6562

Conic Equidistant Projection

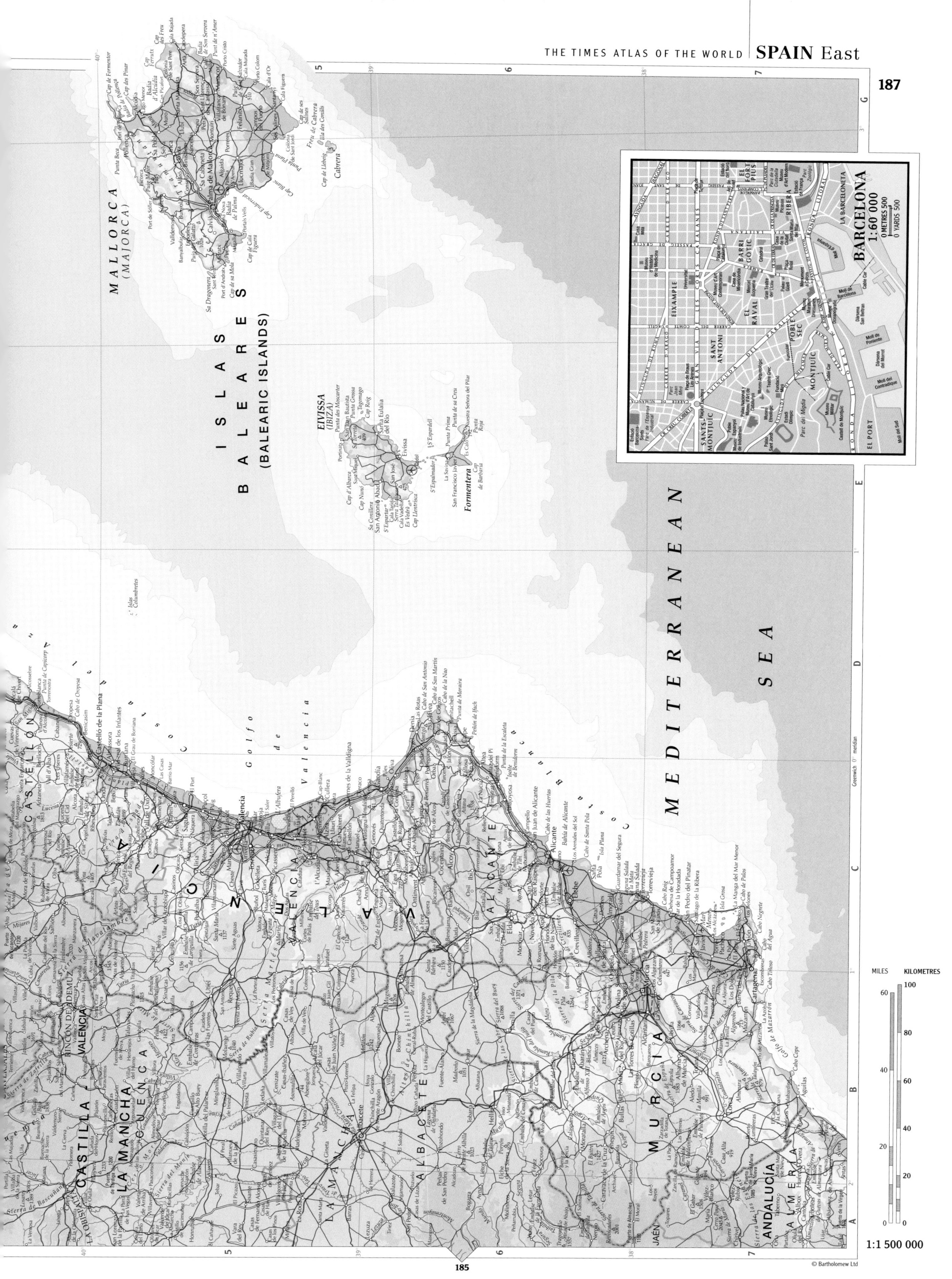

MALLORCA
(MAJORCA)

I S L A S

B A L E A R E S

(BALEARIC ISLANDS)

EIVISSA
(IBIZA)

Formentera

BARCELONA
1:60 000

0 METRES 500
0 YARDS 500

M E D I T E R R A N E A N

S E A

Greenwich 0° meridian

CASTELLÓN

VALENCIA

Golfo de Valencia

Costa del Azahar

Costa Blanca

ALICANTE

MURCIA

CASTILLA
LA MANCHA

CUENCA

ALBACETE

ANDALUCÍA

JAÉN

ALMERÍA

MILES   KILOMETRES

60   100

80

40   60

40

20

20

0   0

1:1 500 000

185

© Bartholomew Ltd

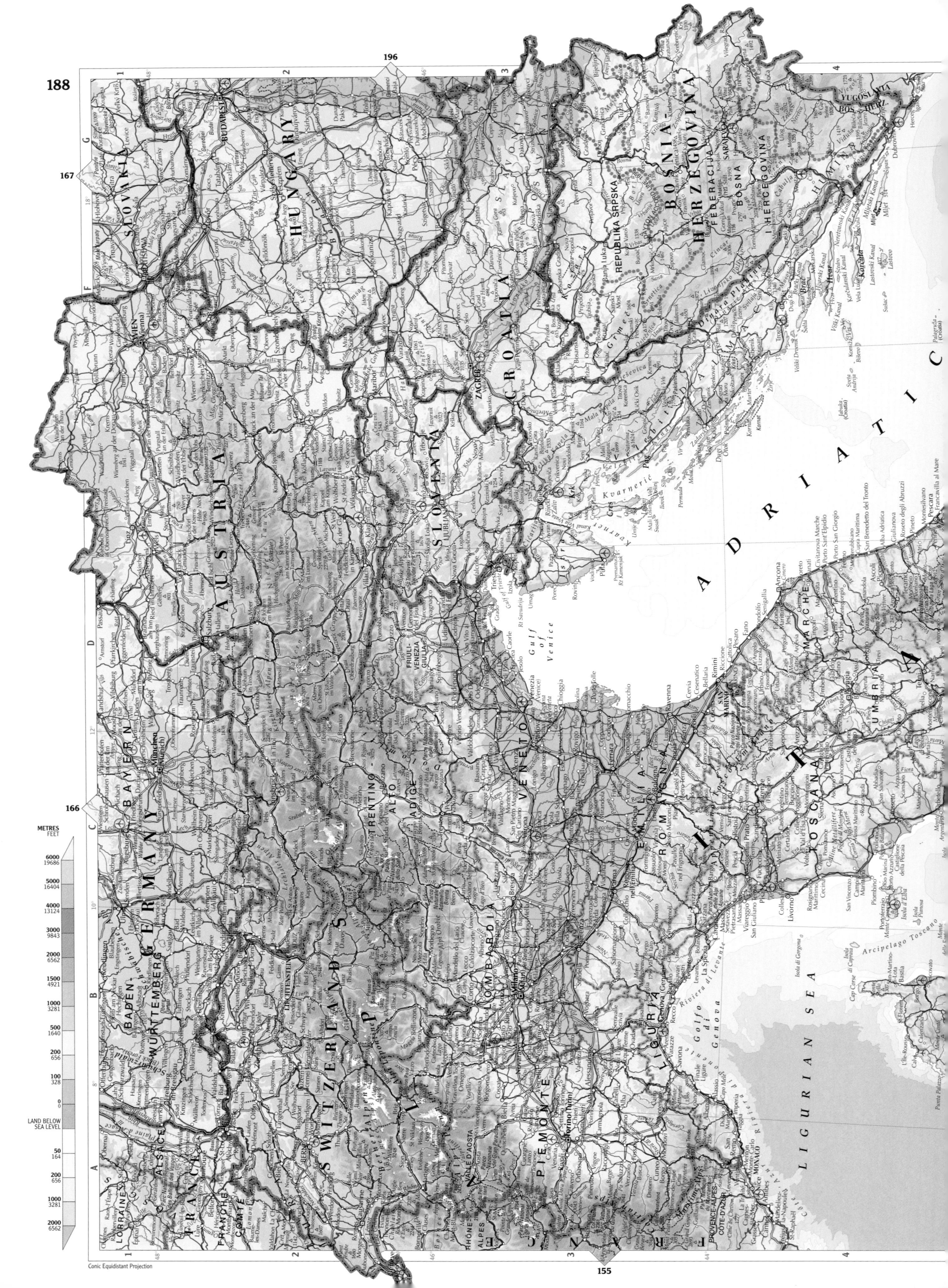

Conic Equidistant Projection

MEDITERRANEAN SEA

IONIAN SEA

TYRRHENIAN SEA

ADRIATIC SEA

SICILIAN CHANNEL

PUGLIA

BASILICATA

CAMPANIA

CALABRIA

MOLISE

LAZIO

SICILIA (SICILY)

SARDEGNA (SARDINIA) (Italy)

CORSE (CORSICA) (France)

TUNISIA

ALGERIA

ROMA

Napoli Naples

Palermo

Catania

Cagliari

Sassari

Bari

Taranto

Crotone

Catanzaro

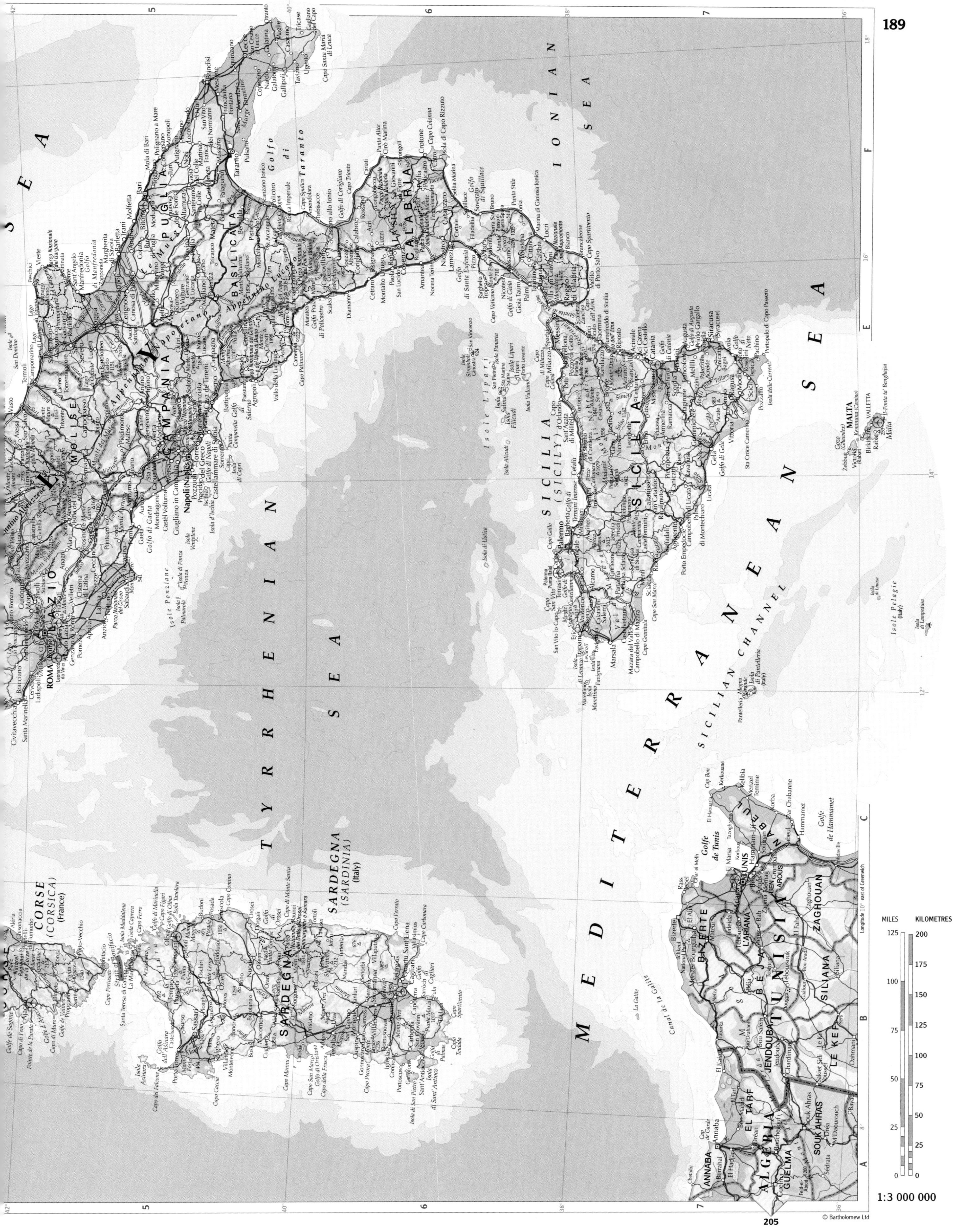

Messina

Siracusa

MALTA

VALLETTA

TUNIS

ANNABA

Golfe de Tunis

Golfe de Hammamet

Isole Eolie o Lipari

Isole Pelagie (Italy)

Isola di Pantelleria (Italy)

Isola di Lampedusa

Longitude 10° east of Greenwich

MILES   KILOMETRES
125   200
100   175
         150
75   125
         100
50   75
25   50
         25
0   0

1 : 3 000 000

FRANCHE-COMTÉ

FRANCE

DOUBS

JURA

SWITZERLAND

FRANCHE-COMTÉ

BERN

FRIBOURG

VAUD

NEUCHÂTEL

SOLOTHURN

BASEL-LANDSCHAFT

AARGAU

ZÜRICH

SCHAFFHAUSEN

THURGAU

SANKT GALLEN

VORARLBERG

LIECHTENSTEIN

VADUZ

LUZERN

ZUG

SCHWYZ

OBWALDEN

NIDWALDEN

GLARUS

URI

GRAUBÜNDEN

TICINO

VALAIS

BAGNES

HAUTE-SAVOIE

RHÔNE-ALPES

VALLE D'AOSTA

SAVOIE

VERBANO

CUSIO-OSSOLA

VERCELLI

BIELLA

NOVARA

VARESE

COMO

LECCO

BERGAMO

LOMBARDIA

BRES...

SONDRIO

ISÈRE

HAUTES-ALPES

FRANCE

TORINO

PIEMONTE

CANAVESE

VERCELLI

Torino (Turin)

ASTI

ALESSANDRIA

PAVIA

LODI

CREMONA

PIACENZA

PARMA

EMILI...

PROVENCE-

CUNEO

GENOVA

LIGURIA

NELLE...

ALPES-DE-

HAUTE-PROVENCE

ALPES-MARITIMES

IMPERIA

SAVONA

MASSA E...

LA SPEZIA

CARRARA

CÔTE D'AZUR

VAR

MONACO

Monte-Carlo

San Remo

Riviera di Levante

Golfo di Genova

Ponente

LIGURIAN SEA

Livorno

LIVORNO

Viareggio

Pietrasanta

Lago di Massaciuccoli

Torre della Meloria

Isola di Gorgona

Rosignano Marittimo

Castiglioncello

Parco Naturale di Migliarino San Rossore-Massaciuccoli

Swiss Cantons not named on the map
1. APPENZELL AUSSER-RHODEN (E1)
2. APPENZELL INNER-RHODEN (E1)
3. FRIBOURG (B2)
4. VAUD (C2)

Conic Equidistant Projection

METRES FEET
6000 19686
5000 16404
4000 13124
3000 9843
2000 6562
1500 4921
1000 3281
500 1640
200 656
100 328
0
LAND BELOW SEA LEVEL
50 164
200 656
1000 3281
2000 6562

191

176

GERMANY

AUSTRIA

SALZBURG

STEIERMARK

TIROL

KÄRNTEN

BOLZANO

TRENTINO

ALTO ADIGE

TRENTO

BELLUNO

FRIULI-
UDINE

PORDENONE

SLOVENIA

VENEZIA GIULIA

VICENZA

TREVISO

VENETO

VERONA

VENEZIA

Gulf of
Trieste

Trieste

GORIZIA

PADOVA

Gulf of
Venice

CROATIA

Rijeka

GORSKI KOTAR

196

ROVIGO

FERRARA

Krk

ROMAGNA

MODENA

BOLOGNA

RAVENNA

ADRIATIC SEA

FORLÌ

Rimini

SAN MARINO

PISTOIA

PRATO

FIRENZE

PESARO
E URBINO

ANCONA

TOSCANA

AREZZO

MARCHE

SIENA

PERUGIA

UMBRIA

MACERATA

MILES KILOMETRES

100

60

80

40

60

20

40

20

0 0

1 : 1 500 000

© Bartholomew Ltd

Longitude 11° east of Greenwich

LIGURIAN
SEA

HAUTE-CORSE

CORSE

CORSE

CORSE
DU SUD

CORSE
(CORSICA)
(France)

Strait of Bonifacio

Golfo
dell'Asinara

SASSARI

NUORO

SARDEGNA

ORISTANO

SARDEGNA
(SARDINIA)
(Italy)

CAGLIARI

Golfo di
Orosei

Golfo di Cagliari

TYRRHENIAN

PISA

LIVORNO

TOSCANA

GROSSETO

SIENA

AREZZO

VITERBO

Isola d'Elba

Arcipelago Toscano

Isola del Giglio

Isola di Montecristo

Civitavecchia

METRES
FEET

6000
19686

5000
16404

4000
13124

3000
9843

2000
6562

1500
4921

1000
3281

500
1640

200
656

100
328

0
0

LAND BELOW
SEA LEVEL

50
164

200
656

1000
3281

2000
6562

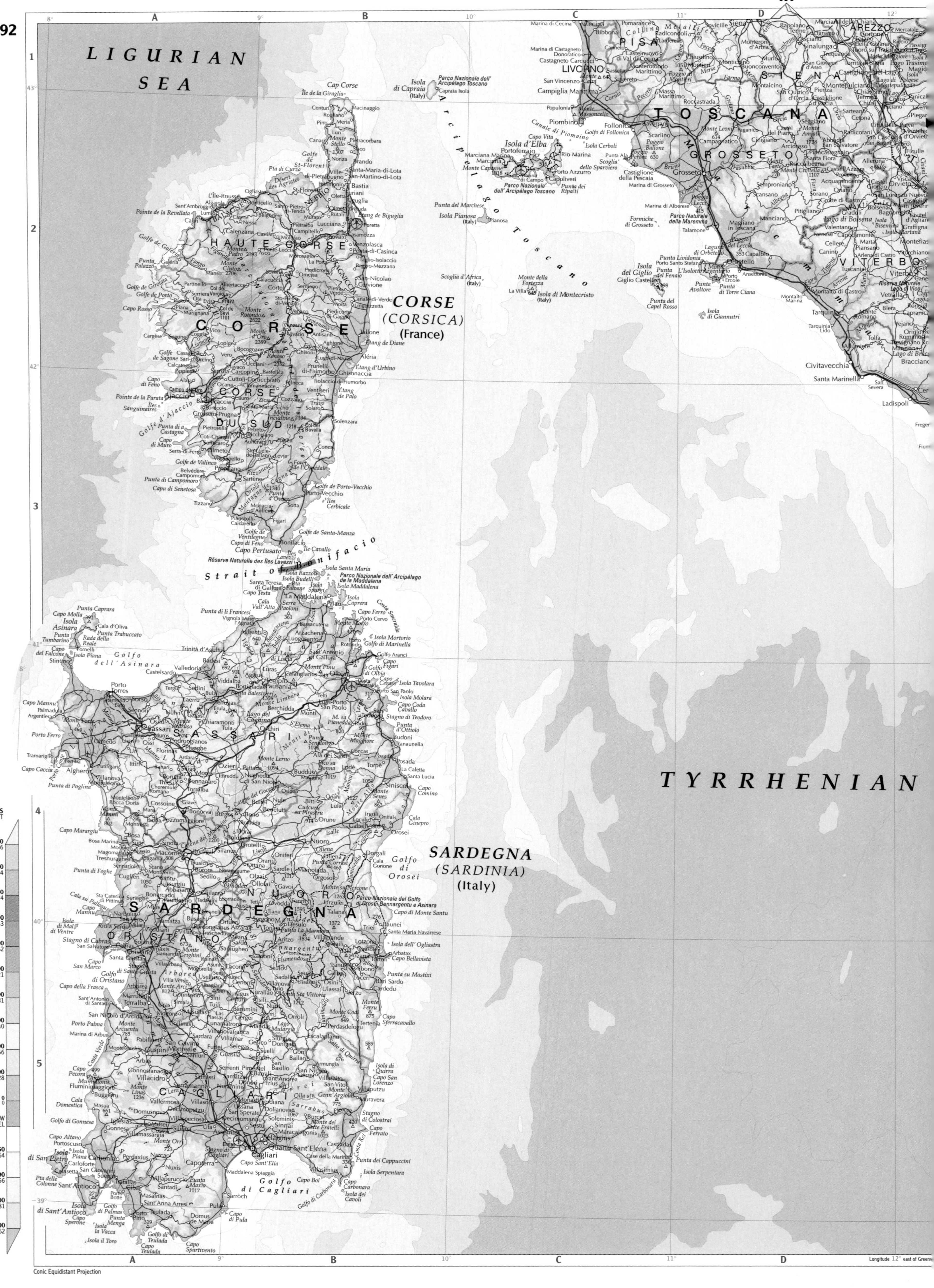

Conic Equidistant Projection

Longitude 12° east of Greenwich

CROATIA

ADRIATIC
SEA

MARCHE

ASCOLI PICENO

TERAMO

ABRUZZO

L'AQUILA

CHIETI

ITALY

ISERNIA
MOLISE

CAMPOBASSO

FOGGIA

PUGLIA

ANZIO

ROMA

LATINA

FROSINONE

CASERTA

BENEVENTO

AVELLINO

BARI

CAMPANIA

NAPOLI
(Naples)

Golfo di Napoli

Golfo
di Gaeta

Golfo
di Salerno

SALERNO

POTENZA

BASILICATA

MATERA

SEA

Isole Ponziane

195

COSENZA

CALABRIA

ROME
1:50 000
0 METRES 500
0 YARDS 500
TRIONFALE

VATICAN
CITY

SALARIO

Villa Borghese

TRASTEVERE

MILES   KILOMETRES

60   100

          80

40   60

          40

20

          20

0   0

1:1 500 000

© Bartholomew Ltd

TYRRHENIAN SEA

SICILIA
(SICILY)

Isole Lipar

SICILIA

TUNISIA

SICILIAN CHANNEL

Golfo di Gela

METRES
FEET

6000
19686

5000
16404

4000
13124

3000
9843

2000
6562

1500
4921

1000
3281

500
1640

200
656

100
328

0
0

LAND BELOW
SEA LEVEL

50
164

200
656

1000
3281

2000
6562

Conic Equidistant Projection

ADRIATIC
SEA

Strait of Otranto

GOLFO
DI
TARANTO

PUGLIA

BASILICATA

SALERNO

POTENZA

MATERA

BRINDISI

TARANTO

LECCE

COSENZA

LA SILA

CROTONE

CALABRIA

CATANZARO

Golfo
di
Santa Eufemia

Golfo
di
Squillace

VIBO VALENTIA

Golfo di Gioia

REGGIO DI CALABRIA

IONIAN

SEA

Golfo
di
Catania

SIRACUSA
(Syracuse)

Golfo
di
Noto

MALTA
1:500 000

Gozo
(Ghawdex)

Kemmuna (Comino)

Malta

MILES   KILOMETRES

60   100

80

40   60

40

20

20

0   0

1:1 500 000

© Bartholomew Ltd

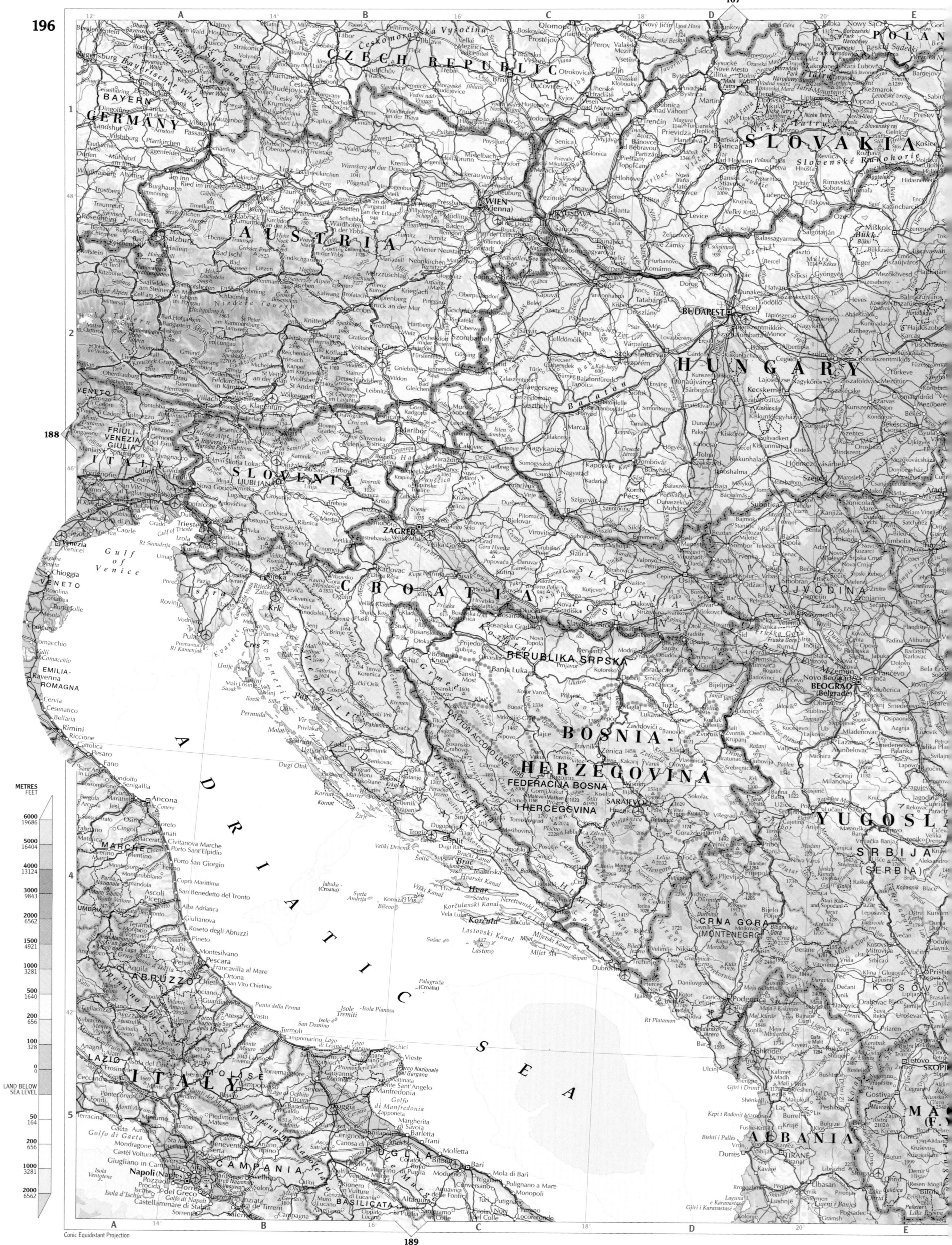

188

METRES FEET
6000 19686
5000 16404
4000 13124
3000 9843
2000 6562
1500 4921
1000 3281
500 1640
200 656
100 328
0 0
LAND BELOW SEA LEVEL
50 164
200 656
1000 3281
2000 6562

Conic Equidistant Projection

1:3 000 000

© Bartholomew Ltd

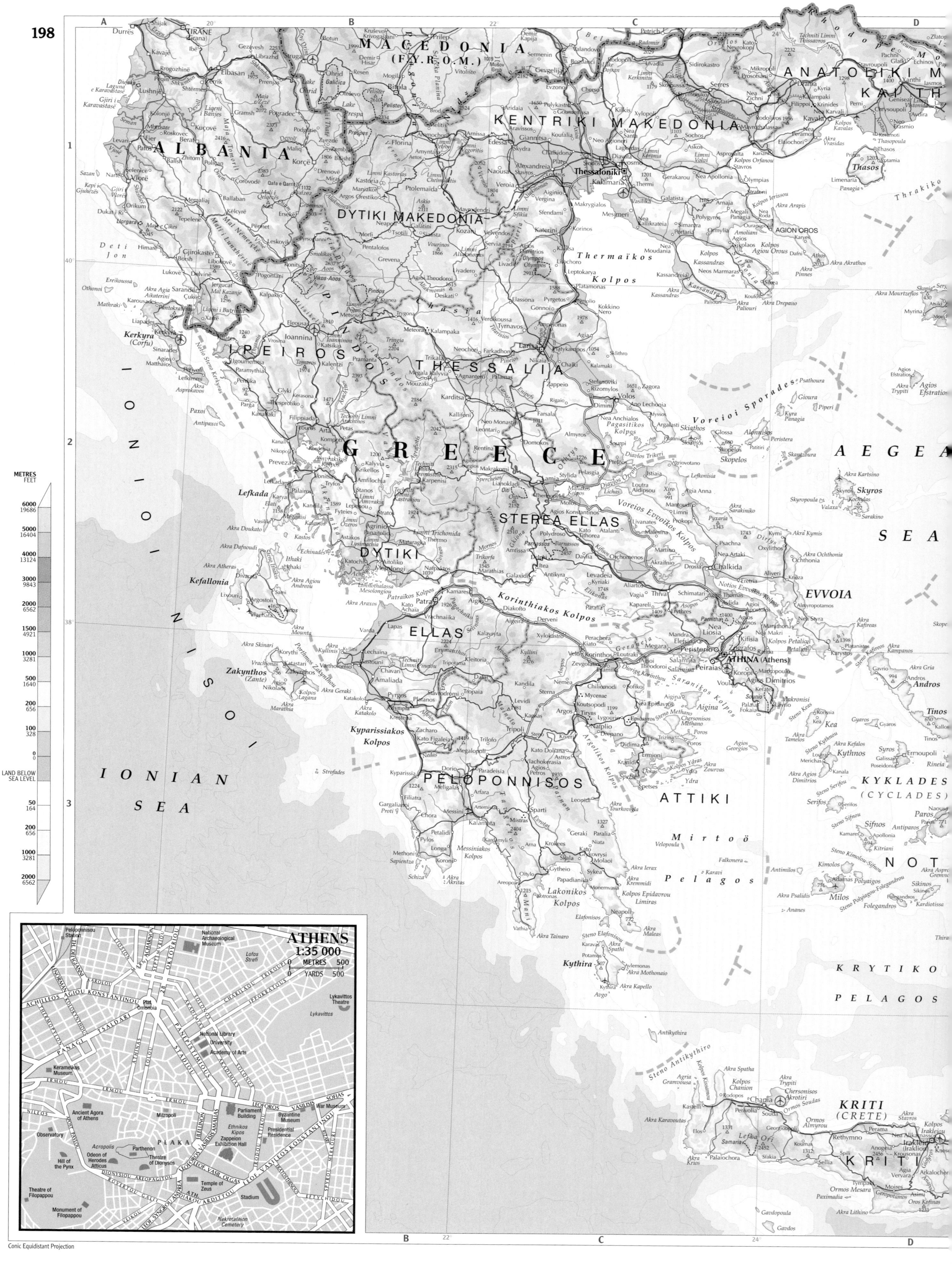

Grid references

A 20° B 22° C 24° D

Country and region labels

MACEDONIA (F.Y.R.O.M.)

ANATOLIKI M KAI TH

KENTRIKI MAKEDONIA

ALBANIA

DYTIKI MAKEDONIA

IPEIROS

THESSALIA

GREECE

STEREA ELLAS

DYTIKI ELLAS

EVVOIA

ATTIKI

PELOPONNISOS

KYKLADES (CYCLADES)

KRITI (CRETE)

IONIAN SEA

IONIO NISOI

AEGEA SEA

THRAKIKO

Thermaïkos Kolpos

Korinthiakos Kolpos

Saronikos Kolpos

Messiniakos Kolpos

Lakonikos Kolpos

Mirtoö Pelagos

KRYTIKO PELAGOS

Voreioi Sporades

Selected settlements

TIRANE (Tiranë), Durrës, Elbasan, Vlorë, Gjirokastër, Ioannina, Kerkyra (Corfu), Larisa, Volos, Thessaloniki, Kalamaria, Veroia, Katerini, Kozani, Trikala, Karditsa, Lamia, Chalkida, Levadeia, Patra, Korinthos, ATHINA (Athens), Peiraias, Tripoli, Sparti, Kalamata, Pyrgos, Zakynthos (Zante), Kefallonia, Lefkada, Ithaki, Skyros, Andros, Tinos, Syros, Ermoupoli, Paros, Naxos, Milos, Sifnos, Serifos, Kythnos, Kea, Chania, Rethymno, Iraklio, Kythira

Elevation key

METRES / FEET
6000 / 19686
5000 / 16404
4000 / 13124
3000 / 9843
2000 / 6562
1500 / 4921
1000 / 3281
500 / 1640
200 / 656
100 / 328
0 / 0
LAND BELOW SEA LEVEL
50 / 164
200 / 656
1000 / 3281
2000 / 6562

Athens inset

ATHENS 1:35 000
METRES 0 500
YARDS 0 500

National Archaeological Museum, Peloponnisou Station, National Library, University, Academy of Arts, Ancient Agora of Athens, Acropolis, Parthenon, Odeon of Herodes Atticus, Theatre of Dionysos, Temple of Zeus, Byzantine Museum, War Museum, Parliament Building, Presidential Residence, Lykavittos, Lykavittos Theatre, Observatory, Hill of the Pynx, Theatre of Filopappou, Monument of Filopappou, Stadium, Keramiekos Museum, Plaka

Conic Equidistant Projection

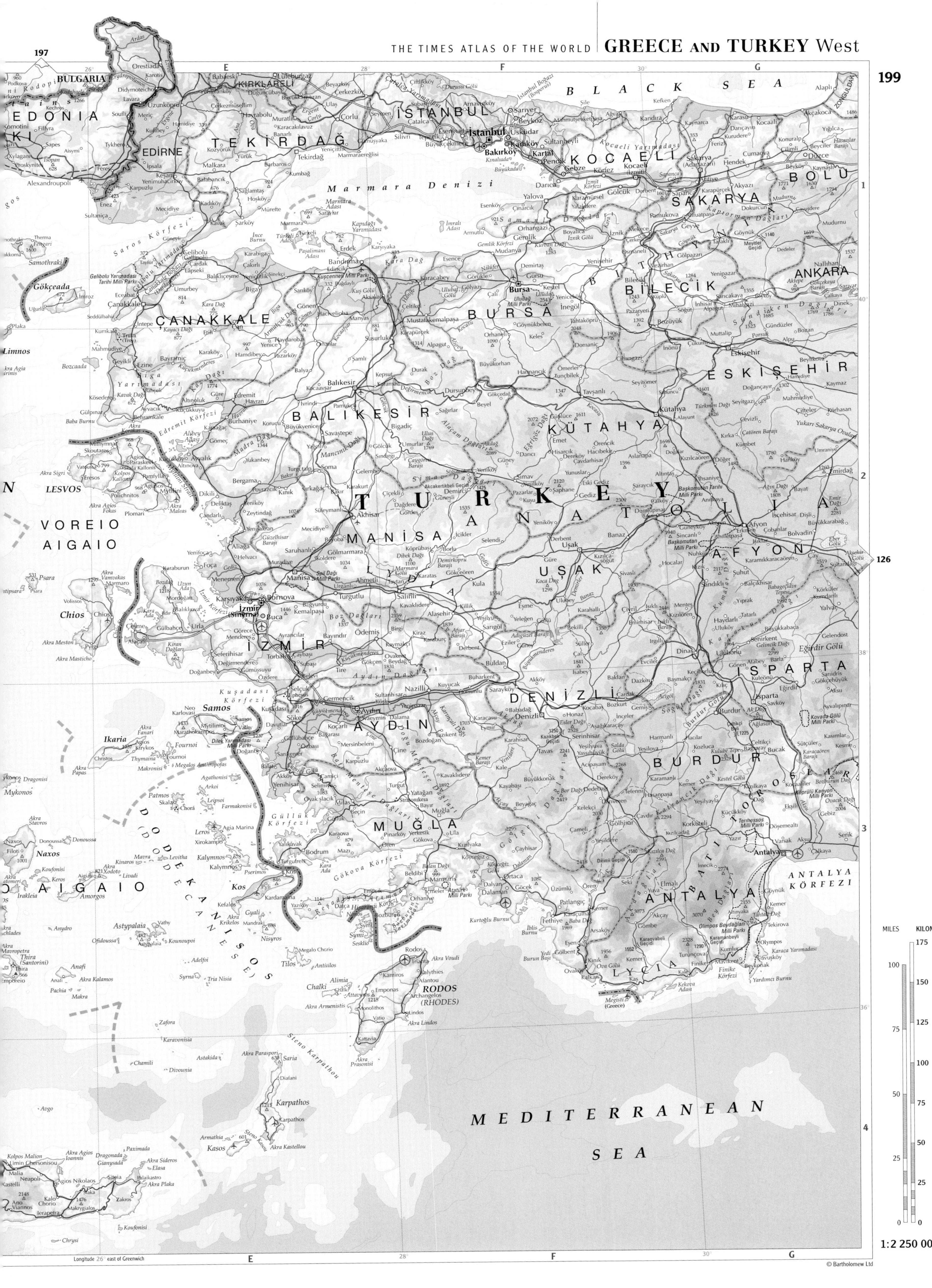

BLACK SEA

BULGARIA

İSTANBUL
TEKİRDAĞ
EDİRNE
KOCAELİ
SAKARYA
BOLU
ANKARA
BİLECİK
BURSA
ESKİŞEHİR
ÇANAKKALE
BALIKESİR
KÜTAHYA
AFYON
MANİSA
UŞAK
İZMİR
DENİZLİ
ISPARTA
AYDIN
BURDUR
MUĞLA
ANTALYA

T U R K E Y

A N A T O L I A

LYDIA

LYCIA

VOREIO AIGAIO

LESVOS

Limnos

Chios

Samos

Ikaria

NOTIO AIGAIO

(DODEKANISOS)

Naxos

Mykonos

RODOS (RHODES)

Karpathos

Kos

Marmara Denizi

Saros Körfezi

Edremit Körfezi

İzmir Körfezi

Kuşadası Körfezi

Güllük Körfezi

Gökova Körfezi

ANTALYA KÖRFEZİ

M E D I T E R R A N E A N

S E A

MILES KILOMETRES
175
150
125
100
100
75
75
50
50
25
25
0   0

A B C D E

EU...
PR...

Pyrenees

Corse

Sardegna

Tyrrhenian Sea

M E D I T...

Alger Bejaïa Skikda
Tanger *Str. of Gibraltar* Oran Ech Chélif Constantine Annaba **Tunis**
Sidi Bel Abbès Sfax
Rabat Fès *Golfe de Gabès*
Casablanca Gabès
MOROCCO Laghouat **TUNISIA** Tripo...
Beni Mellal
Marrakech S Mellal Béchar

Arquipélago dos Açores

A L G E R I A

Arquipélago da Madeira

Canary Islands
(Spain) *Lanzarote*
Tenerife **Las Palmas de Gran Canaria**
Islas *Gran* □Laâyoune
Canarias *Canaria*

Hoggar
Mt Tahat
2918

S A H A...

S A H A R A

WESTERN SAHARA

Ténéré du Tafassâsset

Nouâdhibou

N I G E...

M A U R I T A N I A

Agadez

M A L I
Gao

Nouakchott

Senegal

St Louis Kayes Ségou Mopti **Niamey** Zinder
Niger
Dakar S E N E G A L Kayes Ségou Bamako Niamey Sokoto Kano
Kaolack B U R K I N A
CAPE VERDE THE GAMBIA Banjul **Ouagadougou**
São Tiago **Praia** GUINEA- Bobo-Dioulasso Kaduna Gombé
Fogo BISSAU *Fouta* *Kainji* *Shiroro*
THE GAMBIA *Djalon* **BENIN** *Reservoir* *Reservoir* N I G E R I A
Bissau Tamale Parakou **Abuja**
Santo Antão
Boa Vista G U I N E A Kankan C Ô T E Ogbomoso *Benue*
Conakry D'IVOIRE Bouaké **GHANA** *Niger* Onitsha
SIERRA *Lac* Kumasi Ibadan CAMER...
LEONE *de Kossou* Lagos
Freetown Yamoussoukro *Lake Volta* Warri Nkongsamba
Abidjan **Lomé** *Volta* Port Douala
Monrovia **Accra** Harcourt **Malabo** **Yaound...**
LIBERIA Cape Coast *Bioco*
Gulf EQUATORIAL GUINEA Bata
of SÃO TOMÉ AND PRÍNCIPE *Príncipe*
Guinea São Tomé **Libreville**
São Tomé **São Tomé** **GABO...**

A T L A N T I C

Annobón
(Equatorial Guinea)

Port-Gentil

Pointe-Noire
CABINDA
(Angola)

Ascension
(U.K.)

O C E A N

Namibe

St Helena
(U.K.)

S O U T H

São Francisco

A M E R I C A

Ilha da Trindade *Ilhas*
Martin Vas

Paraná

Tropic of Cancer

Equator

Tropic of Capricorn

45° 30° 15°

30° 15° 0°

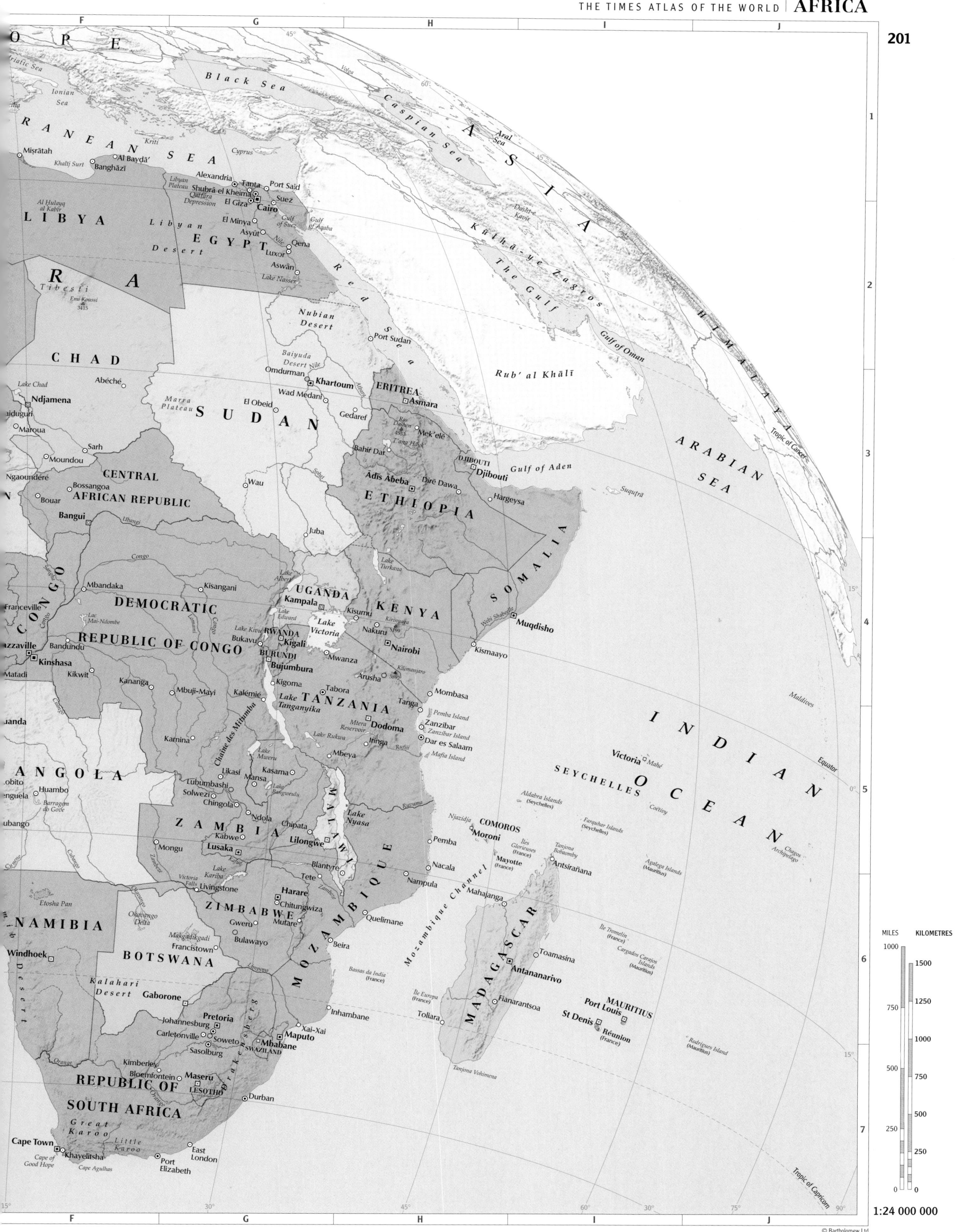

U R O P E

Adriatic Sea

Ionian Sea

Mişrātah

Khalīj Surt   Banghāzī

Al Baydā'

LIBYA

Al Hulayq al Kabīr

Libyan Plateau

Tibesti
Emi Koussi
3415

CHAD

Lake Chad

Ndjamena

Maroua

iduguri

Sarh

Moundou

Ngaoundéré

Bouar

Bossangoa

CENTRAL AFRICAN REPUBLIC

Bangui

Ubangi

CONGO

Franceville

Congo

azzaville

Kinshasa

Matadi   Kikwit

Lac Mai-Ndombe

Mbandaka

Kisangani

DEMOCRATIC REPUBLIC OF CONGO

Bandundu

Kananga

Mbuji-Mayi

Kamina

Chaîne des Mitumba

Kalémie

Likasi

Lubumbashi

Solwezi

Chingola

Ndola

Kabwe

ZAMBIA

Mongu

Lusaka

Kafue

Kasama

Lake Bangweulu

Lake Mweru

Kigoma

Tabora

Mwanza

Dodoma

TANZANIA

Lake Tanganyika

Mtera Reservoir

Iringa

Mbeya

Lake Rukwa

Rufiji

Chipata

Lake Nyasa

MALAWI

Lilongwe

Blantyre

Black Sea

Kriti

Cyprus

Volga

Caspian Sea

Aral Sea

A S I A

Dasht-e Kavir

Kūhhā-ye Zagros

The Gulf

Gulf of Oman

Rub' al Khālī

Kūhhā-ye Zagros

H I M A L A Y A

Alexandria   Tanta   Port Saïd

Shubrā el Kheima   Suez

El Gîza   **Cairo**

Qattara Depression

El Minya

EGYPT

Asyūt   Luxor

Gulf of Suez

Gulf of Aqaba

Qena

Aswān

Red Sea

Lake Nasser

Nubian Desert

Baiyuda Desert   *Nile*

Port Sudan

Omdurman   **Khartoum**

Wad Medani

SUDAN

El Obeid

Marra Plateau

Gedaref

ERITREA

Asmara

Ras Dashen

Mek'ele

T'ana Hayk

Bahir Dar

Wau

Juba

ETHIOPIA

Ādīs Ābeba   Dīre Dawa

DJIBOUTI
Djibouti

Hargeysa

Gulf of Aden

Suquţrā

SOMALIA

Webi Shabeelle

Muqdisho

Kismaayo

ARABIAN SEA

UGANDA

Kampala

Lake Edward

Kisumu

KENYA

Nakuru

Kirinyaga (Kenya)

Nairobi

Lake Albert

Lake Turkana

RWANDA

Bukavu

Kigali

Lake Kivu

BURUNDI

Bujumbura

Lake Victoria

Mwanza

Arusha

Kilimanjaro

Tanga

Serengeti

Mombasa

Pemba Island

Zanzibar

Zanzibar Island

Dar es Salaam

Mafia Island

Ruvuma

COMOROS

Njazidja   **Moroni**

Pemba

Nacala

Nampula

Mayotte (France)

Aldabra Islands (Seychelles)

Farquhar Islands (Seychelles)

Victoria   *Mahé*

SEYCHELLES

Coëtivy

Îles Glorieuses (France)

Antsirañana

Tanjona Bobaomby

Mahajanga

Maldives

I N D I A N   O C E A N

Equator

0°

Agalega Islands (Mauritius)

Chagos Archipelago

Cargados Carajos Islands (Mauritius)

Tropic of Cancer

Toamasina

Antananarivo

MADAGASCAR

Île Tromelin (France)

Flanarantsoa

Île Europa (France)

Toliara

Tanjona Vohimena

Bassas da India (France)

Rodrigues Island (Mauritius)

MAURITIUS

Port Louis

St Denis   *Réunion (France)*

Mozambique Channel

MOZAMBIQUE

Tete

Quelimane

Beira

Inhambane

Xai-Xai

Maputo

Limpopo

Zambezi

Harare

Chitungwiza

ZIMBABWE

Gweru   Mutare

Bulawayo

Francistown

BOTSWANA

Makgadikgadi

Gaborone

Kalahari Desert

ANGOLA

Huambo

enguela

Barragem do Gove

ubango

obito

uanda

Cunene

Cuando

Okavango Delta

Etosha Pan

NAMIBIA

Windhoek

Desert

Orange

Kimberley

Bloemfontein   **Maseru**

LESOTHO

REPUBLIC OF SOUTH AFRICA

Great Karoo

Little Karoo

Cape Town
Khayelitsha

Cape of Good Hope   *Cape Agulhas*

East London

Port Elizabeth

Durban

Drakensberg

Pretoria

Johannesburg

Carletonville   Soweto

Sasolburg

Mbabane

SWAZILAND

Mozambique Channel

Mavinga

Mansa

Livingstone

Lake Kariba

Victoria Falls

Kamina

© Bartholomew Ltd

MILES   KILOMETRES

1000

1500

750

1250

1000

500

750

500

250

250

0   0

1:24 000 000

Tropic of Capricorn

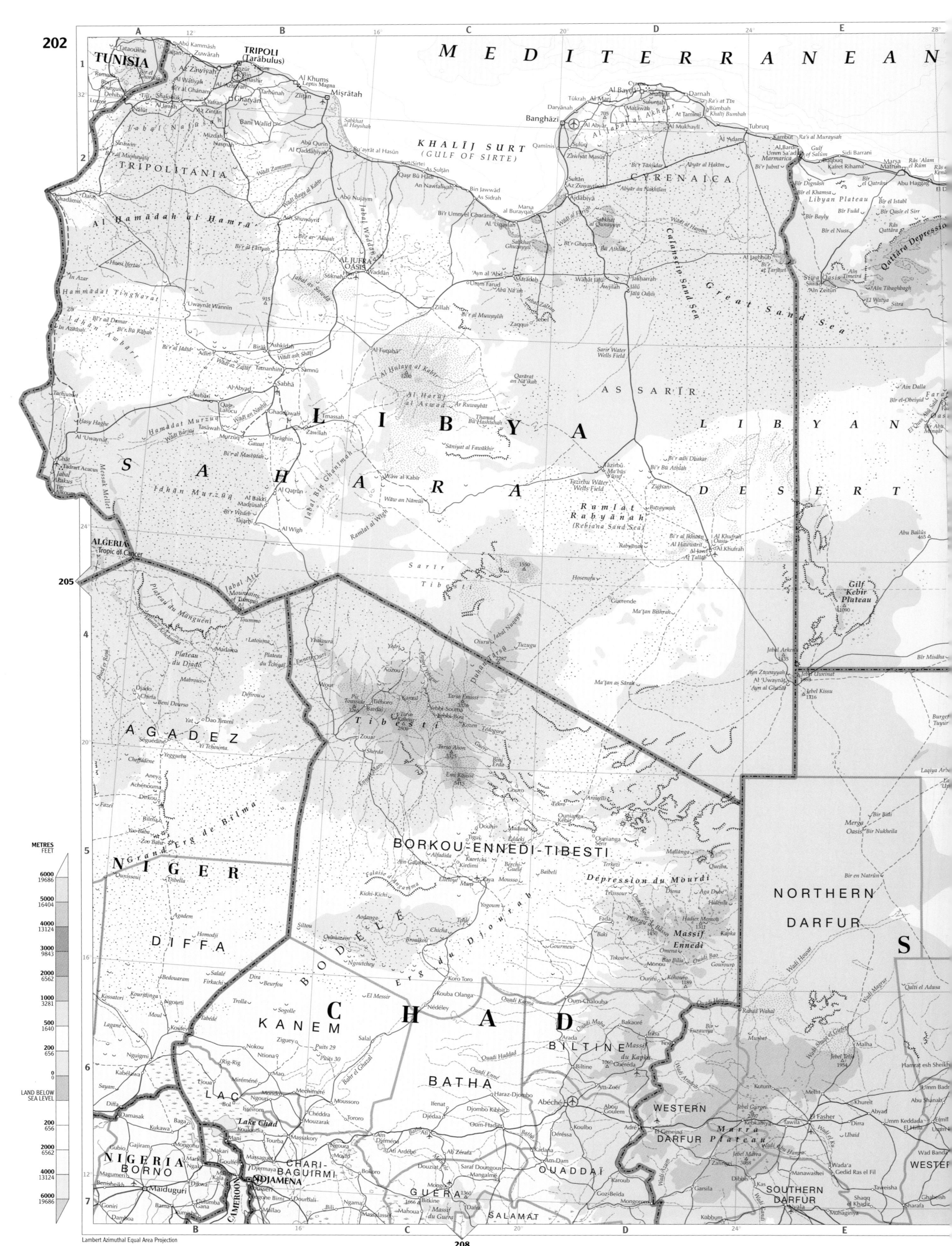

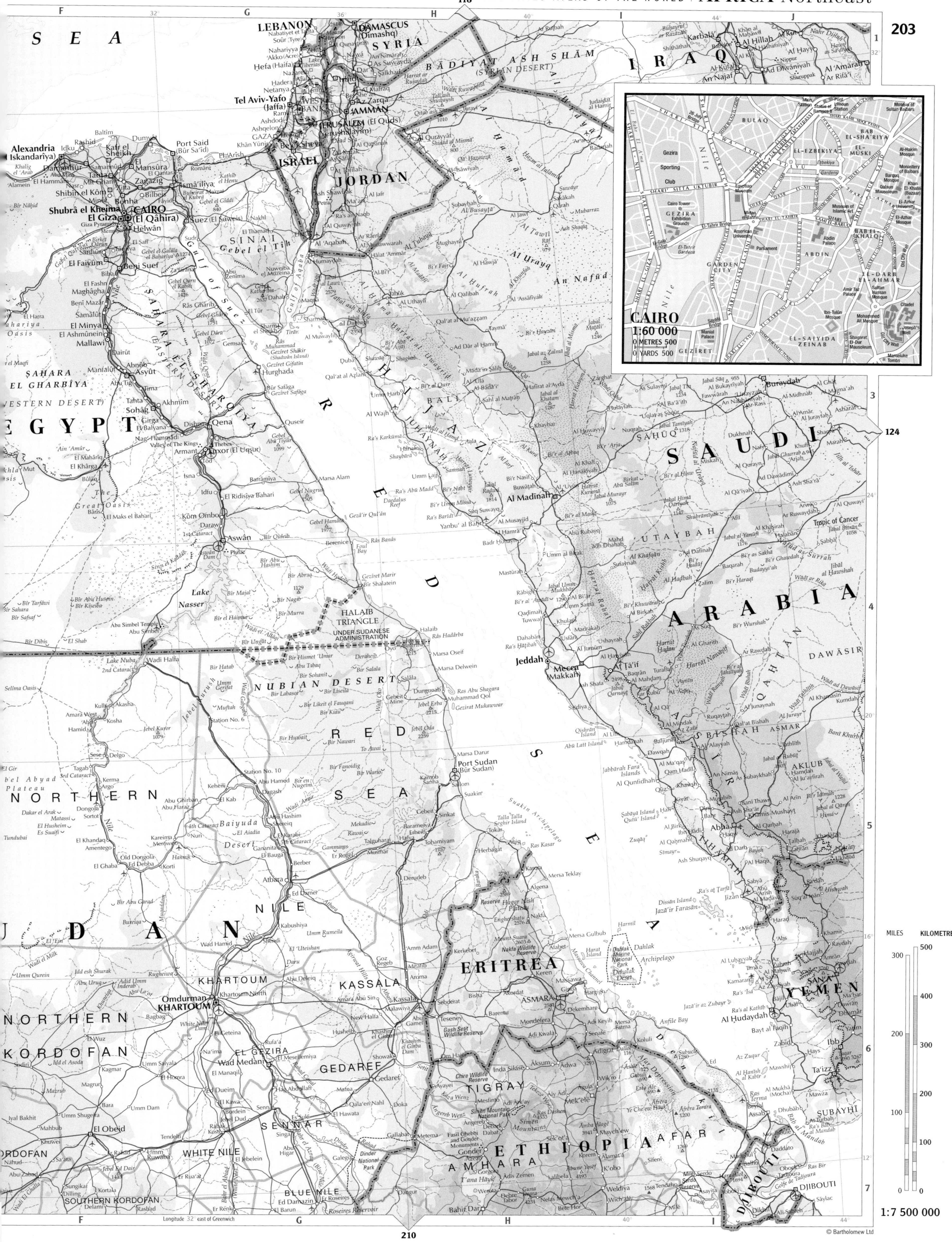

S E A

LEBANON
DAMASCUS
Dimashq
SYRIA
IRAQ

BÄDIYAT ASH SHÄM
(Syrian Desert)

Alexandria
(Iskandarîya)

Port Said
(Bûr Sa'îd)

Tel Aviv-Yafo
(Jaffa)
JERUSALEM (El Quds)
ISRAEL
WEST BANK
GAZA
AMMAN
JORDAN

CAIRO
El Giza
(El Qâhira)
Helwân
Suez (El Suweis)

SINAI
Gebel el Tîh

EGYPT

Gulf of Suez
Gulf of Aqaba

SAHARA EL GHARBIYA
(WESTERN DESERT)

Luxor (El Uqsur)
Thebes
Valley of The Kings

HIJAZ

SAUDI

ARABIA

Aswân
Lake Nasser

Abu Simbel Temple

HALAIB
TRIANGLE
UNDER SUDANESE
ADMINISTRATION

Al Madînah

Jeddah
Mecca
Makkah

NUBIAN DESERT

R E D

S E A

Port Sudan
(Bûr Sudan)

Wadi Halfa

NORTHERN

S U D A N

N I L E

KHARTOUM
Omdurman
KHARTOUM

NORTHERN

KORDOFAN

WHITE NILE

BLUE NILE

El Obeid

SENNAR

EL GEZIRA

GEDAREF

KASSALA

ERITREA

ASMARA

TIGRAY

AMHARA

ETHIOPIA

AFAR

DJIBOUTI
DJIBOUTI

YEMEN
SANA
Al Hudaydah

SOUTHERN KORDOFAN

BULAQ
EL-EZBEKIYA
EL-MUSKI
Gezira
Sporting
Club
GEZIRA
Exhibition
Grounds
Cairo Tower
Egyptian
Museum
El-Tahrir Bridge
American
University
Parliament
GARDEN
CITY
ABDIN
Abdin
Palace
EL-DARB
EL-AHMAR
EL-SAIYIDA
ZEINAB

MILES   KILOMETRES
300   500

200   400

              300

100   200

              100

0   0

1:7 500 000

Longitude 32 east of Greenwich

© Bartholomew Ltd

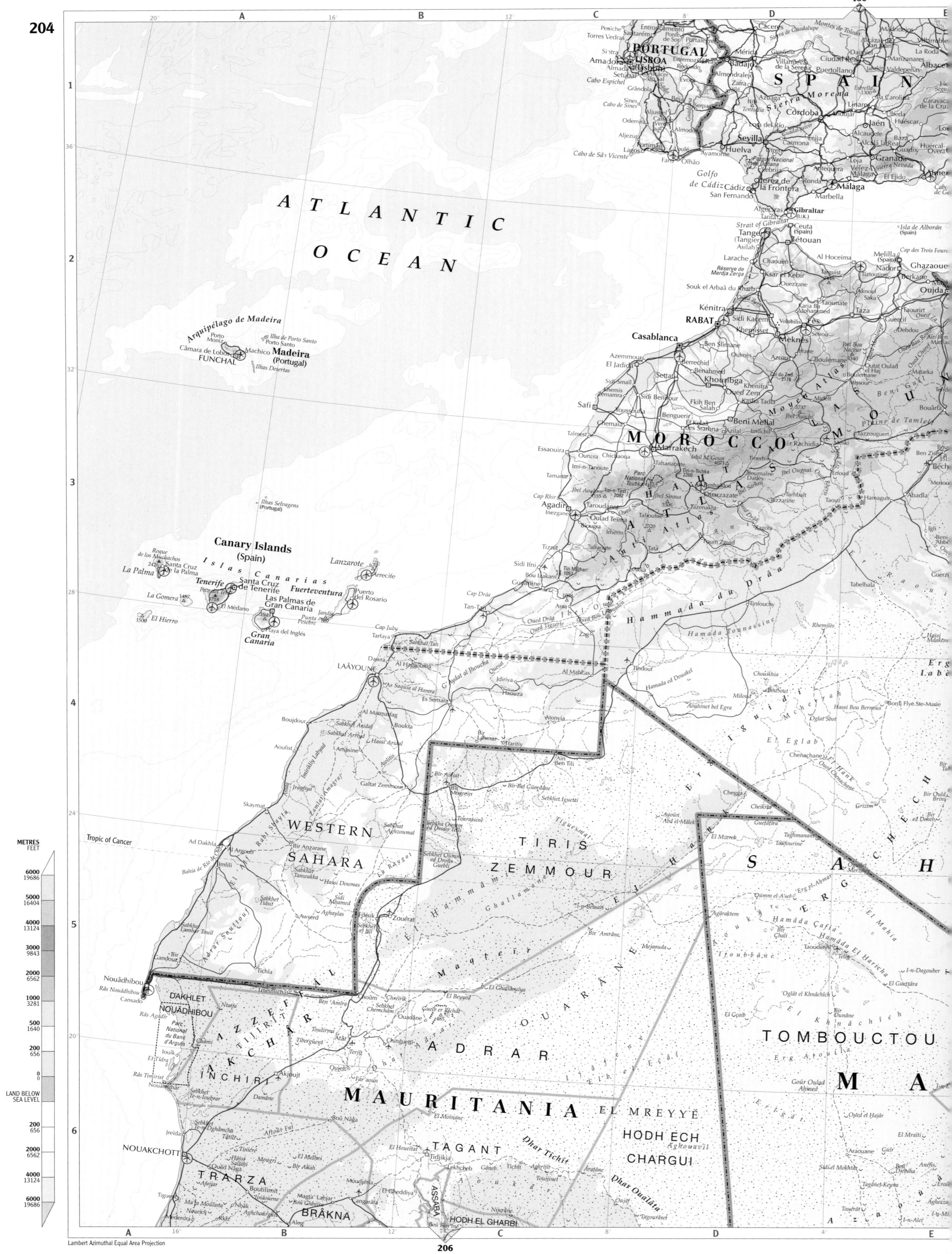

A · T · L · A · N · T · I · C

O · C · E · A · N

PORTUGAL
LISBOA

SPAIN

Córdoba

Sevilla

Huelva

Cádiz
Jerez de la Frontera
San Fernando

Gibraltar (U.K.)
Ceuta (Spain)
Tanger (Tangier)
Tétouan
Al Hoceima
Melilla (Spain)
Nador
Ghazaoue

Oujda

Chaouen
Ksar el Kebir
Larache
Ouezzane

Kénitra
RABAT
Sidi Kacem
Meknès
Fès
Taza

Casablanca

Azemmour
El Jadida
Berrechid
Benahmed
Settat
Khouribga
Khenifra
Midelt

Safi
Sidi Smail
Khemis Zemamra
Sidi Bennour
Oued Zem

Essaouira
Chemaïa
Benguerir
Kelaâ des Srarhna
Beni Mellal

MOROCCO

Marrakech

El Rachidia

Chichaoua
Tahanaoute
Ouarzazate
Zagora

Agadir
Taroudannt
Oulad Teima
Inezgane
Taliouine
Tinghir

Tiznit

Tata

Sidi Ifni
Goulimine

Cap Dráa
Tan-Tan

Arquipélago de Madeira
Porto Moniz
Ilha de Porto Santo
Porto Santo
Câmara de Lobos
Machico
Madeira (Portugal)
FUNCHAL
Ilhas Desertas

Ilhas Selvagens (Portugal)

Canary Islands (Spain)
Islas Canarias
Roque de los Muchachos
Santa Cruz de la Palma
La Palma
Lanzarote
Arrecife
Tenerife
Santa Cruz de Tenerife
Fuerteventura
La Gomera
El Médano
Las Palmas de Gran Canaria
Puerto del Rosario
El Hierro
Gran Canaria
Playa del Inglés
Punta de Jandía

Cap Juby
Tarfaya
Sebkhat Tah
Dawra

LAÂYOUNE
Al Hagounia
As Saguia al Hamra
Es Semara

Boujdour

WESTERN

SAHARA

Al Marmartag
Boukra

Aousert

TIRIS

ZEMMOUR

Bir Anzarane

Ad Dakhla

Argoub

Bahía de Río de Oro

METRES **FEET**

6000 19686
5000 16404
4000 13124
3000 9843
2000 6562
1000 3281
500 1640
200 656
0 0

LAND BELOW SEA LEVEL

200 656
2000 6562
4000 13124
6000 19686

Tropic of Cancer

Zouérat

Nouâdhibou
Râs Nouâdhibou
Cansado

DAKHLET
NOUÂDHIBOU
Râs Agadir

Parc National du Banc d'Arguin

A Z Z E F F A L

A K C H A R

INCHIRI

Râs Timiris

NOUAKCHOTT

TRARZA

BRÂKNA

Atâr
ADRAR

Akjoujt

Chinguetti

Oujeft

MAURITANIA

TAGANT
Tidjikja

ASSABA

HODH EL GHARBI

EL MREYYÉ

HODH ECH
CHARGUI

TOMBOUCTOU

M A

S A H A

Lambert Azimuthal Equal Area Projection

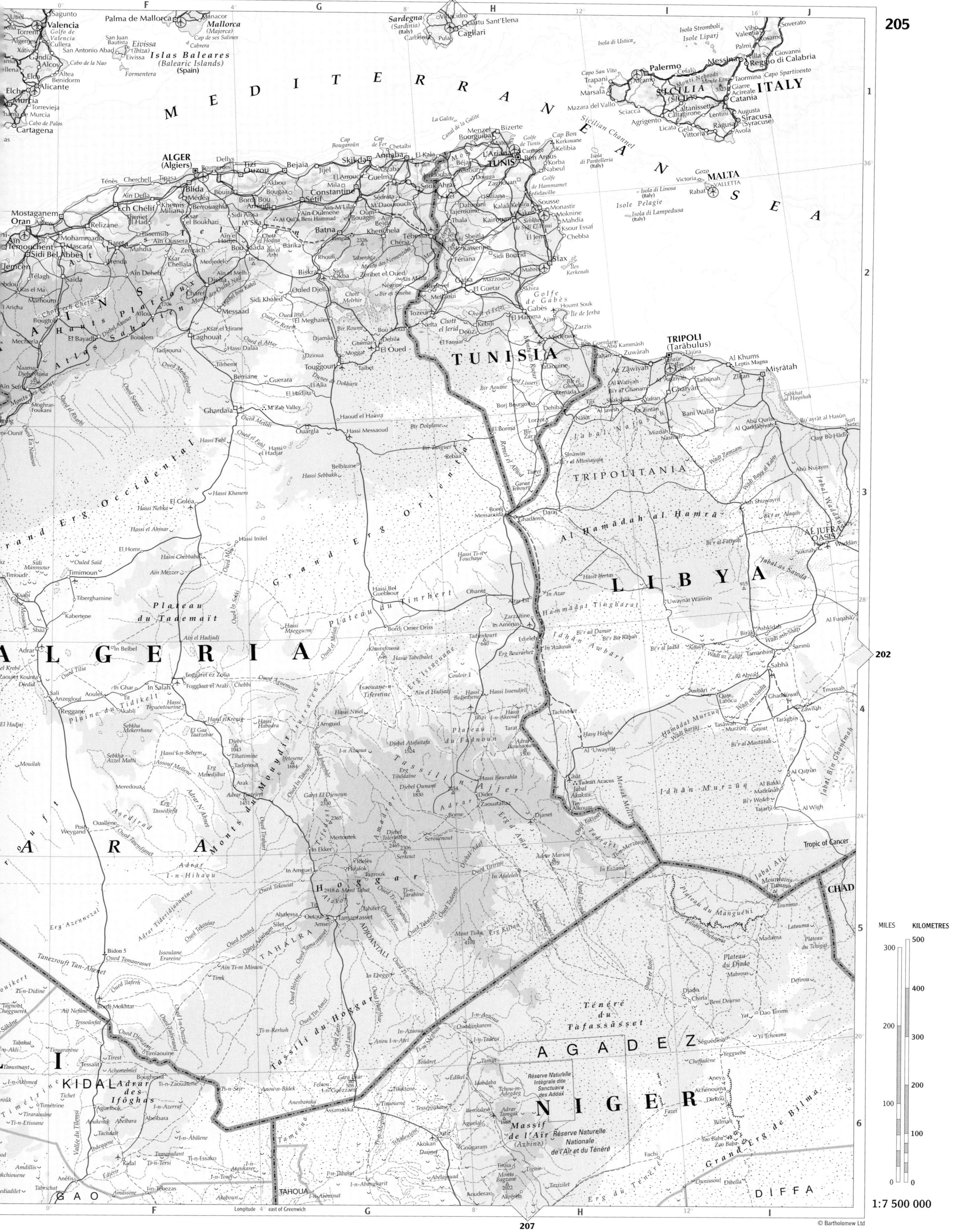

MEDITERRANEAN SEA

SPAIN · Valencia · Alicante · Cartagena · Murcia · Elche · Torrevieja · Mostaganem · Oran

Islas Baleares (Balearic Islands) (Spain) · Mallorca · Palma de Mallorca · Eivissa (Ibiza) · Formentera

Sardegna (Sardinia) (Italy) · Cagliari · Carbonia

SICILIA (SICILY) · Palermo · Trapani · Marsala · Catania · Siracusa (Syracuse) · Ragusa · **ITALY** · Reggio di Calabria · Messina

Isole Liparì · Isola di Ustica

MALTA · VALLETTA · Victoria · Gozo

Isole Pelagie · Isola di Linosa · Isola di Lampedusa

ALGER (Algiers) · Dellys · Tizi Ouzou · Bejaïa · Jijel · Skikda · Annaba · El Kala · L'Ariana · **TUNIS** · Ben Arous

Blida · Médéa · Bouira · Sétif · Constantine · Guelma · Souk Ahras · Dougga · Zaghouan

Ech Chélif · Relizane · Mascara · Sidi Bel Abbès · Tlemcen · Aïn Temouchent

Batna · Khenchela · Tébessa · Kasserine · Sbeitla · Kairouan · Sousse · Monastir · Mahdia · Sfax

Îles Kerkenah · Golfe de Gabès · Gabès · Île de Jerba · Zarzis · Médenine

Biskra · Touggourt · El Oued · Tozeur · Nefta · Chott el Jerid · Douz · Tataouine

TUNISIA

Laghouat · Ghardaïa · Ouargla · Hassi Messaoud

Grand Erg Occidental · Grand Erg Oriental

El Goléa · Timimoun · Plateau du Tademaït · In Salah

ALGERIA · **LIBYA**

TRIPOLI (Ṭarābulus) · Al Khums · Leptis Magna · Mişrātah · Az Zāwiyah · Gharyān · Banī Walīd

TRIPOLITANIA · Al Ḥamādah al Ḥamrā' · Ghadāmis · Darj

Al Jufrah Oasis · Wāddān · Idhān Murzuq · Sabhā · Ghāt · Tadrart Acacus · Jabal Akakus · Murzuq

Reggane · Tidikelt · In Ekker · Tamanrasset · Hoggar · Mont Tahat · Silet · In Guezzam

Tassili n'Ajjer · Djanet · Illizi · Bordj Omar Driss

Tropic of Cancer

CHAD · Plateau du Manguéni · Plateau du Djado

AGADEZ · Ténéré du Tafassâsset

NIGER · Massif de l'Aïr · Réserve Naturelle Nationale de l'Aïr et du Ténéré

KIDAL · Adrar des Ifôghas · **GAO** · Kidal

Tanezrouft Tan-Ahenet · Bordj Mokhtar

TAHOUA · **DIFFA** · Grand Erg de Bilma · Ténéré du Tafassâsset

Longitude 4 east of Greenwich

202

MILES · KILOMETRES · 300 · 500 · 200 · 300 · 100 · 100 · 0 · 0

1:7 500 000

© Bartholomew Ltd

207

A 16 B 12 C 8 D 4 E

1

İNCHIRI ADRAR S A H

DAKHLET NOUADHIBOU
Parc National du Banc d'Arguin
AKCHÂR

M A U R I T A N I A

TRARZA

TAGANT EL MREYYÉ HODH ECH CHARGUI

TOMBOUCTOU

BRÂKNA

ASSABA HODH H'O'D EL GHARBI

NOUAKCHOTT

St-Louis -16°

GORGOL M A L I

DAKAR Thiès
Kaolack
S E N E G A L

GUIDIMAKA

MOPTI

KAYES

THE GAMBIA
BANJUL
Parc National du Delta du Saloum

KOULIKORO SÉGOU

BURKINA

OUAGADOUGOU

GUINEA-BISSAU
BISSAU

MOYENNE-GUINÉE
Fouta Djallon

GUINEA HAUTE-GUINÉE

BAMAKO

SIKASSO

Bobo-Dioulasso

GUINÉE-MARITIME

CONAKRY

UPPER WEST

NORTHERN

FREETOWN
WESTERN AREA
SIERRA LEONE
EASTERN
SOUTHERN

GUINÉE-FORESTIÈRE

CÔTE D'IVOIRE

GHANA
BRONG-AHAFO

ASHANTI
Kumasi

NORTHERN

LIBERIA

MONROVIA

YAMOUSSOUKRO

D'IVOIRE

WESTERN

Abidjan

A T L A N T I C   O C E A N

METRES FEET
6000 19686
5000 16404
4000 13124
3000 9843
2000 6562
1000 3281
500 1640
200 656
0 0
LAND BELOW SEA LEVEL
200 656
2000 6562
4000 13124
6000 19686

CAPE VERDE
AT THE SAME SCALE
24°W

Santo Antão
Mindelo São Vicente
Porto Novo Santa Luzia
Sal Pedra Lume
Santa Maria
Boa Vista
16°N
Ilhas do Cabo Verde
São Tiago Maio
Fogo Brava
PRAIA

Equator

Lambert Azimuthal Equal Area Projection
Longitude 4° west of Greenwich

B 12 C 8 D E

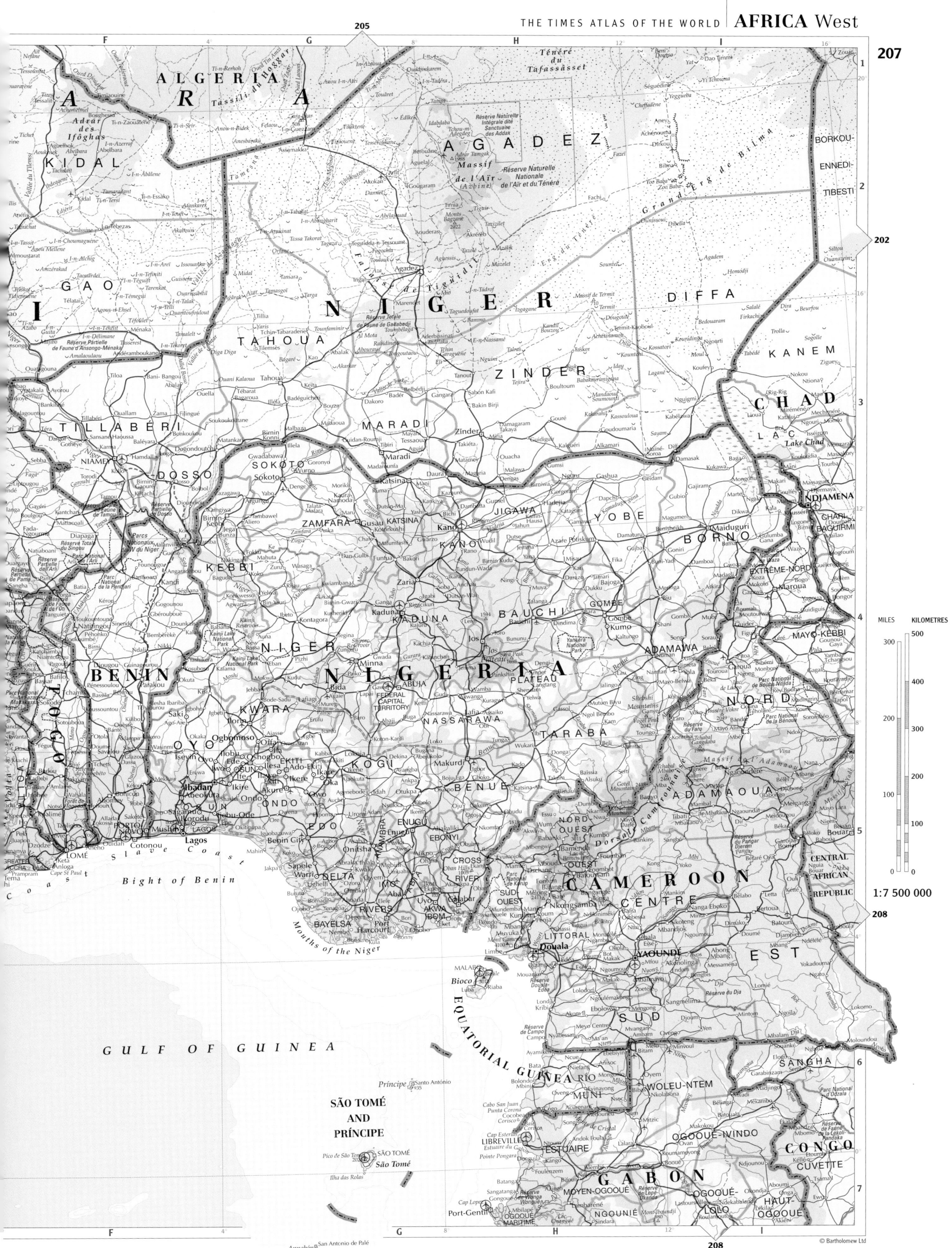

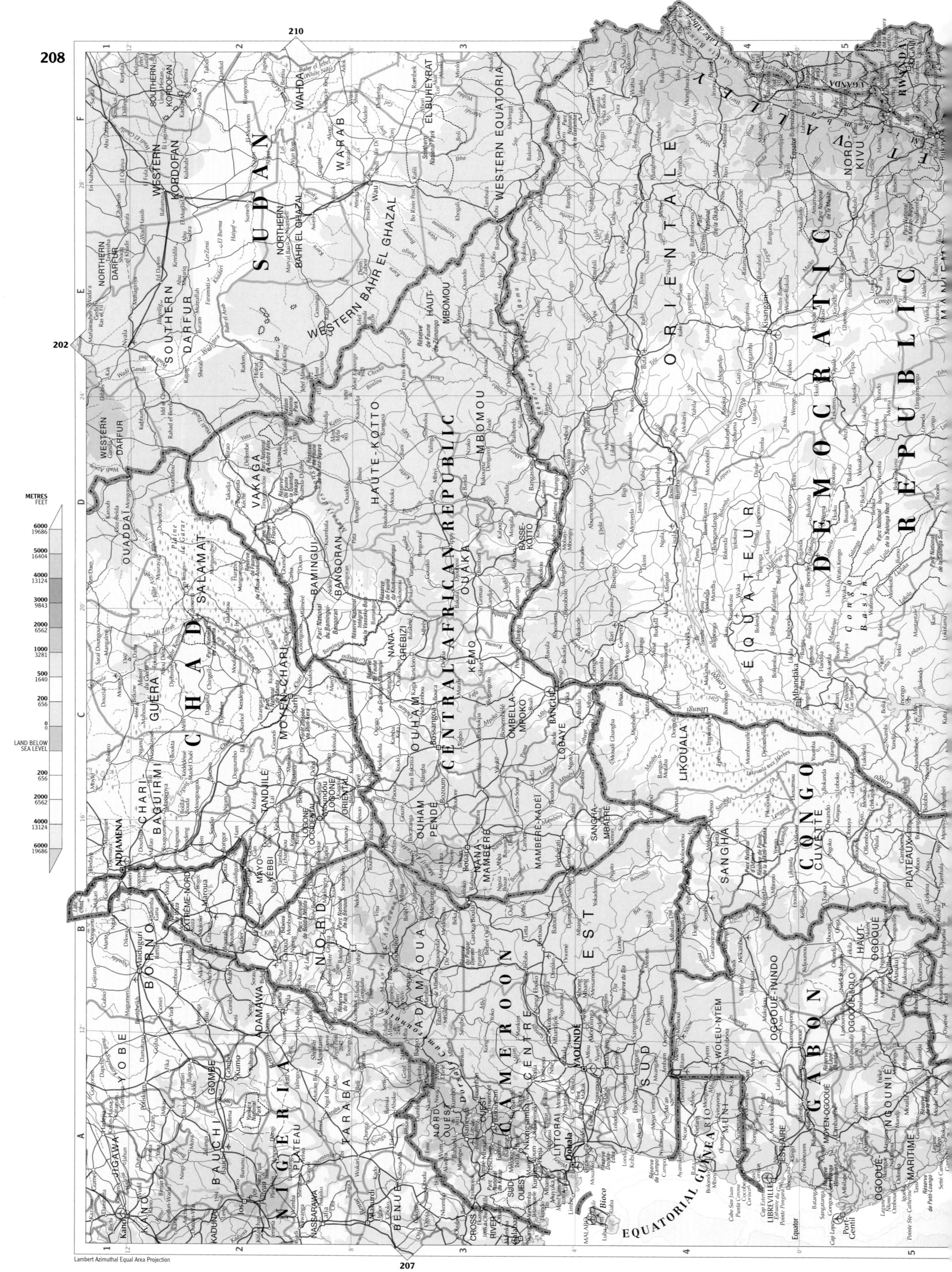

210

202

207

Lambert Azimuthal Equal Area Projection

212

MILES   KILOMETRES

500

300

400

200   300

100   200

100

0   0

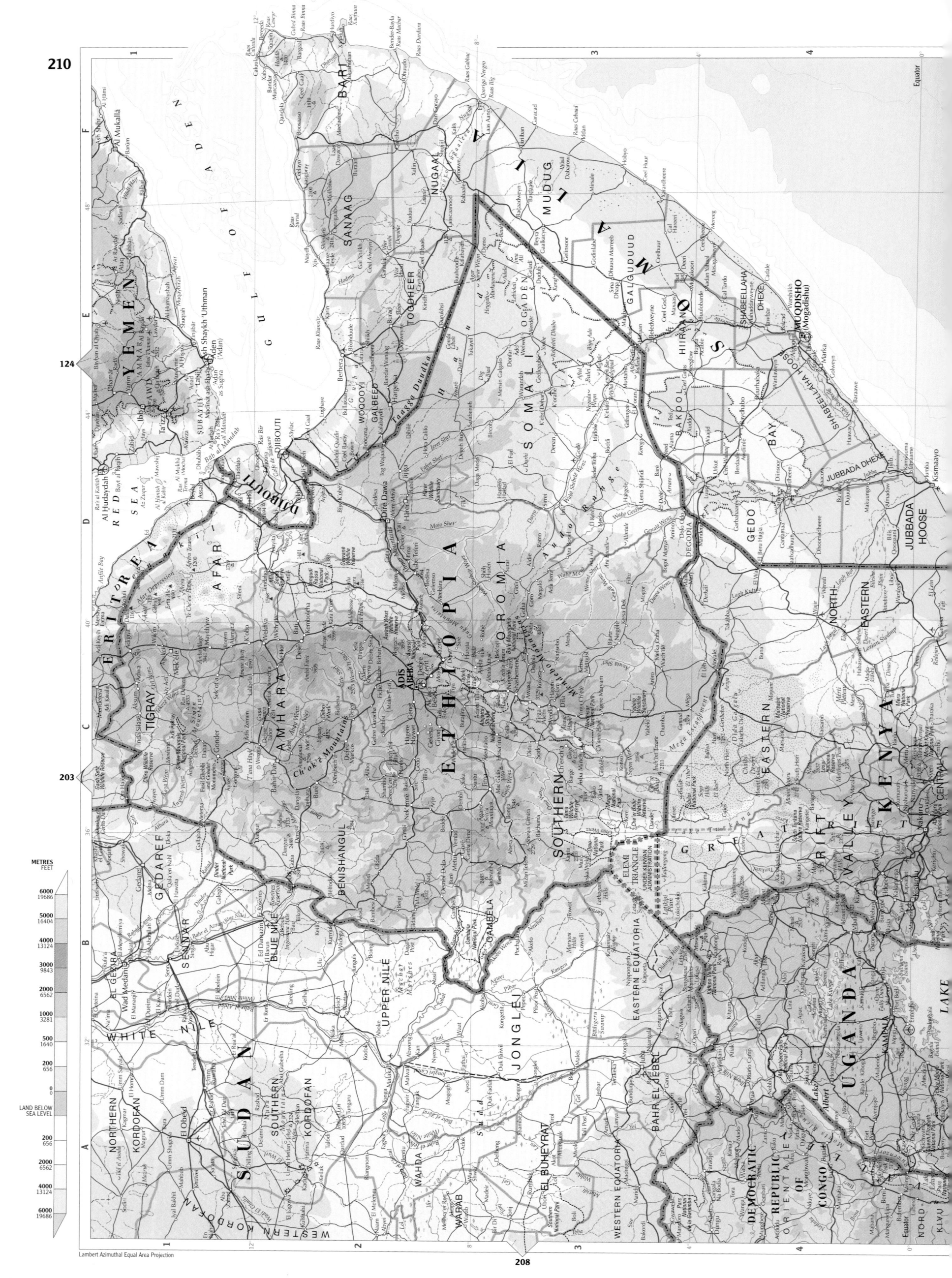

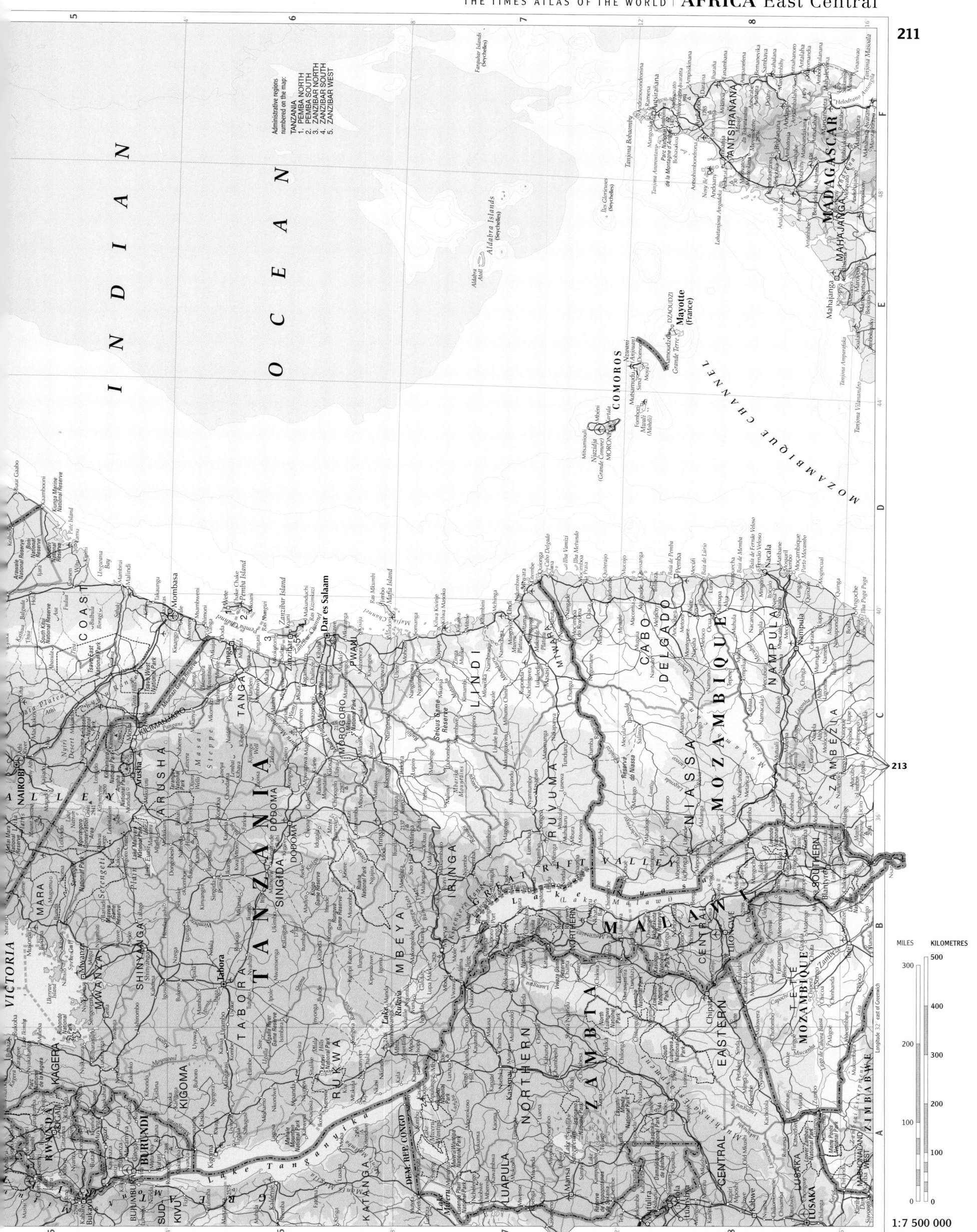

I N D I A N

O C E A N

Farquhar Islands
(Seychelles)

Aldabra Islands
(Seychelles)

Aldabra
Atoll

Îles Glorieuses
(Seychelles)

Administrative regions
numbered on the map:

TANZANIA
1. PEMBA NORTH
2. PEMBA SOUTH
3. ZANZIBAR NORTH
4. ZANZIBAR SOUTH
5. ZANZIBAR WEST

MADAGASCAR

ANTSIRAÑANA

MAHAJANGA

Mahajanga

COMOROS

Njazidja
(Grande Comore)
MORONI

Mayotte
(France)

M O Z A M B I Q U E   C H A N N E L

213

COAST

Mombasa

Pemba Island

Zanzibar Island

Dar es Salaam

Mafia Island

NAIROBI

MARA

KAGERA

SHINYANGA

MWANZA

KIGOMA

RWANDA

BURUNDI

DEM. REP. CONGO

KATANGA

LUAPULA

KILIMANJARO

ARUSHA

TABORA

Tabora

DODOMA

SINGIDA

MOROGORO

PWANI

Selous Game Reserve

LINDI

MTWARA

RUVUMA

CABO
DELGADO

Pemba

NIASSA

NAMPULA

Nacala

Nampula

MOZAMBIQUE

ZAMBEZIA

T A N Z A N I A

MBEYA

IRINGA

G R E A T   R I F T   V A L L E Y

Lake Nyasa
(Lake Malawi)

NORTHERN

M A L A W I

CENTRAL

SOUTHERN

Blantyre

RUKWA

Lake
Tanganyika

Lake Rukwa

NORTHERN

Z A M B I A

CENTRAL

EASTERN

TETE

MOZAMBIQUE

LUSAKA

Katwe

MASHONALAND
WEST

MASHONALAND
CENTRAL

ZIMBABWE

Longitude 32° east of Greenwich

VICTORIA

KIVU

SUD-
KIVU

BUJUMBURA

Lake
Victoria

209

MILES   KILOMETRES

300   500

400

200   300

200

100   100

0   0

1:7 500 000

© Bartholomew Ltd

ATLANTIC

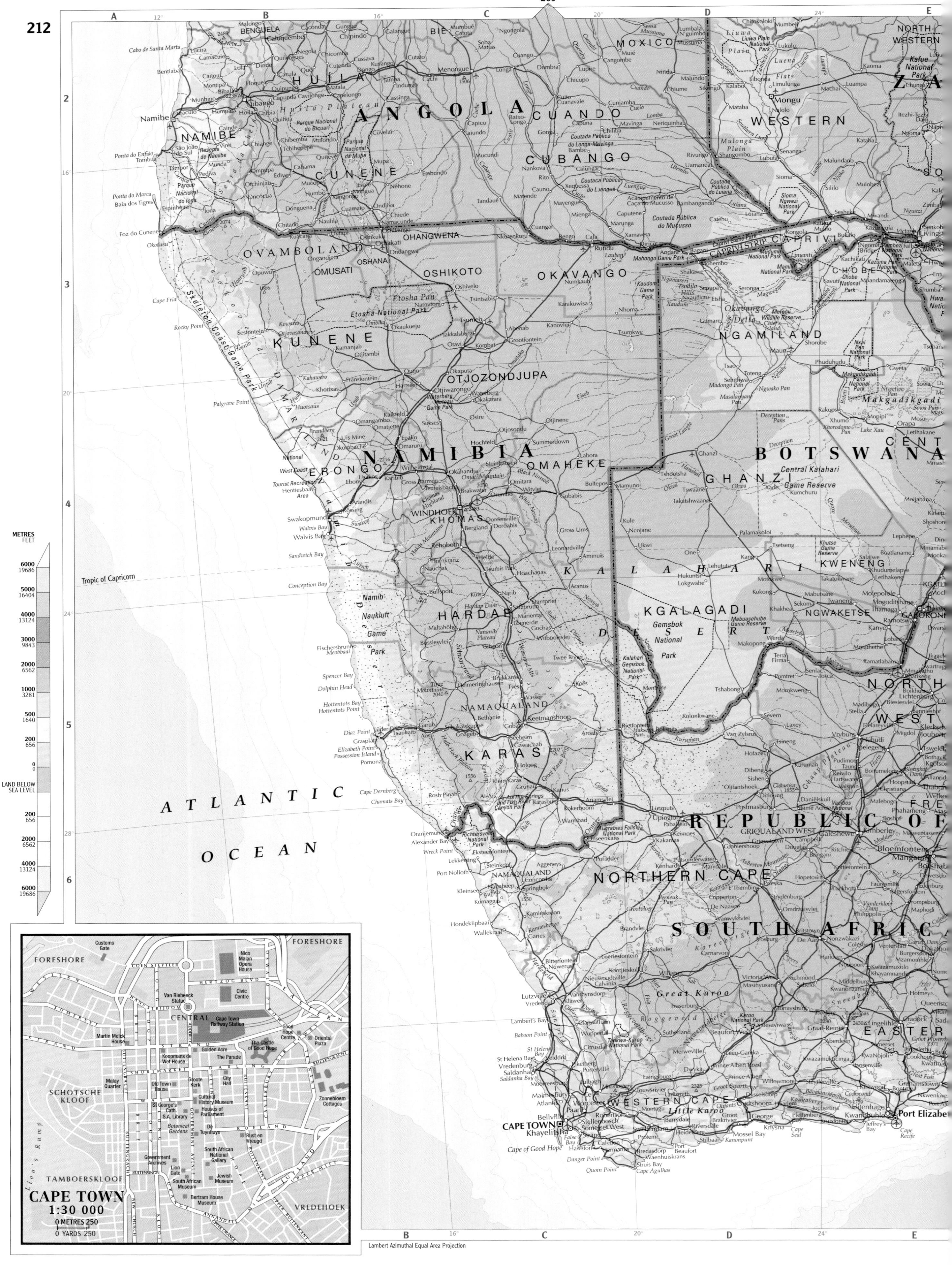

OCEAN

ANGOLA

NAMIBIA

BOTSWANA

REPUBLIC OF

SOUTH AFRICA

METRES / FEET

METRES	FEET
6000	19686
5000	16404
4000	13124
3000	9843
2000	6562
1000	3281
500	1640
200	656
0	0

LAND BELOW SEA LEVEL

200	656
2000	6562
4000	13124
6000	19686

Tropic of Capricorn

BENGUELA

HUILA

NAMIBE

CUNENE

CUANDO CUBANGO

MOXICO

WESTERN

ZA

CAPRIVI

CHOBE

OVAMBOLAND

OHANGWENA

OSHANA

OMUSATI

OSHIKOTO

OKAVANGO

NGAMILAND

Etosha Pan

Etosha National Park

KUNENE

DAMARALAND

OTJOZONDJUPA

GHANZI

CENT

Central Kalahari
Game Reserve

ERONGO

Windhoek

KHOMAS

OMAHEKE

Walvis Bay

KWENENG

KALAHARI

HARDAP

DESERT

KGALAGADI

Gemsbok National Park

NGWAKETSE

GABORONE

KARAS

NAMAQUALAND

KGATL

NORTH WEST

Keetmanshoop

GRIQUALAND WEST

NORTHERN CAPE

Kimberley

FREE

Bloemfontein

Orange

Great Karoo

Little Karoo

WESTERN CAPE

EASTERN

CAPE TOWN

Cape of Good Hope

Port Elizabeth

Cape Agulhas

CAPE TOWN
1:30 000

FORESHORE

FORESHORE

Customs Gate

Nico Malan Opera House

Civic Centre

Van Riebeeck Statue

CENTRAL

Cape Town Railway Station

Martin Melck House

Koopmans de Wet House

Good Hope Centre

Oriental Plaza

Golden Acre

The Parade

The Castle of Good Hope

Old Town House

City Hall

Zonnebloem Cottages

Malay Quarter

SCHOTSCHE KLOOF

St George's Cath.

S.A. Library

Cultural History Museum

De Tuynhuys

Botanical Gardens

Government Archives

Lion Gate

South African National Gallery

South African Museum

Jewish Museum

Bertram House Museum

TAMBOERSKLOOF

VREDEHOEK

Lion's Rump

0 METRES 250
0 YARDS 250

Lambert Azimuthal Equal Area Projection

MILES KILOMETRES

300
400
200
300
100
200
100
0 0

1:7 500 000

MOZAMBIQUE CHANNEL

INDIAN OCEAN

Tropic of Capricorn

MADAGASCAR
AT THE SAME SCALE

© Bartholomew Ltd

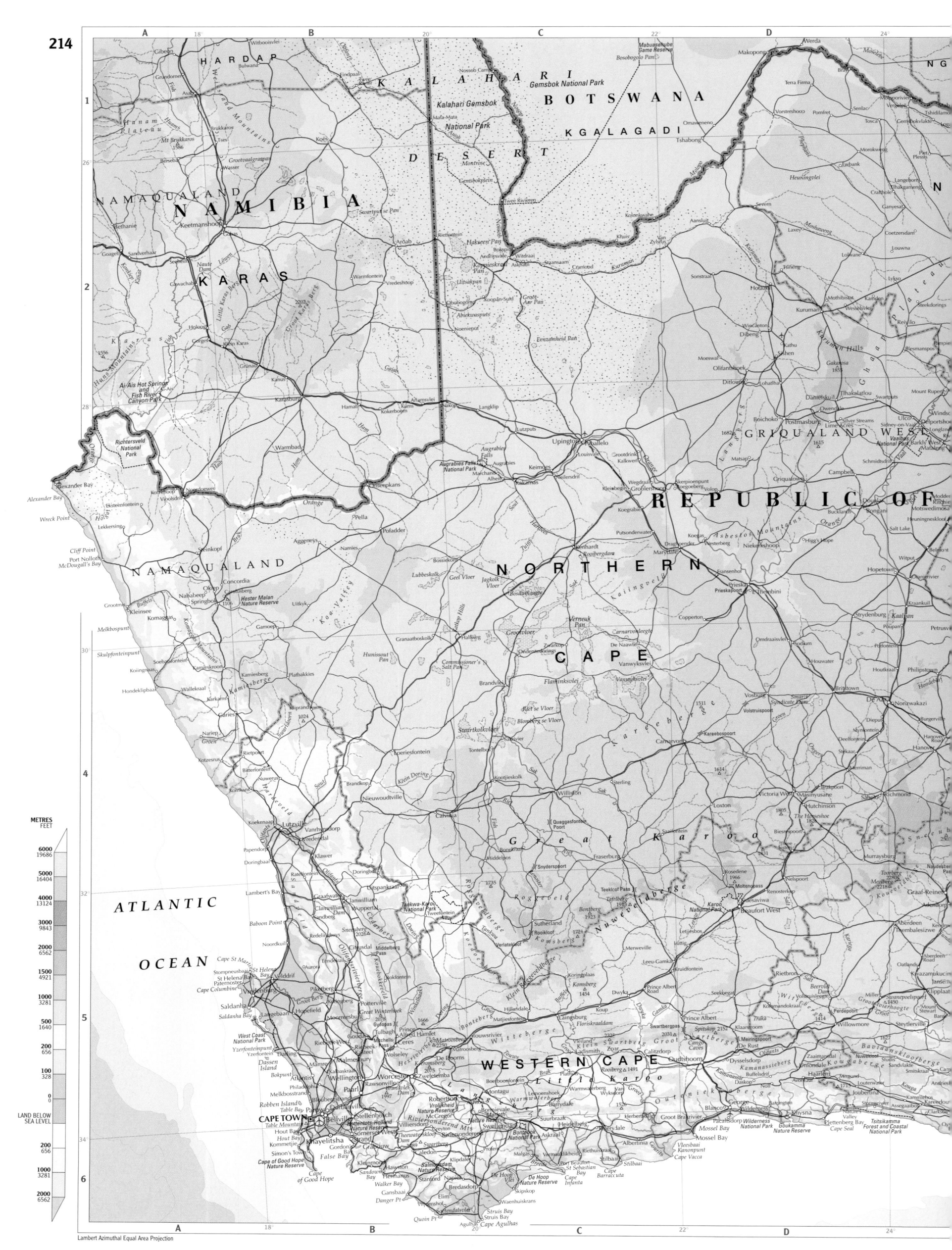

KETSE

NORTH WEST

FREE STATE

SOUTH AFRICA

GAUTENG

PRETORIA

Johannesburg

Soweto

Sasolburg

Klerksdorp

Bloemfontein

MASERU

LESOTHO

MPUMALANGA

SWAZILAND

MBABANE

HHOHHO

MANZINI

SHISELWENI

LUBOMBO

MOZAMBIQUE

MARUTO

MAPUTO

KWAZULU-NATAL

Newcastle

Ladysmith

Pietermaritzburg

Durban

EASTERN CAPE

GRIQUALAND EAST

Umtata

Queenstown

EASTERN CAPE

Mdantsane

East London

King William's Town

Grahamstown

Port Elizabeth

Uitenhage

Cape Recife

Algoa Bay

I N D I A N

O C E A N

Longitude 26° east of Greenwich

MILES

KILOMETRES

125

100

75

50

25

200

175

150

125

100

75

50

25

0

1:3 300 000

© Bartholomew Ltd

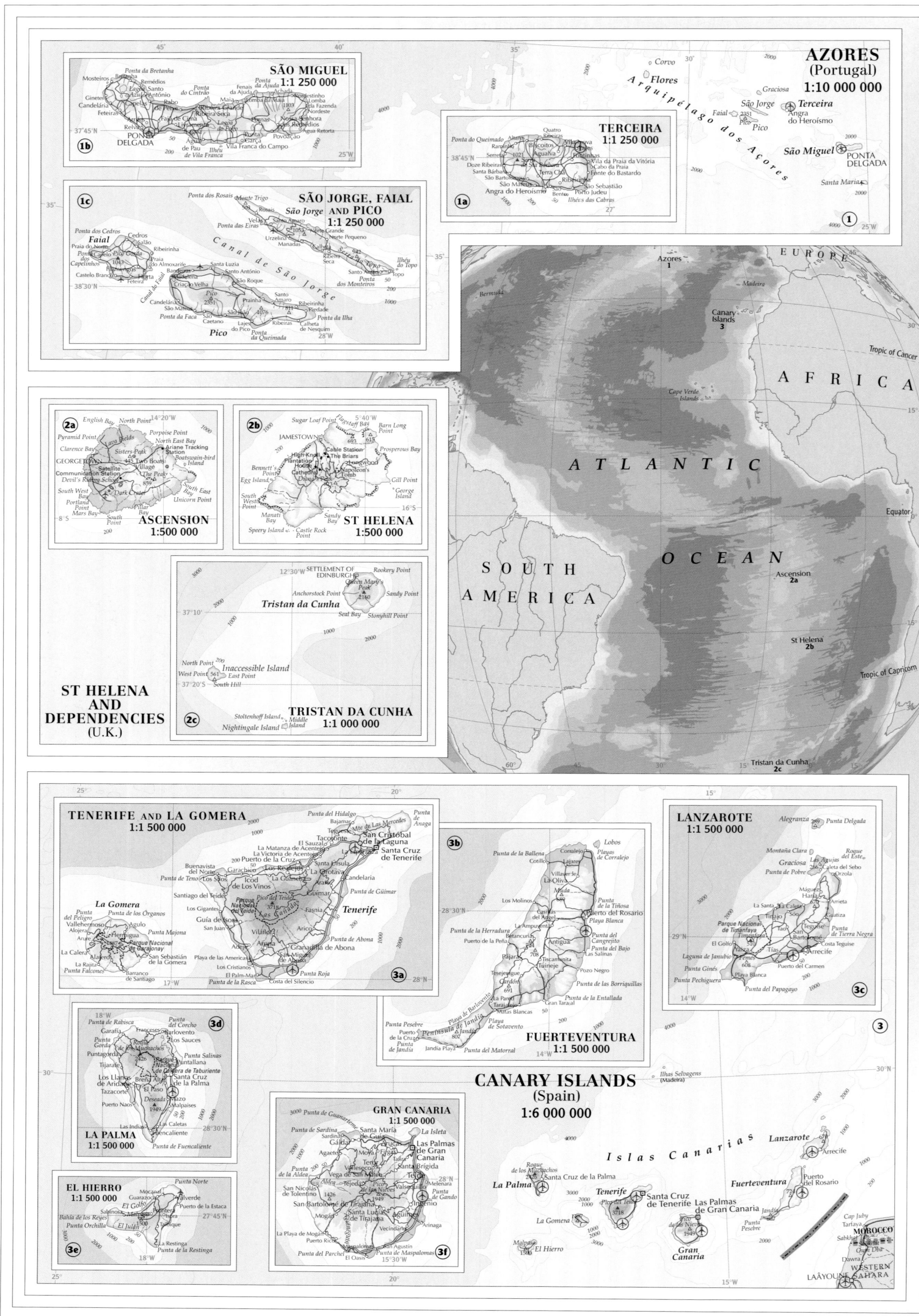

© Bartholomew Ltd

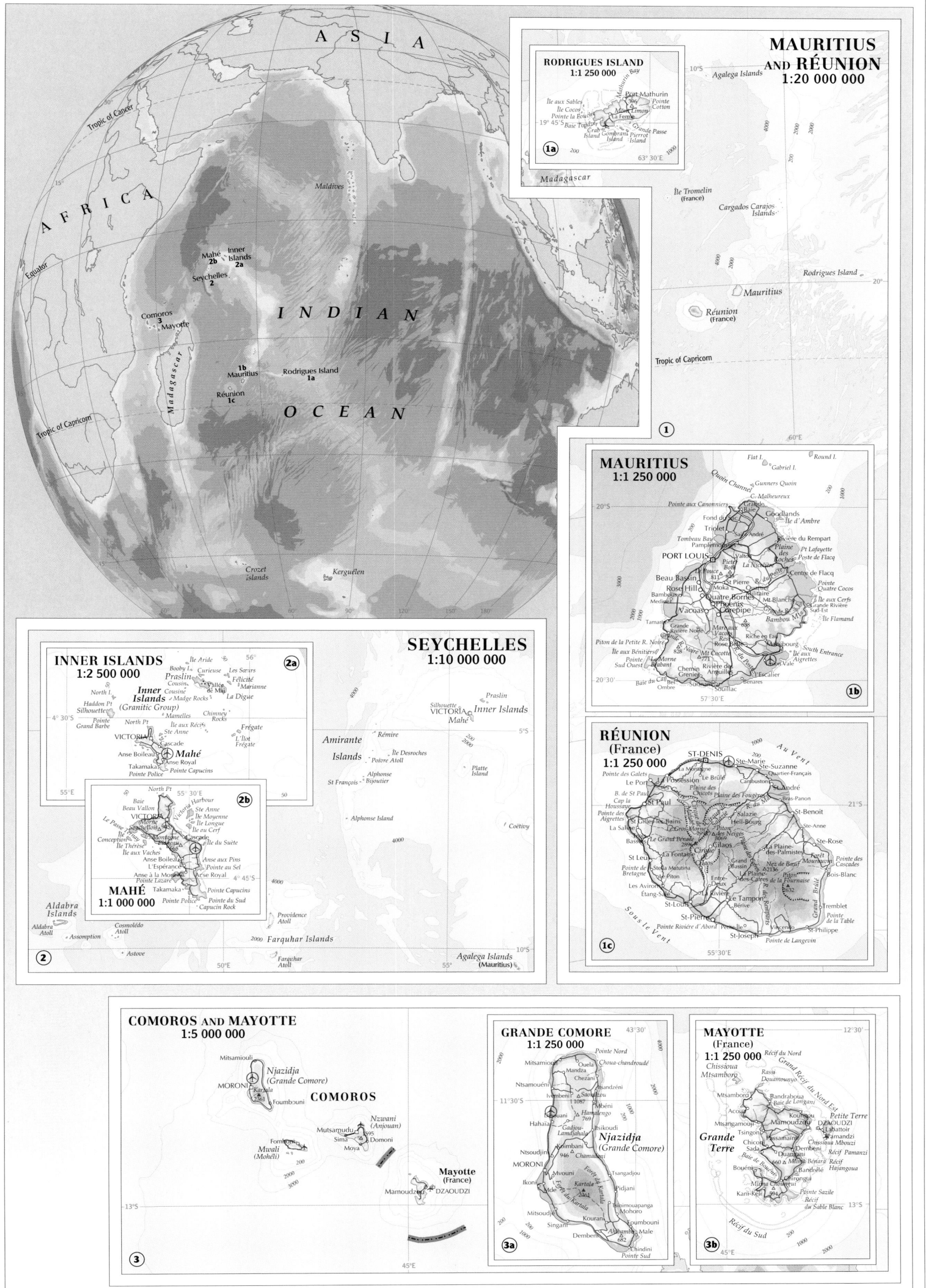

© Bartholomew Ltd

A   B   C   D   E

A S I A

ARCTIC

OCEAN

Arctic Circle

60°   75°   120°   105°   90°

135°

150°

165°

180°

165°

150°

Queen

Prince
Patrick
Island

Elle

Ringnes

Mackenzie
King

Melville Island

McClure Strait   Viscount Melville
Sound

Banks
Island

Stefansson
Island

Sachs Harbour

Amundsen
Gulf

Victoria

Island

Bathurst
Inlet

NU

Coronation
Gulf

Contwoyto L.

Chukchi
Sea

Point
Hope

Barrow

BEAUFORT SEA

Mackenzie
Bay

Inuvik

Richardson
Mountains

Great
Bear
Lake

Napaktulik
Lake

Déline

Hottah L.

BERING

SEA

St Matthew
Island

St Lawrence
Island

Bering Strait

Nome

Norton
Sound

Nunivak
Island

Pribilof
Islands

Brooks Range

ALASKA

Kuskokwim Mts

Mount
McKinley

Alaska
Range

Anchorage

Kenai

Yukon

Ogilvie
Mountains

Mackenzie Mountains

NORTHWEST

TERRITORIES

Yellowknife

Fort
Simpson

Great Slave
Lake

Lac la
Martre

MacKay
Lake

Dubawnt
Lake

Selwyn
Lake

Attu
Island

Aleutian Islands

Andreanof Islands

Fox Islands

Aleutian Range

Bristol Bay

Kodiak
Island

Gulf of
Alaska

Alaska
Range

Wrangell
Mountains

Mount Logan

Kluane
Lake

YUKON

TERRITORY

Whitehorse

Watson
Lake

Cassiar Mountains

Fort
Nelson

Trout
Lake

C   A   N

Uranium City

L. Claire   Lake
Athabasca

Reind

PACIFIC

OCEAN

Tropic of Cancer

Midway
Islands
(U.S.A.)

15°

30°

Alexander
Archipelago

Juneau

Prince Rupert

Queen Charlotte
Islands

Queen Charlotte
Sound

Heart Str.

COAST

BRITISH

COLUMBIA

MOUNTAINS

Dawson
Creek

Williston
Lake

Prince
George

Vancouver
Island

Vancouver

Victoria

Kamloops

Jasper

Lesser
Slave Lake

Grande
Prairie

Fort
McMurray

ALBERTA

Edmonton

Lloydminster

Lac la
Biche

N. Saskatchewan

SASKATCHEWAN

Prince
Albert

Saskatoon

L
Lynn

R
O
C
K

Calgary

Medicine
Hat

Lethbridge

Regina

Winnipeg

Saskatchewan

Seattle

Olympia

WASHINGTON

Spokane

Portland   Columbia

Salem

Eugene

OREGON

Great Falls

Helena

MONTANA

Bitterroot Range

Billings

Bismarc

NO

DA

SO
DA

Pier

Kanai

Honolulu

Oahu

HAWAII

Hawaiian Islands
(U.S.A.)

Maui

Hawaii

Boise

IDAHO

Twin Falls

Bighorn
Mountains

WYOMING

Casper

Rapid
City

Equator

0°

Line Islands

Coast Ranges

Cascade Range

Klamath

Great Salt Lake

Reno

Sacramento

Carson
City

San Francisco

San Jose

Salt Lake City

NEVADA

UTAH

Great
Basin

Mount
Whitney

Sierra Nevada

Uinta
Mountains

Green R.

Cheyenne

COLORADO

Denver

Colorado
Springs

North
Platte

NEB

UNITED   STA

Las Vegas

CALIFORNIA

Los Angeles

San Diego

Tijuana

Ensenada

Mexicali

ARIZONA

Colorado
Plateau

Colorado R.

Albuquerque

Santa Fe

NEW

MEXICO

Phoenix

Tucson

El Paso

Ciudad
Juárez

Rio Grande

Amarillo

Lubbock

T

Sacramento Mts

Eagle
Pa

Guadalupe
(Mexico)

Baja California

Golfo de California

Hermosillo

Chihuahua

Bolsón
de Mapimí

Sierra Madre

Sierra

Villa Insurgentes

Los
Mochis

Torreón

Monter

La Paz

MEXIC

Durango

Occidental

San Luis
Potosí

Mazatlán

Tepic

Islas
Revillagigedo
(Mexico)

Guadalajara

Morelia

Sier

Île Clipperton
(France)

Administrative regions abbreviated on the map:

U.S.A.		CANADA	
CONN.	CONNECTICUT	P.E.I.	PRINCE EDWARD ISLAND
DEL.	DELAWARE		
MD	MARYLAND		
MASS.	MASSACHUSETTS		
N.H.	NEW HAMPSHIRE		
N.J.	NEW JERSEY		
R.I.	RHODE ISLAND		
VER.	VERMONT		
W. VIRG.	WEST VIRGINIA		

A   B   C   D   E

165°   15°   150°   0° 135°   120°   105°

EUROPE

AFRICA

ATLANTIC OCEAN

Greenland
(Kalaallit Nunaat)
(Denmark)

Baffin
Bay

Baffin Island

Davis Strait

Denmark Strait

Iceland

Labrador Sea

HUDSON BAY

CANADA

NEWFOUNDLAND

QUÉBEC

ONTARIO

MANITOBA

MINNESOTA

WISCONSIN

MICHIGAN

IOWA

ILLINOIS INDIANA OHIO

MISSOURI

KENTUCKY

TENNESSEE

ARKANSAS

MISSISSIPPI ALABAMA GEORGIA

LOUISIANA

OF AMERICA

OKLAHOMA

TEXAS

Chicago
Detroit
Cleveland
PENNSYLVANIA
New York
Philadelphia
Washington
VIRGINIA
NORTH CAROLINA
SOUTH CAROLINA
FLORIDA

Appalachian Mountains

Cape Hatteras

Bermuda
(U.K.)

GULF OF MEXICO

Miami

THE BAHAMAS
Nassau

Turks and Caicos Is
(U.K.)

CUBA

La Habana

Hispaniola

HAITI
DOMINICAN REPUBLIC
Port-au-Prince
Santo Domingo

Puerto Rico
(U.S.A.)
San Juan

Jamaica
Kingston

Greater Antilles

Leeward Islands

Virgin Is

ANTIGUA AND BARBUDA
Guadeloupe (France)
DOMINICA
Martinique (France)
ST LUCIA
BARBADOS
ST VINCENT AND THE GRENADINES
GRENADA

TRINIDAD AND TOBAGO
Port of Spain

Windward Islands

Lesser Antilles

CARIBBEAN SEA

Netherlands Antilles
Aruba (Neth.)
Curaçao

MÉXICO

BELIZE
Belmopan

GUATEMALA
Guatemala

HONDURAS
Tegucigalpa

EL SALVADOR
San Salvador

NICARAGUA
Managua

COSTA RICA
San José

PANAMA
Panamá
Colón

SOUTH AMERICA

Equator

Tropic of Cancer

MILES   KILOMETRES
1000
             1500
750   1250
             1000
500   750
             500
250
             250
0   0

BERING
SEA

RUSSIAN
FEDERATION

ARCTIC
OCEAN

BEAUFORT
SEA

U.S.A.

ALASKA

ALEUTIAN ISLANDS

GULF OF ALASKA

PACIFIC

OCEAN

YUKON TERRITORY

NORTHWEST TERRITORIES

C A N

BRITISH COLUMBIA

ALBERTA

SASKATCHEWAN

Edmonton

Calgary

Saskatoon

Regina

Vancouver

WASHINGTON

Seattle

OREGON

IDAHO

MONTANA

NORTH DAK

Boise

UNITED

OF AME

WYOMING

SOUTH DAK

NEBRASK

CALIFORNIA

NEVADA

UTAH

Sacramento

San Francisco

San Jose

Fresno

Reno

METRES
FEET

6000
19686

5000
16404

4000
13124

3000
9843

2000
6562

1000
3281

500
1640

200
656

0

LAND BELOW
SEA LEVEL

200
656

2000
6562

4000
13124

6000
19686

1:15 000 000

MILES   KILOMETRES

© Bartholomew Ltd

Longitude 70° west of Greenwich

A 140° · B · 136° · C · 132° · D · 128° · E · 124° · F · 120° · G · 116° · H

YUKON TERRITORY

NORTHWEST TERRI

Great Bear Lake

MACKENZIE MOUNTAINS

Whitehorse

ALASKA U.S.A.

Alexander Archipelago

Chichagof Island

Baranof Island

Prince of Wales Island

Dixon Entrance

Hecate Strait

Graham Island

Queen Charlotte Islands

Moresby Island

Prince Rupert

Kitimat

COAST

MOUNTAINS

BRITISH

COLUMBIA

ALBERTA

ROCKY

MOUNTAINS

Prince George

Great Slave Lake

Fort Nelson

Fort St. John

Dawson Creek

Grande Prairie

Edmonton

Liard Plateau

Stikine Plateau

Fraser

Plateau

Williams Lake

Quesnel

Columbia Mountains

Cariboo Mountains

Kamloops

Calgary

PACIFIC

OCEAN

Queen Charlotte Sound

Queen Charlotte Strait

Vancouver Island

Vancouver

Victoria

Nanaimo

Abbotsford

Chilliwack

Kelowna

Penticton

Okanagan

WASHINGTON

IDAHO

CANADA
U.S.A.

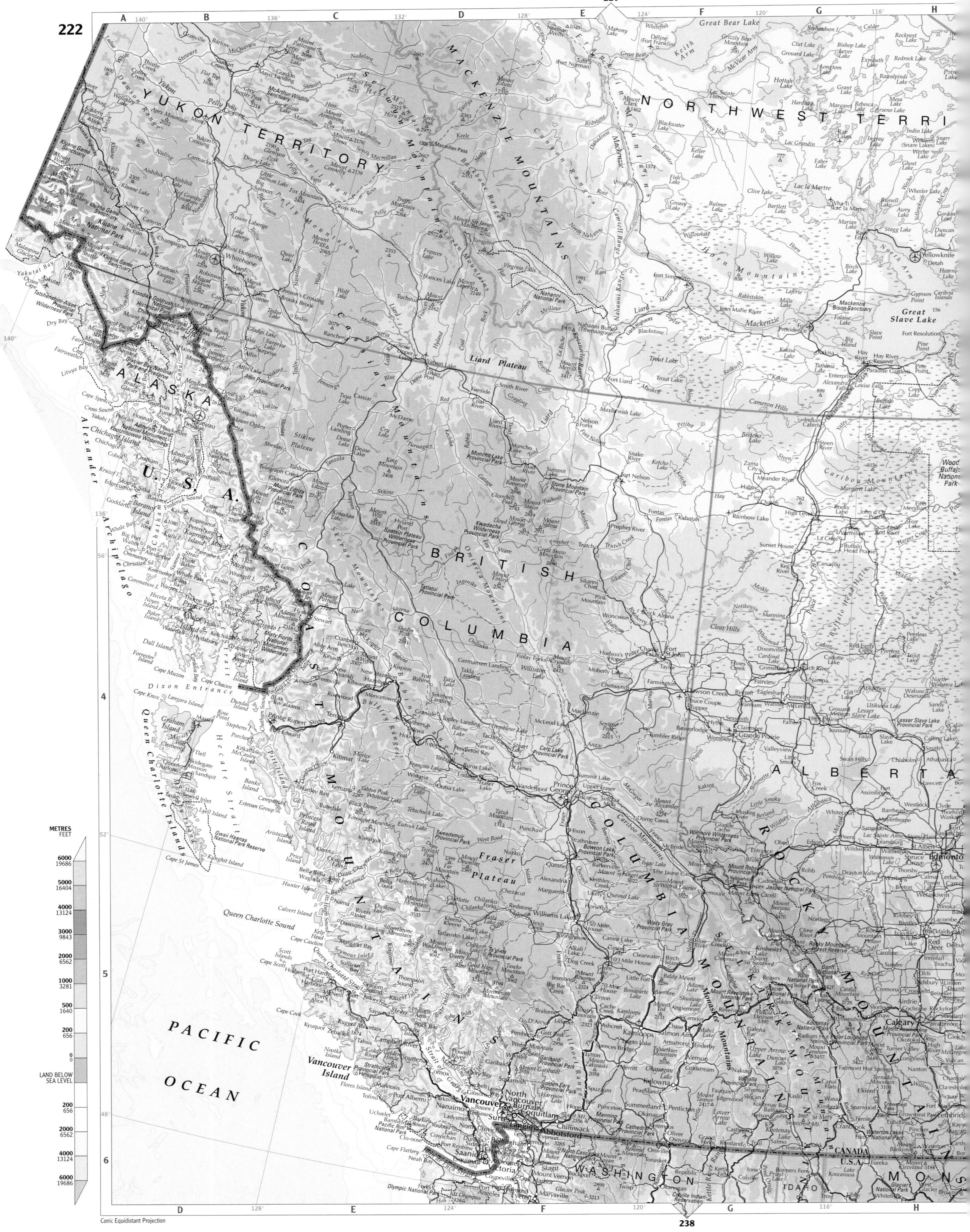

Conic Equidistant Projection

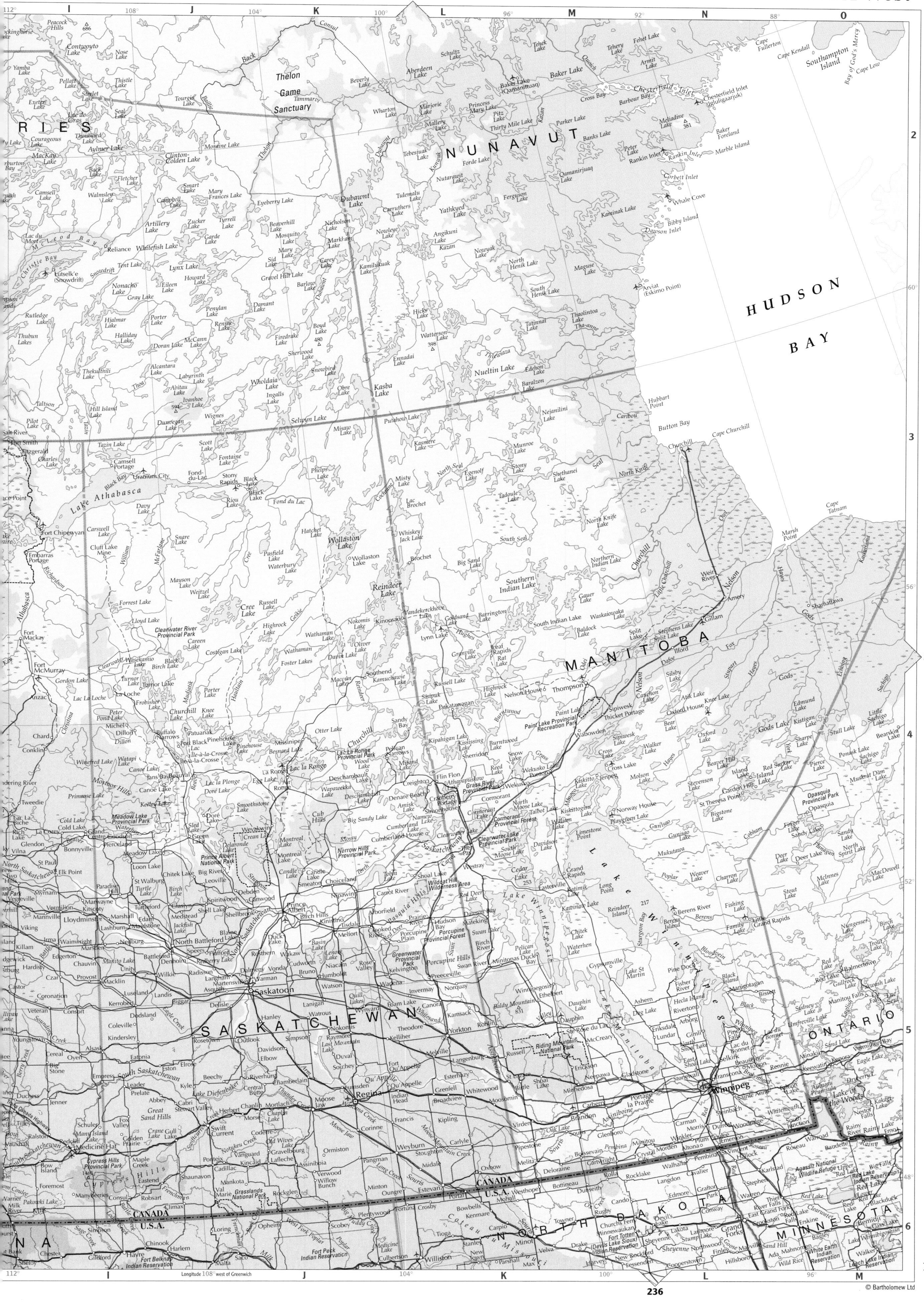

NUNAVUT

HUDSON

BAY

Thelon
Game
Sanctuary

Lake Athabasca

MANITOBA

SASKATCHEWAN

ONTARIO

NORTH DAKOTA

MINNESOTA

CANADA
U.S.A.

Winnipeg

Saskatoon

Regina

Prince Albert

Lake Winnipeg

Lake Winnipegosis

Lake Manitoba

Churchill

Reindeer Lake

Wollaston Lake

Dubawnt Lake

MILES   KILOMETRES

250   400
        350
200   300
        250
150   200
100   150
        100
50   50

0   0

1:6 000 000

Longitude 108° west of Greenwich

© Bartholomew Ltd

224

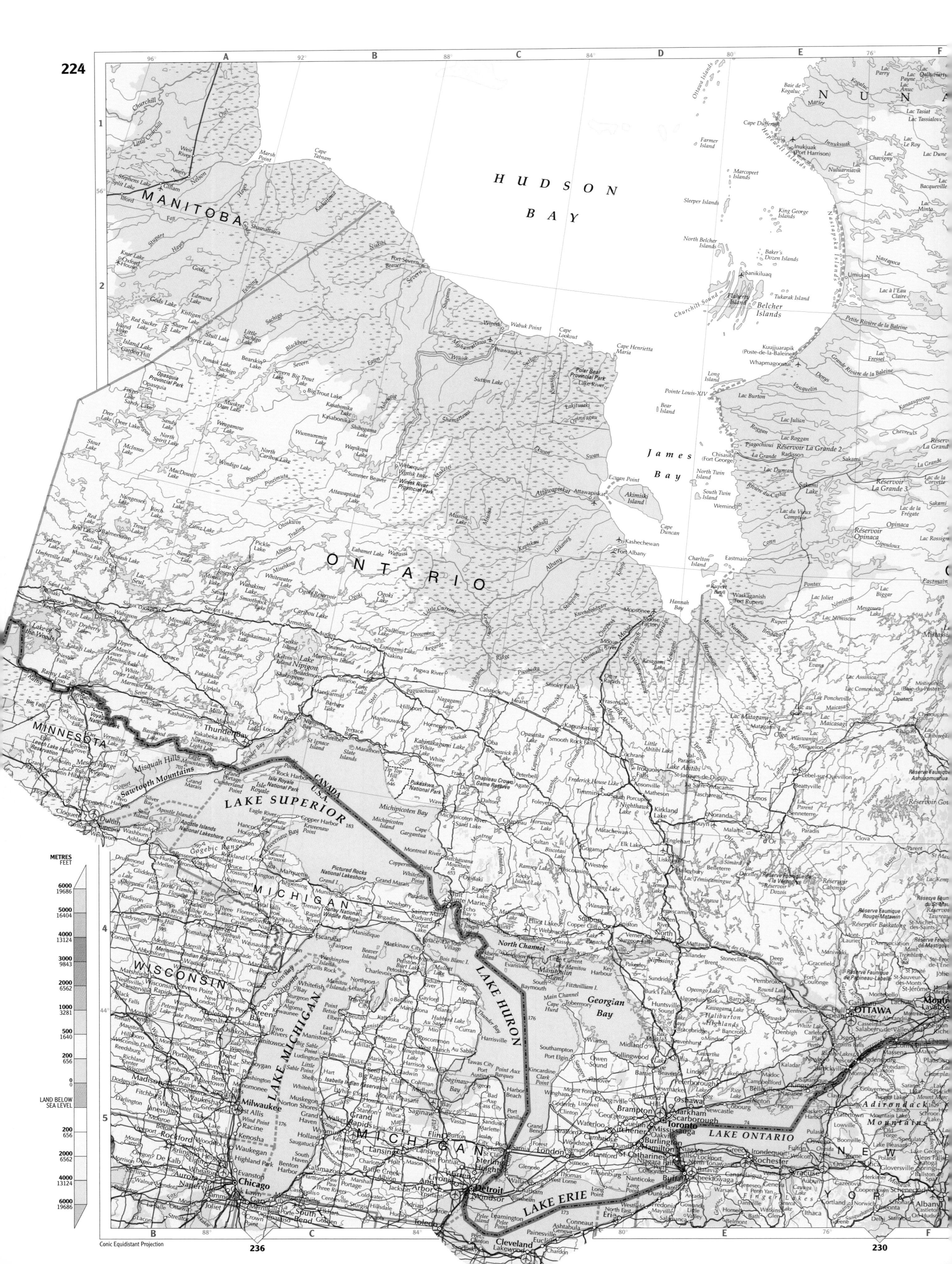

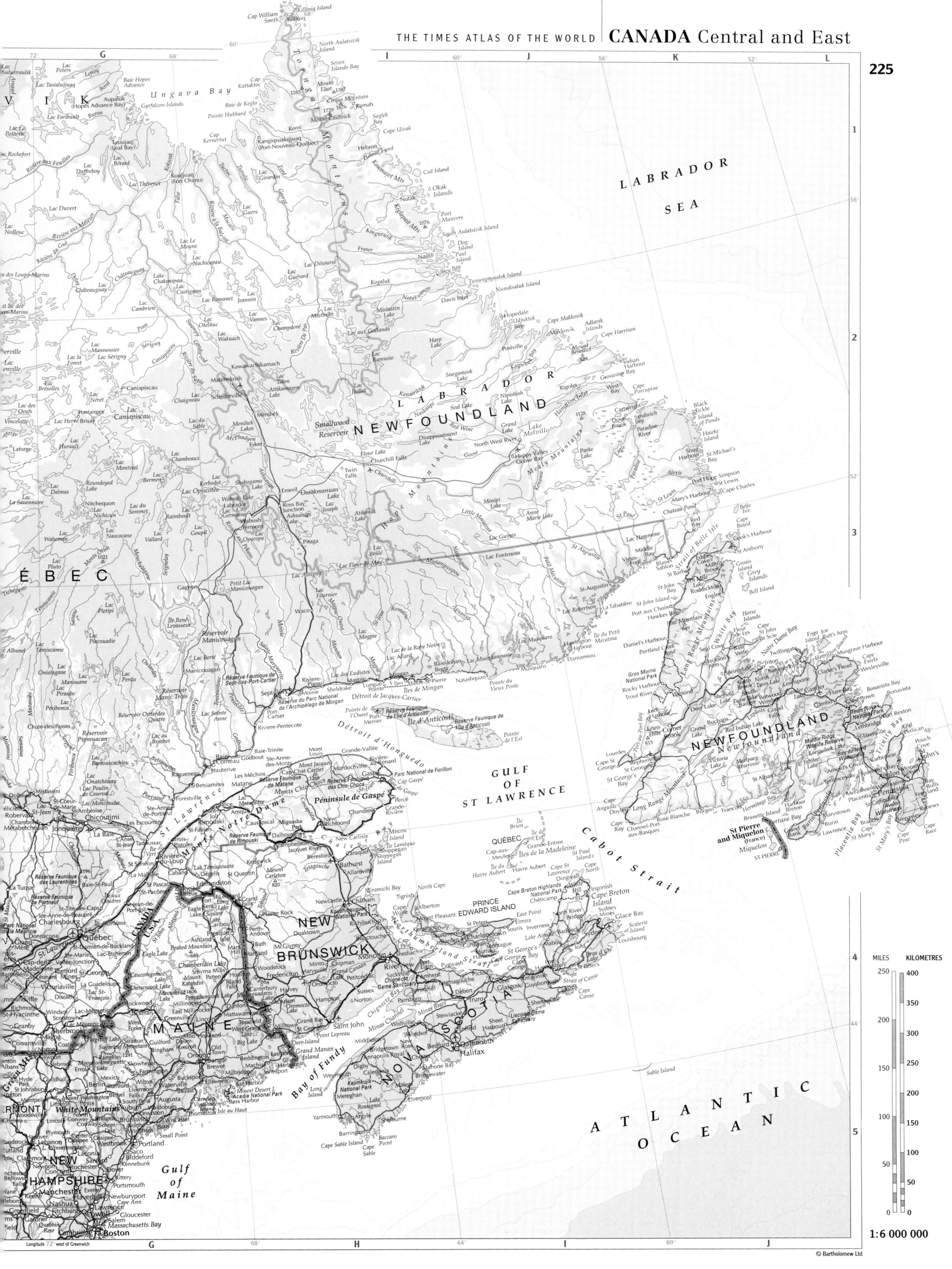

L A B R A D O R

S E A

L A B R A D O R

N E W F O U N D L A N D

NEWFOUNDLAND
Newfoundland

GULF
OF
ST LAWRENCE

Cabot Strait

St Pierre
and Miquelon
(France)
ST-PIERRE

QUÉBEC

Péninsule de Gaspé

Chaleur Bay

PRINCE
EDWARD ISLAND

NEW
BRUNSWICK

NOVA SCOTIA

MAINE

Bay of Fundy

Northumberland Strait

Cape Breton
Island

Halifax

A T L A N T I C

O C E A N

Ungava Bay

ÉBEC

VIK

NEW
HAMPSHIRE

Gulf
of
Maine

RMONT

Boston

Massachusetts Bay

MILES   KILOMETRES

250 — 400

— 350

200 — 300

— 250

150 — 200

— 150

100 —

— 100

50 —

— 50

0 — 0

1:6 000 000

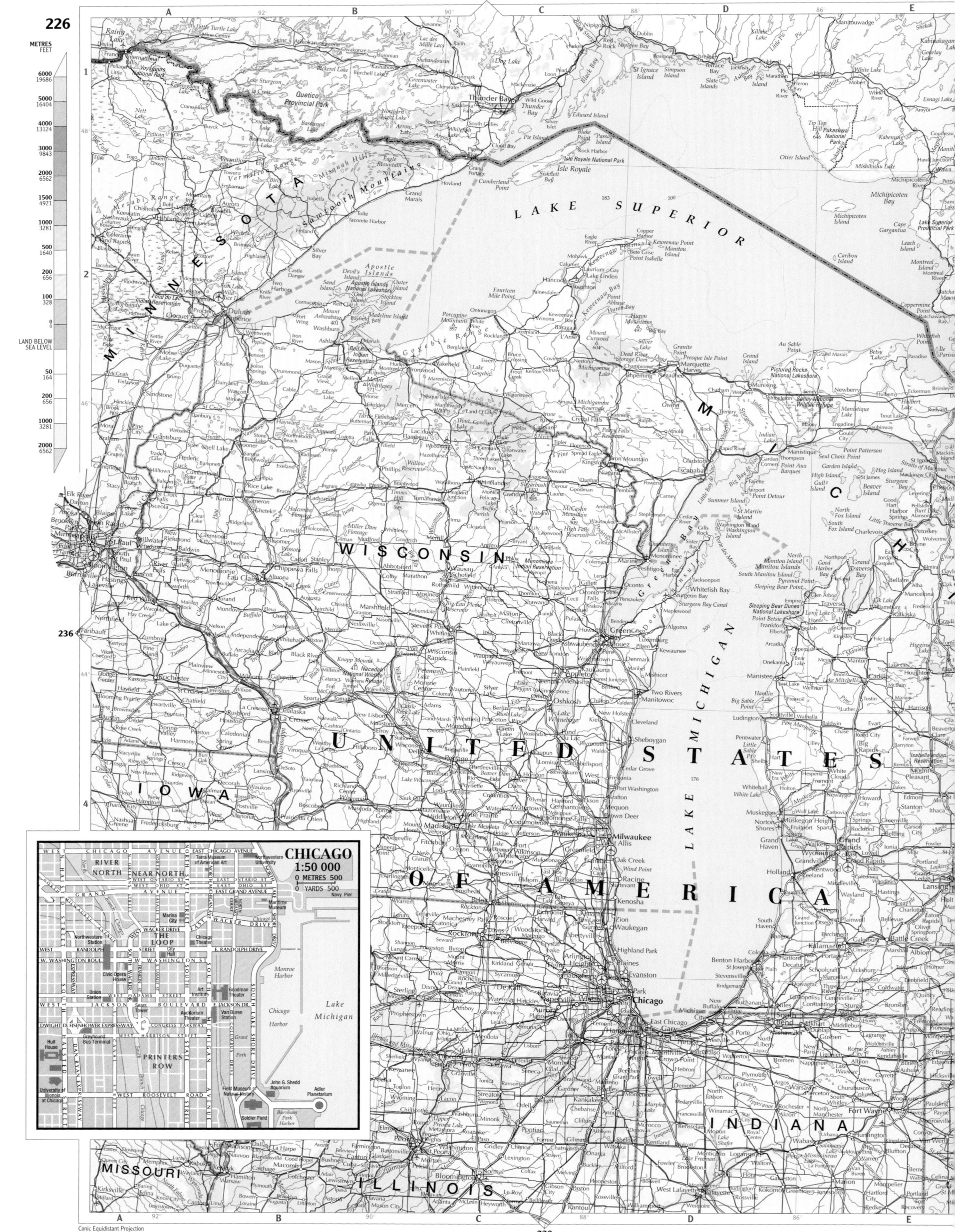

METRES
FEET

6000
19686

5000
16404

4000
13124

3000
9843

2000
6562

1500
4921

1000
3281

500
1640

200
656

100
328

0
0

LAND BELOW
SEA LEVEL

50
164

200
656

1000
3281

2000
6562

LAKE SUPERIOR

MINNESOTA

Quetico
Provincial Park

Thunder Bay

Isle Royale National Park

MICHIGAN

WISCONSIN

Lake
Superior

Duluth

UNITED STATES

LAKE MICHIGAN

Green Bay

OF AMERICA

Milwaukee

IOWA

Madison

Rockford

Chicago

ILLINOIS

MISSOURI

INDIANA

Lake
Michigan

CHICAGO
1:50 000
0 METRES 500
0 YARDS 500

RIVER
NORTH

NEAR NORTH

THE
LOOP

Navy Pier

Maritime
Museum

Marina
City

Chicago
Theater

Art
Institute

Sears
Tower

Auditorium
Theater

Goodman
Theater

Van Buren
Station

Grant
Park

Monroe
Harbor

Chicago
Harbor

Lake
Michigan

Greyhound
Bus Terminal

Hull
House

University of
Illinois at Chicago

PRINTERS
ROW

Field Museum
of Natural History

John G. Shedd
Aquarium

Adler
Planetarium

Soldier Field

Burnham
Park Harbor

Conic Equidistant Projection

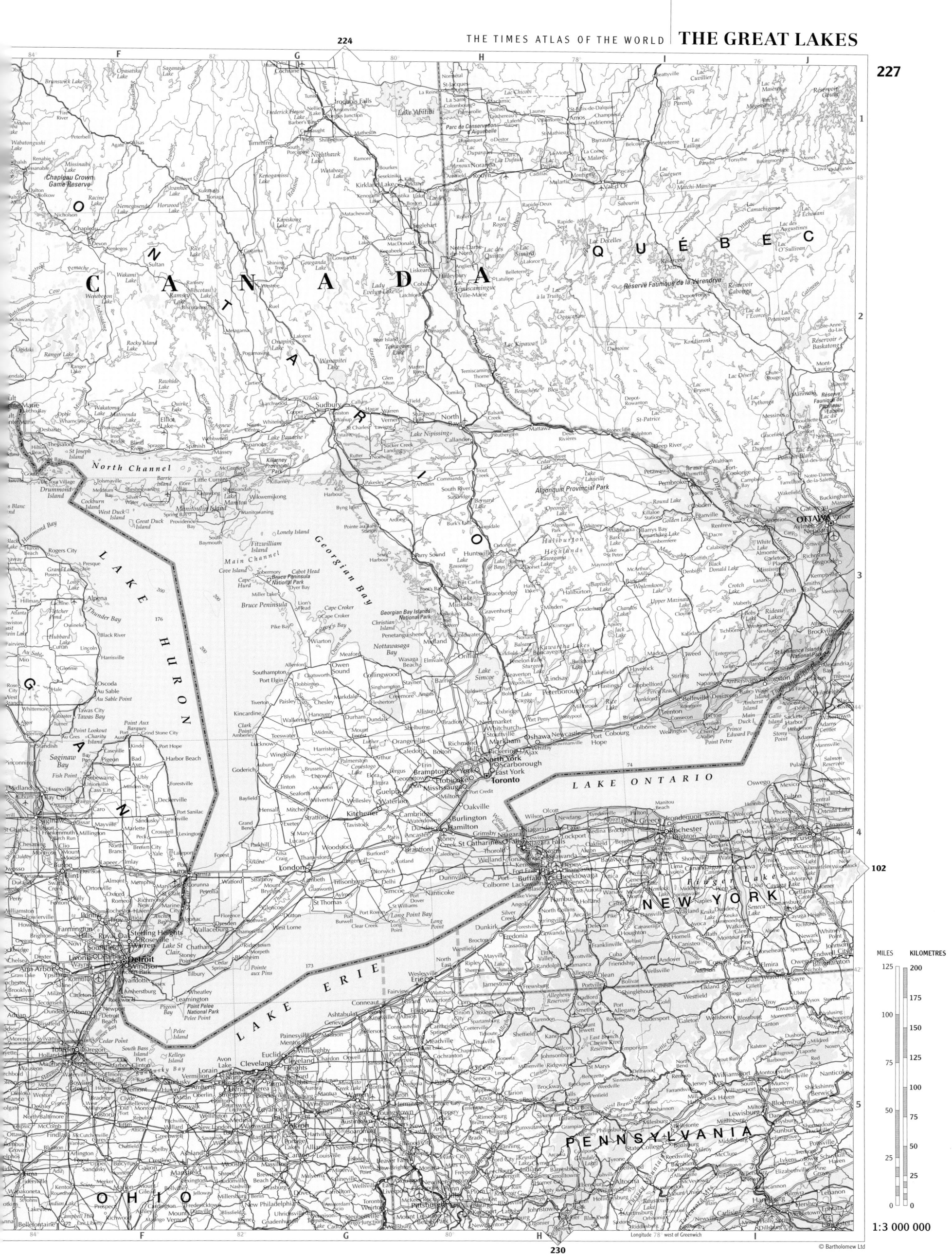

C A N A D A

Q U É B E C

O N T A R I O

M I C H I G A N

LAKE HURON

North Channel

Georgian Bay

Manitoulin Island

Bruce Peninsula

Algonquin Provincial Park

OTTAWA

Sudbury

North Bay

Lake Nipissing

Toronto

Mississauga

Hamilton

LAKE ONTARIO

Buffalo

Rochester

Syracuse

NEW YORK

LAKE ERIE

Detroit

Windsor

Cleveland

Toledo

O H I O

P E N N S Y L V A N I A

MILES   KILOMETRES

125   200

          175

100   150

          125

75   100

          75

50

          50

25   25

0   0

102

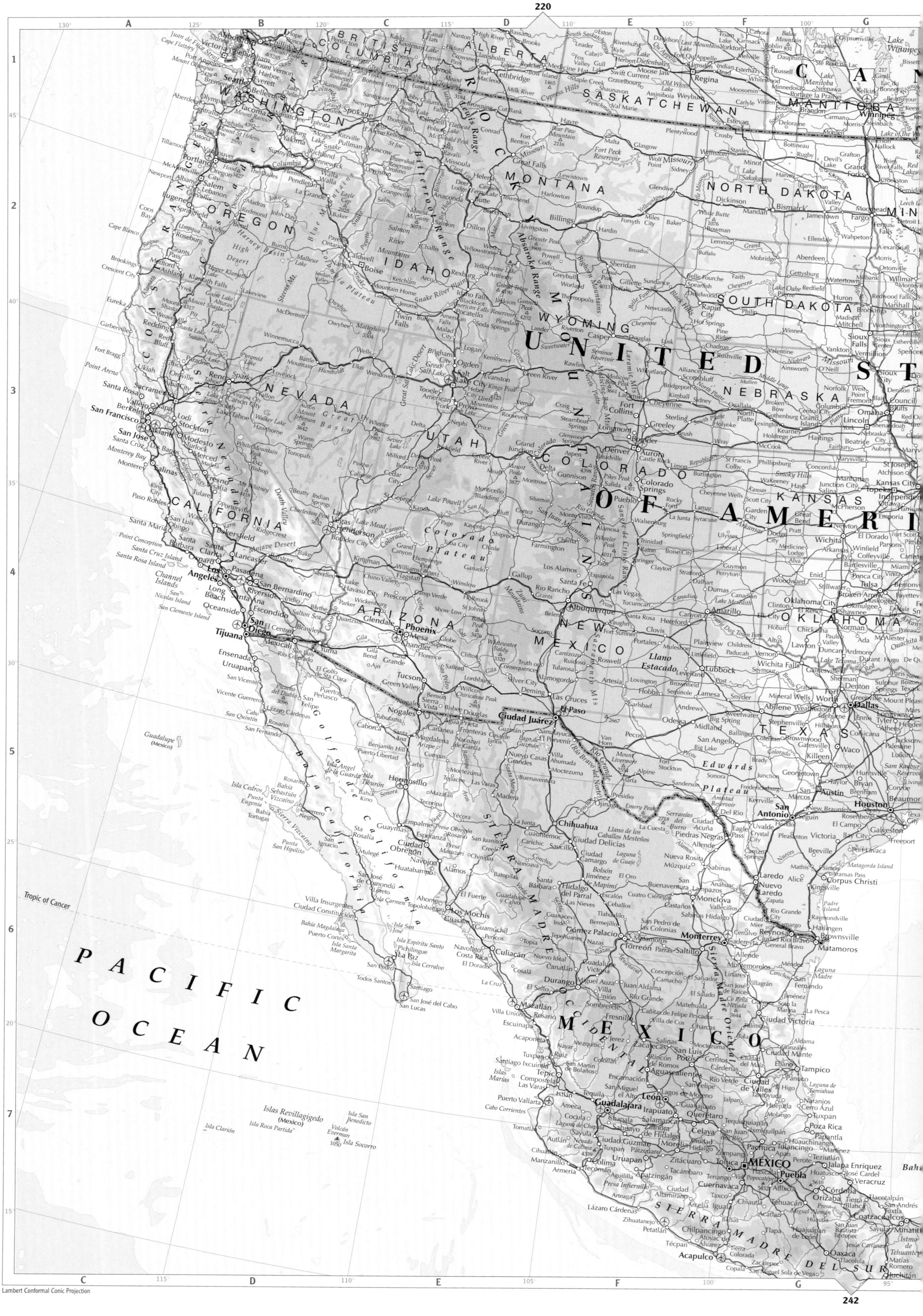
220
BRITISH COLUMBIA
ALBERTA
SASKATCHEWAN
MANITOBA
WASHINGTON
OREGON
IDAHO
MONTANA
NORTH DAKOTA
SOUTH DAKOTA
WYOMING
NEBRASKA
NEVADA
UTAH
COLORADO
KANSAS
CALIFORNIA
ARIZONA
NEW MEXICO
OKLAHOMA
TEXAS
UNITED STATES OF AMERICA
MEXICO
PACIFIC OCEAN
Golfo de California
Baja California
SIERRA MADRE OCCIDENTAL
SIERRA MADRE ORIENTAL
SIERRA MADRE DEL SUR
ROCKY MOUNTAINS
Tropic of Cancer
Great Basin
Colorado Plateau
Llano Estacado
Edwards Plateau
Islas Revillagigedo (Mexico)
Guadalupe (Mexico)
Seattle
Portland
San Francisco
San Jose
Los Angeles
San Diego
Tijuana
Phoenix
Salt Lake City
Denver
El Paso
Ciudad Juárez
Dallas
Houston
San Antonio
Monterrey
Guadalajara
MÉXICO
Winnipeg
Regina
Chihuahua
Acapulco
242

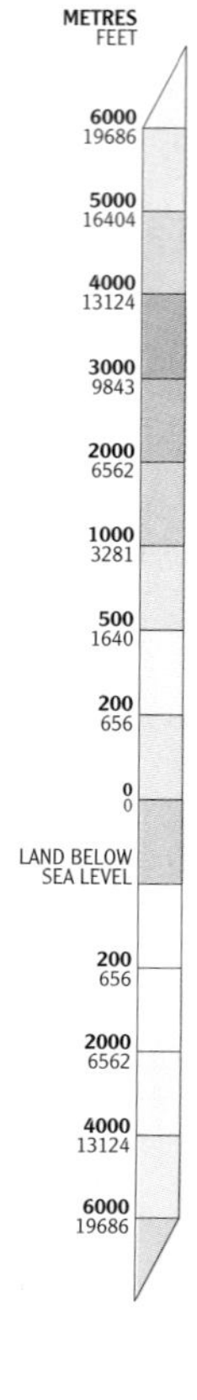
METRES
FEET
6000 19686
5000 16404
4000 13124
3000 9843
2000 6562
1000 3281
500 1640
200 656
0 0
LAND BELOW SEA LEVEL
200 656
2000 6562
4000 13124
6000 19686

Lambert Conformal Conic Projection

GULF OF MEXICO

A T L A N T I C

O C E A N

THE BAHAMAS

CUBA

LA HABANA
(Havana)

WEST INDIES

Turks and
Caicos Islands
(U.K.)

HISPANIOLA

HAITI
PORT-AU-
PRINCE

DOMINICAN
REPUBLIC
SANTO
DOMINGO

Puerto
Rico
(U.S.A.)

Bermuda
(U.K.) ·HAMILTON

JAMAICA
KINGSTON

Cayman Islands
(U.K.)

G R E A T E R A N T I L L E S

C A R I B B E A N   S E A

YUCATÁN

GUATEMALA

BELIZE

Tropic of Cancer

MILES   KILOMETRES
500   800
         700
400   600
         500
300   400
         400
200   300
         200
100
         100
0   0

247

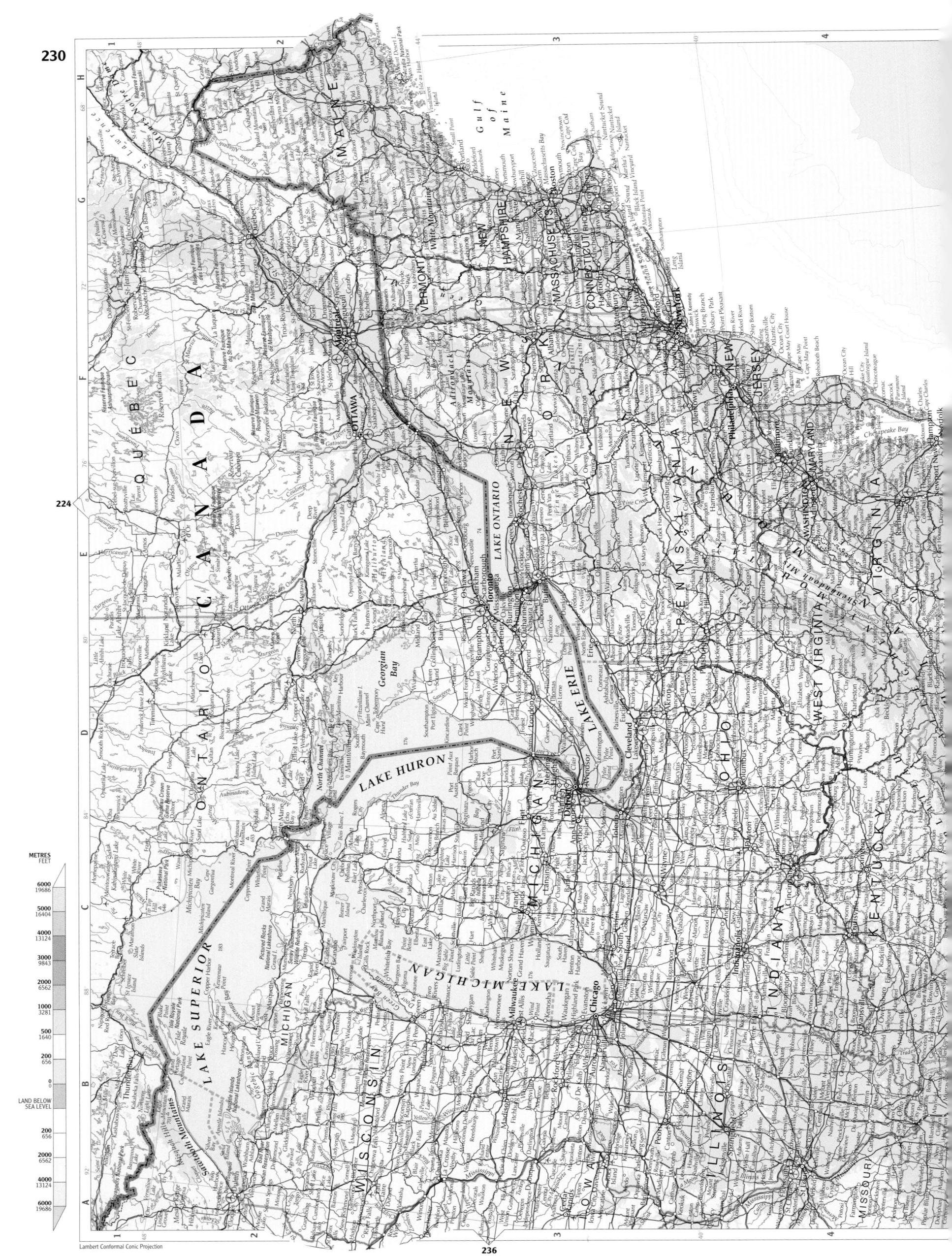

1:6 000 000

© Bartholomew Ltd

METRES
FEET

6000
19686

5000
16404

4000
13124

3000
9843

2000
6562

1500
4921

1000
3281

500
1640

200
656

100
328

0
0

LAND BELOW
SEA LEVEL

200
656

1000
3281

2000
6562

Lambert Conformal Conic Projection

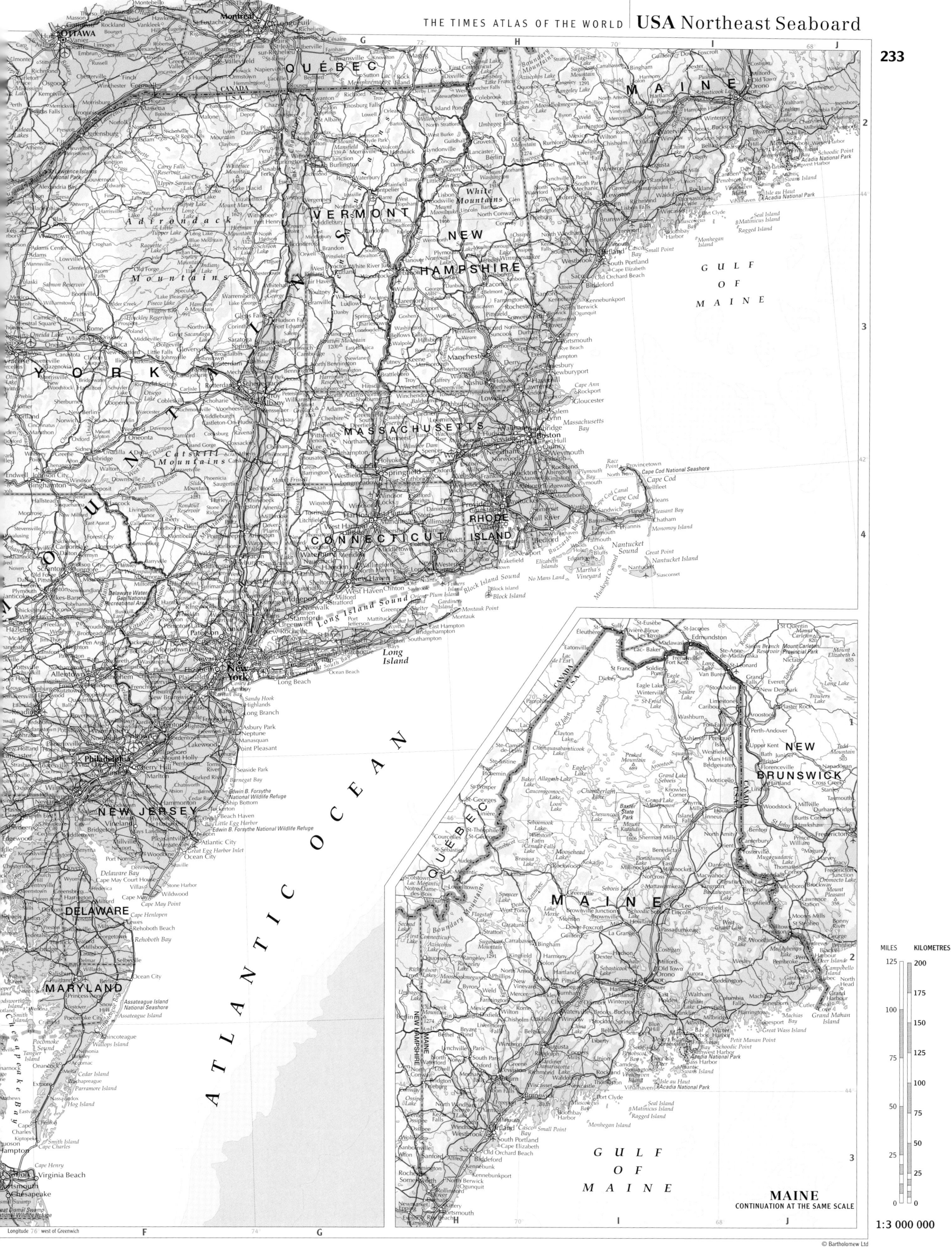

MILES KILOMETRES

MAINE
CONTINUATION AT THE SAME SCALE

1:3 000 000

© Bartholomew Ltd

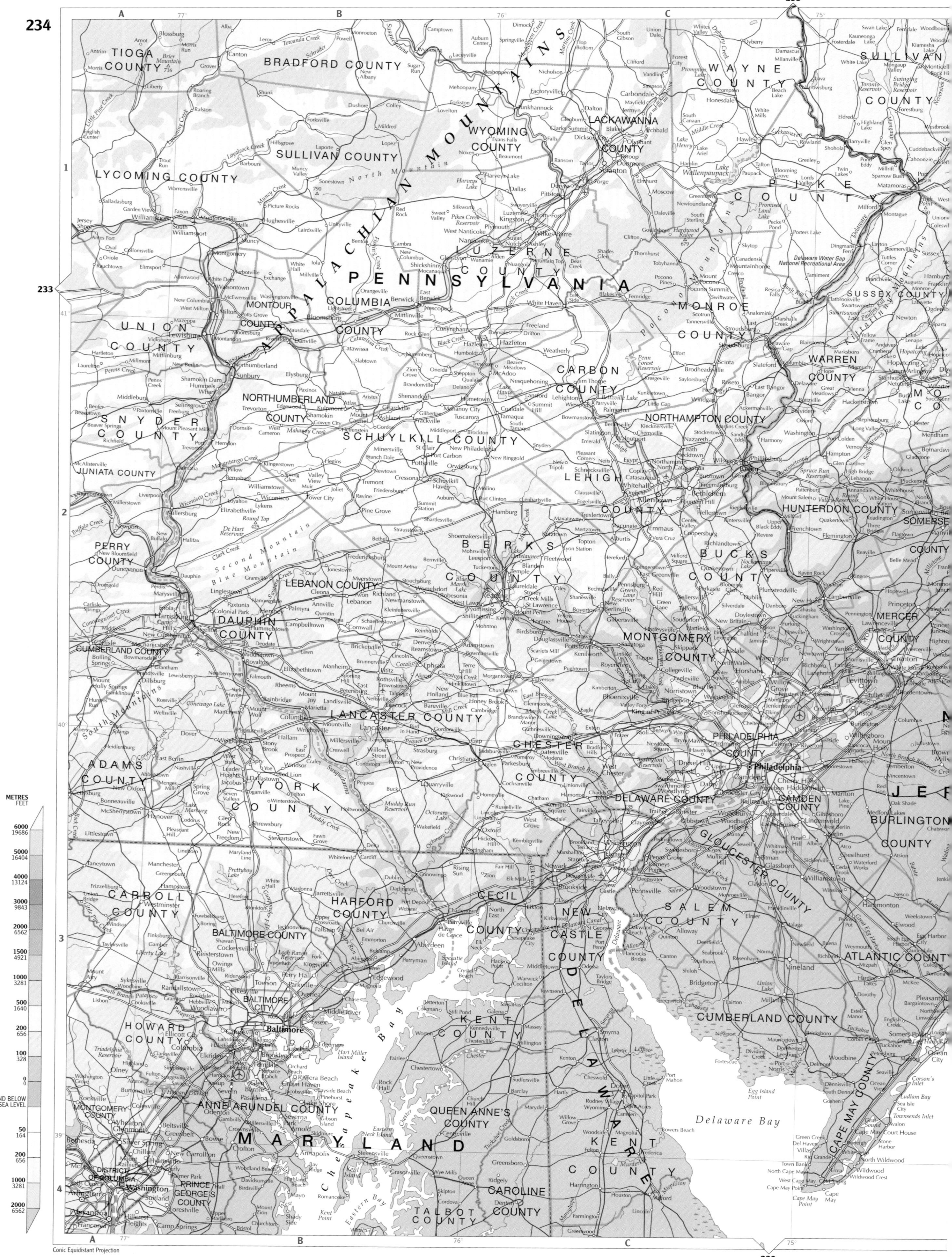

A 77° **B** 76° **C** 75°

TIOGA COUNTY
BRADFORD COUNTY
SULLIVAN COUNTY
WAYNE COUNTY
SULLIVAN COUNTY
LYCOMING COUNTY

1

Brier Mountain 716
Antrim
Arnot
Blossburg
Morris Run
Canton
Grover
Towanda Creek
Leroy
Powell
Monroeton
Camptown
Dimock
Springville
Auburn Center
Union Dale
White Valley
Dyberry
Damascus

WYOMING COUNTY
LACKAWANNA COUNTY
LUZERNE COUNTY
PIKE COUNTY

233
41°

UNION COUNTY
MONTOUR
COLUMBIA COUNTY
NORTHUMBERLAND COUNTY
SNYDER COUNTY
JUNIATA COUNTY
MONROE COUNTY
CARBON COUNTY
SCHUYLKILL COUNTY
WARREN COUNTY
SUSSEX COUNTY
LEHIGH COUNTY
NORTHAMPTON COUNTY
HUNTERDON COUNTY
SOMERSET COUNTY

APPALACHIAN MOUNTAINS
PENNSYLVANIA

2

PERRY COUNTY
BERKS COUNTY
BUCKS COUNTY
LEBANON COUNTY
DAUPHIN COUNTY
MONTGOMERY COUNTY
MERCER COUNTY

Harrisburg
CUMBERLAND COUNTY
Carlisle
Lancaster
LANCASTER COUNTY
CHESTER COUNTY
PHILADELPHIA COUNTY
Philadelphia
CAMDEN COUNTY
BURLINGTON COUNTY

40°

ADAMS COUNTY
YORK COUNTY
DELAWARE COUNTY
GLOUCESTER COUNTY
Trenton

METRES FEET
6000 19686
5000 16404
4000 13124
3000 9843
2000 6562
1500 4921
1000 3281
500 1640
200 656
100 328
0 0
LAND BELOW SEA LEVEL
50 164
200 656
1000 3281
2000 6562

CARROLL COUNTY
HARFORD COUNTY
CECIL COUNTY
NEW CASTLE COUNTY
SALEM COUNTY
ATLANTIC COUNTY

BALTIMORE COUNTY
Baltimore
BALTIMORE CITY
CUMBERLAND COUNTY

3

HOWARD COUNTY
KENT COUNTY
DELAWARE

ANNE ARUNDEL COUNTY
Annapolis
QUEEN ANNE'S COUNTY
KENT COUNTY
CAPE MAY COUNTY

MONTGOMERY COUNTY
DISTRICT OF COLUMBIA
Washington
PRINCE GEORGE'S COUNTY
MARYLAND
Chesapeake Bay
Eastern Bay
Delaware Bay

39°

TALBOT COUNTY
CAROLINE COUNTY

4

Conic Equidistant Projection

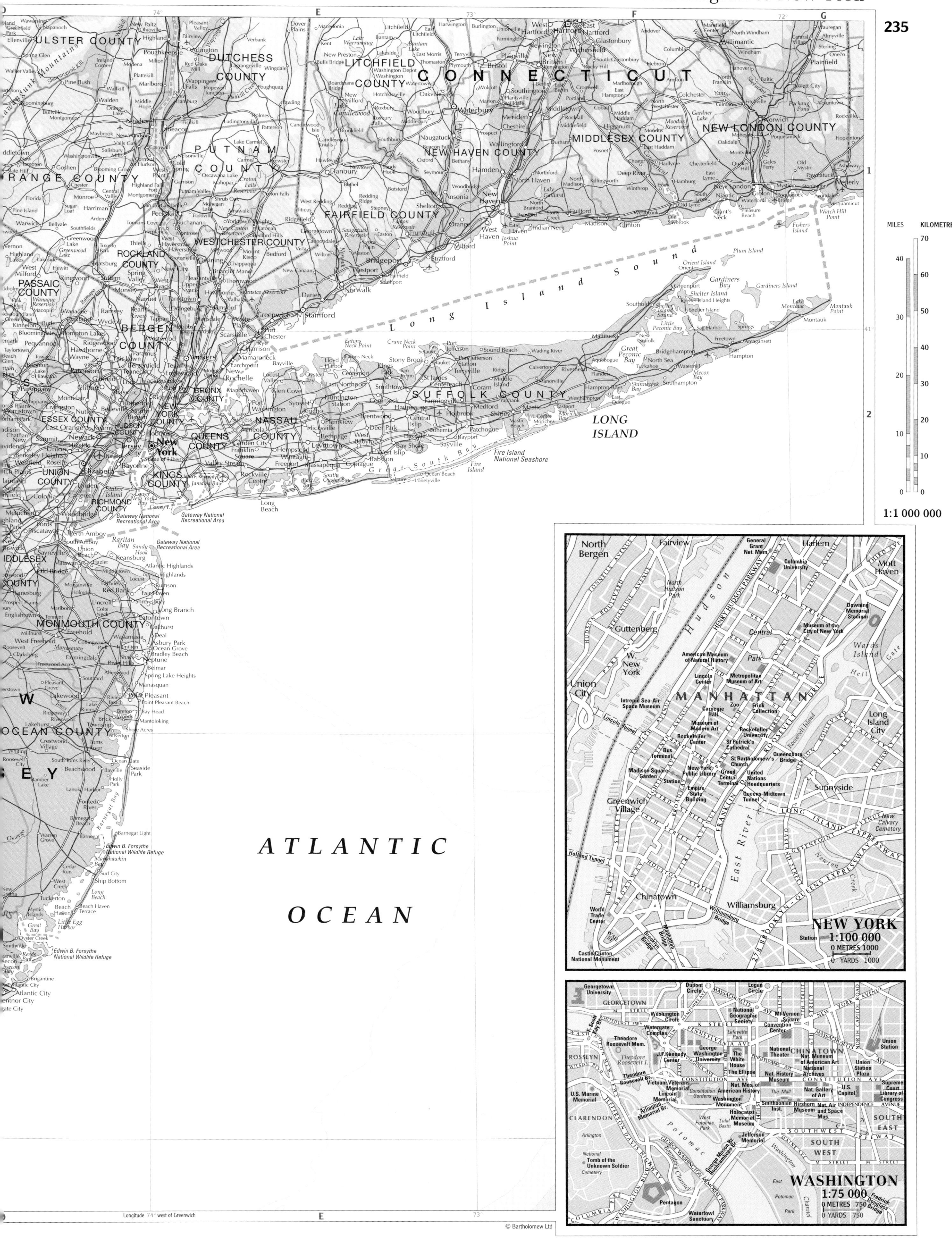

ULSTER COUNTY
DUTCHESS COUNTY
LITCHFIELD COUNTY
CONNECTICUT
ORANGE COUNTY
PUTNAM COUNTY
NEW HAVEN COUNTY
MIDDLESEX COUNTY
NEW LONDON COUNTY
PASSAIC COUNTY
ROCKLAND COUNTY
WESTCHESTER COUNTY
FAIRFIELD COUNTY
BERGEN COUNTY
ESSEX COUNTY
HUDSON COUNTY
NEW YORK COUNTY
BRONX COUNTY
QUEENS COUNTY
NASSAU COUNTY
SUFFOLK COUNTY
UNION COUNTY
KINGS COUNTY
RICHMOND COUNTY
MIDDLESEX COUNTY
MONMOUTH COUNTY
OCEAN COUNTY

New York

Long Island Sound

LONG ISLAND

Gateway National Recreational Area

Fire Island National Seashore

Edwin B. Forsythe National Wildlife Refuge

ATLANTIC OCEAN

MILES   KILOMETRES
70
40   60
50
30   40
20   30
10   20
10
0   0

1:1 000 000

Longitude 74° west of Greenwich

© Bartholomew Ltd

North Bergen
Fairview
General Grant Nat. Mem.
Harlem
Mott Haven
Guttenberg
North Hudson Park
Columbia University
W. New York
American Museum of Natural History
Central Park
Museum of the City of New York
Ward's Island
Union City
MANHATTAN
Metropolitan Museum of Art
Lincoln Center
Hell Gate
Carnegie Hall
Zoo
Frick Collection
Long Island City
Intrepid Sea-Air-Space Museum
Museum of Modern Art
Rockefeller University
Bus Terminal
Rockefeller Center
St Patrick's Cathedral
Queensboro Bridge
Sunnyside
New York Public Library
St Bartholomew's Church
Madison Square Garden
Grand Central Terminal
United Nations Headquarters
Station
Empire State Building
Queens-Midtown Tunnel
Greenwich Village
Franklin
East River
New Calvary Cemetery
Holland Tunnel
LONG ISLAND EXPRESSWAY
Chinatown
Williamsburg
Williamsburg Bridge
World Trade Center
Castle Clinton National Monument

NEW YORK
1:100 000
0 METRES 1000
0 YARDS 1000

Georgetown University
Dupont Circle
Logan Circle
GEORGETOWN
National Geographic Society
Mt Vernon Square Convention Center
Washington Circle
Watergate Complex
Lafayette Square
ROSSLYN
Theodore Roosevelt Mem.
J.F Kennedy Center
George Washington University
The White House
The Ellipse
National Theater
National Archives
CHINATOWN
Union Station
Nat. Museum of American Art
Theodore Roosevelt I.
Vietnam Veterans Memorial
Constitution Gardens
Nat. Gallery of Art
Union Station Plaza
CLARENDON
U.S. Marine Memorial
Lincoln Memorial
Constitution Hall
American History
Washington Monument
Nat. Air and Space Mus.
Supreme Court
U.S. Capitol
Library of Congress
West Potomac Park
Smithsonian Inst.
Hirshhorn Museum
Holocaust Memorial Museum
SOUTH EAST
Arlington
Jefferson Memorial
SOUTH WEST
Tidal Basin
Tomb of the Unknown Soldier
Pentagon
Waterfowl Sanctuary
Potomac Park

WASHINGTON
1:75 000
0 METRES 750
0 YARDS 750

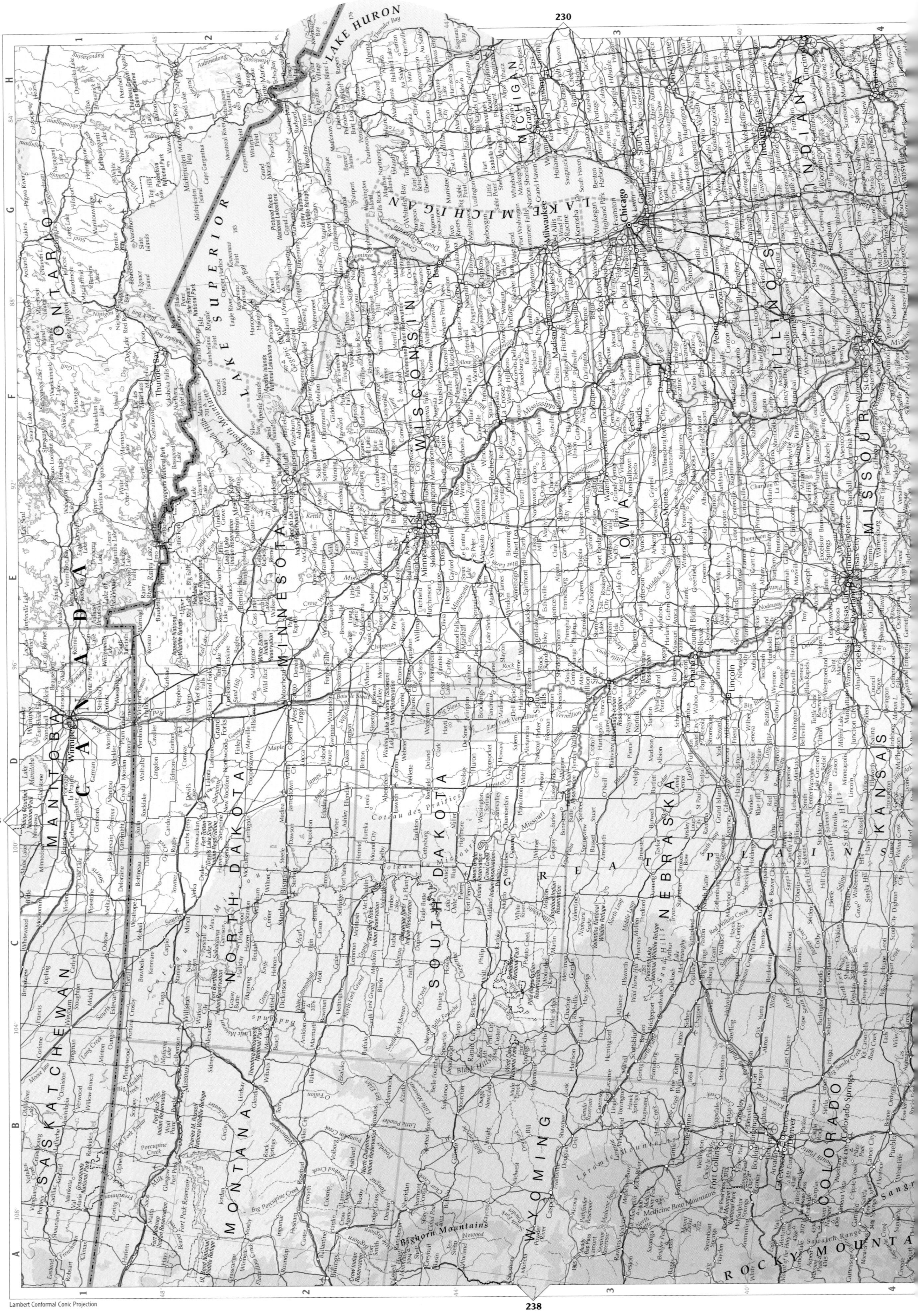

LAKE HURON

LAKE SUPERIOR

LAKE MICHIGAN

CANADA

ONTARIO

MANITOBA

SASKATCHEWAN

MINNESOTA

WISCONSIN

MICHIGAN

INDIANA

ILLINOIS

IOWA

MISSOURI

NORTH DAKOTA

SOUTH DAKOTA

NEBRASKA

KANSAS

MONTANA

WYOMING

COLORADO

GREAT PLAINS

ROCKY MOUNTAINS

Bighorn Mountains

Laramie Mountains

Sawatch Range

Black Hills

Chicago
Milwaukee
Minneapolis
Winnipeg
Sioux Falls
Omaha
Lincoln
Des Moines
Cedar Rapids
Kansas City
Fort Collins
Denver
Colorado Springs
Springfield
Indianapolis

METRES	FEET
6000	19686
5000	16404
4000	13124
3000	9843
2000	6562
1000	3281
500	1640
200	656
0	0
LAND BELOW SEA LEVEL	
200	656
2000	6562
4000	13124
6000	19686

223

Lambert Conformal Conic Projection

1:6 000 000

© Bartholomew Ltd

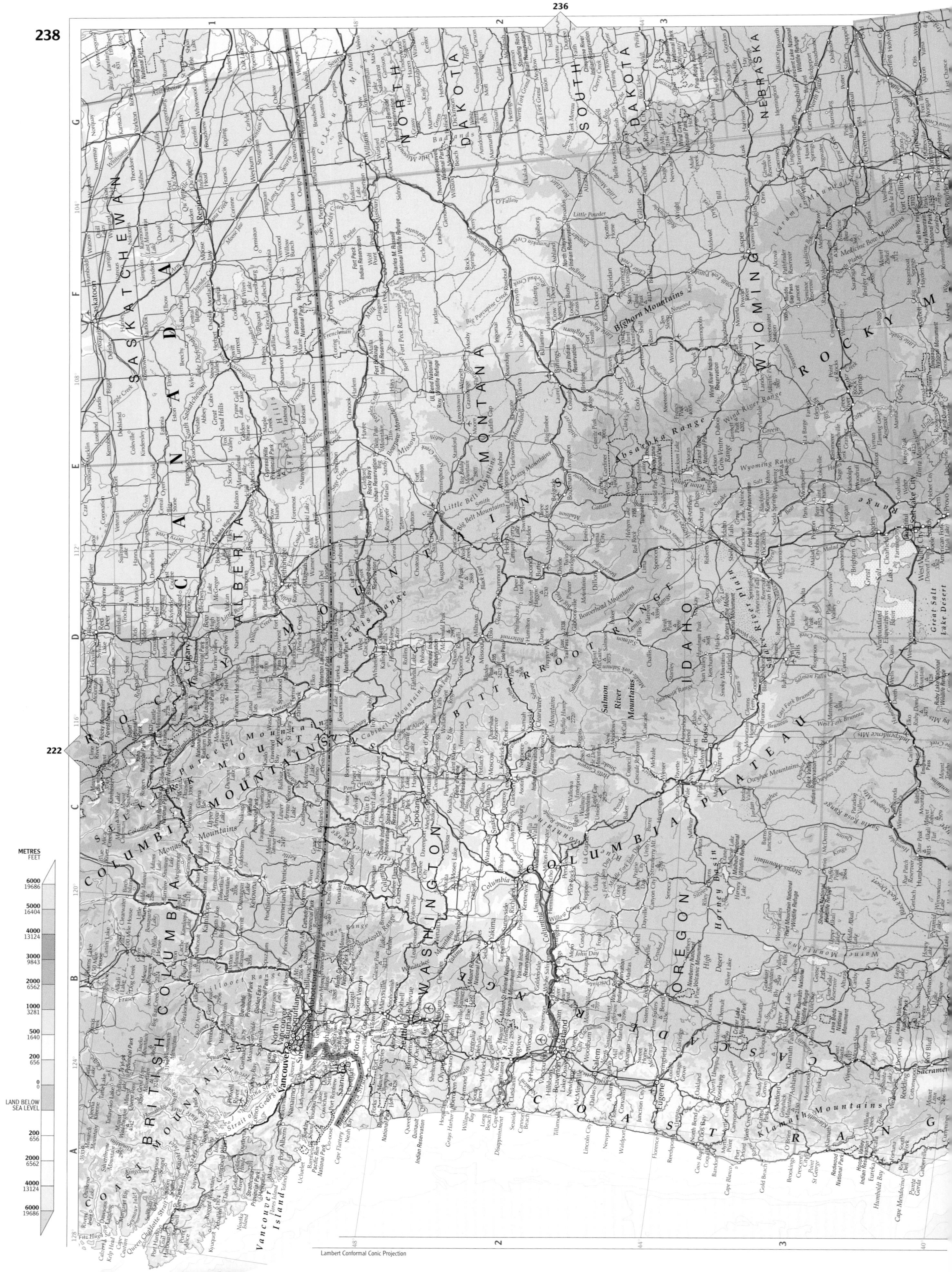

222

METRES
FEET
6000 19686
5000 16404
4000 13124
3000 9843
2000 6562
1000 3281
500 1640
200 656
0
LAND BELOW
SEA LEVEL
200 656
2000 6562
4000 13124
6000 19686

SASKATCHEWAN

ALBERTA

C A N A D A

BRITISH COLUMBIA

NORTH DAKOTA

SOUTH DAKOTA

NEBRASKA

WYOMING

M O N T A N A

I D A H O

W A S H I N G T O N

O R E G O N

R O C K Y   M O U N T A I N S

C O L U M B I A   M O U N T A I N S

COLUMBIA PLATEAU

C A S C A D E   R A N G E

C O A S T   R A N G E

B I T T E R R O O T

Bighorn Mountains

Absaroka Range

Wyoming Range

Bitterroot Range

Lewis Range

Salmon River Mountains

Klamath Mountains

Vancouver Island

Calgary

Red Deer

Saskatoon

Regina

Spokane

Seattle

Vancouver

Portland

Salem

Eugene

Salt Lake City

Great Salt Lake

Great Salt Lake Desert

Missouri

Columbia

Lambert Conformal Conic Projection

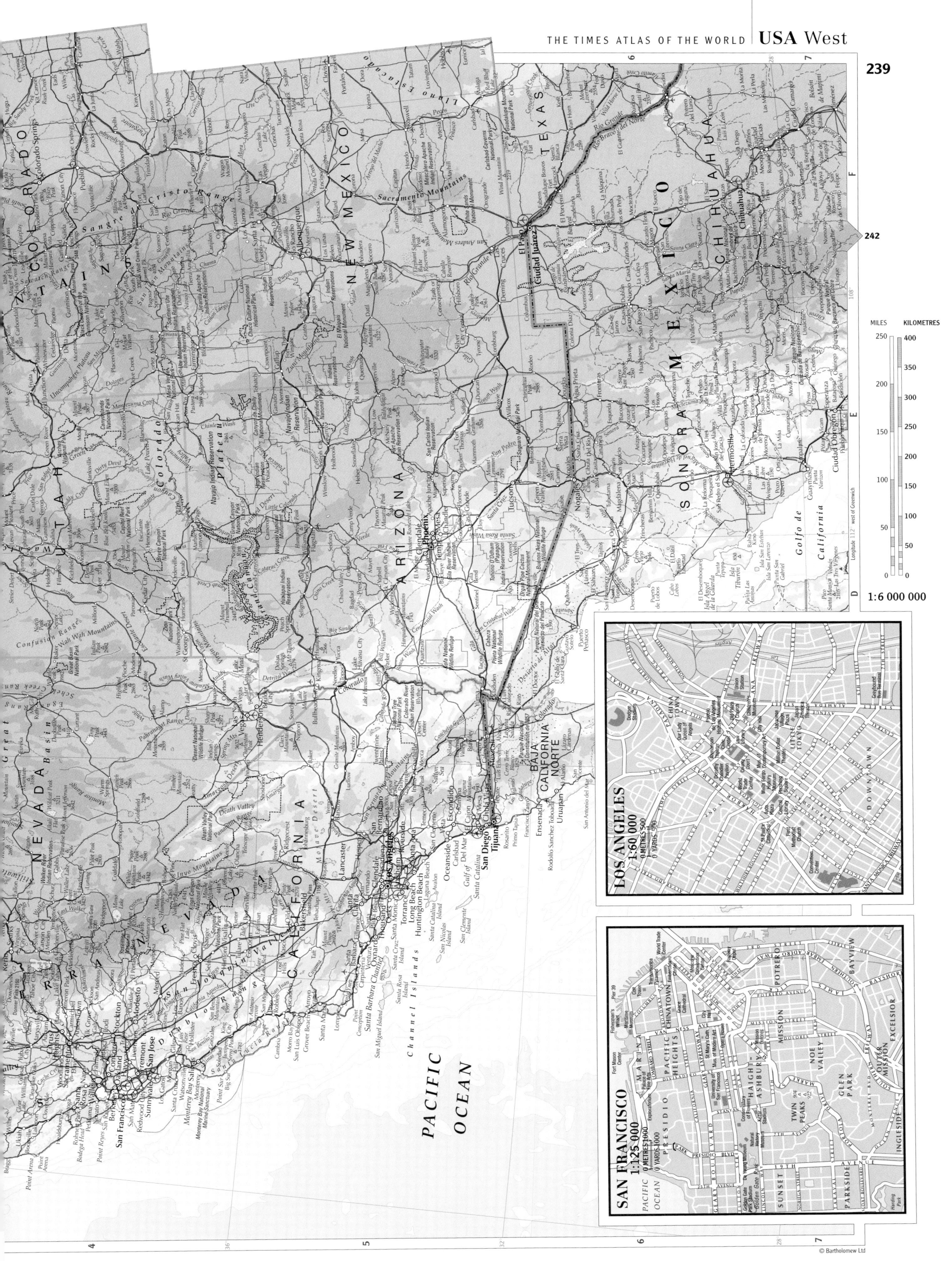

242

MILES   KILOMETRES

250   400

350

200   300

150   250

200

100   150

100

50

50

0   0

1:6 000 000

LOS ANGELES
1:60 000
0 METRES 500
0 YARDS 500

SAN FRANCISCO
1:125 000
0 METRES 1000
0 YARDS 1000

© Bartholomew Ltd

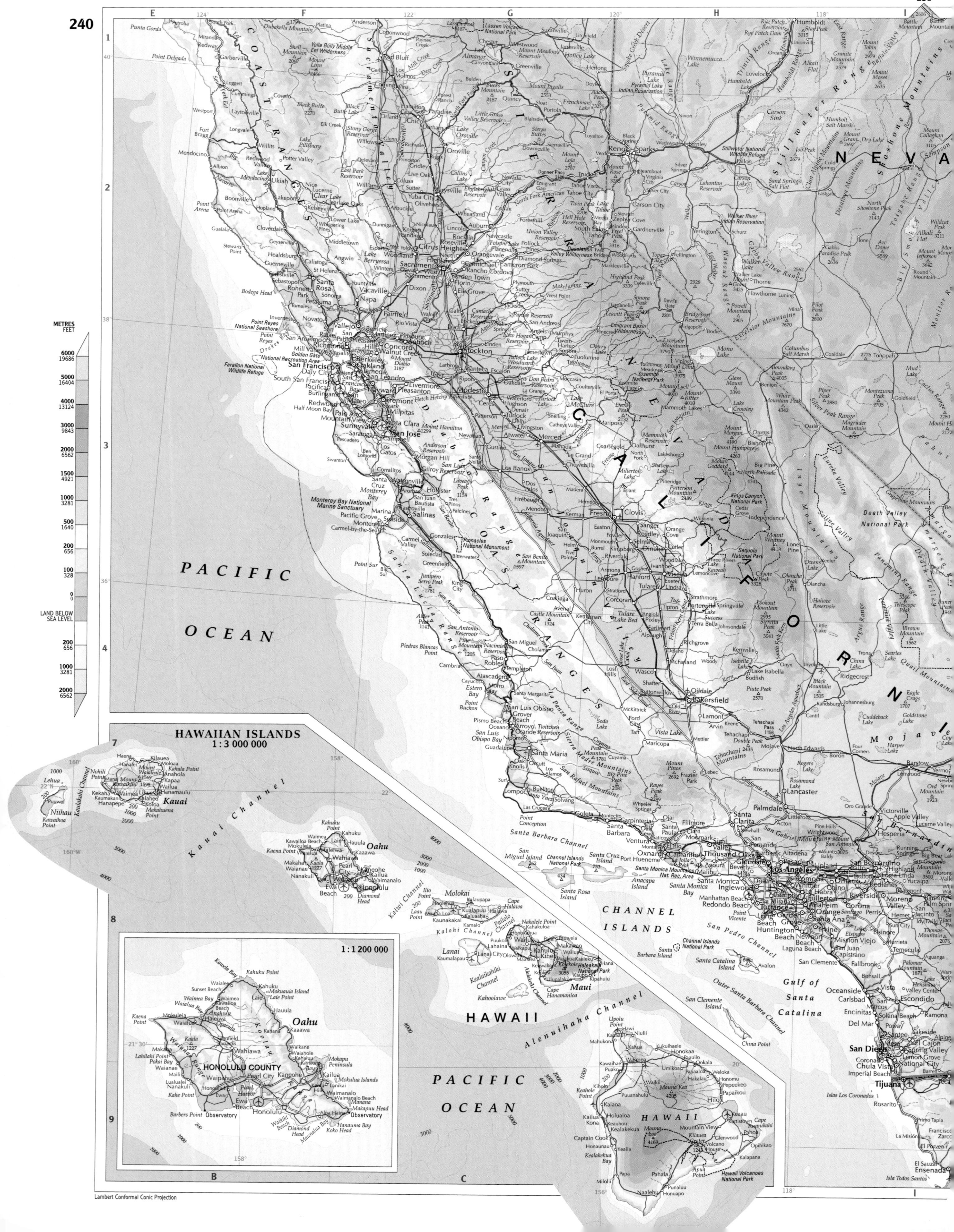

NEVADA

CALIFORNIA

PACIFIC OCEAN

HAWAIIAN ISLANDS
1 : 3 000 000

Kauai

Oahu

Molokai

Lanai

Maui

HAWAII

PACIFIC OCEAN

CHANNEL ISLANDS

Gulf of Santa Catalina

1 : 1 200 000
HONOLULU COUNTY

Oahu

Honolulu

METRES FEET
6000 19686
5000 16404
4000 13124
3000 9843
2000 6562
1500 4921
1000 3281
500 1640
200 656
100 328
0 0
LAND BELOW SEA LEVEL
200 656
1000 3281
2000 6562

Lambert Conformal Conic Projection

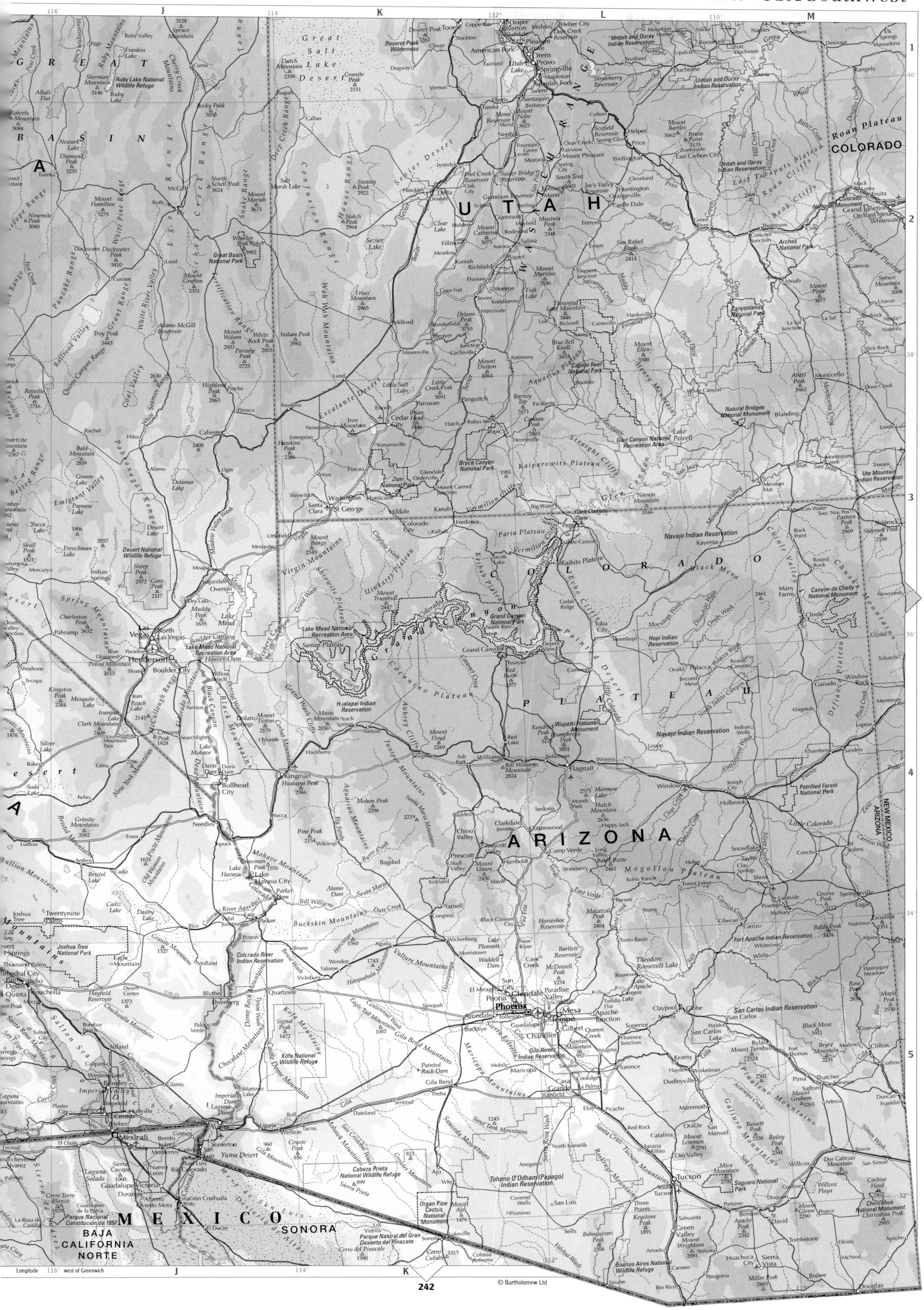

UTAH

ARIZONA

COLORADO

NEW MEXICO

MEXICO

BAJA CALIFORNIA NORTE

SONORA

GREAT BASIN

Great Salt Lake Desert

Great Salt Lake

WASATCH RANGE

COLORADO PLATEAU

Grand Canyon National Park

Navajo Indian Reservation

Hopi Indian Reservation

Lake Mead National Recreation Area

Glen Canyon National Recreation Area

Canyonlands National Park

Petrified Forest National Park

Joshua Tree National Park

Mogollon Plateau

Kaiparowits Plateau

Coconino Plateau

Las Vegas
Phoenix
Mesa
Tempe
Tucson
Flagstaff
St George
Cedar City
Kingman
Bullhead City
Boulder City
Henderson
Provo
Orem
Price
Moab
Mexicali

Lake Mead
Lake Powell
Lake Havasu

Salton Sea

© Bartholomew Ltd

Longitude 116° west of Greenwich

1:3 000 000

MILES   KILOMETRES
125   200
100   175
         150
75   125
         100
50   75
25   50
         25
0   0

239

242

STATES OF AMERICA

TEXAS

MISSISSIPPI

LOUISIANA

ALABAMA

FLORIDA

Dallas
Fort Worth
Abilene
Austin
San Antonio
Houston
Beaumont
New Orleans
Baton Rouge
Mobile
Corpus Christi
Laredo
Nuevo Laredo

GULF OF MEXICO

Tropic of Cancer

Monterrey
NUEVO LEON
TAMAULIPAS
Ciudad Victoria
SAN LUIS POTOSI
San Luis Potosí
Ciudad Madero
Tampico
Veracruz
GUANAJUATO
Guanajuato
QUERÉTARO
Querétaro
HIDALGO
Pachuca
MÉXICO
Toluca
MICHOACÁN
MORELOS
PUEBLA
Puebla
TLAXCALA
Jalapa Enríquez
Veracruz
Córdoba
Bahía de Campeche

Campeche
YUCATÁN
Mérida
QUINTANA ROO
Cancún
Cozumel
Chetumal
CAMPECHE
TABASCO
Villahermosa
Coatzacoalcos
Minatitlán

GUERRERO
OAXACA
SIERRA MADRE DEL SUR
Acapulco
Oaxaca
Golfo de Tehuantepec
Istmo de Tehuantepec

CHIAPAS
Tuxtla Gutiérrez

PACIFIC OCEAN

BELIZE
Belize

GUATEMALA
Guatemala

HONDURAS

EL SALVADOR
SAN SALVADOR

Yucatan Channel

Gulf of Honduras

Longitude 100° west of Greenwich

© Bartholomew Ltd

1:6 600 000

MILES   KILOMETRES
250   400
        350
200   300
        250
150   200
        150
100
        100
50   50
0   0

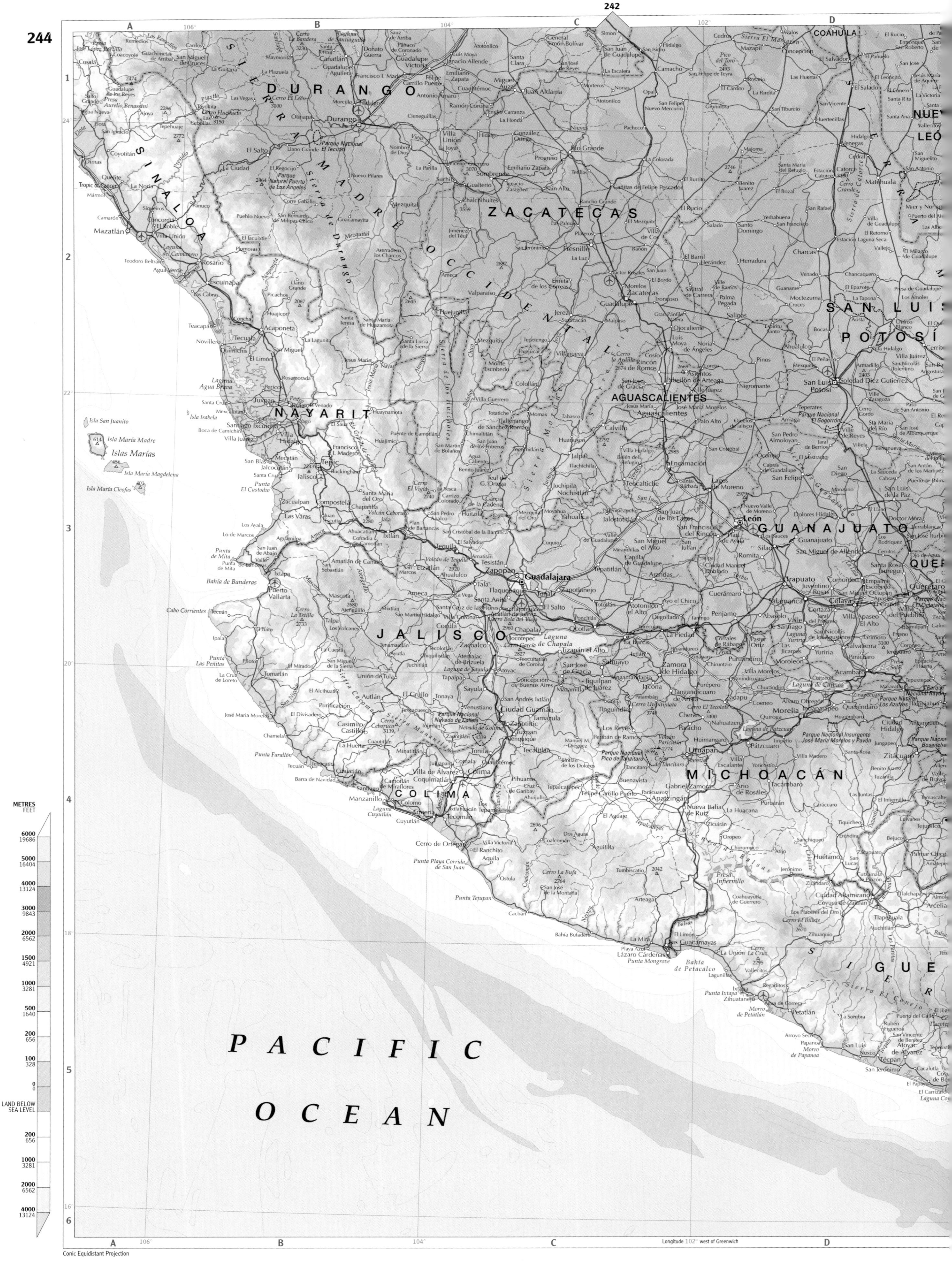

DURANGO

SINALOA

ZACATECAS

NAYARIT

AGUASCALIENTES

SAN LUIS POTOSÍ

JALISCO

GUANAJUATO

COLIMA

MICHOACÁN

COAHUILA

NUEVO LEÓN

QUER

Mazatlán

Durango

Guadalajara

León

San Luis Potosí

Soledad Díez Gutiérrez

Aguascalientes

Zacatecas

Tepic

Colima

Manzanillo

Lázaro Cárdenas

Sierra Madre Occidental

Sierra Madre de Durango

Islas Marías

Isla San Juanito

Isla María Madre

Isla María Magdalena

Isla María Cleofas

Isla Isabela

Laguna de Chapala

Bahía de Banderas

Cabo Corrientes

Puerto Vallarta

Tropic of Cancer

P A C I F I C

O C E A N

Conic Equidistant Projection

Longitude 102° west of Greenwich

METRES / FEET

METRES	FEET
6000	19686
5000	16404
4000	13124
3000	9843
2000	6562
1500	4921
1000	3281
500	1640
200	656
100	328
0	0

LAND BELOW SEA LEVEL

200	656
1000	3281
2000	6562
4000	13124

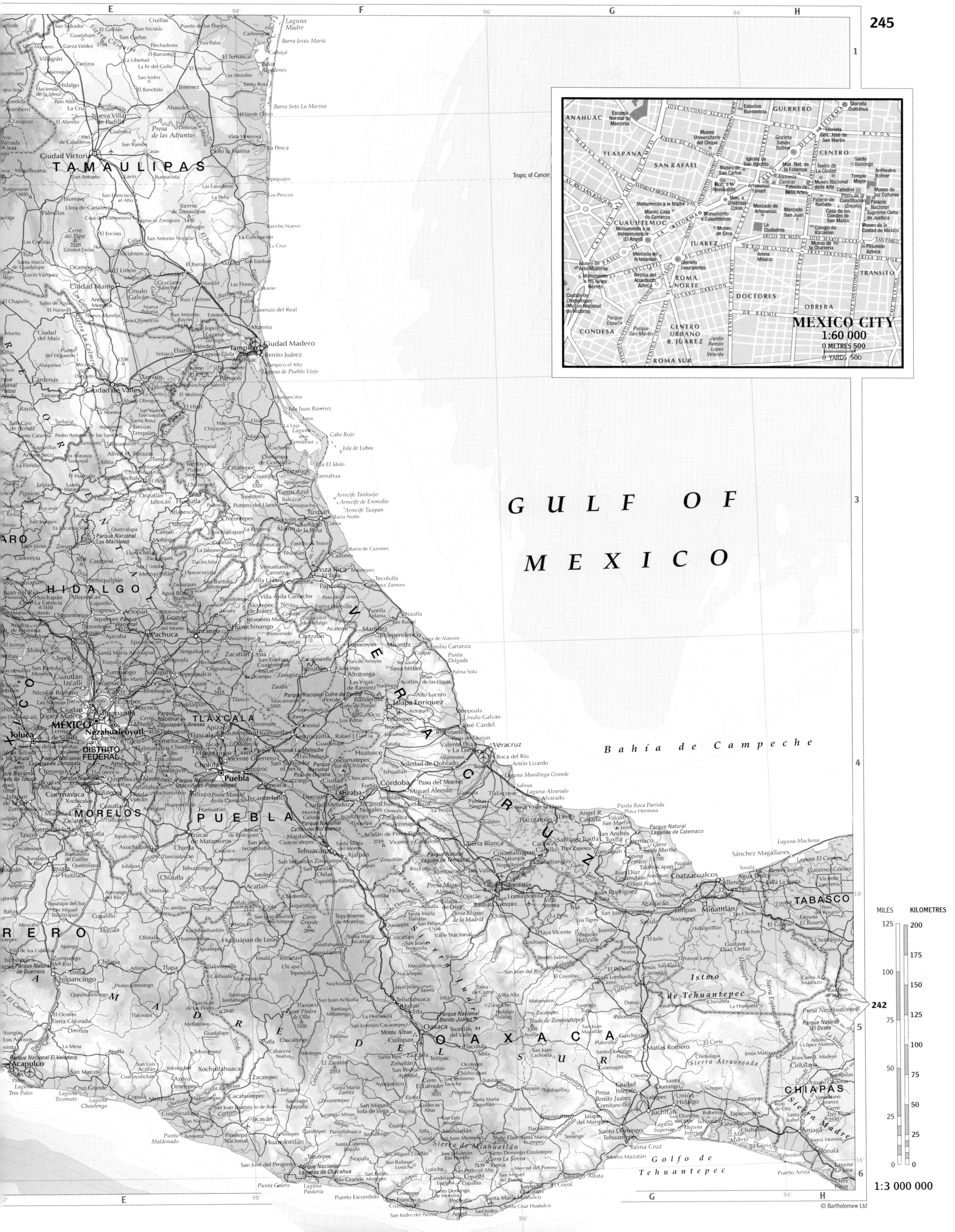

GULF OF MEXICO

MEXICO CITY
1:60 000
0 METRES 500
0 YARDS 500

States / regions:

TAMAULIPAS

HIDALGO

TLAXCALA

DISTRITO FEDERAL

MORELOS

PUEBLA

VERACRUZ

OAXACA

TABASCO

CHIAPAS

Bahía de Campeche

Istmo de Tehuantepec

Golfo de Tehuantepec

Tropic of Cancer

Ciudad Victoria

Tampico
Ciudad Madero

Pachuca

MEXICO
Nezahualcóyotl
Toluca

Puebla
Cholula
Cuernavaca

Jalapa Enríquez

Veracruz
Boca del Río

Orizaba
Córdoba

Coatzacoalcos
Minatitlán

Oaxaca

Acapulco

Chilpancingo

MILES   KILOMETRES
125   200
100   175
        150
75   125
        100
50   75
25   50
        25
0   0

242

1:3 000 000

© Bartholomew Ltd

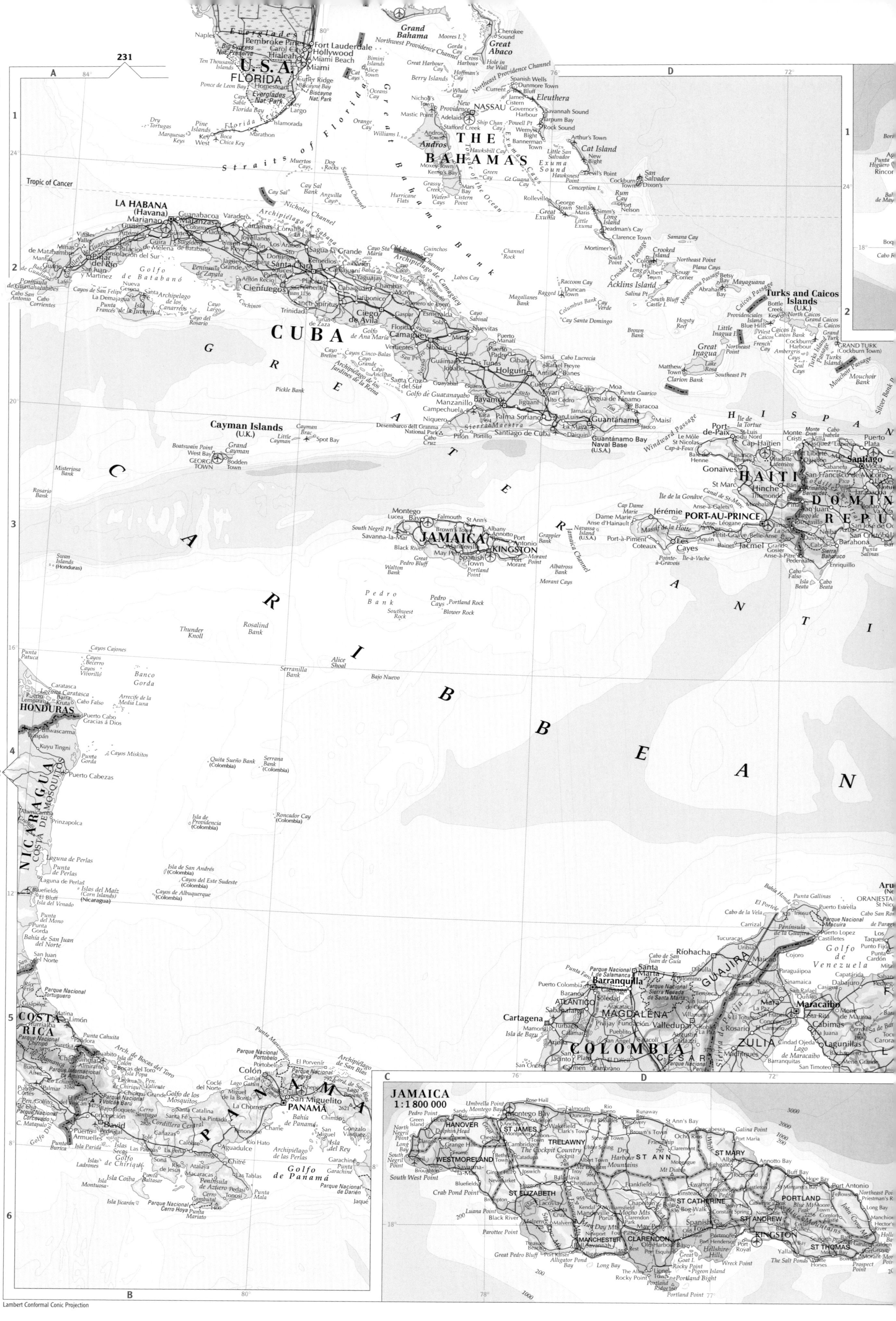

231

242

U.S.A.
FLORIDA
Naples
Everglades
Big Cypress
Pembroke Pines
Carol City
Hialeah
Hollywood
Fort Lauderdale
Miami Beach
Miami
Ten Thousand Islands
Homestead
Ponce de Leon Bay
Cape Sable
Everglades Nat. Park
Key Largo
Florida Bay
Islamorada
Marathon
Key West
Florida Keys
Dry Tortugas
Marquesas Keys
Boca Chica Key

Grand Bahama
Great Abaco
THE BAHAMAS
NASSAU
Andros
Eleuthera
Cat Island
San Salvador
Rum Cay
Long Island
Crooked Island
Acklins Island
Mayaguana
Great Inagua
Little Inagua

Tropic of Cancer
Straits of Florida

LA HABANA (Havana)
Guanabacoa
Marianao
Matanzas
Varadero
Cárdenas
Pinar del Río
Santa Clara
Cienfuegos
Sancti Spíritus
Ciego de Ávila
Camagüey
Las Tunas
Holguín
Bayamo
Manzanillo
Santiago de Cuba
Guantánamo
Guantánamo Bay Naval Base (U.S.A.)

CUBA
GREATER

Cayman Islands (U.K.)
Grand Cayman
GEORGE TOWN
Little Cayman
Cayman Brac

Turks and Caicos Islands (U.K.)
GRAND TURK (Cockburn Town)

HISPAN
HAITI
PORT-AU-PRINCE
Gonaïves
Cap-Haïtien
Jérémie
Les Cayes
Jacmel
DOMIN
REPU
Santiago
Puerto Plata
Barahona

JAMAICA
Montego Bay
KINGSTON
Spanish Town
May Pen
Black River
Savanna-la-Mar
Port Antonio

CARIBBEAN

HONDURAS
Puerto Lempira
Bilwascarma

NICARAGUA
COSTA DE MOSQUITOS
Puerto Cabezas
Prinzapolca
Bluefields
El Bluff
Laguna de Perlas
Isla de San Andrés (Colombia)

Pedro Bank
Rosalind Bank
Thunder Knoll
Alice Shoal
Serranilla Bank
Bajo Nuevo
Quita Sueño Bank (Colombia)
Serrana Bank (Colombia)
Roncador Cay (Colombia)
Isla de Providencia (Colombia)
Cayos de Albuquerque (Colombia)

COSTA RICA
Limón
PANAMÁ
PANAMA
Colón
Golfo de los Mosquitos
Golfo de Panamá
Archipiélago de las Perlas
Península de Azuero

COLOMBIA
Barranquilla
Cartagena
Santa Marta
Ríohacha
Valledupar
Maracaibo
Golfo de Venezuela
GUAJIRA
MAGDALENA
ATLÁNTICO
CESAR
ZULIA
Lago de Maracaibo
Cabimas
Lagunillas

METRES / FEET
6000 / 19686
5000 / 16404
4000 / 13124
3000 / 9843
2000 / 6562
1000 / 3281
500 / 1640
200 / 656
0
LAND BELOW SEA LEVEL
200 / 656
2000 / 6562
4000 / 13124
6000 / 19686

JAMAICA 1:1 800 000
HANOVER
ST JAMES
TRELAWNY
WESTMORELAND
ST ANN
ST MARY
PORTLAND
ST ELIZABETH
MANCHESTER
CLARENDON
ST CATHERINE
ST ANDREW
ST THOMAS
KINGSTON
Montego Bay
Falmouth
Runaway Bay
Ocho Rios
Port Antonio
The Cockpit Country
Blue Mountains

Lambert Conformal Conic Projection

© Bartholomew Ltd

1 : 6 600 000

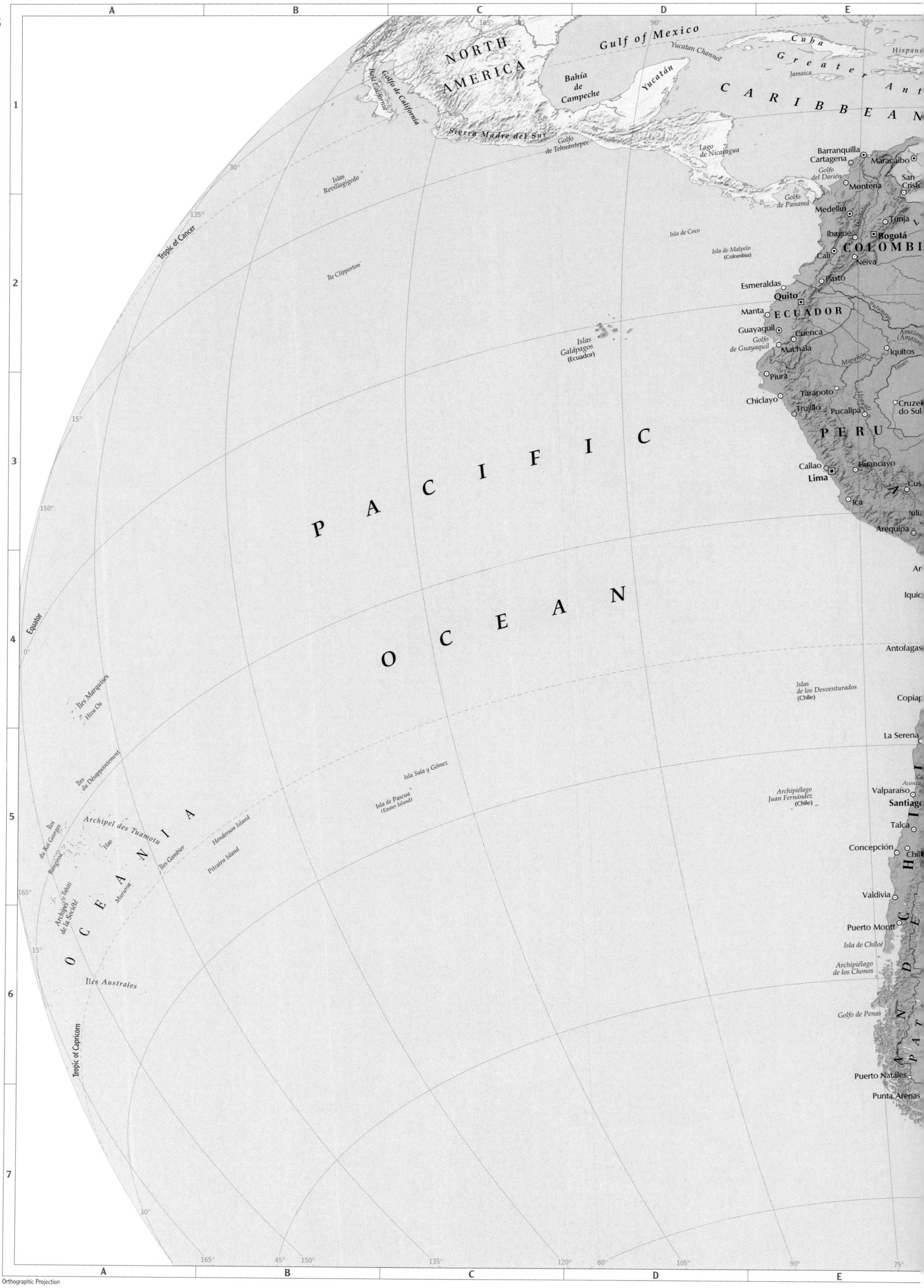

A B C D E

NORTH
AMERICA

Gulf of Mexico

Cuba

Hispan

Yucatan Channel

Greater

Ant

Jamaica

Bahía
de
Campeche

Yucatán

CARIBBEAN

Golfo de California

Baja California

Sierra Madre del Sur

Golfo
de Tehuantepec

Lago
de Nicaragua

Barranquilla
Cartagena

Maracaibo

Golfo
del Darién

Montería

San
Cristo

30°

Islas
Revillagigedo

135°

Tropic of Cancer

Ile Clipperton

Isla de Coco

Golfo
de Panamá

Medellín

Bogotá

Ibagué

COLOMBI

Isla de Malpelo
(Colombia)

Cali

Tunja

V

Neiva

Pasto

Esmeraldas

Quito

Putumayo

Manta

ECUADOR

Amazon
(Amazo

Guayaquil

Cuenca

Islas
Galápagos
(Ecuador)

Golfo
de Guayaquil

Machala

Piura

Iquitos

Marañón

Tarapoto

Chiclayo

Trujillo

Pucallpa

Cruze
do Sul

15°

PERU

P A C I F I C

Callao

Huancayo

A

Cus

Lima

150°

Ica

Julia

Arequipa

Equator

0°

O C E A N

Ar

Iqui

Antofagas

Islas
de los Desventurados
(Chile)

Copiap

Îles Marquises

Hiva Oa

La Serena

Isla Sala y Gómez

Archipiélago
Juan Fernández
(Chile)

Valparaíso

Aconca

Santiago

Îles
du Désappointement

Isla de Pascua
(Easter Island)

Talca

Îles
Rei Georges

Archipel des Tuamotu

Henderson Island

Concepción

Chil

Ila

Rangiroa

Hao

Îles Gambier

Pitcairn Island

Archipel
de la Société

Tahiti

Makatea

O C E A N I A

Valdivia

165°

Puerto Montt

Isla de Chiloé

15°

Archipiélago
de los Chonos

Îles Australes

AND

PA

Golfo de Penas

DE

Tropic of Capricorn

Puerto Natales

HI

Punta Arenas

165° 45° 150° 135° 120° 60° 105° 90° 75°

A B C D E

les

S E A

Puerto Rico
Virgin Is
Anguilla
St Kitts-Nevis
Montserrat
Barbuda
Antigua
Dominica
Guadeloupe

Lesser Antilles

Martinique
St Lucia
St Vincent
and the Grenadines
Grenada
Barbados
Tobago
Trinidad

uba

Curaçao

Valencia
Caracas
Maracay
arquisimeto
Cumaná

Ciudad Bolívar

VENEZUELA
Orinoco
Puerto Ayacucho

GUYANA
Georgetown

SURINAME
Paramaribo
Cayenne
French
Guiana

os

Boa Vista

Orinoco

Negro

Japurá

Tonantins

Manaus

Carauari

Branco

Negro

Madeira

Purus

Macapá

Mouths of the Amazon

Amazonas (Amazon)
Santarém
Xingu
Tapajós
Belém

L V A S

Rio Branco
Porto
Velho

Guaporé

B R A Z I L

Xingu

São Luís

Parnaíba

Maraba
Tocantins
Teresina

Fortaleza

Araguaína

Natal
Fernando
de Noronha
(Brazil)

Palmas

Barragem
de Sobradinho

Floresta
João Pessoa
Recife

Puerto Maldonado

Juàzeiro
Maceió

Lago
Titicaca
La Paz
BOLIVIA
Cochabamba
Santa Cruz

Aracaju

Cuiabá

Araguaia

São Francisco

Salvador

Potosí
Sucre

Brasília
Goiânia

Ilhéus

Tarija

Campo
Grande

Araçatuba
Uberaba

Patos
de Minas

Teófilo
Otôni

PARAGUAY
San Salvador
de Jujuy

Pedro Juan
Caballero

Ribeirão
Preto
Belo
Horizonte

Vitória

Teuco
Gran Chaco
San Miguel
de Tucumán

Paraguay
Asunción
Coronel
Oviedo

Maringá
Campinas
São Paulo
Santos

Nevado
del Salado

Formosa
Encarnación

Paraná

Iguaçu

Rio
de Janeiro

Catamarca
Resistencia

Posadas

Curitiba

La Rioja
Corrientes

Florianópolis

nas Grandes
Salinas
de Ambargasta

Santa Maria

an Juan

Mar Chiquita
Lago

Santa Fé
Concordia
Paraná
Paysandú

Porto Alegre

Lagoa
dos Patos

Córdoba
Rosario

URUGUAY

Rio Grande

Mendoza

San Luis
**Buenos
Aires**

San
Rafael
ARGENTINA
La Plata
Rio de la Plata
Montevideo

Santa Rosa

Neuquén

Viedma
Golfo San Matías

Negro

ONIA
Bahía Blanca
Mar del Plata

Trelew

Comodoro Rivadavia
Golfo de San Jorge

Bahía
Grande
Falkland
Islands
(U.K.)
Stanley
Río Gallegos

a Grande
Tierra del Fuego
Ushuaia

Isla de los Estados

bo de Hornos

rake Passage

South Georgia

South Georgia
and
South Sandwich
Islands
(U.K.)

Shag
Rocks

Traversay Islands
South
Sandwich
Islands
Candlemas Island
Saunders Island
Montagu Island

South Shetland
Islands

South Orkney
Islands

Southern Thule
Island
Bristol Island

Antarctic Peninsula

Tropic of Cancer

Arquipélago
da Madeira

Islas
Canarias

Gran
Canaria

Santo Antão
Ilhas
do Cabo Verde
Boa Vista
São Tiago

A F R I C A

Senegal

Niger

Equator

Gulf
of
Guinea

Ascension

Ilha da Trindade
(Brazil)
Ilhas
Martin Vas
(Brazil)

St Helena

A T L A N T I C

O C E A N

Tropic of Capricorn

Tristan
da Cunha

Orange

Cape of Good Hope

MILES	KILOMETRES
1000	1500
750	1250
	1000
500	750
250	500
	250
0	0

1:27 000 000

© Bartholomew Ltd

A · 80° · B · 76° · C · 72° · D · 68°

CARIBBEAN SEA

Administrative regions numbered on the map:
COLOMBIA
1. SANTAFÉ DE BOGOTÁ (C3)
ECUADOR
2. BOLÍVAR (B5)
3. CHIMBORAZO (B5)
4. TUNGURAHUA (B5)
5. ZAMORA-CHINCHIPE (B5)

PACIFIC OCEAN

PANAMA

GALAPAGOS ISLANDS
(Ecuador)
AT THE SAME SCALE

Isla Culpepper
Isla Wenman
Isla Pinta
Isla Marchena · Isla Genovesa
Roca Redonda
ISLAS GALÁPAGOS Equator
Volcán Wolf
Isla San Salvador
Isla Fernandina
Isla Isabela · Isla Santa Cruz
Cerro Azul · Isla Santa Fé · Puerto Baquerizo Moreno
Puerto Velasco Ibarra · Isla Española
Isla Santa María
92° W

Equator

COLOMBIA

Barranquilla · Cartagena
ATLÁNTICO · MAGDALENA
BOLÍVAR · CÉSAR
SUCRE · CÓRDOBA
ANTIOQUIA · SANTANDER
Medellín · NORTE DE SANTANDER
CHOCÓ · CALDAS · RISARALDA · CUNDINAMARCA · BOYACÁ · CASANARE
QUINDÍO · **BOGOTÁ** · VICHADA
VALLE · TOLIMA · META
Cali · HUILA
CAUCA · GUAINÍA
NARIÑO · PUTUMAYO · CAQUETÁ · GUAVIARE · VAUPÉS
CARCHI
ESMERALDAS · IMBABURA · SUCUMBÍOS
PICHINCHA · ORELLANA · AMAZONAS
QUITO
COTOPAXI · NAPO
MANABÍ · PASTAZA
ECUADOR
LOS RÍOS · MORONA-SANTIAGO
Guayaquil · GUAYAS · CAÑAR
AZUAY · Cuenca
EL ORO · LOJA
TUMBES
PIURA · LAMBAYEQUE · CAJAMARCA
LA LIBERTAD
SAN MARTÍN
ÁNCASH · HUÁNUCO
PERU · LORETO · UCAYALI · ACRE

VENEZUELA
Maracaibo · FALCÓN · Coro · CARACAS · Maracay
ZULIA · LARA · Barquisimeto · ARAGUA
TRUJILLO · MÉRIDA · PORTUGUESA · COJEDES · GUÁRICO
TÁCHIRA · San Cristóbal · BARINAS
NORTE DE SANTANDER · APURE · San Fernando de Apure
ARAUCA

Ríohacha · GUAJIRA
Santa Marta
Maracay · MIRANDA

ORANJESTAD · Aruba (Netherlands) · Curaçao (Netherlands) · WILLEMSTAD · Netherlands Antilles · Bonaire · Lesser Antilles

AMAZONAS

Iquitos

Leticia · Tabatinga

Benjamin Constant

METRES / FEET
6000 / 19686
5000 / 16404
4000 / 13124
3000 / 9843
2000 / 6562
1000 / 3281
500 / 1640
200 / 656
0 / 0
LAND BELOW SEA LEVEL
200 / 656
2000 / 6562
4000 / 13124
6000 / 19686

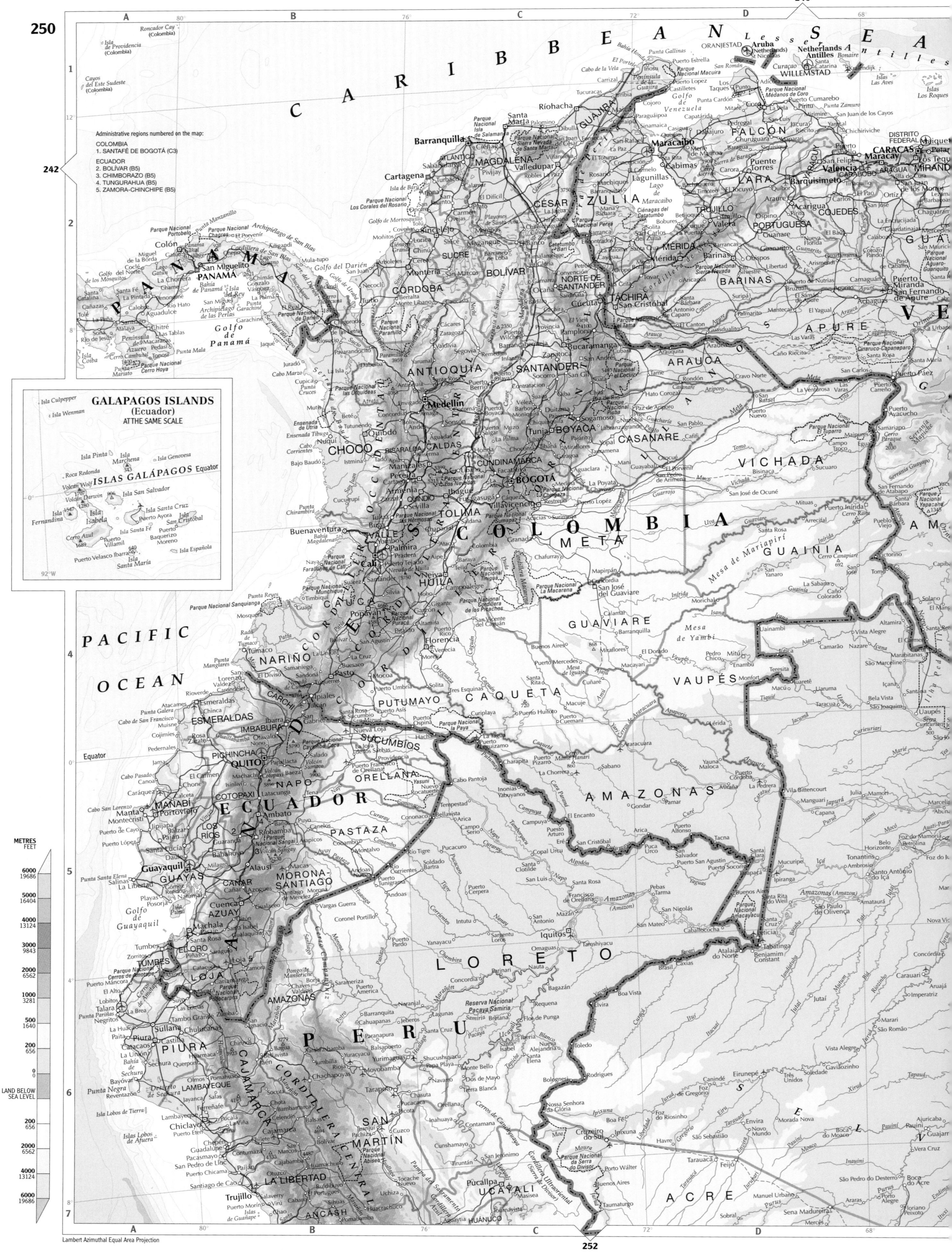

Lambert Azimuthal Equal Area Projection

ATLANTIC OCEAN

MILES KILOMETRES
300 — 500
— 400
200 — 300
— 200
100 — 100
1:7 500 000

GRENADA
ST GEORGE'S
The Grenadines
Mustique
Canouan
Carriacou
Hillsborough
Petite Martinique
Ronde
Grenville

TRINIDAD AND TOBAGO
Tobago
Plymouth
Charlotteville
Scarborough
PORT OF SPAIN
Trinidad
San Fernando

Isla de Margarita
NUEVA ESPARTA
Porlamar
La Asunción
Isla Blanquilla
Isla La Tortuga
Isla Coche
Cumaná
SUCRE
Barcelona
MONAGAS
Maturín
ANZOÁTEGUI
Orinoco
DELTA AMACURO
Ciudad Guayana
Ciudad Bolívar

VENEZUELA
BOLÍVAR
GUIANA HIGHLANDS
Salto del Ángel / Angel Falls
Parque Nacional Canaima
La Gran Sabana
Pakaraima Mountains

GUYANA
GEORGETOWN
Linden
New Amsterdam
Bartica
Kaieteur Falls

SURINAME
PARAMARIBO
Nieuw Nickerie

French Guiana
CAYENNE
St-Laurent-du-Maroni
Kourou
Cabo Orange
Parque Nacional de Cabo Orange

RORAIMA
Boa Vista
Kanuku Mountains
Serra Tumucumaque

AMAPÁ
Macapá
Equator
Mouths of the Amazon
Ilha de Marajó

AMAZONAS
Manaus
Manacapuru
Rio Negro

BRAZIL
Itaituba
Parque Nacional Amazônia
Santarém
Óbidos
Altamira
Tucuruí

PARÁ

RONDÔNIA
Porto Velho

MATO GROSSO

Serra dos Carajás

Longitude 64° west of Greenwich

© Bartholomew Ltd

PACIFIC

OCEAN

PERU

BOLIVIA

AMAZON

ACRE

LORETO

UCAYALI

SAN MARTIN

LA LIBERTAD

ANCASH

HUANUCO

PASCO

JUNIN

LIMA

HUANCAVELICA

ICA

AYACUCHO

APURIMAC

CUSCO

MADRE DE DIOS

PANDO

BENI

LA PAZ

PUNO

AREQUIPA

MOQUEGUA

TACNA

ORURO

COCHABAMBA

SUCRE

TARAPACÁ

POTOSÍ

CHUQUISACA

TARIJA

JUJUY

SALTA

CATAMARCA

TUCUMAN

LA RIOJA

ATACAMA

CHILE

CAJAMARCA

AMAZONAS

Callao
LIMA
Trujillo
Chimbote
Huancayo
Ayacucho
Arequipa
Ica
Nazca
Tacna
Arica
Iquique
Antofagasta
LA PAZ
Cochabamba
Oruro
Potosí
Tarija
Lago Titicaca
Juliaca
Lago de Poopó
Salar de Uyuni
Salar de Atacama

Tropic of Capricorn

Isla San Lorenzo
Islas de Huaurú
Isla San Gallán
Península Paracas
Punta Santa María

Islas de los Desventurados
Isla San Félix
Isla San Ambrosio

JUAN FERNÁNDEZ ISLANDS
(Chile)
AT THE SAME SCALE
San Juan Bautista   Isla
Isla   Robinson
Santa Clara   Crusoe
Alejandro Selkirk
Isla
Archipiélago Juan Fernández

80°W

METRES
FEET
6000 / 19686
5000 / 16404
4000 / 13124
3000 / 9843
2000 / 6562
1000 / 3281
500 / 1640
200 / 656
0 / 0
LAND BELOW SEA LEVEL
200 / 656
2000 / 6562
4000 / 13124
6000 / 19686

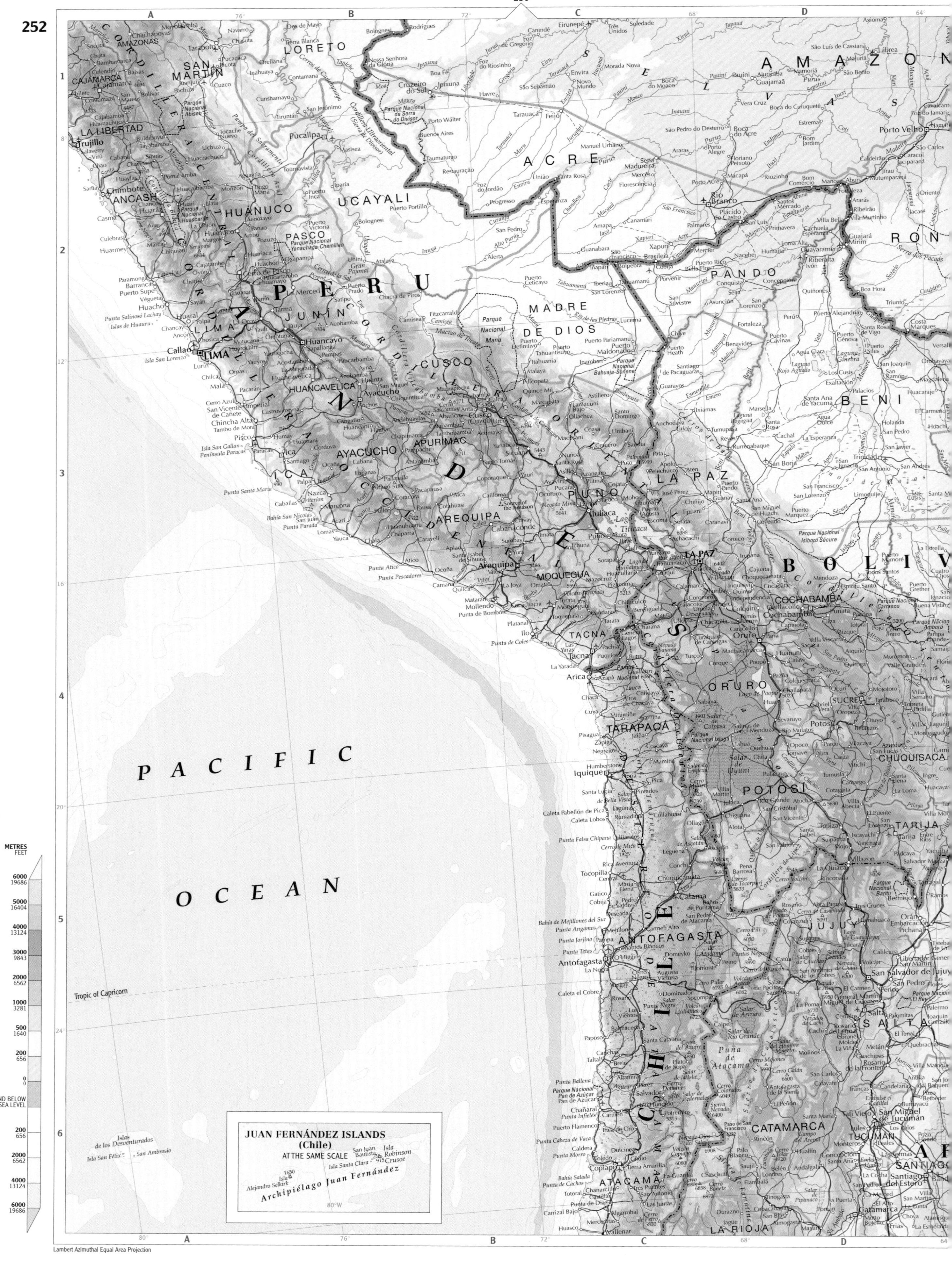

Lambert Azimuthal Equal Area Projection

PARÁ

TOCANTINS

MATO GROSSO

BRAZIL

Planalto do Mato Grosso

SANTA CRUZ

Santa Cruz

GOIÁS

DISTRITO FEDERAL
BRASÍLIA
Goiânia

MINAS GERAIS

Uberlândia
Uberaba

MATO GROSSO DO SUL

Campo Grande

SÃO PAULO

São Paulo
Campinas
Santos
São Bernardo do Campo
São Vicente
Tropic of Capricorn

PARAGUAY

ASUNCIÓN

FORMOSA

CHACO

PARANÁ

Curitiba
Ponta Grossa

SANTA CATARINA

Blumenau
Itajaí
Florianópolis

RIO GRANDE DO SUL

CORRIENTES

MISIONES

ARGENTINA

SANTA FÉ

ATLANTIC OCEAN

MILES — KILOMETRES

300 — 500
400
200 — 300
200
100 — 100
0 — 0

1:7 500 000

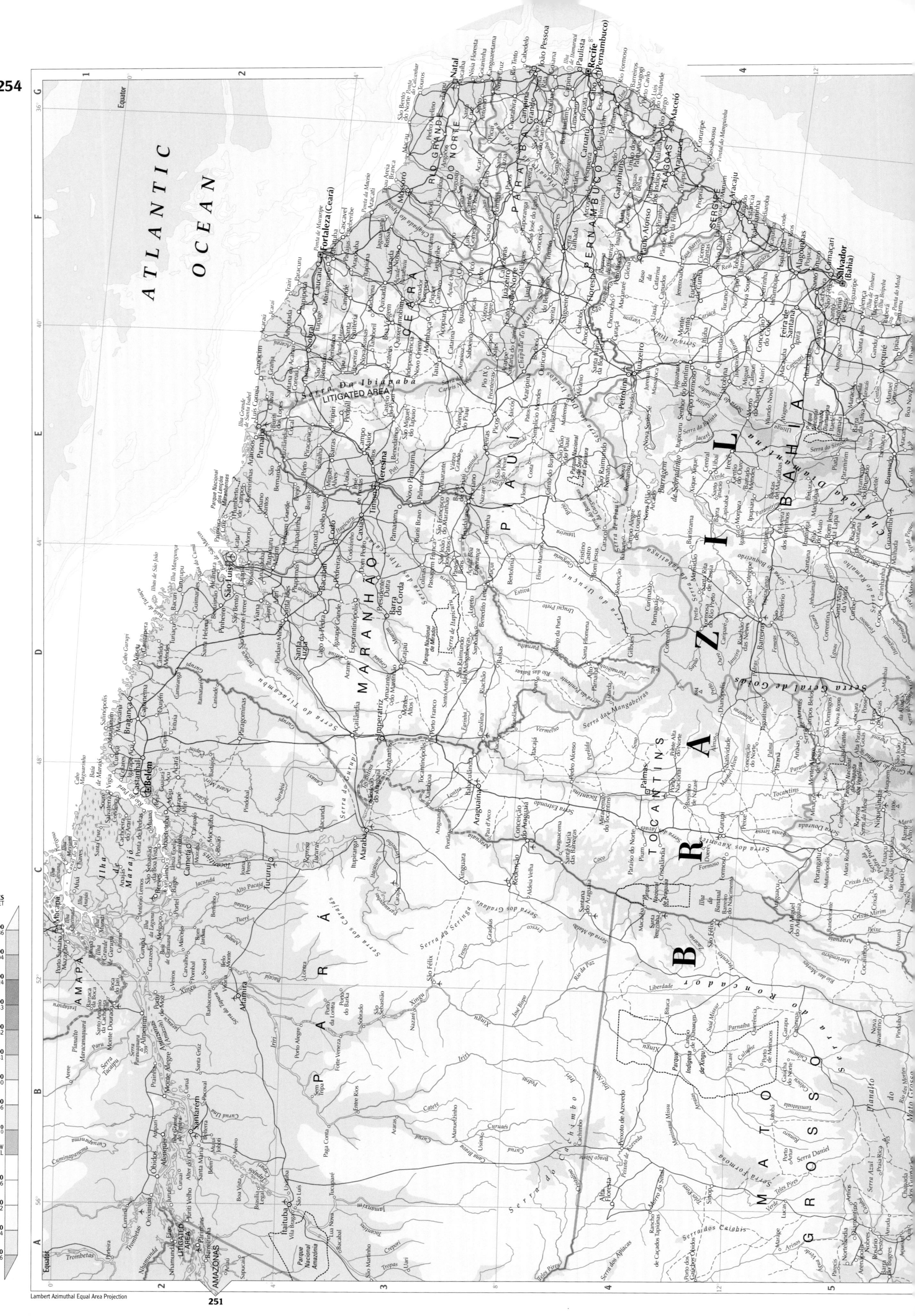

ATLANTIC

OCEAN

B R A Z I L

MARANHÃO

PIAUÍ

CEARÁ

RIO GRANDE DO NORTE

PARAÍBA

PERNAMBUCO

ALAGOAS

SERGIPE

BAHIA

TOCANTINS

PARÁ

AMAPÁ

AMAZONAS

MATO GROSSO

Fortaleza (Ceará)

Teresina

São Luís

Belém

Santarém

Macapá

Recife (Pernambuco)

Natal

João Pessoa

Maceió

Aracaju

Salvador (Bahia)

Palmas

Marabá

Altamira

Araguaína

LITIGATED AREA

Serra Da Ibiapaba

Equator

METRES
FEET

6000	19686
5000	16404
4000	13124
3000	9843
2000	6562
1000	3281
500	1640
200	656
0	0

LAND BELOW
SEA LEVEL

200	656
2000	6562
4000	13124
6000	19686

ATLANTIC

OCEAN

RIO DE JANEIRO
1:125 000
0 METRES 1000
0 YARDS 1000

MINAS GERAIS

ESPÍRITO SANTO

Rio de Janeiro

BRASÍLIA
DISTRITO
FEDERAL

GOIÁS

SÃO PAULO

São Paulo

Santos

PARANÁ

Curitiba

SANTA CATARINA

MATO GROSSO DO SUL

RIO GRANDE DO SUL

Porto Alegre

Lagoa
dos
Patos

PARAGUAY

ARGENTINA

MISIONES

CORRIENTES

URUGUAY

MILES   KILOMETRES
300   500
            400
200   300
            200
100
            100
0   0

1:7 500 000

© Bartholomew Ltd

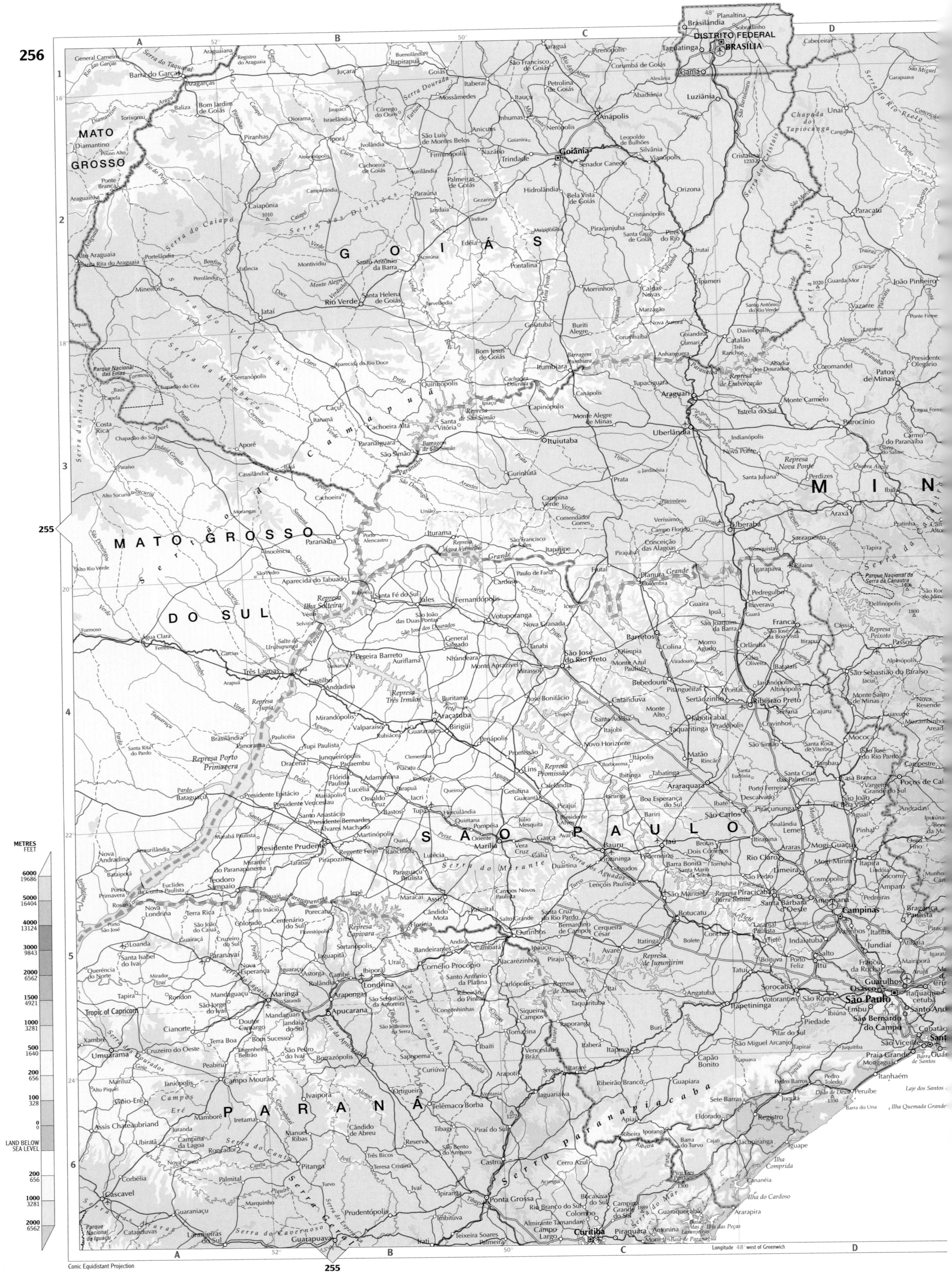

MATO GROSSO

GOIÁS

DISTRITO FEDERAL

BRASÍLIA

MATO GROSSO DO SUL

MIN (MINAS)

SÃO PAULO

PARANÁ

Goiânia

Curitiba

São Paulo

Tropic of Capricorn

METRES / FEET

METRES	FEET
6000	19686
5000	16404
4000	13124
3000	9843
2000	6562
1500	4921
1000	3281
500	1640
200	656
100	328
0	0

LAND BELOW SEA LEVEL

200	656
1000	3281
2000	6562

Longitude 48° west of Greenwich

BAHIA

Planalto

do

Brasil

MINAS GERAIS

ESPIRITO
SANTO

RIO

DE JANEIRO

Rio de Janeiro

ATLANTIC

OCEAN

Tropic of Capricorn

MILES   KILOMETRES

125   200

175

100   150

125

75   100

50   75

50

25
25

0   0

1:3 300 000

SÃO PAULO
1:125 000
0 METRES 1000
0 YARDS 1000

BOM RETIRO

BARRA
FUNDA

PARI

SANTA
CECÍLIA

SANTA
EFIGÊNIA

CONSOLAÇÃO

BRÁS

© Bartholomew Ltd

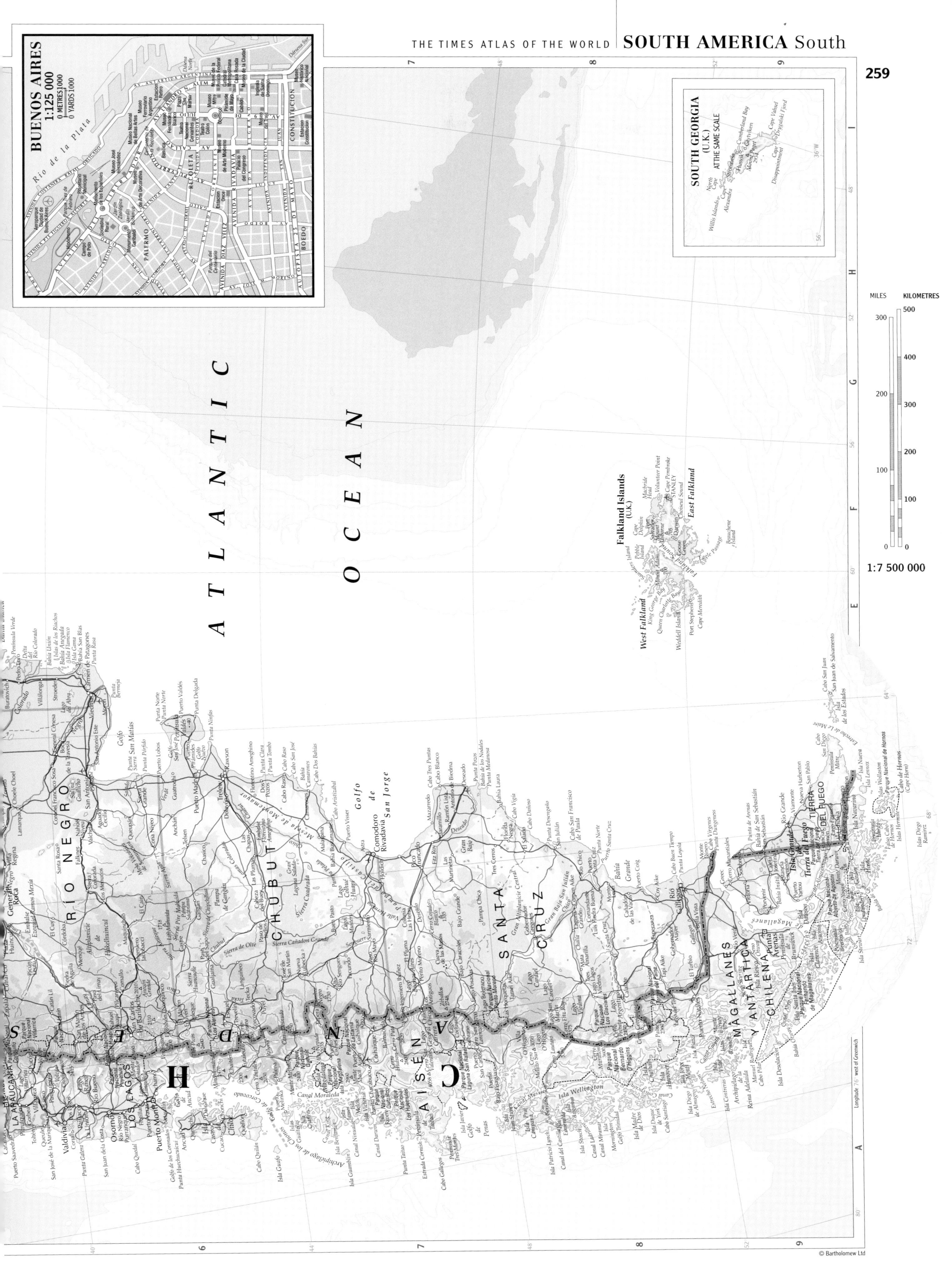

A 72°   B   70°   C   68°   D   66°   E

PACIFIC OCEAN

COQUIMBO

SAN JUAN

LA RIOJA

VALPARAÍSO

SANTIAGO

SAN LUIS

O'HIGGINS

MENDOZA

A R G E N

MAULE

Travesía

Travesía Puntana

PAMPA SECA

C H I L E

A N D E S

BÍOBÍO

Pampa de la Varita

PAMPA

NEUQUÉN

LA PAMPA

LA ARAUCANÍA

RÍO

NEGRO

La Serena
Coquimbo
Ovalle
Illapel
Valparaíso
Viña del Mar
Santiago
San Bernardo
Rancagua
San Fernando
Curicó
Talca
Linares
Chillán
Concepción
Los Ángeles
Temuco

San Juan
San Luis
Mendoza
Godoy Cruz
San Rafael
Malargüe
Neuquén
General Roca
Cipolletti

Cerro Aconcagua 6960
Tupungato
Volcán Maipo
Volcán San José 5830
Volcán Tinguiririca
Volcán Descabezado
Volcán Domuyo 4800
Volcán Tromen
Volcán Llaima
Volcán Villarrica

Salinas Grandes
Salina de Mascasín
Pampa de las Salinas
Embalse del Nihuil
Salina Llancanelo
Embalse Casa de Piedra
Embalse Ezequiel Ramos Mexía

METRES FEET

6000	19686
5000	16404
4000	13124
3000	9843
2000	6562
1500	4921
1000	3281
500	1640
200	656
100	328
0	0

LAND BELOW SEA LEVEL

200	656
1000	3281
2000	6562

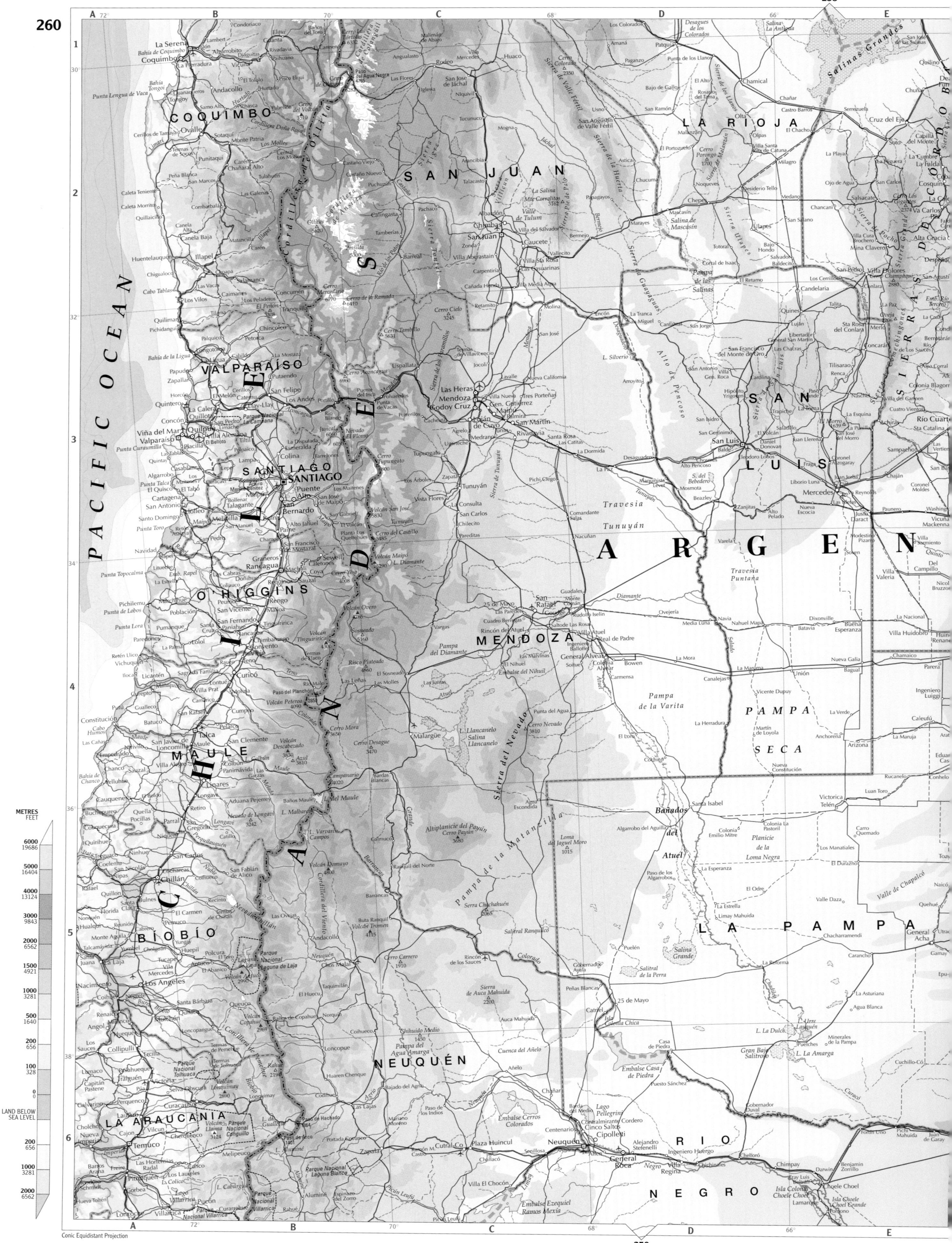

Conic Equidistant Projection

A 72°   B   70°   C   68°   D   66°   E

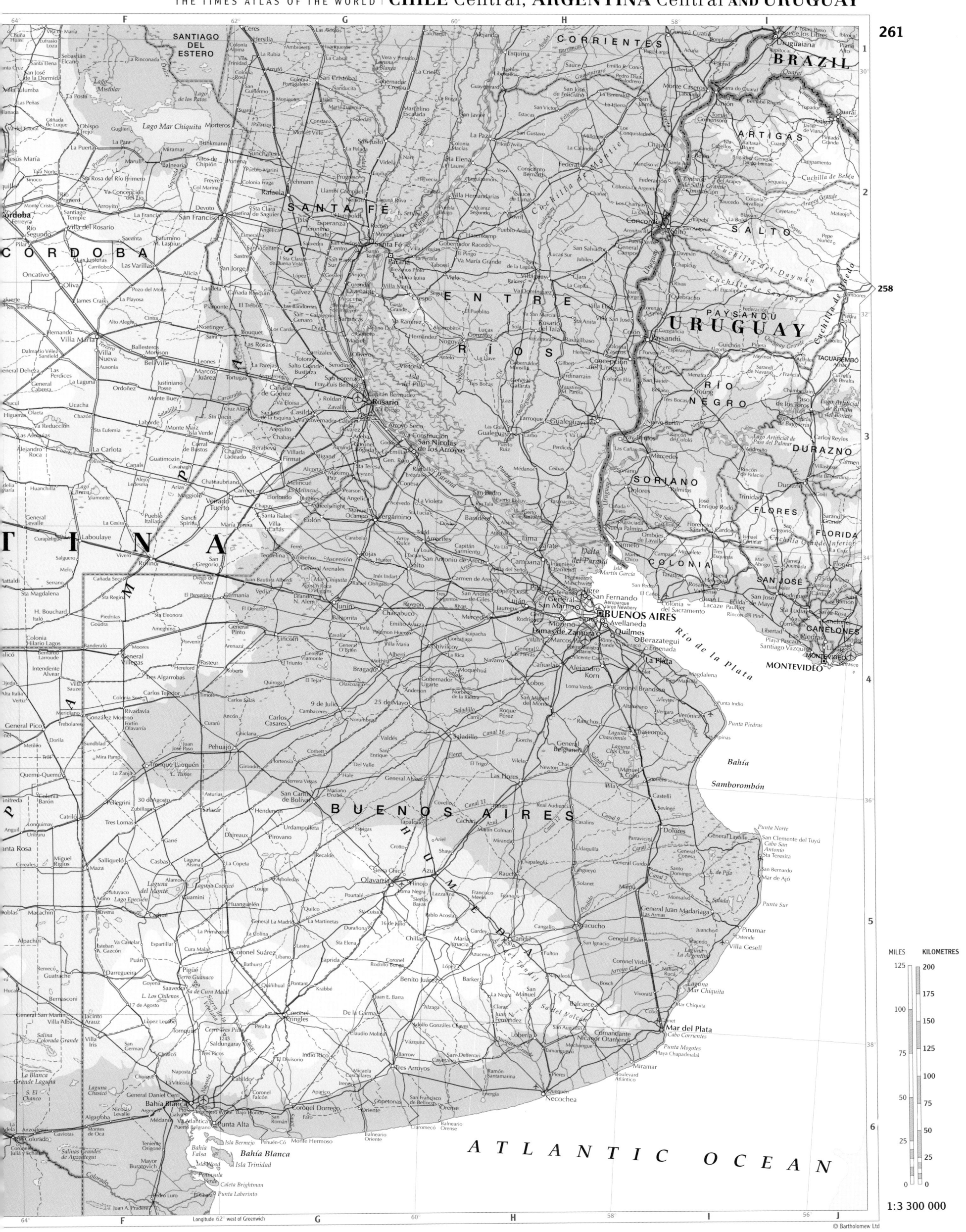

MILES KILOMETRES
125 200
 175
100 150
 125
75 100
 75
50 50
25 25
0 0

1:3 300 000

© Bartholomew Ltd

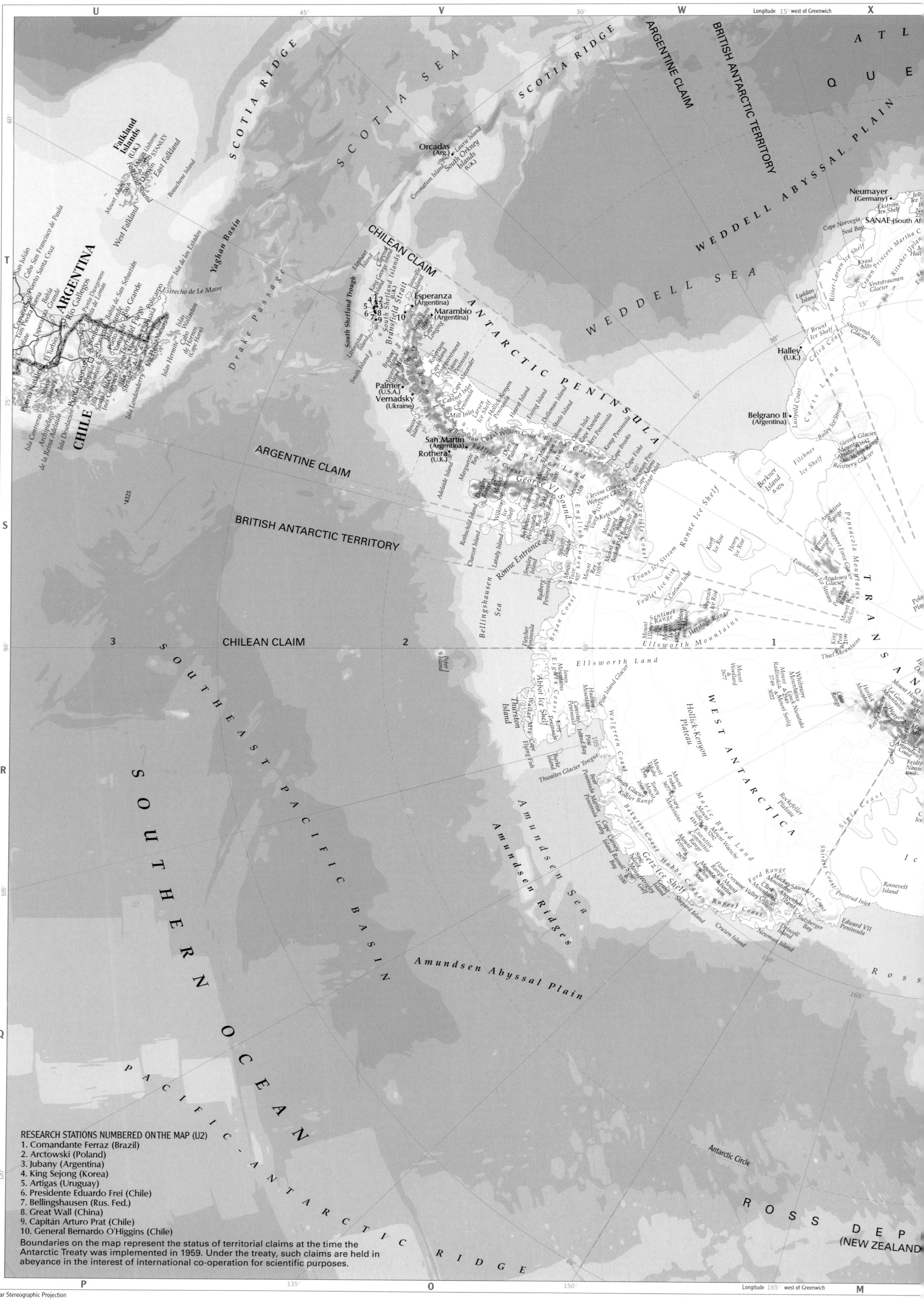

U 45° V 30° W Longitude 15° west of Greenwich X

A T L

Q U E

SCOTIA RIDGE

SCOTIA SEA

SCOTIA RIDGE

ARGENTINE CLAIM

BRITISH ANTARCTIC TERRITORY

60°

Falkland Islands (U.K.)

Port STANLEY

West Falkland
East Falkland

Orcadas (Arg.)
Laurie Island
South Orkney Islands (U.K.)
Coronation Island

Neumayer (Germany)
Ekström Ice Shelf

WEDDELL ABYSSAL PLAIN

SANAE (South Af

Cape Norvegia
Seal Bay

T

San Julián
Cabo San Francisco de Paula
Puerto Santa Cruz
ARGENTINA
Río Gallegos

Yaghan Basin

CHILEAN CLAIM

Elephant Island
King George Island
South Shetland Islands

Esperanza (Argentina)
Marambio (Argentina)

W E D D E L L S E A

Riiser-Larsen Ice Shelf
Cronprinsesse Martha Kyst

Brunt Ice Shelf

75°

CHILE

Estrecho de Le Maire
Tierra del Fuego

Drake Passage

South Shetland Trough

Bransfield Strait

A N T A R C T I C

P E N I N S U L A

Halley (U.K.)

Coats Land

Cabo de Hornos (Cape Horn)
Islas Hermite
Islas Wollaston

Palmer (U.S.A.)
Vernadsky (Ukraine)

Filchner Ice Shelf

Belgrano II (Argentina)

S

ARGENTINE CLAIM

San Martin (Argentina)
Rothera (U.K.)

George VI Sound

Berkner Island

Pensacola Mountains

BRITISH ANTARCTIC TERRITORY

Ronne Ice Shelf

Bellingshausen Sea

Ronne Ice Shelf

T R A N S A N

90° 3 CHILEAN CLAIM 2 1

Ellsworth Land

Ellsworth Mountains

Peter I Island

S O U T H E A S T P A C I F I C B A S I N

WEST ANTARCTICA

Hollick-Kenyon Plateau

Marie Byrd Land

R

Thwaites Glacier Tongue

Amundsen Sea

Amundsen Ridges

Getz Ice Shelf

Rockefeller Plateau

METRES
FEET

S O U T H E R N

O C E A N

Amundsen Abyssal Plain

Roosevelt Island

Ros

Edward VII Peninsula

4000 13124
3000 9843
2000 6562
1000 3281
500 1640
200 656
0 0
LAND BELOW SEA LEVEL
200 656
2000 6562
3000 9843
4000 13124
5000 16404
6000 19686
7000 22967
9000 29529

Q

R O S S

Antarctic Circle

P A C I F I C - A N T A R C T I C

RESEARCH STATIONS NUMBERED ON THE MAP (U2)
1. Comandante Ferraz (Brazil)
2. Arctowski (Poland)
3. Jubany (Argentina)
4. King Sejong (Korea)
5. Artigas (Uruguay)
6. Presidente Eduardo Frei (Chile)
7. Bellingshausen (Rus. Fed.)
8. Great Wall (China)
9. Capitán Arturo Prat (Chile)
10. General Bernardo O'Higgins (Chile)

Boundaries on the map represent the status of territorial claims at the time the Antarctic Treaty was implemented in 1959. Under the treaty, such claims are held in abeyance in the interest of international co-operation for scientific purposes.

R O S S

D E P

(NEW ZEALAND

R I D G E

P 135° O 150° Longitude 165° west of Greenwich M

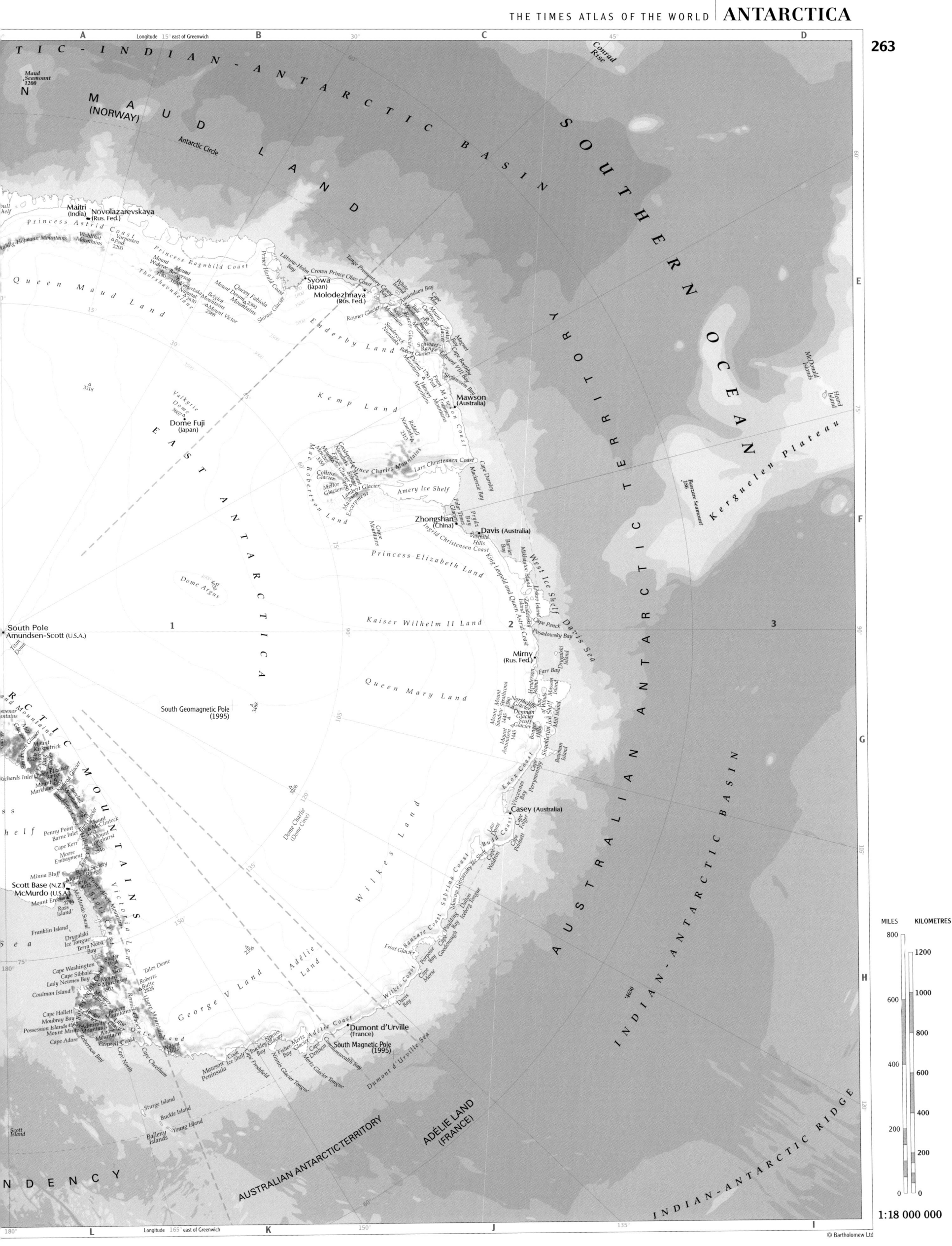

1:18 000 000

© Bartholomew Ltd

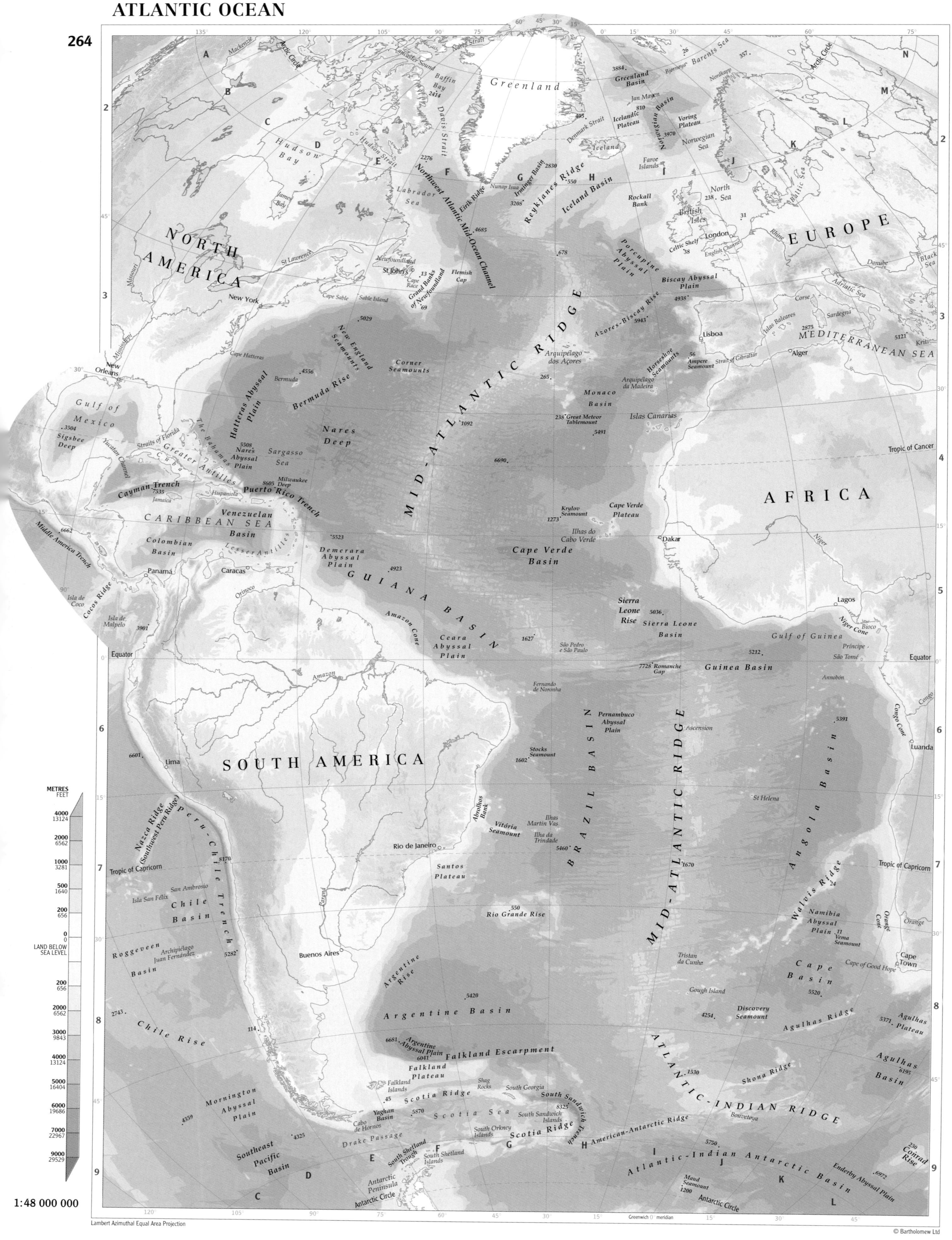

NORTH AMERICA
SOUTH AMERICA
EUROPE
AFRICA
Greenland

Arctic Circle
Mackenzie
Arctic Ridge
Baffin Bay
Lancaster Sound
Nares Strait
Barents Sea
Bjørnøya
Nordkapp
357
26
Greenland Basin
3884
Jan Mayen
810
Norwegian Basin
Icelandic Plateau
Voring Plateau
3970
Norwegian Sea
405
Denmark Strait
Iceland
Faroe Islands
Baltic Sea
North Sea
238
31
Rhine
Danube
Black Sea
Adriatic Sea
Corse
Islas Baleares
Sardegna
2875
MEDITERRANEAN SEA
5121
Kriti
Alger

Hudson Bay
James Bay
Davis Strait
2276
2830
Nunap Isua
Irminger Basin
Eirik Ridge
4685
Reykjanes Ridge
3208
550
Iceland Basin
678
Rockall Bank
British Isles
Celtic Shelf
London
English Channel
Porcupine Abyssal Plain
Biscay Abyssal Plain
4938
Lisboa
Strait of Gibraltar

St Lawrence
Newfoundland
St John's
13
Cape Race
Flemish Cap
Grand Banks of Newfoundland
69
Northwest Atlantic Mid-Ocean Channel
MID-ATLANTIC RIDGE

New York
Cape Sable
Sable Island
5029
Cape Hatteras
New England Seamounts
Bermuda
4556
Corner Seamounts
265
Arquipélago dos Açores
Azores-Biscay Rise
5943
Horseshoe Seamounts
Ampere Seamount
56
Arquipélago da Madeira
Monaco Basin
238 Great Meteor Tablemount
5491
Islas Canarias

New Orleans
Gulf of Mexico
3504
Sigsbee Deep
Hatteras Abyssal Plain
Bermuda Rise
Nares Deep
5508 Nares Abyssal Plain
Sargasso Sea
1092
6690
Tropic of Cancer

Straits of Florida
Yucatan Channel
Cuba
The Bahamas
Greater Antilles
Milwaukee Deep
8605
Puerto Rico Trench
Hispaniola
Jamaica
Cayman Trench
7535
CARIBBEAN SEA
Venezuelan Basin
6662
Colombian Basin
Panamá
Lesser Antilles
Krylov Seamount
1273
Cape Verde Plateau
Ilhas do Cabo Verde
Cape Verde Basin
Dakar
Niger

Isla de Coco
Cocos Ridge
Isla de Malpelo
3901
Caracas
Orinoco
Demerara Abyssal Plain
5523
4923
GUIANA BASIN
Ceara Abyssal Plain
1627
São Pedro e São Paulo
Sierra Leone Rise
5036
Sierra Leone Basin
Gulf of Guinea
Lagos
Niger Cone
Bioco

Middle America Trench
Amazon Cone
Amazon
Equator
7728 Romanche Gap
5212
Guinea Basin
Príncipe
São Tomé
Annobón
Equator

Lima
6601
SOUTH AMERICA
Fernando de Noronha
Pernambuco Abyssal Plain
BRAZIL BASIN
Ascension
Congo
Congo Cone
Luanda
5391
Angola Basin

Stocks Seamount
1602
MID-ATLANTIC RIDGE

Nazca Ridge
Southwest Peru Ridge
5170
Peru-Chile Trench
Abrolhos Bank
Vitória Seamount
Ilhas Martin Vas
Ilha da Trindade
5460
St Helena
6

Tropic of Capricorn
San Ambrosio
Isla San Félix
Chile Basin
Santos Plateau
1670
Walvis Ridge
24
Namibia Abyssal Plain
11 Vema Seamount
Orange Cone
Orange
Tropic of Capricorn

Roggeveen Basin
Archipiélago Juan Fernández
5282
Paraná
Rio Grande Rise
550
Tristan da Cunha
Cape Basin
Cape of Good Hope
Cape Town

Buenos Aires
Argentine Rise
5420
Gough Island
Discovery Seamount
5520
Agulhas Ridge
5371
Agulhas Plateau

2743
Chile Rise
114
Argentine Basin
Argentine Abyssal Plain
6681
6041
Falkland Escarpment
4254
Agulhas Basin
6195

Mornington Abyssal Plain
4359
Falkland Plateau
Falkland Islands
45
Shag Rocks
South Georgia
Scotia Ridge
Scotia Sea
South Sandwich Islands
South Sandwich Trench
8325
1530
Shona Ridge
Bouvetøya
230
Central Rise

Southeast Pacific Basin
4325
Cabo de Hornos
Drake Passage
Yaghan Basin
5870
Scotia Ridge
South Orkney Islands
American-Antarctic Ridge
5750
ATLANTIC-INDIAN RIDGE
Maud Seamount
1200
6972
Enderby Abyssal Plain

Antarctic Peninsula
South Shetland Trough
South Shetland Islands
Antarctic Circle
Atlantic-Indian Antarctic Basin
Antarctic Circle

Lambert Azimuthal Equal Area Projection
1:48 000 000
Greenwich Ō meridian
© Bartholomew Ltd

METRES
FEET
4000 — 13124
2000 — 6562
1000 — 3281
500 — 1640
200 — 656
0 — 0
LAND BELOW SEA LEVEL
200 — 656
2000 — 6562
3000 — 9843
4000 — 13124
5000 — 16404
6000 — 19686
7000 — 22967
9000 — 29529

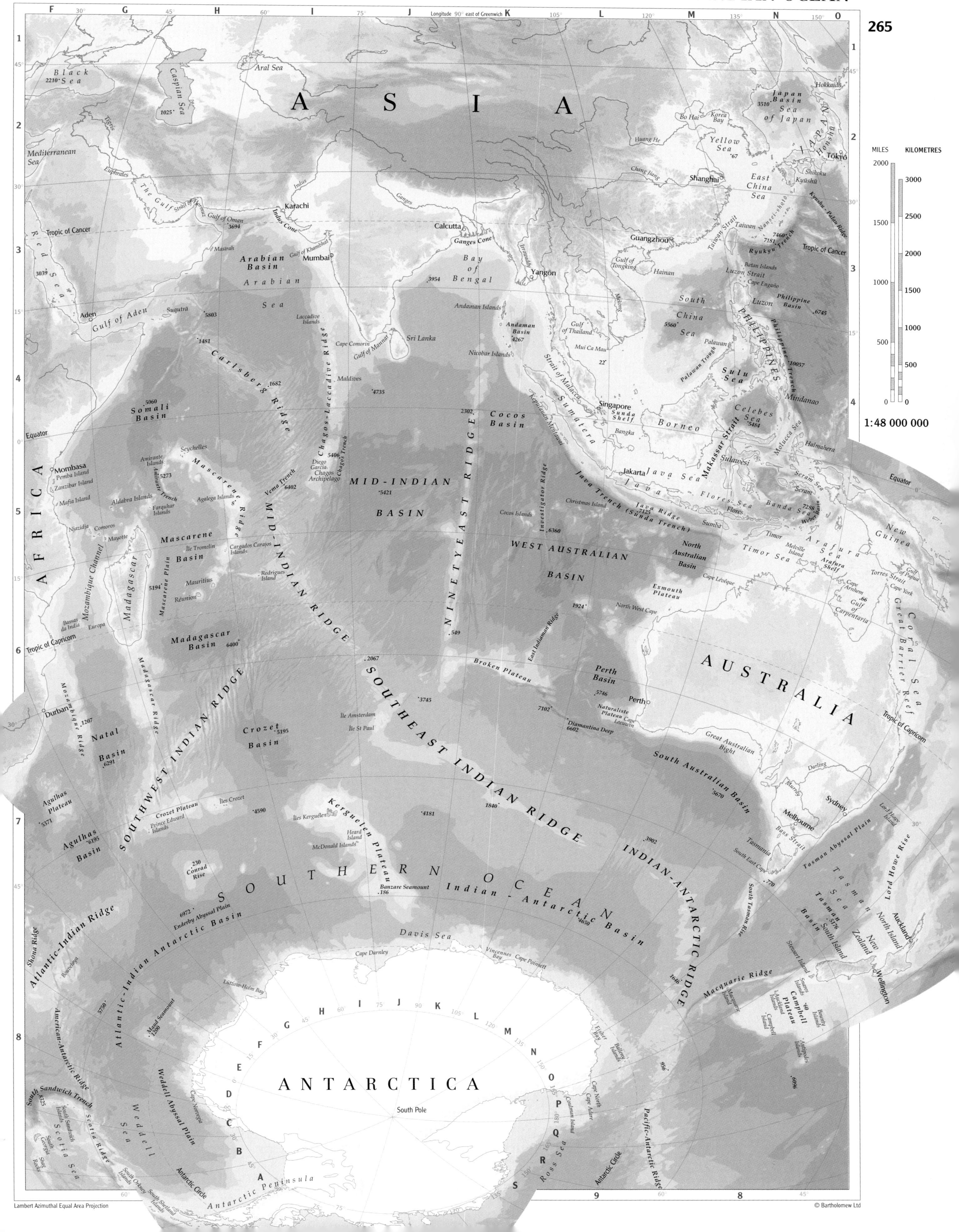

Longitude 90° east of Greenwich

MILES   KILOMETRES

1:48 000 000

A S I A

AFRICA

AUSTRALIA

ANTARCTICA

South Pole

Black Sea
2210
Caspian Sea
1025
Aral Sea
Mediterranean Sea
Red Sea
3039
The Gulf
Euphrates
Tigris
Strait of Hormuz
Gulf of Oman
3694
Karachi
Indus
Indus Cone
Gulf of Khambhat
Mumbai
3954
Ganges
Calcutta
Ganges Cone
Bay of Bengal
Yangon
Irrawaddy
Aden
Gulf of Aden
Suqutra
5803
Arabian Basin
Arabian Sea
Masirah
Laccadive Islands
1481
Carlsberg Ridge
1682
Chagos-Laccadive Ridge
Cape Comorin
Gulf of Mannar
Sri Lanka
Maldives
4735
Andaman Islands
Andaman Basin
4267
Nicobar Islands
Strait of Malacca
Sumatera
Singapore
Sunda Shelf
Mombasa
Pemba Island
Zanzibar Island
Mafia Island
Njazidja
Comoros
Mayotte
Somali Basin
5060
Seychelles
Amirante Islands
Amirante Trench
5273
Mascarene Ridge
Aldabra Islands
Farquhar Islands
Agalega Islands
8
2302
Chagos Trench
Vema Trench
6402
5406
Diego Garcia
Chagos Archipelago
MID-INDIAN BASIN
5421
Cocos Basin
NINETYEAST RIDGE
Cocos Islands
Investigator Ridge
6360
Christmas Island
Java Trench (Sunda Trench)
Java
Jakarta
Java Sea
Sunda
Bangka
Borneo
WEST AUSTRALIAN BASIN
East Indiaman Ridge
1924
North West Cape
North Australian Basin
Cape Lévêque
Exmouth Plateau
Ile Tromelin
Cargados Carajos Islands
Mascarene Basin
Madagascar
Mauritius
Réunion
5194
Rodrigues Island
Mascarene Plain
MID-INDIAN RIDGE
Madagascar Basin
6400
Madagascar Ridge
2067
Broken Plateau
3745
Ile Amsterdam
Ile St Paul
SOUTHEAST INDIAN RIDGE
549
Perth Basin
5746
Perth
Naturaliste Plateau
Cape Leeuwin
7102
Diamantina Deep
6602
Great Australian Bight
South Australian Basin
5670
Darling
Murray
Sydney
Melbourne
Bass Strait
Tasmania
Durban
Mozambique Ridge
1207
Natal Basin
6291
Agulhas Plateau
5371
Agulhas Basin
6195
SOUTHWEST INDIAN RIDGE
Crozet Basin
5195
Crozet Plateau
Prince Edward Islands
4590
Iles Crozet
Iles Kerguelen
Kerguelen Plateau
4181
Heard Island
McDonald Islands
1840
INDIAN-ANTARCTIC RIDGE
3902
South East Cape
South Tasman Rise
770
Tasman Sea
Tasman Basin
5276
South Island
Lord Howe Rise
Tasman Abyssal Plain
Atlantic-Indian Ridge
Shona Ridge
5779
Maud Seamount
1200
6972
Enderby Abyssal Plain
Banzare Seamount
186
Indian-Antarctic Basin
4630
SOUTHERN OCEAN
230 Conrad Rise
Atlantic-Indian Antarctic Basin
Davis Sea
Cape Darnley
Lützow-Holm Bay
Vincennes Bay
Cape Poinsett
956
6096
Macquarie Ridge
Campbell Plateau
Auckland Islands
Campbell Island
Wellington
North Island
Nero Deep
American-Antarctic Ridge
Bouvetøya
South Sandwich Trench
6325
South Sandwich Islands
Scotia Sea
Scotia Ridge
South Georgia
South Orkney Islands
South Shetland Islands
Antarctic Peninsula
Weddell Sea
Weddell Abyssal Plain
Antarctic Circle
Pacific-Antarctic Ridge
Ross Sea
Coulman Island
Cape North
Cape Adare
Balleny Islands
Fisher Bay
Scott Island
Japan Basin
Sea of Japan
3510
Hokkaidō
Honshū
Tokyo
Shikoku
Kyūshū
Kyūshū-Palau Ridge
Bo Hai
Korea Bay
Yellow Sea
67
Huang He
Chang Jiang
Shanghai
East China Sea
Guangzhou
Gulf of Tongking
Hainan
Mekong
Gulf of Thailand
Mui Ca Mau
22
South China Sea
5560
Taiwan Strait
Taiwan
Batan Islands
Luzon Strait
Cape Engaño
Luzon
7460
7181
Ryukyu Trench
Philippine Basin
6745
PHILIPPINES
Philippine Trench
10057
Mindanao
Palawan
Palawan Trough
Sulu Sea
5484
Celebes Sea
Molucca Sea
Halmahera
Sulawesi
Makassar Strait
Flores Sea
Flores
Sumba
Timor
Melville Island
Sumba
Banda Sea
7288
Weber
Seram Sea
Seram
Arafura Sea
Arafura Shelf
Cape Arnhem
Gulf of Carpentaria
66
New Guinea
Gulf of Papua
Torres Strait
Cape York
Coral Sea
Great Barrier Reef
Tropic of Cancer
Tropic of Capricorn
Equator
Tropic of Cancer

Lambert Azimuthal Equal Area Projection

© Bartholomew Ltd

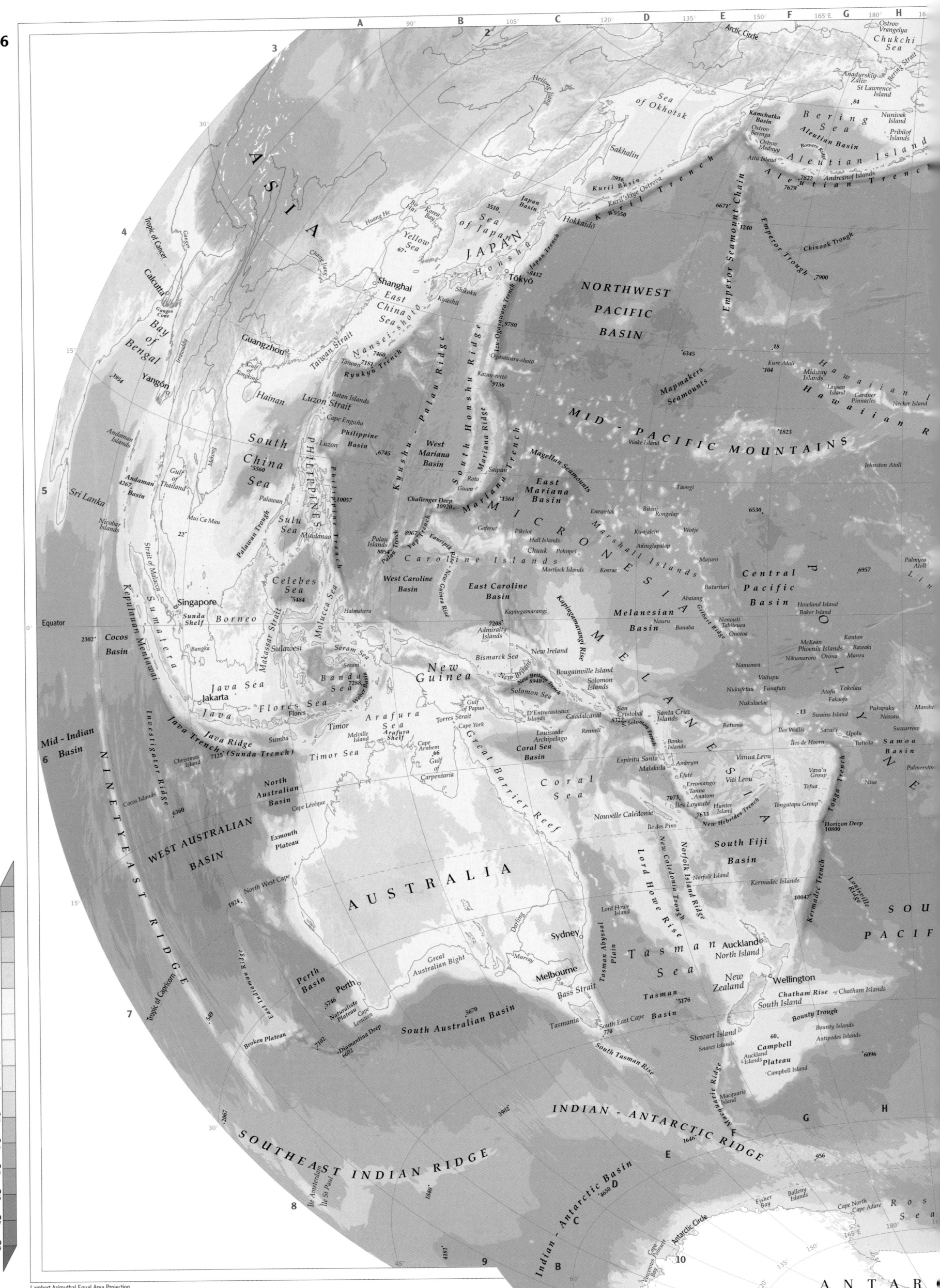

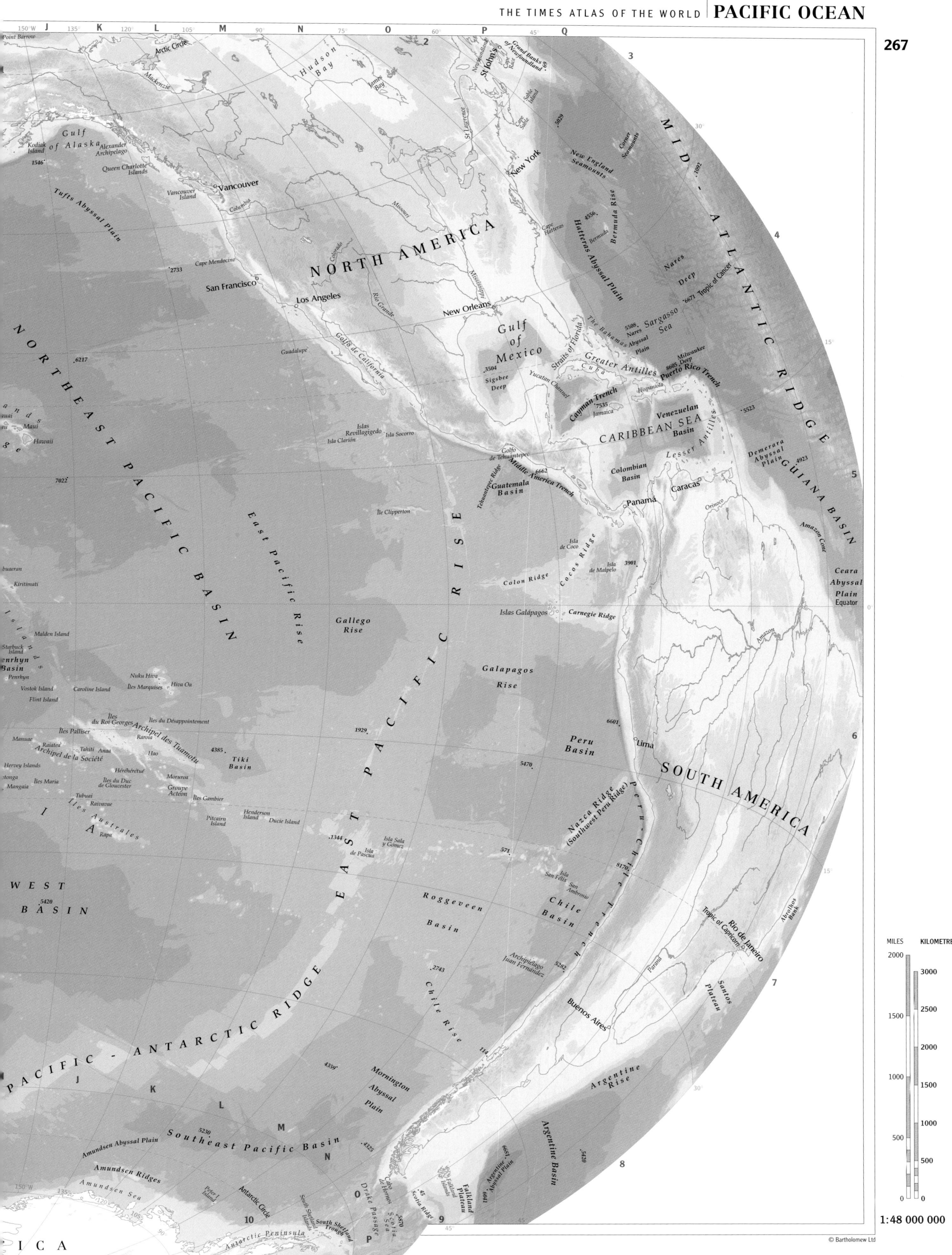

Point Barrow
150°W J 135° K 120° L 105° M 90° N 75° 2 O 60° P 45° Q 3
Arctic Circle
Mackenzie
Hudson Bay
James Bay
Newfoundland
St. John's
Grand Banks of Newfoundland
Cape Race
Cape Sable
MID - ATLANTIC RIDGE 3
Gulf of Alaska
Kodiak Island
Alexander Archipelago
Queen Charlotte Islands
1546
New York
New England Seamounts
Cone Seamounts
Bermuda Rise 4
.2733
Vancouver Island
Vancouver
Columbia
Missouri
Cape Hatteras
Hatteras Abyssal Plain
4556
Bermuda
.1002
NORTHEAST PACIFIC BASIN
Cape Mendocino
San Francisco
Los Angeles
Rio Grande
New Orleans
Colorado
Mississippi
Gulf of Mexico
Straits of Florida
The Bahamas
Nares Abyssal Plain
Sargasso Sea
Nares Deep
.6671 Tropic of Cancer
5508
15°
.6217
Guadalupe
Golfo de California
3504 Sigsbee Deep
Yucatan Channel
Cuba
Greater Antilles
Hispaniola
8605 Milwaukee Deep
Puerto Rico Trench
Milwaukee Deep
MID - ATLANTIC RIDGE
GUIANA BASIN
ai Kauai
Maui Hawaii
Islas Revillagigedo
Isla Socorro
Isla Clarión
Golfo de Tehuantepec
Tehuantepec Ridge
Middle America Trench
6662
Guatemala Basin
Cayman Trench
.7535
Jamaica
CARIBBEAN SEA
Venezuelan Basin
.5523
Demerara Abyssal Plain
.4923
5
7022
Île Clipperton
EAST PACIFIC RISE
Panamá
Colombian Basin
Caracas
Lesser Antilles
Amazon Cone
Isla de Coco
Colón Ridge
Cocos Ridge
Isla de Malpelo
3901.
Orinoco
Ceara Abyssal Plain
Equator 0
Islands
Kiritimati
Gallego Rise
Islas Galápagos
Carnegie Ridge
Amazon
Islands
Malden Island
Galapagos Rise
SOUTH AMERICA
Starbuck Island
enrhyn Basin
Penrhyn
Vostok Island
Flint Island
Nuku Hiva
Îles Marquises
Hiva Oa
Caroline Island
Peru Basin
6601.
Lima
6
Manuae
Raiatea
Tahiti Anaa
Îles du Roi Georges
Raroia
Îles du Désappointement
Archipel des Tuamotu
1929.
5470.
Nazca Ridge (Southwest Peru Ridge)
Hervey Islands
Archipel de la Société
Hao
Hérēhérétue
4385.
Tiki Basin
Peru-Chile Trench
tonga
Îles Maria
Mangaia
Îles du Duc de Gloucester
Moruroa
Groupe Actéon
Îles Gambier
I Îles A Australes
Tubuai
Raivavae
Rapa
Pitcairn Island
Henderson Island
Ducie Island
Isla Sala y Gómez
Isla de Pascua
571.
San Félix
Isla San Ambrosio
8170.
Chile Basin
15°
WEST BASIN
5420
EAST PACIFIC RISE
.1344
Roggeveen Basin
.2743
Archipiélago Juan Fernández
5292.
114
Paraná
Tropic of Capricorn
Rio de Janeiro
Abrolhos Bank
PACIFIC - ANTARCTIC RIDGE
Buenos Aires
Santos Plateau
7
4359.
Mornington Abyssal Plain
Chile Rise
Argentine Rise
Argentine Basin
.5429
J K L M N O P Q
5230
Southeast Pacific Basin
.4225
Parana
Argentine Abyssal Plain
1699.
Amundsen Abyssal Plain
Amundsen Ridges
Peter I Island
Antarctic Circle
Cabo de Hornos
45
Falkland Islands
Falkland Plateau
5579.
8
150°W 135° 120° 105° 90° 75° Drake Passage
South Shetland Islands
South Shetland Trough
Scotia Ridge
Scotia Sea
9
I C A
Antarctic Peninsula
10 P

© Bartholomew Ltd

MILES   KILOMETRES
2000
           3000
1500
           2500
           2000
1000
           1500
           1000
500
           500
0   0

1 : 48 000 000

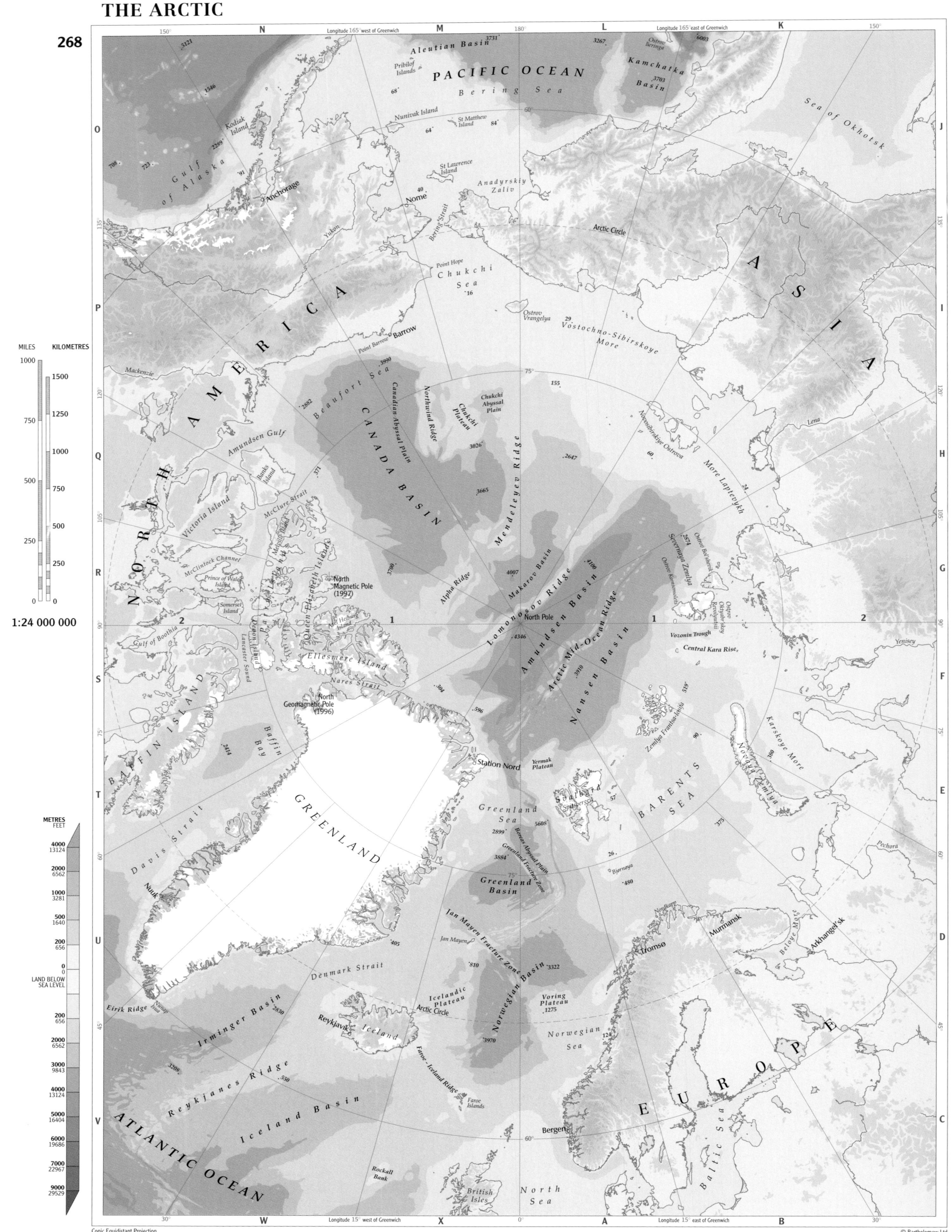

THE ARCTIC

268

MILES | KILOMETRES

1000 | 1500
750 | 1250
| 1000
500 | 750
250 | 500
| 250
0 | 0

1:24 000 000

METRES | FEET

4000 | 13124
2000 | 6562
1000 | 3281
500 | 1640
200 | 656
0 | 0
LAND BELOW SEA LEVEL
200 | 656
2000 | 6562
3000 | 9843
4000 | 13124
5000 | 16404
6000 | 19686
7000 | 22967
9000 | 29529

Conic Equidistant Projection

© Bartholomew Ltd

GLOSSARY

Geographical term	Language	Meaning
A		
-á	Icelandic	river
-å	Danish	river
Āb	Farsi	river
Abajo	Spanish	lower
Abbaye	French	abbey
Abhainn	Gaelic	river
Abyār	Arabic	wells
Açude	Portuguese	reservoir
Adası	Azeri, Turkish	island
Adrar	Berber	hills, mountains
Agia, Agios	Greek	saint
Agioi	Greek	saints
Aiguille	French	peak
Ain, 'Ain, 'Aïn, Aïn, 'Aïn	Arabic	spring, well
Akra	Greek	cape, point
Ala-	Finnish	lower
Allt	Gaelic	river
Alpi	Italian	mountain range
Alpe	Slovene	mountain range
Alpen	German	mountain range
Alpes	French	mountain range
Alt-	German	old
Alta	Italian, Portuguese, Spanish	upper
Altiplanicie	Spanish	high plain
Alto	Italian, Portuguese, Spanish	upper
Alto	Spanish	summit
-älv, -älven	Swedish	river
Ano	Greek	upper
Anou, Ânou	Berber	well
Anse	French	bay
Ao	Thai	bay
Archipel	French	archipelago
Archipiélago	Spanish	archipelago
Arenas	Spanish	sands
Argelanots'	Armenian	reserve
Arkhipelag	Russian	archipelago
Arquipélago	Portuguese	archipelago
Arrecife	Spanish	reef
Arriba	Spanish	upper
Arroio	Portuguese	watercourse
Arroyo	Spanish	watercourse
Augstiene	Latvian	hill region
Aust-	Norwegian	east, eastern
Austur-	Icelandic	east, eastern
Avtonomnaya, Avtonomnyy	Russian	autonomous
Āw	Kurdish	river
'Ayn	Arabic	spring, waterhole, well
B		
Baai, -baai	Afrikaans, Dutch	bay
Bāb	Arabic	strait
Bad	German	spa
Badia	Catalan	bay
Bādiyah	Arabic	desert
Bælt	Danish	strait
Bagh	Gaelic	bay
Bahia	Portuguese	bay
Bahía	Spanish	bay
Bahr, Baḥr, Baḩr	Arabic	bay, lake, canal, river, watercourse
Bahra, Baḩra	Arabic	lagoon, lake
Baía	Portuguese	bay
Baie	French	bay
Baixa, Baixo	Portuguese	lower
Baja	Spanish	lower
Bajja	Maltese	bay
Bajo	Spanish	depression, lower
Bālā	Farsi	upper
Ban	Laotian, Thai	village
Banc	Welsh	hill
Banco	Spanish	shoal
Bandao	Chinese	peninsula
Bandar	Arabic, Farsi, Somali	anchorage, inlet, port, harbour
Bandar	Malay	port, town
Banī	Arabic	desert
Banjaran	Malay	mountain range
Baraj, Barajı	Turkish	dam
Barat	Indonesian, Malay	west, western
Barra	Portuguese, Spanish	sandbank, sandbar, spit
Barrage	French	dam
Barragem	Portuguese	dam, reservoir
Barranco	Spanish	gorge, ravine
Baruun	Mongolian	west, western
Bas, Basse	French	lower
Bassin	French	basin
Bāţin, Baţn	Arabic	depression
-beek	Afrikaans, Dutch	river
Beg, Beag	Gaelic, Irish	small
Bei	Chinese	north, northern
bei	German	at, near
Beinn	Gaelic	mountain
Belogor'ye	Russian	mountain range
Ben	Gaelic	mountain
Bereg	Russian	coastal area
-berg, -berge	German, Norwegian, Swedish, Afrikaans	mountain, mountains
Besar	Indonesian, Malay	big
Bi'ār	Arabic	wells
Bir, Bi'r, Bîr	Arabic	waterhole, well
Birkat	Arabic	waterhole, well
-bjerg	Danish	hill
Boca	Portuguese, Spanish	mouth
Bodden	German	bay
Boğazı	Turkish	strait, pass
Bois	French	forest, wood
Boloto	Russian	marsh
Bol'shaya, Bol'shiye, Bol'shoy, Bol'shoye	Russian	big
-bong	Korean	mountain
Boquerón	Spanish	pass
Bory	Polish	woods
-botn	Norwegian	valley floor
-botten	Swedish	valley floor
Böyük	Azeri	big
Braţul	Romanian	arm, branch
-bre, -breen	Norwegian	glacier
Bredning	Danish	bay
Breg	Croatian, Serbian	hill
-bron	Afrikaans	spring, well
Brücke	German	bridge
Bucht	German	bay
Bugt	Danish	bay
-bugten	Danish	bay
Bukhta	Russian	bay
Bukit	Indonesian, Malay	hill, mountain
-bukt, -bukta	Norwegian	bay
-bukten	Swedish	bay
Bulag	Mongolian	spring
Bulak	Russian, Uighur	spring
Bum, Burun	Burmese	mountain
Burnu, Burun	Turkish	cape, point
Büyük	Turkish	big
Bwlch	Welsh	pass
C		
Cabo	Portuguese, Spanish	cape, point
Cachoeira	Portuguese	waterfall
Caka	Tibetan	salt lake
Cala	Catalan, Italian	bay
Caleta	Spanish	inlet
Câmpia	Romanian	plain
Campo	Italian, Spanish	plain
Cañada, Cañadón	Spanish	ravine, gorge
Canal	French, Portuguese, Spanish	canal, channel
Caño	Spanish	river
Cañon	Spanish	canyon
Caol	Gaelic	hill
Cap	Catalan, French	cape, point
Capo	Italian	cape, point
Carn	Welsh	hill
Castell	Catalan	castle
Causse	French	limestone plateau
Çay, -çay, Çayı, -çayı	Azeri, Turkish	river
Cayo	Spanish	island
Cefn	Welsh	hill, ridge
Cerro	Spanish	hill, mountain, peak
Česká, České, Český	Czech	Czech
Chaco	Spanish	plain
Chāh	Farsi	river
Chaîne	French	mountain range
Cham	Kurdish	river
Chapada	Portuguese	hills, uplands
Château	French	castle, palace
Chau	Chinese	island
Chaung	Burmese	river
Chāy	Kurdish	river
Chhu	Dzongkha (Bhutan)	river
Chiang	Thai	town
Chink	Russian	hill range
Chiyā	Kurdish	mountain, hill range
Chott	Arabic	salt lake
Chuan	Chinese	river
Chuŏr Phnum	Cambodian	mountain range
Ci	Indonesian	river
Ciénaga	Spanish	marshy lake
Cima	Italian	peak
Cime	French	peak
Città	Italian	city
Ciudad	Spanish	town, city
Cnoc	Gaelic	hill
Co	Tibetan	lake
Col	French	pass
Collado	Spanish	mountain
Colle	Italian	pass
Colline	French	hill
Cona	Tibetan	lake
Cordillera	Spanish	mountain range
Corno	Italian	peak
Coronel	Spanish	colonel
Costa	Catalan, Italian, Portuguese, Spanish	coastal area
Côte	French	coast, hill region, slope
Coutada	Portuguese	reserve
Coxilha	Portuguese	mountain pasture
Cratère	French	crater
Creag	Gaelic	mountain
Cruz	Spanish	cross
Cu Lao	Vietnamese	island
Cuchilla	Spanish	mountain range
Cuenca	Spanish	deep valley, river basin
Cueva	Spanish	cave
Cumbre	Spanish	mountain
-cun	Chinese	village
D		
Da	Chinese	big
Da	Vietnamese	river
Dağ, Dağı	Azeri, Turkish	hill(s), mountain(s)
Dāgh	Farsi	mountain(s)
Dağları	Turkish	mountains
-dake	Japanese	hill, mountain
-dal	Afrikaans, Danish, Swedish	valley
-dal, -dalen	Norwegian	valley
-dalur	Icelandic	valley
-dan	Korean	cape, point
Danau	Indonesian, Malay	lake
Dao	Chinese	island
Đao	Vietnamese	island
Daqq	Farsi	salt flat, salt lake
-dara	Tajik	river
Darreh	Farsi	valley
Dar'ya	Russian	river
Daryācheh	Farsi	lake
Dashan	Chinese	mountain
Dasht	Farsi	desert
Dataran Tinggi	Malay	plateau
Davan	Kazakh	pass
Dawḩat	Arabic	bay
Dayr	Arabic	monastery
Dealul	Romanian	hill, mountain
Dealurile	Romanian	hills
Deh	Farsi	village
Deir	Arabic	monastery
Denizi	Turkish	sea
Deresi	Turkish	river
Desierto	Spanish	desert
Détroit	French	channel
-diep	Dutch	channel
Dingzi	Chinese	hill, small mountain
Djebel	Arabic	mountain
-do	Korean	island
Dolna, Dolni	Bulgarian	lower
Dolna, Dolne, Dolny	Polish	lower
Dolní	Czech	lower
Dong	Chinese	east, eastern
-dong	Korean	village
Donja, Donji	Croatian, Serbian	lower
Dorf	German	village
-dorp	Afrikaans, Dutch	village
Druim	Gaelic	hill, mountain
Dund	Mongolian	middle, central
Düzü	Azeri	plain
-dyngja	Icelandic	hill, mountain
Dzüün	Mongolian	east, eastern
E		
Eilean	Gaelic	island
-elv, -elva	Norwegian	river
Embalse	Spanish	reservoir
'Emeq	Hebrew	plain
Ensenada	Spanish	bay
Erg, 'Erg, 'Erg	Arabic	sand dunes
Eski	Turkish	old
Estany	Catalan	pond
Estero	Spanish	estuary, inlet, lagoon
Estrada	Spanish	bay
Estrecho	Spanish	strait
Étang	French	lagoon, lake
-ey, -eyjar	Icelandic	island, islands
-eyri	Icelandic	sandbar
ežeras	Lithuanian	lake
ezers	Latvian	lake
F		
Falaise	French	cliff, escarpment
Farihy	Malagasy	lake
Fayḑat	Arabic	waterhole
-fell	Icelandic	hill, mountain
Fels	German	rock
Feng	Chinese	mountain
Fiume	Italian	river

Geographical term	Language	Meaning
-fjäll, -fjällen, -fjället	Swedish	hill(s), mountain(s)
-fjallgarður	Icelandic	mountains
-fjara	Icelandic	beach
-fjell, -fjellet	Norwegian	mountain
-fjöll	Icelandic	hill(s), mountain(s)
Fjord, -fjord, -fjorden	Danish, Norwegian, Swedish	fjord
-fjörður	Icelandic	fjord
Fliegu	Maltese	channel
-fljót	Icelandic	river
-flói	Icelandic	bay
-főcsatorna	Hungarian	canal
Foel	Welsh	hill
Förde	German	inlet
Forêt	French	forest
Forst	German	forest
-foss	Icelandic	waterfall
-foss, -fossen	Norwegian	rapids, waterfall
Fuente	Spanish	source, well
Fulayj	Arabic	watercourse

G

Geographical term	Language	Meaning
-gan	Japanese	rock
Gang	Dzongkha (Bhutan)	mountain
Gang	Chinese	bay, river
-gang	Korean	river
Gaoyuan	Chinese	plateau
Gardaneh	Farsi	pass
-gat	Dutch	channel
-gata	Japanese	inlet, lagoon, lake
Gau	German	district
Gave	French	torrent
-gawa	Japanese	river
Gebel	Arabic	mountain
Gebergte	Dutch	mountain range
Gebiet	German	district, region
Gebirge	German	mountains
Geodha	Gaelic	inlet
Gezâ'ir	Arabic	islands
Gezirat	Arabic	island
Ghard	Arabic	sand dunes
Ghubba	Arabic	bay
Gjiri	Albanian	bay
Gletscher	German	glacier
Gobernador	Spanish	governor
Gobi	Mongolian	desert
Gol	Mongolian	river
Göl	Azeri	lake
Golets	Russian	mountain
Golf	Catalan	gulf
Golfe	French	bay, gulf
Golfo	Italian, Spanish	bay, gulf
Gölü	Azeri, Turkish	lake
Gora	Bulgarian, Croatian, Russian, Serbian	mountain(s)
Gorges	French	gorge
Górka	Polish	hill
Gornja, Gornje, Gornji	Croatian, Serbian	upper
Gorno-	Russian	mountainous
Gory	Russian	mountains
Góry	Polish	mountains
Gou	Chinese	river
Graben	German	trench
-grad	Bulgarian, Croatian, Russian, Serbian	town
Grand, Grande	French	big
-gród	Polish	town
Groot	Afrikaans, Dutch	big
Gross, Grosse, Grossen, Grosser (also Groß-)	German	big
Grotta	Italian	cave
Grotte	French	cave
Grotte	Italian	caves
Groupe	French	group
Grund	German	ground, valley
Gruppo	Italian	group
Gryada	Russian	mountains
Guan	Chinese	pass
Guba	Russian	bay, gulf
Gubed	Somali	bay
-guntõ	Japanese	islands
Gunung	Indonesian, Malay	mountain
Guri	Albanian	peak

H

Geographical term	Language	Meaning
Ḩafar	Arabic	wells
Hafen	German	port, harbour
Haff	German	bay
Hai	Chinese	lake, sea
Haixia	Chinese	channel, strait
-háls	Icelandic	ridge
-halvøya	Norwegian	peninsula
Hamada, Hammada	Arabic	plateau
-hamn	Norwegian, Swedish	port, harbour
-hamrar	Icelandic	cliffs
Hāmūn	Farsi	marsh, salt pan
-hantō	Japanese	peninsula
Har	Hebrew	mountain
Hara	Belorussian	hill
Hardt	German	wooded hills
Ḩarrat, Ḩarrāt	Arabic	lava field
Hassi	Arabic	well
-haug, -haugen	Norwegian	hill
-havn	Danish, Faroese, Norwegian	bay, harbour, port
Hawr	Arabic	lake, impermanent lake, marsh
Hāyk'	Amharic	lake
He	Chinese	river
-hegység	Hungarian	hills, mountains
-hei	Norwegian	heath, moor
-heide	Dutch	heath, marsh
Heide	German	heath, moor
-heiði	Icelandic	heath

Geographical term	Language	Meaning
Helodrano	Malagasy	bay
Higashi-	Japanese	east, eastern
-hisar	Turkish	castle
Ḩiṣn	Arabic	fort
Hka	Burmese	river
-hnjúkur	Icelandic	hill
-ho	Korean	lake
-hø	Norwegian	peak
Hoch	German	high
Hoek	Dutch	cape, point
-höfði	Icelandic	hill, mountain
-höfn	Icelandic	cove
Hög	Swedish	height, high
-högda	Norwegian	height
Höhe	German	height
Hohen-	German	high
Hoi, Hoi Hap	Chinese	bay, channel, harbour, inlet
-høj, -høje	Danish	hill, hills
Hon	Vietnamese	island
Hoog	Dutch	high
Hora, Hory	Czech, Ukrainian	mountain(s)
-horn	Icelandic	cape, point, peak
Horn, -horn	German	mountain, peak
Horná, Horné, Horní, Horný	Czech	upper
Ḩorvot	Hebrew	ruins
-hot	Mongolian	town
-hrad	Czech	town
-hraun	Icelandic	lava field
Hu	Chinese	lake

I

Geographical term	Language	Meaning
Idd	Arabic	well
Île	French	island
Ilha, Ilhéu	Portuguese	island
Illa	Catalan	island
im	German	in
imeni	Russian	in the name of
Inish	Irish	island
Insel, Inseln	German	island, islands
Insula	Romanian	island
Irq, 'Irq	Arabic	hill, sand dune, sand dunes
Isla	Spanish	island
Iso-	Finnish	big
Isola, Isole	Italian	island, islands
Isolte	Catalan	island
Isthme	French	isthmus
Istmo	Spanish	isthmus
-iwa	Japanese	island

J

Geographical term	Language	Meaning
Jabal	Arabic	mountain
järv	Estonian	lake
-järvi	Finnish	lake
Jasiired	Somali	island
Jaun-	Latvian	new
-jaure	Lappish	lake
Jazirah, Jazïreh, Jazïrat	Arabic	island
Jbel, Jebel	Arabic	mountain
Jezero, jezero	Croatian, Serbian, Slovene	lake
Jezioro	Polish	lake
Jiang	Chinese	river
Jiao	Chinese	cape, point
Jibāl	Arabic	mountains
-jima	Japanese	island
Jing	Chinese	well
-jõgi	Estonian	river
-joki	Finnish	river
-jokka	Lappish	river
-jökull, jökullen	Icelandic, Norwegian	glacier, ice cap

K

Geographical term	Language	Meaning
Kaap	Afrikaans	cape, point
-kai	Japanese	bay, channel
-kaigan	Japanese	coastal area
-kaikyō	Japanese	channel, strait
Kali	Indonesian, Malay	river
kalnas, kalnis	Lithuanian	hill
Kalns	Latvian	hill
Kamen'	Russian	rock
Kamm	German	ridge, crest
Kâmpóng	Cambodian	town, village
-kanaal	Dutch	canal
Kanal	German, Russian	canal
Kanał	Polish	canal
Kanalı	Azeri	canal
Kaôh	Cambodian	island
Kap	Danish	cape, point
Kapp	Norwegian	cape, point
Karang	Indonesian, Malay	reef
Kato	Greek	lower
Kavïr	Farsi	salt desert
-kawa	Japanese	river
Kecil	Indonesian, Malay	small
K'edi	Georgian	hills
Kefar	Hebrew	village
Kepi	Albanian	cape, point
Kepulauan	Indonesian	islands
Keski-	Finnish	middle, central
Khabrah, Khabrat	Arabic	impermanent lake
Khalig, Khalïj	Arabic	bay, gulf
Khao	Thai	peak
Khashm	Arabic	hill
Khawr	Arabic	bay, channel
Khor, Khôr	Arabic	bay
Khowr	Farsi	bay, inlet
Khrebet	Russian	mountain range
Kis-	Hungarian	small
Kita-	Japanese	north, northern
Klein	Afrikaans	small
Klein, Kleine, Kleiner	German	small

Geographical term	Language	Meaning
Klint	Danish	cliff
-kloof	Afrikaans	pass
Knock	Irish	hill
-ko	Japanese	lake
Kɔ	Thai	island
-kōchi, -kōgen	Japanese	plateau
Koh	Farsi	mountain
Kok	Chinese	cape, point
Köl	Kazakh, Kyrgyz	lake
Kolpos	Greek	gulf
Koog	German	polder (reclaimed land)
-kop	Afrikaans	hill, mountain
Kopf	German	hill
Körfezi	Turkish	bay, gulf
kõrgustik	Estonian	upland
Kosa	Russian, Ukrainian	spit
Kou	Chinese	river mouth
-köy	Turkish	village
Kraj	Croatian, Czech, Polish, Serbian	region
Krajcbrazowy	Polish	regional
Kray	Russian	territory
Kryazh	Russian	hills, ridge
Kuala	Malay	river mouth
Küçük	Turkish	small
Kuduk	Uighur	well
Küh	Farsi	mountain
Kühhā	Farsi	mountain range
Kul'	Russian	lake
-kül	Tajik	lake
-küla	Estonian	village
Kum	Russian	sandy desert
-kundo	Korean	islands
Kuppe	German	hill top
kurk	Estonian	channel, strait
K'vemo	Georgian	upper
-kvísl, kvíslar	Icelandic	river, rivers
-kylä	Finnish	village
Kyun	Burmese	island

L

Geographical term	Language	Meaning
La	Tibetan	pass
Lac	French	lake
Lacul	Romanian	lake
Laem	Thai	cape, point
Lago	Italian, Portuguese, Spanish	lake
Lagoa	Portuguese	lagoon
Laguna	Spanish	lagoon, lake
Lagune	French	lagoon
laht	Estonian	bay
-laid	Estonian	island
Lam	Thai	river
Län	Swedish	county
Land	German	province
Lande	French	heath, sandy moor
Las	Polish	wood, forest
Laut	Indonesian, Malay	sea
Lerr	Armenian	mountain
Lerrnashght'a	Armenian	mountains
Lich	Armenian	lake
Liedao	Chinese	islands
Liel-	Latvian	big
Lille	Danish, Norwegian	small
Liman	Russian	bay, lagoon, lake
Limni	Greek	lagoon, lake
Limnothalassa	Greek	inlet, lagoon
Ling	Chinese	mountain range
Liqeni	Albanian	lake
Llano	Spanish	plain, prairie
Llyn	Welsh	lake
Loch, Lochan	Gaelic	lake, small lake
Lohatanjona	Malagasy	cape, point
Loi	Burmese	mountain
looduskaitseala	Estonian	reserve
Luonnonpuisto	Finnish	nature reserve
-luoto	Finnish	rocky island
Lyman	Ukrainian	bay, lake

M

Geographical term	Language	Meaning
Macizo	Spanish	mountain range
Madh	Albanian	big
Madïnat	Arabic	town
Mae, Mae Nam	Thai	river
mägi	Estonian	hill
Măgura	Romanian	hill, mountain
Maḩaṭṭat	Arabic	station
Maja	Albanian	mountain
Mal	Albanian	mountain(s)
Mala	Croatian, Serbian	small
Malá	Czech, Slovak	small
Mali	Albanian	mountain
Mali	Croatian, Serbian, Ukrainian	small
Malo	Croatian, Serbian	small
Maloye	Russian	small
Maly, Malyya	Belorussian	small
-man	Korean	bay
Mar	Spanish	lagoon, lake
Marais	French	marsh, swamp
Mare	Italian	sea
Mare	Romanian	big
marios	Lithuanian	lake
Marsa	Arabic	anchorage, bay, inlet
Marsch	German	fen, marsh
Masabb	Arabic	estuary
Massif	French	mountains, upland
Ma'ţan	Arabic	well
Mayor	Spanish	higher, larger
Maz-	Latvian	small
Meall	Gaelic	hill, mountain
Meer	Dutch, German	lake
Mega, Megalo-	Greek	big
Men	Chinese	gate

Geographical term	Language	Meaning
Menor	Portuguese, Spanish	smaller, lesser
Mersa	Arabic	anchorage, inlet
Mesa, Meseta	Spanish	tableland
Mesto	Croatian, Serbian	town
Město	Czech	town
Mets	Armenian	big
Mezzo	Italian	middle, central
Miao	Chinese	temple
Miasto	Polish	town
Mic, Mica	Romanian	small
Mikra, Mikri	Greek	small
Mīnā'	Arabic	port, harbour
Minami-	Japanese	south, southern
-mine	Japanese	mountain
-misaki	Japanese	cape, point
Mishāsh	Arabic	well
Mittel-, Mitten-	German	middle, central
Moel	Welsh	hill
Monasterio	Spanish	monastery
Moni	Greek	monastery
Mont	French	hill, mountain
Montagna	Italian	mountain
Montagne	French	mountain
Monte	Italian, Portuguese, Spanish	hill, mountain
Monti	Italian	mountains
Moor	German	marsh, moor, swamp
Moos	German	marsh, moss
More	Russian	sea
Mörön	Mongolian	river
Morro	Portuguese	hill
Morro	Spanish	cape, point
-mose	Danish	marsh, moor
Moyen	French	middle, central
Mt'a	Georgian	mountain
Muang	Laotian, Thai	town
Muara	Indonesian, Malay	estuary
Mui	Vietnamese	cape, point
Mun	Chinese	channel
Munţii	Romanian	mountains
Mynydd	Welsh	mountain
-mýri	Icelandic	marsh
Mys	Russian	cape, point

N

na	Croatian, Czech, Russian, Serbian, Slovak, Slovene	on
Nacional	Portuguese, Spanish	national
nacionalinis	Lithuanian	national
nad	Czech, Polish, Slovak	above, over
-nada	Japanese	bay, gulf
Nafūd	Arabic	desert, sand dunes
Nagor'ye	Russian	mountains, plateau
Nagy-	Hungarian	big
Nahr	Arabic	river
Nakhon	Thai	town
Nakrdzali	Georgian	reserve
Nam	Burmese, Laotian	river
Nam	Korean, Vietnamese	south, southern
Nan	Chinese	south, southern
Nanshan	Chinese	mountain range
Narodowy	Polish	national
Nationaal	Dutch	national
Naturreservat	Norwegian, Swedish	nature reserve
Natuurreservaat	Dutch	nature reserve
Naviglio	Italian	canal
Nawa-	Urdu	new
Nazionale	Italian	national
Neder-	Dutch	lower
Nehri	Turkish	river
Nei	Chinese	inner
Nek	Afrikaans	pass
-nes	Icelandic	cape, point
Neu-	German	new
Neuf, Neuve	French	new
Nevado, Nevada	Spanish	snow-covered mountain(s)
Nieder-	German	lower
Nieuw, Nieuwe, Nieuwer	Dutch	new
nina	Estonian	cape, point
Nishi-	Japanese	west, western
Nizhneye, Nizhniy, Nizhniye, Nizhnyaya	Russian	lower
Nizina	Belorussian	lowland
Nízke	Slovak	low
Nizmennost'	Russian	lowland
Nižní	Czech	lower
Nižný	Slovak	lower
Noguera	Catalan	river
Noord	Dutch	north, northern
Nord	French, German	north, northern
Nord-, Nordre	Danish	north, northern
Norður	Icelandic	north, northern
Norra	Swedish	north, northern
Nørre	Danish	north, northern
Norte	Portuguese, Spanish	north, northern
Nos	Bulgarian, Russian	cape, point, spit
Nosy	Malagasy	island
Nou	Romanian	new
Nouveau, Nouvelle	French	new
Nova	Bulgarian, Croatian, Portuguese, Serbian, Slovene, Ukrainian	new
Nová	Czech	new
Novaya	Russian	new
Nové	Czech, Slovak	new
Novi	Bulgarian, Croatian, Serbian, Ukrainian	new
Novo	Portuguese, Slovene	new
Novo-, Novoye	Russian	new
Novy	Belorussian	new
Nový	Czech	new
Novyy, Novyye	Russian, Ukrainian	new
Novyya	Belorussian	new
Nowa, Nowe, Nowy	Polish	new
Nueva, Nuevo	Spanish	new
-numa	Japanese	lake

Geographical term	Language	Meaning
-núpur	Icelandic	hill
Nur	Chinese, Mongolian	lake
Nuruu	Mongolian	mountain range
Nuur	Mongolian	lake
Ny-	Danish, Norwegian, Swedish	new

O

-ø	Danish	island
-ö	Swedish	island
oaivi, oaivve	Lappish	hill, mountain
Obanbari	Tajik	reservoir
Ober-	German	upper
Oblast'	Russian, Ukrainian	administrative division
-odde	Danish, Norwegian	cape, point
Oeste	Spanish	west, western
Okrug	Russian	administrative district
-ön	Swedish	island
Öndör-	Mongolian	upper
-oog	German	island
Oost, Ooster	Dutch	east, eastern
-öræfi	Icelandic	lava field
Oriental	Spanish	east, eastern
Ormos	Greek	bay
Oros	Greek	mountain
-ós	Icelandic	river mouth
Ost-	German	east, eastern
Øster-	Danish, Norwegian	east, eastern
Östra-	Swedish	east, eastern
Ostriv	Ukrainian	island
Ostrov, Ostrova	Russian	island, islands
Oud, Oude, Ouden, Ouder	Dutch	old
Oued	Arabic	watercourse
Ovası	Turkish	plain
Over-	Danish, Dutch	upper
Över-, Övre-	Norwegian, Swedish	upper
-oy	Faroese	island
Ozero	Russian, Ukrainian	lake

P

-pää	Finnish	hill
Pampa	Spanish	plain
Pantà	Catalan	reservoir
Pantanal	Portuguese	marsh
Pao	Chinese	small lake
Parbat	Urdu	mountain
Parc	French	park
Parc Naturel	French	nature reserve
Parco	Italian	park
parkas	Lithuanian	park
Parque	Portuguese, Spanish	park
-pas	Afrikaans	pass
Paso	Spanish	pass
Paß	German	pass
Passage	French	channel
Passe	French	channel
Passo	Italian	pass
Pasul	Romanian	pass
Pegunungan	Indonesian, Malay	mountain range
Pelabuhan	Malay	port, harbour
Pen	Welsh	hill
Peña	Spanish	cliff, rock
Pendi	Chinese	basin
Península	Spanish	peninsula
Péninsule	French	peninsula
Penisola	Italian	peninsula
Pereval	Russian	pass
Pervo-, Pervyy	Russian	first
Peski	Russian	desert
Petit, Petite	French	small
Phou	Laotian	mountain
Phu	Thai, Vietnamese	mountain
Phumĭ	Cambodian	town, village
Pic	Catalan, French	peak
Picacho	Spanish	peak
Pico	Spanish	peak
Pik	Russian	peak
Pingyuan	Chinese	plain
Pivostriv	Ukrainian	peninsula
Pizzo	Italian	peak
-plaat	Dutch	flat, sandbank, shoal
Plage	French	beach
Plaine	French	plain
Planalto	Portuguese	plateau
Planina	Bulgarian, Croatian, Serbian	mountain(s)
Platforma	Romanian	plateau
Plato	Bulgarian, Russian	plateau
Playa	Spanish	beach
Plaza	Spanish	market-place, square
Ploskogor'ye	Russian	plateau
Po	Chinese	lake
pod	Czech, Russian, Slovak	under, sub-, near
Podişul	Romanian	plateau
Pointe	French	cape, point
Pojezierze	Polish	area of lakes
Polje	Croatian, Serbian	plain
Poluostrov	Russian	peninsula
Pont	French	bridge
Ponta	Maltese, Portuguese	cape, point
Ponte	Portuguese	bridge
poolsaar	Estonian	peninsula
Porogi	Russian	rapids
Port	Catalan, French, Maltese, Russian	port, harbour
Portella	Italian	pass
Portillo	Spanish	gap, pass
Porto	Italian, Portuguese, Spanish	bay, port, harbour, pass
Pradesh	Hindi	state

Geographical term	Language	Meaning
Praia	Portuguese	beach, shore
Prêk	Cambodian	lake, river
près	French	near, beside
Presa	Spanish	reservoir
Presqu'île	French	peninsula
Pri-	Russian	near, by
Proliv	Russian	channel, strait
Protoka	Russian	channel, watercourse
Pueblo	Spanish	village
Puente	Spanish	bridge
Puerta	Spanish	narrow pass
Puerto	Spanish	pass, port, harbour
Puig	Catalan	hill, mountain
Puk-	Korean	north, northern
Pulau	Indonesian, Malay	island
Pulau-pulau	Indonesian, Malay	islands
Puncak	Indonesian, Malay	hill, mountain, summit
Punta	Italian, Spanish	cape, point
Punta	Italian	hill, mountain
Puntan	Marshallese	cape, point
Puy	French	peak

Q

Qā'	Arabic	depression, salt flat, impermanent lake
Qabr	Arabic	tomb
Qafa	Albanian	pass
Qala	Maltese	bay
Qalamat	Arabic	well
Qalti	Arabic	well
Qāret	Arabic	hill
Qatorkūhi	Tajik	mountain range
Qi	Chinese	banner (administrative division)
Qiao	Chinese	bridge
Qiryat	Hebrew	town
Qolleh	Farsi	mountain
Qoor, Qooriga	Somali	bay
qoruğu	Azeri	reserve
Qu	Tibetan	river
Quan	Chinese	spring, well
Quebrada	Spanish	ravine, river
Qullai	Tajik	mountain
Qundao	Chinese	islands

R

Raas	Somali	cape, point
Rade	French	harbour
rags	Latvian	cape, point
Rambla	Catalan	river
Ramla	Maltese	bay, harbour
Ramlat	Arabic	sandy desert
-rani	Icelandic	spur
Ras	Arabic, Maltese	cape, point
Ra's	Arabic, Farsi	cape, point
Rās, Räs	Arabic	cape, point
Ravnina	Russian	plain
Récif	French	reef
Represa	Portuguese, Spanish	reservoir
Reserva	Portuguese, Spanish	reserve
Réserve de Faune, Réserve Faunique	French	wildlife reserve
Réserve Naturelle	French	nature reserve
Reshteh	Farsi	mountain range
Respublika	Russian	republic
-rettō	Japanese	island chain, island group
rezervatas	Lithuanian	reserve
-ri	Korean	village
Ri	Tibetan	mountain
Ría	Spanish	estuary, inlet, river mouth
Ribeirão, Ribeiro	Portuguese	river
Rio	Portuguese	river
Río	Spanish	river
Riserva	Italian	reserve
-rivier	Afrikaans	river
Riviera	Italian	coastal area
Rivière	French	river
Roca	Spanish	rock
Rocher	French	rock
Rt	Croatian, Serbian	cape, point
Rū, Rūbār	Kurdish	river
Rubh', Rubha	Gaelic	cape, point
Rūd, Rūdkhāneh	Farsi	river
Rujm	Arabic	hill

S

-saar	Estonian	island
-saari	Finnish	island
Sabkhat, Sabkhet	Arabic	impermanent lake, salt flat, salt marsh
Sadd, Saddat	Arabic	dam
Sagar, Sagara	Hindi	lake
Şaghīr, Şaghīr	Arabic	small
Şaḥrā'	Arabic	desert
-saki	Japanese	cape, point
Salar, Salina	Spanish	salt pan
Salto	Portuguese, Spanish	waterfall
San	Italian, Maltese, Portuguese, Spanish	saint
San	Laotian	mountain
-san	Japanese, Korean	mountain
-sanchi	Japanese	mountain range
-sandur	Icelandic	sandy area
Sankt	German, Russian	saint
-sanmaek	Korean	mountain range
-sanmyaku	Japanese	mountain range
Sant	Catalan	saint
Sant'	Italian	saint

Geographical term	Language	Meaning
Santa	Italian, Portuguese, Spanish	saint
Santo	Italian, Portuguese, Spanish	saint
São	Portuguese	saint
Sar	Kurdish	mountain
Sarīr	Arabic	desert
Satu	Romanian	village
Say	Kyrgyz	river
Schloß	German	castle, mansion
Scoglio	Italian	reef, rock
Sebkha, Sebkhet	Arabic	salt flat, salt marsh
See, -see	German	lake
-şehir	Turkish	town
Selat	Indonesian, Malay	channel, strait
Selatan	Indonesian, Malay	south, southern
-selkä	Finnish	lake, open water, ridge
Selo	Croatian, Russian, Serbian	village
Selva	Portuguese, Spanish	forest
Semenanjung	Indonesian, Malay	peninsula
Seno	Spanish	bay, sound
Serra	Catalan, Portuguese	hills, mountains
Serranía	Spanish	mountain range
-seter	Norwegian	mountain pasture
-seto	Japanese	channel, strait
Severnaya, Severnoye, Severnyy, Severo-	Russian	north, northern
Sfântu	Romanian	saint
Sgeir	Gaelic	island
Sgor, Sgorach, Sgorr, Sgurr	Gaelic	hill
Shahr	Farsi	town
Sha'īb, Sha'īān	Arabic	watercourse
Shamo	Chinese	desert
Shan	Chinese	hill(s), mountain(s)
Shang	Chinese	next to, upper
Shankou	Chinese	pass
Sharm	Arabic	bay
Shaṭṭ	Arabic	estuary, river mouth, watercourse
Shën-	Albanian	saint
Shet'	Amharic	watercourse
Shi	Chinese	city
-shima	Japanese	island
-sho	Japanese	island
-shotō	Japanese	islands
Shui	Chinese	river
Shui Tong	Chinese	reservoir
Shuiku	Chinese	reservoir
Sierra	Spanish	mountain range
Silsiläsi	Azeri	hills
-sjø	Norwegian	lake
-sjö, -sjön	Swedish	lake
-sjór	Icelandic	lake
-sker	Icelandic	island
-skog	Norwegian	wood
Slieau	Manx	hill, mountain
Slieve	Irish	hill, mountain
Sloboda	Russian	large village
Sø	Danish, Norwegian	lake
Söder, Södra	Swedish	south, southern
Solonchak	Russian	salt lake
Sommet	French	peak, summit
Sønder-, Søndre	Danish	south, southern
Sông	Vietnamese	river
Sopka	Russian	hill, mountain, volcano
Sør-	Norwegian	south, southern
Sor	Russian	salt pan
sous	French	under
Sovkhoz	Russian	state farm
Spitze	German	peak
Sredna, Sredno	Bulgarian	middle, central
Sredne-, Sredneye, Sredniy, Srednyaya	Russian	middle, central
Sron	Gaelic	hill
Stac	Gaelic	hill, stack
-stad	Afrikaans, Norwegian, Swedish	town
-stadt	German	town
-staður	Icelandic	town
Stagno	Italian	lagoon, lake
Stara, Stari	Croatian, Serbian, Ukrainian	old
Stará, Staré, Starý	Czech	old
Staraya, Stary, Staryya	Belorussian	old
Staraya, Staroye, Staryy, Staryye	Russian	old
Stare, Staro-, Staryy	Ukrainian	old
Stausee	German	reservoir
Steno	Greek	strait
Step'	Russian	plain, steppe
Stob	Gaelic	hill, mountain
Stœng	Cambodian	river
Stór-, Stóra, Stóri	Icelandic	big
Stor, Stora	Swedish	big
Store	Danish	big
Strand	Danish, German	beach
-strand	Norwegian, Swedish	beach
Straße	German	street
Stretta	Italian	strait
-strönd	Icelandic	beach
Sud	French	south, southern
Süd-, Süder-	German	south, southern
Suður-	Icelandic	south, southern
Suid	Afrikaans	south, southern
-suidō	Japanese	channel, strait
Sul	Portuguese	south, southern
sul, sull'	Italian	on
Sund	Swedish	strait, sound
Sungai	Indonesian, Malay	river
-suo	Finnish	marsh, swamp
Superior	Spanish	upper
Sūq	Arabic	market
Sur	Spanish	south, southern
sur	French	on
Suur	Estonian	big
Sveti	Croatian, Serbian	saint
Syðra, Syðri	Icelandic	south, southern
sýsla	Icelandic	county

Geographical term	Language	Meaning
Szent-	Hungarian	saint
-sziget	Hungarian	island

T

-tag	Uighur	mountain
-take	Japanese	hill, mountain
Tal	German	valley
Tall	Arabic	hill
Tanjona	Malagasy	cape, point
Tanjong, Tanjung	Indonesian, Malay	cape, point
Tao	Chinese	island
Tassili	Berber	plateau
Tau	Russian	mountain(s)
Taung	Burmese	mountain
Tba	Georgian	lake
Techniti Limni	Greek	reservoir
tekojärvi	Finnish	reservoir
Tell	Arabic	hill, mountain
Teluk, Telukan	Indonesian, Malay	bay, gulf
Tengah	Indonesian, Malay	middle, central
Teniente	Spanish	lieutenant
Tepe, Tepesi	Turkish	hill, mountain
Terara	Amharic	mountain
Terre	French	land
Thale	Thai	lake
Thamad	Arabic	well
Tierra	Spanish	land
Timur	Indonesian, Malay	east, eastern
-tind, -tinden	Norwegian	peak
-tindar	Icelandic	peak
-tindur	Faroese, Icelandic	peak
Tir'at	Arabic	canal, river, watercourse
Tizi	Berber	pass
-tjåkkå	Lappish	mountain
-tjärro	Lappish	mountain
-tó	Hungarian	lake
-tō	Japanese	island
-to	Korean	island
-tōge	Japanese	pass
-tong	Korean	village
Tônlé	Cambodian	lake, river
Too	Kyrgyz	mountain range
-topp, -toppen	Norwegian	peak
T'ou	Chinese	cape, point
Tsentral'nyy	Russian	central
Tso	Tibetan	lake
Tsqalsats'avi	Georgian	reservoir
Tsui	Chinese	cape, point
Túnel	Spanish	tunnel
-tunturi	Finnish	treeless mountain

U

Über-	German	upper
-udden	Swedish	cape, point
Ugheltekhili	Georgian	pass
Új-	Hungarian	new
Ujung	Indonesian	cape, point
Unter-, unter	German	below, lower
'Uqlat	Arabic	well
-ura	Japanese	inlet
'Urayq, 'Urūq	Arabic	sand dunes
Ust'-, Ust'ye	Russian	river mouth
Utara	Indonesian, Malay	north, northern
Uttar	Hindi	north, northern
Uul	Mongolian	mountain range
Uval	Russian	hills
'Uyūn	Arabic	springs

V

v	Czech	in
-vaara, -vaarat	Finnish	hill(s), mountain(s)
Vaart, -vaart	Dutch	canal
-vaðall	Icelandic	inlet
-våg	Norwegian	bay
-vágur	Faroese	bay
Väike-	Estonian	small
väin	Estonian	bay, channel, strait
Val	French, Portuguese, Spanish	valley
Vale	Portuguese, Romanian	valley
Vall	Catalan, Spanish	valley
Valle	Italian, Spanish	valley
Vallée	French	valley
Valli	Italian	valleys
Vallon	French	small valley
Vârful	Romanian	hill, mountain
-város	Hungarian	town
-varre	Norwegian	mountain
Väster, Västra	Swedish	west, western
-vatn	Icelandic	lake
-vatn, -vatnet	Norwegian	lake
-vatten, -vattnet	Swedish	lake
Vaux	French	valleys
Vechi	Romanian	old
veehoidla	Estonian	lake
-veld	Afrikaans	field
Velha, Velho	Portuguese	old
Velika	Croatian, Slovene, Serbian	big
Velikaya, Velikiy, Velikiye	Russian	big
Velike	Slovene	big
Veliki	Croatian, Serbian	big
Velká, Velké, Velký	Czech	big
Veľká, Veľké, Veľký	Slovak	big
-vellir	Icelandic	plain
Velyka	Ukrainian	big
Verkhne-, Verkhneye, Verkhniy, Verkhnyaya	Russian	upper
-vesi	Finnish	lake, water
Viaduc	French	viaduct
-vidda	Norwegian	plateau

Geographical term	Language	Meaning
Vieja, Viejo	Spanish	old
Vieux	French	old
Vig	Danish	bay
-vík	Icelandic	bay
-vik	Norwegian	bay, inlet
Vila	Portuguese	small town
Ville	French	town
Vinh	Vietnamese	bay
-víz	Hungarian	river
-víztároló	Hungarian	reservoir
-vlei	Afrikaans	lake, salt pan
-vloer	Afrikaans	salt pan
Voblasts'	Belorussian	province
Vodaskhovishcha	Belorussian	reservoir
Vodná nádrž	Slovak	reservoir
Vodní nádrž	Czech	reservoir
Vodokhranilishche	Russian	reservoir
Vodoskhovyshche	Ukrainian	reservoir
-vogur	Icelandic	bay
Volcán	Spanish	volcano
Vostochno-, Vostochnyy	Russian	east, eastern
-vötn	Icelandic	lakes
Vozvyshennost'	Russian	hills, upland
Vozyera	Belorussian	lake
Vpadina	Russian	depression
Vrchovina	Czech	hills, mountain region
Vrŭkh	Bulgarian	hill, mountain
Vulkan	Russian	volcano
Vyalikaya, Vyalikaye, Vyaliki, Vyalikiya	Belorussian	big
Vyerkhnya	Belorussian	upper
Vysokaya, Vysokoye	Russian	upper

W

-waard	Dutch	polder (reclaimed land)
Wad	Dutch	sandflat
Wadi, Wâdi, Wādī	Arabic	watercourse
Wai	Chinese	outer
Wald	German	forest
Wan	Chinese	bay
-wan	Japanese	bay
Wand	German	cliff
Wasser	German	water
Wāw	Arabic	well
Webi	Somali	river
Wenz	Amharic	river, watercourse
Wielka, Wielki, Wielkie, Wielko-	Polish	big
-woud	Dutch	wood, forest
Wysoka, Wysoki, Wysokie	Polish	upper
Wyżna	Polish	lowland
Wzvyshsha	Belorussian	upland

X

Xé	Vietnamese	river
Xi	Chinese	river, west, western
Xia	Chinese	gorge, lower
Xian	Chinese	county
Xiao	Chinese	small

Y

Yam	Hebrew	lake, sea
-yama	Japanese	mountain
Yang	Chinese	channel
Yangi	Russian	new
Yarımadası	Azeri, Turkish	peninsula
Yazovir	Bulgarian	reservoir
Ye	Burmese	island
Yeni	Turkish	new
Yli-	Finnish	upper
Ynys	Welsh	island
Yoma	Burmese	mountain range
You	Chinese	right
Ytra-, Ytri-	Icelandic	outer
Ytre-	Norwegian	outer
Ytter-	Norwegian, Swedish	outer
Yuan	Chinese	spring
Yumco	Tibetan	lake
Yunhe	Chinese	canal
Yuzhno-, Yuzhnyy	Russian	south, southern

Z

Za-	Russian	behind, beyond
-zaki	Japanese	cape, point
Zalew	Polish	bay
Zaliv	Russian	bay, gulf, inlet
-zan	Japanese	mountain
Zand	Dutch	sandbank, sandhill
Zangbo	Tibetan	river
Zapadnaya, Zapadno-, Zapadnyy	Russian	west, western
Zapavyednik	Belorussian	reserve
Zapovednik	Russian	reserve
Zapovidnyk	Ukrainian	reserve
Zatoka	Polish, Ukrainian	bay, gulf, lagoon
-zee	Dutch	lake, sea
Zemlya	Russian	land
Zemo	Georgian	upper
Zhen	Chinese	town
Zhong	Chinese	middle, central
Zhou	Chinese	island
Zizhiqu	Chinese	autonomous region
Zuid, Zuider	Dutch	south, southern
Zuo	Chinese	left

INTRODUCTION TO THE INDEX

The index includes names shown on the maps in the Atlas of the World. Each entry includes the country or geographical area in which the feature is located, a page number and an alphanumeric reference. Additional details within the entries are explained below. Abbreviations used in the index are explained in the table below.

REFERENCING

Names are referenced by page number, the first element of each entry, and by a grid reference. The grid reference correlates to the alphanumeric values which appear within each map frame. These reflect the graticule on the map – the letter relates to longitude divisions, the number to latitude divisions.

Names are generally referenced to the largest scale map page on which they appear. For large geographical features, including countries, the reference is to the largest scale map on which the feature appears in its entirety, or on which the majority of it appears.

Rivers are referenced to their lowest downstream point – either their mouth or their confluence with another river. The river name will generally be positioned as close to this point as possible, but may not necessarily be in the same grid square.

ALTERNATIVE NAMES

Alternative names or name forms appear as cross-references and refer the user to the entry for the map form of the name.

For rivers with multiple names – for example those which flow through several countries – all alternative name forms are included within the main index entries, with details of the countries in which each form applies. Different types of name used are: alternative forms or spellings currently in use (alt.); English conventional name forms normally used in English-language contexts (conv.); and long names – full forms of names which are most commonly used in the abbreviated form.

ADMINISTRATIVE QUALIFIERS

Entries within the following countries include the main administrative division in which they occur: Australia, Canada, China, India, U.K., U.S.A. and Yugoslavia. Administrative divisions are also included to differentiate duplicate names – entries of exactly the same name and feature type within the one country – where these division names are shown on the maps. In such cases, duplicate names are alphabetized in the order of the administrative division names.

Additional qualifiers are included for names within selected geographical areas, to indicate more clearly their location. In particular, this has been applied to island nations to indicate the island group, or individual island, on which a feature occurs.

DESCRIPTORS

Entries, other than those for towns and cities, include a descriptor indicating the type of geographical feature. Descriptors are not included where the type of feature is implicit in the name itself, unless there is a town or city of exactly the same name.

INSETS

Entries relating to names appearing on insets are indicated by a small box symbol: □, followed by an index number if there is more than one inset on the page, or by a grid reference if the inset has its own alphanumeric values.

NAME FORMS AND ALPHABETICAL ORDER

Name forms are as they appear on the maps, with additional alternative forms included as cross-references. Names appear in full in the index, although they may appear in abbreviated form on the maps.

The Icelandic characters Þ and þ are transliterated and alphabetized as 'Th' and 'th'. The German character ß is alphabetized as 'ss'. Names beginning with Mac or Mc are alphabetized exactly as they appear. The terms Saint, Sainte, etc, are abbreviated to St, Ste, etc, but alphabetized as if in the full form.

Name form policies are explained in the Introduction to the Atlas (pp 66-67).

NUMERICAL ENTRIES

Entries beginning with numerals appear at the beginning of the index, in numerical order. Elsewhere, numerals appear before 'a'.

PERMUTED TERMS

Names beginning with generic, geographical terms are permuted – the descriptive term is placed after, and the index alphabetized by, the main part of the name. For example, Lake Superior is indexed as Superior, Lake; Mount Everest as Everest, Mount. This policy is applied to all languages. Permuting has not been applied to names of towns, cities or administrative divisions beginning with such geographical terms. These remain in their full form, for example, Lake Isabella, California, USA.

The definite article is not permuted in any language.

INDEX ABBREVIATIONS

A.C.T.	Australian Capital Territory	est.	estuary	Moz.	Mozambique	rf	reef
admin. dist.	administrative district	Eth.	Ethiopia	MS	Mississippi	RI	Rhode Island
admin. div.	administrative division	Fin.	Finland	MT	Montana	Rus. Fed.	Russian Federation
admin. reg.	administrative region	FL	Florida	mt.	mountain	S.	South
Afgh.	Afghanistan	for.	forest	mts	mountains	S.A.	South Australia
AK	Alaska	Fr. Guiana	French Guiana	mun.	municipality	Sask.	Saskatchewan
AL	Alabama	Fr. Polynesia	French Polynesia	N.	North	SC	South Carolina
Alg.	Algeria	g.	gulf	N.B.	New Brunswick	SD	South Dakota
alt.	alternative name form	GA	Georgia	NC	North Carolina	sea chan.	sea channel
Alta	Alberta	Gd Bahama	Grand Bahama	ND	North Dakota	Sing.	Singapore
Andhra Prad.	Andhra Pradesh	Ger.	Germany	NE	Nebraska	str.	strait
AR	Arkansas	Guat.	Guatemala	Neth.	Netherlands	Switz.	Switzerland
Arg.	Argentina	hd	headland	Nfld.	Newfoundland	Tajik.	Tajikistan
Arun. Prad.	Arunachal Pradesh	Heilong.	Heilongjiang	NH	New Hampshire	Tanz.	Tanzania
Austr.	Australia	HI	Hawaii	Nic.	Nicaragua	Tas.	Tasmania
aut. comm.	autonomous community	Hima. Prad.	Himachal Pradesh	NJ	New Jersey	terr.	territory
aut. div.	autonomous division	H.K.	Hong Kong	NM	New Mexico	Thai.	Thailand
aut. prov.	autonomous province	Hond.	Honduras	N.S.	Nova Scotia	TN	Tennessee
aut. reg.	autonomous region	i.	island	N.S.W.	New South Wales	Trin. and Tob.	Trinidad and Tobago
aut. rep.	autonomous republic	is	islands	N.T.	Northern Territory	tun.	tunnel
AZ	Arizona	IA	Iowa	NV	Nevada	Turkm.	Turkmenistan
Azer.	Azerbaijan	ID	Idaho	N.W.T.	Northwest Territories	TX	Texas
b.	bay	IL	Illinois	NY	New York	U.A.E.	United Arab Emirates
Bangl.	Bangladesh	imp. l.	impermanent lake	N.Z.	New Zealand	U.K.	United Kingdom
B.C.	British Columbia	IN	Indiana	OH	Ohio	Ukr.	Ukraine
B.I.O.T.	British Indian Ocean Territory	Indon.	Indonesia	OK	Oklahoma	Uru.	Uruguay
Bol.	Bolivia	isth.	isthmus	Ont.	Ontario	U.S.A.	United States of America
Bos.-Herz.	Bosnia-Herzegovina	Kazakh.	Kazakhstan	OR	Oregon	UT	Utah
Bulg.	Bulgaria	KS	Kansas	PA	Pennsylvania	Uttar Prad.	Uttar Pradesh
c.	cape	KY	Kentucky	Pak.	Pakistan	Uzbek.	Uzbekistan
CA	California	Kyrg.	Kyrgyzstan	Para.	Paraguay	VA	Virginia
Can.	Canada	l.	lake	P.E.I.	Prince Edward Island	val.	valley
C.A.R.	Central African Republic	LA	Louisiana	pen.	peninsula	Venez.	Venezuela
CO	Colorado	lag.	lagoon	Phil.	Philippines	Vic.	Victoria
Col.	Colombia	Lith.	Lithuania	plat.	plateau	vol.	volcano
conv.	conventional name form	Lux.	Luxembourg	P.N.G.	Papua New Guinea	vol. crater	volcanic crater
CT	Connecticut	MA	Massachusetts	Pol.	Poland	VT	Vermont
Czech Rep.	Czech Republic	Madag.	Madagascar	Port.	Portugal	W.	West, Western
DC	District of Columbia	Madh. Prad.	Madhya Pradesh	pref.	prefecture	W.A.	Western Australia
DE	Delaware	Mahar.	Maharashtra	prov.	province	WA	Washington
Dem. Rep. Congo	Democratic Republic of Congo	Man.	Manitoba	Qld	Queensland	WI	Wisconsin
depr.	depression	Maur.	Mauritania	Que.	Québec	WV	West Virginia
dept	department	MD	Maryland	r.	river	WY	Wyoming
des.	desert	ME	Maine	r. mouth	river mouth	Y.T.	Yukon Territory
Dom. Rep.	Dominican Republic	Mex.	Mexico	reg.	region	Yugo.	Yugoslavia
E.	East, Eastern	MI	Michigan	Rep.	Republic		
Equat. Guinea	Equatorial Guinea	MN	Minnesota	research stn	research station		
esc.	escarpment	MO	Missouri	resr	reservoir		

1

261 G4 **9 de Julio** Arg.
261 G4 **25 de Mayo** Buenos Aires Arg.
260 D5 **25 de Mayo** La Pampa Arg.
260 C4 **25 de Mayo** Mendoza Arg.
261 I4 **25 de Mayo** Uru.
129 F4 **26 Bakı Komissarı** Azer.
261 F5 **30 de Agosto** Arg.
211 G3 **42nd Hill** S. Africa
222 F5 **70 Mile House** B.C. Can.
222 F5 **100 Mile House** B.C. Can.
222 F4 **150 Mile House** B.C. Can.

A

156 C1 **Aa** r. France
169 B4 **Aa** r. Ger.
169 C4 **Aa** r. Ger.
Aabenraa Denmark see Åbenrå
172 C4 **Aach** Ger.
172 D4 **Aach** Ger.
169 B5 **Aachen** Ger.
190 D1 **Aadorf** Switz.
Aalborg Denmark see Ålborg
173 E3 **Aalen** Ger.
Aalesund Norway see Ålesund
Aaley Lebanon see 'Āley
164 D2 **Aalsmeer** Neth.
165 D4 **Aalst** Belgium
165 E3 **Aalst** Neth.
164 F3 **Aalten** Neth.
165 C3 **Aalter** Belgium
Aanaar Fin. see Inari
140 N3 **Äänekoski** Fin.
214 D2 **Aansluit** S. Africa
Aar r. Switz. see Aare
113 □1 **Aarah** i. N. Male Maldives
190 D1 **Aarau** Switz.
190 C1 **Aarberg** Switz.
190 C1 **Aarburg** Switz.
165 C3 **Aardenburg** Neth.
190 D1 **Aare** r. Switz.
140 M2 **Aareavaara** Sweden
190 D1 **Aargau** canton Switz.
164 E3 **Aarle** Neth.
165 D4 **Aarschot** Belgium
165 D3 **Aartselaar** Belgium
172 B4 **Aarwangen** Switz.
221 M3 **Aasiaat** Greenland
Aath Belgium see Ath
108 B1 **Aba** Sichuan China
208 F4 **Aba** Dem. Rep. Congo
177 H4 **Aba** Hungary
207 G5 **Aba** Nigeria
124 D2 **Abā ad Dūd** Saudi Arabia
251 G6 **Abacaxis** r. Brazil
122 B4 **Ābādān** Iran
122 C4 **Ābādān, Jazīrah** i. Iran/Iraq
122 C4 **Ābādeh** Iran
122 C4 **Ābādeh Tashk** Iran
183 F4 **Abadla** Alg.
256 D3 **Abadia dos Dourados** Brazil
256 C2 **Abadiânia** Brazil
182 C1 **Abadín** Spain
204 E3 **Abadla** Alg.
177 J4 **Abádszalók** Hungary
129 B1 **Abadzekhskaya** Rus. Fed.
257 E3 **Abaeté** Brazil
257 E3 **Abaeté** r. Brazil
254 C2 **Abaetetuba** Brazil
Abagnar Qi Nei Mongol China see Xilinhot
Abag Qi Nei Mongol China see Xin Hot
253 G6 **Abaí** Para.
77 H1 **Abaiang** atoll Kiribati
182 B1 **A Baiuca** Spain
241 M3 **Abajo Peak** UT U.S.A.
207 H5 **Abakaliki** Nigeria
98 F1 **Abakan** Rus. Fed.
98 E1 **Abakanskiy Khrebet** mts Rus. Fed.
208 B5 **Abala** Congo
207 F3 **Abala** Niger
207 G3 **Abalak** Niger
138 H4 **Abalyanka** r. Belarus
126 D2 **Abana** Turkey
183 H4 **Abánades** Spain
252 B3 **Abancay** Peru
208 A5 **Abanga** r. Gabon
187 B6 **Abanilla** Spain
191 G3 **Abano Terme** Italy
252 E4 **Abapó** Bol.
187 B6 **Abarán** Spain
Abariringa i. Phoenix Is Kiribati see Kanton
122 C4 **Abarqū** Iran
182 C2 **A Barqueta** Spain
Abarshahr Iran see Neyshābūr
177 J4 **Abasár** Hungary
129 C2 **Abasha** Georgia
102 L1 **Abashiri** Japan
102 L2 **Abashiri-ko** r. Japan
102 L1 **Abashiri-wan** b. Japan
244 D3 **Abasolo** Guanajuato Mex.
245 E1 **Abasolo del Valle** Mex.
245 G5 **Abasolo** Tamaulipas Mex.
177 K3 **Abaújszántó** Hungary
138 C3 **Abava** r. Latvia
121 H2 **Abay** Karagandinskaya Oblast' Kazakh.
Abay Vostochnyy Kazakhstan Kazakh. see Karaul
Abay Bazar Karagandinskaya Oblast' Kazakh. see Abay
210 B2 **Äbay Wenz** r. Eth.
 alt. Azraq, Bahr el (Sudan), conv. Blue Nile
98 F1 **Abaza** Rus. Fed.
208 B3 **Abba** C.A.R.
192 D2 **Abbadia San Salvatore** Italy
122 D3 **Abbāsābād** Iran
192 A4 **Abbasanta** Sardegna Italy
Abbatis Villa France see Abbeville
156 B2 **Abbeville** France
231 C6 **Abbeville** AL U.S.A.
231 D6 **Abbeville** GA U.S.A.
237 E6 **Abbeville** LA U.S.A.
231 E5 **Abbeville** SC U.S.A.
223 I5 **Abbey** Sask. Can.
147 C4 **Abbeydorney** Rep. of Ireland
147 B4 **Abbeyfeale** Rep. of Ireland
147 D4 **Abbeyleix** Rep. of Ireland
149 F3 **Abbeytown** Cumbria, England U.K.
190 A2 **Abbiategrasso** Italy
140 L2 **Abborrträsk** Sweden
85 F4 **Abbot, Mount** Qld Austr.
85 F3 **Abbot Bay** Qld Austr.
151 F2 **Abbots Bromley** Staffordshire, England U.K.
150 E4 **Abbotsbury** Dorset, England U.K.
222 F5 **Abbotsford** B.C. Can.
226 B3 **Abbotsford** WI U.S.A.
151 G3 **Abbots Langley** Hertfordshire, England U.K.
234 B3 **Abbotstown** PA U.S.A.
239 F4 **Abbott** NM U.S.A.
233 O4 **Abbott** VA U.S.A.
232 C5 **Abbott** WV U.S.A.
123 H3 **Abbottabad** Pak.
262 R2 **Abbott Ice Shelf** Antarctica
164 D2 **Abcoude** Neth.
172 G4 **Abda** Hungary
127 F3 **'Abd al 'Azīz, Jabal** hill Syria
122 A3 **Ābdānān** Iran
120 C1 **Abdulino** Rus. Fed.
202 D6 **Abéché** Chad
105 L4 **Abe-gawa** r. Japan
183 H3 **Abejar** Spain
187 C5 **Abejuela** Spain
207 G5 **Abejukolo** Nigeria
184 B2 **Abela** Port.
165 B4 **Abele** Belgium
Abellinum Italy see Avellino
77 H1 **Abemama** atoll Gilbert Is Kiribati
173 E2 **Abenberg** Ger.
185 I1 **Abengibre** Spain

206 E5 **Abengourou** Côte d'Ivoire
185 F2 **Abenójar** Spain
142 C4 **Åbenrå** Denmark
173 F3 **Abens** r. Ger.
173 F3 **Abensberg** Ger.
207 F5 **Abeokuta** Nigeria
150 C2 **Aberaeron** Ceredigion, Wales U.K.
150 D3 **Aberaman** Rhondda Cynon Taff, Wales U.K.
150 D3 **Aberavon** Neath Port Talbot, Wales U.K.
150 B3 **Abercanaid** Merthyr Tydfil, Wales U.K.
146 F4 **Aberchirder** Aberdeenshire, Scotland U.K.
Abercorn Zambia see Mbala
83 G3 **Abercrombie** r. N.S.W. Austr.
150 D3 **Abercynon** Rhondda Cynon Taff, Wales U.K.
150 D3 **Aberdare** Rhondda Cynon Taff, Wales U.K.
210 C5 **Aberdare National Park** Kenya
150 C2 **Aberdaron** Gwynedd, Wales U.K.
Aberdaugleddau Pembrokeshire, Wales U.K. see Milford Haven
83 G3 **Aberdeen** N.S.W. Austr.
109 □ **Aberdeen** H.K. China
214 E5 **Aberdeen** S. Africa
146 F4 **Aberdeen** Aberdeen, Scotland U.K.
234 B3 **Aberdeen** MD U.S.A.
237 F5 **Aberdeen** MS U.S.A.
232 B5 **Aberdeen** OH U.S.A.
236 D2 **Aberdeen** SD U.S.A.
238 B2 **Aberdeen** WA U.S.A.
223 L1 **Aberdeen Lake** Nunavut Can.
214 E5 **Aberdeen Road** S. Africa
146 F4 **Aberdeenshire** admin. div. Scotland U.K.
150 C2 **Aberdovey** Gwynedd, Wales U.K.
150 C2 **Aberdyfi** Gwynedd, Wales U.K.
210 C1 **Äbeye Yosēf** mt. Eth.
146 F5 **Aberfeldy** Perth and Kinross, Scotland U.K.
150 C1 **Aberffraw** Isle of Anglesey, Wales U.K.
149 H4 **Aberford** West Yorkshire, England U.K.
146 D5 **Aberfoyle** Stirling, Scotland U.K.
150 D3 **Abergavenny** Monmouthshire, Wales U.K.
150 D3 **Abergele** Conwy, Wales U.K.
Abergwaun Pembrokeshire, Wales U.K. see Fishguard
150 D2 **Abergwesyn** Powys, Wales U.K.
150 D2 **Abergynolwyn** Gwynedd, Wales U.K.
Aberhonddu Powys, Wales U.K. see Brecon
150 D3 **Aberkenfig** Bridgend, Wales U.K.
146 F5 **Aberlady** East Lothian, Scotland U.K.
146 F4 **Aberlemno** Angus, Scotland U.K.
146 E5 **Aberlour** Moray, Scotland U.K. see Barmouth
237 C5 **Abernathy** TX U.S.A.
146 E5 **Abernethy** Perth and Kinross, Scotland U.K.
150 C2 **Aberporth** Ceredigion, Wales U.K.
150 D3 **Abersychan** Torfaen, Wales U.K.
176 B1 **Abertamy** Czech Rep.
Abertawe Swansea, Wales U.K. see Swansea
Aberteifi Ceredigion, Wales U.K. see Cardigan
184 E1 **Aberthaw** Blaenau Gwent, Wales U.K.
146 E5 **Aberuthven** Perth and Kinross, Scotland U.K.
150 C2 **Aberystwyth** Ceredigion, Wales U.K.
Abeshr Chad see Abéché
134 M2 **Abez'** Rus. Fed.
124 C4 **Abhā** Saudi Arabia
124 C2 **Abhā, Jabal** hill Saudi Arabia
146 A4 **Abhainnsuidhe** Western Isles, Scotland U.K.
116 E5 **Abhanpur** Madh. Prad. India
122 B3 **Abhar** r. Iran
122 B3 **Abhar Rūd** r. Iran
207 G5 **Abia** state Nigeria
203 G6 **Abiad, Bahr el** r. Sudan/Uganda
 alt. Jebel, Bahr el, conv. White Nile
183 H4 **Abia de la Obispalía** Spain
210 C3 **Abiata Hāyk'** l. Eth.
122 B4 **Abī-i Bazuft** r. Iran
250 B2 **Abibe, Serranía de** mts Col.
206 D3 **Abidjan** Côte d'Ivoire
186 C2 **Abiego** Spain
105 G3 **Abiko** Japan
236 D4 **Abilene** KS U.S.A.
237 D5 **Abilene** TX U.S.A.
159 G5 **Ability** France
151 F3 **Abingdon** Oxfordshire, England U.K.
234 A3 **Abingdon** MD U.S.A.
232 B6 **Abingdon** VA U.S.A.
Abingdon Island Islas Galápagos Ecuador see Pinta, Isla
146 E6 **Abington** South Lanarkshire, Scotland U.K.
233 H3 **Abington** MA U.S.A.
234 C2 **Abington** PA U.S.A.
85 G3 **Abington Reef** Coral Sea Is Terr. Austr.
135 G4 **Abinsk** Rus. Fed.
183 O5 **Ab-i-Panja** r. Afgh./Tajik. see Pyandzh
123 F2 **Ab-i-Safed** r. Afgh.
223 J2 **Abitau Lake** N.W.T. Can.
224 D3 **Abitibi** r. Ont. Can.
224 D3 **Abitibi, Lake** Ont./Que. Can.
Abkhazia aut. rep. Georgia see Apkhazet'i
185 M3 **Abla** Spain
156 B4 **Ablis** France
183 I3 **Ablitas** Spain
46 A4 **Abo Naft** r. Iraq
Åbo Fin. see Turku
116 D4 **Abohar** Punjab India
206 E5 **Aboisso** Côte d'Ivoire
207 F5 **Abomey** Benin
208 C2 **Abong Mbang** Cameroon
94 B1 **Abongabong, Gunung** mt. Indon.
207 I6 **Abonnema** Nigeria
177 J4 **Abony** Hungary
56 D1 **Aboot** Oman
92 A4 **Aborlan** Phil.
208 B2 **Aboumi** Gabon
208 B2 **Abourassén, Mont** mt. C.A.R.
207 F3 **Abouya** r. Niger
146 F4 **Aboyne** Aberdeenshire, Scotland U.K.
125 G5 **Abqaiq** Saudi Arabia
182 B3 **Abragão** Port.
246 D4 **Abraham's Bay** Mayaguana Bahamas
184 A2 **Abrantes** Port.
258 D1 **Abra Pampa** Arg.

137 I5 **Abrau Dyurso** Rus. Fed.
182 C4 **Abraveses** Port.
257 F4 **Abre Campo** Brazil
182 C3 **Abreiro** Port.
186 E3 **Abrera** Spain
157 H4 **Abreschviller** France
160 B2 **Abrest** France
203 F4 **'Abri** Sudan
161 E4 **Abriès** France
257 H3 **Abrolhos, Arquipélago dos** is Brazil
264 G7 **Abrolhos Bank** sea feature S. Atlantic Ocean
139 J2 **Abrosovo** Rus. Fed.
197 F2 **Abrud** Romania
Abruzzi admin. reg. Italy see Abruzzo
193 F2 **Abruzzo** admin. reg. Italy
192 D2 **Abruzzo** admin. reg. Italy
179 I4 **'Abs** Yemen
262 W1 **Absalom, Mount** Antarctica
178 C3 **Absam** Austria
238 E2 **Absaroka Range** mts WY U.S.A.
173 E2 **Absberg** Ger.
179 M3 **Absdorf** Austria
235 G3 **Absecon** NJ U.S.A.
129 F3 **Abşeron Yarımadası** pen. Azer.
179 E3 **Abtenau** Austria
173 D3 **Abtsgmünd** Ger.
126 C4 **Abū al Duhūr** Syria
127 F4 **Abū 'Alī** r. Saudi Arabia
202 E3 **Abū Ballūs** hill Egypt
125 F2 **Abū Dhabi** U.A.E.
128 C4 **Abū Hallūfah, Jabal** hill Jordan
203 G5 **Abu Hamed** Sudan
113 □2 **Abuhera** i. Addu Atoll Maldives
128 A5 **Abu Huwsa, Gebel** hill Egypt
207 G4 **Abuja** Nigeria
127 F4 **Abū Kamāl** Syria
105 L4 **Abukuma-gawa** r. Japan
105 L4 **Abukuma-kōchi** plat. Japan
128 C5 **Abu Mena** tourist site Egypt
127 J7 **Abū Mūsá** i. The Gulf
Abū Mūsā, Jazīreh-ye i. The Gulf see Abu Musa
252 D2 **Abunā** r. Bol./Brazil
252 D2 **Abunā** Brazil
90 C2 **Abuyog** Phil.
203 F6 **Abu Zabad** Sudan
125 F2 **Abū Zabī** U.A.E. see Abu Dhabi
143 G2 **Åby** Sweden
125 D4 **Abyad** governorate Yemen
86 C4 **Abydos** W.A. Austr.
140 M2 **Åbyn** Sweden
Abyssinia country Africa see Ethiopia
120 D1 **Abzakovo** Rus. Fed.
120 D2 **Abzanovo** Rus. Fed.
250 C4 **Acacias** Col.
205 F3 **Acacus, Jabal** mts Libya see Akakus, Jabal
177 I4 **Académian Vernadskiy** research stn Antarctica see Vernadsky
Acadia prov. Can. see Nova Scotia
254 D3 **Acailândia** Brazil
254 F4 **Acajutiba** Brazil
243 H6 **Acajutla** El Salvador
243 G5 **Acala** Mex.
244 D3 **Acamaro** Mex.
254 C2 **Acambay** Mex.
209 D9 **Acampamento de Caça do Mucusso** Angola
243 H4 **Acanceh** Mex.
244 D3 **Acándi** Col.
182 B2 **A Cañiza** Spain
244 B2 **Acaponeta** r. Mex.
245 E5 **Acaponeta** Mex.
254 C2 **Acapulco** r. Mex.
245 G5 **Acapulco** Mex.
 Acapulco de Juárez Mex. see Acapulco
254 C2 **Acará** Brazil
254 C2 **Acará** r. Brazil
254 C2 **Acará Miri** r. Brazil
253 E2 **Acaraú, Represa de** resr Para.
257 E1 **Acari** r. Brazil
252 B3 **Acari** Peru
254 C3 **Acari** Peru
251 G4 **Acari, Serra** hills Brazil/Guyana
250 D2 **Acarigua** Venez.
197 F2 **Acâş** Romania
194 D5 **Acate** Sicilia Italy
245 G3 **Acatepec** Mex.
244 C3 **Acatlán de Juárez** Mex.
245 F5 **Acatlán de Pérez Figueroa** Mex.
245 F5 **Acatzingo** Mex.
245 G4 **Acay, Nevado de** mt. Arg.
245 G5 **Acayucan** Mex.
193 H3 **Accadia** Italy
190 B4 **Acceglio** Italy
193 I4 **Accettura** Italy
174 D2 **Accho** Israel see 'Akko
120 D2 **Accomac** VA U.S.A. see Accomack
233 F6 **Accomac** VA U.S.A.
163 B6 **Accous** France
206 E5 **Accra** Ghana
149 G4 **Accrington** Lancashire, England U.K.
193 F2 **Accumoli** Italy
261 G3 **Aceba** Arg.
182 C3 **Acebo** Spain
184 E1 **Acedera** Spain
183 H2 **Acedo** Spain
258 G3 **Aceguá** Brazil
94 B1 **Aceh** admin. dist. Indon.
182 C3 **Acehuche** Spain
184 C2 **Aceituna** Spain
183 I3 **Acered** Spain
193 H4 **Acerenza** Italy
193 H4 **Acerno** Italy
193 G4 **Acerra** Italy

146 C3 **Achiltibuie** Highland, Scotland U.K.
168 E2 **Achim** Ger.
Achim admin. dist. Indon. see Aceh
131 K4 **Achinsk** Rus. Fed.
126 C4 **Achintee** Highland, Scotland U.K.
260 C3 **Achiras** Arg.
121 G4 **Achisay** Kazakh.
129 E2 **Achisu** Rus. Fed.
129 D2 **Achkhoy-Martan** Rus. Fed.
146 C3 **Achnasheen** Highland, Scotland U.K.
173 G3 **Achslach** Ger.
172 D3 **Achstetten** Ger.
146 B5 **Achosnich** Highland, Scotland U.K.
173 G3 **Achslach** Ger.
172 D3 **Achterwehr** Ger.
195 E1 **Aci Castello** Sicilia Italy
195 E5 **Aci Catena** Sicilia Italy
199 F3 **Acıpayam** Turkey
195 E5 **Acireale** Sicilia Italy
195 E5 **Aci St Antonio** Sicilia Italy
237 F5 **Ackerman** MS U.S.A.
234 C2 **Ackermanville** PA U.S.A.
236 E3 **Ackley** IA U.S.A.
246 D2 **Acklins Island** Bahamas
149 H4 **Ackworth Moor Top** West Yorkshire, England U.K.
151 I2 **Acle** Norfolk, England U.K.
252 B3 **Acobamba** Peru
160 B2 **Acolin** r. France
260 B3 **Aconcagua** r. Chile
260 B3 **Aconcagua, Cerro** mt. Arg.
254 F3 **Acopiara** Brazil
252 A1 **Acora** Peru
216 □1 **Açores, Arquipélago dos** is N. Atlantic Ocean
182 B1 **A Coruña** Spain
182 B1 **A Coruña** prov. Galicia Spain
217 □3a **Acoua** Mayotte
242 □I7 **Acoyapa** Nic.
194 D4 **Acquacalda** Isole Lipari Italy
191 H5 **Acqualagna** Italy
193 F3 **Acquapendente** Italy
192 D2 **Acquappesa** Italy
193 F2 **Acquasanta Terme** Italy
193 F2 **Acquasparta** Italy
191 H5 **Acquaviva Picena** Italy
156 B3 **Acquigny** France
192 A2 **Acqui Terme** Italy
233 F3 **Acra** NY U.S.A.
 Acragas Sicilia Italy see Agrigento
82 C3 **Acraman, Lake** salt flat S.A. Austr.
252 D2 **Acre** r. Brazil
252 C2 **Acre** state Brazil
256 B2 **Acreúna** Brazil
195 F3 **Acri** Italy
177 H4 **Acs** Hungary
177 I4 **Ácsa** Hungary
210 C1 **Adi Kwala** Eritrea
210 B2 **Acton** Suffolk, England U.K.
151 H2 **Acton** Suffolk, England U.K.
240 H4 **Acton** CA U.S.A.
245 E3 **Actopán** Mex.
252 F3 **Açucena** Brazil
245 G4 **Acuña** Mex.
245 F4 **Acultzingo** Mex.
194 A1 **Acunum Acusio** France see Montélimar
207 H6 **Acurenam** Equat. Guinea
253 F3 **Açuruá** Brazil
193 F3 **Acuto** Italy
207 F5 **Ada** Ghana
236 D2 **Ada** MN U.S.A.
237 D5 **Ada** OH U.S.A.
232 B4 **Ada** OK U.S.A.
196 C3 **Ada** Vojvodina, Srbija Yugo.
220 C3 **Adachi** Japan
Adabazar Turkey see Sakarya
137 I5 **Adagum** r. Rus. Fed.
226 D4 **Adahuesca** Spain
183 F3 **Adaïr** IL U.S.A.
140 L2 **Adak** Sweden
140 L2 **Adak** Sweden
220 A4 **Adak Island** AK U.S.A.
220 A4 **Adak Island** AK U.S.A.
128 C1 **Adalı** Turkey
Adalia Turkey see Antalya
125 G4 **Adam** Oman
259 F8 **Adam, Mount** hill Falkland Is
256 B4 **Adamantina** Brazil
207 I5 **Adamaoua** prov. Cameroon
198 D3 **Adamas** Notio Aigaio Greece
197 H3 **Adamclisi** Romania
193 F3 **Adamello** mt. Italy
83 B3 **Adaminaby** N.S.W. Austr.
210 C3 **Adamí Tulu** Eth.
174 B2 **Adamovka** Czech Rep.
120 D2 **Adamovka** Rus. Fed.
175 K4 **Adamów** Pol.
175 K5 **Adamówka** Pol.
136 D3 **Adampil'** Ukr.
232 B5 **Adams** KY U.S.A.
233 J3 **Adams** MA U.S.A.
234 A4 **Adams** NY U.S.A.
233 E3 **Adams** NY U.S.A.
226 C4 **Adams** WI U.S.A.
262 T2 **Adams, Cape** Antarctica
81 C5 **Adams, Mount** South I. N.Z.
233 E3 **Adams Center** NY U.S.A.
234 A3 **Adams County** PA U.S.A.
222 F5 **Adams Mountain** AK U.S.A.
188 □ **Adam's Peak** Sri Lanka see Sri Pada
240 D2 **Adams Peak** CA U.S.A.
147 E4 **Adamstown** Rep. of Ireland
234 B2 **Adamstown** PA U.S.A.
185 F2 **Adamuz** Spain
126 D3 **Adana** Turkey
126 D3 **Adana** prov. Turkey
Adana Yemen see Aden
127 H2 **Adana as Sughra** Yemen
210 C1 **Ädwa** Eth.
149 H4 **Adwick le Street** South Yorkshire, England U.K.
207 G5 **Adadó** Ghana
131 P3 **Adycha** r. Rus. Fed.
129 B1 **Adyge-Khabl'** Rus. Fed.
129 A1 **Adygeya, Respublika** aut. rep. Rus. Fed.
129 A1 **Adygeysk** Rus. Fed.
 Adygeyskaya Avtonomnaya Oblast' aut. rep. Rus. Fed. see Adygeya, Respublika
135 I7 **Adyk** Respublika Kalmykiya - Khalm'g-Tangch Rus. Fed.
204 B5 **Adzel** Spain
206 E5 **Adzopé** Côte d'Ivoire
134 H2 **Adz'va** r. Rus. Fed.
134 H2 **Adz'vavom** Rus. Fed.
198 C2 **Aegean Sea** Greece/Turkey
138 G1 **Aegna** i. Estonia
 Aegviidu Estonia
Aegyptus country Africa see Egypt
189 □ **Aela** Jordan see Al 'Aqabah
 Aelana Jordan see Al 'Aqabah
 Aelia Capitolina Israel/West Bank see Jerusalem

125 D3 **Ad Dilam** Saudi Arabia
149 H4 **Addingham** West Yorkshire, England U.K.
 Addis Ababa Eth. see Ādīs Ābeba
124 C2 **Ad Dir'īyah** Saudi Arabia
124 D3 **Addis Abeba**
 Ad Dīwānīyah Iraq see Ad Qādisīyah
151 G3 **Addlestone** Surrey, England U.K.
215 E5 **Addo** S. Africa
 Addo Atoll Maldives see Addu Atoll
113 □2 **Addu Atoll** Maldives
216 □3a **Adeje** Tenerife Canary Is
231 D6 **Adel** GA U.S.A.
236 E3 **Adel** IA U.S.A.
82 D3 **Adelaide** S.A. Austr.
246 D1 **Adelaide** New Prov. Bahamas
215 F5 **Adelaide** S. Africa
262 T2 **Adelaide Island** Antarctica
84 B2 **Adelaide River** N.T. Austr.
190 C2 **Adelboden** Switz.
86 D2 **Adele Island** W.A. Austr.
195 F1 **Adelfia** Italy
168 F3 **Adelheidsdorf** Ger.
262 □ **Adélie Coast** reg. Antarctica
263 J2 **Adélie Land** reg. Antarctica
172 D3 **Adelmannsfelden** Ger.
83 G3 **Adelong** N.S.W. Austr.
178 C3 **Adelschlag** Ger.
173 F2 **Adelsdorf** Ger.
172 D2 **Adelsheim** Ger.
173 E3 **Adelshofen** Ger.
124 C5 **Ademuz** Spain
187 B4 **Aden** Yemen
124 C5 **Aden, Gulf of** Somalia/Yemen
169 E5 **Adenau** Ger.
168 F2 **Adendorf** Ger.
214 C5 **Adendorp** S. Africa
169 E4 **Adenstedt** Ger.
207 G3 **Aderbissinat** Niger
116 B5 **Adesar** Gujarat India
 Adhamas Notio Aigaio Greece see Adamas
125 G2 **Adhan, Jabal** mt. U.A.E.
124 D5 **Adhanah, Wādī** watercourse Yemen
125 F2 **'Adhiriyāt, Jibāl al** mts Jordan
116 E5 **Adhoi** Gujarat India
206 E5 **Adiaké** Côte d'Ivoire
210 C1 **Ādī Ark'ay** Eth.
184 C2 **Adiça, Serra da** hills Port.
124 B5 **Ad Da'iro** Eth.
191 H3 **Adige** r. Italy
 Adigey Autonomous Oblast aut. rep. Rus. Fed. see Adygeya, Respublika
210 C1 **Ādīgrat** Eth.
 Adi-Kaie Eritrea see Adī K'eyih
203 H6 **Ādī Kelē** Eritrea
210 C1 **Adi K'eyih** Eritrea
210 C1 **Adi Kwala** Eritrea
113 □4 **Adilabad** Andhra Prad. India
127 F3 **Adilcevaz** Turkey
124 C4 **Adin** CA U.S.A.
197 L1 **Adâncata** Romania
 Adâncata Romania
228 A4 **Adinkerke** Belgium
203 F2 **Adirondack Mountains** NY U.S.A.
233 F2 **Adiri** Libya
126 D3 **Adi Ugri** Eritrea see Mendefera
129 A2 **Adjara** Turkey
210 C1 **Ādīs Ābeba** Eth.
124 B5 **Adī Ugri** Eritrea see Mendefera
126 D3 **Adıyaman** Turkey
126 D3 **Adıyaman** prov. Turkey
197 I1 **Adjud** Romania
210 D3 **Adele Land**
197 H2 **Adâncata** Romania
247 □1 **Adjuntas** Puerto Rico
149 H4 **Adlington** Lancashire, England U.K.
190 D1 **Adliswil** Switz.
173 D3 **Adlkofen** Ger.
173 G4 **Adlkofen** Ger.

142 D4 **Ærø** i. Denmark
137 H5 **Aérofotos'kyy** Ukr.
154 C **Aeron** r. Wales U.K.
168 F1 **Æreskøbing** Denmark
169 E3 **Aerzen** Ger.
 Aesernia Italy see Isernia
182 B2 **A Estrada** Spain
137 J2 **Afanas'yevka** Rus. Fed.
134 K4 **Afanas'yevo** Rus. Fed.
82 B1 **Afars, Mount** hill S.A. Austr.
87 D6 **Agnew** W.A. Austr.
147 F2 **Agnew's Hill** hill Northern Ireland U.K.
199 I3 **Afandou** Notio Aigaio Greece see Afantou
199 I3 **Afantou** Notio Aigaio Greece
206 E5 **Agnibilékrou** Côte d'Ivoire
203 I6 **Afar Depression** Eritrea/Eth.
158 D4 **Aff** r. France
206 E5 **Afféri** Côte d'Ivoire
193 E5 **Affile** Italy
173 E3 **Affing** Ger.
190 D1 **Affoltern am Albis** Switz.
205 F4 **Afireville** Alg. see Khemis Miliana
123 F3 **Afghānestān** country Asia
210 E4 **Afgooye** Somalia
124 A3 **Afīf** Saudi Arabia
207 G5 **Afikpo** Nigeria
139 J3 **Afim'ino** Rus. Fed.
137 J5 **Afipskiy** Rus. Fed.
140 J3 **Åfjord** Norway
179 G3 **Aflenz Kurort** Austria
206 F2 **Aflou** Alg.
170 D2 **Afoldern** Ger.
173 D3 **Afonso Cláudio** Brazil
182 C2 **A Forxa** Galicia Spain
182 C2 **A Forxa** Galicia Spain
173 G4 **Afrensdorf** Ger.
210 D1 **Äfrêra Terara** vol. Eth.
200 **Africa** continent
199 **Africa Nova** country Africa see Tunisia
116 B5 **Afsasar** Gujarat India
179 F3 **Afritz** Austria
91 K3 **Agrijan** i. N. Mariana Is
233 F3 **Afton** NY U.S.A.
238 E3 **Afton** NY U.S.A.
146 D6 **Afton Bridgend** East Ayrshire, Scotland U.K.
251 I5 **Afuá** Brazil
127 G2 **'Afula** Israel
199 G2 **Afyon** Turkey
199 G2 **Afyon** prov. Turkey
 Afyonkarahisar Turkey see Afyon
171 H1 **Aga** Ger.
107 G1 **Aga** r. Rus. Fed.
 Aga-Buryat Autonomous Okrug admin. div. Rus. Fed. see Aginskiy Buryatskiy Avtonomnyy Okrug
116 B5 **Adesar** Gujarat India
207 G3 **Agadez** Niger
207 G3 **Agadez** dept Niger
204 C2 **Agadir** Morocco
121 F2 **Agadyr'** Kazakh.
216 □1b **AgadZ** São Miguel Azores
247 □1 **Aguadilla** Puerto Rico
244 E3 **Aguascalientes** Mex.
244 E3 **Aguascalientes** state Mex.
177 I5 **Agárd** Hungary
114 B2 **Agashi** Mahar. India
224 D3 **Agate** Ont. Can.
244 E3 **Agats** Indon.
131 N2 **Agatan** r. Rus. Fed.
220 D1 **Agattu Island** AK U.S.A.
220 A4 **Agattu Strait** AK U.S.A.
206 E5 **Agboville** Côte d'Ivoire
207 I5 **Agbor** Bojibóji Nigeria
129 F5 **Ağcabädi** Azer.
129 E5 **Ağdam** Azer.
129 F5 **Ağdaş** Azer.
129 E3 **Ağdäră** Azer.
161 J6 **Agde** France
161 I6 **Agde, Cap d'** c. France
162 D4 **Agen** France
 Agedabia Libya see Ajdābiyā
163 C4 **Agen** France
209 B8 **Agere Maryam** Eth.
210 C3 **Ageyevo** Rus. Fed.
139 R5 **Agger** r. Ger.
169 H4 **Aghaboy** Rep. of Ireland
124 B5 **Ädwa** Eth.
129 C3 **Aghajari** Iran
147 C5 **Aghada** Rep. of Ireland
129 C3 **Aghada** Rep. of Ireland
147 C7 **Aghagower** Rep. of Ireland

Aelönlaplap atoll Marshall Is see Ailinglapalap
 Aenus Turkey see Enez
232 D2 **Ærø** i. Denmark
142 D4 **Aeron** r. Wales U.K.
123 F3 **Afghānestān** country Asia
210 E4 **Afgooye** Somalia
124 C3 **Afīf** Saudi Arabia
207 G5 **Agege** Nigeria
129 D2 **Agvali** Rus. Fed.
194 D5 **Agira** Sicilia Italy
215 E2 **Agisanang** S. Africa
148 C2 **Agivey** Northern Ireland U.K.
172 C2 **Aglasterhausen** Ger.
199 G3 **Agliana** Italy
192 B3 **Aglié** Sardegna Italy
163 F6 **Agly** r. France
190 E3 **Agnadello** Italy
198 B2 **Agnantero** Greece
189 E2 **Agnano** Greece
199 F3 **Agna** r. Italy
82 B1 **Agnes, Mount** hill S.A. Austr.
87 D6 **Agnew** W.A. Austr.
147 F2 **Agnew's Hill** hill Northern Ireland U.K.
206 E5 **Agnibilékrou** Côte d'Ivoire
191 G3 **Agnita** Romania
190 D1 **Agno** Switz.
193 G3 **Agnone** Italy
104 C4 **Ago** Japan
172 C3 **Ago-Are** Nigeria
190 D3 **Agogna** r. Italy
206 E5 **Agogo** Ghana
 Agoitz Spain see Aoiz
182 B2 **A Golada** Spain
200 E5 **Agona** Ghana
162 C3 **Agonac** France
206 E5 **Agona Junction** Ghana
158 E2 **Agon-Coutainville** France
106 D4 **Agong** Qinghai China
191 H2 **Agordo** Italy
187 C6 **Agost** Spain
163 D5 **Agout** r. France
116 D4 **Agra** Uttar Prad. India
179 G3 **Agrafotis** r. Greece
198 B2 **Agram** Croatia see Zagreb
185 I2 **Agramón** Spain
186 C3 **Agramunt** Spain
190 E3 **Agrate Brianza** Italy
183 I3 **Ágreda** Spain
187 C6 **Agres** Spain
193 I4 **Agri** r. Italy
129 C4 **Ağrı** Turkey
129 C4 **Ağrı** prov. Turkey
129 D4 **Ağrı Dağı** mt. Turkey
 Agrigan i. N. Mariana Is see Agrijan
 Agrigento Sicilia Italy
195 C5 **Agrigento** prov. Sicilia Italy
 Agrigentum Sicilia Italy see Agrigento
91 K3 **Agrijan** i. N. Mariana Is
197 F2 **Agriş** i. Romania
198 B2 **Agrinio** Greece
191 H4 **Agro r.** Italy
193 K4 **Agropoli** Italy
128 E1 **Ağrı Ovası** plain Turkey
190 E3 **Agrisu** Rus. Fed.
199 G2 **Ağrı Tepe** r. Turkey
129 F3 **Ağsu** Azer.
215 E5 **Agter Sneeuberg** S. Africa
215 E4 **Agtertang** S. Africa
260 C4 **Agua Amarga, Pampa del** plain Arg.
245 H4 **Agua Blanca Iturbide** Mex.
257 F2 **Água Boa** Brazil
244 B2 **Agua Brava, Laguna** lag. Mex.
256 A4 **Água Clara** Brazil
246 □ **Aguada** Cuba
247 □1 **Aguada** Puerto Rico
250 C3 **Aguada de Pau** São Miguel Azores
216 □1b **Aguadilla** Puerto Rico
247 □2 **Aguadilla** Puerto Rico
255 C5 **Água Doce do Norte** Brazil
256 C5 **Agua Dulce** Mex.
245 G4 **Agua Dulce** Mex.
242 □J7 **Aguadulce** Panama
185 H4 **Aguadulce** Andalucía Spain
241 H5 **Agua Fria** r. AZ U.S.A.
256 D5 **Aguaí** Brazil
216 □1a **Agualva** Terceira Azores
244 C1 **Aguanaval** r. Mex.
184 C3 **Aguanga** hill Port.
240 C5 **Aguanga** CA U.S.A.
242 □J6 **Aguanquéterique** Hond.
77 L1 **Aguanus** r. Que. Can.
242 □J6 **Aguán** r. Hond.
252 E4 **Aguapei** r. Bol.
256 A4 **Aguapei** r. Brazil
256 A4 **Aguapei, Serra** hills Brazil
256 B4 **Agua Prieta** Mex.
252 E4 **Aguaraguë, Cordillera de** mts Bol.
258 E1 **Aguaray** Arg.
182 B2 **A Guarda** Galicia Spain
216 □1b **Água Retorta** São Miguel Azores
186 B3 **Aguarón** Spain
242 D3 **Aguaruto** Mex.
186 C2 **Aguas** r. Spain
185 I3 **Aguas** r. Spain
254 F4 **Águas Belas** Brazil
182 B5 **Águas Belas** Port.
247 □3 **Aguas Buenas** Puerto Rico
244 C3 **Aguascalientes** Mex.
245 E3 **Aguascalientes** state Mex.
256 C1 **Aguas Corrientes** Uru.
187 C6 **Aguas de Busot** Spain
257 G2 **Águas Formosas** Brazil
182 C3 **Águas Frias** Port.
182 B5 **Águas Vermelhas** Brazil
176 C4 **Aguila** Hungary
214 E3 **Aguaviva** Spain
186 C4 **Aguaza** Spain
195 F4 **Agua Verde** r. Brazil
246 B4 **Agua Verde** Mex.
253 C1 **A Gudiña** Spain
185 P2 **Agudo** Spain
182 B3 **Agudos** Port.
183 G2 **Águeda** r. Port./Spain
186 C3 **Agüera** r. Spain
186 C2 **Agüero** France
254 F4 **Águas Belas** Brazil
182 B5 **Águas Belas** Port.
247 D5 **Aguas Buenas** Puerto Rico
256 C4 **Aguri** Japan
244 C1 **Aguilafuente** Spain
182 D4 **Aguijan** i. N. Mariana Is
183 I4 **Aguila** AZ U.S.A.
241 H5 **Aguila** AZ U.S.A.
185 L5 **Aguilar** Spain
239 L4 **Aguilar** CO U.S.A.
182 D3 **Aguilar de Alfambra** Spain
183 K3 **Aguilar de Campoo** Spain
182 D3 **Aguilar de la Frontera** Spain
183 I5 **Águilas** Spain
185 I3 **Águilas** Spain
244 D4 **Aguililla** Mex.
242 □J6 **Agüín** Spain
182 B4 **Aguié** Niger
216 □3f **Aguimes** Gran Canaria Canary Is
216 □3f **Aguineguín** r. Gran Canaria Canary Is
92 C4 **Aguisan** Phil.
92 C5 **Aguisan** Phil.
183 Q5 **Agüitas** r. Spain
210 C1 **Agula'i** Eth.
214 C6 **Agulhas** S. Africa
214 K9 **Agulhas Basin** sea feature Southern Ocean
214 C6 **Agulhas, Cape** S. Africa
257 F5 **Agulhas Negras** mt. Brazil
264 J8 **Agulhas Plateau** sea feature Southern Ocean
264 J8 **Agulhas Ridge** sea feature S. Atlantic Ocean
216 □3a **Agulo** La Gomera Canary Is
102 □1 **Aguni-jima** i. Japan
 Agunt Italy see San Candido
92 A4 **Agusan** r. Phil.
92 B3 **Agutaya** i. Phil.
199 F1 **Agva** Turkey
129 F5 **Ağvan** Azer.
199 I1 **Agvali** Rus. Fed.
207 G4 **Agwara** Nigeria
91 C3 **Agwei** r. Sudan
194 D5 **Agira** Sicilia Italy see Agira
 Agyrium Sicilia Italy see Agira
147 B5 **Ahascragh** Rep. of Ireland
122 A2 **Ahar** Iran
81 C5 **Ahaura** South I. N.Z.
81 C5 **Ahaura** r. South I. N.Z.

Ahaus to Aleshki

275

169 C3 Ahaus Ger.
168 E2 Ahausen Ger.
147 D4 Ahenny Rep. of Ireland
147 C5 Aherla Rep. of Ireland
147 D4 Aherlow r. Rep. of Ireland
217 □3a Ahibambo mt. Njazidja Comoros
182 D4 Ahigal Spain
182 D3 Ahigal de Villarino Spain
185 F3 Ahillo mt. Spain
184 E2 Ahillones Spain
80 F3 Ahimanawa Range mts North I. N.Z.
80 D1 Ahipara North I. N.Z.
114 D2 Ahiri Mahar. India
80 E3 Ahititi North I. N.Z.
138 F2 Ahja r. Estonia
220 B4 Ahklun Mountains AK U.S.A.
127 F3 Ahlat Turkey
170 F2 Ahlbeck Ger.
168 E3 Ahlden (Aller) Ger.
169 C4 Ahlen Ger.
168 E2 Ahlerstedt Ger.
168 D3 Ahlhorn Ger.
171 C4 Ahlsdorf Ger.
116 C5 Ahmadabad Gujarat India
128 B5 Aḥmad al Bāqir, Jabal mt. Jordan
129 E4 Ähmädbäyli Azer.
114 B2 Ahmadnagar Mahar. India
114 C2 Ahmadpur Mahar. India
123 G4 Ahmadpur East Pak.
123 G4 Ahmadpur Sial Pak.
210 D2 Ahmar Mountains Eth.
Ahmedabad Gujarat India see Ahmadabad
Ahmednagar Mahar. India see Ahmadnagar
199 E2 Ahmetli Turkey
199 G2 Ahmetpaşa Turkey
168 F3 Ahnsbeck Ger.
207 G5 Ahoada Nigeria
147 E2 Ahoghill Northern Ireland U.K.
242 C3 Ahome Mex.
116 C4 Ahore Rajasthan India
169 F5 Ahorn Ger.
178 C3 Ahornspitze mt. Austria
231 E4 Ahoskie NC U.S.A.
169 C5 Ahr r. Ger.
122 B4 Ahram Iran
Ahrâmât el Jîzah tourist site Egypt see Giza Pyramids
137 H5 Ahrarne Ukr.
117 E4 Ahraura Uttar Prad. India
169 B5 Ahrbrück Ger.
168 F1 Ahrensbök Ger.
168 F2 Ahrensburg Ger.
170 E3 Ahrensfelde Ger.
170 D1 Ahrenshagen Ger.
169 C4 Ahse r. Ger.
134 D3 Ähtäri Fin.
138 F2 Ahtme Estonia
243 H6 Ahuachapán El Salvador
244 C3 Ahualulco Jalisco Mex.
244 D2 Ahualulco San Luis Potosí Mex.
162 E2 Ahun France
79 □3 Ahunui atoll Arch. des Tuamotu Fr. Polynesia
81 C6 Ahuriri r. South I. N.Z.
143 F4 Åhus Sweden
122 B4 Ahvāz Iran
Ahvenanmaa is Fin. see Åland
116 C5 Ahwa Gujarat India
124 D5 Aḥwar Yemen
Ahwāz Iran see Ahvāz
101 C4 Ai r. China
250 D4 Aiari r. Brazil
107 F3 Aibag Gol r. China
183 I2 Aibar Spain
179 G4 Aibl Austria
247 □1 Aibonito Puerto Rico
173 F3 Aichach Ger.
172 C3 Aichhalden Ger.
104 D4 Aichi pref. Japan
173 E4 Aichstetten Ger.
232 B5 Aid OH U.S.A.
173 H3 Aidenbach Ger.
169 F5 Aidhausen Ger.
194 D5 Aidone Sicilia Italy
240 □ Aiea HI U.S.A.
193 I5 Aiello Calabro Italy
193 H5 Aieta Italy
162 B2 Aiffres France
198 C2 Aigeira Greece
179 F3 Aigen im Ennstal Austria
179 E2 Aigen im Mühlkreis Austria
128 B2 Aigialousa Cyprus
198 C3 Aigina Greece
198 C3 Aigina i. Greece
198 C1 Aiginio Greece
198 C2 Aigio Greece
190 B2 Aigle Switz.
161 E4 Aigle de Chambeyron mt. France
161 E4 Aiglun France
163 C5 Aignan France
156 E5 Aignay-le-Duc France
161 B4 Aigoual, Mont mt. France
162 C3 Aigre France
162 B2 Aigrefeuille-d'Aunis France
158 E4 Aigrefeuille-sur-Maine France
258 G4 Aiguá Uru.
160 C1 Aigue, Mont hill France
160 E3 Aiguebelle France
160 E3 Aigueblanche France
160 B2 Aigueperse France
161 C4 Aigues r. France
161 C5 Aigues-Mortes France
161 B5 Aigues-Mortes, Golfe d' b. France
161 A5 Aigues-Vives France
161 C5 Aigues-Vives France
163 D6 Aigues-Vives France
161 D4 Aiguille, Mont mt. France
160 F3 Aiguille d'Argentière mt. France/Switz.
160 F3 Aiguille de la Grande Sassière mt. France
161 E3 Aiguille de Péclet mt. France
161 E3 Aiguille de Scolette mt. France/Italy
160 E3 Aiguille du Midi mt. France
161 E4 Aiguilles France
161 E3 Aiguilles d'Arves mts France
160 E3 Aiguilles des Glaciers mts France
160 E3 Aiguille Verte mt. France
163 C4 Aiguillon France
162 D2 Aigurande France
Aihua Yunnan China see Yunxian
Aihui Heilong. China see Heihe
252 A2 Aija Peru
Aijal Mizoram India see Aizawl
105 F3 Aikawa Japan
231 D5 Aiken SC U.S.A.
108 B3 Ailao Shan mts Yunnan China
84 C4 Aileron N.T. Austr.
108 D3 Ailing Guangxi China
Ailinglabelab atoll Marshall Is see Ailinglaplap
266 G6 Ailinglaplap atoll Marshall Is
156 D5 Aillant-sur-Tholon France
163 B4 Aillas France
161 E5 Aille r. France
157 G5 Aillevillers-et-Lyaumont France
156 B2 Ailly-le-Haut-Clocher France
156 C3 Ailly-sur-Noye France
156 C3 Ailly-sur-Somme France
227 G4 Ailsa Craig Ont. Can.
146 C6 Ailsa Craig i. Scotland U.K.
161 C5 Aimargues France
160 E3 Aime France
Aimeo i. Fr. Polynesia see Moorea
258 D3 Aimogasta Arg.
257 G3 Aimorés Brazil
257 G2 Aimorés, Serra dos hills Brazil
160 D2 Ain dept Rhône-Alpes France
160 D3 Ain r. France
160 A2 Ainay-le-Château France
138 E3 Ainaži Latvia
205 G2 Aïn Beïda Alg.
204 E2 Aïn Beni Mathar Morocco
204 C4 'Aïn Ben Tili Maur.
205 F1 Aïn Defla Alg.
205 F2 Aïn Deheb Alg.
173 E3 Aindling Ger.
205 F2 Aïn el Hadjel Alg.
205 G2 Aïn el Melh Alg.
178 D4 Ainet Austria
163 A5 Ainhoa France
205 G1 Aïn-M'Lila Alg.
Aïn Mokra Alg. see Berrahal
205 G2 Aïn Oulmene Alg.
205 F2 Aïn Oussera Alg.
173 G4 Ainring Ger.
186 D2 Ainsa Spain
Ain Salah Alg. see In Salah
149 F4 Ainsdale Merseyside, England U.K.
205 E2 Aïn Sefra Alg.
236 D3 Ainsworth NE U.S.A.
Aintab Turkey see Gaziantep
205 E2 Aïn Temouchent Alg.
149 G4 Aintree Merseyside, England U.K.
183 I3 Ainzón Spain
103 G6 Aioi Japan
250 C4 Aipe Col.
252 D4 Aiquile Bol.
156 B3 Airaines France
190 C4 Airasca Italy
94 B2 Airbangis Sumatera Indon.
146 B4 Aird Asaig Western Isles, Scotland U.K.
146 C4 Aird of Sleat Highland, Scotland U.K.
222 H5 Airdrie Alta Can.
146 E6 Airdrie North Lanarkshire, Scotland U.K.
157 E3 Aire r. France
149 H4 Airedale val. England U.K.
163 B5 Aire-sur-l'Adour France
156 C2 Aire-sur-la-Lys France
95 E3 Airhitam r. Indon.
146 B3 Airidh a'Bhruaich Western Isles, Scotland U.K.
85 G4 Airlie Beach Qld Austr.
86 B4 Airlie Island W.A. Austr.
193 G3 Airola Italy
190 D2 Airolo Switz.
223 J4 Air Ronge Sask. Can.
146 E5 Airth Falkirk, Scotland U.K.
149 G3 Airton North Yorkshire, England U.K.
162 B2 Airvault France
96 A2 Aisatung Mountain Myanmar
173 F2 Aisch r. Ger.
259 B7 Aisén admin. reg. Chile
156 E5 Aisey-sur-Seine France
107 I4 Ai Shan hill Shandong China
222 B2 Aishihik Y.T. Can.
173 E3 Aislingen Ger.
156 D3 Aisne dept Picardie France
157 C3 Aisne r. France
205 E2 Aïssa, Djebel mt. Alg.
160 E1 Aïssey France
160 C1 Aisy-sur-Armançon France
187 C6 Aitana mt. Spain
204 D3 Aït Benhaddou tourist site Morocco
173 G3 Aiterach r. Ger.
173 G3 Aiterhofen Ger.
146 F2 Aith Orkney, Scotland U.K.
236 E2 Aitkin MN U.S.A.
198 B2 Aitoliko Greece
186 D3 Aitona Spain
120 C1 Aitova Rus. Fed.
173 E4 Aitrach Ger.
173 E4 Aitrang Ger.
81 □2 Aitutaki i. Cook Is
197 F2 Aiud Romania
138 E3 Aiviekste r. Latvia
Aix France see Aix-en-Provence
160 C3 Aix r. France
156 D4 Aix-en-Othe France
161 D5 Aix-en-Provence France
162 D3 Aixe-sur-Vienne France
Aix-la-Chapelle Ger. see Aachen
160 D3 Aix-les-Bains France
210 C1 Āīy Ādī Eth.
Aíyina i. Greece see Aigina
Aiyínion Greece see Aiginio
Aíyion Greece see Aigio
Aíyira Greece see Aigeira
117 H5 Aizawl Mizoram India
158 E5 Aizenay France
138 E3 Aizkraukle Latvia
183 I2 Aizpun Spain
138 C3 Aizpute Latvia
103 I5 Aizu-wakamatsu Japan
124 C2 Ajā, Jibāl mts Saudi Arabia
192 A3 Ajaccio Corse France
Ajaccio airport Corse France see Campo dell'Oro
192 A3 Ajaccio, Golfe d' b. Corse France
245 E3 Ajacuba Mex.
116 E4 Ajaigarh Madh. Prad. India
250 C4 Ajajú r. Col.
177 L3 Ajak Hungary
245 F4 Ajalpán Mex.
116 C5 Ajanta Mahar. India
Ajanta Range hills India see Sahyadriparvat Range
207 G5 Ajaokuta Nigeria
Ajaria aut. rep. Georgia see Ach'ara
207 G4 Ajasse Nigeria
162 D3 Ajat France
227 H4 Ajax Ont. Can.
81 D5 Ajax, Mount South I. N.Z.
Ajayameru Rajasthan India see Ajmer
106 B2 Aj Bogd Uul mts Mongolia
202 D2 Ajdābiyā Libya
188 D3 Ajdovščina Slovenia
a-Jiddét des. Oman see Ḥarāsīs, Jiddat al
117 G4 Ajimganj W. Bengal India
177 G4 Ajka Hungary
128 B3 'Ajlūn Jordan
125 F2 Ajman U.A.E.
116 C4 Ajmer Rajasthan India
Ajmer-Merwara Rajasthan India see Ajmer
183 G1 Ajo Spain
241 K5 Ajo AZ U.S.A.
241 K5 Ajo, Mount AZ U.S.A.
183 G5 Ajofrín Spain
78 □3b Ajokwola i. Majuro Marshall Is
114 B2 Ajra Mahar. India
92 B4 Ajuy Phil.
102 K2 Akabira Japan
Akademii Nauk, Khrebet mt. Tajik. see Akademiyai Fanho, Qatorkŭhi
123 G2 Akademiyai Fanho, Qatorkŭhi mt. Tajik.
102 I4 Aka-gawa r. Japan
103 F6 Akagi Japan
105 F2 Akagi-yama vol. Japan
105 E3 Akaishi-dake mt. Japan
105 D4 Akaishi-sanmyaku mts Japan
210 C2 Āk'ak'ī Beseka Eth.
202 A3 Akakus, Jabal mts Libya
114 C2 Akalkot Mahar. India
Akamagaseki Japan see Shimonoseki
207 H5 Akamkpa Nigeria
198 B2 Akarnanika mts Greece
81 D5 Akaroa South I. N.Z.
81 D5 Akaroa Harbour South I. N.Z.
127 E4 Akāshat Iraq
104 A4 Akashi Japan
215 G1 Akasia S. Africa
140 M2 Äkäsjoki r. Fin.
177 I5 Akasztó Hungary
81 E4 Akatarawa North I. N.Z.
121 H3 Akbakay Kazakh.
116 E4 Akbarpur Uttar Prad. India
117 E4 Akbarpur Uttar Prad. India
121 G2 Akbeit Kazakh.
128 C1 Akbez Turkey
205 G1 Akbou Alg.
120 C2 Akbulak Rus. Fed.
129 A3 Akçaabat Turkey
126 E3 Akçadağ Turkey
129 C4 Akça Dağ mt. Turkey
126 E3 Akçakale Turkey
199 G1 Akçakoca Turkey
128 A1 Akçalı Dağları mts Turkey
199 E3 Akçaova Turkey
199 F3 Akçay Antalya Turkey
199 F3 Akçay r. Turkey
122 D1 Akchakaya, Vpadina depr. Turkm.
206 B2 Akchâr reg. Maur.
121 H3 Akchatau Kazakh.
Akchi Kazakh. see Akshiy
129 B4 Akdağ mt. Turkey
199 F2 Akdağ mt. Turkey
199 F3 Akdağ mts Turkey
199 G3 Ak Dağı mt. Turkey
199 F3 Akdağlar mts Turkey
126 D3 Akdağmadeni Turkey
129 C3 Akdam Turkey
122 D1 Akdepe Turkm.
128 A1 Akdere Turkey
129 B4 Akdoğan Dağı mts Turkey
149 G2 Akeld Northumberland, England U.K.
124 B5 Akele Guzai prov. Eritrea
171 D4 Aken Ger.
143 H2 Åkersberga Sweden
142 D1 Akershus county Norway
164 D2 Akersloot Neth.
143 G2 Åkers styckebruk Sweden
208 D4 Aketi Dem. Rep. Congo
Akgyr Erezi hills Turkm. see Akkyr, Gory
129 D2 Akhalgori Georgia
Akhali-Afoni Georgia see Akhali Ap'oni
129 B2 Akhali Ap'oni Georgia
129 C3 Akhalk'alak'i Georgia
Akhal Oblast admin. div. Turkm. see Akhal'skaya Oblast'
122 D2 Akhal'skaya Oblast' admin. div. Turkm.
129 C3 Akhalts'ikhe Georgia
202 D2 Akhḍar, Al Jabal al mts Libya
125 G3 Akhḍar, Jabal mts Oman
Akhelóös r. Greece see Acheloös
197 H4 Akheloy Bulg.
199 E2 Akhisar Turkey
129 D3 Akhk'erp'i Georgia
129 D2 Akhmeta Georgia
129 B1 Akhmetovskaya Rus. Fed.
203 F3 Akhmîm Egypt
116 C2 Akhnoor Jammu and Kashmir
Akhsu Azer. see Ağsu
Akhta Armenia see Hrazdan
127 I6 Akhtar Iran
128 C1 Akhtarīn Syria
135 I6 Akhtubinsk Rus. Fed.
129 E3 Akhty Rus. Fed.
Akhtyrka Ukr. see Okhtyrka
137 J5 Akhtyrskiy Rus. Fed.
120 D1 Akhunovo Rus. Fed.
129 E3 Akhvay, Gora mt. Azer./Rus. Fed.
103 F7 Aki Japan
208 B5 Akiéni Gabon
Akıncılar Turkey see Selçuk
126 E2 Akıncılar Turkey
113 □1 Akinfushi i. N. Male Maldives
143 F4 Åkirkeby Bornholm Denmark
105 F3 Akiruno Japan
105 F3 Akishima Japan
100 E1 Akishma r. Rus. Fed.
102 J4 Akita Japan
102 J4 Akita pref. Japan
80 F4 Akitio North I. N.Z.
105 F2 Akiyama-gawa r. Japan
206 B2 Akjoujt Maur.
204 C3 Akka Morocco
140 L2 Akkajaure l. Sweden
Akkerman Ukr. see Bilhorod-Dnistrovs'kyy
120 D2 Akkermanovka Rus. Fed.
128 B3 'Akko Israel
121 G1 Akkol' Akmolinskaya Oblast' Kazakh.
135 J7 Akkol' Kazakh.
121 G4 Akkol' Kazakh.
199 E3 Akköy Turkey
199 F3 Akköy Turkey
164 E1 Akkrum Neth.
121 I2 Akku Kazakh.
Akkul' Kazakh. see Akkol'
120 F3 Akkum Kazakh.
126 E2 Akkuş Turkey
122 C1 Akkyr, Gory hills Turkm.
120 B3 Akkystau Kazakh.
207 F4 Aklampa Benin
220 E3 Aklavik N.W.T. Can.
116 D4 Aklera Rajasthan India
Ak-Mechet Kazakh. see Kyzylorda
138 D4 Akmena r. Lith.
138 D3 Akmenė Lith.
Akmola Kazakh. see Astana
Akmola Oblast admin. div. Kazakh. see Akmolinskaya Oblast'
Akmolinsk Kazakh. see Astana
121 G2 Akmolinskaya Oblast' admin. div. Kazakh.
138 E3 Aknīste Latvia
204 E2 Aknoul Morocco
103 G6 Akō Japan
210 B3 Akobo Wenz r. Eth./Sudan
116 D5 Akodia Madh. Prad. India
114 B2 Akola Mahar. India
116 D5 Akola Mahar. India
207 H6 Akom II Cameroon
207 I6 Akonolinga Cameroon
203 H6 Akordat Eritrea
199 G2 Akören Afyon Turkey
126 D3 Akören Turkey
116 D5 Akot Mahar. India
206 E5 Akoupé Côte d'Ivoire
221 L3 Akpatok Island Nunavut Can.
110 B3 Akqi Xinjiang China
198 C2 Akraifnio Greece
140 □B2 Akranes Iceland
142 A2 Åkrehamn Norway
236 C3 Akron CO U.S.A.
226 D5 Akron IN U.S.A.
232 D3 Akron NY U.S.A.
232 C4 Akron OH U.S.A.
234 B2 Akron PA U.S.A.
Akrotiri Bay Cyprus see Akrotirion Bay
128 A2 Akrotirion Bay Cyprus
Akrotiriou, Kolpos b. Cyprus see Akrotirion Bay
128 A2 Akrotiri Sovereign Base Area military base Cyprus
111 B5 Aksai Chin terr. Asia
199 F1 Aksakal Turkey
197 H4 Aksakovo Bulg.
135 K5 Aksakovo Rus. Fed.
126 D3 Aksaray Turkey
130 H3 Aksarka Rus. Fed.
129 B2 Aksaut r. Rus. Fed.
110 F4 Aksay Gansu China
120 C2 Aksay Kazakh.
121 H4 Ak-Say r. Kyrg.
135 G7 Aksay Rostovskaya Oblast' Rus. Fed.
135 I7 Aksay Volgogradskaya Oblast' Rus. Fed.
137 J4 Aksay r. Rus. Fed.
126 C3 Akşehir Turkey
199 G2 Akşehir Gölü l. Turkey
126 C3 Akseki Turkey
120 C1 Aksenovo Rus. Fed.
122 C4 Aks-e Rostam r. Iran
107 G1 Aksha Rus. Fed.
120 C2 Akshatau Kazakh.
120 E2 Akshiganak Kazakh.
121 I4 Akshiy Kazakh.
120 B4 Akshukur Kazakh.
110 C3 Aksu Xinjiang China
121 I3 Aksu Almatinskaya Oblast' Kazakh.
121 I1 Aksu Pavlodarskaya Oblast' Kazakh.
121 G1 Aksu Severnyy Kazakhstan Kazakh.
120 C2 Aksu Zapadnyy Kazakhstan Kazakh.
121 I3 Aksu r. Kazakh.
Aksu r. Tajik. see Oksu
199 G3 Aksu Antalya Turkey
199 G3 Aksu Isparta Turkey
199 G3 Aksu r. Turkey
120 F2 Aksuat Kustanayskaya Oblast' Kazakh.
121 J3 Aksuat Vostochnyy Kazakhstan Kazakh.
121 H2 Aksu-Ayuly Kazakh.
135 J5 Aksubayevo Rus. Fed.
121 H3 Aksuek Kazakh.
110 C3 Aksu He r. China
210 C1 Āksum Eth.
111 D4 Aktag mt. Xinjiang China
134 K5 Aktanysh Rus. Fed.
128 C1 Aktaş Turkey
127 G3 Aktaş Dağı mt. Turkey
129 E2 Aktash r. Rus. Fed.
120 F5 Aktash Uzbek.
121 G3 Aktau Karagandinskaya Oblast' Kazakh.
121 H2 Aktau Karagandinskaya Oblast' Kazakh.
120 B4 Aktau Mangistauskaya Oblast' Kazakh.
128 C1 Aktepe Turkey
199 G1 Aktepe hill Turkey
110 B4 Akto Xinjiang China
121 H2 Aktogay Karagandinskaya Oblast' Kazakh.
121 H1 Aktogay Pavlodarskaya Oblast' Kazakh.
121 I3 Aktogay Vostochnyy Kazakhstan Kazakh.
128 C1 Aktoprak Turkey
139 H4 Aktsyabrskaya Belarus
138 G5 Aktsyabrski Homyel'skaya Voblasts' Belarus
138 G4 Aktsyabrski Vitsyebskaya Voblasts' Belarus
121 H4 Ak-Tüz Kyrg.
120 D2 Aktyubinsk Kazakh.
120 D2 Aktyubinskaya Oblast' admin. div. Kazakh.
Aktyubinsk Oblast admin. div. Kazakh. see Aktyubinskaya Oblast'
Aktyuz Kyrg. see Ak-Tüz
221 K3 Akulivik Que. Can.
206 E5 Akumadan Ghana
103 E7 Akune Japan
210 B4 Akur mt. Uganda
129 D3 Akura Georgia
207 G5 Akure Nigeria
140 □C2 Akureyri Iceland
80 E2 Akuroa North I. N.Z.
102 □1 Akuseki-jima i. Japan
129 E2 Akusha Rus. Fed.
220 B4 Akutan AK U.S.A.
207 G5 Akwa Ibom state Nigeria
207 H4 Akwanga Nigeria
207 H5 Akwaya Cameroon
Akyab Myanmar see Sittwe
129 C3 Akyaka Turkey
120 D2 Ak"yar Rus. Fed.
199 G1 Akyazı Turkey
121 H3 Akzhal Karagandinskaya Oblast' Kazakh.
121 J2 Akzhal Vostochnyy Kazakhstan Kazakh.
120 F3 Akzhar Kzyl-Ordinskaya Oblast' Kazakh.
121 J3 Akzhar Vostochnyy Kazakhstan Kazakh.
121 G4 Akzhar Zhambylskaya Oblast' Kazakh.
121 F3 Akzhaykyn, Ozero salt l. Kazakh.
142 C1 Ål Norway
138 G5 Ala r. Belarus
191 G3 Ala Italy
231 C6 Alabama r. AL U.S.A.
231 C5 Alabama state U.S.A.
231 C5 Alabaster AL U.S.A.
227 F3 Alabaster MI U.S.A.
121 G4 Ala-Buka Kyrg.
202 D1 Al Abyār Libya
195 F4 Alaca r. Italy
126 D2 Alaca Turkey
129 B3 Alaca Dağı mt. Turkey
126 E3 Alacahan Turkey
126 D2 Alaçam Turkey
199 F2 Alaçam Dağları mts Turkey
Alacant Spain see Alicante
199 E2 Alaçatı Turkey
243 H4 Alacrán, Arrecife rf Mex.
197 G5 Aladag mt. Bulg.
126 D3 Aladağ Turkey
129 C3 Aladağ mt. Turkey
127 F3 Ala Dağlar mts Turkey
126 D3 Ala Dağları mts Turkey
192 B4 Alà dei Sardi Sardegna Italy
190 C3 Ala di Stura Italy
183 E3 Alaejos Spain
114 C4 Alagapuram Tamil Nadu India
Alagez mt. Armenia see Aragats Lerr
106 B2 Alag Hayrhan Uul mt. Mongolia
129 D2 Alagir Rus. Fed.
190 C3 Alagna Valsesia Italy
161 B3 Alagnon r. France
254 F4 Alagoas state Brazil
254 F5 Alagoinhas Brazil
186 B3 Alagón Spain
182 D5 Alagón r. Spain
129 C3 Alagöz Dağı mt. Turkey
92 C5 Alah r. Phil.
94 C3 Alahanpanjang Sumatera Indon.
140 M3 Alahärmä Fin.
127 H5 Al Aḥmadī Kuwait
163 E5 Alaigne France
186 □ Alaior Spain
123 G2 Alai Range mts Asia
122 C3 Ālaivān Iran
184 D3 Alájar Spain
140 M3 Alajärvi Fin.
216 □3a Alajero La Gomera Canary Is
124 C2 Al Ajfar Saudi Arabia
138 F2 Alajõgi r. Estonia
242 □I7 Alajuela Costa Rica
213 □J4 Alak Ambohimaha Madag.
220 B3 Alakanuk AK U.S.A.
129 B2 Alakhadzi Georgia
129 E3 Alakhundag, Gora mt. Rus. Fed.
116 D3 Alaknanda r. India
121 J3 Alakol', Ozero salt l. Kazakh.
Ala Kul salt l. Kazakh. see Alakol', Ozero
140 O2 Alakurtti Rus. Fed.
251 F5 Alalaú r. Brazil
124 C4 Al 'Alayyah Saudi Arabia
Alalia Corse France see Aléria
182 B2 A Lama Spain
127 F3 Al 'Amādīyah Iraq
91 K3 Alamagan i. N. Mariana Is
Alamaguan i. N. Mariana Is see Alamagan
127 G5 Al 'Amārah Iraq
210 C1 Ālamat'ā Eth.
185 F3 Alameda Spain
240 F3 Alameda CA U.S.A.
185 G1 Alameda de Cervera Spain
183 G4 Alameda de la Sagra Spain
127 G5 Al Amghar waterhole Iraq
185 F2 Alamillo Spain
92 A2 Alaminos Phil.
239 F6 Alamito Creek r. TX U.S.A.
124 C3 Al Amlah Saudi Arabia
245 F3 Álamo Mex.
184 C2 Álamo r. Port.
184 E4 Alamo r. Spain
231 D5 Alamo GA U.S.A.
241 J3 Alamo NV U.S.A.
237 F5 Alamo TN U.S.A.
239 F5 Alamogordo NM U.S.A.
237 D6 Alamo Heights TX U.S.A.
250 A6 Alamor Ecuador
242 C2 Alamos Sonora Mex.
242 C3 Alamos Sonora Mex.
243 E3 Alamos r. Mex.
242 C3 Alamos, Sierra mts Mex.
239 F4 Alamosa CO U.S.A.
239 F5 Alamosa Creek r. NM U.S.A.
114 C3 Alampur Andhra Prad. India
124 D5 Al 'Anad Yemen
140 K2 Alanäs Sweden
127 F4 Al Anbār governorate Iraq
141 L3 Åland is Fin.
170 C2 Aland r. Ger.
114 C2 Aland Karnataka India
122 A2 Aland r. Iran
129 B3 Alan Dağı mt. Turkey
Åland Islands Fin. see Åland
184 C2 Alandroal Port.
141 L4 Ålands Hav sea chan. Fin./Sweden
114 D3 Alandur Tamil Nadu India
184 D2 Alange Spain
184 D2 Alange, Embalse de resr Spain
Alania aut. reg. Georgia see Samkhret' Oset'i
184 E2 Alanís Spain
226 E3 Alanson MI U.S.A.
126 D3 Alanya Turkey
177 H5 Alap Hungary
231 D6 Alapaha r. GA U.S.A.
114 C4 Alapakam Tamil Nadu India
199 G1 Alaplı Turkey
Alappuzha Kerala India see Alleppey
116 D4 Alapur Uttar Prad. India
128 B5 Al 'Aqabah Jordan
124 C3 Al 'Aqīq Saudi Arabia
125 E2 Al 'Arabiyah i. Saudi Arabia
Al 'Arabīyah as Sa'ūdīyah country Asia see Saudi Arabia
183 E4 Alaraz Spain
183 H5 Alarcón Spain
183 H5 Alarcón, Embalse de resr Spain
183 F2 Alar del Rey Spain
187 F5 Alaró Spain
124 D2 Al Arṭāwīyah Saudi Arabia
95 G5 Alas, Selat sea chan. Indon.
199 F2 Alaşehir Turkey
129 D3 Äläsgärli Azer.
Alashiya country Asia see Cyprus
220 D3 Alaska state U.S.A.
213 F3 Alaska Zimbabwe
220 D4 Alaska, Gulf of AK U.S.A.
222 A2 Alaska Highway Can./U.S.A.
220 B4 Alaska Peninsula AK U.S.A.
220 D3 Alaska Range mts AK U.S.A.
190 D4 Alassio Italy
141 M3 Alastaro Fin.
129 F4 Älät Azer.
120 E5 Alat Uzbek.
192 A3 Alata Corse France
187 B5 Alatoz Spain
193 F3 Alatri Italy
129 F3 Älät Tiräsi plat. Azer.
177 J4 Alattyán Hungary
135 I5 Alatyr' Rus. Fed.
135 I5 Alatyr' r. Rus. Fed.
250 B5 Alausí Ecuador
183 H2 Álava prov. País Vasco Spain
129 D3 Alaverdi Armenia
140 N2 Alavieska Fin.
140 M3 Alavus Fin.
125 G3 Al Awābī Oman
82 E3 Alawoona S.A. Austr.
Alay Kyrka Toosu mts Asia see Alai Range
125 F2 Al 'Ayn U.A.E.
Alayskiy Khrebet mts Asia see Alai Range
129 E3 Alazani r. Azer./Georgia
131 Q2 Alazeya r. Rus. Fed.
202 B1 Al 'Azīzīyah Libya
172 C4 Alb r. Ger.
190 D4 Alba Italy
186 B4 Alba Spain
226 E3 Alba MI U.S.A.
234 B1 Alba PA U.S.A.
81 B6 Alba, Mount South I. N.Z.
193 F2 Alba Adriatica Italy
128 C1 Al Bāb Syria
185 I1 Albacete Spain
185 I2 Albacete prov. Castilla - La Mancha Spain
124 B2 Al Badā'i' Saudi Arabia
183 E4 Alba de Tormes Spain
124 D3 Al Badī' Saudi Arabia
127 G5 Al Bādiyah al Janūbīyah hill Iraq
142 D3 Ålbæk Denmark
142 D3 Ålbæk Bugt b. Denmark
192 A5 Albagiara Sardegna Italy
124 C3 Al Bāḥah Egypt
124 C3 Al Bāḥah prov. Saudi Arabia
128 B2 Al Bahlūlīyah Syria
Al Bahrayn country Asia see Bahrain
187 C6 Albaida Spain
197 F2 Alba Iulia Romania
185 H2 Albaladejo Spain
184 D1 Albalá del Caudillo Spain
161 C4 Alba-la-Romaine France
186 C3 Albalate de Arzobispo Spain
186 D3 Albalate de Cinca Spain
183 H4 Albalate de las Nogueras Spain
183 H4 Albalate de Zorita Spain
186 C3 Albalatillo Spain
163 E5 Alban France
185 H3 Albánchez Spain
193 H4 Albanella Italy
196 D5 Albania country Europe
193 I4 Albano di Lucania Italy
193 E3 Albano Laziale Italy
87 C7 Albany W.A. Austr.
224 D2 Albany r. Ont. Can.
246 □ Albany Jamaica
231 C6 Albany GA U.S.A.
236 E3 Albany MO U.S.A.
233 G3 Albany NY U.S.A.
232 B5 Albany OH U.S.A.
238 B2 Albany OR U.S.A.
237 D5 Albany TX U.S.A.
186 F2 Albanyà Spain
85 G5 Albany Downs Qld Austr.
258 G4 Albardão do João Maria coastal area Brazil
202 E2 Al Bardī Libya
260 C2 Albardón Arg.
190 E2 Albaredo per San Marco Italy
161 B4 Albaret-le-Comtal France
190 E4 Albareto Italy
161 B4 Albaret-Ste-Marie France
160 D3 Albarine r. France
161 C5 Albaron France
183 I4 Albarracín Spain
184 D1 Albarragena r. Spain
137 J4 Albasi r. Rus. Fed.
127 G5 Al Baṣrah Iraq
127 G5 Al Baṣrah governorate Iraq
150 C4 Albaston Cornwall, England U.K.
185 I2 Albatana Spain
186 D3 Albatàrrec Spain
187 C6 Albatera Spain
125 G3 Al Bāṭinah admin. reg. Oman
85 E2 Albatross Bay Qld Austr.
83 F5 Albatross Island Tas. Austr.
202 D1 Al Bayḍā' Libya
124 D5 Al Bayḍā' Yemen
124 D5 Al Bayḍā' governorate Yemen
172 C4 Albbruck Ger.
157 H4 Albe r. France
192 D2 Albegna r. Italy
186 D3 Albelda Spain
183 H2 Albelda de Iregua Spain
186 C2 Albella Spain
231 D5 Albemarle NC U.S.A.
Albemarle Island Islas Galápagos Ecuador see Isabela, Isla
231 E5 Albemarle Sound sea chan. NC U.S.A.
183 H4 Albendea Spain
185 F3 Albendín Spain
190 D4 Albenga Italy
160 D3 Albens France
187 C4 Albentosa Spain
183 F5 Alberche r. Spain
253 F6 Alberdi Para.
182 B4 Albergaria-a-Velha Port.
182 B5 Albergaria dos Doze Port.
190 B3 Albergian, Monte mt. Italy
187 C5 Alberic Spain
183 H2 Alberite Spain
179 F2 Alberndorf in der Riedmark Austria
184 C3 Albernoa Port.
186 C2 Albero Alto Spain
195 G2 Alberobello Italy
191 H3 Alberoni Italy
178 A3 Alberschwende Austria
168 E1 Albersdorf Ger.
83 F3 Albert N.S.W. Austr.
84 D3 Albert r. Qld Austr.
156 C3 Albert France
82 D3 Albert, Lake S.A. Austr.
210 A4 Albert, Lake Dem. Rep. Congo/Uganda
222 H4 Alberta prov. Can.
232 E6 Alberta VA U.S.A.
192 A2 Albertacce Corse France
190 E4 Alberta Ligure Italy
261 G4 Alberti Arg.
140 □ Albert I Land reg. Svalbard
214 C6 Albertinia S. Africa
177 I4 Albertirsa Hungary
236 E3 Albert Lea MN U.S.A.
210 B4 Albert Nile r. Sudan/Uganda
225 H4 Alberton P.E.I. Can.
215 G2 Alberton S. Africa
238 D2 Alberton MT U.S.A.
241 J5 Alberto Oviedo Mota Mex.
215 E2 Albertshoek S. Africa
173 E2 Albertshofen Ger.
246 □ Albert Town Jamaica
81 B6 Albert Town South I. N.Z.
Albertville Dem. Rep. Congo see Kalémié
160 E3 Albertville France
231 C5 Albertville AL U.S.A.
186 C3 Alberuela de Tubo Spain
186 D3 Albesa Spain
197 H2 Albeşti Romania
197 H2 Albeşti Romania
157 G4 Albestroff France
163 E5 Albi France
236 E3 Albia IA U.S.A.
163 D4 Albias France
125 E2 Al Bīḍah des. Saudi Arabia
195 F3 Albidona Italy
191 G3 Albignasego Italy
251 H3 Albina Suriname
190 E3 Albino Italy
240 F2 Albion CA U.S.A.
230 C3 Albion IN U.S.A.
226 E4 Albion MI U.S.A.
236 D3 Albion NE U.S.A.
234 D3 Albion NJ U.S.A.
232 D3 Albion NY U.S.A.
232 C4 Albion PA U.S.A.
183 E2 Albires Spain
124 C4 Al Birk Saudi Arabia
172 C2 Albisheim (Pfrimm) Ger.
190 D4 Albisola Marina Italy
190 D4 Albisola Superiore Italy
124 D3 Al Biyāḍh reg. Saudi Arabia
164 D3 Alblasserdam Neth.
187 D4 Albocácer Spain
185 H3 Alboloduy Spain
161 C3 Albon France
185 G4 Albondón Spain
187 B5 Alborea Spain
142 C3 Ålborg Denmark
142 D3 Ålborg Bugt b. Denmark
122 B2 Alborz, Reshteh-ye mts Iran
197 G3 Albota Romania
185 H3 Albox Spain
177 H2 Albrechtice Czech Rep.
150 E2 Albrighton Shropshire, England U.K.
85 F4 Albro Qld Austr.
172 D3 Albstadt Ger.
173 D3 Albuch hills Ger.
125 E2 Al Budayyi Bahrain
184 B3 Albufeira Port.
187 B7 Albujón Spain
124 C2 Al Bukayrīyah Saudi Arabia
190 E2 Albula r. Switz.
190 E2 Albula Alpen mts Switz.
185 G4 Albuñol Spain
185 G4 Albuñuelas Spain
239 F5 Albuquerque NM U.S.A.
246 B4 Albuquerque, Cayos de is Caribbean Sea
125 F2 Al Buraymī Oman
233 G2 Alburg VT U.S.A.
128 B5 Al Burj Jordan
193 H4 Alburno, Monte mt. Italy
184 D1 Alburquerque Spain
234 C2 Alburtis PA U.S.A.
83 F4 Albury N.S.W. Austr.
81 C6 Albury South I. N.Z.
127 F4 Al Buşayrah Syria
128 D4 Al Busayṭā' plain Saudi Arabia
126 E5 Al Busayṭā' plain Saudi Arabia
124 D1 Al Bushūk well Saudi Arabia
160 E3 Alby-sur-Chéran France
252 B3 Alca Peru
184 A2 Alcabideche Port.
187 C5 Alcácer Spain
184 B2 Alcácer do Sal Port.
184 B2 Alcáçovas Port.
184 B2 Alcáçovas r. Port.
185 I2 Alcadozo Spain
186 C4 Alcaine Spain
182 C5 Alcains Port.
187 D4 Alcalá de Chivert Spain
184 E3 Alcalá de Guadaira Spain
186 C2 Alcalá de Gurrea Spain
183 G4 Alcalá de Henares Spain
187 C4 Alcalá de la Selva Spain
187 B5 Alcalá del Júcar Spain
184 E4 Alcalá de los Gazules Spain
184 E3 Alcalá del Río Spain
185 E4 Alcalá del Valle Spain
185 G3 Alcalá la Real Spain
194 B5 Alcamo Sicilia Italy
186 D3 Alcampell Spain
186 D3 Alcanadre r. Spain
186 D4 Alcanar Spain
184 B1 Alcanede Port.
184 B1 Alcanena Port.
184 B1 Alcanhões Port.
182 D3 Alcañices Spain
186 C3 Alcañiz Spain
254 D2 Alcântara Brazil
182 D5 Alcántara Spain
182 D5 Alcántara, Embalse de resr Spain
187 B7 Alcantarilla Spain
183 H4 Alcantud Spain
185 F2 Alcaracejos Spain
194 D4 Alcara li Fusi Sicilia Italy
185 H2 Alcaraz Spain
184 C3 Alcaria do Cume hill Port.
184 C3 Alcaria Ruiva Port.
180 C4 Alcaria Ruiva hill Port.
184 C2 Alcarrache r. Port./Spain
186 D3 Alcarràs Spain
185 F4 Alcaucín Spain
185 F3 Alcaudete Spain
183 F5 Alcaudete de la Jara Spain
163 B5 Alçay-Alçabéhéty-Sunharette France
184 D2 Alcazaba r. Spain
183 H4 Alcázar del Rey Spain
185 G1 Alcázar de San Juan Spain
183 F3 Alcazarén Spain
Alcazarquivir Morocco see Ksar el Kebir
151 F2 Alcester Warwickshire, England U.K.
137 J3 Alchevs'k Ukr.
260 E3 Alcira Arg.
Alcira Spain see Alzira
185 F1 Alcoba Spain
257 H2 Alcobaça Brazil
182 B5 Alcobaça Port.
183 G4 Alcobendas Spain
184 B1 Alcobertas Port.
Alcocebre Spain see Alcossebre
183 H4 Alcocer Spain
183 G2 Alcocero de Mola Spain
184 B2 Alcochete Port.
184 B1 Alcoentre Port.
182 B4 Alcofra Port.
185 F3 Alcolea Andalucía Spain
185 H4 Alcolea Andalucía Spain
185 F2 Alcolea de Calatrava Spain
186 D3 Alcolea de Cinca Spain
183 H3 Alcolea del Pinar Spain
184 E3 Alcolea del Río Spain
186 D3 Alcoletge Spain
184 E1 Alcollarín Spain
184 C2 Alconchel Spain
184 D2 Alconera Spain
185 H3 Alcóntar Spain
84 C4 Alcoota N.T. Austr.
187 C4 Alcora Spain
183 G4 Alcorcón Spain
186 C4 Alcorisa Spain
184 D1 Alcorneo r. Port./Spain
183 I4 Alcoroches Spain
261 G3 Alcorta Arg.
187 D4 Alcossebre Spain
184 C3 Alcoutim Port.
238 F3 Alcova WY U.S.A.
186 E3 Alcover Spain
187 C6 Alcoy Spain
177 H4 Alcsútdobos Hungary
186 C3 Alcubierre Spain
183 G3 Alcubilla de Avellaneda Spain
185 G2 Alcubillas Spain
187 C5 Alcublas Spain
187 G5 Alcúdia Spain
185 F2 Alcudia r. Spain
Alcudia de Carlet Spain see L'Alcudia
185 G3 Alcudia de Guadix Spain
181 E4 Alcudia de Monteagud Spain
184 D1 Alcuéscar Spain
217 □2 Aldabra Atoll Aldabra Is Seychelles
217 □2 Aldabra Islands Seychelles
242 D2 Aldama Chihuahua Mex.
245 E2 Aldama Tamaulipas Mex.
131 N4 Aldan Rus. Fed.
131 N3 Aldan r. Rus. Fed.
151 F3 Aldbourne Wiltshire, England U.K.
149 I4 Aldbrough East Riding of Yorkshire, England U.K.
151 I2 Alde r. England U.K.
216 □3f Aldea r. Gran Canaria Canary Is
184 E1 Aldeacentenera Spain
182 D3 Aldeadávila de la Ribera Spain
184 D1 Aldea del Cano Spain
183 F4 Aldea del Fresno Spain
182 D4 Aldea del Obispo Spain
185 G2 Aldea del Rey Spain
182 E5 Aldea de Trujillo Spain
183 H3 Aldealafuente Spain
183 H3 Aldealpozo Spain
183 F3 Aldeamayor de San Martín Spain
183 E5 Aldeanueva de Barbarroya Spain
182 E3 Aldeanueva de Figueroa Spain
182 E4 Aldeanueva del Camino Spain
183 E5 Aldeanueva de San Bartolomé Spain
185 G2 Aldeaquemada Spain
182 E3 Aldearrodrigo Spain
183 F3 Aldeaseca Spain
182 E4 Aldeatejada Spain
183 F4 Aldeavieja Spain
151 I2 Aldeburgh Suffolk, England U.K.
182 D4 Aldehuela de la Bóveda Spain
182 D4 Aldehuela de Yeltes Spain
184 C1 Aldeia da Mata Port.
182 D4 Aldeia da Ponte Port.
184 C2 Aldeia de Ferreira Port.
182 C4 Aldeia do Bispo Port.
184 B3 Aldeia dos Elvas Port.
184 B3 Aldeia dos Palheiros Port.
182 D4 Aldeia Velha Guarda Port.
184 B1 Aldeia Velha Portalegre Port.
234 B1 Alden PA U.S.A.
151 G3 Aldenham Hertfordshire, England U.K.
169 B5 Aldenhoven Ger.
191 G3 Aldeno Italy
151 F3 Alderbury Wiltshire, England U.K.
233 F3 Alder Creek NY U.S.A.
147 E2 Aldergrove Northern Ireland U.K.
151 F4 Alderholt Dorset, England U.K.
149 G4 Alderley Edge Cheshire, England U.K.
158 D2 Alderney i. Channel Is
240 G4 Alder Peak CA U.S.A.
173 H3 Aldersbach Ger.
151 G3 Aldershot Hampshire, England U.K.
232 C6 Alderson WV U.S.A.
196 E5 Aldinci Macedonia
172 C3 Aldingen Ger.
149 F3 Aldingham Cumbria, England U.K.
151 H3 Aldington Kent, England U.K.
215 H3 Aldinville S. Africa
186 D4 Aldover Spain
151 F2 Aldridge West Midlands, England U.K.
163 A5 Aldudes France
142 E3 Åled Sweden
185 I3 Aledo Spain
236 F3 Aledo IL U.S.A.
206 B2 Aleg Maur.
216 □3c Alegranza i. Canary Is
257 G4 Alegre Espírito Santo Brazil
256 D3 Alegre Minas Gerais Brazil
255 B9 Alegrete Brazil
184 C1 Alegrete Port.
183 H2 Alegría-Dulantzi Spain
239 E5 Alegros Mountain NM U.S.A.
261 H1 Alejandra Arg.
261 H4 Alejandro Korn Arg.
261 F3 Alejandro Roca Arg.
252 □ Alejandro Selkirk, Isla i. S. Pacific Ocean
260 D6 Alejandro Stefenelli Arg.
139 I1 Alekhovshchina Rus. Fed.
Aleksandriya Kirovohrads'ka Oblast' Ukr. see Oleksandriya
139 M5 Aleksandro-Nevskiy Rus. Fed.
Aleksandropol Armenia see Gyumri
139 L3 Aleksandrov Rus. Fed.
196 E4 Aleksandrovac Srbija Yugo.
Aleksandrov Dar Ukr. see Rakhmanivka
120 B2 Aleksandrov Gay Rus. Fed.
135 K5 Aleksandrovka Orenburgskaya Oblast' Rus. Fed.
137 J4 Aleksandrovka Rostovskaya Oblast' Rus. Fed.
197 G4 Aleksandrovo Khaskovo Bulg.
197 G4 Aleksandrovo Lovech Bulg.
134 L4 Aleksandrovsk Rus. Fed.
Aleksandrovsk Ukr. see Zaporizhzhya
Aleksandrovskiy Rus. Fed. see Aleksandrovsk
129 C1 Aleksandrovskoye Stavropol'skiy Kray Rus. Fed.
127 G1 Aleksandrovskoye Stavropol'skiy Kray Rus. Fed.
130 I3 Aleksandrovskoye Tomskaya Oblast' Rus. Fed.
100 G2 Aleksandrovsk-Sakhalinskiy Sakhalin Rus. Fed.
175 I3 Aleksandrów Pol.
174 G3 Aleksandrów Kujawski Pol.
175 H4 Aleksandrów Łódzki Pol.
177 I6 Aleksa Šantić Vojvodina, Srbija Yugo.
129 F3 Alekseyevka Azer.
Alekseyevka Akmolinskaya Oblast' Kazakh. see Akkol'
121 H2 Alekseyevka Pavlodarskaya Oblast' Kazakh.
Alekseyevka Vostochnyy Kazakhstan Kazakh. see Terekty
135 G6 Alekseyevka Belgorodskaya Oblast' Rus. Fed.
135 G6 Alekseyevka Belgorodskaya Oblast' Rus. Fed.
137 K3 Alekseyevo-Lozovskoye Rus. Fed.
135 H6 Alekseyevskaya Rus. Fed.
139 K4 Aleksin Rus. Fed.
197 E4 Aleksinac Srbija Yugo.
143 G3 Ålem Sweden
208 A5 Alèmbé Gabon
210 D2 'Alem Maya Eth.
257 F4 Além Paraíba Brazil
140 J3 Ålen Norway
159 G3 Alençon France
160 B2 Alène r. France
251 H5 Alenquer Brazil
184 B1 Alenquer Port.
184 B1 Alenquer r. Port.
240 □C9 Alenuihaha Channel HI U.S.A.
163 E6 Alénya France
Alep Syria see Ḥalab
206 E5 Alépé Côte d'Ivoire
Aleppo Syria see Ḥalab
114 C2 Aler r. India
173 E3 Alerheim Ger.
192 B2 Aléria Corse France
186 C2 Alerre Spain
221 L1 Alert Nunavut Can.
222 E5 Alert Bay B.C. Can.
161 C4 Alès France
192 A5 Ales Sardegna Italy
197 F2 Aleşd Romania
Aleshki Ukr. see Tsyurupyns'k

Alesia France see Alise-Ste-Reine
Aleşkirt Turkey see Eleşkirt
183 H2 Alesón Spain
190 D4 Alessándria Italy
190 D4 Alessándria prov. Piemonte Italy
195 F3 Alessandria del Carretto Italy
195 H3 Alessano Italy
Alessio Albania see Lezhë
142 C2 Ålestrup Denmark
140 I3 Ålesund Norway
163 E5 Alet-les-Bains France
Aletrium Italy see Alatri
190 C2 Aletschhorn mt. Switz.
266 G2 Aleutian Basin sea feature Bering Sea
220 A4 Aleutian Islands AK U.S.A.
220 C4 Aleutian Range mts AK U.S.A.
266 H2 Aleutian Trench sea feature N. Pacific Ocean
Alevişik Turkey see Samandağı
236 C2 Alexander ND U.S.A.
262 T2 Alexander, Cape Antarctica
84 D2 Alexander, Mount hill N.T. Austr.
87 B4 Alexander, Mount hill W.A. Austr.
220 E4 Alexander Archipelago is AK U.S.A.
214 A3 Alexander Bay b. Namibia/S. Africa
214 A3 Alexander Bay S. Africa
231 C5 Alexander City U.S.A.
262 T2 Alexander Island Antarctica
122 C2 Alexander's Wall tourist site Iran
83 F4 Alexandra Vic. Austr.
84 D3 Alexandra r. Qld Austr.
81 B6 Alexandra South I. N.Z.
259 □ Alexandra, Cape S. Georgia
Alexandra Land i. Zemlya Frantsa-Iosifa Rus. Fed. see Zemlya Aleksandry
198 C1 Alexandreia Greece
Alexandretta Turkey see İskenderun
Alexandria Afgh. see Ghaznī
84 D3 Alexandria N.T. Austr.
222 F4 Alexandria B.C. Can.
224 F4 Alexandria Ont. Can.
202 F2 Alexandria Romania
197 G4 Alexandria S. Africa
215 F5 Alexandria Turkm. see Mary
146 D6 Alexandria West Dunbartonshire, Scotland U.K.
232 A5 Alexandria KY U.S.A.
237 E6 Alexandria LA U.S.A.
236 C2 Alexandria MN U.S.A.
236 D3 Alexandria SD U.S.A.
234 A4 Alexandria VA U.S.A.
Alexandria Arachoton Afgh. see Kandahār
Alexandria Areion Afgh. see Herāt
233 F2 Alexandria Bay NY U.S.A.
Alexandria Prophthasia Afgh. see Farāh
82 D3 Alexandrina, Lake S.A. Austr.
199 D1 Alexandroupoli Greece
256 C2 Alexânia Brazil
225 J2 Alexis r. Nfld. Can.
128 B3 Alexis Creek B.C. Can.
121 J1 'Aley Lebanon
121 J1 Aley r. Rus. Fed.
195 H2 Alezio Italy
169 C5 Alf Ger.
185 G3 Alfacar Spain
187 C5 Alfafar Spain
182 D4 Alfaiates Port.
186 C3 Alfajarín Spain
245 E3 Alfajayucan Mex.
186 B4 Alfambra r. Spain
186 B4 Alfambra Spain
184 B3 Alfambras Port.
186 B3 Alfamén Spain
182 D3 Alfândega da Fé Port.
186 D3 Alfántega Spain
182 E4 Al Fardah Yemen
182 B4 Alfarràs Port.
185 F3 Alfarnate Spain
183 I2 Alfaro Spain
186 D3 Alfarràs Spain
125 C2 Al Farūq reg. Saudi Arabia
127 G5 Al Farwānīyah Kuwait
Al Faro Morocco see Fès
197 H4 Alfatar Bulg.
127 C4 Al Fatḥah Iraq
Al Fayyūm Egypt see El Faiyûm
187 C6 Alfaz del Pi Spain
124 C5 Al Fāzih Yemen
172 D3 Alfdorf Ger.
193 G3 Alfedena Italy
190 B3 Alfeés r. Greece
182 A5 Alfeizerão Port.
169 E4 Alfeld (Leine) Ger.
182 B3 Alfena Port.
257 E4 Alfenas Brazil
184 B3 Alferce Port.
186 C3 Alferrarede Port.
169 C3 Alfhausen Ger.
Alfios r. Greece see Alfeios
177 J5 Alföld plain Hungary
191 H4 Alfonsine Italy
146 F4 Alford Aberdeenshire, Scotland U.K.
149 J4 Alford Lincolnshire, England U.K.
186 D3 Alforja Spain
233 F2 Alfred ME U.S.A.
233 □H3 Alfred ME U.S.A.
87 E5 Alfred and Marie Range hills W.A. Austr.
245 E3 Alfred M. Terrazas Mex.
225 G4 Alfredo Chaves Brazil
80 E4 Alfredton North I. N.Z.
149 H4 Alfreton Derbyshire, England U.K.
141 L3 Alfta Sweden
Al Fujayrah U.A.E. see Fujairah
184 B2 Alfundão Port.
118 D2 Al Furāt r. Iraq/Syria alt. Firat (Turkey), conv. Euphrates
120 D2 Alga Kazakh.
120 C2 Algabas Kazakh.
187 F5 Algaida Spain
192 A2 Algajola Corse France
185 E3 Algámitas Spain
184 E4 Algar Spain
142 B2 Ålgård Norway
185 F3 Algarinejo Spain
261 F6 Algarrobo Arg.
260 B1 Algarrobito Chile
260 B3 Algarrobo Chile
185 F4 Algarrobo Spain
184 B3 Algarve reg. Port.
135 H5 Algasovo Rus. Fed.
185 E4 Algatocín Spain
185 G3 Algeciras Spain
Algeciras, Bahía de b. Gibraltar/Spain see Gibraltar, Bay of
187 C5 Algemesí Spain
205 F1 Alger Alg.
227 E3 Alger MI U.S.A.
205 F3 Algeria country Africa
169 E3 Algermissen Ger.
186 D3 Algerri Spain
183 G4 Algete Spain
129 D3 Alget'i r. Georgia
Algha Kazakh. see Alga
125 G3 Al Ghafāt Oman
Al Ghardaqah Egypt see Hurghada
124 D3 Al Gharīth Saudi Arabia
128 M4 Al Ghawr plain Jordan/West Bank
125 F4 Al Ghaydah Yemen
124 D3 Al Ghazālah Saudi Arabia
192 A4 Alghero Sardegna Italy
125 G3 Al Ghubar Oman
125 D2 Al Ghwaybiyah Saudi Arabia
184 B3 Algibre r. Port.
187 C5 Algimia de Alfara Spain
Algiers Alg. see Alger
187 C5 Alginet Spain

215 E5 Algoa Bay S. Africa
250 D5 Algodón r. Peru
183 G4 Algodonales Spain
183 G5 Algodor r. Spain
226 D3 Algoma WI U.S.A.
236 E3 Algona IA U.S.A.
227 F4 Algonac MI U.S.A.
224 D4 Algonquin Park Ont. Can.
183 H4 Algora Spain
182 D3 Algoso Port.
184 B3 Algoz Port.
157 G3 Algrange France
140 L2 Algutsjö Sweden
184 C3 Alguaire Spain
187 B6 Alguazas Spain
184 A2 Algueirão-Mem Martins Port.
187 C6 Algueña Spain
124 C1 Al Ḩabbānīyah Iraq
185 H4 Alhadas Port.
182 B4 Alhadas Port.
124 B4 Al Ḩadbah reg. Saudi Arabia
124 D3 Al Ḩaddār Saudi Arabia
124 D2 Al Ḩadīthah Saudi Arabia
127 F5 Al Ḩadīthah Iraq
127 F4 Al Ḩadīthah Iraq
128 C2 Al Ḩadr Iraq
127 F4 Al Ḩaffah Syria
125 D2 Al Ḩā'ir Saudi Arabia
125 G3 Al Ḩajar Oman
125 G3 Al Ḩajar al Gharbī mts Oman
125 G3 Al Ḩajar ash Sharqī mts Oman
185 G3 Alhama r. Spain
183 I3 Alhama de Almería Spain
183 I3 Alhama de Aragón Spain
185 G3 Alhama de Granada Spain
187 B7 Alhama de Murcia Spain
124 D3 Al Ḩamad plain Saudi Arabia
202 A2 Al Ḩamrā' plat. Libya
185 G3 Alhambra Spain
125 E5 Al Ḩāmi Yemen
124 B3 Al Ḩamrā' Saudi Arabia
124 C2 Al Ḩamrā' reg. Saudi Arabia
184 C4 Alhándra Port.
124 D3 Al Ḩanīsh al Kabīr i. Yemen
127 G5 Al Ḩanīyah esc. Iraq
124 D3 Al Ḩarīq Saudi Arabia
202 C3 Al Ḩarūj al Aswad hills Libya
127 F3 Al Ḩasakah Syria
124 B1 Al Ḩāshimīyah Iraq
185 F4 Alhaurín el Grande Spain
185 E3 Alhaurín de la Torre Spain
125 G4 Al Ḩawār salt pan Saudi Arabia
125 G3 Al Ḩawiyah Saudi Arabia
127 G4 Al Ḩayy Iraq
124 D4 Al Ḩazm al-Jawf Yemen
214 C3 Alhendín Spain
185 H3 Alhóndiga Spain
127 G4 Al Ḩillah Iraq
124 D3 Al Ḩillah Saudi Arabia
Al Ḩillah governorate Iraq see Bābil
124 D3 Al Ḩilwah Saudi Arabia
125 D2 Al Hindīyah Iraq
124 D4 Al Ḩinnāh Saudi Arabia
124 D4 Al Ḩinw mt. Saudi Arabia
125 E3 Al Ḩishwah hills Yemen
124 A1 Al Ḩismā plain Saudi Arabia
124 D5 Al Ḩisn Jordan
124 C5 Al Ḩisn Yemen
204 C2 Al Hoceima Morocco
180 D5 Al Hoceima prov. Morocco
182 C4 Alhões Port.
183 H4 Alhóndiga Spain
124 C5 Al Ḩudaydah Yemen
124 C5 Al Ḩudaydah governorate Yemen
124 C1 Al Ḩudūd ash Shamālīyah prov. Saudi Arabia
124 B1 Al Ḩufrah reg. Saudi Arabia
125 E2 Al Ḩufūf Saudi Arabia
124 B1 Al Ḩūj hills Saudi Arabia
202 C3 Al Ḩulayq al Kabīr hills Libya
124 D5 Al Ḩumayshah Yemen
125 F3 Al Ḩusayn Oman
125 G3 Al Ḩuwatsah Oman
125 G3 Al Ḩuwaynah Oman
128 C2 Al Ḩuwayz Syria
195 E4 Alì Sicilia Italy
195 E4 Alia Sicilia Italy
156 C3 Aliaga France
158 B4 Aliaga Spain
220 C3 Aliakovak AK U.S.A.
131 Q3 Alaikh-Yun' Rus. Fed.
234 D2 Alamuchy NJ U.S.A.
161 C2 Allan France
147 D2 Allanche France
215 F3 Allandale S. Africa
85 L9 Allanmyo Myanmar
215 F2 Allanridge S. Africa
148 F2 Allanton North Lanarkshire, Scotland U.K.
114 C2 Allapalli Mahar. India
129 F4 Allano Italy
225 H4 Allardville N.B. Can.
182 C2 Alláriz Spain
157 H4 Allarmont France
162 E3 Allassac France
183 H3 Allauch France
125 B4 Alladys S. Africa
190 C1 Alle Switz.
226 E4 Allegan MI U.S.A.
191 H4 Alleghe Italy
233 F4 Allegheny r. PA U.S.A.
232 D4 Allegheny Mountains U.S.A.
232 D4 Allegheny Reservoir PA U.S.A.
161 B3 Allègre France
163 D7 Alleins France
147 D5 Allen Rep. of Ireland
232 A4 Allen MI U.S.A.
147 A3 Allen, Lough l. Rep. of Ireland
81 A7 Allen, Mount hill Stewart I. N.Z.
231 D5 Allendale SC U.S.A.
149 G3 Allendale Town Northumberland, England U.K.
244 D2 Allende Coahuila Mex.
245 E2 Allende Nuevo León Mex.
169 F4 Allendorf Ger.
169 D5 Allendorf (Eder) Ger.
169 D5 Allendorf (Lumda) Ger.
227 I2 Allenford Ont. Can.
149 G3 Allenheads Northumberland, England U.K.
172 E2 Allersbach Ger.
Allenstein Poland see Olsztyn
232 E4 Allensville OH U.S.A.
124 C3 Al Mindak Saudi Arabia
205 G2 Al Mintirib Oman
242 □J7 Almirante Panama
256 C6 Almirante Tamandaré Brazil
Almiró Greece see Almyros
Al-Mirfa U.A.E. see Al Mirfa'
124 E4 Al Mismerīyah Syria
Al Mukallā Yemen
Al Quwayṭirah governorate Syria

(further entries continue)

140 L2 Alitälve mt. Sweden
195 E4 Alì Terme Sicilia Italy
227 H3 Aliveri Greece
219 F4 Aliwal North S. Africa
222 F4 Alix Alta Can.
136 E5 Aliyabe r. Ukr.
156 B3 Alizay France
125 C2 Al Jafūrah des. Saudi Arabia
202 E2 Al Jaghbūb Libya
124 B3 Al Jahrah Kuwait
125 E2 Al Jamalīyah Qatar
184 C3 Aljaraque Spain
124 D2 Al Jauf Saudi Arabia
124 C1 Al Jawb reg. Saudi Arabia
202 D3 Al Jawf Libya
118 D4 Al Jawf Saudi Arabia
124 D3 Al Jawf Iraq
124 B1 Al Jawf prov. Saudi Arabia
124 C1 Al Jawf governorate Yemen
Al Jawlān hills Syria see Golan
124 D3 Al Jaza'ir Alg. see Alger
122 C2 Aljezur Port.
124 C3 Al Jibān des. Saudi Arabia
184 E4 Aljibe mt. Spain
125 G2 Al Jifnah Saudi Arabia
202 B2 Al Jufra Oasis Libya
184 C3 Aljumm Oasis Spain
124 C3 Al Junaynah Saudi Arabia
124 C2 Al Jurayfah Saudi Arabia
124 C2 Al Jurdhāwiyah Saudi Arabia
184 B3 Aljustrel Port.
124 C2 Al Kahfah Saudi Arabia
124 D3 Al Kalbān Oman
222 F5 Alkali Lake B.C. Can.
136 E5 Alkalıya r. Ukr.
125 G3 Al Kāmil Oman
128 B4 Al Karak Jordan
128 B4 Al Karāmah Jordan
127 G4 Al Kāẓimīyah Iraq
165 E4 Alken Belgium
125 G3 Al Khabūrah Oman
124 D3 Al Khafjan salt pan Saudi Arabia
124 D3 Al Khamāsīn Saudi Arabia
124 D3 Al Kharfah Saudi Arabia
124 D3 Al Khārijah Egypt see El Khārga
125 G2 Al Khaşab Oman
124 D3 Al Khaşab Saudi Arabia
125 E2 Al Khatam reg. U.A.E.
124 D4 Al Khaṭīnī vol. Saudi Arabia
125 E2 Al Khawr Qatar
125 E2 Al Khobar Saudi Arabia
202 D3 Al Khufrah Oasis Libya
202 B1 Al Khums Libya
124 B1 Al Khunfah sand area Saudi Arabia
125 E3 Al Khunn Saudi Arabia
125 F3 Al Khuwayr Qatar
125 F3 Al Kīfl Iraq
125 E2 Al Kir'ānah Qatar
164 D2 Alkmaar Neth.
179 F2 Alkoven Austria
172 G4 Al Kūfah Iraq
127 G4 Al Kumayt Iraq
125 H3 Al Kusbah Saudi Arabia
127 G4 Al Kūt Iraq
Al Kuwayt country Asia see Kuwait
124 C1 Al Kuwayt Kuwait
127 F5 Al Labbah plain Saudi Arabia
207 F5 Alada Benin
128 B2 Al Lādhiqīyah Syria
128 B2 Al Lādhiqīyah governorate Syria
114 C3 Allagadda Andhra Prad. India
233 □I1 Allagash r. ME U.S.A.
116 E4 Allahabad Uttar Prad. India
129 D3 Allahüekber Tepe mt. Turkey
193 A3 Al Sardegna Italy
156 C3 Allaines France
156 C3 Allaines-Mervilliers France
158 D4 Allaire France
120 D4 Al Lajā lava field Syria
234 A5 Allakaket AK U.S.A.
131 Q3 Allakh-Yun' Rus. Fed.
161 C2 Allan France
147 D2 Allanche France
215 F3 Allandale S. Africa
85 L9 Allanmyo Myanmar
215 F2 Allanridge S. Africa
148 F2 Allanton North Lanarkshire, Scotland U.K.
114 C2 Allapalli Mahar. India
129 F4 Allano Italy
225 H4 Allardville N.B. Can.
182 C2 Alláriz Spain
157 H4 Allarmont France
162 E3 Allassac France
183 H3 Allauch France
125 B4 Allays S. Africa
190 C1 Alle Switz.
226 E4 Allegan MI U.S.A.
191 H4 Alleghe Italy
233 F4 Allegheny r. PA U.S.A.
232 D4 Allegheny Mountains U.S.A.
232 D4 Allegheny Reservoir PA U.S.A.
161 B3 Allègre France
163 D7 Alleins France
147 D5 Allen Rep. of Ireland
232 A4 Allen MI U.S.A.
147 A3 Allen, Lough l. Rep. of Ireland
81 A7 Allen, Mount hill Stewart I. N.Z.
231 D5 Allendale SC U.S.A.
149 G3 Allendale Town Northumberland, England U.K.
244 D2 Allende Coahuila Mex.
245 E2 Allende Nuevo León Mex.
169 F4 Allendorf Ger.
169 D5 Allendorf (Eder) Ger.
169 D5 Allendorf (Lumda) Ger.
227 I2 Allenford Ont. Can.
149 G3 Allenheads Northumberland, England U.K.
172 E2 Allersbach Ger.
Allenstein Poland see Olsztyn
232 E4 Allensville OH U.S.A.
232 C4 Allensville PA U.S.A.
123 I4 Allentown NJ U.S.A.
179 G2 Allentsteig Austria
112 B4 Alleppey Kerala India
169 G3 Aller r. Ger.
160 D2 Allerey-sur-Saône France
161 B5 Allerona Italy
172 F3 Allershausen Ger.
235 G2 Allevard France
161 C4 Allex France
149 E2 Allhallows Medway, England U.K.
169 H4 Allhallows Ger.
236 D3 Allianci U.S.A. (Alliance)
232 C4 Alliance OH U.S.A.
156 E4 Allibaudières France
Alligany France see Alligny
202 E2 Al Lihabah Yemen
124 C5 Al Lith oasis U.A.E.
125 F3 Al Liwā' oasis U.A.E.
146 C5 Alloa Clackmannanshire, Scotland U.K.
159 I4 Allogny France
149 F3 Allonby Cumbria, England U.K.
162 C1 Allonnes Pays de la Loire France
159 G4 Allonnes Pays de la Loire France
186 B4 Allones France
183 G4 Allora Qld Austr.
161 E4 Alloue France
162 C2 Allouis France
147 C4 Alloway r. Ireland
147 D6 Alloway South Ayrshire, Scotland U.K.
234 D5 Alloway NJ U.S.A.
234 D5 Alloway Creek r. NJ U.S.A.
190 C1 Allschwil Switz.
171 G4 Allstedt Ger.
160 B1 Alluy France
225 G3 Alma Que. Can.
231 D6 Alma GA U.S.A.
236 D3 Alma KS U.S.A.
226 E4 Alma MI U.S.A.
236 D3 Alma NE U.S.A.
Alma-Ata Kazakh. see Almaty
Alma-Ata Oblast' admin. div. Kazakh. see Almatinskaya Oblast'
186 D3 Almacelles Spain
185 H4 Almáchar Spain
184 C4 Almada Port.
185 G3 Almadén Spain
124 B1 Al Madáfi' plat. Saudi Arabia
85 C4 Almaden Qld Austr.
183 H5 Almadén de la Plata Spain
183 G5 Almadenejos Spain
122 A4 Al Madīnah Iraq
124 B2 Al Madīnah Saudi Arabia
124 B2 Al Madīnah prov. Saudi Arabia
128 C3 Al Mafraq Jordan
124 D3 Almaghbe Arg.
125 G2 Al Maghrib reg. U.A.E.
124 D3 Almagre mt. Spain
185 G3 Almagro Spain
204 C4 Al Mahbas Western Sahara
185 G3 Al Mahrah reg. Yemen
124 C5 Al Mahrah reg. Yemen
124 D4 Al Mahwīt governorate Yemen
125 D5 Al Maḩwīt Yemen
124 C5 Al Maḩwīt governorate Yemen
125 D2 Al Majma'ah Saudi Arabia
Al Manāmah Bahrain see Manama
125 E2 Al Manāmah Bahrain
183 G3 Almanazar r. Spain
121 J2 Almanor, Lake CA U.S.A.
184 A2 Almansa Spain
184 B2 Almansil Port.
Al Manṣūrah Egypt see El Manṣûra
183 E2 Almanza Spain
185 H2 Almanzor mt. Spain
185 H2 Almanzora r. Spain
182 C5 Al Ma'qil Iraq
187 B6 Al Ma'rī Iraq
183 H3 Almarjá reg. Saudi Arabia
183 H3 Almaraz Spain
254 D4 Almas Brazil
171 L4 Almaş Romania
197 F2 Almaş r. Romania
256 C1 Almas, Rio das r. Brazil
193 A3 Al Maşna'a Oman
177 H1 Almásfüzitő Hungary
177 I4 Almás-patak r. Hungary
187 D3 Almassora Spain
121 I4 Almatinskaya Oblast' admin. div. Kazakh. see Almatinskaya Oblast'
121 I4 Almaty Kazakh.
Almaty Oblast admin. div. Kazakh. see Almatinskaya Oblast'
Almaty Oblysy admin. div. Kazakh. see Almatinskaya Oblast'
127 F4 Al Mawşil Iraq
127 F4 Al Mayādīn Syria
183 H3 Almazán Spain
131 M1 Almaznyy Rus. Fed.
187 B6 Al Mazrah r. Spain
173 H3 Almbach r. Ger.
169 D4 Alme r. Ger.
Almeirim Brazil see Almassora
187 D5 Almenar Spain
253 F3 Almenara Brazil
185 G2 Almenara hill Spain
187 E3 Almenara Spain
183 H3 Almenara, Sierra de mts Spain
184 D2 Almendra, Embalse de resr Spain
182 C3 Almendra, Embalse de resr Spain
184 D2 Almendralejo Spain
124 C2 Al Mendinejos Spain
164 B4 Almere Neth.
185 H4 Almería Spain
185 I4 Almería, Golfo de b. Spain
135 K5 Al'met'yevsk Rus. Fed.
124 D3 Al Midhnab Saudi Arabia
124 B5 Al Miḩrāḍ reg. Saudi Arabia
187 C6 Almiras Greece see Almyros
184 D5 Almina, Punta pt Ceuta Spain
124 C3 Al Mindak Saudi Arabia
125 G2 Al Mintirib Oman
242 □J7 Almirante Panama
256 C6 Almirante Tamandaré Brazil
Almiró Greece see Almyros
183 H4 Almiskab Saudi Arabia
184 D3 Almodôvar Port.
185 H3 Almodôvar del Campo Spain
183 G5 Almodôvar del Río Spain
182 E4 Almofala Port.
184 A3 Almograve Port.
124 C2 Almoharín Spain
187 C6 Almonacid de la Sierra Spain
183 H3 Almonacid del Marquesado Spain
187 C3 Almonacid de Toledo Spain
184 C3 Almonaster la Real Spain
147 D4 Almonte r. Scotland U.K.
146 F4 Almonte r. Scotland U.K.
183 H3 Almonte Spain
184 D3 Almora Uttar Prad. India
185 H4 Almoradí Spain
177 K4 Almosd Hungary
185 H4 Almoster Port.

143 F4 Allinge-Sandvig Bornholm Denmark
116 D3 Almora Uttar Prad. India
187 C6 Almoradí Spain
185 H4 Almorox Spain
177 K4 Almoster Hungary
182 B4 Almoster Port.
184 D1 Almoster Port.
169 E3 Almoster Ger.
145 E3 Alness r. Scotland U.K.
146 D4 Alness Highland, Scotland U.K.
146 E3 Alness r. Scotland U.K.
149 G1 Alnmouth Northumberland, England U.K.
149 G1 Alnwick Northumberland, England U.K.
187 B4 Alobras Spain
183 H4 Alocén Spain
77 I3 Alofi Niue
77 I3 Alofi, Île i. Wallis and Futuna Is
138 E3 Aloja Latvia
138 E3 Alolya r. Rus. Fed.
117 H3 Along Arun. Prad. India
108 D4 Alonnisos i. Greece
198 C2 Alonnisos i. Greece
256 D6 Alonso r. Brazil
93 C5 Alor i. Indon.
93 C5 Alor, Kepulauan is Indon.
94 C1 Alor Star Malaysia see Alor Setar
186 E2 Alós d'Ensil Spain
164 D4 Alosno Spain
Alost Belgium see Aalst
186 E2 Aloya P.N.G.
159 F5 Alouettes, Mont des hill France
183 H3 Alovera Spain
123 G2 Aloxa-Corton France
87 F5 Aloysius, Mount W.A. Austr.
185 F4 Alozaina Spain
186 E2 Alp Spain
261 F5 Alpachiri Arg.
199 G1 Alpagut Bursa Turkey
184 C1 Alpalhão Port.
197 F2 Alpanseque Spain
240 H4 Alpaugh CA U.S.A.
178 C3 Alpbach Austria
182 C4 Alpedrete Spain
182 B5 Alpedrinha Port.
169 B4 Alpen Ger.
227 F3 Alpena MI U.S.A.
169 C2 Alpenrod Ger.
187 B6 Alpera Spain
261 F6 Alpha r. Qld Austr.
85 H5 Alpha S. Africa
214 B5 Alpha S. Africa
268 F1 Alpha Ridge sea feature Arctic Ocean
164 D2 Alphen Neth.
164 C3 Alphen aan den Rijn Neth.
217 □ Alphonse i. Seychelles
217 □ Alphonse Island Seychelles
184 B1 Alpiarça Port.
Alpi Dolomitiche mts Italy see Dolomiti
191 E6 Alpi Marittime mts France/Italy
173 G3 Alm Berg mt. Ger.
169 D4 Alme r. Ger.
241 M5 Alpine AZ U.S.A.
240 I5 Alpine CA U.S.A.
227 I4 Alpine MI U.S.A.
237 C6 Alpine TX U.S.A.
236 F3 Alpine WY U.S.A.
172 G3 Alpirsbach Ger.
190 D2 Alpnach Switz.
179 H3 Alpokalja mts Hungary
191 I3 Alpone r. Italy
189 I2 Alpone r. Italy
180 C5 Alpu Turkey
187 D5 Alpuente Spain
187 B4 Al Qaddāhīyah Libya
128 C3 Al Qādisīyah governorate Iraq
124 C2 Al Qāhirah Egypt see Cairo
127 F4 Al Qā'im Iraq
205 E2 Al Qal'a' Beni Hammad tourist site Alg.
127 F3 Al Qāmishlī Syria
124 D3 Al Qardah Syria
128 C3 Al Qaryatayn Syria
124 C5 Al Qaşim prov. Saudi Arabia
124 D3 Al Qaṭīf Saudi Arabia
124 C5 Al Qaṭn Yemen
124 C3 Al Qaṭrānah Jordan
124 C2 Al Qaţţ Oman
124 D5 Al Qawwas reg. Saudi Arabia
124 D3 Al Qayṣūmah Saudi Arabia
124 C2 Al Qunaytirah Syria
124 B5 Al Qunfidhah Saudi Arabia
124 C5 Al Qurayyah Saudi Arabia
124 C1 Al Quraytifah Saudi Arabia
124 D2 Al Qurayyah U.A.E.
124 C4 Al Qurayyāt Saudi Arabia
124 D3 Al Qurnah Iraq
125 G3 Al Quwārah Saudi Arabia
124 C2 Al Qusayr Saudi Arabia
124 D5 Al Quwayh Yemen
124 D3 Al Quwārah Jordan
125 F3 Al Quwayʻīyah Saudi Arabia
124 C5 Al Quzah Yemen

172 C2 Alsbach Ger.
169 B5 Alsdorf Ger.
222 B3 Alsek r. AK U.S.A.
169 E5 Alsenborn Ger.
190 C4 Alser Ger.
172 E2 Alsfeld Ger.
169 E5 Alsfeld Ger.
172 C2 Alsheim Ger.
Alsh, Loch sea chan. Scotland U.K.
146 C4 Alsleben (Saale) Ger.
125 C3 Al Subakh Saudi Arabia
177 G3 Alsónémedi Hungary
177 G3 Alsórs Hungary
177 J3 Alsózsolca Hungary
171 A3 Alsterán r. Sweden
143 F3 Alstermo Sweden
157 G3 Alsting France
149 G3 Alston Cumbria, England U.K.
83 H2 Alstonville N.S.W. Austr.
138 D2 Alsunga Latvia
143 J3 Alta Mex.
143 H2 Älta Sweden
190 E1 Altach Austria
191 G2 Altacroce, Monte mt. Italy
173 G3 Altdorf Ger.
170 F2 Altdorf Ger.
Altamira Brazil
Altamira Costa Rica
186 C2 Altamira Mex.
183 F1 Altamira, Cuevas de tourist site Spain
195 I3 Altamira, Sierra de mts Spain
231 D6 Altamonte Springs City FL U.S.A.
107 I1 Altan Bulag Mongolia
107 H1 Altan Emel Nei Mongol China
107 H2 Altan Ovoo mt. China/Mongolia
107 F4 Altan Shiret Nei Mongol China
Altan Xiret Nei Mongol China see Altan Shiret
254 D5 Alta Paraíso de Goiás Brazil
239 E6 Altar r. Mex.
242 B1 Altar, Desierto de des. Mex.
190 D4 Altare Italy
216 □ Altares Terceira Azores
242 D3 Altata Mex.
179 E3 Altaussee Austria
194 D2 Altavilla Irpina Italy
193 H4 Altavilla Silentina Italy
232 D5 Altavista VA U.S.A.
112 H3 Altay Xinjiang China
106 C2 Altay Mongolia
106 F2 Altay, Respublika aut. rep. Rus. Fed.
106 D1 Altay, Respublika aut. rep. Rus. Fed.
Altay Kray admin. div. Rus. Fed. see Altayskiy Kray
Altayskiy Krebet mts Asia see Altai Mountains
121 J2 Altayskiy Kray admin. div. Rus. Fed.
171 F4 Altdöbern Ger.
173 G3 Altdorf Ger.
168 E1 Alte Elde r. Ger.
170 C2 Altea Spain
170 F1 Altefähr Ger.
173 G3 Alteglofsheim Ger.
140 M1 Alteidet Norway
172 G2 Altena Ger.
169 B5 Altena Ger.
172 F2 Altenahr Ger.
169 B5 Altena Ger.
169 D4 Altenbeken Ger.
171 E5 Altenberg Ger.
169 E6 Altenberge Ger.
169 H6 Altenbruch-Westerende Ger.
171 D5 Altenburg Ger.
169 C3 Altenfeld Ger.
169 F5 Altenfelden Austria
172 F2 Altenfelden Austria
170 E1 Altengamme Ger.
172 D3 Altenheim Ger.
169 E4 Altenhof Ger.
169 C5 Altenkirchen (Westerwald) Ger.
168 F1 Altenkrempe Ger.
173 G3 Altenmarkt an der Alz Ger.
179 H3 Altenmarkt an der Triesting Austria
179 F3 Altenmarkt bei St Gallen Austria
179 F3 Altenmarkt im Pongau Austria
169 D6 Altenmünster Ger.
172 C3 Altenstadt Bayern Ger.
173 G3 Altenstadt Bayern Ger.
169 E6 Altenstadt Hessen Ger.
173 G2 Altenstadt an der Waldnaab Ger.
172 C2 Altensteig Ger.
170 F2 Altentreptow Ger.
169 E4 Altenwedddingen Ger.
170 E1 Alte Oder r. Ger.
172 C2 Alter do Chão Port.
184 C1 Alter Pedroso hill Port.
171 E3 Altes Lager Ger.
172 D3 Altglashütten Ger.
140 L1 Altevatnet l. Norway
173 F3 Altheim Ger.
179 E2 Altheim Austria
172 D3 Altheim (Alb) Ger.
172 C3 Althengstett Ger.
173 G4 Althofen Austria
172 D3 Altheim Ger.
169 D4 Altkirchen Ger.
171 D5 Altkirchen Ger.
163 I3 Altkirch France
172 D2 Altlandsberg Ger.
173 H3 Altmannstein Ger.
173 I3 Altmittweida Ger.
172 D3 Altmühl r. Ger.
193 I3 Altmühltal park Ger.
151 F2 Altnaharra Highland, Scotland U.K.
226 B4 Alto MI U.S.A.
191 B3 Alto, Monte hill Italy
256 A2 Alto Araguaia Brazil
209 C7 Alto Cedro Cuba
209 C7 Alto Chicapa Angola
183 H3 Alto Cruz mt. Spain
260 D3 Alto de Cabezas mt. Spain
183 I3 Alto del Moncayo mt. Spain
260 D3 Alto de Pencoso hills Arg.
256 C3 Alto do São João mt. Spain
254 C2 Alto Garças Brazil
184 B2 Alto Garças Brazil
209 B8 Alto Jahuel Chile
200 B3 Alto Ligonha Moz.
213 H2 Alto Molócuè Moz.
138 D3 Altomonte Italy
173 G3 Altomünster Ger.
184 E5 Alton Perth and Kinross, Scotland U.K.
151 G6 Alton Hampshire, England U.K.
151 F2 Alton Staffordshire, England U.K.

236 F4 Alton IL U.S.A.
237 F4 Alton MO U.S.A.
233 □H3 Alton NH U.S.A.
222 B3 Altona B.C. Can.
223 L5 Altona Man. Can.
82 D1 Altona S.A. Austr.
259 B7 Alto Nevado mt. Chile
183 G2 Altofonte Italy
232 A2 Altoona PA U.S.A.
226 B3 Altoona WI U.S.A.
251 L5 Alto Paraíso Brazil
254 D6 Alto Parnaíba Brazil
191 F5 Altopascio Italy
256 A6 Alto Piquiri Brazil
252 C2 Alto Purús r. Peru
182 C3 Alto Rabagão, Barragem do resr Port.
257 F4 Alto Rio Doce Brazil
259 C7 Alto Rio Senguerr Arg.
186 D3 Altorricón Spain
254 E3 Altos Brazil
183 H4 Altos de Cabrejas mts Spain
261 F2 Altos de Chipión Arg.
183 G2 Altotero mt. Spain
245 F4 Altotonga Mex.
173 G3 Altötting Ger.
170 F3 Altranft Ger.
123 I2 Altrich Ger.
149 G4 Altrincham Greater Manchester, England U.K.
170 D3 Alt Ruppin Ger.
Altsasu Spain see Alsasua
82 B1 Alt Schwerin Ger.
172 D4 Altshausen Ger.
190 E1 Altstätten Switz.
129 C2 Altud Rus. Fed.
139 T5 Altukhovo Rus. Fed.
129 B4 Altunhisar Turkey
Altun He r. China see Qinghai China
107 L5 Altun Shan mts China
187 C5 Altura Spain
238 B3 Alturas CA U.S.A.
237 D5 Altus OK U.S.A.
173 H3 Altusried Ger.
169 F3 Alt Wallmoden Ger.
190 F2 Altynivka Ukr.
120 D4 Altynkul' Uzbek.
Altyn-Topkan Tajik. see Oltintopkan
138 E2 Alu Estonia
213 H2 Alua Moz.
126 E2 Alucra Turkey
138 F3 Alūksne Latvia
135 I4 Alum r. Latvia
122 B3 Alūm Iran
232 C5 Alum Bridge WV U.S.A.
260 B6 Alumine Arg.
143 M1 Aluminé Arg.
182 B3 Alumis Sweden
197 G2 Alunga Romania
137 H5 Alupka Ukr.
202 C2 Al 'Uqaylah Libya
Al 'Uqaylah Libya see Al Uqaylah
Al 'Uqayr Saudi Arabia
125 E2 Al 'Uqayr Saudi Arabia
114 C3 Al Uqşur Egypt see El Uqşur
125 E6 Al Urayq des. Saudi Arabia
Al 'Urdun country Asia see Jordan
Alur Setar Malaysia see Alor Setar
137 H1 Alushta Ukr.
183 I4 Alustante Spain
127 E5 Al 'Uwayja Saudi Arabia
124 D2 Al 'Uwaynah Saudi Arabia
127 G5 Al 'Uyūn Saudi Arabia
182 B4 Alva r. Port.
146 E5 Alva Clackmannanshire, Scotland U.K.
237 D4 Alva OK U.S.A.
182 B5 Alvaiázere Port.
184 B3 Alvalade Port.
122 B3 Alvand, Küh-e mt. Iran
199 K3 Alvanley Switz.
129 B4 Alvar Turkey
245 G4 Alvarado Mex.
237 D5 Alvarado TX U.S.A.
251 E4 Álvares Brazil
182 C4 Álvares Port.
257 F3 Álvares Machado Brazil
261 G3 Álvarez Arg.
244 B3 Álvaro Obregón Mex.
141 L3 Älvdalen Sweden
141 L3 Älvdalen val. Sweden
184 B3 Alvechurch Worcestershire, England U.K.
187 Aledo r. Spain
182 B3 Alvega Port.
148 C2 Alveley Shropshire, England U.K.
182 B5 Alverca do Ribatejo Port.
165 D4 Alveringem Belgium
151 H5 Alveslohe Ger.
182 B2 Alvesta Brazil
151 H5 Alveston South Gloucestershire, England U.K.
143 D3 Alviano Italy
146 F1 Alvie Highland, Scotland U.K.
142 C2 Alvignac France
142 B1 Alvik Norway
143 G3 Alvik Sweden
237 E6 Alvin TX U.S.A.
226 C3 Alvin WI U.S.A.
257 F4 Alvinópolis Brazil
193 F3 Alvito Italy
184 C2 Alvito Port.
143 G1 Älvkarleby Sweden
193 H1 Alvo r. Italy
182 B4 Alvoco da Serra Port.
184 C2 Al Wabrah Saudi Arabia
124 B2 Al Wajh Saudi Arabia
125 F3 Al Wakrah Qatar
116 D4 Alwar Rajasthan India
112 B4 Alwaye Kerala India see Aluva
114 B3 Alwernia Pol.
125 F4 Al Widyān plat. Iraq/Saudi Arabia
202 C3 Al Wigh, Ramlat des. Libya
125 G3 Al Wustá admin. reg. Oman
Alxa Youqi Nei Mongol China see Ehen Hudag
Alxa Zuoqi Nei Mongol China see Bayan Hot
84 D2 Alyangula N.T. Austr.
146 E5 Alyth Perth and Kinross, Scotland U.K.
138 E4 Alytus Lith.
173 G3 Alz r. Ger.
211 B5 Alzada MT U.S.A.
181 Alzano Lombardo Italy
165 I5 Alzenau in Unterfranken Ger.
187 C6 Alzey Ger.
161 B5 Alzon France
163 G4 Alzonne France
215 G3 Amabele S. Africa
163 F6 Amadalen France
141 K3 Åmådalen Sweden
84 B5 Amadeus, Lake salt flat N.T. Austr.
221 K3 Amadjuak Lake Nunavut Can.
241 L6 Amado AZ U.S.A.
211 A5 Amadora Port.
184 A2 Amadora Port.
208 B4 Amadror Alg.
250 C2 Amaga Col.
105 L3 Amaga-dake mt. Japan
235 F7 Amagansett NY U.S.A.
104 D4 Amagasaki Japan
143 F5 Amager i. Denmark
105 G3 Amagi Japan
104 C3 Amagi-san vol. Japan
105 E3 Amagi-take mt. Japan
104 C3 Amagoi-dake mt. Japan
245 H5 Amajac r. Mex.
105 D2 Amakazari-yama mt. Japan

103 D7 Amakusa-nada b. Japan
125 F4 Amal Oman
142 E2 Amal Sweden
114 D2 Amalapuram Andhra Prad. India
99 K1 Amalat r. Rus. Fed.
193 G4 Amalfi Italy
215 E2 Amalia S. Africa
198 B3 Amaliada Greece
116 C5 Amalner Mahar. India
253 G5 Amambaí Brazil
253 G5 Amambaí, Serra de hills Brazil/Para.
102 □1 Amami-Ō-shima i. Japan
102 □1 Amami-shotō is Japan
141 K3 Amån r. Sweden
157 G5 Amance r. France
157 G5 Amance r. France
160 E1 Amanda OH U.S.A.
232 B5 Amanda OH U.S.A.
193 F2 Amandola Italy
120 D2 Amangel'dy Aktyubinskaya Oblast' Kazakh.
120 □1 Amangel'dy Kustanayskaya Oblast' Kazakh. see Amangel'dy
120 F1 Amankaragay Kazakh.
159 F3 Amanlis France
   Amankeldi Aktyubinskaya Oblast' Kazakh. see Amangel'dy
   Amankeldi Kustanayskaya Oblast' Kazakh. see Amangel'dy
120 E3 Amanotkel' Kazakh.
   Amanaraghay Kazakh. see Amangel'dy
   Amanarkaragay
193 I5 Amanzimtoti S. Africa
215 H4 Amapá state Brazil
251 I4 Amapá state Brazil
245 F4 Amapa r. Mex.
251 I4 Amapala Hond.
242 □16 Amapari r. Brazil
251 I4 Amapari r. Brazil
197 F3 Amaradia r. Romania
255 B9 Amaral Ferrador Brazil
254 E3 Amarante Brazil
252 B4 Amarante Brazil
254 D3 Amarante do Maranhão Brazil
96 B2 Amarapura Myanmar
114 C4 Amaravati r. India
106 E2 Amardalay Mongolia
182 B3 Amarela, Serra mts Port.
184 C2 Amareleja Port.
182 B3 Amares Port.
184 C2 Amargosa Brazil
241 I3 Amargosa Desert NV U.S.A.
240 I3 Amargosa Range mts CA U.S.A.
241 I3 Amargosa Valley NV U.S.A.
185 G1 Amarguillo r. Spain
   Amargura Island Tonga see Fonualei
237 C5 Amarillo TX U.S.A.
258 C4 Amarillo, Cerro mt. Arg.
116 E5 Amarkantak Madh. Prad. India
116 E5 Amaro, Monte mt. Italy
195 H4 Amaroni Italy
84 D4 Amaroo, Lake salt flat Qld Austr.
117 G5 Amarpur Tripura India
116 D5 Amarwara Madh. Prad. India
116 D5 Amarwara r. India
193 F3 Amaseno Italy
193 F3 Amaseno r. Italy
129 C3 Amasia Armenia
   Amasia Turkey see Amasya
204 B4 Amasine Western Sahara
126 D2 Amasra Turkey
126 D2 Amasya Turkey
82 B1 Amata S.A. Austr.
250 D5 Amataurá Brazil
243 G5 Amatenango Mex.
215 H3 Amatikulu S. Africa
245 H4 Amatlán Mex.
244 B3 Amatlán de Cañas Mex.
195 F4 Amato r. Italy
193 F2 Amatrice Italy
235 E1 Amawalk NY U.S.A.
165 E4 Amay Belgium
183 F2 Amaya mt. Spain
100 B1 Amazar r. Rus. Fed.
100 B1 Amazar Rus. Fed.
251 I4 Amazon r. S. America alt. Amazonas
252 C3 Amazon, Mouths of the Brazil
252 C3 Amazonas state Brazil
250 D5 Amazonas dept Col.
250 B6 Amazonas dept Peru
251 I4 Amazonas r. S. America conv. Amazon
250 D5 Amazonas state Venez.
264 F5 Amazon Cone sea feature S. Atlantic Ocean
210 C1 Amba Ālagē mt. Eth.
114 B2 Ambad Mahar. India
210 C2 Amba Farit mt. Eth.
213 □I4 Ambahikily Madag.
116 C2 Ambajogai Mahar. India
116 D3 Ambala Haryana India
213 □J5 Ambalangoda Sri Lanka
213 □J4 Ambalantota Sri Lanka
213 □J4 Ambalavao Madag.
84 C4 Ambalindum N.T. Austr.
207 H6 Ambam Cameroon
162 B4 Ambarès-et-Lagarve France
258 D2 Ambargasta, Salinas de salt pan Arg.
134 F2 Ambarnyy Rus. Fed.
117 G5 Ambasa Tripura India
183 E2 Ambasaguas Spain
114 C4 Ambasamudram Tamil Nadu India
85 F5 Ambathala Qld Austr.
250 B5 Ambato Ecuador
258 C3 Ambato, Sierra mts Arg.
213 □J3 Ambato Boeny Madag.
116 C2 Ambato Finandrahana Madag.
213 □J3 Ambatolampy Madag.
213 □J3 Ambatomainty Madag.
213 □J3 Ambatomanoina Madag.
213 □K3 Ambatondrazaka Madag.
213 □J3 Ambatosoratra Madag.
162 D3 Ambazac France
   Ambejogai Mahar. India see Ambajogai
   Ambelón Greece see Ampelonas
   Amber Rajasthan India see Amer
173 F2 Amberg Ger.
226 D3 Amberg WI U.S.A.
149 H4 Ambergate Derbyshire, England U.K.
246 E2 Ambergris Cays is Turks and Caicos Is
160 D3 Ambérieu-en-Bugey France
227 G3 Amberley Ont. Can.
81 D5 Amberley South I. N.Z.
165 E4 Amberloup Belgium
160 B3 Ambert France
116 C5 Ambgaon Mahar. India
163 E5 Ambialet France
   Ambianum Ger. see Amiens
206 C3 Ambidédi Mali
160 C2 Ambierle France
160 C2 Ambièvre France
117 E5 Ambikapur Madh. Prad. India
213 □I4 Ambila Madag.
159 G4 Ambillou France
213 □K2 Ambilobe Madag.
222 D3 Ambition, Mount B.C. Can.
213 □I3 Amblainville France
178 B3 Amblainville Austria/Ger.

213 □K4 Ambodiharina Madag.
213 □J3 Ambohidratrimo Madag.
213 □J3 Ambohijanahary Madag.
213 □J4 Ambohimahasoa Madag.
213 □I4 Ambohimahavelona Madag.
162 C1 Amboise France
158 D4 Ambon France
93 D3 Ambon Maluku Indon.
93 C3 Ambon i. Maluku Indon.
213 □J5 Ambondro Madag.
156 E3 Ambonnay France
211 C5 Amboseli National Park Kenya
213 □J4 Ambositra Madag.
213 □J3 Ambovombe Madag.
241 J4 Amboy CA U.S.A.
226 C5 Amboy IL U.S.A.
159 H5 Ambrault France
209 B6 Ambriz Angola
129 C2 Ambrolauri Georgia
160 D2 Ambronay France
151 F3 Ambrosden Oxfordshire, England U.K.
78 □5 Ambrym i. Vanuatu
   Ambrym i. Vanuatu see Ambrym
209 B6 Ambundu Angola
216 □1a Amsterdam i. Indian Ocean
184 C3 Amêndoa Port.
184 C3 Amendoeira Port.
195 F3 Amendolara Italy
195 H5 Amendolea r. Italy
233 G4 Amenia NY U.S.A.
111 A7 Amer Rajasthan India
186 F2 Amer Spain
173 G4 Amerang Ger.
182 C2 A Merca Spain
240 G2 American, North Fork r. CA U.S.A.
256 D5 Americana Brazil
264 H9 American-Antarctic Ridge sea feature S. Atlantic Ocean
238 D3 American Falls ID U.S.A.
241 L1 American Fork UT U.S.A.
78 □2 American Samoa terr. S. Pacific Ocean
231 C5 Americus GA U.S.A.
179 F3 Ameringkogel mt. Austria
164 E3 Amerongen Neth.
164 E3 Amersfoort Neth.
215 H3 Amersfoort S. Africa
151 G3 Amersham Buckinghamshire, England U.K.
223 M3 Amery Man. Can.
236 E3 Ames IA U.S.A.
151 F3 Amesbury Wiltshire, England U.K.
233 H3 Amesbury MA U.S.A.
116 C4 Amet Rajasthan India
116 E4 Amethi Uttar Prad. India
186 A1 Amezketa Spain
182 C2 A Mezquita Spain
198 D2 Amfissa Greece
159 G2 Amfreville-la-Campagne France
95 F3 Amga r. Rus. Fed.
131 O3 Amga Rus. Fed.
107 H1 Amgalang Nei Mongol China
131 T3 Amguema Rus. Fed.
99 O1 Amgu r. Rus. Fed.
210 C2 Amhara admin. reg. Eth.
183 H1 Amurrio Spain
100 D1 Amurskaya Oblast' admin. div. Rus. Fed.
185 H4 Amusco Spain
119 J3 Amuzgi r. Spain
182 E3 Amvisas Spain
173 F4 Amechs Ger.
190 E2 Amer Switz.
   Andegavum France see Angers
190 D1 Andelfingen Switz.
161 J4 Andelle r. France
157 F4 Andelot-Blancheville France
160 D2 Andelot-en-Montagne France
178 A3 Andelsbuch Austria
164 E3 Andelst Neth.
161 B4 Andenes Norway
165 E4 Andenne Belgium
165 D4 Anderlecht Belgium
165 D4 Anderlues Belgium
190 D2 Andermatt Switz.
169 C4 Andernach Ger.
173 K4 Andernos-les-Bains France
143 G1 Andersberg Sweden
207 H4 Andersón AK U.S.A.
98 H1 Anderson AK U.S.A.
84 C5 Anderson CA U.S.A.
86 F4 Anderson IN U.S.A.
230 C4 Anderson MO U.S.A.
237 E4 Anderson SC U.S.A.
231 D5 Anderson Bay Tas. Austr.
83 F5 Anderson Bay Tas. Austr.
169 E1 Andervenne OH U.S.A.
223 K2 Anderson Lake B.C. Can.
250 C3 Andes mts S. America
252 B3 Andes mts S. America
140 L1 Andfjorden sea chan. Norway
141 K3 Ånge Sweden
251 F3 Angel, Salto del waterfall Venez.
242 B2 Ángel de la Guarda, Isla i. Mex.
92 B3 Angeles Phil.
   Angel Falls Venez. see Angel, Salto del
143 M4 Ängelholm Sweden
187 C5 Angelina r. Spain
87 C4 Angelina r. TX U.S.A.
245 G4 Angel R. Cabada Mex.
245 G4 Ángels Camp CA U.S.A.
143 L3 Ängelsberg Sweden
173 G4 Angenstein Ger.
147 D2 Angera r. Rep. of Ireland
147 D2 Angereb Wenz r. Eth.
140 C5 Ångermanälven r. Sweden
170 F2 Angermünde Ger.
159 F2 Angern r. France
146 D6 Angel r. Wales U.K.
187 B5 Anglés Spain
163 D2 Anglesea r. France
159 G4 Anglés-sur-l'Anglin France
155 D6 Anglesey i. Wales U.K.

234 B4 Anne Arundel County county MD U.S.A.
   Anne Arundel Town MD U.S.A. see Annapolis
160 E3 Annecy France
160 E3 Annecy, Lac d' l. France
160 E3 Annecy-le-Vieux France
160 E2 Annemasse France
164 F1 Annen Neth.
198 D4 Annese-et-Beaulieu France
161 C3 Anneyron France
149 N1 Annfield Plain Durham, England U.K.
148 E2 Annick r. Scotland U.K.
85 E2 Annie r. Qld Austr.
128 C3 An Nimārah Syria
124 C4 An Nimāṣ Saudi Arabia
108 B3 Anning Yunnan China
108 B3 Anning He r. Sichuan China
108 M5 Annino Rus. Fed.
231 C5 Anniston AL U.S.A.
207 G7 Annobón i. Equat. Guinea
156 C2 Annœullin France
161 F3 Annonay France
246 □ Annotto Bay Jamaica
148 D3 Annsborough Northern Ireland U.K.
125 C3 An Nu'ayrīyah Saudi Arabia
125 E2 An Nuqay'ah Qatar
232 B6 Annville KY U.S.A.
213 □J4 Annville PA U.S.A.
172 E2 Annweiler am Trifels Ger.
186 A1 Anoeta Spain
198 D4 Anogeia Kriti Greece
226 A3 Anoka MN U.S.A.
198 C2 Ano Lechonia Thessalia Greece
183 I3 Añón Spain
   Anonima atoll Micronesia see Namonuito
139 M4 Anopino Rus. Fed.
164 F3 Anor France
185 F2 Añora Spain
251 F5 Anori Brazil
213 □K3 Anosibe An'Ala Madag.
157 G4 Anould France
183 G5 Añover de Tajo Spain
199 D4 Ano Viannos Kriti Greece
198 D4 Anoyia Kriti Greece see Anogeia
108 C4 Anpu Guangdong China
108 D4 Anpu Gang b. China
109 G4 Anqing Anhui China
107 H4 Anqiu Shandong China
183 H4 Anquela del Ducado Spain
178 D4 Anras Austria
109 E3 Anren Hunan China
   An Rubha pen. Scotland U.K. see Eye Peninsula
165 E4 Ans Belgium
142 C3 Ans Denmark
150 E2 Ansac-sur-Vienne France
108 A3 Ansai Shaanxi China
173 E2 Ansbach Ger.
160 E4 Anse France
246 □ Anse-à-Galets Haiti
246 E3 Anse-à-Pitre Haiti
246 E3 Anse-à-Veau Haiti
247 □ Anse Bertrand Guadeloupe
192 D2 Ansedonia Italy
165 B4 Anseremme Belgium
83 F4 Anser Group is Tas. Austr.
179 F2 Ansfelden Austria
148 E5 An Sgarsoch mt. Scotland U.K.
107 I3 Anshan Liaoning China
108 C3 Anshun Guizhou China
182 B5 Ansião Port.
169 H2 Ansitz Italy
260 C2 Ansina Arg.
260 C2 Ansite, Cordillera de mts Arg.
258 G3 Ansina Arg.
126 E5 An Sirhān, Wādī watercourse Saudi Arabia
143 J5 Ansjö Sweden
148 E5 Ansley NE U.S.A.
186 C2 Ansó Spain
237 E5 Anson TX U.S.A.
84 B2 Anson Bay N.T. Austr.
207 F3 Ansongo Mali
235 E1 Ansonia CT U.S.A.
232 A4 Ansonia OH U.S.A.
224 D3 Ansonville Ont. Can.
171 F5 Ansprung Ger.
232 C5 Ansted WV U.S.A.
148 F5 Anstruther Scotland U.K.
107 K5 Ansu China see Xushui
151 I2 Ant r. England U.K.
116 A4 Anta Peru
252 B4 Antabamba Peru
213 □K2 Antalaha Madag.
199 G3 Antalya Turkey
199 G3 Antalya prov. Turkey
199 G3 Antalya Körfezi g. Turkey
213 □K3 Antanambao Manampotsy Madag.
213 □J3 Antananarivo Madag.
213 □J3 Antananarivo prov. Madag.
213 □J3 Antanimora Atsimo Madag.
   Antão i. Cape Verde see Santo Antão
   An tAonach Rep. of Ireland see Nenagh
262 Antarctica continent
262 T2 Antarctic Peninsula Antarctica
148 F4 Antas Peru
185 I3 Antas Spain
182 C3 Antas de Ulla Spain
260 C2 Antelope CA U.S.A.
146 C4 An Teallach mt. Scotland U.K.
241 F3 Antelope Range mts NV U.S.A.
160 D2 Antenne r. France
178 E3 Anterselva di Sopra Italy
234 A1 Antes Fort PA U.S.A.
161 I3 Anthéor France
178 C5 Anthisnes Belgium
237 D4 Anthony KS U.S.A.
239 K6 Anthony NM U.S.A.
82 F5 Anthony, Lake salt flat W.A. Austr.
84 C4 Anthony Lagoon N.T. Austr.
204 C3 Anti Atlas mts Morocco
161 F5 Antibes France
225 I3 Anticosti, Île d' i. Que. Can.
   Anticosti, Island of i. Que. Can. see Anticosti, Île d'
159 G2 Antifer, Cap d' c. France
227 I4 Antigo WI U.S.A.
246 C2 Antigonish N.S. Can.
247 □2 Antigua i. Antigua and Barbuda
216 □3b Antigua Fuerteventura Canary Is
243 H6 Antigua country West Indies see Antigua and Barbuda
247 □2 Antigua and Barbuda country West Indies
   Antigua Guatemala Guat. see Antigua
   Antiguo-Morelos Mex.
198 C2 Antikyra Greece
198 C4 Antikythiro, Steno sea chan. Greece
   Anti Lebanon mts Lebanon/Syria see Sharqī, Jabal ash
226 D2 Antilla Cuba
159 E3 Antillo Sicilia Italy
198 D3 Antimony r. U.S.A.
241 G2 Antimony UT U.S.A.
   An tInbhear Mór Rep. of Ireland see Arklow
240 O3 Antioch CA U.S.A.
226 C4 Antioch IL U.S.A.
128 A1 Antioch Turkey see Antakya
250 C2 Antioquia Col.
250 C2 Antioquia dept Col.
198 C3 Antiparos i. Greece
198 C4 Antipaxoi i. Greece
193 B3 Antipiano Corse France
192 B2 Antisanti Corse France
237 E5 Antlers OK U.S.A.

Arno to Auckland Islands
279

191 F5 **Arno** *r.* Italy
82 D3 **Arno Bay** *S.A.* Austr.
182 B2 **Arnoia** *r.* Spain
146 B3 **Arnol** *Western Isles, Scotland* U.K.
149 H4 **Arnold** *Nottinghamshire, England* U.K.
234 B3 **Arnold** *MD* U.S.A.
226 D2 **Arnold** *MI* U.S.A.
236 F4 **Arnold** *MO* U.S.A.
225 K4 **Arnold's Cove** *Nfld.* Can.
179 E4 **Arnoldstein** Austria
162 E1 **Arnon** *r.* France
Arnon *r.* Jordan *see* **Mawjib, Wādī al**
177 J3 **Arnót** Hungary
234 A1 **Arnot** *PA* U.S.A.
140 M1 **Arnøya** *i.* Norway
Arnoya *r.* Spain *see* **Arnoia**
224 E4 **Arnprior** *Ont.* Can.
148 E1 **Arnprior** *Stirling, Scotland* U.K.
169 D4 **Arnsberg** Ger.
169 D4 **Arnsberg** *admin. reg. Nordrhein-Westfalen* Ger.
169 D4 **Arnsberger Wald** *hills* Ger.
173 G2 **Arnschwang** Ger.
171 E4 **Arnsdorf bei Dresden** Ger.
169 F5 **Arnstadt** Ger.
227 H3 **Arnstein** *Ont.* Can.
171 A5 **Arnstein** Ger.
173 G3 **Arnstorf** Ger.
227 H1 **Arntfield** *Que.* Can.
183 G1 **Arnuero** Spain
251 E3 **Aro** *r.* Venez.
212 C5 **Aroab** Namibia
261 G3 **Arocena** Arg.
184 D3 **Aroche** Spain
182 B4 **Arões** Port.
182 B3 **Arões** Port.
177 J4 **Ároktő** Hungary
224 C3 **Aroland** *Ont.* Can.
169 E4 **Arolsen** Ger.
203 H6 **Aroma** Sudan
240 G3 **Aromas** *CA* U.S.A.
159 F3 **Aron** France
160 B2 **Aron** *r.* France
159 F3 **Aron** *r.* France
116 D4 **Aron** *Madh. Prad.* India
216 □3a **Arona** *Tenerife* Canary Is
190 D3 **Arona** Italy
233 □J1 **Aroostook** *N.B.* Can.
233 □J1 **Aroostook** *r. ME* U.S.A.
77 H2 **Arorae** *i. Gilbert Is* Kiribati
Arore *i. Gilbert Is* Kiribati *see* **Arorae**
92 B3 **Aroroy** Phil.
242 C2 **Aros** *r.* Mex.
182 B3 **Arosa** Port.
190 E2 **Arosa** Switz.
Arossi *i.* Solomon Is *see* **San Cristobal**
182 B4 **Arouca** Port.
129 D4 **Arp'a** *r.* Armenia
129 C3 **Arpa** *r.* Armenia/Turkey
127 F2 **Arpaçay** Turkey
128 B1 **Arpaçsakarlar** Turkey
156 C4 **Arpajon** France
163 E4 **Arpajon-sur-Cère** France
193 F3 **Arpino** Italy
Arpinum Italy *see* **Arpino**
Arqalyq Kazakh. *see* **Arkalyk**
193 F2 **Arquata del Tronto** Italy
190 D4 **Arquata Scrivia** Italy
163 E6 **Arques** *Languedoc-Roussillon* France
156 C2 **Arques** *Nord - Pas-de-Calais* France
156 B3 **Arques-la-Bataille** France
185 G2 **Arquillos** Spain
123 F5 **Arra** *r.* Pak.
182 B2 **Arrabal** Spain
85 E5 **Arrabury** *Qld* Austr.
173 G2 **Arrach** Ger.
157 G4 **Arracourt** France
158 D4 **Arradon** France
206 E5 **Arrah** Côte d'Ivoire
Arrah *Bihar* India *see* **Ara**
124 D5 **Ar Rāhidah** Yemen
254 D5 **Arraias** Brazil
254 B4 **Arraias** *r.* Brazil
254 D5 **Arraias, Serra de** *hills* Brazil
184 C2 **Arraiolos** Port.
127 F4 **Ar Ramādī** Iraq
147 C4 **Arra Mountains** *hills* Rep. of Ireland
128 C3 **Ar Ramthā** Jordan
146 C6 **Arran** *i. Scotland* U.K.
157 F3 **Arrancy-sur-Crusne** France
184 A2 **Arranhó** Port.
128 D2 **Ar Raqqah** Syria
128 D1 **Ar Raqqah** *governorate* Syria
156 C2 **Arras** France
Arrasate Spain *see* **Mondragón**
163 B6 **Arras-en-Lavedan** France
124 C2 **Ar-Rass** Saudi Arabia
163 C4 **Arrats** *r.* France
163 A5 **Arraute-Charritte** France
124 C3 **Ar Rawḑah** Saudi Arabia
125 D5 **Ar Rawḑah** Yemen
124 D3 **Ar Rayn** Saudi Arabia
125 E2 **Ar Rayyān** Qatar
163 C6 **Arreau** France
250 D4 **Arrecifal** Col.
216 □3c **Arrecife** *Lanzarote* Canary Is
261 G4 **Arrecifes** Arg.
183 G1 **Arredondo** Spain
158 B3 **Arrée, Monts d'** *hills* France
156 E4 **Arrentières** France
Arretium Italy *see* **Arezzo**
179 E4 **Arriach** Austria
245 H5 **Arriagá** Mex.
244 D3 **Arriaga** *San Luis Potosí* Mex.
185 E4 **Arriate** Spain
261 G4 **Arribeños** Arg.
127 G5 **Ar Rifā'ī** Iraq
182 B4 **Arrifana** *Aveiro* Port.
182 B4 **Arrifana** *Coimbra* Port.
182 C4 **Arrifana** *Guarda* Port.
216 □1b **Arrifes** *São Miguel* Azores
156 E4 **Arrigny** France
183 H1 **Arrigorriaga** Spain
127 G5 **Ar Rihāb** *salt flat* Iraq
125 F3 **Ar Rimāl** *des.* Saudi Arabia
232 D6 **Arrington** *VA* U.S.A.
87 B6 **Arrino** *W.A.* Austr.
183 E1 **Arriondas** Spain
Ar Riyāḑ Saudi Arabia *see* **Riyadh**
124 D2 **Ar Riyāḑ** *prov.* Saudi Arabia
185 F1 **Arroba de los Montes** Spain
182 D4 **Arrobuey** *mt.* Spain
146 D5 **Arrochar** *Argyll and Bute, Scotland* U.K.
258 G4 **Arroio Grande** Brazil
159 F2 **Arromanches-les-Bains** France
184 C1 **Arronches** Port.
193 E2 **Arrone** Italy
192 D2 **Arrone** *r.* Italy
193 E3 **Arrone** *r.* Italy
183 H2 **Arroniz** Spain
163 B5 **Arros** *r.* France
190 D4 **Arroscia** *r.* Italy
156 B4 **Arrou** France
160 B2 **Arroux** *r.* France
226 C1 **Arrow** *r. Ont.* Can.
150 E2 **Arrow** *r. England* U.K.
147 C2 **Arrow, Lough** *l.* Rep. of Ireland
238 E2 **Arrow Creek** *r. MT* U.S.A.
81 C5 **Arrowsmith, Mount** *South I.* N.Z.
81 B6 **Arrowtown** *South I.* N.Z.
183 F2 **Arroyal** Spain
261 F2 **Arroyito** Arg.
247 □1 **Arroyo** Puerto Rico
184 D1 **Arroyo de la Luz** Spain
184 D2 **Arroyo de San Serván** Spain
261 I5 **Arroyo Grande** *r.* Arg.
240 G4 **Arroyo Grande** *CA* U.S.A.
184 D2 **Arroyomolinos de León** Spain
261 G3 **Arroyo Seco** Arg.
245 E3 **Arroyo Seco** Mex.
184 A2 **Arruda dos Vinhos** Port.
261 G2 **Arrufó** Arg.
127 G5 **Ar Rumaythah** Iraq
128 C3 **Ar Ruşayfah** Jordan
125 G3 **Ar Rustāq** Oman
127 F4 **Ar Ruţbah** Iraq
124 D3 **Ar Ruwayḑah** Saudi Arabia
157 G3 **Arry** France
142 C3 **Års** Denmark
122 A2 **Ars** Iran
199 F3 **Arsaköy** Turkey
Ărsarybaba Erezi *hills* Turkm. *see* **Irsarybaba, Gory**
186 E2 **Arsèguel** Spain
122 C4 **Arsenajān** Iran
162 A2 **Ars-en-Ré** France
100 E3 **Arsen'yev** Rus. Fed.
139 K5 **Arsen'yevo** Rus. Fed.
138 G4 **Arshanskaye Wzvyshsha** *hills* Belarus
191 G3 **Arsiè** Italy
191 G3 **Arsiero** Italy
114 C3 **Arsikere** *Karnataka* India
129 A3 **Arsin** Turkey
134 J4 **Arsk** Rus. Fed.
193 F2 **Arsoli** Italy
160 C3 **Ars-sur-Formans** France
157 G3 **Ars-sur-Moselle** France
78 □5 **Art, Île** *i.* New Caledonia
198 B2 **Arta** Greece
187 G5 **Artà** Spain
183 I2 **Artajona** Spain
129 D2 **Art'ana** Georgia
187 C5 **Artana** Spain
190 C3 **Artanavaz** *r.* Italy
159 G4 **Artannes-sur-Indre** France
129 D4 **Artashat** Armenia
243 E3 **Arteaga** *Coahuila* Mex.
244 C4 **Arteaga** *Michoacán* Mex.
187 C5 **Arteas de Abajo** *mt.* Spain
100 E4 **Artem** Rus. Fed.
160 D3 **Artemare** France
246 B2 **Artemisa** Cuba
137 I3 **Artemivka** *Kharkivs'ka Oblast'* Ukr.
137 H3 **Artemivka** *Poltavs'ka Oblast'* Ukr.
137 J3 **Artemivs'k** Ukr.
137 J3 **Artemivs'k** Ukr.
Artemovsk Ukr. *see* **Artemivs'k**
131 M4 **Artemovskiy** *Irkutskaya Oblast'* Rus. Fed.
100 E4 **Artemovskiy** *Primorskiy Kray* Rus. Fed.
191 G2 **Artèn** Italy
193 E3 **Artena** Italy
156 B4 **Artenay** France
171 C4 **Artern (Unstrut)** Ger.
186 E3 **Artés** Spain
186 E3 **Artesa de Segre** Spain
241 M5 **Artesia** *AZ* U.S.A.
239 F5 **Artesia** *NM* U.S.A.
190 D1 **Arth** Switz.
163 E5 **Arthès** France
163 B5 **Arthez-d'Asson** France
163 B5 **Arthez-de-Béarn** France
159 H5 **Arthon** France
158 E4 **Arthon-en-Retz** France
87 B5 **Arthur** *r. W.A.* Austr.
227 G4 **Arthur** *Ont.* Can.
236 C3 **Arthur** *NE* U.S.A.
232 B6 **Arthur** *TN* U.S.A.
82 D2 **Arthur, Lake** *salt flat S.A.* Austr.
232 C4 **Arthur, Lake** *PA* U.S.A.
83 F5 **Arthur Lake** *Tas.* Austr.
85 G4 **Arthur Point** *Qld* Austr.
81 C5 **Arthur's Pass** *South I.* N.Z.
246 D1 **Arthur's Town** *Cat I.* Bahamas
148 C2 **Articlave** *Northern Ireland* U.K.
186 C2 **Artieda** Spain
186 D2 **Arties** Spain
148 B3 **Artigarvan** *Northern Ireland* U.K.
262 U2 **Artigas** *research stn* Antarctica
261 I2 **Artigas** Uru.
261 I2 **Artigas** *dept* Uru.
163 D5 **Artigat** France
129 C3 **Art'ik** Armenia
223 I2 **Artillery Lake** *N.W.T.* Can.
163 B5 **Artix** France
138 F1 **Artjärvi** Fin.
168 F2 **Artlenburg** Ger.
190 F3 **Artogne** Italy
127 F3 **Artos Dağı** *mt.* Turkey
126 E2 **Artova** Turkey
Artsakh *aut. reg.* Azer. *see* **Dağlıq Qarabağ**
106 D2 **Arts Bogd Uul** *mts* Mongolia
Artsiz Ukr. *see* **Artsyz**
136 E5 **Artsyz** Ukr.
161 E5 **Artuby** *r.* France
Artur de Paiva Angola *see* **Kuvango**
110 B4 **Artux** *Xinjiang* China
127 F2 **Artvin** Turkey
129 B3 **Artvin** *prov.* Turkey
91 H8 **Aru, Kepulauan** *is* Indon.
182 C2 **A Rúa** Spain
210 A4 **Arua** Uganda
254 C5 **Aruanã** Brazil
247 □9 **Aruba** *terr.* West Indies
216 □3f **Arucas** *Gran Canaria* Canary Is
163 B5 **Arudy** France
256 D5 **Arujá** Brazil
107 J2 **Arun** *r.* China
117 F4 **Arun** *r.* Nepal
117 H4 **Arunachal Pradesh** *state* India
81 C5 **Arundel** *South I.* N.Z.
151 G4 **Arundel** *West Sussex, England* U.K.
Arun Qi *Nei Mongol* China *see* **Naji**
142 D4 **Årup** Denmark
114 C4 **Aruppukkottai** *Tamil Nadu* India
211 C5 **Arusha** Tanz.
211 C5 **Arusha** *admin. reg.* Tanz.
211 C5 **Arusha National Park** Tanz.
95 E3 **Arut** *r.* Indon.
208 D4 **Aruwimi** *r.* Dem. Rep. Congo
236 B4 **Arvada** *CO* U.S.A.
147 D3 **Arvagh** Rep. of Ireland
161 E3 **Arvan** *r.* France
106 D2 **Arvayheer** Mongolia
160 E2 **Arve** *r.* France
162 A3 **Arvert** France
163 B4 **Arveyres** France
116 D5 **Arvi** *Mahar.* India
223 M2 **Arviat** *Nunavut* Can.
230 G1 **Arvida** *Que.* Can.
140 L2 **Arvidsjaur** Sweden
161 A4 **Arvieu** France
161 E4 **Arvieux** France
142 E2 **Arvika** Sweden
240 H4 **Arvin** *CA* U.S.A.
195 F3 **Arvo, Lago** *l.* Italy
232 D6 **Arvonia** *VA* U.S.A.
124 D3 **Arwā'** Saudi Arabia
107 H2 **Arxan** *Nei Mongol* China
Aryanah Tunisia *see* **L'Ariana**
134 K4 **Aryazh** Rus. Fed.
121 G1 **Arykbalyk** Kazakh.
Aryqbayq Kazakh. *see* **Arykbalyk**
121 G4 **Arys'** Kazakh.
121 G4 **Arys'** *r.* Kazakh.
192 B3 **Arzachena** *Sardegna* Italy
163 B5 **Arzacq-Arraziguet** France
135 H5 **Arzamas** Rus. Fed.
192 B5 **Arzana** *Sardegna* Italy
158 C4 **Arzano** France
169 C5 **Arzbach** Ger.
171 D5 **Arzberg** *Bayern* Ger.
171 E4 **Arzberg** *Sachsen* Ger.
163 E5 **Arzens** France
205 E2 **Arzew** Alg.
169 B5 **Arzfeld** Ger.
135 I7 **Arzgir** Rus. Fed.
191 G3 **Arzignano** Italy
Arzila Morocco *see* **Asilah**
178 B3 **Arzl im Pitztal** Austria
161 B3 **Arzon** *r.* France
182 B2 **Arzúa** Spain
165 E3 **As** Belgium
176 B1 **Aš** Czech Rep.
142 D3 **Aså** Denmark
142 E3 **Åsa** Sweden
207 G5 **Asaba** Nigeria
128 D1 **Asad, Buḩayrat al** *resr* Syria
123 G3 **Asadābād** Afgh.
122 B3 **Asadābād** Iran
129 E3 **Aşağı Ağcakänd** Azer.
129 D3 **Aşağı Äskipara** Azer.
129 D3 **Aşağı Ayıblı** Azer.
129 C3 **Aşağı Dağ** *mt.* Turkey
199 F3 **Aşağıkaraçay** Turkey
129 B3 **Aşağıkatıklı** Turkey
129 C4 **Aşağıküpkıran** Turkey
129 E3 **Aşağı Oratağ** Azer.
129 D4 **Aşağısağmallı** Turkey
129 B4 **Aşağısöylemez** Turkey
94 B2 **Asahan** *r.* Indon.
105 G3 **Asahi** Japan
102 I4 **Asahi-dake** *mt.* Japan
102 K2 **Asahi-dake** *vol.* Japan
103 F6 **Asahi-gawa** *r.* Japan
102 K2 **Asahikawa** Japan
105 F1 **Asahi-take** *mt.* Japan
105 F3 **Asaka** Japan
121 H4 **Asaka** Uzbek.
104 C3 **Asake-gawa** *r.* Japan
104 C4 **Asamaga-take** *hill* Japan
206 E5 **Asamankese** Ghana
105 E2 **Asama-yama** *vol.* Japan
206 E5 **Asankranguaa** Ghana
117 F5 **Asansol** *W. Bengal* India
206 E5 **Asanwenso** Ghana
163 B5 **Asasp-Arros** France
Asava *i.* Fiji *see* **Yasawa**
210 D2 **Āsayita** Eth.
169 C5 **Asbach** Ger.
173 E3 **Asbach-Bäumenheim** Ger.
230 G2 **Asbestos** *Que.* Can.
Asbestos Hill *Que.* Can. *see* **Purtuniq**
214 D3 **Asbestos Mountains** S. Africa
210 D2 **Āsbe Teferi** Eth.
143 F2 **Åsbro** Sweden
233 F4 **Asbury Park** *NJ* U.S.A.
163 A5 **Ascain** France
Ascalon Israel *see* **Ashqelon**
193 H4 **Ascea** Italy
261 G4 **Ascensión** Arg.
253 E3 **Ascensión** Bol.
245 E1 **Ascensión** Mex.
Ascension *atoll* Micronesia *see* **Pohnpei**
216 □2a **Ascension** *i.* S. Atlantic Ocean
173 G2 **Ascha** Ger.
173 G2 **Ascha** *r.* Ger.
179 F2 **Aschach an der Donau** Austria
172 D2 **Aschaffenburg** Ger.
178 C3 **Aschau im Zillertal** Austria
173 G4 **Aschau in Chiemgau** Ger.
179 F2 **Aschbach Markt** Austria
169 C4 **Ascheberg** Ger.
168 F1 **Ascheberg (Holstein)** Ger.
173 H3 **Aschenstein** *hill* Ger.
156 C4 **Aschères-le-Marché** France
171 C4 **Aschersleben** Ger.
173 F3 **Aschheim** Ger.
191 G5 **Asciano** Italy
192 B2 **Asco** *Corse* France
193 F2 **Ascoli Piceno** Italy
193 F2 **Ascoli Piceno** *prov. Marche* Italy
193 H3 **Ascoli Satriano** Italy
190 D2 **Ascona** Switz.
151 G3 **Ascot** *Windsor and Maidenhead, England* U.K.
252 C5 **Ascotán, Salar de** *salt flat* Chile
163 D6 **Ascou** France
182 B2 **As Covas** Spain
Asculum Italy *see* **Ascoli Piceno**
Asculum Picenum Italy *see* **Ascoli Piceno**
233 G3 **Ascutney** *VT* U.S.A.
113 □1 **Asdhu** *i. N. Male* Maldives
Asdu *i. N. Male* Maldives *see* **Asdhu**
Āseb Eritrea *see* **Assab**
143 F3 **Åseda** Sweden
205 F4 **Asedjrad** *plat.* Alg.
120 C1 **Asekeyevo** Rus. Fed.
210 C3 **Āsela** Eth.
140 L2 **Åsele** Sweden
141 K3 **Åsen** Sweden
168 E2 **Asendorf** *Niedersachsen* Ger.
168 E3 **Asendorf** *Niedersachsen* Ger.
197 G4 **Asenovgrad** Bulg.
142 B2 **Åseral** Norway
138 F2 **Aseri** Estonia
122 D3 **Aşfāk** Iran
128 C3 **Aşfar, Jabal al** *mt.* Jordan
128 C3 **Aşfar, Tall al** *hill* Syria
156 E3 **Asfeld** France
151 G2 **Asfordby** *Leicestershire, England* U.K.
151 I3 **Ash** *Kent, England* U.K.
151 G3 **Ash** *Surrey, England* U.K.
134 L5 **Asha** Rus. Fed.
104 D2 **Ashahi-dake** *mt.* Japan
206 E5 **Ashanti** *admin. reg.* Ghana
134 L4 **Ashap** Rus. Fed.
124 D2 **Asharat** Saudi Arabia
235 G1 **Ashaway** *RI* U.S.A.
147 E3 **Ashbourne** Rep. of Ireland
149 H4 **Ashbourne** *Derbyshire, England* U.K.
231 D6 **Ashburn** *GA* U.S.A.
87 B4 **Ashburton** *watercourse W.A.* Austr.
81 C5 **Ashburton** *South I.* N.Z.
81 C6 **Ashburton** *r. South I.* N.Z.
150 D4 **Ashburton** *Devon, England* U.K.
84 C3 **Ashburton Range** *hills N.T.* Austr.
151 F3 **Ashbury** *Oxfordshire, England* U.K.
151 F2 **Ashby de la Zouch** *Leicestershire, England* U.K.
150 E3 **Ashchurch** *Gloucestershire, England* U.K.
Ashchysay Kazakh. *see* **Achisay**
150 E3 **Ashcott** *Somerset, England* U.K.
222 F5 **Ashcroft** *B.C.* Can.
128 B4 **Ashdod** Israel
237 E5 **Ashdown** *AR* U.S.A.
151 H3 **Ashdown Forest** *reg. England* U.K.
231 E5 **Asheboro** *NC* U.S.A.
237 D5 **Asher** *OK* U.S.A.
223 L5 **Ashern** *Man.* Can.
231 D5 **Asheville** *NC* U.S.A.
224 C2 **Asheweig** *r. Ont.* Can.
83 G2 **Ashford** *N.S.W.* Austr.
147 E3 **Ashford** Rep. of Ireland
148 C5 **Ashford** *r.* Rep. of Ireland
151 F4 **Ashford** *Hampshire, England* U.K.
151 H3 **Ashford** *Kent, England* U.K.
151 G3 **Ashford** *Surrey, England* U.K.
241 K4 **Ash Fork** *AZ* U.S.A.
122 D2 **Ashgabat** Turkm.
80 E4 **Ashhurst** *North I.* N.Z.
102 K2 **Ashibetsu** Japan
105 F2 **Ashikaga** Japan
151 H2 **Ashill** *Norfolk, England* U.K.
149 H2 **Ashington** *Northumberland, England* U.K.
226 C4 **Ashippun** *WI* U.S.A.
104 B4 **Ashiya** Japan
122 C4 **Ashkazar** Iran
Ashkelon Israel *see* **Ashqelon**
Ashkhabad Turkm. *see* **Ashgabat**
Ashkhabadskaya Oblast' *admin. div.* Turkm. *see* **Akhal'skaya Oblast'**
146 F6 **Ashkirk** *Scottish Borders, Scotland* U.K.
226 D5 **Ashkum** *IL* U.S.A.
231 C5 **Ashland** *AL* U.S.A.
237 D4 **Ashland** *KS* U.S.A.
232 B5 **Ashland** *KY* U.S.A.
233 □I1 **Ashland** *ME* U.S.A.
237 F5 **Ashland** *MS* U.S.A.
238 F2 **Ashland** *MT* U.S.A.
236 D3 **Ashland** *NE* U.S.A.
233 H3 **Ashland** *NH* U.S.A.
232 B4 **Ashland** *OH* U.S.A.
238 B3 **Ashland** *OR* U.S.A.
234 B2 **Ashland** *PA* U.S.A.
232 E6 **Ashland** *VA* U.S.A.
226 B2 **Ashland** *WI* U.S.A.
231 C4 **Ashland City** *TN* U.S.A.
83 G2 **Ashley** *N.S.W.* Austr.
81 D5 **Ashley** *r. South I.* N.Z.
151 H2 **Ashley** *Cambridgeshire, England* U.K.
226 E5 **Ashley** *IN* U.S.A.
226 E4 **Ashley** *MI* U.S.A.
236 D2 **Ashley** *ND* U.S.A.
232 B4 **Ashley** *OH* U.S.A.
234 C1 **Ashley** *PA* U.S.A.
86 D2 **Ashmore and Cartier Islands** *terr.* Austr.
86 D2 **Ashmore Reef** *Ashmore & Cartier Is* Austr.
138 E4 **Ashmyanskaye Wzvyshsha** *hills* Belarus
138 E4 **Ashmyany** *Hrodzyenskaya Voblasts'* Belarus
138 F4 **Ashmyany** *Hrodzyenskaya Voblasts'* Belarus
116 D4 **Ashoknagar** *Madh. Prad.* India
129 C3 **Ashots'k'** Armenia
128 B4 **Ashqelon** Israel
127 F5 **Ash Shabakah** Iraq
127 F3 **Ash Shaddādah** Syria
124 C3 **Ash Shafa** Saudi Arabia
Ash Sham Syria *see* **Damascus**
125 G2 **Ash Sha'm** U.A.E.
127 G5 **Ash Shanāfīyah** Iraq
124 D2 **Ash Sha'rā'** Saudi Arabia
125 D4 **Ash Sharawrah** Saudi Arabia
Ash Shāriqah U.A.E. *see* **Sharjah**
127 F4 **Ash Sharqāţ** Iraq
125 G3 **Ash Sharqīyah** *admin. reg.* Oman
125 G3 **Ash Sharqīyah** *reg.* Oman
125 E3 **Ash Sharqīyah** *prov.* Saudi Arabia
127 G5 **Ash Shaţrah** Iraq
128 B4 **Ash Shawbak** Jordan
124 D5 **Ash Shaykh 'Uthman** Yemen
128 C5 **Ash Shiblīyāt** *hill* Saudi Arabia
125 E5 **Ash Shiḩr** Yemen
125 G2 **Ash Shināş** Oman
124 C2 **Ash Shubaykīyah** Saudi Arabia
125 D2 **Ash Shumlūl** Saudi Arabia
124 C4 **Ash Shuqayq** Saudi Arabia
Ash Shurayf Saudi Arabia *see* **Khaybar**
116 D5 **Ashta** *Madh. Prad.* India
114 B2 **Ashta** *Mahar.* India
232 C4 **Ashtabula** *OH* U.S.A.
129 D3 **Ashtarak** Armenia
114 B2 **Ashti** *Mahar.* India
114 C2 **Ashti** *Mahar.* India
116 D5 **Ashti** *Mahar.* India
214 C5 **Ashton** S. Africa
149 G4 **Ashton** *Cheshire, England* U.K.
238 E2 **Ashton** *ID* U.S.A.
226 C5 **Ashton** *IL* U.S.A.
234 A3 **Ashton** *MD* U.S.A.
215 E6 **Ashton Bay** S. Africa
149 G4 **Ashton-under-Lyne** *Greater Manchester, England* U.K.
225 H2 **Ashuanipi** *r. Nfld.* Can.
230 F1 **Ashuapmushuan** *r. Que.* Can.
Ashur Iraq *see* **Ash Sharqāţ**
151 F4 **Ashurst** *Hampshire, England* U.K.
151 H3 **Ashurst** *Kent, England* U.K.
231 C5 **Ashville** *AL* U.S.A.
233 □I2 **Ashville** *ME* U.S.A.
232 D4 **Ashville** *PA* U.S.A.
226 B2 **Ashwabay, Mount** *hill WI* U.S.A.
226 C3 **Ashwaubenon** *WI* U.S.A.
150 E3 **Ashwick** *Somerset, England* U.K.
128 C2 **'Āṣī** *r.* Lebanon/Syria
128 C1 **Asi** *r.* Turkey *alt.* **'Āṣī, Nahr al (Asia),** *conv.* **Orontes (Lebanon/Syria)**
128 C1 **'Āṣī, Nahr al** *r.* Asia *alt.* **Asi (Turkey),** *conv.* **Orontes (Lebanon/Syria)**
88 **Asia** *continent*
191 G3 **Asiago** Italy
244 C2 **Asientos** Mex.
114 C2 **Asifabad** *Andhra Prad.* India
115 E2 **Asika** *Orissa* India
141 N3 **Asikkala** Fin.
204 D2 **Asilah** Morocco
252 C3 **Asillo** Peru
198 D4 **Asimi** *Kriti* Greece
186 B2 **Asín** Spain
192 A4 **Asinara, Golfo dell'** *b. Sardegna* Italy
192 A3 **Asinara, Isola** *i. Sardegna* Italy
116 C4 **Asind** *Rajasthan* India
130 J4 **Asino** Rus. Fed.
139 H4 **Asintorf** Belarus
138 G5 **Asipovichy** Belarus
124 C4 **'Asīr** *prov.* Saudi Arabia
124 C3 **'Asīr** *reg.* Saudi Arabia
Asisium Italy *see* **Assisi**
138 C1 **Askainen** Fin.
127 F3 **Aşkale** Turkey
137 G4 **Askaniya Nova** Ukr.
120 D1 **Askarovo** Rus. Fed.
147 C4 **Askeaton** Rep. of Ireland
215 F4 **Askeaton** S. Africa
142 D2 **Asker** Norway
129 A4 **Asker Dağı** *mt.* Turkey
149 H4 **Askern** *South Yorkshire, England* U.K.
143 F2 **Askersund** Sweden
214 C2 **Askham** S. Africa
147 C2 **Askill** Rep. of Ireland
142 D2 **Askim** Norway
134 L4 **Askino** Rus. Fed.
198 B1 **Askio** *mt.* Greece
207 I4 **Askira** Nigeria
146 B5 **Askival** *hill Scotland* U.K.
98 F1 **Askiz** Rus. Fed.
141 N3 **Askola** Fin.
143 G2 **Äsköping** Sweden
198 C1 **Askos** *Kentriki Makedonia* Greece
116 E3 **Askot** *Uttar Prad.* India
142 A1 **Askøy** *i.* Norway
214 C6 **Askraal** S. Africa
141 I3 **Askvoll** Norway
129 E4 **Askyaran** Azer.
199 F2 **Aslanapa** Turkey
122 A2 **Aşlāndūz** Iran
138 G5 **Aslik** *r.* Belarus
Aslóközpont Hungary *see* **Mórahalom**
203 H6 **Asmara** Eritrea
Āsmera Eritrea *see* **Asmara**
143 F3 **Åsnen** *l.* Sweden
182 B1 **As Neves** *Galicia* Spain
182 B2 **As Neves** *Galicia* Spain
182 C2 **As Nogais** Spain
193 F1 **Aso** *r.* Italy
190 F3 **Asola** Italy
191 G3 **Asolo** Italy
185 I1 **Asomadilla** *hill* Spain
198 C2 **Asopos** *r.* Greece
198 C3 **Asopos** *r.* Greece
210 B2 **Āsosa** Eth.
103 E7 **Aso-san** *vol.* Japan
203 H4 **Asoteriba, Jebel** *mt.* Sudan
238 C2 **Asotin** *WA* U.S.A.
177 I5 **Ásotthalom** Hungary
134 L4 **Aspa** Rus. Fed.
179 E2 **Aspach** Austria
179 H3 **Aspang-Markt** Austria
122 B2 **Aspar** Iran
121 H4 **Aspara** Kazakh.
179 H2 **Asparn an der Zaya** Austria
197 H4 **Asparukhovo** Bulg.
140 K3 **Aspås** Sweden
149 F3 **Aspatria** *Cumbria, England* U.K.
187 C6 **Aspe** Spain
140 L3 **Äspea** Sweden
239 F4 **Aspen** *CO* U.S.A.
164 E3 **Asperen** Neth.
172 D3 **Asperg** Ger.
237 C5 **Aspermont** *TX* U.S.A.
234 A3 **Aspers** *PA* U.S.A.
163 C5 **Aspet** France
129 C3 **Aspindza** Georgia
161 B5 **Aspiran** France
81 B6 **Aspiring, Mount** *South I.* N.Z.
182 C1 **As Pontes de García Rodríguez** Spain
161 D4 **Aspremont** France
161 D4 **Aspres-sur-Buëch** France
163 E4 **Asprières** France
Aspropotamos *r.* Greece *see* **Acheloös**
198 C1 **Asprovalta** Greece
116 C5 **Aspur** *Rajasthan* India
223 J4 **Asquith** *Sask.* Can.
191 G3 **Assa** *r.* Italy
204 C3 **Assa** Morocco
129 D2 **Assa** *r.* Rus. Fed.
128 C2 **As Sa'an** Syria
203 I6 **Assab** Eritrea
206 C2 **Assaba** *admin. reg.* Maur.
124 C2 **Aš Sab'ān** Saudi Arabia
128 D2 **As Sabkhah** Syria
128 C3 **Aş Şafā** *lava field* Syria
Aş Şafāqis Tunisia *see* **Sfax**
128 B4 **Aş Şāfī** Jordan
128 C1 **As Safīrah** Syria
124 C5 **Aş Şahīf** Yemen
Assake Uzbek. *see* **Asaka**
120 D4 **Assake-Audan, Vpadina** *depr.* Uzbek.
125 D2 **As Salamiyah** Saudi Arabia
127 F4 **Aş Şālihīyah** Syria
128 B3 **As Salţ** Jordan
117 G4 **Assam** *state* India
127 G5 **As Samāwah** Iraq
172 D2 **Assamstadt** Ger.
125 E3 **Aş Şanām** *reg.* Saudi Arabia
163 B5 **Assat** France
124 D3 **As Sawādah** *reg.* Saudi Arabia
165 D4 **Asse** Belgium
161 D5 **Asse** *r.* France
214 E5 **Assegaaibos** S. Africa
192 B5 **Assemini** *Sardegna* Italy
164 F1 **Assen** Neth.
164 D2 **Assendelft** Neth.
165 C3 **Assenede** Belgium
142 C4 **Assens** Denmark
158 D4 **Assérac** France
193 F2 **Assergi** Italy
165 E4 **Assesse** Belgium
163 D4 **Assier** France
223 J5 **Assiniboia** *Sask.* Can.
223 L5 **Assiniboine** *r. Man./Sask.* Can.
222 H5 **Assiniboine, Mount** *Alta/B.C.* Can.
256 B5 **Assis** Brazil
256 A6 **Assis Chateaubriand** Brazil
193 E1 **Assisi** Italy
169 D5 **Aßlar** Ger.
178 D4 **Assling** Austria
173 G4 **Aßling** Ger.
190 E3 **Asso** Italy
206 □ **Assomada** *São Tiago* Cape Verde
217 □2 **Assomption** *i.* Seychelles
163 B5 **Asson** France
194 D5 **Assoro** *Sicilia* Italy
127 G5 **Aş Şubayḩīyah** Kuwait
124 C4 **As Subaykhah** Saudi Arabia
125 E5 **As Sufāl** Yemen
127 G4 **As Sulaymānīyah** Iraq
127 G4 **As Sulaymānīyah** *governorate* Iraq
124 C2 **As Sulaymī** Saudi Arabia
124 D3 **As Sulayyil** Saudi Arabia
125 E2 **Aş Şulb** *reg.* Saudi Arabia
184 C1 **Assumar** Port.
124 D2 **Aş Şummān** *plat.* Saudi Arabia
125 E3 **Aş Şummān** *plat.* Saudi Arabia
As Sūrīyah *country* Asia *see* **Syria**
127 F4 **Aş Şuwar** Syria
128 C3 **As Suwaydā'** Syria
128 C3 **As Suwaydā'** *governorate* Syria
125 G3 **As Suwayḩ** Oman
125 G3 **As Suwayq** Oman
124 C3 **As Suwayriqīyah** Saudi Arabia
As Suways Egypt *see* **El Suweis**
124 D5 **As Suwwādīyah** Yemen
146 C3 **Assynt, Loch** *l. Scotland* U.K.
141 J3 **Asta** *r.* Norway
191 G2 **Asta, Cima d'** *mt.* Italy
Astacus Turkey *see* **Kocaeli**
163 C4 **Astaffort** France
198 B2 **Astakos** Greece
121 G2 **Astana** Kazakh.
122 B2 **Astaneh** Iran
122 B2 **Āstārā** Iran
142 E1 **Åsteby** Sweden
179 F2 **Asten** Austria
165 E3 **Asten** Neth.
Asterabad Iran *see* **Gorgān**
190 D4 **Asti** Italy
190 D4 **Asti** *prov. Piemonte* Italy
191 G3 **Astico** *r.* Italy
177 L4 **Aştileu** Romania
252 C3 **Astillero** Peru
Astin Tag *mts* China *see* **Altun Shan**
Astipálaia *i.* Greece *see* **Astypalaia**
163 D6 **Aston** *r.* France
151 G3 **Aston Clinton** *Buckinghamshire, England* U.K.
116 C2 **Astor** Jammu and Kashmir
123 H3 **Astor** *r.* Pak.
256 B5 **Astorga** Brazil
182 D2 **Astorga** Spain
226 B5 **Astoria** *IL* U.S.A.
238 B2 **Astoria** *OR* U.S.A.
142 E3 **Åstorp** Sweden
217 □2 **Astove** *i.* Seychelles
Astrabad Iran *see* **Gorgān**
Astrakhan' Kazakh. *see* **Astrakhanka**
120 B3 **Astrakhan'** Rus. Fed.
Astrakhan' Bazar Azer. *see* **Cälilabad**
121 G2 **Astrakhanka** Kazakh.
137 H4 **Astrakhanka** Ukr.
Astrakhan Oblast *admin. div.* Rus. Fed. *see* **Astrakhanskaya Oblast'**
120 A3 **Astrakhanskaya Oblast'** *admin. div.* Rus. Fed.
138 E4 **Astravyets** Belarus
129 F3 **Astraxanka** Azer.
Astrida Rwanda *see* **Butare**
78 □5 **Astrolabe, Récifs de l'** *rf* New Caledonia
198 C3 **Astros** Greece
138 E5 **Astryna** Belarus
139 H5 **Astsyer** *r.* Belarus
183 F2 **Astudillo** Spain
193 E3 **Astura** *r.* Italy
182 D1 **Asturias** *airport* Spain
182 D1 **Asturias** *aut. comm.* Spain
Asturica Augusta Spain *see* **Astorga**
151 F2 **Astwood Bank** *Worcestershire, England* U.K.
199 E3 **Astypalaia** *i.* Greece
121 J2 **Asubulak** Kazakh.
Asūbulaq Kazakh. *see* **Asubulak**
239 D6 **Asunción** *r.* Mex.
91 K3 **Asuncion** *i.* N. Mariana Is
253 F6 **Asunción** Para.
243 H6 **Asunción Mita** Guat.
192 A5 **Asuni** *Sardegna* Italy
104 C2 **Asuwa-gawa** *r.* Japan
138 G3 **Asvyeya** Belarus
138 G3 **Asvyeyskaye, Vozyera** *l.* Belarus
210 A4 **Aswa** *r.* Uganda
125 G2 **Aswad** Oman
203 G3 **Aswân** Egypt
124 A2 **Aswân** *governorate* Egypt
203 F3 **Asyûţ** Egypt
126 C6 **Asyûţ** *governorate* Egypt
177 J3 **Aszaló** Hungary
79 □2a **Ata** *i.* Tonga
250 E3 **Atabapo** *r.* Col./Venez.
121 G4 **Atabay** Kazakh.
199 G3 **Atabey** Turkey
258 C2 **Atacama** *admin. reg.* Chile
258 C2 **Atacama, Desierto de** *des.* Chile
252 C5 **Atacama, Salar de** *salt flat* Chile
250 B4 **Atacames** Ecuador
205 G4 **Atafaitafa, Djebel** *mt.* Alg.
81 □1 **Atafu** *atoll* Tokelau
81 □1 **Atafu** *i.* Tokelau
104 B3 **Atago-san** *hill* Japan
105 F3 **Atago-yama** *hill* Japan
128 A5 **Atairtîr el Dahami, Gebel** *mt.* Egypt
128 B1 **Atakent** Turkey
129 F3 **Atakişili** Azer.
205 G5 **Atakor** *mts* Alg.
207 F5 **Atakpamé** Togo
254 G4 **Atalaia** Brazil
184 B2 **Atalaia** *hill* Port.
250 D6 **Atalaia do Norte** Brazil
Atalándi Greece *see* **Atalanti**
198 C2 **Atalanti** Greece
242 □J7 **Atalaya** Panama
252 B2 **Atalaya** Peru
185 I3 **Atalaya Arabe** *hill* Spain
257 G3 **Ataléia** Brazil
105 F3 **Atami** Japan
Ataniya Turkey *see* **Adana**
177 J4 **Átány** Hungary
124 D5 **'Ataq** Yemen
128 A5 **'Ataqa, Gebel** *hill* Egypt
183 F3 **Ataquines** Spain
204 B5 **Atâr** Maur.
96 B3 **Ataran** *r.* Myanmar
Atas *i.* Cocos Is *see* **South Island**
240 G4 **Atascadero** *CA* U.S.A.
121 G2 **Atasu** Kazakh.
111 E4 **Atatan He** *r.* China
Atáviros *mt. Notio Aigaio* Greece *see* **Attavyros**
122 D1 **Atayab** Turkm.
128 A1 **Atayurt** Turkey
203 G5 **Atbara** Sudan
203 G5 **Atbara** *r.* Sudan
121 G2 **Atbasar** Kazakh.
121 H4 **At-Bashy** Kyrg.
236 E4 **Atchison** *KS* U.S.A.
234 D3 **Atco** *NJ* U.S.A.
183 I3 **Atea** Spain
206 E5 **Atebubu** Ghana
183 I3 **Ateca** Spain
182 C3 **Atei** Port.
182 C2 **A Teixeira** Spain
193 G3 **Ateleta** Italy
193 H4 **Atella** Italy
193 H4 **Atella** *r.* Italy
244 C3 **Atemajac de Brizuela** Mex.
105 E1 **Atema-yama** *mt.* Japan
252 C3 **Aten** Bol.
193 H4 **Atena Lucana** Italy
244 B3 **Atengo** *r.* Mex.
244 B3 **Atenguillo** *r.* Mex.
244 C4 **Atenquique** Mex.
Ateransk Kazakh. *see* **Atyrau**
193 F2 **Aterno** *r.* Italy
123 E3 **Āteshkhāneh, Kūh-e** *hill* Afgh.
193 G2 **Atessa** Italy
234 C3 **Atglen** *PA* U.S.A.
165 C4 **Ath** Belgium
222 H4 **Athabasca** *Alta* Can.
222 I3 **Athabasca** *r. Alta* Can.
223 I3 **Athabasca, Lake** *Alberta/Saskatchewan* Can.
117 F5 **Athagarh** *Orissa* India
232 B5 **Athalia** *OH* U.S.A.
147 E3 **Athboy** Rep. of Ireland
147 B4 **Athea** Rep. of Ireland
Athenae Greece *see* **Athina**
147 C3 **Athenry** Rep. of Ireland
227 J3 **Athens** *Ont.* Can.
Athens Greece *see* **Athina**
231 C5 **Athens** *AL* U.S.A.
231 D5 **Athens** *GA* U.S.A.
233 G3 **Athens** *NY* U.S.A.
232 B5 **Athens** *OH* U.S.A.
232 E4 **Athens** *PA* U.S.A.
231 C5 **Athens** *TN* U.S.A.
237 E5 **Athens** *TX* U.S.A.
169 F4 **Athenstedt** Ger.
150 C4 **Atherington** *Devon, England* U.K.
151 F2 **Atherstone** *Warwickshire, England* U.K.
85 F3 **Atherton** *Qld* Austr.
149 G4 **Atherton** *Greater Manchester, England* U.K.
211 C5 **Athi** *r.* Kenya
156 C3 **Athies** France
156 D3 **Athies-sous-Laon** France
198 C3 **Athina** Greece
Athínai Greece *see* **Athina**
211 C5 **Athi River** Kenya
159 F3 **Athis-de-l'Orne** France
156 C4 **Athis-Mons** France
147 C4 **Athlacca** Rep. of Ireland
147 C3 **Athleague** Rep. of Ireland
147 D3 **Athlone** Rep. of Ireland
114 B2 **Athni** *Karnataka* India
81 B6 **Athol** *South I.* N.Z.
233 G3 **Athol** *MA* U.S.A.
146 D5 **Atholl, Forest of** *reg. Scotland* U.K.
198 D1 **Athos** *mt.* Greece
Athos, Mount *admin. div.* Greece *see* **Agion Oros**
127 F4 **Ath Tharthār, Wādī** *r.* Iraq
128 C5 **Ath Thāyat** *mt.* Saudi Arabia
147 E4 **Athy** Rep. of Ireland
202 C6 **Ati** Chad
202 B4 **Ati, Jabal** *mts* Libya
80 F3 **Atiamuri** *North I.* N.Z.
256 D5 **Atibaia** Brazil
252 B4 **Atico** Peru
183 H3 **Atienza** Spain
222 H4 **Atikameg** *Alta* Can.
224 D2 **Atikameg** *r. Ont.* Can.
224 B3 **Atikokan** *Ont.* Can.
92 B3 **Atimonan** Phil.
193 F3 **Atina** Italy
114 C4 **Atirampattinam** *Tamil Nadu* India
243 H6 **Atitlán** Guat.
81 □2 **Atiu** *i.* Cook Is
Atjeh *admin. dist.* Indon. *see* **Aceh**
131 Q3 **Atka** Rus. Fed.
220 A4 **Atka** *AK* U.S.A.
220 A4 **Atka Island** *AK* U.S.A.
177 I4 **Atkár** Hungary
135 I6 **Atkarsk** Rus. Fed.
237 E5 **Atkins** *AR* U.S.A.
245 E4 **Atlacomulco** Mex.
215 F1 **Atlanta** S. Africa
231 C5 **Atlanta** *GA* U.S.A.
226 C5 **Atlanta** *IL* U.S.A.
227 E3 **Atlanta** *MI* U.S.A.
237 E5 **Atlanta** *TX* U.S.A.
126 D3 **Atlantı** Turkey
236 E3 **Atlantic** *IA* U.S.A.
233 □I2 **Atlantic** *ME* U.S.A.
231 E5 **Atlantic** *NC* U.S.A.
233 F5 **Atlantic City** *NJ* U.S.A.
234 D3 **Atlantic County** *county NJ* U.S.A.
235 D2 **Atlantic Highlands** *NJ* U.S.A.
263 H3 **Atlantic-Indian-Antarctic Basin** *sea feature* S. Atlantic Ocean
265 D8 **Atlantic-Indian Ridge** *sea feature* Southern Ocean
250 C2 **Atlántico** *dept* Col.
264 **Atlantic Ocean**
238 E3 **Atlantic Peak** *WY* U.S.A.
214 B5 **Atlantis** S. Africa
245 E3 **Atlapexco** Mex.
234 B2 **Atlas** *PA* U.S.A.
106 C3 **Atlas Bogd** *mt.* Mongolia
Atlas Méditerranéen *mts* Alg. *see* **Atlas Tellien**
204 D3 **Atlas Mountains** Africa
205 F2 **Atlas Saharien** *mts* Alg.
205 F2 **Atlas Tellien** *mts* Alg.
245 E4 **Atlatlahucan** Mex.
222 C3 **Atlin** *B.C.* Can.
128 B3 **'Atlit** Israel
245 E4 **Atlixco** Mex.
114 C3 **Atmakur** *Andhra Prad.* India
114 C3 **Atmakur** *Andhra Prad.* India
231 C6 **Atmore** *AL* U.S.A.
116 D5 **Atner** *Madh. Prad.* India
114 C2 **Atnur** *Karnataka* India
252 D5 **Atocha** Bol.
237 D5 **Atoka** *OK* U.S.A.
245 E3 **Atotonico El Grande** Mex.
244 C3 **Atotonilco el Alto** Mex.
96 D3 **Atouat** *mt.* Laos
184 A1 **Atouguia da Baleia** Port.
244 C3 **Atoyac** Mex.
245 F5 **Atoyac** *r. Oaxaca* Mex.
245 E4 **Atoyac** *r. Puebla* Mex.
245 F4 **Atoyac** *r. Veracruz* Mex.
244 D5 **Atoyac de Álvarez** Mex.
114 B2 **Atpadi** *Mahar.* India
220 C2 **Atqasuk** *AK* U.S.A.
117 G4 **Atrai** *r.* India
122 C2 **Atrak, Rūd-e** *r.* Iran/Turkm. *alt.* **Atrek,** *alt.* **Etrek**
142 E3 **Ätran** *r.* Sweden
116 D4 **Atranh** *Uttar Prad.* India
250 B2 **Atrato** *r.* Col.
245 G5 **Atravesada, Sierra** *mts* Mex.
122 C2 **Atrek** *r.* Iran/Turkm. *alt.* **Atrak, Rūd-e,** *alt.* **Etrek**
193 F2 **Atri** Italy
Atria Italy *see* **Adria**
193 G4 **Atripalda** Italy
Atropatene *country* Asia *see* **Azerbaijan**
129 C2 **Ats'ana** Georgia
234 D3 **Atsion** *NJ* U.S.A.
105 F3 **Atsugi** Japan
128 B4 **Aţ Ţafīlah** Jordan
124 C3 **Aţ Ţā'if** Saudi Arabia
177 H5 **Attala** Hungary
Attalea Turkey *see* **Antalya**
Attalia Turkey *see* **Antalya**
231 C5 **Attalla** *AL* U.S.A.
127 F4 **At Ta'mīm** *governorate* Iraq
202 D1 **At Tamīmī** Libya
148 B5 **Attanagh** Rep. of Ireland
97 D4 **Attapu** Laos
147 B2 **Attavalley** Rep. of Ireland
199 E3 **Attavyros** *mt. Notio Aigaio* Greece
224 D2 **Attawapiskat** *Ont.* Can.
224 D2 **Attawapiskat** *r. Ont.* Can.
203 H2 **Aţ Ţawīl** *mts* Saudi Arabia
124 C1 **At Taysīyah** *plat.* Saudi Arabia
128 B4 **Aţ Ţayyibah** Jordan
80 D4 **Attempt Hill** *hill South I.* N.Z.
169 C4 **Attendorn** Ger.
173 F3 **Attenkirchen** Ger.
215 G1 **Atteridgeville** S. Africa
179 E3 **Attersee** Austria
179 E3 **Attersee** *l.* Austria
165 E5 **Attert** Belgium
165 F5 **Attert** *r.* Lux.
147 E2 **Attica** *Northern Ireland* U.K.
230 C3 **Attica** *IN* U.S.A.
232 D3 **Attica** *NY* U.S.A.
232 B4 **Attica** *OH* U.S.A.
156 D3 **Attichy** France
193 E2 **Attigliano** Italy
160 D2 **Attignat** France
156 E3 **Attigny** France
198 C3 **Attiki** *admin. reg.* Greece
114 C4 **Attingal** *Kerala* India
233 H4 **Attleboro** *MA* U.S.A.
151 I2 **Attleborough** *Norfolk, England* U.K.
151 I2 **Attlebridge** *Norfolk, England* U.K.
179 E2 **Attnang** Austria
123 H3 **Attock City** Pak.
Attopeu Laos *see* **Attapu**
126 E5 **Aţ Ţubayq** *reg.* Saudi Arabia
266 G2 **Attu Island** *AK* U.S.A.
83 G2 **Attunga** *N.S.W.* Austr.
At Tūnisīyah *country* Africa *see* **Tunisia**
114 C4 **Attur** *Tamil Nadu* India
114 C4 **Attur** *Tamil Nadu* India
124 C5 **At Turbah** Yemen
124 D5 **At Turbah** Yemen
147 C3 **Attymon** Rep. of Ireland
125 E5 **Atūd** Yemen
260 D5 **Atuel** *r.* Arg.
162 C3 **Atur** France
143 F2 **Åtvidaberg** Sweden
117 G4 **Atwari** Bangl.
240 G3 **Atwater** *CA* U.S.A.
236 C4 **Atwood** *KS* U.S.A.
135 I5 **Atyashevo** Rus. Fed.
120 B3 **Atyrau** Kazakh.
Atyrau Oblast *admin. div.* Kazakh. *see* **Atyrauskaya Oblast'**
Atyraū Oblysy *admin. div.* Kazakh. *see* **Atyrauskaya Oblast'**
120 B3 **Atyrauskaya Oblast'** *admin. div.* Kazakh.
135 H5 **Atyur'yevo** Rus. Fed.
137 G2 **Atyusha** Ukr.
192 B5 **Atzara** *Sardegna* Italy
179 G2 **Atzenbrugg** Austria
171 C4 **Atzendorf** Ger.
178 A3 **Au** Austria
190 E1 **Au** Switz.
250 E5 **Auati-Paraná** *r.* Brazil
173 E2 **Aub** Ger.
169 E5 **Aubach** *r.* Ger.
161 D5 **Aubagne** France
161 C5 **Aubais** France
165 E5 **Aubange** Belgium
162 D3 **Aubazines** France
159 G3 **Aube** France
156 E4 **Aube** *dept Champagne-Ardenne* France
156 D4 **Aube** *r.* France
213 H3 **Aúbe** Moz.
165 E4 **Aubel** Belgium
161 C4 **Aubenas** France
156 E3 **Aubenton** France
156 B4 **Aubergenville** France
156 E3 **Aubérive** France
157 F5 **Auberive** *Champagne-Ardenne* France
162 C3 **Aubeterre-sur-Dronne** France
156 D4 **Aubetin** *r.* France
156 B3 **Aubevoye** France
163 C5 **Aubiet** France
161 D4 **Aubignan** France
159 G4 **Aubigné-Racan** France
161 D4 **Aubignosc** France
156 C2 **Aubigny-en-Artois** France
159 I4 **Aubigny-sur-Nère** France
163 E4 **Aubin** France
224 D4 **Aubinadong** *r. Ont.* Can.
190 B2 **Aubonne** Switz.
161 C5 **Aubord** France
157 F3 **Auboué** France
161 A4 **Aubrac** *mts* France
157 F3 **Aubreville** France
241 K4 **Aubrey Cliffs** *mts AZ* U.S.A.
220 F3 **Aubry Lake** *N.W.T.* Can.
85 G5 **Auburn** *r. Qld* Austr.
227 G4 **Auburn** *Ont.* Can.
231 C5 **Auburn** *AL* U.S.A.
240 G2 **Auburn** *CA* U.S.A.
236 F4 **Auburn** *IL* U.S.A.
230 C3 **Auburn** *IN* U.S.A.
233 H3 **Auburn** *MA* U.S.A.
233 □H2 **Auburn** *ME* U.S.A.
227 E4 **Auburn** *MI* U.S.A.
236 E3 **Auburn** *NE* U.S.A.
232 E3 **Auburn** *NY* U.S.A.
234 B2 **Auburn** *PA* U.S.A.
238 B2 **Auburn** *WA* U.S.A.
234 B1 **Auburn Center** *PA* U.S.A.
226 B3 **Auburndale** *WI* U.S.A.
85 G5 **Auburn Range** *hills Qld* Austr.
162 E3 **Aubusson** France
156 D2 **Auby** France
260 C5 **Auca Mahuida, Sierra de** *mt.* Arg.
163 D5 **Aucamville** France
138 D3 **Auce** Latvia
163 C5 **Auch** France
146 E5 **Auchallater** *Aberdeenshire, Scotland* U.K.
148 D2 **Auchbraad** *Argyll and Bute, Scotland* U.K.
156 C2 **Auchel** France
146 F5 **Auchenblae** *Aberdeenshire, Scotland* U.K.
146 C6 **Auchenbreck** *Argyll and Bute, Scotland* U.K.
146 E7 **Auchencairn** *Dumfries and Galloway, Scotland* U.K.
146 F6 **Auchencrow** *Scottish Borders, Scotland* U.K.
207 G5 **Auchi** Nigeria
146 D6 **Auchinleck** *East Ayrshire, Scotland* U.K.
146 F5 **Auchmull** *Angus, Scotland* U.K.
146 F4 **Auchnagatt** *Aberdeenshire, Scotland* U.K.
146 E4 **Aucholzie** *Aberdeenshire, Scotland* U.K.
146 F5 **Auchronie** *Angus, Scotland* U.K.
146 E5 **Auchterarder** *Perth and Kinross, Scotland* U.K.
146 E5 **Auchtermuchty** *Fife, Scotland* U.K.
156 C2 **Auchy-au-Bois** France
80 E2 **Auckland** *North I.* N.Z.
80 E2 **Auckland** *admin. reg. North I.* N.Z.
77 G6 **Auckland Islands** N.Z.

Aucun to Bagni di Rabbi
280

163 B6 Aucun France
161 A5 Aude dept Languedoc-Roussillon France
161 B5 Aude r. France
224 C3 Auden Ont. Can.
Audenarde Belgium see Oudenaarde
163 A4 Audenge France
158 E2 Auderville France
233 □H2 Audet Que. Can.
160 D1 Audeux France
158 B3 Audierne France
160 E1 Audincourt France
150 E2 Audlem Cheshire, England U.K.
149 G4 Audley Staffordshire, England U.K.
163 B5 Audon France
210 D3 Audo Range mts Eth.
156 B2 Audresselles France
138 E2 Audru Estonia
156 C2 Audruicq France
236 E3 Audubon IA U.S.A.
234 C3 Audubon NJ U.S.A.
157 F3 Audun-le-Roman France
171 D5 Aue Ger.
168 C2 Aue r. Ger.
169 E3 Aue r. Ger.
169 F3 Aue r. Ger.
173 H3 Auerbach Bayern Ger.
171 D5 Auerbach Sachsen Ger.
171 D5 Auerbach Sachsen Ger.
173 F2 Auerbach in der Oberpfalz Ger.
171 D5 Auersberg mt. Ger.
179 H2 Auersthal Austria
171 D5 Auerswalde Ger.
156 B3 Auffay France
173 G3 Aufhausen Ger.
85 F5 Augathella Qld Austr.
147 D2 Augher Northern Ireland U.K.
147 E2 Aughnacloy Northern Ireland U.K.
147 C3 Aughrim Galway Rep. of Ireland
147 E4 Aughrim Wicklow Rep. of Ireland
149 G4 Aughton Lancashire, England U.K.
149 H4 Aughton South Yorkshire, England U.K.
162 C3 Augignac France
214 C3 Augrabies S. Africa
214 C3 Augrabies Falls S. Africa
227 F3 Au Gres MI U.S.A.
173 E3 Augsburg Ger.
178 B2 Augsburg airport Ger.
138 E3 Augšlīgatne Latvia
138 F3 Augšzemes augstiene hills Latvia
87 B7 Augusta W.A. Austr.
195 E5 Augusta Sicilia Italy
237 F5 Augusta AR U.S.A.
231 D5 Augusta GA U.S.A.
226 B5 Augusta IL U.S.A.
237 D4 Augusta KS U.S.A.
232 A5 Augusta KY U.S.A.
233 □I2 Augusta ME U.S.A.
238 D2 Augusta MT U.S.A.
234 D1 Augusta NJ U.S.A.
226 B3 Augusta WI U.S.A.
232 D5 Augusta WV U.S.A.
195 E5 Augusta, Golfo di b. Sicilia Italy
Augusta Auscorum France see Auch
Augusta Taurinorum Italy see Torino
Augusta Treverorum Ger. see Trier
Augusta Vindelicorum Ger. see Augsburg
168 E1 Augustenborg Denmark
246 D5 Augustin Cadazzi Col.
Augusto Cardosa Moz. see Metangula
257 E3 Augusto de Lima Brazil
Augustodunum France see Autun
254 F3 Augusto Severo Brazil
175 K2 Augustów Pol.
175 L3 Augustowo Pol.
87 C5 Augustus, Mount W.A. Austr.
171 E5 Augustusburg Ger.
86 E2 Augustus Island W.A. Austr.
169 E3 Auhagen Ger.
173 F3 Au in der Hallertau Ger.
157 E4 Aujon r. France
222 C3 Auke Bay AK U.S.A.
78 □6 Auki Malaita Solomon Is
168 E1 Aukrug Ger.
138 D4 Aukštelkai Lith.
140 L2 Auktsjaur Sweden
86 D4 Auld, Lake salt flat W.A. Austr.
146 E4 Auldearn Highland, Scotland U.K.
169 F4 Auleben Ger.
190 E4 Aulella r. Italy
172 D4 Aulendorf Ger.
193 H4 Auletta Italy
Auliye Ata Zhambylskaya Oblast' Kazakh. see Taraz
190 E4 Aulla Italy
192 B3 Aullène Corse France
160 B3 Aulnat France
160 B3 Aulnat airport France
162 B2 Aulnay France
156 C4 Aulnay-sous-Bois France
158 B3 Aulne r. France
157 G4 Aulnois sur-Seille France
156 D2 Aulnoye-Aymeries France
Aulon Albania see Vlorë
163 C5 Aulon France
170 C3 Aulosen Ger.
156 B2 Ault France
146 C4 Aultbea Highland, Scotland U.K.
146 D4 Aultguish Inn Highland, Scotland U.K.
163 D6 Aulus-les-Bains France
171 C5 Auma Ger.
156 B3 Aumale France
160 A2 Aumance r. France
157 F3 Aumetz France
120 E4 Auminzatau, Gory hills Uzbek.
160 D2 Aumont France
161 B4 Aumont-Aubrac France
168 F2 Aumühle Ger.
207 G4 Auna Nigeria
160 B1 Aunay-en-Bazois France
159 F2 Aunay-sur-Odon France
156 B4 Auneau France
156 C3 Auneuil France
142 D3 Auning Denmark
183 H4 Auñón Spain
191 I2 Aupa r. Italy
225 G1 Aupaluk Que. Can.
161 E5 Aups France
141 M3 Aura Fin.
173 E2 Aurach Ger.
178 D3 Aurach bei Kitzbühel Austria
114 C2 Aurad Karnataka India
163 D5 Auradé France
169 E5 Aura im Sinngrund Ger.
116 D4 Auraiya Uttar Prad. India
138 D1 Aurajoki r. Fin.
117 F4 Aurangabad Bihar India
114 B2 Aurangabad Mahar. India
158 D4 Auray France
159 E2 Aure r. France
140 J3 Aure Norway
161 C3 Aurec-sur-Loire France
163 C5 Aureilhan France
161 C5 Aureille France
161 D4 Aurel Provence-Alpes-Côte-d'Azur France
161 D4 Aurel Rhône-Alpes France
244 A1 Aurelio Benassini, Presa resr Mex.
163 B5 Aurensan France
168 C2 Aurich Ger.
256 B4 Auriflama Brazil
163 C5 Aurignac France
Aurigny i. Channel Is see Alderney
256 B2 Aurilândia Brazil
162 E4 Aurillac France
186 C2 Aurín r. Spain
191 G2 Aurino r. Italy
161 D5 Auriol France
191 I3 Aurisina Italy
80 E3 Auroa North I. N.Z.
179 E2 Aurolzmünster Austria
161 E4 Auron France
160 A1 Auron r. France
191 H2 Auronzo di Cadore Italy
92 B5 Aurora Phil.
214 B5 Aurora S. Africa
238 F4 Aurora CO U.S.A.
226 C5 Aurora IL U.S.A.
233 □I2 Aurora ME U.S.A.
226 A2 Aurora MN U.S.A.
237 E4 Aurora MO U.S.A.
236 D3 Aurora NE U.S.A.
232 C4 Aurora OH U.S.A.
241 L2 Aurora UT U.S.A.
Aurora Island Vanuatu see Maéwo
163 B4 Auros France
161 B4 Auroux France
85 E2 Aurukun Qld Austr.
193 F3 Aurunci, Monti mts Italy
114 C2 Ausa Mahar. India
191 I3 Ausa r. Italy
227 F3 Au Sable MI U.S.A.
227 F3 Au Sable r. MI U.S.A.
233 G2 Ausable r. NY U.S.A.
233 G2 Ausable Forks NY U.S.A.
191 I3 Ausa-Corno Italy
Auschwitz Pol. see Oświęcim
Ausculum Italy see Ascoli Satriano
Ausculum Apulum Italy see Ascoli Satriano
183 H2 Ausejo Spain
193 F3 Ausente r. Italy
177 L4 Auşeu Romania
146 F2 Auskerry i. Scotland U.K.
171 C3 Ausleben Ger.
193 F3 Ausoni, Monti mts Italy
193 F3 Ausonia Italy
163 D5 Ausseing Tour hill France
163 E5 Aussillon France
161 E3 Aussois France
163 D5 Aussonne France
163 B5 Aussurucq France
142 C2 Aust-Agder county Norway
140 □C2 Austari-Jökulsá r. Iceland
140 □ Austfonna ice cap Svalbard
226 A4 Austin MN U.S.A.
240 I2 Austin NV U.S.A.
237 D6 Austin TX U.S.A.
87 C5 Austin, Lake salt flat W.A. Austr.
232 C4 Austintown OH U.S.A.
192 B4 Austis Sardegna Italy
84 D4 Austral Downs N.T. Austr.
79 □3 Australes, Îles is Fr. Polynesia
76 C4 Australia country Oceania
263 J2 Australian Antarctic Territory Antarctica
83 G3 Australian Capital Territory admin. div. Austr.
87 B7 Australind W.A. Austr.
179 E3 Austria country Europe
138 D3 Austrumkursas augstiene hills Latvia
140 □D2 Austurland constituency Iceland
140 K1 Austvågøy i. Norway
251 G5 Autazes Brazil
163 D5 Auterive France
Autesiodorum France see Auxerre
160 D1 Autet France
156 B2 Authie r. France
227 H1 Authier Que. Can.
159 F4 Authion r. France
159 G4 Authon Centre France
161 E4 Authon Provence-Alpes-Côte-d'Azur France
159 G3 Authon-du-Perche France
244 B4 Autlán Mex.
183 H2 Autol Spain
161 D3 Autrans France
157 F4 Autreville France
160 D1 Autrey-lès-Gray France
157 E3 Autry France
160 C2 Autun France
156 E3 Auve France
165 D4 Auvelais Belgium
160 B3 Auvergne admin. reg. France
161 A4 Auvergne reg. France
160 A3 Auvergne, Monts d' mts France
159 F4 Auvers-le-Hamon France
156 C3 Auvers-sur-Oise France
162 C3 Auvézère r. France
163 C4 Auvignon r. France
163 C4 Auvillar France
156 E3 Auvillers-les-Forges France
156 D5 Auxerre France
156 C2 Auxi-le-Château France
160 D1 Auxonne France
160 C2 Auxy France
251 F3 Auyan Tepuí plat. Venez.
160 A2 Auzances France
163 D6 Auzat France
161 B3 Auzat-sur-Allier France
162 E3 Auze r. France
163 E4 Auzits France
161 B3 Auzon France
163 C4 Auzoue r. France
121 J2 Auzzov Kazakh.
96 A2 Ava Myanmar
237 E4 Ava MO U.S.A.
233 F3 Ava NY U.S.A.
256 C5 Avaí Brazil
162 C2 Availles-Limouzine France
160 B1 Avallon France
159 F3 Avaloirs, Mont des hill France
240 H5 Avalon CA U.S.A.
234 D3 Avalon NJ U.S.A.
225 K4 Avalon Peninsula Nfld. Can.
261 H2 Avalos r. Arg.
122 A2 Avān Iran
114 C4 Avanashi Tamil Nadu India
182 B4 Avanca Port.
163 C4 Avance r. France
161 E4 Avançon France
251 G3 Avanganna mt. Guyana
114 D2 Avanigadda Andhra Prad. India
126 D3 Avanos Turkey
156 E4 Avant-lès-Ramerupt France
Avarau atoll Cook Is see Palmerston
256 C5 Avaré Brazil
Avaricum France see Bourges
127 G3 Āvārsin Iran
129 E2 Avarskoye Koysu r. Rus. Fed.
81 □3 Avarua Rarotonga Cook Is
140 L2 Avaträsk Sweden
140 L2 Avaviken Sweden
232 B6 Avawam KY U.S.A.
Avdeyevka Ukr. see Avdiyivka
198 D1 Avdira Anatoliki Makedonia kai Thraki Greece
137 I3 Avdiyivka Ukr.
182 B3 Ave r. Port.
151 F3 Avebury Wiltshire, England U.K.
182 D2 A Veiga Galicia Spain
184 B1 Aveiras de Cima Port.
182 B4 Aveiro Port.
182 B4 Aveiro admin. dist. Port.
182 B4 Aveiro, Ria de est. Port.
182 B5 Avelar Port.
182 B3 Aveleda Braga Port.
182 D3 Aveleda Bragança Port.
151 H3 Aveley Thurrock, England U.K.
165 C4 Avelgem Belgium
261 H4 Avellaneda Buenos Aires Arg.
258 F3 Avellaneda Santa Fé Arg.
193 G4 Avellino Italy
193 H4 Avellino prov. Campania Italy
158 C4 Aven r. France
240 G3 Avenal CA U.S.A.
156 E3 Avenay-Val-d'Or France
190 C2 Avenches Switz.
161 B5 Avène France
164 D2 Avenhorn Neth.
182 B1 Avenida do Marqués de Figueroa Spain
Avenio France see Avignon
Aventicum Switz. see Avenches
160 B2 Avermes France
146 D4 Averon r. Scotland U.K.
140 I3 Averøya i. Norway
190 E2 Avers Switz.
193 G4 Aversa Italy
247 G4 Aves i. West Indies
Aves is West Indies see Las Aves, Islas
156 C2 Avesnes-le-Comte France
156 D2 Avesnes-sur-Helpe France
143 G1 Avesta Sweden
190 E4 Aveto r. Italy
195 G2 Avetrano Italy
161 A4 Aveyron dept Midi-Pyrénées France
163 D4 Aveyron r. France
193 F2 Avezzano Italy
186 E2 Avia Spain
182 B2 Avia r. Spain
191 H2 Aviano Italy
258 E2 Aviá Terai Arg.
146 E4 Aviemore Highland, Scotland U.K.
81 C6 Aviemore, Lake South I. N.Z.
190 C3 Avigliana Italy
193 H4 Avigliano Italy
193 E2 Avigliano Umbro Italy
161 C5 Avignon France
163 D5 Avignonet-Lauragais France
183 F4 Ávila Spain
183 F4 Ávila prov. Castilla y León Spain
183 E4 Ávila, Sierra de mts Spain
182 E1 Avilés Spain
160 E1 Avilley France
137 J4 Avilo-Uspenka Rus. Fed.
182 B1 Aviño Spain
182 B3 Avintes Port.
186 E3 Avinyó Spain
191 F3 Avio Italy
156 C2 Avion France
182 B2 Avión mt. Spain
157 F3 Avioth France
184 C1 Avis Port.
191 G2 Avisio r. Italy
156 E4 Avize France
128 A1 Avlama Dağı mt. Turkey
198 C2 Avlida Greece
Avlona Albania see Vlorë
142 C3 Avlum Denmark
134 I3 Avnyugskiy Rus. Fed.
83 F5 Avoca Tas. Austr.
83 E4 Avoca Vic. Austr.
83 E3 Avoca r. Vic. Austr.
147 E4 Avoca Rep. of Ireland
215 H1 Avoca S. Africa
236 E3 Avoca IA U.S.A.
232 E3 Avoca NY U.S.A.
146 D4 Avoch Highland, Scotland U.K.
159 G4 Avoine France
195 E6 Avola Sicilia Italy
87 C6 Avon r. W.A. Austr.
156 C4 Avon France
150 D4 Avon r. Devon, England U.K.
150 E3 Avon r. England U.K.
151 E2 Avon r. England U.K.
151 F4 Avon r. England U.K.
226 B5 Avon IL U.S.A.
232 E3 Avon NY U.S.A.
234 B2 Avon PA U.S.A.
147 E4 Avonbeg r. Rep. of Ireland
149 F2 Avonbridge Falkirk, Scotland U.K.
241 K5 Avondale AZ U.S.A.
234 C3 Avondale PA U.S.A.
235 G1 Avondale RI U.S.A.
84 D4 Avon Downs N.T. Austr.
85 F4 Avon Downs Qld Austr.
232 B4 Avon Lake OH U.S.A.
147 E4 Avonmore r. Rep. of Ireland
150 E3 Avonmouth Bristol, England U.K.
231 D7 Avon Park FL U.S.A.
214 D5 Avontuur S. Africa
160 A1 Avord France
160 E2 Avoriaz France
138 E3 Avoti Latvia
160 E1 Avoudrey France
197 H1 Avrămeni Romania
197 E2 Avram Iancu Romania
158 E3 Avranches France
156 C3 Avre r. France
159 H3 Avre r. France
157 G4 Avricourt France
197 G3 Avrig Romania
157 F3 Avril France
162 A2 Avrillé France
159 F4 Avrillé France
129 B3 Avsek Dağı mt. Turkey
Avveel Fin. see Ivalo
Avvil Fin. see Ivalo
128 B3 A'waj r. Syria
104 A4 Awaji-shima i. Japan
80 F3 Awakeri North I. N.Z.
80 E3 Awakino North I. N.Z.
125 E2 Awālī Bahrain
165 E4 Awans Belgium
80 D1 Awanui North I. N.Z.
210 E2 Āwarē Eth.
81 B7 Awarua South I. N.Z.
210 C3 Āwasa Eth.
210 D2 Āwash Eth.
210 D2 Āwash r. Eth.
110 C3 Awat Xinjiang China
210 C3 Āwatā Shet' r. Eth.
81 E4 Awatere r. South I. N.Z.
202 B3 Awbārī Libya
147 C4 Awbeg r. Rep. of Ireland
146 C5 Awe, Loch l. Scotland U.K.
208 E2 Aweil Sudan
207 G5 Awgu Nigeria
207 G5 Awka Nigeria
204 B4 Awlitis watercourse Western Sahara
93 B3 Awo r. Indon.
150 E3 Awre Gloucestershire, England U.K.
93 C2 Awu vol. Indon.
178 C3 Axams Austria
163 E6 Axat France
150 D4 Axe r. Devon/Dorset, England U.K.
150 E3 Axe r. North Somerset/Somerset, England U.K.
83 F4 Axedale Vic. Austr.
165 C3 Axel Neth.
221 I2 Axel Heiberg Island Nunavut Can.
197 G2 Axente Sever Romania
206 E5 Axim Ghana
198 C1 Axios r. Greece
163 D6 Ax-les-Thermes France
150 E4 Axminster Devon, England U.K.
245 E4 Axochiapan Mex.
183 H1 Axpe-Busturia Spain
168 D2 Axstedt Ger.
Axum Eth. see Āksum
156 E3 Ay France
104 B3 Ayabe Japan
204 D2 Ayachi, Jbel mt. Morocco
261 H5 Ayacucho Arg.
252 B3 Ayacucho Peru
252 B3 Ayacucho dept Peru
121 J3 Ayagoz Kazakh.
Ayaguz Kazakh. see Ayagoz
120 F4 Ayakagytma, Vpadina depr. Uzbek.
120 F4 Ayakkuduk Uzbek.
Ayaköz Kazakh. see Ayagoz
206 E5 Ayamé Côte d'Ivoire
184 C3 Ayamonte Spain
131 O4 Ayan Rus. Fed.
126 D2 Ayancık Turkey
101 C5 Ayang N. Korea
207 G5 Ayangba Nigeria
250 C3 Ayapel, Serranía de mts Col.
126 D2 Ayaş Turkey
105 F3 Ayase Japan
252 C3 Ayaviri Peru
210 C1 Ayayei Eth.
123 G2 Āybak Afgh.
149 H3 Aycliffe Durham, England U.K.
121 G1 Aydabul Kazakh.
137 J2 Aydar Rus. Fed.
137 J3 Aydar r. Ukr.
121 F4 Aydarkul', Ozero l. Uzbek.
120 F3 Aydarly Kazakh.
160 A3 Aydat France
125 F4 'Aydim, Wādī r. Oman
199 E3 Aydın Turkey
199 F3 Aydın prov. Turkey
128 A1 Aydıncık Turkey
199 E2 Aydın Dağları mts Turkey
129 C4 Aydınlar Turkey
129 B3 Aydıntepe Turkey
121 G3 Ayeat, Gora hill Kazakh.
183 H2 Ayedo mt. Spain
210 D2 Āyelu Terara vol. Eth.
162 D3 Ayen France
233 H3 Ayer MA U.S.A.
186 C2 Ayerbe Spain
Ayers Rock hill N.T. Austr. see Uluru
Ayeyarwady r. Myanmar see Irrawaddy
110 D1 Aygulakskiy Khrebet mts Rus. Fed.
Ayiá Greece see Agia
Ayiásos Voreio Aigaio Greece see Agiasos
173 F4 Aying Ger.
Áyion Óros admin. div. Greece see Agion Oros
Áyios Dhimítrios Attiki Greece see Agios Dimitrios
Áyios Evstrátios i. Greece see Agios Efstratios
Áyios Nikólaos Kriti Greece see Agios Nikolaos
210 C1 Āykel Eth.
131 M3 Aykhal Rus. Fed.
134 J3 Aykino Rus. Fed.
81 D5 Aylesbury South I. N.Z.
151 G3 Aylesbury Buckinghamshire, England U.K.
151 H3 Aylesford Kent, England U.K.
151 I3 Aylesham Kent, England U.K.
232 E6 Aylett VA U.S.A.
183 G3 Ayllón Spain
227 G4 Aylmer Ont. Can.
227 J3 Aylmer Que. Can.
223 I1 Aylmer Lake N.W.T. Can.
151 I2 Aylsham Norfolk, England U.K.
120 E2 Aymagambetov Kazakh.
190 C3 Aymavilles Italy
252 B3 Ayna Peru
185 H2 Ayna Spain
121 I3 Aynabulak Kazakh.
163 D4 Aynac France
125 D5 'Ayn Ba Ma'bad Yemen
123 G2 Ayní Tajik.
126 E3 'Ayn 'Īsá Syria
244 C3 Ayo el Chico Mex.
131 R3 Ayon, Ostrov i. Rus. Fed.
182 D2 Ayoo de Vidriales Spain
245 F5 Ayoquezco Mex.
187 B5 Ayora Spain
207 F3 Ayorou Niger
207 I6 Ayos Cameroon
206 C2 'Ayoûn el 'Atroûs Maur.
85 F3 Ayr Qld Austr.
227 G4 Ayr Ont. Can.
146 D6 Ayr South Ayrshire, Scotland U.K.
146 D6 Ayr r. Scotland U.K.
150 D1 Ayr, Point of Wales U.K.
128 C1 Ayran Turkey
126 D3 Ayrancı Turkey
199 E2 Ayrancılar Turkey
129 E3 Äyriçay r. Azer.
159 G5 Ayron France
129 D3 Ayrum Armenia
149 H3 Aysgarth North Yorkshire, England U.K.
210 D2 Āysha Eth.
173 E3 Aystetten Ger.
120 E3 Ayteke Bi Kazakh.
197 H4 Aytos Bulg.
197 H4 Aytoska Reka r. Bulg.
162 A2 Aytré France
93 D2 Ayu, Kepulauan atoll Irian Jaya Indon.
183 H2 Ayuda r. Spain
184 D1 Ayuela r. Spain
125 F4 Ayun Oman
Ayuthia Thai. see Ayutthaya
137 K4 Ayutinskiy Rus. Fed.
245 E5 Ayutla Mex.
97 C4 Ayutthaya Thai.
199 E2 Ayvacık Turkey
126 E3 Ayvalı Turkey
199 E2 Ayvalık Turkey
199 G3 Ayvalıpınar Turkey
165 E4 Aywaille Belgium
125 E4 Aywat al Manāhil, Wādī r. Yemen
125 E4 Aywat aş Şay'ar, Wādī r. Yemen
242 □I6 Azacualpa Hond.
183 I2 Azagra Spain
186 C3 Azaila Spain
Azak Rus. Fed. see Azov
184 B1 Azambuja Port.
184 C2 Azambuja r. Port.
117 E4 Azamgarh Uttar Prad. India
252 C3 Azangaro Peru
196 E3 Azanja Srbija Yugo.
157 F3 Azannes-et-Soumazannes France
186 D3 Azanúy Spain
206 E2 Azaouâd reg. Mali
207 F2 Azaouagh, Vallée de watercourse Mali/Niger
252 C4 Azapa Chile
258 G3 Azara Arg.
Azaran Iran see Hashtrud
Azärbayjan country Asia see Azerbaijan
122 A2 Āžarbāyjān-e Gharbī prov. Iran
122 A2 Āžarbāyjān-e Sharqī prov. Iran
207 H4 Azare Nigeria
184 C2 Azaruja Port.
138 G5 Azarychy Belarus
129 D3 Azatamut Armenia
139 K2 Azatskoye, Ozero l. Rus. Fed.
129 C3 Azavret'i Georgia
159 H5 Azay-le-Ferron France
159 G4 Azay-le-Rideau France
128 C1 A'zāz Syria
Azbine mts Niger see L'Aïr, Massif de
126 D2 Azdavay Turkey
159 F4 Azé France
204 C2 Azemmour Morocco
162 D2 Azerables France
129 F3 Azerbaijan country Asia
Azerbaydzhanskaya S.S.R. country Asia see Azerbaijan
160 C3 Azergues r. France
184 C2 Azevel r. Port.
210 C1 Āzezo Eth.
129 D3 Azhdahak Lerr mt. Armenia
204 D2 Azilal Morocco
227 G2 Azilda Ont. Can.
161 A5 Azille France
156 C2 Azincourt France
184 B1 Azinhaga Port.
184 C3 Azinhal Port.
182 D3 Azinhoso Port.
Azizbekov Armenia see Vayk'
Aziziye Turkey see Pınarbaşı
186 A1 Azkoitia Spain
135 K5 Aznakayevo Rus. Fed.
184 D3 Aznalcázar Spain
184 D3 Aznalcóllar Spain
250 B5 Azogues Ecuador
184 A2 Azóia Port.
216 □1 Azores aut. reg. N. Atlantic Ocean
264 H3 Azores-Biscay Rise sea feature N. Atlantic Ocean
Azotus Israel see Ashdod
135 G7 Azov Rus. Fed.
137 I4 Azov, Sea of Rus. Fed./Ukr.
Azovs'ke More sea Rus. Fed./Ukr. see Azov, Sea of
Azovskoye More sea Rus. Fed./Ukr. see Azov, Sea of
245 E5 Azoyú Mex.
186 A1 Azpeitia Spain
203 G6 Azraq, Bahr el r. Sudan alt. Ābay Wenz (Ethiopia), conv. Blue Nile
204 D2 Azrou Morocco
239 E4 Aztec NM U.S.A.
246 E3 Azua Dom. Rep.
184 E2 Azuaga Spain
186 C3 Azuara Spain
250 B5 Azuay prov. Ecuador
258 C2 Azúcar r. Chile
185 F2 Azuel Spain
183 H2 Azuelo Spain
185 G1 Azuer r. Spain
242 □J8 Azuero, Península de pen. Panama
258 C2 Azufre, Cerro del mt. Chile
261 H5 Azul Arg.
261 H5 Azul r. Arg.
260 B4 Azul vol. Chile
243 H5 Azul r. Mex.
250 □ Azul, Cerro vol. Islas Galápagos Ecuador
252 B2 Azul, Cordillera mts Peru
253 G3 Azul, Serra hills Brazil
102 J5 Azuma-san vol. Japan
105 E2 Azumaya-san mt. Japan
183 G4 Azuqueca de Henares Spain
163 A5 Azur France
182 B3 Azurara Port.
252 D5 Azurduy Bol.
183 E5 Azután Spain
160 B2 Azy-le-Vif France
'Azza Gaza see Gaza
205 G1 Azzaba Alg.
128 C3 Az Zabadānī Syria
125 G3 Az Ẓāhirah admin. reg. Oman
125 E2 Az Ẓahrān Saudi Arabia
125 E2 Az Zallāq Bahrain
191 H3 Azzano Decimo Italy
Az Zaqāzīq Egypt see Zagazig
128 C1 Az Zarbah Syria
128 C3 Az Zarqā' Jordan
202 B1 Az Zāwīyah Libya
124 C5 Az Zaydīyah Yemen
204 B5 Azzeffâl hills Maur./W. Sahara
124 D2 Az Zilfī Saudi Arabia
190 F3 Azzone Italy
127 G5 Az Zubayr Iraq
124 C5 Az Zuhrah Yemen
124 C5 Az Zuqur i. Yemen

B

79 □1a Ba Viti Levu Fiji
78 □5 Baâba i. New Caledonia
95 G2 Baai r. Indon.
128 C2 Ba'albek Lebanon
171 C4 Baalberge Ger.
164 F2 Baalder Neth.
128 B4 Ba'al Ḥazor mt. West Bank
157 F3 Baâlon France
190 D1 Baar Switz.
210 D4 Baardheere Somalia
173 F3 Baar-Ebenhausen Ger.
165 D3 Baarle-Hertog Belgium
165 D3 Baarle-Nassau Neth.
164 E2 Baarn Neth.
116 D4 Bab Uttar Prad. India
197 F4 Baba mt. Bulg.
179 F1 Baba hill Czech Rep.
123 G3 Bābā, Kūh-e mts Afgh.
206 B2 Bababé Maur.
254 D3 Babaçulândia Brazil
197 I3 Babadag Romania
199 F3 Babadağ Turkey
199 F3 Baba Dağ mt. Turkey
197 I3 Babadagului, Podişul plat. Romania
122 E2 Babadaykhan Akhal'skaya Oblast' Turkm.
122 E2 Babadaykhan Akhal'skaya Oblast' Turkm.
199 E1 Babaeski Turkey
199 G2 Babageçidin Tepesi mt. Turkey
250 B5 Babahoyo Ecuador
116 E3 Babai r. Nepal
106 E3 Babai Gaxun Nei Mongol China
127 G3 Bābā Jān Iran
129 D4 Babāk Azer.
92 C5 Babak Phil.
203 I6 Bāb al Mandab str. Africa/Asia
124 C5 Bāb al Mandab, Ra's c. Yemen
93 A3 Babana Sulawesi Selatan Indon.
215 H3 Babanango S. Africa
215 G3 Babangiboni mt. S. Africa
207 H5 Babanki Cameroon
208 E2 Babanusa Sudan
Babao Qinghai China see Qilian
108 C4 Babao Yunnan China
95 F4 Babat Jawa Timur Indon.
211 B6 Babati Tanz.
139 J2 Babayevo Rus. Fed.
137 H3 Babaykivka Ukr.
129 E2 Babayurt Rus. Fed.
150 D4 Babbacombe Bay England U.K.
87 B5 Babbage Island W.A. Austr.
164 F3 Babberich Neth.
92 □ Babeldaob i. Palau
215 G1 Babelegi S. Africa
Babelthuap i. Palau see Babeldaob
173 E3 Babenhausen Bayern Ger.
172 C2 Babenhausen Hessen Ger.
197 G3 Băbeni Romania
116 E4 Baberu Uttar Prad. India
175 H6 Babia Góra mt. Pol.
175 I1 Babiak Warmińsko-Mazurskie Pol.
174 G3 Babiak Wielkopolskie Pol.
108 B4 Babian Jiang r. Yunnan China
176 G2 Babice Czech Rep.
175 H5 Babice Pol.
127 G4 Bābil governorate Iraq
183 E4 Babilafuente Spain
174 D3 Babimost Pol.
85 F3 Babinda Qld Austr.
220 F4 Babine r. B.C. Can.
222 E4 Babine r. B.C. Can.
222 E4 Babine Range mts B.C. Can.
176 G5 Babócsa Hungary
122 C2 Bābol Iran
177 G4 Bábolna Hungary
122 C2 Bābol Sar Iran
214 B5 Baboon Point S. Africa
241 L6 Baboquivari Peak AZ U.S.A.
174 F5 Baborów Pol.
175 I3 Baboszewo Pol.
208 B3 Baboua C.A.R.
138 G5 Babruysk Belarus
138 D4 Babtai Lith.
Babu Guangxi China see Hexian
197 E5 Babuna Planina mts Macedonia
98 I1 Babushkin Rus. Fed.
197 F4 Babušnica Srbija Yugo.
92 A4 Babuyan Phil.
92 B2 Babuyan Channel Phil.
92 B2 Babuyan Islands Phil.
149 I4 Babworth Nottinghamshire, England U.K.
127 G4 Babylon tourist site Iraq
235 E2 Babylon NY U.S.A.
139 J4 Babynino Rus. Fed.
196 D3 Bač Vojvodina, Srbija Yugo.
210 E3 Bacaadweyn Somalia
250 D5 Bacaba r. Brazil
242 C3 Bacabáchi Mex.
254 D3 Bacabal Brazil
251 I5 Bacajá r. Brazil
126 C2 Bacakliyayla Tepesi mt. Turkey
243 H5 Bacalar Mex.
93 C3 Bacan i. Maluku Indon.
163 C6 Bacanère, Pic de mt. France
185 H3 Bacares Spain
92 B2 Bacarra Phil.
197 H2 Bacău Romania
157 G4 Baccarat France
191 H3 Bacchiglione r. Italy
190 D2 Baceno Italy
96 D2 Băc Giang Vietnam
173 G2 Bach an der Donau Ger.
169 C5 Bacharach Ger.
138 G4 Bacheykava Belarus
173 E3 Bachhagel Ger.
239 F6 Bachiniva Mex.
175 K6 Bachórz Pol.
110 B4 Bachu Xinjiang China
175 K3 Baciki Bliższe Pol.
85 E3 Back r. Qld Austr.
223 M1 Back r. N.W.T./Nunavut Can.
146 F2 Backaland Orkney, Scotland U.K.
196 D3 Bačka Palanka Vojvodina, Srbija Yugo.
196 D3 Bačka Topola Vojvodina, Srbija Yugo.
232 D5 Backbone Mountain MD U.S.A.
222 D2 Backbone Ranges mts N.W.T. Can.
140 L3 Backe Sweden
142 E2 Bäckefors Sweden
143 F2 Bäckhammar Sweden
177 H6 Bački Breg Vojvodina, Srbija Yugo.
177 H6 Bački Monoštor Vojvodina, Srbija Yugo.
196 D3 Bački Petrovac Vojvodina, Srbija Yugo.
172 D3 Backnang Ger.
196 E3 Bačko Gradište Vojvodina, Srbija Yugo.
175 J5 Baćkowice Pol.
82 D3 Backstairs Passage S.A. Austr.
150 E3 Backwell North Somerset, England U.K.
97 D5 Bac Liêu Vietnam
96 D2 Băc Ninh Vietnam
92 B2 Bacnotan Phil.
92 B3 Baco, Mount Mindoro Phil.
242 C2 Bacoachi Mex.
242 C3 Bacobampo Mex.
193 G4 Bacoli Italy
92 B4 Bacolod Phil.
Bacou, Pic de mt. France see Guerreys, Pic de
156 A3 Bacqueville-en-Caux France
177 I5 Bácsalmás Hungary
177 I5 Bácsbokod Hungary
177 I5 Bácsborsód Hungary
177 I5 Bács-Kiskun county Hungary
Bactra Afgh. see Balkh
177 I3 Bacúch Slovakia
149 G4 Bacup Lancashire, England U.K.
254 D2 Bacuri Brazil
236 C2 Bad r. SD U.S.A.
Bada Guangxi China see Xilin
210 C3 Bada mt. Eth.
173 G3 Bad Abbach Ger.
114 B4 Badagara Kerala India
173 G4 Bad Aibling Ger.
106 D3 Badain Jaran Shamo des. Nei Mongol China
251 F5 Badajós, Lago l. Brazil
184 D2 Badajoz Spain
184 D2 Badajoz prov. Extremadura Spain
123 G2 Badakhshān prov. Afgh.
Badakhshan aut. rep. Tajik. see Kŭhistoni Badakhshon
Badakhshoni Kŭhí aut. rep. Tajik. see Kŭhistoni Badakhshon
186 F3 Badalona Spain
190 C5 Badalucco Italy
183 G1 Bádames Spain
114 B3 Badami Karnataka India
127 F5 Badanah Saudi Arabia
Badaojiang Jilin China see Baishan
183 H2 Badarán Spain
Badarinath mts India see Badrinath Peaks
117 H4 Badarpur Assam India
179 E3 Bad Aussee Austria
227 F4 Bad Axe MI U.S.A.
169 C3 Bad Bentheim Ger.
168 C3 Badbergen Ger.
172 B2 Bad Bergzabern Ger.
171 C5 Bad Berka Ger.
169 D4 Bad Berleburg Ger.
171 C5 Bad Berneck im Fichtelgebirge Ger.
169 C5 Bad Bertrich Ger.
168 F2 Bad Bevensen Ger.
171 C4 Bad Bibra Ger.
173 H3 Bad Birnbach Ger.
171 C5 Bad Blankenburg Ger.
179 E4 Bad Bleiberg Austria
169 F5 Bad Bocklet Ger.
171 D5 Bad Brambach Ger.
168 E2 Bad Bramstedt Ger.
169 C5 Bad Breisig Ger.
169 E5 Bad Brückenau Ger.
172 D3 Bad Buchau Ger.
169 D5 Bad Camberg Ger.
146 C4 Badcaul Highland, Scotland U.K.
225 I4 Baddeck N.S. Can.
169 F3 Baddeckenstedt Ger.
123 F4 Baddo r. Pak.
170 C1 Bad Doberan Ger.
169 E4 Bad Driburg Ger.
171 D4 Bad Düben Ger.
172 C2 Bad Dürkheim Ger.
171 D4 Bad Dürrenberg Ger.
172 C3 Bad Dürrheim Ger.
171 C4 Badeborn Ger.
162 D3 Badefols-d'Ans France
169 E3 Bad Eilsen Ger.
171 D5 Bad Elster Ger.
Bademli Turkey see Aladağ
169 C5 Bad Ems Ger.
179 H2 Baden Austria
158 D4 Baden France
190 D1 Baden Switz.
186 B3 Badenas Spain
172 C3 Baden-Baden Ger.
169 D5 Bad Endbach Ger.
173 G4 Bad Endorf Ger.
169 F4 Badenhausen Ger.
146 D5 Badenoch reg. Scotland U.K.
146 F4 Badenscoth Aberdeenshire, Scotland U.K.
172 B4 Badenweiler Ger.
172 C3 Baden-Württemberg land Ger.
207 G3 Badér Niger
169 F4 Badersleben Ger.
192 A4 Badesi Sardegna Italy
169 D3 Bad Essen Ger.
173 G4 Bad Feilnbach Ger.
170 F3 Bad Freienwalde Ger.
172 D2 Bad Friedrichshall Ger.
173 H3 Bad Füssing Ger.
179 G4 Bad Gams Austria
169 F4 Bad Gandersheim Ger.
178 E3 Badgastein Austria
225 K3 Badger Nfld. Can.
123 E3 Bādghīs prov. Afgh.
179 G4 Bad Gleichenberg Austria
179 E3 Bad Goisern Austria
179 F2 Bad Großpertholz Austria
169 F4 Bad Grund (Harz) Ger.
179 F2 Bad Hall Austria
178 D3 Bad Häring Austria
169 F4 Bad Harzburg Ger.
173 F4 Bad Heilbrunn Ger.
172 C3 Bad Herrenalb Ger.
169 E5 Bad Hersfeld Ger.
164 D2 Badhoevedorp Neth.
178 E3 Bad Hofgastein Austria
169 D5 Bad Homburg vor der Höhe Ger.
169 C5 Bad Honnef Ger.
206 B4 Badi r. Guinea
191 G2 Badia Italy
191 G3 Badia Calavena Italy
187 F5 Badia Gran Spain
191 G3 Badia Polesine Italy
191 H5 Badia Tedalda Italy
169 D3 Bad Iburg Ger.
183 G4 Badiel r. Spain
210 B3 Badigeru Swamp Sudan
123 G5 Badin Pak.
177 I3 Badín Slovakia
242 D3 Badiraguato Mex.
179 E3 Bad Ischl Austria
126 E4 Bādiyat ash Shām des. Asia
Badje-Sohppar Sweden see Övre Soppero
169 E4 Bad Karlshafen Ger.
169 F5 Bad Kissingen Ger.
170 C2 Bad Kleinen Ger.
179 E4 Bad Kleinkirchheim Austria
171 C5 Bad Klosterlausnitz Ger.
173 F4 Bad Kohlgrub Ger.
172 D2 Bad König Ger.
Bad Königsdorff Pol. see Jastrzębie-Zdrój
169 F5 Bad Königshofen im Grabfeld Ger.
171 C4 Bad Kösen Ger.
179 F2 Bad Kreuzen Austria
172 B2 Bad Kreuznach Ger.
172 B4 Bad Krozingen Ger.
169 D5 Bad Laasphe Ger.
169 D3 Bad Laer Ger.
236 C2 Badlands reg. ND U.S.A.
236 C3 Badlands reg. SD U.S.A.
169 F4 Bad Langensalza Ger.
171 C4 Bad Lauchstädt Ger.
171 D4 Bad Lausick Ger.
169 F4 Bad Lauterberg im Harz Ger.
179 F2 Bad Leonfelden Austria
171 E4 Bad Liebenwerda Ger.
172 C3 Bad Liebenzell Ger.
169 D4 Bad Lippspringe Ger.
146 E3 Badlipster Highland, Scotland U.K.
172 D2 Bad Mergentheim Ger.
179 E3 Bad Mitterndorf Austria
169 E3 Bad Münder am Deister Ger.
172 B2 Bad Münster am Stein-Ebernburg Ger.
169 B5 Bad Münstereifel Ger.
171 F4 Bad Muskau Ger.
169 D5 Bad Nauheim Ger.
116 C5 Badnawar Madh. Prad. India
169 E3 Bad Nenndorf Ger.
169 C5 Bad Neuenahr-Ahrweiler Ger.
169 F5 Bad Neustadt an der Saale Ger.
169 D3 Bad Oeynhausen Ger.
195 F4 Badolato Italy
185 F3 Badolatosa Spain
168 F2 Bad Oldesloe Ger.
108 D2 Badong Hubei China
157 G4 Badonviller France
169 E5 Bad Orb Ger.
207 F5 Badou Togo
196 D3 Badovinci Srbija Yugo.
172 C3 Bad Peterstal Ger.
179 H2 Bad Pirawarth Austria
215 H1 Badplaas S. Africa
169 E4 Bad Pyrmont Ger.
179 G4 Bad Radkersburg Austria
190 E1 Bad Ragaz Switz.
172 D2 Bad Rappenau Ger.
173 G4 Bad Reichenhall Ger.
124 B3 Badr Ḥunayn Saudi Arabia
116 D3 Badrinath Peaks India
169 D3 Bad Rothenfelde Ger.
171 F3 Bad Saarow-Pieskow Ger.
169 F4 Bad Sachsa Ger.
172 B4 Bad Säckingen Ger.
179 F4 Bad St Leonhard im Lavanttal Austria
169 F3 Bad Salzdetfurth Ger.
169 E5 Bad Salzschlirf Ger.
169 D3 Bad Salzuflen Ger.
169 F5 Bad Salzungen Ger.
169 D4 Bad Sassendorf Ger.
179 E2 Bad Schallerbach Austria
171 F5 Bad Schandau Ger.
171 D4 Bad Schmiedeberg Ger.
172 C2 Bad Schönborn Ger.
172 D3 Bad Schussenried Ger.
169 D5 Bad Schwalbach Ger.
168 F2 Bad Schwartau Ger.
168 F2 Bad Segeberg Ger.
151 F2 Badsey Worcestershire, England U.K.
169 E5 Bad Soden-Salmünster Ger.
169 E4 Bad Sooden-Allendorf Ger.
171 C5 Bad Steben Ger.
171 C4 Bad Suderode Ger.
171 C4 Bad Sulza Ger.
170 D1 Bad Sülze Ger.
169 F4 Bad Tennstedt Ger.
173 F4 Bad Tölz Ger.
109 F3 Badu Fujian China
172 D3 Bad Überkingen Ger.
91 J9 Badu Island Qld Austr.
186 B3 Badules Spain
114 D5 Badulla Sri Lanka
172 D3 Bad Urach Ger.
114 C3 Badvel Andhra Prad. India
169 D5 Bad Vilbel Ger.
179 H3 Bad Vöslau Austria
172 D4 Bad Waldsee Ger.
179 H3 Bad Waltersdorf Austria
173 F4 Bad Wiessee Ger.
169 E4 Bad Wildungen Ger.
170 C3 Bad Wilsnack Ger.
172 D2 Bad Wimpfen Ger.
179 E2 Bad Wimsbach-Neydharting Austria
173 E2 Bad Windsheim Ger.
173 E4 Bad Wörishofen Ger.
172 D4 Bad Wurzach Ger.
179 F2 Bad Zell Austria
169 E4 Bad Zwesten Ger.
168 D2 Bad Zwischenahn Ger.
Bae Cinmel Conwy, Wales U.K. see Kinmel Bay
Bae Colwyn Conwy, Wales U.K. see Colwyn Bay
170 C2 Baek Ger.
142 C4 Bække Denmark
142 C3 Bækmarksbro Denmark
165 E4 Baelen Belgium
185 F3 Baena Spain
Bae Penrhyn Conwy, Wales U.K. see Penrhyn Bay
169 B5 Baesweiler Ger.
185 G3 Baeza Spain
207 H5 Bafang Cameroon
206 B3 Bafatá Guinea-Bissau
123 H3 Baffa Pak.
221 L2 Baffin Bay sea Can./Greenland
221 L3 Baffin Island Nunavut Can.
207 H5 Bafia Cameroon
207 F4 Bafilo Togo
206 C3 Bafing r. Guinea/Mali
164 F1 Baflo Neth.
206 C3 Bafoulabé Mali
207 H5 Bafoussam Cameroon
122 C4 Bāfq Iran
126 D2 Bafra Turkey
122 D4 Bāft Iran
208 E4 Bafwasende Dem. Rep. Congo
177 I4 Bag Hungary
186 E2 Bagà Spain
106 D2 Baga Bogd Uul mts Mongolia
117 F4 Bagaha Bihar India
95 G1 Bagahak hill Sabah Malaysia
195 E4 Bagaladi Italy
114 B2 Bagalkot Karnataka India
177 K4 Bagamér Hungary
211 C6 Bagamoyo Tanz.
121 I1 Bagan Rus. Fed.
92 C5 Baganga Phil.
94 C2 Bagansiapiapi Sumatera Indon.
190 F4 Baganza r. Italy
199 E3 Bağarası Turkey
161 C4 Bagard France
207 G3 Bagaroua Niger
209 C5 Bagata Dem. Rep. Congo
241 K4 Bagdad AZ U.S.A.
Bagdadi Georgia see Baghdat'i
258 G3 Bagé Brazil
160 C2 Bâgé-le-Châtel France
168 F1 Bagenkop Denmark
114 C3 Bagepalli Karnataka India
Bagerhat Bangl. see Bagherhat
163 E6 Bages France
116 D3 Bageshwar Uttar Prad. India
114 C2 Bagevadi Karnataka India
143 F2 Baggå Sweden
238 F3 Baggs WY U.S.A.
116 C5 Bagh Madh. Prad. India
Bagh a'Chaisteil Western Isles, Scotland U.K. see Castlebay
122 E2 Baghbaghū Iran
127 G4 Baghdād Iraq
127 G4 Baghdād governorate Iraq
129 C2 Baghdat'i Georgia
117 G5 Bagherhat Bangl.
194 C4 Bagheria Sicilia Italy
122 D4 Bāghīn Iran
123 G2 Baghlān Afgh.
123 G3 Baghlān prov. Afgh.
122 A2 Bāghlī Da hill Iran
129 C3 Baghramyan Armenia
150 D1 Bagillt Flintshire, Wales U.K.
129 A4 Bağırpaşa Dağı mts Turkey
Bağırsak Deresi r. Syria/Turkey see Sājūr, Nahr
129 B4 Bağlar Turkey
236 E2 Bagley MN U.S.A.
117 E3 Baglung Nepal
141 J3 Bagn Norway
191 G4 Bagnacavallo Italy
163 E4 Bagnac-sur-Célé France
195 E4 Bagnara Calabra Italy
190 E4 Bagnaria Italy
191 I3 Bagnaria Arsa Italy
190 D4 Bagnasco Italy
156 C4 Bagneaux-sur-Loing France
163 C5 Bagnères-de-Bigorre France
163 C6 Bagnères-de-Luchon France
190 E2 Bagni di Masino Italy
191 F2 Bagni di Rabbi Italy

191 G5 Bagno di Romagna Italy
159 F3 Bagnoles-de-l'Orne France
193 G3 Bagnoli del Trigno Italy
191 G3 Bagnoli di Sopra Italy
193 H4 Bagnoli Irpino Italy
190 F3 Bagnolo in Piano Italy
190 F3 Bagnolo Mella Italy
161 F4 Bagnolo Piemonte Italy
191 F3 Bagnolo San Vito Italy
161 G5 Bagnols-en-Forêt France
161 B4 Bagnols-les-Bains France
161 G4 Bagnols-sur-Cèze France
190 F4 Bagnone Italy
192 E2 Bagnoregio Italy
117 F4 Bagnuiti r. Nepal
  Bago admin. div. Myanmar see
  Pegu
92 B4 Bago Phil.
176 F5 Bagod Hungary
206 D3 Bagoé r. Côte d'Ivoire/Mali
190 F3 Bagolino Italy
  Bagong Guizhou China see
  Sansui
138 C4 Bagrationovsk Rus. Fed.
  Bagrax Xinjiang China see Bohu
  Bagrax Hu l. China see Bohu
  Bosten Hu
251 I5 Bagre Brazil
199 G3 Bagsaray Burdur Turkey
151 G3 Bagshot Surrey, England U.K.
207 G4 Bagudo Nigeria
186 B3 Báguena Spain
92 B2 Baguio Luzon Phil.
92 C5 Baguio Mindanao Phil.
  Bagur Spain see Begur
176 G4 Bágyogszovát Hungary
199 E2 Bağyurdu Turkey
207 H2 Bagzane, Monts mts Niger
163 A5 Bahabón de Esgueva Spain
117 C7 Bahadurganj Nepal
116 D3 Bahadurgarh Haryana India
  Bahāmābād Iran see Rafsanjān
  Bahamas country West Indies
  see The Bahamas
117 G4 Baharampur W. Bengal India
203 F3 Bahariya Oasis Egypt
137 I4 Bahatyr Ukr.
95 G2 Bahau r. Indon.
94 C2 Bahau Malaysia
123 H4 Bahawalnagar Pak.
123 G4 Bahawalpur Pak.
128 B1 Bahçe Turkey
126 E3 Bahçe Turkey
108 C2 Ba He r. Turkey
  Baharden Turkm. see
  Bakherden
116 D3 Baheri Uttar Prad. India
211 B6 Bahi Tanz.
  Bahia Brazil see Salvador
257 G1 Bahia state Brazil
261 F6 Bahía Blanca Arg.
242 C2 Bahía Kino Mex.
253 F5 Bahía Negra Para.
242 B3 Bahía Tortugas Mex.
183 F2 Bahíllo Spain
210 C2 Bahir Dar Eth.
125 G3 Bahlā Oman
197 H2 Bahlui r. Romania
122 B4 Bahmanshīr, Khowr-e r. Iran
176 G3 Báhoň Slovakia
116 E4 Bahraich Uttar Prad. India
125 E2 Bahrain country Asia
125 E2 Bahrain, Gulf of Asia
122 B2 Bahrāmābād Iran
129 E4 Bahrāmtāpā Azer.
171 C3 Bahrdorf Ger.
210 A3 Bahr el Jebel state Sudan
168 D3 Bahrenborstel Ger.
116 D4 Bahror Rajasthan India
123 E5 Bāhū Kālāt Iran
139 H4 Bahushewsk Belarus
197 H2 Baia Suceava Romania
197 I3 Baia Tulcea Romania
197 F2 Baia de Aramă Romania
197 F2 Baia de Arieș Romania
177 L5 Baia de Criș Romania
199 I3 Baía dos Tigres Angola
209 B8 Baia Farta Angola
197 F2 Baia Mare Romania
251 I5 Baião Brazil
182 B3 Baião Port.
197 F2 Baia Sprie Romania
194 B5 Baiata r. Sicilia Italy
208 B3 Baibokoum Chad
  Baicheng Henan China see
  Xiping
107 I2 Baicheng Jilin China
110 C3 Baicheng Xinjiang China
197 G3 Băicoi Romania
  Baidoa Somalia see Baydhabo
109 F3 Baidu Guangdong China
  Baie-aux-Feuilles Que. Can.
  see Tasiujaq
225 G3 Baie-Comeau Que. Can.
246 D3 Baie de Henne Haiti
  Baie-du-Poste Que. Can. see
  Mistissini
225 I3 Baie-Johan-Beetz Que. Can.
173 F3 Baienfurt Ger.
173 F3 Baiersbronn Ger.
173 G7 Baiersdorf Ger.
225 G4 Baie-St-Paul Que. Can.
225 H3 Baie-Trinité Que. Can.
225 J3 Baie Verte Nfld. Can.
162 B3 Baignes-Ste-Radegonde France
160 C1 Baigneux-les-Juifs France
261 G4 Baigorrita Arg.
107 H4 Baigou r. China
  Baiguan Zhejiang China see
  Shangyu
109 E2 Baiguo Hubei China
183 I2 Baigura mt. Spain
108 A3 Baihanchang Yunnan China
116 C2 Baihar Madh. Prad. India
108 D1 Baihe Jilin China
108 D1 Baihe Shaanxi China
109 E1 Bai He r. China
  Baiji Iraq see Bayjī
116 D2 Baijnath Hima. Prad. India
116 D3 Baijnath Uttar Prad. India
116 E4 Baikanthpur Madh. Prad. India
117 E5 Baikunthpur Madh. Prad. India
107 I2 Bailang Nei Mongol China
149 H4 Baildon West Yorkshire,
  England U.K.
146 B3 Baile Ailein Western Isles,
  Scotland U.K.
  Baile Átha Cliath
  Rep. of Ireland see Dublin
  Baile Átha Luain
  Rep. of Ireland see Athlone
197 G3 Băile Govora Romania
197 F3 Băile Herculane Romania
  Baile Mhartainn Western Isles,
  Scotland U.K. see Balmartin
185 G2 Bailén Spain
197 G3 Băile Olănești Romania
197 F3 Băilești Romania
197 F3 Băileștilor, Câmpia plain
  Romania
197 G2 Băile Tușnad Romania
215 F4 Bailey S. Africa
87 D6 Bailey Range hills W.A. Austr.
83 I2 Baileyton U.S.A.
108 C2 Bailicun Guangxi China
156 B4 Bailleul-le-Pin France
156 C2 Bailleul France
223 J1 Baillie r. Nunavut Can.
147 E3 Baillieborough Rep. of Ireland
165 E4 Baillonville Belgium
186 C2 Bailo Spain
108 C1 Bailong Jiang r. Gansu China
209 B8 Bailundo Angola
108 B1 Baima Qinghai China
  Baima Xizang China see Baxoi
149 I4 Bain r. England U.K.
111 E6 Bainang Xizang China
  Bainbridge Western Isles,
  England U.K.
231 C6 Bainbridge GA U.S.A.
233 F3 Bainbridge NY U.S.A.
232 B5 Bainbridge OH U.S.A.
232 B6 Bainbridge PA U.S.A.
158 E4 Bain-de-Bretagne France
159 D6 Baindt Ger.
114 B3 Bainduru Karnataka India

246 D3 Bainet Haiti
111 E6 Baingoin Xizang China
  Baini Guizhou China see Yuqing
161 B3 Bains France
157 G4 Bains-les-Bains France
158 D4 Bains-sur-Oust France
149 I4 Bainton East Riding of
  Yorkshire, England U.K.
182 B1 Baio Grande Spain
182 B2 Baiona Spain
108 B1 Baiqên Qinghai China
100 C3 Baiquan Heilong. China
117 F4 Bairagnia Bihar India
237 D5 Baird TX U.S.A.
220 C3 Baird Mountains AK U.S.A.
77 H1 Bairiki Kiribati
107 H3 Bairin Qiao Nei Mongol China
  Bairin Youqi Nei Mongol China
  see Daban
  Bairin Zuoqi Nei Mongol China
  see Lindong
121 G4 Bairkum Kazakh.
83 F4 Bairnsdale Vic. Austr.
184 C2 Bairro dos Canaviais Port.
158 E3 Bais Bretagne France
159 F3 Bais Pays de la Loire France
92 B4 Bais Phil.
163 C4 Baïse r. France
160 C2 Baisha Chongqing China
108 D5 Baisha Hainan China
109 E3 Baisha Jiangxi China
108 D2 Baisha Sichuan China
  Baishan Guangxi China see
  Mashan
100 C4 Baishan Jilin China
101 C4 Baishan Jilin China
107 F5 Baishui Shaanxi China
108 C1 Baishui Jiang r. Sichuan China
191 F4 Baiso Italy
163 B6 Bàișoara Romania
138 D4 Baisogala Lith.
177 L5 Bäiţa Romania
108 A1 Baitang Qinghai China
107 H3 Baitie r. China
161 C4 Baïut Romania
161 G4 Baixa France
184 A2 Baixa da Banheira Port.
163 E6 Baixas France
  Baixi Sichuan China see Yibin
107 G4 Baixiang Hebei China
107 I3 Baixingt Nei Mongol China
251 G3 Baixo Guandu Brazil
209 C8 Baixo-Longa Angola
107 H4 Baiyang Dian resr China
110 E3 Baiyanghe Xinjiang China
  Baiyashi Hunan China see
  Dong'an
106 E4 Baiyin Gansu China
108 A2 Baiyü Sichuan China
203 G5 Baiyuda Desert Sudan
177 H5 Baja Hungary
242 B2 Baja California pen. Mex.
242 B2 Baja California Norte
  state Mex.
242 B3 Baja California Sur state Mex.
122 B2 Bājalān Iran
243 E3 Bajan Mex.
196 D3 Baj Baj W. Bengal India
177 H4 Baja Slovakia
124 C5 Bājil Yemen
196 D3 Bajina Bašta Srbija Yugo.
117 G4 Bajitpur Bangl.
100 C3 Bajkovo Rus. Fed.
177 H5 Bajmok Vojvodina, Srbija Yugo.
177 H4 Bajna Hungary
116 C5 Bajna Madh. Prad. India
242 DJ7 Baja Boquete Panama
207 H4 Bajoga Nigeria
95 C2 Bajool Qld Austr.
177 H4 Bajót Hungary
186 E3 Bajoz r. Spain
177 F5 Bajrakot Orissa India
196 E4 Bajram Curri Albania
176 F5 Bak Hungary
177 G4 Bak Slovakia
95 F3 Baka, Bukit mt. Indon.
208 D3 Bakala C.A.R.
175 K1 Bakałarzewo Pol.
134 K5 Bakaly Rus. Fed.
121 I3 Bakanas Kazakh.
191 J3 Bakar Croatia
206 A3 Bakau Gambia
95 G2 Bakayan, Gunung mt. Indon.
137 G2 Bakayivka Ukr.
168 D4 Bakel Neth.
206 B3 Bakel Senegal
241 E4 Baker CA U.S.A.
238 D2 Baker ID U.S.A.
237 F6 Baker LA U.S.A.
238 F2 Baker MT U.S.A.
238 C2 Baker OR U.S.A.
232 D5 Baker WV U.S.A.
238 B1 Baker, Mount vol. WA U.S.A.
241 L4 Baker Butte mt. AZ U.S.A.
87 E5 Baker Island N. Pacific Ocean
223 M1 Baker Lake salt flat W.A. Austr.
223 M1 Baker Lake l. Nunavut Can.
241 M5 Baker Lake Nunavut Can.
233 □11 Baker Lake l. Nunavut Can.
85 G4 Bakers Creek Qld Austr.
231 D7 Bakersfield CA U.S.A.
231 D4 Bakersville N.C. U.S.A.
215 F1 Bakerville S. Africa
149 H4 Bakewell Derbyshire,
  England U.K.
125 G2 Bakha Oman
  Bakharden Turkm. see
  Bakherden
122 D2 Bakhardok Turkm.
124 E2 Bakharz mts Iran
  Bakhchisaray Ukr.
137 G5 Bakhchysaray Ukr.
122 D2 Bakherden Turkm.
100 D2 Bakhirevo Rus. Fed.
137 G2 Bakhmach Ukr.
  Bakhmut Ukr. see Artemivs'k
137 J3 Bakhmut r. Ukr.
  Bākhtarān Iran see
  Kermānshāh
  Bākhtarān prov. Iran see
  Kermānshāh
122 C4 Bakhtegan, Daryācheh-ye
  l. Iran
117 F4 Bakhtiyarpur Bihar India
121 J3 Bakhty Kazakh.
251 G3 Bakhuis Gebergte mts
  Suriname
129 F3 Baki Azer.
183 H1 Baki Spain
199 E2 Bakır r. Turkey
199 F1 Bakırköy Turkey
129 E2 Bakıxanov Azer.
140 □2 Bakkaflói b. Iceland
164 F1 Bakkeveen Neth.
199 F3 Baklan Turkey
116 C2 Bakloh Hima. Prad. India
206 D4 Bako Côte d'Ivoire
210 C3 Bako Oromia Eth.
210 C3 Bako Southern Eth.
177 H4 Bakonszeg Hungary
177 G4 Bakony hills Hungary
177 G4 Bakonybél Hungary
177 G4 Bakonynána Hungary
177 H4 Bakonyszárkány Hungary
177 G4 Bakonyszentkirály Hungary
176 G4 Bakonyszombathely Hungary
210 D3 Bakool admin. reg. Somalia
207 H4 Bakori Nigeria
208 D3 Bakouma C.A.R.
179 H4 Bakovci Slovenia
171 K5 Bakov nad Jizerou
  Czech Rep.
206 C3 Bakoy r. Mali
177 H6 Baksa Hungary
129 D2 Baksan Rus. Fed.
129 D2 Baksan r. Rus. Fed.
177 L4 Baktalórántháza Hungary
  Baku Azer. see Baki
168 D3 Bakum Ger.
129 D3 Bakuriani Georgia
262 P2 Bakutis Coast Antarctica
  Baky Azer. see Baki
131 P3 Baky Uyandino r. Rus. Fed.
199 F2 Balâ Turkey
150 D2 Bala Gwynedd, Wales U.K.
252 D2 Bala, Cerros de mts Bol.

92 A5 Balabac i. Phil.
95 G1 Balabac Strait Malaysia/Phil.
95 G3 Balabalangan, Kepulauan
  atolls Indon.
199 K4 Balabancık Turkey
256 A2 Baliza Brazil
168 E2 Balje Ger.
124 C4 Balk Ger.
164 E2 Balk Neth.
  Balkan Mountains Bulg./Yugo.
  see Stara Planina
  Balkan Oblast admin. div.
  Turkm. see
122 C1 Balkanabat Turkm.
  Balkanskaya Oblast'
  admin. div. Turkm.
177 K4 Balkány Hungary
121 G1 Balkashino Kazakh.
164 F2 Balkbrug Neth.
123 F2 Balkh Afgh.
121 H3 Balkhab r. Afgh.
  Balkhash Kazakh.
121 H3 Balkhash, Ozero l. Kazakh. see
114 C2 Balkonda Andhra Prad. India
120 A3 Balkuduk Kazakh.
190 E3 Ballabio Italy
146 C5 Ballachulish Highland,
  Scotland U.K.
87 D7 Balladonia W.A. Austr.
83 G2 Balladoran N.S.W. Austr.
147 C3 Ballaghaderreen
156 C4 Ballancourt-sur-Essonne
  France
140 L1 Ballangen Norway
159 G4 Ballan-Miré France
238 E2 Ballantine MT U.S.A.
146 E5 Ballantrae South Ayrshire,
  Scotland U.K.
192 B5 Ballao Sardegna Italy
83 E4 Ballarat Vic. Austr.
87 D6 Ballard, Lake salt flat
  W.A. Austr.
114 C2 Ballari Mahar. India
146 E4 Ballater Aberdeenshire,
  Scotland U.K.
206 C3 Ballé Mali
159 F4 Ballée France
146 E6 Ballencleuch Law hill
  Scotland U.K.
263 K2 Balleny Islands Antarctica
159 F2 Balleroy France
142 E4 Ballerup Denmark
261 F3 Ballesteros Arg.
147 B4 Ballia Uttar Prad. India
148 B3 Ballina N.S.W. Austr.
83 B1 Ballina N.S.W. Austr.
147 A3 Ballina Rep. of Ireland
147 D3 Ballinaboy Rep. of Ireland
147 D3 Ballinafad Rep. of Ireland
147 D3 Ballinagar Rep. of Ireland
147 D3 Ballinakill Rep. of Ireland
147 D3 Ballinalack Rep. of Ireland
147 D3 Ballinalee Rep. of Ireland
147 D2 Ballinamallard
  Northern Ireland U.K.
147 C3 Ballinameen Rep. of Ireland
147 D4 Ballinamult Rep. of Ireland
147 C3 Ballinascarthy Rep. of Ireland
147 C4 Ballinasloe Rep. of Ireland
147 E4 Ballinderreen Rep. of Ireland
147 D3 Ballinderry r. Rep. of Ireland
147 E2 Ballinderry
  Northern Ireland U.K.
147 E2 Ballindine Rep. of Ireland
147 C4 Ballindooly Rep. of Ireland
147 C5 Ballineen Rep. of Ireland
147 D4 Ballingarry Tipperary
  Rep. of Ireland
147 B5 Ballingeary Rep. of Ireland
237 D6 Ballinger TX U.S.A.
146 E5 Ballingry Fife, Scotland U.K.
82 E4 Ballinhassig Rep. of Ireland
81 D5 Ballinrobe Rep. of Ireland
237 C6 Ballinspittle Rep. of Ireland
146 B5 Ballinluig Perth and Kinross,
  Scotland U.K.
147 B5 Ballinskelligs Rep. of Ireland
147 C5 Ballinspittle Rep. of Ireland
146 E5 Ballintoy Northern Ireland U.K.
147 B4 Ballinure r. Rep. of Ireland
147 A3 Ballinskelligs Rep. of Ireland
147 D5 Ballintra Rep. of Ireland
173 E3 Ballmertshofen Ger.
186 D6 Ballobar Spain
147 C5 Balloch W. Dunbartonshire,
  Scotland U.K.
159 G3 Ballon France
148 C5 Ballon Rep. of Ireland
83 G2 Ballon d'Alsace mt. France
177 I5 Ballósság Hungary
159 E4 Ballots France
198 A1 Ballsh Albania
82 □2² Ball's Pyramid i.
  Lord Howe I. Austr.
169 F4 Ballstädt Ger.
233 G3 Ballston Spa NY U.S.A.
164 E1 Ballum Neth.
147 C2 Ballure Rep. of Ireland
234 C2 Bally PA U.S.A.
147 C2 Ballybay Rep. of Ireland
147 C3 Ballybofey Rep. of Ireland
147 C3 Ballyboghil Rep. of Ireland
147 C5 Ballybogy Rep. of Ireland
147 A5 Ballybrack Dublin
  Rep. of Ireland
147 B5 Ballybrack Kerry
  Rep. of Ireland
147 D4 Ballybrophy Rep. of Ireland
147 D4 Ballybunnion Rep. of Ireland
147 C5 Ballycahill Rep. of Ireland
147 C5 Ballycanew Rep. of Ireland
147 C5 Ballycarney Rep. of Ireland
147 F2 Ballycarra Rep. of Ireland
147 F2 Ballycastle Northern Ireland U.K.
147 B2 Ballycastle Rep. of Ireland
147 F2 Ballyclare
  Northern Ireland U.K.
147 E2 Ballyclare Northern Ireland U.K.
147 D2 Ballyconnell Cavan
  Rep. of Ireland
147 C2 Ballyconnell Sligo
  Rep. of Ireland
147 C5 Ballycroy Rep. of Ireland
147 B5 Ballycumber Rep. of Ireland
147 C5 Ballydangan Rep. of Ireland
147 C5 Ballydehob Rep. of Ireland
147 B4 Ballydesmond Rep. of Ireland
147 B4 Ballyduff Rep. of Ireland
147 F2 Ballyfarnan Rep. of Ireland
147 C4 Ballyfeard Rep. of Ireland
148 B5 Ballyforan Rep. of Ireland
147 F2 Ballygalley
  Northern Ireland U.K.
147 E2 Ballygar Rep. of Ireland
147 D3 Ballygawley
  Northern Ireland U.K.
147 E1 Ballygowan Mayo Rep. of Ireland
175 H1 Ballyglass Mayo Rep. of Ireland
116 D2 Ballygowan
  Northern Ireland U.K.
146 B6 Ballygrant Argyll and Bute,
  Scotland U.K.
147 C5 Ballyhaise Rep. of Ireland
147 C3 Ballyhahill Rep. of Ireland
147 C4 Ballyhaunis Rep. of Ireland
147 C5 Ballyheige Rep. of Ireland

146 E4 Balintore Highland,
  Scotland U.K.
146 □ Balintore Angus, Scotland U.K.
  Balíra r. Andorra/Spain see
  Valira
95 F4 Bali Sea Indon.
168 E2 Balje Ger.
124 C4 Balje'r Saudi Arabia
164 E2 Balk Neth.
147 B4 Ballyheigue Rep. of Ireland
147 C4 Ballyhooly Rep. of Ireland
147 F2 Ballyhornan
  Northern Ireland U.K.
147 C4 Ballyhoura Mountains hills
  Rep. of Ireland
147 D3 Ballyjamesduff Rep. of Ireland
147 D2 Ballykeeran Rep. of Ireland
147 C5 Ballykelly Northern Ireland U.K.
147 C4 Ballykilleen Rep. of Ireland
147 C4 Ballylanders Rep. of Ireland
147 C3 Ballyleague Rep. of Ireland
147 E2 Ballyleny Northern Ireland U.K.
147 D3 Ballyliffen Rep. of Ireland
147 B4 Ballylongford Rep. of Ireland
147 D4 Ballylynan Rep. of Ireland
147 D4 Ballymacarberry
147 F2 Ballymacelligott
147 E2 Ballymack Rep. of Ireland
148 B3 Ballymackilroy
  Northern Ireland U.K.
147 D4 Ballymacmague
85 E1 Ballymacward Rep. of Ireland
206 D3 Ballymahon Rep. of Ireland
147 D2 Ballymagorry
  Northern Ireland U.K.
147 E2 Ballymena
  Northern Ireland U.K.
147 C3 Ballymoe Rep. of Ireland
147 E1 Ballymoney
  Northern Ireland U.K.
147 D1 Ballymore Donegal
  Rep. of Ireland
147 C4 Ballymore Westmeath
  Rep. of Ireland
147 E4 Ballymote Rep. of Ireland
147 E4 Ballymurphy Rep. of Ireland
147 E4 Ballynaboia Rep. of Ireland
147 E4 Ballynacarriga Rep. of Ireland
147 E4 Ballynacarrigy Rep. of Ireland
148 B4 Ballynacorra Rep. of Ireland
147 D3 Ballynahinch Rep. of Ireland
147 F2 Ballynahinch
  Northern Ireland U.K.
147 C4 Ballynahowen Rep. of Ireland
147 C4 Ballynamona Rep. of Ireland
147 B4 Ballynaskeeva Rep. of Ireland
147 C4 Ballyneety Rep. of Ireland
148 C4 Ballynockan Rep. of Ireland
147 F2 Ballynure Northern Ireland U.K.
147 C5 Ballypreen Rep. of Ireland
147 D4 Ballyragget Rep. of Ireland
147 D4 Ballyroan Rep. of Ireland
147 E2 Ballyronan
  Northern Ireland U.K.
147 B5 Ballysadare Rep. of Ireland
147 C5 Ballyshannon Rep. of Ireland
84 C2 Ballysteen Rep. of Ireland
206 B3 Ballyteige Bay Rep. of Ireland
177 J4 Ballyvaughan Rep. of Ireland
147 F2 Ballyvoy Northern Ireland U.K.
147 D4 Ballyvoyle Rep. of Ireland
147 F2 Ballywalter
147 E4 Ballyward Northern Ireland U.K.
147 E4 Ballywilliam Rep. of Ireland
146 A4 Balmacara Highland,
  Scotland U.K.
259 C7 Balmaceda Chile
85 G5 Balmaha Stirling, Scotland U.K.
254 C2 Balmaceda S.A. Austr.
115 G2 Balmaseda Spain
192 A4 Balmazújváros Hungary
190 C3 Balme Italy
161 D4 Balmedie Aberdeenshire,
  Scotland U.K.
147 D4 Balmer Rajasthan India see
  Barmer
147 B5 Balmerino Fife, Scotland U.K.
82 E4 Balmoral Vic. Austr.
81 D5 Balmoral Qld Austr.
237 C6 Balmorhea TX U.S.A.
190 D3 Balmuccia Italy
146 C4 Balnaguard Highland,
  Scotland U.K.
146 A4 Balnahard Argyll and Bute,
  Scotland U.K.
146 B4 Balnakeil Highland,
  Scotland U.K.
146 F4 Balnapaling Highland,
  Scotland U.K.
261 F2 Balnearia Arg.
190 D3 Balniel Italy
123 F4 Balochistan prov. Pak.
119 I4 Balochistan reg. Pak.
116 E5 Balod Madh. Prad. India
116 E5 Baloda Madh. Prad. India
116 E5 Baloda Bazar Madh. Prad.
  India
159 G4 Ballon France

117 F5 Balumath Bihar India
82 D3 Balumbah S.A. Austr.
138 F3 Balupe r. Latvia
150 F3 Baluran, Gunung mt. Indon.
117 G4 Balurghat W. Bengal India
197 H2 Bălușeni Romania
92 C5 Balut i. Phil.
193 H4 Balvano Italy
100 K2 Balvatnet l. Norway
169 C4 Balve Ger.
138 F3 Balvi Latvia
199 E2 Balya Turkey
107 F1 Balygychan Rus. Fed.
121 H4 Balykchy Kazakh.
120 B3 Balykty-Khem r. Rus. Fed.
  Balyqshy Kazakh. see Balykshi
250 B5 Balzar Ecuador
172 C4 Balzers Liechtenstein
122 D4 Bam Kermān Iran
122 D2 Bam Iran
207 I4 Bama Nigeria
85 I1 Bama Qld Austr.
206 D3 Bamaga Qld Austr.
206 B3 Bamako Mali
208 C3 Bamba r. C.A.R.
206 E2 Bamba Mali
208 B5 Bamba Congo
92 B2 Bambang Phil.
209 D9 Bambangando Angola
221 D3 Bambari C.A.R.
173 E2 Bamberg Ger.
231 D5 Bamberg S.C. U.S.A.
235 D3 Bamber Lake N.J. U.S.A.
206 A3 Bambey Senegal
208 C3 Bambili Dem. Rep. Congo
215 F4 Bamboesberg mts S. Africa
86 D4 Bamboo Creek W.A. Austr.
206 C3 Bambouk reg. Mali
257 F4 Bambuí Brazil
149 H2 Bamburgh Northumberland,
  England U.K.
208 D3 Bamenda Xizang China
122 B4 Bāmdezh Iran
207 H5 Bamenda Cameroon
222 E5 Bamfield B.C. Can.
123 F3 Bāmiān Afgh.
  Bāmiān prov. Afgh.
107 J3 Bamiancheng Liaoning China
  Bamiantong Heilong. China see
  Muling
208 D3 Bamingui C.A.R.
208 C2 Bamingui r. C.A.R.
208 D2 Bamingui-Bangoran
  pref. C.A.R.
123 G3 Bāmiyan r. Afgh.
172 C2 Bammental Ger.
242 C3 Bamoa Mex.
116 E4 Bamor Madh. Prad. India
123 E5 Bam Posht, Kūh-e mts Iran
150 D4 Bampton Devon, England U.K.
151 F3 Bampton Oxfordshire,
  England U.K.
122 E5 Bampūr Iran
122 E3 Bamrūd Iran
84 C2 Bamyili N.T. Austr.
84 B4 Ban Burkina
177 G4 Bana Hungary
77 G2 Banaba i. Kiribati
97 B5 Ban Bang Saphan Yai Thai.
140 J2 Banaguil Norway
263 H2 Banabuiu, Açude resr Brazil
260 D5 Bañados del Atuel marsh Arg.
253 E4 Bañados del Izozog
  swamp Bol.
253 F4 Bañados de Otuquis
  marsh Bol.
92 B3 Banahao, Mount vol.
207 F7 Banahuma, Mount vol.
206 D3 Banamba Mali
108 C2 Banan Chongqing China
206 C3 Banana Qld Austr.
254 C1 Bananal, Ilha do i. Brazil
115 E2 Banavar Karnataka India
192 A4 Banari Sardegna Italy
199 E1 Banarlı Turkey
116 D4 Banas r. India
161 B4 Banassac France
204 C3 Bani, Jbel ridge Morocco
205 H2 Bania C.A.R.
207 F3 Bani-Bangou Niger
206 B3 Bani Mali
246 F3 Bani Dom. Rep.
206 B3 Bani r. Mali
92 A2 Bani Phil.
204 D2 Bani, Jbel ridge Morocco
205 H2 Bania C.A.R.
207 F3 Bani-Bangou Niger
175 K1 Banie Mazurskie Pol.
206 D3 Banifing r. Mali
206 D3 Banifing r. Mali
122 C5 Banī Forūr, Jazīreh-ye i. Iran
124 B4 Banī Khatmah reg.
  Saudi Arabia
124 F5 Banī Khurb hills Saudi Arabia
207 F4 Banikoara Benin
124 D4 Banī Ma'ārid des. Saudi Arabia
125 E3 Banī Mukassir des.
  Saudi Arabia

147 C5 Bandon r. Rep. of Ireland
  Ban Don Thai. see Surat Thani
238 A3 Bandon OR U.S.A.
113 □¹ Bandos i. N. Male Maldives
114 B2 Bandra Mahar. India
217 □3b Bandraboua Mayotte
217 □3b Bandrélé Mayotte
209 C5 Bandundu Dem. Rep. Congo
209 C6 Bandundu admin. reg.
  Dem. Rep. Congo
95 D4 Bandung Jawa Barat Indon.
87 B6 Bandya W.A. Austr.
197 H3 Băneasa Romania
197 H3 Băneasa Romania
122 A3 Bāneh Iran
  Banera Rajasthan India
187 C6 Banes Cuba
246 D2 Banes Cuba
222 G4 Banff Alta Can.
146 F4 Banff Aberdeenshire,
  Scotland U.K.
206 D4 Banfora Burkina
95 F2 Banga, Gunung mt. Indon.
209 B7 Banga Angola
209 D6 Banga Dem. Rep. Congo
92 C5 Banga Phil.
114 C3 Bangalore Karnataka India
114 H2 Bangalow N.S.W. Austr.
114 C3 Banganapalle Andhra Prad.
  India
116 D4 Banganga r. India
207 H5 Bangangté Cameroon
117 G5 Bangaon W. Bengal India
95 F1 Bangar Brunei
92 B2 Bangar Phil.
117 G5 Bangara r. Bangl.
114 C2 Bangarapet Karnataka India
208 D3 Bangassou C.A.R.
96 C3 Bangfai, Xé r. Laos
93 B3 Banggai Indon.
95 G1 Banggi i. Sabah Malaysia
202 D1 Banghāzī Libya
96 D3 Banghiang, Xé r. Laos
95 F4 Bangil Jawa Timur Indon.
94 D3 Bangka i. Indon.
93 B3 Bangka, Selat sea chan.
  Indon.
95 F4 Bangkalan Jawa Timur Indon.
94 C2 Bangko Sumatera Indon.
94 D3 Bangko Sumatera Indon.
97 C4 Bangkok Thai.
97 C4 Bangkok, Bight of b. Thai.
  Bangla state India see
  West Bengal
117 G5 Bangladesh country Asia
108 A4 Bangma Shan mts Yunnan
  China
96 C3 Bang Mun Nak Thai.
140 K2 Bangsberg Sweden
206 D5 Bangolo Côte d'Ivoire
150 C1 Bangor Gwynedd, Wales U.K.
147 F2 Bangor Northern Ireland U.K.
233 □I2 Bangor ME U.S.A.
234 E2 Bangor PA U.S.A.
234 C2 Bangor PA U.S.A.
117 F5 Bangriposi Orissa India
241 H5 Bangs, Mount AZ U.S.A.
140 J2 Bangsund Norway
208 C3 Bangui C.A.R.
92 B2 Bangui Phil.
211 B8 Bangula Malawi
209 F7 Bangweulu, Lake Zambia
206 C3 Banh Norfolk, England U.K.
95 D4 Banham Norfolk, England U.K.
96 C2 Ban Houayxay Laos
96 C2 Ban Houayxay Laos
207 E3 Bani r. Mali
246 E3 Bani Dom. Rep.
206 B3 Bani r. Mali
204 D2 Bani, Jbel ridge Morocco
207 F3 Bani-Bangou Niger
177 J6 Banatsko Veliko Selo
  Vojvodina, Srbija Yugo.
199 F2 Banaz Turkey
199 F2 Banaz r. Turkey
116 F6 Banbar Xizang China
124 D4 Banī Khatmah reg.
  Saudi Arabia
147 E2 Banbridge
  Northern Ireland U.K.
96 B3 Ban Khai Thai.
151 F2 Banbury Oxfordshire,
  England U.K.
97 B4 Ban Khao Yoi Thai.
163 A5 Banca France
147 B4 Banki Orissa India
207 H2 Banchory Aberdeenshire,
  Scotland U.K.
207 B5 Banko B.C. Can.
224 E4 Bancroft Ont. Can.
215 J5 Banko Massif de mt. Guinea
  Bancroft Zambia see
  Chililabombwe
208 A3 Banda Cameroon
116 D4 Banda Madh. Prad. India
116 E4 Banda Uttar Prad. India
94 A1 Banda Aceh Sumatera Indon.
83 H2 Banda Banda, Mount
  N.S.W. Austr.
94 B2 Bandahara, Gunung mt.
  Indon.
206 D4 Bandama Côte d'Ivoire
206 D4 Bandama Blanc r.
  Côte d'Ivoire
122 E4 Bandān Iran
122 E4 Bandān Kūh mts Iran
116 F4 Bandanwara Rajasthan India
213 G3 Bandar Moz.
  Bandarampur Uttar Prad. India
117 H5 Bandar-Abbas Iran
122 C5 Bandar-e 'Abbās Iran
122 B2 Bandar-e Anzalī Iran
122 C5 Bandar-e Chārak Iran
122 C5 Bandar-e Deylam Iran
122 C5 Bandar-e Emām Khomeynī
  Iran
122 C5 Bandar-e Lengeh Iran
122 C5 Bandar-e Maqām Iran
122 C5 Bandar-e Moghūyeh Iran
122 B4 Bandar-e Pahlavi Iran see
  Bandar-e Anzalī
122 C5 Bandar-e Rīg Iran
122 B2 Bandar-e Torkaman Iran
122 B2 Bandar-e Torkeman Iran
  Bandar Lampung Sumatera
  Indon. see
  Tanjungkarang-Telukbetung
95 F1 Bandar Seri Begawan Brunei
93 B3 Banda Sea Indon.
257 F2 Bandeira Brazil
257 G2 Bandeirantes Brazil
257 G1 Bandeiras, Pico das mt. Brazil
234 E3 Bandera Arg.
243 B5 Banderas Mex.
244 D3 Banderas, Bahía de b. Mex.
123 G3 Bandharkh India
116 F4 Bandhi r. Rajasthan India
175 H1 Bandi r. Rajasthan India
114 C3 Bandi r. India
206 E3 Bandiagara Mali
123 G3 Bandipur Afgh.
116 E3 Bandipur Jammu and Kashmir
116 D3 Bandol Glacier
  Jammu and Kashmir
199 E1 Bandırma Turkey
147 C5 Bandon Rep. of Ireland

147 C5 Bandon r. Rep. of Ireland
238 A3 Bandon OR U.S.A.
114 B2 Bandra Mahar. India
217 □3b Bandraboua Mayotte
217 □3b Bandrélé Mayotte
209 C5 Bandundu Dem. Rep. Congo
209 C6 Bandundu admin. reg.
  Dem. Rep. Congo
95 D4 Bandung Jawa Barat Indon.
87 B6 Bandya W.A. Austr.
197 H3 Băneasa Romania
197 H3 Băneasa Romania
122 A3 Bāneh Iran
123 A3 Baneh Iran
187 C6 Banes Cuba
246 D2 Banes Cuba
222 G4 Banff Alta Can.
146 F4 Banff Aberdeenshire,
  Scotland U.K.
206 D4 Banfora Burkina
95 F2 Banga, Gunung mt. Indon.
209 B7 Banga Angola
209 D6 Banga Dem. Rep. Congo
92 C5 Banga Phil.
114 C3 Bangalore Karnataka India
114 H2 Bangalow N.S.W. Austr.
114 C3 Banganapalle Andhra Prad.
  India
116 D4 Banganga r. India
207 H5 Bangangté Cameroon
117 G5 Bangaon W. Bengal India
95 F1 Bangar Brunei
92 B2 Bangar Phil.
117 G5 Bangara r. Bangl.
114 C2 Bangarapet Karnataka India
208 D3 Bangassou C.A.R.
96 C3 Bangfai, Xé r. Laos
93 B3 Banggai Indon.
95 G1 Banggi i. Sabah Malaysia
202 D1 Banghāzī Libya
96 D3 Banghiang, Xé r. Laos
95 F4 Bangil Jawa Timur Indon.
94 D3 Bangka i. Indon.
93 B3 Bangka, Selat sea chan.
  Indon.
95 F4 Bangkalan Jawa Timur Indon.
94 C2 Bangko Sumatera Indon.
94 D3 Bangko Sumatera Indon.
97 C4 Bangkok Thai.
97 C4 Bangkok, Bight of b. Thai.
  Bangla state India see
  West Bengal
117 G5 Bangladesh country Asia
108 A4 Bangma Shan mts Yunnan
  China
96 C3 Bang Mun Nak Thai.
140 K2 Bangsberg Sweden
206 D5 Bangolo Côte d'Ivoire
150 C1 Bangor Gwynedd, Wales U.K.
147 F2 Bangor Northern Ireland U.K.
233 □I2 Bangor ME U.S.A.
234 E2 Bangor PA U.S.A.
234 C2 Bangor PA U.S.A.
117 F5 Bangriposi Orissa India
241 H5 Bangs, Mount AZ U.S.A.
140 J2 Bangsund Norway
208 C3 Bangui C.A.R.
92 B2 Bangui Phil.
211 B8 Bangula Malawi
209 F7 Bangweulu, Lake Zambia
96 C2 Ban Houayxay Laos
96 C2 Ban Houayxay Laos
207 F4 Bani Benin
246 E3 Bani Dom. Rep.
206 B3 Bani r. Mali
204 D2 Bani, Jbel ridge Morocco
186 E2 Bañiera Spain
188 D2 Bāniyās Syria
188 D2 Bāniyās Syria
191 K1 Banja Srbija Yugo.
188 D2 Banja Luka Bos.-Herz.
95 F3 Banjarbaru Kalimantan Selatan
  Indon.
95 F3 Banjarmasin Kalimantan
  Selatan Indon.
206 A3 Banjul Gambia
86 B4 Bankā Bihar India
117 F4 Banka Bihar India
84 D2 Bankapur Karnataka India
114 B3 Bankapur Karnataka India
116 E4 Bankass Mali
143 M3 Bankeryd Sweden
146 F5 Bankfoot Perth and Kinross,
  Scotland U.K.
97 C4 Ban Khai Thai.
97 B4 Ban Khao Yoi Thai.
147 B4 Banki Orissa India
116 D2 Bankhead Qld Austr.
116 D3 Bankhol B.C. Can.
215 J5 Banko, Massif de mt. Guinea
206 C3 Bankol Guinea
222 C3 Banks Island B.C. Can.
220 F2 Banks Island N.W.T. Can.
78 □6 Banks Islands Vanuatu
81 D5 Banks Peninsula South I. N.Z.
83 C5 Banks Strait Tas. Austr.
117 F5 Bankura W. Bengal India
197 F3 Bankya Grad Sofiya Bulg.
96 C2 Ban Lamduan Thai.
108 C3 Banlan Guangxi China
96 B4 Ban Mae Mo Thai.
147 E1 Bann r. Northern Ireland U.K.
96 D3 Bann r. Northern Ireland U.K.
96 D3 Bannalec France
246 A1 Bannerman Town Eleuthera
  Bahamas
199 J8 Bannu admin. div. Pak.
119 K3 Bannu Pak.
119 K3 Bannu admin. div. Pak.
161 D4 Banon France
185 E4 Baños de la Encina Spain
250 B5 Baños Ecuador
182 D5 Baños de Molgas Spain
183 E4 Baños de Montemayor
  Spain
186 D2 Baños de Panticosa Spain
182 D3 Baños de Río Tobía Spain
183 E3 Baños de Valdearados Spain
177 H3 Bánov Slovakia

177 H3 Bánovce nad Bebravou Slovakia
188 G3 Banoviči Bos.-Herz.
96 D3 Ban Phaeng Thai.
96 C3 Ban Phai Thai.
96 D4 Ban Phon Laos
96 B4 Banphot Phisai Thai.
97 B4 Ban Pong Thai.
108 C3 Banqiao Yunnan China
206 B3 Bansang Gambia
96 B3 Ban Saraphi Thai.
97 B5 Ban Sawi Thai.
117 E4 Bansgaon Uttar Prad. India
147 C4 Bansha Rep. of Ireland
116 C4 Bansi Rajasthan India
116 D4 Bansi Uttar Prad. India
117 E4 Bansi Uttar Prad. India
177 I3 Banská Bystrica Slovakia
177 H3 Banská Štiavnica Slovakia
197 F5 Bansko Bulg.
177 I3 Banskobystrický Kraj admin. reg. Slovakia
117 F4 Bansloi r. India
151 G3 Banstead Surrey, England U.K.
114 C2 Banswada Andhra Prad. India
116 C5 Banswara Rajasthan India
164 E2 Bant Neth.
93 A4 Bantaeng Sulawesi Selatan Indon.
235 E1 Bantam CT U.S.A.
207 F4 Bantè Benin
147 C4 Banteer Rep. of Ireland
97 B5 Ban Tha Chang Thai.
97 B5 Ban Tha Kham Thai.
150 D4 Bantham Devon, England U.K.
96 B3 Ban Tha Song Yang Thai.
Banthat mts Cambodia see Cardomom Range
96 C4 Ban Tha Tako Thai.
96 C4 Ban Tha Tum Thai.
97 C6 Ban Thepha Thai.
157 F3 Bantheville France
97 B4 Ban Thung Luang Thai.
147 B5 Bantry Rep. of Ireland
147 B5 Bantry Bay Rep. of Ireland
95 E4 Bantul Indon.
116 B5 Bantva Gujarat India
114 B3 Bantval Karnataka India
150 E3 Banwell North Somerset, England U.K.
94 B2 Banyak, Pulau-pulau is Indon.
187 F5 Banyalbufar Spain
207 H5 Banyo Cameroon
186 F2 Banyoles Spain
94 D3 Banyuasin r. Indon.
163 F6 Banyuls-sur-Mer France
95 E4 Banyumas Jawa Tengah Indon.
95 F5 Banyuwangi Jawa Timur Indon.
263 I2 Banzare Coast Antarctica
265 J8 Banzare Seamount sea feature Indian Ocean
Banzart Tunisia see Bizerte
193 I4 Banzi Italy
170 C2 Banzkow Ger.
Banzyville Dem. Rep. Congo see Mobayi-Mbongo
Bao'an Guangdong China see Shenzhen
106 D5 Bao'an Qinghai China
Bao'an Shaanxi China see Zhidan
107 G3 Baochang Nei Mongol China
Baocheng Hainan China see Baoting
108 C1 Baocheng Shaanxi China
107 H4 Baodi Tianjin China
107 G4 Baoding Hebei China
109 E1 Baofeng Henan China
Baohe Yunnan China see Weixi
107 E5 Baoji Shaanxi China
107 E5 Baoji Shaanxi China
109 D2 Baokang Hubei China
107 I2 Baokang Nei Mongol China
97 D5 Bao Lôc Vietnam
100 E3 Baoqing Heilong. China
208 B3 Baoro C.A.R.
109 G2 Baoshan Shanghai China
108 A3 Baoshan Yunnan China
108 D5 Baoting Hainan China
107 F3 Baotou Nei Mongol China
206 C3 Baoulé r. Mali
206 D3 Baoulé r. Mali
108 B2 Baoxing Sichuan China
108 B4 Baoxiu Yunnan China
109 F1 Baoying Jiangsu China
Baoyou Hainan China see Ledong
116 C4 Bap Rajasthan India
114 D3 Bapatla Andhra Prad. India
156 C2 Bapaume France
Bapu Sichuan China see Meigu
111 F5 Baqên Xizang China
111 F6 Baqên Xizang China
Baqiu Jiangxi China see Xiajiang
Baqty Kazakh. see Bakhty
127 G4 Ba'qūbah Iraq
157 E3 Bar r. France
136 D3 Bar Ukr.
196 D4 Bar Crna Gora Yugo.
207 H4 Bara Nigeria
177 K6 Bara Romania
203 F6 Bara Sudan
210 E4 Baraawe Somalia
95 F3 Barabai Kalimantan Selatan Indon.
116 E4 Bara Banki Uttar Prad. India
177 L3 Barabás Hungary
Barabhas Western Isles, Scotland U.K. see Barvas
117 F5 Barabhum W. Bengal India
130 I4 Barabinsk Rus. Fed.
226 C4 Baraboo WI U.S.A.
226 C4 Baraboo r. WI U.S.A.
206 E3 Baraboulé Burkina
136 F4 Baraboy r. Ukr.
Baracaldo Spain see Barakaldo
246 D2 Baracoa Cuba
177 H5 Baracs Hungary
177 H4 Baracska Hungary
128 C3 Baradá, Nahr r. Syria
261 H3 Baradero Arg.
83 G2 Baradine N.S.W. Austr.
83 G2 Baradine r. N.S.W. Austr.
226 C2 Baraga MI U.S.A.
197 H3 Bărăganului, Câmpia plain Romania
193 H4 Baragiano Italy
250 D2 Baragua, Sierra de mts Venez.
117 G5 Barahanuddin Bangl.
246 E3 Barahona Dom. Rep.
183 H3 Barahona Spain
117 H4 Barail Range mts India
206 E2 Bara Issa r. Mali
183 H4 Barajas de Melo Spain
196 E3 Barajevo Srbija Yugo.
117 H4 Barak r. India
183 H1 Barakaldo Spain
123 G3 Barakī Barak Afgh.
215 E5 Barakke S. Africa
117 F5 Barakot Orissa India
121 F1 Barakpay Kazakh.
85 G5 Baralaba Qld Austr.
129 C3 Baralet'i Georgia
182 C2 Baralla Spain
95 F1 Baram r. Sarawak Malaysia
251 G3 Baramanni Guyana
114 B2 Baramati Mahar. India
85 G5 Barambah r. Qld Austr.
183 H1 Barambio Spain
116 C2 Baramula Jammu and Kashmir
139 H4 Baran' Belarus
116 D4 Baran Rajasthan India
123 G5 Baran r. Pak.
122 E3 Bārān, Kūh-e mts Iran
183 I2 Barañain Spain
138 F5 Baranavichy Belarus
177 K4 Báránd Hungary
193 G3 Baranello Italy
123 E3 Barang, Dasht-i des. Afgh.
131 R3 Baranikha Rus. Fed.
136 D2 Baranivka Ukr.
246 D5 Baranoa Col.
193 F4 Barano d'Ischia Italy
222 C3 Baranof AK U.S.A.
220 E4 Baranof Island AK U.S.A.
Baranovichi Belarus see Baranavichy
120 A1 Baranovka Rus. Fed.
175 K4 Baranów Pol.
174 G4 Baranów Pol.
Baranowicze Belarus see Baranavichy
175 J2 Baranowo Pol.
175 J5 Baranów Sandomierska Pol.
177 H5 Baranya county Hungary
177 H6 Baranyai-dombság hills Hungary
257 F3 Barão de Cocais Brazil
254 E3 Barão de Grajaú Brazil
253 G4 Barão de Melgaço Brazil
184 B3 Barão de São Miguel Port.
197 G2 Baraolt Romania
206 D3 Baraouéli Mali
Baraqbay Kazakh. see Barakpay
165 E4 Baraque de Fraiture hill Belgium
163 E4 Baraqueville France
253 F1 Bararati r. Brazil
136 E2 Barashi Ukr.
93 C4 Barat Daya, Kepulauan is Maluku Indon.
82 D3 Baratta S.A. Austr.
251 F4 Barauaná, Serra mts Brazil
116 D3 Baraut Uttar Prad. India
250 C4 Baraya Col.
257 F4 Barbacena Brazil
184 C2 Barbacena Port.
182 C2 Barbadás Spain
Barba de Puerco Spain see Puerto Seguro
183 G2 Barbadillo de Herreros Spain
183 G2 Barbadillo del Mercado Spain
183 G2 Barbadillo del Pez Spain
247 □4 Barbados country West Indies
192 B4 Barbagia mts Sardegna Italy
191 J3 Barban Croatia
128 A5 Barbar, Gebel el mt. Egypt
191 G3 Barbarano Vicentino Italy
245 F2 Barbarena r. Mex.
199 E1 Barbaros Turkey
163 C4 Barbaste France
186 D2 Barbastro Spain
191 J4 Barbat Croatia
184 E4 Barbate r. Spain
184 E4 Barbate de Franco Spain
158 D5 Barbâtre France
163 C5 Barbazan France
163 C5 Barbazan-Debat France
161 C5 Barbentane France
191 G4 Barberino di Mugello Italy
227 G1 Barber's Bay Ont. Can.
215 H1 Barberton S. Africa
232 C4 Barberton OH U.S.A.
162 B3 Barbezieux-St-Hilaire France
117 F4 Barbigha Bihar India
117 F5 Barbil Orissa India
156 C4 Barbizon France
149 G3 Barbon Cumbria, England U.K.
156 D4 Barbonne-Fayel France
250 C3 Barbosa Col.
163 B5 Barbotan-les-Thermes France
234 B1 Barbours PA U.S.A.
232 B6 Barbourville KY U.S.A.
92 B4 Barboza Phil.
247 □2 Barbuda i. Antigua and Barbuda
151 F2 Barby Northamptonshire, England U.K.
171 C4 Barby (Elbe) Ger.
197 F4 Bârca Romania
183 H3 Barca Spain
186 D2 Barcabo Spain
182 D3 Barca de Alva Port.
85 F4 Barcaldine Qld Austr.
184 D2 Barcarrota Spain
197 E2 Barcău r. Romania
Barce Libya see Al Marj
182 B3 Barcelinhos Port.
195 E4 Barcellona Pozzo di Gotto Sicilia Italy
186 F3 Barcelona Spain
186 E3 Barcelona prov. Cataluña Spain
251 E2 Barcelona Venez.
247 □1 Barceloneta Puerto Rico
163 B5 Barcelonne-du-Gers France
161 E4 Barcelonnette France
251 F5 Barcelos Brazil
182 B3 Barcelos Port.
182 D1 Bárcena del Monasterio Spain
183 F1 Bárcena de Pie de Concha Spain
183 G1 Barcenillas de Cerezos Spain
169 F5 Barchfeld Ger.
175 J1 Barciany Pol.
161 D4 Barcillonnette France
174 F3 Barcin Pol.
Barcino Spain see Barcelona
191 H2 Barcis Italy
234 C3 Barclay MD U.S.A.
Barclay de Tolly atoll Arch. des Tuamotu Fr. Polynesia see Raroia
206 C5 Barclayville Liberia
183 H3 Barcones Spain
Barcoo Creek watercourse Qld/S.A. Austr. see Cooper Creek
182 C3 Barcos Port.
176 G6 Barcs Hungary
163 B5 Barcus France
175 I2 Barczewo Pol.
160 C1 Bard, Montagne de hill France
129 E3 Bärdä Azer.
134 K4 Barda Rus. Fed.
140 □C2 Bárðarbunga mt. Iceland
128 A4 Bardawīl, Sabkhet el lag. Egypt
117 F5 Barddhaman W. Bengal India
177 K2 Bardejov Slovakia
186 B2 Bárdena Spain
171 D3 Bardenitz Ger.
Bardera Somalia see Baardheere
86 D3 Bardi W.A. Austr.
190 E4 Bardi Italy
190 D4 Bardineto Italy
149 I4 Bardney Lincolnshire, England U.K.
174 E5 Bardo Pol.
191 F3 Bardolino Italy
190 B3 Bardonecchia Italy
163 A5 Bardos France
168 F2 Bardowick Ger.
149 F3 Bardsea Cumbria, England U.K.
150 C2 Bardsey Island Wales U.K.
150 C2 Bardsey Sound sea chan. Wales U.K.
122 B3 Bard Shah Iran
122 D4 Bardsīr Iran
230 C4 Bardstown KY U.S.A.
177 G5 Bárdudvarnok Hungary
Barduli Italy see Barletta
237 F4 Bardwell KY U.S.A.
207 H5 Baré Cameroon
81 A6 Bare Cone hill South I. N.Z.
163 C6 Barèges France
116 D3 Bareilly Uttar Prad. India
116 D5 Bareli Madh. Prad. India
83 F3 Barellan N.S.W. Austr.
168 D3 Barenburg Ger.
168 F2 Barendorf Ger.
117 G4 Barengapara Meghalaya India
171 F4 Bärenklau Ger.
171 E5 Bärenstein Ger.
171 E5 Bärenstein Ger.
156 A3 Barentin France
159 F3 Barenton France
Barents Island Svalbard see Barentsøya
140 □ Barentsøya i. Svalbard
268 C1 Barents Sea Arctic Ocean
203 H6 Barentu Eritrea
234 B2 Bareville PA U.S.A.
158 E2 Barfleur France
158 E2 Barfleur, Pointe de pt France
190 F4 Barga Italy
210 F2 Bargaal Somalia
190 E4 Bargagli Italy
234 D3 Bargaintown NJ U.S.A.
85 H5 Bargara Qld Austr.
183 F5 Bargas Spain
190 C4 Barge Italy
161 E5 Bargemon France
168 E1 Bargenstedt Ger.
190 F3 Barghe Italy
116 D5 Bargi Madh. Prad. India
Bargıri Van Turkey see Muradiye
170 E2 Bargischow Ger.
175 K2 Bargłów Kościelny Pol.
150 D3 Bargoed Caerphilly, Wales U.K.
146 D6 Bargrennan Dumfries and Galloway, Scotland U.K.
168 E2 Bargstedt Ger.
168 F2 Bargteheide Ger.
163 C4 Barguelonne r. France
117 G5 Barguna Bangl.
114 C4 Bargur Tamil Nadu India
129 E4 Bärgüşad r. Azer.
117 F4 Barh Bihar India
117 E4 Barhaj Uttar Prad. India
117 E4 Barhalganj Uttar Prad. India
83 F3 Barham N.S.W. Austr.
151 I3 Barham Kent, England U.K.
233 □I2 Bar Harbor ME U.S.A.
117 F4 Barharwa Bihar India
151 H2 Bar Hill Cambridgeshire, England U.K.
116 D4 Bari Rajasthan India
195 F1 Bari Italy
193 I4 Bari prov. Puglia Italy
210 F2 Bari admin. reg. Somalia
97 D5 Ba Ria Vietnam
211 B5 Bariadi Tanz.
123 H4 Bari Doab lowland Pak.
205 G2 Barika Alg.
193 H4 Barile Italy
251 G2 Barima r. Guyana
187 B6 Barinas Spain
250 D2 Barinas Venez.
250 D2 Barinas state Venez.
226 A5 Baring MO U.S.A.
210 C4 Baringo, Lake Kenya
117 F5 Baripada Orissa India
256 C5 Bariri Brazil
116 C4 Bari Sadri Rajasthan India
117 G5 Barisal Bangl.
117 G5 Barisal admin. div. Bangl.
94 C3 Barisan, Pegunungan mts Indon.
192 B5 Barì Sardo Sardegna Italy
193 F2 Barisciano Italy
95 F3 Barito r. Indon.
Barium Italy see Bari
161 C4 Barjac France
161 E5 Barjaude, Montagne de mt. France
161 E5 Barjols France
117 F5 Barjora W. Bengal India
124 B4 Barka prov. Eritrea
125 G3 Barkā Oman
108 B2 Barkam Sichuan China
138 F3 Barkava Latvia
168 E1 Barkelsby Ger.
261 H5 Barker Arg.
87 D6 Barker, Lake salt flat W.A. Austr.
222 F4 Barkerville B.C. Can.
206 B2 Barkéwol el Abiod Maur.
117 F4 Barki Saraiya Bihar India
84 D4 Barkly Downs Qld Austr.
215 F4 Barkly East S. Africa
84 C3 Barkly Tableland reg. N.T. Austr.
214 E3 Barkly West S. Africa
106 B3 Barkol Xinjiang China
116 D3 Barkot Uttar Prad. India
174 F2 Barkowo Pol.
151 H2 Barkway Hertfordshire, England U.K.
199 G2 Barla Turkey
197 H2 Bârlad Romania
197 H2 Bârladului, Podişul plat. Romania
150 E2 Barlaston Staffordshire, England U.K.
149 H4 Barlborough Derbyshire, England U.K.
150 D3 Barle r. England U.K.
171 C3 Barleben Ger.
157 F4 Bar-le-Duc France
87 C6 Barlee, Lake salt flat W.A. Austr.
87 B4 Barlee Range hills W.A. Austr.
161 E4 Barles France
193 I3 Barletta Italy
151 H2 Barley Hertfordshire, England U.K.
156 C2 Barlin France
174 D3 Barlinek Pol.
216 □3d Barlovento La Palma Canary Is
222 B2 Barlow Y.T. Can.
137 G4 Barmashove Ukr.
83 F3 Barmedman N.S.W. Austr.
Barmen-Elberfeld Ger. see Wuppertal
116 B4 Barmer Rajasthan India
82 E3 Barmera S.A. Austr.
127 H5 Barm Fīrūz, Kūh-e mt. Iran
150 C2 Barmouth Gwynedd, Wales U.K.
150 C2 Barmouth Bay Wales U.K.
168 E2 Barmstedt Ger.
147 B3 Barna Rep. of Ireland
177 L6 Bârna Romania
116 C5 Barnagar Madh. Prad. India
116 C3 Barnala Punjab India
222 B3 Barnard, Mount Alaska/B.C. Can./U.S.A.
149 H3 Barnard Castle Durham, England U.K.
83 F2 Barnato N.S.W. Austr.
147 B2 Barnatra Rep. of Ireland
173 G2 Bärnau Ger.
98 D1 Barnaul Rus. Fed.
179 G3 Barnbach Austria
235 D3 Barnegat NJ U.S.A.
235 D3 Barnegat Beach NJ U.S.A.
235 D3 Barnegat Light NJ U.S.A.
232 D4 Barnesboro PA U.S.A.
221 K2 Barnes Icecap Nunavut Can.
231 D5 Barnesville GA U.S.A.
236 D2 Barnesville MN U.S.A.
232 C5 Barnesville OH U.S.A.
151 G3 Barnet Greater London, England U.K.
233 G2 Barnet VT U.S.A.
164 E2 Barneveld Neth.
158 E2 Barneville-Carteret France
170 D3 Barnewitz Ger.
147 C3 Barneycarroll Rep. of Ireland
83 F3 Barneys Lake imp. l. N.S.W. Austr.
241 L3 Barney Top mt. UT U.S.A.
237 C6 Barnhart TX U.S.A.
151 H2 Barningham Suffolk, England U.K.
147 E2 Barnmeen Northern Ireland U.K.
149 G4 Barnoldswick Lancashire, England U.K.
197 H2 Bârnova, Dealul hill Romania
237 D4 Barnsdall OK U.S.A.
149 H4 Barnsley South Yorkshire, England U.K.
233 H4 Barnstable MA U.S.A.
171 C4 Barnstädt Ger.
150 C3 Barnstaple Devon, England U.K.
Barnstaple Bay England U.K. see Bideford Bay
168 D3 Barnstorf Ger.
149 G4 Barnton Cheshire, England U.K.
169 E4 Barntrup Ger.
231 D5 Barnwell SC U.S.A.
207 G4 Baro Nigeria
Baroda Gujarat India see Vadodara
116 D4 Baroda Madh. Prad. India
215 E4 Baroda S. Africa
214 E5 Baroe S. Africa
179 F4 Bärofen mt. Austria
190 D3 Barone, Monte mt. Italy
108 A2 Barong Sichuan China
87 E5 Barons Range hills W.A. Austr.
157 G4 Baronville France
78 □6 Barora Fa i. Solomon Is
78 □6 Barora Ite i. Solomon Is
210 B2 Baro Wenz r. Eth.
138 F4 Barowka Belarus
117 G4 Barpeta Assam India
Bar Pla Soi Thai. see Chon Buri
128 B5 Barqa, Gebel mt. Egypt
187 B7 Barqueros Spain
184 B1 Barquinha Port.
250 D2 Barquisimeto Venez.
157 H4 Barr France
146 D6 Barr South Ayrshire, Scotland U.K.
254 E4 Barra Brazil
146 A5 Barra i. Scotland U.K.
146 A4 Barra, Sound of sea chan. Scotland U.K.
83 G2 Barraba N.S.W. Austr.
256 C5 Barra Bonita Brazil
256 C5 Barra Bonita, Represa resr Brazil
187 C4 Barracas Spain
186 B4 Barrachina Spain
232 C5 Barrackville WV U.S.A.
254 E5 Barra da Estiva Brazil
257 G3 Barra de São Francisco Brazil
253 F3 Barra do Bugres Brazil
254 D3 Barra do Corda Brazil
209 B7 Barra do Cuanza Angola
256 A1 Barra do Garças Brazil
254 E4 Barrado Mendes Brazil
257 F5 Barra do Piraí Brazil
256 C6 Barra do Turvo Brazil
194 D5 Barrafranca Sicilia Italy
Barraigh i. Scotland U.K. see Barra
242 □J6 Barra Kruta Hond.
182 B2 Barral Spain
192 B5 Barrali Sardegna Italy
257 F4 Barra Longa Brazil
257 E5 Barra Mansa Brazil
203 G3 Barrâmîya Egypt
163 C5 Barran France
252 A2 Barranca Peru
250 C3 Barrancabermeja Col.
261 G3 Barrancas Arg.
260 C5 Barrancas r. Corrientes Arg.
261 H2 Barrancas r. Mendoza/Neuquén Arg.
246 D5 Barrancas Col.
250 C2 Barranco de Loba Col.
184 C3 Barranco do Velho Port.
184 D2 Barrancos Port.
185 I2 Barranda Spain
250 C2 Barranquilla Col.
247 □1 Barranquitas Puerto Rico
146 B5 Barrapoll Argyll and Bute, Scotland U.K.
254 E3 Barras Brazil
227 I1 Barraute Que. Can.
185 H1 Barrax Spain
233 G3 Barre MA U.S.A.
233 G2 Barre VT U.S.A.
260 C2 Barreal Arg.
161 B4 Barre-des-Cévennes France
161 E4 Barre des Ecrins mt. France
254 D5 Barreiras Brazil
251 G5 Barreirinha Brazil
254 E2 Barreirinhas Brazil
255 B5 Barreiro r. Brazil
184 A2 Barreiro Port.
254 G4 Barreiros Brazil
161 E5 Barrême France
Barren Island Kiribati see Starbuck Island
256 C4 Barretos Brazil
240 I5 Barrett CA U.S.A.
86 E3 Barrett, Mount hill W.A. Austr.
222 H4 Barrhead Alta Can.
146 D6 Barrhead East Renfrewshire, Scotland U.K.
81 C5 Barrhill South I. N.Z.
146 D6 Barrhill South Ayrshire, Scotland U.K.
186 F3 Barriada Nueva Spain
224 E4 Barrie Ont. Can.
222 F5 Barrière B.C. Can.
82 E2 Barrier Range hills N.S.W. Austr.
243 I5 Barrier Reef Belize
225 H5 Barrington N.S. Can.
214 D5 Barrington S. Africa
83 G3 Barrington, Mount N.S.W. Austr.
Barrington Island Islas Galápagos Ecuador see Santa Fé, Isla
83 F2 Barringun N.S.W. Austr.
187 C7 Barrio del Peral Spain
187 C5 Barrio Mar Spain
182 C3 Barrô Port.
254 C5 Barro Alto Brazil
182 C4 Barroca Port.
182 B2 Barroças e Taias Port.
157 F4 Barrois, Plateau du France
257 H2 Barrolândia Brazil
226 B3 Barron WI U.S.A.
226 B3 Barronett WI U.S.A.
260 A6 Barros Arana Chile
182 B3 Barroselas Port.
257 F4 Barroso Brazil
147 E4 Barrow r. Rep. of Ireland
220 C2 Barrow AK U.S.A.
151 G2 Barrowby Lincolnshire, England U.K.
84 C4 Barrow Creek N.T. Austr.
149 G4 Barrowford Lancashire, England U.K.
149 F3 Barrow-in-Furness Cumbria, England U.K.
86 B4 Barrow Island W.A. Austr.
85 F2 Barrow Point Qld Austr.
87 E5 Barrow Range hills W.A. Austr.
221 I2 Barrow Strait Nunavut Can.
149 I4 Barrow upon Humber North Lincolnshire, England U.K.
87 D5 Barr Smith Range hills W.A. Austr.
182 D3 Barruecopardo Spain
183 F2 Barruelo de Santullan Spain
150 D3 Barry Vale of Glamorgan, Wales U.K.
214 C5 Barrydale S. Africa
83 F4 Barry Mountains Vic. Austr.
224 E4 Barrys Bay Ont. Can.
232 A3 Barryton MI U.S.A.
80 E3 Barryville North I. N.Z.
234 D1 Barryville NY U.S.A.
177 L5 Bârsa Romania
163 B4 Barsac France
206 E3 Barsalogo Burkina
116 C3 Barsalpur Rajasthan India
197 G2 Bârsana Romania
168 F2 Barsbüttel Ger.
121 I2 Barshatas Kazakh.
Barshi Mahar. India see Barsi
114 B2 Barsi Mahar. India
169 E3 Barsinghausen Ger.
168 C2 Barßel Ger.
240 I4 Barstow CA U.S.A.
139 K4 Barsuki Rus. Fed.
114 D2 Barsur Madh. Prad. India
156 E4 Bar-sur-Aube France
156 E4 Bar-sur-Seine France
138 C3 Bārta r. Latvia
123 G2 Bartang r. Tajik.
160 F1 Bartenheim France
172 D2 Bartenstein Ger.
170 D1 Barth Ger.
170 D1 Barthe r. Ger.
172 D3 Bartholomä Ger.
237 E5 Bartholomew, Bayou r. LA U.S.A.
Bartholomew Island Vanuatu see Malo
251 G3 Bartica Guyana
126 D2 Bartın Turkey
85 F3 Bartle Frere, Mount Qld Austr.
232 B5 Bartles OH U.S.A.
241 L2 Bartles, Mount UT U.S.A.
237 D4 Bartlesville OK U.S.A.
236 D3 Bartlett NE U.S.A.
233 H2 Bartlett NH U.S.A.
80 F3 Bartletts North I. N.Z.
175 I2 Bartniki Pol.
149 G4 Barton Lancashire, England U.K.
233 G2 Barton VT U.S.A.
151 G3 Barton-le-Clay Bedfordshire, England U.K.
151 F2 Barton-under-Needwood Staffordshire, England U.K.
149 I4 Barton-upon-Humber North Lincolnshire, England U.K.
226 C5 Bartonville IL U.S.A.
143 I4 Bartoszyce Pol.
231 D7 Bartow FL U.S.A.
138 C3 Bartuva r. Lith.
250 C2 Baru, Isla de i. Col.
175 H3 Baruchowo Pol.
117 G5 Baruipur W. Bengal India
184 C1 Barulho Port.
125 E5 Barūm Yemen
192 B5 Barumini Sardegna Italy
94 C2 Barumun r. Indon.
Barunga N.T. Austr. see Bamyili
94 B2 Barus Sumatera Indon.
171 E3 Baruth Brandenburg Ger.
171 F4 Baruth Sachsen Ger.
106 E1 Baruunharaa Mongolia
106 B1 Baruunturuun Mongolia
107 G2 Baruun Urt Mongolia
115 E2 Baruva Andhra Prad. India
146 B3 Barvas Western Isles, Scotland U.K.
165 E4 Barvaux Belgium
168 D3 Barver Ger.
137 I3 Barvinkove Ukr.
117 F5 Barwa Bihar India
116 D5 Barwah Madh. Prad. India
116 B5 Barwala Gujarat India
116 C3 Barwala Haryana India
116 C5 Barwani Madh. Prad. India
116 D4 Barwa Sagar Uttar Prad. India
168 F3 Barwedel Ger.
Barwéli Mali see Baraouéli
174 E2 Barwice Pol.
83 F2 Barwon r. N.S.W. Austr.
139 J4 Baryatino Rus. Fed.
139 K4 Barybino Rus. Fed.
174 E4 Barycz r. Pol.
Barygaza Gujarat India see Bharuch
138 G4 Barysaw Belarus
135 I5 Barysh Rus. Fed.
137 F2 Baryshivka Ukr.
182 E1 Bárzana Spain
177 L5 Bârzava Romania
97 D5 Basăk, Tônlé r. Cambodia
85 F3 Basalt r. Qld Austr.
208 C4 Basankusu Dem. Rep. Congo
117 F4 Basantpur Bihar India
136 E4 Basarabeasca Moldova
197 I3 Basarabi Romania
Basargechar Armenia see Vardenis
183 H1 Basauri Spain
261 H3 Basavilbaso Arg.
92 B4 Basay Phil.
129 B3 Başçakmak Turkey
197 H3 Bâsca Mică r. Romania
186 F2 Bàscara Spain
157 F3 Bascharage Lux.
150 E2 Baschurch Shropshire, England U.K.
193 F2 Basciano Italy
92 B1 Basco Phil.
183 G2 Basconcillos del Tozo Spain
209 B6 Bas-Congo admin. reg. Dem. Rep. Congo
163 B5 Bascons France
163 C5 Bascous France
183 H4 Bascuñana, Sierra de mts Spain
168 E2 Basdahl Ger.
170 E3 Basdorf Ger.
129 A3 Başdurak Turkey
165 C4 Basècles Belgium
190 C1 Basel Switz.
191 G2 Baselga di Pinè Italy
193 G3 Baselice Italy
190 C1 Baselland canton Switz.
160 F1 Basel-Mulhouse airport France
161 C3 Bas-en-Basset France
193 I4 Basentello r. Italy
193 I4 Basento r. Italy
197 H2 Başeu r. Romania
92 C4 Basey Phil.
122 D5 Bashākerd, Kūhhā-ye mts Iran
Bashan Jiangxi China see Chongren
Bashanta Rus. Fed. see Gorodovikovsk
222 H4 Bashaw Alta Can.
121 K2 Bashchelakskiy Khrebet mts Rus. Fed.
215 G5 Bashee r. S. Africa
215 G4 Bashee Bridge S. Africa
123 G3 Bashgul r. Afgh.
90 F2 Bashi Channel Taiwan
110 D1 Bashkaus r. Rus. Fed.
Bashkiria aut. rep. Rus. Fed. see Bashkortostan, Respublika
Bashkirskaya A.S.S.R. aut. rep. Rus. Fed. see Bashkortostan, Respublika
129 D3 Bashk'oi Georgia
120 D1 Bashkortostan, Respublika aut. rep. Rus. Fed.
135 H5 Bashmakovo Rus. Fed.
137 G4 Bashtanka Ukr.
116 D4 Basi Rajasthan India
117 F5 Basia Bihar India
151 H3 Basildon Essex, England U.K.
237 E6 Basile LA U.S.A.
207 H6 Basile, Pico mt. Equat. Guinea
191 I2 Basiliano Italy
193 H4 Basilicata admin. reg. Italy
238 E2 Basin WY U.S.A.
151 F3 Basingstoke Hampshire, England U.K.
127 G4 Bāsīra r. Iraq
117 G5 Basirhat W. Bengal India
128 B2 Basīţ, Ra's al pt Syria
177 H2 Baška Czech Rep.
127 G3 Başkale Turkey
224 F4 Baskatong, Réservoir resr Que. Can.
86 D3 Baskerville, Cape W.A. Austr.
129 B3 Başköy Turkey
135 I6 Baskunchak, Ozero l. Rus. Fed.
129 E3 Baş Layski Azer.
Basle Switz. see Basel
149 H4 Baslow Derbyshire, England U.K.
199 G3 Başmakçı Turkey
114 C2 Basmat Mahar. India
116 D5 Basoda Madh. Prad. India
190 D2 Basodino mt. Italy/Switz.
208 D4 Basoko Dem. Rep. Congo
209 D6 Basongo Dem. Rep. Congo
129 E3 Baş Qärvänd Azer.
Basque Country aut. comm. Spain see País Vasco
Basra Iraq see Al Başrah
157 H4 Bas-Rhin dept Alsace France
Bass, Îlots de is Îs Australes Fr. Polynesia see Marotiri
192 B3 Bassacutena Sardegna Italy
192 B3 Bassacutena r. Sardegna Italy
223 H5 Bassano Alta Can.
191 G3 Bassano del Grappa Italy
192 E2 Bassano Romano Italy
207 F4 Bassar Togo
265 G6 Bassas da India rf Indian Ocean
114 B3 Bassas de Pedro Padua Bank sea feature India
206 D4 Bassawa Côte d'Ivoire
190 C1 Bassecourt Switz.
158 E4 Basse-Goulaine France
96 A3 Bassein Myanmar
96 A3 Bassein r. Myanmar
208 D3 Basse-Kotto pref. C.A.R.
159 F3 Basse-Normandie admin. reg. France
Basses-Alpes dept Provence-Alpes-Côte-d'Azur France see Alpes-de-Haute-Provence
206 B3 Basse Santa Su Gambia
Basses-Pyrénées dept Aquitaine France see Pyrénées-Atlantiques
247 □2 Basse-Terre Guadeloupe
247 □2 Basse-Terre i. Guadeloupe
247 □2 Basseterre St Kitts and Nevis
236 D3 Bassett NE U.S.A.
232 D6 Bassett VA U.S.A.
241 L5 Bassett Peak AZ U.S.A.
233 □I2 Bass Harbor ME U.S.A.
193 F3 Bassiano Italy
163 D6 Bassiès, Pic Rouge de mt. France
206 D3 Bassikounou Maur.
207 F4 Bassila Benin
151 G2 Bassingbourn Cambridgeshire, England U.K.
149 I4 Bassingham Lincolnshire, England U.K.
202 D5 Basso, Plateau de Chad
163 C5 Bassoues France
146 F5 Bass Rock i. Scotland U.K.
83 F4 Bass Strait Tas./Vic. Austr.
168 D3 Bassum Ger.
160 D3 Bassy France
142 E3 Båstad Sweden
122 C5 Bastak Iran
127 I3 Bastam Iran
122 A2 Bastānābād Iran
193 E2 Bastardo Italy
192 B2 Bastelica Corse France
192 A3 Bastelicaccia Corse France
163 B5 Bastennes France
169 F5 Bastheim Ger.
117 E4 Basti Uttar Prad. India
192 B2 Bastia Corse France
Bastia airport Corse France see Poretta
193 E1 Bastia Italy
232 C6 Bastian VA U.S.A.
165 E4 Bastogne Belgium
170 C1 Bastorf Ger.
256 B4 Bastos Brazil
237 F5 Bastrop LA U.S.A.
237 D6 Bastrop TX U.S.A.
140 M2 Bastuträsk Sweden
136 D1 Bastyn' Belarus
123 F5 Basul r. Pak.
Basuo Hainan China see Dongfang
Basutoland country Africa see Lesotho
139 H5 Basya r. Belarus
128 A1 Başyayla Turkey
Bas-Zaïre admin. reg. Dem. Rep. Congo see Bas-Congo
188 F4 Bat mt. Croatia
125 G3 Bat, Al Khutm and Al Ayn tourist site Oman
207 H6 Bata Equat. Guinea
177 H5 Báta Hungary
177 L5 Bata Romania
92 B3 Bataan Peninsula Phil.
246 B2 Batabanó, Golfo de b. Cuba
92 B2 Batac Phil.
242 C3 Batacosa Mex.
131 O3 Batagay Rus. Fed.
131 O3 Batagay-Alyta Rus. Fed.
256 A4 Bataguaçu Brazil
256 A5 Bataiporã Brazil
197 G5 Batak Bulg.
116 C3 Batala Punjab India
254 E3 Batalha Brazil
182 B5 Batalha Port.
120 D2 Batamshinskiy Kazakh.
Batamshy Kazakh. see Batamshinskiy
108 A2 Batang Sichuan China
95 E4 Batang Jawa Tengah Indon.
208 C3 Batangafo C.A.R.
92 B3 Batangas Phil.
94 D3 Batanghari r. Indon.
92 B1 Batan Islands Phil.
177 K5 Batăr Romania
177 H5 Bátaszék Hungary
256 D4 Batatais Brazil
Batavia Indon. see Jakarta
226 C5 Batavia IL U.S.A.
232 D3 Batavia NY U.S.A.
232 A5 Batavia OH U.S.A.
135 G7 Bataysk Rus. Fed.
227 E2 Batchawana Ont. Can.
227 E2 Batchawana r. Ont. Can.
226 E2 Batchawana Bay Ont. Can.
224 C4 Batchawana Mountain hill Ont. Can.
84 B2 Batchelor N.T. Austr.
97 C4 Bătdâmbâng Cambodia
186 D3 Batea Spain
94 A1 Bateemeucica, Gunung mt. Indon.
209 B5 Batéké, Plateaux Congo
83 G3 Batemans Bay N.S.W. Austr.
185 F2 Baterno Spain
231 D5 Batesburg SC U.S.A.
87 D5 Bates Range hills W.A. Austr.
237 F5 Batesville AR U.S.A.
237 F5 Batesville MS U.S.A.
139 H2 Batetskiy Rus. Fed.
225 H4 Bath N.B. Can.
227 I3 Bath Ont. Can.
150 E3 Bath Bath and North East Somerset, England U.K.
226 B5 Bath IL U.S.A.
233 □I3 Bath ME U.S.A.
232 E3 Bath NY U.S.A.
234 C2 Bath PA U.S.A.
202 C6 Batha pref. Chad
150 E3 Bath and North East Somerset admin. div. England U.K.
150 E3 Batheaston Bath and North East Somerset, England U.K.
150 E3 Bathford Bath and North East Somerset, England U.K.
146 E6 Bathgate West Lothian, Scotland U.K.
116 C3 Bathinda Punjab India
164 F2 Bathmen Neth.
83 G3 Bathurst N.S.W. Austr.
225 H4 Bathurst N.B. Can.
Bathurst Gambia see Banjul
215 F5 Bathurst S. Africa
85 F2 Bathurst Bay Qld Austr.
220 H3 Bathurst Inlet Nunavut Can.
220 H3 Bathurst Inlet inlet Nunavut Can.
84 B1 Bathurst Island N.T. Austr.
221 I2 Bathurst Island Nunavut Can.
210 D2 Batī Eth.
206 E4 Batié Burkina
79 □1 Batiki i. Fiji
157 F3 Batilly France
199 E3 Batı Menteşe Dağları mts Turkey
177 H6 Batina Croatia
254 E4 Batista, Serra da hills Brazil
199 G3 Batı Toroslar mts Turkey
177 J2 Batizovce Slovakia
149 H4 Batley West Yorkshire, England U.K.
83 G3 Batlow N.S.W. Austr.
127 F3 Batman Turkey
205 G2 Batna Alg.
125 E3 Baţn aţ Ţarfā' depr. Saudi Arabia
196 E3 Batočina Srbija Yugo.
209 E9 Batoka Zambia
237 F6 Baton Rouge LA U.S.A.
177 I4 Bátonyterenye Hungary
242 D3 Batopilas Mex.
177 H4 Bátorove Kosihy Slovakia
175 K5 Batorz Pol.
116 C2 Batote Jammu and Kashmir
207 I5 Batouri Cameroon
177 H3 Bátovce Slovakia
Batrā' tourist site Jordan see Petra
124 B2 Batrā, Jabal mt. Saudi Arabia
128 B5 Batrā', Jabal al mt. Jordan
177 L5 Bătrâna, Vârful mt. Romania
128 B2 Batroûn Lebanon
140 O1 Båtsfjord Norway
234 D3 Batsto r. NJ U.S.A.
Battambang Cambodia see Bătdâmbâng
169 D4 Battenberg (Eder) Ger.
190 C1 Bätterkinden Switz.
116 C3 Batti Punjab India
114 D5 Batticaloa Sri Lanka
193 G4 Battipaglia Italy
223 I4 Battle r. Alberta/Saskatchewan Can.
151 H4 Battle East Sussex, England U.K.
84 B2 Battle Creek r. N.T. Austr.
223 I5 Battle Creek r. Can./U.S.A.
226 E4 Battle Creek MI U.S.A.
223 I4 Battleford Sask. Can.
240 I1 Battle Mountain NV U.S.A.
240 I1 Battle Mountain mt. NV U.S.A.
177 K5 Battonya Hungary
210 C3 Batu mt. Eth.
95 F2 Batu, Bukit mt. Sarawak Malaysia
94 B3 Batu, Pulau-pulau is Indon.
95 F2 Batuayau, Bukit mt. Indon.
95 F2 Batu Bora, Bukit mt. Sarawak Malaysia
260 B4 Batuco Chile
94 C1 Batu Gajah Malaysia
92 C5 Batulaki Phil.
95 F2 Batulilangmebang, Gunung mt. Indon.
Batum Georgia see Bat'umi
129 B3 Bat'umi Georgia
94 C2 Batu Pahat Malaysia
94 C1 Batu Puteh, Gunung mt. Malaysia
94 D4 Baturaja Sumatera Indon.
95 E5 Baturetno Jawa Tengah Indon.
137 G2 Baturyn Ukr.
94 C3 Batusangkar Sumatera Indon.
177 H5 Bátya Hungary
175 M5 Batyatychi Ukr.
135 I5 Batyrevo Rus. Fed.
Batys Qazaqstan Oblysy admin. div. Kazakh. see Zapadnyy Kazakhstan
158 D4 Batz-sur-Mer France
251 H6 Bau r. Brazil
93 B4 Baubau Sulawesi Tenggara Indon.
207 H4 Bauchi Nigeria
207 H4 Bauchi state Nigeria
194 C5 Baucina Sicilia Italy
158 C4 Baud France
117 F5 Bauda Orissa India
236 E1 Baudette MN U.S.A.
250 B3 Baudo, Serranía de mts Col.
Baudouinville Dem. Rep. Congo see Moba
161 E5 Bauduen France
190 D2 Bauen Switz.
159 F4 Baugé France
160 E3 Bauges mts France
151 F3 Baughurst Hampshire, England U.K.
160 A1 Baugy France
85 G5 Bauhinia Qld Austr.
158 E4 Baulon France
160 E1 Baume-les-Dames France
172 B2 Baumholder Ger.
169 F6 Baunach Ger.
169 F6 Baunach r. Ger.
192 B4 Baunei Sardegna Italy
147 B4 Baurtregaum hill Rep. of Ireland
256 C5 Bauru Brazil
169 B5 Bausendorf Ger.
125 G3 Baushar Oman
138 E3 Bauska Latvia
120 B3 Bautino Kazakh.
171 F4 Bautzen Ger.
121 G4 Bauyrzhan Momysh-Uly Kazakh.
160 E1 Bavans France
Bavaria land Ger. see Bayern
156 D2 Bavay France
114 B2 Bavda Mahar. India
164 D3 Bavel Neth.
190 D3 Baveno Italy
214 D5 Baviaanskloofberge mts S. Africa
160 E1 Bavilliers France
242 C2 Bavispe r. Mex.
116 C5 Bavla Gujarat India
139 L3 Bavleny Rus. Fed.
135 K5 Bavly Rus. Fed.
176 D2 Bavorov Czech Rep.
116 D3 Bawal Haryana India
151 I2 Bawdeswell Norfolk, England U.K.
151 I2 Bawdsey Suffolk, England U.K.
96 B2 Bawdwin Myanmar
95 F4 Bawean i. Indon.
168 C3 Bawinkel Ger.
203 F2 Bawiti Egypt
206 E4 Bawku Ghana
148 B3 Bawnboy Rep. of Ireland
108 B2 Bawolung Sichuan China
149 H4 Bawtry South Yorkshire, England U.K.
108 B1 Baxi Sichuan China
Baxian Chongqing China see Banan
Baxian Hebei China see Bazhou
110 E4 Baxkorgan Xinjiang China
231 D6 Baxley GA U.S.A.
108 A2 Baxoi Xizang China
Bay Xinjiang China see Baicheng
210 D4 Bay admin. reg. Somalia
206 E5 Baya r. Côte d'Ivoire
189 B8 Bayad Alg.
246 C2 Bayamo Cuba
247 □1 Bayamón Puerto Rico
100 C3 Bayan Heilong. China
Bayan Qinghai China see Hualong
95 G5 Bayan Lombok Indon.
106 D2 Bayan Arhangay Mongolia
106 B2 Bayan Govĭ-Altay Mongolia
107 F1 Bayan Hentiy Mongolia
116 D4 Bayana Rajasthan India
121 H2 Bayanaul Kazakh.
106 C2 Bayanbulag Bayanhongor Mongolia
106 C2 Bayanbulag Bayanhongor Mongolia
107 F2 Bayanbulag Hentiy Mongolia
107 F2 Bayandelger Mongolia
208 C4 Bayanga C.A.R.
208 B3 Bayanga-Didi C.A.R.
Bayan Gol Nei Mongol China see Dengkou
106 B2 Bayangol Mongolia
106 D1 Bayangol Rus. Fed.
106 B5 Bayan Har Shan mts China
106 D2 Bayanhongor Mongolia
106 C2 Bayanhongor prov. Mongolia
106 E4 Bayan Hot Nei Mongol China
106 D2 Bayanhushuu Mongolia
106 E3 Bayan Mod Nei Mongol China
106 E3 Bayan Nuru Nei Mongol China
242 □K7 Bayano, Lago l. Panama
107 F3 Bayan Obo Kuangqu Nei Mongol China
106 A1 Bayan-Ölgiy prov. Mongolia
106 B2 Bayan-Ovoo Mongolia
107 F1 Bayan-Ovoo Mongolia
107 G3 Bayan Qagan Nei Mongol China
106 C2 Bayansayr Mongolia
106 C4 Bayan Shan mt. China
107 H1 Bayan Tohoi Nei Mongol China
107 H2 Bayan Ul Hot Nei Mongol China
185 H3 Bayárcal Spain
236 C3 Bayard NE U.S.A.
232 D5 Bayard WV U.S.A.
157 F4 Bayard-sur-Marne France
183 H2 Bayas r. Spain
107 G2 Bayasgalant Mongolia
199 G2 Bayat Afyon Turkey
Bayat Antalya Turkey see Akçay
92 B4 Bayawan Phil.
122 C4 Bayāẕ Iran
92 C4 Baybay Phil.
231 E5 Bayboro NC U.S.A.
232 B4 Bay Bridge OH U.S.A.
225 K4 Bay Bulls Nfld. Can.
127 F2 Bayburt Turkey
129 B3 Bayburt prov. Turkey
136 E3 Baybuzivka Ukr.
120 C3 Baychunas Kazakh.
227 F4 Bay City MI U.S.A.
237 D6 Bay City TX U.S.A.
149 F3 Baycliff Cumbria, England U.K.
124 B2 Baydā, Jabal al hill Saudi Arabia
130 H3 Baydaratskaya Guba Rus. Fed.
210 D4 Baydhabo Somalia
106 C2 Baydrag Gol r. Mongolia
Baydzhansay Kazakh. see Bayzhansay
156 D4 Baye France
157 E4 Bayel France
207 G5 Bayelsa state Nigeria
173 H3 Bayerbach Ger.
173 G3 Bayerbach bei Ergoldsbach Ger.
173 H2 Bayerisch Eisenstein Ger.
173 G2 Bayerischer Wald mts Ger.
173 G4 Bayerisch Gmain Ger.
171 B5 Bayern land Ger.
173 F4 Bayersoien Ger.
159 F2 Bayeux France
121 J1 Bayevo Rus. Fed.
227 G4 Bayfield Ont. Can.
226 B2 Bayfield WI U.S.A.

121 F3	Baygakum Kazakh.
120 C2	Baygakum Kazakh.
120 E1	Baygora Kazakh.
137 J1	Baygora r. Rus. Fed.
261 I3	Baygorria, Lago Artificial de resr Uru.
124 D5	Bayhan al Qişab Yemen
235 D2	Bay Head NJ U.S.A.
129 E3	Bäyimli Azer.
199 E2	Bayındır Turkey
199 F3	Bayır Turkey
	Bay Islands is Hond. see La Bahía, Islas de
111 F6	Bayizhen Xizang China
127 F4	Bayji Iraq
	Baykadam Kazakh. see Saudakent
106 E1	Baykal, Ozero l. Rus. Fed.
100 D1	Baykal-Amur Magistral Rus. Fed.
	Baykal Range mts Rus. Fed. see Baykal'skiy Khrebet
106 E1	Baykal'sk Rus. Fed.
98 I1	Baykal'skiy Khrebet mts Rus. Fed.
127 F3	Baykan Turkey
135 K3	Baykibashevo Rus. Fed.
131 K3	Baykit Rus. Fed.
120 D1	Baymak Rus. Fed.
231 C6	Bay Minette AL U.S.A.
125 F3	Baynūna'h req. U.A.E.
	Bayo Spain see Baio Grande
80 F2	Bay of Plenty admin. reg. North I. N.Z.
92 B2	Bayombong Phil.
163 A5	Bayon France
	Bayona Spain see Baiona
235 D2	Bayonne France
250 A6	Bayóvar Peru
227 F4	Bay Port MI U.S.A.
235 E2	Bayport NY U.S.A.
	Bayqadam Kazakh. see Saudakent
129 C3	Bayraktutan Turkey
133 F2	Bayramaly Turkm.
199 E2	Bayramiç Turkey
173 F2	Bayreuth Ger.
234 B4	Bay Ridge MD U.S.A.
173 D4	Bayrischzell Ger.
	Bayrūt Lebanon see Beirut
237 F6	Bay St Louis MS U.S.A.
	Bayshonas Kazakh. see Bayshonas
235 E2	Bay Shore NY U.S.A.
233 E7	Bayside Beach MD U.S.A.
237 F6	Bay Springs MS U.S.A.
150 H2	Bayston Hill Shropshire, England U.K.
121 F5	Baysun Uzbek.
121 F5	Baysuntau, Gory mts Uzbek.
124 C5	Bayt al Faqīh Yemen
106 A2	Baytik-Shan mts China
	Bayt Lahm West Bank see Bethlehem
237 E6	Baytown TX U.S.A.
183 H3	Bayubas de Abajo Spain
80 F3	Bay View North I. N.Z.
235 D3	Bayville NJ U.S.A.
235 E2	Bayville NY U.S.A.
	Bayyrqum Kazakh. see Bairkum
123 G4	Bayzhansay Kazakh.
185 H3	Baza Spain
185 H3	Baza r. Spain
185 H3	Baza, Sierra de mts Spain
176 F5	Bázakerettye Hungary
136 D3	Bazaliya Ukr.
136 E2	Bazancourt France
120 B2	Bazarchulan Kazakh.
129 E3	Bazardyuzi, Gora mt. Azer./Rus. Fed.
122 B2	Bāzār-e Māsāl Iran
123 G3	Bazargan Iran
121 G5	Bazarkhanym, Gora mt. Uzbek.
121 H4	Bazar-Korgon Kyrg.
	Bazar Kurgan Kyrg. see Bazar-Korgon
120 A1	Bazarnyy Karabulak Rus. Fed.
135 I5	Bazarnyy Syzgan Rus. Fed.
	Bazarshulan Kazakh. see Bazarchulan
	Bazartobe Kazakh. see Bazartobe
163 D4	Bazas France
137 H4	Bazavluk r. Ukr.
157 E3	Bazeilles France
163 C5	Bazet France
108 C2	Bazhong Sichuan China
107 H4	Bazhou Hebei China
163 C5	Baziège France
163 C5	Bazillac France
224 F4	Bazin r. Que. Can.
206 C4	Baziwenhi Liberia
122 E5	Bazmān Iran
122 E4	Bazmān, Kūh-e mt. Iran
160 B1	Bazoches France
159 F3	Bazoches-au-Houlme France
156 C4	Bazoches-les-Gallerandes France
159 G3	Bazougers France
159 F3	Bazouges France
158 E3	Bazouges-la-Pérouse France
128 C2	Bcharré Lebanon
97 D5	Be r. Vietnam
236 C2	Beach ND U.S.A.
227 I3	Beachburg Ont. Can.
232 C4	Beach City OH U.S.A.
235 D2	Beach Glen NJ U.S.A.
235 D3	Beach Haven NJ U.S.A.
235 D3	Beach Haven Terrace NJ U.S.A.
234 C1	Beach Lake PA U.S.A.
82 E4	Beachport S.A. Austr.
235 D3	Beachwood NJ U.S.A.
151 H4	Beachy Head hd England U.K.
81 C6	Beacon N.W. Austr.
233 G4	Beacon NY U.S.A.
215 F5	Beacon Bay S. Africa
235 E1	Beacon Falls CT U.S.A.
83 F5	Beaconsfield Tas. Austr.
151 G3	Beaconsfield Buckinghamshire, England U.K.
149 H2	Beadnell Northumberland, England U.K.
259 C9	Beagle, Canal sea chan. Arg.
86 D2	Beagle Bank r. W.A. Austr.
86 D3	Beagle Bay W.A. Austr.
84 B2	Beagle Gulf N.T. Austr.
87 B6	Beagle Island W.A. Austr.
213 □K2	Bealanana Madag.
	Béal an Átha Ireland see Ballina
	Béal Átha na Sluaighe Ireland see Ballinasloe
147 C5	Bealnablath Rep. of Ireland
237 C5	Beals Creek r. TX U.S.A.
150 E4	Beaminster Dorset, England U.K.
213 □J5	Beampingaratra mts Madag.
163 I4	Béar, Cap c. France
213 □K2	Beandrarezona Madag.
238 D3	Bear r. ID U.S.A.
147 B5	Beara r. Rep. of Ireland
	Bearalváhki Norway see Berlevåg
234 C1	Bear Creek PA U.S.A.
237 C4	Bear Creek r. KS U.S.A.
224 C3	Beardmore Ont. Can.
236 F3	Beardstown IL U.S.A.
	Bear Island i. Arctic Ocean see Bjørnøya
227 G2	Bear Island Ont. Can.
147 B5	Bear Island r. Rep. of Ireland
182 B2	Beariz Spain
163 I4	Bear Lake mt. France
238 E3	Bear Lake r. ID U.S.A.
116 C4	Beara r. Madh. Prad. India
236 C3	Bear Mountain SD U.S.A.
	Bearnaraigh i. Western Isles, Scotland U.K. see Bernera
238 E1	Bear Paw Mountain MT U.S.A.
238 E1	Bearpaw Mountains MT U.S.A.
262 Q2	Bear Peninsula Antarctica
223 N4	Bearskin Lake Ont. Can.
151 H3	Bearsted Kent, England U.K.
116 C3	Beas r. India

184 D3	Beas Spain
186 A1	Beasain Spain
185 G3	Beas de Granada Spain
185 H2	Beas de Segura Spain
213 F3	Beatrice Zimbabwe
84 D2	Beatrice, Cape N.T. Austr.
146 E6	Beattock Dumfries and Galloway, Scotland U.K.
222 F3	Beatton r. B.C. Can.
240 I3	Beatty NV U.S.A.
224 E3	Beattyville Que. Can.
232 B6	Beattyville KY U.S.A.
161 C5	Beaucaire France
156 B3	Beaucamps-le-Vieux France
161 C4	Beauchastel France
160 I1	Beaucourt France
159 F4	Beaucouzé France
85 H5	Beaudesert Qld Austr.
	Beauduc, Golfe de b. France see Stes Maries, Golfe des
159 G3	Beaufay France
83 E4	Beaufort Vic. Austr.
160 D2	Beaufort Franche-Comté France
160 E3	Beaufort Rhône-Alpes France
147 B4	Beaufort r. Rep. of Ireland
231 E5	Beaufort NC U.S.A.
231 D5	Beaufort SC U.S.A.
128 B3	Beaufort Castle tourist site Lebanon
162 B1	Beaufort-en-Vallée France
160 E3	Beaufortin mts France
220 F2	Beaufort Sea Can./U.S.A.
214 D5	Beaufort West S. Africa
156 B5	Beaugency France
233 G2	Beauharnois Que. Can.
161 E4	Beaujeu Provence-Alpes-Côte-d'Azur France
160 C2	Beaujeu Rhône-Alpes France
160 C2	Beaujolais, Monts du hills France
161 C5	Beaulieu France
159 H4	Beaulieu-lès-Loches France
162 D4	Beaulieu-sur-Dordogne France
160 A1	Beaulieu-sur-Loire France
160 B2	Beaulon France
146 D4	Beauly Highland, Scotland U.K.
146 D4	Beauly r. Scotland U.K.
146 D4	Beauly Firth est. Scotland U.K.
163 C5	Beaumarchés France
150 C1	Beaumaris Isle of Anglesey, Wales U.K.
161 D4	Beaumes-de-Venise France
159 G2	Beaumesnil France
156 B3	Beaumetz-lès-Loges France
157 B5	Beaumont Belgium
163 C4	Beaumont Aquitaine France
160 B3	Beaumont Auvergne France
158 E2	Beaumont Basse-Normandie France
159 G5	Beaumont Poitou-Charentes France
81 B6	Beaumont South I. N.Z.
240 I5	Beaumont CA U.S.A.
237 F6	Beaumont KS U.S.A.
234 C1	Beaumont PA U.S.A.
237 E6	Beaumont TX U.S.A.
163 C5	Beaumont-de-Lomagne France
161 D5	Beaumont-de-Pertuis France
157 F3	Beaumont-en-Argonne France
159 G4	Beaumont-en-Véron France
156 C3	Beaumont-la-Ronce France
159 G2	Beaumont-le-Roger France
159 G3	Beaumont-les-Autels France
168 F3	Beaumont-sur-Oise France
149 I4	Beaumont-sur-Sarthe France
160 C1	Beaune France
156 C4	Beaune La Rolande France
159 F4	Beaupréau France
157 D4	Beauquesne France
165 D4	Beauraing Belgium
161 C3	Beaurepaire France
160 C2	Beaurepaire-en-Bresse France
161 D4	Beaurières France
228 □²	Beausejour Man. Can.
172 C2	Beausoleil France
161 D3	Beausoleil France
156 D3	Beautor France
156 D3	Beauvais France
223 J4	Beauval Sask. Can.
156 B3	Beauval France
161 E4	Beauvezer France
163 C4	Beauville France
156 D5	Beauvoir-sur-Mer France
162 B2	Beauvoir-sur-Niort France
163 D5	Beauvoisin France
161 C3	Beauzac France
163 D5	Beauzelle France
223 J4	Beaver r. Alberta/Saskatchewan Can.
224 C2	Beaver r. Ont. Can.
222 C2	Beaver r. Y.T. Can.
222 B2	Beaver r. Y.T. Can.
237 C4	Beaver OK U.S.A.
241 K2	Beaver UT U.S.A.
232 C4	Beaver r. OK U.S.A.
241 K2	Beaver r. UT U.S.A.
222 A2	Beaver City AK U.S.A.
237 E4	Beaver Creek Y.T. Can.
238 F1	Beaver Creek r. MT U.S.A.
236 C2	Beaver Creek r. ND U.S.A.
236 D3	Beaver Creek r. NE U.S.A.
230 C4	Beaver Dam KY U.S.A.
226 C4	Beaver Dam WI U.S.A.
236 D3	Beaver Falls PA U.S.A.
263 D2	Beaver Glacier Antarctica
238 D2	Beaverhead r. MT U.S.A.
238 E2	Beaverhead Mountains MT U.S.A.
237 E4	Beaver Lake resr AR U.S.A.
222 G4	Beaverlodge Alta Can.
234 D4	Beaver Meadows PA U.S.A.
234 A2	Beaver Springs PA U.S.A.
232 D4	Beaverton Ont. Can.
226 I4	Beaverton MI U.S.A.
238 B3	Beaverton OR U.S.A.
116 C4	Beawar Rajasthan India
177 J5	Beba Vojvodina Srbija
208 C2	Bébédjia Chad
256 C4	Bebedouro Brazil
254 F3	Beberibe Brazil
171 C3	Bebertal Ger.
149 F4	Bebington Merseyside, England U.K.
208 C2	Bébo Chad
169 E5	Bebra Ger.
108 A2	Bêca Qinghai China
160 E3	Becca du Lac mt. France
151 I2	Beccles Suffolk, England U.K.
182 E4	Beceda Spain
193 C3	Beceite Spain
196 I3	Bečej Vojvodina, Srbija Yugo.
182 C2	Becerreá Spain
183 J4	Becerril Spain
183 F2	Becerril de Campos Spain
204 E3	Béchar Alg.
172 B2	Becherbach Ger.
158 E3	Bécherel France
137 N6	Bechevka Rus. Fed.
173 E2	Bechhofen Bayern Ger.
172 B2	Bechhofen Rheinland-Pfalz Ger.
171 F5	Bechlin Czech Rep.
234 C2	Bechtelsville PA U.S.A.
172 C2	Bechtheim Ger.
	Bechuanaland country Africa see Botswana
176 D2	Bečký Czech Rep.
177 K6	Becicherecu Mic Romania
183 E2	Becilla de Valderaduey Spain
199 J3	Beçin Turkey
167 F2	Beckdorf Ger.
169 E3	Beckedorf Ger.
168 D3	Beckeln Ger.
262 T1	Becker, Mount Antarctica
172 A2	Beckingen Ger.
149 I4	Beckingham Nottinghamshire, England U.K.
232 C5	Beckley WV U.S.A.
177 G3	Beckov Slovakia
81 B6	Becks South I. N.Z.
169 D4	Beckum Ger.
241 J2	Becky Peak NV U.S.A.

197 G2	Beclean Romania
159 F4	Bécon-les-Granits France
171 E5	Bečov Czech Rep.
176 E1	Bečov nad Teplou Czech Rep.
176 F5	Becsehely Hungary
177 G2	Bečva r. Czech Rep.
210 D2	Beda Hāykʾ l. Eth.
149 H3	Bedale North Yorkshire, England U.K.
161 B5	Bédarieux France
161 C4	Bédarrides France
169 B5	Bedburg Ger.
169 B4	Bedburg-Hau Ger.
150 D3	Beddau Rhondda Cynon Taff, Wales U.K.
150 C1	Beddgelert Gwynedd, Wales U.K.
151 H4	Beddingham East Sussex, England U.K.
233 □I2	Beddington ME U.S.A.
158 E3	Bédée France
179 K4	Bedekovčina Croatia
210 C2	Bedelē Eth.
168 D2	Bederkesa Ger.
210 D2	Bedesa Eth.
134 L5	Bedeyeva Polyana Rus. Fed.
116 B5	Bedi Gujarat India
129 D3	Bedari Georgia
175 H4	Będków Pol.
149 G4	Bedlington Northumberland, England U.K.
110 F3	Bedlno Pol.
185 G3	Bedmar Spain
188 F2	Bednja r. Croatia
135 I6	Bednodem'yanovsk Rus. Fed.
146 D6	Beith North Ayrshire, Scotland U.K.
128 B4	Beit Jālā West Bank
197 F2	Beiuş Romania
163 E5	Bedous France
241 M2	Bedrock CO U.S.A.
164 F1	Bedum Neth.
150 D3	Bedwas Caerphilly, Wales U.K.
151 F2	Bedworth Warwickshire, England U.K.
175 H5	Będzin Pol.
224 D5	Beech r. IL U.S.A.
247 E5	Beecher Falls VT U.S.A.
83 F4	Beechworth Vic. Austr.
223 J5	Beechy Sask. Can.
168 F3	Beedenbostel Ger.
149 I4	Beeford East Riding of Yorkshire, England U.K.
164 E3	Beek Gelderland Neth.
164 E3	Beek Noord-Brabant Neth.
164 E2	Beekbergen Neth.
171 D3	Beelitz Ger.
234 D1	Beemerville NJ U.S.A.
171 C3	Beendorf Ger.
85 H5	Beenleigh Qld Austr.
170 D2	Beenz Ger.
84 C3	Beer Devon, England U.K.
172 C2	Beerfelden Ger.
87 C6	Beeringnurding, Mount hill W.A. Austr.
165 D3	Beernem Belgium
156 B2	Beernem Belgium
165 D3	Beerse Belgium
165 D4	Beerse Belgium
	Be'er Sheva' Israel see Be'er Sheva'
128 B4	Be'er Sheva' Israel
165 B3	Beerst Belgium
174 C4	Beesenstedt Ger.
196 E3	Beška Vojvodina, Srbija Yugo.
171 F3	Beeskow Ger.
215 F1	Beesten Germany
169 E1	Beesten Ger.
149 G5	Beeston Nottinghamshire, England U.K.
84 C3	Beetaloo N.T. Austr.
262 T2	Beethoven Peninsula Antarctica
151 H2	Beetley Norfolk, England U.K.
164 F1	Beetsterzwaag Neth.
170 D5	Beetzendorf Ger.
85 H5	Beeville TX U.S.A.
177 J3	Bežava Slovakia
176 D1	Beg, Lough l. Rep. of Ireland
176 G1	Běla pod Pradědem Czech Rep.
114 B2	Begari r. Pak.
114 B2	Begampur Mahar. India
94 B2	Bega N.S.W. Austr.
197 E3	Bega r. Romania
183 I2	Begadan France
162 B3	Bégadan France
117 J5	Begamganj Bangl.
158 G3	Bégard France
123 G5	Begari r. Pak.
185 G3	Begíjar Spain
165 D3	Begíjnendijk Belgium
163 B4	Bègles France
199 K5	Beg-Meil France
206 E5	Begoro Ghana
206 E5	Begoro Ghana
116 C4	Begun Rajasthan India
186 D4	Begur Spain
117 F4	Begusarai Bihar India
213 □J5	Behara Madag.
213 □J5	Behbehān Iran
126 B6	Behenna governorate Egypt
168 E2	Behlendorf Ger.
262 T2	Behrendt Mountains Antarctica
157 G3	Behren-lès-Forbach France
173 F6	Behringen Ger.
172 E2	Behnhafr Iran
215 E5	Behulpsaam S. Africa
100 □2	Bei'ao Zhejiang China see Dongtou
108 B4	Beiba Shaanxi China
108 C2	Beibei Sichuan China
108 C2	Beida Libya see Al Bayḑāʾ
107 G5	Beigang Taiwan see Peikang
149 H4	Beighton South Yorkshire, England U.K.
190 D4	Beigua, Monte mt. Italy
108 B4	Beihai Guangxi China
109 F3	Bei Jiang r. China
109 H3	Beijing China
107 H4	Beijing mun. China
164 E2	Beilen Neth.
108 C4	Beiliu Guangxi China
173 F2	Beingriers Ger.
169 C3	Beilrode Ger.
172 D2	Beilstein Ger.
172 D2	Beinstein Ger.
208 B3	Béinamar Chad
190 B1	Beinasco Italy
156 F4	Beine-Nauroy France
109 □5	Beining Liaoning China
107 J3	Beining Liaoning China
146 D2	Beinn an Tuirc hill Scotland U.K.
146 C4	Beinn Bhan hill Scotland U.K.

146 B6	Beinn Bheigeir hill Scotland U.K.
146 C5	Beinn Bhreac hill Argyll and Bute, Scotland U.K.
146 C5	Beinn Bhreac hill Argyll and Bute, Scotland U.K.
146 C6	Beinn Bhreac hill Argyll and Bute, Scotland U.K.
146 B4	Beinn Bhreac hill Highland, Scotland U.K.
146 D5	Beinn Bhuidhe hill Scotland U.K.
146 D4	Beinn Dearg mt. Highland, Scotland U.K.
146 E5	Beinn Dearg mt. Perth and Kinross, Scotland U.K.
146 D1	Beinn Dorain mt. Scotland U.K.
144 E3	Beinn Heasgarnich mt. Scotland U.K.
146 C5	Beinn Ime mt. Scotland U.K.
146 B6	Beinn Leoid hill Scotland U.K.
146 B3	Beinn Mholach hill Scotland U.K.
146 C5	Beinn Mhor hill Scotland U.K.
146 A4	Beinn Mhòr hill Western Isles, Scotland U.K.
146 B4	Beinn Mhòr hill Western Isles, Scotland U.K.
146 D5	Beinn na Lap hill Scotland U.K.
146 C4	Beinn na Seamraig hill Scotland U.K.
146 C5	Beinn Resipol hill Scotland U.K.
146 D4	Beinn Sgritheall hill Scotland U.K.
146 C5	Beinn Squlaird hill Scotland U.K.
146 D4	Beinn Tharsuinn hill Scotland U.K.
146 E5	Beinn Udlamain mt. Scotland U.K.
190 D1	Beinwil Switz.
107 I3	Beipiao Liaoning China
213 G3	Beira Moz.
	Beira prov. Moz. see Sofala
184 C2	Beirã Port.
183 I2	Beire Spain
109 E1	Beir r. China
128 B3	Beirut Lebanon
222 H5	Beiseker Alta Can.
106 C3	Beishan Nei Mongol China
108 B3	Bei Shan mt. Gansu China
106 B3	Bei Shan mts China
213 F4	Beitbridge Zimbabwe
146 D6	Beith North Ayrshire, Scotland U.K.
128 B4	Beit Jālā West Bank
197 F2	Beiuş Romania
184 C2	Beja Port.
183 A3	Beja admin. dist. Port.
205 H1	Béja Tunisia
189 B7	Béja admin. div. Tunisia
182 E5	Bejar Spain
122 D3	Bejestān Iran
123 G4	Beji r. Pak.
187 C5	Bejís Spain
247 E5	Bejuma Venez.
207 I6	Bek r. Cameroon
119 J1	Bekabad Uzbek.
213 □J3	Bekapaika Madag.
94 D3	Bekdash Turkm.
177 K5	Békás Hungary
177 K5	Békés Hungary
177 J5	Békéscsaba Hungary
177 J5	Békéssámson Hungary
177 J5	Békésszentandrás Hungary
137 G4	Bekhtery Ukr.
199 F2	Bekilli Turkey
213 □J5	Bekily Madag.
197 G4	Bekobod Uzbek. see Bekabad
213 □J4	Bekopaka-Antongo Madag.
135 H5	Bekoropoka-Antongo Madag.
207 F4	Bekwai Ghana
117 F4	Bela Uttar Prad. India
116 F4	Bela Uttar Prad. India
123 G5	Bela Pak.
177 H2	Belá Slovakia
123 G4	Belab r. Pak.
213 F5	Bela-Bela S. Africa
207 I5	Bélabo Cameroon
196 E3	Bela Crkva Vojvodina, Srbija Yugo.
177 H3	Beladice Slovakia
177 K2	Belá-Dulice Slovakia
121 J2	Bel'agash Kazakh.
158 D3	Bel Air hill France
234 B3	Bel Air MD U.S.A.
185 E2	Belalcázar Spain
176 B2	Bělá nad Radbuzou Czech Rep.
188 F2	Bela Palanka Srbija Yugo.
177 J3	Bélapátfalva Hungary
176 D1	Bělá pod Bezdězem Czech Rep.
176 G1	Bělá pod Pradědem Czech Rep.
114 B2	Belagavi Mahar. India
93 B3	Belarus country Europe
187 F5	Belasco Spain
183 I2	Belascoáin Spain
197 F5	Belasitsa mts Bulg./Macedonia
209 B6	Bela Vista Bengo Angola
213 □K4	Bela Vista Huambo Angola see Katchiungo
253 F4	Bela Vista Brazil
213 G5	Bela Vista Moz.
256 C2	Bela Vista de Goiás Brazil
94 B2	Belawan Sumatera Indon.
142 D1	Belaya r. Norway
137 J5	Belaya r. Rus. Fed.
137 K3	Belaya r. Rus. Fed.
131 T3	Belaya r. Rus. Fed.
137 G1	Belaya Berezka Rus. Fed.
135 H6	Belaya Glina Rus. Fed.
135 I5	Belaya Kalitva Rus. Fed.
135 H6	Belaya Kholunitsa Rus. Fed.
99 K3	Belayan r. Indon.
95 F7	Belayan, Gunung mt. Indon.
139 L3	Belaya Rechka Rus. Fed.
	Belaya Tserkva Ukr. see Bila Tserkva
231 G3	Belle Glade FL U.S.A.
158 B4	Belle-Île i. France
225 K3	Belle Isle i. Nfld. Can.
225 K3	Belle Isle, Strait of Nfld. Can.
236 E3	Belle Mead NJ U.S.A.
197 H2	Belmac Romania
171 E4	Belgern Ger.
199 G4	Belkaracaören Turkey
	Belgian Congo country Africa see Congo, Democratic Republic of
263 C2	Belgica Mountains Antarctica
	België country Europe see Belgium
	Belgique country Europe see Belgium
165 D4	Belgium country Europe
192 D3	Belgodère Corse France
135 G6	Belgorod-Dnestrovskyy Ukr.
	Belgorod Oblast admin. div. Rus. Fed. see Belgorodskaya Oblast'
135 G6	Belgorodskaya Oblast' admin. div. Rus. Fed.
233 □I2	Belgrade ME U.S.A.
238 E2	Belgrade MT U.S.A.
232 D3	Belgrade NY U.S.A.
	Belgrade Srbija Yugo. see Beograd
262 V1	Belgrano II research stn Antarctica
81 D4	Belgrove South I. N.Z.
163 B4	Béliet France
156 B4	Belhomert-Guéhouville France
206 B4	Beli Guinea-Bissau
207 H5	Beli Nigeria
186 E3	Belianes Spain
179 H4	Belica Croatia
194 B5	Belice r. Sicilia Italy
194 C5	Belici r. Sicilia Italy
188 E3	Beli Drim r. Yugo.
129 F3	Belidzhi Rus. Fed.
	Beliliou i. Palau see Peleliu
188 G3	Beli Lom r. Bulg.
188 G3	Beli Manastir Croatia
163 B4	Belin-Béliet France
183 G4	Belinchón Spain
232 D5	Belington WV U.S.A.
121 I2	Belogorsk Rus. Fed.
262 O1	Belogorsk Ukr. see Bilohirs'k
121 I2	Belogor'ye Kazakh.
137 K2	Belogor'ye Rus. Fed.
213 □J5	Beloha Madag.
257 F3	Belo Horizonte Brazil
236 D4	Beloit KS U.S.A.
226 C4	Beloit WI U.S.A.
254 F4	Belo Jardim Brazil
134 H3	Belokurikha Rus. Fed.
121 K2	Belokurikha Rus. Fed.
134 G4	Belomorsk Rus. Fed.
134 G3	Belomorsk Rus. Fed.
117 H5	Belonia Tripura India
139 L4	Beloomut Rus. Fed.
257 F3	Belo Oriente Brazil
183 D2	Belorado Spain
135 G7	Belorechensk Rus. Fed.
	Belorechenskaya Rus. Fed. see Belorechensk
126 E2	Belören Turkey
120 D1	Beloretsk Rus. Fed.
	Belorussia country Europe see Belarus
	Beloslav Bulg.
	Belostok Pol. see Białystok
197 H4	Belotintsi Bulg.
210 C2	Belo Tsiribihina Madag.
121 J2	Belousovka Kazakh.
139 K4	Belousovo Rus. Fed.
285 E4	Belo Vale Brazil
100 D1	Beloyarovo Rus. Fed.
139 K1	Beloye, Ozero l. Rus. Fed.
134 G4	Beloye More sea Rus. Fed.
139 L4	Beloye, Ozero l. Rus. Fed.
139 L4	Belozërsk Rus. Fed.
	Belozërskoye Ukr. see Bilozerka
190 B5	Belp Switz.
172 B5	Belp airport Switz.
241 F5	Bell Cay rf Qld Austr.
163 D2	Belpech France
149 H4	Belper Derbyshire, England U.K.
232 C5	Belpre OH U.S.A.
171 E4	Belleben Ger.
175 I4	Bełsk Duży Pol.
185 H4	Beltana S. Africa
82 D2	Belt Bay salt flat S.A. Austr.
241 I3	Belted Range mts NV U.S.A.
169 C5	Beltes Gol r. Mongolia
179 I4	Beltinci Slovenia
177 L4	Beltiug Romania
177 L3	Beltra Slovakia
147 D4	Beltra Mayo Rep. of Ireland
147 D3	Beltra Sligo Rep. of Ireland
164 F2	Beltrum Neth.
	Belts Moldova see Bălţi
	Beltsy Moldova see Bălţi
232 C4	Belturbet Rep. of Ireland
192 A5	Belubula r. N.S.W. Austr.
112 Q2	Belukha, Gora mt.
114 B3	Belur Karnataka India
82 D2	Belur India
183 H5	Belvedere CA U.S.A.
240 B2	Belvedere Italy
193 H5	Belvedere Marittimo Italy
187 C6	Belvès France
158 F4	Belvezet France
163 J5	Belvédère-Campomoro Corse France
163 J5	Belvès France
160 G4	Belvèze-du-Razès France
163 J5	Belvédère Corse France

83 H2	Bellingen N.S.W. Austr.
149 G2	Bellingham Northumberland, England U.K.
238 B1	Bellingham WA U.S.A.
262 U2	Bellingshausen research stn Antarctica
	Bellingshausen Island atoll Arch. de la Société Fr. Polynesia see Motu One
164 C1	Bellingwolde Neth.
190 D3	Bellinzago Novarese Italy
190 E2	Bellinzona Switz.
222 D4	Bell Island Hot Springs AK U.S.A.
193 G4	Bellizzi Italy
234 C3	Bellmawr NJ U.S.A.
250 C3	Bello Col.
183 I4	Bello Spain
163 B5	Bellocq France
78 □6	Bellona i. Solomon Is
114 B3	Bellary Karnataka India
233 G3	Bellows Falls VT U.S.A.
186 D6	Bellshill North Lanarkshire, Scotland U.K.
171 D6	Belluno Ger.
191 H2	Belluno prov. Veneto Italy
114 C3	Belluru Karnataka India
235 D1	Bellvale NY U.S.A.
186 E2	Bellver de Cerdanya Spain
261 F3	Bell Ville Arg.
183 H5	Bellville S. Africa
232 B4	Bellville OH U.S.A.
237 D6	Bellville TX U.S.A.
232 D4	Bellwood PA U.S.A.
222 H5	Belly r. Alta Can.
183 I2	Belm Ger.
235 D2	Belmar NJ U.S.A.
177 K5	Belmezőgyer Hungary
185 E2	Bélmez Spain
185 G3	Bélmez de la Moraleda Spain
83 G3	Belmont N.S.W. Austr.
163 C5	Belmont France
214 C5	Belmont S. Africa
146 □H1	Belmont Shetland, Scotland U.K.
233 H3	Belmont ME U.S.A.
232 D3	Belmont NY U.S.A.
160 C2	Belmont-de-la-Loire France
257 H1	Belmonte Brazil
182 C4	Belmonte Port.
184 E3	Belmonte Asturias Spain
183 H5	Belmonte Castilla - La Mancha Spain
193 I5	Belmonte del Sannio Italy
193 E2	Belmonte in Sabina Italy
194 C4	Belmonte Mezzagno Sicilia Italy
161 A5	Belmont-sur-Rance France
243 H5	Belmopan Belize
147 B2	Belmullet Rep. of Ireland
256 E4	Belo Campo Brazil
165 C4	Belœil Belgium
121 I2	Belokurikha Rus. Fed.
	Beloye More sea see Rus. Fed.
83 G2	Belobogsk Rus. Fed.
107 J4	Belobogsk Ukr. see Bilohirs'k
238 B2	Bond OR U.S.A.
215 F4	Bendarag mt. S. Africa
208 B3	Bende Dem. Rep. Congo
83 G2	Bendemeer N.S.W. Austr.
	Bender-Bayla Somalia
210 F2	Bender Moldova see Tighina
226 D3	Benderville WI U.S.A.
	Bendery Moldova see Tighina
168 E2	Bendestorf Ger.
83 G4	Bendoc Vic. Austr.
83 G4	Bendoc Vic. Austr.
169 C5	Bendorf Ger.
	Bendzin Pol. see Będzin
138 E4	Bēne Latvia
164 E3	Beneden-Leeuwen Neth.
225 J2	Benedict, Mount hill Nfld. Can.
233 □I2	Benedicta ME U.S.A.
173 F4	Benediktbeuren Ger.
173 F4	Benediktenwand mt. Ger.
184 B1	Benedita Port.
254 E3	Benedito Brazil
253 E3	Benedito Leite Brazil
163 B5	Benejúzar Spain
187 E3	Benesse-Maremne France
195 B4	Benestroff France
162 B2	Benet France
190 C4	Benevagienna Italy
173 H5	Bénévent-l'Abbaye France
193 G3	Benevento Italy
193 G3	Benevento prov. Campania Italy
	Beneventum Italy see Benevento
232 D4	Benezette PA U.S.A.
157 H4	Benfeld France
234 A2	Benfer PA U.S.A.
107 J2	Benfica do Ribatejo Port.
96 C3	Beng, Nam r. Laos
113 G8	Bengal, Bay of sea Indian Ocean
207 I6	Bengbis Cameroon
109 F1	Bengbu Anhui China
146 B4	Ben Geary hill Scotland U.K.
	Benghazi Libya see Banghāzī
94 C3	Bengkalis Sumatera Indon.
94 C3	Bengkalis i. Indon.
209 B7	Bengo prov. Angola
187 D4	Bengohr Spain
209 B8	Benguela Angola
209 B7	Benguela prov. Angola
187 D6	Benguerir Morocco
203 H2	Benha Egypt
146 B3	Ben Hiant hill Scotland U.K.
146 D2	Ben Hope hill Scotland U.K.
252 D3	Beni r. Bol.
208 E4	Beni Dem. Rep. Congo
204 E3	Beni-Abbès Alg.
186 E5	Benia de Onís Spain
187 E5	Beniarrés Spain
205 H1	Beni Boufrah Morocco
187 D6	Benicarló Spain
187 C6	Benicásim Spain
240 J2	Benicia CA U.S.A.
187 C5	Benidorm Spain
204 E2	Beni Mazâr Egypt
204 E2	Beni Mellal Morocco
207 F4	Benin country Africa
207 G5	Benin r. Nigeria
207 G5	Benin, Bight of g. Africa
207 G5	Benin City Nigeria
205 E2	Beni-Saf Alg.
204 E2	Beni Suef Egypt
183 O3	Benisa Spain
187 E4	Benissa Spain
163 F5	Benissanet Spain
187 F2	Benkoku Japan
189 O6	Benko Dem. Rep. Congo
89 □	Benkovac Croatia
146 C3	Ben Kilbreck hill Scotland U.K.
146 D3	Ben Klibreck hill Scotland U.K.
146 E4	Ben Lawers mt. Scotland U.K.
147 E4	Ben Lomond hill Rep. of Ireland
83 F6	Ben Lomond mt. Tas. Austr.
146 D4	Ben Loyal hill Scotland U.K.
146 D4	Ben Lui mt. Scotland U.K.
146 E4	Ben Macdui mt. Scotland U.K.
146 C4	Ben More hill Scotland U.K.
146 D4	Ben More mt. Scotland U.K.
146 D3	Ben More Assynt hill Scotland U.K.
81 C6	Ben More Assynt Scotland U.K.
146 D3	Ben Nevis mt. Scotland U.K.

175 L5	Bełżec Pol.
171 D3	Belzig Ger.
237 F5	Belzoni MS U.S.A.
175 K5	Bełżyce Pol.
213 □J3	Bemaraha, Plateau du Madag.
209 B6	Bembe Angola
207 F4	Bembèrèkè Benin
185 E3	Bembézar r. Spain
182 D2	Bembibre Castilla y León Spain
182 B1	Bembibre Galicia Spain
151 F4	Bembridge Isle of Wight, England U.K.
236 E2	Bemidji MN U.S.A.
237 F5	Bemis TN U.S.A.
164 E3	Bemmel Neth.
184 B3	Bemposta Bragança Port.
184 B1	Bemposta Santarém Port.
149 I3	Bempton East Riding of Yorkshire, England U.K.
206 D3	Bèna Burkina
209 D6	Bena Dibele Dem. Rep. Congo
187 C5	Benaguasil Spain
185 H4	Benahadux Spain
185 E4	Benahavís Spain
204 D2	Benahmed Morocco
146 B4	Ben Alder hill Scotland U.K.
83 F4	Benalla Vic. Austr.
185 F4	Benalmádena Spain
185 G3	Benalúa de Guadix Spain
185 G3	Benalúa de las Villas Spain
184 E4	Benalup de Sidonia Spain
185 F4	Benamargosa Spain
185 F3	Benamejí Spain
185 H3	Benamocarra Spain
185 E4	Benaocaz Spain
185 E4	Benaoján Spain
	Benares Uttar Prad. India see Varanasi
205 H1	Ben Arous Tunisia
189 B7	Ben Arous admin. div. Tunisia
187 C6	Benasal Spain
186 D2	Benasque Spain
162 C2	Benassay France
176 D1	Benátky nad Jizerou Czech Rep.
184 B2	Benavente Port.
182 E2	Benavente Spain
252 D3	Benavides Bol.
187 C6	Benavides de Órbigo Spain
147 B3	Benbane Head Rep. of Ireland
146 A4	Ben Aoun mt. Scotland U.K.
147 B5	Benbaun hill Rep. of Ireland
146 A4	Benbecula i. Scotland U.K.
147 C2	Benbulbin hill Rep. of Ireland
147 B3	Benburb Rep. of Ireland
147 B3	Benbury hill Rep. of Ireland
184 C2	Bencatel Port.
109 G1	Bencha Jiangsu China
	Bencheng Hebei China see Luannan
146 E5	Ben Chonzie hill Scotland U.K.
147 B3	Bencorr hill Rep. of Ireland
146 B4	Ben Cruachan mt. Scotland U.K.
87 C6	Bencubbin W.A. Austr.
238 B2	Bend OR U.S.A.
215 H4	Bendearg mt. S. Africa
209 C6	Bendera Dem. Rep. Congo
83 G2	Bendemeer N.S.W. Austr.
210 F2	Bender-Bayla Somalia
226 D3	Benderville WI U.S.A.
168 E2	Bendestorf Ger.
83 G4	Bendoc Vic. Austr.
169 C5	Bendorf Ger.
138 E4	Bēne Latvia
164 E3	Beneden-Leeuwen Neth.
225 J2	Benedict, Mount hill Nfld. Can.
233 □I2	Benedicta ME U.S.A.
173 F4	Benediktbeuren Ger.
173 F4	Benediktenwand mt. Ger.
184 B1	Benedita Port.
254 E3	Benedito Brazil
253 E3	Benedito Leite Brazil
163 B5	Benejúzar Spain
187 E3	Benesse-Maremne France
195 B4	Benestroff France
162 B2	Benet France
190 C4	Benevagienna Italy
173 H5	Bénévent-l'Abbaye France
193 G3	Benevento Italy
193 G3	Benevento prov. Campania Italy
	Beneventum Italy see Benevento
232 D4	Benezette PA U.S.A.
157 H4	Benfeld France
234 A2	Benfer PA U.S.A.
107 J2	Benfica do Ribatejo Port.
96 C3	Beng, Nam r. Laos
113 G8	Bengal, Bay of sea Indian Ocean
207 I6	Bengbis Cameroon
109 F1	Bengbu Anhui China
146 B4	Ben Geary hill Scotland U.K.
	Benghazi Libya see Banghāzī
94 C3	Bengkalis Sumatera Indon.
94 C3	Bengkalis i. Indon.
209 B7	Bengo prov. Angola
187 D4	Bengohr Spain
209 B8	Benguela Angola
209 B7	Benguela prov. Angola
187 D6	Benguerir Morocco
203 H2	Benha Egypt
146 B3	Ben Hiant hill Scotland U.K.
146 D2	Ben Hope hill Scotland U.K.
252 D3	Beni r. Bol.
208 E4	Beni Dem. Rep. Congo
204 E3	Beni-Abbès Alg.
186 E5	Benia de Onís Spain
187 E5	Beniarrés Spain
205 H1	Beni Boufrah Morocco
187 D6	Benicarló Spain
187 C6	Benicásim Spain
240 J2	Benicia CA U.S.A.
187 C5	Benidorm Spain
204 E2	Beni Mazâr Egypt
204 E2	Beni Mellal Morocco
207 F4	Benin country Africa
207 G5	Benin r. Nigeria
207 G5	Benin, Bight of g. Africa
207 G5	Benin City Nigeria
205 E2	Beni-Saf Alg.
204 E2	Beni Suef Egypt
187 E4	Benissa Spain
207 F2	Benjak Japan
251 H5	Benjamim Constant Brazil
242 B2	Benjamín Hill Mex.
204 E3	Beni Ounif Alg.
204 E3	Beni Saf Alg.
261 H5	Benito Arg.
223 K5	Benito Man. Can.
247 □2	Benito r. Equat. Guinea see Mbini
261 H5	Benito Juárez Arg.
241 J5	Benito Juárez Mex.

Benito Juárez to Bilauktaung Range
284

245 H4 Benito Juárez Mex.
245 F2 Benito Juárez Mex.
245 G5 Benito Juárez, Presa resr Mex.
92 B2 Benito Soliven Phil.
185 H3 Benizalón Spain
185 I2 Benizar y la Tercia Spain
250 D6 Benjamim Constant Brazil
237 D5 Benjamin TX U.S.A.
259 B7 Benjamín, Isla i. Chile
242 C2 Benjamín Hill Mex.
236 C3 Benkelman NE U.S.A.
190 E1 Benken Switz.
146 D3 Ben Klibreck hill Scotland U.K.
188 E3 Benkovac Croatia
197 H4 Benkovski Bulg.
146 D5 Ben Lawers mt. Scotland U.K.
146 D5 Ben Ledi hill Scotland U.K.
150 C1 Benllech Isle of Anglesey, Wales U.K.
187 D4 Benlloch Spain
83 G2 Ben Lomond mt. N.S.W. Austr.
146 D5 Ben Lomond hill Scotland U.K.
240 F3 Ben Lomond CA U.S.A.
146 D3 Ben Loyal hill Scotland U.K.
146 D5 Ben Lui mt. Scotland U.K.
215 F4 Ben Macdhui mt. Lesotho
144 F3 Ben Macdui mt. Scotland U.K.
189 A7 Ben Mahidi Alg.
84 D3 Benmara N.T. Austr.
81 C5 Ben More mt. South I. N.Z.
146 B5 Ben More hill Scotland U.K.
146 D5 Ben More mt. Scotland U.K.
81 C6 Benmore, Lake South I. N.Z.
146 D3 Ben More Assynt hill Scotland U.K.
81 C6 Benmore Peak South I. N.Z.
171 C4 Benndorf Ger.
164 D2 Bennebroek Neth.
169 F4 Benneckenstein (Harz) Ger.
164 E2 Bennekom Neth.
222 C3 Bennett B.C. Can.
226 B2 Bennett WI U.S.A.
147 D4 Bennettsbridge Rep. of Ireland
231 E5 Bennettsville SC U.S.A.
146 C5 Ben Nevis mt. Scotland U.K.
80 E3 Benneydale North I. N.Z.
233 H3 Bennington NH U.S.A.
233 G3 Bennington VT U.S.A.
171 C4 Bennstedt Ger.
171 C4 Bennungen Ger.
158 B4 Bénodet France
81 B6 Ben Ohau Range mts South I. N.Z.
215 G2 Benoni S. Africa
207 I4 Bénoué r. Cameroon
208 C2 Bénoy Chad
182 C4 Benquerença Port.
163 B5 Benquet France
146 E4 Ben Rinnes hill Scotland U.K.
184 B3 Bensafrim Port.
171 D3 Bensdorf Ger.
169 F5 Benshausen Ger.
172 C2 Bensheim Ger.
204 D2 Ben Slimane Morocco
151 F3 Benson Oxfordshire, England U.K.
241 L6 Benson AZ U.S.A.
236 E2 Benson MN U.S.A.
206 C5 Bensonville Liberia
232 C5 Bens Run WV U.S.A.
146 C5 Ben Starav mt. Scotland U.K.
122 D5 Bent Iran
164 F2 Bentelo Neth.
206 B4 Benti Guinea
209 B8 Bentiaba Angola
180 E5 Ben Tieb Morocco
84 D3 Bentinck Island Qld Austr.
97 B5 Bentinck Island Myanmar
146 E5 Ben Tirran hill Scotland U.K.
208 F2 Bentiu Sudan
128 B3 Bent Jbail Lebanon
222 H4 Bentley Alta Can.
149 H4 Bentley South Yorkshire, England U.K.
232 C4 Bentleyville PA U.S.A.
253 F4 Bento Gomes r. Brazil
233 □J2 Benton N.B. Can.
237 E5 Benton AR U.S.A.
240 H3 Benton CA U.S.A.
236 F4 Benton IL U.S.A.
237 F4 Benton KY U.S.A.
237 E5 Benton LA U.S.A.
237 F4 Benton MO U.S.A.
234 B1 Benton PA U.S.A.
231 C5 Benton TN U.S.A.
Bentong Malaysia see Bentung
226 D4 Benton Harbor MI U.S.A.
237 E4 Bentonville AR U.S.A.
232 B5 Bentonville OH U.S.A.
97 D5 Bên Tre Vietnam
94 C2 Bentung Malaysia
170 D1 Bentwisch Ger.
170 E2 Bentzin Ger.
207 G5 Benue r. Nigeria
207 H5 Benue state Nigeria
94 C2 Benum, Gunung mt. Malaysia
177 I3 Beňuš Slovakia
146 D5 Ben Vorlich hill Argyll and Bute, Scotland U.K.
146 D5 Ben Vorlich hill Perth and Kinross/Stirling, Scotland U.K.
147 B3 Benwee hill Rep. of Ireland
232 C4 Benwood WV U.S.A.
146 D4 Ben Wyvis mt. Scotland U.K.
107 I3 Benxi Liaoning China
196 E3 Beograd Srbija Yugo.
116 E4 Beohari Madh. Prad. India
206 D5 Béoumi Côte d'Ivoire
94 C4 Bepagut, Gunung mt. Indon.
108 C3 Bepian Jiang r. Guizhou China
103 E7 Beppu Japan
79 □1a Beqa i. Fiji
247 □3 Bequia i. St Vincent
254 D2 Bequimão Brazil
117 G4 Bera Bangl.
261 G3 Berabevú Arg.
116 C4 Berach r. India
147 D2 Beragh Northern Ireland U.K.
213 □K2 Beramanja Madag.
196 D4 Berane Crna Gora Yugo.
183 G1 Beranga Spain
183 H1 Berango Spain
183 H2 Berantevilla Spain
116 D5 Berasia Madh. Prad. India
94 B2 Berastagi Sumatera Indon.
198 A1 Berat Albania
163 D5 Bérat France
95 G3 Beratus, Gunung mt. Indon.
173 F2 Beratzhausen Ger.
95 G2 Berau r. Indon.
91 H7 Berau, Teluk b. Indon.
261 H4 Berazategui Arg.
186 C3 Berbegal Spain
203 G5 Berber Sudan
210 E2 Berbera Somalia
208 B3 Berbérati C.A.R.
215 H2 Berbice S. Africa
183 I2 Berbinzana Spain
183 G1 Bercedo Spain
177 I4 Bercel Hungary
156 D4 Bercenay-en-Othe France
183 E3 Bercero Spain
190 E4 Berceto Italy
165 C4 Berchem Belgium
192 B4 Berchidda Sardegna Italy
173 F2 Berching Ger.
120 D2 Berchogur Kazakh.
173 H4 Berchtesgaden Ger.
173 G4 Berchtesgadener Alpen mts Ger.
185 G4 Bérchules Spain
182 E2 Bercianos del Páramo Spain
156 B2 Berck France
129 D3 Berd Armenia
137 I4 Berda r. Ukr.
159 G3 Berd'huis France
Berdichev Ukr. see Berdychiv
131 N3 Berdigestyakh Rus. Fed.
130 J4 Berdsk Rus. Fed.
182 D1 Berducedo Spain
186 C2 Berdún Spain
137 I4 Berdyans'k Ukr.
136 E3 Berdychiv Ukr.
208 C2 Béré Chad
232 A6 Berea KY U.S.A.
232 C4 Berea OH U.S.A.
150 C4 Bere Alston Devon, England U.K.
Béréby Côte d'Ivoire see Grand-Bérébi
210 F2 Bereeda Somalia
150 C4 Bere Ferrers Devon, England U.K.
139 K1 Bereg Rus. Fed.
177 L3 Beregdaróc Hungary
Beregovo Ukr. see Berehove
190 E3 Bereguardo Italy
136 C3 Berehomet Ukr.
136 B3 Berehove Ukr.
179 H5 Berek Croatia
137 I3 Bereka Ukr.
137 I3 Bereka r. Ukr.
177 K4 Berekböszörmény Hungary
213 □J4 Bereketa Madag.
177 J4 Berekfürdő Hungary
211 B6 Bereku Tanz.
206 E5 Berekum Ghana
177 H6 Beremend Hungary
139 L3 Berendeyevo Rus. Fed.
252 C4 Berenguela Bol.
203 G4 Berenice Egypt
Berenice Libya see Banghāzī
223 L4 Berens r. Man. Can.
223 L4 Berens River Man. Can.
213 □J4 Berenty Madag.
150 E4 Bere Regis Dorset, England U.K.
225 H4 Beresford N.B. Can.
236 D3 Beresford SD U.S.A.
136 C2 Berestechko Ukr.
197 H2 Bereşti Romania
137 G2 Berestivka Ukr.
137 H3 Berestova r. Ukr.
137 I4 Berestove Ukr.
137 H3 Berestoven'ka Ukr.
137 G2 Berestovets' Ukr.
136 C2 Berestyane Ukr.
177 K4 Berettyó r. Hungary
177 K4 Berettyóújfalu Hungary
213 □J3 Berevo Madag.
Bereza Belarus see Byaroza
137 F2 Berezan' Ukr.
137 F4 Berezanka Ukr.
137 J5 Berezanskaya Rus. Fed.
139 I3 Berezayka Rus. Fed.
136 D2 Berezdiv Ukr.
197 I2 Berezeni Romania
136 C3 Berezhany Ukr.
Berezino Belarus see Byerazino
137 G2 Berezivka Chernihivs'ka Oblast' Ukr.
137 G4 Berezivka Kirovohrads'ka Oblast' Ukr.
136 F4 Berezivka Odes'ka Oblast' Ukr.
136 D3 Berezivka Zhytomyrs'ka Oblast' Ukr.
136 E2 Berezivka Zhytomyrs'ka Oblast' Ukr.
137 F2 Berezna Ukr.
136 D2 Berezne Ukr.
137 G4 Bereznehuvate Ukr.
134 H3 Bereznik Arkhangel'skaya Oblast' Rus. Fed.
134 L4 Berezniki Rus. Fed.
136 D2 Bereznyky Ukr.
Berezov Rus. Fed. see Berezovo
134 L3 Berezovaya r. Rus. Fed.
136 D2 Berezove Ukr.
Berezovka Belarus see Byarozawka
100 C2 Berezovka Amurskaya Oblast' Rus. Fed.
120 D1 Berezovka Orenburgskaya Oblast' Rus. Fed.
134 L4 Berezovka Permskaya Oblast' Rus. Fed.
Berezovka Odes'ka Oblast' Ukr. see Berezivka
130 H3 Berezovo Rus. Fed.
100 E2 Berezovyy Rus. Fed.
136 E4 Berezyne Ukr.
172 D4 Berg Baden-Württemberg Ger.
171 C5 Berg Bayern Ger.
173 F4 Berg Bayern Ger.
169 B5 Berg Rheinland-Pfalz Ger.
165 F5 Berg Lux.
172 C3 Berg (Pfalz) Ger.
171 C4 Berga Sachsen-Anhalt Ger.
171 D5 Berga Thüringen Ger.
186 E2 Berga Spain
199 E2 Bergama Turkey
190 E3 Bergamo Italy
190 E3 Bergamo prov. Lombardia Italy
186 C4 Bergantes r. Spain
183 H1 Bergara Spain
172 D4 Bergatreute Ger.
173 F2 Berg bei Neumarkt in der Oberpfalz Ger.
179 E2 Berg bei Rohrbach Austria
141 L3 Bergby Sweden
170 C2 Berge Brandenburg Ger.
168 C3 Berge Niedersachsen Ger.
186 C4 Berge Spain
190 D4 Bergeggi Italy
173 G4 Bergen Bayern Ger.
170 E1 Bergen Mecklenburg-Vorpommern Ger.
168 E3 Bergen Niedersachsen Ger.
164 D2 Bergen Neth.
142 A1 Bergen Norway
215 H2 Bergen S. Africa
232 E3 Bergen NY U.S.A.
168 F3 Bergen (Dumme) Ger.
235 D2 Bergen County county NJ U.S.A.
235 E2 Bergenfield NJ U.S.A.
164 D3 Bergen op Zoom Neth.
164 F2 Bergentheim Neth.
163 C4 Bergerac France
156 E4 Bergères-lès-Vertus France
263 B2 Bergerson, Mount Antarctica
160 C2 Bergesserin France
165 E3 Bergeyk Neth.
170 E3 Bergfelde Ger.
164 E3 Bergharen Neth.
172 B3 Berghaupten Ger.
178 E3 Bergheim Austria
173 F3 Bergheim Ger.
169 E4 Bergheim (Edertal) Ger.
169 B5 Bergheim (Erft) Ger.
164 E3 Berghem Neth.
171 E3 Bergholz-Rehbrücke Ger.
172 D3 Berghülen Ger.
178 E4 Berg im Drautal Austria
169 C5 Bergisch Gladbach Ger.
169 C4 Bergkamen Ger.
173 F3 Bergkirchen Ger.
226 C2 Bergland MI U.S.A.
140 L2 Bergnäs Sweden
140 L2 Bergnäsviken Sweden
169 C4 Bergneustadt Ger.
Bergomum Italy see Bergamo
232 C5 Bergoo WV U.S.A.
169 F5 Bergrheinfeld Ger.
143 H2 Bergshamra Sweden
141 L3 Bergsjö Sweden
140 M2 Bergsviken Sweden
173 E2 Bergtheim Ger.
183 G2 Bergüenda Spain
156 C2 Bergues France
164 F1 Bergum Neth.
190 E2 Bergün Switz.
215 G3 Bergville S. Africa
171 D4 Bergwitz Ger.
107 F2 Berh Mongolia
94 C3 Berhala, Selat sea chan. Indon.
Berhampur W. Bengal India see Baharampur
197 H2 Berheci r. Romania
177 H4 Berhida Hungary
257 F2 Berilo Brazil
131 R4 Beringa, Ostrov i. Rus. Fed.
87 C5 Beringarra W.A. Austr.
165 E3 Beringe Neth.
184 C2 Beringel Port.
165 E3 Beringen Belgium
131 S3 Beringovskiy Chukotskiy Avtonomnyy Okrug Rus. Fed.
220 A4 Bering Sea N. Pacific Ocean
220 B3 Bering Strait Rus. Fed./U.S.A.
151 F3 Berinsfield Oxfordshire, England U.K.
Berislav Ukr. see Beryslav
136 F4 Berizky Ukr.
185 H4 Berja Spain
169 F5 Berka Ger.
140 J3 Berkåk Norway
204 E2 Berkane Morocco
164 D3 Berkel Neth.
164 F2 Berkel r. Neth.
86 E2 Berkeley r. W.A. Austr.
150 E3 Berkeley Gloucestershire, England U.K.
240 F3 Berkeley CA U.S.A.
235 D2 Berkeley Heights NJ U.S.A.
232 D5 Berkeley Springs WV U.S.A.
168 F2 Berkenthin Ger.
151 G3 Berkhamsted Hertfordshire, England U.K.
173 E3 Berkheim Ger.
164 E2 Berkhout Neth.
262 U1 Berkner Island Antarctica
197 F4 Berkovitsa Bulg.
234 C2 Berks County county PA U.S.A.
233 G3 Berkshire Hills MA U.S.A.
151 F2 Berkswell West Midlands, England U.K.
164 F2 Berkum Neth.
165 D3 Berlaar Belgium
156 D2 Berlaimont France
222 G4 Berland r. Alta Can.
184 E2 Berlanga Spain
183 H3 Berlanga de Duero Spain
165 D3 Berlare Belgium
140 O1 Berlevåg Norway
164 E3 Berlicum Neth.
164 E1 Berlikum Neth.
170 E3 Berlin Ger.
171 E3 Berlin land Ger.
235 F1 Berlin CT U.S.A.
233 F5 Berlin MD U.S.A.
233 □H2 Berlin NH U.S.A.
234 D3 Berlin NJ U.S.A.
232 C4 Berlin OH U.S.A.
232 D5 Berlin PA U.S.A.
226 C4 Berlin WI U.S.A.
262 O1 Berlin, Mount Antarctica
169 F4 Berlingerode Ger.
81 C4 Berlins South I. N.Z.
234 C2 Berlinsville PA U.S.A.
196 E3 Berlişte Romania
171 C4 Berlstedt Ger.
83 G4 Bermagui N.S.W. Austr.
172 D4 Bermatingen Ger.
122 D2 Berme Turkm.
242 E3 Bermejíllo Mex.
260 D3 Bermejo r. Arg.
258 F2 Bermejo r. Arg./Bol.
252 D5 Bermejo Bol.
261 G6 Bermejo, Isla i. Arg.
183 H1 Bermeo Spain
182 D3 Bermillo de Sayago Spain
231 □1 Bermuda terr. N. Atlantic Ocean
264 E4 Bermuda Rise sea feature N. Atlantic Ocean
190 C2 Bern Switz.
190 C2 Bern canton Switz.
163 C5 Bernac-Dessus France
195 F2 Bernalda Italy
239 F5 Bernalillo NM U.S.A.
256 C5 Bernardino de Campos Brazil
183 F3 Bernardos Spain
234 D2 Bernardsville NJ U.S.A.
176 D2 Bernartice Czech Rep.
261 F5 Bernasconi Arg.
172 C4 Bernau Baden-Württemberg Ger.
170 E3 Bernau Brandenburg Ger.
173 G4 Bernau am Chiemsee Ger.
156 C2 Bernaville France
159 G2 Bernay France
173 E4 Bernbeuren Ger.
171 C4 Bernburg (Saale) Ger.
179 H3 Berndorf Austria
168 D2 Berne Ger.
Berne Switz. see Bern
226 E5 Berne IN U.S.A.
177 H3 Bernecebaráti Hungary
183 H2 Bernedo Spain
190 C2 Berner Alpen mts Switz.
146 A4 Berneray i. Western Isles, Scotland U.K.
146 A5 Berneray i. Western Isles, Scotland U.K.
Bernese Alps mts Switz. see Berner Alpen
182 E2 Bernesga r. Spain
160 E2 Bernex France
173 F2 Berngau Ger.
179 H2 Bernhardsthal Austria
173 G2 Bernhardswald Ger.
87 B5 Bernier Island W.A. Austr.
161 D3 Bernin France
183 H4 Berninches mt. Spain
146 B4 Bernisdale Highland, Scotland U.K.
165 C4 Bernissart Belgium
170 C2 Bernitt Ger.
172 B2 Bernkastel-Kues Ger.
163 B4 Bernos-Beaulac France
173 F4 Bernried Bayern Ger.
173 G3 Bernried Bayern Ger.
171 F4 Bernsdorf Ger.
173 E3 Bernstadt Baden-Württemberg Ger.
171 F4 Bernstadt Sachsen Ger.
232 A6 Bernstadt KY U.S.A.
179 H3 Bernstein Austria
234 B2 Bernville PA U.S.A.
Beroea Greece see Veroia
Beroea Syria see Halab
190 D1 Beromünster Switz.
213 □J4 Beroroha Madag.
176 D2 Beroun Czech Rep.
176 D2 Berounka r. Czech Rep.
197 F5 Berovo Macedonia
191 G4 Berra Italy
189 A7 Berrahal Alg.
161 A5 Berre r. France
161 D5 Berre, Étang de lag. France
204 D2 Berrechid Morocco
161 D5 Berre-l'Étang France
82 E3 Berri S.A. Austr.
205 F2 Berriane Alg.
161 C4 Berrias-et-Casteljau France
183 H1 Berriatúa Spain
83 G4 Berridale N.S.W. Austr.
146 E3 Berriedale Highland, Scotland U.K.
146 E3 Berriedale Water r. Scotland U.K.
158 C3 Berrien France
83 F3 Berrigan N.S.W. Austr.
183 I2 Berriozar Spain
184 D3 Berrocal Spain
260 E3 Berrotarán Arg.
205 F1 Berrouaghia Alg.
150 D3 Berrow Somerset, England U.K.
156 E3 Berru France
83 G3 Berry N.S.W. Austr.
156 D3 Berry-au-Bac France
223 I5 Berry Creek r. Alta Can.
246 C1 Berry Islands Bahamas
234 B2 Berrysburg PA U.S.A.
237 E4 Berryville AR U.S.A.
232 E5 Berryville VA U.S.A.
168 C3 Bersenbrück Ger.
136 E3 Bershad' Ukr.
162 B3 Berson France
191 F3 Bersone Italy
120 E1 Bersuat Rus. Fed.
129 B3 Berta r. Turkey
182 B2 Bertamirans Spain
171 F4 Berthelsdorf Ger.
161 A4 Bertholène France
156 C2 Bertincourt France
191 H4 Bertinoro Italy
165 E4 Bertogne Belgium
254 E3 Bertolínia Brazil
257 G2 Bertópolis Brazil
207 I5 Bertoua Cameroon
165 F5 Bertrange Lux.
157 G4 Bertrichamps France
165 E5 Bertrix Belgium
77 H2 Beru atoll Gilbert Is Kiribati
168 C2 Berumbur Ger.
120 E4 Beruni Uzbek.
251 F5 Beruri Brazil
114 C5 Beruwala Sri Lanka
197 F2 Berveni Romania
146 F5 Bervie Water r. Scotland U.K.
159 G2 Berville-sur-Mer France
83 F4 Berwick Vic. Austr.
233 H3 Berwick ME U.S.A.
227 I5 Berwick PA U.S.A.
149 G2 Berwick-upon-Tweed Northumberland, England U.K.
150 D2 Berwyn hills Wales U.K.
234 C2 Berwyn PA U.S.A.
137 G4 Beryslav Ukr.
Berytus Lebanon see Beirut
197 E3 Berzasca Romania
138 F3 Bērzaune Latvia
138 D4 Beržė r. Lith.
176 G5 Berzence Hungary
175 L1 Berźniki Pol.
185 E1 Berzocana Spain
161 B4 Bès r. France
213 □J3 Besalampy Madag.
186 F2 Besalú Spain
160 E1 Besançon France
183 F2 Besande Spain
95 F3 Besar, Gunung mt. Indon.
94 C1 Besar, Gunung mt. Malaysia
183 F1 Besaya r. Spain
160 B2 Besbre r. France
186 F3 Bescanó Spain
139 H5 Besed' r. Rus. Fed.
169 D5 Beselich-Obertiefenbach Ger.
177 H3 Bešeňov Slovakia
177 J4 Besenyőtelek Hungary
177 J4 Besenyszög Hungary
Beshariq Uzbek. see Besharyk
121 G4 Besharyk Uzbek.
120 F5 Beshkent Uzbek.
122 C4 Beshneh Iran
129 D3 Besht'asheni Georgia
121 G4 Besh-Ter, Gora mt. Kyrg./Uzbek.
Besh-Ter Toosu mt. Kyrg./Uzbek. see Besh-Ter, Gora
Beshtor Toghi mt. Kyrg./Uzbek. see Besh-Ter, Gora
186 D2 Besiberri Sud mt. Spain
127 F3 Beşiri Turkey
175 J6 Beskid Niski hills Pol.
175 I6 Beskid Sądecki mts Pol.
Beskra Alg. see Biskra
129 D2 Beslan Rus. Fed.
197 F5 Beslet mt. Bulg.
197 F4 Besna Kobila mt. Yugo.
126 E3 Besni Turkey
190 D3 Besozzo Italy
Beşparmak Dağları mts Cyprus see Pentadaktylos Range
139 K4 Besputa r. Rus. Fed.
149 H4 Bessacarr South Yorkshire, England U.K.
161 B5 Bessan France
208 B3 Béssao Chad
Bessarabka Moldova see Basarabeasca
121 G4 Bessaye, Gora mt. Kazakh.
160 B2 Bessay-sur-Allier France
147 E2 Bessbrook Northern Ireland U.K.
161 E3 Besse France
160 A3 Besse-et-St-Anastaise France
161 C4 Bessèges France
231 C5 Bessemer AL U.S.A.
226 B2 Bessemer MI U.S.A.
232 C4 Bessemer PA U.S.A.
160 C3 Bessenay France
172 D2 Bessenbach Ger.
159 G4 Bessé-sur-Braye France
161 E5 Besse-sur-Issole France
120 C3 Besshoky, Gora hill Kazakh.
163 D5 Bessières France
162 D2 Bessines-sur-Gartempe France
129 B1 Besskorbnaya Rus. Fed.
135 I5 Bessonovka Rus. Fed.
162 E3 Bessou, Mont de hill France
164 E3 Best Neth.
120 C2 Bestamak Aktyubinskaya Oblast' Kazakh.
121 I2 Bestamak Vostochnyy Kazakhstan Kazakh.
171 E3 Bestensee Ger.
215 G3 Besters S. Africa
121 H1 Bestobe Kazakh.
143 F2 Bestorp Sweden
169 D4 Bestwig Ger.
84 C2 Beswick N.T. Austr.
213 □J3 Betafo Madag.
213 □J3 Betanantanana Madag.
252 D4 Betanzos Bol.
182 B1 Betanzos Spain
207 I5 Bétaré Oya Cameroon
226 D2 Bete Grise MI U.S.A.
186 B1 Betelu Spain
187 C5 Bétera Spain
207 F4 Bétérou Benin
183 H4 Beteta Spain
204 D2 Beth, Oued r. Morocco
215 G2 Bethal S. Africa
212 C5 Bethanie Namibia
235 F1 Bethany CT U.S.A.
236 E3 Bethany MO U.S.A.
237 D5 Bethany OK U.S.A.
177 K6 Bethausen Romania
220 B3 Bethel AK U.S.A.
235 E1 Bethel CT U.S.A.
233 □H2 Bethel ME U.S.A.
232 A5 Bethel OH U.S.A.
234 B2 Bethel PA U.S.A.
169 E3 Betheln Ger.
232 C4 Bethel Park PA U.S.A.
246 □ Bethel Town Jamaica
156 E3 Bétheny France
151 H3 Bethersden Kent, England U.K.
150 C1 Bethesda Gwynedd, Wales U.K.
234 A4 Bethesda MD U.S.A.
232 C4 Bethesda OH U.S.A.
215 E4 Bethesdaweg S. Africa
156 C3 Béthisy-St-Pierre France
80 F2 Bethlehem North I. N.Z.
215 G3 Bethlehem S. Africa
234 C2 Bethlehem PA U.S.A.
128 B4 Bethlehem West Bank
215 E5 Bethlesdorp S. Africa
163 D6 Bethmale France
156 D4 Bethon France
235 E2 Bethpage NY U.S.A.
215 E4 Bethulie S. Africa
156 C2 Béthune France
156 B3 Béthune r. France
257 E3 Betim Brazil
213 □J4 Betioky Madag.
95 F5 Betiri, Gunung mt. Indon.
Bet Lehem West Bank see Bethlehem
139 I4 Betlitsa Rus. Fed.
116 C5 Betma Madh. Prad. India
156 D4 Beton-Bazoches France
97 C6 Betong Thai.
84 E5 Betoota Qld Austr.
210 C2 Beto Shet' r. Eth.
208 C4 Bétou Congo
121 G3 Betpak-Dala plain Kazakh.
213 □J3 Betrandraka Madag.
213 □J4 Betroka Madag.
157 H4 Betschdorf France
128 B3 Bet She'an Israel
225 G3 Betsiamites Que. Can.
225 G3 Betsiamites r. Que. Can.
213 □J2 Betsiboka r. Madag.
104 C2 Betsu-zan mt. Japan
246 D2 Betsy Bay Mayaguana Bahamas
157 G3 Bettelainville France
178 C3 Bettelwurf mt. Austria
165 F5 Bettembourg Lux.
165 F5 Bettendorf Lux.
234 B3 Betterton MD U.S.A.
117 F4 Bettiah Bihar India
215 G2 Bettiesdam S. Africa
172 A2 Bettingen Ger.
143 G2 Bettna Sweden
190 E4 Bettola Italy
158 E3 Betton France
193 E1 Bettona Italy
146 D3 Bettyhill Highland, Scotland U.K.
147 E3 Bettystown Rep. of Ireland
116 D5 Betul Madh. Prad. India
116 D4 Betwa r. India
150 D1 Betws-y-coed Conwy, Wales U.K.
187 C5 Betxi Spain
156 C3 Betz France
169 C5 Betzdorf Ger.
165 F5 Betzdorf Lux.
173 F2 Betzenstein Ger.
173 E4 Betzigau Ger.
209 B6 Béu Angola
161 E4 Beuil France
83 E3 Beulah Vic. Austr.
150 D2 Beulah Powys, Wales U.K.
226 D3 Beulah MI U.S.A.
236 C2 Beulah ND U.S.A.
151 H3 Beult r. England U.K.
164 E3 Beuningen Neth.
169 F4 Beuren Ger.
172 C3 Beuron Ger.
157 E4 Beurville France
Beuthen Pol. see Bytom
160 C2 Beuvray, Mont hill France
160 B1 Beuvron r. France
159 H4 Beuvron r. France
156 C2 Beuvry France
159 G2 Beuzeville France
193 E2 Bevagna Italy
190 B2 Bevaix Switz.
169 C3 Bever r. Ger.
161 F5 Bévéra r. France
87 C7 Beverley W.A. Austr.
149 I4 Beverley East Riding of Yorkshire, England U.K.
233 H3 Beverly MA U.S.A.
234 D2 Beverly NJ U.S.A.
232 C5 Beverly OH U.S.A.
240 H4 Beverly Hills CA U.S.A.
169 E4 Bevern Ger.
168 D2 Beverstedt Ger.
169 E4 Beverungen Ger.
164 D2 Beverwijk Neth.
156 B4 Béville-le-Comte France
150 E2 Bewdley Worcestershire, England U.K.
190 C2 Bex Switz.
172 B2 Bexbach Ger.
151 H4 Bexhill East Sussex, England U.K.
111 D4 Bextograk Xinjiang China
199 F3 Beyağaç Turkey
199 E1 Beyazköy Turkey
Beyce Turkey see Orhaneli
163 B4 Beychac-et-Caillau France
199 G1 Beyciler Bolu Turkey
199 F2 Beydağ Turkey
199 G3 Bey Dağları mts Turkey
171 C3 Beyendorf Ger.
199 G3 Beykonak Turkey
199 G1 Beyköy Turkey
199 F1 Beykoz Turkey
206 C4 Beyla Guinea
Beylagan Azer. see Beyläqan
129 E4 Beyläqan Azer.
199 G2 Beylikova Turkey
203 I6 Beylul Eritrea
163 D4 Beynac-et-Cazenac France
162 D3 Beynat France
165 E4 Beyne-Heusay Belgium
120 C3 Beyneu Kazakh.
160 D3 Beynost France
199 E2 Beyoba Manisa Turkey
103 I8 Beyoneisu Retugan i. Japan
126 C2 Beypazarı Turkey
126 E3 Beypınarı Turkey
114 B4 Beypore Kerala India
122 C5 Beyram Iran
Beyrouth Lebanon see Beirut
126 C3 Beyşehir Turkey
126 C3 Beyşehir Gölü l. Turkey
137 J5 Beysug Rus. Fed.
137 J4 Beysug r. Rus. Fed.
137 J5 Beysuzhek r. Rus. Fed.
127 F3 Beytüşşebap Turkey
161 D4 Bez r. France
187 B4 Bezas Spain
178 A3 Bezau Austria
134 J4 Bezbozhnik Rus. Fed.
196 D3 Bezdan Vojvodina, Srbija Yugo.
160 D1 Bèze France
129 C2 Bezengi Rus. Fed.
176 G4 Bezenye Hungary
138 G3 Bezhanitskaya Vozvyshennost' hills Rus. Fed.
138 G3 Bezhanitsy Rus. Fed.
197 G4 Bezhanovo Bulg.
139 K3 Bezhetsk Rus. Fed.
139 K3 Bezhetskiy Verkh reg. Rus. Fed.
129 E2 Bezhta Rus. Fed.
161 B5 Béziers France
175 I1 Bezledy Pol.
Bezmein Turkm. see Byuzmeyin
161 C5 Bezouce France
177 L3 Bežovce Slovakia
Bezwada Andhra Prad. India see Vijayawada
116 B4 Bhabhar Gujarat India
116 C5 Bhabra Madh. Prad. India
117 E4 Bhabua Bihar India
116 B5 Bhachau Gujarat India
116 B5 Bhadar r. India
116 C2 Bhadarwah Jammu and Kashmir
123 H4 Bhadaur Punjab India
117 F4 Bhadgaon Nepal
117 E4 Bhadohi Uttar Prad. India
116 C3 Bhadra Rajasthan India
114 D2 Bhadrachalam Andhra Prad. India
Bhadrachalam Road Station Andhra Prad. India see Kottagudem
117 F5 Bhadrakh Orissa India
114 B3 Bhadravati Karnataka India
123 F4 Bhag Pak.
111 B5 Bhaga r. India
117 F4 Bhagalpur Bihar India
117 G5 Bhagirathi r. India
114 C2 Bhainsa Andhra Prad. India
116 D5 Bhainsdehi Madh. Prad. India
117 G4 Bhairab Bazar Bangl.
117 E4 Bhairawa Nepal
Bhairawaha Nepal see Bhairawa
119 I4 Bhairi Hol mt. Pak.
123 G4 Bhakkar Pak.
Bhaktapur Nepal see Bhadgaon
114 C2 Bhalki Karnataka India
123 H3 Bhalwal Pak.
116 D5 Bhamgarh Madh. Prad. India
96 B1 Bhamo Myanmar
116 D5 Bhandara Mahar. India
116 D4 Bhander Madh. Prad. India
115 E2 Bhanjanagar Orissa India
116 C4 Bhanpura Madh. Prad. India
116 D5 Bhanrer Range hills Madh. Prad. India
Bharat country Asia see India
116 D4 Bharatpur Rajasthan India
117 H4 Bhareli r. India
123 E5 Bhari r. Pak.
116 D4 Bharthana Uttar Prad. India
116 C5 Bharuch Gujarat India
116 E5 Bhatapara Madh. Prad. India
Bhatinda Punjab India see Bathinda
114 B3 Bhatkal Karnataka India
Bhatnair Rajasthan India see Hanumangarh
117 G5 Bhatpara W. Bengal India
123 H3 Bhaun Gharibwal Pak.
114 C4 Bhavani Tamil Nadu India
114 C4 Bhavani r. India
116 C5 Bhavnagar Gujarat India
123 H4 Bhawana Pak.
115 D2 Bhawanipatna Orissa India
Bhearnaraigh, Eilean i. Western Isles, Scotland U.K. see Berneray
Bheemavaram Andhra Prad. India see Bhimavaram
215 H2 Bhekuzulu S. Africa
123 H3 Bhera Pak.
116 E3 Bheri r. Nepal
116 E5 Bhilai Madh. Prad. India
116 C4 Bhildi Gujarat India
116 C4 Bhilwara Rajasthan India
114 C2 Bhima r. India
114 D2 Bhimavaram Andhra Prad. India
123 H3 Bhimbar Pak.
117 F4 Bhimnagar Bihar India
116 D4 Bhind Madh. Prad. India
116 C4 Bhindar Rajasthan India
116 E4 Bhinga Uttar Prad. India
114 B2 Bhingar Mahar. India
116 C4 Bhinmal Rajasthan India
114 B2 Bhiwandi Mahar. India
116 D3 Bhiwani Haryana India
116 B5 Bhogat Gujarat India
116 C5 Bhokardan Mahar. India
117 G5 Bhola Bangl.
116 D4 Bhongaon Uttar Prad. India
114 C2 Bhongir Andhra Prad. India
215 G4 Bhongweni S. Africa
116 D5 Bhopal Madh. Prad. India
114 D2 Bhopalpatnam Madh. Prad. India
114 B2 Bhor Mahar. India
Bhrigukaccha Gujarat India see Bharuch
117 F5 Bhuban Orissa India
117 F5 Bhubaneshwar Orissa India
Bhubaneswar Orissa India see Bhubaneshwar
116 B5 Bhuj Gujarat India
96 B3 Bhumiphol Dam Thai.
215 H2 Bhunya Swaziland
116 C5 Bhusawal Mahar. India
117 G4 Bhutan country Asia
116 B4 Bhuttewala Rajasthan India
114 C4 Bhuvanagiri Tamil Nadu India
250 E5 Biá r. Brazil
209 E7 Bia, Monts mts Dem. Rep. Congo
96 C3 Bia, Phou mt. Laos
122 D5 Bīabān mts Iran
174 F4 Biadki Pol.
Biafra, Bight of g. Africa see Benin, Bight of
174 F5 Biała Pol.
175 I5 Biała r. Pol.
174 F5 Biała r. Pol.
174 G4 Biała-Parcela Pierwsza Pol.
175 K2 Biała Piska Pol.
175 L3 Biała Podlaska Pol.
175 I4 Biała Rawska Pol.
174 F2 Białe Błota Pol.
175 K4 Białka r. Pol.
175 I4 Białobrzegi Pol.
175 K5 Białobrzegi Pol.
174 D2 Białogard Pol.
174 F2 Białośliwie Pol.
175 L3 Białowieża Pol.
174 E2 Biały Bór Pol.
175 I6 Biały Dunajec Pol.
175 L2 Białystok Pol.
194 D5 Biancavilla Sicilia Italy
195 F4 Bianco Italy
190 C3 Bianco, Corno mt. Italy
Bianco, Monte mt. France/Italy see Mont Blanc
107 I5 Biandan Gang r. mouth China
190 D3 Biandrate Italy
208 D3 Bianga C.A.R.
206 D5 Biankouma Côte d'Ivoire
206 E5 Bianouan Côte d'Ivoire
160 E2 Bians-les-Usiers France
190 D3 Bianzè Italy
Bianzhuang Shandong China see Cangshan
92 C5 Biao Phil.
116 D5 Biaora Madh. Prad. India
187 C6 Biar Spain
122 C2 Bīārjmand Iran
163 A5 Biarritz France
Biarritz airport France see Parme
163 A5 Biarrotte France
162 D4 Biars-sur-Cère France
163 A4 Bias Aquitaine France
163 C4 Bias Aquitaine France
190 D2 Biasca Switz.
177 H4 Biatorbágy Hungary
203 F2 Biba Egypt
102 J2 Bibai Japan
209 B8 Bibala Angola
83 G4 Bibbenluke N.S.W. Austr.
191 G5 Bibbiena Italy
191 F5 Bibbona Italy
207 I4 Bibémi Cameroon
172 C3 Biberach Ger.
172 D3 Biberach an der Riß Ger.
173 E3 Biberbach Ger.
173 E2 Bibert r. Ger.
206 E5 Bibiani Ghana
191 I3 Bibione Italy
117 G4 Bibiyana r. Bangl.
172 C2 Biblis Ger.
Biblos Lebanon see Jbail
136 C3 Bibrka Ukr.
151 F3 Bibury Gloucestershire, England U.K.
257 F4 Bicas Brazil
177 M4 Bicaz Maramureș Romania
197 H2 Bicaz Neamț Romania
193 H3 Biccari Italy
151 F3 Bicester Oxfordshire, England U.K.
210 C2 Bichena Eth.
Bicheng Chongqing China see Bishan
83 G5 Bicheno Tas. Austr.
100 E3 Bichevaya Rus. Fed.
207 H3 Bichi Nigeria
100 F1 Bichi r. Rus. Fed.
173 F4 Bichl Ger.
114 B3 Bicholim Goa India
107 E1 Bichura Rus. Fed.
129 B2 Bichvint'a Georgia
172 C2 Bickenbach Ger.
151 F2 Bickenhill West Midlands, England U.K.
84 D2 Bickerton Island N.T. Austr.
150 C4 Bickleigh Devon, England U.K.
150 D4 Bickleigh Devon, England U.K.
151 H3 Bicknacre Essex, England U.K.
241 L2 Bicknell UT U.S.A.
129 F3 Bico Azer.
187 C5 Bicorp Spain
184 B3 Bicos Port.
177 H4 Bicske Hungary
150 E2 Bicton Shropshire, England U.K.
114 B2 Bid Mahar. India
207 G4 Bida Nigeria
163 A5 Bidache France
114 C2 Bidar Karnataka India
163 A5 Bidart France
116 C4 Bidasar Rajasthan India
125 G3 Bidbid Oman
233 □H3 Biddeford ME U.S.A.
151 H3 Biddenden Kent, England U.K.
164 E2 Biddinghuizen Neth.
149 G4 Biddulph Staffordshire, England U.K.
146 C5 Bidean nam Bian mt. Scotland U.K.
150 C3 Bideford Devon, England U.K.
150 C3 Bideford Bay England U.K.
191 H4 Bidente r. Italy
151 F2 Bidford-on-Avon Warwickshire, England U.K.
122 D4 Bidkhan, Kūh-e mt. Iran
205 F5 Bidon 5 tourist site Alg.
163 B5 Bidos France
163 A5 Bidouze r. France
177 K3 Bidovce Slovakia
100 E3 Bidzhar r. Rus. Fed.
Bié Angola see Kuito
209 C8 Bié prov. Angola
169 E5 Bieber Ger.
172 C2 Biebesheim am Rhein Ger.
175 K2 Biebrza r. Pol.
175 J6 Biecz Pol.
169 D5 Biedenkopf Ger.
171 C3 Biederitz Ger.
186 C2 Biel Spain
190 C1 Biel Switz.
175 K3 Bielany-Żyłaki Pol.
174 E5 Bielawa Pol.
169 D3 Bielefeld Ger.
174 C2 Bielice Pol.
175 I5 Bieliny Kapitulne Pol.
Bielitz Pol. see Bielsko-Biała
190 D3 Biella Italy
190 D3 Biella prov. Piemonte Italy
163 B5 Bielle France
186 D2 Bielsa Spain
175 H3 Bielsk Pol.
175 H6 Bielsko-Biała Pol.
175 L3 Bielsk Podlaski Pol.
169 E4 Bielstein hill Ger.
168 F2 Bienenbüttel Ger.
97 D5 Biên Hoa Vietnam
160 D2 Bienne r. France
Bienne Switz. see Biel
190 F3 Bienno Italy
185 H2 Bienservida Spain
184 D2 Bienvenida Spain
184 D2 Bienvenida hill Spain
183 H4 Bienvenida mt. Spain
251 H4 Bienvenue Fr. Guiana
209 B8 Bié Plateau Angola
177 H1 Bierawa Pol.
174 G5 Bierawka r. Pol.
85 F5 Bierbank Qld Austr.
174 G5 Bierdzany Pol.
171 C4 Biere Ger.
190 B2 Bière Switz.
186 C2 Bierge Spain
159 F4 Bierné France
163 D6 Biert France
175 H5 Bieruń Pol.
174 F4 Bierutów Pol.
174 G3 Bierzwienna-Długa Pol.
174 D2 Bierzwnik Pol.
186 C2 Biescas Spain
170 C3 Biese r. Ger.
170 E3 Biesenthal Ger.
174 E1 Biesiekierz Pol.
215 E2 Biesiesvlei S. Africa
157 F4 Biesles France
214 D4 Biesrespoort S. Africa
173 E4 Biessenhofen Ger.
175 K6 Bieszczady mts Pol.
172 C3 Bietigheim Ger.
172 D3 Bietigheim-Bissingen Ger.
170 E2 Bietikow Ger.
190 C2 Bietschhorn mt. Switz.
165 E5 Bièvre Belgium
175 H3 Bieżuń Pol.
193 H3 Biferno r. Italy
208 A5 Bifoun Gabon
240 F2 Big r. CA U.S.A.
199 E1 Biga Turkey
199 E1 Biga r. Turkey
199 F2 Bigadiç Turkey
261 G3 Bigand Arg.
163 B4 Biganos France
187 C6 Bigastro Spain
199 E2 Biga Yarımadası pen. Turkey
238 E2 Big Baldy Mountain MT U.S.A.
222 F5 Big Bar Creek B.C. Can.
226 D2 Big Bay MI U.S.A.
78 □5 Big Bay b. Vanuatu
226 D3 Big Bay de Noc MI U.S.A.
240 I4 Big Bear Lake CA U.S.A.
238 E2 Big Belt Mountains MT U.S.A.
215 H2 Big Bend Swaziland
237 F5 Big Black r. MS U.S.A.
236 D4 Big Blue r. NE U.S.A.
150 D4 Bigbury-on-Sea Devon, England U.K.
78 □3a Bigej i. Kwajalein Marshall Is
234 C3 Big Elk Creek r. MD U.S.A.
106 C2 Biger Nuur salt l. Mongolia
236 E1 Big Falls MN U.S.A.
226 A1 Big Fork r. MN U.S.A.
223 J4 Biggar Sask. Can.
146 E6 Biggar South Lanarkshire, Scotland U.K.
78 □3a Biggarenn i. Kwajalein Marshall Is
215 G3 Biggarsberg S. Africa
86 E2 Bigge Island W.A. Austr.
85 H5 Biggenden Qld Austr.
222 B3 Bigger, Mount B.C. Can.
78 □3a Biggerann i. Kwajalein Marshall Is
151 H3 Biggin Hill Greater London, England U.K.
151 G2 Biggleswade Bedfordshire, England U.K.
240 G2 Biggs CA U.S.A.
238 B2 Biggs OR U.S.A.
238 D2 Big Hole r. MT U.S.A.
238 F2 Bighorn r. Montana/Wyoming U.S.A.
238 F2 Bighorn Mountains WY U.S.A.
78 □3a Bigi i. Kwajalein Marshall Is
139 L5 Bigil'dino Rus. Fed.
129 E3 Bığır Azer.
232 D6 Big Island VA U.S.A.
237 C6 Big Lake TX U.S.A.
238 D3 Big Lost r. ID U.S.A.
238 F1 Big Muddy Creek r. MT U.S.A.
158 D4 Bignan France
190 D2 Bignasco Switz.
206 A3 Bignona Senegal
209 E6 Bigobo Dem. Rep. Congo
232 D6 Big Otter r. VA U.S.A.
240 H3 Big Pine CA U.S.A.
240 H4 Big Pine Peak CA U.S.A.
238 F2 Big Porcupine Creek r. MT U.S.A.
222 C3 Big Port Walter AK U.S.A.
226 E4 Big Rapids MI U.S.A.
226 C3 Big Rib r. WI U.S.A.
223 J4 Big River Sask. Can.
222 C2 Big Salmon Y.T. Can.
222 C2 Big Salmon r. Y.T. Can.
238 E1 Big Sandy MT U.S.A.
238 E3 Big Sandy r. WY U.S.A.
236 C4 Big Sandy Creek r. CO U.S.A.
236 D3 Big Sioux r. SD U.S.A.
240 I2 Big Smokey Valley NV U.S.A.
237 C5 Big Spring TX U.S.A.
236 C3 Big Springs NE U.S.A.
223 I5 Big Stone Alta Can.
236 D2 Big Stone City SD U.S.A.
232 B6 Big Stone Gap VA U.S.A.
237 F5 Big Sunflower r. MS U.S.A.
240 G3 Big Sur CA U.S.A.
238 E2 Big Timber MT U.S.A.
224 B2 Big Trout Lake Ont. Can.
186 B2 Bigüezal Spain
192 B2 Biguglia Corse France
222 H4 Big Valley Alta Can.
241 L3 Big Water UT U.S.A.
227 H3 Bigwin Ont. Can.
188 E3 Bihać Bos.-Herz.
117 F4 Bihar state India
177 K4 Biharia Romania
117 F4 Bihariganj Bihar India
177 K4 Biharkeresztes Hungary
177 K4 Biharnagybajom Hungary
117 F4 Bihar Sharif Bihar India
177 K5 Biharugra Hungary
177 L5 Bihor county Romania
197 F2 Bihor, Vârful mt. Romania
177 L5 Bihorului, Munții mts Romania
117 H4 Bihpuriagaon Assam India
206 A4 Bijagós, Arquipélago dos is Guinea-Bissau
116 C4 Bijainagar Rajasthan India
116 D4 Bijaipur Madh. Prad. India
114 B2 Bijapur Karnataka India
122 A3 Bījār Iran
114 D2 Bijarpur Madh. Prad. India
116 D4 Bijawar Madh. Prad. India
116 C2 Bijbehara Jammu and Kashmir
188 G3 Bijeljina Bos.-Herz.
188 E3 Bijelolasica mt. Croatia
196 D4 Bijelo Polje Crna Gora Yugo.
108 C3 Bijie Guizhou China
117 G4 Bijni Assam India
116 D3 Bijnor Uttar Prad. India
116 C4 Bijolia Rajasthan India
217 □2 Bijoutier i. Seychelles
125 E2 Bijrān, Khashm hill Saudi Arabia
116 C4 Bikampur Rajasthan India
116 C3 Bikaner Rajasthan India
120 E3 Bikbauli Kazakh.
128 B3 Bikfaiya Lebanon
100 E3 Bikin Rus. Fed.
100 E3 Bikin r. Rus. Fed.
213 F4 Bikita Zimbabwe
208 C5 Bikoro Dem. Rep. Congo
108 C1 Bikou Gansu China
177 I6 Bikovo Vojvodina, Srbija Yugo.
117 F4 Bikramganj Bihar India
137 J3 Bila r. Ukr.
137 J3 Bila r. Ukr.
129 F3 Biläcarı Azer.
125 G3 Bilād Banī Bū 'Alī Oman
125 G3 Bilād Banī Bū Ḩasan Oman
124 C3 Bilād Ghāmid reg. Saudi Arabia
124 C3 Bilād Zahran reg. Saudi Arabia
137 G4 Bila Krynytsya Ukr.
207 E3 Bilanga Burkina
116 C4 Bilara Rajasthan India
116 D3 Bilari Uttar Prad. India
116 D3 Bilaspur Hima. Prad. India
116 E5 Bilaspur Madh. Prad. India
129 F4 Biläsuvar Azer.
136 F3 Bila Tserkva Ukr.
97 B4 Bilauktaung Range mts Myanmar/Thai.

183 H1 Bilbao Spain
203 F2 Bilbeis Egypt
Bilbo Spain see Bilbao
197 G2 Bilbor Romania
146 E3 Bilbster Highland, Scotland U.K.
188 G4 Bileća Bos.-Herz.
199 F1 Bilecik Turkey
199 G1 Bilecik prov. Turkey
196 E3 Biled Romania
129 F4 Bileh Savār Iran
137 I3 Bilen'ke Ukr.
137 H4 Bilen'ke Ukr.
175 K5 Biłgoraj Pol.
211 A5 Bilharamulo Tanz.
116 C4 Bilhaur Uttar Prad. India
136 F4 Bilhorod-Dnistrovs'ky Ukr.
208 D3 Bili r. Dem. Rep. Congo
131 R3 Bilibino Rus. Fed.
96 B3 Bilin Myanmar
93 I4 Bilina Czech Rep.
92 C4 Biliran i. Phil.
198 B1 Bilisht Albania
107 I4 Bilky r. Ukr.
177 M3 Bilky Ukr.
238 F3 Bill WY U.S.A.
87 B5 Billabalong W.A. Austr.
Billabong Creek r. N.S.W. Austr. see Moulamein Creek
87 B5 Billabong Roadhouse W.A. Austr.
142 D3 Billdal Sweden
168 F2 Bille r. Ger.
169 C4 Billerbeck Ger.
163 B5 Billère France
151 H3 Billericay Essex, England U.K.
160 D2 Billiat France
172 D2 Billigheim Ger.
86 E3 Billiluna W.A. Austr.
264 J2 Billingford Norfolk, England U.K.
149 H3 Billingham Stockton-on-Tees, England U.K.
149 I4 Billinghay Lincolnshire, England U.K.
238 E2 Billings MT U.S.A.
151 G3 Billingshurst West Sussex, England U.K.
Billiton i. Indon. see Belitung
151 I2 Billockby Norfolk, England U.K.
150 E4 Bill of Portland hd England U.K.
160 B3 Billom France
142 C4 Billund Denmark
141 J5 Billund airport Denmark
241 J4 Bill Williams r. AZ U.S.A.
241 K4 Bill Williams Mountain AZ U.S.A.
160 B2 Billy France
207 I2 Bilma Niger
85 G5 Biloela Qld Austr.
176 F5 Bilo Gora hills Croatia
137 H5 Bilohirs'k Ukr.
136 D2 Bilohir''ya Ukr.
136 D3 Bilohorodka Khmel'nyts'ka Oblast' Ukr.
136 F2 Bilohorodka Kyivs'ka Oblast' Ukr.
251 G4 Biloku Guyana
137 I3 Bilokurakyne Ukr.
114 C2 Biloli Mahar. India
137 I3 Biloluts'k Ukr.
137 H2 Bilopillya Ukr.
136 D2 Bilotyn Ukr.
177 H2 Bilovec Czech Rep.
136 C2 Bilovice Czech Rep.
137 J3 Bilovods'k Ukr.
237 F6 Biloxi MS U.S.A.
137 G4 Bilozerka Ukr.
137 I3 Bilozers'ke Ukr.
169 F4 Bilshausen Ger.
115 I3 Bil'shivtsi Ukr.
116 D3 Bilsi Uttar Prad. India
137 H2 Bil's'k Ukr.
136 C2 Bil's'ka Volya Ukr.
146 E6 Bilston Midlothian, Scotland U.K.
164 E2 Bilthoven Neth.
202 D6 Biltine Chad
202 D6 Biltine pref. Chad
149 I4 Bilton East Riding of Yorkshire, England U.K.
96 B3 Bilugyun Island Myanmar
137 H3 Bilukhivka Ukr.
93 B2 Bilungala Sulawesi Utara Indon.
136 F4 Bilyayivka Ukr.
175 K6 Bilychi Ukr.
137 H3 Bilyky Ukr.
136 E3 Bilykivka Ukr.
136 E4 Bilyne Ukr.
137 I3 Bilyts'ke Ukr.
165 C4 Bilyy Cheremosh r. Ukr.
137 I2 Bilyy Kolodyaz' Ukr.
163 E4 Bilzen Belgium
208 E4 Bima r. Dem. Rep. Congo
95 G5 Bima Sumbawa Indon.
207 F4 Bimbila Ghana
246 C1 Bimini Islands Bahamas
115 I2 Bimlipatam Andhra Prad. India
129 G3 Bināk Azer.
173 G3 Bina r. Ger.
177 H4 Biña Slovakia
186 D3 Binaced Spain
116 C4 Bina-Etawa Madh. Prad. India
93 D3 Binaija, Gunung mt. Seram Indon.
92 B4 Binalbagan Phil.
122 D2 Binālūd, Kūh-e mts Iran
156 B5 Binas France
236 D2 Binasco Italy
89 F4 Binbee Qld Austr.
126 E3 Binboğa Dağı mt. Turkey
149 I4 Binbrook Lincolnshire, England U.K.
165 C4 Binche Belgium
107 H4 Bincheng Shandong China
108 B3 Binchuan Yunnan China
208 B2 Binder Chad
116 E4 Bindki Uttar Prad. India
173 F2 Bindlach Ger.
85 G5 Bindle Qld Austr.
Bindloe Island Islas Galápagos Ecuador see Marchena, Isla
213 I3 Bindura Zimbabwe
186 D3 Binefar Spain
148 C2 Binevenagh hill Northern Ireland U.K.
213 E3 Binga Zimbabwe
213 G3 Binga, Monte mt. Moz.
83 G2 Bingara N.S.W. Austr.
84 D2 Bing Bong N.T. Austr.
106 D4 Bingcaowan Gansu China
172 D3 Bingen Ger.
172 B2 Bingen am Rhein Ger.
164 F3 Bingerden Neth.
206 E5 Bingerville Côte d'Ivoire
151 G2 Bingham Nottinghamshire, England U.K.
233 □I2 Bingham ME U.S.A.
147 A2 Binghamstown Rep. of Ireland
233 F3 Binghamton NY U.S.A.
202 B3 Bin Ghanīmah, Jabal hills Libya
149 H4 Bingley West Yorkshire, England U.K.
Bingmei Guizhou China see Congjiang
127 F3 Bingöl Turkey
127 E3 Bingöl prov. Turkey
127 F3 Bingöl Dağı mt. Turkey
129 E4 Bingöl Dağları mts Turkey
Bingzi Jiangxi China see Yushan
108 A2 Bingzhongluo Yunnan China
158 D3 Binic France
92 B4 Binicuil Phil.
115 H4 Binika Orissa India
187 F5 Binissalem Spain
94 B2 Binjai Sumatera Indon.
83 G2 Binnaway N.S.W. Austr.
146 D5 Binnein Mor mt. Scotland U.K.
168 E3 Binnen Ger.
92 C3 Binonan Phil.
117 F5 Binpur W. Bengal India
94 C1 Bintan i. Indon.
94 C1 Bintang, Bukit mts Malaysia

92 B3 Bintuan Phil.
94 C4 Bintuhan Sumatera Indon.
95 F2 Bintulu Sarawak Malaysia
92 B3 Binubusan Phil.
100 C3 Binxian Heilong. China
107 T5 Binxian Shaanxi China
Binxian Shandong China see Bincheng
108 D4 Binyang Guangxi China
207 G4 Bin-Yauri Nigeria
172 B4 Binzen Ger.
Binzhou Guangxi China see Binyang
Binzhou Heilong. China see Binxian
107 H4 Binzhou Shandong China
260 A5 Bío Bío admin. reg. Chile
260 A5 Bío Bío r. Chile
207 H6 Bioco i. Equat. Guinea
188 E4 Biograd na Moru Croatia
Bioko i. Equat. Guinea see Bioco
160 D3 Biol France
190 C3 Bionaz Italy
186 E3 Biosca Spain
161 F5 Biot France
186 B2 Biota Spain
168 C3 Bippen Ger.
257 E3 Bîrlad Mold.
Bir Mahr. India see Bid
210 D2 Bir, Ras pt Djibouti
100 C2 Bira r. Rus. Fed.
100 E2 Bira r. Rus. Fed.
123 E5 Bīrag, Kūh-e mts Iran
202 B3 Bīrāk Libya
100 D2 Birakan Rus. Fed.
127 F4 Bi'r al Mulūsī Iraq
202 B2 Birao C.A.R.
117 F4 Biratnagar Nepal
222 H3 Birch r. Alta Can.
223 J4 Birch Hills Sask. Can.
151 I3 Birchington Kent, England U.K.
83 G3 Birchip Vic. Austr.
177 L6 Birchiş Romania
222 G5 Birch Island B.C. Can.
222 H3 Birch Mountains Y.T. Can.
223 K4 Birch River Man. Can.
237 F4 Birch River WV U.S.A.
227 F4 Birch Run MI U.S.A.
226 B3 Birchwood WI U.S.A.
210 D3 Bircot Eth.
175 K6 Bircza Pol.
164 E1 Birdaard Neth.
147 C4 Birdhill Rep. of Ireland
234 B2 Bird in Hand PA U.S.A.
117 F4 Bird Island N. Mariana Is see Farallon de Medinilla
234 C2 Birdsboro PA U.S.A.
241 L2 Birdseye UT U.S.A.
84 D5 Birdsville Qld Austr.
234 B4 Birdsville MD U.S.A.
84 C2 Birdum r. N.T. Austr.
126 E3 Birecik Turkey
Birendranagar Nepal see Surkhet
211 A5 Birenga Rwanda
202 E5 Bir en Natrūn well Sudan
94 B1 Bireun Sumatera Indon.
199 F2 Birgi İzmir Turkey
128 E4 Bīrjand Iran
142 C2 Birkeland Norway
172 C2 Birkenau Ger.
172 C3 Birkenfeld Baden-Württemberg Ger.
172 D2 Birkenfeld Bayern Ger.
172 B2 Birkenfeld Rheinland-Pfalz Ger.
149 F4 Birkenhead Merseyside, England U.K.
169 C5 Birken-Honigsessen Ger.
170 E3 Birkenwerder Berlin Ger.
168 G1 Birket Denmark
203 F2 Birket Qārūn l. Egypt
179 G3 Birkfeld Austria
195 □ Birkirkara Malta
82 B1 Birksgate Range hills S.A. Austr.
169 F4 Birkungen Ger.
137 H2 Birky Ukr.
Bîrlad Romania see Bârlad
121 H3 Birlik Zhambylskaya Oblast' Kazakh.
Birlik Zhambylskaya Oblast' Kazakh. see Brlik
151 F2 Birmingham West Midlands, England U.K.
231 C5 Birmingham AL U.S.A.
117 F5 Birmitrapur Orissa India
204 C4 Bir Mogreïn Maur.
178 D3 Birnhorn mt. Austria
207 F4 Birnin Benin
79 □7a Birnie i. Kiribati
207 F3 Birnin-Gaouré Niger
207 G4 Birnin-Gwari Nigeria
207 G3 Birnin-Kebbi Nigeria
207 G3 Birnin Konni Niger
207 H3 Birnin Kudu Nigeria
207 H3 Birniwa Nigeria
100 E2 Birobidzhan Rus. Fed.
163 C4 Biron France
92 A4 Birong Phil.
117 F4 Birpur Bihar India
147 J3 Birr Rep. of Ireland
169 B5 Birresborn Ger.
83 F2 Birrie r. N.S.W. Austr.
84 B3 Birrindudu N.T. Austr.
197 K3 Bîrsana Romania
145 □ Birsay Orkney, Scotland U.K.
190 C1 Birse r. Switz.
Birshoghyr Kazakh. see Berchogur
134 K5 Birsk Rus. Fed.
151 F2 Birstall Leicestershire, England U.K.
169 E5 Birstein Ger.
138 E4 Birštonas Lith.
85 □2 Birthday Mountain hill Qld Austr.
223 K5 Birtle Man. Can.
149 H3 Birtley Tyne and Wear, England U.K.
111 F6 Biru Xizang China
136 E4 Biruinţa Moldova
Biruinţa Moldova see Ştefan Vodă
114 B3 Birur Karnataka India
Biruxiong Xizang China see Biru
138 E3 Biržai Lith.
195 □ Birżebbuġa Malta
193 H3 Bisaccia Italy
194 C5 Bisacquino Sicilia Italy
104 C3 Bisai Japan
116 D3 Bisalpur Uttar Prad. India
192 B3 Bisaurin mt. Spain
241 M6 Bisbee AZ U.S.A.
194 E6 Biscari Sicilia Italy see Acate
163 A4 Biscarrosse France
163 A4 Biscarrosse et de Parentis, Étang de l. France
163 A4 Biscarrosse-Plage France
158 B5 Biscay, Bay of sea France/Spain
264 I3 Biscay Abyssal Plain sea feature N. Atlantic Ocean
193 I3 Biscéglie Italy
173 E2 Bischberg Ger.
172 D2 Bischbrunn Ger.
157 H4 Bischheim France
169 D5 Bischoffen Ger.
173 E2 Bischofferode Ger.
173 F1 Bischofsgrün Ger.
172 C2 Bischofsheim Ger.
169 F5 Bischofsheim an der Rhön Ger.
178 C5 Bischofshofen Austria
173 H3 Bischofsmais Ger.
173 H3 Bischofsreut Ger.
190 D1 Bischofszell Switz.
157 H4 Bischwiller France
262 T2 Biscoe Islands Antarctica
216 □1a Biscoitos Terceira Azores
224 D4 Biscotasing Ont. Can.

193 F2 Bisenti Italy
134 L4 Biser Rus. Fed.
134 L4 Bisert' r. Rus. Fed.
197 H4 Bisertsi Bulg.
108 B4 Bisezhai Yunnan China
203 H6 Bisha Eritrea
108 C2 Bishan Chongqing China
Bishbek Kyrg. see Bishkek
127 H4 Bisheh Iran
121 H4 Bishkek Kyrg.
117 F5 Bishnupur W. Bengal India
215 F5 Bisho S. Africa
240 H3 Bishop CA U.S.A.
149 H3 Bishop Auckland Durham, England U.K.
146 D6 Bishopbriggs East Dunbartonshire, Scotland U.K.
150 E2 Bishop's Castle Shropshire, England U.K.
150 E3 Bishop's Cleeve Gloucestershire, England U.K.
150 D3 Bishop's Hull Somerset, England U.K.
151 F2 Bishop's Itchington Warwickshire, England U.K.
150 D3 Bishop's Lydeard Somerset, England U.K.
151 H3 Bishop's Stortford Hertfordshire, England U.K.
150 C3 Bishop's Tawton Devon, England U.K.
150 D4 Bishopsteignton Devon, England U.K.
151 F4 Bishop's Waltham Hampshire, England U.K.
146 D6 Bishopton Renfrewshire, Scotland U.K.
231 D5 Bishopville SC U.S.A.
126 E4 Bishri, Jabal hills Syria
196 D5 Bishti i Pallës pt Albania
100 B1 Bishui Heilong. China
Bishui Henan China see Biyang
215 G4 Bisi S. Africa
193 I5 Bisignano Italy
205 G2 Bisingen Ger.
175 K4 Biskupice Lubelskie Pol.
174 G4 Biskupice Opolskie Pol.
177 I3 Biskupice Slovakia
175 H2 Biskupiec Warmińsko-Mazurskie Pol.
175 I2 Biskupiec Warmińsko-Mazurskie Pol.
150 E3 Bisley Gloucestershire, England U.K.
92 C4 Bislig Phil.
236 C2 Bismarck ND U.S.A.
91 K7 Bismarck Archipelago is P.N.G.
76 E2 Bismarck Range mts P.N.G.
91 K7 Bismarck Sea P.N.G.
170 C3 Bismark (Altmark) Ger.
127 F3 Bismil Turkey
141 J3 Bismo Norway
236 C2 Bison SD U.S.A.
122 A3 Bīsotūn Iran
140 L3 Bispgården Sweden
115 D2 Bispingen Ger.
11 B2 Bissamcuttak Orissa India
206 B4 Bissau Guinea-Bissau
207 H5 Bissaula Nigeria
165 F5 Bissen Lux.
170 D3 Bissendorf Ger.
168 D3 Bissendorf (Wedemark) Ger.
223 N5 Bissett Man. Can.
206 C4 Bissikrima Guinea
173 E3 Bissingen Ger.
206 B3 Bissorã Guinea-Bissau
94 □ Bistagno Italy
222 G3 Bistcho Lake Alta Can.
196 C5 Bistra mt. Macedonia
197 J3 Bistra r. Romania
196 I4 Bistra r. Yugo.
197 F2 Bistret Romania
197 J4 Bistrica Slovenia
197 G2 Bistriţa Romania
197 H2 Bistriţa r. Romania
197 H2 Bistriţa Bârgăului Romania
197 G1 Bistriţa, Munţii mts Romania
197 F5 Bistriţa r. Bulg.
116 E4 Biswan Uttar Prad. India
143 I4 Bisztynek Pol.
208 A4 Bitam Gabon
172 A2 Bitburg Ger.
157 H3 Bitche France
195 F1 Bitetto Italy
116 E4 Bithur Uttar Prad. India
208 C2 Bitkine Chad
127 F3 Bitlis Turkey
196 E5 Bitola Macedonia
Bitolj Macedonia see Bitola
195 F1 Bitonto Italy
81 B8 Bitrān, Jabal hill Saudi Arabia
157 H5 Bitschwiller-lès-Thann France
241 M2 Bitter Creek r. UT U.S.A.
238 F3 Bitter Creek r. WY U.S.A.
171 D4 Bitterfeld Ger.
214 B3 Bitterfontein S. Africa
238 D2 Bitterroot r. ID U.S.A.
238 D2 Bitterroot Range mts ID U.S.A.
240 D3 Bitterwater CA U.S.A.
192 B4 Bitti Sardegna Italy
171 C3 Bittkau Ger.
150 D3 Bitton South Gloucestershire, England U.K.
207 E4 Bittou Burkina
93 C2 Bitung Sulawesi Utara Indon.
215 G4 Bityi S. Africa
138 C6 Bityug r. Rus. Fed.
173 D3 Bitz Ger.
207 I4 Biu Nigeria
183 F2 Biurrun Spain
215 H2 Bivane r. S. Africa
190 E2 Bivio Switz.
197 H2 Bivolari Romania
194 E4 Bivona Sicilia Italy
226 A2 Biwabik MN U.S.A.
104 B3 Biwa-ko l. Japan
145 □ Bixad Romania
146 □G1 Bixter Shetland, Scotland U.K.
121 N1 Biya r. Rus. Fed.
113 □7 Biyadhoo i. S. Male Maldives
150 D3 Biyang Torfaen, Wales U.K.
109 L1 Biyang Anhui China see Yixian
121 K1 Biysk Rus. Fed.
127 K6 Bizana S. Africa
161 B5 Bizanos France
161 A5 Bize-Minervois France
103 G6 Bizen Japan
205 H1 Bizerta Tunisia see Bizerte
199 B7 Bizerte Tunisia
199 B7 Bizerte admin. div. Tunisia
140 □A2 Bjargtangar hd Iceland
140 L1 Bjärkey Norway
143 E3 Bjärnum Sweden
143 E4 Bjärsjölagård Sweden
143 D2 Bjästa Sweden
196 I4 Bjelašnica mts Yugo.
188 F3 Bjelolasica mt. Bos.-Herz.
188 F3 Bjelovar Croatia
134 L5 Bjelovar Respublika Bashkortostan Rus. Fed.
141 J5 Bjerkvik Norway
168 F3 Bjerreby Denmark
142 F3 Bjerringbro Denmark
142 B3 Bjerreby Sweden
143 D4 Björkliden Sweden
140 L1 Björkliden Sweden
143 G1 Björklinge Sweden
140 L2 Björksele Sweden
142 A1 Bjørnafjorden b. Norway
142 A1 Bjørnarøen i. Norway
141 I6 Björna Sweden
137 L4 Bjørnevatn Norway
140 L2 Björneborg Fin. see Pori
268 B2 Bjørnøya i. Arctic Ocean
142 E1 Bjørøythorpe Norway
140 L3 Bjørsås Sweden
206 B3 Bla Mali
146 B4 Bla Bheinn hill Scotland U.K.
193 F4 Blace Italy
196 F4 Blace Srbija Yugo.
174 G5 Blachownia Pol.
165 D5 Black r. Man. Can.
226 D3 Black r. Ont. Can.
224 D3 Black r. Ont. Can.

229 H3 Black r. AR U.S.A.
85 F4 Blair WI U.S.A.
146 E5 Blair Athol Qld Austr.
215 F1 Blair Athol Perth and Kinross, Scotland U.K.
146 E5 Blairbeth S. Africa
Blairgowrie Perth and Kinross, Scotland U.K.
85 F5 Blackadder Water r.
224 B2 Blackall Qld Austr.
226 A2 Blackbear r. Ont. Can.
151 F3 Blackberry MN U.S.A.
85 E3 Black Bourton Oxfordshire, England U.K.
148 C4 Black Bull Rep. of Ireland
146 F4 Blackburn Aberdeenshire, Scotland U.K.
149 G4 Blackburn Blackburn with Darwen, England U.K.
146 E6 Blackburn West Lothian, Scotland U.K.
149 G4 Blackburn with Darwen admin. div. England U.K.
85 H5 Blackbutt Qld Austr.
240 F2 Black Butte CA U.S.A.
240 F2 Black Butte Lake CA U.S.A.
241 J4 Black Canyon gorge AZ U.S.A.
151 I2 Black Canyon City AZ U.S.A.
262 T2 Black Coast Antarctica
149 F3 Black Combe hill England U.K.
148 E2 Blackcraig Hill hill Scotland U.K.
226 C3 Black Creek WI U.S.A.
234 B1 Black Creek r. PA U.S.A.
222 E4 Black Creek r. Can.
150 D4 Black Down Hills England U.K.
236 E2 Blackduck MN U.S.A.
222 H4 Blackfalds Alta Can.
151 F4 Blackfield Hampshire, England U.K.
238 D3 Blackfoot ID U.S.A.
238 D2 Black Foot r. MT U.S.A.
146 E5 Blackford Perth and Kinross, Scotland U.K.
Black Forest mts Ger. see Schwarzwald
149 H4 Black Hill hill England U.K.
238 F2 Black Hills SD U.S.A.
146 E6 Blackhope Scar hill Scotland U.K.
146 D4 Black Isle pen. Scotland U.K.
223 J3 Black Lake Sask. Can.
148 B3 Blacklion Rep. of Ireland
146 E5 Blacklunans Perth and Kinross, Scotland U.K.
241 M5 Black Mesa mt. AZ U.S.A.
241 L3 Black Mesa ridge AZ U.S.A.
150 D3 Blackmoor Gate Devon, England U.K.
151 H3 Blackmore Essex, England U.K.
150 D3 Black Mountain hill Wales U.K.
240 H4 Black Mountain CA U.S.A.
232 B6 Black Mountain KY U.S.A.
150 D3 Black Mountains hills Wales U.K.
241 I4 Black Mountains AZ U.S.A.
212 C4 Black Nossob watercourse Namibia
151 H3 Black Notley Essex, England U.K.
149 F4 Blackpool Blackpool, England U.K.
246 □ Black River Jamaica
227 F1 Black River MI U.S.A.
233 F2 Black River NY U.S.A.
Black River r. Vietnam see Đa, Sông
226 B3 Black River Falls WI U.S.A.
161 M5 Black Rock hill Jordan see 'Unāb, Jabal al
147 E3 Blackrock Rep. of Ireland
232 C6 Black Rock Desert NV U.S.A.
232 C6 Blacksburg VA U.S.A.
135 G5 Black Sea Asia/Europe
238 E3 Blacks Fork r. WY U.S.A.
233 J2 Blacks Harbour N.B. Can.
231 D6 Blackshear GA U.S.A.
147 A2 Blacksod Bay Rep. of Ireland
240 H2 Black Springs NV U.S.A.
147 E4 Blackstairs Mountains hills Rep. of Ireland
222 F2 Blackstone r. N.W.T. Can.
232 G5 Blackstone VA U.S.A.
226 C1 Black Sturgeon r. Ont. Can.
83 G2 Black Sugarloaf mt. N.S.W. Austr.
240 D2 Black Tickle Nfld. Can.
147 D2 Blacktown Northern Ireland U.K.
215 H3 Black Umfolozi r. S. Africa
83 G2 Blackville N.S.W. Austr.
206 E4 Black Volta r. Africa alt. Mouhoun, alt. Volta Noire
85 G4 Blackwater Qld Austr.
222 E4 Blackwater r. N.W.T. Can.
147 E4 Blackwater r. Rep. of Ireland
147 E3 Blackwater r. Rep. of Ireland
147 E3 Blackwater r. Cavan/Meath Rep. of Ireland
147 D4 Blackwater r. Rep. of Ireland
151 H3 Blackwater r. England U.K.
146 D3 Black Water r. Highland, Scotland U.K.
146 D4 Black Water r. Highland, Scotland U.K.
232 E4 Blackwater r. VA U.S.A.
161 J4 Blackwater watercourse AZ U.S.A.
83 G3 Blackwater Reservoir Scotland U.K.
148 C3 Blackwatertown Northern Ireland U.K.
87 B7 Blackwood r. W.A. Austr.
150 D3 Blackwood Caerphilly, Wales U.K.
165 D2 Bladel Neth.
150 D3 Blaenau Ffestiniog Gwynedd, Wales U.K.
150 D3 Blaenau Gwent admin. div. Wales U.K.
150 D3 Blaengarw Bridgend, Wales U.K.
150 D3 Blaengwrach Neath Port Talbot, Wales U.K.
140 K2 Blåfjellhatten mt. Norway
150 D3 Blaenavon North Somerset, England U.K.
161 F3 Blagnac France
135 H7 Blagodarnyy Rus. Fed.
197 G3 Blagoevgrad Bulg.
197 G3 Blagoevgrad admin. div. Bulg.
197 H2 Blagoeşti Romania
197 F4 Blagovegrad Bulg.
121 I1 Blagoveshchenka Severnyy Kazakhstan Kazakh.
100 B2 Blagoveshchensk Amurskaya Oblast' Rus. Fed.
134 L5 Blagoveshchensk Respublika Bashkortostan Rus. Fed.
137 G4 Blagoveshchenskoye Severnyy Kazakhstan Kazakh.
121 H4 Blagoveshchenskoye Zhambylskaya Oblast' Kazakh.
137 H4 Blahodatne Mykolayivs'ka Oblast' Ukr.
137 I4 Blahodatne Zaporiz'ka Oblast' Ukr.
137 H4 Blahovishchenka Zaporiz'ka Oblast' Ukr.
173 G3 Blaibach Ger.
146 C5 Blaich Highland, Scotland U.K.
140 L3 Blaiken Sweden
222 H5 Blaikiston, Mount B.C. Can.
158 C5 Blain France
232 E4 Blain PA U.S.A.
180 D2 Blaco Phil.
182 D4 Blair Spain

226 B3 Blair WI U.S.A.
172 B2 Blieskastel Ger.
156 E4 Bligny France
160 C5 Bligny-sur-Ouche France
215 F1 Blijham Neth.
146 E5 Blijham Neth.
182 E1 Blímea Spain
179 F2 Blindenmarkt Austria
170 F2 Blindow Ger.
232 D6 Blind River Ont. Can.
215 F5 Blinkwater S. Africa
82 D2 Bliman S. Austr.
190 D2 Blinnenhorn mt. Italy/Switz.
238 D3 Bliss ID U.S.A.
227 F5 Blissfield MI U.S.A.
232 C4 Blissfield OH U.S.A.
151 G2 Blisworth Northamptonshire, England U.K.
95 J5 Blitar Jawa Timur Indon.
174 G4 Blizanów Pol.
173 G2 Blížkovice Czech Rep.
176 E3 Blizne Pol.
175 I4 Blížyn Pol.
233 H4 Block Island RI U.S.A.
233 H4 Block Island Sound sea chan. RI U.S.A.
157 F2 Blockley Gloucestershire, England U.K.
215 H2 Bloedrivier S. Africa
215 F3 Bloemfontein S. Africa
215 E2 Bloemhof S. Africa
215 E2 Bloemhof Dam S. Africa
159 H4 Blois France
164 H2 Blokzijl Neth.
169 E4 Blomberg Ger.
215 M4 Blomby Ger.
256 D3 Blönduós Iceland
140 □C2 Blönduós l. Iceland
140 □B2 Blöndulón l. Iceland
171 D4 Blönsdorf Ger.
159 G2 Blonville-sur-Mer France
84 B5 Bloods Range mts N.T. Austr.
223 L5 Bloodvein r. Man. Can.
147 C1 Bloody Foreland pt Rep. of Ireland
226 B3 Bloomer WI U.S.A.
227 I4 Bloomfield Ont. Can.
236 E3 Bloomfield IA U.S.A.
230 C4 Bloomfield IN U.S.A.
241 F4 Bloomfield MO U.S.A.
239 J4 Bloomfield NM U.S.A.
85 F2 Bloomfield River Qld Austr.
235 D3 Bloomingdale NJ U.S.A.
230 C3 Bloomingdale IN U.S.A.
235 D1 Blooming Grove NY U.S.A.
234 C1 Blooming Grove PA U.S.A.
226 A4 Blooming Prairie MN U.S.A.
230 C5 Bloomington IL U.S.A.
234 A3 Bloomington IN U.S.A.
226 A4 Bloomington MN U.S.A.
234 C2 Bloomsburg PA U.S.A.
227 I5 Bloomsburg PA U.S.A.
85 G4 Bloomsbury Qld Austr.
234 C2 Bloomsbury NJ U.S.A.
95 E4 Blora Jawa Tengah Indon.
227 I1 Blossburg PA U.S.A.
260 C8 Blossville Kyst coastal area Greenland
160 F1 Blotzheim France
214 B5 Bloubergstrand S. Africa
215 F3 Bloudi? S. Africa
215 C1 Blountstown FL U.S.A.
232 B6 Blountville TN U.S.A.
163 C5 Blousson-Sérian France
176 C2 Blovice Czech Rep.
170 C2 Blowatz Ger.
151 F2 Bloxham Oxfordshire, England U.K.
149 H4 Blubberhouses North Yorkshire, England U.K.
178 A3 Bludenz Austria
178 A3 Bludesch Austria
222 D3 Blue r. B.C. Can.
237 E5 Blue r. OK U.S.A.
148 B4 Blue Ball Rep. of Ireland
234 B4 Blue Ball PA U.S.A.
234 B2 Blue Bell PA U.S.A.
241 L2 Blue Bell Knoll mt. UT U.S.A.
222 F5 Blueberry r. B.C. Can.
215 E5 Blue Cliff S. Africa
Blue Creek r. Mex. see Azul
241 J3 Blue Diamond NV U.S.A.
236 E3 Blue Earth MN U.S.A.
232 C6 Bluefield VA U.S.A.
232 C6 Bluefield WV U.S.A.
244 □ Bluefields Nic.
147 B4 Blueford Rep. of Ireland
215 F4 Bluegums S. Africa
233 □I2 Blue Hill ME U.S.A.
236 D3 Blue Hill NE U.S.A.
117 H5 Blue Mountain India
234 B2 Blue Mountain ridge PA U.S.A.
233 F3 Blue Mountain mt. PA U.S.A.
246 □ Blue Mountain Peak Jamaica
241 L1 Blue Mountains U.T. U.S.A.
83 G4 Blue Mountains N.S.W. Austr.
238 C2 Blue Mountains OR U.S.A.
84 D2 Blue Mud Bay N.T. Austr.
210 B2 Blue Nile r. Eth./Sudan alt. Abay Wenz (Ethiopia), alt. Azraq, Bahr el (Sudan)
210 B2 Blue Nile state Sudan
218 D4 Blue Rapids KS U.S.A.
236 C6 Blue Ridge mts VA U.S.A.
231 C5 Blue Ridge GA U.S.A.
232 F5 Blue Ridge mts VA U.S.A.
222 G4 Blue River B.C. Can.
149 F4 Blue Stack Mountains hills Rep. of Ireland
85 B7 Bluff Qld Austr.
81 B7 Bluff N.Z.
241 M3 Bluff UT U.S.A.
231 C5 Bluff City TN U.S.A.
86 E3 Bluff Face Range hills N.Z.
87 B7 Bluff Knoll mt. W.A. Austr.
87 B7 Bluff Point W.A. Austr.
232 D3 Bluffton OH U.S.A.
232 C3 Bluffton OH U.S.A.
172 H3 Blumau in Steiermark Austria
172 C2 Blumberg Baden-Württemberg Ger.
171 F2 Blumberg Brandenburg Ger.
255 C8 Blumenau Brazil
172 E2 Blumenberg Ger.
170 D2 Blumenholz Ger.
172 F2 Blumberg Ger.
190 C2 Blümlisalp mt. Switz.
236 C2 Blunt SD U.S.A.
222 F5 Blustry Mountain B.C. Can.
81 B7 Bly OR U.S.A.
227 H4 Blyth Ont. Can.
149 H2 Blyth Northumberland, England U.K.
149 G4 Blyth r. England U.K.
151 F2 Blyth Nottinghamshire, England U.K.
151 I2 Blyth Suffolk, England U.K.
170 E4 Blyth Bridge Scottish Borders, Scotland U.K.
241 H4 Blythe Beach S. Africa
241 H4 Blythe CA U.S.A.
237 F4 Blytheville AR U.S.A.
87 B7 Blythe Range hills W.A. Austr.
149 I4 Blyton Lincolnshire, England U.K.
160 A2 Blzheny Ukr. see Blyznyuky
137 I3 Blyzneyuky Ukr.
150 C4 Bo r. Sierra Leone
199 C4 Bo r. China
150 C4 Boa Sierra Leone
206 D5 Boac Phil.
92 B3 Boac Phil.
160 D2 Boada Spain

182 B3 Boalhosa Port.
208 C3 Boali C.A.R.
232 E4 Boalsburg PA U.S.A.
232 C3 Boa Nova Brazil
191 G3 Boara Pisani Italy
232 C4 Boardman OH U.S.A.
235 E1 Boardmans Bridge CT U.S.A.
146 D4 Boath Highland, Scotland U.K.
85 F5 Boatman Qld Austr.
146 E4 Boat of Garten Highland, Scotland U.K.
184 □ Boaventura Madeira
254 F3 Boa Viagem Brazil
251 F4 Boa Vista i. Cape Verde
206 □ Boa Vista i. Cape Verde
251 F3 Boa Vista Brazil
185 F3 Boabadilla Andalucía Spain
183 H2 Boabadilla La Rioja Spain
183 E3 Boabadilla del Campo Spain
108 D4 Boabi Guangxi China
171 J4 Bobai China
115 K2 Bobbili Andhra Prad. India
190 E4 Bobbio Italy
190 C4 Bobbio Pellice Italy
172 C2 Bobenheim-Roxheim Ger.
136 D2 Bober r. Ukr.
136 B3 Boberka Ukr.
182 D1 Bobia mt. Spain
173 F4 Bobigny France
173 E3 Bobingen Ger.
170 C2 Böblingen Ger.
175 M4 Bobly Ukr.
206 E3 Bobo-Dioulasso Burkina
174 E2 Boboliće Pol.
92 C3 Bobon Phil.
213 F4 Bobonong Botswana
182 B2 Boborás Spain
177 L4 Bobota Romania
Bobrov Kuk mt. Yugo. see Durmitor
197 F4 Bobovdol Bulg.
197 L3 Bobove Ukr.
175 I6 Bobowa Pol.
136 C2 Bobowo Pol.
121 G4 Boboyob, Gora mt. Uzbek.
138 G4 Bobr r. Belarus
138 G4 Bobr r. Belarus
174 D3 Bóbr r. Pol.
173 H2 Böbrach Ger.
Bobrik Rus. Fed. see Novomoskovsk
Bobrinets Ukr. see Bobrynets'
135 H6 Bobrov Rus. Fed.
177 I2 Bobrov Slovakia
177 I2 Bobrovec Slovakia
Bobrovytsya Ukr.
137 I2 Bobrovo-Dvorskoye Rus. Fed.
137 F2 Bobrovytsya r. Ukr.
171 I4 Bobrowice Ger.
174 G3 Bobrowniki Kujawsko-Pomorskie Pol.
175 L2 Bobrowniki Podlaskie Pol.
175 H2 Bobrowo Pol.
138 F5 Bobruysk Belarus see Babruysk
136 F4 Bobryk-Druhyy Ukr.
137 G3 Bobrynets' Ukr.
138 F5 Bobrynets' Ukr.
108 B1 Bobso Sichuan China
213 □J4 Boby mt. Madag.
179 G4 Boč hill Slovenia
183 F2 Boca de Huérgano Spain
248 B2 Boca de Acre Brazil
252 D2 Boca do Acre Brazil
Boca Grande r. mouth Trin. and Tob./Venez.
257 E5 Bocaina de Minas Brazil
257 F2 Bocaiúva Brazil
206 C6 Bocanda Côte d'Ivoire
206 D5 Bocanda do Sul Brazil
231 D7 Boca Raton FL U.S.A.
242 □J7 Bocas del Toro Panama
242 □J7 Bocas del Toro, Archipiélago del is Panama
195 F3 Bocchigliero Italy
183 F5 Boceguillas Spain
176 E2 Bochnia Pol.
165 E3 Bocholt Belgium
169 B4 Bocholt Ger.
176 C1 Bochov Czech Rep.
169 C4 Bochum Ger.
213 F4 Bochum S. Africa
169 F3 Bockenem Ger.
207 H4 Bochum Bayern Ger.
168 D2 Bockhorn Niedersachsen Ger.
173 F5 Böckl Pol.
192 B2 Bocognano Corse France
209 B8 Bocoio Angola
177 J4 Bócsa Hungary
197 J5 Bocq r. Belgium
85 H3 Bócsa Hungary
197 J3 Bocsa Romania
197 L4 Bocşa Romania
207 H2 Boda Dalarna Sweden
143 L2 Boda Kalmar Sweden
142 H3 Bodafors Sweden
143 F3 Boda glasbruk Sweden
177 H4 Bodajk Hungary
83 C6 Bodalla W.A. Austr.
163 C6 Bodallin W.A. Austr.
85 H6 Bodaybo Rus. Fed.
146 G4 Boddam Aberdeenshire, Scotland U.K.
146 □G1 Boddam Shetland, Scotland U.K.
170 C3 Boddin Ger.
87 C7 Boddington W.A. Austr.
246 B1 Bodden Town Cayman Is
171 D4 Bode r. Ger.
240 B2 Bodega Head hd CA U.S.A.
164 D2 Bodegraven Neth.
168 D2 Bodelshausen Ger.
150 C4 Bodelwyddan Denbighshire, Wales U.K.
140 M2 Boden Sweden
150 C5 Bodenfelde Ger.
Bodensee l. Europe see Constance, Lake
172 C2 Bodenheim Ger.
169 E2 Bodenkirchen Ger.
173 H4 Bodenmais Ger.
172 F2 Bodenwerder Ger.
169 F3 Bodenwerder Ger.
169 F4 Bodenwöhr Ger.
173 H3 Bodenwöhr Ger.
150 C4 Bodenham Herefordshire, England U.K.
150 B4 Bodedern Isle of Anglesey, Wales U.K.
207 G4 Bode-Sadu Nigeria
240 H1 Bodfish CA U.S.A.
150 C4 Bodffordd Isle of Anglesey, Wales U.K.
116 D2 Bodh Gaya Bihar India
151 F2 Bodicote Oxfordshire, England U.K.
240 H2 Bodie CA U.S.A.
□A3 Bodinayakkanur Tamil Nadu India
269 □ Bodin r. Spain
150 C4 Bodman Ger.
150 C4 Bodmin Cornwall, England U.K.
150 C4 Bodmin Moor moorland England U.K.
140 L3 Bodø Norway
142 K2 Bodoco Brazil
254 F3 Bodocó Brazil
253 F5 Bodoquena Brazil
253 F5 Bodoquena, Serra da hills Brazil
177 K3 Bodrog r. Hungary
177 K3 Bodroghalom Hungary

199 E3 Bodrum Turkey
140 K3 Bodsjö Sweden
140 M2 Bodträskfors Sweden
113 ◻1 Boduhali i. N. Male Maldives
177 J3 Bódva r. Hungary
177 J3 Bódva r. Slovakia
177 J3 Bódvaszilas Hungary
175 I3 Bodzanów Pol.
175 I5 Bodzentyn Pol.
163 C4 Boé France
165 D3 Boechout Belgium
223 K5 Boecillo Spain
183 F2 Boecillo i. Spain
160 E2 Boëge France
214 D3 Boegoeberg S. Africa
164 E3 Boekel Neth.
165 C3 Boekhoute Belgium
160 C3 Boën France
208 D5 Boende Dem. Rep. Congo
214 C5 Boerboonfontein S. Africa
237 D6 Boerne TX U.S.A.
215 F5 Boesmans r. S. Africa
237 F6 Boeuf r. LA U.S.A.
182 D2 Boeza Spain
182 D2 Boeza r. Spain
256 C5 Bofete Brazil
206 B4 Boffa Guinea
161 C4 Boffres France
169 E4 Boffzen Ger.
142 C2 Befjell hill Norway
177 J4 Bogács Hungary
182 D4 Bogajo Spain
96 A3 Bogale Myanmar
96 A4 Bogale r. Myanmar
237 F6 Bogalusa LA U.S.A.
83 F2 Bogan r. N.S.W. Austr.
207 E3 Bogandé Burkina
83 F3 Bogan Gate Qld Austr.
85 F4 Bogantungan Qld Austr.
185 H2 Bogarra Spain
196 D3 Bogatić Srbija Yugo.
134 J4 Bogatye Saby Rus. Fed.
174 C5 Bogatynia Pol.
126 D3 Boğazlıyan Turkey
111 D6 Bogcang Zangbo r. Xizang China
177 K6 Bogda Romania
110 E3 Bogda Feng mt. Xinjiang China
197 G4 Bogdan mt. Bulg.
197 G4 Bogdana Romania
197 F5 Bogdanci Macedonia
177 L4 Bogdand Romania
174 D3 Bogdaniec Pol.
— Bogdanovka Georgia see Ninotsminda
120 C1 Bogdanovka Rus. Fed.
106 A3 Bogda Shan mts China
121 H1 Bogembay Kazakh.
173 H1 Bogen Ger.
140 L1 Bogen Norway
142 D4 Bogense Denmark
83 G2 Boggabilla Qld Austr.
83 G2 Boggabri r. N.S.W. Austr.
78 ◻3a Boggerapp i. Kwajalein Marshall Is
147 B4 Boggeragh Mountains hills Rep. of Ireland
78 ◻3a Boggerik i. Kwajalein Marshall Is
87 C4 Boggola hill W.A. Austr.
247 ◻2 Boggy Peak hill Antigua Antigua and Barbuda
— Boghari Alg. see Ksar el Boukhari
85 F4 Bogie r. Qld Austr.
146 F4 Bogie r. Scotland U.K.
190 E4 Bogliasco Italy
190 D2 Bognanco Italy
159 H5 Bognieère Aberdeenshire, Scotland U.K.
151 G4 Bognor Regis West Sussex, England U.K.
156 E3 Bogny-sur-Meuse France
207 I4 Bogo Cameroon
170 D1 Bogø Denmark
170 D1 Bogø i. Denmark
92 C4 Bogo Phil.
— Bogodukhov Ukr. see Bohodukhiv
121 G1 Bogodukhovka Kazakh.
147 D3 Bog of Allen reg. Rep. of Ireland
121 G1 Bogolyubovo Kazakh.
139 I4 Bogolyubovo Smolenskaya Oblast' Rus. Fed.
139 M3 Bogolyubovo Vladimirskaya Oblast' Rus. Fed.
83 F4 Bogong, Mount Vic. Austr.
94 B3 Bogor Jawa Barat Indon.
175 J5 Bogoria Pol.
139 L5 Bogoroditsk Rus. Fed.
139 J5 Bogoroditskoye Rus. Fed.
134 H4 Bogorodsk Rus. Fed.
100 G1 Bogorodskoye Khabarovsky Kray Rus. Fed.
134 J4 Bogorodskoye Kirovskaya Oblast' Rus. Fed.
250 C3 Bogotá Col.
177 K3 Bogota hill Slovakia
130 J4 Bogota r. Rus. Fed.
134 I4 Bogovarovo Rus. Fed.
— Bogoyavlenskoye Tambovskaya Oblast' Rus. Fed. see Pervomayskiy
117 G4 Bogra Bangl.
131 K4 Boguchany Rus. Fed.
135 H6 Boguchar Rus. Fed.
137 K3 Boguchwał Rus. Fed.
175 J6 Boguchwała Pol.
206 B2 Bogué Maur.
237 F6 Bogue Chitto r. MS U.S.A.
— Boguslav Ukr. see Bohuslav
174 C5 Bogusław Pol.
246 ◻ Bog Walk Jamaica
177 H5 Bogyiszló Hungary
95 ◻ Boh r. Indon.
107 H4 Bo Hai g. China
107 I4 Bohai Haixia sea chan. China
156 D3 Bohain-en-Vermandois France
107 H4 Bohai Wan b. China
158 B3 Bohan France
142 C2 Bohdan Ukr.
137 H1 Bohdanivka Ukr.
179 G2 Böheimkirchen Austria
176 D1 Bohemia reg. Czech Rep.
235 E2 Bohemia NY U.S.A.
86 E3 Bohemia Downs W.A. Austr.
— Bohemian Forest mts Ger. see Böhmer Wald
147 C4 Boher Rep. of Ireland
148 B4 Boheraphuca Rep. of Ireland
207 F5 Bohicon Benin
179 L4 Bohinjska Bistrica Slovenia
179 L4 Bohinjsko jezero l. Slovenia
172 C2 Böhl Ger.
171 D4 Böhlen Ger.
171 H4 Böhlitz-Ehrenberg Ger.
215 D3 Bohlokong S. Africa
168 E3 Böhme Ger.
168 E3 Böhme r. Ger.
— Böhmen reg. Czech Rep. see Bohemia
173 G2 Böhmer Wald mts Ger. see Bohemia
169 J3 Bohmte Ger.
139 G6 Bohodukhiv Ukr.

236 D2 Bois de Sioux r. MN U.S.A.
238 C3 Boise ID U.S.A.
238 C3 Boise r. ID U.S.A.
237 C4 Boise City OK U.S.A.
158 D3 Boisgervilly France
158 B3 Bois-Guillaume France
156 C4 Bois-le-Roi France
161 C5 Boisseron France
163 E4 Boisset France
161 C4 Boisset-et-Gaujac France
223 K5 Boissevain Man. Can.
163 E5 Boisseron France
191 H2 Boite r. Italy
215 E2 Boitumelong S. Africa
256 D5 Boituva Brazil
170 E2 Boitzenburg Ger.
162 C2 Boivre r. France
163 F2 Boize r. France
168 F2 Boizenburg Ger.
174 D4 Bojadła Pol.
193 G3 Bojano Italy
175 J5 Bojanowo Pol.
174 E4 Bojanowo Pol.
92 B2 Bojeador, Cape Phil.
177 H3 Bojná Slovakia
177 H3 Bojnice Slovakia
197 F4 Bojnik Srbija Yugo.
122 D2 Bojnūrd Iran
95 E4 Bojonegoro Jawa Timur Indon.
207 H5 Boju-Ega Nigeria
— Bokaak atoll Marshall Is see Majuro
111 E4 Bokadaban Feng mt. Qinghai/Xinjiang China
117 H4 Bokajan Assam India
117 F5 Bokaro Bihar India
206 B4 Boké Guinea
168 D2 Bokel Ger.
214 B5 Bokfontein S. Africa
83 F2 Bokhara r. N.S.W. Austr.
207 H5 Bokito Cameroon
168 E1 Böklund Ger.
209 B6 Boko Congo
177 H4 Boko Hungary
121 I4 Bökönbaev Kyrg. see Bökönbaev
177 K4 Bököny Hungary
202 C6 Bokoro Chad
209 B6 Boko-Songho Congo
— Bokovo-Antratsit Ukr. see Antratsyt
135 H6 Bokovskaya Rus. Fed.
215 G2 Boksburg S. Africa
139 I2 Boksitogorsk Rus. Fed.
214 C2 Bokspits S. Africa
100 F2 Boktor Rus. Fed.
208 D5 Bokungu Dem. Rep. Congo
— Bokurdak Turkm. see Bakhardok
202 B6 Bol Chad
244 C3 Bola del Viejo, Cerro mt. Mex.
206 B4 Bolama Guinea-Bissau
121 I4 Bolan r. Pak.
208 E3 Bolanda, Jebel mt. Sudan
172 C2 Bolanden Ger.
160 E1 Bolandoz France
190 E4 Bolano Italy
244 B3 Bolaños r. Mex.
185 G2 Bolaños de Calatrava Spain
159 G2 Bolbec France
177 H5 Bölcske Hungary
122 B4 Boldají Iran
170 E2 Boldekow Ger.
168 E1 Bolderslev Denmark
177 K3 Boldogkőváralja Hungary
149 H3 Boldon Tyne and Wear, England U.K.
151 F4 Boldre Hampshire, England U.K.
197 H3 Boldu Romania
120 D3 Boldumsaz Turkm.
177 K6 Boldur Romania
177 J3 Boldva r. Hungary
110 C2 Bole Xinjiang China
206 E4 Bole Ghana
186 C2 Bolea Spain
136 B3 Bolekhiv Ukr.
177 G3 Boleráz Slovakia
175 I5 Bolesław Pol.
174 D4 Bolesławiec Pol.
174 E4 Bolesławiec Pol.
174 C5 Bolesławiec Pol.
135 J5 Bolgar Respublika Tatarstan Rus. Fed.
206 E4 Bolgatanga Ghana
136 E5 Bolhrad Ukr.
100 D3 Boli Heilong. China
140 M2 Boliden Sweden
— Bolifuri i. S. Male Maldives Bolifushi
113 ◻1 Bolifushi i. S. Male Maldives
175 I3 Bolimów Pol.
92 A2 Bolinao Phil.
197 G3 Bolintin-Vale Romania
250 C2 Bolívar dept Col.
252 A1 Bolívar Peru
232 D6 Bolívar MO U.S.A.
234 C2 Bolívar NY U.S.A.
237 F5 Bolívar TN U.S.A.
251 F3 Bolívar state Venez.
252 D4 Bolivia country S. America
— Boljevac Srbija Yugo.
128 A1 Bolkar Dağları mts Turkey
139 K5 Bolkhov Rus. Fed.
227 F1 Bolkow Ont. Can.
170 C1 Bölkow Ger.
170 C1 Bölkow Ger.
170 D3 Boll Ger.
142 E3 Bollebygd Sweden
161 C4 Bollène France
190 C3 Bollengo Italy
168 E1 Bollingstedt Ger.
149 G4 Bollington Cheshire, England U.K.
141 L3 Bollnäs Sweden
83 F2 Bollon Qld Austr.
172 B4 Bollschweil Ger.
166 E3 Bollstedt Ger.
168 F2 Bollwiller France
184 D3 Bollullos Par del Condado Spain
157 H5 Bollwiller France
143 E3 Bolmen l. Sweden
151 G2 Bolnhurst Bedfordshire, England U.K.
129 D3 Bolnisi Georgia
208 C5 Bolobo Dem. Rep. Congo
92 B5 Bolod Islands Phil.
191 G4 Bologna Italy
191 G4 Bologna prov. Emilia-Romagna Italy
157 F4 Bologne France
250 C6 Bolognesi Loreto Peru
252 B2 Bolognesi Ucayali Peru
194 C5 Bolognetta Sicilia Italy
193 F2 Bolognola Italy
139 H3 Bologovo Rus. Fed.
139 J3 Bologoye Rus. Fed.
215 H3 Bolokanang S. Africa
139 H4 Bolokhovo Rus. Fed.
208 D4 Bolomba Dem. Rep. Congo
— Bolon' Rus. Fed. see Achan
183 B2 Boñar Spain
243 H4 Bolonchén de Rejón Mex.
207 H6 Bolondo Equat. Guinea
92 B5 Bolong Phil.
209 B7 Bolongongo Angola
192 A4 Bolotana Sardegna Italy
247 ◻7 Bonasse Trin. and Tob.
193 L2 Bonassola Italy
225 K3 Bonavista Nfld. Can.
82 ◻2 Bon Bon S.A. Austr.
159 F3 Bonchamp-lès-Laval France
149 F4 Bonchester Bridge Scottish Borders, Scotland U.K.
190 C1 Boncourt Switz.
137 J3 Bondarevka Ukr.
139 U5 Bondari Rus. Fed.
191 H4 Bondeno Italy
191 G2 Bondeno Italy
208 E4 Bondo Dem. Rep. Congo
92 B3 Bondoc Peninsula Phil.
172 C3 Bondorf Ger.
206 E4 Bondoukou Côte d'Ivoire
95 H4 Bondowoso Jawa Indon.
231 H7 Bonds Cay i. Bahamas
226 A1 Bonduel WI U.S.A.
156 B3 Bondues France

134 F2 Bol'shaya Imandra, Ozero l. Rus. Fed.
137 I2 Bol'shaya Khalan' Rus. Fed.
135 H7 Bol'shaya Kokshaga r. Rus. Fed.
137 K1 Bol'shaya Lipovitsa Rus. Fed.
135 H7 Bol'shaya Martinovka Rus. Fed.
134 M1 Bol'shaya Novoselka Ukr. see Velyka Novosilka
134 M1 Bol'shaya Oyu r. Rus. Fed.
134 M2 Bol'shaya Rogovaya r. Rus. Fed.
134 L2 Bol'shaya Synya r. Rus. Fed.
— Bol'shaya Tsarevshchina Samarskaya Oblast' Rus. Fed. see Volzhskiy
134 K4 Bol'shaya Usa Rus. Fed.
139 I2 Bol'shaya Vishera Rus. Fed.
121 I2 Bol'shaya Vladimirovka Kazakh.
137 J2 Bol'he Bykovo Rus. Fed.
137 J4 Bol'shekrepinskaya Rus. Fed.
121 K2 Bol'shenarymskoye Kazakh.
139 J3 Bol'she-Ploskoye Rus. Fed.
134 M1 Bol'shetroitskoye Rus. Fed.
131 L2 Bol'shevik, Ostrov i. Severnaya Zemlya Rus. Fed.
134 K2 Bol'shezemel'skaya Tundra lowland Rus. Fed.
120 D3 Bol'shiye Barsuki, Peski des. Kazakh.
137 J4 Bol'shiye Saly Rus. Fed.
121 I4 Bol'shoy Aksau Kazakh.
131 Q3 Bol'shoy Aluy r. Rus. Fed.
131 M2 Bol'shoy Anyuy r. Rus. Fed.
131 M2 Bol'shoy Begichev, Ostrov i. Rus. Fed.
138 G1 Bol'shoy Berezovyy, Ostrov i. Rus. Fed.
121 J2 Bol'shoy Bukon' Kazakh.
137 I2 Bol'shoye Gorodishche Rus. Fed.
135 I5 Bol'shoye Ignatovo Rus. Fed.
135 I5 Bol'shoye Murashkino Rus. Fed.
139 J5 Bol'shoye Polpino Rus. Fed.
134 G3 Bol'shoye Selo Rus. Fed.
137 H2 Bol'shoye Soldatskoye Rus. Fed.
120 C2 Bol'shoy Irk r. Rus. Fed.
120 A2 Bol'shoy Irgiz r. Rus. Fed.
100 E4 Bol'shoy Kamen' Rus. Fed.
— Bol'shoy Kavkaz mts Asia/Europe see Caucasus
139 L5 Bol'shoy Khomutets Rus. Fed.
139 L5 Bol'shoy Patok r. Rus. Fed.
131 O4 Bol'shoy Shantar, Ostrov i. Rus. Fed.
— Bol'shoy Tokmak Kyrg. see Tokmak
— Bol'shoy Tokmak Ukr. see Tokmak
139 H3 Bol'shoy Tuder r. Rus. Fed.
120 B2 Bol'shoy Uzen' r. Kazakh./Rus. Fed.
129 B1 Bol'shoy Zelenchuk r. Rus. Fed.
149 H4 Bolsover Derbyshire, England U.K.
164 E1 Bolsward Neth.
174 G1 Bolszewo Pol.
186 D2 Boltaña Spain
149 H3 Boltby North Yorkshire, England U.K.
190 C2 Boltigen Switz.
227 H4 Bolton Ont. Can.
92 C5 Bolton Phil.
149 G4 Bolton Greater Manchester, England U.K.
149 G3 Bolton-le-Sands Lancashire, England U.K.
137 H3 Boltyshka Ukr.
126 C2 Bolu Turkey
199 G1 Bolu prov. Turkey
110 C2 Bolungarvík Iceland
140 D1 Boluntay Qinghai China
109 E4 Boluo Guangdong China
139 J5 Bolva r. Rus. Fed.
199 G2 Bolvadin Turkey
150 C4 Bolventor Cornwall, England U.K.
177 H6 Bóly Hungary
197 H4 Bolyarovo Bulg.
191 G2 Bolzano Italy
191 G2 Bolzano prov. Trentino - Alto Adige Italy
209 B6 Boma Dem. Rep. Congo
83 G3 Bomaderry N.S.W. Austr.
207 G5 Bomadi Nigeria
108 A2 Bomai Sichuan China
165 E4 Bomal Belgium
83 G4 Bomaderry N.S.W. Austr.
184 A1 Bombarral Port.
— Bombay Mahar. India see Mumbai
80 E2 Bombay North I. N.Z.
241 J6 Bombay Beach CA U.S.A.
91 H7 Bomberai, Semenanjung pen. Indon.
209 B5 Bombo r. Dem. Rep. Congo
257 E3 Bom Despacho Brazil
117 H4 Bomdila Arun. Prad. India
150 E2 Bomere Heath Shropshire, England U.K.
111 F6 Bomi Xizang China
254 G3 Bom Jardim Brazil
256 A2 Bom Jardim de Goiás Brazil
257 E4 Bom Jardim de Minas Brazil
254 D5 Bom Jesus Piauí Brazil
255 C9 Bom Jesus Rio Grande do Sul Brazil
254 E5 Bom Jesus da Gurgueia, Serra do hills Brazil
256 C5 Bom Jesus da Lapa Brazil
256 C5 Bom Jesus de Goiás Brazil
257 G4 Bom Jesus do Itabapoana Brazil
257 G4 Bom Jesus do Norte Brazil
168 E3 Bomlitz Ger.
142 A2 Bømlo i. Norway
208 E4 Bomokandi r. Dem. Rep. Congo
208 C4 Bomongo Dem. Rep. Congo
163 B6 Bompas France
194 C5 Bompensiere Sicilia Italy
194 D5 Bompietro Sicilia Italy
255 C8 Bom Retiro Brazil
257 E4 Bom Sucesso Minas Gerais Brazil
256 B5 Bom Sucesso Paraná Brazil
— Bona Alg. see Annaba
160 B1 Bona France
122 A2 Bonāb Iran
163 G3 Bonac-Irazein France
202 D2 Bonassa Switz.
232 E6 Bon Air VA U.S.A.
247 ◻8 Bonaire i. Neth. Antilles
87 B7 Bonalbo N.S.W. Austr.
195 F4 Bonanza r. Italy
242 ◻16 Bonanza Nic.
83 F3 Bonanza Sardegna Italy
246 E3 Bonao Dom. Rep.
86 E2 Bonaparte Archipelago is W.A. Austr.
183 E2 Boñar Spain
148 B4 Bonar Bridge Highland, Scotland U.K.
248 D3 Bonasila Dome mt. AK U.S.A.
190 C1 Bonaduz Switz.
192 A4 Bonarcado Sardegna Italy
225 K3 Bonavista Nfld. Can.
263 D2 Boothby, Cape Antarctica
221 I2 Boothia, Gulf of Nunavut Can.
169 F4 Bootle Cumbria, England U.K.
149 G4 Bootle Merseyside, England U.K.

93 B4 Bone, Teluk b. Indon.
168 F1 Bönebüttel Ger.
193 G3 Bonefro Italy
214 C4 Bonekraal S. Africa
169 C4 Boñén France
93 B4 Bonerate, Kepulauan is Indon.
146 E5 Bo'ness Falkirk, Scotland U.K.
187 C6 Bonete Spain
185 C6 Bonete i. Spain
92 B3 Bonga Bong r. Phil.
214 D3 Bongani Assam India
208 D4 Bongandanga Dem. Rep. Congo
214 D3 Bongani S. Africa
92 A5 Bongao Phil.
85 D4 Bongaree Qld Austr.
93 C3 Bongka r. Indon.
206 C5 Big Mountains hills Liberia
209 B7 Bongo, Serra do mts Angola
213 ◻J3 Bongolava mts Madag.
208 B2 Bongor Chad
206 D5 Bongouanou Côte d'Ivoire
208 D4 Bongoville Gabon
97 E4 Bông Son Vietnam
237 D5 Bonham TX U.S.A.
140 L3 Bonhamn Sweden
206 E6 Boni Mali
185 C6 Boniches Spain
206 D4 Boniérédougou Côte d'Ivoire
174 G3 Boniewo Pol.
192 B3 Bonifacio Corse France
192 B3 Bonifacio, Bocche di str. France/Italy see Bonifacio, Strait of
192 B3 Bonifacio, Bouches de str. France/Italy see Bonifacio, Strait of
135 I5 Bonifacio, Strait of France/Italy
193 H5 Bonifati Italy
231 D6 Bonifay FL U.S.A.
190 C2 Bönigen Switz.
174 E1 Bonin i. Rus. Fed.
— Bonin Islands N. Pacific Ocean see Ogasawara-shotō
231 D7 Bonita Springs FL U.S.A.
253 E6 Bonito Brazil
146 F6 Bonjedward Scottish Borders, Scotland U.K.
207 F3 Bonkoukou Niger
169 C5 Bonn Ger.
163 C5 Bonna Ger. see Bonn
192 A4 Bonnanaro Sardegna Italy
162 D2 Bonnat France
172 C4 Bonnay France
172 C4 Bonndorf im Schwarzwald Ger.
161 D4 Bonne r. France
160 E2 Bonneveaux PA U.S.A.
233 C5 Bonnefont France
238 C1 Bonners Ferry ID U.S.A.
159 G3 Bonnétable France
156 B4 Bonneval Centre France
161 F3 Bonneval Rhône-Alpes France
163 H3 Bonneval-sur-Arc France
160 E2 Bonneveaux France
161 C4 Bonneville France
82 E4 Bonney, Lake S.A. Austr.
156 B3 Bonnières-sur-Seine France
84 C3 Bonnie Rock W.A. Austr.
161 D5 Bonnieux France
165 C5 Bonnières S. Africa
172 D2 Bönnigheim Ger.
169 B4 Bönningstedt Ger.
163 B5 Bonnut France
207 G5 Bonny Nigeria
215 G4 Bonnybridge Falkirk, Scotland U.K.
215 G4 Bonny Ridge S. Africa
215 I4 Bonnyrigg Midlothian, Scotland U.K.
233 ◻J2 Bonny River N.T. Can.
160 A1 Bonny-sur-Loire France
223 I4 Bonnyville Alta Can.
192 B3 Bono Sardegna Italy
92 A4 Bonobono Phil.
97 D5 Bonom Mhai mt. Vietnam
— Bononia Italy see Bologna
192 A4 Bonorva Sardegna Italy
206 C5 Bonoua Côte d'Ivoire
81 N2 Bonpland, Mount South I. N.Z.
160 E2 Bonsall CA U.S.A.
83 G2 Bonshaw N.S.W. Austr.
160 C3 Bonson France
206 B5 Bonthe Sierra Leone
92 B2 Bontoc Phil.
92 B3 Bontoc mt. S. Africa
93 A4 Bontosunggu Sulawesi Selatan Indon.
215 G4 Bontrand S. Africa
215 G3 Bontruug S. Africa
177 G4 Bóny Hungary
177 H5 Bonyhád Hungary
84 B4 Bonython Range hills N.T. Austr.
143 N4 Boo Sweden
93 D3 Boo, Kepulauan is Irian Jaya Indon.
170 E2 Boock Ger.
84 D4 Bookabie S.A. Austr.
149 J5 Book Cliffs ridge UT U.S.A.
237 C4 Booker TX U.S.A.
206 C4 Boola Guinea
83 G2 Boolba Qld Austr.
147 D4 Booleroo Centre S.A. Austr.
147 D4 Booley Hills Rep. of Ireland
83 F3 Booligal N.S.W. Austr.
87 B7 Boologooro W.A. Austr.
85 B5 Boonah Qld Austr.
236 D3 Boone CO U.S.A.
226 A5 Boone IA U.S.A.
231 D4 Boone NC U.S.A.
232 D6 Booneville AR U.S.A.
232 F7 Booneville KY U.S.A.
237 F5 Booneville MS U.S.A.
215 F3 Boons S. Africa
232 D6 Boonsboro MD U.S.A.
235 D5 Boonton NJ U.S.A.
106 C2 Böön Tsagaan Nuur salt l. Mongolia
138 G4 Boonville CA U.S.A.
230 D4 Boonville IN U.S.A.
236 E4 Boonville MO U.S.A.
234 C2 Boonville NY U.S.A.
213 D4 Boorama Somalia
83 F3 Booroorban N.S.W. Austr.
83 G3 Boorowa N.S.W. Austr.
83 F3 Boort Vic. Austr.
165 H5 Boortmeerbeek Belgium
156 B3 Boos France
156 D3 Boos France
213 I2 Boosaaso Somalia
168 F1 Boostedt Ger.
233 ◻1I3 Boothbay Harbor ME U.S.A.
263 D2 Boothby, Cape Antarctica
221 I2 Boothia, Gulf of Nunavut Can.
169 F4 Bootle Cumbria, England U.K.

129 C5 Boradigah Azer.
213 ◻K3 Boraha, Nosy i. Madag.
238 D2 Borah Peak ID U.S.A.
156 C3 Boran-sur-Oise France
146 C5 Boraraigh i. Western Isles, Scotland U.K. see Boreray
143 E5 Borås Sweden
122 B4 Borāzjān Iran
251 G6 Borba Brazil
184 C2 Borba Port.
254 C2 Borbera r. Italy
256 A2 Borborema Brazil
256 C4 Borborema, Planalto da plat. Brazil
254 F3 Borborema Romania
169 D4 Borchen Ger.
263 K2 Borchgrevink Coast Antarctica
127 F2 Borçka Turkey
84 D3 Borçulo Neth.
86 D3 Borda, Cape S.A. Austr.
256 D5 Borda da Mata Brazil
199 F3 Bor Dağı mt. Turkey
183 H3 Bordalba Spain
213 H4 Bordany Hungary
163 B4 Bordeaux France
116 D5 Bordehi Madh. Prad. India
184 B3 Bordeira Port.
168 D1 Bordelum Ger.
87 C7 Borden r. W.A. Austr.
225 I4 Borden P.E.I. Can.
221 J2 Borden Island N.W.T. Can.
221 J2 Borden Peninsula Nunavut Can.
234 D2 Bordentown NJ U.S.A.
163 C6 Bordères-Louron France
163 C5 Bordères admin. div. Scotland U.K. see Scottish Borders
82 E4 Bordertown S.A. Austr.
163 B5 Bordes Aquitaine France
163 B5 Bordes Midi-Pyrénées France
168 F1 Bordesholm Ger.
190 C5 Bordighera Italy
186 F2 Bordils Spain
194 B5 Bordino r. Sicilia Italy
205 G1 Bordj Bou Arréridj Alg.
186 C4 Bordão Spain
141 G1 Bordoy i. Faroe Is
121 H4 Bordu Kyrg.
— Bordunskiy Kyrg. see Bordu
197 H3 Borduşani Romania
199 G4 Bore Mali
200 E3 Borea Mali
174 F5 Borek Strzeliński Pol.
174 F4 Borek Wielkopolski Pol.
225 G1 Borel r. Que. Can.
146 C6 Boreland r. Scotland U.K.
147 C4 Boreland Rep. of Ireland
146 □ Boreray i. Western Isles, Scotland U.K.
179 H2 Borgafjäll Sweden
172 A2 Borg de Porvoo
160 A1 Borga r. Fin. see Porvoo
179 H2 Borgafjäll Sweden
140 □B2 Borgarnes Iceland
140 L1 Borgentreich Ger.
169 E4 Borger Neth.
237 C5 Borger TX U.S.A.
187 D5 Borges r. Spain
190 E4 Borghetto di Borbera Italy
143 G3 Borgholm Kalmar Sweden
169 D3 Borgholzhausen Ger.
190 F4 Borgia Italy
165 C4 Borgie r. Scotland U.K.
192 B2 Borgo Corse France
190 D3 Borgo a Mozzano Italy
190 D5 Borgo d'Ale Italy
193 F3 Borgoforte Italy
190 D3 Borgofranco d'Ivrea Italy
191 G3 Borgo Grappa Italy
193 H3 Borgo-lavezzaro Italy
190 D4 Borgomanero Italy
190 E5 Borgomaro Italy
190 E4 Borgonovo Val Tidone Italy
191 G4 Borgo Panigale airport Italy
190 D4 Borgo San Dalmazzo Italy
191 G4 Borgo San Lorenzo Italy
190 E4 Borgo Val di Taro Italy
191 G2 Borgo Valsugana Italy
193 D2 Borgo Vercelli Italy
170 E3 Börgstdorf Ger.
168 E1 Borgstedt Ger.
142 F2 Borgsjöbroat mt. Norway
197 G5 Boria Italy
176 G3 Borynya Hungary
84 B4 Bori mts Bos.-Herz.
143 H2 Boo Sweden
93 D3 Boo, Kepulauan is Irian Jaya Indon.
170 E2 Boock Ger.
184 D7 Borgue Dumfries and Galloway, Scotland U.K.
116 D5 Bori India
166 C5 Bori r. India
207 G5 Börili Kazakh. see Burli
139 J3 Borilovo Rus. Fed.
234 B3 Boring MD U.S.A.
197 G5 Boring Italy
139 L5 Borinskoye Rus. Fed.
136 B3 Borislav Ukr. see Boryslav
137 J2 Borisovka Rus. Fed.
177 H1 Börzsöny hills Hungary
101 G1 Borzya r. Rus. Fed.
194 C6 Bosa Sardegna Italy
177 G3 Bošáca Slovakia
121 Borsa Kazakh. see Bosaga
— Borsagınskiy Kazakh. see Bosaga
192 A4 Bosa Marina Sardegna Italy
197 H4 Bosanci Romania
196 B3 Bosanska Dubica Bos.-Herz.
188 F3 Bosanska Gradiška Bos.-Herz.
188 F3 Bosanska Kostajnica Bos.-Herz.
188 F3 Bosanska Krupa Bos.-Herz.
188 G3 Bosanski Brod Bos.-Herz.
188 F3 Bosanski Petrovac Bos.-Herz.
188 G3 Bosanski Šamac Bos.-Herz.
188 F3 Bosansko Grahovo Bos.-Herz.
168 A5 Bosau Ger. de Aguiar Port.
183 C3 Bosque Spain

169 C5 Bornich Ger.
207 I4 Borno state Nigeria
184 I4 Bornos Spain
183 H4 Bornova r. Spain
199 E2 Bornova Turkey
168 F2 Bornsen Ger.
174 C4 Bornstedt Ger.
188 G3 Borodia Spain
95 E4 Borobudur tourist site Indon.
175 L5 Borod Romania
137 H3 Borodayivka Ukr.
184 B3 Borodianka Ukr.
136 D1 Borodianka Ukr.
138 G2 Borodinskoye Rus. Fed.
131 K3 Borodino Rus. Fed.
190 E2 Borodyanka Rus. Fed.
256 C4 Borborema Brazil
256 D1 Borborema, Planalto da plat. Brazil
139 K3 Borok-Sulezhskiy Rus. Fed.
137 H2 Boromlya Ukr.
137 H2 Boromlya r. Ukr.
139 K3 Boromlya Rus. Fed.
206 E4 Boromo Burkina
240 I4 Boron CA U.S.A.
141 Boron Mali
92 C4 Borongan Phil.
175 F4 Boronów Pol.
192 A4 Borore Sardegna Italy
85 G5 Bororen Qld Austr.
175 I5 Borota Pol.
206 D4 Borotou Côte d'Ivoire
149 H3 Boroughbridge North Yorkshire, England U.K.
151 H3 Borough Green Kent, England U.K.
137 I3 Borova Kharkiv's'ka Oblast' Ukr.
136 F2 Borova Kyivs'ka Oblast' Ukr.
137 J3 Borova r. Ukr.
177 F4 Borova Bulg.
176 D2 Borovany Czech Rep.
136 C2 Borove Rivnens'ka Oblast' Ukr.
136 C2 Borove Rivnens'ka Oblast' Ukr.
139 I2 Borovenka Rus. Fed.
139 I2 Borovichi Rus. Fed.
175 F5 Borovnica Slovenia
188 G3 Borovo Selo Croatia
134 J4 Borovoy Kirovskaya Oblast' Rus. Fed.
134 F2 Borovoy Respublika Kareliya Rus. Fed.
134 K3 Borovoy Respublika Komi Rus. Fed.
121 G1 Borovoye Kazakh.
139 K4 Borovsk Rus. Fed.
175 J5 Borowa Pol.
175 I5 Borowie Pol.
183 H4 Borox Spain
257 E3 Borrachudo r. Brazil
254 A2 Borrazópolis Brazil
143 F4 Borrby Sweden
170 D1 Borre Denmark
149 I5 Borrello Italy
238 D5 Borrego Springs CA U.S.A.
162 D4 Borrèze France
187 F4 Borriol Spain
147 D4 Borris-in-Ossory Rep. of Ireland
147 C4 Borrisokane Rep. of Ireland
84 D3 Borroloola N.T. Austr.
149 F3 Borrowdale Cumbria, England U.K.
177 K4 Bors Romania
142 K4 Borş Norway
192 G2 Borşa Romania
197 K3 Borşa Romania
193 J2 Borša Slovakia
116 C3 Borsad Gujarat India
165 D3 Borsbeek Belgium
197 J2 Borsec Romania
169 E4 Börsel Ger.
199 A1 Borsh Albania
137 K2 Borshchevskiye Peski Rus. Fed.
— Borshchiv Ukr.
175 M6 Borshchovochnyy Khrebet mts Rus. Fed.
136 C2 Borshchiv Ukr.
121 I2 Borsippa tourist site Iraq
120 B1 Borský Jur Slovakia
179 I2 Borský Mikuláš Slovakia
177 K3 Borský Svätý Jur Slovakia
177 K3 Borsod-Abaúj-Zemplén county Hungary
177 J3 Borsodnádasd Hungary
177 J3 Borsodszentgyörgy Hungary
165 C3 Borssele Neth.
169 F3 Börßum Ger.
169 D3 Bortenbrock Neth.
171 F5 Börtewitz Ger.
110 C2 Bortala Xinjiang China see Bole
110 C2 Bortala He r. China
150 C2 Borth Ceredigion, Wales U.K.
192 A4 Bortigali Sardegna Italy
183 E3 Bort-les-Orgues France
106 B2 Bor-Üdzüür Mongolia
122 B4 Borūjen Iran
122 B3 Borūjerd Iran
129 D5 Borün Iran
128 D3 Bor Ul Shan mts China
199 G4 Boruth Hungary
142 D4 Borve Highland, Scotland U.K.
136 B3 Boryslav Ukr.
163 C6 Boryspil' Ukr.
159 H2 Borzaya r. Rus. Fed.
177 H1 Börzsöny hills Hungary
101 G1 Borzya r. Rus. Fed.
194 C6 Bosa Sardegna Italy
177 G3 Bošáca Slovakia
121 Bosaga Kazakh.
250 B4 Bosa r. Peru
183 B3 Borja Spain
183 B3 Borja Spain
186 D3 Borjabad Spain
— Borjas Blancas Spain see Les Borges Blanques
129 G3 Borjomi Georgia
138 G4 Borkovichy Belarus
207 G3 Borkou reg. Chad
197 H3 Borkovichy Belarus
169 C2 Borkum Ger.
169 C2 Borkum i. Ger.
143 K3 Borlänge Sweden
190 E3 Bormida r. Italy
191 G2 Bormio Italy
171 E4 Borna Ger.
171 F5 Borna Sachsen Ger.
169 C4 Born am Darß Ger.
169 C4 Born-Berge hill Ger.
168 D1 Borne Neth.
169 E3 Borne r. France
164 E2 Borne France
192 A4 Bornel France
190 E4 Bornes France
137 J2 Bornes de Aguiar Port.
182 C3 Bosque Spain

129 C3 Bornich Ger.
207 I4 Borno state Nigeria
183 H4 Bornova r. Spain
199 E2 Bornova Turkey
174 C4 Bornstedt Ger.
188 G3 Borodia Spain
95 E4 Borobudur tourist site Indon.
175 I3 Borok Czech Rep.
137 I3 Borova Kharkiv's'ka Oblast' Ukr.
136 F2 Borova Kyivs'ka Oblast' Ukr.
137 J3 Borova r. Ukr.
197 L4 Botiz Romania
113 B4 Botkins OH U.S.A.
135 I6 Botkul', Ozero l. Kazakh./Rus. Fed.
129 E2 Botlikh Rus. Fed.
197 G2 Botna r. Moldova
197 H2 Botna r. Moldova (see above)
182 C3 Botorrita Spain
197 J2 Botoroaga Romania
197 H1 Botoșani Romania
195 F4 Botricello Italy
206 D5 Botro Côte d'Ivoire
235 I1 Botsford CT U.S.A.
179 J1 Botsmark Sweden
213 ◻5 Botswana country Africa
195 F3 Botte Donato, Monte mt. Italy
169 D4 Bottendorf (Burgwald) Ger.
168 F3 Bottendorf (Obernholz) Ger.
140 M2 Botttesviken g. Fin./Sweden
151 G2 Bottesford
233 I4 Bottesford North Lincolnshire, England U.K.
151 G2 Bottesford Leicestershire, England U.K.
192 B3 Bottidda Sardegna Italy
236 I1 Bottineau ND U.S.A.
247 G3 Bottom Saba Neth. Antilles
169 B4 Bottrop Ger.
256 C5 Botucatu Brazil
257 F2 Botumirim Brazil
196 B3 Botuna Macedonia
197 H2 Botușhany Moldova state
— Botuceni
225 K3 Botwood Nfld. Can.
168 D2 Bötzingen Ger.
206 D5 Bouaflé Côte d'Ivoire
156 B3 Bouafles France
206 D5 Bouaké Côte d'Ivoire
205 F2 Bouanem Alg.
206 D4 Bouandougou Côte d'Ivoire
208 B3 Bouar C.A.R.
204 D2 Bouarfa Morocco
208 B4 Bouaye France
207 I5 Boubin hill Czech Rep.
176 D2 Boubín hill Czech Rep.
208 B3 Bouca C.A.R.
163 A3 Boucau France
84 C2 Boucaut Bay N.T. Austr.
160 E5 Bouc-Bel-Air France
159 F3 Bouché France
156 D3 Bouchain France
189 F4 Bouchegouf Alg.
159 F4 Bouchemaine France
161 I. L'Oyauté New Caledonia see Tiga
163 G3 Bouchervile Que. Can.
161 Bouches-du-Rhône dept Provence-Alpes-Côte-d'Azur France
227 J2 Bouchette Que. Can.
225 H4 Bouctouche N.B. Can.
180 C5 Boudinar Morocco
190 B2 Boudry Switz.
217 ◻3a Bouéni Mayotte
209 B6 Bouenza admin. reg. Congo
163 C1 Bouesse France
159 H4 Bouessay France
205 G1 Bougaa Alg.
128 A1 Bougainville, Cape W.A. Austr.
89 L2 Bougainville Island P.N.G.
85 F2 Bougainville Reef Coral Sea Is Terr. Austr.
78 ◻6 Bougainville Strait Solomon Is see Bejaia
163 C5 Bougard Mali
159 F4 Bougault France
206 E6 Bouguenais France
159 H5 Bouillac France
247 ◻ Bouillante Guadeloupe
165 D4 Bouillargues France
165 D4 Bouillon Belgium
156 D5 Bouilly France
156 D5 Bouin France
205 F1 Bouira Alg.
204 B3 Bou Izakarn Morocco
163 C6 Boujailles France
163 B5 Boujan-sur-Libron France
204 A3 Boujdour Western Sahara
205 F2 Bou Kahli, Djebel mt. Alg.
207 I5 Boukombé Benin
208 C3 Boukoula C.A.R.
157 G5 Boulay-Moselle France
160 C2 Boulazac France
163 C1 Boulbon France
162 D5 Boulbon France
165 C5 Bouillon Belgium
163 D5 Bouilly France
205 D5 Bou Izakarn Morocco

129 C5 Boradigah Azer.
197 F4 Bosilegrad Srbija Yugo.
197 F4 Bosiljgrad Srbija Yugo. see Bosilegrad
172 C3 Bösingen Ger.
120 E1 Boskol' Kazakh.
164 D2 Boskoop Neth.
176 F2 Boskovice Czech Rep.
197 H4 Bosna r. Bos.-Herz.
188 G3 Bosna hills Bos.-Herz.
197 H4 Bosna hills Bos.-Herz.
— Bosna i Hercegovina country Europe see Bosnia and Herzegovina
— Bosnia-Herzegovina country Europe see Bosnia and Herzegovina
— Bosna Saray Bos.-Herz. see Sarajevo
188 F3 Bosnia and Herzegovina, Federation of aut. div. Bos.-Herz. see Federacija Bosna i Hercegovina
188 F3 Bosnia-Herzegovina country Europe
208 C3 Bosobolo Dem. Rep. Congo
105 ◻3a Bōsō-hantō pen. Japan
179 H1 Bošovice Czech Rep.
215 F2 Bospoort S. Africa
— Bosporus str. Turkey see İstanbul Boğazı
182 B1 Bosque Spain
208 C3 Bossangoa C.A.R.
141 K3 Bössbod Sweden
208 C3 Bossembélé C.A.R.
162 C4 Bosset France
208 C3 Bossentélé C.A.R.
186 C2 Bossòst Spain
237 E5 Bossier City LA U.S.A.
206 D4 Bossora Burkina
186 D2 Bóssost Spain
215 F1 Bospruit S. Africa
86 D3 Bossut, Cape W.A. Austr.
124 B2 Bostān Iran
110 D3 Bosten Hu l. China
110 D3 Bosten Hu l. China
151 G2 Boston Lincolnshire, England U.K.
233 I3 Boston MA U.S.A.
82 C3 Boston Bay S.A. Austr.
227 H1 Boston Creek Ont. Can.
237 E5 Boston Mountains AR U.S.A.
149 H4 Boston Spa West Yorkshire, England U.K.
188 E3 Bosut r. Croatia
226 B5 Boswell IA U.S.A.
232 D5 Boswell PA U.S.A.
116 B5 Botad Gujarat India
208 A3 Botata Liberia
168 D1 Boteld Sweden
197 G3 Boteni Romania
151 I2 Botesdale Suffolk, England U.K.
212 E4 Boteti r. Botswana
135 D8 Botev mt. Bulg.
177 G4 Botfalu Hungary
149 F3 Bothel Cumbria, England U.K.
238 B2 Bothell WA U.S.A.
141 L3 Bothnia, Gulf of Fin./Sweden
83 F5 Bothwell Tas. Austr.
227 G4 Bothwell Ont. Can.
182 C3 Boticas Port.

169 C5 Bornich Ger.
207 I4 Borno state Nigeria
197 L4 Botiz Romania
135 I6 Botkins OH U.S.A.
135 I6 Botkul', Ozero l. Kazakh./Rus. Fed.
129 E2 Botlikh Rus. Fed.
197 G2 Botna r. Moldova
182 C3 Botorrita Spain
197 J2 Botoroaga Romania
197 H1 Botoșani Romania
195 F4 Botricello Italy
206 D5 Botro Côte d'Ivoire
235 I1 Botsford CT U.S.A.
179 J1 Botsmark Sweden
213 ◻5 Botswana country Africa
195 F3 Botte Donato, Monte mt. Italy
169 D4 Bottendorf (Burgwald) Ger.
168 F3 Bottendorf (Obernholz) Ger.
140 M2 Bottenviken g. Fin./Sweden
151 G2 Bottesford North Lincolnshire, England U.K.
233 I4 Bottesford Leicestershire, England U.K.
192 B3 Bottidda Sardegna Italy
236 I1 Bottineau ND U.S.A.
247 G3 Bottom Saba Neth. Antilles
169 B4 Bottrop Ger.
256 C5 Botucatu Brazil
257 F2 Botumirim Brazil
196 B3 Botuna Macedonia
197 H2 Botușhany Moldova
225 K3 Botwood Nfld. Can.
168 D2 Bötzingen Ger.
206 D5 Bouaflé Côte d'Ivoire
156 B3 Bouafles France
206 D5 Bouaké Côte d'Ivoire
205 F2 Bouanem Alg.
206 D4 Bouandougou Côte d'Ivoire
208 B3 Bouar C.A.R.
204 D2 Bouarfa Morocco
208 B4 Bouaye France
176 D2 Boubín hill Czech Rep.
208 B3 Bouca C.A.R.
163 A3 Boucau France
84 C2 Boucaut Bay N.T. Austr.
160 E5 Bouc-Bel-Air France
159 F3 Bouché France
156 D3 Bouchain France
189 F4 Bouchegouf Alg.
159 F4 Bouchemaine France
161 □ Bouches de l'Oyo ... L'Oyauté New Caledonia see Tiga
227 J2 Boucherville Que. Can.
161 Bouches-du-Rhône dept Provence-Alpes-Côte-d'Azur France
225 H4 Bouctouche N.B. Can.
180 C5 Boudinar Morocco
190 B2 Boudry Switz.
217 ◻3a Bouéni Mayotte
209 B6 Bouenza admin. reg. Congo
163 C1 Bouesse France
159 H4 Bouessay France
205 G1 Bougaa Alg.
128 A1 Bougainville, Cape W.A. Austr.
89 L2 Bougainville Island P.N.G.
85 F2 Bougainville Reef Coral Sea Is Terr. Austr.
— Bougainville Strait Solomon Is
163 C5 Bougarï Mali
159 F4 Bougault France
206 E6 Bouguenais France
159 H5 Bouillac France
247 ◻ Bouillante Guadeloupe
165 D4 Bouillargues France
165 D4 Bouillon Belgium
156 D5 Bouilly France
156 D5 Bouin France
205 F1 Bouira Alg.
204 B3 Bou Izakarn Morocco
163 C6 Boujailles France
163 B5 Boujan-sur-Libron France
204 A3 Boujdour Western Sahara
205 F2 Bou Kahli, Djebel mt. Alg.
207 I5 Boukombé Benin
208 C3 Boukoula C.A.R.
157 G5 Boulay-Moselle France
160 C2 Boulazac France
163 C1 Boulbon France
205 D5 Boulemane Morocco

Boulemane to Brodheadsville
287

204 D2 Boulemane Boulemane Morocco
241 I5 Boulevard CA U.S.A.
Boulhaut Morocco see Ben Slimane
84 D4 Boulia Qld Austr.
157 F3 Bouligny France
163 D5 Bouloc France
Boulogne France see Boulogne-sur-Mer
158 E4 Boulogne r. France
156 C4 Boulogne-Billancourt France
163 C5 Boulogne-sur-Gesse France
156 B2 Boulogne-sur-Mer France
159 G4 Bouloire France
208 E3 Boulou r. C.A.R.
77 G4 Bouloupari New Caledonia
161 E5 Boulouris France
206 E3 Boulsa Burkina
149 G4 Boulsworth Hill hill England U.K.
157 E3 Boult-aux-Bois France
156 E3 Boulzicourt France
204 D3 Boumalne Dadès Morocco
208 B5 Boumango Gabon
207 I6 Boumba r. Cameroon
208 B3 Boumbé I r. C.A.R.
205 F1 Boumerdes Alg.
186 E2 Boumort mt. Spain
186 E2 Boumort, Serra del mts Spain
206 E4 Bouna Côte d'Ivoire
204 E2 Bou Naceur, Jbel mt. Morocco
206 B2 Boû Nâga Maur.
233 □H2 Boundary Mountains ME U.S.A.
240 H3 Boundary Peak NV U.S.A.
234 D2 Bound Brook NJ U.S.A.
206 D4 Boundiali Côte d'Ivoire
208 B5 Boundji Congo
96 E3 Boung r. Vietnam
208 D3 Boungou r. C.A.R.
163 C4 Bouniagues France
206 B3 Bounkiling Senegal
238 E3 Bountiful UT U.S.A.
84 D3 Bountiful Island Qld Austr.
77 H6 Bounty Islands N.Z.
266 G9 Bounty Trough sea feature S. Pacific Ocean
261 G3 Bouquet Arg.
78 □5 Bourail New Caledonia
160 C2 Bourbince r. France
Bourbon reg. France see Bourbonnais
Bourbon terr. Indian Ocean see Réunion
160 B2 Bourbon-Lancy France
160 B2 Bourbon-l'Archambault France
160 A2 Bourbonnais reg. France
157 F5 Bourbonne-les-Bains France
156 C2 Bourbourg France
160 D3 Bourbre r. France
158 C3 Bourbriac France
162 A3 Bourcefranc-le-Chapus France
161 D4 Bourdeaux France
162 C3 Bourdeilles France
157 G4 Bourdonnay France
206 E2 Bourem Mali
162 C2 Bouresse France
162 B3 Bourg France
159 G2 Bourg-Achard France
162 D3 Bourganeuf France
161 C3 Bourg-Argental France
158 E4 Bourgbarré France
158 B3 Bourg-Blanc France
161 D3 Bourg-de-Péage France
160 C2 Bourg-de-Thizy France
163 C4 Bourg-de-Visa France
156 A3 Bourg-Dun France
160 D2 Bourg-en-Bresse France
162 E1 Bourges France
233 F2 Bourget Ont. Can.
160 D3 Bourget, Lac du l. France
156 D3 Bourg-et-Comin France
160 A3 Bourg-Lastic France
161 C4 Bourg-lès-Valence France
163 D6 Bourg-Madame France
227 J1 Bourgmont Que. Can.
159 F4 Bourgneuf-en-Mauges France
158 E4 Bourgneuf-en-Retz France
156 E3 Bourgogne France
156 E5 Bourgogne admin. reg. France
160 D3 Bourgoin-Jallieu France
161 C4 Bourg-St-Andéol France
163 D5 Bourg-St-Bernard France
160 E3 Bourg-St-Maurice France
159 G2 Bourgtheroulde-Infreville France
159 F2 Bourguébus France
159 G4 Bourgueil France
83 F2 Bourke N.S.W. Austr.
227 G1 Bourkes Ont. Can.
157 F4 Bourmont France
161 D3 Bourne r. France
151 G2 Bourne Lincolnshire, England U.K.
151 F4 Bournemouth Bournemouth, England U.K.
151 F4 Bournemouth admin. div. England U.K.
159 E5 Bournezeau France
161 B3 Bournoncle-St-Pierre France
182 B3 Bouro Port.
160 E1 Bourogne France
206 E4 Bouroum-Bouroum Burkina
207 I4 Bourrah Cameroon
163 C4 Bourran France
163 B4 Bourriot-Bergonce France
165 F5 Bourscheid Lux.
164 G1 Bourtange Neth.
159 G3 Bourth France
150 E3 Bourton Dorset, England U.K.
151 F3 Bourton-on-the-Water Gloucestershire, England U.K.
206 E3 Bourzanga Burkina
205 G2 Bou Saâda Alg.
189 B7 Bou Salem Tunisia
241 J5 Bouse AZ U.S.A.
162 E2 Boussac France
206 E3 Boussé Burkina
163 C5 Boussens France
160 D1 Boussières France
208 C2 Bousso Chad
156 E2 Boussois France
165 C4 Boussu Belgium
165 D4 Boutersem Belgium
206 B2 Boutilimit Maur.
162 B3 Boutonne r. France
156 B3 Bouttencourt France
Bouvet Island terr. S. Atlantic Ocean see Bouvetøya
264 J9 Bouvetøya terr. S. Atlantic Ocean
161 D4 Bouvières France
158 E4 Bouvron France
157 G4 Bouxières-aux-Dames France
157 H4 Bouxwiller France
156 E3 Bouy France
207 G3 Bouza Niger
159 H5 Bouzanne r. France
157 G3 Bouzonville France
156 E3 Bouzy France
195 E4 Bova Italy
195 F4 Bovalino Italy
195 E5 Bova Marina Italy
179 E4 Bovec Slovenia
182 C2 Bóveda Spain
183 G2 Bóveda Spain
190 F3 Bovegno Italy
169 E4 Bovenden Ger.
Boven Kapuas Mountains Indon./Malaysia see Kapuas Hulu, Pegunungan
164 E2 Bovenkarspel Neth.
164 F2 Bovensmilde Neth.
156 C3 Boves France
190 C4 Boves Italy
150 D4 Bovey r. England U.K.
226 A2 Bovey MN U.S.A.
150 D4 Bovey Tracey Devon, England U.K.
148 C3 Boviel Northern Ireland U.K.
165 E4 Bovigny Belgium
193 F3 Boville Ernica Italy
150 E4 Bovington Camp Dorset, England U.K.
193 H3 Bovino Italy
191 G3 Bovolone Italy
261 H2 Bovril Arg.
168 E1 Bovrup Denmark
137 G3 Bovtyshka Ukr.
86 F3 Bow r. W.A. Austr.
223 I5 Bow r. Alta Can.
Bowa Sichuan China see Muli
236 C1 Bowbells ND U.S.A.
149 H3 Bowburn Durham, England U.K.
232 D5 Bowden WV U.S.A.
Bowditch atoll Tokelau see Fakaofo
260 D4 Bowen Arg.
85 G4 Bowen Qld Austr.
85 F4 Bowen r. Qld Austr.
226 B5 Bowen IL U.S.A.
83 G4 Bowen, Mount Vic. Austr.
85 F4 Bowen Downs Qld Austr.
84 C1 Bowen Strait N.T. Austr.
85 G5 Bowenville Qld Austr.
234 C3 Bowers Beach DE U.S.A.
263 K2 Bowers Mountains Antarctica
266 G2 Bowers Ridge sea feature Bering Sea
149 G3 Bowes Durham, England U.K.
85 F4 Bowie Qld Austr.
241 M5 Bowie AZ U.S.A.
234 B4 Bowie MD U.S.A.
237 D5 Bowie TX U.S.A.
223 I5 Bow Island Alta Can.
122 A2 Bowkan Iran
149 G4 Bowland, Forest of reg. England U.K.
230 C4 Bowling Green KY U.S.A.
236 F4 Bowling Green MO U.S.A.
232 B4 Bowling Green OH U.S.A.
232 E5 Bowling Green VA U.S.A.
85 F3 Bowling Green, Cape Qld Austr.
85 F3 Bowling Green Bay Qld Austr.
236 C2 Bowman ND U.S.A.
222 F5 Bowman, Mount B.C. Can.
262 T2 Bowman Coast Antarctica
263 G2 Bowman Island Antarctica
262 T2 Bowman Peninsula Antarctica
234 B2 Bowmansdale PA U.S.A.
234 C2 Bowmanstown PA U.S.A.
234 B2 Bowmansville PA U.S.A.
227 H4 Bowmanville Ont. Can.
149 G2 Bowmont Water r. England/Scotland U.K.
146 B6 Bowmore Argyll and Bute, Scotland U.K.
149 F3 Bowness-on-Solway Cumbria, England U.K.
149 G3 Bowness-on-Windermere Cumbria, England U.K.
Bowo Sichuan China see Bomai
Bowo Xizang China see Bomi
83 H2 Bowraville N.S.W. Austr.
222 F4 Bowron r. B.C. Can.
150 E3 Box Wiltshire, England U.K.
172 D2 Boxberg Baden-Württemberg Ger.
171 F4 Boxberg Sachsen Ger.
171 E4 Boxdorf Ger.
236 C2 Box Elder SD U.S.A.
236 C2 Box Elder r. SD U.S.A.
143 F2 Boxholm Sweden
107 H4 Boxing Shandong China
164 E3 Boxmeer Neth.
164 E3 Boxtel Neth.
126 D2 Boyabat Turkey
250 C3 Boyaca dept Col.
197 H4 Boyadzhik Bulg.
199 F1 Boyalıca Turkey
Boyalık Turkey see Çiçekdağı
197 F4 Boyana tourist site Bulg.
109 F2 Boyang Jiangxi China
197 H4 Boyanovo Bulg.
87 B7 Boyanup W.A. Austr.
136 F2 Boyarka Ukr.
83 H2 Boyd r. N.S.W. Austr.
87 E5 Boyd Lagoon salt flat W.A. Austr.
232 D6 Boydton VA U.S.A.
236 E3 Boyer r. IA U.S.A.
234 C2 Boyertown PA U.S.A.
232 E6 Boykins VA U.S.A.
222 H4 Boyle Alta Can.
147 C3 Boyle Rep. of Ireland
85 G4 Boyne r. Qld Austr.
85 G5 Boyne r. Qld Austr.
147 E3 Boyne r. Rep. of Ireland
226 E3 Boyne City MI U.S.A.
156 C4 Boynes France
Boysun Uzbek. see Baysun
253 E5 Boyuibe Bol.
129 E3 Böyük Dähnä Azer.
122 A1 Böyük Hinaldağ mt. Azer.
129 E4 Böyük İşıqlı Dağ mt. Armenia
87 C7 Boyup Brook W.A. Austr.
199 G2 Bozan Turkey
129 B3 Bozan Dağı mt. Turkey
Bozashy Tübegi pen. Kazakh. see Buzachi, Poluostrov
199 F3 Bozburun Turkey
199 G3 Bozburun Dağ mt. Turkey
128 C1 Bozdağ mt. Turkey
199 E2 Bozdağ mt. Turkey
199 F2 Boz Dağ mts Turkey
Bozdag, Khrebet hills Azer. see Bozdağ Silsiläsi
199 E2 Boz Dağları mts Turkey
129 E3 Bozdağ Silsiläsi hills Azer.
129 C4 Bozdağ Tepe mt. Turkey
199 F3 Bozdoğan Turkey
151 G2 Bozeat Northamptonshire, England U.K.
161 E3 Bozel France
238 E2 Bozeman MT U.S.A.
Bozen Italy see Bolzano
175 H3 Bożewo Pol.
109 E1 Bozhou Anhui China
176 F3 Božíce Czech Rep.
179 H5 Božjakovina Croatia
126 D3 Bozkır Turkey
Bozköl Kazakh. see Boskol'
199 F3 Bozkurt Turkey
Bozoglan mts Turkey see Bolkar Dağları
161 A4 Bozouls France
208 C3 Bozoum C.A.R.
126 E3 Bozova Turkey
197 F3 Bozovici Romania
122 A2 Bozqūsh, Kūh-e mts Iran
121 H2 Bozshakol' Kazakh.
199 G2 Bozüyük Turkey
128 A1 Bozyazı Turkey
190 F3 Bozzolo Italy
190 C4 Bra Italy
146 E5 Braan r. Scotland U.K.
143 F3 Braås Sweden
262 T2 Brabant Island Antarctica
165 D4 Brabant Wallon prov. Belgium
188 F4 Brač i. Croatia
146 B4 Bracadale Highland, Scotland U.K.
146 B4 Bracadale, Loch b. Scotland U.K.
Bracara Port. see Braga
192 E2 Bracciano Italy
192 E2 Bracciano, Lago di l. Italy
224 E4 Bracebridge Ont. Can.
149 I4 Bracebridge Heath Lincolnshire, England U.K.
162 B3 Brach France
169 C5 Brachbach Ger.
159 H4 Bracieux France
148 B4 Brackagh Rep. of Ireland
140 K3 Bräcke Sweden
168 F2 Brackel Ger.
172 D2 Brackenheim Ger.
237 C6 Brackettville TX U.S.A.
188 F4 Brački Kanal sea chan. Croatia
151 F2 Brackley Northamptonshire, England U.K.
147 D3 Bracknagh Rep. of Ireland
151 G3 Bracknell Bracknell Forest, England U.K.
151 G3 Bracknell Forest admin. div. England U.K.
253 G2 Braço Norte r. Brazil
197 F2 Brad Romania
193 I4 Bradano r. Italy
231 D7 Bradenton FL U.S.A.
227 H3 Bradford Ont. Can.
149 H4 Bradford West Yorkshire, England U.K.
232 A4 Bradford OH U.S.A.
232 D4 Bradford PA U.S.A.
233 G3 Bradford VT U.S.A.
234 B1 Bradford County county PA U.S.A.
234 C2 Bradford Hills PA U.S.A.
150 E3 Bradford-on-Avon Wiltshire, England U.K.
151 F4 Brading Isle of Wight, England U.K.
226 D5 Bradley IL U.S.A.
235 D2 Bradley Beach NJ U.S.A.
232 B4 Bradner OH U.S.A.
150 D4 Bradninch Devon, England U.K.
150 E4 Bradpole Dorset, England U.K.
149 G4 Bradshaw Greater Manchester, England U.K.
232 C6 Bradshaw WV U.S.A.
86 E2 Bradshaw, Mount hill W.A. Austr.
149 H4 Bradwell Derbyshire, England U.K.
151 I2 Bradwell Norfolk, England U.K.
151 H3 Bradwell Waterside Essex, England U.K.
237 D6 Brady TX U.S.A.
237 D6 Brady Creek r. TX U.S.A.
146 □G1 Brae Shetland, Scotland U.K.
146 D4 Braeantra Highland, Scotland U.K.
146 F5 Braehead Angus, Scotland U.K.
82 D3 Braemar S.A. Austr.
146 E4 Braemar Aberdeenshire, Scotland U.K.
194 D5 Braemi r. Sicilia Italy
182 B3 Braga Port.
182 B3 Braga admin. dist. Port.
261 G4 Bragado Arg.
254 D2 Bragança Brazil
182 D3 Bragança Port.
182 D3 Bragança admin. dist. Port.
256 D5 Bragança Paulista Brazil
226 A3 Braham MN U.S.A.
136 F2 Brahin Belarus
136 F2 Brahinka r. Belarus
168 F2 Brahlstorf Ger.
117 I4 Brahmakund Arun. Prad. India
117 G5 Brahmanbaria Bangl.
117 F5 Brahmani r. India
115 E2 Brahmapur Orissa India
111 E7 Brahmaputra r. China/India alt. Dihang (India), alt. Yarlung Zangbo (China)
83 G3 Braidwood N.S.W. Austr.
226 C5 Braidwood IL U.S.A.
197 H3 Brăila Romania
197 H3 Brăilei, Insula Mare a i. Romania
151 F2 Brailsford Derbyshire, England U.K.
156 D3 Braine France
165 D4 Braine-l'Alleud Belgium
165 D4 Braine-le-Comte Belgium
236 E2 Brainerd MN U.S.A.
159 G4 Brain-sur-Allonnes France
151 H3 Braintree Essex, England U.K.
149 F3 Braithwaite Cumbria, England U.K.
84 C1 Braithwaite Point N.T. Austr.
165 E4 Braives Belgium
213 F4 Brak r. Northern S. Africa
214 C5 Brak r. W. Cape S. Africa
168 D2 Brake (Unterweser) Ger.
165 C4 Brakel Belgium
169 E4 Brakel Ger.
164 E3 Brakel Neth.
206 B2 Brâkna admin. reg. Maur.
143 F3 Bräkneån r. Sweden
215 G2 Brakpan S. Africa
214 D4 Brakpoort S. Africa
215 F2 Brakspruit S. Africa
142 E2 Brålanda Sweden
174 F4 Bralin Pol.
190 E4 Brallo di Pregola Italy
222 F5 Bralorne B.C. Can.
163 E5 Bram France
161 E3 Bramans France
178 D3 Bramberg am Wildkogel Austria
82 C3 Bramfield S.A. Austr.
151 I2 Bramford Suffolk, England U.K.
116 D5 Bramhapuri Mahar. India
149 H4 Bramley South Yorkshire, England U.K.
142 C4 Bramming Denmark
224 E5 Brampton Ont. Can.
151 G2 Brampton Cambridgeshire, England U.K.
149 G3 Brampton Cumbria, England U.K.
151 I2 Brampton Suffolk, England U.K.
169 C3 Bramsche Niedersachsen Ger.
169 D3 Bramsche Niedersachsen Ger.
168 D2 Bramstedt Ger.
85 E2 Bramwell Qld Austr.
182 E1 Braña Caballo mt. Spain
171 E5 Braňany Czech Rep.
177 H3 Branč Slovakia
195 F5 Brancaleone Italy
151 H2 Brancaster Norfolk, England U.K.
225 K4 Branch Nfld. Can.
234 B2 Branch Dale PA U.S.A.
234 D1 Branchville NJ U.S.A.
253 E2 Branco r. Mato Grosso Brazil
251 F5 Branco r. Roraima Brazil
206 □ Branco i. Cape Verde
173 F2 Brand Ger.
247 □8 Brandaris hill Bonaire Neth. Antilles
212 B4 Brandberg mt. Namibia
141 L3 Brändbo Sweden
142 D1 Brandbu Norway
142 C4 Brande Denmark
168 E2 Brande-Hörnerkirchen Ger.
178 C3 Brandenberg Austria
171 D3 Brandenburg Ger.
171 E3 Brandenburg land Ger.
230 C4 Brandenburg KY U.S.A.
171 E5 Brand-Erbisdorf Ger.
149 I4 Brandesburton East Riding of Yorkshire, England U.K.
215 F3 Brandfort S. Africa
171 E4 Brandis Brandenburg Ger.
171 D4 Brandis Sachsen Ger.
214 B4 Brandkop S. Africa
179 G2 Brand-Nagelberg Austria
141 M3 Brändö Åland Fin.
192 B2 Brando Corse France
85 F3 Brandon Qld Austr.
223 L5 Brandon Man. Can.
147 A4 Brandon Rep. of Ireland
149 H3 Brandon Durham, England U.K.
151 H2 Brandon Suffolk, England U.K.
237 F5 Brandon MS U.S.A.
236 D3 Brandon SD U.S.A.
233 G3 Brandon VT U.S.A.
147 A4 Brandon Bay Rep. of Ireland
147 E4 Brandon Hill hill Rep. of Ireland
147 A4 Brandon Mountain hill Rep. of Ireland
234 B2 Brandonville PA U.S.A.
232 D5 Brandonville WV U.S.A.
170 E1 Brandshagen Ger.
234 A2 Brandtsville PA U.S.A.
214 C4 Brandvlei S. Africa
176 D1 Brandýs nad Labem-Stará Boleslav Czech Rep.
234 C3 Brandywine Creek, East Branch r. PA U.S.A.
234 C3 Brandywine Creek, West Branch r. DE U.S.A.
234 C2 Brandywine Manor PA U.S.A.
235 F1 Branford CT U.S.A.
231 D6 Branford FL U.S.A.
160 D2 Branges France
179 E5 Branica r. Slovenia
143 H4 Braniewo Pol.
177 L6 Brănişca Romania
156 D5 Branlin r. France
140 M2 Brännberg Sweden
163 B4 Branne France
173 G4 Brannenburg Ger.
183 F2 Branösera Spain
262 T2 Bransfield Strait Antarctica
151 F4 Bransgore Hampshire, England U.K.
175 K3 Brańsk Pol.
237 C4 Branson CO U.S.A.
149 I4 Branston Lincolnshire, England U.K.
175 J3 Brańszczyk Pol.
95 F4 Brantas r. Indon.
224 D5 Brantford Ont. Can.
151 I3 Brantham Suffolk, England U.K.
177 G1 Brantice Czech Rep.
231 C6 Brantley AL U.S.A.
162 C3 Brantôme France
137 H2 Brantsivka Ukr.
226 B3 Brantwood WI U.S.A.
137 F2 Branytsya Ukr.
190 E2 Branzi Italy
183 G3 Braojos Spain
190 F3 Braone Italy
161 D5 Bras France
196 E4 Brasaljce Kosovo, Srbija Yugo.
225 I4 Bras d'Or Lake N.S. Can.
182 B4 Brasfemes Port.
Brasil country S. America see Brazil
257 G2 Brasil, Planalto do plat. Brazil
256 A4 Brasilândia Brazil
256 C1 Brasilândia Brazil
252 C2 Brasileia Brazil
256 D1 Brasília Brazil
257 E2 Brasília de Minas Brazil
138 E3 Brasla r. Latvia
Braslav Belarus see Braslaw
138 F4 Braslaw Belarus
197 G3 Braşov Romania
139 J5 Brasovo Rus. Fed.
257 F4 Brás Pires Brazil
207 G5 Brass Nigeria
163 E5 Brassac France
161 B3 Brassac-les-Mines France
165 D3 Brasschaat Belgium
95 G1 Brassey, Banjaran mts Sabah Malaysia
84 C4 Brassey, Mount N.T. Austr.
87 D5 Brassey Range hills W.A. Austr.
160 B1 Brassy France
142 D2 Brastad Sweden
173 H2 Břasy Czech Rep.
197 G4 Bratan mt. Bulg.
197 F2 Bratca Romania
176 G3 Bratislava Slovakia
176 G3 Bratislavský Kraj admin. reg. Slovakia
175 J5 Bratkowice Pol.
131 L4 Bratsk Rus. Fed.
137 F4 Brats'ke Ukr.
131 L4 Bratskoye Vodokhranilishche resr Rus. Fed.
136 E3 Bratslav Ukr.
233 G3 Brattleboro VT U.S.A.
142 E1 Brattmon Sweden
150 E3 Bratton Wiltshire, England U.K.
140 I3 Brattvåg Norway
188 G3 Bratunac Bos.-Herz.
169 C5 Braubach Ger.
162 B3 Braud-et-St-Louis France
257 F3 Braúnas Brazil
178 E2 Braunau am Inn Austria
172 A2 Brauneberg Ger.
169 D5 Braunfels Ger.
169 F4 Braunlage Ger.
172 C4 Bräunlingen Ger.
172 D2 Braunsbach Ger.
171 C4 Braunsbedra Ger.
169 F3 Braunschweig Ger.
169 E4 Braunschweig admin. reg. Niedersachsen Ger.
151 F2 Braunston Northamptonshire, England U.K.
151 F2 Braunstone Leicestershire, England U.K.
150 C3 Braunton Devon, England U.K.
215 F4 Braunville S. Africa
206 □ Brava i. Cape Verde
185 H3 Bravatas r. Spain
232 C5 Brave PA U.S.A.
136 E4 Bravicea Moldova
252 D4 Bravo, Cerro mt. Bol.
242 F3 Bravo del Norte, Río r. Mex./U.S.A. alt. Rio Grande
241 J5 Brawley CA U.S.A.
147 E3 Bray Rep. of Ireland
214 D1 Bray S. Africa
151 G3 Bray Windsor and Maidenhead, England U.K.
150 D4 Bray r. England U.K.
156 C1 Bray-Dunes France
159 G4 Braye r. France
147 A5 Bray Head hd Rep. of Ireland
136 E3 Brayiliv Ukr.
156 D4 Bray-sur-Seine France
149 H4 Brayton North Yorkshire, England U.K.
185 F2 Brazatortas Spain
222 H4 Brazeau r. Alta Can.
222 G4 Brazeau, Mount Alta Can.
160 D1 Brazey-en-Plaine France
177 L5 Brazii Romania
254 C4 Brazil country S. America
230 C4 Brazil IN U.S.A.
264 H7 Brazil Basin sea feature S. Atlantic Ocean
237 E6 Brazos r. TX U.S.A.
209 B6 Brazzaville Congo
188 G3 Brčko Bos.-Herz.
174 G2 Brda r. Pol.
174 G3 Brdów Pol.
176 C2 Brdy hills Czech Rep.
Bré Rep. of Ireland see Bray
183 I3 Brea Spain
84 D4 Breadalbane Qld Austr.
146 D5 Breadalbane reg. Scotland U.K.
87 E5 Breaden, Lake salt flat W.A. Austr.
183 G4 Brea de Tajo Spain
215 F5 Breakfast Vlei S. Africa
85 H5 Breaksea Spit Qld Austr.
158 E3 Bréal-sous-Montfort France
150 E3 Bream Gloucestershire, England U.K.
80 E1 Bream Bay North I. N.Z.
149 G2 Breamish r. England U.K.
146 A3 Breanais Western Isles, Scotland U.K.
146 B3 Breascleit Western Isles, Scotland U.K.
151 F2 Breaston Derbyshire, England U.K.
159 G2 Bréauté France
197 G3 Breaza Romania
95 E4 Brebes Jawa Tengah Indon.
161 F5 Brec d'Utelle mt. France
158 E3 Brécey France
158 D4 Brech France
156 C3 Brêche r. France
150 C3 Brechfa Carmarthenshire, Wales U.K.
146 F5 Brechin Angus, Scotland U.K.
165 D3 Brecht Belgium
239 F4 Breckenridge CO U.S.A.
236 D2 Breckenridge MN U.S.A.
237 D5 Breckenridge TX U.S.A.
169 C4 Breckerfeld Ger.
151 H2 Breckland lowland England U.K.
259 B9 Brecknock, Península pen. Chile
232 C4 Brecksville OH U.S.A.
176 F3 Břeclav Czech Rep.
150 D3 Brecon Powys, Wales U.K.
150 D3 Brecon Beacons reg. Wales U.K.
150 D3 Brecon Beacons National Park Wales U.K.
164 D3 Breda Neth.
186 F3 Breda Spain
143 E3 Bredaryd Sweden
214 C6 Bredasdorp S. Africa
83 G3 Bredbo N.S.W. Austr.
168 C3 Breddenberg Ger.
170 D3 Breddin Ger.
168 E2 Breddorf Ger.
142 C4 Brede r. Denmark
151 H4 Brede r. England U.K.
165 B3 Bredene Belgium
170 E2 Bredereiche Ger.
150 E2 Bredon Worcestershire, England U.K.
168 D1 Bredstedt Ger.
140 L3 Bredträsk Sweden
140 K2 Bredviken Sweden
120 E1 Bredy Rus. Fed.
165 E3 Bree Belgium
214 C6 Breede r. S. Africa
170 C2 Breese Ger.
164 D2 Breezand Neth.
232 D5 Breezewood PA U.S.A.
172 C4 Breg r. Ger.
197 E5 Bregalnica r. Macedonia
179 G5 Bregana Croatia
191 G3 Breganze Italy
178 A3 Bregenz Austria
168 F1 Bregninge Denmark
197 F3 Bregovo Bulg.
191 F3 Breguzzo Italy
158 E3 Bréhal France
158 D3 Bréhan France
169 F4 Brehme Ger.
171 D4 Brehna Ger.
140 □A2 Breiðafjörður b. Iceland
157 H3 Breidenbach France
169 D5 Breidenbach Ger.
236 C2 Breien ND U.S.A.
168 E1 Breiholz Ger.
190 E2 Breil Switz.
161 F5 Breil-sur-Roya France
215 F4 Breipaal S. Africa
172 B3 Breisach am Rhein Ger.
190 C1 Breitenbach Switz.
169 E5 Breitenbach am Herzberg Ger.
178 C3 Breitenbach am Inn Austria
173 H3 Breitenberg Ger.
173 E3 Breitenbrunn Bayern Ger.
173 F2 Breitenbrunn Bayern Ger.
168 E2 Breitenburg Ger.
168 F2 Breitenfelde Ger.
171 C4 Breitenhagen Ger.
178 B3 Breitenwang Austria
169 F4 Breitenworbis Ger.
178 C3 Breiter Grieskogel mt. Austria
170 E2 Breiter Luzinsee l. Ger.
172 C4 Breitnau Ger.
169 D5 Breitscheid Hessen Ger.
169 C5 Breitscheid Rheinland-Pfalz Ger.
169 F5 Breitungen Ger.
140 M1 Breivikbotn Norway
254 C4 Brejinho de Nazaré Brazil
254 E2 Brejo Brazil
254 E4 Brejo r. Brazil
168 D1 Breklum Ger.
140 J3 Brekstad Norway
158 B3 Brélès France
190 E3 Brembo r. Italy
168 D2 Bremen Ger.
168 D2 Bremen land Ger.
231 C5 Bremen GA U.S.A.
226 D5 Bremen IN U.S.A.
232 B5 Bremen OH U.S.A.
87 C7 Bremer Bay W.A. Austr.
87 C7 Bremer Bay b. W.A. Austr.
168 D2 Bremerhaven Ger.
87 D7 Bremer Range hills W.A. Austr.
Bremersdorp Swaziland see Manzini
238 B2 Bremerton WA U.S.A.
168 E2 Bremervörde Ger.
190 D1 Bremgarten Switz.
169 C5 Bremm Ger.
142 A2 Bremnes Norway
162 A2 Brem-sur-Mer France
175 J5 Breń r. Pol.
216 □3d Breña Alta La Palma Canary Is
150 D3 Brendon Hills England U.K.
184 E3 Brenes Spain
237 D6 Brenham TX U.S.A.
184 C2 Brenhas r. Port.
174 G6 Brenna Pol.
160 D2 Brenne r. France
159 G4 Brenne r. France
191 G2 Brennero Italy
Brennero, Passo di pass Austria/Italy see Brenner Pass
Brennerpaß pass Austria/Italy see Brenner Pass
178 C4 Brenner Pass pass Austria/Italy
190 F3 Breno Italy
160 D2 Brénod France
163 D5 Brens France
172 C2 Brensbach Ger.
224 E4 Brent Ont. Can.
191 H3 Brenta r. Italy
191 F2 Brenta, Gruppo di mts Italy
150 E3 Brent Knoll Somerset, England U.K.
151 H3 Brentwood Essex, England U.K.
235 E2 Brentwood NY U.S.A.
173 E3 Brenz r. Ger.
191 F3 Brenzone Italy
190 F3 Brescia Italy
190 F3 Brescia prov. Lombardia Italy
165 C3 Breskens Neth.
Breslau Pol. see Wrocław
156 B2 Bresle r. France
156 C3 Bresles France
190 E3 Bressana Bottarone Italy
191 G2 Bressanone Italy
146 □G1 Bressay i. Scotland U.K.
163 D5 Bressols France
162 B2 Bressuire France
136 B1 Brest Belarus
158 B3 Brest France
179 G5 Brestanica Slovenia
179 G4 Bresternica Slovenia
Brest-Litovsk Belarus see Brest
Brest Oblast admin. div. Belarus see Brestskaya Voblasts'
197 E4 Brestovac Srbija Yugo.
177 K6 Brestovăț Romania
Brestskaya Oblast' admin. div. Belarus see Brestskaya Voblasts'
138 E5 Brestskaya Voblasts' admin. div. Belarus
158 D3 Bretagne admin. reg. France
163 C5 Bretagne-d'Armagnac France
250 C6 Bretana Peru
216 □1b Bretanha São Miguel Azores
197 H2 Brețcu Romania
158 E3 Breteil France
163 D4 Bretenoux France
159 G3 Breteuil Haute-Normandie France
156 C3 Breteuil Picardie France
158 E5 Brétignolles-sur-Mer France
156 C4 Brétigny-sur-Orge France
171 F4 Bretnig Ger.
182 E3 Bretocino Spain
222 H4 Breton Alta Can.
246 C2 Breton, Cayo i. Cuba
159 G3 Bretoncelles France
237 F6 Breton Sound b. LA U.S.A.
235 D2 Breton Woods NJ U.S.A.
172 C2 Bretten Ger.
150 E1 Bretton Flintshire, Wales U.K.
159 F2 Brettville-sur-Laize France
172 B2 Bretzenheim Ger.
172 D2 Bretzfeld Ger.
252 B2 Breu r. Brazil/Peru
172 D2 Breuberg-Neustadt Ger.
157 G5 Breuches France
157 G5 Breuchin r. France
164 E3 Breugel Neth.
190 C3 Breuil-Cervinia Italy
162 B3 Breuil-Magné France
156 B4 Breuilpont France
164 E2 Breukelen Neth.
169 E4 Breuna Ger.
157 F4 Breuvannes-en-Bassigny France
231 D5 Brevard NC U.S.A.
251 I5 Breves Brazil
142 C2 Brevik Norway
142 E2 Breviken Sweden
160 E2 Brévon r. France
169 E4 Brevörde Ger.
83 F2 Brewarrina N.S.W. Austr.
233 □I2 Brewer ME U.S.A.
206 C5 Brewerville Liberia
150 E2 Brewood Staffordshire, England U.K.
236 D3 Brewster NE U.S.A.
235 E1 Brewster NY U.S.A.
232 C4 Brewster OH U.S.A.
238 C1 Brewster WA U.S.A.
Brewster, Kap c. Greenland see Kangikajik
231 C6 Brewton AL U.S.A.
215 G2 Breyten S. Africa
139 K2 Breytovo Rus. Fed.
177 I2 Breza Slovakia
Brezhnev Rus. Fed. see Naberezhnyye Chelny
176 F3 Březí Czech Rep.
188 E3 Brežice Slovenia
179 H4 Breznica Croatia
176 C2 Březnice Czech Rep.
197 F4 Breznik Bulg.
197 F3 Breznița-Motru Romania
197 F5 Breznitsa Bulg.
171 E5 Březno Czech Rep.
177 I3 Brezno Slovakia
156 B4 Brézolles France
177 G2 Březová Czech Rep.
177 G3 Brezová pod Bradlom Slovakia
177 L3 Brezovec Slovakia
179 F4 Brezovica Slovenia
197 G4 Brezovo Bulg.
188 F3 Brezovo Polje hill Croatia
208 D3 Bria C.A.R.
162 D3 Briance r. France
161 E4 Briançon France
241 K3 Brian Head mt. UT U.S.A.
235 E1 Briarcliff Manor NY U.S.A.
160 A1 Briare France
163 D5 Briatexte France
195 F4 Briatico Italy
85 H5 Bribie Island Qld Austr.
161 F4 Bric Bouchet mt. France/Italy
136 D3 Briceni Moldova
161 E4 Bric Froid mt. France/Italy
Brichany Moldova see Briceni
190 C4 Bricherasio Italy
147 C3 Brickeens Rep. of Ireland
234 B2 Brickerville PA U.S.A.
234 D3 Bricksboro NJ U.S.A.
235 D2 Brick Township NJ U.S.A.
157 E4 Bricon France
158 E2 Bricquebec France
147 D4 Bride r. Rep. of Ireland
161 E3 Brides-les-Bains France
151 I3 Bridge Kent, England U.K.
235 F2 Bridgehampton NY U.S.A.
147 E4 Bridgeland Rep. of Ireland
226 D5 Bridgeman MI U.S.A.
147 D1 Bridgend Rep. of Ireland
146 F5 Bridgend Angus, Scotland U.K.
146 B6 Bridgend Argyll and Bute, Scotland U.K.
150 D3 Bridgend Bridgend, Wales U.K.
146 E4 Bridgend Moray, Scotland U.K.
150 D3 Bridgend admin. div. Wales U.K.
146 E5 Bridge of Allan Stirling, Scotland U.K.
146 D5 Bridge of Balgie Perth and Kinross, Scotland U.K.
146 E5 Bridge of Cally Perth and Kinross, Scotland U.K.
146 E5 Bridge of Craigisla Angus, Scotland U.K.
146 F4 Bridge of Don Aberdeen, Scotland U.K.
146 F5 Bridge of Dun Angus, Scotland U.K.
146 F5 Bridge of Dye Aberdeenshire, Scotland U.K.
146 E5 Bridge of Earn Perth and Kinross, Scotland U.K.
146 E3 Bridge of Forss Highland, Scotland U.K.
146 D5 Bridge of Orchy Argyll and Bute, Scotland U.K.
146 □G1 Bridge of Walls Shetland, Scotland U.K.
146 D6 Bridge of Weir Renfrewshire, Scotland U.K.
231 C5 Bridgeport AL U.S.A.
240 H2 Bridgeport CA U.S.A.
233 G4 Bridgeport CT U.S.A.
227 F4 Bridgeport MI U.S.A.
236 C3 Bridgeport NE U.S.A.
234 C2 Bridgeport PA U.S.A.
237 D5 Bridgeport TX U.S.A.
238 E2 Bridger MT U.S.A.
238 F3 Bridger Peak WY U.S.A.
234 C3 Bridgeton NJ U.S.A.
87 C7 Bridgetown W.A. Austr.
247 □4 Bridgetown Barbados
225 H4 Bridgetown N.S. Can.
147 E4 Bridgetown Rep. of Ireland
233 F5 Bridgeville DE U.S.A.
83 F5 Bridgewater Tas. Austr.
225 H4 Bridgewater N.S. Can.
233 H4 Bridgewater MA U.S.A.
233 □J1 Bridgewater ME U.S.A.
233 F3 Bridgewater NY U.S.A.
232 D5 Bridgewater VA U.S.A.
82 E4 Bridgewater, Cape Vic. Austr.
150 E2 Bridgnorth Shropshire, England U.K.
233 □H2 Bridgton ME U.S.A.
150 D3 Bridgwater Somerset, England U.K.
150 D3 Bridgwater Bay England U.K.
176 G2 Břidličná Czech Rep.
149 I3 Bridlington East Riding of Yorkshire, England U.K.
149 I3 Bridlington Bay England U.K.
83 F5 Bridport Tas. Austr.
150 E4 Bridport Dorset, England U.K.
162 C3 Brie France
156 C4 Brie reg. France
158 C3 Briec France
156 C4 Brie-Comte-Robert France
169 C5 Briedel Ger.
Brieg Pol. see Brzeg
164 D3 Brielle Neth.
156 E4 Brienne-le-Château France
160 C2 Briennon France
156 D4 Brienon-sur-Armançon France
190 D2 Brienz Switz.
193 H4 Brienza Italy
190 D2 Brienzer Rothorn mt. Switz.
190 C2 Brienzer See l. Switz.
234 A1 Brier Mountain hill PA U.S.A.
232 C5 Briery Knob mt. WV U.S.A.
171 F3 Briescht Ger.
170 D3 Brieselang Ger.
171 F3 Briesen Ger.
171 E4 Brieske Ger.
171 F3 Brieskow-Finkenheerd Ger.
171 F4 Briesnig Ger.
168 F2 Brietlingen Ger.
157 E3 Brieuilles-sur-Bar France
183 H2 Brieva de Cameros Spain
157 F3 Briey France
190 C2 Brig Switz.
172 C4 Brigach r. Ger.
235 D3 Brigantine NJ U.S.A.
149 I4 Brigg North Lincolnshire, England U.K.
238 F3 Briggsdale CO U.S.A.
226 C4 Briggsville WI U.S.A.
149 F3 Brigham Cumbria, England U.K.
238 D3 Brigham City UT U.S.A.
149 H4 Brighouse West Yorkshire, England U.K.
151 F4 Brighstone Isle of Wight, England U.K.
83 F4 Bright Vic. Austr.
151 I3 Brightlingsea Essex, England U.K.
227 I3 Brighton Ont. Can.
81 C6 Brighton South I. N.Z.
151 G4 Brighton Brighton and Hove, England U.K.
238 F4 Brighton CO U.S.A.
227 F4 Brighton MI U.S.A.
232 E3 Brighton NY U.S.A.
232 B5 Brighton WV U.S.A.
151 G4 Brighton and Hove admin. div. England U.K.
85 E4 Brighton Downs Qld Austr.
81 D4 Brightwater South I. N.Z.
160 C3 Brignais France
163 C5 Brignemont France
158 B3 Brignogan-Plage France
161 E5 Brignoles France
146 D5 Brig o'Turk Stirling, Scotland U.K.
151 G2 Brigstock Northamptonshire, England U.K.
183 H4 Brihuega Spain
206 A3 Brikama Gambia
226 C3 Brillion WI U.S.A.
157 F4 Brillon-en-Barrois France
169 D4 Brilon Ger.
149 H4 Brimington Derbyshire, England U.K.
226 E2 Brimley MI U.S.A.
226 B2 Brimson MN U.S.A.
247 □2 Brimstone Hill Fortress National Park St Kitts and Nevis
184 C2 Brinches Port.
182 D3 Brincones Spain
195 G2 Brindisi Italy
195 G2 Brindisi prov. Puglia Italy
193 H4 Brindisi Montagna Italy
82 C2 Bring, Lake salt flat S.A. Austr.
188 E3 Brinje Croatia
237 F5 Brinkley AR U.S.A.
261 F2 Brinkmann Arg.
168 C2 Brinkum Niedersachsen Ger.
168 D2 Brinkum Niedersachsen Ger.
82 D3 Brinkworth S.A. Austr.
160 B1 Brinon-sur-Beuvron France
159 I4 Brinon-sur-Sauldre France
149 H4 Brinsley Nottinghamshire, England U.K.
157 G4 Brin-sur-Seille France
149 H4 Brinsworth South Yorkshire, England U.K.
161 B4 Brion France
183 H2 Briones Spain
159 G2 Brionne France
161 B3 Brioude France
162 B2 Brioux-sur-Boutonne France
159 F3 Briouze France
225 G2 Brisay Que. Can.
85 H5 Brisbane Qld Austr.
191 G4 Brisighella Italy
159 F4 Brissac-Quince France
233 □J1 Bristol N.B. Can.
150 E3 Bristol Bristol, England U.K.
150 E3 Bristol admin. div. England U.K.
233 G4 Bristol CT U.S.A.
231 C6 Bristol FL U.S.A.
234 B4 Bristol MD U.S.A.
233 H3 Bristol NH U.S.A.
234 D2 Bristol PA U.S.A.
233 H4 Bristol RI U.S.A.
232 B6 Bristol TN U.S.A.
233 G2 Bristol VT U.S.A.
220 B4 Bristol Bay AK U.S.A.
150 C3 Bristol Channel est. England U.K.
241 I4 Bristol Mountains CA U.S.A.
151 I2 Briston Norfolk, England U.K.
237 D5 Bristow OK U.S.A.
150 E4 Brit r. England U.K.
Britannia Island Î. Loyauté New Caledonia see Maré
182 B3 Britelo Port.
262 S2 British Antarctic Territory Antarctica
222 F5 British Columbia prov. Can.
221 J1 British Empire Range mts Nunavut Can.
British Guiana country S. America see Guyana
British Honduras country Central America see Belize
88 C7 British Indian Ocean Territory terr. Indian Ocean
264 J6 British Isles N. Atlantic Ocean
British Solomon Islands country S. Pacific Ocean see Solomon Islands
179 F4 Britof Slovenia
Brito Godins Angola see Kiwaba N'zogi
215 F1 Brits S. Africa
214 D4 Britstown S. Africa
147 E3 Brittas Rep. of Ireland
147 E4 Brittas Bay Rep. of Ireland
146 B4 Brittle, Loch b. Scotland U.K.
236 D2 Britton SD U.S.A.
170 E3 Britz Ger.
162 D3 Brive-la-Gaillarde France
161 B3 Brives-Charensac France
183 G2 Briviesca Spain
158 E2 Brix France
178 D3 Brixen im Thale Austria
150 D4 Brixham Torbay, England U.K.
Brixia Italy see Brescia
178 C3 Brixlegg Austria
151 G2 Brixworth Northamptonshire, England U.K.
191 I3 Brkini reg. Slovenia
Brlik Zhambylskaya Oblast' Kazakh. see Birlik
121 H4 Brlik Zhambylskaya Oblast' Kazakh.
176 F2 Brněnský kraj admin. reg. Czech Rep.
171 F5 Brniště Czech Rep.
176 F2 Brno Czech Rep.
143 G2 Bro Sweden
Broach Gujarat India see Bharuch
231 D5 Broad r. SC U.S.A.
233 F3 Broadalbin NY U.S.A.
87 D6 Broad Arrow W.A. Austr.
224 E3 Broadback r. Que. Can.
146 B3 Broad Bay Scotland U.K.
150 D4 Broadclyst Devon, England U.K.
83 F4 Broadford Vic. Austr.
147 C4 Broadford Clare Rep. of Ireland
147 C4 Broadford Limerick Rep. of Ireland
146 C4 Broadford Highland, Scotland U.K.
147 B2 Broad Haven b. Rep. of Ireland
150 B3 Broad Haven Pembrokeshire, Wales U.K.
150 E2 Broad Heath Worcestershire, England U.K.
146 E6 Broad Law hill Scotland U.K.
150 E4 Broadmayne Dorset, England U.K.
84 C3 Broadmere N.T. Austr.
151 H4 Broad Oak East Sussex, England U.K.
85 G4 Broad Sound sea chan. Qld Austr.
85 G4 Broad Sound Channel Qld Austr.
85 G4 Broadsound Range hills Qld Austr.
151 I3 Broadstairs Kent, England U.K.
238 F2 Broadus MT U.S.A.
223 K5 Broadview Sask. Can.
83 H2 Broadwater N.S.W. Austr.
236 C3 Broadwater NE U.S.A.
147 E4 Broadway Rep. of Ireland
151 F2 Broadway Worcestershire, England U.K.
232 D5 Broadway VA U.S.A.
150 E4 Broadwey Dorset, England U.K.
150 E4 Broadwindsor Dorset, England U.K.
80 D1 Broadwood North I. N.Z.
168 E1 Broager Denmark
143 F3 Broby Sweden
190 C2 Broc Switz.
163 B4 Brocas France
138 D3 Brocēni Latvia
146 B4 Brochel Highland, Scotland U.K.
223 K3 Brochet Man. Can.
149 G4 Brock r. England U.K.
168 E2 Brockel Niedersachsen Ger.
168 F3 Bröckel Ger.
169 F4 Brocken mt. Ger.
151 F4 Brockenhurst Hampshire, England U.K.
86 C4 Brockman, Mount W.A. Austr.
232 E3 Brockport NY U.S.A.
232 D4 Brockport PA U.S.A.
233 H3 Brockton MA U.S.A.
234 B2 Brockton PA U.S.A.
169 D3 Brockum Ger.
224 F4 Brockville Ont. Can.
233 □J2 Brockway N.B. Can.
232 D4 Brockway PA U.S.A.
150 E3 Brockworth Gloucestershire, England U.K.
232 D3 Brocton NY U.S.A.
196 E5 Brod Macedonia
176 G2 Brodek u Přerova Czech Rep.
170 D1 Broderstorf Ger.
136 E3 Brodets'ke Ukr.
221 J2 Brodeur Peninsula Nunavut Can.
226 C4 Brodhead WI U.S.A.
234 C2 Brodhead r. PA U.S.A.
234 C2 Brodheadsville PA U.S.A.

Brodick to Burstow

288

146 C6 Brodick North Ayrshire, Scotland U.K.
232 D6 Brodnax VA U.S.A.
175 H2 Brodnica Kujawsko-Pomorskie Pol.
174 E3 Brodnica Wielkopolskie Pol.
176 G3 Brodské Slovakia
174 C4 Brody Pol.
136 C2 Brody Ukr.
215 E2 Broedersput S. Africa
164 F3 Broekhuizenvorst Neth.
215 E4 Broekpoort r. S. Africa
159 G2 Broglie France
169 C5 Brohl Ger.
170 E2 Brohm Ger.
160 D1 Broin France
174 D2 Brojce Pol.
175 J3 Brok Pol.
175 J3 Brok r. Pol.
168 E2 Brokdorf Ger.
142 C2 Brokefjell mt. Norway
87 C7 Broke Inlet W.A. Austr.
237 E4 Broken Arrow OK U.S.A.
83 G3 Broken Bay N.S.W. Austr.
236 D3 Broken Bow NE U.S.A.
237 E5 Broken Bow OK U.S.A.
233 E5 Brokenburg VA U.S.A.
223 L5 Brokenhead r. Man. Can.
82 E2 Broken Hill N.S.W. Austr.
Broken Hill Zambia see Kabwe
265 K7 Broken Plateau sea feature Indian Ocean
251 H3 Brokopondo Suriname
Brokopondo Stuwmeer resr Suriname see Professor van Blommestein Meer
168 E2 Brokstedt Ger.
194 D4 Brolo Sicilia Italy
173 E2 Brombachsee l. Ger.
Bromberg Pol. see Bydgoszcz
168 F3 Brome Ger.
150 E2 Bromfield Shropshire, England U.K.
151 G2 Bromham Bedfordshire, England U.K.
150 E3 Bromham Wiltshire, England U.K.
151 G3 Bromley Greater London, England U.K.
161 A4 Brommat France
149 H3 Brompton North Yorkshire, England U.K.
149 H3 Brompton on Swale North Yorkshire, England U.K.
143 G3 Brömsebro Sweden
150 E2 Bromsgrove Worcestershire, England U.K.
169 D4 Bromskirchen Ger.
150 E2 Bromyard Herefordshire, England U.K.
160 C3 Bron France
150 D2 Bronaber Gwynedd, Wales U.K.
183 I4 Bronchales Spain
142 C3 Brønderslev Denmark
206 E5 Brong-Ahafo admin. reg. Ghana
190 E3 Broni Italy
215 G1 Bronkhorstspruit S. Africa
139 L4 Bronnitsy Rus. Fed.
140 K2 Brønnøysund Norway
231 D6 Bronson FL U.S.A.
226 E5 Bronson MI U.S.A.
194 D5 Bronte Sicilia Italy
235 E2 Bronx County county NY U.S.A.
136 D2 Bronyts'ka Huta Ukr.
190 E3 Bronzone, Monte mt. Italy
151 I2 Brooke Norfolk, England U.K.
232 E5 Brooke VA U.S.A.
147 D2 Brookeborough Northern Ireland U.K.
92 A4 Brooke's Point Phil.
235 E1 Brookfield CT U.S.A.
236 E4 Brookfield MO U.S.A.
226 C4 Brookfield WI U.S.A.
237 F6 Brookhaven MS U.S.A.
238 A3 Brookings OR U.S.A.
236 D2 Brookings SD U.S.A.
234 C3 Brookland Terrace DE U.S.A.
233 H3 Brookline MA U.S.A.
226 B5 Brooklyn IL U.S.A.
227 E4 Brooklyn MI U.S.A.
234 B3 Brooklyn Park MD U.S.A.
226 A3 Brooklyn Park MN U.S.A.
232 D6 Brookneal VA U.S.A.
226 A3 Brook Park MN U.S.A.
223 I5 Brooks Alta Can.
233 □I2 Brooks ME U.S.A.
232 C6 Brooks WV U.S.A.
262 T2 Brooks, Cape Antarctica
222 C2 Brooks Brook Y.T. Can.
234 C3 Brookside DE U.S.A.
220 D3 Brooks Range mts AK U.S.A.
226 D5 Brookston IN U.S.A.
226 A2 Brookston MN U.S.A.
231 D6 Brooksville FL U.S.A.
232 A5 Brooksville KY U.S.A.
87 C7 Brookton W.A. Austr.
233 □J2 Brookton ME U.S.A.
230 C4 Brookville IN U.S.A.
232 D4 Brookville PA U.S.A.
146 C4 Broom, Loch inlet Scotland U.K.
86 D3 Broome W.A. Austr.
87 C7 Broomehill W.A. Austr.
147 E2 Broomfield Rep. of Ireland
151 H3 Broomfield Essex, England U.K.
158 D3 Broons France
161 A3 Broquiès France
146 E3 Brora Highland, Scotland U.K.
146 E3 Brora r. Scotland U.K.
143 F4 Brösarp Sweden
150 E2 Broseley Shropshire, England U.K.
136 C3 Broshniv Osada Ukr.
147 B4 Brosna Rep. of Ireland
147 D3 Brosna r. Rep. of Ireland
162 B3 Brossac France
140 L1 Brostadbotn Norway
197 G2 Broșteni Romania
232 D6 Brosville VA U.S.A.
256 C5 Brotas Brazil
184 B2 Brotas Port.
254 E5 Brotas de Macaúbas Brazil
238 E3 Brothers OR U.S.A.
186 C2 Broto Spain
157 F4 Brottes France
149 I3 Brotton Redcar and Cleveland, England U.K.
156 B4 Brou France
149 G3 Brough Cumbria, England U.K.
149 I4 Brough East Riding of Yorkshire, England U.K.
146 E3 Brough Highland, Scotland U.K.
148 B4 Broughal Rep. of Ireland
146 E2 Brough Head hd Scotland U.K.
147 E2 Broughshane Northern Ireland U.K.
150 E1 Broughton Flintshire, Wales U.K.
151 G2 Broughton Northamptonshire, England U.K.
149 I4 Broughton North Lincolnshire, England U.K.
146 E6 Broughton Scottish Borders, Scotland U.K.
151 F2 Broughton Astley Leicestershire, England U.K.
149 F3 Broughton in Furness Cumbria, England U.K.
Broughton Island Nunavut Can. see Qikiqtarjuaq
146 F2 Broughtown Orkney, Scotland U.K.
176 F1 Broumov Czech Rep.
157 E4 Brousseval France
157 G4 Brouvelieures France
164 C3 Brouwershaven Neth.
136 F2 Brovary Ukr.
85 G5 Brovinia Qld Austr.
142 C3 Brovst Denmark
236 E2 Browerville MN U.S.A.
87 C6 Brown, Lake salt flat W.A. Austr.
82 D3 Brown, Mount hill S.A. Austr.
82 C3 Brown, Point S.A. Austr.
227 F4 Brown City MI U.S.A.
85 E3 Brown Creek r. Qld Austr.
226 D4 Brown Deer WI U.S.A.
149 G4 Brown Edge Staffordshire, England U.K.
87 E5 Browne Range hills W.A. Austr.
237 C5 Brownfield TX U.S.A.
151 F2 Brownhills West Midlands, England U.K.
238 D1 Browning MT U.S.A.
240 I4 Brown Mountain CA U.S.A.
226 A4 Brownsdale MN U.S.A.
234 D3 Browns Mills NJ U.S.A.
246 □ Brown's Town Jamaica
230 C4 Brownstown IN U.S.A.
234 B2 Brownstown PA U.S.A.
236 D2 Browns Valley MN U.S.A.
230 C4 Brownsville KY U.S.A.
232 D4 Brownsville PA U.S.A.
237 F5 Brownsville TN U.S.A.
237 D7 Brownsville TX U.S.A.
251 H3 Brownsweg Suriname
233 □I2 Brownville ME U.S.A.
233 □I2 Brownville Junction ME U.S.A.
237 D6 Brownwood TX U.S.A.
86 D2 Browse Island W.A. Austr.
146 E6 Broxburn West Lothian, Scotland U.K.
190 C2 Broye r. Switz.
156 D4 Broyes France
171 F5 Brozany Czech Rep.
182 D5 Brozas Spain
138 G5 Brozha Belarus
190 F3 Brozzo Italy
176 E2 Brtnice Czech Rep.
146 E5 Bruar Water r. Scotland U.K.
156 C2 Bruay-la-Bussière France
237 F5 Bruce MS U.S.A.
226 B3 Bruce WI U.S.A.
86 C4 Bruce, Mount W.A. Austr.
226 E2 Bruce Crossing MI U.S.A.
232 B3 Bruce Peninsula Ont. Can.
87 C6 Bruce Rock W.A. Austr.
157 H4 Bruche r. France
168 E3 Bruchhausen-Vilsen Ger.
169 D5 Bruchköbel Ger.
172 B2 Bruchmühlbach Ger.
172 C2 Bruchsal Ger.
172 B2 Bruchweiler-Bärenbach Ger.
171 D3 Brück Ger.
178 D3 Bruck an der Großglocknerstraße Austria
179 H2 Bruck an der Leitha Austria
179 G3 Bruck an der Mur Austria
173 F3 Bruckberg Ger.
172 D2 Brücken Ger.
172 B2 Brücken (Pfalz) Ger.
172 G2 Bruck in der Oberpfalz Ger.
179 F2 Brückl Austria
173 F4 Bruckmühl Ger.
195 E5 Brucoli Sicilia Italy
175 H3 Brudzeń Duży Pol.
174 G3 Brudzew Pol.
162 B3 Brue r. England U.K.
161 D5 Brue-Auriac France
170 C2 Brüel Ger.
159 I5 Bruère-Allichamps France
165 C4 Brugelette Belgium
Bruges Belgium see Brugge
190 D1 Brugg Switz.
165 C3 Brugge Belgium
169 E3 Brüggen Ger.
169 B4 Brüggen Ger.
194 E6 Brugnato Italy
191 E4 Brugnera Italy
163 D5 Bruguières France
140 I3 Bruhagen Norway
172 C2 Brühl Ger.
169 B5 Brühl Ger.
227 F5 Bruin KY U.S.A.
232 D4 Bruin PA U.S.A.
164 D3 Bruinisse Neth.
241 L2 Bruin Point mt. UT U.S.A.
214 A1 Brukkaros, Mount Namibia
222 G4 Brûlé Alta Can.
226 B2 Brule WI U.S.A.
159 F4 Brûlon France
165 D5 Brûly Belgium
257 E4 Brumadinho Brazil
254 E5 Brumado Brazil
157 H4 Brumath France
164 F2 Brummen Neth.
177 H2 Brumov-Bylnice Czech Rep.
177 G1 Brumovice Czech Rep.
141 J3 Brumunddal Norway
192 C2 Bruna r. Italy
147 E3 Brú Na Bóinne tourist site Meath Rep. of Ireland
170 C3 Brunau Ger.
151 I2 Brundall Norfolk, England U.K.
151 I2 Brundish Suffolk, England U.K.
Brundisium Italy see Brindisi
238 D3 Bruneau ID U.S.A.
238 D3 Bruneau r. ID U.S.A.
238 D3 Bruneau, East Fork r. Idaho/Nevada U.S.A.
238 D3 Bruneau, West Fork r. Idaho/Nevada U.S.A.
156 E3 Brunehamel France
95 F1 Brunei country Asia
Brunei Brunei see Bandar Seri Begawan
95 F1 Brunei Bay Malaysia
183 G4 Brunete Spain
84 C3 Brunette Downs N.T. Austr.
140 K3 Brunflo Sweden
191 G2 Brunico Italy
163 D4 Bruniquel France
179 G4 Brunn Austria
Brünn Czech Rep. see Brno
170 E2 Brunn Ger.
143 G2 Brunna Sweden
179 H2 Brunn am Gebirge Austria
170 D1 Brunnen Switz.
81 C5 Brunner, Lake South I. N.Z.
234 B2 Brunnerville PA U.S.A.
223 J4 Bruno Sask. Can.
226 A2 Bruno MN U.S.A.
168 E2 Brunsbüttel Ger.
165 E4 Brunssum Neth.
157 H5 Brunstatt France
Brunswick Ger. see Braunschweig
231 D6 Brunswick GA U.S.A.
232 E5 Brunswick MD U.S.A.
233 □I3 Brunswick ME U.S.A.
236 E4 Brunswick MO U.S.A.
232 C4 Brunswick OH U.S.A.
259 C9 Brunswick, Peninsula de pen. Chile
86 E2 Brunswick Bay W.A. Austr.
83 H2 Brunswick Head N.S.W. Austr.
87 B7 Brunswick Junction W.A. Austr.
176 G2 Bruntál Czech Rep.
215 H3 Bruntville S. Africa
83 F5 Bruny Island Tas. Austr.
196 E4 Brus Srbija Yugo.
Brusa Turkey see Bursa
178 C4 Brusago Italy
170 C2 Brüsewitz Ger.
236 C3 Brush CO U.S.A.
223 F2 Brushton NY U.S.A.
190 F2 Brusio Switz.
177 I3 Brusno Slovakia
139 J3 Brusovo Rus. Fed.
255 C8 Brusque Brazil
161 A5 Brusque France
Brussel Belgium see Bruxelles
Brussels Belgium see Bruxelles
227 G4 Brussels Ont. Can.
170 F2 Brüssow Ger.
177 L4 Brusturi Romania
197 H2 Brusturi-Drăgănești Romania
174 F2 Brusy Pol.
136 E2 Brusyliv Ukr.
83 F4 Bruthen Vic. Austr.
150 E3 Bruton Somerset, England U.K.
169 C5 Bruttig-Fankel Ger.
165 D4 Bruxelles Belgium
157 G4 Bruyères France
156 D3 Bruyères-et-Montbérault France
158 E3 Bruz France
177 H2 Brvniště Slovakia
175 I3 Brwinów Pol.
236 G3 Bryan OH U.S.A.
237 D6 Bryan TX U.S.A.
82 D3 Bryan, Mount hill S.A. Austr.
262 S2 Bryan Coast Antarctica
137 J3 Bryanka Ukr.
139 J5 Bryansk Rus. Fed.
139 I5 Bryanskaya Oblast' admin. div. Rus. Fed.
Bryansk Oblast admin. div. Rus. Fed. see Bryanskaya Oblast'
129 E1 Bryanskoye Rus. Fed.
237 E5 Bryant AR U.S.A.
226 C3 Bryant WI U.S.A.
237 E4 Bryant Creek r. MO U.S.A.
233 □H2 Bryant Pond ME U.S.A.
241 M5 Bryce Mountains AZ U.S.A.
150 □ Bryher i. England U.K.
137 G4 Brylivka Ukr.
150 D1 Brymbo Wrexham, Wales U.K.
150 D3 Brynamman Carmarthenshire, Wales U.K.
142 A2 Bryne Norway
150 D1 Brynford Flintshire, Wales U.K.
175 H5 Brynica r. Pol.
135 G7 Bryn'kovskaya Rus. Fed.
150 D3 Brynmawr Blaenau Gwent, Wales U.K.
234 C2 Bryn Mawr PA U.S.A.
231 D5 Bryson City NC U.S.A.
135 G7 Bryukhovetskaya Rus. Fed.
136 B3 Bryukhovychi Ukr.
196 E3 Brzava r. Yugo.
175 F5 Brzeg Pol.
174 E4 Brzeg Dolny Pol.
175 G3 Brześć Kujawski Pol.
174 G3 Brześć nad Bugiem Belarus see Brest
175 I6 Brzesko Pol.
175 H6 Brzeszcze Pol.
174 G3 Brzezie Pol.
175 H4 Brzeziny Łódzkie Pol.
175 J6 Brzeziny Podkarpackie Pol.
174 G4 Brzeziny Wielkopolskie Pol.
175 H6 Brzeźnica Pol.
175 J5 Brzeźnica Pol.
174 G4 Brzeźnio Pol.
175 L4 Brzeźno Pol.
174 G3 Brzeźno Pol.
174 D2 Brzeźno Pol.
175 I4 Brzeźno Pol.
175 J6 Brzostek Pol.
177 J3 Brzotín Slovakia
175 J4 Brzóza Pol.
175 K6 Brzozów Pol.
175 K2 Brzozówka r. Pol.
175 H2 Brzuze Pol.
175 K5 Brzyska Wola Pol.
156 B4 Bû France
124 D4 Bū well Yemen
142 E3 Bua Sweden
158 C3 Buais France
78 □6 Buala Sta Isabel Solomon Is
Bouandougou Côte d'Ivoire see Bouandougou
182 B4 Buarcos Port.
94 C2 Buatan Sumatera Indon.
206 B4 Buba Guinea-Bissau
211 A5 Bubanza Burundi
173 F2 Bubenreuth Ger.
213 F4 Bubi r. Zimbabwe
158 C4 Bubry France
149 I4 Bubwith East Riding of Yorkshire, England U.K.
199 E2 Buca Turkey
199 G3 Bucak Turkey
177 G3 Bučany Slovakia
250 C3 Bucaramanga Col.
92 C4 Bucas Grande i. Phil.
86 D3 Buccaneer Archipelago is W.A. Austr.
194 D5 Buccheri Sicilia Italy
193 G4 Bucchianico Italy
194 D2 Bucciana, Monte mt. Italy
190 E3 Buccinasco Italy
193 H4 Buccino Italy
197 H2 Bucecea Romania
197 G3 Bucegi, Munții mts Romania
182 A4 Bucelas Port.
160 D1 Bucey-lès-Gy France
173 E3 Buch Ger.
136 C3 Buchach Ukr.
173 G3 Buch am Erlbach Ger.
83 G4 Buchan Vic. Austr.
206 C5 Buchanan Liberia
231 C5 Buchanan GA U.S.A.
226 D5 Buchanan MI U.S.A.
235 E1 Buchanan NY U.S.A.
232 D6 Buchanan VA U.S.A.
85 F4 Buchanan, Lake salt flat Qld Austr.
87 D5 Buchanan, Lake salt flat W.A. Austr.
225 J3 Buchans Nfld. Can.
Bucharest Romania see București
173 G3 Buchbach Ger.
169 C5 Büchel Ger.
168 F2 Büchen Ger.
172 D2 Buchen (Odenwald) Ger.
172 C4 Buchenbach Baden-Württemberg Ger.
173 F2 Büchenbach Ger.
173 E4 Buchenberg Ger.
172 B2 Büchenbeuren Ger.
168 D3 Bucholz Ger.
168 E3 Buchholz (Aller) Ger.
169 C5 Buchholz (Westerwald) Ger.
179 F2 Buchkirchen Austria
173 H3 Büchlberg Ger.
173 E3 Bucholoe Ger.
176 G2 Buchlovice Czech Rep.
146 D5 Buchlyvie Stirling, Scotland U.K.
168 E2 Bucholz in der Nordheide Ger.
190 E1 Buchs Switz.
260 A5 Buchupureo Chile
156 B3 Buchy France
191 G5 Bucine Italy
234 B3 Buck PA U.S.A.
151 G2 Buckden Cambridgeshire, England U.K.
149 G3 Buckden North Yorkshire, England U.K.
169 E3 Bückeburg Ger.
168 E3 Bücken Ger.
241 K5 Buckeye AZ U.S.A.
150 D4 Buckfastleigh Devon, England U.K.
232 C5 Buckhannon WV U.S.A.
232 C5 Buckhannon r. WV U.S.A.
146 E5 Buckhaven Fife, Scotland U.K.
227 H3 Buckhorn Ont. Can.
146 F4 Buckie Moray, Scotland U.K.
227 J3 Buckingham Que. Can.
151 G2 Buckingham Buckinghamshire, England U.K.
234 C2 Buckingham PA U.S.A.
232 D6 Buckingham VA U.S.A.
84 C2 Buckingham Bay N.T. Austr.
151 G3 Buckinghamshire admin. div. England U.K.
220 B3 Buckland AK U.S.A.
214 D3 Bucklands S. Africa
85 G5 Buckland Tableland reg. Qld Austr.
82 D3 Buckleboo S.A. Austr.
151 F3 Bucklebury West Berkshire, England U.K.
263 K2 Buckle Island Antarctica
150 D1 Buckley Flintshire, Wales U.K.
226 C5 Buckley IL U.S.A.
237 D4 Bucklin KS U.S.A.
170 F3 Buckow Märkische Schweiz Ger.
146 F4 Bucksburn Aberdeen, Scotland U.K.
234 C2 Bucks County county PA U.S.A.
241 K4 Buckskin Mountains AZ U.S.A.
240 G2 Bucks Mountain CA U.S.A.
233 □I2 Bucksport ME U.S.A.
170 D3 Bückwitz Ger.
176 G2 Bučovice Czech Rep.
209 B6 Buco-Zau Angola
177 K4 Bucsa Hungary
197 G3 Bucșani Romania
197 H3 București Romania
156 D3 Bucy-lès-Pierrepont France
232 B4 Bucyrus OH U.S.A.
175 H6 Buczek Pol.
186 D4 Buda, Illa de i. Spain
139 H5 Buda-Koshalyova Belarus
177 H4 Budakeszi Hungary
96 A2 Budalin Myanmar
177 H4 Budaörs Hungary
177 H4 Budapest Hungary
116 D3 Budaun Uttar Prad. India
87 B6 Budd, Mount hill W.A. Austr.
83 F2 Budda N.S.W. Austr.
263 H2 Budd Coast Antarctica
171 C3 Büddenstedt Ger.
234 D2 Budd Lake NJ U.S.A.
192 B4 Budduso Sardegna Italy
150 C4 Bude Cornwall, England U.K.
237 F6 Bude MS U.S.A.
150 C4 Bude Bay England U.K.
176 D2 Budějovický kraj admin. reg. Czech Rep.
165 E3 Budel Neth.
168 E1 Büdelsdorf Ger.
136 C3 Budenets' Ukr.
169 D5 Budenheim Ger.
129 D1 Budennovsk Rus. Fed.
Budennoye Belgorodskaya Oblast' Rus. Fed. see Krasnogvardeyskoye
184 B3 Budens Port.
85 H5 Buderim Qld Austr.
197 H3 Budești Romania
135 G6 Budhiya, Gebel mt. Egypt
128 A5 Budhlada Punjab India
183 H4 Budia Spain
169 E5 Büdingen Ger.
179 H4 Budinšćina Croatia
177 G2 Budišov nad Budišovkou Czech Rep.
174 F5 Budkowiczanka r. Pol.
150 D4 Budleigh Salterton Devon, England U.K.
139 I2 Budogoshch' Rus. Fed.
191 H2 Budoia Italy
106 B5 Budongquan Qinghai China
192 B4 Budoni Sardegna Italy
191 G4 Budrio Italy
175 J1 Budry Pol.
Búdszentmihály Hungary see Tiszavasvári
125 E3 Budū', Sabkhat al salt pan Saudi Arabia
197 F2 Budureasa Romania
177 L4 Buduslău Romania
196 D4 Budva Crna Gora Yugo.
Budweis Czech Rep. see České Budějovice
171 F5 Budyně nad Ohří Czech Rep.
175 H4 Budziszewice Pol.
175 H6 Budzów Pol.
174 E3 Budzyń Pol.
207 H5 Buea Cameroon
161 D4 Buëch r. France
240 G4 Buellton CA U.S.A.
186 B4 Bueña Spain
242 D3 Buena NJ U.S.A.
183 H5 Buenache de Alarcón Spain
183 H4 Buenache de la Sierra Spain
260 E4 Buena Esperanza Arg.
250 B4 Buenaventura Col.
242 D2 Buenaventura Mex.
183 G3 Buenaventura Spain
244 C4 Buenavista Mex.
Buena Vista i. N. Mariana Is see Tinian
92 B3 Buenavista Phil.
239 F4 Buena Vista CO U.S.A.
231 C5 Buena Vista GA U.S.A.
232 D6 Buena Vista VA U.S.A.
216 □3a Buenavista del Norte Tenerife Canary Is
183 F2 Buenavista de Valdavia Spain
183 H4 Buendia Spain
183 H4 Buendia, Embalse de resr Spain
209 B6 Buenga r. Angola
209 B6 Buengas Angola
257 B5 Buenópolis Brazil
261 E4 Buenos Aires Arg.
261 G5 Buenos Aires prov. Arg.
250 D5 Buenos Aires Col.
259 B7 Buenos Aires, Lago l. Arg./Chile
255 F5 Buerarema Brazil
250 B4 Buesaco Col.
160 E2 Buet, Le Mont mt. France
182 B2 Bueu Spain
185 G2 Bueuy, Cabeza de mt. Spain
242 D3 Bufa Mex.
222 H2 Buffalo r. Alta/N.W.T. Can.
236 E2 Buffalo MN U.S.A.
236 E4 Buffalo MO U.S.A.
237 E4 Buffalo NY U.S.A.
232 D3 Buffalo NY U.S.A.
232 B5 Buffalo OH U.S.A.
237 D4 Buffalo OK U.S.A.
236 C2 Buffalo SD U.S.A.
237 D6 Buffalo TX U.S.A.
226 B3 Buffalo WI U.S.A.
238 F2 Buffalo WY U.S.A.
237 E5 Buffalo r. AR U.S.A.
231 C5 Buffalo r. TN U.S.A.
226 B3 Buffalo r. WI U.S.A.
234 A2 Buffalo Creek r. PA U.S.A.
222 G3 Buffalo Head Hills Y.T. Can.
223 H4 Buffalo Head Prairie Alta Can.
238 D2 Buffalo Hump mt. ID U.S.A.
223 I4 Buffalo Narrows Sask. Can.
213 F4 Buffalo Range Zimbabwe
246 □ Buff Bay Jamaica
215 H3 Buffels r. Kwazulu-Natal S. Africa
214 C5 Buffels r. W. Cape S. Africa
214 D5 Buffelsdrif S. Africa
213 E4 Buffels Drift S. Africa
160 C2 Bufflières France
168 D3 Buffleben Ger.
231 C5 Buford GA U.S.A.
197 G3 Buftea Romania
175 L4 Bug r. Pol.
250 B4 Buga Col.
106 B2 Buga Mongolia
Buga Buga i. Vanuatu see Toga
177 I5 Bugac Hungary
210 B5 Bugala Island Uganda
83 G2 Bugaldie N.S.W. Austr.
207 G5 Bugana Nigeria
107 E1 Bugant Mongolia
163 E6 Bugarach, Pic de mt. France
Bugaz Ukr. see Zatoka
151 F2 Bugbrooke Northamptonshire, England U.K.
199 E1 Buğdaylı Balıkesir Turkey
122 C2 Bugdayli Turkm.
162 D3 Bugeat France
165 D5 Buggenhout Belgium
192 A5 Buggerru Sardegna Italy
172 B4 Buggingen Ger.
184 □ Bugio i. Madeira
193 F2 Bugnara Italy
163 B5 Bugnein France
188 F3 Bugojno Bos.-Herz.
107 I1 Bugt Nei Mongol China
92 B2 Buguey Phil.
135 K5 Bugul'ma Rus. Fed.
120 E3 Bugun' Kazakh.
Bügür Xinjiang China see Luntai
120 C1 Buguruslan Rus. Fed.
177 I4 Bugyi Hungary
122 C4 Buḩābād Iran
199 F3 Buharkent Turkey
213 F3 Buhera Zimbabwe
106 C4 Buh He r. China
92 B3 Buhi Phil.
238 E3 Buhl ID U.S.A.
226 A2 Buhl MN U.S.A.
172 C3 Bühlertal Ger.
172 D2 Bühlertann Ger.
172 D2 Bühlerzell Ger.
169 F3 Bühne Ger.
136 D2 Buhryn Ukr.
127 F3 Bühtan r. Turkey
211 B6 Buhu r. Tanz.
197 H2 Buhuși Romania
191 I2 Buia Italy
222 F3 Buick B.C. Can.
146 C5 Buie, Loch b. Scotland U.K.
150 D3 Builth Wells Powys, Wales U.K.
260 B3 Buin Chile
135 I5 Buinsk Rus. Fed.
107 H2 Buir Nur l. Mongolia
161 D4 Buis-les-Baronnies France
164 F1 Buitenpost Neth.
183 G4 Buitrago del Lozoya Spain
185 F3 Bujalance Spain
197 E4 Bujanovac Srbija Yugo.
186 C3 Bujaraloz Spain
197 G4 Bujoru Romania
211 A5 Bujumbura Burundi
179 H3 Bük Hungary
174 E3 Buk Pol.
99 K1 Bukachacha Rus. Fed.
209 E7 Bukama Dem. Rep. Congo
121 J1 Bukanskoye Rus. Fed.
120 F4 Bukantau, Gory hills Uzbek.
208 F5 Bukavu Dem. Rep. Congo
211 B6 Bukene Tanz.
120 F5 Bukhara Uzbek.
Bukhara Oblast admin. div. Uzbek. see Bukharskaya Oblast'
120 E4 Bukharskaya Oblast' admin. div. Uzbek.
Bukhoro Uzbek. see Bukhara
Bukhoro Wiloyati admin. div. Uzbek. see Bukharskaya Oblast'
121 K2 Bukhtarminskoye Vodokhranilishche resr Kazakh.
94 □ Bukit Timah hill Sing.
94 C3 Bukittinggi Sumatera Indon.
177 J3 Bükk mts Hungary
177 J4 Bükkábrány Hungary
177 J4 Bükkalja hills Hungary
114 C3 Bukkapatnam Andhra Prad. India
177 G5 Bükkösd Hungary
177 J4 Bükkszérc Hungary
171 D4 Buko Ger.
211 A5 Bukoba Tanz.
177 H2 Bukovec Czech Rep.
177 L2 Bukovské vrchy hills Slovakia
175 K5 Bukowa r. Pol.
174 F3 Bukowe Pol.
174 F4 Bukowice Pol.
174 G2 Bukowiec Pol.
171 G3 Bukowiec hill Pol.
174 F1 Bukowina Pol.
175 I6 Bukowina Tatrzańska Pol.
175 I6 Bukowno Pol.
174 F5 Bukowno Pol.
175 K6 Bukowsko Pol.
Bükreș Romania see București
136 F3 Buky Ukr.
122 C4 Būl, Kūh-e mt. Iran
206 B3 Bula Guinea-Bissau
209 B7 Bula Atumba Angola
190 D1 Bülach Switz.
107 F1 Bulag Mongolia
107 E1 Bulagtay Mongolia
83 H3 Bulahdelal N.S.W. Austr.
92 B3 Bulan Phil.
198 E2 Bulancak Turkey
116 D3 Bulandshahr Uttar Prad. India
127 F3 Bulanık Turkey
120 C1 Bulanovo Rus. Fed.
93 B2 Bulawa, Gunung mt. Indon.
213 F4 Bulawayo Zimbabwe
121 G1 Bulayevo Kazakh.
126 E3 Bulbul Syria
199 F2 Buldan Turkey
116 D5 Buldana Mahar. India
252 A2 Buldibuyo Peru
120 C2 Buldurta Kazakh.
Buldyrty Kazakh. see Buldurta
210 E3 Bulei well Eth.
215 H1 Bulembu Swaziland
151 F3 Bulford Wiltshire, England U.K.
106 D1 Bulgan Bulgan Mongolia
Bulgan Hovd Mongolia see Bürenhayrhan
106 B2 Bulgan Hovd Mongolia
106 D1 Bulgan Hövsgöl Mongolia
106 D2 Bulgan Ömnögovĭ Mongolia
106 D1 Bulgan prov. Mongolia
106 A2 Bulgan Gol r. Mongolia
Bulgar Respublika Tatarstan Rus. Fed. see Bolgar
197 I4 Bŭlgarevo Bulg.
197 G4 Bulgaria country Europe
Bŭlgariya country Europe see Bulgaria
193 H4 Bulgheria, Monte mt. Italy
157 F4 Bulgnéville France
129 C3 Bulgurlu Turkey
137 G5 Bulhanak r. Ukr.
168 D2 Bülkau Ger.
151 F2 Bulkington Warwickshire, England U.K.
222 D4 Bulkley Ranges mts B.C. Can.
175 I3 Bulkowo Pol.
185 F2 Bullaque r. Spain
183 H3 Bullas Spain
85 E5 Bullawarra, Lake salt flat Qld Austr.
169 C5 Bullay Ger.
190 C2 Bulle Switz.
83 E2 Bullea, Lake salt flat N.S.W. Austr.
81 C4 Buller r. South I. N.Z.
87 C6 Bullfinch W.A. Austr.
241 J4 Bullhead City AZ U.S.A.
83 G3 Bulli N.S.W. Austr.
165 F4 Büllingen Belgium
241 I4 Bullion Mountains CA U.S.A.
140 M2 Bullmark Sweden
84 B2 Bullo r. N.T. Austr.
183 H4 Bullones r. Spain
83 E2 Bulloo Downs Qld Austr.
83 E2 Bulloo Lake salt flat Qld Austr.
80 E4 Bulls North I. N.Z.
83 E5 Bulls Bridge CT U.S.A.
235 E1 Bullsville NY U.S.A.
156 C2 Bully-les-Mines France
84 C2 Bulman N.T. Austr.
84 C2 Bulman Gorge N.T. Austr.
151 F2 Bulmer Tye Essex, England U.K.
260 A5 Bulnes Chile
83 E4 Buloke, Lake dry lake Vic. Austr.
196 E5 Bulqizë Albania
192 B4 Bultei Sardegna Italy
215 F3 Bultfontein S. Africa
95 G2 Bulu, Gunung mt. Indon.
92 C5 Buluan Phil.
93 B4 Bulukumba Sulawesi Selatan Indon.
209 C6 Bulungu Bandundu Dem. Rep. Congo
209 D6 Bulungu Kasai Occidental Dem. Rep. Congo
121 F5 Bulungur Uzbek.
92 C3 Bulusan Phil.
215 G3 Bulwer S. Africa
171 F4 Bulz Romania
192 A4 Bulzi Sardegna Italy
78 □6 Buma Malaita Solomon Is
209 C6 Bumba Bandundu Dem. Rep. Congo
208 D4 Bumba Équateur Dem. Rep. Congo
106 E2 Bumbat Mongolia
197 F3 Bumbești-Jiu Romania
206 C4 Bumbuna Sierra Leone
96 B1 Bumpha Bum mt. Myanmar
147 C3 Bunacurry Rep. of Ireland
147 C1 Bunbeg Rep. of Ireland
87 B7 Bunbury W.A. Austr.
149 G4 Bunbury Cheshire, England U.K.
147 E4 Bunclody Rep. of Ireland
147 D1 Buncrana Rep. of Ireland
211 B5 Bunda Tanz.
85 H5 Bundaberg Qld Austr.
83 F2 Bundaleer Qld Austr.
83 G2 Bundarra N.S.W. Austr.
168 C2 Bunde Niedersachsen Ger.
169 D3 Bünde Ger.
172 B2 Bundenbach Ger.
168 C2 Bunderhee Ger.
116 C4 Bundi Rajasthan India
210 A4 Bundibugyo Uganda
147 C2 Bundoran Rep. of Ireland
117 F5 Bundu Bihar India
196 D5 Bunë r. Albania/Yugo.
207 H3 Bunga r. Nigeria
104 B3 Bunga-dake mt. Japan
94 B3 Bungalaut, Selat sea chan. Indon.
151 I2 Bungay Suffolk, England U.K.
96 C4 Bung Boraphet l. Thai.
83 G3 Bungendore N.S.W. Austr.
263 G2 Bunger Hills Antarctica
85 G5 Bungil Creek r. Qld Austr.
209 B6 Bungo Angola
210 B4 Bungoma Kenya
103 F7 Bungo-suidō sea chan. Japan
103 E7 Bungo-takada Japan
Bunguran, Kepulauan is Indon. see Natuna, Kepulauan
Bunguran, Pulau i. Indon. see Natuna Besar
208 F4 Bunia Dem. Rep. Congo
183 G2 Buniel Spain
177 L6 Bunila Romania
87 D6 Buningonia well W.A. Austr.
207 I4 Buni-Yadi Nigeria
116 C2 Bunji Jammu and Kashmir
237 F4 Bunker MO U.S.A.
85 H4 Bunker Group atolls Qld Austr.
209 E7 Bunkeya Dem. Rep. Congo
237 E6 Bunkie LA U.S.A.
141 K3 Bunkris Sweden
147 D4 Bunmahon Rep. of Ireland
147 B2 Bunnahowen Rep. of Ireland
147 C2 Bunnanadden Rep. of Ireland
231 D6 Bunnell FL U.S.A.
164 E2 Bunnik Neth.
147 B2 Bunnyconnellan Rep. of Ireland
80 E4 Bunnythorpe North I. N.Z.
187 C5 Buñol Spain
164 E2 Bunschoten-Spakenburg Neth.
177 L5 Bunteşti Romania
87 C6 Buntine W.A. Austr.
151 G3 Buntingford Hertfordshire, England U.K.
183 I3 Buñuel Spain
207 H4 Bununu Nigeria
126 D3 Bünyan Turkey
187 F5 Bunyola Spain
207 G3 Bunza Nigeria
188 F3 Buoač Bos.-Herz.
193 H4 Buonabitacolo Italy
193 G4 Buonalbergo Italy
192 D1 Buonconvento Italy
97 E4 Buôn Mê Thuôt Vietnam
193 H5 Buonvicino Italy
111 D6 Buqayq Saudi Arabia see Abqaiq
Buqtyrma Bögeni resr Kazakh. see Bukhtarminskoye Vodokhranilishche
210 F2 Buraan Somalia
87 C6 Burakin W.A. Austr.
121 K2 Buran Kazakh.
257 H2 Buranhaém r. Brazil
120 C2 Burannoye Rus. Fed.
192 B2 Burano r. Italy
210 E2 Burao Somalia
92 C4 Burauen Phil.
116 C5 Buray r. India
124 C2 Buraydah Saudi Arabia
134 K5 Burayevo Rus. Fed.
169 D5 Burbach Ger.
151 F3 Burbage Wiltshire, England U.K.
186 B3 Burbáguena Spain
240 H4 Burbank CA U.S.A.
192 B5 Burcei Sardegna Italy
137 H4 Burchak Ukr.
222 E4 Burchell Lake Ont. Can.
83 F3 Burcher N.S.W. Austr.
85 F3 Burdekin r. Qld Austr.
85 F4 Burdekin Falls Qld Austr.
160 D2 Burdet, Mont mt. France
Burdigala France see Bordeaux
165 E4 Burdinne Belgium
199 G3 Burdur Turkey
199 G3 Burdur prov. Turkey
199 G3 Burdur Gölü l. Turkey
Burdwan W. Bengal India see Barddhaman
210 C2 Burē Amhara Eth.
210 B2 Burē Oromia Eth.
151 I2 Bure r. England U.K.
161 D4 Bure, Pic de mt. France
140 M2 Bureå Sweden
100 E2 Bureinskiy Khrebet mts Rus. Fed.
183 F2 Burejo r. Spain
169 D4 Büren Ger.
164 E3 Buren Neth.
190 C1 Büren an der Aare Switz.
106 A2 Bürenhayrhan Hovd Mongolia
107 F2 Bürentsogt Mongolia
260 A5 Bureo r. Chile
151 I2 Bures Suffolk, England U.K.
100 D2 Bureya r. Rus. Fed.
Bureya-Pristan' Rus. Fed. see Novobureyskiy
Bureya Range mts Rus. Fed. see Bureinskiy Khrebet
227 G4 Burford Ont. Can.
151 F3 Burford Oxfordshire, England U.K.
163 C5 Burg France
171 F4 Burg Ger.
168 E2 Burg (Dithmarschen) Ger.
106 E1 Burgaltay Mongolia
182 E3 Burganes de Valverde Spain
197 H4 Burgas Bulg.
179 H3 Burgau Austria
173 E3 Burgau Ger.
184 B3 Burgau Port.
170 C1 Burg auf Fehmarn Ger.
231 E5 Burgaw NC U.S.A.
171 C3 Burg bei Magdeburg Ger.
173 E4 Burgberg im Allgäu Ger.
173 F3 Burgbernheim Ger.
169 C5 Burgbrohl Ger.
169 F3 Burgdorf Ger.
169 F3 Burgdorf Niedersachsen Ger.
190 C1 Burgdorf Switz.
172 E2 Burgebrach Ger.
171 C5 Bürgel Ger.
179 H3 Burgenland land Austria
225 J4 Burgeo Nfld. Can.
215 F4 Burgersdorp S. Africa
213 F5 Burgersfort S. Africa
214 E4 Burgerville S. Africa
87 D6 Burges, Mount hill W.A. Austr.
233 E6 Burgess VA U.S.A.
151 G4 Burgess Hill West Sussex, England U.K.
173 E2 Burghaslach Ger.
169 E5 Burghaun Ger.
173 G3 Burghausen Ger.
149 F3 Burgh by Sands Cumbria, England U.K.
151 F3 Burghclere Hampshire, England U.K.
146 E4 Burghead Moray, Scotland U.K.
173 F3 Burgheim Ger.
151 F3 Burghfield Common West Berkshire, England U.K.
164 C3 Burgh-Haamstede Neth.
150 E2 Burghill Herefordshire, England U.K.
149 J4 Burgh le Marsh Lincolnshire, England U.K.
194 C5 Burgio Sicilia Italy
194 D5 Burgio, Serra di hill Sicilia Italy
178 E2 Burgkirchen Austria
173 G3 Burgkirchen an der Alz Ger.
173 E2 Burgkunstadt Ger.
190 E1 Bürglen Thurgau Switz.
190 D2 Bürglen Uri Switz.
173 G2 Burglengenfeld Ger.
172 E2 Burgoberbach Ger.
183 G2 Burgohondo Spain
192 A4 Burgos Sardegna Italy
243 F3 Burgos Mex.
183 G2 Burgos Spain
183 G2 Burgos prov. Castilla y León Spain
169 F5 Burgpreppach Ger.
172 D3 Burgrieden Ger.
173 F2 Burgsalach Ger.
169 E5 Burgsinn Ger.
171 D4 Burgstädt Ger.
171 D5 Burgstädt Ger.
170 E2 Burg Stargard Ger.
143 H3 Burgsvik Gotland Sweden
173 F2 Burgthann Ger.
169 F4 Burgtonna Ger.
186 B2 Burguete Spain
186 B2 Burgui Spain
184 E3 Burguillos Spain
184 D2 Burguillos del Cerro Spain
173 E2 Burgwindheim Ger.
117 F5 Burhabalanga r. India
106 B5 Burhan Budai Shan mts China
199 E2 Burhaniye Turkey
116 D5 Burhanpur Madh. Prad. India
116 E5 Burhar-Dhanpuri Madh. Prad. India
168 D2 Burhave (Butjadingen) Ger.
117 F4 Burhi Gandak r. India
158 D2 Burhou i. Channel Is
256 C5 Buri Brazil
92 B3 Burias i. Phil.
190 C4 Buriasco Italy
Buriat-Mongol Republic aut. rep. Rus. Fed. see Buryatiya, Respublika
120 D2 Buribay Rus. Fed.
162 B3 Burie France
117 E4 Buri Gandak r. Nepal
225 K4 Burin Nfld. Can.
225 K4 Burin Peninsula Nfld. Can.
96 C4 Buriram Thai.
256 B4 Buritama Brazil
254 E2 Buriti Brazil
253 F3 Buriti r. Brazil
256 C3 Buriti Alegre Brazil
254 E3 Buriti Bravo Brazil
254 E2 Buriti dos Lopes Brazil
254 E4 Buritirama Brazil
255 D5 Buritis Brazil
257 E2 Buritizeiro Brazil
187 C5 Burjassot Spain
187 L6 Burjuc Romania
173 E2 Burk Ger.
121 I4 Burkan-Suu r. Kyrg.
169 E5 Burkardroth Ger.
237 D5 Burkburnett TX U.S.A.
84 D4 Burke watercourse Qld Austr.
236 D3 Burke SD U.S.A.
262 Q2 Burke Island Antarctica
81 C6 Burke Pass South I. N.Z.
230 C4 Burkesville KY U.S.A.
84 D3 Burketown Qld Austr.
232 D6 Burkeville VA U.S.A.
131 P3 Burkhala Rus. Fed.
206 E4 Burkina country Africa
Burkina Faso country Africa see Burkina
224 E4 Burk's Falls Ont. Can.
121 I1 Burla Rus. Fed.
121 I1 Burla r. Rus. Fed.
183 I2 Burlada Spain
172 D3 Burladingen Ger.
163 F5 Burlats France
85 E4 Burleigh Qld Austr.
234 D3 Burleigh NJ U.S.A.
151 F4 Burley Hampshire, England U.K.
238 D3 Burley ID U.S.A.
150 E2 Burley Gate Herefordshire, England U.K.
149 H4 Burley in Wharfedale West Yorkshire, England U.K.
120 E1 Burli Kazakh.
121 J2 Burlin Kazakh.
240 F3 Burlingame CA U.S.A.
224 E5 Burlington Ont. Can.
236 C4 Burlington CO U.S.A.
235 F1 Burlington CT U.S.A.
230 B3 Burlington IA U.S.A.
226 D5 Burlington IN U.S.A.
236 E4 Burlington KS U.S.A.
236 G4 Burlington KY U.S.A.
231 E4 Burlington NC U.S.A.
234 D2 Burlington NJ U.S.A.
233 G2 Burlington VT U.S.A.
238 B1 Burlington WA U.S.A.
226 C4 Burlington WI U.S.A.
234 D3 Burlington County county NJ U.S.A.
120 D1 Burly Rus. Fed.
Burma country Asia see Myanmar
134 J4 Burmakino Kirovskaya Oblast' Rus. Fed.
139 M3 Burmakino Yaroslavskaya Oblast' Rus. Fed.
178 D3 Bürmoos Austria
222 F5 Burnaby B.C. Can.
148 B5 Burnchurch Rep. of Ireland
146 F2 Burness Orkney, Scotland U.K.
237 D6 Burnet TX U.S.A.
85 H5 Burnett r. Qld Austr.
85 H5 Burnett Heads Qld Austr.
238 B3 Burney CA U.S.A.
259 B9 Burney, Monte vol. Chile
147 C4 Burnfoot Rep. of Ireland
147 E2 Burnfoot Northern Ireland U.K.
81 D5 Burnham South I. N.Z.
151 G3 Burnham Buckinghamshire, England U.K.
233 □I2 Burnham ME U.S.A.
232 E4 Burnham PA U.S.A.
151 H2 Burnham Market Norfolk, England U.K.
151 H3 Burnham-on-Crouch Essex, England U.K.
150 E3 Burnham-on-Sea Somerset, England U.K.
148 E2 Burnhouse North Ayrshire, Scotland U.K.
83 F5 Burnie Tas. Austr.
232 B6 Burning Springs KY U.S.A.
149 I3 Burniston North Yorkshire, England U.K.
149 G4 Burnley Lancashire, England U.K.
146 F6 Burnmouth Scottish Borders, Scotland U.K.
149 H3 Burnopfield Durham, England U.K.
Burnoye Kazakh. see Bauyrzhan Momysh-Uly
238 C3 Burns OR U.S.A.
220 H3 Burnside r. Nunavut Can.
87 D5 Burnside, Lake salt flat W.A. Austr.
238 C3 Burns Junction OR U.S.A.
222 E4 Burns Lake B.C. Can.
226 A3 Burnsville MN U.S.A.
232 C5 Burnsville WV U.S.A.
238 C2 Burnt r. OR U.S.A.
146 E5 Burntisland Fife, Scotland U.K.
223 L4 Burntwood r. Man. Can.
151 F2 Burntwood Green Staffordshire, England U.K.
225 G1 Buron r. Que. Can.
183 E1 Burón Spain
190 D3 Buronzo Italy
163 B5 Burons France
120 E4 Burovoy Uzbek.
170 E2 Burow Ger.
110 D2 Burqin Xinjiang China
110 D2 Burqin r. China
128 D3 Burqu' Jordan
82 D3 Burra S.A. Austr.
146 F1 Burra i. Scotland U.K.
146 □G1 Burravoe Shetland, Scotland U.K.
146 F3 Burray i. Scotland U.K.
196 E5 Burrel Albania
240 H3 Burrel CA U.S.A.
146 E5 Burrelton Perth and Kinross, Scotland U.K.
147 B3 Burren Rep. of Ireland
147 B3 Burren reg. Rep. of Ireland
148 C3 Burren Northern Ireland U.K.
83 G3 Burrendong Reservoir N.S.W. Austr.
83 G2 Burren Junction N.S.W. Austr.
83 G3 Burrewarra Point N.S.W. Austr.
187 C5 Burriana Spain
83 G3 Burrinjuck Reservoir N.S.W. Austr.
226 B4 Burr Oak IA U.S.A.
147 B3 Burron Rep. of Ireland
148 E3 Burrow Head hd Scotland U.K.
84 B2 Burrundie N.T. Austr.
150 C3 Burry Port Carmarthenshire, Wales U.K.
178 A3 Burs Austria
199 F1 Bursa Turkey
199 F1 Bursa prov. Turkey
203 G2 Būr Safājah Egypt
203 G2 Būr Sa'īd Egypt
126 D5 Būr Sa'īd governorate Egypt
149 G4 Burscough Lancashire, England U.K.
149 G4 Burscough Bridge Lancashire, England U.K.
169 E4 Burscheid Ger.
136 C3 Burshtyn Ukr.
172 C2 Bürstadt Ger.
151 G3 Burstow Surrey, England U.K.

Būr Sudan to Camisea
289

Būr Sudan Sudan see Port Sudan
82 E3 Burta N.S.W. Austr.
173 E3 Burtenbach Ger.
138 E3 Burtnieku ezers l. Latvia
151 F4 Burton Dorset, England U.K.
227 F4 Burton MI U.S.A.
150 E4 Burton Bradstock Dorset, England U.K.
149 G3 Burton-in-Kendal Cumbria, England U.K.
151 G2 Burton Latimer Northamptonshire, England U.K.
149 H3 Burton Leonard North Yorkshire, England U.K.
147 C2 Burtonport Rep. of Ireland
234 B3 Burtonsville MD U.S.A.
149 I4 Burton upon Stather North Lincolnshire, England U.K.
151 F2 Burton upon Trent Staffordshire, England U.K.
140 M2 Burträsk Sweden
233 □J1 Burtts Corner N.B. Can.
83 E3 Burtundy N.S.W. Austr.
84 C4 Burt Well N.T. Austr.
93 C3 Buru i. Maluku Indon.
183 F5 Burujón Spain
137 H5 Burul'cha r. Ukr.
126 C5 Burullus, Bahra el lag. Egypt
Burullus, Lake lag. Egypt see Burullus, Bahra el
Burultokay Xinjiang China see Fuhai
211 A5 Burundi country Africa
Burunniy Rus. Fed. see Tsagan Aman
211 A5 Bururi Burundi
150 E2 Burwarton Shropshire, England U.K.
151 H4 Burwash East Sussex, England U.K.
222 B2 Burwash Landing Y.T. Can.
151 H2 Burwell Cambridgeshire, England U.K.
236 D3 Burwell NE U.S.A.
146 F3 Burwick Orkney, Scotland U.K.
149 G4 Bury Greater Manchester, England U.K.
Buryatia aut. rep. Rus. Fed. see Buryatiya, Respublika
106 G1 Buryatiya, Respublika aut. rep. Rus. Fed.
Buryatskaya Mongolskaya A.S.S.R. aut. rep. Rus. Fed. see Buryatiya, Respublika
137 G2 Buryn' Ukr.
151 H2 Bury St Edmunds Suffolk, England U.K.
174 G4 Burzenin Pol.
161 C4 Burzet France
192 A4 Busachi Sardegna Italy
190 D4 Busalla Italy
Busan S. Korea see Pusan
190 F4 Busana Italy
238 F2 Busby MT U.S.A.
190 C4 Busca Italy
179 H2 Buschberg hill Austria
170 D3 Buschow Ger.
168 E1 Busdorf Ger.
Buseire Syria see Al Buşayrah
194 B4 Buseto Palizzolo Sicilia Italy
148 C2 Bush r. Northern Ireland U.K.
136 E3 Busha Ukr.
136 D2 Bushcha Ukr.
122 B4 Būshehr Iran
122 B4 Būshehr prov. Iran
210 A5 Bushenyi Uganda
151 G3 Bushey Hertfordshire, England U.K.
Bushire Iran see Būshehr
234 C1 Bushkill PA U.S.A.
234 D1 Bush Kill r. PA U.S.A.
147 E1 Bushmills Northern Ireland U.K.
231 D6 Bushnell FL U.S.A.
226 B5 Bushnell IL U.S.A.
196 E5 Bushtricë Albania
210 B4 Busia Kenya
156 D2 Busigny France
177 I3 Bušince Slovakia
208 D4 Businga Dem. Rep. Congo
208 C5 Busira r. Dem. Rep. Congo
136 C3 Bus'k Ukr.
142 C1 Buskerud county Norway
175 I5 Busko-Zdrój Pol.
Buskul' Kazakh. see Boskol'
157 G5 Bussang France
87 B7 Busselton W.A. Austr.
193 H4 Bussento r. Italy
190 F3 Busseto Italy
162 C3 Bussière-Badil France
162 D2 Bussière-Dunoise France
162 D3 Bussière-Galant France
162 C2 Bussière-Poitevine France
190 B2 Bussigny Switz.
193 F2 Bussi sul Tirino Italy
171 C5 Büßleben Ger.
191 F3 Bussolengo Italy
190 C3 Bussoleno Italy
164 E2 Bussum Neth.
156 D4 Bussy-en-Othe France
160 C1 Bussy-le-Grand France
243 E3 Bustamante Mex.
197 G3 Buşteni Romania
261 G3 Bustinza Arg.
190 D3 Busto Arsizio Italy
92 A3 Busuanga Phil.
92 A3 Busuanga i. Phil.
168 D1 Büsum Ger.
191 I2 But r. Italy
208 E4 Buta Dem. Rep. Congo
210 C2 Butajīra Eth.
197 F4 Butan Bulg.
97 B6 Butang Group is Thai.
211 A5 Butare Rwanda
266 G6 Butaritari atoll Kiribati
146 C6 Bute i. Scotland U.K.
146 C6 Bute, Sound of sea chan. Scotland U.K.
197 H2 Butea Romania
222 D4 Butedale B.C. Can.
208 F4 Butembo Dem. Rep. Congo
177 L5 Buteni Romania
194 D5 Butera Sicilia Italy
165 F4 Bütgenbach Belgium
215 G3 Butha Buthe Lesotho
Butha Qi Nei Mongol China see Zalantun
96 A2 Buthidaung Myanmar
160 F3 Buthier di Valpelline r. Italy
255 C9 Butiá Brazil
210 A4 Butiaba Uganda
237 F5 Butler AL U.S.A.
231 C5 Butler GA U.S.A.
226 E5 Butler IN U.S.A.
232 A5 Butler KY U.S.A.
236 E4 Butler MO U.S.A.
235 D1 Butler NJ U.S.A.
232 D4 Butler PA U.S.A.
147 D2 Butlers Bridge Rep. of Ireland
93 B4 Buton i. Indon.
136 E4 Butor Moldova
137 I2 Butovo Rus. Fed.
170 D2 Bütow Ger.
184 D2 Butrera mt. Spain
198 B2 Butrintit, Liqeni i l. Albania
175 I2 Butryny Pol.
190 E1 Bütschwil Switz.
175 M4 Butsyn Ukr.
237 F5 Buttahatchee r. MS U.S.A.
238 D2 Butte MT U.S.A.
236 D3 Butte NE U.S.A.
172 C2 Büttelborn Ger.
171 C4 Buttelstedt Ger.
173 F2 Buttenheim Ger.
173 E3 Buttenwiesen Ger.
149 F3 Buttermere Cumbria, England U.K.
226 B2 Butternut WI U.S.A.
149 I3 Butterwick North Yorkshire, England U.K.
94 C1 Butterworth Malaysia
215 G5 Butterworth S. Africa
240 G2 Buttes, Sierra mt. CA U.S.A.
147 C4 Buttevant Rep. of Ireland
172 D2 Bütthard Ger.
146 B3 Butt of Lewis hd Scotland U.K.
240 H4 Buttonwillow CA U.S.A.
171 C4 Buttstädt Ger.
169 F4 Büttstedt Ger.
87 D7 Butty Head hd W.A. Austr.
234 C2 Buttzville NJ U.S.A.
92 C4 Butuan Phil.
136 E4 Butuceni Moldova
108 B3 Butuo Sichuan China
135 H6 Buturlinovka Rus. Fed.
117 E4 Butwal Nepal
Butysh Rus. Fed. see Kama
169 D5 Butzbach Ger.
170 C2 Bützow Ger.
234 C2 Butztown PA U.S.A.
210 E4 Buulobarde Somalia
Buurakan r. Kyrg. see Burkan-Suu
211 D5 Buur Gaabo Somalia
210 E4 Buurhabaka Somalia
164 F2 Buurse Neth.
210 B4 Buvuma Island Uganda
128 B5 Buwārah, Jabal mt. Saudi Arabia
124 B2 Buwāţah Saudi Arabia
117 F4 Buxar Bihar India
159 G5 Buxerolles France
173 F3 Buxheim Ger.
160 A2 Buxières-les-Mines France
151 H4 Buxted East Sussex, England U.K.
168 E2 Buxtehude Ger.
149 H4 Buxton Derbyshire, England U.K.
160 C2 Buxy France
134 H4 Buy Rus. Fed.
134 K4 Buy r. Rus. Fed.
106 C2 Buyant Bayanhongor Mongolia
106 A1 Buyant Bayan-Ölgiy Mongolia
107 F2 Buyant Hentiy Mongolia
106 A1 Buyant Gol r. Mongolia
106 C2 Buyant Gol r. Mongolia
107 F2 Buyant-Uhaa Mongolia
226 A1 Buyck MN U.S.A.
129 E2 Buynaksk Rus. Fed.
206 D5 Buyo Côte d'Ivoire
108 B4 Buyuan Jiang r. Yunnan China
127 G3 Büyük Ağrı Dağı mt. Turkey
129 C3 Büyükçatak Turkey
199 F1 Büyükçekmece Turkey
199 G2 Büyükkabaca Turkey
199 G2 Büyükkarabağ Turkey
199 E1 Büyükkarıştıran Turkey
199 F3 Büyükkonak Turkey
199 E3 Büyükmenderes r. Turkey
199 F2 Büyükorhan Turkey
128 C1 Büyükşahinbey Turkey
199 E2 Büyükyenice Balıkesir Turkey
107 I3 Buyun Shan mt. Liaoning China
120 B3 Buzachi, Poluostrov pen. Kazakh.
162 D2 Buzançais France
157 E3 Buzancy France
197 H3 Buzău Romania
197 H3 Buzău r. Romania
197 H3 Buzău r. Romania
135 K5 Buzdyak Rus. Fed.
191 I3 Buzet Croatia
163 C4 Buzet-sur-Baïse France
163 D5 Buzet-sur-Tarn France
139 M4 Buzha r. Rus. Fed.
213 G3 Búzi Moz.
213 G3 Búzi r. Moz.
197 E3 Buziaş Romania
177 K3 Buzica Slovakia
Büzmeyin Turkm. see Byuzmeyin
129 G3 Buzovna Azer.
120 C1 Buzuluk Rus. Fed.
135 H6 Buzuluk r. Rus. Fed.
163 B5 Buzy France
233 H4 Buzzards Bay MA U.S.A.
Bwcle Flintshire, Wales U.K. see Buckley
114 B3 Byadgi Karnataka India
138 G4 Byahoml' Belarus
197 G4 Byala Ruse Bulg.
197 H4 Byala Varna Bulg.
199 E1 Byala Reka r. Bulg.
197 F4 Byala Slatina Bulg.
138 G5 Byalynichy Belarus
Byam Martin atoll Arch. des Tuamotu Fr. Polynesia see Ahunui
138 E5 Byarezina r. Belarus
138 H5 Byarezina r. Belarus
138 E5 Byaroza Belarus
138 E5 Byarozawka Belarus
175 K4 Bychawa Pol.
174 G5 Bycina Pol.
174 G4 Byczyna Pol.
174 G2 Bydgoszcz Pol.
138 E5 Byelaazyorsk Belarus
136 D2 Byelavusha Belarus
139 H5 Byelitsk Belarus
Byelorussia country Europe see Belarus
175 N1 Byenyakoni Belarus
Byerastavitsa Belarus see Pahranichny
138 G5 Byerazino Belarus
238 F4 Byers CO U.S.A.
138 G4 Byeshankovichy Belarus
232 C5 Byesville OH U.S.A.
139 H5 Byesyedz' r. Belarus
85 G4 Byfield Qld Austr.
151 F2 Byfield Northamptonshire, England U.K.
151 G3 Byfleet Surrey, England U.K.
140 M2 Bygdeå Sweden
140 M2 Bygdsiljum Sweden
142 B2 Bygland Norway
171 F4 Byhleguhre Ger.
137 I3 Byk r. Ukr.
139 H5 Bykhaw Belarus
Bykhov Belarus see Bykhaw
136 D2 Bykivka Ukr.
142 B2 Bykle Norway
135 I6 Bykovo Rus. Fed.
241 L5 Bylas AZ U.S.A.
150 D1 Bylchau Conwy, Wales U.K.
168 E1 Bylderup-Bov Denmark
221 K2 Bylot Island Nunavut Can.
129 C2 Bylym Rus. Fed.
227 G3 Byng Inlet Ont. Can.
85 E3 Bynoe r. Qld Austr.
84 B2 Bynoe Harbour N.T. Austr.
107 H1 Byrka Rus. Fed.
137 G2 Byrlivka Ukr.
83 F2 Byrock N.S.W. Austr.
226 C4 Byron IL U.S.A.
233 □H2 Byron ME U.S.A.
232 B3 Byron MI U.S.A.
83 H2 Byron, Cape N.S.W. Austr.
83 H2 Byron Bay N.S.W. Austr.
Byron Island Gilbert Is Kiribati see Nikunau
131 K2 Byrranga, Gory mts Rus. Fed.
137 G1 Byryne Ukr.
136 E2 Byshiv Ukr.
176 D1 Byšice Czech Rep.
140 M2 Byske Sweden
140 M2 Byskeälven r. Sweden
100 D1 Byssa r. Rus. Fed.
175 H6 Bystra Pol.
177 I2 Bystrá mt. Slovakia
176 F2 Bystré Czech Rep.
177 K2 Bystré Slovakia
177 H3 Bystričany Slovakia
177 H2 Bystřice Czech Rep.
176 D2 Bystřice Czech Rep.
176 E1 Bystřice r. Czech Rep.
176 F2 Bystřice nad Pernštejnem Czech Rep.
177 G2 Bystřice pod Hostýnem Czech Rep.
107 F1 Bystrinskiy Golets, Gora mt. Rus. Fed.
Bystrovka Kyrg. see Kemin
136 C3 Bystrytsya Ukr.
136 B3 Bystrytsya r. Ukr.
121 K1 Bystryy Istok Rus. Fed.
134 K5 Bystryy Tanyp r. Rus. Fed.
174 F5 Bystrzyca Pol.
174 E4 Bystrzyca r. Pol.
175 K4 Bystrzyca r. Pol.
174 E5 Bystrzyca Kłodzka Pol.
176 F1 Bystrzyckie, Góry mts Czech Rep./Pol.
131 O3 Bytantay r. Rus. Fed.
177 H2 Bytča Slovakia
174 D3 Bytnica Pol.
174 G5 Bytom Pol.
174 D4 Bytom Odrzański Pol.
139 J5 Bytosh' Rus. Fed.
143 G4 Bytów Pol.
211 A5 Byumba Rwanda
122 D2 Byuzmeyin Turkm.
143 G3 Byxelkrok Kalmar Sweden
Byzantium Turkey see İstanbul
176 G3 Bzenec Czech Rep.
129 B2 Bzip'i r. Georgia
129 B2 Bzip'is K'edi hills Georgia
175 I3 Bzura r. Pol.

C

96 D3 Ca, Sông r. Vietnam
253 F6 Caacupé Para.
253 F6 Caaguazú Para.
253 G6 Caaguazú, Cordillera de hills Para.
209 B8 Caála Angola
251 F5 Caapiranga Brazil
255 B7 Caarapó Brazil
253 F6 Caazapá Para.
253 F3 Cabaçal r. Brazil
246 C2 Cabaiguán Cuba
163 B6 Caballiros, Pic de mt. France
252 B3 Caballas Peru
185 G3 Caballo mt. Spain
250 D5 Caballococha Peru
252 A2 Cabana Peru
163 C5 Cabanac France
163 B4 Cabanac-et-Villagrains France
252 C3 Cabanaconde Peru
182 B3 Cabana Maior Port.
182 E1 Cabañaquinta Spain
184 C3 Cabanas Port.
185 H3 Cabañas mt. Spain
182 E5 Cabañas del Castillo Spain
182 C4 Cabanas de Viriato Port.
182 D2 Cabañas Raras Spain
92 B3 Cabanatuan Phil.
163 D5 Cabanères hill France
187 D4 Cabanes Spain
161 C5 Cabannes France
225 G4 Cabano Que. Can.
188 E3 Čabar Croatia
161 E5 Cabasse France
186 D3 Cabassers Spain
182 C2 Cabe r. Spain
184 C3 Cabeça Gorda Port.
184 B2 Cabeção Port.
256 D1 Cabeceiras Brazil
182 C3 Cabeceiras de Basto Port.
184 C1 Cabeço de Vide Port.
182 C5 Cabeço Rainha mt. Port.
254 G3 Cabedelo Brazil
163 E6 Cabestany France
177 L5 Căbeşti Romania
182 D3 Cabeza de Framontanos Spain
185 E2 Cabeza del Buey Spain
182 D3 Cabeza del Caballo Spain
184 D2 Cabeza la Vaca Spain
183 G5 Cabezamesada Spain
185 F2 Cabezarados Spain
253 E4 Cabezas Bol.
183 E4 Cabezas del Villar Spain
247 □1 Cabezas de San Juan pt Puerto Rico
184 C3 Cabezas Rubias Spain
183 I3 Cabezo de Morés mt. Spain
187 B6 Cabezo de Torres Spain
184 C3 Cabezo Gordo hill Spain
183 F3 Cabezón Spain
183 H2 Cabezón de Cameros Spain
183 F1 Cabezón de la Sal Spain
183 F1 Cabezón de Liébana Spain
182 E4 Cabezuela del Valle Spain
261 G6 Cabildo Arg.
250 D2 Cabimas Venez.
209 B6 Cabinda Angola
209 B6 Cabinda prov. Angola
238 D1 Cabinet Mountains MT U.S.A.
Cabistra Turkey see Ereğli
226 B2 Cable WI U.S.A.
254 G4 Cabo Brazil
216 □1a Cabo da Praia Terceira Azores
213 H2 Cabo Delgado prov. Moz.
257 F5 Cabo Frio Brazil
183 H3 Cabolafuente Spain
237 E4 Cabool MO U.S.A.
85 H5 Caboolture Qld Austr.
242 B2 Caborca Mex.
225 I4 Cabot Strait Nfld./N.S. Can.
159 F2 Cabourg France
Cabo Verde country N. Atlantic Ocean see Cape Verde
206 □ Cabo Verde, Ilhas do is N. Atlantic Ocean
Cabo Yubi Morocco see Tarfaya
185 F3 Cabra Spain
185 F3 Cabra r. Spain
182 B3 Cabração Port.
186 E3 Cabra del Camp Spain
185 G3 Cabra del Santo Cristo Spain
187 C4 Cabra de Mora Spain
246 E3 Cabral Dom. Rep.
257 E2 Cabral, Serra do mts Brazil
192 A5 Cabras Sardegna Italy
185 F3 Cabras mt. Spain
192 A5 Cabras, Stagno di l. Sardegna Italy
129 E4 Cäbrayıl Azer.
183 H3 Cabrejas, Sierra de mts Spain
183 H3 Cabrejas del Pinar Spain
184 B2 Cabrela Port.
184 B2 Cabrela r. Port.
246 E3 Cabrera Dom. Rep.
187 F5 Cabrera i. Spain
185 F2 Cabrera r. Spain
163 D4 Cabrerets France
223 I5 Cabri Sask. Can.
183 I5 Cabriel r. Spain
161 D5 Cabrières-d'Aigues France
182 C4 Cabril Port.
182 D2 Cabrillanes Spain
182 D4 Cabrillas Spain
183 H4 Cabrillas r. Spain
254 F4 Cabrobó Brazil
92 B2 Cabugao Phil.
188 F4 Čabulja mt. Bos.-Herz.
182 D2 Cacabelos Spain
255 C8 Caçador Brazil
Cacagoin Sichuan China see Qagca
245 E5 Cacahuatepec Mex.
196 E4 Čačak Srbija Yugo.
257 E5 Cacapava Brazil
255 B9 Cacapava do Sul Brazil
232 D5 Cacapon r. WV U.S.A.
182 D3 Caçarelhos Port.
250 C3 Cácares Col.
194 C5 Caccamo Sicilia Italy
193 I3 Caccia, Monte hill Italy
195 F3 Caccuri Italy
184 A2 Cacém Port.
255 B9 Cacequi Brazil
253 F4 Cáceres Brazil
184 D1 Cáceres Spain
182 D5 Cáceres prov. Extremadura Spain
261 H5 Cachari Arg.
237 F4 Cache r. IL U.S.A.
206 A3 Cacheau r. Guinea-Bissau
222 F5 Cache Creek B.C. Can.
240 G2 Cache Creek r. CA U.S.A.
238 F3 Cache la Poudre r. CO U.S.A.
238 D3 Cache Peak ID U.S.A.
206 A3 Cacheu Guinea-Bissau
258 D2 Cachi Arg.
258 D2 Cachi, Nevados de mts Arg.
254 B4 Cachimbo, Serra do hills Brazil
209 D7 Cachimo Angola
258 C2 Cachina r. Chile
209 C8 Cachingues Angola
254 F5 Cachoeira Bahia Brazil
256 B3 Cachoeira Mato Grosso do Sul Brazil
256 B3 Cachoeira Alta Brazil
256 B2 Cachoeira de Goiás Brazil
254 C2 Cachoeira do Arari Brazil
257 E3 Cachoeira dos Macacos Brazil
255 B9 Cachoeira do Sul Brazil
257 E5 Cachoeira Paulista Brazil
257 F5 Cachoeiras de Macacu Brazil
257 G4 Cachoeiro de Itapemirim Brazil
184 C3 Cachopo Port.
177 G3 Čachtice Slovakia
182 B4 Cacia Port.
185 G3 Cacín Spain
185 F3 Cacín r. Spain
206 B4 Cacine Guinea-Bissau
209 C7 Cacolo Angola
244 B3 Cacoma, Sierra mts Mex.
209 B8 Caconda Angola
209 B6 Cacongo Angola
237 C4 Cactus TX U.S.A.
240 I3 Cactus Range mts NV U.S.A.
256 B3 Caçu Brazil
209 B7 Cacuaco Angola
209 C7 Caculama Angola
254 E5 Caculé Brazil
257 H2 Cacumba, Ilha i. Brazil
209 B7 Cacuso Angola
184 A1 Cadafais Port.
150 D2 Cadair Idris hills Wales U.K.
163 D5 Cadalen France
183 F4 Cadalso de los Vidrios Spain
148 B4 Cadamstown Rep. of Ireland
186 G2 Cadaqués Spain
184 A1 Cadaval Port.
177 H2 Čadca Slovakia
210 D2 Caddabassa l. Eth.
151 G3 Caddington Bedfordshire, England U.K.
191 F4 Cadelbosco di Sopra Italy
84 C2 Cadell r. N.T. Austr.
190 D2 Cadenazzo Switz.
168 E2 Cadenberge Ger.
161 D5 Cadenet France
190 E4 Cadeo Italy
243 E3 Cadereyta Nuevo León Mex.
245 E3 Cadereyta Querétaro Mex.
Cader Idris hills Wales U.K. see Cadair Idris
161 C4 Caderousse France
Cadí mt. Spain see Torre de Cadí
186 E2 Cadí, Túnel de tun. Spain
185 G4 Cádiar Spain
82 C2 Cadibarrawirracanna, Lake salt flat S.A. Austr.
92 B3 Cadig Mountains Phil.
227 H1 Cadillac Que. Can.
223 J5 Cadillac Sask. Can.
163 B4 Cadillac France
226 E3 Cadillac MI U.S.A.
129 C3 Çadır Dağı mt. Turkey
129 B4 Çadırkaya Turkey
92 B4 Cadiz Phil.
184 D4 Cádiz Spain
184 E4 Cádiz prov. Andalucía Spain
241 J4 Cadiz CA U.S.A.
230 C4 Cadiz KY U.S.A.
232 C4 Cadiz OH U.S.A.
184 C4 Cádiz, Golfo de g. Spain
173 E2 Cadolzburg Ger.
222 G4 Cadomin Alta Can.
191 G3 Cadoneghe Italy
226 B3 Cadott WI U.S.A.
222 G3 Cadotte r. Alta Can.
222 G3 Cadotte Lake Alta Can.
163 D5 Cadours France
87 C6 Cadoux W.A. Austr.
254 E4 Caém Brazil
159 F2 Caen France
159 F2 Caen, Plaine de plain France
150 D3 Caerau Cardiff, Wales U.K.
Caerdydd Cardiff, Wales U.K. see Cardiff
Caere Italy see Cerveteri
Caerffili Caerphilly, Wales U.K. see Caerphilly
Caerfyrddin Carmarthenshire, Wales U.K. see Carmarthen
150 D1 Caergwrle Flintshire, Wales U.K.
Caergybi Isle of Anglesey, Wales U.K. see Holyhead
150 D1 Caerhun Conwy, Wales U.K.
150 E3 Caerleon Newport, Wales U.K.
150 C1 Caernarfon Gwynedd, Wales U.K.
150 C1 Caernarfon Bay Wales U.K.
150 C1 Caernarfon Castle tourist site Wales U.K.
Caernarvon Gwynedd, Wales U.K. see Caernarfon
150 D3 Caerphilly Caerphilly, Wales U.K.
150 D3 Caerphilly admin. div. Wales U.K.
150 D2 Caersws Powys, Wales U.K.
150 E3 Caerwent Monmouthshire, Wales U.K.
Caesaraugusta Spain see Zaragoza
Caesarea Alg. see Cherchell
128 B3 Caesarea tourist site Israel
Caesarea Cappadociae Turkey see Kayseri
Caesarea Philippi Syria see Bāniyās
Caesarodunum France see Tours
Caesaromagus Essex, England U.K. see Chelmsford
257 F3 Caeté Brazil
252 C2 Caeté r. Brazil
254 E5 Caetité Brazil
190 C3 Cafasse Italy
258 D2 Cafayate Arg.
256 C4 Cafelândia Brazil
Caffa Ukr. see Feodosiya
251 G4 Cafuini r. Brazil
92 B2 Cagayan r. Phil.
92 C4 Cagayan de Oro Phil.
92 B4 Cagayan Islands Phil.
193 H4 Caggiano Italy
191 H5 Cagli Italy
192 B5 Cagliari Sardegna Italy
192 B5 Cagliari prov. Sardegna Italy
192 B5 Cagliari, Golfo di b. Sardegna Italy
163 E5 Cagnac-les-Mines France
193 H3 Cagnano Varano Italy
161 F5 Cagnes-sur-Mer France
250 C5 Caguán r. Col.
247 □1 Caguas Puerto Rico
147 B5 Caha hill Rep. of Ireland
231 C5 Cahaba r. AL U.S.A.
209 B9 Cahama Angola
147 B5 Caha Mountains hills Rep. of Ireland
147 C4 Caher Rep. of Ireland
147 A5 Cahermore Rep. of Ireland
147 A5 Cahersiveen Rep. of Ireland
147 D4 Cahir Rep. of Ireland
Cahirciveen Rep. of Ireland see Cahersiveen
234 D1 Cahoonzie NY U.S.A.
163 D4 Cahors France
250 B6 Cahuapanas Peru
136 E5 Cahul Moldova
163 D5 Cahuzac-sur-Vère France
213 G3 Caia Moz.
184 C2 Caia Port.
184 C2 Caia r. Port.
184 C1 Caia, Barragem do resr Port.
253 F3 Caiabis, Serra dos hills Brazil
256 B1 Caiapó r. Brazil
256 A2 Caiapó, Serra do mts Brazil
256 B2 Caiapônia Brazil
193 G3 Caiazzo Italy
246 C2 Caibarién Cuba
96 D2 Cai Bâu, Đao i. Vietnam
97 D5 Cai Be Vietnam
254 F3 Caicó Brazil
246 E2 Caicos Islands Turks and Caicos Is
246 D2 Caicos Passage Bahamas/Turks and Caicos Is
109 E2 Caidian Hubei China
Caidu Henan China see Shangcai
87 E7 Caiguna W.A. Austr.
108 D2 Caihua Hubei China
252 C3 Cailloma Peru
244 A2 Caimanero, Laguna del lag. Mex.
260 B2 Caimanes Chile
209 B8 Caimbambo Angola
183 I4 Caimodorro mt. Spain
136 E4 Căinar r. Moldova
209 B8 Cainde Angola
197 G3 Câineni Romania
241 L2 Caineville UT U.S.A.
108 B1 Cainnyigoin Sichuan China
182 B1 Caión Spain
161 C4 Cairanne France
262 W1 Caird Coast Antarctica
146 A4 Cairinis Western Isles, Scotland U.K.
146 C5 Cairnbaan Argyll and Bute, Scotland U.K.
146 D5 Cairndow Argyll and Bute, Scotland U.K.
146 E5 Cairneyhill Fife, Scotland U.K.
146 E4 Cairn Gorm mt. Scotland U.K.
146 E4 Cairngorm Mountains Scotland U.K.
146 C7 Cairnryan Dumfries and Galloway, Scotland U.K.
85 F3 Cairns Qld Austr.
146 D6 Cairnsmore of Carsphairn hill Scotland U.K.
146 D7 Cairnsmore of Fleet hill Scotland U.K.
146 E4 Cairn Toul mt. Scotland U.K.
203 F2 Cairo Egypt
231 C6 Cairo GA U.S.A.
237 F4 Cairo IL U.S.A.
193 F3 Cairo, Monte mt. Italy
190 D4 Cairo Montenotte Italy
Caisleán an Bharraigh Rep. of Ireland see Castlebar
161 C5 Caissargues France
146 C6 Caisteal Abhail hill Scotland U.K.
151 I2 Caister-on-Sea Norfolk, England U.K.
149 I4 Caistor Lincolnshire, England U.K.
146 E3 Caithness reg. Scotland U.K.
209 B8 Caitou Angola
209 C8 Caiundo Angola
83 F2 Caiwarro Qld Austr.
109 F3 Caixi Fujian China
Caiyuanzhen Zhejiang China see Shengsi
252 D5 Caiza Bol.
109 F2 Caizi Hu l. China
252 A1 Cajabamba Peru
252 A1 Cajamarca Peru
250 B6 Cajamarca dept Peru
254 D2 Cajapió Brazil
163 D4 Cajarc France
254 D2 Cajari Brazil
252 A2 Cajatambo Peru
254 F3 Cajàzeiras Brazil
196 D4 Čajetina Srbija Yugo.
92 B3 Cajidiocan Phil.
177 H3 Čajkov Slovakia
188 G4 Čajniče Bos.-Herz.
260 A6 Cajon Chile
245 G5 Cajonos r. Mex.
252 D4 Cajuata Bol.
256 D4 Cajuru Brazil
197 G2 Cajvana Romania
106 C4 Caka Qinghai China
177 H3 Čakajovce Slovakia
Caka'lho Xizang China see Yanjing
129 A4 Çakırkaş Turkey
129 C3 Çakmak Turkey
129 C4 Çakmak Dağı mts Turkey
188 F2 Čakovec Croatia
199 F2 Çal Turkey
Çal Turkey see Çukurca
215 F4 Cala S. Africa
184 D3 Cala Spain
184 D3 Cala r. Spain
207 H5 Calabar Nigeria
187 B7 Calabardina Spain
227 I3 Calabogie Ont. Can.
193 I6 Calabria admin. reg. Italy
186 D3 Calaceite Spain
192 B2 Calacuccia Corse France
186 □ Cala d'Alcaufar Spain
192 A3 Cala d'Oliva Sardegna Italy
187 G5 Cala d'Or Spain
186 □ Cala en Porter Spain
186 E3 Calaf Spain
197 F4 Calafat Romania
259 B8 Calafate Arg.
186 E3 Calafell Spain
187 G5 Cala Figuera Spain
197 H2 Calafindeşti Romania
193 H3 Calaggio r. Italy
192 B4 Cala Gonone Sardegna Italy
92 B3 Calagua Islands Phil.
Calagurris Spain see Calahorra
185 G4 Calahonda Spain
183 I2 Calahorra Spain
209 C9 Calai Angola
156 B2 Calais France
233 □J2 Calais ME U.S.A.
258 D2 Calalasteo, Sierra de mts Arg.
78 □3b Calalin i. Majuro Marshall Is
191 H2 Calalzo di Cadore Italy
252 C5 Calama Chile
190 D4 Calamandrana Italy
250 C2 Calamar Col.
92 A4 Calamian Group is Phil.
187 G5 Cala Millor Spain
186 B4 Calamocha Spain
184 D2 Calamonte Spain
187 G5 Cala Murada Spain
197 F3 Călan Romania
146 B3 Calanais Western Isles, Scotland U.K.
184 D3 Calañas Spain
190 E2 Calancasca r. Switz.
186 C4 Calanda Spain
209 C7 Calandula Angola
94 A1 Calang Sumatera Indon.
192 B4 Calangianus Sardegna Italy
195 E4 Calanna Italy
202 D2 Calanscio Sand Sea des. Libya
92 B3 Calapan Phil.
187 G5 Cala Rajada Spain
185 H3 Calar Alta mt. Spain
136 E4 Călăraşi Moldova
197 H3 Călăraşi Romania
186 □ Cala Santa Galdana Spain
194 D5 Calascibetta Sicilia Italy
192 A5 Calasetta Sardegna Italy
185 I2 Calasparra Spain
194 B5 Calatafimi Sicilia Italy
183 H3 Calatañazor Spain
187 E6 Cala Tarida Spain
183 I3 Calatayud Spain
183 I3 Calatorao Spain
171 E4 Calau Ger.
92 B3 Calauag Phil.
187 E6 Cala Vadella Spain
185 E2 Calaveruela hill Spain
92 C3 Calbayog Phil.
171 C4 Calbe (Saale) Ger.
169 F3 Calberlah Ger.
92 C4 Calbiga Phil.
252 C3 Calca Peru
243 G2 Calcasieu r. LA U.S.A.
192 A2 Calcatoggio Corse France
190 F5 Calci Italy
193 I4 Calciano Italy
190 F3 Calcinato Italy
190 E3 Calcio Italy
251 I4 Calçoene Brazil
117 G5 Calcutta W. Bengal India
197 G3 Căldăraru Romania
193 F1 Caldarola Italy
191 G2 Caldaro sulla Strada del Vino Italy
250 C3 Caldas dept Col.
184 A1 Caldas da Rainha Port.
Caldas de Mombuy Spain see Caldes de Montbui
184 B3 Caldas de Monchique Port.
182 B2 Caldas de Reis Spain
182 B3 Caldas de Vizela Port.
256 C2 Caldas Novas Brazil
149 F3 Caldbeck Cumbria, England U.K.
186 C2 Caldearenas Spain
151 G2 Caldecott Rutland, England U.K.
182 B3 Caldelas Port.
182 B3 Caldelas Taipas Port.
169 E4 Calden Ger.
222 G1 Calder r. N.W.T. Can.
258 C2 Caldera Chile
146 E6 Caldercruix North Lanarkshire, Scotland U.K.
183 I4 Caldereros, Sierra de mts Spain
85 F5 Caldervale Qld Austr.
186 F3 Caldes de Montbui Spain
186 F3 Caldes d'Estrac Spain
149 G3 Caldew r. England U.K.
150 C3 Caldey Island Wales U.K.
150 E3 Caldicot Monmouthshire, Wales U.K.
129 C4 Çaldıran Van Turkey
127 F3 Çaldıran Van Turkey
191 G3 Caldogno Italy
191 G2 Caldonazzo Italy
149 H3 Caldwell North Yorkshire, England U.K.
238 C3 Caldwell ID U.S.A.
237 D4 Caldwell KS U.S.A.
232 C5 Caldwell OH U.S.A.
237 D6 Caldwell TX U.S.A.
227 H4 Caledon Ont. Can.
215 F4 Caledon r. Lesotho/S. Africa
214 B6 Caledon S. Africa
148 C3 Caledon Northern Ireland U.K.
84 D2 Caledon Bay N.T. Austr.
225 H4 Caledonia N.S. Can.
227 H4 Caledonia Ont. Can.
Caledonia admin. div. U.K. see Scotland
226 E4 Caledonia MI U.S.A.
226 B4 Caledonia MN U.S.A.
232 E3 Caledonia NY U.S.A.
186 F3 Calella Spain
85 G4 Calen Qld Austr.
182 B3 Calendário Port.
192 A2 Calenzana Corse France
191 G5 Calenzano Italy
231 C5 Calera AL U.S.A.
184 D2 Calera de León Spain
183 E5 Calera y Chozas Spain
183 G3 Caleruega Spain
260 B4 Caletones Chile
260 E4 Caleufú Arg.
241 J5 Calexico CA U.S.A.
148 E3 Calf of Man i. Isle of Man
146 F2 Calfsound Orkney, Scotland U.K.
222 H5 Calgary Alta Can.
146 B5 Calgary Argyll and Bute, Scotland U.K.
216 □1c Calheta São Jorge Azores
184 □ Calheta Madeira
216 □1c Calheta de Nesquim Pico Azores
231 C5 Calhoun GA U.S.A.
230 C4 Calhoun KY U.S.A.
250 B4 Cali Col.
199 F1 Çalı Turkey
114 B4 Calicut Kerala India
241 J3 Caliente NV U.S.A.
236 E4 California MO U.S.A.
240 F1 California state U.S.A.
242 B2 California, Golfo de g. Mex.
186 D4 Cálig Spain
163 C4 Calignac France
129 F4 Cälilabad Azer.
258 D1 Calilegua Arg.
197 G3 Călimăneşti Romania
197 G2 Călimani, Munţii mts Romania
195 H2 Calimera Italy
260 C2 Calingasta Arg.
Calininsc Moldova see Cupcina
241 J5 Calipatria CA U.S.A.
240 F2 Calistoga CA U.S.A.
193 H4 Calitri Italy
214 C5 Calitzdorp S. Africa
190 D4 Calizzano Italy
199 G3 Çalkaya Turkey
243 H4 Calkiní Mex.
199 G2 Çalköy Turkey
82 E2 Callabonna, Lake salt flat S.A. Austr.
158 C3 Callac France
232 C6 Callaghan VA U.S.A.
240 I2 Callaghan, Mount NV U.S.A.
231 D6 Callahan FL U.S.A.
147 D4 Callan Rep. of Ireland
148 C3 Callan r. Northern Ireland U.K.
224 E4 Callander Ont. Can.
146 D5 Callander Stirling, Scotland U.K.
232 D6 Callands VA U.S.A.
92 B2 Callang Phil.
Callanish Western Isles, Scotland U.K. see Calanais
164 D2 Callantsoog Neth.
252 A3 Callao Peru
241 K2 Callao UT U.S.A.
161 E5 Callas France
163 B4 Callen France
182 E1 Callezuela Spain
161 E5 Callian France
190 D3 Calliano Italy
233 F4 Callicoon NY U.S.A.
85 G5 Callide Qld Austr.
222 H4 Calling Lake Alta Can.
150 C4 Callington Cornwall, England U.K.
85 G5 Calliope Qld Austr.
Callipolis Turkey see Gelibolu
187 C6 Callosa d'En Sarrià Spain
187 C6 Callosa de Segura Spain
227 G2 Callum Ont. Can.
87 B5 Callyharra Springs W.A. Austr.
222 H4 Calmar Alta Can.
226 B4 Calmar IA U.S.A.
197 G4 Călmăţui r. Romania
163 D5 Calmont Midi-Pyrénées France
163 E4 Calmont Midi-Pyrénées France
245 E3 Calnali Mex.
150 E3 Calne Wiltshire, England U.K.
197 G3 Câlniştea r. Romania
190 E3 Calolziocorte Italy
183 I4 Calomarde Spain
186 G3 Calonge Spain
163 C4 Calonges France
156 C2 Calonne-Ricouart France
231 D7 Caloosahatchee r. FL U.S.A.
193 G3 Calore Italy
193 G3 Calore r. Italy
193 H4 Calore r. Italy
243 H4 Calotmul Mex.
85 H5 Caloundra Qld Austr.
177 G4 Čalovec Slovakia
Čalovo Slovakia see Veľký Meder
187 D6 Calpe Spain
245 E4 Calpulálpan Mex.
224 C3 Calstock Ont. Can.
194 C5 Caltabellotta Sicilia Italy
194 D5 Caltagirone Sicilia Italy
194 D5 Caltagirone r. Sicilia Italy
194 D5 Caltanissetta Sicilia Italy
194 C5 Caltanissetta prov. Sicilia Italy
194 C5 Caltavuturo Sicilia Italy
128 A1 Çaltıbozkır Turkey
190 D3 Caltignaga Italy
183 H3 Caltojar Spain
147 C3 Caltraghlea Rep. of Ireland
160 C3 Caluire-et-Cuire France
209 B7 Calulo Angola
226 C2 Calumet MI U.S.A.
226 A2 Calumet MN U.S.A.
209 D8 Calunda Angola
209 B8 Caluquembe Angola
190 C3 Caluso Italy
210 F2 Caluula Somalia
159 F2 Calvados dept Basse-Normandie France
182 B4 Calvão Port.
182 B3 Calvario Spain
182 E4 Calvarrasa de Abajo Spain
182 E4 Calvarrasa de Arriba Spain
193 H4 Calvello Italy
149 H4 Calver Derbyshire, England U.K.
147 E3 Calverstown Rep. of Ireland
84 D3 Calvert r. N.T. Austr.
84 D3 Calvert Hills N.T. Austr.
235 F2 Calverton NY U.S.A.
87 D4 Calvert Range hills W.A. Austr.
192 A2 Calvi Corse France
192 C1 Calvi, Monte hill Italy
187 F5 Calvià Spain
193 E2 Calvi dell'Umbria Italy
163 D4 Calvignac France
244 C3 Calvillo Mex.
146 E5 Calvine Perth and Kinross, Scotland U.K.
163 E4 Calvinet France
214 B4 Calvinia S. Africa
193 G3 Calvi Risorta Italy
161 C5 Calvisson France
182 E4 Calvitero mt. Spain
194 D6 Calvo, Monte hill Sicilia Italy
193 H3 Calvo, Monte mt. Italy
171 C3 Calvörde Ger.
182 C3 Calvos Spain
172 C3 Calw Ger.
185 G2 Calzada de Calatrava Spain
182 E3 Calzada de Valdunciel Spain
182 D4 Calzadilla Spain
151 H2 Cam r. England U.K.
209 B7 Camabatela Angola
254 F5 Camaçari Brazil
184 □ Camacha Madeira
224 E4 Camachigama r. Que. Can.
244 C1 Camacho Mex.
209 B8 Camacuio Angola
209 C8 Camacupa Angola
250 E2 Camaguán Venez.
246 C2 Camagüey Cuba
246 C2 Camagüey, Archipiélago de is Cuba
94 C1 Camah, Gunung mt. Malaysia
190 F5 Camaiore Italy
251 G6 Camaiú r. Brazil
246 C2 Camajuaní Cuba
Çamalan Turkey see Gülek
191 G5 Camaldoli Italy
183 F1 Camaleño Spain
254 F5 Camamu Brazil
252 B4 Camana Peru
252 B4 Camaná r. Peru
186 B4 Camañas Spain
209 D7 Camanongue Angola
255 B6 Camapuã Brazil
255 C9 Camaquã Brazil
255 C9 Camaquã r. Brazil
197 F2 Camăr Romania
184 □ Câmara de Lobos Madeira
253 F3 Camararé r. Brazil
186 D3 Camarasa Spain
183 F4 Camarena Spain
187 B4 Camarena r. Spain
187 B4 Camarena de la Sierra Spain
161 A5 Camarès France
161 C4 Camaret-sur-Aigues France
158 B3 Camaret-sur-Mer France
243 F3 Camargo Mex.
161 C5 Camargue reg. France
240 H4 Camarillo CA U.S.A.
182 A1 Camariñas Spain
186 D4 Camarles Spain
259 D7 Camarones, Bahía b. Arg.
147 E4 Camaross Rep. of Ireland
182 D2 Camarzana de Tera Spain
184 D3 Camas Spain
238 B2 Camas WA U.S.A.
238 D3 Camas r. ID U.S.A.
238 D3 Camas Creek r. ID U.S.A.
146 C5 Camasnacroise Highland, Scotland U.K.
194 C5 Camastra Sicilia Italy
97 D5 Ca Mau Vietnam
209 C7 Camaxilo Angola
182 B2 Cambados Spain
256 B5 Cambará Brazil
Cambay Gujarat India see Khambhat
Cambay, Gulf of India see Khambhat, Gulf of
256 B5 Cambé Brazil
151 G3 Camberley Surrey, England U.K.
163 B4 Cambes France
97 D4 Cambodia country Asia
163 A5 Cambo-les-Bains France
163 E5 Cambon France
255 C8 Camboriú Brazil
150 B4 Camborne Cornwall, England U.K.
234 B1 Cambra PA U.S.A.
82 D3 Cambrai S.A. Austr.
156 D2 Cambrai France
182 B1 Cambre Spain
159 G2 Cambremer France
182 C3 Cambres Port.
214 E5 Cambria S. Africa
Cambria admin. div. U.K. see Wales
240 G4 Cambria CA U.S.A.
150 D2 Cambrian Mountains hills Wales U.K.
224 D5 Cambridge Ont. Can.
246 □ Cambridge Jamaica
80 E2 Cambridge North I. N.Z.
151 H2 Cambridge Cambridgeshire, England U.K.
236 F3 Cambridge IL U.S.A.
233 H3 Cambridge MA U.S.A.
233 E5 Cambridge MD U.S.A.
226 A3 Cambridge MN U.S.A.
233 G3 Cambridge NY U.S.A.
232 C4 Cambridge OH U.S.A.
234 C2 Cambridge PA U.S.A.
233 G2 Cambridge VT U.S.A.
226 C4 Cambridge WI U.S.A.
221 H3 Cambridge Bay Nunavut Can.
86 F2 Cambridge Gulf W.A. Austr.
151 H2 Cambridgeshire admin. div. England U.K.
232 C4 Cambridge Springs PA U.S.A.
186 E3 Cambrils de Mar Spain
156 C2 Cambrin France
156 B2 Cambron France
170 C2 Cambs Ger.
256 D5 Cambuí Brazil
209 D6 Cambulo Angola
209 C7 Cambundi-Catembo Angola
257 E4 Cambuquira Brazil
171 C4 Camburg Ger.
250 A3 Cambutal, Cerro mt. Panama
83 G3 Camden N.S.W. Austr.
231 C5 Camden AL U.S.A.
237 E5 Camden AR U.S.A.
234 C3 Camden DE U.S.A.
233 □I2 Camden ME U.S.A.
231 E4 Camden NC U.S.A.
234 C3 Camden NJ U.S.A.
233 F3 Camden NY U.S.A.
232 A5 Camden OH U.S.A.
231 D5 Camden SC U.S.A.
237 F4 Camden TN U.S.A.
234 C3 Camden County county NJ U.S.A.
86 E2 Camden Sound sea chan. W.A. Austr.
236 E4 Camdenton MO U.S.A.
209 D7 Cameia Angola
150 C4 Camelford Cornwall, England U.K.
199 F3 Çameli Turkey
136 E3 Camenca Moldova
191 I5 Camerano Italy
193 F1 Camerino Italy
Camerinum Italy see Camerino
241 L4 Cameron AZ U.S.A.
237 E6 Cameron LA U.S.A.
236 E4 Cameron MO U.S.A.
237 D6 Cameron TX U.S.A.
226 B3 Cameron WI U.S.A.
232 C5 Cameron WV U.S.A.
94 C1 Cameron Highlands Malaysia
94 C1 Cameron Highlands mts Malaysia
222 G3 Cameron Hills Y.T. Can.
81 A7 Cameron Mountains South I. N.Z.
240 G2 Cameron Park CA U.S.A.
207 I5 Cameroon country Africa
193 H4 Camerota Italy
Caméroun country Africa see Cameroon
207 H5 Cameroun, Mont vol. Cameroon
149 F3 Camerton Cumbria, England U.K.
251 I5 Cametá Brazil
84 B3 Camfield r. N.T. Austr.
199 E3 Çamiçi Muğla Turkey
193 F2 Camicia, Monte mt. Italy
92 B2 Camiguin i. Phil.
128 B1 Camili Turkey
92 B3 Camiling Phil.
231 C6 Camilla GA U.S.A.
168 F2 Camin Ger.
252 C4 Camiña Chile
182 B3 Caminha Port.
182 D4 Caminomorisco Spain
186 B4 Caminreal Spain
252 E5 Camiri Bol.
252 B2 Camisea r. Peru

Carrazedo de Montenegro to Central, Cordillera 291

182 C3 Carrazedo de Montenegro Port.
86 F3 Carr Boyd Range hills W.A. Austr.
146 E4 Carrbridge Highland, Scotland U.K.
182 B3 Carreço Port.
184 B1 Carregado Port.
182 C4 Carregal do Sal Port.
182 B5 Carregueiros Port.
182 B1 Carreira Spain
184 C3 Carreiros r. Port.
183 F1 Carreña de Cabrales Spain
260 C5 Carrero, Cerro mt. Arg.
163 B5 Carresse-Cassaber France
Carrhae Turkey see Harran
183 G1 Carriazo Spain
147 C2 Carrick Donegal Rep. of Ireland
147 E4 Carrick Wexford Rep. of Ireland
146 D6 Carrick reg. Scotland U.K.
147 D4 Carrickbeg Rep. of Ireland
147 D3 Carrickboy Rep. of Ireland
147 F2 Carrickfergus Northern Ireland U.K.
147 E3 Carrickmacross Rep. of Ireland
147 D2 Carrickmore Northern Ireland U.K.
147 C3 Carrick-on-Shannon Rep. of Ireland
147 D4 Carrick-on-Suir Rep. of Ireland
182 B5 Carriço Port.
82 D3 Carrieton S.A. Austr.
147 C5 Carrigaline Rep. of Ireland
147 D3 Carrigallen Rep. of Ireland
147 B5 Carriganimmy Rep. of Ireland
147 D2 Carrigans Rep. of Ireland
147 B4 Carrigkerry Rep. of Ireland
147 C5 Carrigtwohill Rep. of Ireland
242 E3 Carrillo Mex.
236 D2 Carrington ND U.S.A.
182 B1 Carrio Spain
183 F2 Carrion r. Spain
185 G1 Carrión de Calatrava Spain
184 D3 Carrión de los Céspedes Spain
183 F2 Carrión de los Condes Spain
261 G3 Carrizales Arg.
241 L4 Carrizo AZ U.S.A.
237 C4 Carrizo Creek r. TX U.S.A.
182 E2 Carrizo de la Ribera Spain
185 H2 Carrizosa Spain
237 D6 Carrizo Springs TX U.S.A.
239 F5 Carrizozo NM U.S.A.
185 H1 Carro hill Spain
236 E3 Carroll IA U.S.A.
234 A3 Carroll County county MD U.S.A.
237 F5 Carrollton AL U.S.A.
231 C5 Carrollton GA U.S.A.
236 F4 Carrollton IL U.S.A.
230 C4 Carrollton KY U.S.A.
236 E4 Carrollton MO U.S.A.
237 F5 Carrollton MS U.S.A.
232 C4 Carrollton OH U.S.A.
232 D4 Carrolltown PA U.S.A.
85 E3 Carron r. Qld Austr.
146 D4 Carron r. Highland, Scotland U.K.
146 C4 Carron, Loch inlet Scotland U.K.
146 E6 Carronbridge Dumfries and Galloway, Scotland U.K.
161 F5 Carros France
223 K4 Carrot r. Sask. Can.
223 K4 Carrot River Sask. Can.
159 F3 Carrouges France
147 D1 Carrowkeel Rep. of Ireland
147 C3 Carrowmore Rep. of Ireland
147 C2 Carrowneden Rep. of Ireland
232 E6 Carrsville VA U.S.A.
190 C4 Carrù Italy
237 F4 Carruthersville MO U.S.A.
147 F2 Carryduff Northern Ireland U.K.
161 D5 Carry-le-Rouet France
162 B3 Cars France
163 D4 Carsac-Aillac France
146 C5 Carsaig Argyll and Bute, Scotland U.K.
126 E2 Çarşamba Turkey
129 A3 Çarşıbaşı Turkey
193 F2 Carsoli Italy
86 E2 Carson r. W.A. Austr.
236 C2 Carson ND U.S.A.
240 H2 Carson r. NV U.S.A.
226 E4 Carson City MI U.S.A.
240 H2 Carson City NV U.S.A.
86 E2 Carson Escarpment W.A. Austr.
240 H2 Carson Lake NV U.S.A.
227 F4 Carsonville MI U.S.A.
160 F1 Carspach France
146 D6 Carsphairn Dumfries and Galloway, Scotland U.K.
146 E6 Carstairs South Lanarkshire, Scotland U.K.
Carstensz-top mt. Indon. see Jaya, Puncak
260 B3 Cartagena Chile
250 C2 Cartagena Col.
187 C7 Cartagena Spain
250 C3 Cartago Col.
242 □J7 Cartago Costa Rica
185 F4 Cártama Spain
184 B1 Cartaxo Port.
184 C3 Cartaya Spain
162 B3 Cartelègue France
85 E2 Carter, Mount hill Qld Austr.
158 E2 Carteret France
235 D2 Carteret NJ U.S.A.
Carteret Island Solomon Is see Malaita
231 C5 Cartersville GA U.S.A.
81 E4 Carterton North I. N.Z.
151 F3 Carterton Oxfordshire, England U.K.
183 F1 Cartes Spain
205 H1 Carthage tourist site Tunisia
226 B5 Carthage IL U.S.A.
237 E4 Carthage MO U.S.A.
231 B5 Carthage MS U.S.A.
231 E5 Carthage NC U.S.A.
233 F3 Carthage NY U.S.A.
231 C4 Carthage TN U.S.A.
237 E5 Carthage TX U.S.A.
Carthago tourist site Tunisia see Carthage
Carthago Nova Spain see Cartagena
227 G2 Cartier Ont. Can.
86 D2 Cartier Island Ashmore & Cartier Is Austr.
149 G3 Cartmel Cumbria, England U.K.
191 H5 Cartoceto Italy
223 L5 Cartwright Man. Can.
225 J2 Cartwright Nfld. Can.
254 G4 Caruarú Brazil
182 D2 Carucedo Spain
193 G3 Carunchio Italy
197 H2 Cărunta, Vârful mt. Romania
251 F2 Carúpano Venez.
254 D2 Carutapera Brazil
182 B5 Carvalhal Santarém Port.
184 B2 Carvalhal Setúbal Port.
182 C3 Carvalho de Egas Port.
232 B6 Carver KY U.S.A.
182 D3 Carviçais Port.
156 C2 Carvin France
184 A1 Carvoeira Port.
184 B3 Carvoeiro Port.
184 A1 Carvoeiro, Cabo c. Port.
85 F5 Carwell Qld Austr.
129 F3 Çarxı Azer.
231 E5 Cary NC U.S.A.
83 E2 Caryapundy Swamp Qld Austr.
232 A6 Caryville TN U.S.A.
226 B3 Caryville WI U.S.A.
185 I3 Casa Alta hill Spain
185 F4 Casabermeja Spain
258 D1 Casabindo, Cerro de mt. Arg.
260 B3 Casablanca Chile
204 D2 Casablanca Morocco
256 D4 Casa Branca Brazil
184 B2 Casa Branca Évora Port.
184 C2 Casa Branca Portalegre Port.
193 G3 Casacalenda Italy
242 C2 Casa de Janos Mex.
185 F2 Casa de Michos Spain
260 D6 Casa de Piedra, Embalse resr Arg.
193 G3 Casagiove Italy
192 A2 Casaglione Corse France
241 L5 Casa Grande AZ U.S.A.
195 H2 Casa l'Abate Italy
193 G2 Casalanguida Italy
183 H2 Casalarreina Spain
193 G2 Casalbordino Italy
193 H3 Casalbore Italy
193 H4 Casalbuono Italy
190 E3 Casalbuttano ed Uniti Italy
190 D4 Casàl Cermelli Italy
191 G4 Casalecchio di Reno Italy
190 D3 Casale Monferrato Italy
193 H4 Casaletto Spartano Italy
191 G4 Casalfiumanese Italy
191 F4 Casalgrande Italy
190 C4 Casalgrasso Italy
184 B1 Casalinho Port.
190 F4 Casalmaggiore Italy
193 H3 Casalnuovo Monterotaro Italy
190 E3 Casalpusterlengo Italy
193 H3 Casalvecchio di Puglia Italy
193 H4 Casàl Velino Italy
206 A3 Casamance r. Senegal
195 F2 Casamassima Italy
192 B2 Casamozza Corse France
250 D3 Casanare dept Col.
250 D3 Casanare r. Col.
185 F4 Casarabonela Spain
195 H2 Casarano Italy
182 D5 Casar de Cáceres Spain
182 D4 Casar de Palomero Spain
183 G3 Casarejos Spain
185 E4 Casares Spain
182 D4 Casares de las Hurdes Spain
185 F3 Casariche Spain
183 F4 Casarrubios del Monte Spain
191 H3 Casarsa della Delizia Italy
190 E4 Casarza Ligure Italy
187 B4 Casas Altas Spain
185 H1 Casas de Benitez Spain
185 E1 Casas de Don Pedro Spain
185 H1 Casas de Fernando Alonso Spain
185 H1 Casas de Haro Spain
187 B5 Casas de Juan Gil Spain
185 I1 Casas de Juan Núñez Spain
185 H2 Casas de Lázaro Spain
182 E4 Casas del Monte Spain
185 H1 Casas de los Pinos Spain
187 B6 Casas del Puerto Spain
182 D5 Casas de Millán Spain
187 B5 Casas de Ves Spain
242 D2 Casas Grandes Mex.
242 D2 Casas Grandes r. Mex.
185 I1 Casas-Ibáñez Spain
185 H1 Casasimarro Spain
184 C2 Casas Novas de Mares Port.
183 E3 Casasola de Arión Spain
182 E5 Casatejada Spain
190 E3 Casatenovo Italy
183 F4 Casavieja Spain
261 F5 Casbas Arg.
255 B9 Casca Brazil
87 D7 Cascade W.A. Austr.
81 B6 Cascade r. South I. N.Z.
236 F3 Cascade IA U.S.A.
238 C2 Cascade ID U.S.A.
238 E2 Cascade MT U.S.A.
228 B2 Cascade Range mts Can./U.S.A.
184 A2 Cascais Port.
242 □I7 Cascal, Paso del pass Nic.
183 I2 Cascante Spain
187 B4 Cascante del Río Spain
225 H3 Cascapédia r. Que. Can.
254 F3 Cascavel Ceará Brazil
256 A6 Cascavel Paraná Brazil
193 F2 Cascia Italy
191 F5 Casciana Terme Italy
190 F5 Cascina Italy
197 H3 Căscioarele Romania
226 D3 Casco WI U.S.A.
233 □I3 Casco Bay ME U.S.A.
184 B2 Casebres Port.
183 I2 Cáseda Spain
192 B5 Case della Marina Sardegna Italy
190 D3 Casei Gerola Italy
170 F2 Casekow Ger.
190 D4 Casella Italy
193 H4 Caselle in Pittari Italy
190 C3 Caselle Torinese Italy
195 F2 Case Perrone Italy
186 E2 Caserras Spain
193 G3 Caserta Italy
193 G3 Caserta prov. Campania Italy
184 B3 Casével Port.
227 F4 Caseville MI U.S.A.
263 H2 Casey research stn Antarctica
210 F2 Caseyr, Raas c. Somalia
147 D1 Cashel Donegal Rep. of Ireland
147 C3 Cashel Galway Rep. of Ireland
147 B3 Cashel Galway Rep. of Ireland
147 D4 Cashel Laois Rep. of Ireland
147 D4 Cashel Tipperary Rep. of Ireland
147 C3 Cashla Rep. of Ireland
147 A3 Cashleen Rep. of Ireland
85 G5 Cashmere Qld Austr.
226 B4 Cashton WI U.S.A.
92 B2 Casiguran Phil.
261 G3 Casilda Arg.
183 F4 Casillas Spain
182 D4 Casillas de Flores Spain
197 I3 Casimcea Romania
197 I3 Casimcea r. Romania
244 B4 Casimiro Castillo Mex.
257 F5 Casimiro de Abreu Brazil
190 F4 Casina Italy
83 H2 Casino N.S.W. Austr.
187 C5 Casinos Spain
176 E2 Čáslav Czech Rep.
252 A2 Casma Peru
Casnewydd Newport, Wales U.K. see Newport
226 E4 Casnovia MI U.S.A.
182 D2 Casoio r. Spain
190 F4 Casola in Lunigiana Italy
191 G4 Casola Valsenio Italy
191 G5 Casole d'Elsa Italy
193 G2 Casoli Italy
193 G4 Casoria Italy
186 C3 Caspe Spain
238 F3 Casper WY U.S.A.
226 C2 Caspian MI U.S.A.
Caspian Lowland Kazakh./Rus. Fed. see Prikaspiyskaya Nizmennost'
120 B3 Caspian Sea Asia/Europe
232 D5 Cass WV U.S.A.
227 F4 Cass r. MI U.S.A.
213 G2 Cassacatiza Moz.
232 D3 Cassadaga NY U.S.A.
186 F3 Cassà de la Selva Spain
163 C5 Cassagnabère-Tournas France
163 E4 Cassagnes-Bégonhès France
209 D7 Cassai Angola
209 D8 Cassamba Angola
163 E4 Cassaniouze France
193 I5 Cassano allo Ionio Italy
195 F2 Cassano delle Murge Italy
190 D3 Cassano Magnano Italy
190 D4 Cassano Spinola Italy
194 D5 Cassaro Sicilia Italy
227 F4 Cass City MI U.S.A.
156 C2 Cassel France
224 F4 Casselman Ont. Can.
236 D2 Casselton ND U.S.A.
163 C4 Casseneuil France
256 D4 Cássia Brazil
222 D3 Cassiar B.C. Can.
222 D3 Cassiar Mountains B.C. Can.
195 E6 Cassibile Sicilia Italy
195 E6 Cassibile r. Sicilia Italy
256 B3 Cassilândia Brazil
83 G3 Cassilis N.S.W. Austr.
190 D4 Cassine Italy
193 F3 Cassino Italy
161 D5 Cassis France
236 E2 Cass Lake MN U.S.A.
146 D4 Cassley r. Scotland U.K.
191 G3 Cassola Italy
209 B7 Cassongue Angola
226 D5 Cassopolis MI U.S.A.
161 A4 Cassuéjouls France
237 E4 Cassville MO U.S.A.
176 G3 Častá Slovakia
190 D3 Castagliona Olona Italy
191 G3 Castagnaro Italy
192 C1 Castagneto Carducci Italy
190 D4 Castagnole delle Lanze Italy
190 D4 Castagnole Monferrato Italy
187 C6 Castalla Spain
183 E5 Castañar de Ibor Spain
183 H2 Castañares de Rioja Spain
163 D5 Castanet-Tolosan France
254 D2 Castanhal Brazil
182 C4 Castanheira Port.
182 B4 Castanheira de Pêra Port.
260 C2 Castaño r. Arg.
190 D3 Castano Primo Italy
243 E3 Castaños Mex.
190 E2 Castasegna Switz.
190 E3 Casteggio Italy
183 I2 Castejón Spain
186 D3 Castejón del Puente Spain
186 C3 Castejón de Monegros Spain
186 D2 Castejón de Sos Spain
186 C3 Castejón de Valdejasa Spain
193 H3 Castèl Baronia Italy
191 I5 Castelbellino Italy
191 G4 Castèl Bolognese Italy
194 D5 Castelbuono Sicilia Italy
193 H4 Castelcivita Italy
194 C4 Casteldaccia Sicilia Italy
191 F3 Castèl d'Ario Italy
190 C4 Casteldelfino Italy
193 F2 Castèl del Monte Italy
192 D2 Castèl del Piano Italy
191 G4 Castèl del Rio Italy
194 D5 Castèl di Iudica Sicilia Italy
193 F2 Castèl di Lama Italy
194 D5 Castèl di Lucio Sicilia Italy
193 G3 Castèl di Sangro Italy
182 C4 Casteleiro Port.
191 I5 Castelfidardo Italy
191 F5 Castelfiorentino Italy
186 C3 Castelflorite Spain
191 G5 Castèl Focognano Italy
193 F3 Castelforte Italy
193 H4 Castelfranci Italy
191 G5 Castelfranco di Sopra Italy
191 F5 Castelfranco di Sotto Italy
191 G4 Castelfranco Emilia Italy
193 H3 Castelfranco in Miscano Italy
191 G3 Castelfranco Veneto Italy
193 G2 Castèl Frentano Italy
192 D2 Castèl Giorgio Italy
190 F3 Castèl Goffredo Italy
193 H4 Castelgrande Italy
163 C4 Casteljaloux France
173 E2 Castell Ger.
190 D4 Castell'Alfero Italy
193 F2 Castellalto Italy
194 B4 Castellammare, Golfo di b. Sicilia Italy
194 B4 Castellammare del Golfo Sicilia Italy
193 G4 Castellammare di Stabia Italy
190 C3 Castellamonte Italy
195 G2 Castellana Grotte Italy
161 E5 Castellane France
195 F2 Castellaneta Italy
195 F2 Castellaneta Marina Italy
185 H2 Castellanos mt. Spain
183 F2 Castellanos de Castro Spain
185 E4 Castellar de la Frontera Spain
183 I4 Castellar de la Muela Spain
186 E2 Castellar de la Ribera Spain
185 G2 Castellar de Santiago Spain
185 G2 Castellar de Santisteban Spain
190 E4 Castell'Arquato Italy
192 D2 Castell'Azzara Italy
190 D4 Castellazzo Bormida Italy
186 D3 Castelldans Spain
186 G3 Castell d'Aro Spain
186 D4 Castell de Cabres Spain
187 C6 Castell de Castells Spain
186 E3 Castelldefels Spain
185 G4 Castell de Ferro Spain
190 E3 Castelleone Italy
190 D3 Castelletto sopra Ticino Italy
186 F2 Castellfollit de la Roca Spain
186 C4 Castellfort Spain
261 I5 Castelli Buenos Aires Arg.
258 E2 Castelli Chaco Arg.
191 G5 Castellina in Chianti Italy
191 F5 Castellina Marittima Italy
193 F3 Castelliri Italy
Castell-nedd Neath Port Talbot, Wales U.K. see Neath
Castell Newydd Emlyn Ceredigion, Wales U.K. see Newcastle Emlyn
187 C5 Castellnovo Spain
191 G4 Castello d'Argile Italy
Castello de Ampurias Spain see Castellò d'Empúries
187 C5 Castelló de la Plana Spain
186 G2 Castellò d'Empúries Spain
187 C6 Castelló de Rugat Spain
190 D4 Castello di Annone Italy
187 C4 Castellón prov. Valencia Spain
Castellón de la Plana Spain see Castelló de la Plana
186 C4 Castellote Spain
191 G2 Castello Tesino Italy
186 D3 Castellserà Spain
186 F3 Castellterçol Spain
191 F3 Castellucchio Italy
193 H3 Castelluccio dei Sauri Italy
193 H4 Castelluccio Inferiore Italy
193 H3 Castellucio Valmaggiore Italy
194 D4 Castell'Umberto Sicilia Italy
194 B4 Castelluzzo Sicilia Italy
193 E3 Castèl Madama Italy
191 G4 Càstel Maggiore Italy
190 C4 Castelmagno Italy
191 G3 Castelmassa Italy
163 C4 Castelmoron-sur-Lot France
194 D1 Castel Morrone Italy
163 D5 Castelnau France
163 C5 Castelnau-Barbarens France
163 D5 Castelnaudary France
163 C5 Castelnau-d'Auzan France
163 C4 Castelnaud-de-Gratecambe France
163 E5 Castelnau-de-Brassac France
162 B3 Castelnau-de-Médoc France
163 D5 Castelnau-de-Montmiral France
163 D5 Castelnau d'Estréfonds France
161 B5 Castelnau-le-Lez France
163 C5 Castelnau-Magnoac France
163 D4 Castelnau-Montratier France
163 B5 Castelnau-Rivière-Basse France
191 F4 Castelnovo di Sotto Italy
190 F4 Castelnovo ne'Monti Italy
191 G5 Castelnuovo Berardenga Italy
193 H3 Castelnuovo della Daunia Italy
190 F4 Castelnuovo di Garfagnana Italy
192 C1 Castelnuovo di Val di Cecina Italy
190 C3 Castelnuovo Don Bosco Italy
190 D4 Castelnuovo Scrivia Italy
257 G4 Castelo Brazil
182 D4 Castelo Bom Port.
216 □1c Castelo Branco Faial Azores
182 D3 Castelo Branco Bragança Port.
182 C5 Castelo Branco Castelo Branco Port.
182 C4 Castelo Branco admin. dist. Port.
182 B5 Castelo de Bode, Barragem do resr Port.
182 B3 Castelo de Paiva Port.
184 C1 Castelo de Vide Port.
182 B3 Castelo do Neiva Port.
254 E3 Castelo do Piauí Brazil
182 B3 Castelões Port.
182 C3 Castelo Melhor Port.
182 D4 Castelo Mendo Port.
182 D4 Castelo Rodrigo Port.
191 I5 Castelplanio Italy
191 I5 Castelraimondo Italy
193 E2 Castèl Ritaldi Italy
191 G2 Castelrotto Italy
163 C4 Castelsagrat France
190 E3 Castèl San Giovanni Italy
191 G5 Castèl San Niccolò Italy
191 G4 Castèl San Pietro Terme Italy
193 F2 Castèl Sant'Angelo Italy
193 F2 Castelsantangelo sul Nera Italy
193 H4 Castelsaraceno Italy
192 A4 Castelsardo Sardegna Italy
163 D4 Castelsarrasin France
186 C4 Castelseras Spain
194 C5 Casteltermini Sicilia Italy
190 E3 Castelverde Italy
193 G3 Castelvetere in Val Fortore Italy
194 B5 Castelvetrano Sicilia Italy
190 E3 Castelvetro Placentino Italy
192 E2 Castèl Viscardo Italy
193 F3 Castèl Volturno Italy
191 G4 Castenaso Italy
163 C5 Castéra-Verduzan France
82 E4 Casterton Vic. Austr.
163 B5 Castetnau-Camblong France
163 A5 Castets France
192 B5 Castiadas Sardegna Italy
187 B4 Castielfabib Spain
186 C2 Castiello de Jaca Spain
192 B2 Castifao Corse France
190 F5 Castiglioncello Italy
191 G4 Castiglione dei Pepoli Italy
192 E1 Castiglione del Lago Italy
192 C2 Castiglione della Pescaia Italy
190 F3 Castiglione della Stiviere Italy
192 D1 Castiglione d'Orcia Italy
192 E2 Castiglione in Teverina Italy
193 G3 Castiglione Messer Marino Italy
191 G5 Castiglion Fiorentino Italy
193 F2 Castignano Italy
185 E1 Castilblanco Spain
184 E3 Castilblanco de los Arroyos Spain
232 D3 Castile NY U.S.A.
256 B4 Castilho Brazil
183 I2 Castiliscar Spain
250 A6 Castilla Peru
183 G5 Castilla - La Mancha aut. comm. Spain
183 F3 Castilla y León aut. comm. Spain
184 D3 Castilleja de la Cuesta Spain
185 H3 Castillejar Spain
183 E3 Castillejo hill Spain
182 D4 Castillejo de Martin Viejo Spain
183 G3 Castillejo de Mesleón Spain
183 G3 Castillejo de Robledo Spain
250 D2 Castilletes Col.
260 C3 Castillo, Cerro del mt. Arg.
259 C7 Castillo, Pampa del hills Arg.
183 F4 Castillo de Bayuela Spain
183 H5 Castillo de Garcimuñoz Spain
185 G3 Castillo de Locubín Spain
163 D6 Castillon-en-Couserans France
163 B4 Castillon-la-Bataille France
163 C4 Castillonnès France
186 B2 Castillo-Nuevo Spain
258 G4 Castillos Uru.
258 G4 Castillos, Lago de l. Uru.
183 H3 Castilruiz Spain
190 F3 Castione della Presolana Italy
178 E5 Castiòns di Strada Italy
147 B3 Castlebar Rep. of Ireland
146 A5 Castlebay Western Isles, Scotland U.K.
147 E3 Castlebellingham Rep. of Ireland
147 C3 Castleblakeney Rep. of Ireland
147 E2 Castleblayney Rep. of Ireland
151 F2 Castle Bromwich West Midlands, England U.K.
149 G3 Castle Carrock Cumbria, England U.K.
150 E3 Castle Cary Somerset, England U.K.
147 D4 Castlecomer Rep. of Ireland
147 C4 Castleconnell Rep. of Ireland
147 B2 Castleconor Rep. of Ireland
241 L2 Castle Dale UT U.S.A.
226 B2 Castle Danger MN U.S.A.
147 E2 Castledawson Northern Ireland U.K.
147 D2 Castlederg Northern Ireland U.K.
147 E4 Castledermot Rep. of Ireland
241 J5 Castle Dome Mountains AZ U.S.A.
151 F2 Castle Donington Leicestershire, England U.K.
146 E7 Castle Douglas Dumfries and Galloway, Scotland U.K.
147 E4 Castleellis Rep. of Ireland
147 D2 Castlefinn Rep. of Ireland
149 H4 Castleford West Yorkshire, England U.K.
147 C5 Castlefreke Rep. of Ireland
147 C2 Castlegal Rep. of Ireland
222 G5 Castlegar B.C. Can.
147 A4 Castlegregory Rep. of Ireland
147 B2 Castlehill Rep. of Ireland
246 D2 Castle Island Bahamas
147 B4 Castleisland Rep. of Ireland
148 B4 Castlejordan Rep. of Ireland
146 D7 Castle Kennedy Dumfries and Galloway, Scotland U.K.
147 C4 Castlelyons Rep. of Ireland
83 F4 Castlemaine Vic. Austr.
147 B4 Castlemaine Rep. of Ireland
150 B3 Castlemartin Pembrokeshire, Wales U.K.
147 C5 Castlemartyr Rep. of Ireland
222 H5 Castle Mountain Alta Can.
240 G4 Castle Mountain CA U.S.A.
81 F4 Castlepoint North I. N.Z.
147 D3 Castlepollard Rep. of Ireland
147 C3 Castlerea Rep. of Ireland
83 F2 Castlereagh r. N.S.W. Austr.
147 F2 Castlereagh Northern Ireland U.K.
147 E1 Castlerock Northern Ireland U.K.
239 F4 Castle Rock CO U.S.A.
238 B2 Castle Rock WA U.S.A.
147 E1 Castleroe Northern Ireland U.K.
149 H3 Castleside Durham, England U.K.
246 □ Castleton Jamaica
149 I3 Castleton North Yorkshire, England U.K.
233 G3 Castleton-On-Hudson NY U.S.A.
148 E3 Castletown Isle of Man
147 B3 Castletown Clare Rep. of Ireland
147 C5 Castletown Cork Rep. of Ireland
147 D4 Castletown Laois Rep. of Ireland
147 E3 Castletown Meath Rep. of Ireland
146 E3 Castletown Highland, Scotland U.K.
147 C4 Castletownroche Rep. of Ireland
147 B3 Castleville Rep. of Ireland
147 F2 Castlewellan Northern Ireland U.K.
223 I4 Castor Alta Can.
224 E2 Castor, Rivière du r. Que. Can.
237 E6 Castor Creek r. LA U.S.A.
Castra Regina Ger. see Regensburg
183 F2 Castrejón de la Peña Spain
182 C3 Castrelo do Val Spain
163 E5 Castres France
164 D2 Castricum Neth.
161 B5 Castries France
247 □3 Castries St Lucia
195 H3 Castrignano del Capo Italy
185 H3 Castril Spain
185 H3 Castril r. Spain
183 F3 Castrillo de Don Juan Spain
183 F3 Castrillo de Duero Spain
183 G3 Castrillo de la Reina Spain
183 G3 Castrillo de la Vega Spain
183 F2 Castrillo de Villavega Spain
183 F3 Castrillo Tejeriego Spain
256 C6 Castro Brazil
259 B6 Castro Chile
195 H2 Castro Italy
182 C2 Castro Spain
182 A1 Castro r. Spain
254 F5 Castro Alves Brazil
183 G1 Castrobarto Spain
182 E2 Castrocalbón Spain
182 C2 Castro Caldelas Spain
191 G4 Castrocaro Terme Italy
182 D2 Castrocontrigo Spain
182 C4 Castro Daire Port.
193 F3 Castro dei Volsci Italy
185 F3 Castro del Río Spain
182 C1 Castro de Ouro Spain
182 C1 Castro de Rei Spain
194 C5 Castrofilippo Sicilia Italy
182 E3 Castrogonzalo Spain
183 F2 Castrojeriz Spain
182 B2 Castro Laboreiro Port.
184 C3 Castro Marim Port.
183 F2 Castromocho Spain
183 E3 Castromonte Spain
182 E3 Castronuevo Spain
183 E3 Castronuño Spain
194 C5 Castronuovo di Sicilia Sicilia Italy
193 G3 Castropignano Italy
182 D2 Castropodame Spain
182 C1 Castropol Spain
169 C4 Castrop-Rauxel Ger.
195 E4 Castroreale Sicilia Italy
183 G1 Castro-Urdiales Spain
182 B2 Castrove hill Spain
184 B3 Castro Verde Port.
182 C1 Castroverde Spain
183 E3 Castroverde de Campos Spain
193 I5 Castrovillari Italy
240 G3 Castroville CA U.S.A.
252 B3 Castrovirreyna Peru
184 E2 Castuera Spain
106 A1 Cast Uul mt. Mongolia
86 E2 Casuarina, Mount hill W.A. Austr.
127 F3 Çat Turkey
209 C8 Catabola Angola
242 □I6 Catacamas Hond.
250 A6 Catacaos Peru
250 B6 Catacocha Ecuador
187 C5 Catadau Spain
257 F4 Cataguases Brazil
92 B3 Catainğan Phil.
127 F3 Çatak Turkey
256 D3 Catalão Brazil
199 F1 Çatalca Turkey
199 F1 Çatalca Yarımadası pen. Turkey
241 L5 Catalina AZ U.S.A.
Catalonia aut. comm. Spain see Cataluña
186 E3 Cataluña aut. comm. Spain
Catalunya aut. comm. Spain see Cataluña
126 D2 Çatalzeytin Turkey
258 D3 Catamarca Arg.
258 D2 Catamarca prov. Arg.
Catambia Moz. see Catandica
Catana Sicilia Italy see Catania
92 B3 Catanauan Phil.
213 G3 Catandica Moz.
92 C3 Catanduanes i. Phil.
256 C4 Catanduva Brazil
256 A6 Catanduvas Brazil
195 E5 Catania Sicilia Italy
194 D5 Catania prov. Sicilia Italy
195 E5 Catania, Golfo di g. Sicilia Italy
195 F4 Catanzaro Italy
195 F4 Catanzaro prov. Calabria Italy
195 F4 Catanzaro Marina Italy
226 B3 Cataract WI U.S.A.
254 F3 Catarina Brazil
237 D6 Catarina TX U.S.A.
92 C3 Catarman Phil.
187 C5 Catarroja Spain
234 C2 Catasauqua PA U.S.A.
82 C3 Catastrophe, Cape S.A. Austr.
226 B3 Catawba WI U.S.A.
231 D5 Catawba r. SC U.S.A.
227 I5 Catawissa PA U.S.A.
234 B2 Catawissa Creek r. PA U.S.A.
96 D2 Cat Ba, Đao i. Vietnam
92 C4 Catbalogan Phil.
246 C1 Cat Cays is Bahamas
92 C5 Cateel Phil.
245 G4 Catemaco Mex.
245 G4 Catemaco, Laguna l. Mex.
260 B3 Catemu Chile
194 D5 Catenanuova Sicilia Italy
209 B8 Catengue Angola
151 G3 Caterham Surrey, England U.K.
192 A2 Cateri Corse France
209 B7 Catete Angola
251 H6 Catete r. Brazil
83 G4 Cathcart N.S.W. Austr.
215 F5 Cathcart S. Africa
241 I5 Cathedral City CA U.S.A.
215 G3 Cathedral Peak Lesotho
147 A5 Catherdaniel Rep. of Ireland
231 C5 Catherine AL U.S.A.
241 K2 Catherine, Mount UT U.S.A.
240 G3 Catheys Valley CA U.S.A.
238 B2 Cathlamet WA U.S.A.
186 D4 Catí Spain
193 F2 Catignano Italy
206 B4 Catió Guinea-Bissau
246 D1 Cat Island Bahamas
182 C4 Cativelos Port.
232 B5 Catlettsburg KY U.S.A.
243 I4 Catoche, Cabo c. Mex.
182 B2 Catoira Spain
254 F3 Catolé do Rocha Brazil
149 G3 Caton Lancashire, England U.K.
195 E4 Catona r. Italy
234 B3 Catonsville MD U.S.A.
244 D2 Catorce Mex.
244 D2 Catorce, Sierra de mts Mex.
182 D2 Catoute mt. Spain
187 C6 Catral Spain
191 H5 Catria, Monte mt. Italy
260 D5 Catriel Arg.
261 F5 Catriló Arg.
251 F4 Catrimani r. Brazil
146 D6 Catrine East Ayrshire, Scotland U.K.
150 E2 Catshill Worcestershire, England U.K.
233 G3 Catskill NY U.S.A.
233 F3 Catskill Mountains NY U.S.A.
157 G3 Cattenom France
169 F5 Catterfeld Ger.
149 H3 Catterick North Yorkshire, England U.K.
149 H3 Catterick Camp North Yorkshire, England U.K.
146 F5 Catterline Aberdeenshire, Scotland U.K.
81 C6 Cattle Creek South I. N.Z.
191 H5 Cattolica Italy
194 C5 Cattolica Eraclea Sicilia Italy
213 G2 Catur Moz.
163 D4 Catus France
194 C5 Catuso, Monte mt. Sicilia Italy
177 L4 Căuaș Romania
254 C2 Cauaxi r. Brazil
92 B4 Cauayan Phil.
225 I1 Caubvick, Mount Nfld. Can.
250 B4 Cauca dept Col.
250 C2 Cauca r. Col.
254 F2 Caucaia Brazil
250 C3 Caucasia Col.
129 B2 Caucasus mts Asia/Europe
260 C2 Caucete Arg.
158 C4 Caudan France
162 C4 Caudau r. France
159 G2 Caudebec-en-Caux France
163 C4 Caudecoste France
187 C6 Caudete Spain
187 B5 Caudete de las Fuentes Spain
187 C5 Caudiel Spain
163 E6 Caudiès de-Fenouillèdes France
156 D2 Caudry France
163 D5 Caujac France
158 D3 Caulnes France
195 F4 Caulonia Italy
163 D4 Caumont Midi-Pyrénées France
163 D5 Caumont Midi-Pyrénées France
159 F2 Caumont-l'Éventé France
161 C5 Caumont-sur-Durance France
246 C2 Caunao r. Cuba
163 E5 Caunes-Minervois France
209 C7 Caungula Angola
260 A4 Cauquenes Chile
251 E3 Caura r. Venez.
251 F5 Caurés r. Brazil
192 A3 Cauro Corse France
225 H3 Causapscal Que. Can.
136 E4 Căușeni Moldova
147 B4 Causeway Rep. of Ireland
147 E1 Causeway Head Northern Ireland U.K.
163 D4 Caussade France
252 D3 Cautário r. Brazil
163 B6 Cauterets France
246 C2 Cauto r. Cuba
129 F3 Cavad Azer.
193 G4 Cava de'Tirreni Italy
182 B3 Cávado r. Port.
190 D3 Cavaglià Italy
161 D5 Cavaillon France
161 E5 Cavalaire-sur-Mer France
254 D5 Cavalcante Brazil
184 B3 Cavaleiro Port.
191 G2 Cavalese Italy
236 D1 Cavalier ND U.S.A.
190 C4 Cavallermaggiore Italy
191 H3 Cavallino Italy
206 D5 Cavally r. Côte d'Ivoire
190 E3 Cava Manara Italy
147 D3 Cavan Rep. of Ireland
147 D3 Cavan county Rep. of Ireland
190 E2 Cavargna Italy
191 H3 Cavarzere Italy
191 I2 Cavazzo Carnico Italy
199 F2 Çavdarhisar Turkey
199 F3 Çavdır Turkey
81 C6 Cave South I. N.Z.
237 F4 Cave City AR U.S.A.
230 C4 Cave City KY U.S.A.
241 L5 Cave Creek AZ U.S.A.
191 I2 Cave del Predil Italy
161 C5 Caveirac France
87 F5 Cavenagh Range hills W.A. Austr.
83 E4 Cavendish Vic. Austr.
255 B9 Cavera, Serra do hills Brazil
256 A6 Cavernoso, Serra do mts Brazil
150 E2 Caverswall Staffordshire, England U.K.
182 C3 Cavês Port.
191 G4 Cavezzo Italy
251 I4 Caviana, Ilha i. Brazil
162 B3 Cavignac France
92 B3 Cavite Phil.
191 J3 Čavle Croatia
197 F2 Cavnic Romania
193 E3 Cavo, Monte hill Italy
195 F2 Cavone r. Italy
190 C4 Cavour Italy
226 C3 Cavour WI U.S.A.
191 F4 Cavriago Italy
191 G5 Cavriglia Italy
126 C3 Çavuşçu Turkey
199 G3 Çavuşköy Turkey
146 E4 Cawdor Highland, Scotland U.K.
83 E3 Cawndilla Lake imp. l. N.S.W. Austr.
Cawnpore Uttar Prad. India see Kanpur
149 H4 Cawood North Yorkshire, England U.K.
232 B6 Cawood KY U.S.A.
151 I2 Cawston Norfolk, England U.K.
257 E4 Caxambu Brazil
182 B5 Caxarias Port.
254 E3 Caxias Brazil
255 C9 Caxias do Sul Brazil
209 B7 Caxito Angola
251 I5 Caxiuana, Baía de l. Brazil
199 G2 Çay Turkey
129 C3 Çayarası Turkey
199 E2 Çaybaşı İzmir Turkey
Çaybaşı Turkey see Çayeli
231 D5 Cayce SC U.S.A.
126 D2 Çaycuma Turkey
127 F2 Çayeli Turkey
251 H3 Cayenne Fr. Guiana
156 B2 Cayeux-sur-Mer France
247 □1 Cayey Puerto Rico
126 D3 Çayhan Turkey
199 F3 Çayhisar Turkey
126 C2 Çayırhan Turkey
129 B4 Çayırlı Turkey
129 B3 Çaykara Turkey
163 D4 Caylus France
246 C3 Cayman Brac i. Cayman Is
246 B3 Cayman Islands terr. West Indies
264 D4 Cayman Trench sea feature Caribbean Sea
210 E2 Caynabo Somalia
150 E2 Caynham Shropshire, England U.K.
161 B4 Cayres France
246 B2 Cay Sal i. Bahamas
246 B2 Cay Sal Bank sea feature Bahamas
246 D2 Cay Santa Domingo i. Bahamas
149 I4 Caythorpe Lincolnshire, England U.K.
149 I3 Cayton North Yorkshire, England U.K.
240 G4 Cayucos CA U.S.A.
227 H4 Cayuga Ont. Can.
232 E3 Cayuga Heights NY U.S.A.
246 D2 Cay Verde i. Bahamas
209 D7 Cazage Angola
Cazaje Angola see Cazage
183 F4 Cazalegas Spain
184 E3 Cazalla de la Sierra Spain
163 D4 Cazals Midi-Pyrénées France
163 D4 Cazals Midi-Pyrénées France
197 H3 Căzănești Romania
163 B5 Cazaubon France
163 A4 Cazaux et de Sanguinet, Étang de l. France
233 F3 Cazenovia NY U.S.A.
163 D5 Cazères France
163 D4 Cazes-Mondenard France
163 E5 Cazilhac France
188 F3 Čazma Croatia
209 D7 Cazombo Angola
245 F3 Cazones Mex.
245 F3 Cazones r. Mex.
185 H3 Cazorla Spain
185 G3 Cazorla, Sierra de mts Spain
163 D4 Cazoulès France
213 G2 Cazula Moz.
183 F2 Cea Castilla y León Spain
182 C2 Cea Galicia Spain
183 E2 Cea r. Spain
Ceadâr-Lunga Moldova see Ciadîr-Lunga
Ceanannus Mór Meath Rep. of Ireland see Kells
146 A4 Ceann a'Bháigh Western Isles, Scotland U.K.
183 H1 Ceanuri Spain
Ceará Brazil see Fortaleza
254 F3 Ceará state Brazil
264 G6 Ceara Abyssal Plain sea feature S. Atlantic Ocean
146 B3 Cearsiadair Western Isles, Scotland U.K.
197 I3 Ceatalchioi Romania
Ceatharlach Rep. of Ireland see Carlow
159 F3 Ceaucé France
161 B3 Céaux-d'Allègre France
242 D3 Ceballos Mex.
128 A1 Cebireis Dağı mt. Turkey
182 C5 Cebolais de Cima Port.
183 F5 Cebolla Spain
244 B4 Ceboruco, Cerro mt. Mex.
244 B3 Ceboruco, Volcán vol. Mex.
177 I3 Čebovce Slovakia
183 F4 Cebreros Spain
92 B4 Cebu Phil.
92 B4 Cebu i. Phil.
193 F3 Ceccano Italy
177 H5 Cece Hungary
178 C4 Cece, Cima di mt. Italy
177 K3 Čečejovce Slovakia
176 E2 Čechtice Czech Rep.
177 H3 Čechynce Slovakia
226 C3 Cecil WI U.S.A.
234 C3 Cecil County county MD U.S.A.
85 G5 Cecil Plains Qld Austr.
87 D5 Cecil Rhodes, Mount hill W.A. Austr.
234 C3 Cecilton MD U.S.A.
191 F5 Cecina Italy
191 F5 Cecina r. Italy
195 F3 Cecita, Lago di l. Italy
182 D5 Ceclavín Spain
182 C3 Cedães Port.
226 E4 Cedar r. MI U.S.A.
236 C2 Cedar r. ND U.S.A.
236 D3 Cedar r. NE U.S.A.
214 B5 Cedarberg mts S. Africa
232 C6 Cedar Bluff VA U.S.A.
234 D3 Cedar Brook NJ U.S.A.
241 K3 Cedar City UT U.S.A.
239 F4 Cedaredge CO U.S.A.
236 E3 Cedar Falls IA U.S.A.
240 H3 Cedar Grove CA U.S.A.
226 D4 Cedar Grove WI U.S.A.
232 C5 Cedar Grove WV U.S.A.
223 K4 Cedar Lake Man. Can.
230 B3 Cedar Rapids IA U.S.A.
241 L3 Cedar Ridge AZ U.S.A.
226 D3 Cedar River MI U.S.A.
235 D3 Cedar Run NJ U.S.A.
227 F4 Cedar Springs Ont. Can.
226 E4 Cedar Springs MI U.S.A.
231 C5 Cedartown GA U.S.A.
215 G4 Cedarville S. Africa
226 C4 Cedarville IL U.S.A.
227 E3 Cedarville MI U.S.A.
232 B5 Cedarville OH U.S.A.
190 F2 Cedegolo Italy
182 B1 Cedeira Spain
182 B1 Cedeira hill Spain
183 F5 Cedena r. Spain
182 C5 Cedillo Spain
183 G4 Cedillo del Condado Spain
244 D2 Cedral Mex.
186 C4 Cedrillas Spain
192 B4 Cedrino r. Sardegna Italy
254 F3 Cedro Brazil
216 □1c Cedros Faial Azores
244 D1 Cedros Mex.
242 B2 Cedros, Isla i. Mex.
174 G1 Cedry Wielkie Pol.
82 C3 Ceduna S.A. Austr.
174 C3 Cedynia Pol.
182 A2 Cée Spain
210 E3 Ceelbuur Somalia
210 E2 Ceerigaabo Somalia
177 K5 Cefa Romania
194 D4 Cefalù Sicilia Italy
Cefn Bychan Caerphilly, Wales U.K. see Newbridge
150 D2 Cefn-mawr Wrexham, Wales U.K.
183 F3 Cega r. Spain
191 H3 Ceggia Italy
177 I4 Cegléd Hungary
177 I4 Ceglédbercel Hungary
195 G2 Ceglie Messapica Italy
175 J3 Cegłów Pol.
196 E5 Čegrane Macedonia
177 L4 Cehal Romania
185 I2 Cehegín Spain
108 C3 Ceheng Guizhou China
196 D4 Čehotina r. Yugo.
197 F2 Cehu Silvaniei Romania
247 □1 Ceiba Puerto Rico
177 L5 Ceica Romania
161 B5 Ceilhes-et-Rocozels France
Ceinewydd Ceredigion, Wales U.K. see New Quay
183 E2 Ceinos de Campos Spain
157 G4 Ceintrey France
182 B4 Ceira Port.
182 B4 Ceira r. Port.
176 F3 Čejč Czech Rep.
177 K3 Cejkov Slovakia
179 H2 Čejkovice Czech Rep.
174 G2 Cekcyn Pol.
126 D2 Çekerek Turkey
174 G4 Ceków-Kolonia Pol.
186 B4 Celadas Spain
94 C1 Celah, Gunung mt. Malaysia
176 D1 Čelákovice Czech Rep.
193 F2 Celano Italy
182 C2 Celanova Spain
244 D3 Celaya Mex.
147 E3 Celbridge Rep. of Ireland
163 D4 Célé r. France
Celebes i. Indon. see Sulawesi
93 B2 Celebes Sea Indon./Phil.
129 C4 Çelebibağı Turkey
182 B3 Celeiros Port.
250 B6 Celendín Peru
193 G3 Celenza Valfortore Italy
195 F3 Celico Italy
236 G3 Celina OH U.S.A.
231 C4 Celina TN U.S.A.
188 E2 Celje Slovenia
186 B4 Cella Spain
176 G4 Celldömölk Hungary
168 F3 Celle Ger.
192 D2 Cellere Italy
165 C4 Celles Belgium
163 D6 Celles France
162 B2 Celles-sur-Belle France
160 B3 Celles-sur-Durolle France
156 E4 Celles-sur-Ource France
159 H4 Cellettes France
191 H2 Cellina r. Italy
193 F2 Cellino Attanasio Italy
195 G2 Cellino San Marco Italy
193 F3 Cellole Italy
193 H3 Celone r. Italy
182 C4 Celorico da Beira Port.
182 C3 Celorico de Basto Port.
Celovec Austria see Klagenfurt
186 F2 Celrà Spain
145 D6 Celtic Sea Rep. of Ireland/U.K.
264 I2 Celtic Shelf sea feature N. Atlantic Ocean
199 G3 Çeltikçi Turkey
199 F1 Çeltikçi Turkey
129 C4 Çem r. Turkey
95 F2 Cemaru, Gunung mt. Indon.
191 G2 Cembra Italy
126 D2 Cemilbey Turkey
126 E3 Çemişgezek Turkey
150 D2 Cemmaes Powys, Wales U.K.
179 F4 Čemšeniška planina mt. Slovenia
163 D4 Cénac-et-St-Julien France
196 E2 Cenad Romania
191 G2 Cencenighe Agordino Italy
161 C4 Cendras France
162 C4 Cendrieux France
196 E3 Cenei Romania
191 G3 Ceneselli Italy
190 D4 Cengio Italy
183 H2 Cenicero Spain
183 F4 Ceniclentos Spain
185 I1 Cenizate Spain
190 F4 Ceno r. Italy
163 B4 Cenon France
196 E3 Čenta Vojvodina, Srbija Yugo.
190 C4 Centallo Italy
Centane S. Africa see Kentani
81 B6 Centaur Peak South I. N.Z.
Centellas Spain see Centelles
186 F3 Centelles Spain
260 C6 Centenario Arg.
256 B5 Centenário do Sul Brazil
213 F3 Centenary Zimbabwe
236 C2 Center ND U.S.A.
236 D3 Center NE U.S.A.
237 E6 Center TX U.S.A.
232 B4 Centerburg OH U.S.A.
235 E2 Centereach NY U.S.A.
235 F2 Center Moriches NY U.S.A.
233 □H3 Center Ossipee NH U.S.A.
231 C5 Center Point AL U.S.A.
235 E2 Centerport NY U.S.A.
234 C2 Center Square PA U.S.A.
234 C2 Center Valley PA U.S.A.
231 C5 Centerville AL U.S.A.
236 E3 Centerville IA U.S.A.
237 F4 Centerville MO U.S.A.
232 B5 Centerville OH U.S.A.
232 D4 Centerville PA U.S.A.
232 D4 Centerville PA U.S.A.
231 C5 Centerville TN U.S.A.
237 E6 Centerville TX U.S.A.
232 C5 Centerville WV U.S.A.
191 G4 Cento Italy
193 H4 Centola Italy
Centrafricaine, République country Africa see Central African Republic
212 E4 Central admin. dist. Botswana
254 E4 Central Brazil
206 E5 Central admin. reg. Ghana
210 C5 Central prov. Kenya
211 B8 Central admin. reg. Malawi
239 E5 Central NM U.S.A.
209 F8 Central prov. Zambia
252 D4 Central, Cordillera mts Bol.
250 B4 Central, Cordillera mts Col.
246 E3 Central, Cordillera mts Dom. Rep.
242 □J7 Central, Cordillera mts Panama

252 A2 Central, Cordillera *mts* Peru
92 B2 Central, Cordillera *mts* Phil.
247 □1 Central, Cordillera *mts*
Puerto Rico
Central African Empire
country Africa *see*
Central African Republic
208 D3 Central African Republic
country Africa
123 F4 Central Brahui Range
mts Pak.
223 J5 Central Butte *Sask.* Can.
236 F3 Central City *IA* U.S.A.
236 D3 Central City *NE* U.S.A.
232 D4 Central City *PA* U.S.A.
257 G3 Central de Minas Brazil
233 H4 Central Falls *RI* U.S.A.
236 H4 Centralia *IL* U.S.A.
238 B2 Centralia *WA* U.S.A.
235 E2 Central Islip *NY* U.S.A.
123 F5 Central Makran Range
mts Pak.
84 C4 Central Mount Stuart *hill*
N.T. Austr.
84 B4 Central Mount Wedge
N.T. Austr.
266 G5 Central Pacific Basin
sea feature Pacific Ocean
Central Provinces *state* India
see Madhya Pradesh
215 G3 Central Range *mts* Lesotho
91 J7 Central Range P.N.G.
Central Russian Upland *hills*
Rus. Fed. *see* Sredne-
Russkaya Vozvyshennost'
Central Siberian Plateau
Rus. Fed. *see* Sredne-
Sibirskoye Ploskogor'ye
233 E3 Central Square *NY* U.S.A.
235 D1 Central Valley *NY* U.S.A.
235 G1 Central Village *CT* U.S.A.
207 H5 Centre *prov.* Cameroon
162 D1 Centre *admin. reg.* France
231 C5 Centre *AL* U.S.A.
234 B3 Centreville *MD* U.S.A.
226 E5 Centreville *MI* U.S.A.
232 E5 Centreville *VA* U.S.A.
192 B2 Centuri *Corse* France
215 G1 Centurion S. Africa
194 D5 Centuripe *Sicilia* Italy
231 C6 Century *FL* U.S.A.
109 D4 Cenxi *Guangxi* China
Ceos *i.* Greece *see* Kea
146 B3 Ceos *Western Isles,*
Scotland U.K.
163 D4 Céou *r.* France
193 G2 Cepagatti Italy
Cephaloedium *Sicilia* Italy *see*
Cefalù
Cephalonia *i.* Greece *see*
Kefallonia
188 G3 Čepin Croatia
182 C4 Cepões Port.
156 C4 Cepoy France
194 D1 Ceppaloni Italy
193 F3 Ceprano Italy
95 E4 Cepu *Jawa Tengah* Indon.
196 D3 Cer *hills* Yugo.
Ceram *i. Maluku* Indon. *see*
Seram
194 D5 Cerami *Sicilia* Italy
194 D5 Cerami *r. Sicilia* Italy
Ceram Sea Indon. *see*
Seram Sea
190 D3 Cerano Italy
175 K3 Ceranów Pol.
159 G4 Cérans-Foulletourte France
195 E4 Cerasi Italy
193 H4 Ceraso Italy
161 L6 Cerbăl Romania
241 J4 Cerbat Mountains *AZ* U.S.A.
163 F6 Cerbère France
186 G2 Cerbère, Cap *c.* France/Spain
Cerb, Cap *c.* France *see* Servol
184 B1 Cercal Lisboa Port.
184 B3 Cercal Setúbal Port.
184 B3 Cercal *hill* Port.
176 D2 Čerčany Czech Rep.
183 F4 Cercedilla Spain
182 B2 Cercedo Spain
193 F2 Cercemaggiore Italy
193 F2 Cerchio Italy
176 B2 Čerchov *mt.* Czech Rep.
160 B2 Cercy-la-Tour France
194 C5 Cerda *Sicilia* Italy
186 F3 Cerdanyola del Vallès Spain
182 C4 Cerdeira Port.
159 I4 Cerdon France
163 D4 Cère *r.* France
193 G2 Cerea Italy
223 I5 Cereal *Alta* Can.
177 I3 Cered Hungary
150 D2 Ceredigion *admin. div.*
Wales U.K.
191 G3 Ceregnano Italy
174 T3 Cerekwica Pol.
158 E3 Cérences France
195 F3 Cerenzia Italy
261 G1 Ceres Arg.
254 C5 Ceres Brazil
190 C3 Ceres Italy
214 B5 Ceres S. Africa
240 G3 Ceres *CA* U.S.A.
190 C3 Ceresole Reale Italy
159 G2 Ceresone *r.* Italy
161 D5 Cèreste France
163 E6 Céret France
250 C2 Cereté Col.
183 G3 Cerezo de Abajo Spain
183 G3 Cerezo de Arriba Spain
183 G2 Cerezo de Riotirón Spain
165 D4 Cerfontaine Belgium
177 K2 Čergov *mts* Slovakia
153 G3 Cergy France
171 G5 Cerhenice Czech Rep.
190 C4 Ceriale Italy
190 C5 Ceriana Italy
193 H3 Cerignola Italy
Cerigo *i.* Greece *see* Kythira
126 D3 Çerikli Turkey
160 A2 Cérilly France
156 D4 Cerisiers France
159 F2 Cerisy-la-Forêt France
158 G2 Cerisy-la-Salle France
159 F5 Cerizay France
191 J3 Cerk *mt.* Slovenia
126 D2 Çerkeş Turkey
199 F1 Çerkezköy Turkey
199 E1 Çerkezmillen Turkey
179 H4 Çerklje Slovenia
188 E3 Cerknica Slovenia
179 E4 Cerkno Slovenia
129 C3 Çerme Turkey
197 E2 Cermei Romania
193 F2 Cermignano Italy
126 E3 Çermik Turkey
197 I3 Černa Romania
197 F3 Cerna *r.* Romania
197 F3 Cerna *r.* Romania
197 G3 Cerna *r.* Romania
182 B5 Cernache do Bonjardim
Port.
176 F2 Černá Hora Czech Rep.
176 D3 Černá Hora *mt.* Czech Rep.
197 H3 Cernat Romania
Cernăuți *Chernivts'ka Oblast'*
Ukr. *see* Chernivtsi
197 I3 Cernavodă Romania
157 H5 Cernay France
176 C1 Černčice Czech Rep.
156 C2 Cerney-en-Dormois France
176 C1 Černčice Czech Rep.
183 G2 Cernégula Spain
179 H4 Černelavci Slovenia
190 D1 Cernier Switz.
177 L2 Černiny *hill* Slovakia
190 E3 Cernobbio Italy
176 D2 Černošice Czech Rep.
176 B2 Černovice Czech Rep.
176 C2 Černovice Czech Rep.
163 D4 Cérou *r.* France
256 C5 Cerqueira César Brazil
182 D4 Cerralbo Spain
243 F3 Cerralvo Mex.
131 B2 Cerro d'Esi Italy
193 E2 Cerreto Sannita Italy
193 G3 Cerro Sannita Italy
150 D1 Cerrigydrudion *Conwy,*
Wales U.K.
196 D5 Cërrik Albania
258 D2 Cerrillos Arg.

244 D2 Cerritos Mex.
193 G3 Cerro al Volturno Italy
256 C6 Cerro Azul Brazil
245 F3 Cerro Azul Mex.
252 A3 Cerro Azul Peru
258 C2 Cerro Bonete *mt.* Arg.
188 E3 Cerro de Hierro Spain
244 C4 Cerro de Ortega Mex.
252 A2 Cerro de Pasco Peru
185 G4 Cerrón *mt.* Spain
250 D2 Cerrón, Cerro *mt.* Venez.
260 C6 Cerros Colorados, Embalse
resr Arg.
159 F4 Cersay France
193 I4 Cersosimo Italy
191 G5 Certaldo Italy
177 G3 Certeju de Sus Romania
190 D3 Certosa di Pavia Italy
190 C4 Certosa di Pesio Italy
182 C3 Cerva Port.
182 B3 Cervães Port.
193 H4 Cervaro *mt.* Spain
87 B6 Cervantes *W.A.* Austr.
259 B8 Cervantes, Cerro *mt.* Arg.
193 F3 Cervaro Italy
193 H3 Cervaro *r.* Italy
191 M4 Cervati, Monte *mt.* Italy
183 F2 Cervatos de la Cueza Spain
176 F1 Červená Voda Czech Rep.
171 G5 Červené Pečky Czech Rep.
197 G2 Cervenia Romania
176 D2 Červenka Czech Rep.
186 E3 Cervera Spain
183 I3 Cervera de la Cañada Spain
183 F4 Cervera de Llano Spain
183 F4 Cervera de los Montes Spain
183 I2 Cervera del Río Alhama Spain
183 F2 Cervera de Pisuerga Spain
192 E3 Cerveteri Italy
193 I2 Cervia Italy
193 H4 Cervialto, Monte *mt.* Italy
191 I3 Cervignano del Friuli Italy
191 G2 Cervina, Punta *mt.* Italy
193 G3 Cervinara Italy
176 E2 Červivá Řečice Czech Rep.
182 B2 Cervione *Corse* France
190 D5 Cervo Italy
190 D3 Cervo *r.* Italy
182 C1 Cervo Spain
160 B1 Cervon France
193 I5 Cerzeto Italy
191 I5 Cesano *r.* Italy
250 C2 César *dept* Col.
250 C2 César *r.* Col.
96 C4 Cesa *r.* Thai.
261 I2 Cesar Arg.
178 D5 Cesen, Monte *mt.* Italy
123 G4 Cesar *r.* Pak.
213 F3 Cesari Zimbabwe
211 C6 Chake Chake Tanz.
117 E4 Chakia *Uttar Prad.* India
222 H5 Chak Jhumra Pak.
117 F5 Chakradharpur *Bihar* India
117 F5 Chakulia *Bihar* India
129 B3 Ch'ak'vi Georgia
123 H3 Chakwal Pak.
252 B3 Chala Peru
163 B6 Chalabre France
162 C3 Chalais France
190 C2 Chalais Switz.
161 E3 Chalamont France
123 F3 Chalap Dalan *mts* Afgh.
160 C2 Chalaronne *r.* France
242 □H6 Chalatenango El Salvador
213 H3 Chalaua Moz.
244 C2 Chalchihuites Mex.
245 E4 Chalco Mex.
151 F4 Chale *Isle of Wight,*
England U.K.
162 C3 Chalais France
161 C4 Chaleon France
111 F4 Chalengkou *Qinghai* China
156 C4 Châlette-sur-Loing France
225 H3 Chaleur Bay *inlet*
N.B./Que. Can.
Chaleurs, Baie de *inlet*
N.B./Que. Can. *see* Chaleur Bay
234 C2 Chalfont *PA* U.S.A.
150 E3 Chalford *Gloucestershire,*
England U.K.
Chalgrove *Oxfordshire,*
England U.K.
259 C8 Chalia *r.* Arg.
175 H3 Chalin Pol.
157 F5 Chalindrey France
109 C3 Chaling *Hunan* China
116 C5 Chalisgaon *Maharashtra* India
114 C4 Chalisseri *Kerala* India
160 A2 Chalivoy-Milon France
Chalkar, Ozero *salt l.* Kazakh. *see* Shalkar, Ozero
198 C2 Chalki *Thessalia* Greece
199 E3 Chalki *i.* Greece
198 C2 Chalkida Greece
198 C1 Chalkidona *Kentriki Makedonia*
Greece
121 I4 Chalkudysu Kazakh.
114 C3 Challakere *Karnataka* India
116 D3 Challapata Bol.
252 D4 Challapata Bol.
266 E5 Challenger Deep *sea feature*
N. Pacific Ocean
156 E3 Challerange France
162 B3 Challes-les-Eaux France
183 F3 Challis *ID* U.S.A.
237 F6 Chalmette *LA* U.S.A.
160 B2 Chalmoux France
160 C2 Chaloire *r.* France
162 B1 Chalonnes-sur-Loire France
156 E4 Châlons-en-Champagne
France
Châlons-sur-Marne France *see*
Châlons-en-Champagne
160 C2 Chalon-sur-Saône France
129 C2 Chaloyan Georgia
116 C1 Chalt *Jammu and Kashmir*
137 J4 Chaltyr' Rus. Fed.
97 C4 Chaltyr' Rus. Fed.
215 I5 Chalumna S. Africa
162 C3 Chalus France

226 A2 Chaffey *WI* U.S.A.
173 G2 Chamerau Ger.
156 E5 Chamesson France
162 D3 Chameyrat France
260 D2 Chamical Arg.
120 F3 Chamgan *Kyzl-Ordinskaya Oblast'*
Kazakh.
210 C3 Ch'amo Hāyk' *l.* Eth.
190 C3 Chamonix Italy
Chamoli *Uttar Prad.* India *see*
Gopeshwar
160 E3 Chamonix-Mont-Blanc
France
Chamouchouane *r.* Que. Can.
see Ashuapmushuan
161 D4 Chamouse, Montagne de *mt.*
France
160 E3 Chamoux-sur-Gelon France
117 E5 Champa *Madh. Prad.* India
162 E3 Champagnac France
162 C3 Champagnac-de-Belair
France
161 B3 Champagne Y.T. Can.
222 B2 Champagne Y.T. Can.
159 G3 Champagné France
156 E4 Champagne-Ardenne
admin. reg. France
215 G3 Champagne Castle *mt.*
S. Africa
160 D3 Champagne-en-Valromey
France
162 C3 Champagne-Mouton France
159 G3 Champagne-sur-Oise France
156 C4 Champagne-sur-Seine France
157 G5 Champagney France
160 D2 Champagnole France
86 E2 Champagny Islands
W.A. Austr.
230 B3 Champaign *IL* U.S.A.
149 F2 Champany *Falkirk,*
Scotland U.K.
260 E2 Champaqui, Cerro *mt.* Arg.
252 A2 Champan *r.* Peru
97 D4 Champasak Laos
156 D4 Champaubert France
162 C3 Champcevinel France
162 B2 Champdeniers-St-Denis
France
160 C1 Champ-d'Oiseau France
157 H4 Champ du Feu *mt.* France
160 B3 Champeix France
190 B2 Champéry Switz.
157 G7 Champforgeuil France
159 F3 Champgenéteux France
117 H5 Champhai *Mizoram* India
161 D3 Champier France
159 F4 Champigné France
162 C3 Champigneulles France
159 G4 Champigny France
156 E4 Champignol-lez-Mondeville
France
156 C4 Champigny France
222 H1 Champion Alta Can.
226 D2 Champion *MI* U.S.A.
233 G2 Champlain *NY* U.S.A.
232 E5 Champlain *VA* U.S.A.
233 G2 Champlain, Lake *Can./U.S.A.*
252 A2 Chao Peru
160 B3 Chao Spain
107 H4 Chaobai *r.* China
109 F2 Chaohu *Anhui* China
109 F2 Chao Hu *l.* China
97 C4 Chao Phraya *r.* Thai.
Chaor *Nei Mongol* China *see*
Zalantun
204 D2 Chaouèn *prov.* Morocco
204 C2 Chaouèn Morocco
158 C3 Chaource France
109 F4 Chaoyang *Guangdong* China
107 H4 Chaoyang *Guangdong* China *see*
Jiayin
Chaoyang *Liaoning* China *see*
Huinan
107 I1 Chaoyang *Liaoning* China
107 I1 Chaoyang *Nei Mongol* China
113 D2 Chaozhou *Guangdong* China
253 G3 Chapada dos Guimarães
Brazil
255 B6 Chapadão do Sul Brazil
254 E2 Chapadinha Brazil
224 C3 Chapais Que. Can.
244 D4 Chanak Turkey *see* Çanakkale
243 G5 Chanal Mex.
260 E5 Chañar Arg.
258 C2 Chañar *r.* Port./Spain
244 B3 Chapala Mex.
122 D2 Chañarán Iran
261 F3 Chañar Ladeado Arg.
251 F3 Chanaro, Cerro *mt.* Venez.
161 C3 Chanas France
184 C1 Chanca Port.
Chança *r.* Port./Spain *see*
Chanza
160 C1 Chanceaux France
159 G4 Chanceaux-sur-Choisille
France
182 B5 Chancelaria Port.
247 □2 Chances Peak *vol.* Montserrat
260 A4 Chanco Chile
Chanda *Mahar.* India *see*
Chandrapur
220 D3 Chandalar *r. AK* U.S.A.
116 D3 Chandausi *Uttar Prad.* India
117 F5 Chandbali Orissa India
116 B5 Chanderi *Madh. Prad.* India
116 D3 Chandia *Madh. Prad.* India
116 D3 Chandigarh *Chandigarh* India
117 F5 Chandil *Bihar* India
225 H3 Chandler Que. Can.
241 G5 Chandler *AZ* U.S.A.
237 D5 Chandler *OK* U.S.A.
122 E3 Chandler *r.* Brazil
224 D4 Chapleau Ont. Can.
223 J5 Chaplin *Sask.* Can.
137 K5 Chaplygin Rus. Fed.
137 H5 Chaplyivka Ukr.
139 L5 Chaplynka Ukr.
137 G4 Chaplynka Ukr.
222 F4 Chapman, Mount B.C. Can.
232 D4 Chapmanville *PA* U.S.A.
232 B6 Chapmanville *WV* U.S.A.
125 □ Chapman's Peak *vol.* S. Africa
83 F5 Chappell Islands *Tas.* Austr.
162 A2 Chapra *Bihar* India *see*
Chhapra
258 F2 Charadai Arg.
252 A4 Charagua Bol.
252 C4 Charaña Bol.
258 E2 Charata Arg.
160 C2 Charbonnat France
162 D3 Charbonnel, Pointe de *mt.*
France
244 D2 Charcas Mex.
160 B1 Charcenne France
160 D2 Charchilla France
262 S2 Charcot Island Antarctica
223 I4 Chard Alta Can.
150 E4 Chard *Somerset, England* U.K.
Chardara Kazakh. *see*
Shardara
121 G4 Chardarinskoye
Vodokhranilishche *resr*
Kazakh./Uzbek.
232 C4 Chardon *OH* U.S.A.
150 E4 Chardstock *Devon,*
England U.K.
159 F4 Chardzhev Turkm. *see*
Chardzhou
Chardzhev Turkm. *see* Chardzhev

161 D3 Chamechaude *mt.* France
156 E5 Chamelet France
162 D3 Champeix France
260 D2 Champagnat France
107 H3 Changping *Beijing* China
109 F4 Changpu *Hunan* China *see*
Suining
109 E2 Changsha *Hunan* China
109 F2 Changshan *Zhejiang* China
107 I4 Changshan Qundao *is* China
108 C3 Changshi *Guizhou* China
108 C2 Changshou *Chongqing* China
109 D3 Changshou *Hunan* China *see*
Dongxiang
109 G2 Changshu *Jiangsu* China
156 C3 Changsong S. Korea
109 D3 Changshou *Hunan* China *see*
Changde
101 C5 Changting *Fujian* China
100 D3 Changting *Heilong.* China
101 C4 Changting *Liaoning* China
242 □J7 Changuinola Panama
100 C4 Ch'angwön S. Korea
107 E5 Changwu *Shaanxi* China
109 F2 Changxing *Zhejiang* China
101 C5 Changyi *Shandong* China
107 H4 Changyi *Shandong* China
101 C5 Changyön N. Korea
101 C5 Changyuan *Chongqing* China *see*
Rongchang
107 G5 Changyuan *Henan* China
108 C4 Changzhi *Shanxi* China
107 G4 Changzhi *Shanxi* China
109 F2 Changzhou *Jiangsu* China
198 D4 Chania *Kriti* Greece
162 B3 Chaniers France
198 C4 Chanion, Kolpos *b. Kriti*
Greece
161 G3 Chankou Gansu China
133 D4 Channagiri *Karnataka* India
114 C3 Channapatna *Karnataka* India
120 E5 Channel Islands English Chan.
240 H5 Channel Islands *CA* U.S.A.
225 J4 Channel-Port-aux-Basques
Nfld. Can.
246 C2 Channel Rock *i.* Bahamas
145 H6 Channel Tunnel France/U.K.
160 B3 Channing *MI* U.S.A.
237 C5 Channing *TX* U.S.A.
182 C3 Chantada Spain
131 S3 Chantal'skiy *mt.* Rus. Fed.
162 B2 Chantelle France
158 E3 Chantepie France
162 A2 Chantonnay France
160 E1 Chantrans France
159 F3 Chanu France
161 G3 Chanute *KS* U.S.A.
130 I4 Chany, Ozero *salt l.* Rus. Fed.
252 A2 Chao Peru
160 B3 Chao Spain
107 H4 Chaobai *r.* China
109 F2 Chaohu *Anhui* China
109 F2 Chao Hu *l.* China
97 C4 Chao Phraya *r.* Thai.
Chaor *Nei Mongol* China *see*
Zalantun
204 D2 Chaouèn *prov.* Morocco
204 C2 Chaouèn Morocco
158 C3 Chaource France
109 F4 Chaoyang *Guangdong* China
107 H4 Chaoyang *Guangdong* China *see*
Jiayin
Chaoyang *Liaoning* China *see*
Huinan
107 I1 Chaoyang *Liaoning* China
107 I1 Chaoyang *Nei Mongol* China
113 D2 Chaozhou *Guangdong* China
253 G3 Chapada dos Guimarães
Brazil
160 E1 Charquemont France
120 C2 Charrat Switz.
162 B2 Charrée France
160 B2 Charrin France
162 C2 Charroux France
156 E3 Chars France
160 B1 Charron France
131 S3 Charsadda Pak.
232 B5 Charters *KY* U.S.A.
85 F4 Charters Towers *Qld* Austr.
151 I3 Chartham *Kent, England* U.K.
156 B4 Chartres France
121 G4 Charvakskoye
Vodokhranilishche *resr*
Kazakh./Uzbek.
96 C4 Charvensod Italy
161 D4 Charvonne France
234 C2 Charwelton *Northants,*
England U.K.
161 C4 Chasais France
157 F5 Charmont France
157 G4 Charny *r.* Rus. Fed.
195 F3 Charya *Rajasthan* India
161 C4 Charysh *r.* Rus. Fed.
185 B5 Charyshskoye Rus. Fed.
157 F5 Chârost France
160 E1 Charquemont France
190 C2 Charrat Switz.
160 E2 Charmey France
180 F2 Chas *Bihar* India
182 B4 Chascomús Arg.
226 A2 Chase *B.C.* Can.
224 D3 Chase *MD* U.S.A.
226 E4 Chase *MI* U.S.A.
232 D6 Chase City *VA* U.S.A.
138 G4 Chashniki Belarus
198 B2 Chasia *reg.* Greece
116 B4 Chaska *MN* U.S.A.
236 E2 Chaska *MN* U.S.A.
81 B7 Chaslands Mistake *c.*
South I. N.Z.
156C3 Chaulnes France
160 D2 Chaumergy France
185 B8 Chaumont France
156 C4 Chaumont-en-Vexin France
159 F4 Chaumont-Porcien France
157 H4 Chaumont-sur-Aire France
159 H4 Chaumont-sur-Loire France
162 C2 Chaunay France
161 B4 Chauny France

116 D4 Charkhari *Uttar Prad.* India
116 D3 Charkhi Dadri *Haryana* India
Charklik *Xinjiang* China *see*
Ruoqiang
151 F3 Charlbury *Oxfordshire,*
England U.K.
215 G2 Charl Cilliers S. Africa
231 E7 Charlemont
Northern Ireland U.K.
165 D4 Charleroi Belgium
222 G4 Charlesbourg Que. Can.
236 C3 Charles City *IA* U.S.A.
232 E6 Charles City *VA* U.S.A.
156 C3 Charles de Gaulle *airport*
France
Charles Island *Islas Galápagos*
Ecuador *see* Santa María, Isla
84 B2 Charles Point *N.T.* Austr.
81 C4 Charleston *South I.* N.Z.
237 E5 Charleston *AR* U.S.A.
226 B6 Charleston *IL* U.S.A.
236 F4 Charleston *IL* U.S.A.
231 E5 Charleston *MO* U.S.A.
237 I4 Charleston *MO* U.S.A.
231 E5 Charleston *SC* U.S.A.
232 C5 Charleston *WV* U.S.A.
247 □2 Charleston St Kitts and Nevis
234 J3 Charleston Peak *NV* U.S.A.
147 C3 Charlestown Rep. of Ireland
101 C5 Charlestown S. Africa
247 □2 Charlestown St Kitts and Nevis
162 C2 Charlestown of Aberlour
Moray, Scotland U.K. *see*
Aberlour
85 F5 Charleville *Qld* Austr.
Charleville Rep. of Ireland *see*
Rathluirc
156 E3 Charleville-Mézières France
222 F3 Charlevoix B.C. Can.
226 E4 Charlevoix *MI* U.S.A.
233 H4 Charlestown *RI* U.S.A.
232 E5 Charles Town *VA* U.S.A.
232 D5 Charlotte *MI* U.S.A.
247 F3 Charlotte Amalie
Virgin Is (U.S.A.)
232 D6 Charlotte Court House
VA U.S.A.
142 E2 Charlottenberg Sweden
232 E4 Charlottesville *VA* U.S.A.
225 I4 Charlottetown *P.E.I.* Can.
247 □5 Charlotteville Trin. and Tob.
83 E4 Charlton *Vic.* Austr.
151 F3 Charlton *Hampshire,*
England U.K.
150 E3 Charlton *Wiltshire, England* U.K.
150 E3 Charlton Kings
Gloucestershire, England U.K.
151 G3 Charlwood *Surrey,*
England U.K.
156 C4 Charme France
157 G4 Charmé France
161 C4 Charmes-sur-Rhône France
190 C2 Charmey Switz.
151 F4 Charminster *Dorset,*
England U.K.
157 G4 Charmois-l'Orgueilleux
France
156 E4 Charmont-sous-Barbuise
France
157 G4 Charmouth *Dorset,*
England U.K.
156 D5 Charnay France
157 G4 Charnay-lès-Mâcon France
184 C2 Charneca Port.
139 H4 Charneka *r.* Belarus
86 B3 Charnley *r. W.A.* Austr.
121 G4 Charni France
237 F6 Chatom *AL* U.S.A.
117 F4 Chatra *Bihar* India
157 F3 Charny-sur-Meuse France
157 G4 Charolles France
159 I5 Chârost France
160 E1 Charquemont France
190 C2 Charrat Switz.
160 E2 Charmey Switz.

162 B3 Châteauneuf-sur-Charente
France
159 I5 Châteauneuf-sur-Cher France
156 C5 Châteauneuf-sur-Loire France
159 F4 Châteauneuf-sur-Sarthe
France
160 B1 Châteauneuf-Val-de-Bargis
France
162 D2 Châteauponsac France
156 E3 Château-Porcien France
161 E4 Châteauredon France
156 C5 Châteaurenard France
161 C5 Châteaurenard France
159 G4 Château-Renault France
162 D2 Châteauroux France
161 E5 Châteauroux France
156 D3 Château-Salins France
156 E3 Château-Thierry France
157 E4 Châteauvillain France
222 G3 Chatek Alta Can.
162 B3 Châtelaillon-Plage France
158 D3 Châtelaudren France
160 B1 Châtel-Censoir France
165 D4 Châteldon France
162 C3 Châtelet Belgium
160 C1 Châtel-Gérard France
215 G1 Châtelostwn S. Africa
247 □2 Châtelet France
162 C2 Châtellerault France
162 D2 Châtel-Montagne France
162 D2 Châtelperron France
161 C4 Châtel-St-Denis Switz.
190 B2 Châtel-St-Denis Switz.
157 G4 Châtel-sur-Moselle France
162 E2 Châtelus-Malvaleix France
157 H4 Châtenois France
161 E1 Châtenois France
160 E1 Châtenois-les-Forges France
162 C2 Châtenoy-le-Royal France
226 A4 Chatfield *MN* U.S.A.
232 B4 Chatfield *OH* U.S.A.
225 H4 Chatham *N.B.* Can.
151 H3 Chatham *Medway,*
England U.K.
222 C3 Chatham *AK* U.S.A.
233 I4 Chatham *MA* U.S.A.
226 D2 Chatham *MI* U.S.A.
235 D2 Chatham *NJ* U.S.A.
233 G3 Chatham *NY* U.S.A.
234 C3 Chatham *PA* U.S.A.
232 D6 Chatham *VA* U.S.A.
259 B8 Chatham, Isla *i.* Chile
Chatham Island *Islas*
Galápagos Ecuador *see*
San Cristóbal, Isla
Chatham Island Samoa *see*
Savai'i
80 □ Chatham Islands
S. Pacific Ocean
266 H8 Chatham Rise *sea feature*
S. Pacific Ocean
222 C3 Chatham Strait *AK* U.S.A.
165 E5 Châtillon Belgium
190 C3 Châtillon Italy
156 C5 Châtillon-Coligny France
160 C1 Châtillon-en-Bazois France
161 D4 Châtillon-en-Diois France
160 C2 Châtillon-en-Michaille France
160 B3 Châtillon-la-Palud France
160 C2 Châtillon-sur-Chalaronne
France
159 F3 Châtillon-sur-Colmont France
160 D2 Châtillon-sur-Indre France
160 A1 Châtillon-sur-Loire France
157 E4 Châtillon-sur-Marne France
159 F4 Châtillon-sur-Seine France
159 F5 Châtillon-sur-Thouet France
121 G4 Chatkal *mt.* Kyrg.
121 G4 Chatkal *r.* Kyrg.
237 F6 Chatom *AL* U.S.A.
117 F4 Chatra *Bihar* India
233 H3 Chatsworth *Ont.* Can.
231 C5 Chatsworth *GA* U.S.A.
226 C5 Chatsworth *IL* U.S.A.
234 D3 Chatsworth *NJ* U.S.A.
Chattagam Bangl. *see*
Chittagong
231 C6 Chattahoochee *FL* U.S.A.
231 C5 Chattahoochee *r.* U.S.A.
231 C5 Chattanooga *TN* U.S.A.
161 D3 Chatte France
151 H2 Chatteris *Cambridgeshire,*
England U.K.
81 B6 Chatto Creek *South I.* N.Z.
149 H2 Chatton *Northumberland,*
England U.K.
96 C4 Chatturat Thai.
161 D4 Chatuzange-le-Goubet France
234 C3 Chatwood *PA* U.S.A.
Chatyr-Kël' *l.* Kyrg. *see*
Chatyr-Köl
121 H4 Chatyr-Köl *l.* Kyrg.
185 G3 Chauchina Spain
157 F5 Chaudenay France
161 B4 Chaudes-Aigues France
165 B4 Chaudeyrac France
165 E4 Chaudfontaine Belgium
97 D5 Châu Đốc Vietnam
159 F4 Chaudron-en-Mauges France
160 C2 Chauffailles France
161 E4 Chauffayer France
116 B4 Chauhtan *Rajasthan* India
96 A2 Chauk Myanmar
116 E4 Chauka *r.* India
Chaukhamba *mts* India *see*
Badrinath Peaks
156C3 Chaulnes France
160 D2 Chaumergy France
185 B8 Chaumont France
156 C4 Chaumont-en-Vexin France
159 F4 Chaumont-Porcien France
157 H4 Chaumont-sur-Aire France
159 H4 Chaumont-sur-Loire France
162 C2 Chaunay France
161 B4 Chauny France
121 H4 Chauvay Kyrg.
162 C2 Chauvency Kyrg.
223 I4 Chauvin *Alta* Can.
160 D1 Chaux, Forêt de *for.* France
158 E5 Chavagnes-en-Paillers
France
114 C4 Chavakacheri Sri Lanka
254 C2 Chaval Brazil
161 C3 Chavanay France
156 E4 Chavanges France
161 C4 Chavaniac-Lafayette France
190 A2 Chavannes France
122 D4 Chavár Iran
198 B3 Chavari *Dytiki Ellas* Greece
157 G4 Chavelot France
161 C5 Chavasy Belarus
159 H5 Chavusy Belarus
123 F4 Chawal *r.* Pak.
96 D2 Chây *r.* Vietnam
Chayan *see* Shayan
252 D4 Chayanta *r.* Bol.
133 K2 Chaybukha Rus. Fed.
134 C4 Chaykovskiy Rus. Fed.
233 G2 Chazy *NY* U.S.A.
149 G4 Cheadle *Greater Manchester,*
England U.K.
151 F2 Cheadle *Staffordshire,*
England U.K.
232 D5 Cheat *r. WV* U.S.A.
176 C1 Cheb Czech Rep.
226 E3 Chebanse *IL* U.S.A.
205 H2 Chebba Tunisia
134 J4 Cheboksary Rus. Fed.
226 E3 Cheboygan *MI* U.S.A.
183 I4 Checa Spain
204 C2 Chechel'nyk Ukr.
Chechen', Ostrov *i.* Rus. Fed.
109 G4 Ch'ech'eng Taiwan
129 D2 Chechenskaya Respublika
aut. rep. Rus. Fed.

Chechnya to Christianshåb 293

Chechnya aut. rep. Rus. Fed. see Chechenskaya Respublika
101 D5 Chech'ŏn S. Korea
136 C3 Chechva r. Ukr.
175 I5 Chęciny Pol.
237 E5 Checotah OK U.S.A.
156 C5 Chécy France
151 H2 Chedburgh Suffolk, England U.K.
150 E3 Cheddar Somerset, England U.K.
149 G4 Cheddleton Staffordshire, England U.K.
96 A3 Cheduba Island Myanmar
157 E4 Chée r. France
147 E4 Cheekpoint Rep. of Ireland
232 D3 Cheektowaga NY U.S.A.
224 D3 Cheepash r. Ont. Can.
85 F5 Cheepie Qld Austr.
263 K2 Cheetham, Cape Antarctica
162 B2 Chef-Boutonne France
Chefoo Shandong China see Yantai
220 B3 Chefornak AK U.S.A.
100 E2 Chegdomyn Rus. Fed.
Chegem 1 Rus. Fed. see Chegem Pervyy
129 C2 Chegem r. Rus. Fed.
129 C2 Chegem Pervyy Rus. Fed.
204 D4 Chegga Maur.
213 F3 Chegutu Zimbabwe
238 B2 Chehalis WA U.S.A.
238 B2 Chehalis r. WA U.S.A.
127 G4 Cheharız tourist site Iraq
122 A3 Chehel Chashmeh, Kūh-e hill Iran
122 E4 Chehel Dokhtarān, Kūh-e mt. Iran
198 B1 Cheimaditis, Limni l. Greece
161 E5 Cheiron, Cime du mt. France
101 C6 Cheju S. Korea
101 C6 Cheju-do i. S. Korea
101 C6 Cheju-haehyŏp sea chan. S. Korea
139 K4 Chekalin Rus. Fed.
134 K5 Chekan Rus. Fed.
Chek Chue H.K. China see Stanley
139 K4 Chekhov Moskovskaya Oblast' Rus. Fed.
100 G3 Chekhov Sakhalin Rus. Fed.
Chekiang prov. China see Zhejiang
109 □ Chek Lap Kok i. H.K. China
134 H4 Chekshino Rus. Fed.
209 B9 Chela, Serra da mts Angola
163 C5 Chélan France
238 B2 Chelan WA U.S.A.
238 B1 Chelan, Lake WA U.S.A.
137 J4 Chelbas r. Rus. Fed.
137 J5 Chelbasskaya Rus. Fed.
184 A2 Cheleiros Port.
184 A2 Cheleiros r. Port.
122 C2 Cheleken Turkm.
184 C2 Cheles Spain
120 D3 Chelkar Kazakh.
187 C5 Chella Spain
175 L4 Chełm Pol.
175 H5 Chełmek Pol.
151 H3 Chelmer r. England U.K.
175 I6 Chełmiec Pol.
174 G2 Chełmno Pol.
174 G3 Chełmno Pol.
151 H3 Chelmsford Essex, England U.K.
233 H3 Chelmsford MA U.S.A.
174 G2 Chełmża Pol.
227 E4 Chelsea MI U.S.A.
233 G3 Chelsea VT U.S.A.
80 E4 Cheltenham North I. N.Z.
150 E3 Cheltenham Gloucestershire, England U.K.
234 C2 Cheltenham PA U.S.A.
187 C5 Chelva Spain
130 H4 Chelyabinsk Rus. Fed.
120 E1 Chelyabinskaya Oblast' admin. div. Rus. Fed.
Chelyabinsk Oblast admin. div. Rus. Fed. see Chelyabinskaya Oblast'
232 C5 Chelyan WV U.S.A.
131 L2 Chelyuskin, Mys c. Rus. Fed.
204 C2 Chemaïa Morocco
243 I4 Chemax Mex.
159 F4 Chemazé France
213 G3 Chemba Moz.
209 F7 Chembe Zambia
136 D3 Chemerivtsi Ukr.
159 H4 Chémery France
157 E3 Chémery-sur-Bar France
162 B1 Chemillé France
160 D2 Chemin France
157 E4 Cheminon France
159 F4 Chemiré-le-Gaudin France
Chemmis Egypt see Akhmîm
171 D5 Chemnitz Ger.
171 D5 Chemnitz admin. reg. Sachsen Ger.
Chemulpo S. Korea see Inch'ŏn
238 B3 Chemult OR U.S.A.
227 I5 Chemung r. NY U.S.A.
116 B3 Chenab r. India/Pak.
233 F3 Chenango r. NY U.S.A.
233 F3 Chenango Bridge NY U.S.A.
160 C2 Chénas France
210 C3 Ch'ench'a Eth.
Chendir r. Turkm. see Chandyr
160 D1 Chenecey-Buillon France
162 E2 Chénérailles France
114 D3 Chengalpattu Tamil Nadu India
114 C3 Chengam Tamil Nadu India
107 G4 Cheng'an Hebei China
108 D3 Chengbu Hunan China
107 F5 Chengcheng Shaanxi China
Chengchow Henan China see Zhengzhou
107 H3 Chengde Hebei China
108 C2 Chengdu Sichuan China
108 B3 Chenggong Yunnan China
109 F4 Chenghai Guangdong China
Chengjiang Jiangxi China see Taihe
108 B3 Chengjiang Yunnan China
108 D2 Chengkou Chongqing China
108 D5 Chengmai Hainan China
Chengqiao Shanghai China see Chongming
Chengshou Sichuan China see Yingshan
Chengtu Sichuan China see Chengdu
107 G5 Chengwu Shandong China
108 C1 Chengxian Gansu China
Chengxian Guizhou China see Fuquan
Chengxiang Chongqing China see Wuxi
Chengxiang Jiangxi China see Quannan
Chengxiang Sichuan China see Mianning
Chengxiang Sichuan China see Tianquan
Chengxiang Sichuan China see Qingshen
Chengyang Shandong China see Juxian
Chengzhong Guangxi China see Ningming
Chengzi Yunnan China see Longchuan
157 G4 Cheniménil France
114 D3 Chennai Tamil Nadu India
226 C5 Chenoa IL U.S.A.
159 H4 Chenonceaux France
160 D1 Chenôve France
Chenstokhov Pol. see Częstochowa
107 E1 Chentejn Nuruu mts Mongolia
108 D3 Chenxi Hunan China
156 D5 Cheny France
Chenyang Hunan China see Chenxi
Chenying Jiangxi China see Wannian
109 E3 Chenzhou Hunan China
Cheom Ksan Cambodia see Chŏâm Khsant
197 G5 Chepelare Bulg.
250 B6 Chepén Peru
260 D2 Chepes Arg.
137 I3 Chepil' Ukr.
242 □K7 Chepo Panama
150 E3 Chepstow Monmouthshire, Wales U.K.
134 J4 Cheptsa r. Rus. Fed.
156 E4 Chepy France
159 I4 Cher dept Centre France
162 C1 Cher r. France
Chera state India see Kerala
187 C5 Chera Spain
162 B3 Chérac France
160 D3 Chéran r. France
244 D4 Cherán Mex.
190 C4 Cherasco Italy
163 B5 Chéraute France
231 E5 Cheraw SC U.S.A.
158 E2 Cherbourg France
205 F1 Cherchell Alg.
Cherchen Xinjiang China see Qiemo
135 J5 Cherdakly Rus. Fed.
134 L3 Cherdyn' Rus. Fed.
158 E4 Chère r. France
177 L4 Cherechiu Romania
129 D2 Cherek r. Rus. Fed.
138 G3 Cherekha r. Rus. Fed.
135 G6 Cheremisinovo Rus. Fed.
98 H1 Cheremkhovo Rus. Fed.
121 J1 Cheremnoye Rus. Fed.
100 E3 Cheremshany Rus. Fed.
134 J4 Cheremukhovka Rus. Fed.
192 A4 Cheremule Sardegna Italy
130 J4 Cherepanovo Rus. Fed.
Cherepkovo Moldova see Ciripcău
139 K2 Cherepovets Rus. Fed.
134 I3 Cherevkovo Rus. Fed.
205 E2 Chergui, Chott ech imp. l. Alg.
205 G2 Chéria Alg.
114 C2 Cherial Andhra Prad. India
190 E3 Cherio r. Italy
151 F3 Cheriton Hampshire, England U.K.
233 F6 Cheriton VA U.S.A.
136 F3 Cherkas'ka Oblast' admin. div. Ukr.
137 H3 Cherkas'ke Ukr.
137 I3 Cherkas'ke Ukr.
Cherkas'ke Ukr. see Zymohir"ya
Cherkasskaya Oblast' admin. div. Ukr. see Cherkas'ka Oblast'
Cherkasskoye Ukr. see Zymohir"ya
Cherkassy Ukr. see Cherkasy
137 G3 Cherkasy Ukr.
Cherkasy Oblast admin. div. Ukr. see Cherkas'ka Oblast'
129 C1 Cherkessk Rus. Fed.
139 L3 Cherkutino Rus. Fed.
114 D2 Cherla Andhra Prad. India
121 H1 Cherlak Rus. Fed.
136 D3 Cherlenivka Ukr.
129 D2 Chermen Rus. Fed.
134 L4 Chermoz Rus. Fed.
139 K5 Chern' Rus. Fed.
139 K5 Chern' r. Rus. Fed.
121 G4 Chernak Kazakh.
139 L5 Chernava Lipetskaya Oblast' Rus. Fed.
139 L5 Chernava Ryazanskaya Oblast' Rus. Fed.
134 L1 Chernaya r. Rus. Fed.
138 F2 Chernaya r. Rus. Fed.
137 K2 Chernaya Kalitva r. Rus. Fed.
134 J4 Chernaya Kholunitsa Rus. Fed.
137 G2 Chernecha Sloboda Ukr.
Chernenko Moldova see Şoldăneşti
137 H3 Čherneshchyna Ukr.
Chernigov Ukr. see Chernihiv
100 E3 Chernigovka Rus. Fed.
Chernigov Oblast admin. div. Ukr. see Chernihivs'ka Oblast'
129 A1 Chernigovskaya Rus. Fed.
Chernigovskaya Oblast' admin. div. Ukr. see Chernihivs'ka Oblast'
129 A1 Chernigovskoye Rus. Fed.
137 F2 Chernihiv Ukr.
Chernihiv Oblast admin. div. Ukr. see Chernihivs'ka Oblast'
137 G2 Chernihivs'ka Oblast' admin. div. Ukr.
197 G4 Cherni Lom r. Bulg.
137 I4 Cherninivka Ukr.
136 D3 Chernivets'ka Oblast' admin. div. Ukr.
Chernivetskaya Oblast' admin. div. Ukr. see Chernivets'ka Oblast'
197 F4 Cherni Vrŭkh mt. Bulg.
136 C3 Chernivtsi Chernivets'ka Oblast' Ukr.
136 E3 Chernivtsi Vinnyts'ka Oblast' Ukr.
Chernivtsi Oblast admin. div. Ukr. see Chernivets'ka Oblast'
136 C3 Cherniyiv Ukr.
Chernobyl' Ukr. see Chornobyl'
98 F1 Chernogorsk Rus. Fed.
129 C1 Chernolesskoye Rus. Fed.
134 K3 Chernorechenskiy Rus. Fed.
121 I1 Chernoretskoye Kazakh.
134 I4 Chernovskoye Rus. Fed.
Chernovtsy Chernivets'ka Oblast' Ukr. see Chernivtsi
Chernovtsy Oblast admin. div. Ukr. see Chernivets'ka Oblast'
Chernoye More sea Asia/Europe see Black Sea
134 L4 Chernushka Rus. Fed.
136 E2 Chernyakhiv Ukr.
138 C4 Chernyakhovsk Rus. Fed.
135 G6 Chernyanka Rus. Fed.
99 K1 Chernyshevsk Rus. Fed.
131 M3 Chernyshevskiy Rus. Fed.
135 H6 Chernyshkovskiy Rus. Fed.
135 I7 Chernyye Zemli reg. Rus. Fed.
Chernyy Irtysh r. China/Kazakh. see Ertix He
120 C2 Chernyy Otrog Rus. Fed.
134 F3 Chernyy Porog Rus. Fed.
Chernyy Rynok Rus. Fed. see Kochubey
135 I6 Chernyy Yar Rus. Fed.
236 E3 Cherokee IA U.S.A.
237 D4 Cherokee OK U.S.A.
231 D4 Cherokee Lake TN U.S.A.
237 E4 Cherokees, Lake o' the OK U.S.A.
246 C1 Cherokee Sound Gt Abaco Bahamas
156 D4 Chéroy France
260 A6 Cherquenco Chile
117 G4 Cherrapunji Meghalaya India
149 I4 Cherry Burton East Riding of Yorkshire, England U.K.
236 C2 Cherry Creek r. SD U.S.A.
241 J1 Cherry Creek Mountains NV U.S.A.
233 □J2 Cherryfield ME U.S.A.
234 C3 Cherry Hill NJ U.S.A.
77 G3 Cherry Island Solomon Is
227 I4 Cherry Valley Ont. Can.
234 C2 Cherryville PA U.S.A.
149 I4 Cherry Willingham Lincolnshire, England U.K.
131 R3 Cherskiy Rus. Fed.
Cherskiy Range mts Chitinskaya Oblast' Rus. Fed. see Cherskogo, Khrebet
107 F1 Cherskogo, Khrebet mts Chitinskaya Oblast' Rus. Fed.
131 P3 Cherskogo, Khrebet mts Respublika Sakha (Yakutiya) Rus. Fed.
198 C1 Cherso Kentriki Makedonia Greece
190 C4 Chersogno, Monte mt. Italy
186 D4 Chert Spain
Cherta Spain see Xerta
Cherthala Kerala India see Shertally
Chertkov Ukr. see Chortkiv
135 H6 Chertkovo Rus. Fed.
81 C5 Chertsey South I. N.Z.
151 G3 Chertsey Surrey, England U.K.
139 M4 Cherusti Rus. Fed.
162 D3 Cherveix-Cubas France
197 G4 Cherven Bryag Bulg.
162 B3 Cherves-Richemont France
129 D2 Chervlennaya Rus. Fed.
129 D1 Chervlennyye Buruny Rus. Fed.
137 G3 Chervona Kam"yanka Ukr.
137 H2 Chervone Sums'ka Oblast' Ukr.
136 E3 Chervone Zhytomyrs'ka Oblast' Ukr.
137 I4 Chervone Pole Ukr.
137 F2 Chervoni Partyzany Ukr.
Chervonoarmeyskoye Ukr. see Vil'nyans'k
Chervonoarmiys'k Ukr. see Krasnoarmiys'k
Chervonoarmiys'k Ukr. see Radyvyliv
136 E2 Chervonoarmiys'k Ukr.
Chervonograd Ukr. see Chervonohrad
136 C2 Chervonohrad Ukr.
137 H4 Chervonohryhorivka Ukr.
137 I3 Chervonooskil's'ke Vodoskhovyshche resr Ukr.
Chervonopartizansk Ukr. see Chervonopartyzans'k
137 J3 Chervonopartyzans'k Ukr.
137 G2 Chervonozavods'ke Ukr.
136 F4 Chervonoznam"yanka Ukr.
137 I3 Chervonyy Donets' Ukr.
137 G4 Chervonyy Mayak Ukr.
138 G5 Chervyen' Belarus
151 F3 Cherwell r. England U.K.
139 H5 Cherykaw Belarus
227 E4 Chesaning MI U.S.A.
233 E6 Chesapeake VA U.S.A.
234 B4 Chesapeake Bay MD/VA U.S.A.
232 E5 Chesapeake Beach MD U.S.A.
234 C3 Chesapeake City MD U.S.A.
151 G3 Chesham Buckinghamshire, England U.K.
149 G4 Cheshire admin. div. England U.K.
235 F1 Cheshire CT U.S.A.
233 G3 Cheshire MA U.S.A.
149 G4 Cheshire Plain England U.K.
134 I2 Cheshskaya Guba b. Rus. Fed.
151 G3 Cheshunt Hertfordshire, England U.K.
150 E4 Chesil Beach England U.K.
234 D3 Chesilhurst NJ U.S.A.
227 G3 Chesley Ont. Can.
156 E5 Chesley France
120 E1 Chesma Rus. Fed.
Chesnokovka Rus. Fed. see Novoaltaysk
156 D4 Chessy-les-Prés France
187 C5 Cheste Spain
225 H4 Chester N.S. Can.
149 G4 Chester Cheshire, England U.K.
240 G1 Chester CA U.S.A.
235 F1 Chester CT U.S.A.
236 F4 Chester IL U.S.A.
234 B4 Chester MD U.S.A.
238 E1 Chester MT U.S.A.
234 D2 Chester NJ U.S.A.
235 D1 Chester NY U.S.A.
232 C5 Chester OH U.S.A.
234 C3 Chester PA U.S.A.
231 D5 Chester SC U.S.A.
232 E6 Chester VA U.S.A.
234 B4 Chester r. MD U.S.A.
246 □ Chester Castle Jamaica
234 C2 Chester County county PA U.S.A.
149 H4 Chesterfield Derbyshire, England U.K.
235 F1 Chesterfield CT U.S.A.
236 F4 Chesterfield MO U.S.A.
231 D5 Chesterfield SC U.S.A.
232 E6 Chesterfield VA U.S.A.
77 F3 Chesterfield, Îles is New Caledonia
223 N2 Chesterfield Inlet Nunavut Can.
223 M2 Chesterfield Inlet inlet Nunavut Can.
149 H3 Chester-le-Street Durham, England U.K.
146 F6 Chesters Scottish Borders, Scotland U.K.
234 B3 Chestertown MD U.S.A.
233 G3 Chestertown NY U.S.A.
233 F2 Chesterville Ont. Can.
234 C3 Chesterville MD U.S.A.
232 D4 Chestnut Ridge PA U.S.A.
234 C3 Cheswold DE U.S.A.
226 B3 Chetek WI U.S.A.
225 I4 Chéticamp N.S. Can.
237 E4 Chetopa KS U.S.A.
243 H5 Chetumal Mex.
222 F4 Chetwynd B.C. Can.
109 □ Cheung Chau H.K. China
109 □ Cheung Chau H.K. China
161 E4 Cheval Blanc, Sommet du mt. France
162 B3 Chevanceaux France
156 D5 Chevannes France
241 L4 Chevelon Creek r. AZ U.S.A.
177 K6 Chevereşu Mare Romania
234 B4 Cheverly MD U.S.A.
160 D1 Chevigny-St-Sauveur France
157 F4 Chevillon France
156 B4 Chevilly France
81 D5 Cheviot South I. N.Z.
232 A5 Cheviot OH U.S.A.
149 G2 Cheviot Hills England U.K.
85 E5 Cheviot Range hills Qld Austr.
224 F2 Chevreulx r. Que. Can.
156 C4 Chevreuse France
210 C3 Che'w Bahir salt l. Eth.
238 C1 Chewelah WA U.S.A.
150 E3 Chew Magna Bath and North East Somerset, England U.K.
237 D5 Cheyenne OK U.S.A.
238 F3 Cheyenne WY U.S.A.
236 C2 Cheyenne r. SD U.S.A.
236 C4 Cheyenne Wells CO U.S.A.
161 A3 Cheylade France
87 C7 Cheyne Bay W.A. Austr.
114 D3 Cheyur Tamil Nadu India
114 C3 Cheyyar r. India
222 E4 Chezacut B.C. Can.
159 I5 Chezal-Benoît France
163 B6 Chèze France
116 D4 Chhabra Rajasthan India
116 C4 Chhapar Rajasthan India
117 F4 Chhapra Bihar India
116 D4 Chhata Uttar Prad. India
117 G4 Chhatak Bangl.
117 F4 Chhatarpur Bihar India
116 D4 Chhatarpur Madh. Prad. India
115 E2 Chhatrapur Orissa India
97 C5 Chhay Arêng, Stœng r. Cambodia
116 D4 Chhibramau Uttar Prad. India
116 D5 Chhindwara Madh. Prad. India
116 D4 Chhipa Barod Rajasthan India
97 D4 Chhlong, Prêk r. Cambodia
116 D5 Chhota Chhindwara Madh. Prad. India
116 C5 Chhota Udepur Gujarat India
116 E5 Chhuikhadan Madh. Prad. India
Chhuk Cambodia see Phumĭ Chhuk
117 G4 Chhukha Bhutan
257 F4 Chiador Brazil
109 G4 Chiai Taiwan
191 G3 Chiampo Italy
191 G3 Chiampo r. Italy
192 D1 Chianciano Terme Italy
209 B8 Chiange Angola
96 C3 Chiang Kham Thai.
96 C3 Chiang Khan Thai.
96 B3 Chiang Mai Thai.
96 B3 Chiang Rai Thai.
192 E2 Chiani r. Italy
191 F5 Chianni Italy
243 G5 Chiapa Mex.
245 H5 Chiapas state Mex.
194 D5 Chiaramonte Gulfi Sicilia Italy
192 A4 Chiaramonti Sardegna Italy
191 I5 Chiaravalle Italy
195 F4 Chiaravalle Centrale Italy
190 E3 Chiari Italy
193 I4 Chiaromonte Italy
191 I2 Chiarso r. Italy
191 H5 Chiascio r. Italy
190 E3 Chiasso Italy
129 C2 Chiat'ura Georgia
245 E4 Chiautempan Mex.
245 E4 Chiautla Mex.
245 E4 Chiautzingo Mex.
190 E4 Chiavari Italy
190 E3 Chiavenna r. Italy
190 E2 Chiavenno Italy
105 G3 Chiba Japan
105 G3 Chiba pref. Japan
213 G4 Chibabava Moz.
209 B8 Chibemba Angola
Chibi Zimbabwe see Chivi
209 B8 Chibia Angola
Chibizovka Rus. Fed. see Zherdevka
213 G4 Chiboma Moz.
224 F3 Chibougamau Que. Can.
224 F3 Chibougamau r. Que. Can.
213 G5 Chibuto Moz.
209 F8 Chibwe Zambia
Chicacole Andhra Prad. India see Srikakulam
226 D5 Chicago IL U.S.A.
226 D5 Chicago Heights IL U.S.A.
209 D6 Chicapa r. Angola
245 E2 Chicayán r. Mex.
225 H3 Chic-Chocs, Monts mts Que. Can.
197 G3 Chicera Hamba hill Romania
222 B3 Chichagof AK U.S.A.
220 E4 Chichagof Island AK U.S.A.
123 F5 Chichak r. Pak.
204 C3 Chichaoua Morocco
252 D5 Chichas, Cordillera de mts Bol.
159 F5 Chiché France
107 G3 Chicheng Hebei China
Chicheng Sichuan China see Pengxi
243 H4 Chichén Itzá tourist site Mex.
151 G4 Chichester West Sussex, England U.K.
86 C4 Chichester Range mts W.A. Austr.
116 E5 Chichgarh Mahar. India
105 F3 Chichibu Japan
105 F2 Chichibu-gawa r. Japan
245 E5 Chichihualco Mex.
103 □3 Chichi-jima i. Japan
103 □3 Chichijima-rettō is Japan
116 D5 Chicholi Madh. Prad. India
232 E6 Chickahominy r. VA U.S.A.
231 C5 Chickamauga Lake TN U.S.A.
237 F6 Chickasawhay r. MS U.S.A.
237 D5 Chickasha OK U.S.A.
150 E4 Chickerell Dorset, England U.K.
184 D4 Chiclana de la Frontera Spain
250 B6 Chiclayo Peru
261 G6 Chico r. Buenos Aires Arg.
259 C6 Chico r. Chubut Arg.
259 D7 Chico r. Chubut Arg.
259 C8 Chico r. Santa Cruz Arg.
244 C2 Chico r. Mex.
240 G2 Chico CA U.S.A.
Chicobea i. Fiji see Cikobia
209 B8 Chicomba Angola
243 G6 Chicomucelo Mex.
217 □3b Chiconi Mayotte
211 B8 Chiconono Moz.
245 E3 Chicontepec Mex.
233 G3 Chicopee MA U.S.A.
92 B2 Chico Sapocoy, Mount Luzon Phil.
225 G3 Chicoutimi Que. Can.
225 G3 Chicoutimi r. Que. Can.
209 C8 Chicupo Angola
114 C4 Chidambaram Tamil Nadu India
151 G3 Chiddingfold Surrey, England U.K.
111 F6 Chido Xizang China
101 C6 Chido S. Korea
209 C9 Chiede Angola
231 D6 Chiefland FL U.S.A.
212 D3 Chief's Island Botswana
173 G4 Chiemgauer Alpen mts Ger.
173 G4 Chieming Ger.
173 G4 Chiemsee l. Ger.
191 G2 Chienes Italy
209 F7 Chiengi Zambia
Chiengmai Thai. see Chiang Mai
191 I5 Chienti r. Italy
190 C3 Chieri Italy
157 F3 Chiers r. France
190 E2 Chiesa in Valmalenco Italy
177 L4 Chieşd Romania
191 F3 Chiese r. Italy
193 G2 Chieti Italy
193 G2 Chieti prov. Abruzzo Italy
193 H3 Chieuti Italy
151 F3 Chieveley West Berkshire, England U.K.
165 C4 Chièvres Belgium
107 H3 Chifeng Nei Mongol China
257 G2 Chifre, Serra do mts Brazil
213 G2 Chifunde Moz.
121 H3 Chiganak Kazakh.
105 F3 Chigasaki Japan
220 C4 Chiginagak Volcano, Mount AK U.S.A.
137 K2 Chigla r. Rus. Fed.
220 C4 Chignik AK U.S.A.
160 E3 Chignin France
250 B3 Chigorodó Col.
252 D5 Chiguana Bol.
111 E6 Chigu Co l. China
151 H3 Chigwell Essex, England U.K.
242 D2 Chihuahua Mex.
242 D2 Chihuahua state Mex.
260 C6 Chihuido Medio mt. Arg.
121 F3 Chiili Kazakh.
106 C3 Chijinpu Gansu China
129 D3 Chikaani Georgia
116 D5 Chikalda Mahar. India
108 D4 Chikan Guangdong China
237 D4 Chikaskia r. KS U.S.A.
114 C3 Chik Ballapur Karnataka India
138 G3 Chikhachevo Rus. Fed.
116 D5 Chikhali Kalan Parasia Madh. Prad. India
116 D5 Chikhli Mahar. India
114 B3 Chikmagalur Karnataka India
114 B2 Chikodi Karnataka India
114 B2 Chikodi Road Karnataka India
129 C2 Chikola Rus. Fed.
106 E1 Chikoy Rus. Fed.
107 E1 Chikoy r. Rus. Fed.
103 E7 Chikugo Japan
105 E1 Chikuma-gawa r. Japan
103 E7 Chikushino Japan
211 B8 Chikwawa Malawi
245 E2 Chila, Laguna l. Mex.
222 F4 Chilanko r. B.C. Can.
222 E4 Chilanko Forks B.C. Can.
245 E5 Chilapa Mex.
116 C2 Chilas Jammu and Kashmir
114 C5 Chilaw Sri Lanka
252 A3 Chilca Peru
187 C5 Chilches Spain
150 E3 Chilcompton Somerset, England U.K.
222 F5 Chilcotin r. B.C. Can.
85 G3 Chilcott Island Coral Sea Is Terr. Austr.
85 H5 Childers Qld Austr.
237 C5 Childress TX U.S.A.
151 F3 Childrey Oxfordshire, England U.K.
259 B7 Chile country S. America
267 N8 Chile Basin sea feature S. Pacific Ocean
259 C7 Chile Chico Chile
258 D3 Chilecito Arg.
209 B8 Chilengue, Serra do mts Angola
267 N8 Chile Rise sea feature S. Pacific Ocean
252 A1 Chilete Peru
135 I7 Chilgir Rus. Fed.
151 H3 Chilham Kent, England U.K.
232 C6 Chilhowie VA U.S.A.
Chilia-Nouă Ukr. see Kiliya
197 I3 Chilia Veche Romania
121 I4 Chilik Kazakh.
121 I4 Chilik r. Kazakh.
115 E2 Chilika Lake India
209 E8 Chililabombwe Zambia
198 C3 Chiliomodi Greece
222 C3 Chilkat r. Can./U.S.A.
222 F4 Chilko r. B.C. Can.
85 F3 Chillagoe Qld Austr.
260 A5 Chillán Chile
260 A5 Chillán r. Chile
260 B5 Chillán, Nevado mts Chile
261 H5 Chillar Arg.
156 C4 Chilleurs-aux-Bois France
226 C5 Chillicothe IL U.S.A.
236 E4 Chillicothe MO U.S.A.
232 B5 Chillicothe OH U.S.A.
116 C1 Chillinji Jammu and Kashmir
222 F5 Chilliwack B.C. Can.
185 F2 Chillón Spain
185 G2 Chilluévar Spain
234 B4 Chillum MD U.S.A.
122 C1 Chil'mamedkum, Peski des. Turkm.
117 G4 Chilmari Bangl.
259 B6 Chiloé, Isla de i. Chile
Chiloé, Isla Grande de i. Chile see Chiloé, Isla de
183 G4 Chiloeches Spain
238 B3 Chiloquin OR U.S.A.
245 E5 Chilpancingo Mex.
232 B3 Chilson MI U.S.A.
83 F4 Chiltern Vic. Austr.
151 G3 Chiltern Hills England U.K.
226 C3 Chilton WI U.S.A.
209 D7 Chiluage Angola
209 F7 Chilubi Zambia
211 B7 Chilumba Malawi
109 G3 Chilung Taiwan
211 B7 Chimala Tanz.
243 H6 Chimaltenango Guat.
213 G3 Chimanimani Zimbabwe
165 D4 Chimay Belgium
165 D4 Chimay, Bois de for. Belgium
260 B4 Chimbarongo Chile
260 C2 Chimbas Arg.
120 D4 Chimbay Uzbek.
252 A2 Chimbote Peru
Chimboy Uzbek. see Chimbay
185 G3 Chimeneas Spain
123 H4 Chimian Pak.
250 C2 Chimichaguá Col.
121 G4 Chimion Uzbek.
Chimishliya Moldova see Cimişlia
Chimkent Kazakh. see Shymkent
Chimkentskaya Oblast' admin. div. Kazakh. see Yuzhnyy Kazakhstan
213 G3 Chimoio Moz.
185 F2 Chimorra hill Spain
260 D6 Chimpay Arg.
123 G2 Chimtargha, Qullai mt. Tajik.
Chimtorga, Gora mt. Tajik. see Chimtargha, Qullai
96 A2 Chin state Myanmar
98 E4 China country Asia
243 F3 China Mex.
China, Republic of country Asia see Taiwan
China Bakir r. Myanmar see To
245 G4 Chinameca Mex.
245 F3 Chinampa de Gorostiza Mex.
190 C4 Chinanale Italy
242 □I6 Chinandega Nic.
239 F6 Chinati Peak TX U.S.A.
121 G4 Chinaz Uzbek.
252 A3 Chincha Alta Peru
222 G3 Chinchaga r. Alta Can.
85 G5 Chinchilla Qld Austr.
185 I2 Chinchilla de Monte Aragón Spain
114 C2 Chincholi Karnataka India
183 G4 Chinchón Spain
243 I5 Chinchorro, Banco sea feature Mex.
260 B3 Chincolco Chile
233 F6 Chincoteague VA U.S.A.
233 F6 Chincoteague Bay MD/VA U.S.A.
213 H3 Chinde Moz.
101 C6 Chindo S. Korea
101 C6 Chin-do i. S. Korea
160 D3 Chindrieux France
108 A1 Chindu Qinghai China
96 A2 Chindwin r. Myanmar
116 C2 Chineni Jammu and Kashmir
Chinese Turkestan aut. reg. China see Xinjiang Uygur Zizhiqu
151 G3 Chingford Greater London, England U.K.
Chinghai prov. China see Qinghai
101 C5 Chinghwa N. Korea
120 C2 Chingirlau Kazakh.
121 I2 Chingiz-Tau, Khrebet mts Kazakh.
Chingleput Tamil Nadu India see Chengalpattu
209 E8 Chingola Zambia
209 C8 Chinguar Angola
204 B5 Chinguețți Maur.
101 D6 Chinhae S. Korea
213 F3 Chinhoyi Zimbabwe
Chini Hima. Prad. India see Kalpa
252 C3 Chiñijo Bol.
Chining Shandong China see Jining
123 H4 Chiniot Pak.
242 C3 Chinipas Mex.
97 D4 Chinit, Stœng r. Cambodia
101 D6 Chinju S. Korea
208 D3 Chinko r. C.A.R.
241 M3 Chinle AZ U.S.A.
109 F3 Chinmen Taiwan
109 F3 Chinmen Tao i. Taiwan
114 D3 Chinna Ganjam Andhra Prad. India
114 C4 Chinnamanur Tamil Nadu India
Chinnamp'o N. Korea see Namp'o
114 C4 Chinna Salem Tamil Nadu India
151 G3 Chinnor Oxfordshire, England U.K.
114 C2 Chinnur Andhra Prad. India
105 E3 Chino Japan
240 I4 Chino CA U.S.A.
87 C7 Chinocup, Lake salt flat W.A. Austr.
162 C1 Chinon France
238 E1 Chinook MT U.S.A.
266 H3 Chinook Trough sea feature N. Pacific Ocean
241 K4 Chino Valley AZ U.S.A.
Chinoz Uzbek. see Chinaz
211 B7 Chinsali Zambia
114 D2 Chintalnar Madh. Prad. India
114 C3 Chintamani Karnataka India
197 F2 Chinteni Romania
211 B7 Chintheche Malawi
250 C2 Chinú Col.
165 E5 Chiny Belgium
165 E5 Chiny, Forêt de for. Belgium
213 G3 Chioco Moz.
191 H3 Chioggia Italy
190 B3 Chiomonte Italy
199 E2 Chios Voreio Aigaio Greece
199 D2 Chios i. Greece
211 B8 Chipata Zambia
111 B5 Chip Chap r. China/India
259 C6 Chipchihua, Sierra de mts Arg.
209 F7 Chipili Zambia
209 B8 Chipindo Angola
107 H4 Chiping Shandong China
Chipinga Zimbabwe see Chipinge
213 G4 Chipinge Zimbabwe
184 D4 Chipiona Spain
231 C6 Chipley FL U.S.A.
114 B2 Chiplun Mahar. India
225 H4 Chipman N.B. Can.
150 E3 Chippenham Wiltshire, England U.K.
213 G3 Chipperone, Monte mt. Moz.
236 E2 Chippewa r. MN U.S.A.
226 A3 Chippewa r. WI U.S.A.
226 B3 Chippewa Falls WI U.S.A.
151 F2 Chipping Campden Gloucestershire, England U.K.
151 F3 Chipping Norton Oxfordshire, England U.K.
151 H3 Chipping Ongar Essex, England U.K.
150 E3 Chipping Sodbury South Gloucestershire, England U.K.
190 C2 Chippis Switz.
186 C3 Chiprana Spain
197 F4 Chiprovtsi Bulg.
Chipuriro Zimbabwe see Guruve
115 D2 Chipurupalle Andhra Prad. India
115 D2 Chipurupalle Andhra Prad. India
243 H6 Chiquimula Guat.
250 C3 Chiquinquira Col.
261 G4 Chiquita, Mar l. Arg.
245 E1 Chiquita, Sierra mts Mex.
244 D4 Chiquito r. Mex.
253 E4 Chiquitos Jesuit Missions tourist site Brazil
135 H6 Chir r. Rus. Fed.
161 B4 Chirac France
114 D3 Chirada Andhra Prad. India
211 B8 Chiradzulu Malawi
129 F3 Chirakhchay r. Rus. Fed.
114 B4 Chirakkal Kerala India
114 D3 Chirala Andhra Prad. India
213 G3 Chiramba Moz.
111 A6 Chirawa Rajasthan India
150 D2 Chirbury Shropshire, England U.K.
121 G4 Chirchik Uzbek.
121 G4 Chirchik r. Uzbek.
213 F4 Chiredzi Zimbabwe
250 E2 Chirgua r. Venez.
241 M6 Chiricahua Peak AZ U.S.A.
250 C2 Chiriguaná Col.
250 B6 Chirinos Peru
242 □J7 Chiriquí, Golfo de b. Panama
242 □J7 Chiriquí, Laguna de b. Panama
242 □J7 Chiriquí Grande Panama
101 C6 Chiri-san mt. S. Korea
185 H3 Chirivel Spain
129 D2 Chiri-Yurt Rus. Fed.
150 D2 Chirk Wrexham, Wales U.K.
146 F6 Chirnside Scottish Borders, Scotland U.K.
217 □3b Chirongui Mayotte
160 C2 Chiroubles France
197 G4 Chirpan Bulg.
104 D3 Chiryū Japan
209 F8 Chisamba Zambia
209 E8 Chisasa Zambia
224 E2 Chisasibi Que. Can.
243 H6 Chisec Guat.
151 F3 Chiseldon Swindon, England U.K.
197 H3 Chiselet Romania
Chishima-retto is Rus. Fed. see Kuril Islands
135 K5 Chishmy Rus. Fed.
222 H4 Chisholm Alta Can.
233 □H2 Chisholm ME U.S.A.
226 A2 Chisholm MN U.S.A.
123 H4 Chishtian Mandi Pak.
108 C2 Chishui Guizhou China
108 C3 Chishuihe Sichuan China
108 C2 Chishui He r. China
Chisimaio Somalia see Kismaayo
136 E4 Chişinău Moldova
177 L5 Chişindia Romania
197 E2 Chişineu-Criş Romania
177 L4 Chişlaz Romania
190 C4 Chisola r. Italy
190 C4 Chisone r. Italy
134 J5 Chistopol' Rus. Fed.
121 F1 Chistopol'ye Kazakh.
Chistyakovo Ukr. see Torez
121 G1 Chistyakovskoye Kazakh.
252 D5 Chita Bol.
104 C4 Chita Japan
99 J1 Chita Rus. Fed.
104 C4 Chita-hantō pen. Japan
Chitaldrug Karnataka India see Chitradurga
116 B4 Chitalwana Rajasthan India
Chita Oblast admin. div. Rus. Fed. see Chitinskaya Oblast'
209 D6 Chitato Angola
223 J4 Chitek Lake Sask. Can.
209 C8 Chitembo Angola
191 G5 Chitignano Italy
100 A2 Chitinskaya Oblast' admin. div. Rus. Fed.
211 B7 Chitipa Malawi
213 G4 Chitobe Moz.
209 D8 Chitokoloki Zambia
Chitor Rajasthan India see Chittaurgarh
102 J2 Chitose Japan
114 C3 Chitradurga Karnataka India
116 E4 Chitrakut Uttar Prad. India
123 G3 Chitral Pak.
123 G3 Chitral r. Pak.
114 C3 Chitravati r. India
242 □J8 Chitré Panama
116 B5 Chitrod Gujarat India
117 G5 Chittagong Bangl.
117 G5 Chittagong admin. div. Bangl.
117 F5 Chittaranjan W. Bengal India
116 C4 Chittaurgarh Rajasthan India
114 C3 Chittoor Andhra Prad. India
Chittorgarh Rajasthan India see Chittaurgarh
114 C4 Chittur Kerala India
213 F3 Chitungwiza Zimbabwe
211 C7 Chiulezi r. Moz.
Chiu Lung H.K. China see Kowloon
209 D8 Chiume Angola
213 H2 Chiúre Novo Moz.
190 E2 Chiuro Italy
191 G2 Chiusa Italy
190 C4 Chiusa di Pesio Italy
191 I2 Chiusaforte Italy
194 C5 Chiusa Sclafani Sicilia Italy
190 C5 Chiusavecchia Italy
192 D1 Chiusdino Italy
190 C3 Chiusella r. Italy
192 D1 Chiusi Italy
191 G5 Chiusi della Verna Italy
213 G2 Chiúta Moz.
187 C5 Chiva Spain
190 C3 Chivasso Italy
252 C3 Chivay Peru
252 C3 Chive Bol.
213 F3 Chivhu Zimbabwe
213 F4 Chivi Zimbabwe
261 G4 Chivilcoy Arg.
162 B2 Chizé France
120 B2 Chizha Vtoraya Kazakh.
Chkalov Rus. Fed. see Orenburg
137 H4 Chkalove Ukr.
121 G1 Chkalovo Kazakh.
Chkalovo Rus. Fed. see Kurchaloy
134 H4 Chkalovsk Rus. Fed.
Chkalovskaya Oblast' admin. div. Rus. Fed. see Orenburgskaya Oblast'
137 I3 Chkalovs'ke Ukr.
100 E3 Chkalovskoye Rus. Fed.
177 G2 Chlebičov Czech Rep.
177 I2 Chlebnice Slovakia
Chlef Alg. see Ech Chélif
175 I4 Chlewiska Pol.
177 K3 Chlmec r. Slovakia
175 K6 Chłopice Pol.
241 J4 Chloride AZ U.S.A.
174 E3 Chludowo Pol.
173 H2 Chlumčany Czech Rep.
176 C1 Chlumec Czech Rep.
176 E1 Chlumec nad Cidlinou Czech Rep.
176 D3 Chlum u Třeboně Czech Rep.
177 H2 Chmeľová hill Slovakia
175 I5 Chmielnik Pol.
175 K4 Chmiel Pierwszy Pol.
97 D4 Chŏâm Khsant Cambodia
260 B2 Choapa r. Chile
212 E3 Chobe admin. dist. Botswana
174 D3 Chobienice Pol.
245 F4 Chocamán Mex.
247 □3 Choc Bay St Lucia
176 F1 Choceň Czech Rep.
175 H3 Choceń Pol.
101 C5 Choch'iwŏn S. Korea
177 G3 Chocholná-Velčice Slovakia
174 D4 Chocianów Pol.
174 D2 Chociwel Pol.
250 B3 Choco dept Col.
241 J5 Chocolate Mountains AZ/CA U.S.A.
250 C3 Chocontá Col.
231 C6 Choctawhatchee r. FL U.S.A.
174 F4 Chocz Pol.
174 F1 Choczewo Pol.
114 D2 Chodavaram Andhra Prad. India
175 H3 Chodecz Pol.
175 K4 Chodel Pol.
175 J4 Chodelka r. Pol.
176 B1 Chodov Czech Rep.
176 B2 Chodová Planá Czech Rep.
175 K3 Chodów Pol.
175 H3 Chodów Pol.
174 E3 Chodzież Pol.
260 E6 Choele Choel Arg.
105 F3 Chōfu Japan
223 J4 Choiceland Sask. Can.
78 □6 Choiseul i. Solomon Is
259 F8 Choiseul Sound sea chan. Falkland Is
160 E3 Choisy France
242 C3 Choix Mex.
174 C3 Chojna Pol.
174 F2 Chojnice Pol.
174 D4 Chojnów Pol.
102 J4 Chōkai-san vol. Japan
210 C2 Ch'ok'ē Mountains Eth.
129 C2 Ch'okhatauri Georgia
121 H4 Chokpar Kazakh.
Chokue Moz. see Chókwé
131 P2 Chokurdakh Rus. Fed.
213 G5 Chókwé Moz.
240 G4 Cholame CA U.S.A.
240 G4 Cholame Creek r. CA U.S.A.
108 A1 Chola Shan mts Sichuan China
260 A6 Cholchol Chile
162 B1 Cholet France
242 □I6 Choloma Hond.
121 I4 Cholpon-Ata Kyrg.
151 F3 Cholsey Oxfordshire, England U.K.
245 E4 Cholula Mex.
242 □I6 Choluteca Hond.
209 E9 Choma Zambia
101 D5 Chŏmch'ŏn S. Korea
161 B3 Chomelix France
161 C4 Chomérac France
Chomo Xizang China see Yadong
111 E6 Chomo Ganggar mt. Xizang China
117 G4 Chomo Lhari mt. Bhutan
116 C4 Chomun Rajasthan India
176 C1 Chomutov Czech Rep.
176 C1 Chomutovka r. Czech Rep.
131 L3 Chona r. Rus. Fed.
101 C5 Ch'ŏnan S. Korea
97 C4 Chon Buri Thai.
259 B6 Chonchi Chile
250 A5 Chone Ecuador
Chong'an Fujian China see Wuyishan
101 C5 Ch'ŏngch'ŏn-gang r. N. Korea
101 D6 Ch'ongdo S. Korea
Chonggye Xizang China see Qonggyai
103 D6 Chŏngja S. Korea
101 D4 Ch'ŏngjin N. Korea
101 C5 Chŏngju N. Korea
101 C5 Ch'ŏngju S. Korea
108 A2 Chongkü Xizang China
107 G3 Chongli Hebei China
Chonglong Sichuan China see Zizhong
109 G2 Chongming Shanghai China
109 G2 Chongming Dao i. China
209 B8 Chongoroi Angola
101 C5 Chŏngp'yŏng N. Korea
108 C2 Chongqing Chongqing China
Chongqing Sichuan China see Chongzhou
108 C2 Chongqing mun. China
109 E3 Chongren Jiangxi China
101 C6 Chŏngŭp S. Korea
209 F8 Chongwe Zambia
109 E2 Chongyang Hubei China
109 F3 Chongyang Xi r. China
109 E3 Chongyi Jiangxi China
108 B2 Chongzhou Sichuan China
108 C4 Chongzuo Guangxi China
101 C6 Chŏnju S. Korea
245 H5 Chontalpa Mex.
117 F3 Cho Oyu mt. China/Nepal
157 E2 Chooz France
136 B3 Chop Ukr.
117 E4 Chopan Uttar Prad. India
116 C5 Chopda Mahar. India
97 D5 Chơ Phước Hai Vietnam
255 B8 Chopimzinho Brazil
136 E2 Chopovychi Ukr.
233 E5 Choptank r. MD U.S.A.
252 D4 Choquecamata Bol.
198 B3 Chora Greece
199 E3 Chorá tourist site Greece
161 E4 Chorges France
149 G4 Chorley Lancashire, England U.K.
151 G3 Chorleywood Hertfordshire, England U.K.
136 E4 Chorna Ukr.
137 G5 Chorna r. Ukr.
136 C3 Chorna Tysa Ukr.
175 M5 Chorniyiv Ukr.
137 G3 Chornobay Ukr.
136 F2 Chornobyl' Ukr.
177 L3 Chornoholova Ukr.
137 F4 Chornomors'ke Ukr.
135 F7 Chornomors'ke Ukr.
136 E3 Chornorudka Ukr.
137 G2 Chornukhy Ukr.
137 F3 Chornyy Tashlyk r. Ukr.
129 B3 Chorokhi r. Georgia/Turkey
175 K2 Choroszcz Pol.
85 E4 Chorregon Qld Austr.
254 F4 Chorrochó Brazil
136 C3 Chortkiv Ukr.
116 B5 Chorwad Gujarat India
101 C5 Ch'ŏrwŏn S. Korea
175 I2 Chorzele Pol.
174 G5 Chorzów Pol.
101 C4 Ch'osan N. Korea
105 G3 Chōshi Japan
259 B5 Choshuenco, Volcán vol. Chile
260 B5 Chos Malal Arg.
174 D2 Choszczno Pol.
250 B6 Chota Peru
238 D2 Choteau MT U.S.A.
176 E2 Chotěboř Czech Rep.
173 H2 Chotěšov Czech Rep.
116 B5 Chotila Gujarat India
177 H4 Chotín Slovakia
217 □3a Choua-chandroudé i. Comoros
156 E3 Chouilly France
204 B5 Choûm Maur.
184 B1 Chouto Port.
159 H4 Chouzy-sur-Cisse France
240 G3 Chowchilla CA U.S.A.
114 B4 Chowghat Kerala India
222 G4 Chown, Mount Alta Can.
121 K2 Choya Rus. Fed.
107 G2 Choybalsan Mongolia
160 D1 Choye France
107 F2 Choyr Mongolia
182 E2 Chozas de Abajo Spain
Chozas de la Sierra Spain see Soto del Real
176 E2 Chrast Pardubický kraj Czech Rep.
176 C2 Chrást Czech Rep.
176 D1 Chrastava Czech Rep.
171 F5 Chřibská Czech Rep.
176 G2 Chřiby hills Czech Rep.
236 G4 Chrisman IL U.S.A.
215 H2 Chrissiesmeer S. Africa
81 D5 Christchurch South I. N.Z.
151 F4 Christchurch Dorset, England U.K.
246 □ Christiana Jamaica
215 E2 Christiana S. Africa
234 C3 Christiana PA U.S.A.
Christiania Norway see Oslo
232 C6 Christiansburg VA U.S.A.
142 C4 Christiansfeld Denmark
Christianshåb Greenland see Qasigiannguit

Christiansted to Cognin

294

247 F3 Christiansted Virgin Is (U.S.A.)
226 B3 Christie WI U.S.A.
223 I3 Christina r. Alta Can.
81 B6 Christina, Mount South I. N.Z.
149 G4 Christleton Cheshire, England U.K.
86 E3 Christmas Creek W.A. Austr.
86 E3 Christmas Creek r. W.A. Austr.
86 □1 Christmas Island terr. Indian Ocean
149 H2 Christon Bank Northumberland, England U.K.
87 E5 Christopher, Lake salt flat W.A. Austr.
176 E2 Chrudim Czech Rep.
175 H3 Chruślin Pol.
198 D1 Chrysoupoli Greece
148 E2 Chryston North Lanarkshire, Scotland U.K.
175 H5 Chrzanów Pol.
174 F4 Chrząstowa Wielka Pol.
174 G5 Chrząstowice Pol.
174 E3 Chrzypsko Wielkie Pol.
Chu Kazakh. see Shu
121 F3 Chu r. Kazakh.
117 G5 Chuadanga Bangl.
109 G2 Chuansha Shanghai China
108 A2 Chubalung Sichuan China
137 I4 Chubarivka Ukr.
Chubarovka Ukr. see Polohy
Chubartau Kazakh. see Barshatas
238 D3 Chubbuck ID U.S.A.
137 J4 Chuburka r. Rus. Fed.
259 C6 Chubut prov. Arg.
259 D6 Chubut r. Arg.
177 H2 Chuchelná Czech Rep.
135 H5 Chuchkovo Rus. Fed.
241 J5 Chuckwalla Mountains CA U.S.A.
242 □K7 Chucunaque r. Panama
150 D4 Chudleigh Devon, England U.K.
136 E2 Chudniv Ukr.
174 G5 Chudoba Pol.
139 H2 Chudovo Rus. Fed.
Chudskoye, Ozero l. Estonia/Rus. Fed. see Peipus, Lake
220 D3 Chugach Mountains AK U.S.A.
103 F6 Chūgoku-sanchi mts Japan
Chugqênsumdo Qinghai China see Jigzhi
Chuguchak Xinjiang China see Tacheng
Chuguyev Ukr. see Chuhuyiv
100 E3 Chuguyevka Rus. Fed.
238 F3 Chugwater WY U.S.A.
Chuhai Guangdong China see Zhuhai
137 I3 Chuhuyiv Ukr.
121 H3 Chu-Iliyskiye Gory mts Kazakh.
108 A2 Chuka Xizang China
Chukai Malaysia see Cukai
Chukchi Peninsula Rus. Fed. see Chukotskiy Poluostrov
268 M1 Chukchi Plateau sea feature Arctic Ocean
220 A3 Chukchi Sea Rus. Fed./U.S.A.
134 H4 Chukhloma Rus. Fed.
131 T3 Chukotskiy Poluostrov pen. Rus. Fed.
137 G4 Chulakivka Ukr.
Chulakkurgan Kazakh. see Shollakorgan
Chulaktau Kazakh. see Karatau
240 I5 Chula Vista CA U.S.A.
187 C5 Chulilla Spain
150 D4 Chulmleigh Devon, England U.K.
250 A6 Chulucanas Peru
123 I3 Chulung Pass Pak.
106 D1 Chuluut Gol r. Mongolia
130 J4 Chulym Rus. Fed.
110 D1 Chulyshman r. Rus. Fed.
252 C3 Chuma Bol.
137 H4 Chumaky Ukr.
258 D3 Chumbicha Arg.
108 A1 Chumda Qinghai China
197 G4 Chumerna mt. Bulg.
100 E1 Chumikan Rus. Fed.
129 D3 Ch'umlaqi Georgia
96 C3 Chum Phae Thai.
97 B5 Chumphon Thai.
96 C4 Chum Saeng Thai.
260 E2 Chuña Arg.
131 K4 Chuna r. Rus. Fed.
109 F2 Chun'an Zhejiang China
140 P2 Chuna-Tundra plain Rus. Fed.
101 C5 Ch'unch'ŏn S. Korea
121 I4 Chundzha Kazakh.
209 E8 Chunga Zambia
Chung-hua Jen-min Kung-ho-kuo country Asia see China
Chung-hua Min-kuo country Asia see Taiwan
101 C5 Ch'ungju S. Korea
Chungking Chongqing China see Chongqing
Ch'ungmu S. Korea see T'ongyŏng
101 C5 Chŭngsan N. Korea
109 G4 Chungyang Shanmo mts Taiwan
100 D4 Chunhua Jilin China
243 H5 Chunhuhux Mex.
Chunxi Jiangsu China see Gaochun
131 K3 Chunya r. Rus. Fed.
211 B7 Chunya Tanz.
97 D4 Chuŏr Phnum Dângrêk mts Cambodia/Thai.
Chuosijia Sichuan China see Guanyinqiao
134 F2 Chupa Rus. Fed.
137 H2 Chupakhivka Ukr.
122 A2 Chūplū Iran
136 F3 Chupyra Ukr.
252 C5 Chuquicamata Chile
252 D5 Chuquisaca dept Bol.
Chuqung Qinghai China see Chindu
134 K4 Chur Rus. Fed.
190 E2 Chur Switz.
117 H4 Churachandpur Manipur India
131 O3 Churapcha Rus. Fed.
134 K5 Churayevo Rus. Fed.
151 H2 Church End Essex, England U.K.
148 B3 Church Hill Rep. of Ireland
234 C3 Church Hill MD U.S.A.
232 B6 Church Hill TN U.S.A.
223 M3 Churchill Man. Can.
223 M3 Churchill r. Man. Can.
225 I2 Churchill r. Nfld. Can.
225 I2 Churchill Falls Nfld. Can.
263 K1 Churchill Mountains Antarctica
222 E3 Churchill Peak B.C. Can.
149 G4 Church Lawton Cheshire, England U.K.
236 D1 Churchs Ferry ND U.S.A.
150 E2 Church Stretton Shropshire, England U.K.
234 B4 Churchton MD U.S.A.
147 C4 Churchtown Cork Rep. of Ireland
147 C5 Churchtown Cork Rep. of Ireland
234 C2 Churchtown PA U.S.A.
234 B3 Churchville MD U.S.A.
232 D5 Churchville VA U.S.A.
106 A1 Chureg-Tag, Gora mt. Rus. Fed.
117 F4 Churia Ghati Hills Nepal
252 A2 Churin Peru
129 E2 Churkey Rus. Fed.
129 E2 Churkeyskoye Vodokhranilishche resr Rus. Fed.
134 I4 Churov Rus. Fed.
137 G1 Churovichi Rus. Fed.
116 C3 Churu Rajasthan India
Churubay Nura Karagandinskaya Oblast' Kazakh. see Abay
226 E5 Churubusco IN U.S.A.
250 D2 Churuguara Venez.
190 E2 Churwalden Switz.
116 D2 Chushul Jammu and Kashmir
241 M3 Chuska Mountains NM U.S.A.
134 L4 Chusovaya r. Rus. Fed.
134 L4 Chusovoy Rus. Fed.
Chust Ukr. see Khust
121 G4 Chust Uzbek.
225 G3 Chute-des-Passes Que. Can.
227 I2 Chute-Rouge Que. Can.
137 H3 Chutove Ukr.
109 G3 Chutung Taiwan
78 □4a Chuuk is Micronesia
Chuvashia aut. rep. Rus. Fed. see Chuvashskaya Respublika
Chuvashskaya A.S.S.R. aut. rep. Rus. Fed. see Chuvashskaya Respublika
135 I5 Chuvashskaya Respublika aut. rep. Rus. Fed.
108 B3 Chuxiong Yunnan China
121 H4 Chüy admin. div. Kyrg.
258 G4 Chuy Uru.
97 E4 Chư Yang Sin mt. Vietnam
Chuyskaya Oblast' admin. div. Kyrg. see Chüy
160 C3 Chuzelles France
109 F1 Chuzhou Anhui China
176 D3 Chvalšiny Czech Rep.
127 G4 Chwārtā Iraq
174 G1 Chwaszczyno Pol.
Chwitffordd Flintshire, Wales U.K. see Whitford
174 G6 Chybie Pol.
136 F4 Chychykliya r. Ukr.
121 G3 Chyganak Kazakh.
137 G3 Chyhyryn Ukr.
Chymyshliya Moldova see Cimișlia
136 B3 Chynadiyeve Ukr.
171 F5 Chyňava Czech Rep.
175 J4 Chynów Pol.
Chystyakove Ukr. see Torez
211 C5 Chyulu Range mts Kenya
175 M6 Chyzhykiv Ukr.
196 E3 Ciacova Romania
Ciadâr-Lunga Moldova see Ciadîr-Lunga
136 E4 Ciadîr-Lunga Moldova
163 C5 Ciadoux France
193 H5 Ciagola, Monte mt. Italy
247 □1 Ciales Puerto Rico
192 B3 Ciamannacce Corse France
95 E4 Ciamis Jawa Barat Indon.
193 E3 Ciampino Italy
193 E3 Ciampino airport Italy
194 C5 Cianciana Sicilia Italy
94 D4 Cianjur Jawa Barat Indon.
256 A5 Cianorte Brazil
161 F5 Cians r. France
174 G5 Ciasna Pol.
174 F3 Ciążeń Pol.
94 D4 Cibadak Jawa Barat Indon.
177 J5 Cibakháza Hungary
95 E4 Cibatu Jawa Barat Indon.
241 L4 Cibecue AZ U.S.A.
94 D4 Cibinong Jawa Barat Indon.
211 A5 Cibitoke Burundi
237 D6 Cibolo Creek r. TX U.S.A.
184 B2 Ciborro Port.
94 D4 Ci Buni r. Indon.
242 C2 Cibuta, Sierra mt. Mex.
190 E4 Cicagna Italy
188 D3 Čićarija mts Croatia
193 G4 Cicciano Italy
126 D3 Çiçekdağı Turkey
128 B1 Çiçekli Turkey
199 F2 Çiçekli Turkey
193 H4 Cicerale Italy
226 D5 Cicero IL U.S.A.
254 F4 Cícero Dantas Brazil
196 E4 Ćićevac Srbija Yugo.
174 E4 Cicha Woda r. Pol.
175 L3 Cicibór Duży Pol.
177 G4 Čičov Slovakia
183 I2 Cidacos r. Spain
126 D2 Cide Turkey
176 E1 Cidlina r. Czech Rep.
183 H3 Cidones Spain
247 □1 Cidra Puerto Rico
175 I3 Ciechanów Pol.
175 K3 Ciechanowiec Pol.
174 G3 Ciechocinek Pol.
246 C2 Ciego de Avila Cuba
175 I4 Cielądz Pol.
260 C3 Cielo, Cerro mt. Arg.
183 G4 Ciempozuelos Spain
250 C2 Ciénaga Col.
246 B2 Cienfuegos Cuba
174 F3 Cienin Zaborny Pol.
175 J4 Ciepielów Pol.
174 E5 Ciepłowody Pol.
163 C6 Cier-de-Luchon France
177 G3 Čierna Voda Slovakia
177 K3 Čierna voda r. Slovakia
177 H3 Čierne Kľačany Slovakia
177 I3 Čierny Balog Slovakia
163 C6 Cierp-Gaud France
174 F2 Cierznie Pol.
175 L5 Cieszanów Pol.
174 F4 Cieszków Pol.
174 G6 Cieszyn Śląskie Pol.
174 F4 Cieszyn Wielkopolskie Pol.
163 C5 Cieutat France
162 D3 Cieux France
187 B6 Cieza Spain
175 I6 Ciężkowice Pol.
128 C1 Çiflikköy Turkey
199 G2 Çifteler Turkey
Çiftlik Turkey see Kelkit
129 B4 Çiftlikköy Turkey
199 F1 Çiftlikköy Turkey
183 H4 Cifuentes Spain
183 F3 Cigales Spain
177 K3 Cigánd Hungary
190 D3 Cigliano Italy
183 G5 Cigüela r. Spain
126 D3 Cihanbeyli Turkey
199 F2 Cihangazi Turkey
244 B4 Cihuatlán Mex.
185 F1 Cijara, Embalse de resr Spain
177 J6 Čik r. Yugo.
Cikai Yunnan China see Gongshan
198 A1 Çikes, Maja e mt. Albania
79 □1 Cikobia i. Fiji
188 F4 Čikola r. Croatia
95 E4 Cilacap Jawa Tengah Indon.
127 F2 Çıldır Turkey
127 F2 Çıldır Gölü l. Turkey
95 E4 Ciledug Jawa Barat Indon.
109 D2 Cili Hunan China
197 G4 Cilieni Romania
199 G1 Cilimli Turkey
Cill Airne Rep. of Ireland see Killarney
183 I4 Cillas Spain
Cill Chainnigh Rep. of Ireland see Kilkenny
146 A4 Cille Bhrighde Western Isles, Scotland U.K.
182 D4 Cilleros Spain
Cill Mhantáin Rep. of Ireland see Wicklow
127 G3 Cilo Dağı mt. Turkey
129 G3 Çiloy Azer.
150 D3 Cilybebyll Neath Port Talbot, Wales U.K.
150 D2 Cilycwm Carmarthenshire, Wales U.K.
241 J4 Cima CA U.S.A.
94 D4 Cimahi Jawa Barat Indon.
182 E2 Cimanes del Tejar Spain
237 C4 Cimarron KS U.S.A.
239 F4 Cimarron NM U.S.A.
237 D4 Cimarron r. OK U.S.A.
239 F4 Cimarron Creek r. CO U.S.A.
183 I3 Cimballa Spain
194 C5 Ciminna Sicilia Italy
192 E2 Cimino, Monte mt. Italy
136 E4 Cimișlia Moldova
191 H2 Cimolais Italy
191 F4 Cimone, Monte mt. Italy
Cîmpeni Romania see Câmpeni
Cîmpia Turzii Romania see Câmpia Turzii
Cîmpina Romania see Câmpina
Cîmpulung Romania see Câmpulung
Cîmpulung la Tisa Romania see Câmpulung la Tisa
Cîmpulung Moldovenesc Romania see Câmpulung Moldovenesc
127 F3 Çınar Turkey
199 F1 Çınarcık Turkey
250 E3 Cinaruco r. Venez.
186 D3 Cinca r. Spain
186 D2 Cinca, Canal de r. Spain
188 F4 Cincar mt. Bos.-Herz.
236 G4 Cincinnati OH U.S.A.
233 F3 Cincinnatus NY U.S.A.
185 G1 Cinco Casas Spain
Cinco de Outubro Angola see Xá-Muteba
260 C6 Cinco Saltos Arg.
186 C4 Cinctorres Spain
197 G3 Cincu Romania
150 E3 Cinderford Gloucestershire, England U.K.
199 F3 Çine Turkey
199 E3 Çine r. Turkey
182 E2 Ciñera Spain
165 E4 Ciney Belgium
182 B3 Cinfães Port.
191 I5 Cingoli Italy
192 D2 Cinigiano Italy
190 E3 Cinisello Balsamo Italy
194 C4 Cinisi Sicilia Italy
177 I3 Cinobaňa Slovakia
159 G4 Cinq-Mars-la-Pile France
195 F4 Cinquefrondi Italy
190 E4 Cinque Terre reg. Italy
245 H5 Cintalapa Mex.
163 D5 Cintegabelle France
192 A2 Cinto, Monte mt. France
157 F5 Cintrey France
183 I2 Cintruénigo Spain
215 G5 Cintsa S. Africa
256 B5 Cinzas r. Brazil
197 H3 Ciolpani Romania
177 L6 Ciordan, Dealul hill Romania
188 F4 Čiovo i. Croatia
Ciping Jiangxi China see Jinggangshan
254 F4 Cipó Brazil
257 E3 Cipo r. Brazil
260 D6 Cipolletti Arg.
257 F4 Cipotânea Brazil
187 C4 Cirat Spain
182 E2 Cirbanal mt. Spain
193 G3 Circello Italy
193 F3 Circeo, Monte hill Italy
220 D3 Circle AK U.S.A.
238 F2 Circle MT U.S.A.
232 B5 Circleville OH U.S.A.
241 K2 Circleville UT U.S.A.
95 E4 Cirebon Jawa Barat Indon.
151 F3 Cirencester Gloucestershire, England U.K.
Cirene tourist site Libya see Cyrene
157 E4 Cirey-sur-Blaise France
157 G4 Cirey-sur-Vezouze France
183 I3 Ciria Spain
190 C3 Ciriè Italy
193 I4 Cirigliano Italy
136 E3 Ciripcău Moldova
195 G3 Cirò Italy
177 K3 Cirocha r. Slovakia
195 G3 Cirò Marina Italy
163 B4 Ciron r. France
225 I1 Cirque Mountain Nfld. Can.
Cirta Alg. see Constantine
183 G5 Ciruelos Spain
160 C2 Ciry-le-Noble France
190 D4 Cisano sul Neva Italy
241 M2 Cisco UT U.S.A.
178 C4 Cismòn r. Italy
175 K6 Cisna Pol.
197 G3 Cisnădie Romania
183 F2 Cisneros Spain
191 H3 Cisòn di Valmarino Italy
159 G5 Cissé France
193 E3 Cisterna di Latina Italy
195 G2 Cisternino Italy
183 E2 Cistierna Spain
246 D3 Citadelle Laferrière tourist site Haiti
191 H5 Citerna Italy
245 F3 Citlaltepec Mex.
Citlaltépetl vol. Mex. see Orizaba, Pico de
188 F4 Čitluk Bos.-Herz.
163 E5 Citou France
237 F6 Citronelle AL U.S.A.
214 B5 Citrusdal S. Africa
240 G2 Citrus Heights CA U.S.A.
191 G3 Cittadella Italy
192 E2 Città della Pieve Italy
191 H5 Città di Castello Italy
190 C3 Citta di Torino airport Italy
193 E2 Cittaducale Italy
195 F4 Cittanova Italy
193 F2 Cittareale Italy
193 G2 Città Sant'Angelo Italy
190 D3 Cittiglio Italy
147 D1 City of Derry airport Northern Ireland U.K.
197 G3 Ciucaș, Vârful mt. Romania
197 F2 Ciucea Romania
243 E2 Ciudad Acuña Mex.
244 D4 Ciudad Altamirano Mex.
251 F2 Ciudad Bolívar Venez.
242 D3 Ciudad Camargo Mex.
242 C3 Ciudad Constitución Mex.
243 H6 Ciudad Cuauhtémoc Mex.
243 H5 Ciudad del Carmen Mex.
253 G6 Ciudad del Este Para.
242 D2 Ciudad Delicias Mex.
245 E2 Ciudad del Maíz Mex.
245 E3 Ciudad de Valles Mex.
251 F2 Ciudad Guayana Venez.
244 C4 Ciudad Guzmán Mex.
244 D4 Ciudad Hidalgo Mex.
245 G5 Ciudad Ixtepec Mex.
242 D2 Ciudad Juárez Mex.
242 E3 Ciudad Lerdo Mex.
245 E4 Ciudad López Mateos Mex.
245 F2 Ciudad Madero Mex.
245 E2 Ciudad Mante Mex.
244 D3 Ciudad Manuel Doblado Mex.
245 F4 Ciudad Mendoza Mex.
243 F3 Ciudad Mier Mex.
242 C3 Ciudad Obregón Mex.
185 G2 Ciudad Real Spain
185 G2 Ciudad Real prov. Castilla - La Mancha Spain
243 F3 Ciudad Río Bravo Mex.
182 D4 Ciudad Rodrigo Spain
245 F4 Ciudad Serdán Mex.
Ciudad Trujillo Dom. Rep. see Santo Domingo
245 E2 Ciudad Victoria Mex.
197 E3 Ciudanovița Romania
177 L4 Ciuhoi Romania
136 D4 Ciuhur r. Moldova
136 E4 Ciulucal de Mijloc r. Moldova
197 G2 Ciumani Romania
177 K5 Ciumeghiu Romania
186 □ Ciutadella de Menorca Spain
162 C2 Civaux France
191 H2 Civetta, Monte mt. Italy
191 I2 Cividale del Friuli Italy
193 I5 Civita Italy
193 E2 Civita Castellana Italy
193 F3 Civita d'Antino Italy
191 I5 Civitanova Marche Italy
193 F2 Civitaquana Italy
192 D2 Civitavecchia Italy
192 D2 Civitella, Monte mt. Italy
193 F2 Civitella Casanova Italy
192 E2 Civitella d'Agliano Italy
191 G4 Civitella di Romagna Italy
191 G5 Civitella in Val di Chiana Italy
193 F3 Civitella Roveto Italy
159 I5 Civray Centre France
162 C2 Civray Poitou-Charentes France
199 F2 Çivril Turkey
192 B5 Cixerri r. Sardegna Italy
109 G2 Cixi Zhejiang China
107 G4 Cixian Hebei China
177 L4 Cizer Romania
Cizhou Hebei China see Cixian
171 F5 Čížkovice Czech Rep.
127 F3 Cizre Turkey
176 C2 Čkyně Czech Rep.
146 B5 Clabhach Argyll and Bute, Scotland U.K.
146 C6 Clachan Argyll and Bute, Scotland U.K.
146 B4 Clachan Highland, Scotland U.K.
238 B2 Clackamas r. OR U.S.A.
146 E5 Clackmannanshire admin. div. Scotland U.K.
151 I3 Clacton-on-Sea Essex, England U.K.
146 C5 Cladich Argyll and Bute, Scotland U.K.
148 B3 Clady Northern Ireland U.K.
147 E2 Clady Northern Ireland U.K.
146 C5 Claggan Highland, Scotland U.K.
162 C2 Clain r. France
163 C4 Clairac France
223 H3 Claire, Lake Alta Can.
222 G4 Clairmont Alta Can.
156 C3 Clairoix France
163 E4 Clairvaux-d'Aveyron France
160 D2 Clairvaux-les-Lacs France
162 C2 Claise r. France
161 D3 Claix France
160 B1 Clamecy France
226 B2 Clam Lake WI U.S.A.
148 B3 Clanabogan Northern Ireland U.K.
240 I2 Clan Alpine Mountains NV U.S.A.
81 C6 Clandeboye South I. N.Z.
147 E3 Clane Rep. of Ireland
151 F3 Clanfield Oxfordshire, England U.K.
161 F4 Clans France
231 C5 Clanton AL U.S.A.
215 F4 Clanville S. Africa
214 B5 Clanwilliam S. Africa
146 C6 Claonaig Argyll and Bute, Scotland U.K.
151 G2 Clapham Bedfordshire, England U.K.
149 G3 Clapham North Yorkshire, England U.K.
261 H2 Clara Arg.
85 E3 Clara r. Qld Austr.
147 D3 Clara Rep. of Ireland
85 E3 Claraville Qld Austr.
149 I4 Clarborough Nottinghamshire, England U.K.
83 E3 Clare N.S.W. Austr.
82 D3 Clare S.A. Austr.
147 C4 Clare county Rep. of Ireland
147 B3 Clare r. Rep. of Ireland
151 H2 Clare Suffolk, England U.K.
226 E4 Clare MI U.S.A.
147 C4 Clarecastle Rep. of Ireland
147 D3 Clareen Rep. of Ireland
147 C3 Claregalway Rep. of Ireland
147 A3 Clare Island Rep. of Ireland
246 □ Claremont Jamaica
233 G3 Claremont NH U.S.A.
85 E2 Claremont Isles Qld Austr.
237 E4 Claremore OK U.S.A.
147 C3 Claremorris Rep. of Ireland
83 H2 Clarence r. N.S.W. Austr.
81 D5 Clarence South I. N.Z.
81 D5 Clarence r. South I. N.Z.
259 C9 Clarence, Isla i. Chile
262 U2 Clarence Island Antarctica
84 B1 Clarence Strait N.T. Austr.
222 C3 Clarence Strait AK U.S.A.
246 D2 Clarence Town Long I. Bahamas
246 □ Clarendon parish Jamaica
81 C7 Clarendon South I. N.Z.
237 F5 Clarendon AR U.S.A.
232 D4 Clarendon PA U.S.A.
237 C5 Clarendon TX U.S.A.
246 □ Clarendon Park Jamaica
215 G3 Clarens S. Africa
225 K3 Clarenville Nfld. Can.
222 H5 Claresholm Alta Can.
161 B5 Claret Languedoc-Roussillon France
161 D4 Claret Provence-Alpes-Côte-d'Azur France
187 C5 Clariano r. Spain
85 E3 Clarina Creek r. Qld Austr.
236 E3 Clarinda IA U.S.A.
232 C5 Clarington OH U.S.A.
236 E3 Clarion IA U.S.A.
232 D4 Clarion PA U.S.A.
232 D4 Clarion r. PA U.S.A.
246 D2 Clarion Bank sea feature Bahamas
80 E2 Claris North I. N.Z.
236 D2 Clark SD U.S.A.
222 F1 Clark, Mount N.W.T. Can.
234 B2 Clark Creek r. PA U.S.A.
241 K4 Clarkdale AZ U.S.A.
85 F3 Clarke r. Qld Austr.
215 G4 Clarkebury S. Africa
85 F4 Clarke Range mts Qld Austr.
85 F3 Clarke River Qld Austr.
85 E3 Clarkes Creek r. Qld Austr.
225 K3 Clarke's Head Nfld. Can.
231 D5 Clarkesville GA U.S.A.
238 C1 Clark Fork r. ID U.S.A.
238 C1 Clark Fork r. MT U.S.A.
231 D5 Clark Hill Reservoir Georgia/S. Carolina U.S.A.
241 J4 Clark Mountain CA U.S.A.
262 O1 Clark Mountains Antarctica
235 D2 Clarksburg NJ U.S.A.
232 C5 Clarksburg WV U.S.A.
237 F5 Clarksdale MS U.S.A.
238 E2 Clark's Fork Yellowstone r. MT U.S.A.
81 C6 Clarks Junction South I. N.Z.
214 E6 Clarkson S. Africa
234 C1 Clarks Summit PA U.S.A.
238 C2 Clarkston WA U.S.A.
246 □ Clark's Town Jamaica
237 E5 Clarksville AR U.S.A.
234 B3 Clarksville MD U.S.A.
231 C4 Clarksville TN U.S.A.
237 E5 Clarksville TX U.S.A.
232 D6 Clarksville VA U.S.A.
256 B1 Claro r. Mato Grosso Brazil
256 B3 Claro r. Goiás Brazil
190 E2 Claro Switz.
156 D2 Clary France
146 D4 Clashmore Highland, Scotland U.K.
146 C3 Clashnessie Highland, Scotland U.K.
238 B2 Clatskanie OR U.S.A.
237 C5 Claude TX U.S.A.
257 E4 Cláudio Brazil
147 D2 Claudy Northern Ireland U.K.
171 E5 Clausnitz Ger.
234 C2 Claussville PA U.S.A.
169 F4 Clausthal-Zellerfeld Ger.
191 H2 Claut Italy
191 H2 Clauzetto Italy
92 B2 Claveria Phil.
151 H3 Clavering Essex, England U.K.
150 E2 Claverley Shropshire, England U.K.
165 E4 Clavier Belgium
231 D5 Claxton GA U.S.A.
234 B2 Clay PA U.S.A.
232 C5 Clay WV U.S.A.
233 G2 Clayburg NY U.S.A.
236 D4 Clay Center KS U.S.A.
236 D3 Clay Center NE U.S.A.
232 B6 Clay City KY U.S.A.
149 H4 Clay Cross Derbyshire, England U.K.
151 I2 Claydon Suffolk, England U.K.
156 C4 Claye-Souilly France
234 C3 Claymont DE U.S.A.
149 I4 Claypole Lincolnshire, England U.K.
241 L5 Claypool AZ U.S.A.
241 L4 Clay Springs AZ U.S.A.
151 G4 Clayton West Sussex, England U.K.
231 C6 Clayton AL U.S.A.
234 C3 Clayton DE U.S.A.
231 D5 Clayton GA U.S.A.
234 C3 Clayton NJ U.S.A.
237 C4 Clayton NM U.S.A.
233 E2 Clayton NY U.S.A.
237 E5 Clayton OK U.S.A.
233 □I1 Clayton Lake ME U.S.A.
149 G4 Clayton-le-Moors Lancashire, England U.K.
261 H3 Clé r. Arg.
146 B5 Cleadale Highland, Scotland U.K.
149 H3 Cleadon Tyne and Wear, England U.K.
147 B5 Cleady Rep. of Ireland
147 B5 Clear, Cape Rep. of Ireland
232 C5 Clearco WV U.S.A.
227 G4 Clear Creek Ont. Can.
241 L2 Clear Creek UT U.S.A.
241 L4 Clear Creek r. AZ U.S.A.
238 F2 Clear Creek r. WY U.S.A.
232 D4 Clearfield PA U.S.A.
238 D3 Clearfield UT U.S.A.
237 D5 Clear Fork Brazos r. TX U.S.A.
222 G3 Clear Hills Y.T. Can.
147 B5 Clear Island Rep. of Ireland
236 E3 Clear Lake IA U.S.A.
236 D2 Clear Lake SD U.S.A.
226 A3 Clear Lake WI U.S.A.
240 F2 Clearlake Oaks CA U.S.A.
238 F2 Clearmont WY U.S.A.
232 E5 Clear Spring MD U.S.A.
222 G5 Clearwater B.C. Can.
223 I3 Clearwater r. Alberta/Saskatchewan Can.
222 H4 Clearwater r. Alta Can.
231 D7 Clearwater FL U.S.A.
238 C2 Clearwater r. ID U.S.A.
236 D2 Clearwater r. MN U.S.A.
226 C3 Clearwater Lake WI U.S.A.
238 D2 Clearwater Mountains ID U.S.A.
149 F3 Cleator Moor Cumbria, England U.K.
237 D5 Cleburne TX U.S.A.
159 F3 Clécy France
158 B3 Cléder France
150 E2 Cleehill Shropshire, England U.K.
238 B2 Cle Elum WA U.S.A.
149 I4 Cleethorpes North East Lincolnshire, England U.K.
157 F4 Clefmont France
158 C4 Cléguer France
158 C3 Cléguérec France
150 E2 Clehonger Herefordshire, England U.K.
197 G3 Clejani Romania
161 D4 Clelles France
165 E5 Clémency Lux.
256 B4 Clementina Brazil
231 D5 Clemson SC U.S.A.
232 C5 Clendenin WV U.S.A.
168 F3 Clenze Ger.
150 E2 Cleobury Mortimer Shropshire, England U.K.
156 B3 Cléon France
234 B2 Cleona PA U.S.A.
161 C4 Cléon-d'Andran France
92 A4 Cleopatra Needle mt. Palawan Phil.
159 G4 Cléré-les-Pins France
156 B3 Clères France
156 E4 Clérey France
Clerf Lux. see Clervaux
227 H1 Cléricy Que. Can.
161 C3 Clérieux France
81 A6 Clerke, Mount South I. N.Z.
86 C3 Clerke Reef W.A. Austr.
160 C2 Clermain France
85 F4 Clermont Qld Austr.
163 D5 Clermont Midi-Pyrénées France
156 C3 Clermont Picardie France
215 H3 Clermont S. Africa
231 D6 Clermont FL U.S.A.
159 F4 Clermont-Créans France
162 C4 Clermont-de-Beauregard France
Clermont de Tonnère atoll Arch. des Tuamotu Fr. Polynesia see Reao
157 F3 Clermont-en-Argonne France
160 B3 Clermont-Ferrand France
161 B5 Clermont-l'Hérault France
160 E1 Clerval France
165 F4 Clervaux Lux.
165 F5 Clervé r. Lux.
156 C4 Cléry r. France
156 B5 Cléry-St-André France
191 G2 Cles Italy
82 D3 Cleve S.A. Austr.
150 E3 Clevedon North Somerset, England U.K.
231 D5 Cleveland GA U.S.A.
237 F5 Cleveland MS U.S.A.
232 C4 Cleveland OH U.S.A.
231 C5 Cleveland TN U.S.A.
237 E6 Cleveland TX U.S.A.
241 L2 Cleveland UT U.S.A.
232 B6 Cleveland VA U.S.A.
226 D4 Cleveland WI U.S.A.
85 F3 Cleveland, Cape Qld Austr.
238 D1 Cleveland, Mount MT U.S.A.
85 F3 Cleveland Bay Qld Austr.
232 C4 Cleveland Heights OH U.S.A.
149 H3 Cleveland Hills England U.K.
255 B8 Clevelândia Brazil
149 F4 Cleveleys Lancashire, England U.K.
Cleves Ger. see Kleve
147 B3 Clew Bay Rep. of Ireland
215 G1 Clewer S. Africa
231 D7 Clewiston FL U.S.A.
81 A7 Clifden South I. N.Z.
147 A3 Clifden Rep. of Ireland
84 D3 Cliffdale r. Qld Austr.
151 H3 Cliffe Medway, England U.K.
151 H3 Cliffe Woods Medway, England U.K.
147 C2 Cliffonoy Rep. of Ireland
215 F4 Clifford S. Africa
234 C1 Clifford PA U.S.A.
232 C5 Clifftop WV U.S.A.
85 G5 Clifton Qld Austr.
151 G2 Clifton Bedfordshire, England U.K.
241 M5 Clifton AZ U.S.A.
226 D5 Clifton IL U.S.A.
236 D4 Clifton KS U.S.A.
235 D2 Clifton NJ U.S.A.
234 C1 Clifton PA U.S.A.
85 F3 Clifton Beach Qld Austr.
232 D6 Clifton Forge VA U.S.A.
82 D1 Clifton Hills S.A. Austr.
233 G3 Clifton Park NY U.S.A.
223 I5 Climax Sask. Can.
226 E4 Climax MI U.S.A.
232 B6 Clinch r. TN U.S.A.
232 B6 Clinchco VA U.S.A.
232 B6 Clinch Mountain mts TN/VA U.S.A.
232 B6 Clinchport VA U.S.A.
222 G4 Cline River Alta Can.
165 D3 Clinge Neth.
169 F4 Clingen Ger.
222 F5 Clinton B.C. Can.
224 D5 Clinton Ont. Can.
81 B7 Clinton South I. N.Z.
237 E5 Clinton AR U.S.A.
235 F1 Clinton CT U.S.A.
230 B3 Clinton IA U.S.A.
236 F3 Clinton IL U.S.A.
237 F4 Clinton KY U.S.A.
237 F6 Clinton LA U.S.A.
233 □I2 Clinton ME U.S.A.
227 F4 Clinton MI U.S.A.
236 E4 Clinton MO U.S.A.
237 F5 Clinton MS U.S.A.
231 E5 Clinton NC U.S.A.
233 F3 Clinton NY U.S.A.
232 C4 Clinton OH U.S.A.
237 D5 Clinton OK U.S.A.
231 C4 Clinton TN U.S.A.
223 J1 Clinton-Colden Lake N.W.T. Can.
226 C3 Clintonville WI U.S.A.
232 C6 Clintonville WV U.S.A.
232 B6 Clintwood VA U.S.A.
231 C6 Clio AL U.S.A.
227 F4 Clio MI U.S.A.
159 H5 Clion France
218 E7 Clipperton, Île terr. N. Pacific Ocean
146 B4 Clisham hill Scotland U.K.
158 E4 Clisson France
149 G4 Clitheroe Lancashire, England U.K.
80 F3 Clive North I. N.Z.
252 D4 Cliza Bol.
87 B4 Cloates, Point W.A. Austr.
215 F3 Clocolan S. Africa
147 D4 Clogh Kilkenny Rep. of Ireland
147 E4 Clogh Wexford Rep. of Ireland
147 E2 Clogh Northern Ireland U.K.
147 D2 Cloghan Donegal Rep. of Ireland
147 D3 Cloghan Offaly Rep. of Ireland
148 B4 Cloghan Westmeath Rep. of Ireland
147 A4 Cloghane Rep. of Ireland
147 C2 Cloghboy Rep. of Ireland
147 D4 Clogheen Rep. of Ireland
147 B3 Clogher Rep. of Ireland
147 D2 Clogher Northern Ireland U.K.
147 E3 Clogherhead Rep. of Ireland
147 E1 Clogh Mills Northern Ireland U.K.
147 F2 Cloghy Northern Ireland U.K.
147 E4 Clohamon Rep. of Ireland
158 C4 Clohars-Carnoët France
85 E4 Clonagh Qld Austr.
147 C5 Clonakilty Rep. of Ireland
147 D3 Clonare Rep. of Ireland
148 B4 Clonaslee Rep. of Ireland
84 E4 Cloncurry Qld Austr.
85 E3 Cloncurry r. Qld Austr.
147 E3 Clondalkin Rep. of Ireland
147 D4 Clonea Rep. of Ireland
147 E3 Clonee Rep. of Ireland
147 D4 Cloneen Rep. of Ireland
147 E4 Clonegal Rep. of Ireland
147 D2 Clones Rep. of Ireland
147 D1 Clonmany Rep. of Ireland
147 D4 Clonmel Rep. of Ireland
147 D3 Clonmellon Rep. of Ireland
147 E4 Clonmore Carlow Rep. of Ireland
147 D4 Clonmore Tipperary Rep. of Ireland
147 D3 Clonopy Rep. of Ireland
147 D4 Clonoulty Rep. of Ireland
147 E4 Clonroche Rep. of Ireland
147 E3 Clontarf Rep. of Ireland
147 E2 Clontibret Rep. of Ireland
147 D3 Clonygowan Rep. of Ireland
147 C2 Cloonacool Rep. of Ireland
147 B4 Cloonbannin Rep. of Ireland
147 B3 Cloonboo Rep. of Ireland
147 D3 Cloone Rep. of Ireland
148 B4 Clooneagh Rep. of Ireland
147 C3 Cloonfad Roscommon Rep. of Ireland
147 C3 Cloonfad Roscommon Rep. of Ireland
147 B3 Cloonkeen Rep. of Ireland
147 C3 Cloontia Rep. of Ireland
222 E5 Clo-oose B.C. Can.
168 D3 Cloppenburg Ger.
226 A2 Cloquet MN U.S.A.
226 A2 Cloquet r. MN U.S.A.
258 F2 Clorinda Arg.
146 E6 Closeburn Dumfries and Galloway, Scotland U.K.
226 C1 Cloud Bay Ont. Can.
238 F2 Cloud Peak WY U.S.A.
81 E4 Cloudy Bay South I. N.Z.
162 C2 Clouère r. France
147 F2 Clough Northern Ireland U.K.
149 I3 Cloughton North Yorkshire, England U.K.
146 □G1 Clousta Shetland, Scotland U.K.
224 F3 Clova Que. Can.
146 E5 Clova Angus, Scotland U.K.
150 C3 Clovelly Devon, England U.K.
146 F6 Clovenfords Scottish Borders, Scotland U.K.
241 K1 Clover UT U.S.A.
240 F2 Cloverdale CA U.S.A.
240 H3 Clovis CA U.S.A.
237 C5 Clovis NM U.S.A.
146 C5 Clovullin Highland, Scotland U.K.
149 H4 Clowne Derbyshire, England U.K.
156 B5 Cloyes-sur-le-Loir France
227 I3 Cloyne Ont. Can.
147 C5 Cloyne Rep. of Ireland
Cluain Meala Rep. of Ireland see Clonmel
146 C4 Cluanie, Loch l. Scotland U.K.
223 I3 Cluff Lake Mine Sask. Can.
162 D2 Cluis France
197 F2 Cluj-Napoca Romania
161 E4 Clumanc France
150 D2 Clun Shropshire, England U.K.
150 E2 Clun r. England U.K.
146 D5 Clunes Highland, Scotland U.K.
84 D5 Cluny Qld Austr.
160 C2 Cluny France
160 E2 Cluses France
Clusium Italy see Chiusi
190 E3 Clusone Italy
232 D6 Cluster Springs VA U.S.A.
81 B7 Clutha r. South I. N.Z.
87 E5 Clutterbuck Hills hill W.A. Austr.
150 E3 Clutton Bath and North East Somerset, England U.K.
150 D1 Clwydian Range hills Wales U.K.
150 D3 Clydach Swansea, Wales U.K.
150 D3 Clydach Vale Rhondda Cynon Taff, Wales U.K.
222 H4 Clyde Alta Can.
81 B6 Clyde South I. N.Z.
146 D6 Clyde r. Scotland U.K.
232 E3 Clyde NY U.S.A.
232 B4 Clyde OH U.S.A.
146 D6 Clyde, Firth of est. Scotland U.K.
146 D6 Clydebank West Dunbartonshire, Scotland U.K.
221 L2 Clyde River Nunavut Can.
146 E6 Clydesdale val. Scotland U.K.
81 B7 Clydevale South I. N.Z.
226 C4 Clyman WI U.S.A.
232 D4 Clymer PA U.S.A.
150 C3 Clynderwen Carmarthenshire, Wales U.K.
150 D2 Clyro Powys, Wales U.K.
175 J5 Ćmielów Pol.
146 E4 Cnoc Fraing hill Scotland U.K.
146 C6 Cnoc Moy hill Scotland U.K.
Cnossus tourist site Greece see Knosos
182 C3 Côa r. Port.
245 E4 Coacalco Mex.
241 I5 Coachella CA U.S.A.
147 C5 Coachford Rep. of Ireland
147 E2 Coagh Northern Ireland U.K.
242 E3 Coahuila state Mex.
222 E3 Coal r. Y.T. Can.
146 E6 Coalburn South Lanarkshire, Scotland U.K.
226 C5 Coal City IL U.S.A.
244 C4 Coalcomán r. Mex.
223 H5 Coaldale Alta Can.
240 I2 Coaldale NV U.S.A.
234 C2 Coaldale PA U.S.A.
237 D5 Coalgate OK U.S.A.
232 B5 Coal Grove OH U.S.A.
222 E5 Coal Harbour B.C. Can.
240 G3 Coalinga CA U.S.A.
147 E2 Coalisland Northern Ireland U.K.
232 D4 Coalport PA U.S.A.
222 E3 Coal River B.C. Can.
215 G2 Coalville S. Africa
151 F2 Coalville Leicestershire, England U.K.
238 E3 Coalville UT U.S.A.
247 □1 Coamo Puerto Rico
182 D1 Coaña Spain
251 F6 Coari Brazil
251 F6 Coari r. Brazil
251 F6 Coari, Lago l. Brazil
163 B5 Coarraze France
240 H3 Coarsegold CA U.S.A.
252 C3 Coasa Peru
211 D5 Coast prov. Kenya
Coast admin. reg. Tanz. see Pwani
197 H1 Coasta Ibăneștilor ridge Romania
237 E6 Coastal Plain U.S.A.
222 E4 Coast Mountains B.C. Can.
85 G5 Coast Range hills Qld Austr.
240 F1 Coast Ranges mts CA U.S.A.
146 D6 Coatbridge North Lanarkshire, Scotland U.K.
245 F4 Coatepec Mex.
245 E4 Coatepec Harinas Mex.
243 H6 Coatepeque Guat.
234 C3 Coatesville PA U.S.A.
225 G4 Coaticook Que. Can.
221 J3 Coats Island Nunavut Can.
262 V1 Coats Land reg. Antarctica
245 G4 Coatzacoalcos Mex.
245 G4 Coatzacoalcos r. Mex.
245 F3 Coatzintla Mex.
197 I3 Cobadin Romania
227 H2 Cobalt Ont. Can.
235 F1 Cobalt CT U.S.A.
243 H6 Cobán Guat.
129 D3 Çobandağ hill Azer./Georgia
199 G2 Çobanlar Turkey
83 F2 Cobar N.S.W. Austr.
83 G4 Cobargo N.S.W. Austr.
87 E5 Cobb, Lake salt flat W.A. Austr.
83 E4 Cobden Vic. Austr.
227 I3 Cobden Ont. Can.
183 G4 Cobeja Spain
183 H4 Cobeta Spain
147 C5 Cóbh Rep. of Ireland
223 M4 Cobham r. Man./Ont. Can.
151 G3 Cobham Surrey, England U.K.
252 C2 Cobija Bol.
Coblenz Ger. see Koblenz
233 F3 Cobleskill NY U.S.A.
148 C4 Coblinstown Rep. of Ireland
222 C3 Cobol AK U.S.A.
224 E5 Cobourg Ont. Can.
84 C1 Cobourg Peninsula N.T. Austr.
260 A5 Cobquecura Chile
87 C5 Cobra W.A. Austr.
83 F3 Cobram Vic. Austr.
184 C3 Cobres r. Port.
211 B8 Cóbuè Moz.
169 F5 Coburg Ger.
183 F3 Coca Spain
252 C4 Cocachacra Peru
254 E2 Cocal Brazil
234 B2 Cocalico Creek r. PA U.S.A.
254 C5 Cocalinho Brazil
Cocanada Andhra Prad. India see Kakinada
252 D4 Cocapata Bol.
193 H4 Coccovello, Monte mt. Italy
187 C6 Cocentaina Spain
252 D4 Cochabamba Bol.
252 D4 Cochabamba dept Bol.
259 B6 Cochamó Chile
260 A5 Cocharcas Chile
169 C5 Cochem Ger.
114 C4 Cochin Kerala India
241 M5 Cochise AZ U.S.A.
241 M5 Cochise Head mt. AZ U.S.A.
231 D5 Cochran GA U.S.A.
222 H5 Cochrane Alta Can.
224 D3 Cochrane Ont. Can.
223 K3 Cochrane r. Sask. Can.
232 C4 Cochranton PA U.S.A.
234 C3 Cochranville PA U.S.A.
171 C4 Cochstedt Ger.
177 L5 Cociuba Mare Romania
82 C3 Cockaleechie S.A. Austr.
146 E4 Cock Bridge Aberdeenshire, Scotland U.K.
82 E3 Cockburn S.A. Austr.
246 E2 Cockburn Harbour Turks and Caicos Is
146 F6 Cockburnspath Scottish Borders, Scotland U.K.
246 D1 Cockburn Town San Salvador Bahamas
Cockburn Town Turks and Caicos Is see Grand Turk
149 H2 Cockenheugh hill England U.K.
146 F6 Cockenzie and Port Seton East Lothian, Scotland U.K.
149 F3 Cocker r. England U.K.
149 G4 Cockerham Lancashire, England U.K.
149 F3 Cockermouth Cumbria, England U.K.
150 D3 Cockett Swansea, Wales U.K.
234 B3 Cockeysville MD U.S.A.
87 E7 Cocklebiddy W.A. Austr.
215 E5 Cockscomb mt. S. Africa
254 C4 Coco r. Brazil
242 □J6 Coco r. Hond./Nic.
267 N5 Coco, Isla de i. N. Pacific Ocean
208 A4 Cocobeach Gabon
115 G3 Coco Channel India
241 K4 Coconino Plateau AZ U.S.A.
83 F3 Cocoparra Range hills N.S.W. Austr.
250 C3 Cocorná Col.
254 D5 Cocos Brazil
265 K4 Cocos Basin sea feature Indian Ocean
86 □2 Cocos Islands terr. Indian Ocean
267 N5 Cocos Ridge sea feature N. Pacific Ocean
244 C3 Cocula Mex.
163 C4 Cocumont France
233 H4 Cod, Cape MA U.S.A.
197 H2 Codăești Romania
251 F5 Codajás Brazil
149 H3 Cod Beck r. England U.K.
151 I2 Coddenham Suffolk, England U.K.
149 I4 Coddington Nottinghamshire, England U.K.
223 J5 Coderre Sask. Can.
191 H3 Codevigo Italy
81 A7 Codfish Island Stewart I. N.Z.
192 B5 Codi, Monte hill Sardegna Italy
151 G3 Codicote Hertfordshire, England U.K.
191 H4 Codigoro Italy
197 G3 Codlea Romania
149 H4 Codnor Derbyshire, England U.K.
254 E3 Codó Brazil
190 E3 Codogno Italy
187 E6 Codol airport Spain
234 B3 Codorus PA U.S.A.
183 I3 Codos Spain
263 D2 Codrington, Mount Antarctica
191 H3 Codroipo Italy
192 A4 Codrongianos Sardegna Italy
136 E4 Codru Moldova
177 L5 Codru-Moma, Munții mts Romania
150 E2 Codsall Staffordshire, England U.K.
238 E2 Cody WY U.S.A.
232 B6 Coeburn VA U.S.A.
215 E5 Coega S. Africa
260 A5 Coelemu Chile
254 E3 Coelho Neto Brazil
85 E2 Coen Qld Austr.
85 E2 Coen r. Qld Austr.
244 D4 Coeneo Mex.
215 E5 Coerney S. Africa
251 G4 Coeroeni r. Suriname
169 C4 Coesfeld Ger.
217 □2 Coëtivy i. Seychelles
214 E2 Coetzersdam S. Africa
238 C2 Coeur d'Alene ID U.S.A.
238 C2 Coeur d'Alene r. ID U.S.A.
164 F2 Coevorden Neth.
158 E5 Coëx France
215 G4 Coffee Bay S. Africa
222 B2 Coffee Creek Y.T. Can.
237 F5 Coffeeville MS U.S.A.
237 E4 Coffeyville KS U.S.A.
82 C3 Coffin Bay S.A. Austr.
82 C3 Coffin Bay b. S.A. Austr.
83 H2 Coffs Harbour N.S.W. Austr.
215 F5 Cofimvaba S. Africa
245 F4 Cofre de Perote mt. Mex.
187 B5 Cofrentes Spain
Cogălniceanu airport Romania see Kogălniceanu
197 I3 Cogealac Romania
183 F3 Cogeces del Monte Spain
151 H3 Coggeshall Essex, England U.K.
192 A2 Coggia Corse France
190 D3 Coggiola Italy
192 A4 Coghinas r. Sardegna Italy
192 B4 Coghinas, Lago del l. Sardegna Italy
215 G4 Coghlan S. Africa
86 E3 Coghlan, Mount hill W.A. Austr.
186 D2 Cogigar r. Spain
162 B3 Cognac France
162 D3 Cognac-la-Forêt France
190 C3 Cogne Italy
160 D3 Cognin France

207 H6 Cogo Equat. Guinea
190 D4 Cogoleto Italy
161 E5 Cogolin France
183 G2 Cogollos Spain
183 G4 Cogollos r. Spain
185 G3 Cogollos Vega Spain
183 G4 Cogolludo Spain
234 C3 Cohagula Port.
Čohkkiras Sweden see Jukkasjärvi
232 E2 Cohocton r. NJ U.S.A.
233 G3 Cohoes NY U.S.A.
83 F3 Cohuna Vic. Austr.
242 ☐J8 Coiba, Isla i. Panama
262 T3 Coig r. Arg.
146 C3 Coigeach, Rubha pt Scotland U.K.
259 B7 Coihaique Chile
260 A5 Coihue Chile
114 C4 Coimbatore Tamil Nadu India
260 A5 Coihueco Chile
182 B4 Coimbra Port.
182 B4 Coimbra admin. dist. Port.
181 C4 Coin Spain
156 D3 Coincy France
252 C4 Coipasa, Salar de salt flat Bol.
Coire Switz. see Chur
160 C3 Coise r. France
182 C4 Coja Port.
197 G3 Cojasca Romania
250 D2 Cojedes state Venez.
259 C7 Cojudo Blanco, Cerro mt. Arg.
177 J6 Čoka Vojvodina, Srbija Yugo.
238 E3 Cokeville WY U.S.A.
83 E4 Colac Vic. Austr.
81 A7 Colac South I. N.Z.
260 C1 Colangüil, Cordillera de mts Arg.
254 C2 Colares Brazil
257 G3 Colatina Brazil
163 C4 Colayrac-St-Cirq France
169 D5 Cölbe Ger.
Colberg Ger. see Kołobrzeg
171 C3 Colbitz Germany
191 H5 Colbordolo Italy
227 I4 Colborne Ont. Can.
260 B4 Colbún Chile
236 C4 Colby KS U.S.A.
226 C3 Colby WI U.S.A.
252 B3 Colca r. Peru
197 H3 Colceag Romania
215 E5 Colchester S. Africa
151 H3 Colchester Essex, England U.K.
235 F1 Colchester CT U.S.A.
226 B5 Colchester IL U.S.A.
224 C4 Cold Bay AK U.S.A.
151 F4 Colden Common Hampshire, England U.K.
146 F6 Coldingham Scottish Borders, Scotland U.K.
171 D4 Colditz Germany
223 I4 Cold Lake Alta Can.
234 D4 Cold Spring NJ U.S.A.
235 E1 Cold Spring NY U.S.A.
237 E6 Coldspring TX U.S.A.
240 I2 Cold Springs NV U.S.A.
222 G5 Coldstream B.C. Can.
81 C6 Coldstream South I. N.Z.
146 F6 Coldstream Scottish Borders, Scotland U.K.
227 H3 Coldwater Ont. Can.
236 C4 Coldwater KS U.S.A.
232 B3 Coldwater MI U.S.A.
237 E4 Coldwater r. MS U.S.A.
237 C4 Coldwater Creek r. OK U.S.A.
226 D1 Coldwell Ont. Can.
233 H2 Colebrook NH U.S.A.
215 G3 Coleford S. Africa
150 E3 Coleford Gloucestershire, England U.K.
150 E3 Coleford Somerset, England U.K.
85 E2 Coleman r. Qld Austr.
234 B3 Coleman MD U.S.A.
226 C4 Coleman MI U.S.A.
237 D6 Coleman TX U.S.A.
226 C4 Coleman WI U.S.A.
Çölemerik Turkey see Hakkâri
215 G3 Colenso S. Africa
197 G3 Colentina r. Romania
262 T2 Cole Peninsula Antarctica
84 E4 Coleraine Vic. Austr.
147 E1 Coleraine Northern Ireland U.K.
226 A2 Coleraine MN U.S.A.
81 C5 Coleridge, Lake South I. N.Z.
150 E3 Colerne Wiltshire, England U.K.
252 C4 Coles, Punta de pt Peru
83 G5 Coles Bay Tas. Austr.
215 E4 Colesberg S. Africa
151 F2 Coleshill Warwickshire, England U.K.
234 A3 Colesville MD U.S.A.
234 D1 Colesville NJ U.S.A.
223 I5 Coleville Sask. Can.
240 H2 Coleville CA U.S.A.
240 G2 Colfax CA U.S.A.
226 C5 Colfax IL U.S.A.
237 E6 Colfax LA U.S.A.
238 C2 Colfax WA U.S.A.
226 B3 Colfax WI U.S.A.
146 ☐H1 Colgrave Sound str. Scotland U.K.
259 C7 Colhué Huapi, Lago l. Arg.
197 G3 Colibași Romania
190 E2 Colico Italy
160 D2 Coligny France
215 F2 Coligny S. Africa
164 C3 Colijnsplaat Neth.
244 C4 Colima Mex.
244 C4 Colima state Mex.
244 C4 Colima, Nevado de vol. Mex.
260 B3 Colina Chile
254 C3 Colinas Brazil
183 G1 Colindres Spain
146 C2 Colintraive Argyll and Bute, Scotland U.K.
254 B5 Coliseu r. Brazil
146 B5 Coll i. Scotland U.K.
183 I4 Collado Bajo mt. Spain
183 G3 Collado Hermoso Spain
183 G4 Collado Villalba Spain
190 F4 Collagna Italy
181 ☐I Colla Micheri r. Austria/Italy
181 E2 Collanzo Spain
83 G2 Collarenebri N.S.W. Austr.
193 F2 Collarmele Italy
190 F4 Collecchio Italy
193 G3 Colle di Val d'Elsa Italy
213 F4 Colleen Dawn Zimbabwe
193 F3 Colleferro Italy
231 C5 College Park GA U.S.A.
237 D6 College Station TX U.S.A.
224 C3 Collegeville PA U.S.A.
190 C3 Collegno Italy
191 G2 Colle Isarco Italy
193 F3 Collelongo Italy
193 F3 Collepardo Italy
195 H3 Collepasso Italy
193 F3 Collesalvetti Italy
193 G3 Colle Sannita Italy
194 C5 Collesano Sicilia Italy
193 F3 Colletorto Italy
151 F3 Colley PA U.S.A.
193 H4 Colli a Volturno Italy
193 G3 Colli a Volturno Italy
83 G2 Collie N.S.W. Austr.
87 C7 Collie W.A. Austr.
86 E3 Collier Bay W.A. Austr.
84 B2 Collier Range hills W.A. Austr.
237 F5 Collierville TN U.S.A.
146 G4 Collieston Aberdeenshire, Scotland U.K.
146 E6 Collin Dumfries and Galloway, Scotland U.K.
192 A5 Collina Sardegna Italy
158 C2 Collinée France
149 I4 Collingham Nottinghamshire, England U.K.
168 C2 Collinghorst (Rhauderfehn) Ger.
227 G3 Collingwood Ont. Can.
81 D5 Collingwood South I. N.Z.
235 D2 Collingwood Park NJ U.S.A.
237 F6 Collins MS U.S.A.

221 H2 Collinson Peninsula Nunavut Can.
85 F4 Collinsville Qld Austr.
231 C5 Collinsville AL U.S.A.
237 E4 Collinsville OK U.S.A.
232 D6 Collinsville VA U.S.A.
178 B5 Collio Italy
163 F6 Collioure France
260 A5 Collipulli Chile
171 E4 Collmberg hill Ger.
161 E5 Collobrières France
190 B2 Collombey Switz.
234 A1 Collomsville PA U.S.A.
147 D5 Collon Rep. of Ireland
160 D2 Collonges France
162 D3 Collonges-la-Rouge France
147 C2 Collooney Rep. of Ireland
157 H4 Colmar France
161 E4 Colmars France
173 E2 Colmberg Ger.
182 D4 Colmeal Port.
185 F4 Colmenar Spain
182 E4 Colmenar de Montemayor Spain
183 G4 Colmenar de Oreja Spain
183 G4 Colmenar Viejo Spain
160 B1 Colmery France
146 D6 Colmonell South Ayrshire, Scotland U.K.
151 F3 Coln r. England U.K.
146 E4 Colnabaichin Aberdeenshire, Scotland U.K.
151 G3 Colnbrook Windsor and Maidenhead, England U.K.
149 G4 Colne Lancashire, England U.K.
151 H3 Colne r. England U.K.
151 G3 Colney Heath Hertfordshire, England U.K.
168 D3 Colnrade Ger.
83 G3 Colo r. N.S.W. Austr.
195 F2 Cologna r. Italy
191 G3 Cologna Veneta Italy
234 D3 Cologne NJ U.S.A.
226 D4 Cologne IN U.S.A.
226 C3 Cologne WI U.S.A.
Cologne Ger. see Köln
159 F2 Colombelles France
160 E3 Colombey-les-Belles France
157 F4 Colombey-les-Deux-Églises France
256 C4 Colômbia Brazil
250 C3 Colombia Col.
264 D5 Colombian Basin sea feature S. Atlantic Ocean
190 B2 Colombier Switz.
160 E3 Colombier, Mont mt. France
163 E4 Colombier France
156 C6 Colombo Brazil
114 C5 Colombo Sri Lanka
227 H1 Colombourg Que. Can.
183 F1 Colombres Spain
185 I3 Colomera r. Spain
183 G3 Colomera Spain
186 B3 Colomiers France
163 D5 Colomers Spain
261 G3 Colón Buenos Aires Arg.
261 H3 Colón Entre Ríos Arg.
246 B2 Colón Cuba
244 D3 Colón Mex.
242 ☐K7 Colón Panama
226 E5 Colon MI U.S.A.
Colón, Archipiélago de is Pacific Ocean see Galápagos, Islas
82 C2 Colona S.A. Austr.
116 E4 Colonelganj Uttar Prad. India
246 D2 Colonel Hill Bahamas
258 E2 Colonia Switz.
261 4 Colonia dept Uru.
261 4 Colonia Uru.
235 D2 Colonia Agrippina Ger. see Köln
260 D4 Colonia Alvear Arg.
261 F5 Colonia Barón Arg.
260 E3 Colonia Biagorria Arg.
261 H3 Colonia Caseros Arg.
260 E6 Colonia Choele Choel, Isla i. Arg.
261 I4 Colonia del Sacramento Uru.
187 G5 Colònia de Sant Jordi Spain
187 G5 Colònia de Sant Pere Spain
258 E3 Colonia Dora Arg.
261 F4 Colonia Hilario Lagos Arg.
Colonia Julia Fenestris Italy see Fano
259 C7 Colonia Las Heras Arg.
232 E6 Colonial Heights VA U.S.A.
234 D4 Colonial Park PA U.S.A.
195 G3 Colonna, Capo c. Italy
193 F2 Colonnella Italy
267 M5 Colón Ridge sea feature Pacific Ocean
146 B5 Colonsay i. Scotland U.K.
260 B5 Colorado r. Arg.
258 D3 Colorado r. La Rioja Arg.
260 C2 Colorado r. San Juan Arg.
258 B5 Colorado r. Brazil
260 B4 Colorado r. Chile
245 F5 Colorado r. Mex./U.S.A.
237 D6 Colorado r. TX U.S.A.
241 M4 Colorado state U.S.A.
260 D2 Colorado, Cerro mt. Arg.
259 C5 Colorado, Delta del Río Arg.
241 K3 Colorado City AZ U.S.A.
237 C5 Colorado City TX U.S.A.
241 M3 Colorado Desert CA U.S.A.
241 M3 Colorado Plateau CO U.S.A.
258 C2 Colorados, Cerro mt. Arg.
239 F4 Colorado Springs CO U.S.A.
190 F4 Colorno Italy
184 B4 Colos Port.
Colossae Turkey see Honaz
161 G3 Colostre r. France
245 F6 Colotepec r. Mex.
244 C2 Colotlán Mex.
170 E2 Cölpin Ger.
252 D4 Colquechaca Bol.
146 E6 Colquhar Scottish Borders, Scotland U.K.
252 D4 Colquiri Bol.
231 C5 Colquitt GA U.S.A.
157 H4 Colroy-la-Grande France
232 B6 Colson KY U.S.A.
151 G2 Colsterworth Lincolnshire, England U.K.
149 I5 Colston r. England U.K.
238 F2 Colstrip MT U.S.A.
151 I2 Coltishall Norfolk, England U.K.
240 I4 Colton CA U.S.A.
241 L2 Colton UT U.S.A.
235 D2 Colts Neck NJ U.S.A.
187 B7 Colubres hill Spain
235 F1 Columbia CT U.S.A.
230 C4 Columbia KY U.S.A.
237 E5 Columbia LA U.S.A.
234 B4 Columbia MD U.S.A.
237 F5 Columbia MO U.S.A.
237 F6 Columbia MS U.S.A.
234 B2 Columbia NC U.S.A.
234 B4 Columbia PA U.S.A.
231 D5 Columbia SC U.S.A.
230 C5 Columbia TN U.S.A.
222 K1 Columbia, Cape Nunavut Can.
222 G4 Columbia, Mount Alta/B.C. Can.
242 B2 Columbia, Sierra mts Mex.
230 C4 Columbia City IN U.S.A.
234 B1 Columbia County county PA U.S.A.
233 G4 Columbia Falls ME U.S.A.
238 D1 Columbia Falls MT U.S.A.
222 F4 Columbia Mountains B.C. Can.
232 C4 Columbiana OH U.S.A.
222 G4 Columbia Plateau U.S.A.
214 A5 Columbine, Cape S. Africa
231 C5 Columbus GA U.S.A.

237 E4 Columbus KS U.S.A.
237 F5 Columbus MS U.S.A.
238 E2 Columbus MT U.S.A.
231 D5 Columbus NC U.S.A.
234 D2 Columbus NE U.S.A.
239 F6 Columbus NM U.S.A.
232 B5 Columbus OH U.S.A.
237 D6 Columbus TX U.S.A.
232 A4 Columbus WI U.S.A.
226 C4 Columbus Grove OH U.S.A.
257 G3 Coluna Brazil
183 E1 Coluña Spain
240 F2 Colusa CA U.S.A.
80 E2 Colville North I. N.Z.
238 D3 Colville WA U.S.A.
220 C2 Colville r. AK U.S.A.
80 E2 Colville, Cape North I. N.Z.
87 E6 Colville, Lake salt flat W.A. Austr.
80 E2 Colville Channel North I. N.Z.
220 F3 Colville Lake N.W.T. Can.
151 F2 Colwich Staffordshire, England U.K.
150 D1 Colwyn Bay Conwy, Wales U.K.
162 D3 Coly France
150 D4 Colyton Devon, England U.K.
191 H4 Comacchio Italy
191 H4 Comacchio, Valli di lag. Italy
111 E6 Comai Xizang China
244 C4 Comala Mex.
243 G5 Comalcalco Mex.
245 E3 Comales r. Mex.
161 A3 Comana Romania
197 H3 Comana Romania
197 L3 Comana Romania
237 D6 Comanche TX U.S.A.
262 U2 Comandante Ferraz research stn Antarctica
258 F2 Comandante Fontana Arg.
259 C8 Comandante Luis Piedra Buena Arg.
261 I6 Comandante Nicanor Otamendi Arg.
197 H2 Comăneşti Romania
186 E2 Comapedrosa, Pic de mt. Andorra
197 G3 Comarnic Romania
242 ☐I6 Comayagua Hond.
231 D5 Combahee r. SC U.S.A.
157 F5 Combeaufontaine France
160 E3 Combe de Savoie val. France
150 C3 Combe Martin Devon, England U.K.
147 F2 Comber Northern Ireland U.K.
227 I3 Combermere Ont. Can.
96 A3 Combermere Bay Myanmar
151 H2 Comberton Cambridgeshire, England U.K.
150 E4 Combe St Nicholas Somerset, England U.K.
156 E4 Comblain-au-Pont Belgium
160 C1 Comblanchien France
156 C2 Combles France
190 F2 Combloux, Monte mt. Italy/Switz.
156 E3 Combourg France
158 B4 Combrailles reg. France
160 B3 Combronde France
260 E3 Comechingones, Sierra de mts Arg.
193 I5 Comegliàns Italy
191 H2 Comelico Superiore Italy
184 B1 Comenda Port.
256 C3 Comendador Gomes Brazil
256 D3 Comércio Brazil
247 ☐1 Comerío Puerto Rico
191 H5 Comero, Monte mt. Italy
85 G4 Comet r. Qld Austr.
237 D6 Comfort TX U.S.A.
232 C5 Comfort WV U.S.A.
117 G5 Comilla Bangl.
183 F1 Comillas Spain
165 B4 Comines Belgium
Comino i. Malta see Kemmuna
194 D6 Comino Sicilia Italy
245 G5 Comitancillo Mex.
243 G5 Comitán de Domínguez Mex.
194 C5 Comitini Sicilia Italy
177 J6 Comloşu Mare Romania
235 E2 Commack NY U.S.A.
227 H3 Commanda Ont. Can.
147 D2 Commeen Rep. of Ireland
160 D2 Commenailles France
163 B4 Commensacq France
160 A2 Commentry France
159 F5 Commequiers France
157 F4 Commercy France
214 B4 Commissioner's Salt Pan S. Africa
221 J3 Committee Bay Nunavut Can.
215 H2 Commondale S. Africa
Commonwealth Territory admin. div. Austr. see Jervis Bay Territory
146 B5 Comonsay i. Scotland U.K.
190 E3 Como Italy
190 E3 Como prov. Lombardia Italy
190 E3 Como, Lago di l. Italy
190 E3 Como, Lake Italy see Como, Lago di
245 G4 Comoapan Mex.
260 B3 Comodoro Arturo Merino Benítez airport Chile
259 D7 Comodoro Rivadavia Arg.
Comoé r. Côte d'Ivoire see Komoé
244 D3 Comonfort Mex.
Comores country Africa see Comoros
217 ☐3 Comoros country Africa
222 E5 Comox B.C. Can.
185 G4 Cómpeta Spain
190 C4 Compiano Italy
156 C3 Compiègne France
156 C3 Compigny France
184 B2 Comporta Port.
244 B3 Compostela Mex.
92 C5 Compostela Phil.
162 D3 Compreignac France
256 D6 Comprida, Ilha i. Brazil
161 E5 Comps-sur-Artuby France
240 H5 Compton CA U.S.A.
226 C5 Compton IL U.S.A.
136 E4 Comrat Moldova
146 E5 Comrie Perth and Kinross, Scotland U.K.
237 C6 Comstock TX U.S.A.
193 F2 Comunanza Italy
194 D5 Comunelli r. Sicilia Italy
96 D3 Con, Sông r. Vietnam
111 F7 Cona Xizang China
128 C1 Cona Turkey
206 B4 Conakry Guinea
250 B5 Conambo r. Ecuador
83 F5 Conara Junction Tas. Austr.
192 B4 Conca Corse France
191 H5 Conca r. Italy
258 E5 Concarán Arg.
158 C4 Concarneau France
192 B4 Conca Sardegna Italy
256 E3 Conceição r. Brazil
257 H3 Conceição Brazil
257 ☐3 Conceição da Barra Brazil
254 D5 Conceição das Alagoas Brazil
257 E4 Conceição de Macabu Brazil
254 B3 Conceição do Araguaia Brazil
254 C5 Conceição do Coité Brazil
257 E4 Conceição do Mato Dentro Brazil
257 E4 Conceição do Rio Verde Brazil
258 F3 Concepción Arg.
250 C4 Concepción Arg.
252 D5 Concepción Bol.
260 B4 Concepción Chile
244 D3 Concepción Mex.
258 E3 Concepción Para.
246 D4 Concepción Panama
261 H1 Concepción del Uruguay Arg.
212 B4 Conception Bay Namibia
246 D1 Conception Island Bahamas
190 F3 Concesio Italy

213 F3 Concession Zimbabwe
183 G1 Concha Spain
256 C5 Conchas Brazil
239 F5 Conchas NM U.S.A.
162 D4 Conches-en-Ouche France
241 H4 Concho AZ U.S.A.
237 D6 Concho r. TX U.S.A.
242 D2 Conchos r. Chihuahua Mex.
243 F3 Conchos r. Nuevo León/Tamaulipas Mex.
260 B3 Concón Chile
240 F3 Concord CA U.S.A.
226 E4 Concord MI U.S.A.
231 D5 Concord NC U.S.A.
233 H3 Concord NH U.S.A.
226 C4 Concord OH U.S.A.
232 D6 Concord VA U.S.A.
261 H3 Concordia Arg.
252 C2 Concórdia Brazil
244 A2 Concordia Mex.
215 B7 Concordia S. Africa
236 D4 Concordia KS U.S.A.
123 H2 Concord Peak Afgh.
160 A3 Concorès France
163 D4 Concots France
250 C6 Concumén r. Chile
260 B2 Concumén Chile
85 G5 Condamine Qld Austr.
85 G5 Condamine r. Qld Austr.
161 A3 Condat France
163 D4 Condat-sur-Vienne France
156 D3 Condé-en-Brie France
242 ☐I6 Condega Nic.
182 B4 Condeixa-a-Nova Port.
159 G3 Condé-sur-Huisne France
159 F3 Condé-sur-l'Escaut France
159 F3 Condé-sur-Noireau France
159 E2 Condé-sur-Vire France
255 E5 Condeúba Brazil
191 F3 Condino Italy
83 F3 Condobolin N.S.W. Austr.
195 E4 Condofuri Italy
163 C5 Condom France
238 D3 Condon OR U.S.A.
183 D3 Condor, Cordillera del mts Ecuador/Peru
150 C2 Condover Shropshire, England U.K.
231 C6 Conecuh r. AL U.S.A.
191 H2 Conegliano Italy
239 F4 Conejos CO U.S.A.
92 C4 Conejo r. Colorado/New Mexico U.S.A.
227 H5 Conemaugh r. PA U.S.A.
191 I5 Conero, Monte mt. Italy
261 G3 Conesa Arg.
259 B8 Conestoga PA U.S.A.
234 C4 Conestoga Creek r. PA U.S.A.
162 D1 Contres France
161 F4 Coney r. France
235 E2 Coney Island NY U.S.A.
157 F3 Confolens France
157 F3 Conflans-en-Jarnisy France
157 F4 Conflans-sur-Lanterne France
193 I5 Conflenti Italy
91 L9 Conflict Group is P.N.G.
232 D5 Confluence PA U.S.A.
Confoederatio Helvetica country Europe see Switzerland
162 C2 Confolens France
241 K2 Confusion Range mts UT U.S.A.
253 F6 Confuso r. Para.
147 B3 Cong Rep. of Ireland
150 C4 Congdon's Shop Cornwall, England U.K.
Congdü Xizang China see Nyalam
109 L4 Conghua Guangdong China
108 D3 Congjiang Guizhou China
149 G4 Congleton Cheshire, England U.K.
208 B5 Congo country Africa
209 B6 Congo r. Congo/Dem. Rep. Congo
Congo (Brazzaville) country Africa see Congo, Republic of
Congo (Kinshasa) country Africa see Congo, Democratic Republic of
208 D5 Congo, Democratic Republic of country Africa
208 B5 Congo, Republic of country Africa
208 D5 Congo Basin Dem. Rep. Congo
264 J6 Congo Cone sea feature S. Atlantic Ocean
Congo Free State country Africa see Congo, Democratic Republic of
257 F4 Congonhas Brazil
254 B5 Congonhinhas Brazil
182 D2 Congosto Spain
182 D2 Congosto de Valdavia Spain
150 D3 Congresbury North Somerset, England U.K.
241 K4 Congress AZ U.S.A.
159 E4 Congrier France
243 H5 Conhuas Mex.
81 C6 Conical Peak hill South I. N.Z.
184 B4 Conil de la Frontera Spain
149 I4 Coningsby Lincolnshire, England U.K.
149 H4 Conisbrough South Yorkshire, England U.K.
84 C4 Coniston N.T. Austr.
224 D4 Coniston Ont. Can.
149 F3 Coniston Cumbria, England U.K.
85 F3 Conjuboy Qld Austr.
185 G4 Conjuros hill Spain
243 H4 Conkal Mex.
223 I4 Conklin Alta Can.
260 D3 Conlara Arg.
159 F3 Conlie France
160 D2 Conliège France
147 F2 Conlig Northern Ireland U.K.
224 D2 Conn r. Que. Can.
147 B2 Conn, Lough l. Rep. of Ireland
147 B2 Connacht reg. Rep. of Ireland see Connaught
150 D1 Connah's Quay Flintshire, Wales U.K.
156 D4 Connantre France
227 I1 Connaught Ont. Can.
150 C4 Connaught reg. Rep. of Ireland see Connacht
151 F3 Coombe Bissett Wiltshire, England U.K.
83 G2 Conneaut OH U.S.A.
232 D3 Conneaut Lake PA U.S.A.
235 F1 Connecticut r. CT U.S.A.
233 I4 Connecticut state U.S.A.
146 C4 Connel Argyll and Bute, Scotland U.K.
232 D4 Connellsville PA U.S.A.
85 B5 Connemara Qld Austr.
147 B3 Connemara reg. Rep. of Ireland
84 B5 Conner, Mount hill N.T. Austr.
159 G3 Connerré France
230 C4 Connersville IN U.S.A.
147 B3 Connolly Rep. of Ireland
222 C2 Connolly, Mount Y.T. Can.
146 B7 Connor Northern Ireland U.K.
85 F4 Connors Range hills Qld Austr.
83 F3 Conoble N.S.W. Austr.
234 B3 Conococheague Creek r. PA U.S.A.
250 C2 Cononaco r. Ecuador
146 D3 Conon Bridge Highland, Scotland U.K.
177 K6 Conop Romania
177 I6 Čonoplja Vojvodina, Srbija Yugo.
226 C2 Conover WI U.S.A.
170 E2 Conow Ger.
226 B3 Conowingo MD U.S.A.
163 G5 Conques France
163 C5 Conques-sur-Orbiel France
256 B3 Conquista Brazil
185 F2 Conquista Spain
238 E1 Conrad MT U.S.A.

264 L9 Conrad Rise sea feature Southern Ocean
237 E6 Conroe TX U.S.A.
191 G4 Consandolo Italy
258 C2 Conscripto Bernardi Arg.
165 F5 Consdorf Lux.
227 I3 Consecon Ont. Can.
257 G3 Conselheiro Lafaiete Brazil
257 G3 Conselheiro Pena Brazil
191 G4 Conselice Italy
187 F5 Consell Spain
157 F3 Consenvoye France
149 H3 Consett Durham, England U.K.
234 C2 Conshohocken PA U.S.A.
246 B2 Consolación del Sur Cuba
97 D5 Côn Son i. Vietnam
223 I4 Consort Alta Can.
Constance Ger. see Konstanz
Constance, Lake Ger./Switz. see Bodensee
184 B1 Constância Port.
197 I3 Constanța Romania
Constanța airport Romania see Mihail Kogălniceanu
Constantia tourist site Cyprus see Salamis
Constantina Ger. see Konstanz
182 D3 Constantim Bragança Port.
182 C3 Constantim Vila Real Port.
184 E3 Constantina Spain
205 G1 Constantine Alg.
150 B4 Constantine Cornwall, England U.K.
226 E5 Constantine MI U.S.A.
Constantinople Turkey see Istanbul
260 A4 Constanza Chile
261 I2 Constitución Chile
185 G1 Constitución Uru.
185 G1 Consuegra Spain
85 G5 Consuelo Qld Austr.
223 I5 Consul Sask. Can.
223 K1 Consul r. Nunavut Can.
258 D3 Consul NV U.S.A.
257 G3 Contagalo Brazil
257 E3 Contagem Brazil
252 B1 Contamana Peru
191 H3 Contarina Italy
254 F5 Contas r. Brazil
215 E3 Content S. Africa
260 B1 Contessa Entellina Sicilia Italy
190 C2 Contessa Italy
193 E2 Contigliano Italy
146 D4 Contin Highland, Scotland U.K.
232 A4 Continental OH U.S.A.
163 E4 Contis-Plage France
233 H3 Contoocook r. NH U.S.A.
243 I4 Contratación Col.
259 B8 Contreras, Isla i. Chile
162 D1 Contres France
157 F4 Contrexéville France
231 ☐1a Contumo Chile
252 A1 Contumazá Peru
193 H4 Contursi Terme Italy
223 I1 Contwoyto Lake N.W.T./Nunavut Can.
156 C3 Conty France
237 F6 Convent LA U.S.A.
260 B4 Convento Viejo Chile
195 G2 Conversano Italy
232 A4 Convoy OH U.S.A.
215 E4 Conway S. Africa
237 E5 Conway AR U.S.A.
230 C4 Conway KY U.S.A.
236 D1 Conway ND U.S.A.
233 H3 Conway NH U.S.A.
231 E5 Conway SC U.S.A.
85 G5 Conway, Cape Qld Austr.
82 C2 Conway, Lake salt flat S.A. Austr.
234 D1 Conway Springs KS U.S.A.
150 C1 Conwy Conwy, Wales U.K.
150 D1 Conwy admin. div. Wales U.K.
150 C1 Conwy r. Wales U.K.
150 D1 Conwy Bay Wales U.K.
234 B2 Conyngham PA U.S.A.
85 G5 Coober Pedy S.A. Austr.
222 B2 Cook, Mount Can./U.S.A.
Cook, Mount South I. N.Z. see Aoraki
Cook Atoll Kiribati see Tarawa
156 C5 Cookes Peak NM U.S.A.
231 G4 Cookeville TN U.S.A.
151 G3 Cookham Windsor and Maidenhead, England U.K.
215 E5 Cookhouse S. Africa
220 C3 Cook Inlet sea chan. AK U.S.A.
81 C1 Cook Islands terr. S. Pacific Ocean
150 C2 Cookley Worcestershire, England U.K.
233 F3 Cooksburg NY U.S.A.
146 E4 Cook's Cairn hill Scotland U.K.
225 K3 Cook's Harbour Nfld. Can.
85 F2 Cooks Passage Qld Austr.
Cookstown Northern Ireland U.K.
81 E4 Cook Strait South I. N.Z.
234 A3 Cooksville MD U.S.A.
85 F2 Cooktown Qld Austr.
83 F2 Coolabah N.S.W. Austr.
83 F3 Coolah N.S.W. Austr.
83 F3 Coolamon N.S.W. Austr.
147 B3 Coolaney Rep. of Ireland
84 B2 Coolawanyah W.A. Austr.
241 L5 Coolidge AZ U.S.A.
87 C7 Coolimba W.A. Austr.
147 D3 Coolock Rep. of Ireland
147 C4 Coolroebeg Rep. of Ireland
84 B5 Cooma N.S.W. Austr.
83 G4 Cooma N.S.W. Austr.
147 E3 Coomacarrea hill Rep. of Ireland
83 E3 Coombah N.S.W. Austr.
150 C4 Coombe Cornwall, England U.K.
151 F3 Coombe Bissett Wiltshire, England U.K.
87 C6 Coomberdale W.A. Austr.
83 F2 Coonabarabran N.S.W. Austr.
83 E3 Coonalpyn S.A. Austr.
83 F2 Coonamble N.S.W. Austr.
87 C6 Coonana W.A. Austr.
82 E1 Coonawarra S.A. Austr.
Coondapoor Karnataka India see Kundapura
86 C4 Coongan r. W.A. Austr.
82 E1 Coongie Qld Austr.
84 C2 Coongoola Qld Austr.
85 F4 Coon Rapids MN U.S.A.
85 F2 Cooper r. N.T. Austr.
237 E5 Cooper TX U.S.A.
82 E1 Cooper Creek watercourse Qld/S.A. Austr.
85 H5 Coopernook N.S.W. Austr.
233 ☐12 Coopers Mills ME U.S.A.
246 D2 Cooper's Town Bahamas
234 C2 Cooperstown NY U.S.A.
236 D2 Cooperstown ND U.S.A.
226 D3 Cooperville MI U.S.A.
83 G5 Coosa r. Qld Austr.
238 A3 Coos Bay OR U.S.A.
83 G3 Cootamundra N.S.W. Austr.
147 D3 Cootehill Rep. of Ireland
83 F5 Cooyar Qld Austr.
84 C2 Cooyar Qld Austr.

245 E5 Copala Mex.
245 E4 Copalillo Mex.
245 F6 Copalito r. Mex.
242 ☐H6 Copán tourist site Hond.
195 H4 Copanello Italy
236 G4 Cope CO U.S.A.
226 E3 Copemish MI U.S.A.
Copenhagen Denmark see København
195 H2 Copertino Italy
261 G6 Copetonas Arg.
96 D3 Co Pi, Phou mt. Laos/Vietnam
157 F3 Copinsay i. Scotland U.K.
258 C2 Copiapó Chile
258 C2 Copiapó r. Chile
260 B1 Copiapó, Volcán vol. Chile
234 C2 Copley PA U.S.A.
82 B2 Copley S.A. Austr.
149 H3 Copley Durham, England U.K.
149 H3 Copmanthorpe York, England U.K.
186 E3 Copons Spain
190 E3 Copons Spain
191 G4 Copparo Italy
234 C3 Coppename r. Suriname
251 G4 Coppename r. Suriname
169 E9 Coppengrave Ger.
209 E8 Copperbelt prov. Zambia
160 D1 Copperbelt Ont. Can.
85 E3 Copperfield r. Qld Austr.
226 D2 Copper Harbor MI U.S.A.
Coppermine Nunavut Can. see Kugluktuk
220 G3 Coppermine r. Nunavut Can.
214 D3 Copperton S. Africa
241 K1 Copperton UT U.S.A.
150 D4 Copplestone Devon, England U.K.
111 D6 Coqên Xizang China
247 ☐1 Coqui Puerto Rico
Coquilhatville Dem. Rep. Congo see Mbandaka
Coquille i. Micronesia see Pikelot
238 A3 Coquille OR U.S.A.
260 B1 Coquimbo Chile
260 B1 Coquimbo admin. reg. Chile
260 B1 Coquimbo, Bahía de b. Chile
195 G2 Coquimbo Spain
197 G2 Copşa Mică Romania
151 G3 Copthorne Surrey, England U.K.
151 F4 Copythorne Hampshire, England U.K.
257 E3 Coração de Jesus Brazil
252 A1 Coracora Peru
83 H2 Coraki N.S.W. Austr.
87 B4 Coral Bay W.A. Austr.
231 D7 Coral Gables FL U.S.A.
221 J3 Coral Harbour Nunavut Can.
78 ☐5 Coral Heights Bahamas
266 F6 Coral Sea S. Pacific Ocean
77 F3 Coral Sea Basin S. Pacific Ocean
77 F3 Coral Sea Islands Territory terr. Austr.
147 D3 Coralstown Rep. of Ireland
235 E2 Coram NY U.S.A.
83 E4 Corangamite, Lake Vic. Austr.
232 C4 Coraopolis PA U.S.A.
129 F3 Çorat Azer.
193 I3 Corato Italy
147 B3 Corbally Rep. of Ireland
156 C4 Corbeil-Essonnes France
156 C4 Corbeilles France
163 C5 Corbelin France
157 G3 Corbény France
186 E3 Corbera de Terra Alta Spain
156 C3 Corbie France
191 H3 Corbola Italy
183 G3 Corbonar Spain
157 F4 Corbridge Northumberland, England U.K.
149 I3 Corbu Azer.
151 G2 Corby Northamptonshire, England U.K.
186 D3 Corça Spain
184 C3 Corcaigh Rep. of Ireland see Cork
186 F2 Corcelles-lès-Cîteaux France
160 D1 Corciano Italy
160 D1 Corcieux France
185 G1 Córcoles r. Spain
240 H3 Corcoran CA U.S.A.
182 B1 Corcoran CA U.S.A.
259 B6 Corcovado, Golfo de sea chan. Chile
182 A2 Corcubión Spain
147 C3 Corcyra i. Greece see Kerkyra
147 B5 Cordal Rep. of Ireland
257 H5 Cordeiro Brazil
257 H5 Cordele GA U.S.A.
240 G2 Cordell OK U.S.A.
158 C3 Cordemais France
193 H3 Cordenòns Italy
163 C4 Cordes France
187 E5 Cordevole r. Italy
188 D4 Cordido r. Spain
182 B2 Cordillera Range mts Phil.
82 E1 Cordillo Downs S.A. Austr.
184 C3 Córdoba Arg.
184 B3 Córdoba Mex.
185 E4 Córdoba Spain
185 E4 Córdoba prov. Andalucía Spain
220 D3 Córdoba, Sierras de mts Arg.
184 D1 Cordobilla de Lácara Spain
252 B2 Cordova Peru
220 D3 Cordova AK U.S.A.
234 A4 Cordova MD U.S.A.

Corinth, Gulf of sea chan. Greece see Korinthiakos Kolpos
Corinthus Greece see Korinthos
257 E3 Corinto Brazil
242 ☐I6 Corinto Nic.
185 E4 Coripe Spain
253 F4 Corixa Grande r. Bol./Brazil
253 F4 Corixinha r. Brazil
147 C5 Cork Rep. of Ireland
147 C4 Cork county Rep. of Ireland
158 B4 Corlay France
147 C3 Corlee Rep. of Ireland
194 C5 Corleone Sicilia Italy
193 I4 Corleto Perticara Italy
199 E1 Çorlu Turkey
199 E1 Çorlu r. Turkey
160 C2 Cormaranche-en-Bugey France
159 G2 Cormeilles France
182 B2 Cormery France
156 C3 Cormicy France
191 I3 Cormòns Italy
161 G4 Cormorant Man. Can.
193 H3 Cornacchia, Monte mt. Italy
147 C3 Cornafulla Rep. of Ireland
147 B3 Cornamona Rep. of Ireland
190 D3 Cornaredo Italy
161 C4 Cornas France
168 D2 Cornau Ger.
169 E4 Cornberg Ger.
159 F4 Corné France
191 G2 Cornedo all'Isarco Italy
163 E6 Cornellà-del-Vercol France
215 G2 Cornelia S. Africa
256 B5 Cornélio Procópio Brazil
226 B3 Cornell WI U.S.A.
186 F3 Cornellà de Llobregat Spain
186 F2 Cornellà de Terri Spain
182 D1 Cornellana Spain
225 J3 Corner Brook Nfld. Can.
83 F3 Corner Inlet b. Vic. Austr.
185 I3 Corneros r. Spain
264 F3 Corner Seamounts sea feature N. Atlantic Ocean
136 E4 Corneşti Italy see Tarquinia
191 G3 Cornetto KY U.S.A.
191 J2 Cornetto Italy
177 I3 Corna mt. Italy
190 F4 Corniglio Italy
156 E3 Cornimont France
237 E4 Corning AR U.S.A.
240 F2 Corning CA U.S.A.
236 E3 Corning IA U.S.A.
232 E3 Corning NY U.S.A.
232 B5 Corning OH U.S.A.
Corn Islands is Nic. see Maíz, Islas del
193 G3 Corno r. Italy
193 F2 Corno, Monte mt. Italy
190 F2 Corno al Campo mt. Italy/Switz.
226 B2 Cornucopia WI U.S.A.
191 H3 Cornuda Italy
183 G2 Cornudilla Spain
161 B5 Cornus France
224 F3 Cornwall Ont. Can.
225 ☐ Cornwall P.E.I. Can.
150 C4 Cornwall admin. div. England U.K.
235 D1 Cornwall NY U.S.A.
234 C2 Cornwall PA U.S.A.
221 I2 Cornwallis Island Nunavut Can.
221 I1 Cornwall Island Nunavut Can.
235 D1 Cornwall on Hudson NY U.S.A.
82 D3 Corny Point S.A. Austr.
250 E2 Coroacá Brazil
257 ☐ Coroatá Brazil
252 C4 Corocoro Bol.
231 E2 Corocoro, Isla i. Venez.
80 E2 Coroglen North I. N.Z.
250 C2 Coroglin Rep. of Ireland
92 B4 Coron Phil.
92 B4 Coron Bay Phil.
256 D3 Coromandel Brazil
80 E2 Coromandel North I. N.Z.
114 D4 Coromandel Coast India
114 C4 Coromandel Peninsula North I. N.Z.
80 E2 Coromandel Range hills North I. N.Z.
80 E2 Corona Spain
159 F4 Corona NM U.S.A.
92 B4 Corona P. Phil.
184 B2 Coron P. Port.
240 I5 Corona CA U.S.A.
240 I5 Coronado CA U.S.A.
242 ☐J7 Coronado, Bahía de b. Costa Rica
223 I4 Coronation Alta Can.
220 G3 Coronation Gulf Nunavut Can.
262 U2 Coronation Island S. Orkney Is Atlantic Ocean
86 E2 Coronation Islands W.A. Austr.
210 B3 Coronda Arg.
261 H4 Coronda Arg.
260 B3 Coronel Bogado Arg.
261 H4 Coronel Brandsen Arg.
261 F3 Coronel Dorrego Arg.
257 F3 Coronel Fabriciano Brazil
258 D2 Coronel Moldes Arg.
257 F2 Coronel Murta Brazil
261 G5 Coronel Oviedo Para.
261 G5 Coronel Pringles Arg.
253 G5 Coronel Sapucaia Mato Grosso do Sul Brazil

245 E5 Copala Mex.
245 E4 Copalillo Mex.
247 ☐1 Coqui Puerto Rico
227 C4 Corbin City NJ U.S.A.
226 E2 Corbin KY U.S.A.
232 A6 Corbin KY U.S.A.
235 D1 Corbin City NJ U.S.A.
186 D3 Corbins Spain
234 B2 Corbins PA U.S.A.
151 G4 Corbones r. Spain
149 G3 Corbridge Northumberland, England U.K.
186 D3 Corça Spain
82 D3 Corny Point S.A. Austr.
250 D2 Coroacá Brazil
257 G2 Coroatá Brazil
252 C4 Corocoro Bol.
257 F2 Corocoro Bol.
147 B4 Coroglen North I. N.Z.
92 B4 Coron Phil.
184 B2 Corona Port.
184 B3 Corona r. Port.
240 I5 Corona CA U.S.A.
240 I5 Coronado CA U.S.A.
256 D3 Coromandel Brazil
114 B4 Coromandel Coast India
88 C4 Coromandel Peninsula North I. N.Z.
80 E2 Coromandel Range hills North I. N.Z.
159 E4 Coron France
92 B3 Coron Phil.
184 B2 Corona Port.
240 I5 Corona CA U.S.A.
182 B3 Coronda Brazil
257 F2 Coronel João Sá Brazil
253 G5 Coronel Murta Brazil
261 G5 Coronel Suárez Arg.
261 I5 Coronel Vidal Arg.
81 B6 Coronet Peak South I. N.Z.
198 B1 Çorovodë Albania
83 F3 Corowa N.S.W. Austr.
243 H5 Corozal Belize
161 C3 Corps France
158 E3 Corps-Nuds France
252 D7 Corpus Arg.
237 D7 Corpus Christi TX U.S.A.
252 D4 Corque Bol.
259 B5 Corral Chile
182 A2 Corral mt. Spain
183 G3 Corral de Almaguer Spain
261 F3 Corral de Bustos Arg.
185 G2 Corral de Calatrava Spain
184 E4 Corral de Cantos mt. Spain
183 G3 Corrales Spain
246 B2 Corralillo Cuba
240 D2 Corralitos, Monte mt. Arg.
261 B5 Corral Nuevo Mex.
185 I2 Corral-Rubio Spain
87 B5 Corrandibby Range hills W.A. Austr.
213 H2 Corrane Moz.
92 C3 Corregidor i. Phil.
258 B5 Corrêgo do Ouro Brazil
257 G2 Córrego Novo Brazil
254 D4 Corrente Brazil
254 F2 Corrente r. Bahia Brazil
254 C4 Corrente r. Piauí Brazil
256 D2 Corrente r. Minas Gerais Brazil
255 F3 Corrente Grande r. Brazil
258 C2 Corrientes r. Arg.
254 D5 Correntina Brazil
Correntina r. Brazil see Éguas

Culebras to Dashköpri
297

252 A2 Culebras Peru
247 □1 Culebrinas r. Puerto Rico
164 E3 Culemborg Neth.
129 D4 Culfa Azer.
242 D3 Culiacán Mex.
92 A4 Culion Phil.
92 A4 Culion i. Phil.
148 B3 Culkey Northern Ireland U.K.
187 C4 Culla Spain
148 B5 Cullahill Rep. of Ireland
185 H3 Cullar r. Spain
185 H3 Cúllar-Baza Spain
147 E2 Cullaville Northern Ireland U.K.
147 B2 Culleens Rep. of Ireland
146 F4 Cullen Moray, Scotland U.K.
237 E5 Cullen LA U.S.A.
85 E1 Cullen Point Qld Austr.
187 C5 Cullera Spain
146 D4 Cullicudden Highland, Scotland U.K.
147 B3 Cullin Rep. of Ireland
215 G1 Cullinan S. Africa
146 C5 Cullipool Argyll and Bute, Scotland U.K.
146 □G1 Cullivoe Shetland, Scotland U.K.
231 C5 Cullman AL U.S.A.
150 D4 Cullompton Devon, England U.K.
190 B2 Cully Switz.
147 E2 Cullybackey Northern Ireland U.K.
147 E2 Cullyhanna Northern Ireland U.K.
146 C3 Cul Mor hill Scotland U.K.
147 D1 Culmore Northern Ireland U.K.
150 D4 Culmstock Devon, England U.K.
146 C4 Culnacraig Highland, Scotland U.K.
146 B4 Culnaknock Highland, Scotland U.K.
160 D3 Culoz France
232 E5 Culpeper VA U.S.A.
250 □ Culpepper, Isla i. Islas Galápagos Ecuador
146 D4 Culrain Highland, Scotland U.K.
146 □G1 Culswick Shetland, Scotland U.K.
146 E6 Culter Fell hill Scotland U.K.
146 F4 Cults Aberdeen, Scotland U.K.
254 B4 Culuene r. Brazil
226 D5 Culver IN U.S.A.
87 E7 Culver, Point W.A. Austr.
81 D5 Culverden South I. N.Z.
146 D6 Culzean Bay Scotland U.K.
254 D2 Cumã, Baía do inlet Brazil
129 C4 Cumaçay Turkey
251 E2 Cumaná Venez.
199 G1 Cumaova Turkey
256 C3 Cumari Brazil
250 B4 Cumbal, Nevado de vol. Col.
232 B6 Cumberland KY U.S.A.
232 D5 Cumberland MD U.S.A.
232 C5 Cumberland OH U.S.A.
232 D6 Cumberland VA U.S.A.
226 A3 Cumberland WI U.S.A.
232 A6 Cumberland r. KY U.S.A.
259 □ Cumberland Bay S. Georgia
234 C3 Cumberland County county NJ U.S.A.
234 A2 Cumberland County county PA U.S.A.
223 K4 Cumberland House Sask. Can.
85 G4 Cumberland Islands Qld Austr.
232 B6 Cumberland Mountain mts KY/TN U.S.A.
221 L3 Cumberland Peninsula Nunavut Can.
231 C5 Cumberland Plateau Kentucky/Tennessee U.S.A.
221 L3 Cumberland Sound sea chan. Nunavut Can.
146 E6 Cumbernauld North Lanarkshire, Scotland U.K.
256 D5 Cumbica airport São Paulo Brazil
183 F5 Cumbre Alta mt. Spain
259 C7 Cumbre Negro mt. Arg.
184 D2 Cumbres de San Bartolomé Spain
184 D2 Cumbres Mayores Spain
149 F3 Cumbria admin. div. England U.K.
114 C3 Cumbum Andhra Prad. India
184 B3 Cumeada Port.
190 C4 Cumiana Italy
182 C3 Cumieira Port.
251 H5 Cuminapanema r. Brazil
146 F4 Cuminestown Aberdeenshire, Scotland U.K.
170 C2 Cumlosen Ger.
231 C5 Cumming GA U.S.A.
240 F2 Cummings CA U.S.A.
82 C3 Cummins S.A. Austr.
86 E3 Cummins Range hills W.A. Austr.
83 G3 Cumnock N.S.W. Austr.
146 D6 Cumnock East Ayrshire, Scotland U.K.
151 F3 Cumnor Oxfordshire, England U.K.
242 C2 Cumpas Mex.
260 B4 Cumpeo Chile
126 D3 Çumra Turkey
159 F4 Cunault France
260 A6 Cunco Chile
87 C6 Cunderdin W.A. Austr.
250 C3 Cundinamarca dept Col.
215 G3 Cundycleugh S. Africa
163 C4 Cunegès France
209 B9 Cunene prov. Angola
209 B9 Cunene r. Angola/Namibia alt. Kunene
190 C4 Cuneo Italy
190 C4 Cuneo prov. Piemonte Italy
171 F4 Cunewalde Ger.
156 E4 Cunfin France
82 C3 Cungena S.A. Austr.
97 E4 Cung Sơn Vietnam
126 E3 Çüngüş Turkey
257 E5 Cunha Brazil
182 C4 Cunha Port.
209 C8 Cunhinga Angola
136 E4 Cunicea Moldova
186 E3 Cunit Spain
160 B3 Cunlhat France
83 F2 Cunnamulla Qld Austr.
146 □G1 Cunningsburgh Shetland, Scotland U.K.
182 B2 Cuntis Spain
197 E3 Cununa mt. Romania
140 N1 Čuokkaraš'ša mt. Norway
190 C3 Cuorgnè Italy
146 E5 Cupar Fife, Scotland U.K.
251 H5 Cupari r. Brazil
177 L4 Cupari, Dealul hill Romania
136 D3 Cupcina Moldova
193 G2 Cupello Italy
193 F1 Cupra Marittima Italy
191 I5 Cupramontana Italy
196 E4 Ćuprija Srbija Yugo.
242 C3 Cupula, Pico mt. Mex.
163 D5 Cuq-Toulza France
254 F4 Curaçá Brazil
250 D6 Curaçá r. Brazil
247 □10 Curaçao i. Neth. Antilles
260 B6 Curacautín Chile
260 E6 Curacó r. Arg.
258 B5 Curanilahue Chile
252 C2 Curanja r. Peru
250 C5 Curaray r. Ecuador
260 B6 Curarrehue Chile
177 L5 Curățele Romania
258 F3 Curaya r. Arg.
82 D2 Curdlawidny Lagoon salt flat S.A. Austr.
250 D5 Curé r. Col.
160 B1 Cure r. France
190 D3 Cureggio Italy
260 A4 Curepto Chile
160 C2 Curgy France
Curia Switz. see Chur
260 B4 Curicó Chile
250 E5 Curicuriari, Serra hill Brazil
250 E5 Curieuriari r. Brazil
254 D4 Curimata Brazil
195 F4 Curinga Italy
256 C6 Curitiba Brazil
255 C8 Curitibanos Brazil
256 B6 Curiúva Brazil
83 G2 Curlewis N.S.W. Austr.
82 D2 Curnamona S.A. Austr.
209 A8 Curoca r. Angola
190 D3 Curone r. Italy
191 F2 Curon Venosta Italy
182 C3 Curopos Port.
83 G2 Currabubula N.S.W. Austr.
147 E4 Curracloe Rep. of Ireland
147 E3 Curragh Rep. of Ireland
147 C3 Curraghroe Rep. of Ireland
147 C3 Curragh West Rep. of Ireland
147 C4 Curraglass Rep. of Ireland
184 □ Curral das Freiras Madeira
251 I5 Curralinho Brazil
227 F3 Curran MI U.S.A.
241 J2 Currant NV U.S.A.
83 F2 Curranyalpa N.S.W. Austr.
182 B2 Currás Spain
85 E5 Currawilla Qld Austr.
237 F4 Current r. MO U.S.A.
83 E4 Currie Tas. Austr.
241 J1 Currie NV U.S.A.
231 E4 Currituck NC U.S.A.
147 C3 Curry Rep. of Ireland
150 E3 Curry Rivel Somerset, England U.K.
195 H2 Cursi Italy
177 L6 Curtea Romania
197 G3 Curtea de Argeș Romania
196 E2 Curtici Romania
87 D6 Curtin W.A. Austr.
85 H5 Curtis Channel Qld Austr.
83 F4 Curtis Group is Tas. Austr.
85 G4 Curtis Island Qld Austr.
77 I5 Curtis Island N.Z.
177 L4 Curtuișeni Romania
251 H6 Curuá r. Brazil
251 I4 Curuá, Ilha i. Brazil
254 B3 Curuaés r. Brazil
251 H5 Curuapanema r. Brazil
251 H5 Curuá Una r. Brazil
254 D2 Curuçá Brazil
94 C3 Curup Sumatera Indon.
251 E4 Curupira, Serra mts Brazil/Venez.
253 E3 Cururú Bol.
253 F1 Cururu r. Brazil
254 D2 Cururupu Brazil
251 F3 Curutú, Cerro mt. Venez.
261 H1 Curuzú Cuatiá Arg.
257 E3 Curvelo Brazil
226 C2 Curwood, Mount hill MI U.S.A.
193 G3 Cusano Mutri Italy
252 C3 Cusco Peru
252 B3 Cusco dept Peru
147 E1 Cushendall Northern Ireland U.K.
147 E1 Cushendun Northern Ireland U.K.
148 B4 Cushina Rep. of Ireland
237 D4 Cushing OK U.S.A.
190 F4 Cusna, Monte mt. Italy
162 C3 Cussac France
162 B3 Cussac-Fort-Médoc France
161 B4 Cussac-sur-Loire France
160 B2 Cusset France
231 C5 Cusseta GA U.S.A.
160 C1 Cussy-les-Forges France
238 F2 Custer MT U.S.A.
236 C3 Custer SD U.S.A.
157 G4 Custines France
194 B4 Custonaci Sicilia Italy
238 D1 Cut Bank MT U.S.A.
238 D1 Cut Bank Creek r. MT U.S.A.
231 C6 Cuthbert GA U.S.A.
84 C2 Cuthbertson Falls N.T. Austr.
191 F4 Cutigliano Italy
240 H3 Cutler CA U.S.A.
233 □J2 Cutler ME U.S.A.
231 D7 Cutler Ridge FL U.S.A.
194 D5 Cutò r. Sicilia Italy
237 F6 Cut Off LA U.S.A.
260 C6 Cutral-Co Arg.
195 F3 Cutro Italy
195 H2 Cutrofiano Italy
83 F2 Cuttaburra Creek r. Qld Austr.
117 F5 Cuttack Orissa India
192 A3 Cuttoli-Corticchiato Corse France
244 D4 Cutzamala r. Mex.
209 B8 Cuvelai Angola
208 B5 Cuvette admin. reg. Congo
87 B5 Cuvier, Cape W.A. Austr.
163 E5 Cuxac-Cabardès France
161 A5 Cuxac-d'Aude France
129 F4 Çuxanlı Azer.
168 D2 Cuxhaven Ger.
232 C4 Cuyahoga Falls OH U.S.A.
240 H4 Cuyama CA U.S.A.
240 G4 Cuyama r. CA U.S.A.
92 B3 Cuyapo Phil.
92 B4 Cuyo Phil.
92 B4 Cuyo East Passage Phil.
92 B4 Cuyo Islands Phil.
92 B4 Cuyo West Passage Phil.
251 G3 Cuyuni r. Guyana
244 B4 Cuyutlán Mex.
162 D4 Cuzance France
Cuzco Peru see Cusco
185 F2 Cuzna r. Spain
163 C4 Cuzorn France
171 F5 Cvikov Czech Rep.
150 D3 Cwm Blaenau Gwent, Wales U.K.
150 D3 Cwmafan Neath Port Talbot, Wales U.K.
150 D2 Cwmbach Powys, Wales U.K.
150 D3 Cwmbran Torfaen, Wales U.K.
150 D3 Cwmllynfell Neath Port Talbot, Wales U.K.
211 A5 Cyangugu Rwanda
174 C3 Cybinka Pol.
Cyclades dept Greece see Kyklades
Cyclades is Greece see Kyklades
175 L4 Cyców Pol.
Cydonia Kriti Greece see Chania
Cydweli Carmarthenshire, Wales U.K. see Kidwelly
83 F5 Cygnet Tas. Austr.
232 B4 Cygnet OH U.S.A.
Cymru admin. div. U.K. see Wales
150 D2 Cynghordy Carmarthenshire, Wales U.K.
150 C3 Cynin r. Wales U.K.
232 A5 Cynthiana KY U.S.A.
150 C3 Cynwyl Elfed Carmarthenshire, Wales U.K.
223 I5 Cypress Hills Sask. Can.
128 A2 Cyprus country Asia
202 D3 Cyrenaica reg. Libya
202 D1 Cyrene tourist site Libya
156 D2 Cysoing France
Cythera i. Greece see Kythira
150 C3 Cywyn r. Wales U.K.
174 E3 Czacz Pol.
174 G4 Czajków Pol.
174 E2 Czaplinek Pol.
223 I4 Czar Alta Can.
175 J5 Czarna Podkarpackie Pol.
175 K5 Czarna Podkarpackie Pol.
175 H4 Czarna r. Pol.
175 H5 Czarna r. Pol.
175 J5 Czarna r. Pol.
175 L2 Czarna Białostocka Pol.
174 F1 Czarna Dąbrówka Pol.
175 K6 Czarna Górna Pol.
175 L2 Czarna Hańcza r. Pol.
175 I5 Czarna Nida r. Pol.
174 G3 Czarna Struga r. Pol.
174 G2 Czarna Woda Pol.
175 H5 Czarnca Pol.
174 E2 Czarne Pol.
175 J2 Czarnia Pol.
174 E3 Czarnków Pol.
174 G4 Czarnożyły Pol.
175 H6 Czarny Dunajec Pol.
177 I2 Czarny Dunajec r. Pol.
174 G4 Czastary Pol.
175 I6 Czchów Pol.
175 H6 Czechowice-Dziedzice Pol.
176 E2 Czech Republic country Europe
175 J4 Czekarzewice Pol.
175 K4 Czemierniki Pol.
174 E3 Czempiń Pol.
175 L3 Czeremcha Pol.
174 F4 Czermin Pol.
174 D4 Czerna Mała r. Pol.
174 D4 Czerna Wielka r. Pol.
174 F4 Czernica Pol.
174 E2 Czernica r. Pol.
175 I2 Czernice Borowe Pol.
174 F3 Czerniejewo Pol.
175 I4 Czerniewice Pol.
174 G3 Czernikowo Pol.
174 E4 Czernina Pol.
Czernowitz Chernivets'ka Oblast' Ukr. see Chernivtsi
174 F2 Czersk Pol.
174 D3 Czerwieńsk Pol.
175 J3 Czerwin Pol.
175 I3 Czerwińsk nad Wisłą Pol.
174 G5 Czerwionka-Leszczyny Pol.
174 E3 Czerwonak Pol.
171 G4 Czerwona Woda Pol.
175 J3 Czerwonka Włościańska Pol.
175 H4 Czestków Pol.
175 H5 Częstochowa Pol.
174 F4 Czeszów Pol.
174 E2 Człopa Pol.
174 F2 Człuchów Pol.
174 F3 Czmoń Pol.
171 F4 Czorneboh hill Ger.
175 I3 Czosnów Pol.
175 J6 Czudec Pol.
175 L3 Czyże Pol.
175 K3 Czyżew-Osada Pol.

D

96 D2 Đa, Sông r. Vietnam
169 C5 Daaden Ger.
107 J2 Da'an Jilin China
92 B4 Daanbantayan Phil.
164 F2 Daarle Neth.
128 B4 Ḍabāb, Jabal aḍ mt. Jordan
211 B7 Dabaga Tanz.
250 D2 Dabajuro Venez.
206 D4 Dabakala Côte d'Ivoire
107 H3 Daban Nei Mongol China
106 D4 Daban Shan mts China
108 B2 Dabao Sichuan China
177 I4 Dabas Hungary
108 D1 Daba Shan mts China
210 C1 Dabat Eth.
Dabba Sichuan China see Daocheng
250 B3 Dabeiba Col.
96 B3 Dabein Myanmar
170 C2 Dabel Ger.
116 C5 Dabhoi Gujarat India
114 B2 Dabhol Mahar. India
174 D3 Dąbie Pol.
174 G3 Dąbie Pol.
174 C2 Dąbie, Jezioro l. Pol.
109 E2 Dabie Shan mts China
143 G4 Dąbki Pol.
157 H4 Dabo France
116 D4 Daboh Madh. Prad. India
206 C4 Dabola Guinea
206 D5 Dabou Côte d'Ivoire
206 E4 Daboya Ghana
107 F4 Dabqig Nei Mongol China
116 D4 Dabra Madh. Prad. India
174 G3 Dąbroszyn Pol.
174 F3 Dąbrowa Kujawsko-Pormorskie Pol.
174 F5 Dąbrowa Opolskie Pol.
174 F5 Dąbrowa Opolskie Pol.
175 L2 Dąbrowa Białostocka Pol.
174 G3 Dąbrowa Biskupia Pol.
174 G2 Dąbrowa Chełmińska Pol.
175 H5 Dąbrowa Górnicza Pol.
175 I5 Dąbrowa Tarnowska Pol.
175 H3 Dąbrowice Pol.
174 D3 Dąbrówka Wielkopolska Pol.
175 I2 Dąbrówno Pol.
109 F3 Dabu Guangdong China
197 G4 Dăbuleni Romania
Dacca Bangl. see Dhaka
173 F3 Dachau Ger.
173 F3 Dachauer Moos marsh Ger.
106 D4 Dachechang Nei Mongol China
107 H3 Dachengzi Liaoning China
114 C2 Dachepalle Andhra Prad. India
175 L5 Dachnów Pol.
169 F4 Dachrieden Ger.
173 E2 Dachsbach Ger.
108 C2 Dachuan Sichuan China
176 E2 Dačice Czech Rep.
227 I3 Dacre Ont. Can.
149 G3 Dacre Cumbria, England U.K.
177 H4 Dad Hungary
129 B4 Dadaş Turkey
126 D2 Daday Turkey
210 D1 Daddato Djibouti
231 D6 Dade City FL U.S.A.
231 C5 Dadeville AL U.S.A.
Dadong Liaoning China see Donggang
163 D5 Dadou r. France
116 C5 Dadra Dadra India
Dadra Mahar. India see Achalpur
116 C5 Dadra and Nagar Haveli union terr. India
123 F5 Dadu Pak.
108 B2 Dadu He r. Sichuan China
97 D5 Đa Dung r. Vietnam
92 B3 Daet Phil.
108 C3 Dafang Guizhou China
109 G1 Dafeng Jiangsu China
117 H4 Dafla Hills India
198 C3 Dafni Dytiki Ellas Greece
223 M4 Dafoe r. Man. Can.
226 E2 Dafter MI U.S.A.
177 H4 Dág Hungary
116 C5 Dag Rajasthan India
199 G3 Dağ Antalya Turkey
210 D3 Daga Medo Eth.
206 B2 Dagana Senegal
183 G4 Daganzo de Arriba Spain
106 D5 Dagcangihamo Gansu China
129 D3 Dağ Cäyir Azer.
129 C3 Dağcı Turkey
138 F3 Dagda Latvia
199 F2 Dağdere Manisa Turkey
Dage Hebei China see Fengning
168 D1 Dagebüll Ger.
Dagenraad atoll Arch. des Tuamotu Fr. Polynesia see Manihi
129 E2 Dagestan, Respublika aut. rep. Rus. Fed.
Dagestanskaya A.S.S.R. aut. rep. Rus. Fed. see Dagestan, Respublika
129 F2 Dagestanskiye Ogni Rus. Fed.
Dagezhen Hebei China see Fengning
215 E5 Daggaboersnek S. Africa
Daghestan aut. rep. Rus. Fed. see Dagestan, Respublika
163 D4 Daglan France
129 E4 Dağlıq Qarabağ aut. reg. Azer.
190 C1 Dagmersellen Switz.
Dagö i. Estonia see Hiiumaa
Dagon Myanmar see Yangôn
81 B6 Dagon mt. South I. N.Z.
129 C3 Dağpınar Turkey
111 D6 Dagrag Zangbo r. Xizang China
107 H4 Dagu Tianjin China
107 I4 Dagu r. China
108 B3 Daguan Yunnan China
100 D3 Daguokui Shan hill Heilong. China
92 B2 Dagupan Phil.
84 B3 Daguragu N.T. Austr.
Dagxoi Sichuan China see Sowa
Dagxoi Sichuan China see Yidun
111 E6 Dagzê Xizang China
124 B3 Dahabān Saudi Arabia
222 E2 Dahadinni r. N.W.T. Can.
Dahalach, Isole is Eritrea see Dahlak Archipelago
Dahana des. Saudi Arabia see Ad Dahnā'
114 B2 Dahanu Mahar. India
Dahe Guangxi China see Ziyuan
107 F3 Dahei r. China
100 D3 Daheiding Shan mt. China
106 B3 Dahei Shan mt. Xinjiang China
109 F3 Daheng Fujian China
Daheyan Xinjiang China see Turpan Zhan
100 E3 Dahezhen Heilong. China
107 H3 Da Hinggan Ling mts China
114 B2 Dahivadi Mahar. India
203 I6 Dahlak Archipelago is Eritrea
169 B5 Dahlem Ger.
171 E4 Dahlen Ger.
168 F2 Dahlenburg Ger.
171 E4 Dahlener Heide reg. Ger.
171 C3 Dahlenwarsleben Ger.
231 D5 Dahlonega GA U.S.A.
171 E3 Dahlwitz-Hoppegarten Ger.
205 H2 Dahmani Tunisia
171 E4 Dahme Brandenburg Ger.
170 C1 Dahme Schleswig-Holstein Ger.
171 E3 Dahme r. Ger.
172 B2 Dahn Ger.
116 C5 Dahod Gujarat India
Dahomey country Africa see Benin
Dahra Senegal see Dara
168 F3 Dähre Ger.
127 F3 Dahūk Iraq
127 F3 Dahūk governorate Iraq
125 E4 Ḍaḥyah, Wādī r. Yemen
105 E3 Daibosatsu-rei mt. Japan
107 H4 Daicheng Hebei China
Daido r. N. Korea see Taedong-gang
105 G2 Daigo Japan
78 □6 Dai Island Solomon Is
140 L2 Daikanvik Sweden
96 B3 Daik-u Myanmar
146 B3 Dail Bho Thuath Western Isles, Scotland U.K.
232 D5 Dailey WV U.S.A.
146 D6 Dailly South Ayrshire, Scotland U.K.
122 D3 Daim Iran
103 F5 Daimanji-san hill Japan
185 G1 Daimiel Spain
105 E3 Daimugen-zan mt. Japan
147 D3 Daingean Rep. of Ireland
237 E5 Daingerfield TX U.S.A.
104 C2 Dainichiga-take vol. Japan
104 C2 Dainichi-gawa r. Japan
104 C2 Dainichi-zan mt. Japan
108 A1 Dainkog Sichuan China
85 F3 Daintree Qld Austr.
156 C2 Dainville France
157 F4 Dainville-Bertheléville France
261 G5 Daireaux Arg.
Dairen Liaoning China see Dalian
146 F5 Dairsie Fife, Scotland U.K.
203 F3 Dairût Egypt
235 D1 Dairyland NY U.S.A.
226 A2 Dairyland WI U.S.A.
103 F6 Dai-sen vol. Japan
109 G2 Daishan Zhejiang China
104 B4 Daitō Japan
105 F2 Daiya-gawa r. Japan
Daiyue Shanxi China see Shanyin
109 F3 Daiyun Shan mts China
246 E3 Dajabón Dom. Rep.
84 D4 Dajarra Qld Austr.
Dajie Yunnan China see Jiangchuan
108 B2 Dajin Chuan r. Sichuan China
106 D4 Dajing Gansu China
106 B4 Da Juh Qinghai China
206 A3 Dakar Senegal
Dakhla Western Sahara see Ad Dakhla
203 F3 Dakhla Oasis Egypt
204 A5 Dakhlet Nouâdhibou admin. reg. Maur.
129 B1 Dakhovskaya Rus. Fed.
97 D4 Đak Nghe r. Vietnam
138 G5 Dakol'ka r. Belarus
116 C5 Dakor Gujarat India
207 G3 Dakoro Niger
236 E3 Dakota City IA U.S.A.
236 D3 Dakota City NE U.S.A.
196 E4 Đakovica Kosovo, Srbija Yugo.
188 G3 Đakovo Croatia
209 D7 Dala Angola
177 J5 Đala Vojvodina, Srbija Yugo.
178 B3 Dalaas Austria
206 B4 Dalaba Guinea
146 A4 Dalabrog Western Isles, Scotland U.K.
Dalad Qi Nei Mongol China see Shulinzhao
Dalai Jilin China see Da'an
106 D3 Dalain Hob Nei Mongol China
122 A3 Dālā Khānī, Kūh-e mt. Iran
122 B4 Dālakī Iran
122 B4 Dalaki, Rūd-e r. Iran
128 A5 Dalal, Gebel mt. Egypt
143 G1 Dalälven r. Sweden
199 F3 Dalama Aydın Turkey
107 G3 Dalamamiao Nei Mongol China
199 F3 Dalaman Turkey
199 F3 Dalaman r. Turkey
106 E3 Dalandzadgad Mongolia
92 B4 Dalanganem Islands Phil.
110 C3 Dalaoba Xinjiang China
Dalap-Uliga-Darrit Majuro Marshall Is see Delap-Uliga-Djarrit
143 F1 Dalarna county Sweden
141 K3 Dalarna reg. Sweden
97 E5 Đa Lat Vietnam
Dalatando Angola see N'dalatando
106 D3 Dalay Mongolia
146 E7 Dalbeattie Dumfries and Galloway, Scotland U.K.
85 F4 Dalbeg Qld Austr.
170 C2 Dalberg-Wendelstorf Ger.
226 A3 Dalbo MN U.S.A.
142 E2 Dalbosjön l. Sweden
85 G5 Dalby Qld Austr.
142 E4 Dalby Sweden
259 B6 Dalcahue Chile
142 A1 Dale Hordaland Norway
141 I3 Dale Sogn og Fjordane Norway
150 B3 Dale Pembrokeshire, Wales U.K.
232 E5 Dale City VA U.S.A.
169 B5 Daleiden Ger.
164 F2 Dalen Neth.
215 G2 Daleside S. Africa
175 I5 Daleszyce Pol.
231 C6 Daleville AL U.S.A.
234 C1 Daleville PA U.S.A.
141 K3 Dalfors Sweden
164 F2 Dalfsen Neth.
87 C5 Dalgaranger, Mount hill W.A. Austr.
83 G4 Dalgety N.S.W. Austr.
87 B5 Dalgety r. W.A. Austr.
146 E5 Dalgety Bay Fife, Scotland U.K.
151 H2 Dalham Suffolk, England U.K.
237 C4 Dalhart TX U.S.A.
225 H3 Dalhousie N.B. Can.
116 D2 Dalhousie Hima. Prad. India
107 F5 Dali Shaanxi China
108 B3 Dali Yunnan China
107 F4 Dali r. China
107 I4 Dalian Liaoning China
Daliang Guangdong China see Shunde
106 D4 Daliang Qinghai China
108 B2 Daliang Shan mts Sichuan China
185 H4 Dalías Spain
Daliburgh Western Isles, Scotland U.K. see Dalabrog
129 E4 Dälidağ mt. Azer.
175 H4 Dalików Pol.
129 E3 Dälilär Azer.
129 E3 Dälimämmädli Azer.
107 I3 Dalin Nei Mongol China
107 I3 Daling r. China
Dalinghe Liaoning China see Linhai
101 C4 Dalizi Jilin China
188 G3 Dalj Croatia
146 E6 Dalkeith Midlothian, Scotland U.K.
117 F4 Dalkola W. Bengal India
85 H5 Dallarnil Qld Austr.
146 E4 Dallas Moray, Scotland U.K.
238 B2 Dallas OR U.S.A.
234 C1 Dallas PA U.S.A.
237 D5 Dallas TX U.S.A.
226 B5 Dallas City IL U.S.A.
234 B3 Dallastown PA U.S.A.
Dalles City OR U.S.A. see The Dalles
170 E3 Dallgow Ger.
220 E4 Dall Island AK U.S.A.
210 D1 Dallol vol. Eth.
188 E3 Dalmacija reg. Croatia
146 D5 Dalmally Argyll and Bute, Scotland U.K.
116 E4 Dalman Uttar Prad. India
177 H5 Dalmand Hungary
Dalmatia reg. Croatia see Dalmacija
234 B2 Dalmatia PA U.S.A.
146 D6 Dalmellington East Ayrshire, Scotland U.K.
223 J4 Dalmeny Sask. Can.
190 E3 Dalmine Italy
146 D4 Dalnavie Highland, Scotland U.K.
100 E3 Dal'negorsk Rus. Fed.
100 E3 Dal'nerechensk Rus. Fed.
134 I5 Dal'neye Konstantinovo Rus. Fed.
Dalny Liaoning China see Dalian
206 D5 Daloa Côte d'Ivoire
85 G1 Daloloia Group is P.N.G.
108 C3 Dalou Shan mts China
171 D5 Dalovice Czech Rep.
146 D6 Dalry North Ayrshire, Scotland U.K.
146 D6 Dalrymple East Ayrshire, Scotland U.K.
85 F4 Dalrymple, Lake Qld Austr.
85 G4 Dalrymple, Mount Qld Austr.
138 D1 Dalsbruk Fin.
142 E2 Dals Långed Sweden
157 G3 Dalstein France
149 G3 Dalston Cumbria, England U.K.
117 F4 Daltenganj Bihar India
224 C3 Dalton Ont. Can.
215 H3 Dalton S. Africa
231 C5 Dalton GA U.S.A.
233 G3 Dalton MA U.S.A.
232 C4 Dalton OH U.S.A.
234 C1 Dalton PA U.S.A.
Daltonganj Bihar India see Daltenganj
149 F3 Dalton-in-Furness Cumbria, England U.K.
227 E1 Dalton Mills Ont. Can.
147 C4 Dalua r. Rep. of Ireland
94 C2 Daludalu Sumatera Indon.
161 E4 Daluis France
109 E4 Daluo Shan mt. Guangdong China
140 □C2 Dalvík Iceland
87 C6 Dalwallinu W.A. Austr.
146 D5 Dalwhinnie Highland, Scotland U.K.
84 B2 Daly r. N.T. Austr.
199 F3 Dalyan Turkey
240 F3 Daly City CA U.S.A.
84 B2 Daly River N.T. Austr.
147 C3 Dalystown Rep. of Ireland
84 C3 Daly Waters N.T. Austr.
136 B2 Damachava Belarus
207 H3 Damagaram Takaya Niger
129 C3 Damal Turkey
116 C5 Daman Daman India
116 B5 Daman and Diu union terr. India
138 E5 Damanava Belarus
122 B3 Dāmaneh Iran
203 F2 Damanhûr Egypt
Damão Daman India see Daman
122 B3 Damaq Iran
129 B3 Damar Turkey
208 C3 Damara C.A.R.
212 C4 Damaraland reg. Namibia
Damas Syria see Damascus
207 I3 Damasak Nigeria
157 G4 Damas-aux-Bois France
128 C3 Damascus Syria
232 E5 Damascus MD U.S.A.
234 C1 Damascus PA U.S.A.
232 C6 Damascus VA U.S.A.
174 F3 Damasławek Pol.
207 H4 Damaturu Nigeria
122 C3 Damāvand Iran
122 C3 Damāvand, Qolleh-ye mt. Iran
163 C4 Damazan France
209 B6 Damba Angola
157 H4 Dambach-la-Ville France
207 F4 Dambai Ghana
207 H3 Dambatta Nigeria
170 C2 Dambeck Ger.
207 I4 Damboa Nigeria
179 H1 Dambořice Czech Rep.
197 G3 Dâmbovița r. Romania
117 H4 Damchara Assam India
120 F2 Damdy Kustanayskaya Oblast' Kazakh.
157 G4 Damelevières France
246 D3 Dame Marie Haiti
151 F4 Damerham Hampshire, England U.K.
148 B5 Damerstown Rep. of Ireland
156 D3 Damery France
158 D4 Damgan France
122 C2 Damghan Iran
147 E1 Damhead Northern Ireland U.K.
163 D5 Damiatte France
Damietta Egypt see Dumyât
159 G3 Damigny France
107 G4 Daming Hebei China
108 D4 Daming Shan mt. Guangxi China
108 A1 Damjong Qinghai China
Dammam Saudi Arabia see Ad Dammām
156 B4 Dammarie France
190 D2 Dammastock mt. Switz.
165 C3 Damme Belgium
168 D3 Damme Ger.
174 F1 Damnica Pol.
174 F1 Damno Pol.
116 D5 Damoh Madh. Prad. India
206 E4 Damongo Ghana
128 B3 Damour Lebanon
168 E1 Damp Ger.
94 C2 Dampar, Tasik l. Malaysia
160 D1 Damparis France
86 C4 Dampier W.A. Austr.
86 C4 Dampier Archipelago is W.A. Austr.
160 D1 Dampierre France
156 C5 Dampierre-en-Burly France
160 E1 Dampierre-sur-Linotte France
160 D1 Dampierre-sur-Salon France
93 D3 Dampir, Selat sea chan. Irian Jaya Indon.
160 E1 Damprichard France
Damqoq Zangbo r. Xizang China see Maquan He
111 F5 Dam Qu r. Qinghai China
97 D5 Dâmrei, Chuŏr Phnum mts Cambodia
117 H3 Damroh Arun. Prad. India
171 D3 Damsdorf Ger.
170 C2 Damshagen Ger.
170 D1 Damsholte Denmark
190 B1 Damvant Switz.
156 B4 Damville France
157 F3 Damvillers France
164 F1 Damwoude Neth.
Damxoi Xizang China see Comai
111 E6 Damxung Xizang China
231 E4 Dan r. NC U.S.A.
240 H3 Dana, Mount CA U.S.A.
129 E3 Danaçı Azer.
185 G2 Dañador r. Spain
Danakil reg. Eritrea/Eth. see Denakil
206 C5 Danané Côte d'Ivoire
96 E3 Đa Năng Vietnam
106 B3 Dananhu Xinjiang China
92 C4 Danao Phil.
108 B2 Danba Sichuan China
234 C2 Danboro PA U.S.A.
151 H3 Danbury Essex, England U.K.
233 G4 Danbury CT U.S.A.
231 D4 Danbury NC U.S.A.
233 H3 Danbury NH U.S.A.
226 A2 Danbury WI U.S.A.
149 I3 Danby North Yorkshire, England U.K.
233 G3 Danby VT U.S.A.
109 E1 Dancheng Henan China
Dancheng Zhejiang China see Xiangshan
87 B6 Dandaragan W.A. Austr.
209 B7 Dande r. Angola
116 E3 Dandel'dhura Nepal
114 B3 Dandeli Karnataka India
149 F2 Danderhall Midlothian, Scotland U.K.
101 C4 Dandong Liaoning China
104 D3 Dando-san mt. Japan
231 D4 Dandridge TN U.S.A.
138 C4 Danė r. Lith.
149 G4 Dane r. England U.K.
151 H3 Danehill East Sussex, England U.K.
147 D3 Danesfort Rep. of Ireland
197 G4 Daneți Romania
Dänew Turkm. see Dyanev
108 D1 Danfeng Shaanxi China
Danfeng Yunnan China see Shizong
233 □J2 Danforth ME U.S.A.
Dangara Tajik. see Danghara
100 D3 Dangbizhen Rus. Fed.
106 E5 Dangchang Gansu China
Dangchengwan Gansu China see Subei
209 B6 Dange Angola
Danger Islands atoll Cook Is see Pukapuka
84 B1 Danger Point N.T. Austr.
214 B6 Danger Point S. Africa
162 C2 Dangé-St-Romain France
123 G2 Danghara Tajik.
106 B4 Danghe Nanshan mts China
210 C2 Dangila Eth.
Dangla Shan mts Xizang China see Tanggula Shan
117 H4 Dangori Assam India
111 E6 Dangqên Xizang China
243 H5 Dangriga Belize
107 H5 Dangshan Anhui China
109 F2 Dangtu Anhui China
207 G4 Dan-Gulbi Nigeria
210 B2 Dangur mt. Eth.
109 D2 Dangyang Hubei China
174 G5 Daniec Pol.
238 E3 Daniel WY U.S.A.
254 B5 Daniel, Serra hills Brazil
225 J3 Daniel's Harbour Nfld. Can.
214 D3 Daniëlskuil S. Africa
233 H4 Danielson CT U.S.A.
215 G2 Danielsrus S. Africa
231 D5 Danielsville GA U.S.A.
134 H4 Danilov Rus. Fed.
196 D4 Danilovgrad Crna Gora Yugo.
121 G1 Danilovka Kazakh.
135 I6 Danilovka Rus. Fed.
134 G4 Danilovskaya Vozvyshennost' hills Rus. Fed.
107 F4 Daning Shanxi China
129 F3 Dänizkänarı Azer.
Danjiang Guizhou China see Leishan
109 D1 Danjiangkou Hubei China
160 E1 Danjoutin France
125 G3 Ḍank Oman
124 C5 Ḍankalia prov. Eritrea
171 C4 Dankerode Ger.
169 F5 Dankmarshausen Ger.
139 L5 Dankov Rus. Fed.
121 I4 Dankova, Pik mt. Kyrg.
108 B2 Danleng Sichuan China
242 □I6 Danlí Hond.
221 P1 Danmark Fjord inlet Greenland
169 F3 Danndorf Ger.
168 G1 Dannemare Denmark
160 F1 Dannemarie France
233 G2 Dannemora NY U.S.A.
170 C2 Dannenberg (Elbe) Ger.
170 E2 Dannenwalde Ger.
80 F4 Dannevirke North I. N.Z.
168 E1 Dannewerk Ger.
215 H3 Dannhauser S. Africa
206 E4 Dano Burkina
Danshui Taiwan see Tanshui
232 E3 Dansville NY U.S.A.
116 C4 Danta Gujarat India
232 B6 Dante VA U.S.A.
114 D2 Dantewara Madh. Prad. India
Dantu Jiangsu China see Zhenjiang
197 I3 Danube r. Europe alt. Donau (Austria/Germany), alt. Duna (Hungary), alt. Dunaj (Slovakia), alt. Dunărea (Romania), alt. Dunav (Yugoslavia)
Danube Delta Romania see Dunării, Delta
96 A3 Danubyu Myanmar
237 E5 Danville AR U.S.A.
230 C3 Danville IL U.S.A.
230 C4 Danville IN U.S.A.
230 C4 Danville KY U.S.A.
232 B4 Danville OH U.S.A.
227 I5 Danville PA U.S.A.
232 D6 Danville VA U.S.A.
233 G2 Danville VT U.S.A.
Danxian Hainan China see Danzhou
109 F2 Danyang Jiangsu China
108 C3 Danzhai Guizhou China
108 D3 Danzhou Guangxi China
108 D5 Danzhou Hainan China
Danzhou Shaanxi China see Yichuan
Danzig Pol. see Gdańsk
Danzig, Gulf of Pol./Rus. Fed. see Gdańsk, Gulf of
92 B4 Dao Phil.
182 B4 Dão r. Port.
108 B2 Daocheng Sichuan China
Daojiang Hunan China see Daoxian
Daokou Henan China see Huaxian
159 F4 Daon France
108 D2 Daoshiping Hubei China
106 D4 Daotanghe Qinghai China
Dao Tay Sa is S. China Sea see Paracel Islands
Daoud Alg. see Aïn Beïda
206 E5 Daoukro Côte d'Ivoire
158 B3 Daoulas France
109 D3 Daoxian Hunan China
108 C2 Daozhen Guizhou China
92 C4 Dapa Phil.
207 F4 Dapaong Togo
117 I4 Daphabum mt. Arun. Prad. India
Daphnae tourist site Egypt see Kawm Dafanah
231 C6 Daphne AL U.S.A.
92 B4 Dapiak, Mount Mindanao Phil.
Dapingdi Sichuan China see Yanbian
92 B4 Dapitan Phil.
Dapu Guangxi China see Liucheng
126 C5 Daqahlîya governorate Egypt
111 F4 Da Qaidam Zhen Qinghai China
108 B3 Daqiao Yunnan China
100 C3 Daqing Heilong. China
107 I3 Daqin Tal Nei Mongol China
109 F3 Daqiu Fujian China
110 F3 Daquan Gansu China
106 B3 Daquanwan Xinjiang China
127 G4 Dāqūq Iraq
206 B3 Dara Senegal
128 C3 Dar'ā Syria
128 C3 Dar'ā governorate Syria
203 G3 Dâra, Gebel mt. Egypt
251 E5 Daraá r. Brazil
122 C4 Dārāb Iran
197 H1 Darabani Romania
92 B3 Daraga Phil.
138 G5 Darahanava Belarus
122 B3 Dārān Iran
97 E4 Đa Răng, Sông r. Vietnam
177 G6 Darány Hungary
99 J1 Darasun Rus. Fed.
Daraut-Kurgan Kyrg. see Daroot-Korgan
196 E4 Đaravica mt. Yugo.
203 G3 Daraw Egypt
207 H4 Darazo Nigeria
Darband Uzbek. see Derbent
122 D4 Darband, Kūh-e mt. Iran
138 C3 Darbėnai Lith.
180 D5 Dar Ben Karricha el Behri Morocco
117 F4 Darbhanga Bihar India
238 D2 Darby MT U.S.A.
234 C3 Darby PA U.S.A.
147 A4 Darby's Bridge Rep. of Ireland
108 A1 Darcang Sichuan China
189 C7 Dar Chabanne Tunisia
180 D5 Dar Chaoui Morocco
222 F5 D'Arcy B.C. Can.
188 G3 Darda Croatia
237 E5 Dardanelle AR U.S.A.
240 H2 Dardanelle CA U.S.A.
169 F4 Dardesheim Ger.
Dardo Sichuan China see Kangding
191 F2 Darè Italy
Dar el Beida Morocco see Casablanca
126 E3 Darende Turkey
211 C6 Dar es Salaam Tanz.
83 E3 Dareton N.S.W. Austr.
81 D5 Darfield South I. N.Z.
190 F3 Darfo Boario Terme Italy
123 E1 Darganata Turkm.
80 D1 Dargaville North I. N.Z.
175 J1 Dargin, Jezioro l. Pol.
83 F4 Dargo Vic. Austr.
207 F3 Dargol Niger
170 D2 Dargun Ger.
106 E1 Darhan Mongolia
Darhan Muminggan Lianheqi Nei Mongol China see Bailingmiao
199 F1 Darıca Turkey
199 G1 Darıçayırı Sakarya Turkey
199 F2 Darıcı Turkey
235 E1 Darien CT U.S.A.
231 D6 Darien GA U.S.A.
250 B2 Darién, Golfo del g. Col.
242 □K7 Darién, Serranía del mts Panama
129 A4 Darıkent Turkey
121 H2 Dar'inskiy Kazakh.
120 B2 Dar'inskoye Kazakh.
242 □I6 Darío Nic.
199 F3 Darıveren Denizli Turkey
Darīya Kazakh. see Dar'inskiy
Darjeeling W. Bengal India see Darjiling
117 G4 Darjiling W. Bengal India
87 C7 Darkan W.A. Austr.
82 D3 Darke Peak S.A. Austr.
147 E2 Darkley Northern Ireland U.K.
108 A1 Darlag Qinghai China
83 E3 Darling r. N.S.W. Austr.
214 B5 Darling S. Africa
85 G5 Darling Downs hills Qld Austr.
169 F4 Darlingerode Ger.
87 B7 Darling Range hills W.A. Austr.
149 H3 Darlington Darlington, England U.K.
149 H3 Darlington admin. div. England U.K.
234 B3 Darlington MD U.S.A.
231 E5 Darlington SC U.S.A.
226 B4 Darlington WI U.S.A.
83 F3 Darlington Point N.S.W. Austr.
87 D5 Darlot, Lake salt flat W.A. Austr.
143 G4 Darłówko Pol.
143 G4 Darłowo Pol.
197 H2 Dărmănești Romania
114 C2 Darmaraopet Andhra Prad. India
172 C2 Darmstadt Ger.
169 D6 Darmstadt admin. reg. Hessen Ger.
116 C5 Darna r. India
202 D1 Darnah Libya
215 H3 Darnall S. Africa
156 B3 Darnétal France
157 G4 Darney France
83 E3 Darnick N.S.W. Austr.
157 G4 Darnieulles France
186 F2 Darnius Spain
263 E2 Darnley, Cape Antarctica
186 G2 Daró r. Spain
183 I3 Daroca Spain
121 H5 Daroot-Korgan Kyrg.
134 I4 Darovskoy Rus. Fed.
182 B3 Darque Port.
146 F4 Darra Aberdeenshire, Scotland U.K.
147 B4 Darragh Rep. of Ireland
261 F5 Darregueira Arg.
122 D2 Darreh Gaz Iran
Darreh Gozaru r. Iran see Gīzeh Rūd
122 C4 Darreh-ye Bāhābād Iran
123 G3 Darreh-ye Shekārī r. Afgh.
123 G3 Darreh-ye Shekārī r. Afgh.
185 G3 Darro Spain
114 C3 Darsi Andhra Prad. India
170 D1 Darß pen. Ger.
150 D4 Dart r. England U.K.
128 C1 Dār Ta'izzah Syria
Dartang Xizang China see Baqên
151 H3 Dartford Kent, England U.K.
150 D4 Dartington Devon, England U.K.
150 D4 Dartmeet Devon, England U.K.
82 E4 Dartmoor Vic. Austr.
150 C4 Dartmoor hills England U.K.
150 D4 Dartmoor National Park England U.K.
225 I4 Dartmouth N.S. Can.
150 D4 Dartmouth Devon, England U.K.
85 F5 Dartmouth, Lake salt flat Qld Austr.
83 F4 Dartmouth Reservoir Vic. Austr.
149 H4 Darton South Yorkshire, England U.K.
91 J8 Daru P.N.G.
206 C5 Daru Sierra Leone
104 A3 Daruga-mine mt. Japan
188 F3 Daruvar Croatia
122 D1 Darvaza Turkm.
146 D6 Darvel East Ayrshire, Scotland U.K.
Darvi Hovd Mongolia see Bulgan
123 G2 Darvoz, Qatorkŭhi mts Tajik.
149 G4 Darwen Blackburn with Darwen, England U.K.
213 F3 Darwendale Zimbabwe
116 D5 Darwha Mahar. India
84 B2 Darwin N.T. Austr.
259 F8 Darwin Falkland Is
259 C9 Darwin, Monte mt. Chile
250 □ Darwin, Volcán vol. Islas Galápagos Ecuador
Darwin Island Islas Galápagos Ecuador see Culpepper, Isla
123 G4 Darya Khan Pak.
120 F3 Dar'yalyktakyr, Ravnina plain Kazakh.
202 D1 Daryānah Libya
Dar"yoi Amu r. Asia see Amudar'ya
Dar"yoi Sir r. Asia see Syrdar'ya
122 D4 Dārzīn Iran
116 B5 Dasada Gujarat India
107 G4 Dasha r. China
175 M6 Dashava Ukr.
107 G1 Dashbalbar Mongolia
Dashhowuz Turkm. see Dashkhovuz
107 I3 Dashiqiao Liaoning China
106 A3 Dashitou Xinjiang China
136 E3 Dashiv Ukr.
107 I2 Dashizhai Nei Mongol China
Dashkesan Azer. see Daşkäsän
122 D1 Dashkhovuz Turkm.
Dashkhovuz Oblast admin. div. Turkm. see Dashkhovuzskaya Oblast'
122 D1 Dashkhovuzskaya Oblast' admin. div. Turkm.
Dashköpri Turkm. see Tashkepri

Dasht to **Diamante**

122 D2	Dasht Iran
123 E5	Dasht r. Pak.
122 C4	Dasht-e Palang r. Iran
176 E1	Dašice Czech Rep.
173 F3	Dasing Ger.
123 H3	Daska Pak.
129 E3	Daşkäsän Azer.
214 D5	Daskop S. Africa
170 D1	Dassow Ger.
108 C3	Dasongshu Yunnan China
123 H2	Daspar mt. Pak.
207 F5	Dassa Benin
168 F2	Dassel Ger.
168 F2	Dassendorf Ger.
214 B5	Dassen Island S. Africa
168 F2	Dassow Ger.
129 E4	Dastakert Armenia
100 D4	Da Suifen He r. China
116 C3	Dasuya Punjab India
215 G2	Dasville S. Africa
175 H3	Daszyna Pol.
199 E3	Datça Turkey
102 J2	Date Japan
242 K5	Dateland AZ U.S.A.
116 C5	Datha Gujarat India
116 D4	Datia Madh. Prad. India
109 F3	Datian Fujian China
109 D4	Datian Ding mt. Guangdong China
239 F5	Datil NM U.S.A.
	Datong Fujian China see Tong'an
100 C3	Datong Heilong. China
106 D4	Datong Qinghai China
107 G3	Datong Shanxi China
106 C4	Datong He r. China
106 C4	Datong Shan mts China
169 C4	Dätteln Ger.
169 F4	Datterode (Ringgau) Ger.
92 C5	Datu Piang Phil.
123 G3	Daud Khel Pak.
117 F4	Daudnagar Bihar India
138 E4	Daugai Lith.
138 E3	Daugava r. Latvia
	alt. Zakhodnyaya Dzvina,
	alt. Zapadnaya Dvina,
	conv. Western Dvina
138 F4	Daugavpils Latvia
138 D3	Daugyvenė r. Lith.
123 F2	Daulatabad Afgh.
	Daulatabad Iran see Malāyer
117 G5	Daulatpur Bangl.
250 B5	Daule Ecuador
163 D5	Daumazan-sur-Arize France
159 F4	Daumeray France
169 B5	Daun Ger.
114 B2	Daund Mahar. India
96 A2	Daunggyi r. Myanmar
223 K5	Daund Man. Can.
161 E5	Dauphin France
234 B2	Dauphin PA U.S.A.
234 B2	Dauphin County county PA U.S.A.
161 D4	Dauphiné, Alpes du mts France
207 H3	Daura Nigeria
87 B5	Daurie Creek r. W.A. Austr.
107 H1	Dauriya Rus. Fed.
116 D4	Dausa Rajasthan India
169 D5	Dautphetal-Friedensdorf Ger.
169 D5	Dautphetal-Holzhausen Ger.
146 E4	Dava Moray, Scotland U.K.
129 F3	Däväçi Azer.
114 B3	Davangere Karnataka India
92 C5	Davao Gulf Phil.
123 E5	Dāvar Panāh Iran
215 G2	Davel S. Africa
233 B3	Davenport IA U.S.A.
233 D3	Davenport NY U.S.A.
238 C2	Davenport WA U.S.A.
85 E5	Davenport Downs Qld Austr.
84 C4	Davenport Range hills N.T. Austr.
151 F2	Daventry Northamptonshire, England U.K.
215 G2	Daveyton S. Africa
161 C3	Davézieux France
242 J7	David Panama
238 D3	David City NE U.S.A.
223 J5	Davidson Sask. Can.
84 B4	Davidson, Mount hill N.T. Austr.
234 B4	Davidsonville MD U.S.A.
82 B1	Davies, Mount S.A. Austr.
256 D1	Davinópolis Brazil
146 D4	Davis research stn Antarctica
263 F2	Davis research stn Antarctica
86 D4	Davis r. W.A. Austr.
240 G2	Davis CA U.S.A.
233 D5	Davis WV U.S.A.
232 D5	Davis, Mount hill PA U.S.A.
241 J4	Davis Dam AZ U.S.A.
225 I2	Davis Inlet Nfld. Can.
227 F4	Davis Mts U.S.A.
263 I2	Davis Sea Antarctica
221 M3	Davis Strait Can./Greenland
135 K5	Davlekanovo Rus. Fed.
198 C2	Davlia Greece
177 H5	Dávod Hungary
195 F4	Davoli Italy
190 E2	Davos Switz.
199 E3	Davutlar Turkey
232 C6	Davy WV U.S.A.
136 D1	Davyd-Haradok Belarus
175 M6	Davydiv Ukr.
137 G4	Davyd Brid Ukr.
137 H4	Davydivka Ukr.
	Davydkovo Rus. Fed. see Tolbukhino
137 J2	Davydovka Rus. Fed.
107 I3	Dawa Liaoning China
	Dawahaidy atoll Arch. des Tuamotu Fr. Polynesia see Ravahéré
210 D3	Dawa Wenz r. Eth.
111 D6	Dawaxung Xizang China
108 B2	Dawê Sichuan China
	Dawei Myanmar see Tavoy
	Dawei b. Myanmar see Tavoy
107 I4	Dawen r. China
150 D4	Dawlish Devon, England U.K.
96 B3	Dawna Range mts Myanmar/Thai.
125 F4	Dawqah Oman
124 D5	Dawran Yemen
85 G4	Dawson r. Qld Austr.
220 E3	Dawson Y.T. Can.
231 C6	Dawson GA U.S.A.
236 D2	Dawson ND U.S.A.
259 C9	Dawson, Isla i. Chile
222 G5	Dawson, Mount B.C. Can.
222 F3	Dawson Creek B.C. Can.
222 A2	Dawson Range mts Y.T. Can.
224 E5	Dawsons Landing B.C. Can.
231 C5	Dawsonville GA U.S.A.
109 E2	Dawu Hubei China
	Dawu Qinghai China see Maqên
108 B2	Dawu Sichuan China
	Dawu Taiwan see Tawu
	Dawukou Ningxia China see Shizuishan
109 E2	Dawu Shan hill Hubei China
125 G3	Dawwah Oman
163 A5	Dax France
	Daxian Sichuan China see Daxin
108 C4	Daxin Guangdong China
108 C3	Daxing Yunnan China see Ninglang
	Daxing Yunnan China see Lüchun
108 E3	Daxue Zhejiang China see Wencheng
108 B2	Daxue Shan mts Sichuan China
108 B3	Dayan Yunnan China see Lijiang
107 I4	Dayang r. China
111 F7	Dayang r. China
107 J1	Dayangshu Nei Mongol China
108 B3	Dayao Yunnan China
109 E2	Daye Hubei China
108 A3	Dayang Jiang r. China
	Dayishan Jiangsu China see Guanyun
129 D2	Daykhokh, Gora mt. Rus. Fed.
83 F4	Daylesford Vic. Austr.
261 H2	Daymán r. Uru.
261 I2	Daymán, Cuchilla del hills Uru.

108 E2	Dayong Hunan China
128 B3	Dayr Abū Sa'id Jordan
127 F4	Dayr az Zawr Syria
128 C1	Dayr Ḥāfir Syria
223 H4	Daysland Alta Can.
226 A3	Dayton MN U.S.A.
232 A5	Dayton OH U.S.A.
231 C5	Dayton TN U.S.A.
237 E6	Dayton TX U.S.A.
232 D5	Dayton VA U.S.A.
238 C2	Dayton WA U.S.A.
231 D6	Daytona Beach FL U.S.A.
109 E3	Dayu Jiangxi China
109 E3	Dayu Ling mts China
107 H5	Da Yunhe canal China
238 C2	Dayville OR U.S.A.
103 E7	Dazaifu Japan
122 A2	Dazgir Iran
	Dazhe Guangdong China see Pingyuan
	Dazhongji Jiangsu China see Dafeng
108 C2	Dazhu Sichuan China
108 C2	Dazu Chongqing China
108 C2	Dazu Rock Carvings tourist site Chongqing China
214 E4	De Aar S. Africa
147 C4	Dead r. Rep. of Ireland
233 □H2	Dead r. ME U.S.A.
226 D2	Dead r. MI U.S.A.
246 D2	Deadman's Cay Long I. Bahamas
241 J4	Dead Mountains NV U.S.A.
128 B4	Dead Sea salt l. Asia
236 C2	Deadwood SD U.S.A.
84 C2	Deaf Adder Creek r. N.T. Austr.
87 F6	Deakin W.A. Austr.
151 I3	Deal Kent, England U.K.
215 E3	Dealesville S. Africa
222 E4	Dean r. B.C. Can.
109 E2	De'an Jiangxi China
150 E3	Dean, Forest of England U.K.
260 E2	Deán Funes Arg.
146 E5	Dean Water r. Scotland U.K.
227 F4	Dearborn MI U.S.A.
149 F3	Dearham Cumbria, England U.K.
149 H4	Dearne r. England U.K.
238 C2	Deary ID U.S.A.
222 D3	Dease r. B.C. Can.
220 F3	Dease Arm b. N.W.T. Can.
222 D3	Dease Lake B.C. Can.
220 H3	Dease Strait Nunavut Can.
240 I3	Death Valley CA U.S.A.
240 I3	Death Valley depr. CA U.S.A.
241 I3	Death Valley Junction CA U.S.A.
159 G2	Deauville France
238 E2	Deaver WY U.S.A.
129 E3	Deavgay, Gora mt. Rus. Fed.
117 G5	Debagram W. Bengal India
137 J3	Debal'tseve Ukr.
	Debal'tsove Ukr. see Debal'tseve
108 C4	Debao Guangxi China
196 C5	Debar Macedonia
223 J4	Debark Eth.
223 J4	Debden Sask. Can.
204 E2	Debesa Morocco
129 D3	Debed r. Armenia
151 I2	Deben r. England U.K.
151 I2	Debenham Suffolk, England U.K.
225 I4	Debert N.S. Can.
134 K4	Debesy Rus. Fed.
175 J5	Debica Pol.
174 C3	Debno Pol.
206 D3	Débo, Lac l. Mali
87 C6	Deborah East, Lake salt flat W.A. Austr.
87 C6	Deborah West, Lake salt flat W.A. Austr.
175 I4	Deborzeczka Pol.
175 L4	Debowa Kłoda Pol.
175 H2	Dębowa Łąka Pol.
175 K4	Dębrno Pol.
174 F1	Dębnica Kaszubska Pol.
176 I6	Debrno Pol.
174 C3	Debno Pol.
196 C2	Debrc Serbia Yugo.
210 C2	Debre Birhan Eth.
177 K4	Debrecen Hungary
210 C2	Debre Markos Eth.
196 C2	Debrešte Macedonia
210 C2	Debre Tabor Eth.
210 C2	Debre Werk' Eth.
196 C4	Debre Zeyit Eth.
174 F2	Dębrzno Pol.
	Deçan Kosovo, Srbija Yugo.
	Dečani
196 B3	Deçani Kosovo, Srbija Yugo.
231 C3	Decatur AL U.S.A.
231 C5	Decatur GA U.S.A.
230 B3	Decatur IL U.S.A.
230 C3	Decatur IN U.S.A.
226 E4	Decatur MI U.S.A.
231 C5	Decatur MS U.S.A.
237 D5	Decatur TN U.S.A.
237 F5	Decatur TX U.S.A.
163 E4	Decazeville France
114 C2	Deccan plat. India
85 H5	Deception Bay Qld Austr.
84 D2	Deception West, Lake salt flat W.A. Austr.
	Deception Island Vanuatu see Moso
212 D4	Deception Pans salt pan Botswana
108 B3	Dechang Sichuan China
	Decheng Guangdong China see Deqing
177 I5	Dechtice Slovakia
192 A5	Decimomannu Sardegna Italy
192 A5	Decimoputzu Sardegna Italy
176 D1	Děčín Czech Rep.
160 B2	Decize France
238 F2	Decker MT U.S.A.
226 I5	Deckerville MI U.S.A.
164 D1	De Cocksdorp Neth.
195 F3	Decollatura Italy
226 B4	Decorah IA U.S.A.
84 C1	De Courcy Head hd N.T. Austr.
177 H5	Decs Hungary
	Dedang Yunnan China see Yongde
199 C6	Dedebağı Turkey
199 E6	Dedegöl Dağları mts Turkey
169 F3	Dedeleben Ger.
169 F3	Dedelstorf Ger.
170 F2	Dedelow Ger.
168 F3	Dedelstorf Ger.
210 C2	Dedemsvaart Neth.
177 J3	Dédestapolcány Hungary
151 I3	Dedham Essex, England U.K.
139 U6	Dedovo Rus. Fed.
256 L2	Dedo de Deus mt. Brazil
227 J4	Dedovaichi Rus. Fed.
129 E3	Dedoplis'tsqaro Georgia
206 E3	Dédougou Burkina Faso
138 I3	Dedovichi Rus. Fed.
100 C3	Dedu Heilong. China
120 C2	Dedua Turkey
188 B2	Dedza Malawi
213 G2	Dedza Mountain Malawi
150 D1	Dee est. Wales U.K.
149 F4	Dee r. England/Wales U.K.
146 F4	Dee r. Scotland U.K.
146 D6	Dee r. Scotland U.K.
147 C5	Deel r. Cork/Limerick Rep. of Ireland
147 D4	Deel r. Mayo Rep. of Ireland
147 E4	Deel r. Meath/Westmeath Rep. of Ireland
147 B2	Deele r. Rep. of Ireland
214 C3	Deelfontein S. Africa
164 B4	Deensen Ger.
85 E5	Deep Creek Range mts UT U.S.A.
151 G2	Deeping St Nicholas Lincolnshire, England U.K.
224 E4	Deep River Ont. Can.

235 F1	Deep River CT U.S.A.
83 G2	Deepwater N.S.W. Austr.
234 C3	Deepwater NJ U.S.A.
240 F2	Deer Creek r. CA U.S.A.
234 B3	Deer Creek r. MD U.S.A.
234 C3	Deerfield NJ U.S.A.
226 E2	Deerfield MI U.S.A.
210 E3	Deeri Somalia
87 F5	Deering, Mount W.A. Austr.
233 □I2	Deer Isle ME U.S.A.
225 J4	Deer Lake Nfld. Can.
224 B3	Deer Lake Ont. Can.
165 C4	Deerlijk Belgium
238 D2	Deer Lodge MT U.S.A.
235 F2	Deer Park NY U.S.A.
238 C2	Deer Park WA U.S.A.
	Deesa Gujarat India see Disa
235 H1	Deetz Ger.
171 D3	Deetz Ger.
137 J5	Defanovka Rus. Fed.
	Defeng Guizhou China see Liping
236 D3	Defiance OH U.S.A.
241 M4	Defiance Plateau AZ U.S.A.
231 C6	De Funiak Springs FL U.S.A.
163 D4	Dégagnac France
116 C4	Degana Rajasthan India
182 D2	Degaña Spain
192 D2	Degano r. Italy
191 H2	Degani Bur Eth.
150 D1	Degannwy Conwy, Wales U.K.
108 A2	Dêgê Sichuan China
184 C2	Degebe r. Port.
143 F4	Degeberga Sweden
210 D2	Degeh Bur Eth.
225 G4	Dégelis Que. Can.
207 G5	Degema Nigeria
143 F2	Degerfors Sweden
173 O3	Deggendorf Ger.
172 D3	Deggingen Ger.
123 H4	Degh r. Pak.
128 C1	Değirmenbaşı Turkey
199 J1	Değirmenci r. Turkey
199 E2	Değirmendere Turkey
128 C1	Değirmenlik Cyprus see Kythrea
190 D2	Dego Italy
244 C3	Degollado Mex.
86 C4	De Grey r. W.A. Austr.
86 C4	De Grey r. W.A. Austr.
133 L2	De Gyda Rus. Fed.
165 C3	De Haan Belgium
203 I6	Dehalak Deset i. Eritrea
122 C4	Deh Bid Iran
122 B4	Deh-e Kohneh Iran
183 F2	Dehesa de Campoamor Spain
183 F7	Dehesa de Montejo Spain
183 G2	Dehesas de Guadix Spain
122 A3	Deh Golān Iran
122 A3	Dehkvoŭneh Iran
78 □1b	Dehpehk i. Pohnpei Micronesia
	Dehqonobod Uzbek. see Dekhkanabad
116 D3	Dehra Dun Uttar Prad. India
117 F4	Dehri Bihar India
109 F3	Dehua Fujian China
100 C3	Dehui Jilin China
172 C2	Deidesheim Ger.
185 Q3	Deifontes Spain
182 D3	Deilão Port.
173 F7	Deining Ger.
173 E3	Deiningen Ger.
165 C4	Deinze Belgium
128 C4	Deir el Qamar Lebanon
	Deir-ez-Zor Syria see Dayr az Zawr
	Deißlingen Ger.
172 C3	Deißlingen Ger.
191 J1	Deiva Marina Italy
197 J2	Dej Romania
196 E5	Dejë, Mal mt. Albania
210 C2	Dejen Eth.
175 J1	Dejguny, Jezioro l. Pol.
	Deji Xizang China see Rinbung
108 D2	Dejiang Guizhou China
237 C5	De Kalb IL U.S.A.
237 F5	De Kalb MS U.S.A.
237 F5	De Kalb TX U.S.A.
233 F2	De Kalb Junction NY U.S.A.
191 I3	Dekani Slovenia
203 I6	Dekemhare Eritrea
78 □4b	Deke Sokehs i. Pohnpei Micronesia
121 F5	Dekhkanabad Uzbek.
207 I4	Dekina Nigeria
165 D6	De Klinge Belgium
208 C3	Dékoa C.A.R.
164 D1	De Koog Neth.
164 D2	De Kooy Neth.
164 C2	De Krim Neth.
150 C4	Delabole Cornwall, England U.K.
261 G5	De la Garma Arg.
84 B2	Delamere N.T. Austr.
149 G4	Delamere Cheshire, England U.K.
234 D2	Delancey NY U.S.A.
231 D6	De Land FL U.S.A.
240 H4	Delano CA U.S.A.
234 B2	Delano PA U.S.A.
241 K2	Delano Peak UT U.S.A.
78 □3b	Delap i. Majuro Marshall Is
78 □3b	Delap-Uliga-Djarrit Majuro Marshall Is
215 E2	Delareyville S. Africa
220 A4	Delarof Islands AK U.S.A.
235 G3	Delaware r. U.S.A.
232 A4	Delaware OH U.S.A.
236 E4	Delaware r. KS U.S.A.
235 F3	Delaware r. NJ/PA U.S.A.
96 C3	Delaware state U.S.A.
233 F4	Delaware, East Branch r. NY U.S.A.
233 F4	Delaware, West Branch r. NY U.S.A.
235 G3	Delaware Bay DE/NJ U.S.A.
234 C3	Delaware City DE U.S.A.
234 D2	Delaware County county PA U.S.A.
234 C3	Delaware Water Gap PA U.S.A.
225 G4	Delay r. Que. Can.
196 B2	Delbarton WV U.S.A.
222 F4	Del Bonita Alta Can.
169 E3	Delbrück Ger.
176 C2	Del Campillo Arg.
197 P5	Delčevo Macedonia
164 F2	Delden Neth.
83 G4	Delegate N.S.W. Austr.
182 E5	Deleitosa Spain
196 D3	Đelekovec Croatia
190 B2	Delémont Switz.
141 M3	Delet Teili D. Fin.
197 N4	Delena r. Romania
164 E1	Delfzijl Neth.
256 H3	Delfinópolis Brazil
213 G3	Delgado, Cabo c. Moz.
106 D1	Delger Mörön r. Mongolia
234 D3	Del Haven NJ U.S.A.
227 G4	Delhi Ont. Can.
231 D6	Delhi Qinghai China
116 D3	Delhi Delhi India
116 D3	Delhi admin. div. India
240 G3	Delhi CA U.S.A.
239 L4	Delhi CO U.S.A.
237 F5	Delhi LA U.S.A.
233 F3	Delhi NY U.S.A.
194 C5	Delia Sicilia Italy
194 C5	Delia r. Sicilia Italy
195 □	Delianuova Italy
236 E4	Delia Turkey
146 F5	Deli Rep. of Ireland
251 H3	Délices Fr. Guiana
193 P4	Delicato Italy
138 J3	Delijan Iran
223 J4	Delijes Turkey
222 F1	Deline N.W.T. Can.
168 F2	Delingsdorf Ger.
106 D4	Delingha Qinghai China
223 J4	Delisle Sask. Can.
171 E3	Delitzsch Ger.
178 E4	Dellach Austria

178 E4	Dellach im Drautal Austria
160 F1	Delle France
169 E4	Delligsen Ger.
190 F3	Dello Italy
236 D3	Dell Rapids SD U.S.A.
205 F1	Dellys Alg.
240 I5	Del Mar CA U.S.A.
233 F5	Delmar DE U.S.A.
235 A3	Delmas S. Africa
157 G4	Delme France
214 B3	Delmenhorst Ger.
234 D3	Delmont NJ U.S.A.
232 D4	Delmont PA U.S.A.
188 E3	Delnice Croatia
239 F4	Del Norte CO U.S.A.
108 C4	Delong Guangxi China
131 Q2	De-Longa, Ostrova is Novosibirskiye O-va Rus. Fed. see De-Longa, Ostrova
220 B3	De Long Islands Novosibirskiye O-va Rus. Fed. see De-Longa, Ostrova
220 B3	De Long Mountains AK U.S.A.
	De Long Strait Rus. Fed. see Longa, Proliv
83 F5	Deloraine Tas. Austr.
223 K5	Deloraine Man. Can.
198 C2	Delphi tourist site Greece
230 C3	Delphi IN U.S.A.
232 A4	Delphos OH U.S.A.
214 D3	Delportshoop S. Africa
231 D7	Delray Beach FL U.S.A.
242 C2	Del Rio Mex.
237 C6	Del Rio TX U.S.A.
141 L3	Delsbo Sweden
207 G5	Delta state Nigeria
239 E4	Delta CO U.S.A.
232 A4	Delta OH U.S.A.
234 B3	Delta PA U.S.A.
241 K2	Delta UT U.S.A.
251 F2	Delta Amacuro state Venez.
85 E3	Delta Downs Qld Austr.
220 D3	Delta Junction AK U.S.A.
231 D6	Delton FL U.S.A.
83 G2	Delungra N.S.W. Austr.
164 G2	De Lutte Neth.
116 B5	Delvada Gujarat India
147 D3	Delvin Rep. of Ireland
198 B2	Delvinë Albania
136 C3	Delyatyn Ukr.
120 C1	Dema r. Rus. Fed.
95 H4	Demak Jawa Tengah Indon.
157 F4	Demange-aux-Eaux France
160 C3	Demavend mt. Iran see Damāvand, Qolleh-ye
209 D6	Demba Dem. Rep. Congo
209 C7	Demba Chio Angola
182 B1	Dembava Lith.
210 C2	Dembech'a Eth.
217 □3b	Dembeni Njazidja Comoros
217 □3b	Dembeni Mayotte
210 B2	Dembi Dolo Eth.
177 K3	Demecser Hungary
164 E2	De Meern Neth.
170 D2	Demen Ger.
165 D3	Demer r. Belgium
264 F5	Demerara Abyssal Plain sea feature S. Atlantic Ocean
137 H5	Demerdzhi mt. Ukr.
160 C2	Demigny France
239 F5	Deming NM U.S.A.
251 F5	Demini r. Brazil
251 F4	Demini, Serras do mts Brazil
199 F2	Demirci Manisa Turkey
129 A3	Demirci Trabzon Turkey
196 D5	Demir Hisar Macedonia
128 D2	Demir Kapija Macedonia
197 M5	Demirköy Turkey
199 F2	Demirler r. Turkey
128 C1	Demirözü Turkey
215 K3	Demistkraal S. Africa
170 E2	Demmin Ger.
190 C4	Demonte Italy
231 C5	Demopolis AL U.S.A.
230 B3	Demotte IN U.S.A.
207 G4	Dempo, Gunung vol. Indon.
87 D7	Dempster, Point W.A. Austr.
163 C5	Demu France
137 I3	Demuryne Ukr.
	Dem'yanovka Kustanayskaya Oblast' Kazakh. see Lenínskoye
134 I3	Dem'yanovo Rus. Fed.
139 Y3	Dem'yanovo Rus. Fed.
136 C2	Demydivka Ukr.
136 C2	Demydove Ukr.
136 D2	Demydiv Ukr.
214 C4	De Naawte S. Africa
156 D2	Denain France
240 D3	Denair CA U.S.A.
223 I3	Denali AK U.S.A.
223 I3	Denali reg. Eritrea/Eth.
223 K4	Denare Beach Sask. Can.
163 E5	Dénat France
164 D2	Den Burg Neth.
151 F2	Denby Derby, England U.K.
211 F5	Dencik Tanz.
205 D7	Dendâra Maur.
165 D5	Denderleeuw Belgium
165 D5	Dendermonde Belgium
165 D3	Den Dolder Neth.
165 D3	Dendre r. Belgium
213 F4	Dendron S. Africa
164 E3	Den Dungen Neth.
196 E4	Deneba Eth.
164 C2	Denekamp Neth.
196 C3	Đeneral Janković Kosovo, Srbija Yugo.
143 L3	Denezhkin Kamen', Gora mt. Rus. Fed.
207 H3	Dengas Niger
207 H3	Denge Nigeria
207 H4	Dengi Nigeria
	Dengjiabu Jiangxi China see Yujiang
	Dêngka Gansu China see Têwo
	Dêngkagoin Gansu China see Têwo
107 D3	Dêngkagoin Gansu China see Têwo
111 G4	Dêngqên Xizang China
109 E4	Dengta Guangdong China
109 E1	Dengxian Henan China
	Dengzhou Henan China see Dengxian
	Dengzhou Shandong China see Penglai
	Den Haag Neth. see 's-Gravenhage
87 B5	Denham W.A. Austr.
86 F2	Denham r. W.A. Austr.
151 G3	Denham Buckinghamshire, England U.K.
246 □	Denham, Mount hill Jamaica
84 D3	Denham Island Qld Austr.
85 D3	Denham Range mts Qld Austr.
87 B5	Denham Sound sea chan. W.A. Austr.
164 D2	Den Helder Neth.
185 G3	Denia Spain
83 D4	Deniliquin N.S.W. Austr.
238 D3	Denio NV U.S.A.
236 D3	Denison IA U.S.A.
237 D5	Denison TX U.S.A.
263 J2	Denison, Cape Antarctica

86 F2	Denison Plains W.A. Austr.
	Denisovka Kazakh. see Ordzhonikidze
199 F3	Denizli Turkey
199 F3	Denizli prov. Turkey
161 E4	Denjuan, Sommet de mt. France
172 D3	Denkendorf Baden-Württemberg Ger.
173 F3	Denkendorf Bayern Ger.
172 C3	Denkingen Baden-Württemberg Ger.
172 D3	Denkingen Baden-Württemberg Ger.
173 E4	Denklingen Ger.
169 F3	Denkte Ger.
83 G3	Denman N.S.W. Austr.
87 C8	Denmark W.A. Austr.
142 F3	Denmark country Europe
226 C3	Denmark WI U.S.A.
221 P3	Denmark Fjord inlet Greenland
	Denmark Strait Greenland/Iceland
151 I4	Denmead Hampshire, England U.K.
215 L2	Dennilton S. Africa
235 C3	Dennington Suffolk, England U.K.
86 F4	Dennis, Lake salt flat W.A. Austr.
232 A4	Dennison OH U.S.A.
210 D3	Dennsville S. Africa
146 E5	Denny Falkirk, Scotland U.K.
164 E2	Den Oever Neth.
	Denow Uzbek. see Denau
95 F5	Denpasar Bali Indon.
234 C2	Densor Ger.
190 C2	Dent Blanche mt. Switz.
161 C4	Dent de Rez hill France
165 C4	Dentergem Belgium
173 E2	Dentlein am Forst Ger.
149 G4	Denton Greater Manchester, England U.K.
234 C4	Denton MD U.S.A.
237 D5	Denton TX U.S.A.
161 E3	Dent Parrachée mt. France
87 B7	D'Entrecasteaux, Point W.A. Austr.
77 G3	D'Entrecasteaux, Récifs rf New Caledonia
91 L8	D'Entrecasteaux Islands P.N.G.
190 B3	Dents du Midi mt. Switz.
151 H2	Denver Norfolk, England U.K.
239 L4	Denver CO U.S.A.
234 B2	Denver PA U.S.A.
224 C4	Denys r. Que. Can.
172 D3	Denzlingen Ger.
117 F4	Deo Eth.
116 D3	Deoband Uttar Prad. India
115 D2	Deobhog Madh. Prad. India
114 C3	Deodar PA U.S.A.
116 C4	Deodate PA U.S.A.
117 F5	Deogarh Orissa India
116 C4	Deogarh Rajasthan India
116 C4	Deogarh mt. Madh. Prad. India
116 D5	Deoli Madh. Prad. India
162 D3	Déols France
117 E4	Deoria Uttar Prad. India
116 C4	Deori Madh. Prad. India
117 E4	Deoria Uttar Prad. India
115 D3	Deosai, Plains of reg. Jammu and Kashmir
100 C1	Dep r. Rus. Fed.
116 C5	Depalpur Madh. Prad. India
165 B3	De Panne Belgium
226 C3	De Pere WI U.S.A.
233 D2	Depew NY U.S.A.
227 I2	Depot-Forbes Que. Can.
227 I2	Depot-Rowanton Que. Can.
106 B3	Depsang Point hill Aksai Chin
226 C5	Depue IL U.S.A.
131 O3	Deputatskiy Rus. Fed.
	Dêqên Xizang China see Dagzê
111 E6	Dêqên Xizang China
108 A2	Dêqên Yunnan China
109 D2	Deqing Guangdong China
109 G2	Deqing Zhejiang China
237 E5	De Queen AR U.S.A.
238 C2	De Quincy LA U.S.A.
123 G4	Dera r. Pak.
123 G4	Dera Bugti Pak.
123 G3	Dera Ghazi Khan Pak.
123 G3	Dera Ismail Khan Pak.
263 D2	Deram, Mount Antarctica
129 B1	Derazhne Ukr.
136 D2	Derazhnya Ukr.
129 F3	Derben Rus. Fed.
129 F2	Derbent Kocaeli Turkey
199 F1	Derbent Manisa Turkey
121 F5	Derbent Uzbek.
129 F2	Derbesiye Turkey see Şenyurt
100 B2	Derbur Nei Mongol China
83 F3	Derby Tas. Austr.
86 D3	Derby W.A. Austr.
215 I5	Derby S. Africa
151 F2	Derby Derby, England U.K.
235 H3	Derby CT U.S.A.
213 G5	Derby KS U.S.A.
233 G3	Derby Line VT U.S.A.
149 H4	Derbyshire admin. div. England U.K.
147 H4	Derecske Hungary
128 C1	Dereçine Turkey
199 F2	Dereköy Turkey
199 F2	Dereköy Turkey
199 C6	Dereköy Kütahya Turkey
169 F4	Derenburg Ger.
136 E2	Derental Ger.
137 H3	Derezuvate Ukr.
147 F4	Derg, Lough l. Rep. of Ireland/U.K.
147 C4	Derg, Lough l. Rep. of Ireland
147 C4	Derg r. Rep. of Ireland/U.K.
121 U3	Dergachi Rus. Fed.
97 I3	Dergachi Ukr. see Derhachi
137 H3	Derhachi Ukr.
237 E6	De Ridder LA U.S.A.
164 C3	De Rijp Neth.
129 D2	Derik Turkey
128 C1	Derinkuyu Turkey
137 J3	Deriyivka Ukr.
100 C2	Derkul r. Rus. Fed./Ukr.
179 I3	Dermbach Ger.
204 B3	Derna Libya see Darnah
199 L5	Dernieh Rus. Fed.
170 H2	Derneburg Ger.
179 I3	Derneburg Ger.
147 E6	Derreen Rep. of Ireland
147 C5	Derreendaragh Rep. of Ireland
	Derreeny Bridge Rep. of Ireland
147 B5	Derry r. Rep. of Ireland
147 E5	Derry Rep. of Ireland
	Derry Northern Ireland U.K. see Londonderry
233 H3	Derry NH U.S.A.
147 C5	Derrybeg Rep. of Ireland
147 D5	Derrybrien Rep. of Ireland
147 E6	Derryerglinna Rep. of Ireland
147 C4	Derrygonnelly Northern Ireland U.K.
147 C4	Derrygrogan Rep. of Ireland
147 D4	Derrykeevan Rep. of Ireland
147 B4	Derrylin Northern Ireland U.K.
147 B5	Derrymore Rep. of Ireland
147 B4	Derrynacreevy Rep. of Ireland
147 C6	Derrynasaggart Mountains hills Rep. of Ireland
147 B5	Derrynawilt Northern Ireland U.K.
147 B5	Derryrush Rep. of Ireland
147 B5	Derrytrasna Rep. of Ireland
147 D5	Derryveagh Mountains hills Rep. of Ireland
116 C3	Dera Nanak Punjab India
124 B4	Dersa Eritrea
151 I2	Dersingham Norfolk, England U.K.
106 D2	Derst Mongolia
237 D5	Des Arc AR U.S.A.
128 D1	Derua Italy see Deruta
100 B2	Derxi Nei Mongol China see Dersum
237 D5	Dêrub Xizang China see Rutog

203 H5	Derudeb Sudan
214 D5	De Rust S. Africa
193 E2	Deruta Italy
146 B5	Dervaig Argyll and Bute, Scotland U.K.
158 E4	Derval France
198 C2	Derveni Peloponnisos Greece
188 F3	Derventa Bos.-Herz.
190 E2	Dervio Italy
83 F5	Derwent r. Tas. Austr.
151 F2	Derwent r. Derbyshire, England U.K.
149 I4	Derwent r. England U.K.
149 F3	Derwent Water l. England U.K.
	Derweze Turkm. see Darvaza
139 U7	Derza r. Rus. Fed.
120 C1	Derzhavino Rus. Fed.
121 F2	Derzhavinsk Kazakh.
	Derzhavinskiy Kazakh. see Derzhavinsk
197 N6	Desa Romania
260 C4	Desaguadero r. Arg.
260 C4	Desaguadero r. Bol.
260 C4	Desagües, Cerro mt. Arg.
161 C4	Désaignes France
190 D3	Desana Italy
79 □	Désappointement, Îles du is Arch. des Tuamotu Fr. Polynesia
237 F5	Desarc AR U.S.A.
240 I2	Desatoya Mountains NV U.S.A.
227 F2	Desbarats Ont. Can.
151 G2	Desborough Northamptonshire, England U.K.
116 D5	Desa Madh. Prad. India
260 B4	Descabezado, Volcán vol. Chile
256 D4	Descalvado Brazil
182 D4	Descargamaría Spain
162 C2	Descartes France
223 K4	Deschambault Lake Sask. Can.
238 B3	Deschutes r. OR U.S.A.
210 C2	Desē Eth.
216 □3d	Deseada vol. La Palma Canary Is
259 C7	Deseado Arg.
259 D7	Deseado r. Arg.
246 C3	Desembarco del Granma National Park tourist site Granma Cuba
242 B2	Desemboque Mex.
191 F3	Desenzano del Garda Italy
241 K2	Deseret UT U.S.A.
241 K1	Deseret Peak UT U.S.A.
227 I3	Deseronto Ont. Can.
190 C3	Desertas, Ilhas i. Madeira
184 □	Desertas, Ilhas i. Madeira
241 J5	Desert Center CA U.S.A.
241 I5	Desert Hot Springs CA U.S.A.
160 A2	Désertines France
148 C3	Desertmartin Northern Ireland U.K.
241 L3	Desert View AZ U.S.A.
185 G2	Desesperada mt. Spain
161 B3	Desges France
225 H4	Deshaies i. Guadeloupe
227 H4	Deshler OH U.S.A.
116 C4	Deshnok Rajasthan India
187 D3	Desi mt. Eth.
250 A6	Desierto de Sechura des. Peru
190 D3	Desio Italy
198 B2	Deskati Greece
179 I5	Deskle Slovenia
236 D2	De Smet SD U.S.A.
236 C4	Des Moines r. U.S.A.
236 E3	Des Moines IA U.S.A.
239 L4	Des Moines NM U.S.A.
136 C1	Desna r. Rus. Fed./Ukr.
137 D2	Desna r. Rus. Fed.
176 B1	Desná Czech Rep.
136 C1	Desna r. Ukr.
197 H2	Desnățui r. Romania
138 L4	Desnogorsk Rus. Fed.
259 C9	Desolación, Isla i. Chile
131 O3	Desolación, Isla i. Chile
215 H5	Despatch S. Africa
106 D1	Despen Rus. Fed.
260 E2	Despeñaderos Arg.
226 B5	Desplaines IL U.S.A.
187 C3	Despoblado r. Spain
217 □1b	Desroches, Île i. Seychelles
171 D3	Dessau Ger.
171 D3	Dessau admin. reg. Sachsen-Anhalt Ger.
165 D5	Destelbergen Belgium
227 I1	Destor Que. Can.
82 D3	D'Estrees Bay S.A. Austr.
222 F4	Destruction Bay Y.T. Can.
192 B8	Desulo Sardegna Italy
160 C2	Desvres France
177 I5	Deszk Hungary
196 J2	Deta Romania
222 J2	Detah N.W.T. Can.
139 H4	Detchino Rus. Fed.
213 F3	Dete Zimbabwe
168 E4	Detern Ger.
198 A1	Deti Jon b. Albania/Greece
196 A3	Detinja r. Yugo.
177 J4	Detk Hungary
169 E4	Detmold Ger.
169 E4	Detmold admin. reg. Nordrhein-Westfalen Ger.
227 H4	Detroit MI U.S.A.
227 H4	Detroit Beach MI U.S.A.
236 E2	Detroit Lakes MN U.S.A.
173 I4	Dettelbach Ger.
172 D3	Dettingen an der Erms Ger.
172 D3	Dettingen an der Iller Ger.
170 D1	Dettmannsdorf Ger.
172 E3	Dettum Ger.
173 E4	Dettwiller France
97 D4	Det Udom Thai.
177 I3	Detva Slovakia
164 F2	Deuben Ger.
156 C2	Deûle r. France
164 F2	Deurne Neth.
169 B5	Deutsch Evern Ger.
178 B2	Deutschfeistritz Austria
179 L5	Deutsch Goritz Austria
179 L6	Deutsch-Griffen Austria
170 D3	Deutschhof Ger.
179 I4	Deutsch Kaltenbrunn Austria
	Deutschland country Europe see Germany
173 H2	Deutsch Kreutz Austria
179 L4	Deutschneudorf Ger.
179 N3	Deutsch-Wagram Austria
166 G3	Deutzen Ger.
227 H1	Deux-Rivières Ont. Can.
162 C3	Deux-Sèvres dept France
	Poitou-Charentes France
197 P3	Deva Romania
182 D1	Deva r. Spain
149 G5	Deva Cheshire, England U.K. see Chester
114 C3	Devakottai Tamil Nadu India
114 C2	Devanhalli Karnataka India
163 D4	Dévargaï r. Romania
177 K5	Devaványa Hungary
129 C6	Develi Turkey
164 F2	Deventer Neth.
146 F3	Deveron r. Scotland U.K.
197 P6	Devesel Romania
197 M3	Devetaş Romania
176 E1	Devét Skal hill Czech Rep.
116 C5	Devgadh Bariya Gujarat India
129 B6	Devgeçidi Barajı Turkey
114 A2	Devgarh Mahar. India
116 B4	Devikot Rajasthan India
156 F3	Deville France
177 K4	Devil River Peak South I. N.Z.
	Devils r. TX U.S.A.
80 □3	Devil's Backbone mt. South I. N.Z.

147 D4	Devil's Bit Mountain hill Rep. of Ireland
150 D2	Devil's Bridge Ceredigion, Wales U.K.
236 D1	Devils Lake ND U.S.A.
220 E4	Devils Paw mt. AK U.S.A.
240 H3	Devils Peak CA U.S.A.
246 D1	Devil's Point Cat I. Bahamas
222 C3	Devil's Thumb mt. Alaska/B.C. Can./U.S.A.
197 G5	Devin Bulg.
237 D6	Devine TX U.S.A.
237 □2	Devitsa r. Rus. Fed.
151 F3	Devizes Wiltshire, England U.K.
116 C4	Devli Rajasthan India
226 A1	Devlin Ont. Can.
197 N3	Devnya Bulg.
196 D5	Devoll r. Albania
161 C4	Dévoluy mts France
227 F2	Devon r. Can.
215 G2	Devon S. Africa
146 E4	Devon admin. div. England U.K.
149 L1	Devon r. England U.K.
146 E5	Devon r. Scotland U.K.
221 I2	Devon Island Nunavut Can.
83 F5	Devonport Tas. Austr.
240 I4	Devore CA U.S.A.
129 C6	Devrek Turkey
135 F8	Devrekâni Turkey
126 D2	Devrez r. Turkey
116 C5	Devrukh Mahar. India
117 H4	Dewangani Bangl.
116 D5	Dewas Madh. Prad. India
215 F3	Dewetsdorp S. Africa
247 □2	Dewey Puerto Rico
164 F2	De Wijk Neth.
237 F5	De Witt AR U.S.A.
233 E3	De Witt NY U.S.A.
149 H4	Dewsbury West Yorkshire, England U.K.
109 F2	Dexing Jiangxi China
233 □I2	Dexter ME U.S.A.
233 F2	Dexter NY U.S.A.
226 A4	Dexter MN U.S.A.
237 F4	Dexter MO U.S.A.
239 F5	Dexter NM U.S.A.
233 E2	Dexter NY U.S.A.
108 C2	Deyang Sichuan China
82 B2	Dey-Dey Lake salt flat S.A. Austr.
137 H2	Deykalivka Ukr.
143 I4	Deyma r. Rus. Fed.
	Deyneka Turkm. see Dyanev
122 B4	Dez r. Iran
122 B4	Deza Spain
182 B2	Deza r. Spain
222 B2	Dezadeash Y.T. Can.
122 B3	Dezful Iran
107 H4	Dezhou Shandong China
	Dezhou Sichuan China see Dechang
	Dezh Shāhpūr Iran see Marīvān
175 N1	Dezna Romania
190 F3	Dezzo r. Italy
128 B3	Dhahab, Wādi adh r. Syria
128 B4	Dhāhiriya West Bank
124 D2	Dhahlān, Jabal hill Saudi Arabia
	Dhahran Saudi Arabia see Aẓ Ẓahrān
117 G5	Dhaka Bangl.
117 G5	Dhaka admin. div. Bangl.
114 B3	Dhalbhum reg. India
124 E5	Dhamār Yemen
124 D5	Dhamār governorate Yemen
116 C5	Dhamnod Madh. Prad. India
116 D5	Dhampur Uttar Prad. India
116 C5	Dhamtari Madh. Prad. India
117 F5	Dhanbad Jharkhand India
116 C4	Dhandhuka Gujarat India
116 C4	Dhanera Gujarat India
117 F4	Dhang Range mts Nepal
117 F3	Dhankuta Nepal
116 B5	Dhar Adrar hills Maur.
206 B3	Dhar Adrar hills Maur.
116 B5	Dharampur Gujarat India
117 H4	Dharan Bazar Nepal
116 C5	Dharangaon Mahar. India
114 C3	Dharapuram Tamil Nadu India
116 B5	Dhari Gujarat India
117 H4	Dharmanagar Tripura India
117 E5	Dharmapuri Tamil Nadu India
114 C3	Dharmavaram Andhra Prad. India
116 D5	Dharmjaygarh Madh. Prad. India
116 D2	Dharmkot Punjab India
206 B2	Dhar Oualâta hills Maur.
206 C2	Dhar Tichît hills Maur.
114 C2	Dharur Mahar. India
114 B3	Dharwad Karnataka India
	Dharwar Karnataka India see Dharwad
116 D3	Dhasa Gujarat India
116 C5	Dhasan r. Madh. Prad. India
116 E3	Dhaulagiri I mt. Nepal
116 E4	Dhaulpur Uttar Prad. India
116 E4	Dhaurahra Uttar Prad. India
	Dhávlia Greece see Davlia
	Dhawlagiri mt. Nepal see Dhaulagiri I
	Dhebar Lake India see Jaisamand
128 A2	Dhekelia Sovereign Base Area military base Cyprus
117 H4	Dhekiajuli Assam India
117 F5	Dhenkanal Orissa India
	Dheskáti Greece see Deskati
	Dhiakoptón Greece see Diakopto
	Dhībān Jordan
128 B4	Dhībān Jordan
	Dhídhima Greece see Didima
	Dhidhimótikhon Greece see Didymoteicho
113 □	Dhiffushi i. N. Male Maldives
113 □	Dhigufinolhu i. S. Male Maldives
117 H4	Dhing Assam India
124 □1	Dhi Qar governorate Iraq
	Dhodhekánisos is Greece see Dodekanisos
	Dhofar admin. reg. Oman see Zufār
116 C5	Dhola Gujarat India
116 C5	Dholka Gujarat India
	Dhomokós Greece see Domokos
114 C3	Dhone Andhra Prad. India
116 B5	Dhoraji Gujarat India
116 B5	Dhori Gujarat India
116 B5	Dhrangadhra Gujarat India
116 B5	Dhrol Gujarat India
172 A2	Dhron Ger.
	Dhrosia Greece see Drosia
117 H4	Dhubri Assam India
116 C5	Dhule Mahar. India
	Dhulia Mahar. India see Dhule
117 F4	Dhulian Bihar India
116 D4	Dhuma Madh. Prad. India
210 F2	Dhuudo Somalia
210 E2	Dhuusa Marreeb Somalia
206 B2	Dhuwaybān basin Saudi Arabia
	Dhytikí Ellás admin. reg. Greece see Dytiki Ellas
	Dhytiki Makedhonía admin. reg. Greece see Dytiki Makedonia
198 B2	Dia i. Greece
161 F4	Diable, Cime du mt. France
240 C3	Diablo, Mount CA U.S.A.
240 D3	Diablo, Picacho del mt. Mex.
240 B3	Diablo Range mts CA U.S.A.
211 C7	Diaca Moz.
206 B3	Diafarabé Mali
206 B3	Diakon Mali
175 K2	Diakoftó Greece
176 F3	Diakovce Slovakia
206 B3	Dialafara Mali
206 B3	Dialakoto Senegal
206 B3	Diallassagou Mali
261 G3	Diamante Arg.
260 D4	Diamante r. Arg.
193 H5	Diamante Italy

Diamante, Pampa del to Donskoye

299

260 C4 Diamante, Pampa del plain Arg.
85 D5 Diamantina watercourse Qld Austr.
257 F3 Diamantina Brazil
254 E5 Diamantina, Chapada plat. Brazil
265 K7 Diamantina Deep sea feature Indian Ocean
85 E4 Diamantina Lakes Qld Austr.
256 A2 Diamantino Mato Grosso Brazil
253 F3 Diamantino Mato Grosso Brazil
256 A2 Diamantino r. Brazil
117 G5 Diamond Harbour W. Bengal India
85 G3 Diamond Islets Coral Sea Is Terr. Austr.
241 J2 Diamond Peak NV U.S.A.
240 G2 Diamond Springs CA U.S.A.
238 E3 Diamondville WY U.S.A.
206 C3 Diamou Mali
206 B3 Diamounguél Senegal
109 D4 Dianbai Guangdong China
Dianbu Anhui China see Feidong
108 B3 Diancang Shan mt. Yunnan China
85 G2 Diane Bank sea feature Coral Sea Is Terr. Austr.
206 C3 Diangounté Kamara Mali
206 C5 Diani r. Guinea
108 C2 Dianjiang Chongqing China
190 D4 Diano d'Alba Italy
190 D5 Diano Marina Italy
254 D4 Dianópolis Brazil
206 D4 Dianra Côte d'Ivoire
Dianyang Yunnan China see Shidian
Diaobingshan Liaoning China see Tiefa
100 D3 Diaoling Heilong. China
207 F3 Diapaga Burkina
128 A2 Diarizos r. Cyprus
206 C4 Diatifèrè Guinea
198 C1 Diavata Kentriki Makedonia Greece
115 G3 Diavolo, Mount hill Andaman & Nicobar Is India
261 G3 Diaz Arg.
125 G2 Dibā al Ḥiṣn U.A.E.
125 G3 Ḍibab Oman
Dibang r. India see Dingba Qu
209 D6 Dibaya Dem. Rep. Congo
209 C6 Dibaya-Lubwe Dem. Rep. Congo
151 F4 Dibden Hampshire, England U.K.
199 F2 Dibek Dağı mt. Turkey
214 D2 Dibeng S. Africa
136 E2 Dibrova Kyivs'ka Oblast' Ukr.
136 D2 Dibrova Zhytomyrs'ka Oblast' Ukr.
117 H4 Dibrugarh Assam India
182 B2 Dices Spain
168 D3 Dickel Ger.
237 C5 Dickens TX U.S.A.
233 □I1 Dickey ME U.S.A.
236 C2 Dickinson ND U.S.A.
231 C4 Dickson TN U.S.A.
234 C1 Dickson City PA U.S.A.
140 □ Dickson Land reg. Svalbard
127 F3 Dicle r. Turkey alt. Dijlah, Nahr (Iraq/Syria), conv. Tigris
191 G5 Dicomano Italy
164 F3 Didam Neth.
151 F3 Didcot Oxfordshire, England U.K.
169 F3 Didderse Ger.
129 D2 Didi Borbalo, Mt'a Georgia
206 C3 Didiéni Mali
129 C2 Didi Jikhaishi Georgia
129 D3 Didi Lilo Georgia
198 C3 Didima Greece
136 E2 Didivshchyna Ukr.
222 H5 Didsbury Alta Can.
116 C4 Didwana Rajasthan India
213 □K3 Didy Madag.
199 E1 Didymoteicho Greece
138 F4 Didžiasalis Lith.
161 D4 Die France
215 H1 Die Berg mt. S. Africa
215 H1 Die Berg mt. S. Africa
169 C5 Dieblich Ger.
206 E4 Diébougou Burkina
172 C2 Dieburg Ger.
177 L5 Dieci Romania
Diedenhofen France see Thionville
173 E3 Diedorf Bayern Ger.
169 F4 Diedorf Thüringen Ger.
223 I5 Diefenbaker, Lake Sask. Can.
162 E3 Diège r. France
183 E4 Diego Alvaro Spain
259 B8 Diego de Almagro, Isla i. Chile
265 I5 Diego Garcia i. B.I.O.T.
247 □7 Diego Martin Trin. and Tob.
259 C9 Diego Ramirez, Islas is Chile
Diégo Suarez Madag. see Antsirañana
206 C5 Diéké Guinea
170 D2 Diekhof Ger.
169 E3 Diekholzen Ger.
165 F5 Diekirch Lux.
165 E5 Diekirch admin. dist. Lux.
190 D1 Dielsdorf Switz.
206 C3 Diéma Mali
206 A3 Diembéreng Senegal
169 E4 Diemel r. Ger.
164 D2 Diemen Neth.
160 D3 Diémoz France
172 C2 Dienheim Ger.
161 A3 Dienne France
138 E3 Dienvidsusēja r. Latvia
156 E4 Dienville France
169 D3 Diepenau Ger.
165 E4 Diepenbeek Belgium
164 F2 Diepenheim Neth.
164 F2 Diepenveen Neth.
168 D3 Diepholz Ger.
156 B3 Dieppe France
247 □2 Dieppe Bay Town St Kitts and Nevis
214 D4 Dieput S. Africa
169 C5 Dierdorf Ger.
164 F2 Dieren Neth.
237 E5 Dierks AR U.S.A.
106 E4 Di'er Nonchang Qu r. China
100 C3 Di'er Songhua Jiang r. China
168 F3 Diesdorf Ger.
171 D4 Dieskau Ger.
173 E2 Diespeck Ger.
164 E3 Diessen Neth.
173 F4 Dießen am Ammersee Ger.
190 D1 Diessenhofen Switz.
165 E4 Diest Belgium
179 F2 Dietachdorf Austria
173 E3 Dietenheim Ger.
173 E2 Dietenhofen Ger.
173 G3 Dietersburg Ger.
173 F2 Dietfurt an der Altmühl Ger.
190 D1 Dietikon Switz.
172 C3 Dietingen Ger.
179 F2 Dietmanns Niederösterreich Austria
179 G2 Dietmanns Niederösterreich Austria
173 E4 Dietmannsried Ger.
173 F4 Dietramszell Ger.
169 D5 Dietzenbach Ger.
169 D5 Dietzhölztal-Ewersbach Ger.
157 F3 Dieue-sur-Meuse France
161 D4 Dieulefit France
157 G4 Dieulouard France
157 G4 Dieuze France
164 F2 Diever Neth.
169 D5 Diez Ger.
185 G3 Diezma Spain
207 I3 Diffa Niger
207 I2 Diffa dept Niger
165 E5 Differdange Lux.
115 E2 Digapahandi Orissa India
117 H4 Digboi Assam India
225 H4 Digby N.S. Can.
141 K3 Digerbergen hill Sweden
142 E1 Digerberget hill Sweden
116 C4 Diggi Rajasthan India
129 D3 Dighomi Georgia
236 C4 Dighton KS U.S.A.
114 C2 Diglur Mahar. India
162 C3 Dignac France
191 H2 Dignano Italy
161 E4 Digne-les-Bains France
156 B4 Digny France
160 B2 Digoin France
191 H2 Digòn r. Italy
129 C3 Digor Turkey
129 D2 Digora Rus. Fed.
92 C5 Digos Phil.
116 D5 Digras Mahar. India
123 G5 Digri Pak.
91 I8 Digul r. Indon.
111 F7 Dihang r. India alt. Yarlung Zangbo (China), conv. Brahmaputra
175 M5 Dihtiv Ukr.
137 G2 Dihtyari Ukr.
210 D4 Diinsoor Somalia
127 G5 Dijlah, Nahr r. Iraq/Syria alt. Dicle (Turkey), conv. Tigris
165 D4 Dijle r. Belgium
160 D1 Dijon France
Dijon airport France see Longvic
140 L2 Dikanäs Sweden
116 C4 Diken Madh. Prad. India
210 D2 Dikhil Djibouti
117 H4 Dikho r. India
199 E2 Dikili Turkey
165 B4 Dikkebus Belgium
129 D2 Diklosmta mt. Rus. Fed.
129 C3 Dikmeköyü Turkey
206 D4 Dikodougou Côte d'Ivoire
114 B2 Diksal Mahar. India
165 B3 Diksmuide Belgium
130 J2 Dikson Rus. Fed.
207 I3 Dikwa Nigeria
210 C3 Dīla Eth.
185 G3 Dilar Spain
185 G3 Dilar r. Spain
122 D4 Dilaram Iran
165 D4 Dilbeek Belgium
129 B3 Dilek Dağı mt. Turkey
93 C5 Dili East Timor
129 D3 Dilijan Armenia
81 D5 Dilion Cone mt. South I. N.Z.
129 C3 Dilip'i Georgia
Dilizhan Armenia see Dilijan
169 D5 Dillenburg Ger.
237 D6 Dilley TX U.S.A.
206 D3 Dilli Mali
142 D2 Dilling Norway
203 F6 Dilling Sudan
172 A2 Dillingen (Saar) Ger.
173 E3 Dillingen an der Donau Ger.
220 C4 Dillingham AK U.S.A.
223 I4 Dillon Sask. Can.
223 I4 Dillon r. Alberta/Saskatchewan Can.
238 D2 Dillon MT U.S.A.
231 E5 Dillon SC U.S.A.
227 I5 Dillsburg PA U.S.A.
232 D6 Dillwyn VA U.S.A.
209 D7 Dilolo Dem. Rep. Congo
165 E3 Dilsen Belgium
127 G4 Diltāwa Iraq
207 I5 Dimako Cameroon
117 H4 Dimapur Nagaland India
191 F2 Dimaro Italy
244 A2 Dimas Mex.
Dimashq Syria see Damascus
128 C3 Dimashq governorate Syria
209 D6 Dimbelenge Dem. Rep. Congo
206 D5 Dimbokro Côte d'Ivoire
83 E4 Dimboola Vic. Austr.
85 F3 Dimbulah Qld Austr.
198 C2 Dimini Thessalia Greece
Dimitrov Ukr. see Dymytrov
197 G4 Dimitrovgrad Bulg.
135 J5 Dimitrovgrad Rus. Fed.
197 F4 Dimitrovgrad Srbija Yugo.
Dimitrovo Bulg. see Pernik
237 C5 Dimmitt TX U.S.A.
234 C1 Dimock PA U.S.A.
128 B4 Dīmona Israel
92 C4 Dinagat i. Phil.
117 G4 Dinajpur Bangl.
195 F4 Dinami Italy
158 D3 Dinan France
116 C2 Dinanagar Punjab India
165 D4 Dinant Belgium
117 F4 Dinapur Bihar India
199 G2 Dinar Turkey
122 B4 Dīnār, Kūh-e mt. Iran
188 F3 Dinara mt. Bos.-Herz.
188 F3 Dinara Planina mts Bos.-Herz./Croatia
158 D3 Dinard France
Dinaric Alps mts Bos.-Herz./Croatia see Dinara Planina
150 D3 Dinas Powys Vale of Glamorgan, Wales U.K.
Dinbych Denbighshire, Wales U.K. see Denbigh
Dinbych-y-Pysgod Pembrokeshire, Wales U.K. see Tenby
209 B8 Dinde Angola
203 G6 Dinder r. Sudan
124 A5 Dinder el Agaliyin r. Sudan
114 C2 Dindi r. India
114 C4 Dindigul Tamil Nadu India
207 H4 Dindima Nigeria
116 E5 Dindori Madh. Prad. India
116 C5 Dindori Mahar. India
158 B3 Dinéault France
199 G2 Dinek Eskişehir Turkey
126 D3 Dinek Konya Turkey
209 C6 Dinga Dem. Rep. Congo
123 H3 Dinga Pak.
108 D5 Ding'an Hainan China
117 H4 Dingba Qu r. India
107 E4 Dingbian Shaanxi China
109 E2 Dingbujie Anhui China
Dingcheng Hainan China see Ding'an
158 E3 Dingé France
169 F4 Dingelstädt Ger.
94 C3 Dingin, Bukit mt. Indon.
147 A4 Dingle Rep. of Ireland
147 A4 Dingle pen. Rep. of Ireland
147 A4 Dingle Bay Rep. of Ireland
234 D1 Dingmans Ferry PA U.S.A.
109 E3 Dingnan Jiangxi China
85 G4 Dingo Qld Austr.
173 G3 Dingolfing Ger.
Dingping Sichuan China see Linshui
92 B2 Dingras Phil.
107 G5 Dingtao Shandong China
206 C4 Dinguiraye Guinea
225 I4 Dingwall N.S. Can.
146 D4 Dingwall Highland, Scotland U.K.
106 E5 Dingxi Gansu China
Dingxian Hebei China see Dingzhou
107 G4 Dingxiang Shanxi China
106 C3 Dingxin Gansu China
107 G4 Dingxing Hebei China
109 F1 Dingyuan Anhui China
107 G4 Dingzhou Hebei China
110 F4 Dingzikou Qinghai China
117 G4 Dinhata W. Bengal India
96 D2 Dinh Lâp Vietnam
147 D4 Dinin r. Rep. of Ireland
164 F2 Dinkel r. Neth.
173 E2 Dinkelsbühl Ger.
173 E3 Dinkelscherben Ger.
168 D3 Dinklage Ger.
146 F4 Dinnet Aberdeenshire, Scotland U.K.
111 D6 Dinngyê Xizang China
149 H4 Dinnington South Yorkshire, England U.K.
241 M1 Dinosaur CO U.S.A.
137 J5 Dinskaya Rus. Fed.
169 B4 Dinslaken Ger.
164 D3 Dinteloord Neth.
164 E3 Dinther Neth.
240 H3 Dinuba CA U.S.A.
232 E6 Dinwiddie VA U.S.A.
164 F3 Dinxperlo Neth.
206 D3 Dioïla Mali
161 D4 Diois, Massif du mts France
206 C4 Dion r. Guinea
257 F3 Dionísio Brazil
255 B8 Dionísio Cerqueira Brazil
161 C5 Dions France
256 B2 Diorama Brazil
Dioscurias Georgia see Sokhumi
177 H4 Diósd Hungary
197 F2 Diosig Romania
177 I4 Diósjenő Hungary
Diospolis Magna tourist site Egypt see Thebes
160 B2 Diou France
206 A3 Diouloulou Senegal
207 F3 Dioundiou Niger
206 D3 Dioura Mali
206 A3 Diourbel Senegal
123 H4 Dipalpur Pak.
116 E3 Dipayal Nepal
117 H4 Diphu Assam India
193 I5 Dipignano Italy
Dipkarpaz Cyprus see Rizokarpason
123 G5 Diplo Pak.
92 B4 Dipolog Phil.
165 F5 Dippach Lux.
169 E5 Dipperz Ger.
171 E5 Dippoldiswalde Ger.
81 B6 Dipton South I. N.Z.
Dipu Zhejiang China see Anji
117 H4 Dirang Arun. Prad. India
206 E2 Diré Mali
85 E2 Direction, Cape Qld Austr.
210 D2 Dirē Dawa Eth.
242 □I7 Diriamba Nic.
209 D9 Dirico Angola
194 D5 Dirillo r. Sicilia Italy
158 B3 Dirinon France
87 B5 Dirk Hartog Island W.A. Austr.
164 D2 Dirkshorn Neth.
164 D3 Dirksland Neth.
173 E3 Dirlewang Ger.
172 C2 Dirmstein Ger.
83 G2 Dirranbandi Qld Austr.
149 G2 Dirrington Great Law hill Scotland U.K.
124 C4 Ḍirs Saudi Arabia
Dirschau Pol. see Tczew
241 L3 Dirty Devil r. UT U.S.A.
116 C4 Disa Gujarat India
117 H4 Disang r. India
262 T2 Disappointment, Cape Antarctica
259 □ Disappointment, Cape S. Georgia
87 D4 Disappointment, Lake salt flat W.A. Austr.
Disappointment Islands Arch. des Tuamotu Fr. Polynesia see Désappointement, Îles du
173 E3 Dischingen Ger.
82 E4 Discovery Bay Vic. Austr.
264 J8 Discovery Seamounts sea feature S. Atlantic Ocean
190 D2 Disentis Muster Switz.
190 E2 Disgrazia, Monte mt. Italy
203 G3 Dishna Egypt
Disko i. Greenland see Qeqertarsuaq
Disko Bugt b. Greenland see Qeqertarsuup Tunua
199 G2 Dişli Turkey
84 E3 Dismal Creek r. Qld Austr.
263 D2 Dismal Mountains Antarctica
156 C4 Disneyland Paris tourist site France
195 H2 Diso Italy
165 E4 Dison Belgium
112 H6 Dispur Assam India
232 E6 Disputanta VA U.S.A.
225 G4 Disraëli Que. Can.
151 I2 Diss Norfolk, England U.K.
159 G5 Dissay France
159 G4 Dissay-sous-Courcillon France
169 D3 Dissen am Teutoburger Wald Ger.
206 E4 Dissin Burkina
149 F3 Distington Cumbria, England U.K.
256 D1 Distrito Federal admin. dist. Brazil
245 E4 Distrito Federal admin. dist. Mex.
250 E2 Distrito Federal admin. dist. Venez.
126 C5 Disûq Egypt
171 C4 Ditfurt Ger.
214 D3 Ditloung S. Africa
194 E5 Dittaino r. Sicilia Italy
169 F5 Dittelbrunn Ger.
173 E2 Dittenheim Ger.
151 H3 Ditton Kent, England U.K.
172 D3 Ditzingen Ger.
116 B5 Diu Daman India
92 C4 Diuata Mountains Phil.
179 E5 Divača Slovenia
122 A3 Dīvān Darreh Iran
Divehi country Indian Ocean see Maldives
208 B5 Divénié Congo
190 D2 Diveria r. Italy
159 F2 Dives r. France
159 F2 Dives-sur-Mer France
135 H5 Diveyevo Rus. Fed.
Divichi Azer. see Däväçi
238 D2 Divide MT U.S.A.
234 C3 Dividing Creek NJ U.S.A.
195 E4 Divieto Sicilia Italy
177 I3 Divín Slovakia
177 H2 Divina Slovakia
257 F4 Divinésia Brazil
257 E4 Divinópolis Brazil
156 C2 Divion France
256 B2 Divisões, Serra das mts Brazil
Divisor, Sierra de mts Peru see Ultraoriental, Cordillera
135 H7 Divnoye Rus. Fed.
206 D5 Divo Côte d'Ivoire
160 E2 Divonne-les-Bains France
184 B2 Divor r. Port.
126 E3 Divriği Turkey
134 L4 Div'ya Rus. Fed.
Diwaniyah Iraq see Ad Dīwānīyah
206 E5 Dixcove Ghana
233 □H2 Dixfield ME U.S.A.
156 D4 Dixmont France
233 □I2 Dixmont ME U.S.A.
240 G2 Dixon CA U.S.A.
226 C5 Dixon IL U.S.A.
238 D2 Dixon MT U.S.A.
220 E4 Dixon Entrance sea chan. Can./U.S.A.
222 G3 Dixonville Alta Can.
233 H2 Dixville Que. Can.
127 F3 Diyadin Turkey
127 G4 Diyālá governorate Iraq
127 G4 Diyālá, Nahr r. Iraq
127 F3 Diyarbakır Turkey
116 B4 Diyodar Gujarat India
Dizak Iran see Dāvar Panāh
207 H6 Dizangué Cameroon
Dize Turkey see Yüksekova
232 B6 Dizney KY U.S.A.
156 D3 Dizy France
156 E3 Dizy-le-Gros France
207 I6 Dja r. Cameroon
202 B4 Djado, Plateau du Niger
Djakarta Indon. see Jakarta
Djakovica Kosovo, Srbija Yugo. see Đakovica
205 G2 Djamâa Alg.
208 B5 Djambala Congo
205 H4 Djanet Alg.
78 □3b Djarrit i. Majuro Marshall Is
Djarrit-Uliga-Dalap Majuro Marshall Is see Delap-Uliga-Djarrit
205 F4 Djebr mt. Alg.
202 C6 Djédaa Chad
205 F2 Djelfa Alg.
208 E3 Djéma C.A.R.
Djeneral Jankovič Kosovo, Srbija Yugo. see Đeneral Janković
206 D3 Djenné Mali
202 B6 Djermaya Chad
206 E3 Djibo Burkina
206 D4 Djiborosso Côte d'Ivoire
210 D2 Djibouti country Africa
210 D2 Djibouti Djibouti
Djidjelli Alg. see Jijel
206 C3 Djiguéni Maur.
207 I5 Djohong Cameroon
208 B4 Djoua r. Congo/Gabon
147 E3 Djouce Mountain hill Rep. of Ireland
207 F4 Djougou Benin
207 I6 Djoum Cameroon
143 F1 Djurås Sweden
116 C3 Dlairi Punjab India
177 K3 Dlhé Klčovo Slovakia
177 H2 Dlhé Pole Slovakia
176 G2 Dlouhá Loučka Czech Rep.
174 G5 Dłubnia r. Pol.
174 F4 Długołęka Pol.
175 K2 Długołęka Pol.
175 J3 Długosiodło Pol.
175 H4 Dłutów Pol.
120 B1 Dmitriyevka Samarskaya Oblast' Rus. Fed.
135 H5 Dmitriyevka Tambovskaya Oblast' Rus. Fed.
135 F5 Dmitriyev-L'govskiy Rus. Fed.
Dmitriyevsk Donets'ka Oblast' Ukr. see Makiyivka
139 K3 Dmitrov Rus. Fed.
139 L4 Dmitrovskiy Pogost Rus. Fed.
139 J5 Dmitrovsk-Orlovskiy Rus. Fed.
137 J1 Dmitryashevka Rus. Fed.
137 G2 Dmytrivka Chernihivs'ka Oblast' Ukr.
137 H4 Dmytrivka Dnipropetrovs'ka Oblast' Ukr.
137 I3 Dmytrivka Dnipropetrovs'ka Oblast' Ukr.
137 G3 Dmytrivka Kirovohrads'ka Oblast' Ukr.
137 F4 Dmytrivka Mykolayivs'ka Oblast' Ukr.
137 I4 Dmytrivka Zaporiz'ka Oblast' Ukr.
Dmytriyevs'k Donets'ka Oblast' Ukr. see Makiyivka
139 H4 Dnepr r. Rus. Fed. alt. Dnipro (Ukraine), alt. Dnyapro (Belarus), conv. Dnieper
Dneprodzerzhinsk Ukr. see Dniprodzerzhyns'k
Dnepropetrovsk Ukr. see Dnipropetrovs'k
Dnepropetrovskaya Oblast' admin. div. Ukr. see Dnipropetrovs'ka Oblast'
Dnepropetrovsk Oblast admin. div. Ukr. see Dnipropetrovs'ka Oblast'
Dneprorudnoye Ukr. see Dniprorudne
136 E4 Dnestrovsc Moldova
135 F7 Dnieper r. Europe alt. Dnepr (Rus. Fed.), alt. Dnipro (Ukraine), alt. Dnyapro (Belarus)
136 E3 Dniester r. Ukr. alt. Dnister (Ukraine), alt. Nistru (Moldova)
137 G4 Dnipro r. Ukr. alt. Dnepr (Rus. Fed.), alt. Dnyapro (Belarus), conv. Dnieper
137 H3 Dniprodzerzhyns'k Ukr.
137 G3 Dniprodzerzhyns'ke Vodoskhovyshche resr Ukr.
137 H3 Dnipropetrovs'k Ukr.
137 H3 Dnipropetrovs'ka Oblast' admin. div. Ukr.
Dnipropetrovsk Oblast admin. div. Ukr. see Dnipropetrovs'ka Oblast'
137 H4 Dniprorudne Ukr.
137 H4 Dniprovka Ukr.
137 H3 Dniprovs'ke Vodoskhovyshche resr Ukr.
137 G4 Dnipryany Ukr.
136 E3 Dnister r. Ukr. alt. Nistru (Moldova), conv. Dniester
136 F4 Dnistrov'ky Lyman l. Ukr.
138 G3 Dno Rus. Fed.
139 H5 Dnyapro r. Belarus alt. Dnepr (Rus. Fed.), alt. Dnipro (Ukraine), conv. Dnieper
213 G3 Doa Moz.
147 E2 Doagh Northern Ireland U.K.
225 H4 Doaktown N.B. Can.
213 □K2 Doany Madag.
163 B5 Doazit France
208 C2 Doba Chad
Doba Xizang China see Toiba
177 L4 Doba Romania
138 H5 Dobasna r. Belarus
170 D2 Dobbertin Ger.
191 H2 Dobbiaco Italy
227 G3 Dobbinton Ont. Can.
235 E1 Dobbs Ferry NY U.S.A.
175 I6 Dobczyce Pol.
138 D3 Dobele Latvia
171 E4 Döbeln Ger.
91 H7 Doberai, Jazirah pen. Indon.
Doberai Peninsula Indon. see Doberai, Jazirah
171 E4 Doberlug-Kirchhain Ger.
171 F4 Döbern Ger.
179 G2 Dobersberg Austria
168 F1 Dobersdorf Ger.
171 F4 Dobershau Ger.
174 D3 Dobiegniew Pol.
175 J4 Dobieszyn Pol.
179 G4 Dobl Austria
261 E5 Doblas Arg.
188 G3 Doboj Bos.-Herz.
122 C4 Do Borjī Iran
177 K5 Doboz Hungary
175 I6 Dobra Małopolskie Pol.
174 G4 Dobra Wielkopolskie Pol.
174 C2 Dobra Zachodniopomorskie Pol.
174 D2 Dobra Zachodniopomorskie Pol.
177 L6 Dobra Romania
171 C5 Döbraberg hill Ger.
177 I3 Dobrá Niva Slovakia
176 C2 Dobřany Czech Rep.
179 F2 Dobrá Voda Czech Rep.
174 G3 Dobre Kujawsko-Pomorskie Pol.
175 J3 Dobre Mazowieckie Pol.
137 G4 Dobre Ukr.
143 I4 Dobre Miasto Pol.
197 F2 Dobrești Romania
197 H4 Dobrich Bulg.
135 H5 Dobrinka Rus. Fed.
176 D2 Dobříš Czech Rep.
171 D3 Dobritz Ger.
173 H2 Dobřív Czech Rep.
183 G2 Dobro Spain
174 G5 Dobrodzień Pol.
177 H5 Döbrököz Hungary
174 E5 Dobromierz Pol.
136 B3 Dobromyl' Ukr.
175 H4 Dobroń Pol.
177 L3 Dobron' Ukr.
176 E2 Dobronín Czech Rep.
137 I3 Dobropillya Ukr.
Dobropol'ye Ukr. see Dobropillya
175 L5 Dobrosyn Ukr.
174 F4 Dobroszyce Pol.
197 G3 Dobrotești Romania
175 M5 Dobrotvir Ukr.
197 H2 Dobrovăț Romania
171 F5 Dobrovice Czech Rep.
179 H4 Dobrovnik Slovenia
175 I5 Dobrowoda Pol.
139 L5 Dobroye Rus. Fed.
197 H4 Dobrudzhansko Plato plat. Bulg.
197 G3 Dobrun Romania
137 F1 Dobrush Belarus
176 F1 Dobruška Czech Rep.
134 L4 Dobryanka Rus. Fed.
137 F1 Dobryanka Ukr.
139 K4 Dobrynikha Rus. Fed.
175 I3 Dobrzankowo Pol.
174 D2 Dobrzany Pol.
174 F5 Dobrzeń Wielki Pol.
174 F4 Dobrzyca Pol.
174 E2 Dobrzyca r. Pol.
175 H3 Dobrzyków Pol.
175 H3 Dobrzyń nad Wisłą Pol.
177 J3 Dobšiná Slovakia
175 J1 Dobskie, Jezioro l. Pol.
81 C5 Dobson South I. N.Z.
81 B6 Dobson r. South I. N.Z.
231 D4 Dobson NC U.S.A.
150 C4 Dobwalls Cornwall, England U.K.
177 J5 Dóc Hungary
257 H3 Doce r. Espírito Santo Brazil
256 B3 Doce r. Goiás Brazil
146 D5 Dochart r. Scotland U.K.
146 D4 Dochgarroch Highland, Scotland U.K.
151 H2 Docking Norfolk, England U.K.
169 B5 Dockweiler Ger.
Doc Penfro Pembrokeshire, Wales U.K. see Pembroke Dock
244 D2 Doctor Arroyo Mex.
242 D2 Doctor Belisario Domínguez Mex.
87 E6 Doctor Hicks Range hills W.A. Austr.
244 D3 Doctor Mora Mex.
Doctor Petru Groza Romania see Ştei
114 C3 Dod Ballapur Karnataka India
151 H3 Doddinghurst Essex, England U.K.
149 G2 Doddington Northumberland, England U.K.
Dodecanese is Greece see Dodekanisos
199 E4 Dodekanisos is Greece
164 E3 Dodewaard Neth.
226 A3 Dodge Center MN U.S.A.
237 C4 Dodge City KS U.S.A.
226 B4 Dodgeville WI U.S.A.
191 G3 Dodici, Cima mt. Italy
211 B6 Dodoma Tanz.
211 B6 Dodoma admin. reg. Tanz.
223 I5 Dodsland Sask. Can.
232 B5 Dodsonville OH U.S.A.
164 F2 Doesburg Neth.
164 F3 Doetinchem Neth.
197 G3 Doftana r. Romania
224 B3 Dog r. Ont. Can.
111 E5 Dogai Coring salt l. China
111 E5 Dogaicoring Qangco salt l. China
199 E3 Doğanbey Turkey
199 E2 Doğanbey Turkey
199 G2 Doğançayır Eskişehir Turkey
126 E3 Doğanşehir Turkey
129 C4 Doğansu Turkey
222 F5 Dog Creek B.C. Can.
149 I4 Dogdyke Lincolnshire, England U.K.
199 G2 Döğer Turkey
172 C4 Dogern Ger.
224 B3 Dog Lake Ont. Can.
190 C4 Dogliani Italy
197 E3 Dognecea Romania
103 F5 Dōgo i. Japan
206 D4 Dogo Mali
207 G3 Dogondoutchi Niger
103 F6 Dōgo-yama mt. Japan
246 C1 Dog Rocks is Bahamas
127 G3 Doğubeyazıt Turkey
129 B3 Doğu Karadenız Dağları mts Turkey
199 F3 Doğu Menteşe Dağları mts Turkey
111 D6 Dogxung Zangbo r. Xizang China
125 E2 Doha Qatar
Dohad Gujarat India see Dahod
171 C5 Döhlau Ger.
171 E5 Dohna Ger.
215 F5 Dohne S. Africa
168 C3 Dohren Ger.
111 C7 Dohrighat Uttar Prad. India
77 I4 Doi i. Fiji
111 E6 Doilungdêqên Xizang China
Doïranis, Limni l. Greece/Macedonia see Dojran, Lake
Doire Northern Ireland U.K. see Londonderry
96 B3 Doi Saket Thai.
117 F5 Doisanagar Bihar India
165 D4 Doische Belgium
256 C5 Dois Córregos Brazil
254 E4 Dois Irmãos, Serra dos hills Brazil
184 A1 Dois Portos Port.
176 G3 Dojč Slovakia
197 F5 Dojran, Lake Greece/Macedonia
Dojransko Ezero l. Greece/Macedonia see Dojran, Lake
205 G2 Dokhara, Dunes de des. Alg.
141 J3 Dokka Norway
140 M2 Dokkas Sweden
164 E1 Dokkum Neth.
164 E1 Dokkumer Ee r. Neth.
123 G5 Dokri Pak.
Dokshukino Rus. Fed. see Nartkala
138 F4 Dokshytsy Belarus
176 D1 Doksy Liberecký kraj Czech Rep.
171 F5 Doksy Středočeský kraj Czech Rep.
120 F2 Dokuchayevka Kazakh.
137 I4 Dokuchayevs'k Ukr.
199 G1 Dokurcun Sakarya Turkey
236 D2 Doland SD U.S.A.
150 D2 Dolanog Powys, Wales U.K.
241 J4 Dolan Springs AZ U.S.A.
259 D6 Dolavón Arg.
225 F3 Dolbeau Que. Can.
150 C2 Dolbenmaen Gwynedd, Wales U.K.
190 C5 Dolceacqua Italy
158 E3 Dol-de-Bretagne France
160 D1 Dole France
160 F3 Dolent, Mont mt. France/Italy
150 D2 Dolfor Powys, Wales U.K.
150 D1 Dolgarrog Conwy, Wales U.K.
150 D2 Dolgellau Gwynedd, Wales U.K.
170 E2 Dolgen Ger.
233 F3 Dolgeville NY U.S.A.
137 H2 Dolgiye Budy Rus. Fed.
175 I1 Dolgorukovo Kaliningradskaya Oblast' Rus. Fed.
139 L5 Dolgorukovo Lipetskaya Oblast' Rus. Fed.
135 G5 Dolgoye Rus. Fed.
197 H2 Dolhasca Romania
175 M5 Dołhobyczów Pol.
192 B5 Dolianova Sardegna Italy
174 D2 Dolice Pol.
Dolina Ukr. see Dolyna
129 C1 Dolinovka Rus. Fed.
100 G3 Dolinsk Sakhalin Rus. Fed.
Dolisie Congo see Loubomo
197 E4 Doljevac Srbija Yugo.
147 C4 Dolla Rep. of Ireland
146 E5 Dollar Clackmannanshire, Scotland U.K.
168 C2 Dollart Ger.
171 C3 Dolle Ger.
262 T2 Dolleman Island Antarctica
157 H5 Doller r. France
168 E2 Dollern Ger.
171 D4 Döllnitz Ger.
173 F3 Dollnstein Ger.
159 G3 Dollon France
169 F4 Döllstädt Ger.
169 F5 Dolmar hill Ger.
121 G1 Dolmatovo Kazakh.
197 G4 Dolna Lipnitska Bulg.
177 H3 Dolné Vestenice Slovakia
177 H2 Dolní Benešov Czech Rep.
171 F5 Dolní Beřkovice Czech Rep.
179 I2 Dolní Bojanovice Czech Rep.
176 E1 Dolní Bousov Czech Rep.
179 F1 Dolní Bukovsko Czech Rep.
197 H4 Dolni Chiflik Bulg.
197 G4 Dolni Dŭbnik Bulg.
179 H2 Dolní Dunajovice Czech Rep.
176 D3 Dolní Dvořiště Czech Rep.
176 F2 Dolní Kounice Czech Rep.
177 G3 Dolní Němčí Czech Rep.
176 D1 Dolní Podluží Czech Rep.
171 F5 Dolní Poustevna Czech Rep.
176 F2 Dolní Újezd Czech Rep.
176 B1 Dolní Žandov Czech Rep.
197 F4 Dolno Kamartsi Bulg.
197 G4 Dolno Levski Bulg.
174 E4 Dolnośląskie prov. Pol.
177 I2 Dolný Kubín Slovakia
Dolný Peter Slovakia see Svätý Peter
177 H3 Dolný Pial Slovakia
177 G4 Dolný Štál Slovakia
191 H3 Dolo Italy
190 F4 Dolo r. Italy
78 □4b Dolohmwar hill Pohnpei Micronesia
160 D3 Dolomieu France
Dolomites mts Italy see Dolomiti
191 G3 Dolomiti mts Italy
Dolonnur Nei Mongol China see Duolun
210 D3 Dolo Odo Eth.
261 I5 Dolores Arg.
243 H5 Dolores Guat.
242 C3 Dolores Mex.
187 C6 Dolores Spain
261 H3 Dolores Uru.
241 M2 Dolores r. CO U.S.A.
244 D3 Dolores Hidalgo Mex.
196 E3 Dolovo Vojvodina, Srbija Yugo.
220 G3 Dolphin and Union Strait Nunavut Can.
149 F2 Dolphinton South Lanarkshire, Scotland U.K.
178 D4 Dölsach Austria
174 F4 Dolsk Pol.
175 K3 Dołubowo Pol.
162 A3 Dolus-d'Oléron France
136 B3 Dolyna Ukr.
137 G3 Dolyns'ka Ukr.
137 I4 Dolzhanskaya Rus. Fed.
137 H2 Dolzhenkovo Rus. Fed.
91 I7 Dom, Gunung mt. Indon.
177 J3 Domaháza Hungary
199 F2 Domaniç Turkey
175 K3 Domanice Pol.
193 I5 Domanico Italy
175 H3 Domaniewice Łódzkie Pol.
175 I4 Domaniewice Mazowieckie Pol.
177 H2 Domaniža Slovakia
117 G4 Domar Bangl.
Domartang Xizang China see Banbar
156 C2 Domart-en-Ponthieu France
179 H4 Domašinec Croatia
177 J5 Domaszek Hungary
174 E5 Domaszków Pol.
174 F4 Domaszowice Pol.
190 E2 Domat Ems Switz.
156 D4 Domats France
176 B2 Domažlice Czech Rep.
111 F5 Domba Qinghai China
120 D2 Dombarovskiy Rus. Fed.
141 J3 Dombås Norway
157 F3 Dombasle-en-Argonne France
157 F4 Dombasle-en-Xaintois France
157 G4 Dombasle-sur-Meurthe France
129 B2 Dombay Rus. Fed.
213 G3 Dombe Moz.
209 B8 Dombe Grande Angola
177 K5 Dombegyház Hungary
177 H5 Dombóvár Hungary
177 K3 Dombrád Hungary
Dombrau Pol. see Dąbrowa Górnicza
190 B1 Dombresson Switz.
Dombrovitsa Rivnens'ka Oblast' Ukr. see Dubrovytsya
Dombrowa Pol. see Dąbrowa Górnicza
164 C3 Domburg Neth.
257 F3 Dom Cavati Brazil
Domda Qinghai China see Qingshuihe
160 A3 Dôme, Monts mts France
263 F1 Dome Argus ice feature Antarctica
263 H2 Dome Charlie ice feature Antarctica
Dome Circe ice feature Antarctica see Dome Charlie
222 F4 Dome Creek B.C. Can.
263 C2 Dome Fuji research stn Antarctica
178 D4 Domegge di Cadore Italy
138 D4 Domeikava Lith.
161 D3 Domène France
160 A2 Domérat France
241 J5 Dome Rock Mountains AZ U.S.A.
171 C3 Domersleben Ger.
86 F2 Domett, Cape W.A. Austr.
81 D4 Domett, Mount South I. N.Z.
157 F4 Domèvre-en-Haye France
157 G4 Domèvre-sur-Vezouze France
258 C3 Domeyko Chile
163 B5 Domezaine-Berraute France
255 B9 Dom Feliciano Brazil
159 F3 Domfront France
157 F4 Domgermain France
257 G4 Domingos Martins Brazil
182 C4 Dominguiso Port.
247 □2 Dominica country West Indies
242 □J7 Dominical Costa Rica
Dominicana, República country West Indies see Dominican Republic
246 E3 Dominican Republic country West Indies
247 □2 Dominica Passage Dominica/Guadeloupe
Dominique i. Fr. Polynesia see Hiva Oa
170 C2 Dömitz Ger.
257 F3 Dom Joaquim Brazil
157 E4 Dommartin-le-Franc France
156 E4 Dommartin-Varimont France
163 D4 Domme France
164 E3 Dommel r. Neth.
169 C5 Dommershausen Ger.
171 D4 Dommitzsch Ger.
197 G3 Domnești Romania
197 G3 Domnești Romania
170 C3 Dömnitz r. Ger.
210 E3 Domo Eth.
139 K4 Domodedovo Rus. Fed.
190 D2 Domodossola Italy
198 C2 Domokos Greece
217 □3 Domoni Comoros
156 C3 Domont France
177 H4 Dömös Hungary
157 G4 Dompaire France
157 F4 Dompcevrin France
255 B9 Dom Pedrito Brazil
254 D3 Dom Pedro Brazil
160 C2 Dompierre-les-Ormes France
160 B2 Dompierre-sur-Besbre France
162 A2 Dompierre-sur-Mer France
158 E5 Dompierre-sur-Yon France
95 G5 Dompu Sumbawa Indon.
157 F4 Domrémy-la-Pucelle France
177 I4 Dömsöd Hungary
170 C2 Domsühl Ger.
192 A6 Domus de Maria Sardegna Italy
192 A5 Domusnovas Sardegna Italy
260 B5 Domuyo, Volcán vol. Arg.
137 H4 Domuzla r. Ukr.
83 G2 Domville, Mount hill Qld Austr.
188 E2 Domžale Slovenia
85 G3 Don r. Qld Austr.
158 E4 Don r. France
114 C2 Don r. India
242 C3 Don Mex.
139 L5 Don r. Rus. Fed.
146 F4 Don r. Scotland U.K.
96 D4 Don, Xé r. Laos
147 E3 Donabate Rep. of Ireland
191 H3 Donada Italy
147 D2 Donagh Northern Ireland U.K.
147 F2 Donaghadee Northern Ireland U.K.
147 E2 Donaghcloney Northern Ireland U.K.
147 D4 Donaghmore Laois Rep. of Ireland
147 E3 Donaghmore Meath Rep. of Ireland
147 E2 Donaghmore Northern Ireland U.K.
83 E4 Donald Vic. Austr.
237 F6 Donaldsonville LA U.S.A.
258 C2 Donalnes, Cerro mt. Chile
231 C6 Donalsonville GA U.S.A.
184 D2 Don Álvaro Spain
185 F3 Doña Mencía Spain
147 E3 Donard Rep. of Ireland
260 B2 Doña Rosa, Cordillera mts Chile
244 B1 Donato Guerra Mex.
178 I2 Donau r. Austria/Ger. alt. Duna (Hungary), alt. Dunaj (Slovakia), alt. Dunărea (Romania), alt. Dunav (Yugoslavia), conv. Danube
172 C4 Donaueschingen Ger.
173 G2 Donaustauf Ger.
173 E3 Donauwörth Ger.
184 E2 Don Benito Spain
149 H4 Doncaster South Yorkshire, England U.K.
157 E3 Donchery France
209 B7 Dondo Angola
136 D3 Donduşeni Moldova
Dondyushany Moldova see Donduşeni
147 C2 Donegal Rep. of Ireland
147 C2 Donegal county Rep. of Ireland
147 C2 Donegal Bay Rep. of Ireland
Dönenbay Kazakh. see Dunenbay
137 J3 Donetsk Rus. Fed.
137 I4 Donets'k Ukr.
137 I3 Donets'ka Oblast' admin. div. Ukr.
Donetskaya Oblast' admin. div. Ukr. see Donets'ka Oblast'
137 I2 Donetskaya Seymitsa r. Rus. Fed.
Donetsko-Amrovsiyevka Ukr. see Amvrosiyivka
Donetsk Oblast admin. div. Ukr. see Donets'ka Oblast'
137 J3 Donets'kyy Ukr.
137 J3 Donets'kyy Kryazh hills Rus. Fed./Ukr.
207 H4 Donga r. Cameroon/Nigeria
207 H5 Donga Nigeria
109 D3 Dong'an Hunan China
87 B6 Dongara W.A. Austr.
116 E5 Dongargaon Madh. Prad. India
116 E5 Dongargarh Madh. Prad. India
110 F3 Dongbatu Gansu China
Dongbo Xizang China see Mêdog
Dongchuan Yunnan China see Yao'an
108 B3 Dongchuan Yunnan China
Dongcun Shandong China see Haiyang
Dongcun Shanxi China see Lanxian
107 H4 Dong'e Shandong China
164 D3 Dongen Neth.
158 D4 Donges France
108 D5 Dongfang Hainan China
100 E3 Dongfanghong Heilong. China
100 C4 Dongfeng Jilin China
93 A3 Donggala Sulawesi Tengah Indon.
101 C5 Donggang Liaoning China
Donggou Liaoning China see Donggang
109 E3 Donggu Jiangxi China
109 E4 Dongguan Guangdong China
96 D3 Đông Ha Vietnam
107 H5 Donghai Jiangsu China
Dong Hai sea N. Pacific Ocean see East China Sea
108 C2 Dong He r. China
96 D3 Đông Hôi Vietnam
109 E4 Dong Jiang r. China
100 D3 Dongjingcheng Heilong. China
108 D3 Dongkou Hunan China
108 C3 Donglan Guangxi China
106 D4 Dongle Gansu China
107 I3 Dongliao r. China
110 E4 Donglük Xinjiang China
Dongmen Guangxi China see Luocheng
107 G5 Dongming Shandong China
100 D3 Dongning Heilong. China
209 B8 Dongo Angola
190 E2 Dongo Italy
203 F5 Dongola Sudan
210 B3 Dongotona Mountains Sudan
208 C4 Dongou Congo
96 C3 Dong Phraya Fai mts Thai.
96 C4 Dong Phraya Yen esc. Thai.
109 E4 Dongping Guangdong China
Dongping Hunan China see Anhua
107 H5 Dongping Shandong China
107 H4 Dongping Hu l. China
Dongpo Sichuan China see Meishan
111 E6 Dongqiao Xizang China
109 F4 Dongshan Fujian China
Dongshan Jiangsu China see Jiangning
109 G2 Dongshan Jiangsu China
Dongshan Jiangxi China see Shangyou
109 E3 Dongshao Jiangxi China
107 F4 Dongsheng Nei Mongol China
Dongshuan Yunnan China see Tangdan
109 G1 Dongtai Jiangsu China
109 G1 Dongtai r. China
109 E2 Dongting Hu l. China
109 G3 Dongtou Zhejiang China
Dong Ujimqin Qi Nei Mongol China see Uliastai
Dongxiang Sichuan China see Xuanhan
108 C4 Dongxing Guangxi China
100 C3 Dongxing Heilong. China
109 G2 Dongyang Zhejiang China
107 H4 Dongying Shandong China
106 D4 Dongzhen Gansu China
109 F2 Dongzhi Anhui China
260 B4 Doñihue Chile
151 G2 Donington Lincolnshire, England U.K.
237 F4 Doniphan MO U.S.A.
196 E4 Donja Dubnica Kosovo, Srbija Yugo.
179 H4 Donja Dubrava Croatia
179 H4 Donja Konjšćina Croatia
179 G5 Donja Stubica Croatia
179 H4 Donja Višnjica Croatia
222 A2 Donjek r. Y.T. Can.
157 F4 Donjeux France
188 G3 Donji Miholjac Croatia
197 F3 Donji Milanovac Srbija Yugo.
188 F3 Donji Vakuf Bos.-Herz.
188 E3 Donji Zemunik Croatia
164 F1 Donkerbroek Neth.
215 E4 Donkerpoort S. Africa
140 K2 Dønna i. Norway
225 G4 Donnacona Que. Can.
194 D6 Donnalucata Sicilia Italy
190 C3 Donnas Italy
222 G4 Donnelly Alta Can.
80 D1 Donnellys Crossing North I. N.Z.
156 D4 Donnemarie-Dontilly France
179 F3 Donnersbach Austria
172 B2 Donnersberg hill Ger.
173 E2 Donnersdorf Ger.
150 E2 Donnington Telford and Wrekin, England U.K.
87 B7 Donnybrook W.A. Austr.
147 C4 Donohill Rep. of Ireland
157 H4 Donon mt. France
192 B5 Donori Sardegna Italy
186 B1 Donostia - San Sebastián Spain
147 C5 Donoughmore Rep. of Ireland
199 D3 Donoussa i. Greece
226 D5 Donovan IL U.S.A.
137 I4 Dons'ke Ukr.
137 K4 Donskoy Rostovskaya Oblast' Rus. Fed.
139 L5 Donskoy Tul'skaya Oblast' Rus. Fed.
139 L5 Donskoye Lipetskaya Oblast' Rus. Fed.
135 H7 Donskoye Stavropol'skiy Kray Rus. Fed.

137 J2 Donskoye Belogor'ye hills Rus. Fed.
92 B3 Donsol Phil.
96 B3 Donthami r. Myanmar
158 E3 Donville-les-Bains France
163 C4 Donzac France
172 D3 Donzdorf Ger.
162 D3 Donzenac France
161 C4 Donzère France
160 B1 Donzy France
147 A3 Dooagh Rep. of Ireland
147 C2 Doocastle Rep. of Ireland
147 A3 Dooega Rep. of Ireland
147 B3 Doogbeg Rep. of Ireland
147 A2 Doogort Rep. of Ireland
147 B2 Doohooma Rep. of Ireland
148 B3 Dooish Northern Ireland U.K.
86 C4 Dooleena hill W.A. Austr.
84 D3 Doomadgee Qld Austr.
147 C4 Doon r. Rep. of Ireland
146 D6 Doon r. Scotland U.K.
146 D6 Doon, Loch l. Scotland U.K.
147 A2 Doonbeg Rep. of Ireland
146 B4 Doonbeg r. Rep. of Ireland
147 A4 Doonbeg r. Rep. of Ireland
147 A3 Doonloughan Rep. of Ireland
147 A4 Doonmanagh Rep. of Ireland
164 E2 Doorn Neth.
226 D3 Door Peninsula WI U.S.A.
174 E3 Dopiewo Pol.
108 B2 Do Qu r. Sichuan China
237 C5 Dora NM U.S.A.
86 D4 Dora, Lake salt flat W.A. Austr.
190 D3 Dora Baltea r. Italy
160 E3 Dora di Ferret r. Italy
160 F3 Dora di Veny r. Italy
190 C3 Dora Riparia r. Italy
Dorbiljin Xinjiang China see Emin
234 D3 Dorbod Heilong. China see Taikang
Dorbod Qi Nei Mongol China see Ulan Hua
196 E4 Đorče Petrov Macedonia
150 E4 Dorchester Dorset, England U.K.
234 D3 Dorchester NJ U.S.A.
156 C4 Dordives France
162 C3 Dordogne dept Aquitaine France
160 A3 Dordogne r. France
151 F2 Dordon Warwickshire, England U.K.
164 D3 Dordrecht Neth.
215 F4 Dordrecht S. Africa
160 B2 Dore r. France
160 A3 Dore, Monts mts France
223 J4 Doré Lake Sask. Can.
161 B3 Doré-l'Église France
178 A3 Doren Austria
169 E3 Dörentrup Ger.
146 D4 Dores r. Highland, Scotland U.K.
257 F3 Dores de Guanhães Brazil
257 E3 Dores do Indaiá Brazil
173 G3 Dorfen Ger.
178 E3 Dorfgastein Austria
168 E3 Dorfmark Ger.
170 C2 Dorf Mecklenburg Ger.
192 B4 Dorgali Sardegna Italy
106 B1 Dörgön Mongolia
177 K5 Dorgoş Romania
123 H4 Dori r. Afgh.
207 E3 Dori Burkina
214 B4 Doring r. S. Africa
214 B5 Doring r. S. Africa
214 B4 Doringbaai S. Africa
214 B4 Doringbos S. Africa
198 B3 Dorio Peloponnisos Greece
84 B2 Dorisvale N.T. Austr.
151 G3 Dorking Surrey, England U.K.
157 H4 Dorlisheim France
206 E5 Dormaa-Ahenkro Ghana
146 E4 Dorman Ger.
177 J4 Dormánd Hungary
156 D3 Dormans France
190 D3 Dormelletto Italy
172 C3 Dormettingen Ger.
100 E3 Dormidontovka Rus. Fed.
114 D2 Dornakal Andhra Prad. India
179 G4 Dornava Slovenia
169 E4 Dörnberg (Habichtswald) Ger.
178 A3 Dornbirn Austria
171 C4 Dornburg (Saale) Ger.
169 D5 Dornburg-Frickhofen Ger.
168 E2 Dornbusch Ger.
169 F5 Dorndorf Ger.
171 C4 Dorndorf-Steudnitz Ger.
182 C3 Dornelas Port.
160 B2 Dornes France
169 E4 Dörnhagen (Fuldabrück) Ger.
172 C3 Dornhan Ger.
146 C4 Dornie Highland, Scotland U.K.
171 D3 Dörnitz Ger.
190 D3 Dorno Italy
146 D4 Dornoch Highland, Scotland U.K.
146 D4 Dornoch Firth est. Scotland U.K.
107 G1 Dornod prov. Mongolia
107 F2 Dornogovĭ prov. Mongolia
234 B2 Dornsife PA U.S.A.
172 D3 Dornstadt Ger.
172 C3 Dornstetten Ger.
168 C2 Dornum Ger.
169 E4 Dornumersiel Ger.
208 E2 Doro Mali
197 H3 Dorobanţu Romania
177 H4 Dorog Hungary
177 I3 Dorogháza Hungary
139 I4 Dorogobuzh Rus. Fed.
197 H2 Dorohoi Romania
175 L4 Dorohusk Pol.
139 K4 Dorokhovo Rus. Fed.
177 L4 Doroliţ Romania
137 F3 Doroshivka Ukr.
Dorostol Bulg. see Silistra
136 C2 Dorosyny Ukr.
140 L2 Dorotea Sweden
234 D3 Dorothy NJ U.S.A.
Dorpat Estonia see Tartu
168 C3 Dörpen Ger.
87 B5 Dorre Island W.A. Austr.
83 H2 Dorrigo N.S.W. Austr.
238 B3 Dorris CA U.S.A.
207 H5 Dorsale Camerounaise slope Cameroon/Nigeria
227 H3 Dorset Ont. Can.
150 E4 Dorset admin. div. England U.K.
232 C4 Dorset OH U.S.A.
169 F3 Dorstadt Ger.
169 B4 Dorsten Ger.
160 D2 Dortan France
169 C4 Dortmund Ger.
232 B6 Dorton KY U.S.A.
126 E3 Dörtyol Turkey
174 C4 Dorochów Pol.
129 C4 Dorukdibi Turkey
168 E3 Dörverden Ger.
Doryleum Turkey see Eskişehir
172 E2 Dörzbach Ger.
187 C5 Dos Aguas Spain
131 S3 Do Sări Iran
183 G5 Dosbarrios Spain
241 M5 Dos Cabezas Mountains AZ U.S.A.
250 C6 Dos de Mayo Peru
199 G3 Döşemealtı Turkey
123 J4 Doshakh, Koh-i- mt. Afgh.
184 E3 Dos Hermanas Spain
243 H5 Dos Lagunos Guat.
96 D2 Đo Son Vietnam
240 G3 Dos Palos CA U.S.A.
197 G5 Dospat Bulg.
197 G5 Dospat r. Bulg.
185 I3 Dos Picos mt. Spain
170 D3 Dosse r. Ger.
172 C2 Dossenheim Ger.
208 C2 Dosso, Bahr r. Chad
207 F3 Dosso Niger
207 F3 Dosso dept Niger
190 D2 Dossola, Val val. Italy
120 C3 Dossor Kazakh.
185 F2 Dos Torres Spain
121 J3 Dostyk Kazakh.
Dostyq Kazakh. see Dostyk
231 C6 Dothan AL U.S.A.
168 D3 Dötlingen Ger.
172 C3 Dotternhausen Ger.

199 D1 Döttingen Switz.
156 D2 Douai France
207 H5 Douala Cameroon
158 B3 Douarnenez France
85 H5 Double Island Point Qld Austr.
237 C5 Double Mountain Fork r. TX U.S.A.
240 H4 Double Peak CA U.S.A.
85 J3 Double Point Qld Austr.
231 C5 Double Springs AL U.S.A.
176 E2 Doubrava r. Czech Rep.
160 E2 Doubs France
160 E1 Doubs dept Franche-Comté France
160 D2 Doubs r. France/Switz.
86 E2 Doubtful Bay W.A. Austr.
87 C7 Doubtful Island Bay W.A. Austr.
81 A6 Doubtful Sound South I. N.Z.
81 A6 Doubtful Sound inlet South I. N.Z.
156 D5 Douchy France
156 D2 Douchy-les-Mines France
160 D2 Doucier France
159 G2 Doudeville France
162 B1 Doué-la-Fontaine France
206 D3 Douentza Mali
148 D2 Dougarie North Ayrshire, Scotland U.K.
205 H1 Dougga tourist site Tunisia
147 C2 Dough Mountain hill Rep. of Ireland
145 E4 Douglas Isle of Man
80 E3 Douglas North I. N.Z.
147 C5 Douglas Rep. of Ireland
214 D3 Douglas S. Africa
146 E6 Douglas South Lanarkshire, Scotland U.K.
222 C3 Douglas AZ U.S.A.
241 M6 Douglas AZ U.S.A.
231 D6 Douglas GA U.S.A.
236 E4 Douglas WY U.S.A.
148 B3 Douglas Bridge Northern Ireland U.K.
241 M1 Douglas Creek r. CO U.S.A.
262 T2 Douglas Range mts Antarctica
234 C2 Douglassville PA U.S.A.
146 F5 Douglastown Angus, Scotland U.K.
231 C5 Douglasville GA U.S.A.
Douhudi Hubei China see Gong'an
157 H4 Doulaincourt-Saucourt France
Douliu Taiwan see Touliu
156 C2 Doullens France
206 D3 Doumé Benin
207 I5 Doumé Cameroon
207 I5 Doumé r. Cameroon
109 E4 Doumen Guangdong China
146 E2 Dounby Orkney, Scotland U.K.
146 D5 Doune Stirling, Scotland U.K.
146 D5 Doune Hill hill Scotland U.K.
207 F4 Doundoussa Benin
146 E3 Dounreay Highland, Scotland U.K.
176 C1 Doupovské Hory mts Czech Rep.
165 C4 Dour Belgium
256 C3 Dourada, Cachoeira waterfall Brazil
256 B2 Dourada, Serra hills Brazil
254 C5 Dourada, Serra mts Brazil
255 B7 Dourados Brazil
255 B7 Dourados r. Brazil
208 B2 Dourbali Chad
161 B4 Dourbie r. France
161 B4 Dourbies France
161 A4 Dourdou r. France
161 A5 Dourdou r. France
156 E3 Dourgne France
156 D2 Douriez France
182 B3 Douro r. Port.
  alt. Duero (Spain)
160 D3 Doussard France
256 A5 Doutor Camargo Brazil
158 E3 Douvaine France
158 E2 Douvres France
159 F2 Douvres-la-Délivrande France
161 C3 Douvre r. France
205 H1 Douz Tunisia
168 B5 Douze r. France
162 C3 Douzillac France
157 F3 Douzy France
191 G4 Dovadola Italy
136 E2 Dovbysh Ukr.
151 F2 Dove r. Derbyshire/Staffordshire, England U.K.
149 I3 Dove r. North Yorkshire, England U.K.
151 I2 Dove Brook Nfld. Can.
225 J2 Dove Bugt b. Greenland
221 P2 Dove Creek CO U.S.A.
241 M3 Dove Creek CO U.S.A.
83 F5 Dover Tas. Austr.
151 I3 Dover Kent, England U.K.
234 C3 Dover DE U.S.A.
234 D3 Dover NJ U.S.A.
232 C4 Dover OH U.S.A.
234 B3 Dover NH U.S.A.
231 C4 Dover TN U.S.A.
87 C7 Dover, Point W.A. Austr.
145 H6 Dover, Strait of France/U.K.
233 I2 Dover-Foxcroft ME U.S.A.
151 F2 Doveridge Derbyshire, England U.K.
235 E1 Dover Plains NY U.S.A.
Dovey r. Wales U.K. see Dyfi
122 B4 Doveyrich, Rüd-e r. Iran/Iraq
136 D3 Dovhe Ukr.
136 C2 Dovhoshyyi Ukr.
175 L1 Dovinė r. Lith.
141 J3 Dovrefjell mts Norway
137 H2 Dovzhyk Ukr.
Dow, Lake Botswana see Xau, Lake
211 B8 Dowa Malawi
226 D5 Dowagiac MI U.S.A.
146 E5 Dowally Perth and Kinross, Scotland U.K.
123 G2 Dowdeshwar Afgh.
122 B4 Dowlatābād Afgh.
123 E2 Dowlatābād Iran
147 E2 Down county Northern Ireland U.K.
240 H5 Downey CA U.S.A.
151 H2 Downham Market Norfolk, England U.K.
240 G2 Downieville CA U.S.A.
226 A5 Downing MO U.S.A.
234 C2 Downingtown PA U.S.A.
147 F2 Downpatrick Northern Ireland U.K.
236 D4 Downs KS U.S.A.
233 F3 Downsville NY U.S.A.
235 B3 Downsville WI U.S.A.
151 F4 Downton Wiltshire, England U.K.
222 E4 Downton, Mount B.C. Can.
147 C2 Dowra Rep. of Ireland
122 A3 Dow Sar Iran
122 C3 Dow Rūd Iran
151 I2 Dowsby Lincolnshire, England U.K.
160 A2 Doyet France
240 A1 Doyle CA U.S.A.
234 C2 Doylestown PA U.S.A.
197 G3 Doyrentsi Bulg.
122 D5 Dozdān r. Iran
103 F5 Dōzen is Japan
216 □1b Doze Ribeiras Terceira Azores
159 F2 Dozulé France
137 G3 Drabiv Ukr.
161 D3 Drac r. France
256 B4 Dracena Brazil
196 B4 Dračevo Macedonia
171 H4 Drachhausen Ger.
173 H2 Drachselsried Ger.
164 F1 Drachten Neth.
147 G2 Dracula r. Ukr.
161 C4 Dragalina r. Romania
177 L5 Drăganeşti Romania
83 F4 Draganeşti-Olt Romania
197 G3 Drăganeşti-Vlaşca Romania

197 G3 Drăgăşani Romania
168 F2 Drage Ger.
177 L5 Drăgeşti Romania
214 D3 Draghoender S. Africa
197 F4 Dragoana, Isla i. Spain see Sa Dragonera
193 G3 Dragoni Italy
247 □7 Dragon's Mouths str. Trin. and Tob./Venez.
241 L5 Dragoon AZ U.S.A.
162 E2 Draguignan France
197 H1 Drăguşeni Romania
197 H3 Drăguşeni Romania
176 G2 Drahanovice Czech Rep.
136 C1 Drahichyn Belarus
171 E4 Drahnsdorf Ger.
83 H2 Drake N.S.W. Austr.
236 C2 Drake ND U.S.A.
168 E3 Drakenburg Ger.
215 H4 Drakensberg mts Lesotho/S. Africa
213 F5 Drakensberg mts S. Africa
215 G3 Drakensberg Garden S. Africa
215 G4 Draken's Rock mt. S. Africa
264 E9 Drake Passage S. Atlantic Ocean
240 F3 Drakes Bay CA U.S.A.
129 D3 Drakhtik Armenia
136 E5 Drakulya r. Ukr.
198 D1 Drama Greece
142 D2 Drammen Norway
156 C4 Drancy France
97 D4 Đrăng, Prêk r. Cambodia
140 □B2 Drangajökull ice cap Iceland
147 D4 Drangan Rep. of Ireland
142 C2 Drangedal Norway
116 C4 Drangme Chhu r. Bhutan
168 D2 Drangstedt Ger.
174 D3 Dranse r. France
170 D2 Dranse r. France
169 E4 Dransfeld Ger.
171 E2 Dranske Ger.
241 L1 Draper UT U.S.A.
222 B3 Draper, Mount AK U.S.A.
147 E2 Draperstown Northern Ireland U.K.
Drapsaca Afgh. see Kondūz
116 C2 Dras Jammu and Kashmir
179 H2 Draßhofen Austria
179 H3 Draßmarkt Austria
178 F4 Drau r. Austria
  alt. Drava (Croatia),
  alt. Dráva (Hungary)
188 G3 Drava r. Croatia/Slovenia
  alt. Drau (Austria),
  alt. Dráva (Hungary)
188 G3 Dráva r. Hungary
  alt. Drau (Austria),
  alt. Drava (Croatia)
177 G6 Drávafok Hungary
188 F2 Dravograd r. Slovenia
174 D3 Drawa r. Pol.
174 D2 Drawno Pol.
174 D2 Drawsko Pol.
174 D2 Drawsko Pomorskie Pol.
151 I2 Drayton Norfolk, England U.K.
151 F3 Drayton Oxfordshire, England U.K.
222 H4 Drayton Valley Alta Can.
175 J2 Drążdżewo Pol.
189 A7 Dréa Alg.
168 D3 Drebber Ger.
171 F4 Drebkau Ger.
160 C2 Drée r. France
147 B4 Dreenagh Rep. of Ireland
170 D3 Dreetz Ger.
150 C3 Drefach Carmarthenshire, Wales U.K.
177 I3 Drégelypalánk Hungary
146 D6 Dreghorn North Ayrshire, Scotland U.K.
169 D5 Dreieich Ger.
178 D3 Dreiherrnspitze mt. Austria
171 C3 Dreileben Ger.
172 A2 Dreis Ger.
172 B3 Dreisam r. Ger.
173 H3 Dreisesselberg mt. Ger.
169 E4 Dreistelzberge hill Ger.
173 F4 Dreitorspitze mt. Ger.
175 K4 Drelów Pol.
168 E1 Drelsdorf Ger.
149 G1 Drem East Lothian, Scotland U.K.
191 I2 Drenchia Italy
188 G3 Drenovci Croatia
197 B1 Drenova Bulg.
170 E2 Drense Ger.
164 E2 Drensteinfurt Ger.
164 F2 Drenthe prov. Neth.
198 C3 Drepano Peloponnisos Greece
227 F4 Dresden Ont. Can.
171 F4 Dresden Ger.
171 F4 Dresden admin. reg. Sachsen Ger.
237 F4 Dresden TN U.S.A.
156 B4 Dreux France
176 F2 Dřevnice r. Czech Rep.
175 I3 Drewitz Ger.
174 G1 Drewnica Pol.
232 E6 Drewryville VA U.S.A.
234 C3 Drexel Hill PA U.S.A.
232 A3 Dreyahna Ger.
232 C4 Dřiteč Czech Rep.
176 D2 Dříteň Czech Rep.
234 B3 Driebergen Neth.
183 G4 Driebes Spain
169 D5 Driedorf Ger.
177 K3 Drienov Slovakia
151 F3 Driffield Gloucestershire, England U.K.
234 C2 Drifton PA U.S.A.
232 D4 Driftwood PA U.S.A.
235 B2 Driggs ID U.S.A.
191 F2 Drimaivka Ukr.
147 D3 Drimmo Rep. of Ireland
146 C5 Drimnin Highland, Scotland U.K.
84 C1 Drimolague Rep. of Ireland
196 C4 Drin r. Albania
188 G3 Drina r. Bos.-Herz./Yugo.
197 B3 Drincea r. Romania
196 C4 Drini i Zi r. Albania
196 D5 Drinit, Gjiri i b. Albania
108 B1 Drinjača r. Albania
232 B6 Drip Rock KY U.S.A.
147 C5 Dripsey Rep. of Ireland
262 O1 Driscoll Island Antarctica
182 D2 Drissa Belarus see Vyerkhnyadzvinsk
182 B2 Duas Igrejas Port.
207 □3b Duaqua-Nkwanta Ghana
176 D1 Dubá Czech Rep.
188 F4 Dubá Saudi Arabia
125 F2 Dubai U.A.E.
240 E3 Dubakella Mountain CA U.S.A.
177 L5 Dubăsari Moldova
177 L5 Dubăsari r. Moldova
136 C2 Dubatovka Ukr.
223 I2 Dubawnt r. Nunavut Can.
223 K2 Dubawnt Lake N.W.T./Nunavut Can.
124 C2 Dubayy U.A.E. see Dubai
124 C2 Dubbagh, Jabal ad mt. Saudi Arabia
83 G3 Dubbo N.S.W. Austr.
206 D5 Dube r. Liberia
136 C2 Dubeczno Pol.
171 D4 Düben Ger.
171 D4 Dübener Heide reg. Ger.
212 E4 Dubenki Rus. Fed.
106 E1 Dulaanhaan Mongolia
237 C5 Dulac LA U.S.A.
106 C1 Dulan Qinghai China
242 □P11 Dulce r. Arg.
241 J3 Dulce NM U.S.A.
183 F3 Dulce r. Spain
190 C2 Dulce Nombre de Culmí Hond.
107 G1 Duldurga Rus. Fed.
147 E3 Duleek Rep. of Ireland
131 O3 Dulgalakh r. Rus. Fed.
197 H4 Dülgopol Bulg.
85 L1 Dulhunty r. Qld Austr.
95 F2 Dulit, Pegunungan mts Sarawak Malaysia
108 D3 Dulia Jiang r. China
117 H4 Dullabchara Assam India
151 H2 Dullingham Cambridgeshire, England U.K.
215 H2 Dullstroom S. Africa
164 C3 Dülmen Ger.
146 C4 Dulnain r. Scotland U.K.
146 C4 Dulnain Bridge Highland, Scotland U.K.
197 H4 Dulovo Bulg.
226 B2 Duluth MN U.S.A.
236 E2 Duluth/Superior airport MN U.S.A.
150 D3 Dulverton Somerset, England U.K.
139 M3 Dulyapino Rus. Fed.
92 B2 Dumaguete Phil.
94 C2 Dumai Sumatera Indon.
129 C3 Dumanlı Turkey
129 B4 Dumanlı Tepe mt. Turkey
83 G2 Dumaresq r. N.S.W. Austr.
237 C5 Dumas TX U.S.A.
146 D6 Dumbarton West Dunbartonshire, Scotland U.K.
215 H2 Dumbe S. Africa
78 □6 Dumbéa New Caledonia
177 I3 Ďumbier mt. Slovakia
146 C5 Dumbuck W.A. Austr.
87 C7 Dumbleyung, Lake salt flat W.A. Austr.
177 L6 Dumbrava Romania
177 L3 Dumbrăveni Romania
197 H3 Dumbrăveni Romania
197 G3 Dumbrăviţa Romania
177 K6 Dumbrăviţa Romania
182 A1 Dumbría Spain
177 H4 Dum Duma Assam India
197 H2 Dumeşti Romania
197 I2 Dumeşti Romania
136 D2 Dumfries and Galloway admin. div. Scotland U.K.
136 D2 Dumfries Dumfries and Galloway, Scotland U.K.
197 G2 Dumitra Romania
117 F4 Dumka Bihar India
129 B3 Dumlu Turkey
129 B3 Dumlu Daği mt. Turkey
128 A1 Dumlupınar Turkey
114 D2 Dummagudem Andhra Prad. India
151 H2 Dümmer l. Ger.
224 C4 Dumoine r. Que. Can.
263 J2 Dumont d'Urville research stn Antarctica
169 B5 Dümpelfeld Ger.
117 H4 Dumra Bihar India
203 F2 Dumyât Egypt
126 C5 Dumyât governorate Egypt
169 F4 Dün ridge Ger.
188 D3 Duna r. Hungary
  alt. Donau (Austria/Germany),
  alt. Dunaj (Slovakia),
  alt. Dunărea (Romania),
  conv. Danube
177 J3 Dunaalmás Hungary
138 F4 Dünaburg Latvia see Daugavpils
177 H5 Dunabogdány Hungary
177 H5 Dunaföldvár Hungary
177 I4 Dunaharaszti Hungary
188 F2 Dunaj r. Slovakia
  alt. Donau (Austria/Germany),
  alt. Duna (Hungary),
  alt. Dunărea (Romania),
  conv. Danube
175 I5 Dunajec r. Slovakia
177 I4 Dunajská Lužná Slovakia
177 G4 Dunajská Streda Slovakia
177 H4 Dunakeszi Hungary
176 G4 Dunakiliti Hungary
83 F7 Dunalley Tas. Austr.
83 G2 Dunapataj Hungary
197 I3 Dunărea r. Romania
  alt. Donau (Austria/Germany),
  alt. Duna (Hungary),
  alt. Dunaj (Slovakia),
  conv. Danube
197 I3 Dunării, Delta Romania
177 H5 Dunaszeg Hungary
177 H5 Dunaszekcső Hungary
177 H5 Dunaszentgyörgy Hungary
176 G4 Dunaszentmiklós Hungary
177 H5 Dunatetétlen Hungary
177 H5 Dunaújváros Hungary
191 I4 Dunav r. Yugo.
  alt. Donau (Austria/Germany),
  alt. Duna (Hungary),
  alt. Dunaj (Slovakia),
  conv. Danube
177 H5 Dunavecse Hungary
197 H4 Dunavtsi Bulg.
136 C3 Dunayivtsi Khmel'nyts'ka Oblast' Ukr.
136 C3 Dunayivtsi Khmel'nyts'ka Oblast' Ukr.
223 J4 Dunblane Man. Can.
221 J5 Dunblane Stirling, Scotland U.K.
147 E4 Dunboyne Rep. of Ireland
147 C4 Dunbrody Abbey Rep. of Ireland
108 D1 Du He r. China
163 B3 Duhort-Bachen France
202 C4 Duhūn Tārsū mts Chad/Libya
85 F2 Duifken Point Qld Austr.
117 I4 Duijen Neth.
213 B4 Duiwelskloof S. Africa
215 I2 Duiwelskloof S. Africa
246 □ Duncansby Jamaica
146 E2 Duncansby Head hd Scotland U.K.
147 F4 Duncannon Rep. of Ireland
234 A2 Duncannon PA U.S.A.
147 D4 Duncormick Rep. of Ireland
115 G4 Duncan Passage Andaman & Nicobar Is India
246 □ Duncans Jamaica
146 F2 Duncansby Head hd Scotland U.K.

131 O3 Dulgalakh r. Rus. Fed.
197 H4 Dulbyiv Ukr.
129 E2 Dubki Rus. Fed.
226 D1 Dublin Ont. Can.
147 E3 Dublin Rep. of Ireland
147 E3 Dublin county Rep. of Ireland
233 D5 Dublin GA U.S.A.
234 C2 Dublin MD U.S.A.
232 C6 Dublin VA U.S.A.
147 D2 Dublin Northern Ireland U.K.
147 E3 Dublin Bay Rep. of Ireland
136 D2 Dubliany L'viv.s'ka Oblast' Ukr.
136 D3 Dubliany L'viv.s'ka Oblast' Ukr.
138 F3 Dubna r. Latvia
139 K3 Dubna Moskovskaya Oblast' Rus. Fed.
139 K4 Dubna Tul'skaya Oblast' Rus. Fed.
176 G3 Dubňany Czech Rep.
176 D3 Dubné Czech Rep.
177 H3 Dubnica nad Váhom Slovakia
136 C2 Dubno Ukr.
232 D4 Du Bois PA U.S.A.
238 E3 Dubois WY U.S.A.
Dubossary Moldova see Dubăsari
136 B3 Dubove Ukr.
177 J2 Dubovica Slovakia
136 E3 Dubovica Ukr.
135 I6 Dubovka Volgogradskaya Oblast' Rus. Fed.
Dubovo Moldova see Dubău
139 M4 Dubovskoye Rus. Fed.
135 H7 Dubovskoye Rus. Fed.
137 G2 Dubov''yazivka Ukr.
137 F3 Dübbar Daği mt. Azer.
178 G5 Dubrava Croatia
179 H5 Dubrava Croatia
179 I3 Dubravica Croatia
179 I3 Dubrávy Slovakia
206 B4 Dubréka Guinea
Dubris Kent, England U.K. see Dover
179 H5 Dubrovčki Croatia
139 L4 Dubrovichi Rus. Fed.
139 I5 Dubrovka Rus. Fed.
188 G4 Dubrovnik Croatia
121 G1 Dubrovnoye Kazakh.
175 L6 Dubrovytsya Ukr.
136 D2 Dubrovytsya Rivnens'ka Oblast' Ukr.
136 D2 Dubrowna Belarus
139 H4 Dubrowna Belarus
121 J4 Dubun Kazakh.
138 D4 Dubysa r. Lith.
79 □3 Duc de Gloucester, Îles du is Fr. Polynesia
158 B2 Ducey France
109 F2 Duchang Jiangxi China
170 C2 Ducherow Ger.
241 L1 Duchesne UT U.S.A.
241 M1 Duchesne r. UT U.S.A.
84 D4 Duchess Qld Austr.
223 I5 Duchess Alta Can.
176 D1 Duchcov Czech Rep.
79 I5 Ducie r. Qld Austr.
267 K7 Ducie Island Pitcairn Is
Ducie Island Kiribati see McKean
223 K4 Duck r. TN U.S.A.
223 K4 Duck Bay Man. Can.
161 H3 Duck Creek r. W.A. Austr.
223 J4 Duck Lake Sask. Can.
161 H3 Duck End Essex, England U.K.
241 J3 Duckwall Mountain CA U.S.A.
241 J2 Duckwater NV U.S.A.
241 J2 Duckwater Peak NV U.S.A.
114 C2 Duda r. India
115 B3 Dudareva Rus. Fed.
250 C3 Duda r. Col.
137 G4 Dudchany Ukr.
149 G2 Duddo Northumberland, England U.K.
147 E3 Duddon r. England U.K.
165 F3 Dudelange Lux.
169 B6 Dudeldorf Ger.
169 F4 Duderstadt Ger.
117 F4 Dudhi Uttar Prad. India
117 H3 Dudhnai Assam India
117 H3 Dudhnoi Assam India
169 B5 Düdinghausen Ger.
190 C2 Düdingen Switz.
130 D3 Dudinka Rus. Fed.
150 E2 Dudley West Midlands, England U.K.
235 G3 Dudley PA U.S.A.
169 B6 Dudweiler Ger.
241 L5 Dudleyville AZ U.S.A.
114 C2 Dudna r. India
215 E3 Dudu Rajasthan India
188 F2 Dudváh r. Slovakia
146 F4 Dudwick, Hill of hill Scotland U.K.
206 D5 Duékoué Côte d'Ivoire
129 E2 Duen, Bukit vol. Indon.
183 F3 Dueñas Spain
254 C2 Dueré Brazil
182 B2 Duerna r. Spain
182 D3 Duero r. Spain
  alt. Douro (Portugal)
191 J3 Duelfe Belgium
165 D3 Duffel Belgium
238 D3 Duffer Peak NV U.S.A.
151 F2 Duffield Derbyshire, England U.K.
232 B5 Duffield VA U.S.A.
78 □6 Duff Islands Solomon Is
146 E4 Dufftown Moray, Scotland U.K.
190 C3 Dufourspitze mt. Italy/Switz.
223 I5 Dufrost Man. Can.
136 D3 Dunayivtsi Khmel'nyts'ka Oblast' Ukr.
136 C3 Dunayivtsi Khmel'nyts'ka Oblast' Ukr.
223 I5 Dunbar Qld Austr.
149 G1 Dunbar East Lothian, Scotland U.K.
238 E3 Dunbar WI U.S.A.
146 E5 Dunbeath Highland, Scotland U.K.
146 E2 Dunblane Stirling, Scotland U.K.
147 E4 Dunboyne Rep. of Ireland
147 B.C. Can.
147 E2 Duncan B.C. Can.
115 G4 Duncan Passage Andaman & Nicobar Is India
241 M5 Duncan AZ U.S.A.
237 D5 Duncan OK U.S.A.
221 J3 Duncan r. B.C. Can.
114 C2 Duncan, Cape Nunavut Can.
224 D2 Duncan, Lake Que. Can.
227 H3 Duncannon Rep. of Ireland
236 A2 Duncan Town Bahamas
151 F2 Dunchurch Warwickshire, England U.K.
146 F5 Duncrub hill Scotland U.K.
138 F3 Dundaga Latvia
146 C5 Dun da Ghaoithe hill Scotland U.K.
147 E3 Dundalk Rep. of Ireland
234 B3 Dundalk MD U.S.A.
147 E3 Dundalk Bay Rep. of Ireland
224 E4 Dundas Ont. Can.
223 F2 Dundas, Lake salt flat W.A. Austr.
225 F2 Dundas Island B.C. Can.
147 F3 Dundas Strait N.T. Austr.
107 F2 Dundbürd Mongolia
108 C2 Dun Dealgan Rep. of Ireland see Dundalk
215 H3 Dundee S. Africa
146 E5 Dundee Dundee, Scotland U.K.
146 E5 Dundee admin. div. Scotland U.K.
235 G2 Dundee NY U.S.A.
232 C4 Dundee OH U.S.A.
106 D1 Dundgovĭ prov. Mongolia
107 H3 Dund Hot Nei Mongol China
106 C2 Dund-Us Mongolia
213 B4 Dundonald Rep. of Ireland
84 B4 Dundoo Qld Austr.
147 D3 Dundrennan Dumfries and Galloway, Scotland U.K.

131 O3 Dulgalakh r. Rus. Fed.
197 H4 Dundrum Dublin Rep. of Ireland
147 C4 Dundrum Tipperary Rep. of Ireland
147 F2 Dundrum Northern Ireland U.K.
147 F2 Dundrum Bay Northern Ireland U.K.
116 E4 Dundwa Range mts India/Nepal
146 E6 Duneaton Water r. Scotland U.K.
81 C6 Dunedin South I. N.Z.
231 D6 Dunedin FL U.S.A.
83 G3 Dunedoo N.S.W. Austr.
149 F5 Dunes France
148 B2 Dunfanaghy Rep. of Ireland
146 E5 Dunfermline Fife, Scotland U.K.
147 E2 Dungannon Northern Ireland U.K.
Dún Garbhán Waterford Rep. of Ireland see Dungarvan
116 C3 Dungargarh Rajasthan India
116 C5 Dungarpur Rajasthan India
147 D4 Dungarvan Kilkenny Rep. of Ireland
147 D4 Dungarvan Waterford Rep. of Ireland
151 H4 Dungeness hd England U.K.
169 C5 Düngenheim Ger.
147 C2 Dungiven Northern Ireland U.K.
147 C2 Dunglow Rep. of Ireland
83 G3 Dungog N.S.W. Austr.
147 C5 Dungourney Rep. of Ireland
208 F4 Dungu Dem. Rep. Congo
94 C1 Dungun Malaysia
149 I4 Dunholme Lincolnshire, England U.K.
Dunhou Jiangxi China see Ji'an
100 C1 Dunhua Jilin China
110 F3 Dunhuang Gansu China
161 C3 Dunières France
85 G5 Dunkeld Qld Austr.
83 C3 Dunkeld Vic. Austr.
146 E5 Dunkeld Perth and Kinross, Scotland U.K.
147 C3 Dunkellin r. Rep. of Ireland
179 G2 Dunkelsteiner Wald for. Austria
156 C1 Dunkerque France
147 A4 Dunkerrin Rep. of Ireland
150 D3 Dunkery Beacon hill England U.K.
Dunkirk France see Dunkerque
151 H3 Dunkirk Kent, England U.K.
232 D3 Dunkirk NY U.S.A.
232 A4 Dunkirk OH U.S.A.
206 E5 Dunkwa Ghana
147 D4 Dún Laoghaire Rep. of Ireland
147 E3 Dunlavin Rep. of Ireland
147 E3 Dunleer Rep. of Ireland
162 D2 Dun-le-Palestel France
160 C1 Dun-les-Places France
148 B2 Dunlewy Rep. of Ireland
147 E1 Dunloy Northern Ireland U.K.
145 G2 Dunluce tourist site Northern Ireland U.K.
177 H4 Dunaalmás Hungary
224 E4 Dunmanus Rep. of Ireland
147 B5 Dunmanus Bay Rep. of Ireland
147 B5 Dunmanway Rep. of Ireland
147 C3 Dunmore Rep. of Ireland
234 C1 Dunmore PA U.S.A.
232 D5 Dunmore WV U.S.A.
147 C5 Dunmore East Rep. of Ireland
246 C1 Dunmore Town Eleuthera Bahamas
147 E2 Dunmurry Northern Ireland U.K.
231 E5 Dunn NC U.S.A.
147 D2 Dunnamanagh Northern Ireland U.K.
147 D1 Dunnellon FL U.S.A.
146 E5 Dunnet Highland, Scotland U.K.
240 C2 Dunnigan CA U.S.A.
236 D3 Dunning NE U.S.A.
149 I4 Dunnington York, England U.K.
87 E2 Dunns Range hills W.A. Austr.
227 H4 Dunnville Ont. Can.
83 D3 Dunolly Vic. Austr.
146 C5 Dunoon Argyll and Bute, Scotland U.K.
147 A4 Dunquin Rep. of Ireland
146 E6 Dun Rig hill Scotland U.K.
146 E6 Duns Scottish Borders, Scotland U.K.
81 C6 Dunsandel South I. N.Z.
87 B7 Dunsborough W.A. Austr.
226 B5 Dunseith ND U.S.A. (see Dumseith)
240 C1 Dunsmuir CA U.S.A.
151 G3 Dunstable Bedfordshire, England U.K.
81 B6 Dunstan Mountains South I. N.Z.
150 D3 Dunster Somerset, England U.K.
160 A2 Dun-sur-Auron France
157 F3 Dun-sur-Meuse France
81 C6 Duntroon South I. N.Z.
168 C2 Dunum Ger.
146 D6 Dunure South Ayrshire, Scotland U.K.
150 C4 Dunvant Swansea, Wales U.K.
146 B4 Dunvegan Highland, Scotland U.K.
146 B4 Dunvegan, Loch b. Scotland U.K.
84 D3 Dunwich Qld Austr.
146 A4 Dunyapur Pak.
107 J1 Duobukur r. China
107 H3 Duolun Nei Mongol China
108 A2 Duolun Nei Mongol China
109 D3 Dupang Ling mts China
227 J2 Duparquet Que. Can.
179 H4 Duplica Slovenia
197 F4 Dupnitsa Bulg.
236 C2 Dupree SD U.S.A.
185 H4 Dupuy, Cape W.A. Austr.
Duque de Bragança Angola see Calandula
256 D3 Duque de Caxias Brazil
259 B8 Duque de York, Isla i. Chile
138 C3 Durāji Latvia
188 D3 Durandarra r. Bulg.
210 C2 Dura r. Eth.
204 E3 Dūrā West Bank
191 H2 Dura, Cima mt. Italy
124 D3 Durac Rus. Fed.
32 E3 Durack r. W.A. Austr.
86 E3 Durack Range hills W.A. Austr.
As Sālihīyah
126 E4 Durağan Turkey
199 L3 Durak Turkey
199 J5 Durana Spain
163 C4 Durance r. France
161 D4 Durance r. France
227 F4 Durand MI U.S.A.
226 B3 Durand WI U.S.A.
185 F2 Durana r. Spain
241 J5 Durango state Mex.
244 B1 Durango Durango Mex.
244 B1 Durango state Mex.
183 E1 Durango Spain
241 J3 Durango CO U.S.A.
244 B2 Durango, Sierra de mts Mex.
197 I4 Duranulak Bulg.
191 J2 Duranno, Monte mt. Italy
237 F5 Durant MS U.S.A.
237 D5 Durant OK U.S.A.
163 C4 Duras France
183 F3 Duratón r. Spain

Duravel to Ejeda
301

163 D4 Duravel France
261 I3 Durazno Uru.
261 I3 Durazno dept Uru.
Durazzo Albania see Durrës
172 C3 Durbach Ger.
163 D5 Durban France
215 H3 Durban S. Africa
161 A6 Durban-Corbières France
214 B5 Durbanville S. Africa
172 C3 Dürbheim Ger.
232 D5 Durbin WV U.S.A.
157 G4 Durbion r. France
165 E4 Durbuy Belgium
185 G4 Dúrcal Spain
185 G4 Dúrcal r. Spain
177 H2 Ďurčiná Slovakia
160 A2 Durdat-Larequille France
159 G2 Durdent r. France
188 F2 Đurđevac Croatia
110 E2 Düre Xinjiang China
169 B5 Düren Ger.
122 D3 Dūren Iran
161 B5 Durfort France
116 E5 Durg Madh. Prad. India
117 G4 Durgapur Bangl.
117 F5 Durgapur W. Bengal India
227 G3 Durham Ont. Can.
149 H3 Durham Durham, England U.K.
149 G3 Durham admin. div. England U.K.
240 G2 Durham CA U.S.A.
235 F1 Durham CT U.S.A.
231 E5 Durham NC U.S.A.
233 □H3 Durham NH U.S.A.
233 □J1 Durham Bridge N.B. Can.
85 E5 Durham Downs Qld Austr.
94 C2 Duri Sumatera Indon.
146 E6 Durisdeer Dumfries and Galloway, Scotland U.K.
Durlas Rep. of Ireland see Thurles
136 E4 Durleşti Moldova
156 D1 Durme r. Belgium
172 D3 Dürmentingen Ger.
172 C3 Durmersheim Ger.
196 D4 Durmitor mt. Yugo.
146 D3 Durness Highland, Scotland U.K.
179 H2 Dürnkrut Austria
Durocortorum France see Reims
85 G5 Durong South Qld Austr.
Durostorum Bulg. see Silistra
Durovernum Kent, England U.K. see Canterbury
196 D5 Durrës Albania
84 E5 Durrie Qld Austr.
173 E3 Dürrlauingen Ger.
171 F4 Dürröhrsdorf-Dittersbach Ger.
147 D4 Durrow Rep. of Ireland
173 E2 Dürrwangen Ger.
147 A5 Dursey Island Rep. of Ireland
150 E3 Dursley Gloucestershire, England U.K.
199 F2 Dursunbey Turkey
159 F4 Durtal France
Duru Guizhou China see Wuchuan
208 F4 Duru r. Dem. Rep. Congo
183 H3 Duruelo de la Sierra Spain
122 E3 Dūruh Iran
210 E2 Durukhsi Somalia
128 C3 Durūz, Jabal ad mt. Syria
80 D4 D'Urville Island South I. N.Z.
234 C1 Duryea PA U.S.A.
146 □G1 Dury Voe inlet Scotland U.K.
138 E4 Dusetos Lith.
122 D2 Dushak Turkm.
108 C3 Dushan Guizhou China
123 G2 Dushanbe Tajik.
110 D2 Dushanzi Xinjiang China
129 D2 Dushet'i Georgia
227 I5 Dushore PA U.S.A.
138 D4 Dusia l. Lith.
177 H5 Dusnok Hungary
174 G2 Dusocin Pol.
86 F2 Dussejour, Cape W.A. Austr.
169 B4 Düsseldorf Ger.
169 B4 Düsseldorf admin. reg. Nordrhein-Westfalen Ger.
164 D3 Dussen Neth.
172 D3 Dußlingen Ger.
171 D4 Düßnitz Ger.
123 G2 Dusti Tajik.
121 G4 Dustlik Uzbek.
238 C2 Dusty WA U.S.A.
174 E3 Duszniki Pol.
174 E5 Duszniki-Zdrój Pol.
Dutch East Indies country Asia see Indonesia
234 E1 Dutchess County county NY U.S.A.
Dutch Guiana country S. America see Suriname
220 B4 Dutch Harbor AK U.S.A.
241 K1 Dutch Mountain UT U.S.A.
Dutch New Guinea prov. Indon. see Irian Jaya
Dutch West Indies terr. West Indies see Netherlands Antilles
179 E5 Dutovlje Slovenia
207 H4 Dutsan-Wai Nigeria
207 H4 Dutse Nigeria
207 G3 Dutsin-Ma Nigeria
85 E4 Dutton r. Qld Austr.
227 G4 Dutton Ont. Can.
238 E2 Dutton MT U.S.A.
82 D2 Dutton, Lake salt flat S.A. Austr.
241 K2 Dutton, Mount UT U.S.A.
223 J5 Duval Sask. Can.
134 L5 Duvan Rus. Fed.
137 J3 Duvanka r. Ukr.
Duvannyy Azer. see Qobustan
140 K3 Duved Sweden
246 E3 Duvergé Dom. Rep.
Duvno Bos.-Herz. see Tomislavgrad
127 G3 Duwin Iraq
108 C3 Duyun Guizhou China
199 G1 Düzce Turkey
129 D3 Düz Cırdaxan Azer.
Duzdab Iran see Zāhedān
129 A3 Düzköy Turkey
136 D1 Dvarets Belarus
197 G4 Dve Mogili Bulg.
Dvinsk Latvia see Daugavpils
134 G2 Dvinskaya Guba g. Rus. Fed.
139 H3 Dvin'ye, Ozero l. Rus. Fed.
136 D2 Dvirets' Ukr.
175 M5 Dvirtsi Ukr.
188 F3 Dvor Croatia
177 G2 Dvorce Czech Rep.
137 I3 Dvorichna Ukr.
177 H4 Dvory nad Žitavou Slovakia
176 E1 Dvůr Králové Czech Rep.
211 B8 Dwangwa Malawi
116 B5 Dwarka Gujarat India
212 E5 Dwarsberg S. Africa
87 C7 Dwellingup W.A. Austr.
215 H4 Dweshula S. Africa
226 C5 Dwight IL U.S.A.
175 J5 Dwikozy Pol.
164 F2 Dwingeloo Neth.
214 C5 Dwyka S. Africa
214 C5 Dwyka r. S. Africa
137 K3 D'yachenkovo Rus. Fed.
134 H4 D'yakonovo Rus. Fed.
137 J4 Dyakove Ukr.
148 C3 Dyan Northern Ireland U.K.
123 E2 Dyanev Turkm.
197 H4 Dyankovo Bulg.
139 J5 Dyat'kovo Rus. Fed.
234 C1 Dyberry PA U.S.A.
234 C1 Dyberry Creek r. PA U.S.A.
146 F4 Dyce Aberdeen, Scotland U.K.
175 K6 Dydnia Pol.
221 L3 Dyer, Cape Nunavut Can.
227 G3 Dyer Bay Ont. Can.
262 T2 Dyer Plateau Antarctica
237 F4 Dyersburg TN U.S.A.
81 E4 Dyeville North I. N.Z.
Dyffryn Isle of Anglesey, Wales U.K. see Valley
150 D2 Dyfi r. Wales U.K.
174 D1 Dygowo Pol.
167 H4 Dyje r. Austria/Czech Rep.
137 H3 Dykan'ka Ukr.
146 E4 Dyke Moray, Scotland U.K.
146 E5 Dykehead Angus, Scotland U.K.
129 C2 Dykh-Tau, Gora mt. Rus. Fed.
165 D4 Dyle r. Belgium
176 B2 Dyleň hill Czech Rep.
175 J2 Dylewo Pol.
175 H2 Dylewska Góra hill Pol.
129 E2 Dylym Rus. Fed.
151 H3 Dymchurch Kent, England U.K.
136 F2 Dymer Ukr.
150 E3 Dymock Gloucestershire, England U.K.
138 G1 Dymovka r. Rus. Fed.
137 I3 Dymytrov Ukr.
137 G3 Dymytrove Ukr.
142 C1 Dyna mt. Norway
83 F2 Dynevor Downs Qld Austr.
175 K6 Dynów Pol.
160 C2 Dyo France
215 G4 Dyoki S. Africa
Dyrrhachium Albania see Durrës
85 G4 Dysart Qld Austr.
150 D1 Dyserth Denbighshire, Wales U.K.
173 H2 Dýšina Czech Rep.
138 F4 Dysna r. Lith.
138 F4 Dysnų ežeras l. Lith.
214 D5 Dysselsdorp S. Africa
198 B2 Dytiki Ellas admin. reg. Greece
198 B1 Dytiki Makedonia admin. reg. Greece
197 H4 Dyulino Bulg.
129 E3 Dyul'tydag, Gora mt. Rus. Fed.
134 K5 Dyurtyuli Rus. Fed.
136 E5 Dyviziya Ukr.
175 I2 Dywity Pol.
106 D2 Dzaanhushuu Mongolia
106 C2 Dzag Gol r. Mongolia
217 □3b Dzaoudzi Mayotte
Dzaudzhikau Rus. Fed. see Vladikavkaz
106 B1 Dzavhan prov. Mongolia
106 B1 Dzavhan Gol r. Mongolia
176 C1 Džbán mts Czech Rep.
106 D2 Dzegstey Mongolia
136 D3 Dzelentsi Ukr.
106 E1 Dzelter Mongolia
Dzerzhinsk Belarus see Dzyarzhynsk
134 H4 Dzerzhinsk Rus. Fed.
Dzerzhinskoye Kazakh. see Kabanbay
137 I3 Dzerzhyns'k Ukr.
136 D2 Dzerzhyns'k Ukr.
100 D1 Dzhagdy, Khrebet mts Rus. Fed.
Dzhaksy Kazakh. see Zhaksy
120 F3 Dzhalagash Kazakh.
Dzhalalabad Azer. see Cälilabad
Dzhalal-Abad Kyrg. see Jalal-Abad
Dzhalal-Abadskaya Oblast' admin. div. Kyrg. see Jalal-Abad
134 K5 Dzhalil' Rus. Fed.
100 B1 Dzhalinda Rus. Fed.
Dzhaltyr Kazakh. see Zhaltyr
Dzhambeyty Zapadnyy Kazakhstan Kazakh. see Zhympity
Dzhambul Zhambylskaya Oblast' Kazakh. see Taraz
Dzhambulskaya Oblast' admin. div. Kazakh. see Zhambylskaya Oblast'
Dzhandari Georgia see Jandari
122 C1 Dzhanga Turkm.
120 B2 Dzhangala Kazakh.
120 E4 Dzhangel'dy Uzbek.
Dzhankel'dy Uzbek. see Dzhangel'dy
137 H5 Dzhankoy Ukr.
121 I3 Dzhansugurov Kazakh.
120 A2 Dzhanybek Kazakh.
Dzhaparidze Georgia see Jap'aridze
Dzharkent Kazakh. see Zharkent
121 F5 Dzharkurgan Uzbek.
131 O3 Dzhebariki-Khaya Rus. Fed.
197 G5 Dzhebel Bulg.
122 C2 Dzhebel Turkm.
Dzhergalan Kyrg. see Jyrgalang
Dzhermuk Armenia see Jermuk
Dzhetygara Kazakh. see Zhitikara
120 F4 Dzhetymtau, Gory hills Uzbek.
Dzhetysay Kazakh. see Zhetysay
120 E5 Dzheykhun Turkm.
Dzhezdy Kazakh. see Zhezdy
Dzhezkazgan Karagandinskaya Oblast' Kazakh. see Zhezkazgan
106 E1 Dzhida Rus. Fed.
106 E1 Dzhida r. Rus. Fed.
106 D1 Dzhidinskiy, Khrebet mts Mongolia/Rus. Fed.
Dzhingil'dy Uzbek. see Dzhangel'dy
Dzhirgatal' Tajik. see Jirgatol
121 F4 Dzhizak Uzbek.
Dzhizak Oblast admin. div. Uzbek. see Dzhizakskaya Oblast'
121 F4 Dzhizakskaya Oblast' admin. div. Uzbek.
Dzhokhar Ghala Rus. Fed. see Groznyy
Dzhordzhiashvili Georgia see Jorjiashvili
135 G7 Dzhubga Rus. Fed.
131 O4 Dzhugdzhur, Khrebet mts Rus. Fed.
Dzhul'fa Azer. see Culfa
136 E3 Dzhulynka Ukr.
121 F5 Dzhuma Uzbek.
121 I3 Dzhungarskiy Alatau, Khrebet mts China/Kazakh.
129 E2 Dzhurmut r. Rus. Fed.
Dzhurun Kazakh. see Zhuryn
136 E3 Dzhuryn Ukr.
120 F3 Dzhusaly Kzyl-Ordinskaya Oblast' Kazakh.
175 K3 Dziadkowice Pol.
174 F4 Dziadowa Kłoda Pol.
175 H2 Działdówka r. Pol.
175 I2 Działdowo Pol.
175 I5 Działoszyce Pol.
174 G4 Działoszyn Pol.
175 H2 Działyń Pol.
243 H5 Dzibalchén Mex.
174 F1 Dziemiany Pol.
174 G5 Dziergowice Pol.
175 I3 Dzierzążnia Pol.
175 H2 Dzierzgoń Pol.
175 I2 Dzierzgowo Pol.
174 E5 Dzierżoniów Pol.
175 J1 Dzietrzychowo Pol.
174 F3 Dziewierzewo Pol.
243 H4 Dzilam de Bravo Mex.
138 G4 Dzisna Belarus
243 H4 Dzitás Mex.
138 E5 Dzitva r. Belarus
136 C2 Dzivin Belarus
174 C2 Dziwna r. Pol.
207 F5 Dzodze Ghana
107 E2 Dzogsool Mongolia
106 C1 Dzöölön Mongolia
129 D3 Dzoraget r. Armenia
Dzungarian Basin China see Junggar Pendi
106 B1 Dzur Mongolia
107 F2 Dzüünbayan Mongolia
106 E2 Dzuunmod Mongolia
106 B2 Dzüyl Mongolia
175 I2 Dźwierzuty Pol.
174 C1 Dzwinów Pol.
175 K5 Dzwola Pol.
175 H5 Dzwonowice Pol.
138 F5 Dzyaniskavichy Belarus
139 I5 Dzyarazhnya r. Belarus
138 F5 Dzyarzhynsk Belarus
138 E5 Dzyatlava Belarus
136 D1 Dzyatlavichy Belarus
138 F4 Dzyerkawshchyna Belarus

E

236 C4 Eads CO U.S.A.
241 M4 Eagar AZ U.S.A.
225 J2 Eagle r. Nfld. Can.
220 D3 Eagle AK U.S.A.
239 F4 Eagle CO U.S.A.
234 C2 Eagle PA U.S.A.
236 C2 Eagle Butte SD U.S.A.
238 C2 Eagle Cap mt. OR U.S.A.
240 I4 Eagle Crags mt. CA U.S.A.
223 J4 Eagle Creek r. Sask. Can.
233 □I1 Eagle Lake ME U.S.A.
241 J5 Eagle Mountain CA U.S.A.
226 B2 Eagle Mountain hill MN U.S.A.
237 C6 Eagle Pass TX U.S.A.
259 F9 Eagle Passage Falkland Is
239 F6 Eagle Peak TX U.S.A.
220 E3 Eagle Plain Y.T. Can.
226 C2 Eagle River MI U.S.A.
226 C3 Eagle River WI U.S.A.
232 D6 Eagle Rock VA U.S.A.
149 H3 Eaglescliffe Stockton-on-Tees, England U.K.
146 E6 Eaglesfield Dumfries and Galloway, Scotland U.K.
222 G4 Eaglesham Alta Can.
146 D6 Eaglesham East Renfrewshire, Scotland U.K.
241 K5 Eagle Tail Mountains AZ U.S.A.
234 C2 Eagleville PA U.S.A.
151 G3 Ealing Greater London, England U.K.
Eap i. Micronesia see Yap
87 D5 Earaheedy W.A. Austr.
149 G4 Earby Lancashire, England U.K.
150 D2 Eardisley Herefordshire, England U.K.
223 M5 Ear Falls Ont. Can.
151 H2 Earith Cambridgeshire, England U.K.
240 H4 Earlimart CA U.S.A.
81 A6 Earl Mountains South I. N.Z.
151 G2 Earls Barton Northamptonshire, England U.K.
151 H3 Earls Colne Essex, England U.K.
151 F2 Earl Shilton Leicestershire, England U.K.
146 D5 Earl's Seat hill Scotland U.K.
146 F6 Earlston Scottish Borders, Scotland U.K.
151 I2 Earl Stonham Suffolk, England U.K.
227 H2 Earlton Ont. Can.
146 E5 Earn r. Scotland U.K.
81 B6 Earnscleugh South I. N.Z.
81 B6 Earnslaw, Mount South I. N.Z.
241 J4 Earp CA U.S.A.
146 A5 Earsairidh Western Isles, Scotland U.K.
237 C5 Earth TX U.S.A.
146 C5 Easdale Argyll and Bute, Scotland U.K.
151 G4 Easebourne West Sussex, England U.K.
149 H3 Easington Durham, England U.K.
149 J4 Easington East Riding of Yorkshire, England U.K.
149 H3 Easingwold North Yorkshire, England U.K.
147 C2 Easky Rep. of Ireland
231 D5 Easley SC U.S.A.
87 D6 East, Mount hill W.A. Austr.
84 C2 East Alligator r. N.T. Austr.
263 H1 East Antarctica reg. Antarctica
233 F4 East Ararat PA U.S.A.
232 D3 East Aurora NY U.S.A.
146 D6 East Ayrshire admin. div. Scotland U.K.
84 B2 East Baines r. N.T. Austr.
234 C2 East Bangor PA U.S.A.
East Bengal country Asia see Bangladesh
151 I3 East Bergholt Suffolk, England U.K.
235 F1 East Berlin CT U.S.A.
234 B3 East Berlin PA U.S.A.
234 B1 East Berwick PA U.S.A.
81 E4 Eastbourne North I. N.Z.
151 H4 Eastbourne East Sussex, England U.K.
232 D4 East Brady PA U.S.A.
233 F4 East Branch NY U.S.A.
151 G2 East Bridgford Nottinghamshire, England U.K.
149 I4 Eastburn East Riding of Yorkshire, England U.K.
246 E2 East Caicos i. Turks and Caicos Is
80 G2 East Cape North I. N.Z.
241 L2 East Carbon City UT U.S.A.
266 E5 East Caroline Basin sea feature N. Pacific Ocean
226 D5 East Chicago IN U.S.A.
99 M5 East China Sea N. Pacific Ocean
80 E2 East Coast Bays North I. N.Z.
150 E4 East Coker Somerset, England U.K.
223 H5 East Coulee Alta Can.
151 H4 East Dean East Sussex, England U.K.
151 H2 East Dereham Norfolk, England U.K.
146 D6 East Dunbartonshire admin. div. Scotland U.K.
223 I5 Eastend Sask. Can.
87 B6 Easter Group is W.A. Austr.
Easter Island S. Pacific Ocean see Pascua, Isla de
206 E5 Eastern admin. reg. Ghana
210 C5 Eastern prov. Kenya
206 C4 Eastern prov. Sierra Leone
211 A8 Eastern prov. Zambia
215 F4 Eastern Cape prov. S. Africa
85 E4 Eastern Creek r. Qld Austr.
Eastern Desert Egypt see Şaḩara el Sharqîya
210 B3 Eastern Equatoria state Sudan
114 C4 Eastern Ghats mts India
Eastern Lesser Sunda Islands prov. Indon. see Nusa Tenggara Timur
Eastern Samoa terr. S. Pacific Ocean see American Samoa
Eastern Sayan Mountains Rus. Fed. see Vostochnyy Sayan
Eastern Taurus plat. Turkey see Güneydoğu Toroslar
Eastern Transvaal prov. S. Africa see Mpumalanga
146 □G1 Easter Quarff Shetland, Scotland U.K.
146 D4 Easter Ross reg. Scotland U.K.
223 L4 Easterville Man. Can.
259 F9 East Falkland i. Falkland Is
233 H4 East Falmouth MA U.S.A.
149 J4 East Fen reg. England U.K.
149 I3 Eastfield North Yorkshire, England U.K.
East Flanders prov. Belgium see Oost-Vlaanderen
East Frisian Islands Ger. see Ostfriesische Inseln
149 G3 Eastgate Durham, England U.K.
240 I2 Eastgate NV U.S.A.
236 D2 East Grand Forks MN U.S.A.
226 E4 East Grand Rapids MI U.S.A.
234 C2 East Greenville PA U.S.A.
151 G3 East Grinstead West Sussex, England U.K.
235 F1 East Haddam CT U.S.A.
235 F1 East Hampton CT U.S.A.
233 G3 Easthampton MA U.S.A.
235 F2 East Hampton NY U.S.A.
151 F3 East Hanney Oxfordshire, England U.K.
151 H2 East Harling Norfolk, England U.K.
235 F1 East Hartford CT U.S.A.
235 F1 East Haven CT U.S.A.
85 E3 East Haydon Qld Austr.
233 □I2 East Holden ME U.S.A.
151 G3 East Horsley Surrey, England U.K.
150 E3 East Huntspill Somerset, England U.K.
265 K6 East Indiaman Ridge sea feature Indian Ocean
233 G3 East Jamaica VT U.S.A.
226 E3 East Jordan MI U.S.A.
East Kazakhstan Oblast admin. div. Kazakh. see Vostochnyy Kazakhstan
149 J4 East Keal Lincolnshire, England U.K.
146 D6 East Kilbride South Lanarkshire, Scotland U.K.
226 D3 East Lake MI U.S.A.
237 D5 Eastland TX U.S.A.
226 E4 East Lansing MI U.S.A.
151 F4 Eastleigh Hampshire, England U.K.
232 B4 East Liberty OH U.S.A.
146 F6 East Linton East Lothian, Scotland U.K.
235 E1 East Litchfield CT U.S.A.
232 C4 East Liverpool OH U.S.A.
146 B3 East Loch Roag inlet Scotland U.K.
146 B4 East Loch Tarbert inlet Scotland U.K.
215 F5 East London S. Africa
233 G3 East Longmeadow MA U.S.A.
150 C4 East Looe Cornwall, England U.K.
146 F6 East Lothian admin. div. Scotland U.K.
235 F1 East Lyme CT U.S.A.
224 E2 Eastmain Que. Can.
224 E2 Eastmain r. Que. Can.
151 H3 East Malling Kent, England U.K.
233 G2 Eastman Que. Can.
231 D5 Eastman GA U.S.A.
266 F5 East Mariana Basin sea feature Pacific Ocean
149 I4 East Markham Nottinghamshire, England U.K.
85 F4 Eastmere Qld Austr.
233 G3 East Middlebury VT U.S.A.
151 F2 East Midlands airport England U.K.
233 □I2 East Millinocket ME U.S.A.
235 E1 East Morris CT U.S.A.
231 D7 East Naples FL U.S.A.
235 E2 East Northport NY U.S.A.
149 I4 Eastoft North Lincolnshire, England U.K.
150 E4 Easton Dorset, England U.K.
240 H3 Easton CA U.S.A.
235 E1 Easton CT U.S.A.
233 E5 Easton MD U.S.A.
234 C2 Easton PA U.S.A.
150 E3 Easton-in-Gordano North Somerset, England U.K.
235 D2 East Orange NJ U.S.A.
267 L8 East Pacific Ridge S. Pacific Ocean
267 L4 East Pacific Rise sea feature N. Pacific Ocean
East Pakistan country Asia see Bangladesh
232 C4 East Palestine OH U.S.A.
226 C5 East Peoria IL U.S.A.
234 B2 East Petersburg PA U.S.A.
233 □J2 Eastport ME U.S.A.
226 E3 Eastport MI U.S.A.
235 F2 Eastport NY U.S.A.
151 G4 East Preston West Sussex, England U.K.
234 B3 East Prospect PA U.S.A.
235 F2 East Quogue NY U.S.A.
240 I1 East Range mts NV U.S.A.
146 D6 East Renfrewshire admin. div. Scotland U.K.
East Retford Nottinghamshire, England U.K. see Retford
231 C5 East Ridge TN U.S.A.
149 I4 East Riding of Yorkshire admin. div. England U.K.
146 E7 Eastriggs Dumfries and Galloway, Scotland U.K.
151 I3 Eastry Kent, England U.K.
230 B4 East St Louis IL U.S.A.
East Sea N. Pacific Ocean see Japan, Sea of
235 E2 East Setauket NY U.S.A.
234 C1 East Side PA U.S.A.
240 H4 East Side Canal r. CA U.S.A.
83 G4 East Sister Island Tas. Austr.
234 C1 East Stroudsburg PA U.S.A.
151 H4 East Sussex admin. div. England U.K.
232 B2 East Tawas MI U.S.A.
93 C5 East Timor terr. Asia
117 F4 East Tons r. India
83 F2 East Toorale N.S.W. Austr.
226 C4 East Troy WI U.S.A.
241 L4 East Verde r. AZ U.S.A.
Eastview Ont. Can. see Vanier
233 F6 Eastville VA U.S.A.
240 H2 East Walker r. NV U.S.A.
151 G4 East Wittering West Sussex, England U.K.
149 H4 Eastwood Nottinghamshire, England U.K.
151 F3 East Woodhay Hampshire, England U.K.
227 H4 East York Ont. Can.
87 B7 Eaton W.A. Austr.
238 F3 Eaton CO U.S.A.
230 C4 Eaton OH U.S.A.
151 G3 Eaton Bray Bedfordshire, England U.K.
223 I5 Eatonia Sask. Can.
226 E4 Eaton Rapids MI U.S.A.
235 E2 Eatons Neck NY U.S.A.
151 G2 Eaton Socon Cambridgeshire, England U.K.
231 D5 Eatonton GA U.S.A.
235 D2 Eatontown NJ U.S.A.
233 □I1 Eatonville Que. Can.
238 B2 Eatonville WA U.S.A.
226 B3 Eau Claire WI U.S.A.
226 B3 Eau Claire r. WI U.S.A.
156 B3 Eaulne r. France
163 D5 Eaunes France
91 J5 Eauripik atoll Micronesia
266 E5 Eauripik Rise-New Guinea Rise sea feature N. Pacific Ocean
Eaurypyg atoll Micronesia see Eauripik
163 B6 Eaux-Bonnes France
163 C5 Eauze France
78 □3a Ebadon i. Kwajalein Marshall Is
85 E2 Ebagoola Qld Austr.
207 G4 Eban Nigeria
245 E2 Ebano Mex.
178 D3 Ebbs Austria
150 D3 Ebbw Vale Blaenau Gwent, Wales U.K.
207 H6 Ebebiyin Equat. Guinea
169 F4 Ebeleben Ger.
142 D3 Ebeltoft Denmark
178 C3 Eben am Achensee Austria
215 G5 Ebende S. Africa
179 E4 Ebene Reichenau Austria
179 H3 Ebenfurth Austria
179 E3 Eben im Pongau Austria
232 D4 Ebensburg PA U.S.A.
179 E3 Ebensee Austria
169 F5 Ebensfeld Ger.
179 F4 Ebenthal Austria
172 D4 Ebenweiler Ger.
179 H3 Eberau Austria
172 C2 Eberbach Ger.
169 F4 Ebergötzen Ger.
172 D3 Eberhardzell Ger.
173 F2 Ebermannsdorf Ger.
173 F2 Ebermannstadt Ger.
169 F5 Ebern Ger.
179 F4 Eberndorf Austria
171 E4 Ebersbach Sachsen Ger.
171 F4 Ebersbach Sachsen Ger.
172 D3 Ebersbach an der Fils Ger.
173 F3 Ebersberg Ger.
179 E2 Eberschwang Austria
179 G3 Ebersdorf Austria
168 E2 Ebersdorf Niedersachsen Ger.
171 C5 Ebersdorf Thüringen Ger.
157 H4 Ebersmunster France
179 F4 Eberstein Austria
170 E3 Eberswalde-Finow Ger.
234 C2 Ebervale PA U.S.A.
177 K4 Ebes Hungary
102 J2 Ebetsu Japan
78 □3a Ebeye Kwajalein Marshall Is
172 C3 Ebhausen Ger.
108 B2 Ebian Sichuan China
190 D1 Ebikon Switz.
105 F3 Ebina Japan
103 E7 Ebino Japan
Ebi Nor salt l. China see Ebinur Hu
110 C2 Ebinur Hu salt l. China
128 C2 Ebla tourist site Syria
190 E1 Ebnat-Kappel Switz.
209 B7 Ebo Angola
208 D4 Ebola r. Dem. Rep. Congo
193 H4 Eboli Italy
207 H6 Ebolowa Cameroon
207 H5 Ebonyi state Nigeria
173 E2 Ebrach Ger.
Ebre r. Spain see Ebro
179 H3 Ebreichsdorf Austria
160 B2 Ébreuil France
183 H3 Ebrillos r. Spain
172 B4 Ebringen Ger.
183 4 Ebro r. Spain
183 G1 Ebro, Embalse del resr Spain
187 B4 Ebrón r. Spain
169 D5 Ebsdorfergrund-Dreihausen Ger.
169 D5 Ebsdorfergrund-Rauischholzhausen Ger.
168 F2 Ebstorf Ger.
Eburacum York, England U.K. see York
Eburodunum France see Embrun
Ebusus i. Spain see Eivissa
245 E4 Ecatepec Mex.
165 D4 Écaussinnes-d'Enghien Belgium
Ecbatana Iran see Hamadān
146 E6 Ecclefechan Dumfries and Galloway, Scotland U.K.
149 G4 Eccles Greater Manchester, England U.K.
146 F6 Eccles Scottish Borders, Scotland U.K.
232 C6 Eccles WV U.S.A.
149 H4 Ecclesfield South Yorkshire, England U.K.
150 E2 Eccleshall Staffordshire, England U.K.
149 G4 Eccleston Lancashire, England U.K.
199 E1 Eceabat Turkey
92 B2 Echague Phil.
190 B2 Echallens Switz.
246 B5 Echandi, Cerro mt. Costa Rica
183 I2 Echarri Spain
183 H2 Echarri-Aranaz Spain
159 G3 Échauffour France
205 F1 Ech Chélif Alg.
Echeng Hubei China see Ezhou
160 E1 Échenoz-la-Méline France
242 B2 Echeverria, Pico mt. Mex.
162 B3 Échillais France
198 B2 Echinades i. Greece
173 F3 Eching Bayern Ger.
173 G3 Eching Bayern Ger.
198 D1 Echinos Greece
162 B2 Échiré France
161 D3 Échirolles France
105 E3 Echizen-dake mt. Japan
Echmiadzin Armenia see Ejmiatsin
238 C2 Echo OR U.S.A.
83 F5 Echo, Lake Tas. Austr.
220 G3 Echo Bay N.W.T. Can.
224 C4 Echo Bay Ont. Can.
241 L3 Echo Cliffs esc. AZ U.S.A.
223 M4 Echoing r. Man./Ont. Can.
162 C3 Échourgnac France
179 G2 Echsenbach Austria
165 E3 Echt Neth.
146 F4 Echt Aberdeenshire, Scotland U.K.
169 F4 Echte Ger.
165 F5 Echternach Lux.
83 F4 Echuca Vic. Austr.
169 D5 Echzell Ger.
185 E3 Écija Spain
261 I4 Ecilda Paullier Uru.
148 E1 Eck, Loch l. Scotland U.K.
196 E3 Ečka Vojvodina, Srbija Yugo.
171 C4 Eckartsberga Ger.
157 H4 Eckbolsheim France
173 F2 Eckental Ger.
226 E2 Eckerman MI U.S.A.
168 E1 Eckernförde Ger.
141 L3 Eckerö Åland Fin.
173 F2 Eckersdorf Ger.
146 F6 Eckford Scottish Borders, Scotland U.K.
149 H4 Eckington Derbyshire, England U.K.
150 E2 Eckington Worcestershire, England U.K.
232 C6 Eckman WV U.S.A.
222 H4 Eckville Alta Can.
168 D2 Eckwarden (Butjadingen) Ger.
157 E4 Éclaron-Braucourt-Ste-Livière France
159 G4 Écommoy France
257 G3 Ecoporanga Brazil
156 B3 Écos France
159 F3 Écouché France
159 F4 Écouflant France
156 B3 Écouis France
157 F4 Écrouves France
177 G4 Écs Hungary
177 I4 Ecséd Hungary
177 I4 Ecseg Hungary
177 J4 Ecsegfalva Hungary
177 I4 Ecser Hungary
250 B5 Ecuador country S. America
162 D1 Écueillé France
160 C2 Écuisses France
156 E4 Écury-sur-Coole France
203 I6 Ed Eritrea
142 D2 Ed Sweden
223 I4 Edam Sask. Can.
164 E2 Edam Neth.
146 F2 Eday i. Scotland U.K.
203 F6 Ed Dair, Jebel mt. Sudan
210 B2 Ed Damazin Sudan
203 G5 Ed Damer Sudan
203 F5 Ed Debba Sudan
168 E2 Eddelak Ger.
171 C4 Edderitz Ger.
146 D4 Edderton Highland, Scotland U.K.
225 J3 Eddies Cove Nfld. Can.
203 G6 Ed Dueim Sudan
83 G5 Eddystone Point Tas. Austr.
237 F4 Eddyville KY U.S.A.
164 E2 Ede Neth.
207 G5 Ede Nigeria
207 H6 Edéa Cameroon
165 D3 Edegem Belgium
256 C2 Edéia Brazil
177 J3 Edelény Hungary
179 G3 Edelschrott Austria
169 F3 Edemissen Ger.
83 G4 Eden N.S.W. Austr.
148 D3 Eden Northern Ireland U.K.
149 F3 Eden r. England U.K.
232 D6 Eden NC U.S.A.
237 D6 Eden TX U.S.A.
238 E3 Eden WY U.S.A.
151 H3 Edenbridge Kent, England U.K.
215 E3 Edenburg S. Africa
81 B7 Edendale South I. N.Z.
215 H3 Edendale S. Africa
147 D3 Edenderry Rep. of Ireland
149 G4 Edenfield Lancashire, England U.K.
82 E4 Edenhope Vic. Austr.
172 C2 Edenkoben Ger.
226 A3 Eden Prairie MN U.S.A.
231 E4 Edenton NC U.S.A.
215 G2 Edenvale S. Africa
215 F2 Edenville S. Africa
169 E4 Eder r. Ger.
169 E4 Edermünde Ger.
147 D2 Ederny Northern Ireland U.K.
198 C1 Edessa Greece
Edessa Turkey see Şanlıurfa
140 K3 Edevik Sweden
168 C2 Edewecht Ger.
168 C2 Edewechterdamm Ger.
Edfu Egypt see Idfu
236 D3 Edgar NE U.S.A.
86 D4 Edgar, Mount hill W.A. Austr.
86 D3 Edgar Ranges hills W.A. Austr.
233 H4 Edgartown MA U.S.A.
80 F2 Edgecumbe North I. N.Z.
80 F3 Edgecumbe, Mount hill North I. N.Z.
Edgecumbe Island Solomon Is see Utupua
231 D5 Edgefield SC U.S.A.
Edge Island Svalbard see Edgeøya
236 D2 Edgeley ND U.S.A.
234 B3 Edgemere MD U.S.A.
236 C3 Edgemont SD U.S.A.
140 □ Edgeøya i. Svalbard
223 I4 Edgerton Alta Can.
232 A4 Edgerton OH U.S.A.
232 E6 Edgerton VA U.S.A.
226 C4 Edgerton WI U.S.A.
222 G5 Edgewood B.C. Can.
234 B3 Edgewood MD U.S.A.
234 B2 Edgewood PA U.S.A.
147 D3 Edgeworthstown Rep. of Ireland
78 □3a Edgigen i. Kwajalein Marshall Is
150 E2 Edgmond Telford and Wrekin, England U.K.
Édhessa Greece see Edessa
81 B6 Edievale South I. N.Z.
169 C5 Ediger-Eller Ger.
129 C3 Edik'ilisa Georgia
236 E3 Edina MO U.S.A.
232 C4 Edinboro PA U.S.A.
237 D7 Edinburg TX U.S.A.
232 D5 Edinburg VA U.S.A.
146 E6 Edinburgh Edinburgh, Scotland U.K.
146 E6 Edinburgh admin. div. Scotland U.K.
199 E1 Edincik Turkey
136 D3 Edineţ Moldova
172 C2 Edingen-Neckarhausen Ger.
126 B2 Edirne Turkey
199 E1 Edirne prov. Turkey
234 C2 Edison PA U.S.A.
129 D1 Edissiya Rus. Fed.
231 D5 Edisto r. SC U.S.A.
238 E2 Edith, Mount MT U.S.A.
82 D3 Edithburgh S.A. Austr.
222 G4 Edith Cavell, Mount Alta Can.
87 D5 Edith Withnell, Lake salt flat W.A. Austr.
87 D6 Edjudina W.A. Austr.
173 G3 Edling Ger.
149 H2 Edlingham Northumberland, England U.K.
179 H3 Edlitz Austria
237 D5 Edmond OK U.S.A.
238 B2 Edmonds WA U.S.A.
147 C3 Edmondstown Rep. of Ireland
85 F3 Edmonton Qld Austr.
222 H4 Edmonton Alta Can.
230 C4 Edmonton KY U.S.A.
226 E4 Edmore MI U.S.A.
236 D1 Edmore ND U.S.A.
149 H3 Edmundbyres Durham, England U.K.
225 G4 Edmundston N.B. Can.
237 D6 Edna TX U.S.A.
222 C4 Edna Bay AK U.S.A.
Edo Japan see Tōkyō
207 G5 Edo state Nigeria
105 F3 Edo-gawa r. Japan
190 F2 Edolo Italy
128 B4 Edom reg. Israel/Jordan
199 E2 Edremit Turkey
199 E2 Edremit Körfezi b. Turkey
106 C2 Edrengiyn Nuruu mts Mongolia
182 D3 Edrosa Port.
182 D3 Edroso Port.
143 H2 Edsbro Sweden
143 G2 Edsbruk Sweden
141 K3 Edsbyn Sweden
140 L3 Edsele Sweden
222 G4 Edson Alta Can.
260 E4 Eduardo Castex Arg.
222 D1 Eduni, Mount N.W.T. Can.
83 F3 Edward r. N.S.W. Austr.
85 E2 Edward r. Qld Austr.
208 F5 Edward, Lake Dem. Rep. Congo/Uganda
262 T1 Edward, Mount Antarctica
86 F4 Edward, Mount N.T. Austr.
Edwardesabad Pak. see Bannu
84 C2 Edward Island N.T. Austr.
233 F2 Edwards NY U.S.A.
237 C6 Edwards Plateau TX U.S.A.
236 F4 Edwardsville IL U.S.A.
262 N1 Edward VII Peninsula Antarctica
149 H4 Edwinstowe Nottinghamshire, England U.K.
222 D3 Edziza, Mount B.C. Can.
Edzo N.W.T. Can. see Rae-Edzo
164 F2 Eefde Neth.
165 C3 Eeklo Belgium
240 E1 Eel r. CA U.S.A.
240 F1 Eel, South Fork r. CA U.S.A.
164 F1 Eelde-Paterswolde Neth.
164 E2 Eem r. Neth.
164 E2 Eemnes Neth.
214 B5 Eendekuil S. Africa
164 F1 Eenrum Neth.
164 F2 Eerbeek Neth.
165 C3 Eernegem Belgium
165 E3 Eersel Neth.
Eesti country Europe see Estonia
78 □5 Éfaté i. Vanuatu
179 F2 Eferding Austria
Efes tourist site Turkey see Ephesus
173 F2 Effeltrich Ger.
226 A2 Effie MN U.S.A.
151 G3 Effingham Surrey, England U.K.
236 F4 Effingham IL U.S.A.
234 C2 Effort PA U.S.A.
190 D1 Effretikon Switz.
126 D2 Eflâni Turkey
172 B4 Efringen-Kirchen Ger.
Efsus Turkey see Afşin
197 F3 Eftimie Murgu Romania
107 F1 Eg Mongolia
183 I2 Ega r. Spain
241 J2 Egan Range mts NV U.S.A.
227 I3 Eganville Ont. Can.
187 C6 Egea hill Spain
Egedesminde Greenland see Aasiaat
171 C4 Egeln Ger.
173 F3 Egenhofen Ger.
171 D5 Eger r. Ger.
173 E3 Eger r. Ger.
177 J4 Eger Hungary
177 J4 Egerbakta Hungary
177 J3 Egercsehi Hungary
168 E1 Egernsund Denmark
142 B2 Egersund Norway
87 C5 Egerton, Mount hill W.A. Austr.
176 F5 Egervár Hungary
168 F2 Egestorf Ger.
178 A3 Egg Austria
168 E1 Eggebek Ger.
142 C2 Eggedøla r. Norway
169 D4 Eggegebirge hills Ger.
179 G2 Eggenburg Austria
173 G3 Eggenfelden Ger.
172 C2 Eggenstein-Leopoldshafen Ger.
168 C3 Eggermühlen Ger.
171 C4 Eggersdorf Ger.
179 G3 Eggersdorf bei Graz Austria
170 E3 Eggersdorf bei Strausberg Ger.
170 F2 Eggesin Ger.
226 D3 Egg Harbor WI U.S.A.
234 D3 Egg Harbor City NJ U.S.A.
172 C4 Eggingen Ger.
190 C2 Eggiwil Switz.
173 H3 Egglham Ger.
173 F2 Eggolsheim Ger.
173 G4 Eggstätt Ger.
151 G3 Egham Surrey, England U.K.
165 D4 Eghezée Belgium
Egiarreta Spain see Eguiarreta
146 F2 Egilsay i. Scotland U.K.
140 □D2 Egilsstaðir Iceland
Eğin Turkey see Kemaliye
86 C4 Eginbah W.A. Austr.
Egindibulaq Kazakh. see Yegindybulak
173 H3 Eging am See Ger.
199 G3 Eğirdir Turkey
199 G3 Eğirdir Gölü l. Turkey
106 D1 Egiyn Gol r. Mongolia
162 E3 Égletons France
173 F4 Egling Ger.
173 E3 Egling an der Paar Ger.
149 H2 Eglingham Northumberland, England U.K.
147 D1 Eglinton Northern Ireland U.K.
172 C4 Eglisau Switz.
148 C3 Eglish Northern Ireland U.K.
173 F2 Egloffstein Ger.
150 D2 Eglwys Fach Ceredigion, Wales U.K.
150 C2 Eglwyswrw Pembrokeshire, Wales U.K.
164 D2 Egmond aan Zee Neth.
164 D2 Egmond-Binnen Neth.
80 D3 Egmont, Cape North I. N.Z.
Egmont, Mount vol. North I. N.Z. see Taranaki, Mount
80 E3 Egmont Village North I. N.Z.
191 G2 Egna Italy
149 F3 Egremont Cumbria, England U.K.
199 F2 Eğrigöz Dağı mts Turkey
156 D4 Égriselles-le-Bocage France
149 I3 Egton North Yorkshire, England U.K.
142 C4 Egtved Denmark
254 D5 Éguas r. Brazil
183 I2 Eguiarreta Spain
161 D5 Éguilles France
156 E4 Éguilly-sous-Bois France
157 H4 Eguisheim France
162 D2 Éguzon-Chantôme France
131 T3 Egvekinot Rus. Fed.
177 J4 Egyek Hungary
179 H3 Egyházasfalu Hungary
177 H5 Egyházaskozár Hungary
176 F4 Egyházasrádóc Hungary
203 F2 Egypt country Africa
234 C2 Egypt PA U.S.A.
173 E2 Ehebach r. Ger.
173 F3 Ehekirchen Ger.
106 D4 Ehen Hudag Nei Mongol China
103 F7 Ehime pref. Japan
173 E2 Ehingen Ger.
172 D3 Ehingen (Donau) Ger.
171 C3 Ehle r. Ger.
169 E4 Ehlen (Habichtswald) Ger.
172 C3 Ehningen Ger.
168 F3 Ehra-Lessien Ger.
241 J5 Ehrenberg AZ U.S.A.
84 B4 Ehrenberg Range hills N.T. Austr.
169 F5 Ehrenberg-Wüstensachsen Ger.
168 D3 Ehrenburg Ger.
179 G4 Ehrenhausen Austria
169 D5 Ehringshausen Ger.
178 B3 Ehrwald Austria
79 □3 Eiao i. Fr. Polynesia
183 H1 Eibar Spain
173 E2 Eibelstadt Ger.
171 D5 Eibenstock Ger.
164 F2 Eibergen Neth.
179 G4 Eibiswald Austria
172 C2 Eich Ger.
173 F3 Eichenau Ger.
171 C3 Eichenbarleben Ger.
169 E5 Eichenberg hill Ger.
172 D2 Eichenbühl Ger.
173 G3 Eichendorf Ger.
169 E5 Eichenzell Ger.
179 G2 Eichgraben Austria
171 D5 Eichigt Ger.
173 F3 Eichstätt Ger.
172 B3 Eichstetten Ger.
171 E3 Eichwalde Ger.
171 C4 Eickendorf Ger.
168 F3 Eicklingen Ger.
140 I3 Eide Norway
168 D1 Eider r. Ger.
142 B1 Eidfjord Norway
140 J3 Eidsvåg Norway
85 G5 Eidsvold Qld Austr.
142 D1 Eidsvoll Norway
140 □ Eidsvollfjellet mt. Svalbard
169 B5 Eifel hills Ger.
172 C4 Eigeltingen Ger.
190 D2 Eiger mt. Switz.
142 A2 Eigerøya i. Norway
146 B5 Eigg i. Scotland U.K.
146 B5 Eigg, Sound of sea chan. Scotland U.K.
114 B5 Eight Degree Channel India/Maldives
262 R2 Eights Coast Antarctica
86 D3 Eighty Mile Beach W.A. Austr.
165 E4 Eijsden Neth.
142 A1 Eikelandsosen Norway
142 B2 Eiken Norway
146 C5 Eil, Loch inlet Scotland U.K.
Eilat Israel see Elat
83 F4 Eildon Vic. Austr.
83 F4 Eildon, Lake Vic. Austr.
171 D4 Eilenburg Ger.
171 C4 Eilenstedt Ger.
251 G4 Eilerts de Haan Gebergte mts Suriname
92 □ Eil Malk i. Palau
171 C3 Eilsleben Ger.
169 E3 Eime Ger.
169 E4 Eimen Ger.
Eimeo i. Fr. Polynesia see Moorea
168 F3 Eimke Ger.
146 B3 Einacleit Western Isles, Scotland U.K.
85 F3 Einasleigh Qld Austr.
85 E3 Einasleigh r. Qld Austr.
169 E4 Einbeck Ger.
165 E3 Eindhoven Neth.
171 C4 Eine r. Ger.
172 C2 Einhausen Ger.
146 D4 Einig r. Scotland U.K.
171 D5 Einsiedel Ger.
190 D1 Einsiedeln Switz.
157 G4 Einville-au-Jard France
Éire country Europe see Ireland, Republic of
264 G2 Eirik Ridge sea feature N. Atlantic Ocean
Eiriosgaigh i. Scotland U.K. see Eriskay
250 D6 Eiru r. Brazil
250 D6 Eirunepé Brazil
169 E4 Eisberg hill Ger.
165 F5 Eisch r. Lux.
165 E4 Eisden Belgium
169 F4 Eisdorf Ger.
173 G3 Eiselfing Ger.
169 F5 Eisenach Ger.
172 C4 Eisenbach (Hochschwarzwald) Ger.
171 C5 Eisenberg Ger.
172 C2 Eisenberg (Pfalz) Ger.
179 F3 Eisenerz Austria
Eisenhower, Mount Alta Can. see Castle Mountain
179 E4 Eisenhut mt. Austria
171 F3 Eisenhüttenstadt Ger.
179 F4 Eisenkappel Austria
179 H3 Eisenstadt Austria
169 F5 Eisfeld Ger.
146 C4 Eishort, Loch inlet Scotland U.K.
138 E4 Eišiškės Lith.
171 C4 Eisleben Lutherstadt Ger.
172 D3 Eislingen (Fils) Ger.
80 E2 Eistow North I. N.Z.
173 F3 Eitensheim Ger.
169 E5 Eiterfeld Ger.
169 C5 Eitorf Ger.
169 E3 Eitzum (Despetal) Ger.
141 I3 Eivinvik Norway
187 E6 Eivissa Spain
187 E5 Eivissa i. Spain
182 C2 Eixe, Serra do mts Spain
182 B4 Eixo Port.
182 B3 Eja Port.
186 B2 Ejea de los Caballeros Spain
213 □J5 Ejeda Madag.

Ejin Horo Qi to Epworth

302

Ejin Horo Qi Nei Mongol China see Altan Shiret
Ejin Qi Nei Mongol China see Dalain Hob
Ejmiadzin Armenia see Ejmiatsin
129 D3 Ejmiatsin Armenia
186 C4 Ejulve Spain
206 E5 Ejura Ghana
238 F2 Ekalaka MT U.S.A.
207 H5 Ekang Nigeria
215 G1 Ekangala S. Africa
141 M4 Ekenäs Fin.
142 E2 Ekenäs Sweden
165 D3 Ekeren Belgium
143 G2 Ekerö Sweden
207 G5 Eket Nigeria
80 E4 Eketahuna North I. N.Z.
Ekhínos Greece see Echinos
Ekhmîm Egypt see Akhmîm
121 H2 Ekibastuz Kazakh.
100 E1 Ekimchan Rus. Fed.
128 D1 Ekinyazı Turkey
207 G5 Ekiti state Nigeria
207 H5 Ekondo Titi Cameroon
140 P2 Ekostrovskaya Imandra, Ozero l. Rus. Fed.
207 G5 Ekpoma Nigeria
165 C3 Eksaarde Belgium
165 E3 Eksel Belgium
Eksere Turkey see Gündoğmuş
142 E1 Ekshärad Sweden
199 G3 Ekşili Turkey
143 F3 Eksjö Sweden
214 A3 Eksteenfontein S. Africa
140 L2 Ekträsk Sweden
224 D2 Ekwan r. Ont. Can.
96 B3 Ela Myanmar
El Aaiún Western Sahara see Laâyoune
244 C4 El Aguaje Mex.
198 D1 Elaiochori Anatoliki Makedonia kai Thraki Greece
187 C7 El Algar Spain
189 B7 El Alia Tunisia
184 C3 El Almendro Spain
185 H4 El Alquián Spain
250 A6 El Alto Peru
126 C5 El 'Amirîya Egypt
156 B4 Élancourt France
215 H1 Elands r. S. Africa
213 F5 Elands r. S. Africa
215 F5 Elandsberg mt. S. Africa
215 G1 Elandsdoorn S. Africa
215 E5 Elandsdrif S. Africa
215 H3 Elandskraal S. Africa
215 G3 Elandslaagte S. Africa
215 F1 Elandsputte S. Africa
150 D2 Elan Village Powys, Wales U.K.
Elar Armenia see Abovyan
184 E3 El Arahal Spain
El Araïche Morocco see Larache
242 B2 El Arco Mex.
183 E4 El Arenal Castilla y León Spain
El Arenal Islas Baleares Spain see S'Arenal
85 F3 El Arish Qld Austr.
203 G2 El 'Arîsh Egypt
205 G1 El Arrouch Alg.
203 F3 El Ashmûnein Egypt
El Asnam Alg. see Ech Chélif
198 C2 Elassona Greece
183 G1 El Astillero Spain
128 B5 Elat Israel
204 B5 El 'Aṭf reg. Western Sahara
198 B2 Elati mt. Ionioi Nisoi Greece
91 K5 Elato atoll Micronesia
126 E3 Elazığ Turkey
129 A4 Elazığ prov. Turkey
231 C6 Elba AL U.S.A.
192 C2 Elba, Isola d' i. Italy
128 A5 El Bahr El Ahmar governorate Egypt
185 H2 El Ballestero Spain
203 F3 El Balyana Egypt
100 F2 El'ban Rus. Fed.
250 C2 El Banco Col.
182 E4 El Barco de Ávila Spain
El Barco de Valdeorras Spain see O Barco
183 F4 El Barraco Spain
242 D2 El Barreal salt l. Mex.
244 C2 El Barril Mex.
196 E5 Elbasan Albania
126 D3 Elbaşı Turkey
205 F2 El Bayadh Alg.
168 E2 Elbe r. Ger. alt. Labe (Czech Rep.)
238 B2 Elbe WA U.S.A.
206 C2 'Elb el Fçâl des. Maur.
260 B3 El Belloto airport Valparaíso Chile
169 C3 Elbergen Ger.
183 G4 El Berrueco Spain
226 D3 Elberta MI U.S.A.
241 L2 Elberta UT U.S.A.
231 D5 Elberton GA U.S.A.
156 B3 Elbeuf France
128 C1 Elbeyli Turkey
244 D4 El Billete, Cerro mt. Mex.
Elbing Pol. see Elbląg
169 F4 Elbingerode (Harz) Ger.
126 E3 Elbistan Turkey
143 H4 Elbląg Pol.
242 □J6 El Bluff Nic.
182 D4 El Bodón Spain
El Bollo Spain see O Bolo
259 C6 El Bolsón Arg.
185 H2 El Bonillo Spain
185 E4 El Bosque Spain
El Boulaïda Alg. see Blida
223 J5 Elbow Sask. Can.
231 E7 Elbow Cay i. Bahamas
236 D2 Elbow Lake MN U.S.A.
129 C2 El'brus Rus. Fed.
129 C2 Elbrus mt. Rus. Fed.
208 F3 El Buheyrat state Sudan
185 I2 El Buitre mt. Spain
185 F1 El Bullaque Spain
164 E2 Elburg Neth.
185 F4 El Burgo Spain
183 H2 Elburgo Spain
186 C3 El Burgo de Ebro Spain
183 G3 El Burgo de Osma Spain
183 E2 El Burgo Ranero Spain
Elburz Mountains Iran see Alborz, Reshteh-ye
183 I3 El Buste Spain
137 J4 El'buzd r. Rus. Fed.
182 D4 El Cabaco Spain
185 I3 El Cabildo y la Campana Spain
185 H4 El Cabo de Gata Spain
240 I5 El Cajon CA U.S.A.
251 F3 El Callao Venez.
El Caló Spain see Es Caló
245 D5 El Camotal, Sierra mts Mex.
183 E5 El Campillo de la Jara Spain
El Campo Spain see Campo Lugar
237 D6 El Campo TX U.S.A.
183 E4 El Campo de Peñaranda Spain
183 H5 El Cañavate Spain
237 C7 El Capulin r. Mex.
258 D2 El Carmen Arg.
252 E3 El Carmen Bol.
260 B5 El Carmen Chile
250 B5 El Carmen Ecuador
187 C5 El Caroche mt. Spain
185 F3 El Carpio Spain
183 F5 El Carpio de Tajo Spain
183 G4 El Casar Spain
183 F4 El Casar de Escalona Spain
187 C4 El Castellar Spain
184 D3 El Castillo de las Guardas Spain
243 G6 El Cebú, Cerro mt. Mex.
185 G2 El Centenillo Spain
241 J5 El Centro CA U.S.A.
253 E4 El Cerro Bol.
184 D3 El Cerro de Andévalo Spain
187 C6 Elche Spain
185 H2 Elche de la Sierra Spain
243 G5 El Chichónal vol. Mex.
173 E3 Elchingen Ger.
226 C3 Elcho WI U.S.A.
84 C1 Elcho Island N.T. Austr.
183 H2 Elciego Spain
El Coca Ecuador see Puerto Francisco de Orellana
185 F2 El Collado hill Spain
244 B4 El Colomo Mex.
244 D5 El Conejo, Sierra mts Mex.
186 F3 El Congost r. Spain
184 E3 El Coronil Spain
245 G5 El Corte r. Mex.
246 B2 El Cotorro Cuba
245 G6 El Coyol Mex.
182 D4 El Cubo de Don Sancho Spain
182 E3 El Cubo de Tierra del Vino Spain
184 D4 El Cuervo Spain
187 C6 Elda Spain
210 B4 Eldama Ravine Kenya
170 C2 Elde r. Ger.
227 H2 Eldee Ont. Can.
170 C2 Eldena Ger.
226 C5 Eldena IL U.S.A.
226 C3 Elderon WI U.S.A.
140 □C3 Eldhraun lava field Iceland
250 C2 El Difícil Col.
131 O3 El'dikan Rus. Fed.
168 F3 Eldingen Ger.
El Djezair Alg. see Alger
236 E4 Eldon MO U.S.A.
236 E3 Eldora IA U.S.A.
234 D3 Eldora NJ U.S.A.
258 G2 Eldorado Arg.
256 C6 Eldorado Brazil
242 D3 El Dorado Mex.
237 E5 El Dorado AR U.S.A.
237 D4 El Dorado KS U.S.A.
237 C6 Eldorado TX U.S.A.
241 J4 Eldorado Mountains NV U.S.A.
210 B4 Eldoret Kenya
234 D1 Eldred NY U.S.A.
232 C5 Eleanor WV U.S.A.
238 E2 Electric Peak MT U.S.A.
198 C2 Elefsina Greece
204 D4 El Eglab plat. Alg.
138 D3 Eleja Latvia
185 H4 El Ejido Spain
177 K5 Elek Hungary
Elek r. Rus. Fed. see Ilek
138 E4 Elektrėnai Lith.
139 L4 Elektrogorsk Rus. Fed.
139 L4 Elektrostal' Rus. Fed.
139 L4 Elektrougli Rus. Fed.
207 G5 Elele Nigeria
210 B3 Elemi Triangle terr. Africa
197 G4 Elena Bulg.
169 F4 Elend Ger.
198 B2 Eleousa Ipeiros Greece
114 B2 Elephanta Caves tourist site Mahar. India
239 F5 Elephant Butte Reservoir NM U.S.A.
262 U2 Elephant Island Antarctica
183 F4 El Escorial Spain
197 F5 Eleshnitsa Bulg.
127 F3 Eleşkirt Turkey
183 F4 El Espinar Spain
243 H6 El Estor Guat.
187 C7 El Estrecho Spain
246 C1 Eleuthera i. Bahamas
226 B3 Eleva WI U.S.A.
237 F4 Eleven Point r. MO U.S.A.
189 B7 El Fahs Tunisia
203 F2 El Faiyûm Egypt
126 C5 El Faiyûm governorate Egypt
202 E6 El Fasher Sudan
203 F2 El Fashn Egypt
180 D5 El Fendek Morocco
El Ferrol Spain see Ferrol
El Ferrol del Caudillo Spain see Ferrol
169 E5 Elfershausen Ger.
183 F4 El Fresno Spain
241 M6 Elfrida AZ U.S.A.
210 D3 El Fud Eth.
242 C3 El Fuerte Mex.
208 F2 El Fula Sudan
185 H3 El Gabar mt. Spain
184 D3 El Garrobo Spain
185 E4 El Gastor Spain
202 D6 El Geneina Sudan
169 E4 Elgershausen (Schauenburg) Ger.
183 H1 Elgeta Spain
203 G6 El Geteina Sudan
203 G6 El Gezira state Sudan
206 C2 El Gheddiya Maur.
142 D2 Elgheia hill Norway
El Ghor plain Jordan/West Bank see Al Ghawr
146 E4 Elgin Moray, Scotland U.K.
226 C4 Elgin IL U.S.A.
236 C2 Elgin ND U.S.A.
241 J3 Elgin NV U.S.A.
238 C2 Elgin OR U.S.A.
237 D6 Elgin TX U.S.A.
85 F4 Elgin Down Qld Austr.
131 P3 El'ginskiy Rus. Fed.
203 F2 El Gîza Egypt
126 C5 El Gîza governorate Egypt
183 H1 Elgoibar Spain
146 B4 Elgol Highland, Scotland U.K.
205 F3 El Goléa Alg.
216 □3e El Golfo b. El Hierro Canary Is
210 B4 Elgon, Mount Uganda
140 O1 Elgoras, Gora hill Rus. Fed.
141 J3 Elgpiggen mt. Norway
186 D2 El Grado Spain
184 C3 El Granado Spain
187 C5 El Grau de Borriana Spain
244 B4 El Grullo Mex.
245 H5 El Guanal Mex.
205 H2 El Guetar Tunisia
131 M3 El'gyay Rus. Fed.
189 A7 El Hadjar Alg.
205 H2 El Hamma Tunisia
203 F2 El Hammâm Egypt
204 C5 El Ḥammâmi reg. Maur.
204 D4 El Hank reg. Alg.
204 C5 El Ḥank esc. Mali/Maur.
203 F2 El Harra Egypt
242 □J7 El Hato del Volcán Panama
203 G6 El Hawata Sudan
126 C5 El Heiz Egypt
216 □3e El Hierro i. Canary Is
245 E3 El Higo Mex.
183 H5 El Hito Spain
183 F4 El Hoyo de Pinares Spain
246 E3 Elías Piña Dom. Rep.
193 F2 Elice Italy
Elichpur Mahar. India see Achalpur
232 A4 Elida OH U.S.A.
146 F5 Elie Fife, Scotland U.K.
209 E5 Elila r. Dem. Rep. Congo
214 B6 Elim S. Africa
220 B3 Elim AK U.S.A.
138 F1 Elimäki Fin.
Elimberrum France see Auch
234 A1 Elimsport PA U.S.A.
151 F4 Eling Hampshire, England U.K.
197 F4 Elin Pelin Bulg.
129 D2 Elin-Yurt Rus. Fed.
193 H3 Elio, Monte d' hill Italy
225 I1 Eliot, Mount Nfld. Can.
186 B1 Eliozondo Spain
Élisabethville Dem. Rep. Congo see Lubumbashi
254 E4 Eliseu Martins Brazil
El Iskandarîya Egypt see Alexandria
126 C5 El Iskandarîya governorate Egypt
135 I7 Elista Rus. Fed.
178 E3 Elixhausen Austria
233 F4 Elizabeth NJ U.S.A.
232 C5 Elizabeth WV U.S.A.
86 E3 Elizabeth, Mount hill W.A. Austr.
233 □J1 Elizabeth, Mount hill N.B. Can.
231 E4 Elizabeth City NC U.S.A.
84 D3 Elizabeth Creek r. Qld Austr.
Elizabeth Island Pitcairn Is see Henderson Island
77 F4 Elizabeth Reef Austr.
232 B6 Elizabethton TN U.S.A.
237 F4 Elizabethtown IL U.S.A.
230 C4 Elizabethtown KY U.S.A.
231 E5 Elizabethtown NC U.S.A.
233 G2 Elizabethtown NY U.S.A.
234 B2 Elizabethtown PA U.S.A.
227 I5 Elizabethville PA U.S.A.
204 C2 El Jadida Morocco
242 D3 El Jaralito Mex.
182 D4 Eljas Spain
205 H2 El Jem Tunisia
222 H5 Elk r. B.C. Can.
175 K2 Ełk Pol.
175 K2 Ełk r. Pol.
234 C3 Elk r. MD U.S.A.
231 C5 Elk r. TN U.S.A.
El Kaa Lebanon see Qaa
236 F3 Elkader IA U.S.A.
205 H1 El Kala Alg.
138 E3 Elkas kalns hill Latvia
232 B6 Elkatawa KY U.S.A.
237 D5 Elk City OK U.S.A.
240 F2 Elk Creek CA U.S.A.
84 C4 Elkedra N.T. Austr.
204 D2 El Kelaâ des Srarhna Morocco
169 C5 Elkenroth Ger.
210 D3 Ēl Kerē Eth.
222 H5 Elkford B.C. Can.
240 G2 Elk Grove CA U.S.A.
El Khalil West Bank see Hebron
203 F5 El Khandaq Sudan
203 F3 El Khârga Egypt
230 C3 Elkhart IN U.S.A.
237 C4 Elkhart KS U.S.A.
El Khartûm Sudan see Khartoum
El Khenachich esc. Mali see El Khnâchîch
204 D5 El Khnâchîch esc. Mali
226 C4 Elkhorn WI U.S.A.
236 D3 Elkhorn r. NE U.S.A.
232 B6 Elkhorn City KY U.S.A.
129 D2 El'khotovo Rus. Fed.
197 H4 Elkhovo Bulg.
Elki Turkey see Beytüşşebap
231 D4 Elkin NC U.S.A.
232 D5 Elkins WV U.S.A.
234 C2 Elkins Park PA U.S.A.
224 D4 Elk Lake Ont. Can.
232 E4 Elkland PA U.S.A.
234 C3 Elk Mills MD U.S.A.
238 F3 Elk Mountain WY U.S.A.
234 C3 Elk Neck MD U.S.A.
222 H5 Elko B.C. Can.
238 D3 Elko NV U.S.A.
223 I4 Elk Point Alta Can.
236 D3 Elk Point SD U.S.A.
234 B3 Elkridge MD U.S.A.
226 A3 Elk River MN U.S.A.
241 M1 Elk Springs CO U.S.A.
230 C4 Elkton KY U.S.A.
234 C3 Elkton MD U.S.A.
232 D5 Elkton VA U.S.A.
232 C5 Elkview WV U.S.A.
245 F5 El Labrador, Cerro mt. Mex.
143 H1 Ellan Sweden
129 E3 Elläryoğu Dağı hill Azer.
Ellas country Europe see Greece
87 B5 Ellavalla W.A. Austr.
231 C5 Ellaville GA U.S.A.
178 C3 Ellbögen Austria
158 C4 Ellé r. France
171 D5 Ellefeld Ger.
221 H2 Ellef Ringnes Island Nunavut Can.
128 C1 Ellek Turkey
87 C7 Elleker W.A. Austr.
241 L2 Ellen, Mount UT U.S.A.
116 C3 Ellenabad Haryana India
173 E2 Ellenberg Ger.
232 C5 Ellenboro WV U.S.A.
233 G2 Ellenburg Depot NY U.S.A.
233 F5 Ellendale DE U.S.A.
236 D2 Ellendale ND U.S.A.
238 B2 Ellensburg WA U.S.A.
235 D1 Ellenville NY U.S.A.
244 B1 El León, Cerro mt. Mex.
78 □3a Eller i. Kwajalein Marshall Is
168 E2 Ellerau Ger.
168 E2 Ellerbek Ger.
168 E2 Ellerhoop Ger.
81 D5 Ellesmere South I. N.Z.
150 E2 Ellesmere Shropshire, England U.K.
81 D5 Ellesmere, Lake South I. N.Z.
221 J2 Ellesmere Island Nunavut Can.
149 G4 Ellesmere Port Cheshire, England U.K.
262 S1 Ellesworth Mountains Antarctica
165 C4 Ellezelles Belgium
158 C4 Elliant France
221 H3 Ellice r. Nunavut Can.
Ellice Island atoll Tuvalu see Funafuti
Ellice Islands country S. Pacific Ocean see Tuvalu
234 B3 Ellicott City MD U.S.A.
232 D3 Ellicottville NY U.S.A.
231 C5 Ellijay GA U.S.A.
244 B2 El Limón Mex.
245 E2 El Limón Mex.
173 E2 Ellingen Ger.
149 H2 Ellingham Northumberland, England U.K.
149 H2 Ellington Northumberland, England U.K.
84 C3 Elliot N.T. Austr.
215 F4 Elliot S. Africa
85 F3 Elliot, Mount Qld Austr.
215 G4 Elliotdale S. Africa
232 D5 Elliot Knob mt. VA U.S.A.
224 D4 Elliot Lake Ont. Can.
238 D2 Ellis ID U.S.A.
236 D4 Ellis KS U.S.A.
213 E4 Ellisras S. Africa
82 C3 Elliston S.A. Austr.
232 C6 Elliston VA U.S.A.
237 F6 Ellisville MS U.S.A.
182 C1 El Llano Spain
178 D3 Ellmau Austria
146 F4 Ellon Aberdeenshire, Scotland U.K.
116 C5 Ellora Caves tourist site Mahar. India
142 D2 Ellös Sweden
182 E4 El Losar del Barco Spain
149 I4 Elloughton East Riding of Yorkshire, England U.K.
169 F4 Ellrich Ger.
236 D4 Ellsworth KS U.S.A.
233 □I2 Ellsworth ME U.S.A.
236 C3 Ellsworth NE U.S.A.
226 A3 Ellsworth WI U.S.A.
262 R1 Ellsworth Land reg. Antarctica
173 E3 Ellwangen (Jagst) Ger.
232 C4 Ellwood City PA U.S.A.
168 D2 Ellwürden Ger.
168 E2 Elm Ger.
190 E2 Elm Switz.
151 H2 Elm Cambridgeshire, England U.K.
175 I1 Elma r. Pol.
247 E3 El Macao Dom. Rep.
204 E5 El Mahia reg. Mali
259 C6 El Maitén Arg.
129 C4 Elmakaya Turkey
128 A1 Elmakuz Dağı mt. Turkey
199 F3 Elmalı Turkey
203 G6 El Manaqil Sudan
203 F2 El Mansûra Egypt
180 D5 El Manzla Morocco
189 C7 El Marsa Tunisia
186 D3 El Masroig Spain
205 G2 El Meghaïer Alg.
260 B3 El Melón Chile
170 C2 Elmenhorst Mecklenburg-Vorpommern Ger.
170 D1 Elmenhorst Mecklenburg-Vorpommern Ger.
170 E1 Elmenhorst Mecklenburg-Vorpommern Ger.
168 F2 Elmenhorst Schleswig-Holstein Ger.
168 F2 Elmenhorst Schleswig-Holstein Ger.
234 C3 Elmer NJ U.S.A.
234 C1 Elmhurst PA U.S.A.
206 E5 Elmina Ghana
128 B2 El Mīna Lebanon
203 F2 El Minya Egypt
126 C5 El Minya governorate Egypt
227 G4 Elmira Ont. Can.
225 I4 Elmira P.E.I. Can.
226 E3 Elmira MI U.S.A.
227 I4 Elmira NY U.S.A.
245 E4 El Mirador, Cerro mt. Mex.
241 K5 El Mirage AZ U.S.A.
183 G4 El Molar Spain
185 F1 El Molinillo Spain
185 H3 El Moral Spain
83 F4 Elmore Vic. Austr.
232 B4 Elmore OH U.S.A.
186 E3 El Morell Spain
260 E3 El Morro mt. Arg.
235 E1 Elmsford NY U.S.A.
168 E2 Elmshorn Ger.
172 B2 Elmstein Ger.
151 H2 Elmswell Suffolk, England U.K.
208 E2 El Muglad Sudan
187 B6 El Mugrón mt. Spain
227 H3 Elmvale Ont. Can.
226 C5 Elmwood IL U.S.A.
226 A3 Elmwood WI U.S.A.
244 C4 El Naranjo r. Mex.
163 E6 Elne France
140 I3 Elnesvågen Norway
92 A4 El Nido Phil.
203 F6 El Obeid Sudan
227 G4 Elora Ont. Can.
158 B3 Elorn r. France
250 B5 El Oro prov. Ecuador
242 E3 El Oro Coahuila Mex.
244 D4 El Oro México Mex.
183 H1 Elorrio Spain
261 G3 Elortondo Arg.
183 I2 Elorz Spain
183 F4 El Oso Spain
177 H5 Előszállás Hungary
244 A2 Elota r. Mex.
205 G2 El Oued Alg.
245 E3 Eloxochitlán Mex.
241 L5 Eloy AZ U.S.A.
157 G4 Éloyes France
185 F4 El Palo Spain
250 D2 El Pao Venez.
242 □I6 El Paraíso Hond.
245 G5 El Paraíso Mex.
216 □3d El Paso La Palma Canary Is
226 C5 El Paso IL U.S.A.
El Paso KS U.S.A. see Derby
239 F6 El Paso TX U.S.A.
182 D4 El Payo Spain
185 H1 El Pedernoso Spain
245 E2 El Pedregoso r. Mex.
184 E3 El Pedroso Spain
183 E3 El Pedroso de la Armuña Spain
260 B3 El Peñón mt. Chile
183 I5 El Peral Spain
182 E3 El Perdigón Spain
186 D4 El Perelló Spain
187 C5 El Perelló Spain
168 E1 Elpersbüttel Ger.
147 C3 Elphin Rep. of Ireland
146 C3 Elphin Highland, Scotland U.K.
185 H1 El Picazo Spain
Elpin Armenia see Yelp'in
186 D3 El Pinell de Bray Spain
182 E3 El Piñero Spain
186 E3 El pla de Santa Maria Spain
260 B3 El Plomo, Nevado mt. Chile
186 C4 El Pobo Spain
183 I4 El Pobo de Dueñas Spain
187 C5 El Port Spain
240 H3 El Portal CA U.S.A.
186 G2 El Port de la Selva Spain
240 I5 El Porvenir Baja California Norte Mex.
242 D2 El Porvenír Mex.
242 □K7 El Porvenír Panama
186 F3 El Prat de Llobregat Spain
243 H6 El Progreso Guat.
185 H1 El Provencio Spain
183 G1 El Puente Spain
183 E5 El Puente de Arzobispo Spain
El Puerto de Andraitx Spain see Port d'Andratx
184 D4 El Puerto de Santa María Spain
128 A5 El Qâ' val. Egypt
El Qâhira Egypt see Cairo
126 C5 El Qâhira governorate Egypt
128 B3 El Qasimiye r. Lebanon
203 F3 El Qasr Egypt
El Quds Israel/West Bank see Jerusalem
258 D2 El Quebrachal Arg.
260 B1 Elqui r. Chile
260 B3 El Quisco Chile
244 C4 El Ranchito Mex.
183 H2 El Rasillo Spain
184 D3 El Real de la Jara Spain
183 F4 El Real de San Vicente Spain
183 H4 El Recuenco Spain
244 D3 El Refugio Mex.
237 D5 El Reno OK U.S.A.
203 G3 El Ridisîya Bahari Egypt
240 H4 El Rio CA U.S.A.
244 A2 El Roble Mex.
185 F1 El Robledo Spain
184 D3 El Rocío Spain
183 G5 El Romeral Spain
184 C3 El Rompido Spain
184 D3 El Ronquillo Spain
223 I5 Elrose Sask. Can.
226 B4 Elroy WI U.S.A.
183 H3 El Royo Spain
185 F3 El Rubio Spain
244 C2 El Rucio Mex.
222 C2 Elsa Y.T. Can.
194 D5 Elsa r. Sicilia Italy
191 F5 Elsa r. Italy
186 B2 El Sabinar Aragón Spain
185 H2 El Sabinar Murcia Spain
203 F2 El Saff Egypt
242 B2 El Sahuaro Mex.
244 D1 El Salado Mex.
187 C5 El Saler Spain
126 D5 El Sâlhîya Egypt
185 I2 El Salobral Spain
244 B2 El Salto Durango Mex.
244 C3 El Salto Jalisco Mex.
243 H6 El Salvador country Central America
258 C2 El Salvador Chile
244 D1 El Salvador Mex.
92 C4 El Salvador Phil.
186 D3 Els Arcs Spain
227 F1 Elsas Ont. Can.
Elsass reg. France see Alsace
185 E3 El Saucejo Spain
182 D4 El Saugo Spain
242 D2 El Sauz Mex.
216 □3a El Sauzal Tenerife Canary Is
240 I6 El Sauzal Mex.
172 D2 Elsava r. Ger.
178 E3 Elsbethen Austria
149 G2 Elsdon Northumberland, England U.K.
168 E2 Elsdorf Niedersachsen Ger.
169 B5 Elsdorf Nordrhein-Westfalen Ger.
168 E1 Elsdorf-Westermühlen Ger.
169 D3 Else r. Ger.
247 E3 El Seibo Dom. Rep.
165 F4 Elsenborn Belgium
173 F3 Elsendorf Ger.
172 D2 Elsenfeld Ger.
172 C2 Elsenz r. Ger.
186 E2 El Serrat Andorra
84 C2 Elsey N.T. Austr.
168 D2 Elsfleth Ger.
84 C2 El Sharana N.T. Austr.
226 E4 Elsie MI U.S.A.
Elsinore Denmark see Helsingør
240 I5 Elsinore CA U.S.A.
241 K2 Elsinore UT U.S.A.
165 E4 Elsloo Neth.
234 C3 Elsmere DE U.S.A.
171 D4 Elsnig Ger.
171 D4 Elsnigk Ger.
186 D3 El Soleràs Spain
164 E2 Elspeet Neth.
186 E3 Els Prats de Rei Spain
164 E3 Elst Gelderland Neth.
164 E3 Elst Utrecht Neth.
151 G3 Elstead Surrey, England U.K.
171 D4 Elster Ger.
171 D5 Elsterberg Ger.
171 E4 Elsterwerda Ger.
151 G3 Elstree Hertfordshire, England U.K.
242 D2 El Sueco Mex.
203 G2 El Suweis Egypt
128 A5 El Suweis governorate Egypt
260 B3 El Tabo Chile
245 F3 El Tajín tourist site Mex.
205 H1 El Tarf Alg.
189 B7 El Tarf prov. Alg.
244 D4 El Tecolote, Cerro mt. Mex.
182 D2 El Teleno mt. Spain
245 E1 El Temascal Mex.
179 H3 Eltendorf Austria
171 D5 Elterlein Ger.
80 E3 Eltham North I. N.Z.
183 F4 El Tiemblo Spain
251 E2 El Tigre Venez.
173 E2 Eltmann Ger.
183 H5 El Toboso Spain
250 D2 El Tocuyo Venez.
147 C4 Elton Rep. of Ireland
120 A2 El'ton Rus. Fed.
151 G2 Elton Cambridgeshire, England U.K.
149 G4 Elton Cheshire, England U.K.
120 A2 El'ton, Ozero l. Rus. Fed.
238 C2 Eltopia WA U.S.A.
182 E4 El Torno Spain
261 G3 El Trébol Arg.
245 E5 El Treinta Mex.
185 F1 El Trincheto Spain
242 C4 El Triunfo Mex.
184 D3 El Tumbalejo Spain
203 G2 El Tûr Egypt
186 D2 El Turbón mt. Spain
169 D5 Eltville am Rhein Ger.
203 G3 El Uqşur Egypt
114 D2 Eluru Andhra Prad. India
138 F2 Elva Estonia
146 E6 Elvanfoot South Lanarkshire, Scotland U.K.
Elvanlı Turkey see Tömük
184 C2 Elvas Port.
158 D4 Elven France
186 E3 El Vendrell Spain
234 C2 Elverson PA U.S.A.
141 J3 Elverum Norway
250 C3 El Viejo mt. Col.
242 □I6 El Viejo Nic.
244 B3 El Vigía, Cerro mt. Mex.
149 I4 Elvington York, England U.K.
86 F3 Elvire r. W.A. Austr.
185 F2 El Viso Spain
184 E3 El Viso del Alcor Spain
190 D3 Elvo r. Italy
126 B6 El Wâdi El Jadid governorate Egypt
226 C5 Elwood IL U.S.A.
230 C3 Elwood IN U.S.A.
236 D3 Elwood NE U.S.A.
234 D3 Elwood NJ U.S.A.
169 F4 Elxleben Ger.
151 H2 Ely Cambridgeshire, England U.K.
150 D3 Ely Cardiff, Wales U.K.
226 B2 Ely MN U.S.A.
241 J2 Ely NV U.S.A.
232 B4 Elyria OH U.S.A.
227 I5 Elysburg PA U.S.A.
169 D5 Elz Ger.
172 B3 Elz r. Ger.
245 F5 El Zacatón, Cerro mt. Mex.
172 C3 Elzach Ger.
169 E3 Elze Ger.
168 E3 Elze (Wedemark) Ger.
78 □5 Émaé i. Vanuatu
160 D1 Émagny France
138 F2 Emajõgi r. Estonia
122 D2 Emām Qolī Iran
122 C2 Emāmrūd Iran
123 G2 Emām Şaḩēb Afgh.
143 G3 Emån r. Sweden
215 I2 Emangusi S. Africa
78 □5 Émao i. Vanuatu
121 J3 Emazar Kazakh.
120 D2 Emba Kazakh.
120 C3 Emba r. Kazakh.
215 G2 Embalenhle S. Africa
258 D1 Embarcación Arg.
223 I3 Embarras Portage Alta Can.
226 A2 Embarrass MN U.S.A.
Embi Kazakh. see Emba
183 I4 Embid Spain
183 I3 Embid de Ariza Spain
Embira r. Brazil see Envira
149 H2 Embleton Northumberland, England U.K.
146 E4 Embo Highland, Scotland U.K.
Émbonas Notio Aigaio Greece see Emponas
256 D3 Emborcação, Represa de resr Brazil
Emborion Greece see Emporeio
172 C4 Embrach Switz.
234 C3 Embreeville PA U.S.A.
233 F2 Embrun Ont. Can.
161 E4 Embrun France
168 F2 Embsen Ger.
256 D5 Embu Brazil
210 C5 Embu Kenya
113 □1 Embudhu i. S. Male Maldives
113 □1 Embudhu Finolhu i. S. Male Maldives
168 C2 Emden Ger.
199 E3 Emecik Turkey
Emei Sichuan China see Emeishan
108 B2 Emeishan Sichuan China
108 B2 Emei Shan mt. Sichuan China
121 J3 Emel' r. Kazakh.
85 G4 Emerald Qld Austr.
83 F4 Emerald Vic. Austr.
234 C2 Emerald PA U.S.A.
225 H2 Emeril Nfld. Can.
Emerita Augusta Spain see Mérida
252 D3 Emero r. Bol.
223 L5 Emerson Man. Can.
232 B5 Emerson KY U.S.A.
241 L2 Emery UT U.S.A.
Emesa Syria see Ḩimş
199 F2 Emet Turkey
215 H1 eMgwenya S. Africa
240 G2 Emigrant Gap CA U.S.A.
241 J3 Emigrant Valley NV U.S.A.
215 H1 eMijindini S. Africa
202 C5 Emi Koussi mt. Chad
222 G2 Emile r. N.W.T. Can.
243 H5 Emiliano Zapata Chiapas Mex.
244 C1 Emiliano Zapata Durango Mex.
244 C2 Emiliano Zapata Zacatecas Mex.
190 G4 Emilia-Romagna admin. reg. Italy
261 G4 Emilio Ayarza Arg.
245 F4 Emilio Carranza Mex.
190 C3 Emilius, Monte mt. Italy
110 C2 Emin Xinjiang China
237 F4 Eminence MO U.S.A.
110 C2 Emin He r. China
197 H4 Eminska Planina hills Bulg.
199 G2 Emirdağ Turkey
199 G2 Emir Dağı mt. Turkey
199 F2 Emirhisar Turkey
83 F5 Emita Tas. Austr.
168 E1 Emkendorf Ger.
232 D4 Emlenton PA U.S.A.
168 B3 Emlichheim Ger.
147 C4 Emly Rep. of Ireland
143 F3 Emmaboda Sweden
Emmahaven Sumatera Indon. see Telukbayur
139 K3 Emmaus Rus. Fed.
234 C2 Emmaus PA U.S.A.
83 G2 Emmaville N.S.W. Austr.
190 C1 Emme r. Switz.
164 E2 Emmeloord Neth.
168 D1 Emmelsbüll-Horsbüll Ger.
169 C5 Emmelshausen Ger.
164 F2 Emmen Neth.
172 C4 Emmen Switz.
172 B3 Emmendingen Ger.
169 E3 Emmer r. Ger.
164 G2 Emmer-Compascuum Neth.
164 F2 Emmer-Erfscheidenveen Neth.
169 B4 Emmerich Ger.
173 F3 Emmering Ger.
173 G3 Emmerting Ger.
85 F5 Emmet Qld Austr.
236 E3 Emmetsburg IA U.S.A.
238 C3 Emmett ID U.S.A.
232 B3 Emmett MI U.S.A.
114 C3 Emmiganuru Andhra Prad. India
232 E5 Emmitsburg MD U.S.A.
234 B3 Emmorton MD U.S.A.
151 H2 Emneth Norfolk, England U.K.
223 M5 Emo Ont. Can.
177 J4 Emőd Hungary
Emona Slovenia see Ljubljana
237 E5 Emory TX U.S.A.
237 C6 Emory Peak TX U.S.A.
206 B4 Empada Guinea-Bissau
242 C3 Empalme Mex.
244 D3 Empalme Escobedo Mex.
181 E4 Empanadas mt. Spain
215 H3 Empangeni S. Africa
258 F2 Empedrado Arg.
260 A4 Empedrado Chile
164 E3 Empel Neth.
266 G2 Emperor Seamount Chain sea feature N. Pacific Ocean
266 G2 Emperor Trough sea feature N. Pacific Ocean
172 C3 Empfingen Ger.
Empingham Reservoir England U.K. see Rutland Water
226 D3 Empire MI U.S.A.
191 F5 Empoli Italy
199 E3 Emponas Notio Aigaio Greece
199 D3 Emporeio Greece
236 D4 Emporia KS U.S.A.
232 E6 Emporia VA U.S.A.
232 D4 Emporium PA U.S.A.
223 I5 Empress Alta Can.
213 F3 Empress Mine Zimbabwe
165 E4 Emptinne Belgium
Empty Quarter des. Saudi Arabia see Rub' al Khālī
161 C3 Empurany France
168 C2 Ems r. Ger.
169 C3 Emsbüren Ger.
227 H3 Emsdale Ont. Can.
169 C3 Emsdetten Ger.
173 E2 Emskirchen Ger.
164 E2 Emst Neth.
168 D3 Emstek Ger.
151 G4 Emsworth Hampshire, England U.K.
215 H1 Emthonjeni S. Africa
168 D3 Emtinghausen Ger.
85 E3 Emu Creek r. Qld Austr.
138 F2 Emumägi hill Estonia
85 G4 Emu Park Qld Austr.
100 C1 Emur r. China
147 E2 Emyvale Rep. of Ireland
215 G2 Emzinoni S. Africa
104 D3 Ena Japan
140 K3 Enafors Sweden
250 D4 Enambú Col.
141 L3 Enånger Sweden
104 D3 Ena-san mt. Japan
186 D4 Encanadé mt. Spain
255 B9 Encantadas, Serra das hills Brazil
245 H5 Encantado r. Mex.
92 B3 Encanto, Cape Phil.
244 C3 Encarnación Mex.
253 G6 Encarnación Para.
206 E5 Enchi Ghana
185 I1 Encina r. Spain
186 B3 Encinacorba Spain
237 D6 Encinal TX U.S.A.
185 G2 Encinas mt. Spain
183 E4 Encinas de Abajo Spain
184 D2 Encinasola Spain
185 F3 Encinas Reales Spain
182 D2 Encinedo Spain
240 I5 Encinitas CA U.S.A.
239 F5 Encino NM U.S.A.
183 H2 Enciso Spain
82 D3 Encounter Bay S.A. Austr.
255 E5 Encruzilhada Brazil
255 B9 Encruzilhada do Sul Brazil
177 K3 Encs Hungary
177 L4 Encsencs Hungary
222 E4 Endako B.C. Can.
94 C2 Endau r. Malaysia
85 E1 Endeavour Strait Qld Austr.
142 D4 Endelave i. Denmark
77 I2 Enderbury i. Kiribati
222 G5 Enderby B.C. Can.
Enderby atoll Micronesia see Puluwat
151 F2 Enderby Leicestershire, England U.K.
264 L9 Enderby Abyssal Plain sea feature Southern Ocean
86 C4 Enderby Island W.A. Austr.
263 D2 Enderby Land reg. Antarctica
220 C3 Endicott Mountains AK U.S.A.
252 D2 Endimari r. Brazil
172 B3 Endingen Ger.
207 I6 Endom Cameroon
177 I3 Endrefalva Hungary
182 E4 Endrinal Spain
163 D6 Endron, Pique d' mt. France
227 I4 Endwell NY U.S.A.
252 B2 Ene r. Peru
87 B6 Eneabba W.A. Austr.
142 D2 Enebakk Norway
191 G3 Enego Italy
137 J5 Enem Rus. Fed.
EnenKio N. Pacific Ocean see Wake Atoll
121 I4 Energeticheskiy Kazakh.
120 D2 Energetik Rus. Fed.
Energodar Ukr. see Enerhodar
137 H4 Enerhodar Ukr.
176 G4 Enese Hungary
266 G6 Enewetak atoll Marshall Is
199 E1 Enez Turkey
182 B2 Enfesta Spain
225 I4 Enfield N.S. Can.
151 G3 Enfield Greater London, England U.K.
231 E4 Enfield NC U.S.A.
226 E2 Engadine MI U.S.A.
140 J3 Engan Norway
265 M3 Engaño, Cape Phil.
Engaños, Río de los r. Col. see Yari
215 F4 Engcobo S. Africa
169 C3 Engden Ger.
190 D2 Engelberg Switz.
231 F5 Engelhard NC U.S.A.
179 H2 Engelhartstetten Austria
179 E2 Engelhartszell Austria
168 D3 Engeln Ger.
120 A2 Engel's Saratovskaya Oblast' Rus. Fed.
173 G3 Engelsberg Ger.
164 D1 Engelschmangat sea chan. Neth.
171 D4 Engelsdorf Ger.
169 C5 Engelskirchen Ger.
172 C4 Engen Ger.
256 A5 Engenheiro Beltrão Brazil
257 F2 Engenheiro Navarro Brazil
169 D3 Enger Ger.
141 J3 Engerdal Norway
170 C3 Engersen Ger.
168 D1 Enge-Sande Ger.
94 C4 Enggano i. Indon.
203 H5 Enghershatu mt. Eritrea
165 D4 Enghien Belgium
222 C3 Engineer B.C. Can.
165 E4 Engis Belgium
149 H5 England admin. div. U.K.
225 K3 Englee Nfld. Can.
156 D2 Englefontaine France
224 E4 Englehart Ont. Can.
231 D7 Englewood FL U.S.A.
235 E2 Englewood NJ U.S.A.
232 A5 Englewood OH U.S.A.
223 M5 English r. Ont. Can.
230 C4 English IN U.S.A.
English Bazar W. Bengal India see Ingraj Bazar
234 A1 English Center PA U.S.A.
145 G7 English Channel France/U.K.
262 S2 English Coast Antarctica
234 D3 English Creek NJ U.S.A.
247 □2 English Harbour Town Antigua and Barbuda
235 D2 Englishtown NJ U.S.A.
163 D6 Engomer France
134 F2 Engozero Rus. Fed.
172 D3 Engstingen Ger.
187 C6 Enguera Spain
183 I5 Enguidanos Spain
138 D3 Engure Latvia
129 B2 Enguri r. Georgia
215 H3 Enhlalakahle S. Africa
237 D4 Enid OK U.S.A.
78 □3b Enigu i. Majuro Marshall Is
172 D3 Eningen unter Achalm Ger.
198 C2 Enipefs r. Greece
102 J2 Eniwa Japan
Eniwetok atoll Marshall Is see Enewetak
185 H4 Enix Spain
Enkeldoorn Zimbabwe see Chivhu
157 H3 Enkenbach Ger.
164 E2 Enkhuizen Neth.
172 B2 Enkirch Ger.
143 G2 Enköping Sweden
Enle Yunnan China see Zhenyuan
194 D5 Enna Sicilia Italy
194 D5 Enna prov. Sicilia Italy
190 E3 Enna r. Italy
203 F6 En Nahud Sudan
202 D5 Ennedi, Massif mts Chad
147 D3 Ennell, Lough l. Rep. of Ireland
169 C4 Ennepetal Ger.
215 F2 Ennerdale S. Africa
157 G3 Ennery France
246 D3 Ennery Haiti
160 B3 Ennezat France
83 F2 Enngonia N.S.W. Austr.
169 D4 Ennigerloh Ger.
123 H3 Enninabad Pak.
236 C2 Enning SD U.S.A.
147 C4 Ennis Rep. of Ireland
238 E2 Ennis MT U.S.A.
237 D5 Ennis TX U.S.A.
147 E4 Enniscorthy Rep. of Ireland
147 C5 Enniskean Rep. of Ireland
147 E3 Enniskerry Rep. of Ireland
147 D2 Enniskillen Northern Ireland U.K.
147 B4 Ennistymon Rep. of Ireland
78 □3a Enniwetak i. Kwajalein Marshall Is
128 B3 Enn Nâqoûra Lebanon
179 F2 Enns Austria
179 F2 Enns r. Austria
78 □3a Ennubuj i. Kwajalein Marshall Is
78 □3a Ennumennet i. Kwajalein Marshall Is
78 □3a Ennylabagan i. Kwajalein Marshall Is
140 O3 Eno Fin.
241 K3 Enoch UT U.S.A.
234 B2 Enola PA U.S.A.
140 O3 Enonkoski Fin.
140 M1 Enontekiö Fin.
231 D5 Enoree r. SC U.S.A.
233 G2 Enosburg Falls VT U.S.A.
109 E4 Enping Guangdong China
92 B2 Enrile Phil.
246 E3 Enriquillo Dom. Rep.
164 E2 Ens Neth.
83 F4 Ensay Vic. Austr.
164 F2 Enschede Neth.
173 F2 Ensdorf Ger.
169 D4 Ense Ger.
261 I4 Ensenada Arg.
242 A2 Ensenada Baja California Norte Mex.
242 C4 Ensenada Baja California Sur Mex.
247 □1 Ensenada Puerto Rico
172 B2 Ensheim Ger.
108 D2 Enshi Hubei China
104 D4 Enshū-nada g. Japan
157 H5 Ensisheim France
231 C6 Ensley FL U.S.A.
151 F3 Enstone Oxfordshire, England U.K.
161 D5 Ensuès-la-Redonne France
210 B4 Entebbe Uganda
164 F2 Enter Neth.
146 E6 Enterkinfoot Dumfries and Galloway, Scotland U.K.
222 G2 Enterprise N.W.T. Can.
227 I3 Enterprise Ont. Can.
231 C6 Enterprise AL U.S.A.
238 C2 Enterprise OR U.S.A.
241 K3 Enterprise UT U.S.A.
95 F2 Entimau, Bukit hill Sarawak Malaysia
190 D2 Entlebuch Switz.
190 C4 Entracque Italy
184 B3 Entradas Port.
161 C4 Entraigues-sur-Sorgues France
160 B1 Entrains-sur-Nohain France
159 F4 Entrammes France
222 G4 Entrance Alta Can.
84 B2 Entrance Island N.T. Austr.
161 E4 Entraunes France
161 A4 Entraygues-sur-Truyère France
261 H3 Entre Ríos prov. Arg.
252 D5 Entre Ríos Bol.
254 F4 Entre Rios Brazil
Entre Rios Moz. see Malema
257 E4 Entre Rios de Minas Brazil
161 E5 Entrevaux France
184 B1 Entroncamento Port.
215 H3 Entumeni S. Africa
207 G5 Enugu Nigeria
207 G5 Enugu state Nigeria
131 T3 Enurmino Rus. Fed.
182 C5 Envendos Port.
156 B3 Envermeu France
250 C3 Envigado Col.
252 C1 Envira Brazil
252 C1 Envira r. Brazil
177 H5 Enying Hungary
81 C5 Enys, Mount South I. N.Z.
172 D2 Enz r. Ger.
190 F4 Enza r. Italy
105 E3 Enzan Japan
179 H2 Enzersdorf an der Fischa Austria
172 C3 Enzklösterle Ger.
182 C1 Eo r. Spain
Eochaill Rep. of Ireland see Youghal
232 B6 Eolia KY U.S.A.
Eooa i. Tonga see Eua
146 B3 Eoropaidh Western Isles, Scotland U.K.
159 G2 Épaignes France
190 B2 Epalignes Switz.
245 E3 Epazoyucan Mex.
164 E2 Epe Neth.
207 F5 Epe Nigeria
208 C4 Epéna Congo
177 J5 Eperjes Hungary
156 D3 Épernay France
156 B4 Épernon France
172 C3 Epfendorf Ger.
199 E3 Ephesus tourist site Turkey
241 L2 Ephraim UT U.S.A.
234 B2 Ephrata PA U.S.A.
238 C2 Ephrata WA U.S.A.
78 □5 Épi i. Vanuatu
Epidamnus Albania see Durrës
198 C3 Epidavros tourist site Greece
156 B5 Épieds-en-Beauce France
161 E3 Épierre France
181 F2 Épila Spain
160 C2 Épinac France
157 G4 Épinal France
Epirus admin. reg. Greece see Ipeiros
160 B1 Epiry France
128 A2 Episkopi Cyprus
160 C1 Époisses France
193 F4 Epomeo, Monte hill Italy
172 A2 Eppelborn Ger.
172 C2 Eppelheim Ger.
172 B2 Eppenbrunn Ger.
171 E5 Eppendorf Ger.
172 C2 Eppertshausen Ger.
156 D3 Eppeville France
151 H3 Epping Essex, England U.K.
233 □H3 Epping NH U.S.A.
172 C2 Eppingen Ger.
173 E3 Eppishausen Ger.
169 D5 Eppstein Ger.
150 D2 Eppynt, Mynydd hills Wales U.K.
151 G3 Epsom Surrey, England U.K.
156 B3 Epte r. France
159 G4 Épuisay France
149 I4 Epworth North Lincolnshire, England U.K.

122 C4 Eqlīd Iran
208 D4 Équateur admin. reg. Dem. Rep. Congo
207 H6 Equatorial Guinea country Africa
158 I4 Équeurdreville-Hainneville France
191 F5 Era r. Italy
191 H3 Eraclea Italy
191 H3 Eraclea Mare Italy
186 B1 Eracurri mt. Spain
92 A4 Eran Phil.
183 H1 Erandio Spain
116 C5 Erandol Mahar. India
215 G1 Erasmia S. Africa
Erawadi r. Myanmar see Irrawaddy
190 E3 Erba Italy
203 H4 Erba, Jebel mt. Sudan
126 E2 Erbaa Turkey
172 D3 Erbach Baden-Württemberg Ger.
172 D2 Erbach Hessen Ger.
173 G2 Erbendorf Ger.
172 B2 Erbeskopf hill Ger.
190 D3 Erbognone r. Italy
158 E4 Erbray France
128 A2 Ercan airport Cyprus
163 D6 Ercé France
127 F3 Erçek Turkey
260 A6 Ercilla Chile
127 F3 Erciş Turkey
126 D3 Erciyes Daği mt. Turkey
177 H4 Ercsi Hungary
177 H4 Érd Hungary
140 N1 Erdalsfjellet hill Norway
Erdaobaihe Jilin China see Baihe
106 B5 Erdaogou Qinghai China
100 C4 Erdao Jiang r. China
171 C4 Erdeborn Ger.
199 E1 Erdek Turkey
126 D3 Erdemli Turkey
106 C1 Erdenet Hövsgöl Mongolia
106 E1 Erdenet Orhon Mongolia
106 D2 Erdenetsogt Bayanhongor Mongolia
106 E3 Erdenetsogt Ömnögovi Mongolia
158 C4 Erdeven France
173 F3 Erding Ger.
171 E5 Erdmannsdorf Ger.
135 I7 Erdniyevskiy Rus. Fed.
158 E4 Erdre r. France
172 D4 Erdweg Ger.
256 A6 Eré, Campos hills Brazil
158 D3 Éréac France
251 E3 Erebato r. Venez.
263 L1 Erebus, Mount vol. Antarctica
127 G5 Erech tourist site Iraq
255 B8 Erechim Brazil
107 G1 Erentsav Mongolia
126 D3 Ereğli Turkey
126 C2 Ereğli Turkey
194 D5 Erego Moz. see Errego
194 D5 Erei, Monti mts Sicilia Italy
Erementaú Kazakh. see Yeremyentau
110 D3 Erenhaberga Shan mts China
107 G3 Erenhot Nei Mongol China
196 E4 Erenik r. Yugo.
122 D3 Erentepe Turkey
183 F3 Eresma r. Spain
199 D2 Eresos Voreio Aigaio Greece
198 C2 Eretria Greece
Erevan Armenia see Yerevan
168 E1 Erfde Ger.
204 D3 Erfoud Morocco
169 B5 Erftstadt Ger.
171 C5 Erfurt Ger.
127 E3 Ergani Turkey
204 D5 'Erg Atouila des. Mali
205 H4 'Erg Chech des. Alg./Mali
205 H4 Erg d' Amer des. Alg.
202 C6 Erg du Djourab des. Chad
207 H2 Erg du Ténéré des. Niger
107 F3 Ergel Mongolia
169 E2 Ergersheim Ger.
204 E4 Erg Iabes des. Alg.
204 D4 Erg Iguidi des. Alg./Maur.
205 E5 'Erg I-n-Sâkâne des. Mali
205 G4 Erg Issaouane des. Alg.
143 L2 Ergli Latvia
173 G3 Ergolding Ger.
173 G3 Ergoldsbach Ger.
158 B3 Ergué-Gabéric France
208 B2 Erguig r. Chad
107 I1 Erguil Nei Mongol China
Ergun he r. China/Rus. Fed. see Argun'
Ergun Youqi Nei Mongol China see Ergun
173 G3 Erharting Ger.
182 E2 Eria r. Spain
146 D3 Eribol Highland, Scotland U.K.
146 D3 Eribol, Loch inlet Scotland U.K.
164 F2 Erica Neth.
194 C5 Erice Sicilia Italy
163 I2 Erice Spain
184 A2 Ericeira Port.
146 E5 Ericht r. Scotland U.K.
146 E4 Ericht, Loch l. Scotland U.K.
223 L5 Erickson Man. Can.
237 E4 Erie KS U.S.A.
232 C3 Erie PA U.S.A.
227 G4 Erie, Lake Can./U.S.A.
Erieddu r. N. Male Maldives see Eriyadhu
206 D2 'Erigât des. Mali
130 D2 Erik Eriksenstretet sea chan. Svalbard
223 L5 Eriksdale Man. Can.
143 F3 Eriksmåla Sweden
185 E2 Erillas hill Spain
231 C4 Erin TN U.S.A.
173 H3 Ering Ger.
143 F3 Eringsboda Sweden
146 A4 Eriskay i. Scotland U.K.
172 D4 Eriskirch Ger.
151 H2 Eriswell Suffolk, England U.K.
190 C1 Eriswil Switz.
Erithraí Greece see Erythres
Erithropótamos r. Greece see Erydropotamos
203 H6 Eritrea country Africa
213 □1 Eriyadhu i. N. Male Maldives
Eriyadu i. N. Male Maldives see Eriyadhu
169 B4 Erkelenz Ger.
156 C2 Erkelsbrugge France
169 E4 Erker-Shakhar Rus. Fed.
173 E3 Erkheim Ger.
199 G2 Erkmen Afyon Turkey
171 E3 Erkner Ger.
178 D3 Erl Austria
186 C2 Erla Spain
190 C1 Erlach Switz.
173 F2 Erlangen Ger.
109 D1 Erlangping Henan China
173 H2 Erlau r. Austria
179 G2 Erlauf Austria
179 G2 Erlauf r. Austria
84 C5 Erldunda N.T. Austr.
169 D5 Erlenbach am Main Ger.
190 D4 Erii Italy
100 D4 Erlong Shan mt. China
234 D4 Erma N.J. U.S.A.
Ermak Pavlodarskaya Oblast' Kazakh. see Aksu
164 E2 Ermelo Neth.
215 I2 Ermelo S. Africa
199 D5 Ermenek Turkey
128 A1 Ermenek r. Turkey
199 G5 Ermenek Turkey
184 B2 Ermidas do Sado Port.
191 G2 Ermioni Greece
244 C2 Ermita de los Correas Mex.
173 D3 Erms r. Germany
183 H1 Ermua Spain
114 C4 Ernakulam Kerala India

169 D5 Erndtebrück Ger.
147 C2 Erne r. Rep. of Ireland/U.K.
159 F3 Ernée France
159 F3 Ernée r. France
87 D5 Ernest Giles Range hills W.A. Austr.
179 H2 Ernstbrunn Austria
172 A2 Ernz Noire r. Lux.
114 C4 Erode Tamil Nadu India
78 □3b Eroj i. Majuro Marshall Is
173 E3 Erolzheim Ger.
85 E5 Eromanga Qld Austr.
212 B4 Erongo admin. reg. Namibia
164 B3 Erp Neth.
177 K4 Érpatak Hungary
169 C5 Erpel Ger.
106 B3 Erpu Xinjiang China
Erqu Shaanxi China see Zhouzhi
165 D4 Erquelinnes Belgium
158 D3 Erquy France
204 D3 Er Rachidia Morocco
203 F6 Er Rahad Sudan
146 B5 Erraid i. Scotland U.K.
204 E3 Er Raoui des. Alg.
183 C5 Errazu Spain
147 C5 Errego r. Italy
147 D2 Errigal hill Rep. of Ireland
147 D4 Erril Rep. of Ireland
170 C1 Errindlev Denmark
190 D4 Erro r. Italy
186 B2 Erro r. Spain
149 F3 Errochty Water r. Scotland U.K.
146 D4 Erogie Highland, Scotland U.K.
80 F3 Erskdale North I. N.Z.
146 E6 Erskine Scotland U.K.
225 H2 Erskine Nfld. Can.
137 I3 Eskhar Ukr.
140 □ Eskifjörður Iceland
199 F2 Eski Gediz Turkey
170 C1 Eskilstrup Denmark
143 G2 Eskilstuna Sweden
220 E3 Eskimo Lakes N.W.T. Can.
Eskimo Point Nunavut Can. see Arviat
127 F3 Eski Mosul Iraq
121 H4 Eski-Nookat Kyrg.
126 D2 Eskipazar Turkey
199 G2 Eskişehir Turkey
199 G2 Eskişehir prov. Turkey
183 D3 Esla r. Spain
122 A3 Eslāmābād-e Gharb Iran
173 G2 Eslarn Ger.
183 J2 Eslava Spain
199 F3 Esler Daği mt. Turkey
169 D4 Eslohe (Sauerland) Ger.
142 E4 Eslöv Sweden
199 F2 Eşme Turkey
129 C3 Eşmeçayır Turkey
244 B3 Esmeralda Chile
246 G2 Esmeralda Cuba
259 B8 Esmeralda, Isla i. Chile
257 E3 Esmeraldas Brazil
250 B4 Esmeraldas Ecuador
250 B4 Esmeraldas prov. Ecuador
252 D3 Esmeraldo r. Bol.
186 □ Es Migjorn Gran Spain
232 D6 Esmont VA U.S.A.
182 B4 Esmoriz Port.
156 D2 Esnes France
165 D4 Esneux Belgium
187 C5 Espadán r. Spain
182 D2 Espadañedo Spain
122 E5 Espakeh Iran
161 A4 Espalion France
161 B3 Espaly-St-Marcel France
São Francisco
171 E5 Erzgebirge mts Czech Rep./Ger.
100 C2 Erzhan Heilong. China
106 B1 Erzin Rus. Fed.
126 E3 Erzin Turkey
129 A4 Erzincan prov. Turkey
127 F3 Erzincan Turkey
127 F3 Erzurum Turkey
129 A3 Erzurum prov. Turkey
191 H1 Esanatoglia Italy
195 G3 Esaro r. Italy
193 I5 Esaro r. Italy
102 J4 Esashi Japan
143 E5 Esbjerg Denmark
142 C4 Esbjerg airport Denmark
156 C4 Esblye France
Esbo Fin. see Espoo
254 G4 Escada Brazil
182 C2 Escairón Spain
183 G1 Escalante Phil.
241 L3 Escalante UT U.S.A.
241 L3 Escalante r. UT U.S.A.
182 D4 Escalhão Port.
163 A5 Escaliers, Pic des mt. France
186 C1 Escaló Spain
187 E6 Es Caló Spain
240 C3 Escalón Mex.
183 F4 Escalona Spain
183 F3 Escalona del Prado Spain
182 C5 Escalos de Baixo Port.
182 C5 Escalos de Cima Port.
183 H3 Escalote r. Spain
231 C6 Escambia r. AL U.S.A.
183 H4 Escamilla Spain
226 D3 Escanaba MI U.S.A.
161 B5 Escandorgue ridge France
184 C4 Escañuela Spain
182 C4 Escarabote Spain
186 C2 Escarcega Mex.
183 F1 Escaro France
165 C4 Escaut r. Belgium
184 E3 Escalona France
257 F2 Espinosa, Serra do mts Brazil
182 B4 Espinhal Port.
184 D2 Espinheira hill Angola
182 B3 Espinho Port.
255 B9 Espinho, Serra do hills Brazil
183 F1 Espinilla Spain
250 E3 Espinosa Brazil
183 F1 Espinosa de Cerrato Spain
183 F3 Espinosa de Henares Spain
183 F1 Espinosa de los Monteros Spain
183 F5 Espinoso del Rey Spain
163 F6 Espira-de-l'Agly France
182 B2 Espirito Santo Brazil
257 G3 Espírito Santo state Brazil
184 C3 Espírito Santo Spain
92 B2 Espiritu Phil.
78 □ Espiritu Santo i. Vanuatu
243 I5 Espíritu Santo, Bahía del b. Mex.
243 H4 Espita Mex.
254 F4 Esplanada Brazil
187 H3 Espluges de Llobregat Spain
186 D3 Esplús Spain
186 D2 Espolla Spain
182 B4 Espondeilham France
140 Q3 Espoo Fin.
141 N3 Espoo Fin.
182 C4 Espoon Port.

165 D3 Essen Belgium
169 C4 Essen Congo
208 B4 Etoumbi Congo
235 D2 Etra NJ U.S.A.
156 C4 Étréchy France
183 F4 Étrek r. Iran/Turkm. see Atrek
156 B3 Étrépagny France
159 G2 Étretat France
159 E3 Étreux France
156 B3 Étrœungt France
159 F3 Évreux France
198 C3 Evrotas r. Greece
196 C4 Évry France
198 D2 Evvoia i. Greece
198 C1 Evzonoi Kentriki Makedonia Greece
240 □ Ewa HI U.S.A.
240 □ Ewa Beach HI U.S.A.
85 F3 Ewan Qld Austr.
182 C3 Ewbank S. Africa
171 C4 Ewarton Jamaica
210 D4 Ewaso Ngiro r. Kenya
172 C3 Ewbank S. Africa
146 C4 Ewe, Loch b. Scotland U.K.
151 G3 Ewell Surrey, England U.K.
226 C2 Ewen MI U.S.A.
Ewenkizu Zizhiqi Nei Mongol China see Bayan Tohoi
151 G3 Ewhurst Surrey, England U.K.
234 C2 Ewing NJ U.S.A.
262 T2 Ewing Island Antarctica
208 B5 Ewo Congo
198 C5 Examilia Peloponnisos Greece
215 F3 Excelsior S. Africa
240 H2 Excelsior Mountains CA U.S.A.
236 E4 Excelsior Springs MO U.S.A.
182 D3 Exuma Pa Can.
232 C6 Exchange PA U.S.A.
150 C4 Excideuil France
150 D3 Exe r. England U.K.
150 D3 Exebridge Somerset, England U.K.
262 P1 Executive Committee Range mts Antarctica
226 B3 Exeland WI U.S.A.
83 G3 Exeter N.S.W. Austr.
227 G4 Exeter Ont. Can.
150 D4 Exeter Devon, England U.K.
233 □H3 Exeter NH U.S.A.
240 H3 Exeter CA U.S.A.
233 □H3 Exeter NH U.S.A.
161 E3 Exilles Italy
164 F2 Exloo Neth.
159 G3 Exmes France
150 D4 Exminster Devon, England U.K.
151 I3 Exmouth, Mouth of the England U.K.
86 A4 Exmouth W.A. Austr.
150 D4 Exmouth Devon, England U.K.
86 A4 Exmouth Gulf W.A. Austr.
265 L6 Exmouth Plateau sea feature Indian Ocean
85 G5 Expedition Range mts Australia
225 K3 Exploits r. Nfld. Can.
225 H2 Exshaw Alta Can.
239 □ Exton PA U.S.A.
245 I3 Extoraz r. Mex.
245 G5 Extremadura aut. comm. Spain
207 I4 Extrême-Nord prov. Cameroon
182 B3 Extremo Port.
246 C1 Exuma Cays i. Bahamas
246 D1 Exuma Sound sea chan. Bahamas
135 G7 Eya r. Rus. Fed.
149 H4 Eyam Derbyshire, England U.K.
211 B5 Eyasi, Lake salt l. Tanz.
Eyawadi r. Myanmar see Irrawaddy
161 D3 Eybens France
162 D3 Eybouleuf France
163 D6 Eycheil France
142 C2 Eydehavn Norway
168 D3 Eydelstedt Ger.
85 G2 Eyeigh Qld Austr.
151 I2 Eye Suffolk, England U.K.
146 F6 Eyemouth Scottish Borders, Scotland U.K.
146 B3 Eye Peninsula Scotland U.K.
147 D4 Eyeries Rep. of Ireland
161 D4 Eyguians France
161 D5 Eyguières France
162 E3 Eygurande France
162 D3 Eygurande-et-Gardedeuil France
140 □ Eyjafjallajökull ice cap Iceland
140 □ Eyjafjörður inlet Iceland
210 F3 Eyl Somalia
210 E3 Eylau Rus. Fed. see Bagrationovsk
156 B3 Eyn r. England U.K.
164 D3 Eurville-Bienville France
169 B5 Euskirchen Ger.
165 E4 Eußenheim Ger.
178 E2 Eustis FL U.S.A.
231 D6 Eustis FL U.S.A.
223 H4 Euston N.S.W. Austr.
231 C5 Eutaw AL U.S.A.
168 F1 Eutin Ger.
172 C3 Eutingen im Gäu Ger.
171 D4 Eutzsch Ger.
158 C2 Euville France
84 C3 Euving Downs N.T. Austr.
190 D3 Evançon r. Italy
215 G2 Evander S. Africa
236 F4 Evans, Mount CO U.S.A.
221 H4 Evansburg Alta Can.
76 D4 Evans, Mount N.T. Austr.
234 B1 Evans Falls PA U.S.A.
221 J3 Evans Strait Nunavut Can.
226 B5 Evanston IL U.S.A.
238 D6 Evanston WY U.S.A.
234 □ Evansville IN U.S.A.
226 C4 Evansville WI U.S.A.
226 C4 Evansville WI U.S.A.
237 D6 Evant TX U.S.A.
146 D4 Evanton Highland, Scotland U.K.
161 B3 Évaux-les-Bains France
164 E4 Evart MI U.S.A.
215 F2 Évaton S. Africa
160 A2 Évaux-les-Bains France
122 C5 Evaz Iran
129 D4 Evci Turkey
199 F2 Evciler Turkey
128 B1 Evcili Turkey
165 E4 Evelith MN U.S.A.
141 N3 Evenes Norway
140 L1 Evenskjær Norway
82 C2 Everard, Lake salt flat S.A. Austr.
84 C4 Everard, Mount N.T. Austr.
82 C1 Everard Range hills S.A. Austr.
84 C4 Everard, Mount N.T. Austr.
156 B4 Évergem Belgium
150 E3 Evercreech Somerset, England U.K.
164 E3 Everdingen Neth.
235 H2 Everett N.B. Can.
117 F4 Everest, Mount China/Nepal
233 □J1 Everett MA U.S.A.
234 C4 Everett PA U.S.A.
239 □ Evergem swamp FL U.S.A.
231 C7 Everglades City FL U.S.A.
231 C6 Evergreen AL U.S.A.
150 □2 Evie Orkney, Scotland U.K.
228 F1 Evergreen CO U.S.A.
151 F3 Evington England U.K.
159 G3 Évian-les-Bains France
164 M3 Evijärvi Fin.
185 H2 Évinos r. Greece
184 B3 Évora Spain
142 C2 Evje Norway

212 C3 Etosha Pan salt pan Namibia
208 B4 Etoumbi Congo
235 D2 Etra NJ U.S.A.
156 C4 Étrechy France
183 F4 Étrek r. Iran/Turkm. see Atrek
156 B3 Étrépagny France
159 G2 Étretat France
159 E3 Étreux France
156 B3 Étrœungt France
161 F2 Ettal Ger.
146 E6 Ettelbruck Lux.
146 E6 Ettrick Scottish Borders, Scotland U.K.
149 G2 Ettrickbridge Scottish Borders, Scotland U.K.
146 E6 Ettrick Forest reg. Scotland U.K.
146 C5 Ettrick Water r. Scotland U.K.
169 E6 Ettringen Ger.
172 D3 Etwall Derbyshire, England U.K.
186 B1 Etxalar Spain
Etxarri Spain see Echarri
Etxarri-Aranatz Spain see Echarri-Aranaz
244 B3 Etzatlán Mex.
223 I5 Etzicom Coulee r. Alta Can.
156 B2 Eu France
79 □2a Eua i. Tonga
83 F3 Euabalong N.S.W. Austr.
156 C2 Eubigheim Ger.
Euboea i. Greece see Evvoia
87 F6 Eucla W.A. Austr.
232 C4 Euclid OH U.S.A.
254 F4 Euclides da Cunha Brazil
256 A5 Euclides da Cunha Paulista Brazil
83 G4 Eucumbene, Lake N.S.W. Austr.
237 F5 Eudora AR U.S.A.
84 D3 Eudunda S.A. Austr.
231 C6 Euerbach Ger.
169 F5 Euerdorf Ger.
231 C6 Eufaula AL U.S.A.
237 E5 Eufaula OK U.S.A.
237 E5 Eufaula Lake resr OK U.S.A.
165 F4 Eupen Belgium
172 D2 Eupora MS U.S.A.
118 D2 Euphrates r. Asia
alt. Al Furāt (Iraq/Syria), alt. Firat (Turkey)
237 F5 Eupora MS U.S.A.
141 M3 Eura Fin.
173 F3 Eurasburg Bayern Ger.
173 F4 Eurasburg Bayern Ger.
179 F2 Euratsfeld Austria
156 B3 Eure dept Haute-Normandie France
156 B3 Eure r. France
156 B4 Eure-et-Loir dept Centre France
168 D3 Eurohansa Ger.
164 D3 Europoort reg. Neth.
183 E1 Europa, Île i. Indian Ocean
183 E1 Europa, Picos de mts Spain
132 Europe continent
213 □4b Eramanga i. Vanuatu

234 C1 Factoryville PA U.S.A.
184 C1 Fadagosa Port.
207 H3 Fada-Ngourma Burkina
177 H5 Fadd Hungary
205 H4 Fadnoun, Plateau du Alg.
191 I2 Faedis Italy
191 G4 Faenza Italy
Færoerne terr.
N. Atlantic Ocean see Faroe Islands
Faeroes see Faroe Islands
Faesulae Italy see Fiesole
192 D2 Faete, Monte hill Italy
208 C3 Fafa r. C.A.R.
182 B3 Fafe Port.
191 I2 Fagagna Italy
197 G3 Fågăraş Romania
Fagatau atoll Arch. des Tuamotu Fr. Polynesia see Fangatau
78 □7 Fagatogo American Samoa
141 J3 Fagernes Norway
143 F2 Fagersta Sweden
197 F3 Făget Romania
193 I5 Fagnano Castello Italy
192 A2 Fagnano, Lago i. Arg./Chile
156 E4 Fagnes reg. Belgium
206 D2 Faguibine, Lac l. Mali
148 B2 Fahan Rep. of Ireland
168 E1 Fahrdorf Ger.
172 F3 Fahrenkrug Ger.
172 F3 Fährenzhausen Ger.
173 F3 Fahland Ger.
125 G3 Fahūd, Jabal hill Oman
216 □1a Faial i. Azores
184 □ Faial Madeira
216 □1c Faial, Canal do sea chan. Azores
193 G3 Faicchio Italy
78 □1a Faichuk i. Chuuk Micronesia
169 C5 Faid Ger.
190 D3 Faido Switz.
162 D3 Faide Port.
168 E4 Faines Belgium
160 C1 Fains-les-Montbard France
157 F4 Fains-Véel France
220 D3 Fairbanks AK U.S.A.
232 A5 Fairborn OH U.S.A.
234 C3 Fairbury NE U.S.A.
226 B3 Fairchild WI U.S.A.
81 B7 Fairfax South I. N.Z.
232 E5 Fairfax VA U.S.A.
233 G2 Fairfax VT U.S.A.
233 F3 Fairfield CT U.S.A.
236 D3 Fairfield IA U.S.A.
238 D3 Fairfield ID U.S.A.
232 A5 Fairfield OH U.S.A.
237 D6 Fairfield TX U.S.A.
241 K1 Fairfield VA U.S.A.
232 D6 Fairfield VA U.S.A.
151 F3 Fairford Gloucestershire, England U.K.
227 F4 Fairgrove MI U.S.A.
233 H4 Fairhaven MA U.S.A.
227 G4 Fair Haven NJ U.S.A.
233 G3 Fair Haven VT U.S.A.
234 C3 Fair Hill MD U.S.A.
235 G2 Fair Lawn NJ U.S.A.
232 C5 Fairlea MD U.S.A.
233 F3 Fairless Hills PA U.S.A.
81 C6 Fairlie South I. N.Z.
146 D5 Fairlie North Ayrshire, Scotland U.K.
85 D7 Fairlight Qld Austr.
151 H4 Fairlight East Sussex, England U.K.
236 E3 Fairmont MN U.S.A.
232 C5 Fairmont WV U.S.A.
222 H5 Fairmont Hot Springs B.C. Can.
151 F4 Fair Oak Hampshire, England U.K.
237 F5 Fair Oaks AR U.S.A.
226 D4 Fair Plain MI U.S.A.
239 F4 Fairplay CO U.S.A.
234 D1 Fairport NY U.S.A.
234 C3 Fairview NJ U.S.A.
85 F7 Fairview Qld Austr.
222 G3 Fairview Alta Can.
235 G1 Fairview IL U.S.A.
227 K7 Fairview KY U.S.A.
227 F3 Fairview MI U.S.A.
239 H2 Fairview NJ U.S.A.
235 G1 Fairview NY U.S.A.
237 D4 Fairview OK U.S.A.
232 C4 Fairview PA U.S.A.
241 J1 Fairview UT U.S.A.
226 B4 Fairview WI U.S.A.
234 D4 Fairview WV U.S.A.
222 B2 Fairweather, Mount Alaska/B.C. Can./U.S.A.
91 J5 Fais i. Micronesia
123 H4 Faisalabad Pak.
156 E3 Faissault France
236 C3 Faith SD U.S.A.
193 L2 Faito, Monte mt. Italy
123 H3 Faizabad Afgh. see Feyzābād
116 E4 Faizabad Uttar Prad. India
116 E4 Fajã da Ovelha Madeira
216 □1b Fajã do Cima São Miguel Azores
182 B2 Fajão Port.
184 B2 Fajarda Port.
247 K1 Fajardo Puerto Rico
175 H5 Fajsz Hungary
81 □1 Fakaofo atoll Tokelau
Fakaofu atoll Tokelau see Fakaofo
79 □3 Fakarava atoll Arch. des Tuamotu Fr. Polynesia
151 H2 Fakenham Norfolk, England U.K.
140 K3 Fåker Sweden
117 G4 Fakiragram Assam India
197 H3 Fakiyska Reka r. Bulg.
142 E4 Fakse Denmark
142 E4 Fakse Bugt b. Denmark
100 C4 Faku Liaoning China
206 B4 Falaba Sierra Leone
150 C4 Fal r. England U.K.
191 G2 Falconara Marittima Italy
193 I5 Falconara Sicilia Italy
Falconara Tonga see Fonuafo'ou
234 B1 Falcon Lake Man. Can.
243 M5 Falcon Lake i. Mex./U.S.A.
193 G3 Falconara Italy
184 D3 Faldeiro Port.
206 B3 Falékourou Senegal
193 D5 Falerii Italy
193 F1 Falerone Italy
195 G5 Faleşti Moldova see Făleşti
197 L1 Făleşti Moldova
237 D7 Falfurrias TX U.S.A.
222 G4 Falher Alta Can.
171 D5 Falkenberg Bayern Ger.
171 F4 Falkenberg Brandenburg Ger.
171 F4 Falkenberg Brandenburg Ger.
142 E4 Falkenberg Sweden

Falkenhagen to Flekkerøy
304

170 D2 Falkenhagen Ger.
171 D4 Falkenhain Ger.
170 E3 Falkensee Ger.
173 G2 Falkenstein Bayern Ger.
171 D5 Falkenstein Sachsen Ger.
170 E3 Falkenthal Ger.
146 E6 Falkirk Falkirk, Scotland U.K.
146 E6 Falkirk admin. div. Scotland U.K.
236 E5 Falkland Fife, Scotland U.K.
264 F9 Falkland Escarpment sea feature S. Atlantic Ocean
259 F8 Falkland Islands terr. S. Atlantic Ocean
264 F9 Falkland Plateau sea feature S. Atlantic Ocean
259 E9 Falkland Sound sea chan. Falkland Is
142 E2 Falköping Sweden
175 I4 Fałków Pol.
237 E4 Fall r. KS U.S.A.
232 B6 Fall Branch TN U.S.A.
240 I5 Fallbrook CA U.S.A.
226 B3 Fall Creek WI U.S.A.
190 C3 Fallère, Monte mt. Italy
158 E5 Falleron France
140 M2 Fällfors Sweden
262 T2 Fallieres Coast Antarctica
146 E5 Fallin Stirling, Scotland U.K.
168 E3 Fallingbostel Ger.
147 A2 Fallmore Rep. of Ireland
215 F5 Fallodon S. Africa
240 H2 Fallon NV U.S.A.
233 H4 Fall River MA U.S.A.
234 C1 Falls PA U.S.A.
234 A4 Falls Church VA U.S.A.
236 E3 Falls City NE U.S.A.
232 D4 Falls Creek PA U.S.A.
234 D2 Fallsington PA U.S.A.
234 B3 Fallston MD U.S.A.
190 D2 Falmenta Italy
246 □ Falmouth Jamaica
150 B4 Falmouth Cornwall, England U.K.
232 A5 Falmouth KY U.S.A.
233 H4 Falmouth MA U.S.A.
233 □H3 Falmouth ME U.S.A.
234 B2 Falmouth PA U.S.A.
232 E5 Falmouth VA U.S.A.
150 B4 Falmouth Bay England U.K.
247 □2 Falmouth Harbour Antigua and Barbuda
206 D3 Falo Mali
206 D3 Falou Mali
261 F6 Falsa, Bahía b. Arg.
225 G1 False r. Que. Can.
214 B6 False Bay S. Africa
220 B4 False Pass AK U.S.A.
117 F5 False Point India
186 D3 Falset Spain
259 C9 Falso Cabo de Hornos c. Chile
142 D4 Falster i. Denmark
149 G2 Falstone Northumberland, England U.K.
197 H2 Fălticeni Romania
143 F1 Falun Sweden
93 D3 Fam, Kepulauan is Irian Jaya Indon.
Famagusta Cyprus see Ammochostos
Famagusta Bay Cyprus see Ammochostos Bay
182 C4 Famalicão Port.
258 D3 Famatina Arg.
258 C3 Famatina, Sierra de mts Arg.
169 F5 Fambach Ger.
157 G3 Fameck France
122 B3 Famenin Iran
165 D4 Famenne val. Belgium
86 B4 Fame Range hills W.A. Austr.
86 E4 Family Well W.A. Austr.
206 D3 Fana Mali
78 □4a Fanaik i. Chuuk Micronesia
78 □4a Fanan i. Chuuk Micronesia
191 F4 Fanano Italy
78 □4a Fanapanges i. Chuuk Micronesia
109 F2 Fanchang Anhui China
213 □J4 Fandriana Madag.
147 E3 Fane r. Rep. of Ireland
96 B3 Fang Thai.
79 □3 Fangatau atoll Arch. des Tuamotu Fr. Polynesia
79 □3 Fangataufa atoll Arch. des Tuamotu Fr. Polynesia
Fangcheng Guangxi China see Fangchenggang
109 E1 Fangcheng Henan China
108 D4 Fangchenggang Guangxi China
108 D2 Fangdou Shan mts China
109 G4 Fangliao Taiwan
192 A2 Fango r. Corse France
109 G4 Fangshan Taiwan
108 D1 Fangxian Hubei China
100 D3 Fangzheng Heilong. China
196 D5 Fani i Vogël r. Albania
138 F5 Fanipal' Belarus
163 E5 Fanjeaux France
108 D2 Fankuai Sichuan China
Fankuaidian Sichuan China see Fankuai
109 □ Fanling H.K. China
186 C2 Fanlo Spain
146 C4 Fannich, Loch l. Scotland U.K.
140 J3 Fannrem Norway
120 D5 Fannūj Iran
142 C4 Fanø i. Denmark
191 I5 Fano Italy
142 C4 Fanø Bugt b. Denmark
78 □4a Fanos i. Chuuk Micronesia
Fanoualie i. Tonga see Fonualei
109 F2 Fanshan Anhui China
109 G3 Fanshan Zhejiang China
106 E4 Fanshi Shanxi China
96 C2 Fan Si Pan mt. Vietnam
177 K5 Fântâna Rece hill Romania
177 K5 Fântânele Romania
Fanum Fortunae Italy see Fano
107 G5 Fanxian Henan China
182 B3 Fão Port.
Farab Turkm. see Farap
206 C3 Faraba Mali
Farab-Pristan' Turkm. see Dzheykhun
208 F4 Faradje Dem. Rep. Congo
Faradofay Madag. see Tôlañaro
213 □J4 Farafangana Madag.
206 B3 Farafenni Gambia
193 G2 Fara Filiorum Petri Italy
202 C3 Farafra Oasis Egypt
123 E3 Farāh Afgh.
123 E3 Farāh prov. Afgh.
Farahābād Iran see Khezerābād
213 □K2 Farahalana Madag.
193 E2 Fara in Sabina Italy
91 K3 Farallon de Medinilla i. N. Mariana Is
91 J2 Farallon de Pajaros vol. N. Mariana Is
182 E3 Faramontanos de Tábara Spain
206 C4 Faranah Guinea
197 H2 Faraoani Romania
123 F2 Farap Turkm.
125 F4 Fararah Oman
124 C4 Farasān, Jazā'ir is Saudi Arabia
193 G2 Fara San Martino Italy
186 B2 Farasdues Spain
213 □J3 Faratsiho Madag.
91 J5 Faraulep atoll Micronesia
197 G2 Farcău, Vârful mt. Romania
173 F4 Farchant Ger.
165 D4 Farciennes Belgium
177 L6 Fârdea Romania
185 H3 Fardes r. Spain
147 D3 Fardrum Rep. of Ireland
157 G3 Farébersviller France
151 F4 Fareham Hampshire, England U.K.
156 D4 Faremoutiers France
Farewell, Cape Greenland see Nunap Isua
80 D4 Farewell, Cape South I. N.Z.
80 D4 Farewell Spit South I. N.Z.
193 E2 Farfa r. Italy
142 E2 Färgelanda Sweden
Farghona Uzbek. see Fergana
Farghona Wiloyati admin. div. Uzbek. see Ferganskaya Oblast'
231 D6 Fargo GA U.S.A.
236 D2 Fargo ND U.S.A.
163 E4 Fargues France
163 F5 Fargues-sur-Ourbise France
168 E1 Fårhus Denmark
236 E2 Faribault MN U.S.A.
116 D3 Faridabad Haryana India
116 C3 Faridkot Punjab India
117 G5 Faridpur Bangl.
116 D3 Faridpur Uttar Prad. India
122 D2 Fārīg Iran
141 K3 Färila Sweden
206 B3 Farim Guinea-Bissau
122 D3 Farīmān Iran
151 F3 Faringdon Oxfordshire, England U.K.
149 G4 Farington Lancashire, England U.K.
254 D3 Farinha r. Brazil
190 E4 Farini Italy
182 D3 Fariza de Sayago Spain
143 G3 Färjestaden Kalmar Sweden
198 C2 Farkadhon Greece
Farkhar Afgh. see Farkhato
123 G2 Farkhato Afgh.
123 G2 Farkhor Tajik.
211 B6 Farkwa Tanz.
85 G4 Farleigh Qld Austr.
151 F3 Farleigh Wallop Hampshire, England U.K.
186 C3 Farlete Spain
192 D1 Farma r. Italy
199 E3 Farmakonisi i. Greece
150 E3 Farmborough Bath and North East Somerset, England U.K.
226 C5 Farmer City IL U.S.A.
237 E5 Farmerville LA U.S.A.
235 D2 Farmingdale NJ U.S.A.
222 F4 Farmington B.C. Can.
235 F1 Farmington CT U.S.A.
234 C4 Farmington DE U.S.A.
226 B5 Farmington IL U.S.A.
233 □H2 Farmington ME U.S.A.
237 F4 Farmington MO U.S.A.
233 □H3 Farmington NH U.S.A.
239 E4 Farmington NM U.S.A.
238 E3 Farmington UT U.S.A.
232 B3 Farmington Hills MI U.S.A.
235 E2 Farmingville NY U.S.A.
177 I4 Farmos Hungary
222 E4 Far Mountain B.C. Can.
232 D6 Farmville VA U.S.A.
177 H3 Farná Slovakia
151 G3 Farnborough Hampshire, England U.K.
149 G4 Farndon Cheshire, England U.K.
149 I4 Farndon Nottinghamshire, England U.K.
149 H2 Farne Islands England U.K.
192 B2 Farnese Italy
233 G2 Farnham Que. Can.
151 G3 Farnham Surrey, England U.K.
232 E6 Farnham VA U.S.A.
87 E5 Farnham, Lake salt flat W.A. Austr.
222 G5 Farnham, Mount B.C. Can.
151 G3 Farnham Royal Buckinghamshire, England U.K.
171 C4 Farnstädt Ger.
149 G4 Farnworth Greater Manchester, England U.K.
251 G5 Faro Brazil
207 I4 Faro r. Cameroon
222 C2 Faro Y.T. Can.
184 C3 Faro Port.
184 B3 Faro admin. dist. Port.
182 C2 Faro mt. Spain
143 H3 Fårö Gotland Sweden
182 C2 Faro, Serra do mts Spain
144 D1 Faroe Islands terr. N. Atlantic Ocean
190 C3 Faroma, Monte mt. Italy
143 H3 Fårösund Gotland Sweden
217 □2 Farquhar Atoll Seychelles
217 □2 Farquhar Islands Seychelles
87 D5 Farquharson Tableland hills W.A. Austr.
146 D4 Farr Highland, Scotland U.K.
191 H2 Farra d'Alpago Italy
232 E4 Farrandsville PA U.S.A.
147 B4 Farranfore Rep. of Ireland
146 D4 Farrar r. Scotland U.K.
124 C4 Farrāsh, Jabal al hill Saudi Arabia
122 C4 Farrāshband Iran
227 J3 Farrellton Que. Can.
122 D3 Farrokhī Iran
Farrukhabad Uttar Prad. India see Fatehgarh
122 C4 Fārs prov. Iran
129 B1 Fars r. Rus. Fed.
122 C3 Farsakh Iran
198 C3 Farsala Greece
198 C2 Farsaliotis r. Greece
127 H6 Fārsī, Jazīreh-ye i. Iran
142 C3 Farsø Denmark
238 E3 Farson WY U.S.A.
142 B2 Farsund Norway
197 H3 Fărtănești Romania
256 B2 Fartura r. Brazil
255 B8 Fartura, Serra da mts Brazil
142 C3 Fårvang Denmark
Farvel, Kap c. Greenland see Nunap Isua
226 E4 Farwell MI U.S.A.
237 C5 Farwell TX U.S.A.
123 F2 Fāryāb prov. Afgh.
122 D4 Fāryāb Iran
138 G4 Farynava Belarus
122 C4 Fasā Iran
195 G2 Fasano Italy
137 J3 Fashchivka Ukr.
210 C1 Fasil Ghebbi and Gonder Monuments tourist site Eth.
216 □3a Fasnia Tenerife Canary Is
168 F3 Faßberg Ger.
136 E2 Fastiv Ukr.
Fastov Ukr. see Fastiv
208 F4 Fataki Dem. Rep. Congo
193 F3 Fate, Monte delle mt. Italy
116 C3 Fatehabad Haryana India
116 D4 Fatehgarh Madh. Prad. India
116 D4 Fatehgarh Uttar Prad. India
116 C4 Fatehnagar Rajasthan India
116 E4 Fatehpur Uttar Prad. India
116 D4 Fatehpur Sikri Uttar Prad. India
182 C4 Fatela Port.
215 F3 Fateng Tse Ntsho S. Africa
137 H1 Fatezh Rus. Fed.
122 C4 Fathābād Iran
206 A3 Fatick Senegal
182 B5 Fátima Port.
Fattoilep atoll Micronesia see Faraulep
Fatuhiva i. Fr. Polynesia see Fatu Hiva
79 □3 Fatu Hiva i. Fr. Polynesia
78 □6 Fauabu Malaita Solomon Is
157 G5 Faucogney-et-la-Mer France
163 E5 Faugères France
147 D1 Faughan r. Northern Ireland U.K.
190 F5 Fauglia Italy
163 C4 Fauguerolles France
172 D2 Faulbach Ger.
146 E6 Fauldhouse West Lothian, Scotland U.K.
170 D2 Faulenrost Ger.
236 D2 Faulkton SD U.S.A.
157 G3 Faulquemont France
156 C2 Fauquembergues France
227 G5 Fauquier B.C. Can.
87 F5 Faure Island W.A. Austr.
215 E3 Fauresmith S. Africa
78 □6 Fauro i. Solomon Is
140 K2 Fauske Norway
222 H4 Faust Alta Can.
156 C2 Fauville-en-Caux France
163 C4 Faux France
162 D3 Faux-la-Montagne France
182 C3 Favaios Port.
190 E4 Favale di Malvaro Italy
191 H5 Favalto, Monte mt. Italy
195 E5 Favara Sicilia Italy
187 C5 Favara Spain
160 E3 Faverges France
157 G4 Faverney France
158 E4 Faverolles France
151 H3 Faversham Kent, England U.K.
157 F4 Favières France
194 B5 Favignana Sicilia Italy
194 B5 Favignana, Isola i. Sicilia Italy
222 H4 Fawcett Alta Can.
151 F4 Fawley Hampshire, England U.K.
224 B2 Fawn r. Ont. Can.
234 B3 Fawn Grove PA U.S.A.
215 H3 Fawnleas S. Africa
124 C2 Fawwārah Saudi Arabia
140 □B2 Faxaflói b. Iceland
140 L3 Faxälven r. Sweden
234 B1 Faxon PA U.S.A.
202 C5 Faya Chad
78 □5 Fayaoué Î. Loyauté New Caledonia
156 C5 Fay-aux-Loges France
163 D4 Faycelles France
158 D4 Fay-de-Bretagne France
161 E5 Fayence France
231 C5 Fayette AL U.S.A.
226 D3 Fayette MI U.S.A.
236 E4 Fayette MO U.S.A.
237 F6 Fayette MS U.S.A.
232 A4 Fayette OH U.S.A.
237 E4 Fayetteville AR U.S.A.
231 C5 Fayetteville GA U.S.A.
231 E5 Fayetteville NC U.S.A.
233 E3 Fayetteville NY U.S.A.
232 E5 Fayetteville PA U.S.A.
231 C5 Fayetteville TN U.S.A.
232 C5 Fayetteville WV U.S.A.
127 H5 Faylakah i. Kuwait
157 F5 Fayl-la-Forêt France
157 G5 Faymont France
186 D3 Fayón Spain
161 C4 Fay-sur-Lignon France
91 L5 Fayu i. Micronesia
191 I4 Fažana Croatia
151 F2 Fazeley Staffordshire, England U.K.
116 C3 Fazilka Punjab India
125 E2 Fazrān, Jabal hill Saudi Arabia
204 B5 Fdérik Maur.
147 B4 Feale r. Rep. of Ireland
146 C4 Fearnmore Highland, Scotland U.K.
163 B5 Féas France
234 C2 Feasterville PA U.S.A.
240 G2 Feather r. CA U.S.A.
240 G2 Feather, North Fork r. CA U.S.A.
81 E4 Featherston North I. N.Z.
150 E2 Featherstone Staffordshire, England U.K.
149 H4 Featherstone West Yorkshire, England U.K.
159 G2 Fécamp France
192 D1 Feccia r. Italy
157 H4 Fecht r. France
188 G3 Federacija Bosna i Hercegovina aut. div. Bos.-Herz.
261 I2 Federación Arg.
261 H2 Federal Arg.
207 G4 Federal Capital Territory admin. div. Nigeria
Federal District admin. dist. Brazil see Distrito Federal
Federal District admin. dist. Mex. see Distrito Federal
Federal District admin. dist. Venez. see Distrito Federal
233 F5 Federalsburg MD U.S.A.
Federated Malay States country Asia see Malaysia
144 J1 Fedje Norway
137 H4 Fedorivka Ukr.
Fedorov Zapadnyy Kazakhstan Kazakh. see Fedorovka
120 E1 Fedorovka Kustanayskaya Oblast' Kazakh.
121 I1 Fedorovka Pavlodarskaya Oblast' Kazakh.
120 B2 Fedorovka Zapadnyy Kazakhstan Kazakh.
120 C1 Fedorovka Respublika Bashkortostan Rus. Fed.
137 J4 Fedorovka Rostovskaya Oblast' Rus. Fed.
120 B1 Fedorovka Samarskaya Oblast' Rus. Fed.
135 I6 Fedorovka Saratovskaya Oblast' Rus. Fed.
137 J5 Fedorovskaya Rus. Fed.
146 D4 Feehlin r. Scotland U.K.
147 D2 Feeny Northern Ireland U.K.
78 □4a Fefan i. Chuuk Micronesia
158 D4 Fégréac France
177 J4 Fegyvernek Hungary
177 L4 Fehérgyarmat Hungary
177 J4 Fehér-Körös r. Hungary
177 H4 Fehérvárcsurgó Hungary
170 C1 Fehmarn i. Ger.
Fehmarn Belt str. Denmark/Ger. see Femer Bælt
170 D3 Fehrbellin Ger.
179 H4 Fehring Austria
257 G4 Feia, Lagoa lag. Brazil
Feicheng Shandong China see Feixian
109 F2 Feidong Anhui China
156 D2 Feignies France
252 C2 Feijó Brazil
184 A2 Feijó Port.
172 B2 Feilbingert Ger.
81 E4 Feilding North I. N.Z.
171 C5 Feilitzsch Ger.
160 C2 Feillens France
Feio r. Brazil see Aguapeí
Feira Zambia see Luangwa
254 F5 Feira de Santana Brazil
182 B3 Feira do Monte Spain
128 B5 Feirāni, Gebel mt. Egypt
160 E3 Feissons-sur-Isère France
179 F4 Feistritz im Rosental Austria
179 G4 Feistritz ob Bleiburg Austria
184 C3 Feiteira Port.
109 F2 Feixi Anhui China
107 H5 Feixian Shandong China
107 G4 Feixiang Hebei China
177 H4 Fejér county Hungary
142 D4 Fejø i. Denmark
126 D3 Feke Turkey
177 K3 Fekete-Körös r. Hungary
187 G5 Felanitx Spain
172 F2 Felchow Ger.
169 F5 Felda r. Ger.
173 F4 Feldafing Ger.
179 F4 Feld am See Austria
179 G4 Feldbach Austria
160 F1 Feldbach France
170 E2 Feldberg Ger.
172 C4 Feldberg mt. Ger.
168 E1 Felde Ger.
177 J4 Feldebrő Hungary
178 A3 Feldkirch Austria
172 D4 Feldkirch admin. reg. Austria
173 F3 Feldkirchen Ger.
179 G3 Feldkirchen bei Graz Austria
179 F4 Feldkirchen in Kärnten Austria
173 F4 Feldkirchen-Westerham Ger.
197 G2 Feldru Romania
182 D3 Felgar Port.
182 B3 Felgueiras Port.
177 J5 Felgyő Hungary
261 H2 Feliciano r. Arg.
232 A5 Felicity OH U.S.A.
113 D11 Felidhu Atoll Maldives
150 D2 Felindre Powys, Wales U.K.
161 B3 Felines France
190 F4 Felino Italy
244 B1 Felipe Carrillo Puerto Durango Mex.
244 C4 Felipe Carrillo Puerto Michoacán Mex.
243 H5 Felipe C. Puerto Mex.
193 H4 Felitto Italy
185 H4 Félix Spain
179 H3 Felixdorf Austria
257 E3 Felixlândia Brazil
151 I3 Felixstowe Suffolk, England U.K.
215 H3 Felixton S. Africa
190 D4 Felizzano Italy
172 A2 Fell Ger.
146 E6 Fell, Loch hill Scotland U.K.
191 I2 Fella r. Italy
172 D3 Fellbach Ger.
162 E3 Felletin France
149 H3 Felling Tyne and Wear, England U.K.
246 □ Fellowship Jamaica
232 D5 Fellowsville WV U.S.A.
168 F1 Felm Ger.
177 K5 Felnac Romania
Fels Lux. see Larochette
169 E4 Felsberg Ger.
Felsina Italy see Bologna
177 K3 Felsődobsza Hungary
177 I4 Felsőlajos Hungary
177 H5 Felsőnyék Hungary
177 G6 Felsőszentmárton Hungary
177 J4 Felsőtárkány Hungary
179 H4 Felső-Válicka r. Hungary
177 J3 Felsőzsolca Hungary
168 E1 Felsted Denmark
151 H3 Felsted Essex, England U.K.
149 H2 Felton Northumberland, England U.K.
234 C3 Felton DE U.S.A.
234 B3 Felton PA U.S.A.
191 G2 Feltre Italy
151 H2 Feltwell Norfolk, England U.K.
193 F2 Fema, Monte mt. Italy
254 D5 Femeas r. Brazil
168 F1 Femer Bælt str. Denmark/Ger.
216 □3c Femés hill Lanzarote Canary Is
195 F3 Femminamorta, Monte mt. Italy
142 D4 Femø i. Denmark
107 F5 Fen r. China
147 E4 Fenagh Carlow Rep. of Ireland
147 D3 Fenagh Leitrim Rep. of Ireland
216 □1b Fenais da Ajuda São Miguel Azores
160 D1 Fénay France
163 D5 Fendeille France
225 F3 Fenelon Falls Ont. Can.
78 □4a Fenepi i. Chuuk Micronesia
Fénérive Madag. see Fenoarivo Atsinanana
129 A3 Fenerköyü Turkey
190 C3 Fenestrelle Italy
157 H4 Fénétrange France
159 F4 Feneu France
136 G2 Fenevychi Ukr.
199 D1 Fengari mt. Anatoliki Makedonia kai Thraki Greece
Fengcheng Fujian China see Anxi
Fengcheng Fujian China see Lianjiang
Fengcheng Fujian China see Yongding
Fengcheng Guangdong China see Xinfeng
Fengcheng Guangxi China see Fengshan
109 E2 Fengcheng Jiangxi China
101 C4 Fengcheng Liaoning China
Fengchuan Jiangxi China see Fengxin
108 C2 Fengdu Chongqing China
Fenggang Fujian China see Shaxian
108 C3 Fenggang Guizhou China
Fenggang Jiangxi China see Yihuang
109 G2 Fenghua Zhejiang China
108 D3 Fenghuang Hunan China
Fengjiaba Sichuan China see Wangcang
108 D2 Fengjie Chongqing China
109 D4 Fengkai Guangdong China
109 G4 Fenglin Taiwan
Fengming Shaanxi China see Qishan
107 H4 Fengnan Hebei China
107 H3 Fengning Hebei China
Fengqi Shaanxi China see Luochuan
108 A4 Fengqing Yunnan China
107 G5 Fengqiu Henan China
107 H4 Fengrun Hebei China
Fengshan Fujian China see Luoyuan
108 C3 Fengshan Guangxi China
Fengshan Hubei China see Luotian
Fengshan Yunnan China see Fengqing
100 B1 Fengshui Shan mt. Heilong. China
109 F1 Fengtai Anhui China
Fengwei Yunnan China see Zhenkang
Fengweiba Yunnan China see Zhenkang
107 H5 Fengxian Jiangsu China
108 C1 Fengxian Shaanxi China
109 G2 Fengxian Shanghai China
Fengxiang Heilong. China see Luobei
Fengxiang Yunnan China see Lincang
109 E2 Fengxin Jiangxi China
109 F1 Fengyang Anhui China
Fengyi Guizhou China see Zheng'an
Fengyi Sichuan China see Maoxian
109 G3 Fengyüan Taiwan
107 G3 Fengzhen Nei Mongol China
117 G5 Feni Bangl.
162 B2 Fenioux France
190 C3 Fenis Italy
147 B4 Fenit Rep. of Ireland
150 D4 Feniton Devon, England U.K.
117 G5 Fenny r. Bangl./India
213 □K3 Fenoarivo Atsinanana Madag.
213 □J3 Fenoarivo Be Madag.
163 D5 Fenouillet France
151 G2 Fenstanton Cambridgeshire, England U.K.
173 G2 Fensterbach r. Ger.
227 F4 Fenton MI U.S.A.
81 □1 Fenua Loa i. Tokelau
81 □1 Fenua Loa i. Tokelau
Fenua Ura atoll Arch. de la Société Fr. Polynesia see Manuae
146 D6 Fenwick East Ayrshire, Scotland U.K.
149 H2 Fenwick Northumberland, England U.K.
232 C5 Fenwick WV U.S.A.
107 F4 Fenyang Shanxi China
177 L3 Fényeslitke Hungary
109 E3 Fenyi Jiangxi China
150 B4 Feock Cornwall, England U.K.
137 H5 Feodosiya Ukr.
146 B6 Feolin Ferry Argyll and Bute, Scotland U.K.
147 C4 Feonanagh Rep. of Ireland
78 □6 Fera i. Solomon Is
Férai Greece see Feres
147 D3 Ferbane Rep. of Ireland
171 D3 Ferchland Ger.
195 F4 Ferdinandea Italy
172 E2 Ferdinandshof Ger.
122 D3 Ferdows Iran
156 D4 Fère-Champenoise France
156 D3 Fère-en-Tardenois France
158 D4 Férel France
193 F4 Ferentillo Italy
193 F3 Ferentino Italy
199 E1 Feres Greece
185 I2 Férez Spain
121 G4 Fergana Uzbek.
Fergana Oblast admin. div. Uzbek. see Ferganskaya Oblast'
Fergana Range mts Kyrg. see Fergana Too Tizmegi
121 H4 Fergana Too Tizmegi mts Kyrg.
121 G4 Ferganskaya Oblast' admin. div. Uzbek.
Ferganskiy Khrebet mts Kyrg. see Fergana Too Tizmegi
227 G4 Fergus Ont. Can.
147 C4 Fergus r. Rep. of Ireland
236 D2 Fergus Falls MN U.S.A.
84 B2 Fergusson r. N.T. Austr.
205 H2 Feriana Tunisia
199 G1 Ferizli Turkey
206 D4 Ferkessédougou Côte d'Ivoire
194 D5 Ferla Sicilia Italy
179 F4 Ferlach Austria
147 D2 Fermanagh county Northern Ireland U.K.
182 B4 Fermelã Port.
182 B4 Fermentelos Port.
191 H5 Fermignano Italy
193 F1 Fermo Italy
225 H2 Fermont Que. Can.
182 D3 Fermoselle Spain
147 C4 Fermoy Rep. of Ireland
185 G1 Fernáncaballero Spain
250 □ Fernandina, Isla i. Islas Galápagos Ecuador
231 D6 Fernandina Beach FL U.S.A.
264 G6 Fernando de Noronha i. Brazil
256 C3 Fernandópolis Brazil
Fernando Poó i. Equat. Guinea see Bioco
185 F3 Fernán Núñez Spain
213 I2 Fernão Veloso Moz.
234 B3 Ferndale MD U.S.A.
234 D1 Ferndale NY U.S.A.
238 B1 Ferndale WA U.S.A.
179 E4 Ferndorf Austria
151 F4 Ferndown Dorset, England U.K.
146 E4 Ferness Highland, Scotland U.K.
160 E2 Ferney-Voltaire France
80 F3 Fernhill North I. N.Z.
150 E2 Fernhill Heath Worcestershire, England U.K.
151 G3 Fernhurst West Sussex, England U.K.
222 H5 Fernie B.C. Can.
179 G4 Fernitz Austria
83 F2 Fernlee Qld Austr.
240 H2 Fernley NV U.S.A.
234 C1 Fernridge PA U.S.A.
147 E4 Ferns Rep. of Ireland
238 C2 Fernwood ID U.S.A.
195 F4 Feroleto Antico Italy
Ferozepore Punjab India see Firozpur
161 A5 Ferrals-les-Corbières France
195 F2 Ferrandina Italy
191 G4 Ferrara Italy
191 G4 Ferrara prov. Emilia-Romagna Italy
191 H4 Ferrarese r. Italy
193 G3 Ferrazzano Italy
182 C1 Ferreira Spain
184 B2 Ferreira do Alentejo Port.
182 B5 Ferreira do Zêzere Port.
251 I4 Ferreira-Gomes Brazil
184 A1 Ferrel Port.
232 B5 Ferrellsburg WV U.S.A.
250 B6 Ferreñafe Peru
182 D3 Ferreras de Abajo Spain
182 D3 Ferreras de Arriba Spain
190 C4 Ferrere Italy
186 □ Ferreries Spain
186 B3 Ferreruela de Huerva Spain
182 D3 Ferreruela de Tábara Spain
160 F1 Ferrette France
261 E2 Ferreyra Arg.
237 F6 Ferriday LA U.S.A.
190 E4 Ferriere Italy
156 E2 Ferrière-la-Grande France
165 E4 Ferrières Belgium
156 C4 Ferrières France
161 B3 Ferrières-St-Mary France
163 D6 Ferrières-sur-Ariège France
194 D5 Ferro r. Sicilia Italy
195 F3 Ferro r. Italy
182 B1 Ferrol Spain
241 L2 Ferron UT U.S.A.
257 F3 Ferros Brazil
192 B5 Ferru, Monte hill Sardegna Italy
232 C6 Ferrum VA U.S.A.
147 E4 Ferrycarrig Rep. of Ireland
146 F5 Ferryden Angus, Scotland U.K.
149 H3 Ferryhill Durham, England U.K.
225 K4 Ferryland Nfld. Can.
Ferryville Tunisia see Menzel Bourguiba
172 A2 Ferschweiler Ger.
120 D1 Fershampenuaz Rus. Fed.
192 A4 Fertilia Sardegna Italy
179 H3 Fertő l. Austria/Hungary
179 H3 Fertőd Hungary
179 H3 Fertőrákos Hungary
176 F4 Fertőszentmiklós Hungary
176 F4 Fertőszéplak Hungary
182 B3 Fervença Port.
164 E1 Ferwerd Neth.
139 K4 Ferzikovo Rus. Fed.
202 A1 Fès Morocco
209 C6 Feshi Dem. Rep. Congo
146 E4 Feshiebridge Highland, Scotland U.K.
236 D2 Fessenden ND U.S.A.
157 H5 Fessenheim France
156 D3 Festieux France
216 □1c Feteira Faial Azores
216 □1b Feteira São Miguel Azores
197 H3 Fetești Romania
197 H3 Fetești-Gară Romania
147 D4 Fethard Tipperary Rep. of Ireland
147 E4 Fethard Wexford Rep. of Ireland
Fethiye Malatya Turkey see Yazıhan
199 F3 Fethiye Muğla Turkey
146 □H1 Fetlar i. Scotland U.K.
146 F5 Fettercairn Aberdeenshire, Scotland U.K.
173 F2 Feucht Ger.
173 E2 Feuchtwangen Ger.
163 C4 Feugarolles France
225 G1 Feuilles, Rivière aux r. Que. Can.
156 B3 Feuquières France
156 B2 Feuquières-en-Vimeu France
160 C3 Feurs France
100 D1 Fevral'sk Rus. Fed.
126 E3 Fevzipaşa Turkey
162 D3 Feytiat France
123 G2 Feyzābād Afgh.
Fez Morocco see Fès
150 D2 Ffestiniog Gwynedd, Wales U.K.
150 C2 Ffostrasol Ceredigion, Wales U.K.
163 D5 Fiac France
258 D2 Fiambalá Arg.
258 D2 Fiambalá r. Arg.
193 F2 Fiamignano Italy
206 E4 Fian Ghana
213 □J4 Fianarantsoa Madag.
213 □J4 Fianarantsoa prov. Madag.
208 B2 Fianga Chad
190 C3 Fiano Italy
193 E2 Fiano Romano Italy
191 I5 Fiastra r. Italy
190 F2 Fiavè Italy
184 C3 Ficalho hill Port.
194 C4 Ficarazzi Sicilia Italy
191 G4 Ficarolo Italy
210 C2 Fichē Eth.
173 F2 Fichtelberg Ger.
171 D5 Fichtelgebirge hills Ger.
173 G2 Fichtelnaab r. Ger.
172 D3 Fichtenberg Ger.
215 F3 Ficksburg S. Africa
192 E2 Ficulle Italy
194 D5 Ficuzza r. Sicilia Italy
194 C4 Ficuzza Sicilia Italy
146 E4 Fiddich r. Scotland U.K.
147 D4 Fiddown Rep. of Ireland
190 F4 Fidenza Italy
176 G2 Fidlův Kopec hill Czech Rep.
206 C4 Fié r. Guinea
178 C4 Fié allo Sciliar Italy
178 D3 Fieberbrunn Austria
193 F1 Fiegni, Monte mt. Italy
222 G5 Field B.C. Can.
227 G2 Field Ont. Can.
232 B6 Field KY U.S.A.
84 C2 Field Island N.T. Austr.
138 F3 Fiemanka r. Latvia
197 G3 Fieni Romania
198 A1 Fier Albania
160 D3 Fier r. France
178 C4 Fiera di Primiero Italy
84 C2 Fiery Creek r. Qld Austr.
196 E4 Fierzës, Liqeni i resr Albania
190 D2 Fiesch Switz.
191 G5 Fiesole Italy
191 G4 Fiesso Umbertiano Italy
146 F5 Fife admin. div. Scotland U.K.
226 E3 Fife Lake MI U.S.A.
146 F5 Fife Ness pt Scotland U.K.
83 F3 Fifield N.S.W. Austr.
226 B3 Fifield WI U.S.A.
203 G5 Fifth Cataract rapids Sudan
222 H3 Fifth Meridian Alta Can.
161 E5 Figanières France
192 A2 Figarella r. Corse France
192 B3 Figari Corse France
163 E4 Figeac France
191 G5 Figline Valdarno Italy
184 B2 Figueira r. Port.
182 B4 Figueira da Foz Port.
182 D4 Figueira de Castelo Rodrigo Port.
184 B2 Figueira dos Cavaleiros Port.
184 C1 Figueira e Barros Port.
182 C4 Figueiredo de Alva Port.
184 C1 Figueiró Port.
182 C4 Figueiró da Granja Port.
182 B5 Figueiró dos Vinhos Port.
Figueras Spain see Figueres
186 F2 Figueres Spain
182 D3 Figueruela de Arriba Spain
205 E2 Figuig Morocco
207 I4 Figuil Cameroon
213 □J3 Fihaonana Madag.
79 □1 Fiji country S. Pacific Ocean
164 D3 Fijnaart Neth.
213 F3 Filabusi Zimbabwe
242 □I7 Filadelfia Costa Rica
195 F4 Filadelfia Italy
253 E5 Filadélfia Para.
177 I3 Fiľakovo Slovakia
206 D4 Filamana Mali
191 F4 Filattiera Italy
262 V1 Filchner Ice Shelf Antarctica
193 F3 Filettino Italy
149 I3 Filey North Yorkshire, England U.K.
193 H4 Filiano Italy
197 F3 Filiași Romania
198 B2 Filiates Greece
198 B3 Filiatra Greece
Filibe Bulg. see Plovdiv
195 E4 Filicudi, Isola i. Isole Lipari Italy
194 D4 Filicudi Porto Isole Lipari Italy
207 F3 Filingué Niger
199 D1 Filiouri r. Greece
Filipinas country Asia see Philippines
175 K1 Filipów Pol.
198 B3 Filippiada Greece
198 D1 Filippoi tourist site Greece
143 F2 Filipstad Sweden
190 E2 Filisur Switz.
140 J3 Fillan Norway
156 C2 Fillièvres France
160 E2 Fillinges France
Fillira Greece see Fillyra
240 H4 Fillmore CA U.S.A.
241 K2 Fillmore UT U.S.A.
151 F2 Fillongley Warwickshire, England U.K.
199 D1 Fillyra Greece
245 F3 Filomeno Mata Mex.
199 D3 Filoti Notio Aigaio Greece
191 I5 Filottrano Italy
172 D3 Fils r. Ger.
168 C2 Filsum Ger.
150 E3 Filton South Gloucestershire, England U.K.
210 D3 Filtu Eth.
179 E3 Filzmoos Austria
149 I3 Fimber East Riding of Yorkshire, England U.K.
194 D4 Finale Sicilia Italy
191 G4 Finale Emilia Italy
190 D4 Finale Ligure Italy
185 H3 Fiñana Spain
146 F5 Finavon Angus, Scotland U.K.
232 D6 Fincastle VA U.S.A.
233 F2 Finch Ont. Can.
210 C2 Finch'a'ā Hāyk' l. Eth.
151 G3 Finchampstead Wokingham, England U.K.
85 G4 Finch Hatton Qld Austr.
151 H3 Finchingfield Essex, England U.K.
151 F2 Findern Derbyshire, England U.K.
146 E4 Findhorn Moray, Scotland U.K.
146 E4 Findhorn r. Scotland U.K.
127 F3 Fındık Turkey
129 B3 Fındıklı Turkey
232 B4 Findlay OH U.S.A.
146 F4 Findochty Moray, Scotland U.K.
151 G4 Findon West Sussex, England U.K.
233 F2 Fine NY U.S.A.
151 G2 Finedon Northamptonshire, England U.K.
195 F2 Finese, Monte hill Italy
187 C6 Finestrat Spain
83 G5 Fingal Tas. Austr.
233 E3 Finger Lakes NY U.S.A.
116 E5 Fingeshwar Madh. Prad. India
213 G2 Fingoè Moz.
163 D5 Finhan France
161 B4 Finiels, Sommet de mt. France
199 G3 Finike Turkey
199 G3 Finike Körfezi b. Turkey
177 L5 Finiș Romania
158 C3 Finistère dept Bretagne France
Finisterre Spain see Fisterra
Finisterre, Cabo c. Spain see Fisterra, Cabo
Finisterre, Cape Spain see Fisterra, Cabo
84 C5 Finke N.T. Austr.
84 C5 Finke watercourse N.T. Austr.
82 C2 Finke, Mount hill S.A. Austr.
84 B2 Finke Bay N.T. Austr.
178 C3 Finkenberg Austria
179 E4 Finkenstein Austria
234 B3 Finksburg MD U.S.A.
140 N3 Finland country Europe
226 B2 Finland MN U.S.A.
140 M3 Finland, Gulf of Europe
222 E3 Finlay r. B.C. Can.
222 E3 Finlay, Mount B.C. Can.
222 E3 Finlay Forks B.C. Can.
226 A2 Finlayson MN U.S.A.
83 F3 Finley N.S.W. Austr.
236 D2 Finley ND U.S.A.
226 C1 Finmark Ont. Can.
147 D2 Finn r. Rep. of Ireland
143 F1 Finnbodarna Sweden
171 C4 Finne ridge Ger.
147 C3 Finnea Rep. of Ireland
169 C4 Finnentrop Ger.
143 F2 Finnerödja Sweden
85 F2 Finnigan, Mount Qld Austr.
151 I2 Finningham Suffolk, England U.K.
149 I4 Finningly South Yorkshire, England U.K.
84 B2 Finniss r. N.T. Austr.
82 C3 Finniss, Cape S.A. Austr.
140 N1 Finnmark county Norway
140 M1 Finnmarksvidda reg. Norway
140 L1 Finnsnes Norway
170 E3 Finowfurt Ger.
173 F3 Finsing Ger.
143 F2 Finspång Sweden
190 D2 Finsteraarhorn mt. Switz.
171 E4 Finsterwalde Ger.
164 E2 Finsterwolde Neth.
146 E2 Finstown Orkney, Scotland U.K.
141 L3 Finström Åland Fin.
168 E2 Fintel Ger.
177 K2 Fintice Slovakia
Fintinele Romania see Fântânele
147 D2 Fintona Northern Ireland U.K.
147 C2 Fintown Rep. of Ireland
146 D5 Fintry Stirling, Scotland U.K.
85 E4 Finucane Range hills Qld Austr.
147 B4 Finuge Rep. of Ireland
147 E1 Finvoy Northern Ireland U.K.
193 E2 Fionchi, Monte mt. Italy
146 C5 Fionn Loch l. Scotland U.K.
146 B5 Fionnphort Argyll and Bute, Scotland U.K.
192 D2 Fiora r. Italy
191 F4 Fiorano Modense Italy
190 E4 Fiorenzuola d'Arda Italy
193 F2 Fiori, Montagna dei mt. Italy
118 D2 Fırat r. Turkey alt. Al Furāt (Iraq/Syria), conv. Euphrates
129 A4 Fırat Nehri r. Turkey
240 G3 Firebaugh CA U.S.A.
235 E2 Fire Island NY U.S.A.
191 G5 Firenze Italy
191 G5 Firenze prov. Toscana Italy
191 G4 Firenzuola Italy
227 F1 Fire River Ont. Can.
222 E3 Fireside B.C. Can.
236 D3 Firesteel Creek r. SD U.S.A.
216 □3f Firgas Gran Canaria Canary Is
175 K4 Firlej Pol.
261 G3 Firmat Arg.
163 E4 Firmi France
256 B2 Firminópolis Brazil
161 C3 Firminy France
193 I5 Firmo Italy
Firmum Italy see Fermo
Firmum Picenum Italy see Fermo
139 I3 Firovo Rus. Fed.
116 D4 Firozabad Uttar Prad. India
116 D4 Firozpur Haryana India
116 C3 Firozpur Punjab India
168 C2 Firrel Ger.
203 G3 First Cataract rapids Egypt
85 F2 First Three Mile Opening sea chan. Qld Austr.
146 □G1 Firth Shetland, Scotland U.K.
Fīrūzābād Baluchestān va Sīstān Iran see Rāsk
122 C4 Fīrūzābād Iran
122 D2 Fīrūzeh Iran
122 D2 Fīrūzkūh Iran
122 D2 Firyuza Turkm.
186 C2 Fiscal Spain
173 E3 Fischach Ger.
179 H2 Fischamend Markt Austria
179 G3 Fischbach Austria
172 B2 Fischbach Ger.
173 F4 Fischbachau Ger.
172 B2 Fischbach bei Dahn Ger.
170 D3 Fischbeck Ger.
173 E4 Fischen im Allgäu Ger.
212 C6 Fish watercourse Namibia
214 C4 Fish r. S. Africa
149 H3 Fishburn Durham, England U.K.
82 B2 Fisher S.A. Austr.
223 L5 Fisher River Man. Can.
221 J3 Fisher Strait Nunavut Can.
232 D5 Fishersville VA U.S.A.
150 C3 Fishguard Pembrokeshire, Wales U.K.
150 C2 Fishguard Bay Wales U.K.
233 E5 Fishing Creek MD U.S.A.
234 B2 Fishing Creek r. PA U.S.A.
235 E1 Fishkill NY U.S.A.
235 E1 Fishkill Creek r. NY U.S.A.
151 H2 Fishtoft Lincolnshire, England U.K.
141 I3 Fiská Norway
262 T2 Fiske, Cape Antarctica
156 D3 Fismes France
182 A2 Fisterra Spain
182 A2 Fisterra, Cabo c. Spain
233 H3 Fitchburg MA U.S.A.
226 C4 Fitchburg WI U.S.A.
235 F1 Fitchville CT U.S.A.
232 B4 Fitchville OH U.S.A.
183 I2 Fitero Spain
146 □G2 Fitful Head hd Scotland U.K.
Fitiai Greece see Fyteies
142 A2 Fitjar Norway
78 □2 Fito, Mount vol. Samoa
163 E6 Fitou France
252 B2 Fitzcarrald Peru
223 I3 Fitzgerald Alta Can.
231 D6 Fitzgerald GA U.S.A.
156 C3 Fitz-James France
84 B2 Fitzmaurice r. N.T. Austr.
85 G4 Fitzroy r. Qld Austr.
86 D3 Fitzroy r. W.A. Austr.
259 B8 Fitz Roy, Cerro mt. Arg.
86 E3 Fitzroy Crossing W.A. Austr.
193 F3 Fiuggi Italy
191 F4 Fiumalbo Italy
193 H3 Fiumarella r. Italy
Fiume Croatia see Rijeka
193 I5 Fiumefreddo Bruzio Italy
195 E5 Fiumefreddo di Sicilia Sicilia Italy
191 H3 Fiume Veneto Italy
192 E3 Fiumicino Italy
192 B3 Fium'Orbo r. Corse France
146 C5 Fiunary Highland, Scotland U.K.
81 C6 Five Forks South I. N.Z.
147 D2 Fivemiletown Northern Ireland U.K.
240 G3 Five Points CA U.S.A.
81 B6 Five Rivers South I. N.Z.
190 F4 Fivizzano Italy
161 B3 Fix-St-Geneys France
209 F6 Fizi Dem. Rep. Congo
Fizuli Azer. see Füzuli
140 L2 Fjällsjönäs Sweden
143 G2 Fjärdhundra reg. Sweden
142 A1 Fjell Norway
142 C3 Fjerritslev Denmark
204 D2 Fkih Ben Salah Morocco
142 C1 Flå Norway
179 E3 Flachau Austria
173 E2 Flachslanden Ger.
168 C2 Flachsmeer Ger.
146 □G1 Fladdabister Shetland, Scotland U.K.
142 C4 Fladså r. Denmark
169 F5 Fladungen Ger.
163 E4 Flagnac France
215 G4 Flagstaff S. Africa
241 L4 Flagstaff AZ U.S.A.
233 □H2 Flagstaff Lake ME U.S.A.
234 D2 Flagtown NJ U.S.A.
224 E1 Flaherty Island Nunavut Can.
160 E2 Flaine France
140 M2 Flakaberg Sweden
158 E2 Flamanville France
197 H2 Flămânzi Romania
226 B3 Flambeau r. WI U.S.A.
149 I3 Flamborough East Riding of Yorkshire, England U.K.
149 I3 Flamborough Head hd England U.K.
259 E6 Flamenco, Isla i. Arg.
216 □1c Flamengos Faial Azores
186 D2 Flamicell r. Spain
171 D3 Fläming hills Ger.
223 M4 Flanagan r. Ont. Can.
235 F2 Flanders NY U.S.A.
156 C2 Flandre reg. France
236 D2 Flandreau SD U.S.A.
146 B3 Flannan Isles Scotland U.K.
140 K2 Flåsjön l. Sweden
161 E5 Flassans-sur-Issole France
222 E2 Flat r. N.W.T. Can.
226 E4 Flat r. MI U.S.A.
233 F1 Flatbrookville NJ U.S.A.
140 □C2 Flateyjardalsheiði reg. Iceland
220 G5 Flathead r. MT U.S.A.
238 D2 Flatiron mt. ID U.S.A.
90 E4 Flat Island S. China Sea
232 B6 Flat Lick KY U.S.A.
81 A6 Flat Mountain South I. N.Z.
178 E4 Flattach Austria
85 F2 Flattery, Cape Qld Austr.
179 F4 Flattnitz Austria
222 B2 Flat Top mt. Y.T. Can.
238 F2 Flatwillow Creek r. MT U.S.A.
232 B5 Flatwoods KY U.S.A.
232 C5 Flatwoods WV U.S.A.
178 C3 Flaurling Austria
157 G4 Flavigny-sur-Moselle France
160 C1 Flavigny-sur-Ozerain France
161 A4 Flavin France
190 E1 Flawil Switz.
161 E5 Flayosc France
171 C3 Flechtingen Ger.
168 E1 Fleckeby Ger.
170 D2 Flecken Zechlin Ger.
151 F2 Fleckney Leicestershire, England U.K.
151 G3 Fleet Hampshire, England U.K.
146 D4 Fleet r. Scotland U.K.
170 C3 Fleetmark Ger.
85 F4 Fleetwood Qld Austr.
149 F4 Fleetwood Lancashire, England U.K.
234 C2 Fleetwood PA U.S.A.
172 D2 Flein Ger.
142 B2 Flekkefjord Norway
142 C2 Flekkerøy i. Norway

Flémalle to Freyburg (Unstrut)

305

165 E4 Flémalle Belgium
232 B5 Flemingsburg KY U.S.A.
234 D2 Flemington NJ U.S.A.
264 G2 Flemish Cap sea feature N. Atlantic Ocean
151 H2 Flempton Suffolk, England U.K.
143 G2 Flen Sweden
168 E1 Flensborg Fjord inlet Denmark/Ger.
168 E1 Flensburg Ger.
Flensburger Förde inlet Denmark/Ger. see Flensborg Fjord
165 E4 Fléron Belgium
159 F3 Flers France
227 G3 Flesherton Ont. Can.
170 C3 Flessau Ger.
262 S2 Fletcher Peninsula Antarctica
163 C5 Fleurance France
225 J3 Fleur de Lys Nfld. Can.
162 C2 Fleuré France
160 C2 Fleurie France
190 B2 Fleurier Switz.
165 D4 Fleurus Belgium
161 B5 Fleury France
156 B5 Fleury-les-Aubrais France
156 B3 Fleury-sur-Andelle France
159 F2 Fleury-sur-Orne France
157 F3 Fléville-Lixières France
164 E2 Flevoland prov. Neth.
150 C4 Flexbury Cornwall, England U.K.
169 E5 Flieden Ger.
178 B3 Fließ Austria
149 F3 Flimby Cumbria, England U.K.
190 E2 Flims Switz.
151 H3 Flimwell East Sussex, England U.K.
85 E3 Flinders r. Qld Austr.
87 B7 Flinders Bay W.A. Austr.
85 F2 Flinders Group is Qld Austr.
82 C3 Flinders Island S.A. Austr.
83 G4 Flinders Island Tas. Austr.
85 G3 Flinders Passage Qld Austr.
82 D3 Flinders Ranges mts S.A. Austr.
85 G3 Flinders Reefs Coral Sea Is Terr. Austr.
156 D2 Flines-lez-Raches France
223 K4 Flin Flon Man. Can.
150 D1 Flint Flintshire, Wales U.K.
227 F4 Flint MI U.S.A.
231 C6 Flint r. GA U.S.A.
227 F4 Flint r. MI U.S.A.
168 F1 Flintbek Ger.
267 I6 Flint Island Kiribati
85 G5 Flinton Qld Austr.
150 D1 Flintshire admin. div. Wales U.K.
232 D5 Flintstone MD U.S.A.
157 F4 Flirey France
142 E1 Flisa Norway
141 K3 Flisa r. Norway
142 B2 Fliseggi mt. Norway
151 G2 Flitwick Bedfordshire, England U.K.
186 D3 Flix Spain
156 C2 Flixecourt France
156 E3 Flize France
142 E3 Floda Sweden
149 G2 Flodden Northumberland, England U.K.
156 D5 Flogny-la-Chapelle France
171 E5 Flöha Ger.
171 E5 Flöha r. Ger.
157 E3 Floing France
163 B4 Floirac France
262 P1 Flood Range mts Antarctica
226 A2 Floodwood MN U.S.A.
149 G3 Flookburgh Cumbria, England U.K.
84 B2 Flora r. N.T. Austr.
226 D5 Flora IN U.S.A.
161 B4 Florac France
231 C6 Florala AL U.S.A.
157 G3 Florange France
85 F3 Flora Reef Coral Sea Is Terr. Austr.
84 D3 Floraville Qld Austr.
165 D4 Floreffe Belgium
227 F4 Florence Ont. Can.
Florence Italy see Firenze
231 C5 Florence AL U.S.A.
241 L5 Florence AZ U.S.A.
239 F4 Florence CO U.S.A.
236 D4 Florence KS U.S.A.
234 D2 Florence NJ U.S.A.
238 A3 Florence OR U.S.A.
231 E5 Florence SC U.S.A.
226 C3 Florence WI U.S.A.
241 L5 Florence Junction AZ U.S.A.
233 □J1 Florenceville N.B. Can.
250 C4 Florencia Col.
261 I3 Florencio Sánchez Uru.
165 D4 Florennes Belgium
161 B5 Florensac France
Florentia Italy see Firenze
165 E5 Florenville Belgium
261 H4 Flores r. Arg.
216 □1 Flores i. Azores
254 F3 Flores Pernambuco Brazil
254 E3 Flores Piauí Brazil
243 H5 Flores Guat.
93 B5 Flores i. Indon.
261 I3 Flores dept Uru.
183 E4 Flores de Ávila Spain
254 D5 Flores de Goiás Brazil
Floreshty Moldova see Floreşti
93 A4 Flores Sea Indon.
254 F4 Floresta Brazil
194 D5 Floresta Sicilia Italy
136 E4 Floreşti Moldova
256 B5 Florestópolis Brazil
237 D6 Floresville TX U.S.A.
235 D2 Florham Park NJ U.S.A.
254 E3 Floriano Brazil
255 C8 Florianópolis Brazil
252 E4 Florida Bol.
260 A5 Florida Chile
246 C2 Florida Cuba
247 □1 Florida Puerto Rico
261 I4 Florida Uru.
261 I4 Florida dept Uru.
235 D1 Florida NY U.S.A.
231 D6 Florida state U.S.A.
231 D7 Florida, Straits of Bahamas/U.S.A.
231 D7 Florida Bay FL U.S.A.
182 E3 Florida de Liébana Spain
78 □6 Florida Islands Solomon Is
231 D7 Florida Keys is FL U.S.A.
256 B4 Flórida Paulista Brazil
195 E5 Floridia Sicilia Italy
237 B7 Florido r. Mex.
197 F2 Florii, Vârful hill Romania
240 G2 Florin CA U.S.A.
198 B1 Florina Greece
192 A4 Florinas Sardegna Italy
256 B5 Florínia Brazil
236 F4 Florissant MO U.S.A.
141 I3 Florø Norway
169 E5 Flörsbach Ger.
169 D5 Flörsheim am Main Ger.
172 C2 Flörsheim-Dalsheim Ger.
169 D5 Florstadt Ger.
173 G2 Floß Ger.
173 G2 Flossenbürg Ger.
146 E3 Flotta i. Scotland U.K.
163 E5 Floure France
226 A4 Floyd IA U.S.A.
232 C6 Floyd VA U.S.A.
241 K4 Floyd, Mount AZ U.S.A.
237 C5 Floydada TX U.S.A.
178 B4 Fluchthorn mt. Austria/Switz.
190 D2 Flüelen Switz.
190 D2 Flühli Switz.
186 C3 Flúmen r. Spain
192 B5 Flumendosa r. Sardegna Italy
193 H3 Flumeri Italy
160 E3 Flumet France
192 B4 Flumineddu r. Sardegna Italy
192 B5 Flumineddu r. Sardegna Italy
192 A5 Fluminimaggiore Sardegna Italy
190 E1 Flums Switz.
Flushing Neth. see Vlissingen
232 B3 Flushing MI U.S.A.
232 C4 Flushing OH U.S.A.
192 A4 Flussio Sardegna Italy
186 G2 Fluvià r. Spain
91 J8 Fly r. P.N.G.
262 R2 Flying Fish, Cape Antarctica
86 □1 Flying Fish Cove Christmas I.
84 C2 Flying Fox Creek r. N.T. Austr.
79 □2 Foa i. Tonga
223 K5 Foam Lake Sask. Can.
190 D3 Fobello Italy
188 G4 Foča Bos.-Herz.
199 E2 Foça Turkey
165 E4 Focant Belgium
191 H3 Focce dell'Adige r. mouth Italy
146 E4 Fochabers Moray, Scotland U.K.
215 F2 Fochville S. Africa
168 E1 Fockbek Ger.
197 H3 Focşani Romania
197 H2 Focuri Romania
159 I4 Foëcy France
84 D2 Foelsche r. N.T. Austr.
109 E4 Fogang Guangdong China
84 B2 Fog Bay N.T. Austr.
234 C2 Fogelsville PA U.S.A.
193 H3 Foggia Italy
193 H3 Foggia prov. Puglia Italy
191 H5 Foglia r. Italy
141 M3 Föglö Åland Fin.
206 □ Fogo i. Cape Verde
121 G4 Fogoleva Kazakh.
179 F3 Fohnsdorf Austria
168 D1 Föhr i. Ger.
171 D3 Fohrde Ger.
172 A2 Föhren Ger.
184 B3 Fóia hill Port.
191 G5 Foiano della Chiana Italy
177 L4 Foieni Romania
147 A5 Foilclough hill Rep. of Ireland
146 D3 Foinaven hill Scotland U.K.
163 D6 Foix France
186 E3 Foix r. Spain
139 J5 Fokino Rus. Fed.
207 G4 Fokku Nigeria
177 H5 Foktő Hungary
142 B1 Folarskarnuten mt. Norway
140 K2 Folda sea chan. Norway
177 J5 Földeák Hungary
177 K4 Földes Hungary
140 J2 Foldfjorden sea chan. Norway
198 D3 Folegandros i. Greece
231 C6 Foley AL U.S.A.
236 E2 Foley MN U.S.A.
224 D3 Foleyet Ont. Can.
85 G4 Foleyvale Qld Austr.
Folgares Angola see Capelongo
191 G3 Folgarìa Italy
263 H2 Folger, Cape Antarctica
182 C2 Folgoso de Courel Spain
182 D2 Folgoso de la Ribera Spain
193 F2 Folignano Italy
193 E2 Foligno Italy
151 I3 Folkestone Kent, England U.K.
151 G2 Folkingham Lincolnshire, England U.K.
231 D6 Folkston GA U.S.A.
141 J3 Folldal Norway
191 H3 Follina Italy
140 K3 Föllinge Sweden
192 C2 Follonica Italy
150 C4 Folly Gate Devon, England U.K.
157 G3 Folschviller France
232 C5 Folsom WV U.S.A.
217 □3 Fomboni Comoros
246 C2 Fómento Cuba
135 H7 Fomin Rus. Fed.
134 H5 Fominki Rus. Fed.
134 H4 Fominskoye Rus. Fed.
183 G2 Foncea hill Spain
233 F3 Fonda NY U.S.A.
223 J3 Fond-du-Lac Sask. Can.
223 J3 Fond du Lac r. Sask. Can.
226 C4 Fond du Lac WI U.S.A.
232 B6 Fonde KY U.S.A.
182 B3 Fondevila Spain
193 F3 Fondi Italy
185 H4 Fondón Spain
185 G3 Fonelas Spain
186 B3 Fonfría Spain
182 D3 Fonfría Spain
206 C4 Fon Going ridge Guinea
192 B4 Fonni Sardegna Italy
163 C4 Fonroque France
Fonsagrada Spain see A Fonsagrada
250 C2 Fonseca Col.
163 D5 Fonsorbes France
157 G5 Fontaine Franche-Comté France
161 D3 Fontaine Rhône-Alpes France
156 C4 Fontainebleau France
160 D1 Fontaine-Française France
156 B3 Fontaine-le-Bourg France
159 G2 Fontaine-le-Dun France
160 D1 Fontaine-lès-Dijon France
157 G5 Fontaine-lès-Luxeuil France
165 D4 Fontaine-l'Évêque Belgium
160 C2 Fontaines Bourgogne France
156 D5 Fontaines Bourgogne France
161 F4 Fontan France
234 B2 Fontana PA U.S.A.
183 G4 Fontanar Spain
185 F1 Fontanarejo Spain
190 F4 Fontanellato Italy
193 F3 Fontanelle r. Italy
161 C5 Fontanès France
225 G2 Fontanges Que. Can.
190 E4 Fontanigorda Italy
161 B3 Fontannes France
185 F2 Fontanosas Spain
222 F3 Fontas B.C. Can.
222 F3 Fontas r. B.C. Can.
Font Blanca, Pic de mt. France/Spain see Port, Pic du
251 E5 Fonte Boa Brazil
193 F2 Fontecchio Italy
193 F2 Fontecellese, Monte mt. Italy
216 □1a Fonte do Bastardo Terceira Azores
207 H5 Fontem Cameroon
162 B2 Fontenay-le-Comte France
156 C4 Fontenay-Trésigny France
160 B1 Fontenoy France
157 G5 Fontenoy-le-Château France
157 F4 Fontenoy-sur-Moselle France
182 B5 Fontes Port.
159 G4 Fontevraud-l'Abbaye France
159 G5 Fontgombault France
191 G3 Fonti, Cima mt. Italy
216 □1a Fontinhas Terceira Azores
183 F4 Fontiveros Spain
157 F3 Fontoy France
163 E6 Font-Romeu-Odeillo-Via France
147 E3 Fontstown Rep. of Ireland
140 □D2 Fontur pt Iceland
161 C5 Fontvieille France
79 □2 Fonuafo'ou i. Tonga
Fonuafu'u i. Tonga see Fonuafo'ou
77 I3 Fonualei i. Tonga
78 □4a Fonuchu i. Chuuk Micronesia
177 G5 Fonyód Hungary
186 D2 Fonz Spain
191 G2 Fonzaso Italy
Foochow Fujian China see Fuzhou
227 H3 Foot's Bay Ont. Can.
108 D1 Foping Shaanxi China
190 E2 Foppolo Italy
193 E2 Forano Italy
122 C3 Forat Iran
Foraulep atoll Micronesia see Faraulep
157 G3 Forbach France
172 C3 Forbach Ger.
83 G3 Forbes N.S.W. Austr.
222 G4 Forbes, Mount Alta Can.
81 A6 Forbes, Mount South I. N.Z.
117 F4 Forbesganj Bihar India
161 E5 Forcalcueiret France
186 C4 Forcall Spain
161 D5 Forcalquier France
182 B2 Forcarei Spain
Forcary Spain see Forcarei
193 F2 Force Italy
172 B3 Forchheim Baden-Württemberg Ger.
173 F2 Forchheim Bayern Ger.
172 D2 Forchtenberg Ger.
179 H3 Forchtenstein Austria
225 H1 Ford r. Que. Can.
146 C5 Ford Argyll and Bute, Scotland U.K.
149 G2 Ford Northumberland, England U.K.
226 D3 Ford r. MI U.S.A.
84 B2 Ford, Cape N.T. Austr.
240 H4 Ford City CA U.S.A.
232 D4 Ford City PA U.S.A.
141 I3 Førde Norway
80 E3 Fordell North I. N.Z.
171 C4 Förderstedt Ger.
151 H2 Fordham Cambridgeshire, England U.K.
151 F4 Fordingbridge Hampshire, England U.K.
192 A5 Fordongianus Sardegna Italy
146 F5 Fordoun Aberdeenshire, Scotland U.K.
262 O1 Ford Range mts Antarctica
235 D2 Fords NJ U.S.A.
83 F2 Fords Bridge N.S.W. Austr.
147 E3 Fordstown Rep. of Ireland
146 F4 Fordyce Aberdeenshire, Scotland U.K.
237 E5 Fordyce AR U.S.A.
206 B4 Forécariah Guinea
221 O3 Forel, Mont mt. Greenland
151 F4 Foreland hd England U.K.
237 E5 Foreman AR U.S.A.
223 I5 Foremost Alta Can.
193 H4 Forenza Italy
222 E4 Foresight Mountain B.C. Can.
224 D5 Forest Ont. Can.
237 F5 Forest MS U.S.A.
232 B4 Forest OH U.S.A.
232 D6 Forest VA U.S.A.
223 H4 Forestburg Alta Can.
234 D1 Forestburg NY U.S.A.
234 C1 Forest City PA U.S.A.
85 E3 Forest Creek r. Qld Austr.
83 F3 Forest Hill N.S.W. Austr.
85 F5 Forest Hill Qld Austr.
240 G2 Foresthill CA U.S.A.
83 G5 Forestier Peninsula Tas. Austr.
226 C3 Forest Junction WI U.S.A.
226 A3 Forest Lake MN U.S.A.
241 L4 Forest Lakes AZ U.S.A.
231 C5 Forest Park GA U.S.A.
240 G2 Forest Ranch CA U.S.A.
151 H3 Forest Row East Sussex, England U.K.
225 G3 Forestville Que. Can.
240 F2 Forestville CA U.S.A.
234 B4 Forestville MD U.S.A.
227 F4 Forestville MI U.S.A.
232 D3 Forestville NY U.S.A.
142 A2 Føresvik Norway
160 B3 Forez, Monts du mts France
160 B3 Forez, Plaine du plain France
146 F5 Forfar Angus, Scotland U.K.
237 C4 Forgan OK U.S.A.
156 B3 Forges-les-Eaux France
173 E4 Forggensee l. Ger.
146 E4 Forgie Moray, Scotland U.K.
193 G4 Forino Italy
193 F4 Forio Italy
171 C5 Föritz Ger.
182 B3 Forjães Port.
234 B3 Fork MD U.S.A.
237 F5 Forked Deer r. TN U.S.A.
233 F5 Forked River NJ U.S.A.
147 E2 Forkhill Northern Ireland U.K.
238 A2 Forks WA U.S.A.
234 B1 Forkston PA U.S.A.
234 B1 Forksville PA U.S.A.
232 D6 Fork Union VA U.S.A.
191 H4 Forlì Italy
191 H5 Forlì prov. Emilia-Romagna Italy
191 H4 Forlimpopoli Italy
236 D2 Forman ND U.S.A.
190 D2 Formazza Italy
149 F4 Formby Merseyside, England U.K.
187 E6 Formentera i. Spain
187 G5 Formentor, Cap de c. Spain
156 B3 Formerie France
Former Yugoslav Republic of Macedonia country Europe see Macedonia
193 F3 Formia Italy
187 C4 Formiche Alto Spain
193 G3 Formicola Italy
257 E4 Formiga Brazil
191 F4 Formigine Italy
191 G4 Formignana Italy
163 E6 Formiguères France
258 F2 Formosa Arg.
258 F2 Formosa prov. Arg.
Formosa country Asia see Taiwan
255 D5 Formosa Brazil
253 G3 Formosa, Serra hills Brazil
254 D4 Formosa do Rio Preto Brazil
Formosa Strait China/Taiwan see Taiwan Strait
182 B4 Formoselha Port.
254 D5 Formoso Minas Gerais Brazil
254 C4 Formoso Tocantins Brazil
254 D5 Formoso r. Bahia Brazil
256 A3 Formoso r. Goiás Brazil
254 C4 Formoso r. Tocantins Brazil
147 B3 Formoyle Rep. of Ireland
192 A3 Fornelli Sardegna Italy
186 □ Fornells Spain
186 F3 Fornells de la Selva Spain
191 H2 Forni Avoltri Italy
191 H2 Forni di Sopra Italy
191 H2 Forni di Sotto Italy
190 C3 Forno Alpi Graie Italy
178 D4 Forno di Zoldo Italy
182 D3 Fornos Port.
182 C4 Fornos de Algodres Port.
190 F4 Fornovo di Taro Italy
193 G2 Foro r. Italy
140 J3 Forolshogna mt. Norway
137 G5 Foros Ukr.
184 B2 Foros de Vale Figueira Port.
184 B1 Foros do Arrão Port.
Føroyar terr. N. Atlantic Ocean see Faroe Islands
177 I5 Forráskút Hungary
146 E4 Forres Moray, Scotland U.K.
87 F6 Forrest W.A. Austr.
86 F2 Forrest r. W.A. Austr.
226 C5 Forrest IL U.S.A.
262 U1 Forrestal Range mts Antarctica
237 F5 Forrest City AR U.S.A.
87 F6 Forrest Lakes salt flat W.A. Austr.
226 C4 Forreston IL U.S.A.
Forrest River Mission W.A. Austr. see Oombulgurri
177 K3 Forró Hungary
162 B2 Fors France
142 B2 Forsand Norway
85 E3 Forsayth Qld Austr.
150 E2 Forsbrook Staffordshire, England U.K.
142 E2 Forshaga Sweden
146 E3 Forsinard Highland, Scotland U.K.
140 L2 Forsnäs Sweden
141 M3 Forssa Fin.
172 C2 Forst Baden-Württemberg Ger.
171 F4 Forst Brandenburg Ger.
83 H3 Forster N.S.W. Austr.
173 F3 Forstern Ger.
173 F3 Forstinning Ger.
231 D5 Forsyth GA U.S.A.
237 E4 Forsyth MO U.S.A.
238 F2 Forsyth MT U.S.A.
227 I1 Forsythe Que. Can.
84 D3 Forsyth Islands Qld Austr.
85 E4 Forsyth Range hills Qld Austr.
123 H4 Fort Abbas Pak.
224 D2 Fort Albany Ont. Can.
252 D2 Fortaleza Bol.
254 F2 Fortaleza Brazil
186 C4 Fortanete Spain
Fort Archambault Chad see Sarh
232 D5 Fort Ashby WV U.S.A.
222 H4 Fort Assiniboine Alta Can.
226 C4 Fort Atkinson WI U.S.A.
146 D4 Fort Augustus Highland, Scotland U.K.
222 E4 Fort Babine B.C. Can.
215 F5 Fort Beaufort S. Africa
238 E2 Fort Benton MT U.S.A.
223 J4 Fort Black Sask. Can.
Fort Brabant N.W.T. Can. see Tuktoyaktuk
240 F2 Fort Bragg CA U.S.A.
Fort Carillon NY U.S.A. see Ticonderoga
Fort Carnot Madag. see Ikongo
Fort Charlet Alg. see Djanet
Fort Chimo Que. Can. see Kuujjuaq
223 I3 Fort Chipewyan Alta Can.
238 F3 Fort Collins CO U.S.A.
85 E4 Fort Constantine Qld Austr.
224 E4 Fort-Coulonge Que. Can.
233 F2 Fort Covington NY U.S.A.
Fort Crampel C.A.R. see Kaga Bandoro
Fort-Dauphin Madag. see Tôlañaro
237 C6 Fort Davis TX U.S.A.
247 □3 Fort-de-France Martinique
Fort de Kock Sumatera Indon. see Bukittinggi
Fort de Polignac Alg. see Illizi
231 C5 Fort Deposit AL U.S.A.
236 E3 Fort Dodge IA U.S.A.
215 G4 Fort Donald S. Africa
241 M1 Fort Duchesne UT U.S.A.
182 B2 Forte Spain
192 A4 Forte, Monte hill Sardegna Italy
233 G3 Fort Edward NY U.S.A.
227 H4 Fort Erie Ont. Can.
86 C4 Fortescue r. W.A. Austr.
234 C3 Fortescue NJ U.S.A.
191 G2 Fortezza Italy
192 C2 Fortezza, Monte della hill Italy
233 □J1 Fort Fairfield ME U.S.A.
Fort Foureau Cameroon see Kousséri
226 A1 Fort Frances Ont. Can.
Fort Franklin N.W.T. Can. see Déline
231 C6 Fort Gaines GA U.S.A.
239 F4 Fort Garland CO U.S.A.
232 B5 Fort Gay WV U.S.A.
Fort George Que. Can. see Chisasibi
220 F3 Fort Good Hope N.W.T. Can.
Fort Gouraud Maur. see Fdérik
146 E6 Forth South Lanarkshire, Scotland U.K.
144 F3 Forth r. Scotland U.K.
146 E5 Forth, Firth of est. Scotland U.K.
Fort Hall Kenya see Muranga
239 F6 Fort Hancock TX U.S.A.
215 F5 Fort Hare S. Africa
241 J2 Fortification Range mts NV U.S.A.
245 F4 Fortín Mex.
253 E5 Fortín Ávalos Sánchez Para.
253 F5 Fortín Carlos Antonio López Para.
253 F5 Fortín Coronel Bogado Para.
253 E5 Fortín Coronel Eugenio Garay Para.
146 D5 Fortingall Perth and Kinross, Scotland U.K.
253 E5 Fortín General Mendoza Para.
253 E5 Fortín Hernandarías Para.
253 E5 Fortín Infante Rivarola Para.
253 F5 Fortín Juan de Zalazar Para.
253 F5 Fortín Presidente Ayala Para.
253 E5 Fortín Teniente Juan Echauri López Para.
184 C1 Fortios Port.
Fort Jameson Zambia see Chipata
Fort Johnston Malawi see Mangochi
233 □I1 Fort Kent ME U.S.A.
238 B3 Fort Klamath OR U.S.A.
Fort Lamy Chad see Ndjamena
Fort Laperrine Alg. see Tamanrasset
238 F3 Fort Laramie WY U.S.A.
231 D7 Fort Lauderdale FL U.S.A.
235 E2 Fort Lee NJ U.S.A.
222 F2 Fort Liard N.W.T. Can.
246 E3 Fort Liberté Haiti
232 E5 Fort Loudon PA U.S.A.
223 I3 Fort Mackay Alta Can.
222 H5 Fort Macleod Alta Can.
226 B5 Fort Madison IA U.S.A.
156 B2 Fort-Mahon-Plage France
Fort Manning Malawi see Mchinji
226 B3 Fort McCoy WI U.S.A.
223 I3 Fort McMurray Alta Can.
220 E3 Fort McPherson N.W.T. Can.
235 E1 Fort Montgomery NY U.S.A.
236 C3 Fort Morgan CO U.S.A.
215 H3 Fort Mtombeni S. Africa
231 D7 Fort Myers FL U.S.A.
222 F3 Fort Nelson B.C. Can.
222 F3 Fort Nelson r. B.C. Can.
Fort Norman N.W.T. Can. see Tulít'a
Fort Orange NY U.S.A. see Albany
193 H3 Fortore r. Italy
231 C5 Fort Payne AL U.S.A.
238 F1 Fort Peck MT U.S.A.
238 F2 Fort Peck Reservoir MT U.S.A.
231 D7 Fort Pierce FL U.S.A.
236 C2 Fort Pierre SD U.S.A.
210 A4 Fort Portal Uganda
222 G2 Fort Providence N.W.T. Can.
223 K5 Fort Qu'Appelle Sask. Can.
Fort Randall AK U.S.A. see Cold Bay
232 A4 Fort Recovery OH U.S.A.
222 H2 Fort Resolution N.W.T. Can.
213 F3 Fort Rixon Zimbabwe
81 B7 Fortrose South I. N.Z.
146 D4 Fortrose Highland, Scotland U.K.
Fort Rosebery Zambia see Mansa
Fort Rousset Congo see Owando
Fort Rupert Que. Can. see Waskaganish
222 E4 Fort St James B.C. Can.
222 F3 Fort St John B.C. Can.
Fort Sandeman Pak. see Zhob
222 H4 Fort Saskatchewan Alta Can.
237 E4 Fort Scott KS U.S.A.
224 C1 Fort Severn Ont. Can.
120 B3 Fort-Shevchenko Kazakh.
222 F2 Fort Simpson N.W.T. Can.
223 H2 Fort Smith N.W.T. Can.
237 E5 Fort Smith AR U.S.A.
238 F2 Fort Smith MT U.S.A.
237 C6 Fort Stockton TX U.S.A.
239 F5 Fort Sumner NM U.S.A.
237 D4 Fort Supply OK U.S.A.
241 M5 Fort Thomas AZ U.S.A.
Fort Trinquet Maur. see Bîr Mogreïn
187 B6 Fortuna Spain
238 A3 Fortuna CA U.S.A.
236 C1 Fortuna ND U.S.A.
225 K4 Fortune Bay Nfld. Can.
150 E4 Fortuneswell Dorset, England U.K.
231 D5 Fort Valley GA U.S.A.
222 G3 Fort Vermilion Alta Can.
Fort Victoria Zimbabwe see Masvingo
Fort Walton FL U.S.A. see Fort Walton Beach
231 C6 Fort Walton Beach FL U.S.A.
Fort Ware B.C. Can. see Ware
234 C2 Fort Washington PA U.S.A.
230 C3 Fort Wayne IN U.S.A.
251 G3 Fort Wellington Guyana
146 C5 Fort William Highland, Scotland U.K.
239 E5 Fort Wingate NM U.S.A.
237 D5 Fort Worth TX U.S.A.
236 C2 Fort Yates ND U.S.A.
234 C1 Forty Fort PA U.S.A.
Forty-Second Hill S. Africa see 42nd Hill
220 D3 Fort Yukon AK U.S.A.
Forum Iulii France see Fréjus
122 C5 Forūr, Jazīreh-ye i. Iran
140 K2 Forvik Norway
195 E5 Forza d'Agrò Sicilia Italy
163 C6 Fos France
190 F4 Fosdinovo Italy
109 E4 Foshan Guangdong China
141 K3 Foskvallen Sweden
140 J3 Fosna pen. Norway
206 E5 Foso Ghana
193 G2 Fossacesia Italy
178 D5 Fossalta di Portogruaro Italy
190 C4 Fossano Italy
191 H5 Fossato di Vico Italy
162 C3 Fossemagne France
165 D4 Fosses-la-Ville Belgium
160 D2 Fossiat France
238 B2 Fossil OR U.S.A.
86 E3 Fossil Downs W.A. Austr.
191 H5 Fossombrone Italy
161 C5 Fos-sur-Mer France
83 F4 Foster Vic. Austr.
232 A5 Foster KY U.S.A.
222 C3 Foster, Mount Alaska/B.C. Can./U.S.A.
221 P2 Foster Bugt b. Greenland
234 D1 Fosterdale NY U.S.A.
233 □J2 Fosterville N.B. Can.
232 B4 Fostoria OH U.S.A.
177 I4 Fót Hungary
213 □J5 Fotadrevo Madag.
149 I4 Fotherby Lincolnshire, England U.K.
Fotuna i. Vanuatu see Futuna
156 B3 Foucarmont France
160 D1 Foucherans France
158 B4 Fouesnant France
157 F4 Foug France
208 A5 Fougamou Gabon
158 E3 Fougères France
157 G5 Fougerolles France
159 F3 Fougerolles-du-Plessis France
156 C3 Fouilloy France
146 □F1 Foula i. Scotland U.K.
157 F4 Foulain France
206 B3 Foulamôri Guinea
163 C4 Foulayronnes France
146 F6 Foulden Scottish Borders, Scotland U.K.
208 A5 Foulenzem Gabon
147 E4 Foulkesmill Rep. of Ireland
149 G4 Foulridge Lancashire, England U.K.
81 C4 Foulwind, Cape South I. N.Z.
207 H5 Foumban Cameroon
207 H5 Foumbot Cameroon
217 □3a Foumbouni Njazidja Comoros
204 D3 Foum Zguid Morocco
206 A3 Foundiougne Senegal
232 B6 Fount KY U.S.A.
226 A4 Fountain MN U.S.A.
147 B4 Fountain Cross Rep. of Ireland
241 L2 Fountain Green UT U.S.A.
234 C2 Fountain Hill PA U.S.A.
149 H3 Fountains Abbey tourist site England U.K.
184 C3 Foupana r. Port.
162 A3 Fouras France
163 C5 Fourcès France
160 B1 Fourchambault France
157 F4 Fourches, Mont des hill France
240 I4 Four Corners CA U.S.A.
151 H3 Four Elms Kent, England U.K.
215 G3 Fouriesburg S. Africa
151 F3 Four Marks Hampshire, England U.K.
156 E2 Fourmies France
161 B4 Fournels France
199 E3 Fournoi Greece
199 E3 Fournoi i. Greece
151 H4 Four Oaks East Sussex, England U.K.
161 C5 Fourques Languedoc-Roussillon France
163 E6 Fourques Languedoc-Roussillon France
163 C4 Fourques-sur-Garonne France
160 B2 Fours France
203 G5 Fourth Cataract rapids Sudan
206 B4 Fouta Djallon reg. Guinea
81 A7 Foveaux Strait South I. N.Z.
234 B3 Fowbelsburg MD U.S.A.
150 C4 Fowey Cornwall, England U.K.
150 C4 Fowey r. England U.K.
231 E7 Fowl Cay i. Bahamas
240 H3 Fowler CA U.S.A.
239 F4 Fowler CO U.S.A.
230 C3 Fowler IN U.S.A.
226 E4 Fowler MI U.S.A.
82 C2 Fowlers Bay S.A. Austr.
82 C3 Fowlers Bay b. S.A. Austr.
227 E4 Fowlerville MI U.S.A.
127 H3 Fowman Iran
150 E2 Fownhope Herefordshire, England U.K.
222 E3 Fox r. B.C. Can.
223 M3 Fox r. Man. Can.
226 C5 Fox r. IL U.S.A.
226 C4 Fox r. WI U.S.A.
182 B1 Foxas Spain
85 F4 Fox Creek r. Qld Austr.
222 G4 Fox Creek Alta Can.
221 K3 Foxe Basin g. Nunavut Can.
221 J3 Foxe Channel Nunavut Can.
221 K3 Foxe Peninsula Nunavut Can.
147 B3 Foxford Rep. of Ireland
81 C5 Fox Glacier South I. N.Z.
220 B4 Fox Islands AK U.S.A.
222 H3 Fox Lake Alta Can.
226 C4 Fox Lake IL U.S.A.
222 C2 Fox Mountain Y.T. Can.
238 F3 Foxpark WY U.S.A.
80 E4 Foxton North I. N.Z.
80 E4 Foxton Beach North I. N.Z.
223 I5 Fox Valley Sask. Can.
146 D4 Foyers Highland, Scotland U.K.
148 B4 Foygh Rep. of Ireland
147 D2 Foyle r. Rep. of Ireland/U.K.
147 D1 Foyle, Lough b. Rep. of Ireland/U.K.
147 B4 Foynes Rep. of Ireland
184 B1 Foz Port.
182 C1 Foz Spain
184 A1 Foz do Arelho Port.
209 A9 Foz do Cunene Angola
255 B8 Foz do Iguaçu Brazil
182 C5 Foz Giraldo Port.
190 C4 Frabosa Soprana Italy
175 L2 Frącki Pol.
227 I5 Frackville PA U.S.A.
182 E4 Frades de la Sierra Spain
186 D3 Fraga Spain
195 G2 Fragagnano Italy
179 F2 Fraham Austria
258 G4 Fraile Muerto Uru.
185 G3 Frailes Spain
165 D4 Fraire Belgium
160 D1 Fraisans France
161 A5 Fraisse-sur-Agout France
157 H4 Fraize France
262 Q1 Frakes, Mount Antarctica
165 C4 Frameries Belgium
151 H4 Framfield East Sussex, England U.K.
233 H3 Framingham MA U.S.A.
151 I2 Framlingham Suffolk, England U.K.
143 G1 Främlingshem Sweden
169 E5 Frammersbach Ger.
263 E2 Framnes Mountains Antarctica
263 D2 Fram Peak Antarctica
175 K5 Frampol Pol.
151 G2 Frampton Lincolnshire, England U.K.
150 E3 Frampton on Severn Gloucestershire, England U.K.
256 D4 Franca Brazil
193 G2 Francavilla al Mare Italy
195 E5 Francavilla di Sicilia Sicilia Italy
195 G2 Francavilla Fontana Italy
193 I4 Francavilla in Sinni Italy
154 F3 France country Europe
82 E4 Frances S.A. Austr.
222 D2 Frances r. Y.T. Can.
163 C4 Francescas France
222 D2 Frances Lake Y.T. Can.
226 D5 Francesville IN U.S.A.
208 B5 Franceville Gabon
157 G5 Franche-Comté admin. reg. France
223 K5 Francis Sask. Can.
Francis atoll Gilbert Is Kiribati see Beru
Francisco de Orellana Ecuador see Puerto Francisco de Orellana
250 C5 Francisco de Orellana Peru
242 E3 Francisco I. Madero Mex.
244 B1 Francisco I. Madero Mex.
244 B3 Francisco I. Madero Mex.
257 F2 Francisco Sá Brazil
242 A1 Francisco Zarco Mex.
213 E4 Francistown Botswana
182 C3 Franco Port.
256 D5 Franco da Rocha Brazil
194 D5 Francofonte Sicilia Italy
225 J4 Francois Nfld. Can.
186 E3 Francolí r. Spain
234 A4 Franconia VA U.S.A.
165 E4 Francorchamps Belgium
163 D4 Francoulès France
238 E3 Francs Peak WY U.S.A.
164 E1 Franeker Neth.
160 D2 Frangy France
169 D4 Frankenau Ger.
171 E5 Frankenberg Ger.
169 D4 Frankenberg (Eder) Ger.
179 E2 Frankenburg am Hausruck Austria
179 G3 Frankenfels Austria
169 F5 Frankenhain Ger.
169 F5 Frankenheim Ger.
179 E3 Frankenmarkt Austria
227 F4 Frankenmuth MI U.S.A.
172 C2 Frankenthal (Pfalz) Ger.
171 C5 Frankenwald mts Ger.
246 □ Frankfield Jamaica
227 I3 Frankford Ont. Can.
215 G2 Frankfort S. Africa
230 C3 Frankfort IN U.S.A.
230 C4 Frankfort KY U.S.A.
226 D3 Frankfort MI U.S.A.
232 B5 Frankfort OH U.S.A.
169 D5 Frankfurt am Main Ger.
171 F3 Frankfurt an der Oder Ger.
173 E3 Fränkische Alb hills Ger.
173 F2 Fränkische Rezat r. Ger.
169 E5 Fränkische Saale r. Ger.
173 F2 Fränkische Schweiz reg. Ger.
87 C7 Frankland r. W.A. Austr.
83 F4 Frankland, Cape Tas. Austr.
150 E2 Frankley Worcestershire, England U.K.
215 G4 Franklin S. Africa
241 M5 Franklin AZ U.S.A.
231 C5 Franklin GA U.S.A.
230 C4 Franklin IN U.S.A.
230 C4 Franklin KY U.S.A.
237 F6 Franklin LA U.S.A.
233 H3 Franklin MA U.S.A.
233 □I2 Franklin ME U.S.A.
231 D5 Franklin NC U.S.A.
236 D3 Franklin NE U.S.A.
233 H3 Franklin NH U.S.A.
234 D1 Franklin NJ U.S.A.
232 A5 Franklin OH U.S.A.
232 D4 Franklin PA U.S.A.
231 C5 Franklin TN U.S.A.
237 D6 Franklin TX U.S.A.
232 E6 Franklin VA U.S.A.
226 C4 Franklin WI U.S.A.
232 D5 Franklin WV U.S.A.
234 A2 Franklinburg PA U.S.A.
228 C1 Franklin D. Roosevelt Lake WA U.S.A.
232 B5 Franklin Furnace OH U.S.A.
226 C5 Franklin Grove IL U.S.A.
82 D3 Franklin Harbor b. S.A. Austr.
263 L1 Franklin Island Antarctica
222 F2 Franklin Mountains N.W.T. Can.
81 A6 Franklin Mountains South I. N.Z.
234 D2 Franklin Park NJ U.S.A.
83 F5 Franklin Sound sea chan. Tas. Austr.
235 E2 Franklin Square NY U.S.A.
221 I2 Franklin Strait Nunavut Can.
237 F6 Franklinton LA U.S.A.
234 C3 Franklinville NJ U.S.A.
232 D3 Franklinville NY U.S.A.
175 I1 Frankowo Pol.
140 K3 Frankrike Sweden
83 F4 Frankston Vic. Austr.
81 B6 Frankton South I. N.Z.
160 D1 Franois France
214 D3 Fransenhof S. Africa
141 L3 Fränsta Sweden
176 B1 Františkovy Lázně Czech Rep.
224 C3 Franz Ont. Can.
170 D1 Franzburg Ger.
81 C5 Franz Josef Glacier South I. N.Z.
Franz Josef Land is Rus. Fed. see Zemlya Frantsa-Iosifa
173 F3 Franz Josef Strauss airport Ger.
194 D5 Frasca, Monte hill Sicilia Italy
193 E3 Frascati Italy
193 I5 Frascineto Italy
173 G4 Frasdorf Ger.
86 D3 Fraser r. W.A. Austr.
222 F5 Fraser r. B.C. Can.
225 I1 Fraser r. Nfld. Can.
87 C5 Fraser, Mount hill W.A. Austr.
214 C4 Fraserburg S. Africa
146 F4 Fraserburgh Aberdeenshire, Scotland U.K.
224 D3 Fraserdale Ont. Can.
85 H5 Fraser Island Qld Austr.
87 B4 Fraser Island W.A. Austr.
222 E4 Fraser Lake B.C. Can.
222 E4 Fraser Plateau B.C. Can.
87 D7 Fraser Range W.A. Austr.
87 D7 Fraser Range hills W.A. Austr.
80 F3 Frasertown North I. N.Z.
160 E2 Frasne France
165 C4 Frasnes-lez-Buissenal Belgium
165 D4 Frasnes-lez-Gosselies Belgium
191 F4 Frassinoro Italy
193 G3 Frasso Telesino Italy
178 A3 Frastanz Austria
182 C5 Fratel Port.
194 D4 Fratello r. Sicilia Italy
226 E2 Frater Ont. Can.
197 G4 Frăteşti Romania
191 G3 Fratta r. Italy
191 G3 Fratta Polesine Italy
193 E2 Fratta Todina Italy
190 C1 Fraubrunnen Switz.
173 H3 Frauenau Ger.
190 D1 Frauenfeld Switz.
179 H3 Frauenkirchen Austria
171 E5 Frauenstein Ger.
179 G4 Frauental an der Laßnitz Austria
169 F5 Frauenwald Ger.
173 F3 Fraunberg Ger.
171 D5 Fraureuth Ger.
261 H3 Fray Bentos Uru.
261 G3 Fray Luis Beltrán Arg.
258 G4 Fray Marcos Uru.
163 D4 Frayssinet-le-Gélat France
234 C2 Frazer PA U.S.A.
232 B4 Frazeysburg OH U.S.A.
240 H4 Frazier Park CA U.S.A.
182 B3 Freamunde Port.
197 I3 Frecăţei Romania
161 B5 Frech, Mont mt. France
182 C3 Frechas Port.
169 B5 Frechen Ger.
183 F2 Frechilla Spain
149 G4 Freckleton Lancashire, England U.K.
169 E4 Freden (Leine) Ger.
168 E2 Fredenbeck Ger.
226 E3 Frederic MI U.S.A.
226 A3 Frederic WI U.S.A.
234 C3 Frederica DE U.S.A.
142 C4 Fredericia Denmark
87 C5 Frederick r. W.A. Austr.
232 E5 Frederick MD U.S.A.
237 D5 Frederick OK U.S.A.
226 A4 Fredericksburg IA U.S.A.
234 B2 Fredericksburg PA U.S.A.
237 D6 Fredericksburg TX U.S.A.
232 E5 Fredericksburg VA U.S.A.
237 F4 Fredericktown MO U.S.A.
232 B4 Fredericktown OH U.S.A.
225 H4 Fredericton N.B. Can.
233 □J2 Fredericton Junction N.B. Can.
142 E4 Frederiksborg county Denmark
Frederikshåb Greenland see Paamiut
142 D3 Frederikshavn Denmark
142 E4 Frederikssund Denmark
247 F3 Frederiksted Virgin Is (U.S.A.)
142 E4 Frederiksværk Denmark
170 E3 Fredersdorf Ger.
241 K3 Fredonia AZ U.S.A.
237 E4 Fredonia KS U.S.A.
232 D3 Fredonia NY U.S.A.
232 C4 Fredonia PA U.S.A.
226 D4 Fredonia WI U.S.A.
140 L2 Fredrika Sweden
143 F1 Fredriksberg Sweden
Fredrikshamn Fin. see Hamina
142 D2 Fredrikstad Norway
Fredriksvern Norway see Stavern
175 K6 Fredropol Pol.
234 B2 Freeburg PA U.S.A.
233 F4 Freehold NJ U.S.A.
234 C1 Freeland PA U.S.A.
82 D3 Freeling S.A. Austr.
84 C4 Freeling, Mount hill N.T. Austr.
82 D2 Freeling Heights hill S.A. Austr.
240 H2 Freel Peak CA U.S.A.
236 D3 Freeman SD U.S.A.
234 C2 Freemansburg PA U.S.A.
231 C6 Freeport FL U.S.A.
226 C4 Freeport IL U.S.A.
233 □H3 Freeport ME U.S.A.
235 E2 Freeport NY U.S.A.
232 D4 Freeport PA U.S.A.
237 E6 Freeport TX U.S.A.
231 E7 Freeport City Bahamas
237 D7 Freer TX U.S.A.
226 D3 Freesoil MI U.S.A.
215 F3 Free State prov. S. Africa
206 B4 Freetown Sierra Leone
235 F2 Freetown NY U.S.A.
235 D2 Freewood Acres NJ U.S.A.
217 □2a Frégate i. Inner Islands Seychelles
184 D2 Fregenal de la Sierra Spain
192 E3 Fregene Italy
186 D4 Freginals Spain
82 C1 Fregon S.A. Austr.
158 D3 Fréhel France
171 E5 Freiberg Ger.
171 D4 Freiberger Mulde r. Ger.
172 C4 Freiburg admin. reg. Baden-Württemberg Ger.
Freiburg Switz. see Fribourg
168 E2 Freiburg (Elbe) Ger.
172 B3 Freiburg im Breisgau Ger.
169 E5 Freiensteinau Ger.
168 E1 Freienwill Ger.
257 G2 Frei Gonzaga Brazil
173 F2 Freihung Ger.
257 G3 Frei Inocêncio Brazil
185 H3 Freila Spain
173 G4 Freilassing Ger.
172 C2 Freinsheim Ger.
260 A6 Freire Chile
172 B2 Freisen Ger.
173 F3 Freising Ger.
161 E4 Freissinières France
179 F2 Freistadt Austria
157 G3 Freistroff France
171 E5 Freital Ger.
182 C4 Freixedas Port.
182 B5 Freixianda Port.
182 C3 Freixiel Port.
182 C4 Freixiosa Port.
182 B3 Freixo Port.
182 D3 Freixo de Espada à Cinta Port.
163 E5 Fréjairolles France
161 E5 Fréjus France
161 E5 Fréjus, Golfe de b. France
161 E3 Fréjus Tunnel France/Italy
142 A1 Frekhaug Norway
169 F3 Frellstedt Ger.
87 B7 Fremantle W.A. Austr.
173 E3 Fremdingen Ger.
150 C3 Fremington Devon, England U.K.
240 G3 Fremont CA U.S.A.
226 E5 Fremont IN U.S.A.
226 E4 Fremont MI U.S.A.
236 D3 Fremont NE U.S.A.
232 B4 Fremont OH U.S.A.
226 C3 Fremont WI U.S.A.
241 L2 Fremont r. UT U.S.A.
241 L2 Fremont Junction UT U.S.A.
232 B6 Frenchburg KY U.S.A.
246 D2 French Cay i. Turks and Caicos Is
French Congo country Africa see Congo
232 D4 French Creek r. PA U.S.A.
251 H4 French Guiana terr. S. America
French Guinea country Africa see Guinea
83 F4 French Island Vic. Austr.
238 F1 Frenchman r. MT U.S.A.
233 □I2 Frenchman Bay ME U.S.A.
236 C3 Frenchman Creek r. NE U.S.A.
81 D4 French Pass South I. N.Z.
79 □3 French Polynesia terr. S. Pacific Ocean
French Somaliland country Africa see Djibouti
73 G6 French Southern and Antarctic Lands terr. Indian Ocean
French Sudan country Africa see Mali
French Territory of the Afars and Issas country Africa see Djibouti
234 C2 Frenchtown NJ U.S.A.
233 □I1 Frenchville ME U.S.A.
156 B2 Frencq France
205 F2 Frenda Alg.
156 B3 Freneuse France
173 E2 Frensdorf Ger.
151 G3 Frensham Surrey, England U.K.
177 H2 Frenštát pod Radhoštěm Czech Rep.
193 G3 Frentani, Monti dei mts Italy
215 G3 Frere S. Africa
169 C3 Freren Ger.
179 E4 Fresach Austria
193 G3 Fresagrandinaria Italy
251 I6 Fresco r. Brazil
206 D5 Fresco Côte d'Ivoire
263 K2 Freshfield, Cape Antarctica
147 D4 Freshford Rep. of Ireland
151 F4 Freshwater Isle of Wight, England U.K.
150 C3 Freshwater East Pembrokeshire, Wales U.K.
156 B4 Fresnay-l'Evêque France
159 G3 Fresnay-sur-Sarthe France
185 G2 Fresnedas r. Spain
185 F2 Fresnedillas hill Spain
160 D1 Fresne-St-Mamès France
157 F3 Fresnes-en-Woëvre France
157 F5 Fresnes-sur-Apance France
156 D2 Fresnes-sur-Escaut France
244 C2 Fresnillo Mex.
240 H3 Fresno CA U.S.A.
240 G3 Fresno r. CA U.S.A.
182 E4 Fresno Alhándiga Spain
182 E3 Fresno de la Ribera Spain
182 E3 Fresno de Sayago Spain
183 E3 Fresno el Viejo Spain
156 B3 Fresnoy-Folny France
156 D3 Fresnoy-le-Grand France
156 B2 Fressenneville France
157 G5 Fresse-sur-Moselle France
151 I2 Fressingfield Suffolk, England U.K.
141 I3 Fresvikbreen glacier Norway
146 E3 Freswick Highland, Scotland U.K.
160 D1 Fretigney-et-Velloreille France
172 D2 Freudenberg Baden-Württemberg Ger.
173 F2 Freudenberg Bayern Ger.
169 C5 Freudenberg Nordrhein-Westfalen Ger.
172 A2 Freudenburg Ger.
172 C3 Freudenstadt Ger.
156 C2 Frévent France
232 D3 Frewsburg NY U.S.A.
171 C4 Freyburg (Unstrut) Ger.

Garopaba to Giza
307

255 C9 Garopaba Brazil
116 C4 Garoth Madh. Prad. India
206 E2 Garou, Lac l. Mali
207 I4 Garoua Cameroon
207 I5 Garoua Boulai Cameroon
143 F2 Garphyttan Sweden
Garqêntang Xizang China see Sog
182 E2 Garrafe de Torio Spain
163 A6 Garralda Spain
147 B5 Garrane Rep. of Ireland
183 H3 Garray Spain
168 D3 Garrel Ger.
226 E5 Garrett IN U.S.A.
147 C2 Garrison Northern Ireland U.K.
232 B5 Garrison KY U.S.A.
236 E2 Garrison MN U.S.A.
236 C2 Garrison ND U.S.A.
235 E1 Garrison NY U.S.A.
147 E3 Garristown Rep. of Ireland
129 C3 Garrnarrich Armenia
147 F1 Garronpoint Northern Ireland U.K.
182 D5 Garrovillas Spain
185 I3 Garrucha Spain
146 D4 Garry r. Scotland U.K.
146 D4 Garry, Loch l. Highland, Scotland U.K.
122 D2 Garrygala Turkm.
146 B3 Garrynahine Western Isles, Scotland U.K.
215 F4 Garryowen S. Africa
147 C5 Garryvoe Rep. of Ireland
173 G3 Gars am Inn Ger.
179 G2 Gars am Kamp Austria
149 G3 Garsdale Head Cumbria, England U.K.
143 F4 Gärsnäs Sweden
149 G4 Garstang Lancashire, England U.K.
168 F2 Garstedt Ger.
179 F2 Garsten Austria
81 B6 Garston South I. N.Z.
Gartar Sichuan China see Qianning
162 C2 Gartempe r. France
150 D2 Garth Powys, Wales U.K.
150 D2 Garthmyl Powys, Wales U.K.
146 D5 Gartocharn West Dunbartonshire, Scotland U.K.
Gartog Xizang China see Markam
170 C2 Gartow Ger.
172 C3 Gärtringen Ger.
170 F2 Gartz Ger.
95 D4 Garut Jawa Barat Indon.
147 D3 Garvagh Rep. of Ireland
147 E2 Garvagh Northern Ireland U.K.
147 D2 Garvaghy Northern Ireland U.K.
146 F6 Garvald East Lothian, Scotland U.K.
146 D4 Garvamore Highland, Scotland U.K.
184 B3 Garvão Port.
146 B5 Garvard Argyll and Bute, Scotland U.K.
146 D4 Garve Highland, Scotland U.K.
81 B6 Garvie Mountains South I. N.Z.
117 E4 Garwa Bihar India
175 J4 Garwolin Pol.
230 C3 Gary IN U.S.A.
232 C6 Gary WV U.S.A.
108 A2 Garyi Sichuan China
103 F6 Garyū-zan mt. Japan
170 E1 Garz Ger.
258 E3 Garza Arg.
111 B5 Gar Zangbo r. China
108 A2 Garzê Sichuan China
250 C4 Garzón Col.
Gasan-Kuli Turkm. see Esenguly
174 F3 Gąsawa Pol.
178 B4 Gaschurn Austria
171 D4 Gaschwitz Ger.
163 B5 Gascogne reg. France
154 C5 Gascogne, Golfe de g. France/Spain
236 F4 Gasconade r. MO U.S.A.
Gascony reg. France see Gascogne
Gascony, Gulf of France/Spain see Gascogne, Golfe de
87 B5 Gascoyne r. W.A. Austr.
87 C5 Gascoyne, Mount hill W.A. Austr.
87 B5 Gascoyne Junction W.A. Austr.
183 H4 Gascueña Spain
Gascuña, Golfo de g. France/Spain see Gascogne, Golfe de
113 □1 Gasfinolhu i. N. Male Maldives
124 B5 Gash and Setit prov. Eritrea
116 D2 Gasherbrum mt. Jammu and Kashmir
123 E5 Gasht Iran
207 H3 Gashua Nigeria
175 K2 Gąski Pol.
156 B3 Gasny France
175 I3 Gąsocin Pol.
246 C2 Gaspar Cuba
94 D3 Gaspar, Selat sea chan. Indon.
225 H3 Gaspé Que. Can.
225 H3 Gaspé, Péninsule de pen. Que. Can.
195 F4 Gasperina Italy
179 E2 Gaspoltshofen Austria
206 E3 Gassan Burkina
102 J4 Gassan vol. Japan
206 B3 Gassane Senegal
232 C5 Gassaway WV U.S.A.
164 F2 Gasselte Neth.
164 F2 Gasselternijveen Neth.
161 E5 Gassin France
207 H4 Gassol Nigeria
241 J3 Gass Peak NV U.S.A.
Gasteiz Spain see Vitoria-Gasteiz
100 G2 Gastello Sakhalin Rus. Fed.
179 G2 Gastern Austria
163 A4 Gastes France
232 E6 Gaston NC U.S.A.
231 D5 Gastonia NC U.S.A.
198 B3 Gastouni Greece
182 D4 Gata Spain
185 H4 Gata, Cabo de c. Spain
182 D4 Gata, Sierra de mts Spain
187 D6 Gata de Gorgos Spain
222 E3 Gataga r. B.C. Can.
196 E3 Gătaia Romania
139 H2 Gatchina Rus. Fed.
232 B6 Gate City VA U.S.A.
146 D7 Gatehouse of Fleet Dumfries and Galloway, Scotland U.K.
177 I5 Gátér Hungary
171 C4 Gatersleben Ger.
149 H3 Gateshead Tyne and Wear, England U.K.
231 E4 Gatesville NC U.S.A.
237 D6 Gatesville TX U.S.A.
241 M2 Gateway CO U.S.A.
224 F4 Gatineau Que. Can.
224 F4 Gatineau r. Que. Can.
185 F2 Gato r. Spain
Gatong Xizang China see Jomda
Gatooma Zimbabwe see Kadoma
187 C5 Gátova Spain
179 H2 Gattendorf Austria
191 H4 Gatteo a Mare Italy
161 F5 Gattières France
190 D3 Gattinara Italy
85 H5 Gatton Qld Austr.
242 □J7 Gatún, Lago l. Panama
122 B3 Gatvand Iran
151 G3 Gatwick airport England U.K.
79 □1 Gau i. Fiji
172 C2 Gau-Algesheim Ger.
156 D3 Gauchy France
185 E4 Gaucín Spain
123 E4 Gaud-i-Zirreh depr. Afgh.
Gauhati Assam India see Guwahati
138 E3 Gauja r. Latvia
138 E4 Gauja r. Lith.
172 D2 Gaukönigshofen Ger.
Gaul country Europe see France
184 □ Gaula Madeira
140 J3 Gaula r. Norway
232 C5 Gauley Bridge WV U.S.A.
172 C2 Gau-Odernheim Ger.
141 I3 Gaupne Norway
Gaurdak Turkm. see Govurdak
116 E5 Gaurella Madh. Prad. India
114 C3 Gauribidanur Karnataka India
117 G5 Gaurnadi Bangl.
142 C2 Gausta mt. Norway
215 G2 Gauteng prov. S. Africa
173 F3 Gauting Ger.
186 C3 Gautizalema r. Spain
186 F3 Gavà Spain
190 F3 Gavardo Italy
163 B6 Gavarnie France
Gavarr Armenia see Kamo
123 E5 Gavāter Iran
177 K3 Gávavencsellő Hungary
122 C5 Gāvbandī Iran
122 C5 Gāvbūs, Kūh-e mts Iran
163 A5 Gave r. France
182 B2 Gave Port.
163 B5 Gave d'Arrens r. France
163 B5 Gave d'Aspe r. France
163 A5 Gave d'Oloron r. France
163 B5 Gave d'Ossau r. France
122 A3 Gāveh Rūd r. Iran
165 C4 Gavere Belgium
190 D4 Gavi Italy
255 E5 Gavião r. Brazil
184 C1 Gavião Port.
190 D3 Gavirate Italy
143 G1 Gävle Sweden
143 F1 Gävleborg county Sweden
143 G1 Gävlebukten b. Sweden
192 B4 Gavoi Sardegna Italy
192 C2 Gavorrano Italy
158 E3 Gavray France
135 H5 Gavrilovka Vtoraya Rus. Fed.
139 M3 Gavrilov Posad Rus. Fed.
139 L3 Gavrilov-Yam Rus. Fed.
117 F4 Gawan Bihar India
179 H2 Gaweinstal Austria
116 D5 Gawilgarh Hills India
82 D3 Gawler S.A. Austr.
82 C3 Gawler Ranges hills S.A. Austr.
175 K1 Gawliki Wielkie Pol.
174 D4 Gaworzyce Pol.
149 G4 Gawsworth Cheshire, England U.K.
149 G3 Gawthrop Cumbria, England U.K.
207 G4 Gawu Nigeria
120 D2 Gay Rus. Fed.
226 C2 Gay MI U.S.A.
100 D4 Gaya r. China
117 F4 Gaya Bihar India
207 F4 Gaya Niger
Gayá r. Spain see Gaià
148 B4 Gaybrook Rep. of Ireland
204 C4 G'Aydat al Jhoucha ridge Western Sahara
137 I5 Gayduk Rus. Fed.
207 F3 Gayéri Burkina
226 E3 Gaylord MI U.S.A.
236 E2 Gaylord MN U.S.A.
85 G5 Gayndah Qld Austr.
134 K3 Gayny Rus. Fed.
Gaysin Ukr. see Haysyn
151 H2 Gayton Norfolk, England U.K.
134 G4 Gayutino Rus. Fed.
Gayvoron Ukr. see Hayvoron
128 B4 Gaza terr. Asia
128 B4 Gaza Gaza
213 G4 Gaza prov. Moz.
123 E1 Gaz-Achak Turkm.
121 G4 Gazalkent Uzbek.
122 C2 Gazandzhyk Turkm.
207 I4 Gazawa Cameroon
126 E3 Gaziantep Turkey
128 C1 Gaziantep prov. Turkey
Gazibenli Turkey see Yahyalı
129 C3 Gaziler Turkey
Gazimağusa Cyprus see Ammochostos
100 B1 Gazimur r. Rus. Fed.
100 A2 Gazimurskiy Khrebet mts Rus. Fed.
126 D3 Gazipaşa Turkey
120 E4 Gazli Uzbek.
Gazojak Turkm. see Gaz-Achak
183 I2 Gazolaz Spain
191 F3 Gazoldo degli Ippoliti Italy
191 G3 Gazzo Veronese Italy
191 F3 Gazzuolo Italy
206 D5 Gbaaka Liberia
206 B5 Gbangbatok Sierra Leone
206 C5 Gbarnga Liberia
206 C5 Gbatala Liberia
177 H4 Gbelce Slovakia
176 G3 Gbely Slovakia
207 F4 Gbéroubouè Benin
207 H5 Gboko Nigeria
143 H4 Gdańsk Pol.
175 H1 Gdańsk, Gulf of Pol./Rus. Fed.
Gdańska, Zatoka g. Pol./Rus. Fed. see Gdańsk, Gulf of
Gdingen Pol. see Gdynia
138 F2 Gdov Rus. Fed.
175 I6 Gdów Pol.
143 H4 Gdynia Pol.
146 D4 Geal Charn hill Highland, Scotland U.K.
146 E4 Geal Charn hill Highland, Scotland U.K.
163 E6 Géant, Pic du mt. France
238 B3 Gearhart Mountain OR U.S.A.
Gearraidh na h-Aibhne Western Isles, Scotland U.K. see Garrynahine
148 B4 Geashill Rep. of Ireland
163 B5 Geaune France
169 F4 Gebesee Ger.
169 C5 Gebhardshain Ger.
199 G3 Gebiz Turkey
210 C2 Gebre Guracha Eth.
199 F1 Gebze Turkey
Gecheng Chongqing China see Chengkou
172 C3 Gechingen Ger.
94 C3 Gedang, Gunung mt. Indon.
138 E4 Gedanonių kalnas hill Lith.
203 G6 Gedaref Sudan
203 G6 Gedaref state Sudan
151 G2 Geddington Northamptonshire, England U.K.
177 H5 Géderlak Hungary
169 E5 Gedern Ger.
165 D5 Gedinne Belgium
199 F2 Gediz Turkey
199 E2 Gediz r. Turkey
151 H2 Gedney Drove End Lincolnshire, England U.K.
210 D4 Gedo admin. reg. Somalia
163 C6 Gèdre France
142 D4 Gedser Denmark
142 C3 Gedsted Denmark
Gedzheti Georgia see Gejet'i
165 E3 Geel Belgium
83 F4 Geelong Vic. Austr.
87 B6 Geelvink Channel W.A. Austr.
165 E4 Geer r. Belgium
164 D3 Geertruidenberg Neth.
168 C3 Geeste Ger.
168 D2 Geeste r. Ger.
164 F2 Geesteren Neth.
170 C3 Geestgottberg Ger.
168 F2 Geesthacht Ger.
165 E4 Geetbets Belgium
171 C5 Gefell Ger.
210 C2 Gefersa Eth.
164 E3 Geffen Neth.
171 C5 Gefrees Ger.
138 C4 Gėgė r. Lith.
Gegechkori Georgia see Martvili
177 K3 Gégény Hungary
129 D3 Geghadir Armenia
129 D3 Geghama Lerrnashght'a mts Armenia
111 C5 Gê'gyai Xizang China
78 □3a Gehh i. Kwajalein Marshall Is
168 D3 Gehrde Ger.
169 E3 Gehrden Ger.
171 C5 Gehren Ger.
109 F2 Ge Hu l. China
207 H3 Geidam Nigeria
172 D2 Geiersberg hill Ger.
173 G2 Geiersthal Ger.
234 C2 Geigertown PA U.S.A.
223 K3 Geikie r. Sask. Can.
85 E2 Geikie Range hills Qld Austr.
169 B5 Geilenkirchen Ger.
142 C1 Geilo Norway
169 E5 Geisa Ger.
169 E5 Geiselbach Ger.
173 G3 Geiselhöring Ger.
173 E2 Geiselwind Ger.
173 F3 Geisenfeld Ger.
173 G3 Geisenhausen Ger.
172 B2 Geisenheim Ger.
171 E5 Geising Ger.
172 C4 Geisingen Ger.
169 F4 Geisleden Ger.
172 C3 Geislingen Ger.
172 D3 Geislingen an der Steige Ger.
169 F4 Geismar Ger.
157 H4 Geispolsheim France
178 D3 Geißstein mt. Austria
179 G3 Geistthal Austria
211 B5 Geita Tanz.
171 D4 Geithain Ger.
140 K2 Geittind mt. Norway
129 C2 Gejet'i Georgia
108 B4 Gejiu Yunnan China
122 D2 Gekdepe Turkm.
210 A3 Gel r. Sudan
194 D5 Gela Sicilia Italy
194 D5 Gela r. Sicilia Italy
194 D5 Gela, Golfo di g. Sicilia Italy
111 E5 Geladaindong mt. Qinghai China
210 E3 Geladī Eth.
211 C5 Gelai vol. Tanz.
161 F4 Gélas, Cime du mt. France/Italy
170 D1 Gelbensande Ger.
173 E2 Gelchsheim Ger.
164 F2 Gelderland prov. Neth.
164 E3 Geldermalsen Neth.
169 B4 Geldern Ger.
169 F5 Geldersheim Ger.
165 E3 Geldrop Neth.
165 E4 Geleen Neth.
199 E2 Gelembe Turkey
210 D2 Gelemso Eth.
171 D5 Gelenau Ger.
199 G2 Gelendost Turkey
135 G7 Gelendzhik Rus. Fed.
117 G4 Gelephu Bhutan
199 E1 Gelibolu Turkey
199 E1 Gelibolu Yarımadası pen. Turkey
199 G2 Gelincik Dağı mt. Turkey
163 C4 Gelise r. France
176 F5 Gellénháza Hungary
150 D3 Gelligaer Caerphilly, Wales U.K.
78 □3a Gellinam i. Kwajalein Marshall Is
169 E5 Gelnhausen Ger.
177 J3 Gelnica Slovakia
163 B5 Gelos France
163 B5 Geloux r. France
142 C4 Gels r. Denmark
186 C3 Gelsa Spain
176 F5 Gelse Hungary
169 C4 Gelsenkirchen Ger.
173 F3 Geltendorf Ger.
168 E1 Gelting Ger.
171 D3 Geltow Ger.
165 D4 Gembloux Belgium
207 H5 Gembu Nigeria
160 D1 Gemeaux France
208 C4 Gemena Dem. Rep. Congo
161 D5 Gémenos France
126 E3 Gemerek Turkey
177 J3 Gemerská Hôrka Slovakia
177 J3 Gemerská Poloma Slovakia
164 E3 Gemert Neth.
199 F3 Gemiş Turkey
199 F1 Gemlik Turkey
172 C2 Gemmingen Ger.
191 I2 Gemona del Friuli Italy
162 B3 Gémozac France
203 G3 Gemsa Egypt
212 D5 Gemsbok National Park Botswana
214 E1 Gemsbokvlakte S. Africa
172 B2 Gemünden Ger.
169 D5 Gemünden (Wohra) Ger.
169 E5 Gemünden am Main Ger.
107 H1 Gen r. China
185 E4 Genal r. Spain
210 D3 Genalē Wenz r. Eth.
165 D4 Genappe Belgium
185 H2 Génave Spain
193 E3 Genazzano Italy
129 B4 Genç Turkey
162 C2 Gençay France
176 F4 Gencsapáti Hungary
124 B5 Gendoa r. Eth.
160 D1 Gendrey France
164 F3 Gendringen Neth.
164 E3 Gendt Neth.
160 C2 Génelard France
164 F2 Genemuiden Neth.
260 E5 General Acha Arg.
261 G5 General Alvear Buenos Aires Arg.
260 D4 General Alvear Mendoza Arg.
261 G4 General Arenales Arg.
253 F6 General Artigas Para.
261 H4 General Belgrano Arg.
General Belgrano II research stn Antarctica see Belgrano II
262 U2 General Bernardo O'Higgins research stn Antarctica
261 F3 General Cabrera Arg.
261 H2 General Campos Arg.
256 A1 General Carneiro Brazil
259 B7 General Carrera, Lago l. Arg./Chile
261 F6 General Daniel Cerri Arg.
261 F3 General Deheza Arg.
General Freire Angola see Muxaluando
261 H3 General Galarza Arg.
260 C3 General Gutiérrez Arg.
258 F2 General José de San Martín Arg.
261 I5 General Juan Madariaga Arg.
252 C4 General Lagos Chile
261 H4 General Las Heras Arg.
261 I5 General Lavalle Arg.
261 F4 General Levalle Arg.
92 C4 General Luna Phil.
92 C4 General MacArthur Phil.
General Machado Angola see Camacupa
258 D2 General Martín Miguel de Güemes Arg.
261 F4 General Pico Arg.
261 G4 General Pinto Arg.
261 I5 General Pirán Arg.
260 D6 General Roca Arg.
261 H4 General Rodriguez Arg.
261 G3 General Rojo Arg.
253 E4 General Saavedra Bol.
256 B4 General Salgado Brazil
General San Martín research stn Antarctica see San Martín
261 H4 General San Martín Arg.
261 F5 General San Martín Arg.
92 C5 General Santos Phil.
244 C1 General Simón Bolívar Mex.
243 F3 General Terán Mex.
197 I4 General Toshevo Bulg.
261 F4 General Villegas Arg.
232 E4 Genesee PA U.S.A.
232 E3 Genesee r. NY U.S.A.
232 E3 Geneseo NY U.S.A.
182 D1 Genestoso Spain
210 C2 Genet Eth.
158 E3 Genêts France
215 F2 Geneva S. Africa
Geneva Switz. see Genève
231 C6 Geneva AL U.S.A.
226 C5 Geneva IL U.S.A.
236 D3 Geneva NE U.S.A.
232 E3 Geneva NY U.S.A.
232 C4 Geneva OH U.S.A.
Geneva, Lake France/Switz. see Léman, Lac
190 B2 Genève Switz.
160 E2 Genève canton Switz.
183 H2 Genevilla Spain
160 E2 Genevois mts France
Genf Switz. see Genève
191 H5 Genga Italy
108 B1 Gengda Sichuan China
172 C3 Gengenbach Ger.
109 E4 Genglou Guangdong China
108 A4 Gengma Yunnan China
Gengqing Sichuan China see Dêgê
Gengxuan Yunnan China see Gengma
210 B3 Geni r. Sudan
Genichesk Ukr. see Heniches'k
185 E3 Genil r. Spain
198 D1 Genisea Greece
163 B4 Génissac France
165 E4 Genk Belgium
160 D1 Genlis France
192 B5 Gennargentu, Monti del mts Sardegna Italy
192 B5 Genn'Argiolas, Monte hill Sardegna Italy
164 E3 Gennep Neth.
162 B1 Gennes France
83 G4 Genoa Vic. Austr.
Genoa Italy see Genova
226 C4 Genoa IL U.S.A.
161 B4 Génolhac France
192 B5 Genoni Sardegna Italy
162 D2 Genouillac France
162 C2 Genouillé France
159 H4 Genouilly France
190 D4 Genova Italy
190 E4 Genova prov. Liguria Italy
190 D4 Genova, Golfo di g. Italy
187 C6 Genovés Spain
250 □ Genovesa, Isla i. Islas Galápagos Ecuador
163 C4 Gensac France
165 C3 Gent Belgium
171 D3 Genthin Ger.
254 E4 Gentio do Ouro Brazil
162 E3 Gentioux, Plateau de France
162 D3 Gentioux-Pigerolles France
Genua Italy see Genova
193 I4 Genzano di Lucania Italy
193 E3 Genzano di Roma Italy
197 F2 Geoagiu r. Romania
87 B7 Geographe Bay W.A. Austr.
87 B5 Geographe Channel W.A. Austr.
Geok-Tepe Turkm. see Gekdepe
86 C4 George r. W.A. Austr.
225 H1 George r. Que. Can.
214 D5 George S. Africa
83 G3 George, Lake N.S.W. Austr.
82 D4 George, Lake S.A. Austr.
86 D4 George, Lake salt flat W.A. Austr.
210 A4 George, Lake Uganda
233 G3 George, Lake NY U.S.A.
84 B4 George Gills Range mts N.T. Austr.
150 C3 Georgeham Devon, England U.K.
George Land i. Zemlya Frantsa-Iosifa Rus. Fed. see Zemlya Georga
173 G2 Georgenberg Ger.
173 F2 Georgensgmünd Ger.
233 G3 Georges Mills NH U.S.A.
85 E3 Georgetown Qld Austr.
83 F5 George Town Tas. Austr.
246 D2 George Town Gt Exuma Bahamas
224 E5 Georgetown Ont. Can.
246 B3 George Town Cayman Is
206 B3 Georgetown Gambia
251 G3 Georgetown Guyana
94 C1 George Town Malaysia
235 E1 Georgetown CT U.S.A.
233 F5 Georgetown DE U.S.A.
231 C6 Georgetown GA U.S.A.
230 C4 Georgetown KY U.S.A.
232 B5 Georgetown OH U.S.A.
231 E5 Georgetown SC U.S.A.
237 D6 Georgetown TX U.S.A.
262 T2 George VI Sound sea chan. Antarctica
263 K2 George V Land reg. Antarctica
237 D6 George West TX U.S.A.
129 C3 Georgia country Asia
231 D5 Georgia state U.S.A.
222 E5 Georgia, Strait of B.C. Can.
231 C6 Georgiana AL U.S.A.
224 D4 Georgian Bay Ont. Can.
Georgi Traykov Bulg. see Dolni Chiflik
Georgiu-Dezh Rus. Fed. see Liski
120 D2 Georgiyevka Aktyubinskaya Oblast' Kazakh.
121 J2 Georgiyevka Vostochnyy Kazakhstan Kazakh.
Georgiyevka Zhambylskaya Oblast' Kazakh. see Korday
129 C1 Georgiyevsk Rus. Fed.
134 I4 Georgiyevskoye Kostromskaya Oblast' Rus. Fed.
129 A1 Georgiyevskoye Krasnodarskiy Kray Rus. Fed.
168 C3 Georgsdorf Ger.
168 C2 Georgsheil Ger.
169 D3 Georgsmarienhütte Ger.
Georg von Neumayer research stn Antarctica see Neumayer
163 B5 Ger Aquitaine France
159 F3 Ger Basse-Normandie France
186 E2 Ger Spain
171 D5 Gera Ger.
165 C4 Geraardsbergen Belgium
169 F5 Geraberg Ger.
172 D2 Gerabronn Ger.
195 F4 Gerace Italy
195 F4 Gerace r. Italy
194 D5 Geraci Siculo Sicilia Italy
147 B5 Gerahies Rep. of Ireland
198 C1 Gerakarou Greece
198 C3 Geraki Greece
256 B6 Geral, Serra mts Brazil
254 D4 Geral de Goiás, Serra hills Brazil
81 C6 Geraldine South I. N.Z.
254 D5 Geral do Paraná, Serra hills Brazil
87 B6 Geraldton W.A. Austr.
157 G4 Gérardmer France
179 G2 Geras Austria
179 H2 Gerasdorf bei Wien Austria
122 C5 Gerāsh Iran
156 E4 Géraudot France
240 F1 Gerber CA U.S.A.
157 G4 Gerbéviller France
161 C4 Gerbier de Jonc mt. France
171 C4 Gerbstedt Ger.
176 G4 Gérce Hungary
172 D2 Gerchsheim Ger.
127 F3 Gercüş Turkey
168 F3 Gerdau Ger.
215 F2 Gerdau S. Africa
Gerdauen Kaliningradskaya Oblast' Rus. Fed. see Zheleznodorozhnyy
126 D2 Gerede Turkey
126 D2 Gerede r. Turkey
184 D3 Gerena Spain
177 J5 Gerendás Hungary
182 B3 Gerês, Serra do mts Port.
177 H5 Geresdlak Hungary
123 F4 Gereshk Afgh.
178 D2 Geretsberg Austria
173 F4 Geretsried Ger.
185 H3 Gérgal Spain
129 E2 Gergebil' Rus. Fed.
192 B5 Gergei Sardegna Italy
177 K3 Gergely-hegy hill Hungary
160 C2 Gergy France
173 E2 Gerhardshofen Ger.
122 D3 Gerīmenj Iran
183 F5 Gerindote Spain
236 C3 Gering NE U.S.A.
171 D4 Geringswalde Ger.
177 J4 Gerje r. Hungary
177 H5 Gerjen Hungary
238 C3 Gerlach NV U.S.A.
177 J2 Gerlachovský štít mt. Slovakia
172 D3 Gerlingen Ger.
261 F4 Germania Arg.
Germania country Europe see Germany
Germanicea Turkey see Kahramanmaraş
222 E4 Germansen Landing B.C. Can.
German South-West Africa country Africa see Namibia
232 E5 Germantown MD U.S.A.
232 A5 Germantown OH U.S.A.
237 F5 Germantown TN U.S.A.
226 C4 Germantown WI U.S.A.
166 E3 Germany country Europe
173 E4 Germaringen Ger.
157 F4 Germay France
199 E3 Germencik Turkey
173 F3 Germering Ger.
172 C2 Germersheim Ger.
156 C5 Germigny-des-Prés France
183 H1 Gernika-Lumo Spain
171 C4 Gernrode Sachsen-Anhalt Ger.
169 F4 Gernrode Thüringen Ger.
172 C3 Gernsbach Ger.
172 C2 Gernsheim Ger.
190 E2 Gerola Alta Italy
171 C5 Geroldsgrün Ger.
173 F3 Gerolsbach Ger.
169 B5 Gerolstein Ger.
173 E2 Gerolzhofen Ger.
Gerona Spain see Girona
198 D4 Geropotamos r. Kriti Greece
191 J3 Gerovo Croatia
165 D4 Gerpinnes Belgium
151 G3 Gerrards Cross Buckinghamshire, England U.K.
192 B5 Gerrei reg. Sardegna Italy
Gerri Spain see Guerri de la Sal
163 C5 Gers dept Midi-Pyrénées France
163 C4 Gers r. France
190 D2 Gersau Switz.
169 E5 Gersfeld (Rhön) Ger.
172 B2 Gersheim Ger.
114 B3 Gersoppa Karnataka India
171 E4 Gerste r. Ger.
168 C3 Gersten Ger.
173 E3 Gerstetten Ger.
157 H4 Gerstheim France
173 E3 Gersthofen Ger.
169 F5 Gerstungen Ger.
170 E2 Gerswalde Ger.
161 D4 Gervanne r. France
171 C3 Gerwisch Ger.
Géryville Alg. see El Bayadh
160 B3 Gerzat France
111 D5 Gêrzê Xizang China
126 D2 Gerze Turkey
173 G3 Gerzen Ger.
169 C4 Gescher Ger.
179 H3 Geschriebenstein hill Austria
169 F5 Geschwenda Ger.
169 D4 Geseke Ger.
192 B5 Gesico Sardegna Italy
Gesoriacum France see Boulogne-sur-Mer
157 E3 Gespunsart France
173 E3 Gessertshausen Ger.
190 C4 Gesso r. Italy
187 C5 Gestalgar Spain
159 E4 Gesté France
192 B5 Gesturi Sardegna Italy
193 H3 Gesualdo Italy
165 E4 Gesves Belgium
177 K5 Geszt Hungary
177 K4 Geszteréd Hungary
141 L3 Geta Åland Fin.
183 G4 Getafe Spain
165 E4 Gete r. Belgium
197 F3 Getic, Podişul plat. Romania
158 E4 Gétigné France
129 D3 Getik r. Armenia
168 E1 Gettorf Ger.
234 A3 Gettysburg PA U.S.A.
236 D2 Gettysburg SD U.S.A.
108 C3 Getu He r. China
256 C4 Getulina Brazil
262 P2 Getz Ice Shelf Antarctica
165 E4 Geul r. Neth.
94 B2 Geumapang r. Indon.
94 B1 Geureudong, Gunung vol. Indon.
83 G3 Geurie N.S.W. Austr.
127 F3 Gevaş Turkey
169 C4 Gevelsberg Ger.
158 E3 Gévezé France
197 F5 Gevgelija Macedonia
184 C1 Gévora r. Spain
114 B2 Gevrai Mahar. India
160 C1 Gevrey-Chambertin France
160 E2 Gex France
Gexianzhuang Hebei China see Qinghe
183 H1 Gexto Spain
Gey Iran see Nīkshahr
171 D5 Geyer Ger.
199 E2 Geyikli Turkey
215 E2 Geysdorp S. Africa
240 F2 Geyserville CA U.S.A.
199 G1 Geyve Turkey
256 C2 Gezarina Brazil
198 B1 Gezavesh Albania
179 G2 Gföhl Austria
214 D2 Ghaap Plateau S. Africa
127 F4 Ghadaf, Wādī al watercourse Iraq
Ghadamés Libya see Ghadāmis
202 A2 Ghadāmis Libya
122 C2 Ghaem Shahr Iran
117 F4 Ghaghara r. India
78 □6 Ghaghe i. Solomon Is
117 F5 Ghaghra Bihar India
120 E2 Ghalkarteniz, Solonchak salt marsh Kazakh.
Ghallaorol Uzbek. see Gallyaaral
206 E4 Ghana country Africa
116 C4 Ghanliala Rajasthan India
116 B5 Ghantwar Gujarat India
212 D4 Ghanzi Botswana
212 D4 Ghanzi admin. dist. Botswana
Ghap'an Armenia see Kapan
124 C3 Gharāmīl, Jabal al hill Saudi Arabia
126 C5 Gharbîya governorate Egypt
205 F2 Ghardaïa Alg.
189 B7 Ghardimaou Tunisia
117 E5 Gharghoda Madh. Prad. India
203 G2 Ghârib, Gebel mt. Egypt
123 G2 Gharm Tajik.
125 G4 Gharm, Wādī r. Oman
123 F5 Gharo Pak.
202 B1 Gharyān Libya
202 A3 Ghāt Libya
116 E4 Ghatampur Uttar Prad. India
117 F5 Ghatgan Orissa India
116 C5 Ghatol Rajasthan India
117 F5 Ghatsila Bihar India
123 G4 Ghauspur Pak.
Għawdex i. Malta see Gozo
202 C6 Ghazal, Bahr el watercourse Chad
208 F2 Ghazal, Bahr el r. Sudan
Ghazalkent Uzbek. see Gazalkent
204 E2 Ghazaouet Alg.
116 D3 Ghaziabad Uttar Prad. India
117 E4 Ghazipur Uttar Prad. India
Ghazna Afgh. see Ghaznī
123 G3 Ghaznī Afgh.
123 F3 Ghaznī prov. Afgh.
123 F3 Ghazni r. Afgh.
124 C2 Ghazzālah Saudi Arabia
190 F3 Ghedi Italy
197 F3 Ghelari Romania
197 H3 Ghelința Romania
Ghent Belgium see Gent
232 C6 Ghent WV U.S.A.
Gheorghe Gheorghiu-Dej Romania see Onești
197 H3 Gheorghe Lazăr Romania
197 G2 Gheorgheni Romania
114 B2 Gherdi Mahar. India
197 F2 Gherla Romania
190 D3 Ghiffa Italy
Ghijduwon Uzbek. see Gizhduvan
192 A4 Ghilarza Sardegna Italy
177 K5 Ghioroc Romania
197 F3 Ghioroiu Romania
177 K6 Ghiroda Romania
165 C4 Ghislenghien Belgium
192 B2 Ghisonaccia Corse France
192 B2 Ghisoni Corse France
116 C1 Ghizar Jammu and Kashmir
177 K6 Ghizela Romania
78 □6 Ghizunabeana Islands Solomon Is
114 B2 Ghod Mahar. India
114 B2 Ghod r. India
116 C5 Gholvad Mahar. India
123 G3 Ghorband r. Afgh.
116 B4 Ghotaru Rajasthan India
123 G5 Ghotki Pak.
123 F3 Ghowr prov. Afgh.
117 F4 Ghuari r. India
Ghudamis Libya see Ghadāmis
114 C2 Ghugus Mahar. India
Ghukasyan Armenia see Ashots'k'
128 C4 Ghurayfah hill Saudi Arabia
123 E3 Ghurian Afgh.
124 D2 Ghurrab, Jabal hill Saudi Arabia
124 C3 Ghurūb, Jabal hill Saudi Arabia
202 C2 Ghuzayyil, Sabkhat salt marsh Libya
Ghuzor Uzbek. see Guzar
156 C1 Ghyvelde France
97 D5 Gia Đinh Vietnam
135 H7 Giaginskaya Rus. Fed.
128 A2 Gialias r. Cyprus
96 D3 Giang r. Vietnam
198 C1 Giannitsa Greece
192 D2 Giannutri, Isola di i. Italy
193 E2 Giano dell'Umbria Italy
215 G3 Giant's Castle mt. S. Africa
147 E1 Giant's Causeway lava field Northern Ireland U.K.
235 F1 Giant's Neck CT U.S.A.
95 F5 Gianyar Bali Indon.
195 E5 Giardini-Naxos Sicilia Italy
196 E3 Giarmata Romania
194 D5 Giarratana Sicilia Italy
195 E5 Giarre Sicilia Italy
162 E3 Giat France
192 A4 Giave Sardegna Italy
190 C3 Giaveno Italy
190 C3 Giavino, Monte mt. Italy
192 A5 Giba Sardegna Italy
184 E4 Gibalbín hill Spain
246 C2 Gibara Cuba
184 E3 Gibarrayo hill Spain
86 E2 Gibb r. W.A. Austr.
236 D3 Gibbon NE U.S.A.
238 D2 Gibbonsville ID U.S.A.
86 E3 Gibb River W.A. Austr.
234 D3 Gibbsboro NJ U.S.A.
234 C3 Gibbstown NJ U.S.A.
194 B5 Gibellina Nuova Sicilia Italy
212 C5 Gibeon Namibia
159 F2 Giberville France
162 A2 Giboule r. France
184 D3 Gibraleón Spain
185 E4 Gibraltar Europe
185 □ Gibraltar, Bay of Gibraltar/Spain
184 E4 Gibraltar, Campo de reg. Spain
204 D2 Gibraltar, Strait of Morocco/Spain
87 D7 Gibson W.A. Austr.
231 D5 Gibson GA U.S.A.
226 C5 Gibson City IL U.S.A.
87 D5 Gibson Desert W.A. Austr.
234 B3 Gibson Island MD U.S.A.
222 F5 Gibsons B.C. Can.
175 L1 Giby Pol.
129 F3 Gicäki Dağı mt. Azer.
106 B2 Gichgeniyn Nuruu mts Mongolia
210 B2 Gidda Eth.
114 C3 Giddalur Andhra Prad. India
203 G2 Gîddi, Gebel el hill Egypt
237 D6 Giddings TX U.S.A.
Giddi Pass hill Egypt see Gîddi, Gebel el
140 L3 Gideälven r. Sweden
175 H5 Gidle Pol.
210 C3 Gīdolē Eth.
172 D2 Giebelstadt Ger.
169 F4 Gieboldehausen Ger.
175 H4 Gieczno Pol.
168 F1 Giekau Ger.
164 E1 Giekerk Neth.
167 K3 Giełczew r. Pol.
175 I4 Gielniów Pol.
170 D2 Gielow Ger.
156 C5 Gien France
173 E3 Giengen an der Brenz Ger.
161 D3 Gières France
165 D3 Gierle Belgium
171 C4 Giersleben Ger.
169 F4 Gierstädt Ger.
175 I2 Gierzwałd Pol.
169 E4 Gieselwerder (Oberweser) Ger.
169 D5 Gießen Ger.
169 D5 Gießen admin. reg. Hessen Ger.
164 F1 Gieten Neth.
175 I2 Gietrzwałd Pol.
159 H4 Gièvres France
122 D2 Gīfan Iran
149 G2 Gifford East Lothian, Scotland U.K.
163 E4 Giffou r. France
160 E2 Giffre r. France
169 F3 Gifhorn Ger.
222 H4 Gift Lake Alta Can.
104 C3 Gifu Japan
104 C3 Gifu pref. Japan
135 H7 Gigant Rus. Fed.
242 C3 Giganta, Cerro mt. Mex.
250 C4 Gigante Col.
185 I3 Gigante mt. Spain
161 B5 Gigean France
146 C6 Gigha i. Scotland U.K.
146 C6 Gigha, Sound of sea chan. Scotland U.K.
197 F4 Gighera Romania
192 C2 Giglio, Isola del i. Italy
192 C2 Giglio Castello Italy
161 B5 Gignac Languedoc-Roussillon France
161 D5 Gignac Provence-Alpes-Côte-d'Azur France
190 C3 Gignod Italy
161 D4 Gigondas France
182 E1 Gijón Spain
163 E5 Gijou r. France
211 A5 Gikongoro Rwanda
241 J5 Gila r. AZ U.S.A.
241 K5 Gila Bend AZ U.S.A.
241 K5 Gila Bend Mountains AZ U.S.A.
241 J5 Gila Mountains AZ U.S.A.
122 B2 Gīlān prov. Iran
122 A3 Gīlān-e Gharb Iran
197 F2 Gilău Romania
129 F3 Giläzi Azer.
149 I4 Gilberdyke East Riding of Yorkshire, England U.K.
85 E3 Gilbert r. Qld Austr.
241 L5 Gilbert AZ U.S.A.
226 A2 Gilbert MN U.S.A.
232 C6 Gilbert WV U.S.A.
Gilbert Islands country Pacific Ocean see Kiribati
234 B2 Gilberton PA U.S.A.
85 E3 Gilbert Range mts Qld Austr.
266 G6 Gilbert Ridge sea feature Pacific Ocean
85 E3 Gilbert River Qld Austr.
234 C2 Gilbertsville PA U.S.A.
232 B4 Gilboa OH U.S.A.
254 D4 Gilbués Brazil
173 F3 Gilching Ger.
238 E1 Gildford MT U.S.A.
213 H3 Gilé Moz.
185 F3 Gilena Spain
87 C6 Giles, Lake salt flat W.A. Austr.
84 B3 Giles Creek r. N.T. Austr.
87 F5 Giles Meteorological Station W.A. Austr.
84 B4 Giles Range mts N.T. Austr.
161 F5 Gilette France
202 E4 Gilf Kebir Plateau Egypt
147 E2 Gilford Northern Ireland U.K.
83 G2 Gilgai N.S.W. Austr.
83 G2 Gilgandra N.S.W. Austr.
83 G2 Gil Gil Creek r. N.S.W. Austr.
116 C2 Gilgit Jammu and Kashmir
116 C2 Gilgit r. Jammu and Kashmir
83 F3 Gilgunnia N.S.W. Austr.
95 F5 Gilimanuk Bali Indon.
Gılındire Turkey see Aydıncık
147 C2 Gill, Lough l. Rep. of Ireland
223 M3 Gillam Man. Can.
149 I3 Gillamoor North Yorkshire, England U.K.
142 E3 Gilleleje Denmark
87 E5 Gillen, Lake salt flat W.A. Austr.
169 B5 Gillenfeld Ger.
82 D3 Gilles, Lake salt flat S.A. Austr.
232 E4 Gillett PA U.S.A.
226 C3 Gillett WI U.S.A.
238 F2 Gillette WY U.S.A.
140 K3 Gillhov Sweden
85 E4 Gilliat Qld Austr.
85 E4 Gilliat r. Qld Austr.
150 E3 Gillingham Dorset, England U.K.
151 H3 Gillingham Medway, England U.K.
149 H3 Gilling West North Yorkshire, England U.K.
146 E3 Gills Highland, Scotland U.K.
226 D3 Gills Rock WI U.S.A.
160 E3 Gilly-sur-Isère France
160 B2 Gilly-sur-Loire France
235 F1 Gilman CT U.S.A.
226 D5 Gilman IL U.S.A.
226 B3 Gilman WI U.S.A.
237 E5 Gilmer TX U.S.A.
146 E5 Gilmerton Perth and Kinross, Scotland U.K.
197 F3 Gilort r. Romania
240 G3 Gilroy CA U.S.A.
169 E5 Gilserberg Ger.
149 G3 Gilsland Northumberland, England U.K.
146 F6 Gilston Scottish Borders, Scotland U.K.
168 E3 Gilten Ger.
91 J8 Giluwe, Mount P.N.G.
150 D3 Gilwern Monmouthshire, Wales U.K.
164 D3 Gilze Neth.
210 B2 Gīmbī Eth.
247 □3 Gimie, Mount vol. St Lucia
195 F4 Gimigliano Italy
223 L5 Gimli Man. Can.
143 H1 Gimo Sweden
163 D5 Gimone r. France
163 C5 Gimont France
160 B2 Gimouille France
161 D5 Ginasservis France
203 H6 Ginda Eritrea
85 G4 Gindie Qld Austr.
252 D3 Ginebra, Laguna l. Bol.
128 A5 Gineina, Râs el mt. Egypt
161 A5 Ginestas France
216 □1b Ginetes São Miguel Azores
114 D5 Gin Ganga r. Sri Lanka
114 C3 Gingee Tamil Nadu India
165 E4 Gingelom Belgium
172 D3 Gingen an der Fils Ger.
85 G5 Gin Gin Qld Austr.
87 B6 Gingin W.A. Austr.
215 H3 Gingindlovu S. Africa
92 C4 Gingoog Phil.
170 E1 Gingst Ger.
210 D3 Ginīr Eth.
138 D4 Ginkūnai Lith.
163 E6 Ginoles France
195 F2 Ginosa Italy
195 E4 Ginostra Isole Lipari Italy
Ginzo de Limia Spain see Xinzo de Limia
184 C3 Giões Port.
198 D4 Giofyros r. Kriti Greece
193 H4 Gioi Italy
195 E4 Gioia, Golfo di b. Italy
193 F3 Gioia dei Marsi Italy
195 F2 Gioia del Colle Italy
193 G3 Gioia Sannitica Italy
195 E4 Gioia Tauro Italy
195 F4 Gioiosa Ionica Italy
194 D4 Gioiosa Marea Sicilia Italy
190 D2 Giornico Switz.
198 D2 Gioura i. Greece
193 F2 Giovenco r. Italy
191 F2 Gioveretto mt. Italy
191 G5 Giovi, Monte hill Italy
193 I3 Giovinazzo Italy
224 F2 Gipouloux r. Que. Can.
83 F4 Gippsland reg. Vic. Austr.
113 □1 Giraavaru i. N. Male Maldives
116 B4 Girab Rajasthan India
177 K2 Giraltovce Slovakia
157 G4 Girancourt France
122 D4 Gīrān Rīg mt. Iran
116 D5 Girar Mahar. India
237 E4 Girard KS U.S.A.
232 C4 Girard OH U.S.A.
232 C3 Girard PA U.S.A.
234 B2 Girardville PA U.S.A.
192 B5 Girasole Sardegna Italy
Giravaru i. N. Male Maldives see Giraavaru
123 F5 Girdar Dhor r. Pak.
123 E4 Girdi Iran
207 I4 Girei Nigeria
126 E2 Giresun Turkey
203 F3 Girga Egypt
Girgenti Sicilia Italy see Agrigento
208 C4 Giri r. Dem. Rep. Congo
117 F4 Giridih Bihar India
195 F4 Girifalco Italy
83 F2 Girilambone N.S.W. Austr.
177 K4 Girişu de Criş Romania
136 D4 Gîrla Mare r. Moldova
116 C5 Girna r. India
Girne Cyprus see Keryneia
177 K6 Giroc Romania
169 C5 Girod Ger.
157 G5 Giromagny France
250 B5 Girón Ecuador
Giron Sweden see Kiruna
186 F3 Girona Spain
186 F2 Girona prov. Cataluña Spain
163 B4 Gironde dept Aquitaine France
162 B3 Gironde est. France
163 B4 Gironde-sur-Dropt France
186 E2 Gironella Spain
163 D5 Girou r. France
163 D5 Giroussens France
151 H2 Girton Cambridgeshire, England U.K.
255 B9 Giruá Brazil
146 D6 Girvan South Ayrshire, Scotland U.K.
134 F3 Girvas Rus. Fed.
80 G3 Gisborne North I. N.Z.
80 G3 Gisborne admin. reg. North I. N.Z.
149 G4 Gisburn Lancashire, England U.K.
222 F4 Giscome B.C. Can.
211 A5 Gisenyi Rwanda
142 E3 Gislaved Sweden
156 B3 Gisors France
Gissar Tajik. see Hisor
123 F2 Gissar Range mts Tajik./Uzbek.
Gissarskiy Khrebet mts Tajik./Uzbek. see Gissar Range
193 G2 Gissi Italy
165 B3 Gistel Belgium
190 D2 Giswil Switz.
211 A5 Gitarama Rwanda
211 A5 Gitega Burundi
169 F4 Gittelde Ger.
Giuba r. Somalia see Jubba
197 F3 Giubega Romania
190 E2 Giubiasco Switz.
191 F3 Giudicarie, Valli val. Italy
193 G4 Giugliano in Campania Italy
193 F3 Giuliano di Roma Italy
193 F2 Giulianova Italy
190 F4 Giuncugnano Italy
197 G2 Giurgeului, Munții mts Romania
197 G4 Giurgiu Romania
122 D2 Givar Iran
142 C4 Give Denmark
156 B3 Giverny France
157 E2 Givet France
160 C3 Givors France
165 D4 Givry Belgium
160 C2 Givry France
157 E4 Givry-en-Argonne France
213 F4 Giyani S. Africa
210 C2 Giyon Eth.
Giza Egypt see El Gîza

Govĭ Altayn Nuruu to Groß-Enzersdorf 309

106 C2 Govĭ Altayn Nuruu mts Mongolia
116 E4 Govindgarh Madh. Prad. India
123 F2 Govurdak Turkm.
81 D4 Gowanbridge South I. N.Z.
232 D3 Gowanda NY U.S.A.
85 F5 Gowan Range hills Qld Austr.
175 I4 Gowarczów Pol.
234 B2 Gowen City PA U.S.A.
150 C3 Gower pen. Wales U.K.
227 G2 Gowganda Ont. Can.
174 F1 Gowidlino Pol.
174 C2 Gowienica r. Pol.
147 D3 Gowna, Lough l. Rep. of Ireland
175 J3 Goworowo Pol.
147 D4 Gowran Rep. of Ireland
Gowurdak Turkm. see Govurdak
149 G4 Gowy r. England U.K.
149 I4 Goxhill North Lincolnshire, England U.K.
258 F3 Goya Arg.
247 □2 Goyave Guadeloupe
129 E3 Göyçay Azer.
129 E3 Göyçay r. Azer.
84 C2 Goyder r. N.T. Austr.
84 C5 Goyder watercourse N.T. Austr.
82 D1 Goyder Lagoon salt flat S.A. Austr.
Goymatdag hills Turkm. see Koymatdag, Gory
199 G3 Göynük Turkey
127 F3 Göynük Turkey
199 G1 Göynük Turkey
199 G1 Göynük r. Turkey
199 F2 Göynükbelen Turkey
102 J4 Goyō-zan mt. Japan
129 F4 Göytäpä Azer.
202 D6 Goz-Beïda Chad
128 B1 Gözcüler Turkey
175 J4 Gózd Pol.
174 D4 Gozdnica Pol.
126 E3 Gözene Turkey
111 C5 Gozha Co salt l. China
195 □ Gozo i. Malta
190 D3 Gozzano Italy
214 E5 Graaf-Reinet S. Africa
214 B5 Graafwater S. Africa
172 C2 Graben-Neudorf Ger.
173 G4 Grabenstätt Ger.
169 F5 Grabfeld plain Ger.
175 G4 Grabia r. Pol.
175 H4 Grabica Pol.
206 D5 Grabo Côte d'Ivoire
214 B6 Grabouw S. Africa
197 F3 Grabovica Srbija Yugo.
121 H1 Grabovo Kazakh.
170 C2 Grabow Mecklenburg-Vorpommern Ger.
171 C3 Grabow Sachsen-Anhalt Ger.
175 H3 Grabów Pol.
143 G4 Grabowa r. Pol.
170 D2 Grabowhöfe Ger.
175 L5 Grabowiec Lubelskie Pol.
175 J4 Grabowiec Mazowieckie Pol.
175 J4 Grabów nad Pilicą Pol.
174 G4 Grabów nad Prosną Pol.
174 F2 Grabówno Pol.
174 F4 Grabowno Wielkie Pol.
175 K2 Grabowo Podlaskie Pol.
175 K1 Grabowo Warmińsko-Mazurskie Pol.
190 E1 Grabs Switz.
188 E3 Gračac Croatia
188 G3 Gračanica Bos.-Herz.
162 D1 Graçay France
87 C7 Grace, Lake salt flat W.A. Austr.
224 E4 Gracefield Que. Can.
165 E4 Grâce-Hollogne Belgium
85 G4 Gracemere Qld Austr.
158 C3 Grâces France
139 M5 Grachevka Lipetskaya Oblast' Rus. Fed.
120 C1 Grachevka Orenburgskaya Oblast' Rus. Fed.
121 I2 Grachi Kazakh.
245 E2 Graciano Sánchez Mex.
242 □H6 Gracías Hond.
216 □1c Graciosa i. Azores
216 □3c Graciosa i. Canary Is
188 G3 Gradačac Bos.-Herz.
191 H5 Gradara Italy
254 C4 Gradaús, Serra dos hills Brazil
183 E2 Gradefes Spain
197 H4 Gradets Bulg.
163 B4 Gradignan France
197 H4 Gradishte hill Bulg.
Gradiška Bos.-Herz. see Bosanska Gradiška
188 G3 Gradište Croatia
197 H3 Grădiştea Romania
191 I3 Grado Italy
182 D1 Grado Spain
192 D2 Gradoli Italy
237 C5 Grady NM U.S.A.
146 E3 Graemsay i. Scotland U.K.
185 G3 Graena Spain
173 F3 Gräfelfing Ger.
173 F2 Gräfenberg Ger.
169 E5 Gräfendorf Ger.
179 G3 Grafendorf bei Hartberg Austria
171 D4 Gräfenhainichen Ger.
172 C4 Grafenhausen Ger.
169 F5 Gräfenroda Ger.
179 F4 Grafenstein Austria
171 C5 Gräfenthal Ger.
169 F4 Gräfentonna Ger.
173 F2 Grafenwöhr Ger.
179 G2 Grafenworth Austria
192 E2 Graffignano Italy
169 F3 Grafhorst Ger.
171 C5 Gräfinau-Angstedt Ger.
173 F3 Grafing bei München Ger.
142 C1 Gråfjell mt. Norway
173 G3 Grafling Ger.
173 F3 Grafrath Ger.
140 K3 Gräftåvallen Sweden
83 H2 Grafton N.S.W. Austr.
236 D1 Grafton ND U.S.A.
232 B4 Grafton OH U.S.A.
226 D4 Grafton WI U.S.A.
232 C5 Grafton WV U.S.A.
85 F3 Grafton, Cape Qld Austr.
241 J2 Grafton, Mount NV U.S.A.
85 F3 Grafton Passage Qld Austr.
142 C1 Grågalten hill Norway
193 G4 Gragnano Italy
231 E4 Graham NC U.S.A.
237 D5 Graham TX U.S.A.
241 M5 Graham, Mount AZ U.S.A.
Graham Bell Island Zemlya Frantsa-Iosifa Rus. Fed. see Greem-Bell, Ostrov
222 C4 Graham Island B.C. Can.
221 I2 Graham Island Nunavut Can.
262 T2 Graham Land reg. Antarctica
215 F5 Grahamstown S. Africa
Grahovo Bos.-Herz. see Bosansko Grahovo
148 C5 Graigue Rep. of Ireland
147 E4 Graiguenamanagh Rep. of Ireland
151 H3 Grain Medway, England U.K.
151 H3 Grain, Isle of pen. England U.K.
173 F4 Grainau Ger.
173 H3 Grainet Ger.
161 A4 Graissac France
161 B5 Graissessac France
183 I5 Graja de Iniesta Spain
183 E2 Grajal de Campos Spain
254 D3 Grajaú Brazil
254 D2 Grajaú r. Brazil
175 K2 Grajewo Pol.
134 J4 Grakhovo Rus. Fed.
179 G4 Gralla Austria
142 C4 Gram Denmark
197 F4 Gramada mt. Yugo.
179 F2 Gramastettan Austria
163 D4 Gramat France
163 D4 Gramat, Causse de hills France
197 H4 Gramatikovo Bulg.
179 H2 Gramatneusiedl Austria
161 D5 Grambois France
170 F2 Grambow Ger.
170 C2 Gramkow Ger.
170 D1 Grammendorf Ger.
194 D5 Grammichele Sicilia Italy
Grammont Belgium see Geraardsbergen
190 C5 Grammont, Mont mt. Italy
198 B1 Grámmos mt. Greece
232 D4 Grampian PA U.S.A.
146 D5 Grampian Mountains Scotland U.K.
83 E4 Grampians, The mts Vic. Austr.
150 C4 Grampound Cornwall, England U.K.
164 F2 Gramsbergen Neth.
196 E5 Gramsh Albania
170 F2 Gramzow Ger.
Gran Hungary see Esztergom
190 C4 Grana r. Italy
190 D3 Grana r. Italy
214 B4 Granaatboskolk S. Africa
147 E3 Granabeg Rep. of Ireland
250 C4 Granada Col.
242 □I7 Granada Nic.
185 G3 Granada Spain
185 G3 Granada prov. Andalucía Spain
236 C4 Granada CO U.S.A.
216 □3a Granadilla de Abona Tenerife Canary Is
184 C3 Granado hill Spain
147 D3 Granard Rep. of Ireland
191 G4 Granarolo dell'Emilia Italy
178 D3 Granatspitze mt. Austria
185 G2 Granátula de Calatrava Spain
259 D7 Gran Bajo depr. Arg.
260 D6 Gran Bajo Salitroso salt flat Arg.
237 D5 Granbury TX U.S.A.
225 F4 Granby Que. Can.
238 F3 Granby CO U.S.A.
216 □3f Gran Canaria i. Canary Is
157 F5 Grancey-le-Château-Nouvelle France
253 E6 Gran Chaco reg. Arg./Para.
157 F4 Grand France
230 C3 Grand r. MO U.S.A.
236 C2 Grand r. SD U.S.A.
236 C2 Grand, North Fork r. SD U.S.A.
236 C2 Grand, South Fork r. SD U.S.A.
161 D4 Grand Armet mt. France
182 D1 Grandas de Salime Spain
Grand Atlas mts Morocco see Haut Atlas
246 C1 Grand Bahama i. Bahamas
157 H5 Grand Ballon mt. France
225 K4 Grand Bank Nfld. Can.
264 F3 Grand Banks of Newfoundland sea feature N. Atlantic Ocean
206 E5 Grand-Bassam Côte d'Ivoire
225 H4 Grand Bay N.B. Can.
237 F6 Grand Bay AL U.S.A.
217 □1c Grand Bénare mt. Réunion
224 D5 Grand Bend Ont. Can.
161 E4 Grand Bérard mt. France
206 D5 Grand-Bérébi Côte d'Ivoire
232 B3 Grand Blanc MI U.S.A.
246 E2 Grand Caicos i. Turks and Caicos Is
159 E2 Grandcamp-Maisy France
Grand Canal China see Da Yunhe
Grand Canary i. Canary Is see Gran Canaria
241 K3 Grand Canyon AZ U.S.A.
241 K3 Grand Canyon gorge AZ U.S.A.
246 B3 Grand Cayman i. Cayman Is
223 I4 Grand Centre Alta Can.
206 C5 Grand Cess Liberia
158 D4 Grand-Champ France
160 E1 Grand-Charmont France
160 D3 Grand Colombier mt. France
190 C3 Grand Combin mt. Switz.
238 C2 Grand Coulee WA U.S.A.
156 B3 Grand-Couronne France
226 C5 Grand Detour IL U.S.A.
260 C5 Grande r. Arg.
252 E4 Grande r. Santa Cruz Bol.
253 E4 Grande r. Santa Cruz Bol.
254 E4 Grande r. Bahia Brazil
256 B3 Grande r. São Paulo Brazil
194 C5 Grande r. Sicilia Italy
245 H5 Grande r. Chiapas Mex.
244 C4 Grande r. Jalisco/Michoacán Mex.
245 F5 Grande r. Oaxaca Mex.
245 G5 Grande r. Oaxaca Mex.
242 □J6 Grande r. Nic.
252 B3 Grande r. Peru
187 C5 Grande r. Spain
185 F4 Grande r. Spain
185 G2 Grande r. Spain
259 C8 Grande, Bahía b. Arg.
245 F5 Grande, Cerro mt. Oaxaca Mex.
244 D2 Grande, Cerro mt. San Luis Potosí Mex.
257 E5 Grande, Ilha i. Brazil
194 B5 Grande, Montagna hill Sicilia Italy
260 D5 Grande, Salina salt flat Arg.
253 E2 Grande, Serra hills Brazil
251 F4 Grande, Serra mt. Brazil
260 E2 Grande, Sierra mts Arg.
247 □2 Grande Anse Guadeloupe
217 □1b Grande Baie Mauritius
222 G4 Grande Cache Alta Can.
Grande Comore i. Comoros see Njazidja
225 I4 Grande-Entree Que. Can.
163 B4 Grande Leyre r. France
222 G4 Grande Prairie Alta Can.
207 I2 Grand Erg de Bilma des. Niger
205 E3 Grand Erg Occidental des. Alg.
205 G3 Grand Erg Oriental des. Alg.
225 H3 Grande-Rivière Que. Can.
217 □1b Grande Rivière Noire r. Mauritius
217 □1b Grande Rivière South East r. Mauritius
217 □1b Grande Rivière Sud-Est r. Mauritius
190 C3 Grande Rochère mt. Italy
238 C2 Grande Ronde r. OR U.S.A.
260 E2 Grandes, Salinas salt marsh Arg.
160 A1 Grande Sauldre r. France
160 F3 Grandes Jorasses mts France/Italy
156 C1 Grande-Synthe France
247 □2 Grande-Terre i. Guadeloupe
217 □3b Grande Terre i. Mayotte
161 D4 Grande Tête de l'Obiou mt. France
158 D5 Grand Etier r. France
190 C3 Grande Tournalin mt. Italy
163 E4 Grande-Vabre France
225 H3 Grande-Vallée Que. Can.
190 C3 Grand Eyvia r. Italy
225 H4 Grand Falls N.B. Can.
225 K3 Grand Falls Nfld. Can.
222 G5 Grand Forks B.C. Can.
236 D2 Grand Forks ND U.S.A.
156 C1 Grand-Fort-Philippe France
158 E4 Grand-Fougeray France
163 B6 Grand Gabizos mt. France
233 F3 Grand Gorge NY U.S.A.
246 E3 Grand Gosier Haiti
225 H4 Grand Harbour N.B. Can.
226 D4 Grand Haven MI U.S.A.
236 D3 Grand Island NE U.S.A.
237 F6 Grand Isle LA U.S.A.
233 □I1 Grand Isle ME U.S.A.
241 M2 Grand Junction CO U.S.A.
226 D4 Grand Junction MI U.S.A.
206 D5 Grand-Lahou Côte d'Ivoire
159 E5 Grand Lay r. France
226 E4 Grand Ledge MI U.S.A.
158 E4 Grand-Lieu, Lac de l. France
159 E5 Grand Maine r. France
225 H4 Grand Manan Island N.B. Can.
226 E2 Grand Marais MI U.S.A.
226 B2 Grand Marais MN U.S.A.
226 C4 Grand Marsh WI U.S.A.
225 F4 Grand-Mère Que. Can.
156 C4 Grand Morin r. France
184 B2 Grândola Port.
184 B2 Grândola r. Port.
184 B2 Grândola, Serra de mts Port.
161 D3 Grand Pic de Belledonne mt. France
226 C2 Grand Portage MN U.S.A.
157 E3 Grandpré France
156 C4 Grandpuits-Bailly-Carrois France
223 L4 Grand Rapids Man. Can.
226 E4 Grand Rapids MI U.S.A.
226 A2 Grand Rapids MN U.S.A.
78 □5 Grand Récif de Cook rf New Caledonia
161 C5 Grand Rhône r. France
161 B4 Grandrieu France
160 C2 Grandris France
161 E3 Grand Roc Noir mt. France
Grand St Bernard, Col du pass Italy/Switz. see Great St Bernard Pass
251 H3 Grand Santi Fr. Guiana
190 B2 Grandson Switz.
238 E3 Grand Teton mt. WY U.S.A.
226 E3 Grand Traverse Bay MI U.S.A.
246 E2 Grand Turk Turks and Caicos Is
246 E2 Grand Turk i. Turks and Caicos Is
160 E1 Grandvelle-et-le-Perrenot France
226 B2 Grand View WI U.S.A.
160 E1 Grandvillars France
226 E4 Grandville MI U.S.A.
157 G4 Grandvillers France
156 B3 Grandvilliers France
241 J4 Grand Wash Cliffs mts AZ U.S.A.
226 A3 Grandy MN U.S.A.
161 C4 Grane France
186 C3 Grañén Spain
260 B4 Graneros Chile
147 E3 Grange Louth Rep. of Ireland
147 C2 Grange Sligo Rep. of Ireland
147 D5 Grange Waterford Rep. of Ireland
160 E2 Grange, Mont de mt. France
147 E3 Grangebellow Rep. of Ireland
147 E4 Grangeford Rep. of Ireland
246 □ Grange Hill Jamaica
146 E5 Grangemouth Falkirk, Scotland U.K.
149 G3 Grange-over-Sands Cumbria, England U.K.
238 E3 Granger WY U.S.A.
143 F1 Grängesberg Sweden
157 G4 Granges-sur-Vologne France
150 D3 Grangetown Cardiff, Wales U.K.
238 C2 Grangeville ID U.S.A.
140 M2 Granhult Sweden
161 D3 Granier, Mont mt. France
222 E4 Granisle B.C. Can.
234 B3 Granite MD U.S.A.
236 F4 Granite City IL U.S.A.
236 E2 Granite Falls MN U.S.A.
240 I1 Granite Mountain NV U.S.A.
241 J4 Granite Mountains CA U.S.A.
241 J5 Granite Mountains CA U.S.A.
238 E2 Granite Peak MT U.S.A.
241 K1 Granite Peak UT U.S.A.
Granitic Group is Seychelles see Inner Islands
121 H4 Granitogorsk Kazakh.
194 B5 Granitola, Capo c. Sicilia Italy
194 B5 Granitola-Torretta Sicilia Italy
81 C4 Granity South I. N.Z.
254 E2 Granja Brazil
184 C2 Granja Port.
182 E3 Granja de Moreruela Spain
184 E2 Granja de Torrehermosa Spain
182 B4 Granja do Ulmeiro Port.
259 D7 Gran Laguna Salada l. Arg.
143 F2 Gränna Sweden
186 F3 Granollers Spain
174 E3 Granowo Pol.
252 B2 Gran Pajonal plain Peru
190 C3 Gran Paradiso mt. Italy
178 C4 Gran Pilastro mt. Austria/Italy
Gran San Bernardo, Colle del pass Italy/Switz. see Great St Bernard Pass
193 F2 Gran Sasso d'Italia mts Italy
171 D4 Granschütz Ger.
170 E2 Gransee Ger.
148 C3 Gransha Northern Ireland U.K.
236 C3 Grant NE U.S.A.
240 H2 Grant, Mount NV U.S.A.
240 I2 Grant, Mount NV U.S.A.
236 E3 Grant City MO U.S.A.
151 G2 Grantham Lincolnshire, England U.K.
234 B2 Grantham PA U.S.A.
262 P2 Grant Island Antarctica
84 C1 Grant Island N.T. Austr.
226 B3 Granton WI U.S.A.
146 E4 Grantown-on-Spey Highland, Scotland U.K.
226 D5 Grant Park IL U.S.A.
241 J2 Grant Range mts NV U.S.A.
239 F5 Grants NM U.S.A.
226 A3 Grantsburg WI U.S.A.
146 F6 Grantshouse Scottish Borders, Scotland U.K.
238 B3 Grants Pass OR U.S.A.
232 C5 Grantsville WV U.S.A.
234 B2 Grantville PA U.S.A.
222 B2 Granville Y.T. Can.
158 E3 Granville France
241 M5 Granville AZ U.S.A.
226 C5 Granville IL U.S.A.
233 G3 Granville NY U.S.A.
232 B4 Granville OH U.S.A.
142 B1 Granvin Norway
170 C2 Granzin Ger.
257 F2 Grão Mogol Brazil
240 I3 Grapevine Mountains NV U.S.A.
191 G3 Grappa, Monte mt. Italy
223 I1 Gras, Lac de l. N.W.T. Can.
168 D2 Grasberg Ger.
213 F5 Graskop S. Africa
171 C3 Grasleben Ger.
142 E1 Gräsmarken Sweden
149 F3 Grasmere Cumbria, England U.K.
234 B4 Grasonville MD U.S.A.
223 L3 Grass r. Man. Can.
233 F2 Grass r. NY U.S.A.
193 I4 Grassano Italy
173 G4 Grassau Ger.
161 E5 Grasse France
232 D4 Grassflat PA U.S.A.
149 H3 Grassington North Yorkshire, England U.K.
227 E4 Grass Lake MI U.S.A.
87 D7 Grass Patch W.A. Austr.
238 E2 Grassrange MT U.S.A.
240 G2 Grass Valley CA U.S.A.
83 F5 Grassy Tas. Austr.
236 C2 Grassy Butte ND U.S.A.
246 C2 Grassy Creek r. Andros Bahamas
168 E1 Gråsten Denmark
142 E2 Grästorp Sweden
186 D3 Gratallops Spain
163 D5 Gratens France
163 D5 Gratentour France
226 B4 Gratiot WI U.S.A.
179 G3 Gratkorn Austria
140 L2 Gråträsk Sweden
194 C5 Gratteri Sicilia Italy
179 G3 Gratwein Austria
190 E2 Graubünden canton Switz.
Graudenz Pol. see Grudziądz
169 C5 Grauer Kopf hill Ger.
163 D5 Graulhet France
171 E4 Graupa Ger.
186 D2 Graus Spain
183 I2 Grávalos Spain
254 G4 Gravata Brazil
255 C9 Gravataí Brazil
140 K1 Gravdal Norway
164 E3 Grave Neth.
190 E2 Gravedona Italy
223 J5 Gravelbourg Sask. Can.
156 C2 Gravelines France
190 D3 Gravellona Toce Italy
157 G3 Gravelotte France
224 E4 Gravenhurst Ont. Can.
169 D5 Grävenwiesbach Ger.
238 D2 Grave Peak ID U.S.A.
83 G2 Gravesend N.S.W. Austr.
151 H3 Gravesend Kent, England U.K.
237 E4 Gravette AR U.S.A.
156 B3 Gravigny France
193 I4 Gravina r. Italy
195 F2 Gravina di Matera r. Italy
193 I4 Gravina in Puglia Italy
192 A3 Gravona r. Corse France
226 E3 Grawn MI U.S.A.
160 D1 Gray France
231 D5 Gray GA U.S.A.
232 A6 Gray KY U.S.A.
233 □H3 Gray ME U.S.A.
232 B6 Gray TN U.S.A.
162 A3 Grayan-et-l'Hôpital France
238 B3 Grayback Mountain OR U.S.A.
222 E3 Grayling r. B.C. Can.
226 E3 Grayling MI U.S.A.
149 G3 Grayrigg Cumbria, England U.K.
151 H3 Grays Thurrock, England U.K.
151 G3 Grayshott Hampshire, England U.K.
232 B5 Grayson KY U.S.A.
230 C4 Grayville IL U.S.A.
137 H2 Grayvoron Rus. Fed.
179 G3 Graz Austria
161 C3 Grazac France
185 E4 Grazalema Spain
175 H2 Grążawy Pol.
194 D1 Grazzanise Italy
197 F4 Grdelica Srbija Yugo.
186 B4 Grea de Albarracín Spain
163 D4 Gréalou France
246 □ Great r. Jamaica
246 C1 Great Abaco i. Bahamas
76 C5 Great Australian Bight g. Austr.
149 H3 Great Ayton North Yorkshire, England U.K.
151 H3 Great Baddow Essex, England U.K.
246 C1 Great Bahama Bank sea feature Bahamas
80 E2 Great Barrier Island North I. N.Z.
85 F1 Great Barrier Reef Qld Austr.
233 G3 Great Barrington MA U.S.A.
151 H2 Great Barton Suffolk, England U.K.
241 I2 Great Basin NV U.S.A.
222 E1 Great Bear r. N.W.T. Can.
222 G1 Great Bear Lake N.W.T. Can.
Great Belt sea chan. Denmark see Store Bælt
236 D4 Great Bend KS U.S.A.
233 F4 Great Bend PA U.S.A.
151 I3 Great Bentley Essex, England U.K.
146 B3 Great Bernera i. Scotland U.K.
151 H2 Great Bircham Norfolk, England U.K.
147 A4 Great Blasket Island Rep. of Ireland
149 H3 Great Broughton North Yorkshire, England U.K.
149 F3 Great Clifton Cumbria, England U.K.
97 A4 Great Coco Island Cocos Is
151 H2 Great Cornard Suffolk, England U.K.
148 E2 Great Cumbrae i. Scotland U.K.
76 E5 Great Dividing Range mts Austr.
149 F3 Great Dodd hill England U.K.
149 I3 Great Driffield East Riding of Yorkshire, England U.K.
227 F3 Great Duck Island Ont. Can.
151 H3 Great Dunmow Essex, England U.K.
Great Eastern Erg des. Alg. see Grand Erg Oriental
149 G4 Great Eccleston Lancashire, England U.K.
234 D3 Great Egg Harbor r. NJ U.S.A.
151 H2 Great Ellingham Norfolk, England U.K.
246 B2 Greater Antilles is Caribbean Sea
Greater Khingan Mountains China see Da Hinggan Ling
151 G3 Greater London admin. div. England U.K.
149 G4 Greater Manchester admin. div. England U.K.
125 F2 Greater Tunb i. The Gulf
246 D2 Great Exuma i. Bahamas
238 E2 Great Falls MT U.S.A.
215 F5 Great Fish r. S. Africa
213 E7 Great Fish Point S. Africa
80 E4 Greatford North I. N.Z.
117 F4 Great Gandak r. India
Great Ganges atoll Cook Is see Manihiki
151 F2 Great Glen Leicestershire, England U.K.
151 G2 Great Gonerby Lincolnshire, England U.K.
151 G2 Great Gransden Cambridgeshire, England U.K.
246 C1 Great Guana Cay i. Bahamas
231 E7 Great Guana Cay i. Bahamas
151 G3 Greatham Hampshire, England U.K.
149 H3 Greatham Hartlepool, England U.K.
150 E2 Great Hanwood Shropshire, England U.K.
246 C1 Great Harbour Cay i. Bahamas
149 G4 Great Harwood Lancashire, England U.K.
151 F2 Great Haywood Staffordshire, England U.K.
151 H3 Great Horkesley Essex, England U.K.
246 D2 Great Inagua i. Bahamas
147 C5 Great Island Rep. of Ireland
214 D5 Great Karoo plat. S. Africa
215 G5 Great Kei r. S. Africa
85 G4 Great Keppel Island Qld Austr.
83 F5 Great Lake Tas. Austr.
151 G2 Great Linford Milton Keynes, England U.K.
150 E2 Great Malvern Worcestershire, England U.K.
149 F4 Great Marton Blackpool, England U.K.
234 D2 Great Meadows NJ U.S.A.
264 H4 Great Meteor Tablemount sea feature N. Atlantic Ocean
232 A5 Great Miami r. OH U.S.A.
151 G3 Great Missenden Buckinghamshire, England U.K.
115 G5 Great Nicobar i. Andaman & Nicobar Is India
150 D1 Great Ormes Head hd Wales U.K.
151 H2 Great Ouse r. England U.K.
83 G5 Great Oyster Bay Tas. Austr.
85 F3 Great Palm Island Qld Austr.
221 K3 Great Plain of the Koukdjuak Nunavut Can.
236 C3 Great Plains NE U.S.A.
151 G2 Great Ponton Lincolnshire, England U.K.
Great Rann of Kachchh marsh India see Rann of Kachchh
150 D2 Great Rhos hill Wales U.K.
210 B5 Great Rift Valley Africa
211 C6 Great Ruaha r. Tanz.
160 F3 Great St Bernard Pass Italy/Switz.
231 E7 Great Sale Cay i. Bahamas
149 G3 Great Salkeld Cumbria, England U.K.
238 D3 Great Salt Lake UT U.S.A.
241 K1 Great Salt Lake Desert UT U.S.A.
247 □2 Great Salt Pond l. St Kitts and Nevis
151 H3 Great Sampford Essex, England U.K.
223 I5 Great Sand Hills Sask. Can.
202 E2 Great Sand Sea des. Egypt/Libya
86 D4 Great Sandy Desert W.A. Austr.
Great Sandy Island Qld Austr. see Fraser Island
151 H2 Great Shelford Cambridgeshire, England U.K.
222 H2 Great Slave Lake N.W.T. Can.
231 C5 Great Smoky Mountains N. Carolina/Tennessee U.S.A.
222 E3 Great Snow Mountain B.C. Can.
151 I3 Great Stour r. England U.K.
148 C4 Great Sugar Loaf hill Rep. of Ireland
150 C4 Great Torrington Devon, England U.K.
Great Usutu r. Africa see Usutu
87 F6 Great Victoria Desert W.A. Austr.
151 H3 Great Wakering Essex, England U.K.
262 U2 Great Wall research stn Antarctica
107 H3 Great Wall tourist site China
151 H3 Great Waltham Essex, England U.K.
Great Western Erg des. Alg. see Grand Erg Occidental
83 F5 Great Western Tiers mts Tas. Austr.
149 H3 Great Whernside hill England U.K.
214 B5 Great Winterhoek mt. S. Africa
150 E2 Great Wyrley Staffordshire, England U.K.
151 I2 Great Yarmouth Norfolk, England U.K.
151 H2 Great Yeldham Essex, England U.K.
Great Zab r. Iraq see Zāb al Kabīr, Nahr az
213 F4 Great Zimbabwe National Monument tourist site Zimbabwe
142 D2 Grebbestad Sweden
169 E5 Grebenau Ger.
169 F4 Grebendorf (Meinhard) Ger.
169 E5 Grebenhain Ger.
Grebenkovskiy Ukr. see Hrebinka
129 E2 Grebenskaya Rus. Fed.
Grebenski Rus. Fed. see Grebenskaya
169 E4 Grebenstein Ger.
168 F1 Grebin Ger.
175 J3 Grębków Pol.
174 E4 Grębocice Pol.
174 G2 Grębocin Pol.
175 J5 Grębów Pol.
Grebyonka Ukr. see Hrebinka
193 E2 Greccio Italy
193 H3 Greci Italy
197 I3 Greci, Vârful hill Romania
189 D5 Greco, Monte mt. Italy
173 F2 Greding Ger.
182 E4 Gredos, Sierra de mts Spain
198 B2 Greece country Europe
232 E3 Greece NY U.S.A.
238 F3 Greeley CO U.S.A.
234 D1 Greeley PA U.S.A.
236 D3 Greely Center NE U.S.A.
221 J1 Greely Fiord inlet Nunavut Can.
130 H1 Greem-Bell, Ostrov i. Zemlya Frantsa-Iosifa Rus. Fed.
229 M1 Green r. N.B. Can.
230 C4 Green r. KY U.S.A.
236 C2 Green r. ND U.S.A.
241 M2 Green r. WY U.S.A.
226 C3 Green Bay WI U.S.A.
226 D3 Green Bay b. WI U.S.A.
234 B3 Greenbelt MD U.S.A.
232 C6 Greenbrier r. WV U.S.A.
87 C7 Greenbushes W.A. Austr.
83 G4 Green Cape N.S.W. Austr.
231 E7 Greencastle Bahamas
147 E1 Greencastle Rep. of Ireland
147 D2 Greencastle Northern Ireland U.K.
147 E2 Greencastle Northern Ireland U.K.
230 C4 Greencastle IN U.S.A.
232 E5 Greencastle PA U.S.A.
246 C1 Green Cay i. Bahamas
231 D6 Green Cove Springs FL U.S.A.
234 D3 Green Creek NJ U.S.A.
169 E4 Greene Ger.
226 A4 Greene IA U.S.A.
233 □H2 Greene ME U.S.A.
233 F3 Greene NY U.S.A.
231 D4 Greeneville TN U.S.A.
240 G3 Greenfield CA U.S.A.
236 E3 Greenfield IA U.S.A.
230 C4 Greenfield IN U.S.A.
233 G3 Greenfield MA U.S.A.
237 E4 Greenfield MO U.S.A.
232 B5 Greenfield OH U.S.A.
226 C4 Greenfield WI U.S.A.
235 D1 Greenfield Park NY U.S.A.
148 F2 Greengairs North Lanarkshire, Scotland U.K.
151 F3 Greenham West Berkshire, England U.K.
234 B3 Green Haven MD U.S.A.
87 B6 Green Head W.A. Austr.
87 B6 Green Head hd W.A. Austr.
149 G3 Greenhead Northumberland, England U.K.
84 C1 Greenhill Island N.T. Austr.
81 B7 Greenhills South I. N.Z.
147 F2 Greenisland Northern Ireland U.K.
223 J4 Green Lake Sask. Can.
226 C4 Green Lake WI U.S.A.
221 N2 Greenland terr. N. America
226 C2 Greenland MI U.S.A.
268 X2 Greenland Basin sea feature Arctic Ocean
218 G1 Greenland Sea Greenland/Svalbard
234 C2 Green Lane PA U.S.A.
146 F6 Greenlaw Scottish Borders, Scotland U.K.
146 E5 Greenloaning Perth and Kinross, Scotland U.K.
146 E6 Green Lowther hill Scotland U.K.
82 C3 Greenly Island S.A. Austr.
234 B3 Greenmount MD U.S.A.
233 G2 Green Mountains VT U.S.A.
146 D6 Greenock Inverclyde, Scotland U.K.
149 F3 Greenodd Cumbria, England U.K.
147 E2 Greenore Rep. of Ireland
87 B6 Greenough W.A. Austr.
87 B6 Greenough r. W.A. Austr.
235 D1 Green Pond NJ U.S.A.
233 G4 Greenport NY U.S.A.
241 L2 Green River UT U.S.A.
238 E3 Green River WY U.S.A.
231 C5 Greensboro AL U.S.A.
231 D5 Greensboro GA U.S.A.
234 C4 Greensboro MD U.S.A.
231 E4 Greensboro NC U.S.A.
230 C4 Greensburg IN U.S.A.
237 D4 Greensburg KS U.S.A.
230 C4 Greensburg KY U.S.A.
237 F6 Greensburg LA U.S.A.
232 D4 Greensburg PA U.S.A.
241 M4 Greens Peak NM U.S.A.
146 C4 Greenstone Point Scotland U.K.
226 E5 Greentown IN U.S.A.
234 C1 Greentown PA U.S.A.
236 F4 Greenup IL U.S.A.
232 B5 Greenup KY U.S.A.
85 F3 Greenvale Qld Austr.
233 F2 Green Valley Ont. Can.
241 L6 Green Valley AZ U.S.A.
222 D4 Greenville B.C. Can.
206 C5 Greenville Liberia
231 C6 Greenville AL U.S.A.
240 G1 Greenville CA U.S.A.
231 D6 Greenville FL U.S.A.
231 C5 Greenville GA U.S.A.
236 F4 Greenville IL U.S.A.
230 C4 Greenville KY U.S.A.
233 □I2 Greenville ME U.S.A.
226 E4 Greenville MI U.S.A.
237 F4 Greenville MO U.S.A.
237 F5 Greenville MS U.S.A.
231 E5 Greenville NC U.S.A.
233 H3 Greenville NH U.S.A.
236 G3 Greenville OH U.S.A.
232 C4 Greenville PA U.S.A.
231 D5 Greenville SC U.S.A.
237 D5 Greenville TX U.S.A.
232 D5 Greenville VA U.S.A.
150 C3 Greenway Pembrokeshire, Wales U.K.
Greenwich atoll Micronesia see Kapingamarangi
151 G3 Greenwich Greater London, England U.K.
235 E1 Greenwich CT U.S.A.
234 C3 Greenwich NJ U.S.A.
233 G3 Greenwich NY U.S.A.
232 B4 Greenwich OH U.S.A.
237 E5 Greenwood AR U.S.A.
234 C4 Greenwood DE U.S.A.
230 C4 Greenwood IN U.S.A.
237 F5 Greenwood MS U.S.A.
231 D5 Greenwood SC U.S.A.
226 B3 Greenwood WI U.S.A.
235 D1 Greenwood Lake NY U.S.A.
231 D5 Greer SC U.S.A.
148 C5 Greese r. Rep. of Ireland
168 C2 Greetsiel (Krummhörn) Ger.
250 D6 Gregório r. Brazil
84 D3 Gregory r. Qld Austr.
227 E4 Gregory MI U.S.A.
236 D3 Gregory SD U.S.A.
82 D2 Gregory, Lake salt flat S.A. Austr.
86 E4 Gregory, Lake salt flat W.A. Austr.
87 C5 Gregory, Lake salt flat W.A. Austr.
84 D3 Gregory Downs Qld Austr.
85 E3 Gregory Range hills Qld Austr.
86 D4 Gregory Range hills W.A. Austr.
178 E4 Greifenburg Austria
171 E4 Greifendorf Ger.
190 D1 Greifensee l. Switz.
169 D5 Greifenstein Ger.
170 E2 Greiffenberg Ger.
170 E1 Greifswald Ger.
170 E1 Greifswalder Bodden b. Ger.
179 F2 Grein Austria
171 D5 Greiz Ger.
168 F1 Gremersdorf Ger.
134 G1 Gremikha Rus. Fed.
134 L4 Gremyachinsk Rus. Fed.
137 J2 Gremyach'ye Rus. Fed.
142 D3 Grenå Denmark
237 F5 Grenada MS U.S.A.
247 □6 Grenada country West Indies
163 D5 Grenade France
163 B5 Grenade-sur-l'Adour France
157 F5 Grenant France
190 C1 Grenchen Switz.
83 G3 Grenfell N.S.W. Austr.
223 K5 Grenfell Sask. Can.
161 D3 Grenoble France
247 □6 Grenville Grenada
85 E1 Grenville, Cape Qld Austr.
Grenville Island Fiji see Rotuma
172 B4 Grenzach-Wyhlen Ger.
161 D5 Gréoux-les-Bains France
170 D1 Gresenhorst Ger.
238 B2 Gresham OR U.S.A.
95 F4 Gresik Jawa Timur Indon.
190 C3 Gressan Italy
161 D3 Gresse r. France
168 F2 Gresse Ger.
161 D4 Gresse-en-Vercors France
190 C3 Gressoney-la-Trinite Italy
179 G3 Gresten Austria
160 D3 Grésy-sur-Aix France
160 E3 Grésy-sur-Isère France
149 G3 Greta r. England U.K.
192 D2 Gretano r. Italy
146 E7 Gretna Dumfries and Galloway, Scotland U.K.
237 F6 Gretna LA U.S.A.
232 D6 Gretna VA U.S.A.
173 E2 Grettstadt Ger.
169 F4 Greußen Ger.
157 F4 Greux France
191 G5 Greve r. Italy
191 G5 Greve in Chianti Italy
164 C3 Grevelingen sea chan. Neth.
168 F2 Greven Mecklenburg-Vorpommern Ger.
169 C3 Greven Nordrhein-Westfalen Ger.
198 B1 Grevena Greece
165 E3 Grevenbicht Neth.
169 B4 Grevenbroich Ger.
165 F5 Grevenmacher Lux.
165 F5 Grevenmacher admin. dist. Lux.
170 C2 Grevesmühlen Ger.
225 J4 Grey r. Nfld. Can.
81 C5 Grey r. South I. N.Z.
84 D2 Grey, Cape N.T. Austr.
147 F2 Greyabbey Northern Ireland U.K.
238 E2 Greybull WY U.S.A.
238 E2 Greybull r. WY U.S.A.
222 C2 Grey Hunter Peak Y.T. Can.
215 G2 Greylingstad S. Africa
233 G3 Greylock, Mount MA U.S.A.
81 C5 Greymouth South I. N.Z.
83 E2 Grey Range hills Qld Austr.
87 B5 Grey's Plains W.A. Austr.
149 G3 Greystoke Cumbria, England U.K.
147 E3 Greystones Rep. of Ireland
214 B6 Greyton S. Africa
81 E4 Greytown North I. N.Z.
215 H3 Greytown S. Africa
165 D4 Grez-Doiceau Belgium
159 F4 Grez-en-Bouère France
191 G3 Grezzana Italy
146 B3 Griais Western Isles, Scotland U.K.
135 H6 Gribanovskiy Rus. Fed.
208 C2 Gribingui r. C.A.R.
240 G2 Gridley CA U.S.A.
226 C5 Gridley IL U.S.A.
171 C3 Grieben Ger.
183 I4 Griegos Spain
157 H4 Gries France
178 C3 Gries am Brenner Austria
172 C3 Griesbach Ger.
173 H3 Griesbach im Rottal Ger.
172 C2 Griesheim Ger.
179 E2 Grieskirchen Austria
171 F4 Grießen Ger.
173 G4 Griesstätt Ger.
179 F4 Griffen Austria
231 C5 Griffin GA U.S.A.
83 F3 Griffith N.S.W. Austr.
227 I3 Griffith Ont. Can.
232 C5 Griffithsville WV U.S.A.
Grigan i. N. Mariana Is see Agrihan
192 A5 Grighini, Monte hill Sardegna Italy
Grigioni canton Switz. see Graubünden
138 E4 Grigiškės Lith.
190 E3 Grigna mt. Italy
190 F3 Grigna r. Italy
161 C4 Grignan France
191 G2 Grigno Italy
191 G2 Grigno r. Italy
163 B4 Grignols France
160 C3 Grigny France
136 E4 Grigoriopol Moldova
183 F2 Grijota Spain
164 F1 Grijpskerk Neth.
161 C4 Grillon France
83 F5 Grim, Cape Tas. Austr.
193 I5 Grimaldi Italy
208 D3 Grimari C.A.R.
161 E5 Grimaud France
171 D4 Grimma Ger.
170 E1 Grimmen Ger.
179 E3 Grimming mt. Austria
149 J4 Grimoldby Lincolnshire, England U.K.
146 A4 Grimsay i. Scotland U.K.
227 H4 Grimsby Ont. Can.
149 I4 Grimsby North East Lincolnshire, England U.K.
140 □C2 Grímsey i. Iceland
222 G3 Grimshaw Alta Can.
142 C2 Grimstad Norway
151 H2 Grimston Norfolk, England U.K.
142 A2 Grindafjord Norway
141 J3 Grindaheim Norway
140 □B3 Grindavík Iceland
190 D2 Grindelwald Switz.
142 C4 Grindsted Denmark
227 F3 Grind Stone City MI U.S.A.
197 H3 Grindu Ialomiţa Romania
197 I3 Grindu Tulcea Romania
197 H2 Grinduşu, Vârful mt. Romania
139 I5 Grinevo Rus. Fed.
149 I4 Gringley on the Hill Nottinghamshire, England U.K.
236 E3 Grinnell IA U.S.A.
183 G4 Griñón Spain
178 B3 Grins Austria
197 G2 Grinţieş Romania
188 E2 Grintovec mt. Slovenia
178 C3 Grinzens Austria
183 I3 Grío r. Spain
Griomasaigh i. Scotland U.K. see Grimsay
215 G4 Griqualand East reg. S. Africa
214 D3 Griqualand West reg. S. Africa
214 D3 Griquatown S. Africa
Grischun canton Switz. see Graubünden
221 J2 Grise Fiord Nunavut Can.
186 B3 Grisén Spain
Grishino Ukr. see Krasnoarmiys'k
191 G3 Grisignano di Zocco Italy
156 B2 Gris Nez, Cap c. France
193 H5 Grisolia Italy
163 D5 Grisolles France
Grisons canton Switz. see Graubünden
143 H1 Grisslehamn Sweden
146 F3 Gritley Orkney, Scotland U.K.
137 J5 Grivenskaya Rus. Fed.
149 F3 Grizebeck Cumbria, England U.K.
222 F1 Grizzly Bear Mountain hill N.W.T. Can.
188 F3 Grmeč mts Bos.-Herz.
165 D3 Grobbendonk Belgium
173 F3 Gröbenzell Ger.
171 D4 Gröbers Ger.
138 C3 Grobiņa Latvia
215 G1 Groblersdal S. Africa
214 D3 Groblershoop S. Africa
179 E3 Gröbming Austria
171 C4 Gröbzig Ger.
196 E3 Grocka Srbija Yugo.
175 K4 Gródek Pol.
175 L2 Gródek Pol.
100 D3 Grodekovo Rus. Fed.
171 E4 Gröden Ger.
178 E3 Grödig Austria
171 E4 Gröditz Ger.
175 I2 Gródki Pol.
174 F5 Grodków Pol.
Grodnenskaya Oblast' admin. div. Belarus see Hrodzyenskaya Voblasts'
Grodnenskaya Vozvyshennost' hills Belarus see Hrodnyendskaye Wzvyshsha
Grodno Belarus see Hrodna
Grodno Oblast admin. div. Belarus see Hrodzyenskaya Voblasts'
175 H2 Grodziczno Pol.
174 G3 Grodziec Pol.
175 K3 Grodzisk Pol.
175 I3 Grodzisk Mazowiecki Pol.
174 E3 Grodzisk Wielkopolski Pol.
164 F2 Groenlo Neth.
215 H2 Groenvlei S. Africa
237 D6 Groesbeck TX U.S.A.
164 E3 Groesbeek Neth.
85 F3 Groganville Qld Austr.
169 E3 Grohnde (Emmerthal) Ger.
177 L6 Grohot, Vârful hill Romania
171 D4 Groitzsch Ger.
158 C4 Groix France
158 C4 Groix, Île de i. France
175 I4 Grójec Pol.
175 I2 Grom Pol.
174 D4 Gromadka Pol.
189 C7 Grombalia Tunisia
168 F1 Grömitz Ger.
175 I6 Gromnik Pol.
190 E3 Gromo Italy
168 D1 Grønå r. Denmark
169 E3 Gronau (Leine) Ger.
169 C3 Gronau (Westfalen) Ger.
193 I5 Grondo r. Italy
173 E4 Grönenbach Ger.
140 K2 Grong Norway
171 C4 Gröningen Ger.
164 F1 Groningen Neth.
164 F1 Groningen prov. Neth.
251 H3 Groningen Suriname
Grønland terr. N. America see Greenland
175 H1 Gronowo Markusy Pol.
143 F3 Grönskåra Sweden
237 C5 Groom TX U.S.A.
147 F2 Groomsport Northern Ireland U.K.
214 E5 Groot r. E. Cape S. Africa
214 B5 Groot r. W. Cape S. Africa
214 C5 Groot r. W. Cape S. Africa
214 C2 Groot-Aar Pan salt pan S. Africa
214 B5 Groot Berg r. S. Africa
215 E4 Groot Brak r. S. Africa
214 D6 Groot Brakrivier S. Africa
215 G2 Grootdraaidam dam S. Africa
214 C3 Grootdrink S. Africa
164 E2 Grootebroek Neth.
84 D2 Groote Eylandt i. N.T. Austr.
164 F1 Grootegast Neth.
212 C3 Grootfontein Namibia
212 C5 Groot Karas Berg plat. Namibia
213 F4 Groot Letaba r. S. Africa
215 F1 Groot Marico S. Africa
214 A3 Grootmis S. Africa
215 F1 Grootpan S. Africa
214 C5 Groot Swartberge mts S. Africa
215 G2 Grootvlei S. Africa
215 F5 Groot Winterberg mt. S. Africa
190 D3 Gropello Cairoli Italy
197 H3 Gropeni Romania
161 E5 Gros Bessillon hill France
160 C1 Grosbois-en-Montagne France
161 F3 Groscavallo Italy
190 F2 Grosio Italy
247 □3 Gros Islet St Lucia
247 □3 Gros-Morne Martinique
160 C2 Grosne r. France
178 B4 Grosotto Italy
247 □3 Gros Piton mt. St Lucia
173 E3 Großaitingen Ger.
169 E4 Großalmerode Ger.
171 C3 Groß Ammensleben Ger.
178 E3 Großarl Austria
169 F4 Großbartloff Ger.
171 E3 Großbeeren Ger.
168 C3 Groß Berßen Ger.
172 C2 Groß-Bieberau Ger.
169 F4 Großbodungen Ger.
171 D4 Großbothen Ger.
172 D3 Großbottwar Ger.
171 C5 Großbreitenbach Ger.
169 E3 Großburgwedel (Burgwedel) Ger.
169 F4 Großburschla Ger.
170 E3 Groß Dölln Ger.
171 F4 Großdubrau Ger.
172 C3 Große Enz r. Ger.
173 G3 Große Laaber r. Ger.
172 D3 Große Lauter r. Ger.
169 F3 Groß Elbe (Elbe) Ger.
172 C3 Grosselfingen Ger.
168 E2 Großenaspe Ger.
170 C1 Großenbrode Ger.
169 D5 Großen-Buseck Ger.
169 F4 Großenehrich Ger.
179 H2 Groß Engersdorf Austria
169 F4 Großengottern Ger.
171 E4 Großenhain Ger.
168 D3 Großenkneten Ger.
169 E5 Großenlüder Ger.
168 F2 Großensee Ger.
171 D5 Großenstein Ger.
168 E1 Großenwiehe Ger.
179 H2 Groß-Enzersdorf Austria

173 H2 Großer Arber mt. Ger.
169 F5 Großer Beerberg hill Ger.
169 F5 Grosser Bösenstein mt. Austria
169 F5 Großer Breitenberg hill Ger.
179 F3 Grosser Buchstein mt. Austria
172 B2 Großer Eyberg hill Ger.
169 F5 Großer Gleichberg hill Ger.
171 D5 Großer Kornberg hill Ger.
170 E2 Großer Landgraben r. Ger.
172 B2 Grosser Löffler mt. Austria
171 E4 Große Röder r. Ger.
176 C2 Grosser Osser mt. Czech Rep./Ger.
168 F1 Großer Plöner See l. Ger.
179 F3 Großer Rachel mt. Austria
179 H3 Großer Rachel mt. Ger.
171 E3 Großer Selchower See l. Ger.
179 F4 Grosser Speikkofel mt. Austria
179 F4 Grosser Speikkogel mt. Austria
168 C2 Großer Meer l. Ger.
178 D3 Großes Wiesbachhorn mt. Austria
192 D2 Grosseto Italy
192 D2 Grosseto prov. Toscana Italy
192 A3 Grosseto-Prugna Corse France
193 G3 Große Vils r. Ger.
170 E2 Groß Fredenwalde Ger.
169 F4 Großfurra Ger.
170 C3 Groß Garz Ger.
172 C2 Groß-Gerau Ger.
179 F2 Groß-Gerungs Austria
169 E3 Groß Giesen Ger.
171 E4 Groß Glienicke Ger.
178 D3 Großglockner mt. Austria
173 G4 Großgmain Ger.
171 E4 Groß Godems Ger.
172 G2 Großgöttfritz Austria
168 F2 Groß Grönau Ger.
173 E2 Großhabersdorf Ger.
168 F2 Großhansdorf Ger.
179 F2 Großharras Austria
169 F3 Groß Heere (Heere) Ger.
171 F5 Großhennersdorf Ger.
171 C4 Großheringen Ger.
168 C3 Groß-Hesepe Ger.
172 D2 Großheubach Ger.
173 G4 Großinzemoos Ger.
173 G4 Großkarolinenfeld Ger.
171 C4 Großkayna Ger.
170 E1 Groß Kiesow Ger.
179 G4 Großklein Austria
171 D4 Großkorbetha Ger.
171 D5 Groß Köris Ger.
171 F4 Großkoschen Ger.
171 D3 Groß Kreutz Ger.
179 H2 Großkrut Austria
168 F1 Groß Kummerfeld Ger.
170 C3 Groß Laasch Ger.
169 F3 Groß Lafferde (Lahstedt) Ger.
173 E2 Großlangheim Ger.
171 D4 Großlehna Ger.
171 F3 Groß Leuthen Ger.
171 F3 Groß Lindow Ger.
189 B5 Großlittgen Ger.
169 F4 Großlohra Ger.
171 E4 Großmehlen Ger.
173 F3 Großmehring Ger.
170 D1 Groß Miltzow Ger.
171 C4 Großmonra Ger.
172 C4 Großmühlingen Ger.
171 C4 Großnaundorf Ger.
171 E4 Groß Nemerow Ger.
168 F3 Groß Oesingen Ger.
171 E5 Großolbersdorf Ger.
171 C4 Großörner Ger.
172 D2 Großostheim Ger.
179 H3 Großpetersdorf Austria
170 D2 Groß Plasten Ger.
171 C4 Groß Quenstedt Ger.
179 F3 Großraming Austria
171 F4 Großräschen Ger.
172 D2 Großrinderfeld Ger.
171 F4 Großröhrsdorf Ger.
171 C4 Groß Rosenburg Ger.
172 A2 Großrosseln Ger.
171 C4 Großrudestedt Ger.
179 H2 Groß Rußbach Austria
179 G4 Groß St Florian Austria
171 F4 Groß Särchen Ger.
171 F4 Groß Schacksdorf Ger.
171 E5 Großschirma Ger.
179 G4 Großschönau Austria
171 F5 Großschönau Ger.
170 E3 Groß Schönebeck Ger.
170 C3 Groß Schwechten Ger.
169 F3 Groß Schwülper (Schwülper) Ger.
179 F3 Groß-Sieghartls Austria
168 E1 Großsolt Ger.
168 C3 Groß Stavern Ger.
171 D4 Großsteinberg Ger.
171 D4 Groß Stieten Ger.
171 D4 Großtreben Ger.
169 F3 Groß Twülpstedt Ger.
172 C2 Groß-Umstadt Ger.
178 D3 Großvenediger mt. Austria
190 D1 Grosswangen Switz.
170 D2 Groß Warnow Ger.
169 F4 Großweikersdorf Austria
172 C2 Großwallstadt Ger.
179 G2 Großwilfersdorf Austria
168 E1 Groß Wittensee Ger.
170 D2 Groß Wokern Ger.
170 D3 Großwudicke Ger.
170 D2 Groß Wüstenfelde Ger.
170 E3 Groß Ziethen Ger.
172 C3 Groß-Zimmern Ger.
157 G4 Grostenquin France
188 E3 Grosuplje Slovenia
263 L1 Grosvenor Mountains Antarctica
238 C3 Gros Ventre Range mts WY U.S.A.
165 D3 Grote Nete r. Belgium
235 F1 Groton CT U.S.A.
233 E3 Groton NY U.S.A.
236 D2 Groton SD U.S.A.
193 I2 Grottaferrata Italy
195 G2 Grottaglie Italy
193 F2 Grottammare Italy
193 F1 Grottazzolina Italy
194 C5 Grotte Sicilia Italy
192 D3 Grotte di Castro Italy
195 F4 Grotteria Italy
232 D5 Grottoes VA U.S.A.
195 F2 Grottole Italy
222 G4 Grouard Mission Alta Can.
206 E5 Groumania Côte d'Ivoire
224 D3 Groundhog r. Ont. Can.
164 E1 Grouw Neth.
237 E4 Grove OK U.S.A.
232 B5 Grove City OH U.S.A.
232 C4 Grove City PA U.S.A.
231 C6 Grove Hill AL U.S.A.
141 K3 Grövelsjön Sweden
263 F2 Grove Mountains Antarctica
234 B1 Grover PA U.S.A.
240 G4 Grover Beach CA U.S.A.
233 H2 Groveton NH U.S.A.
237 G6 Groveton TX U.S.A.
234 D2 Groveville NJ U.S.A.
241 K5 Growler Mountains AZ U.S.A.
197 H4 Grozd'ovo Bulg.
129 D2 Groznyy Rus. Fed.
171 C5 Grub am Forst Ger.
145 F3 Grubbafjället mt. Norway
165 F3 Grubbenvorst Neth.
170 C1 Grube Ger.
188 F3 Grubišno Polje Croatia
174 D2 Gruczno Pol.
190 C4 Grudovo Bulg. see Sredets
175 I2 Gruda Pol.
174 D2 Grudusk Pol.
174 G2 Grudziądz Pol.
190 D4 Grue r. Italy
157 G4 Gruey-lès-Surance France
190 C3 Grugliasco Italy
146 B6 Gruinart, Loch inlet Scotland U.K.
161 B5 Grüissan France
182 D1 Grullos Spain
197 H2 Grumăzeşti Romania
171 F4 Grumbach Ger.

193 H4 Grumento Nova Italy
195 F1 Grumo Appula Italy
142 E2 Grums Sweden
179 G3 Grünau Austria
179 G2 Grünau Austria
179 G3 Grünau Austria
179 G3 Grünbach am Schneeberg Austria
169 D5 Grünberg Ger.
Grünberg Pol. see Zielona Góra
179 F3 Grünburg Austria
141 K3 Grundagssätern Sweden
141 K3 Grundforsen Sweden
169 F3 Grundhof Ger.
140 L3 Grundsunda Sweden
232 B6 Grundy VA U.S.A.
236 E3 Grundy Center IA U.S.A.
170 E3 Grüneberg Ger.
168 E2 Grünendeich Ger.
178 E2 Grünewald Ger.
171 E4 Grünewalde Ger.
171 E3 Grünheide Ger.
172 D4 Grünkraut Ger.
171 F3 Grunow Ger.
174 D2 Grünstadt Ger.
172 C2 Grünstadt Ger.
160 B2 Grury France
174 G2 Gruta Pol.
146 □2 Grutness Shetland, Scotland U.K.
237 C4 Gruver TX U.S.A.
190 C2 Gruyères Switz.
138 D3 Gruzdžiai Lith.
Gruzinskaya S.S.R. country Asia see Georgia
139 L5 Gryazi Rus. Fed.
139 L4 Gryazovets Rus. Fed.
175 I6 Grybów Pol.
174 D2 Gryfice Pol.
174 D2 Gryfino Pol.
174 C2 Gryfów Śląski Pol.
140 L1 Gryllefjord Norway
142 A2 Grytenuten hill Norway
143 G1 Gryttjom Sweden
259 □ Grytviken S. Georgia
175 I2 Gryźliny Pol.
174 E2 Grzegorzew Pol.
174 E2 Grzmiąca Pol.
174 E2 Grzywna Pol.
179 E3 Gschwandt Austria
173 D3 Gschwend Ger.
190 C2 Gstaad Switz.
173 G4 Gstadt am Chiemsee Ger.
190 C2 Gsteig Switz.
117 F5 Gua Bihar India
191 G3 Gua r. Italy
242 □J7 Guabito Panama
246 C2 Guacanayabo, Golfo de b. Cuba
247 F5 Guacara Venez.
250 D3 Guacharía r. Col.
258 D2 Guachipas Arg.
257 G4 Guaçuí Brazil
185 G3 Guadahortuna Spain
185 H3 Guadahortuna r. Spain
184 D3 Guadaira r. Spain
184 E3 Guadairilla r. Spain
184 D2 Guadajira r. Spain
184 E3 Guadajoz r. Spain
185 F3 Guadajoz r. Spain
244 B3 Guadalajara Mex.
183 G4 Guadalajara Spain
183 H4 Guadalajara prov. Castilla - La Mancha Spain
187 B4 Guadalaviar r. Spain
184 E3 Guadalbacar r. Spain
185 G3 Guadalbullón r. Spain
78 □3 Guadalcanal i. Solomon Is
184 E2 Guadalcanal Spain
185 E3 Guadalcázar Spain
184 E2 Guadalén r. Spain
185 H3 Guadalentín r. Spain
185 I3 Guadalentín r. Spain
184 D4 Guadalete r. Spain
185 F4 Guadalhorce r. Spain
185 E3 Guadalimar r. Spain
185 E3 Guadalmazán r. Spain
185 G3 Guadalmellato r. Spain
185 F2 Guadalmez r. Spain
185 F2 Guadalope r. Spain
185 F3 Guadalquivir r. Spain
216 □1c Guadalupe Graciosa Azores
254 E3 Guadalupe Brazil
245 E5 Guadalupe Guerrero Mex.
243 Guadalupe Nuevo León Mex.
245 F4 Guadalupe Puebla Mex.
244 C2 Guadalupe Zacatecas Mex.
242 Guadalupe i. Mex.
250 B6 Guadalupe Peru
185 E1 Guadalupe Spain
241 L5 Guadalupe AZ U.S.A.
240 G4 Guadalupe CA U.S.A.
237 D6 Guadalupe r. TX U.S.A.
237 D6 Guadalupe r. TX U.S.A.
184 E1 Guadalupe, Sierra de mts Spain
244 B1 Guadalupe Aguilera Mex.
239 F6 Guadalupe Bravos Mex.
237 B6 Guadalupe Peak TX U.S.A.
241 J5 Guadalupe Victoria Baja California Norte Mex.
244 B1 Guadalupe Victoria Durango Mex.
185 E3 Guadalvacarejo r. Spain
183 H4 Guadamajud r. Spain
185 E2 Guadamatilla r. Spain
184 E2 Guadamez r. Spain
183 F5 Guadamur Spain
183 F3 Guadarrama Spain
183 F3 Guadarrama r. Spain
183 F3 Guadarrama, Sierra de mts Spain
183 I5 Guadassuar r. Spain
247 □2 Guadeloupe terr. West Indies
247 □2 Guadeloupe Passage Caribbean Sea
184 D4 Guadiamar r. Spain
185 D3 Guadiana r. Port./Spain
185 D3 Guadiana Menor r. Spain
185 E3 Guadiato r. Spain
183 H4 Guadiela r. Spain
185 G3 Guadix Spain
259 B6 Guafo, Isla i. Chile
255 C9 Guaíba Brazil
250 B4 Guaillabamba r. Ecuador
246 C2 Guáimaro Cuba
250 D4 Guainía dept Col.
250 D4 Guainía r. Col./Venez.
251 E1 Guaiquinima, Cerro mt. Venez.
255 B8 Guaíra Brazil
256 C4 Guaíra São Paulo Brazil
256 A5 Guaiçuí Brazil
259 B6 Guaitecas, Islas is Chile
252 D2 Guajará Mirim Brazil
250 B4 Guajara r. Brazil
254 □ Guajaraçá Brazil
260 D2 Guayaquil, Sierra de mts Arg.
247 □1 Guajataca r. Puerto Rico
242 E3 Guaje, Llano de plain Mex.
247 □1 Guají depr Col.
250 B5 Guálaco Ecuador
243 H6 Gualán Guat.
250 B5 Gualaquiza Ecuador
193 E2 Gualdo Cattaneo Italy
191 H5 Gualdo Tadino Italy
191 H3 Gualeguay Arg.
259 E5 Gualeguay r. Arg.
259 E5 Gualeguaychu Arg.
252 C4 Gualillos r. Chile
193 F3 Gualtieri Italy
191 F4 Gualtieri Italy
91 J4 Guam terr. N. Pacific Ocean
120 D4 Gubadag Turkm.
134 L4 Gubakha Rus. Fed.
92 C3 Gubat Phil.
210 B2 Guba Eth.
120 D4 Gubadag Turkm.
191 H5 Gubbio Italy
161 C4 Gubbin Rep. of Ireland
242 H6 Gu'an Hebei China
171 F4 Guben Ger.
197 G4 Gŭbene Bulg.
246 B2 Guanabacoa Cuba

242 □I7 Guanacaste, Cordillera de mts Costa Rica
242 D3 Guanacevi Mex.
261 F5 Guanaco, Cerro hill Arg.
246 A2 Guanahacabibes, Península de pen. Cuba
242 □I5 Guanaja Hond.
246 B2 Guanajay Cuba
244 D3 Guanajuato Mex.
244 D3 Guanajuato state Mex.
244 D3 Guanajuato, Sierra de mts Mex.
254 E5 Guanambi Brazil
250 E7 Guanape, Islas de is Peru
250 D2 Guanare Venez.
250 D2 Guanare Viejo r. Venez.
250 D2 Guanarito Venez.
250 D2 Guanarito r. Venez.
252 D3 Guanay Bol.
107 F4 Guand Shan mt. Shanxi China
257 G3 Guandu r. Brazil
109 E3 Guandu Guangdong China
246 A2 Guane Cuba
109 F3 Guang'an Sichuan China
109 F2 Guangchang Jiangxi China
110 F2 Guangde Anhui China
109 E4 Guangdong prov. China
109 E2 Guangfeng Jiangxi China
108 C2 Guanghai Guangdong China
108 C2 Guanghan Hubei China see Laohekou
107 G4 Guanglin Shanxi China
108 B3 Guangmao Shan mt. Yunnan China
Guangming Sichuan China see Xide
109 F2 Guangming Ding mt. Anhui China
108 C3 Guangnan Yunnan China
109 E4 Guangning Guangdong China
Guangning Liaoning China see Beining
107 H4 Guangrao Shandong China
109 E2 Guangshan Henan China
109 E2 Guangshui Hubei China
Guangxi Zhuangzu Zizhiqu aut. reg. China see Guangxi Zhuangzu Zizhiqu
108 D4 Guangxi Zhuangzu Zizhiqu aut. reg. China
108 C1 Guangyuan Sichuan China
109 E3 Guangze Fujian China
109 E4 Guangzhou Guangdong China
107 G4 Guangzong Hebei China
257 F3 Guanhães Brazil
257 F3 Guanhães r. Brazil
107 H5 Guanhe Kou r. mouth China
247 □ Guaniguanico, Cordillera de mts Cuba
251 F2 Guanipa r. Venez.
108 C3 Guanling Guizhou China
108 D3 Guanman Shan mts China
108 D1 Guanpo Henan China
Guanshui Guizhou China see Guanling
260 B1 Guanta Chile
251 E2 Guanta Venez.
246 D2 Guantánamo Cuba
246 D3 Guantánamo Bay Naval Base military base Cuba
107 G4 Guantao Hebei China
Guanxian Sichuan China see Dujiangyan
109 D3 Guanyang Guangxi China
109 E4 Guanyinqiao Sichuan China
109 H5 Guanyun Jiangsu China
252 C3 Guapay r. Santa Cruz Bol. see Grande
257 E4 Guapé Brazil
250 B4 Guapi Col.
256 C6 Guápiara Brazil
242 □J7 Guápiles Costa Rica
252 D3 Guaporé r. Bol./Brazil
255 C9 Guaporé state Brazil see Rondônia
252 C4 Guaqui Bol.
256 D4 Guará r. Brazil
256 D5 Guará r. Brazil
186 C2 Guara, Sierra de mts Spain
254 G3 Guarabira Brazil
257 F4 Guaraciaba Brazil
250 B5 Guaranda Ecuador
257 F4 Guaraní Brazil
257 F4 Guaraniaçu Brazil
256 B4 Guaranta Brazil
257 G4 Guarapari Brazil
256 C6 Guarapuava Brazil
256 C6 Guaraqueçaba Brazil
256 B4 Guararapes Brazil
257 H2 Guaratinga Brazil
257 E5 Guaratinguetá Brazil
256 D6 Guaratuba Brazil
252 C3 Guarayos r. Bol.
193 F3 Guarcino Italy
182 C4 Guarda Port.
182 C4 Guarda admin. dist. Port.
Guardafui, Cape Somalia see Gwardafuy, Gees
185 H3 Guardal r. Spain
186 D2 Guardamar del Segura Spain
256 D2 Guarda Mor Brazil
195 F4 Guardavalle Italy
193 G2 Guardiagrele Italy
193 G3 Guardia Perticara Italy
191 H4 Guardia Piemontese Italy
193 G3 Guardia Sanframondi Italy
185 H4 Guardias Viejas Spain
186 E2 Guardiola de Berguedà Spain
183 F2 Guardo Spain
182 C5 Guardunha, Serra de mts Port.
184 D2 Guareña Spain
183 D3 Guareña r. Spain
186 C2 Guárico r. Brazil
253 E1 Guariba r. Brazil
250 E2 Guárico state Venez.
185 F4 Guaro Spain
251 E1 Guárico r. Col.
185 I3 Guarromán Spain
256 D5 Guarujá Brazil
256 D5 Guarulhos Brazil
244 C2 Guasave Mex.
192 B5 Guasila Sardegna Italy
191 F4 Guastalla Italy
Guastatoya Guat. see El Progreso
117 G5 Guásuba r. India
243 H6 Guatemala country Central America
243 H6 Guatemala Guat.
243 Guatemala, Golfo de g. Guat.
261 M5 Guatemala Basin sea feature Pacific Ocean
Guatemala City Guat. see Guatemala
251 E1 Guatope, Parque Nacional nat. park Venez.
258 C2 Guatrache Arg.
250 D4 Guaviare dept Col.
250 D4 Guaviare r. Col.
252 □2 Guaxupé Brazil
258 A5 Guayabero r. Col.
260 D2 Guayacán Chile
250 B6 Guayaquil Ecuador
250 A5 Guayaquil, Golfo de g. Ecuador
252 D2 Guayaramerín Bol.
250 A5 Guayas prov. Ecuador
244 □ Guaymas Mex.
250 □ Guaynabo Puerto Rico
247 □1 Guayo Arg.
245 G4 Guayama r. Mex.
250 □ Guayama Puerto Rico
250 E3 Guayape, Serranía mts Venez.

175 J1 Guber r. Pol.
201 □ Gubio Nigeria
135 G6 Gubkin Rus. Fed.
107 G4 Gucheng Hebei China
109 D1 Gucheng Hubei China
129 D2 Gudalur Tamil Nadu India
Gudanaqris K'edi hills Georgia
186 C4 Gudar Orissa India
115 D2 Gudari Orissa India
186 A1 Gudaut'a prov. Pais Vasco
141 J3 Gudbrandsdalen val. Norway
142 D3 Gudenå r. Denmark
169 E4 Gudensberg Ger.
168 E1 Gudermes Rus. Fed.
143 F4 Gudhjem Bornholm Denmark
201 □ Gudi Nigeria
114 D2 Gudivada Andhra Prad. India
114 C3 Gudiyattam Tamil Nadu India
142 D4 Gudme Denmark
157 F4 Gudmont-Villiers France
100 C4 Gudong r. China
115 E3 Gudri r. Pak.
126 D2 Güdül Turkey
114 C3 Gudur Andhra Prad. India
114 C2 Gudur Andhra Prad. India
100 C2 Gudzhal r. Rus. Fed.
225 G1 Guè, Rivière du r. Que. Can.
157 H5 Guebwiller France
206 C4 Guéckédou Guinea
158 D4 Guégon France
185 G3 Güéjar-Sierra Spain
200 B2 Guelb er Rîchât hill Maur.
208 D2 Guélengdeng Chad
205 G1 Guelma Alg.
189 A7 Guelma prov. Alg.
204 C3 Guelmine Morocco
224 D5 Guelph Ont. Can.
157 H4 Guémar France
157 F4 Guémené-Penfao France
158 C3 Guémené-sur-Scorff France
245 E2 Guémez Mex.
157 G3 Guénange France
207 F4 Guéné Benin
183 F3 Güeñes Spain
158 E4 Guenroet France
206 B3 Guènt Paté Senegal
158 D4 Guer France
208 C2 Guéra pref. Chad
208 C2 Guéra, Massif du mts Chad
158 D4 Guérande France
205 G2 Guerara Alg.
204 C2 Guercif Morocco
202 D6 Guéréda Chad
156 E4 Guérigny France
160 B1 Guérigny France
240 F2 Guerin-Kouka Togo
240 F2 Guerneville CA U.S.A.
183 G2 Guernica Spain see Gernika-Lumo
158 D2 Guernsey terr. Channel Is
238 F3 Guernsey WY U.S.A.
206 C2 Guérou Maur.
184 C3 Guerreiros do Rio Port.
237 C6 Guerrero Coahuila Mex.
243 F3 Guerrero Tamaulipas Mex.
184 D2 Guerrero r. Spain
242 B3 Guerrero Negro Mex.
163 C6 Guerryes, Pic de mt. France
186 E2 Guerri de la Sal Spain
160 C2 Guéret France
206 D5 Guéyo Côte d'Ivoire
109 F2 Gufeng Fujian China see Pingnan
100 Gufu Hubei China see Xingshan
135 H7 Gugark' Armenia
210 C3 Gugê mt. Eth.
78 □3a Gugegwe i. Kwajalein Marshall Is
172 C2 Guglingen Ger.
193 G3 Guglionesi Italy
91 K3 Guguan i. N. Mariana Is
109 F2 Guhe Anhui China
122 D5 Gūh Kūh mt. Iran
170 D2 Gühlen-Glienicke Ger.
100 C4 Guhuai Henan China see Pingyu
182 B5 Guia Port.
216 □3a Guía de Isora Tenerife Canary Is
184 C4 Guiana Basin sea feature N. Atlantic Ocean
250 E3 Guiana Highlands mts S. America
206 D5 Guibéroua Côte d'Ivoire
158 E4 Guichainville France
158 E4 Guichen France
82 D4 Guichen Bay S.A. Austr.
109 F2 Guichi Anhui China
245 G5 Guichicovi Mex.
261 D6 Guichón Uru.
172 □ Guidan Chad
106 D5 Guide Qinghai China
158 C4 Guidel France
205 F2 Guidjiba Chad
206 B2 Guiglo Côte d'Ivoire
156 C4 Guignen France
156 D3 Guignicourt France
213 G5 Guija Moz.
108 D4 Gui Jiang r. China
109 F1 Guiji Shan mts China
182 D4 Guijo de Coria Spain
182 D4 Guijo de Galisteo Spain
182 D4 Guijo de Granadilla Spain
182 E4 Guijuelo Spain
161 F4 Guil r. France
151 G3 Guildford Surrey, England U.K.
233 H2 Guildhall VT U.S.A.
149 F5 Guildtown Perth and Kinross, Scotland U.K.
158 B3 Guilers France
235 F1 Guilford CT U.S.A.
233 □2 Guilford ME U.S.A.
161 C4 Guilherand France
211 B8 Guilherme Capelo Angola see Cacongo
182 B3 Guilhofrei Port.
109 D3 Guilin Guangxi China
161 E4 Guillaumes France
161 F4 Guillestre France
158 D2 Guilliers France
158 C4 Guilvinec France
199 G2 Güimar Tenerife Canary Is
254 D2 Guimarães Brazil
182 B3 Guimarães Port.
92 B4 Guimaras i. Phil.
107 H5 Guimeng Ding mt. Shandong China
207 F4 Guinagourou Benin
106 C5 Guinan Qinghai China
209 B8 Guinas r. Namibia
206 A4 Guinea country Africa
207 G6 Guinea, Gulf of Africa
223 I4 Guinea Basin sea feature N. Atlantic Ocean
206 A3 Guinea-Bissau country Africa
206 B4 Guinea-Conakry country Africa see Guinea
Guinea Equatorial country Africa see Equatorial Guinea
Guiné-Bissau country Africa see Guinea-Bissau
Guinée country Africa see Guinea

206 C4 Guinée-Forestière admin. reg. Guinea
206 B4 Guinée-Maritime admin. reg. Guinea
246 B2 Güines Cuba
156 B2 Guînes France
159 C3 Guingamp France
206 B3 Guinguinéo Senegal
158 B3 Guipavas France
108 C4 Guiping Guangxi China
158 E4 Guipry France
186 A1 Guipúzcoa prov. País Vasco Spain
246 B2 Güira de Melena Cuba
255 B6 Guiratinga Brazil
251 I3 Guisanbourg Fr. Guiana
183 E4 Guisando Spain
161 E4 Guisane r. France
148 C3 Guisborough Redcar and Cleveland, England U.K.
156 D3 Guiscard France
158 C3 Guiscriff France
156 D3 Guise France
149 H4 Guiseley West Yorkshire, England U.K.
158 B3 Guissény France
158 A4 Guist Norfolk, England U.K.
161 C5 Guîtres France
162 B3 Güîtres France
206 D5 Guitri Côte d'Ivoire
92 C4 Guiuan Phil.
247 N1 Guíva Hill Fiji
108 D3 Guixi Chongqing China see Dianjiang
109 F3 Guixi Jiangxi China
108 C3 Guiyang Guizhou China
109 E3 Guiyang Hunan China
108 C3 Guiyang Hunan China
224 D5 Guizhou prov. China
157 H4 Guébwiller France
173 H3 Gujan-Mestras France
162 B4 Gujan-Mestras France
116 C5 Gujarat state India
123 H3 Gujar Khan Pak.
123 H3 Gujarat state India see Gujarat
123 H3 Gujrat r. Pak.
128 B2 Gujba Nigeria
206 B3 Gujranwala India
114 C2 Gukovo Rus. Fed.
135 G6 Gukovo Rus. Fed.
116 D2 Gulabgarh Jammu and Kashmir
120 D4 Gulabie Uzbek.
106 D4 Gulang Gansu China
83 G2 Gulargambone N.S.W. Austr.
199 E1 Gul'bakhor Uzbek.
121 G4 Gul'bakhor Uzbek.
114 C2 Gulbarga Karnataka India
138 G4 Gulbene Latvia
121 G4 Gul'cha Kyrg. see Gülchö
154 H4 Gülchö Kyrg.
129 B3 Gül daği mt. Turkey
170 C1 Guldborg Denmark
126 D3 Güle Turkey
100 Gulf of Chihli China see Bo Hai
237 F6 Gulfport MS U.S.A.
231 C6 Gulf Shores AL U.S.A.
83 G3 Gulgong N.S.W. Austr.
113 □1 Gulhi i. S. Male Maldives see Gulhi
100 B1 Gulian Heilong. China
108 C3 Gulin Sichuan China
121 G4 Gulistan Uzbek.
Guliston Uzbek. see Gulistan
170 C2 Gülitz Ger.
107 I1 Guliya Shan mt. Nei Mongol China
Gulja Hubei China see Yining
135 H7 Gul'kevichi Rus. Fed.
224 E3 Gull r. Ont. Can.
148 C4 Gull r. Ont. Can.
148 C3 Gulladuff Northern Ireland U.K.
146 F5 Gullane East Lothian, Scotland U.K.
223 I5 Gull Lake Sask. Can.
143 F2 Gullspång Sweden
199 F2 Güllü Uşak Turkey
199 G3 Güllübahçe Turkey
126 D3 Güllük Azer.
199 E4 Güllük Turkey
199 E3 Güllük Körfezi b. Turkey
116 C2 Gulmarg Jammu and Kashmir
191 G3 Gülsen Bursa Turkey
199 F1 Gülşehir Turkey
126 C2 Gülşehir Turkey
129 D2 Gülşad Kazakh.
126 D3 Gülşehir Turkey
210 B4 Gulu Uganda
197 G4 Gülübovo Bulg.
85 G5 Guluguba Qld Austr.
207 I4 Gulumba Gana Nigeria
207 I4 Gulwe Tanz.
129 B1 Gulyantsi Bulg.
170 D2 Gülzow Ger.
Guma Xinjiang China see Pishan
123 G4 Gumal r. Pak.
212 D3 Gumare Botswana
135 I5 Gumbinnen Rus. Fed. see Gusev
210 A3 Gumbiri mt. Sudan
122 C2 Gumdag Turkm.
207 H3 Gumel Nigeria
199 F1 Gümüldür Turkey see Varto
183 G3 Gumiel de Hizán Spain
183 G3 Gumiel de Mercado Spain
117 F5 Gumla Bihar India
105 J2 Gumma pref. Japan
169 E4 Gummersbach Ger.
94 B1 Gumpang r. Indon.
169 F5 Gumpelstadt Ger.
139 H4 Gumtow Ger.
126 E2 Gümüşhacıköy Turkey
199 G2 Gümüşsuyu Turkey
199 F1 Gümüşyaka Turkey
120 A3 Guna Madh. Prad. India
108 C3 Gunan Chongqing China see Qijiang
184 E2 Gunarós Vojvodina, Srbija Yugo.
210 C2 Guna Terara mt. Eth.
161 F4 Gunb r. France
83 G2 Gundabooka National Park N.S.W. Austr.
172 B3 Gundelfingen Ger.
173 G4 Gundelfingen an der Donau Ger.
172 D2 Gundelfingen Baden-Württemberg Ger.
169 E5 Gundelsheim Bayern Ger.
114 C3 Gunderi Karnataka India
157 H4 Gundershoffen France
114 C2 Gundlakamma r. India
114 C3 Gundlupet Karnataka India
169 C4 Gündogdu Turkey
170 D2 Gundorovka Rus. Fed. see Donetsk
199 F2 Gündüzler Turkey
199 F2 Güney Turkey
199 G2 Güney Turkey
199 F2 Güney Turkey
199 G2 Güneydoğu Toroslar plat. Turkey
199 G2 Güneyköy Afyon Turkey
199 B3 Güneyköy Turkey
128 A1 Güneysu Turkey
209 C6 Gungu Dem. Rep. Congo
209 B8 Gungue Angola
135 H6 Gunib Rus. Fed.
199 F2 Günlüce Turkey
140 L2 Gunna i. Scotland U.K.
140 M2 Gunnarn Sweden
85 F5 Gunnawarra Qld Austr.
221 P2 Gunnbjørn Fjeld nunatak Greenland
83 H2 Gunnedah N.S.W. Austr.

170 D2 Gutow Ger.
190 D2 Guttannen Switz.
179 F4 Guttaring Austria
236 F3 Guttenberg IA U.S.A.
213 F3 Guttenberg IA U.S.A.
170 E2 Gützkow Ger.
170 E2 Gützkow Ger.
129 B4 Güveçli Turkey
140 L2 Guvertfjället mts Sweden
117 G4 Guwahati Assam India
127 F3 Güwêr Iraq
Guwlumayak Turkm. see Kuuli-Mayak
169 E4 Guxhagen Ger.
109 E3 Guxian Jiangxi China
251 G3 Guyana country S. America
Guyane Française terr. S. America see French Guiana
172 C2 Guyang Nei Mongol China see Guzhang
107 F3 Guyang Nei Mongol China
160 C2 Guye r. France
107 H2 Guyi Guangxi China see Sanjiang
237 C4 Guymon OK U.S.A.
122 C4 Guyom Iran
Guyong Guizhou China see Jiangle
83 J2 Guyra N.S.W. Austr.
225 H4 Guysborough N.S. Can.
107 G3 Guyuan Hebei China
106 E5 Guyuan Ningxia China
121 F5 Guzar Uzbek.
128 B1 Güzelbağ Turkey
Güzelhisar Turkey see Morfou
108 D2 Guzhang Hunan China
109 F1 Guzhen Anhui China
Guizhou Guizhou China see Rongjiang
242 D2 Guzmán, Lago de l. Mex.
138 C4 Gvardeysk Rus. Fed.
Gvardeyskoye Rus. Fed. see Elin-Yurt
137 K2 Gvozd Ukr.
83 G2 Gwabegar N.S.W. Austr.
207 G4 Gwada Nigeria
207 G3 Gwadabawa Nigeria
123 G5 Gwadar Pak.
123 G5 Gwadar West Bay Pak.
123 G5 Gwadar Pak. see Gwadar
116 D4 Gwalior Madh. Prad. India
213 F4 Gwanda Zimbabwe
207 G4 Gwarzo Nigeria
150 D3 Gwaun-Cae-Gurwen Neath Port Talbot, Wales U.K.
213 E3 Gwayi r. Zimbabwe
174 E2 Gwda r. Pol.
147 C2 Gweebarra Bay Rep. of Ireland
147 C1 Gweedore Rep. of Ireland
213 F3 Gwelo Zimbabwe see Gweru
212 E4 Gweta Botswana
226 D2 Gwinn MI U.S.A.
236 D2 Gwinner ND U.S.A.
147 C4 Gwithian Cornwall, England U.K.
207 I4 Gwoza Nigeria
83 G2 Gwydir r. N.S.W. Austr.
150 C1 Gwynedd admin. div. Wales U.K.
150 D1 Gwytherin Conwy, Wales U.K.
63 Gy France
111 F6 Gyaca Xizang China
Gyaʼgya Xizang China see Saga
Gyaijêpozhanggê Qinghai China see Zhidoi
108 A1 Gyai Qu r. Xizang China
111 G6 Gyaisi Qinghai China
Gyaisi Sichuan China see Jiulong
177 I4 Gyál Hungary
199 E3 Gyali i. Greece
Gyamotang Xizang China see Dêngqên
Gyandzha Azer. see Gäncä
111 D6 Gyangrang Xizang China
111 D6 Gyangzê Xizang China
106 C5 Gyaring Qinghai China
111 E6 Gyaring Co l. China
106 C5 Gyaring Hu l. Qinghai China
176 G4 Gyarmat Hungary
199 □ Gyaros i. Greece
Gyaurs ʼTurkm. see Sakhra
130 I2 Gydan, Khrebet mts Rus. Fed. see Kolymskiy, Khrebet
Gydanskiy Poluostrov pen. Rus. Fed.
176 G5 Gyékényes Hungary
177 H4 Gyermely Hungary
156 E4 Gyé-sur-Seine France
Zabqung
Gyhum Ger.
111 F6 Gyigang Xizang China see Zayü
111 D6 Gyimda Xizang China
111 D6 Gyirong Xizang China
108 A2 Gyitang Xizang China
Gyixong Xizang China see Gonggar
111 F5 Gyiza Qinghai China
142 F5 Gyldenløveshøj hill Denmark
147 C6 Gyleen Rep. of Ireland
140 M2 Gyljen Sweden
85 G5 Gympie Qld Austr.
96 B2 Gyobingauk Myanmar
105 F2 Gyoda Japan
177 J5 Gyomaendrőd Hungary
177 J4 Gyömöre Hungary
177 I4 Gyömrő Hungary
177 H5 Gyöngyös Hungary
177 I5 Gyöngyös r. Hungary
177 H5 Gyöngyös Hungary
177 H4 Gyöngyöshalász Hungary
177 H4 Gyöngyöspata Hungary
177 H5 Gyönk Hungary
176 G4 Győr Hungary
176 G4 Győr-Moson-Sopron county Hungary
177 H5 Győrság Hungary
177 H4 Győrszentmárton Hungary see Pannonhalma
177 H4 Győrtelek Hungary
177 H4 Győrújbarát Hungary
177 H4 Gypsumville Man. Can.
223 J5 Gytheio Greece
197 K5 Gyula Hungary
177 L5 Gyulafehérvár Romania see Alba Iulia
177 J2 Gyulaháza Hungary
177 H5 Gyulaj Hungary
129 F3 Gyul'gerychay r. Rus. Fed.
Gyümai Qinghai China see Darlag
129 C3 Gyumri Armenia
122 D2 Gyunyar Bair hill Turkm.
129 D2 Gyyzylarbat Turkm.
139 J4 Gzhatsk Rus. Fed. see Gagarin
175 I3 Gzy Pol.

117 G4 Ha Bhutan
138 E2 Haabneeme Estonia
165 D4 Haacht Belgium
179 F2 Haag Austria
179 E2 Haag am Hausruck Austria
173 H3 Haag in Oberbayern Ger.
140 □ Haakon VII Land reg. Svalbard
164 F2 Haaksbergen Neth.
164 F2 Haaltert Belgium
164 D3 Haamstede Neth.
106 E1 Haanhöhiy Uul mts Mongolia
79 □ Haʼano i. Tonga
79 □7 Haʼapai Group is Tonga
134 N2 Haapajärvi Fin.
134 N2 Haapavesi Fin.
138 E2 Haapsalu Estonia
173 F3 Haar Ger.

Ha 'Arava to Hase 311

Ha 'Arava *watercourse* Israel/Jordan *see* **'Arabah, Wādī al**
173 H3 **Haarbach** Ger.
172 B2 **Haardt** *hills* Ger.
172 B2 **Haardtkopf** *hill* Ger.
164 D2 **Haarlem** Neth.
214 D5 **Haarlem** S. Africa
169 C4 **Haarstrang** *ridge* Ger.
81 B5 **Haast** *South I.* N.Z.
81 B5 **Haast** *r. South I.* N.Z.
84 B4 **Haast Bluff** *N.T.* Austr.
81 B6 **Haast Range** *mts South I.* N.Z.
164 D3 **Haastrecht** Neth.
123 F5 **Hab** *r.* Pak.
173 F4 **Habach** Ger.
110 D1 **Habahe** *Xinjiang* China
Habai Group *is* Tonga *see* **Ha'apai Group**
Habana Cuba *see* **La Habana**
173 G1 **Habartov** Czech Rep.
163 B5 **Habas** France
222 G3 **Habay** *Alta* Can.
165 E5 **Habay-la-Neuve** Belgium
124 D5 **Ḩabbān** Yemen
127 F4 **Ḩabbānīyah, Hawr al** *l.* Iraq
124 C4 **Habhab ash Shaykh, Ḩarrāt** *lava field* Saudi Arabia
178 C3 **Habicht** *mt.* Austria
117 G4 **Habiganj** Bangl.
104 B4 **Habikino** Japan
128 B4 **Ḩabīs, Wādī al** *r.* Jordan
143 F3 **Habo** Sweden
177 I2 **Habovka** Slovakia
117 G5 **Habra** *W. Bengal* India
176 E2 **Habry** Czech Rep.
157 H5 **Habsheim** France
125 E4 **Ḩabshīyah, Jabal** *mts* Yemen
169 C5 **Hachenburg** Ger.
105 E2 **Hachibuse-yama** *mt.* Japan
104 D2 **Hachimori-yama** *mt.* Japan
102 J3 **Hachinohe** Japan
105 F3 **Hachiōji** Japan
199 F2 **Hacıbekir** Turkey
126 D3 **Hacıbektaş** Turkey
129 C4 **Hacıhalit** Turkey
Hacıköy Turkey *see* **Çekerek**
183 G3 **Hacinas** Spain
128 C1 **Hacıpaşa** Turkey
129 F4 **Hacıqāhrämanlı** Azer.
129 F3 **Hacı Zeynalabdin** Azer.
82 D2 **Hack, Mount** *S.A.* Austr.
241 K4 **Hackberry** *AZ* U.S.A.
172 B2 **Hackenheim** Ger.
235 D2 **Hackensack** *NJ* U.S.A.
232 C5 **Hacker Valley** *WV* U.S.A.
147 E4 **Hacketstown** Rep. of Ireland
234 D2 **Hackettstown** *NJ* U.S.A.
151 G2 **Hackleton** *Northamptonshire, England* U.K.
151 I3 **Hacklinge** *Kent, England* U.K.
149 I3 **Hackness** *North Yorkshire, England* U.K.
234 C3 **Hack Point** *MD* U.S.A.
213 G4 **Hacufera** Moz.
175 J6 **Haczów** Pol.
125 E3 **Hadabat al Budū** *plain* Saudi Arabia
114 B3 **Hadagalli** *Karnataka* India
169 D5 **Hadamar** Ger.
123 F4 **Hada Mountains** Afgh.
124 C3 **Ḩaḑan, Ḩarrat** *lava field* Saudi Arabia
105 F3 **Hadano** Japan
151 G3 **Haddenham** *Buckinghamshire, England* U.K.
146 F6 **Haddington** *East Lothian, Scotland* U.K.
151 I2 **Haddiscoe** *Norfolk, England* U.K.
234 C3 **Haddonfield** *NJ* U.S.A.
207 H3 **Hadejia** Nigeria
142 D1 **Hadeland** *reg.* Norway
128 B3 **Ḩadera** Israel
128 B3 **Ḩadera** *r.* Israel
142 C4 **Haderslev** Denmark
142 C3 **Haderup** Denmark
114 C2 **Hadgaon** *Mahar.* India
124 C3 **Ḩādhah** Saudi Arabia
125 E3 **Ḩādh Banī Zaynān** *des.* Saudi Arabia
113 D11 **Hadhdhunmathi Atoll** Maldives
Hadhramaut *reg.* Yemen *see* **Ḩaḑramawt**
125 F5 **Hadīboh** *Suquṭrā* Yemen
111 D4 **Hadilik** *Xinjiang* China
126 D3 **Hadım** Turkey
202 D5 **Hadjer Momou** *mt.* Chad
151 H2 **Hadleigh** *Suffolk, England* U.K.
150 E2 **Hadley** *Telford and Wrekin, England* U.K.
221 H2 **Hadley Bay** *Nunavut* Can.
235 F1 **Hadlyme** *CT* U.S.A.
171 C4 **Hadmersleben** Ger.
157 G4 **Hadol** France
125 E4 **Ḩaḑramawt** *governorate* Yemen
125 D5 **Ḩaḑramawt** *reg.* Yemen
Hadranum *Sicilia* Italy *see* **Adrano**
179 H2 **Hadres** Austria
Hadria Italy *see* **Adria**
149 G2 **Hadrian's Wall** *tourist site England* U.K.
Hadrumetum Tunisia *see* **Sousse**
129 E4 **Hadrut** Azer.
140 K1 **Hadseløy** *i.* Norway
142 D3 **Hadsten** Denmark
142 D3 **Hadsund** Denmark
137 G2 **Hadyach** Ukr.
102 □2 **Haebaru** Japan
261 I3 **Haedo, Cuchilla de** *hills* Uru.
101 C5 **Haeju** N. Korea
101 C5 **Haeju-man** *b.* N. Korea
165 E3 **Haelen** Neth.
240 □B7 **Haena** *HI* U.S.A.
101 C6 **Haenam** S. Korea
124 D1 **Ḩafar al Bāṭin** Saudi Arabia
223 J4 **Hafford** *Sask.* Can.
126 E3 **Hafik** Turkey
124 B2 **Hafirat al'Aydā** Saudi Arabia
124 D2 **Hafirat Nasah** Saudi Arabia
125 F3 **Ḩafīt** Oman
125 F2 **Ḩafīt, Jabal** *mt.* U.A.E.
123 H3 **Hafizabad** Pak.
117 H4 **Haflong** *Assam* India
140 □B2 **Hafnarfjörður** Iceland
179 G2 **Hafnerbach** Austria
129 F4 **Haftoni** Azer.
140 □B2 **Hafursfjörður** *b.* Iceland
Haga Myanmar *see* **Haka**
203 G6 **Hag Abdullah** Sudan
215 G5 **Haga-Haga** S. Africa
179 H5 **Haganj** Croatia
227 G2 **Hagar** *Ont.* Can.
114 C3 **Hagari** *r.* India
203 H5 **Hagar Nish Plateau** Eritrea
78 □1 **Hagåtña** Guam
143 G3 **Hagbyån** *r.* Sweden
168 C2 **Hage** Ger.
171 D3 **Hagelberg** *hill* Ger.
169 C4 **Hagen** Ger.
91 J8 **Hagen, Mount** P.N.G.
169 C3 **Hagen am Teutoburger Wald** Ger.
172 C2 **Hagenbach** Ger.
169 E3 **Hagenburg** Ger.
168 D2 **Hagen im Bremischen** Ger.
170 C2 **Hagenow** Ger.
222 E4 **Hagensborg** *B.C.* Can.
171 F4 **Hagenwerder** Ger.
210 C2 **Hāgere Hiywet** Eth.
210 C3 **Hāgere Selam** Eth.
232 B6 **Hagerhill** *KY* U.S.A.
232 E5 **Hagerstown** *MD* U.S.A.
163 B5 **Hagetaubin** France
163 B5 **Hagetmau** France
143 E1 **Hagfors** Sweden
140 K3 **Häggenås** Sweden
238 D2 **Haggin, Mount** *MT* U.S.A.
140 K3 **Häggsjön** Sweden
140 K3 **Häggsjövik** Sweden
103 E6 **Hagi** Japan
96 D2 **Ha Giang** Vietnam
97 E4 **Ha Giao, Sông** *r.* Vietnam
150 E2 **Hagley** *Herefordshire, England* U.K.
150 E2 **Hagley** *Worcestershire, England* U.K.
HaGolan *hills* Syria *see* **Golan**
157 G3 **Hagondange** France
147 B4 **Hag's Head** *hd* Rep. of Ireland
233 G3 **Hague** *NY* U.S.A.
157 H4 **Haguenau** France
217 □3a **Hahaïa** *Njazidja* Comoros
103 □3 **Hahajima-rettō** *is* Japan
169 F4 **Hahausen** Ger.
173 F2 **Hahnbach** Ger.
172 C2 **Hähnlein** Ger.
169 D5 **Hahnstätten** Ger.
176 F5 **Hahót** Hungary
107 H4 **Hai** *r.* China
211 C5 **Hai** Tanz.
109 G1 **Hai'an** *Jiangsu* China
172 D2 **Haibach** *Bayern* Ger.
173 G2 **Haibach** *Bayern* Ger.
105 E4 **Haibara** Japan
Haicheng *Guangdong* China *see* **Haifeng**
107 I3 **Haicheng** *Liaoning* China
Haicheng *Ningxia* China *see* **Haiyuan**
116 E4 **Haidargarh** *Uttar Prad.* India
173 G2 **Haidenaab** *r.* Ger.
179 F2 **Haidershofen** Austria
173 H3 **Haidmühle** Ger.
96 D2 **Hai Dương** Vietnam
Haifa Israel *see* **Ḩefa**
128 B3 **Haifa, Bay of** Israel
109 E4 **Haifeng** *Guangdong* China
87 E6 **Haig** *W.A.* Austr.
169 D5 **Haiger** Ger.
172 C3 **Haigerloch** Ger.
Haikakan *country* Asia *see* **Armenia**
Haikang *Guangdong* China *see* **Leizhou**
108 D4 **Haikou** *Hainan* China
124 C2 **Ḩā'il** Saudi Arabia
124 C2 **Ḩā'il** *prov.* Saudi Arabia
117 H4 **Hailakandi** *Assam* India
107 H1 **Hailar** *Nei Mongol* China
107 H1 **Hailar** *r.* China
238 D3 **Hailey** *ID* U.S.A.
224 E4 **Haileybury** *Ont.* Can.
100 D3 **Hailin** *Heilong.* China
Hailong *Jilin* China *see* **Meihekou**
151 H4 **Hailsham** *East Sussex, England* U.K.
100 C3 **Hailun** *Heilong.* China
140 N2 **Hailuoto** Fin.
109 G2 **Haimen** *Jiangsu* China
173 F3 **Haimhausen** Ger.
178 B3 **Haiming** Austria
173 G3 **Haiming** Ger.
169 F5 **Haina** Ger.
169 D4 **Haina (Kloster)** Ger.
108 D5 **Hainan** *i.* China
99 I8 **Hainan** *prov.* China
Hainan Strait China *see* **Qiongzhou Haixia**
165 D4 **Hainaut** *prov.* Belgium
179 H2 **Hainburg an der Donau** Austria
206 C5 **Haindi** Liberia
220 E4 **Haines** *AK* U.S.A.
231 D6 **Haines City** *FL* U.S.A.
222 B2 **Haines Junction** *Y.T.* Can.
234 D3 **Hainesport** *NJ* U.S.A.
222 B2 **Haines Road** Can./U.S.A.
179 G2 **Hainfeld** Austria
169 F4 **Hainich** *ridge* Ger.
171 E5 **Hainichen** Ger.
169 F4 **Hainleite** *ridge* Ger.
Haiphong Vietnam *see* **Hai Phong**
96 D2 **Hai Phong** Vietnam
100 E3 **Haiqing** *Heilong.* China
106 D3 **Hairhan Namag** *Nei Mongol* China
157 F4 **Haironville** France
172 C3 **Haiterbach** Ger.
246 D3 **Haiti** *country* West Indies
179 G2 **Haitzendorf** Austria
106 D4 **Haiyan** *Qinghai* China
109 G2 **Haiyan** *Zhejiang* China
Haiyang *Anhui* China *see* **Xiuning**
107 I4 **Haiyang** *Shandong* China
Haiyou *Zhejiang* China *see* **Sanmen**
106 E4 **Haiyuan** *Ningxia* China
107 H5 **Haizhou Wan** *b.* China
122 C3 **Ḩāj Ali Qoli, Kavīr-e** *salt l.* Iran
177 K4 **Hajdú-Bihar** *county* Hungary
177 K4 **Hajdúböszörmény** Hungary
177 K4 **Hajdúdorog** Hungary
177 K4 **Hajdúhadház** Hungary
177 K4 **Hajdúnánás** Hungary
177 K4 **Hajdúsámson** Hungary
177 K4 **Hajdúszoboszló** Hungary
177 K4 **Hajdúszovát** Hungary
125 F5 **Ḩajhir** *mt. Suquṭrā* Yemen
117 F4 **Hajipur** *Bihar* India
125 E2 **Hajir** *reg.* Saudi Arabia
124 C5 **Ḩajjah** Yemen
124 C4 **Ḩajjah** *governorate* Yemen
122 C4 **Ḩājjīābād** Iran
122 C4 **Ḩājjīābād** Iran
177 H4 **Hajmáskér** Hungary
175 L3 **Hajnówka** Pol.
117 G4 **Hajo** *Assam* India
177 I5 **Hajós** Hungary
124 C3 **Ḩajrah** Saudi Arabia
177 G3 **Hájske** Slovakia
96 A2 **Haka** Myanmar
240 □D9 **Hakalau** *HI* U.S.A.
129 E4 **Häkäri** *r.* Azer.
103 I5 **Hakase-yama** *mt.* Japan
81 C6 **Hakataramea** *South I.* N.Z.
81 C5 **Hakatere** *South I.* N.Z.
Hakatere *r. South I.* N.Z. *see* **Ashburton**
259 C6 **Hakelhuincul, Altiplanicie de** *plat.* Arg.
Hakha Myanmar *see* **Haka**
128 B4 **Hakippa, Har** *hill* Israel
127 F3 **Hakkârı** Turkey
140 M2 **Hakkas** Sweden
104 B4 **Hakken-zan** *mt.* Japan
102 J3 **Hakkōda-san** *mt.* Japan
105 E4 **Hakkō-san** *hill* Japan
102 K1 **Hako-dake** *mt.* Japan
102 J3 **Hakodate** Japan
212 C4 **Hakos Mountains** Namibia
129 B4 **Haksever** Turkey
104 C2 **Hakui** Japan
104 C2 **Haku-san** *vol.* Japan
Hal Belgium *see* **Halle**
123 G5 **Hala** Pak.
128 B4 **Ḩalā', Jabal al** *mt.* Jordan
128 C1 **Ḩalab** Syria
128 C1 **Ḩalab** *governorate* Syria
124 D3 **Halabān** Saudi Arabia
127 G4 **Halabja** Iraq
Halach Turkm. *see* **Khalach**
243 H4 **Halachó** Mex.
100 C3 **Halahai** *Jilin* China
136 D3 **Halahora de Sus** Moldova
203 G4 **Halaib Triangle** *terr.* Egypt/Sudan
128 A4 **Halâl, Gebel** *hill* Egypt
125 G4 **Ḩalāniyāt, Juzur al** *is* Oman
176 G4 **Halászi** Hungary
197 H2 **Hălăucești** Romania
143 F2 **Hålaveden** *hills* Sweden
240 □C8 **Halawa** *HI* U.S.A.
128 C2 **Halba** Lebanon
106 C1 **Halban** *Hövsgöl* Mongolia
171 E3 **Halbe** Ger.
179 G4 **Halbenrain** Austria
171 C4 **Halberstadt** Ger.
150 D4 **Halberton** *Devon, England* U.K.
173 E4 **Halblech** Ger.
179 H3 **Halbturn** Austria
92 B3 **Halcon, Mount** *Mindoro* Phil.
215 G4 **Halcyon Drift** S. Africa
142 D2 **Halden** Norway
171 C3 **Haldensleben** Ger.
173 E4 **Haldenwang** Ger.
117 G5 **Haldi** *r. W. Bengal* India
117 G5 **Haldia** *W. Bengal* India
117 G4 **Haldibari** *W. Bengal* India
116 D3 **Haldwani** *Uttar Prad.* India
149 G4 **Hale** *Greater Manchester, England* U.K.
227 F3 **Hale** *MI* U.S.A.
87 C5 **Hale, Mount** *hill W.A.* Austr.
129 C3 **Halefoğlu** Turkey
122 C5 **Hāleh** Iran
240 □ **Haleiwa** *HI* U.S.A.
165 E4 **Halen** Belgium
177 H2 **Halenkov** Czech Rep.
Haleparki Deresi *r.* Syria/Turkey *see* **Quwayq, Nahr**
151 I2 **Hales** *Norfolk, England* U.K.
150 E2 **Halesowen** *West Midlands, England* U.K.
151 I2 **Halesworth** *Suffolk, England* U.K.
234 B3 **Halethorpe** *MD* U.S.A.
149 G4 **Halewood** *Merseyside, England* U.K.
231 C5 **Haleyville** *AL* U.S.A.
206 E5 **Half Assini** Ghana
126 E3 **Halfeti** Turkey
173 G4 **Halfing** Ger.
81 B7 **Halfmoon Bay** *Stewart I.* N.Z.
240 F3 **Half Moon Bay** *CA* U.S.A.
82 C2 **Half Moon Lake** *salt flat S.A.* Austr.
222 F3 **Halfway** *r. B.C.* Can.
232 E5 **Halfway** *MD* U.S.A.
164 D2 **Halfweg** Neth.
214 C4 **Halfweg** S. Africa
142 E1 **Halgån** *r.* Sweden
107 H2 **Halhgol** Mongolia
227 H3 **Haliburton** *Ont.* Can.
224 E4 **Haliburton Highlands** *hills Ont.* Can.
177 I3 **Halič** Slovakia
Halicarnassus Turkey *see* **Bodrum**
225 I4 **Halifax** *N.S.* Can.
149 H4 **Halifax** *West Yorkshire, England* U.K.
231 E4 **Halifax** *NC* U.S.A.
234 B2 **Halifax** *PA* U.S.A.
232 D6 **Halifax** *VA* U.S.A.
85 F3 **Halifax, Mount** *Qld* Austr.
85 F3 **Halifax Bay** *Qld* Austr.
138 D1 **Halikko** Fin.
129 B4 **Halilçavuş** Turkey
128 C2 **Ḩalīmah** *mt.* Lebanon/Syria
82 B2 **Halinor Lake** *salt flat S.A.* Austr.
Haliut *Nei Mongol* China *see* **Urad Zhongqi**
114 B3 **Haliyal** *Karnataka* India
146 E3 **Halkirk** *Highland, Scotland* U.K.
150 D1 **Halkyn** *Flintshire, Wales* U.K.
Hall *atoll Gilbert Is* Kiribati *see* **Maiana**
143 H3 **Hall** *Gotland* Sweden
148 E2 **Hall** *East Renfrewshire, Scotland* U.K.
234 B4 **Hall** *MD* U.S.A.
140 L3 **Hälla** Sweden
144 F2 **Halladale** *r. Scotland* U.K.
234 B2 **Hallam** *PA* U.S.A.
142 E3 **Halland** *county* Sweden
151 H4 **Halland** *East Sussex, England* U.K.
142 E3 **Hallandsåsen** *hills* Sweden
101 C6 **Halla-san** *mt.* S. Korea
221 J3 **Hall Beach** *Nunavut* Can.
173 F3 **Hallbergmoos** Ger.
165 D3 **Halle** *Antwerpen* Belgium
165 D4 **Halle** *Vlaams Brabant* Belgium
169 E4 **Halle** Ger.
171 C4 **Halle** *admin. reg. Sachsen-Anhalt* Ger.
171 C4 **Halle (Saale)** Ger.
169 D3 **Halle (Westfalen)** Ger.
143 F2 **Hällefors** Sweden
143 G2 **Hälleforsnäs** Sweden
178 E3 **Hallein** Austria
140 K3 **Hallen** *Jämtland* Sweden
143 G1 **Hållen** *Uppsala* Sweden
169 D4 **Hallenberg** Ger.
156 B3 **Hallencourt** France
171 C4 **Halle-Neustadt** Ger.
173 E2 **Hallerndorf** Ger.
263 L2 **Hallett, Cape** Antarctica
237 D6 **Hallettsville** *TX* U.S.A.
142 D2 **Hälleviksstrand** Sweden
262 W1 **Halley** *research stn* Antarctica
262 X2 **Hallgreen, Mount** Antarctica
236 C2 **Halliday** *ND* U.S.A.
168 D1 **Halligen** *is* Ger.
142 C1 **Hallingdal** *val.* Norway
142 C2 **Hallingdalselva** *r.* Norway
143 G3 **Hallingeberg** Sweden
178 C3 **Hall in Tirol** Austria
266 F5 **Hall Islands** Micronesia
138 E2 **Halliste** *r.* Estonia
140 L2 **Hällnäs** Sweden
236 D1 **Hallock** *MN* U.S.A.
150 E2 **Hallow** *Worcestershire, England* U.K.
221 L3 **Hall Peninsula** *Nunavut* Can.
86 E2 **Hall Point** *W.A.* Austr.
234 B1 **Halls** *PA* U.S.A.
143 F2 **Hallsberg** Sweden
86 E3 **Halls Creek** *W.A.* Austr.
227 H3 **Halls Lake** *Ont.* Can.
173 E2 **Hallstadt** Ger.
179 E3 **Hallstatt** Austria
179 E3 **Hallstätter See** *l.* Austria
143 H1 **Hallstavik** Sweden
233 F4 **Hallstead** *PA* U.S.A.
147 E3 **Halltown** Rep. of Ireland
165 C4 **Halluin** Belgium
164 E1 **Hallum** Neth.
140 L2 **Hällvik** Sweden
140 K3 **Hallviken** Sweden
190 D1 **Hallwiler See** *l.* Switz.
150 C4 **Hallworthy** *Cornwall, England* U.K.
177 L5 **Hălmăgel** Romania
177 L5 **Hălmagiu** Romania
93 D2 **Halmahera** *i. Maluku* Indon.
93 D3 **Halmahera Sea** *Maluku* Indon.
177 L4 **Halmășd** Romania
197 F2 **Halmeu** Romania
142 E3 **Halmstad** Sweden
116 C5 **Halol** *Gujarat* India
188 E2 **Haloze** *reg.* Slovenia
142 D3 **Hals** Denmark
195 □ **Hal Saflieni Hypogeum** *tourist site* Malta
171 E5 **Halsbrücke** Ger.
169 C5 **Halsenbach** Ger.
Hälsingborg Sweden *see* **Helsingborg**
151 H3 **Halstead** *Essex, England* U.K.
168 E2 **Halstenbek** Ger.
164 D3 **Halsteren** Neth.
157 G3 **Halstroff** France
140 N3 **Halsua** Fin.
106 B4 **Haltang** *r.* China
169 C4 **Haltern** Ger.
151 G3 **Halton** *Buckinghamshire, England* U.K.
149 G3 **Halton** *Lancashire, England* U.K.
149 G4 **Halton** *admin. div. England* U.K.
149 G3 **Halton Gill** *North Yorkshire, England* U.K.
149 G3 **Haltwhistle** *Northumberland, England* U.K.
116 B5 **Halvad** *Gujarat* India
169 C4 **Halver** Ger.
150 D4 **Halwell** *Devon, England* U.K.
136 C3 **Halych** Ukr.
137 G2 **Halytsya** Ukr.
176 B2 **Halže** Czech Rep.
156 D3 **Ham** France
146 □F1 **Ham** *Shetland, Scotland* U.K.
103 F6 **Hamada** Japan
204 D5 **Ḩamâda Çafia** *des.* Mali
204 D4 **Hamada ed Douakel** *plat.* Alg.
204 D5 **Ḩamâda El Ḩaricha** *des.* Mali
122 B3 **Hamadān** Iran
122 B3 **Hamadān** *prov.* Iran
202 B3 **Ḩamādat Murzuq** *plat.* Libya
204 D3 **Hamada Tounassine** *des.* Alg.
204 E3 **Hamaguir** Alg.
128 C2 **Ḩamāh** Syria
128 C2 **Ḩamāh** *governorate* Syria
105 D4 **Hamakita** Japan
217 □3a **Hamalengo** *mt. Njazidja* Comoros
104 D4 **Hamamatsu** Japan
104 D4 **Hamana-ko** *l.* Japan
184 E2 **Hamapega** *hill* Spain
141 J3 **Hamar** Norway
140 K1 **Hamarøy** Norway
140 K1 **Hamarøy** *i.* Norway
124 B5 **Hamasien** *prov.* Eritrea
203 G3 **Hamâta, Gebel** *mt.* Egypt
157 H3 **Hambach** France
114 D5 **Hambantota** Sri Lanka
168 F2 **Hamberge** Ger.
168 D2 **Hambergen** Ger.
151 G3 **Hambleden** *Buckinghamshire, England* U.K.
151 F4 **Hamble-le-Rice** *Hampshire, England* U.K.
149 G4 **Hambleton** *Lancashire, England* U.K.
232 D5 **Hambleton** *WV* U.S.A.
149 H3 **Hambleton Hills** *England* U.K.
172 C2 **Hambrücken** Ger.
168 E3 **Hambühren** Ger.
168 E2 **Hamburg** Ger.
168 E2 **Hamburg** *land* Ger.
215 F5 **Hamburg** S. Africa
237 F5 **Hamburg** *AR* U.S.A.
235 F1 **Hamburg** *CT* U.S.A.
236 E3 **Hamburg** *IA* U.S.A.
234 D1 **Hamburg** *NJ* U.S.A.
232 D3 **Hamburg** *NY* U.S.A.
234 C2 **Hamburg** *PA* U.S.A.
142 D2 **Hamburgsund** Sweden
158 E3 **Hambye** France
124 C4 **Ḩamḑah** Saudi Arabia
207 F3 **Hamdallay** Niger
124 C4 **Ḩamdānah** Saudi Arabia
233 G4 **Hamden** *CT* U.S.A.
199 E2 **Hamdibey** Turkey
128 B1 **Hamdili** Turkey
168 E1 **Hamdorf** Ger.
141 M3 **Hämeenkangas** *moorland* Fin.
138 E1 **Hämeenkoski** *Etelä-Suomi* Fin.
141 M3 **Hämeenkoski** *Länsi-Suomi* Fin.
141 M3 **Hämeenkyrö** Fin.
141 N3 **Hämeenlinna** Fin.
HaMelaḩ, Yam *salt l.* Asia *see* **Dead Sea**
168 E3 **Hämelhausen** Ger.
87 B5 **Hamelin** *W.A.* Austr.
87 B7 **Hamelin, Cape** *W.A.* Austr.
87 B5 **Hamelin Pool** *b. W.A.* Austr.
169 E3 **Hameln** Ger.
171 C3 **Hamersleben** Ger.
86 C4 **Hamersley** *W.A.* Austr.
87 C6 **Hamersley Lakes** *salt flat W.A.* Austr.
86 C4 **Hamersley Range** *mts W.A.* Austr.
170 C3 **Hämerten** Ger.
101 C5 **Hamhŭng** N. Korea
106 B3 **Hami** *Xinjiang* China
122 B4 **Ḩamīd** Iran
199 E1 **Hamidiye** Turkey
84 E4 **Hamilton** *Qld* Austr.
84 C5 **Hamilton** *S.A.* Austr.
231 □1 **Hamilton** Bermuda
224 E5 **Hamilton** *Ont.* Can.
Hamilton *r. Nfld.* Can. *see* **Churchill**
80 E2 **Hamilton** *North I.* N.Z.
146 D6 **Hamilton** *South Lanarkshire, Scotland* U.K.
231 C5 **Hamilton** *AL* U.S.A.
231 C5 **Hamilton** *GA* U.S.A.
226 B5 **Hamilton** *IL* U.S.A.
238 D2 **Hamilton** *MT* U.S.A.
235 D2 **Hamilton** *NJ* U.S.A.
233 F3 **Hamilton** *NY* U.S.A.
232 A5 **Hamilton** *OH* U.S.A.
237 D6 **Hamilton** *TX* U.S.A.
240 G3 **Hamilton, Mount** *CA* U.S.A.
241 J2 **Hamilton, Mount** *NV* U.S.A.
81 B6 **Hamilton Burn** *South I.* N.Z.
240 F2 **Hamilton City** *CA* U.S.A.
84 C4 **Hamilton Downs** *N.T.* Austr.
225 J2 **Hamilton Inlet** *Nfld.* Can.
233 F3 **Hamilton Mountain** *hill NY* U.S.A.
148 C3 **Hamilton's Bawn** *Northern Ireland* U.K.
141 N3 **Hamina** Fin.
116 D3 **Hamirpur** *Hima. Prad.* India
116 E4 **Hamirpur** *Uttar Prad.* India
Hamitabat Turkey *see* **Isparta**
231 E5 **Hamlet** *NC* U.S.A.
82 D3 **Hamley Bridge** *S.A.* Austr.
234 C1 **Hamlin** *PA* U.S.A.
237 C5 **Hamlin** *TX* U.S.A.
232 B5 **Hamlin** *WV* U.S.A.
169 C4 **Hamm** *Nordrhein-Westfalen* Ger.
172 C2 **Hamm** *Rheinland-Pfalz* Ger.
169 C5 **Hamm (Sieg)** Ger.
204 C3 **Hammada du Drâa** *plat.* Alg.
202 A2 **Hammādat Tingharat** *des.* Libya
168 E2 **Hammah** Ger.
127 F3 **Ḩammām al 'Alīl** Iraq
181 F5 **Hammam Boughrara** Alg.
189 C7 **Hammamet** Tunisia
205 H1 **Hammamet, Golfe de** *g.* Tunisia
189 C7 **Hammam-Lif** Tunisia
215 G1 **Hammanskraal** S. Africa
127 G5 **Ḩammār, Hawr al** *imp. l.* Iraq
141 L3 **Hammarland** *Åland* Fin.
215 H3 **Hammarsdale** S. Africa
140 L3 **Hammarstrand** Sweden
165 D3 **Hamme** Belgium
142 C3 **Hammel** Denmark
169 E5 **Hammelburg** Ger.
170 E2 **Hammelspring** Ger.
165 D4 **Hamme-Mille** Belgium
171 D5 **Hammerbrücke** Ger.
140 K3 **Hammerdal** Sweden
140 M1 **Hammerfest** Norway
151 F2 **Hammerwich** *Staffordshire, England* U.K.
169 B4 **Hamminkeln** Ger.
82 D3 **Hammond** *S.A.* Austr.
230 C3 **Hammond** *IN* U.S.A.
237 F6 **Hammond** *LA* U.S.A.
238 F2 **Hammond** *MT* U.S.A.
227 E3 **Hammond Bay** *MI* U.S.A.
232 E3 **Hammondsport** *NY* U.S.A.
234 D3 **Hammonton** *NJ* U.S.A.
146 □G1 **Hamnavoe** *Shetland, Scotland* U.K.
146 □G1 **Hamnavoe** *Shetland, Scotland* U.K.
146 □G1 **Hamnavoe** *Shetland, Scotland* U.K.
165 E4 **Hamoir** Belgium
165 E4 **Hamois** Belgium
165 E3 **Hamont** Belgium
234 C3 **Hamorton** *PA* U.S.A.
81 C6 **Hampden** *South I.* N.Z.
233 □I2 **Hampden Highlands** *ME* U.S.A.
232 D6 **Hampden Sydney** *VA* U.S.A.
114 C3 **Hampi** *Karnataka* India
140 M2 **Håmpjåkk** Sweden
157 G4 **Hampont** France
151 F4 **Hampreston** *Dorset, England* U.K.
151 F3 **Hampshire** *admin. div. England* U.K.
234 B3 **Hampstead** *MD* U.S.A.
225 H4 **Hampton** *N.B.* Can.
237 E5 **Hampton** *AR* U.S.A.
236 E3 **Hampton** *IA* U.S.A.
233 □H3 **Hampton** *NH* U.S.A.
234 D2 **Hampton** *NJ* U.S.A.
231 D5 **Hampton** *SC* U.S.A.
233 E6 **Hampton** *VA* U.S.A.
235 F2 **Hampton Bays** *NY* U.S.A.
87 E7 **Hampton Tableland** *reg. W.A.* Austr.
195 □ **Hamrun** Malta
238 E3 **Hams Fork** *r. WY* U.S.A.
157 G3 **Ham-sous-Varsberg** France
151 H3 **Hamstreet** *Kent, England* U.K.
165 D4 **Ham-sur-Heure** Belgium
97 D5 **Ham Tân** Vietnam
122 D5 **Hāmūn-e Jaz Mūrīān** *salt marsh* Iran
123 E4 **Hāmūn Helmand** *salt flat* Afgh./Iran
123 F4 **Hamun-i-Lora** *dry lake* Pak.
123 E4 **Hamun-i-Mashkel** *salt flat* Pak.
127 F3 **Hamur** Turkey
105 F3 **Hamura** Japan
Hamwic *Southampton, England* U.K. *see* **Southampton**
Hamza Uzbek. *see* **Khamza**
128 A1 **Hamzalar** Turkey
176 G2 **Haná** *r.* Czech Rep.
240 □C8 **Hana** *HI* U.S.A.
246 B2 **Hanábana** *r.* Cuba
129 C3 **Hanak** Turkey
Hanakpınar Turkey *see* **Çınar**
124 B2 **Ḩanalc** Saudi Arabia
240 □B7 **Hanalei** *HI* U.S.A.
102 J4 **Hanamaki** Japan
240 □B8 **Hanamaulu** *HI* U.S.A.
211 B6 **Hanang** *mt.* Tanz.
Hananui *hill Stewart I.* N.Z. *see* **Anglem, Mount**
240 □B8 **Hanapepe** *HI* U.S.A.
169 D5 **Hanau** Ger.
Hâncești Moldova *see* **Hîncești**
107 F5 **Hancheng** *Shaanxi* China
156 B4 **Hanches** France
109 E2 **Hanchuan** *Hubei* China
232 D5 **Hancock** *MD* U.S.A.
226 C2 **Hancock** *MI* U.S.A.
233 F4 **Hancock** *NY* U.S.A.
234 C3 **Hancocks Bridge** *NJ* U.S.A.
104 C4 **Handa** Japan
146 C3 **Handa Island** *Scotland* U.K.
107 G4 **Handan** *Hebei* China
168 E2 **Handeloh** Ger.
211 C6 **Handeni** Tanz.
168 E1 **Handewitt** Ger.
Handian *Shanxi* China *see* **Changzhi**
177 H3 **Handlová** Slovakia
168 F2 **Handorf** Ger.
168 C3 **Handrup** Ger.
105 F3 **Haneda** *airport* Japan
HaNegev *des.* Israel *see* **Negev**
168 E1 **Hanerau-Hademarschen** Ger.
Hanfeng *Chongqing* China *see* **Kaixian**
240 H3 **Hanford** *CA* U.S.A.
114 B3 **Hangal** *Karnataka* India
101 C5 **Han-gang** *r.* S. Korea
106 C1 **Hangayn Nuruu** *mts* Mongolia
Hangchow *Zhejiang* China *see* **Hangzhou**
Hangchuan *Fujian* China *see* **Guangze**
171 E3 **Hangelsberg** Ger.
Hanggin Houqi *Nei Mongol* China *see* **Xamba**
Hanggin Qi *Nei Mongol* China *see* **Xin**
Hangö Fin. *see* **Hanko**
107 H4 **Hangu** *Tianjin* China
123 G3 **Hangu** Pak.
109 G2 **Hangzhou** *Zhejiang* China
109 G2 **Hangzhou Wan** *b.* China
150 E3 **Hanham** *South Gloucestershire, England* U.K.
127 F3 **Hani** Turkey
125 E2 **Ḩanīdh** Saudi Arabia
199 F1 **Hanife** *r.* Turkey
177 K3 **Haniska** Slovakia
Hanjia *Chongqing* China *see* **Pengshui**
Hanjiang *Jiangsu* China *see* **Yangzhou**
109 F4 **Han Jiang** *r.* China
106 E4 **Hanjiaoshui** *Ningxia* China
140 N3 **Hankasalmi** Fin.
168 F3 **Hankensbüttel** Ger.
215 E5 **Hankey** S. Africa
141 M4 **Hanko** Fin.
199 G2 **Hanköy** Turkey
241 L2 **Hanksville** *UT* U.S.A.
116 D2 **Hanle** Jammu and Kashmir
223 J5 **Hanley** *Sask.* Can.
150 E2 **Hanley Castle** *Worcestershire, England* U.K.
81 D5 **Hanmer Springs** *South I.* N.Z.
85 F2 **Hann** *r. Qld* Austr.
86 E3 **Hann** *r. W.A.* Austr.
86 E2 **Hann, Mount** *hill W.A.* Austr.
223 I5 **Hanna** *Alta* Can.
175 L4 **Hanna** Pol.
241 M5 **Hannagan Meadow** *AZ* U.S.A.
236 F4 **Hannibal** *MO* U.S.A.
232 E3 **Hannibal** *NY* U.S.A.
232 C5 **Hannibal** *OH* U.S.A.
137 G3 **Hannivka** Ukr.
105 F3 **Hannō** Japan
157 F3 **Hannonville-sous-les-Côtes** France
169 E3 **Hannover** Ger.
169 E3 **Hannover** *admin. reg. Niedersachsen* Ger.
169 E4 **Hannoversch Münden** Ger.
84 C4 **Hann Range** *mts N.T.* Austr.
165 E4 **Hannut** Belgium
143 F4 **Hanöbukten** *b.* Sweden
Hanoi Vietnam *see* **Ha Nôi**
96 D2 **Ha Nôi** Vietnam
224 D4 **Hanover** *Ont.* Can.
Hanover Ger. *see* **Hannover**
246 □ **Hanover** *parish* Jamaica
214 E4 **Hanover** S. Africa
235 F1 **Hanover** *CT* U.S.A.
233 G3 **Hanover** *NH* U.S.A.
232 B4 **Hanover** *OH* U.S.A.
234 B3 **Hanover** *PA* U.S.A.
232 E6 **Hanover** *VA* U.S.A.
259 B8 **Hanover, Isla** *i.* Chile
234 B2 **Hanoverdale** *PA* U.S.A.
214 E4 **Hanover Road** S. Africa
176 G4 **Hanság** *hill* Hungary
165 C3 **Hansbeke** Belgium
263 D2 **Hansen Mountains** Antarctica
170 C2 **Hanshagen** Ger.
109 D2 **Hanshou** *Hunan* China
109 E2 **Han Shui** *r.* China
116 D3 **Hansi** *Haryana* India
151 G2 **Hanslope** *Milton Keynes, England* U.K.
140 L1 **Hansnes** Norway
82 D2 **Hanson, Lake** *salt flat S.A.* Austr.
232 B6 **Hansonville** *VA* U.S.A.
168 F2 **Hanstedt** *Niedersachsen* Ger.
168 F2 **Hanstedt** *Niedersachsen* Ger.
142 C3 **Hanstholm** Denmark
107 H2 **Han Sum** *Nei Mongol* China
157 G4 **Han-sur-Nied** France
Hantengri Feng *mt.* Kazakh./Kyrg. *see* **Khan-Tengri, Pik**
177 H5 **Hantos** Hungary
138 F5 **Hantsavichy** Belarus
116 E4 **Hanumana** *Madh. Prad.* India
116 C3 **Hanumangarh** *Rajasthan* India
177 K2 **Hanušovce nad Topľou** Slovakia
176 F1 **Hanušovice** Czech Rep.
106 D1 **Hanuy Gol** *r.* Mongolia
158 B3 **Hanvec** France
83 F3 **Hanwwod** *N.S.W.* Austr.
Hanyang *Hubei* China *see* **Caidian**
108 D1 **Hanyin** *Shaanxi* China
105 F2 **Hanyū** Japan
Hanyuan *Gansu* China *see* **Xihe**
108 B2 **Hanyuan** *Sichuan* China
108 C1 **Hanzhong** *Shaanxi* China
79 □3 **Hao** *atoll Arch. des Tuamotu* Fr. Polynesia
Haomen *Qinghai* China *see* **Menyuan**
117 G5 **Haora** *W. Bengal* India
185 E5 **Haouz, Jebel el** *hill* Morocco
140 N2 **Haparanda** Sweden
165 E3 **Hapert** Neth.
117 H4 **Hapoli** *Arun. Prad.* India
173 F2 **Happburg** Ger.
151 I2 **Happisburgh** *Norfolk, England* U.K.
241 L4 **Happy Jack** *AZ* U.S.A.
225 I2 **Happy Valley - Goose Bay** *Nfld.* Can.
164 E3 **Haps** Neth.
101 D4 **Hapsu** N. Korea
116 D3 **Hapur** *Uttar Prad.* India
126 D5 **Ḩaql** Saudi Arabia
210 D2 **Hara Alol** *mt.* Djibouti
124 C4 **Ḩaraḑ** Yemen
128 B5 **Ḩarad, Jabal al** *mt.* Jordan
124 D3 **Haradah** Saudi Arabia
125 E2 **Ḩaraḑh** Saudi Arabia
138 G4 **Haradok** Belarus
138 G4 **Haradotskaye Wzvyshsha** *hills* Belarus
140 M2 **Harads** Sweden
138 F5 **Haradzishcha** Belarus
138 F5 **Haradzyeya** Belarus
117 E4 **Haraiya** *Uttar Prad.* India
124 C4 **Ḩarajā** Saudi Arabia
102 J5 **Haramachi** Japan
116 C2 **Haramukh** *mt.* Jammu and Kashmir
Haran Turkey *see* **Harran**
138 G4 **Harany** Belarus
123 H4 **Harappa Road** Pak.
213 F3 **Harare** Zimbabwe
215 E3 **Ha Rasebi** S. Africa
125 F4 **Ḩarāsīs, Jiddat al** *des.* Oman
175 K5 **Harasiuki** Pol.
122 C4 **Harāt** Iran
208 D2 **Haraze-Mangueigne** Chad
169 E4 **Harbarnsen** Ger.
206 C5 **Harbel** Liberia
100 C3 **Harbin** *Heilong.* China
171 C3 **Harbke** Ger.
151 I3 **Harbledown** *Kent, England* U.K.
123 F4 **Harboi Hills** Pak.
156 C3 **Harbonnières** France
227 F4 **Harbor Beach** *MI* U.S.A.
226 E3 **Harbor Springs** *MI* U.S.A.
225 K4 **Harbour Breton** *Nfld.* Can.
173 E3 **Harburg (Schwaben)** Ger.
151 F2 **Harbury** *Warwickshire, England* U.K.
241 K5 **Harcuvar Mountains** *AZ* U.S.A.
178 A3 **Hard** Austria
125 E4 **Ḩarḑah, Wādī** *r.* Yemen
116 D5 **Harda Khas** *Madh. Prad.* India
142 B1 **Hardanger** *reg.* Norway
142 A2 **Hardangerfjorden** *sea chan.* Norway
212 C5 **Hardap** *admin. reg.* Namibia
212 C5 **Hardap Dam** Namibia
141 I3 **Hardbakke** Norway
231 D5 **Hardeeville** *SC* U.S.A.
179 G2 **Hardegg** Austria
169 E4 **Hardegsen** Ger.
156 B2 **Hardelot-Plage** France
95 F1 **Harden, Bukit** *mt.* Indon.
164 F2 **Hardenberg** Neth.
164 E2 **Harderwijk** Neth.
87 C4 **Hardey** *r. W.A.* Austr.
172 D2 **Hardheim** Ger.
236 F4 **Hardin** *IL* U.S.A.
238 F2 **Hardin** *MT* U.S.A.
86 C4 **Harding** *r. W.A.* Austr.
215 G4 **Harding** S. Africa
234 D3 **Harding Lakes** *NJ* U.S.A.
87 C5 **Harding Range** *hills W.A.* Austr.
151 G2 **Hardingstone** *Northamptonshire, England* U.K.
164 D3 **Hardinxveld-Giessendam** Neth.
223 I4 **Hardisty** *Alta* Can.
116 E4 **Hardoi** *Uttar Prad.* India
172 C3 **Hardt** Ger.
Hardwar *Uttar Prad.* India *see* **Haridwar**
231 D5 **Hardwick** *GA* U.S.A.
233 G2 **Hardwick** *VT* U.S.A.
234 C1 **Hardwood Ridge** *PA* U.S.A.
237 F4 **Hardy** *AR* U.S.A.
Hardy, Mount *North I.* N.Z. *see* **Rangipoua**
225 K3 **Hare Bay** *Nfld.* Can.
151 G3 **Harefield** *Greater London, England* U.K.
149 F2 **Hare Hill** *hill Scotland* U.K.
140 I3 **Hareid** Norway
165 C4 **Harelbeke** Belgium
164 F1 **Haren** Neth.
168 C3 **Haren (Ems)** Ger.
210 D2 **Hārer** Eth.
151 H3 **Hare Street** *Hertfordshire, England* U.K.
149 H4 **Harewood** *West Yorkshire, England* U.K.
128 B3 **Harf el Mreffi** *mt.* Lebanon
159 G2 **Harfleur** France
234 B3 **Harford County** *county MD* U.S.A.
107 H1 **Hargant** *Nei Mongol* China
Hargeisa Somalia *see* **Hargeysa**
172 B2 **Hargesheim** Ger.
210 E2 **Hargeysa** Somalia
197 G2 **Harghita, Munții** *mts* Romania
197 G2 **Harghita-Mădăraș, Vârful** *mt.* Romania
203 H6 **Hargigo** Eritrea
165 E4 **Hargimont** Belgium
157 E2 **Hargnies** France
106 C4 **Har Hu** *l. Qinghai* China
216 □3c **Haría** *Lanzarote* Canary Is
124 D5 **Ḩarīb** Yemen
116 D3 **Haridwar** *Uttar Prad.* India
128 B4 **Harif, Har** *mt.* Israel
114 B3 **Harihar** *Karnataka* India
81 C5 **Harihari** *South I.* N.Z.
114 B3 **Hariharpur** *Karnataka* India
116 B5 **Harij** *Gujarat* India
138 D2 **Hari kurk** *sea chan.* Estonia
128 C1 **Ḩārim** Syria
104 A4 **Harima-nada** *b.* Japan
117 G5 **Haringhat** *r.* Bangl.
164 D3 **Haringvliet** *est.* Neth.
104 D2 **Harinoki-dake** *mt.* Japan
114 C4 **Haripad** *Kerala* India
123 H3 **Haripur** Pak.
128 C3 **Ḩarīr, Wādī adh** *r.* Syria
123 E2 **Hari Rūd** *r.* Afgh./Iran
141 K3 **Härjåsjön** Sweden
141 M3 **Harjavalta** Fin.
141 K3 **Härjedalen** *reg.* Sweden
176 F4 **Harka** Hungary
177 I5 **Harkakötöny** Hungary
140 K3 **Hårkan** *r.* Sweden
177 H6 **Harkány** Hungary
236 E3 **Harlan** *IA* U.S.A.
232 B6 **Harlan** *KY* U.S.A.
197 H2 **Hârlău** Romania
150 C2 **Harlech** *Gwynedd, Wales* U.K.
238 E1 **Harlem** *MT* U.S.A.
151 I2 **Harleston** *Norfolk, England* U.K.
234 C2 **Harleysville** *PA* U.S.A.
164 E1 **Harlingen** Neth.
237 D7 **Harlingen** *TX* U.S.A.
151 G3 **Harlington** *Bedfordshire, England* U.K.
151 H3 **Harlow** *Essex, England* U.K.
238 E2 **Harlowton** *MT* U.S.A.
156 D3 **Harly** France
232 D5 **Harman** *WV* U.S.A.
199 F2 **Harmancık** Turkey
199 F3 **Harmanlı** Turkey
179 H2 **Harmannsdorf** Austria
234 B3 **Harmans** *MD* U.S.A.
164 D2 **Harmelen** Neth.
233 □I2 **Harmony** *ME* U.S.A.
226 A4 **Harmony** *MN* U.S.A.
234 C2 **Harmony** *NJ* U.S.A.
168 F1 **Harmsdorf** *Schleswig-Holstein* Ger.
168 F2 **Harmsdorf** *Schleswig-Holstein* Ger.
114 C3 **Harnahalli** *Karnataka* India
114 B2 **Harnai** *Mahar.* India
123 F4 **Harnai** Pak.
156 C2 **Harnes** France
238 C3 **Harney Basin** *OR* U.S.A.
140 L3 **Härnösand** Sweden
106 B1 **Har Nuur** *l.* Mongolia
183 H2 **Haro** Spain
232 B6 **Harold** *KY* U.S.A.
146 □H1 **Haroldswick** *Shetland, Scotland* U.K.
157 G4 **Haroué** France
114 B3 **Harpanahalli** *Karnataka* India
151 G3 **Harpenden** *Hertfordshire, England* U.K.
206 D5 **Harper** Liberia
237 D4 **Harper** *KS* U.S.A.
222 H3 **Harper Creek** *r. Alta* Can.
232 E5 **Harpers Ferry** *WV* U.S.A.
151 G2 **Harpole** *Northamptonshire, England* U.K.
168 D3 **Harpstedt** Ger.
Harqin Qi *Nei Mongol* China *see* **Jinshan**
Harqin Zuoqi Mongolzu Zizhixian *Liaoning* China *see* **Dachengzi**
241 K5 **Harquahala Mountains** *AZ* U.S.A.
116 D5 **Harrai** *Madh. Prad.* India
128 D1 **Harran** Turkey
124 C3 **Ḩarrāt Kishb** *lava field* Saudi Arabia
146 E2 **Harray, Loch of** *l. Scotland* U.K.
224 E3 **Harricanaw** *r. Ont./Que.* Can.
146 E5 **Harrietfield** *Perth and Kinross, Scotland* U.K.
151 H3 **Harrietsham** *Kent, England* U.K.
235 D1 **Harriman** *NY* U.S.A.
83 H2 **Harrington** *N.S.W.* Austr.
234 C4 **Harrington** *DE* U.S.A.
233 □J2 **Harrington** *ME* U.S.A.
225 J3 **Harrington Harbour** *Que.* Can.
146 B4 **Harris** *reg. Scotland* U.K.
82 C2 **Harris, Lake** *salt flat S.A.* Austr.
84 B5 **Harris, Mount** *N.T.* Austr.
146 A4 **Harris, Sound of** *sea chan. Scotland* U.K.
215 F2 **Harrisburg** S. Africa
237 F5 **Harrisburg** *AR* U.S.A.
237 F4 **Harrisburg** *IL* U.S.A.
236 C3 **Harrisburg** *NE* U.S.A.
232 B5 **Harrisburg** *OH* U.S.A.
227 I5 **Harrisburg** *PA* U.S.A.
168 E1 **Harrislee** Ger.
87 C7 **Harrismith** *W.A.* Austr.
215 G3 **Harrismith** S. Africa
81 B6 **Harris Mountains** *South I.* N.Z.
237 E4 **Harrison** *AR* U.S.A.
226 E3 **Harrison** *MI* U.S.A.
236 C3 **Harrison** *NE* U.S.A.
235 E2 **Harrison** *NY* U.S.A.
237 F6 **Harrisonburg** *LA* U.S.A.
232 D5 **Harrisonburg** *VA* U.S.A.
234 B3 **Harrisonville** *MD* U.S.A.
236 E4 **Harrisonville** *MO* U.S.A.
227 G4 **Harriston** *Ont.* Can.
227 F3 **Harrisville** *MI* U.S.A.
233 F2 **Harrisville** *NY* U.S.A.
232 C5 **Harrisville** *WV* U.S.A.
Harrodsville *North I.* N.Z. *see* **Otorohanga**
149 H4 **Harrogate** *North Yorkshire, England* U.K.
232 B6 **Harrogate** *TN* U.S.A.
227 I3 **Harrowsmith** *Ont.* Can.
141 K3 **Harsa** Sweden
106 C5 **Har Sai Shan** *mt. Qinghai* China
177 J4 **Harsány** Hungary
168 E2 **Harsefeld** Ger.
197 G3 **Hârsești** Romania
169 D4 **Harsewinkel** Ger.
122 A3 **Harsīn** Iran
126 E2 **Harşit** *r.* Turkey
171 C4 **Harsleben** Ger.
197 H3 **Hârșova** Romania
140 L2 **Harsprånget** Sweden
140 L1 **Harstad** Norway
151 H2 **Harston** *Cambridgeshire, England* U.K.
116 D5 **Harsud** *Madh. Prad.* India
169 E3 **Harsum** Ger.
220 E3 **Hart** *r. Y.T.* Can.
226 D4 **Hart** *MI* U.S.A.
82 D2 **Hart, Lake** *salt flat S.A.* Austr.
86 E3 **Hart, Mount** *hill W.A.* Austr.
177 I5 **Harta** Hungary
107 I3 **Hartao** *Liaoning* China
215 F2 **Hartbeesfontein** S. Africa
215 F1 **Hartbeespoort** S. Africa
179 G3 **Hartberg** Austria
142 B1 **Harteigan** *mt.* Norway
168 F2 **Hartenholm** Ger.
156 D3 **Hartennes-et-Taux** France
171 D5 **Hartenstein** Ger.
149 G3 **Harter Fell** *hill England* U.K.
151 H3 **Hartfield** *East Sussex, England* U.K.
206 C5 **Hartford** Liberia
233 G4 **Hartford** *CT* U.S.A.
230 C4 **Hartford** *KY* U.S.A.
226 D4 **Hartford** *MI* U.S.A.
236 D3 **Hartford** *SD* U.S.A.
226 C4 **Hartford** *WI* U.S.A.
230 C3 **Hartford City** *IN* U.S.A.
171 D4 **Hartha** Ger.
172 C2 **Harthausen** Ger.
172 B4 **Hartheim** Ger.
149 F2 **Harthill** *North Lanarkshire, Scotland* U.K.
197 G3 **Hârtibaciu** *r.* Romania
178 C3 **Hart im Zillertal** Austria
236 D3 **Hartington** *NE* U.S.A.
179 E2 **Hartkirchen** Austria
225 H4 **Hartland** *N.B.* Can.
150 C4 **Hartland** *Devon, England* U.K.
233 □I2 **Hartland** *ME* U.S.A.
150 C3 **Hartland Point** *England* U.K.
150 E2 **Hartlebury** *Worcestershire, England* U.K.
149 H3 **Hartlepool** *Hartlepool, England* U.K.
149 H3 **Hartlepool** *admin. div. England* U.K.
234 A2 **Hartleton** *PA* U.S.A.
151 H3 **Hartley** *Kent, England* U.K.
237 C5 **Hartley** *TX* U.S.A.
Hartley Zimbabwe *see* **Chegutu**
222 D4 **Hartley Bay** *B.C.* Can.
151 G3 **Hartley Wintney** *Hampshire, England* U.K.
234 C3 **Hartly** *DE* U.S.A.
173 H2 **Hartmanice** Czech Rep.
171 C5 **Hartmannsdorf** Ger.
141 N3 **Hartola** Fin.
214 E3 **Harts** *r.* S. Africa
235 E1 **Hartsdale** *NY* U.S.A.
231 C5 **Hartselle** *AL* U.S.A.
173 E3 **Härtsfeld** *hills* Ger.
151 F2 **Hartshill** *Warwickshire, England* U.K.
151 F2 **Hartshorne** *Derbyshire, England* U.K.
237 E5 **Hartshorne** *OK* U.S.A.
84 C4 **Harts Range** *N.T.* Austr.
84 C4 **Harts Range** *mts N.T.* Austr.
231 D5 **Hartsville** *SC* U.S.A.
231 C4 **Hartsville** *TN* U.S.A.
215 E2 **Hartswater** S. Africa
237 E4 **Hartville** *MO* U.S.A.
232 C4 **Hartville** *OH* U.S.A.
151 G2 **Hartwell** *Northamptonshire, England* U.K.
231 D5 **Hartwell** *GA* U.S.A.
231 D5 **Hartwell Reservoir** *Georgia/S. Carolina* U.S.A.
114 C3 **Harur** *Tamil Nadu* India
106 B2 **Har Us Nuur** *l.* Mongolia
106 B1 **Har Us Nuur** *salt l.* Mongolia
106 E1 **Haruuhin Gol** *r.* Mongolia
226 C4 **Harvard** *IL* U.S.A.
239 F4 **Harvard, Mount** *CO* U.S.A.
87 B7 **Harvey** *W.A.* Austr.
225 H4 **Harvey** *N.B.* Can.
226 D2 **Harvey** *MI* U.S.A.
236 C2 **Harvey** *ND* U.S.A.
234 B1 **Harveys Lake** *PA* U.S.A.
151 F2 **Harvington** *Worcestershire, England* U.K.
151 F3 **Harwell** *Oxfordshire, England* U.K.
151 I3 **Harwich** *Essex, England* U.K.
233 H4 **Harwich Port** *MA* U.S.A.
235 E1 **Harwington** *CT* U.S.A.
83 H2 **Harwood** *N.S.W.* Austr.
149 H4 **Harworth** *Nottinghamshire, England* U.K.
116 D3 **Haryana** *state* India
136 D1 **Haryn'** *r.* Belarus
Haryn' *r.* Ukr. *see* **Horyn'**
169 F4 **Harz** *hills* Ger.
171 C4 **Harzgerode** Ger.
129 B3 **Hasan Dağı** *mt.* Turkey
126 D3 **Hasan Dağı** *mts* Turkey
Hasan Guli Turkm. *see* **Esenguly**
127 F3 **Hasankeyf** Turkey
122 D5 **Ḩasan Langī** Iran
114 C2 **Hasanparti** *Andhra Prad.* India
199 F3 **Hasanpaşa** *Burdur* Turkey
122 A2 **Ḩasan Sālārān** Iran
114 C4 **Hasanur** *Tamil Nadu* India
128 B3 **Hasbaïya** Lebanon
126 D4 **Hasbani** *r.* Lebanon
126 D3 **Hasbek** Turkey
169 C3 **Hasbergen** Ger.
146 □H1 **Hascosay** *i. Scotland* U.K.
116 E5 **Hasdo** *r. Madh. Prad.* India
169 C3 **Hase** *r.* Ger.

168 E2	**Haseldorf** Ger.
168 C3	**Haselünne** Ger.
261 H2	**Hasenkamp** Arg.
169 F5	**Hasenkopf** hill Ger.
190 C1	**Hasenmatt** mt. Switz.
106 E2	**Hashaat** Mongolia
104 C3	**Hashima** Japan
104 B4	**Hashimoto** Japan
122 B3	**Hashtgerd** Iran
122 B2	**Hashtpar** Gīlān Iran
	Hashtpar Gīlān Iran see **Tālesh**
122 A2	**Hashtrud** Iran
	Hašić Bos.-Herz. see **Srnice**
123 H4	**Hasilpur** Pak.
237 D5	**Haskell** TX U.S.A.
129 C3	**Hasköy** Turkey
179 F2	**Haslach an der Mühl** Austria
172 C3	**Haslach im Kinzigtal** Ger.
149 H4	**Hasland** Derbyshire, England U.K.
143 F4	**Hasle** Bornholm Denmark
190 C1	**Hasle** Switz.
151 Q3	**Haslemere** Surrey, England U.K.
142 D4	**Haslev** Denmark
149 G4	**Haslingden** Lancashire, England U.K.
168 E2	**Hasloh** Ger.
177 L5	**Hăşmaş** Romania
197 G2	**Hăşmaşul Mare** mt. Romania
163 A5	**Hasparren** France
137 H5	**Haspra** Ukr.
129 C4	**Hasretpınar** Turkey
128 C1	**Haşş, Jabal** al hills Syria
128 C1	**Hassa** Turkey
114 C3	**Hassan** Karnataka India
169 F5	**Haßberge** hills Ger.
168 E3	**Haßbergen** Ger.
168 E3	**Hassel** (Weser) Ger.
169 F4	**Hasselfelde** Ger.
165 E4	**Hasselt** Belgium
164 F2	**Hasselt** Neth.
169 F5	**Haßfurt** Ger.
204 B4	**Hassi Aridal** well Western Sahara
204 B5	**Hassi Doughà** well Western Sahara
205 G3	**Hassi Messaoud** Alg.
170 E2	**Haßleben** Ger.
171 C6	**Haßleben** Ger.
143 E3	**Hässleholm** Sweden
172 C2	**Haßloch** Ger.
172 D2	**Haßmersheim** Ger.
143 G1	**Hästbo** Sweden
169 E3	**Haste** Ger.
165 D4	**Hastière-Lavaux** Belgium
83 F4	**Hastings** Vic. Austr.
83 H2	**Hastings** Qld Austr.
227 I3	**Hastings** Ont. Can.
80 F3	**Hastings** North I. N.Z.
151 H4	**Hastings** East Sussex, England U.K.
226 E4	**Hastings** MI U.S.A.
226 A3	**Hastings** MN U.S.A.
236 D3	**Hastings** NE U.S.A.
105 F3	**Hasuda** Japan
177 H2	**Hať** Czech Rep.
177 L3	**Hať** Slovakia
117 E4	**Hata** Uttar Prad. India
106 D2	**Hatansuudal** Mongolia
	Hatay Turkey see **Antakya**
128 C1	**Hatay** prov. Turkey
234 C2	**Hatboro** PA U.S.A.
241 K3	**Hatch** UT U.S.A.
84 C4	**Hatches Creek** N.T. Austr.
237 F5	**Hatchie** r. TN U.S.A.
197 F3	**Haţeg** Romania
81 F4	**Hatepe** North I. N.Z.
102 □1	**Hateruma-jima** i. Japan
83 E3	**Hatfield** N.S.W. Austr.
151 G3	**Hatfield** Hertfordshire, England U.K.
149 I4	**Hatfield** South Yorkshire, England U.K.
234 C2	**Hatfield** PA U.S.A.
151 H3	**Hatfield Broad Oak** Essex, England U.K.
151 H3	**Hatfield Peverel** Essex, England U.K.
106 D1	**Hatgal** Mongolia
150 C4	**Hatherleigh** Devon, England U.K.
151 F2	**Hathern** Leicestershire, England U.K.
149 H4	**Hathersage** Derbyshire, England U.K.
116 D4	**Hathras** Uttar Prad. India
97 D5	**Ha Tiên** Vietnam
96 D3	**Ha Tinh** Vietnam
	Hatisar Bhutan see **Gelephu**
250 D3	**Hato** Curaçao Col.
247 E3	**Hato Mayor** Dom. Rep.
116 D5	**Hat Piplia** Madh. Prad. India
	Hatra Iraq see **Al Ḩaḑr**
103 F6	**Hatsukaichi** Japan
116 D4	**Hatta** Madh. Prad. India
116 E5	**Hatta** Madh. Prad. India
83 E3	**Hattah** Vic. Austr.
164 F2	**Hattem** Neth.
173 F3	**Hattenhofen** Ger.
231 F5	**Hatteras, Cape** NC U.S.A.
264 E4	**Hatteras Abyssal Plain** sea feature S. Atlantic Ocean
169 D5	**Hattersheim am Main** Ger.
169 C5	**Hattert** Ger.
140 K2	**Hattfjelldal** Norway
115 D2	**Hatti** r. India
237 F6	**Hattiesburg** MS U.S.A.
169 C4	**Hattingen** Ger.
146 G4	**Hatton** Aberdeenshire, Scotland U.K.
151 F2	**Hatton** Derbyshire, England U.K.
95 G1	**Hatton, Gunung** hill Sabah Malaysia
169 F4	**Hattorf am Harz** Ger.
100 C4	**Hattori-gawa** r. Japan
97 B4	**Hattras Passage** Myanmar
168 E1	**Hattstedt** Ger.
141 N3	**Hattula** Fin.
177 I4	**Hatvan** Hungary
97 C6	**Hat Yai** Thai.
172 C2	**Hatzenbühl** Ger.
179 H4	**Hatzendorf** Austria
169 D5	**Hatzfeld (Eder)** Ger.
156 C2	**Haubourdin** France
210 E2	**Haud** reg. Eth.
172 B2	**Hauenstein** Ger.
142 B2	**Hauge** Norway
142 A2	**Haugesund** Norway
150 E2	**Haughton** Staffordshire, England U.K.
97 D5	**Hàu Giang, Sông** r. Vietnam
179 H2	**Haugsdorf** Austria
141 N3	**Hauho** Fin.
80 E3	**Hauhungaroa** mt. North I. N.Z.
80 E3	**Hauhungaroa Range** mts North I. N.Z.
140 N2	**Haukipudas** Fin.
140 O3	**Haukivesi** l. Fin.
141 N3	**Haukivuori** Fin.
164 F1	**Haulerwijk** Neth.
223 J4	**Haultain** r. Sask. Can.
80 F3	**Haumoana** North I. N.Z.
235 G2	**Hauppauge** NY U.S.A.
170 F3	**Hauptgraben** r. Ger.
215 F2	**Hauptrus** S. Africa
171 E4	**Hauptspree** r. Ger.
80 F3	**Haupuni Point** North I. N.Z.
81 A7	**Hauroko, Lake** South I. N.Z.
179 E3	**Haus** Austria
172 A3	**Hausach** Ger.
171 D4	**Hausdorf** Ger.
173 F2	**Hausen** Bayern Ger.
173 H2	**Hausen** Bayern Ger.
173 E1	**Hausen bei Würzburg** Ger.
172 H4	**Hausen im Wiesental** Ger.
172 C4	**Häusern** Ger.
173 H4	**Hausham** Ger.
138 E1	**Hausjärvi** Fin.
173 K4	**Hausleiten** Austria
179 G4	**Hausmannstätten** Austria
190 E2	**Hausstock** mt. Switz.
204 D3	**Haut Atlas** mts Morocco
	Haut-Congo prov. Dem. Rep. Congo see **Orientale**
157 G3	**Haut-du-Them-Château-Lambert** France
157 F5	**Haute-Amance** France
192 B2	**Haute-Corse** dept Corse France
160 D2	**Hautecourt-Romanèche** France

162 D2	**Hautefort** France
163 D5	**Haute-Garonne** dept Midi-Pyrénées France
206 C4	**Haute-Guinée** admin. reg. Guinea
208 D3	**Haute-Kotto** pref. C.A.R.
161 B3	**Haute-Loire** dept Auvergne France
160 E3	**Hauteluce** France
157 F4	**Haute-Marne** dept Champagne-Ardenne France
156 B3	**Haute-Normandie** admin. reg. France
225 G3	**Hauterive** Que. Can.
161 D3	**Hauterives** France
161 E4	**Hautes-Alpes** dept Provence-Alpes-Côte-d'Azur France
157 G5	**Haute-Saône** dept Franche-Comté France
157 F5	**Haute-Saône, Plateau de** la France
160 E2	**Haute-Savoie** dept Rhône-Alpes France
165 F4	**Hautes Fagnes** moorland Belgium
163 C5	**Hautes-Pyrénées** dept Midi-Pyrénées France
162 B2	**Hauteurs de la Gâtine** reg. France
162 D3	**Haute-Vienne** dept Limousin France
156 D3	**Hautevillers** France
206 E4	**Haute-Volta** country Africa see **Burkina**
165 E4	**Haut-Fays** Belgium
160 C2	**Haut-Folin** hill France
208 E3	**Haut-Mbomou** pref. C.A.R.
156 D2	**Hautmont** France
208 B5	**Haut-Ogooué** prov. Gabon
157 H5	**Haut-Rhin** dept Alsace France
159 I3	**Hauts-de-Seine** dept France
205 E2	**Hauts Plateaux** Alg.
	Haut-Zaïre admin. reg. Dem. Rep. Congo see **Orientale**
240 □	**Hauula** HI U.S.A.
	Hauvo Fin. see **Nagu**
81 A4	**Hauwai** South I. N.Z.
163 B5	**Haux** France
173 H3	**Hauzenberg** Ger.
226 B5	**Havana** Cuba see **La Habana**
151 G4	**Havana** IL U.S.A.
197 H1	**Havârna** Romania
171 C3	**Havel** r. Ger.
165 E4	**Havelange** Belgium
170 D3	**Havelberg** Ger.
123 H4	**Haveli** Pak.
123 H3	**Haveliān** Pak.
170 D3	**Havelländisches Luch** marsh Ger.
227 I3	**Havelock** Ont. Can.
81 D4	**Havelock** South I. N.Z.
81 C5	**Havelock** r. South I. N.Z.
	Havelock Swaziland see **Bulembu**
231 E5	**Havelock** NC U.S.A.
84 C2	**Havelock Falls** N.T. Austr.
80 F3	**Havelock North** North I. N.Z.
164 F2	**Havelte** Neth.
234 D4	**Haven** KS U.S.A.
142 E3	**Haverdal** Sweden
151 H2	**Haverfordwest** Pembrokeshire, Wales U.K.
151 H2	**Haverhill** Suffolk, England U.K.
233 H3	**Haverhill** MA U.S.A.
114 B3	**Haveri** Karnataka India
169 F3	**Haverlah** Ger.
141 K3	**Haverö** Sweden
165 E4	**Haversin** Belgium
235 E1	**Haverstraw** NY U.S.A.
234 C2	**Havertown** PA U.S.A.
	Havîrna Romania see **Havârna**
177 H2	**Havířov** Czech Rep.
169 C4	**Havixbeck** Ger.
176 G2	**Havlíčkův Brod** Czech Rep.
140 N1	**Havøysund** Norway
177 J2	**Havran** mt. Slovakia
199 G2	**Havran** Turkey
199 E2	**Havran** r. Turkey
165 D4	**Havré** Belgium
238 E1	**Havre** MT U.S.A.
225 I4	**Havre Aubert** Que. Can.
234 B3	**Havre de Grace** MD U.S.A.
225 I3	**Havre-St-Pierre** Que. Can.
137 I3	**Havrylivka** Dnipropetrovs'ka Oblast' Ukr.
137 I3	**Havrylivka** Kharkivs'ka Oblast' Ukr.
197 H5	**Havsa** Turkey
128 B1	**Havutlu** Turkey
199 E2	**Havza** Turkey
240 □B1	**Hawaii** i. HI U.S.A.
240 □D1	**Hawaii** state U.S.A.
266 H4	**Hawaiian Islands** N. Pacific Ocean
266 H4	**Hawaiian Ridge** sea feature N. Pacific Ocean
127 H5	**Ḩawallī** Kuwait
	Hawar i. The Gulf see **Huwār**
150 D1	**Hawarden** Flintshire, Wales U.K.
81 B6	**Hawea, Lake** South I. N.Z.
80 D3	**Hawera** North I. N.Z.
149 G3	**Hawes** North Yorkshire, England U.K.
230 C4	**Hawesville** KY U.S.A.
146 F6	**Hawick** Scottish Borders, Scotland U.K.
81 B6	**Hawkdun Range** mts South I. N.Z.
80 F3	**Hawke Bay** North I. N.Z.
82 D2	**Hawker** S.A. Austr.
82 E2	**Hawkers Gate** N.S.W. Austr.
225 J3	**Hawke's Bay** Nfld. Can.
80 F3	**Hawke's Bay** admin. reg. North I. N.Z.
83 F2	**Hawkesbury** Qld Austr.
241 L4	**Hawkesbury** South Gloucestershire, England U.K.
226 B4	**Hawkeye** IA U.S.A.
151 H3	**Hawkhurst** Kent, England U.K.
241 K4	**Hawk Inlet** AK U.S.A.
226 F1	**Hawk Junction** Ont. Can.
231 C5	**Haw Knob** mt. N. Carolina/Tennessee U.S.A.
246 C1	**Hawksbill Cay** i. Bahamas
233 □J2	**Hawkshaw** N.B. Can.
149 G3	**Hawkshead** Cumbria, England U.K.
238 F3	**Hawk Springs** WY U.S.A.
81 D5	**Hawkswood** South I. N.Z.
151 H3	**Hawkwell** Essex, England U.K.
85 G5	**Hawkwood** Qld Austr.
	Hawler Iraq see **Arbīl**
151 G3	**Hawley** Hampshire, England U.K.
234 C1	**Hawley** PA U.S.A.
235 E1	**Hawleyville** CT U.S.A.
138 E5	**Hawnby** North Yorkshire, England U.K.
149 H4	**Haworth** West Yorkshire, England U.K.
151 G4	**Haxby** York, England U.K.
149 I4	**Haxey** North Lincolnshire, England U.K.
83 F3	**Hay** N.S.W. Austr.
222 F2	**Hay** r. Can.
84 C5	**Hay** r. N.T. Austr.
140 L2	**Hay, Mount** N.T. Austr.
100 A4	**Hayachine-san** mt. Japan
106 D3	**Haya-gawa** r. Japan
103 F6	**Haya-kawa** r. Japan
105 F3	**Hayama** Japan
157 G3	**Hayange** France
156 D3	**Haybes** France
137 I4	**Haychur** r. Ukr.
226 A3	**Hay Creek** MN U.S.A.

128 B4	**Haydān, Wādī al** r. Jordan
122 A2	**Ḩaydarābād** Iran
199 G2	**Haydarlı** Turkey
199 G2	**Haydaroba** Turkey
241 L5	**Hayden** AZ U.S.A.
238 F3	**Hayden** CO U.S.A.
238 C2	**Hayden** ID U.S.A.
149 G4	**Haydock** Merseyside, England U.K.
149 G3	**Haydon Bridge** Northumberland, England U.K.
151 F3	**Haydon Wick** Swindon, England U.K.
223 M3	**Hayes** r. Man. Can.
221 I3	**Hayes** r. Nunavut Can.
236 D3	**Hayes Center** NE U.S.A.
84 B2	**Hayes Creek** N.T. Austr.
221 M2	**Hayes Halvø** pen. Greenland
231 D5	**Hayesville** NC U.S.A.
149 H4	**Hayfield** Derbyshire, England U.K.
226 A4	**Hayfield** MN U.S.A.
172 D3	**Hayingen** Ger.
125 G2	**Hayl** Oman
107 G2	**Haylaastay** Mongolia
150 B4	**Hayle** Cornwall, England U.K.
150 B4	**Hayle** r. England U.K.
124 C2	**Haymā'** Oman
126 D3	**Haymana** Turkey
85 G4	**Hayman Island** Qld Austr.
199 H5	**Haymarket** VA U.S.A.
138 G4	**Haynauz** r. Belarus
237 E5	**Haynesville** LA U.S.A.
234 A4	**Haynesville** AL U.S.A.
128 B3	**Hefa** Israel
150 D2	**Hay-on-Wye** Powys, Wales U.K.
	Hayotboshi Toghi mt. Uzbek. see **Khayatbashi, Gora**
199 E1	**Hayrabolu** Turkey
129 B3	**Hayrat** Turkey
222 H2	**Hay River** N.W.T. Can.
222 H2	**Hay River Reserve** N.W.T. Can.
236 D4	**Hays** KS U.S.A.
238 E1	**Hays** MT U.S.A.
124 C5	**Hays** Yemen
202 B2	**Haysyah, Sabkhat al** salt pan Libya
232 B6	**Haysi** VA U.S.A.
262 N1	**Hays Mountains** Antarctica
236 C3	**Hay Springs** NE U.S.A.
237 D4	**Haysville** KS U.S.A.
136 D3	**Haysyn** Ukr.
143 D1	**Haytî** SD U.S.A.
149 G3	**Hayton** Cumbria, England U.K.
149 I4	**Hayton** East Riding of Yorkshire, England U.K.
136 E3	**Hayvoron** Ukr.
240 F3	**Hayward** CA U.S.A.
226 B2	**Hayward** WI U.S.A.
151 G4	**Haywards Heath** West Sussex, England U.K.
123 F3	**Hazarajat** reg. Afgh.
232 B6	**Hazard** KY U.S.A.
117 F5	**Hazaribag** Bihar India
117 F5	**Hazaribagh Range** mts Bihar India
122 D2	**Hazar Masjed, Kūh-e** mts Iran
156 C2	**Hazebrouck** France
149 G4	**Hazel Grove** Greater Manchester, England U.K.
226 C3	**Hazelhurst** WI U.S.A.
222 E4	**Hazelton** B.C. Can.
236 C2	**Hazelton** ND U.S.A.
221 C2	**Hazen Strait** N.W.T./Nunavut Can.
231 D6	**Hazlehurst** GA U.S.A.
237 F6	**Hazlehurst** MS U.S.A.
151 G3	**Hazlemere** Buckinghamshire, England U.K.
235 D2	**Hazlet** NJ U.S.A.
234 C2	**Hazleton** PA U.S.A.
86 F4	**Hazlett, Lake** salt flat W.A. Austr.
177 K2	**Hažín** Slovakia
176 B1	**Hazro** Czech Rep.
123 H3	**Hazro** Pak.
127 F3	**Hazro** Turkey
261 F4	**H. Bouchard** Arg.
151 H2	**Headcorn** Kent, England U.K.
151 H3	**Headley** Hampshire, England U.K.
147 B3	**Headford** Rep. of Ireland
84 D4	**Headingly** Qld Austr.
151 G3	**Headley** Hampshire, England U.K.
82 B2	**Head of Bight** b. S.A. Austr.
146 D4	**Heads of Ayr** hd Scotland U.K.
226 C3	**Headford Junction** WI U.S.A.
86 B4	**Healabhal Bheag** hill Scotland U.K.
240 F2	**Healdsburg** CA U.S.A.
237 D5	**Healdton** OK U.S.A.
83 F4	**Healesville** Vic. Austr.
149 H4	**Healing** North East Lincolnshire, England U.K.
232 D6	**Healing Springs** VA U.S.A.
149 H4	**Heanor** Derbyshire, England U.K.
81 E4	**Heaphy Track** South I. N.Z.
150 C3	**Heanton Punchardon** Devon, England U.K.
226 E4	**Hearne** TX U.S.A.
224 D4	**Hearst** Ont. Can.
262 T2	**Heart Island** Antarctica
236 C2	**Heart** r. ND U.S.A.
252 C3	**Heath** r. Bol./Peru
149 H4	**Heath Derbyshire, England U.K.**
83 F4	**Heathcote** Vic. Austr.
151 H4	**Heathfield** East Sussex, England U.K.
151 G3	**Heathrow airport** England U.K.
232 E6	**Heathsville** VA U.S.A.
237 E5	**Heavener** OK U.S.A.
237 D7	**Hebbronville** TX U.S.A.
85 G2	**Hebbville** Qld Austr.
149 G4	**Hebden Bridge** West Yorkshire, England U.K.
107 G4	**Hebei** prov. China
83 F2	**Hebel** Qld Austr.
224 L4	**Heber** AZ U.S.A.
241 J5	**Heber** AZ U.S.A.
237 E5	**Heber Springs** AR U.S.A.
173 G3	**Herbertsfelden** Ger.
173 E2	**Hebertshausen** Ger.
107 G5	**Hebi** Henan China
146 B3	**Hebrides, Sea of the** Scotland U.K.
225 I1	**Hebron** Nfld. Can.
235 F1	**Hebron** CT U.S.A.
230 C5	**Hebron** IN U.S.A.
233 F5	**Hebron** MD U.S.A.
236 C2	**Hebron** ND U.S.A.
236 D3	**Hebron** NE U.S.A.
128 B4	**Hebron** West Bank
	Hebros r. Greece/Turkey see **Evros**
143 G2	**Heby** Sweden
222 D4	**Hecate Strait** B.C. Can.
243 H4	**Hecelchakán** Mex.
	Hecheng Jiangxi China see **Zixi**
	Hecheng Zhejiang China see **Qingtian**
108 C2	**Hechi** Guangxi China
172 C3	**Hechingen** Ger.
186 C2	**Hecho** Spain
165 E3	**Hechtel** Belgium
173 G3	**Hechthausen** Ger.
108 C2	**Hechuan** Chongqing China
	Hechuan Jiangxi China see **Yongxing**
197 H2	**Heckelberg** Ger.
151 G2	**Heckington** Lincolnshire, England U.K.
171 C4	**Hecklingen** Ger.
128 B2	**Hecktown** PA U.S.A.
236 C2	**Hector** MN U.S.A.
232 E1	**Hector, Mount** North I. N.Z.
81 E4	**Hector, Mount** North I. N.Z.
143 D1	**Hede** Jiangsu China see **Sheyang**
143 F2	**Hede** Sweden
141 K3	**Hede** Sweden
164 E2	**Hedel** Neth.
143 J4	**Hedemora** Sweden

140 M2	**Hedenäset** Sweden
142 C4	**Hedensted** Denmark
169 F3	**Hedeper** Ger.
171 C4	**Hedersleben** Ger.
143 G1	**Hedesunda** Sweden
238 C2	**He Devil Mountain** ID U.S.A.
151 F4	**Hedge End** Hampshire, England U.K.
81 B7	**Hedgehope** South I. N.Z.
142 D1	**Hedmark** county Norway
149 I4	**Hedon** East Riding of Yorkshire, England U.K.
168 C1	**Heede** Ger.
164 E2	**Heeg** Neth.
169 C3	**Heek** Ger.
165 E3	**Heel** Neth.
168 D2	**Heemsen** Ger.
164 D2	**Heemskerk** Neth.
164 D2	**Heemstede** Neth.
165 D3	**Heer** Belgium
164 F2	**Heerde** Neth.
164 C2	**Heerenveen** Neth.
164 D2	**Heerhugowaard** Neth.
140 □	**Heer Land** reg. Svalbard
165 E4	**Heerlen** Neth.
165 E3	**Heers** Belgium
164 E3	**Heesch** Neth.
168 E2	**Heeslingen** Ger.
169 E3	**Heeßen** Ger.
164 E3	**Heeswijk** Neth.
168 D2	**Heeze** Neth.
128 B3	**Hefa** Israel
107 F2	**Hefei** Anhui China
108 D2	**Hefeng** Hubei China
234 C3	**Heflin** AL U.S.A.
100 D3	**Hegang** Heilong. China
114 C3	**Heggadadevankote** Karnataka India
141 J3	**Heggenes** Norway
169 E4	**Hehlen** Ger.
	Heidan r. Jordan see **Haydān, Wādī al**
171 C4	**Heidberg** hill Ger.
168 E1	**Heide** Ger.
173 F2	**Heideck** Ger.
172 C2	**Heidelberg** Ger.
215 G2	**Heidelberg** Gauteng S. Africa
214 C6	**Heidelberg** W. Cape S. Africa
169 D4	**Heiden** Ger.
190 E1	**Heiden** Switz.
168 E2	**Heidenau** Niedersachsen Ger.
171 E5	**Heidenau** Sachsen Ger.
173 E2	**Heidenheim** Ger.
173 E3	**Heidenheim an der Brenz** Ger.
179 G2	**Heidenreichstein** Austria
215 J2	**Heidelberg** PA U.S.A.
102 J4	**Hei-gawa** r. Japan
169 H3	**Heigenbrücken** Ger.
149 H3	**Heighington** Darlington, England U.K.
149 I4	**Heighington** Lincolnshire, England U.K.
100 C2	**Heihe** Heilong. China
168 F1	**Heikendorf** Ger.
215 F2	**Heilbron** S. Africa
172 D2	**Heilbronn** Ger.
164 D2	**Heiloo** Neth.
173 E2	**Heilsbronn** Ger.
157 E4	**Heiltz-le-Maurupt** France
	Heilungkiang prov. China see **Heilongjiang**
164 D2	**Heiloo** Neth.
165 E3	**Heinberg** Belgium
173 F2	**Heimbach** Ger.
179 G4	**Heimbuchenthal** Ger.
169 F4	**Heimburg** Ger.
172 D4	**Heimenkirch** Ger.
173 G3	**Heimertingen** Ger.
179 G4	**Heimschuh** Austria
169 E4	**Heimsen** Ger.
164 E4	**Heinade** Ger.
173 G3	**Heinäveden** Fin.
169 E4	**Heinebach (Alheim)** Ger.
168 E2	**Heinebrück** Ger.
171 F3	**Heinersdorf** Ger.
169 F3	**Heinersreuth** Ger.
165 D3	**Heinkenszand** Neth.
164 F2	**Heino** Neth.
141 N3	**Heinola** Fin.
137 I6	**Heinrichswalde** Rus. Fed. see **Slavsk**
169 B4	**Heinsberg** Ger.
97 B4	**Heinze Islands** Myanmar
173 H3	**Heishan** Liaoning China
107 H1	**Heishantou** Nei Mongol China
108 B1	**Heishui** Sichuan China
128 B3	**Heisker Islands** Scotland U.K. see **Monach Islands**
165 D3	**Heist-op-den-Berg** Belgium
108 E2	**Heitan, Gebel** hill Egypt
172 B4	**Heitersheim** Ger.
107 G4	**Heituo Shan** mt. Shanxi China
107 □	**Hejaz** reg. Saudi Arabia see **Hijaz**
107 H4	**Hejian** Hebei China
108 C2	**Hejiang** Sichuan China
109 D2	**He Jiang** r. China
107 F3	**Hejin** Shanxi China
107 G5	**Hebi** Henan China
146 B3	**Hejnice** Czech Rep.
177 N7	**Hejőbába** Hungary
156 E2	**Hekelgem** Belgium
126 E3	**Hekimhan** Turkey
104 C4	**Hekla** vol. Iceland
104 C3	**Heko-san** mt. Japan
108 C2	**Hekou** Gansu China
109 D2	**Hekou** Hubei China
190 D1	**Hekou** Jiangxi China see **Yanshan**
	Hekou Sichuan China see **Yajiang**
108 B4	**Hekou** Yunnan China
215 H4	**Hekpoort** S. Africa
143 H4	**Hel** Pol.
188 G3	**Helagsfjället** mt. Sweden
164 D2	**Helden** Neth.
146 A3	**Helen** i. Palau
241 M1	**Helen, Mount** NV U.S.A.
188 F3	**Helena** AL U.S.A.
232 B4	**Helena** MT U.S.A.
113 □1	**Helengeli** i. N. Male Maldives
146 D5	**Helen's Bay** Northern Ireland U.K.
146 D5	**Hensburgh** Argyll and Bute, Scotland U.K.
179 F3	**Helenschlag** Austria
80 □	**Helensville** North I. N.Z.
142 C3	**Helgenæs** pen. Denmark
168 C1	**Helgoland** i. Ger.

168 C1	**Helgoland** i. Ger.
168 D1	**Helgoländer Bucht** b. Ger.
140 L3	**Helgum** Sweden
151 H2	**Helhoughton** Norfolk, England U.K.
	Heligoland i. Ger. see **Helgoland**
	Heligoland Bight b. Ger. see **Helgoländer Bucht**
	Helixi Anhui China see **Ningguo**
	Hellas country Europe see **Greece**
122 B4	**Helleh** r. Iran
164 F2	**Hellendoorn** Neth.
169 B5	**Hellenthal** Ger.
169 C3	**Hellern** Ger.
164 D3	**Hellevoetsluis** Neth.
149 G3	**Hellifield** North Yorkshire, England U.K.
185 I2	**Hellín** Spain
151 H4	**Hellingly** East Sussex, England U.K.
	Hell-Ville Madag. see **Andoany**
240 O3	**Hellwege** Ger.
123 E4	**Helmand** r. Afgh.
123 E4	**Helmand** prov. Afgh.
	Helmantica Spain see **Salamanca**
171 C5	**Helmbrechts** Ger.
171 C4	**Helme** r. Ger.
164 E3	**Helmond** Neth.
146 E3	**Helmsdale** Highland, Scotland U.K.
146 E2	**Helmsdale** r. Scotland U.K.
149 H3	**Helmsley** North Yorkshire, England U.K.
172 D2	**Helmstadt** Ger.
171 C3	**Helmstedt** Ger.
213 □K2	**Helodrano Antongila** b. Madag.
100 D4	**Helong** Jilin China
156 F2	**Helpe** r. France
241 L2	**Helper** UT U.S.A.
215 H3	**Helpmekaar** S. Africa
151 G2	**Helpringham** Lincolnshire, England U.K.
169 E3	**Helpsen** Ger.
	Helter Berge hills Ger.
149 H3	**Helsby** Cheshire, England U.K.
168 E2	**Helse** Ger.
143 D3	**Helsingborg** Sweden
142 E3	**Helsinge** Denmark
	Helsingfors Fin. see **Helsinki**
141 N3	**Helsinki** Fin.
150 B4	**Helston** Cornwall, England U.K.
172 B2	**Heltersberg** Ger.
199 E2	**Helvacı** Turkey
149 F3	**Helvellyn** hill England U.K.
	Helvetic Republic country Europe see **Switzerland**
164 E3	**Helvoirt** Neth.
203 F2	**Helwân** Egypt
156 D2	**Hem** France
173 F2	**Hemau** Ger.
	Hembudu i. S. Male Maldives see **Embudhu**
151 G3	**Hemel Hempstead** Hertfordshire, England U.K.
169 C4	**Hemer** Ger.
240 I5	**Hemet** CA U.S.A.
173 E2	**Hemhofen** Ger.
236 C3	**Hemingford** NE U.S.A.
151 G2	**Hemingford Grey** Cambridgeshire, England U.K.
226 E1	**Hemlo** Ont. Can.
168 E1	**Hemme** Ger.
168 E2	**Hemmingen** Ger.
233 G2	**Hemmingford** Que. Can.
168 E1	**Hemmingstedt** Ger.
168 D3	**Hemsloh** Ger.
149 H4	**Hemsworth** West Yorkshire, England U.K.
150 D4	**Hemyock** Devon, England U.K.
107 F4	**Henan** prov. China
106 D5	**Henan** prov. China
109 E1	**Henan** prov. China
140 □	**Henån** Sweden
158 B2	**Hénanbihen** France
183 I3	**Henarejos** Spain
183 I4	**Henares** r. Spain
84 A5	**Hencida** Hungary
177 H4	**Hencida** Hungary
199 G1	**Hendek** Turkey
261 G1	**Henderson** Arg.
231 E4	**Henderson** KY U.S.A.
232 A4	**Henderson** KY U.S.A.
231 E4	**Henderson** NC U.S.A.
233 D2	**Henderson** NV U.S.A.
235 F1	**Henderson** NY U.S.A.
231 C5	**Henderson** TN U.S.A.
237 E5	**Henderson** TX U.S.A.
263 G2	**Henderson Island** Antarctica
267 K7	**Henderson Island** Pitcairn Is
231 D5	**Hendersonville** NC U.S.A.
231 C4	**Hendersonville** TN U.S.A.
	Henderville atoll Gilbert Is Kiribati see **Aranuka**
151 G3	**Hendon** Greater London, England U.K.
122 C2	**Hendorābī** i. Iran
122 C5	**Hendrik-Ido-Ambacht** Neth.
215 H1	**Hendriksdal** S. Africa
215 H3	**Hendrina** S. Africa
	Henegouwen prov. Belgium see **Hainaut**
151 G4	**Henfield** West Sussex, England U.K.
80 D1	**Hengam** Jazīreh-ye i. Iran
109 E3	**Hengch'un** Taiwan
108 A2	**Hengdong** Hunan China
108 A2	**Hengduan Shan** mts Xizang China
164 F2	**Hengelo** Gelderland Neth.
164 G2	**Hengelo** Overijssel Neth.
173 H2	**Hengersberg** Ger.
164 E2	**Hengevelde** Neth.
190 D1	**Henggart** Switz.
	Hengnan Hunan China see **Hengyang**
108 B2	**Hengshan** Hunan China
109 L2	**Hengshan** Hunan China
106 C4	**Heng Shan** mt. Hunan China
107 G4	**Heng Shan** mt. Shanxi China
107 G4	**Hengshui** Hebei China
	Hengshui Jiangxi China see **Chongyi**
108 C3	**Hengxian** Guangxi China
109 E2	**Hengyang** Hunan China
109 E2	**Hengyang** Hunan China
	Hengzhou Guangxi China see **Hengxian**
137 K6	**Heniches'k** Ukr.
156 C2	**Hénin-Beaumont** France
156 C2	**Hénin-Liétard** France see **Hénin-Beaumont**
150 D4	**Henley** South I. N.Z.
151 G3	**Henley-in-Arden** Warwickshire, England U.K.
151 G3	**Henley-on-Thames** Oxfordshire, England U.K.
	Henlopen, Cape DE U.S.A.
231 G4	**Henlow** Central Bedfordshire, England U.K.
179 I2	**Henndorf am Wallersee** Austria
158 C2	**Hennebont** France
169 C5	**Hennef (Sieg)** Ger.
215 F2	**Hennenman** S. Africa
237 D4	**Hennessey** OK U.S.A.

171 E3	**Hennickendorf** Brandenburg Ger.
171 E3	**Hennickendorf** Brandenburg Ger.
170 E3	**Hennigsdorf Berlin** Ger.
233 H3	**Henniker** NH U.S.A.
168 E1	**Hennstedt** Ger.
162 E1	**Henneweiler** Ger.
162 E1	**Henrichemont** France
87 G4	**Henry** r. W.A. Austr.
226 C5	**Henry** IL U.S.A.
237 E5	**Henry** OK U.S.A.
262 T1	**Henry Ice Rise** Antarctica
262 □1	**Henryk Arctowski** research stn Antarctica see **Arctowski**
174 F5	**Henrykowo** Pol.
241 L2	**Henry Mountains** UT U.S.A.
238 G4	**Henrys Fork** r. ID U.S.A.
227 G4	**Hensall** Ont. Can.
86 F3	**Hensman, Mount** hill W.A. Austr.
168 E2	**Henstedt-Ulzburg** Ger.
150 E4	**Henstridge** Somerset, England U.K.
107 F2	**Hentiy** prov. Mongolia
96 A3	**Henzada** Myanmar
	Heping Guizhou China see **Huishui**
	Heping Guizhou China see **Yanhe**
	Hepo Guangdong China see **Jiexi**
169 E3	**Heppen** Belgium
172 C2	**Heppenheim (Bergstraße)** Ger.
238 C2	**Heppner** OR U.S.A.
168 E2	**Hepstedt** Ger.
	Heptanesus is Greece see **Ionioi Nisoi**
108 D1	**Hepu** Guangxi China
108 B3	**Heqing** Yunnan China
107 F4	**Hequ** Shanxi China
	Heraclea Turkey see **Ereğli**
	Heraclea Pontica Turkey see **Ereğli**
	Heraklion Kriti Greece see **Irakleio**
85 G2	**Herald Cays** atolls Coral Sea Is Terr. Austr.
244 C2	**Herańdez** Mex.
80 E3	**Herangi** hill North I. N.Z.
123 E3	**Herāt** Afgh.
123 E3	**Herāt** prov. Afgh.
113 □2	**Heratera** i. Addu Atoll Maldives
161 B5	**Hérault** dept Languedoc-Roussillon France
159 I3	**Hérault** r. France
161 C3	**Herbasse** r. France
159 H4	**Herbault** France
85 F3	**Herbert** r. Qld Austr.
223 J5	**Herbert** Sask. Can.
81 C6	**Herbert** South I. N.Z.
84 D4	**Herbert Downs** Qld Austr.
172 D3	**Herbertingen** Ger.
85 F3	**Herberton** Qld Austr.
214 C6	**Herbertsdale** S. Africa
147 C4	**Herbertstown** Rep. of Ireland
80 F4	**Herbertville** North I. N.Z.
87 E5	**Herbert Wash** salt flat W.A. Austr.
165 D5	**Herbeumont** Belgium
158 B2	**Herbignac** France
172 D3	**Herbolzheim** Ger.
169 D5	**Herborn** Ger.
173 E3	**Herbrechtingen** Ger.
169 F4	**Herbsleben** Ger.
169 E5	**Herbstein** Ger.
174 G4	**Herby** Pol.
183 H2	**Herce** Spain
	Hercegfalva Hungary see **Mezőfalva**
177 H4	**Herceghalom** Hungary
	Herceg-Novi Crna Gora Yugo.
177 H6	**Hercegszántó** Hungary
256 B4	**Herculândia** Brazil
262 Q1	**Hercules Dome** ice feature Antarctica
169 C4	**Herdecke** Ger.
168 C5	**Herdorf** Ger.
180 E1	**Herdwangen-Schönach** Ger.
185 M1	**Herencia** Spain
177 G4	**Herend** Hungary
165 D4	**Herentals** Belgium
165 D3	**Herenthout** Belgium
161 B5	**Hérépian** France
172 D4	**Herford** Ger.
172 D4	**Hergatz** Ger.
267 □4	**Hergest Island** Fr. Polynesia see **Motu Iti**
190 D2	**Hergiswil** Switz.
184 I1	**Herguijuela** Spain
158 D2	**Héric** France
160 C1	**Héricourt** France
161 D4	**Hérimoncourt-en-Caux** France
156 E1	**Hérin** Belgium
185 P5	**Herne** Germany
169 C4	**Herne** Ger.
151 I3	**Herne Bay** Kent, England U.K.
142 C3	**Herning** Denmark
244 B2	**Heroica Nogales** Mex. see **Nogales**
173 F2	**Heroldsbach** Ger.
173 F2	**Heroldsberg** Ger.
165 E4	**Héron** Belgium
106 B2	**Heron** Qld Austr.
109 E2	**Herong** Hubei China
85 G4	**Heron Island** Qld Austr.
159 F2	**Hérouville-St-Clair** France
	Herowābād Iran see **Khalkhāl**
177 H5	**Herpenyó** r. Hungary
169 F5	**Herpf** Ger.
258 F2	**Herradura** Arg.
244 C2	**Herradura** Mex.
183 J2	**Herramélluri** Spain
163 B5	**Herré** France
236 C2	**Herreid** SD U.S.A.
172 C3	**Herrenberg** Ger.
258 E3	**Herrera** Arg.
185 F3	**Herrera** Spain
186 B3	**Herrera** mt. Spain
185 E1	**Herrera de Duque** Spain
186 B3	**Herrera de los Navarros** Spain
183 F2	**Herrera de Pisuerga** Spain
183 I4	**Herrería** Spain
184 D1	**Herreruela** Spain
236 F4	**Herrilden** IL U.S.A.
175 K4	**Herrlishied** Ger.
157 H4	**Herrlisheim** France
142 E2	**Herrljunga** Sweden
173 F4	**Herrsching am Ammersee** Ger.
143 H3	**Hervik** Gotland Sweden
160 A1	**Héry** France
173 F2	**Hers** r. France
173 F2	**Hersbruck** Ger.
165 C4	**Herschbach** Ger.
215 F4	**Herschel** S. Africa
173 F2	**Herschweiler-Pettersheim** Ger.
165 D3	**Herselt** Belgium
157 F3	**Herseranges** France
227 I5	**Hershey** PA U.S.A.
261 G2	**Hersilia** Arg.
165 D4	**Herstal** Belgium
151 H4	**Herstmonceux** East Sussex, England U.K.
146 E3	**Herston** Orkney, Scotland U.K.
226 A3	**Hertel** WI U.S.A.
169 C4	**Herten** Ger.
151 G3	**Hertford** Hertfordshire, England U.K.
231 E4	**Hertford** NC U.S.A.
151 H3	**Hertfordshire** admin. div. England U.K.
136 D3	**Hertsa** Ukr.
215 E3	**Hertzogville** S. Africa
168 E4	**Herzberg** Ger.
182 D3	**Herzberg** S. Africa
169 E4	**Herzberg am Harz** Ger.
169 D4	**Herzebrock-Clarholz** Ger.
156 E1	**Herzele** Belgium
171 F3	**Herzfelde** Ger.
168 E2	**Herzhorn** Ger.
128 B3	**Herzliyya** Israel
190 C2	**Herzogenaurach** Ger.
179 G2	**Herzogenbuchsee** Switz.
170 E2	**Herzogenrath** Austria
122 B3	**Ḩeşār** Iran
156 C2	**Hesdin** France
108 D4	**Heshan** Guangxi China
109 C2	**Heshengqiao** Hubei China
107 F3	**Heshui** Gansu China
107 C5	**Heshun** Shanxi China
240 I4	**Hesperia** CA U.S.A.
226 D4	**Hesperia** MI U.S.A.
222 E5	**Hesquiat** B.C. Can.
173 E2	**Heßdorf** Ger.
	Heßdorf Ger. see **Hessen**
226 E2	**Hessel** MI U.S.A.
173 E2	**Hesselberg** hill Ger.
169 D5	**Hessen** land Ger.
173 E2	**Hessen** land Ger.
169 D4	**Hessisch Oldendorf** Ger.
222 C2	**Hess Mountains** Y.T. Can.
169 E3	**Hessisch Lichtenau** Ger.
169 E3	**Hestern (Adenbüttel)** Ger.
149 E4	**Heswall** Merseyside, England U.K.
151 □	**Het** r. Laos
235 E1	**Heteren** Neth.
177 H5	**Hetés** Hungary
151 12	**Hethersett** Norfolk, England U.K.
149 H3	**Hetlingen** Ger.
157 J2	**Hettange-Grande** France
157 E3	**Hettenleidelheim** Ger.
172 D3	**Hettenshausen** Ger.
172 D3	**Hettingen** Ger.
149 G3	**Hetton** North Yorkshire, England U.K.
149 H3	**Hetton-le-Hole** Tyne and Wear, England U.K.
169 E4	**Hettstedt** Ger.
173 G2	**Hetzerath** Ger.
168 E3	**Heuback** Ger.
169 D5	**Heuchelheim** Ger.
164 E3	**Heuchin** France
164 E3	**Heukelum** Neth.
214 E3	**Heuningkloof** S. Africa
215 F2	**Heuningspruit** S. Africa
164 E3	**Heusden** Neth.
169 G4	**Heustreu** Ger.
169 G4	**Heuweler** Lux.
233 F2	**Heuvelton** NY U.S.A.
177 J4	**Heves** Hungary
177 J4	**Heves** county Hungary
177 I5	**Héviz** Hungary
176 F3	**Hevlín** Czech Rep.
	Hewei Guangdong China see **Hebu**
235 I1	**Hewitt** NJ U.S.A.
178 B3	**Hewlett** NY U.S.A.
178 B3	**Hexham** Northumberland, England U.K.
	Hexian Anhui China
108 C2	**Hexian** Guangxi China
	Hexigten Qi Nei Mongol China see **Jingpeng**
106 D4	**Hexipu** Gansu China
151 H3	**Hextable** Kent, England U.K.
	Heyang Guangdong China see **Nanhe**
151 H3	**Heybridge** Essex, England U.K.
153 □	**Heydebreck-Cosel** Pol. see **Kędzierzyn-Koźle**
214 E4	**Heydon** S. Africa
169 E3	**Heyen** Ger.

Heyin to Hornád
313

Heyin Qinghai China see Guide
171 E4 Heynitz Ger.
160 D3 Heyrieux France
149 G3 Heysham Lancashire, England U.K.
215 H2 Heyshope Dam S. Africa
165 E3 Heythuysen Neth.
109 E4 Heyuan Guangdong China
82 E4 Heywood Vic. Austr.
149 G4 Heywood Greater Manchester, England U.K.
226 C5 Heyworth IL U.S.A.
107 G5 Heze Shandong China
108 C3 Hezhang Guizhou China
106 D5 Hezheng Gansu China
106 D5 Hezuozhen Gansu China
231 D7 Hialeah FL U.S.A.
Hiau i. Fr. Polynesia see Eiao
231 D5 Hiawassee GA U.S.A.
236 E4 Hiawatha KS U.S.A.
149 I4 Hibaldstow North Lincolnshire, England U.K.
215 H4 Hibberdene S. Africa
226 A2 Hibbing MN U.S.A.
83 F5 Hibbs, Point Tas. Austr.
86 D2 Hibernia Reef Ashmore & Cartier Is Austr.
237 F4 Hickman KY U.S.A.
231 D5 Hickory NC U.S.A.
234 C3 Hickory Hill PA U.S.A.
80 G2 Hicks Bay North I. N.Z.
235 E2 Hicksville NY U.S.A.
232 A4 Hicksville OH U.S.A.
237 D5 Hico TX U.S.A.
104 D3 Hida-gawa r. Japan
104 B5 Hidaka-gawa r. Japan
102 K2 Hidaka-sanmyaku mts Japan
104 C2 Hida-kōchi plat. Japan
243 F3 Hidalgo Coahuila Mex.
244 B1 Hidalgo Durango Mex.
245 E1 Hidalgo Tamaulipas Mex.
245 E3 Hidalgo state Mex.
242 D3 Hidalgo del Parral Mex.
177 H5 Hidas Hungary
104 D2 Hida-sanmyaku mts Japan
177 K3 Hidasnémeti Hungary
169 D3 Hiddenhausen Ger.
170 E1 Hiddensee Ger.
170 E1 Hiddensee i. Ger.
85 F3 Hidden Valley Qld Austr.
128 B1 Hıdırlı Turkey
197 F2 Hidişelu de Sus Romania
142 B2 Hidra i. Norway
256 C2 Hidrolândia Brazil
254 C5 Hidrolina Brazil
179 F3 Hieflau Austria
183 H3 Hiendelaencina Spain
78 □5 Hienghène New Caledonia
159 F4 Hière r. France
Hierosolyma Israel/West Bank see Jerusalem
183 G4 Hierro, Cabeza de mt. Spain
162 B3 Hiersac France
103 F6 Higashi-Hiroshima Japan
105 F2 Higashi-matsuyama Japan
105 F3 Higashimurayama Japan
102 J4 Higashine Japan
104 B4 Higashi-ōsaka Japan
103 D7 Higashi-suidō sea chan. Japan
105 D2 Higashi-yama mt. Japan
235 F1 Higganum CT U.S.A.
237 C4 Higgins TX U.S.A.
233 F3 Higgins Bay NY U.S.A.
214 D3 Higg's Hope S. Africa
151 H3 Higham Kent, England U.K.
151 G2 Higham Ferrers Northamptonshire, England U.K.
150 C4 Highampton Devon, England U.K.
High Atlas mts Morocco see Haut Atlas
149 G3 High Bentham North Yorkshire, England U.K.
146 D6 High Blantyre South Lanarkshire, Scotland U.K.
150 E3 Highbridge Somerset, England U.K.
234 D2 High Bridge NJ U.S.A.
151 F3 Highclere Hampshire, England U.K.
238 B3 High Desert OR U.S.A.
149 H3 High Etherley Durham, England U.K.
215 H4 Highflats S. Africa
151 H3 High Garrett Essex, England U.K.
246 □ Highgate Jamaica
151 H3 High Halden Kent, England U.K.
149 I3 High Hawsker North Yorkshire, England U.K.
149 G3 High Hesket Cumbria, England U.K.
237 E6 High Island TX U.S.A.
146 D4 Highland admin. div. Scotland U.K.
240 I4 Highland CA U.S.A.
234 B3 Highland MD U.S.A.
226 B2 Highland MN U.S.A.
235 E1 Highland NY U.S.A.
226 B4 Highland WI U.S.A.
234 B4 Highland Beach MD U.S.A.
235 E1 Highland Falls NY U.S.A.
234 D1 Highland Lake NY U.S.A.
235 D1 Highland Lakes NJ U.S.A.
226 D4 Highland Park IL U.S.A.
232 B3 Highland Park MI U.S.A.
235 D2 Highland Park NJ U.S.A.
240 H2 Highland Peak CA U.S.A.
241 J3 Highland Peak NV U.S.A.
235 E2 Highlands NJ U.S.A.
232 E6 Highland Springs VA U.S.A.
149 G4 High Legh Cheshire, England U.K.
222 G3 High Level Alta Can.
150 E2 Highley Shropshire, England U.K.
149 F3 High Lorton Cumbria, England U.K.
236 D2 Highmore SD U.S.A.
150 E3 Highnam Gloucestershire, England U.K.
149 H4 High Peak hill England U.K.
231 E5 High Point NC U.S.A.
234 D1 High Point hill NJ U.S.A.
222 G4 High Prairie Alta Can.
222 H5 High River Alta Can.
231 E7 High Rock Bahamas
83 F5 High Rocky Point Tas. Austr.
149 G3 High Seat hill England U.K.
231 D6 High Springs FL U.S.A.
High Tatras mts Pol./Slovakia see Tatry
235 D2 Hightstown NJ U.S.A.
151 F3 Highworth Swindon, England U.K.
151 G3 High Wycombe Buckinghamshire, England U.K.
242 D3 Higuera de Abuya Mex.
185 G3 Higuera de Arjona Spain
184 E2 Higuera de la Serena Spain
184 D3 Higuera de la Sierra Spain
184 D2 Higuera de Vargas Spain
184 D2 Higuera la Real Spain
247 □1 Higüero, Punta pt Puerto Rico
187 B6 Higueruela Spain
187 C5 Higueruelas Spain
247 E3 Higüey Dom. Rep.
105 F3 Higuri-gawa r. Japan
77 I3 Hihifo Tonga
210 E3 Hiiraan admin. reg. Somalia
138 D2 Hiiumaa i. Estonia
186 C3 Híjar Spain
94 C3 Hijau, Gunung mt. Indon.
124 B2 Hijaz reg. Saudi Arabia
105 E3 Hijiri-dake mt. Japan
92 C5 Hijo Phil.
183 H1 Hijuela r. Spain
105 E2 Hikabo-yama mt. Japan
103 E7 Hikari Japan
104 B5 Hiki-gawa r. Japan
241 J3 Hiko NV U.S.A.
104 C3 Hikone Japan
103 E7 Hiko-san mt. Japan
80 E1 Hikurangi North I. N.Z.
80 G2 Hikurangi mt. North I. N.Z.
129 F3 Hil Azer.
263 K1 Hilary Coast Antarctica
171 E5 Hilbersdorf Ger.
169 D5 Hilchenbach Ger.
241 K3 Hildale UT U.S.A.
169 F5 Hildburghausen Ger.
169 B4 Hilden Ger.
151 H3 Hildenborough Kent, England U.K.
169 F5 Hilders Ger.
149 I3 Hilderthorpe East Riding of Yorkshire, England U.K.
169 E3 Hildesheim Ger.
151 H2 Hilgay Norfolk, England U.K.
168 E3 Hilgermissen Ger.
173 F3 Hilgertshausen Ger.
117 G4 Hili Bangl.
168 C3 Hilkenbrook Ger.
87 B6 Hill r. W.A. Austr.
247 □4 Hillaby, Mount hill Barbados
Hillah Iraq see Al Ḥillah
214 C5 Hillandale S. Africa
232 B4 Hillard OH U.S.A.
236 D4 Hill City KS U.S.A.
236 C3 Hill City SD U.S.A.
241 M2 Hill Creek r. UT U.S.A.
234 B4 Hillcrest Heights MD U.S.A.
169 D3 Hille Ger.
164 D2 Hillegom Neth.
83 G3 Hill End N.S.W. Austr.
142 E4 Hillerød Denmark
81 D4 Hillersden South I. N.Z.
169 F3 Hillerse Ger.
143 E3 Hillerstorp Sweden
169 B5 Hillesheim Ger.
85 F3 Hillgrove Qld Austr.
227 F3 Hillman MI U.S.A.
87 C6 Hillman, Lake salt flat W.A. Austr.
236 F4 Hillsboro IL U.S.A.
236 F4 Hillsboro MO U.S.A.
236 D2 Hillsboro ND U.S.A.
233 H3 Hillsboro NH U.S.A.
239 F5 Hillsboro NM U.S.A.
232 B5 Hillsboro OH U.S.A.
238 B2 Hillsboro OR U.S.A.
237 D5 Hillsboro TX U.S.A.
226 B4 Hillsboro WI U.S.A.
247 □3 Hillsborough Grenada
147 E2 Hillsborough Northern Ireland U.K.
231 E4 Hillsborough NC U.S.A.
85 G4 Hillsborough, Cape Qld Austr.
169 C5 Hillscheid Ger.
226 E5 Hillsdale MI U.S.A.
233 G3 Hillsdale NY U.S.A.
227 I5 Hillsgrove PA U.S.A.
86 C4 Hillside W.A. Austr.
146 F5 Hillside Angus, Scotland U.K.
146 □G1 Hillside Shetland, Scotland U.K.
235 D2 Hillside NJ U.S.A.
224 C3 Hillsport Ont. Can.
83 F3 Hillston N.S.W. Austr.
232 C6 Hillsville VA U.S.A.
146 □G1 Hillswick Shetland, Scotland U.K.
147 E2 Hilltown Northern Ireland U.K.
240 □D9 Hilo HI U.S.A.
150 E3 Hilperton Wiltshire, England U.K.
173 F2 Hilpoltstein Ger.
157 H4 Hilsenheim France
169 D3 Hilter am Teutoburger Wald Ger.
84 D4 Hilton Qld Austr.
215 H3 Hilton S. Africa
151 F2 Hilton Derbyshire, England U.K.
232 E3 Hilton NY U.S.A.
227 F2 Hilton Beach Ont. Can.
231 D5 Hilton Head Island SC U.S.A.
173 F2 Hiltpoltstein Ger.
126 E3 Hilvan Turkey
164 E3 Hilvarenbeek Neth.
164 E2 Hilversum Neth.
172 C4 Hilzingen Ger.
116 D3 Himachal Pradesh state India
124 C2 Ḥimā Ḍarīyah, Jabal mt. Saudi Arabia
116 D2 Himalaya mts Asia
140 M2 Himanka Fin.
198 A1 Himarë Albania
80 E4 Himatangi North I. N.Z.
80 E4 Himatangi Beach North I. N.Z.
116 C5 Himatnagar Gujarat India
179 H2 Himberg Austria
168 F2 Himbergen Ger.
105 D1 Hime-gawa r. Japan
103 G6 Himeji Japan
102 J4 Himekami-dake mt. Japan
177 H5 Himesháza Hungary
215 G3 Himeville S. Africa
104 C2 Himi Japan
113 □1 Himmafushi i. N. Male Maldives
179 F4 Himmelberg Austria
142 C3 Himmelbjerget hill Denmark
168 E2 Himmelpforten Ger.
124 B5 Himora Eth.
128 C2 Ḥimṣ Syria
128 D2 Ḥimṣ governorate Syria
81 E4 Hinakura North I. N.Z.
92 C4 Hinatuan Phil.
136 E4 Hînceşti Moldova
246 D3 Hinche Haiti
85 F3 Hinchinbrook Island Qld Austr.
151 F2 Hinckley Leicestershire, England U.K.
226 C5 Hinckley IL U.S.A.
233 □I2 Hinckley ME U.S.A.
226 A2 Hinckley MN U.S.A.
241 K2 Hinckley UT U.S.A.
209 B6 Hinda Congo
111 B6 Hindan r. India
129 E3 Hindarx Azer.
116 D4 Hindaun Rajasthan India
173 E4 Hindelang Ger.
170 C3 Hindenburg Ger.
Hindenburg Pol. see Zabrze
149 I3 Hinderwell North Yorkshire, England U.K.
151 G3 Hindhead Surrey, England U.K.
149 G4 Hindley Greater Manchester, England U.K.
232 B6 Hindman KY U.S.A.
83 E4 Hindmarsh, Lake dry lake Vic. Austr.
117 F5 Hindola Orissa India
116 C4 Hindoli Rajasthan India
150 E3 Hindon Wiltshire, England U.K.
116 D5 Hindoria Madh. Prad. India
114 C3 Hindri r. India
81 C6 Hinds South I. N.Z.
142 D4 Hindsholm pen. Denmark
123 F3 Hindu Kush mts Afgh./Pak.
114 C3 Hindupur Andhra Prad. India
222 G3 Hines Creek Alta Can.
231 D6 Hinesville GA U.S.A.
116 D5 Hinganghat Mahar. India
151 H2 Hingham Norfolk, England U.K.
123 F5 Hingol r. Pak.
Hingol r. Pak. see Girdar Dhor
127 F3 Hınıs Turkey
234 B2 Hinkletown PA U.S.A.
140 □ Hinlopenstretet str. Svalbard
140 K1 Hinnøya i. Norway
105 F3 Hino Japan
92 B4 Hinobaan Phil.
104 C2 Hino-gawa r. Japan
104 C3 Hino-gawa r. Japan
182 D5 Hinojal Spain
184 D2 Hinojales Spain
185 H3 Hinojares Spain
185 F2 Hinojasas de Calatrava Spain
183 H3 Hinojedo mt. Spain
261 G5 Hinojo Arg.
184 D3 Hinojos Spain
183 I3 Hinojosa Spain
182 D4 Hinojosa de Duero Spain
186 C4 Hinojosa de Jarque Spain
185 E2 Hinojosa del Duque Spain
180 D2 Hinojosa de San Vicente Spain
233 G3 Hinsdale NH U.S.A.
168 C2 Hinte Ger.
178 C3 Hinteres Sonnenwendjoch mt. Austria
171 F5 Hinterhermsdorf Ger.
169 F5 Hinternah Ger.
190 E2 Hinterrhein Switz.
190 E2 Hinterrhein r. Switz.
173 H3 Hinterschmiding Ger.
170 F2 Hintersee Ger.
172 B2 Hinterweidenthal Ger.
172 C4 Hinterzarten Ger.
Hinthada Myanmar see Henzada
220 G4 Hinton Alta Can.
237 D5 Hinton OK U.S.A.
232 C6 Hinton WV U.S.A.
80 E2 Hinuera North I. N.Z.
190 D1 Hinwil Switz.
163 B5 Hinx France
Hiort i. Western Isles, Scotland U.K. see Hirta
178 C3 Hippach Austria
164 D2 Hippolytushoef Neth.
Hipponium Italy see Vibo Valentia
Hippo Regius Alg. see Annaba
Hippo Zarytus Tunisia see Bizerte
168 D2 Hipstedt Ger.
127 G3 Hirabit Dağ mt. Turkey
103 D7 Hirado Japan
150 D1 Hiraethog, Mynydd hills Wales U.K.
105 F1 Hiraga-take mt. Japan
104 B4 Hirakata Japan
117 E5 Hirakud Reservoir India
102 □1 Hirara Japan
103 F6 Hirata Japan
105 F3 Hiratsuka Japan
114 B3 Hirekerur Karnataka India
206 D5 Hiré-Watta Côte d'Ivoire
114 C3 Hiriyur Karnataka India
Hîrlău Romania see Hârlău
210 D2 Hīrna Eth.
137 I3 Hirnyk Donets'ka Oblast' Ukr.
175 M5 Hirnyk L'vivs'ka Oblast' Ukr.
102 J3 Hirosaki Japan
103 F6 Hiroshima Japan
103 F6 Hiroshima airport Japan
103 F6 Hiroshima pref. Japan
172 C3 Hirrlingen Ger.
173 F2 Hirschaid Ger.
173 F2 Hirschau Ger.
171 C5 Hirschberg Ger.
173 F4 Hirschberg mt. Ger.
Hirschberg Pol. see Jelenia Góra
173 G3 Hirschenstn mt. Ger.
171 E4 Hirschfeld Ger.
171 F5 Hirschfelde Ger.
172 C2 Hirschhorn (Neckar) Ger.
160 F1 Hirsingue France
137 H4 Hirsivka Ukr.
137 J3 Hirs'ke Ukr.
136 F3 Hirs'kyy Tikych r. Ukr.
156 E3 Hirson France
Hîrşova Romania see Hârşova
146 □ Hirta i. Western Isles, Scotland U.K.
179 H3 Hirtenberg Austria
142 C3 Hirtshals Denmark
105 F3 Hiruga-take mt. Japan
150 D3 Hirwaun Rhondda Cynon Taff, Wales U.K.
169 E5 Hirzenhain Ger.
104 C4 Hisai Japan
116 C3 Hisar Haryana India
199 F2 Hisarcık Turkey
Hisarköy Turkey see Domaniç
126 D2 Hisarönü Turkey
199 E3 Hisarönü Körfezi b. Turkey
123 G2 Hisor Tajik.
Hisor Tizmasi mts Tajik./Uzbek. see Gissar Range
Hispalis Spain see Sevilla
Hispania country Europe see Spain
246 D2 Hispaniola i. Caribbean Sea
Hissar Haryana India see Hisar
117 F4 Hisua Bihar India
127 F4 Hīt Iraq
103 E7 Hita Japan
183 G4 Hita Spain
105 G2 Hitachi Japan
105 G2 Hitachinaka Japan
105 G2 Hitachi-ōta Japan
113 □2 Hitaddu Addu Atoll Maldives
113 □2 Hitaddu i. Addu Atoll Maldives
151 G3 Hitchin Hertfordshire, England U.K.
Hithadhoo i. Addu Atoll Maldives see Hitaddu
103 E7 Hitoyoshi Japan
140 J3 Hitra i. Norway
178 A3 Hittisau Austria
170 C2 Hitzacker Ger.
179 G3 Hitzendorf Austria
173 F3 Hitzhofen Ger.
168 E2 Hitzhusen Ger.
190 D1 Hitzkirch Switz.
78 □5 Hiu i. Vanuatu
105 F2 Hiuchiga-take vol. Japan
79 □3 Hiva Oa i. Fr. Polynesia
222 F4 Hixon B.C. Can.
85 H4 Hixson Cay rf Qld Austr.
226 B3 Hixton WI U.S.A.
175 L5 Hiyche Ukr.
127 F3 Hizan Bitlis Turkey
142 D3 Hjallerup Denmark
143 F2 Hjälmaren l. Sweden
142 C2 Hjartdøld r. Norway
142 B2 Hjelmeland Norway
143 F2 Hjo Sweden
168 E1 Hjordkær Denmark
142 D3 Hjørring Denmark
142 D3 Hjuvik Sweden
96 B2 Hka, Nam r. Myanmar
96 B1 Hkakabo Razi mt. Myanmar
96 B2 Hkok r. Myanmar
96 B1 Hkring Bum mt. Myanmar
215 H3 Hlabisa S. Africa
96 B3 Hlaing r. Myanmar
Hlako Kangri mt. Xizang China see Lhagoi Kangri
215 H2 Hlatikulu Swaziland
176 F5 Hlebine Croatia
96 B3 Hlegu Myanmar
136 F2 Hlevakha Ukr.
136 E4 Hlinaia Moldova
177 H3 Hliník nad Hronom Slovakia
177 K3 Hlinné Slovakia
176 E2 Hlinsko Czech Rep.
197 H2 Hlipiceni Romania
191 J4 Hlm hill Croatia
137 G3 Hlobyne Ukr.
215 F3 Hlohlowane S. Africa
176 F3 Hlohovec Czech Rep.
177 G3 Hlohovec Slovakia
215 G3 Hlotse Lesotho
176 G2 Hlubočky Czech Rep.
176 D2 Hluboká nad Vltavou Czech Rep.
177 H2 Hlučín Czech Rep.
215 I3 Hluhluwe S. Africa
177 G3 Hluk Czech Rep.
137 G2 Hlukhiv Ukr.
136 E3 Hlukhivtsi Ukr.
138 G5 Hlusha Belarus
138 G5 Hlusk Belarus
136 C3 Hlyboka Ukr.
138 F4 Hlybokaye Belarus
136 D2 Hlynne Ukr.
137 G3 Hlyns'k Ukr.
136 C3 Hlynyany Ukr.
177 J2 Hniezdné Slovakia
177 J3 Hnilec r. Slovakia
136 E3 Hnivan' Ukr.
175 M6 Hnizdychiv Ukr.
136 C3 Hnizna r. Ukr.
177 I3 Hnúšťa Slovakia
136 C3 Hnyla Lypa r. Ukr.
137 I2 Hnylytsya Ukr.
136 F3 Hnylyy Tikych r. Ukr.
137 F4 Hnylyy Yelanets' r. Ukr.
207 F5 Ho Ghana
96 D2 Hoa Binh Vietnam
96 C2 Hoang Liên Son mts Vietnam
Hoang Sa is S. China Sea see Paracel Islands
83 F5 Hobart Tas. Austr.
237 D5 Hobart OK U.S.A.
237 C5 Hobbs NM U.S.A.
262 P1 Hobbs Coast Antarctica
129 B4 Höbek Dağı mt. Turkey
231 D7 Hobe Sound FL U.S.A.
215 F3 Hobhouse S. Africa
235 D2 Hoboken NJ U.S.A.
110 D2 Hoboksar Xinjiang China
177 G5 Hobol Hungary
142 D2 Hobøl Norway
107 G3 Hobor Nei Mongol China
Hobot Xar Qi Nei Mongol China see Xin Bulag
142 C3 Hobro Denmark
165 E5 Hobscheid Lux.
143 H3 Hoburg Gotland Sweden
210 F3 Hobyo Somalia
199 F2 Hocalar Turkey
178 D3 Hocharn mt. Austria
172 D2 Höchberg Ger.
179 F2 Hochbira hill Austria
168 E1 Hochdonn Ger.
172 D3 Hochdorf Ger.
190 D1 Hochdorf Switz.
172 C4 Höchenschwand Ger.
Hochfeiler mt. Austria/Italy see Gran Pilastro
179 E3 Hochfeind mt. Austria
157 H4 Hochfelden France
Hochgall mt. Austria/Italy see Collalto
173 G4 Hochgern mt. Ger.
179 E3 Hochgolling mt. Austria
169 F5 Höchheim Ger.
169 D5 Hochheim am Main Ger.
97 D5 Hô Chi Minh Vietnam
Ho Chi Minh City Vietnam see Hô Chi Minh
173 G4 Hochkalter mt. Ger.
178 E3 Hochkönig mt. Austria
179 F4 Hochobir mt. Austria
179 G3 Hochschwab mt. Austria
179 F3 Hochschwab mts Austria
172 B2 Hochspeyer Ger.
172 C2 Hochstadt (Pfalz) Ger.
173 E2 Höchstadt an der Aisch Ger.
173 E3 Höchstädt an der Donau Ger.
172 B2 Hochstetten-Dhaun Ger.
172 C2 Höchst im Odenwald Ger.
179 F3 Hochtor mt. Austria
178 C3 Hochunnutz mt. Austria
190 E2 Hochwang mt. Switz.
Hochwilde mt. Austria/Italy see L'Altissima
172 C2 Hockenheim Ger.
232 C5 Hocking r. OH U.S.A.
151 H3 Hockley Essex, England U.K.
151 F2 Hockley Heath West Midlands, England U.K.
175 K6 Hoczew Pol.
175 K6 Hoczewka r. Pol.
116 D4 Hodal Haryana India
177 L4 Hodász Hungary
104 C2 Hōdatsu-san hill Japan
210 F2 Hodda mt. Somalia
149 G4 Hodder r. England U.K.
151 G3 Hoddesdon Hertfordshire, England U.K.
Hodeidah Yemen see Al Ḥudaydah
177 J3 Hodejov Slovakia
168 E3 Hodenhagen Ger.
232 C5 Hodgesville WV U.S.A.
84 C2 Hodgson Downs N.T. Austr.
206 D2 Hodh Ech Chargui admin. reg. Maur.
206 C2 Hodh El Gharbi admin. reg. Maur.
177 J5 Hódmezővásárhely Hungary
205 G2 Hodna, Chott el salt l. Alg.
150 E2 Hodnet Shropshire, England U.K.
177 M4 Hodod Romania
179 H2 Hodonice Czech Rep.
176 G3 Hodonín Czech Rep.
197 G2 Hodoşa Romania
106 C1 Hödrögö Mongolia
215 G3 Hodsons Peak Lesotho
165 C3 Hoek Neth.
164 D3 Hoek van Holland Neth.
157 H4 Hœnheim France
165 E4 Hoensbroek Neth.
157 H4 Hœrdt France
100 D4 Hoeryŏng N. Korea
165 E4 Hoeselt Belgium
164 E2 Hoevelaken Neth.
164 D3 Hoeven Neth.
101 C5 Hoeyang N. Korea
171 C5 Hof Bayern Ger.
169 D5 Hof Rheinland-Pfalz Ger.
179 H3 Hof am Leithaberge Austria
178 E3 Hof bei Salzburg Austria
169 E5 Hofbieber Ger.
178 B3 Höfen Austria
168 F3 Höfer Ger.
233 G3 Hoffman Mountain NY U.S.A.
246 C1 Hoffman's Cay i. Bahamas
169 E4 Hofgeismar Ger.
169 D5 Hofheim am Taunus Ger.
169 F5 Hofheim in Unterfranken Ger.
173 H3 Hofkirchen Ger.
215 E4 Hofmeyr S. Africa
140 □D2 Höfn Iceland
143 G1 Hofors Sweden
140 □C2 Hofsjökull ice cap Iceland
103 E6 Hōfu Japan
Hofūf Saudi Arabia see Al Hufūf
142 E3 Höganäs Sweden
83 F4 Hogan Group is Tas. Austr.
233 F2 Hogansburg NY U.S.A.
85 F5 Hoganthulla Creek r. Qld Austr.
84 D4 Hogarth, Mount hill N.T. Austr.
222 C2 Hogg, Mount Y.T. Can.
205 G5 Hoggar plat. Alg.
143 G3 Högsby Sweden
143 F2 Högsjö Sweden
141 I3 Høgste Breakulen mt. Norway
149 J4 Hogsthorpe Lincolnshire, England U.K.
177 H5 Hőgyész Hungary
238 A2 Hoh r. WA U.S.A.
172 B3 Hohberg Ger.
171 D4 Hohburg Ger.
179 E4 Hohe Leier mt. Austria
178 E4 Hohe Leiten mt. Austria
173 E3 Hohen-Altheim Ger.
168 E2 Hohenaspe Ger.
173 H3 Hohenau Ger.
179 H2 Hohenau an der March Austria
179 G3 Hohenberg Austria
171 F4 Hohenbocka Ger.
179 H4 Hohenbrugg-Weinberg Austria
173 F3 Hohenbrunn Ger.
171 E4 Hohenbucko Ger.
173 F2 Hohenburg Ger.
171 C3 Hohendodeleben Ger.
170 E1 Hohendorf Ger.
169 F4 Hohenebra Ger.
179 G2 Hoheneich Austria
178 A3 Hohenems Austria
173 F2 Hohenfels Ger.
173 E4 Hohenfurch Ger.
170 D3 Hohengöhren Ger.
169 F3 Hohenhameln Ger.
173 F3 Hohenkammer Ger.
168 C2 Hohenkirchen Ger.
171 E4 Hohenleipisch Ger.
171 D5 Hohenleuben Ger.
173 F3 Hohenlinden Ger.
168 E2 Hohenlockstedt Ger.
172 D2 Hohenloher Ebene plain Ger.
170 E2 Hohenmocker Ger.
171 D4 Hohenmölsen Ger.
170 D3 Hohennauen Ger.
170 E3 Hohen Neuendorf Berlin Ger.
179 F3 Hohe Nock mt. Austria
169 E5 Hohenroda-Ransbach Ger.
169 F5 Hohenroth Ger.
170 F3 Hohensaaten Ger.
Hohensalza Pol. see Inowrocław
171 D3 Hohenseeden Ger.
171 D5 Hohenstein-Ernstthal Ger.
172 D3 Hohentengen Ger.
172 C4 Hohentengen am Hochrhein Ger.
173 G3 Hohenthann Ger.
171 D4 Hohenthurm Ger.
231 C5 Hohenwald TN U.S.A.
170 D2 Hohen Wangelin Ger.
173 F3 Hohenwart Ger.
173 G2 Hohenwarth Ger.
168 E1 Hohenwestedt Ger.
170 C3 Hohenwulsch Ger.
179 E2 Hohenzell Austria
179 E3 Hoher Dachstein mt. Austria
Hoh Ereg Nei Mongol China see Wuchuan
178 E3 Hoher Göll mt. Austria/Ger.
169 E5 Hohe Rhön mts Ger.
178 B3 Hoher Ifen mt. Austria/Ger.
178 D3 Hohe Salve mt. Austria
169 E4 Hohes Gras hill Ger.
169 F4 Hohes Kreuz Ger.
178 D3 Hohe Tauern mts Austria
165 F4 Hohe Venn moorland Belgium
190 C2 Hohgant mt. Switz.
Hohhot Nei Mongol China see Huhhot
172 C3 Hohloh hill Ger.
169 C5 Höhn Ger.
168 E1 Hohn Schleswig-Holstein Ger.
168 F3 Hohne Ger.
157 H4 Hohneck mt. France
168 F2 Hohnstorf (Elbe) Ger.
207 F5 Hohoe Ghana
137 G3 Hoholeve Ukr.
137 F2 Hoholiv Ukr.
137 H4 Hoholivka Ukr.
168 F1 Hohwacht (Ostsee) Ger.
111 E5 Hoh Xil Shan mts China
96 E4 Hôi An Vietnam
210 A4 Hoima Uganda
168 F2 Hoisdorf Ger.
236 D4 Hoisington KS U.S.A.
106 C4 Hoit Taria Qinghai China
117 H4 Hojai Assam India
Hojambaz Turkm. see Khodzhambaz
168 D1 Højer Denmark
103 F7 Hōjo Japan
96 C2 Hok r. Myanmar
143 E3 Hökensås hills Sweden
80 D1 Hokianga Harbour North I. N.Z.
105 G2 Hōki-gawa r. Japan
80 E4 Hokio Beach North I. N.Z.
81 C5 Hokitika South I. N.Z.
100 G4 Hokkaidō i. Japan
102 K2 Hokkaidō pref. Japan
142 C2 Hokksund Norway
122 D2 Hokmābād Iran
81 B7 Hokonui South I. N.Z.
81 B6 Hokonui Hills South I. N.Z.
129 D3 Hoktemberyan Armenia
105 E1 Hokura-gawa r. Japan
142 C1 Hol Buskerud Norway
140 L1 Hol Nordland Norway
177 J3 Hoľa mt. Slovakia
114 C3 Holalkere Karnataka India
137 G4 Hola Prystan' Ukr.
142 D4 Holbæk Denmark
215 H2 Holbank S. Africa
151 H2 Holbeach Lincolnshire, England U.K.
222 D5 Holberg B.C. Can.
168 E1 Holbøl Denmark
85 G3 Holborne Island Qld Austr.
83 F3 Holbrook N.S.W. Austr.
151 I3 Holbrook Suffolk, England U.K.
241 L4 Holbrook AZ U.S.A.
235 E2 Holbrook NY U.S.A.
226 B3 Holcombe WI U.S.A.
223 H4 Holden Alta Can.
149 G4 Holden Lancashire, England U.K.
241 K2 Holden UT U.S.A.
237 D5 Holdenville OK U.S.A.
149 I4 Holderness pen. England U.K.
168 D3 Holdorf Ger.
236 D3 Holdrege NE U.S.A.
168 G1 Holeby Denmark
114 C3 Hole Narsipur Karnataka India
177 G2 Holešov Czech Rep.
232 A4 Holgate OH U.S.A.
182 D5 Holguera Spain
246 C2 Holguín Cuba
176 G3 Holíč Slovakia
176 E1 Holice Czech Rep.
137 G2 Holinka Ukr.
141 K3 Höljes Sweden
179 H2 Hollabrunn Austria
169 C3 Hollage (Wallenhorst) Ger.
Holland country Europe see Netherlands
226 D4 Holland MI U.S.A.
232 D3 Holland NY U.S.A.
232 B4 Holland OH U.S.A.
237 F5 Hollandale MS U.S.A.
Hollandia Irian Jaya Indon. see Jayapura
151 I3 Holland-on-Sea Essex, England U.K.
164 F2 Hollandscheveld Neth.
146 F2 Hollandstoun Scotland U.K.
165 E5 Hollange Belgium
169 F3 Holle Ger.
171 C4 Holleben Ger.
173 F3 Hollenbach Ger.
168 F2 Hollenbek Ger.
179 G4 Hollenegg Austria
168 E2 Hollenstedt Ger.
179 F3 Hollenstein an der Ybbs Austria
232 D3 Holley NY U.S.A.
173 F2 Hollfeld Ger.
262 T2 Hollick-Kenyon Peninsula Antarctica
262 Q1 Hollick-Kenyon Plateau Antarctica
232 D4 Hollidaysburg PA U.S.A.
168 E1 Hollingstedt Ger.
151 H4 Hollington East Sussex, England U.K.
149 H4 Hollingworth Greater Manchester, England U.K.
222 C4 Hollis AK U.S.A.
237 D5 Hollis OK U.S.A.
240 G3 Hollister CA U.S.A.
177 K3 Hollóháza Hungary
141 N3 Hollola Fin.
164 E1 Hollum Neth.
227 F4 Holly MI U.S.A.
148 E2 Hollybush East Ayrshire, Scotland U.K.
150 E2 Hollybush Worcestershire, England U.K.
81 A6 Hollyford r. South I. N.Z.
235 D3 Holly Park NJ U.S.A.
237 F5 Holly Springs MS U.S.A.
147 E3 Hollywood Rep. of Ireland
231 D7 Hollywood FL U.S.A.
168 E2 Holm Ger.
136 E4 Hol'ma Ukr.
220 G2 Holman N.W.T. Can.
235 D2 Holmdel NJ U.S.A.
215 G2 Holmdene S. Africa
149 I4 Holme-on-Spalding-Moor East Riding of Yorkshire, England U.K.
235 E1 Holmes NY U.S.A.
149 G4 Holmes Chapel Cheshire, England U.K.
149 H4 Holmesfield Derbyshire, England U.K.
85 F3 Holmes Reef Coral Sea Is Terr. Austr.
142 D2 Holmestrand Norway
232 C4 Holmesville OH U.S.A.
149 H4 Holmfirth West Yorkshire, England U.K.
Holmgard Rus. Fed. see Velikiy Novgorod
140 M3 Holmsund Sweden
141 L3 Holmsveden Sweden
136 C2 Holoby Ukr.
177 L5 Holod Romania
197 F2 Holod r. Romania
136 C3 Holohory hills Ukr.
128 B3 Ḥolon Israel
86 E2 Holothuria Banks rf W.A. Austr.
173 H2 Holoubkov Czech Rep.
136 F3 Holovanivs'k Ukr.
136 B3 Holovets'ko Ukr.
137 G3 Holovkivka Ukr.
175 M4 Holovne Ukr.
136 E2 Holovyne Ukr.
85 E2 Holroyd r. Qld Austr.
142 E3 Holsljunga Sweden
215 G2 Holspruit r. S. Africa
168 D2 Holste Ger.
142 C3 Holstebro Denmark
142 C4 Holsted Denmark
190 C1 Hölstein Switz.
236 E3 Holstein IA U.S.A.
Holsteinsborg Greenland see Sisimiut
232 B6 Holston r. TN U.S.A.
150 C4 Holsworthy Devon, England U.K.
151 I2 Holt Norfolk, England U.K.
150 E3 Holt Wiltshire, England U.K.
150 E1 Holt Wrexham, Wales U.K.
226 E4 Holt MI U.S.A.
164 F2 Holten Neth.
168 C2 Holtgast Ger.
170 C2 Holthusen Ger.
168 C2 Holtland Ger.
236 E4 Holton KS U.S.A.
226 D4 Holton MI U.S.A.
149 I4 Holton le Clay Lincolnshire, England U.K.
168 C2 Holtrop (Großefehn) Ger.
168 E1 Holtsee Ger.
241 J5 Holtville CA U.S.A.
234 B3 Holtwood PA U.S.A.
240 □D9 Holualoa HI U.S.A.
137 H3 Holubivka Ukr.
164 E1 Holwerd Neth.
164 F1 Holwierde Neth.
147 D4 Holycross Rep. of Ireland
220 C3 Holy Cross AK U.S.A.
239 F4 Holy Cross, Mount of the CO U.S.A.
150 C1 Holyhead Isle of Anglesey, Wales U.K.
150 C1 Holyhead Bay Wales U.K.
149 H2 Holy Island England U.K.
146 C6 Holy Island Scotland U.K.
150 C1 Holy Island Wales U.K.
236 C3 Holyoke CO U.S.A.
233 G3 Holyoke MA U.S.A.
Holy See Europe see Vatican City
150 D1 Holywell Flintshire, Wales U.K.
147 D2 Holywell Northern Ireland U.K.
146 E6 Holywood Dumfries and Galloway, Scotland U.K.
147 F2 Holywood Northern Ireland U.K.
169 C5 Holzappel Ger.
171 E4 Holzdorf Ger.
169 E4 Holzen Ger.
172 D3 Holzgerlingen Ger.
171 D4 Holzhausen Ger.
169 C5 Holzhausen an der Haide Ger.
173 E3 Holzheim Bayern Ger.
173 E3 Holzheim Bayern Ger.
173 E3 Holzheim Bayern Ger.
169 D5 Holzheim Hessen Ger.
173 F4 Holzkirchen Ger.
169 E4 Holzminden Ger.
169 F4 Holzthaleben Ger.
171 D4 Holzweißig Ger.
169 C4 Holzwickede Ger.
210 B5 Homa Bay Kenya
96 A1 Homalin Myanmar
222 E5 Homathko r. B.C. Can.
Homāyūnshahr Iran see Khomeynīshahr
169 E4 Homberg (Efze) Ger.
169 D5 Homberg (Ohm) Ger.
156 C3 Hombleux France
206 E3 Hombori Mali
157 G3 Hombourg-Budange France
157 G3 Hombourg-Haut France
172 B2 Homburg Ger.
221 L3 Home Bay Nunavut Can.
157 F3 Homécourt France
85 F3 Home Hill Qld Austr.
86 □2 Home Island Cocos Is
182 B3 Homem r. Port.
220 C4 Homer AK U.S.A.
231 D5 Homer GA U.S.A.
237 E5 Homer LA U.S.A.
226 E4 Homer MI U.S.A.
233 E3 Homer NY U.S.A.
232 D4 Homer City PA U.S.A.
151 I2 Homersfield Suffolk, England U.K.
231 D6 Homerville GA U.S.A.
85 F4 Homestead Qld Austr.
231 D7 Homestead FL U.S.A.
234 C2 Hometown PA U.S.A.
234 C3 Homeville PA U.S.A.
81 E4 Homewood North I. N.Z.
231 C5 Homewood AL U.S.A.
140 J3 Hommelvik Norway
114 C2 Homnabad Karnataka India
197 H2 Homocea Romania
177 I5 Homokmégy Hungary
177 G5 Homokszentgyörgy Hungary
177 M4 Homoroade Romania
177 L3 Homorod r. Romania
Homs Libya see Al Khums
Homs Syria see Ḥimṣ
137 F1 Homyel' Belarus
Homyel Oblast admin. div. Belarus see Homyel'skaya Voblasts'
139 G5 Homyel'skaya Voblasts' admin. div. Belarus
232 C6 Honaker VA U.S.A.
Honan prov. China see Henan
240 □D9 Honaunau HI U.S.A.
114 C3 Honavalli Karnataka India
114 B3 Honavar Karnataka India
199 F3 Honaz Turkey
136 F2 Honcharivs'ke Ukr.
250 C3 Honda Col.
117 F5 Honda Orissa India
117 F5 Hondapa Orissa India
186 B1 Hondarribia Spain
214 E4 Hondeblaf r. S. Africa
214 A4 Hondeklipbaai S. Africa
243 H5 Hondo r. Belize/Mex.
103 E7 Hondo Japan
239 F5 Hondo NM U.S.A.
237 D6 Hondo TX U.S.A.
239 F5 Hondo r. NM U.S.A.
187 C6 Hondón de las Nieves Spain
187 C6 Hondón de los Frailes Spain
156 C2 Hondschoote France
246 A4 Honduras country Central America
242 □I5 Honduras, Gulf of Belize/Hond.
190 C3 Hône Italy
142 D1 Hønefoss Norway
232 E3 Honeoye Falls NY U.S.A.
234 C1 Honesdale PA U.S.A.
234 C2 Honey Brook PA U.S.A.
159 G2 Honfleur France
96 D2 Hong, Mouths of the Vietnam
96 D2 Hông, Sông r. Vietnam
109 E2 Hong'an Hubei China
101 C5 Hongch'ŏn S. Korea
96 D2 Hông Gai Vietnam
110 E4 Honggouzi Qinghai China
96 D1 Hongguo Guizhou China
109 E4 Honghai Wan b. China
108 B4 Honghe Yunnan China
109 E1 Hong He r. China
109 E2 Honghu Hubei China
Hongjialou Shandong China see Licheng
108 D3 Hongjiang Hunan China
Hongjiang Sichuan China see Wangcang
109 □ Hong Kong H.K. China
109 E4 Hong Kong special admin. reg. China
107 F4 Hongliu r. China
Hongliuwan Gansu China see Aksay
110 F3 Hongliuyuan Gansu China
97 D5 Hông Ngư Vietnam
Hongqiao Hunan China see Qidong
109 G2 Hongqiao airport China
Hongqizhen Hainan China see Tongshi
108 A2 Hongshan Yunnan China
108 D4 Hongshui He r. China
107 F4 Hongtong Shanxi China
225 H3 Honguedo, Détroit d' sea chan. Que. Can.
Hongwansi Gansu China see Sunan
101 C4 Hongwŏn N. Korea
108 B1 Hongyuan Sichuan China
109 F1 Hongze Jiangsu China
109 F1 Hongze Hu l. China
78 □6 Honiara Guadalcanal Solomon Is
150 D4 Honiton Devon, England U.K.
102 J4 Honjō Japan
105 F2 Honjō Japan
141 M3 Honkajoki Fin.
149 H4 Honley West Yorkshire, England U.K.
114 B3 Honnali Karnataka India
140 N1 Honningsvåg Norway
240 □D8 Honokaa HI U.S.A.
240 □C8 Honokahua HI U.S.A.
80 F2 Honokawa mt. North I. N.Z.
240 □ Honolulu HI U.S.A.
240 □ Honolulu County county HI U.S.A.
240 □D9 Honomu HI U.S.A.
226 D3 Honor MI U.S.A.
240 □ Honouliuli HI U.S.A.
174 B3 Hönow Ger.
183 H5 Honrubia Spain
183 G3 Honrubia de la Cuesta Spain
103 F6 Honshū i. Japan
183 H5 Hontacillas Spain
183 F3 Hontalbilla Spain
183 H5 Hontanaya Spain
163 B5 Hontanx France
177 H3 Hontianske Nemce Slovakia
183 G2 Hontoria de la Cantera Spain
183 G3 Hontoria del Pinar Spain
183 G3 Hontoria de Valdearados Spain
240 □D9 Honuapo HI U.S.A.
114 B2 Honwad Karnataka India
151 H3 Hoo Medway, England U.K.
238 B2 Hood, Mount vol. OR U.S.A.
222 C3 Hood Bay AK U.S.A.
Hood Island Islas Galápagos Ecuador see Española, Isla
87 C7 Hood Point W.A. Austr.
238 B2 Hood River OR U.S.A.
164 D2 Hoofddorp Neth.
168 D1 Hooge Ger.
165 D3 Hoogerheide Neth.
164 F2 Hoogersmilde Neth.
164 F2 Hoogeveen Neth.
164 F1 Hoogezand-Sappemeer Neth.
164 D3 Hooge Zwaluwe Neth.
164 F2 Hooghalen Neth.
Hooghly r. mouth India see Hugli
164 E2 Hoogkarspel Neth.
164 F3 Hoog-Keppel Neth.
164 F1 Hoogkerk Neth.
164 E2 Hoogland Neth.
168 B3 Hoogstede Ger.
165 D3 Hoogstraten Belgium
164 D3 Hoogvliet Neth.
149 I4 Hook East Riding of Yorkshire, England U.K.
151 G3 Hook Hampshire, England U.K.
237 C4 Hooker OK U.S.A.
151 F3 Hook Norton Oxfordshire, England U.K.
Hook of Holland Neth. see Hoek van Holland
85 H5 Hook Point Qld Austr.
85 G3 Hook Reef Qld Austr.
168 D2 Hooksiel Ger.
240 □C8 Hoolehua HI U.S.A.
220 E4 Hoonah AK U.S.A.
220 B3 Hooper Bay AK U.S.A.
226 D5 Hoopeston IL U.S.A.
215 E2 Hoopstad S. Africa
142 E4 Höör Sweden
164 E2 Hoorn Neth.
77 I3 Hoorn, Îles de is Wallis and Futuna Is
164 D3 Hoornaar Neth.
105 E3 Hōō-san mt. Japan
233 G3 Hoosick NY U.S.A.
241 J3 Hoover Dam AZ/NV U.S.A.
106 D2 Höövör Mongolia
140 □B2 Hóp lag. Iceland
127 F2 Hopa Turkey
234 D2 Hopatcong NJ U.S.A.
234 C1 Hop Bottom PA U.S.A.
222 F5 Hope B.C. Can.
81 D4 Hope South I. N.Z.
81 D5 Hope r. South I. N.Z.
150 D1 Hope Flintshire, Wales U.K.
237 E5 Hope AR U.S.A.
234 D2 Hope NJ U.S.A.
82 D2 Hope, Lake salt flat S.A. Austr.
87 D7 Hope, Lake salt flat W.A. Austr.
146 D3 Hope, Loch l. Scotland U.K.
246 □ Hope Bay Jamaica
225 I2 Hopedale Nfld. Can.
237 F6 Hopedale LA U.S.A.
214 B5 Hopefield S. Africa
Hopei prov. China see Hebei
243 H5 Hopelchén Mex.
146 E4 Hopeman Moray, Scotland U.K.
140 □ Hopen i. Svalbard
Hopes Advance Bay Que. Can. see Aupaluk
83 E3 Hopetoun Vic. Austr.
87 D7 Hopetoun W.A. Austr.
214 E3 Hopetown S. Africa
85 F2 Hope Vale Qld Austr.
233 H4 Hope Valley RI U.S.A.
234 D2 Hopewell NJ U.S.A.
232 E6 Hopewell VA U.S.A.
235 E1 Hopewell Junction NY U.S.A.
178 D3 Hopfgarten im Brixental Austria
83 E4 Hopkins r. Vic. Austr.
87 F5 Hopkins, Lake salt flat W.A. Austr.
230 C4 Hopkinsville KY U.S.A.
235 G1 Hopkinton RI U.S.A.
240 F2 Hopland CA U.S.A.
172 B2 Hoppstädten Ger.
169 C3 Hopsten Ger.
151 I2 Hopton Norfolk, England U.K.
151 H2 Hopton Suffolk, England U.K.
150 E2 Hoptonheath Shropshire, England U.K.
238 B2 Hoquiam WA U.S.A.
106 D5 Hor Qinghai China
136 F2 Hora Ukr.
129 E4 Horadiz Azer.
104 D4 Hōraiji-san hill Japan
151 H4 Horam East Sussex, England U.K.
127 F2 Horasan Turkey
176 C2 Horažďovice Czech Rep.
172 C3 Horb am Neckar Ger.
170 D1 Horbelev Denmark
151 G2 Horbling Lincolnshire, England U.K.
157 H4 Horbourg-Wihr France
178 A3 Hörbranz Austria
143 E4 Hörby Sweden
183 E3 Horcajo de las Torres Spain
185 F1 Horcajo de los Montes Spain
183 H5 Horcajo de Santiago Spain
183 E4 Horcajo Medianero Spain
183 G4 Horche Spain
185 F2 Horcón hill Spain
258 D2 Horcones r. Arg.
142 B1 Hordaland county Norway
169 F4 Hörden Ger.
151 F4 Hordle Hampshire, England U.K.
150 C2 Horeb Ceredigion, Wales U.K.
80 D1 Horeke North I. N.Z.
197 F3 Horezu Romania
173 E3 Horgau Ger.
190 D1 Horgen Switz.
172 D4 Horgenzell Ger.
106 C1 Horgo Mongolia
196 D2 Horgoš Vojvodina, Srbija Yugo.
136 B3 Horhany mts Ukr.
106 E3 Hörh Uul mts Mongolia
197 I3 Horia Romania
176 E1 Hořice Czech Rep.
226 C4 Horicon WI U.S.A.
107 F3 Horinger Nei Mongol China
179 H3 Horitschon Austria
106 D2 Horiult Mongolia
266 H7 Horizon Deep sea feature S. Pacific Ocean
171 F4 Horka Ger.
139 H4 Horki Belarus
151 G3 Horley Surrey, England U.K.
262 Q1 Horlick Mountains Antarctica
171 E4 Hörlitz Ger.
137 J3 Horlivka Ukr.
122 E4 Hormak Iran
247 □1 Hormigueros Puerto Rico
183 H2 Hormilla Spain
122 D5 Hormoz i. Iran
122 C5 Hormoz, Kūh-e mt. Iran
122 D5 Hormozgan prov. Iran
122 C5 Hormūd-e Bāgh Iran
122 D5 Hormuz, Strait of Iran/Oman
179 G2 Horn Austria
222 G2 Horn r. N.W.T. Can.
140 □B2 Horn c. Iceland
Horn, Cape Chile see Hornos, Cabo de
184 D2 Hornachos Spain
185 E3 Hornachuelos Spain
Hornád r. Hungary/Slovakia see Hernád

176 G3 Horná Potôň Slovakia
177 H3 Horná Štubňa Slovakia
140 L2 Hornavan l. Sweden
172 B2 Hornbach Ger.
169 D4 Horn-Bad Meinberg Ger.
237 E6 Hornbeck LA U.S.A.
172 C3 Hornberg Ger.
238 B3 Hornbrook CA U.S.A.
169 F3 Hornburg Ger.
149 G3 Hornby Lancashire, England U.K.
149 I4 Horncastle Lincolnshire, England U.K.
143 G1 Horndal Sweden
151 F4 Horndean Hampshire, England U.K.
 Horne, Îles de is Wallis and Futuna Is see Hoorn, Îles de
168 E2 Horneburg Ger.
140 L3 Hörnefors Sweden
232 E3 Hornell NY U.S.A.
224 C3 Hornepayne Ont. Can.
238 D2 Hornerstown NJ U.S.A.
177 G3 Horné Saliby Slovakia
177 H2 Horné Srnie Slovakia
147 C1 Horn Head hd Rep. of Ireland
177 H2 Horní Bečva Czech Rep.
177 G2 Horní Benešov Czech Rep.
177 F5 Horní Bělkovice Czech Rep.
176 C2 Horní Bříza Czech Rep.
176 C1 Horní Jiřetín Czech Rep.
242 C3 Hornillos Mex.
176 G2 Horní Moštěnice Czech Rep.
141 I3 Horníndal Norway
151 I2 Horning Norfolk, England U.K.
176 D3 Horní Planá Czech Rep.
171 F5 Horní Počaply Czech Rep.
172 C3 Hornindge mt. Ger.
85 E1 Horn Island Qld Austr.
176 B1 Horní Slavkov Czech Rep.
176 D3 Horní Stropnice Czech Rep.
222 F2 Horn Mountains N.W.T. Can.
185 H2 Hornos Spain
259 D9 Hornos, Cabo de c. Chile
137 F1 Hornostayivka Chernihivs'ka Oblast' Ukr.
137 G4 Hornostayivka Khersons'ka Oblast' Ukr.
171 F4 Hornow Ger.
156 B3 Hornoy-le-Bourg France
222 D2 Horn Peak Y.T. Can.
83 G3 Hornsby N.S.W. Austr.
149 I4 Hornsea East Riding of Yorkshire, England U.K.
141 L3 Hornslandet pen. Sweden
142 D3 Hornslet Denmark
170 C2 Hornstorf Ger.
168 D1 Hörnum Ger.
177 L4 Horoatu Crasnei Romania
136 C3 Horodenka Ukr.
136 D2 Horodets' Ukr.
175 M5 Horodlo Pol.
137 F2 Horodnya Ukr.
136 D2 Horodnytsya Ukr.
136 D3 Horodok Khmel'nyts'ka Oblast' Ukr.
136 B3 Horodok L'vivs'ka Oblast' Ukr.
137 F3 Horodyshche Cherkas'ka Oblast' Ukr.
137 F2 Horodyshche Chernihivs'ka Oblast' Ukr.
137 J3 Horodyshche Luhans'ka Oblast' Ukr.
136 C3 Horodyshche Ternopils'ka Oblast' Ukr.
136 C2 Horokhiv Ukr.
137 I3 Horokhvatka Ukr.
171 F5 Horoměřice Czech Rep.
177 L3 Horonda Ukr.
110 C3 Horo Shan mts China
102 K1 Horoshiri-dake mt. Japan
102 K1 Horoshiri-yama mt. Japan
176 C2 Horovice Czech Rep.
107 I3 Horqin Shadi reg. China
 Horqin Youyi Qianqi Nei Mongol China see Ulanhot
 Horqin Zuoyi Houqi Nei Mongol China see Ganjig
 Horqin Zuoyi Zhongqi Nei Mongol China see Baokang
253 F5 Horqueta Para.
150 C4 Horrabridge Devon, England U.K.
170 C1 Horreby Denmark
142 E3 Horred Sweden
151 H2 Horringer Suffolk, England U.K.
87 B6 Horrocks W.A. Austr.
111 E6 Horru Xizang China
179 F2 Hörsching Austria
238 F3 Horse Creek r. WY U.S.A.
222 F4 Horsefly B.C. Can.
227 I4 Horseheads NY U.S.A.
149 H3 Horsehouse North Yorkshire, England U.K.
169 F4 Hörsel r. Ger.
147 C3 Horseleap Galway Rep. of Ireland
147 D3 Horseleap Westmeath Rep. of Ireland
142 C4 Horsens Denmark
84 C5 Horseshoe Bend N.T. Austr.
238 C3 Horseshoe Bend ID U.S.A.
241 L4 Horseshoe Reservoir AZ U.S.A.
264 K3 Horseshoe Seamounts sea feature N. Atlantic Ocean
151 I2 Horsford Norfolk, England U.K.
149 H4 Horsforth West Yorkshire, England U.K.
83 E4 Horsham Vic. Austr.
151 G3 Horsham West Sussex, England U.K.
234 C2 Horsham PA U.S.A.
136 E2 Horshchyk Ukr.
171 C3 Hörsingen Ger.
168 G1 Horslunde Denmark
151 H3 Horsmonden Kent, England U.K.
176 B2 Horšovský Týn Czech Rep.
169 F5 Horst Neth.
165 F3 Horst Neth.
168 E2 Horst (Holstein) Ger.
151 I2 Horstead Norfolk, England U.K.
168 E2 Horstedt Ger.
169 C3 Hörstel Ger.
169 C3 Horstmar Ger.
199 F3 Horsunlu Aydın Turkey
177 I4 Hort Hungary
216 □1 Horta Faial Azores
142 D2 Horten Norway
182 D2 Hortezuela Spain
183 G2 Hortigüela Spain
177 K4 Hortobágy Hungary
220 F3 Horton r. N.W.T. Can.
151 F4 Horton Heath Hampshire, England U.K.
149 G3 Horton in Ribblesdale North Yorkshire, England U.K.
168 E1 Heruphav Denmark
190 D1 Horw Switz.
149 D1 Horwich Greater Manchester, England U.K.
136 D2 Horyn' r. Ukr.
175 L5 Horyniec Pol.
175 L5 Horyszów Pol.
210 O3 Hosa'ina Eth.
151 H5 Hösbach Ger.
114 C3 Hosdurga Karnataka India
95 F2 Hose, Pegunungan mts Sarawak Malaysia
171 F4 Hosena Ger.
169 E5 Hosenfeld Ger.
116 D5 Hoshangabad Madh. Prad. India
136 D2 Hoshcha Ukr.
116 C3 Hoshiarpur Punjab India
106 A1 Höshööt Mongolia
165 H4 Hosingen Lux.
199 E1 Hoşköy Turkey
114 C3 Hospet Karnataka India
163 C6 Hospice de France France
 Hospitalet Cataluña Spain see L'Hospitalet de l'Infant
 Hospitalet Cataluña Spain see L'Hospitalet de Llobregat
163 F3 Hosségor France

207 I4 Hosséré Vokre mt. Cameroon
172 D4 Hoßkirch Ger.
177 K4 Hosszúpályi Hungary
177 H4 Hosszúpereszteg Hungary
186 F3 Hostalric Spain
 Hostalric Spain see Hostalric
259 C9 Hoste, Isla i. Chile
163 B4 Hostens France
176 F3 Hostěradice Czech Rep.
177 H3 Hostie Slovakia
176 E1 Hostinné Czech Rep.
176 D1 Hostivice Czech Rep.
171 F5 Hošťka Czech Rep.
176 E1 Hostomice Czech Rep.
173 G2 Hošťoun Czech Rep.
168 E1 Hostruspav Denmark
114 C3 Hosur Tamil Nadu India
140 K3 Hotagen r. Sweden
104 D2 Hotaka Japan
105 F2 Hotaka-yama mt. Japan
111 C4 Hotan China
214 D2 Hotazel S. Africa
235 E1 Hotchkissville CT U.S.A.
241 I2 Hot Creek r. NV U.S.A.
241 I2 Hot Creek Range mts NV U.S.A.
171 C3 Hötensleben Ger.
87 C7 Hotham r. W.A. Austr.
84 B2 Hotham, Cape N.T. Austr.
140 L2 Hoting Sweden
179 G4 Hotinja vas Slovenia
237 E5 Hot Springs AR U.S.A.
 Hot Springs NM U.S.A. see Truth or Consequences
236 C3 Hot Springs SD U.S.A.
238 F3 Hot Sulphur Springs CO U.S.A.
222 C2 Hottah Lake N.W.T. Can.
212 B5 Hottentots Bay Namibia
165 E4 Hotton Belgium
78 □5 Houaïlu New Caledonia
156 C2 Houdain France
156 B4 Houdan France
157 F4 Houdelaincourt France
163 C4 Houeillès France
163 C5 Houeydets France
165 E4 Houffalize Belgium
85 F3 Houghton r. Qld Austr.
149 G3 Houghton Cumbria, England U.K.
226 C2 Houghton MI U.S.A.
232 D3 Houghton NY U.S.A.
226 E3 Houghton Lake MI U.S.A.
149 H3 Houghton le Spring Tyne and Wear, England U.K.
151 G3 Houghton Regis Bedfordshire, England U.K.
96 C2 Houie Moc, Phou mt. Laos
159 F2 Houlgate France
157 I5 Houlton ME U.S.A.
107 F5 Houma Shanxi China
237 F6 Houma LA U.S.A.
109 E4 Houmen Guangdong China
205 H2 Houmt Souk Tunisia
206 B4 Houndé Burkina
146 F6 Houndwood Scottish Borders, Scotland U.K.
156 C2 Houplines France
146 C4 Hourn, Loch inlet Scotland U.K.
162 A3 Hourtin France
162 A3 Hourtin et de Carcans, Étang d' l. France
162 A3 Hourtin-Plage France
233 G3 Housatonic MA U.S.A.
235 E1 Housatonic r. CT U.S.A.
241 K2 House Range mts UT U.S.A.
149 E6 Housesteads tourist site England U.K.
222 E4 Houston B.C. Can.
234 C4 Houston DE U.S.A.
226 B4 Houston MN U.S.A.
237 F4 Houston MO U.S.A.
233 H3 Houston MS U.S.A.
237 E6 Houston TX U.S.A.
214 B6 Hout Bay S. Africa
164 E2 Houten Neth.
165 B3 Houthalen Belgium
185 B4 Houthulst Belgium
214 E4 Houtkraal S. Africa
87 B6 Houtman Abrolhos is W.A. Austr.
146 F3 Houton Orkney, Scotland U.K.
141 M3 Houtskär Fin.
214 D4 Houwater S. Africa
165 E4 Houyet Belgium
 Houzhai Guangdong China see Nan'ao
104 D4 Hov Denmark
142 D1 Hov Norway
143 F2 Hova Sweden
106 A2 Hovd Hovd Mongolia
106 D2 Hovd Övörhangay Mongolia
106 A2 Hovd Mongolia
106 C2 Hovdefjell hill Norway
106 B1 Hovd Gol r. Mongolia
151 G4 Hove Brighton and Hove, England U.K.
169 D4 Hövelhof Ger.
136 C3 Hovera, Hora mt. Ukr.
149 H3 Hoveton Norfolk, England U.K.
122 B4 Hoveyzeh Iran
149 I3 Hovingham North Yorkshire, England U.K.
226 C2 Hovland MN U.S.A.
143 F3 Hovmantorp Sweden
129 G3 Hövsan Azer.
107 F3 Hövsgöl Mongolia
106 D1 Hövsgöl prov. Mongolia
106 D1 Hövsgöl Nuur l. Mongolia
137 G3 Hovtva r. Ukr.
137 G3 Hovtva r. Ukr.
124 C5 Howakil Bay Eritrea
202 E5 Howar, Wadi watercourse Sudan
85 H5 Howard Qld Austr.
237 D4 Howard KS U.S.A.
236 D2 Howard SD U.S.A.
226 C3 Howard WI U.S.A.
226 E4 Howard City MI U.S.A.
234 B2 Howard County county MD U.S.A.
149 H3 Howardian Hills England U.K.
84 C2 Howard Island N.T. Austr.
84 B2 Howard Springs N.T. Austr.
149 I4 Howden East Riding of Yorkshire, England U.K.
226 E5 Howe IN U.S.A.
83 G4 Howe, Cape Vic. Austr.
262 O1 Howe, Mount Antarctica
227 F4 Howell MI U.S.A.
146 F5 Howe of the Mearns reg. Scotland U.K.
236 C2 Howes SD U.S.A.
233 G2 Howick Que. Can.
215 H3 Howick S. Africa
82 D1 Howitt, Lake salt flat Austr.
233 □I2 Howland ME U.S.A.
77 I1 Howland Island N. Pacific Ocean
83 F3 Howlong N.S.W. Austr.
 Howlwadaag Somalia see Haora
147 E4 Howth Rep. of Ireland
236 C4 Hoxie KS U.S.A.
169 E4 Höxter Ger.
110 D2 Hoxtolgay Xinjiang China
146 E3 Hoy i. Scotland U.K.
168 D3 Hoya Ger.
105 F3 Höya Japan
185 I2 Hoya Gonzalo Spain
141 I3 Høyanger Norway
171 F4 Hoyerswerda Ger.
149 H4 Hoylake Merseyside, England U.K.
149 H4 Hoyland South Yorkshire, England U.K.
140 K2 Høylandet Norway
227 I3 Hoyle Ont. Can.
171 C4 Hoym Ger.
183 J3 Hoyo de Manzanares Spain
182 D4 Hoyos Spain
182 D4 Hoyos del Espino Spain
199 M6 Hoyran Turkey
136 E3 Hoziat Turkey
185 L4 Hozgarganta r. Spain
104 B3 Hozu-gawa r. Japan
136 E2 Hrabove Ukr.

176 E1 Hradec Králové Czech Rep.
177 G2 Hradec nad Moravicí Czech Rep.
176 F2 Hradec nad Svitavou Czech Rep.
176 C1 Hrádek Czech Rep.
176 D1 Hrádek nad Nisou Czech Rep.
176 F3 Hradešice Czech Rep.
176 C1 Hradiště Czech Rep.
177 H3 Hradiště Slovakia
137 G3 Hradyz'k Ukr.
138 G5 Hradzyanka Belarus
176 B1 Hranice Olomoucký kraj Czech Rep.
176 G2 Hranice Olomoucký kraj Czech Rep.
136 E2 Hranitne Ukr.
179 H3 Hranovnica Slovakia
188 G4 Hrasnica Bos.-Herz.
179 G4 Hrastnik Slovenia
140 □D2 Hraun slope Iceland
129 D3 Hrazdan Armenia
137 F5 Hrazenyi hill Czech Rep.
136 F3 Hrebinka r. Ukr.
137 F3 Hrebinka Ukr.
137 G1 Hrem"yach Ukr.
137 G4 Hreyhove Ukr.
177 H3 Hriňová Slovakia
136 E3 Hristovaia Moldova
137 E5 Hrób Ukr.
117 I3 Hrochot' Slovakia
176 E2 Hrochův Týnec Czech Rep.
138 D5 Hrodna Belarus
 Hrodna Oblast admin. div. Belarus see Hrodzyenskaya Voblasts'
175 L2 Hrodnyendskaye Wzvyshsha hills Belarus
138 E5 Hrodzyenskaya Voblasts' admin. div. Belarus
137 H4 Hromivka Ukr.
173 H2 Hromnice Czech Rep.
177 H4 Hron r. Slovakia
177 I3 Hronec Slovakia
176 F1 Hronov Czech Rep.
177 H3 Hronský Beňadik Slovakia
176 F2 Hrotovice Czech Rep.
171 D5 Hroznětín Czech Rep.
175 L5 Hrubieszów Pol.
175 M4 Hrudky Ukr.
137 H2 Hrun' Ukr.
137 H2 Hrun' Ukr.
177 I3 Hrushuvakha Ukr.
176 F3 Hruško Ukr.
176 F3 Hrušky Czech Rep.
177 H1 Hrušovany u Brna Czech Rep.
177 I2 Hruštín Slovakia
175 K3 Hrusznew Pol.
 Hrvatska Europe country see Croatia
 Hrvatska Kostajnica Croatia see Bosanska Kostajnica
188 F3 Hrvatska Grahovo Bos.-Herz. see Bosansko Grahovo
137 G2 Hryhorivka Chernihivs'ka Oblast' Ukr.
137 G2 Hryhorivka Dnipropetrovs'ka Oblast' Ukr.
137 G4 Hryhorivka Khersons'ka Oblast' Ukr.
136 D3 Hrymayliv Ukr.
136 C4 Hrynyava Ukr.
136 E3 Hryshivtsi Ukr.
136 D3 Hrytsiv Ukr.
96 B2 Hsi-hseng Myanmar
96 B2 Hsin, Nam r. Myanmar
 Hsin-chia-p'o country Asia see Singapore
 Hsin-chia-p'o Sing. see Singapore
109 G3 Hsinchu Taiwan
 Hsinking Jilin China see Changchun
109 G4 Hsinying Taiwan
 Hsi-sha Ch'un-tao is S. China Sea see Paracel Islands
109 G3 Hsüeh Shan mt. Taiwan
109 G3 Hua'an Fujian China
252 A2 Huacaibamba Peru
252 E5 Huacaraje Bol.
252 E5 Huacaya Bol.
252 E5 Huacaya Bol.
107 F4 Huachi Gansu China
252 A2 Huacho Peru
252 B2 Huachón Peru
100 D3 Huachuan Heilong. China
241 L6 Huachuca City AZ U.S.A.
260 C2 Huaco Arg.
252 A2 Huacrachuco Peru
107 G3 Huade Nei Mongol China
100 C4 Huadian Jilin China
109 E4 Huadu Guangdong China
109 E1 Huafeng Fujian China
107 H4 Huaian Hebei China
109 F1 Huai'an Jiangsu China
109 F1 Huaibei Anhui China
109 E1 Huaibin Henan China
 Huaicheng Guangdong China see Huaiji
 Huaide Jilin China see Gongzhuling
 Huaidian Henan China see Shenqiu
109 F1 Huai He r. China
108 D3 Huaihua Hunan China
109 E4 Huaiji Guangdong China
107 G3 Huailai Hebei China
96 C3 Huai Luang r. Thai.
109 F2 Huainan Anhui China
109 F2 Huaining Anhui China
107 G4 Huairen Shanxi China
107 H3 Huairou Beijing China
97 A4 Huai Samran r. Thai.
109 E1 Huaiyang Henan China
109 F1 Huaiyin Jiangsu China
109 F1 Huaiyuan Anhui China
108 D3 Huaiyuan Guangxi China
245 J5 Huajicori Mex.
245 F5 Huajuápan de León Mex.
243 F5 Huajuápan de León Mex.
109 G3 Hualien Taiwan
252 B3 Hualla Peru
252 A2 Huallaga r. Peru
250 O6 Huallanca Peru
224 D4 Hualqui Chile
252 A1 Huamachuco Peru
245 F4 Huamantla Mex.
209 B8 Huambo Angola
209 B8 Huambo prov. Angola
100 D3 Huanan Heilong. China
252 B3 Huancabamba Peru
255 E6 Huancane Peru
252 B3 Huancapi Peru
252 B3 Huancavelica Peru
252 B3 Huancavelica dept Peru
252 A2 Huancayo Peru
107 F4 Huanchaca Gansu China
136 C3 Hrabove

109 F2 Huangshan Anhui China
108 B1 Huangshengguan China see Shexian
109 E2 Huangshi Hubei China
 Huangshi Guangdong China see Huilai
107 E4 Huangtu Gaoyuan plat. China
261 G5 Huanguelén Arg.
107 I4 Huangxian Shandong China
106 D4 Huangyan Zhejiang China
106 D4 Huangyuan Qinghai China
107 I3 Huangzhong Qinghai China
 Huangzhou Hubei China see Huanggang
108 B3 Huaning Yunnan China
108 D3 Huanjiang Guangxi China
103 D3 Huanren Liaoning China
107 E4 Huanren Liaoning China
 Huanshan Zhejiang China see Yuhuan
252 B3 Huanta Peru
107 H4 Huantai Shandong China
252 A2 Huánuco Peru
252 A2 Huánuco dept Peru
244 C3 Huanusco Mex.
107 E4 Huanxian Gansu China
107 F4 Huaojian Jilin China
252 A2 Huaráz Peru
252 B3 Huari Peru
252 A2 Huarmey Peru
252 A3 Huarochiri Peru
183 I2 Huarte-Araquil Spain
250 B5 Huasaga r. Peru
107 I3 Huashan China
107 F5 Hua Shan mt. Shaanxi China
106 C5 Huashixia Qinghai China
242 C3 Huatabampo Mex.
245 F4 Huatusco Mex.
245 E3 Huauchinango Mex.
252 A2 Huaura, Islas de is Peru
245 F4 Huautla Mex.
107 G5 Huaxian Henan China
107 F5 Huaxian Shaanxi China
 Huayang Anhui China see Jixi
252 A2 Huaylas Peru
 Huayuan Hubei China see Xiaochang
108 D2 Huayuan Hunan China
 Huazangsi Gansu China see Tianzhu
106 D4 Huazhaizi Gansu China
108 D4 Huazhou Guangdong China
245 F5 Huazolotitlán Mex.
109 E2 Hubei prov. China
114 B3 Hubli Karnataka India
177 I2 Hubová Slovakia
137 H3 Hubynykha Ukr.
101 C4 Huch'ang N. Korea
169 D3 Hüde (Oldenburg) Ger.
168 D2 Hude (Oldenburg) Ger.
107 I1 Hude Hulin Czech Rep.
197 H1 Hudeşti Romania
113 □1 Huduvelli i. N. Male Maldives
141 L3 Hudiksvall Sweden
233 H3 Hudson MA U.S.A.
233 E5 Hudson MD U.S.A.
233 □I2 Hudson ME U.S.A.
232 E5 Hudson NH U.S.A.
233 H3 Hudson NH U.S.A.
233 G3 Hudson NY U.S.A.
226 A2 Hudson r. NY U.S.A.
233 G4 Hudson r. NY U.S.A.
 Hudson, Baie d' sea Can. see Hudson Bay
259 B7 Hudson, Cerro mt. Chile
 Hudson, Détroit d' str. Nunavut/Que. Can. see Hudson Strait
237 E4 Hudson, Lake OK U.S.A.
223 K4 Hudson Bay Sask. Can.
221 J4 Hudson Bay sea Can.
235 D2 Hudson County county NJ U.S.A.
233 G3 Hudson Falls NY U.S.A.
 Hudson Island Tuvalu see Nanumanga
221 P2 Hudson Land reg. Greenland
262 R2 Hudson Mountains Antarctica
222 F3 Hudson's Hope B.C. Can.
221 K3 Hudson Strait Nunavut/Que. Can.
96 D3 Huê Vietnam
182 D4 Huebra r. Spain
183 I3 Huebra r. Spain
183 I3 Huécija Spain
197 J3 Huedin Romania
184 E3 Huélago Spain
158 C2 Huelgoat France
186 A3 Huelma Spain
184 D3 Huelva Spain
184 C4 Huelva prov. Andalucía Spain
184 D3 Huelva r. Spain
184 H3 Huelves Spain
184 F4 Huércal de Almería Spain
185 I3 Huércal-Overa Spain
239 F4 Huerfano r. CO U.S.A.
183 I4 Huérguina Spain
183 I3 Huermeces Spain
183 G5 Huerta de Valdecarábanos Spain
183 H4 Huertahernando Spain
183 H4 Huerto Spain
186 C4 Huerva r. Spain
186 C3 Huesa Spain
185 I3 Huesa del Común Spain
186 C4 Huesca Spain
186 C3 Huesca prov. Aragón Spain
186 A3 Huéscar Spain
244 D4 Huetamo Mex.
183 H3 Huete Spain
184 F3 Huétor-Tájar Spain
85 H4 Hueytown AL U.S.A.
231 C6 Hueytown AL U.S.A.
183 G5 Huéznar r. Spain
172 C4 Hüfingen Ger.
209 B8 Hufrane Angola
142 A1 Huftarøy i. Norway
149 I4 Huggate East Riding of Yorkshire, England U.K.
85 F4 Hughenden Qld Austr.
261 D5 Hughes Arg.
82 B2 Hughes S.A. Austr.
218 C3 Hughes r. Can.
232 D5 Hughesville PA U.S.A.
240 □ Hughson CA U.S.A.

245 E3 Huichapán Mex.
101 C4 Huich'ŏn N. Korea
 Huichang Anhui China see Shexian
109 E2 Huichang China
 Huicheng Guangdong China see Huilai
109 E3 Huidong Guangdong China
108 B3 Huidong Sichuan China
100 C4 Huifa He r. China
101 H1 Huihe Nei Mongol China
165 D3 Huijbergen Neth.
209 B8 Huila Angola
209 B8 Huila prov. Angola
250 C3 Huila dept Col.
250 C4 Huila, Nevado de vol. Col.
108 B3 Huilai Guangdong China
209 B8 Huila Plateau Angola
108 B3 Huili Sichuan China
 Huilong Jiangsu China see Qidong
108 C3 Huishui Guizhou China
146 A4 Huisinis Western Isles, Scotland U.K.
160 C5 Huisne r. France
159 H4 Huisseau-sur-Cosson France
164 E3 Huissen Neth.
141 M3 Huittinen Fin.
244 D4 Huitzila Mex.
245 F5 Huitzuco Mex.
245 F5 Huixtla Mex.
243 G6 Huixtla Mex.
 Huiyang Guangdong China see Huizhou
108 B3 Huize Yunnan China
164 E2 Huizen Neth.
109 E4 Huizhou Guangdong China
 Huizhou Guangdong China see Hubei
106 E2 Hüjirt Arhangay Mongolia
106 E2 Hüjirt Övörhangay Mongolia
106 E2 Hüjirt Töv Mongolia
80 E4 Hukanui North I. N.Z.
106 B5 Hukawng Valley Myanmar
212 D4 Hukuntsi Botswana
100 C3 Hulan r. China
100 C3 Hulan Heilong. China
107 I2 Hulan Ergi Heilong. China
124 C2 Hulayfä' Saudi Arabia
226 E2 Hulbert MI U.S.A.
232 B6 Hulen KY U.S.A.
 Huliao Guangdong China see Dabu
169 D3 Hüllhorst Ger.
169 D3 Hülsede Ger.
165 E4 Hulsberg Neth.
165 D3 Hulshout Belgium
165 C3 Hulst Neth.
143 G1 Hulterstad Kalmar Sweden
143 F3 Hultsfred Sweden
168 E5 Hüpstedt Ger.
101 H3 Huludao Liaoning China
113 □1 Huluk i. N. Male Maldives
 Hulumeedhoo i. Addu Atoll Maldives see Midu
 Hulun Nei Mongol China see Hailar
 Hulwän Egypt see Helwân
137 I4 Hulyaypole Ukr.
100 C2 Huma Heilong. China
107 I3 Huma Heilong. China
106 D2 Humacao Puerto Rico
253 E4 Humaitá Brazil
253 F6 Humaitá Para.
183 G4 Humanes de Mohernando Spain
215 C8 Humansdorp S. Africa
252 B3 Humay Peru
124 D2 Humayyän, Jabal hill Saudi Arabia
209 B9 Humbe Angola
209 B8 Humbe, Serra do mts Angola
149 J4 Humber, Mouth of the England U.K.
149 I4 Humberside airport England U.K.
149 I4 Humberston North East Lincolnshire, England U.K.
254 E2 Humberto de Campos Brazil
149 G2 Humbie East Lothian, Scotland U.K.
168 F1 Humble Denmark
261 H3 Humboldt Arg.
223 J4 Humboldt Sask. Can.
241 K6 Humboldt AZ U.S.A.
236 E3 Humboldt NE U.S.A.
240 H1 Humboldt r. NV U.S.A.
78 □5 Humboldt, Mount New Caledonia
238 A3 Humboldt Bay CA U.S.A.
81 B6 Humboldt Mountain mts South I. N.Z.
240 H1 Humboldt Range mts NV U.S.A.
85 F5 Humeburn Qld Austr.
261 G5 Humeda plain Arg.
252 C3 Humedo Bol.
140 J2 Humeda Norway
177 K7 Humenné Slovakia
83 F3 Hume Reservoir N.S.W. Austr.
157 F5 Humes-Jorquenay France
185 H3 Humilladero Spain
232 D4 Hummeltown PA U.S.A.
234 B2 Hummels Wharf PA U.S.A.
81 C6 Hummock Hill South I. N.Z.
179 H4 Hum na Sutli Croatia
209 B8 Humpata Angola
 Humphrey Island atoll Cook Is see Manihiki
240 H3 Humphreys, Mount CA U.S.A.
261 L4 Humphreys Peak AZ U.S.A.
176 L4 Humpolec Czech Rep.
176 F2 Humpolec Czech Rep.
149 H3 Humshaugh Northumberland, England U.K.
210 F2 Hurdiyo Somalia
107 I3 Hure Nei Mongol China
106 D2 Hürement Mongolia
 Huri r. Nei Mongol China see Hure
203 G3 Hurghada Egypt
210 C4 Huri r. Kenya
128 D2 Huri Ger.
137 G3 Hurka Ukr.
226 C1 Hurkett Ont. Can.
147 C4 Hurler's Cross Rep. of Ireland

197 F3 Hunedoara Romania
169 E5 Hünfeld Ger.
169 E5 Hünfelden-Kirberg Ger.
177 H4 Hungary country Europe
169 D5 Hungen Ger.
173 F3 Hungerberg hill Ger.
83 F7 Hungerford Qld Austr.
151 F3 Hungerford West Berkshire, England U.K.
106 B1 Hüngiy Gol r. Mongolia
101 C5 Hüngnam N. Korea
147 B5 Hungry Hill hill Rep. of Ireland
114 C2 Hungund Karnataka India
234 C2 Hungund
 Hunjiang Jilin China see Baishan
149 I3 Hunmanby North Yorkshire, England U.K.
142 D2 Hunnebostrand Sweden
165 E3 Hunsel Neth.
212 B3 Huns Mountains Namibia
157 H4 Hunspach France
151 H2 Hunstanton Norfolk, England U.K.
123 H2 Hunstein mt. Austria
168 D3 Hunte r. Ger.
83 J5 Hunter r. N.S.W. Austr.
81 A7 Hunter r. South I. N.Z.
224 C3 Hunters Run PA U.S.A.
80 E2 Hunterville North I. N.Z.
234 C5 Huntingburg IN U.S.A.
232 E4 Huntingdon TN U.S.A.
230 C3 Huntingdon PA U.S.A.
150 G2 Huntingdon Cambridgeshire, England U.K.
232 E4 Huntingdon TN U.S.A.
234 C1 Huntingdon UT U.S.A.
232 B5 Huntington WV U.S.A.
240 H5 Huntington Beach CA U.S.A.
227 I4 Huntington Creek r. NV U.S.A.
235 J2 Huntington Station PA U.S.A.
80 E2 Huntly North I. N.Z.
146 F3 Huntly Aberdeenshire, Scotland U.K.
226 C1 Hunt's Quay Argyll and Bute, Scotland U.K.
234 A2 Hunters Run PA U.S.A.
237 E4 Huntsville AL U.S.A.
231 C5 Huntsville AR U.S.A.
227 E4 Huntsville MO U.S.A.
227 I3 Huntsville TX U.S.A.
124 D2 Hunayti'ah Saudi Arabia
107 J5 Hunya Hungary
137 I3 Hunyani r. Moz./Zimbabwe see Manyame
107 G4 Hunyuan Shanxi China
116 C2 Hunza Jammu and Kashmir
123 H3 Hunza r. Pak.
164 F1 Hunze r. Neth.
110 C2 Huocheng Xinjiang China
107 G5 Huojia Henan China
100 C2 Huolongmen Heilong. China
 Huolu Hebei China see Luquan
96 D3 Huong Thuy Vietnam
83 F5 Huonville Tas. Austr.
109 F1 Huoqiu Anhui China
109 F2 Huoshan Anhui China
100 D2 Huo Shan mt. Hubei China
107 F4 Huoxian Shanxi China
222 D3 Hupalivka Ukr.
137 H3 Hupalivka Ukr.
135 M3 Huppy France
222 D3 Hupsel Neth.
169 F4 Hüpstedt Ger.
124 C4 Hüth Yemen
100 E3 Hutou Heilong. China
87 B6 Hutt r. W.A. Austr.
178 E3 Hüttau Austria
179 F4 Hüttenberg Austria
172 D2 Hüttenberg hill Ger.
169 D5 Hüttenberg-Hochelheim Ger.
169 F4 Hüttenrode Ger.
173 H3 Hutthurm Ger.
149 J4 Hüttlingen Ger.
150 E3 Hutton North Somerset, England U.K.
85 G5 Hutton, Mount hill Qld Austr.
149 I4 Hutton Cranswick East Riding of Yorkshire, England U.K.
87 D5 Hutton Range hills W.A. Austr.
149 H3 Hutton Rudby North Yorkshire, England U.K.
190 C1 Huttwil Switz.
110 D2 Hutubi Xinjiang China
110 D2 Hutubi He r. China
107 H4 Hutuo r. China
168 F2 Hützel Ger.
130 D11 Huvadhu Atoll Maldives
123 H3 Hüvär Iran
168 G3 Hüven Ger.
122 D5 Hüvián, Küh-e mts Iran
125 E2 Huwär i. The Gulf
175 K6 Huwniki Pol.
122 D5 Huwwah Iran
101 C6 Huxley, Mount South I. N.Z.
86 B3 Huxley, Mount hill W.A. Austr.
165 B1 Huxley, Mount South I. N.Z.
165 B4 Huy Belgium
149 G4 Huyton Merseyside, England U.K.
136 C4 Huyva Ukr.
109 G2 Huzhen Zhejiang China
109 G2 Huzhou Zhejiang China
106 D4 Huzhu Qinghai China
114 C2 Huzurnagar Andhra Prad. India
233 F3 Hvannadalshnúkur vol. Iceland
140 □B2 Hvannadalshnúkur vol. Iceland
199 H4 Hvar Croatia
188 F4 Hvar i. Croatia
137 H5 Hvardiys'ke Ukr.
188 F4 Hvarski Kanal sea chan. Croatia
140 □B2 Hveragerði Iceland
142 E5 Hvide Sande Denmark
142 □D3 Hvíta r. Iceland
142 D1 Hvittingfoss Norway
136 D3 Hvizdets' Ukr.
137 G2 Hvyntove Ukr.
134 L4 Hwadae N. Korea
212 E3 Hwange Zimbabwe
101 C5 Hwang Ho r. China see Huang He
101 C5 Hwangju N. Korea
213 F3 Hwedza Zimbabwe
104 B3 Hwlffordd Pembrokeshire, Wales U.K. see Haverfordwest
233 H4 Hyannis MA U.S.A.
236 C3 Hyannis NE U.S.A.
106 B1 Hyargas Nuur salt l. Mongolia
81 B8 Hyattsville MD U.S.A.
222 C4 Hydaburg AK U.S.A.
81 C6 Hyde South I. N.Z.
149 G4 Hyde Greater Manchester, England U.K.
232 C7 Hyde AK U.S.A.
232 B6 Hyde KY U.S.A.
233 G2 Hyde Park VT U.S.A.
222 D4 Hyder AK U.S.A.
114 C2 Hyderabad Andhra Prad. India
123 G5 Hyderabad Pak.
161 E5 Hyères France
161 E5 Hyères, Îles d' is France
101 D4 Hyesan N. Korea
222 D3 Hyland r. Can.
84 B2 Hyland, Mount N.S.W. Austr.
222 D3 Hyland Post B.C. Can.
141 I3 Hyllestad Norway
143 F4 Hyltebruk Sweden
157 G4 Hymont France
104 A3 Hyndman PA U.S.A.
146 B5 Hynish Argyll and Bute, Scotland U.K.
104 A3 Hyōgo pref. Japan
103 D5 Hyōno-sen mt. Japan
140 O2 Hyrynsalmi Fin.
222 G4 Hyrynsalmi Iran see Gorgán
238 F2 Hysham MT U.S.A.
222 G4 Hythe Alta Can.
151 F4 Hythe Hampshire, England U.K.
151 I3 Hythe Kent, England U.K.
141 N3 Hyvinkää Fin.
175 K6 Hyżne Pol.

I

97 E4 Ia Dun r. Vietnam
256 C4 Iaçanga Brazil
252 C2 Iaco r. Brazil
197 G2 Iacobeni Sibiu Romania
197 G2 Iacobeni Suceava Romania
256 B4 Iacri Brazil
254 E5 Iaçu Brazil
232 C6 Iaeger WV U.S.A.
213 □J4 Iakora Madag.
 Ialbuzi Rus. Fed. see El'brus
136 C5 Ialomița r. Romania
197 I3 Ialomița r. Romania
197 H3 Ialomiței, Balta marsh Romania
136 E4 Ialoveni Moldova
197 I3 Ialpug r. Moldova
197 G3 Ianca Romania
197 I2 Iana Romania
129 C2 Ianet'i Georgia
257 F3 Iapu Brazil
251 F3 Iauaretê Brazil
251 F3 Iauaretê Brazil
197 H2 Iaşi Romania
199 H6 Iasmos Greece
92 A3 Iba Phil.
206 D5 Ibadan Nigeria
250 C2 Ibagué Col.
250 C3 Ibagué Col.
184 E1 Ibahernando Spain
256 C5 Ibaiti Brazil
197 G3 Ibănești Romania
197 H2 Ibăneşti Romania
196 D4 Ibar r. Serbia
104 F3 Ibaraki Osaka Japan
105 G2 Ibaraki pref. Japan
250 B4 Ibarra Ecuador
256 B4 Ibarra Brazil
258 E3 Ibarreta Arg.
124 D5 Ibb Yemen
206 C4 Ibb governorate Yemen
169 D3 Ibbenbüren Ger.
183 G3 Ibdes Spain
198 A1 Ibeas de Juarros Spain
258 F2 Iberá, Esteros del marsh Arg.
251 G4 Iberia Peru
250 D4 Iberia Madre de Dios Peru
257 F4 Ibertioga Brazil
225 F2 Iberville, Lac d' l. Que. Can.
140 L1 Ibestad Norway
94 F1 Ibi Sumatera Indon.
207 G4 Ibi Nigeria
185 K3 Ibi Spain
257 E3 Ibiá Brazil
254 D4 Ibiapaba, Serra da hills Brazil
257 F2 Ibiaí Brazil
182 D1 Ibias r. Spain
255 A9 Ibicuí r. Brazil

Ibie to 'Irq Subay 315

161 C4 Ibie r. France
104 C3 Ibi-gawa r. Japan
254 F4 Ibimirim Brazil
208 F4 Ibina r. Dem. Rep. Congo
256 B5 Ibiporã Brazil
256 C4 Ibirá Brazil
257 G3 Ibiraçu Brazil
254 E5 Ibitiara Brazil
256 C4 Ibitinga Brazil
256 D5 Ibiúna Brazil
Ibiza Spain see Eivissa
Ibiza i. Spain see Eivissa
194 D5 Iblei, Monti mts Sicilia Italy
163 B5 Ibos France
254 E5 Ibotirama Brazil
208 A5 Iboundji Gabon
208 A5 Iboundji, Mont hill Gabon
125 G3 Ibrā' Oman
Ibrala Turkey see Yeşildere
135 I5 Ibresi Rus. Fed.
125 G3 Ibrī Oman
185 G2 Ibros Spain
151 F2 Ibstock Leicestershire, England U.K.
104 C3 Ibuki-yama mt. Japan
103 E8 Ibusuki Japan
250 E5 Içá r. Brazil
252 B3 Ica Peru
252 B3 Ica dept Peru
250 E4 Içana r. Brazil
Icaria i. Greece see Ikaria
254 D2 Icatu Brazil
241 J3 Iceberg Canyon gorge NV U.S.A.
126 D3 İçel İçel Turkey
128 A1 İçel prov. Turkey
221 Q3 Iceland country Europe
264 H2 Iceland Basin sea feature N. Atlantic Ocean
264 I1 Icelandic Plateau sea feature N. Atlantic Ocean
256 C4 Icem Brazil
117 F4 Ichak Bihar India
114 B2 Ichalkaranji Mahar. India
115 E2 Ichchapuram Andhra Prad. India
173 E3 Ichenhausen Ger.
172 B3 Ichenheim Ger.
105 G3 Ichihara Japan
105 F3 Ichikawa Japan
104 A4 Ichi-kawa r. Japan
105 E3 Ichikawadaimon Japan
252 D4 Ichilo r. Bol.
104 C3 Ichinomiya Aichi Japan
104 D4 Ichinomiya Aichi Japan
102 J4 Ichinoseki Japan
131 Q4 Ichinskiy, Vulkan vol. Rus. Fed.
Ichkeria aut. rep. Rus. Fed. see Chechenskaya Respublika
137 G2 Ichnya Ukr.
101 C5 Ich'ŏn N. Korea
101 C5 Ich'ŏn S. Korea
165 C3 Ichtegem Belgium
169 F5 Ichtershausen Ger.
199 F2 İçikler Turkey
173 F4 Icking Ger.
151 H4 Icklesham East Sussex, England U.K.
151 H2 Icklingham Suffolk, England U.K.
199 F3 İçmeler Turkey
254 F3 Icó Brazil
216 □3a Icod de los Vinos Tenerife Canary Is
257 G4 Iconha Brazil
Iconium Turkey see Konya
Icosium Alg. see Alger
Iculisma France see Angoulême
İd Turkey see Narman
81 C6 Ida, Mount South I. N.Z.
237 E5 Idabel OK U.S.A.
236 E3 Ida Grove IA U.S.A.
207 G5 Idah Nigeria
238 D2 Idaho state U.S.A.
238 D3 Idaho City ID U.S.A.
238 D3 Idaho Falls ID U.S.A.
238 B2 Idanha OR U.S.A.
186 C2 Idanha-a-Nova Port.
116 C5 Idar Gujarat India
172 B2 Idar-Oberstein Ger.
81 B6 Ida Valley South I. N.Z.
147 D2 Idefjorden inlet Norway/Sweden
170 C3 Iden Ger.
106 C1 Ider Mongolia
106 D1 Ideriyn Gol r. Mongolia
170 C1 Idestrup Denmark
203 G3 Idfu Egypt
202 A3 Idhān Awbārī des. Libya
202 B3 Idhān Murzūq des. Libya
Idhra i. Greece see Ydra
Idi Amin Dada, Lake Dem. Rep. Congo/Uganda see Edward, Lake
186 A1 Idiazabal Spain
191 G4 Idice r. Italy
209 C6 Idiofa Dem. Rep. Congo
220 C3 Iditarod AK U.S.A.
140 M1 Idivuoma Sweden
203 F2 Idkū Egypt
149 I4 Idle r. England U.K.
128 C2 Idlib Syria
128 C2 Idlib governorate Syria
151 F3 Idmiston Wiltshire, England U.K.
183 I2 Idocin Spain
177 J6 Idoš Vojvodina, Srbija Yugo.
Idra i. Greece see Ydra
84 C5 Idracowra N.T. Austr.
141 K3 Idre Sweden
188 F2 Idrija Slovenia
188 D2 Idrijca r. Slovenia
138 G3 Idritsa Rus. Fed.
190 F3 Idro Italy
163 B5 Idron-Ousse-Sendets France
168 E1 Idstedt Ger.
169 D5 Idstein Ger.
114 C4 Idukki Kerala India
215 G5 Idutywa S. Africa
240 I5 Idyllwild CA U.S.A.
Idzhevan Armenia see Ijevan
102 □2 Ie Japan
138 E3 Iecava Latvia
138 D3 Iecava r. Latvia
102 □2 Ie-jima i. Japan
255 B5 Iepê Brazil
165 B4 Ieper Belgium
197 F2 Ier r. Romania
199 D4 Ierapetra Kriti Greece
211 C7 Ifakara Tanz.
91 J5 Ifalik atoll Micronesia
Ifaluk atoll Micronesia see Ifalik
213 □J4 Ifanadiana Madag.
213 □J4 Ifanirea Madag.
207 G5 Ife Nigeria
202 C6 Ifenat Chad
207 H2 Iferouâne Niger
205 G4 Ifetesene mt. Alg.
173 F4 Iffeldorf Ger.
158 D3 Iffendic France
172 C3 Iffezheim Ger.
85 E3 Iffley Qld Austr.
207 F2 Ifôghas, Adrar des hills Mali
207 G5 Ifon Nigeria
82 C2 Ifould Lake salt flat S.A. Austr.
204 D2 Ifrane Morocco
159 F2 Ifs France
169 F4 Ifta Ger.
179 F5 Ig Slovenia
207 G4 Igabi Nigeria
177 G5 Igal Hungary
196 D4 Igalo Crna Gora Yugo.
95 E2 Igan r. Sarawak Malaysia
210 B4 Iganga Uganda
177 H5 Igar Hungary
256 D4 Igarapava Brazil
254 D2 Igarape Açú Brazil
254 D3 Igarapé Grande Brazil
254 C2 Igarapé Miri Brazil
256 D5 Igaratá Brazil
130 J3 Igarka Rus. Fed.
253 G6 Igatimi Para.
116 D5 Igatpuri Mahar. India
207 G4 Igbeti Nigeria
207 F4 Igboho Nigeria
207 H5 Igbor Nigeria
127 G3 Iğdır Turkey
129 D4 Iğdır prov. Turkey
159 G3 Igé France
183 H2 Igea Spain
172 A2 Igel Ger.
173 F2 Igensdorf Ger.
172 D2 Igersheim Ger.
172 C2 Iggelheim Ger.
173 H3 Iggensbach Ger.
141 L3 Iggesund Sweden
197 F2 Ighiu Romania
190 E2 Igis Switz.
192 A5 Iglesias Sardegna Italy
192 B5 Iglesiente reg. Sardegna Italy
204 E3 Igli Alg.
173 E3 Igling Ger.
134 L5 Iglino Rus. Fed.
221 J3 Igloolik Nunavut Can.
Igluligaarjuk Nunavut Can. see Chesterfield Inlet
128 A5 'Igma, Gebel el plat. Egypt
125 G3 Ignace Ont. Can.
244 B1 Ignacio Allende Mex.
245 G4 Ignacio de la Llave Mex.
242 D2 Ignacio Zaragosa Mex.
138 F4 Ignalina Lith.
197 B2 İğneada Turkey
177 L5 Ignești Romania
157 G4 Igney France
160 D1 Ignon r. France
211 A6 Igombe r. Tanz.
139 I4 Igorevskaya Rus. Fed.
160 C1 Igornay France
183 H1 Igorre Spain
198 D3 Igoumenitsa Greece
134 K4 Igra Rus. Fed.
182 B2 Igrexa Spain
182 B2 Igrexario Spain
186 C2 Igriés Spain
130 H3 Igrim Rus. Fed.
256 B4 Iguaçu r. Brazil
255 E5 Iguaí Brazil
250 C4 Iguaje, Mesa de hills Col.
245 E4 Iguala Mex.
186 E3 Igualada Spain
185 F4 Igualeja Spain
256 D6 Iguape Brazil
256 B5 Iguaraçu Brazil
257 E4 Igarapé Brazil
257 E4 Iguatama Brazil
255 B7 Iguatemi Brazil
255 B7 Iguatemi r. Brazil
254 F3 Iguatu Brazil
182 D2 Iguëña Spain
182 C2 Iguerande France
211 B6 Igunga Tanz.
207 G5 Iguobazuwa Nigeria
Iguvium Italy see Gubbio
213 □K2 Iharaña Madag.
176 G5 Iharosberény Hungary
114 B5 Ihavandhippolhu Atoll Maldives
107 E3 Ihbulag Mongolia
102 □1 Iheya-jima i. Japan
106 E2 Ihhayrhan Mongolia
207 G5 Ihiala Nigeria
177 J2 Ihľany Slovakia
168 C2 Ihlowerhörn (Ihlow) Ger.
136 E2 Ihnatpil' Ukr.
160 B4 Iholdy France
213 □J4 Ihosy Madag.
168 C2 Ihrhove Ger.
172 B3 Ihringen Ger.
173 F3 Ihrlerstein Ger.
199 G2 İhsaniye Turkey
106 E1 Ihsuuj Mongolia
107 I3 Ih Tal Nei Mongol China
105 D3 Iida Japan
102 I5 Iide-san mt. Japan
140 O3 Iijoki r. Fin.
140 N3 Iisalmi Fin.
138 F1 Iitti Fin.
105 E2 Iiyama Japan
103 E7 Iizuka Japan
207 F5 Ijebu-Ode Nigeria
129 D3 Ijevan Armenia
164 E1 IJlst Neth.
164 D3 IJmuiden Neth.
204 D5 Ijoubbâne des. Mali
164 E2 IJssel r. Neth.
164 D2 IJsselmeer l. Neth.
164 E2 IJsselmuiden Neth.
164 E3 IJsselstein Neth.
255 B9 Ijuí Brazil
253 G8 Ijuí r. Brazil
165 C3 IJzendijke Neth.
165 B3 IJzer r. Belgium alt. Yser (France)
Ikaahuk N.W.T. Can. see Sachs Harbour
141 M3 Ikaalinen Fin.
215 F3 Ikageleng S. Africa
215 F2 Ikageng S. Africa
213 □J3 Ikahavo hill Madag.
213 □J4 Ikalamavony Madag.
81 C5 Ikamatua South I. N.Z.
207 H5 Ikang Nigeria
207 H4 Ikara Nigeria
207 G5 Ikare Nigeria
199 E3 Ikaria i. Greece
104 B4 Ikaruga Japan
142 C3 Ikast Denmark
81 C6 Ikawai South I. N.Z.
80 E4 Ikawhenua Range mts North I. N.Z.
104 B3 Ikeda Japan
104 C4 Ikegoya-yama mt. Japan
207 F5 Ikeja Nigeria
208 D5 Ikela Dem. Rep. Congo
208 C4 Ikelemba r. Dem. Rep. Congo
207 G5 Ikem Nigeria
207 G5 Ikere Nigeria
Ikerre Nigeria see Ikere
176 F4 Ikervár Hungary
197 F4 Ikhtiman Bulg.
215 E3 Ikhutseng S. Africa
103 D7 Iki i. Japan
128 D1 İkiağız Turkey
135 I7 Iki-Burul Rus. Fed.
207 G5 Ikire Nigeria
129 B3 İkizdere Turkey
207 H5 Ikom Nigeria
184 B4 Ikoma Japan
213 □J4 Ikongo Madag.
217 □3a Ikoni Njazidja Comoros
129 B1 Ikon-Khalk Rus. Fed.
213 □J3 Ikopa r. Madag.
137 J2 Ikorets r. Rus. Fed.
207 F5 Ikorodu Nigeria
207 G5 Ikot Ekpene Nigeria
205 H4 Ikouhaouene, Adrar mt. Alg.
177 G4 Ikrény Hungary
101 C6 Iksan S. Korea
211 B6 Ikungi Tanz.
211 B6 Ikungu Tanz.
136 C2 Ikva r. Ukr.
207 G4 Ila Nigeria
92 B2 Ilagan Phil.
114 C4 Ilaiyankudi Tamil Nadu India
213 □K3 Ilaka Atsinanana Madag.
122 A3 Īlām Iran
122 A3 Īlām prov. Iran
117 F4 Ilam Nepal
109 G3 Ilan Taiwan
174 C3 Iłanka r. Pol.
190 E2 Ilanz Switz.
137 H3 Ilarionove Ukr.
207 F5 Ilaro Nigeria
252 C4 Ilave Peru
175 H2 Iława Pol.
207 G5 Ilawe-Ekiti Nigeria
122 D4 Ilazārān, Kūh-e mt. Iran
106 C2 Il Bogd Uul mts Mongolia
192 B5 Ilbono Sardegna Italy
150 E4 Ilchester Somerset, England U.K.
Ile r. China/Kazakh. see Ili
223 J4 Île-à-la-Crosse Sask. Can.
209 D6 Ilebo Dem. Rep. Congo
156 C4 Île-de-France admin. reg. France
211 B7 Ileje Tanz.
120 C2 Ilek Kazakh.
120 C2 Ilek r. Rus. Fed.
137 H2 Ilek-Pen'kovka Rus. Fed.
147 B5 Ilen r. Rep. of Ireland
Ilerda prov. Cataluña Spain see Lérida
Île Royale i. N.S. Can. see Cape Breton Island
207 G5 Ilesa Nigeria
Ilesha Nigeria see Ilesa
207 F4 Ilesha Ibariba Nigeria
134 J5 Ilet' r. Rus. Fed.
134 H3 Ileza Rus. Fed.
169 F4 Ilfeld Ger.
223 M3 Ilford Man. Can.
151 H3 Ilford Greater London, England U.K.
85 F4 Ilfracombe Qld Austr.
150 C3 Ilfracombe Devon, England U.K.
126 D2 Ilgaz Turkey
126 C3 Ilgın Turkey
257 E5 Ilhabela Brazil
257 E5 Ilha Grande, Baía da b. Brazil
255 B7 Ilha Grande, Represa resr Brazil
256 B4 Ilha Solteira, Represa resr Brazil
182 B4 Ílhavo Port.
255 F5 Ilhéus Brazil
121 I3 Ili r. China/Kazakh.
Ili Kazakh. see Kapchagay
197 F3 Ilia Romania
220 C4 Iliamna Lake AK U.S.A.
126 E3 İliç Turkey
129 B4 Iliça Turkey
129 B4 Iliça Turkey
121 G4 Il'ich Kazakh.
Il'ichevsk Azer. see Şärur
Il'ichevsk Ukr. see Illichivs'k
Ilici Spain see Elche
92 C4 Iligan Phil.
92 C4 Iligan Bay Phil.
Ili He r. China/Kazakh. see Ili
188 G4 Ilijaš Bos.-Herz.
221 P2 Ilimananngip Nunaa i. Greenland
131 L3 Ilimpeya r. Rus. Fed.
120 D2 Il'inka Kazakh.
121 H2 Il'inka Rus. Fed.
139 H4 Il'ino Rus. Fed.
134 K4 Il'inskiy Rus. Fed.
139 I1 Il'inskiy Rus. Fed.
100 G3 Il'inskiy Sakhalin Rus. Fed.
134 I3 Il'insko-Podomskoye Rus. Fed.
137 J4 Il'inskoye Rus. Fed.
139 J5 Il'inskoye Rus. Fed.
139 K3 Il'inskoye Rus. Fed.
139 L5 Il'inskoye Rus. Fed.
139 I3 Il'inskoye Rus. Fed.
139 L3 Il'inskoye-Khovanskoye Rus. Fed.
Il'intsy Ukr. see Illintsi
233 F3 Ilion NY U.S.A.
188 E3 Ilirska Bistrica Slovenia
Ilium tourist site Turkey see Truva
138 F4 Iliya r. Belarus
Iliysk Kazakh. see Kapchagay
177 L3 Ilk Hungary
114 B3 Ilkal Karnataka India
151 F2 Ilkeston Derbyshire, England U.K.
149 H4 Ilkley West Yorkshire, England U.K.
157 H4 Ill r. France
183 H4 Illana Spain
92 B5 Illana Bay Phil.
260 B2 Illapel Chile
260 B2 Illapel r. Chile
185 H4 Illar Spain
191 G3 Illasi r. Italy
163 B4 Illats France
82 C1 Illbillee, Mount hill S.A. Austr.
158 E3 Ille r. France
158 E3 Ille-et-Vilaine dept Bretagne France
207 G3 Illéla Niger
207 G3 Illela Nigeria
173 E3 Iller r. Ger.
173 D3 Illerrieden Ger.
173 E3 Illertissen Ger.
173 E3 Illesas Spain
163 E6 Ille-sur-Têt France
136 F4 Illichivs'k Ukr.
156 B4 Illiers-Combray France
252 D4 Illimani, Nevado de mt. Bol.
172 C3 Illingen Baden-Württemberg Ger.
172 B2 Illingen Saarland Ger.
136 F4 Illinka Ukr.
226 B5 Illinois r. IL U.S.A.
226 B5 Illinois state U.S.A.
236 F4 Illintsi Ukr.
205 H4 Illizi Alg.
157 H4 Illkirch-Graffenstaden France
172 D4 Illmensee Ger.
179 H3 Illmitz Austria
185 G3 Illora Spain
192 A4 Illorai Sardegna Italy
172 D2 Illschwang Ger.
183 I3 Illueca Spain
157 H5 Illzach France
171 I3 Ilm r. Ger.
171 C4 Ilm r. Ger.
173 F3 Ilm r. Ger.
87 E6 Ilma, Lake salt flat W.A. Austr.
124 D4 'Ilmān, Jabal al hill Saudi Arabia
139 H2 Il'men', Ozero l. Rus. Fed.
169 F5 Ilmenau Ger.
168 F2 Ilmenau r. Ger.
150 E4 Ilminster Somerset, England U.K.
136 B3 Il'nytsya Ukr.
252 C4 Ilo Peru
207 G5 Ilobu Nigeria
92 B4 Iloilo Phil.
140 O3 Ilomantsi Fin.
207 G4 Ilorin Nigeria
188 F3 Ilova r. Croatia
135 I6 Ilovatka Rus. Fed.
137 J4 Ilovays'k Ukr.
197 F5 Ilovica Macedonia
137 J2 Ilovka Rus. Fed.
136 F4 Ilovlya Rus. Fed.
135 H6 Ilovlya r. Rus. Fed.
175 I3 Iłów Pol.
174 D3 Iłowa Pol.
175 I2 Iłowo Osada Pol.
164 D2 Ilpendam Neth.
131 R3 Il'pyrskiy Rus. Fed.
Il'pyrskoye Rus. Fed. see Il'pyrskiy
141 L3 Ilsbo Sweden
170 C2 Ilse r. Ger.
169 F3 Ilsede Ger.
169 F3 Ilsenburg (Harz) Ger.
172 D3 Ilsfeld Ger.
172 C2 Ilshofen Ger.
150 D4 Ilsington Devon, England U.K.
137 J5 Il'skiy Rus. Fed.
138 F4 Ilūkste Latvia
221 M3 Ilulissat Greenland
Ilva i. Italy see Elba, Isola d'
158 F4 Il'ya Belarus
Il'yaly Turkm. see Yylanly
134 L3 Il'ych r. Rus. Fed.
179 G3 Ilz Austria
173 H3 Ilz r. Ger.
175 H2 Iłża Pol.
175 J4 Iłżanka r. Pol.
103 F6 Imabari Japan
102 I3 Imabetsu Japan
251 G5 Imabú r. Brazil
105 F2 Imaichi Japan
213 H2 Imala Moz.
127 G5 Imām al Ḩamzah Iraq
126 D3 İmamoğlu Turkey
Iman Rus. Fed. see Dal'nerechensk
100 E3 Iman r. Rus. Fed.
121 G1 Imantau, Ozero l. Kazakh.
103 D7 Imari Japan
206 E3 Imasgo Burkina
Imassogo Burkina see Imasgo
251 F3 Imataca, Serranía de mts Venez.
141 O3 Imatra Fin.
250 B4 Imbabura prov. Ecuador
255 C9 Imbituba Brazil
256 B6 Imbituva Brazil
177 H4 Imeľ Slovakia
imeni 26 Bakinskikh Komissarov Azer. see 26 Bakı Komissarı
122 C2 imeni 26 Bakinskikh Komissarov Turkm.
134 H4 imeni Babushkina Rus. Fed.
123 E2 imeni C. A. Niyazova Turkm.
imeni Chapayevka Turkm. see imeni C. A. Niyazova
131 P3 imeni Gastello Rus. Fed.
imeni G. I. Petrovskogo Cherkas'ka Oblast' Ukr. see Horodyshche
139 M3 imeni Gor'kogo Rus. Fed.
imeni G. Ya. Sedova Ukr. see Syedove
137 H2 imeni Karla Libknekhta Rus. Fed.
imeni Khamzy Khakikmzade Uzbek. see Khamza
imeni Kirova Kazakh. see Kopbirlik
imeni Kirova Donets'ka Oblast' Ukr. see Kirove
imeni Kirova Donets'ka Oblast' Ukr. see Kirovs'k
imeni L. M. Kaganovicha Ukr. see Popasna
134 I4 imeni M. I. Kalinina Rus. Fed.
imeni Petra Stuchki Latvia see Aizkraukle
100 F1 imeni Poliny Osipenko Rus. Fed.
139 K2 imeni Zhelyabova Rus. Fed.
137 H3 Imeny Lenina, Ozero l. Ukr.
191 G2 Imèr Italy
194 D5 Imera r. Sicilia Italy
251 E4 Imeri, Serra mts Brazil
210 D3 Īmī Eth.
204 C3 Imi-n-Tanoute Morocco
204 B4 Imirikliy Labyad reg. Western Sahara
Imishli Azer. see İmişli
129 F4 İmişli Azer.
101 C5 Imjin-gang r. N. Korea/S. Korea
227 F4 Imlay City MI U.S.A.
169 F5 Immelborn Ger.
172 C4 Immendingen Ger.
169 E4 Immenhausen Ger.
173 F2 Immenreuth Ger.
172 D4 Immenstaad am Bodensee Ger.
173 E4 Immenstadt im Allgäu Ger.
149 I4 Immingham North East Lincolnshire, England U.K.
231 D7 Immokalee FL U.S.A.
207 G5 Imo state Nigeria
191 G4 Imola Italy
188 F4 Imotski Croatia
215 G3 Impendle S. Africa
254 D3 Imperatriz Brazil
190 D5 Imperia Italy
190 C4 Imperia prov. Liguria Italy
260 A6 Imperial r. Chile
252 A3 Imperial Peru
241 J5 Imperial CA U.S.A.
236 C3 Imperial NE U.S.A.
241 J5 Imperial Beach CA U.S.A.
86 C3 Imperieuse Reef W.A. Austr.
208 C4 Impfondo Congo
117 H4 Imphal Manipur India
160 B2 Imphy France
151 H2 Impington Cambridgeshire, England U.K.
191 G5 Impruneta Italy
177 I5 Imrehegy Hungary
199 D1 İmroz Çanakkale Turkey
İmroz i. Turkey see Gökçeada
İmrun Turkey see Pütürge
101 C6 Imsil S. Korea
178 B3 Imst Austria
242 C2 Imuris Mex.
205 E5 Imzouren Morocco
100 E2 In r. Rus. Fed.
105 D3 Ina Japan
174 C2 Ina r. Pol.
92 A4 Inagauan Phil.
104 E4 Ina-gawa r. Japan
147 B4 Inagh Rep. of Ireland
105 F3 Inagi Japan
254 F4 Inajá Brazil
253 H2 Inaja r. Brazil
252 C3 Inambari Peru
252 C3 Inambari r. Peru
177 H3 Ináncs Hungary
215 H3 Inanda S. Africa
81 C4 Inangahua Junction South I. N.Z.
252 C4 Iñapari Peru
140 N1 Inari Fin.
140 N1 Inarijärvi l. Fin.
140 N1 Inarijoki r. Fin./Norway
252 D2 Inauini r. Brazil
103 J5 Inawashiro-ko l. Japan
105 G2 Inazawa Japan
187 F5 Inca Spain
199 F3 İnceler Turkey
147 B4 Inch Kerry Rep. of Ireland
147 E4 Inch Wexford Rep. of Ireland
146 F5 Inchbare Angus, Scotland U.K.
81 D5 Inchbonnie South I. N.Z.
122 D2 İncheh Iran
173 F3 Inchenhofen Ger.
156 B2 Incheville France
147 B5 Inchigeelagh Rep. of Ireland
210 C3 Inch'īnī Terara mt. Eth.
146 D6 Inchinnan Renfrewshire, Scotland U.K.
204 B5 Inchiri admin. reg. Maur.
101 C5 Inch'ŏn S. Korea
213 G3 Inchope Moz.
146 E5 Inchture Perth and Kinross, Scotland U.K.
183 G2 Incinillas Spain
Incio Spain see A Cruz de Incio
Incirli Sakarya Turkey see Karasu
213 G5 Incomati r. Moz.
165 D4 Incourt Belgium
192 B3 Incudine, Monte mt. France
138 E3 Inčukalns Latvia
146 B6 Indaal, Loch b. Scotland U.K.
257 E3 Indaiá r. Brazil
256 A3 Indaiá Grande r. Brazil
256 D5 Indaiatuba Brazil
140 L3 Indalsälven r. Sweden
141 I3 Indalstø Norway
244 D4 Indaparapeo Mex.
116 D4 Indargarh Madh. Prad. India
116 D4 Indargarh Rajasthan India
210 C1 Inda Silasē Eth.
242 D3 Indé Mex.
Indefatigable Island Islas Galápagos Ecuador see Santa Cruz, Isla
240 H3 Independence CA U.S.A.
236 F3 Independence IA U.S.A.
237 E4 Independence KS U.S.A.
230 C4 Independence KY U.S.A.
226 A2 Independence MN U.S.A.
236 E4 Independence MO U.S.A.
232 C6 Independence VA U.S.A.
226 B3 Independence WI U.S.A.
238 C3 Independence Mountains NV U.S.A.
252 D4 Independencia Bol.
254 E3 Independência Brazil
245 F3 Independencia Mex.
197 H3 Independența Romania
197 I4 Independența Romania
197 I3 Independența Romania
107 I2 Inder Nei Mongol China
120 B2 Inderborskiy Kazakh.
114 C2 Indi Karnataka India
113 H6 India country Asia
226 D2 Indian r. MI U.S.A.
232 D4 Indiana PA U.S.A.
226 D5 Indiana state U.S.A.
246 P9 Indian-Antarctic Basin sea feature Southern Ocean
265 L8 Indian-Antarctic Ridge sea feature Southern Ocean
230 C4 Indianapolis IN U.S.A.
222 G3 Indian Cabins Alta Can.
Indian Desert India/Pak. see Thar Desert
232 B6 Indian Fields KY U.S.A.
225 J2 Indian Harbour Nfld. Can.
223 K5 Indian Head Sask. Can.
233 F3 Indian Lake NY U.S.A.
235 F1 Indian Neck CT U.S.A.
213 □G5 Indian Ocean OCEAN
236 E3 Indianola IA U.S.A.
237 F5 Indianola MS U.S.A.
256 D3 Indianópolis Brazil
241 K2 Indian Peak UT U.S.A.
226 E3 Indian River MI U.S.A.
241 J3 Indian Springs NV U.S.A.
241 L4 Indian Wells AZ U.S.A.
256 B2 Indiara Brazil
254 F4 Indiaroba Brazil
247 □1 Indiera Alta Puerto Rico
131 P2 Indigirka r. Rus. Fed.
196 E3 Inđija Vojvodina, Srbija Yugo.
242 □J7 Indio r. Nic.
241 I5 Indio CA U.S.A.
261 G6 Indio Rico Arg.
78 □6 Indispensable Strait Solomon Is
137 H5 Indol r. Ukr.
139 K1 Indomanka r. Rus. Fed.
90 D7 Indonesia country Asia
116 C5 Indore Madh. Prad. India
94 C3 Indragiri r. Indon.
95 E4 Indramayu Jawa Barat Indon.
Indrapura, Gunung vol. Indon. see Kerinci, Gunung
115 D2 Indravati r. India
159 H5 Indre dept Centre France
162 C1 Indre r. France
159 G4 Indre-et-Loire dept Centre France
82 C1 Indulkana S.A. Austr.
Indur Andhra Prad. India see Nizamabad
114 C2 Indurti Andhra Prad. India
116 E2 Indus r. China/Pak. alt. Shiquan He (China)
123 F5 Indus, Mouths of the Pak.
265 I3 Indus Cone sea feature Indian Ocean
215 F4 Indwe S. Africa
215 F5 Indwe r. S. Africa
197 H4 Indzhe Voyvoda Bulg.
126 D2 İnebolu Turkey
199 F1 İnegöl Turkey
93 B5 Inerie vol. Flores Indon.
197 E2 Ineu Arad Romania
177 L4 Ineu Bihor Romania
Inevi Turkey see Cihanbeyli
232 B6 Inez KY U.S.A.
204 C3 Inezgane Morocco
214 C6 Infanta, Cape S. Africa
Infantes Spain see Villanueva de los Infantes
245 G5 Inferior, Laguna lag. Mex.
253 E2 Inferno, Cachoeira waterfall Brazil
244 D4 Infiernillo, Presa resr Mex.
183 E1 Infiesto Spain
96 C2 Ing, Mae Nam r. Thai.
209 B6 Inga Dem. Rep. Congo
141 N3 Ingå Fin.
207 G2 Ingal Niger
240 G2 Ingalls, Mount CA U.S.A.
151 H3 Ingatestone Essex, England U.K.
172 D2 Ingelfingen Ger.
172 C2 Ingelheim am Rhein Ger.
165 C4 Ingelmunster Belgium
143 F3 Ingelstad Sweden
208 C5 Ingende Dem. Rep. Congo
258 E1 Ingeniero Guillermo Nueva Juárez Arg.
260 D6 Ingeniero Huergo Arg.
259 C6 Ingeniero Jacobacci Arg.
260 E4 Ingeniero Luiggi Arg.
261 H4 Ingeniero Maschwitz Arg.
261 H4 Ingeniero Otamendi Arg.
222 E3 Ingenika r. B.C. Can.
216 □3f Ingenio Gran Canaria Canary Is
252 B3 Ingenio r. Peru
224 D5 Ingersoll Ont. Can.
106 D1 Ingettolgoy Mongolia
85 F3 Ingham Qld Austr.
120 F5 Ingichka Uzbek.
183 H2 Inglares r. Spain
149 G3 Ingleborough hill England U.K.
149 H3 Ingleton Durham, England U.K.
149 G3 Ingleton North Yorkshire, England U.K.
149 G4 Inglewhite Lancashire, England U.K.
83 G2 Inglewood Qld Austr.
83 E4 Inglewood Vic. Austr.
80 E3 Inglewood North I. N.Z.
240 H5 Inglewood CA U.S.A.
149 G3 Inglewood Forest England U.K.
84 D2 Inglis Island N.T. Austr.
107 G1 Ingoda r. Rus. Fed.
96 B1 Ingoka Pum mt. Myanmar
172 D3 Ingoldingen Ger.
149 J4 Ingoldmells Lincolnshire, England U.K.
173 F3 Ingolstadt Ger.
82 C2 Ingomar S.A. Austr.
238 F2 Ingomar MT U.S.A.
225 I4 Ingonish N.S. Can.
117 G4 Ingraj Bazar W. Bengal India
146 G6 Ingram Northumberland, England U.K.
232 D6 Ingram VA U.S.A.
226 B3 Ingram WI U.S.A.
159 F4 Ingrandes Pays de la Loire France
159 G5 Ingrandes Poitou-Charentes France
252 E5 Ingre Bol.
156 B5 Ingré France
263 F2 Ingrid Christensen Coast Antarctica
158 C4 Inguiniel France
Ingul r. Ukr. see Inhul
Ingulets Ukr. see Inhulets'
Ingushetia aut. rep. Rus. Fed. see Ingushskaya Respublika
129 D2 Ingushskaya Respublika aut. rep. Rus. Fed.
215 I2 Ingwavuma S. Africa
Ingwavuma r. Swaziland see Ngwavuma
157 H4 Ingwiller France
213 G4 Inhambane Moz.
213 G4 Inhambane prov. Moz.
254 F4 Inhambupe Brazil
213 G3 Inhaminga Moz.
257 F3 Inhapim Brazil
213 G4 Inhassoro Moz.
205 F5 I-n-Hihaou, Adrar hills Alg.
199 G1 İnhisar Turkey
137 F4 Inhul r. Ukr.
137 G4 Inhulets' Ukr.
137 G4 Inhulets' r. Ukr.
256 C2 Inhumas Brazil
93 B5 Inielika vol. Flores Indon.
185 I1 Iniesta Spain
257 E3 Inimutaba Brazil
138 C1 Iniö Fin.
250 E4 Inírida r. Col.
Inis Rep. of Ireland see Ennis
Inis Córthaidh Rep. of Ireland see Enniscorthy
147 A3 Inishark i. Rep. of Ireland
147 A3 Inishbofin i. Rep. of Ireland
147 B3 Inisheer i. Rep. of Ireland
147 B3 Inishmaan i. Rep. of Ireland
147 B3 Inishmore i. Rep. of Ireland
147 C2 Inishmurray i. Rep. of Ireland
147 D1 Inishowen pen. Rep. of Ireland
147 E1 Inishowen Head hd Rep. of Ireland
147 D1 Inishtrahull i. Rep. of Ireland
147 D1 Inishtrahull Sound sea chan. Rep. of Ireland
147 A3 Inishturk i. Rep. of Ireland
107 H2 Injgan Sum Nei Mongol China
210 C2 Injibara Eth.
85 G5 Injune Qld Austr.
120 F3 Inkardar'ya Kazakh.
151 F3 Inkberrow Worcestershire, England U.K.
176 G5 Inke Hungary
85 E3 Inkerman Qld Austr.
137 G5 Inkerman Ukr.
222 C3 Inklin B.C. Can.
222 C3 Inklin r. B.C. Can.
81 D5 Inland Kaikoura Range mts South I. N.Z.
Inland Sea Japan see Seto-naikai
233 F3 Inlet NY U.S.A.
173 E5 Inn r. Europe
103 E7 Innai Japan
82 E1 Innamincka S.A. Austr.
140 K2 Inndyr Norway
146 D6 Innellan Argyll and Bute, Scotland U.K.
217 □2a Inner Islands Seychelles
146 E6 Innerleithen Scottish Borders, Scotland U.K.
173 H3 Innernzell Ger.
146 C4 Inner Sound sea chan. Scotland U.K.
190 D2 Innertkirchen Switz.
173 F3 Inning am Ammersee Ger.
85 F3 Innisfail Qld Austr.
222 H4 Innisfail Alta Can.
147 C5 Innishannon Rep. of Ireland
147 E2 Inniskeen Rep. of Ireland
100 D2 Innokent'yevka Rus. Fed.
103 F6 Innoshima Japan
178 C3 Innsbruck Austria
191 G1 Innsbruck airport Austria
224 E1 Innuksuak r. Que. Can.
147 A5 Inny r. Kerry Rep. of Ireland
147 D3 Inny r. Longford/Westmeath Rep. of Ireland
256 B3 Inocência Brazil
208 C5 Inongo Dem. Rep. Congo
199 G2 İnönü Turkey
Inoucdjouac Que. Can. see Inukjuak
177 H3 Inovec mt. Slovakia
175 I4 Inowłódz Pol.
174 G3 Inowrocław Pol.
129 C1 Inozemtsevo Rus. Fed.
252 D4 Inquisivi Bol.
190 C1 Ins Switz.
205 F4 In Salah Alg.
135 I5 Insar Rus. Fed.
146 F4 Insch Aberdeenshire, Scotland U.K.
87 B5 Inscription, Cape W.A. Austr.
96 B3 Insein Myanmar
174 D2 Ińsko Pol.
157 G4 Insming France
Insterburg Rus. Fed. see Chernyakhovsk
129 E3 Institut Azer.
138 C4 Instruch r. Rus. Fed.
197 H3 Însurăței Romania
213 E3 Insuza r. Zimbabwe
134 M2 Inta Rus. Fed.
261 F4 Intendente Alvear Arg.
199 E1 İntepe Turkey
Interamna Italy see Teramo
190 C2 Interlaken Switz.
226 A1 International Falls MN U.S.A.
197 H3 Intorsura Buzăului Romania
190 E3 Introbio Italy
250 C5 Intutu Peru
224 E1 Inukjuak Que. Can.
220 E3 Inuvik N.W.T. Can.
252 B2 Inuya r. Peru
104 C3 Inuyama Japan
134 L4 In'va r. Rus. Fed.
147 C2 Inver Rep. of Ireland
146 C4 Inveralligin Highland, Scotland U.K.
146 G4 Inverallochy Aberdeenshire, Scotland U.K.
147 B3 Inveran Rep. of Ireland
146 C5 Inveraray Argyll and Bute, Scotland U.K.
146 F5 Inverarity Angus, Scotland U.K.
146 D5 Inverarnan Argyll and Bute, Scotland U.K.
146 F5 Inverbervie Aberdeenshire, Scotland U.K.
81 B7 Invercargill South I. N.Z.
146 D6 Inverclyde admin. div. Scotland U.K.
83 G2 Inverell N.S.W. Austr.
146 E5 Inverey Aberdeenshire, Scotland U.K.
146 D4 Invergarry Highland, Scotland U.K.
146 D4 Invergordon Highland, Scotland U.K.
146 C5 Inverinan Argyll and Bute, Scotland U.K.
146 F5 Inverkeilor Angus, Scotland U.K.
146 E5 Inverkeithing Fife, Scotland U.K.
146 C3 Inverkirkaig Highland, Scotland U.K.
146 C4 Inverlael Highland, Scotland U.K.
85 E3 Inverleigh Qld Austr.
223 K5 Invermay Sask. Can.
146 D4 Invermoriston Highland, Scotland U.K.
225 I4 Inverness N.S. Can.
146 D4 Inverness Highland, Scotland U.K.
240 F2 Inverness CA U.S.A.
231 D6 Inverness FL U.S.A.
146 C5 Invernoaden Argyll and Bute, Scotland U.K.
146 D5 Inversnaid Stirling, Scotland U.K.
146 F4 Inverurie Aberdeenshire, Scotland U.K.
84 B3 Inverway N.T. Austr.
97 B4 Investigator Channel Myanmar
82 C3 Investigator Group is S.A. Austr.
265 K5 Investigator Ridge sea feature Indian Ocean
82 D3 Investigator Strait S.A. Austr.
232 D5 Inwood WV U.S.A.
215 G4 Inxu r. S. Africa
Inyanga Zimbabwe see Nyanga
213 G3 Inyangani mt. Zimbabwe
Inyati Zimbabwe see Nyathi
Inyazura Zimbabwe see Nyazura
240 I4 Inyokern CA U.S.A.
240 H3 Inyo Mountains CA U.S.A.
211 B6 Inyonga Tanz.
135 I5 Inza Rus. Fed.
173 G4 Inzell Ger.
120 D1 Inzer Rus. Fed.
134 L5 Inzer r. Rus. Fed.
135 H5 Inzhavino Rus. Fed.
178 C3 Inzing Austria
158 C4 Inzinzac-Lochrist France
198 B2 Ioannina Greece
198 B2 Ioanninon, Limni l. Greece
191 I2 Iôf di Montasio mt. Italy
103 □3 Iō-jima i. Japan
134 G2 Iokanga r. Rus. Fed.
237 E4 Iola KS U.S.A.
234 B1 Iola PA U.S.A.
226 C3 Iola WI U.S.A.
Iolotan' Turkm. see Yeloten
209 B9 Iona Angola
225 I4 Iona N.S. Can.
146 B5 Iona i. Scotland U.K.
146 B5 Iona Abbey tourist site Scotland U.K.
240 I2 Ione NV U.S.A.
238 C1 Ione WA U.S.A.
197 G3 Ionești Romania
226 E4 Ionia MI U.S.A.
Ionian Islands Greece see Ionioi Nisoi
198 A2 Ionian Sea Greece/Italy
Ionio prov. Puglia Italy see Taranto
198 A2 Ionioi Nisoi is Greece
Iori r. Azer. see Qabırrı
129 E3 Iori r. Georgia
198 D3 Ios Greece
199 D3 Ios i. Greece
Iō-tō i. Japan see Iō-jima
102 □1 Iō-Tori-jima i. Japan
206 A2 Iouîk Maur.
236 E3 Iowa r. IA U.S.A.
236 E3 Iowa state U.S.A.
236 F3 Iowa City IA U.S.A.
236 E3 Iowa Falls IA U.S.A.
104 C2 Iō-zan hill Japan
136 E1 Ipa r. Belarus
256 C2 Ipameri Brazil
257 G3 Ipanema Brazil
254 F4 Ipanema r. Brazil
252 B2 Iparía Peru
257 F3 Ipatinga Brazil
135 H7 Ipatovo Rus. Fed.
256 C5 Ipauçu Brazil
226 B5 Ipava IL U.S.A.
198 B2 Ipeiros admin. reg. Greece
177 H4 Ipeľ r. Slovakia
177 I3 Ipeľ r. Slovakia
215 E2 Ipelegeng S. Africa
177 H4 Ipeľská pahorkatina mts Slovakia
173 E2 Iphofen Ger.
256 C3 Ipiaçu Brazil
250 B4 Ipiales Col.
254 F5 Ipiaú Brazil
254 F5 Ipirá Brazil
256 B6 Ipiranga Brazil
Ípiros admin. reg. Greece see Ipeiros
78 □4a Ipis i. Chuuk Micronesia
252 B1 Ipixuna Brazil
252 B1 Ipixuna r. Amazonas Brazil
251 F6 Ipixuna r. Amazonas Brazil
94 C1 Ipoh Malaysia
177 H4 Ipoly r. Hungary/Slovakia
215 E3 Ipopeng S. Africa
256 B2 Iporá Brazil
256 C6 Iporanga Brazil
194 D6 Ippari r. Sicilia Italy
173 E2 Ippesheim Ger.
150 D4 Ipplepen Devon, England U.K.
208 D3 Ippy C.A.R.
199 E1 İpsala Turkey
173 E2 Ipsheim Ger.
149 H4 Ipstones Staffordshire, England U.K.
85 H5 Ipswich Qld Austr.
151 I2 Ipswich Suffolk, England U.K.
236 D2 Ipswich SD U.S.A.
254 E3 Ipu Brazil
256 C4 Ipuã Brazil
256 C4 Ipueiras Brazil
256 D5 Ipuiúna Brazil
254 E4 Ipupiara Brazil
139 H5 Iput' r. Rus. Fed.
137 F1 Iputs' r. Belarus
221 L3 Iqaluit Nunavut Can.
111 F4 Iqe He r. China
253 F3 Iquê r. Brazil
252 C5 Iquique Chile
Iquiri r. Brazil see Ituxi
250 C5 Iquitos Peru
102 □1 Irabu-jima i. Japan
251 H3 Iracoubo Fr. Guiana
104 C4 Irago-suidō str. Japan
255 B8 Iraí Brazil
198 C1 Irakleia Greece
199 D3 Irakleia i. Greece
198 D4 Irakleio Kriti Greece
198 D4 Irakleiou, Kolpos b. Kriti Greece
Iráklia i. Greece see Irakleia
Iraklion Kriti Greece see Irakleio
254 E5 Iramaia Brazil
122 C4 Iran country Asia
95 F2 Iran, Pegunungan mts Indon.
156 D5 Irancy France
122 A2 Īrānshāh Iran
122 E5 Īrānshahr Iran
244 D3 Irapuato Mex.
127 F4 Iraq country Asia
205 G4 Irarrarene reg. Alg.
233 G2 Irasville VT U.S.A.
251 H5 Irataparu r. Brazil
178 D1 Irati Brazil
183 I2 Irati r. Spain
177 K5 Iratoşu Romania
134 K2 Irayel' Rus. Fed.
242 □J7 Irazú, Volcán vol. Costa Rica
138 D3 Irbe r. Latvia
Irbes šaurums sea chan. Estonia/Latvia see Irbe Strait
138 D3 Irbe Strait Estonia/Latvia
Irbe väin sea chan. Estonia/Latvia see Irbe Strait
128 B3 Irbid Jordan
Irbil Iraq see Arbīl
130 H4 Irbit Rus. Fed.
151 G2 Irchester Northamptonshire, England U.K.
179 F3 Irdning Austria
137 F3 Irdyn' Ukr.
254 E4 Irecê Brazil
177 H5 Iregszemcse Hungary
183 H2 Iregua r. Spain
147 D3 Ireland, Republic of country Europe
235 D1 Ireland Corners NY U.S.A.
147 E3 Ireland's Eye i. Rep. of Ireland
134 L4 Iren' r. Rus. Fed.
81 A6 Irene, Mount South I. N.Z.
251 G4 Ireng r. Guyana/Venez.
256 A6 Iretama Brazil
120 D1 Irgakly Rus. Fed.
129 D3 Irganch'ai Georgia
199 F2 Irgıllı Turkey
120 E2 Irgiz Kazakh.
120 E2 Irgiz r. Kazakh.
192 B4 Irgoli Sardegna Italy
204 C3 Irherm Morocco
204 D3 Irhil M'Goun mt. Morocco
Iri S. Korea see Iksan
Irian Barat prov. Indon. see Irian Jaya
93 D3 Irian Jaya prov. Indon.
91 I7 Irian Jaya reg. Indon.
202 D6 Iriba Chad
251 G4 Iricoumé, Serra hills Brazil
122 A2 Īrī Dāgh mt. Iran
196 D3 Irig Vojvodina, Srbija Yugo.
92 B3 Iriga Phil.
160 C3 Irigny France
120 D2 Iriklinskiy Rus. Fed.
211 B6 Iringa Tanz.
211 B7 Iringa admin. reg. Tanz.
114 C4 Irinjalakuda Kerala India
102 □1 Iriomote-jima i. Japan
251 H5 Iriri r. Brazil
254 B4 Iriri Novo r. Brazil
Irish Free State country Europe see Ireland, Republic of
145 E5 Irish Sea Rep. of Ireland/U.K.
163 A5 Irissarry France
254 D2 Irituia Brazil
182 B2 Irixo Spain
137 J5 Irkliyevskaya Rus. Fed.
137 G3 Irkliyiv Ukr.
98 H1 Irkutsk Rus. Fed.
98 H1 Irkutskaya Oblast' admin. div. Rus. Fed.
Irkutsk Oblast admin. div. Rus. Fed. see Irkutskaya Oblast'
173 G3 Irlbach Ger.
223 I4 Irma Alta Can.
226 C3 Irma WI U.S.A.
126 D3 Irmak Turkey
264 G2 Irminger Basin sea feature N. Atlantic Ocean
194 D6 Irminio r. Sicilia Italy
231 D5 Irmo SC U.S.A.
164 E1 Irnsum Neth.
208 C2 Iro, Lac l. Chad
158 E3 Irodouër France
158 B3 Iroise, Mer d' g. France
82 D3 Iron Baron S.A. Austr.
227 F2 Iron Bridge Ont. Can.
150 E2 Ironbridge Telford and Wrekin, England U.K.
232 E3 Irondequoit NY U.S.A.
226 A2 Iron Junction MN U.S.A.
82 D3 Iron Knob S.A. Austr.
226 C3 Iron Mountain MI U.S.A.
241 K3 Iron Mountain mt. UT U.S.A.
85 F2 Iron Mountains hills Rep. of Ireland
226 C2 Iron River MI U.S.A.
226 B2 Iron River WI U.S.A.
237 F4 Ironton MO U.S.A.
232 B5 Ironton OH U.S.A.
226 B2 Ironwood MI U.S.A.
233 F2 Iroquois Ont. Can.
226 C5 Iroquois r. IN U.S.A.
224 D3 Iroquois Falls Ont. Can.
92 C3 Irosin Phil.
Irpen' Ukr. see Irpin'
136 F2 Irpin' Ukr.
136 F2 Irpin' r. Ukr.
125 D2 'Irq al Ḩarūrī des. Saudi Arabia
124 C2 'Irq al Mazhūr des. Saudi Arabia
124 D2 'Irq ath Thāmām des. Saudi Arabia
124 D2 'Irq Banbān des. Saudi Arabia
125 D2 'Irq Jahām des. Saudi Arabia
124 C5 'Irq Subay des. Saudi Arabia

Jarud *Nei Mongol* China *see* Lubei
196 E4 Jarut r.m. Yugo.
138 E2 Järvakandi Estonia
141 N3 Järvenpää Fin.
157 G4 Jarville-la-Malgrange France
75 I4 Jarvis Island *terr.* N. Pacific Ocean
140 K2 Järvsand Sweden
141 L3 Järvsö Sweden
117 E4 Jarwa *Uttar Prad.* India
159 F4 Jarzé France
250 B6 Jasdan *Gujarat* India
161 D5 Jas de la Laure *hill* France
177 I3 Jasenie Slovakia
177 K3 Jasenov Slovakia
117 F5 Jashpurnagar *Madh. Prad.* India
174 D4 Jasień Pol.
174 F1 Jasień Pol.
175 J3 Jasienica Pol.
175 J6 Jasieniec Pol.
207 F5 Jasikan Ghana
175 J6 Jasiołka r. Pol.
175 K5 Jasionka Pol.
175 I5 Jasionna Pol.
122 D5 Jāsk Iran
122 D5 Jāsk-e Kohneh Iran
175 J6 Jasło Pol.
176 F2 Jasové Bohunice Slovakia
138 E4 Jašiūnai Lith.
170 E1 Jasmund *pen.* Ger.
262 T2 Jason Peninsula Antarctica
177 J3 Jasová Slovakia
177 H4 Jasová Slovakia
262 G4 Jasper *Alta* Can.
231 C5 Jasper *AL* U.S.A.
237 E4 Jasper *AR* U.S.A.
231 C6 Jasper *FL* U.S.A.
230 C4 Jasper *GA* U.S.A.
230 C4 Jasper *IN* U.S.A.
231 C5 Jasper *NY* U.S.A.
232 B5 Jasper *OH* U.S.A.
231 C5 Jasper *TN* U.S.A.
237 E6 Jasper *TX* U.S.A.
160 C3 Jassans-Riottier France
160 D2 Jasseron France
Jassy Romania *see* Iaşi
143 H4 Jastarnia Pol.
188 E3 Jastrebarsko Croatia
174 E4 Jastrowie Pol.
175 I4 Jastrząb Pol.
174 G1 Jastrzębia Góra Pol.
174 G6 Jastrzębie-Zdrój Pol.
175 K2 Jaświły Pol.
177 J4 Jászapáti Hungary
177 J4 Jászárokszállás Hungary
177 I4 Jászberény Hungary
177 I4 Jászboldogháza Hungary
177 I4 Jászfényszaru Hungary
177 J4 Jászkarajenő Hungary
177 J4 Jászkisér Hungary
177 I4 Jászladány Hungary
177 J4 Jász-Nagykun-Szolnok *county* Hungary
177 I5 Jászszentandrás Hungary
177 J4 Jászszentlászló Hungary
177 J4 Jásztelek Hungary
183 H1 Jata, Monte *hill* Spain
256 B2 Jataí Brazil
251 G4 Jatar Spain
185 G4 Jatar Spain
116 D4 Jatara *Madh. Prad.* India
123 G5 Jati Pak.
95 E4 Jatibarang *Jawa Barat* Indon.
246 C2 Jatibonico Cuba
Játiva Spain *see* Xàtiva
95 E4 Jatiwangi *Jawa Barat* Indon.
194 C4 Jato r. *Sicilia* Italy
141 M5 Jättendal Sweden
170 E2 Jatznick Ger.
170 E2 Jatzke Ger.
256 C5 Jaú Brazil
255 F5 Jaú r. Brazil
255 F5 Jaueperi r. Brazil
246 D2 Jauco Cuba
252 B2 Jauja Peru
186 C3 Jaulín Spain
245 G2 Jaumave Mex.
162 F2 Jaun Switz.
251 E6 Jauna r. Brazil
162 C2 Jaunay-Clan France
138 F4 Jaunjelgava Latvia
138 D3 Jaunmārupe Latvia
138 F3 Jaunpiebalga Latvia
138 E3 Jaunpils Latvia
117 E4 Jaunpur *Uttar Prad.* India
252 B2 Jauquara r. Brazil
161 A5 Jaur r. France
261 H4 Jauregui Arg.
186 B3 Jaurietta Spain
253 F4 Jauru r. Brazil
161 E4 Jauru r. Brazil
Java i. Indon. *see* Jawa
254 C4 Javadi Hills India
129 C3 Javakhet'is K'edi *hills* Armenia/Georgia
187 B4 Javalambre *mt.* Spain
187 B4 Javalambre, Sierra de *mts* Spain
183 I4 Javalón *mt.* Spain
250 D6 Javari r. Brazil/Peru
  alt. Yavari
265 L5 Java Ridge *sea feature* Indian Ocean
107 U1 Javarthushuu Mongolia
95 E4 Java Sea Indon.
265 K5 Java Trench *sea feature* Indian Ocean
187 D6 Jávea-Xàbia Spain
170 C3 Jävenitz Ger.
185 F3 Javerero *mt.* Spain
162 C2 Javerlhac-et-la-Chapelle-St-Robert France
129 C4 Javier Armenia
185 G7 Javier, Isla i. Chile
196 E4 Javor *mts* Yugo.
177 I3 Javorie *mt.* Slovakia
196 D4 Javorje *mt.* Yugo.
176 E2 Javořice *hill* Czech Rep.
177 I3 Javorníky *mts* Slovakia
177 H2 Javorníky *mts* Slovakia
140 M2 Jävre Sweden
159 F3 Javron-les-Chapelles France
95 D5 Jawa i. Indon.
94 C4 Jawa Barat *prov.* Indon.
116 D4 Jawad *Madh. Prad.* India
114 D4 Jawala r. India
116 D3 Jawala Mukhi *Hima. Prad.* India
116 D5 Jawar *Madh. Prad.* India
95 E4 Jawa Tengah *prov.* Indon.
95 E4 Jawa Timur *prov.* Indon.
128 C1 Jawbān Bayk Syria
124 E7 Jawf, Wādī al *watercourse* Yemen
114 B2 Jawhar *Mahar.* India
210 E4 Jawhar Somalia
174 E4 Jawor Pol.
175 J4 Jawor Pol.
175 K6 Jaworki Pol.
175 J3 Jawornik Polski Pol.
174 E4 Jawor Solecki Pol.
175 I4 Jaworze Pol.
175 H5 Jaworzno Pol.
174 E4 Jaworzyna *mt.* Pol.
175 H6 Jaworzyna Śląska Pol.
237 E4 Jay *OK* U.S.A.
94 17 Jaya, Puncak *mt.* Indon.
114 B2 Jayakwadi Sagar l. India
250 B6 Jayanca Peru
94 12 Jayanti India
95 D4 Jayapura *Irian Jaya* Indon.
185 G4 Jayena Spain
117 G4 Jaynagar *Bihar* India
114 D4 Jaynagar *W. Bengal* India
115 D2 Jaypur *Orissa* India
128 C3 Jayrūd Syria
247 □1 Jayuya Puerto Rico
125 F2 Jazirah, Jabal al *hill* U.A.E.
124 J4 Jazeneuil France
237 F6 Jeanerette *LA* U.S.A.

122 F2 Jean Marie River *N.W.T.* Can.
122 D4 Jean Bārez, Kūh-e *mts* Iran
207 G4 Jebba Nigeria
196 E3 Jebel Romania
Jebel Turkm. *see* Dzhebel
210 A2 Jebel, Bahr el r. Sudan/Uganda
  alt. Abiad, Bahr el, *conv.* White Nile
203 F5 Jebel Abyad Plateau Sudan
Jebel Ali U.A.E. *see* Mina Jebel Ali
250 B6 Jéberos Peru
180 D5 Jebha Morocco
157 H4 Jebsheim France
146 F6 Jedburgh *Scottish Borders, Scotland* U.K.
124 B3 Jeddah Saudi Arabia
189 B7 Jedeida Tunisia
175 K4 Jedlanka Pol.
174 E5 Jedlicze Pol.
174 E5 Jedlina-Zdrój Pol.
175 J4 Jedlińsk Pol.
175 J4 Jedlnia-Letnisko Pol.
175 J5 Jednorożec Pol.
175 I5 Jędrzejów Pol.
184 E4 Jedrze Pol.
175 K2 Jedwabne Pol.
175 I2 Jedwabno Pol.
175 K5 Jeetze r. Ger.
231 D5 Jefferson *GA* U.S.A.
237 E4 Jefferson *NC* U.S.A.
232 C6 Jefferson *NC* U.S.A.
232 C4 Jefferson *OH* U.S.A.
237 E5 Jefferson *TX* U.S.A.
232 C4 Jefferson *WI* U.S.A.
238 E2 Jefferson r. *MT* U.S.A.
240 I2 Jefferson, Mount *NV* U.S.A.
238 B2 Jefferson, Mount *vol. OR* U.S.A.
236 E4 Jefferson City *MO* U.S.A.
232 E5 Jeffersonton *VA* U.S.A.
231 D5 Jeffersonville *GA* U.S.A.
230 C4 Jeffersonville *IN* U.S.A.
232 B6 Jeffersonville *KY* U.S.A.
232 B5 Jeffersonville *OH* U.S.A.
232 E6 Jeffrey *WV* U.S.A.
215 E6 Jeffrey's Bay S. Africa
207 G3 Jega Nigeria
163 C5 Jegun France
231 D5 Jegun China *see* Jinghe
Jelai r. Indon.
168 D1 Jejsing Denmark
138 E3 Jékabpils Latvia
174 F4 Jelcz-Laskowice Pol.
177 H3 Jelenec Slovakia
174 D5 Jelenia Góra Pol.
175 K1 Jeleniewo Pol.
175 H6 Jelenin Pol.
138 D3 Jelgava Latvia
177 G3 Jelka Slovakia
232 A6 Jellico *TN* U.S.A.
224 C3 Jellicoe *Ont.* Can.
80 E2 Jellicoe Channel *North I.* N.Z.
142 C4 Jelling Denmark
177 J3 Jelšava Slovakia
193 K3 Jelsi Italy
99 F5 Jembe r. Indon.
169 F3 Jembke Ger.
165 D4 Jemeppe Belgium
239 F5 Jemez Pueblo *NM* U.S.A.
168 C2 Jemgum Ger.
174 E4 Jemielno Pol.
174 D2 Jemielnica Pol.
110 D2 Jeminay (Topterek) China/Kyrg.
107 H3 Jixiang China
108 A3 Jenbach Austria
223 I5 Jenner *Alta* Can.
179 H4 Jennersdorf Austria
247 L6 Jennings Antigua and Barbuda
222 C3 Jennings *r. B.C.* Can.
237 E6 Jennings *LA* U.S.A.
223 L4 Jenpeg *Man.* Can.
241 M1 Jensen *UT* U.S.A.
95 E4 Jepara *Jawa Tengah* Indon.
83 E4 Jeparit *Vic.* Austr.
254 E5 Jequié Brazil
257 E2 Jequitaí Brazil
257 E2 Jequitaí r. Brazil
254 E2 Jequitinhonha Brazil
257 H1 Jequitinhonha r. Brazil
171 C3 Jerchel Ger.
83 G1 Jerécuaro Mex.
129 D4 Jérémie Haiti
244 C2 Jeremoabo Brazil
244 C2 Jerez r. Mex.
184 D4 Jerez de la Frontera Spain
185 G3 Jerez del Marquesado Spain
184 D2 Jerez de los Caballeros Spain
140 L2 Jerfojaur Sweden
198 B2 Jergucat Albania
187 C5 Jérica Spain
85 F4 Jericho *Qld* Austr.
235 F2 Jericho *NY* U.S.A.
128 C4 Jericho West Bank
173 I3 Jerichow Ger.
205 H2 Jerid, Chott el *salt l.* Tunisia
83 E6 Jerilderie *N.S.W.* Austr.
174 E4 Jerka Pol.
129 D4 Jermuk Armenia
244 C1 Jermyn *PA* U.S.A.
241 X4 Jerome *AZ* U.S.A.
238 D4 Jerome *ID* U.S.A.
232 D4 Jerome *PA* U.S.A.
261 G2 Jeromenin Norte Arg.
87 C7 Jerramungup *W.A.* Austr.
175 J4 Jersbek Ger.
158 B2 Jersey *terr.* Channel Is
235 F3 Jersey City *NJ* U.S.A.
235 G3 Jersey Shore *PA* U.S.A.
174 E4 Jerseyville *IL* U.S.A.
182 E6 Jerte Spain
182 E5 Jerte r. Spain
128 B4 Jerusalem Israel/West Bank
80 E3 Jerusalem *North I.* N.Z.
83 G3 Jervis Bay *Jervis Bay* Austr.
83 G3 Jervis Bay b. *Jervis Bay* Austr.
83 G3 Jervis Bay Territory *admin. div.* Austr.
84 C4 Jervis Range *hills N.T.* Austr.
169 I3 Jerxheim Ger.
174 F4 Jerzmanowa Pol.
192 B5 Jerzu *Sardegna* Italy
176 C1 Jesberg Ger.

244 B3 Jesús María r. Mex.
116 B5 Jetalsar *Gujarat* India
Jethro *tourist site* Saudi Arabia *see* Maghā'ir Shu'ayb
236 D4 Jetmore *KS* U.S.A.
173 E3 Jettingen-Scheppach Ger.
173 F3 Jetzendorf Ger.
168 E1 Jeumont France
168 C2 Jever Ger.
176 F3 Jevíčko Czech Rep.
176 F3 Jevišovice Czech Rep.
87 D4 Jevišovka r. Czech Rep.
142 D1 Jevnaker Norway
234 A4 Jewett *OH* U.S.A.
232 C6 Jewell Ridge *VA* U.S.A.
235 G1 Jewett City *CT* U.S.A.
Jewish Autonomous Oblast *admin. div. Rus. Fed. see* Yevreyskaya Avtonomnaya Oblast'
173 H2 Jexhof *tourist site* Ger.
173 H2 Jezerní Stěna *mt.* Ger.
174 G2 Jeziorak, Jezioro l. Pol.
175 J3 Jeziorany Pol.
174 G4 Jeziorko, Jezioro l. Pol.
175 K4 Jeziorzany Pol.
175 K5 Jeżów Pol.
128 B3 Jezzine Lebanon
116 C5 Jhabua *Madh. Prad.* India
117 F4 Jha Jha *Bihar* India
170 D3 Jhajjar *Haryana* India
116 C4 Jhajju *Rajasthan* India
114 G5 Jhal Pak.
117 G5 Jhalakati Bangl.
116 C4 Jhalawar *Rajasthan* India
123 H4 Jhang Pak.
117 F4 Jhanjharpur *Bihar* India
116 D4 Jhansi *Uttar Prad.* India
111 F7 Jhanzi r. India
117 F5 Jhargram *W. Bengal* India
117 F5 Jharia *Bihar* India
115 E1 Jharsuguda *Orissa* India
123 G4 Jhatpat Pak.
116 C3 Jhelum r. India/Pak.
123 H3 Jhelum Pak.
Jhenaidaha Bangl. *see* Jhenida
117 G5 Jhenida Bangl.
116 B5 Jhinjhuvada *Gujarat* India
117 F5 Jhinkpani *Bihar* India
123 G5 Jhudo Pak.
117 F4 Jhumritilaiya *Bihar* India
116 C3 Jhunjhunun *Rajasthan* India
116 E4 Jhusi *Uttar Prad.* India
108 C1 Jiachuan *Sichuan* China
Jiachuanzhen *Sichuan* China *see* Jiachuan
109 G2 Jiading *Jiangxi* China
Jiading *Shanghai* China *see* Xinhe
108 B2 Jiahe *Hunan* China
108 C2 Jialing Jiang r. *Sichuan* China
Jiaji *Hainan* China *see* Qionghai
109 E1 Jiamusi *Heilong.* China
109 E3 Ji'an *Jiangxi* China
101 C4 Ji'an *Jilin* China
Jiancaohu *Xinjiang* China *see* Nanchang
107 H3 Jianchang *Liaoning* China
108 A3 Jianchuan *Yunnan* China
Jiandaoyu *Hubei* China *see* Zigui
109 F2 Jiande *Zhejiang* China
108 C2 Jiang'an *Sichuan* China
Jiangbei *Chongqing* China *see* Yubei
108 B2 Jiangcheng *Yunnan* China
108 B3 Jiangcheng *Yunnan* China
108 C2 Jiangcun *Hunan* China
109 F1 Jiangdu *Jiangsu* China
109 E3 Jianggang *Jiangxi* China
106 A2 Jianggumiao *Xinjiang* China
109 E3 Jiangkou *Guangdong* China *see* Fengkai
108 C1 Jiangkou *Shaanxi* China
108 C2 Jiangle *Fujian* China
Jiangling *Hubei* China *see* Jingzhou
109 F3 Jiangluozhen *Gansu* China
109 E4 Jiangmen *Guangdong* China
Jiangna *Yunnan* China *see* Yanshan
109 F2 Jiangning *Jiangsu* China
109 E3 Jiangshan *Zhejiang* China
108 C2 Jiangshui *Guizhou* China
Dejiang
109 F1 Jiangsu prov. China
109 E3 Jiangxi prov. China
109 H3 Jiangxia *Hubei* China
Jiangxigou *Qinghai* China *see* Wuchang
107 F5 Jiangyan *Shandong* China
109 G1 Jiangyan *Jiangsu* China
108 B2 Jiangyong *Hunan* China
108 C2 Jiangyou *Sichuan* China
Jianhu *Jiangsu* China *see* Yongshou
100 C4 Jianli *Jilin* China
106 C4 Jianli *Gansu* China
109 F3 Jianli *Hubei* China
109 F1 Jian'ou *Fujian* China
108 B3 Jianping *Liaoning* China
107 H3 Jianping *Liaoning* China
108 A1 Jianshe *Qinghai* China
108 B2 Jianshi *Hubei* China
107 H4 Jianshui *Yunnan* China
100 C3 Jiao'ao *Jilin* China
110 I3 Jiaohe *Jilin* China
109 H3 Jiaojiang *Zhejiang* China *see* Taizhou
107 F4 Jiaokou *Yunnan* China *see* Yiliang
107 H3 Jiaolai r. China
109 H3 Jiaolai r. China
107 I3 Jiaonan *Shandong* China
100 C4 Jiaotong *Shandong* China
107 H5 Jiaozhou *Shandong* China
107 G4 Jiaozuo *Henan* China
108 B3 Jiasa *Yunnan* China
Mingguang
107 H3 Jiashi *Xinjiang* China
107 I4 Jiaxian *Henan* China
107 H3 Jiaxian *Shaanxi* China
109 G2 Jiaxing *Zhejiang* China
109 G2 Jiayin *Heilong.* China
109 D2 Jiayu *Hubei* China
106 C4 Jiayuguan *Gansu* China
114 C2 Jiazi *Guangdong* China
197 H3 Jibou *Romania* China
109 F3 Jibu *Hunan* China

108 B3 Jinyang *Sichuan* China
Jinyuan *Sichuan* China *see* Dayi
109 E4 Jinyun *Zhejiang* China
109 E4 Jinzhai *Anhui* China
109 E1 Jinzhou *Liaoning* China
138 D1 Jiesia r. Lith.
138 C4 Jieznas Lith.
207 H3 Jigawa *state* Nigeria
87 D4 Jiggalong *W.A.* Austr.
246 C2 Jiguaní Cuba
244 C4 Jiguan de Juárez Mex.
245 H5 Jiquipilas Mex.
123 G2 Jirgatol Tajik.
117 H4 Jiri r. India
210 E3 Jirin Gol *Nei Mongol* China
176 E1 Jirkov Czech Rep.
107 C1 Jirny Czech Rep.
122 D4 Jiroft Iran
210 F3 Jirriiban Somalia
107 F5 Jishan *Shanxi* China
108 C2 Jishi *Qinghai* China *see* Xunhua
108 B2 Jishou *Hunan* China
108 B2 Jishui *Jiangxi* China *see* Yongfeng
128 C2 Jisr ash Shughūr Syria
176 D2 Jistebnice Czech Rep.
Jitian *Guangdong* China *see* Lianshan
210 D4 Jilib Somalia
100 C4 Jilin China
107 J3 Jilin prov. China
100 C4 Jilin Hada Ling *mts* China
100 B2 Jiliu r. China
183 I3 Jiloca r. Spain
176 E1 Jílové *Czech Rep.*
176 D2 Jílové u Prahy Czech Rep.
210 C3 Jima Eth.
246 E3 Jimani Haiti
196 E3 Jimbolia Romania
108 B3 Jimda *Sichuan* China *see* Zindo
185 G3 Jimena Spain
184 E5 Jimena de la Frontera Spain
242 D2 Jiménez Mex.
245 E1 Jiménez Mex.
245 E1 Jiménez Mex.
107 I3 Jiménez Mex.
84 D2 Jim Jim Creek r. *N.T.* Austr.
Jimo *Shandong* China *see* Jimo
176 F2 Jimramov Czech Rep.
110 E3 Jimsar *Xinjiang* China
234 C2 Jim Thorpe *PA* U.S.A.
197 F3 Jina Romania
107 H4 Jin'an *Shandong* China
125 F4 Jiz, Wādī al r. Yemen
123 H5 Jīzān Saudi Arabia
176 D1 Jizera r. Czech Rep.
176 E1 Jizerské Hory *mts* Czech Rep.
107 H3 Jizhou *Hebei* China
105 F2 Jizō-dake *mt.* Japan
Jizzakh Uzbek. *see* Dzhizak
Jizzakh Wiloyati admin. div. Uzbek. *see* Dzhizakskaya Oblast'
255 C8 Joaçaba Brazil
170 D3 Joachimsthal Ger.
257 G2 Joaíma Brazil
206 A3 Joal-Fadiout Senegal
182 B3 Joane Port.
254 E3 João Belo Moz. *see* Xai-Xai
116 D3 João Haryana India
254 G3 João Monlevade Brazil
250 D2 João Pessoa Brazil
256 D3 João Pinheiro Brazil
257 D2 Joaquim Felício Brazil
245 G1 Joaquín V. González Arg.
182 B3 Jobabo Cuba
116 C5 Jobat *Madh. Prad.* India
177 I4 Jobbágyi Hungary
92 C5 José Bispo r. Brazil
240 I2 Job Peak *NV* U.S.A.
178 D5 Jochberg Austria
171 D5 Jöcketal Ger.
172 C2 Jockgrim Ger.
244 B3 Jocotepec Mex.
245 E4 Jocotitlán, Volcán vol. Mex.
108 B3 Jocón Honduras
165 D4 Jodhpur *Rajasthan* India
165 D4 Jodoigne Belgium
92 D6 Joe Batt's Arm *Nfld.* Can.
240 H2 Joe's Valley Reservoir *UT* U.S.A.
140 N2 Joesjö Sweden
105 E1 Jōetsu Japan
213 E3 Jofane Moz.
123 I5 Joffre, Mount *Alta/B.C.* Can.
104 D2 Jōgaguri r. Japan
117 F4 Jogbani *Bihar* India
138 F2 Jõgeva Estonia
216 D2 Joghatay, Kūh-ye *hill* Iran
116 D3 Jogindarnagar *Hima. Prad.* India
Jogjakarta Indon. *see* Yogyakarta
215 I4 Johannesburg S. Africa
171 I4 Johanngeorgenstadt Ger.
173 J3 Johanniskirchen Ger.
116 E5 Johilla r. *Madh. Prad.* India
86 B3 John, Mount *hill W.A.* Austr.
238 C2 John Day *OR* U.S.A.
178 D5 John Day r. *OR* U.S.A.
238 C2 John Day, Middle Fork r. *OR* U.S.A.
238 C2 John Day, North Fork r. *OR* U.S.A.
222 H3 John d'Or Prairie *Alta* Can.
233 G4 John F. Kennedy airport *NY* U.S.A.
222 D3 John Jay, Mount *Alaska/B.C.* Can./U.S.A.

141 M3 Jokioinen Fin.
140 L2 Jokkmokk Sweden
140 □B2 Jökulbrúargil *hill* Iceland
140 □C2 Jökulfjörðir *inlet* Iceland
140 □C2 Jökulsá á Fjöllum r. Iceland
191 G4 Jolanda di Savoia Italy
254 C4 Jolarpettai *Tamil Nadu* India
127 G3 Jolfa Iran
226 C5 Joliet *IL* U.S.A.
234 B2 Joliet *PA* U.S.A.
224 F4 Joliette *Que.* Can.
92 B5 Jolo Phil.
92 B5 Jolo i. Phil.
160 E3 Joly, Mont mt. France
138 D1 Jomala Åland Fin.
95 H4 Jombang *Jawa Timur* Indon.
108 A2 Jomda *Xizang* China
142 C2 Jomfruland i. Norway
100 F2 Jōmine-san mt. Japan
190 D1 Jona Switz.
122 C5 Jonāb Iran
232 B6 Jonancy *KY* U.S.A.
160 C2 Joncy France
142 H4 Jondal Norway
106 D3 Jonê *Gansu* China
104 D2 Jōnen-dake *mt.* Japan
237 F5 Jonesboro *AR* U.S.A.
226 B5 Jonesboro *IL* U.S.A.
237 E5 Jonesboro *LA* U.S.A.
233 □J2 Jonesboro *ME* U.S.A.
232 B6 Jonesboro *TN* U.S.A.
232 B4 Jones Mills *PA* U.S.A.
262 P2 Jones Mountains Antarctica
233 □J2 Jonesport *ME* U.S.A.
221 J2 Jones Sound *sea chan.* Nunavut Can.
234 B2 Jonestown *PA* U.S.A.
237 F6 Jonesville *LA* U.S.A.
232 B6 Jonesville *VA* U.S.A.
210 B3 Jonglei *state* Sudan
175 I3 Joniec Pol.
138 D3 Joniškėlis Lith.
138 D3 Joniškis Lith.
117 E5 Jonk r. India
143 J4 Jönköping Sweden
143 I3 Jönköping *county* Sweden
175 I2 Jonkowo Pol.
225 G4 Jonquière *Que.* Can.
161 C4 Jonquières France
162 B3 Jonzac France
237 E4 Joplin *MO* U.S.A.
245 E2 Jopoy Mex.
Joppa Israel *see* Tel Aviv-Yafo
234 B3 Joppatowne *MD* U.S.A.
191 M3 Joppolo Italy
116 D4 Jora *Madh. Prad.* India
186 B3 Jorcas Spain
  Jordan *country* Asia
186 C1 Jordán r. Spain
238 F3 Jordan *MT* U.S.A.
235 F3 Jordan *NY* U.S.A.
238 C3 Jordan r. *OR* U.S.A.
241 L1 Jordan r. *UT* U.S.A.
257 C1 Jordânia Brazil
161 A1 Jordane r. France
175 H6 Jordanów Pol.
174 G5 Jordanów Śląski Pol.
238 D3 Jordan Valley *OR* U.S.A.
142 H4 Jørgenfjord Norway
142 C4 Jørgenberd Denmark
117 H4 Jorhat *Assam* India
129 D3 Jorjiashvili Georgia
168 E2 Jork Ger.
142 J2 Jörlanda Sweden
139 S3 Jorma r. Norway
168 K5 Jormvattnet Sweden
140 M2 Jörn Sweden
141 N3 Jorpeland Norway
185 N3 Jorquera r. Chile
206 B4 Jos Nigeria
92 C5 Jose Abad Santos Phil.
254 B4 José Bispo r. Brazil
245 F4 José Cardel Mex.
259 C7 José de Freitas Brazil
259 C7 José de San Martín Arg.
261 I3 José Enrique Rodó Uru.
171 G5 Josefův Důl Czech Rep.
245 G4 José López Portillo, Presa resr Mex.
244 C3 José María Morelos Mex.
92 D7 José Pañganiban Phil.
258 F4 José Pedro Varela Uru.
86 F2 Joseph Bonaparte Gulf W.A. Austr.
241 L4 Joseph City *AZ* U.S.A.
225 H3 Joseph, Lac l. Nfld. Can.
115 F3 Joshimath *Uttar Prad.* India
117 F5 Joshipur *Orissa* India
254 C4 Joshua Tree *CA* U.S.A.
105 G2 Jōsō Japan
171 I5 Jössen Ger.
142 H1 Josephsberg *glacier* Norway
165 D4 Jostedalsbreen *glacier* Norway
138 D1 Josvainiai Lith.
141 N6 Jotunheimen *mts* Norway
182 B2 Jou Port.
159 H4 Jouanne r. France
215 I2 Joubertina S. Africa
215 H2 Joubertson S. Africa
212 C3 Jouberton S. Africa
162 C3 Jouberton S. Africa
158 C3 Jouë-lès-Tours France
160 A1 Jougne France
161 C5 Jouques France
160 D3 Jounié Lebanon
161 G3 Jouques France
164 C2 Joure Neth.
222 H4 Journial France
222 H4 Joussard *Alta* Can.
141 M3 Joutsa Fin.
141 S3 Joutseno Fin.
160 B1 Joux-la-Ville France
157 I5 Jouy-aux-Arches France
156 B5 Jouy-le-Potier France
156 D3 Jouy-le-Rams France
146 E6 Jovellanos Cuba
117 H4 Jowai *Meghalaya* India
226 C3 Joy, Mount *Y.T.* Can.
254 C3 Joyce's Country reg. Rep. of Ireland
161 C4 Joyeuse France
105 B6 Jōyō Japan
161 B4 Jožeňov Pol.
171 H5 Jözefów Pol.
140 N3 Jozini S. Africa
215 J3 Jreïda Maur.
206 A3 Juà r. Brazil
250 E3 Juan Aldama Mex.
244 C1 Juancheng *Shandong* China
256 C2 Juan de Fuca Strait
222 E5 Juan de Nova i. France
250 □3 Juan de Nova i. Indian Ocean

242 A1 Juárez, Sierra de *mts* Mex.
254 E4 Juazeiro Brazil
254 F3 Juazeiro do Norte Brazil
206 C5 Juazohn Liberia
Jubba r. Somalia *see* Jubba
210 D5 Juba Sudan
124 D5 Juban Yemen
262 U2 Jubany research stn Antarctica
210 D5 Jubba r. Somalia
210 D4 Jubbada Dhexe admin. reg. Somalia
210 D4 Jubbada Hoose admin. reg. Somalia
116 C3 Jubbulpore Madh. Prad. India *see* Jabalpur
168 E1 Jübek Ger.
87 B6 Jubilee Lake *salt flat* W.A. Austr.
159 F3 Jublains France
183 J3 Júcar r. Spain
256 E1 Jucás r. Brazil
187 C5 Júcar-Turia, Canal r. Spain
254 F3 Jucás Brazil
169 B4 Jüchen Ger.
244 C3 Juchipila Mex.
244 C3 Juchipila r. Mex.
245 G5 Juchitán Mex.
175 L2 Juchnowiec Dolny Pol.
169 F5 Jüchsen Ger.
257 E2 Jucuruçu Brazil
257 H2 Jucuruçu r. Brazil
142 J2 Jucurutu Brazil
142 H5 Judaberg Norway
127 F5 Judaidat al Hamir Iraq
126 E4 Judaydah Syria
171 G5 Judenbach Ger.
179 I3 Judenburg Austria
108 A3 Judian *Yunnan* China
179 I3 Judith r. MT U.S.A.
238 E2 Judith Gap *MT* U.S.A.
Juegang *Jiangsu* China *see* Rudong
185 G2 Juego de Bolos *mt.* Spain
142 D4 Juelsminde Denmark
183 I4 Juez mt. Spain
251 F5 Jufari r. Brazil
158 D3 Jugon-les-Lacs France
  Jugoslavia *country* Europe *see* Yugoslavia
107 H4 Juh *Nei Mongol* China
169 E4 Jühnde Ger.
178 C3 Juifen *mt.* Austria
242 □I6 Juigalpa Nic.
159 F3 Juigné-sur-Loire France
162 D3 Juillac France
163 C5 Juillan France
156 C3 Juilly France
255 F3 Juína Brazil
256 C4 Juina r. Brazil
168 C2 Juist i. Ger.
257 F3 Juiz de Fora Brazil
94 C3 Jujuhan r. Indon.
161 C5 Jujurieux France
258 D1 Jujuy prov. Arg.
140 M2 Jukkasjärvi Sweden
179 F2 Julbach Austria
173 J3 Julbach Ger.
108 B2 Julearsden r. Brazil
156 C4 Julianadorp Neth.
85 D4 Julia Creek *Qld* Austr.
85 E4 Julia Creek r. *Qld* Austr.
240 I5 Julian *CA* U.S.A.
164 D2 Julianadorp Neth.
  Julian Alps *mts* Slovenia *see* Julijske Alpe
251 G3 Julianatop *mt.* Indon. *see* Mandala, Puncak
251 G3 Juliana Top *mt.* Suriname
140 □ Julianehåb Greenland *see* Qaqortoq
147 D3 Julianstown Rep. of Ireland
169 B5 Jülich Ger.
160 C2 Julienas France
160 C2 Juliénas France
160 C2 Julien, Mont *hill* France
188 F2 Julijske Alpe *mts* Slovenia
255 B9 Júlio de Castilhos Brazil
  Juliomagus France *see* Angers
256 C5 Júlio Mesquita Brazil
84 D4 Julius, Lake *Qld* Austr.
158 D3 Jullouville France
158 E3 Jullundur *Punjab* India *see* Jalandhar
251 E6 Juma r. Brazil
107 G4 Juma r. China
  Juma *Uzbek.* China *see* Dzhuma
108 A1 Jumanggoin *Sichuan* China
206 D5 Jumbilla Peru
161 B1 Jumeaux France
163 B4 Jumilhac-le-Grand France
187 B6 Jumilla Spain
116 E3 Jumla Nepal
  Jumna r. India *see* Yamuna
114 B2 Jumner r. India
226 B4 Junagadh *Gujarat* India
115 D2 Junagarh *Orissa* India
107 H2 Jun Bulen *Nei Mongol* China
182 B2 Juncal mt. Chile
182 B2 Juncal r. Port.
247 □1 Juncos Puerto Rico
237 D6 Junction *TX* U.S.A.
241 G2 Junction *UT* U.S.A.
84 D1 Junction Bay *N.T.* Austr.
236 D4 Junction City *KS* U.S.A.
238 B3 Junction City *OR* U.S.A.
256 D3 Jundiaí Brazil
256 D3 Jundiaí Brazil
226 A3 Juneau *AK* U.S.A.
83 F3 Junee *N.S.W.* Austr.
  Jungar Qi *Nei Mongol* China *see* Shagedu
190 C3 Jungfrau mt. Switz.
110 C2 Junggar Pendi basin China
172 E3 Jungingen Ger.
165 J5 Junglinster Lux.
227 I5 Juniata r. *PA* U.S.A.
234 A3 Juniata r. *PA* U.S.A.
196 E4 Junik *Kosovo, Srbija* Yugo.
260 C3 Junín Arg.
260 C3 Junín Arg.
252 B3 Junín Mendoza Arg.
252 B2 Junín Peru
252 D2 Junín del Guía Peru
233 □J2 Junín Mt. U.S.A.
241 K4 Juniper Mountains *AZ* U.S.A.
240 G3 Junipero Serro Peak *CA* U.S.A.
156 C3 Junisville France
108 C5 Junkerath Ger.
108 B3 Junlian *Sichuan* China
237 C6 Juno *TX* U.S.A.
141 N3 Junnar *Mahar.* India
143 N2 Junosuando Sweden
143 L3 Junqueirópolis Brazil
140 L3 Junsele Sweden
238 D3 Juntura *OR* U.S.A.
108 A1 Junxi *Fujian* China *see* Datian
  Ju'nyung *Sichuan* China *see* Ju'nyung
138 F3 Juodšiliai Lith.
138 E3 Juodkrantė Lith.
138 E3 Juodupė Lith.
138 E3 Juozapinės kalnas *hill* Lith.
159 G3 Jupilles France
231 E7 Jupiter *FL* U.S.A.
156 D6 Jupille Belgium
256 D3 Jupiá, Represa resr Brazil
256 D5 Juquiá Brazil
256 D5 Juquiá r. Brazil
160 D2 Jura *dept Franche-Comté* France
161 D1 Jura r. France/Switz.
146 D5 Jura i. Scotland U.K.
190 C1 Jura *canton* Switz.
146 C5 Jura, Sound of sea chan. Scotland U.K.

Jura, Sound of to **Kapran**
318

146 C6 **Jura, Sound of** sea chan. Scotland U.K.
250 B3 **Juradó** Col.
257 F2 **Juramento** Brazil
163 B5 **Jurançon** France
256 A6 **Juranda** Brazil
138 D4 **Jurbarkas** Lith.
165 C4 **Jurbise** Belgium
170 C2 **Jürgenshagen** Ger.
170 D2 **Jürgenstorf** Ger.
86 D3 **Jurgurra** r. W.A. Austr.
107 I2 **Jurh** Nei Mongol China
111 E5 **Jurhen Ul Shan** mts China
138 E2 **Jüri** Estonia
87 B6 **Jurien** W.A. Austr.
87 B6 **Jurien Bay** W.A. Austr.
162 B3 **Jurignac** France
197 I3 **Jurilovca** Romania
251 G5 **Juriti Velho** Brazil
191 J4 **Jurjevo** Croatia
138 D3 **Jūrmala** Latvia
184 C2 **Juromenha** Port.
109 F2 **Jurong** Jiangsu China
94 □ **Jurong** Sing.
Jur pri Bratislave Slovakia see Svätý Jur
251 E5 **Juruá** Brazil
250 E5 **Juruá** r. Brazil
253 F3 **Juruena** Brazil
253 F1 **Juruena** r. Brazil
256 C5 **Jurumirim, Represa de** resr Brazil
253 G2 **Juruna** r. Brazil
252 C1 **Jurupari** r. Brazil
251 G5 **Juruti** Brazil
140 M3 **Jurva** Fin.
162 E4 **Jussac** France
157 F5 **Jussey** France
232 C6 **Justice** WV U.S.A.
261 F3 **Justiniano Posse** Arg.
260 E3 **Justo Daract** Arg.
177 G5 **Juta** Hungary
250 D6 **Jutaí** Brazil
250 E5 **Jutaí** r. Brazil
171 E4 **Jüterbog** Ger.
255 B7 **Juti** Brazil
243 H6 **Jutiapa** Guat.
242 □I6 **Jutiapa** Hond.
242 □I6 **Juticalpa** Hond.
Jutland pen. Denmark see Jylland
174 F4 **Jutrosin** Pol.
140 O3 **Juuka** Fin.
141 N3 **Juupajoki** Fin.
141 N3 **Juva** Fin.
244 D3 **Juventino Rosas** Mex.
159 E3 **Juvigné** France
159 E3 **Juvigny-le-Tertre** France
159 F3 **Juvigny-sous-Andaine** France
95 E4 **Juwana** Jawa Tengah Indon.
107 H5 **Juxian** Shandong China
107 H5 **Juye** Shandong China
122 D3 **Jūymand** Iran
122 C4 **Jūyom** Iran
157 E4 **Juzennecourt** France
163 C6 **Juzet-d'Izaut** France
Južnoukrajinsk Ukr. see Yuzhnoukrayinsk
212 E5 **Jwaneng** Botswana
142 D4 **Jyderup** Denmark
142 C3 **Jylland** pen. Denmark
121 I4 **Jyrgalang** Kyrg.
141 N3 **Jyväskylä** Fin.

K

116 D2 **K2** mt. China/Jammu and Kashmir
207 G4 **Ka** r. Nigeria
240 □ **Kaaawa** HI U.S.A.
Kaakhka Turkm. see **Kaka**
240 □ **Kaala** mt. HI U.S.A.
78 □5 **Kaala-Gomen** New Caledonia
215 H1 **Kaalrug** S. Africa
215 H1 **Kaapamuiden** S. Africa
Kaapstad S. Africa see **Cape Town**
141 M3 **Kaarina** Fin.
170 C2 **Kaarßen** Ger.
169 B4 **Kaarst** Ger.
206 C3 **Kaarta** reg. Mali
164 E3 **Kaatsheuvel** Neth.
140 O3 **Kaavi** Fin.
Kaba Xinjiang China see Habahe
121 K3 **Kaba** r. China/Kazakh.
177 K4 **Kaba** Hungary
123 E2 **Kabakly** Turkm.
129 C3 **Kabak Tepe** mt. Turkey
206 C4 **Kabala** Sierra Leone
211 A5 **Kabale** Uganda
Kabalega Falls National Park Uganda see **Murchison Falls National Park**
209 E6 **Kabalo** Dem. Rep. Congo
209 E6 **Kabambare** Dem. Rep. Congo
121 F1 **Kaban'** Kazakh.
121 J3 **Kabanbay** Kazakh.
94 B2 **Kabanjahe** Sumatera Indon.
120 B1 **Kabanovka** Rus. Fed.
Kabanye Ukr. see **Krasnorichens'ke**
79 □1 **Kabara** i. Fiji
137 I5 **Kabardinka** Rus. Fed.
Kabardino-Balkarskaya A.S.S.R. aut. rep. Rus. Fed. see Kabardino-Balkarskaya Respublika
129 C2 **Kabardino-Balkarskaya Respublika** aut. rep. Rus. Fed.
208 F5 **Kabare** Dem. Rep. Congo
Kabarega National Park Uganda see **Murchison Falls National Park**
92 B5 **Kabasalan** Phil.
105 G2 **Kaba-san** hill Japan
96 B3 **Kabaung** r. Myanmar
96 A2 **Kabaw Valley** Myanmar
207 G5 **Kabba** Nigeria
114 C3 **Kabbani** r. India
140 M2 **Kåbdalis** Sweden
177 G4 **Kab-hegy** hill Hungary
224 C3 **Kabinakagami** r. Ont. Can.
224 C3 **Kabinakagami Lake** Ont. Can.
209 E6 **Kabinda** Dem. Rep. Congo
128 B2 **Kabīr** r. Syria
122 A3 **Kabīrkūh** mts Iran
129 E4 **Kābirli** Azer.
123 G4 **Kabirwala** Pak.
116 D5 **Kabneshwar** Mahar. India
208 C3 **Kabo** C.A.R.
123 G2 **Kabodiyen** Tajik.
Kabodiyon Tajik. see Kabodiyen
209 E8 **Kabompo** Zambia
209 D8 **Kabompo** r. Zambia
209 E6 **Kabongo** Dem. Rep. Congo
207 F4 **Kabou** Togo
206 A3 **Kabrousse** Senegal
122 D2 **Kabūd Gonbad** Iran
122 B3 **Kabūd Rāhang** Iran
92 B2 **Kabugao** Phil.
123 G3 **Kābul** Afgh.
123 G3 **Kābul** prov. Afgh.
123 H3 **Kabul** r. Afgh.
209 F8 **Kabunda** Dem. Rep. Congo
105 F2 **Kabura-gawa** r. Japan
209 F8 **Kabwe** Zambia
120 E2 **Kabyrga** r. Kazakh.
196 E4 **Kačanik** Kosovo, Srbija Yugo.
137 G5 **Kacha** r. Ukr.
210 B4 **Kachagalau** mt. Kenya
Kachagani Georgia see Qach'aghani
123 E4 **Kacha Kuh** mts Iran/Pak.
135 I6 **Kachalinskaya** Rus. Fed.
116 B5 **Kachchh, Gulf of** Gujarat India
116 C4 **Kachhola** Rajasthan India
117 E4 **Kachhwa** Uttar Prad. India
207 G4 **Kachia** Nigeria
96 B1 **Kachin** state Myanmar
121 I1 **Kachiry** Kazakh.
211 A8 **Kacholola** Zambia
98 I1 **Kachug** Rus. Fed.
171 E5 **Kačice** Czech Rep.
127 F2 **Kaçkar Dağı** mt. Turkey
129 C4 **Kaçmaz** Turkey
167 H3 **Kaczawa** r. Pol.
174 E2 **Kaczory** Pol.
114 C4 **Kadaiyanallur** Tamil Nadu India
210 B4 **Kadam** mt. Uganda
176 C1 **Kadaň** Czech Rep.
123 F4 **Kadanai** r. Afgh./Pak.
97 B4 **Kadan Kyun** i. Myanmar
177 G5 **Kadarkút** Hungary
116 D4 **Kadaura** Uttar Prad. India
79 □1 **Kadavu** i. Fiji
79 □1a **Kadavu Passage** Fiji
107 H1 **Kadaya** Rus. Fed.
206 E5 **Kade** Ghana
87 E5 **Kadgo, Lake** salt flat W.A. Austr.
Kādhimain Iraq see Al Kāẓimīyah
116 C5 **Kadi** Gujarat India
206 D4 **Kadiana** Mali
114 C4 **Kadiapattanam** Tamil Nadu India
Kadijica mt. Bulg. see **Kadiytsa**
199 E1 **Kadıköy** Turkey
199 F1 **Kadıköy** Turkey
82 D3 **Kadina** S.A. Austr.
96 C3 **Kading** r. Laos
126 D3 **Kadınhanı** Turkey
206 D4 **Kadiolo** Mali
206 C4 **Kadiondola, Mount** Guinea
114 C3 **Kadiri** Andhra Prad. India
126 E3 **Kadirli** Turkey
Kadiyevka Ukr. see Stakhanov
197 F5 **Kadiytsa** mt. Bulg.
207 F5 **Kadjebi** Ghana
114 B4 **Kadmat** i. India
134 H4 **Kadnikov** Rus. Fed.
207 H5 **Kado** Nigeria
94 C1 **Kadok** Malaysia
236 C3 **Kadoka** SD U.S.A.
135 H5 **Kadom** Rus. Fed.
213 F3 **Kadoma** Zimbabwe
138 F2 **Kadrina** Estonia
208 F2 **Kadugli** Sudan
207 G4 **Kaduna** Nigeria
207 G4 **Kaduna** r. Nigeria
207 G4 **Kaduna** state Nigeria
114 C3 **Kadur** Karnataka India
108 A2 **Kadusam** mt. China/India
139 K2 **Kaduy** Rus. Fed.
134 H4 **Kadyy** Rus. Fed.
Kadzharan Armenia see K'ajaran
134 K2 **Kadzherom** Rus. Fed.
Kadzhi-Say Kyrg. see **Kajy-Say**
175 J2 **Kadzidło** Pol.
101 C5 **Kaechon** N. Korea
206 B2 **Kaédi** Maur.
207 I4 **Kaélé** Cameroon
240 □C8 **Kaeleku** HI U.S.A.
80 D1 **Kaeo** North I. N.Z.
168 E1 **Kær** Denmark
101 C5 **Kaesŏng** N. Korea
Kafa Ukr. see **Feodosiya**
209 D7 **Kafakumba** Dem. Rep. Congo
Kafan Armenia see **Kapan**
207 H4 **Kafanchan** Nigeria
215 F3 **Kafferrivier** S. Africa
207 H3 **Kaffin-Hausa** Nigeria
215 E3 **Kaffir** r. S. Africa
206 B3 **Kaffrine** Senegal
Kafirnigan Tajik. see Kofarnihon
206 D4 **Kafolo** Côte d'Ivoire
203 F2 **Kafr el Sheikh** Egypt
126 C5 **Kafr el Sheikh** governorate Egypt
210 B4 **Kafu** r. Uganda
209 F8 **Kafue** Zambia
209 F8 **Kafue** r. Zambia
104 C2 **Kaga** Japan
208 C3 **Kaga Bandoro** C.A.R.
137 J4 **Kagal'nik** Rus. Fed.
137 J4 **Kagal'nik** r. Rus. Fed.
135 H7 **Kagal'nitskaya** Rus. Fed.
120 F5 **Kagan** Uzbek.
106 D5 **Kagang** Qinghai China
Kaganovich Rus. Fed. see **Tovarkovskiy**
Kaganovichabad Tajik. see **Kolkhozobod**
Kaganovichi Pervyye Ukr. see **Polis'ke**
Kagarlyk Ukr. see **Kaharlyk**
103 G6 **Kagawa** pref. Japan
227 F3 **Kagawong** Ont. Can.
140 M2 **Kåge** Sweden
211 A5 **Kagera** admin. reg. Tanz.
127 F2 **Kağızman** Turkey
103 E8 **Kagoshima** Japan
102 □1 **Kagoshima** pref. Japan
Kagul Moldova see **Cahul**
240 □C8 **Kahakuloa** HI U.S.A.
240 □ **Kahaluu** HI U.S.A.
211 B5 **Kahama** Tanz.
136 F3 **Kaharlyk** Ukr.
95 F3 **Kahayan** r. Indon.
209 C6 **Kahemba** Dem. Rep. Congo
81 A6 **Kaherekoau Mountains** South I. N.Z.
169 D5 **Kahl** r. Ger.
171 C5 **Kahla** Ger.
169 E5 **Kahl am Main** Ger.
222 F3 **Kahntah** B.C. Can.
Kahnu Iran see **Kahnūj**
122 D5 **Kahnūj** Iran
80 D1 **Kahoe** North I. N.Z.
236 F3 **Kahoka** MO U.S.A.
240 □C8 **Kahoolawe** i. HI U.S.A.
130 D3 **Kahperusvaarat** mts Fin.
126 E3 **Kahramanmaraş** Turkey
123 G4 **Kahror** Pak.
126 E3 **Kahta** Turkey
240 □D8 **Kahua** HI U.S.A.
240 □ **Kahuku** HI U.S.A.
136 E5 **Kahul, Ozero** l. Ukr.
Kahulaui i. HI U.S.A. see Kahoolawe
240 □C8 **Kahului** HI U.S.A.
122 D4 **Kahūrak** Iran
80 D4 **Kahurangi Point** South I. N.Z.
123 H3 **Kahuta** Pak.
91 H8 **Kai, Kepulauan** is Indon.
210 A3 **Kaia** r. Sudan
80 D1 **Kaiaka** North I. N.Z.
207 F4 **Kaiama** Nigeria
81 D5 **Kaiapoi** South I. N.Z.
241 K3 **Kaibab** AZ U.S.A.
106 C4 **Kaibamardang** Qinghai China
91 H8 **Kai Besar** i. Indon.
241 L3 **Kaibito Plateau** AZ U.S.A.
78 □6 **Kaichui, Mount** Guadalcanal Solomon Is
110 D3 **Kaidu He** r. China
251 G3 **Kaieteur Falls** Guyana
107 G5 **Kaifeng** Henan China
107 G5 **Kaifeng** Henan China
80 D1 **Kaihu** North I. N.Z.
Kaihua Yunnan China see Wenshan
109 F2 **Kaihua** Zhejiang China
214 C3 **Kaiingveld** reg. S. Africa
108 C2 **Kaijiang** Sichuan China
91 H8 **Kai Kecil** i. Indon.
80 D1 **Kaikohe** North I. N.Z.
81 D5 **Kaikoura** South I. N.Z.
206 C4 **Kailahun** Sierra Leone
Kailas mt. Xizang China see **Kangrinboqê Feng**
Kailas Range mts Xizang China see **Gangdisê Shan**
108 C3 **Kaili** Guizhou China
107 I3 **Kailu** Nei Mongol China
240 □ **Kailua** HI U.S.A.
240 □D9 **Kailua Kona** HI U.S.A.
80 E2 **Kaimai** North I. N.Z.
80 E2 **Kaimai Range** hills North I. N.Z.
80 E3 **Kaimanawa Mountains** North I. N.Z.
108 A1 **Kaimar** Qinghai China
81 C5 **Kaimata** South I. N.Z.
116 D4 **Kaimganj** Uttar Prad. India
103 E8 **Kaimon-dake** hill Japan
116 E4 **Kaimur Range** hills India
138 D2 **Käina** Estonia
104 B4 **Kainan** Japan
Kainda Kyrg. see **Kayyngdy**
Kaindy Kyrg. see **Kayyngdy**
80 F3 **Kaingaroa Forest** North I. N.Z.
207 F3 **Kaingiwa** Nigeria
207 G4 **Kainji Reservoir** Nigeria
117 F5 **Kaintaragarh** Orissa India
140 M2 **Kainulasjärvi** Sweden
80 E2 **Kaipara Flats** North I. N.Z.
80 E2 **Kaipara Harbour** North I. N.Z.
241 L3 **Kaiparowits Plateau** UT U.S.A.
109 E4 **Kaiping** Guangdong China
Kaiping Yunnan China see **Dêqên**
Kaira Gujarat India see **Kheda**
80 F3 **Kairakau Beach** North I. N.Z.
116 D3 **Kairana** Uttar Prad. India
205 H2 **Kairouan** Tunisia
140 L1 **Kaisepakte** Sweden
172 B2 **Kaiserslautern** Ger.
263 F2 **Kaiser Wilhelm II Land** reg. Antarctica
100 D4 **Kaishantun** Jilin China
173 E3 **Kaisheim** Ger.
138 E4 **Kaišiadorys** Lith.
80 D1 **Kaitaia** North I. N.Z.
81 B7 **Kaitangata** South I. N.Z.
80 F3 **Kaitawa** North I. N.Z.
116 D5 **Kaitha** Madh. Prad. India
116 D3 **Kaithal** Haryana India
Kaitong Jilin China see **Tongyu**
140 M2 **Kaitum** Sweden
140 M2 **Kaitumälven** r. Sweden
240 □C8 **Kaiwi Channel** HI U.S.A.
108 D2 **Kaixian** Chongqing China
108 C3 **Kaiyang** Guizhou China
107 J3 **Kaiyuan** Liaoning China
108 B4 **Kaiyuan** Yunnan China
104 B4 **Kaizuka** Japan
140 N2 **Kajaani** Fin.
84 E4 **Kajabbi** Qld Austr.
94 C2 **Kajang** Malaysia
129 E4 **K'ajaran** Armenia
177 H5 **Kajdacs** Hungary
176 D3 **Kájov** Czech Rep.
122 A2 **Kaju** Iran
207 G4 **Kajuru** Nigeria
121 I4 **Kajy-Say** Kyrg.
122 D2 **Kaka** Turkm.
224 B3 **Kakabeka Falls** Ont. Can.
129 D3 **Kakabet'i** Georgia
92 C5 **Kakal** r. Phil.
214 C3 **Kakamas** S. Africa
210 B4 **Kakamega** Kenya
104 C3 **Kakamigahara** Japan
209 A6 **Kakamoéka** Congo
188 G3 **Kakanj** Bos.-Herz.
81 C6 **Kakanui Mountains** South I. N.Z.
80 E3 **Kakaramea** North I. N.Z.
80 E3 **Kakaramea** vol. North I. N.Z.
177 H5 **Kakasd** Hungary
206 C5 **Kakata** Liberia
80 E3 **Kakatahi** North I. N.Z.
117 H4 **Kakching** Manipur India
222 C3 **Kake** AK U.S.A.
105 E4 **Kakegawa** Japan
209 D6 **Kakenge** Dem. Rep. Congo
168 E2 **Kakenstorf** Ger.
170 C3 **Kakerbeck** Ger.
102 □1 **Kakeroma-jima** i. Japan
129 B2 **Kakhat'i** Georgia
129 D2 **Kakhet'is K'edi** hills Georgia
Kakhi Azer. see **Qax**
129 E2 **Kakhib** Rus. Fed.
137 G4 **Kakhovka** Ukr.
137 G4 **Kakhovs'ke Vodoskhovyshche** resr Ukr.
Kakhul Moldova see **Cahul**
122 B4 **Kākī** Iran
114 D2 **Kakinada** Andhra Prad. India
196 D4 **Kakinjës, Maja e** mt. Albania
222 G2 **Kakisa** N.W.T. Can.
222 G2 **Kakisa** r. N.W.T. Can.
104 A4 **Kakogawa** Japan
104 A4 **Kako-gawa** r. Japan
175 K4 **Kąkolewnica Wschodnia** Pol.
174 E4 **Kąkolewo** Pol.
116 D4 **Kakrala** Uttar Prad. India
206 B4 **Kakrima** r. Guinea
119 L1 **Kakshaal-Too** mts China/Kyrg.
220 D2 **Kaktovik** AK U.S.A.
177 I4 **Kakucs** Hungary
102 J5 **Kakuda** Japan
95 F2 **Kakus** r. Sarawak Malaysia
222 G4 **Kakwa** r. Alta Can.
188 E3 **Kal** hill Croatia
177 J4 **Kál** Hungary
211 A7 **Kala** Tanz.
205 H2 **Kalaâ Kebira** Tunisia
Kalaallit Nunaat terr. N. America see **Greenland**
123 G3 **Kalabagh** Pak.
Kalabak mt. Bulg./Greece see Radomir
Kalabáka Greece see Kalampaka
Kalabákion Greece see Kalampaki
114 C2 **Kalabgur** Andhra Prad. India
82 E2 **Kalabity** S.A. Austr.
209 D8 **Kalabo** Zambia
135 H6 **Kalach** Rus. Fed.
135 H6 **Kalach-na-Donu** Rus. Fed.
96 A2 **Kaladan** r. India/Myanmar
224 E4 **Kaladar** Ont. Can.
114 B2 **Kaladgi** Karnataka India
93 B3 **Kalaena** r. Indon.
212 D4 **Kalahari Desert** Africa
214 C1 **Kalahari Gemsbok National Park** S. Africa
240 □B8 **Kalaheo** HI U.S.A.
Kalaikhum Tajik. see Qal'aikhum
Kalai-Khumb Tajik. see Qal'aikhum
123 E3 **Kala-I-Mor** Turkm.
140 M2 **Kalajoki** Fin.
140 M2 **Kalajoki** r. Fin.
197 H4 **Kalakoch** hill Bulg.
207 F4 **Kalalé** Benin
116 D5 **Kalam** Mahar. India
Kalámai Greece see **Kalamata**
212 E4 **Kalamare** Botswana
198 C1 **Kalamaria** Greece
198 C3 **Kalamata** Greece
226 E4 **Kalamazoo** MI U.S.A.
226 D4 **Kalamazoo** r. MI U.S.A.
114 C2 **Kalamnuri** Mahar. India
198 B2 **Kalampaka** Greece
198 D1 **Kalampaki** Greece
206 C4 **Kalana** Mali
111 B6 **Kalanaur** Haryana India
116 C3 **Kalanaur** Punjab India
137 G4 **Kalanchak** Ukr.
Kalandula Angola see Calandula
210 B5 **Kalangala** Uganda
107 H1 **Kalanguy** Rus. Fed.
87 C6 **Kalannie** W.A. Austr.
116 C3 **Kalanwali** Haryana India
240 □D9 **Kalaoa** HI U.S.A.
92 C5 **Kalaong** Phil.
114 C4 **Kala Oya** r. Sri Lanka
240 □D9 **Kalapana** HI U.S.A.
Kalarash Moldova see **Călăraşi**
139 J3 **Kalashnikovo** Rus. Fed.
96 C3 **Kalasin** Thai.
Kalāt Iran see **Kabūd Gonbad**
123 F4 **Kalat** Pak.
122 D3 **Kalat, Kūh-e** mt. Iran
240 □C8 **Kalaupapa** HI U.S.A.
135 I7 **Kalaus** r. Rus. Fed.
116 B5 **Kalavad** Gujarat India
198 C2 **Kalavryta** Greece
125 G2 **Kalbā** U.A.E.
129 E3 **Kälbäcär** Azer.
87 B5 **Kalbarri** W.A. Austr.
214 B5 **Kalbaskraal** S. Africa
170 C3 **Kalbe (Milde)** Ger.
121 J2 **Kalbinskiy Khrebet** mts Kazakh.
173 F2 **Kalchreuth** Ger.
137 I4 **Kal'chyk** r. Ukr.
176 G4 **Káld** Hungary
128 B1 **Kaldırım** Turkey
120 C2 **Kaldygayty** r. Kazakh.
199 F3 **Kale** Denizli Turkey
129 A3 **Kale** Gümüşhane Turkey
129 A3 **Kale** r. Turkey
126 D2 **Kalecik** Turkey
169 F4 **Kalefeld** Ger.
122 B2 **Kaleh Sarai** Iran
209 E6 **Kalema** Dem. Rep. Congo
209 F6 **Kalémié** Dem. Rep. Congo
96 A2 **Kalemyo** Myanmar
188 G3 **Kalesija** Bos.-Herz.
174 G5 **Kalety** Pol.
140 O2 **Kalevala** Respublika Kareliya Rus. Fed.
96 A2 **Kalewa** Myanmar
146 F6 **Kale Water** r. Scotland U.K.
107 H1 **Kalga** Rus. Fed.
87 C7 **Kalgan** r. W.A. Austr.
Kalgan Hebei China see Zhangjiakou
114 B3 **Kalghatgi** Karnataka India
87 D6 **Kalgoorlie** W.A. Austr.
188 E3 **Kali** Croatia
116 E3 **Kali** r. India/Nepal
94 D4 **Kalianda** Sumatera Indon.
92 B4 **Kalibo** Phil.
232 A4 **Kalida** OH U.S.A.
117 F4 **Kali Gandaki** r. Nepal
114 C3 **Kaligiri** Andhra Prad. India
Kalikata W. Bengal India see Calcutta
139 L5 **Kalikino** Rus. Fed.
208 E5 **Kalima** Dem. Rep. Congo
95 E3 **Kalimantan** reg. Indon.
95 E2 **Kalimantan Barat** prov. Indon.
95 F3 **Kalimantan Selatan** prov. Indon.
95 F3 **Kalimantan Tengah** prov. Indon.
95 G2 **Kalimantan Timur** prov. Indon.
Kálimnos i. Greece see Kalymnos
117 G4 **Kalimpang** W. Bengal India
114 B3 **Kalinadi** r. India
116 E4 **Kali Nadi** r. India
115 E2 **Kalingapatnam** Andhra Prad. India
Kalinin Rus. Fed. see **Tver'**
Kalinin Turkm. see **Boldumsaz**
Kalininabad Tajik. see Kalininobod
138 C4 **Kaliningrad** Rus. Fed.
Kaliningrad Oblast admin. div. Rus. Fed. see **Kaliningradskaya Oblast'**
138 C4 **Kaliningradskaya Oblast'** admin. div. Rus. Fed.
138 B4 **Kaliningradskiy Zaliv** b. Rus. Fed.
129 D3 **Kalininkänd** Azer.
Kalinino Armenia see **Tashir**
134 H4 **Kalinino** Kostromskaya Oblast' Rus. Fed.
137 J5 **Kalinino** Krasnodarskiy Kray Rus. Fed.
121 H1 **Kalinino** Omskaya Oblast' Rus. Fed.
134 L4 **Kalinino** Permskaya Oblast' Rus. Fed.
123 G2 **Kalininobod** Tajik.
Kalininsk Moldova see Cupcina
135 I6 **Kalininsk** Rus. Fed.
135 G7 **Kalininskaya** Rus. Fed.
Kalininskaya Oblast' admin. div. Rus. Fed. see **Tverskaya Oblast'**
137 G4 **Kalinins'ke** Ukr.
116 C5 **Kalinjara** Rajasthan India
136 E1 **Kalinkavichy** Belarus
Kalinkovichi Belarus see Kalinkavichy
129 F4 **Kalinovka** Azer.
120 C2 **Kalinovka** Kazakh.
Kalinovka Vinnyts'ka Oblast' Ukr. see **Kalynivka**
129 D2 **Kalinovskaya** Rus. Fed.
174 G4 **Kalinowa** Pol.
175 K2 **Kalinowo** Pol.
210 F2 **Kalis** Somalia
95 F5 **Kalisat** Jawa Timur Indon.
Kalisch Pol. see **Kalisz**
114 C1 **Kali Sindh** r. India
174 G2 **Kaliska** Pol.
238 D1 **Kalispell** MT U.S.A.
176 D3 **Kaliště** hill Czech Rep.
174 G4 **Kalisz** Pol.
174 D2 **Kalisz Pomorski** Pol.
135 H6 **Kalitva** r. Rus. Fed.
140 M2 **Kalix** Sweden
140 M2 **Kalixälven** r. Sweden
116 D3 **Kalka** Haryana India
137 I4 **Kalka** r. Ukr.
199 F3 **Kalkan** Turkey
129 B3 **Kalkandere** Turkey
169 B4 **Kalkar** Ger.
84 B3 **Kalkaringi** N.T. Austr.
226 E3 **Kalkaska** MI U.S.A.
212 C4 **Kalkfeld** Namibia
170 C2 **Kalkhorst** Ger.
214 C3 **Kalkwerf** S. Africa
169 B5 **Kall** Ger.
114 C4 **Kallakkurichchi** Tamil Nadu India
140 L2 **Kallaktjåkkå** mt. Sweden
114 C2 **Kallam** Mahar. India
138 F2 **Kallaste** Estonia
140 N3 **Kallavesi** l. Fin.
140 K3 **Kållberget** Sweden
140 M2 **Kallfjärden** b. Sweden
179 E2 **Kallham** Austria
198 B2 **Kallifoni** Greece
143 F3 **Kallinge** Sweden
196 D5 **Kallmet i Madh** Albania
173 F2 **Kallmünz** Ger.
177 K4 **Kállósemjén** Hungary
140 K3 **Kallsjön** l. Sweden
114 C2 **Kallur** Karnataka India
177 K4 **Kálmánháza** Hungary
121 J1 **Kalmanka** Rus. Fed.
143 G3 **Kalmar** Sweden
143 G3 **Kalmar** county Sweden
143 G3 **Kalmarsund** sea chan. Sweden
172 C2 **Kalmit** hill Ger.
137 I4 **Kal'mius** r. Ukr.
165 D3 **Kalmthout** Belgium
114 D5 **Kalmunai** Sri Lanka
Kalmykia aut. rep. Rus. Fed. see **Kalmykiya - Khalm'g-Tangch, Respublika**
135 I7 **Kalmykiya - Khalm'g-Tangch, Respublika** aut. rep. Rus. Fed.
Kalmykovo Kazakh. see **Taypak**
Kalmytskaya Avtonomnaya Oblast' aut. rep. Rus. Fed. see Kalmykiya - Khalm'g-Tangch, Respublika
117 E5 **Kalnai** Madh. Prad. India
177 H3 **Kalná nad Hronom** Slovakia
138 D3 **Kalnciems** Latvia
117 G4 **Kalni** r. Bangl.
188 F2 **Kalnik** mts Croatia
199 D4 **Kalo Chorio** Kriti Greece
177 H5 **Kalocsa** Hungary
136 D2 **Kalodnaye** Belarus
116 C5 **Kalol** Gujarat India
116 C5 **Kalol** Gujarat India
209 E9 **Kalomo** Zambia
222 E4 **Kalone Peak** B.C. Can.
128 A2 **Kalopanagiotis** Cyprus
78 □6 **Kalourat, Mount** Malaita Solomon Is
122 A2 **Kalow** r. Iran
177 H5 **Káloz** Hungary
116 D3 **Kalpa** Hima. Prad. India
114 C4 **Kalpetta** Kerala India
116 D4 **Kalpi** Uttar Prad. India
110 B3 **Kalpin** Xinjiang China
Kalquduq Uzbek. see **Kulkuduk**
178 D3 **Kals am Großglockner** Austria
179 G4 **Kalsdorf bei Graz** Austria
122 D2 **Kāl-Shūr, Rūd-e** r. Iran
220 C3 **Kaltag** AK U.S.A.
134 K5 **Kaltasy** Rus. Fed.
190 E1 **Kaltbrunn** Switz.
178 C3 **Kaltenbach** Austria
168 E2 **Kaltenkirchen** Ger.
169 F5 **Kaltennordheim** Ger.
169 F5 **Kaltensundheim** Ger.
169 F5 **Kaltenwestheim** Ger.
84 B5 **Kaltukatjara** N.T. Austr.
207 H4 **Kaltungo** Nigeria
116 C3 **Kalu** Rajasthan India
114 B2 **Kalu** r. India
240 □C8 **Kaluaaha** HI U.S.A.
196 E3 **Kaluđerica** Srbija Yugo.
139 K4 **Kaluga** Rus. Fed.
Kaluga Oblast admin. div. Rus. Fed. see **Kaluzhskaya Oblast'**
137 G4 **Kaluha** Ukr.
95 F2 **Kalulong, Bukit** mt. Sarawak Malaysia
209 F8 **Kalulushi** Zambia
86 E2 **Kalumburu** W.A. Austr.
142 D4 **Kalundborg** Denmark
123 G3 **Kalur Kot** Pak.
136 C3 **Kalush** Ukr.
175 J3 **Kałuszyn** Pol.
114 C5 **Kalutara** Sri Lanka
139 J4 **Kaluzhskaya Oblast'** admin. div. Rus. Fed.
116 C5 **Kalvan** Mahar. India
138 D4 **Kalvarija** Lith.
138 E4 **Kalveliai** Lith.
134 C3 **Kälviä** Fin.
141 N3 **Kalvola** Fin.
114 C2 **Kalwakurti** Andhra Prad. India
179 F3 **Kalwang** Austria
175 H6 **Kalwaria Zebrzydowska** Pol.
134 L3 **Kal'ya** Rus. Fed.
114 B2 **Kalyan** Mahar. India
114 C3 **Kalyandurg** Andhra Prad. India
114 C2 **Kalyani** Karnataka India
115 D2 **Kalyansingapuram** Orissa India
139 K3 **Kalyazin** Rus. Fed.
199 E3 **Kalymnos** Greece
199 E3 **Kalymnos** i. Greece
136 F2 **Kalynivka** Kyivs'ka Oblast' Ukr.
137 H5 **Kalynivka** Respublika Krym Ukr.
136 E3 **Kalynivka** Vinnyts'ka Oblast' Ukr.
137 F2 **Kalyta** Ukr.
199 F3 **Kalythies** Notio Aigaio Greece
198 B2 **Kalyvia** Dytiki Ellas Greece
209 E5 **Kama** Dem. Rep. Congo
96 A3 **Kama** Myanmar
134 K4 **Kama** Rus. Fed.
134 K4 **Kama** r. Rus. Fed.
105 F3 **Kamagaya** Japan
102 J4 **Kamaishi** Japan
105 F3 **Kamakura** Japan
206 B4 **Kamakwie** Sierra Leone
114 C3 **Kamalapuram** Andhra Prad. India
123 H4 **Kamalia** Pak.
240 □C8 **Kamalo** HI U.S.A.
116 D4 **Kaman** Rajasthan India
126 D3 **Kaman** Turkey
105 E3 **Kamanashi-gawa** r. Japan
105 E3 **Kamanashi-yama** mt. Japan
214 D5 **Kamanassie** r. S. Africa
124 C5 **Kamaran** Yemen
124 C5 **Kamarān** i. Yemen
Kamaran Island Yemen see Kamarān
138 E3 **Kamarde** Latvia
114 C2 **Kamareddi** Andhra Prad. India
198 B2 **Kamares** Greece
129 D3 **Kämärli** Azer.
Kamarlu Armenia see **Artashat**
136 F2 **Kamaryn** Belarus
121 F5 **Kamashi** Uzbek.
213 E3 **Kamativi** Zimbabwe
207 F4 **Kamba** Nigeria
87 D6 **Kambalda** W.A. Austr.
114 C4 **Kambam** Tamil Nadu India
Kambara i. Fiji see **Kabara**
Kambara Japan see **Kanbara**
134 K4 **Kambarka** Rus. Fed.
206 B4 **Kambia** Sierra Leone
Kambo-san mt. N. Korea see Kwanmo-bong
209 E7 **Kambove** Dem. Rep. Congo
93 B3 **Kambuno, Bukit** mt. Indon.
197 H4 **Kamburovo** Bulg.
202 E2 **Kambūt** Libya
131 R4 **Kamchatka** r. Rus. Fed.
131 Q4 **Kamchatka, Poluostrov** pen. Rus. Fed.
266 G2 **Kamchatka Basin** sea feature Bering Sea
Kamchatka Peninsula Rus. Fed. see Kamchatka, Poluostrov
131 R4 **Kamchatskiy Proliv** str. Rus. Fed.
131 R4 **Kamchatskiy Zaliv** b. Rus. Fed.
197 H4 **Kamchiya** r. Bulg.
197 H4 **Kamchiyska Planina** hills Bulg.
214 D2 **Kamden** S. Africa
120 B1 **Kamelik** r. Rus. Fed.
197 G4 **Kamen** Bulg.
169 C4 **Kamen** Ger.
131 K3 **Kamen', Gory** mts Rus. Fed.
209 E6 **Kamende** Dem. Rep. Congo
176 D3 **Kamenec** mt. Czech Rep.
Kamenets-Podol'skiy Ukr. see **Kam"yanets'-Podil's'kyy**
177 J2 **Kamenica** Slovakia
197 F4 **Kamenica** Srbija Yugo.
176 E2 **Kamenice nad Lipou** Czech Rep.
171 F5 **Kamenický Šenov** Czech Rep.
177 H4 **Kameničná** Slovakia
177 H4 **Kamenín** Slovakia
126 A2 **Kamenitsa** mt. Bulg.
197 G4 **Kamenitsa** r. Bulg.
177 H6 **Kamenjak** hill Croatia
120 B2 **Kamenka** Kazakh.
Kamenka Moldova see Camenca
134 I2 **Kamenka** Arkhangel'skaya Oblast' Rus. Fed.
135 I5 **Kamenka** Penzenskaya Oblast' Rus. Fed.
100 F3 **Kamenka** Primorskiy Kray Rus. Fed.
135 G6 **Kamenka** Voronezhskaya Oblast' Rus. Fed.
Kamenka Ukr. see **Kam"yanka**
Kamenka-Bugskaya Ukr. see **Kam"yanka-Buz'ka**
Kamenka-Shevchenkovskaya Ukr. see **Kam"yanka**
Kamen'-Kashirskiy Ukr. see **Kamin'-Kashyrs'kyy**
Kamenka-Strumilovskaya Ukr. see **Kam"yanka-Buz'ka**
130 J4 **Kamen'-na-Obi** Rus. Fed.
134 G4 **Kamenniki** Rus. Fed.
138 G1 **Kamennogorsk** Rus. Fed.
129 B1 **Kamennomostskiy** Rus. Fed.
176 D2 **Kamenný Přívoz** Czech Rep.
176 D3 **Kamenný Újezd** Czech Rep.
197 H4 **Kameno** Bulg.
137 K4 **Kamenolomni** Rus. Fed.
Kamenongue Angola see Camanongue
100 E3 **Kamen'-Rybolov** Rus. Fed.
135 I6 **Kamenskiy** Rus. Fed.
131 R3 **Kamenskoye** Koryakskiy Avtonomnyy Okrug Rus. Fed.
139 L5 **Kamenskoye** Lipetskaya Oblast' Rus. Fed.
Kamenskoye Ukr. see **Dniprodzerzhyns'k**
135 H6 **Kamensk-Shakhtinskiy** Rus. Fed.
130 H4 **Kamensk-Ural'skiy** Rus. Fed.
171 F4 **Kamenz** Ger.
104 B3 **Kameoka** Japan
170 D3 **Kamern** Ger.
146 C6 **Kames** Argyll and Bute, Scotland U.K.
139 M3 **Kameshkovo** Rus. Fed.
111 B6 **Kamet** mt. Xizang China
104 C4 **Kameyama** Japan
196 D5 **Kamëz** Albania
238 C2 **Kamiah** ID U.S.A.
104 D2 **Kamichi** Japan
175 L4 **Kamień** Pol.
175 K5 **Kamień** Pol.
175 I6 **Kamienica** Pol.
174 E3 **Kamieniec** Pol.
174 E5 **Kamieniec Ząbkowicki** Pol.
174 F2 **Kamień Krajeński** Pol.
175 J4 **Kamienna** r. Pol.
174 E5 **Kamienna Gora** Pol.
174 F5 **Kamiennik** Pol.
174 C2 **Kamień Pomorski** Pol.
175 H4 **Kamieńsk** Pol.
170 F3 **Kamień Wielkie** Pol.
214 B4 **Kamiesberg** S. Africa
214 B4 **Kamiesberge** mts S. Africa
214 A4 **Kamieskroon** S. Africa
105 F3 **Kamifukuoka** Japan
84 E3 **Kamileroi** Qld Austr.
209 E7 **Kamina** Dem. Rep. Congo
136 C2 **Kamin'-Kashyrs'kyy** Ukr.
102 □1 **Kaminone-jima** i. Japan
102 J4 **Kaminoyama** Japan
188 E2 **Kaminške in Savinjske Alpe** mts Slovenia
139 M3 **Kaminskiy** Rus. Fed.
175 I3 **Kamion** Mazowieckie Pol.
175 I4 **Kamion** Mazowieckie Pol.
175 K4 **Kamionka** Pol.
199 E3 **Kamiros** Notio Aigaio Greece
209 F5 **Kamituga** Dem. Rep. Congo
121 G3 **Kamkaly** Kazakh.
117 F4 **Kamla** r. India
117 H4 **Kamla** r. India
222 F5 **Kamloops** B.C. Can.
173 E3 **Kammel** r. Ger.
214 E5 **Kammiebos** S. Africa
173 E3 **Kammlach** Ger.
104 C3 **Kammuri-yama** mt. Japan
188 E2 **Kamnik** Slovenia
129 D3 **Kamo** Armenia
80 E1 **Kamo** North I. N.Z.
105 G3 **Kamogawa** Japan
123 H4 **Kamoke** Pak.
179 G2 **Kamp** r. Austria
169 C5 **Kamp** Ger.
210 B4 **Kampala** Uganda
94 C2 **Kampar** r. Indon.
94 C1 **Kampar** Malaysia
138 D3 **Kamparkalns** hill Latvia
94 C2 **Kamparkiri** r. Indon.
168 D1 **Kampen** Ger.
164 E2 **Kampen** Neth.
209 E5 **Kampene** Dem. Rep. Congo
172 C3 **Kämpfelbach** Ger.
96 B3 **Kamphaeng Phet** Thai.
175 I3 **Kampinos** Pol.
114 C3 **Kampli** Karnataka India
169 B4 **Kamp-Lintfort** Ger.
97 D5 **Kâmpóng Cham** Cambodia
97 D4 **Kâmpóng Chhnăng** Cambodia
97 D4 **Kâmpóng Khleăng** Cambodia
Kâmpóng Saôm Cambodia see Sihanoukville
97 D5 **Kâmpóng Spoe** Cambodia
97 D4 **Kâmpóng Thum** Cambodia
97 D5 **Kâmpôt** Cambodia
206 E4 **Kampti** Burkina
Kampuchea country Asia see Cambodia
223 K5 **Kamsack** Sask. Can.
206 B4 **Kamsar** Guinea
171 C5 **Kamsdorf** Ger.
135 J5 **Kamskoye Ust'ye** Rus. Fed.
134 L4 **Kamskoye Vodokhranilishche** resr Rus. Fed.
116 E5 **Kamtha** Mahar. India
102 K2 **Kamui-dake** mt. Japan
210 B4 **Kamuli** Uganda
177 J5 **Kamut** Hungary
136 D2 **Kam"yane** Ukr.
137 H2 **Kam"yane** Ukr.
136 D3 **Kam"yanets'-Podil's'kyy** Ukr.
137 G3 **Kam"yanka** Ukr.
137 I3 **Kam"yanka** Ukr.
137 G3 **Kam"yanka** r. Ukr.
136 C2 **Kam"yanka-Buz'ka** Ukr.
137 H4 **Kam"yanka-Dniprovs'ka** Ukr.
136 E5 **Kam"yans'ke** Ukr.
137 H4 **Kam"yans'ke** Ukr.
138 D5 **Kamyanyets** Belarus
122 A3 **Kāmyārān** Iran
135 G7 **Kamyshevatskaya** Rus. Fed.
135 I6 **Kamyshin** Rus. Fed.
135 K5 **Kamyshla** Rus. Fed.
120 E3 **Kamyshlybash** Kazakh.
Kamyshnaya r. Rus. Fed./Ukr. see **Komyshna**
120 E2 **Kamysknoye** Kazakh.
Kamyslybas Kazakh. see Kamyshlybash
120 E3 **Kamyslybas, Ozero** l. Kazakh.
120 B3 **Kamyzyak** Rus. Fed.
125 G2 **Kamzar** Oman
131 K4 **Kan** r. Rus. Fed.
213 E3 **Kana** r. Zimbabwe
95 F2 **Kana, Bukit** mt. Sarawak Malaysia
224 E2 **Kanaaupscow** r. Que. Can.
241 K3 **Kanab** UT U.S.A.
241 K3 **Kanab Creek** r. AZ U.S.A.
220 A4 **Kanaga Island** AK U.S.A.
105 F3 **Kanagawa** pref. Japan
225 J2 **Kanairiktok** r. Nfld. Can.
114 C3 **Kanakapura** Karnataka India
179 E4 **Kanal** Slovenia
198 B2 **Kanallaki** Greece
140 K2 **Kanan** Sweden
215 F2 **Kanana** S. Africa
209 D6 **Kananga** Dem. Rep. Congo
Kanarak Orissa India see Konarka
241 K3 **Kanarraville** UT U.S.A.
134 I5 **Kanash** Rus. Fed.
232 B5 **Kanawha** r. WV U.S.A.
104 C2 **Kanazawa** Japan
96 A2 **Kanbalu** Myanmar
105 E3 **Kanbara** Japan
97 B4 **Kanchanaburi** Thai.
Kanchanjanga mt. India/Nepal see **Kangchenjunga**
114 C3 **Kanchipuram** Tamil Nadu India
175 K6 **Kańczuga** Pol.
123 F4 **Kand** mt. Pak.
123 F4 **Kandahār** Afgh.
123 F4 **Kandahār** prov. Afgh.
114 C2 **Kandahar** Mahar. India
140 P2 **Kandalaksha** Rus. Fed.
134 F2 **Kandalakshskiy Zaliv** g. Rus. Fed.
95 F3 **Kandangan** Kalimantan Selatan Indon.
138 D3 **Kandava** Latvia
Kandavu Passage Fiji see Kadavu Passage
207 F4 **Kandé** Togo
172 C2 **Kandel** Ger.
172 C3 **Kandel** mt. Ger.
170 E1 **Kandelin** Ger.
190 C2 **Kander** r. Switz.
172 B4 **Kandern** Ger.
190 C2 **Kandersteg** Switz.
123 G4 **Kandhkot** Pak.
207 F4 **Kandi** Benin
123 G5 **Kandiaro** Pak.
198 B2 **Kandila** Dytiki Ellas Greece
198 C3 **Kandila** Peloponnisos Greece
129 C4 **Kandil Dağı** mt. Turkey
129 B4 **Kandilli** Turkey
199 G1 **Kandıra** Turkey
116 B5 **Kandla** Gujarat India
113 □1 **Kandooma Fushi** i. S. Male Maldives
83 G3 **Kandos** N.S.W. Austr.
115 E1 **Kandra** Bihar India
213 □J3 **Kandreho** Madag.
117 E5 **Kandri** Madh. Prad. India
114 C3 **Kandukur** Andhra Prad. India
114 D5 **Kandy** Sri Lanka
120 D2 **Kandyagash** Kazakh.
232 D4 **Kane** PA U.S.A.
221 L2 **Kane Bassin** b. Greenland
202 B6 **Kanem** pref. Chad
240 □ **Kaneohe** HI U.S.A.
Kanev Ukr. see **Kaniv**
135 G7 **Kanevskaya** Rus. Fed.
206 B4 **Kanfarande** Guinea
212 D4 **Kang** Botswana
117 G5 **Kanga** r. Bangl.
221 M3 **Kangaatsiaq** Greenland
206 C4 **Kangaba** Mali
126 E3 **Kangal** Turkey
131 N3 **Kangalassy** Rus. Fed.
122 C5 **Kangān** Iran
94 C1 **Kangar** Malaysia
206 C4 **Kangaré** Mali
82 D3 **Kangaroo Island** S.A. Austr.
251 G3 **Kangaruma** Guyana
141 N3 **Kangasala** Fin.
140 O3 **Kangaslampi** Fin.
141 N3 **Kangasniemi** Fin.
122 A3 **Kangāvar** Iran
114 C4 **Kangayam** Tamil Nadu India
107 G3 **Kangbao** Hebei China
117 G4 **Kangchenjunga** mt. India/Nepal
108 B2 **Kangding** Sichuan China
95 F4 **Kangean, Kepulauan** is Indon.
210 B3 **Kangen** r. Sudan
221 M3 **Kangerlussuaq** Greenland
221 P2 **Kangertittivaq** sea chan. Greenland
101 C4 **Kanggye** N. Korea
221 P2 **Kangikajik** c. Greenland
225 H1 **Kangiqsualujjuaq** Que. Can.
221 K3 **Kangiqsujuaq** Que. Can.
221 K3 **Kangirsuk** Que. Can.
106 D5 **Kangle** Gansu China
Kangle Jiangxi China see Wanzai
108 A1 **Kanglong** Qinghai China
111 E6 **Kangmar** Xizang China
101 D5 **Kangnŭng** S. Korea
208 A4 **Kango** Gabon
140 M2 **Kangos** Sweden
107 I3 **Kangping** Liaoning China
116 D2 **Kangra** Hima. Prad. India
111 C6 **Kangrinboqê Feng** mt. Xizang China
Kangsangdobdê Xizang China see **Xainza**
111 F7 **Kangto** mt. China/India
111 D5 **Kangtog** Xizang China
108 C1 **Kangxian** Gansu China
96 A3 **Kangyidaung** Myanmar
116 D5 **Kanhan** r. India
117 E4 **Kanhar** r. Bihar India
114 C2 **Kanhargaon** Mahar. India
206 D4 **Kani** Côte d'Ivoire
104 D3 **Kani** Japan
96 A2 **Kani** Myanmar
209 E6 **Kaniama** Dem. Rep. Congo
123 G1 **Kanibadam** Tajik.
95 G1 **Kanibongan** Sabah Malaysia
81 C5 **Kaniere** South I. N.Z.
206 A3 **Kanifing** Gambia
113 □1 **Kanifinolhu** i. N. Male Maldives
114 C3 **Kanigiri** Andhra Prad. India
217 □3b **Kani-Kéli** Mayotte
120 F4 **Kanimekh** Uzbek.
134 I2 **Kanin, Poluostrov** pen. Rus. Fed.
134 H1 **Kanin Nos, Mys** c. Rus. Fed.
134 H2 **Kaninskiy Bereg** coastal area Rus. Fed.
178 A3 **Kanisfluh** mt. Austria
137 F3 **Kaniv** Ukr.
82 E4 **Kaniva** Vic. Austr.
117 E3 **Kanjiroba** mt. Nepal
196 E2 **Kanjiža** Vojvodina, Srbija Yugo.
141 M3 **Kankaanpää** Fin.
226 D5 **Kankakee** IL U.S.A.
226 C5 **Kankakee** r. IL U.S.A.
206 C4 **Kankan** Guinea
116 E5 **Kanker** Madh. Prad. India
114 D4 **Kankesanturai** Sri Lanka
207 G3 **Kankiya** Nigeria
206 C3 **Kankossa** Maur.
97 B5 **Kanmaw Kyun** i. Myanmar
103 F6 **Kanmuri-yama** mt. Japan
Kanmuri-yama mt. Japan see Kammuri-yama
116 C5 **Kannad** Mahar. India
105 F2 **Kanna-gawa** r. Japan
231 D5 **Kannapolis** NC U.S.A.
116 D4 **Kannauj** Uttar Prad. India
171 C4 **Kannawurf** Ger.
114 C4 **Kanniyakumari** Tamil Nadu India
116 D5 **Kannod** Madh. Prad. India
140 N3 **Kannonkoski** Fin.
Kannur Kerala India see Cannanore
140 M3 **Kannus** Fin.
207 H3 **Kano** Nigeria
207 H4 **Kano** r. Nigeria
207 H4 **Kano** state Nigeria
105 E3 **Kano-gawa** r. Japan
121 I2 **Kanonerka** Kazakh.
103 F6 **Kan-onji** Japan
116 C4 **Kanor** Rajasthan India
236 C4 **Kanorado** KS U.S.A.
241 K2 **Kanosh** UT U.S.A.
103 E8 **Kanoya** Japan
116 E4 **Kanpur** Uttar Prad. India
123 G4 **Kanpur** Pak.
104 B4 **Kansai** airport Japan
209 E8 **Kansanshi** Zambia
236 E4 **Kansas** r. KS U.S.A.
236 D4 **Kansas** state U.S.A.
236 E4 **Kansas City** KS U.S.A.
236 E4 **Kansas City** MO U.S.A.
131 K4 **Kansk** Rus. Fed.
Kansu prov. China see **Gansu**
210 B3 **Kanta** mt. Eth.
97 B6 **Kantang** Thai.
128 A2 **Kantara** hill Cyprus
97 D4 **Kantaralak** Thai.
129 B4 **Kantarkaya** Turkey
Kantavu i. Fiji see **Kadavu**
207 F3 **Kantchari** Burkina
135 G6 **Kantemirovka** Rus. Fed.
164 F1 **Kantens** Neth.
116 D3 **Kanth** Uttar Prad. India
117 F4 **Kanti** Bihar India
117 F5 **Kantilo** Orissa India
220 C3 **Kantishna** r. AK U.S.A.
111 A6 **Kantli** r. India
105 F3 **Kantō-heiya** plain Japan
77 I2 **Kanton** i. Phoenix Is Kiribati
Kan-Too, Pik mt. Kazakh./Kyrg. see **Khan-Tengri, Pik**
105 E3 **Kanto-sanchi** mts Japan
147 C4 **Kanturk** Rep. of Ireland
251 G4 **Kanuku Mountains** Guyana
105 F2 **Kanuma** Japan
114 C3 **Kanur** Andhra Prad. India
91 J8 **Kanuwe** r. P.N.G.
Kanyakubja Uttar Prad. India see **Kannauj**
215 H1 **KaNyamazane** S. Africa
212 E5 **Kanye** Botswana
207 G3 **Kao** Niger
79 □2 **Kao** i. Tonga
109 G4 **Kaohsiung** Taiwan
212 B3 **Kaokoveld** plat. Namibia
206 A3 **Kaolack** Senegal
209 E8 **Kaoma** Zambia
240 □B7 **Kapaa** HI U.S.A.
240 □D8 **Kapaau** HI U.S.A.
121 I3 **Kapal** Kazakh.
196 D4 **Kapa Moračka** mt. Yugo.
129 E4 **Kapan** Armenia
198 C2 **Kapareli** Greece
136 E1 **Kapatkyevichy** Belarus
211 A7 **Kapatu** Zambia
121 I4 **Kapchagay** Kazakh.
121 I4 **Kapchagayskoye Vodokhranilishche** resr Kazakh.
210 B4 **Kapchorwa** Uganda
164 C3 **Kapelle** Neth.
165 D3 **Kapellen** Belgium
143 H2 **Kapellskär** Sweden
Kapelskär Sweden see Kapellskär
210 B4 **Kapenguria** Kenya
179 G3 **Kapfenberg** Austria
179 G4 **Kapfenstein** Austria
199 E1 **Kapıdağı Yarımadası** pen. Turkey
117 G4 **Kapili** r. India
77 F1 **Kapingamarangi** atoll Micronesia
266 F5 **Kapingamarangi Rise** sea feature N. Pacific Ocean
199 G1 **Kapıorman Dağları** mts Turkey
209 F8 **Kapiri Mposhi** Zambia
123 G3 **Kāpīsā** prov. Afgh.
224 D2 **Kapiskau** r. Ont. Can.
137 F3 **Kapitanivka** Ukr.
81 E4 **Kapiti Island** North I. N.Z.
202 D6 **Kapka, Massif du** mts Chad
93 C3 **Kaplamada, Gunung** mt. Buru Indon.
122 C1 **Kaplankyr, Chink** hills Turkm./Uzbek.
176 D3 **Kaplice** Czech Rep.
97 B5 **Kapoe** Thai.
210 B3 **Kapoeta** Sudan
177 J4 **Kápolna** Hungary
80 E3 **Kaponga** North I. N.Z.
196 D2 **Kapos** r. Romania
177 G5 **Kaposfő** Hungary
177 H5 **Kaposszekcső** Hungary
177 G5 **Kaposvár** Hungary
172 B2 **Kappel** Ger.
179 F4 **Kappel am Krappfeld** Austria
172 B3 **Kappel-Grafenhausen** Ger.
168 E1 **Kappeln** Ger.
172 C3 **Kappelrodeck** Ger.
178 B3 **Kappl** Austria
116 D4 **Kapran** Rajasthan India

Kaprun to Kelso
319

178 D3 Kaprun Austria
210 B4 Kapsabet Kenya
101 D4 Kapsan N. Korea
139 I2 Kapsha r. Rus. Fed.
Kapsukas Lith. see Marijampolė
117 H5 Kaptai Bangl.
107 H1 Kaptsegaytuy Rus. Fed.
136 E1 Kaptsevichy Belarus
95 E3 Kapuas r. Indon.
95 F3 Kapuas r. Indon.
95 F2 Kapuas Hulu, Pegunungan mts Indon./Malaysia
82 D3 Kapunda S.A. Austr.
116 C4 Kapuriya Rajasthan India
116 C3 Kapurthala Punjab India
177 K2 Kapušany Slovakia
224 D3 Kapuskasing Ont. Can.
224 D3 Kapuskasing r. Ont. Can.
135 I6 Kapustin Yar Rus. Fed.
137 F2 Kapustyntsi Kyivs'ka Oblast' Ukr.
137 H2 Kapustyntsi Sums'ka Oblast' Ukr.
209 F7 Kaputa Zambia
83 G2 Kaputar mt. N.S.W. Austr.
176 G4 Kapuvár Hungary
Kapydzhik, Gora mt. Armenia/Azer. see Qazangödağ
138 F5 Kapyl' Belarus
101 C5 Kap'yŏng S. Korea
111 F6 Ka Qu r. Xizang China
116 E4 Kara Uttar Prad. India
134 N1 Kara r. Rus. Fed.
207 F4 Kara Togo
199 F1 Kara r. Turkey
127 F3 Kara r. Turkey
199 E2 Karaağaç Balıkesir Turkey
126 D3 Karaali Turkey
Karaaul Vostochnyy Kazakhstan Kazakh. see Karaul
121 H4 Kara-Balta Kyrg.
139 L3 Karabanovo Rus. Fed.
121 H2 Karabas Kazakh.
Karabekaul Turkm. see Garabekevyul
129 B4 Karabey Turkey
199 E1 Karabiga Turkey
123 E2 Karabil', Vozvyshennost' hills Turkm.
129 B4 Karaboğa Dağları mts Turkey
122 C1 Kara-Bogaz-Gol, Proliv sea chan. Turkm.
122C1 Kara-Bogaz-Gol, Zaliv b. Turkm.
Karaboynak Turkm. see Atayab
129 E2 Karabudakhkent Rus. Fed.
126 D2 Karabük Turkey
121 I3 Karabulak Almatinskaya Oblast' Kazakh.
121 K3 Karabulak Vostochnyy Kazakhstan Kazakh.
129 D2 Karabulak Rus. Fed.
121 H2 Karabulakskaya Kazakh.
Karabura Xinjiang China see Yumin
199 F2 Karaburç İzmir Turkey
199 E2 Karaburun Turkey
120 E2 Karabutak Kazakh.
199 F1 Karacabey Turkey
199 E1 Karacakılavuz Turkey
126 C2 Karacaköy Turkey
127 E3 Karacalı Dağ mt. Turkey
128 A1 Karaçal Tepe mt. Turkey
199 F3 Karacasu Turkey
Karachay-Cherkess Republic aut. rep. Rus. Fed. see Karachayevo-Cherkesskaya Respublika
Karachayevo-Cherkesskaya A.S.S.R. aut. rep. Rus. Fed. see Karachayevo-Cherkesskaya Respublika
129 B2 Karachayevo-Cherkesskaya Respublika aut. rep. Rus. Fed.
129 B2 Karachayevsk Rus. Fed.
139 J5 Karachev Rus. Fed.
123 F5 Karachi Pak.
127 F3 Karaçoban Turkey
199 F3 Karaçulha Turkey
Karacurun Turkey see Hilvan
177 G5 Karád Hungary
114 B2 Karad Mahar. India
128 D1 Kara Dağ hill Turkey
199 E1 Kara Dağ hill Turkey
199 F1 Kara Dağ hills Turkey
126 D3 Kara Dağ mt. Turkey
121 H4 Kara-Darya r. Kyrg.
Kara-Dar'ya Uzbek. see Payshanba
Kara Deniz sea Asia/Europe see Black Sea
206 E4 Karaga Ghana
121 H2 Karaganda Kazakh.
121 H2 Karagandinskaya Oblast' admin. div. Kazakh.
129 D1 Karagas Rus. Fed.
121 I3 Karagash Kazakh.
134 K4 Karagay Rus. Fed.
121 H2 Karagayly Kazakh.
131 R4 Karaginskiy, Ostrov i. Rus. Fed.
120 B4 Karagiye, Vpadina depr. Kazakh.
129 B4 Karagöl Dağları mts Turkey
211 A5 Karagwe Tanz.
197 H5 Karahalil Turkey
199 F2 Karahallı Turkey
126 D3 Karahasanlı Turkey
199 F3 Karahisar Turkey
134 L5 Karaidel' Rus. Fed.
114 C4 Karaikal Pondicherry India
114 C4 Karaikkudi Tamil Nadu India
121 K3 Kara Irtysh r. Kazakh.
126 D3 Karaisalı Turkey
122 B3 Karaj Iran
Karak Jordan see Al Karak
Kara-Kala Turkm. see Garrygala
Karakalli Turkey see Özalp
120 D4 Karakalpakistan, Respublika aut. rep. Uzbek.
120 D3 Karakalpakiya Uzbek.
Karakalpakskaya Respublika aut. rep. Uzbek. see Karakalpakistan, Respublika
Karakalpakstan aut. rep. Uzbek. see Karakalpakistan, Respublika
120 F4 Karakatinskaya, Vpadina depr. Uzbek.
Karakax Xinjiang China see Moyu
111 C4 Karakax He r. China
111 C5 Karakax Shan mts Xinjiang China
129 C4 Karakaya r. Turkey
129 B4 Karakaya Tepe mt. Turkey
126 E3 Karakeçi Turkey
126 D3 Karakeçili Turkey
93 C1 Karakelong i. Indon.
Karaklis Armenia see Vanadzor
127 F3 Karakoçan Turkey
121 G1 Karakoga Kazakh.
120 C2 Karakol' Kazakh.
121 H4 Kara-Köl Kyrg.
121 I4 Karakol Kyrg.
Karaköprü Turkey see Karaçoban
123 H2 Karakoram mts Asia
116 D2 Karakoram Pass China/Jammu and Kashmir
210 C2 Kara K'orē Eth.
206 B3 Karakoro r. Mali/Maur.
Karaköse Turkey see Ağrı
128 B1 Karaköse Turkey
129 E2 Karakoysu r. Rus. Fed.
129 D4 Karakoyunlu Turkey
Karakubbud Ukr. see Komsomol's'ke
Kara-Kuga Kazakh. see Karakoga
Kara Kul' Kyrg. see Kara-Köl
120 E5 Karakul' Bukharskaya Oblast' Uzbek.
120 E5 Karakul' Bukharskaya Oblast' Uzbek.
Karakul', Ozero l. Tajik. see Qarokŭl
Kara-Kul'dzha Kyrg. see Kara-Kulja
134 K4 Karakulino Rus. Fed.
121 H4 Kara-Kulja Kyrg.
120 E1 Karakul'skoye Rus. Fed.
120 C3 Karakum, Peski des. Kazakh.
Karakum Desert Turkm. see Karakumy, Peski
123 E2 Karakumskiy Kanal canal Turkm.
122 E2 Karakumy, Peski des. Turkm.
127 F2 Karakurt Kars Turkey
199 E2 Karakurt Manisa Turkey
199 G2 Karakuş Dağı ridge Turkey
87 C5 Karalundi W.A. Austr.
93 A3 Karama r. Indon.
199 F2 Karaman Balıkesir Turkey
126 D3 Karaman Karaman Turkey
128 A1 Karaman prov. Turkey
199 F3 Karamanlı Turkey
110 D2 Karamay Xinjiang China
81 D4 Karamea South I. N.Z.
81 D4 Karamea r. South I. N.Z.
81 C4 Karamea Bight b. South I. N.Z.
199 G2 Karamıkkaracaören Turkey
111 D4 Karamiran Xinjiang China
111 D4 Karamiran He r. China
131 Q3 Karamken Rus. Fed.
199 F1 Karamürsel Turkey
138 G3 Karamyshevo Rus. Fed.
123 G2 Karan r. Afgh.
Karan state Myanmar see Kayin
177 I3 Karancsalja Hungary
177 I3 Karancskeszi Hungary
177 I3 Karancsság Hungary
206 A3 Karang Senegal
81 B5 Karangarua South I. N.Z.
95 F5 Karangasem Bali Indon.
95 E5 Karangbolong, Tanjung pt Indon.
93 C2 Karangetang vol. Indon.
208 B4 Karangoua r. Congo
116 D5 Karanja Mahar. India
114 C2 Karanja r. India
117 F5 Karanjia Orissa India
116 C3 Karanpura Rajasthan India
121 I1 Karaoba Kazakh.
199 E3 Karaova Turkey
121 H3 Karaoy Almatinskaya Oblast' Kazakh.
121 H3 Karaoy Almatinskaya Oblast' Kazakh.
197 H4 Karapelit Bulg.
126 D3 Karapınar Turkey
199 F2 Karapürçek Turkey
199 G1 Karapürçek Turkey
212 C5 Karas admin. reg. Namibia
214 A2 Karas mts Namibia
126 C2 Karaşar Turkey
111 C4 Karasay Xinjiang China
212 C6 Karasburg Namibia
Kara Sea Rus. Fed. see Karskoye More
139 L3 Karash Rus. Fed.
121 H2 Karashoky Kazakh.
188 G3 Karašica r. Croatia
177 H6 Karasica r. Hungary/Romania
137 H5 Karasivka r. Ukr.
140 N1 Kárášjohka Norway
140 N1 Kárášjohka r. Norway
Karasjok Norway see Kárášjohka
Karasjokka r. Norway see Kárášjohka
121 G1 Karasor, Ozero l. Kazakh.
Kara Strait Rus. Fed. see Karskiye Vorota, Proliv
120 E2 Karasu Kustanayskaya Oblast' Kazakh.
120 F1 Karasu Kustanayskaya Oblast' Kazakh.
121 H1 Karasu r. Kazakh.
128 C1 Karasu r. Syria/Turkey
Karasu Bitlis Turkey see Hizan
199 G1 Karasu Sakarya Turkey
127 F3 Karasu r. Turkey
Karasubazar Ukr. see Bilohirs'k
105 F2 Karasu-gawa r. Japan
121 I1 Karasuk Rus. Fed.
136 E5 Karasulak r. Ukr.
121 H4 Kara-Suu Kyrg.
136 C2 Karasyn Ukr.
122 E3 Karāt Iran
129 E2 Karata Rus. Fed.
121 K3 Karatan Kazakh.
126 D3 Karataş Turkey
128 C1 Karataş Turkey
199 F2 Karataş Manisa Turkey
121 G4 Karatau Kazakh.
121 F3 Karatau, Khrebet mts Kazakh.
114 C4 Karativu i. Sri Lanka
120 C2 Karatobe Kazakh.
120 D2 Karatogay Kazakh.
121 I3 Karatol r. Kazakh.
120 C3 Karaton Kazakh.
140 L2 Karats Sweden
103 D7 Karatsu Japan
106 A2 Karatünggü Xinjiang China
120 F2 Kara-Turgey r. Kazakh.
121 I2 Karaul Vostochnyy Kazakhstan Kazakh.
120 F5 Karaulbazar Uzbek.
116 D4 Karauli Rajasthan India
Karaulkel'dy Kazakh. see Bayganin
127 F2 Karaurgan Turkey
120 D4 Karauzyak Uzbek.
Karavan Kyrg. see Kerben
196 D5 Karavastasë, Gjiri i b. Albania
139 M3 Karavayevo Rus. Fed.
94 D4 Karawang Jawa Barat Indon.
Karaxahar r. China see Kaidu He
129 C4 Karayazı Turkey
128 C1 Karayılan Turkey
121 G2 Karazhal Kazakh.
120 D4 Karazhar Uzbek.
127 G4 Karbalā' Iraq
127 F4 Karbalā' governorate Iraq
169 D5 Karben Ger.
170 D2 Karbow-Vietlübbe Ger.
121 H2 Karbushevka Kazakh.
168 E1 Karby Ger.
177 J4 Karcag Hungary
177 K3 Karcsa Hungary
175 J3 Karczew Pol.
175 K4 Karczmiska Pol.
197 I4 Kardam Bulg.
199 E3 Kardamaina Notio Aigaio Greece
179 F1 Kardašova Řečice Czech Rep.
Kardeljevo Croatia see Ploče
169 C5 Karden Ger.
Kardhaámaina Notio Aigaio Greece see Kardamaina
Kardhítsa Greece see Karditsa
140 M2 Kardis Sweden
198 B2 Karditsa Greece
138 D2 Kärdla Estonia
177 J5 Kardos Hungary
179 H3 Kardos-ér r. Hungary
177 J5 Kardoskút Hungary
139 I4 Kardymovo Rus. Fed.
129 D2 Kardzhin Rus. Fed.
215 F3 Karee S. Africa
214 C4 Kareeberge mts S. Africa
214 E5 Kareedouw S. Africa
180 D5 Kareha, Jebel mt. Morocco
203 F5 Kareima Sudan
129 C3 K'areli Georgia
116 D5 Kareli Madh. Prad. India
Karelia aut. rep. Rus. Fed. see Kareliya, Respublika
138 F5 Karelichy Belarus
134 F3 Kareliya, Respublika aut. rep. Rus. Fed.
Karel'skaya A.S.S.R. aut. rep. Rus. Fed. see Kareliya, Respublika
134 F2 Karel'skiy Bereg coastal area Rus. Fed.
211 B6 Karema Dodoma Tanz.
211 A6 Karema Rukwa Tanz.
Karen state Myanmar see Kayin
99 K1 Karenga r. Rus. Fed.
116 D4 Karera Madh. Prad. India
140 M1 Karesuando Sweden
122 E5 Kārevāndar Iran
120 C2 Kargala Rus. Fed.
129 E2 Kargalinskaya Rus. Fed.
Kargalinski Rus. Fed. see Kargalinskaya
120 D2 Kargalinskoye Kazakh.
127 F3 Kargapazarı Dağları mts Turkey
Karghalik Xinjiang China see Yecheng
126 D2 Kargı Turkey
116 D2 Kargil Jammu and Kashmir
Kargilik Xinjiang China see Yecheng
128 B1 Kargıpınarı Turkey
134 G3 Kargopol' Rus. Fed.
174 D3 Kargowa Pol.
116 D4 Karhal Uttar Prad. India
143 G1 Karholmsbruk Sweden
207 H4 Kari Nigeria
204 D2 Karia Ba Mohammed Morocco
137 K1 Karian Rus. Fed.
213 F3 Kariba Zimbabwe
209 E9 Kariba, Lake resr Zambia/Zimbabwe
209 F9 Kariba Dam Zambia/Zimbabwe
102 I2 Kariba-yama vol. Japan
212 B4 Karibib Namibia
214 D5 Kariega r. S. Africa
80 D1 Karikari, Cape North I. N.Z.
95 E3 Karimata i. Indon.
95 E3 Karimata, Pulau-pulau is Indon.
95 E3 Karimata, Selat str. Indon.
117 H4 Karimganj Assam India
114 C2 Karimnagar Andhra Prad. India
95 E4 Karimunjawa, Pulau-pulau is Indon.
210 E2 Karin Somalia
141 M3 Karinainen Fin.
199 F3 Karınçalı Dağı mts Turkey
141 K3 Käringsjön Sweden
215 H1 Karino S. Africa
80 E2 Karioi hill North I. N.Z.
141 M3 Karis Fin.
211 A5 Karisimbi, Mont vol. Rwanda
Káristos Greece see Karystos
198 C1 Karitsa Greece
104 C4 Kariya Japan
Karjaa Fin. see Karis
138 D1 Karjalohja Fin.
116 C5 Karjan Gujarat India
114 B2 Karjat Mahar. India
117 F5 Karkai r. Bihar India
114 B3 Karkal Karnataka India
114 B2 Karkamb Mahar. India
214 A4 Karkams S. Africa
121 H2 Karkaralinsk Kazakh.
92 C5 Karkaralong, Kepulauan is Indon.
122 A4 Karkheh, Rūdkhāneh-ye r. Iran
137 G5 Karkinits'ka Zatoka g. Ukr.
141 N3 Karkkila Fin.
141 N3 Kärkölä Fin.
138 E2 Karksi-Nuia Estonia
106 B3 Karlik Shan mt. Xinjiang China
174 D1 Karlino Pol.
127 F3 Karlıova Turkey
137 H3 Karlivka Ukr.
129 C4 Karlıyayla Turkey
123 H2 Karl Marks, Qullai mt. Tajik.
Karl-Marx-Stadt Ger. see Chemnitz
Karlo-Libknekhtovsk Ukr. see Soledar
188 E3 Karlovac Croatia
176 B1 Karlovarský kraj admin. reg. Czech Rep.
176 G1 Karlovice Czech Rep.
Karlovka Ukr. see Karlivka
197 G4 Karlovo Bulg.
176 B1 Karlovy Vary Czech Rep.
172 C3 Karlsbad Ger.
141 K3 Karlsberg Sweden
143 F2 Karlsborg Sweden
170 E2 Karlsburg Ger.
Karlsburg Romania see Alba Iulia
172 C2 Karlsdorf-Neuthard Ger.
173 F3 Karlsfeld Ger.
170 E1 Karlshagen Ger.
143 F3 Karlshamn Sweden
168 E2 Karlshöfen Ger.
173 F3 Karlshuld Ger.
143 F2 Karlskoga Sweden
173 F3 Karlskron Ger.
143 F3 Karlskrona Sweden
172 C2 Karlsruhe Ger.
172 C3 Karlsruhe admin. reg. Baden-Württemberg Ger.
142 E2 Karlstad Sweden
236 D1 Karlstad MN U.S.A.
172 D2 Karlstadt Ger.
169 E5 Karlstein am Main Ger.
179 G2 Karlstein an der Thaya Austria
179 G2 Karlstetten Austria
220 C4 Karluk AK U.S.A.
139 H5 Karma Belarus
207 F3 Karma Niger
114 B2 Karmala Mahar. India
139 J4 Karmanovo Rus. Fed.
140 L2 Karmas Sweden
Karmir Armenia see Chambarak
Karmona Spain see Córdoba
142 A2 Karmøy i. Norway
120 F5 Karnabchul', Step' plain Uzbek.
117 H5 Karnafuli Reservoir Bangl.
116 D3 Karnal Haryana India
116 E3 Karnali r. Nepal
117 G5 Karnaphuli r. Bangl.
116 D3 Karnaprayag Uttar Prad. India
114 B3 Karnataka state India
137 H3 Karnaukhivka Ukr.
237 D6 Karnes City TX U.S.A.
174 D1 Karnice Pol.
175 I3 Karniewo Pol.
178 D4 Karnische Alpen mts Austria
197 H4 Karnobat Bulg.
179 E4 Kärnten land Austria
213 F3 Karoi Zimbabwe
191 I3 Karojba Croatia
177 H2 Karolinka Czech Rep.
117 H4 Karong Manipur India
211 B7 Karonga Malawi
87 D6 Karonie W.A. Austr.
214 D5 Karoo National Park S. Africa
82 D3 Karoonda S.A. Austr.
123 G4 Karor Pak.
Káros i. Greece see Keros
199 E1 Karotis Greece
198 A2 Karousades Ionioi Nisoi Greece
170 D2 Karow Mecklenburg-Vorpommern Ger.
171 D3 Karow Sachsen-Anhalt Ger.
174 D5 Karpacz Pol.
128 B2 Karpasia pen. Cyprus
Karpas Peninsula Cyprus see Karpasia
199 E4 Karpathos Notio Aigaio Greece
199 E4 Karpathos i. Greece
199 E3 Karpathou, Steno sea chan. Greece
Karpaty mts Europe see Carpathian Mountains
198 B2 Karpenisi Greece
Karpilovka Homyel'skaya Voblasts' Belarus see Aktsyabrski
134 M4 Karpinsk Rus. Fed.
134 I2 Karpogory Rus. Fed.
199 E3 Karpuzlu Aydın Turkey
199 E1 Karpuzlu Edirne Turkey
136 F2 Karpylivka Chernihivs'ka Oblast' Ukr.
137 G2 Karpylivka Chernihivs'ka Oblast' Ukr.
136 D2 Karpylivka Rivnens'ka Oblast' Ukr.
86 C4 Karratha W.A. Austr.
170 C2 Karrenzin Ger.
215 F4 Karringmelkspruit S. Africa
Karroo plat. S. Africa see Great Karoo
123 E3 Karrukh Afgh.
127 F2 Kars Turkey
129 C3 Kars prov. Turkey
129 C3 Kars r. Turkey
121 F3 Karsakpay Kazakh.
140 N3 Kärsämäki Fin.
138 F3 Kārsava Latvia
171 C4 Karsdorf Ger.
120 F5 Karshi Uzbek.
120 F5 Karshinskaya Step' plain Uzbek.
129 B3 Karşıköy Turkey
174 F2 Karsin Pol.
199 F1 Karşıyaka Turkey
199 E2 Karşıyaka Turkey
117 G4 Karsiyang W. Bengal India
130 G3 Karskiye Vorota, Proliv str. Rus. Fed.
130 I2 Karskoye More sea Rus. Fed.
170 C2 Karstädt Ger.
170 C2 Karstädt Ger.
134 D3 Karstula Fin.
135 I5 Karsun Rus. Fed.
177 I4 Kartal Hungary
199 F1 Kartal Turkey
217 □3a Kartala vol. Njazidja Comoros
120 E1 Kartaly Rus. Fed.
116 C3 Kartarpur Punjab India
138 C4 Kartena Lith.
232 D4 Karthaus PA U.S.A.
129 D2 K'art'lis K'edi hills Georgia
Kartsa Rus. Fed. see Oktyabr'skoye
140 N3 Karttula Fin.
143 H4 Kartuzy Pol.
209 F8 Karubwe Zambia
102 J3 Karumai Japan
85 E3 Karumba Qld Austr.
122 B4 Karun, Kūh-e hill Iran
122 B4 Kārūn, Rūd-e r. Iran
114 C4 Karunagapalli Kerala India
140 M2 Karungi Sweden
86 E3 Karunjie W.A. Austr.
142 C3 Karup Denmark
142 C3 Karup r. Denmark
114 C4 Karur Tamil Nadu India
211 A5 Karuzi Burundi
114 C3 Karvetnagar Andhra Prad. India
141 M3 Karvia Fin.
177 H2 Karviná Czech Rep.
136 E2 Karvynivka Ukr.
114 B3 Karwar Karnataka India
116 E4 Karwi Uttar Prad. India
175 J2 Karwica Pol.
170 C2 Karwitz Ger.
198 B2 Karya Ionioi Nisoi Greece
Karyagino Azer. see Füzuli
99 J1 Karymskoye Rus. Fed.
120 C4 Karynzharyk, Peski des. Kazakh.
198 D2 Karystos Greece
199 F3 Kaş Turkey
114 B2 Kasa Mahar. India
Kasaba Turkey see Turgutlu
224 B2 Kasabonika Ont. Can.
104 D2 Kasaga-dake mt. Japan
104 D3 Kasagi-yama mt. Japan
209 C5 Kasai r. Dem. Rep. Congo
104 A4 Kasai Japan
209 D6 Kasai, Plateau du Dem. Rep. Congo
209 D6 Kasai Occidental admin. reg. Dem. Rep. Congo
209 E6 Kasai Oriental admin. reg. Dem. Rep. Congo
209 D7 Kasaji Dem. Rep. Congo
105 G2 Kasama Japan
211 A7 Kasama Zambia
104 C3 Kasamatsu Japan
120 F5 Kasan Uzbek.
212 E3 Kasane Botswana
211 A7 Kasanga Tanz.
209 B6 Kasangulu Dem. Rep. Congo
121 G4 Kasansay Uzbek.
114 B3 Kasaragod Kerala India
138 D2 Kasari r. Estonia
104 C4 Kasatori-yama hill Japan
223 K2 Kasba Lake Can.
204 D2 Kasba Tadla Morocco
103 E8 Kaseda Japan
176 C2 Kasejovice Czech Rep.
209 E8 Kasempa Zambia
171 C5 Kasendorf Ger.
209 F7 Kasenga Dem. Rep. Congo
210 A4 Kasese Uganda
Kasevo Rus. Fed. see Neftekamsk
116 D4 Kasganj Uttar Prad. India
Kasha Xizang China see Gonjo
224 B3 Kashabowie Ont. Can.
122 B3 Kāshān Iran
135 H6 Kashary Rus. Fed.
224 D2 Kashechewan Ont. Can.
Kashgar Xinjiang China see Kashi
110 B4 Kashi Xinjiang China
104 B4 Kashiba Japan
104 B4 Kashihara Japan
105 G3 Kashima Ibaraki Japan
103 E7 Kashima Saga Japan
105 G2 Kashima-nada b. Japan
104 D2 Kashimayaria-dake mt. Japan
139 K3 Kashin Rus. Fed.
139 K3 Kashinka r. Rus. Fed.
116 D3 Kashipur Uttar Prad. India
139 L4 Kashira Rus. Fed.
139 L4 Kashirka r. Rus. Fed.
137 J2 Kashirskoye Rus. Fed.
209 F8 Kashitu Zambia
105 F3 Kashiwa Japan
104 B4 Kashiwara Japan
103 I5 Kashiwazaki Japan
121 F5 Kashkadar'inskaya Oblast' admin. div. Uzbek.
123 F2 Kashkadar'ya r. Uzbek.
Kashkadarya Oblast admin. div. Uzbek. see Kashkadar'inskaya Oblast'
129 C2 Kashkhatau Kabardino-Balkarskaya Respublika Rus. Fed.
137 I4 Kashlahach r. Ukr.
122 D3 Kāshmar Iran
Kashmir terr. Asia see Jammu and Kashmir
116 C2 Kashmir, Vale of val. India
123 G4 Kashmor Pak.
209 E6 Kashyukulu Dem. Rep. Congo
Kasi Uttar Prad. India see Varanasi
117 E4 Kasia Uttar Prad. India
199 G3 Kasımlar Turkey
135 H5 Kasimov Rus. Fed.
179 H5 Kašina Croatia
177 I5 Kaskantyú Hungary
236 F4 Kaskaskia r. IL U.S.A.
223 N3 Kaskattama r. Man. Can.
121 I4 Kaskelen Kazakh.
141 M3 Kaskinen Fin.
Kas Klong i. Cambodia see Kŏng, Kaôh
Kaskö Fin. see Kaskinen
222 G5 Kaslo B.C. Can.
139 J4 Kasnya r. Rus. Fed.
209 E6 Kasongo Dem. Rep. Congo
209 C6 Kasongo-Lunda Dem. Rep. Congo
199 E4 Kasos i. Greece
176 C2 Kašperské Hory Czech Rep.
129 D3 Kaspi Georgia
Kaspīy Mangy Oypaty lowland Kazakh./Rus. Fed. see Prikaspiyskaya Nizmennost'
129 E2 Kaspiysk Rus. Fed.
Kaspiyskiy Rus. Fed. see Lagan'
Kaspiyskoye More sea Asia/Europe see Caspian Sea
139 H4 Kasplya Rus. Fed.
139 H4 Kasplya r. Rus. Fed.
116 C5 Kasrawad Madh. Prad. India
Kasrik Turkey see Gürpınar
129 E3 Kasristsqali Georgia
Kassa Slovakia see Košice
138 D2 Kassaare laht b. Estonia
203 H6 Kassala Sudan
203 G6 Kassala state Sudan
198 C1 Kassandra pen. Greece
198 C1 Kassandras, Kolpos b. Greece
198 C1 Kassandreia Greece
168 F1 Kasseedorf Ger.
169 E4 Kassel Ger.
169 E4 Kassel admin. reg. Hessen Ger.
205 H2 Kasserine Tunisia
226 A3 Kasson MN U.S.A.
126 D2 Kastamonu Turkey
169 C5 Kastellaun Ger.
198 C4 Kastelli Kriti Greece
199 D4 Kastelli Kriti Greece
Kastéllion Kriti Greece see Kastelli
Kastellorizon i. Greece see Megisti
165 D3 Kasterlee Belgium
173 F2 Kastl Bayern Ger.
173 G3 Kastl Bayern Ger.
168 F2 Kastorf Ger.
198 B1 Kastoria Greece
198 B1 Kastorias, Limni l. Greece
135 G6 Kastornoye Rus. Fed.
139 I5 Kastsyukovichy Belarus
139 H5 Kastsyukowka Belarus
104 C3 Kasugai Japan
105 F3 Kasukabe Japan
215 F5 Kasuka Road S. Africa
211 A6 Kasulu Tanz.
105 G2 Kasumiga-ura l. Japan
129 F3 Kasumkent Rus. Fed.
211 B8 Kasungu Malawi
123 H4 Kasur Pak.
177 J5 Kaszaper Hungary
207 H3 Katagum Nigeria
233 □I2 Katahdin, Mount ME U.S.A.
116 D2 Kataklik Jammu and Kashmir
210 B4 Katakwi Uganda
209 D6 Katanda Dem. Rep. Congo
209 E7 Katanga admin. reg. Dem. Rep. Congo
116 D5 Katangi Madh. Prad. India
116 D5 Katangi Madh. Prad. India
100 G2 Katangli Sakhalin Rus. Fed.
87 C7 Katanning W.A. Austr.
104 B4 Katano Japan
122 B2 Kata Pusht Iran
105 F2 Katashina-gawa r. Japan
198 B3 Katastari Ionioi Nisoi Greece
211 A6 Katavi National Park Tanz.
115 G5 Katchall i. Andaman & Nicobar Is India
207 F4 Katchamba Togo
209 C8 Katchiungo Angola
209 E6 Katea Dem. Rep. Congo
198 C1 Katerini Greece
136 F3 Katerynopil' Ukr.
147 E2 Katesbridge Northern Ireland U.K.
211 B6 Katesh Tanz.
220 E4 Kate's Needle mt. Alaska/B.C. Can./U.S.A.
211 B8 Katete Zambia
129 E3 Katex Azer.
117 E5 Katghora Madh. Prad. India
96 B1 Katha Myanmar
203 G2 Katherîna, Gebel mt. Egypt
84 C2 Katherine N.T. Austr.
84 B2 Katherine r. N.T. Austr.
116 C5 Kathi Mahar. India
116 B5 Kathiawar pen. Gujarat India
128 A4 Kathîb el Henu hill Egypt
215 G2 Kathlehong S. Africa
171 F4 Kathlow Ger.
117 F4 Kathmandu Nepal
214 D2 Kathu S. Africa
116 C2 Kathua Jammu and Kashmir
206 C3 Kati Mali
95 F2 Katibas r. Sarawak Malaysia
177 K4 Kati-ér r. Hungary
117 F4 Katihar Bihar India
80 E2 Katikati North I. N.Z.
215 F5 Kati-Kati S. Africa
212 E3 Katima Mulilo Namibia
206 D4 Katiola Côte d'Ivoire
Kā Tiritiri o te Moana mts South I. N.Z. see Southern Alps
136 E5 Katlabukh, Ozero l. Ukr.
169 F4 Katlenburg-Lindau Ger.
177 G3 Kátlovce Slovakia
111 D4 Katma Xinjiang China
Katmandu Nepal see Kathmandu
198 B2 Kato Achaïa Greece
198 B2 Katochi Greece
198 C3 Kato Doliana Peloponnisos Greece
198 B3 Kato Figaleia Greece
198 C3 Kato Glykovrysi Greece
116 D5 Katol Mahar. India
235 E1 Katonah NY U.S.A.
209 F8 Katondwe Zambia
198 C1 Kato Nevrokopi Greece
210 A4 Katonga r. Uganda
121 K2 Katon-Karagay Kazakh.
Katonqaraghay Kazakh. see Katon-Karagay
83 G3 Katoomba N.S.W. Austr.
93 B3 Katoposa, Gunung mt. Indon.
116 C5 Katosan Gujarat India
198 C2 Kato Tithorea Greece
Kåtotjåkka mt. Sweden see Godučohkka
176 C2 Katovice Czech Rep.
175 H5 Katowice Pol.
117 G5 Katoya W. Bengal India
116 C5 Katpur Gujarat India
199 F3 Katrancık Dağı mts Turkey
146 D5 Katrine, Loch l. Scotland U.K.
143 G2 Katrineholm Sweden
179 F2 Katsdorf Austria
198 B2 Katsikas Greece
207 G3 Katsina Nigeria
207 G4 Katsina state Nigeria
207 H5 Katsina-Ala Nigeria
105 F3 Katsura-gawa r. Japan
104 B4 Katsuragi-san hill Japan
105 G3 Katsuura Japan
104 C2 Katsuyama Japan
121 F5 Kattakurgan Uzbek.
86 E4 Kattamudda Well W.A. Austr.
Kattaqŭrghon Uzbek. see Kattakurgan
123 F3 Kattasang Hills Afgh.
142 D3 Kattegat str. Denmark/Sweden
140 L2 Kattisavan Sweden
Kattowitz Pol. see Katowice
114 C4 Kattuputtur Tamil Nadu India
211 B7 Katumbi Malawi
110 D1 Katun' r. Rus. Fed.
134 I4 Katunino Rus. Fed.
110 D1 Katunskiy Khrebet mts Rus. Fed.
Katwa W. Bengal India see Katoya
164 D2 Katwijk aan Zee Neth.
175 J2 Kąty Pol.
Katyk Ukr. see Shakhtars'k
177 I5 Katymár Hungary
174 E4 Kąty Wrocławskie Pol.
173 G2 Katzbach r. Ger.
179 H3 Katzelsdorf Austria
172 D2 Katzenbuckel hill Ger.
169 C5 Katzenelnbogen Ger.
171 C5 Katzhütte Ger.
172 B2 Katzweiler Ger.
240 □B7 Kauai i. HI U.S.A.
240 □B8 Kauai Channel HI U.S.A.
169 C5 Kaub Ger.
173 E4 Kaufbeuren Ger.
173 E3 Kaufering Ger.
237 D5 Kaufman TX U.S.A.
169 E4 Kaufungen Ger.
141 M3 Kauhajoki Fin.
140 M3 Kauhava Fin.
226 C3 Kaukauna WI U.S.A.
96 B1 Kaukkwè Hills Myanmar
240 □B8 Kaulakahi Channel HI U.S.A.
165 E3 Kaulille Belgium
171 C5 Kaulsdorf Ger.
80 E4 Kaumai North I. N.Z.
225 I1 Kaumajet Mountains Nfld. Can.
240 □B8 Kaumakani HI U.S.A.
240 □C8 Kaumalapau HI U.S.A.
240 □C8 Kaunakakai HI U.S.A.
138 D4 Kaunas Lith.
234 D1 Kauneonga Lake NY U.S.A.
117 G4 Kaunia Bangl.
140 M2 Kaunisvaara Sweden
138 E4 Kauno marios l. Lith.
81 C5 Kaupiri South I. N.Z.
240 □C8 Kaupo HI U.S.A.
207 G3 Kaura-Namoda Nigeria
Kaushany Moldova see Căușeni
140 M3 Kaustinen Fin.
165 F5 Kautenbach Lux.
140 M1 Kautokeino Norway
179 G2 Kautzen Austria
197 F5 Kavadarci Macedonia
196 D5 Kavajë Albania
199 E1 Kavak anakkale Turkey
126 E2 Kavak Samsun Turkey
199 E2 Kavak Dağı hill Turkey
199 F2 Kavaklıdere Turkey
199 F3 Kavaklıdere Turkey
198 D1 Kavala Greece
100 E3 Kavalerovo Rus. Fed.
114 D3 Kavali Andhra Prad. India
114 C4 Kavalpatnam Tamil Nadu India
122 C4 Kavār Iran
114 B4 Kavaratti Lakshadweep India
197 I4 Kavarna Bulg.
138 E4 Kavarskas Lith.
170 D2 Kavelstorf Ger.
206 B4 Kavendou, Mont mt. Guinea
114 C4 Kaveri r. India
114 C3 Kaveripatnam Tamil Nadu India
116 C5 Kavi Gujarat India
91 L7 Kavieng New Ireland P.N.G.
122 C3 Kavīr, Dasht-e des. Iran
122 C4 Kavīr-e Abarkuh des. Iran
122 D3 Kavīr-i-Namak salt flat Iran
129 C1 Kavkazskiy Rus. Fed.
175 L6 Kavs'ke Ukr.
251 H3 Kaw Fr. Guiana
104 C1 Kawachi-dake hill Japan
104 B4 Kawachi-nagano Japan
105 F3 Kawagoe Japan
105 F3 Kawaguchi Japan
240 □D8 Kawaihae HI U.S.A.
240 □B7 Kawaikini, Mount HI U.S.A.
240 □ Kawailoa Beach HI U.S.A.
80 E1 Kawakawa North I. N.Z.
209 F7 Kawambwa Zambia
104 B3 Kawanishi Japan
105 F2 Kawarazawa-gawa r. Japan
116 E5 Kawardha Madh. Prad. India
105 F3 Kawasaki Japan
225 H2 Kawawachikamach Que. Can.
80 F3 Kaweka mt. North I. N.Z.
80 F3 Kaweka Range mts North I. N.Z.
226 B1 Kawene Ont. Can.
80 F3 Kawerau North I. N.Z.
80 E3 Kawhia North I. N.Z.
80 E3 Kawhia Harbour North I. N.Z.
241 I3 Kawich Peak NV U.S.A.
241 I3 Kawich Range mts NV U.S.A.
96 B3 Kawkareik Myanmar
96 A2 Kawlin Myanmar
128 A4 Kawm Dafanah tourist site Egypt
Kawthoolei state Myanmar see Kayin
Kawthule state Myanmar see Kayin
Kaxgar Xinjiang China see Kashi
110 B4 Kaxgar He r. China
110 C3 Kax He r. China
111 C4 Kaxtax Shan mts China
206 E3 Kaya Burkina
129 C3 Kayaaltı Turkey
199 E2 Kayacı Dağı hill Turkey
126 E3 Kayadibi Turkey
105 E3 Kayaga-take mt. Japan
96 B3 Kayah state Myanmar
129 E2 Kayakent Rus. Fed.
211 A7 Kayambi Zambia
95 E3 Kayan r. Indon.
95 G2 Kayan r. Indon.
96 B3 Kayan Myanmar
211 A5 Kayanaza Burundi
92 □ Kayangel atoll Palau
114 C4 Kayankulam Kerala India
114 C2 Kayar Mahar. India
93 C2 Kayasa Halmahera Indon.
129 D1 Kayasula Rus. Fed.
238 F3 Kaycee WY U.S.A.
Kaydanovo Belarus see Dzyarzhynsk
241 L3 Kayenta AZ U.S.A.
209 B6 Kayes Congo
206 C3 Kayes Mali
206 C3 Kayes admin. reg. Mali
120 F2 Kayga Kazakh.
Kaygy Kazakh. see Kayga
96 B3 Kayin state Myanmar
165 F5 Kayl Lux.
199 F2 Kaymakçı İzmir Turkey
121 H1 Kaymanachikha Kazakh.
199 G2 Kaymaz Turkey
171 D5 Kayna Ger.
121 I2 Kaynar Kazakh.
126 E3 Kaynar Turkey
199 G1 Kaynarca Turkey
197 H5 Kaynarlı r. Turkey
199 G1 Kaynaşlı Turkey
Kayrakkum Tajik. see Qayroqqum
Kayrakkumskoye Vodokhranilishche resr Tajik. see Obanbori Qayroqqum
121 H2 Kayrakty Kazakh.
126 D3 Kayseri Turkey
157 H4 Kaysersberg France
94 D3 Kayuagung Sumatera Indon.
130 J3 Kayyerkan Rus. Fed.
121 H4 Kayyngdy Kyrg.
139 L5 Kazachka Rus. Fed.
131 O2 Kazach'ye Rus. Fed.
Kazakh Azer. see Qazax
Kazakhskaya S.S.R. country Asia see Kazakhstan
121 G2 Kazakhskiy Melkosopochnik plain Kazakh.
120 C4 Kazakhskiy Zaliv b. Kazakh.
120 J2 Kazakhstan country Asia
Kazakhstan Kazakh. see Aksay
139 L5 Kazaki Rus. Fed.
Kazakstan country Asia see Kazakhstan
120 E3 Kazalinsk Kazakh.
223 M2 Kazan r. Nunavut Can.
134 J5 Kazan' Rus. Fed.
129 C4 Kazan Turkey
126 D3 Kazancı Turkey
Kazandzhik Turkm. see Gazandzhyk
198 B2 Kazanje, Mal mt. Albania
134 J5 Kazanka r. Rus. Fed.
137 G4 Kazanka Ukr.
128 B1 Kazanlı Turkey
197 G4 Kazanlŭk Bulg.
139 L5 Kazanovka Rus. Fed.
175 J4 Kazanów Pol.
103 □3 Kazan-rettō is N. Pacific Ocean
135 H6 Kazanskaya Rus. Fed.
Kazatin Ukr. see Kozyatyn
120 D2 Kazatskiy Kazakh.
210 C1 Kaza Wenz r. Eth.
Kazbegi Georgia see Qazbegi
129 D2 Kazbek mt. Georgia/Rus. Fed.
199 E2 Kaz Dağı mts Turkey
122 B4 Kāzerūn Iran
121 G1 Kazgorodok Kazakh.
134 J3 Kazhim Rus. Fed.
123 E5 Kazhmak r. Pak.
Kazi Magomed Azer. see Qazımämmäd
175 I5 Kazimierza Wielka Pol.
174 G3 Kazimierz Biskupi Pol.
175 J4 Kazimierz Dolne Pol.
177 J3 Kazincbarcika Hungary
137 I2 Kazinka Belgorodskaya Oblast' Rus. Fed.
139 L5 Kazinka Lipetskaya Oblast' Rus. Fed.
139 L5 Kazinka Ryazanskaya Oblast' Rus. Fed.
137 K2 Kazinka Voronezhskaya Oblast' Rus. Fed.
138 E5 Kazlowshchyna Belarus
138 D4 Kazlų Rūda Lith.
174 E3 Kaźmierz Pol.
176 C2 Kaznějov Czech Rep.
105 F2 Kazo Japan
120 B2 Kaztalovka Kazakh.
209 D6 Kazumba Dem. Rep. Congo
209 E9 Kazungula Zambia
102 J3 Kazuno Japan
122 D2 Kazy Turkm.
121 G4 Kazygurt Yuzhnyy Kazakhstan Kazakh.
130 H3 Kazym r. Rus. Fed.
196 D4 Kçirë Albania
174 F3 Kcynia Pol.
176 C2 Kdyně Czech Rep.
198 D3 Kea i. Greece
240 □D9 Keaau HI U.S.A.
147 E2 Keady Northern Ireland U.K.
146 B5 Keal, Loch na b. Scotland U.K.
240 □C8 Kealaikahiki Channel HI U.S.A.
240 □D9 Kealakekua HI U.S.A.
240 □D9 Kealia HI U.S.A.
147 B5 Kealkill Rep. of Ireland
241 L4 Keams Canyon AZ U.S.A.
Kéamu i. Vanuatu see Anatom
235 D2 Keansburg NJ U.S.A.
147 F2 Kearney Northern Ireland U.K.
236 D3 Kearney NE U.S.A.
232 E5 Kearneysville WV U.S.A.
241 L5 Kearny AZ U.S.A.
235 D2 Kearny NJ U.S.A.
215 H3 Keate's Drift S. Africa
240 □D9 Keauhou HI U.S.A.
240 □C8 Keawakapu HI U.S.A.
126 E3 Keban Turkey
126 E3 Keban Barajı resr Turkey
207 F3 Kebbi state Nigeria
206 A3 Kébémèr Senegal
207 I4 Kébi r. Cameroon
205 H2 Kebili Tunisia
128 B2 Kebīr, Nahr al r. Lebanon/Syria
140 L2 Kebnekaise mt. Sweden
146 B3 Kebock Head hd Scotland U.K.
210 E3 K'ebrī Dehar Eth.
95 E4 Kebumen Jawa Tengah Indon.
177 I5 Kecel Hungary
210 C3 K'ech'a Terara mt. Eth.
222 E3 Kechika r. B.C. Can.
199 G3 Keçiborlu Turkey
177 I5 Kecskemét Hungary
94 C1 Kedah state Malaysia
138 D4 Kėdainiai Lith.
Kedairu Passage Fiji see Kadavu Passage
111 B6 Kedarnath Peak Uttar Prad. India
225 H4 Kedgwick N.B. Can.
109 E2 Kedian Hubei China
151 H2 Kedington Suffolk, England U.K.
95 F4 Kediri Jawa Timur Indon.
100 C3 Kedong Heilong. China
206 B3 Kédougou Senegal
134 K2 Kedva r. Rus. Fed.
174 G5 Kędzierzyn-Koźle Pol.
149 I4 Keelby Lincolnshire, England U.K.
222 E1 Keele r. Y.T. Can.
149 G4 Keele Staffordshire, England U.K.
222 D2 Keele Peak Y.T. Can.
240 I3 Keeler CA U.S.A.
Keeling Islands terr. Indian Ocean see Cocos Islands
Keelung Taiwan see Chilung
146 F5 Keen, Mount hill Scotland U.K.
147 D3 Keenagh Rep. of Ireland
240 H4 Keene CA U.S.A.
233 G3 Keene NH U.S.A.
232 C4 Keene OH U.S.A.
84 B2 Keep r. N.T. Austr.
165 D4 Keerbergen Belgium
215 F3 Keeromsberg mt. Free State S. Africa
214 B5 Keeromsberg mt. W. Cape S. Africa
85 E2 Keer-weer, Cape Qld Austr.
212 C5 Keetmanshoop Namibia
223 M5 Keewatin Ont. Can.
226 A2 Keewatin MN U.S.A.
Kefallinía i. Greece see Kefallonia
198 B2 Kefallonia i. Greece
199 E3 Kefalos Notio Aigaio Greece
Kefe Ukr. see Feodosiya
169 E5 Kefenrod Ger.
179 F2 Kefermarkt Austria
207 G4 Keffi Nigeria
199 G1 Kefken Kocaeli Turkey
140 □B2 Keflavík Iceland
114 D5 Kegalla Sri Lanka
Kegayli Uzbek. see Kegeyli
121 I4 Kegen Kazakh.
120 D4 Kegeyli Uzbek.
222 G3 Keg River Alta Can.
135 I7 Kegul'ta Rus. Fed.
138 E3 Ķegums Latvia
151 F2 Kegworth Leicestershire, England U.K.
172 B3 Kehl Ger.
165 F5 Kehlen Lux.
138 E2 Kehra Estonia
169 C5 Kehrig Ger.
138 E2 Kehtna Estonia
137 H3 Kehychivka Ukr.
241 K3 Keibab Plateau AZ U.S.A.
149 H4 Keighley West Yorkshire, England U.K.
138 E2 Keila Estonia
138 E2 Keila r. Estonia
214 C3 Keimoes S. Africa
215 G5 Kei Mouth S. Africa
215 F5 Kei Road S. Africa
215 F5 Keiskama r. S. Africa
215 F5 Keiskammahoek S. Africa
146 E3 Keiss Highland, Scotland U.K.
207 G3 Keïta Niger
208 C2 Kéita, Bahr r. Chad
140 N3 Keitele Fin.
140 N3 Keitele l. Fin.
82 E4 Keith S.A. Austr.
146 F4 Keith Moray, Scotland U.K.
84 B1 Keith, Cape N.T. Austr.
222 F1 Keith Arm b. N.W.T. Can.
222 F4 Keithley Creek B.C. Can.
104 D2 Kekachi-yama mt. Japan
240 □B8 Kekaha HI U.S.A.
138 E3 Ķekava Latvia
177 L3 Kékcse Hungary
81 D5 Kekerengu South I. N.Z.
177 J4 Kékes mt. Hungary
116 C4 Kekri Rajasthan India
Kěk-Tash Kyrg. see Kök-Tash
210 E3 K'elafo Eth.
114 B5 Kelai atoll Maldives
107 F4 Kelan Shanxi China
94 C2 Kelang Malaysia
94 C1 Kelantan r. Malaysia
94 C1 Kelantan state Malaysia
93 A4 Kelara r. Indon.
122 B2 Kelārdasht Iran
169 B5 Kelberg Ger.
171 C4 Kelbra (Kyffhäuser) Ger.
177 G2 Kelč Czech Rep.
198 B1 Këlcyrë Albania
129 C3 Kel Dağı mt. Turkey
177 I5 Kelebia Hungary
199 F3 Kelekçi Turkey
199 F2 Keles Turkey
121 G4 Keles Uzbek.
173 F3 Kelheim Ger.
205 H1 Kelibia Tunisia
123 F2 Kelif Turkm.
123 E2 Kelifskiy Uzboy marsh Turkm.
169 D5 Kelkheim (Taunus) Ger.
126 E2 Kelkit Turkey
126 E2 Kelkit r. Turkey
172 A2 Kell Ger.
81 A6 Kellard, Mount South I. N.Z.
146 E4 Kellas Moray, Scotland U.K.
138 F2 Kellavere hill Estonia
208 B5 Kéllé Congo
170 C1 Kellenhusen Ger.
87 C6 Kellerberrin W.A. Austr.
121 G1 Kellerovka Kazakh.
223 K5 Kelliher Sask. Can.
168 E2 Kellinghusen Ger.
173 E3 Kellmünz an der Iller Ger.
238 C2 Kellogg ID U.S.A.
147 A5 Kells Kerry Rep. of Ireland
147 D4 Kells Kilkenny Rep. of Ireland
147 E3 Kells Meath Rep. of Ireland
147 E2 Kells Northern Ireland U.K.
147 E2 Kells r. Northern Ireland U.K.
147 C3 Kellysgrove Rep. of Ireland
138 D4 Kelmė Lith.
136 D3 Kel'mentsi Ukr.
165 F4 Kelmis Belgium
208 B2 Kelo Chad
78 □6 Keloma i. Solomon Is
222 G5 Kelowna B.C. Can.
149 G4 Kelsall Cheshire, England U.K.
226 A2 Kelsey MN U.S.A.
240 F2 Kelseyville CA U.S.A.
81 B6 Kelso South I. N.Z.

Kilmaurs to Koartac
321

148 E2 Kilmaurs East Ayrshire, Scotland U.K.
148 C4 Kilmeague Rep. of Ireland
147 B3 Kilmeena Rep. of Ireland
146 C5 Kilmelford Argyll and Bute, Scotland U.K.
134 J4 Kil'mez' Rus. Fed.
134 J4 Kil'mez' r. Rus. Fed.
150 D4 Kilmington Devon, England U.K.
147 C5 Kilmona Rep. of Ireland
83 F4 Kilmore Vic. Austr.
147 C4 Kilmore Clare Rep. of Ireland
147 E4 Kilmore Wexford Rep. of Ireland
147 E4 Kilmore Quay Rep. of Ireland
147 B4 Kilmorna Rep. of Ireland
146 C6 Kilmory Argyll and Bute, Scotland U.K.
146 B4 Kilmory Highland, Scotland U.K.
147 C4 Kilmurry Rep. of Ireland
148 C5 Kilmyshall Rep. of Ireland
147 D3 Kilnaleck Rep. of Ireland
147 E4 Kilnamanagh Rep. of Ireland
146 B5 Kilninian Argyll and Bute, Scotland U.K.
146 C5 Kilninver Argyll and Bute, Scotland U.K.
147 C3 Kilnock Rep. of Ireland
146 B5 Kiloran Argyll and Bute, Scotland U.K.
211 C6 Kilosa Tanz.
147 E4 Kilquiggin Rep. of Ireland
147 E2 Kilrea Northern Ireland U.K.
147 C2 Kilrean Rep. of Ireland
147 C3 Kilreekill Rep. of Ireland
147 B3 Kilronan Rep. of Ireland
147 D2 Kilross Donegal Rep. of Ireland
147 C4 Kilross Tipperary Rep. of Ireland
147 B4 Kilrush Rep. of Ireland
147 C3 Kilsallagh Rep. of Ireland
148 C4 Kilsaran Rep. of Ireland
147 E3 Kilskeer Rep. of Ireland
148 B3 Kilskeery Northern Ireland U.K.
146 D6 Kilsyth North Lanarkshire, Scotland U.K.
147 C3 Kiltartan Rep. of Ireland
147 E4 Kiltealy Rep. of Ireland
148 C4 Kilteel Rep. of Ireland
147 C3 Kiltimagh Rep. of Ireland
147 E4 Kiltogan Rep. of Ireland
147 C3 Kiltoom Rep. of Ireland
147 C3 Kiltullagh Rep. of Ireland
137 I4 Kil'tychchya r. Ukr.
148 A3 Kiltyclogher Rep. of Ireland
209 F7 Kilwa Dem. Rep. Congo
211 C7 Kilwa Kivinje Tanz.
211 C7 Kilwa Masoko Tanz.
147 F2 Kilwaughter Northern Ireland U.K.
146 D6 Kilwinning North Ayrshire, Scotland U.K.
147 C4 Kilworth Rep. of Ireland
Kilyazi Azer. see Giläzi
116 C5 Kim r. India
237 C4 Kim CO U.S.A.
211 C7 Kimambi Tanz.
82 D3 Kimba S.A. Austr.
236 C3 Kimball NE U.S.A.
232 B4 Kimball OH U.S.A.
91 L8 Kimbe New Britain P.N.G.
222 H5 Kimberley B.C. Can.
215 E3 Kimberley S. Africa
151 I2 Kimberley Norfolk, England U.K.
86 E3 Kimberley Downs W.A. Austr.
86 E3 Kimberley Plateau W.A. Austr.
87 C5 Kimberley Range hills W.A. Austr.
234 C2 Kimberton PA U.S.A.
151 G2 Kimbolton Cambridgeshire, England U.K.
101 D4 Kimch'aek N. Korea
101 D5 Kimch'ŏn S. Korea
101 D6 Kimhae S. Korea
Kími Greece see Kymi
141 M3 Kimito Fin.
105 F3 Kimitsu Japan
101 C6 Kimje S. Korea
221 L3 Kimmirut Nunavut Can.
198 D3 Kimolos i. Greece
209 B6 Kimongo Congo
139 L5 Kimovsk Tul'skaya Oblast' Rus. Fed.
206 D3 Kimparana Mali
232 B6 Kimper KY U.S.A.
209 B6 Kimpese Dem. Rep. Congo
102 I4 Kimpoku-san mt. Japan
151 G3 Kimpton Hertfordshire, England U.K.
139 K3 Kimry Rus. Fed.
222 E4 Kimsquit B.C. Can.
143 F2 Kimstad Sweden
209 B6 Kimvula Dem. Rep. Congo
95 G1 Kinabalu, Gunung mt. Sabah Malaysia
95 G1 Kinabatangan r. Sabah Malaysia
211 C6 Kinango Kenya
199 E3 Kinaros i. Greece
175 M6 Kinashiv Ukr.
222 G4 Kinbasket Lake B.C. Can.
146 E3 Kinbrace Highland, Scotland U.K.
223 J5 Kincaid Sask. Can.
224 D4 Kincardine Ont. Can.
149 F1 Kincardine Fife, Scotland U.K.
146 F4 Kincardine O'Neil Aberdeenshire, Scotland U.K.
96 B1 Kinchang Myanmar
222 D4 Kincolith B.C. Can.
146 E4 Kincraig Highland, Scotland U.K.
177 H4 Kincses Hungary
209 E7 Kinda Dem. Rep. Congo
209 B5 Kindamba Congo
96 A2 Kindat Myanmar
179 G3 Kindberg Austria
227 F4 Kinde MI U.S.A.
171 C4 Kindelbrück Ger.
237 E6 Kinder LA U.S.A.
169 C5 Kinderbeuern Ger.
164 D3 Kinderdijk Neth.
149 H4 Kinder Scout hill England U.K.
223 I5 Kindersley Sask. Can.
206 B4 Kindia Guinea
173 F3 Kinding Ger.
172 B2 Kindsbach Ger.
209 E5 Kindu Dem. Rep. Congo
135 J5 Kinel' Rus. Fed.
120 B1 Kinel'-Cherkasy Rus. Fed.
134 H4 Kineshma Rus. Fed.
151 F3 Kineton Gloucestershire, England U.K.
84 C1 King r. N.T. Austr.
84 C2 King r. N.T. Austr.
86 F2 King r. W.A. Austr.
87 D5 King, Lake salt flat W.A. Austr.
232 E6 King and QueenCourthouse VA U.S.A.
85 G5 Kingaroy Qld Austr.
147 C2 Kingarrow Rep. of Ireland
146 C6 Kingarth Argyll and Bute, Scotland U.K.
240 G3 King City CA U.S.A.
222 E5 Kingcome r. B.C. Can.
86 E2 King Edward r. W.A. Austr.
157 H5 Kingersheim France
233 □H2 Kingfield ME U.S.A.
237 D5 Kingfisher OK U.S.A.
232 E5 King George VA U.S.A.
259 E8 King George Bay Falkland Is
262 U2 King George Island Antarctica
King George Islands Arch. des Tuamotu Fr. Polynesia see Roi Georges, Îles du
87 C7 King George Sound b. W.A. Austr.
86 D4 King Hill hill W.A. Austr.
146 E5 Kinghorn Fife, Scotland U.K.
146 C4 Kingie r. Scotland U.K.
138 G2 Kingisepp Rus. Fed.
83 E4 King Island Tas. Austr.
King Island Myanmar see Kadan Kyun
Kingisseppa Estonia see Kuressaare
227 H1 King Kirkland Ont. Can.
263 F2 King Leopold and Queen Astrid Coast Antarctica
86 E3 King Leopold Ranges hills W.A. Austr.
241 J4 Kingman AZ U.S.A.
237 D4 Kingman KS U.S.A.
233 □I2 Kingman ME U.S.A.
75 I3 Kingman Reef N. Pacific Ocean
222 D3 King Mountain B.C. Can.
237 C6 King Mountain hill TX U.S.A.
234 C2 King of Prussia PA U.S.A.
82 C2 Kingoonya S.A. Austr.
262 S1 King Peak Antarctica
262 R2 King Peninsula Antarctica
147 D4 Kings r. Rep. of Ireland
240 G3 Kings r. CA U.S.A.
238 C3 Kings r. NV U.S.A.
146 F5 Kingsbarns Fife, Scotland U.K.
150 D4 Kingsbridge Devon, England U.K.
240 H3 Kingsburg CA U.S.A.
151 F2 Kingsbury Warwickshire, England U.K.
150 E4 Kingsbury Episcopi Somerset, England U.K.
84 B5 Kings Canyon N.T. Austr.
151 F3 Kingsclere Hampshire, England U.K.
82 D3 Kingscote S.A. Austr.
235 E2 Kings County county NY U.S.A.
147 E3 Kingscourt Rep. of Ireland
151 I3 Kingsdown Kent, England U.K.
80 E2 Kingseat North I. N.Z.
262 U2 King Sejong research stn Antarctica
226 C3 Kingsford MI U.S.A.
146 D5 Kingshouse Stirling, Scotland U.K.
150 D4 Kingskerswell Devon, England U.K.
231 D6 Kingsland GA U.S.A.
226 E5 Kingsland IN U.S.A.
151 G3 Kings Langley Hertfordshire, England U.K.
215 H2 Kingsley S. Africa
149 H4 Kingsley Staffordshire, England U.K.
226 E3 Kingsley MI U.S.A.
151 H2 King's Lynn Norfolk, England U.K.
77 H2 Kingsmill Group is Gilbert Is Kiribati
151 H3 Kingsnorth Kent, England U.K.
86 D3 King Sound b. W.A. Austr.
235 E2 Kings Park NY U.S.A.
238 E3 Kings Peak UT U.S.A.
232 B6 Kingsport TN U.S.A.
151 F2 King's Sutton Northamptonshire, England U.K.
150 D4 Kingsteignton Devon, England U.K.
150 E3 Kingsthorne Herefordshire, England U.K.
83 F5 Kingston Tas. Austr.
224 E4 Kingston Ont. Can.
246 □ Kingston Jamaica
81 B6 Kingston South I. N.Z.
146 E4 Kingston Moray, Scotland U.K.
233 H4 Kingston MA U.S.A.
236 E4 Kingston MO U.S.A.
233 F4 Kingston NY U.S.A.
232 B5 Kingston OH U.S.A.
234 C1 Kingston PA U.S.A.
231 C5 Kingston TN U.S.A.
232 C6 Kingston WV U.S.A.
151 F3 Kingston Bagpuize Oxfordshire, England U.K.
150 E2 Kingstone Herefordshire, England U.K.
241 J4 Kingston Peak CA U.S.A.
150 E3 Kingston Seymour North Somerset, England U.K.
82 D4 Kingston South East S.A. Austr.
149 I4 Kingston upon Hull Kingston upon Hull, England U.K.
149 I4 Kingston upon Hull admin. div. England U.K.
151 G3 Kingston upon Thames Greater London, England U.K.
247 □3 Kingstown St Vincent
231 E5 Kingstree SC U.S.A.
234 B3 Kingsville MD U.S.A.
237 D7 Kingsville TX U.S.A.
150 D4 Kingswear Devon, England U.K.
150 E3 Kingswood South Gloucestershire, England U.K.
151 G3 Kingswood Surrey, England U.K.
151 F3 King's Worthy Hampshire, England U.K.
150 D2 Kington Herefordshire, England U.K.
209 C6 Kingungi Dem. Rep. Congo
225 I1 Kingurutik r. Nfld. Can.
146 D4 Kingussie Highland, Scotland U.K.
232 E6 King William VA U.S.A.
221 I3 King William Island Nunavut Can.
Kingwilliamstown Rep. of Ireland see Ballydesmond
215 F5 King William's Town S. Africa
237 E6 Kingwood TX U.S.A.
232 D5 Kingwood WV U.S.A.
209 F7 Kiniama Dem. Rep. Congo
199 F3 Kınık Turkey
199 E2 Kınık Turkey
215 G4 Kinirapoort S. Africa
223 J4 Kinistino Sask. Can.
137 H4 Kinka r. Ukr.
209 B6 Kinkala Congo
80 E3 Kinleith North I. N.Z.
81 B6 Kinloch South I. N.Z.
146 B4 Kinloch Highland, Scotland U.K.
146 C3 Kinlochbervie Highland, Scotland U.K.
146 C5 Kinlocheil Highland, Scotland U.K.
146 C4 Kinlochewe Highland, Scotland U.K.
146 C4 Kinloch Hourn Highland, Scotland U.K.
146 D5 Kinlochleven Highland, Scotland U.K.
146 D5 Kinloch Rannoch Perth and Kinross, Scotland U.K.
146 E4 Kinloss Moray, Scotland U.K.
147 C2 Kinlough Rep. of Ireland
150 D1 Kinmel Bay Conwy, Wales U.K.
Kinmen Taiwan see Chinmen
227 H3 Kinmount Ont. Can.
142 E3 Kinna Sweden
147 B3 Kinnadoohy Rep. of Ireland
81 B5 Kinnaird, Mount South I. N.Z.
114 D2 Kinnarasani r. India
147 D3 Kinnegad Rep. of Ireland
235 D1 Kinnelon NJ U.S.A.
Kinneret, Yam l. Israel see Tiberias, Lake
147 D3 Kinnitty Rep. of Ireland
114 D4 Kinniyai Sri Lanka
140 N3 Kinnula Fin.
224 D2 Kinoje r. Ont. Can.
104 B4 Kino-kawa r. Japan
223 K3 Kinoosao Sask. Can.
Kinpoku-san mt. Japan see Kimpoku-san
165 E3 Kinrooi Belgium
215 G2 Kinross S. Africa
146 E5 Kinross Perth and Kinross, Scotland U.K.
147 C5 Kinsale Rep. of Ireland
232 E5 Kinsale VA U.S.A.
142 B1 Kinsarvik Norway
209 B6 Kinshasa Dem. Rep. Congo
209 C6 Kinshasa admin. reg. Dem. Rep. Congo
137 I4 Kins'ki Rozdory Ukr.
237 D4 Kinsley KS U.S.A.
232 C4 Kinsman OH U.S.A.
231 E5 Kinston NC U.S.A.
138 C4 Kintai Lith.
206 E4 Kintampo Ghana
151 F3 Kintbury West Berkshire, England U.K.
234 C2 Kintersville PA U.S.A.
84 B4 Kintore N.T. Austr.
146 F4 Kintore Aberdeenshire, Scotland U.K.
82 B1 Kintore, Mount S.A. Austr.
86 F4 Kintore Range hills N.T. Austr.
146 B6 Kintour Argyll and Bute, Scotland U.K.
146 C6 Kintyre pen. Scotland U.K.
96 A2 Kinu Myanmar
105 G3 Kinu-gawa r. Japan
105 F2 Kinunuma-yama mt. Japan
224 D2 Kinushseo r. Ont. Can.
222 H4 Kinuso Alta Can.
147 C3 Kinvara Rep. of Ireland
147 B3 Kinvarra Rep. of Ireland
150 E2 Kinver Staffordshire, England U.K.
114 C2 Kinwat Mahar. India
211 B6 Kinyangiri Tanz.
210 B4 Kinyeti mt. Sudan
172 B3 Kinzig r. Ger.
169 D5 Kinzig r. Ger.
211 B6 Kiomboi Tanz.
129 C2 Kion-Khokh, Gora mt. Rus. Fed.
227 H2 Kiosk Ont. Can.
239 F4 Kiowa CO U.S.A.
237 D4 Kiowa KS U.S.A.
238 F3 Kiowa Creek r. CO U.S.A.
240 □C8 Kipahulu HI U.S.A.
Kiparissía Greece see Kyparissia
134 G4 Kipelovo Rus. Fed.
138 G2 Kipen' Rus. Fed.
211 B7 Kipengere Range mts Tanz.
173 F3 Kipfenberg Ger.
211 A6 Kipili Tanz.
223 K5 Kipling Sask. Can.
Kipling Station Sask. Can. see Kipling
149 H4 Kippax West Yorkshire, England U.K.
190 C2 Kippel Switz.
146 D5 Kippen Stirling, Scotland U.K.
172 B3 Kippenheim Ger.
147 E3 Kippure hill Rep. of Ireland
121 J1 Kiprino Rus. Fed.
134 I4 Kipshenga Rus. Fed.
137 F2 Kipti Ukr.
233 F6 Kiptopeke VA U.S.A.
Kipungo Angola see Quipungo
209 E7 Kipushi Dem. Rep. Congo
209 F8 Kipushia Dem. Rep. Congo
117 E4 Kirakat Uttar Prad. India
78 □6 Kirakira San Cristobal Solomon Is
177 J3 Király Hungary
177 G5 Királyegyháza Hungary
177 J5 Királyhegyes Hungary
199 E2 Kiran Dağları hills Turkey
114 D2 Kirandul Madh. Prad. India
206 C3 Kirané Mali
128 A1 Kıravga Turkey
138 G5 Kirawsk Belarus
199 F2 Kiraz Turkey
237 E6 Kirbyville TX U.S.A.
173 G4 Kirchanschöring Ger.
172 C2 Kirchardt Ger.
178 E4 Kirchbach Austria
179 G4 Kirchbach in Steiermark Austria
173 H3 Kirchberg Bayern Ger.
171 D5 Kirchberg Sachsen Ger.
190 C1 Kirchberg Bern Switz.
190 E1 Kirchberg Sankt Gallen Switz.
172 B2 Kirchberg (Hunsrück) Ger.
179 G2 Kirchberg am Wagram Austria
179 G2 Kirchberg am Walde Austria
179 G3 Kirchberg am Wechsel Austria
173 E3 Kirchberg an der Iller Ger.
172 D2 Kirchberg an der Jagst Ger.
179 G2 Kirchberg an der Pielach Austria
179 G4 Kirchberg an der Raab Austria
178 D3 Kirchberg in Tirol Austria
178 D3 Kirchbichl Austria
169 E4 Kirchbrak Ger.
170 C2 Kirchdorf Mecklenburg-Vorpommern Ger.
168 D3 Kirchdorf Niedersachsen Ger.
173 G3 Kirchdorf am Inn Ger.
173 F3 Kirchdorf an der Amper Ger.
179 F3 Kirchdorf an der Krems Austria
173 H3 Kirchdorf im Wald Ger.
178 D3 Kirchdorf in Tirol Austria
173 F2 Kirchehrenbach Ger.
169 C5 Kirchen (Sieg) Ger.
171 C5 Kirchenlamitz Ger.
173 F2 Kirchenpingarten Ger.
173 F2 Kirchensittenbach Ger.
172 D3 Kirchentellinsfurt Ger.
173 F2 Kirchenthumbach Ger.
169 D5 Kirchhain Ger.
169 F4 Kirchheilingen Ger.
172 D2 Kirchheim Bayern Ger.
169 E5 Kirchheim Hessen Ger.
172 D2 Kirchheim am Neckar Ger.
173 F3 Kirchheim bei München Ger.
172 C2 Kirchheim-Bolanden Ger.
173 E3 Kirchheim in Schwaben Ger.
172 D3 Kirchheim unter Teck Ger.
169 D4 Kirchhundem Ger.
170 C2 Kirch Jesar Ger.
169 F5 Kirchlauter Ger.
168 E3 Kirchlinteln Ger.
170 C2 Kirch Mulsow Ger.
169 E3 Kirchohsen (Emmerthal) Ger.
173 G3 Kirchroth Ger.
179 H3 Kirchschlag in der Buckligen Welt Austria
168 D3 Kirchseelte Ger.
168 E2 Kirchtimke Ger.
168 E2 Kirchwalsede Ger.
173 G3 Kirchweidach Ger.
168 D2 Kirchwistedt Ger.
169 F4 Kirchworbis Ger.
172 B4 Kirchzarten Ger.
172 D2 Kirchzell Ger.
129 C3 Kırdamı Turkey
131 L4 Kirensk Rus. Fed.
139 K5 Kireyevsk Rus. Fed.
Kirghizia country Asia see Kyrgyzstan
121 H4 Kirghiz Range mts Asia
120 C1 Kirgiz-Miyaki Rus. Fed.
Kirgizskaya S.S.R. country Asia see Kyrgyzstan
Kirgizskiy Khrebet mts Asia see Kirghiz Range
Kirgizstan country Asia see Kyrgyzstan
Kíria Greece see Kyria
Kiriákion Greece see Kyriaki
77 J2 Kiribati country Pacific Ocean
105 E2 Kiriga-mine mt. Japan
126 E3 Kırıkhan Turkey
126 D3 Kırıkkale Turkey
106 A2 Kirikkuduk Xinjiang China
80 E1 Kirikopuni North I. N.Z.
139 L2 Kirillov Rus. Fed.
Kirin Jilin China see Jilin
Kirin prov. China see Jilin
210 C5 Kirinyaga mt. Kenya
139 I2 Kirishi Rus. Fed.
103 E8 Kirishima-yama vol. Japan
267 I5 Kiritimati i. Kiribati
199 G2 Kırka Turkey
199 E2 Kırkağaç Turkey
146 E7 Kirkbean Dumfries and Galloway, Scotland U.K.
149 F3 Kirkbride Cumbria, England U.K.
122 A2 Kirk Bulāg Dāgi mt. Iran
149 H4 Kirkburton West Yorkshire, England U.K.
149 G4 Kirkby Merseyside, England U.K.
149 H4 Kirkby in Ashfield Nottinghamshire, England U.K.
149 G3 Kirkby Lonsdale Cumbria, England U.K.
149 H3 Kirkby Malzeard North Yorkshire, England U.K.
149 I3 Kirkbymoorside North Yorkshire, England U.K.
149 G3 Kirkby Stephen Cumbria, England U.K.
149 G3 Kirkby Thore Cumbria, England U.K.
146 E5 Kirkcaldy Fife, Scotland U.K.
146 C7 Kirkcolm Dumfries and Galloway, Scotland U.K.
146 E6 Kirkconnel Dumfries and Galloway, Scotland U.K.
146 D7 Kirkcowan Dumfries and Galloway, Scotland U.K.
147 F2 Kirkcubbin Northern Ireland U.K.
146 D7 Kirkcudbright Dumfries and Galloway, Scotland U.K.
148 E3 Kirkcudbright Bay Scotland U.K.
172 B2 Kirkel-Neuhäusel Ger.
142 E1 Kirkenær Norway
140 O1 Kirkenes Norway
227 H3 Kirkfield Ont. Can.
149 G4 Kirkham Lancashire, England U.K.
146 D7 Kirkinner Dumfries and Galloway, Scotland U.K.
146 D6 Kirkintilloch East Dunbartonshire, Scotland U.K.
141 N3 Kirkkonummi Fin.
241 K4 Kirkland AZ U.S.A.
226 C4 Kirkland IL U.S.A.
224 D3 Kirkland Lake Ont. Can.
129 A4 Kırklar Dağı mt. Turkey
129 B3 Kırklar Dağı mt. Turkey
126 B2 Kırklareli Turkey
199 E1 Kırklareli prov. Turkey
149 H3 Kirklevington Stockton-on-Tees, England U.K.
146 E6 Kirkliston Edinburgh, Scotland U.K.
81 C6 Kirkliston Range mts South I. N.Z.
148 E3 Kirk Michael Isle of Man
146 E5 Kirkmichael Perth and Kinross, Scotland U.K.
146 D6 Kirkmichael South Ayrshire, Scotland U.K.
146 E6 Kirkmuirhill South Lanarkshire, Scotland U.K.
149 G3 Kirkoswald Cumbria, England U.K.
146 D6 Kirkoswald South Ayrshire, Scotland U.K.
197 G5 Kirkovo Bulg.
129 B4 Kırköy Turkey
263 L1 Kirkpatrick, Mount Antarctica
146 E6 Kirkpatrick-Fleming Dumfries and Galloway, Scotland U.K.
149 H4 Kirk Sandall South Yorkshire, England U.K.
236 E3 Kirksville MO U.S.A.
148 D1 Kirkton Argyll and Bute, Scotland U.K.
146 F4 Kirkton of Durris Aberdeenshire, Scotland U.K.
146 F5 Kirkton of Menmuir Angus, Scotland U.K.
146 F4 Kirktown of Auchterless Aberdeenshire, Scotland U.K.
146 F4 Kirktown of Deskford Moray, Scotland U.K.
127 G4 Kirkūk Iraq
146 F3 Kirkwall Orkney, Scotland U.K.
215 E5 Kirkwood S. Africa
234 C3 Kirkwood DE U.S.A.
234 B3 Kirkwood PA U.S.A.
149 G2 Kirk Yetholm Scottish Borders, Scotland U.K.
Kirman Iran see Kermān
126 C2 Kırmır r. Turkey
129 A4 Kırmızıköprü Turkey
172 B2 Kirn Ger.
Kırobası Turkey see Mağara
Kīrov Kazakh. see Balpyk Bi
Kirov Kyrg. see Kyzyl-Adyr
139 J4 Kirov Kaluzhskaya Oblast' Rus. Fed.
134 J4 Kirov Kirovskaya Oblast' Rus. Fed.
Kirova, Zaliv b. Azer. see Qızılağac Körfäzi
Kirovabad Azer. see Gäncä
Kirovabad Tajik. see Panj
Kirovakan Armenia see Vanadzor
137 I3 Kirove Donets'ka Oblast' Ukr.
137 G3 Kirove Kirovohrads'ka Oblast' Ukr.
137 H4 Kirove Zaporiz'ka Oblast' Ukr.
120 C2 Kirovo Kazakh.
Kirovo Donets'ka Oblast' Ukr. see Kirove
Kirovo Kirovohrads'ka Oblast' Ukr. see Kirovohrad
Kirovo Uzbek. see Besharyk
Kirov Oblast admin. div. Rus. Fed. see Kirovskaya Oblast'
134 J4 Kirovo-Chepetsk Rus. Fed.
Kirovo-Chepetskiy Rus. Fed. see Kirovo-Chepetsk
Kirovograd Kirovohrads'ka Oblast' Ukr. see Kirovohrad
Kirovograd Oblast admin. div. Ukr. see Kirovohrads'ka Oblast'
Kirovogradskaya Oblast' admin. div. Ukr. see Kirovohrads'ka Oblast'
137 G3 Kirovohrad Kirovohrads'ka Oblast' Ukr.
Kirovohrad Oblast admin. div. Ukr. see Kirovohrads'ka Oblast'
136 G3 Kirovohrads'ka Oblast' admin. div. Ukr.
129 F4 Kirovsk Azer.
139 H2 Kirovsk Leningradskaya Oblast' Rus. Fed.
134 F2 Kirovsk Murmanskaya Oblast' Rus. Fed.
Kirovsk Turkm. see Babadaykhan
137 I3 Kirovs'k Donets'ka Oblast' Ukr.
137 J3 Kirovs'k Ukr.
137 K4 Kirovskaya Rus. Fed.
134 J4 Kirovskaya Oblast' admin. div. Rus. Fed.
137 H3 Kirovs'ke Dnipropetrovs'ka Oblast' Ukr.
137 J3 Kirovs'ke Donets'ka Oblast' Ukr.
137 H5 Kirovs'ke Respublika Krym Ukr.
Kirovskiy Kazakh. see Balpyk Bi
137 I2 Kirovskiy Kurskaya Oblast' Rus. Fed.
100 E3 Kirovskiy Primorskiy Kray Rus. Fed.
Kirovskoye Kyrg. see Kyzyl-Adyr
Kirovskoye Dnipropetrovs'ka Oblast' Ukr. see Kirovs'ke
Kirovskoye Donets'ka Oblast' Ukr. see Kirovs'ke
Kirovskoye Respublika Krym Ukr. see Kirovs'ke
Kırpaşa pen. Cyprus see Karpasia
137 J5 Kirpili r. Rus. Fed.
137 J5 Kirpil'skaya Rus. Fed.
146 E5 Kirriemuir Angus, Scotland U.K.
134 K4 Kirs Rus. Fed.
135 H5 Kirsanov Rus. Fed.
172 B2 Kirschweiler Ger.
126 D3 Kırşehir Turkey
175 L1 Kirsna r. Lith.
207 F3 Kirtachi Niger
123 F5 Kirthar Range mts Pak.
151 F3 Kirtlington Oxfordshire, England U.K.
151 G2 Kirton Lincolnshire, England U.K.
151 I2 Kirton Suffolk, England U.K.
149 I4 Kirton in Lindsey North Lincolnshire, England U.K.
169 E5 Kirtorf Ger.
129 C2 Kirts'khi Georgia
140 M2 Kiruna Sweden
211 A5 Kirundo Burundi
262 X2 Kirwan Escarpment Antarctica
135 I5 Kirya Rus. Fed.
105 F2 Kiryū Japan
139 L3 Kirzhach Rus. Fed.
143 F3 Kisa Sweden
211 C6 Kisaki Tanz.
208 E4 Kisangani Dem. Rep. Congo
211 C6 Kisangire Tanz.
177 L3 Kisar Hungary
94 B2 Kisaran Sumatera Indon.
211 C6 Kisarawe Tanz.
105 F3 Kisarazu Japan
128 D1 Kısas Turkey
177 H4 Kisbér Hungary
98 E1 Kiselevsk Rus. Fed.
188 G4 Kiseljak Bos.-Herz.
139 I1 Kisel'nya Rus. Fed.
177 J3 Kisgyőr Hungary
117 F4 Kishanganj Bihar India
116 B4 Kishangarh Rajasthan India
116 C4 Kishangarh Rajasthan India
116 C2 Kishen Ganga r. India/Pak.
104 B4 Kishi-gawa r. Japan
Kishinev Moldova see Chişinău
Kishiözen r. Kazakh./Rus. Fed. see Malyy Uzen'
104 B4 Kishiwada Japan
121 H1 Kishkenekol' Kazakh.
117 G4 Kishorganj Bangl.
146 C4 Kishorn, Loch inlet Scotland U.K.
116 C2 Kishtwar Jammu and Kashmir
207 F4 Kisi Nigeria
175 H2 Kisielice Pol.
175 K2 Kisielnica Pol.
211 B6 Kisigo r. Tanz.
210 B5 Kisii Kenya
211 C6 Kisiju Tanz.
129 C3 Kısır Dağı mt. Turkey
220 A4 Kiska Island AK U.S.A.
141 M3 Kisko Fin.
177 J4 Kisköre Hungary
177 I5 Kiskőrös Hungary
177 I5 Kiskunfélegyháza Hungary
177 I5 Kiskunhalas Hungary
177 I4 Kiskunlacháza Hungary
177 I5 Kiskunmajsa Hungary
177 H5 Kisláng Hungary
177 K4 Kisléta Hungary
177 G4 Kislőd Hungary
129 C2 Kislovodsk Rus. Fed.
137 J4 Kislyakovskaya Rus. Fed.
210 D5 Kismaayo Somalia
177 K4 Kismarja Hungary
Kismayu Somalia see Kismaayo
104 C3 Kiso-gawa r. Japan
105 E3 Kiso-gawa r. Japan
211 A5 Kisoro Uganda
105 D3 Kiso-sanmyaku mts Japan
179 F4 Kisovec Slovenia
222 E4 Kispiox B.C. Can.
222 E4 Kispiox r. B.C. Can.
Kisseraing Island Myanmar see Kanmaw Kyun
206 C4 Kissidougou Guinea
231 D6 Kissimmee FL U.S.A.
231 D7 Kissimmee r. FL U.S.A.
173 E3 Kissing Ger.
172 D4 Kißlegg Ger.
202 E4 Kissu, Jebel mt. Sudan
177 I5 Kisszállás Hungary
172 D2 Kist Ger.
188 E4 Kistanje Croatia
177 I5 Kistelek Hungary
135 H5 Kistendey Rus. Fed.
Kistna r. India see Krishna
177 J3 Kistokaj Hungary
177 J4 Kisújszállás Hungary
103 F6 Kisuki Japan
210 B5 Kisumu Kenya
177 L3 Kisvárda Hungary
Kisykkamys Kazakh. see Dzhangala
174 F3 Kiszkowo Pol.
177 J5 Kiszombor Hungary
210 A3 Kit r. Sudan
206 C3 Kita Mali
121 F5 Kitab Uzbek.
104 C3 Kitagata Japan
105 G2 Kitaibaraki Japan
103 □3 Kita-Iō-jima vol. Kazan-rettō Japan
104 A4 Kitajima Japan
102 J4 Kitakami Japan
102 J4 Kitakami-gawa r. Japan
102 I5 Kitakata Japan
103 E7 Kita-Kyūshū Japan
210 B4 Kitale Kenya
102 K2 Kitami Japan
102 K1 Kitami-sanchi mts Japan
105 F2 Kitamoto Japan
104 B5 Kitayama-gawa r. Japan
236 C4 Kit Carson CO U.S.A.
224 D5 Kitchener Ont. Can.
224 E3 Kitchigama r. Que. Can.
140 O3 Kitee Fin.
210 B4 Kitgum Uganda
Kíthira i. Greece see Kythira
Kíthnos i. Greece see Kythnos
222 D4 Kitimat B.C. Can.
140 N2 Kitinen r. Fin.
222 D4 Kitkatla B.C. Can.
Kitob Uzbek. see Kitab
139 M3 Kitovo Rus. Fed.
222 D4 Kitsault B.C. Can.
223 I4 Kitscoty Alta Can.
136 C3 Kitsman' Ukr.
103 E7 Kitsuki Japan
232 D4 Kittanning PA U.S.A.
234 D2 Kittatinny Mountains hills NJ U.S.A.
233 □H3 Kittery ME U.S.A.
140 N2 Kittilä Fin.
105 G1 Kittoya-yama hill Fukushima Japan
179 I2 Kittsee Austria
114 B3 Kittur Karnataka India
231 F4 Kitty Hawk NC U.S.A.
211 C5 Kitui Kenya
211 C5 Kitumbeine vol. Tanz.
211 B6 Kitunda Tanz.
222 D4 Kitwanga B.C. Can.
209 F8 Kitwe Zambia
178 D3 Kitzbühel Austria
178 D3 Kitzbüheler Alpen mts Austria
178 D3 Kitzbüheler Horn mt. Austria
179 G4 Kitzeck im Sausal Austria
171 D4 Kitzen Ger.
173 E2 Kitzingen Ger.
171 D4 Kitzscher Ger.
178 D3 Kitzsteinhorn mt. Austria
175 H5 Kiucze Pol.
141 M3 Kiukainen Fin.
91 J8 Kiunga P.N.G.
140 N3 Kiuruvesi Fin.
140 N2 Kivalo ridge Fin.
198 C3 Kiveri Greece
139 K3 Kiverichi Rus. Fed.
136 C2 Kivertsi Ukr.
140 N3 Kivijärvi Fin.
143 F4 Kivik Sweden
138 F2 Kiviõli Estonia
137 I3 Kivsharivka Ukr.
208 F5 Kivu, Lake Dem. Rep. Congo/Rwanda
209 C7 Kiwaba N'zogi Angola
175 I1 Kiwity Pol.
Kiyev Ukr. see Kyiv
121 G2 Kiyevka Kazakh.
Kiyevskaya Oblast' admin. div. Ukr. see Kyivs'ka Oblast'
139 K4 Kiyevskiy Rus. Fed.
Kiyevskoye Vodokhranilishche resr Ukr. see Kyyivs'ke Vodoskhovyshche
197 I5 Kıyıköy Turkey
121 F2 Kiyma Kazakh.
105 G3 Kiyosumi-yama hill Japan
105 E1 Kiyotsu-gawa r. Japan
134 L4 Kizel Rus. Fed.
134 I3 Kizema Rus. Fed.
134 F3 Kizhi, Ostrov i. Rus. Fed.
199 G2 Kızık Afyon Turkey
128 A1 Kızılalan Turkey
199 F3 Kızılcadağ Turkey
199 F3 Kızılca Dağ mt. Turkey
126 D2 Kızılcahamam Turkey
199 G2 Kızılcaören Turkey
199 F2 Kızılca-söğüt Turkey
129 C4 Kızılcaziyaret Dağı mt. Turkey
128 B1 Kızıldağ mt. Turkey
128 A1 Kızıldağ mt. Turkey
126 E3 Kızıl Dağı mt. Turkey
126 D2 Kızılırmak Turkey
126 D2 Kızılırmak r. Turkey
199 G3 Kızılkaya Turkey
199 G2 Kızılören Turkey
126 D3 Kızılören Turkey
120 D1 Kizil'skoye Rus. Fed.
127 F3 Kızıltepe Turkey
128 A1 Kızılyaka Turkey
199 F3 Kızılyaka Turkey
129 E2 Kizil"yurt Rus. Fed.
128 B1 Kızkalesi Turkey
129 E2 Kizlyar Respublika Dagestan Rus. Fed.
129 D2 Kizlyar Respublika Severnaya Osetiya Rus. Fed.
134 J4 Kizner Rus. Fed.
104 B4 Kizu-gawa r. Japan
Kizyl-Arbat Turkm. see Gyzylarbat
123 F2 Kizylayak Turkm.
142 C3 Kjellerup Denmark
140 N1 Kjøllefjord Norway
140 L1 Kjøpsvik Norway
214 D5 Klaarstroom S. Africa
164 D3 Klaaswaal Neth.
176 C2 Klabava r. Czech Rep.
143 E1 Klacken hill Sweden
177 H3 Kľačno Slovakia
188 G3 Kladanj Bos.-Herz.
170 C3 Kläden Ger.
176 D1 Kladno Czech Rep.
197 F3 Kladovo Srbija Yugo.
176 B2 Kladruby Czech Rep.
179 F4 Klagenfurt Austria
191 J2 Klagenfurt airport Austria
241 M4 Klagetoh AZ U.S.A.
138 C4 Klaipėda Lith.
175 I6 Kłaj Pol.
177 H3 Kľak mt. Slovakia
177 I2 Kľak mt. Slovakia
Klaksvig Faroe Is see Klaksvík
144 D1 Klaksvík Faroe Is
238 A3 Klamath CA U.S.A.
238 A3 Klamath r. CA U.S.A.
238 B3 Klamath Falls OR U.S.A.
238 B3 Klamath Mountains CA U.S.A.
191 J3 Klana Croatia
Klang Malaysia see Kelang
168 D1 Klanxbüll Ger.
222 D3 Klappan r. B.C. Can.
142 E2 Klarälven r. Sweden
140 L3 Klärke Sweden
177 H3 Klasov Slovakia
142 E2 Klässbol Sweden
176 C1 Klášterec nad Ohří Czech Rep.
95 E4 Klaten Jawa Tengah Indon.
176 C2 Klatovy Czech Rep.
179 F3 Klaus an der Pyhrnbahn Austria
171 E3 Klausdorf Brandenburg Ger.
170 E1 Klausdorf Mecklenburg-Vorpommern Ger.
168 F1 Klausdorf Schleswig-Holstein Ger.
172 A2 Klausen Ger.
179 H2 Klausen Leopoldsdorf Austria
136 F2 Klavdiyevo-Tarasove Ukr.
214 B4 Klawer S. Africa
220 E4 Klawock AK U.S.A.
164 F2 Klazienaveen Neth.
206 C5 Kle Liberia
179 E4 Kleblach-Lind Austria
234 C2 Klecknersville PA U.S.A.
174 F3 Kłecko Pol.
174 G3 Kleczew Pol.
222 E5 Kleena Kleene B.C. Can.
214 C3 Kleinbegin S. Africa
168 C3 Klein Berßen Ger.
172 B2 Kleinblittersdorf Ger.
170 E2 Klein Bünzow Ger.
247 □10 Klein Curaçao i. Neth. Antilles
214 B4 Klein Doring r. S. Africa
171 E4 Kleine Elster r. Ger.
140 J3 Kleinegga mt. Norway
173 G3 Kleine Laaber r. Ger.
173 F3 Kleine Paar r. Ger.
170 E1 Kleiner Jasmunder Bodden b. Ger.
178 C3 Kleiner Solstein mt. Austria
171 F4 Kleine Spree r. Ger.
173 G3 Kleine Vils r. Ger.
234 B2 Kleinfeltersville PA U.S.A.
172 D2 Kleinheubach Ger.
171 C4 Kleinjena Ger.
171 D3 Klein Kreutz Ger.
171 E3 Kleinmachnow Ger.
214 B6 Kleinmond S. Africa
168 E2 Klein Nordende Ger.
172 D1 Kleinostheim Ger.
171 C4 Kleinpaschleben Ger.
172 D2 Kleinrinderfeld Ger.
214 C5 Klein Roggeveldberge mts S. Africa
168 F2 Klein Rönnau Ger.
179 F4 Klein Sankt Paul Austria
214 A3 Kleinsee S. Africa
214 C5 Klein Swartberg mt. S. Africa
215 F3 Klein-Vet r. S. Africa
172 D2 Kleinwallstadt Ger.
171 C3 Klein Wanzleben Ger.
169 F3 Kleinwinnigstedt (Winnigstedt) Ger.
198 C3 Kleitoria Greece
175 L3 Klejniki Pol.
188 F3 Klekovača mt. Bos.-Herz.
136 E3 Klembivka Ukr.
222 D4 Klemtu B.C. Can.
176 B2 Klenčí pod Čerchovem Czech Rep.
174 D4 Klenica Pol.
177 I3 Klenovec Slovakia
176 G2 Klenovice na Hané Czech Rep.
177 I3 Klenovský Vepor mt. Slovakia
175 L2 Kleosin Pol.
175 L2 Klepacze Pol.
137 K2 Klepovka Rus. Fed.
142 A2 Kleppe Norway
142 A1 Kleppestø Norway
174 D3 Klępsk Pol.
215 F2 Klerksdorp S. Africa
215 F2 Klerkskraal S. Africa
136 D2 Klesiv Ukr.
175 L3 Kleszczele Pol.
174 F3 Kleszczewo Pol.
175 H4 Kleszczów Pol.
139 I5 Kletnya Rus. Fed.
Kletsk Belarus see Klyetsk
135 H6 Kletskaya Rus. Fed.
Kletskiy Rus. Fed. see Kletskaya
171 E4 Klettwitz Ger.
136 C2 Klevan' Ukr.
169 B4 Kleve Ger.
137 G2 Kleven' r. Rus. Fed.
138 G5 Klichaw Belarus
107 H1 Klichka Rus. Fed.
171 D4 Klieken Ger.
215 E5 Klienpoort S. Africa
170 D3 Klietz Ger.
139 H5 Klimavichy Belarus
197 H4 Kliment Bulg.
177 H2 Klimkovice Czech Rep.
134 J4 Klimkovka Rus. Fed.
175 I5 Klimontów Pol.
175 J5 Klimontów Pol.
Klimovichi Belarus see Klimavichy
135 F5 Klimovo Rus. Fed.
139 K4 Klimovsk Rus. Fed.
140 K2 Klimpfjäll Sweden
139 K3 Klin Rus. Fed.
177 I2 Klin Slovakia
196 E4 Klina Kosovo, Srbija Yugo.
222 E5 Klinaklini r. B.C. Can.
92 C5 Kling Phil.
171 E5 Klingenberg Ger.
172 D2 Klingenberg am Main Ger.
171 D5 Klingenthal Ger.
234 B2 Klingerstown PA U.S.A.
95 E2 Klingkang, Banjaran mts Indon./Malaysia
170 D2 Klink Ger.
176 C1 Klínovec mt. Czech Rep.
139 K3 Klinsko-Dmitrovskaya Gryada ridge Rus. Fed.
143 H3 Klintehamn Gotland Sweden
120 B2 Klintsovka Rus. Fed.
139 I5 Klintsy Rus. Fed.
215 G2 Klip r. S. Africa
214 B6 Klipdale S. Africa
215 E5 Klipfontein S. Africa
168 E1 Kliplev Denmark
142 E3 Klippan Sweden
214 E5 Klipplaat S. Africa
214 B4 Kliprand S. Africa
215 H1 Klipskool S. Africa
188 F4 Klis Croatia
197 F4 Klisura Srbija Yugo.
142 C3 Klitmøller Denmark
Klitória Greece see Kleitoria
171 F4 Klitten Ger.
168 D1 Klixbüll Ger.
177 I6 Kljajićevo Vojvodina, Srbija Yugo.
188 F3 Ključ Bos.-Herz.
176 F3 Klobouky Czech Rep.
174 G5 Kłobuck Pol.
179 G4 Klöch Austria
175 J4 Kłoczew Pol.
170 G3 Kłodawa Pol.
174 G3 Kłodawa Pol.
174 E5 Kłodzko Pol.
142 D1 Kløfta Norway
175 H5 Kłomnice Pol.
174 G4 Klonowa Pol.
138 E2 Klooga Estonia
164 F2 Kloosterhaar Neth.
165 D3 Kloosterzande Neth.
177 J3 Kloptaň mt. Slovakia
179 H5 Kloštar Ivanić Croatia
176 G6 Kloštar Podravski Croatia
170 E3 Klosterfelde Ger.
171 C4 Klosterhäseler Ger.
173 E3 Klosterlechfeld Ger.
171 C4 Klostermansfeld Ger.
179 H2 Klosterneuburg Austria
190 E2 Klosters Switz.
171 F4 Klosterwasser r. Ger.
171 E3 Kloster Zinna Ger.
172 C4 Kloten Switz.
169 C5 Klotten Ger.
170 C3 Klötze (Altmark) Ger.
222 B2 Kluane r. Y.T. Can.
Kluang Malaysia see Keluang
174 G5 Kluczbork Pol.
175 H5 Kluczewsko Pol.
Klukhori Rus. Fed. see Karachayevsk
175 H4 Kluki Pol.
175 K3 Klukowo Pol.
220 E4 Klukwan AK U.S.A.
164 D3 Klundert Neth.
95 F5 Klungkung Bali Indon.
123 G5 Klupro Pak.
168 C3 Kluse Ger.
175 K2 Klusy Pol.
170 C2 Klütz Ger.
175 I4 Klwów Pol.
138 G5 Klyava r. Belarus
135 K5 Klyavlino Rus. Fed.
139 M3 Klyaz'ma r. Rus. Fed.
138 F5 Klyetsk Belarus
137 H3 Klymivka Ukr.
137 G2 Klyshky Ukr.
131 R4 Klyuchevskaya, Sopka vol. Rus. Fed.
121 I1 Klyuchi Altayskiy Kray Rus. Fed.
131 R4 Klyuchi Kamchatskaya Oblast' Rus. Fed.
78 □6 Kmagha Sta Isabel Solomon Is
215 F4 Knapdaar S. Africa
81 B7 Knapdale South I. N.Z.
146 C6 Knapdale reg. Scotland U.K.
226 B3 Knapp Mound hill WI U.S.A.
142 E3 Knäred Sweden
149 H3 Knaresborough North Yorkshire, England U.K.
143 F1 Knästen hill Sweden
149 H3 Knayton North Yorkshire, England U.K.
151 G3 Knebworth Hertfordshire, England U.K.
168 F3 Knesebeck Ger.
165 C3 Knesselare Belgium
169 F6 Knetzgau Ger.
188 G3 Kneževi Vinogradi Croatia
177 H6 Kneževo Croatia
197 G4 Knezha Bulg.
171 G5 Kněžmost Czech Rep.
196 E4 Knić Srbija Yugo.
236 C2 Knife r. ND U.S.A.
226 B2 Knife River MN U.S.A.
150 D2 Knighton Powys, Wales U.K.
240 G2 Knights Landing CA U.S.A.
188 F3 Knin Croatia
143 F3 Knislinge Sweden
179 F3 Knittelfeld Austria
172 C2 Knittlingen Ger.
143 G2 Knivsta Sweden
176 D3 Knížecí stolec mt. Czech Rep.
197 G5 Knizhovnik Bulg.
197 F4 Knjaževac Srbija Yugo.
87 B6 Knobby Head hd W.A. Austr.
Knob Lake Nfld. Can. see Schefferville
86 F2 Knob Peak hill W.A. Austr.
147 B4 Knock Clare Rep. of Ireland
147 C3 Knock Mayo Rep. of Ireland
146 C5 Knock Argyll and Bute, Scotland U.K.
147 B5 Knockaboy hill Rep. of Ireland
147 B4 Knockacummer hill Rep. of Ireland
147 C2 Knockalongy hill Rep. of Ireland
147 B4 Knockalough Rep. of Ireland
148 C5 Knockananna Rep. of Ireland
148 C5 Knockanarrigan Rep. of Ireland
146 E4 Knockandhu Moray, Scotland U.K.
147 B4 Knockanefune hill Rep. of Ireland
146 D4 Knockban Highland, Scotland U.K.
147 E4 Knockbrandon Rep. of Ireland
147 E3 Knockbridge Rep. of Ireland
147 D4 Knockbrit Rep. of Ireland
147 C3 Knockcroghery Rep. of Ireland
146 F4 Knock Hill hill Scotland U.K.
147 C3 Knock International airport Rep. of Ireland
147 E1 Knocklayd hill Northern Ireland U.K.
147 C4 Knocklong Rep. of Ireland
147 C4 Knockmealdown Mountains hills Rep. of Ireland
147 B2 Knockmore Rep. of Ireland
147 C3 Knockmoyle Rep. of Ireland
147 B4 Knocknaboul Rep. of Ireland
148 C2 Knocknacarry Northern Ireland U.K.
147 B4 Knocknagree Rep. of Ireland
147 C4 Knocknaskagh hill Rep. of Ireland
147 C5 Knockraha Rep. of Ireland
147 C5 Knocks Rep. of Ireland
165 C3 Knokke-Heist Belgium
170 E2 Knorrendorf Ger.
198 D4 Knosos tourist site Greece
Knossós tourist site Greece see Knosos
149 H4 Knottingley West Yorkshire, England U.K.
151 F2 Knowle West Midlands, England U.K.
262 T2 Knowles, Cape Antarctica
233 □I1 Knowles Corner ME U.S.A.
233 G2 Knowlton Que. Can.
230 C3 Knox IN U.S.A.
232 D4 Knox PA U.S.A.
Knox Atoll Kiribati see Tarawa
226 A5 Knox City MO U.S.A.
263 G2 Knox Coast Antarctica
231 D5 Knoxville GA U.S.A.
236 E3 Knoxville IA U.S.A.
231 D5 Knoxville TN U.S.A.
146 C4 Knoydart mts Scotland U.K.
150 D2 Knucklas Powys, Wales U.K.
221 L2 Knud Rasmussen Land reg. Greenland
169 E4 Knüllwald-Remsfeld Ger.
174 G5 Knurów Pol.
149 G4 Knutsford Cheshire, England U.K.
134 I5 Knyaginino Rus. Fed.
138 F4 Knyahinin Belarus
137 G4 Knyaze-Hryhorivka Ukr.
175 M5 Knyazhe Ukr.
214 D6 Knysna S. Africa
175 K2 Knyszyn Pol.
100 F3 Ko, Gora mt. Rus. Fed.
208 F2 Koalib, Jebel mt. Sudan
211 C6 Koani Tanz.
Koartac Que. Can. see Quaqtaq

94 D3 Koba Indon.
179 E4 Kobarid Slovenia
103 E8 Kobayashi Japan
104 B4 Kōbe Japan
137 H3 Kobelyaky Ukr.
142 E4 København Denmark
142 E4 København mun. Denmark
206 C3 Kobenni Maur.
179 F3 Kobenz Austria
179 H3 Kobersdorf Austria
175 H4 Kobiele Wielkie Pol.
174 E5 Kobierzyce Pol.
174 G5 Kobiór Pol.
102 □1 Kōbi-sho i. Japan
169 C5 Koblenz Ger.
169 C5 Koblenz admin. reg. Rheinland-Pfalz Ger.
137 F4 Kobleve Ukr.
210 C1 K'obo Eth.
210 A4 Koboko Uganda
139 K2 Kobozha r. Rus. Fed.
134 J4 Kobra Rus. Fed.
Kobrin Belarus see Kobryn
91 H8 Kobroör i. Indon.
170 C2 Kobrow Ger.
136 C1 Kobryn Belarus
129 B3 K'obulet'i Georgia
105 E3 Kobushiga-take mt. Japan
131 N3 Kobyay Rus. Fed.
174 F4 Kobyla Góra Pol.
174 C2 Kobylanka Pol.
136 C3 Kobylets'ka Polyana Ukr.
176 F3 Kobylí Czech Rep.
174 F4 Kobylin Pol.
175 K2 Kobylin-Borzymy Pol.
175 J3 Kobyłka Pol.
174 F1 Kobylnica Pol.
175 I3 Kobylniki Pol.
199 F1 Kocaafşar r. Turkey
199 G1 Kocaali Turkey
199 G3 Kocaaliler Turkey
199 E2 Kocaavşar Turkey
199 F3 Kocabaş Denizli Turkey
199 F2 Koca Dağ mt. Turkey
199 F1 Kocaeli Turkey
199 F1 Kocaeli prov. Turkey
199 F1 Kocaeli Yarımadası pen. Turkey
129 C3 Kocaköy Turkey
197 F5 Kočani Macedonia
129 C4 Kocapınar Turkey
199 E3 Koçarlı Turkey
129 C4 Kocasu r. Turkey
199 F1 Kocasu r. Turkey
128 C1 Kocatepe Turkey
129 C4 Koçbaşı Tepe mt. Turkey
196 D3 Koceljevo Srbija Yugo.
188 E3 Kočevje Slovenia
101 C6 Koch'ang S. Korea
174 G5 Kochanowice Pol.
117 G4 Koch Bihar W. Bengal India
173 F4 Kochel am See Ger.
173 F4 Kochelsee l. Ger.
172 D2 Kocher r. Ger.
137 H3 Kocherezhky Ukr.
197 F4 Kocherinovo Bulg.
136 E2 Kocheriv Ukr.
137 I2 Kochetovka Rus. Fed.
134 K4 Kochevo Rus. Fed.
Kochi Kerala India see Cochin
103 F7 Kōchi Japan
103 F7 Kōchi pref. Japan
Koçhisar Turkey see Kızıltepe
120 E1 Kochkar' Rus. Fed.
121 H4 Kochkor Kyrg.
Kochkorka Kyrg. see Kochkor
135 I5 Kochkurovo Rus. Fed.
129 E1 Kochubey Rus. Fed.
129 B1 Kochubeyevskoye Rus. Fed.
198 D2 Kochylas hill Sterea Ellas Greece
175 K4 Kock Pol.
129 D3 Koçkıran Turkey
129 C3 Koçköyü Turkey
170 C3 Köckte Ger.
177 G3 Kočovce Slovakia
177 H4 Kocs Hungary
177 I4 Kocsér Hungary
177 H5 Kocsola Hungary
174 F2 Koczała Pol.
114 B3 Kod Karnataka India
114 C4 Kodaikanal Tamil Nadu India
105 F3 Kodaira Japan
102 □1 Kodakara-jima i. Japan
136 F2 Kodaky Ukr.
115 E2 Kodala Orissa India
117 F4 Kodarma Bihar India
175 L4 Kodeń Pol.
137 J2 Kodentsovo Rus. Fed.
171 F4 Kodersdorf Ger.
220 C4 Kodiak AK U.S.A.
220 C4 Kodiak Island AK U.S.A.
116 B5 Kodinar Gujarat India
134 G3 Kodino Rus. Fed.
138 C1 Kodisjoki Fin.
171 C5 Köditz Ger.
114 C4 Kodiyakkarai Tamil Nadu India
176 G4 Kodó r. Hungary
102 J3 Kodomari Japan
129 B2 Kodori r. Georgia
129 B2 Kodoris K'edi hills Georgia
136 E2 Kodra Ukr.
175 H4 Kodrąb Pol.
114 C3 Kodumuru Andhra Prad. India
136 E3 Kodyma Ukr.
136 F3 Kodyma r. Ukr.
197 G5 Kodzhaele mt. Bulg./Greece
Kodzhori Georgia see Kojori
214 D3 Koegas S. Africa
214 C3 Koegrabie S. Africa
164 F2 Koekange Neth.
165 B3 Koekelare Belgium
214 B4 Koekenaap S. Africa
212 C5 Koës Namibia
165 C3 Koewacht Neth.
241 K5 Kofa Mountains AZ U.S.A.
123 G2 Kofarnihon Tajik.
123 G2 Kofarnihon r. Tajik.
197 H5 Kofçaz Turkey
173 G3 Köfering Ger.
215 E3 Koffiefontein S. Africa
198 D4 Kofinas, Oros mt. Kriti Greece
179 G3 Köflach Austria
206 E5 Koforidua Ghana
105 E3 Kōfu Japan
105 F2 Koga Japan
197 I3 Kogălniceanu airport Romania
224 E1 Kogaluc r. Que. Can.
225 I1 Kogaluk r. Nfld. Can.
85 G5 Kogan Qld Austr.
105 F3 Koganei Japan
142 E4 Køge Denmark
142 E4 Køge Bugt b. Denmark
134 L3 Kogel' r. Rus. Fed.
207 G4 Kogi state Nigeria
Kogon Uzbek. see Kagan
123 G3 Kohat Pak.
138 E2 Kohila Estonia
117 H4 Kohima Nagaland India
78 □6 Kohinggo i. New Georgia Is Solomon Is
122 B4 Kohkīlūyeh va Būyer Aḥmadī prov. Iran
173 G2 Kohlberg Ger.
168 D2 Köhlen Ger.
262 Q2 Kohler Range mts Antarctica
241 L4 Kohls Ranch AZ U.S.A.
138 F2 Kohtla-Järve Estonia
80 E2 Kohukohunui hill North I. N.Z.
81 C6 Kohurau mt. South I. N.Z.
136 E5 Kohyl'nyk r. Ukr.
222 A2 Koidern Y.T. Can.
222 A2 Koidern Mountain Y.T. Can.
Koidu Sierra Leone see Sefadu
214 A4 Koiingnaas S. Africa
114 C2 Koilkonda Andhra Prad. India
114 C3 Koilkuntla Andhra Prad. India
217 □3a Koimbani Njazidja Comoros
134 J3 Koin r. Rus. Fed.
127 G3 Koi Sanjaq Iraq
140 O3 Koitere l. Fin.
105 F3 Koito-gawa r. Japan
101 D6 Kŏje-do i. S. Korea
176 G2 Kojetín Czech Rep.
87 C7 Kojonup W.A. Austr.
129 D3 Kojori Georgia
96 C2 Kok r. Thai.
177 I4 Kóka Hungary
233 □I2 Kokadjo ME U.S.A.
105 G3 Kokai-gawa r. Japan
120 F2 Kokalaat Kazakh.
121 G4 Kokand Uzbek.
Kokankishlak Uzbek. see Pakhtaabad
141 M4 Kökar Åland Fin.
138 C2 Kökarsfjärden b. Fin.
81 C5 Kokatahi South I. N.Z.
177 I3 Kokava nad Rimavicou Slovakia
123 G2 Kokcha r. Afgh.
Kokchetav Kazakh. see Kokshetau
141 M3 Kokemäki Fin.
138 G4 Kokhanava Belarus
139 M3 Kokhma Rus. Fed.
206 B3 Koki Senegal
121 H4 Kök-Janggak Kyrg.
140 M3 Kokkola Fin.
138 E3 Koknese Latvia
207 G4 Koko Nigeria
206 C3 Kokofata Mali
206 D5 Kokolo-Pozo Côte d'Ivoire
230 C3 Kokomo IN U.S.A.
139 J5 Kokorevka Rus. Fed.
139 K4 Kokoshkino Rus. Fed.
215 F2 Kokosi S. Africa
206 B4 Kokou mt. Guinea
121 J2 Kokpekti Kazakh.
179 F4 Kokra r. Slovenia
179 F4 Kokrica Slovenia
101 C5 Koksan N. Korea
121 G4 Koksaray Kazakh.
Kokshaal-Tau, Khrebet mts China/Kyrg. see Kakshaal-Too
134 I4 Koksharka Rus. Fed.
121 G1 Kokshetau Kazakh.
165 B3 Koksijde Belgium
225 G1 Koksoak r. Que. Can.
215 G4 Kokstad S. Africa
121 I3 Koksu Almatinskaya Oblast' Kazakh.
121 G4 Koksu Yuzhnyy Kazakhstan Kazakh.
121 I3 Koktal Kazakh.
121 H4 Kök-Tash Kyrg.
121 I3 Kokterek Kazakh.
Koktokay Xinjiang China see Fuyun
103 E8 Kokubu Japan
105 E3 Kokushiga-take mt. Japan
Kok-Yangak Kyrg. see Kök-Janggak
121 J2 Kokzhayyk Kazakh.
140 P1 Kola Rus. Fed.
140 P1 Kola r. Rus. Fed.
Kolab r. India see Sabari
117 F5 Kolabira Orissa India
123 F5 Kolachi r. Pak.
175 H4 Kołacin Pol.
175 L4 Kołacze Pol.
174 F3 Kołaczkowo Pol.
175 J6 Kołaczyce Pol.
117 F5 Kolaghat W. Bengal India
116 C2 Kolahoi mt. Jammu and Kashmir
206 C4 Kolahun Liberia
93 B4 Kolaka Sulawesi Tenggara Indon.
175 K2 Kołaki Kościelne Pol.
92 B4 Kolambugan Phil.
97 B6 Ko Lanta Thai.
Kola Peninsula Rus. Fed. see Kol'skiy Poluostrov
114 C3 Kolar Karnataka India
114 D2 Kolar Madh. Prad. India
116 D4 Kolaras Madh. Prad. India
114 C3 Kolar Gold Fields Karnataka India
140 M2 Kolari Fin.
Kolarovgrad Bulg. see Shumen
177 G4 Kolárovo Slovakia
140 K3 Kolåsen Sweden
196 D4 Kolašin Crna Gora Yugo.
116 C4 Kolayat Rajasthan India
143 G2 Kolbäck Sweden
170 F2 Kołbacz Pol.
174 C2 Kołbaskowo Pol.
Kolberg Pol. see Kołobrzeg
173 G4 Kolbermoor Ger.
175 J3 Kołbiel Pol.
142 D2 Kolbotn Norway
174 G1 Kolbudy Górne Pol.
175 J5 Kolbuszowa Pol.
139 L3 Kol'chugino Rus. Fed.
137 G5 Kol'chuhyne Ukr.
136 B3 Kol'chyne Ukr.
177 L3 Kölcse Hungary
174 F1 Kołczygłowy Pol.
206 B3 Kolda Senegal
199 E2 Koldere Turkey
142 C4 Kolding Denmark
240 □C8 Kolekole mt. HI U.S.A.
100 G1 Kolendo Sakhalin Rus. Fed.
140 M2 Koler Sweden
177 H5 Kölesd Hungary
134 J1 Kolguyev, Ostrov i. Rus. Fed.
117 F5 Kolhan reg. Bihar India
114 B2 Kolhapur Mahar. India
141 N3 Kolho Fin.
113 D11 Kolhumadulu Atoll Maldives
206 B3 Koliba r. Guinea/Guinea-Bissau
Kolikata W. Bengal India see Calcutta
140 N3 Kolima l. Fin.
176 E1 Kolín Czech Rep.
176 C2 Kolinec Czech Rep.
210 C3 K'olīto Eth.
173 E2 Kolitzheim Ger.
Kolkata W. Bengal India see Calcutta
177 H6 Kölked Hungary
Kolkhozabad Khatlon Tajik. see Kolkhozobod
123 G2 Kolkhozobod Tajik.
171 F4 Kolkwitz Ger.
136 C2 Kolky Ukr.
Kollam Kerala India see Quilon
173 H3 Kollbach r. Ger.
171 C4 Kölleda Ger.
114 C3 Kollegal Karnataka India
173 G2 Kollnburg Ger.
168 E2 Kölln-Reisiek Ger.
207 F3 Kollo Niger
164 F1 Kollum Neth.
168 E1 Kollund Denmark
169 B5 Köln Ger.
169 B5 Köln admin. reg. Nordrhein-Westfalen Ger.
169 C5 Köln-Bonn airport Ger.
175 L2 Kolnica Pol.
175 J2 Kolno Podlaskie Pol.
175 I2 Kolno Warmińsko-Mazurskie Pol.
209 B6 Kolo Dem. Rep. Congo
174 G3 Koło Pol.
211 B6 Kolo Tanz.
240 □B8 Koloa HI U.S.A.
139 M3 Kolobovo Rus. Fed.
143 F4 Kołobrzeg Pol.
171 E4 Kolochau Ger.
136 B3 Kolochava Ukr.
139 K2 Kolodenskoye, Ozero l. Rus. Fed.
137 J2 Kolodeznyy Rus. Fed.
136 C3 Kolodne Ukr.
134 I4 Kologriv Rus. Fed.
206 C3 Kolokani Mali
139 M3 Koloksha r. Rus. Fed.
137 H3 Kolomak Ukr.
137 H3 Kolomak r. Ukr.
78 □6 Kolombangara i. New Georgia Is Solomon Is
Kolomea Ukr. see Kolomyya
139 L4 Kolomna Rus. Fed.
Kołomyja Ukr. see Kolomyya
136 C3 Kolomyya Ukr.
206 D4 Kolondiéba Mali
93 B3 Kolonedale Sulawesi Tengah Indon.
78 □4b Kolonia Pohnpei Micronesia
196 D5 Kolonjë Albania
174 G5 Kolonowskie Pol.
137 H3 Kolontayiv Ukr.
139 J1 Koloshma r. Rus. Fed.
140 P1 Kolozero, Ozero l. Rus. Fed.
Kolozsvár Romania see Cluj-Napoca
139 K2 Kolp' r. Rus. Fed.
139 M4 Kolp' r. Rus. Fed.
130 J4 Kolpashevo Rus. Fed.
139 H2 Kolpino Rus. Fed.
135 G5 Kolpny Rus. Fed.
178 C3 Kolsass Austria
121 J4 Kol'shat Kazakh.
139 M3 Kolshevo Rus. Fed.
134 F2 Kol'skiy Poluostrov pen. Rus. Fed.
174 D4 Kolsko Pol.
143 F2 Kolsva Sweden
141 K3 Kölsvallen Sweden
177 H3 Kolta Slovakia
120 B1 Koltubanovskiy Rus. Fed.
196 E3 Kolubara r. Yugo.
Kölük Turkey see Kahta
203 I6 Koluli Eritrea
175 H4 Koluszki Pol.
121 G2 Koluton Kazakh.
134 L2 Kolva r. Rus. Fed.
134 L3 Kolva r. Rus. Fed.
140 J2 Kolvereid Norway
134 F2 Kolvitskoye, Ozero l. Rus. Fed.
209 E7 Kolwezi Dem. Rep. Congo
114 B2 Kolya r. India
139 L5 Kolybel'skoye Rus. Fed.
131 R3 Kolyma r. Rus. Fed.
Kolyma Lowland Rus. Fed. see Kolymskaya Nizmennost'
Kolyma Range mts Rus. Fed. see Kolymskiy, Khrebet
131 Q3 Kolymskaya Nizmennost' lowland Rus. Fed.
131 R3 Kolymskiy, Khrebet mts Rus. Fed.
131 P3 Kolymskoye Vodokhranilische resr Rus. Fed.
135 I5 Kolyshley Rus. Fed.
131 T3 Kolyuchinskaya Guba b. Rus. Fed.
121 J2 Kolyvan' Rus. Fed.
197 F4 Kom mt. Bulg.
177 K4 Komádi Hungary
105 F3 Komae Japan
105 D3 Komaga-dake mt. Japan
105 D3 Komagane Japan
105 F1 Komaga-take mt. Japan
102 J2 Komaga-take vol. Japan
214 A3 Komaggas S. Africa
214 A3 Komaggas Mountains S. Africa
104 C3 Komaki Japan
175 K6 Komańcza Pol.
100 F2 Komandnaya, Gora mt. Rus. Fed.
131 R4 Komandorskiye Ostrova is Rus. Fed.
139 J5 Komarichi Rus. Fed.
196 D4 Komarnica r. Yugo.
177 H4 Komárno Slovakia
136 B3 Komarno Ukr.
177 H4 Komárom Hungary
177 H4 Komárom-Esztergom county Hungary
176 C2 Komárov Czech Rep.
136 C2 Komarove Ukr.
138 G1 Komarovo Rus. Fed.
175 K4 Komarówka Podlaska Pol.
175 L5 Komarów Osada Pol.
215 H1 Komati r. Swaziland
215 H1 Komatipoort S. Africa
104 C2 Komatsu Japan
104 A4 Komatsushima Japan
212 C3 Kombat Namibia
206 E3 Kombissiri Burkina
Kombótion Greece see Kompoti
94 D3 Komering r. Indon.
215 F5 Komga S. Africa
134 J3 Komi, Respublika aut. rep. Rus. Fed.
Komi A.S.S.R. aut. rep. Rus. Fed. see Komi, Respublika
179 H4 Komin Croatia
Komintern Ukr. see Marhanets'
136 F4 Kominternivs'ke Ukr.
Komi-Permyak Autonomous Okrug admin. div. Rus. Fed. see Komi-Permyatskiy Avtonomnyy Okrug
134 K3 Komi-Permyatskiy Avtonomnyy Okrug admin. div. Rus. Fed.
188 F4 Komiža Croatia
177 H3 Komjatice Slovakia
177 I2 Komjatná Slovakia
214 B4 Komkans S. Africa
177 H5 Komló Baranya Hungary
177 J4 Kömlő Heves Hungary
214 D5 Kommandokraal S. Africa
214 B6 Kommetjie S. Africa
215 F3 Kommissiepoort S. Africa
Kommuna Turkm. see Babadaykhan
134 H4 Kommunar Kostromskaya Oblast' Rus. Fed.
139 H2 Kommunar Leningradskaya Oblast' Rus. Fed.
139 M3 Kommunar Vladimirskaya Oblast' Rus. Fed.
Kommunarsk Ukr. see Alchevs'k
Kommunizm, Qullai mt. Tajik. see Garmo, Qullai
Kommunizma, Pik mt. Tajik. see Garmo, Qullai
93 A5 Komodo i. Indon.
206 C4 Komodou Guinea
206 E5 Komoé r. Côte d'Ivoire
203 G3 Kôm Ombo Egypt
209 B5 Komono Congo
91 I8 Komoran i. Indon.
174 E3 Komorniki Pol.
177 L3 Komoró Hungary
105 E2 Komoro Japan
175 J3 Komorowo Pol.
174 G4 Komorzno Pol.
199 D1 Komotini Greece
137 G3 Kompaniyivka Ukr.
177 I5 Kömpöc Hungary
Kompong Cham Cambodia see Kâmpóng Cham
Kompong Chhnang Cambodia see Kâmpóng Chhnăng
Kompong Kleang Cambodia see Kâmpóng Khleăng
Kompong Som Cambodia see Sihanoukville
Kompong Speu Cambodia see Kâmpóng Spoe
Kompong Thom Cambodia see Kâmpóng Thum
198 B2 Kompoti Greece
174 F5 Komprachcice Pol.
Komrat Moldova see Comrat
214 C5 Komsberg mt. S. Africa
214 C5 Komsberg mts S. Africa
Komsomol Kazakh. see Komsomolets
Komsomol Turkm. see Komsomol'sk
120 E1 Komsomolets Kazakh.
131 K1 Komsomolets, Ostrov i. Severnaya Zemlya Rus. Fed.
139 M3 Komsomol'sk Rus. Fed.
123 E2 Komsomol'sk Turkm.
137 G3 Komsomol's'k Ukr.
137 J4 Komsomol's'ke Ukr.
137 I3 Komsomol's'ke Ukr.
131 S3 Komsomol'skiy Rus. Fed.
Komsomol'skiy Rus. Fed. see Yugorsk
129 E2 Komsomol'skiy Rus. Fed.
135 I7 Komsomol'skiy Rus. Fed.
135 I5 Komsomol'skiy Respublika Mordoviya Rus. Fed.
100 F2 Komsomol'sk-na-Amure Rus. Fed.
120 E2 Komsomol'skoye Kazakh.
197 G5 Komuniga Bulg.
128 C1 Kömürçukuru Turkey
127 F2 Kömürlü Turkey
137 G4 Komyshany Ukr.
137 J3 Komyshna r. Rus. Fed./Ukr.
137 G2 Komyshnya Ukr.
137 H4 Komyshuvakha Ukr.
137 F3 Komyshuvate Ukr.
137 I4 Komysh-Zorya Ukr.
117 E4 Kon Uttar Prad. India
128 B1 Konacık Turkey
115 D2 Konada Andhra Prad. India
129 C4 Konakkuran Turkey
139 K3 Konakovo Rus. Fed.
104 C3 Kōnan Japan
123 G3 Konar prov. Afgh.
Konarak Orissa India see Konarka
115 E2 Konarka Orissa India
175 K2 Konarzyce Pol.
174 F2 Konarzyny Pol.
116 D4 Konch Uttar Prad. India
139 J2 Konchanskoye-Suvorovskoye Rus. Fed.
134 F3 Konchezero Rus. Fed.
136 C1 Konchytsy Belarus
114 D2 Kondagaon Madh. Prad. India
129 E4 Köndälänçay r. Azer.
114 D2 Kondapalle Andhra Prad. India
114 D2 Kondavid Andhra Prad. India
87 C7 Kondinin W.A. Austr.
Kondinskoye Khanty-Mansiyskiy Avtonomnyy Okrug Rus. Fed. see Oktyabr'skoye
130 H3 Kondinskoye Khanty-Mansiyskiy Avtonomnyy Okrug Rus. Fed.
211 B6 Kondoa Tanz.
135 I5 Kondol' Rus. Fed.
129 D3 Kondoli Georgia
134 F3 Kondopoga Rus. Fed.
177 J5 Kondoros Hungary
174 E5 Kondratowice Pol.
139 J4 Kondrovo Rus. Fed.
123 G2 Kondūz Afgh.
123 G2 Kondūz prov. Afgh.
78 □5 Koné New Caledonia
197 F5 Konečka Planina mts Macedonia
Köneürgench Turkm. see Keneurgench
206 D4 Kong Côte d'Ivoire
97 C5 Kŏng, Kaôh i. Cambodia
97 D4 Kông, Tônlé r. Cambodia
96 D4 Kong, Xé r. Laos
221 O3 Kong Christian IX Land reg. Greenland
221 P2 Kong Christian X Land reg. Greenland
142 C4 Kongeå r. Denmark
Kongelab atoll Marshall Is see Rongelap
142 E4 Kongens Lyngby Denmark
221 M3 Kong Frederik IX Land reg. Greenland
221 P2 Kong Frederik VIII Land reg. Greenland
221 N3 Kong Frederik VI Kyst coastal area Greenland
140 □ Kong Karls Land is Svalbard
95 G2 Kong Kat hill Indon.
95 G2 Kongkemul mt. Indon.
104 D2 Kongōdo-san mt. Japan
209 E6 Kongolo Dem. Rep. Congo
221 P2 Kong Oscars Fjord inlet Greenland
206 E3 Kongoussi Burkina
142 C2 Kongsberg Norway
140 □ Kongsøya i. Svalbard
142 E1 Kongsvinger Norway
110 A4 Kongur Shan mt. Xinjiang China
211 C6 Kongwa Tanz.
221 P2 Kong Wilhelm Land reg. Greenland
Konibodom Tajik. see Kanibadam
176 F2 Konice Czech Rep.
175 H5 Koniecpol Pol.
172 D2 Königheim Ger.
Königsberg Rus. Fed. see Kaliningrad
169 F5 Königsberg in Bayern Ger.
171 C3 Königsborn Ger.
173 E3 Königsbronn Ger.
171 E4 Königsbrück Ger.
173 E3 Königsbrunn Ger.
173 F4 Königsdorf Ger.
171 C5 Königsee Ger.
173 F2 Königsfeld Ger.
172 C3 Königsfeld im Schwarzwald Ger.
171 E3 Königsgraben r. Ger.
171 F4 Königshain Ger.
171 C4 Königshofen Ger.
Königshütte Pol. see Chorzów
169 F3 Königslutter am Elm Ger.
173 F3 Königsmoos Ger.
173 G4 Königssee Ger.
173 F2 Königstein Ger.
171 F5 Königstein Ger.
172 C2 Königstuhl hill Ger.
171 E5 Königswalde Ger.
171 F4 Königswartha Ger.
179 F2 Königswiesen Austria
169 C5 Königswinter Ger.
171 E3 Königs Wusterhausen Ger.
Konimekh Uzbek. see Kanimekh
174 G3 Konin Pol.
100 F1 Konin r. Rus. Fed.
198 B1 Konitsa Greece
171 C5 Könitz Ger.
190 C2 Köniz Switz.
188 F4 Konj mt. Bos.-Herz.
188 F4 Konjic Bos.-Herz.
188 G3 Konjuh mts Bos.-Herz.
140 M1 Könkämäeno r. Fin./Sweden
139 L5 Kon'-Kolodez' Rus. Fed.
206 E3 Konna Mali
232 C6 Konnarock VA U.S.A.
171 C4 Könnern Ger.
171 D5 Konnersreuth Ger.
140 N3 Konnevesi Fin.
137 F3 Kononcha Ukr.
206 E5 Konongo Ghana
137 G2 Kononivka Ukr.
177 I1 Konopiska Pol.
175 I2 Konopki Pol.
136 F4 Konoplyane Ukr.
134 H3 Konosha Rus. Fed.
105 F2 Kōnosu Japan
137 G2 Konotop Ukr.
110 E3 Konqi He r. China
171 C5 Konradsreuth Ger.
175 I4 Końskie Pol.
167 K3 Końskowola Pol.
210 C3 Konso Eth.
175 J3 Konstancin-Jeziorna Pol.
Konstantinograd Ukr. see Krasnohrad
100 C2 Konstantinovka Rus. Fed.
Konstantinovka Donets'ka Oblast' Ukr. see Kostyantynivka
Konstantinovka Kharkivs'ka Oblast' Ukr. see Kostyantynivka
Konstantinovka Khersons'ka Oblast' Ukr. see Kostyantynivka
Konstantinovka Zaporiz'ka Oblast' Ukr. see Kostyantynivka
139 L3 Konstantinovo Rus. Fed.
135 H7 Konstantinovsk Rus. Fed.
139 L3 Konstantinovskiy Rus. Fed.
176 B2 Konstantinovy Lázně Czech Rep.
175 L3 Konstantynów Pol.
175 H4 Konstantynów Łódzki Pol.
172 D4 Konstanz Ger.
207 G4 Kontagora Nigeria
140 O3 Kontiolahti Fin.
140 O2 Kontiomäki Fin.
97 D4 Kon Tum Vietnam
97 E4 Kontum, Plateau du Vietnam
Könugard Ukr. see Kyiv
199 G1 Konuralp Bolu Turkey
126 D3 Konya Turkey
177 K4 Konyár Hungary
121 H3 Konyrat Karagandinskaya Oblast' Kazakh.
121 I3 Konyrolen Kazakh.
137 H2 Konyshevka Rus. Fed.
120 C2 Konystanu Kazakh.
121 G1 Konyukhovo Kazakh.
172 A2 Konz Ger.
173 G2 Konzell Ger.
134 L4 Konzhakovskiy Kamen', Gora mt. Rus. Fed.
87 D6 Kookynie W.A. Austr.
86 D2 Koolan Island W.A. Austr.
87 C4 Kooline W.A. Austr.
84 D5 Koolivoo, Lake salt flat Qld Austr.
82 D2 Koolkootinnie, Lake salt flat S.A. Austr.
82 D3 Koolunga S.A. Austr.
87 C6 Koolyanobbing W.A. Austr.
83 F3 Koondrook Vic. Austr.
82 C2 Koonibba S.A. Austr.
214 C2 Koopan-Suid S. Africa
83 G3 Koorawatha N.S.W. Austr.
87 C6 Koorda W.A. Austr.
86 B4 Koordarrie W.A. Austr.
241 L2 Koosharem UT U.S.A.
238 C2 Kooskia ID U.S.A.
222 G5 Kootenay r. B.C. Can.
222 G5 Kootenay Bay B.C. Can.
222 G5 Kootenay Lake B.C. Can.
83 G2 Kootingal N.S.W. Austr.
214 C4 Kootjieskolk S. Africa
164 E2 Kootwijkerbroek Neth.
121 H4 Kopa Kazakh.
177 I2 Kopa mt. Slovakia
129 C4 Kopal Turkey
137 H4 Kopani Ukr.
135 I7 Kopanovka Rus. Fed.
137 J4 Kopanskaya Rus. Fed.
196 E4 Kopaonik mts Yugo.
114 B2 Kopargaon Mahar. India
136 D3 Kopayhorod Ukr.
121 I3 Kopbirlik Kazakh.
176 G3 Kopčany Slovakia
188 D3 Koper Slovenia
142 A2 Kopervik Norway
122 D2 Kopet Dag mts Iran/Turkm.
Kopet-Dag, Khrebet mts Iran/Turkm. see Kopet Dag
176 F4 Kópháza Hungary
174 F5 Kopice Pol.
176 E1 Kopidlno Czech Rep.
143 G2 Köping Sweden
196 D4 Koplik Albania
140 L3 Köpmanholmen Sweden
114 B3 Koppa Karnataka India
114 C3 Koppal Karnataka India
141 J3 Koppang Norway
196 D2 Koppány r. Romania
143 F2 Kopparberg Sweden
Kopparberg county Sweden see Dalarna
Koppeh Dāgh mts Iran/Turkm. see Kopet Dag
169 C5 Köppel hill Ger.
100 G2 Koppi r. Rus. Fed.
215 F2 Koppies S. Africa
214 C2 Koppieskraal Pan salt pan S. Africa
178 E3 Koppl Austria
188 F2 Koprivnica Croatia
126 C3 Köprü r. Turkey
199 F2 Köprübaşı Manisa Turkey
129 B3 Köprübaşı Trabzon Turkey
129 B4 Köprüköy Turkey
126 D3 Köprülü Turkey
175 J5 Koprzywianka r. Pol.
175 J5 Koprzywnica Pol.
215 F4 Kopshorn mt. S. Africa
165 F5 Kopstal Lux.
139 H4 Koptsi Belarus
138 E2 Kõpu r. Estonia
80 E2 Kopu North I. N.Z.
80 F3 Kopuawhara North I. N.Z.
136 C3 Kopychyntsi Ukr.
Kopyl' Belarus see Kapyl'
116 E4 Kora Uttar Prad. India
196 E5 Korab mts Albania/Macedonia
139 M5 Korablino Rus. Fed.
210 E3 K'orahē Eth.
111 D4 Koramlik Xinjiang China
188 E3 Korana r. Bos.-Herz./Croatia
114 C2 Korangal Andhra Prad. India
115 D2 Koraput Orissa India
Korat Thai. see Nakhon Ratchasima
114 C2 Koratla Andhra Prad. India
117 E5 Korba Madh. Prad. India
205 H1 Korba Tunisia
169 D4 Korbach Ger.
129 C2 Korbouli Georgia
94 C1 Korbu, Gunung mt. Malaysia
198 B1 Korçë Albania
121 J1 Korchino Rus. Fed.
136 D3 Korchivka Ukr.
170 C2 Körchow Ger.
136 D2 Korchyk r. Ukr.
188 F4 Korčula Croatia
188 F4 Korčula i. Croatia
188 F4 Korčulanski Kanal sea chan. Croatia
175 K3 Korczew Pol.
175 J6 Korczyna Pol.
121 H4 Korday Zhambylskaya Oblast' Kazakh.
172 A2 Kordel Ger.
136 E3 Kordelivka Ukr.
122 A3 Kordestān prov. Iran
127 H4 Kord Khvord Iran
122 C2 Kord Kūy Iran
134 L4 Kordon Rus. Fed.
101 C4 Korea, North country Asia
101 C5 Korea, South country Asia
101 C5 Korea Bay g. China/N. Korea
103 D6 Korea Strait Japan/S. Korea
114 B2 Koregaon Mahar. India
136 C3 Korelychi Ukr.
210 C1 Korem Eth.
137 I2 Koren' r. Rus. Fed.
137 H2 Korenevo Rus. Fed.
176 E1 Kořenov Czech Rep.
135 G7 Korenovsk Rus. Fed.
Korenovskaya Rus. Fed. see Korenovsk
206 C3 Koréra-Koré Mali
136 D2 Korets' Ukr.
131 R3 Korf Rus. Fed.
174 F5 Korfantów Pol.
199 F1 Körfez Turkey
262 T1 Korff Ice Rise Antarctica
100 E2 Korfovskiy Rus. Fed.
110 C2 Korgas Xinjiang China
140 K2 Korgen Norway
129 F3 Korgöz Azer.
199 G2 Körhasan Turkey
206 D4 Korhogo Côte d'Ivoire
206 C5 Koribundu Sierra Leone
116 B5 Kori Creek inlet Gujarat India
214 B5 Koringberg S. Africa
214 C5 Koringplaas S. Africa
80 E3 Koriniti North I. N.Z.
198 C1 Korinos Greece
142 D4 Korinth Denmark
198 C2 Korinthiakos Kolpos sea chan. Greece
198 C3 Korinthos Greece
177 G4 Kőris-hegy hill Hungary
Koritsa Albania see Korçë
103 J5 Kōriyama Japan
122 D2 Korkī Iran
130 H4 Korkino Rus. Fed.
131 Q3 Korkodon r. Rus. Fed.
199 G2 Körküler Turkey
199 G3 Korkuteli Turkey
110 D3 Korla Xinjiang China
169 E4 Körle Ger.
196 D4 Korman mt. Yugo.
176 F4 Körmend Hungary
175 L6 Kornalovychi Ukr.
188 E4 Kornat i. Croatia
169 F4 Körner Ger.
Korneshty Moldova see Cornești
179 H2 Korneuburg Austria
121 H2 Korneyevka Karagandinskaya Oblast' Kazakh.
121 G1 Korneyevka Severnyy Kazakhstan Kazakh.
120 B2 Korneyevka Rus. Fed.
174 F3 Kórnik Pol.
121 J1 Kornilovo Rus. Fed.
Kornisi Georgia see Qornisi
172 D3 Kornwestheim Ger.
177 H4 Környe Hungary
136 E2 Kornyn Ukr.
206 D4 Koro Côte d'Ivoire
79 □1 Koro i. Fiji
93 B3 Koro r. Indon.
206 E3 Koro Mali
225 H1 Koroc r. Que. Can.
135 G6 Korocha Rus. Fed.
137 I2 Korocha r. Rus. Fed.
126 D2 Köroğlu Dağları mts Turkey
126 D2 Köroğlu Tepesi mt. Turkey
211 C6 Korogwe Tanz.
136 B3 Koroleve Ukr.
81 □3 Koromiri i. Rarotonga Cook Is
198 B3 Koroni Greece
198 C1 Koronia, Limni l. Greece
174 F2 Koronowo Pol.
137 G2 Korop Ukr.
198 C3 Koropi Greece
92 □ Koror Palau
196 E2 Körös r. Romania
177 I5 Kőrös-ér r. Hungary
177 K5 Körösladány Hungary
177 K4 Körösszakál Hungary
177 K5 Köröstarcsa Hungary
136 E2 Korosten' Ukr.
136 E2 Korostyshiv Ukr.
134 M1 Korotaikha r. Rus. Fed.
196 E4 Korotnik mt. Albania
135 G6 Korotoyak Rus. Fed.
Korovino Rus. Fed. see Solntsevo
79 □1a Korovou Viti Levu Fiji
137 G2 Korovyntsi Ukr.
139 L3 Korozhechna r. Rus. Fed.
172 A2 Körperich Ger.
141 N3 Korpilahti Fin.
140 M2 Korpilombolo Sweden
141 M3 Korpo Fin.
Korppoo Fin. see Korpo
129 E4 Korrnidzor Armenia
137 H4 Korsak r. Ukr.
100 G3 Korsakov Sakhalin Rus. Fed.
139 K5 Korsakovo Rus. Fed.
143 F3 Korsberga Sweden
137 K2 Korshevo Rus. Fed.
141 K3 Korskrogen Sweden
140 M3 Korsnäs Fin.
138 E1 Korso Fin.
142 D4 Korsør Denmark
137 F3 Korsun'-Shevchenkivs'kyy Ukr.
Korsun'-Shevchenkovskiy Ukr. see Korsun'-Shevchenkivs'kyy
143 I4 Korsze Pol.
136 C2 Kortelisy Ukr.
165 C3 Kortemark Belgium
140 M3 Kortesjärvi Fin.
165 E4 Kortessem Belgium
164 C3 Kortgene Neth.
203 F5 Korti Sudan
134 J3 Kortkeros Rus. Fed.
165 C4 Kortrijk Belgium
134 H4 Kortsovo Rus. Fed.
128 A1 Korualan Turkey
199 E2 Korucu Turkey
83 F4 Korumburra Vic. Austr.
116 D4 Korwai Madh. Prad. India
131 Q4 Koryakskaya, Sopka vol. Rus. Fed.
131 S3 Koryakskiy Khrebet mts Rus. Fed.
134 I3 Koryazhma Rus. Fed.
176 G2 Koryčany Czech Rep.
175 L2 Korycin Pol.
104 B4 Kōryō Japan
101 D6 Koryŏng S. Korea
175 J3 Korytnica Pol.
137 G2 Koryukivka Ukr.
175 I6 Korzenna Pol.
120 C2 Korzhun Kazakh.
199 E3 Kos Notio Aigaio Greece
199 E3 Kos i. Greece
134 K4 Kosa Rus. Fed.
134 K3 Kosa r. Rus. Fed.
136 F2 Kosachivka Ukr.
120 E2 Kosagal Kazakh.
104 D4 Kosai Japan
174 G1 Kosakowo Pol.
101 C5 Kosan N. Korea
138 E5 Kosava Belarus
139 K4 Kosaya Gora Rus. Fed.
120 C3 Koschagyl Kazakh.
173 F3 Kösching Ger.
179 F4 Koschutnikturm mt. Austria/Slovenia
174 E3 Kościan Pol.
174 G3 Kościelec Pol.
174 G4 Kościelna Wieś Pol.
143 G4 Kościerzyna Pol.
237 F5 Kosciusko MS U.S.A.
Kosciusko, Mount N.S.W. Austr. see Kosciuszko, Mount
83 G4 Kosciuszko, Mount N.S.W. Austr.
138 E2 Kose Estonia
129 A3 Köse Turkey
177 H2 Košeca Slovakia
128 A1 Köseçobanlı Turkey
129 C4 Köse Dağı mt. Turkey
126 E2 Köse Dağı mt. Turkey
199 E2 Kösedere Turkey
168 E1 Kosel Ger.
177 K4 Kösély r. Hungary
170 F1 Koserow Ger.
114 C2 Kosgi Andhra Prad. India
106 A1 Kosh-Agach Rus. Fed.
120 B2 Koshankol' Kazakh.
105 F3 Koshigaya Japan
103 D8 Koshikijima-rettō is Japan
103 D8 Koshiki-kaikyō sea chan. Japan
122 E3 Koshkak Iran
135 J5 Koshki Rus. Fed.
120 E4 Koshkupyr Uzbek.
136 D3 Koshlyaky Ukr.
137 H3 Koshmanivka Ukr.
105 E2 Kōshoku Japan
121 F4 Koshrabad Uzbek.
116 D4 Kosi Uttar Prad. India
116 D3 Kosi r. India
177 K3 Košice Slovakia
177 K3 Košický Kraj admin. reg. Slovakia
114 C3 Kosigi Andhra Prad. India
117 F4 Kosi Reservoir Nepal
120 D2 Kos-Istek Kazakh.
136 C3 Kosiv Ukr.
137 G3 Kosivka Ukr.
196 D4 Kosjerić Srbija Yugo.
199 F3 Köşk Turkey
Koski Fin. see Hämeenkoski
140 M2 Koskullskulle Sweden
134 J3 Koslan Rus. Fed.
Köslin Pol. see Koszalin
134 J2 Kosma r. Rus. Fed.
171 F5 Kosmonosy Czech Rep.
139 M3 Kosmynino Rus. Fed.
188 G3 Košnica r. Croatia
174 F2 Kosobudy Pol.
Koson Uzbek. see Kasan
101 D5 Kosŏng N. Korea
Kosonsoy Uzbek. see Kasansay
Kosova prov. Yugo. see Kosovo
196 E4 Kosovo prov. Yugo.
Kosovo-Metohija prov. Yugo. see Kosovo
196 E4 Kosovo Polje Kosovo, Srbija Yugo.
196 E4 Kosovo Polje plain Yugo.
197 E4 Kosovska Kamenica Kosovo, Srbija Yugo.
196 E4 Kosovska Mitrovica Kosovo, Srbija Yugo.
175 K3 Kosów Lacki Pol.
266 F5 Kosrae atoll Micronesia
128 B1 Kösreli Turkey
171 E4 Koßdorf Ger.
173 F2 Kösseine hill Ger.
178 D3 Kössen Austria
173 H3 Kößlar r. Ger.
206 D5 Kossou, Lac de l. Côte d'Ivoire
Kosta-Khetagurovo Rus. Fed. see Nazran'
120 E1 Kostanay Kazakh.
176 D2 Kostelec nad Černými Lesy Czech Rep.
171 F5 Kostelec nad Labem Czech Rep.
176 F1 Kostelec nad Orlicí Czech Rep.
197 F4 Kostenets Bulg.
215 F1 Koster S. Africa
139 L4 Kosterevo Rus. Fed.
203 G6 Kosti Sudan
179 H2 Kostice Czech Rep.
197 F4 Kostinbrod Bulg.
130 J3 Kostino Rus. Fed.
196 E3 Kostolac Srbija Yugo.
174 E4 Kostomłoty Pol.
140 O2 Kostomuksha Rus. Fed.
136 D2 Kostopil' Ukr.
Kostopol' Ukr. see Kostopil'
139 M3 Kostroma Rus. Fed.
134 H4 Kostroma r. Rus. Fed.
Kostroma Oblast admin. div. Rus. Fed. see Kostromskaya Oblast'
134 H4 Kostromskaya Oblast' admin. div. Rus. Fed.
174 C3 Kostrzyn Lubuskie Pol.
174 F3 Kostrzyn Wielkopolskie Pol.
175 K3 Kostrzyń r. Pol.
137 I3 Kostyantynivka Donets'ka Oblast' Ukr.
137 H3 Kostyantynivka Kharkivs'ka Oblast' Ukr.
137 G4 Kostyantynivka Khersons'ka Oblast' Ukr.
137 H4 Kostyantynivka Zaporiz'ka Oblast' Ukr.
Kostyukovichi Belarus see Kastsyukovichy
177 L3 Kosyny Ukr.
134 L2 Kos'yu r. Rus. Fed.
143 G4 Koszalin Pol.
174 G5 Koszęcin Pol.
176 F4 Kőszeg Hungary
179 H3 Kőszegi-hegység hill Hungary
175 I5 Koszyce Pol.
114 D3 Kota Andhra Prad. India
116 E5 Kota Madh. Prad. India
116 C4 Kota Rajasthan India
94 D4 Kotaagung Sumatera Indon.
Kota Baharu Malaysia see Kota Bharu
95 G3 Kotabaru Kalimantan Selatan Indon.
94 C1 Kota Bharu Malaysia
94 D4 Kotabumi Sumatera Indon.
123 G4 Kot Addu Pak.
95 G1 Kota Kinabalu Sabah Malaysia
93 C2 Kotamobagu Sulawesi Utara Indon.
222 E2 Kotaneelee Range mts N.W.T./Y.T. Can.
121 I3 Kotanemel', Gora mt. Kazakh.
94 C2 Kotapinang Sumatera Indon.
116 E4 Kotar Madh. Prad. India
116 C4 Kotari r. India
95 E2 Kota Samarahan Sarawak Malaysia
94 C2 Kota Tinggi Malaysia
117 G5 Kotchandpur Bangl.
222 F3 Kotcho r. B.C. Can.
123 G5 Kot Diji Pak.
116 D3 Kotdwara Uttar Prad. India
177 K5 Kötegyán Hungary
197 H4 Kotel Bulg.
177 J4 Kőtelek Hungary
134 J4 Kotel'nich Rus. Fed.
135 H7 Kotel'nikovo Rus. Fed.
131 O2 Kotel'nyy, Ostrov i. Novosibirskiye O-va Rus. Fed.
170 E2 Kotelow Ger.
137 H2 Kotel'va Ukr.
80 F3 Kotemaori North I. N.Z.
115 D2 Kotgar Orissa India
116 D3 Kotgarh Hima. Prad. India
Kothagudem Andhra Prad. India see Kottagudem
171 C4 Köthen (Anhalt) Ger.
116 E4 Kothi Madh. Prad. India
206 B3 Kotiari Naoude Senegal
210 B4 Kotido Uganda
141 N3 Kotka Fin.
116 C3 Kot Kapura Punjab India
174 E4 Kotla Pol.
134 I3 Kotlas Rus. Fed.
123 H3 Kotli Pak.
220 B3 Kotlik AK U.S.A.
174 F4 Kotlin Pol.
175 J5 Kotlina Sandomierska basin Pol.
138 G2 Kotly Rus. Fed.
207 G4 Koton-Karifi Nigeria
196 D4 Kotor Crna Gora Yugo.
179 H4 Kotoriba Croatia
207 G3 Kotorkoshi Nigeria
139 L3 Kotorosl' r. Rus. Fed.
188 G3 Kotorsko Bos.-Herz.
188 F3 Kotor Varoš Bos.-Herz.
137 H3 Kotovka Ukr.
135 I6 Kotovo Rus. Fed.
Kotovsk Moldova see Hîncești
135 H5 Kotovsk Rus. Fed.
136 E4 Kotovs'k Ukr.
116 D4 Kot Putli Rajasthan India
138 E5 Kotra r. Belarus
114 D2 Kotri r. India
123 G5 Kotri Pak.
178 E4 Kötschach Austria
114 D2 Kottagudem Andhra Prad. India
114 C4 Kottayam Kerala India
114 B4 Kottayam Pondicherry India
Kotte Sri Lanka see Sri Jayewardenepura Kotte
169 C5 Kottenheim Ger.
179 G2 Kottes Austria
179 F4 Köttmannsdorf Austria
208 D3 Kotto r. C.A.R.
114 C3 Kotturu Karnataka India
79 □2 Kotu Group is Tonga
175 K3 Kotuń Pol.
122 C2 Koturdepe Turkm.
131 L2 Kotuy r. Rus. Fed.
117 E5 Kotwar Peak Madh. Prad. India
Kotyuzhany Moldova see Cotiujeni
173 E3 Kötz Ger.
220 B3 Kotzebue AK U.S.A.
220 B3 Kotzebue Sound sea chan. AK U.S.A.
214 A3 Kotzehoop S. Africa
214 A4 Kotzesrus S. Africa
173 G2 Kötzting Ger.
208 D3 Kouango C.A.R.
206 C4 Koubia Guinea
166 A3 Koudekerke Neth.
206 E3 Koudougou Burkina
164 E2 Koudum Neth.
198 C1 Koufalia Greece
199 D3 Koufonisi i. Greece
214 E5 Kouga r. S. Africa
214 D5 Kougaberge mts S. Africa
208 B3 Koui C.A.R.
206 D5 Kouibli Côte d'Ivoire
209 A6 Kouilou admin. reg. Congo
206 D4 Kouka Burkina
208 C3 Koukourou r. C.A.R.
208 B5 Koulamoutou Gabon
206 D3 Koulikoro Mali
206 D3 Koulikoro admin. reg. Mali
207 I4 Koum Cameroon
208 C3 Kouma r. C.A.R.
78 □5 Koumac New Caledonia
85 G4 Koumala Qld Austr.
206 E4 Koumbia Burkina
206 B4 Koumbia Guinea
208 C2 Koumra Chad
206 B3 Koundâra Guinea
206 C3 Koundian Mali
206 D4 Koundougou Burkina
206 B3 Koungheul Senegal
217 □3b Koungou Mayotte
206 B3 Kounkané Senegal
121 H3 Kounradskiy Karagandinskaya Oblast' Kazakh.
Kounradskiy Karagandinskaya Oblast' Kazakh. see Konyrat
206 B4 Kounsitél Guinea
237 E6 Kountze TX U.S.A.
214 C5 Koup S. Africa
206 E3 Koupéla Burkina
Kouqian Jilin China see Yongji
217 □3a Kourani Njazidja Comoros
176 D2 Kouřim Czech Rep.
251 H3 Kourou Fr. Guiana
198 D1 Kourou r. Greece
206 C2 Koûroudjél Maur.
206 C4 Kouroussa Guinea
206 B3 Koussanar Senegal
206 C3 Koussané Mali
207 I3 Kousséri Cameroon
207 F4 Koussountou Togo
206 D3 Koutiala Mali
173 G2 Kout na Šumav Czech Rep.
206 D4 Kouto Côte d'Ivoire
198 C3 Koutsopodi Peloponnisos Greece
141 N3 Kouvola Fin.
208 C5 Kouyou r. Congo

196 E3 Kovačica Vojvodina, Srbija Yugo.
177 H5 Kővágószőlős Hungary
136 F3 Kovalivka Ukr.
134 B2 Kovalberget Sweden
177 H3 Kovarce Slovakia
176 C1 Kovářská Czech Rep.
137 F2 Kovchyn Ukr.
134 G2 Kovdor Rus. Fed.
136 C2 Kovel' Ukr.
134 H4 Kovernino Rus. Fed.
196 E3 Kovilj Vojvodina, Srbija Yugo.
114 C4 Kovilpatti Tamil Nadu India
196 E3 Kovin Vojvodina, Srbija Yugo.
134 Lith. see Kaunas
134 J2 Kovriga, Gora hill Rus. Fed.
139 M3 Kovrov Rus. Fed.
137 J3 Kovsuh r. Ukr.
137 H3 Kov''yahy Ukr.
135 H5 Kovylkino Rus. Fed.
139 K1 Kovzhskoye, Ozero l. Rus. Fed.
175 H3 Kowal Pol.
174 G4 Kowale Pol.
175 K1 Kowale Oleckie Pol.
174 G4 Kowale-Pańskie Pol.
174 G2 Kowalewo Pomorskie Pol.
85 F2 Kowanyama Qld Austr.
174 D5 Kowary Pol.
81 C5 Kowhitirangi South I. N.Z.
175 I4 Kowiesy Pol.
109 Kowloon H.K. China
109 Kowloon Peninsula H.K. China
206 C5 Koyama Guinea
199 F3 Köyceğiz Turkey
134 J3 Koygorodok Rus. Fed.
122 C1 Koymatdag, Gory hills Turkm.
197 G4 Koynare Bulg.
134 L3 Koyp, Gora mt. Rus. Fed.
220 C3 Koyukuk r. AK U.S.A.
126 E2 Koyulhisar Turkey
207 I4 Koza Cameroon
134 G4 Koza Rus. Fed.
137 I2 Kozacha Lopan' Ukr.
   Kozağacı Turkey see Günyüzü
126 D3 Kozan Turkey
198 B1 Kozani Greece
188 F3 Kozara mts Bos.-Herz.
177 H5 Kozármisleny Hungary
137 F2 Kozarr Ukr.
177 H3 Kozárovce Slovakia
   Kozarska Dubica Bos.-Herz. see Bosanska Dubica
137 G4 Kozats'ke Ukr.
137 G2 Kozats'ke Ukr.
137 F2 Kozelets' Ukr.
139 J4 Kozel'sk Rus. Fed.
120 E3 Kozhabakhy Kazakh.
136 E3 Kozhanka Ukr.
   Kozhikode Kerala India see Calicut
134 L3 Kozhim-Iz, Gora mt. Rus. Fed.
135 H7 Kozhukhiv Ukr.
134 L2 Kozhva r. Rus. Fed.
134 L2 Kozhym r. Rus. Fed.
175 H5 Koziegłowy Pol.
174 C2 Kozielice Pol.
175 J4 Kozienice Pol.
137 H2 Koziivka Ukr.
176 C2 Kožlany Czech Rep.
197 F4 Kozloduy Bulg.
177 H2 Kozlovice Czech Rep.
134 J5 Kozlovka Chuvashskaya Respublika Rus. Fed.
135 I5 Kozlovka Respublika Mordoviya Rus. Fed.
135 H6 Kozlovka Voronezhskaya Oblast' Rus. Fed.
137 K2 Kozlovka Voronezhskaya Oblast' Rus. Fed.
139 K3 Kozlovo Rus. Fed.
175 I3 Kozłów Pol.
175 I3 Kozłów Biskupi Pol.
175 I2 Kozłowo Pol.
126 C2 Kozluk Turkey
188 G3 Kozluk Bos.-Herz.
174 F4 Kozmin Pol.
174 G4 Koźminek Pol.
134 I4 Koz''modem''yansk Kazakh.
197 F4 Koznitsa mt. Bulg.
136 C3 Kozova Ukr.
175 K4 Kozubszczyzna Pol.
174 D4 Kożuchów Pol.
197 F5 Kožuf mts Greece/Macedonia
135 I5 Kozyatyn Ukr.
137 G2 Kozyatyn Ukr.
136 F2 Kozyuliv Ukr.
137 F3 Kozyuliv Turkey
199 E1 Kozyörük Turkey
174 E2 Kożyńska Ukr.
207 F5 Kpalimé Togo
207 F5 Kpandae Ghana
207 F5 Kpandu Ghana
207 F5 Kpedze Ghana
97 B5 Kra, Isthmus of Thai.
215 F4 Kraai r. S. Africa
214 E3 Kraankuil S. Africa
165 D3 Krabbendijke Neth.
97 B5 Krabi Thai.
95 B5 Kra Buri Thai.
97 A5 Kraôh Cambodia
114 K3 Kräckelbäcken Sweden
170 F2 Krackow Ger.
139 J3 Kraftino, Ozero l. Rus. Fed.
171 C5 Kraftsdorf Ger.
95 E4 Kragan Jawa Tengah Indon.
164 E3 Kragerø Norway
164 F2 Kraggenburg Neth.
196 E3 Kragujevac Srbija Yugo.
173 G3 Kraiburg an Inn Ger.
172 C2 Kraichbach r. Ger.
178 F3 Krajenka Pol.
94 D4 Krakatau i. Indon.
   Krakau Ger. see Kraków
136 B3 Krakovets' Ukr.
175 H5 Kraków Pol.
226 C3 Krakow WI U.S.A.
122 C1 Krakovodnoye Zaliv b. Turkm.
170 D2 Krakow am See Ger.
170 D2 Krakower See l. Ger.
175 G4 Krakowsko-Częstochowska, Wyżyna plat. Pol.
97 B5 Kra Lenya r. Myanmar
176 F1 Kralíky Czech Rep.
188 E3 Kraljevica Croatia
196 E4 Kraljevo Srbija Yugo.
177 J3 Kráľova hoľa mt. Slovakia
177 G3 Kráľova nad Váhom Slovakia
177 G3 Kráľov Brod Slovakia
176 E1 Královéhradecký kraj admin. reg. Czech Rep.
176 C2 Kralovice Czech Rep.
177 K3 Kráľovský Chlmec Slovakia
176 D1 Kralupy nad Vltavou Czech Rep.
176 D2 Králův Dvůr Czech Rep.
137 J3 Kramators'k Ukr.
137 I3 Kramators'k Ukr.
140 L3 Kramfors Sweden
187 C7 Krammer est. Neth.
173 H6 Kramsach Austria
169 B4 Kranenburg Ger.
198 C3 Kranidi Greece
188 E2 Kranj Slovenia
188 D3 Kranjska Gora Slovenia
215 G3 Kransfontein S. Africa
215 H3 Kranskop r. S. Africa
173 F3 Kranzberg Ger.
188 F2 Krapanj Croatia
188 E3 Krapina Croatia
188 E2 Krapinske Toplice Croatia
175 G5 Krapkowice Pol.
179 E5 Kras plat. Slovenia
137 G3 Krasavino Rus. Fed.
135 K6 Krasiczyn Pol.
   Krasilov Ukr. see Krasyliv
   Krasilovka Chernihiv'ska Oblast' Ukr. see Krasylivka
   Krasilovka Zhytomyrs'ka Oblast' Ukr. see Krasylivka
175 L6 Krasiv Ukr.

136 C3 Krasiyiv Ukr.
100 D4 Kraskino Rus. Fed.
138 F4 Kräslava Latvia
176 B1 Kraslice Czech Rep.
171 F5 Krásná Lípa Czech Rep.
139 H5 Krasnapolye Belarus
137 I4 Krasna Polyana Ukr.
136 F3 Krasna Slobidka Ukr.
138 E5 Krasnasyel'ski Belarus
139 H5 Krasnaya Gorbatka Rus. Fed.
121 H2 Krasnaya Polyana Kazakh.
129 B2 Krasnaya Polyana Rus. Fed.
138 F5 Krasnaya Slabada Belarus
137 H2 Krasnaya Yaruga Rus. Fed.
139 K5 Krasnaya Zarya Rus. Fed.
175 I3 Krasne Mazowieckie Pol.
175 K5 Krasne Podkarpackie Pol.
137 F2 Krasne Chernihiv'ska Oblast' Ukr.
137 G2 Krasne Chernihiv'ska Oblast' Ukr.
136 C3 Krasne Ivano-Frankivs'ka Oblast' Ukr.
137 G4 Krasne Khersons'ka Oblast' Ukr.
136 C3 Krasne L'vivs'ka Oblast' Ukr.
136 D3 Krasne Ternopils'ka Oblast' Ukr.
136 E3 Krasne Vinnyts'ka Oblast' Ukr.
175 L5 Krasiczyn Pol.
175 K5 Krasnik Pol.
136 E4 Krasni Okny Ukr.
139 L3 Krasnoarmeysk Moskovskaya Oblast' Rus. Fed.
135 I6 Krasnoarmeysk Saratovskaya Oblast' Rus. Fed.
   Krasnoarmeysk Ukr. see Krasnoarmiys'k
131 S3 Krasnoarmeyskiy Chukotskiy Avtonomnyy Okrug Rus. Fed.
135 H7 Krasnoarmeyskiy Rostovskaya Oblast' Rus. Fed. see Urus-Martan
137 I3 Krasnoarmiys'k Ukr.
134 I3 Krasnoborsk Rus. Fed.
175 L5 Krasnobród Pol.
135 G7 Krasnodar Rus. Fed.
   Krasnodar Kray admin. div. see Krasnodarskiy Kray
129 A1 Krasnodarskiy Kray admin. div. Rus. Fed.
137 J3 Krasnodon Luhans'ka Oblast' Ukr.
137 J3 Krasnodon Luhans'ka Oblast' Ukr.
139 H2 Krasnofarfornyy Rus. Fed.
   Krasnogorka Kazakh. see Ul'ken Sulutar
138 G3 Krasnogorodskoye Rus. Fed.
139 K4 Krasnogorsk Moskovskaya Oblast' Rus. Fed.
100 G2 Krasnogorsk Sakhalin Rus. Fed.
121 K1 Krasnogorskoye Altayskiy Kray Rus. Fed.
134 K4 Krasnogorskoye Udmurtskaya Respublika Rus. Fed.
   Krasnograd Ukr. see Krasnohrad
139 M3 Krasnogvardeyskiy Rus. Fed.
137 J2 Krasnogvardeyskoye Belgorodskaya Oblast' Rus. Fed.
137 J5 Krasnogvardeyskoye Respublika Adygeya Rus. Fed.
135 H7 Krasnogvardeyskoye Stavropol'skiy Kray Rus. Fed.
137 I3 Krasnohorivka Ukr.
137 H3 Krasnohrad Ukr.
137 H5 Krasnohvardiys'ke Ukr.
107 H1 Krasnokamensk Rus. Fed.
134 K4 Krasnokamsk Rus. Fed.
120 C2 Krasnokholm Rus. Fed.
   Krasnokutsk Pavlodarskaya Oblast' Kazakh. see Aktogay
137 H2 Krasnokutsk Rus. Fed.
   Krasnokutskoye Pavlodarskaya Oblast' Kazakh. see Aktogay
135 G6 Krasnolesnyy Rus. Fed.
138 D4 Krasnoles'ye Rus. Fed.
137 J2 Krasnolip'ye Rus. Fed.
137 J3 Krasnomayskiy Rus. Fed.
177 H2 Krasno nad Kysucou Slovakia
113 I3 Krasnopavlivka Ukr.
137 G5 Krasnoperekops'k Ukr.
136 E3 Krasnopil' Ukr.
137 H2 Krasnopillia Ukr.
137 H2 Krasnorechenskiy Rus. Fed.
100 E3 Krasnorechenskoye Rus. Fed.
171 D4 Krasnosiele Ger.
169 B5 Kreuzau Ger.
136 D3 Krasnosilka Vinnyts'ka Oblast' Ukr.
136 D3 Krasnosilka Zhytomyrs'ka Oblast' Ukr.
135 H5 Krasnoslobodsk Rus. Fed.
134 K4 Krasnoslobodnoye Rus. Fed.
100 H4 Krasnotur'insk Rus. Fed.
134 L4 Krasnoufimsk Rus. Fed.
120 D1 Krasnousol'skiy Rus. Fed.
134 L3 Krasnovishersk Rus. Fed.
   Turkmenbashi
   Krasnovodskaya Oblast' admin. div. Turkm. see Balkanskaya Oblast'
122 C1 Krasnovodskiy Zaliv b. Turkm.
122 C1 Krasnovodskoye Plato plat. Turkm.
121 J2 Krasnoyar Kazakh.
100 D2 Krasnoyarovo Rus. Fed.
131 K4 Krasnoyarsk Rus. Fed.
120 D2 Krasnoyarskiy Rus. Fed.
98 F1 Krasnoyarskiy Kray admin. div. Rus. Fed. see
   Krasnoyarsk Kray admin. div. Rus. Fed. see
   Krasnoyarskiy Kray
135 G6 Krasnoyarskoye Belgorodskaya Oblast' Rus. Fed.
139 I5 Krasnoye Belgorodskaya Oblast' Rus. Fed.
134 I4 Krasnoye Bryanskaya Oblast' Rus. Fed.
137 G4 Krasnoye Lipetskaya Oblast' Rus. Fed.
137 J4 Krasnoye Krasnodarskiy Kray Rus. Fed.
175 L5 Krasnoye Lipetskaya Respublika Kalmykiya-Khalm'g-Tangch Rus. Fed.
140 H4 Ulan Erge
131 S3 Krasnoye, Ozero l. Rus. Fed.
139 M4 Krasnoye-na-Volge Rus. Fed.
137 J3 Krasnoye Plamya Rus. Fed.
137 J3 Krasnoye Znamya Rus. Fed.
143 G5 Krasnyil's'k Ukr.
138 D4 Krasnoznamensk Rus. Fed.
   Krasnoznamenka Norway
137 G2 Krasnoznamens'k
   Krasnoznam"yanka Ukr. see
121 G2 Krasnoznamyanskoye Kazakh.
137 G4 Krasnoznam"yanka Ukr.
175 I5 Krasnozyersk Rus. Fed.
139 J4 Krasnyy Rus. Fed.
215 L6 Krasnyy Chikoy Rus. Fed.
138 F4 Krasnyye Baki Rus. Fed.
139 I7 Krasnyye Barrikady Rus. Fed.
164 D2 Krasnyye Ocheti Rus. Fed.
137 G2 Krasnyy Kamyshanik Rus. Fed.
   Rus. Fed. see Komsomol'skiy

139 K2 Krasnyy Kholm Rus. Fed.
120 A2 Krasnyy Kut Rus. Fed.
137 J2 Krasnyy Liman Rus. Fed.
139 H3 Krasnyy Luch Rus. Fed.
137 J3 Krasnyy Luch Rus. Fed.
137 I3 Krasnyy Lyman Rus. Fed.
139 L3 Krasnyy Oktyabr' Rus. Fed.
139 M3 Krasnyy Profintern Rus. Fed.
137 K4 Krasnyy Sulin Rus. Fed.
135 I6 Krasnyy Tekstil'shchik Rus. Fed.
121 G1 Krasnyy Yar Kazakh.
120 B3 Krasnyy Yar Astrakhanskaya Oblast' Rus. Fed.
120 B1 Krasnyy Yar Samarskaya Oblast' Rus. Fed.
135 I6 Krasnyy Yar Volgogradskaya Oblast' Rus. Fed.
175 I5 Krasocin Pol.
136 E2 Krasyatychi Ukr.
136 D3 Krasyliv Ukr.
137 F2 Krasylivka Chernihiv'ska Oblast' Ukr.
136 E2 Krasylivka Zhytomyrs'ka Oblast' Ukr.
174 G4 Kraszewice Pol.
175 I1 Kraszewo Pol.
177 L3 Krasznar r. Hungary
197 F4 Kratie Cambodia see Krâchéh
197 G3 Kratovo Macedonia
172 D3 Krauchenwies Ger.
138 F4 Krauja Latvia
262 X2 Kraul Mountains Antarctica
171 F4 Krauschwitz Ger.
177 I2 Krauthenn Ger.
   Krǎvanh, Chuŏr Phnum mts Cambodia see Cardamom Range
177 H2 Kravaře Czech Rep.
129 E2 Kraynovka Rus. Fed.
171 F4 Kreba-Neudorf Ger.
169 F4 Krebeck Ger.
139 H2 Krechevitsy Rus. Fed.
169 B4 Krefeld Ger.
169 E4 Kreiensen Ger.
164 E2 Krielekoord Neth.
171 C5 Kreischa Ger.
138 E4 Krekenava Lith.
198 B2 Kremaston, Techniti Limni resr Greece
188 E3 Kremen mt. Croatia
   Kremenchug Ukr. see Kremenchuk
137 G3 Kremenchuk Ukr.
137 G3 Kremenchuts'ka Vodoskhovyshche resr Ukr.
136 C2 Kremenets' Ukr.
139 K4 Kremenki Rus. Fed.
176 E2 Kŕemešník hill Czech Rep.
137 J3 Kreminna Ukr.
136 C3 Kremidtsi Ukr.
   Kreml' Rus. Fed. see Solovetskiy
170 E3 Kremmen Ger.
238 F3 Kremmling CO U.S.A.
176 E1 Kremnica Slovakia
196 E4 Kremnú Albania
179 G2 Krems r. Austria
179 F2 Krems an der Donau Austria
179 F2 Kremsmünster Austria
176 E2 Kŕepice Czech Rep.
137 J4 Krepkaya r. Rus. Fed./Ukr.
197 E3 Krepolin PA U.S.A.
234 C2 Kresgeville PA U.S.A.
171 F5 Křešice Czech Rep.
177 F5 Kresna Bulg.
   Kressbronn am Bodensee Ger.
131 T3 Kresta, Zaliv g. Rus. Fed.
198 B3 Krestena Greece
132 I3 Krest-Khal'dzhayy Rus. Fed.
131 Q3 Krestsy Rus. Fed.
138 C4 Kretinga r. Lith.
171 D4 Kretzschau Ger.
173 F4 Kreuth Ger.
169 B5 Kreuzau Ger.
196 E4 Kreuzeck mt. Austria
178 C3 Kreuzjoch mt. Austria
190 E1 Kreuzlingen Switz.
169 C5 Kreuztal Ger.
172 D2 Kreuzwertheim Ger.
207 H6 Kribi Cameroon
170 F2 Krichim Bulg.
179 G3 Krieglach Austria
190 C1 Kriegstetten Switz.
215 E4 Kriel S. Africa
170 E2 Krien Ger.
190 D1 Kriens Switz.
141 M5 Krievukalns hill Latvia
198 B3 Krikellos Greece
172 D2 Krikovo Moldova see Cricova
179 F5 Krim r. Slovenia
208 B2 Krim–Krim Chad
164 D3 Krimpen aan de IJssel Neth.
176 I1 Křinec Czech Rep.
198 D1 Krinides Greece
137 J4 Kripka r. Rus. Fed./Ukr. see Krynka
175 M5 Krippenstein mt. Austria
114 D2 Krishna r. India
114 C3 Krishna, Mouths of the India
114 C3 Krishnagiri Tamil Nadu India
114 D4 Krishnai r. India
114 C5 Krishnanagar W. Bengal India
114 C3 Krishnarajpet Karnataka India
143 G3 Kristdala Sweden
   Kristiania Norway see Oslo
142 B2 Kristiansand Norway
143 F3 Kristianstad Sweden
140 I3 Kristiansund Norway
   Kristiinankaupunki Fin. see Kristinestad
143 F2 Kristinehamn Sweden
141 M3 Kristinestad Fin.
   Kristinopol' Ukr. see Chervonohrad
198 D4 Kriti admin. reg. Greece
171 I1 Kriti i. Greece
170 D1 Kritzmow Ger.
139 L4 Krivača mt. Yugo.
188 G3 Krivaja r. Bos.-Herz.
139 K6 Krivodol Bulg.
137 F4 Krivorozhzhya Ukr.
137 F3 Krivoy Rog Ukr. see Kryvyy Rih
137 G4 Kryvyy Rih Ukr.
196 F2 Križanovce Czech Rep.
188 F2 Križevci Croatia
188 E3 Krk i. Croatia
188 E3 Krk i. Croatia
176 F2 Krka r. Croatia
188 E3 Krka r. Slovenia
188 F2 Krka r. Slovenia
175 H3 Krnov Czech Rep.
175 G4 Krobia Pol.
175 I5 Kroczyce Pol.
206 D5 Krommodoke Liberia
170 E1 Kröpelin Ger.
174 G4 Krokowa Mała Pol.
143 G4 Krokek Sweden
140 J3 Krokom Sweden
143 H2 Krokstadøra Norway
137 G2 Krolevets' Ukr.
175 G4 Królewska Huta Pol. see Chorzów
174 G2 Królowy Most Pol.
175 L2 Kru r. Pol.
175 I7 Krupa r. S. Africa
216 E6 Krom r. S. Africa
204 D2 Krom, r. S. Africa
175 G2 Kromów Pol.
175 H2 Kronowit Mała Pol.
175 I2 Kromnów Pol.
175 K6 Krzywcza Pol.
143 G2 Krzywiń Pol.
174 C5 Krzywiń Pol.
175 J2 Krzyż Wielkopolski Pol.
198 D3 Krytiko Pelagos sea Greece
137 G3 Kryva Ruda Ukr.
137 F4 Kryvchnaka Ukr.
137 G5 Krychchy Belarus
137 G4 Kryvyy Rih Ukr.
136 E4 Kryzhopil' Ukr.
196 B4 Kržanovice Pol.
188 F3 Krška i. Croatia
188 E3 Krka i. Croatia

139 J5 Kromy Rus. Fed.
171 C5 Kronach Ger.
172 C2 Kronau Ger.
169 D5 Kronberg im Taunus Ger.
142 C2 Kronfjell hill Norway
97 C5 Krŏng Kaôh Kŏng Cambodia
   Kronoberg county Sweden
139 M3 Kronshtadt Rus. Fed.
131 R4 Kronotskiy Zaliv b. Rus. Fed.
221 P1 Kronprins Christian Land reg. Greenland
221 O3 Kronprins Frederik Bjerge nunataks Greenland
168 D2 Kronprinzenkoog Ger.
168 F1 Kronshagen Ger.
138 G2 Kronshtadt Rus. Fed.
   Kronstadt Romania see Braşov
   Kronstadt Rus. Fed. see Kronshtadt
179 F2 Kronstorf Austria
215 F2 Kroonstad S. Africa
170 C1 Kröpelin Ger.
169 E1 Kröppelshagen-Fahrendorf Ger.
168 E1 Kropp Ger.
169 C1 Kroppenstedt Ger.
171 D4 Kropstädt Ger.
175 I6 Krościenko nad Dunajcem Pol.
170 E1 Kröslin Ger.
174 F4 Krośnice Pol.
175 H3 Krośniewice Pol.
175 J6 Krosno Pol.
175 J6 Krosno Odrzańskie Pol.
174 D4 Krosno Odrzańskie Pol.
95 C1 Kuala Terengganu Malaysia
94 C3 Kualatungal Sumatera Indon.
95 G1 Kuamut r. Sabah Malaysia
107 H3 Kuancheng Hebei China
101 C4 Kuandian Liaoning China
   Kuandian Yunnan China see Yiliang
109 G4 Kuanshan Taiwan
94 C2 Kuantan Malaysia
80 E2 Kuaotuou North I. N.Z.
94 C1 Kuba Azer. see Quba
129 C2 Kuba Rus. Fed.
129 E2 Kubachi Rus. Fed.
129 B1 Kuban' r. Rus. Fed.
129 A1 Kubanskaya Rus. Fed.
127 E2 Kubär Dayr az Zawr Syria
127 E4 Kubär Dayr az Zawr Syria
125 G3 Kubärah Oman
140 L3 Kubbe Sweden
137 J5 Kübekháza Hungary
134 G4 Kubenskoye, Ozero l. Rus. Fed.
139 K4 Kubinka Rus. Fed.
190 E2 Küblis Switz.
134 J5 Kublych r. Ukr.
197 H4 Kubrat Bulg.
170 L3 Kubrinsk Rus. Fed.
197 E3 Kučevo Srbija Yugo.
188 E3 Kučevo Srbija Yugo.
114 C4 Kuchaman Rajasthan India
81 G5 Kuchera Rajasthan India
114 C4 Kuchera Rajasthan India
137 J2 Kucherivka Ukr.
95 E2 Kuching Sarawak Malaysia
111 G5 Kuchinoerabu-shima i. Japan
178 E3 Kuchl Austria
134 G4 Kuchurhan r. Ukr.
   Kucing Sarawak Malaysia see Kuching
175 H4 Kuciny Pol.
170 F2 Kückelberge hill Ger.
198 A1 Kuçovë Albania
128 C1 Küçükağrı Dağı mt. Turkey
199 G3 Küçükköy Turkey
199 E2 Küçükköy Turkey
199 E1 Küçükkuyu anakkale Turkey
199 E3 Küçükmenderes r. Turkey
199 E3 Küçükmenderes r. Turkey
175 I2 Kuczbork-Osada Pol.
116 B5 Kuda Gujarat India
114 B2 Kudachi Karnataka India
114 B4 Kudal Mahar. India
113 Maldives
114 B4 Kudal Mahar. India
113 Kudalhi I. N. Male Maldives
103 E7 Kudamatsu Japan
114 G5 Kudara-Somon Rus. Fed.
168 F2 Kudowa-Zdrój Pol.
114 G3 Kuddewörde Ger.
138 D3 Kudever r. Rus. Fed.
196 E5 Kukës Albania
187 I3 Kudremukh mt. Karnataka India
95 E4 Kudus Jawa Tengah Indon.
134 K4 Kudymkar Rus. Fed.
178 D3 Kufstein Austria
138 E4 Kugala Kazakh.
134 I4 Kugesi Rus. Fed.
187 H4 Kugey Rus. Fed.
220 G2 Kugluktuk Nunavut Can.
136 D2 Kugo-Eya r. Rus. Fed.
135 H7 Kugul'ta Rus. Fed.
103 F3 Kuh, Ras al pt Iran
123 F5 Kühbonän Iran
96 B1 Kumon Range mts Myanmar
180 E3 Kumotori-yama mt. Japan
101 E4 Kumozu r. Japan
138 E4 Kumphawapi Thai.
129 F2 Kumpurtuntur hill Fin.
179 D3 Kum see chan.

175 I5 Książ Wielki Pol.
174 F3 Książ Wielkopolski Pol.
175 K5 Książpol Pol.
122 C1 Kskyrbulak Yuzhnyy, Gora hill Turkm.
205 E4 Ksour, Monts des mts Alg.
205 H2 Ksour, Monts des mts Tunisia
205 H2 Ksour Essaf Tunisia
134 I4 Kstovo Rus. Fed.
125 D2 Kū', Jabal al hill Saudi Arabia
   Kuaidamao Jilin China see Tonghua
95 F1 Kuala Belait Brunei
94 C1 Kuala Dungun Malaysia see Dungun
94 C1 Kuala Kangsar Malaysia
95 F3 Kualakapuas Kalimantan Indon.
94 C1 Kuala Kerai Malaysia
95 G1 Kuala Kinabatangan r. mouth Sabah Malaysia
94 C1 Kuala Lipis Malaysia
94 C2 Kuala Lumpur Malaysia
95 F3 Kualapembuang Kalimantan Tengah Indon.
94 C1 Kuala Pilah Malaysia
   Kuala Simpang Sumatera Indon.
240 □C8 Kuaapau HI U.S.A.
94 B1 Kualasimpang Sumatera Indon.
138 D4 Kulautuva Lith.
137 H2 Kul'baki Rus. Fed.
138 C3 Kuldīga Latvia
   Kuldja Xinjiang China see Yining
100 D2 Kul'dur Rus. Fed.
120 E4 Kul'dzhuktau, Gory Uzbek.
135 H5 Kulebaki Rus. Fed.
199 G3 Kuleönü Turkey
137 J4 Kuleshovka Rus. Fed.
175 K2 Kulesze Pol.
175 K1 Kulesze Kościelne Pol.
139 L5 Kulikovo Arkhangel'skaya Oblast' Rus. Fed.
139 L5 Kulikovo Lipetskaya Oblast' Rus. Fed.
94 C1 Kulim Malaysia
87 C7 Kulin W.A. Austr.
114 C4 Kulittalai Tamil Nadu India
136 E4 Kulkuduk Uzbek.
141 M3 Kullaa Fin.
169 F4 Küllstedt Ger.
116 D3 Kullu Hima. Prad. India
173 F2 Kulmain Ger.
114 D3 Kulmbach Ger.
123 G2 Kŭlob Tajik.
139 I2 Kulotino Rus. Fed.
134 H3 Kuloy Rus. Fed.
134 H2 Kuloy r. Rus. Fed.
127 F3 Kuluba Turkey
82 D3 Kulpara S.A. Austr.
234 B2 Kulpmont PA U.S.A.
120 C3 Kul'sary Kazakh.
172 D2 Külsheim Ger.
126 D3 Kulu Turkey
199 G3 Kulübe Tepe mt. Turkey
120 E1 Kulunda Rus. Fed.
121 I1 Kulunda r. Rus. Fed.
121 H1 Kulundinskaya Step' plain Kazakh./Rus. Fed.
121 I1 Kulundinskoye, Ozero salt l. Rus. Fed.
83 E3 Kulwin Vic. Austr.
123 H2 Kulyab Tajik. see Kŭlob
134 G4 Kulykivka r. Ukr.
139 K4 Kubinka Rus. Fed.
190 D2 Küma r. Rus. Fed.
105 F2 Kumagaya Japan
95 E3 Kumai, Teluk b. Indon.
120 D2 Kumak r. Rus. Fed.
131 J4 Kumalar Dağı mts Turkey
102 C1 Kumamoto Japan
104 C5 Kumamoto pref. Japan
197 E4 Kumanovo Macedonia
81 C5 Kumara r. Rus. Fed.
81 C5 Kumara South I. N.Z.
88 E5 Kumarkhali Bangl.
206 E5 Kumasi Ghana
215 G4 Ku-Mayima S. Africa
207 H5 Kumayri Armenia see Gyumri
199 E1 Kumbağ Turkey
114 C4 Kumbakonam Tamil Nadu India
179 G3 Kumberg Austria
199 G2 Kumbet Turkey
114 B2 Kumbharli Ghat mt. India
207 H5 Kumbo Cameroon
138 D3 Kumbri Latvia
124 D3 Kumdah Saudi Arabia
199 G2 Kumdanlı Isparta Turkey
102 □1 Kume-jima i. Japan
134 H4 Kumeny Rus. Fed.
136 C2 Kumertau Rus. Fed.
96 C1 Kumkuy r. Ukr.

138 D4 Kulautuva Lith.
137 H2 Kul'baki Rus. Fed.
138 C3 Kuldīga Latvia
100 C1 Kul'dur Rus. Fed.
120 E4 Kul'dzhuktau, Gory Uzbek.
135 H5 Kulebaki Rus. Fed.
199 F3 Kuling Hima. Prad. India
173 F2 Kulmain Ger.
199 G3 Kuleönü Turkey
181 J4 Kuleshovka Rus. Fed.
175 K2 Kulesze Pol.
175 K1 Kulesze Kościelne Pol.
106 A4 Kunlun Shan mts China
177 I4 Kunmadaras Hungary
108 B3 Kunming Yunnan China
116 D4 Kunnu r. India
175 G3 Kunowice Pol.
174 F4 Kunowo Pol.
177 I4 Kunpeszér Hungary
176 G2 Kunovice Czech Rep.
101 C6 Kunsan S. Korea
109 G2 Kunshan Jiangsu China
177 I4 Kunštát Czech Rep.
177 I5 Kunszállás Hungary
177 I4 Kunszentmárton Hungary
177 H4 Kunszentmiklós Hungary
86 F2 Kununurra W.A. Austr.
223 L2 Kunwak r. Nunavut Can.
116 D4 Kunwari r. India
139 H3 Kun'ya r. Rus. Fed.
139 H3 Kun'ya r. Rus. Fed.
   Kunyang Henan China see Yexian
   Kunyang Zhejiang China see Pingyang
   Kunya-Urgench Turkm. see Köneurgench
137 I3 Kun'ye Ukr.
176 E2 Kunžak Czech Rep.
169 E5 Künzell Ger.
172 D2 Künzelsau Ger.
171 C4 Künzels-Berg hill Ger.
173 H3 Künzing Ger.
109 G2 Kuocang Shan mts China
140 N5 Kuopio Fin.
141 N3 Kuorevesi Fin.
174 F5 Kup Pol.
188 F3 Kupa r. Croatia/Slovenia
93 B5 Kupang Timor Indon.
114 D2 Kupari Orissa India
116 C2 Kupchino Moldova see Cupcina
171 C5 Kun'ye Ukr.
176 E2 Kupferberg Ger.
172 D2 Kupferzell Ger.
137 I2 Kupino Rus. Fed.
171 C4 Kupiškis Lith.
191 J3 Kupjak Croatia
188 F3 Kupreanof AK U.S.A.
220 E4 Kupreanof Island AK U.S.A.
171 C5 Küps Ger.
116 C2 Kupwara Jammu and Kashmir
137 I3 Kup"yans'k Ukr.
137 I3 Kup"yans'k-Vuzlovyy Ukr.
136 C2 Kupychiv Ukr.
110 C3 Kuqa Xinjiang China
129 F4 Kür r. Azer.
129 C3 Kür r. Georgia
129 E2 Kür r. Rus. Fed.
100 C2 Kur r. Rus. Fed.
126 C3 Kura r. Turkey
129 C2 Kura r. Azer./Georgia
129 C2 Kura r. Turkey
87 C5 Kurabuka r. W.A. Austr.
121 H4 Kuragaty Kazakh.
104 D2 Kuragino Rus. Fed.
139 L3 Kuragino Rus. Fed.
137 I4 Kuragino Rus. Fed.
113 J3 Kurakhovo Ukr. see Kurakhove
113 I3 Kurakhovo Ukr. see
   Kurakhove
   Kura kurk sea chan. Estonia/Latvia see Irbe Strait
104 A4 Kuragino Rus. Fed.
85 B5 Kuranda Qld Austr.
104 D2 Kurashasayskiy Kazakh.
116 E5 Kurasia Madh. Prad. India
103 F6 Kurashiki Japan
104 A2 Kurayoshi Japan
103 A6 Kurayskiy Khrebet mts Rus. Fed.
104 B4 Kurba Rus. Fed.
126 C2 Kurban Dağı mt. Turkey
137 J2 Kurban Rus. Fed.
196 E2 Kurca r. Romania
197 J2 Kurchaloy Rus. Fed.
196 C3 Kurchatov Rus. Fed.
121 J2 Kurchum r. Kazakh.
114 C4 Kurduvadi Mahar. India
177 H5 Kürdämir Azer.
143 G2 Kurday Kazakh.
129 F5 Kürdzhali Bulg.
103 F6 Kurdzhinovo Rus. Fed.
103 E6 Kure Japan
114 C5 Kuré Atoll HI U.S.A.
138 E2 Kuressaare Estonia
138 D2 Kurgan Rus. Fed.
266 E2 Kuril Basin sea feature Sea of Okhotsk
101 C6 Kurihama Japan
170 L4 Kurile, Mal mt. Albania
99 Q3 Kuril'sk Kuril'skiye O-va Rus. Fed.
120 D2 Kuril'skiye Ostrova is Rus. Fed. see Kuril Islands
266 E3 Kuril Trench sea feature N. Pacific Ocean
129 A1 Kürim Czech Rep.
176 F2 Kuřim Czech Rep.
129 A1 Kurinskaya Rus. Fed.
210 B4 Kurkçü Turkey see Sarıkavak
84 E2 Kuridala Qld Austr.
114 A1 Kurigram Bangl.
140 M3 Kürin Fin.
266 E2 Kuril Basin sea feature

114 C3 Kunie i. New Caledonia see Pins, Île des
114 C3 Kunigal Karnataka India
104 C2 Kunimi-dake mt. Japan
103 E7 Kunimi-dake mt. Japan
177 G2 Kunín Czech Rep.
95 E4 Kuningan Jawa Barat Indon.
174 G5 Kuniów Pol.
199 G3 Kunkeni Turkey
234 C2 Kunkletown PA U.S.A.
116 B5 Kunlavav Gujarat India
116 C3 Kunlui r. India/Nepal
106 A4 Kunlun Shan mts China
177 I4 Kunmadaras Hungary
108 B3 Kunming Yunnan China
116 D3 Kunnu r. India
175 G3 Kunowice Pol.
174 F4 Kunowo Pol.
177 I4 Kunpeszér Hungary
176 G2 Kunovice Czech Rep.
101 C6 Kunsan S. Korea
109 G2 Kunshan Jiangsu China
177 I4 Kunštát Czech Rep.
177 I5 Kunszállás Hungary
177 I4 Kunszentmárton Hungary
177 H4 Kunszentmiklós Hungary
86 F2 Kununurra W.A. Austr.
223 L2 Kunwak r. Nunavut Can.
116 D4 Kunwari r. India
139 H3 Kun'ya r. Rus. Fed.
139 H3 Kun'ya r. Rus. Fed.
   Kunyang Henan China see Yexian
   Kunyang Zhejiang China see Pingyang
   Kunya-Urgench Turkm. see Köneurgench
137 I3 Kun'ye Ukr.
176 E2 Kunžak Czech Rep.
169 E5 Künzell Ger.
172 D2 Künzelsau Ger.
171 C4 Künzels-Berg hill Ger.
173 H3 Künzing Ger.
109 G2 Kuocang Shan mts China
140 N5 Kuopio Fin.
141 N3 Kuorevesi Fin.
174 F5 Kup Pol.
188 F3 Kupa r. Croatia/Slovenia
93 B5 Kupang Timor Indon.
114 D2 Kupari Orissa India
116 C2 Kupchino Moldova see Cupcina
171 C5 Kupferberg Ger.
172 D2 Kupferzell Ger.
137 I2 Kupino Rus. Fed.
171 C4 Kupiškis Lith.
191 J3 Kupjak Croatia
188 F3 Kupres Bos.-Herz.
220 E4 Kupreanof AK U.S.A.
171 C5 Kupreanof Island AK U.S.A.
116 C2 Küps Ger.
137 I3 Kupwara Jammu and Kashmir
137 I3 Kup"yans'k Ukr.
136 C2 Kup"yans'k-Vuzlovyy Ukr.
110 C3 Kupychiv Ukr.
129 F4 Kuqa Xinjiang China
129 C3 Kür r. Azer.
129 E2 Kür r. Georgia
100 C2 Kür r. Rus. Fed.
126 C3 Kür r. Rus. Fed.
129 C2 Kura r. Turkey
129 C2 Kura r. Azer./Georgia
87 C5 Kura r. Turkey
121 H4 Kurabuka r. W.A. Austr.
104 D2 Kuragaty Kazakh.
139 L3 Kuragino Rus. Fed.
137 I4 Kurakhove Ukr.
113 I3 Kurakhovo Ukr. see Kurakhove
104 A4 Kurashki Japan
85 B5 Kuranda Qld Austr.
104 D2 Kurashasayskiy Kazakh.
116 E5 Kurasia Madh. Prad. India
103 F6 Kurashiki Japan
104 A2 Kurayoshi Japan
103 A6 Kurayskiy Khrebet mts Rus. Fed.
104 B4 Kurba Rus. Fed.
126 C2 Kurban Dağı mt. Turkey
137 J2 Kurban Rus. Fed.
196 E2 Kurca r. Romania
197 J2 Kurchaloy Rus. Fed.
196 C3 Kurchatov Rus. Fed.
121 J2 Kurchum r. Kazakh.
114 C4 Kurduvadi Mahar. India
177 H5 Kürdämir Azer.
143 G2 Kurday Kazakh.
129 F5 Kürdzhali Bulg.
103 F6 Kurdzhinovo Rus. Fed.
103 E6 Kure Japan
114 C5 Kuré Atoll HI U.S.A.
138 E2 Kuressaare Estonia
138 D2 Kurgan Rus. Fed.
266 E2 Kuril Basin sea feature Sea of Okhotsk
101 C6 Kurihama Japan
170 L4 Kurile, Mal mt. Albania
99 Q3 Kuril'sk Kuril'skiye O-va Rus. Fed.
120 D2 Kuril'skiye Ostrova is Rus. Fed. see Kuril Islands
266 E3 Kuril Trench sea feature N. Pacific Ocean
129 A1 Kurim Czech Rep.
176 F2 Kuřim Czech Rep.
129 A1 Kurinskaya Rus. Fed.
210 B4 Kurkçü Turkey see Sarıkavak
84 E2 Kuridala Qld Austr.
114 A1 Kurigram Bangl.
104 H4 Kuroshio Japan
102 □1 Kuroshima i. Japan
100 C1 Kurovskiy Rus. Fed.
139 L4 Kurovskoye Rus. Fed.

Kurovychi to Laï
324

175 M6 Kurovychi Ukr.
81 C6 Kurow South I. N.Z.
175 K4 Kurów Pol.
175 H4 Kurowice Pol.
123 G3 Kurram r. Afgh./Pak.
83 G3 Kurri Kurri N.S.W. Austr.
129 C1 Kursavka Rus. Fed.
138 D3 Kuršėnai Lith.
124 C3 Kursh, Jabal hill Saudi Arabia
Kürshim Kazakh. see Kurchum
Kurshskiy Zaliv b. Lith./Rus. Fed. see Courland Lagoon
Kuršių marios b. Lith./Rus. Fed. see Courland Lagoon
135 G6 Kursk Rus. Fed.
129 D1 Kurskaya Rus. Fed.
135 G6 Kurskaya Oblast' admin. div. Rus. Fed.
Kurskiy Zaliv b. Lith./Rus. Fed. see Courland Lagoon
Kursk Oblast admin. div. Rus. Fed. see Kurskaya Oblast'
137 H2 Kurskoye Vodokhranilishche resr Rus. Fed.
196 E4 Kuršumlija Srbija Yugo.
126 D2 Kurşunlu Turkey
127 F3 Kurtalan Turkey
199 E1 Kurtbey Edirne Turkey
Kürti r. Kazakh. see Kurtty
240 □D9 Kurtistown HI U.S.A.
129 D3 K'urt'lari Georgia
128 B1 Kurtpınar Turkey
128 B1 Kurttepe Turkey
121 I3 Kurtty r. Kazakh.
Kurty r. Kazakh. see Kurtty
141 M3 Kuru Fin.
Kurú r. Greece see Kourou
117 F5 Kuru Bihar India
126 D2 Kurucaşile Turkey
116 E5 Kurud Madh. Prad. India
199 G1 Kurudere Turkey
116 D3 Kurukshetra Haryana India
110 D3 Kuruktag mts China
214 D2 Kuruman S. Africa
103 E7 Kurume Japan
99 J1 Kurumkan Rus. Fed.
210 B3 Kurun r. Sudan
114 B2 Kurundvad Mahar. India
114 D5 Kurunegala Sri Lanka
107 H1 Kurunzulay Rus. Fed.
115 D2 Kurupam Andhra Prad. India
203 F4 Kurush, Jebel hills Sudan
121 J2 Kur'ya Rus. Fed.
137 J3 Kuryachivka Ukr.
120 B4 Kuryk Kazakh.
137 H3 Kurylivka Ukr.
175 K5 Kuryłówka Pol.
175 H5 Kurzelów Pol.
175 I4 Kurzeszyn Pol.
175 H2 Kurzętnik Pol.
199 E3 Kuşadası Turkey
199 E3 Kuşadası Körfezi b. Turkey
Kusaie atoll Micronesia see Kosrae
128 C1 Kuşalanı Turkey
Kusary Azer. see Qusar
104 B3 Kusatsu Japan
172 B2 Kusel Ger.
170 C3 Kusey Ger.
116 C5 Kushalgarh Rajasthan India
139 K3 Kushalino Rus. Fed.
122 D3 Kūshank Iran
135 G7 Kushchevskaya Rus. Fed.
207 G4 Kusheriki Nigeria
104 C4 Kushida-gawa r. Japan
103 E8 Kushikino Japan
103 E8 Kushima Japan
102 L2 Kushiro Japan
Kushka Turkm. see Gushgy
120 F1 Kushmurun Kazakh.
120 F1 Kushmurun, Ozero salt l. Kazakh.
134 K5 Kushnarenkovo Rus. Fed.
114 C3 Kushtagi Karnataka India
117 G5 Kushtia Bangl.
137 H4 Kushuhum Ukr.
106 E4 Kushui r. China
120 B2 Kushum Kazakh.
120 B2 Kushum r. Kazakh.
128 A1 Kuskan Turkey
220 B3 Kuskokwim r. AK U.S.A.
220 B4 Kuskokwim Bay AK U.S.A.
220 C3 Kuskokwim Mountains AK U.S.A.
Kuşluyan Turkey see Gölköy
190 D1 Küsnacht Switz.
101 C5 Kusŏng N. Korea
102 L2 Kussharo-ko l. Japan
190 D1 Küssnacht Switz.
Kustanay Kazakh. see Kostanay
Kustanay Oblast admin. div. Kazakh. see Kustanayskaya Oblast'
120 E1 Kustanayskaya Oblast' admin. div. Kazakh.
141 M3 Kustavi Fin.
170 C3 Küsten Ger.
Küstence Romania see Constanța
172 D3 Kusterdingen Ger.
Kustia Bangl. see Kushtia
136 D3 Kustivtsi Ukr.
93 C2 Kusu Halmahera Indon.
104 C4 Kusu Japan
199 F2 Kuşu Kütahya Turkey
97 C5 Kut, Ko i. Thai.
94 B2 Kutacane Sumatera Indon.
199 F2 Kütahya Turkey
199 F2 Kütahya prov. Turkey
129 A1 Kutais Rus. Fed.
129 C2 K'ut'aisi Georgia
Kut-al-Imara Iraq see Al Kūt
129 E1 Kutan Rus. Fed.
Kutaraja Sumatera Indon. see Banda Aceh
80 F3 Kutarere North I. N.Z.
128 D4 Kutayfat Ţurayf vol. Saudi Arabia
Kutch, Gulf of Gujarat India see Kachchh, Gulf of
Kutch, Rann of marsh India see Rann of Kachchh
127 H4 Kūt-e Gapu tourist site Iran
168 E2 Kutenholz Ger.
137 J4 Kuteynykove Ukr.
188 F3 Kutina Croatia
188 F3 Kutjevo Croatia
215 F2 Kutloanong S. Africa
176 E2 Kutná Hora Czech Rep.
175 H3 Kutno Pol.
140 M1 Kuttainen Sweden
208 C5 Kutu Dem. Rep. Congo
202 E6 Kutum Sudan
Kutuzov Moldova see Ialoveni
176 G3 Kúty Slovakia
173 E3 Kutzenhausen Ger.
234 C2 Kutztown PA U.S.A.
220 G2 Kuujjua r. N.W.T. Can.
225 G1 Kuujjuaq Que. Can.
224 E2 Kuujjuarapik Que. Can.
122 C1 Kuuli-Mayak Turkm.
165 C4 Kuurne Belgium
138 E2 Kuusalu Estonia
140 O2 Kuusamo Fin.
141 N3 Kuusankoski Fin.
138 D1 Kuusjoki Fin.
138 F2 Kuutse mägi hill Estonia
134 K4 Kuva Rus. Fed.
120 D2 Kuvandyk Rus. Fed.
209 C8 Kuvango Angola
139 J3 Kuvshinovo Rus. Fed.
Kuwaé i. Vanuatu see Tongoa
127 G5 Kuwait country Asia
Kuwajleen atoll Marshall Is see Kwajalein
104 C3 Kuwana Japan
Küybyshev Kazakh. see Kuybyshevskiy
130 I4 Kuybyshev Novosibirskaya Oblast' Rus. Fed.
Kuybyshev Respublika Tatarstan Rus. Fed. see Bolgar
Kuybyshev Samarskaya Oblast' Rus. Fed. see Samara
137 I4 Kuybysheve Donets'ka Oblast' Ukr.
137 I4 Kuybysheve Zaporiz'ka Oblast' Ukr.
Kuybyshevka-Vostochnaya Rus. Fed. see Belogorsk
Kuybyshevo Kazakh. see Zhyngyldy
137 J4 Kuybyshevo Rus. Fed.
Kuybyshevskaya Oblast' admin. div. Rus. Fed. see Samarskaya Oblast'
121 F1 Kuybyshevskiy Kazakh.
135 J5 Kuybyshevskoye Vodokhranilishche resr Rus. Fed.
107 F4 Kuye r. China
134 K4 Kuyeda Rus. Fed.
121 H3 Kuygan Kazakh.
106 B3 Küysu Xinjiang China
110 D2 Kuytun Xinjiang China
110 C2 Kuytun He r. China
199 F3 Kuyucak Turkey
128 B1 Kuyuluk Turkey
251 G4 Kuyuwini r. Guyana
137 I3 Kuzemivka Ukr.
137 H2 Kuzemyn Ukr.
134 J4 Kuzhener Rus. Fed.
139 I3 Kuzhenkino Rus. Fed.
129 B1 Kuzhorskaya Rus. Fed.
138 D4 Kužiai Lith.
Kuzik'end Armenia see Garrnarrich
177 K3 Kuzmice Slovakia
175 K6 Kuźmina Pol.
139 H1 Kuz'molovskiy Rus. Fed.
138 G1 Kuznechnoye Rus. Fed.
120 A1 Kuznetsk Rus. Fed.
136 C2 Kuznetsovs'k Ukr.
174 G5 Kuźnia Raciborska Pol.
175 L2 Kuźnica Pol.
135 I5 Kuzovatovo Rus. Fed.
139 L5 Kuzovka Rus. Fed.
102 J3 Kuzumaki Japan
104 C2 Kuzuryū-gawa r. Japan
140 M1 Kvænangen sea chan. Norway
142 D4 Kværndrup Denmark
168 E1 Kværs Denmark
140 L1 Kvaløya i. Norway
140 M1 Kvaløya i. Norway
140 M1 Kvalsund Norway
Kvareli Georgia see Qvareli
120 D1 Kvarkeno Rus. Fed.
141 K3 Kvarnberg Sweden
188 E3 Kvarner g. Croatia
188 E3 Kvarnerić sea chan. Croatia
176 G2 Kvasice Czech Rep.
136 C3 Kvasy Ukr.
136 D2 Kvasyliv Ukr.
129 C3 K'veda Nasakirali Georgia
138 C4 Kvėdarna Lith.
129 D2 K'vemo Alvani Georgia
129 D3 K'vemo Bodbe Georgia
129 D3 K'vemo Bolnisi Georgia
140 L2 Kvikkjokk Sweden
143 F3 Kvillsfors Sweden
142 B2 Kvinesdal Norway
141 L3 Kvissleby Sweden
141 I3 Kvitanosi mt. Norway
141 I3 Kvitegga mt. Norway
142 C2 Kviteseid Norway
140 □ Kvitøya ice feature Svalbard
142 A2 Kvitsøy Norway
209 C5 Kwa r. Dem. Rep. Congo
165 E3 Kwaadmechelen Belgium
Kwabhaca S. Africa see Mount Frere
215 H2 KwaChibukhulu S. Africa
215 G2 KwaDela S. Africa
Kwadelen atoll Marshall Is see Kwajalein
215 G1 KwaGuga S. Africa
78 □3a Kwajalein atoll Marshall Is
78 □3a Kwajalein i. Marshall Is
251 H3 Kwakoegron Suriname
251 G3 Kwakwani Guyana
215 F2 Kwakwatse S. Africa
211 C6 Kwale Kenya
207 G5 Kwale Nigeria
215 H3 KwaMashu S. Africa
215 I3 Kwa-Mbonambi S. Africa
206 E5 Kwame Danso Ghana
215 G1 KwaMhlanga S. Africa
211 B6 Kwa Mtoro Tanz.
Kwangchow Guangdong China see Guangzhou
101 C6 Kwangju S. Korea
209 C5 Kwango r. Dem. Rep. Congo
Kwangsi Chuang Autonomous Region aut. reg. China see Guangxi Zhuangzu Zizhiqu
Kwangtung prov. China see Guangdong
101 D4 Kwanmo-bong mt. N. Korea
215 E5 Kwanobuhle S. Africa
215 E5 KwaNojoli S. Africa
215 F5 Kwanonqubela S. Africa
215 E4 Kwanonzame S. Africa
Kwanza r. Angola see Cuanza
215 F5 Kwa-Pita S. Africa
207 F4 Kwara state Nigeria
215 H2 KwaThandeka S. Africa
215 F5 Kwatinidubu S. Africa
215 G2 KwaZamokhule S. Africa
214 E5 Kwazamukucinga S. Africa
215 E4 Kwazamuxolo S. Africa
215 G2 KwaZanele S. Africa
215 H3 Kwazulu-Natal prov. S. Africa
Kweichow prov. China see Guizhou
Kweiyang Guizhou China see Guiyang
213 F3 Kwekwe Zimbabwe
212 E4 Kweneng admin. dist. Botswana
209 C6 Kwenge r. Dem. Rep. Congo
224 D3 Kwetabohigan r. Ont. Can.
215 F4 Kwezi-Naledi S. Africa
174 G2 Kwidzyn Pol.
220 B4 Kwigillingok AK U.S.A.
174 E3 Kwilcz Pol.
209 C5 Kwilu r. Angola/Dem. Rep. Congo
87 B7 Kwinana W.A. Austr.
174 D4 Kwisa r. Pol.
251 G4 Kwitaro r. Guyana
91 H7 Kwoka mt. Indon.
208 E3 Kwoungo, Mont mt. C.A.R.
208 C2 Kyabé Chad
85 E5 Kyabra Qld Austr.
83 F4 Kyabram Vic. Austr.
96 A3 Kyaiklat Myanmar
96 B3 Kyaikto Myanmar
106 E1 Kyakhta Rus. Fed.
83 E3 Kyalite N.S.W. Austr.
82 C3 Kyancutta S.A. Austr.
96 A3 Kyangin Myanmar
96 B3 Kyaukhnyat Myanmar
96 A2 Kyaukpadaung Myanmar
96 A3 Kyaukpyu Myanmar
96 B2 Kyaukse Myanmar
96 B3 Kyauktan Myanmar
96 A3 Kyaunggon Myanmar
138 D4 Kybartai Lith.
83 G4 Kybeyan Range mts N.S.W. Austr.
82 E4 Kybybolite S.A. Austr.
96 D2 Ky Cung, Sông r. Vietnam
81 C6 Kyeburn South I. N.Z.
211 B7 Kyela Tanz.
116 D2 Kyelang Hima. Prad. India
206 E5 Kyeraa Ghana
121 H3 Kyeylbelen, Gora hill Kazakh.
96 B3 Kyidaunggan Myanmar
106 D4 Kyikug Qinghai China
207 E4 Kyinderi Ghana
136 F2 Kyiv Ukr.
136 F2 Kyivs'ka Oblast' admin. div. Ukr.
176 G2 Kyjov Czech Rep.
198 D3 Kyklades dept Greece
126 B3 Kyklades is Greece
223 I5 Kyle Sask. Can.
149 H3 Kyle r. England U.K.
146 C4 Kyleakin Highland, Scotland U.K.
146 C4 Kyle of Lochalsh Highland, Scotland U.K.
146 D3 Kyle of Tongue inlet Scotland U.K.
146 C4 Kylerhea Highland, Scotland U.K.
146 C6 Kyles of Bute sea chan. Scotland U.K.
146 B4 Kyles Scalpay Western Isles, Scotland U.K.
146 C3 Kylestrome Highland, Scotland U.K.
169 B6 Kyll r. Ger.
169 B5 Kyllburg Ger.
198 C3 Kyllini mt. Greece
141 M3 Kylmäkoski Fin.
198 D2 Kymi Greece
138 F1 Kymijoki r. Fin.
83 F4 Kyneton Vic. Austr.
142 E1 Kynna r. Norway
176 B1 Kynšperk nad Ohří Czech Rep.
85 E4 Kynuna Qld Austr.
210 B4 Kyoga, Lake Uganda
104 C2 Kyōga-dake mt. Japan
105 D3 Kyōga-dake mt. Japan
104 B3 Kyōga-misaki pt Japan
83 H2 Kyogle N.S.W. Austr.
85 F4 Kyong Qld Austr.
101 C5 Kyŏnggi-man b. S. Korea
101 D6 Kyŏngju S. Korea
96 A3 Kyonpyaw Myanmar
104 B4 Kyōto Japan
104 B3 Kyōto pref. Japan
102 J4 Kyōwa Japan
198 B3 Kyparissia Greece
198 B3 Kyparissiakos Kolpos b. Greece
Kypros country Asia see Cyprus
107 G1 Kyra Rus. Fed.
198 D2 Kyra Panagia i. Greece
Kyrenia Cyprus see Keryneia
Kyrenia Mountains Cyprus see Pentadaktylos Range
121 H4 Kyrgyzstan country Asia
136 E5 Kyrhyzh-Kytay r. Ukr.
198 D1 Kyria Greece
198 C2 Kyriaki Greece
170 D3 Kyritz Ger.
142 B2 Kyrkjenuten mt. Norway
140 J3 Kyrksæterøra Norway
136 E3 Kyrnasivka Ukr.
136 E5 Kyrnychky Ukr.
137 H2 Kyrykivka Ukr.
137 H4 Kyrylivka Ukr.
137 I3 Kyseli Ukr.
136 C3 Kyseliv Ukr.
137 F2 Kyselivka Ukr.
136 D2 Kyshyy Ukr.
177 H2 Kysucké Nové Mesto Slovakia
131 O3 Kytalyktakh Rus. Fed.
136 E5 Kytay, Ozero l. Ukr.
137 H3 Kytayhorod Ukr.
198 C3 Kythira i. Greece
198 D3 Kythnos i. Greece
128 A2 Kythrea Cyprus
121 G4 Kyumyush-Tak, Pik mt. Kyrg.
222 E5 Kyuquot B.C. Can.
Kyurdamir Azer. see Kürdämir
103 E8 Kyūshū i. Japan
266 E4 Kyushu-Palau Ridge sea feature N. Pacific Ocean
103 E7 Kyūshū-sanchi mts Japan
197 F4 Kyustendil Bulg.
96 B3 Kywebwe Myanmar
83 F3 Kywong N.S.W. Austr.
Kyyev Ukr. see Kyiv
Kyyiv Ukr. see Kyiv
136 F2 Kyyivs'ke Vodoskhovyshche resr Ukr.
140 N3 Kyyjärvi Fin.
120 C3 Kyzan Kazakh.
129 C2 Kyzburun Tretiy Rus. Fed.
120 D4 Kyzketken Uzbek.
Kyzyl Moldova see Ştefan Vodă
98 F1 Kyzyl Rus. Fed.
121 G4 Kyzyl-Adyr Kyrg.
121 I3 Kyzylagash Kazakh.
Kyzyl-Burun Azer. see Siyäzän
Kyzyl-Kiya Kyrg. see Kyzyl-Kyya
Kyzylkum, Peski des. Kazakh./Uzbek. see Kyzylkum Desert
120 F4 Kyzylkum Desert Kazakh./Uzbek.
121 H4 Kyzyl-Kyya Kyrg.
98 F1 Kyzyl-Mazhalyk Rus. Fed.
120 F3 Kyzylorda Kazakh.
Kyzyl-Orda Oblast admin. div. Kazakh. see Kzyl-Ordinskaya Oblast'
120 C4 Kyzylsay Kazakh.
121 I4 Kyzyl-Suu Kyrg.
121 G5 Kyzyl-Suu r. Kyrg.
121 H3 Kyzyltau Kazakh.
121 G2 Kyzylzhar Kazakh.
Kzyl-Dzhar Kazakh. see Kyzylzhar
Kzyl-Orda Kazakh. see Kyzylorda
120 E3 Kzyl-Ordinskaya Oblast' admin. div. Kazakh.
120 F3 Kzyl-Ordinskoye Vodokhranilishche resr Kazakh.
Kzyltu Kazakh. see Kishkenekol'

L

179 H2 Laa an der Thaya Austria
173 F2 Laaber Ger.
170 D2 Laage Ger.
138 E2 Laagri Estonia
182 D4 La Alberca Castilla y León Spain
187 B7 La Alberca Murcia Spain
183 H5 La Alberca de Záncara Spain
182 D4 La Alberguería de Argañán Spain
184 D2 La Albuera Spain
183 E4 La Aldehuela Spain
184 D3 La Algaba Spain
183 E4 La Aliseda de Tormes Spain
187 B7 La Aljorra Spain
183 H5 La Almarcha Spain
186 C3 La Almolda Spain
183 I3 La Almunia de Doña Godina Spain
260 E6 La Amarga, Lago l. Arg.
243 G6 La Angostura, Presa de resr Mex.
184 C3 La Antilla Spain
260 A6 La Araucania admin. reg. Chile
244 C2 La Ardilla, Cerro mt. Mex.
179 E3 Laarkirchen Austria
165 C3 Laarne Belgium
210 E2 Laascaanood Somalia
210 F2 Laasgoray Somalia
170 C2 Laaslich Ger.
251 F2 La Asunción Venez.
182 C5 La Atalaya de Santiago hill Spain
169 E3 Laatzen Ger.
190 E2 Laax Switz.
204 B4 Laâyoune Western Sahara
187 B7 La Azohía Spain
196 E4 Lab r. Yugo.
129 B1 Laba r. Rus. Fed.
242 E2 La Babia Mex.
159 F3 La Baconnière France
242 □I5 La Bahía, Islas de is Hond.
225 G3 La Baie Que. Can.
183 F4 Labajos Spain
224 E2 La Baleine, Grande Rivière de r. Que. Can.
224 E2 La Baleine, Petite Rivière de r. Que. Can.
225 H1 La Baleine, Rivière à r. Que. Can.
160 E3 La Balme-de-Sillingy France
258 D2 La Banda Arg.
244 B1 La Bandera, Cerro mt. Mex.
182 E2 La Bañeza Spain
Labao Guangxi China see Liujiang
244 C3 La Barca Mex.
238 E3 La Barge WY U.S.A.
158 D5 La Barre-de-Monts France
159 G3 La Barre-en-Ouche France
163 C5 La Barthe-de-Neste France
163 C5 Labarthe-Rivière France
79 □1 Labasa Vanua Levu Fiji
156 C2 La Bassée France
163 A5 La Bastide-Clairence France
163 D5 Labastide-d'Anjou France
163 B5 Labastide-d'Armagnac France
163 D5 La Bastide-de Bousignac France
163 D5 La Bastide-de-Sérou France
161 D5 La Bastide-des-Jourdans France
163 E4 La Bastide-l'Évêque France
163 D4 Labastide-Murat France
161 B4 La Bastide-Puylaurent France
161 A5 Labastide-Rouairoux France
163 D5 Labastide-St-Pierre France
163 D6 La Bastide-sur-l'Hers France
160 E3 La Bâthie France
161 E4 La Bâtie-Neuve France
217 □3b Labattoir Mayotte
163 B5 Labatut France
163 C5 Labatut-Rivière France
158 D4 La Baule-Escoublac France
159 G3 La Bazoche-Gouet France
159 G3 La Bazoge France
190 B2 L'Abbaye Switz.
176 D1 Labe r. Czech Rep. alt. Elbe (Germany)
206 B4 Labé Guinea
161 C4 La Bégude-de-Mazenc France
163 C5 Labéjan France
224 F4 Labelle Que. Can.
231 D7 La Belle FL U.S.A.
163 A5 Labenne France
161 E4 La Bérarde France
160 D1 Labergement-lès-Seurre France
161 E5 La Bernarde, Sommet de mt. France
158 D4 La Bernerie-en-Retz France
190 C2 La Berra mt. Switz.
173 G3 Laberweinting Ger.
222 F3 La Biche r. N.W.T. Can.
223 H4 La Biche, Lac l. Alta Can.
188 E3 Labin Croatia
129 B1 Labinsk Rus. Fed.
160 D3 La Biolle France
94 C2 Labis Malaysia
186 D3 La Bisbal de Falset Spain
186 E3 La Bisbal del Penedès Spain
186 G3 La Bisbal d'Empordà Spain
174 F3 Łabiszyn Pol.
161 C4 Lablachère France
261 F6 La Blanca Grande Laguna l. Arg.
92 B3 Labo Phil.
182 D1 La Bobia, Sierra de mts Spain
129 C2 Laboda, Gora mt. Georgia/Rus. Fed.
183 H3 La Bodera mt. Spain
168 F1 Laboe Ger.
156 B4 La Bonneville-sur-Iton France
261 F3 Laborde Arg.
177 K3 Laborec r. Slovakia
87 C5 Labouchere, Mount hill W.A. Austr.
158 E3 La Bouëxière France
163 B4 Labouheyre France
161 D5 La Bouilladisse France
261 F4 Laboulaye Arg.
160 A3 La Bourboule France
158 E3 La Boussac France
163 E5 Laboutarie France
183 E3 La Bóveda de Toro Spain
175 I6 Łabowa Pol.
225 I2 Labrador reg. Nfld. Can.
225 H2 Labrador City Nfld. Can.
221 M3 Labrador Sea Can./Greenland
Labrang Gansu China see Xiahe
250 C3 Labranzagrande Col.
252 D1 Lábrea Brazil
247 □7 La Brea Trin. and Tob.
163 B4 La Brède France
161 E4 La Bréole France
157 G4 La Bresse France
160 D3 La Bridoire France
163 B4 Labrit France
157 H4 La Broque France
158 E4 La Bruffière France
163 E5 Labruguière France
184 A1 Labrujeira Port.
159 F5 L'Absie France
95 F1 Labuan Malaysia
Labudalin Nei Mongol China see Ergun
244 C4 La Bufa, Cerro mt. Mex.
94 D4 Labuhan Jawa Barat Indon.
94 C2 Labuhanbilik Sumatera Indon.
94 B2 Labuhanruku Sumatera Indon.
161 D3 La Buisse France
95 G1 Labuk r. Sabah Malaysia
93 C3 Labuna Maluku Indon.
175 L5 Łabunie Pol.
156 C5 La Bussière France
96 A3 Labutta Myanmar
143 G1 Läby Sweden
82 C2 Labyrinth, Lake salt flat S.A. Austr.
130 H3 Labytnangi Rus. Fed.
196 D5 Laç Albania
202 B6 Lac pref. Chad
183 G4 La Cabrera Spain
182 D2 La Cabrera, Sierra de mts Spain
161 D5 La Cadière-d'Azur France
159 F5 La Caillère-St-Hilaire France
185 G3 Lacalahorra Spain
185 G1 La Calderina mt. Spain
185 G1 La Calderina, Sierra de mts Spain
260 E2 La Calera Arg.
216 □3a La Calera La Gomera Canary Is
260 B3 La Calera Chile
192 B4 La Caletta Sardegna Italy
225 I3 Lac Allard Que. Can.
La Calle Alg. see El Kala
161 A4 Lacalm France
161 C5 La Calmette France
183 E5 La Calzada de Oropesa Spain
185 E3 La Campana Spain
185 H4 La Cañada de San Urbano Spain
186 C4 La Cañada de Verich Spain
162 A4 Lacanau France
162 A3 Lacanau-Océan France
160 C1 Lacanche France
La Cañiza Spain see A Cañiza
161 B4 La Canourgue France
243 H5 Lacantún r. Mex.
156 D3 La Capelle France
161 A4 Lacapelle-Barrès France
163 D4 Lacapelle-Marival France
163 E4 Lacapelle-Viescamp France
184 D2 Lácara r. Spain
196 D3 Laćarak Vojvodina, Srbija Yugo.
182 D1 La Caridad Spain
261 F3 La Carlota Arg.
92 B4 La Carlota Phil.
185 F3 La Carlota Spain
185 G2 La Carolina Spain
163 A5 Lacarre France
161 A5 Lacaune France
161 A5 Lacaune, Monts de mts France
186 D4 La Cava Spain
183 G1 La Cavada Spain
161 B4 La Cavalerie France
163 D4 Lacave France
163 E5 Lacaze France
233 □I1 Lac-Baker N.B. Can.
Laccadive, Minicoy and Amindivi Islands union terr. India see Lakshadweep
114 B4 Laccadive Islands India
193 F4 Lacco Ameno Italy
223 L5 Lac du Bonnet Man. Can.
226 C3 Lac du Flambeau WI U.S.A.
149 I4 Laceby North East Lincolnshire, England U.K.
Lacedaemon Greece see Sparti
193 H3 Lacedonia Italy
242 □I6 La Ceiba Hond.
186 F3 La Cellera de Ter Spain
159 G4 La Celle-St-Avant France
156 C4 La Celle-St-Cloud France
La Cenia Spain see La Sènia
82 D4 Lacepede Bay S.A. Austr.
86 D3 Lacepede Islands W.A. Austr.
183 G2 La Cerca Spain
186 C4 La Cerollera Spain
191 F2 Laces Italy
225 G4 Lac-Etchemin Que. Can.
234 B1 Laceyville PA U.S.A.
233 □H1 Lac Frontière Que. Can.
134 G3 Lacha, Ozero l. Rus. Fed.
161 B3 La Chaise-Dieu France
158 E5 La Chaize-le-Vicomte France
161 E3 La Chambre France
160 A2 La Chapelaude France
157 F3 La Chapelle France
162 D3 La Chapelle-Aubareil France
157 G4 La Chapelle-aux-Bois France
162 D4 La Chapelle-aux-Saints France
160 E2 La Chapelle-d'Abondance France
159 F4 La Chapelle-d'Aligné France
159 F3 La Chapelle-d'Andaine France
159 I4 La Chapelle-d'Angillon France
158 E3 La Chapelle-des-Fougeretz France
158 D4 La-Chapelle-des-Marais France
161 E4 La Chapelle-en-Valgaudémar France
161 D4 La Chapelle-en-Vercors France
156 C4 La Chapelle-la-Reine France
161 B3 La Chapelle-Laurent France
160 B1 La Chapelle-St-André France
159 F5 La Chapelle-St-Laurent France
156 E4 La Chapelle-St-Luc France
156 B5 La Chapelle-St-Mesmin France
160 D1 La Chapelle-St-Quillain France
159 I4 La Chapelle-St-Ursin France
161 C4 Lachapelle-sous-Aubenas France
158 E4 La Chapelle-sur-Erdre France
160 B1 La Charité-sur-Loire France
159 G4 La Chartre-sur-le-Loir France
161 D3 La Chartreuse, Massif de mts France
162 B2 La Châtaigneraie France
162 D2 La Châtre France
162 D2 La Châtre-Langlin France
157 E5 La Chaume France
157 F3 Lachaussée, Étang de l. France
159 H4 La Chaussée-St-Victor France
156 E4 La Chaussée-sur-Marne France
190 B1 La Chaux-de-Fonds Switz.
160 D2 La Chaux-du-Dombief France
190 D1 Lachen Switz.
168 F3 Lachendorf Ger.
161 E5 Lachens, Montagne de mt. France
172 C2 Lachen-Speyerdorf Ger.
156 E3 La Cheppe France
158 E4 La Chevrolière France
158 D3 La Chèze France
227 F3 Lachine MI U.S.A.
83 E3 Lachlan r. N.S.W. Austr.
250 C5 La Chorrera Col.
242 □K7 La Chorrera Panama
175 K2 Lachowo Pol.
168 F3 Lachte r. Ger.
117 G4 Lachung Sikkim India
224 F4 Lachute Que. Can.
138 F4 Lāči Latvia
183 I4 La Cierva Spain
129 E4 Laçın Azer.
161 D5 La Ciotat France
183 F3 La Cisterniga Spain
244 B2 La Ciudad Mex.
175 H3 Łąck Pol.
148 B3 Lack Northern Ireland U.K.
232 D3 Lackawanna NY U.S.A.
234 C1 Lackawanna r. PA U.S.A.
234 C1 Lackawanna County county PA U.S.A.
234 D1 Lackawaxen r. PA U.S.A.
175 I6 Łącko Pol.
223 I4 Lac La Biche Alta Can.
Lac la Martre N.W.T. Can. see Wha Ti
160 C2 La Clayette France
160 E3 La Clusaz France
161 D4 La Cluse France
160 E2 La Cluse-et-Mijoux France
225 G4 Lac-Mégantic Que. Can.
258 D2 La Cocha Arg.
150 E3 Lacock Wiltshire, England U.K.
184 C1 La Codosera Spain
186 D3 La Cogulla mt. Spain
233 G2 Lacolle Que. Can.
161 F5 La Colle-sur-Loup France
245 E2 La Colmena, Sierra mts Mex.
242 C2 La Colorada Mex.
222 H4 Lacombe Alta Can.
226 C5 Lacon IL U.S.A.
183 G1 La Concha Spain
243 G5 La Concordia Mex.
161 E4 La Condamine-Châtelard France
192 B5 Laconi Sardegna Italy
233 H3 Laconia NH U.S.A.
260 C3 La Consulta Arg.
161 B5 La Coquillade hill France
162 C3 La Coquille France
223 I4 La Corey Alta Can.
227 I1 La Corne Que. Can.
185 E2 La Coronada Andalucía Spain
184 E2 La Coronada Extremadura Spain
La Coruña Spain see A Coruña
La Coruña prov. Galicia Spain see A Coruña
161 D5 Lacoste France
161 D3 La Côte-St-André France
162 A2 La-Couarde-sur-Mer France
162 C3 La Couronne France
163 D6 Lacourt France
162 E3 La Courtine France
156 B4 La Couture-Boussey France
161 B5 La Couvertoirade France
246 □ Lacovia Jamaica
163 B5 Lacq France
161 E5 La Crau France
162 B2 La Crèche France
226 B4 La Crescent MN U.S.A.
222 G3 La Crete Alta Can.
186 D4 La Creu de Santos hill Spain
261 G2 La Criolla Arg.
161 A4 Lacroix-Barrez France
159 E3 La Croixille France
156 C3 Lacroix-St-Ouen France
161 E5 La Croix-Valmer France
236 D4 La Crosse KS U.S.A.
232 D6 La Crosse VA U.S.A.
226 B4 La Crosse WI U.S.A.
163 E5 Lacrouzette France
258 F3 La Cruz Arg.
250 B4 La Cruz Col.
242 □I7 La Cruz Costa Rica
242 D4 La Cruz Sinaloa Mex.
245 E1 La Cruz Tamaulipas Mex.
242 □I6 La Cruz Nic.
244 D5 La Cruz, Cerro mt. Mex.
242 E2 La Cuesta Mex.
182 D3 La Culebra, Sierra de mts Spain
260 E2 La Cumbre Arg.
184 E1 La Cumbre Spain
183 H2 Lacunza Spain
236 E4 La Cygne KS U.S.A.
175 J4 Łaczany Pol.
175 I5 Łęczna Pol.
174 F5 Łącznik Pol.
175 K5 Łada r. Pol.
257 G2 Ladainha Brazil
116 D2 Ladakh Range mts India
137 G2 Ladan Ukr.
177 I4 Ladánybene Hungary
169 C3 Ladbergen Ger.
177 H2 Ladce Slovakia
226 C5 Ladd IL U.S.A.
174 F3 Lądek Pol.
174 E5 Lądek-Zdrój Pol.
168 E1 Ladelund Ger.
246 B2 La Demajagua Cuba
183 G2 La Demanda, Sierra de mts Spain
172 C2 Ladenburg Ger.
158 D2 La Déroute, Passage de str. Channel Is/France
247 □2 La Désirade i. Guadeloupe
146 C4 Ladhar Bheinn mt. Scotland U.K.
162 D3 Ladignac-le-Long France
217 □2a La Digue i. Inner Islands Seychelles
126 D2 Ladik Turkey
179 F4 Ladinger Spitz mt. Austria
163 E4 Ladinhac France
214 C5 Ladismith S. Africa
192 E3 Ladispoli Italy
123 E4 Lādīz Iran
116 C4 Ladnun Rajasthan India
182 C5 Ladoeiro Port.
190 B2 La Dôle mt. Switz.
156 C4 Ladon France
198 B3 Ladon r. Greece
108 D3 Ladong Guangxi China
139 H1 Ladozhskoye Ozero l. Rus. Fed.
182 C1 Ladra r. Spain
Ladrones terr. N. Pacific Ocean see Northern Mariana Islands
242 □J8 Ladrones, Islas is Panama
117 H4 Ladu mt. Arun. Prad. India
222 A2 Ladue r. Can./U.S.A.
138 C4 Ladushkin Rus. Fed.
134 F3 Ladva Rus. Fed.
134 F3 Ladva-Vetka Rus. Fed.
116 D3 Ladwa Haryana India
146 E5 Ladybank Fife, Scotland U.K.
83 G5 Lady Barron Tas. Austr.
215 F3 Ladybrand S. Africa
215 F4 Lady Frere S. Africa
215 F4 Lady Grey S. Africa
136 D3 Ladyhy Ukr.
148 E2 Lady Isle i. Scotland U.K.
146 F6 Ladykirk Scottish Borders, Scotland U.K.
146 F4 Ladysford Aberdeenshire, Scotland U.K.
222 F5 Ladysmith B.C. Can.
215 G3 Ladysmith S. Africa
226 B3 Ladysmith WI U.S.A.
121 G2 Ladyzhenka Kazakh.
136 E3 Ladyzhyn Ukr.
136 F3 Ladyzhynka Ukr.
175 H4 Ładzice Pol.
91 K8 Lae P.N.G.
261 G3 La Emilia Arg.
97 C4 Laem Ngop Thai.
187 C6 La Encina Spain
169 C3 Laer Ger.
183 E2 La Ercina Spain
141 I3 Lærdalsøyri Norway
192 A4 Laerru Sardegna Italy
La Escala Spain see L'Escala
142 D3 Læsø i. Denmark
142 D3 Læsø Rende sea chan. Denmark
253 E3 La Esperanza Bol.
216 □3a La Esperanza Tenerife Canary Is
242 □H6 La Esperanza Hond.
242 □I6 La Esperanza, Sierra de mts Hond.
182 D1 La Espina Spain
245 E3 La Estancia, Cerro mt. Mex.
183 E5 La Estrella Spain
260 E2 La Falda Arg.
161 D5 La Fare-les-Oliviers France
226 B4 La Farge WI U.S.A.
233 F2 La Fargeville NY U.S.A.
161 E5 La Farlède France
186 D3 La Fatarrella Spain
161 D4 La Faurie France
162 A2 La Faute-sur-Mer France
Lafayette Alg. see Bougaa
231 C5 Lafayette AL U.S.A.
240 F3 Lafayette CA U.S.A.
238 F4 Lafayette CO U.S.A.
231 C5 La Fayette GA U.S.A.
230 C3 Lafayette IN U.S.A.
237 E6 Lafayette LA U.S.A.
234 D1 Lafayette NJ U.S.A.
232 B5 Lafayette OH U.S.A.
231 C4 Lafayette TN U.S.A.
246 A2 Lafé Cuba
185 I1 La Felipa Spain
156 D3 La Fère France
158 E5 La Ferrière France
159 F3 La Ferrière-aux-Etangs France
227 H1 Laferté Que. Can.
222 G2 Laferte r. N.W.T. Can.
156 C4 La Ferté-Alais France
159 G3 La Ferté-Bernard France
159 G3 La Ferté-Frênel France
156 D4 La Ferté-Gaucher France
159 H4 La Ferté-Imbault France
156 D5 La Ferté-Loupièrre France
159 F3 La Ferté-Macé France
156 D3 La-Ferté-Milon France
156 B5 La Ferté-St-Aubin France
156 B5 La Ferté-St-Cyr France
156 D4 La Ferté-sous-Jouarre France
157 F5 Laferté-sur-Amance France
157 E4 Laferté-sur-Aube France
159 G3 La Férte-Vidame France
156 B5 La Ferté-Villeneuil France
207 H4 Lafia Nigeria
207 G4 Lafiagi Nigeria
163 C5 Lafitole France
224 E3 Laflamme r. Que. Can.
223 J5 Lafleche Sask. Can.
159 F4 La Flèche France
182 D1 La Florida Spain
162 A2 La Flotte France
179 H3 Lafnitz Austria
179 H4 Lafnitz r. Austria
78 □5 La Foa New Caledonia
232 A6 La Follette TN U.S.A.
226 E5 La Fontaine IN U.S.A.
159 G4 La Fontaine-St-Martin France
187 C6 La Font de la Figuera Spain
161 E4 La Font Sancte, Pic de mt. France
227 H2 Laforce Que. Can.
163 C4 La Force France
227 G2 Laforest Ont. Can.
158 C4 La Forêt-Fouesant France
159 F5 La Forêt-sur-Sèvre France
225 F2 Laforge Que. Can.
225 F2 Laforge r. Que. Can.
157 G4 La Forge France
186 D2 Lafortunada Spain
163 E4 La Fouillade France
160 C3 La Fouillouse France
237 F6 Lafourche, Bayou r. LA U.S.A.
161 E4 La Foux-d'Allos France
163 D4 Lafrançaise France
156 E3 La Francheville France
261 F2 La Francia Arg.
182 D4 La Fregeneda Spain
159 G3 La Fresnaye-sur-Chédouat France
157 H4 Lafrimbolle France
183 H4 La Frontera Spain
122 C5 Lāft Iran
182 D4 La Fuente de San Esteban Spain
186 E3 La Fuliola Spain
158 D4 La Gacilly France
186 D4 La Galera del Pla Spain
205 H1 La Galite, Canal de sea chan. Tunisia
258 E3 La Gallareta Arg.
256 D3 Lagamar Brazil
120 A3 Lagan' Rus. Fed.
143 E3 Lagan r. Sweden
147 F2 Lagan r. Northern Ireland U.K.
161 E5 La Garde France
161 C4 La Garde-Adhémar France
161 E5 La Garde-Freinet France
163 D5 Lagardelle-sur-Lèze France
182 C3 Lagarelhos Port.
182 C4 Lagares da Beira Port.
185 F2 La Garganta Spain
158 E5 La Garnache France
186 F3 La Garriga Spain
163 E5 Lagarrigue France
184 D2 La Garrovilla Spain
183 E5 Lagartera Spain
254 F4 Lagarto Brazil
256 A5 Lagarto, Serra do hills Brazil
159 E5 La Gaubretière France
148 C2 Lagavara Northern Ireland U.K.
206 B3 Lagbar Senegal
169 B3 Lage Niedersachsen Ger.
169 D4 Lage Nordrhein-Westfalen Ger.
165 E3 Lage Mierde Neth.
142 C1 Lågen r. Norway
142 D2 Lågen r. Norway
168 E2 Lägerdorf Ger.
146 C6 Lagg North Ayrshire, Scotland U.K.
146 D4 Laggan Highland, Scotland U.K.
146 D4 Laggan Highland, Scotland U.K.
146 D5 Laggan, Loch l. Scotland U.K.
148 C2 Laggan Bay Scotland U.K.
146 B5 Lagganulva Argyll and Bute, Scotland U.K.
147 C2 Laghey Rep. of Ireland
123 G3 Laghmān prov. Afgh.
205 F2 Laghouat Alg.
147 C3 Laghtgeorge Rep. of Ireland
174 E5 Łagiewniki Pol.
185 I1 La Gineta Spain
198 C1 Lagkadas Greece
158 E2 La Glacerie France
250 C2 La Gloria Col.
160 D3 Lagnieu France
156 C4 Lagny-sur-Marne France
193 I5 Lago Italy
Lago prov. Moz. see Niassa
216 □1b Lagoa São Miguel Azores
182 D3 Lagoa Bragança Port.
184 B3 Lagoa Faro Port.
182 D3 Lagoaça Port.
257 E4 Lagoa da Prata Brazil
257 E4 Lagoa Dourada Brazil
256 D3 Lagoa Formosa Brazil
257 F3 Lagoa Santa Brazil
255 C9 Lagoa Vermelha Brazil
254 D3 Lago da Pedra Brazil
129 E3 Lagodekhi Georgia
187 G5 Lago Menor Spain
216 □3a La Gomera i. Canary Is
243 H6 La Gomera Guat.
246 D3 La Gonâve, Île de i. Haiti
193 H4 Lagonegro Italy
92 B3 Lagonoy Gulf Phil.
84 D3 Lagoon Creek r. Qld Austr.
Lagoon Island atoll Arch. des Tuamotu Fr. Polynesia see Tematangi
163 B5 Lagor France
162 B3 Lagorce Aquitaine France
161 C4 Lagorce Rhône-Alpes France
262 O1 La Gorce Mountains Antarctica
162 A2 Lagord France
186 E3 La Gornal Spain
244 C3 Lagos r. Mex.
207 F5 Lagos Nigeria
207 F5 Lagos state Nigeria
184 B3 Lagos Port.
211 A6 Lagosa Tanz.
191 H4 Lagosanto Italy
244 D3 Lagos de Moreno Mex.
174 D3 Łagów Pol.
175 J5 Łagów Pol.
140 □ Lågøya i. Svalbard
183 H2 Lagrán Spain
184 D3 La Granada de Riotinto Spain
186 D3 La Granadella Spain
160 C3 La Grand-Croix France
224 E2 La Grande r. Que. Can.
238 C2 La Grande OR U.S.A.
224 E2 La Grande 2, Réservoir resr Que. Can.
224 F2 La Grande 3, Réservoir resr Que. Can.
224 F2 La Grande 4, Réservoir resr Que. Can.
161 E3 La Grande Casse, Pointe de mt. France
161 C4 La Grande-Combe France
161 C5 La Grande-Motte France
86 D3 Lagrange W.A. Austr.
240 G3 La Grange CA U.S.A.
231 C5 La Grange GA U.S.A.
230 C3 Lagrange IN U.S.A.
230 C4 La Grange KY U.S.A.
233 □I2 La Grange ME U.S.A.
237 D6 La Grange TX U.S.A.
86 D3 Lagrange Bay W.A. Austr.
235 E1 Lagrangeville NY U.S.A.
186 D3 La Granja d'Escarp Spain
185 E2 La Granjuela Spain
251 F3 La Gran Sabana plat. Venez.
161 A5 Lagrasse France
161 E3 La Grave France
163 D4 La Grésigne, Forêt de reg. France
190 C2 La Gruyère, Lac de l. Switz.
225 G4 La Guadeloupe Que. Can.
250 D2 La Guajira, Península de pen. Col.
216 □3a La Guancha Tenerife Canary Is
184 E2 La Guarda Spain
183 G5 La Guardia Castilla - La Mancha Spain
La Guardia Galicia Spain see A Guardia
183 H2 Laguardia Spain
185 G3 La Guardia de Jaén Spain
186 C2 Laguarta Spain
La Gudiña Spain see A Gudiña
162 D3 Laguenne France
163 D4 Laguépie France
158 E4 La Guerche-de-Bretagne France
160 A2 La Guerche-sur-l'Aubois France
158 D5 La Guérinière France
160 C2 La Guiche France
161 A4 Laguiole France
255 C9 Laguna Brazil
239 F5 Laguna NM U.S.A.
251 I5 Laguna, Ilha da i. Brazil
240 I5 Laguna Beach CA U.S.A.
182 E2 Laguna Dalga Spain
183 F3 Laguna de Duero Spain
182 E2 Laguna de Negrillos Spain
242 □J6 Laguna de Perlas Nic.
241 I5 Laguna Mountains CA U.S.A.
250 C6 Lagunas Peru
258 E2 Laguna Yema Arg.
191 G2 Lagundo Italy
182 E4 Lagunilla Spain
252 E4 Lagunillas Bol.
250 D2 Lagunillas Venez.
107 J1 Laha Heilong. China
184 E2 La Haba Spain
246 B2 La Habana Cuba
240 I5 La Habra CA U.S.A.
95 G1 Lahad Datu Sabah Malaysia
158 E2 La Hague, Cap de c. France
240 □C8 Lahaina HI U.S.A.
116 D4 Lahar Madh. Prad. India
147 B2 Lahardaun Rep. of Ireland
226 B5 La Harpe IL U.S.A.
116 E4 Laharpur Uttar Prad. India
234 C2 Lahaska PA U.S.A.
94 C3 Lahat Sumatera Indon.
158 E2 La Haye-du-Puits France
158 E3 La Haye-Pesnel France
168 C3 Lähden Ger.
260 B2 La Herradura Chile
185 H2 La Herrera Spain
159 G2 La Hève, Cap de c. France
157 F4 Laheycourt France
129 F3 Lahıc Azer.
187 B6 La Higuera Spain
124 D5 Laḩij Yemen
124 D5 Laḩij governorate Yemen
118 F2 Lāhījān Iran
147 B4 Lahinch Rep. of Ireland
182 E3 La Hiniesta Spain
136 C1 Lahishyn Belarus
168 C3 Lahn Ger.
169 C5 Lahn r. Ger.
169 D5 Lahnau Ger.
169 C5 Lahnstein Ger.
169 D5 Lahntal-Goßfelden Ger.
142 E3 Laholm Sweden
142 E3 Laholmsbukten b. Sweden
183 E4 La Horcajada Spain
123 H4 Lahore Pak.
183 G3 La Horra Spain
246 D3 La Hotte, Massif de mts Haiti
138 F4 Lahoysk Belarus
172 B3 Lahr (Schwarzwald) Ger.
141 N3 Lahti Fin.
250 A6 La Huaca Peru
244 D4 La Huacana Mex.
244 B4 La Huerta Mex.
260 D2 La Huerta, Sierra de mts Arg.
208 C2 Laï Chad

109 F1 Lai'an Anhui China
Laibach Slovenia see Ljubljana
108 D4 Laibin Guangxi China
172 D3 Laichingen Ger.
146 C4 Laide Highland, Scotland U.K.
85 H5 Laidley Qld Austr.
146 D5 Laidon, Loch l. Scotland U.K.
240 □C8 Laie HI U.S.A.
108 D2 Laifeng Hubei China
156 E3 Laifour France
159 G3 L'Aigle France
163 F4 La Iglesuela Spain
186 C4 La Iglesuela del Cid Spain
156 E5 Laignes France
190 D5 Laigueglia Italy
162 A2 L'Aiguillon-sur-Mer France
140 M3 Laihia Fin.
140 M2 Lainioälven r. Sweden
141 T2 Lainitz r. Austria
232 A5 Lair KY U.S.A.
207 H2 L'Aïr, Massif de mts Niger
234 B1 Lairdsville PA U.S.A.
146 E3 Lairg Highland, Scotland U.K.
185 H3 La Iruela Spain
94 C3 Lais Sumatera Indon.
92 C5 Lais Phil.
246 B2 La Isabela Cuba
140 L2 Laisälven r. Sweden
134 J5 Laishevo Rus. Fed.
161 A4 La Isleta pen. Gran Canaria Canary Is
216 □1 Laissac France
140 L2 Laisvall Sweden
141 M3 Laitila Fin.
141 U7 Lai'ut Georgia
191 G2 Laives Italy
107 H4 Laiwu Shandong China
107 I4 Laixi Shandong China
107 I4 Laiyang Shandong China
107 G4 Laiyuan Hebei China
159 F2 Laize r. France
107 H4 Laizhou Shandong China
107 H4 Laizhou Wan b. China
159 F2 Laizon r. France
260 B5 Laja, Laguna de l. Chile
84 B3 Lajamanu N.T. Austr.
184 D4 La Jana Spain
162 A2 La Jarrie France
191 F5 Lajatico Italy
162 A2 La Javie France
255 B9 Lajeado Brazil
254 F4 Lajedo Brazil
256 D6 Laje dos Santos i. Brazil
182 D4 Lajeosa Guarda Port.
182 C4 Lajeosa Port.
182 C4 Lajeosa do Mondego Port.
256 C2 Lajes Terceira Azores
255 C8 Lajes Brazil
216 □1c Lajes Brazil
216 □3c Lajes do Pico Pico Azores
219 Brazil
196 E3 Lajkovac Srbija Yugo.
240 H4 La Jolla Peak hill CA U.S.A.
162 D2 La Jonchère-St-Maurice France
163 C4 La Jonquera Spain
177 H5 Lajoskomárom Hungary
177 I4 Lajosmizse Hungary
160 D2 La Joux, Forêt de for. France
242 C4 La Joya Chihuahua Mex.
244 C2 La Joya Durango Mex.
252 C4 La Joya Peru
176 G4 Lajta r. Austria/Hungary
159 F4 La Jumellière France
La Junquera Spain see
La Junquera
236 C4 La Junta CO U.S.A.
246 B2 La Juventud, Isla de i. Cuba
116 B5 Lakadiya Gujarat India
124 C4 Lakathah Saudi Arabia
123 □3c Lakato Madag.
140 M2 Lakaträsk Sweden
232 B6 Lake KY U.S.A.
238 E2 Lake WY U.S.A.
80 E4 Lake Alice North l. N.Z.
236 D3 Lake Andes SD U.S.A.
126 C5 Lake Ariel FN U.S.A.
237 E6 Lake Arthur LA U.S.A.
83 E4 Lake Bolac Vic. Austr.
231 D6 Lake Butler FL U.S.A.
83 F3 Lake Cargelligo N.S.W. Austr.
233 F3 Lake Carmel NY U.S.A.
237 E6 Lake Charles LA U.S.A.
237 F5 Lake City AR U.S.A.
239 F4 Lake City CO U.S.A.
231 D6 Lake City FL U.S.A.
236 E3 Lake City IA U.S.A.
226 E3 Lake City MI U.S.A.
236 A3 Lake City MN U.S.A.
231 E5 Lake City SC U.S.A.
233 F2 Lake Clear NY U.S.A.
81 C6 Lake Coleridge South l. N.Z.
222 E5 Lake Cowichan B.C. Can.
137 J4 Lakedemonovka Rus. Fed.
149 T3 Lake District National Park England U.K.
81 E4 Lake Ferry North l. N.Z.
83 C7 Lakefield Qld Austr.
224 E4 Lakefield Ont. Can.
241 M1 Lake Fork r. CO U.S.A.
226 C4 Lake Geneva WI U.S.A.
233 G3 Lake George NY U.S.A.
87 C7 Lake Grace W.A. Austr.
Lake Harbour Nunavut Can. see Kimmirut
241 J4 Lake Havasu City AZ U.S.A.
235 D2 Lake Hiawatha NJ U.S.A.
234 D2 Lake Hopatcong NJ U.S.A.
234 C2 Lakehurst NJ U.S.A.
241 H4 Lake Isabella CA U.S.A.
237 E6 Lake Jackson TX U.S.A.
87 C7 Lake King W.A. Austr.
85 F2 Lakeland FL U.S.A.
231 D7 Lakeland FL U.S.A.
234 D2 Lakeland GA U.S.A.
234 D2 Lake Lenape NJ U.S.A.
226 C2 Lake Linden MI U.S.A.
222 D5 Lake Louise Alta Can.
211 B5 Lake Manyara National Park Tanz.
236 E3 Lake Mills IA U.S.A.
84 D4 Lake Nash N.T. Austr.
151 H2 Lakenheath Suffolk, England U.K.
238 B2 Lake Oswego OR U.S.A.
226 C2 Lake Paragina South l. N.Z.
234 D3 Lake Pine NJ U.S.A.
231 D7 Lake Placid FL U.S.A.
233 G2 Lake Placid NY U.S.A.
233 F3 Lake Pleasant NY U.S.A.
240 F2 Lakeport CA U.S.A.
227 F4 Lakeport MI U.S.A.
235 G2 Lake Providence LA U.S.A.
81 C6 Lake Pukaki South l. N.Z.
240 H1 Lake Range mts NV U.S.A.
224 D2 Lake River Ont. Can.
235 D2 Lake Riviera NJ U.S.A.
226 C2 Lake Rockwell l. OH U.S.A.
222 G5 Lake's Entrance Vic. Austr.
240 H3 Lakeshore CA U.S.A.
234 B3 Lake Shore MD U.S.A.
241 M4 Lakeside CA U.S.A.
240 15 Lakeside CA U.S.A.
235 E1 Lakeside CT U.S.A.
235 D1 Lakeside CT U.S.A.
235 E2 Lake Success NY U.S.A.
83 J4 Lake Tabourie N.S.W. Austr.
81 C6 Lake Tekapo South l. N.Z.
235 D2 Lake Telemark NJ U.S.A.
232 D3 Lakeview OH U.S.A.
238 B2 Lakeview OR U.S.A.
138 B3 Lakeview VA U.S.A.
226 A3 Lake Village AR U.S.A.
226 E3 Lakeville MN U.S.A.
232 B3 Lake Wales FL U.S.A.
234 D2 Lakewood CO U.S.A.
235 D2 Lakewood NJ U.S.A.
233 F4 Lakewood NY U.S.A.
232 D3 Lakewood OH U.S.A.
232 C5 Lakewood WV U.S.A.
141 O2 Lakhdenpokh'ya Rus. Fed.
Lakhimpur Assam India see
North Lakhimpur
116 H4 Lakhimpur Uttar Prad. India
117 H4 Lakhisarai Bihar India see
Luckeesarai

128 B4 Lakhish r. Israel
116 D5 Lakhnadon Madh. Prad. India
116 B5 Lakhpat Gujarat India
116 B5 Lakhtar Gujarat India
139 H5 Lakhva r. Belarus
129 E3 Läki r. Pol.
129 E3 Läki Azer.
174 F2 Lakin Pol.
236 C4 Lakin KS U.S.A.
139 L3 Lakinsk Rus. Fed.
Lakinskiy Rus. Fed. see
Lakinsk
177 I5 Lakitelek Hungary
224 D2 Lakitusaki r. Ont. Can.
129 D2 Lakkha-Nevre Rus. Fed.
123 G3 Lakki Pak.
198 C3 Lakonikos Kolpos b. Greece
175 H2 Łakorz Pol.
236 D1 Lakota Côte d'Ivoire
206 D5 Lakota ND U.S.A.
140 N1 Laksefjorden sea chan. Norway
140 N1 Lakselv Norway
114 B4 Lakshadweep is India see
Laccadive Islands
117 G5 Laksham Bangl.
114 C2 Lakshettipet Andhra Prad. India
114 B3 Lakshmeshwar Karnataka India
117 G5 Lakshmipur Bangl.
261 F3 La Laguna Arg.
242 C4 La Laguna, Picacho de mt. Mex.
260 A5 La Laja r. Chile
244 D3 La Laja r. Mex.
123 H3 Lala Musa Pak.
245 G3 Lalana r. Mex.
185 E3 La Lantejuela Spain
184 D2 La Lapa Spain
213 F3 Lalapanzi Zimbabwe
197 H5 Lalapaşa Turkey
213 H2 Lalaua Moz.
186 D3 L'Albagés Spain
161 F3 L'Albaron mt. France
158 C3 La Lébègue France
187 C5 L'Alcúdia Spain
160 C3 La Léchère France
85 G4 Laleham Qld Austr.
122 D4 Läleh Zär, Küh-e mt. Iran
170 D2 Lalendorf Ger.
159 D3 Laleston Bridgend, Wales U.K.
161 G4 Lalevade-d'Ardèche France
117 F4 Lalganj Bihar India
91 G2 Lamon Bay Phil.
191 G1 Lamon r. Italy
191 H4 Lamone r. Italy
95 F4 Lamongan Jawa Timur Indon.
163 C6 La Mongie France
236 E3 Lamoni IA U.S.A.
160 B3 La Monnerie-le-Montel France
240 H4 Lamont CA U.S.A.
159 C6 La Montagne France
158 E4 La Montagne France
163 C4 Lamontzie-St-Martin France
156 C3 Lamothe France
162 A2 La Mothe-Achard France
163 D4 Lamothe-Capdeville France
163 C4 Lamothe-Cassel France
163 C4 Lamothe-Landerron France
162 B2 La Mothe-St-Héray France
91 K5 Lamotrek atoll Micronesia
227 H1 La Motte Que. Can.
161 E5 La Motte France
159 I4 Lamotte-Beuvron France
159 I4 La Motte-Chalancon France
157 F3 La Motte-d'Aveillans France
157 F3 La Motte-du-Caire France
160 D3 La Motte-Servolex France
162 D2 La Moure ND U.S.A.
260 B3 Lampa Chile
96 B3 Lampang Thai.
96 C3 Lam Pao Reservoir Thai.
237 D6 Lampasas TX U.S.A.
237 D6 Lampasas r. TX U.S.A.
158 A3 Lampaul France
158 B3 La Loye France
161 E3 L'Apra-d'Huez France
116 B5 Lalpur Gujarat India
134 I3 Lal'sk Rus. Fed.
116 D4 Lalsot Rajasthan India
178 C4 L'Altissima mt. Austria/Italy
186 C3 Lalueza Spain
185 E5 La Luisiana Spain
186 C3 Laluque France
173 H2 Lam Ger.
117 H5 Lama Bangl.
193 G2 Lama Italy
234 B3 La Machine France
97 G4 Lam Plai Mat r. Thai.
151 G2 Lamport Northamptonshire, England U.K.
178 D3 Lamprechtshausen Austria
159 C3 Lampaulus Turkey see Lâpseki
94 D4 Lampung r. Indon.
94 C4 Lampung prov. Indon.
94 D4 Lam Si Bai r. Thai.

156 D2 Lambres-lez-Douai France
190 E3 Lambro r. Italy
172 C2 Lambsheim Ger.
96 C4 Lam Chi r. Thai.
97 C4 Lam Chi r. Thai.
238 F2 Lame Deer MT U.S.A.
182 C2 Lamego Port.
161 E3 La Meije mt. France
158 E4 La Meilleraye-de-Bretagne France
182 D4 Lameiras Port.
247 □ Lamentin Guadeloupe
258 D3 La Merced Arg.
252 B4 La Merced Peru
82 E3 Lameroo S.A. Austr.
82 E3 Lameroo S.A. Austr.
193 F3 La Merta mt. Italy
154 I5 La Mesa CA U.S.A.
237 C5 Lamesa TX U.S.A.
149 H3 Lamesley Tyne and Wear, England U.K.
186 D4 L'Ametlla de Mar Spain
193 I6 Lamezia Italy
187 B5 Lamiable Span
158 C4 Landevant France
158 B3 Landevisiau France
165 F4 Landgraaf Neth.
94 C3 Landik, Gunung mt. Indon.
182 B3 Landim Port.
234 D2 Landing NJ U.S.A.
156 E4 Landiras France
163 B4 Landiras France
223 I4 Landis S. Can.
234 B2 Landisville PA U.S.A.
158 C4 Landivant France
158 B3 Landivisiau France
165 F4 Landivy France
170 C1 Landkirchen auf Fehmarn Ger.
140 K3 Landögssjön l. Sweden
140 O2 Land O' Lakes WI U.S.A.
169 F4 Landolfshausen Ger.
140 K3 Landön Sweden
87 C5 Landor W.A. Austr.
150 D3 Landore Swansea, Wales U.K.
161 A6 Landos France
190 E2 Landquart Switz.
190 E2 Landquart r. Switz.
157 D2 Landrecies France
157 F3 Landres France
157 F3 Landres-et-St-Georges France
231 D5 Landrienne Que. Can.
182 C1 Landro r. Spain
Landrove r. Spain see Landro
231 D5 Landrum SC U.S.A.
160 E3 Landry France
171 D4 Landsberg Ger.
81 B5 Landsborough r. South l. N.Z.
169 B6 Landscheid Ger.
150 □ Land's End pt England U.K.
173 G3 Landshut Ger.
142 E4 Landskrona Sweden
164 D2 Landsmeer Neth.
172 B2 Landstuhl Ger.
175 H5 Lándok r. Que. Can.
197 H3 Laniel Que. Can.
175 H3 Łandyt Pol.
169 D5 Lanigan r. Spain
197 F3 La Nedei mt. Romania
147 D3 Lanesborough Rep. of Ireland
158 C4 Lanester France
231 C5 Lanett AL U.S.A.
159 G3 La Neuve-Lyre France
159 C1 La Neuville France
157 F3 Laneuville-sur-Meuse France
Lanfeng Henan China see
Lankao
96 B1 Langa, Nam r. Myanmar
142 C3 Langå Denmark
183 F3 Langa Spain
97 D5 La Nga r. Vietnam
129 F3 Längäbiz Silsiläsi hills Azer.
183 G3 Langa de Duero Spain
Langadas Greece see
Lagkadas
117 H4 Langanr. India
140 X3 Langan r. Sweden
100 D1 Langang France
121 F5 Langar Kashkadar'inskaya Oblast' Uzbek.
Langar Navoiyskaya Oblast'
Uzbek. see Lyangar
143 F3 Långasjö Sweden
146 B3 Langavat, Loch l. Scotland U.K.
168 E1 Langballig Ger.
214 D3 Langberg mts S. Africa
236 D1 Langdon ND U.S.A.
173 H2 Langdorf Ger.
161 B3 Langeac France
161 C1 Langeais France
214 E5 Langebaan S. Africa
214 D5 Langeberg mts S. Africa
162 D3 Langedijk Neth.
142 C4 Langeland i. Denmark
142 C4 Langeland Baelt str. Denmark
141 N3 Längelmäki Fin.
169 F4 Langeln Ger.
169 H4 Langelsheim Ger.
169 K3 Langemark Belgium
172 C2 Langen Hessen Ger.
168 I2 Langen Niedersachsen Ger.
168 I2 Langenaltheim Ger.
173 J5 Langenaltheim Ger.
173 I4 Langenau Ger.
169 D6 Langenaubach Ger.
178 G3 Langenbach Ger.
178 G3 Langen bei Bregenz Austria
169 I5 Langenberg Ger.
171 H4 Langenberg hill Ger.
173 I3 Langenburg Ger.
223 J4 Langenburg Sask. Can.
169 K4 Langenfeld (Rheinland) Ger.
171 D5 Langenhahn Ger.
172 C3 Langenhahn Ger.
168 J2 Langenhagen Ger.
170 D4 Langenhessen Ger.
169 I4 Langenholtensen Ger.
178 H3 Langenlois Austria
173 K3 Langennaudorf Ger.
173 K3 Langennaunhof Ger.
173 J4 Langenmosen Ger.
173 K5 Langenneufnach Ger.
173 G5 Langenorla Ger.
169 H5 Langenpreising Ger.
158 D2 Langenselbold Ger.
158 D3 Langensendelbach Ger.
172 C2 Langenstein Ger.
173 F3 Langenthal Switz.
173 J3 Langenzenn Ger.
173 G3 Langeoog Ger.
173 G3 Langeoog i. Ger.
216 □3c Langer Berg hill Ger.
173 D3 Langerwehe Ger.
171 E3 Langewiesen Ger.
142 C3 Langeskov Denmark
142 F2 Langesund Norway
172 D3 Langfang Hebei China
151 O2 Langford Bedfordshire, England U.K.
169 I4 Langfurth Ger.
107 F5 Langgapayung Sumatera Indon.
169 H5 Langgöns Ger.
170 D2 Langhagen Ger.
223 J4 Langham Sask. Can.
151 G2 Langham Rutland, England U.K.
143 F3 Langhem Sweden
190 E1 Langhirano Italy
215 I5 Langholm S. Africa
146 F6 Langholm Dumfries and Galloway, Scotland U.K.
147 D4 Langholt hill N.T. Austr.
216 □3a Langholt Iceland
234 D1 Langhorne PA U.S.A.
193 E3 Langhranesflói b. Iceland
193 C3 Langi Kalelinjo i. Indon.
97 B5 Lang Kha Toek, Khao mt. Thai.

158 C3 Landeleau France
165 E4 Landen Belgium
238 E3 Lander WY U.S.A.
158 B3 Landerneau France
157 H4 Landersheim France
163 B5 Landes dept Aquitaine France
163 B4 Landes reg. France
163 B4 Landes France
96 D3 Langong, Xê r. Laos
163 B4 Landesbergen Ger.
158 D4 Landes de Lanvaux reg. France
158 D3 Landes du Mené reg. France
261 F3 Landeta Arg.
187 B5 Landete Spain
158 C4 Landévant France
158 B3 Landévennec France
165 F4 Landgraaf Neth.
94 C3 Landik, Gunung mt. Indon.
182 B3 Landim Port.
234 D2 Landing NJ U.S.A.
156 E4 Landiras France
163 B4 Landiras France
223 I4 Landis S. Can.
234 B2 Landisville PA U.S.A.
158 C4 Landivant France
158 B3 Landivisiau France
165 F4 Landivy France
170 C1 Landkirchen auf Fehmarn Ger.
140 K3 Landögssjön l. Sweden
140 O2 Land O' Lakes WI U.S.A.
190 C2 Langnau Switz.
168 G1 Langa Denmark
161 B4 Langoire France
163 B4 Langoiran France
96 D3 Langon, Xê r. Laos
206 E4 Laoudi-Ba Côte d'Ivoire
163 B4 Langon France
163 B3 Landesbergen Ger.
140 K1 Langøya i. Norway
150 E3 Langport Somerset, England U.K.
109 F3 Langqi Fujian China
173 G3 Langquaid Ger.
182 E1 Langreo Spain
157 F5 Langres France
157 F5 Langres, Plateau de France
94 B1 Langsa Sumatera Indon.
179 F2 Langschlag Austria
107 E3 Längsele Sweden
107 E3 Langshan Nei Mongol China
107 E3 Langshan China
143 G1 Långshyttan Sweden
96 D2 Lang Son Vietnam
149 G3 Langstrothdale Chase hills England U.K.
172 A2 Langsur Ger.
207 H4 Langtang Nigeria
117 I3 Langtang National Park Nepal
149 I3 Langtoft East Riding of Yorkshire, England U.K.
140 M2 Langträsk Sweden
237 C6 Langtry TX U.S.A.
161 A6 Languedoc-Roussillon admin. reg. France
158 C3 Langueux France
Languiaru r. Brazil see Iquê
158 C4 Languidic France
183 G3 Languilla Spain
169 F4 Langula Ger.
134 C2 Langvatnet Sweden
143 I3 Langvinds druk Sweden
168 D2 Langwarden (Butjadingen) Ger.
149 G3 Langwathby Cumbria, England U.K.
168 E3 Langwedel Niedersachsen Ger.
168 E1 Langwedel Schleswig-Holstein Ger.
173 F3 Langweid am Lech Ger.
107 G4 Langya Shan mt. Hebei China
108 C2 Langzhong Sichuan China
168 B3 Lanheses Port.
158 B3 Lanhouarneau France
227 H2 Laniel Que. Can.
175 H3 Łanięta Pol.
158 C4 Lanigan r. Spain
197 F3 La Nedei mt. Romania
147 D3 Lanesborough Rep. of Ireland
136 D3 Lanivtsi Ukr.
95 E2 Lanjak, Bukit mt. Sarawak Malaysia
185 H4 Lanjarón Spain
116 E5 Lanji Madh. Prad. India
187 B7 La Pinilla Spain
216 □3c La Pine OR U.S.A.
176 D4 Lapithos Cyprus see Lapta
92 C3 Lapinig Phil.
187 B7 La Pinilla Spain
140 N3 Lapinlahti Fin.
199 L6 Lapithos Cyprus see Lapta
194 D5 La Pizzuta mt. Sicilia Italy
237 F6 Lapke r. Thai.
160 B3 La Plagne France
158 D4 La-Plaine-sur-Mer France
236 C2 La Plant SD U.S.A.
226 I4 La Plata Arg.
232 E5 La Plata MD U.S.A.
261 I4 La Plata Arg.
238 B3 La Plata CO U.S.A.
261 I4 La Plata, Rio de sea chan. Arg./Uru.

190 C2 Langnau Switz.
168 G1 Langa Denmark
161 B4 Langoire France
163 B4 Langoiran France
163 B4 Langon France
96 D3 Langon, Xê r. Laos
96 D3 Langong, Xê r. Laos
163 B4 Landesbergen Ger.
140 K1 Langøya i. Norway
150 E3 Langport Somerset, England U.K.
109 F3 Langqi Fujian China
173 G3 Langquaid Ger.
182 E1 Langreo Spain
157 F5 Langres France
157 F5 Langres, Plateau de France
94 B1 Langsa Sumatera Indon.
179 F2 Langschlag Austria
107 E3 Längsele Sweden
107 E3 Langshan Nei Mongol China
107 E3 Langshan China
143 G1 Långshyttan Sweden
96 D2 Lang Son Vietnam
149 G3 Langstrothdale Chase hills England U.K.
172 A2 Langsur Ger.
207 H4 Langtang Nigeria
117 I3 Langtang National Park Nepal
149 I3 Langtoft East Riding of Yorkshire, England U.K.
140 M2 Langträsk Sweden
237 C6 Langtry TX U.S.A.
161 A6 Languedoc-Roussillon admin. reg. France
158 C3 Langueux France
158 C4 Languidic France
183 G3 Languilla Spain
169 F4 Langula Ger.
134 C2 Langvatnet Sweden
143 I3 Langvinds druk Sweden
168 D2 Langwarden (Butjadingen) Ger.
149 G3 Langwathby Cumbria, England U.K.
168 E3 Langwedel Niedersachsen Ger.
168 E1 Langwedel Schleswig-Holstein Ger.
173 F3 Langweid am Lech Ger.
107 G4 Langya Shan mt. Hebei China
108 C2 Langzhong Sichuan China
168 B3 Lanheses Port.
158 B3 Lanhouarneau France
227 H2 Laniel Que. Can.
175 H3 Łanięta Pol.
197 F3 La Nedei mt. Romania
95 E2 Lanjak, Bukit mt. Sarawak Malaysia
185 H4 Lanjarón Spain
116 E5 Lanji Madh. Prad. India
108 A2 Lanping Yunnan China
211 A5 Lans, Montagne de mts France
161 C5 Lansargues France
234 C2 Lansdale PA U.S.A.
234 B3 Lansdowne MD U.S.A.
116 D3 Lansdowne Uttar Prad. India
226 C2 L'Anse MI U.S.A.
227 I5 L'Anse-St-Jean Que. Can.
221 H4 Lansford ND U.S.A.
166 L5 Lansing r. Y.T. Can.
236 E3 Lansing IA U.S.A.
226 E4 Lansing MI U.S.A.
226 D3 Lansing MI U.S.A.
140 M2 Lansjärv Sweden
140 L3 Lappland reg. Europe
161 D5 Lansley rain Ger.
169 G4 Lansleburg-Mont-Cenis France
160 D3 Lanslebourg-Mont-Cenis France
199 E1 Lâpseki Turkey
183 D7 Lapta Cyprus
131 S3 Laptevykh, More sea Rus. Fed.
140 M3 Lapua r. Fin.
140 M3 Lapuanjoki r. Fin.
183 H2 La Puebla Spain see Sa Pobla
161 F5 La Puebla de Almoradiel Spain
183 H2 La Puebla de Arganzón Spain
185 D4 La Puebla de Cazalla Spain
186 D3 La Puebla de Híjar Spain
185 C4 La Puebla de los Infantes Spain
184 D3 La Puebla del Río Spain
183 H3 La Puebla del Montalbán Spain
183 F4 La Puebla de Valdavia Spain
183 G3 La Puebla de Valverde Spain
183 F4 La Pueblanueva Spain
100 C3 Lanjat Heilong. China
92 C3 Laoi Phil.
190 F2 La Punt Switz.
216 □3c Lanzarote i. Canary Is
197 P5 Lăpuș Romania
252 E2 Lăpușna r. Romania
106 C4 Lanzhou Gansu China
107 F4 Lanzijing Jilin China
190 B2 Lanzo Torinese Italy
96 C2 Lao Cai Vietnam
108 D3 Laoibe Shan mts Yunnan China
108 D3 Laodong Guangxi China
96 C2 Laos country Asia
107 I4 Laoshan Shandong China

190 C2 Langnau Switz.
190 C2 Langnau Switz.
Laotieshan Shuidao sea chan.
China see Bohai Haixia
100 D4 Laotougou Jilin China
101 C4 Laotuding Shan hill Liaoning China
180 D5 Laou, Oued r. Morocco
100 C4 Laoye Ling mts China
255 C6 Lapa Brazil
185 I3 La Paca Spain
160 B2 La Pacaudière France
207 G4 Lapai Nigeria
160 B2 Lapalisse France
162 A2 La Palice France
216 □3d La Palma i. Canary Is
250 C3 La Palma Col.
242 □K7 La Palma Panama
185 C4 La Palma Spain
241 L5 La Palma AZ U.S.A.
184 D3 La Palma del Condado Spain
161 A6 La Palme France
258 C4 La Paloma Uru.
161 E5 La Palud-sur-Verdon France
260 E5 La Pampa prov. Arg.
175 I6 Łapanów Pol.
260 G4 La Panza Range mts CA U.S.A.
261 F2 La Parejas Arg.
184 D2 La Parra Spain
183 H5 La Parra de Las Vegas Spain
183 H3 La Parrilla hill Spain
182 B5 Lapas Port.
258 C3 La Paz Entre Ríos Arg.
258 D3 La Paz Mendoza Arg.
252 E4 La Paz Bol.
252 E4 La Paz dept Bol.
242 □16 La Paz Hond.
242 C3 La Paz Mex.
261 I4 La Paz Uru.
226 D5 Lapaz IN U.S.A.
250 D5 La Pedrera Col.
158 D3 La Pellerine France
161 E5 La Penne France
158 D4 La Penne-sur-Huveaune France
161 E5 La Peraleja Spain
242 D2 La Perla Mex.
102 J1 La Pérouse Strait Japan/Rus. Fed.
245 F2 La Pesca Mex.
157 H4 La Petite-Pierre France
185 G3 La Peza Spain
150 D4 La Piedad Mex.
238 B3 La Pine OR U.S.A.
92 C3 Lapinig Phil.
187 B7 La Pinilla Spain
140 N3 Lapinlahti Fin.
199 L6 Lapithos Cyprus see Lapta
194 D5 La Pizzuta mt. Sicilia Italy
237 F6 Lapke r. Thai.
160 B3 La Plagne France
158 D4 La-Plaine-sur-Mer France
236 C2 La Plant SD U.S.A.
226 I4 La Plata Arg.
232 E5 La Plata MD U.S.A.
261 I4 La Plata Arg.
238 B3 La Plata CO U.S.A.
261 I4 La Plata, Rio de sea chan. Arg./Uru.
182 D1 La Plaza Spain
162 E3 Lapleau France
163 C4 La Pléaine France
138 D3 Lapmežciems Latvia
186 E3 La Pobla de Lillet Spain
186 D2 La Pobla de Segur Spain
186 E2 La Pobla de Gordon Spain
159 F4 La Pommeraye France
192 B2 La Porta Corse France
230 C3 La Porte IN U.S.A.
227 I5 Laporte PA U.S.A.
226 C5 Laporte, Mount Y.T. Can.
186 D4 La Portellada Spain
187 B5 La Portera Spain
93 A4 Laposo, Bukit mt. Indon.
261 F2 La Posta Arg.
159 I4 La Pouèze France
196 D3 Lapovo Srbija Yugo.
156 C4 La Poyata Col.
143 F2 Lappe Sweden
141 O3 Lappeenranta Fin.
173 G2 Lappersdorf Ger.
141 M3 Lappi Fin.
140 N2 Lappi prov. Fin.
141 O3 Lappland reg. Europe
173 M2 Lapptäsk Sweden
227 G2 La Prairie Que. Can.
159 E4 La Prenée France
261 G5 Lapridá Arg.
183 H2 La Proveda de Soria Spain
237 D6 La Pryor TX U.S.A.
199 E1 Lâpseki Turkey
133 V3 Laptev Sea Rus. Fed. see
Laptevykh, More
Laptev Sea Rus. Fed. see
Laptevykh, More
131 N2 Laptevykh, More sea Rus. Fed.
140 M3 Lapua r. Fin.
140 M3 Lapuanjoki r. Fin.

143 H3 Lärbro Gotland Sweden
163 A5 Larcevaux-Arros-Cibits France
159 E3 Larchamp France
156 C4 Larchant France
162 D3 Larche France
161 E4 Larche Provence-Alpes-Côte-d'Azur France
235 E2 Larchmont NY U.S.A.
227 G2 Larchwood Ont. Can.
191 F3 Lardaro Italy
165 D5 L'Ardenne, Plateau de Belgium
191 F5 Larderello Italy
227 H1 Larder Lake Ont. Can.
182 C5 Lardosa Port.
183 G1 Laredo Spain
237 D7 Laredo TX U.S.A.
161 A5 La Redorte France
259 B9 La Reina Adelaida, Archipiélago de is Chile
227 H1 La Reine Que. Can.
164 F2 Laren Gelderland Neth.
164 E2 Laren Noord-Holland Neth.
163 B4 La Réole France
247 □1 Lares Puerto Rico
147 C2 Largan Rep. of Ireland
Largeau Chad see Faya
161 C4 Largentière France
161 E4 L'Argentière-la-Bessée France
231 D7 Largo FL U.S.A.
146 F5 Largoward Fife, Scotland U.K.
146 D3 Largs North Ayrshire, Scotland U.K.
186 B1 La Rhune hill Spain
191 F5 Lari Italy
205 H3 L'Ariana Tunisia
189 C7 L'Ariana admin. div. Tunisia
93 A3 Lariang r. Indon.
183 H3 La Riba de Escalote Spain
161 C3 La Ricamarie France
236 D1 Larimore ND U.S.A.
184 E3 La Rinconada Spain
193 G3 Larino Italy
258 D3 La Rioja Arg.
258 D3 La Rioja prov. Arg.
183 H2 La Rioja aut. comm. Spain
198 C2 Larisa Greece
Larissa Greece see Larisa
163 D6 L'Arize, Massif de mts France
123 G5 Larkana Pak.
146 E6 Larkhall South Lanarkshire, Scotland U.K.
225 I2 Lark Harbour Nfld. Can.
151 F3 Larkhill Wiltshire, England U.K.
85 F2 Lark Passage Qld Austr.
151 I2 Larling Norfolk, England U.K.
160 E2 Larmont mt. France/Switz.
158 C4 Larmor-Plage France
147 F2 Larne Larne Northern Ireland U.K.
128 A2 Larnaca Cyprus see Larnaka
147 F2 Larne Larne Northern Ireland U.K.
236 D4 Larned KS U.S.A.
147 F2 Larne Lough inlet Northern Ireland U.K.
182 C2 La Roba Spain
184 D1 La Roca de la Sierra Spain
190 C2 La Roche Switz.
159 F4 La Roche France
158 D4 La Roche-Bernard France
162 D3 La Roche-Canillac France
162 C3 La Roche-Chalais France
158 E4 La Roche-de-Rame France
158 D3 La Roche-Derrien France
158 E4 La Roche-des-Arnauds France
165 E4 La Roche-en-Ardenne Belgium
162 C3 La Rochefoucauld France
162 A2 La Rochelle France
159 G5 La Roche-Posay France
160 C2 La Rochepot France
230 C5 Laroche-St-Cydroine France
160 E2 La Roche-sur-Foron France
159 F4 La Roche-sur-Yon France
165 F5 Larochette Lux.
185 H1 La Roda Spain
185 E3 La Roda de Andalucía Spain
159 H4 La Roë France
147 E3 La Romana Dom. Rep.
163 C6 La Romana Spain
223 J4 La Ronge Sask. Can.
161 A4 La Ronge, Lac l. Sask. Can.
161 C5 Laroquebrou France
183 H2 La Roquebrussanne France
161 D5 La Roque-d'Anthéron France
161 D5 La Roque-Gageac France
161 D6 La Roque-Ste-Marguerite France
162 E3 La Roque-Timbaut France
243 E3 La Rosa Mex.
184 C4 La Rosita Mex.
234 A4 La Rouquette France
163 B6 Laruns France
145 F3 Larvik Norway
142 E2 Larvik Norway
137 J4 Larwik Ukr.
161 B4 Larzac, Causse du plat. France
191 F2 Lasa Italy
254 □ La Sabana Arg.
245 C2 Las Adjuntas, Presa de resr Mex.
216 □3d Las Adjuntas i. Canary Is
241 M2 La Sal UT U.S.A.
252 E4 La Sal, Cerros de mts Peru
260 C2 La Salina salt pan Arg.
224 C5 La Salle Junction Ont. Can.
226 B5 La Salle IL U.S.A.
161 A4 La Salle France
190 C3 La Salle les Alpes France
163 C4 La Salle France
161 A5 La Salvetat-St-Gilles France
161 A5 La Salvetat-sur-Agout France
236 C4 Las Animas CO U.S.A.
84 A4 Lasanod Somalia see Laascaanood
190 F1 La Sarine r. Switz.
216 □3c La Sarre Ont. Can.
161 B1 Las Asejas Arg.
162 E4 Lasarte-Oria Spain
161 C5 Las Asejuelas P.G.
183 G2 Las Aves, Islas is West Indies
182 D2 La Savina Spain
246 C3 Las Avispas Mex.
179 F3 Lasberg Austria
258 C3 Las Berlanas Spain
142 C3 Lasby Denmark
258 C3 La Selle Haiti
260 C2 Las Cabras Chile
187 K4 Las Cabras de San Juan Spain
260 C2 Las Cabras Chile
216 □3a Las Cañadas vol. crater Tenerife Canary Is
194 C3 Lascari Sicilia Italy
187 C5 Las Casas Spain
260 C2 Las Casuarinas Arg.

225 K3 La Scie Nfld. Can.
240 G4 Las Cruces CA U.S.A.
239 F5 Las Cruces NM U.S.A.
186 D2 Lascuarre Spain
183 F3 La Seca Spain
183 F4 La Séguinière France
246 E3 La Selle mt. Haiti
186 E3 La Selva del Camp Spain
163 E4 La Selve France
186 D4 La Sènia Spain
161 B5 La Séranne, Montagne de ridge France
260 B1 La Serena Chile
185 E2 La Serena, Embalse de resr Spain
160 D1 La Serre, Massif de hills France
243 E3 Las Esperanças Mex.
185 H3 Las Estancias, Sierra de mts Spain
161 D5 La Seyne-sur-Mer France
261 H5 Las Flores Arg.
244 C4 Las Guacamayas Mex.
123 E5 Lāshār r. Iran
223 I4 Lashburn Sask. Can.
260 C3 Las Heras Arg.
183 F5 Las Herencias Spain
261 E3 Las Higueras Arg.
123 F4 Lashkar Gāh Afgh.
260 A6 Las Hortensias Chile
175 H2 Łasin Pol.
245 F5 La Sirena, Cerro mt. Mex.
244 D3 Las Jicamas Mex.
261 F2 Las Junturas Arg.
175 J4 Łaskarzew Pol.
136 C3 Laskivtsi Ukr.
179 G4 Laško Slovenia
175 I6 Laskowa Pol.
174 G2 Łaskowice Pol.
185 G1 Las Labores Spain
260 B6 Las Lajas Arg.
260 B4 Las Leñas Arg.
250 A6 Las Lomas Peru
258 E2 Las Lomitas Arg.
183 H4 Las Marismas marsh Spain
182 D2 Las Médulas tourist site Castilla y León Spain
185 H3 Las Menas Spain
250 E2 Las Mercedes Venez.
216 □3a La Mercedes, Monte de hill Tenerife Canary Is
185 H1 Las Mesas Spain
243 H6 Las Minas, Sierra de mts Guat.
Las Mulatas is Panama see San Blas, Archipiélago de
245 E4 Las Navajas, Cerro mt. Mex.
185 E3 Las Navas de la Concepción Spain
183 F4 Las Navas del Marqués Spain
165 D4 Lasne Belgium
185 I4 Las Negras Spain
242 D1 Las Nieves Mex.
216 □3f Las Nieves, Pico de mt. Gran Canaria Canary Is
242 E3 Las Nopaleras, Cerro mt. Mex.
79 □3 La Société, Archipel de is Fr. Polynesia
185 G2 La Solana Spain
161 C4 La Somme, Baie de b. France
162 D2 La Souterraine France
174 G5 Lasowice Małe Pol.
258 F2 Las Palmas Arg.
216 □3f Las Palmas de Gran Canaria Gran Canaria Canary Is
244 D4 Las Parotas r. Mex.
185 H1 Las Pedroñeras Spain
261 F3 Las Perdices Arg.
242 □K7 Las Perlas, Archipiélago de is Panama
253 F4 Las Petas Bol.
190 E4 La Spezia Italy
190 E4 La Spezia prov. Italy
261 I4 Las Piedras Uru.
252 C3 Las Piedras, Río de r. Peru
193 H4 La Spina, Monte mt. Italy
192 A5 Las Plassas Sardegna Italy
186 D2 Laspuña Spain
123 H2 Laspur Pak.
261 G3 Las Rosas Arg.
187 D6 Las Rotas Spain
138 D4 Las Rozas de Madrid Spain
168 F2 Lassahn Ger.
260 D2 Las Salinas, Pampa de salt pan Arg.
170 A2 Lassan Ger.
256 C3 Lassance Brazil
159 F3 Lassay-les-Châteaux France
240 G1 Lassen Peak vol. CA U.S.A.
163 B5 Lasseube France
156 C3 Lassigny France
179 F3 Lassing Austria
242 □J8 Las Tablas Panama
236 C4 Last Chance CO U.S.A.
191 G3 Lastebasse Italy
191 G2 Lastè delle Sute mt. Italy
185 I3 Las Termas Arg.
187 D6 Las Torres de Cotillas Spain
260 C1 Las Tórtolas, Cerro mt. Chile
163 E5 Lastours France
208 B5 Lastoursville Gabon
188 F4 Lastovo i. Croatia
188 F4 Lastovski Kanal sea chan. Croatia
191 G5 Lastra a Signa Italy
183 F3 Lastras de Cuéllar Spain
242 B3 Las Tres Virgenes, Volcán vol. Mex.
168 C3 Lastrup Ger.
246 C2 Las Tunas Cuba
159 G4 La Suze-sur-Sarthe France
242 D4 Las Varas Chihuahua Mex.
244 B3 Las Varas Nayarit Mex.
261 F2 Las Varillas Arg.
239 F5 Las Vegas NM U.S.A.
241 J3 Las Vegas NV U.S.A.
182 E4 Las Veguillas Spain
183 F5 Las Ventas con Peña Aguilera Spain
183 E4 Las Ventas de San Julián Spain
245 F4 Las Villuercas mt. Spain
252 C4 Las Yaras Peru
175 L5 Łaszczów Pol.
175 K5 Łaszki Pol.
Lászlófalva Hungary see Szentkirály
225 J3 La Tabatière Que. Can.
250 B5 Latacunga Ecuador
262 S2 Latady Island Antarctica
160 C2 La Tagnière France
161 C3 La Talaudière France
159 F3 La Tannière France
227 H2 Latchford Ont. Can.
151 H3 Latchingdon Essex, England U.K.
79 □2 Late i. Vava'u Gp Tonga
117 F5 Latehar Bihar India
177 H3 La Teignouse, Passage de str. France
191 G2 Latemar mt. Italy
163 F2 Laterza Italy
165 F4 La Teste France
244 B3 La Tetilla, Cerro mt. Mex.
138 F3 Latgales augstiene reg. Latvia
87 C6 Latham W.A. Austr.
168 C3 Lathen Ger.
146 E3 Latheron Highland, Scotland U.K.
116 B5 Lathi Gujarat India
240 B3 Lathrop CA U.S.A.
190 B3 La Thuile Italy
162 C2 Latina France
140 L2 Latikberg Sweden
193 E3 Latina Italy
193 E3 Latina prov. Lazio Italy
191 I3 Latisana Italy
141 N6 Latnaya Rus. Fed.
195 F2 Lato r. Italy
260 E3 La Toma Arg.
177 K3 Latorica r. Slovakia
190 C2 La Tornette mt. Switz.

186 D2 La Torre de Cabdella Spain
251 E2 La Tortuga, Isla i. Venez.
136 B3 Latoryts'ya r. Ukr.
86 D3 Latouche Treville, Cape W.A. Austr.
162 C3 La Tour-Blanche France
161 D5 La Tour-d'Aigues France
160 A3 La Tour-d'Auvergne France
163 D6 Latour-de-Carol France
163 E6 Latour-de-France France
163 D3 La Tour-du-Crieu France
160 C3 La Tour-du-Pin France
161 B5 La Tour-sur-Orb France
161 E3 La Toussuire France
175 J3 Latowicz Pol.
163 I4 Latronico Italy
163 I4 Latronquière France
258 C3 La Troya r. Arg.
139 L2 Łatyhów Pol.
193 I5 Latterico Italy
Latte Island Vava'u Gp Tonga see Late
161 B5 Lattes France
164 F2 Lattrop Neth.
227 H2 Latulipe Que. Can.
225 F4 La Tuque Que. Can.
114 C2 Latur Mahar. India
158 D4 La Turballe France
138 D3 Latvia country Europe
Latvia country Europe see Latvia
Latviyskaya S.S.R. country Europe see Latvia
114 Lau Nigeria
207 H4 Lau Nigeria
210 A3 Lau r. Sudan
117 F5 Lauba r. Madh. Prad. India
169 D5 Laubach Hessen Ger.
173 E4 Laubach Rheinland-Pfalz Ger.
173 E4 Lauben Bayern Ger.
173 E4 Lauben Bayern Ger.
174 C4 Lauca (Unstrut) Ger.
172 D3 Laucherт r. Ger.
172 D2 Lauchhammer Ger.
173 E3 Lauchheim Ger.
172 C2 Lauda-Königshofen Ger.
172 D2 Laudenbach Ger.
146 F6 Lauder Scottish Borders, Scotland U.K.
234 D3 Lauderdale NJ U.S.A.
161 C4 Laudun France
169 E3 Lauenau Ger.
168 F2 Lauenbrücke Ger.
168 F2 Lauenburg (Elbe) Ger.
168 D3 Lauenförde Ger.
171 F. Lauer r. Ger.
172 C3 Lauf Ger.
172 C3 Laufach Ger.
173 F2 Lauf an der Pegnitz Ger.
190 C1 Laufen Switz.
190 D1 Laufenberg Switz.
172 C4 Laufenburg (Baden) Ger.
221 L2 Lauge Koch Kyst reg. Greenland
150 C3 Laugharne Carmarthenshire, Wales U.K.
84 C4 Laughlen, Mount N.T. Austr.
239 F4 Laughlin Peak NM U.S.A.
163 C4 Lauhaus France
173 E3 Lauingen (Donau) Ger.
185 H4 Laujar de Andarax Spain
140 N3 Laukaa Fin.
123 A4 Laukaa Lith.
97 Laun Thai.
163 D5 Launac France
227 H1 Launay Que. Can.
83 F5 Launceston Tas. Austr.
150 C4 Launceston Cornwall, England U.K.
147 B4 Laune r. Rep. of Ireland
97 B4 Laungion Bok Islands Myanmar
253 E5 La Unión Chile
250 D4 La Unión Col.
242 □I6 La Unión El Salvador
244 D5 La Unión Mex.
252 A2 La Unión Huánuco Peru
250 A6 La Unión Piura Peru
187 D6 La Unión Spain
250 B1 La Unión Venez.
157 F5 La Woëvre, Plaine de plain France
157 H4 La Wontzenau France
206 E4 Lawra Ghana
81 B6 Lawrence South I. N.Z.
81 C5 Lawrence r. South I. N.Z.
236 E4 Lawrence KS U.S.A.
233 H3 Lawrence MA U.S.A.
231 C5 Lawrenceburg TN U.S.A.
233 □J2 Lawrence Station N.B. Can.
147 E2 Lawrencetown Northern Ireland U.K.
230 C4 Lawrenceville IL U.S.A.
234 D2 Lawrenceville NJ U.S.A.
232 E4 Lawrenceville VA U.S.A.
232 E6 Lawrenceville VA U.S.A.
87 D5 Lawrence Wells, Mount hill W.A. Austr.
175 K2 Ławsk Pol.
237 D5 Lawton OK U.S.A.
95 E4 Lawu, Gunung vol. Indon.
124 A1 Lawz, Jabal al mt. Saudi Arabia
143 F2 Laxá Sweden
182 B1 Laxe Spain
148 E3 Laxey Isle of Man
214 D2 Laxey S. Africa
146 C3 Laxford Bridge Highland, Scotland U.K.
222 F4 Lax Kw'alaams B.C. Can.
146 □ Laxo Shetland, Scotland U.K.
157 G4 Laxou France
143 K3 Laxsjö Sweden
143 F2 Laxsjön l. Sweden
134 J4 Laxvega r. Rus. Fed.
162 A2 Lay r. France
134 L2 Laya r. Rus. Fed.
186 D2 Layana Spain
124 B3 Laylá Saudi Arabia
161 E5 Laye r. France
183 F5 Layos Spain
163 C4 Layrac France
149 L6 Lays r. England U.K.
175 H2 Łazdoj Pol.
234 D1 Layton NJ U.S.A.
240 F2 Layton U.S.A.
Layturi Georgia see Lat'uri
182 D2 Laza Spain
234 C2 La Zacatosa, Picacho mt. Mex.
161 A4 Laze Spain
195 K2 Lazagurria Spain
177 L5 Lazagurria Spain
100 D1 Lazarev Rus. Fed.
196 F3 Lazarevac Srbija Yugo.
242 C4 Lázaro, Sierra de San mts Mex.
242 B2 Lázaro Cárdenas Mex.
244 C5 Lázaro Cárdenas Mex.
258 C4 Lazcano Uru.
138 D4 Lazdijai Lith.
193 F2 Lazio admin. reg. Italy
191 F3 Lazise Italy
176 F1 Łázně Bělohrad Czech Rep.
176 E1 Lázně Bohdaneč Czech Rep.
176 C1 Lázně Kynžvart Czech Rep.
100 D4 Lazo Primorskiy Kray Rus. Fed.
131 O3 Lazo Respublika Sakha (Yakutiya) Rus. Fed.
149 G3 Lazonby Cumbria, England U.K.
Lazovsk Moldova see Sîngerei

177 L4 Lazuri Romania
177 L5 Lazuri de Beiuş Romania
137 G4 Lazurne Ukr.
175 H5 Łazy Pol.
190 E4 Lazzaro, Monte hill Italy
220 H5 Leacock PA U.S.A.
146 E6 Leadburn Midlothian, Scotland U.K.
149 I4 Leadenham Lincolnshire, England U.K.
223 I5 Leader Sask. Can.
234 B3 Leader Heights PA U.S.A.
146 F6 Leader Water r. Scotland U.K.
146 E6 Leadhills South Lanarkshire, Scotland U.K.
83 G3 Leadville N.S.W. Austr.
239 I4 Leadville CO U.S.A.
237 F6 Leaf r. MS U.S.A.
Leaf Bay Que. Can. see Tasiujaq
223 K3 Lear Rapids Man. Can.
199 B4 Leahy, Cape Antarctica
86 E3 Leake, Mount hill W.A. Austr.
84 E5 Leakesville MS U.S.A.
237 D6 Leakey TX U.S.A.
149 I4 Leakanville NC U.S.A. see Eden
86 C4 Leal, Mount hill W.A. Austr.
258 D2 Leales Arg.
224 D5 Leamington Ont. Can.
151 F2 Leamington Spa, Royal Warwickshire, England U.K.
109 E3 Le'an Jiangxi China
215 G2 Leandra S. Africa
261 G4 Leandro N. Alem Arg.
258 C2 Leandro N. Alem Arg.
147 B4 Leane, Lough l. Rep. of Ireland
215 □J2 Leanja Madag.
117 I4 Leányfalu Hungary
147 B5 Leap Rep. of Ireland
86 B4 Learmonth W.A. Austr.
149 I4 Leasingham Lincolnshire, England U.K.
151 G3 Leatherhead Surrey, England U.K.
165 D4 L'Eau d'Heure l. Belgium
165 D4 L'Eau d'Heure r. Belgium
149 I3 Leaving North Yorkshire, England U.K.
236 E4 Leavenworth KS U.S.A.
238 B3 Leavenworth WA U.S.A.
240 H2 Leavitt Peak CA U.S.A.
136 C4 Leba Pol.
174 F1 Łeba r. Pol.
174 G1 Łeba r. Pol.
172 A2 Lebach Ger.
92 C5 Lebak Phil.
62 E2 Lebaleng S. Africa
208 A5 Lébamba Gabon
197 I4 Lebane Srbija Yugo.
128 B3 Lebanon country Asia
230 C4 Lebanon IN U.S.A.
236 E4 Lebanon KS U.S.A.
237 G4 Lebanon KY U.S.A.
231 I5 Lebanon MO U.S.A.
233 G3 Lebanon NH U.S.A.
234 D3 Lebanon NJ U.S.A.
232 A5 Lebanon OH U.S.A.
234 B2 Lebanon PA U.S.A.
227 I5 Lebanon TN U.S.A.
231 C4 Lebanon VA U.S.A.
232 D6 Lebanon VA U.S.A.
234 B2 Lebanon County county PA U.S.A.
157 G3 Le-Ban-St-Martin France
175 G4 Łebawa Pol.
136 C4 Łebawa Pol.
Lebap Oblast admin. div. Turkm. see Lebapskaya Oblast'
123 C4 Lebapskaya Oblast' admin. div. Turkm.
163 F6 Le Barcarès France
155 K7 Le Barp France
165 C7 Lebbeke Belgium
Lebda tourist site Libya see Leptis Magna
161 C4 Le Béage France
161 D5 Le Beausset France
159 G2 Le Bec-Hellouin France
139 L5 Lebedyan' Ukr. see Lebedyn
137 H2 Lebedyan' Rus. Fed.
137 F2 Lebedyn Ukr.
224 E3 Lebel-sur-Quévillon Que. Can.
171 E4 Lebendorf Ger.
159 F3 Le Bény-Bocage France
176 G3 Lébénymiklós Hungary
163 B5 Le Bez France
156 B2 Le Biot France
162 D2 Le Blanc France
162 D1 Le Bleymard France
174 G1 Łebno Pol.
160 C3 Le Bois-d'Oingt France
162 A2 Le Bois-Plage-en-Ré France
215 I2 Lebombo hills Moz.
215 G2 Lebomboberg hills Moz.
215 I2 Lebombomtsberg hills Moz.
215 I2 Lebonfok Pol.
160 C2 Le Breuil Bourgogne France
156 D4 Le Breuil Champagne-Ardenne France
160 E3 Le Brévent mt. France
179 L6 Lebring-St Margarethen Austria
163 C5 Le Brouilh-Monbert France
161 E4 Le Brusquet France
94 C1 Lebu Gunung vol. Indon.
258 B5 Lebu Chile
182 C3 Lebução Port.
158 C2 Le Faou France
158 C2 Le Faouët France
158 C3 Le Fauga France
197 G4 Lefedzha r. Bulg.
162 C5 Le Fenouiller France
156 B2 Lefferinckoucke France
172 F3 Le Folgoët France
162 B2 Le Folgoët France
147 D4 Le Fouet France
215 F5 Lebotswana S. Africa
214 C3 Lebowakgomo S. Africa
163 C4 Lebrade Ger.
183 H4 Lebrija Spain
127 E5 Lebukan i. Phil.
161 C3 Lebulf S. Africa
214 D5 Leeuwkop r. S. Africa
140 N3 Leivonmäki Fin.

Leningradskaya to Lincoln

327

135 G7 Leningradskaya Rus. Fed.
139 I2 Leningradskaya Oblast' admin. div. Rus. Fed.
131 S3 Leningradskiy Rus. Fed.
Leningradskiy Tajik. see Leningrad
137 F2 Leninivka Ukr.
129 E2 Leninkent Rus. Fed.
Lenino Respublika Krym Ukr. see Lenine
Leninobod Tajik. see Khŭjand
123 G2 Leninobod admin. div. Tajik.
Leninobod Uzbek. see Leninabad
Lenīnogor Kazakh. see Leninogorsk
121 J2 Leninogorsk Kazakh.
135 K5 Leninogorsk Rus. Fed.
121 H5 Lenin Peak Kyrg./Tajik.
121 G4 Leninpol' Kyrg.
135 I6 Leninsk Rus. Fed.
Leninsk Turkm. see Akdepe
Leninsk Uzbek. see Asaka
137 H4 Lenins'ke Ukr.
137 H5 Lenins'ke Ukr.
120 D2 Leninskiy Kazakh.
139 K4 Leninskiy Rus. Fed.
130 J4 Leninsk-Kuznetskiy Rus. Fed.
120 F1 Leninskoye Kustanayskaya Oblast' Kazakh.
Leninskoye Yuzhnyy Kazakhstan Kazakh. see Kazygurt
120 B2 Leninskoye Zapadnyy Kazakhstan Kazakh.
134 I4 Leninskoye Kirovskaya Oblast' Rus. Fed.
100 E3 Leninskoye Yevreyskaya Avtonomnaya Oblast' Rus. Fed.
163 B4 Le Nizan France
190 C2 Lenk Switz.
136 D3 Lenkivtsi Ukr.
Lenkoran' Azer. see Länkäran
86 E3 Lennard r. W.A. Austr.
169 E4 Lenne Ger.
169 C4 Lenne r. Ger.
169 D4 Lennestadt Ger.
172 D3 Lenningen Ger.
259 D9 Lennox, Isla i. Chile
146 D6 Lennoxtown East Dunbartonshire, Scotland U.K.
190 F3 Leno Italy
231 D5 Lenoir NC U.S.A.
231 C5 Lenoir City TN U.S.A.
190 B1 Le Noirmont Switz.
193 F3 Lenola Italy
232 B6 Lenore WV U.S.A.
156 D2 Le Nouvion-en-Thiérache France
233 G3 Lenox MA U.S.A.
165 C4 Lens Belgium
156 C2 Lens France
168 F1 Lensahn Ger.
131 M3 Lensk Rus. Fed.
160 D2 Lent France
164 E3 Lent Neth.
129 C2 Lentekhi Georgia
168 E2 Lentföhrden Ger.
176 F5 Lenti Hungary
191 H2 Lentiai Italy
173 F3 Lenting Ger.
195 E5 Lentini Sicilia Italy
195 E5 Lentini r. Sicilia Italy
Lentvaravas Lith. see Lentvaris
138 E4 Lentvaris Lith.
139 K2 Lent'yevo Rus. Fed.
240 I4 Lenwood CA U.S.A.
190 D1 Lenzburg Switz.
170 C2 Lenzen Ger.
179 E3 Lenzing Austria
172 C4 Lenzkirch Ger.
206 E4 Léo Burkina
191 F4 Leo r. Italy
179 G3 Leoben Austria
179 H2 Leobendorf Austria
179 H3 Leobersdorf Austria
Leodhais, Eilean i. Scotland U.K. see Lewis, Isle of
246 D3 Léogane Haiti
178 D3 Leogang Austria
163 B4 Léognan France
236 D2 Leola SD U.S.A.
150 E2 Leominster Herefordshire, England U.K.
233 H3 Leominster MA U.S.A.
163 A5 Léon France
244 D3 León Mex.
242 □I6 León Nic.
182 E2 León Spain
182 E2 León prov. Castilla y León Spain
236 E3 Leon IA U.S.A.
237 D6 Leon r. TX U.S.A.
182 D2 León, Montes de mts Spain
237 D5 Leonard TX U.S.A.
193 E3 Leonardo da Vinci airport Italy
232 E5 Leonardtown MD U.S.A.
212 C4 Leonardville Namibia
172 D3 Leonberg Ger.
161 D4 Léoncel France
Leondárion Greece see Leontari
179 F2 Leonding Austria
190 D2 Leone, Monte mt. Italy/Switz.
261 F3 Leones Arg.
193 E2 Leonessa Italy
194 D5 Leonforte Sicilia Italy
83 F4 Leongatha Vic. Austr.
192 D2 Leoni, Monte hill Italy
198 C3 Leonidi Greece
100 G2 Leonidovo Sakhalin Rus. Fed.
87 D6 Leonora W.A. Austr.
198 C2 Leontari Greece
86 E3 Leopold r. W.A. Austr.
232 C5 Leopold WV U.S.A.
86 E3 Leopold Downs W.A. Austr.
Léopold II, Lac l. Dem. Rep. Congo see Mai-Ndombe, Lac
257 F4 Leopoldina Brazil
256 C2 Leopoldo de Bulhões Brazil
165 E3 Leopoldsburg Belgium
179 H2 Leopoldsdorf im Marchfelde Austria
170 E2 Leopoldshagen Ger.
169 D3 Leopoldshöhe Ger.
Léopoldville Dem. Rep. Congo see Kinshasa
236 C4 Leoti KS U.S.A.
136 E4 Leova Moldova
223 J4 Leoville Sask. Can.
Leovo Moldova see Leova
158 C4 Le Palais France
162 D3 Le Palais-sur-Vienne France
158 E4 Le Pallet France
156 C2 Le Parcq France
163 C4 Le Passage France
156 D4 Le Pavillon-Ste-Julie France
184 C3 Lepe Spain
161 C3 Le Péage-de-Roussillon France
162 D2 Le Pêchereau France
Lepel' Belarus see Lyepyel'
158 E4 Le Pellerin France
198 B2 Lepenou Greece
161 D4 Le Périer France
163 E6 Le Perthus France
159 E3 Le Pertre France
156 B3 Le Petit-Quevilly France
215 E4 Lephoi S. Africa
162 B4 Le Pian-Médoc France
159 G3 Le Pin-au-Haras France
156 E4 L'Épine France
161 D4 L'Épine France
109 F2 Leping Jiangxi China
159 G3 Le Pin-la-Garenne France
162 C3 Le Pizou France
163 D5 Le Plan France
156 C3 Le Plessis-Belleville France
134 M3 Lep'lya r. Rus. Fed.
161 D4 Le Poët France
188 F2 Lepoglava Croatia
159 H5 Le Poinçonnet France
158 E5 Le Poiré-sur-Vie France
160 D3 Le Pont-de-Beauvoisin France
161 D3 Le Pont-de-Claix France
161 B4 Le Pont-de-Monvert France
161 C5 Le Pontet France
190 D2 Lepontine, Alpi mts Italy/Switz.
195 G2 Leporano Italy
163 A4 Le Porge France
163 A4 Le Porge-Océan France
156 B2 Le Portel France
196 E4 Leposavić Kosovo, Srbija Yugo.
161 B5 Le Pouget France
158 C4 Le Pouldu France
158 D4 Le Pouliguen France
161 C4 Le Pouzin France
140 N3 Leppävesi Fin.
140 N3 Leppävirta Fin.
161 E5 Le Pradet France
Lepsa Kazakh. see Lepsy
Lepsa r. Kazakh. see Lepsy
177 H4 Lepseny Hungary
Lepsi Kazakh. see Lepsinsk
121 J3 Lepsinsk Kazakh.
121 I3 Lepsy Kazakh.
121 I3 Lepsy r. Kazakh.
202 B1 Leptis Magna tourist site Libya
198 C1 Leptokarya Greece
156 B4 Le Puiset France
161 B3 Le-Puy-en-Velay France
159 F4 Le Puy-Notre-Dame France
161 D5 Le Puy-Ste-Réparade France
206 B2 Leqçeïba Maur.
156 D2 Le Quesnoy France
206 D4 Léraba r. Burkina/Côte d'Ivoire
156 C4 Le Raincy France
213 E4 Lerala Botswana
163 D6 Léran France
215 F3 Leratswana S. Africa
194 C5 Lercara Friddi Sicilia Italy
245 G4 Lerdo Mex.
208 B2 Léré Chad
160 A1 Léré France
206 D3 Léré Mali
207 H4 Lere Nigeria
158 B3 Le Relecq-Kerhuon France
182 B2 Lérez r. Spain
158 E3 Le Rheu France
190 E4 Lerici Italy
250 D5 Lérida Col.
Lérida Spain see Lleida
Lérida prov. Cataluña Spain see Lleida
129 F4 Lerik Azer.
183 I2 Lerín Spain
243 H5 Lerma Mex.
244 C3 Lerma r. Mex.
183 G2 Lerma Spain
245 E4 Lerma de Vilada Mex.
163 B4 Lerm-et Musset France
129 C1 Lermontov Rus. Fed.
100 E3 Lermontovka Rus. Fed.
Lermontovskiy Rus. Fed. see Lermontov
192 B4 Lerno, Monte mt. Sardegna Italy
160 E3 Le Roignais mt. France
199 E3 Leros i. Greece
163 E4 Le Rouget France
157 F4 Lérouville France
226 C5 Le Roy IL U.S.A.
226 A4 Le Roy MN U.S.A.
232 E3 Le Roy NY U.S.A.
234 B1 Leroy PA U.S.A.
161 B4 Le Rozier France
157 G4 Lerrain France
190 D4 Lerrone r. Italy
142 E3 Lerum Sweden
160 E1 Le Russey France
146 □G1 Lerwick Shetland, Scotland U.K.
163 C6 Lés Spain
190 D3 Lesa Italy
160 D3 Les Abrets France
247 □2 Les Abymes Guadeloupe
186 B1 Lesaca Spain
161 E5 Les Adrets-de-l'Estérel France
186 F3 Les Agudes mt. Spain
247 □3 Le St-Esprit Martinique
160 A1 Les Aix-d'Angillon France
160 A3 Les Ancizes-Comps France
156 B3 Les Andelys France
161 C5 Les Angles Languedoc-Roussillon France
163 E6 Les Angles Languedoc-Roussillon France
159 G3 Le Sap France
161 E5 Les Arcs Provence-Alpes-Côte-d'Azur France
160 E3 Les Arcs Rhône-Alpes France
159 F5 Les Aubiers France
161 E4 Le Sauze-Super-Sauze France
186 D3 Les Avellanes Spain
160 D3 Les Avenières France
161 B4 Les Bondons France
156 C5 Les Bordes France
163 D5 Les Bordes-sur-Arize France
186 D3 Les Borges Blanques Spain
186 E3 Les Borges del Camp Spain
Lesbos i. Greece see Lesvos
160 D2 Les Bouchoux France
149 H2 Lesbury Northumberland, England U.K.
163 D6 Les Cabannes France
186 G2 L'Escala Spain
161 E4 L'Escale France
163 E5 Les Cammazes France
163 B5 Lescar France
161 F5 L'Escarène France
160 E2 Les Carroz-d'Arâches France
186 D4 Les Cases d'Alcanar Spain
246 D3 Les Cayes Haiti
179 F4 Lesce Slovenia
159 F3 Les Coëvrons hills France
158 B4 Lesconil France
160 E3 Les Contamines-Montjoie France
160 E2 Les Cornettes de Bise mts France/Switz.
163 E5 Lescure-d'Albigeois France
161 E3 Les Deux-Alpes France
190 C2 Les Diablerets mts Switz.
208 D4 Lese r. Dem. Rep. Congo
195 F3 Lese r. Italy
161 D3 Les Échelles France
158 E2 Les Écréhou is Channel Is
162 B3 Les Églisottes-et-Chalaures France
161 E4 Le Seignus-d'Allos France
158 E4 Le Sel-de-Bretagne France
163 B4 Le Sen France
176 G5 Lesencetomaj Hungary
190 B2 Le Sentier Switz.
157 F3 Les Éparges France
159 F5 Les Epesses France
186 E2 Les Escaldes Andorra
225 G3 Les Escoumins Que. Can.
160 D2 Les Essards-Taignevaux France
158 E5 Les Essarts France
233 □I1 Les Étroits Que. Can.
186 E2 Le Seu d'Urgell Spain
163 D4 Les Eyzies-de-Tayac-Sireuil France
160 E1 Les Fins France
157 G4 Les Forges France
160 E2 Les Fourgs France
160 E2 Les Gets France
108 B2 Leshan Sichuan China
157 E3 Les Hautes-Rivières France
137 I2 Leshchinka r. Rus. Fed.
162 A2 Les Herbiers France
Leshou Hebei China see Xianxian
160 E3 Les Houches France
134 I2 Leshukonskoye Rus. Fed.
129 C2 Lesichine Georgia
156 C4 Lésigny France
190 E4 Lesima, Monte mt. Italy
193 H3 Lesina Italy
193 H3 Lesina, Lago di lag. Italy
161 E5 Les Issambres France
141 J3 Lesja Norway
143 F2 Lesjöfors Sweden
163 D4 Les Junies France
161 E3 Les Karellis France
129 C2 Lesken Rus. Fed.
Leskhimstroy Ukr. see Syeverodonets'k
175 K6 Lesko Pol.
197 E4 Leskovac Srbija Yugo.
198 B1 Leskovik Albania
263 F2 Leskov Island Antarctica
137 G3 Les'ky Ukr.
159 E5 Les Landes-Genusson France
162 C3 Les Lèches France
161 D5 Les Lecques France
146 E5 Leslie Fife, Scotland U.K.
226 E4 Leslie MI U.S.A.
158 E5 Les Lucs-sur-Boulogne France
146 E6 Lesmahagow South Lanarkshire, Scotland U.K.
160 D1 Les Maillys France
160 E3 Les Marches France
160 B3 Les Martres-de-Veyre France
161 B5 Les Matelles France
156 E3 Les Mazures France
225 H3 Les Méchins Que. Can.
161 D4 Les Mées France
161 E3 Les Menuires France
158 D3 Les Minquiers is Channel Is
161 E4 Les Monges mt. France
156 E4 Lesmont France
156 B4 Les Mureaux France
177 G2 Lešná Czech Rep.
174 D4 Leśna Pol.
175 L3 Leśna r. Pol.
158 B3 Lesneven France
174 G5 Leśnica Pol.
156 E4 Les Noës-près-Troyes France
134 K4 Lesnoy Kirovskaya Oblast' Rus. Fed.
Lesnoy Murmanskaya Oblast' Rus. Fed. see Umba
139 M4 Lesnoy Ryazanskaya Oblast' Rus. Fed.
139 J2 Lesnoye Rus. Fed.
134 K4 Lesnyye Polyany Rus. Fed.
100 G2 Lesogorsk Sakhalin Rus. Fed.
138 G1 Lesogorskiy Rus. Fed.
161 C4 Les Ollières-sur-Eyrieux France
100 E3 Lesopil'noye Rus. Fed.
161 E4 Les Orres France
131 K4 Lesosibirsk Rus. Fed.
215 G3 Lesotho country Africa
215 G3 Lesotho Highlands Water Scheme Lesotho
100 E3 Lesozavodsk Rus. Fed.
162 B3 Lesparre-Médoc France
162 B3 Les Peintures France
161 D5 Les Pennes-Mirabeau France
163 A5 Lesperon France
156 E3 Les Petites-Loges France
197 F2 Lespezi hill Romania
158 E2 Les Pieux France
161 B5 Lespignan France
186 D4 L'Espina mt. Spain
163 E5 Lespinassière France
161 A5 L'Espinouse, Monts de mts France
160 E2 Les Planches-en-Montagne France
186 E3 L'Espluga Calba Spain
186 E3 L'Espluga de Francolí Spain
162 B1 Les Ponts-de-Cé France
190 B1 Les Ponts-de-Martel Switz.
186 F2 Les Preses Spain
163 C5 Lespugue France
156 E5 Les Riceys France
159 F4 Les Rosiers France
160 E2 Les Rousses France
162 A2 Les Sables-d'Olonne France
161 C4 Les Salles-du-Gardon France
158 E2 Lessay France
165 D4 Lesse r. Belgium
247 F4 Lesser Antilles is Caribbean Sea
Lesser Caucasus mts Asia see Malyy Kavkaz
116 D3 Lesser Himalaya mts India/Nepal
Lesser Khingan Mountains China see Xiao Hinggan Ling
222 H4 Lesser Slave Lake Alta Can.
125 F2 Lesser Tunb i. The Gulf
156 D4 Les Sièges France
165 C4 Lessines Belgium
215 F3 Lessingskop mt. S. Africa
158 E4 Les Sorinières France
163 B5 Lestelle-Bétharram France
232 C6 Lester WV U.S.A.
161 B3 Les Ternes France
156 B3 Les Thilliers-en-Vexin France
161 E4 Les Thuiles France
140 N3 Lestijärvi Fin.
140 M2 Lestijoki r. Fin.
161 A4 Lestrade France
159 G4 Les Trois-Moutiers France
161 A4 Les Trucs d'Aubrac mt. France
86 E2 Lesueur Island W.A. Austr.
156 C4 Les Ulis France
95 F2 Lesung, Bukit mt. Indon.
187 C4 Les Useres Spain
161 C4 Les Vans France
161 B4 Les Vignes France
199 D2 Lesvos i. Greece
175 K4 Leszkowice Pol.
175 I3 Leszno Mazowieckie Pol.
174 E4 Leszno Wielkopolskie Pol.
174 D4 Leszno Górne Pol.
161 D3 Le Taillefer mt. France
186 C2 Le Taillon mt. Spain
159 F5 Le Tallud France
143 F2 Letälven r. Sweden
161 C4 Le Tanargue mt. France
177 K4 Létavértes Hungary
151 G3 Letchworth Hertfordshire, England U.K.
163 A4 Le Teich France
161 C4 Le Teil France
159 F3 Le Teilleul France
160 C1 Le Télégraphe hill France
163 B4 Le Temple France
161 E3 L'Étendard, Pic de mt. France
176 F5 Letenye Hungary
116 D4 Leteri Madh. Prad. India
215 F1 Lethabile S. Africa
96 A2 Letha Range mts Myanmar
222 H5 Lethbridge Alta Can.
225 K3 Lethbridge Nfld. Can.
168 D2 Lethe r. Ger.
159 G3 Le Theil France
158 E4 Le-Theil-de-Bretagne France
251 G4 Lethem Guyana
151 I2 Letheringsett Norfolk, England U.K.
157 G5 Le Thillot France
157 G4 Le Tholy France
161 E5 Le Thoronet France
93 C5 Leti, Kepulauan is Maluku Indon.
250 D6 Leticia Col.
107 H4 Leting Hebei China
193 G3 Letino Italy
214 D5 Letjiesbos S. Africa
177 H4 Letkés Hungary
212 E4 Letlhakane Botswana
212 E5 Letlhakeng Botswana
134 F2 Letnerechenskiy Rus. Fed.
191 H2 Le Tofane mt. Italy
195 E5 Letoianni Sicilia Italy
179 H1 Letonice Czech Rep.
156 B2 Le Touquet-Paris-Plage France
161 B5 Le Tour d'Arre hill France
161 D3 Le Touvet France
176 F2 Letovice Czech Rep.
96 A3 Letpadan Myanmar
156 B2 Le Tréport France
161 A4 Le Truel France
141 K3 Letsbo Sweden
170 F3 Letschin Ger.
215 E2 Letsopa S. Africa
Lette Island Vava'u Gp Tonga see Late
148 B3 Letterbreen Northern Ireland U.K.
147 B3 Lettercallow Rep. of Ireland
147 B5 Letterfinish Rep. of Ireland
147 B3 Letterfrack Rep. of Ireland
147 D2 Letterkenny Rep. of Ireland
150 C3 Letterston Pembrokeshire, Wales U.K.
185 H2 Letur Spain
163 B4 Le Tuzan France
136 D3 Letychiv Ukr.
Lëtzebuerg country Europe see Luxembourg
171 C3 Letzlingen Ger.
197 G3 Leu Romania
209 D7 Léua Angola
171 E4 Leuben Ger.
171 C4 Leubingen Ger.
163 E5 Leuc France
Leucas Ionioi Nisoi Greece see Lefkada
163 F6 Leucate France
146 F5 Leuchars Fife, Scotland U.K.
173 G2 Leuchtenberg Ger.
170 E3 Leuenberg Ger.
157 E5 Leuglay France
190 C2 Leuk Switz.
Leukas Ionioi Nisoi Greece see Lefkada
190 C2 Leukerbad Switz.
146 B3 Leumrabhagh Western Isles, Scotland U.K.
169 D5 Leun Ger.
241 L4 Leupp AZ U.S.A.
85 G4 Leura Qld Austr.
164 E2 Leusden Neth.
94 B2 Leuser, Gunung mt. Indon.
178 C3 Leutasch Austria
171 C5 Leutenberg Ger.
173 E2 Leutershausen Ger.
169 C5 Leutesdorf Ger.
173 E4 Leutkirch im Allgäu Ger.
165 D4 Leuven Belgium
165 C4 Leuze-en-Hainaut Belgium
198 C2 Levadeia Greece
161 E5 Le Val France
157 G5 Le Val-d'Ajol France
157 F5 Le Vallinot-Longeau-Percey France
158 E3 Le Val-St-Père France
198 A1 Levan Albania
241 L2 Levan UT U.S.A.
140 J3 Levanger Norway
190 D4 Levante, Riviera di coastal area Italy
190 E4 Levanto Italy
194 B5 Levanzo Sicilia Italy
194 B4 Levanzo, Isola di i. Sicilia Italy
129 E2 Levashi Rus. Fed.
247 □3 Le Vauclin Martinique
137 J2 Levaya Rossosh' Rus. Fed.
176 G4 Levél Hungary
237 C5 Levelland TX U.S.A.
81 C6 Levels South I. N.Z.
149 I4 Leven East Riding of Yorkshire, England U.K.
146 F5 Leven Fife, Scotland U.K.
146 C5 Leven, Loch inlet Scotland U.K.
146 E5 Leven, Loch l. Scotland U.K.
161 F5 Levens France
149 G3 Levens Cumbria, England U.K.
190 D2 Leventina, Valle val. Switz.
146 □G2 Levenwick Shetland, Scotland U.K.
86 D3 Lévêque, Cape W.A. Austr.
195 H2 Leverano Italy
146 A4 Leverburgh Western Isles, Scotland U.K.
162 A3 Le-Verdon-sur-Mer France
226 E3 Levering MI U.S.A.
169 B4 Leverkusen Ger.
163 D5 Le Vernet France
156 B4 Lèves France
159 I5 Levet France
161 A4 Lévézou mts France
177 H3 Levice Slovakia
191 G2 Levico Terme Italy
198 C3 Levidi Greece
192 B3 Levie Corse France
160 E2 Levier France
161 B5 Le Vigan France
163 D5 Lévignac France
163 C4 Lévignac-de-Guyanne France
163 A4 Lévignacq France
191 H5 Le Ville Italy
80 E4 Levin North I. N.Z.
225 G4 Lévis Que. Can.
199 E3 Levitha i. Greece
Levittown NJ U.S.A. see Willingboro
235 E2 Levittown NY U.S.A.
234 D2 Levittown PA U.S.A.
158 E3 Le-Vivier-sur-Mer France
197 H5 Levka Bulg.
Levkás i. Greece see Lefkada
Levkímmi Ionioi Nisoi Greece see Lefkimmi
177 J2 Levoča Slovakia
177 J2 Levočské vrchy mts Slovakia
162 D2 Levroux France
197 G4 Levski Bulg.
Levskigrad Bulg. see Karlovo
139 L5 Lev Tolstoy Rus. Fed.
79 □1a Levuka Ovalau Fiji
96 B3 Lewe Myanmar
151 H4 Lewes East Sussex, England U.K.
233 F5 Lewes DE U.S.A.
174 F5 Lewin Brzeski Pol.
241 M3 Lewis CO U.S.A.
237 D4 Lewis KS U.S.A.
238 B2 Lewis r. WA U.S.A.
146 B3 Lewis, Isle of i. Scotland U.K.
84 C4 Lewis, Lake salt flat N.T. Austr.
234 B2 Lewisberry PA U.S.A.
232 A5 Lewisburg OH U.S.A.
227 I5 Lewisburg PA U.S.A.
231 C5 Lewisburg TN U.S.A.
232 C6 Lewisburg WV U.S.A.
222 D3 Lewis Cass, Mount Alaska/B.C. Can./U.S.A.
225 J3 Lewis Hills hill Nfld. Can.
81 D5 Lewis Pass South I. N.Z.
225 K3 Lewisporte Nfld. Can.
86 F4 Lewis Range hills W.A. Austr.
238 D1 Lewis Range mts MT U.S.A.
231 C5 Lewis Smith, Lake AL U.S.A.
238 C2 Lewiston ID U.S.A.
233 □H2 Lewiston ME U.S.A.
227 E3 Lewiston MI U.S.A.
226 B4 Lewiston MN U.S.A.
232 D3 Lewiston NY U.S.A.
226 B5 Lewistown IL U.S.A.
226 B5 Lewistown MO U.S.A.
238 E2 Lewistown MT U.S.A.
232 E4 Lewistown PA U.S.A.
237 E5 Lewisville AR U.S.A.
232 C5 Lewisville OH U.S.A.
93 B5 Lewotobi, Gunung vol. Flores Indon.
231 D5 Lexington GA U.S.A.
226 C5 Lexington IL U.S.A.
230 C4 Lexington KY U.S.A.
227 F4 Lexington MI U.S.A.
236 E4 Lexington MO U.S.A.
237 F5 Lexington MS U.S.A.
231 D5 Lexington NC U.S.A.
236 D3 Lexington NE U.S.A.
232 B4 Lexington OH U.S.A.
231 D5 Lexington SC U.S.A.
237 F5 Lexington TN U.S.A.
232 D6 Lexington VA U.S.A.
232 E5 Lexington Park MD U.S.A.
149 H3 Leyburn North Yorkshire, England U.K.
Leyden Neth. see Leiden
108 C3 Leye Guangxi China
122 A2 Leyla Dāgh mt. Iran
149 G4 Leyland Lancashire, England U.K.
163 D4 Leyme France
151 H3 Leysdown-on-Sea Kent, England U.K.
190 C2 Leysin Switz.
92 C4 Leyte i. Phil.
92 C4 Leyte Gulf Phil.
190 C2 Leytron Switz.
163 D6 Lez r. France
183 H2 Leza r. Spain
175 K5 Leżajsk Pol.
161 C4 Lézan France
158 C3 Lézardrieux France
163 D5 Lézat-sur-Lèze France
162 B2 Lezay France
163 D5 Lèze r. France
196 D5 Lezhë Albania
108 C2 Lezhi Sichuan China
139 M3 Lezhnevo Rus. Fed.
161 A5 Lézignan-Corbières France
160 B3 Lezoux France
185 H2 Lezuza Spain
185 H1 Lezuza r. Spain
175 H4 Lgota Wielka Pol.
135 F6 L'gov Rus. Fed.
111 D6 Lhagoi Kangri mt. Xizang China
146 E4 Lhanbryde Moray, Scotland U.K.
111 F6 Lhari Xizang China
Lharigarbo Xizang China see Amdo
111 E6 Lhasa Xizang China
111 E6 Lhasa He r. China
108 A2 Lhatog Xizang China
156 C4 L'Hay-les-Roses France
111 D6 Lhazê Xizang China
179 F1 Lhenice Czech Rep.
163 D5 Lherm France
162 B2 L'Hermenault France
158 E3 L'Hermitage France
113 □1 Lhohifushi i. N. Male Maldives
94 B1 Lhokseumawe Sumatera Indon.
94 B1 Lhoksukon Sumatera Indon.
163 D4 L'Honor-de-Cos France
111 F6 Lhorong Xizang China
163 D4 L'Hospitalet France
186 D4 L'Hospitalet de l'Infant Cataluña Spain
186 F3 L'Hospitalet de Llobregat Cataluña Spain
161 B5 L'Hospitalet-du-Larzac France
163 D6 L'Hospitalet-près-l'Andorre France
186 D4 L'Hostal del Alls Spain
162 A2 L'Houmeau France
111 E6 Lhozhag Xizang China
160 D3 Lhuis France
159 F3 L'Huisserie France
156 E4 Lhuître France
111 F6 Lhünzê Xizang China
111 E6 Lhünzhub Xizang China
96 B3 Li, Mae r. Thai.
192 A2 Liamone r. Corse France
247 □2 Liamuiga, Mount vol. St Kitts and Nevis
109 F3 Liancheng Fujian China
Liancheng Guizhou China see Qinglong
Liancheng Yunnan China see Guangnan
156 C3 Liancourt France
101 D5 Liancourt Rocks i. N. Pacific Ocean
156 B2 Liane r. France
Lianfeng Fujian China see Liancheng
92 C4 Lianga Phil.
109 E2 Liangaz Hu l. China
107 G3 Liangcheng Nei Mongol China
108 C1 Liangdang Gansu China
108 D3 Liangfeng Guangxi China
108 A3 Lianghe Yunnan China
108 C1 Lianghekou Gansu China
108 B2 Lianghekou Sichuan China
Liangjiayoufang Shanxi China see Youyu
108 C2 Liangping Chongqing China
95 F2 Liangpran, Bukit mt. Indon.
Liangshan Chongqing China see Liangping
96 B1 Liang Shan mt. Myanmar
Liangshi Hunan China see Shaodong
94 C2 Liang Timur, Gunung mt. Malaysia
108 B3 Liangwang Shan mts Yunnan China
107 F4 Liangzhen Shaanxi China
Liangzhou Gansu China see Wuwei
Lianhe Chongqing China see Qianjiang
109 E3 Lianhua Jiangxi China
109 F3 Lianjiang Fujian China
108 D4 Lianjiang Guangdong China
Lianjiang Jiangxi China see Xingguo
109 E3 Lianjiangkou Guangdong China
108 C3 Lian Jiang r. China
109 E3 Liannan Guangdong China
198 C2 Lianokladi Sterea Ellas Greece
109 E3 Lianping Guangdong China
Lianran Yunnan China see Anning
109 E3 Lianshan Guangdong China
107 I3 Lianshan Liaoning China
Liantang Jiangxi China see Nanchang
109 D2 Liantuo Hubei China
Lianxian Guangdong China see Lianzhou
100 B1 Lianyin Heilong. China
109 D3 Lianyuan Hunan China
107 H5 Lianyungang Jiangsu China
109 E3 Lianzhou Guangdong China
Lianzhou Guangxi China see Hepu
100 D3 Lianzhushan Heilong. China
107 I3 Liao r. China
107 G4 Liaocheng Shandong China
107 I3 Liaodong Bandao pen. China
107 I3 Liaodong Wan b. China
106 B3 Liaodun Xinjiang China
106 B3 Liaodunzhan Xinjiang China
107 I3 Liaoning prov. China
107 I3 Liaoyang Liaoning China
100 C4 Liaoyuan Jilin China
107 I3 Liaozhong Liaoning China
198 A2 Liapades Ionioi Nisoi Greece
123 G3 Liaqatabad Pak.
222 F2 Liard r. Can.
222 F2 Liard Highway N.W.T. Can.
222 E2 Liard Plateau Y.T. Can.
222 E3 Liard River B.C. Can.
156 E3 Liart France
146 C4 Liathach mt. Scotland U.K.
143 F3 Liatorp Sweden
Liban country Asia see Lebanon
176 E1 Libáň Czech Rep.
128 C2 Liban, Jebel mts Lebanon
250 C3 Libano Col.
Libau Latvia see Liepāja
146 E6 Libberton South Lanarkshire, Scotland U.K.
238 D1 Libby MT U.S.A.
176 C1 Libčeves Czech Rep.
171 F5 Libčice nad Vltavou Czech Rep.
208 C4 Libenge Dem. Rep. Congo
175 I2 Liberadz Pol.
237 C4 Liberal KS U.S.A.
257 E5 Liberdade Brazil
252 C1 Liberdade r. Amazonas Brazil
254 B4 Liberdade r. Mato Grosso Brazil
176 E1 Liberec Czech Rep.
176 E1 Liberecký kraj admin. reg. Czech Rep.
206 C5 Liberia country Africa
242 □I7 Liberia Costa Rica
247 □2 Liberta Antigua and Barbuda
261 I4 Libertad Uru.
258 D1 Libertador General San Martin Arg.
215 F3 Libertase S. Africa
230 C4 Liberty IN U.S.A.
230 C4 Liberty KY U.S.A.
233 □I2 Liberty ME U.S.A.
236 E4 Liberty MO U.S.A.
233 F4 Liberty NY U.S.A.
234 A1 Liberty PA U.S.A.
237 E6 Liberty TX U.S.A.
232 A4 Liberty Center OH U.S.A.
226 D4 Libertyville IL U.S.A.
171 F5 Liběšice Czech Rep.
175 H5 Libiąż Pol.
176 E1 Libice nad Cidlinou Czech Rep.
165 E5 Libin Belgium
176 D3 Libín mt. Czech Rep.
176 G2 Libina Czech Rep.
92 B3 Libmanan Phil.
128 A4 Libni, Gebel hill Egypt
108 C3 Libo Guizhou China
171 F5 Libochovice Czech Rep.
215 G4 Libode S. Africa
198 B1 Libohovë Albania
171 F5 Libouchec Czech Rep.
163 B4 Libourne France
86 E4 Libral Well W.A. Austr.
165 E5 Libramont Belgium
196 E5 Librazhd Albania
242 C2 Libre, Sierra mts Mex.
245 F4 Libres Mex.
208 A4 Libreville Gabon
187 B7 Librilla Spain
187 B4 Libros Spain
92 C5 Libuganon r. Phil.
202 C3 Libya country Africa
202 E3 Libyan Desert Egypt/Libya
202 E2 Libyan Plateau Egypt
260 A4 Licantén Chile
194 C5 Licata Sicilia Italy
190 F4 Licciana Nardi Italy
127 F3 Lice Turkey
193 E2 Licenza Italy
183 G3 Liceras Spain
169 D5 Lich Ger.
Licheng Fujian China see Xianyou
Licheng Guangxi China see Lipu
107 H4 Licheng Shandong China
107 G4 Licheng Shanxi China
80 E3 Lichfield North I. N.Z.
151 F2 Lichfield Staffordshire, England U.K.
211 B8 Lichinga Moz.
177 G1 Lichnov Czech Rep.
174 G1 Lichnowy Pol.
171 C5 Lichte Ger.
172 C3 Lichtenau Baden-Württemberg Ger.
173 E2 Lichtenau Bayern Ger.
169 D4 Lichtenau Nordrhein-Westfalen Ger.
179 G2 Lichtenau im Waldviertel Austria
171 C5 Lichtenberg Bayern Ger.
171 E5 Lichtenberg Sachsen Ger.
215 F2 Lichtenburg S. Africa
171 C5 Lichtenfels Ger.
171 D5 Lichtenstein Ger.
164 F3 Lichtenvoorde Neth.
179 H3 Lichtenwörth Austria
170 E3 Lichterfelde Ger.
165 C3 Lichtervelde Belgium
108 D2 Lichuan Hubei China
109 F3 Lichuan Jiangxi China
213 H3 Liciro Moz.
232 A5 Licking r. KY U.S.A.
188 E3 Lički Osik Croatia
194 D5 Licodia Eubea Sicilia Italy
163 B5 Licq-Athérey France
156 B2 Licques France
Licun Shandong China see Laoshan
139 J2 Lid' r. Rus. Fed.
138 E5 Lida Belarus
142 E2 Lidan r. Sweden
149 G2 Liddel r. England/Scotland U.K.
215 F5 Liddleton S. Africa
177 H2 Lidečko Czech Rep.
142 E3 Lidhult Sweden
143 H2 Lidingö Sweden
142 E2 Lidköping Sweden
191 H3 Lido Italy
191 H4 Lido Adriano Italy
191 H4 Lido di Classe Italy
193 E3 Lido di Foce Verde Italy
191 H3 Lido di Jesolo Italy
195 F2 Lido di Metaponto Italy
193 E3 Lido di Ostia Italy
193 H3 Lido di Siponto Italy
191 H4 Lido di Spina Italy
140 K2 Lidsjöberg Sweden
175 H2 Lidzbark Pol.
143 I4 Lidzbark Warmiński Pol.
179 F2 Liebenau Austria
169 E4 Liebenau Hessen Ger.
168 E3 Liebenau Niedersachsen Ger.
215 G2 Liebenbergs Vlei r. S. Africa
169 F3 Liebenburg Ger.
179 F4 Liebenfels Austria
170 E3 Liebenwalde Ger.
171 F4 Lieberose Ger.
171 D4 Liebertwolkwitz Ger.
84 B4 Liebig, Mount N.T. Austr.
196 E3 Liebling Romania
179 G4 Lieboch Austria
171 E5 Liebstadt Ger.
172 D4 Liechtenstein country Europe
183 I2 Liédena Spain
165 E4 Liège Belgium
165 E4 Liège prov. Belgium
Liegnitz Pol. see Legnica
140 O3 Lieksa Fin.
138 E3 Lielupe r. Latvia
138 E3 Lielvārde Latvia
164 E3 Liempde Neth.
140 L3 Lien Sweden
164 E3 Lienden Neth.
169 C3 Lienen Ger.
178 D4 Lienz Austria
138 C3 Liepāja Latvia
Liepaya Latvia see Liepāja
170 E3 Liepe Ger.
170 E2 Liepen Ger.
170 F2 Liepgarten Ger.
165 D3 Lier Belgium
160 C1 Liernais France
165 E4 Lierneux Belgium
Lierre Belgium see Lier
177 I2 Liesek Slovakia
172 B2 Lieser Ger.
164 E3 Lieshout Neth.
178 F3 Liesing r. Austria
165 E3 Liessel Neth.
156 D3 Liesse-Notre-Dame France
190 C1 Liestal Switz.
177 H3 Liešťany Slovakia
138 D1 Lieto Fin.
185 I2 Liétor Spain
Lietuva country Europe see Lithuania
159 G2 Lieurey France
141 N3 Lievestuore Fin.
156 C2 Liévin France
224 F4 Lièvre r. Que. Can.
179 F3 Liezen Austria
148 C4 Liffey r. Rep. of Ireland
157 F4 Liffol-le-Grand France
147 D2 Lifford Rep. of Ireland
158 E3 Liffré France
259 C6 Lifi Mahuida mt. Arg.
78 □5 Lifou i. Î. Loyauté New Caledonia
150 C4 Lifton Devon, England U.K.
Lifu i. Î. Loyauté New Caledonia see Lifou
Lifudzin Rus. Fed. see Rudnyy
79 □2 Lifuka i. Tonga
92 B3 Ligao Phil.
163 C4 Ligardes France
138 E3 Līgatne Latvia
87 D6 Lightfoot Lake salt flat W.A. Austr.
83 F2 Lightning Ridge N.S.W. Austr.
234 B1 Lightstreet PA U.S.A.
179 G4 Ligist Austria
191 I3 Lignano Pineta Italy
191 I3 Lignano Sabbiadoro Italy
158 E4 Ligné France
158 E5 Ligneron r. France
165 F4 Ligneuville Belgium
159 I5 Lignières France
160 B3 Lignon r. France
161 C3 Lignon r. France
157 F4 Ligny-en-Barrois France
156 D5 Ligny-le-Châtel France
156 B5 Ligny-le-Ribault France
190 F4 Ligonchio Italy
213 H3 Ligonha r. Moz.
226 E5 Ligonier IN U.S.A.
232 D4 Ligonier PA U.S.A.
Ligoúrion Greece see Lygourio
175 H3 Ligowo Pol.
82 C3 Liguanea Island S.A. Austr.
159 G4 Ligueil France
162 C2 Ligugé France
242 C3 Ligui Mex.
Ligure, Mar sea France/Italy see Ligurian Sea
190 D4 Liguria admin. reg. Italy
188 B4 Ligurian Sea France/Italy
Ligurienne, Mer sea France/Italy see Ligurian Sea
241 J5 Ligurta AZ U.S.A.
142 C3 Lihme Denmark
85 G3 Lihou Reef and Cays Coral Sea Is Terr. Austr.
240 □B7 Lihue HI U.S.A.
138 D2 Lihula Estonia
Liivi laht b. Estonia/Latvia see Riga, Gulf of
185 H3 Lijar Spain
108 B3 Lijiang Yunnan China
Lijiang Yunnan China see Yuanjiang
96 E1 Li Jiang r. China
109 E2 Lijiazhai Henan China
96 C3 Lik, Nam r. Laos
188 E3 Lika reg. Croatia
122 B4 Likak Iran
209 E7 Likasi Dem. Rep. Congo
208 E4 Likati r. Dem. Rep. Congo
222 F4 Likely B.C. Can.
Likhachevo Ukr. see Pervomays'kyy
Likhachyovo Ukr. see Pervomays'kyy
139 J3 Likhoslavl' Rus. Fed.
137 K3 Likhovskoy Rus. Fed.
139 L4 Likino-Dulevo Rus. Fed.
116 E5 Likma Madh. Prad. India
208 C4 Likouala admin. reg. Congo
208 C5 Likouala r. Congo
208 C5 Likouala aux Herbes r. Congo
134 H4 Likurga Rus. Fed.
159 G4 L'Île-Bouchard France
192 A2 L'Île-Rousse Corse France
179 G2 Lilienfeld Austria
168 D2 Lilienthal Ger.
109 E3 Liling Hunan China
138 F1 Liljendal Fin.
123 H3 Lilla Pak.
142 E2 Lilla Edet Sweden
140 M2 Lilla Luleälven r. Sweden
140 L2 Lillblaiken hill Sweden
165 D3 Lille Belgium
156 D2 Lille France
142 C4 Lille Bælt sea chan. Denmark
159 G2 Lillebonne France
141 J3 Lillehammer Norway
156 C2 Lillers France
142 C2 Lillesand Norway
150 E2 Lilleshall Telford and Wrekin, England U.K.
142 D2 Lillestrøm Norway
226 E4 Lilley MI U.S.A.
87 E5 Lillian, Point hill W.A. Austr.
146 F6 Lilliesleaf Scottish Borders, Scotland U.K.
231 E5 Lillington NC U.S.A.
183 G5 Lillo Spain
222 F5 Lillooet B.C. Can.
222 F5 Lillooet r. B.C. Can.
222 F5 Lillooet Range mts B.C. Can.
208 E5 Lilo r. Dem. Rep. Congo
117 H4 Lilong Manipur India
211 B8 Lilongwe Malawi
92 B4 Liloy Phil.
226 C3 Lily WI U.S.A.
82 D3 Lilydale S.A. Austr.
83 F5 Lilydale Tas. Austr.
196 D4 Lim r. Yugo.
261 H4 Lima Arg.
191 F4 Lima r. Italy
253 F5 Lima Para.
252 A3 Lima Peru
252 A2 Lima dept Peru
226 B5 Lima IL U.S.A.
238 D2 Lima MT U.S.A.
232 E3 Lima NY U.S.A.
232 A4 Lima OH U.S.A.
257 F4 Lima Duarte Brazil
125 G2 Līmah Oman
120 A3 Liman Rus. Fed.
178 D4 Limana Italy
175 I6 Limanowa Pol.
260 B2 Limarí r. Chile
Limassol Cyprus see Lemesos
147 E1 Limavady Northern Ireland U.K.
260 D6 Limay r. Arg.
156 B3 Limay France
172 D2 Limbach Baden-Württemberg Ger.
172 A2 Limbach Saarland Ger.
171 D5 Limbach Sachsen Ger.
171 D5 Limbach-Oberfrohna Ger.
195 E4 Limbadi Italy
95 F1 Limbang r. Sarawak Malaysia
252 C3 Limbani Peru
138 E3 Limbaži Latvia
116 B5 Limbdi Gujarat India
207 H5 Limbe Cameroon
211 B8 Limbe Malawi
93 B2 Limboto Sulawesi Utara Indon.
165 E4 Limbourg Belgium
213 H3 Limbuè Moz.
84 B3 Limbunya N.T. Austr.
165 E3 Limburg prov. Belgium
165 E3 Limburg prov. Neth.
169 D5 Limburg an der Lahn Ger.
172 C2 Limburgerhof Ger.
214 D3 Lime Acres S. Africa
141 K3 Limedsforsen Sweden
81 B7 Limehills South I. N.Z.
256 D5 Limeira Brazil
149 F1 Limekilns Fife, Scotland U.K.
198 D1 Limenaria Anatoliki Makedonia kai Thraki Greece
147 C4 Limerick Rep. of Ireland
147 C4 Limerick county Rep. of Ireland
226 A4 Lime Springs IA U.S.A.
233 □J1 Limestone ME U.S.A.
142 C3 Limfjorden sea chan. Denmark
182 B3 Limia r. Spain
199 D4 Limin Chersonisou Kriti Greece
140 K2 Limingen Norway
233 □H3 Limington ME U.S.A.
140 N2 Liminka Fin.
142 E3 Limmared Sweden
164 D2 Limmen Neth.
84 D2 Limmen Bight b. N.T. Austr.
84 C2 Limmen Bight River r. N.T. Austr.
198 C2 Limni Greece
199 D2 Limnos i. Greece
254 G3 Limoeiro Brazil
233 F2 Limoges Ont. Can.
162 D3 Limoges France
163 D4 Limogne, Causse de hills France
163 D4 Limogne-en-Quercy France
242 □J7 Limón Costa Rica
242 □I6 Limón Hond.
236 C4 Limon CO U.S.A.
190 C4 Limone Piemonte Italy
160 C3 Limonest France
191 F3 Limone sul Garda Italy
184 D2 Limonetes r. Spain
126 D3 Limonlu Turkey
Limonum France see Poitiers
252 D3 Limoquije Bol.
193 G3 Limosano Italy
162 D3 Limousin admin. reg. France
162 D3 Limousin, Monts du hills France
162 D3 Limousin, Plateaux du France
163 E5 Limoux France
213 G5 Limpopo r. S. Africa/Zimbabwe
108 D3 Limu Guangxi China
209 D8 Limulunga Zambia
140 M2 Linaälven r. Sweden
140 O1 Linakhamari Rus. Fed.
Lin'an Yunnan China see Jianshui
109 F2 Lin'an Zhejiang China
92 A4 Linapacan Strait Phil.
162 D3 Linards France
260 B4 Linares Chile
243 F3 Linares Mex.
185 G2 Linares Spain
187 C4 Linares de Mora Spain
182 E4 Linares de Riofrío Spain
192 A5 Linas, Monte mt. Sardegna Italy
190 E3 Linate airport Italy
95 F2 Linau Balui plat. Sarawak Malaysia
108 B4 Lincang Yunnan China
165 E4 Lincent Belgium
Lincheng Hainan China see Lingao
Lincheng Hunan China see Huitong
109 F3 Linchuan Jiangxi China
262 R1 Linck Nunataks nunataks Antarctica
261 G4 Lincoln Arg.
81 D5 Lincoln South I. N.Z.
149 I4 Lincoln Lincolnshire, England U.K.
240 G2 Lincoln CA U.S.A.
234 C4 Lincoln DE U.S.A.
230 B3 Lincoln IL U.S.A.
236 D4 Lincoln KS U.S.A.
233 □I2 Lincoln ME U.S.A.
227 F3 Lincoln MI U.S.A.
236 D3 Lincoln NE U.S.A.
233 H2 Lincoln NH U.S.A.

328

Lugela to Mağara Dağı

330

213 H3 Lugela Moz.
213 H3 Lugela r. Moz.
213 H1 Lugenda r. Moz.
150 E2 Lugg r. Wales U.K.
81 B6 Luggate South I. N.Z.
111 E6 Luggudontsen mt. Xizang China
163 B4 Luglon France
193 E2 Lugnano in Teverina Italy
160 C2 Lugny France
160 C2 Lugny-lès-Charolles France
191 G4 Lugo Italy
182 C1 Lugo Spain
182 C2 Lugo prov. Galicia Spain
192 B2 Lugo-di-Nazza Corse France
197 E3 Lugoj Romania
182 E1 Lugones Spain
162 B4 Lugon-et-l'Île-du-Carnay France
163 B4 Lugos France
139 K3 Lugovaya Rus. Fed.
Lugovaya Proleyka Volgogradskaya Oblast' Rus. Fed. see Primorsk
121 H4 Lugovoy Kazakh.
121 H4 Lugovoye Kazakh.
160 E2 Lugrin France
185 G3 Lugros Spain
136 C2 Luha r. Ukr.
177 G2 Luhačovice Czech Rep.
137 J3 Luhan' r. Ukr.
137 J3 Luhanchyk r. Ukr.
141 N3 Luhanka Fin.
137 J3 Luhans'k Ukr.
137 J3 Luhans'ka Oblast' admin. div. Ukr.
Luhansk Oblast admin. div. Ukr. see Luhans'ka Oblast'
169 E3 Luhden Ger.
109 F1 Luhe Jiangsu China
168 F2 Luhe r. Ger.
173 G2 Luhe-Wildenau Ger.
107 H2 Luhin Sum Nei Mongol China
Luhit r. China/India see Zayü Qu
96 A1 Luhit r. India
170 E1 Lühmannsdorf Ger.
Luhua Sichuan China see Heishui
108 B2 Luhuo Sichuan China
136 E2 Luhyny Ukr.
209 D7 Luia Angola
209 D6 Luia r. Angola
213 G3 Luia r. Moz.
209 D9 Luiana Angola
209 D9 Luiana r. Angola
197 H3 Luica Romania
146 D4 Luichart, Loch l. Scotland U.K.
Luichow Peninsula China see Leizhou Bandao
Luik Belgium see Liège
208 D5 Luilaka r. Dem. Rep. Congo
Luimbale Angola see Londuimbali
Luimneach Rep. of Ireland see Limerick
146 C5 Luing i. Scotland U.K.
190 D3 Luino Italy
182 C2 Luintra Spain
209 D8 Luio r. Angola
140 N2 Luiro r. Fin.
156 B4 Luisant France
254 E2 Luís Correia Brazil
241 I5 Luis Echeverría Álvarez Mex.
254 F3 Luís Gomes Brazil
209 E7 Luishia Dem. Rep. Congo
242 D2 Luis L. León, Presa resr Mex.
244 C2 Luis Moya Mex.
262 V1 Luitpold Coast Antarctica
209 D6 Luiza Dem. Rep. Congo
209 E6 Luizi Dem. Rep. Congo
261 H4 Luján Arg.
261 H4 Lujan r. Arg.
260 C3 Luján de Cuyo Arg.
109 F2 Lujiang Anhui China
137 G2 Luka Ukr.
177 G3 Lukáčovce Slovakia
176 F4 Lukácsháza Hungary
209 B6 Lukala Dem. Rep. Congo
209 E8 Lukanga Swamps Zambia
Lukapa Angola see Lucapa
188 G3 Lukavac Bos.-Herz.
175 L5 Łukawiec Pol.
87 C5 Luke, Mount hill W.A. Austr.
209 C5 Lukenie r. Dem. Rep. Congo
147 D4 Lukeswell Rep. of Ireland
241 K6 Lukeville AZ U.S.A.
134 H4 Lukh Rus. Fed.
134 H4 Lukh r. Rus. Fed.
139 L4 Lukhovitsy Rus. Fed.
197 G5 Lŭki Bulg.
136 C2 Lukiv Ukr.
109 □ Luk Keng H.K. China
208 C5 Lukolela Dem. Rep. Congo
Lukou Hunan China see Zhuzhou
188 G3 Lukovac r. Bos.-Herz.
198 A2 Lukovë Albania
197 G4 Lukovit Bulg.
139 J3 Lukovnikovo Rus. Fed.
175 K4 Łuków Pol.
175 K3 Łukowisko Pol.
135 I5 Lukoyanov Rus. Fed.
138 D4 Lukšiai Lith.
209 E6 Lukuga r. Dem. Rep. Congo
209 B6 Lukula Dem. Rep. Congo
211 C7 Lukuledi Tanz.
209 D8 Lukulu Zambia
209 F8 Lukusashi r. Zambia
136 B3 Luky Ukr.
209 D5 Lula r. Dem. Rep. Congo
192 B4 Lula Sardegna Italy
140 M2 Luleå Sweden
140 M2 Luleälven r. Sweden
199 E1 Lüleburgaz Turkey
258 D2 Lules Arg.
108 B3 Luliang Yunnan China
107 F4 Lüliang Shan mts China
237 D6 Luling TX U.S.A.
147 E3 Lullymore Rep. of Ireland
107 H4 Lulong Hebei China
208 C4 Lulonga r. Dem. Rep. Congo
208 D4 Lulu r. Dem. Rep. Congo
Luluabourg Dem. Rep. Congo see Kananga
111 D6 Lülung Xizang China
87 C5 Lulworth, Mount hill W.A. Austr.
111 D6 Lumachomo Xizang China
260 A6 Lumaco Chile
95 F5 Lumajang Jawa Timur Indon.
111 C5 Lumajangdong Co salt l. China
Lumbala Moxico Angola see Lumbala Kaquengue
Lumbala Moxico Angola see Lumbala N'guimbo
209 D8 Lumbala Kaquengue Angola
209 D8 Lumbala N'guimbo Angola
209 D9 Lumbe r. Zambia
231 E5 Lumber r. SC U.S.A.
231 E5 Lumberton NC U.S.A.
183 I2 Lumbier Spain
213 I2 Lumbo Moz.
182 D4 Lumbrales Spain
183 H2 Lumbreras Spain
156 C2 Lumbres France
117 H4 Lumding Assam India
211 B7 Lumecha Tanz.
190 F3 Lumezzane Italy
140 N2 Lumijoki Fin.
197 I3 Lumina Romania
257 E4 Luminárias Brazil
192 A2 Lumio Corse France
143 H3 Lummelunda Gotland Sweden
165 E4 Lummen Belgium
141 M3 Lumparland Åland Fin.
146 F4 Lumphanan Aberdeenshire, Scotland U.K.
97 D4 Lumphăt Cambodia
186 B3 Lumpiaque Spain
231 C5 Lumpkin GA U.S.A.
223 J5 Lumsden Sask. Can.
81 B6 Lumsden South I. N.Z.
95 F3 Lumut, Gunung mt. Indon.
106 E2 Lün Mongolia
92 B2 Luna Phil.
186 C2 Luna Spain
184 E4 Luna hill Spain
182 E2 Luna r. Spain
241 M5 Luna NM U.S.A.
156 C4 Lunain r. France
192 A5 Lunamatrona Sardegna Italy
108 B3 Lunan Yunnan China
227 F5 Luna Pier MI U.S.A.
161 B5 Lunas France
116 C5 Lunavada Gujarat India
124 B2 Lunayyir, Ḥarrāt lava field Saudi Arabia
177 L5 Lunca Bihor Romania
197 G4 Lunca Teleorman Romania
197 G2 Lunca Bradului Romania
177 L6 Lunca Cernii de Jos Romania
197 G2 Lunca Ilvei Romania
146 E5 Luncarty Perth and Kinross, Scotland U.K.
197 G3 Luncavăț r. Romania
177 L5 Luncoiu de Jos Romania
142 E4 Lund Sweden
241 J2 Lund NV U.S.A.
241 K2 Lund UT U.S.A.
209 C7 Lunda Norte prov. Angola
223 L5 Lundar Man. Can.
209 D7 Lunda Sul prov. Angola
211 B8 Lundazi Zambia
222 H5 Lundbreck Alta Can.
168 F1 Lundby Denmark
142 C4 Lunde Denmark
168 E1 Lunden Ger.
Lundi r. Zimbabwe see Runde
146 F5 Lundin Links Fife, Scotland U.K.
226 C3 Lunds WI U.S.A.
150 C3 Lundy Island England U.K.
168 D2 Lune r. Ger.
149 G3 Lune r. England U.K.
169 B5 Lünebach Ger.
215 H2 Luneberg S. Africa
168 F2 Lüneburg Ger.
168 E2 Lüneburg admin. reg. Niedersachsen Ger.
161 C5 Lunel France
161 F3 Lunella, Punta mt. Italy
161 C5 Lunel-Viel France
169 C4 Lünen Ger.
232 D6 Lunenburg VA U.S.A.
159 I5 Lunery France
168 D2 Lunestedt Ger.
157 G4 Lunéville France
213 I2 Lunga Moz.
209 E8 Lunga r. Zambia
190 D2 Lungern Switz.
111 C6 Lunggar Xizang China
206 B4 Lungi Sierra Leone
Lungleh Mizoram India see Lunglei
117 H5 Lunglei Mizoram India
111 D6 Lungmari mt. Xizang China
147 E4 Lungnaquilla Mountain hill Rep. of Ireland
193 I5 Lungro Italy
209 D8 Lungué-Bungo r. Angola
209 D8 Lungwebungu r. Zambia
116 B4 Luni r. India
123 G4 Luni r. Pak.
Luninets Belarus see Luninyets
240 H2 Luning NV U.S.A.
135 I5 Lunino Rus. Fed.
136 D1 Luninyets Belarus
163 D5 L'Union France
116 C3 Lunkaransar Rajasthan India
116 C3 Lunkha Rajasthan India
123 H2 Lunkho mt. Afgh./Pak.
146 □G1 Lunna Ness hd Scotland U.K.
169 C3 Lünne Ger.
170 F3 Lunow Ger.
206 B4 Lunsar Sierra Leone
209 F8 Lunsemfwa r. Zambia
213 F5 Lunsklip S. Africa
110 D3 Luntai Xinjiang China
164 E2 Lunteren Neth.
198 B1 Lunxhërisë, Mali i ridge Albania
171 D5 Lunzenau Ger.
107 G5 Luo r. Henan China
107 F5 Luo r. Shaanxi China
100 D3 Luobei Heilong. China
110 E4 Luobuzhuang Xinjiang China
Luocheng Fujian China see Hui'an
106 C4 Luocheng Gansu China
108 D3 Luocheng Guangxi China
107 F5 Luochuan Shaanxi China
108 C3 Luodian Guizhou China
109 D4 Luoding Guangdong China
192 B3 Luogosanto Sardegna Italy
109 E1 Luohe Henan China
108 D4 Luo Jiang r. China
107 F5 Luonan Shaanxi China
107 F5 Luoning Henan China
108 C3 Luoping Yunnan China
141 N3 Luopioinen Fin.
109 E1 Luoshan Henan China
109 E2 Luotian Hubei China
140 M3 Luoto Fin.
Luoxiong Yunnan China see Luoping
Luoyang Guangdong China see Boluo
107 G5 Luoyang Henan China
Luoyang Zhejiang China see Taishun
109 F3 Luoyuan Fujian China
209 B6 Luozi Dem. Rep. Congo
100 D4 Luozigou Jilin China
211 B7 Lupa Market Tanz.
213 E3 Lupane Zimbabwe
108 C3 Lupanshui Guizhou China
95 E2 Lupar r. Sarawak Malaysia
143 G4 Łupawa r. Pol.
173 F2 Lupburg Ger.
184 C1 Lupe r. Port.
197 G2 Lupeni Harghita Romania
197 F3 Lupeni Hunedoara Romania
246 E3 Luperón Dom. Rep.
172 C3 Lupfen hill Ger.
163 C5 Lupiac France
211 B7 Lupilichi Moz.
186 C2 Lupiñén Spain
185 G3 Lupión Spain
209 C8 Lupire Angola
175 K6 Łupków Pol.
191 J3 Lupoglav Croatia
92 C5 Lupon Phil.
171 D4 Luppa Ger.
157 G4 Luppy France
241 M4 Lupton AZ U.S.A.
134 K3 Lup'ya r. Rus. Fed.
Luqiao Sichuan China see Luding
106 D5 Luqu Gansu China
Lu Qu r. China see Tao He
107 G4 Luquan Hebei China
108 B3 Luquan Yunnan China
185 F3 Luque Spain
209 C7 Luquembo Angola
247 □1 Luquillo Puerto Rico
192 B4 Luras Sardegna Italy
226 B5 Luray MO U.S.A.
232 D5 Luray VA U.S.A.
163 B5 Lurbe-St-Christau France
160 A2 Lurcy-Lévis France
157 G5 Lure France
161 D4 Lure, Montagne de mt. France
161 D4 Lure, Sommet de mt. France
211 C8 Lureco r. Moz.
209 C7 Luremo Angola
147 E2 Lurgan Northern Ireland U.K.
192 B2 Luri Corse France
210 A3 Luri r. Sudan
252 D4 Luribay Bol.
252 A3 Lurín Peru
Luring Xizang China see Gêrzê
213 I2 Lúrio Moz.
213 I2 Lurio r. Moz.
140 K2 Lurøy Norway
161 D5 Lurs France
159 I4 Lury-sur-Arnon France
209 F8 Lusaka Zambia
209 F8 Lusaka prov. Zambia
209 D6 Lusambo Dem. Rep. Congo
209 E6 Lusangi Dem. Rep. Congo
194 D2 Lusciano Italy
223 I4 Luseland Sask. Can.
190 C4 Luserna San Giovanni Italy
86 E3 Lush, Mount hill W.A. Austr.
108 B2 Lushan Sichuan China
Lushar Qinghai China see Huangzhong
107 F5 Lushi Henan China
196 D5 Lushnjë Albania
211 C6 Lushoto Tanz.
108 A3 Lushui Yunnan China
107 I4 Lushunkou Liaoning China
109 G1 Lüsi Jiangsu China
95 E4 Lusi r. Indon.
162 C2 Lusignan France
160 B2 Lusigny France
156 E4 Lusigny-sur-Barse France
215 G4 Lusikisiki S. Africa
147 E3 Lusk Rep. of Ireland
238 F3 Lusk WY U.S.A.
161 D4 Lus-la-Croix-Haute France
Luso Angola see Luena
182 B4 Luso Port.
146 D5 Luss Argyll and Bute, Scotland U.K.
162 B4 Lussac France
162 C2 Lussac-les-Châteaux France
162 D2 Lussac-les-Églises France
148 D2 Lussa Loch l. Scotland U.K.
161 C4 Lussan France
168 F3 Lüßberg hill Ger.
170 D2 Lüssow Ger.
146 B4 Lusta Highland, Scotland U.K.
172 C2 Lustadt Ger.
190 E1 Lustenau Austria
215 H2 Lusushwana r. Swaziland
Lusutufu r. Africa see Usutu
175 H3 Luszyn Pol.
Lut, Bahrat salt l. Asia see Dead Sea
122 D4 Lut, Dasht-e des. Iran
191 G2 Lutago Italy
Lutai Tianjin China see Ninghe
168 F2 Lütau Ger.
256 B5 Lutécia Brazil
Lutetia France see Paris
122 D4 Lūt-e Zangī Aḥmad des. Iran
226 E3 Luther MI U.S.A.
232 D4 Luthersburg PA U.S.A.
171 D4 Lutherstadt Wittenberg Ger.
176 G2 Lutín Czech Rep.
168 F1 Lütjenburg Ger.
168 F2 Lütjensee Ger.
175 H3 Lutocin Pol.
175 H4 Lutomiersk Pol.
151 G3 Luton Luton, England U.K.
151 G3 Luton admin. div. England U.K.
95 F1 Lutong Sarawak Malaysia
213 F3 Lutope r. Zimbabwe
175 K6 Lutowiska Pol.
175 I1 Lutry Pol.
223 I2 Łutselk'e N.W.T. Can.
136 C2 Luts'k Ukr.
169 F4 Lutter am Barenberge Ger.
157 H5 Lutterbach France
151 F2 Lutterworth Leicestershire, England U.K.
214 D5 Luttig S. Africa
140 O1 Lutto r. Fin./Rus. Fed. alt. Lotta
209 D8 Lutuai Angola
137 J3 Lutuhyne Ukr.
174 G4 Lututów Pol.
174 F3 Lutynia r. Pol.
231 D6 Lutz FL U.S.A.
171 D4 Lützen Ger.
169 C5 Lutzerath Ger.
173 E3 Lutzingen Ger.
170 C2 Lützow Ger.
214 C3 Lutzputs S. Africa
171 D4 Lützschena Ger.
214 B4 Lutzville S. Africa
141 N3 Luumäki Fin.
210 D4 Luuq Somalia
231 C6 Luverne AL U.S.A.
236 D3 Luverne MN U.S.A.
141 M3 Luvia Fin.
209 E6 Luvua r. Dem. Rep. Congo
209 D8 Luvuei Angola
213 F4 Luvuvhu r. S. Africa
211 C7 Luwegu r. Tanz.
210 B4 Luwero Uganda
209 F7 Luwingu Zambia
93 B3 Luwuk Sulawesi Tengah Indon.
160 D1 Lux France
165 E4 Luxembourg prov. Belgium
165 F5 Luxembourg country Europe
165 F5 Luxembourg Lux.
165 F5 Luxembourg admin. dist. Lux.
Luxemburg country Europe see Luxembourg
226 D3 Luxemburg WI U.S.A.
163 A5 Luxe-Sumberraute France
157 G5 Luxeuil-les-Bains France
163 B4 Luxey France
108 D2 Luxi Hunan China
108 A3 Luxi Yunnan China
108 B3 Luxi Yunnan China
108 C2 Luxian Sichuan China
215 E4 Luxolweni S. Africa
Luxor Egypt see El Uqṣur
150 C4 Luxulyan Cornwall, England U.K.
163 A5 Luy r. France
Luyang Sichuan China see Lushan
163 B5 Luy de Béarn r. France
163 B5 Luy de France r. France
182 D2 Luyego de Somoza Spain
109 E1 Luyi Henan China
165 E3 Luyksgestel Neth.
159 G4 Luynes France
Luyuan Shaanxi China see Gaoling
216 □1c Luz Graciosa Azores
257 E3 Luz Brazil
184 C2 Luz Évora Port.
184 B3 Luz Faro Port.
184 C3 Luz Faro Port.
182 D3 Luz hill Port.
134 I3 Luza Rus. Fed.
134 I3 Luza r. Rus. Fed.
134 L2 Luza r. Rus. Fed.
183 H4 Luzaga Spain
156 C3 Luzarches France
163 B6 Luz-Ardiden France
176 F2 Luže Czech Rep.
163 D4 Luzech France
176 D1 Lužec nad Vltavou Czech Rep.
190 D1 Luzern Switz.
190 D1 Luzern canton Switz.
234 C1 Luzerne PA U.S.A.
234 B1 Luzerne County county PA U.S.A.
139 K4 Luzha r. Rus. Fed.
108 D3 Luzhai Guangxi China
Luzhang Yunnan China see Lushui
108 C3 Luzhi Guizhou China
108 C2 Luzhou Sichuan China
184 B3 Luzianes Port.
256 D2 Luziânia Brazil
176 D1 Lužické Hory mts Czech Rep.
254 E2 Luzilândia Brazil
174 G1 Luzino Pol.
183 F1 Luzmela Spain
176 C1 Lužná Czech Rep.
175 J6 Łużna Pol.
176 D2 Lužnice r. Czech Rep.
92 B3 Luzon i. Phil.
183 H3 Luzón Spain
92 B1 Luzon Strait Phil.
163 C6 Luz-St-Sauveur France
160 B2 Luzy France
174 G4 Łużyca r. Pol.
191 F4 Luzzara Italy
193 I5 Luzzi Italy
136 D1 L'va r. Ukr.
136 C3 L'viv Ukr.
Lviv Oblast admin. div. Ukr. see L'vivs'ka Oblast'
136 C2 L'vivs'ka Oblast' admin. div. Ukr.
L'vov Ukr. see L'viv
Lvov Oblast admin. div. Ukr. see L'vivs'ka Oblast'
L'vovskaya Oblast' admin. div. Ukr. see L'vivs'ka Oblast'
139 K4 L'vovskiy Rus. Fed.
Lwów Ukr. see L'viv
174 E3 Lwówek Pol.
174 D4 Lwówek Śląski Pol.
136 D3 Lyadova r. Ukr.
138 G2 Lyady Rus. Fed.
138 F5 Lyakhavichy Belarus
Lyakhovichi Belarus see Lyakhavichy
131 P2 Lyakhovskiye Ostrova is Novosibirskiye O-va Rus. Fed.
81 A6 Lyall, Mount South I. N.Z.
Lyallpur Pak. see Faisalabad
121 F5 Lyal'mikar Uzbek.
135 I5 Lyambir' Rus. Fed.
134 L4 Lyamino Rus. Fed.
Lyangar Kashkadar'inskaya Oblast' Uzbek. see Langar
121 F4 Lyangar Navoiyskaya Oblast' Uzbek.
134 M3 Lyapin r. Rus. Fed.
137 G3 Lyashivka Ukr.
141 O3 Lyaskelya Rus. Fed.
197 G4 Lyaskovets Bulg.
138 E5 Lyasnaya Belarus
138 D5 Lyasnaya r. Belarus
175 L3 Lyasnaya Lyevaya r. Belarus
177 L3 Lybokhora Ukr.
146 E3 Lybster Highland, Scotland U.K.
175 M4 Lybytiv Ukr.
170 E2 Lychen Ger.
137 H3 Lychkove Ukr.
139 I3 Lychkovo Rus. Fed.
Lyck Pol. see Ełk
140 L2 Lycksele Sweden
234 A1 Lycoming County county PA U.S.A.
234 A1 Lycoming Creek r. PA U.S.A.
Lycopolis Egypt see Asyûṭ
151 H4 Lydd Kent, England U.K.
Lydda Israel see Lod
262 W2 Lyddan Island Antarctica
213 F5 Lydenburg S. Africa
150 C4 Lydford Devon, England U.K.
150 E3 Lydney Gloucestershire, England U.K.
175 I3 Łydynia r. Pol.
138 E5 Lyebyada r. Belarus
136 E2 Lyel'chytsy Belarus
240 H3 Lyell, Mount CA U.S.A.
84 B4 Lyell Brown, Mount hill N.T. Austr.
81 D4 Lyell Range mts South I. N.Z.
138 G4 Lyepyel' Belarus
198 C3 Lygourio Greece
137 I3 Lyhivka Ukr.
227 I5 Lykens PA U.S.A.
137 F2 Lykhachiv Ukr.
137 G3 Lykhivka Ukr.
139 I2 Lykoshino Rus. Fed.
214 E2 Lykso S. Africa
226 A4 Lyle MN U.S.A.
136 E5 Lyman Ukr.
238 E3 Lyman WY U.S.A.
137 I3 Lyman, Ozero l. Ukr.
136 E4 Lymans'ke Ukr.
150 E4 Lyme Bay England U.K.
150 E4 Lyme Regis Dorset, England U.K.
151 I3 Lyminge Kent, England U.K.
151 F4 Lymington Hampshire, England U.K.
149 G4 Lymm Warrington, England U.K.
151 I3 Lympne Kent, England U.K.
150 D4 Lympstone Devon, England U.K.
143 I4 Łyna r. Pol.
232 B6 Lynch KY U.S.A.
231 C5 Lynchburg TN U.S.A.
232 D6 Lynchburg VA U.S.A.
231 E5 Lynches r. SC U.S.A.
232 D6 Lynch Station VA U.S.A.
233 □H2 Lynchville ME U.S.A.
85 E3 Lynd r. Qld Austr.
238 B1 Lynden WA U.S.A.
85 F3 Lyndhurst Qld Austr.
82 D2 Lyndhurst S.A. Austr.
151 F4 Lyndhurst Hampshire, England U.K.
87 B4 Lyndon W.A. Austr.
87 B4 Lyndon r. W.A. Austr.
236 E4 Lyndon KS U.S.A.
226 C4 Lyndon Station WI U.S.A.
232 D3 Lyndonville NY U.S.A.
233 G2 Lyndonville VT U.S.A.
149 F3 Lyne r. England U.K.
151 F3 Lyneham Wiltshire, England U.K.
149 H2 Lynemouth Northumberland, England U.K.
146 E3 Lyness Orkney, Scotland U.K.
142 B2 Lyngdal Norway
140 M1 Lyngen sea chan. Norway
140 M1 Lyngseidet Norway
150 C4 Lynher r. England U.K.
86 D2 Lynher Reef W.A. Austr.
150 D3 Lynmouth Devon, England U.K.
Lynn Norfolk, England U.K. see King's Lynn
233 H3 Lynn MA U.S.A.
241 K2 Lynndyl UT U.S.A.
231 C6 Lynn Haven FL U.S.A.
223 K3 Lynn Lake Man. Can.
137 H2 Lynove Ukr.
137 G2 Lynovytsya Ukr.
87 B6 Lynton W.A. Austr.
150 D3 Lynton Devon, England U.K.
138 F4 Lyntupy Belarus
223 J2 Lynx Lake N.W.T. Can.
226 B4 Lynxville WI U.S.A.
160 C3 Lyon France
Lyon airport France see Satolas
146 E5 Lyon r. Scotland U.K.
146 D5 Lyon, Loch l. Scotland U.K.
233 G2 Lyon Mountain NY U.S.A.
160 C3 Lyonnais, Monts du hills France
82 C2 Lyons S.A. Austr.
87 B5 Lyons r. W.A. Austr.
Lyons France see Lyon
231 D5 Lyons GA U.S.A.
236 D4 Lyons KS U.S.A.
232 E3 Lyons NY U.S.A.
233 F3 Lyons Falls NY U.S.A.
156 B3 Lyons-la-Forêt France
235 E1 Lyons Plain CT U.S.A.
234 C2 Lyon Station PA U.S.A.
139 H4 Lyozna Belarus
136 C2 Lypa r. Ukr.
136 E2 Lypnyky Ukr.
137 G2 Lypova Dolyna Ukr.
136 E3 Lypovets' Ukr.
137 I2 Lyptsi Ukr.
156 D2 Lys r. France
190 C3 Lys r. Italy
168 F1 Lysabild Denmark
177 H2 Lysá Hora mt. Czech Rep.
137 F3 Lysa Hora Ukr.
171 F5 Lysá nad Labem Czech Rep.
177 H2 Lysá pod Makytou Slovakia
175 J2 Łyse Pol.
142 B2 Lysekammen mt. Norway
142 D2 Lysekil Sweden
175 I5 Łysica hill Pol.
176 F2 Lysice Czech Rep.
198 B2 Lysimachia, Limni l. Greece
174 G5 Lyski Pol.
134 I4 Lyskovo Rus. Fed.
137 J4 Lysogorka Rus. Fed.
174 G2 Łysomice Pol.
190 C1 Lyss Switz.
142 D3 Lystrup Denmark
134 L4 Lys'va Rus. Fed.
142 E1 Lysvik Sweden
136 F3 Lysyanka Ukr.
137 J3 Lysychans'k Ukr.
135 I6 Lysyye Gory Rus. Fed.
175 H4 Łyszkowice Pol.
150 E4 Lytchett Matravers Dorset, England U.K.
150 E4 Lytchett Minster Dorset, England U.K.
146 E3 Lyth Highland, Scotland U.K.
149 F4 Lytham St Anne's Lancashire, England U.K.
139 K4 Lytkarino Rus. Fed.
175 M5 Lytovezh Ukr.
81 D5 Lyttelton South I. N.Z.
81 D5 Lyttelton Harbour South I. N.Z.
222 F5 Lytton B.C. Can.
138 G5 Lyuban' Belarus
139 H2 Lyuban' Rus. Fed.
136 D3 Lyubar Ukr.
136 F4 Lyubashivka Ukr.
137 H1 Lyubazh Rus. Fed.
138 F5 Lyubcha Belarus
136 F2 Lyubech Ukr.
139 K4 Lyubertsy Rus. Fed.
136 C2 Lyubeshiv Ukr.
134 H4 Lyubim Rus. Fed.
197 H5 Lyubimets Bulg.
137 H2 Lyubimovka Rus. Fed.
138 E5 Lyubishchytsy Belarus
139 J2 Lyubitovo Rus. Fed.
175 I1 Lyublino Rus. Fed.
175 M4 Lyublynets' Ukr.
139 J5 Lyubokhna Rus. Fed.
175 M4 Lyubokhyny Ukr.
137 H2 Lyubostan' Rus. Fed.
Lyubotin Ukr. see Lyubotyn
137 H3 Lyubotyn Ukr.
137 I4 Lyubymivka Ukr.
175 L6 Lyubyntsi Ukr.
139 I2 Lyubytino Rus. Fed.
139 J5 Lyudinovo Rus. Fed.
197 H4 Lyulyakovo Bulg.
134 I4 Lyunda r. Rus. Fed.
138 F5 Lyusina Belarus
134 L2 Lyzha r. Rus. Fed.
138 G3 Lža r. Latvia
138 G3 Lzha r. Rus. Fed.

M

96 B2 Ma r. Myanmar
96 C2 Ma, Nam r. Laos
96 D3 Ma, Sông r. Vietnam
113 □1 Maabadi i. N. Male Maldives
Maafushi i. S. Male Maldives see Mafushi
240 □C8 Maalaea HI U.S.A.
114 B5 Maalhosmadulu Atoll Maldives
147 B3 Maam Rep. of Ireland
Maamakundhoo i. N. Male Maldives see Makunudhoo
209 E9 Maamba Zambia
147 B3 Maam Cross Rep. of Ireland
207 H6 Ma'an Cameroon
128 B4 Ma'an Jordan
140 N3 Maaninka Fin.
109 F2 Ma'anshan Anhui China
106 D1 Maanyt Bulgan Mongolia
107 E2 Maanyt Töv Mongolia
138 E2 Maardu Estonia
165 E3 Maarheeze Neth.
Maarianhamina Åland Fin. see Mariehamn
164 E2 Maarn Neth.
128 C2 Ma'arrat an Nu'mān Syria
164 E2 Maarssen Neth.
164 E2 Maarssenbroek Neth.
164 E2 Maartensdijk Neth.
164 D3 Maas r. Neth. alt. Meuse (Belgium/France)
147 C2 Maas Rep. of Ireland
165 E3 Maasbracht Neth.
165 F3 Maasbree Neth.
164 D3 Maasdam Neth.
165 E3 Maaseik Belgium
92 C4 Maasin Phil.
164 D3 Maasland Neth.
165 E4 Maasmechelen Belgium
164 D3 Maassluis Neth.
165 E4 Maastricht Neth.
83 F5 Maatsuyker Group is Tas. Austr.
Maba Guangdong China see Qujiang
109 F1 Maba Jiangsu China
215 F1 Mabaalstad North West S. Africa
215 F1 Mabaalstad North West S. Africa
92 B3 Mabalacat Phil.
208 A5 Mabanda Gabon
124 D5 Ma'bar Yemen
251 G2 Mabaruma Guyana
Mabating Yunnan China see Hongshan
82 C2 Mabel Creek S.A. Austr.
86 E3 Mabel Downs W.A. Austr.
224 B3 Mabella Ont. Can.
227 I3 Maberly Ont. Can.
108 B2 Mabian Sichuan China
149 J4 Mablethorpe Lincolnshire, England U.K.
160 C2 Mably France
215 G1 Mabopane S. Africa
225 I4 Mabou N.S. Can.
128 B4 Mabrak, Jabal mt. Jordan
214 E1 Mabule Botswana
212 D5 Mabutsane Botswana
259 B7 Macá, Monte mt. Chile
261 F5 Macachín Arg.
87 C5 Macadam Plains W.A. Austr.
84 B2 Macadam Range hills N.T. Austr.
257 G5 Macaé Brazil
185 H3 Macael Spain
254 G3 Macaíba Brazil
254 E5 Macajuba Brazil
211 B8 Macaloge Moz.
224 E3 Macamic Que. Can.
Macan, Kepulauan atolls Indon. see Taka'Bonerate, Kepulauan
186 F2 Maçanet de Cabrenys Spain
Macao Macau China see Macau
182 C5 Mação Port.
251 I4 Macapá Brazil
Macar Turkey see Gebiz
250 B6 Macará Ecuador
255 E5 Macarani Brazil
250 C4 Macarena, Cordillera mts Col.
251 F2 Macareo, Caño r. Venez.
83 E4 Macarthur Vic. Austr.
250 B5 Macas Ecuador
182 D3 Maçãs r. Port./Spain
Macassar Sulawesi Selatan Indon. see Ujung Pandang
Macassar Strait Indon. see Makassar Strait
187 C5 Macastre Spain
254 F3 Macau Brazil
109 E4 Macau Macau China
162 B3 Macau France
252 C2 Macauã r. Brazil
254 E5 Macaúbas Brazil
77 I5 Macauley Island N.Z.
190 D2 Maccagno Italy
213 G5 Maccaretane Moz.
195 E5 Macchia r. Sicilia Italy
193 G3 Macchiagodena Italy
231 D6 Macclenny FL U.S.A.
149 G4 Macclesfield Cheshire, England U.K.
224 B3 Macdiarmid Ont. Can.
86 F4 Macdonald, Lake salt flat W.A. Austr.
84 B4 Macdonnell Ranges mts N.T. Austr.
146 F4 Macduff Aberdeenshire, Scotland U.K.
177 K5 Macea Romania
182 C2 Maceda Spain
182 D3 Macedo de Cavaleiros Port.
Macedon country Europe see Macedonia
197 E5 Macedonia country Europe
235 E1 Macedonia CT U.S.A.
254 G4 Maceió Brazil
182 C4 Maceira Guarda Port.
182 B5 Maceira Leiria Port.
206 C4 Macenta Guinea
191 I5 Macerata Italy
191 I5 Macerata prov. Marche Italy
191 H5 Macerata Feltria Italy
82 D3 Macfarlane, Lake salt flat S.A. Austr.
147 B5 Macgillycuddy's Reeks mts Rep. of Ireland
148 C3 MacGregor's Corner Northern Ireland U.K.
123 F4 Mach Pak.
257 G2 Machacalis Brazil
252 D4 Machacamarca Bol.
250 B5 Machachi Ecuador
253 E2 Machadinho r. Brazil
257 E4 Machado Brazil
215 H1 Machadodorp S. Africa
184 C2 Machados Port.
211 C5 Machakos Kenya
250 B5 Machala Ecuador
260 B4 Machali Chile
Machali Qinghai China see Madoi
213 G4 Machanga Moz.
253 E5 Macharetí Bol.
210 B2 Machar Marshes Sudan
84 D5 Machattie, Lake salt flat Qld Austr.
156 E3 Machault France
Machaze Moz. see Chitobe
158 E5 Machecoul France
165 D4 Machelen Belgium
150 D3 Machen Caerphilly, Wales U.K.
109 E2 Macheng Hubei China
157 G3 Macheren France
114 C2 Macherla Andhra Prad. India
171 D4 Machern Ger.
185 F1 Machero mt. Spain
226 C4 Machesney Park IL U.S.A.
116 D3 Machhiwara Punjab India
116 E4 Machhlishahr Uttar Prad. India
233 □J2 Machias ME U.S.A.
232 D3 Machias NY U.S.A.
233 □I1 Machias r. ME U.S.A.
184 □ Machico Madeira
105 F3 Machida Japan
114 D2 Machilipatnam Andhra Prad. India
211 B8 Machinga Malawi
250 C2 Machiques Venez.
146 B6 Machir Bay Scotland U.K.
Machiwara Punjab India see Machhiwara
245 H4 Machona, Laguna lag. Mex.
146 C6 Machrihanish Argyll and Bute, Scotland U.K.
137 H3 Machukhy Ukr.
252 B3 Machupicchu tourist site Peru
252 D3 Machupo r. Bol.
150 D2 Machynlleth Powys, Wales U.K.
213 G5 Macia Moz.
Macias Nguema i. Equat. Guinea see Bioco
175 J4 Maciejowice Pol.
261 G3 Maciel Arg.
197 I3 Măcin Romania
192 B2 Macinaggio Corse France
83 G2 Macintyre r. N.S.W. Austr.
83 G2 Macintyre Brook r. Qld Austr.
252 B3 Macizo de Tocate mts Peru
241 M2 Mack CO U.S.A.
129 A3 Maçka Turkey
85 G4 Mackay Qld Austr.
223 I3 MacKay r. Alta Can.
238 D2 Mackay ID U.S.A.
86 F4 Mackay, Lake salt flat W.A. Austr.
223 I2 MacKay Lake N.W.T. Can.
262 O1 Mackay Mountains Antarctica
172 B2 Mackenbach Ger.
169 F4 Mackenrode Ger.
85 G4 Mackenzie r. Qld Austr.
222 F4 Mackenzie B.C. Can.
226 C1 Mackenzie Ont. Can.
222 E1 Mackenzie r. N.W.T. Can.
Mackenzie Guyana see Linden
Mackenzie atoll Micronesia see Ulithi
220 E3 Mackenzie Bay Y.T. Can.
222 G2 Mackenzie Highway N.W.T. Can.
221 G2 Mackenzie King Island N.W.T. Can.
222 C1 Mackenzie Mountains N.W.T./Y.T. Can.
Mackillop, Lake salt flat Qld Austr. see Yamma Yamma, Lake
226 E3 Mackinac Island MI U.S.A.
226 C5 Mackinaw r. IL U.S.A.
226 E3 Mackinaw City MI U.S.A.
223 I4 Macklin Sask. Can.
83 H2 Macksville N.S.W. Austr.
83 H2 Maclean N.S.W. Austr.
215 F5 Macleantown S. Africa
215 G4 Maclear S. Africa
83 H2 Macleay r. N.S.W. Austr.
MacLeod Alta Can. see Fort Macleod
87 B5 MacLeod, Lake imp. l. W.A. Austr.
222 C2 Macmillan r. Y.T. Can.
209 C6 Macocola Angola
226 B5 Macomb IL U.S.A.
192 A4 Macomer Sardegna Italy
211 D8 Macomia Moz.
160 C2 Mâcon France
231 D5 Macon GA U.S.A.
236 E4 Macon MO U.S.A.
237 F5 Macon MS U.S.A.
232 B5 Macon OH U.S.A.
237 F6 Macon, Bayou r. LA U.S.A.
235 D1 Macopin NJ U.S.A.
213 G3 Macossa Moz.
183 E4 Macotera Spain
213 G4 Macovane Moz.
Macpherson Robertson Land reg. Antarctica see Mac. Robertson Land
83 F2 Macquarie r. N.S.W. Austr.
83 F5 Macquarie r. Tas. Austr.
83 G3 Macquarie, Lake b. N.S.W. Austr.
83 F5 Macquarie Harbour Tas. Austr.
82 □3 Macquarie Island S. Pacific Ocean
83 F2 Macquarie Marshes N.S.W. Austr.
83 G3 Macquarie Mountain N.S.W. Austr.
266 F9 Macquarie Ridge sea feature S. Pacific Ocean
81 C6 Macraes Flat South I. N.Z.
263 E2 Mac. Robertson Land reg. Antarctica
147 C5 Macroom Rep. of Ireland
243 H5 Mactún Mex.
190 C3 Macugnaga Italy
196 E5 Macukull Albania
82 C1 Macumba S.A. Austr.
234 C2 Macungie PA U.S.A.
254 F4 Macururé Brazil
252 C3 Macusani Peru
243 G5 Macuspana Mex.
233 □I2 Macwahoc ME U.S.A.
177 K3 Mád Hungary
128 B4 Mādabā Jordan
215 H2 Madadeni S. Africa
213 □ Madagascar i. Africa
265 H6 Madagascar Basin sea feature Indian Ocean
265 G7 Madagascar Ridge sea feature Indian Ocean
207 I4 Madagli Nigeria
124 B2 Madā'in Ṣāliḥ Saudi Arabia
216 □1c Madalena Pico Azores
254 F3 Madalena Brazil
197 G5 Madan Bulg.
114 C3 Madanapalle Andhra Prad. India
91 K8 Madang P.N.G.
116 D4 Madaora Uttar Prad. India
207 G3 Madaoua Niger
177 I5 Madaras Hungary
197 E2 Mădăraș Romania
117 G5 Madaripur Bangl.
207 G3 Madarounfa Niger
227 I3 Madawaska Ont. Can.
224 E4 Madawaska r. Ont. Can.
233 □I1 Madawaska ME U.S.A.
96 B2 Madaya Myanmar
192 B5 Maddalena Spiaggia Sardegna Italy
193 G3 Maddaloni Italy
114 D2 Madded Madh. Prad. India
114 C3 Maddur Karnataka India
164 D3 Made Neth.
251 G5 Madeira r. Brazil
184 □ Madeira terr. N. Atlantic Ocean
184 □ Madeira, Arquipélago da is N. Atlantic Ocean
Madeira, Arquipélago da terr. N. Atlantic Ocean see Madeira
184 □ Madeira, Ilha da i. Madeira
Madeira Islands N. Atlantic Ocean see Madeira, Arquipélago da
253 E2 Madeirinha r. Brazil
150 E2 Madeley Staffordshire, England U.K.
150 E2 Madeley Telford and Wrekin, England U.K.
236 E2 Madelia MN U.S.A.
126 E3 Maden Turkey
242 C2 Madera Mex.
185 H2 Madera r. Spain
240 G3 Madera CA U.S.A.
183 F3 Maderano r. Spain
178 B3 Madererspitze mt. Austria
183 G3 Maderuelo Spain
114 B3 Madgaon Goa India
116 B5 Madhavpur Gujarat India
117 F4 Madhepura Bihar India
111 C7 Madhoganj Uttar Prad. India
117 F4 Madhubani Bihar India
114 C3 Madhugiri Karnataka India
116 D5 Madhya Pradesh state India
95 F2 Madi, Dataran Tinggi plat. Indon.
215 E2 Madibogo S. Africa
82 D2 Madigan Gulf salt flat S.A. Austr.
114 B3 Madikeri Karnataka India
237 D5 Madill OK U.S.A.
209 B6 Madimba Dem. Rep. Congo
206 D4 Madinani Côte d'Ivoire
124 D5 Madīnat ash Sha'b Yemen
128 D2 Madīnat ath Thawrah Syria
157 F4 Madine, Lac de l. France
209 A6 Madingo-Kayes Congo
209 B6 Madingou Congo
252 D3 Madini r. Bol.
163 B5 Madiran France
213 □J3 Madirovalo Madag.
231 C5 Madison AL U.S.A.
235 F1 Madison CT U.S.A.
231 D6 Madison FL U.S.A.
231 D5 Madison GA U.S.A.
230 C4 Madison IN U.S.A.
233 □I2 Madison ME U.S.A.
236 D2 Madison MN U.S.A.
236 D3 Madison NE U.S.A.
235 D2 Madison NJ U.S.A.
232 C4 Madison OH U.S.A.
236 D2 Madison SD U.S.A.
232 D5 Madison VA U.S.A.
226 C4 Madison WI U.S.A.
232 C5 Madison WV U.S.A.
238 E2 Madison r. MT U.S.A.
232 D6 Madison Heights VA U.S.A.
230 C4 Madisonville KY U.S.A.
231 C5 Madisonville TN U.S.A.
237 E6 Madisonville TX U.S.A.
95 E4 Madiun Jawa Timur Indon.
150 E2 Madley Herefordshire, England U.K.
87 D5 Madley, Mount hill W.A. Austr.
224 E4 Madoc Ont. Can.
177 H5 Madocsa Hungary
106 C5 Madoi Qinghai China
157 G4 Madon r. France
138 F3 Madona Latvia
194 C5 Madonie mts Sicilia Italy
234 B3 Madonna MD U.S.A.
191 F2 Madonna di Campiglio Italy
199 E2 Madra Dağı mts Turkey
124 B3 Madrakah Saudi Arabia
Madras Tamil Nadu India see Chennai
Madras state India see Tamil Nadu
238 B2 Madras OR U.S.A.
245 F1 Madre, Laguna lag. Mex.
237 D7 Madre, Laguna lag. TX U.S.A.
245 H5 Madre, Sierra mts Mex.
92 B2 Madre, Sierra mt. Phil.
Madre de Chiapas, Sierra mts Mex. see Madre, Sierra
257 E4 Madre de Deus de Minas Brazil
252 C2 Madre de Dios dept Peru
259 B8 Madre de Dios, Isla i. Chile
244 D4 Madre del Sur, Sierra mts Mex.
244 B1 Madre Occidental, Sierra mts Mex.
244 D1 Madre Oriental, Sierra mts Mex.
163 E6 Madrès, Pic de mt. France
92 C4 Madrid Phil.
183 G4 Madrid Spain
183 G4 Madrid aut. comm. Spain
92 B4 Madridejos Phil.
185 G1 Madridejos Spain
183 F3 Madrigal de las Altas Torres Spain
183 E4 Madrigal de la Vera Spain
183 G2 Madrigal del Monte Spain
184 E1 Madrigalejo Spain
185 I1 Madrigueras Spain
178 A4 Madrisahorn mt. Austria/Switz.
150 □ Madron Cornwall, England U.K.
184 E1 Madroñera Spain
185 I2 Madroño mt. Spain
246 B2 Madruga Cuba
113 □1 Madu i. S. Male Maldives
209 B6 Maduda Dem. Rep. Congo
115 D2 Madugula Andhra Prad. India
87 E6 Madura W.A. Austr.
95 F4 Madura i. Indon.
95 F4 Madura, Selat sea chan. Indon.
114 C4 Madurai Tamil Nadu India
114 C3 Madurantakam Tamil Nadu India
122 C4 Madvār, Kūh-e mt. Iran
116 E4 Madwas Madh. Prad. India
129 E2 Madzhalis Rus. Fed.
197 G5 Madzharovo Bulg.
213 F3 Madziwa Mine Zimbabwe
191 H2 Maè r. Italy
Maé i. Vanuatu see Émaé
105 F2 Maebashi Japan
96 B3 Mae Hong Son Thai.
158 C3 Maël-Carhaix France
142 C2 Mælefjell mt. Norway
186 D3 Maella Spain
183 F4 Maello Spain
150 C3 Maenclochog Pembrokeshire, Wales U.K.
150 D2 Maentwrog Gwynedd, Wales U.K.
193 F3 Maenza Italy
96 B3 Mae Ramat Thai.
96 B3 Mae Rim Thai.
197 F2 Măeriște Romania
96 B3 Mae Sariang Thai.
146 E3 Maes Howe tourist site Scotland U.K.
96 B3 Mae Sot Thai.
150 D3 Maesteg Bridgend, Wales U.K.
246 C3 Maestra, Sierra mts Cuba
185 E3 Maestre hill Spain
183 H2 Maestu Spain
96 B3 Mae Suai Thai.
213 □J3 Maevatanana Madag.
78 □5 Maéwo i. Vanuatu
223 K4 Mafeking Man. Can.
Mafeking S. Africa see Mafikeng
215 F3 Mafeteng Lesotho
83 F4 Maffra Vic. Austr.
211 C7 Mafia Channel Tanz.
211 C6 Mafia Island Tanz.
215 E1 Mafikeng S. Africa
211 B7 Mafinga Tanz.
255 C8 Mafra Brazil
184 A2 Mafra Port.
Mafraq Jordan see Al Mafraq
113 □1 Mafushi i. S. Male Maldives
215 H4 Magabeni S. Africa
184 E2 Magacela hill Spain
131 Q4 Magadan Rus. Fed.
161 B5 Magalas France
215 F1 Magaliesberg mts S. Africa
215 F1 Magaliesburg S. Africa
Magallanes Chile see Punta Arenas
92 B3 Magallanes Phil.
259 C9 Magallanes, Estrecho de sea chan. Chile
259 B9 Magallanes y Antártica Chilena admin. reg. Chile
183 I3 Magallón Spain
187 F5 Magalluf Spain
183 H3 Magaña Spain
147 E4 Maganey Rep. of Ireland
250 C2 Magangue Col.
126 D3 Mağara Turkey
129 C3 Mağara tourist site Turkey
128 A1 Mağara Dağı mt. Turkey

Mağarali to Mangoky
331

128 D1 Mağarali Turkey
129 F3 Magaramkent Rus. Fed.
207 H3 Magaria Niger
Magas Iran see Zābolī
92 B2 Magat r. Phil.
183 F3 Magaz Spain
237 E5 Magazine Mountain hill AR U.S.A.
194 C5 Magazzolo r. Sicilia Italy
206 C4 Magburaka Sierra Leone
100 C1 Magdagachi Rus. Fed.
171 C5 Magdala Ger.
261 I4 Magdalena Arg.
252 D3 Magdalena Bol.
250 C2 Magdalena dept Col.
250 C2 Magdalena r. Col.
242 C2 Magdalena Mex.
242 C2 Magdalena r. Mex.
239 F5 Magdalena NM U.S.A.
259 B7 Magdalena, Isla i. Chile
245 F4 Magdalena Cuayucatepec Mex.
Magdalena Island Fr. Polynesia see Fatu Hiva
95 G1 Magdalene, Gunung mt. Sabah Malaysia
171 C3 Magdeburg Ger.
171 C3 Magdeburg admin. reg. Sachsen-Anhalt Ger.
171 D3 Magdeburgerforth Ger.
85 G3 Magdelaine Cays atoll Coral Sea Is Terr. Austr.
237 F6 Magee MS U.S.A.
95 E4 Magelang Jawa Tengah Indon.
Magellan, Strait of Chile see Magallanes, Estrecho de
266 E4 Magellan Seamounts sea feature N. Pacific Ocean
190 D3 Magenta Italy
87 C7 Magenta, Lake salt flat W.A. Austr.
140 N1 Magerøya i. Norway
163 A5 Magescq France
177 L4 Măgeşti Romania
190 D2 Maggia Switz.
190 D2 Maggia r. Switz.
261 F3 Maggiolo Arg.
190 E4 Maggiorasca, Monte mt. Italy
190 D3 Maggiore, Lago l. Italy
Maggiore, Lake Italy see Maggiore, Lago
192 B4 Maggiore, Monte hill Sardegna Italy
193 G3 Maggiore, Monte mt. Italy
246 □ Maggotty Jamaica
203 F2 Maghâgha Egypt
128 B5 Maghā'ir Shu'ayb tourist site Saudi Arabia
206 B3 Maghama Maur.
147 B5 Maghanlawaun Rep. of Ireland
128 A4 Maghâra, Gebel hill Egypt
147 C2 Maghera Rep. of Ireland
147 E2 Maghera Northern Ireland U.K.
147 E2 Magherafelt Northern Ireland U.K.
148 C3 Magheralin Northern Ireland U.K.
147 D2 Magheramason Northern Ireland U.K.
147 E2 Maghery Northern Ireland U.K.
204 E2 Maghnia Alg.
149 G4 Maghull Merseyside, England U.K.
148 C2 Magilligan Northern Ireland U.K.
185 G3 Mágina mt. Spain
192 E1 Magione Italy
195 F3 Magisano Italy
Magitang Qinghai China see Jainca
188 G3 Maglaj Bos.-Herz.
160 E2 Magland France
197 F3 Maglavit Romania
193 F2 Magliano de'Marsi Italy
192 D2 Magliano in Toscana Italy
193 E2 Magliano Sabina Italy
195 H2 Maglie Italy
177 I4 Maglód Hungary
241 L5 Magma AZ U.S.A.
162 D2 Magnac-Laval France
162 C3 Magnac-sur-Touvre France
194 B6 Magna Grande hill Italy
195 E5 Magna Grande mt. Sicilia Italy
162 B2 Magné France
85 F3 Magnetic Island Qld Austr.
85 F3 Magnetic Passage Qld Austr.
134 F1 Magnetity Rus. Fed.
157 G4 Magnières France
139 J5 Magnitnyy Rus. Fed.
120 D1 Magnitogorsk Rus. Fed.
237 E5 Magnolia AR U.S.A.
234 C3 Magnolia DE U.S.A.
234 B3 Magnolia MD U.S.A.
237 F6 Magnolia MS U.S.A.
175 J4 Magnuszew Pol.
160 B2 Magny-Cours France
156 B3 Magny-en-Vexin France
100 G1 Mago Rus. Fed.
177 H5 Mágocs Hungary
177 J5 Mágocs-ér r. Hungary
213 F2 Màgoé Moz.
225 F4 Magog Que. Can.
192 A4 Magomadas Sardegna Italy
Magosa Cyprus see Ammochostos
209 E8 Magoye Zambia
245 F3 Magozal Mex.
225 H3 Magpie Que. Can.
224 C4 Magpie r. Ont. Can.
225 H3 Magpie r. Que. Can.
225 H3 Magpie-Ouest r. Que. Can.
190 E4 Magra r. Italy
222 H5 Magrath Alta Can.
187 C5 Magre r. Spain
240 I3 Magruder Mountain NV U.S.A.
206 B2 Magṭa' Laḥjar Maur.
211 B5 Magu Tanz.
108 C4 Maguan Yunnan China
213 G5 Magude Moz.
215 H2 Magudu S. Africa
182 C3 Magueija Port.
184 E2 Maguilla Spain
147 D2 Maguiresbridge Northern Ireland U.K.
207 I3 Magumeri Nigeria
233 □J2 Magundy N.B. Can.
117 G5 Magura Bangl.
177 H3 Magura mt. Slovakia
136 D4 Măgura, Dealul hill Moldova
197 F2 Măgura Mare, Vârful hill Romania
197 F3 Măgurii, Vârful mt. Romania
215 F5 Magwali S. Africa
Magway Myanmar see Magwe
Magway admin. div. Myanmar see Magwe
96 A2 Magwe Myanmar
96 A2 Magwe admin. div. Myanmar
177 K4 Magy Hungary
177 G5 Magyaratád Hungary
177 H6 Magyarbóly Hungary
Magyarkanizsa Vojvodina, Srbija Yugo. see Kanjiža
Magyar Köztársaság country Europe see Hungary
177 H5 Magyarszék Hungary
122 A2 Mahābād Iran
114 B2 Mahabaleshwar Mahar. India
116 F4 Mahabharat Range mts Nepal
213 □J4 Mahabo Madag.
114 B2 Mahad Mahar. India
210 E4 Mahaddayweyne Somalia
116 D5 Mahadeo Hills Madh. Prad. India
114 D2 Mahadeopur Andhra Prad. India
232 D4 Mahaffey PA U.S.A.
251 G3 Mahaicony Guyana
213 □J2 Mahajamba r. Madag.
116 C3 Mahajan Rajasthan India
213 □J2 Mahajanga Madag.
213 □J3 Mahajanga prov. Madag.
95 G3 Mahakam r. Indon.
213 E4 Mahalapye Botswana
211 A6 Mahale Mountain National Park Tanz.
213 □K2 Mahalevona Madag.
122 B3 Mahallāt Iran
116 D3 Maham Haryana India
122 D4 Māhān Iran
117 F5 Mahanadi r. India
213 □K3 Mahanoro Madag.
234 B2 Mahanoy City PA U.S.A.
234 B2 Mahanoy Creek r. PA U.S.A.
234 B2 Mahantango Creek r. PA U.S.A.
117 F4 Maharajganj Bihar India
116 E4 Maharajganj Uttar Prad. India
116 D4 Maharajpur Madh. Prad. India
114 B2 Maharashtra state India
122 C4 Mahārlū, Daryācheh-ye salt l. Iran
96 C3 Maha Sarakham Thai.
128 C4 Maḥaṭṭat Ḍab'ah Jordan
247 □2 Mahault, Baie b. Guadeloupe
213 □J2 Mahavavy r. Madag.
114 D4 Mahaweli Ganga r. Sri Lanka
213 □J3 Mahazoma Madag.
114 D2 Mahbubabad Andhra Prad. India
114 C2 Mahbubnagar Andhra Prad. India
124 C3 Mahd adh Dhahab Saudi Arabia
125 F2 Maḥḍah Oman
137 H3 Mahdalynivka Ukr.
205 F2 Mahdia Alg.
251 G3 Mahdia Guyana
205 H2 Mahdia Tunisia
114 B4 Mahe Pondicherry India
217 □2b Mahé i. Inner Islands Seychelles
217 □1b Mahébourg Mauritius
116 D3 Mahendragarh Haryana India
115 E2 Mahendragiri mt. Orissa India
211 C7 Mahenge Tanz.
81 C6 Maheno South I. N.Z.
175 L5 Maheriv Ukr.
116 C5 Mahesana Gujarat India
116 C5 Maheshwar Madh. Prad. India
125 F5 Maḥfirhīn Suquṭrā Yemen
116 D4 Mahgawan Madh. Prad. India
116 C5 Mahi r. Rajasthan India
80 F3 Mahia North I. N.Z.
80 F3 Mahia Peninsula North I. N.Z.
182 D3 Mahíde Spain
78 □6 Mahige Island Solomon Is
139 H5 Mahilyow Belarus
Mahilyow Oblast admin. div. Belarus see Mahilyowskaya Voblasts'
139 H5 Mahilyowskaya Voblasts' admin. div. Belarus
114 B2 Mahim Mahar. India
206 C3 Mahina Mali
140 K2 Mahkene mt. Sweden
215 H3 Mahlabatini S. Africa
96 A2 Mahlaing Myanmar
215 H2 Mahlangasi S. Africa
215 F3 Mahlatswetsa S. Africa
172 B3 Mahlberg Ger.
171 E3 Mahlow Ger.
170 C3 Mahlsdorf Ger.
171 C3 Mahlwinkel Ger.
116 E4 Mahmudabad Uttar Prad. India
122 C2 Mahmudabad Iran
123 G3 Maḥmūd-e 'Erāqī Afgh.
197 I3 Mahmudia Romania
199 E2 Mahmudiye anakkale Turkey
199 G2 Mahmudiye Eskişehir Turkey
128 A1 Mahmutlar Turkey
199 F1 Mahmutşevketpaşa Turkey
236 D2 Mahnomen MN U.S.A.
116 D4 Mahoba Uttar Prad. India
80 E3 Mahoenui North I. N.Z.
116 E4 Maholi Uttar Prad. India
186 □ Mahón Spain
225 H4 Mahone Bay N.S. Can.
235 E1 Mahopac NY U.S.A.
185 I1 Mahora Spain
206 D3 Mahou Mali
125 E4 Mahrāt, Wādī r. Yemen
116 D4 Mahrauni Uttar Prad. India
173 G2 Mähring Ger.
122 E3 Māhrūd Iran
Mahsana Gujarat India see Mahesana
111 F4 Mahuanggou Qinghai China
240 □D8 Mahukona HI U.S.A.
117 H4 Mahur Assam India
114 C2 Mahur Mahar. India
207 G4 Mahuta Nigeria
211 C7 Mahuta Tanz.
116 B5 Mahuva Gujarat India
116 D4 Mahwa Rajasthan India
197 H5 Mahya Dağı mt. Turkey
Mai i. Vanuatu see Émaé
78 □2 Maia American Samoa
216 □1b Maia São Miguel Azores
182 B3 Maia Port.
Maiaia Moz. see Nacala
186 D3 Maials Spain
77 H1 Maiana atoll Gilbert Is Kiribati
117 H4 Maibang Assam India
250 C2 Maicao Col.
224 E3 Maicasagi r. Que. Can.
224 E3 Maicasagi, Lac l. Que. Can.
160 E1 Maîche France
251 F6 Maici r. Brazil
251 H5 Maicuru r. Brazil
195 F4 Maida Italy
150 E3 Maiden Bradley Wiltshire, England U.K.
234 C2 Maiden Creek r. PA U.S.A.
151 G3 Maidenhead Windsor and Maidenhead, England U.K.
150 E4 Maiden Newton Dorset, England U.K.
226 A3 Maiden Rock WI U.S.A.
146 D6 Maidens South Ayrshire, Scotland U.K.
223 I4 Maidstone Sask. Can.
151 H3 Maidstone Kent, England U.K.
207 I4 Maiduguri Nigeria
190 E1 Maienfeld Switz.
195 F4 Maierato Italy
173 E4 Maierhöfen Ger.
197 G2 Maieru Romania
187 C6 Maigmó mt. Spain
156 C3 Maignelay-Montigny France
210 C3 Mai Gudo mt. Eth.
147 C4 Maigue r. Rep. of Ireland
116 E4 Maihar Madh. Prad. India
80 E3 Maihiihi North I. N.Z.
117 G5 Maijdi Bangl.
108 C1 Maiji Shan mt. Gansu China
116 E5 Maikala Range hills Madh. Prad. India
172 C2 Maikammer Ger.
208 E4 Maiko r. Dem. Rep. Congo
117 E5 Mailan Hill mt. Madh. Prad. India
116 E3 Mailani Uttar Prad. India
240 □ Maili HI U.S.A.
163 B4 Maillas France
156 B4 Maillebois France
162 B2 Maillezais France
160 B1 Mailly-la-Ville France
156 E4 Mailly-le-Camp France
156 C2 Mailly-Maillet France
123 H4 Mailsi Pak.
169 D5 Main r. Ger.
124 D4 Ma'īn tourist site Yemen
117 G4 Mainaguri W. Bengal India
172 D2 Mainaschaff Ger.
173 E2 Mainbernheim Ger.
225 K3 Main Brook Nfld. Can.
173 F3 Mainburg Ger.
114 C2 Maindargi Mahar. India
208 C5 Mai-Ndombe, Lac l. Dem. Rep. Congo
227 I4 Main Duck Island Ont. Can.
159 F4 Maine r. France
233 □I2 Maine state U.S.A.
233 □I3 Maine, Gulf of U.S.A.
159 F4 Maine-et-Loire dept Pays de la Loire France
250 C5 Mainé Hanari, Cerro hill Col.
207 I3 Maïné-Soroa Niger
96 B1 Maingkwan Myanmar
147 E3 Mainham Rep. of Ireland
172 D2 Mainhardt Ger.
92 C4 Mainit Phil.
108 A2 Mainkung Xizang China
146 E2 Mainland i. Orkney, Scotland U.K.
146 □G1 Mainland i. Shetland, Scotland U.K.
171 C5 Mainleus Ger.
111 F6 Mainling Xizang China
84 C2 Mainoru N.T. Austr.
84 C2 Mainoru r. N.T. Austr.
117 E5 Mainpat reg. Madh. Prad. India
116 D4 Mainpuri Uttar Prad. India
162 E2 Mainsat France
156 B4 Maintenon France
213 □J3 Maintirano Madag.
156 B4 Mainvilliers France
169 D5 Mainz Ger.
206 □ Maio i. Cape Verde
191 I5 Maiolati Spontini Italy
184 B1 Maior r. Port.
182 B4 Maiorca Port.
182 B5 Maiorga Port.
194 D2 Maiori Italy
260 B3 Maipó r. Chile
260 C4 Maipó, Volcán vol. Chile
261 I5 Maipú Arg.
260 C3 Maipú Arg.
260 B3 Maipú Chile
250 E2 Maiquetía Venez.
111 D6 Maiqu Zangbo r. Xizang China
190 C4 Maira r. Italy
184 E3 Mairena del Alcor Spain
254 E4 Mairi Brazil
256 D5 Mairiporã Brazil
256 C2 Mairipotaba Brazil
173 F3 Maisach Ger.
173 F3 Maisach r. Ger.
178 D3 Maishofen Austria
246 D2 Maisí Cuba
138 E4 Maišiagala Lith.
156 C4 Maisons-Laffitte France
179 G2 Maissau Austria
156 C4 Maisse France
165 E5 Maissin Belgium
Maitea i. Arch. de la Société Fr. Polynesia see Mehetia
173 G3 Maitenbeth Ger.
213 E4 Maitengwe Botswana
117 F5 Maithon Bihar India
83 G3 Maitland N.S.W. Austr.
82 D3 Maitland S.A. Austr.
86 C4 Maitland r. W.A. Austr.
95 G1 Maitland, Banjaran mts Sabah Malaysia
87 D5 Maitland, Lake salt flat W.A. Austr.
263 A2 Maitri research stn Antarctica
Maiwo i. Vanuatu see Maéwo
84 C2 Maiwok r. N.T. Austr.
84 B3 Maiyu, Mount hill N.T. Austr.
242 □J6 Maíz, Islas del is Nic.
111 E6 Maizhokunggar Xizang China
156 D4 Maizières-la-Grande-Paroisse France
157 G3 Maizières-lès-Metz France
104 B3 Maizuru Japan
184 E4 Majaceite r. Spain
183 G4 Majadahonda Spain
182 E5 Majadas de Tiétar Spain
196 D4 Maja Jezercë mt. Albania
114 C2 Majalgaon Mahar. India
251 F4 Majari r. Brazil
125 E5 Majdaḥah Yemen
175 J5 Majdan Królewski Pol.
175 L5 Majdan Niepryski Pol.
197 E3 Majdanpek Srbija Yugo.
257 F5 Majé Brazil
93 A3 Majene Sulawesi Selatan Indon.
188 G3 Majevica mts Bos.-Herz.
116 E4 Majhgawan Madh. Prad. India
116 D5 Majholi Madh. Prad. India
107 H4 Majia r. China
109 D4 Majiang Guangxi China
108 C3 Majiang Guizhou China
Majōl country N. Pacific Ocean see Marshall Islands
Majorca i. Spain see Mallorca
Mājro atoll Marshall Is see Majuro
177 H6 Majs Hungary
117 H4 Majuli Island India
Majunga Madag. see Mahajanga
78 □3b Majuro atoll Marshall Is
215 F3 Majwemasweu S. Africa
206 B3 Maka Senegal
209 B5 Makabana Congo
177 H4 Makád Hungary
240 □ Makaha HI U.S.A.
207 H6 Makak Cameroon
93 A3 Makale Sulawesi Selatan Indon.
117 F4 Makalu mt. China/Nepal
211 A6 Makamba Burundi
121 J3 Makanchi Kazakh.
211 B8 Makanjila Malawi
211 C6 Makanya Tanz.
208 C4 Makanza Dem. Rep. Congo
81 B7 Makarewa South I. N.Z.
207 I3 Makari Cameroon
Makari Mountain National Park Tanz. see Mahale Mountain National Park
136 E2 Makariv Ukr.
81 B6 Makarora r. South I. N.Z.
100 G2 Makarov Sakhalin Rus. Fed.
268 M1 Makarov Basin sea feature Arctic Ocean
136 B3 Makarove Ukr.
135 H5 Makarovo Rus. Fed.
188 F4 Makarska Croatia
134 J4 Makar'ye Rus. Fed.
134 H4 Makar'yev Rus. Fed.
Makassar Sulawesi Selatan Indon. see Ujung Pandang
93 A3 Makassar Strait Indon.
120 C3 Makat Kazakh.
215 I2 Makatini Flats lowland S. Africa
240 □C8 Makawao HI U.S.A.
213 □J4 Makay, Massif du mts Madag.
Makedonija country Europe see Macedonia
215 F3 Makeleketla S. Africa
79 □3 Makemo atoll Arch. des Tuamotu Fr. Polynesia
206 B4 Makeni Sierra Leone
211 B7 Makete Tanz.
Makeyevka Donets'ka Oblast' Ukr. see Makiyivka
212 E4 Makgadikgadi salt pan Botswana
129 E2 Makhachkala Rus. Fed.
215 F4 Makhaleng r. Lesotho
120 B3 Makhambet Kazakh.
124 C2 Makhāmīr, Jabal al hill Saudi Arabia
Makharadze Georgia see Ozurget'i
215 G3 Makheka mt. Lesotho
128 D2 Makhfar al Ḥammām Syria
129 D1 Makhmud-Mekteb Rus. Fed.
127 F4 Makhmūr Iraq
121 G1 Makhorovka Kazakh.
114 C2 Makhtal Andhra Prad. India
125 E4 Makhyah, Wādī r. Yemen
93 C2 Makian vol. Maluku Indon.
105 E2 Makihata-yama mt. Japan
81 C6 Makikihi South I. N.Z.
Makima atoll Arch. des Tuamotu Fr. Polynesia see Makemo
Makin atoll Kiribati see Butaritari
121 G1 Makinsk Kazakh.
Makira i. Solomon Is see San Cristobal
136 D3 Makiv Ukr.
137 F2 Makiyivka Chernihivs'ka Oblast' Ukr.
137 I3 Makiyivka Donets'ka Oblast' Ukr.
Makkah Saudi Arabia see Mecca
124 C3 Makkah prov. Saudi Arabia
225 J2 Makkovik Nfld. Can.
164 E1 Makkum Neth.
177 J5 Makó Hungary
251 G4 Makoa, Serra hills Brazil
79 □1 Makogai i. Fiji
208 B4 Makokou Gabon
215 F2 Makokskraal S. Africa
211 C7 Makonde Plateau Tanz.
Makongai i. Fiji see Makogai
211 B7 Makongolosi Tanz.
212 D5 Makopong Botswana
80 F4 Makotuku North I. N.Z.
208 B5 Makoua Congo
177 H2 Makov Slovakia
188 E3 Makovnik mt. Croatia
175 I4 Maków Pol.
174 F2 Mąkowarsko Pol.
175 J3 Maków Mazowiecki Pol.
175 H6 Maków Podhalański Pol.
198 C2 Makrakomi Greece
116 C4 Makrana Rajasthan India
Makran Coast Range mts Pak. see Talar-i-Band
198 D3 Makronisi i. Greece
198 C1 Makrygialos Kentriki Makedonia Greece
139 J3 Maksatikha Rus. Fed.
116 D5 Maksi Madh. Prad. India
100 F3 Maksimovka Rus. Fed.
116 D5 Maksudangarh Madh. Prad. India
174 G2 Maksymilianowo Pol.
122 A2 Mākū Iran
117 H4 Makum Assam India
211 B7 Makumbako Tanz.
209 D6 Makumbi Dem. Rep. Congo
Makundu i. N. Male Maldives see Makunudhoo
211 C6 Makunduchi Tanz.
109 F4 Makung Taiwan
211 C7 Makunguwiro Tanz.
113 □1 Makunudhoo i. N. Male Maldives
103 E8 Makurazaki Japan
207 H5 Makurdi Nigeria
80 E4 Makuri North I. N.Z.
215 E2 Makwassie S. Africa
117 G4 Mal W. Bengal India
252 A3 Mala Peru
Mala Rep. of Ireland see Mallow
Mala i. Solomon Is see Malaita
185 G3 Malá Spain
140 L2 Malå Sweden
92 C5 Malabang Phil.
114 B3 Malabar Coast India
137 H4 Mala Bilozerka Ukr.
207 H6 Malabo Equat. Guinea
177 I5 Mala Bosna Vojvodina, Srbija Yugo.
92 A4 Malabuñgan Phil.
Malaca Spain see Málaga
257 F2 Malacacheta Brazil
Malacca Malaysia see Melaka
Malacca state Malaysia see Melaka
94 B1 Malacca, Strait of Indon./Malaysia
176 G3 Malacky Slovakia
238 D3 Malad r. ID U.S.A.
238 D3 Malad City ID U.S.A.
137 G2 Mala Divytsya Ukr.
138 F4 Maladzyechna Belarus
177 H2 Malá Fatra mts Slovakia
185 F4 Málaga Spain
185 F4 Málaga prov. Andalucía Spain
234 C3 Malaga NJ U.S.A.
239 F5 Malaga NM U.S.A.
232 C5 Malaga OH U.S.A.
211 A6 Malagarasi r. Burundi/Tanz.
211 A6 Malagarasi Tanz.
185 G1 Malagón Spain
184 C3 Malagon r. Spain
147 E3 Malahide Rep. of Ireland
213 □J4 Malaimbandy Madag.
174 D2 Mała Ina r. Pol.
78 □6 Malaita i. Solomon Is
95 G5 Malaka mt. Sumbawa Indon.
210 A2 Malakal Sudan
114 D2 Malakanagiri Orissa India
188 E3 Mala Kapela mts Croatia
188 E3 Mala Kladuša Bos.-Herz.
78 □6 Malakobi Island Solomon Is
78 □5 Malakula i. Vanuatu
123 H3 Malakwal Pak.
191 G4 Malalbergo Italy
137 G4 Mala Lepetykha Ukr.
93 B3 Malamala Sulawesi Tenggara Indon.
191 H3 Malamocco Italy
136 C2 Mala Moshchanytsya Ukr.
157 F3 Malancourt France
95 F4 Malang Jawa Timur Indon.
Malange Angola see Malanje
209 C7 Malanje Angola
209 C7 Malanje prov. Angola
174 G4 Malanów Pol.
158 D4 Malansac France
207 F4 Malanville Benin
260 D2 Malanzán, Sierra de mts Arg.
137 H3 Mala Pereshchepyna Ukr.
114 C4 Malappuram Kerala India
143 G2 Mälaren l. Sweden
260 C4 Malargüe Arg.
224 E3 Malartic Que. Can.
136 C2 Malaryta Belarus
176 E1 Malá Skála Czech Rep.
222 E5 Malaspina Strait B.C. Can.
179 H4 Mala Subotica Croatia
137 H3 Mala Ternivka r. Ukr.
126 E3 Malatya Turkey
161 D4 Malaucène France
156 B3 Malaunay France
163 B5 Malaussanne France
116 C3 Malaut Punjab India
114 C3 Malavalli Karnataka India
136 F3 Mala Vil'shanka Ukr.
137 F3 Mala Vyska Ukr.
207 H3 Malawa Niger
174 F3 Mała Wełna r. Pol.
211 B7 Malawi country Africa
Malawi, Lake Africa see Nyasa, Lake
140 M3 Malax Fin.
Malaya pen. Malaysia see Malaysia, Semenanjung
129 E1 Malaya Areshevka Rus. Fed.
134 K2 Malaya Pera Rus. Fed.
139 I2 Malaya Vishera Rus. Fed.
92 C4 Malaybalay Phil.
122 B3 Malāyer Iran
156 D4 Malay-le-Grand France
85 G3 Malay Reef Coral Sea Is Terr. Austr.
94 C1 Malaysia country Asia
94 C2 Malaysia, Semenanjung pen. Malaysia
127 F3 Malazgirt Turkey
225 G4 Malbaie r. Que. Can.
207 G3 Malbaza Niger
84 E4 Malbon Qld Austr.
175 H1 Malbork Pol.
172 A2 Malborn Ger.
161 B4 Malbouzon France
160 E2 Malbuisson France
182 C4 Malcata, Serra de mts Port.
191 F3 Malcesine Italy
137 K3 Mal'chevskaya Rus. Fed.
170 D2 Malchin Ger.
170 D2 Malchiner See l. Ger.
170 D2 Malchow Ger.
177 K3 Malčice Slovakia
184 E2 Malcocinado Spain
87 D6 Malcolm W.A. Austr.
87 D7 Malcolm, Point W.A. Austr.
177 K2 Malcov Slovakia
174 E4 Malczyce Pol.
165 C3 Maldegem Belgium
164 E3 Malden Neth.
237 F4 Malden MO U.S.A.
267 I6 Malden Island Kiribati
186 D2 Malditos, Montes mts Spain
113 D10 Maldives country Indian Ocean
83 F4 Maldon Vic. Austr.
151 H3 Maldon Essex, England U.K.
258 G4 Maldonado Uru.
175 H2 Małdyty Pol.
217 □3a Male Njazidja Comoros
191 F2 Malè Italy
113 □1 Male N. Male Maldives
113 □1 Male Atoll Maldives
215 E3 Malebogo S. Africa
174 E1 Malechowo Pol.
114 C2 Malegaon Mahar. India
116 C5 Malegaon Mahar. India
183 I3 Maleján Spain
176 G3 Malé Karpaty hills Slovakia
122 E4 Malek Sīāh, Kūh-e mt. Afgh.
209 B6 Malele Dem. Rep. Congo
213 H2 Malema Moz.
161 D4 Malemort-du-Comtat France
162 D3 Malemort-sur-Corrèze France
168 F1 Malente Ger.
215 G1 Maleoskop S. Africa
143 F3 Målerås Sweden
116 C3 Maler Kotla Punjab India
190 D2 Malesco Italy
197 F5 Maleševske Planine mts Bulg./Macedonia
156 C4 Malesherbes France
198 C2 Malesina Greece
158 D4 Malestroit France
107 F1 Maleta Rus. Fed.
194 D5 Maletto Sicilia Italy
139 L5 Malevka Rus. Fed.
194 D4 Malfa Isole Lipari Italy
214 C6 Malgas S. Africa
173 G3 Malgersdorf Ger.
129 D2 Malgobek Rus. Fed.
140 L2 Malgomaj l. Sweden
186 F3 Malgrat de Mar Spain
254 E5 Malhada Brazil
182 D3 Malhadas Port.
124 D2 Malham Saudi Arabia
116 C4 Malhargarh Madh. Prad. India
238 C2 Malheur r. OR U.S.A.
206 D3 Mali country Africa
206 B3 Mali Guinea
199 D4 Malia Kriti Greece
107 E5 Malian r. China
215 G3 Malibamatso r. Lesotho
240 H4 Malibu CA U.S.A.
159 F4 Malicorne-sur-Sarthe France
156 D5 Maligny France
111 C7 Malihabad Uttar Prad. India
96 B1 Mali Hka r. Myanmar
177 I6 Mali Iđoš Vojvodina, Srbija Yugo.
161 E4 Malijai France
123 E4 Malik Naro mt. Pak.
97 B4 Mali Kyun i. Myanmar
93 B3 Malili Sulawesi Selatan Indon.
143 F3 Målilla Sweden
188 E3 Mali Lošinj Croatia
209 F6 Malimba, Monts mts Dem. Rep. Congo
175 L6 Mali Mokryany Ukr.
147 D1 Malin Rep. of Ireland
Malin Ukr. see Malyn
147 C2 Malin Beg Rep. of Ireland
211 D5 Malindi Kenya
177 I3 Málinec Slovakia
Malines Belgium see Mechelen
208 B5 Malinga Gabon
147 D1 Malin Head hd Rep. of Ireland
197 H2 Mălini Romania
147 C2 Malin More Rep. of Ireland
139 L4 Malino Rus. Fed.
93 B2 Malino, Gunung mt. Indon.
100 E3 Malinovka r. Rus. Fed.
121 I2 Malinovoye Ozero Altayskiy Kray Rus. Fed.
191 J3 Malinska Croatia
211 C7 Malinyi Tanz.
108 C4 Malipo Yunnan China
198 B1 Maliq Albania
188 E3 Mali Raginac mt. Croatia
92 C5 Malita Phil.
92 C4 Malitbog Phil.
116 B5 Maliya Gujarat India
137 G4 Maliyivka Ukr.
196 D3 Mali Zvornik Srbija Yugo.
129 C2 Malka Rus. Fed.
129 D2 Malka r. Rus. Fed.
114 B2 Malkapur Mahar. India
116 D5 Malkapur Mahar. India
199 E1 Malkara Turkey
138 F5 Mal'kavichy Belarus
175 K3 Małkinia Górna Pol.
197 H5 Malko Tŭrnovo Bulg.
83 G4 Mallacoota Vic. Austr.
83 G4 Mallacoota Inlet b. Vic. Austr.
146 C5 Mallaig Highland, Scotland U.K.
203 F3 Mallawi Egypt
140 M1 Mållejus hill Norway
161 D5 Mallemort France
183 I3 Mallén Spain
170 C2 Mallentin Ger.
190 E2 Mallero r. Italy
173 G3 Mallersdorf Ger.
191 F2 Malles Venosta Italy
255 C8 Mallét Brazil
Mallia Kriti Greece see Malia
170 C2 Mallıß Ger.
260 B4 Malloa Chile
187 F5 Mallorca i. Spain
147 C4 Mallow Rep. of Ireland
86 E4 Mallowa Well W.A. Austr.
150 D2 Mallwyd Gwynedd, Wales U.K.
140 J2 Malm Norway
123 E3 Malman Rūd r. Afgh.
140 M2 Malmberget Sweden
165 F4 Malmédy Belgium
214 B5 Malmesbury S. Africa
150 E3 Malmesbury Wiltshire, England U.K.
143 G2 Malmköping Sweden
142 E4 Malmö Sweden
142 E4 Malmö-Sturup airport Sweden
143 F2 Malmslätt Sweden
134 J4 Malmyzh Rus. Fed.
190 D3 Malnate Italy
191 G3 Malo Italy
78 □5 Malo i. Vanuatu
139 K5 Maloarkhangel'sk Rus. Fed.
196 E3 Malo Crniće Srbija Yugo.
175 I5 Małogoszcz Pol.
92 B3 Malolos Phil.
174 D4 Małomice Pol.
137 I3 Malomykhaylivka Ukr.
183 I3 Malón Spain
190 C3 Malone r. Italy
233 F2 Malone NY U.S.A.
108 B3 Malong Yunnan China
209 D7 Malonga Dem. Rep. Congo
190 F2 Malonno Italy
176 D3 Malonty Czech Rep.
175 I5 Małopolska, Wyżyna hills Pol.
175 I6 Małopolskie prov. Pol.
Malorita Belarus see Malaryta
134 G3 Maloshuyka Rus. Fed.
197 F3 Malovăţ Romania
Malovata Moldova see Molovata
141 I3 Måløy Norway
139 K4 Maloyaroslavets Rus. Fed.
139 K2 Maloye Borisovo Rus. Fed.
175 I1 Maloye-Lugovoye Rus. Fed.
134 J2 Malozemel'skaya Tundra lowland Rus. Fed.
182 D4 Malpartida Port.
184 D1 Malpartida de Cáceres Spain
184 E2 Malpartida de la Serena Spain
182 D5 Malpartida de Plasencia Spain
149 G4 Malpas Cheshire, England U.K.
150 D3 Malpas Newport, Wales U.K.
216 □3e Malpaso mt. El Hierro Canary Is
267 N5 Malpelo, Isla de i. N. Pacific Ocean
182 B1 Malpica Spain
183 F5 Malpica de Tajo Spain
182 C5 Malpica do Tejo Port.
138 E3 Mālpils Latvia
114 C2 Malprabha r. India
116 C4 Malpura Rajasthan India
172 C3 Malsch Ger.
176 D3 Malše r. Czech Rep.
169 E4 Malsfeld Ger.
114 B2 Malsiras Mahar. India
179 E4 Malta Austria
189 E8 Malta country Europe
138 F3 Malta Latvia
138 F3 Malta r. Latvia
195 □ Malta i. Malta
182 C4 Malta Port.
238 D3 Malta ID U.S.A.
238 F1 Malta MT U.S.A.
212 C5 Maltahöhe Namibia
207 I3 Maltam Cameroon
149 H4 Maltby South Yorkshire, England U.K.
149 J4 Maltby le Marsh Lincolnshire, England U.K.
172 B3 Malterdingen Ger.
172 C4 Malters Switz.
149 I3 Malton North Yorkshire, England U.K.
183 I3 Maluenda Spain
Malukken is Indon. see Maluku
93 C3 Maluku is Indon.
93 D3 Maluku prov. Indon.
93 C2 Maluku, Kepulauan is Indon.
197 F2 Malului, Vârful hill Romania
207 G4 Malumfashi Nigeria
143 E1 Malung Sweden
175 H5 Maluszyn Pol.
215 G3 Maluti Mountains Lesotho
183 E3 Malva Spain
190 D2 Malvaglia Switz.
114 B2 Malvan Mahar. India
184 A2 Malveira Port.
Malvern Worcestershire, England U.K. see Great Malvern
237 E5 Malvern AR U.S.A.
232 C4 Malvern OH U.S.A.
150 E2 Malvern Link Worcestershire, England U.K.
Malvinas, Islas terr. S. Atlantic Ocean see Falkland Islands
171 F4 Malxe r. Ger.
177 H4 Malý Dunaj r. Slovakia
177 K3 Malý Horeš Slovakia
177 J3 Mályi Hungary
131 M3 Malykay Rus. Fed.
136 E2 Malyn Ukr.
137 I3 Malynivka Ukr.
136 D2 Malyns'k Ukr.
175 K2 Mały Płock Pol.
131 R3 Malyy Anyuy r. Rus. Fed.
177 L3 Malyy Bereznyy Ukr.
135 I7 Malyye Derbety Rus. Fed.
Malyye Kotyuzhany Moldova see Cotiujenii Mici
135 J5 Malyy Irgiz r. Rus. Fed.
129 C3 Malyy Kavkaz mts Asia
107 E1 Malyy Kunaley Rus. Fed.
136 D2 Malyy Stydyn Ukr.
120 B2 Malyy Uzen' r. Kazakh./Rus. Fed.
129 B1 Malyy Zelenchuk r. Rus. Fed.
131 P3 Mama r. Rus. Fed.
134 J5 Mamadysh Rus. Fed.
215 G2 Mamafubedu S. Africa
215 F3 Mamahabane S. Africa
79 □1 Mamanuca-i-Cake Group is Fiji
Mamanutha-i-Thake Group is Fiji see Mamanuca-i-Cake Group
80 D1 Mamaranui North I. N.Z.
235 E2 Mamaroneck NY U.S.A.
93 A3 Mamasa Sulawesi Selatan Indon.
254 D5 Mambai Brazil
92 C4 Mambajao Phil.
208 C4 Mambéré r. C.A.R.
208 B3 Mambéré-Kadéï pref. C.A.R.
208 C4 Mambili r. Congo
206 B4 Mambolo Sierra Leone
256 A6 Mamborê Brazil
183 G3 Mambrilla de Castejón Spain
92 B3 Mamburao Phil.
129 F2 Mamedkala Rus. Fed.
215 G1 Mamelodi S. Africa
159 G3 Mamers France
207 H5 Mamfé Cameroon
250 E5 Mamirauá, Reserve de Desenvolvimento Sustentável nature res. Brazil
160 E1 Mamirolle France
121 G1 Mamlyutka Kazakh.
173 F3 Mammendorf Ger.
173 G3 Mamming Ger.
195 F4 Mammola Italy
241 L5 Mammoth AZ U.S.A.
240 H3 Mammoth Lakes CA U.S.A.
192 B4 Mamoiada Sardegna Italy
192 B4 Mamone Sardegna Italy
138 B4 Mamonovo Rus. Fed.
121 J1 Mamontovo Rus. Fed.
234 D3 Mamora NJ U.S.A.
252 D2 Mamoré r. Bol./Brazil
206 B4 Mamou Guinea
217 □3b Mamoudzou Mayotte
Mamoutsou Mayotte see Mamoudzou
213 □J3 Mampikony Madag.
206 E5 Mampong Ghana
214 B5 Mamre S. Africa
175 J1 Mamry, Jezioro l. Pol.
93 A3 Mamuju Sulawesi Selatan Indon.
122 B3 Māmūnīyeh Iran
196 D5 Mamuras Albania
102 J4 Mamurogawa Japan
Mamutzu Mayotte see Mamoudzou
206 D5 Man Côte d'Ivoire
114 B2 Man r. India
232 C6 Man WV U.S.A.
251 H3 Mana Fr. Guiana
177 H3 Maňa Slovakia
240 □B7 Mana HI U.S.A.
250 B5 Manabí prov. Ecuador
250 C3 Manacacias r. Col.
251 F5 Manacapuru Brazil
187 G5 Manacor Spain
216 □1c Manadas São Jorge Azores
93 C2 Manado Sulawesi Utara Indon.
165 D4 Manage Belgium
242 □I6 Managua Nic.
242 □I6 Managua, Lago de l. Nic.
125 G3 Manaḥ Oman
80 E3 Manaia North I. N.Z.
213 □J4 Manakara Madag.
80 E4 Manakau North I. N.Z.
81 D5 Manakau mt. South I. N.Z.
124 C5 Manākhah Yemen
116 D2 Manali Hima. Prad. India
Manama Bahrain see Al Manāmah
114 C4 Manamadurai Tamil Nadu India
213 □J3 Manambaho r. Madag.
213 □J4 Manambondro Madag.
114 C4 Manamelkudi Tamil Nadu India
251 F2 Manamo, Caño r. Venez.
213 □J4 Mananantañana r. Madag.
213 □J4 Mananara r. Madag.
213 □K3 Mananara Avaratra Madag.
83 E3 Manangatang Vic. Austr.
84 D3 Manangoora N.T. Austr.
213 □K4 Mananjary Madag.
206 D4 Manankoro Mali
206 C3 Manantali, Lac de l. Mali
114 C4 Manantavadi Kerala India
78 □6 Manaoba Island Solomon Is
81 A6 Manapouri South I. N.Z.
81 A6 Manapouri, Lake South I. N.Z.
114 C4 Manapparai Tamil Nadu India
213 □J3 Manarantsandry Madag.
183 H1 Mañaria Spain
110 D2 Manas Xinjiang China
117 G4 Manas r. India
142 E1 Månäs Sweden
121 G4 Manas, Gora mt. Uzbek.
116 C4 Manasa Madh. Prad. India
110 D2 Manas He r. China
110 D2 Manas Hu l. China
129 E2 Manaskent Rus. Fed.
117 F3 Manaslu mt. Nepal
235 D2 Manasquan NJ U.S.A.
235 D2 Manasquan r. NJ U.S.A.
232 E5 Manassas VA U.S.A.
Manastir Macedonia see Bitola
177 L6 Mănăştiur Romania
247 □1 Manatí Puerto Rico
247 □1 Manati, Río Grande de r. Puerto Rico
Man-aung Kyun i. Myanmar see Cheduba Island
251 F5 Manaus Brazil
126 C3 Manavgat Turkey
226 C3 Manawa WI U.S.A.
116 C5 Manawar Madh. Prad. India
80 E2 Manawaru North I. N.Z.
80 E4 Manawatu r. North I. N.Z.
80 E3 Manawatu-Wanganui admin. reg. North I. N.Z.
92 C5 Manay Phil.
117 F5 Manbazar W. Bengal India
128 C1 Manbij Syria
149 J4 Manby Lincolnshire, England U.K.
226 E3 Mancelona MI U.S.A.
183 E4 Mancera de Abajo Spain
114 B2 Manchar Mahar. India
185 G3 Mancha Real Spain
158 E3 Manche dept Basse-Normandie France
246 □ Manchester parish Jamaica
149 G4 Manchester Greater Manchester, England U.K.
233 G4 Manchester CT U.S.A.
236 F3 Manchester IA U.S.A.
232 B6 Manchester KY U.S.A.
234 B3 Manchester MD U.S.A.
227 E4 Manchester MI U.S.A.
233 H3 Manchester NH U.S.A.
232 B5 Manchester OH U.S.A.
234 B2 Manchester PA U.S.A.
231 C5 Manchester TN U.S.A.
233 G3 Manchester VT U.S.A.
173 F3 Manching Ger.
246 □ Manchioneal Jamaica
184 D2 Manchita Spain
192 D2 Manciano Italy
163 C5 Manciet France
199 E2 Mancınık Dağı mts Turkey
239 E4 Mancos CO U.S.A.
241 M3 Mancos r. CO U.S.A.
122 B4 Mand, Rūd-e r. Iran
208 E2 Manda, Jebel mt. Sudan
213 □J4 Mandabe Madag.
256 A5 Mandaguaçu Brazil
256 B5 Mandaguari Brazil
116 B5 Mandal Gujarat India
116 C4 Mandal Rajasthan India
106 D1 Mandal Mongolia
142 B2 Mandal Norway
91 J7 Mandala, Puncak mt. Indon.
96 B2 Mandalay Myanmar
96 A2 Mandalay admin. div. Myanmar
Mandale Myanmar see Mandalay
Mandale admin. div. Myanmar see Mandalay
116 C4 Mandalgarh Rajasthan India
106 E2 Mandalgovĭ Mongolia
142 B2 Mandalselva r. Norway
107 G3 Mandalt Nei Mongol China
236 C2 Mandan ND U.S.A.
195 E4 Mandanici Sicilia Italy
92 B3 Mandaon Phil.
114 C4 Mandapam Tamil Nadu India
192 B5 Mandas Sardegna Italy
195 F3 Mandatoriccio Italy
116 B5 Mandav Hills Gujarat India
123 H4 Mandawa Rajasthan India
183 H4 Mandayona Spain
160 C2 Mandé, Mont de hill France
Mandeghughusu i. New Georgia Is Solomon Is see Simbo
172 B2 Mandelbachtal-Ormesheim Ger.
161 E5 Mandelieu-la-Napoule France
190 E3 Mandello del Lario Italy
182 B1 Mandeo r. Spain
210 D4 Mandera Kenya
241 K2 Manderfield UT U.S.A.
169 B5 Manderscheid Ger.
160 E1 Mandeure France
246 □ Mandeville Jamaica
81 B6 Mandeville South I. N.Z.
116 B4 Mandha Rajasthan India
Mandhoúdhion Greece see Mantoudi
116 D3 Mandi Hima. Prad. India
206 D3 Mandiakui Mali
206 C4 Mandiana Guinea
123 H4 Mandi Burewala Pak.
Mandidzuzure Zimbabwe see Chimanimani
213 G3 Mandié Moz.
213 G2 Mandimba Moz.
208 A5 Mandji Gabon
116 E5 Mandla Madh. Prad. India
177 L3 Mándok Hungary
116 C4 Mandor Rajasthan India
86 D3 Mandora W.A. Austr.
84 B2 Mandorah N.T. Austr.
213 □J3 Mandoro Madag.
207 F4 Mandouri Togo
198 C2 Mandra Greece
213 □J5 Mandrare r. Madag.
Mandrenska r. Bulg. see Sredetska Reka
157 F4 Mandres-en-Barrois France
213 □K2 Mandritsara Madag.
213 □J4 Mandrosonoro Madag.
116 C4 Mandsaur Madh. Prad. India
161 C5 Manduel France
87 B7 Mandurah W.A. Austr.
195 G2 Manduria Italy
116 B5 Mandvi Gujarat India
116 C5 Mandvi Gujarat India
114 C3 Mandya Karnataka India
163 C5 Mane Midi-Pyrénées France
161 D5 Mane Provence-Alpes-Côte-d'Azur France
142 C2 Måne r. Norway
151 H2 Manea Cambridgeshire, England U.K.
169 F5 Manebach Ger.
116 B5 Manekwara Gujarat India
122 D2 Maneli Iran
116 E5 Manendragarh Madh. Prad. India
117 F4 Maner Bihar India
114 C2 Maner r. India
190 F3 Manerbio Italy
183 I2 Mañeru Spain
122 A3 Manesht Kūh mt. Iran
197 G3 Măneşti Romania
176 C2 Manětín Czech Rep.
136 C2 Manevychi Ukr.
203 F3 Manfalût Egypt
193 H3 Manfredonia Italy
193 I3 Manfredonia, Golfo di g. Italy
254 E5 Manga Brazil
206 E4 Manga Burkina
254 D4 Mangabeiras, Serra das hills Brazil
209 C6 Mangai Dem. Rep. Congo
81 □2 Mangaia i. Cook Is
80 E3 Mangakino North I. N.Z.
114 D2 Mangalagiri Andhra Prad. India
117 H4 Mangaldai Assam India
197 I4 Mangalia Romania
202 C6 Mangalmé Chad
114 B3 Mangalore Karnataka India
114 B2 Mangalvedha Mahar. India
81 D5 Mangamaunu South I. N.Z.
80 E3 Mangamingi North I. N.Z.
80 D1 Mangamuka North I. N.Z.
182 E3 Manganeses de la Lampreana Spain
182 E2 Manganeses de la Polvorosa Spain
80 D1 Manganui r. North I. N.Z.
114 B2 Mangaon Mahar. India
114 D2 Mangapet Andhra Prad. India
80 D4 Mangarakau South I. N.Z.
257 E5 Mangaratiba Brazil
79 □3 Mangareva i. Arch. des Tuamotu Fr. Polynesia
Mangareva Islands Arch. des Tuamotu Fr. Polynesia see Gambier, Îles
80 E4 Mangatainoka North I. N.Z.
80 E2 Mangatawhiri North I. N.Z.
215 F3 Mangaung S. Africa
116 E4 Mangawan Madh. Prad. India
80 E3 Mangaweka North I. N.Z.
80 F3 Mangaweka mt. North I. N.Z.
80 E2 Mangawhai North I. N.Z.
Mangde Chhu r. Bhutan see Trongsa Chhu
Ma'ngê Gansu China see Luqu
Mangea i. Cook Is see Mangaia
141 I3 Manger Norway
147 B5 Mangerton Mountain hill Rep. of Ireland
173 G4 Mangfall r. Ger.
173 F4 Mangfallgebirge mts Ger.
95 E3 Manggar Indon.
Mangghyshlaq Kazakh. see Mangistau
Mangghystaū Kazakh. see Mangistau
Mangghystaū Oblysy admin. div. Kazakh. see Mangistauskaya Oblast'
Mangghyt Uzbek. see Mangit
Manghit Uzbek. see Mangit
157 F3 Mangiennes France
120 B4 Mangistau Kazakh.
120 B3 Mangistau, Gory hills Kazakh.
120 C4 Mangistauskaya Oblast' admin. div. Kazakh.
120 E4 Mangit Uzbek.
95 F3 Mangkutup r. Indon.
129 D3 Manglisi Georgia
111 E4 Mangnai Qinghai China
211 B8 Mangochi Malawi
206 D4 Mangodara Burkina
213 □I4 Mangoky r. Toliara Madag.
213 □J4 Mangoky r. Toliara Madag.

332
Mangole to Marston Moretaine

93 C3 **Mangole** *i.* Indon.
114 B2 **Mangoli** *Karnataka* India
213 □I4 **Mangolovolo** Madag.
80 D1 **Mangonui** *North I.* N.Z.
213 □K3 **Mangoro** *r.* Madag.
150 E3 **Mangotsfield** *South Gloucestershire, England* U.K.
Mangqystaū Shyghanaghy *b.* Kazakh. *see* **Mangyshlakskiy Zaliv**
Mangra *Qinghai* China *see* **Guinan**
116 B5 **Mangral** *Gujarat* India
116 D4 **Mangrol** *Rajasthan* India
231 E7 **Mangrove Cay** *i.* Bahamas
116 D5 **Mangrul** *Mahar.* India
Mangshi *Yunnan* China *see* **Luxi**
182 C4 **Mangualde** Port.
258 G4 **Mangueira, Lago** *l.* Brazil
255 B8 **Mangueirinha** Brazil
205 H5 **Manguéni, Plateau du** Niger
100 B2 **Mangui** *Nei Mongol* China
Mangula Zimbabwe *see* **Mhangura**
242 □I6 **Mangulile** Hond.
237 D5 **Mangum** *OK* U.S.A.
254 D2 **Mangunça, Ilha** *i.* Brazil
107 G1 **Mangut** Rus. Fed.
Mangyshlak Kazakh. *see* **Mangistau**
120 B3 **Mangyshlak, Poluostrov** *pen.* Kazakh.
Mangyshlak Oblast *admin. div.* Kazakh. *see* **Mangistauskaya Oblast'**
Mangyshlakskaya Oblast' *admin. div.* Kazakh. *see* **Mangistauskaya Oblast'**
120 B3 **Mangyshlakskiy Zaliv** *b.* Kazakh.
Manhan Mongolia *see* **Tögrög**
179 G2 **Manhartsberg** *hill* Austria
236 D4 **Manhattan** *KS* U.S.A.
240 H5 **Manhattan Beach** *CA* U.S.A.
165 E4 **Manhay** Belgium
234 B2 **Manheim** *PA* U.S.A.
213 G5 **Manhica** Moz.
257 F4 **Manhuaçu** Brazil
257 G3 **Manhuaçu** *r.* Brazil
157 F3 **Manhuelles** France
257 G4 **Manhumirim** Brazil
250 C3 **Mani** Col.
198 C3 **Mani** *pen.* Greece
207 G3 **Mani** Nigeria
213 □J3 **Mania** *r.* Madag.
194 D5 **Maniace** *Sicilia* Italy
191 H2 **Maniago** Italy
198 B1 **Maniakoi** Greece
213 G3 **Manica** Moz.
213 G3 **Manica** *prov.* Moz.
213 G3 **Manicaland** *prov.* Zimbabwe
251 F6 **Manicoré** Brazil
251 F6 **Manicoré** *r.* Brazil
225 G3 **Manicouagan** *Que.* Can.
225 G3 **Manicouagan** *r. Que.* Can.
225 G3 **Manicouagan, Réservoir** *resr Que.* Can.
225 G3 **Manic Trois, Réservoir** *resr Que.* Can.
208 E5 **Maniema** *admin. reg.* Dem. Rep. Congo
125 E2 **Manīfah** Saudi Arabia
108 A2 **Maniganggo** *Sichuan* China
223 L5 **Manigotagan** *Man.* Can.
117 F4 **Manihari** *Bihar* India
79 □3 **Manihi** *atoll Arch. des Tuamotu* Fr. Polynesia
81 □2 **Manihiki** *atoll* Cook Is
221 M3 **Maniitsoq** Greenland
123 F5 **Maniji** *r.* Pak.
117 H5 **Manikchhari** Bangl.
117 G5 **Manikganj** Bangl.
Manikgarh *Mahar.* India *see* **Rajura**
116 E4 **Manikpur** *Uttar Prad.* India
92 B3 **Manila** Phil.
238 E3 **Manila** *UT* U.S.A.
92 B3 **Manila Bay** Phil.
83 G3 **Manildra** *N.S.W.* Austr.
83 G2 **Manilla** *N.S.W.* Austr.
185 E4 **Manilva** Spain
131 R3 **Manily** Rus. Fed.
84 C2 **Maningrida** *N.T.* Austr.
Manipur *Manipur* India *see* **Imphal**
117 H4 **Manipur** *state* India
96 A2 **Manipur** *r.* India/Myanmar
199 E2 **Manisa** Turkey
199 F2 **Manisa** *prov.* Turkey
187 C5 **Manises** Spain
254 B4 **Manissauá Missu** *r.* Brazil
226 D3 **Manistee** *MI* U.S.A.
226 D3 **Manistee** *r. MI* U.S.A.
226 D3 **Manistique** *MI* U.S.A.
223 L4 **Manitoba** *prov.* Can.
223 L5 **Manitoba, Lake** *Man.* Can.
223 L5 **Manitou** *Man.* Can.
225 H3 **Manitou** *r. Que.* Can.
232 E3 **Manitou Beach** *NY* U.S.A.
223 M5 **Manitou Falls** *Ont.* Can.
224 D4 **Manitoulin Island** *Ont.* Can.
224 C3 **Manitouwadge** *Ont.* Can.
227 G3 **Manitowaning** *Ont.* Can.
226 C2 **Manitowish Waters** *WI* U.S.A.
226 D3 **Manitowoc** *WI* U.S.A.
224 F4 **Maniwaki** *Que.* Can.
113 □1 **Maniyafushi** *i. S. Male* Maldives
250 C3 **Manizales** Col.
213 □J4 **Manja** Madag.
213 G5 **Manjacaze** Moz.
213 □J3 **Manjak** Madag.
114 B3 **Manjarabad** *Karnataka* India
114 C4 **Manjeri** *Kerala* India
101 C4 **Man Jiang** *r.* China
122 B2 **Manjil** Iran
87 C7 **Manjimup** *W.A.* Austr.
207 H5 **Manjo** Cameroon
114 C2 **Manjra** *r.* India
179 G2 **Mank** Austria
117 G4 **Mankachar** *Assam* India
Mankanza Dem. Rep. Congo *see* **Makanza**
236 D4 **Mankato** *KS* U.S.A.
236 E2 **Mankato** *MN* U.S.A.
136 F3 **Man'kivka** Ukr.
137 J3 **Man'kivka** Ukr.
136 E3 **Man'kivka** Ukr.
206 D4 **Mankono** Côte d'Ivoire
223 J5 **Mankota** *Sask.* Can.
160 C1 **Manlay** France
186 F3 **Manlleu** Spain
236 E3 **Manly** *IA* U.S.A.
116 C5 **Manmad** *Mahar.* India
84 C2 **Mann** *r. N.T.* Austr.
78 □3a **Mann** *i. Kwajalein* Marshall Is
84 B5 **Mann, Mount** *N.T.* Austr.
94 C4 **Manna** *Sumatera* Indon.
82 D3 **Mannahill** *S.A.* Austr.
114 C4 **Mannar** Sri Lanka
114 C4 **Mannar, Gulf of** India/Sri Lanka
114 C4 **Mannargudi** *Tamil Nadu* India
172 C4 **Männedorf** Switz.
179 H3 **Mannersdorf am Leithagebirge** Austria
179 H3 **Mannersdorf an der Rabnitz** Austria
114 D3 **Manneru** *r.* India
172 C2 **Mannheim** Ger.
Mannicolo Islands Solomon Is *see* **Vanikoro Islands**
222 G3 **Manning** *Alta* Can.
236 C2 **Manning** *ND* U.S.A.
231 D5 **Manning** *SC* U.S.A.
78 □6 **Manning Strait** Solomon Is
232 C5 **Mannington** *WV* U.S.A.
151 I3 **Manningtree** *Essex, England* U.K.
190 C2 **Männlifluh** *mt.* Switz.
84 B5 **Mann Ranges** *mts S.A.* Austr.
233 E3 **Mannsville** *NY* U.S.A.
192 A4 **Mannu** *r. Sardegna* Italy
192 A5 **Mannu** *r. Sardegna* Italy
192 B4 **Mannu** *r. Sardegna* Italy
192 B5 **Mannu** *r. Sardegna* Italy
192 A4 **Mannu, Monte** *hill Sardegna* Italy
223 I4 **Mannville** *Alta* Can.
206 C5 **Mano** *r.* Liberia/Sierra Leone
206 B5 **Mano** Sierra Leone
Man-of-War Rocks *is HI* U.S.A. *see* **Gardner Pinnacles**
111 B7 **Manoharpur** *Rajasthan* India
116 D4 **Manohar Thana** *Rajasthan* India
220 C4 **Manokotak** *AK* U.S.A.
186 G2 **Manol** *r.* Spain
197 H2 **Manoleasa** Romania
213 □K3 **Manompana** Madag.
209 E6 **Manono** Dem. Rep. Congo
150 C3 **Manorbier** *Pembrokeshire, Wales* U.K.
235 E2 **Manorhaven** *NY* U.S.A.
206 C5 **Mano River** Liberia
235 F2 **Manorville** *NY* U.S.A.
161 D5 **Manosque** France
174 E1 **Manowo** Pol.
101 C4 **Manp'o** N. Korea
116 C5 **Manpur** *Madh. Prad.* India
77 I2 **Manra** *i. Phoenix Is* Kiribati
186 E3 **Manresa** Spain
116 C5 **Mansa** *Gujarat* India
116 C3 **Mansa** *Punjab* India
209 F7 **Mansa** Zambia
206 B3 **Mansabá** Guinea-Bissau
206 B3 **Mansa Konko** Gambia
170 F3 **Manschnow** Ger.
123 H3 **Mansehra** Pak.
221 K3 **Mansel Island** *Nunavut* Can.
140 O2 **Mansel'kya** *ridge* Fin./Rus. Fed.
171 C4 **Mansfeld** Ger.
83 F4 **Mansfield** *Vic.* Austr.
149 H4 **Mansfield** *Nottinghamshire, England* U.K.
237 E5 **Mansfield** *AR* U.S.A.
237 E5 **Mansfield** *LA* U.S.A.
233 H3 **Mansfield** *MA* U.S.A.
232 B4 **Mansfield** *OH* U.S.A.
232 E4 **Mansfield** *PA* U.S.A.
233 G2 **Mansfield, Mount** *VT* U.S.A.
235 F1 **Mansfield Center** *CT* U.S.A.
149 H4 **Mansfield Woodhouse** *Nottinghamshire, England* U.K.
254 E4 **Mansidão** Brazil
183 H2 **Mansilla** Spain
183 E2 **Mansilla de las Mulas** Spain
162 C3 **Mansle** France
Manso *r. Tocantins* Brazil *see* **Mortes, Rio das**
192 A2 **Manso** *Corse* France
206 E5 **Manso-Nkwanta** Ghana
163 C4 **Mansonville** France
182 B4 **Mansores** Port.
150 E4 **Manston** *Dorset, England* U.K.
127 H5 **Manşūrī** Iran
126 D3 **Mansurlu** Turkey
250 A5 **Manta** Ecuador
92 A4 **Mantalingajan, Mount** *Palawan* Phil.
252 B3 **Mantaro** *r.* Peru
240 G3 **Manteca** *CA* U.S.A.
182 C4 **Manteigas** Port.
173 G2 **Mantel** Ger.
257 G3 **Mantena** Brazil
226 D5 **Manteno** *IL* U.S.A.
231 F5 **Manteo** *NC* U.S.A.
165 F5 **Manternach** Lux.
156 B4 **Mantes-la-Jolie** France
156 B4 **Mantes-la-Ville** France
114 C2 **Manthani** *Andhra Prad.* India
159 G4 **Manthelan** France
241 L2 **Manti** *UT* U.S.A.
257 D5 **Mantiqueira, Serra da** *mts* Brazil
160 D1 **Mantoche** France
235 D2 **Mantoloking** *NJ* U.S.A.
226 E3 **Manton** *MI* U.S.A.
198 C2 **Mantoudi** Greece
191 F3 **Mantova** Italy
191 F3 **Mantova** *prov. Lombardia* Italy
141 N3 **Mäntsälä** Fin.
141 N3 **Mänttä** Fin.
246 A2 **Mantua** Cuba
Mantua Italy *see* **Mantova**
234 C3 **Mantua** *NJ* U.S.A.
232 C4 **Mantua** *OH* U.S.A.
85 F5 **Mantuan Downs** *Qld* Austr.
134 I4 **Manturovo** *Kostromskaya Oblast'* Rus. Fed.
137 I2 **Manturovo** *Kurskaya Oblast'* Rus. Fed.
141 N3 **Mäntyharju** Fin.
Manu *r.* Bol. *see* **Mapiri**
252 C3 **Manú** *r.* Peru
81 □2 **Manuae** *i.* Cook Is
79 □3 **Manuae** *atoll Arch. de la Société* Fr. Polynesia
78 □2 **Manua Islands** American Samoa
215 G5 **Manubi** S. Africa
187 C5 **Manuel** Spain
254 C4 **Manuel Alves** *r.* Brazil
261 I4 **Manuel J. Cobo** Arg.
261 G3 **Manuel Ocampo** Arg.
256 B6 **Manuel Ribas** Brazil
259 B9 **Manuel Rodriguez, Isla** *i.* Chile
252 C2 **Manuel Urbano** Brazil
254 E5 **Manuel Vitorino** Brazil
122 D5 **Manūjān** Iran
92 B4 **Manukan** Phil.
80 E2 **Manukau** *North I.* N.Z.
80 E2 **Manukau Harbour** *North I.* N.Z.
147 B3 **Manulla** Rep. of Ireland
252 D2 **Manupari** *r.* Bol.
252 D2 **Manurimi** *r.* Bol.
252 D2 **Manuripi** *r.* Bol.
80 F3 **Manutuke** *North I.* N.Z.
114 C3 **Manvi** *Karnataka* India
234 D2 **Manville** *NJ* U.S.A.
114 C2 **Manwat** *Mahar.* India
237 E6 **Many** *LA* U.S.A.
213 F2 **Manyame** *r.* Moz./Zimbabwe
211 B5 **Manyara, Lake** *salt l.* Tanz.
199 E1 **Manyas** Turkey
197 F4 **Manyashki Vrŭkh** *hill* Bulg.
215 F3 **Manyatseng** S. Africa
223 I5 **Manyberries** *Alta* Can.
137 K4 **Manychskaya** Rus. Fed.
241 M3 **Many Farms** *AZ* U.S.A.
136 D3 **Manykivtsi** Ukr.
211 B6 **Manyoni** Tanz.
85 G5 **Many Peaks** *Qld* Austr.
87 C7 **Many Peaks, Mount** *hill W.A.* Austr.
162 C3 **Manzac-sur-Vern** France
128 A4 **Manzala, Bahra el** *lag.* Egypt
Manzala, Lake *lag.* Egypt *see* **Manzala, Bahra el**
182 D3 **Manzanal de Arriba** Spain
182 D2 **Manzanal del Puerto** Spain
185 G1 **Manzanares** Spain
183 G4 **Manzanares** *r.* Spain
183 G4 **Manzanares el Real** Spain
182 C2 **Manzaneda** Spain
182 C2 **Manzaneda, Cabeza de** *mt.* Spain
183 G2 **Manzanedo** Spain
183 G5 **Manzaneque** Spain
187 C4 **Manzanera** Spain
246 C2 **Manzanillo** Cuba
244 B4 **Manzanillo** Mex.
191 I3 **Manzano** Italy
209 F6 **Manzanza** Dem. Rep. Congo
122 B3 **Manzarīyeh** Iran
160 A3 **Manzat** France
107 H1 **Manzhouli** *Nei Mongol* China
192 E2 **Manziana** Italy
160 C2 **Manziat** France
215 H2 **Manzini** Swaziland
215 H2 **Manzini** *admin. dist.* Swaziland
Manzovka Rus. Fed. *see* **Sibirtsevo**
202 B6 **Mao** Chad
246 E3 **Mao** Dom. Rep.
Maó Spain *see* **Mahón**
Mao, Nam *r.* Myanmar *see* **Shweli**
108 C3 **Maoba** *Guizhou* China
108 D2 **Maoba** *Hubei* China
109 E2 **Maocifan** *Hubei* China
108 B1 **Mao'ergai** *Sichuan* China
91 I7 **Maoke, Pegunungan** *mts* Indon.
215 F2 **Maokeng** S. Africa
101 B4 **Maokui Shan** *mt. Liaoning* China
106 D4 **Maomao Shan** *mt. Gansu* China
108 D4 **Maoming** *Guangdong* China
108 B3 **Maotou Shan** *mt. Yunnan* China
Maowen *Sichuan* China *see* **Maoxian**
108 B2 **Maoxian** *Sichuan* China
93 B3 **Mapane** *Sulawesi Tengah* Indon.
209 E9 **Mapanza** Zambia
243 G6 **Mapastepec** Mex.
215 E4 **Maphodi** S. Africa
91 I8 **Mapi** *r.* Indon.
250 E3 **Mapiche, Serranía** *mts* Venez.
242 E3 **Mapimí** Mex.
242 D3 **Mapimí, Bolsón de** *des.* Mex.
252 C3 **Mapiri** Bol.
252 D2 **Mapiri** *r.* Bol.
250 C4 **Mapirpán** Col.
80 E3 **Mapiu** *North I.* N.Z.
236 E3 **Maple** *r. IA* U.S.A.
226 E4 **Maple** *r. MI* U.S.A.
236 D2 **Maple** *r. ND* U.S.A.
236 D2 **Maple** *r. ND* U.S.A.
223 I5 **Maple Creek** *Sask.* Can.
241 M5 **Maple Peak** *AZ* U.S.A.
236 E3 **Mapleton** *IA* U.S.A.
241 L1 **Mapleton** *UT* U.S.A.
226 D3 **Maplewood** *WI* U.S.A.
266 G4 **Mapmakers Seamounts** *sea feature* N. Pacific Ocean
85 E1 **Mapoon** *Qld* Austr.
215 F3 **Mapoteng** Lesotho
114 B3 **Mapuca** *Goa* India
251 G5 **Mapuera** *r.* Brazil
215 H3 **Mapumulo** S. Africa
213 G5 **Maputo** Moz.
213 G5 **Maputo** *prov.* Moz.
213 G5 **Maputo** *r.* Moz./S. Africa
215 F3 **Maputsoe** Lesotho
Maqanshy Kazakh. *see* **Makanchi**
Maqat Kazakh. *see* **Makat**
106 D5 **Maqên** *Qinghai* China
106 C5 **Maqên Gangri** *mt. Qinghai* China
128 B5 **Maqla, Jabal al** *mt.* Saudi Arabia
204 C5 **Maqteïr** *reg.* Maur.
108 B1 **Maqu** *Gansu* China
Ma Qu *r.* China *see* **Huang He**
111 D6 **Maquan He** *r. Xizang* China
183 F4 **Maqueda** Spain
209 B6 **Maquela do Zombo** Angola
259 C6 **Maquinchao** Arg.
236 F3 **Maquoketa** *IA* U.S.A.
236 F3 **Maquoketa** *r. IA* U.S.A.
142 C2 **Mår** *r.* Norway
123 F5 **Mar** *r.* Pak.
182 B3 **Mar** Port.
257 F5 **Mar, Serra do** *mts* Brazil
256 C6 **Mar, Serra do** *mts Paraná* Brazil
257 E5 **Mar, Serra do** *mts Rio de Janeiro/São Paulo* Brazil
255 C9 **Mar, Serra do** *mts Rio Grande do Sul/Santa Catarina* Brazil
251 G3 **Mara** Guyana
117 E5 **Mara** *Madh. Prad.* India
192 A4 **Mara** *Sardegna* Italy
211 B5 **Mara** *admin. reg.* Tanz.
246 E5 **Mara** Venez.
251 E5 **Maraã** Brazil
254 C3 **Maraba** Brazil
256 B5 **Marabá Paulista** Brazil
157 F5 **Marac** France
251 I5 **Maracá** *r.* Brazil
251 F4 **Maracá, Ilha** *i.* Brazil
251 I4 **Maracá, Ilha de** *i.* Brazil
256 B5 **Maracaí** Brazil
250 D2 **Maracaibo** Venez.
250 D2 **Maracaibo, Lago de** *l.* Venez.
Maracaibo, Lake Venez. *see* **Maracaibo, Lago de**
253 G5 **Maracaju** Brazil
253 G5 **Maracaju, Serra de** *hills* Brazil
192 B5 **Maracalagonis** *Sardegna* Italy
254 D2 **Maracanã** Brazil
251 H5 **Maracanaquará, Planalto** *plat.* Brazil
Maracanda Uzbek. *see* **Samarkand**
254 E5 **Maracás** Brazil
254 E5 **Maracás, Chapada de** *hills* Brazil
250 E2 **Maracay** Venez.
Maradhoo *i. Addu Atoll* Maldives *see* **Maradu**
207 G3 **Maradi** Niger
207 G3 **Maradi** *dept* Niger
113 □2 **Maradu** *i. Addu Atoll* Maldives
129 F3 **Maraga** Rus. Fed.
122 A2 **Marāgheh** Iran
254 G4 **Maragogi** Brazil
92 B3 **Maragondon** Phil.
124 D2 **Marah** Saudi Arabia
251 E4 **Marahuaca, Cerro** *mt.* Venez.
158 D5 **Marais breton** *marsh* France
236 E4 **Marais des Cygnes** *r. KS* U.S.A.
254 C2 **Marajó, Baía de** *est.* Brazil
251 I5 **Marajó, Ilha de** *i.* Brazil
77 H1 **Marakei** *atoll Gilbert Is* Kiribati
Maraki *atoll Gilbert Is* Kiribati *see* **Marakei**
114 C3 **Marakkanam** *Tamil Nadu* India
Maralaba *i.* Vanuatu *see* **Mere Lava**
210 C4 **Maralal** Kenya
Maralbashi *Xinjiang* China *see* **Bachu**
129 C3 **Maralik** Armenia
82 B2 **Maralinga** *S.A.* Austr.
Maralwexi *Xinjiang* China *see* **Bachu**
78 □6 **Maramasike** *i.* Solomon Is
Maramba Zambia *see* **Livingstone**
262 U2 **Marambio** *research stn* Antarctica
197 G2 **Maramureşului, Munţii** *mts* Romania
123 F4 **Maran** *mt.* Pak.
122 A3 **Marāna** Iraq
241 L5 **Marana** *AZ* U.S.A.
183 H3 **Maranchón** Spain
122 A2 **Marand** Iran
Marandellas Zimbabwe *see* **Marondera**
191 F4 **Maranello** Italy
157 G3 **Marange-Silvange** France
254 F2 **Maranguape** Brazil
254 C5 **Maranhão** *r.* Brazil
254 D3 **Maranhão** *state* Brazil
184 C1 **Maranhão** Port.
184 C1 **Maranhão, Barragem do** *resr* Port.
191 G4 **Marano** Italy
191 I3 **Marano, Laguna di** *lag.* Italy
85 G5 **Maranoa** *r. Qld* Austr.
194 D2 **Marano di Napoli** Italy
250 C6 **Marañón** *r.* Peru
191 F4 **Marano sul Panaro** Italy
162 B2 **Marans** France
157 E4 **Maranville** France
182 C3 **Marão** *mt.* Port.
182 B3 **Marão, Serra do** *mts* Port.
206 D5 **Maraoué** *r.* Côte d'Ivoire
78 □6 **Marapa** *i.* Solomon Is
254 D2 **Marapanim** Brazil
81 A6 **Mararoa** *r. South I.* N.Z.
Maraş Cyprus *see* **Varosia**
Maraş Turkey *see* **Kahramanmaraş**
197 H3 **Mărăşeşti** Romania
197 H3 **Mărașu** Romania
193 H5 **Maratea** Italy
184 B2 **Marateca** Port.
199 E3 **Marathokampos** *Voreio Aigaio* Greece
224 C3 **Marathon** *Ont.* Can.
Marathón Greece *see* **Marathonas**
231 D7 **Marathon** *FL* U.S.A.
233 E3 **Marathon** *NY* U.S.A.
237 C6 **Marathon** *TX* U.S.A.
226 C3 **Marathon** *WI* U.S.A.
198 C2 **Marathonas** Greece
251 E5 **Marauiá** *r.* Brazil
161 B5 **Maraussan** France
202 D1 **Marāwah** Libya
92 C4 **Marawi** Phil.
156 D4 **Maraye-en-Othe** France
129 F3 **Märäzä** Azer.
150 B4 **Marazion** *Cornwall, England* U.K.
171 E4 **Marbach** Ger.
190 C2 **Marbach** Switz.
172 D3 **Marbach am Neckar** Ger.
185 F4 **Marbella** Spain
185 F4 **Marbella, Ensenada de** *b.* Spain
86 C4 **Marble Bar** *W.A.* Austr.
241 L3 **Marble Canyon** *AZ* U.S.A.
213 F5 **Marble Hall** S. Africa
237 F4 **Marble Hill** *MO* U.S.A.
160 D2 **Marboz** France
215 H4 **Marburg** S. Africa
Marburg Slovenia *see* **Maribor**
169 D5 **Marburg an der Lahn** Ger.
177 L4 **Marca** Romania
176 G4 **Marcal** *r.* Hungary
176 G5 **Marcali** Hungary
176 G4 **Marcaltő** Hungary
191 I4 **Marčana** Croatia
194 B5 **Marcanzotta** *r. Sicilia* Italy
252 C3 **Marcapata** Peru
191 F3 **Marcaria** Italy
261 G2 **Marcelino Escalada** Arg.
193 E2 **Marcellina** Italy
226 E4 **Marcellus** *MI* U.S.A.
233 E3 **Marcellus** *NY* U.S.A.
177 H4 **Marcelová** Slovakia
162 B3 **Marcenais** France
161 A3 **Marcenat** France
179 H2 **March** *r.* Austria *alt.* **Morava (Europe)**
151 H2 **March** *Cambridgeshire, England* U.K.
214 C3 **Marchand** S. Africa
82 D3 **Marchant Hill** *hill S.A.* Austr.
191 H5 **Marche** *admin. reg.* Italy
165 E4 **Marche-en-Famenne** Belgium
179 H2 **Marchegg** Austria
185 E3 **Marchena** Spain
250 □ **Marchena, Isla** *i. Islas Galápagos* Ecuador
156 B5 **Marchenoir** France
163 B4 **Marcheprime** France
156 D2 **Marchiennes** France
260 B4 **Marchihue** Chile
165 E4 **Marchin** Belgium
84 D1 **Marchinbar Island** *N.T.* Austr.
151 F2 **Marchington** *Staffordshire, England* U.K.
261 F2 **Mar Chiquita, Lago** *l.* Arg.
261 I5 **Mar Chiquita, Lago** *l.* Arg.
179 F2 **Marchtrenk** Austria
150 E1 **Marchwiel** *Wrexham, Wales* U.K.
137 H2 **Marchykhyna Buda** Ukr.
163 C5 **Marciac** France
192 C2 **Marciana** Italy
192 C2 **Marciana Marina** Italy
193 G3 **Marcianise** Italy
191 G5 **Marciano della Chiana** Italy
138 F3 **Mārciena** Latvia
160 C2 **Marcigny** France
163 D4 **Marcilhac-sur-Célé** France
162 B3 **Marcillac** France
162 E3 **Marcillac-la-Croisille** France
163 E4 **Marcillac-Vallon** France
160 A2 **Marcillat-en-Combraille** France
159 H4 **Marcilly-en-Gault** France
156 C5 **Marcilly-en-Villette** France
156 D4 **Marcilly-le-Hayer** France
156 B4 **Marcilly-sur-Eure** France
175 I6 **Marcinkowice** Pol.
174 E5 **Marciszów** Pol.
156 B2 **Marck** France
157 H4 **Marckolsheim** France
182 B3 **Marco de Canaveses** Port.
156 D2 **Marcoing** France
253 F2 **Marcolino** *r.* Brazil
191 H3 **Marcòn** Italy
252 B3 **Marcona** Peru
191 H3 **Marco Polo** *airport* Italy
261 F3 **Marcos Juárez** Arg.
261 H4 **Marcos Paz** Arg.
161 E4 **Marcoux** France
156 D2 **Marcq-en-Barœul** France
233 G2 **Marcy, Mount** *NY* U.S.A.
129 G3 **Märdäkan** Azer.
123 H3 **Mardan** Pak.
136 E4 **Mardarivka** Ukr.
261 I5 **Mar de Ajó** Arg.
261 I5 **Mar del Plata** Arg.
150 E2 **Marden** *Herefordshire, England* U.K.
151 H3 **Marden** *Kent, England* U.K.
156 D3 **Mardeuil** France
86 B4 **Mardie** *W.A.* Austr.
127 F3 **Mardın** Turkey
140 L2 **Mårdsele** Sweden
140 M2 **Mårdudden** Sweden
106 D2 **Mardzad** Mongolia
160 C3 **Mare** *r.* France
78 □5 **Maré** *i. Î. Loyauté* New Caledonia
191 G2 **Marebbe** Italy
191 H4 **Marecchia** *r.* Italy
186 □ **Mare de Déu del Toro** *hill* Spain
146 C4 **Maree, Loch** *l. Scotland* U.K.
85 F3 **Mareeba** *Qld* Austr.
149 I4 **Mareham le Fen** *Lincolnshire, England* U.K.
192 C1 **Maremma** *reg.* Italy
206 C3 **Maréna** Mali
207 G2 **Marendet** Niger
236 E3 **Marengo** *IA* U.S.A.
226 C4 **Marengo** *IL* U.S.A.
226 B2 **Marengo** *WI* U.S.A.
226 C2 **Marenisco** *MI* U.S.A.
162 A3 **Marennes** France
195 F4 **Marepotamo** *r.* Italy
151 H4 **Maresfield** *East Sussex, England* U.K.
86 E2 **Maret Islands** *W.A.* Austr.
194 B5 **Marettimo** *Sicilia* Italy
194 B5 **Marettimo, Isola** *i. Sicilia* Italy
162 C3 **Mareuil** France
159 I5 **Mareuil-sur-Arnon** France
156 E3 **Mareuil-sur-Ay** France
162 A2 **Mareuil-sur-Lay-Dissais** France
139 I3 **Marevo** Rus. Fed.
160 D1 **Marey-sur-Tille** France
239 F6 **Marfa** *TX* U.S.A.
150 D3 **Margam** *Neath Port Talbot, Wales* U.K.
Marganets Kazakh. *see* **Zhezdy**
Marganets Ukr. *see* **Marhanets'**
Margao *Goa* India *see* **Madgaon**
86 E3 **Margaret** *r. W.A.* Austr.
86 C4 **Margaret, Mount** *hill W.A.* Austr.
222 E5 **Margaret Bay** *B.C.* Can.
87 B7 **Margaret River** *W.A.* Austr.
233 F3 **Margaretville** *NY* U.S.A.
251 F2 **Margarita, Isla de** *i.* Venez.
137 J4 **Margaritovo** Rus. Fed.
215 H4 **Margate** S. Africa
151 I3 **Margate** *Kent, England* U.K.
235 D3 **Margate City** *NJ* U.S.A.
197 F2 **Mărgău** Romania
162 B3 **Margaux** France
177 K3 **Margecany** Slovakia
156 E4 **Margerie-Hancourt** France
149 H4 **Margery Hill** *hill England* U.K.
172 D2 **Margetshöchheim** Ger.
117 H4 **Margherita** *Assam* India
193 I3 **Margherita di Savoia** Italy
208 F4 **Margherita Peak** Dem. Rep. Congo/Uganda
Marghilon Uzbek. *see* **Margilan**
197 F2 **Marghita** Romania
121 G4 **Margilan** Uzbek.
177 L6 **Margina** Romania
197 G2 **Marginea** Romania
156 C3 **Margny-lès-Compiègne** France
123 E4 **Margo, Dasht-i** *des.* Afgh.
190 C3 **Margone** Italy
174 F3 **Margonin** Pol.
92 B5 **Margosatubig** Phil.
165 E4 **Margraten** Neth.
222 F4 **Marguerite** *B.C.* Can.
Marguerite, Pic *mt.* Dem. Rep. Congo/Uganda *see* **Margherita Peak**
161 C5 **Marguerittes** France
157 F3 **Margut** France
127 G4 **Marhaj Khalīl** Iraq
151 H2 **Marham** *Norfolk, England* U.K.
127 F3 **Marhan Dāgh** *hill* Iraq
137 H4 **Marhanets'** Ukr.
205 E2 **Marhoum** Alg.
252 D1 **Mari** *r.* Brazil
255 B7 **Maria** *r.* Brazil
79 □3 **Maria** *atoll Arch. des Tuamotu* Fr. Polynesia
79 □3 **Maria** *atoll Îs Australes* Fr. Polynesia
185 H3 **María** Spain
179 G2 **Maria Anzbach** Austria
161 C4 **Mariac** France
252 C5 **María Elena** Chile
142 C3 **Mariager** Denmark
261 H5 **María Ignacia** Arg.
84 C2 **Maria Island** *N.T.* Austr.
83 G5 **Maria Island** *Tas.* Austr.
179 G3 **Maria Lankowitz** Austria
182 C4 **Marialva** Port.
85 G4 **Marian** *Qld* Austr.
257 F4 **Mariana** Brazil
183 H4 **Mariana** Spain
246 B2 **Marianao** Cuba
266 E4 **Mariana Ridge** *sea feature* N. Pacific Ocean
266 E5 **Mariana Trench** *sea feature* N. Pacific Ocean
117 H4 **Mariani** *Assam* India
Mariánica, Cordillera *mts* Spain *see* **Morena, Sierra**
237 F5 **Marianna** *AR* U.S.A.
231 C6 **Marianna** *FL* U.S.A.
143 F3 **Mariannelund** Sweden
190 E3 **Mariano Comense** Italy
258 F3 **Mariano Loza** Arg.
Mariano Machado Angola *see* **Ganda**
194 C5 **Marianopoli** *Sicilia* Italy
174 D2 **Marianowo** Pol.
176 B2 **Mariánské Lázně** Czech Rep.
179 E3 **Mariapfarr** Austria
250 D4 **Mariapirí, Mesa de** *hills* Col.
256 B4 **Mariápolis** Brazil
179 F4 **Maria Rain** Austria
238 E2 **Marias** *r. MT* U.S.A.
244 A3 **Marías, Islas** *is* Mex.
179 F4 **Maria Saal** Austria
261 G4 **María Teresa** Arg.
80 D1 **Maria van Diemen, Cape** *North I.* N.Z.
179 F4 **Maria Wörth** Austria
179 G3 **Mariazell** Austria
124 D5 **Ma'rib** Yemen
124 D5 **Ma'rib** *governorate* Yemen
226 D3 **Maribel** *WI* U.S.A.
142 D4 **Maribo** Denmark
188 E2 **Maribor** Slovenia
257 F5 **Maricá** Brazil
Marica *r.* Bulg. *see* **Maritsa**
247 □1 **Maricao** Puerto Rico
241 K5 **Maricopa** *AZ* U.S.A.
240 H4 **Maricopa** *CA* U.S.A.
241 K5 **Maricopa Mountains** *AZ* U.S.A.
Maricourt *Que.* Can. *see* **Kangiqsujuaq**
208 F3 **Maridi** Sudan
250 E5 **Marié** *r.* Brazil
262 P1 **Marie Byrd Land** *reg.* Antarctica
143 G2 **Mariefred** Sweden
247 □2 **Marie-Galante** *i.* Guadeloupe
141 L3 **Mariehamn** *Åland* Fin.
Mari El *aut. rep.* Rus. Fed. *see* **Mariy El, Respublika**
254 C5 **Mariembero** *r.* Brazil
165 D4 **Mariembourg** Belgium
Marienbad Czech Rep. *see* **Mariánské Lázně**
171 E5 **Marienberg** Ger.
Marienburg Pol. *see* **Malbork**
168 C2 **Marienhafe** Ger.
169 E3 **Marienhagen** Ger.
169 C4 **Marienheide** Ger.
169 F3 **Mariental** Ger.
212 C5 **Mariental** Namibia
232 D4 **Marienville** *PA* U.S.A.
Marienwerder Pol. *see* **Kwidzyn**
143 E2 **Mariestad** Sweden
224 E1 **Mariet** *r. Que.* Can.
231 C5 **Marietta** *GA* U.S.A.
232 C5 **Marietta** *OH* U.S.A.
237 D5 **Marietta** *OK* U.S.A.
234 B2 **Marietta** *PA* U.S.A.
233 G2 **Marieville** *Que.* Can.
207 G4 **Mariga** *r.* Nigeria
193 G4 **Marigliano** Italy
192 A2 **Marignana** *Corse* France
161 D5 **Marignane** France
159 G4 **Marigné-Laillé** France
160 E2 **Marignier** France
158 E2 **Marigny** France
156 D4 **Marigny-le-Châtel** France
160 B1 **Marigny-l'Église** France
247 □2 **Marigot** Dominica
247 G3 **Marigot** *St Maarten* West Indies
120 E1 **Mariinskoye** Rus. Fed.
138 D4 **Marijampolė** Lith.
215 F1 **Marikand** S. Africa
197 F5 **Marikostinovo** Bulg.
256 C5 **Marília** Brazil
86 C4 **Marillana** *W.A.* Austr.
256 A6 **Mariluz** Brazil
209 C7 **Marimba** Angola
182 B2 **Marín** Spain
240 G3 **Marina** *CA* U.S.A.
192 D2 **Marina di Alberese** Italy
195 F3 **Marina di Amendolara** Italy
192 A5 **Marina di Arbus** *Sardegna* Italy
193 H4 **Marina di Camerota** Italy
192 C2 **Marina di Campo** Italy
192 C1 **Marina di Castagneto Donoratico** Italy
190 F5 **Marina di Cecina** Italy
193 H3 **Marina di Chieuti** Italy
195 F2 **Marina di Ginosa** Italy
195 F4 **Marina di Gioiosa Ionica** Italy
192 C2 **Marina di Grosseto** Italy
195 H3 **Marina di Leuca** Italy
190 F4 **Marina di Massa** Italy
194 C5 **Marina di Palma** *Sicilia* Italy
195 G2 **Marina di Pulsano** Italy
194 D6 **Marina di Ragusa** *Sicilia* Italy
191 H4 **Marina di Ravenna** Italy
Mar'ina Gorka Belarus *see* **Mar"ina Horka**
138 G5 **Mar"ina Horka** Belarus
185 F3 **Marinaleda** Spain
193 F1 **Marina Palmense** Italy
191 H4 **Marina Romea** Italy
195 F3 **Marina Schiavonea** Italy
92 B3 **Marinduque** *i.* Phil.
227 F4 **Marine City** *MI* U.S.A.
194 B5 **Marinella** *Sicilia* Italy
194 C5 **Marineo** *Sicilia* Italy
156 B3 **Marines** France
187 C5 **Marines** Spain
226 D3 **Marinette** *WI* U.S.A.
256 B5 **Maringá** Brazil
208 C4 **Maringa** *r.* Dem. Rep. Congo
232 B4 **Maringo** *OH* U.S.A.
213 G3 **Maringué** Moz.
160 B3 **Maringues** France
182 B4 **Marinha das Ondas** Port.
182 B5 **Marinha Grande** Port.
184 B1 **Marinhais** Port.
182 B3 **Marinhas** Port.
191 J3 **Marinići** Croatia
129 C1 **Mar'in Kolodtsy** Rus. Fed.
193 E3 **Marino** Italy
Marino Alejandro Selkirk, Isla *i.* S. Pacific Ocean *see* **Alejandro Selkirk, Isla**
231 C5 **Marion** *AL* U.S.A.
237 F5 **Marion** *AR* U.S.A.
235 F1 **Marion** *CT* U.S.A.
237 F4 **Marion** *IL* U.S.A.
230 C3 **Marion** *IN* U.S.A.
236 D4 **Marion** *KS* U.S.A.
237 F4 **Marion** *KY* U.S.A.
226 E3 **Marion** *MI* U.S.A.
231 D5 **Marion** *NC* U.S.A.
232 B4 **Marion** *OH* U.S.A.
231 E5 **Marion** *SC* U.S.A.
232 C6 **Marion** *VA* U.S.A.
226 C3 **Marion** *WI* U.S.A.
82 D3 **Marion Bay** *S.A.* Austr.
84 D4 **Marion Downs** *Qld* Austr.
85 H3 **Marion Reef** *Coral Sea Is Terr.* Austr.
193 I3 **Mariotto** Italy
205 H5 **Mariou, Adrar** *mt.* Alg.
251 H4 **Maripasoula** Fr. Guiana
240 H3 **Mariposa** *CA* U.S.A.
240 G3 **Mariposa** *r. CA* U.S.A.
253 E5 **Mariscal Estigarribia** Para.
197 F2 **Mărişel** Romania
197 G2 **Mărişelu** Romania
161 E4 **Maritime Alps** *mts* France/Italy
Maritime Kray *admin. div.* Rus. Fed. *see* **Primorskiy Kray**
Maritsa Bulg. *see* **Simeonovgrad**
197 H5 **Maritsa** *r.* Bulg.
134 J4 **Mari-Turek** Rus. Fed.
137 I4 **Mariupol'** Ukr.
251 F2 **Mariusa, Isla** *i.* Venez.
127 G4 **Marīvān** Iran
134 J4 **Mariy El, Respublika** *aut. rep.* Rus. Fed.
Mariyskaya A.S.S.R. *aut. rep.* Rus. Fed. *see* **Mariy El, Respublika**
160 C2 **Marizy** France
183 G5 **Marjaliza** Spain
138 E2 **Märjamaa** Estonia
128 B3 **Marjayoûn** Lebanon
150 E3 **Mark** *Somerset, England* U.K.
210 E4 **Marka** Somalia
121 K2 **Markakol', Ozero** *l.* Kazakh.
206 D3 **Markala** Mali
108 A2 **Markam** *Xizang* China
129 D4 **Mārkān** Iran
114 C3 **Markapur** *Andhra Prad.* India
143 E3 **Markaryd** Sweden
122 B3 **Markazī** *prov.* Iran
227 G3 **Markdale** *Ont.* Can.
172 D4 **Markdorf** Ger.
164 F2 **Markelo** Neth.
213 F4 **Marken** S. Africa
164 E2 **Markermeer** *l.* Neth.
171 D5 **Markersdorf bei Burgstädt** Ger.
151 F2 **Market Bosworth** *Leicestershire, England* U.K.
151 G2 **Market Deeping** *Lincolnshire, England* U.K.
150 E2 **Market Drayton** *Shropshire, England* U.K.
151 G2 **Market Harborough** *Leicestershire, England* U.K.
147 E2 **Markethill** *Northern Ireland* U.K.
151 F3 **Market Lavington** *Wiltshire, England* U.K.
149 I4 **Market Rasen** *Lincolnshire, England* U.K.
149 H4 **Market Warsop** *Nottinghamshire, England* U.K.
149 I4 **Market Weighton** *East Riding of Yorkshire, England* U.K.
151 F2 **Markfield** *Leicestershire, England* U.K.
172 D3 **Markgröningen** Ger.
131 M3 **Markha** *r.* Rus. Fed.
224 E5 **Markham** *Ont.* Can.
263 K1 **Markham, Mount** Antarctica
121 H4 **Markhamet** Uzbek.
175 J3 **Marki** Pol.
137 J2 **Marki** Rus. Fed.
183 H1 **Markina-Xemein** Spain
146 E5 **Markinch** *Fife, Scotland* U.K.
171 E3 **Märkisch Buchholz** Ger.
110 B4 **Markit** *Xinjiang* China
140 M2 **Markitta** Sweden
137 J3 **Markivka** Ukr.
136 E3 **Markivka** *r.* Ukr.
171 D4 **Markkleeberg** Ger.
240 H2 **Markleeville** *CA* U.S.A.
232 D5 **Markleysburg** *PA* U.S.A.
173 G3 **Marklkofen** Ger.
168 E3 **Marklohe** Ger.
164 E2 **Marknesse** Neth.
171 D5 **Markneukirchen** Ger.
177 G4 **Márkó** Hungary
198 C3 **Markopoulo** Greece
208 C3 **Markounda** C.A.R.
179 H5 **Markovac Trojstveni** Croatia
131 S3 **Markovo** *Chukotskiy Avtonomnyy Okrug* Rus. Fed.
139 M3 **Markovo** *Ivanovskaya Oblast'* Rus. Fed.
137 H2 **Markovo** *Kurskaya Oblast'* Rus. Fed.
207 F3 **Markoye** Burkina
171 D4 **Markranstädt** Ger.
120 A2 **Marks** Rus. Fed.
237 F5 **Marks** *MS* U.S.A.
234 D2 **Marksboro** *NJ* U.S.A.
151 H3 **Marks Tey** *Essex, England* U.K.
169 F5 **Marksuhl** Ger.
237 E6 **Marksville** *LA* U.S.A.
179 H3 **Markt Allhau** Austria
173 E2 **Marktbergel** Ger.
173 E2 **Markt Berolzheim** Ger.
173 E2 **Markt Bibart** Ger.
173 E2 **Marktbreit** Ger.
173 E2 **Markt Erlbach** Ger.
179 G3 **Markt Hartmannsdorf** Austria
172 D2 **Marktheidenfeld** Ger.
173 F3 **Markt Indersdorf** Ger.
173 G3 **Marktl** Ger.
171 C5 **Marktleugast** Ger.
171 D5 **Marktleuthen** Ger.
173 E4 **Marktoberdorf** Ger.
173 E3 **Marktoffingen** Ger.
222 E5 **Marktosis** *B.C.* Can.
179 H3 **Markt Piesting** Austria
173 G1 **Marktredwitz** Ger.
173 E4 **Markt Rettenbach** Ger.
171 C5 **Marktrodach** Ger.
179 F2 **Markt St Florian** Austria
179 H3 **Markt St Martin** Austria
173 H4 **Marktschellenberg** Ger.
173 F3 **Markt Schwaben** Ger.
173 E2 **Marktseft** Ger.
173 E3 **Markt Wald** Ger.
175 K4 **Markuszów** Pol.
151 G3 **Markyate** *Hertfordshire, England* U.K.
169 C4 **Marl** Ger.
82 C1 **Marla** *S.A.* Austr.
87 C6 **Marlandy Hill** *hill W.A.* Austr.
234 C3 **Marlboro** *NJ* U.S.A.
235 D2 **Marlboro** *NJ* U.S.A.
235 E1 **Marlboro** *NY* U.S.A.
85 G4 **Marlborough** *Qld* Austr.
81 D4 **Marlborough** *admin. reg. South I.* N.Z.
151 F3 **Marlborough** *Wiltshire, England* U.K.
235 F1 **Marlborough** *CT* U.S.A.
233 H3 **Marlborough** *MA* U.S.A.
233 G3 **Marlborough** *NH* U.S.A.
151 F3 **Marlborough Downs** *hills England* U.K.
150 D4 **Marldon** *Devon, England* U.K.
156 D3 **Marle** France
191 G2 **Marlengo** Italy
157 H4 **Marlenheim** France
227 F4 **Marlette** *MI* U.S.A.
161 C3 **Marlhes** France
160 D2 **Marlieux** France
237 D6 **Marlin** *TX* U.S.A.
232 C5 **Marlinton** *WV* U.S.A.
171 C5 **Marlishausen** Ger.
83 G4 **Marlo** *Vic.* Austr.
170 D1 **Marlow** Ger.
151 G3 **Marlow** *Buckinghamshire, England* U.K.
234 D3 **Marlton** *NJ* U.S.A.
157 G3 **Marly** *Lorraine* France
156 D2 **Marly** *Nord - Pas-de-Calais* France
190 C2 **Marly** Switz.
156 C3 **Marly-la-Ville** France
114 B3 **Marmagao** *Goa* India
160 C2 **Marmagne** *Bourgogne* France
159 I4 **Marmagne** *Centre* France
163 C4 **Marmande** France
199 E1 **Marmara** Turkey
Marmara, Sea of *g.* Turkey *see* **Marmara Denizi**
199 E1 **Marmara Adası** *i.* Turkey
199 F1 **Marmara Denizi** *g.* Turkey
199 E1 **Marmaraereğlisi** Turkey
202 E2 **Marmarica** *reg.* Libya
199 F3 **Marmaris** Turkey
199 E2 **Marmaro** *Voreio Aigaio* Greece
236 C2 **Marmarth** *ND* U.S.A.
184 C2 **Marmelar** Port.
184 B1 **Marmeleira** Port.
184 B3 **Marmelete** Port.
251 F6 **Marmelos** *r.* Brazil
232 C5 **Marmet** *WV* U.S.A.
87 D6 **Marmion, Lake** *salt l. W.A.* Austr.
191 F3 **Marmirolo** Italy
191 G2 **Marmolada** *mt.* Italy
185 F2 **Marmolejo** Spain
190 C3 **Marmore** *r.* Italy
157 H4 **Marmoutier** France
160 D1 **Marnay** France
160 E2 **Marnaz** France
156 E3 **Marne** *dept Champagne-Ardenne* France
156 C4 **Marne** *r.* France
168 E2 **Marne** Ger.
157 F5 **Marne, Source de la** *tourist site* France
156 C4 **Marne-la-Vallée** France
129 D3 **Marneuli** Georgia
172 C2 **Marnheim** Ger.
150 E4 **Marnhull** *Dorset, England* U.K.
170 C2 **Marnitz** Ger.
83 E4 **Marnoo** *Vic.* Austr.
208 C2 **Maro** Chad
213 □K2 **Maroambihy** Madag.
213 □K2 **Maroantsetra** Madag.
257 H2 **Maroba** *r.* Brazil
194 D5 **Maroglio** *r. Sicilia* Italy
79 □3 **Marokau** *atoll Arch. des Tuamotu* Fr. Polynesia
80 E3 **Marokopa** *North I.* N.Z.
116 D2 **Marol** Jammu and Kashmir
213 □K4 **Marolambo** Madag.
169 F5 **Maroldsweisach** Ger.
159 G3 **Marolles-les-Braults** France
156 B3 **Maromme** France
213 □K2 **Maromokotro** *mt.* Madag.
213 F3 **Marondera** Zimbabwe
251 H3 **Maroni** *r.* Fr. Guiana
162 D3 **Maronne** *r.* France
85 H5 **Maroochydore** *Qld* Austr.
87 B4 **Maroonah** *W.A.* Austr.
239 F4 **Maroon Peak** *CO* U.S.A.
246 □ **Maroon Town** Jamaica
93 A4 **Maros** *Sulawesi Selatan* Indon.
93 A4 **Maros** *r.* Indon.
196 E2 **Maros** *r.* Romania
177 J5 **Maros-Körös Köze** *plain* Hungary
177 J5 **Maroslele** Hungary
191 G3 **Marostica** Italy
Marosvásárhely Romania *see* **Târgu Mureş**
79 □3 **Marotiri** *is Îs Australes* Fr. Polynesia
213 □K2 **Marotolana** Madag.
207 I4 **Maroua** Cameroon
158 D3 **Maroué** France
213 □J5 **Marovato** Madag.
213 □J3 **Marovoay** *Mahajanga* Madag.
213 □K3 **Marovoay** *Toamasina* Madag.
251 H3 **Marowijne** *r.* Suriname
172 B2 **Marpingen** Ger.
149 G4 **Marple** *Greater Manchester, England* U.K.
127 F4 **Marqādah** Syria
Marqaköl *l.* Kazakh. *see* **Markakol', Ozero**
108 B1 **Mar Qu** *r. Sichuan* China
215 F3 **Marquard** S. Africa
173 G4 **Marquartstein** Ger.
245 E5 **Marquelia** Mex.
Marquesas Islands Fr. Polynesia *see* **Marquises, Îles**
257 F5 **Marquês de Valença** Brazil
226 D2 **Marquette** *MI* U.S.A.
237 D6 **Marquez** *TX* U.S.A.
156 D2 **Marquion** France
156 B2 **Marquise** France
79 □3 **Marquises, Îles** *is* Fr. Polynesia
163 E6 **Marquixanes** France
83 E2 **Marra** *N.S.W.* Austr.
83 F2 **Marra** *r. N.S.W.* Austr.
202 E6 **Marra, Jebel** *mt.* Sudan
213 G5 **Marracuene** Moz.
191 G4 **Marradi** Italy
204 D3 **Marrakech** Morocco
Marrakesh Morocco *see* **Marrakech**
202 E6 **Marra Plateau** Sudan
83 F5 **Marrawah** *Tas.* Austr.
82 D2 **Marree** *S.A.* Austr.
237 F6 **Marrero** *LA* U.S.A.
213 G3 **Marromeu** Moz.
192 A5 **Marrubiu** *Sardegna* Italy
164 E1 **Marrum** Neth.
211 C8 **Marrupa** Moz.
82 C1 **Marryat** *S.A.* Austr.
161 A3 **Mars** *r.* France
232 C4 **Mars** *PA* U.S.A.
203 G3 **Marsa Alam** Egypt
202 C2 **Marsa al Burayqah** Libya
210 C4 **Marsabit** Kenya
160 B3 **Marsac-en-Livradois** France
158 E4 **Marsac-sur-Don** France
190 E4 **Marsaglia** Italy
157 G4 **Marsal** France
194 B5 **Marsala** *Sicilia* Italy
202 E2 **Marsa Matrûh** Egypt
160 C1 **Marsannay-la-Côte** France
161 C4 **Marsanne** France
206 B3 **Marsassoum** Senegal
195 □ **Marsaxlokk** Malta
169 D4 **Marsberg** Ger.
168 F2 **Marschacht** Ger.
193 E2 **Marsciano** Italy
83 F3 **Marsden** *N.S.W.* Austr.
223 I4 **Marsden** *Sask.* Can.
149 H4 **Marsden** *West Yorkshire, England* U.K.
164 D2 **Marsdiep** *sea chan.* Neth.
161 B5 **Marseillan** France
161 D5 **Marseille** France
Marseille *airport* France *see* **Provence**
156 B3 **Marseille-en-Beauvaisis** France
Marseilles France *see* **Marseille**
226 C5 **Marseilles** *IL* U.S.A.
140 K2 **Marsfjället** *mt.* Sweden
128 B5 **Marshah, Jabal** *mt.* Saudi Arabia
223 I4 **Marshall** *Sask.* Can.
237 E5 **Marshall** *AR* U.S.A.
230 C4 **Marshall** *IL* U.S.A.
226 E4 **Marshall** *MI* U.S.A.
236 E2 **Marshall** *MN* U.S.A.
236 E4 **Marshall** *MO* U.S.A.
231 D5 **Marshall** *NC* U.S.A.
237 E5 **Marshall** *TX* U.S.A.
232 E5 **Marshall** *VA* U.S.A.
266 F5 **Marshall Islands** *country* N. Pacific Ocean
234 C1 **Marshalls Creek** *PA* U.S.A.
234 C3 **Marshallton** *DE* U.S.A.
236 E3 **Marshalltown** *IA* U.S.A.
150 E3 **Marshfield** *South Gloucestershire, England* U.K.
237 E4 **Marshfield** *MO* U.S.A.
226 B3 **Marshfield** *WI* U.S.A.
231 E7 **Marsh Harbour** Bahamas
233 □J1 **Mars Hill** *ME* U.S.A.
222 C2 **Marsh Lake** *Y.T.* Can.
122 B2 **Marshūn** Iran
161 C5 **Marsillargues** France
238 C3 **Marsing** *ID* U.S.A.
149 H3 **Marske-by-the-Sea** *Redcar and Cleveland, England* U.K.
157 F3 **Mars-la-Tour** France
156 E4 **Marson** France
163 E5 **Marssac-sur-Tarn** France
143 G2 **Märsta** Sweden
142 D4 **Marstal** Denmark
190 E1 **Märstetten** Switz.
151 F3 **Marston** *Oxfordshire, England* U.K.
150 E4 **Marston Magna** *Somerset, England* U.K.
151 G2 **Marston Moretaine** *Bedfordshire, England* U.K.

Marsugalt to Mechtersen
333

78 □3a **Marsugalt** *i. Kwajalein* Marshall Is
117 F4 **Marsyangdi** *r.* Nepal
234 C4 **Marsyhope** *r. MD* U.S.A.
192 D2 **Marta** Italy
192 D2 **Marta** *r.* Italy
96 B3 **Martaban** Myanmar
96 B3 **Martaban, Gulf of** Myanmar
195 H2 **Martano** Italy
193 E2 **Martano, Monte** *mt.* Italy
95 F3 **Martapura** *Kalimantan Selatan* Indon.
94 D4 **Martapura** *Sumatera* Indon.
207 I3 **Marte** Nigeria
162 D4 **Martel** France
232 B4 **Martel** *OH* U.S.A.
162 D4 **Martel, Causse de** *hills* France
165 E5 **Martelange** Belgium
191 H3 **Martellago** Italy
191 F2 **Martello** Italy
177 J5 **Mártély** Hungary
224 E4 **Marten River** *Ont.* Can.
223 J4 **Martensville** *Sask.* Can.
187 C5 **Martés** *mt.* Spain
168 E3 **Martfeld** Ger.
177 J4 **Martfű** Hungary
151 I2 **Martham** *Norfolk, England* U.K.
233 H4 **Martha's Vineyard** *i. MA* U.S.A.
162 C3 **Marthon** France
246 C2 **Martí** Cuba
182 D4 **Martiago** Spain
191 I2 **Martignacco** Italy
163 B4 **Martignas-sur-Jalles** France
159 F4 **Martigné-Briand** France
158 E4 **Martigné-Ferchaud** France
159 F3 **Martigné-sur-Mayenne** France
190 C2 **Martigny** Switz.
160 C2 **Martigny-le-Comte** France
157 F4 **Martigny-les-Bains** France
157 F4 **Martigny-les-Gerbonvaux** France
183 F4 **Martiherrero** Spain
185 E5 **Martil** Morocco
163 B4 **Martillac** France
184 C3 **Martim Longo** Port.
182 E1 **Martimporra** Spain
Martim Vaz, Ilhas *is* S. Atlantic Ocean *see* Martin Vas, Ilhas
222 F2 **Martin** *r. N.W.T.* Can.
177 H2 **Martin** Slovakia
186 C3 **Martín** *r.* Spain
236 C3 **Martin** *SD* U.S.A.
195 G2 **Martina Franca** Italy
81 E4 **Martinborough** *North I.* N.Z.
182 B5 **Martinchel** Port.
185 F3 **Martín de la Jara** Spain
182 D4 **Martín de Yeltes** Spain
190 E3 **Martinengo** Italy
186 E2 **Martinet** Spain
245 F3 **Martínez** Mex.
240 F2 **Martinez** *CA* U.S.A.
231 D5 **Martinez** *GA* U.S.A.
241 J5 **Martinez Lake** *AZ* U.S.A.
169 F4 **Martinfeld** Ger.
182 B5 **Martingança** Port.
257 E3 **Martinho Campos** Brazil
247 □3 **Martinique** *terr.* West Indies
247 □2 **Martinique Passage** Dominica/Martinique
183 F3 **Martín Muñoz de las Posadas** Spain
198 C2 **Martino** Greece
256 B5 **Martinópolis** Brazil
262 Q2 **Martin Peninsula** Antarctica
179 G2 **Martinsberg** Austria
232 B4 **Martinsburg** *OH* U.S.A.
232 D4 **Martinsburg** *PA* U.S.A.
232 E5 **Martinsburg** *WV* U.S.A.
234 C2 **Martins Creek** *PA* U.S.A.
234 C1 **Martins Creek** *r. PA* U.S.A.
232 C4 **Martins Ferry** *OH* U.S.A.
193 F2 **Martinsicuro** Italy
147 C4 **Martinstown** Rep. of Ireland
230 C4 **Martinsville** *IN* U.S.A.
232 D6 **Martinsville** *VA* U.S.A.
264 H7 **Martin Vas, Ilhas** *is* S. Atlantic Ocean
Martin Vaz Islands S. Atlantic Ocean *see* Martin Vas, Ilhas
192 A4 **Martis** *Sardegna* Italy
159 H5 **Martizay** France
151 I2 **Martlesham** *Suffolk, England* U.K.
150 E2 **Martley** *Worcestershire, England* U.K.
150 E4 **Martock** *Somerset, England* U.K.
Martök Kazakh. *see* **Martuk**
80 E4 **Marton** *North I.* N.Z.
177 H4 **Martonvásar** Hungary
186 E3 **Martorell** Spain
185 G3 **Martos** Spain
163 D5 **Martres-Tolosane** France
141 M3 **Marttila** Fin.
120 D2 **Martuk** Kazakh.
129 D3 **Martuni** Armenia
129 C2 **Martvili** Georgia
137 G2 **Martynivka** Ukr.
136 E2 **Martynovychi** Ukr.
207 G3 **Maru** Nigeria
103 F6 **Marugame** Japan
183 F4 **Marugán** Spain
195 G2 **Maruggio** Italy
81 D4 **Maruia** *r. South I.* N.Z.
254 F4 **Maruim** Brazil
105 E2 **Maruko** Japan
83 G3 **Marulan** *N.S.W.* Austr.
261 F2 **Marull** Arg.
164 F1 **Marum** Neth.
78 □5 **Marum, Mount** *vol.* Vanuatu
122 B4 **Mārūn** *r.* Iran
104 C2 **Maruoka** Japan
175 J4 **Maruszów** Pol.
175 J5 **Maruszów** Pol.
79 □3 **Marutea** *atoll Arch. des Tuamotu* Fr. Polynesia
79 □3 **Marutea** *atoll Arch. des Tuamotu* Fr. Polynesia
104 A3 **Maruyama-gawa** *r.* Japan
184 C1 **Marvão** Port.
122 C4 **Marvast** Iran
122 C4 **Marv Dasht** Iran
161 B4 **Marvejols** France
87 C6 **Marvel Loch** *W.A.* Austr.
157 F3 **Marville** France
241 L2 **Marvine, Mount** *UT* U.S.A.
116 C4 **Marwar Junction** *Rajasthan* India
223 I4 **Marwayne** *Alta* Can.
173 E3 **Marxheim** Ger.
Marxwalde Ger. *see* Neuhardenberg
172 C3 **Marxzell** Ger.
84 B2 **Mary** *r. N.T.* Austr.
85 H5 **Mary** *r. Qld* Austr.
86 E3 **Mary** *r. W.A.* Austr.
123 E2 **Mary** Turkm.
175 M5 **Mar"yanivka** Ukr.
137 I4 **Mar"yanivka** Ukr.
136 D2 **Mar"yanivka** Ukr.
137 J5 **Mar'yanskaya** Rus. Fed.
Mary A.S.S.R. *aut. rep.* Rus. Fed. *see* **Mariy El, Respublika**
146 D4 **Marybank** *Highland, Scotland* U.K.
85 H5 **Maryborough** *Qld* Austr.
83 E4 **Maryborough** *Vic.* Austr.
214 D3 **Marydale** S. Africa
234 C3 **Marydel** *MD* U.S.A.
120 B1 **Mar'yevka** Rus. Fed.
146 □G1 **Maryfield** *Shetland, Scotland* U.K.
137 I4 **Mar"yinka** Ukr.
Maryino Rus. Fed. *see* **Pristen'**
137 H4 **Mar"yivka** Ukr.
146 F5 **Marykirk** *Aberdeenshire, Scotland* U.K.
234 B4 **Maryland** *state* U.S.A.
234 B3 **Maryland Line** *MD* U.S.A.
Mary Oblast *admin. div.* Turkm. *see* **Maryyskaya Oblast'**
146 E4 **Marypark** *Moray, Scotland* U.K.
149 F3 **Maryport** *Cumbria, England* U.K.
225 K2 **Mary's Harbour** *Nfld.* Can.
225 K4 **Marystown** *Nfld.* Can.
241 K2 **Marysvale** *UT* U.S.A.
83 F4 **Marysville** *Vic.* Austr.
225 H4 **Marysville** *N.B.* Can.
240 G2 **Marysville** *CA* U.S.A.
236 D4 **Marysville** *KS* U.S.A.
227 F4 **Marysville** *MI* U.S.A.
232 B4 **Marysville** *OH* U.S.A.
234 B2 **Marysville** *PA* U.S.A.
238 B1 **Marysville** *WA* U.S.A.
84 C5 **Maryvale** *N.T.* Austr.
85 F3 **Maryvale** *Qld* Austr.
236 E3 **Maryville** *MO* U.S.A.
231 D5 **Maryville** *TN* U.S.A.
146 F4 **Marywell** *Aberdeenshire, Scotland* U.K.
122 E2 **Maryyskaya Oblast'** *admin. div.* Turkm.
191 G4 **Marzabotto** Italy
256 C2 **Marzagão** Brazil
171 D3 **Marzahna** Ger.
171 D3 **Marzahne** Ger.
195 E6 **Marzamemi** *Sicilia* Italy
158 D4 **Marzan** France
191 G4 **Marzeno** *r.* Italy
173 F3 **Marzling** Ger.
160 B2 **Marzy** France
183 G2 **Masa** Spain
242 □I7 **Masachapa** Nic.
128 B4 **Masada** *tourist site* Israel
Más Afuera *i.* S. Pacific Ocean *see* **Alejandro Selkirk, Isla**
122 C4 **Masāhūn, Kūh-e** *mt.* Iran
211 B5 **Masai Mara National Reserve** *nature res.* Kenya
192 A5 **Masainas** *Sardegna* Italy
211 C6 **Masai Steppe** *plain* Tanz.
210 A5 **Masaka** Uganda
215 F4 **Masakhane** S. Africa
187 C5 **Masalavés** Spain
129 F4 **Masallı** Azer.
93 B3 **Masamba** *Sulawesi Selatan* Indon.
93 B3 **Masamba** *mt.* Indon.
101 D6 **Masan** S. Korea
137 H5 **Masandra** Ukr.
211 C7 **Masasi** Tanz.
Más á Tierra *i.* S. Pacific Ocean *see* **Robinson Crusoe, Isla**
253 E4 **Masavi** Bol.
242 □I7 **Masaya** Nic.
242 □I6 **Masaya, Volcán** *vol.* Nic.
92 B3 **Masbate** Phil.
92 B3 **Masbate** *i.* Phil.
163 E5 **Mas-Cabardès** France
195 E5 **Mascali** *Sicilia* Italy
195 E5 **Mascalucia** *Sicilia* Italy
205 F2 **Mascara** Alg.
183 G5 **Mascaraque** Spain
265 H6 **Mascarene Basin** *sea feature* Indian Ocean
265 H6 **Mascarene Plain** *sea feature* Indian Ocean
265 H5 **Mascarene Ridge** *sea feature* Indian Ocean
182 C3 **Mascarenhas** Port.
260 D2 **Mascasín, Salina de** *salt pan* Arg.
193 H4 **Maschito** Italy
163 D4 **Masclat** France
244 B3 **Mascota** Mex.
244 B3 **Mascota** *r.* Mex.
230 F2 **Mascouche** *Que.* Can.
186 C2 **Mascún** *r.* Spain
186 D4 **Mas de Barberans** Spain
186 C4 **Mas de las Matas** Spain
183 H4 **Masegosa** Spain
185 H2 **Masegoso** Spain
183 H4 **Masegoso de Tajuña** Spain
172 D3 **Maselheim** Ger.
210 B4 **Maseno** Kenya
190 D2 **Masera** Italy
178 D5 **Maserada sul Piave** Italy
215 F3 **Maseru** Lesotho
157 G5 **Masevaux** France
141 I3 **Masfjorden** Norway
163 D5 **Mas-Grenier** France
Mashaba Zimbabwe *see* Mashava
149 H3 **Masham** *North Yorkshire, England* U.K.
108 D4 **Mashan** *Guangxi* China
213 F4 **Mashava** Zimbabwe
116 D2 **Masherbrum** *mt.* Jammu and Kashmir
137 G1 **Masheve** Ukr.
122 D2 **Mashhad** Iran
116 C4 **Mashi** *r.* India
122 A2 **Mashīrān** Iran
137 H3 **Mashivka** Ukr.
123 E5 **Mashket** *r.* Pak.
123 E5 **Māshkīd** *r.* Iran
213 F3 **Mashonaland Central** *prov.* Zimbabwe
213 F3 **Mashonaland East** *prov.* Zimbabwe
213 F3 **Mashonaland West** *prov.* Zimbabwe
Mashtagi Azer. *see* **Maştağa**
242 C3 **Masiáca** Mex.
215 F4 **Masibambane** S. Africa
182 B2 **Maside** Spain
215 F3 **Masilo** S. Africa
209 C6 **Masi-Manimba** Dem. Rep. Congo
210 A4 **Masindi** Uganda
92 A3 **Masinloc** Phil.
190 E2 **Masino** *r.* Italy
214 D4 **Masinyusane** S. Africa
Masira, Gulf of Oman *see* Maşīrah, Khalīj
125 G3 **Maşīrah, Jazīrat** *i.* Oman
125 G4 **Maşīrah, Khalīj** *b.* Oman
Masira Island Oman *see* Maşīrah, Jazīrat
129 D3 **Masis** Armenia
252 B2 **Masisea** Peru
191 G4 **Masi Torello** Italy
93 D3 **Masiwang** *r. Maluku* Indon.
215 G3 **Masjaing** S. Africa
122 B4 **Masjed Soleymān** Iran
147 B3 **Mask, Lough** *l.* Rep. of Ireland
128 D1 **Maskanah** Syria
122 D5 **Maskūtān** Iran
163 B5 **Maslacq** France
177 K5 **Maşloc** Romania
137 I2 **Maslova Pristan'** Rus. Fed.
137 J2 **Maslovka** Rus. Fed.
175 H4 **Masłowice** Pol.
182 C1 **Masma** *r.* Spain
125 E5 **Masna'ah** Yemen
191 G2 **Maso** *r.* Italy
213 □K2 **Masoala, Tanjona** *c.* Madag.
226 E4 **Mason** *MI* U.S.A.
232 A5 **Mason** *OH* U.S.A.
237 D6 **Mason** *TX* U.S.A.
226 B2 **Mason** *WI* U.S.A.
232 B5 **Mason** *WV* U.S.A.
87 C5 **Mason, Lake** *salt flat W.A.* Austr.
236 E3 **Mason City** *IA* U.S.A.
226 C5 **Mason City** *IL* U.S.A.
190 D4 **Masone** Italy
81 D5 **Masons Flat** *South I.* N.Z.
232 D5 **Masontown** *PA* U.S.A.
232 D5 **Masontown** *WV* U.S.A.
Masqaţ Oman *see* **Muscat**
125 G3 **Masqaţ** *governorate* Oman
190 F4 **Massa** Italy
233 G3 **Massachusetts** *state* U.S.A.
233 H3 **Massachusetts Bay** *MA* U.S.A.
190 F5 **Massaciuccoli, Lago di** *l.* Italy
241 M1 **Massadona** *CO* U.S.A.
190 E4 **Massa e Carrara** *prov. Toscana* Italy
191 H4 **Massa Fiscaglia** Italy
195 G2 **Massafra** Italy
202 B6 **Massaguet** Chad
161 B4 **Mas-St-Chély** France
202 B6 **Massakory** Chad
191 G4 **Massa Lombarda** Italy
193 G4 **Massa Lubrense** Italy
187 C5 **Massamagrell** Spain
192 C1 **Massa Marittimo** Italy
193 E2 **Massa Martana** Italy
208 A5 **Massana** Gabon
213 G4 **Massangena** Moz.
209 C7 **Massango** Angola
213 G2 **Massangulo** Moz.
235 E2 **Massapequa** *NY* U.S.A.
190 F5 **Massarosa** Italy
163 D6 **Massat** France
203 H6 **Massawa** Eritrea
203 H5 **Massawa Channel** Eritrea
159 H4 **Massay** France
169 F5 **Maßbach** Ger.
171 E4 **Massen** Ger.
233 F2 **Massena** *NY* U.S.A.
208 C2 **Massenya** Chad
162 D3 **Masseret** France
195 G2 **Masseria Risana** *hill* Italy
222 C4 **Masset** *B.C.* Can.
163 C5 **Masseube** France
224 D4 **Massey** *Ont.* Can.
234 C3 **Massey** *MD* U.S.A.
161 B3 **Massiac** France
193 F3 **Massico, Monte** *hill* Italy
232 B5 **Massieville** *OH* U.S.A.
161 B3 **Massif Central** *mts* France
206 D4 **Massigui** Mali
Massilia France *see* **Marseille**
232 C4 **Massillon** *OH* U.S.A.
190 D4 **Massimino** Italy
206 D3 **Massina** Mali
173 G3 **Massing** Ger.
227 J3 **Masson** *Que.* Can.
192 C2 **Massoncello, Monte** *hill* Italy
263 G2 **Masson Island** Antarctica
156 C4 **Massy** France
129 F3 **Maştağa** Azer.
169 C5 **Mastershausen** Ger.
81 E4 **Masterton** *North I.* N.Z.
235 F2 **Mastic** *NY* U.S.A.
235 F2 **Mastic Beach** *NY* U.S.A.
246 C1 **Mastic Point** *Andros* Bahamas
144 J1 **Mastrevik** Norway
123 H2 **Mastuj** Pak.
123 F4 **Mastung** Pak.
124 B3 **Mastūrah** Saudi Arabia
138 E5 **Masty** Belarus
192 A5 **Masua** *Sardegna* Italy
103 E6 **Masuda** Japan
Masuku Gabon *see* **Franceville**
Masulipatam *Andhra Prad.* India *see* **Machilipatnam**
192 A5 **Masullas** *Sardegna* Italy
Masuna *i.* American Samoa *see* **Tutuila**
94 C3 **Masurai, Bukit** *mt.* Indon.
213 F4 **Masvingo** Zimbabwe
213 F4 **Masvingo** *prov.* Zimbabwe
211 B5 **Maswe** Tanz.
128 C2 **Maşyāf** Syria
136 B2 **Masyevichy** Belarus
174 C3 **Maszewo** *Lubuskie* Pol.
174 F1 **Maszewo** *Pomorskie* Pol.
174 D2 **Maszewo** *Zachodniopomorskie* Pol.
196 D5 **Mat** *r.* Albania
96 D3 **Mat, Nam** *r.* Laos
80 G2 **Mata** *r. North I.* N.Z.
251 E3 **Mata, Serranía de** *mts* Venez.
213 E3 **Matabeleland North** *prov.* Zimbabwe
213 F4 **Matabeleland South** *prov.* Zimbabwe
117 G4 **Matabhanga** *W. Bengal* India
183 G3 **Matabuena** Spain
184 D2 **Matachel** *r.* Spain
224 D4 **Matachewan** *Ont.* Can.
209 B6 **Matadi** Dem. Rep. Congo
237 C5 **Matador** *TX* U.S.A.
186 F3 **Matagalls** *mt.* Spain
242 □I6 **Matagalpa** Nic.
224 E3 **Matagami** *Que.* Can.
224 E3 **Matagami, Lac** *l. Que.* Can.
237 D6 **Matagorda** *TX* U.S.A.
254 F4 **Mata Grande** Brazil
80 E3 **Matahiwi** *North I.* N.Z.
Mataigou *Ningxia* China *see* **Taole**
80 F2 **Matakana Island** *North I.* N.Z.
81 D4 **Matakitaki** *South I.* N.Z.
209 B8 **Matala** Angola
184 D3 **Matalascañas** Spain
114 D5 **Matale** Sri Lanka
183 H3 **Matalebreras** Spain
214 E3 **Mataleng** S. Africa
124 C2 **Maţāli', Jabal** *hill* Saudi Arabia
183 E2 **Matallana de Valmadrigal** Spain
206 B3 **Matam** Senegal
183 H3 **Matamala de Almazán** Spain
80 E2 **Matamata** *North I.* N.Z.
214 C1 **Mata-Mata** S. Africa
80 F4 **Matamau** *North I.* N.Z.
207 H3 **Matamey** Niger
234 D1 **Matamoras** *PA* U.S.A.
242 E3 **Matamoros** *Coahuila* Mex.
243 F3 **Matamoros** *Tamaulipas* Mex.
183 F2 **Matamorosa** Spain
182 B5 **Mata Mourisca** Port.
211 C7 **Matandu** *r.* Tanz.
225 H3 **Matane** *Que.* Can.
213 □J4 **Matanga** Madag.
80 E2 **Matangi** *North I.* N.Z.
246 B2 **Matanzas** Cuba
256 C4 **Matão** Brazil
254 C4 **Matão, Serra do** *hills* Brazil
174 G5 **Mata Panew** *r.* Pol.
183 F2 **Mataporquera** Spain
183 F3 **Matapozuelos** Spain
260 A4 **Mataquito** *r.* Chile
114 D5 **Matara** Sri Lanka
198 B2 **Mataragka** Greece
95 G5 **Mataram** *Lombok* Indon.
Matarånga Greece *see* **Mataragka**
252 B4 **Matarani** Peru
84 C2 **Mataranka** *N.T.* Austr.
186 F3 **Mataró** Spain
80 E3 **Mataroa** *North I.* N.Z.
93 B3 **Matarombea** *r.* Indon.
186 D3 **Matarraña** *r.* Spain
196 E4 **Mataruška Banja** *Srbija* Yugo.
215 G4 **Matatiele** S. Africa
116 D4 **Matatila Dam** India
80 E3 **Matau** *North I.* N.Z.
81 B7 **Mataura** *South I.* N.Z.
81 B7 **Mataura** *r. South I.* N.Z.
77 I3 **Matā'utu** Wallis and Futuna Is
78 □2 **Matavanu, Mount** *vol.* Samoa
80 F3 **Matawai** *North I.* N.Z.
80 D1 **Matawaia** *North I.* N.Z.
235 D2 **Matawan** *NJ* U.S.A.
230 F2 **Matawin** *r. Que.* Can.
121 I3 **Matay** Kazakh.
253 E3 **Mategua** Bol.
244 D2 **Matehuala** Mex.
197 G2 **Matei** Romania
191 I5 **Matelica** Italy
247 □7 **Matelot** Trin. and Tob.
211 C7 **Matemanga** Tanz.
80 E3 **Matemateaonga Range** *hills North I.* N.Z.
213 G2 **Matenge** Moz.
195 F2 **Matera** Italy
193 I4 **Matera** *prov. Basilicata* Italy
193 G3 **Matese, Monti del** *mts* Italy
177 L4 **Mátészalka** Hungary
205 H1 **Mateur** Tunisia
257 E3 **Mateus Leme** Brazil
232 B6 **Matewan** *WV* U.S.A.
162 B3 **Matha** France
160 E1 **Mathay** France
224 D3 **Matheson** *Ont.* Can.
233 E6 **Mathews** *VA* U.S.A.
190 C3 **Mathi** Italy
232 D5 **Mathias** *WV* U.S.A.
113 □1 **Mathidahura** *i. N. Male* Maldives
237 D6 **Mathis** *TX* U.S.A.
83 F3 **Mathoura** *N.S.W.* Austr.
116 D4 **Mathura** *Uttar Prad.* India
92 C5 **Mati** Phil.
207 F3 **Matiacoali** Burkina
117 G4 **Matiali** *W. Bengal* India
109 E3 **Matianxu** *Hunan* China
123 G5 **Matiari** Pak.
257 F4 **Matias Barbosa** Brazil
254 E5 **Matias Cardoso** Brazil
245 G5 **Matías Romero** Mex.
213 I2 **Matibane** Moz.
158 D3 **Matignon** France
156 D3 **Matigny** France
225 H2 **Matimekosh** *Que.* Can.
195 H2 **Matino** Italy
108 B1 **Matizi** *Sichuan* China
214 C5 **Matjiesfontein** S. Africa
129 C2 **Mat'khoji** Georgia
117 G5 **Matla** *r.* India
123 G5 **Matli** Pak.
149 H4 **Matlock** *Derbyshire, England* U.K.
149 H4 **Matlock Bath** *Derbyshire, England* U.K.
215 F2 **Matlwangtlwang** S. Africa
251 E3 **Mato** *r.* Venez.
251 E3 **Mato, Cerro** *mt.* Venez.
232 C6 **Matoaka** *WV* U.S.A.
213 F4 **Matobo Hills** Zimbabwe
256 A2 **Mato Grosso** *state* Brazil
254 B5 **Mato Grosso, Planalto do** *plat.* Brazil
256 A4 **Mato Grosso do Sul** *state* Brazil
Matopo Hills Zimbabwe *see* **Matobo Hills**
252 D3 **Matos** *r.* Bol.
182 B3 **Matosinhos** Port.
Matou *Guangxi* China *see* Pingguo
160 C2 **Matour** France
257 E3 **Matozinhos** Brazil
177 I4 **Mátra** *mts* Hungary
177 J4 **Matraballa** Hungary
125 G3 **Maţraḩ** Oman
177 I3 **Mátraterenye** Hungary
177 I4 **Mátraverebély** Hungary
178 C3 **Matrei am Brenner** Austria
178 D3 **Matrei in Osttirol** Austria
214 B5 **Matroosberg** S. Africa
214 B5 **Matroosberg** *mt.* S. Africa
215 F1 **Matrooster** S. Africa
126 B5 **Matrûh** *governorate* Egypt
147 E3 **Matry** Rep. of Ireland
214 D3 **Matsap** S. Africa
129 A2 **Matsesta** Rus. Fed.
213 □J4 **Matsiatra** *r.* Madag.
104 B4 **Matsubara** Japan
105 F3 **Matsuda** Japan
105 F3 **Matsudo** Japan
103 F6 **Matsue** Japan
105 D2 **Matsumoto** Japan
104 C4 **Matsusaka** Japan
109 G3 **Matsu Tao** *i.* Taiwan
103 D7 **Matsuura** Japan
103 F7 **Matsuyama** Japan
190 E2 **Matt** Switz.
224 D3 **Mattagami** *r. Ont.* Can.
157 G4 **Mattaincourt** France
261 E4 **Mattaldi** Arg.
224 E4 **Mattawa** *Ont.* Can.
233 □I2 **Mattawamkeag** *ME* U.S.A.
190 C3 **Matterhorn** *mt.* Italy/Switz.
238 D3 **Matterhorn** *mt. NV* U.S.A.
179 H3 **Mattersburg** Austria
Matthew *atoll Gilbert Is* Kiribati *see* **Marakei**
77 H4 **Matthew Island** S. Pacific Ocean
231 D5 **Matthews** *NC* U.S.A.
210 C4 **Matthews Peak** Kenya
246 D2 **Matthew Town** *Gt Inagua* Bahamas
125 F3 **Maţţī, Sabkhat** *salt pan* Saudi Arabia
178 E2 **Mattighofen** Austria
193 I3 **Mattinata** Italy
151 I2 **Mattishall** *Norfolk, England* U.K.
235 F2 **Mattituck** *NY* U.S.A.
140 K3 **Mattmar** Sweden
104 C2 **Mattō** Japan
236 F4 **Mattoon** *IL* U.S.A.
178 E3 **Mattsee** Austria
178 E3 **Mattsee** *l.* Austria
141 K3 **Mattsmyra** Sweden
140 M2 **Måttsund** Sweden
Matturai Sri Lanka *see* **Matara**
252 A2 **Matucana** Peru
114 D5 **Matugama** Sri Lanka
79 □1 **Matuku** *i.* Fiji
191 J3 **Matulji** Croatia
209 C8 **Matumbo** Angola
Matun Afgh. *see* **Khowst**
251 F2 **Maturín** Venez.
183 H3 **Matute** *mt.* Spain
257 E3 **Matutina** Brazil
120 C1 **Matveyevka** Rus. Fed.
137 J4 **Matveyev Kurgan** Rus. Fed.
137 F4 **Matviyivka** *Mykolayivs'ka Oblast'* Ukr.
137 H4 **Matviyivka** *Zaporiz'ka Oblast'* Ukr.
215 F3 **Matwabeng** S. Africa
137 J1 **Matyra** *r.* Rus. Fed.
139 L5 **Matyrskiy** Rus. Fed.
139 L5 **Matyrskoye Vodokhranilishche** *resr* Rus. Fed.
116 D4 **Mau** *Madh. Prad.* India
116 E4 **Mau** *Uttar Prad.* India
117 E4 **Mau** *Uttar Prad.* India
213 H2 **Maúa** Moz.
116 E4 **Mau Aimma** *Uttar Prad.* India
186 D2 **Maubermé, Pic de** *mt.* France/Spain
156 E3 **Maubert-Fontaine** France
156 D2 **Maubeuge** France
115 G2 **Maubin** Myanmar
163 C5 **Maubourguet** France
162 A3 **Maubuisson** France
146 D6 **Mauchline** *East Ayrshire, Scotland* U.K.
146 F4 **Maud** *Aberdeenshire, Scotland* U.K.
87 B4 **Maud, Point** *W.A.* Austr.
116 E4 **Maudaha** *Uttar Prad.* India
83 F3 **Maude** *N.S.W.* Austr.
264 J10 **Maud Seamount** *sea feature* S. Atlantic Ocean
179 H2 **Mauerbach** Austria
178 E2 **Mauerkirchen** Austria
173 F3 **Mauern** Ger.
173 E4 **Mauerstetten** Ger.
251 G5 **Maués** *r.* Brazil
116 E4 **Mauganj** *Madh. Prad.* India
91 K2 **Maug Islands** N. Mariana Is
161 C5 **Mauguio** France
240 □C8 **Maui** *i. HI* U.S.A.
81 □2 **Mauke** *i.* Cook Is
172 C3 **Maulbronn** Ger.
157 H5 **Maulburg** Ger.
162 D3 **Maulde** *r.* France
151 G2 **Maulden** *Bedfordshire, England* U.K.
260 B4 **Maule** Chile
260 A4 **Maule** *admin. reg.* Chile
260 A4 **Maule** *r.* Chile
260 B5 **Maule, Lago del** *l.* Chile
162 B2 **Mauléon** France
163 C6 **Mauléon-Barousse** France
163 B5 **Mauléon-d'Armagnac** France
163 B5 **Mauléon-Licharre** France
159 F4 **Maulévrier** France
259 B6 **Maullín** Chile
117 G4 **Maulvi Bazar** Bangl.
147 B2 **Maumakeogh** *hill* Rep. of Ireland
80 E2 **Maumaupaki** *hill North I.* N.Z.
232 B4 **Maumee** *OH* U.S.A.
232 B4 **Maumee** *r. OH* U.S.A.
147 B3 **Maumturk Mountains** *hills* Rep. of Ireland
212 D3 **Maun** Botswana
247 □1 **Maunabo** Puerto Rico
240 □D9 **Mauna Kea** *vol. HI* U.S.A.
240 □C8 **Mauna Loa** *HI* U.S.A.
240 □D9 **Mauna Loa** *vol. HI* U.S.A.
213 E4 **Maunatlala** Botswana
80 F3 **Maungaharuru Range** *mts North I.* N.Z.
80 F3 **Maungahaumi** *mt. North I.* N.Z.
80 F3 **Maungapohatu** *mt. North I.* N.Z.
80 E3 **Maungarau** *hill North I.* N.Z.
80 F3 **Maungataniwha** *mt. North I.* N.Z.
80 E1 **Maungatapere** *North I.* N.Z.
80 E2 **Maungaturoto** *North I.* N.Z.
96 A2 **Maungdaw** Myanmar
97 B4 **Maungmagan Islands** Myanmar
79 □3 **Maupihaa** *atoll Arch. de la Société* Fr. Polynesia
238 B2 **Maupin** *OR* U.S.A.
142 D1 **Maura** Norway
116 D4 **Mau Rampur** *Uttar Prad.* India
116 E4 **Maurawan** *Uttar Prad.* India
158 E4 **Maure-de-Bretagne** France
163 E6 **Maureillas-las-Illas** France
162 C4 **Maurens** France
237 F6 **Maurepas, Lake** *LA* U.S.A.
161 E5 **Maures, Massif des** *hills* France
252 C4 **Mauri** *r.* Bol.
163 B4 **Mauriac** *Aquitaine* France
162 E3 **Mauriac** *Auvergne* France
Maurice *country* Indian Ocean *see* **Mauritius**
234 C3 **Maurice** *r. NJ* U.S.A.
82 B2 **Maurice, Lake** *salt flat S.A.* Austr.
234 D3 **Mauricetown** *NJ* U.S.A.
164 E3 **Maurik** Neth.
204 C6 **Mauritania** *country* Africa
Mauritanie *country* Africa *see* Mauritania
217 □1b **Mauritius** *country* Indian Ocean
193 G3 **Mauro, Monte** *mt.* Italy
158 D3 **Mauron** France
182 C3 **Mauros** *mt.* Spain
163 D4 **Mauroux** France
163 E4 **Maurs** France
163 E6 **Maury** France
234 B2 **Mausdale** *PA* U.S.A.
161 C5 **Maussanne-les-Alpilles** France
226 B4 **Mauston** *WI* U.S.A.
179 G2 **Mautern an der Donau** Austria
179 E3 **Mauterndorf** Austria
179 F3 **Mautern in Steiermark** Austria
173 H3 **Mauth** Ger.
179 F2 **Mauthausen** Austria
178 E4 **Mauthen** Austria
Mauti *i.* Cook Is *see* **Mauke**
157 F4 **Mauvages** France
161 C3 **Mauves** France
163 C5 **Mauvezin** France
162 B2 **Mauzé-sur-le-Mignon** France
251 E4 **Mavaca** *r.* Venez.
211 C8 **Mavago** Moz.
209 C9 **Mavengue** Angola
199 G3 **Mavikent** Turkey
209 D8 **Mavinga** Angola
232 B6 **Mavisdale** *VA* U.S.A.
213 G3 **Mavita** Moz.
193 F2 **Mavone** *r.* Italy
198 B1 **Mavrodendri** *Dytiki Makedonia* Greece
198 C1 **Mavrothalassa** Greece
215 F4 **Mavuya** S. Africa
95 F2 **Mawa, Bukit** *mt.* Indon.
124 D3 **Māwān, Khashm** *hill* Saudi Arabia
116 D3 **Mawana** *Uttar Prad.* India
209 C6 **Mawanga** Dem. Rep. Congo
109 F3 **Mawei** *Fujian* China
81 C5 **Mawheraiti** *South I.* N.Z.
Māwheranui *r. South I.* N.Z. *see* Grey
124 D5 **Māwiyah** Yemen
128 B4 **Mawjib, Wādī al** *r.* Jordan
96 A2 **Mawlaik** Myanmar
Mawlamyaing Myanmar *see* Moulmein
Mawlamyine Myanmar *see* Moulmein
150 B4 **Mawnan** *Cornwall, England* U.K.
117 G4 **Mawphlang** *Meghalaya* India
124 C2 **Mawqaq** Saudi Arabia
203 I6 **Mawshij** Yemen
263 E2 **Mawson** *research stn* Antarctica
263 E2 **Mawson Coast** Antarctica
263 E2 **Mawson Escarpment** Antarctica
263 K2 **Mawson Peninsula** Antarctica
97 B5 **Maw Taung** *mt.* Myanmar
124 C5 **Mawza** Yemen
236 C2 **Max** *ND* U.S.A.
234 C2 **Maxatawny** *PA* U.S.A.
158 D4 **Maxent** France
173 G2 **Maxhütte-Haidhof** Ger.
192 A5 **Maxia, Punta** *mt. Sardegna* Italy
182 C5 **Maxieira** Port.
261 G3 **Máximo Paz** Arg.
197 H3 **Măxineni** Romania
213 G4 **Maxixe** Moz.
140 M3 **Maxmo** Fin.
169 C5 **Maxsain** Ger.
233 F2 **Maxville** *Ont.* Can.
80 E3 **Maxwell** *North I.* N.Z.
85 E4 **Maxwelton** *Qld* Austr.
86 D3 **May** *r. W.A.* Austr.
146 F5 **May, Isle of** *i. Scotland* U.K.
131 O3 **Maya** *r.* Rus. Fed.
186 B1 **Maya** Spain
137 H3 **Mayachka** Ukr.
135 K5 **Mayachnyy** Rus. Fed.
246 D2 **Mayaguana** *i.* Bahamas
247 □1 **Mayagüez** Puerto Rico
207 G3 **Mayahi** Niger
120 C2 **Mayak** Rus. Fed.
Mayakovskiy Georgia *see* Baghdat'i
123 G2 **Mayakovskogo** *mt.* Tajik.
Mayakovskogo, Pik *mt.* Tajik. *see* **Mayakovskogo**
121 G4 **Mayakum** Kazakh.
136 E3 **Mayaky** Ukr.
Mayals Spain *see* **Maials**
209 B5 **Mayama** Congo
122 C2 **Mayamey** Iran
243 H5 **Maya Mountains** Belize/Guat.
108 D3 **Mayang** *Hunan* China
Mayaqum Kazakh. *see* Mayakum
146 E5 **Mayar** *hill Scotland* U.K.
246 D2 **Mayarí** Cuba
104 B4 **Maya-san** *hill* Japan
102 I4 **Maya-san** *mt.* Japan
238 E3 **Maybell** *CO* U.S.A.
232 C6 **Maybeury** *WV* U.S.A.
146 D6 **Maybole** *South Ayrshire, Scotland* U.K.
235 D1 **Maybrook** *NY* U.S.A.
210 C1 **Maych'ew** Eth.
123 G3 **Maydā Shahr** Afgh.
83 F5 **Maydena** *Tas.* Austr.
210 E2 **Maydh** Somalia
Maydos Turkey *see* **Eceabat**
169 C5 **Mayen** Ger.
159 F3 **Mayenne** France
159 F3 **Mayenne** *dept Pays de la Loire* France
159 F4 **Mayenne** *r.* France
241 K4 **Mayer** *AZ* U.S.A.
111 D5 **Mayêr Kangri** *mt. Xizang* China
237 F5 **Mayersville** *MS* U.S.A.
222 H4 **Mayerthorpe** *Alta* Can.
159 G4 **Mayet** France
125 D5 **Mayfa'ah** Yemen
81 C5 **Mayfield** *South I.* N.Z.
149 H4 **Mayfield** *Staffordshire, England* U.K.
237 F4 **Mayfield** *KY* U.S.A.
234 C1 **Mayfield** *PA* U.S.A.
241 L2 **Mayfield** *UT* U.S.A.
106 D2 **Mayhan** Mongolia
239 F5 **Mayhill** *NM* U.S.A.
100 D3 **Mayi** *r.* China
121 H2 **Maykain** Kazakh.
123 G2 **Maykhura** Tajik.
129 B1 **Maykop** Rus. Fed.
134 K4 **Maykor** Rus. Fed.
121 H4 **Mayluu-Suu** Kyrg.
Mayly-Say Kyrg. *see* Mayluu-Suu
121 K1 **Mayma** Rus. Fed.
121 G4 **Maymak** Kazakh.
96 B2 **Maymyo** Myanmar
98 F1 **Mayna** *Respublika Khakasiya* Rus. Fed.
135 I5 **Mayna** *Ul'yanovskaya Oblast'* Rus. Fed.
231 D4 **Maynardville** *TN* U.S.A.
114 B2 **Mayni** *Mahar.* India
227 I3 **Maynooth** *Ont.* Can.
147 E3 **Maynooth** Rep. of Ireland
222 C2 **Mayo** *Y.T.* Can.
239 E7 **Mayo** *r.* Mex.
252 A1 **Mayo** *r.* Peru
147 B3 **Mayo** Rep. of Ireland
147 B3 **Mayo** *county* Rep. of Ireland
231 D6 **Mayo** *FL* U.S.A.
234 B4 **Mayo** *MD* U.S.A.
207 I4 **Mayo Alim** Cameroon
207 I4 **Mayo-Belwa** Nigeria
147 E2 **Mayobridge** *Northern Ireland* U.K.
208 B2 **Mayo-Kébbi** *pref.* Chad
208 B5 **Mayoko** Congo
Mayo Landing *Y.T.* Can. *see* Mayo
92 B3 **Mayon** *vol. Luzon* Phil.
183 H4 **Mayor** *r.* Spain
183 I2 **Mayor** *r.* Spain
Mayor, Puig *mt.* Spain *see* Puig Major
261 F6 **Mayor Buratovich** Arg.
183 E2 **Mayorga** Spain
253 E4 **Mayor Pablo Lagerenza** Para.
217 □3b **Mayotte** *terr.* Africa
246 □ **May Pen** Jamaica
Mayqayyng Kazakh. *see* Maykain
247 □3 **Mayreau** *i.* St Vincent
161 C4 **Mayres** France
163 D5 **Mayreville** France
178 C3 **Mayrhofen** Austria
128 B4 **Maysah, Tall al** *mt.* Jordan
127 G5 **Maysān** *governorate* Iraq
169 C5 **Mayschoß** Ger.
175 I1 **Mayskaya** *r.* Rus. Fed.
137 I2 **Mayskiy** *Belgorodskaya Oblast'* Rus. Fed.
129 D2 **Mayskiy** *Kabardino-Balkarskaya Respublika* Rus. Fed.
134 K4 **Mayskiy** *Permskaya Oblast'* Rus. Fed.
137 K4 **Mayskiy** *Rostovskaya Oblast'* Rus. Fed.
121 I2 **Mayskoye** Kazakh.
234 D3 **Mays Landing** *NJ* U.S.A.
232 B5 **Maysville** *KY* U.S.A.
236 E4 **Maysville** *MO* U.S.A.
Maytag *Xinjiang* China *see* **Dushanzi**
96 A2 **Mayu** *r.* Myanmar
209 A5 **Mayumba** Gabon
114 C4 **Mayuram** *Tamil Nadu* India
227 F4 **Mayville** *MI* U.S.A.
236 D2 **Mayville** *ND* U.S.A.
232 D3 **Mayville** *NY* U.S.A.
236 C3 **Maywood** *NE* U.S.A.
131 O3 **Mayya** Rus. Fed.
261 F5 **Maza** Arg.
139 K2 **Maza** Rus. Fed.
209 E8 **Mazabuka** Zambia
Mazaca Turkey *see* **Kayseri**
Mazagan Morocco *see* **El Jadida**
251 I5 **Mazagão** Brazil
184 D3 **Mazagón** Spain
156 E3 **Mazagran** France
138 E3 **Maza Jugla** *r.* Latvia
186 D3 **Mazaleón** Spain
163 E5 **Mazamet** France
244 C4 **Mazamitla** Mex.
161 D4 **Mazan** France
250 C5 **Mazán** Peru
122 B2 **Māzandarān** *prov.* Iran
161 C4 **Mazan-l'Abbaye** France
244 D1 **Mazapil** Mex.
123 F3 **Mazar, Koh-i-** *mt.* Afgh.
194 B5 **Mazara, Val di** *val. Sicilia* Italy
194 B5 **Mazara del Vallo** *Sicilia* Italy
183 F5 **Mazarambroz** Spain
123 F2 **Mazār-e Sharīf** Afgh.
183 H4 **Mazarete** Spain
194 B5 **Mazaro** *r. Sicilia* Italy
187 B7 **Mazarrón** Spain
187 B7 **Mazarrón, Golfo de** *b.* Spain
110 B4 **Mazartag** *mt. Xinjiang* China
251 G3 **Mazaruni** *r.* Guyana
242 C2 **Mazatán** Mex.
245 F4 **Mazateca, Sierra** *mts* Mex.
243 H6 **Mazatenango** Guat.
244 A2 **Mazatlán** Mex.
241 L4 **Mazatzal Peak** *AZ* U.S.A.
159 F4 **Mazé** France
215 G5 **Mazeepa Bay** S. Africa
104 D3 **Maze-gawa** *r.* Japan
138 D3 **Mažeikiai** Lith.
234 B2 **Mazeppa** *PA* U.S.A.
163 D5 **Mazères** France
163 B5 **Mazerolles** France
161 C3 **Mazet-St-Voy** France
163 D4 **Mazeyrolles** France
129 A4 **Mazgirt** Turkey
199 E3 **Mazı** Turkey
138 F3 **Mazīča** *r.* Latvia
232 B5 **Mazie** *KY* U.S.A.
162 B2 **Mazières-en-Gâtine** France
216 □3d **Mazo** *La Palma* Canary Is
242 C2 **Mazocahui** Mex.
252 C4 **Mazocruz** Peru
Mazoe Zimbabwe *see* **Mazowe**
226 C4 **Mazomanie** *WI* U.S.A.
106 C3 **Mazong Shan** *mt. Gansu* China
106 B3 **Mazong Shan** *mts* China
213 F3 **Mazowe** Zimbabwe
213 G3 **Mazowe** *r.* Zimbabwe
175 I4 **Mazowiecka** *reg.* Pol.
175 J3 **Mazowieckie** *prov.* Pol.
138 E3 **Mazsalaca** Latvia
122 B3 **Māzū** Iran
175 I2 **Mazurskie, Pojezierze** *reg.* Pol.
136 E1 **Mazyr** Belarus
190 F3 **Mazzano** Italy
193 E2 **Mazzano Romano** Italy
194 D5 **Mazzarino** *Sicilia* Italy
194 D5 **Mazzarrone** *Sicilia* Italy
178 B4 **Mazzo di Valtellina** Italy
Mba *Viti Levu* Fiji *see* **Ba**
215 H2 **Mbabane** Swaziland
206 B3 **Mbacké** Senegal
208 C4 **Mbaéré** *r.* C.A.R.
206 B2 **Mbagne** Maur.
206 D5 **Mbahiakro** Côte d'Ivoire
208 C4 **Mbaïki** C.A.R.
211 A7 **Mbala** Zambia
207 I6 **Mbalam** Cameroon
210 B4 **Mbale** Uganda
207 H6 **Mbalmayo** Cameroon
207 H5 **Mbam** *r.* Cameroon
208 C5 **Mbandaka** Dem. Rep. Congo
207 H5 **Mbandjok** Cameroon
207 I6 **Mbang** Cameroon
207 H5 **Mbanga** Cameroon
78 □6 **Mbanika** *i.* Solomon Is
209 B6 **M'banza Congo** Angola
209 B6 **Mbanza-Ngungu** Dem. Rep. Congo
206 B3 **Mbar** Senegal
210 A5 **Mbarara** Uganda
208 D3 **Mbari** *r.* C.A.R.
211 C7 **Mbarika Mountains** Tanz.
215 I2 **Mbaswana** S. Africa
208 C4 **Mbata** C.A.R.
211 A7 **Mbati** Zambia
Mbatiki *i.* Fiji *see* **Batiki**
78 □6 **Mbava** *i. New Georgia Is* Solomon Is
207 I5 **Mbé** Cameroon
211 C7 **Mbemkuru** *r.* Tanz.
Mbengga *i.* Fiji *see* **Beqa**
207 H5 **Mbengwi** Cameroon
217 □3a **Mbéni** *Njazidja* Comoros
213 F4 **Mberengwa** Zimbabwe
209 F7 **Mbereshi** Zambia
211 B7 **Mbeya** Tanz.
211 B7 **Mbeya** *admin. reg.* Tanz.
207 I5 **Mbi** *r.* Cameroon
208 C3 **Mbi** *r.* C.A.R.
208 A5 **Mbigou** Gabon
196 D4 **Mbilqethit, Maja e** *mt.* Albania
208 B5 **Mbinda** Congo
211 B7 **Mbinga** Tanz.
207 H6 **Mbini** Equat. Guinea
207 H6 **Mbini** *r.* Equat. Guinea
78 □6 **Mbita'ama** *Malaita* Solomon Is
211 A7 **Mbizi Mountains** Tanz.
208 E3 **Mboki** C.A.R.
208 B4 **Mbomo** Congo
208 D3 **Mbomou** *pref.* C.A.R.
208 D3 **Mbomou** *r.* C.A.R./Dem. Rep. Congo
78 □6 **Mborokua** *i.* Solomon Is
207 H5 **Mbouda** Cameroon
206 A3 **Mbour** Senegal
206 B2 **Mbout** Maur.
211 B7 **Mbozi** Tanz.
208 C3 **Mbrès** C.A.R.
198 A1 **Mbrostar** Albania
209 D6 **Mbuji-Mayi** Dem. Rep. Congo
78 □6 **Mbulo** *i. New Georgia Is* Solomon Is
211 B5 **Mbulu** Tanz.
215 H2 **Mbuluzana** *r.* Swaziland
215 I2 **Mbuluzi** *r.* Swaziland
258 F3 **Mburucuyá** Arg.
225 H4 **McAdam** *N.B.* Can.
234 C2 **McAdoo** *PA* U.S.A.
234 D1 **McAfee** *NJ* U.S.A.
237 E5 **McAlester** *OK* U.S.A.
234 A2 **McAlisterville** *PA* U.S.A.
237 D7 **McAllen** *TX* U.S.A.
226 D3 **McAllister** *WI* U.S.A.
84 D2 **McArthur** *r. N.T.* Austr.
232 B5 **McArthur** *OH* U.S.A.
227 I3 **McArthur Mills** *Ont.* Can.
226 E3 **McBain** *MI* U.S.A.
222 F4 **McBride** *B.C.* Can.
238 C2 **McCall** *ID* U.S.A.
237 C6 **McCamey** *TX* U.S.A.
238 D3 **McCammon** *ID* U.S.A.
226 C3 **McCaslin Mountain** *hill WI* U.S.A.
263 K1 **McClintock, Mount** Antarctica
221 H2 **McClintock Channel** *Nunavut* Can.
86 E3 **McClintock Range** *hills W.A.* Austr.
84 C1 **McCluer Island** *N.T.* Austr.
232 B4 **McClure** *OH* U.S.A.
232 E4 **McClure** *PA* U.S.A.
220 G2 **McClure Strait** *N.W.T.* Can.
236 C2 **McClusky** *ND* U.S.A.
237 F6 **McComb** *MS* U.S.A.
232 B4 **McComb** *OH* U.S.A.
232 E5 **McConnellsburg** *PA* U.S.A.
232 C5 **McConnelsville** *OH* U.S.A.
236 C3 **McCook** *NE* U.S.A.
231 D5 **McCormick** *SC* U.S.A.
232 C6 **McCoy** *VA* U.S.A.
222 H2 **McCrea** *r. N.W.T.* Can.
223 L5 **McCreary** *Man.* Can.
241 J4 **McCullough Range** *mts NV* U.S.A.
232 B4 **McCutchenville** *OH* U.S.A.
222 D3 **McDame** *B.C.* Can.
238 C3 **McDermitt** *NV* U.S.A.
232 B5 **McDermott** *OH* U.S.A.
265 I8 **McDonald Islands** Indian Ocean
238 D2 **McDonald Peak** *MT* U.S.A.
231 C5 **McDonough** *GA* U.S.A.
241 L5 **McDowell Peak** *AZ* U.S.A.
234 B1 **McEwensville** *PA* U.S.A.
240 H4 **McFarland** *CA* U.S.A.
226 C4 **McFarland** *WI* U.S.A.
223 J3 **McFarlane** *r. Sask.* Can.
81 B5 **McFarlane, Mount** *South I.* N.Z.
241 J2 **McGill** *NV* U.S.A.
225 H4 **McGivney** *N.B.* Can.
220 C3 **McGrath** *AK* U.S.A.
226 A2 **McGrath** *MN* U.S.A.
222 F4 **McGregor** *r. B.C.* Can.
214 B5 **McGregor** S. Africa
226 A2 **McGregor** *MN* U.S.A.
227 G2 **McGregor Bay** *Ont.* Can.
85 E5 **McGregor Range** *hills Qld* Austr.
238 D2 **McGuire, Mount** *ID* U.S.A.
129 D2 **Mchadijvari** Georgia
204 D4 **Mcherrah** *reg.* Alg.
211 C7 **Mchinga** Tanz.
211 B8 **Mchinji** Malawi
85 E2 **McIlwraith Range** *hills Qld* Austr.
236 C2 **McIntosh** *SD* U.S.A.
86 D4 **McKay Range** *hills W.A.* Austr.
77 I2 **McKean** *i. Phoenix Is* Kiribati
232 A6 **McKee** *KY* U.S.A.
234 D3 **McKee** *NJ* U.S.A.
232 D4 **McKeesport** *PA* U.S.A.
232 C4 **McKees Rocks** *PA* U.S.A.
232 E6 **McKenney** *VA* U.S.A.
237 F4 **McKenzie** *TN* U.S.A.
238 B2 **McKenzie** *r. OR* U.S.A.
85 E4 **McKinlay** *Qld* Austr.
85 E4 **McKinlay** *r. Qld* Austr.
220 C3 **McKinley, Mount** *AK* U.S.A.
237 D5 **McKinney** *TX* U.S.A.
240 H4 **McKittrick** *CA* U.S.A.
236 C2 **McLaughlin** *SD* U.S.A.
226 C5 **McLean** *IL* U.S.A.
234 A4 **McLean** *VA* U.S.A.
236 F4 **McLeansboro** *IL* U.S.A.
222 G4 **McLennan** *Alta* Can.
222 H4 **McLeod** *r. Alta* Can.
222 F4 **McLeod Lake** *B.C.* Can.
238 B2 **McMinnville** *OR* U.S.A.
231 C5 **McMinnville** *TN* U.S.A.
263 L1 **McMurdo** *research stn* Antarctica
241 M4 **McNary** *AZ* U.S.A.
226 C3 **McNaughton** *WI* U.S.A.
McNaughton Lake *B.C.* Can. *see* **Kinbasket Lake**
241 M6 **McNeal** *AZ* U.S.A.
225 H2 **McPhadyen** *r. Nfld.* Can.
236 D4 **McPherson** *KS* U.S.A.
83 H2 **McPherson Range** *mts N.S.W.* Austr.
222 B2 **McQuesten** *r. Y.T.* Can.
231 D5 **McRae** *GA* U.S.A.
232 B6 **McRoberts** *KY* U.S.A.
234 A3 **McSherrystown** *PA* U.S.A.
220 G3 **McTavish Arm** *b. N.W.T.* Can.
232 E4 **McVeytown** *PA* U.S.A.
222 F1 **McVicar Arm** *b. N.W.T.* Can.
232 C5 **McWhorter** *WV* U.S.A.
139 I2 **Mda** *r.* Rus. Fed.
215 F5 **Mdantsane** S. Africa
205 G1 **M'Daourouch** Alg.
217 □3a **Mde** *Njazidja* Comoros
180 D5 **Mdiq** Morocco
241 J3 **Mead, Lake** *resr NV* U.S.A.
237 C4 **Meade** *KS* U.S.A.
220 C2 **Meade** *r. AK* U.S.A.
87 B5 **Meadow** *W.A.* Austr.
236 C2 **Meadow** *SD* U.S.A.
241 K2 **Meadow** *UT* U.S.A.
232 C6 **Meadow Bridge** *WV* U.S.A.
223 I4 **Meadow Lake** *Sask.* Can.
241 J3 **Meadow Valley Wash** *r. NV* U.S.A.
232 C6 **Meadowview** *VA* U.S.A.
237 F6 **Meadville** *MS* U.S.A.
232 C4 **Meadville** *PA* U.S.A.
227 G3 **Meaford** *Ont.* Can.
102 L2 **Meaken** *vol.* Japan
146 D4 **Meal Fuar-mhonaidh** *hill Scotland* U.K.
182 B4 **Mealhada** Port.
146 A3 **Mealisval** *hill Scotland* U.K.
146 D5 **Meall Chuaich** *hill Scotland* U.K.
146 D4 **Meall Dubh** *hill Scotland* U.K.
149 F3 **Mealsgate** *Cumbria, England* U.K.
225 J2 **Mealy Mountains** *Nfld.* Can.
192 B5 **Meana Sardo** *Sardegna* Italy
85 G5 **Meandarra** *Qld* Austr.
222 G3 **Meander River** *Alta* Can.
150 E3 **Meare** *Somerset, England* U.K.
151 F2 **Mease** *r. England* U.K.
151 F2 **Measham** *Leicestershire, England* U.K.
147 E3 **Meath** *county* Rep. of Ireland
160 A2 **Meaulne** France
156 C3 **Méaulte** France
156 C4 **Meaux** France
163 D4 **Meauzac** France
209 B6 **Mebridege** *r.* Angola
117 H3 **Mebu** *Arun. Prad.* India
213 G2 **Mecanhelas** Moz.
244 B3 **Mecatán** Mex.
124 B3 **Mecca** Saudi Arabia
241 I5 **Mecca** *CA* U.S.A.
232 C4 **Mecca** *OH* U.S.A.
233 □H2 **Mechanic Falls** *ME* U.S.A.
232 B4 **Mechanicsburg** *OH* U.S.A.
234 A2 **Mechanicsburg** *PA* U.S.A.
232 C6 **Mechanicsburg** *VA* U.S.A.
232 E6 **Mechanicsville** *VA* U.S.A.
233 G3 **Mechanicville** *NY* U.S.A.
210 D2 **Mechāra** Eth.
165 D3 **Mechelen** Belgium
165 E4 **Mechelen** Neth.
Mecherchar *i.* Palau *see* **Eil Malk**
205 E2 **Mecheria** Alg.
169 B5 **Mechernich** Ger.
135 H7 **Mechetinskaya** Rus. Fed.
202 B6 **Mechiméré** Chad
197 G4 **Mechka** *r.* Bulg.
168 F2 **Mechtersen** Ger.

Mechterstädt to Michigan
334

169 F5 Mechterstädt Ger.
199 E1 Mecidiye Edirne Turkey
199 E2 Mecidiye Manisa Turkey
176 C2 Měčín Czech Rep.
185 G4 Mecina-Bombarón Spain
174 E4 Męcinka Pol.
126 D2 Mecitözü Turkey
172 D4 Meckenbeuren Ger.
169 C5 Meckenheim Ger.
172 C2 Meckesheim Ger.
170 C1 Mecklenburger Bucht b. Ger.
170 D2 Mecklenburg-Vorpommern land Ger.
Mecklenburg - West Pomerania land Ger. see Mecklenburg-Vorpommern
183 G4 Meco Spain
213 H2 Meconta Moz.
177 H5 Mecsek mts Hungary
177 H5 Mecseknádasd Hungary
213 I2 Mecubúri r. Moz.
213 I2 Mecúfi Moz.
211 C8 Mecula Moz.
86 D3 Meda r. W.A. Austr.
182 C4 Meda Port.
182 C2 Meda mt. Spain
114 C2 Medak Andhra Prad. India
94 B2 Medan Sumatera Indon.
261 F6 Médanos Arg.
226 D5 Medaryville IN U.S.A.
182 B3 Medas Port.
114 C2 Medchal Andhra Prad. India
172 B2 Meddersheim Ger.
164 F2 Meddo Neth.
190 D3 Mede Italy
205 F1 Médéa Alg.
169 D4 Medebach Ger.
257 G2 Medeiros Neto Brazil
182 C4 Medelim Port.
250 C3 Medellín Col.
184 E2 Medellín Spain
168 D2 Medem r. Ger.
164 E2 Medemblik Neth.
149 I4 Meden r. England U.K.
205 H2 Medenine Tunisia
Medenitsa Ukr. see Medenychi
136 B3 Medenychi Ukr.
124 C5 Meder Eritrea
206 B2 Mederdra Maur.
190 F4 Medesano Italy
233 G4 Medford NY U.S.A.
237 D4 Medford OK U.S.A.
238 B3 Medford OR U.S.A.
226 B3 Medford WI U.S.A.
234 D3 Medford Lakes NJ U.S.A.
197 I3 Medgidia Romania
177 J5 Medgyesbodzás Hungary
177 K5 Medgyesegyháza Hungary
113 □1 Medhufinolhu i. N. Male Maldives
234 C3 Media PA U.S.A.
186 C3 Mediana Spain
197 G2 Mediaş Romania
238 C2 Medical Lake WA U.S.A.
191 G4 Medicina Italy
238 F3 Medicine Bow WY U.S.A.
238 F3 Medicine Bow r. WY U.S.A.
238 F3 Medicine Bow Mountains WY U.S.A.
238 F3 Medicine Bow Peak WY U.S.A.
223 I5 Medicine Hat Alta Can.
237 D4 Medicine Lodge KS U.S.A.
257 G2 Medina Brazil
Medina Saudi Arabia see Al Madīnah
236 D2 Medina ND U.S.A.
232 D3 Medina NY U.S.A.
232 C4 Medina OH U.S.A.
237 D6 Medina r. TX U.S.A.
183 H3 Medinaceli Spain
184 D2 Medina de las Torres Spain
183 F3 Medina del Campo Spain
183 G2 Medina de Pomar Spain
183 E3 Medina de Rioseco Spain
206 B3 Medina Gounas Senegal
184 E4 Medina-Sidonia Spain
117 F5 Medinipur W. Bengal India
Mediolanum Italy see Milano
162 B3 Médis France
132 F7 Mediterranean Sea
161 B5 Méditerranée airport France
176 G2 Medlov Czech Rep.
120 D2 Mednogorsk Rus. Fed.
139 J3 Mednoye Rus. Fed.
131 R4 Mednyy, Ostrov i. Rus. Fed.
162 A3 Médoc reg. France
111 F6 Mêdog Xizang China
191 G4 Medolla Italy
236 C2 Medora ND U.S.A.
208 A4 Médouneu Gabon
260 C3 Medrano Arg.
175 I5 Mędrzechów Pol.
223 I4 Medstead Sask. Can.
151 F3 Medstead Hampshire, England U.K.
Medu Kongkar Xizang China see Maizhokunggar
191 I4 Medulin Croatia
191 H3 Meduna r. Italy
191 H2 Meduno Italy
Meduro atoll Marshall Is see Majuro
197 E4 Medveđa Srbija Yugo.
134 I4 Medvedevo Rus. Fed.
135 H6 Medveditsa r. Rus. Fed.
188 E3 Medvednica mts Croatia
134 J4 Medvedok Rus. Fed.
137 J5 Medvedovskaya Rus. Fed.
138 D4 Medvėgalio kalnis hill Lith.
137 I2 Medvenka Rus. Fed.
134 F3 Medvezh'yegorsk Rus. Fed.
179 F4 Medvode Slovenia
151 H3 Medway admin. div. England U.K.
151 H3 Medway r. England U.K.
175 K6 Medyka Pol.
139 J4 Medyn' Rus. Fed.
136 D3 Medzhybizh Ukr.
177 K2 Medzilaborce Slovakia
87 B5 Meeberrie W.A. Austr.
164 F1 Meeden Neth.
169 F5 Meeder Ger.
87 C5 Meekatharra W.A. Austr.
238 F3 Meeker CO U.S.A.
232 B4 Meeker OH U.S.A.
240 G2 Meeks Bay CA U.S.A.
214 E5 Meelberg mt. S. Africa
147 C3 Meelick Rep. of Ireland
147 C2 Meenacross Rep. of Ireland
147 C2 Meenanarwa Rep. of Ireland
147 C2 Meentullynagarn Rep. of Ireland
165 D3 Meer Belgium
171 D5 Meerane Ger.
169 E3 Meerbeck Ger.
169 B4 Meerbusch Ger.
165 E3 Meerhout Belgium
164 D3 Meerkerk Neth.
165 D3 Meerle Belgium
164 F3 Meerlo Neth.
172 D4 Meersburg Ger.
165 E4 Meerssen Neth.
113 □1 Meerufenfushi i. N. Male Maldives
116 D3 Meerut Uttar Prad. India
163 A5 Mées France
238 E2 Meeteetse WY U.S.A.
Me'etia i. Arch. de la Société Fr. Polynesia see Mehetia
165 C3 Meetkerke Belgium
165 E3 Meeuwen Belgium
210 C3 Mēga Eth.
210 C3 Mega Escarpment Eth./Kenya
198 B2 Megala Kalyvia Greece
198 C1 Megali Panagia Greece
210 D3 Megalo Eth.
198 C3 Megalopoli Greece
198 C2 Megara Greece
164 E3 Megen Neth.
160 E3 Megève France
210 C2 Megezez mt. Eth.
117 G4 Meghalaya state India
117 F5 Meghasani mt. Orissa India
117 G5 Meghna r. Bangl.
129 E4 Meghri Armenia
Meghrut Armenia see Gugark'
130 I3 Megion Rus. Fed.
199 F3 Megisti i. Greece
139 J2 Meglino, Ozero l. Rus. Fed.
139 J1 Megra r. Rus. Fed.
Megri Armenia see Meghri
Megrut Armenia see Gugark'
197 F3 Mehadica Romania
165 E4 Mehaigne r. Belgium
140 N1 Mehamn Norway
123 F5 Mehar Pak.
87 C4 Meharry, Mount W.A. Austr.
Mehdia Tunisia see Mahdia
168 E2 Mehe r. Ger.
143 G1 Mehedeby Sweden
116 D5 Mehekar Mahar. India
117 G5 Meherpur Bangl.
232 D6 Meherrin VA U.S.A.
232 E6 Meherrin r. VA U.S.A.
79 □3 Mehetia i. Arch. de la Société Fr. Polynesia
116 C5 Mehidpur Madh. Prad. India
167 J5 Méhkerék Hungary
171 D5 Mehltheuer Ger.
236 F4 Mehlville MO U.S.A.
116 C5 Mehmadabad Gujarat India
117 E4 Mehndawal Uttar Prad. India
234 B1 Mehoopany PA U.S.A.
122 A2 Mehrābān Iran
169 B5 Mehren Ger.
172 A2 Mehring Ger.
171 C4 Mehringen Ger.
179 E2 Mehrnbach Austria
172 D3 Mehrstetten Ger.
123 G3 Mehtar Lām Afgh.
162 E1 Mehun-sur-Yèvre France
256 C3 Meia Ponte r. Brazil
Meicheng Anhui China see Qianshan
Meicheng Fujian China see Minqing
109 D2 Meichengzhen Hunan China
150 C3 Meidrim Carmarthenshire, Wales U.K.
207 I5 Meiganga Cameroon
148 C3 Meigh Northern Ireland U.K.
146 E5 Meigle Perth and Kinross, Scotland U.K.
108 B2 Meigu Sichuan China
100 C4 Meihekou Jilin China
165 E3 Meijel Neth.
Meijiang Jiangxi China see Ningdu
109 E3 Mei Jiang r. China
109 E3 Meikeng Guangdong China
222 G3 Meikle r. Alta Can.
148 E1 Meikle Bin hill Scotland U.K.
148 D2 Meikle Kilmory Argyll and Bute, Scotland U.K.
146 E5 Meikleour Perth and Kinross, Scotland U.K.
146 F6 Meikle Says Law hill Scotland U.K.
96 A2 Meiktila Myanmar
190 D1 Meilen Switz.
163 B5 Meilhan France
163 C4 Meilhan-sur-Garonne France
Meilin Jiangxi China see Ganxian
158 E3 Meillac France
160 A2 Meillant France
160 E2 Meillerie France
222 E2 Meilleur r. N.W.T. Can.
Meilü Guangdong China see Wuchuan
182 C4 Meimoa Port.
190 D3 Meina Italy
169 F3 Meine Ger.
169 F3 Meinersen Ger.
169 C4 Meinerzhagen Ger.
178 A3 Meiningen Austria
169 F5 Meiningen Ger.
182 C1 Meira Spain
182 C1 Meira, Serra de mts Spain
190 D2 Meiringen Switz.
171 C4 Meisdorf Ger.
172 B2 Meisenheim Ger.
Meishan Anhui China see Jinzhai
108 B2 Meishan Sichuan China
171 E4 Meißen Ger.
168 E3 Meißendorf Ger.
172 B3 Meißenheim Ger.
222 D2 Meister r. Y.T. Can.
108 C3 Meitan Guizhou China
173 E3 Meitingen Ger.
165 E5 Meix-devant-Virton Belgium
100 D3 Meixi Heilong. China
Meixian Guangdong China see Meizhou
107 E5 Meixian Shaanxi China
Meixing Sichuan China see Xiaojin
109 F3 Meizhou Guangdong China
116 D4 Mej r. India
161 C4 Méjan, Sommet de mt. France
78 □3a Mejatto i. Kwajalein Marshall Is
161 B4 Méjean, Causse plat. France
189 B7 Mejez el Bab Tunisia
258 D3 Mejicana mt. Arg.
252 C5 Mejillones Chile
183 F4 Mejorada Spain
183 G4 Mejorada del Campo Spain
208 B4 Mékambo Gabon
199 G1 Mekece Turkey
210 C1 Mek'elē Eth.
206 A3 Mékhé Senegal
129 E2 Mekhel'ta Rus. Fed.
210 C2 Mekī Eth.
179 F4 Mekinje Slovenia
207 F5 Mekkaw Nigeria
204 D2 Meknès Morocco
108 B4 Mekong r. Asia alt. Lancang Jiang
97 D5 Mekong, Mouths of the Vietnam
191 H2 Mel Italy
208 D2 Méla, Mont hill C.A.R.
260 B4 Melado r. Chile
94 C2 Melaka Malaysia
94 C2 Melaka state Malaysia
193 H4 Melandro r. Italy
266 F6 Melanesia is Oceania
266 F5 Melanesian Basin sea feature Pacific Ocean
191 G3 Melara Italy
95 E2 Melawi r. Indon.
160 C2 Melay Bourgogne France
157 F5 Melay Champagne-Ardenne France
159 F4 Melay Pays de la Loire France
190 D4 Melazzo Italy
168 F2 Melbeck Ger.
151 H2 Melbourn Cambridgeshire, England U.K.
83 F4 Melbourne Vic. Austr.
151 F2 Melbourne Derbyshire, England U.K.
237 F4 Melbourne AR U.S.A.
231 D6 Melbourne FL U.S.A.
140 K1 Melbu Norway
146 □G1 Melby Shetland, Scotland U.K.
259 B7 Melchor, Isla i. Chile
243 H5 Melchor de Mencos Guat.
170 E3 Melchow Ger.
140 J3 Meldal Norway
191 H4 Meldola Italy
168 E1 Meldorf Ger.
232 B6 Meldrum KY U.S.A.
224 D4 Meldrum Bay Ont. Can.
190 D4 Mele Italy
139 K3 Melech r. Rus. Fed.
190 E3 Melegnano Italy
176 G4 Meleg-víz r. Hungary
Melekess Rus. Fed. see Dimitrovgrad
139 M3 Melekhovo Rus. Fed.
196 E3 Melenci Vojvodina, Srbija Yugo.
126 D3 Melendiz Dağı mt. Turkey
195 H2 Melendugno Italy
135 H5 Melenki Rus. Fed.
158 E3 Melesse France
Melet Turkey see Mesudiye
120 C1 Meleuz Rus. Fed.
225 G1 Mélèzes, Rivière aux r. Que. Can.
193 F3 Melfa r. Italy
233 F6 Melfa VA U.S.A.
208 C2 Mélfi Chad
193 H4 Melfi Italy
223 J4 Melfort Sask. Can.
251 I5 Melgaço Brazil
182 B2 Melgaço Port.
183 G5 Melgar r. Spain
183 E2 Melgar de Arriba Spain
183 F2 Melgar de Fernamental Spain
182 D3 Melgar de Tera Spain
158 C4 Melgven France
140 J3 Melhus Norway
95 G1 Meliau, Gunung mt. Sabah Malaysia
165 F3 Melick Neth.
195 F4 Melicucco Italy
182 C2 Melide Spain
184 B2 Melides Port.
198 B3 Meligalas Greece
129 C3 Melikköyü Turkey
181 E5 Melilla N. Africa
195 E5 Melilli Sicilia Italy
259 B7 Melimoyu, Monte mt. Chile
81 B6 Melina, Mount South I. N.Z.
261 G3 Melincué Arg.
137 H3 Melioratyvne Ukr.
260 B6 Melipeuco Chile
260 B3 Melipilla Chile
157 G5 Mélisey France
164 C3 Meliskerke Neth.
195 G3 Melissa Italy
223 K5 Melita Man. Can.
Melitene Turkey see Malatya
198 B1 Meliti Dytiki Makedonia Greece
195 E5 Melito r. Italy
195 E5 Melito di Porto Salvo Italy
137 H4 Melitopol' Ukr.
179 G2 Melk Austria
179 G2 Melk r. Austria
215 E5 Melk r. S. Africa
214 B5 Melkbosstrand S. Africa
150 E3 Melksham Wiltshire, England U.K.
190 F3 Mella r. Italy
158 C4 Mellac France
140 L3 Mellansel Sweden
141 K3 Mellansjö Sweden
140 L2 Mellanström Sweden
178 A3 Mellau Austria
165 C3 Melle Belgium
162 B2 Melle France
169 D3 Melle Ger.
170 C2 Mellen Ger.
226 B2 Mellen WI U.S.A.
168 E3 Mellendorf (Wedemark) Ger.
171 E3 Mellensee Ger.
142 E2 Mellerud Sweden
236 D2 Mellette SD U.S.A.
Mellid Spain see Melide
195 □ Mellieħa Malta
168 F3 Mellin Ger.
171 C5 Mellingen Ger.
168 D3 Mellinghausen Ger.
259 B8 Mellizo Sur, Cerro mt. Chile
169 F5 Mellrichstadt Ger.
150 D3 Mellte r. Wales U.K.
78 □3a Mellu i. Kwajalein Marshall Is
168 D2 Mellum i. Ger.
149 G3 Melmerby Cumbria, England U.K.
215 H3 Melmoth S. Africa
176 D1 Mělník Czech Rep.
136 D3 Mel'nytsya-Podil's'ka Ukr.
258 G4 Melo Uru.
213 H2 Meloco Moz.
215 F3 Meloding S. Africa
182 B2 Melón Spain
207 H5 Mélong Cameroon
Melovoye Ukr. see Milove
220 C3 Melozitna r. AK U.S.A.
158 C4 Melrand France
182 B3 Melres Port.
205 G2 Melrhir, Chott salt l. Alg.
87 D5 Melrose W.A. Austr.
146 F6 Melrose Scottish Borders, Scotland U.K.
236 E2 Melrose MN U.S.A.
190 E1 Mels Switz.
169 C5 Melsbach Ger.
168 F1 Melsdorf Ger.
Melsetter Zimbabwe see Chimanimani
149 H3 Melsonby North Yorkshire, England U.K.
169 E4 Melsungen Ger.
Melta, Mount Sabah Malaysia see Meliau, Gunung
149 H4 Meltham West Yorkshire, England U.K.
83 F4 Melton Vic. Austr.
151 I2 Melton Suffolk, England U.K.
151 G2 Melton Mowbray Leicestershire, England U.K.
211 C8 Meluco Moz.
156 C4 Melun France
114 C4 Melur Tamil Nadu India
146 C4 Melvaig Highland, Scotland U.K.
146 E3 Melvich Highland, Scotland U.K.
223 K5 Melville Sask. Can.
85 F2 Melville, Cape Qld Austr.
84 D2 Melville Bay N.T. Austr.
Melville Bugt b. Greenland see Qimusseriarsuaq
84 B1 Melville Island N.T. Austr.
221 H2 Melville Island N.W.T./Nunavut Can.
221 J3 Melville Peninsula Nunavut Can.
226 C5 Melvin IL U.S.A.
147 C2 Melvin, Lough l. Rep. of Ireland/U.K.
177 I5 Mélykút Hungary
190 E3 Melzo Italy
198 A1 Memaliaj Albania
213 I2 Memba Moz.
91 I7 Memberamo r. Indon.
160 D1 Membrey France
185 G2 Membrilla Spain
182 C5 Membrío Spain
Memel Lith. see Klaipėda
215 G2 Memel S. Africa
138 E3 Mēmele r. Latvia
138 F4 Memiakalnis hill Lith.
173 E2 Memmelsdorf Ger.
173 E4 Memmingen Ger.
173 E4 Memmingerberg Ger.
156 E3 Mémorial Américain hill France
126 C5 Memphis tourist site Egypt
227 F4 Memphis MI U.S.A.
236 E3 Memphis MO U.S.A.
237 F5 Memphis TN U.S.A.
237 C5 Memphis TX U.S.A.
146 F4 Memsie Aberdeenshire, Scotland U.K.
102 K2 Memuro-dake mt. Japan
137 G2 Mena Ukr.
137 G2 Mena r. Ukr.
237 E5 Mena AR U.S.A.
213 □J4 Menabe mts Madag.
190 E2 Menaggio Italy
191 G3 Menago r. Italy
150 C1 Menai Bridge Isle of Anglesey, Wales U.K.
150 C1 Menai Strait Wales U.K.
207 F3 Ménaka Mali
164 E1 Menaldum Neth.
98 I8 Mènam Khong r. Laos/Thai.
213 □J5 Menarandra r. Madag.
237 D6 Menard TX U.S.A.
156 B5 Menars France
183 F5 Menasalbas Spain
160 A2 Menat France
191 H4 Menata Italy
157 F4 Menaucourt France
185 G3 Mencal mt. Spain
116 B5 Mendarda Gujarat India
183 H1 Mendaro Spain
186 B1 Mendaur mt. Spain
183 H2 Mendavia Spain
95 F3 Mendawai r. Indon.
161 B4 Mende France
210 C3 Mendebo Mountains Eth.
203 H6 Mendefera Eritrea
268 M1 Mendeleyev Ridge sea feature Arctic Ocean
134 K5 Mendeleyevsk Rus. Fed.
169 C4 Menden (Sauerland) Ger.
237 F6 Mendenhall MS U.S.A.
199 E2 Menderes Turkey
243 F3 Méndez Mex.
245 E2 Méndez Mex.
92 B3 Mendez-Nuñez Phil.
234 D2 Mendham NJ U.S.A.
210 B2 Mendī Eth.
91 J8 Mendi P.N.G.
183 I2 Mendigorría Spain
150 E3 Mendip Hills England U.K.
163 B5 Menditte France
240 F2 Mendocino CA U.S.A.
238 A3 Mendocino, Cape CA U.S.A.
194 C5 Mendola r. Sicilia Italy
194 C5 Mendola r. Sicilia Italy
226 E4 Mendon MI U.S.A.
83 G2 Mendooran N.S.W. Austr.
240 G3 Mendota CA U.S.A.
226 C5 Mendota IL U.S.A.
260 C3 Mendoza Arg.
260 C4 Mendoza prov. Arg.
260 C3 Mendoza r. Arg.
190 D3 Mendrisio Switz.
87 D7 Mends, Lake salt flat W.A. Austr.
158 D3 Ménéac France
250 D2 Mene de Mauroa Venez.
190 E4 Menegosa, Monte mt. Italy
199 E2 Menemen Turkey
165 C4 Menen Belgium
161 D5 Ménerbes France
162 C3 Ménesplet France
160 C1 Ménessaire France
161 A3 Menet France
159 I4 Menetou-Salon France
158 C3 Menez Bré hill France
158 B3 Menez Hom hill France
194 B5 Menfi Sicilia Italy
108 B4 Mengban Yunnan China
109 F1 Mengcheng Anhui China
172 D3 Mengen Ger.
126 D2 Mengen Turkey
169 D5 Mengerskirchen Ger.
179 F4 Mengeš Slovenia
234 B3 Menges Mills PA U.S.A.
94 D4 Menggala Sumatera Indon.
108 B4 Menghai Yunnan China
185 G3 Mengíbar Spain
121 F1 Mengisor, Ozero salt l. Kazakh.
95 E2 Mengkiang r. Indon.
173 G3 Mengkofen Ger.
93 B3 Mengkoka, Gunung mt. Indon.
108 B4 Mengla Yunnan China
Menglang Yunnan China see Lancang
108 A4 Menglian Yunnan China
Menglie Yunnan China see Jiangcheng
Mengmeng Yunnan China see Shuangjiang
108 D3 Mengshan Guangxi China
Mengxian Henan China see Mengzhou
Mengyang Sichuan China see Mingshan
107 H5 Mengyin Shandong China
107 G5 Mengzhou Henan China
108 B4 Mengzi Yunnan China
150 C4 Menheniot Cornwall, England U.K.
162 B2 Ménigoute France
225 H2 Menihek Nfld. Can.
157 F4 Ménil-la-Tour France
157 G4 Ménil-sur-Belvitte France
Menin Belgium see Menen
179 H1 Měnín Czech Rep.
83 E3 Menindee N.S.W. Austr.
83 E3 Menindee Lake N.S.W. Austr.
82 D3 Meningie S.A. Austr.
147 B3 Menlough Rep. of Ireland
124 B5 Menna r. Eth.
156 C4 Mennecy France
159 H4 Mennetou-sur-Cher France
226 D3 Menominee MI U.S.A.
226 D3 Menominee r. WI U.S.A.
226 C4 Menomonee Falls WI U.S.A.
226 B3 Menomonie WI U.S.A.
209 C8 Menongue Angola
187 C7 Menor, Mar lag. Spain
186 □ Menorca i. Spain
160 B1 Menou France
161 D4 Mens France
162 C3 Mensignac France
168 C3 Menslage Ger.
149 H4 Menston West Yorkshire, England U.K.
Mentakab Malaysia see Mentekab
193 E2 Mentana Italy
92 A5 Mentapok mt. Sabah Malaysia
95 G2 Mentarang r. Indon.
94 B3 Mentawai, Kepulauan is Indon.
94 C3 Mentawai, Selat sea chan. Indon.
95 F3 Mentaya r. Indon.
182 C3 Mente r. Port./Spain
146 D5 Menteith, Lake of Scotland U.K.
94 C2 Mentekab Malaysia
87 B7 Mentelle, Cape W.A. Austr.
169 F4 Menteroda Ger.
199 G2 Menteş Afyon Turkey
160 E3 Menthon-St-Bernard France
184 C2 Mentiras hill Port.
185 H2 Mentiras mt. Spain
241 M4 Mentmore NM U.S.A.
94 D3 Mentok Indon.
161 F5 Menton France
237 C6 Mentone TX U.S.A.
232 C4 Mentor OH U.S.A.
183 F4 Méntrida Spain
95 F3 Mentuba r. Indon.
Menufia governorate Egypt see Minûfiya
95 G2 Menyapa, Gunung mt. Indon.
106 D4 Menyuan Qinghai China
107 F1 Menza r. Rus. Fed.
205 H1 Menzel Bourguiba Tunisia
134 K5 Menzelinsk Rus. Fed.
189 C7 Menzel Temime Tunisia
87 D6 Menzies W.A. Austr.
263 E2 Menzies, Mount Antarctica
190 D1 Menznau Switz.
159 H5 Méobecq France
191 H3 Meolo Italy
242 D2 Meoqui Mex.
161 D5 Méounes-les-Montrieux France
129 C3 Mep'istsqaro, Mt'a Georgia
211 B8 Meponda Moz.
164 F2 Meppel Neth.
168 C3 Meppen Ger.
215 F3 Meqheleng S. Africa
253 E3 Mequéns r. Brazil
186 D3 Mequinenza Spain
186 D3 Mequinenza, Embalse de resr Spain
226 D4 Mequon WI U.S.A.
156 B5 Mer France
190 E2 Mera r. Italy
94 D4 Merak Jawa Barat Indon.
140 J3 Meråker Norway
82 C2 Meramangye, Lake salt flat S.A. Austr.
236 F4 Meramec r. MO U.S.A.
191 G2 Merano Italy
95 E4 Merapi, Gunung vol. Jawa Indon.
95 F5 Merapi, Gunung vol. Jawa Indon.
94 C3 Merapi, Gunung vol. Sumatera Indon.
163 B5 Méraq France
251 F3 Merari, Serra mt. Brazil
225 K4 Merasheen Nfld. Can.
140 M2 Merasjärvi Sweden
190 E3 Merate Italy
212 E4 Meratswe r. Botswana
95 F3 Meratus, Pegunungan mts Indon.
91 J8 Merauke Irian Jaya Indon.
83 E3 Merbein Vic. Austr.
165 D4 Merbes-le-Château Belgium
Merca Somalia see Marka
186 □ Mercadal Spain
129 B4 Mercan Turkey
129 A4 Mercan Dağları mts Turkey
191 H5 Mercatale Italy
191 H5 Mercatello sul Metauro Italy
191 H5 Mercatino Conca Italy
193 G4 Mercato San Severino Italy
191 H5 Mercato Saraceno Italy
240 G3 Merced CA U.S.A.
240 G3 Merced r. CA U.S.A.
260 B2 Mercedario, Cerro mt. Arg.
261 H4 Mercedes Buenos Aires Arg.
258 F3 Mercedes Corrientes Arg.
260 E3 Mercedes San Luis Arg.
261 H3 Mercedes Uru.
233 □I2 Mercer ME U.S.A.
232 A4 Mercer OH U.S.A.
232 C4 Mercer PA U.S.A.
226 B2 Mercer WI U.S.A.
234 D2 Mercer County county NJ U.S.A.
232 E5 Mercersburg PA U.S.A.
234 D2 Mercerville NJ U.S.A.
257 F4 Mercês Brazil
173 E3 Merching Ger.
165 D4 Merchtem Belgium
128 B1 Mercimek Turkey
162 D3 Mercœur France
193 G4 Mercogliano Italy
163 D4 Mercuès France
160 C2 Mercurey France
160 E3 Mercury France
241 J3 Mercury NV U.S.A.
80 E2 Mercury Bay North I. N.Z.
80 E2 Mercury Islands North I. N.Z.
163 D6 Mercus-Garrabet France
Merdenik Turkey see Göle
172 B3 Merdingen Ger.
158 D3 Merdrignac France
165 C4 Mere Belgium
150 E3 Mere Wiltshire, England U.K.
159 I4 Méreau France
233 H3 Meredith NH U.S.A.
137 I3 Merefa Ukr.
78 □5 Mere Lava i. Vanuatu
165 C4 Merelbeke Belgium
80 E2 Meremere North I. N.Z.
140 M3 Merenkurkku str. Fin./Sweden
163 D6 Mérens-les-Vals France
156 C4 Méréville France
139 K2 Merezha Rus. Fed.
202 E5 Merga Oasis Sudan
120 B2 Mergenevo Kazakh.
190 D3 Mergozzo Italy
97 B4 Mergui Myanmar
97 B5 Mergui Archipelago is Myanmar
192 B2 Meria Corse France
82 E3 Meribah S.A. Austr.
161 E3 Méribel-les-Allues France
Meriç r. Greece/Turkey see Evros
199 E1 Meriç Turkey
156 C2 Méricourt France
243 H4 Mérida Mex.
184 D2 Mérida Spain
250 D2 Mérida Venez.
250 D2 Mérida state Venez.
250 D3 Mérida, Cordillera de mts Venez.
151 F2 Meriden West Midlands, England U.K.
233 G4 Meriden CT U.S.A.
237 F5 Meridian MS U.S.A.
237 D6 Meridian TX U.S.A.
163 B4 Mérignac France
140 N2 Merijärvi Fin.
141 M3 Merikarvia Fin.
83 G4 Merimbula N.S.W. Austr.
176 E2 Měřín Czech Rep.
Merín, Laguna l. Brazil/Uru. see Mirim, Lagoa
160 A3 Mérinchal France
85 G4 Merinda Qld Austr.
161 D5 Mérindol France
215 F2 Merindol S. Africa
173 E3 Mering Ger.
207 I4 Meringa Nigeria
82 E3 Meringur Vic. Austr.
91 H6 Merir i. Palau
85 F5 Merivale r. Qld Austr.
177 L4 Mérk Hungary
121 H4 Merke Kazakh.
237 C5 Merkel TX U.S.A.
179 G4 Merkendorf Austria
173 E2 Merkendorf Ger.
138 E4 Merkinė Lith.
176 C2 Merklín Czech Rep.
172 D3 Merklingen Ger.
165 D3 Merksplas Belgium
175 M1 Merkys r. Lith.
191 G3 Merlara Italy
Merlav i. Vanuatu see Mere Lava
158 C4 Merlevenez France
162 E3 Merlines France
260 E3 Merlo Arg.
137 H3 Merlo r. Ukr.
85 E2 Merluna Qld Austr.
86 C3 Mermaid Reef W.A. Austr.
177 G5 Mernye Hungary
182 B1 Mero r. Spain
87 D6 Merolia W.A. Austr.
128 B3 Meron, Har mt. Israel
197 E4 Merošina Srbija Yugo.
203 F5 Merowe Sudan
87 C6 Merredin W.A. Austr.
157 F4 Merrey France
226 E5 Merriam IN U.S.A.
146 D6 Merrick hill Scotland U.K.
227 J3 Merrickville Ont. Can.
227 E4 Merrill MI U.S.A.
226 C3 Merrill WI U.S.A.
222 E2 Merrill, Mount Y.T. Can.
226 B3 Merrillan WI U.S.A.
230 C3 Merrillville IN U.S.A.
214 D4 Merriman S. Africa
236 C3 Merriman NE U.S.A.
150 E4 Merriott Somerset, England U.K.
222 F5 Merritt B.C. Can.
231 D6 Merritt Island FL U.S.A.
83 G3 Merriwa N.S.W. Austr.
83 G2 Merrygoen N.S.W. Austr.
203 I6 Mersa Fatma Eritrea
165 F5 Mersch Lux.
171 E4 Merschwitz Ger.
192 D1 Merse r. Italy
151 H3 Mersea Island England U.K.
171 C4 Merseburg (Saale) Ger.
149 G4 Mersey est. England U.K.
149 F4 Merseyside admin. div. England U.K.
Mersin İçel Turkey see İçel
129 A3 Mersin Trabzon Turkey
94 C2 Mersing Malaysia
95 F2 Mersing, Bukit mt. Sarawak Malaysia
156 B2 Mers-les-Bains France
138 D3 Mērsrags Latvia
116 C4 Merta Rajasthan India
116 C4 Merta Road Rajasthan India
165 F5 Mertert Lux.
172 A2 Mertesdorf Ger.
150 D3 Merthyr Tydfil Merthyr Tydfil, Wales U.K.
150 D3 Merthyr Tydfil admin. div. Wales U.K.
210 C4 Merti Kenya
173 E3 Mertingen Ger.
210 C4 Merti Plateau Kenya
169 C5 Mertloch Ger.
184 C3 Mértola Port.
237 C6 Mertzon TX U.S.A.
234 C2 Mertztown PA U.S.A.
157 H4 Mertzwiller France
156 C3 Méru France
210 C4 Meru Kenya
211 C5 Meru vol. Tanz.
182 B2 Merufe Port.
210 C4 Meru National Park Kenya
Merv Turkm. see Mary
160 D2 Mervans France
162 B2 Mervent France
163 D5 Merville Midi-Pyrénées France
156 C2 Merville Nord - Pas-de-Calais France
159 F2 Merville-Franceville-Plage France
214 C5 Merweville S. Africa
Merya Turkey see Veliköy
156 D4 Méry-sur-Seine France
169 C3 Merzen Ger.
126 D2 Merzifon Turkey
172 A2 Merzig Ger.
262 T2 Merz Peninsula Antarctica
215 F2 Mesa S. Africa
183 I3 Mesa r. Spain
241 L5 Mesa AZ U.S.A.
239 F5 Mesa NM U.S.A.
226 A2 Mesabi Range hills MN U.S.A.
195 G2 Mesagne Italy
158 E4 Mésanger France
182 C3 Mesão Frio Port.
198 D4 Mesara, Ormos b. Kriti Greece
169 D4 Meschede Ger.
162 B3 Meschers-sur-Gironde France
129 B3 Mescit Dağları mts Turkey
140 L2 Meselefors Sweden
78 □4a Meseong i. Chuuk Micronesia
156 D4 Mesgrigny France
134 J5 Mesha r. Rus. Fed.
139 J4 Meshchovsk Rus. Fed.
Meshed Iran see Mashhad
135 H6 Meshkovskaya Rus. Fed.
234 B1 Meshoppen PA U.S.A.
234 B1 Meshoppen Creek r. PA U.S.A.
226 E3 Mesick MI U.S.A.
188 F4 Mesihovina Bos.-Herz.
195 E4 Mesima r. Italy
198 C1 Mesimeri Greece
129 B3 Meskhet'is K'edi hills Georgia
159 F4 Meslay-du-Maine France
160 D2 Mesnay France
190 E2 Mesocco Switz.
191 H4 Mesola Italy
198 B2 Mesolongi Greece
Mesolóngion Greece see Mesolongi
Mesón del Viente Spain see Mesón do Vento
182 B1 Mesón do Vento Spain
195 F3 Mesoraca Italy
172 D2 Mespelbrunn Ger.
158 D4 Mesquer France
257 F3 Mesquita Brazil
241 J3 Mesquite NV U.S.A.
237 D5 Mesquite TX U.S.A.
205 F2 Messaad Alg.
158 E4 Messac France
202 A3 Messak Mellet hills Libya
211 D7 Messalo r. Moz.
207 I6 Messaména Cameroon
Messana Sicilia Italy see Messina
165 E5 Messancy Belgium
163 A5 Messanges France
170 C3 Meßdorf Ger.
159 F3 Messei France
160 A3 Messeix France
184 B3 Messejana Port.
172 C2 Messel Ger.
195 E4 Messina Sicilia Italy
194 D5 Messina prov. Sicilia Italy
213 F4 Messina S. Africa
Messina, Strait of Italy see Messina, Stretta di
195 E4 Messina, Stretta di str. Italy
157 F3 Messincourt France
227 I2 Messines Que. Can.
169 C3 Messingen Ger.
149 I4 Messingham North Lincolnshire, England U.K.
198 C3 Messini Greece
198 C3 Messiniakos Kolpos b. Greece
172 D4 Meßkirch Ger.
140 K3 Messlingen Sweden
172 C3 Meßstetten Ger.
197 G5 Mesta r. Bulg.
Mesta r. Greece see Nestos
185 H2 Mesta r. Spain
185 F2 Mestanza Spain
176 E1 Městec Králové Czech Rep.
Mestghanem Alg. see Mostaganem
129 C2 Mestia Georgia
170 C2 Mestlin Ger.
177 G1 Město Albrechtice Czech Rep.
173 H2 Město Touškov Czech Rep.
191 H3 Mestre Italy
126 E2 Mesudiye Turkey
94 D4 Mesuji r. Indon.
160 A1 Mesves-sur-Loire France
160 C2 Mesvres France
160 C2 Mesvrin r. France
250 C4 Meta dept Col.
250 E3 Meta r. Col./Venez.
193 G4 Meta Italy
225 G3 Métabetchouan Que. Can.
160 E2 Métabief France
227 G2 Metagama Ont. Can.
221 L3 Meta Incognita Peninsula Nunavut Can.
237 F6 Metairie LA U.S.A.
197 F2 Metaliferi, Munţii mts Romania
191 F5 Metallifere, Colline mts Italy
139 H2 Metallostroy Rus. Fed.
226 C5 Metamora IL U.S.A.
258 D2 Metán Arg.
210 C2 Metanara Eth.
211 B8 Metangula Moz.
243 H6 Metapan El Salvador
191 I5 Metauro r. Italy
225 H4 Meteghan N.S. Can.
169 C3 Metelen Ger.
138 D4 Metelys l. Lith.
210 C1 Metema Eth.
198 B2 Meteora tourist site Greece
85 G5 Meteor Creek r. Qld Austr.
151 I2 Metfield Suffolk, England U.K.
149 I4 Metheringham Lincolnshire, England U.K.
146 F4 Methlick Aberdeenshire, Scotland U.K.
198 B3 Methoni Greece
233 H3 Methuen MA U.S.A.
86 E2 Methuen, Mount hill W.A. Austr.
81 C5 Methven South I. N.Z.
146 E5 Methven Perth and Kinross, Scotland U.K.
151 H2 Methwold Norfolk, England U.K.
188 F4 Metković Croatia
222 D4 Metlakatla AK U.S.A.
205 H2 Metlaoui Tunisia
188 E3 Metlika Slovenia
179 F4 Metnitz Austria
179 F4 Metnitz r. Austria
213 H2 Metoro Moz.
195 F4 Metramo r. Italy
94 D4 Metro Sumatera Indon.
237 F4 Metropolis IL U.S.A.
Metsada tourist site Israel see Masada
170 D2 Metschow Ger.
164 F1 Metslawier Neth.
198 B2 Metsovo Greece
173 G3 Metten Ger.
172 A2 Mettendorf Ger.
173 G3 Mettenheim Ger.
231 D5 Metter GA U.S.A.
179 G4 Mettersdorf am Saßbach Austria
165 D4 Mettet Belgium
169 C3 Mettingen Ger.
172 A2 Mettlach Ger.
240 H4 Mettler CA U.S.A.
179 E2 Mettmach Austria
169 B4 Mettmann Ger.
159 G4 Mettray France
114 C4 Mettuppalaiyam Tamil Nadu India
114 C4 Mettur Tamil Nadu India
210 B2 Metu Eth.
235 D2 Metuchen NJ U.S.A.
176 E1 Metuje r. Czech Rep.
157 G3 Metz France
157 H4 Metzeral France
157 G3 Metzervisse France
172 D3 Metzingen Ger.
245 E3 Metzquititlán Mex.
158 E3 Meu r. France
169 C5 Meudt Ger.
94 B1 Meulaboh Sumatera Indon.
156 B3 Meulan France
165 C4 Meulebeke Belgium
156 B5 Meung-sur-Loire France
160 C2 Meursault France
157 G4 Meurthe r. France
157 G4 Meurthe-et-Moselle dept Lorraine France
165 E4 Meuse r. Belgium/France alt. Maas (Neth.)
157 F3 Meuse dept Lorraine France
171 D4 Meuselwitz Ger.
162 D3 Meuzac France
160 D2 Meuzin r. France
150 C4 Mevagissey Cornwall, England U.K.
108 B1 Mêwa Sichuan China
149 H4 Mexborough South Yorkshire, England U.K.
237 D6 Mexia TX U.S.A.
251 I4 Mexiana, Ilha i. Brazil
242 B1 Mexicali Mex.
241 M3 Mexican Hat UT U.S.A.
241 M3 Mexican Water AZ U.S.A.
242 B2 Mexico country Central America
245 E4 México Mex.
245 E4 México state Mex.
233 □H2 Mexico ME U.S.A.
236 F4 Mexico MO U.S.A.
233 E3 Mexico NY U.S.A.
229 G6 Mexico, Gulf of Mex./U.S.A.
Mexico City Mex. see México
184 B3 Mexilhoeira Grande Port.
160 D3 Meximieux France
146 E3 Mey Highland, Scotland U.K.
122 C3 Meybod Iran
170 D2 Meyenburg Ger.
222 C4 Meyers Chuck AK U.S.A.
232 D5 Meyersdale PA U.S.A.
215 G2 Meyerton S. Africa
161 D3 Meylan France
162 E3 Meymac France
123 F3 Meymaneh Afgh.
131 S3 Meynypil'gyno Rus. Fed.
161 D5 Meyrargues France
161 D5 Meyreuil France
161 E4 Meyronnes France
161 B4 Meyrueis France
162 D3 Meyssac France
161 C4 Meysse France
160 E3 Meythet France
160 C3 Meyzieu France
Mezada tourist site Israel see Masada
182 D4 Mezas mt. Spain
245 E5 Mezcala r. Mex.
243 G5 Mezcalapa r. Mex.
197 F4 Mezdra Bulg.
161 B5 Mèze France
161 E5 Mézel France
134 I2 Mezen' Rus. Fed.
134 I2 Mezen' r. Rus. Fed.
161 C4 Mézenc, Mont mt. France
134 H2 Mezenskaya Guba b. Rus. Fed.
160 D2 Mézériat France
139 H4 Mezha r. Rus. Fed.
98 E1 Mezhdurechensk Kemerovskaya Oblast' Rus. Fed.
134 J3 Mezhdurechensk Respublika Komi Rus. Fed.
130 H4 Mezhdurechenskiy Rus. Fed.
Mezhdurechnye Rus. Fed. see Shali
130 G2 Mezhdusharskiy, Ostrov i. Novaya Zemlya Rus. Fed.
137 I3 Mezhova Ukr.
120 D1 Mezhozernyy Rus. Fed.
137 H2 Mezhyrich Ukr.
176 C1 Meziboří Czech Rep.
179 F4 Mežica Slovenia
159 F2 Mézidon-Canon France
159 H5 Mézières-en-Brenne France
162 C2 Mézières-sur-Issoire France
161 C4 Mézilhac France
156 D5 Mézilles France
176 F1 Meziměstí Czech Rep.
163 C4 Mézin France
139 M4 Mezinovskiy Rus. Fed.
182 C4 Mezio Port.
128 B1 Mezitli Turkey
177 K5 Mezőberény Hungary
177 J4 Mezőcsát Hungary
177 H5 Mezőfalva Hungary
177 K5 Mezőgyán Hungary
177 J5 Mezőhegyes Hungary
177 J4 Mezőkeresztes Hungary
177 H5 Mezőkomárom Hungary
177 J5 Mezőkovácsháza Hungary
177 J4 Mezőkövesd Hungary
177 G4 Mezőörs Hungary
163 A4 Mézos France
177 J4 Mezőszemere Hungary
177 H5 Mezőszilas Hungary
177 J4 Mezőtárkány Hungary
177 J5 Mezőtúr Hungary
186 C4 Mezquita de Jarque Spain
244 B2 Mezquital Mex.
244 B3 Mezquital r. Mex.
244 C2 Mezquitic Mex.
128 C1 Mezraaköy Turkey
191 F2 Mezzana Italy
190 E4 Mezzanego Italy
191 G2 Mezzano Italy
191 G2 Mezzocorona Italy
194 C5 Mezzojuso Sicilia Italy
190 E2 Mezzoldo Italy
191 G2 Mezzolombardo Italy
207 H6 Mfou Cameroon
209 B6 Mfouati Congo
211 A8 Mfuwe Zambia
100 G2 Mgachi Sakhalin Rus. Fed.
195 □ Mġarr Gozo Malta
195 □ Mġarr Malta
207 G5 Mgbidi Nigeria
139 I5 Mglin Rus. Fed.
215 G4 Mgwali r. S. Africa
213 F3 Mhangura Zimbabwe
184 E5 Mharhar, Oued r. Morocco
114 B2 Mhasvad Mahar. India
215 H2 Mhlambanyatsi Swaziland
215 H2 Mhlume Swaziland
215 G1 Mhluzi S. Africa
116 C5 Mhow Madh. Prad. India
107 H4 Mi r. China
96 A2 Mi r. Myanmar
146 B3 Miabhaig Western Isles, Scotland U.K.
245 E4 Miacatlan Mex.
175 L5 Miączyn Pol.
245 F5 Miahuatlán Mex.
184 E1 Miajadas Spain
162 C3 Mialet France
241 L5 Miami AZ U.S.A.
231 D7 Miami FL U.S.A.
237 E4 Miami OK U.S.A.
237 C5 Miami TX U.S.A.
231 D7 Miami Beach FL U.S.A.
232 A5 Miamisburg OH U.S.A.
106 C5 Miancaowan Qinghai China
123 H4 Mian Chanmun Pak.
107 F5 Mianchi Henan China
122 A2 Miandowāb Iran
213 □J3 Miandrivazo Madag.
107 I1 Mianduhe Nei Mongol China
122 A2 Mīāneh Iran
108 B2 Mianning Sichuan China
123 G3 Mianwali Pak.
108 C1 Mianxian Shaanxi China
Mianyang Hubei China see Xiantao
108 C2 Mianyang Sichuan China
108 C2 Mianzhu Sichuan China
107 I4 Miaodao Qundao is China
110 C2 Miao'ergou Xinjiang China
Miaogao Zhejiang China see Suichang
109 G3 Miaoli Taiwan
213 □J3 Miarinarivo Madag.
130 H4 Miass Rus. Fed.
174 F2 Miasteckzo Krajeńskie Pol.
174 E1 Miastko Pol.
175 J4 Miastków Kościelny Pol.
175 J2 Miastkowo Pol.
105 D3 Mibu-gawa r. Japan
252 C5 Mica, Cerro de mt. Chile
222 G4 Mica Creek B.C. Can.
241 L5 Mica Mountain AZ U.S.A.
108 C1 Micang Shan mts China
177 K3 Michaľany Slovakia
177 I3 Michalová Slovakia
177 K3 Michalovce Slovakia
175 I5 Michałów Pol.
175 J4 Michałów Górny Pol.
175 H5 Michałowice Pol.
174 F5 Michałowice Pol.
175 L2 Michałowo Pol.
223 I4 Michel Sask. Can.
171 C5 Michelau in Oberfranken Ger.
172 D2 Michelbach an der Bilz Ger.
179 F4 Micheldorf Austria
179 F3 Micheldorf in Oberösterreich Austria
172 D2 Michelfeld Ger.
220 D5 Michelson, Mount AK U.S.A.
172 D2 Michelstadt Ger.
171 E3 Michendorf Ger.
Micheng Yunnan China see Midu
247 E3 Miches Dom. Rep.
236 F2 Michigan state U.S.A.

Michigan, Lake to Mkata Plain
335

226 D4 Michigan, Lake MI/WI U.S.A.
230 C3 Michigan City IN U.S.A.
208 B2 Michika Nigeria
224 C4 Michipicoten Bay Ont. Can.
224 C4 Michipicoten River Ont. Can.
244 C4 Michoacán state Mex.
175 K4 Michów Pol.
Michurin Bulg. see Tsarevo
135 H5 Michurinsk Rus. Fed.
149 G3 Mickleton Durham, England U.K.
151 F2 Mickleton Gloucestershire, England U.K.
242 □I6 Mico r. Nic.
247 □3 Micoud St Lucia
266 E5 Micronesia is Pacific Ocean
91 L6 Micronesia, Federated States of country N. Pacific Ocean
197 F2 Micula Romania
223 K5 Midale Sask. Can.
264 F4 Mid-Atlantic Ridge sea feature Atlantic Ocean
264 H8 Mid-Atlantic Ridge sea feature Atlantic Ocean
146 F2 Midbea Orkney, Scotland U.K.
165 E3 Middelbeers Neth.
164 C3 Middelburg Neth.
215 E4 Middelburg E. Cape S. Africa
215 G1 Middelburg Mpumalanga S. Africa
142 C4 Middelfart Denmark
164 D3 Middelharnis Neth.
165 B3 Middelkerke Belgium
214 C4 Middelpos S. Africa
164 F1 Middelstum Neth.
213 E5 Middelwit S. Africa
164 E2 Middenmeer Neth.
267 M5 Middle America Trench sea feature N. Pacific Ocean
115 G3 Middle Andaman i. Andaman & Nicobar Is India
Middle Atlas mts Morocco see Moyen Atlas
151 F3 Middle Barton Oxfordshire, England U.K.
225 J3 Middle Bay Que. Can.
233 H4 Middleboro MA U.S.A.
230 D4 Middlebourne WV U.S.A.
227 I5 Middleburg PA U.S.A.
232 E5 Middleburg VA U.S.A.
233 F3 Middleburgh NY U.S.A.
235 E1 Middlebury CT U.S.A.
226 E5 Middlebury IN U.S.A.
233 G2 Middlebury VT U.S.A.
237 C6 Middle Concho r. TX U.S.A.
Middle Congo country Africa see Congo
85 E3 Middle Creek r. Qld Austr.
234 C1 Middle Creek r. PA U.S.A.
235 F1 Middlefield CT U.S.A.
235 F1 Middle Haddam CT U.S.A.
149 H3 Middleham North Yorkshire, England U.K.
235 D1 Middle Hope NY U.S.A.
235 F2 Middle Island NY U.S.A.
236 D3 Middle Loup r. NE U.S.A.
150 E4 Middlemarsh Dorset, England U.K.
85 G4 Middlemount Qld Austr.
232 B5 Middleport OH U.S.A.
234 B2 Middleport PA U.S.A.
236 E3 Middle Raccoon r. IA U.S.A.
149 I4 Middle Rasen Lincolnshire, England U.K.
234 B3 Middle River MD U.S.A.
232 B6 Middlesboro KY U.S.A.
149 H3 Middlesbrough Middlesbrough, England U.K.
149 H3 Middlesbrough admin. div. England U.K.
232 E3 Middlesex NY U.S.A.
234 A2 Middlesex PA U.S.A.
235 F1 Middlesex County county CT U.S.A.
235 D2 Middlesex County county NJ U.S.A.
149 H3 Middlesmoor North Yorkshire, England U.K.
85 E4 Middleton Qld Austr.
225 H4 Middleton N.S. Can.
215 E5 Middleton S. Africa
149 G4 Middleton Greater Manchester, England U.K.
151 H2 Middleton Norfolk, England U.K.
232 A3 Middleton MI U.S.A.
226 C4 Middleton WI U.S.A.
151 F2 Middleton Cheney Northamptonshire, England U.K.
149 G3 Middleton in Teesdale Durham, England U.K.
151 G4 Middleton-on-Sea West Sussex, England U.K.
149 I4 Middleton-on-the-Wolds East Riding of Yorkshire, England U.K.
77 F4 Middleton Reef Austr.
151 F3 Middleton Stoney Oxfordshire, England U.K.
147 E2 Middletown Northern Ireland U.K.
240 F2 Middletown CA U.S.A.
235 F1 Middletown CT U.S.A.
234 C3 Middletown DE U.S.A.
232 E5 Middletown MD U.S.A.
235 D2 Middletown NJ U.S.A.
233 F4 Middletown NY U.S.A.
232 A5 Middletown OH U.S.A.
227 I5 Middletown PA U.S.A.
232 D5 Middletown VA U.S.A.
226 E4 Middleville MI U.S.A.
233 F3 Middleville NY U.S.A.
149 G4 Middlewich Cheshire, England U.K.
81 B6 Mid Dome mt. South I. N.Z.
204 D2 Midelt Morocco
80 E3 Midhirst North I. N.Z.
151 G4 Midhurst West Sussex, England U.K.
124 C4 Mīdī Yemen
163 E5 Midi, Canal du France
163 C6 Midi de Bigorre, Pic du mt. France
163 B6 Midi d'Ossau, Pic du mt. France
265 J5 Mid-Indian Basin sea feature Indian Ocean
265 I6 Mid-Indian Ridge sea feature Indian Ocean
161 A4 Midi-Pyrénées admin. reg. France
224 E4 Midland Ont. Can.
241 J5 Midland CA U.S.A.
227 E4 Midland MI U.S.A.
236 C2 Midland SD U.S.A.
237 C5 Midland TX U.S.A.
87 B6 Midland Junction W.A. Austr.
213 F3 Midlands prov. Zimbabwe
147 C5 Midleton Rep. of Ireland
146 E6 Midlothian admin. div. Scotland U.K.
237 D5 Midlothian TX U.S.A.
232 E6 Midlothian VA U.S.A.
168 D2 Midlum Ger.
227 G3 Midmay Ont. Can.
Midnapore W. Bengal India see Medinipur
213 □J4 Midongy Atsimo Madag.
103 E7 Midori-gawa r. Japan
163 B5 Midou r. France
163 B5 Midouze r. France
266 F4 Mid-Pacific Mountains sea feature N. Pacific Ocean
215 G1 Midrand S. Africa
92 C5 Midsayap Phil.
150 E3 Midsomer Norton Bath and North East Somerset, England U.K.
140 I3 Midsund Norway
108 B3 Midu Yunnan China
113 □2 Midu i. Addu Atoll Maldives
238 C2 Midvale ID U.S.A.
Midway Oman see Thamarīt
241 L1 Midway UT U.S.A.
75 H2 Midway Islands N. Pacific Ocean
87 D4 Midway Well W.A. Austr.
238 F3 Midwest WY U.S.A.
237 D5 Midwest City OK U.S.A.
164 G1 Midwolda Neth.
127 F3 Midyat Turkey
Midye Turkey see Kıyıköy
146 □G1 Mid Yell Shetland, Scotland U.K.
197 F4 Midzhur mt. Bulg./Yugo.
104 C4 Mie pref. Japan
175 I5 Miechów Pol.
177 L1 Mieczka r. Pol.
178 C3 Mieders Austria
183 I3 Miedes Spain
175 I5 Miedziana Góra Pol.
174 D3 Miedzichowo Pol.
175 K3 Miedzna Mazowieckie Pol.
175 H6 Miedźna Pol.
174 G5 Miedźno Pol.
174 F4 Międzybórz Pol.
174 D3 Międzychód Pol.
174 E5 Międzylesie Pol.
175 K4 Międzyrzec Podlaski Pol.
174 D3 Międzyrzecz Pol.
174 C2 Międzyzdroje Pol.
141 N3 Miehikkälä Fin.
169 C5 Miehlen Ger.
175 J6 Miejsce Piastowe Pol.
174 E4 Miejska-Górka Pol.
174 E4 Miękinia Pol.
163 C5 Miélan France
161 D4 Miélandre, Montagne de mt. France
175 J5 Mielec Pol.
174 F3 Mieleszyn Pol.
168 F1 Mielkendorf Ger.
175 L3 Mielnik Pol.
174 E1 Mielno Pol.
211 C7 Miembwe Tanz.
178 C3 Mieming Austria
175 G3 Mień r. Pol.
83 F5 Miena Tas. Austr.
209 F8 Miengwe Zambia
183 G1 Miera r. Spain
197 G2 Miercurea-Ciuc Romania
182 E1 Mieres Spain
Mieres del Camín Spain see Mieres
Mieres del Camino Spain see Mieres
165 E3 Mierlo Neth.
174 E5 Mieroszów Pol.
163 D4 Miers France
244 D2 Mier y Noriaga Mex.
175 I5 Mierzawa r. Pol.
143 H4 Mierzeja Helska pen. Pol.
143 H4 Mierzeja Wiślana spit Pol.
172 B2 Miesau Ger.
173 F4 Miesbach Ger.
174 F3 Mieścisko Pol.
172 B2 Miesenbach Ger.
210 D2 Mī'ēso Eth.
171 C3 Mieste Ger.
171 C3 Miesterhorst Ger.
174 F3 Mieszków Pol.
174 C3 Mieszkowice Pol.
172 D3 Mietingen Ger.
141 M3 Mietoinen Fin.
160 E2 Mieussy France
182 D3 Mieza Spain
232 B4 Mifflin OH U.S.A.
227 I5 Mifflinburg PA U.S.A.
232 E4 Mifflintown PA U.S.A.
234 B1 Mifflinville PA U.S.A.
106 E5 Migang Shan mt. Gansu China
215 E2 Migdol S. Africa
156 D5 Migennes France
191 G4 Migliarino Italy
191 G4 Migliaro Italy
195 F2 Miglionica Italy
162 C2 Mignaloux-Beauvoir France
193 F3 Mignano Monte Lungo Italy
192 D2 Mignone r. Italy
160 E2 Mignovillard France
225 H3 Miguasha Park tourist site N.B. Can.
245 F4 Miguel Alemán Mex.
245 F4 Miguel Alemán, Presa resr Mex.
254 E3 Miguel Alves Brazil
244 C1 Miguel Auza Mex.
254 E4 Miguel Calmon Brazil
245 F5 Miguel de la Madrid, Presa resr Mex.
183 G5 Miguel Esteban Spain
257 F5 Miguel Pereira Brazil
261 F5 Miguel Riglos Arg.
185 G2 Miguelturra Spain
197 G3 Mihăileşti Romania
176 G5 Miháld Hungary
199 G1 Mihalgazi Turkey
126 C3 Mihaliççık Turkey
176 G4 Mihályi Hungary
103 F6 Mihara Japan
105 F4 Mihara-yama vol. Japan
Mihidjan W. Bengal India see Chittaranjan
117 F5 Mihijam Bihar India
169 F4 Mihla Ger.
183 F4 Mijares Spain
187 C4 Mijares r. Spain
185 F4 Mijas Spain
185 F4 Mijas mt. Spain
164 D2 Mijdrecht Neth.
105 F1 Mijōga-take mt. Japan
160 E2 Mijoux France
102 J2 Mikasa Japan
136 D1 Mikashevichy Belarus
177 K4 Mikepércs Hungary
138 F5 Mikhanavichy Belarus
Mikha Tskhakaia Georgia see Senaki
Mikhaykovskiy Rus. Fed. see Prozorovo
139 L4 Mikhaylov Rus. Fed.
Mikhaylovgrad Bulg. see Montana
121 I1 Mikhaylovka Pavlodarskaya Oblast' Kazakh.
Mikhaylovka Zhambylskaya Oblast' Kazakh. see Sarykemer
100 A2 Mikhaylovka Chitinskaya Oblast' Rus. Fed.
137 H1 Mikhaylovka Kurskaya Oblast' Rus. Fed.
100 E4 Mikhaylovka Primorskiy Kray Rus. Fed.
Mikhaylovka Tul'skaya Oblast' Rus. Fed. see Kimovsk
135 H6 Mikhaylovka Volgogradskaya Oblast' Rus. Fed.
197 F4 Mikhaylovo Bulg.
137 K3 Mikhaylovo-Aleksandrovskiy Rus. Fed.
121 I2 Mikhaylovskiy Altayskiy Kray Rus. Fed.
Mikhaylovskiy Altayskiy Kray Rus. Fed. see Malinovoye Ozero
Mikhaylovskoye Rus. Fed. see Shpakovskoye
263 F2 Mikhaytov Island Antarctica
139 K4 Mikhnevo Rus. Fed.
104 A4 Miki Japan
Mikínes tourist site Greece see Mycenae
117 H4 Mikir Hills India
141 N3 Mikkeli Fin.
141 N3 Mikkelin mlk Fin.
222 H3 Mikkwa r. Alta Can.
179 G4 Miklavž Slovenia
175 J2 Mikołajki Pol.
175 H2 Mikołajki Pomorskie Pol.
174 G5 Mikołów Pol.
Míkonos i. Greece see Mykonos
174 G1 Mikoszewo Pol.
Mikoyan Armenia see Yeghegnadzor
Mikoyanovka Rus. Fed. see Oktyabr'skiy
198 C1 Mikropoli Greece
174 F4 Mikstat Pol.
171 F5 Mikulasovice Czech Rep.
176 G3 Mikulčice Czech Rep.
176 F3 Mikulov Czech Rep.
176 G1 Mikulovice Czech Rep.
211 C6 Mikumi Tanz.
211 C6 Mikumi National Park Tanz.
134 J3 Mikun' Rus. Fed.
105 E2 Mikuni-sanmyaku mts Japan
105 E3 Mikuni-yama mt. Japan
205 G1 Mila Alg.
236 E2 Milaca MN U.S.A.
114 B5 Miladhunmadulu Atoll Maldives
254 F3 Milagres Brazil
250 B5 Milagro Ecuador
183 I2 Milagro Spain
183 G3 Milagros Spain
175 I1 Miłakowo Pol.
Milan Italy see Milano
227 F4 Milan MI U.S.A.
236 E3 Milan MO U.S.A.
232 B4 Milan OH U.S.A.
209 C7 Milando Angola
82 D3 Milang S.A. Austr.
213 G3 Milange Moz.
190 E3 Milano Italy
190 E3 Milano prov. Lombardia Italy
190 D3 Milano (Malpensa) airport Italy
191 H4 Milano Marittima Italy
Milanovce Slovakia see Veľký Kýr
175 K4 Milanów Pol.
175 I3 Milanówek Pol.
234 C1 Milanville PA U.S.A.
197 G2 Milaş Romania
199 E3 Milas Turkey
195 E4 Milazzo Sicilia Italy
236 D2 Milbank SD U.S.A.
150 E4 Milborne Port Somerset, England U.K.
150 E4 Milborne St Andrew Dorset, England U.K.
233 □J2 Milbridge ME U.S.A.
170 C3 Milde r. Ger.
151 H2 Mildenhall Suffolk, England U.K.
227 I5 Mildred PA U.S.A.
168 E1 Mildstedt Ger.
83 E3 Mildura Vic. Austr.
129 E3 Mil Düzü lowland Azer.
108 B3 Mile Yunnan China
210 D2 Milē Eth.
148 D3 Milebush Northern Ireland U.K.
151 H3 Mile End Essex, England U.K.
246 □ Mile Gully Jamaica
175L3 Milejczyce Pol.
175 H1 Milejewo Pol.
175 K4 Milejów Pol.
194 C5 Milena Sicilia Italy
85 G5 Miles Qld Austr.
232 E4 Milesburg PA U.S.A.
238 F2 Miles City MT U.S.A.
176 C1 Milešovka hill Czech Rep.
147 C4 Milestone Rep. of Ireland
197 H2 Miletin r. Romania
195 F4 Mileto Italy
193 G3 Miletto, Monte mt. Italy
87 C5 Mileura W.A. Austr.
176 D2 Milevsko Czech Rep.
149 G2 Milfield Northumberland, England U.K.
184 B3 Milfontes Port.
147 C4 Milford Cork Rep. of Ireland
147 D1 Milford Donegal Rep. of Ireland
151 G3 Milford Surrey, England U.K.
235 E1 Milford CT U.S.A.
234 C4 Milford DE U.S.A.
226 D5 Milford IL U.S.A.
233 H3 Milford MA U.S.A.
234 B3 Milford MD U.S.A.
233 □I2 Milford ME U.S.A.
232 B3 Milford MI U.S.A.
236 D3 Milford NE U.S.A.
233 H3 Milford NH U.S.A.
234 C2 Milford NJ U.S.A.
234 D1 Milford PA U.S.A.
241 K2 Milford UT U.S.A.
232 E5 Milford VA U.S.A.
150 B3 Milford Haven Pembrokeshire, Wales U.K.
151 F4 Milford on Sea Hampshire, England U.K.
81 A6 Milford Sound South I. N.Z.
81 A6 Milford Sound inlet South I. N.Z.
234 C2 Milford Square PA U.S.A.
85 E3 Milgarra Qld Austr.
87 C5 Milgun W.A. Austr.
Milḩ, Baḩr al l. Iraq see Razāzah, Buḩayrat ar
182 D3 Milhão Port.
161 C5 Milhaud France
174 F4 Milicz Pol.
Milid Turkey see Malatya
84 B1 Milikapiti N.T. Austr.
87 C6 Miling W.A. Austr.
84 C2 Milingimbi N.T. Austr.
192 A4 Milis Sardegna Italy
194 D5 Militello in Val di Catania Sicilia Italy
158 B3 Milizac France
238 F1 Milk r. MT U.S.A.
203 F5 Milk, Wadi el watercourse Sudan
171 F4 Milkel Ger.
175 J2 Miłki Pol.
131 Q4 Mil'kovo Rus. Fed.
174 E4 Miłkowice Pol.
223 H5 Milk River Alta Can.
164 E3 Mill Neth.
85 F3 Millaa Millaa Qld Austr.
226 A5 Millard MO U.S.A.
187 C5 Millares Spain
161 B4 Millau France
160 C2 Millay France
232 D6 Millboro VA U.S.A.
227 H3 Millbrook Ont. Can.
150 C4 Millbrook Cornwall, England U.K.
231 C5 Millbrook AL U.S.A.
233 G4 Millbrook NY U.S.A.
146 E4 Mill Buie hill Scotland U.K.
238 B2 Mill City OR U.S.A.
232 D5 Mill Creek WV U.S.A.
240 F1 Mill Creek r. CA U.S.A.
234 B3 Mill Creek r. PA U.S.A.
235 F1 Milldale CT U.S.A.
231 D5 Milledgeville GA U.S.A.
226 C5 Milledgeville IL U.S.A.
236 E2 Mille Lacs lakes MN U.S.A.
224 B3 Mille Lacs, Lac des l. Ont. Can.
231 D5 Millen GA U.S.A.
214 D5 Miller S. Africa
236 D2 Miller SD U.S.A.
227 G3 Miller Lake Ont. Can.
135 H6 Millerovo Rus. Fed.
241 L6 Miller Peak AZ U.S.A.
227 E3 Millersburg MI U.S.A.
232 C4 Millersburg OH U.S.A.
227 I5 Millersburg PA U.S.A.
82 D2 Millers Creek S.A. Austr.
232 B6 Millers Creek KY U.S.A.
233 G3 Millers Falls MA U.S.A.
81 B6 Millers Flat South I. N.Z.
232 B5 Millersport OH U.S.A.
234 A2 Millerstown PA U.S.A.
234 B3 Millersville MD U.S.A.
234 B3 Millersville PA U.S.A.
233 G4 Millerton NY U.S.A.
162 E3 Millevaches France
162 D3 Millevaches, Plateau de France
147 E2 Millford Northern Ireland U.K.
232 E4 Mill Hall PA U.S.A.
235 D2 Millhurst NJ U.S.A.
82 E4 Millicent S.A. Austr.
157 F4 Millières France
164 F3 Millingen aan de Rijn Neth.
234 C3 Millington MD U.S.A.
227 F4 Millington MI U.S.A.
237 F5 Millington TN U.S.A.
233 □I2 Millinocket ME U.S.A.
252 C5 Milliri, Cerro mt. Bol.
263 G2 Mill Island Antarctica
147 F2 Millisle Northern Ireland U.K.
85 G5 Millmerran Qld Austr.
234 A2 Millmont PA U.S.A.
149 F3 Millom Cumbria, England U.K.
146 D6 Millport North Ayrshire, Scotland U.K.
234 D1 Millrift PA U.S.A.
233 F5 Millsboro DE U.S.A.
179 E4 Millstatt Austria
179 E4 Millstätter See l. Austria
226 B3 Millston WI U.S.A.
232 B6 Millstone KY U.S.A.
232 C5 Millstone WV U.S.A.
234 D2 Millstone r. NJ U.S.A.
86 C4 Millstream W.A. Austr.
147 B4 Millstreet Rep. of Ireland
225 H4 Milltown N.B. Can.
148 B3 Milltown Cavan Rep. of Ireland
147 C3 Milltown Galway Rep. of Ireland
147 B4 Milltown Kerry Rep. of Ireland
148 C4 Milltown Kildare Rep. of Ireland
146 F4 Milltown Aberdeenshire, Scotland U.K.
148 C3 Milltown Northern Ireland U.K.
238 D2 Milltown MT U.S.A.
226 A3 Milltown WI U.S.A.
147 B4 Milltown Malbay Rep. of Ireland
146 F4 Milltown of Rothiemay Moray, Scotland U.K.
85 E3 Millungera Qld Austr.
215 F1 Millvale S. Africa
240 F3 Mill Valley CA U.S.A.
233 □J1 Millville N.B. Can.
234 C3 Millville NJ U.S.A.
234 B1 Millville PA U.S.A.
235 E1 Millwood NY U.S.A.
237 E5 Millwood Lake AR U.S.A.
156 C4 Milly-la-Forêt France
160 C2 Milly-Lamartine France
87 C5 Milly Milly W.A. Austr.
183 I3 Milmarcos Spain
170 E2 Milmersdorf Ger.
165 E4 Milmort Belgium
146 E5 Milnathort Perth and Kinross, Scotland U.K.
Milne Land i. Greenland see Ilimananngip Nunaa
146 D6 Milngavie East Dunbartonshire, Scotland U.K.
149 G4 Milnrow Greater Manchester, England U.K.
149 G3 Milnthorpe Cumbria, England U.K.
206 C4 Milo r. Guinea
195 E5 Milo Sicilia Italy
233 □I2 Milo ME U.S.A.
100 E4 Milogradovo Rus. Fed.
240 □D9 Milolii HI U.S.A.
175 H2 Miłomłyn Pol.
174 G1 Miłoradz Pol.
198 D3 Milos i. Greece
139 L5 Miloslavskoye Rus. Fed.
174 F3 Miłosław Pol.
146 B4 Milovaig Highland, Scotland U.K.
137 K3 Milove Ukr.
171 F5 Milovice Czech Rep.
171 D3 Milow Brandenburg Ger.
170 C2 Milow Mecklenburg-Vorpommern Ger.
175 H6 Milówka Pol.
83 E2 Milparinka N.S.W. Austr.
240 G3 Milpitas CA U.S.A.
232 E4 Milroy PA U.S.A.
173 G2 Miltach Ger.
172 D2 Miltenberg Ger.
83 G3 Milton N.S.W. Austr.
227 H4 Milton Ont. Can.
81 B7 Milton South I. N.Z.
146 D4 Milton Highland, Scotland U.K.
146 E5 Milton Perth and Kinross, Scotland U.K.
233 F5 Milton DE U.S.A.
231 C6 Milton FL U.S.A.
233 □H3 Milton NH U.S.A.
235 E1 Milton NY U.S.A.
234 B1 Milton PA U.S.A.
233 G2 Milton VT U.S.A.
232 B5 Milton WV U.S.A.
150 C4 Milton Abbot Devon, England U.K.
238 C2 Milton-Freewater OR U.S.A.
151 G2 Milton Keynes Milton Keynes, England U.K.
151 G2 Milton Keynes admin. div. England U.K.
170 E1 Miltzow Ger.
109 E2 Miluo Hunan China
227 G4 Milverton Ont. Can.
150 D3 Milverton Somerset, England U.K.
226 D4 Milwaukee WI U.S.A.
264 E4 Milwaukee Deep sea feature Caribbean Sea
120 E2 Mily Kazakh.
135 H6 Milyutinskaya Rus. Fed.
169 F5 Milz Ger.
163 B5 Mimbaste France
82 C1 Mimili S.A. Austr.
114 C4 Mimisal Tamil Nadu India
163 A4 Mimizan France
163 A4 Mimizan-Plage France
176 D1 Mimoň Czech Rep.
208 A5 Mimongo Gabon
257 G4 Mimoso do Sul Brazil
103 G6 Mimuro-yama mt. Japan
243 E3 Mina Mex.
240 H2 Mina NV U.S.A.
252 C3 Mina, Nevado mt. Peru
122 D5 Mīnāb Iran
122 D5 Mīnāb r. Iran
260 E2 Mina Clavero Arg.
184 C3 Mina de São Domingos Port.
223 L4 Minago r. Man. Can.
93 B2 Minahasa, Semenanjung pen. Indon.
Minahassa Peninsula Indon. see Minahasa, Semenanjung
125 F2 Mina Jebel Ali U.A.E.
Minaker B.C. Can. see Prophet River
223 M5 Minaki Ont. Can.
103 E7 Minamata Japan
84 C2 Minamia N.T. Austr.
105 F3 Minamiashigara Japan
104 C4 Minamichita Japan
104 B3 Minami-gawa r. Japan
103 □3 Minami-Iō-jima vol. Kazan-rettō Japan
Min'an Hunan China see Longshan
146 C5 Minard Argyll and Bute, Scotland U.K.
81 B6 Minaret Peaks South I. N.Z.
246 C2 Minas Cuba
94 C2 Minas Sumatera Indon.
258 G4 Minas Uru.
127 H5 Mīnā' Sa'ūd Kuwait
225 H4 Minas Channel N.S. Can.
258 G3 Minas de Corrales Uru.
246 B2 Minas de Matahambre Cuba
184 D3 Minas de Riotinto Spain
256 D3 Minas Gerais state Brazil
257 F2 Minas Novas Brazil
185 I2 Minateda Spain
244 B4 Minatitlán Mex.
245 G4 Minatitlán Mex.
185 H1 Minaya Spain
96 A2 Minbu Myanmar
123 H4 Minchinabad Pak.
259 B6 Minchinmávida vol. Chile
146 E6 Minch Moor hill Scotland U.K.
191 F3 Mincio r. Italy
129 E4 Mincivan Azer.
92 C5 Mindanao i. Phil.
92 C5 Mindanao r. Phil.
82 E3 Mindarie S.A. Austr.
182 B5 Minde Port.
173 E3 Mindel r. Ger.
173 E3 Mindelheim Ger.
206 □ Mindelo Cape Verde
182 B3 Mindelo Port.
173 F3 Mindelstetten Ger.
224 E4 Minden Ont. Can.
169 D3 Minden Ger.
237 E5 Minden LA U.S.A.
236 D3 Minden NE U.S.A.
240 H2 Minden NV U.S.A.
227 F4 Minden City MI U.S.A.
165 D3 Minderhout Belgium
86 B4 Minderoo W.A. Austr.
92 B3 Mindoro i. Phil.
92 A3 Mindoro Strait Phil.
209 B6 Mindouli Congo
177 J5 Mindszent Hungary
177 H5 Mindszentgodisa Hungary
257 E4 Minduri Brazil
120 D1 Mindyak Rus. Fed.
Mindzhivan Azer. see Mincivan
103 E6 Mine Japan
226 A1 Mine Centre Ont. Can.
147 D5 Mine Head Rep. of Ireland
150 D3 Minehead Somerset, England U.K.
124 A3 Mineiga, Gebel mts Egypt/Sudan
256 A2 Mineiros Brazil
194 D5 Mineo Sicilia Italy
235 E2 Mineola NY U.S.A.
237 E5 Mineola TX U.S.A.
150 D1 Minera Wrexham, Wales U.K.
232 E5 Mineral VA U.S.A.
129 C1 Mineral'nyye Vody Rus. Fed.
226 B4 Mineral Point WI U.S.A.
237 D5 Mineral Wells TX U.S.A.
232 C5 Mineralwells WV U.S.A.
191 G4 Minerbio Italy
234 B2 Minersville PA U.S.A.
241 K2 Minersville UT U.S.A.
Minerva atoll Arch. des Tuamotu Fr. Polynesia see Reao
232 C4 Minerva OH U.S.A.
193 I3 Minervino Murge Italy
161 A5 Minervois, Monts du hills France
172 C2 Minfeld Ger.
111 C4 Minfeng Xinjiang China
209 E7 Minga Dem. Rep. Congo
129 E3 Mingäçevir Azer.
129 E3 Mingäçevir Su Anbarı resr Azer.
208 D3 Mingala C.A.R.
225 H3 Mingan Que. Can.
225 I3 Mingan, Îles de is Que. Can.
193 H4 Mingardo r. Italy
82 E3 Mingary S.A. Austr.
Mingechaur Azer. see Mingäçevir
Mingechaurskoye Vodokhranilishche resr Azer. see Mingäçevir Su Anbarı
85 F3 Mingela Qld Austr.
87 B6 Mingenew W.A. Austr.
Mingfeng Hubei China see Yuan'an
109 E1 Minggang Henan China
109 F1 Mingguang Anhui China
96 A2 Mingin Myanmar
96 A2 Mingin Range mts Myanmar
121 H4 Ming-Kush Kyrg.
183 I5 Minglanilla Spain
232 C4 Mingo Junction OH U.S.A.
183 F4 Mingorría Spain
211 C7 Mingoyo Tanz.
Mingshan Chongqing China see Fengdu
108 B2 Mingshan Sichuan China
100 C3 Mingshui Heilong. China
146 A5 Mingulay i. Scotland U.K.
213 I2 Mingùri Moz.
109 F3 Mingxi Fujian China
Mingzhou Hebei China see Weixian
Mingzhou Shaanxi China see Suide
Minhe Jiangxi China see Jinxian
112 J4 Minhe Qinghai China
96 A3 Minhla Magwe Myanmar
96 A3 Minhla Pegu Myanmar
109 F3 Minhou Fujian China
158 E3 Miniac-Morvan France
114 B4 Minicoy i. India
87 D6 Minigwal, Lake salt flat W.A. Austr.
179 H4 Minihof-Liebau Austria
138 C4 Minija r. Lith.
87 B4 Minilya W.A. Austr.
87 B4 Minilya r. W.A. Austr.
260 A5 Mininco Chile
206 D4 Mininian Côte d'Ivoire
183 H3 Ministra mt. Spain
183 H3 Ministra, Sierra mts Spain
223 K4 Minitonas Man. Can.
Minjian Sichuan China see Mabian
108 C2 Min Jiang r. Sichuan China
109 F3 Min Jiang r. China
84 C1 Minjilang N.T. Austr.
129 E4 Minkänd Azer.
Min-Kush Kyrg. see Ming-Kush
82 D3 Minlaton S.A. Austr.
106 D4 Minle Gansu China
207 G4 Minna Nigeria
263 L1 Minna Bluff pt Antarctica
102 □1 Minna-shima i. Japan
141 K3 Minne Sweden
236 D4 Minneapolis KS U.S.A.
226 A3 Minneapolis MN U.S.A.
223 L5 Minnedosa Man. Can.
232 D5 Minnehaha Springs WV U.S.A.
237 C4 Minneola KS U.S.A.
236 E2 Minnesota r. MN U.S.A.
236 E2 Minnesota state U.S.A.
226 B3 Minnesota City MN U.S.A.
236 D1 Minnewaukan ND U.S.A.
87 B4 Minnie Creek W.A. Austr.
146 D7 Minnigaff Dumfries and Galloway, Scotland U.K.
82 C3 Minnipa S.A. Austr.
104 C3 Mino Japan
182 B3 Miño r. Port./Spain
105 E3 Minobu-san mt. Japan
105 E4 Minobu-sanchi mts Japan
104 D3 Minokamo Japan
104 D3 Mino-Mikawa-kōgen reg. Japan
226 B2 Minong WI U.S.A.
226 C5 Minonk IL U.S.A.
104 B4 Minoo Japan
Minorca i. Spain see Menorca
160 C1 Minot France
236 C1 Minot ND U.S.A.
106 D4 Minqin Gansu China
109 F3 Minqing Fujian China
234 C3 Minquadale DE U.S.A.
107 G5 Minquan Henan China
168 C2 Minsen Ger.
108 B1 Min Shan mts Sichuan China
138 F5 Minsk Belarus
Minskaya Oblast' admin. div. Belarus see Minskaya Voblasts'
138 F5 Minskaya Voblasts' admin. div. Belarus
175 J3 Mińsk Mazowiecki Pol.
Minsk Oblast admin. div. Belarus see Minskaya Voblasts'
151 H3 Minster Kent, England U.K.
151 I3 Minster Kent, England U.K.
232 A4 Minster OH U.S.A.
150 E2 Minsterley Shropshire, England U.K.
207 I5 Minta Cameroon
108 B1 Mintang Qinghai China
146 G4 Mintlaw Aberdeenshire, Scotland U.K.
225 H4 Minto N.B. Can.
Minto atoll Arch. des Tuamotu Fr. Polynesia see Tenarunga
263 L2 Minto, Mount Antarctica
220 G2 Minto Inlet N.W.T. Can.
223 J5 Minton Sask. Can.
173 G3 Mintraching Ger.
239 F4 Minturn CO U.S.A.
Minturnae Italy see Minturno
193 F3 Minturno Italy
190 F4 Minucciano Italy
203 F2 Minûf Egypt
126 C5 Minûfîya governorate Egypt
98 F1 Minusinsk Rus. Fed.
190 D2 Minusio Switz.
108 A2 Minutang Arun. Prad. India
208 B4 Minvoul Gabon
106 E5 Minxian Gansu China
Minya Konka mt. Sichuan China see Gongga Shan
134 L5 Minyar Rus. Fed.
83 E4 Minyip Vic. Austr.
227 E3 Mio MI U.S.A.
196 E3 Mionica Srbija Yugo.
160 C3 Mionnay France
160 C3 Mions France
163 B4 Mios France
84 D5 Mipia, Lake salt flat Qld Austr.
110 D3 Miquan Xinjiang China
224 E3 Miquelon Que. Can.
225 J4 Miquelon i. St Pierre and Miquelon
245 E2 Miquihuana Mex.
138 F5 Mir Belarus
250 B4 Mira r. Col.
191 H3 Mira Italy
182 B4 Mira Port.
184 B3 Mira r. Port.
183 I5 Mira Spain
183 I5 Mira r. Spain
161 D5 Mirabeau France
233 F2 Mirabel Que. Can.
163 D4 Mirabel France
182 D5 Mirabel Spain
257 E2 Mirabela Brazil
161 D4 Mirabel-aux-Baronnies France
194 D5 Mirabella Imbaccari Sicilia Italy
257 F4 Miracema Brazil
Miracema do Norte Brazil see Miracema do Tocantins
254 C4 Miracema do Tocantins Brazil
Mirada Hills CA U.S.A. see La Mirada
182 B5 Mira de Aire Port.
257 F4 Miradouro Brazil
163 C5 Miradoux France
250 C3 Miraflores Col.
183 G4 Miraflores de la Sierra Spain
257 F4 Miraí Brazil
114 B2 Miraj Mahar. India
261 I6 Miramar Buenos Aires Arg.
261 F2 Miramar Córdoba Arg.
191 H4 Miramare Italy
161 D5 Miramas France
162 B3 Mirambeau France
186 C4 Mirambel Spain
163 C4 Miramont-de-Guyenne France
163 B5 Miramont-Sensacq France
110 E4 Miran Xinjiang China
253 F5 Miranda Brazil
253 F4 Miranda r. Brazil
Miranda Moz. see Macaloge
240 F1 Miranda CA U.S.A.
250 E2 Miranda state Venez.
87 D5 Miranda, Lake salt flat W.A. Austr.
183 I2 Miranda de Arga Spain
183 H2 Miranda de Ebro Spain
182 E4 Miranda del Castañar Spain
182 B4 Miranda do Corvo Port.
182 D3 Miranda do Douro Port.
163 C5 Mirande France
182 C3 Mirandela Port.
184 D1 Mirandilla Spain
191 G4 Mirandola Italy
163 E4 Mirandol-Bourgnounac France
256 B4 Mirandópolis Brazil
191 H3 Mirano Italy
256 B5 Mirante, Serra do hills Brazil
256 B5 Mirante do Paranapanema Brazil
198 B1 Miras Albania
256 C4 Mirassol Brazil
182 D2 Miravalles mt. Spain
182 E5 Miravete hill Spain
Mir-Bashir Azer. see Tärtär
125 F4 Mirbāţ Oman
129 F4 Mircälal Azer.
175 L5 Mircze Pol.
246 D3 Mirebalais Haiti
160 D1 Mirebeau Bourgogne France
162 C2 Mirebeau Poitou-Charentes France
157 G4 Mirecourt France
163 D5 Miremont France
179 E5 Miren Slovenia
163 D5 Mirepoix France
161 B5 Mireval France
117 F4 Mirganj Bihar India
Mirgorod Ukr. see Myrhorod
95 F1 Miri Sarawak Malaysia
123 E4 Miri mt. Pak.
207 H3 Miria Niger
114 C2 Mirialguda Andhra Prad. India
85 G5 Miriam Vale Qld Austr.
117 H4 Miri Hills India
258 G4 Mirim, Lagoa l. Brazil/Uru.
Mírina Voreio Aigaio Greece see Myrina
114 B3 Mirjan Karnataka India
123 E4 Mīrjāveh Iran
197 G4 Mirkovo Bulg.
188 D3 Mirna r. Croatia
179 G5 Mirna Slovenia
179 G5 Mirna r. Slovenia
263 G2 Mirny research stn Antarctica
134 H3 Mirnyy Arkhangel'skaya Oblast' Rus. Fed.
139 H5 Mirnyy Bryanskaya Oblast' Rus. Fed.
131 M3 Mirnyy Respublika Sakha (Yakutiya) Rus. Fed.
129 D1 Mirnyy Stavropol'skiy Kray Rus. Fed.
197 F3 Miroč hills Yugo.
174 D4 Mirocin Górny Pol.
81 D5 Miromiro mt. South I. N.Z.
Mironovka Kharkivs'ka Oblast' Ukr. see Myronivka
Mironovka Kyivs'ka Oblast' Ukr. see Myronivka
179 H2 Miroslav Czech Rep.
174 E2 Mirosławiec Pol.
176 C2 Mirošov Czech Rep.
171 G4 Mirostowice Dolne Pol.
176 D2 Mirovice Czech Rep.
170 D2 Mirow Ger.
123 H3 Mirpur Pak.
123 G5 Mirpur Batoro Pak.
123 G5 Mirpur Khas Pak.
123 F5 Mirpur Sakro Pak.
222 H4 Mirror Alta Can.
110 D3 Mirsali Xinjiang China
174 D5 Mirsk Pol.
85 F4 Mirtna Qld Austr.
Mirtoan Sea Greece see Mirtoö Pelagos
195 F3 Mirto Crosia Italy
198 C3 Mirtoö Pelagos sea Greece
183 E4 Mirueña de los Infanzones Spain
213 F2 Miruro Moz.
Miryalaguda Andhra Prad. India see Mirialguda
101 D6 Miryang S. Korea
Mirzachul Uzbek. see Gulistan
117 E4 Mirzapur Uttar Prad. India
175 J4 Mirzec Pol.
191 I5 Misa r. Italy
104 B4 Misaki Japan
191 H5 Misano Adriatico Italy
245 F4 Misantla Mex.
105 F3 Misato Japan
207 H4 Misau Nigeria
102 J3 Misawa Japan
177 K5 Mişca Romania
193 G3 Miscano r. Italy
179 H3 Mischendorf Austria
224 B3 Misehkow r. Ont. Can.
160 D1 Miserey-Salines France
116 C1 Misgar Jammu and Kashmir
214 D5 Misgund S. Africa
122 D3 Mīsh, Kūh-e hill Iran
224 C2 Mishamattawa r. Ont. Can.
100 D3 Mishan Heilong. China
226 D5 Mishawaka IN U.S.A.
139 L4 Misheronskiy Rus. Fed.
226 D3 Mishicot WI U.S.A.
105 E3 Mishima Japan
134 L5 Mishkino Rus. Fed.
124 D3 Mishlah, Khashm hill Saudi Arabia
117 H3 Mishmi Hills India
194 C4 Misilmeri Sicilia Italy
258 G2 Misiones prov. Arg.
124 C2 Miskah Saudi Arabia
177 I5 Miske Hungary
242 □J6 Miskitos, Cayos is Nic.
Miskitos, Costa de coastal area Nic. see Costa de Mosquitos
177 J3 Miskolc Hungary
179 G4 Mislinja Slovenia
188 E2 Mislinja r. Slovenia
124 C2 Mismā, Jibāl al mts Saudi Arabia
128 C3 Mismā, Tall al hill Jordan
161 D4 Mison France
93 D3 Misoöl i. Irian Jaya Indon.
234 C4 Mispillion r. DE U.S.A.
226 B2 Misquah Hills MN U.S.A.
235 G1 Misquamicut RI U.S.A.
Misr country Africa see Egypt
Misraç Turkey see Kurtalan
202 B1 Mişrātah Libya
116 E4 Misrikh Uttar Prad. India
227 E1 Missanabie Ont. Can.
193 I4 Missanello Italy
158 D4 Missillac France
224 D3 Missinaibi r. Ont. Can.
223 J4 Missinipe Sask. Can.
85 E2 Mission r. Qld Austr.
236 C3 Mission SD U.S.A.
237 D7 Mission TX U.S.A.
85 F3 Mission Beach Qld Austr.
240 I5 Mission Viejo CA U.S.A.
206 B3 Missira Senegal
224 C2 Missisa r. Ont. Can.
224 E3 Missisicabi r. Que. Can.
224 D4 Mississagi r. Ont. Can.
224 E5 Mississauga Ont. Can.
224 E4 Mississippi r. Ont. Can.
237 F6 Mississippi r. U.S.A.
237 F5 Mississippi state U.S.A.
237 F6 Mississippi Delta LA U.S.A.
237 F6 Mississippi Sound sea chan. MS U.S.A.
Missolonghi Greece see Mesolongi
238 D2 Missoula MT U.S.A.
204 E2 Missour Morocco
236 F4 Missouri r. U.S.A.
236 E4 Missouri state U.S.A.
236 E3 Missouri Valley IA U.S.A.
84 B3 Mistake Creek N.T. Austr.
85 F4 Mistake Creek r. Qld Austr.
225 I3 Mistanipisipou r. Que. Can.
225 F3 Mistassibi r. Que. Can.
225 F3 Mistassini Que. Can.
225 F3 Mistassini r. Que. Can.
224 F3 Mistassini, Lac l. Que. Can.
179 H2 Mistelbach Austria
173 F2 Mistelgau Ger.
195 E5 Misterbianco Sicilia Italy
149 I4 Misterton Nottinghamshire, England U.K.
224 F3 Mistissini Que. Can.
137 J3 Mistky Ukr.
261 F2 Mistolar, Lago l. Arg.
198 C3 Mistras tourist site Greece
194 D5 Mistretta Sicilia Italy
Misuratah Libya see Mişrātah
191 H2 Misurina Italy
140 K2 Misvær Norway
105 F3 Mitaka Japan
213 G2 Mitande Moz.
251 H4 Mitaraca hill Suriname
150 E3 Mitcheldean Gloucestershire, England U.K.
85 F5 Mitchell Qld Austr.
83 H2 Mitchell r. N.S.W. Austr.
85 E2 Mitchell r. Qld Austr.
83 F4 Mitchell r. Vic. Austr.
227 G4 Mitchell Ont. Can.
238 B2 Mitchell OR U.S.A.
236 D3 Mitchell SD U.S.A.
231 D5 Mitchell, Mount NC U.S.A.
Mitchell Island Cook Is see Nassau
Mitchell Island Tuvalu see Nukulaelae
84 B1 Mitchell Point N.T. Austr.
232 D5 Mitchelltown VA U.S.A.
147 C4 Mitchelstown Rep. of Ireland
203 F2 Mīt Ghamr Egypt
116 B5 Mithapur Gujarat India
123 H3 Mitha Tiwano Pak.
123 G5 Mithi Pak.
Míthimna Greece see Mithymna
199 E2 Mithymna Greece
81 □2 Mitiaro i. Cook Is
Mitiero i. Cook Is see Mitiaro
Mitilíni Voreio Aigaio Greece see Mytilini
80 D2 Mititai North I. N.Z.
104 D4 Mito Aichi Japan
105 G2 Mito Ibaraki Japan
80 E4 Mitre mt. North I. N.Z.
77 H3 Mitre Island Solomon Is
81 A6 Mitre Peak South I. N.Z.
135 G6 Mitrofanovka Rus. Fed.
Mitrovica Kosovo, Srbija Yugo. see Kosovska Mitrovica
156 C4 Mitry-Mory France
217 □3a Mitsamiouli Njazidja Comoros
213 □J3 Mitsinjo Madag.
Mits'iwa Eritrea see Massawa
217 □3a Mitsoudjé Njazidja Comoros
105 F2 Mitsukaidō Japan
103 I5 Mitsuke Japan
104 D2 Mitsumatarenge-dake mt. Japan
105 E3 Mitsutōge-yama mt. Japan
83 G3 Mittagong N.S.W. Austr.
83 F4 Mitta Mitta Vic. Austr.
178 B3 Mittelberg Austria
173 E2 Mittelberg hill Ger.
172 D3 Mittelbiberach Ger.
173 E2 Mittelfranken admin. reg. Bayern Ger.
171 C4 Mittelhausen Ger.
169 E5 Mittelkalbach Ger.
169 E5 Mittelsinn Ger.
173 G4 Mittelspitze mt. Ger.
173 F4 Mittenwald Ger.
170 E2 Mittenwalde Brandenburg Ger.
171 E3 Mittenwalde Brandenburg Ger.
179 G3 Mitterdorf im Mürztal Austria
173 G3 Mitterfels Ger.
157 G4 Mittersheim France
178 D3 Mittersill Austria
173 G3 Mitterskirchen Ger.
173 G2 Mitterteich Ger.
Mittimatalik Nunavut Can. see Pond Inlet
171 D5 Mittweida Ger.
250 D4 Mitú Col.
250 D4 Mituas Col.
209 E7 Mitumba, Chaîne des mts Dem. Rep. Congo
208 F5 Mitumba, Monts mts Dem. Rep. Congo
209 E7 Mitwaba Dem. Rep. Congo
171 C5 Mitwitz Ger.
208 A4 Mitzic Gabon
Miughalaigh i. Scotland U.K. see Mingulay
105 F3 Miura Japan
105 F3 Miura-hantō pen. Japan
135 G7 Mius r. Rus. Fed.
137 J4 Miusskiy Liman est. Rus. Fed.
137 J3 Miusyns'k Ukr.
Mixian Henan China see Xinmi
245 E4 Mixteco r. Mex.
104 D2 Miya-gawa r. Japan
104 C4 Miya-gawa r. Japan
102 J4 Miyagi pref. Japan
102 J4 Miyako Japan
102 J5 Miyakoji Japan
102 □1 Miyako-jima i. Japan
103 E8 Miyakonojō Japan
108 B2 Miyaluo Sichuan China
120 C2 Miyaly Kazakh.
Miyang Yunnan China see Mile
116 B5 Miyani Gujarat India
103 E8 Miyanojō Japan
102 □1 Miyanoura-dake mt. Japan
103 E8 Miyazaki Japan
103 E7 Miyazaki pref. Japan
104 B3 Miyazu Japan
108 B3 Miyi Sichuan China
103 F6 Miyoshi Japan
107 H3 Miyun Beijing China
210 B3 Mīzan Teferī Eth.
Mizar Turkey see Karakeçi
147 B5 Mizen Head hd Cork Rep. of Ireland
147 E4 Mizen Head hd Wicklow Rep. of Ireland
136 B3 Mizhhir"ya Ukr.
107 F4 Mizhi Shaanxi China
197 H3 Mizil Romania
197 F4 Miziya Bulg.
136 D2 Mizoch Ukr.
195 F3 Mizofato r. Italy
Mizo Hills state India see Mizoram
117 H5 Mizoram state India
234 D3 Mizpah NJ U.S.A.
252 D4 Mizque Bol.
252 D4 Mizque r. Bol.
105 E3 Mizugaki-yama mt. Japan
105 F3 Mizuho Japan
104 D3 Mizunami Japan
105 F2 Mizuno-gawa r. Japan
102 J4 Mizusawa Japan
143 F2 Mjölby Sweden
142 D2 Mjøndalen Norway
142 D1 Mjøsa l. Norway
215 G4 Mkambati S. Africa
211 C6 Mkata Tanz.
211 C6 Mkata Plain Tanz.

Mkhondvo to Montgomery

336

215 H2 Mkhondvo r. Swaziland
211 C6 Mkoani Tanz.
211 C6 Mkokotoni Tanz.
211 C6 Mkomazi Tanz.
209 F8 Mkushi Zambia
215 I2 Mkuze S. Africa
215 I2 Mkuze r. S. Africa
176 D1 Mladá Boleslav Czech Rep.
176 D2 Mladá Vožice Czech Rep.
176 E1 Mladé Buky Czech Rep.
196 E3 Mladenovac Srbija Yugo.
197 E4 Mlado Nagoričane Macedonia
211 A6 Mlala Hills Tanz.
215 I2 Mlaula r. Swaziland
196 E3 Mlava r. Yugo.
175 I2 Mława Pol.
175 I3 Mławka r. Pol.
217 □3b Mlima Bénara mt. Mayotte
217 □3b Mlima Choungui mt. Mayotte
188 F4 Mljet i. Croatia
188 F4 Mljetski Kanal sea chan. Croatia
137 I2 Mlodat' r. Rus. Fed.
175 I3 Młodzieszyn Pol.
215 H1 Mlumati r. S. Africa
215 F4 Mlungisi S. Africa
175 H1 Młynary Pol.
175 J3 Młynarze Pol.
136 C2 Mlyniv Ukr.
175 M6 Mlynys'ka Ukr.
215 E1 Mmabatho S. Africa
213 E4 Mmadinare Botswana
176 D2 Mnichovice Czech Rep.
176 D1 Mnichovo Hradiště Czech Rep.
175 I5 Mnichów Pol.
175 I4 Mniów Pol.
177 J3 Mníšek nad Hnilcom Slovakia
175 J4 Mniszew Pol.
175 I4 Mniszków Pol.
215 H2 Mnjoli Dam Swaziland
100 F1 Mnogovershinnyy Rus. Fed.
141 I3 Mo Norway
252 B1 Moa r. Brazil
246 D2 Moa Cuba
93 D5 Moa i. Maluku Indon.
241 M2 Moab UT U.S.A.
208 A5 Moabi Gabon
252 C1 Moaco r. Brazil
91 J9 Moa Island Qld Austr.
79 □1 Moala i. Fiji
213 G5 Moamba Moz.
81 C5 Moana South I. N.Z.
182 B2 Moaña Spain
208 B5 Moanda Gabon
241 J3 Moapa NV U.S.A.
147 D3 Moate Rep. of Ireland
213 G3 Moatize Moz.
209 F6 Moba Dem. Rep. Congo
105 G3 Mobara Japan
208 D3 Mobaye C.A.R.
Mobayembongo Dem. Rep. Congo see Mobayi-Mbongo
208 D3 Mobayi-Mbongo Dem. Rep. Congo
149 G4 Mobberley Cheshire, England U.K.
236 E4 Moberly MO U.S.A.
222 F4 Moberly Lake B.C. Can.
226 E1 Mobert Ont. Can.
231 B6 Mobile AL U.S.A.
241 K5 Mobile AZ U.S.A.
237 F6 Mobile Bay AL U.S.A.
92 B3 Mobo Phil.
236 C2 Mobridge SD U.S.A.
Mobutu, Lake Dem. Rep. Congo/Uganda see Albert, Lake
Mobutu Sese Seko, Lake Dem. Rep. Congo/Uganda see Albert, Lake
246 E3 Moca Dom. Rep.
254 C2 Mocajuba Brazil
Moçambique country Africa see Mozambique
213 I2 Moçambique Moz.
Moçâmedes Angola see Namibe
234 B1 Mocanaqua PA U.S.A.
184 B1 Moçarria Port.
240 G3 Moccasin CA U.S.A.
232 B6 Moccasin Gap VA U.S.A.
183 G5 Mocejón Spain
177 G3 Močenok Slovakia
139 K4 Mocha r. Rus. Fed.
Mocha Yemen see Al Mukhā
258 B5 Mocha, Isla i. Chile
183 I3 Mochales Spain
175 H3 Mochowo Pol.
212 E5 Mochudi Botswana
174 E3 Mochy Pol.
211 D7 Mocimboa da Praia Moz.
211 C7 Mocimboa do Rovuma Moz.
197 G2 Mociu Romania
171 C3 Möckern Ger.
172 D2 Möckmühl Ger.
171 D4 Mockrehna Ger.
231 D5 Mocksville NC U.S.A.
185 G3 Moclín Spain
185 F4 Moclinejo Spain
250 E5 Mocó r. Brazil
250 B4 Mocoa Col.
256 D4 Mococa Brazil
261 I2 Mocoretá r. Arg.
242 D3 Mocorito Mex.
242 D2 Moctezuma Chihuahua Mex.
244 D2 Moctezuma San Luis Potosí Mex.
242 C2 Moctezuma Sonora Mex.
245 E3 Moctezuma r. Mex.
239 E6 Moctezuma r. Mex.
213 H3 Mocuba Moz.
109 E4 Mocun Guangdong China
161 E3 Modane France
116 C5 Modasa Gujarat India
165 E4 Modave Belgium
150 D4 Modbury Devon, England U.K.
215 E3 Modder r. S. Africa
214 E3 Modderivier S. Africa
191 F4 Modena Italy
191 F4 Modena prov. Emilia-Romagna Italy
235 D1 Modena NY U.S.A.
234 C3 Modena PA U.S.A.
241 K3 Modena UT U.S.A.
157 H4 Moder r. France
240 G3 Modesto CA U.S.A.
194 D6 Modica Sicilia Italy
191 G4 Modigliana Italy
194 B5 Modione r. Sicilia Italy
175 K5 Modliborzyce Pol.
179 H2 Mödling Austria
175 I4 Modliszewice Pol.
192 A4 Modolo Sardegna Italy
107 F2 Modot Mongolia
176 G3 Modra Slovakia
188 G3 Modriča Bos.-Herz.
176 F2 Modřice Czech Rep.
179 F4 Mödringberg mt. Austria
177 I3 Modrý Kameň Slovakia
195 F1 Modugno Italy
83 F4 Moe Vic. Austr.
213 H3 Moebase Moz.
80 E2 Moehau hill North I. N.Z.
158 C4 Moëlan-sur-Mer France
150 D1 Moel Famau hill Wales U.K.
150 C1 Moelfre Isle of Anglesey, Wales U.K.
150 D2 Moel Sych hill Wales U.K.
141 J3 Moelv Norway
215 F3 Moemaneng S. Africa
Moen i. Chuuk Micronesia see Weno
140 L1 Moen Norway
191 G2 Moena Italy
251 H3 Moengo Suriname
241 L3 Moenkopi AZ U.S.A.
241 L4 Moenkopi Wash r. AZ U.S.A.
165 C3 Moerbeke Belgium
80 E1 Moerewa North I. N.Z.
164 E3 Moergestel Neth.
165 C3 Moerkerke Belgium
Moero, Lake Dem. Rep. Congo/Zambia see Mweru, Lake
169 B4 Moers Ger.
190 E2 Moesa r. Switz.
214 D2 Moeswal S. Africa
78 □6 Moetambe, Mount Choiseul Solomon Is
146 E6 Moffat Dumfries and Galloway, Scotland U.K.
182 D3 Mofreita Port.
177 L4 Moftin Romania
116 C3 Moga Punjab India
Mogadishu Somalia see Muqdisho
Mogador Morocco see Essaouira
182 D3 Mogadouro Port.
182 D3 Mogadouro, Serra de mts Port.
213 F4 Mogalakwena r. S. Africa
114 D2 Mogalturra Andhra Prad. India
102 I4 Mogami-gawa r. Japan
216 □3f Mogán Gran Canaria Canary Is
213 F5 Moganyaka S. Africa
96 B1 Mogaung Myanmar
147 C5 Mogeely Rep. of Ireland
170 D3 Mögelin Ger.
168 D1 Møgeltønder Denmark
179 H4 Mogersdorf Austria
191 I2 Moggio Udinese Italy
172 D3 Mögglingen Ger.
175 I4 Mogielnica Pol.
175 I6 Mogielnica mt. Pol.
256 D5 Mogi-Guaçu Brazil
196 E5 Mogila Macedonia
175 H6 Mogilany Pol.
Mogilev Belarus see Mahilyow
Mogilev Oblast admin. div. Belarus see Mahilyowskaya Voblasts'
Mogilev Podol'skiy Ukr. see Mohyliv Podil's'kyy
Mogilevskaya Oblast' admin. div. Belarus see Mahilyowskaya Voblasts'
174 E3 Mogilnica r. Pol.
174 F3 Mogilno Pol.
256 D5 Mogi-Mirim Brazil
213 I2 Mogincual Moz.
191 F4 Moglia Italy
191 I5 Mogliano Italy
191 H3 Mogliano Veneto Italy
172 D3 Möglingen Ger.
100 A1 Mogocha Rus. Fed.
139 K3 Mogocha r. Rus. Fed.
205 H1 Mogod mts Tunisia
212 E5 Mogoditshane Botswana
182 B4 Mogofores Port.
96 B2 Mogok Myanmar
241 L4 Mogollon Plateau AZ U.S.A.
185 G2 Mogón Spain
Mogontiacum Ger. see Mainz
192 A5 Mogorella Sardegna Italy
192 A5 Mogoro Sardegna Italy
192 A5 Mogoro r. Sardegna Italy
197 H2 Mogoşeşti Romania
175 I3 Mogowo Pol.
107 G1 Mogoytuy Rus. Fed.
208 B2 Mogroum Chad
184 D3 Moguer Spain
107 I2 Moguqi Nei Mongol China
215 F1 Mogwase S. Africa
177 I4 Mogyoród Hungary
177 H6 Mohács Hungary
80 F3 Mohaka r. North I. N.Z.
116 E5 Mohala Madh. Prad. India
215 F4 Mohale's Hoek Lesotho
236 C1 Mohall ND U.S.A.
Moḩammadābād Iran see Darreh Gaz
205 F2 Mohammadia Alg.
116 E3 Mohan r. India/Nepal
116 D4 Mohana Madh. Prad. India
117 G4 Mohanganj Bangl.
185 I2 Moharque Spain
241 J4 Mohave Mountains AZ U.S.A.
226 C2 Mohawk MI U.S.A.
233 G3 Mohawk r. NY U.S.A.
241 K5 Mohawk Mountains AZ U.S.A.
100 B1 Mohe Heilong. China
141 L3 Mohed Sweden
143 F3 Moheda Sweden
182 D4 Mohedas de Granadilla Spain
235 F1 Mohegan CT U.S.A.
235 E1 Mohegan Lake NY U.S.A.
Mohéli i. Comoros see Mwali
176 F2 Mohelnice Czech Rep.
176 F2 Mohelno Czech Rep.
123 G5 Mohenjo Daro tourist site Pak.
147 B4 Moher, Cliffs of Rep. of Ireland
183 G4 Mohernando Spain
147 D4 Mohil Rep. of Ireland
137 I4 Mohila Bel'mak, Hora hill Ukr.
147 D3 Mohill Rep. of Ireland
215 F2 Mohlakeng S. Africa
171 D4 Möhlau Ger.
169 C4 Möhne r. Ger.
234 B2 Mohnton PA U.S.A.
252 C3 Moho Peru
114 B2 Mohol Mahar. India
241 K4 Mohon Peak AZ U.S.A.
177 I4 Mohora Hungary
171 E5 Mohorn Ger.
217 □3a Mohoro Njazidja Comoros
211 C7 Mohoro Tanz.
173 E2 Möhrendorf Ger.
168 E1 Mohrkirch Ger.
234 C2 Mohrsville PA U.S.A.
136 D3 Mohyliv Podil's'kyy Ukr.
136 D2 Mohylyany Ukr.
142 B2 Moi Norway
186 F3 Moià Cataluña Spain
194 D1 Moiano Italy
146 C5 Moidart reg. Scotland U.K.
212 E4 Moijabana Botswana
182 C4 Moimenta da Beira Port.
159 E4 Moine r. France
197 H2 Moineşti Romania
160 C3 Moingt France
Moinkum des. Kazakh. see Moyynkum, Peski
Mointy Kazakh. see Moyynty
147 E2 Moira Northern Ireland U.K.
Moírai Kriti Greece see Moires
140 K2 Mo i Rana Norway
117 H4 Moirang Manipur India
160 D2 Moirans-en-Montagne France
163 C4 Moirax France
198 D4 Moires Kriti Greece
138 E2 Mõisaküla Estonia
168 E2 Moisburg Ger.
158 E4 Moisdon-la-Rivière France
197 G2 Moisei Romania
261 G2 Moisés Ville Arg.
225 H3 Moisie Que. Can.
225 H3 Moisie r. Que. Can.
156 C3 Moislains France
163 D4 Moissac France
161 E5 Moissac-Bellevue France
208 C2 Moïssala Chad
160 D1 Moissey France
192 B2 Moïta Corse France
182 B4 Moita Aveiro Port.
184 B2 Moita Setúbal Port.
187 C6 Moixent-Mogente Spain
185 I3 Mojácar Spain
183 F3 Mojados Spain
240 H4 Mojave CA U.S.A.
240 I4 Mojave r. CA U.S.A.
240 I4 Mojave Desert CA U.S.A.
108 B4 Mojiang Yunnan China
256 D5 Moji das Cruzes Brazil
256 C4 Moji-Guaçu r. Brazil
103 E7 Mojikō Japan
185 G2 Mojina mt. Spain
196 D4 Mojkovac Crna Gora Yugo.
252 D5 Mojo Bol.
210 C2 Mojo Eth.
95 F4 Mojokerto Jawa Timur Indon.
185 G3 Mojón Alto mt. Spain
183 H5 Mojón Alto mt. Spain
258 D2 Mojones, Cerro mt. Arg.
252 D3 Mojos, Llanos de plain Bol.
210 D3 Mojo Shet' r. Eth.
252 D4 Mojotoro Bol.
254 C2 Moju Brazil
105 G2 Mōka Japan
80 E3 Mokai North I. N.Z.
117 F4 Mokama Bihar India
209 F8 Mokambo Dem. Rep. Congo
80 E3 Mokau North I. N.Z.
80 E3 Mokau r. North I. N.Z.
208 B4 Mokéko Congo
240 G2 Mokelumne r. CA U.S.A.
215 G3 Mokhotlong Lesotho
139 K5 Mokhovoye Rus. Fed.
131 N3 Mokhsogollokh Rus. Fed.
136 D2 Mokiyivtsi Ukr.
205 H2 Moknine Tunisia
175 K3 Mokobody Pol.
Mokogai i. Fiji see Makogai
117 H4 Mokokchung Nagaland India
207 I4 Mokolo Cameroon
213 E4 Mokolo r. S. Africa
81 B7 Mokoreta South I. N.Z.
81 B7 Mokoreta hill South I. N.Z.
81 B7 Mokotua South I. N.Z.
101 C6 Mokp'o S. Korea
196 E4 Mokra Gora mts Yugo.
137 F3 Mokra Kalyhirka Ukr.
177 K3 Mokrance Slovakia
196 E3 Mokrin Vojvodina, Srbija Yugo.
137 I4 Mokri Yaly r. Ukr.
120 A2 Mokrous Rus. Fed.
135 H5 Moksha r. Rus. Fed.
135 I5 Mokshan Rus. Fed.
Môktama Myanmar see Martaban
240 □ Mokuleia HI U.S.A.
Mokundurra Rajasthan India see Mukandwara
Mokvin Pershotravnevoye Ukr. see Mokvyn
136 D2 Mokvyn Ukr.
207 G4 Mokwa Nigeria
215 F2 Mokwallo S. Africa
165 E3 Mol Belgium
177 J6 Mol Vojvodina, Srbija Yugo.
195 G1 Mola di Bari Italy
163 D5 Molandier France
245 E3 Molango Mex.
198 C3 Molaoi Greece
190 D4 Molare Italy
188 E3 Molat i. Croatia
187 B6 Molatón mt. Spain
168 C3 Molbergen Ger.
179 F4 Mölbling Austria
150 D1 Mold Flintshire, Wales U.K.
177 J3 Moldava nad Bodvou Slovakia
Moldavia country Europe see Moldova
Moldavskaya S.S.R. country Europe see Moldova
140 I3 Molde Norway
140 K2 Moldjord Norway
136 E4 Moldova country Europe
197 H2 Moldova r. Romania
197 E3 Moldova Nouă Romania
197 G3 Moldoveanu, Vârful mt. Romania
197 G1 Moldovei, Podişul plat. Romania
136 D4 Moldovei Centrale, Podişul plat. Moldova
136 D4 Moldovei de Nord, Cîmpia lowland Moldova
136 D3 Moldovei de Nord, Podişul plat. Moldova
136 E4 Moldovei de Sud, Cîmpia plain Moldova
197 G2 Moldoviţa Romania
129 A2 Moldovka Rus. Fed.
150 D4 Mole r. England U.K.
108 A3 Mole Chaung r. Myanmar
182 B3 Moledo Viana do Castelo Port.
182 C4 Moledo Viseu Port.
182 B4 Molelos Port.
215 G2 Molen r. S. Africa
165 D4 Molenbeek-St-Jean Belgium
212 E5 Molepolole Botswana
149 I4 Molescroft East Riding of Yorkshire, England U.K.
156 E5 Molesmes France
138 E4 Molėtai Lith.
193 I3 Molfetta Italy
168 F1 Molfsee Ger.
140 L3 Moliden Sweden
163 D4 Molières France
163 D4 Molières France
161 C4 Molières-sur-Cèze France
163 A5 Moliets-et-Maa France
260 B4 Molina Chile
193 F2 Molina Aterno Italy
183 I4 Molina de Aragón Spain
187 B6 Molina de Segura Spain
191 F3 Molina di Ledro Italy
193 G3 Molinara Italy
182 D2 Molinaseca Spain
236 F3 Moline IL U.S.A.
237 D4 Moline KS U.S.A.
191 G4 Molinella Italy
161 E4 Molines-en-Queyras France
160 B2 Molinet France
160 D2 Molinges France
185 H2 Molinicos Spain
191 G2 Molini di Tures Italy
231 C6 Molino FL U.S.A.
234 B2 Molino PA U.S.A.
186 C2 Molino de Villobas Spain
186 C4 Molinos Spain
186 F3 Molins de Rei Spain
209 F7 Moliro Dem. Rep. Congo
193 G3 Molise admin. reg. Italy
193 H4 Moliterno Italy
163 E6 Molitg-les-Bains France
177 L5 Moliviş mt. Romania
171 D4 Mölkau Ger.
143 E2 Molkom Sweden
178 E4 Möll r. Austria
122 B3 Mollā Bodāgh Iran
129 F3 Mollakänd Azer.
142 C4 Møllebjerg hill Denmark
183 F1 Molledo Spain
117 H4 Mol Len mt. Nagaland India
170 E2 Möllenbeck Ger.
252 C4 Mollendo Peru
170 D2 Möllenhagen Ger.
87 C6 Mollerin, Lake salt flat W.A. Austr.
186 D3 Mollerussa Spain
160 B2 Molles France
186 F3 Mollet del Vallès Spain
156 C3 Molliens-Dreuil France
185 F3 Mollina Spain
190 E1 Mollis Switz.
179 F3 Molln Austria
170 E2 Mölln Ger.
168 F2 Mölln Ger.
186 F2 Molló Spain
143 F2 Mölltorp Sweden
142 E3 Mölnlycke Sweden
240 □B7 Moloaa HI U.S.A.
137 H4 Molochans'k Ukr.
137 H4 Molochna r. Ukr.
134 G4 Molochnoye Rus. Fed.
134 F1 Molochnyy Rus. Fed.
Molodechno Belarus see Maladzyechna
263 D2 Molodezhnaya research stn Antarctica
137 G3 Molodizhne Kirovohrads'ka Oblast' Ukr.
137 H5 Molodizhne Respublika Krym Ukr.
121 G1 Molodogvardeyskoye Kazakh.
139 I3 Molodoy Tud Rus. Fed.
139 K2 Mologa r. Rus. Fed.
240 □C8 Molokai i. HI U.S.A.
139 K2 Molokovo Rus. Fed.
134 J4 Moloma r. Rus. Fed.
161 B3 Molompize France
83 G3 Molong N.S.W. Austr.
212 D6 Molopo watercourse Botswana/S. Africa
198 C2 Molos Greece
Molotov Rus. Fed. see Perm'
Molotovo Rus. Fed. see Oktyabr'skoye
Molotovsk Kyrg. see Kayyngdy
Molotovsk Arkhangel'skaya Oblast' Rus. Fed. see Severodvinsk
Molotovsk Kirovskaya Oblast' Rus. Fed. see Nolinsk
Molotovskaya Oblast' admin. div. Rus. Fed. see Permskaya Oblast'
207 I6 Moloundou Cameroon
136 E4 Molovata Moldova
160 C1 Moloy France
169 F4 Molschleben Ger.
157 H4 Molsheim France
223 L5 Molson Man. Can.
215 F4 Molteno S. Africa
192 B2 Moltifao Corse France
Moluccas is Indon. see Maluku
93 C3 Molucca Sea Indon.
183 I5 Moluengo mt. Spain
213 H2 Molumbo Moz.
191 F2 Molveno Italy
213 H3 Moma Moz.
83 E2 Momba N.S.W. Austr.
254 F3 Mombaça Brazil
190 D4 Mombaldone Italy
211 C5 Mombasa Kenya
184 B2 Mombeja Port.
183 E4 Mombeltrán Spain
190 D4 Mombercelli Italy
Mombetsu Japan see Monbetsu
208 C5 Momboyo r. Dem. Rep. Congo
169 E5 Mömbris Ger.
256 A3 Mombuca, Serra da hills Brazil
182 D2 Mombuey Spain
197 G5 Momchilgrad Bulg.
226 D5 Momence IL U.S.A.
165 D4 Momignies Belgium
242 □I6 Momotombo, Volcán vol. Nic.
250 C2 Mompós Col.
131 P3 Momskiy Khrebet mts Rus. Fed.
163 B5 Momuy France
142 E4 Møn i. Denmark
117 H4 Mon Nagaland India
96 B3 Mon state Myanmar
241 L2 Mona UT U.S.A.
232 C4 Monaca PA U.S.A.
146 A4 Monach, Sound of sea chan. Scotland U.K.
185 G3 Monachil Spain
185 G3 Monachil r. Spain
146 A4 Monach Islands Scotland U.K.
192 B3 Monacia-d'Aullène Corse France
161 F5 Monaco country Europe
264 H4 Monaco Basin sea feature N. Atlantic Ocean
146 D4 Monadhliath Mountains Scotland U.K.
251 F2 Monagas state Venez.
147 E2 Monaghan Rep. of Ireland
147 E2 Monaghan county Rep. of Ireland
237 C6 Monahans TX U.S.A.
147 E4 Monamolin Rep. of Ireland
247 E3 Mona Passage Dom. Rep./Puerto Rico
213 I2 Monapo Moz.
209 C7 Mona Quimbundo Angola
146 C4 Monar, Loch l. Scotland U.K.
222 E5 Monarch Mountain B.C. Can.
222 G5 Monashee Mountains B.C. Can.
195 F4 Monasterace Italy
147 D3 Monasterevan Rep. of Ireland
183 H2 Monasterio de Suso tourist site Spain
128 A5 Monastery of St Catherine tourist site Egypt
128 A5 Monastery of St Anthony tourist site Egypt
128 A5 Monastery of St Paul tourist site Egypt
192 B5 Monastir Sardegna Italy
Monastir Macedonia see Bitola
205 H2 Monastir Tunisia
175 M6 Monastyrets' Ukr.
Monastyrishche Ukr. see Monastyryshche
139 H4 Monastyrshchina Rus. Fed.
136 E3 Monastyryshche Ukr.
136 C3 Monastyrys'ka Ukr.
207 H5 Monatélé Cameroon
81 C6 Monavale South I. N.Z.
79 □1a Monavatu mt. Viti Levu Fiji
147 D4 Monavullagh Mountains hills Rep. of Ireland
163 C4 Monbahus France
163 C4 Monbazillac France
163 D5 Monbéqui France
102 K1 Monbetsu Japan
163 D5 Monbrun France
187 C5 Moncada Spain
190 C3 Moncalieri Italy
190 D3 Moncalvo Italy
182 D2 Moncalvo mt. Spain
182 B2 Monção Port.
184 C3 Moncarapacho Port.
163 C4 Moncaut France
183 I3 Moncayo, Sierra del mts Spain
159 G4 Moncé-en-Belin France
157 G4 Moncel-sur-Seille France
190 D2 Mönch mt. Switz.
140 P2 Monchegorsk Rus. Fed.
169 B4 Mönchengladbach Ger.
179 H3 Mönchhof Austria
190 F4 Monchio delle Corti Italy
184 B3 Monchique Port.
184 B3 Monchique, Serra de mts Port.
173 E3 Mönchsdeggingen Ger.
231 D5 Moncks Corner SC U.S.A.
163 C4 Monclar France
163 D5 Monclar-de-Quercy France
243 E3 Monclova Mex.
187 C5 Moncófar Spain
158 D3 Moncontour Bretagne France
159 F5 Moncontour Poitou-Charentes France
159 F5 Moncoutant France
163 C4 Moncrabeau France
225 H4 Moncton N.B. Can.
185 F4 Monda Spain
255 B8 Mondai Brazil
182 B2 Mondariz Spain
182 B2 Mondariz-Balneario Spain
163 D5 Mondavezan France
191 H5 Mondavio Italy
182 B4 Mondego r. Port.
182 B4 Mondego, Cabo c. Port.
183 G4 Mondéjar Spain
194 C4 Mondello Sicilia Italy
159 F2 Mondeville France
182 C3 Mondim de Basto Port.
215 H2 Mondlo S. Africa
202 B6 Mondo Chad
191 I5 Mondolfo Italy
182 C1 Mondoñedo Spain
165 F5 Mondorf-les-Bains Lux.
159 G4 Mondoubleau France
190 C4 Mondovì Italy
226 B3 Mondovi WI U.S.A.
161 C4 Mondragon France
183 H1 Mondragón Spain
193 F3 Mondragone Italy
179 E3 Mondsee Austria
179 E3 Mondsee l. Austria
211 C5 Monduli Tanz.
187 C5 Mondúver hill Spain
246 □ Moneague Jamaica
177 L5 Moneasa Romania
226 D5 Monee IL U.S.A.
147 C3 Moneen Rep. of Ireland
190 E4 Moneglia Italy
186 C3 Monegrillo Spain
163 B5 Monein France
232 D4 Monessen PA U.S.A.
184 D2 Monesterio Spain
161 D4 Monestier-de-Clermont France
163 E4 Monestiés France
227 J1 Monet Que. Can.
232 D6 Moneta VA U.S.A.
238 F3 Moneta WY U.S.A.
156 D5 Monéteau France
237 E4 Monett MO U.S.A.
147 D4 Moneygall Rep. of Ireland
146 B7 Moneyglass Northern Ireland U.K.
147 E2 Moneymore Northern Ireland U.K.
148 C3 Moneyneany Northern Ireland U.K.
148 D3 Moneyreagh Northern Ireland U.K.
191 I3 Monfalcone Italy
193 G4 Monfecorvino Rovella Italy
163 C4 Monflanquin France
250 D4 Monfort Col.
163 C5 Monfort France
184 C1 Monforte Port.
182 C2 Monforte Spain
182 C5 Monforte da Beira Port.
190 C4 Monforte d'Alba Italy
187 C6 Monforte del Cid Spain
186 C3 Monforte de Moyuela Spain
182 D4 Monfortinho Port.
184 B2 Monfurado hill Port.
256 D6 Mongaguá Brazil
208 C4 Mongala r. Dem. Rep. Congo
117 G4 Mongar Bhutan
234 D1 Mongaup r. NY U.S.A.
234 D1 Mongaup Valley NY U.S.A.
208 F4 Mongbwalu Dem. Rep. Congo
96 D2 Mông Cai Vietnam
87 C6 Mongers Lake salt flat W.A. Austr.
78 □6 Mongga New Georgia Is Solomon Is
191 G4 Monghidoro Italy
Monghyr Bihar India see Munger
202 C6 Mongo Chad
Mongó hill Spain see Montgó
106 D2 Mongolia country Asia
Mongolküre Xinjiang China see Zhaosu
Mongol Uls country Asia see Mongolia
207 H6 Mongomo Equat. Guinea
86 E2 Mongona, Mount hill W.A. Austr.
207 I3 Mongonu Nigeria
123 H3 Mongora Pak.
208 C4 Mongoumba C.A.R.
146 F5 Mongour hill Scotland U.K.
190 D3 Mongrando Italy
209 D8 Mongu Zambia
206 B2 Mônguel Maur.
191 H2 Monguelfo Italy
106 D2 Mönhbulag Mongolia
173 E3 Monheim Ger.
106 A2 Mönh Hayrhan Uul mt. Mongolia
146 E6 Moniaive Dumfries and Galloway, Scotland U.K.
226 C3 Monico WI U.S.A.
161 D4 Monieux France
146 F5 Monifieth Angus, Scotland U.K.
148 B4 Monilea Rep. of Ireland
250 C3 Moniquirá Col.
161 B4 Monistrol-d'Allier France
186 E3 Monistrol de Montserrat Spain
161 C3 Monistrol-sur-Loire France
240 I2 Monitor Mountain NV U.S.A.
240 I2 Monitor Range mts NV U.S.A.
257 E3 Monjolos Brazil
168 F1 Mönkeberg Ger.
211 B8 Monkey Bay Malawi
87 B5 Monkey Mia W.A. Austr.
175 K2 Mońki Pol.
84 E5 Monkira Qld Austr.
150 C4 Monkokehampton Devon, England U.K.
208 D5 Monkoto Dem. Rep. Congo
151 H2 Monks Eleigh Suffolk, England U.K.
227 G4 Monkton Ont. Can.
234 B3 Monkton MD U.S.A.
187 C4 Monleón r. Spain
163 C5 Monléon-Magnoac France
150 E3 Monmouth Monmouthshire, Wales U.K.
240 H3 Monmouth CA U.S.A.
236 F3 Monmouth IL U.S.A.
235 D2 Monmouth County county NJ U.S.A.
234 D2 Monmouth Junction NJ U.S.A.
222 F5 Monmouth Mountain B.C. Can.
150 E3 Monmouthshire admin. div. Wales U.K.
159 G4 Monnaie France
232 B4 Monnett OH U.S.A.
164 E2 Monnickendam Neth.
150 E3 Monnow r. England/Wales U.K.
207 F5 Mono r. Togo
78 □6 Mono Island Solomon Is
177 K3 Monok Hungary
226 D5 Monon IN U.S.A.
226 B4 Monona IA U.S.A.
195 G2 Monopoli Italy
177 I4 Monor Hungary
232 D4 Monorgahela r. PA U.S.A.
177 K4 Monostorpályi Hungary
187 C6 Monóvar Spain
81 A6 Monowai, Lake South I. N.Z.
163 C4 Monpazier France
183 I2 Monreal Spain
185 H1 Monreal r. Spain
186 B4 Monreal del Campo Spain
194 C4 Monreale Sicilia Italy
146 D7 Monreith Dumfries and Galloway, Scotland U.K.
231 D5 Monroe GA U.S.A.
236 E3 Monroe IA U.S.A.
237 E5 Monroe LA U.S.A.
227 F5 Monroe MI U.S.A.
231 D5 Monroe NC U.S.A.
234 D1 Monroe NJ U.S.A.
235 D1 Monroe NY U.S.A.
241 K2 Monroe UT U.S.A.
232 D6 Monroe VA U.S.A.
238 B2 Monroe WA U.S.A.
226 C4 Monroe WI U.S.A.
226 C3 Monroe Center WI U.S.A.
236 F4 Monroe City MO U.S.A.
234 C1 Monroe County county PA U.S.A.
227 I5 Monroeton PA U.S.A.
231 C6 Monroeville AL U.S.A.
226 E5 Monroeville IN U.S.A.
234 C3 Monroeville NJ U.S.A.
232 B4 Monroeville OH U.S.A.
206 C5 Monrovia Liberia
182 D5 Monroy Spain
186 C4 Monroyo Spain
165 C4 Mons Belgium
161 A5 Mons Languedoc-Roussillon France
161 E5 Mons Provence-Alpes-Côte-d'Azur France
193 F2 Monsampolo del Tronto Italy
182 C4 Monsanto Port.
184 C2 Monsaraz Port.
169 B5 Monschau Ger.
162 C3 Monsec France
163 B5 Monségur France
163 C4 Monségur France
191 G3 Monselice Italy
163 C4 Monsempron-Libos France
156 D2 Mons-en-Barœul France
235 D1 Monsey NY U.S.A.
172 C3 Mönsheim Ger.
172 C2 Monsheim Rheinland-Pfalz Ger.
160 C2 Monsols France
233 □I2 Monson ME U.S.A.
164 D2 Monster Neth.
143 G3 Mönsterås Sweden
191 F5 Monsummano Terme Italy
190 C4 Monta Italy
169 C5 Montabaur Ger.
187 C6 Montaberner Spain
163 F5 Montady France
161 B5 Montagnac France
191 G3 Montagnana Italy
162 B4 Montagne France
160 D1 Montagney France
161 B5 Montagnol France
160 C2 Montagny France
162 C3 Montagrier France
214 C5 Montagu S. Africa
225 I4 Montague P.E.I. Can.
234 D1 Montague NJ U.S.A.
237 D5 Montague TX U.S.A.
87 C5 Montague Range hills W.A. Austr.
86 E2 Montague Sound b. W.A. Austr.
Montagu Island Vanuatu see Nguna
158 E5 Montaigu France
163 D4 Montaigu-de-Quercy France
160 A2 Montaigut France
163 D5 Montaigut-sur-Save France
191 F5 Montaione Italy
95 F3 Montalat r. Indon.
186 C4 Montalbán Spain
185 F3 Montalbán de Córdoba Spain
195 E4 Montalbano Elicona Sicilia Italy
195 F2 Montalbano Jonico Italy
183 H5 Montalbo Spain
192 D1 Montalcino Italy
191 G5 Montale Italy
182 C3 Montalegre Port.
160 D3 Montalieu-Vercieu France
162 A3 Montalivet-les-Bains France
194 C5 Montallegro Sicilia Italy
195 E4 Montalto mt. Italy
193 F2 Montalto delle Marche Italy
192 D2 Montalto di Castro Italy
192 D2 Montalto Marina Italy
193 I5 Montalto Uffugo Italy
182 C5 Montalvão Port.
240 H4 Montalvo CA U.S.A.
182 E3 Montamarta Spain
197 F4 Montana Bulg.
190 C2 Montana Switz.
238 E2 Montana state U.S.A.
Montañana Spain see Puente de Montañana
242 □I6 Montañas de Colón mts Hond.
184 D1 Montánchez hill Spain
184 D1 Montánchez, Sierra de mts Spain
234 B2 Montandon PA U.S.A.
187 C4 Montanejos Spain
163 B5 Montaner France
257 G3 Montanha Brazil
193 H4 Montano Antilia Italy
163 D5 Montans France
193 G3 Montaquila Italy
184 B1 Montargil Port.
156 C5 Montargis France
163 D5 Montastruc-la-Conseillère France
156 C3 Montataire France
163 D4 Montauban France
158 D3 Montauban-de-Bretagne France
163 E5 Montaud, Pic de mt. France
159 F3 Montaudin France
233 H4 Montauk NY U.S.A.
163 C4 Montauriol France
161 E5 Montauroux France
163 B5 Montaut Aquitaine France
163 B5 Montaut Aquitaine France
163 D5 Montaut Midi-Pyrénées France
163 C5 Montaut-les-Crénaux France
215 G3 Mont-aux-Sources mt. Lesotho
163 C4 Montayral France
193 G3 Montazzoli Italy
160 C1 Montbard France
160 D1 Montbarrey France
163 D5 Montbartier France
163 E4 Montbazens France
161 B5 Montbazin France
159 G4 Montbazon France
160 E1 Montbéliard France
160 E2 Montbenoît France
163 C5 Montbernard France
163 D4 Montbeton France
161 B5 Montblanc France
160 E3 Mont Blanc mt. France/Italy
186 E3 Montblanc Spain
Montblanch Spain see Montblanc
160 E3 Mont Blanc Tunnel France/Italy
161 C4 Montboucher-sur-Jaberon France
160 E1 Montbozon France
186 E3 Montbrió del Camp Spain
160 C3 Montbrison France
162 C3 Montbron France
163 D4 Montbrun France
161 D4 Montbrun-les-Bains France
232 C6 Montcalm WV U.S.A.
163 C4 Montcaret France
156 B2 Montcavrel France
160 C2 Montceau-les-Mines France
160 C2 Montcenis France
160 C2 Montchanin France
235 D2 Montclair NJ U.S.A.
156 E3 Montcornet France
156 C5 Montcresson France
163 D4 Montcuq France
156 E3 Montcy-Notre-Dame France
161 B5 Montdardier France
161 E4 Mont-Dauphin France
163 B5 Mont-de-Marsan France
156 C3 Montdidier France
160 A3 Mont-Dore France
261 F5 Monte, Lago del l. Arg.
193 H5 Montea mt. Italy
252 D4 Monteagudo Bol.
183 I3 Monteagudo Spain
183 I5 Monteagudo de las Salinas Spain
183 H3 Monteagudo de las Vicarías Spain
260 A5 Monte Aguila Chile
245 F5 Monte Alban tourist site Oaxaca Mex.
251 H5 Monte Alegre Brazil
256 B2 Monte Alegre r. Brazil
254 D5 Monte Alegre de Goiás Brazil
187 B6 Montealegre del Castillo Spain
256 C3 Monte Alegre de Minas Brazil
256 C4 Monte Alto Brazil
256 C4 Monte Aprazível Brazil
255 E5 Monte Azul Brazil
256 C4 Monte Azul Paulista Brazil
224 F4 Montebello Que. Can.
195 E5 Montebello Ionico Italy
86 B4 Montebello Islands W.A. Austr.
191 G3 Montebello Vicentino Italy
191 H3 Montebelluna Italy
158 E2 Montebourg France
190 E4 Montebruno Italy
261 F3 Monte Buey Arg.
191 H5 Montecalvo in Foglia Italy
258 G2 Montecarlo Arg.
161 F5 Monte-Carlo Monaco
256 D3 Monte Carmelo Brazil
261 I2 Monte Caseros Arg.
191 I5 Montecassiano Italy
193 E2 Monte Castello di Vibio Italy
193 E2 Montecastrilli Italy
191 F5 Montecatini Terme Italy
191 F5 Montecatini Val di Cecina Italy
191 H5 Montecchio Italy
190 F4 Montecchio Emilia Italy
191 G3 Montecchio Maggiore Italy
163 D5 Montech France
190 D3 Montechiaro d'Asti Italy
184 B3 Montechoro Port.
213 E4 Monte Christo S. Africa
193 G3 Montecilfone Italy
240 H4 Montecito CA U.S.A.
182 C5 Monte Claro Port.
182 B3 Monte Córdova Port.
193 G4 Montecorice Italy
193 I4 Monte Cotugna, Lago di l. Italy
191 H2 Montecreale Valcellina Italy
191 F4 Montecreto Italy
246 E3 Monte Cristi Dom. Rep.
250 A5 Montecristi Ecuador
253 E3 Monte Cristo Bol.
184 C1 Monte da Pedra Port.
184 B3 Monte da Rocha, Barragem do resr Port.
182 C2 Montederramo Spain
193 G4 Monte di Procida Italy
184 C2 Monte do Trigo Port.
251 H5 Monte Dourado Brazil
244 C2 Monte Escobedo Mex.
193 G4 Montefalcione Italy
193 E2 Montefalco Italy
193 G3 Montefalcone Italy
193 H3 Montefalcone di Val Fortore Italy
191 I5 Montefano Italy
191 H5 Montefelcino Italy
192 E2 Montefiascone Italy
193 F1 Montefiore dell'Aso Italy
191 F4 Montefiorino Italy
193 G4 Monteforte Irpino Italy
193 F2 Montefortino Italy
193 E2 Montefranco Italy
185 F3 Montefrío Spain
195 F2 Montegiordano Italy
193 F1 Montegiorgio Italy
246 □ Montego Bay Jamaica
246 □ Montego Bay b. Jamaica
184 C3 Monte Gordo Port.
191 I5 Montegranaro Italy
163 C5 Montégut-Arros France
261 G6 Monte Hermoso Arg.
182 D4 Montehermoso Spain
195 G2 Monteiasi Italy
163 D4 Monteils France
254 F3 Monteiro Brazil
185 E4 Montejaque Spain
185 G3 Montejícar Spain
84 B3 Montejinnie N.T. Austr.
183 G3 Montejo de la Sierra Spain
184 A1 Montejunto, Serra de hill Port.
191 H5 Montelabbate Italy
193 F3 Montelanico Italy
184 A2 Montelavar Port.
160 A3 Montel-de-Gelat France
193 H3 Monteleone di Puglia Italy
193 E2 Monteleone di Spoleto Italy
192 E2 Monteleone d'Orvieto Italy
192 A4 Monteleone Rocca Doria Sardegna Italy
193 E2 Monteleone Sabino Italy
194 C4 Montelepre Sicilia Italy
193 E2 Montelibretti Italy
161 D4 Montélier France
161 C4 Montélimar France
253 F5 Monte Lindo r. Para.
193 H4 Montella Italy
184 E3 Montellano Spain
226 C4 Montello WI U.S.A.
163 D5 Montels France
191 G5 Montelupo Fiorentino Italy
191 I5 Montelupone Italy
194 C5 Montemaggiore Belsito Sicilia Italy
261 F3 Monte Maíz Arg.
193 H4 Montemarano Italy
191 I5 Montemarciano Italy
185 H2 Montemayon r. Spain
185 F3 Montemayor Spain
259 D7 Montemayor, Meseta de plat. Arg.
183 F3 Montemayor de Pililla Spain
162 C3 Montemboeuf France
195 G2 Montemesola Italy
193 H3 Montemilone Italy
184 D2 Montemolín Spain
193 F2 Montemonaco Italy
243 F3 Montemorelos Mex.
184 B2 Montemor-o-Novo Port.
182 B4 Montemor-o-Velho Port.
191 G5 Montemurlo Italy
182 B3 Montemuro, Serra de mts Port.
193 H4 Montemurro Italy
159 F3 Montenay France
162 B3 Montendre France
Montenegro aut. rep. Yugo. see Crna Gora
183 H2 Montenegro de Cameros Spain
193 G3 Montenero di Bisaccia Italy
193 G2 Monteneroodomo Italy
195 G2 Monteparano Italy
260 B2 Monte Patria Chile
247 E3 Monte Plata Dom. Rep.
191 I5 Monte Porzio Italy
193 F2 Monteprandone Italy
211 C8 Montepuez Moz.
211 D8 Montepuez r. Moz.
192 D1 Montepulciano Italy
258 E2 Monte Quemado Arg.
158 D4 Monterblanc France
191 H5 Monterchi Italy
182 B5 Monte Real Port.
193 F2 Montereale Italy
156 C4 Montereau-faut-Yonne France
182 B5 Monte Redondo Port.
191 G4 Monterenzio Italy
Monterey Nuevo León Mex. see Monterrey
240 G3 Monterey CA U.S.A.
232 D5 Monterey VA U.S.A.
240 F3 Monterey Bay CA U.S.A.
250 C2 Montería Col.
191 G5 Monteriggioni Italy
253 E4 Montero Bol.
193 G3 Monteroduni Italy
192 D2 Monte Romano Italy
191 G5 Monteroni d'Arbia Italy
195 H2 Monteroni di Lecce Italy
258 D2 Monteros Arg.
193 E2 Monterosi Italy
190 E4 Monterosso al Mare Italy
194 D5 Monterosso Almo Sicilia Italy
195 F4 Monterosso Calabro Italy
193 E2 Monterotondo Italy
192 C1 Monterotondo Marittimo Italy
182 C3 Monterrei Spain
241 J5 Monterrey Baja California Norte Mex.
243 E3 Monterrey Nuevo León Mex.
182 C2 Monterroso Spain
185 E2 Monterrubio de la Serena Spain
193 F1 Monterubbiano Italy
187 C6 Montesa Spain
254 D3 Montes Altos Brazil
193 F3 Monte San Biagio Italy
193 F3 Monte San Giovanni Campano Italy
238 B2 Montesano WA U.S.A.
195 H3 Montesano Salentino Italy
193 H4 Montesano sulla Marcellana Italy
191 G5 Monte San Savino Italy
191 H5 Monte Santa Maria Tiberina Italy
193 H3 Monte Sant'Angelo Italy
254 F4 Monte Santo Brazil
256 D4 Monte Santo de Minas Brazil
193 G3 Montesarchio Italy
195 F2 Montescaglioso Italy
257 F2 Montes Claros Brazil
183 F4 Montesclaros Spain
191 F5 Montescudaio Italy
191 F4 Montese Italy
193 G2 Montesilvano Italy
163 D4 Montesquieu France
163 D5 Montesquieu-Volvestre France
163 C5 Montesquiou France
163 C5 Montestruc-sur-Gers France
184 B3 Montes Velhos Port.
161 C4 Monteux France
194 B5 Montevago Sicilia Italy
191 G5 Montevarchi Italy
192 A5 Montevecchia Sardegna Italy
261 G2 Monte Vera Arg.
193 H3 Monteverde Italy
261 I4 Montevideo Uru.
261 I4 Montevideo dept Uru.
236 E2 Montevideo MN U.S.A.
184 B2 Montevil Port.
239 F4 Monte Vista CO U.S.A.
236 E3 Montezuma IA U.S.A.
237 C4 Montezuma KS U.S.A.
241 M3 Montezuma Creek UT U.S.A.
241 M3 Montezuma Creek r. CO U.S.A.
240 I3 Montezuma Peak NV U.S.A.
163 D4 Montfaucon Midi-Pyrénées France
159 E4 Montfaucon Pays de la Loire France
157 F3 Montfaucon-d'Argonne France
161 C3 Montfaucon-en-Velay France
163 C5 Montferran-Savès France
161 E5 Montferrat France
163 D6 Montferrier France
164 D2 Montfoort Neth.
163 B5 Montfort Aquitaine France
158 E3 Montfort Bretagne France
163 B5 Montfort-en-Chalosse France
156 B4 Montfort-l'Amaury France
159 G3 Montfort-le-Gesnois France
159 G2 Montfort-sur-Risle France
186 D3 Montgai Spain
163 C5 Montgaillard Midi-Pyrénées France
163 C5 Montgaillard Midi-Pyrénées France
163 D6 Montgaillard Midi-Pyrénées France
161 E4 Montgenèvre France
156 C4 Montgeron France
163 D5 Montgiscard France
159 H5 Montgivray France
187 D6 Montgó hill Spain
150 D2 Montgomery Powys, Wales U.K.
231 C5 Montgomery AL U.S.A.
235 D1 Montgomery NY U.S.A.
232 A5 Montgomery OH U.S.A.
227 I5 Montgomery PA U.S.A.
232 C5 Montgomery WV U.S.A.

234 F4 Montgomery City MO U.S.A.
234 A3 Montgomery County county MD U.S.A.
234 C2 Montgomery County county PA U.S.A.
86 D2 Montgomery Islands W.A. Austr.
162 B3 Montguyon France
156 E3 Monthermé France
190 B2 Monthey Switz.
156 E3 Monthois France
157 F4 Monthureux-sur-Saône France
192 B4 Monti Sardegna Italy
191 H3 Monticano r. Italy
190 E3 Monticelli d'Ongina Italy
192 A2 Monticello Corse France
237 F5 Monticello AR U.S.A.
231 D6 Monticello FL U.S.A.
236 F3 Monticello GA U.S.A.
236 D5 Monticello IL U.S.A.
230 C3 Monticello IN U.S.A.
231 E6 Monticello KY U.S.A.
236 C3 Monticello ME U.S.A.
236 F3 Monticello MO U.S.A.
237 D6 Monticello MS U.S.A.
234 D1 Monticello NY U.S.A.
241 H3 Monticello UT U.S.A.
190 F3 Montichiari Italy
192 D1 Montichiari Italy
185 H2 Montiel Spain
185 H2 Montiel, Cuchilla de hills Arg.
261 H2 Montiers France
159 H5 Montiers-sur-Saulx France
156 E4 Montier-en-Der France
192 C1 Montieri Italy
157 F2 Montiers-sur-Saulx France
162 B2 Montignac France
156 D5 Montignies-le-Tilleul Belgium
190 F4 Montignoso Italy
156 D5 Montigny France
156 D5 Montigny-la-Resie France
215 H3 Montigny-lès-Metz France
160 D1 Montigny-Mornay-Villeneuve-sur-Vingeanne France
157 F2 Montigny-sur-Aube France
184 B2 Montijo Port.
184 D2 Montijo Spain
185 F3 Montilla Spain
185 H4 Montillana Spain
183 E4 Montivel France
256 B2 Montividiu Brazil
185 G2 Montivilliers France
185 G2 Montizón Spain
161 A4 Montjean France
159 F3 Montjean-sur-Loire France
225 G3 Mont-Joli Que. Can.
190 C3 Montjovet Italy
161 C4 Montlauer France
224 F4 Mont-Laurier Que. Can.
162 C3 Montlhéry France
225 H3 Mont-Louis Que. Can.
163 E6 Mont-Louis France
162 D3 Montlouis-sur-Loire France
160 D3 Montluel France
160 A2 Montmagny Que. Can.
221 K5 Montmagny Que. Can.
160 C2 Montmarault France
160 D4 Montmartin-sur-Mer France
157 E3 Montmédy France
157 F3 Montmélian France
160 C2 Montmerle-sur-Saône France
161 C4 Montmeyran France
156 D4 Montmirail Champagne-Ardenne France
159 D3 Montmirail Pays de la Loire France
160 D1 Montmirey-le-Château France
162 C3 Montmoreau-St-Cybard France
226 D5 Montmorenci SC U.S.A.
230 G2 Montmorency Que. Can.
161 C2 Montmorillon France
162 C2 Montmort France
160 C1 Montmorot France
156 D4 Montmort-Lucy France
186 F3 Montmpre de Lievant hill Spain
85 G5 Monto Qld Austr.
158 D4 Montoir-de-Bretagne France
158 C4 Montoire-sur-le-Loir France
156 D4 Montois slope France
159 C4 Montoison France
184 C2 Montoito Port.
183 E3 Montón Spain
183 I3 Montón Spain
191 H4 Monte r. Italy
193 E2 Montoro Italy
185 F2 Montoro r. Spain
185 G2 Montoro r. Spain
233 G2 Montour County county PA U.S.A.
234 B1 Montour County county PA U.S.A.
232 E3 Montour Falls NY U.S.A.
159 F5 Montournais France
227 I5 Montourville PA U.S.A.
246 □1 Montpelier Jamaica
238 E3 Montpelier ID U.S.A.
226 E5 Montpelier OH U.S.A.
230 A4 Montpelier OH U.S.A.
233 G2 Montpelier VT U.S.A.
161 B5 Montpellier France
163 C4 Montpeyroux France
163 C4 Montpezat Aquitaine France
163 C5 Montpezat-de-Quercy France
163 E4 Montpezat-sous-Bauzon France
162 C3 Montpon-Ménestérol France
160 C2 Montpont-en-Bresse France
159 H4 Mont-près-Chambord France
Montréal can. see
Montréal
224 F4 Montreal r. Que. Can.
224 E4 Montreal r. Ont. Can.
160 C5 Montréal France
163 C4 Montréal France
163 E5 Montréal France
163 C5 Montréal VI U.S.A.
224 F4 Montréal-Dorval airport Que. Can.
160 D2 Montréal-la-Cluse France
223 J4 Montreal Lake Sask. Can.
224 F4 Montréal-Mirabel airport Que. Can.
224 F4 Montreal River Ont. Can.
163 E5 Montredon-Labessonnié France
161 C3 Montrégeau France
162 D3 Montrejeau France
159 F4 Montrésor France
192 A4 Montresta Sardegna Italy
160 D2 Montret France
160 D2 Montreuil Île-de-France France
156 B2 Montreuil Nord - Pas-de-Calais France
159 E3 Montreuil-Bellay France
157 F3 Montreuil-Juigné France
190 B2 Montreux Switz.
162 D2 Montrevault France
159 H4 Montrevel-en-Bresse France
159 H4 Montrichard France
160 C3 Montricoux France
160 C3 Montriond France
160 C3 Montrodat France
161 A5 Montrodre mt. France
160 C3 Montrond France
160 C3 Montrond-les-Bains France
146 F5 Montrose Angus, Scotland U.K.
159 H4 Montrose CO U.S.A.
241 F4 Montrose CO U.S.A.
227 H4 Montrose MI U.S.A.
235 E1 Montrose NY U.S.A.
232 D5 Montrose WV U.S.A.
187 C5 Montrose VA U.S.A.
156 D1 Monts France
156 B3 Mont-St-Aignan France
156 D4 Mont-St-Jean France
157 F3 Mont-St-Martin France

158 E3 Mont-St-Michel, Baie du b. France
156 D5 Mont-St-Sulpice France
160 C2 Mont-St-Vincent France
163 E4 Montsalvy France
186 D3 Montsant r. Spain
160 C1 Montsauche-les-Settons France
163 C3 Montsaunès France
163 D6 Montségur France
163 B5 Montseny Spain
247 □2 Montserrat terr. West Indies
159 G4 Montsoreau France
163 B5 Montsûrs France
160 D2 Mont-sous-Vaudrey France
159 G5 Monts-sur-Guesnes France
Mont St Michel tourist site France see Le Mont-St-Michel
159 F3 Montsuzain France
187 F5 Montúiri Spain
242 □J8 Montuosa, Isla i. Panama
163 D6 Montuque Spain
232 D6 Montvale France
163 D4 Montvalent France
156 D3 Montville France
235 F1 Montville CT U.S.A.
165 E4 Montzen Belgium
157 E3 Montzéville France
241 L3 Monument Valley reg. AZ U.S.A.
215 F2 Monyakeng S. Africa
96 A2 Monywa Myanmar
190 D3 Monza Italy
209 E9 Monze Zambia
Monze, Cape cp Pak. see Muari, Ras
172 B2 Monzelfeld Ger.
172 B2 Monzingen Ger.
252 A2 Monzón Peru
186 D3 Monzón de Campos Spain
235 F1 Moodus CT U.S.A.
215 H3 Mooi r. Kwazulu-Natal S. Africa
215 F2 Mooi r. North West S. Africa
215 H3 Moirivriet S. Africa
164 E3 Mook Neth.
212 E4 Mookane Botswana
82 D2 Moolawatana S.A. Austr.
82 E2 Moomba S.A. Austr.
83 G2 Moomin Creek r. N.S.W. Austr.
82 C2 Moomaree S.A. Austr.
83 G2 Moonbi Range mts N.S.W. Austr.
147 D4 Mooncoin Rep. of Ireland
84 E5 Moonda Lake salt flat Qld Austr.
147 E4 Moone Rep. of Ireland
85 G5 Moonie Qld Austr.
83 G2 Moonie r. N.S.W./Qld Austr.
82 D3 Moonta S.A. Austr.
82 C6 Moora W.A. Austr.
85 E5 Mooraberree Qld Austr.
171 C5 Moorbad Lobenstein Ger.
238 F2 Moorcroft WY U.S.A.
168 C2 Moordorf (Südbrookmerland) Ger.
164 D3 Moordrecht Neth.
87 B6 Moore r. W.A. Austr.
238 E2 Moore MT U.S.A.
87 C6 Moore, Lake salt flat W.A. Austr.
79 □3a Moorea i. Fr. Polynesia
232 D5 Moorefield WV U.S.A.
231 D7 Moore Haven FL U.S.A.
149 I4 Moorends South Yorkshire, England U.K.
173 F3 Moorenweis Ger.
85 G3 Moore Reef Coral Sea Is Terr. Austr.
234 B2 Mooresburg PA U.S.A.
246 C1 Moores Island Bahamas
233 □J2 Moores Mills N.B. Can.
234 D3 Moorestown NJ U.S.A.
86 E4 Moore Town Jamaica
148 C3 Moorfields Northern Ireland U.K.
146 E6 Moorfoot Hills Scotland U.K.
236 D2 Moorhead MN U.S.A.
83 E3 Moornanyah Lake imp. l. N.S.W. Austr.
82 E3 Mooroock S.A. Austr.
84 C1 Mooroongga Island N.T. Austr.
83 F4 Mooroopna Vic. Austr.
240 H4 Moorpark CA U.S.A.
214 B5 Moorreesburg S. Africa
165 C4 Moorslede Belgium
168 C2 Moorweg Ger.
172 C4 Moos Baden-Württemberg Ger.
173 G3 Moos Bayern Ger.
179 F4 Moosbach Ger.
173 F3 Moosburg an der Isar Ger.
224 D3 Moose r. Ont. Can.
224 D3 Moose Factory Ont. Can.
233 □J1 Moosehead Lake ME U.S.A.
83 □5 Moose Jaw Sask. Can.
223 J5 Moose Jaw r. Sask. Can.
226 A2 Moose Lake MN U.S.A.
223 K5 Moose Mountain Creek r. Sask. Can.
224 D3 Moose River Ont. Can.
233 H2 Moosilauke, Mount NH U.S.A.
173 F3 Moosinning Ger.
179 G4 Moosskirchen Austria
223 K5 Moosomin Sask. Can.
224 D3 Moosonee Ont. Can.
173 F4 Moosthenning Ger.
213 F4 Mopane S. Africa
213 G3 Mopeia Moz.
Mopelia atoll Arch. de la Société Fr. Polynesia see Maupihaa
212 E4 Mopipi Botswana
206 D3 Mopti Mali
206 D3 Mopti admin. reg. Mali
140 N1 Mor r. Fin.
82 B3 Morgam-Viibus hill Fin.
231 D6 Moquegua Peru
252 C4 Moquegua dept Peru
261 H4 Moquehuá Arg.
177 H4 Mór Hungary
207 I4 Mora Cameroon
184 B2 Mora Port.
183 G5 Mora Spain
141 K3 Mora Sweden
236 A2 Mora MN U.S.A.
236 G5 Mora NM U.S.A.
239 F3 Mora r. NM U.S.A.
187 E4 Morača r. Yugo.
138 F5 Morach r. Belarus
213 F4 Moradabad Uttar Prad. India
254 F3 Morada Nova Brazil
257 E3 Morada Nova de Minas Brazil
186 E3 Móra d'Ebre Spain
187 G4 Mora de Rubielos Spain
183 □J3 Moradinho Brazil
175 H2 Morag Pol.
186 D3 Mora la Nova Spain
149 F3 Moralambu Madag.
226 E4 Moram Mahar. India
213 □J3 Moramanga Madag.
226 E3 Moran MI U.S.A.
238 E3 Moran WY U.S.A.
117 H4 Moranhat Assam India
193 I5 Morano Calabro Italy
190 D3 Morano sul Po Italy
246 D3 Morant Bay Jamaica
114 C2 Morappur Tamil Nadu India
114 C5 Morar Highland, Scotland U.K.
146 C5 Morar, Loch l. Scotland U.K.
142 E3 Mörar Sweden
182 D3 Morasverdes Spain

183 I3 Morata de Jalón Spain
183 G4 Morata de Tajuña Spain
185 I2 Moratalla Spain
114 C5 Moratuwa Sri Lanka
179 H2 Morava r. Europe
alt. March (Austria)
179 I1 Morava r. Czech Rep.
177 K3 Morava Slovakia
213 □K2 Moravato Madag.
232 E3 Moravia NY U.S.A.
196 E4 Moravica r. Yugo.
197 I4 Moravica r. Yugo.
177 G2 Moravice r. Czech Rep.
177 H2 Morávka r. Czech Rep.
176 E3 Moravská Dyje r. Czech Rep.
176 E1 Moravská Nová Ves Czech Rep.
176 F2 Moravská Třebová Czech Rep.
176 E2 Moravské Budějovice Czech Rep.
177 H2 Moravskoslezské Beskydy mts Czech Rep.
176 G2 Moravský Beroun Czech Rep.
Moravský Ján Slovakia see Moravský Svätý Ján
176 D3 Moravský Písek Czech Rep.
176 G3 Moravský Svätý Ján Slovakia
87 A8 Morawa W.A. Austr.
175 I5 Morawica r. Pol.
146 E4 Moray admin. div. Scotland U.K.
84 B2 Moray Downs Qld Austr.
146 D4 Moray Firth b. Scotland U.K.
84 B2 Moray Range hills N.T. Austr.
178 B2 Morbach Ger.
190 C2 Morbegno Italy
116 B5 Morbi Gujarat India
160 E2 Morbier France
158 D4 Morbihan dept Bretagne France
179 H3 Morchain See Austria
143 G3 Mörbylånga Kalmar Sweden
195 H3 Morciano di Leuca Italy
191 H5 Morciano di Romagna Italy
100 B2 Mordaga Nei Mongol China
127 G3 Mor Dağ mt. Turkey
158 E3 Mordelles France
126 L5 Morden Man. Can.
199 E2 Mordoğan Turkey
135 I5 Mordovo Rus. Fed.
183 I3 Mordovo Rus. Fed.
Mordoviya A.S.S.R. rep. Rus. Fed. see Mordoviya, Respublika
135 I5 Mordoviya, Respublika aut. rep. Rus. Fed.
139 I4 Mordves Rus. Fed.
Mordvinia aut. rep. Rus. Fed. see Mordoviya, Respublika
137 H4 Mordvynivka Ukr.
175 K3 Mordy Pol.
158 D4 Moréac France
184 C3 Moreanes Port.
114 B3 Moreau r. SD U.S.A.
236 C2 Moreau, South Fork r. SD U.S.A.
146 F6 Morebattle Scottish Borders, Scotland U.K.
149 G3 Morecambe Lancashire, England U.K.
149 F3 Morecambe Bay England U.K.
182 E1 Moreda Spain
183 H2 Moreda de Álava Spain
83 G2 Moree N.S.W. Austr.
156 B5 Morée France
232 B5 Morehead KY U.S.A.
231 E5 Morehead City NC U.S.A.
182 B3 Moreira do Rio Port.
116 D4 Morel r. India
190 D2 Mörel Switz.
244 D4 Morelia Mex.
186 E3 Morella Spain
194 D5 Morella r. Sicilia Italy
244 C2 Morelos Mex.
245 E4 Morelos state Mex.
116 D4 Morena Madh. Prad. India
190 D5 Morena, Sierra mts Spain
241 H5 Morenci AZ U.S.A.
227 E5 Morenci MI U.S.A.
197 L2 Moreni Romania
261 H4 Moreno Arg.
242 C2 Moreno Mex.
240 I5 Moreno Valley CA U.S.A.
183 H2 Morentin Spain
140 □ Mere og Romsdal county Norway
253 F2 Moreru r. Brazil
183 H2 Moreruela de Tábara Spain
192 A4 Mores Sardegna Italy
149 F3 Moresby Cumbria, England U.K.
220 E4 Moresby Island B.C. Can.
222 C4 Moresby Island B.C. Can.
85 H5 Moreton Bay Qld Austr.
150 D4 Moretonhampstead Devon, England U.K.
151 F3 Moreton-in-Marsh Gloucestershire, England U.K.
85 H5 Moreton Island Qld Austr.
150 E2 Moreton Say Shropshire, England U.K.
156 C4 Morêt-sur-Loing France
190 C4 Moretta Italy
189 C5 Moreuil France
134 L1 Moreyu r. Rus. Fed.
160 E2 Morez France
223 J5 Morfa Nefyn Gwynedd, Wales U.K.
190 E4 Morfasso Italy
172 C2 Mörfelden Ger.
128 A2 Morfou Cyprus
128 A2 Morfou Bay Cyprus
140 N1 Morgam-Viibus hill Fin.
82 B3 Morgan S.A. Austr.
236 C3 Morgan GA U.S.A.
232 A5 Morgan KY U.S.A.
84 A2 Morgan, Mount CA U.S.A.
237 F6 Morgan City LA U.S.A.
230 C4 Morganfield KY U.S.A.
231 D5 Morgan Hill CA U.S.A.
231 D5 Morganton NC U.S.A.
230 C4 Morgantown KY U.S.A.
232 D5 Morgantown WV U.S.A.
235 D5 Morganville NJ U.S.A.
158 B3 Morgat France
190 B2 Morges Switz.
157 G4 Morhange France
157 G4 Morhange France
190 C2 Mori Xinjiang China
104 A3 Mori Italy
105 D4 Mori Japan
241 J2 Moriah, Mount NV U.S.A.
239 F5 Moriarty's Range hills Qld Austr.
215 G3 Moriate S. Africa
151 F3 Mortimer West Berkshire, England U.K.
206 B3 Morba Guinea
149 F3 Moricambe Bay England U.K.
160 B2 Morienval France
193 J5 Moricone Italy
104 B4 Morienval France
106 B3 Moriki Nigeria
185 F3 Morila Lesotho
207 G3 Moriki Nigeria
185 F3 Morín Dawa Nei Mongol China see Nirji
149 E4 Moringen Ger.
193 F3 Morino Italy
226 C5 Morino Rus. Fed.
238 B2 Morişca r. Romania
159 G3 Moris Antr. N.S.W. Austr.
165 D3 Morishige Austria
144 C4 Moristown r. Scotland U.K.
171 F1 Moritzburg Ger.
105 H2 Moriyama Japan
104 C3 Moriyoshi-zan vol. Japan
140 M2 Morjärv Sweden
91 P1 Morki r. Pak.
101 J4 Morki Rus. Fed.
139 K3 Morkiny Gory Rus. Fed.
165 D4 Morlaix France
165 B5 Morlanwelz Belgium

172 C2 Mörlenbach Ger.
222 H5 Morley Alta Can.
157 F4 Morley France
149 H4 Morley West Yorkshire, England U.K.
193 I5 Mormanno Italy
156 C4 Mormant France
161 D4 Mormoiron France
Mormugao Goa India see Marmagao
160 C3 Mornand France
160 C3 Mornant France
161 C4 Moranas France
247 □2 Morne-à-l'Eau Guadeloupe
247 □2 Morne Constant hill Guadeloupe
190 D4 Mornese Italy
85 E5 Morney Qld Austr.
259 B8 Mornington, Isla i. Chile
264 D9 Mornington Abyssal Plain sea feature S. Atlantic Ocean
84 D3 Mornington Island Qld Austr.
198 B2 Mornos r. Greece
173 F3 Mörnsheim Ger.
123 F5 Moro Pak.
204 D3 Moro country Africa
116 B5 Morocco Africa
136 C2 Morochne Ukr.
237 E5 Moro Creek r. AR U.S.A.
211 C6 Morogoro Tanz.
211 C7 Morogoro admin. reg. Tanz.
92 B5 Moro Gulf Phil.
215 F3 Morojaneng S. Africa
214 D2 Morokweng S. Africa
81 C6 Morgiel South I. N.Z.
232 D4 Moshannon PA U.S.A.
213 □J4 Morolón Cuba
193 F3 Morolo Italy
106 D1 Mörön Mongolia
190 C1 Moron mt. Switz.
252 C5 Morona Ecuador
252 C4 Morona r. Peru
250 B6 Morona-Santiago prov. Ecuador
213 □J4 Morondava Madag.
183 H3 Morón de Almazán Spain
185 E3 Morón de la Frontera Spain
210 B4 Morogo Côte d'Ivoire
240 I4 Morongo Valley CA U.S.A.
217 □3a Moroni Njazidja Comoros
241 L2 Moroni UT U.S.A.
106 D1 Moron Us He r. Qinghai China
183 I3 Moros Spain
183 F3 Moros r. Spain
192 B2 Morosaglia Corse France
93 D2 Morotai i. Maluku Indon.
210 B4 Moroto Uganda
210 B4 Moroto, Mount Uganda
135 I5 Morozovsk Japan
196 D3 Morava Vojvodina, Srbija Yugo.
247 □1 Morovis Puerto Rico
81 A6 Morowai South I. N.Z.
139 H2 Morozova Rus. Fed.
137 J2 Morozovka Rus. Fed.
135 H6 Morozovsk Rus. Fed.
190 C4 Morozzo Italy
254 E4 Morpara Brazil
149 H2 Morpeth Northumberland, England U.K.
256 C6 Morretes Brazil
232 A4 Morrill KY U.S.A.
236 C3 Morrill NE U.S.A.
237 E5 Morrilton AR U.S.A.
256 C2 Morrinhos Brazil
80 E2 Morrinsville North I. N.Z.
223 L5 Morris Man. Can.
226 C5 Morris IL U.S.A.
236 D2 Morris MN U.S.A.
227 I5 Morris PA U.S.A.
233 F2 Morris County county NJ U.S.A.
221 O1 Morris Jesup, Kap c. Greenland
261 F3 Morrison Arg.
226 C5 Morrison IL U.S.A.
81 C6 Morrisons South I. N.Z.
235 I2 Morris Plains NJ U.S.A.
235 I2 Morris Run PA U.S.A.
150 D3 Morriston Swansea, Wales U.K.
241 K5 Morristown AZ U.S.A.
235 J2 Morristown NJ U.S.A.
233 F2 Morristown NY U.S.A.
231 D4 Morristown TN U.S.A.
235 H3 Morrisville NY U.S.A.
234 D2 Morrisville PA U.S.A.
233 G2 Morrisville VT U.S.A.
192 B3 Morro, Monte hill Sardegna Italy
256 D2 Morro Agudo Brazil
254 D2 Morro Bay CA U.S.A.
256 D2 Morro da Águila hill Spain
254 E4 Morro do Chapéu Brazil
257 G4 Morro do Coco Brazil
250 C2 Morro do Sinal hills Brazil
245 G5 Morro Mazatán Mex.
193 F2 Morrone, Monte mt. Italy
254 D2 Morros Brazil
191 I5 Morrovalle Italy
213 G3 Morrumbala Moz.
169 E5 Morsbach Ger.
172 C2 Morsberg hill Ger.
169 F4 Morschen Ger.
223 J5 Morse Sask. Can.
237 C6 Morse TX U.S.A.
233 F2 Morse Reservoir NY U.S.A.
263 I2 Morse, Cape Antarctica
135 H5 Morshanka Rus. Fed.
Morshanka Rus. Fed. see Morshanka
135 I5 Morshyn Ukr.
101 D3 Morshyn Ukr.
161 D4 Morsleben Ger.
157 G4 Morsum Ger.
157 G4 Mortagne r. France
159 G3 Mortagne-au-Perche France
162 B3 Mortagne-sur-Gironde France
159 E2 Mortagne-sur-Sèvre France
184 B4 Mortágua Port.
159 F3 Mortain France
190 D3 Mortara Italy
160 D1 Morte r. France
161 E1 Morteau France
157 F3 Morteau-Coulibœuf France
156 C3 Mortefontaine France
193 I1 Mortegliano Italy
150 C3 Mortehoe Devon, England U.K.
195 E4 Mortelle Sicilia Italy
261 G2 Morteros Arg.
135 H5 Mortes, Rio das r. Minas Gerais Brazil
254 C4 Mortes, Rio das r. Tocatins Brazil
215 E5 Mortimer S. Africa
151 F3 Mortimer West Berkshire, England U.K.
150 E2 Mortimer's Cross England U.K.
223 J5 Mortlach Sask. Can.
83 A6 Mortlake Vic. Austr.
266 F5 Mortlock Islands Micronesia
Mortlock Islands P.N.G. see Tauu Islands
151 C3 Morton Lincolnshire, England U.K.
149 I4 Morton Lincolnshire, England U.K.
149 E4 Morton Lincolnshire, England U.K.
226 C6 Morton IL U.S.A.
237 C5 Morton TX U.S.A.
238 B2 Morton WA U.S.A.
159 G3 Morton N.S.W. Austr.
178 B3 Mörtschach Austria
165 D3 Mortsel Belgium
210 B4 Morundava r. uganda
104 D3 Morungole mt. Uganda
227 E4 Moruroa atoll Arch. des Tuamotu Fr. Polynesia see Mururoa
160 B1 Morvan hills France
85 C5 Morven Qld Austr.
146 E4 Morven hill Aberdeenshire, Scotland U.K.

146 E3 Morven hill Highland, Scotland U.K.
146 C5 Morvern reg. Scotland U.K.
150 D2 Morville Shropshire, England U.K.
83 F4 Morwell Vic. Austr.
150 C4 Morwenstow Cornwall, England U.K.
174 C3 Moryń Pol.
164 D2 Morzeszczyn Pol.
139 J4 Mosal'sk Rus. Fed.
136 D3 Moşana Moldova
172 D2 Mosbach Ger.
149 H4 Mosborough South Yorkshire, England U.K.
238 F2 Mosby MT U.S.A.
184 A2 Moscavide Port.
191 G5 Moscia r. Italy
193 F2 Mosciano Sant'Angelo Italy
238 C2 Moscow ID U.S.A.
234 C1 Moscow Rus. Fed. admin. div. see Moskva
198 B2 Mornos r. Greece
Moskovskaya Oblast'
171 C5 Mosel Ger.
169 C5 Mosel r. Ger.
232 E6 Moselle r. U.S.A.
157 G3 Moselle dept Lorraine France
157 G3 Moselle r. France
169 C5 Möser Ger.
240 I1 Moses, Mount NV U.S.A.
238 C2 Moses Lake WA U.S.A.
212 E4 Mosetse Botswana
81 C6 Mosgiel South I. N.Z.
232 D4 Moshannon PA U.S.A.
211 C5 Moshenskoye Rus. Fed.
137 J2 Moshenka r. Ukr.
207 G4 Moshi r. Nigeria
211 C5 Moshi Tanz.
137 F3 Moshny Ukr.
174 D3 Mosina Pol.
214 C5 Mosinee WI U.S.A.
215 E2 Mosita S. Africa
140 K2 Mosjøen Norway
140 K2 Mosjøen Norway
140 K2 Moskenesøy i. Norway
140 M1 Moskkugáisi mt. Norway
175 H5 Moskorzew Pol.
140 L2 Moskosel Sweden
123 G2 Moskva Tajik.
139 L4 Moskva r. Rus. Fed.
Moskovskaya Oblast' admin. div. Rus. Fed. see Shakhrikan
137 J2 Moskovka r. Rus. Fed.
139 K4 Moskva r. Rus. Fed.
139 L4 Moskva r. Rus. Fed.
123 G2 Moskva Tajik.
Moskovskaya Oblast' admin. div. Rus. Fed. see Shakhrikhan
196 B3 Mosležel N.S.W. Austr.
215 J3 Mossel S. Africa
172 D3 Mössingen Ger.
148 D3 Mossley Northern Ireland U.K.
85 F3 Mossman Qld Austr.
254 F3 Mossoró Brazil
147 E1 Moss-side Northern Ireland U.K.
146 E4 Mosstodloch Moray, Scotland U.K.
213 □2 Mossuril Moz.
83 G3 Moss Vale N.S.W. Austr.
223 J4 Most Bulg.
176 C1 Most Czech Rep.
195 □ Mosta Malta
205 F2 Mostaganem Alg.
184 D4 Mostar Bos.-Herz.
184 C2 Mosteiro Galicia Port.
182 C1 Mosteiro Galicia Spain
216 □3b Mosteiros São Miguel Azores
197 Q3 Moşteni Romania
175 I2 Mostkowo Pol.
183 J3 Móstoles Spain
136 B5 Mostova r. Ukr.
129 F5 Mostovskoy Rus. Fed.
175 J3 Mostówka r. Pol.
Mosty Belarus see Masty
175 H5 Mosty Pol.
175 L6 Mostys'ka Druha Ukr.
128 C4 Mosul Iraq see Al Mawşil
140 J3 Mosvik Norway
175 M4 Mosyr Ukr.
177 H4 Moszczenica Pol.
210 C2 Mot'a Eth.
78 □7a Mota i. Vanuatu
208 C4 Motaba r. Congo
185 H1 Mota del Cuervo Spain
182 D3 Mota del Marqués Spain
136 C1 Motal' Belarus
143 H2 Motala Sweden
210 D3 Motal Eth.
78 □5 Mota Lava i. Vanuatu
174 D3 Motarzyno Pol.
197 H2 Motca Romania
215 H4 Motete S. Africa
197 F3 Motetema S. Africa
156 C3 Motfontaine France
146 E6 Motherwell North Lanarkshire, Scotland U.K.
214 D2 Mothibistad S. Africa
195 E4 Motilla del Palancar Spain
185 H2 Motilla del Palancar Spain
141 M4 Motjärnshyttan Sweden
101 B4 Motian Ling hill Liaoning China
102 C2 Motloutse r. Botswana
214 E2 Motokwe Botswana
183 I4 Motos Spain
135 J3 Motovskiy Zaliv sea chan. Rus. Fed.
243 P6 Motozintla Mex.
83 K4 Motril Spain
266 F5 Mott ND U.S.A.
243 □ Mott Bihar India
185 H2 Motilla del Palancar Spain
101 B4 Motian Ling hill Liaoning China
102 C2 Motloutse r. Botswana
214 E2 Motokwe Botswana
183 I4 Motos Spain
135 J3 Motovskiy Zaliv sea chan. Rus. Fed.
243 P6 Motozintla Mex.
83 K4 Motril Spain
266 F5 Mott ND U.S.A.
79 □3a Motu One atoll Arch. de la Société Fr. Polynesia
79 □3a Motu Iti i. Fr. Polynesia
243 H4 Motul Mex.
79 □3a Motu Nui i. Fr. Polynesia
80 D1 Motuoapa North I. N.Z.
79 □3 Motu Iti i. Fr. Polynesia
81 C6 Motueka South I. N.Z.
81 C6 Motueka r. South I. N.Z.
87 C4 Motu Fakataua i. Tokelau
81 □1 Motu Fakataua i. Tokelau
83 B1 Motuihe i. N.Z.
81 □1 Motuloa i. Tokelau
79 □3 Motu One i. Fr. Polynesia
81 □1 Motuloa i. Tokelau
80 E3 Motuoapa North I. N.Z.
232 C5 Mott WV U.S.A.
87 C4 Mount Newman W.A. Austr.

146 E3 Morven hill Highland, Scotland U.K.
178 B3 Mötz Austria
142 D3 Mou Denmark
96 D3 Mouan, Nam r. Laos
207 H6 Mouanko Cameroon
161 E5 Mouans-Sartoux France
225 G3 Mouasker r. Que. Can. see Mascara
225 G3 Mouchalagane r. Que. Can.
159 E5 Mouchamps France
163 C5 Mouchan France
160 D2 Mouchard France
161 B4 Mouchet, Mont mt. France
246 E2 Mouchoir Bank sea feature Turks and Caicos Is
246 E2 Mouchoir Passage Turks and Caicos Is
182 C3 Mouda Port.
108 B3 Mouding Yunnan China
206 B2 Moudjéria Maur.
190 B2 Moudon Switz.
161 F5 Mougins France
141 M3 Mouhijärvi Fin.
206 E4 Mouhoun r. Africa
alt. Volta Noire,
conv. Black Volta
208 A5 Mouila Gabon
159 F5 Mouilleron-en-Pareds France
83 F3 Moulamein N.S.W. Austr.
83 E3 Moulamein Creek r. N.S.W. Austr.
163 E4 Moularès France
Moulavibazar Bangl. see Maulvi Bazar
159 F3 Moule France
247 □2 Moule Guadeloupe
209 A5 Moulèngui Binza Gabon
163 C4 Mouleydier France
159 G4 Mouliherne France
159 D6 Moulin France
160 B2 Moulins France
159 G3 Moulins-Engilbert France
159 G3 Moulins-la-Marche France
163 D6 Moulis France
162 C2 Moulis-en-Médoc France
159 G4 Moulismes France
190 C4 Moulle de Jaut, Pic du mt. France
96 A3 Moulmein Myanmar
96 A3 Moulmeingyun Myanmar
204 E2 Moulouya, Oued r. Morocco
151 G4 Moulton Lincolnshire, England U.K.
151 F2 Moulton Northamptonshire, England U.K.
151 H2 Moulton Suffolk, England U.K.
231 C5 Moulton AL U.S.A.
262 P1 Moulton, Mount Antarctica
233 H3 Moultonborough NH U.S.A.
231 D6 Moultrie GA U.S.A.
Moumou-Nounitu i. Solomon Is see San Jorge
237 F4 Mound City IL U.S.A.
236 E4 Mound City KS U.S.A.
236 E3 Mound City MO U.S.A.
236 C2 Mound City SD U.S.A.
232 C5 Moundsville WV U.S.A.
211 D6 Moundsville WV U.S.A.
232 C5 Moundville AL U.S.A.
231 C5 Moundville AL U.S.A.
232 D5 Mountain Lake Park MD U.S.A.
235 D2 Mountain Lakes NJ U.S.A.
233 L1 Mountain Pass CA U.S.A.
234 C1 Mountain Top PA U.S.A.
237 E4 Mountain View AR U.S.A.
240 □D9 Mountain View HI U.S.A.
220 B3 Mountain Village AK U.S.A.
235 J1 Mountain Dale NY U.S.A.
231 D6 Mountain Ash Rhondda Cynon Taff, Wales U.K.
231 C5 Mountain Brook AL U.S.A.
232 E3 Mountain City TN U.S.A.
237 E4 Mountain Grove MO U.S.A.
237 E4 Mountain Home AR U.S.A.
238 D3 Mountain Home ID U.S.A.
224 L1 Mountainhome PA U.S.A.
226 A2 Mountain Iron MN U.S.A.
232 D5 Mountain Lake Park MD U.S.A.
83 G3 Mossgiel N.S.W. Austr.
215 J3 Mossiesdal S. Africa
172 D3 Mössingen Ger.
148 D3 Mossley Northern Ireland U.K.
85 F3 Mossman Qld Austr.
226 B3 Mossinee WI U.S.A.
146 F4 Mossat Aberdeenshire, Scotland U.K.
81 B6 Mossburn South I. N.Z.
214 D3 Mossel Bay S. Africa
209 B5 Mossendjo Congo
163 E6 Mosset France
83 F3 Mossgiel N.S.W. Austr.
234 E4 Mount Aetna PA U.S.A.
237 E4 Mountain Grove MO U.S.A.
239 F3 Mountain View NM U.S.A.
242 □Q10 Mountain View AK U.S.A.
225 H4 Mount Carmel PA U.S.A.
230 C4 Mount Carmel IL U.S.A.
234 C2 Mount Carmel PA U.S.A.
232 B6 Mount Carmel TN U.S.A.
241 K3 Mount Carmel Junction UT U.S.A.
226 C6 Mount Carroll IL U.S.A.
84 C1 Mount Cavenagh N.T. Austr.
147 C2 Mountcharles Rep. of Ireland
147 F3 Mount Clere W.A. Austr.
147 E3 Mountcollins Rep. of Ireland
147 E5 Mount Coolum Qld Austr.
85 H4 Mount Coolon Qld Austr.
213 F3 Mount Darwin Zimbabwe
84 C1 Mount Denison N.T. Austr.
82 C2 Mount Eba S.A. Austr.
210 C2 Mount Edgecumbe N.T. Austr.
222 C3 Mount Edgecumbe AK U.S.A.
237 E6 Mount Enterprise TX U.S.A.
226 E5 Mount Etna IL U.S.A.
148 B3 Mountfield Northern Ireland U.K.
147 C4 Mount Forest S. Africa
224 D5 Mount Forest Ont. Can.
215 J4 Mount Frere S. Africa
82 E4 Mount Gambier S.A. Austr.
147 D3 Mount Garnet Qld Austr.
234 E5 Mount Gay WV U.S.A.
215 F5 Mount Gilead S. Africa
91 J8 Mount Hagen P.N.G.
235 J3 Mount Hamilton N.T. Austr.
234 D3 Mount Holly NJ U.S.A.
231 D5 Mount Holly Springs PA U.S.A.
234 B3 Mount Holly Springs PA U.S.A.
83 G2 Mount Hope N.S.W. Austr.
82 C3 Mount Hope S.A. Austr.
232 C6 Mount Hope WV U.S.A.
232 C6 Mount Horeb WI U.S.A.
85 E4 Mount Howitt Qld Austr.
87 C6 Mount House W.A. Austr.
84 C3 Mount Hutt South I. N.Z.
237 E5 Mount Ida AR U.S.A.
187 D4 Mount Isa Qld Austr.

81 E2 Mount Norris Northern Ireland U.K.
147 D3 Mount Nugent Rep. of Ireland
232 A5 Mount Olivet KY U.S.A.
232 B5 Mount Orab OH U.S.A.
225 K4 Mount Pearl Nfld. Can.
234 C2 Mount Penn PA U.S.A.
85 G5 Mount Perry Qld Austr.
81 B6 Mount Pisa South I. N.Z.
82 D3 Mount Pleasant S.A. Austr.
225 H4 Mount Pleasant P.E.I. Can.
226 E4 Mount Pleasant MI U.S.A.
234 E4 Mount Pleasant MI U.S.A.
232 D4 Mount Pleasant PA U.S.A.
231 E5 Mount Pleasant SC U.S.A.
237 E5 Mount Pleasant TX U.S.A.
241 L2 Mount Pleasant UT U.S.A.
234 A2 Mount Pleasant Mills PA U.S.A.
234 C1 Mount Pocono PA U.S.A.
234 B4 Mount Rainier MD U.S.A.
147 D3 Mount Shannon Rep. of Ireland
81 D1 Mount Richmond Forest Park nature res. South I. N.Z.
214 E3 Mount Salem S. Africa
234 D2 Mount Sanford N.T. Austr.
84 B3 Mount Sandford N.T. Austr.
147 C4 Mountshannon Rep. of Ireland
238 B3 Mount Shasta CA U.S.A.
81 C5 Mount Somers South I. N.Z.
151 F2 Mountsorrel Leicestershire, England U.K.
236 F4 Mount Sterling IL U.S.A.
232 B5 Mount Sterling KY U.S.A.
232 B5 Mount Sterling OH U.S.A.
214 E5 Mount Stewart S. Africa
232 D5 Mount Storm WV U.S.A.
147 B5 Mount Surprise Qld Austr.
84 C4 Mount Swan N.T. Austr.
147 C3 Mount Talbot Rep. of Ireland
232 E4 Mount Union PA U.S.A.
233 F3 Mount Upton NY U.S.A.
87 C5 Mount Vernon W.A. Austr.
237 F6 Mount Vernon AL U.S.A.
231 D5 Mount Vernon GA U.S.A.
236 F4 Mount Vernon IL U.S.A.
230 C4 Mount Vernon IN U.S.A.
232 A6 Mount Vernon KY U.S.A.
236 E4 Mount Vernon MO U.S.A.
235 E2 Mount Vernon NY U.S.A.
232 B4 Mount Vernon OH U.S.A.
237 E5 Mount Vernon TX U.S.A.
238 B1 Mount Vernon WA U.S.A.
234 B2 Mountville PA U.S.A.
232 A6 Mount Washington KY U.S.A.
87 B7 Mount Wedge W.A. Austr.
234 B2 Mount Wolf PA U.S.A.
234 B4 Mount Zion MD U.S.A.
184 C2 Moura Brazil
253 F3 Moura Brazil
184 C3 Moura Port.
202 D5 Mourdi, Dépression du depr. Chad
206 D3 Mourdiah Mali
182 B3 Mourenx France
161 C5 Mouriès France
182 B4 Mourisca do Vouga Port.
156 E3 Mourmelon-le-Grand France
165 D5 Mouscron Belgium
165 C4 Mouscron dept Belgium
208 C2 Mousgougou Chad
232 B6 Mousie KY U.S.A.
161 A5 Mousac France
157 H4 Moussey France
202 C6 Moussoro Chad
163 E5 Moussoulens France
160 B3 Mousey France
156 D3 Moustéru France
161 E5 Moustiers-Ste-Marie France
161 F5 Mouthe France
160 E2 Mouthier-en-Bresse France
161 F4 Mouthier-Haute-Pierre France
160 E2 Mouthoumet France
190 B1 Moutier Switz.
160 E3 Moutier-d'Ahun France
161 E4 Moûtiers France
161 C5 Moutiers-les-Mauxfaits France
179 H4 Moutnice Czech Rep.
207 I4 Moutourwa Cameroon
161 A5 Moux France
156 C3 Moux-en-Morvan France
209 F4 Mouyondzi Congo
198 B2 Mouzaki Greece
202 B6 Mouzarak Chad
157 F3 Mouzon France
161 C4 Mouzon r. France
242 C3 Movas Mex.
197 M3 Movila Miresii Romania
194 C5 Movila Sierra Leone
147 A3 Moycullen Rep. of Ireland
147 D3 Moy r. Rep. of Ireland
147 D3 Moy Northern Ireland U.K.
210 C3 Moyale Eth.
211 B5 Moyale Eth.
206 B4 Moyamba Sierra Leone
206 E2 Moyen Atlas mts Morocco
208 C2 Moyen-Chari pref. Chad
Moyen Congo country Africa see Congo
215 F6 Moyeni Lesotho
157 G4 Moyenmoutier France
206 A3 Moyenne-Guinée admin. reg. Guinea
156 B2 Moyenneville France
208 A5 Moyen-Ogooué prov. Gabon
157 G3 Moyeuvre-Grande France
206 A3 Moygashel Northern Ireland U.K.
147 E2 Moylaw Rep. of Ireland
147 D2 Moylough Rep. of Ireland
147 E2 Moynalty Rep. of Ireland
147 E3 Moynalvey Rep. of Ireland
147 H3 Moyne Rep. of Ireland
250 B6 Moyobamba Peru
196 A2 Moyowosi r. Tanz.
140 N1 Moyvalley Rep. of Ireland
108 A1 Moyu Xinjiang China
213 G3 Moyvalley Rep. of Ireland
143 G3 Moyynkum Kazakh.
143 G3 Moyynkum, Peski des. Kazakh.
143 H3 Moynty Kazakh.
160 B2 Moza Arg. country China
213 I4 Mozambique country Africa
265 G6 Mozambique Channel Africa
Mozambique Ridge sea feature Indian Ocean
182 B4 Mozárbez Spain
122 E2 Mozdūrān Iran
232 B6 Mozelle KY U.S.A.

Mozelos to Naga Hills

338

182 C4 Mozelos Port.
137 I3 Mozh r. Ukr.
138 G4 Mozha r. Belarus
139 K4 Mozhaysk Rus. Fed.
134 K4 Mozhga Rus. Fed.
108 A1 Mozhong Qinghai China
179 F4 Mozirje Slovenia
179 F4 Mozirske Planine mts Slovenia
137 G3 Mozoliyivka Ukr.
183 F3 Mozoncillo Spain
177 G5 Mozsgó Hungary
Mozyr' Belarus see Mazyr
206 A3 Mpal Senegal
211 A6 Mpanda Tanz.
215 H2 Mpemvana S. Africa
206 D3 Mpessoba Mali
215 G5 Mpetu S. Africa
210 B4 Mpigi Uganda
211 A7 Mpika Zambia
208 C3 Mpoko r. C.A.R.
215 H3 Mpolweni S. Africa
209 F7 Mporokoso Zambia
215 I3 Mposa S. Africa
208 C5 Mpouya Congo
211 A7 Mpulungu Zambia
215 H3 Mpumalanga S. Africa
215 G2 Mpumalanga prov. S. Africa
211 C6 Mpwapwa Tanz.
215 G4 Mqanduli S. Africa
Mqinvartsveri mt. Georgia/Rus. Fed. see Kazbek
175 J2 Mrągowo Pol.
173 G2 Mrákov Czech Rep.
135 L5 Mrakovo Rus. Fed.
Mrewa Zimbabwe see Murehwa
188 E3 Mrežnica r. Croatia
188 F3 Mrkonjić-Grad Bos.-Herz.
191 J3 Mrkopalj Croatia
174 F2 Mrocza Pol.
174 F4 Mroczeń Pol.
175 I4 Mroczków Pol.
175 H2 Mroczno Pol.
175 H4 Mroga r. Pol.
175 J3 Mrozy Pol.
137 F2 Mryn Ukr.
205 H2 M'Saken Tunisia
211 C6 Msambweni Kenya
211 C6 Msata Tanz.
174 E1 Mścice Pol.
176 D1 Mšeno Czech Rep.
138 G2 Mshinskaya Rus. Fed.
205 G2 M'Sila Alg.
139 J3 Msta Rus. Fed.
139 H2 Msta r. Rus. Fed.
Mstislavl' Belarus see Mstsislaw
175 H5 Mstów Pol.
139 H4 Mstsislaw Belarus
215 I2 Msunduze r. S. Africa
175 I6 Mszana Dolna Pol.
175 I4 Mszczonów Pol.
211 C7 Mtama Tanz.
210 B4 Mtelo Kenya
211 B6 Mtera Reservoir Tanz.
Mtoko Zimbabwe see Mutoko
215 H3 Mtonjaneni S. Africa
Mtorashanga Zimbabwe see Mutorashanga
217 □3b Mtsamboro Mayotte
217 □3b Mtsangamouji Mayotte
139 K5 Mtsensk Rus. Fed.
129 D3 Mts'khet'a Georgia
213 G6 Mtubatuba S. Africa
215 H3 Mtunzini S. Africa
211 D7 Mtwara Tanz.
211 C7 Mtwara admin. reg. Tanz.
96 A2 Mu r. Myanmar
184 B3 Mu hill Port.
211 C8 Muaguide Moz.
213 G2 Mualadzi Moz.
213 H3 Mualama Moz.
254 C2 Muana Brazil
209 B6 Muanda Dem. Rep. Congo
96 D3 Muang Khammouan Laos
97 D4 Muang Không Laos
96 D4 Muang Khôngxédôn Laos
97 B5 Muang Luang r. Thai.
96 C3 Muang Pakxan Laos
96 C3 Muang Phôn-Hông Laos
96 D4 Muang Sam Sip Thai.
96 C2 Muang Sing Laos
Muang Thai country Asia see Thailand
96 C3 Muang Xaignabouri Laos
213 G3 Muanza Moz.
94 C2 Muar Malaysia
94 C2 Muar r. Malaysia
94 C3 Muarabeliti Sumatera Indon.
94 C3 Muarabungo Sumatera Indon.
94 D4 Muaradua Sumatera Indon.
94 C3 Muaraenim Sumatera Indon.
94 C3 Muaratebo Sumatera Indon.
94 C3 Muaratembesi Sumatera Indon.
95 F3 Muarateweh Kalimantan Tengah Indon.
Muara Tuang Sarawak Malaysia see Kota Samarahan
123 F5 Muari, Ras pt Pak.
116 C3 Muazzam Punjab India
128 B5 Mubārak, Jabal mt. Jordan/Saudi Arabia
117 E4 Mubarakpur Uttar Prad. India
120 F5 Mubarek Uzbek.
210 A4 Mubende Uganda
207 I4 Mubi Nigeria
Muborak Uzbek. see Mubarek
209 B6 Mucaba Angola
251 F4 Mucajaí r. Brazil
251 F4 Mucajaí, Serra do mts Brazil
225 H1 Mucalic r. Que. Can.
213 F2 Mucanha r. Moz.
196 E4 Mučanj mt. Yugo.
86 D4 Muccan W.A. Austr.
193 F1 Muccia Italy
169 C5 Much Ger.
175 H6 Mucharz Pol.
87 B6 Muchea W.A. Austr.
171 C4 Mücheln (Geiseltal) Ger.
Mucheng Henan China see Wuzhi
211 A8 Muchinga Escarpment Zambia
253 E4 Muchiri Bol.
135 H6 Muchkapskiy Rus. Fed.
170 C2 Muchow Ger.
175 I6 Muchówka Pol.
108 B2 Muchuan Sichuan China
150 E2 Much Wenlock Shropshire, England U.K.
183 F3 Mucientes Spain
146 B5 Muck i. Scotland U.K.
171 F4 Mücka Ger.
85 G5 Muckadilla Qld Austr.
169 E5 Mücke Große-Eichen Ger.
169 E5 Mücke-Nieder-Ohmen Ger.
147 C1 Muckish Mountain hill Rep. of Ireland
146 □G1 Muckle Roe i. Scotland U.K.
250 D3 Muco r. Col.
211 D8 Mucojo Moz.
209 D7 Muconda Angola
195 F3 Mucone r. Italy
209 B9 Mucope Angola
177 H5 Mucsi-hegy hill Hungary
177 J3 Múcsony Hungary
213 H3 Mucubela Moz.
251 F5 Mucucuaú r. Brazil
251 E6 Mucuim r. Brazil
213 F3 Mucumbura Moz.
126 D3 Mucur Turkey
257 H3 Mucuri Brazil
257 H3 Mucuri r. Brazil
257 G3 Mucurici Brazil
216 □3b Muda hill Fuerteventura Canary Is
94 C1 Muda r. Malaysia
114 B3 Mudabidri Karnataka India
100 D3 Mudanjiang Heilong. China
100 D3 Mudan Jiang r. China
199 F1 Mudanya Turkey
172 D2 Mudau Ger.
128 C4 Mudaysīsāt, Jabal al hill Jordan
114 C2 Muddebihal Karnataka India
241 J3 Muddy r. NV U.S.A.
237 E5 Muddy Boggy Creek r. OK U.S.A.
234 B3 Muddy Creek r. PA U.S.A.
241 L2 Muddy Creek r. UT U.S.A.
241 J3 Muddy Peak NV U.S.A.
215 H3 Muden S. Africa
168 F3 Müden (Aller) Ger.
168 F3 Müden (Örtze) Ger.
169 C5 Mudersbach Ger.
114 C3 Mudgal Karnataka India
83 G3 Mudgee N.S.W. Austr.
114 B2 Mudhol Karnataka India
114 B3 Mudigere Karnataka India
223 J3 Mudjatik r. Sask. Can.
114 C2 Mudkhed Mahar. India
116 C3 Mudki Punjab India
96 B3 Mudon Myanmar
Mudraya country Africa see Egypt
210 E3 Mudug admin. reg. Somalia
199 G1 Mudurnu Turkey
199 G1 Mudurnu r. Turkey
134 G3 Mud'yuga Rus. Fed.
213 H2 Muecate Moz.
211 C7 Mueda Moz.
186 B3 Muel Spain
186 C4 Muela de Arés mt. Spain
183 G2 Muela de Quintanilla hill Spain
182 E3 Muelas del Pan Spain
86 E3 Mueller Range hills W.A. Austr.
245 G5 Muerto, Mar lag. Mex.
246 B1 Muertos Cays is Bahamas
147 D1 Muff Rep. of Ireland
203 G4 Muftah well Sudan
209 F8 Mufulira Zambia
209 E8 Mufumbwe Zambia
109 E2 Mufu Shan mts China
186 G2 Muga r. Spain
182 D3 Muga de Sayago Spain
129 F3 Muğan Azer.
129 F4 Muğan Düzü lowland Azer.
182 B1 Mugardos Spain
184 B1 Muge Port.
184 B1 Muge r. Port.
171 E4 Mügeln Ger.
171 E4 Mügeln Ger.
172 C3 Muggensturm Ger.
191 I3 Muggia Italy
Mughalbhin Pak. see Jati
117 E4 Mughal Sarai Uttar Prad. India
122 C3 Mūghār Iran
123 G2 Mughsu r. Tajik.
Mugia Spain see Muxía
209 F6 Mugila, Monts mts Dem. Rep. Congo
199 F3 Muğla Turkey
199 F3 Muğla prov. Turkey
120 D3 Mugodzhary, Gory mts Kazakh.
106 B5 Mug Qu r. Qinghai China
163 B5 Mugron France
211 C8 Muguia Moz.
116 E3 Mugu Karnali r. Nepal
211 B5 Mugumu Tanz.
106 A1 Mugur-Aksy Rus. Fed.
111 F5 Mugxung Qinghai China
Muhala Xinjiang China see Yutian
117 E4 Muhammadabad Uttar Prad. India
Muhammarah Iran see Khorramshahr
124 D3 Muḩayriqah Saudi Arabia
211 C6 Muheza Tanz.
172 C3 Mühlacker Ger.
171 D4 Mühlanger Ger.
170 E2 Mühlbach r. Ger.
171 E4 Mühlberg Ger.
169 F5 Mühlberg Ger.
173 G3 Mühldorf am Inn Ger.
179 F3 Mühlen Austria
170 D1 Mühlen hill Ger.
170 E3 Mühlenbeck Ger.
170 C2 Mühlen-Eichsen Ger.
172 C2 Mühlhausen Ger.
173 F2 Mühlhausen Ger.
169 F4 Mühlhausen (Thüringen) Ger.
169 D5 Mühlheim am Main Ger.
172 C3 Mühlheim an der Donau Ger.
263 A2 Mühlig-Hofmann Mountains Antarctica
172 D4 Mühlingen Ger.
171 C5 Mühltroff Ger.
140 N2 Muhos Fin.
128 C2 Muḩradah Syria
173 E2 Muhr am See Ger.
138 D2 Muhu i. Estonia
213 H2 Muhula Moz.
210 B3 Mui Eth.
164 E2 Muiden Neth.
156 B3 Muids France
209 D8 Muié Angola
Muineachán Rep. of Ireland see Monaghan
147 E4 Muine Bheag Rep. of Ireland
182 C3 Muiños Spain
226 E4 Muir MI U.S.A.
234 B2 Muir PA U.S.A.
146 F5 Muirdrum Angus, Scotland U.K.
146 E5 Muirhead Angus, Scotland U.K.
146 D6 Muirkirk East Ayrshire, Scotland U.K.
146 B3 Muirneag hill Scotland U.K.
146 F4 Muir of Fowlis Aberdeenshire, Scotland U.K.
146 D4 Muir of Ord Highland, Scotland U.K.
250 B4 Muisne Ecuador
213 H2 Muite Moz.
156 D3 Muizon France
95 F2 Mujong r. Sarawak Malaysia
101 C5 Muju S. Korea
Mukačevo Ukr. see Mukacheve
136 B3 Mukacheve Ukr.
Mukachevo Ukr. see Mukacheve
95 F2 Mukah r. Sarawak Malaysia
Mukalla Yemen see Al Mukallā
116 C4 Mukandgarh Rajasthan India
116 D4 Mukandwara Rajasthan India
102 J2 Mu-kawa r. Japan
96 D3 Mukdahan Thai.
Mukden Liaoning China see Shenyang
116 C3 Mukerian Punjab India
224 C2 Muketei r. Ont. Can.
175 M3 Mukhavyets r. Belarus
100 F2 Mukhen Rus. Fed.
107 F1 Mukhorshibir' Rus. Fed.
Mukhtuya Rus. Fed. see Lensk
87 C6 Mukinbudin W.A. Austr.
104 B4 Mukō Japan
94 C3 Mukomuko Sumatera Indon.
210 B4 Mukono Uganda
123 F2 Mukry Turkm.
Muksu r. Tajik. see Mughsu
116 C3 Muktsar Punjab India
209 F8 Mukuku Zambia
120 C3 Mukur Atyrauskaya Oblast' Kazakh.
121 J2 Mukur Vostochnyy Kazakhstan Kazakh.
223 L4 Mukutawa r. Man. Can.
226 C4 Mukwonago WI U.S.A.
116 D5 Mul Mahar. India
114 B2 Mula r. India
123 F4 Mula r. Pak.
187 B6 Mula Spain
185 I2 Mula r. Spain
113 D11 Mulakatholhu Atoll Maldives
Mulaku atoll Maldives see Mulakatholhu Atoll
100 D3 Mulan Heilong. China
92 B3 Mulanay Phil.
211 B8 Mulanje Malawi
213 G2 Mulanje, Mount Malawi
82 D2 Mulapula, Lake salt flat S.A. Austr.
190 E4 Mulazzo Italy
114 C3 Mulbagal Karnataka India
151 I2 Mulbarton Norfolk, England U.K.
116 D2 Mulbekh Jammu and Kashmir India
146 E4 Mulben Moray, Scotland U.K.
237 E5 Mulberry AR U.S.A.
220 C3 Mulchatna r. AK U.S.A.
260 A5 Mulchén Chile
171 E5 Mulda Ger.
171 D4 Mulde r. Ger.
171 D4 Muldenstein Ger.
211 A5 Muleba Tanz.
238 F3 Mule Creek WY U.S.A.
242 B3 Mulegé Mex.
237 C5 Muleshoe TX U.S.A.
213 H3 Mulevala Moz.
172 D2 Mulfingen Ger.
86 C4 Mulga Downs W.A. Austr.
84 B5 Mulga Park N.T. Austr.
82 C2 Mulgathing S.A. Austr.
185 G3 Mulhacén mt. Spain
Mülhausen France see Mulhouse
169 B4 Mülheim an der Ruhr Ger.
169 C5 Mülheim-Kärlich Ger.
157 H5 Mulhouse France
108 B3 Muli Sichuan China
113 □2 Mulikadu i. Addu Atoll Maldives
100 D3 Muling Heilong. China
100 D3 Muling Heilong. China
100 E3 Muling r. China
146 C5 Mull i. Scotland U.K.
146 B5 Mull, Sound of sea chan. Scotland U.K.
122 B2 Mulla Ali Iran
148 C4 Mullagh Cavan Rep. of Ireland
147 B4 Mullagh Clare Rep. of Ireland
147 B3 Mullagh Mayo Rep. of Ireland
147 E3 Mullagh Meath Rep. of Ireland
147 B4 Mullaghareirk hill Rep. of Ireland
147 B4 Mullaghareirk Mountains hills Rep. of Ireland
147 D2 Mullaghcarn hill Northern Ireland U.K.
147 E3 Mullaghcleevaun hill Rep. of Ireland
147 D2 Mullaghcloga hill Northern Ireland U.K.
147 C2 Mullaghmore Rep. of Ireland
114 D4 Mullaittivu Sri Lanka
83 G2 Mullaley N.S.W. Austr.
147 E2 Mullan Rep. of Ireland
147 D2 Mullan Northern Ireland U.K.
146 C4 Mullardoch, Loch l. Scotland U.K.
147 F2 Mullartown Northern Ireland U.K.
236 C3 Mullen NE U.S.A.
83 F2 Mullengudgery N.S.W. Austr.
232 C6 Mullens WV U.S.A.
95 F2 Muller, Pegunungan mts Indon.
87 B6 Mullewa W.A. Austr.
172 B4 Müllheim Ger.
234 D3 Mullica r. NJ U.S.A.
234 C3 Mullica Hill NJ U.S.A.
147 D4 Mullinavat Rep. of Ireland
147 D3 Mullingar Rep. of Ireland
231 E5 Mullins SC U.S.A.
150 B4 Mullion Cornwall, England U.K.
83 G3 Mullion Creek N.S.W. Austr.
145 E4 Mull of Galloway c. Scotland U.K.
146 C6 Mull of Kintyre hd Scotland U.K.
146 B6 Mull of Oa hd Scotland U.K.
135 J5 Mullovka Rus. Fed.
171 F3 Müllrose Ger.
143 E3 Mullsjö Sweden
209 E9 Mulobezi Zambia
209 D9 Mulonga Plain Zambia
209 E6 Mulongo Dem. Rep. Congo
147 B3 Mulrany Rep. of Ireland
159 G4 Mulsanne France
116 D5 Multai Madh. Prad. India
123 G4 Multan Pak.
140 N3 Multia Fin.
95 F1 Mulu, Gunung mt. Sarawak Malaysia
114 C2 Mulug Andhra Prad. India
209 E7 Mulumbe, Monts mts Dem. Rep. Congo
122 E5 Mūmān Iran
114 B2 Mumbai Mahar. India
83 G3 Mumbil N.S.W. Austr.
209 B7 Mumbondo Angola
209 E8 Mumbwa Zambia
Muminabad Tajik. see Leningrad
Mu'minobod Tajik. see Leningrad
190 C1 Mümliswil Switz.
120 A3 Mumra Rus. Fed.
96 D4 Mun, Mae Nam r. Thai.
243 H4 Muna Mex.
131 N3 Muna r. Rus. Fed.
123 G5 Munabao Pak.
114 C2 Munagala Andhra Prad. India
103 E7 Munakata Japan
183 E4 Muñana Spain
120 C3 Munayly Kazakh.
120 C4 Munayshy Kazakh.
171 C5 Münchberg Ger.
171 F3 Müncheberg Ger.
173 F3 München Ger.
München airport Ger. see Franz Josef Strauss
171 C5 Münchenbernsdorf Ger.
190 C1 Münchenbuchsee Switz.
München-Gladbach Ger. see Mönchengladbach
169 D5 Münchhausen Ger.
222 E3 Muncho Lake B.C. Can.
101 C5 Munch'ŏn N. Korea
173 F3 Münchsmünster Ger.
173 E2 Münchsteinach Ger.
172 B2 Münchweiler an der Rodalb Ger.
190 E1 Münchwilen Switz.
230 C3 Muncie IN U.S.A.
84 D5 Muncoonie West, Lake salt flat Qld Austr.
227 I5 Muncy PA U.S.A.
234 B1 Muncy Creek r. PA U.S.A.
234 B1 Muncy Valley PA U.S.A.
183 H1 Mundaka Spain
207 H5 Mundemba Cameroon
178 E2 Munderfing Austria
172 D3 Munderkingen Ger.
151 I2 Mundesley Norfolk, England U.K.
151 H2 Mundford Norfolk, England U.K.
87 D4 Mundiwindi W.A. Austr.
85 E3 Mundjura Creek r. Qld Austr.
185 I2 Mundo r. Spain
157 H4 Mundolshiem France
254 E4 Mundo Novo Brazil
116 B5 Mundra Gujarat India
87 E6 Mundrabilla W.A. Austr.
241 L4 Munds Park AZ U.S.A.
85 G5 Mundubbera Qld Austr.
116 C4 Mundwa Rajasthan India
183 I3 Munebrega Spain
185 H1 Munera Spain
114 D2 Muneru r. India
230 C4 Munfordville KY U.S.A.
85 F5 Mungallala Qld Austr.
83 F2 Mungallala Creek r. Qld Austr.
85 F3 Mungana Qld Austr.
116 D4 Mungaoli Madh. Prad. India
213 G3 Mungári Moz.
116 E5 Mungeli Madh. Prad. India
117 F4 Munger Bihar India
227 F4 Munger MI U.S.A.
82 D2 Mungeranie S.A. Austr.
Mu Nggava i. Solomon Is see Rennell
183 H1 Mungia Spain
Mu Ngiki i. Solomon Is see Bellona
83 G2 Mungindi N.S.W. Austr.
117 G5 Mungla Bangl.
209 C7 Mungo Angola
147 C4 Mungret Rep. of Ireland
211 A7 Mungwi Zambia
101 C5 Mun'gyŏng S. Korea
209 B8 Munhino Angola
256 D5 Munhoz Brazil
Munich Ger. see München
183 E4 Muñico Spain
186 C3 Muniesa Spain
183 H2 Munilla Spain
226 D2 Munising MI U.S.A.
257 G4 Muniz Freire Brazil
Munkács Ukr. see Mukacheve
142 D2 Munkedal Sweden
140 K3 Munkflohögen Sweden
142 E2 Munkfors Sweden
106 D1 Munku-Sardyk, Gora mt. Mongolia/Rus. Fed.
165 C4 Munkzwalm Belgium
146 D4 Munlochy Highland, Scotland U.K.
169 F5 Münnerstadt Ger.
173 E3 Munningen Ger.
183 F4 Muñogalindo Spain
83 G5 Munro, Mount Tas. Austr.
117 G5 Munshiganj Bangl.
173 F4 Münsing Ger.
172 D3 Münsingen Ger.
190 C2 Münsingen Switz.
178 C3 Münster Austria
157 H4 Munster France
172 C2 Münster Ger.
168 F3 Münster Ger.
169 C4 Münster Ger.
169 C4 Münster admin. reg. Nordrhein-Westfalen Ger.
147 C4 Munster reg. Rep. of Ireland
190 D2 Münster Switz.
168 E2 Münsterdorf Ger.
173 E3 Münsterhausen Ger.
169 C5 Münstermaifeld Ger.
169 C3 Münster-Osnabrück airport Ger.
87 C6 Muntadgin W.A. Austr.
178 D3 Muntanitz mt. Austria
197 F2 Muntele Mare, Vârful mt. Romania
164 F1 Muntendam Neth.
197 H3 Munteni Romania
Munyal-Par sea feature India see Bassas de Pedro Padua Bank
213 F3 Munyati r. Zimbabwe
215 G4 Munyu S. Africa
169 D5 Münzenberg Ger.
179 E2 Münzkirchen Austria
140 M2 Muodoslompolo Sweden
140 M2 Muonio Fin.
140 M2 Muonioälven r. Fin./Sweden
140 M2 Muonionalusta Sweden
Muonionjoki r. Fin./Sweden see Muonioälven
190 D2 Muotathal Switz.
209 B9 Mupa Angola
213 F3 Mupfure r. Zimbabwe
107 I4 Muping Shandong China
124 D5 Muqaybirah Yemen
210 E4 Muqdisho Somalia
125 F4 Muqshin, Wādī r. Oman
129 F3 Müqtädir Azer.
257 G4 Muqui Brazil
Muqyr Atyrauskaya Oblast' Kazakh. see Mukur
179 H4 Mur r. Austria alt. Mura (Croatia/Slovenia)
179 H4 Mura r. Croatia/Slovenia alt. Mur (Austria)
173 G2 Murach r. Ger.
182 C5 Muradal, Serra do mts Port.
199 E2 Muradiye Manisa Turkey
127 F3 Muradiye Van Turkey
136 E3 Murafa r. Ukr.
102 I4 Murakami Japan
176 F5 Murakeresztúr Hungary
259 B8 Murallón, Cerro mt. Chile
211 A5 Muramvya Burundi
177 J3 Muráň Slovakia
177 J3 Muráň r. Slovakia
210 C5 Muranga Kenya
191 H3 Murano Italy
182 C1 Muras Spain
134 J4 Murashi Rus. Fed.
161 A5 Murasson France
176 F5 Muraszemenye Hungary
161 A3 Murat France
129 B4 Murat r. Turkey
127 E3 Murat r. Turkey
129 B4 Muratgören Turkey
199 E1 Muratlı Turkey
192 B2 Murato Corse France
161 A5 Murat-sur-Vèbre France
179 F3 Murau Austria
175 M3 Murava Belarus
192 B5 Muravera Sardegna Italy
102 J4 Murayama Japan
124 C2 Murayr, Jabal hill Saudi Arabia
190 D4 Murazzano Italy
157 H5 Murbach France
182 C3 Murça Port.
183 I2 Murchante Spain
170 E2 Murchin Ger.
83 F4 Murchison Vic. Austr.
87 B5 Murchison watercourse W.A. Austr.
81 D4 Murchison South I. N.Z.
263 L2 Murchison, Mount Antarctica
87 C5 Murchison, Mount hill W.A. Austr.
81 C5 Murchison, Mount South I. N.Z.
210 A4 Murchison Falls National Park Uganda
84 C4 Murchison Range hills N.T. Austr.
187 B7 Murcia Spain
185 I3 Murcia aut. comm. Spain
174 F3 Murczyn Pol.
161 A4 Mur-de-Barrez France
158 D3 Mûr-de-Bretagne France
234 C3 Murderkill r. DE U.S.A.
159 H4 Mur-de-Sologne France
236 C3 Murdo SD U.S.A.
225 H3 Murdochville Que. Can.
179 G4 Mureck Austria
199 E1 Mürefte Turkey
213 F3 Murehwa Zimbabwe
184 C2 Mures r. Port.
196 E2 Mureş r. Romania
163 D5 Muret France
Murewa Zimbabwe see Murehwa
140 K2 Murfjället mt. Norway
237 E5 Murfreesboro AR U.S.A.
231 E4 Murfreesboro NC U.S.A.
231 C5 Murfreesboro TN U.S.A.
172 C4 Murg Ger.
172 C3 Murg r. Ger.
123 H2 Murgab r. Tajik.
123 E2 Murgap Turkm.
123 E2 Murgap r. Turkm.
84 C1 Murgenella Creek r. N.T. Austr.
197 I2 Murgeni Romania
190 C1 Murgenthal Switz.
195 G2 Murge Tarantine hills Italy
123 E3 Murghab r. Afgh.
Murghob Turkm. see Murgap
Murghob r. Turkm. see Murgap
129 D3 Murghuz Lerr mt. Armenia
193 I4 Murgia Sant'Elia hill Italy
85 G5 Murgon Qld Austr.
87 C5 Murgoo W.A. Austr.
183 H2 Murguía Spain
129 B3 Murgul Turkey
106 C4 Muri Qinghai China
117 F5 Muri Bihar India
122 D2 Mūrī Iran
190 D1 Muri Aargau Switz.
190 C2 Muri Bern Switz.
95 E4 Muria, Gunung mt. Indon.
257 F4 Muriaé Brazil
182 D2 Murias de Paredes Spain
183 G1 Muriedas Spain
209 D7 Muriege Angola
102 K2 Murii-dake mt. Japan
226 C1 Murillo Ont. Can.
183 I2 Murillo el Fruto Spain
190 D3 Murisengo Italy
170 D2 Müritz l. Ger.
80 F3 Muriwai North I. N.Z.
40 M2 Murjek Sweden
1 18 B3 Murley Northern Ireland U.K.
192 D1 Murlo Italy
140 P1 Murmansk Rus. Fed.
140 P1 Murmanskaya Oblast' admin. div. Rus. Fed.
134 F1 Murmanskiy Bereg coastal area Rus. Fed.
Murmansk Oblast admin. div. Rus. Fed. see Murmanskaya Oblast'
140 P1 Murmashi Rus. Fed.
139 M4 Murmino Rus. Fed.
173 G4 Murn r. Ger.
173 F4 Murnau am Staffelsee Ger.
147 E4 Murntown Rep. of Ireland
182 B3 Muro Port.
187 G5 Muro Spain
187 G5 Muro r. Spain
187 C6 Muro de Alcoy Spain
160 A3 Murol France
195 H2 Muro Leccese Italy
193 H4 Muro Lucano Italy
134 H5 Murom Rus. Fed.
104 D2 Muromagi-gawa r. Japan
162 B2 Muron France
177 K5 Murony Hungary
102 J2 Muroran Japan
192 A4 Muros Sardegna Italy
182 D1 Muros Asturias Spain
182 A2 Muros Galicia Spain
103 G7 Muroto Japan
175 M5 Murovane Ukr.
136 D3 Murovani Kurylivtsi Ukr.
129 E3 Murovdağ Silsiläsi hills Azer.
174 F5 Murów Pol.
174 F3 Murowana-Goślina Pol.
238 C3 Murphy ID U.S.A.
231 D5 Murphy NC U.S.A.
240 G2 Murphys CA U.S.A.
83 F2 Murra Murra Qld Austr.
203 G2 Murrat el Kubra, Buheirat l. Egypt
128 A4 Murrat el Sughra, Buheirat l. Egypt
82 D3 Murray r. S.A. Austr.
87 B7 Murray r. W.A. Austr.
222 F3 Murray r. B.C. Can.
237 F4 Murray KY U.S.A.
91 J8 Murray, Lake P.N.G.
222 D2 Murray, Mount Y.T. Can.
82 D3 Murray Bridge S.A. Austr.
232 B5 Murray City OH U.S.A.
84 C4 Murray Downs N.T. Austr.
225 I4 Murray Harbour P.E.I. Can.
87 F5 Murray Range hills W.A. Austr.
214 D4 Murraysburg S. Africa
82 E3 Murrayville Vic. Austr.
123 H3 Murree Pak.
172 D3 Murrhardt Ger.
240 I5 Murrieta CA U.S.A.
83 G3 Murringo N.S.W. Austr.
147 B3 Murrisk reg. Rep. of Ireland
147 B3 Murrooghi Rep. of Ireland
83 G3 Murrumbateman N.S.W. Austr.
83 E3 Murrumbidgee r. N.S.W. Austr.
213 H2 Murrupula Moz.
83 G2 Murrurundi N.S.W. Austr.
159 F4 Mûrs-Erigné France
117 G4 Murshidabad W. Bengal India
188 F2 Murska Sobota Slovenia
179 H4 Mursko Središće Croatia
116 D5 Murtajapur Mahar. India
185 G4 Murtas Spain
182 B4 Murtede Port.
190 C2 Murten Switz.
190 C2 Murtensee l. Switz.
188 E4 Murter Croatia
188 E4 Murter i. Croatia
83 E4 Murtoa Vic. Austr.
182 B4 Murtosa Port.
252 C2 Muru r. Brazil
114 B2 Murud Mahar. India
95 F2 Murud, Gunung mt. Indon.
183 H1 Murueta Spain
95 F3 Murui r. Indon.
95 F3 Murung r. Indon.
95 F3 Murung r. Indon.
120 F4 Muruntau Uzbek.
80 F3 Murupara North I. N.Z.
79 □3 Mururoa atoll Arch. des Tuamotu Fr. Polynesia
Murviedro Spain see Sagunto
161 B5 Murviel-lès-Béziers France
116 E5 Murwara Madh. Prad. India
83 H2 Murwillumbah N.S.W. Austr.
134 J4 Murygino Rus. Fed.
179 G3 Mürz r. Austria
202 B3 Murzūq Libya
174 D3 Murzynowo Pol.
179 G3 Mürzzuschlag Austria
127 F3 Muş Turkey
129 B4 Muş prov. Turkey
138 E3 Mūša r. Latvia/Lith.
124 A1 Mûsa, Gebel mt. Egypt
124 C5 Musa Āli Terara vol. Africa
117 F5 Musabani Bihar India
128 C1 Musabeyli Turkey
123 G4 Musa Khel Bazar Pak.
197 F4 Musala mt. Bulg.
128 B1 Musalı Turkey
101 D4 Musan N. Korea
125 G2 Musandam admin. reg. Oman
123 F3 Musa Qala, Rūd-i r. Afgh.
105 F3 Musashino Japan
Musay'īd Qatar see Umm Sa'id
124 D5 Musaymir Yemen
150 D4 Musbury Devon, England U.K.
125 G3 Muscat Oman
Muscat and Oman country Asia see Oman
236 F3 Muscatine IA U.S.A.
171 D4 Muschwitz Ger.
226 B4 Muscoda WI U.S.A.
234 C2 Musconetcong r. NJ U.S.A.
138 E4 Musė r. Lith.
192 A5 Musei Sardegna Italy
85 E2 Musgrave Qld Austr.
81 C5 Musgrave, Mount South I. N.Z.
225 K3 Musgrave Harbour Nfld. Can.
82 B1 Musgrave Ranges mts S.A. Austr.
209 C5 Mushie Dem. Rep. Congo
207 F5 Mushin Nigeria
137 G3 Mushuryn Rig Ukr.
114 C2 Musi r. India
94 D3 Musi r. Indon.
196 E5 Musica mt. Macedonia
241 K4 Music Mountain AZ U.S.A.
191 H3 Musile di Piave Italy
241 L2 Musinia Peak UT U.S.A.
222 F2 Muskeg r. N.W.T. Can.
233 H4 Muskeget Channel MA U.S.A.
226 D4 Muskegon MI U.S.A.
226 D4 Muskegon r. MI U.S.A.
226 D4 Muskegon Heights MI U.S.A.
222 G4 Muskeg River Alta Can.
232 C5 Muskingum r. OH U.S.A.
237 E5 Muskogee OK U.S.A.
227 H3 Muskoka Ont. Can.
222 F3 Muskwa r. B.C. Can.
Muslim-Croat Federation aut. div. Bos.-Herz. see Federacija Bosna i Hercegovina
134 K5 Muslyumovo Rus. Fed.
211 B5 Musoma Tanz.
191 I5 Musone r. Italy
225 I3 Musquaro Que. Can.
91 K7 Mussau Island P.N.G.
146 E6 Musselburgh East Lothian, Scotland U.K.
164 G2 Musselkanaal Neth.
238 F2 Musselshell r. MT U.S.A.
209 C7 Mussende Angola
209 B6 Musserra Angola
162 C3 Mussidan France
194 C5 Mussomeli Sicilia Italy
165 E5 Musson Belgium
116 D3 Mussoorie Uttar Prad. India
209 D8 Mussuma Angola
209 D8 Mussuma r. Angola
156 E5 Mussy-sur-Seine France
116 E4 Mustafabad Uttar Prad. India
199 F1 Mustafakemalpaşa Turkey
210 E3 Mustahīl Eth.
190 F2 Müstair Switz.
110 D2 Mustau, Gora mt. Xinjiang China
120 C2 Mustayevo Rus. Fed.
259 C7 Musters, Lago l. Arg.
247 □3 Mustique i. St Vincent
138 F3 Mustjõgi r. Estonia
138 E2 Mustla Estonia
138 F2 Mustvee Estonia
83 G3 Muswellbrook N.S.W. Austr.
175 I2 Muszaki Pol.
175 I6 Muszyna Pol.
203 F3 Mut Egypt
126 D3 Mut Turkey
179 G4 Muta Slovenia
209 E8 Mutanda Zambia
213 G3 Mutare Zimbabwe
124 D3 Mutarjim, Khashm hill Saudi Arabia
179 I2 Mutěnice Czech Rep.
146 E5 Muthill Perth and Kinross, Scotland U.K.
183 I2 Mutilva Baja Spain
Mutina Italy see Modena
93 C5 Mutis, Gunung mt. Timor Indon.
134 K2 Mutnyy Materik Rus. Fed.
213 G3 Mutoko Zimbabwe
82 E3 Mutooroo S.A. Austr.
213 F3 Mutorashanga Zimbabwe
193 G3 Mutria, Monte mt. Italy
217 □3 Mutsamudu Comoros
209 E7 Mutshatsha Dem. Rep. Congo
102 J3 Mutsu Japan
102 J3 Mutsu-wan b. Japan
85 F4 Muttaburra Qld Austr.
199 G2 Muttalip Turkey
178 B3 Muttekopf mt. Austria
190 C1 Muttenz Switz.
178 C3 Mutters Austria
172 C2 Mutterstadt Ger.
81 A7 Muttonbird Islands Stewart I. N.Z.
81 B7 Muttonbird Islands Stewart I. N.Z.
114 D3 Muttukuru Andhra Prad. India
114 C4 Muttupet Tamil Nadu India
213 H2 Mutuali Moz.
257 G3 Mutum Brazil
250 D6 Mutum r. Brazil
207 H4 Mutum Biyu Nigeria
254 C5 Mutunópolis Brazil
114 D4 Mutur Sri Lanka
187 C6 Mutxamel Spain
137 G2 Mutyn Ukr.
157 H4 Mutzig France
171 D4 Mutzschen Ger.
141 N3 Muurame Fin.
141 M3 Muurla Fin.
140 N2 Muurola Fin.
107 F4 Mu Us Shamo des. China
209 B7 Muxaluando Angola
129 E3 Muxax Azer.
Muxi Sichuan China see Muchuan
182 A1 Muxía Spain
209 B7 Muxima Angola
134 F3 Muyezerskiy Rus. Fed.
211 A5 Muyinga Burundi
120 D4 Muynak Uzbek.
Muynoq Uzbek. see Muynak
211 B7 Muyombe Zambia
207 H5 Muyuka Cameroon
209 E6 Muyumba Dem. Rep. Congo
121 G3 Muyunkum, Peski des. Kazakh.
121 H4 Muyunkym Kazakh.
108 D2 Muyuping Hubei China
123 H3 Muzaffarabad Pak.
123 G4 Muzaffargarh Pak.
116 D3 Muzaffarnagar Uttar Prad. India
117 F4 Muzaffarpur Bihar India
256 D4 Muzambinho Brazil
110 C3 Muzat He r. China
213 F2 Muze Moz.
158 D4 Muzillac France
250 C3 Muzo Col.
243 E3 Múzquiz Mex.
111 C5 Muztag mt. Xinjiang China
111 D4 Muztag mt. Xinjiang China
110 A4 Muztagata mt. Xinjiang China
Muztor Kyrg. see Toktogul
191 I3 Muzzana del Turgnano Italy
207 H6 Mvangan Cameroon
211 C6 Mvomero Tanz.
208 B4 Mvoung r. Gabon
217 □3a Mvouni Njazidja Comoros
209 B6 Mvouti Congo
213 F3 Mvuma Zimbabwe
217 □3 Mwali i. Comoros
211 C5 Mwanga Tanz.
211 B8 Mwanza Malawi
211 B5 Mwanza Tanz.
211 B5 Mwanza admin. reg. Tanz.
209 D6 Mweka Dem. Rep. Congo
209 F7 Mwenda Zambia
209 D6 Mwene-Ditu Dem. Rep. Congo
213 F4 Mwenezi Zimbabwe
213 F4 Mwenezi r. Zimbabwe
209 F7 Mweru, Lake Dem. Rep. Congo/Zambia
211 C7 Mweru Plateau Tanz.
209 E7 Mwinilunga Zambia
138 F4 Myadzyel Belarus
116 B4 Myajlar Rajasthan India
136 D2 M"yakoty Ukr.
96 A3 Myanaung Myanmar
96 A2 Myanmar country Asia
139 J4 Myatlevo Rus. Fed.
131 P3 Myaundzha Rus. Fed.
96 A3 Myaungmya Myanmar
146 E3 Mybster Highland, Scotland U.K.
198 C3 Mycenae tourist site Greece
Myeik Myanmar see Mergui
232 B5 Myers KY U.S.A.
234 B2 Myerstown PA U.S.A.
96 A2 Myingyan Myanmar
97 B4 Myinmoletkat mt. Myanmar
96 A2 Myinmu Myanmar
96 B1 Myitkyina Myanmar
96 B2 Myittha Myanmar
115 G1 Myittha r. Myanmar
177 G3 Myjava Slovakia
176 F3 Myjava r. Slovakia
137 G3 Mykhaylivka Cherkas'ka Oblast' Ukr.
137 I3 Mykhaylivka Kharkivs'ka Oblast' Ukr.
137 H3 Mykhaylivka Poltavs'ka Oblast' Ukr.
137 H4 Mykhaylivka Zaporiz'ka Oblast' Ukr.
137 H4 Mykhaylivka Zaporiz'ka Oblast' Ukr.
137 F2 Mykhaylo-Kotsyubyns'ke Ukr.
136 D2 Mykhaylyuchka Ukr.
136 B3 Mykolayiv L'vivs'ka Oblast' Ukr.
175 M5 Mykolayiv L'vivs'ka Oblast' Ukr.
137 G4 Mykolayiv Mykolayivs'ka Oblast' Ukr.
137 H4 Mykolayivka Dnipropetrovs'ka Oblast' Ukr.
137 I3 Mykolayivka Dnipropetrovs'ka Oblast' Ukr.
137 I3 Mykolayivka Donets'ka Oblast' Ukr.
137 H4 Mykolayivka Khersons'ka Oblast' Ukr.
136 F4 Mykolayivka Odes'ka Oblast' Ukr.
136 F5 Mykolayivka Odes'ka Oblast' Ukr.
137 I4 Mykolayivka Zaporiz'ka Oblast' Ukr.
136 E4 Mykolayivka-Novorosiys'ka Ukr.
Mykolayiv Oblast admin. div. Ukr. see Mykolayivs'ka Oblast'
137 G4 Mykolayivs'ka Oblast' admin. div. Ukr.
199 D3 Mykonos Notio Aigaio Greece
199 D3 Mykonos i. Greece
136 C3 Mykulyntsi Ukr.
134 J2 Myla r. Rus. Fed.
Mylae Sicilia Italy see Milazzo
Mylasa Turkey see Milas
171 D5 Mylau Ger.
138 F1 Myllykoski Fin.
150 B4 Mylor Cornwall, England U.K.
Mymensing Bangl. see Mymensingh
117 G4 Mymensingh Bangl.
138 C1 Mynäjoki r. Fin.
141 M3 Mynämäki Fin.
214 D4 Mynfontein S. Africa
105 E2 Myōgi-san mt. Japan
96 A2 Myohaung Myanmar
104 A4 Myōken-yama hill Japan
160 D1 Myon France
101 D4 Myŏnggan N. Korea
138 F4 Myory Belarus
103 J8 Myozin-sho i. Japan
140 □C3 Mýrdalsjökull ice cap Iceland
140 □C3 Mýrdalssandur sand area Iceland
140 K1 Myre Norway
140 M2 Myrheden Sweden
137 G3 Myrhorod Ukr.
198 D2 Myrina Voreio Aigaio Greece
137 G3 Myrivs'ke Ukr.
140 L1 Myrlandshaugen Norway
223 I4 Myrnam Alta Can.
137 I4 Myrne Donets'ka Oblast' Ukr.
137 G4 Myrne Khersons'ka Oblast' Ukr.
137 F2 Myrne Kyivs'ka Oblast' Ukr.
175 M5 Myrne Volyns'ka Oblast' Ukr.
137 H4 Myrne Zaporiz'ka Oblast' Ukr.
136 E4 Myrnopillya Ukr.
137 G5 Myrnyy Ukr.
137 I3 Myronivka Kharkivs'ka Oblast' Ukr.
136 F3 Myronivka Kyivs'ka Oblast' Ukr.
136 D2 Myropil' Ukr.
137 H2 Myropillya Ukr.
141 N3 Myrskylä Fin.
231 E5 Myrtle Beach SC U.S.A.
238 B3 Myrtle Creek OR U.S.A.
83 F4 Myrtleford Vic. Austr.
238 A3 Myrtle Point OR U.S.A.
121 G4 Myrzakent Kazakh.
142 D2 Mysen Norway
148 C5 Myshall Rep. of Ireland
138 E5 Myshanka r. Belarus
139 L3 Myshkin Rus. Fed.
Myshkino Rus. Fed. see Myshkin
137 I5 Myskhako Rus. Fed.
174 C3 Myśla r. Pol.
Mys Lazareva Rus. Fed. see Lazarev
175 H6 Myślenice Pol.
174 C3 Myślibórz Pol.
175 H2 Myślice Pol.
175 H5 Mysłowice Pol.
Myslowitz Pol. see Mysłowice
96 E4 My Son tourist site Vietnam
114 C3 Mysore Karnataka India
Mysore state India see Karnataka
Mysovsk Rus. Fed. see Babushkin
131 T3 Mys Shmidta Rus. Fed.
235 G1 Mystic CT U.S.A.
235 D3 Mystic Islands NJ U.S.A.
175 H1 Myszewo Pol.
175 H5 Myszków Pol.
175 J2 Myszyneic Pol.
134 H4 Myt Rus. Fed.
97 D5 My Tho Vietnam
Mytilene i. Greece see Lesvos
199 E2 Mytilini Voreio Aigaio Greece
199 E3 Mytilinioi Voreio Aigaio Greece
126 B3 Mytilini Strait Greece/Turkey
139 K4 Mytishchi Rus. Fed.
177 I3 Mýtna Slovakia
176 C2 Mýto Czech Rep.
241 L1 Myton UT U.S.A.
137 G3 Mytrofanivka Ukr.
140 □C2 Mývatn l. Iceland
140 □C2 Mývatnsöræfi lava field Iceland
136 C2 Myzove Ukr.
205 F2 M'Zab Valley tourist site Alg.
215 F4 Mzamomhle S. Africa
176 B2 Mže r. Czech Rep.
211 B7 Mzimba Malawi
213 F4 Mzingwani r. Zimbabwe
211 B7 Mzuzu Malawi
129 A2 Mzymta r. Rus. Fed.

N

96 C2 Na, Nam r. China/Vietnam
173 G2 Naab r. Ger.
164 D3 Naaldwijk Neth.
240 □D9 Naalehu HI U.S.A.
205 E2 Naama Alg.
141 M3 Naantali Fin.
164 E2 Naarden Neth.
179 F2 Naarn im Machlande Austria
147 E3 Naas Rep. of Ireland
214 A3 Nababeep S. Africa
Nabadwip W. Bengal India see Navadwip
182 B5 Nabão r. Port.
115 D2 Nabarangapur Orissa India
104 C4 Nabari Japan
104 C4 Nabari-gawa r. Japan
92 B4 Nabas Phil.
128 B3 Nabatiyet et Tahta Lebanon
87 D5 Nabberu, Lake salt flat W.A. Austr.
173 G2 Nabburg Ger.
211 C6 Naberera Tanz.
137 J2 Naberezhnoye Rus. Fed.
134 K5 Naberezhnyye Chelny Rus. Fed.
120 A2 Naberezhnyy Uvekh Rus. Fed.
205 H1 Nabeul Tunisia
189 C7 Nabeul admin. div. Tunisia
116 D3 Nabha Punjab India
129 E3 Näbiağalı Azer.
253 F5 Nabileque r. Brazil
117 F4 Nabinagar Bihar India
128 B3 Nāblus West Bank
206 E4 Nabolo Ghana
213 F5 Naboomspruit S. Africa
79 □1 Nabouwalu Vanua Levu Fiji
116 D2 Nabra r. India
177 L3 Nábrád Hungary
Nābulus West Bank see Nāblus
243 G5 Nacajuca Mex.
213 I2 Nacala Moz.
242 □I6 Nacaome Hond.
213 H2 Nacaroa Moz.
176 D2 Načeradec Czech Rep.
138 G4 Nacha r. Belarus
120 B3 Nachalovo Rus. Fed.
238 B2 Naches WA U.S.A.
211 C7 Nachingwea Tanz.
116 B4 Nachna Rajasthan India
176 F1 Náchod Czech Rep.
260 A5 Nacimiento Chile
185 H3 Nacimiento Spain
185 H4 Nacimiento r. Spain
170 D3 Nackel Ger.
172 C2 Nackenheim Ger.
237 E6 Nacogdoches TX U.S.A.
242 C2 Nacozari de García Mex.
175 I3 Nacpolsk Pol.
Nada Hainan China see Danzhou
222 C2 Nadaleen r. Y.T. Can.
176 F5 Nádasd Hungary
177 H4 Nádasdladány Hungary
116 D4 Nadbai Rajasthan India
151 F3 Nadder r. England U.K.
137 G4 Naddnipryans'ke Ukr.
Nådendal Fin. see Naantali
120 E1 Nadezhdinka Kazakh.
Nadezhdinskiy Kazakh. see Nadezhdinka
79 □1a Nadi Viti Levu Fiji
116 C5 Nadiad Gujarat India
196 E2 Nădlac Romania
204 E2 Nador Morocco
180 E5 Nador prov. Morocco
197 F3 Nădrag Romania
129 D2 Nadterechnaya Rus. Fed.
177 K4 Nádudvar Hungary
195 □ Nadur Gozo Malta
122 C3 Nadūshan Iran
136 C3 Nadvirna Ukr.
Nadvornaya Ukr. see Nadvirna
130 I3 Nadym Rus. Fed.
116 C4 Naenwa Rajasthan India
142 D4 Næstved Denmark
117 H5 Naf r. Bangl./Myanmar
128 B5 Nafas, Râs el mt. Egypt
190 E1 Näfels Switz.
149 I3 Nafferton East Riding of Yorkshire, England U.K.
128 B4 Nafḩa, Har hill Israel
198 B2 Nafpaktos Greece
198 C3 Nafplio Greece
Naft r. Iraq see Āb Nafţ
129 E3 Naftalan Azer.
124 D3 Nafūd ad Daḩl des. Saudi Arabia
124 C2 Nafūd al 'Urayq des. Saudi Arabia
124 D2 Nafūd as Sirr des. Saudi Arabia
124 C3 Nafūd as Surrah des. Saudi Arabia
124 D2 Nafūd Qunayfidhah des. Saudi Arabia
202 A2 Nafūsah, Jabal hills Libya
124 C2 Nafy Saudi Arabia
92 B3 Naga Phil.
224 C3 Nagagami r. Ont. Can.
104 C3 Nagahama Japan
117 H4 Naga Hills India

Naga Hills to Neftegorsk 339

Naga Hills state India see Nagaland
102 J4 Nagai Japan
105 E3 Nagaizumi Japan
117 H4 Nagaland state India
83 F4 Nagambie Vic. Austr.
105 E2 Nagano Japan
105 D2 Nagano pref. Japan
103 I5 Nagaoka Japan
117 H4 Nagaon Assam India
Nagapatam Tamil Nadu India see Nagappattinam
114 C4 Nagappattinam Tamil Nadu India
117 G4 Nagar r. Bangl./India
116 D2 Nagar Hima. Prad. India
114 B3 Nagar Karnataka India
116 D4 Nagar Rajasthan India
104 C3 Nagara-gawa r. Japan
114 D2 Nagaram Andhra Prad. India
105 F3 Nagareyama Japan
114 C2 Nagar Karnul Andhra Prad. India
242 □16 Nagarote Nic.
111 E6 Nagarzê Xizang China
103 D7 Nagasaki Japan
103 D7 Nagasaki pref. Japan
103 E6 Nagato Japan
116 C4 Nagaur Rajasthan India
115 D2 Nagavali r. India
116 C5 Nagda Madh. Prad. India
173 F2 Nagel Ger.
164 E2 Nagele Neth.
114 C4 Nagercoil Tamil Nadu India
203 G3 Nag' Hammâdi Egypt
116 D3 Nagina Uttar Prad. India
147 C4 Nagles Mountains hills Rep. of Ireland
175 I5 Nagłowice Pol.
116 E4 Nagod Madh. Prad. India
172 C3 Nagold Ger.
172 C3 Nagold r. Ger.
Nagong Chu r. China see Parlung Zangbo
183 I2 Nagore Spain
Nagorno-Karabakh aut. reg. Azer. see Dağlıq Qarabağ
Nagornyy Karabakh aut. reg. Azer. see Dağlıq Qarabağ
134 J4 Nagorsk Rus. Fed.
139 L3 Nagor'ye Rus. Fed.
191 F3 Nago-Torbole Italy
104 C3 Nagoya Japan
116 D5 Nagpur Mahar. India
111 F6 Nagqu Xizang China
111 F6 Nag Qu r. Xizang China
141 M3 Nagu Fin.
247 E3 Nagua Dom. Rep.
247 □1 Naguabo Puerto Rico
129 C1 Nagutskoye Rus. Fed.
176 G5 Nagyatád Hungary
177 G5 Nagybajom Hungary
177 J5 Nagybánhegyes Hungary
177 H5 Nagybaracska Hungary
Nagybecskerek Vojvodina, Srbija Yugo. see Zrenjanin
177 H5 Nagyberény Hungary
177 H5 Nagyberki Hungary
176 F4 Nagycenk Hungary
177 J4 Nagycsécs Hungary
177 K4 Nagycserkesz Hungary
177 L3 Nagydobos Hungary
177 H5 Nagydorog Hungary
177 L4 Nagyecsed Hungary
Nagyenyed Romania see Aiud
177 J4 Nagyfüged Hungary
177 K3 Nagyhalász Hungary
177 H6 Nagyharsány Hungary
177 K4 Nagyhegyes Hungary
177 H4 Nagyigmánd Hungary
177 J4 Nagyiván Hungary
177 K4 Nagykálló Hungary
177 K5 Nagykamarás Hungary
176 F5 Nagykanizsa Hungary
176 F5 Nagykapornak Hungary
177 H5 Nagykarácsony Hungary
177 I4 Nagykáta Hungary
177 K4 Nagykereki Hungary
177 H5 Nagykónyi Hungary
177 I4 Nagykőrös Hungary
177 H4 Nagykovácsi Hungary
177 J5 Nagylak Hungary
177 I3 Nagylóc Hungary
176 F4 Nagylózs Hungary
177 J5 Nagymágocs Hungary
177 H5 Nagymányok Hungary
177 H4 Nagymaros Hungary
177 K3 Nagy-Milic hill Hungary/Slovakia
177 H6 Nagynyárád Hungary
177 I4 Nagyoroszi Hungary
177 K4 Nagyrábé Hungary
176 G5 Nagyrécse Hungary
176 G4 Nagysimonyi Hungary
177 J5 Nagyszénás Hungary
177 G4 Nagyszentjános Hungary
177 H5 Nagyszokoly Hungary
177 I4 Nagytarcsa Hungary
177 J5 Nagytőke Hungary
Nagyvárad Romania see Oradea
177 L3 Nagyvarsány Hungary
177 G5 Nagyvázsony Hungary
177 H5 Nagyvenyim Hungary
102 □2 Naha Japan
116 D3 Nahan Hima. Prad. India
123 E5 Nahang r. Iran/Pak.
222 F2 Nahanni Butte N.W.T. Can.
222 F2 Nahanni Range mts N.W.T. Can.
128 B3 Nahariyya Israel
183 H4 Naharros Spain
122 B3 Nahāvand Iran
168 F2 Nahe Ger.
172 B2 Nahe r. Ger.
205 F4 N'Ahnet, Adrar mts Alg.
159 H4 Nahon r. France
124 B2 Nahr, Jabal hill Saudi Arabia
168 F2 Nahrendorf Ger.
244 D4 Nahuatzen Mex.
231 D6 Nahunta GA U.S.A.
92 B3 Naic Phil.
242 D3 Naica Mex.
117 G4 Naik Murad Bangl.
171 C5 Naila Ger.
163 D5 Nailloux France
150 E3 Nailsea North Somerset, England U.K.
150 E3 Nailsworth Gloucestershire, England U.K.
Naiman Qi Nei Mongol China see Daqin Tal
225 I1 Nain Nfld. Can.
116 E4 Naina Uttar Prad. India
116 D3 Naini Tal Uttar Prad. India
116 E5 Nainpur Madh. Prad. India
159 G5 Naintré France
79 □1 Nairai i. Fiji
146 E4 Nairn Highland, Scotland U.K.
146 E4 Nairn r. Scotland U.K.
227 G2 Nairn Centre Ont. Can.
211 C5 Nairobi Kenya
Naissus Srbija Yugo. see Niš
210 C5 Naivasha Kenya
157 F4 Naives-Rosières France
158 D4 Naizin France
100 C4 Naizishan Jilin China
163 D4 Najac France
122 B3 Najafābād Iran
246 C2 Najasa r. Cuba
124 C2 Najd reg. Saudi Arabia
183 H2 Nájera Spain
183 H2 Najerilla r. Spain
107 I1 Naji Nei Mongol China
116 D3 Najibabad Uttar Prad. India
183 H3 Nájima r. Spain
101 D4 Najin N. Korea
Najitun Nei Mongol China see Naji
125 E2 Najmah Saudi Arabia
124 D4 Najrān Saudi Arabia
124 D4 Najrān prov. Saudi Arabia
113 □1 Nakachchaafushi i. N. Male Maldives
105 G2 Naka-gawa r. Japan
103 G7 Naka-gawa r. Japan
102 □2 Nakagusuku Japan
Nakahchaafushi i. N. Male Maldives see Nakachchaafushi
103 E7 Nakama Japan
206 E4 Nakambé watercourse Burkina/Ghana alt. Nakanbe, alt. Volta Blanche, conv. White Volta
103 F7 Nakamura Japan
Nakanbé watercourse Burkina/Ghana see White Volta
105 E2 Nakano Japan
102 □1 Nakano-shima i. Japan
105 F1 Nakano-take mt. Japan
211 C7 Nakapanya Tanz.
210 B4 Nakasongola Uganda
Nakatchafushi i. N. Male Maldives see Nakachchaafushi
102 K1 Nakatonbetsu-chō hill Japan
103 E7 Nakatsu Japan
104 D3 Nakatsugawa Japan
105 E2 Nakatsu-gawa r. Japan
113 □1 Nakatuku Fushi i. N. Male Maldives
203 H5 Nakfa Eritrea
Nakhichevan' Azer. see Naxçıvan
Nakhichevan' aut. reg. Azer. see Naxçıvan
100 E4 Nakhodka Rus. Fed.
117 H4 Nakhola Assam India
97 C4 Nakhon Nayok Thai.
97 C4 Nakhon Pathom Thai.
96 D3 Nakhon Phanom Thai.
97 C4 Nakhon Ratchasima Thai.
96 C4 Nakhon Sawan Thai.
97 B5 Nakhon Si Thammarat Thai.
Nakhrachi Khanty-Mansiyskiy Avtonomnyy Okrug Rus. Fed. see Kondinskoye
116 B5 Nakhtarana Gujarat India
224 C3 Nakina Ont. Can.
222 C3 Nakina r. B.C. Can.
129 C2 Nakip'u Georgia
174 F1 Nakla Pol.
176 G2 Náklo Czech Rep.
175 H5 Nakło Pol.
179 F4 Naklo Slovenia
174 F2 Nakło nad Notecią Pol.
220 C4 Naknek AK U.S.A.
116 C3 Nakodar Punjab India
175 J1 Nakomiady Pol.
211 B7 Nakonde Zambia
138 D3 Nākotne Latvia
177 J6 Nakovo Vojvodina, Srbija Yugo.
207 E4 Nakpanduri Ghana
142 D4 Nakskov Denmark
140 K3 Näkten l. Sweden
101 D6 Naktong-gang r. S. Korea
210 C5 Nakuru Kenya
222 G5 Nakusp B.C. Can.
123 F5 Nal r. Pak.
107 E2 Nalayh Mongolia
172 A2 Nalbach Ger.
117 G4 Nalbari Assam India
129 C2 Nal'chik Rus. Fed.
183 H2 Nalda Spain
114 C2 Naldurg Mahar. India
175 K4 Nałęczów Pol.
177 J3 Nálepkovo Slovakia
206 E4 Nalerigu Ghana
114 C2 Nalgonda Andhra Prad. India
117 F4 Nalhati W. Bengal India
117 G4 Nalitabari Bangl.
116 D5 Nalkhera Madh. Prad. India
114 C3 Nallamala Hills India
162 A2 Nalliers France
199 G1 Nallıhan Turkey
121 G1 Nalobino Kazakh.
209 D8 Nalolo Zambia
182 D1 Nalón r. Spain
202 A2 Nālūt Libya
176 C2 Nalžovské Hory Czech Rep.
213 G5 Namaacha Moz.
209 B9 Namacunde Angola
213 H3 Namacurra Moz.
215 G2 Namahadi S. Africa
114 C4 Namakkal Tamil Nadu India
122 D4 Namakzar-e Shadad salt flat Iran
121 G4 Namangan Uzbek.
Namangan Oblast admin. div. Uzbek. see Namanganskaya Oblast'
121 G4 Namanganskaya Oblast' admin. div. Uzbek.
Namangan Wiloyati admin. div. Uzbek. see Namanganskaya Oblast'
211 A6 Namanyere Tanz.
213 H2 Namapa Moz.
212 C5 Namaqualand reg. Namibia
214 A3 Namaqualand reg. S. Africa
213 H2 Namarrói Moz.
117 H4 Nambol Manipur India
172 B2 Namborn Ger.
85 H5 Nambour Qld Austr.
Nambouwalu Vanua Levu Fiji see Nabouwalu
183 G5 Nambroca Spain
83 H2 Nambucca Heads N.S.W. Austr.
Namcha Barwa mt. Xizang China see Namjagbarwa Feng
117 F4 Namche Bazar Nepal
101 C5 Namch'ŏn N. Korea
140 K2 Namdalen val. Norway
140 J2 Namdalseid Norway
96 D2 Nam Định Vietnam
226 B3 Namekagon r. WI U.S.A.
Namen Belgium see Namur
104 D2 Namerikawa Japan
176 F2 Náměšť nad Oslavou Czech Rep.
177 I2 Námestovo Slovakia
213 H2 Nametil Moz.
101 C5 Nam-gang r. N. Korea
101 C6 Namhae-do i. S. Korea
213 H2 Namialo Moz.
212 B5 Namib Desert Namibia
209 B8 Namibe Angola
209 B8 Namibe prov. Angola
212 B4 Namibia country Africa
264 J8 Namibia Abyssal Plain sea feature N. Atlantic Ocean
213 H3 Namidobe Moz.
214 B3 Namies S. Africa
122 B2 Namīn Iran
211 B8 Namitete Malawi
111 F6 Namjagbarwa Feng mt. Xizang China
Namka Xizang China see Doilungdêqên
96 B2 Namlang r. Myanmar
111 E6 Namling Xizang China
96 C3 Nam Ngum Reservoir Laos
83 G2 Namoi r. N.S.W. Austr.
91 K5 Namonuito atoll Micronesia
222 G3 Nampa Alta Can.
116 E3 Nampa mt. Nepal
238 C3 Nampa ID U.S.A.
206 D3 Nampala Mali
101 C5 Namp'o N. Korea
213 H2 Nampula Moz.
213 H2 Nampula prov. Moz.
96 C3 Nam Pung Reservoir Thai.
117 H4 Namrup Assam India
117 H4 Namsi Arun. Prad. India
140 J2 Namsos Norway
140 K2 Namsskogan Norway
131 N3 Namtsy Rus. Fed.
96 B2 Namtu Myanmar
222 E5 Namu B.C. Can.
Namuka i. Tonga see Nomuka
213 H2 Namuli, Monte mt. Moz.
213 H2 Namuno Moz.
165 D4 Namur Belgium
165 D4 Namur prov. Belgium
209 E8 Namwala Zambia
101 C6 Namwŏn S. Korea
90 D4 Namyit Island S. China Sea
174 F4 Namysłów Pol.
96 C3 Nan Thai.
96 C4 Nan, Mae Nam r. Thai.
208 B3 Nana r. C.A.R.
177 H4 Nána Slovakia
208 C3 Nana Barya r. C.A.R./Chad
208 C3 Nana-Grébizi pref. C.A.R.
222 F5 Nanaimo B.C. Can.
240 □ Nanakuli HI U.S.A.
208 B3 Nana-Mambéré pref. C.A.R.
109 F3 Nan'an Fujian China
85 H5 Nanango Qld Austr.
109 F4 Nan'ao Guangdong China
Nan'ao Jiangxi China see Dayu
104 C1 Nanao Japan
104 C2 Nanatsuka Japan
250 C5 Nanay r. Peru
Nanbai Guizhou China see Zunyi
Nanbin Chongqing China see Shizhu
108 C2 Nanbu Sichuan China
260 B4 Nancagua Chile
159 I4 Nançay France
100 D3 Nancha Heilong. China
109 E2 Nanchang Jiangxi China
109 E2 Nanchang Jiangxi China
Nanchangshan Shandong China see Changdao
109 F3 Nancheng Jiangxi China
245 G4 Nanchital Mex.
108 C2 Nanchong Sichuan China
108 C2 Nanchuan Chongqing China
183 H2 Nanclares de la Oca Spain
222 E4 Nancut B.C. Can.
157 G4 Nancy France
116 E3 Nanda Devi mt. Uttar Prad. India
116 E3 Nanda Kot mt. Uttar Prad. India
108 C3 Nandan Guangxi China
114 C2 Nanded Mahar. India
Nander Mahar. India see Nanded
83 G2 Nandewar Range mts N.S.W. Austr.
116 C5 Nandgaon Mahar. India
114 D2 Nandigama Andhra Prad. India
114 C3 Nandikotkur Andhra Prad. India
108 A4 Nanding He r. Yunnan China
116 C5 Nandod Gujarat India
165 E4 Nandrin Belgium
108 D4 Nandu Jiang r. China
116 D5 Nandura Mahar. India
116 C5 Nandurbar Mahar. India
114 C3 Nandyal Andhra Prad. India
197 H3 Nănești Romania
109 D4 Nanfeng Guangdong China
109 F3 Nanfeng Jiangxi China
111 F6 Nang Xizang China
211 C7 Nangade Moz.
207 I5 Nanga Eboko Cameroon
95 E3 Nangahpinoh Kalimantan Barat Indon.
84 C2 Nangalala N.T. Austr.
116 C2 Nanga Parbat mt. Jammu and Kashmir
123 G3 Nangarhār prov. Afgh.
95 E3 Nangatayap Kalimantan Barat Indon.
156 D4 Nangis France
101 C4 Nangnim N. Korea
101 C4 Nangnim-sanmaek mts N. Korea
107 G4 Nangong Hebei China
108 A1 Nangqên Qinghai China
211 C7 Nangulangwa Tanz.
114 C4 Nanguneri Tamil Nadu India
107 G4 Nanhe Hebei China
110 F4 Nanhu Gansu China
108 B3 Nanhua Yunnan China
109 G2 Nanhui Shanghai China
221 J2 Nanisivik Nunavut Can.
114 C3 Nanjangud Karnataka India
108 B3 Nanjian Yunnan China
108 C1 Nanjiang Sichuan China
Nanjie Guangdong China see Guangning
109 F3 Nanjing Fujian China
109 F1 Nanjing Jiangsu China
108 A4 Nanka Jiang r. Yunnan China
109 E3 Nankang Jiangxi China
Nankang Jiangxi China see Xingzi
Nanking Jiangsu China see Nanjing
103 F7 Nankoku Japan
209 C9 Nankova Angola
108 A4 Nanlan He r. Yunnan China
78 □4b Nanlaud hill Pohnpei Micronesia
107 G4 Nanle Henan China
108 A4 Nanlei He r. Yunnan China
109 F2 Nanling Anhui China
109 D3 Nan Ling mts China
108 D4 Nanliu Jiang r. China
Nanlong Sichuan China see Nanbu
Nanma Shandong China see Yiyuan
Nanmulingzue Xizang China see Namling
87 C5 Nannine W.A. Austr.
108 D4 Nanning Guangxi China
87 B7 Nannup W.A. Austr.
96 C3 Na Noi Thai.
221 N3 Nanortalik Greenland
Nanouki atoll Gilbert Is Kiribati see Nonouti
Nanouti atoll Gilbert Is Kiribati see Nonouti
108 C3 Nanpan Jiang r. China
116 E4 Nanpara Uttar Prad. India
107 H4 Nanpi Hebei China
107 I3 Nanpiao Liaoning China
109 F3 Nanping Fujian China
108 C1 Nanping Sichuan China
Nanpu Fujian China see Pucheng
109 F3 Nanpu Xi r. China
Nanqiao Shanghai China see Fengxian
183 F1 Nansa r. Spain
104 C4 Nansei Japan
102 □1 Nansei-shotō is Japan
268 B1 Nansen Basin sea feature Arctic Ocean
221 N1 Nansen Land reg. Greenland
221 I1 Nansen Sound sea chan. Nunavut Can.
90 E4 Nanshan Island S. China Sea
106 B3 Nanshankou Xinjiang China
Nansha Qundao is S. China Sea see Spratly Islands
211 B5 Nansio Tanz.
161 D5 Nans-les-Pins France
161 B4 Nant France
105 G2 Nantai-san hill Japan
105 F2 Nantai-san mt. Japan
150 D3 Nant Bran r. Wales U.K.
156 C4 Nanterre France
158 E4 Nantes France
162 A1 Nantes Atlantique airport France
156 C3 Nanteuil-le-Haudouin France
162 D2 Nantiat France
224 D5 Nanticoke Ont. Can.
233 F5 Nanticoke MD U.S.A.
234 B1 Nanticoke PA U.S.A.
233 F5 Nanticoke r. MD U.S.A.
104 C4 Nantō Japan
222 H5 Nanton Alta Can.
109 G1 Nantong Jiangsu China
109 G2 Nantong Jiangsu China
109 □ Nantou Guangdong China
109 G4 Nant'ou Taiwan
160 D2 Nantua France
233 H4 Nantucket MA U.S.A.
233 I4 Nantucket Island MA U.S.A.
233 H4 Nantucket Sound g. MA U.S.A.
211 C8 Nantulo Moz.
149 G4 Nantwich Cheshire, England U.K.
150 D3 Nantyglo Blaenau Gwent, Wales U.K.
232 D4 Nanty Glo PA U.S.A.
235 D1 Nanuet NY U.S.A.
Nanumaga i. Tuvalu see Nanumanga
77 H2 Nanumanga i. Tuvalu
77 H2 Nanumea i. Tuvalu
257 G2 Nanuque Brazil
93 C1 Nanusa, Kepulauan is Indon.
87 B4 Nanutarra Roadhouse W.A. Austr.
108 C2 Nanxi Sichuan China
109 E2 Nanxian Hunan China
109 E3 Nanxiong Guangdong China
109 G3 Nanyandang Shan mt. Zhejiang China
109 E1 Nanyang Henan China
102 J4 Nanyō Japan
210 C5 Nanyuki Kenya
107 J3 Nanzamu Liaoning China
109 D2 Nanzhang Hubei China
Nanzhao Fujian China see Zhao'an
109 E1 Nanzhao Henan China
108 C1 Nanzheng Shaanxi China
Nanzhou Hunan China see Nanxian
117 G4 Naogaon Bangl.
123 G5 Naokot Pak.
100 E3 Naoli r. China
122 E3 Naomid, Dasht-e des. Afgh./Iran
116 C2 Naoshera Jammu and Kashmir
198 C1 Naousa Kentriki Makedonia Greece
198 D3 Naousa Notio Aigaio Greece
240 F2 Napa CA U.S.A.
233 □J1 Napadogan N.B. Can.
213 H2 Napaha Moz.
220 C3 Napaimiut AK U.S.A.
210 B4 Napak mt. Uganda
220 G3 Napaktulik Lake Nunavut Can.
224 E4 Napanee Ont. Can.
235 D1 Napanoch NY U.S.A.
116 C4 Napasar Rajasthan India
220 B3 Napaskiak AK U.S.A.
226 C5 Naperville IL U.S.A.
190 C1 Napf mt. Switz.
80 F3 Napier North I. N.Z.
214 B6 Napier S. Africa
86 E2 Napier Broome Bay W.A. Austr.
263 D2 Napier Mountains Antarctica
84 C2 Napier Peninsula N.T. Austr.
86 E3 Napier Range hills W.A. Austr.
233 G2 Napierville Que. Can.
175 I2 Napiwoda Pol.
177 K4 Napkor Hungary
Naples Italy see Napoli
231 D7 Naples FL U.S.A.
233 □H3 Naples ME U.S.A.
232 E3 Naples NY U.S.A.
241 M1 Naples UT U.S.A.
108 C4 Napo Guangxi China
250 B5 Napo prov. Ecuador
250 C5 Napo r. Ecuador
194 B5 Napola Sicilia Italy
236 D2 Napoleon ND U.S.A.
232 A4 Napoleon OH U.S.A.
216 □2b Napoleon's Tomb tourist site St Helena
237 F6 Napoleonville LA U.S.A.
193 G4 Napoli Italy
193 G4 Napoli prov. Campania Italy
193 G4 Napoli, Golfo di b. Italy
261 F6 Naposta r. Arg.
226 E5 Nappanee IN U.S.A.
84 C4 Napperby N.T. Austr.
122 A2 Naqadeh Iran
128 A5 Naqb Malha mt. Egypt
124 D5 Naqūb Yemen
187 C5 Náquera Spain
104 B4 Nara Japan
104 B4 Nara pref. Japan
206 D3 Nara Mali
139 K4 Nara r. Rus. Fed.
138 F4 Narach Belarus
138 F4 Narach r. Belarus
82 E4 Naracoorte S.A. Austr.
83 F3 Naradhan N.S.W. Austr.
176 F4 Nárai Hungary
105 D2 Narai-gawa r. Japan
117 G5 Narail Bangl.
116 C4 Naraina Rajasthan India
107 G1 Naranbulag Dornod Mongolia
106 B1 Naranbulag Uvs Mongolia
250 B5 Naranjal Ecuador
247 □1 Naranjito Puerto Rico
245 F3 Naranjos Mex.
122 B3 Naraq Iran
115 E2 Narasannapeta Andhra Prad. India
114 D2 Narasapur Andhra Prad. India
114 D2 Narasaraopet Andhra Prad. India
105 G3 Narashino Japan
117 F5 Narasinghapur Orissa India
107 G1 Narasun Rus. Fed.
97 C6 Narathiwat Thai.
110 C3 Narat Shan mts China
237 C5 Nara Visa NM U.S.A.
117 G5 Narayanganj Bangl.
116 E5 Narayanganj Madh. Prad. India
114 B2 Narayangaon Mahar. India
114 C2 Narayanpet Andhra Prad. India
175 M6 Narayiv Ukr.
175 M6 Narayivka r. Ukr.
Narbada r. India see Narmada
150 C3 Narberth Pembrokeshire, Wales U.K.
Narbo France see Narbonne
192 A4 Narbolia Sardegna Italy
161 B5 Narbonne France
161 B5 Narbonne-Plage France
151 F2 Narborough Leicestershire, England U.K.
151 H2 Narborough Norfolk, England U.K.
Narborough Island Islas Galápagos Ecuador see Fernandina, Isla
192 A5 Narcao Sardegna Italy
182 D1 Narcea r. Spain
160 B1 Narcy France
122 C2 Nardin Iran
195 H2 Nardò Italy
123 G4 Narechi r. Pak.
114 B3 Naregal Karnataka India
87 C7 Narembeen W.A. Austr.
116 D3 Narendranagar Uttar Prad. India
264 E4 Nares Abyssal Plain sea feature S. Atlantic Ocean
264 E4 Nares Deep sea feature N. Atlantic Ocean
221 K2 Nares Strait Can./Greenland
87 E6 Naretha W.A. Austr.
175 L3 Narew Pol.
175 I3 Narew r. Pol.
175 L3 Narewka Pol.
175 L3 Narewka r. Pol.
123 F4 Nari r. Pak.
214 A4 Nariep S. Africa
129 F4 Närimanabad Azer.
129 F3 Närimankänd Azer.
120 A3 Narimanov Rus. Fed.
121 K2 Narimskiy Khrebet mts Kazakh.
126 E3 Narince Turkey
250 B4 Nariño dept Col.
105 G3 Narita Japan
105 G3 Narita airport Japan
140 M2 Narken Sweden
139 M4 Narma r. Rus. Fed.
116 C5 Narmada r. India
129 B3 Narman Turkey
116 D3 Narnaul Haryana India
193 E2 Narni Italy
Narnia Italy see Narni
194 C5 Naro Sicilia Italy
194 C5 Naro r. Sicilia Italy
134 M2 Narodnaya, Gora mt. Rus. Fed.
136 E2 Narodychi Ukr.
139 K4 Naro-Fominsk Rus. Fed.
211 B5 Narok Kenya
83 G4 Narooma N.S.W. Austr.
135 H5 Narovchat Rus. Fed.
136 E2 Narowlya Belarus
141 M3 Närpes Fin.
83 G2 Narrabri N.S.W. Austr.
233 H4 Narragansett Bay RI U.S.A.
83 F2 Narran r. N.S.W. Austr.
83 F3 Narrandera N.S.W. Austr.
83 F2 Narran Lake N.S.W. Austr.
87 C7 Narrogin W.A. Austr.
83 G3 Narromine N.S.W. Austr.
163 A5 Narrosse France
232 C6 Narrows VA U.S.A.
234 C1 Narrowsburg NY U.S.A.
114 C2 Narsapur Andhra Prad. India
221 N3 Narsaq Greenland
171 D4 Narsdorf Ger.
116 D5 Narsimhapur Madh. Prad. India
117 G5 Narsingdi Bangl.
116 D5 Narsinghgarh Madh. Prad. India
115 D2 Narsipatnam Andhra Prad. India
107 G3 Nart Nei Mongol China
106 E1 Nart Mongolia
179 H5 Narta Croatia
198 A1 Nartë Albania
129 C2 Nartkala Rus. Fed.
161 E5 Nartuby r. France
175 I3 Naruszewo Pol.
104 A4 Naruto Japan
138 G2 Narva Estonia
138 G2 Narva r. Estonia/Rus. Fed.
138 F2 Narva Bay Estonia/Rus. Fed.
92 B2 Narvacan Phil.
138 G2 Narva-Jõesuu Estonia
Narva laht b. Estonia/Rus. Fed. see Narva Bay
Narva Reservoir Estonia/Rus. Fed. see Narvskoye Vodokhranilishche
140 L1 Narvik Norway
Narvskiy Zaliv b. Estonia/Rus. Fed. see Narva Bay
138 G2 Narvskoye Vodokhranilishche resr Estonia/Rus. Fed.
116 D3 Narwana Haryana India
116 D4 Narwar Madh. Prad. India
84 C4 Narwietooma N.T. Austr.
134 K2 Nar'yan-Mar Rus. Fed.
121 H4 Naryn Kyrg.
121 H4 Naryn admin. div. Kyrg.
121 H4 Naryn r. Kyrg./Uzbek.
106 B1 Naryn Rus. Fed.
121 J4 Narynkol Kazakh.
Naryn Oblast admin. div. Kyrg. see Naryn
Narynqol Kazakh. see Narynkol
Narynskaya Oblast' admin. div. Kyrg. see Naryn
139 J5 Naryshkino Rus. Fed.
190 C4 Narzole Italy
140 L3 Näsåker Sweden
197 G2 Năsăud Romania
176 E2 Nasavrky Czech Rep.
161 B4 Nasbinals France
143 G3 Näsby Kalmar Sweden
81 C6 Naseby South I. N.Z.
116 C5 Nashik Mahar. India
226 A4 Nashua IA U.S.A.
233 H3 Nashua NH U.S.A.
237 E5 Nashville AR U.S.A.
231 D6 Nashville GA U.S.A.
236 F4 Nashville IL U.S.A.
231 E5 Nashville NC U.S.A.
232 B4 Nashville OH U.S.A.
234 B3 Nashville PA U.S.A.
231 C4 Nashville TN U.S.A.
226 A2 Nashwauk MN U.S.A.
188 G3 Našice Croatia
175 I3 Nasielsk Pol.
141 M3 Näsijärvi l. Fin.
Nasik Mahar. India see Nashik
Nasirabad Bangl. see Mymensingh
116 C4 Nasirabad Rajasthan India
123 G4 Nasirabad Pak.
225 I2 Naskaupi r. Nfld. Can.
117 F4 Nasmganj Bihar India
194 D4 Naso Sicilia Italy
194 D4 Naso r. Sicilia Italy
209 E7 Nasondoye Dem. Rep. Congo
226 B3 Nasonville WI U.S.A.
79 □1 Nasorolevu mt. Vanua Levu Fiji
Nasosnyy Azer. see Hacı Zeynalabdin
203 F2 Nasr Egypt
122 B3 Naşrābād Iran
122 D3 Naşrābād Iran
128 C3 Naşrānī, Jabal an mts Syria
Nasratabad Iran see Zābol
222 D4 Nass r. B.C. Can.
207 G4 Nassarawa Nigeria
207 H4 Nassarawa state Nigeria
85 E2 Nassau r. Qld Austr.
246 C1 Nassau Bahamas
81 □2 Nassau i. Cook Is
169 C5 Nassau Rheinland-Pfalz Ger.
171 E5 Nassau Sachsen Ger.
233 G3 Nassau NY U.S.A.
235 E2 Nassau County county NY U.S.A.
233 F6 Nassawadox VA U.S.A.
170 E3 Nassenheide Ger.
203 G4 Nasser, Lake resr Egypt
178 B3 Nassereith Austria
206 E4 Nassian Côte d'Ivoire
143 F3 Nässjö Sweden
165 E4 Nassogne Belgium
224 E1 Nastapoca r. Que. Can.
169 C5 Nastätten Ger.
138 E1 Nastola Fin.
105 F1 Nasu-dake vol. Japan
92 B3 Nasugbu Phil.
175 K4 Nasutów Pol.
139 H3 Nasva Rus. Fed.
139 H3 Nasva r. Rus. Fed.
141 L3 Nasviken Sweden
177 H4 Naszály Hungary
212 E4 Nata Botswana
254 G3 Natal Brazil
94 B2 Natal Sumatera Indon.
Natal prov. S. Africa see Kwazulu-Natal
265 G7 Natal Basin sea feature Indian Ocean
234 B2 Natalie PA U.S.A.
122 B3 Naţanz Iran
225 I3 Natashquan Que. Can.
225 I3 Natashquan r. Newfoundland/Québec Can.
81 □1 Na Taulaga i. Tokelau
237 F6 Natchez MS U.S.A.
237 E6 Natchitoches LA U.S.A.
149 G3 Nateby Cumbria, England U.K.
190 C2 Naters Switz.
83 F4 Nathalia Vic. Austr.
116 C3 Nathana Punjab India
84 C2 Nathan River N.T. Austr.
116 C4 Nathdwara Rajasthan India
140 □ Nathorst Land reg. Svalbard
207 F4 Natiaboani Burkina
240 I5 National City CA U.S.A.
80 E3 National Park North I. N.Z.
191 I3 Natisone r. Italy
207 F4 Natitingou Benin
257 G4 Natividade Rio de Janeiro Brazil
254 D4 Natividade Tocantins Brazil
222 D2 Natla r. N.W.T. Can.
96 A2 Natogyi Myanmar
117 G4 Nator Bangl.
102 J4 Natori Japan
211 C5 Natron, Lake salt l. Tanz.
105 G1 Natsui-gawa r. Japan
96 A3 Nattalin Myanmar
114 C4 Nattam Tamil Nadu India
96 B3 Nattaung mt. Myanmar
140 M2 Nattavaara Sweden
140 M2 Nattavaara by Sweden
179 E2 Natternback Austria
173 E3 Nattheim Ger.
137 I5 Natukhayevskaya Rus. Fed.
95 D1 Natuna, Kepulauan is Indon.
95 E1 Natuna Besar i. Indon.
232 D6 Natural Bridge VA U.S.A.
87 B7 Naturaliste, Cape W.A. Austr.
87 A5 Naturaliste Channel W.A. Austr.
265 L7 Naturaliste Plateau sea feature Indian Ocean
214 D5 Nature's Valley S. Africa
241 M2 Naturita CO U.S.A.
191 F2 Naturno Italy
Nau Tajik. see Nov
226 E2 Naubinway MI U.S.A.
163 E4 Naucelle France
162 E4 Naucelles France
178 B4 Nauders Austria
170 D3 Nauen Ger.
171 C4 Nauendorf Ger.
235 E1 Naugatuck CT U.S.A.
235 E1 Naugatuck r. CT U.S.A.
172 C2 Nauheim Ger.
162 A3 Naujac-sur-Mer France
92 B3 Naujan Phil.
138 D3 Naujoji Akmenė Lith.
116 C4 Naukh Rajasthan India
147 E3 Naul Rep. of Ireland
169 E4 Naumburg (Hessen) Ger.
171 C4 Naumburg (Saale) Ger.
171 E4 Naundorf Sachsen Ger.
171 E5 Naundorf Sachsen Ger.
169 C5 Nauroth Ger.
129 D2 Naurskaya Rus. Fed.
77 G2 Nauru i. Nauru
77 G2 Nauru country S. Pacific Ocean
123 G5 Naushahro Firoz Pak.
123 G5 Naushara Pak.
106 E1 Naushki Rus. Fed.
141 I3 Naustdal Norway
250 C6 Nauta Peru
Nautaca Uzbek. see Karshi
214 A2 Naute Dam Namibia
245 F3 Nautla Mex.
117 E4 Nautonwa Uttar Prad. India
226 B5 Nauvoo IL U.S.A.
208 E4 Nava r. Dem. Rep. Congo
183 E1 Nava Spain
Navabad Tajik. see Novobod
183 E4 Navacepeda de Tormes Spain
183 F4 Navacerreda Spain
185 G4 Navachica mt. Spain
182 E4 Navaconcejo Spain
183 F4 Nava de Arévalo Spain
183 F3 Nava de la Asunción Spain
183 E3 Nava del Rey Spain
183 E4 Nava de Sotrobal Spain
117 G5 Navadwip W. Bengal India
183 G3 Navafría Spain
183 F5 Navahermosa Spain
129 F3 Navahı Azer.
138 E5 Navahrudak Belarus
138 E5 Navahrudskaye Wzvyshsha hills Belarus
187 C5 Navajas Spain
239 F4 Navajo r. CO U.S.A.
241 L3 Navajo Mountain UT U.S.A.
183 E2 Navajos hill Spain
92 C4 Naval Phil.
186 D2 Naval Spain
183 F4 Navalagamella Spain
183 H3 Navalcaballo Spain
183 E4 Navalcán Spain
183 F4 Navalcarnero Spain
183 H3 Navalero Spain
183 F3 Navalmanzano Spain
183 F4 Navalmoral Spain
182 E5 Navalmoral de la Mata Spain
183 E4 Navalonguilla Spain
183 F4 Navalosa Spain
183 F4 Navalperal de Pinares Spain
185 F1 Navalpino Spain
183 F4 Navaluenga Spain
183 E5 Navalvillar de Ibor Spain
185 E1 Navalvillar de Pela Spain
183 F4 Navamorcuende Spain
147 E3 Navan Rep. of Ireland
Navangar Gujarat India see Jamnagar
138 G4 Navapolatsk Belarus
186 E3 Navarcles Spain
186 B2 Navardún Spain
131 S3 Navarin, Mys c. Rus. Fed.
259 D9 Navarino, Isla i. Chile
183 I2 Navarra aut. comm. Spain
83 E4 Navarre Vic. Austr.
Navarre aut. comm. Spain see Navarra
182 D4 Navarredonda de la Rinconada Spain
163 B5 Navarrenx France
187 C5 Navarrés Spain
183 H2 Navarrete Spain
261 H4 Navarro Arg.
240 F2 Navarro r. CA U.S.A.
186 E3 Navàs Spain
163 B6 Navasa Spain
185 F1 Navas de Estrena Spain
182 D5 Navas del Madroño Spain
183 F4 Navas del Rey Spain
183 F3 Navas de Oro Spain
185 G2 Navas de San Juan Spain
186 B2 Navaseués Spain
182 D4 Navasfrías Spain
134 H5 Navashino Rus. Fed.
237 D6 Navasota TX U.S.A.
237 D6 Navasota r. TX U.S.A.
246 D3 Navassa Island terr. West Indies
186 F2 Navata Spain
183 F4 Navatalgordo Spain
138 E5 Navayel'nya Belarus
190 F3 Nave Italy
184 B3 Nave Port.
182 C2 Navea r. Spain
182 D4 Nave de Haver Port.
148 C2 Nave Island Scotland U.K.
193 F2 Navelli Italy
160 E1 Navenne France
146 D3 Naver r. Scotland U.K.
146 D3 Naver, Loch l. Scotland U.K.
184 B3 Nave Redonda Port.
142 D2 Naverstad Sweden
162 D3 Naves France
186 E3 Navès Spain
139 K5 Navesnoye Rus. Fed.
138 E2 Navesti r. Estonia
185 E1 Navezuelas Spain
182 D1 Navia Spain
182 D1 Navia r. Spain
260 B3 Navidad Chile
237 D6 Navidad r. TX U.S.A.
247 E2 Navidad Bank sea feature Caribbean Sea
160 D2 Navilly France
255 B7 Naviraí Brazil
79 □1 Naviti i. Fiji
136 C2 Naviz Ukr.
139 J5 Navlya Rus. Fed.
139 J5 Navlya r. Rus. Fed.
197 I3 Năvodari Romania
120 F4 Navoi Uzbek.
120 E4 Navoiyskaya Oblast' admin. div. Uzbek.
242 C3 Navojoa Mex.
242 D3 Navolato Mex.
79 □1 Navotuvotu hill Vanua Levu Fiji
Navoy Oblast admin. div. Uzbek. see Navoiyskaya Oblast'
Návpaktos Greece see Nafpaktos
Návplion Greece see Nafplio
143 F3 Nävragöl Sweden
142 B2 Navrestad hill Norway
206 E4 Navrongo Ghana
Navşar Turkey see Şemdinli
116 C5 Navsari Gujarat India
116 C4 Nawa Rajasthan India
128 C3 Nawá Syria
117 G4 Nawabganj Bangl.
98 D6 Nawabganj Uttar Prad. India
111 C7 Nawabganj Uttar Prad. India
123 G5 Nawabshah Pak.
117 F4 Nawada Bihar India
116 C4 Nawalgarh Rajasthan India
111 B6 Nawashahr Punjab India
124 C3 Nawāşīf, Ḩarrāt lava field Saudi Arabia
96 B2 Nawnghkio Myanmar
96 B2 Nawngleng Myanmar
Nawoiy Uzbek. see Navoi
Nawoiy Wiloyati admin. div. Uzbek. see Navoiyskaya Oblast'
175 I6 Nawojowa Pol.
129 D4 Naxçıvan Azer.
129 D4 Naxçıvan aut. reg. Azer.
129 D4 Naxçıvançay r. Azer.
108 C2 Naxi Sichuan China
199 D3 Naxos Notio Aigaio Greece
199 D3 Naxos i. Greece
250 B4 Naya Col.
117 F5 Nayagarh Orissa India
244 B2 Nayarit state Mex.
122 D3 Nāy Band, Kūh-e mt. Iran
163 B5 Nay-Bourdettes France
108 C3 Nayong Guizhou China
102 K1 Nayoro Japan
114 C3 Nayudupeta Andhra Prad. India
254 E3 Nazare Brazil
182 A5 Nazaré Port.
242 E3 Nazareno Mex.
114 C4 Nazareth Tamil Nadu India
128 B3 Nazareth Israel
234 C2 Nazareth PA U.S.A.
256 C2 Nazário Brazil
242 D3 Nazas Mex.
242 D3 Nazas r. Mex.
252 B3 Nazca Peru
267 N7 Nazca Ridge sea feature S. Pacific Ocean
102 □1 Naze Japan
151 H3 Nazeing Essex, England U.K.
159 G4 Nazelles-Négron France
122 A2 Nāzīk Iran
199 F3 Nazilli Turkey
127 E3 Nazımiye Turkey
Nazinon r. Burkina/Ghana see Red Volta
117 H4 Nazira Assam India
117 G5 Nazir Hat Bangl.
129 E3 Näzirli Azer.
139 H2 Naziya Rus. Fed.
222 F4 Nazko B.C. Can.
222 F4 Nazko r. B.C. Can.
122 A2 Nāzlū r. Iran
129 D2 Nazran' Rus. Fed.
210 C2 Nazrēt Eth.
125 G3 Nazwá Oman
130 I4 Nazyvayevsk Rus. Fed.
206 B2 Nbâk Maur.
215 E5 Ncanaha S. Africa
209 F7 Nchelenge Zambia
Ncheu Malawi see Ntcheu
212 D4 Ncojane Botswana
215 F4 Ncora S. Africa
207 H6 Ncue Equat. Guinea
211 B6 Ndala Tanz.
209 B7 N'dalatando Angola
207 F4 Ndali Benin
208 D2 Ndélé C.A.R.
207 I5 Ndélélé Cameroon
208 A5 Ndendé Gabon
Ndende i. Santa Cruz Is Solomon Is see Ndeni
78 □6 Ndeni i. Santa Cruz Is Solomon Is
207 H5 Ndikiniméki Cameroon
206 B3 Ndioum Guènt Senegal
202 B6 Ndjamena Chad
N'Djamena Chad see Ndjamena
208 D3 Ndji r. C.A.R.
207 H5 Ndjim r. Cameroon
208 A5 Ndjolé Gabon
Ndjouani i. Comoros see Nzwani
206 B3 Ndofane Senegal
Ndoi i. Fiji see Doi
209 F8 Ndola Zambia
206 D4 Ndorola Burkina
210 C4 Ndoto mt. Kenya
208 A5 Ndougou Gabon
78 □6 Ndovele New Georgia Is Solomon Is
Nduke i. New Georgia Is Solomon Is see Kolombangara
211 C7 Ndumbwe Tanz.
215 I2 Ndumu S. Africa
215 H3 Ndwedwe S. Africa
162 B3 Né r. France
163 C6 Né, Mont mt. France
198 D4 Nea Alikarnassos Kriti Greece
198 C2 Nea Anchialos Greece
198 C1 Nea Apollonia Greece
198 C2 Nea Artaki Greece
85 F5 Neabul Creek r. Qld Austr.
198 C3 Nea Epidavros Greece
147 E2 Neagh, Lough l. Northern Ireland U.K.
238 A1 Neah Bay WA U.S.A.
197 G3 Neajlov r. Romania
198 C1 Nea Kallikrateia Greece
198 D1 Nea Karvali Greece
147 B3 Neale Rep. of Ireland
84 B5 Neale, Lake salt flat N.T. Austr.
198 C2 Nea Liosia Greece
198 C2 Nea Makri Greece
198 C1 Nea Moudania Greece
197 H2 Neamţ r. Romania
198 D1 Nea Peramos Greece
198 B1 Neapoli Dytiki Makedonia Greece
199 D4 Neapoli Kriti Greece
198 C3 Neapoli Peloponnisos Greece
Neapolis Italy see Napoli
149 G3 Near Sawrey Cumbria, England U.K.
198 C1 Nea Santa Greece
150 D3 Neath Neath Port Talbot, Wales U.K.
150 D3 Neath r. Wales U.K.
150 D3 Neath Port Talbot admin. div. Wales U.K.
198 C1 Nea Zichni Greece
210 A4 Nebbi Uganda
168 D1 Nebel Ger.
173 E4 Nebelhorn mt. Ger.
110 C3 Nebesnaya, Gora mt. Xinjiang China
163 E6 Nébias France
83 F2 Nebine Creek r. Qld Austr.
122 C2 Nebitdag Turkm.
85 G4 Nebo Qld Austr.
241 L2 Nebo, Mount UT U.S.A.
139 I2 Nebolchi Rus. Fed.
171 C4 Nebra (Unstrut) Ger.
236 C3 Nebraska state U.S.A.
236 E3 Nebraska City NE U.S.A.
183 G3 Nebreda Spain
194 D5 Nebrodi, Monti mts Sicilia Italy
139 L3 Nebyloye Rus. Fed.
245 F3 Necaxa r. Mex.
226 B3 Necedah WI U.S.A.
176 E1 Nechanice Czech Rep.
137 F4 Nechayane Ukr.
237 E6 Neches r. TX U.S.A.
250 C2 Nechí r. Col.
185 G4 Nechite r. Spain
172 C2 Neckar r. Ger.
172 C2 Neckarbischofsheim Ger.
172 C2 Neckargemünd Ger.
172 C2 Neckarsteinach Ger.
172 D2 Neckarsulm Ger.
75 H2 Necker Island HI U.S.A.
261 H6 Necochea Arg.
250 B2 Necoclí Col.
151 H2 Necton Norfolk, England U.K.
182 B1 Neda Spain
136 F2 Nedanchychi Ukr.
198 B3 Nedas r. Greece
177 H2 Nedašov Czech Rep.
170 E2 Neddemin Ger.
197 G5 Nedelino Bulg.
188 F2 Nedelišće Croatia
Nederland country Europe see Netherlands
Nederlandse Antillen terr. West Indies see Netherlands Antilles
164 E2 Nederlangbroek Neth.
164 E3 Neder Rijn r. Neth.
170 C1 Neder Vindinge Denmark
165 E3 Nederweert Neth.
Nédha r. Greece see Nedas
171 D3 Nedlitz Ger.
136 D3 Nedoboyivtsi Ukr.
111 E6 Nêdong Xizang China
140 M1 Nedre Soppero Sweden
137 G2 Nedryhayliv Ukr.
142 A2 Nedstrandsfjorden sea chan. Norway
208 F4 Neduka r. Dem. Rep. Congo
176 F2 Nedvědice Czech Rep.
174 G5 Nędza Pol.
105 E2 Neeba-san mt. Japan
164 F2 Neede Neth.
233 H3 Needham MA U.S.A.
151 I2 Needham Market Suffolk, England U.K.
151 G2 Needingworth Cambridgeshire, England U.K.
241 J4 Needles CA U.S.A.
232 D5 Needmore PA U.S.A.
Neemuch Madh. Prad. India see Nimach
226 C3 Neenah WI U.S.A.
223 L5 Neepawa Man. Can.
165 F3 Neer Neth.
164 E3 Neerijnen Neth.
168 C2 Neermoor Ger.
165 E3 Neeroeteren Belgium
165 E3 Neerpelt Belgium
168 F2 Neetze Ger.
234 C2 Neffs PA U.S.A.
234 B2 Neffsville PA U.S.A.
205 G2 Nefta Tunisia
129 F4 Neftçala Azer.
129 G3 Neft Daşları Azer.
Neftechala Azer. see 26 Bakı Komissarı
Neftechala Azer. see Neftçala
129 A1 Neftegorsk Krasnodarskiy Kray Rus. Fed.
100 G1 Neftegorsk Sakhalin Rus. Fed.

Neftegorsk to Niagara-on-the-Lake
340

120 B1 Neftegorsk Samarskaya Oblast' Rus. Fed.
134 K4 Neftekamsk Rus. Fed.
129 D1 Neftekumsk Rus. Fed.
190 D1 Neftenbach Switz.
130 I3 Nefteyugansk Rus. Fed.
Neftezavodsk Turkm. see Seydi
Neftyanyye Kamni Azer. see Neft Daşları
150 C2 Nefyn Gwynedd, Wales U.K.
209 B6 Negage Angola
206 C3 Négala Mali
95 F5 Negara Bali Indon.
95 F3 Negara Kalimantan Selatan Indon.
95 F3 Negara r. Indon.
226 D2 Negaunee MI U.S.A.
210 C3 Negëlê Oromīya Eth.
210 C3 Negëlê Oromīya Eth.
94 C2 Negeri Sembilan state Malaysia
128 B4 Negev des. Israel
211 C7 Negomane Moz.
114 C5 Negombo Sri Lanka
197 F3 Negotin Srbija Yugo.
196 E5 Negotino Macedonia
197 F5 Negotino Macedonia
252 A2 Negra, Cordillera mts Peru
258 G4 Negra, Lago l. Uru.
250 A6 Negra, Punta pt Peru
257 F3 Negra, Serra mts Brazil
253 E3 Negra, Serrania de mts Bol.
191 F3 Negrar Italy
163 D6 Negre, Pic de mt. Andorra
183 H3 Negredo Spain
182 B2 Negreira Spain
163 D4 Nègrepelisse France
197 H2 Negreşti Romania
197 F2 Negreşti-Oaş Romania
260 A5 Negrete Chile
84 B3 Negri r. N.T. Austr.
197 H2 Negri Romania
246 □ Negril Jamaica
Negri Sembilan state Malaysia see Negeri Sembilan
250 A6 Negritos Peru
260 D6 Negro r. Arg.
253 F4 Negro r. Brazil
253 F6 Negro r. Para.
251 G5 Negro r. S. America
182 D2 Negro r. Spain
261 H3 Negro r. Uru.
261 I3 Negro r. Paysandú/Río Negro Uru.
180 D5 Negro, Cabo c. Morocco
Negroponte i. Greece see Evvoia
92 B4 Negros i. Phil.
197 I4 Negru Vodă Romania
238 B2 Nehalem r. OR U.S.A.
122 B3 Nehavand Iran
122 E4 Nehbandān Iran
107 J1 Nehe Heilong. China
197 H3 Nehoiu Romania
209 C9 Nehone Angola
79 □2 Neiafu Vava'u Gp Tonga
246 E3 Neiba Dom. Rep.
157 H4 Neiderbronn-les-Bains France
157 G3 Neid Française r. France
108 C2 Neijiang Sichuan China
223 I4 Neilburg Sask. Can.
214 C3 Neilersdrif S. Africa
226 B3 Neillsville WI U.S.A.
107 D3 Nei Mongol Zizhiqu aut. reg. China
171 C4 Neinstedt Ger.
107 G4 Neiqiu Hebei China
171 G3 Neiße r. Ger./Pol.
250 C4 Neiva Col.
182 B3 Neiva r. Port.
190 D4 Neive Italy
109 D1 Neixiang Henan China
244 C4 Neixpa r. Mex.
Nejd reg. Saudi Arabia see Najd
176 B1 Nejdek Czech Rep.
122 C2 Neka Iran
122 C2 Neka r. Iran
210 C2 Nek'emtē Eth.
135 H6 Nekhayevskaya Rus. Fed.
Nekhayevskiy Rus. Fed. see Nekhayevskaya
137 G2 Nekhayivka Ukr.
174 F3 Nekla Pol.
139 M4 Neklyudovo Rus. Fed.
136 E3 Nekrasove Ukr.
139 K3 Nekrasovskiy Rus. Fed.
139 M3 Nekrasovskoye Rus. Fed.
143 F4 Neksø Bornholm Denmark
182 G2 Nela r. Spain
114 C3 Nelamangala Karnataka India
182 C4 Nelas Port.
139 K2 Nelazskoye Rus. Fed.
85 E4 Nelia Qld Austr.
139 I3 Nelidovo Rus. Fed.
236 G3 Neligh NE U.S.A.
131 O4 Nel'kan Rus. Fed.
131 P3 Nel'kan Rus. Fed.
78 □3a Nell i. Kwajalein Marshall Is
227 G1 Nellie Lake Ont. Can.
172 D3 Nellingen Ger.
114 C3 Nellore Andhra Prad. India
261 G2 Nelson Arg.
222 G5 Nelson B.C. Can.
223 M3 Nelson r. Man. Can.
81 D4 Nelson South I. N.Z.
81 D4 Nelson admin. reg. South I. N.Z.
149 G4 Nelson Lancashire, England U.K.
241 K4 Nelson AZ U.S.A.
236 D3 Nelson NE U.S.A.
241 J4 Nelson NV U.S.A.
226 A3 Nelson WI U.S.A.
82 E4 Nelson, Cape Vic. Austr.
83 H3 Nelson Bay N.S.W. Austr.
81 C5 Nelson Creek South I. N.Z.
222 F3 Nelson Forks B.C. Can.
223 L4 Nelson House Man. Can.
233 F6 Nelsonia VA U.S.A.
235 E1 Nelsonville NY U.S.A.
214 D5 Nelspoort S. Africa
215 H1 Nelspruit S. Africa
134 K3 Nem r. Rus. Fed.
206 D2 Néma Maur.
134 J4 Nema Rus. Fed.
226 A2 Nemadji r. MN U.S.A.
Neman r. Belarus/Lith. see Nyoman
138 D4 Neman Rus. Fed.
138 D4 Neman r. Rus. Fed.
Nemausus France see Nîmes
207 G5 Nembe Nigeria
190 E3 Nembro Italy
177 I3 Nemce Slovakia
134 H4 Nemda r. Rus. Fed.
198 C3 Nemea Greece
227 F2 Nemegos Ont. Can.
138 E4 Nemenčine Lith.
205 G2 Nementcha, Monts des mts Alg.
198 B1 Nëmerçkë, Mal ridge Albania
176 G4 Nemesszalók Hungary
176 G5 Nemesvid Hungary
177 H5 Nemetkér Hungary
Nemetocenna France see Arras
Nemirov Vinnyts'ka Oblast' Ukr. see Nemyriv
224 E3 Némiscau r. Que. Can.
136 F2 Nemishayeve Ukr.
107 J1 Nemor r. China
Nemours Alg. see Ghazaouet
156 C4 Nemours France
127 F3 Nemrut Dağı mt. Turkey
171 C4 Nemsdorf-Göhrendorf Ger.
177 H3 Nemšová Slovakia
100 E2 Nemta r. Rus. Fed.
136 C4 Nemunas r. Lith.
138 E3 Nemunėlis r. Lith.
102 L2 Nemuro Japan
102 L2 Nemuro-kaikyō sea chan. Japan/Rus. Fed.
136 B2 Nemyriv L'vivs'ka Oblast' Ukr.
136 E3 Nemyriv Vinnyts'ka Oblast' Ukr.
147 C4 Nenagh Rep. of Ireland
220 D3 Nenana AK U.S.A.
190 C2 Nendaz Switz.
151 H2 Nene r. England U.K.
Nenets Autonomous Okrug admin. div. Rus. Fed. see Nenetskiy Avtonomnyy Okrug
134 K2 Nenetskiy Avtonomnyy Okrug admin. div. Rus. Fed.
177 I3 Nenince Slovakia
107 J1 Nenjiang Heilong. China
107 J2 Nen Jiang r. China
168 C2 Nenndorf Ger.
170 D3 Nennhausen Ger.
173 F2 Nennslingen Ger.
169 E4 Nentershausen Hessen Ger.
169 C5 Nentershausen Rheinland-Pfalz Ger.
149 G3 Nenthead Cumbria, England U.K.
178 A3 Nenzing Austria
198 C1 Neo Agioneri Kentriki Makedonia Greece
78 □4a Neoch atoll Chuuk Micronesia
198 B2 Neochori Greece
198 D1 Neo Erasmio Anatoliki Makedonia kai Thraki Greece
104 C3 Neo-gawa r. Japan
199 E3 Neo Karlovasi Voreio Aigaio Greece
Neokhórion Greece see Neochori
241 L1 Neola UT U.S.A.
198 C2 Neo Monastiri Greece
192 A4 Neoneli Sardegna Italy
Néon Karlovásion Voreio Aigaio Greece see Neo Karlovasi
226 C3 Neopit WI U.S.A.
237 E4 Neosho MO U.S.A.
237 E4 Neosho r. KS U.S.A.
198 C1 Neos Marmaras Greece
161 E5 Néoules France
186 D2 Néouvielle, Pic de mt. France
116 E3 Nepal country Asia
116 E3 Nepalganj Nepal
116 D5 Nepanagar Madh. Prad. India
224 F4 Nepean Ont. Can.
241 L2 Nephi UT U.S.A.
147 B2 Nephin hill Rep. of Ireland
147 B2 Nephin Beg Range hills Rep. of Ireland
193 E2 Nepi Italy
221 L5 Nepisiguit r. N.B. Can.
176 C2 Nepomuk Czech Rep.
139 L5 Nepryadva r. Rus. Fed.
235 D2 Neptune NJ U.S.A.
82 D3 Neptune Islands S.A. Austr.
175 G3 Ner r. Pol.
193 E2 Nera r. Italy
163 C4 Nérac France
114 B2 Neral Mahar. India
85 H5 Nerang Qld Austr.
176 D1 Neratovice Czech Rep.
177 J6 Nerău Romania
138 E4 Neravai Lith.
171 D4 Nerchau Ger.
99 K1 Nerchinsk Rus. Fed.
100 A2 Nerchinskiy Zavod Rus. Fed.
162 B3 Nercillac France
192 B4 Nercone, Monte su mt. Sardegna Italy
162 B3 Néré France
197 H3 Nereju Romania
139 M3 Nerekhta Rus. Fed.
173 E3 Neresheim Ger.
138 E3 Nereta Latvia
193 F2 Nereto Italy
188 F4 Neretva r. Bos.-Herz./Croatia
175 I4 Neretva r. Ukr.
188 F4 Neretvanski Kanal sea chan. Croatia
191 J4 Nerezine Croatia
116 D5 Neri Mahar. India
209 D8 Neriquinha Angola
138 D4 Neris r. Lith.
160 A2 Néris-les-Bains France
185 G4 Nerja Spain
139 M3 Nerl' Rus. Fed.
139 K3 Nerl' r. Rus. Fed.
139 L3 Nerl' r. Rus. Fed.
139 L3 Nero, Ozero l. Rus. Fed.
160 C3 Néronde France
160 A2 Nérondes France
256 C2 Nerópolis Brazil
169 B5 Neroth Ger.
134 L2 Neroyka, Gora mt. Rus. Fed.
116 D5 Ner Pinglai Mahar. India
185 H2 Nerpio Spain
162 C3 Nersac France
173 E3 Nersingen Ger.
136 F4 Nerubays'ke Ukr.
139 K5 Neruch' r. Rus. Fed.
175 H3 Nerussa r. Rus. Fed.
184 D3 Nerva Spain
191 H3 Nervesa della Battaglia Italy
161 C5 Nervieux France
183 H1 Nervión r. Spain
190 C3 Nery, Monte mt. Italy
131 N4 Neryungri Rus. Fed.
164 E1 Nes Neth.
134 H2 Nes' Rus. Fed.
134 I2 Nes' r. Rus. Fed.
142 C1 Nesbyen Norway
171 F4 Neschwitz Ger.
234 D3 Nesco NJ U.S.A.
234 B1 Nescopeck PA U.S.A.
234 B1 Nescopeck Creek r. PA U.S.A.
197 H4 Nesebŭr Bulg.
234 D2 Neshaminy Creek r. PA U.S.A.
140 □D2 Neskaupstaður Iceland
156 C3 Nesle France
177 H2 Nesluša Slovakia
140 K2 Nesna Norway
176 G2 Nesovice Czech Rep.
161 C4 Nesque r. France
234 C2 Nesquehoning PA U.S.A.
114 B2 Nesri Mahar. India
146 D4 Ness r. Scotland U.K.
146 D4 Ness, Loch l. Scotland U.K.
192 A2 Nessa Corse France
236 D4 Ness City KS U.S.A.
168 C2 Nesse Ger.
169 F5 Nesse r. Ger.
222 C3 Nesselrode, Mount Alaska/B.C. Can./U.S.A.
173 E4 Nesselwang Ger.
190 E1 Nesslau Switz.
163 C5 Neste r. France
138 D4 Nesterov Rus. Fed.
Nesterov Ukr. see Zhovkva
149 F4 Neston Cheshire, England U.K.
193 E2 Nestore r. Italy
191 H5 Nestore r. Italy
223 M5 Nestor Falls Ont. Can.
226 C2 Nestoria MI U.S.A.
198 D1 Nestos r. Greece
Nesvizh Belarus see Nyasvizh
128 B3 Netanya Israel
117 F5 Netarhat Bihar India
234 D2 Netcong NJ U.S.A.
169 E4 Nethe r. Ger.
164 E2 Netherlands country Europe
247 E4 Netherlands Antilles terr. West Indies
146 F4 Netherley Aberdeenshire, Scotland U.K.
150 D3 Nether Stowey Somerset, England U.K.
149 G2 Netherton Northumberland, England U.K.
146 E4 Nethy Bridge Highland, Scotland U.K.
213 H2 Netia Moz.
106 D2 Netishyn Ukr.
195 G3 Neto r. Italy
176 D2 Netolice Czech Rep.
169 D5 Netphen Ger.
169 F4 Netra (Ringgau) Ger.
117 G4 Netrakona Bangl.
116 C5 Netrang Gujarat India
190 E1 Netstal Switz.
157 E4 Nettancourt France
169 B5 Nettersheim Ger.
169 B4 Nettetal Ger.
221 K3 Nettilling Lake Nunavut Can.
149 I4 Nettleham Lincolnshire, England U.K.
193 E3 Nettuno Italy
170 E1 Netzschkau Ger.
173 G2 Neualbenreuth Ger.
169 D5 Neu-Anspach Ger.
210 B3 Neubari r. Sudan
168 E1 Neuberend Ger.
179 G3 Neuberg an der Mürz Austria
173 G4 Neubeuern Ger.
173 F3 Neubiberg Ger.
168 C3 Neubörger Ger.
170 E2 Neubrandenburg Ger.
168 D3 Neubruchhausen Ger.
172 D2 Neubrunn Ger.
170 C1 Neubukow Ger.
172 C3 Neubulach Ger.
173 H3 Neuburg am Inn Ger.
172 C3 Neuburg am Rhein Ger.
173 F3 Neuburg an der Donau Ger.
173 E3 Neuburg an der Kammel Ger.
170 C2 Neuburg-Steinhausen Ger.
171 E4 Neuburxdorf Ger.
190 B2 Neuchâtel Switz.
190 B1 Neuchâtel canton Switz.
190 B2 Neuchâtel, Lac de l. Switz.
168 F2 Neu Darchau Ger.
169 F5 Neudietendorf Ger.
179 H3 Neudorf Austria
171 D5 Neudorf Ger.
171 C5 Neudrossenfeld Ger.
172 C3 Neuenbürg Ger.
172 B4 Neuenburg am Rhein Ger.
173 E2 Neuendettelsau Ger.
170 F3 Neuenhagen Ger.
170 E3 Neuenhagen Berlin Ger.
169 B3 Neuenhaus Ger.
172 C4 Neuenhof Switz.
190 D1 Neuenkirch Switz.
170 E1 Neuenkirchen Mecklenburg-Vorpommern Ger.
170 E1 Neuenkirchen Mecklenburg-Vorpommern Ger.
168 D2 Neuenkirchen Niedersachsen Ger.
168 D2 Neuenkirchen Niedersachsen Ger.
168 D3 Neuenkirchen Niedersachsen Ger.
168 E2 Neuenkirchen Niedersachsen Ger.
169 C3 Neuenkirchen Niedersachsen Ger.
169 C3 Neuenkirchen Nordrhein-Westfalen Ger.
168 E1 Neuenkirchen Schleswig-Holstein Ger.
169 D3 Neuenkirchen (Oldenburg) Ger.
169 C5 Neuenkirchen-Seelscheid Ger.
169 C4 Neuenrade Ger.
172 D3 Neuenstadt am Kocher Ger.
172 D2 Neuenstein Ger.
168 D2 Neuenwalde Ger.
169 B5 Neuerburg Ger.
173 F3 Neufahrn bei Freising Ger.
173 G3 Neufahrn in Niederbayern Ger.
157 H4 Neuf-Brisach France
165 E5 Neufchâteau Belgium
157 F4 Neufchâteau France
161 E3 Neufchâtel-en-Bray France
159 G3 Neufchâtel-en-Saosnois France
156 B2 Neufchâtel-Hardelot France
156 E3 Neufchâtel-sur-Aisne France
168 E2 Neufeld Ger.
179 H3 Neufeld an der Leitha Austria
179 F2 Neufelden Austria
172 D3 Neuffen Ger.
157 E3 Neufmanil France
172 D3 Neufra Ger.
171 C4 Neugattersleben Ger.
171 F5 Neugersdorf Ger.
170 E2 Neuglobsow Ger.
170 F3 Neuhardenberg Ger.
168 C2 Neuharlingersiel Ger.
179 F4 Neuhaus Austria
168 F2 Neuhaus (Elbe) Ger.
168 E2 Neuhaus (Oste) Ger.
173 H3 Neuhaus am Inn Ger.
179 H4 Neuhaus am Klausenbach Austria
171 C5 Neuhaus am Rennweg Ger.
173 F2 Neuhaus an der Pegnitz Ger.
172 C3 Neuhausen Baden-Württemberg Ger.
171 E5 Neuhausen Sachsen Ger.
Neuhausen Rus. Fed. see Gur'yevsk
190 D1 Neuhausen Switz.
172 C4 Neuhausen ob Eck Ger.
171 C5 Neuhaus-Schierschnitz Ger.
169 E5 Neuhof Ger.
173 E2 Neuhof an der Zenn Ger.
179 F2 Neuhofen an der Krems Austria
179 F2 Neuhofen an der Ybbs Austria
159 G4 Neuillé-Pont-Pierre France
160 B1 Neuilly France
156 C3 Neuilly-en-Thelle France
160 B2 Neuilly-le-Réal France
157 F5 Neuilly-l'Évêque France
156 D3 Neuilly-St-Front France
156 C4 Neuilly-sur-Seine France
169 D5 Neu-Isenburg Ger.
170 D2 Neukalen Ger.
170 C2 Neu Kaliß Ger.
168 C2 Neukamperfehn Ger.
171 D4 Neukieritzsch Ger.
172 D4 Neukirch Baden-Württemberg Ger.
171 F4 Neukirch Sachsen Ger.
169 E5 Neukirchen Hessen Ger.
171 D5 Neukirchen Sachsen Ger.
171 D5 Neukirchen Sachsen Ger.
170 C1 Neukirchen Schleswig-Holstein Ger.
168 D1 Neukirchen Schleswig-Holstein Ger.
178 D3 Neukirchen am Großvenediger Austria
178 E2 Neukirchen an der Enknach Austria
179 E2 Neukirchen an der Vöckla Austria
173 G2 Neukirchen-Balbini Ger.
173 F2 Neukirchen bei Sulzbach-Rosenberg Ger.
173 H3 Neukirchen vorm Wald Ger.
170 C2 Neukloster Ger.
Neukuhren Kaliningradskaya Oblast' Rus. Fed. see Pionerskiy
168 C2 Neulehe Ger.
179 G2 Neulengbach Austria
173 E3 Neuler Ger.
170 F3 Neulewin Ger.
160 C3 Neulise France
186 F2 Neulós, Pic mt. Spain
171 E3 Neu Lübbenau Ger.
172 A2 Neumagen Ger.
171 D5 Neumark Sachsen Ger.
171 C4 Neumark Thüringen Ger.
179 F2 Neumarkt im Mühlkreis Austria
173 F2 Neumarkt in der Oberpfalz Ger.
179 F3 Neumarkt in Steiermark Austria
173 G3 Neumarkt-St Veit Ger.
262 X2 Neumayer research stn Antarctica
168 E1 Neumünster Ger.
96 D3 Neun, Nam r. Laos
173 H3 Neunburg vorm Wald Ger.
171 D5 Neundorf Ger.
159 H4 Neung-sur-Beuvron France
190 D1 Neunkirch Switz.
179 H3 Neunkirchen Austria
169 D5 Neunkirchen Nordrhein-Westfalen Ger.
172 B2 Neunkirchen Saarland Ger.
173 F2 Neunkirchen am Sand Ger.
173 G3 Neuötting Ger.
171 F4 Neupetershain Ger.
260 C6 Neuquén Arg.
260 C6 Neuquén prov. Arg.
260 D6 Neuquén r. Arg.
173 H3 Neureichenau Ger.
172 D2 Neuried Ger.
170 D3 Neuruppin Ger.
171 F4 Neusalza-Spremberg Ger.
Neu Sandez Pol. see Nowy Sącz
173 E3 Neusäß Ger.
173 H3 Neuschönau Ger.
231 E5 Neuse r. NC U.S.A.
171 D3 Neuseddin Ger.
173 H3 Neusiedl am See Austria
179 H3 Neusiedler See l. Austria/Hungary
173 F2 Neusorg Ger.
169 B4 Neuss Ger.
161 A3 Neussargues-Moissac France
172 C4 Neustadt Baden-Württemberg Ger.
170 D3 Neustadt Brandenburg Ger.
171 C5 Neustadt Thüringen Ger.
169 F4 Neustadt (Harz) Ger.
169 E5 Neustadt (Hessen) Ger.
169 C5 Neustadt (Wied) Ger.
173 F2 Neustadt am Kulm Ger.
169 F5 Neustadt am Rennsteig Ger.
169 E3 Neustadt am Rübenberge Ger.
173 E2 Neustadt an der Aisch Ger.
173 F3 Neustadt an der Donau Ger.
Neustadt an der Hardt Ger. see Neustadt an der Weinstraße
173 G2 Neustadt an der Waldnaab Ger.
172 C2 Neustadt an der Weinstraße Ger.
171 C5 Neustadt bei Coburg Ger.
170 C2 Neustadt-Glewe Ger.
168 F1 Neustadt in Holstein Ger.
171 F4 Neustadt in Sachsen Ger.
178 C3 Neustift im Stubaital Austria
170 E2 Neustrelitz Ger.
173 G3 Neutraubling Ger.
170 F3 Neutrebbin Ger.
173 E3 Neu-Ulm Ger.
163 F3 Neuvéglise France
157 G4 Neuves-Maisons France
162 C3 Neuvic Aquitaine France
162 E3 Neuvic Limousin France
156 C4 Neuville-aux-Bois France
159 G5 Neuville-de-Poitou France
156 D3 Neuville-les-Dames France
156 B3 Neuville-lès-Dieppe France
160 C3 Neuville-sur-Saône France
159 G3 Neuville-sur-Sarthe France
157 F3 Neuvilly-en-Argonne France
160 B2 Neuvy-Grandchamp France
159 G4 Neuvy-le-Roi France
159 H5 Neuvy-Pailloux France
159 H5 Neuvy-St-Sépulchre France
156 D4 Neuvy-Sautour France
159 I4 Neuvy-sur-Barangeon France
171 C3 Neuwegersleben Ger.
172 C3 Neuweiler Ger.
168 D2 Neuwerk i. Ger.
169 C5 Neuwied Ger.
168 F1 Neuwittenbek Ger.
168 E2 Neu Wulmstorf Ger.
171 D5 Neuwürschnitz Ger.
171 F4 Neu Zauche Ger.
171 F3 Neuzelle Ger.
171 E3 Neu Zittau Ger.
161 E3 Névache France
236 E3 Nevada IA U.S.A.
237 E4 Nevada MO U.S.A.
240 I2 Nevada state U.S.A.
258 C2 Nevada, Sierra mt. Arg.
185 G3 Nevada, Sierra mts Spain
240 G1 Nevada, Sierra mts CA U.S.A.
240 G2 Nevada City CA U.S.A.
260 C4 Nevado, Cerro mt. Arg.
260 C5 Nevado, Sierra del mts Arg.
245 E4 Nevado de Toluca, Volcán vol. Mex.
185 E2 Nevalo r. Spain
114 B2 Nevasa Mahar. India
Nevdubstroy Leningradskaya Oblast' Rus. Fed. see Kirovsk
209 B8 Neve, Serra da mts Angola
176 D2 Neveklov Czech Rep.
138 G3 Nevel' Rus. Fed.
165 C3 Nevele Belgium
100 G3 Nevel'sk Sakhalin Rus. Fed.
183 I4 Nevera mt. Spain
132 A1 Neverkino Rus. Fed.
150 C2 Nevern Pembrokeshire, Wales U.K.
138 E4 Neveronys Lith.
160 B1 Nevers France
234 D1 Neversink r. NY U.S.A.
83 F2 Nevertire N.S.W. Austr.
257 F5 Neves Brazil
188 G4 Nevesinje Bos.-Herz.
158 C4 Névez France
138 D4 Nevėžis r. Lith.
161 A5 Névian France
195 H2 Neviano Italy
159 G2 Néville France
129 B1 Nevinnomyssk Rus. Fed.
247 □2 Nevis i. St Kitts and Nevis
146 C4 Nevis, Loch inlet Scotland U.K.
247 □2 Nevis Peak St Kitts and Nevis
126 D3 Nevşehir Turkey
241 J5 New r. CA U.S.A.
232 C6 New r. WV U.S.A.
146 E7 New Abbey Dumfries and Galloway, Scotland U.K.
146 F4 New Aberdour Aberdeenshire, Scotland U.K.
151 G3 New Addington Greater London, England U.K.
222 D4 New Aiyansh B.C. Can.
211 C7 Newala Tanz.
230 C4 New Albany IN U.S.A.
237 F5 New Albany MS U.S.A.
234 B1 New Albany PA U.S.A.
226 C3 Newald WI U.S.A.
151 F3 New Alresford Hampshire, England U.K.
251 G3 New Amsterdam Guyana
83 F2 New Angledool N.S.W. Austr.
215 H3 Newark S. Africa
240 F3 Newark CA U.S.A.
234 C3 Newark DE U.S.A.
233 F4 Newark NJ U.S.A.
232 E3 Newark NY U.S.A.
232 B4 Newark OH U.S.A.
233 F4 Newark airport NJ U.S.A.
149 I4 Newark-on-Trent Nottinghamshire, England U.K.
227 I4 Newark Valley NY U.S.A.
151 H3 New Ash Green Kent, England U.K.
237 F6 New Augusta MS U.S.A.
226 E4 Newaygo MI U.S.A.
233 H4 New Bedford MA U.S.A.
238 B2 Newberg OR U.S.A.
233 F3 New Berlin NY U.S.A.
234 B2 New Berlin PA U.S.A.
234 C2 New Berlinville PA U.S.A.
231 E5 New Bern NC U.S.A.
226 E2 Newberry MI U.S.A.
231 D5 Newberry SC U.S.A.
240 I4 Newberry Springs CA U.S.A.
234 B2 Newberrytown PA U.S.A.
234 C2 New Bethlehem PA U.S.A.
149 H2 Newbiggin-by-the-Sea Northumberland, England U.K.
146 E6 Newbigging South Lanarkshire, Scotland U.K.
147 D2 Newbliss Rep. of Ireland
227 I5 New Bloomfield PA U.S.A.
224 E4 Newboro Ont. Can.
233 H3 New Boston MA U.S.A.
232 B5 New Boston OH U.S.A.
237 E5 New Boston TX U.S.A.
237 D6 New Braunfels TX U.S.A.
147 C3 Newbridge Galway Rep. of Ireland
147 E3 Newbridge Kildare Rep. of Ireland
147 C4 Newbridge Limerick Rep. of Ireland
150 D3 Newbridge Caerphilly, Wales U.K.
150 D2 Newbridge on Wye Powys, Wales U.K.
232 C4 New Brighton PA U.S.A.
91 K8 New Britain i. P.N.G.
235 F1 New Britain CT U.S.A.
234 C2 New Britain PA U.S.A.
266 F6 New Britain Trench sea feature Pacific Ocean
225 H4 New Brunswick prov. Can.
233 F4 New Brunswick NJ U.S.A.
226 D5 New Buffalo MI U.S.A.
234 B2 New Buffalo PA U.S.A.
147 D2 New Buildings Northern Ireland U.K.
232 E4 Newburg PA U.S.A.
227 I3 Newburgh Ont. Can.
146 F4 Newburgh Aberdeenshire, Scotland U.K.
146 E5 Newburgh Fife, Scotland U.K.
146 E6 Newburgh Scottish Borders, Scotland U.K.
233 F4 Newburgh NY U.S.A.
151 F3 Newbury West Berkshire, England U.K.
Newbury admin. div. England U.K. see West Berkshire
233 H3 Newburyport MA U.S.A.
207 G4 New Bussa Nigeria
149 G3 Newby Bridge Cumbria, England U.K.
146 F4 New Byth Aberdeenshire, Scotland U.K.
78 □5 New Caledonia terr. S. Pacific Ocean
266 F7 New Caledonia Trough sea feature Tasman Sea
235 E1 New Canaan CT U.S.A.
225 H3 New Carlisle Que. Can.
232 A5 New Carlisle OH U.S.A.
234 B4 New Carrollton MD U.S.A.
83 G3 Newcastle N.S.W. Austr.
225 H4 Newcastle N.B. Can.
224 E5 Newcastle Ont. Can.
246 □ Newcastle Jamaica
147 E3 Newcastle Dublin Rep. of Ireland
147 C3 Newcastle Galway Rep. of Ireland
147 D4 Newcastle Tipperary Rep. of Ireland
147 E3 Newcastle Wicklow Rep. of Ireland
215 G2 Newcastle S. Africa
147 F2 Newcastle Northern Ireland U.K.
150 D2 Newcastle Shropshire, England U.K.
240 G2 Newcastle CA U.S.A.
234 C3 New Castle DE U.S.A.
230 C4 New Castle IN U.S.A.
230 C4 New Castle KY U.S.A.
233 □I2 Newcastle ME U.S.A.
232 C4 New Castle PA U.S.A.
241 K3 New Castle UT U.S.A.
232 C6 New Castle VA U.S.A.
238 F3 Newcastle WY U.S.A.
234 C3 New Castle County county DE U.S.A.
84 C3 Newcastle Creek r. N.T. Austr.
150 C2 Newcastle Emlyn Ceredigion, Wales U.K.
146 F6 Newcastleton Scottish Borders, Scotland U.K.
149 G4 Newcastle-under-Lyme Staffordshire, England U.K.
149 H3 Newcastle upon Tyne Tyne and Wear, England U.K.
84 C3 Newcastle Waters N.T. Austr.
147 B4 Newcastle West Rep. of Ireland
147 C5 Newcestown Rep. of Ireland
233 F6 New Church VA U.S.A.
Newchwang Liaoning China see Yingkou
235 E1 New City NY U.S.A.
234 B1 New Columbia PA U.S.A.
234 B1 New Columbus PA U.S.A.
241 M3 Newcomb NM U.S.A.
232 C4 Newcomerstown OH U.S.A.
232 C5 New Concord OH U.S.A.
234 B2 New Cumberland PA U.S.A.
146 D6 New Cumnock East Ayrshire, Scotland U.K.
146 F4 New Deer Aberdeenshire, Scotland U.K.
87 C7 Newdegate W.A. Austr.
116 D3 New Delhi Delhi India
233 □J1 New Denmark N.B. Can.
149 H4 New Earswick York, England U.K.
234 D2 New Egypt NJ U.S.A.
172 A2 Newel Ger.
85 F3 Newell Qld Austr.
236 C2 Newell SD U.S.A.
232 C4 Newell WV U.S.A.
87 E5 Newell, Lake salt flat W.A. Austr.
83 G2 New England Range mts N.S.W. Austr.
264 F3 New England Seamounts sea feature N. Atlantic Ocean
150 E3 Newent Gloucestershire, England U.K.
226 D4 New Era MI U.S.A.
232 D3 Newfane NY U.S.A.
233 G3 Newfane VT U.S.A.
233 G3 Newfield NJ U.S.A.
225 J3 Newfoundland i. Nfld. Can.
225 J2 Newfoundland prov. Can.
235 D1 Newfoundland NJ U.S.A.
234 C1 Newfoundland PA U.S.A.
238 D3 Newfoundland Evaporation Basin salt l. UT U.S.A.
234 B3 New Freedom PA U.S.A.
146 D6 New Galloway Dumfries and Galloway, Scotland U.K.
78 □6 New Georgia i. New Georgia Is Solomon Is
78 □6 New Georgia Islands Solomon Is
78 □6 New Georgia Sound sea chan. Solomon Is
226 C4 New Glarus WI U.S.A.
225 I4 New Glasgow N.S. Can.
147 E3 Newgrange Rep. of Ireland
145 D5 Newgrange Tomb tourist site Rep. of Ireland
235 D3 New Gretna NJ U.S.A.
91 J8 New Guinea i. Indon./P.N.G.
203 G6 New Halfa Sudan
240 H4 Newhall CA U.S.A.
235 E1 New Hamburg NY U.S.A.
233 H2 New Hampshire state U.S.A.
226 A4 New Hampton IA U.S.A.
235 D1 New Hampton NY U.S.A.
215 H3 New Hanover S. Africa
233 F3 New Hartford NY U.S.A.
151 H4 Newhaven East Sussex, England U.K.
233 G4 New Haven CT U.S.A.
226 A4 New Haven IA U.S.A.
226 E5 New Haven IN U.S.A.
227 F4 New Haven MI U.S.A.
232 C5 New Haven WV U.S.A.
235 F1 New Haven County county CT U.S.A.
222 E4 New Hazelton B.C. Can.
New Hebrides country S. Pacific Ocean see Vanuatu
266 G7 New Hebrides Trench sea feature Pacific Ocean
New Holland country Oceania see Australia
234 B2 New Holland PA U.S.A.
226 C4 New Holstein WI U.S.A.
234 D2 New Hope PA U.S.A.
237 F6 New Iberia LA U.S.A.
151 H4 Newick East Sussex, England U.K.
151 H3 Newington Kent, England U.K.
235 F1 Newington CT U.S.A.
148 B4 New Inn Cavan Rep. of Ireland
147 D4 New Inn Laois Rep. of Ireland
147 D4 Newinn Rep. of Ireland
91 L7 New Ireland i. P.N.G.
234 D3 New Jersey state U.S.A.
232 D4 New Kensington PA U.S.A.
232 E6 New Kent VA U.S.A.
147 C4 New Kildimo Rep. of Ireland
239 F5 Newkirk NM U.S.A.
237 D4 Newkirk OK U.S.A.
146 E6 New Lanark tourist site Scotland U.K.
231 D4 Newland NC U.S.A.
87 D6 Newland Range hills W.A. Austr.
146 F4 New Leeds Aberdeenshire, Scotland U.K.
232 B5 New Lexington OH U.S.A.
226 B4 New Lisbon WI U.S.A.
224 E4 New Liskeard Ont. Can.
233 G4 New London CT U.S.A.
232 B4 New London OH U.S.A.
226 C3 New London WI U.S.A.
235 F1 New London County county CT U.S.A.
146 D7 New Luce Dumfries and Galloway, Scotland U.K.
150 □ Newlyn Cornwall, England U.K.
146 F4 Newmachar Aberdeenshire, Scotland U.K.
237 F4 New Madrid MO U.S.A.
87 C4 Newman W.A. Austr.
80 E4 Newman North I. N.Z.
240 G3 Newman CA U.S.A.
262 O1 Newman Island Antarctica
234 B2 Newmanstown PA U.S.A.
224 E4 Newmarket Ont. Can.
246 □ Newmarket Jamaica
147 B4 Newmarket Cork Rep. of Ireland
147 D4 Newmarket Kilkenny Rep. of Ireland
151 H2 Newmarket Suffolk, England U.K.
146 B3 Newmarket Western Isles, Scotland U.K.
233 □H3 Newmarket NH U.S.A.
232 D5 New Market VA U.S.A.
147 C4 Newmarket-on-Fergus Rep. of Ireland
178 E3 Newmarkt am Wallersee Austria
232 C5 New Martinsville WV U.S.A.
238 C2 New Meadows ID U.S.A.
239 F5 New Mexico state U.S.A.
232 A5 New Miami OH U.S.A.
235 E1 New Milford CT U.S.A.
233 F4 New Milford PA U.S.A.
146 F4 Newmill Moray, Scotland U.K.
149 G4 New Mills Derbyshire, England U.K.
146 D6 Newmilns East Ayrshire, Scotland U.K.
151 F4 New Milton Hampshire, England U.K.
151 I3 New Mistley Essex, England U.K.
232 B5 New Moorefield OH U.S.A.
231 C5 Newnan GA U.S.A.
150 E3 Newnham Gloucestershire, England U.K.
87 C6 New Norcia W.A. Austr.
83 F5 New Norfolk Tas. Austr.
237 F6 New Orleans LA U.S.A.
234 A3 New Oxford PA U.S.A.
233 F4 New Paltz NY U.S.A.
226 E5 New Paris IN U.S.A.
232 A5 New Paris OH U.S.A.
232 C4 New Philadelphia OH U.S.A.
234 B2 New Philadelphia PA U.S.A.
146 F4 New Pitsligo Aberdeenshire, Scotland U.K.
80 E3 New Plymouth North I. N.Z.
150 C4 New Polzeath Cornwall, England U.K.
147 B3 Newport Mayo Rep. of Ireland
147 C4 Newport Tipperary Rep. of Ireland
151 H3 Newport Essex, England U.K.
146 E3 Newport Highland, Scotland U.K.
151 F4 Newport Isle of Wight, England U.K.
150 D3 Newport Newport, Wales U.K.
150 C2 Newport Pembrokeshire, Wales U.K.
150 E2 Newport Telford and Wrekin, England U.K.
150 E3 Newport admin. div. Wales U.K.
237 F5 Newport AR U.S.A.
234 C3 Newport DE U.S.A.
230 C4 Newport IN U.S.A.
233 □I2 Newport ME U.S.A.
227 F5 Newport MI U.S.A.
233 G3 Newport NH U.S.A.
234 C3 Newport NJ U.S.A.
238 A2 Newport OR U.S.A.
234 A2 Newport PA U.S.A.
233 H4 Newport RI U.S.A.
231 D5 Newport TN U.S.A.
233 G2 Newport VT U.S.A.
238 C1 Newport WA U.S.A.
150 C2 Newport Bay Wales U.K.
240 I5 Newport Beach CA U.S.A.
232 E6 Newport News VA U.S.A.
146 F5 Newport-on-Tay Fife, Scotland U.K.
151 G2 Newport Pagnell Milton Keynes, England U.K.
231 D6 New Port Richey FL U.S.A.
147 E2 Newport Trench Northern Ireland U.K.
235 E1 New Preston CT U.S.A.
246 C1 New Providence i. Bahamas
235 D2 New Providence NJ U.S.A.
234 B3 New Providence PA U.S.A.
150 C2 New Quay Ceredigion, Wales U.K.
150 B4 Newquay Cornwall, England U.K.
150 D2 New Radnor Powys, Wales U.K.
225 H3 New Richmond Que. Can.
232 A5 New Richmond OH U.S.A.
226 A3 New Richmond WI U.S.A.
234 C2 New Ringgold PA U.S.A.
241 K5 New River AZ U.S.A.
237 F6 New Roads LA U.S.A.
235 E2 New Rochelle NY U.S.A.
236 D2 New Rockford ND U.S.A.
151 H4 New Romney Kent, England U.K.
225 H4 New Ross N.S. Can.
147 E4 New Ross Rep. of Ireland
84 B3 Newry N.T. Austr.
147 E2 Newry Northern Ireland U.K.
226 B4 Newry WI U.S.A.
146 E5 New Scone Perth and Kinross, Scotland U.K.
New Siberia Islands Rus. Fed. see Novosibirskiye Ostrova
231 D6 New Smyrna Beach FL U.S.A.
83 F3 New South Wales state Austr.
232 D4 New Stanton PA U.S.A.
235 F2 New Suffolk NY U.S.A.
232 B6 New Tazewell TN U.S.A.
146 C5 Newton Argyll and Bute, Scotland U.K.
149 G4 Newton Lancashire, England U.K.
231 C6 Newton GA U.S.A.
236 E3 Newton IA U.S.A.
226 C6 Newton IL U.S.A.
236 D4 Newton KS U.S.A.
233 H3 Newton MA U.S.A.
237 F5 Newton MS U.S.A.
231 D5 Newton NC U.S.A.
234 D1 Newton NJ U.S.A.
237 E6 Newton TX U.S.A.
150 D4 Newton Abbot Devon, England U.K.
149 H3 Newton Aycliffe Durham, England U.K.
233 F2 Newton Falls NY U.S.A.
150 C4 Newton Ferrers Devon, England U.K.
146 F4 Newtonhill Aberdeenshire, Scotland U.K.
149 G4 Newton-le-Willows Merseyside, England U.K.
151 G3 Newton Longville Buckinghamshire, England U.K.
146 D6 Newton Mearns East Renfrewshire, Scotland U.K.
146 D4 Newtonmore Highland, Scotland U.K.
150 D4 Newton Poppleford Devon, England U.K.
150 D4 Newton St Cyres Devon, England U.K.
146 D7 Newton Stewart Dumfries and Galloway, Scotland U.K.
140 □ Newtontoppen mt. Svalbard
147 C4 Newtown Cork Rep. of Ireland
147 D4 Newtown Laois Rep. of Ireland
147 C3 Newtown Roscommon Rep. of Ireland
147 C4 Newtown Tipperary Rep. of Ireland
147 D4 Newtown Waterford Rep. of Ireland
150 E2 Newtown Herefordshire, England U.K.
150 D2 Newtown Powys, Wales U.K.
235 E1 Newtown CT U.S.A.
236 C1 New Town ND U.S.A.
234 D2 Newtown PA U.S.A.
234 D2 Newtown PA U.S.A.
147 F2 Newtownabbey Northern Ireland U.K.
147 F2 Newtownards Northern Ireland U.K.
Newtownbarry Rep. of Ireland see Bunclody
147 D2 Newtownbutler Northern Ireland U.K.
148 C3 Newtown Crommelin Northern Ireland U.K.
147 D2 Newtowncunningham Rep. of Ireland
147 D3 Newtown Forbes Rep. of Ireland
147 D2 Newtown Gore Rep. of Ireland
147 E2 Newtownhamilton Northern Ireland U.K.
147 D2 Newtownlow Rep. of Ireland
147 E3 Newtownmountkennedy Rep. of Ireland
146 F6 Newtown St Boswells Scottish Borders, Scotland U.K.
147 B4 Newtown Sandes Rep. of Ireland
234 C3 Newtown Square PA U.S.A.
147 D2 Newtownstewart Northern Ireland U.K.
150 D3 New Tredegar Caerphilly, Wales U.K.
234 C2 New Tripoli PA U.S.A.
146 E5 Newtyle Angus, Scotland U.K.
236 E2 New Ulm MN U.S.A.
232 B5 New Vienna OH U.S.A.
232 E4 Newville PA U.S.A.
233 □H2 New Vineyard ME U.S.A.
149 I4 New Waltham North East Lincolnshire, England U.K.
234 A3 New Windsor MD U.S.A.
235 D1 New Windsor NY U.S.A.
233 F3 New Woodstock NY U.S.A.
233 G4 New York NY U.S.A.
233 F3 New York state U.S.A.
235 E2 New York County county NY U.S.A.
80 New Zealand country Oceania
245 E4 Nexapa r. Mex.
162 D3 Nexon France
134 H4 Neya Rus. Fed.
134 H4 Neya r. Rus. Fed.
104 B4 Neyagawa Japan
122 D4 Ney Bīd Iran
150 C3 Neyland Pembrokeshire, Wales U.K.
122 C4 Neyrīz Iran
122 D2 Neyshābūr Iran
114 C4 Neyyattinkara Kerala India
245 E4 Nezahualcóyotl Mex.
245 H5 Nezahualcóyotl, Presa resr Mex.
176 C2 Nezamyslice Czech Rep.
176 D2 Nežárka r. Czech Rep.
137 I2 Nezhegol' r. Rus. Fed.
Nezhin Ukr. see Nizhyn
129 C1 Nezlobnaya Rus. Fed.
238 C2 Nezperce ID U.S.A.
177 I4 Nézsa Hungary
176 C2 Nezvěstice Czech Rep.
136 C3 Nezvys'ko Ukr.
95 E2 Ngabang Kalimantan Barat Indon.
209 C5 Ngabé Congo
97 B4 Nga Chong, Khao mt. Myanmar/Thai.
80 E1 Ngaiotonga North I. N.Z.
207 I3 Ngala Nigeria
208 C2 Ngama Chad
80 E3 Ngamatapouri North I. N.Z.
207 H5 Ngambé Cameroon
108 A2 Ngamda Xizang China
212 D3 Ngamiland admin. dist. Botswana
111 D6 Ngamring Xizang China
116 F3 Ngangla Ringco salt l. China
111 C5 Nganglong Kangri mt. Xizang China
111 C5 Nganglong Kangri mts Xizang China
111 D6 Ngangzê Co salt l. China
95 E4 Nganjuk Jawa Timur Indon.
108 C5 Ngan Sau, Sông r. Vietnam
96 B3 Ngao Thai.
207 I5 Ngaoundal Cameroon
207 I5 Ngaoundéré Cameroon
80 E3 Ngapuke North I. N.Z.
211 A5 Ngara Tanz.
Ngarrab Xizang China see Gyaca
80 E2 Ngaruawahia North I. N.Z.
80 F3 Ngaruroro r. North I. N.Z.
80 E3 Ngataki North I. N.Z.
80 F3 Ngatapa North I. N.Z.
80 E2 Ngatea North I. N.Z.
96 A3 Ngathainggyaung Myanmar
Ngawa Sichuan China see Aba
97 B4 Ngawan Chaung r. Myanmar
95 E4 Ngawi Jawa Timur Indon.
Ngcheangel atoll Palau see Kayangel
Ngeaur i. Palau see Angaur
91 H5 Ngeruangel i. Palau
Nggamea i. Fiji see Qamea
78 □6 Nggatokae i. New Georgia Is Solomon Is
78 □6 Nggela Sule i. Solomon Is
Nggelelevu i. Fiji see Qelelevu
212 D4 Nghabe r. Botswana
96 C3 Ngiap r. Laos
95 F4 Ngimbang Jawa Timur Indon.
Ngiva Angola see Ondjiva
96 D4 Ngoc Linh mt. Vietnam
207 I6 Ngoko r. Cameroon/Congo
209 E8 Ngoma Zambia
209 B6 Ngoma Tsé-Tsé Congo
215 H2 Ngome S. Africa
111 G6 Ngom Qu r. Qinghai China
80 E3 Ngongotaha North I. N.Z.
111 D5 Ngoqumaima Xizang China
106 C5 Ngoring Qinghai China
106 C5 Ngoring Hu l. Qinghai China
211 B5 Ngorongoro Conservation Area nature res. Tanz.
211 B5 Ngorongoro Crater Tanz.
207 H6 Ngoulémakong Cameroon
207 H6 Ngoumou Cameroon
208 A5 Ngounié prov. Gabon
208 A5 Ngounié r. Gabon
208 B5 Ngouoni Gabon
202 C6 Ngoura Chad
202 D6 Ngouri Chad
207 I3 Ngourti Niger
211 A5 Ngozi Burundi
215 G4 Ngqeleni S. Africa
215 G4 Ngqungqu S. Africa
207 I3 Nguigmi Niger
84 B1 Nguiu N.T. Austr.
84 C2 Ngukurr N.T. Austr.
91 I5 Ngulu atoll Micronesia
96 C3 Ngum, Nam r. Laos
78 □5 Nguna i. Vanuatu
Ngunza Angola see Sumbe
Ngunza-Kabolu Angola see Sumbe
207 H3 Nguru Nigeria
211 C6 Nguru Mountains Tanz.
212 E5 Ngwaketse admin. dist. Botswana
Ngwane country Africa see Swaziland
215 F2 Ngwathe S. Africa
215 I2 Ngwavuma r. Swaziland
215 H3 Ngwelezana S. Africa
215 H2 Ngwempisi r. S. Africa
209 E9 Ngwezi r. Zambia
213 G3 Nhamatanda Moz.
251 G5 Nhamundá Brazil
251 G5 Nhamundá r. Brazil
256 B4 Nhandeara Brazil
209 C7 N'harea Angola
97 E4 Nha Trang Vietnam
82 E4 Nhill Vic. Austr.
215 H2 Nhlangano Swaziland
215 H3 Nhlazatshe S. Africa
96 D2 Nho Quan Vietnam
Nhow i. Fiji see Gau
84 D2 Nhulunbuy N.T. Austr.
206 E5 Niablé Ghana
223 J4 Niacam Sask. Can.
206 E3 Niafounké Mali
226 D3 Niagara WI U.S.A.
224 E5 Niagara Falls Ont. Can.
232 D3 Niagara Falls NY U.S.A.
227 H4 Niagara-on-the-Lake Ont. Can.

Niagassola to North Rona

341

206 C3 **Niagassola** Guinea
206 C4 **Niagouelé, Mont du** hill Guinea
206 D4 **Niakaramandougou** Côte d'Ivoire
207 F3 **Niamey** Niger
206 D3 **Niamina** Mali
207 F4 **Niamtougou** Togo
Nianbai Qinghai China see Ledu
206 C4 **Niandan** r. Guinea
206 C4 **Niandankoro** Guinea
211 C6 **Niangandu** Tanz.
208 E4 **Niangara** Dem. Rep. Congo
206 E3 **Niangay, Lac** l. Mali
206 D4 **Niangoloko** Burkina
237 E4 **Niangua** r. MO U.S.A.
Niangxi Hunan China see Xinshao
206 D4 **Niankorodougou** Burkina
235 F1 **Niantic** CT U.S.A.
107 I2 **Nianzishan** Heilong. China
209 B5 **Niari** admin. reg. Congo
94 B2 **Nias** i. Indon.
213 H2 **Niassa** prov. Moz.
Niassa, Lago l. Africa see Nyasa, Lake
Niaur i. Palau see **Angaur**
163 D6 **Niaux** France
190 E4 **Nibbiano** Italy
86 E4 **Nibil Well** W.A. Austr.
129 E3 **Nic** Azer.
195 G3 **Nicà** r. Italy
138 C3 **Nīca** Latvia
Nicaea Turkey see **İznik**
246 A4 **Nicaragua** country Central America
242 □I7 **Nicaragua, Lago de** l. Nic.
Nicaragua, Lake Nic. see Nicaragua, Lago de
246 D2 **Nicaro** Cuba
195 F4 **Nicastro** Italy
161 F5 **Nice** France
Nice airport France see Côte d'Azur
240 F2 **Nice** CA U.S.A.
Nicephorium Syria see Ar Raqqah
231 C6 **Niceville** FL U.S.A.
190 C3 **Nichelino** Italy
103 E8 **Nichinan** Japan
117 E4 **Nichlaul** Uttar Prad. India
246 B2 **Nicholas Channel** Bahamas/Cuba
230 C4 **Nicholasville** KY U.S.A.
246 C1 **Nicholl's Town** Andros Bahamas
233 E3 **Nichols** NY U.S.A.
86 F3 **Nicholson** W.A. Austr.
84 D3 **Nicholson** r. Qld Austr.
227 F2 **Nicholson** Ont. Can.
234 C1 **Nicholson** PA U.S.A.
87 C5 **Nicholson Range** hills W.A. Austr.
233 F2 **Nicholville** NY U.S.A.
179 I3 **Nickelsdorf** Austria
232 B6 **Nickelsville** VA U.S.A.
115 G4 **Nicobar Islands** Andaman & Nicobar Is India
197 I3 **Nicolae Bălcescu** Romania
243 H5 **Nicolás Bravo** Mex.
245 E4 **Nicolás Romero** Mex.
240 G2 **Nicolaus** CA U.S.A.
195 E5 **Nicolosi** Sicilia Italy
Nicomedia Turkey see **Kocaeli**
Nicopolis Bulg. see **Nikopol**
Nicosia Cyprus see **Lefkosia**
194 D5 **Nicosia** Sicilia Italy
195 E4 **Nicotera** Italy
242 □I7 **Nicoya** Costa Rica
242 □I7 **Nicoya, Península de** pen. Costa Rica
233 □J1 **Nictau** N.B. Can.
197 I3 **Niculițel** Romania
138 C4 **Nida** Lith.
175 I2 **Nida** r. Pol.
175 I5 **Nida** r. Pol.
114 D2 **Nidadavole** Andhra Prad. India
114 C2 **Nidagunda** Andhra Prad. India
190 C1 **Nidau** Switz.
149 H3 **Nidd** r. England U.K.
169 E5 **Nidda** Ger.
169 D5 **Nidda** r. Ger.
169 D5 **Nidder** r. Ger.
149 H3 **Nidderdale** val. England U.K.
142 C2 **Nidelva** r. Norway
190 D2 **Nidwalden** canton Switz.
197 E5 **Nidže** mt. Greece/Macedonia
175 I2 **Nidzica** Pol.
175 I5 **Nidzica** r. Pol.
164 F1 **Niebert** Neth.
184 D3 **Niebla** Spain
175 I3 **Nieborów** Pol.
168 D1 **Niebüll** Ger.
175 J6 **Niebylec** Pol.
174 F3 **Niechanowo** Pol.
175 H4 **Niechcice** Pol.
175 I2 **Niechłonin** Pol.
174 E4 **Niechlów** Pol.
157 G3 **Nied** r. France
157 G3 **Nied Allemande** r. France
169 E4 **Niedenstein** Ger.
173 G3 **Niederaichbach** Ger.
165 F5 **Niederanven** Lux.
169 E5 **Niederaula** Ger.
173 G3 **Niederbayern** admin. reg. Bayern Ger.
190 C1 **Niederbipp** Switz.
169 D5 **Niederbrechen** Ger.
172 C3 **Niedereschach** Ger.
179 E3 **Niedere Tauern** mts Austria
170 E3 **Niederfinow** Ger.
169 C5 **Niederfischbach** Ger.
169 E5 **Nieder-Gemünden** Ger.
171 D4 **Niedergörsdorf** Ger.
169 C5 **Niederkassel** Ger.
172 B2 **Niederkirchen** Ger.
169 B4 **Niederkrüchten** Ger.
168 C3 **Niederlangen** Ger.
171 E3 **Niederlehme** Ger.
171 C3 **Niederndodeleben** Ger.
178 D3 **Niederndorf** Austria
169 D5 **Niederneisen** Ger.
172 D2 **Niedernhall** Ger.
169 D5 **Niedernhausen** Ger.
178 D3 **Niedernsill** Austria
169 E3 **Niedernwöhren** Ger.
172 C2 **Nieder-Olm** Ger.
169 F4 **Niederorschel** Ger.
179 G2 **Niederösterreich** land Austria
169 E5 **Nieder-Rodenbach** Ger.
171 C4 **Niederroßla** Ger.
168 D3 **Niedersachsen** land Ger.
169 F4 **Niedersachswerfen** Ger.
169 D5 **Niederselters** Ger.
172 D2 **Niederstetten** Ger.
173 E3 **Niederstotzingen** Ger.
171 C4 **Niedertrebra** Ger.
190 E1 **Niederurnen** Switz.
173 G3 **Niederviehbach** Ger.
169 F5 **Niederwerrn** Ger.
171 E5 **Niederwiesa** Ger.
173 G3 **Niederwinkling** Ger.
172 B2 **Niederwörresbach** Ger.
169 C5 **Niederzissen** Ger.
175 K4 **Niedrzwica Duża** Pol.
175 K2 **Niedźwiadna** Pol.
175 I6 **Niedźwiedź** Pol.
207 H6 **Niefang** Equat. Guinea
172 C3 **Niefern-Öschelbronn** Ger.
175 J1 **Niegocin, Jezioro** l. Pol.
174 D4 **Niegosławice** Pol.
175 H5 **Niegowa** Pol.
171 C3 **Niegripp** Ger.
169 E4 **Nieheim** Ger.
164 F1 **Niekerk** Neth.
214 D3 **Niekerkshoop** S. Africa
175 I4 **Niekłań Wielki** Pol.
165 D3 **Niel** Belgium
175 L5 **Nielisz** Pol.
206 D4 **Niellé** Côte d'Ivoire
209 F6 **Niemba** Dem. Rep. Congo
171 D4 **Niemberg** Ger.
175 K4 **Niemce** Pol.
174 E5 **Niemcza** Pol.
171 D3 **Niemegk** Ger.
140 M2 **Niemisel** Sweden
174 F5 **Niemodlin** Pol.
174 G4 **Niemysłów** Pol.
206 D4 **Niéna** Mali
175 K5 **Nienadówka** Pol.
168 E1 **Nienborstel** Ger.
171 C4 **Nienburg (Saale)** Ger.
168 E3 **Nienburg (Weser)** Ger.
168 F3 **Nienhagen** Ger.
169 E3 **Nienstädt** Ger.
170 D1 **Niepars** Ger.
175 I5 **Niepołomice** Pol.
175 J3 **Nieporęt** Pol.
156 C2 **Nieppe** France
169 A4 **Niers** r. Ger.
172 C2 **Nierstein** Ger.
171 F4 **Niesky** Ger.
169 E4 **Nieste** Ger.
175 I4 **Nieświń** Pol.
174 G3 **Nieszawa** Pol.
175 J5 **Nietulisko Duże** Pol.
162 D3 **Nieul** France
162 A2 **Nieul-le-Dolent** France
162 A2 **Nieul-sur-Mer** France
251 H3 **Nieuw Amsterdam** Suriname
164 F3 **Nieuw-Bergen** Neth.
164 E2 **Nieuwegein** Neth.
164 D2 **Nieuwe-Niedorp** Neth.
164 F1 **Nieuwe Pekela** Neth.
164 D3 **Nieuwerkerk** Neth.
164 D3 **Nieuwerkerk aan de IJssel** Neth.
165 E4 **Nieuwerkerken** Belgium
164 G1 **Nieuweschans** Neth.
164 D3 **Nieuwe-Tonge** Neth.
164 F2 **Nieuw-Heeten** Neth.
164 D2 **Nieuwkoop** Neth.
164 F2 **Nieuwlande** Neth.
164 F2 **Nieuwleusen** Neth.
164 E2 **Nieuw-Loosdrecht** Neth.
164 E2 **Nieuw-Milligen** Neth.
165 D3 **Nieuw-Namen** Neth.
251 G3 **Nieuw Nickerie** Suriname
164 F1 **Nieuwolda** Neth.
214 B4 **Nieuwoudtville** S. Africa
165 B3 **Nieuwpoort** Belgium
164 D2 **Nieuwveen** Neth.
164 D2 **Nieuw-Vennep** Neth.
164 D3 **Nieuw-Vossemeer** Neth.
164 F2 **Nieuw-Weerdinge** Neth.
169 C5 **Nievern** Ger.
244 C2 **Nieves** Mex.
Nieves Galicia Spain see As Neves
160 B1 **Nièvre** dept Bourgogne France
160 B1 **Nièvre** r. France
160 B2 **Nièvre de Champlemy** r. France
175 K4 **Niewęgłosz** Pol.
126 D3 **Niğde** Turkey
215 G2 **Nigel** S. Africa
207 H2 **Niger** country Africa
207 G5 **Niger** r. Africa
207 G4 **Niger** state Nigeria
207 G5 **Niger, Mouths of the** Nigeria
206 C4 **Niger, Source of the** tourist site Guinea
264 J5 **Niger Cone** sea feature S. Atlantic Ocean
207 G4 **Nigeria** country Africa
146 D4 **Nigg Bay** Scotland U.K.
116 E3 **Nighasan** Uttar Prad. India
81 B6 **Nightcaps** South I. N.Z.
224 D3 **Nighthawk Lake** Ont. Can.
85 E2 **Night Island** Qld Austr.
182 B2 **Nigrán** Spain
198 C1 **Nigrita** Greece
244 D2 **Nigromante** Mex.
185 G4 **Nigüelas** Spain
138 E2 **Nigula looduskaitseala** nature res. Estonia
159 H5 **Niherne** France
Nihommatsu Japan see Nihonmatsu
Nihon country Asia see **Japan**
102 J5 **Nihonmatsu** Japan
102 I5 **Niigata** Japan
105 E1 **Niigata** pref. Japan
105 E2 **Niigata-yake-yama** vol. Japan
103 F7 **Niihama** Japan
240 □A8 **Niihau** i. HI U.S.A.
103 F6 **Niimi** Japan
102 I5 **Niitsu** Japan
185 H4 **Níjar** Spain
164 F2 **Nijeveen** Neth.
164 E2 **Nijkerk** Neth.
165 D3 **Nijlen** Belgium
164 E3 **Nijmegen** Neth.
164 F2 **Nijverdal** Neth.
198 C2 **Nikaia** Greece
140 O1 **Nikel'** Rus. Fed.
120 D2 **Nikel'tau** Kazakh.
121 J2 **Nikitinka** Kazakh.
137 J2 **Nikitovka** Rus. Fed.
140 L2 **Nikkaluokta** Sweden
207 F4 **Nikki** Benin
105 F2 **Nikkō** Japan
179 G3 **Niklasdorf** Austria
134 I4 **Nikola** Rus. Fed.
197 G4 **Nikolaevo** Bulg.
Nikolayev Mykolayivs'ka Oblast' Ukr. see **Mykolayiv**
121 F1 **Nikolayevka** Kazakh.
120 E1 **Nikolayevka** Chelyabinskaya Oblast' Rus. Fed.
100 E2 **Nikolayevka** Khabarovskiy Kray Rus. Fed.
137 J4 **Nikolayevka** Rostovskaya Oblast' Rus. Fed.
135 I5 **Nikolayevka** Ul'yanovskaya Oblast' Rus. Fed.
Nikolayev Oblast admin. div. Ukr. see **Mykolayivs'ka Oblast'**
135 I6 **Nikolayevsk** Rus. Fed.
Nikolayevskaya Oblast' admin. div. Ukr. see **Mykolayivs'ka Oblast'**
Nikolayevskiy Rus. Fed. see Nikolayevsk
100 G1 **Nikolayevsk-na-Amure** Rus. Fed.
Nikolayevskoye Respublika Adygeya Rus. Fed. see **Krasnogvardeyskoye**
135 I5 **Nikol'sk** Rus. Fed.
134 I4 **Nikol'sk** Rus. Fed.
Nikol'skaya Pestravka Rus. Fed. see **Nikol'sk**
Nikol'skiy Kazakh. see Satpayev
139 J1 **Nikol'skiy** Rus. Fed.
131 R4 **Nikol'skoye** Rus. Fed.
139 M3 **Nikol'skoye** Rus. Fed.
139 L5 **Nikol'skoye** Rus. Fed.
120 C1 **Nikol'skoye** Rus. Fed.
Nikol'skoye Rus. Fed. see Sheksna
139 K2 **Nikol'skoye** Rus. Fed.
197 G4 **Nikopol** Bulg.
137 H4 **Nikopol'** Ukr.
122 B2 **Nīk Pey** Iran
126 E2 **Niksar** Turkey
122 E5 **Nīkshahr** Iran
196 D4 **Nikšić** Crna Gora Yugo.
77 I2 **Nikumaroro** i. Phoenix Is Kiribati
77 H2 **Nikunau** i. Gilbert Is Kiribati
Nīl, Bahr el r. Africa see **Nile**
93 D4 **Nila** vol. Maluku Indon.
117 F5 **Nilagiri** Orissa India
114 C4 **Nilakkottai** Tamil Nadu India
114 C4 **Nilambur** Kerala India
241 J5 **Niland** CA U.S.A.
113 D11 **Nilandhoo Atoll** Maldives
114 C2 **Nilanga** Mahar. India
114 D4 **Nilaveli** Sri Lanka
203 F2 **Nile** r. Africa
203 G5 **Nile** state Sudan
226 D5 **Niles** MI U.S.A.
232 C4 **Niles** OH U.S.A.
114 B3 **Nileswaram** Kerala India
124 B5 **Nili** r. Eth.
140 M2 **Nilivaara** Sweden
110 C3 **Nilka** Xinjiang China
257 F5 **Nilópolis** Brazil
117 G4 **Nilphamari** Bangl.
140 O3 **Nilsiä** Fin.
199 F1 **Nilüfer** r. Turkey
157 G3 **Nilvange** France
142 C4 **Nim** Denmark
116 C4 **Nimach** Madh. Prad. India
116 C4 **Nimaj** Rajasthan India
100 E2 **Niman** r. Rus. Fed.
Nimba, Monts mts Africa see Nimba Mountains
116 C4 **Nimbahera** Rajasthan India
114 B2 **Nimbal** Karnataka India
206 C4 **Nimba Mountains** Africa
86 D4 **Nimberra Well** W.A. Austr.
Nimbhera Rajasthan India see Nimbahera
100 F1 **Nimelen** r. Rus. Fed.
161 C5 **Nîmes** France
191 I2 **Nimis** Italy
116 C4 **Nimka Thana** Rajasthan India
83 G4 **Nimmitabel** N.S.W. Austr.
222 E5 **Nimpkish** r. B.C. Can.
123 E4 **Nīmrūz** prov. Afgh.
116 D2 **Nimu** Jammu and Kashmir
Nimwegen Neth. see **Nijmegen**
78 □3a **Ninai** i. Kwajalein Marshall Is
127 F4 **Nīnawá** governorate Iraq
127 F3 **Nīnawá** tourist site Iraq
83 G2 **Nindigully** Qld Austr.
168 E1 **Nindorf** Ger.
114 B4 **Nine Degree Channel** India
Ninemile Bar Dumfries and Galloway, Scotland U.K. see Crocketford
83 E2 **Nine Mile Lake** salt flat N.S.W. Austr.
241 I2 **Ninemile Peak** NV U.S.A.
265 J7 **Ninetyeast Ridge** sea feature Indian Ocean
83 F4 **Ninety Mile Beach** Vic. Austr.
80 D1 **Ninety Mile Beach** North I. N.Z.
Nineveh tourist site Iraq see Nīnawá
151 H4 **Ninfield** East Sussex, England U.K.
100 D3 **Ning'an** Heilong. China
109 G2 **Ningbo** Zhejiang China
107 H3 **Ningcheng** Nei Mongol China
109 F3 **Ningde** Fujian China
109 E3 **Ningdu** Jiangxi China
Ning'er Yunnan China see **Pu'er**
109 F2 **Ningguo** Anhui China
109 G2 **Ninghai** Zhejiang China
107 H4 **Ninghe** Tianjin China
Ninghsia Hui Autonomous Region aut. reg. China see **Ningxia Huizu Zizhiqu**
109 F3 **Ninghua** Fujian China
207 H4 **Ningi** Nigeria
Ningjiang Jilin China see Songyuan
108 A2 **Ningjing Shan** mts Xizang China
108 B3 **Ninglang** Yunnan China
107 G5 **Ningling** Henan China
108 C4 **Ningming** Guangxi China
108 B3 **Ningnan** Sichuan China
108 C1 **Ningqiang** Shaanxi China
108 D1 **Ningshan** Shaanxi China
107 G4 **Ningwu** Shanxi China
Ningxia aut. reg. China see **Ningxia Huizu Zizhiqu**
106 E4 **Ningxia Huizu Zizhiqu** aut. reg. China
107 E5 **Ningxian** Gansu China
109 E2 **Ningxiang** Hunan China
107 H5 **Ningyang** Shandong China
109 D3 **Ningyuan** Hunan China
Ningzhou Yunnan China see Huaning
96 D2 **Ninh Binh** Vietnam
97 E4 **Ninh Hoa** Vietnam
260 A5 **Ninhue** Chile
91 J7 **Ninigo Group** is P.N.G.
102 J3 **Ninohe** Japan
129 C3 **Ninotsminda** Georgia
165 D4 **Ninove** Belgium
129 C1 **Niny** Rus. Fed.
253 G5 **Nioaque** Brazil
236 D3 **Niobrara** r. NE U.S.A.
208 C5 **Nioki** Dem. Rep. Congo
206 D3 **Niono** Mali
206 C3 **Nioro** Mali
206 B3 **Nioro du Rip** Senegal
162 B2 **Niort** France
114 B2 **Nipani** Karnataka India
260 A5 **Ñipas** Chile
223 J4 **Nipawin** Sask. Can.
116 C5 **Niphad** Mahar. India
224 B3 **Nipigon** Ont. Can.
236 F1 **Nipigon** r. Ont. Can.
224 B3 **Nipigon, Lake** Ont. Can.
227 H2 **Nipissing** Ont. Can.
224 E4 **Nipissing, Lake** Ont. Can.
240 G4 **Nipomo** CA U.S.A.
Nippon country Asia see **Japan**
Nippon Hai sea N. Pacific Ocean see Japan, Sea of
127 G4 **Nippur** tourist site Iraq
241 J4 **Nipton** CA U.S.A.
254 C5 **Niquelândia** Brazil
260 B5 **Niquen** Chile
246 C2 **Niquero** Cuba
122 A2 **Nir** Iran
114 B2 **Nira** r. India
105 E3 **Nirasaki** Japan
260 A4 **Nirivilo** Chile
107 J1 **Nirji** Nei Mongol China
114 C2 **Nirmal** Andhra Prad. India
117 F4 **Nirmali** Bihar India
114 C2 **Nirmal Range** hills India
197 E4 **Niš** Srbija Yugo.
182 C5 **Nisa** Port.
182 C5 **Nisa** r. Port.
124 D5 **Niṣāb** Yemen
197 E4 **Nišava** r. Yugo.
146 F6 **Nisbet** Scottish Borders, Scotland U.K.
194 D5 **Niscemi** Sicilia Italy
Nīshāpūr Iran see **Neyshābūr**
138 G4 **Nishcha** r. Belarus
102 L2 **Nishibetsu-gawa** r. Japan
104 B4 **Nishinomiya** Japan
102 □1 **Nishino-omote** Japan
103 □3 **Nishino-shima** vol. Japan
104 D4 **Nishio** Japan
103 D7 **Nishi-Sonogi-hantō** pen. Japan
104 A4 **Nishiwaki** Japan
254 G3 **Nísia Floresta** Brazil
Nisibis Turkey see **Nusaybin**
103 E7 **Nisi-mera** Japan
Nísiros i. Greece see **Nisyros**
233 G3 **Niskayuna** NY U.S.A.
224 B1 **Niskibi** r. Ont. Can.
175 K5 **Nisko** Pol.
222 B2 **Nisling** r. Y.T. Can.
165 D4 **Nismes** Belgium
165 D4 **Nismes, Forêt de** for. Belgium
136 E4 **Nisporeni** Moldova
142 E3 **Nissan** r. Sweden
161 B5 **Nissan-lez-Enserune** France
104 D3 **Nisshin** Japan
194 D5 **Nissoria** Sicilia Italy
142 C3 **Nissum Bredning** b. Denmark
164 E3 **Nistelrode** Neth.
136 F4 **Nistru** r. Moldova alt. **Dnister (Ukraine)**, conv. **Dniester**
136 E4 **Nistrului Inferior, Cîmpia** lowland Moldova
222 C2 **Nisutlin** r. Y.T. Can.
199 E3 **Nisyros** i. Greece
103 F6 **Nita** Japan
225 G2 **Nitchequon** Que. Can.
Nitendi i. Santa Cruz Is Solomon Is see **Ndeni**
257 F5 **Niterói** Brazil
146 E6 **Nith** r. Scotland U.K.
146 E6 **Nithsdale** val. Scotland U.K.
177 H3 **Nitra** Slovakia
177 H4 **Nitra** r. Slovakia
177 H3 **Nitrianske Pravno** Slovakia
177 H3 **Nitriansky Kraj** admin. reg. Slovakia
232 C5 **Nitro** WV U.S.A.
156 D5 **Nitry** France
142 D1 **Nittedal** Norway
172 A2 **Nittel** Ger.
173 G2 **Nittenau** Ger.
173 F2 **Nittendorf** Ger.
Niua i. Vanuatu see **Aniwa**
77 I3 **Niuafo'ou** i. Tonga
Niuafu i. Tonga see **Niuafo'ou**
77 I3 **Niuatoputopu** i. Tonga
110 F4 **Niubiziliang** Qinghai China
81 □4 **Niue** terr. S. Pacific Ocean
Niujing Yunnan China see Binchuan
77 H3 **Niulakita** i. Tuvalu
108 B3 **Niulan Jiang** r. Yunnan China
240 □D8 **Niulii** HI U.S.A.
Niushan Jiangsu China see Donghai
77 H2 **Niutao** i. Tuvalu
109 F2 **Niutoushan** Anhui China
107 I3 **Niuzhuang** Liaoning China
140 N3 **Nivala** Fin.
163 A5 **Nive** r. France
85 F5 **Nive Downs** Qld Austr.
165 D4 **Nivelles** Belgium
175 I1 **Nivenskoye** Rus. Fed.
158 D4 **Nivillac** France
156 C3 **Nivillers** France
160 D3 **Nivolas-Vermelle** France
140 P2 **Nivskiy** Rus. Fed.
116 C4 **Niwai** Rajasthan India
116 D4 **Niwari** Madh. Prad. India
116 E5 **Niwas** Madh. Prad. India
175 J5 **Niwiska** Pol.
157 F3 **Nixéville-Blercourt** France
Nixia Sichuan China see **Sêrxu**
240 H2 **Nixon** NV U.S.A.
Niya Xinjiang China see **Minfeng**
111 C4 **Niya He** r. China
129 F3 **Niyazoba** Azer.
95 E2 **Niyut, Gunung** mt. Indon.
105 F3 **Niza** Japan
114 C2 **Nizamabad** Andhra Prad. India
114 D3 **Nizampatnam** Andhra Prad. India
176 D2 **Nižbor** Czech Rep.
134 I4 **Nizhegorodskaya Oblast'** admin. div. Rus. Fed.
131 L4 **Nizhneangarsk** Rus. Fed.
137 I5 **Nizhnebakanskiy** Rus. Fed.
135 G6 **Nizhnedevitsk** Rus. Fed.
121 K1 **Nizhnekamenka** Rus. Fed.
134 J5 **Nizhnekamsk** Rus. Fed.
134 K5 **Nizhnekamskoye Vodokhranilishche** resr Rus. Fed.
98 G1 **Nizhneudinsk** Rus. Fed.
130 I3 **Nizhnevartovsk** Rus. Fed.
Nizhnevolzhsk Rus. Fed. see Narimanov
131 O2 **Nizhneyansk** Rus. Fed.
134 L4 **Nizhni Irginski** Rus. Fed.
135 I6 **Nizhniy Baskunchak** Rus. Fed.
129 C2 **Nizhniy Chegem** Rus. Fed.
135 H6 **Nizhniy Chir** Rus. Fed.
129 E2 **Nizhniy Dzhengutay** Rus. Fed.
Nizhniye Kresty Rus. Fed. see **Cherskiy**
Nizhniye Ustriki Pol. see Ustrzyki Dolne
137 J2 **Nizhniy Karabut** Rus. Fed.
137 K2 **Nizhniy Kislyay** Rus. Fed.
129 D2 **Nizhniy Kurp** Rus. Fed.
135 H5 **Nizhniy Lomov** Rus. Fed.
137 K2 **Nizhniy Mamon** Rus. Fed.
134 H4 **Nizhniy Novgorod** Rus. Fed.
Nizhniy Novgorod Oblast admin. div. Rus. Fed. see Nizhegorodskaya Oblast'
134 K3 **Nizhniy Odes** Rus. Fed.
137 J2 **Nizhniy Ol'shan** Rus. Fed.
130 G4 **Nizhniy Tagil** Rus. Fed.
107 G1 **Nizhniy Tsasuchey** Rus. Fed.
134 I4 **Nizhniy Yenangsk** Rus. Fed.
134 K3 **Nizhnyaya Omra** Rus. Fed.
140 P2 **Nizhnyaya Pirenga, Ozero** l. Rus. Fed.
131 K4 **Nizhnyaya Poyma** Rus. Fed.
121 I1 **Nizhnyaya Suyetka** Rus. Fed.
131 J3 **Nizhnyaya Tunguska** r. Rus. Fed.
130 G4 **Nizhnyaya Tura** Rus. Fed.
137 J2 **Nizhnyaya Veduga** Rus. Fed.
137 F2 **Nizhyn** Ukr.
175 I3 **Nizina** reg. Pol.
126 E3 **Nizip** Turkey
177 K2 **Nízke Beskydy** hills Slovakia
177 I3 **Nízke Tatry** mts Slovakia
100 E4 **Nizmennyy, Mys** pt Rus. Fed.
177 J3 **Nižná Slaná** Slovakia
177 K3 **Nižný Hrušov** Slovakia
177 K3 **Nižný Žipov** Slovakia
Nizwā Oman see **Nazwá**
Nizza France see **Nice**
195 E5 **Nizza di Sicilia** Sicilia Italy
190 D4 **Nizza Monferrato** Italy
217 □3a **Njazidja** i. Comoros
196 D4 **Njegoš** mts Yugo.
211 C7 **Njinjo** Tanz.
191 J3 **Njivice** Croatia
209 E9 **Njoko** r. Zambia
211 B7 **Njombe** Tanz.
211 B6 **Njombe** r. Tanz.
78 □6 **Njoroveto** New Georgia Is Solomon Is
141 L3 **Njurundabommen** Sweden
141 L3 **Njutånger** Sweden
207 H5 **Nkambe** Cameroon
215 H3 **Nkandla** S. Africa
211 A6 **Nkasi** Tanz.
206 E5 **Nkawkaw** Ghana
211 B7 **Nkhata Bay** Malawi
211 B8 **Nkhotakota** Malawi
207 H5 **Nkongsamba** Cameroon
206 E5 **Nkoranza** Ghana
207 I5 **Nkoteng** Cameroon
215 F4 **Nkululeko** S. Africa
210 A4 **Nkusi** r. Uganda
215 H3 **Nkwalini** S. Africa
207 F4 **Nkwanta** Ghana
215 F5 **Nkwenkwezi** S. Africa
96 B1 **Nmai Hka** r. Myanmar
117 I4 **Noa Dihing** r. India
163 B4 **Noaillan** France
156 C3 **Noailles** France
163 A6 **Noain** Spain
117 G5 **Noakhali** Bangl.
191 H3 **Noale** Italy
185 G3 **Noalejo** Spain
117 F5 **Noamundi** Bihar India
190 C3 **Noasca** Italy
220 B3 **Noatak** r. AK U.S.A.
148 C4 **Nobber** Rep. of Ireland
103 E7 **Nobeoka** Japan
171 D5 **Nobitz** Ger.
183 G5 **Noblejas** Spain
230 C3 **Noblesville** IN U.S.A.
215 F4 **Nobokwe** S. Africa
102 J2 **Noboribetsu** Japan
253 F3 **Nobres** Brazil
85 E5 **Noccundra** Qld Austr.
159 G3 **Nocé** France
191 G2 **Noce** r. Italy
193 H5 **Noce** r. Italy
182 D2 **Noceda** Spain
193 G4 **Nocera Inferiore** Italy
193 I5 **Nocera Terinese** Italy
193 E1 **Nocera Umbra** Italy
190 F4 **Noceto** Italy
244 C3 **Nochistlán** Mex.
195 G2 **Noci** Italy
175 M1 **Nočia** r. Belarus/Lith.
195 H2 **Nociglia** Italy
85 E5 **Nockatunga** Qld Austr.
237 D5 **Nocona** TX U.S.A.
105 F3 **Noda** Japan
236 E4 **Nodaway** r. MO U.S.A.
142 B2 **Nodeland** Norway
160 E1 **Nods** France
163 D5 **Noé** France
224 D4 **Noelville** Ont. Can.
214 C2 **Noenieput** S. Africa
193 I4 **Noepoli** Italy
168 F1 **Noer** Ger.
261 F3 **Noetinger** Arg.
156 C2 **Nœux-les-Mines** France
183 F5 **Noez** Spain
183 F5 **Noez, Pico de** mt. Spain
183 G2 **Nofuentes** Spain
242 C2 **Nogales** Mex.
184 D2 **Nogales** Spain
239 E6 **Nogales** AZ U.S.A.
191 G3 **Nogara** Italy
163 B5 **Nogaro** France
174 H1 **Nogat** r. Pol.
103 E7 **Nōgata** Japan
Nogaysk Ukr. see **Prymors'ke**
129 E1 **Nogayskaya Step'** reg. Rus. Fed.
120 C2 **Nogayty** Kazakh.
157 F4 **Nogent** France
159 G3 **Nogent-le-Bernard** France
156 B4 **Nogent-le-Roi** France
159 G3 **Nogent-le-Rotrou** France
156 E4 **Nogent-sur-Aube** France
156 C4 **Nogent-sur-Marne** France
156 C3 **Nogent-sur-Oise** France
156 D4 **Nogent-sur-Seine** France
156 C5 **Nogent-sur-Vernisson** France
131 K3 **Noginsk** Evenkiyskiy Avtonomnyy Okrug Rus. Fed.
139 L4 **Noginsk** Moskovskaya Oblast' Rus. Fed.
100 G2 **Nogliki** Sakhalin Rus. Fed.
85 G5 **Nogo** r. Qld Austr.
85 G4 **Nogoa** r. Qld Austr.
104 C3 **Nōgōhaku-san** mt. Japan
261 H3 **Nogoyá** Arg.
261 H3 **Nogoya** r. Arg.
177 I4 **Nógrád** Hungary
177 I4 **Nógrád** county Hungary
183 H3 **Nograles** Spain
104 D2 **Noguchigorō-dake** mt. Japan
182 D3 **Nogueira, Serra de** mts Port.
183 I4 **Noguera** Spain
186 D2 **Noguera de Tor** r. Spain
186 D2 **Noguera Pallaresa** r. Spain
186 D3 **Noguera Ribagorçana** r. Spain
163 B5 **Noguères** France
187 C4 **Nogueruelas** Spain
160 A1 **Nohain** r. France
159 H5 **Nohant-Vic** France
116 C3 **Nohar** Rajasthan India
172 B2 **Nohfelden** Ger.
163 D5 **Nohic** France
182 B2 **Noia** Galicia Spain
195 F1 **Noicattaro** Italy
160 E1 **Noidans-lès-Vesoul** France
163 C5 **Noilhan** France
161 B4 **Noir, Causse** plat. France
227 I3 **Noire** r. Que. Can.
163 E5 **Noire, Montagne** mts France
158 C3 **Noires, Montagnes** hills France
160 B3 **Noirétable** France
158 D5 **Noirmoutier, Île de** i. France
158 D4 **Noirmoutier-en-l'Île** France
157 G3 **Noisseville** France
183 G1 **Noja** Spain
232 E5 **Nokesville** VA U.S.A.
116 C4 **Nokha** Rajasthan India
122 E5 **Nokhowch, Kūh-e** mt. Iran
141 M3 **Nokia** Fin.
Nökis Uzbek. see **Nukus**
223 J5 **Nokomis** Sask. Can.
202 B6 **Nokou** Chad
117 G4 **Nokrek Peak** Meghalaya India
142 E3 **Nol** Sweden
208 C4 **Nola** C.A.R.
194 D2 **Nola** Italy
160 C2 **Nolay** France
190 D4 **Noli** Italy
231 D4 **Nolichuky** r. TN U.S.A.
134 J4 **Nolinsk** Kirovskaya Oblast' Rus. Fed.
214 D5 **Noll** S. Africa
183 F4 **Nombela** Spain
220 B3 **Nome** AK U.S.A.
157 G4 **Nomeny** France
157 G4 **Nomexy** France
Nomoi Islands Micronesia see **Mortlock Islands**
215 F4 **Nomonde** S. Africa
78 □4a **Nomoneas** is Chuuk Micronesia
106 E1 **Nomto** Rus. Fed.
79 □2 **Nomuka** i. Tonga
79 □2 **Nomuka Group** is Tonga
91 L5 **Nomwin** atoll Micronesia
134 H4 **Nomzha** Rus. Fed.
223 I2 **Nonacho Lake** N.W.T. Can.
156 B4 **Nonancourt** France
159 G3 **Nonant-le-Pin** France
191 G4 **Nonantola** Italy
186 D3 **Nonaspe** Spain
215 H3 **Nondweni** S. Africa
156 C3 **Nonette** r. France
100 C3 **Nong'an** Jilin China
97 C4 **Nong Hong** Thai.
Nonghui Sichuan China see Guang'an
96 C3 **Nong Khai** Thai.
215 H2 **Nongoma** S. Africa
117 G4 **Nongstoin** Meghalaya India
161 C4 **Nonières** France
172 B3 **Nonnenweier** Ger.
Nonni r. China see **Nen Jiang**
82 D3 **Nonning** S.A. Austr.
172 A2 **Nonnweiler** Ger.
255 B8 **Nonoai** Brazil
242 D3 **Nonoava** Mex.
77 H2 **Nonouti** atoll Gilbert Is Kiribati
101 C5 **Nonsan** S. Korea
97 C4 **Nonthaburi** Thai.
162 C3 **Nontron** France
192 B2 **Nonza** Corse France
214 E4 **Nonzwakazi** S. Africa
138 F2 **Nõo** Estonia
87 C5 **Nookawarra** W.A. Austr.
82 D1 **Noolyeanna Lake** salt flat S.A. Austr.
84 B2 **Noonamah** N.T. Austr.
87 C6 **Noondie, Lake** salt flat W.A. Austr.
86 E3 **Noonkanbah** W.A. Austr.
164 F1 **Noordbergum** Neth.
164 C3 **Noordbeveland** i. Neth.
164 E3 **Noord-Brabant** prov. Neth.
164 F1 **Noordbroek-Uiterburen** Neth.
164 D2 **Noord-Holland** prov. Neth.
215 H1 **Noordkaap** S. Africa
214 B5 **Noordkuil** S. Africa
164 E2 **Noordoost Polder** Neth.
164 D2 **Noordwijk aan Zee** Neth.
164 D2 **Noordwijk-Binnen** Neth.
164 D2 **Noordwijkerhout** Neth.
164 F2 **Noordwolde** Neth.
141 M3 **Noormarkku** Fin.
220 B3 **Noorvik** AK U.S.A.
85 H5 **Noosa Heads** Qld Austr.
164 D2 **Nootdorp** Neth.
245 F5 **Nopala** Mex.
245 F4 **Nopaltepec** Mex.
209 B6 **Nóqui** Angola
193 G2 **Nora** r. Italy
100 D2 **Nora** r. Rus. Fed.
143 F2 **Nora** Sweden
192 A4 **Noragugume** Sardegna Italy
123 G2 **Norak** Tajik.
Norakert Armenia see Baghramyan
92 C5 **Norala** Phil.
224 E3 **Noranda** Que. Can.
Nor-Bayazet Armenia see Kamo
143 F1 **Norberg** Sweden
193 F2 **Norcia** Italy
233 □I2 **Norcross** ME U.S.A.
207 I4 **Nord** prov. Cameroon
156 D2 **Nord** dept Nord - Pas-de-Calais France
140 □ **Nordaustlandet** i. Svalbard
142 C4 **Nordborg** Denmark
142 D4 **Nordby** Denmark
168 C2 **Norddeich** Ger.
168 D1 **Norddorf** Ger.
222 G4 **Nordegg** Alta Can.
168 C2 **Norden** Ger.
173 E3 **Nordendorf** Ger.
168 D2 **Nordenham** Ger.
131 K2 **Nordenshel'da, Arkhipelag** is Rus. Fed.
222 B2 **Nordenskiold** r. Y.T. Can.
140 □ **Nordenskiøld Land** reg. Svalbard
Nordenskjold Archipelago is Rus. Fed. see Nordenshel'da, Arkhipelag
168 D1 **Norder Hever** sea chan. Ger.
168 C2 **Norderney** Ger.
168 C2 **Norderney** i. Ger.
168 D1 **Norderoogsand** i. Ger.
168 F2 **Norderstedt** Ger.
216 □1b **Nordeste** São Miguel Azores
216 □1b **Nordestinho** São Miguel Azores
141 I3 **Nordfjord** reg. Norway
141 I3 **Nordfjordeid** Norway
168 D1 **Nordfriesische Inseln** is Ger.
168 D1 **Nordfriesland** reg. Ger.
171 C3 **Nordgermersleben** Ger.
171 C5 **Nordhalben** Ger.
168 E1 **Nordhastedt** Ger.
169 F4 **Nordhausen** Ger.
172 D2 **Nordheim** Ger.
168 D2 **Nordholz** Ger.
169 C3 **Nordhorn** Ger.
142 A2 **Nordhuglo** Norway
142 C3 **Nordjylland** county Denmark
Nord Kap c. Iceland see **Horn**
140 N1 **Nordkapp** c. Norway
169 C4 **Nordkirchen** Ger.
208 F5 **Nord-Kivu** admin. reg. Dem. Rep. Congo
140 L1 **Nord-Kvaløy** i. Norway
140 N1 **Nordkynhalvøya** i. Norway
140 K2 **Nordland** county Norway
168 D2 **Nordleda** Ger.
140 K2 **Nordli** Norway
173 E3 **Nördlingen** Ger.
140 L3 **Nordmaling** Sweden
207 H5 **Nord-Ouest** prov. Cameroon
156 C2 **Nord - Pas-de-Calais** admin. reg. France
169 C4 **Nordrhein-Westfalen** land Ger.
169 E3 **Nordstemmen** Ger.
168 D1 **Nordstrand** i. Ger.
140 K2 **Nord-Trøndelag** county Norway
140 □C2 **Norðurland eystra** constituency Iceland
140 □B2 **Norðurland vestra** constituency Iceland
140 J3 **Nordvika** Norway
169 C3 **Nordwalde** Ger.
147 E4 **Nore** r. Rep. of Ireland
163 E5 **Nore, Pic de** mt. France
Noreg country Europe see Norway
138 D4 **Noreikiškės** Lith.
182 E1 **Noreña** Spain
142 C1 **Noresund** Norway
151 H2 **Norfolk** admin. div. England U.K.
236 D3 **Norfolk** NE U.S.A.
233 F2 **Norfolk** NY U.S.A.
233 E6 **Norfolk** VA U.S.A.
82 □1 **Norfolk Island** terr. S. Pacific Ocean
266 G7 **Norfolk Island Ridge** sea feature Tasman Sea
164 F1 **Norg** Neth.
Norge country Europe see Norway
149 G2 **Norham** Northumberland, England U.K.
142 B1 **Norheimsund** Norway
244 D2 **Noria de Ángeles** Mex.
104 D2 **Norikura-dake** vol. Japan
130 J3 **Noril'sk** Rus. Fed.
Norkyung Xizang China see Bainang
227 H3 **Norland** Ont. Can.
193 E3 **Norma** Italy
234 C3 **Norma** NJ U.S.A.
226 C5 **Normal** IL U.S.A.
85 E3 **Norman** r. Qld Austr.
237 D5 **Norman** OK U.S.A.
231 D5 **Norman, Lake** resr NC U.S.A.
85 F2 **Normanby** r. Qld Austr.
80 E3 **Normanby** North I. N.Z.
85 G4 **Normanby Range** hills Qld Austr.
Normandes, Îles is English Chan. see Channel Islands
251 G4 **Normandia** Brazil
159 F3 **Normandie** reg. France
159 F3 **Normandie, Collines de** hills France
215 G2 **Normandien** S. Africa
Normandy reg. France see Normandie
85 E3 **Normanton** Qld Austr.
149 H4 **Normanton** West Yorkshire, England U.K.
82 D3 **Normanville** S.A. Austr.
222 E1 **Norman Wells** N.W.T. Can.
227 H1 **Normétal** Que. Can.
87 C7 **Nornalup** W.A. Austr.
160 E1 **Noroy-le-Bourg** France
223 K5 **Norquay** Sask. Can.
140 M2 **Norra Bredåker** Sweden
140 M3 **Norra Gloppet** b. Fin.
140 K2 **Norråker** Sweden
140 M3 **Norra Kvarken** str. Fin./Sweden
140 L2 **Norrbotten** county Sweden
142 C3 **Nørreå** r. Denmark
142 D4 **Nørre Alslev** Denmark
168 G1 **Nørreballe** Denmark
142 D4 **Nørre Lyndelse** Denmark
142 C4 **Nørre Nebel** Denmark
156 C2 **Norrent-Fontes** France
142 C4 **Nørre Snede** Denmark
140 M2 **Norrfjärden** Sweden
143 F3 **Norrhult-Klavreström** Sweden
234 C2 **Norristown** PA U.S.A.
143 G2 **Norrköping** Sweden
141 L3 **Norrsundet** Sweden
143 H2 **Norrtälje** Sweden
87 D7 **Norseman** W.A. Austr.
80 F4 **Norsewood** North I. N.Z.
140 L2 **Norsjö** Sweden
100 D1 **Norsk** Rus. Fed.
251 I4 **Norte, Canal do** sea chan. Brazil
253 F2 **Norte, Serra do** hills Brazil
250 C2 **Norte de Santander** dept Col.
216 □1c **Norte Grande** São Jorge Azores
253 F3 **Nortelândia** Brazil
169 E4 **Nörten-Hardenberg** Ger.
216 □1c **Norte Pequeno** São Jorge Azores
263 L2 **North, Cape** Antarctica
233 G3 **North Adams** MA U.S.A.
149 H3 **Northallerton** North Yorkshire, England U.K.
87 C6 **Northam** W.A. Austr.
150 C3 **Northam** Devon, England U.K.
218 **North America** continent
233 □J2 **North Amity** ME U.S.A.
87 B6 **Northampton** W.A. Austr.
151 G2 **Northampton** Northamptonshire, England U.K.
233 G3 **Northampton** MA U.S.A.
234 C2 **Northampton** PA U.S.A.
234 C2 **Northampton County** county PA U.S.A.
85 F5 **Northampton Downs** Qld Austr.
151 G2 **Northamptonshire** admin. div. England U.K.
115 G3 **North Andaman** i. Andaman & Nicobar Is India
232 E6 **North Anna** r. VA U.S.A.
233 □I2 **North Anson** ME U.S.A.
265 L5 **North Australian Basin** sea feature Indian Ocean
146 D6 **North Ayrshire** admin. div. Scotland U.K.
151 F4 **North Baddesley** Hampshire, England U.K.
232 B4 **North Baltimore** OH U.S.A.
223 I4 **North Battleford** Sask. Can.
224 E4 **North Bay** Ont. Can.
224 E1 **North Belcher Islands** Nunavut Can.
238 A3 **North Bend** OR U.S.A.
232 E4 **North Bend** PA U.S.A.
233 G3 **North Bennington** VT U.S.A.
235 D2 **North Bergen** NJ U.S.A.
146 F5 **North Berwick** East Lothian, Scotland U.K.
233 □H3 **North Berwick** ME U.S.A.
North Borneo state Malaysia see Sabah
237 D6 **North Bosque** r. TX U.S.A.
83 F2 **North Bourke** N.S.W. Austr.
227 F4 **North Branch** MI U.S.A.
226 A3 **North Branch** MN U.S.A.
234 D2 **North Branch** NJ U.S.A.
235 F1 **North Branford** CT U.S.A.
246 E2 **North Caicos** i. Turks and Caicos Is
237 E5 **North Canadian** r. OK U.S.A.
North Cape c. Norway see Nordkapp
80 D1 **North Cape** c. North I. N.Z.
259 □ **North Cape** c. S. Georgia
226 C4 **North Cape** WI U.S.A.
234 D4 **North Cape May** NJ U.S.A.
231 E4 **North Carolina** state U.S.A.
234 C2 **North Catasauqua** PA U.S.A.
149 I4 **North Cave** East Riding of Yorkshire, England U.K.
224 D4 **North Channel** lake channel Ont. Can.
146 B6 **North Channel** Northern Ireland/Scotland U.K.
231 E5 **North Charleston** SC U.S.A.
150 E3 **North Cheriton** Somerset, England U.K.
87 C7 **Northcliffe** W.A. Austr.
232 D3 **North Collins** NY U.S.A.
237 C6 **North Concho** r. TX U.S.A.
233 □H2 **North Conway** NH U.S.A.
North Cousin Islet i. Inner Islands Seychelles see **Cousin**
222 F5 **North Cowichan** B.C. Can.
149 H3 **North Cowton** North Yorkshire, England U.K.
233 G3 **North Creek** NY U.S.A.
236 C2 **North Dakota** state U.S.A.
151 G3 **North Downs** hills England U.K.
149 I4 **North Duffield** North Yorkshire, England U.K.
213 E4 **North East** admin. dist. Botswana
234 C3 **North East** MD U.S.A.
232 D3 **North East** PA U.S.A.
85 H4 **North East Cay** rf Coral Sea Is Terr. Austr.
210 D4 **North-Eastern** prov. Kenya
North-East Frontier Agency state India see Arunachal Pradesh
149 I4 **North East Lincolnshire** admin. div. England U.K.
267 I4 **Northeast Pacific Basin** sea feature Pacific Ocean
246 C1 **Northeast Providence Channel** Bahamas
240 I4 **North Edwards** CA U.S.A.
169 E4 **Northeim** Ger.
151 H2 **North Elmham** Norfolk, England U.K.
206 E4 **Northern** admin. reg. Ghana
211 B7 **Northern** admin. reg. Malawi
213 F4 **Northern** prov. S. Africa
206 C4 **Northern** prov. Sierra Leone
203 F4 **Northern** state Sudan
209 F7 **Northern** prov. Zambia
Northern Aegean admin. reg. Greece see **Voreio Aigaio**
123 H2 **Northern Areas** admin. div. Pak.
208 E2 **Northern Bahr el Ghazal** state Sudan
214 B3 **Northern Cape** prov. S. Africa
81 □2 **Northern Cook Islands** Cook Is
202 E5 **Northern Darfur** state Sudan
Northern Donets r. Rus. Fed. see **Severskiy Donets**
Northern Dvina r. Rus. Fed. see **Severnaya Dvina**
147 E2 **Northern Ireland** prov. U.K.
203 F6 **Northern Kordofan** state Sudan
77 I3 **Northern Lau Group** is Fiji
91 J3 **Northern Mariana Islands** terr. N. Pacific Ocean
Northern Pindus Mountains Greece see **Voreia Pindos**
Northern Rhodesia country Africa see **Zambia**
Northern Sporades is Greece see **Voreioi Sporades**
84 C3 **Northern Territory** admin. div. Austr.
Northern Transvaal prov. S. Africa see **Northern**
146 F5 **North Esk** r. Angus, Scotland U.K.
146 E6 **North Esk** r. Midlothian/Scottish Borders, Scotland U.K.
236 F4 **North Fabius** r. MO U.S.A.
149 I4 **North Ferriby** East Riding of Yorkshire, England U.K.
233 G3 **Northfield** MA U.S.A.
226 A3 **Northfield** MN U.S.A.
234 D3 **Northfield** NJ U.S.A.
233 G2 **Northfield** VT U.S.A.
226 B3 **Northfield** WI U.S.A.
151 H3 **Northfleet** Kent, England U.K.
235 F1 **Northford** CT U.S.A.
151 I3 **North Foreland** c. England U.K.
240 H3 **North Fork** CA U.S.A.
235 F1 **North Franklin** CT U.S.A.
224 D3 **North French** r. Ont. Can.
North Frisian Islands Ger. see **Nordfriesische Inseln**
268 T1 **North Geomagnetic Pole** Arctic Ocean
149 I3 **North Grimston** North Yorkshire, England U.K.
235 F1 **North Haven** CT U.S.A.
233 □J2 **North Head** N.B. Can.
233 G2 **North Hero** VT U.S.A.
240 G2 **North Highlands** CA U.S.A.
233 G3 **North Hudson** NY U.S.A.
149 I4 **North Hykeham** Lincolnshire, England U.K.
151 G2 **Northill** Bedfordshire, England U.K.
84 D2 **North Island** N.T. Austr.
87 B6 **North Island** W.A. Austr.
80 D3 **North Island** N.Z.
241 L4 **North Jadito Canyon** gorge AZ U.S.A.
226 D5 **North Judson** IN U.S.A.
North Kazakhstan Oblast admin. div. Kazakh. see Severnyy Kazakhstan
85 F2 **North Kennedy** r. Qld Austr.
146 D4 **North Kessock** Highland, Scotland U.K.
232 C4 **North Kingsville** OH U.S.A.
223 M3 **North Knife** r. Man. Can.
117 E4 **North Koel** r. Bihar India
241 L5 **North Komelik** AZ U.S.A.
117 H4 **North Lakhimpur** Assam India
146 E6 **North Lanarkshire** admin. div. Scotland U.K.
80 E1 **Northland** admin. reg. North I. N.Z.
North Land is Rus. Fed. see Severnaya Zemlya
241 J3 **North Las Vegas** NV U.S.A.
151 F3 **Northleach** Gloucestershire, England U.K.
226 D5 **North Liberty** IN U.S.A.
232 C4 **North Lima** OH U.S.A.
149 I4 **North Lincolnshire** admin. div. England U.K.
237 E5 **North Little Rock** AR U.S.A.
236 D3 **North Loup** r. NE U.S.A.
222 C2 **North Macmillan** r. Y.T. Can.
235 F1 **North Madison** CT U.S.A.
221 H2 **North Magnetic Pole** Nunavut Can.
113 □1 **North Male Atoll** Maldives
239 F4 **North Mam Peak** CO U.S.A.
226 E5 **North Manchester** IN U.S.A.
232 A5 **North Middletown** KY U.S.A.
150 D3 **North Molton** Devon, England U.K.
234 B1 **North Mountain** mts PA U.S.A.
86 B4 **North Muiron Island** W.A. Austr.
222 F2 **North Nahanni** r. N.W.T. Can.
227 G5 **North Olmsted** OH U.S.A.
236 E2 **Northome** MN U.S.A.
North Ossetia aut. rep. Rus. Fed. see Severnaya Osetiya, Respublika
240 H3 **North Palisade** mt. CA U.S.A.
236 C3 **North Platte** NE U.S.A.
236 C3 **North Platte** r. NE U.S.A.
87 B6 **North Point** W.A. Austr.
268 A1 **North Pole** Arctic Ocean
231 C5 **Northport** AL U.S.A.
231 D7 **North Port** FL U.S.A.
226 E3 **Northport** MI U.S.A.
149 F1 **North Queensferry** Fife, Scotland U.K.
North Rhine - Westphalia land Ger. see Nordrhein-Westfalen
241 K3 **North Rim** AZ U.S.A.
225 I4 **North River Bridge** N.S. Can.
146 □G1 **North Roe** Shetland, Scotland U.K.
North Rona i. Western Isles, Scotland U.K. see **Rona**

342
North Ronaldsay to Oakey

146 F2 **North Ronaldsay** *i.* *Scotland* U.K.
146 F2 **North Ronaldsay Firth** *sea chan.* *Scotland* U.K.
238 B2 **North Santiam** *r.* *OR* U.S.A.
222 J4 **North Saskatchewan** *r.* *Alberta/Saskatchewan* Can.
241 J2 **North Schell Peak** *NV* U.S.A.
144 H3 **North Sea** *sea* Europe
235 F2 **North Sea** *NY* U.S.A.
223 L3 **North Seal** *r.* *Man.* Can.
149 H2 **North Shields** *Tyne and Wear, England* U.K.
240 I2 **North Shoshone Peak** *NV* U.S.A.
North Siberian Lowland Rus. Fed. *see* **Severo-Sibirskaya Nizmennost'**
North Sinai *governorate* Egypt *see* **Shamâl Sînâ'**
220 D3 **North Slope** *plain* *AK* U.S.A.
149 J4 **North Somercotes** *Lincolnshire, England* U.K.
150 E3 **North Somerset** *admin. div.* *England* U.K.
147 B3 **North Sound** *sea chan.* Rep. of Ireland
85 H5 **North Stradbroke Island** *Qld* Austr.
233 H2 **North Stratford** *NH* U.S.A.
149 H2 **North Sunderland** *Northumberland, England* U.K.
80 E3 **North Taranaki Bight** *b.* *North I.* N.Z.
222 F5 **North Thompson** *r.* *B.C.* Can.
149 I4 **North Thoresby** *Lincolnshire, England* U.K.
151 F3 **North Tidworth** *Wiltshire, England* U.K.
146 A4 **Northton** *Western Isles, Scotland* U.K.
232 D3 **North Tonawanda** *NY* U.S.A.
233 G2 **North Troy** *VT* U.S.A.
233 H3 **North Truro** *MA* U.S.A.
149 G3 **North Tyne** *r.* *England* U.K.
146 G4 **North Ugie** *r.* *Scotland* U.K.
146 A4 **North Uist** *i.* *Scotland* U.K.
149 G2 **Northumberland** *admin. div.* *England* U.K.
234 B2 **Northumberland** *PA* U.S.A.
234 B2 **Northumberland County** *county* *PA* U.S.A.
85 G4 **Northumberland Isles** *Qld* Austr.
149 G2 **Northumberland National Park** *England* U.K.
225 H4 **Northumberland Strait** Can.
238 B3 **North Umpqua** *r.* *OR* U.S.A.
222 F5 **North Vancouver** *B.C.* Can.
233 F3 **Northville** *NY* U.S.A.
234 C2 **North Wales** *PA* U.S.A.
151 I2 **North Walsham** *Norfolk, England* U.K.
233 □H2 **North Waterford** *ME* U.S.A.
151 H3 **North Weald Bassett** *Essex, England* U.K.
215 E2 **North West** *prov.* S. Africa
264 F1 **North West Atlantic Mid-Ocean Channnel** *sea chan.* N. Atlantic Ocean
86 B4 **North West Cape** *W.A.* Austr.
235 F1 **North Westchester** *CT* U.S.A.
209 D8 **North-Western** *prov.* Zambia
123 G3 **North West Frontier** *prov.* Pak.
266 F3 **Northwest Pacific Basin** *sea feature* N. Pacific Ocean
246 C1 **Northwest Providence Channel** Bahamas
225 J2 **North West River** *Nfld.* Can.
222 J2 **Northwest Territories** *admin. div.* Can.
149 G4 **Northwich** *Cheshire, England* U.K.
237 D5 **North Wichita** *r.* *TX* U.S.A.
234 D3 **North Wildwood** *NJ* U.S.A.
235 F1 **North Windham** *CT* U.S.A.
233 □H3 **North Windham** *ME* U.S.A.
268 N1 **Northwind Ridge** *sea feature* Arctic Ocean
149 H4 **North Wingfield** *Derbyshire, England* U.K.
151 F4 **Northwood** *Isle of Wight, England* U.K.
236 E3 **Northwood** *IA* U.S.A.
236 D2 **Northwood** *ND* U.S.A.
233 H3 **Northwood** *NH* U.S.A.
226 B3 **Northwoods Beach** *WI* U.S.A.
227 H4 **North York** *Ont.* Can.
149 I3 **North York Moors** *moorland* *England* U.K.
149 I3 **North York Moors National Park** *England* U.K.
149 H3 **North Yorkshire** *admin. div.* *England* U.K.
168 C2 **Nortmoor** Ger.
225 H4 **Norton** *N.B.* Can.
149 I3 **Norton** *North Yorkshire, England* U.K.
151 H2 **Norton** *Suffolk, England* U.K.
236 D4 **Norton** *KS* U.S.A.
232 B6 **Norton** *VA* U.S.A.
233 H2 **Norton** *VT* U.S.A.
213 F3 **Norton** Zimbabwe
149 H5 **Norton Canes** *Staffordshire, England* U.K.
Norton de Matos Angola *see* **Balombo**
150 D3 **Norton Fitzwarren** *Somerset, England* U.K.
226 D4 **Norton Shores** *MI* U.S.A.
220 B3 **Norton Sound** *sea chan.* *AK* U.S.A.
168 E1 **Nortorf** Ger.
168 C3 **Nortrup** Ger.
158 E4 **Nort-sur-Erdre** France
262 X2 **Norvegia, Cape** Antarctica
235 E1 **Norwalk** *CT* U.S.A.
232 B4 **Norwalk** *OH* U.S.A.
226 B4 **Norwalk** *WI* U.S.A.
235 E1 **Norwalk** *r.* *CT* U.S.A.
141 J3 **Norway** *country* Europe
233 □H2 **Norway** *ME* U.S.A.
227 I3 **Norway Bay** *Que.* Can.
223 L4 **Norway House** *Man.* Can.
264 I1 **Norwegian Basin** *sea feature* N. Atlantic Ocean
221 I2 **Norwegian Bay** *Nunavut* Can.
264 J1 **Norwegian Sea** N. Atlantic Ocean
227 G4 **Norwich** *Ont.* Can.
151 I2 **Norwich** *Norfolk, England* U.K.
233 G4 **Norwich** *CT* U.S.A.
233 F3 **Norwich** *NY* U.S.A.
146 □H1 **Norwick** *Shetland, Scotland* U.K.
233 H3 **Norwood** *MA* U.S.A.
231 D5 **Norwood** *NC* U.S.A.
233 F2 **Norwood** *NY* U.S.A.
232 A5 **Norwood** *OH* U.S.A.
92 B3 **Norzagaray** Phil.
102 J3 **Noshiro** Japan
137 F2 **Nosivka** Ukr.
136 D3 **Noskivtsi** Ukr.
214 C1 **Nosop** *watercourse* Africa *alt.* **Nossob**
Nosovka Ukr. *see* **Nosivka**
122 D4 **Noşratābād** Iran
146 □G1 **Noss, Isle of** *i.* *Scotland* U.K.
142 E2 **Nossan** *r.* Sweden
184 B2 **Nossa Senhora da Boa Fé** Port.
184 C1 **Nossa Senhora da Graça de Póvoa e Meadas** Port.
184 C2 **Nossa Senhora da Graça do Divor** Port.
184 C2 **Nossa Senhora das Neves** Port.
184 B2 **Nossa Senhora da Torega** Port.
184 C2 **Nossa Senhora de Machede** Port.
253 F3 **Nossa Senhora do Livramento** Brazil
216 □1b **Nossa Senhora dos Remédios** *São Miguel* Azores
142 E2 **Nossebro** Sweden
171 E4 **Nossen** Ger.
170 D2 **Nossendorf** Ger.
170 D2 **Nossentiner Hütte** Ger.
214 C2 **Nossob** *watercourse* Africa *alt.* **Nosop**
214 C1 **Nossob Camp** S. Africa
206 D3 **Nossombougou** Mali
213 □K4 **Nosy Varika** Madag.
176 G4 **Noszlop** Hungary
177 J4 **Noszvaj** Hungary
140 O1 **Nota** *r.* Fin./Rus. Fed.
225 I1 **Notakwanon** *r.* *Nfld.* Can.
193 F2 **Notaresco** Italy
241 K2 **Notch Peak** *UT* U.S.A.
174 D3 **Noteć** *r.* Pol.
198 B2 **Notia Pindos** *mts* Greece
222 G3 **Notikewin** *r.* *Alta* Can.
177 I4 **Nőtincs** Hungary
198 E3 **Notio Aigaio** *admin. reg.* Greece
Nótion Aiyaíon *admin. reg.* Greece *see* **Notio Aigaio**
198 C2 **Notios Evvoïkos Kolpos** *sea chan.* Greece
195 E6 **Noto** *Sicilia* Italy
195 E6 **Noto, Golfo di** *g.* *Sicilia* Italy
142 C2 **Notodden** Norway
104 C1 **Noto-hantō** *pen.* Japan
102 L1 **Notoro-ko** *l.* Japan
179 F5 **Notranje Gorice** Slovenia
225 G4 **Notre Dame, Monts** *mts* *Que.* Can.
225 K3 **Notre Dame Bay** *Nfld.* Can.
159 G2 **Notre-Dame-de-Gravenchon** France
Notre-Dame-de-Koartac *Que.* Can. *see* **Quaqtaq**
227 J3 **Notre-Dame-de-la-Salette** *Que.* Can.
158 D5 **Notre-Dame-de-Monts** France
158 E5 **Notre-Dame-de-Riez** France
162 C3 **Notre-Dame-de-Sanilhac** France
233 □H2 **Notre-Dame-des-Bois** *Que.* Can.
159 G4 **Notre-Dame-d'Oé** France
227 J2 **Notre-Dame-du-Laus** *Que.* Can.
227 H2 **Notre-Dame-du-Nord** *Que.* Can.
179 E4 **Nötsch im Gailtal** Austria
207 F5 **Notsé** Togo
102 L2 **Notsuke-suidō** *sea chan.* Japan/Rus. Fed.
227 G3 **Nottawasaga Bay** *Ont.* Can.
224 E3 **Nottaway** *r.* *Que.* Can.
168 E2 **Nottensdorf** Ger.
151 F2 **Nottingham** *Nottingham, England* U.K.
151 F2 **Nottingham** *admin. div.* *England* U.K.
234 B3 **Nottingham** *PA* U.S.A.
215 H3 **Nottingham Road** S. Africa
149 I4 **Nottinghamshire** *admin. div.* *England* U.K.
232 D6 **Nottoway** *VA* U.S.A.
232 E6 **Nottoway** *r.* *VA* U.S.A.
169 C4 **Nottuln** Ger.
223 J5 **Notukeu Creek** *r.* *Sask.* Can.
204 A5 **Nouâdhibou** Maur.
206 B2 **Nouakchott** Maur.
206 A2 **Nouâmghâr** Maur.
159 I4 **Nouan-le-Fuzelier** France
159 H4 **Nouans-les-Fontaines** France
157 F3 **Nouart** France
78 □5 **Nouméa** New Caledonia
207 H5 **Noun** *r.* Cameroon
206 E3 **Nouna** Burkina
215 E4 **Noupoort** S. Africa
Nouveau-Comptoir *Que.* Can. *see* **Wemindji**
Nouvelle Anvers Dem. Rep. Congo *see* **Makanza**
78 □5 **Nouvelle Calédonie** *i.* S. Pacific Ocean
Nouvelle Calédonie *terr.* S. Pacific Ocean *see* **New Caledonia**
Nouvelles Hébrides *country* S. Pacific Ocean *see* **Vanuatu**
156 B2 **Nouvion** France
158 E3 **Nouvoitou** France
159 G4 **Nouzilly** France
156 E3 **Nouzonville** France
123 G1 **Nov** Tajik.
176 F5 **Nova** Hungary
257 G4 **Nova Almeida** Brazil
254 C5 **Nova América** Brazil
256 A5 **Nova Andradina** Brazil
137 J3 **Nova Astrakhan'** Ukr.
256 C3 **Nova Aurora** Brazil
Novabad Tajik. *see* **Novobod**
Novabad Tajik. *see* **Novobod**
177 H3 **Nová Baňa** Slovakia
136 E2 **Nova Borova** Ukr.
176 E2 **Nová Bystřice** Czech Rep.
209 B6 **Nova Caipemba** Angola
256 A6 **Nova Cantu** Brazil
Nova Chaves Angola *see* **Muconda**
197 F3 **Novaci** Romania
196 E3 **Nova Crnja** *Vojvodina, Srbija* Yugo.
254 G3 **Nova Cruz** Brazil
177 H3 **Nová Dubnica** Slovakia
257 F3 **Nova Era** Brazil
Nova Esperança Angola *see* **Buengas**
256 A5 **Nova Esperança** Brazil
191 H5 **Novafeltria** Italy
Nova Freixa Moz. *see* **Cuamba**
257 F5 **Nova Friburgo** Brazil
Nova Gaia Angola *see* **Cambundi-Catembo**
Nova Goa *Goa* India *see* **Panaji**
213 G4 **Nova Golegã** Moz.
188 D3 **Nova Gorica** Slovenia
188 F3 **Nova Gradiška** Croatia
256 C4 **Nova Granada** Brazil
137 G3 **Nova Haleshchyna** Ukr.
257 F5 **Nova Iguaçu** Brazil
137 G4 **Nova Kakhovka** Ukr.
137 G4 **Nova Kam"yanka** Ukr.
177 H3 **Nováky** Slovakia
160 D3 **Novalaise** France
186 C2 **Novales** Spain
191 G2 **Nova Levante** Italy
257 F3 **Nova Lima** Brazil
Nova Lisboa Angola *see* **Huambo**
191 J4 **Novalja** Croatia
256 A5 **Nova Londrina** Brazil
177 J2 **Nová Ľubovňa** Slovakia
138 G4 **Novalukoml'** Belarus
213 G4 **Nova Mambone** Moz.
137 G4 **Nova Mayachka** Ukr.
137 F4 **Nova Odesa** Ukr.
176 E1 **Nová Paka** Czech Rep.
137 H3 **Nova Parafiyivka** Ukr.
196 E3 **Nova Pazova** *Vojvodina, Srbija* Yugo.
254 E4 **Nova Pilão Arcado** Brazil
256 D3 **Nova Ponte** Brazil
137 G3 **Nova Praha** Ukr.
190 D3 **Novara** Italy
190 D2 **Novara** *prov.* *Piemonte* Italy
195 E4 **Novara di Sicilia** *Sicilia* Italy
254 E4 **Nova Remanso** Brazil
256 D4 **Nova Resende** Brazil
171 D5 **Nová Role** Czech Rep.
254 D5 **Nova Roma** Brazil
254 E3 **Nova Russas** Brazil
225 H5 **Nova Scotia** *prov.* Can.
254 E4 **Nova Sento Sé** Brazil
257 E3 **Nova Serrana** Brazil
Nova Sintra Angola *see* **Catabola**
195 F2 **Nova Siri** Italy
137 H2 **Nova Sloboda** Ukr.
254 F4 **Nova Soure** Brazil
190 E2 **Novate Mezzola** Italy
240 F2 **Novato** *CA* U.S.A.
188 F3 **Nova Topola** Bos.-Herz.
134 I3 **Novator** Rus. Fed.
136 D3 **Nova Ushytsya** Ukr.
196 D4 **Nova Varoš** *Srbija* Yugo.
179 G1 **Nová Včelnice** Czech Rep.
257 G3 **Nova Venécia** Brazil
171 G5 **Nová Ves I** Czech Rep.
257 H2 **Nova Viçosa** Brazil
137 H3 **Nova Vodolaha** Ukr.
254 B5 **Nova Xavantino** Brazil
137 K2 **Novaya Chigla** Rus. Fed.
Novaya Kakhovka Ukr. *see* **Nova Kakhovka**
137 K2 **Novaya Kalitva** Rus. Fed.
120 B2 **Novaya Kazanka** Kazakh.
139 I1 **Novaya Ladoga** Rus. Fed.
Novaya Odessa Ukr. *see* **Nova Odesa**
Novaya Pismyanka Rus. Fed. *see* **Leninogorsk**
131 P2 **Novaya Sibir', Ostrov** *i.* *Novosibirskiye O-va* Rus. Fed.
137 J2 **Novaya Usman'** Rus. Fed.
Novaya Volodaga Ukr. *see* **Nova Vodolaha**
130 G2 **Novaya Zemlya** *is* Rus. Fed.
Novaya Zhizn *Lipetskaya Oblast'* Rus. Fed. *see* **Kazinka**
197 H4 **Nova Zagora** Bulg.
137 G4 **Nova Zbur"yivka** Ukr.
137 G3 **Nove** Ukr.
176 D3 **Nové Hrady** Czech Rep.
187 C6 **Novelda** Spain
191 F4 **Novellara** Italy
176 F1 **Nové Město nad Metuj** Czech Rep.
177 G3 **Nové Mesto nad Váhom** Slovakia
176 F2 **Nové Město na Moravé** Czech Rep.
175 K6 **Nove Misto** Ukr.
176 B6 **Noventa di Piave** Italy
191 G3 **Noventa Vicentina** Italy
161 C5 **Noves** France
183 F4 **Novés** Spain
171 D5 **Nové Sedlo** Czech Rep.
171 E5 **Nové Strašecí** Czech Rep.
177 H4 **Nové Zámky** Slovakia
Novgorod Rus. Fed. *see* **Velikiy Novgorod**
Novgorod Oblast *admin. div.* Rus. Fed. *see* **Novgorodskaya Oblast'**
Novgorod-Severskiy Ukr. *see* **Novhorod-Sivers'kyy**
139 I2 **Novgorodskaya Oblast'** *admin. div.* Rus. Fed.
Novgorod-Volynskiy Ukr. *see* **Novohrad-Volyns'kyy**
Novgradets Bulg. *see* **Suvorovo**
137 G3 **Novhorodka** Ukr.
137 G2 **Novhorod-Sivers'kyy** Ukr.
137 I3 **Novhorods'ke** Ukr.
227 F4 **Novi** *MI* U.S.A.
196 E3 **Novi Bečej** *Vojvodina, Srbija* Yugo.
136 E2 **Novi Bilokorovychi** Ukr.
137 F2 **Novi Borovychi** Ukr.
136 C2 **Novi Chervyshcha** Ukr.
121 J1 **Novichikha** Rus. Fed.
191 F4 **Novi di Modena** Italy
183 H3 **Noviergas** Spain
Novi Grad Bos.-Herz. *see* **Bosanski Novi**
191 I3 **Novigrad** Croatia
176 F5 **Novigrad Podravski** Croatia
197 F4 **Novi Iskŭr** Bulg.
177 J5 **Novi Kneževac** *Vojvodina, Srbija* Yugo.
100 G3 **Novikovo** *Sakhalin* Rus. Fed.
196 E3 **Novi Kozarci** *Vojvodina, Srbija* Yugo.
Novi Kritsim Bulg. *see* **Stamboliyski**
190 D4 **Novi Ligure** Italy
160 E1 **Novillars** France
165 D4 **Noville** Belgium
244 B2 **Novillero** Mex.
188 F2 **Novi Marof** Croatia
137 G2 **Novi Mlyny** Ukr.
156 E3 **Novion-Porcien** France
197 H4 **Novi Pazar** Bulg.
196 E4 **Novi Pazar** *Srbija* Yugo.
196 D3 **Novi Sad** *Vojvodina, Srbija* Yugo.
137 H3 **Novi Sanzhary** Ukr.
175 M6 **Novi Strilyshcha** Ukr.
188 F3 **Novi Travnik** Bos.-Herz.
188 E3 **Novi Vinodolski** Croatia
139 M3 **Novki** Rus. Fed.
100 G3 **Novoaleksandropov** *Sakhalin* Rus. Fed.
137 J2 **Novoaleksandrovka** Rus. Fed.
135 H7 **Novoaleksandrovsk** Rus. Fed.
Novoalekseyevka Kazakh. *see* **Khobda**
98 D1 **Novoaltaysk** Rus. Fed.
137 J4 **Novoamvrosiyivs'ke** Ukr.
135 H6 **Novoanninskiy** Rus. Fed.
251 F6 **Novo Aripuanã** Brazil
136 F3 **Novoarkhanhel's'k** Ukr.
137 J3 **Novoaydar** Ukr.
137 J4 **Novoazovs'k** Ukr.
137 J4 **Novobataysk** Rus. Fed.
137 J3 **Novobelaya** Rus. Fed.
196 E3 **Novo Beograd** *Srbija* Yugo.
137 J5 **Novobeysugskaya** Rus. Fed.
137 J3 **Novobila** Ukr.
123 G2 **Novobod** Tajik.
123 G2 **Novobod** Tajik.
Novobogatinsk Kazakh. *see* **Novobogatinskoye**
120 B3 **Novobogatinskoye** Kazakh.
137 H4 **Novobohdanivka** Ukr.
137 J3 **Novoborove** Ukr.
100 D2 **Novobureyskiy** Rus. Fed.
134 I4 **Novocheboksarsk** Rus. Fed.
135 J5 **Novocheremshansk** Rus. Fed.
135 H7 **Novocherkassk** Rus. Fed.
257 G2 **Novo Cruzeiro** Brazil
137 H4 **Novodanylivka** Ukr.
137 J4 **Novoderevyankovskaya** Rus. Fed.
136 D3 **Novodnistrovs'k** Ukr.
121 H2 **Novodolinka** Kazakh.
137 I3 **Novodonets'ke** Ukr.
137 J3 **Novodruzhes'k** Ukr.
139 J4 **Novodugino** Rus. Fed.
134 H2 **Novodvinsk** *Arkhangel'skaya Oblast'* Rus. Fed.
Novoekonomicheskoye Ukr. *see* **Dymytrov**
136 E3 **Novofastiv** Ukr.
137 F4 **Novofedorivka** Ukr.
Novogroznenskiy Rus. Fed. *see* **Oyskhara**
Novogrudok Belarus *see* **Navahrudak**
139 K4 **Novogurovskiy** Rus. Fed.
255 C9 **Novo Hamburgo** Brazil
137 H4 **Novohorivka** Ukr.
256 C4 **Novo Horizonte** Brazil
137 G4 **Novohradivka** Ukr.
176 D3 **Novohradské Hory** *mts* Czech Rep.
136 D2 **Novohrad-Volyns'kyy** Ukr.
137 I3 **Novohrodivka** Ukr.
137 H4 **Novohryhorivka** Ukr.
137 H4 **Novoivanivka** Ukr.
129 D3 **Novoivanovka** Azer.
120 D1 **Novokaolinovyy** Rus. Fed.
129 E2 **Novokayakent** Rus. Fed.
Novokazalinsk Kazakh. *see* **Ayteke Bi**
135 H6 **Novokhopersk** Rus. Fed.
100 D2 **Novokiyevskiy Uval** Rus. Fed.
137 F4 **Novokostyantynivka** Ukr.
137 F3 **Novokrasne** Ukr.
137 J3 **Novokrasnyanka** Ukr.
135 H7 **Novokubansk** Rus. Fed.
Novokubanskiy Rus. Fed. *see* **Novokubansk**
120 B1 **Novokuybyshevsk** Rus. Fed.
130 J4 **Novokuznetsk** Rus. Fed.
137 G4 **Novokyyivka** Ukr.
129 E2 **Novolakskoye** Rus. Fed.
263 A2 **Novolazarevskaya** *research stn* Antarctica
137 J5 **Novoleushkovskaya** Rus. Fed.
Novolukoml' Belarus *see* **Novalukoml'**
139 L5 **Novol'vovsk** Rus. Fed.
137 J5 **Novomalorossiyskaya** Rus. Fed.
121 H2 **Novomarkovka** Kazakh.
137 H3 **Novomar"yivka** Ukr.
137 K2 **Novomelovatka** Rus. Fed.
188 E3 **Novo Mesto** Slovenia
139 L4 **Novomichurinsk** Rus. Fed.
135 G7 **Novomikhaylovskiy** Rus. Fed.
196 E3 **Novo Miloševo** *Vojvodina, Srbija* Yugo.
137 J4 **Novominskaya** Rus. Fed.
Novomirgorod Ukr. *see* **Novomyrhorod**
139 L4 **Novomoskovsk** Rus. Fed.
137 H3 **Novomoskovs'k** Ukr.
137 H4 **Novomykhaylivka** Ukr.
137 J3 **Novomykil's'ke** Ukr.
137 H3 **Novomykolayivka** *Dnipropetrovs'ka Oblast'* Ukr.
137 G4 **Novomykolayivka** *Khersons'ka Oblast'* Ukr.
137 H4 **Novomykolayivka** *Khersons'ka Oblast'* Ukr.
137 H4 **Novomykolayivka** *Zaporiz'ka Oblast'* Ukr.
137 F3 **Novomyrhorod** Ukr.
137 G4 **Novonatalivka** Ukr.
Novonazyvayevka Rus. Fed. *see* **Nazyvayevsk**
121 G4 **Novonikolayevka** Kazakh.
Novonikolayevsk Rus. Fed. *see* **Novosibirsk**
137 J5 **Novonikolayevskaya** Rus. Fed.
135 H6 **Novonikolayevskiy** Rus. Fed.
137 H4 **Novooleksandrivka** Ukr.
137 H4 **Novooleksiyivka** Ukr.
251 G5 **Novo Olinda do Norte** Brazil
177 I6 **Novo Orahovo** *Vojvodina, Srbija* Yugo.
254 E3 **Novo Oriente** Brazil
120 D2 **Novoorsk** Rus. Fed.
137 G2 **Novoorzhyts'ke** Ukr.
137 G5 **Novoozerne** Ukr.
136 E2 **Novoozeryanka** Ukr.
254 E3 **Novo Parnarama** Brazil
Novopashiyskiy *Permskaya Oblast'* Rus. Fed. *see* **Gornozavodsk**
137 I3 **Novopavlivka** *Dnipropetrovs'ka Oblast'* Ukr.
136 F4 **Novopavlivka** *Mykolayivs'ka Oblast'* Ukr.
107 F1 **Novopavlovka** Rus. Fed.
129 C2 **Novopavlovsk** Rus. Fed.
Novopavlovskaya Rus. Fed. *see* **Novopavlovsk**
137 H3 **Novopetrivka** Ukr.
137 H3 **Novopidkryazh** Ukr.
120 F1 **Novopokrovka** *Kustanayskaya Oblast'* Kazakh.
121 F1 **Novopokrovka** *Severnyy Kazakhstan* Kazakh.
121 J2 **Novopokrovka** *Vostochnyy Kazakhstan* Kazakh.
100 E3 **Novopokrovka** *Primorskiy Kray* Rus. Fed.
137 K1 **Novopokrovka** *Tambovskaya Oblast'* Rus. Fed.
137 H3 **Novopokrovka** Ukr.
135 H7 **Novopokrovskaya** Rus. Fed.
Novopolotsk Belarus *see* **Navapolatsk**
137 G4 **Novopoltavka** *Mykolayivs'ka Oblast'* Ukr.
137 I4 **Novopoltavka** *Zaporiz'ka Oblast'* Ukr.
137 J3 **Novopskov** Ukr.
Novo Redondo Angola *see* **Sumbe**
120 B2 **Novorepnoye** Rus. Fed.
135 G7 **Novorossiysk** Rus. Fed.
Novorossiyskiy Kazakh. *see* **Novorossiyskoye**
120 D2 **Novorossiyskoye** Kazakh.
137 J5 **Novorozhdestvenskaya** Rus. Fed.
121 F1 **Novorybinka** Kazakh.
138 G3 **Novorzhev** Rus. Fed.
136 E4 **Novosamarka** Ukr.
129 D3 **Novosaratovka** Azer.
171 E5 **Novosedlice** Czech Rep.
176 F3 **Novosedly** Czech Rep.
129 C1 **Novoselitskoye** Rus. Fed.
136 E4 **Novoselivka** Ukr.
137 G5 **Novoselivs'ke** Ukr.
197 F5 **Novo Selo** Macedonia
139 L3 **Novoselovo** Rus. Fed.
Novoselskoye Rus. Fed. *see* **Achkhoy-Martan**
138 G2 **Novosel'ye** Rus. Fed.
136 D3 **Novoselytsya** Ukr.
120 C1 **Novosergiyevka** Rus. Fed.
135 G7 **Novoshakhtinsk** Rus. Fed.
100 E3 **Novoshakhtinskiy** Rus. Fed.
137 J4 **Novoshcherbinovskaya** Rus. Fed.
135 J5 **Novosheshminsk** Rus. Fed.
130 J4 **Novosibirsk** Rus. Fed.
131 P2 **Novosibirskiye Ostrova** *is* Rus. Fed.
139 K5 **Novosil'** Rus. Fed.
137 J2 **Novosil'skoye** Rus. Fed.
137 G4 **Novosofiyivka** Ukr.
139 H3 **Novosokol'niki** Rus. Fed.
120 A1 **Novospasskoye** Rus. Fed.
137 J3 **Novosvitlivka** Ukr.
177 I2 **Novoť** Slovakia
137 J5 **Novotitarovskaya** Rus. Fed.
120 D2 **Novotroitsk** Rus. Fed.
Novotroitskoye Kazakh. *see* **Tole Bi**
137 I4 **Novotroyits'ke** Ukr.
137 H4 **Novotroyits'ke** Ukr.
137 H4 **Novotroyits'ke** Ukr.
Novoukrainka *Kirovohrads'ka Oblast'* Ukr. *see* **Novoukrayinka**
Novoukrainka *Rivnens'ka Oblast'* Ukr. *see* **Novoukrayinka**
137 F3 **Novoukrayinka** *Kirovohrads'ka Oblast'* Ukr.
136 C2 **Novoukrayinka** *Rivnens'ka Oblast'* Ukr.
120 D2 **Novoural'sk** Rus. Fed.
120 B2 **Novouzensk** Rus. Fed.
121 H1 **Novovarshavka** Rus. Fed.
137 H4 **Novovasylivka** *Zaporiz'ka Oblast'* Ukr.
137 I4 **Novovasylivka** *Zaporiz'ka Oblast'* Ukr.
136 C2 **Novovolyns'k** Ukr.
135 G6 **Novovoronezh** Rus. Fed.
Novovoronezhskiy Rus. Fed. *see* **Novovoronezh**
137 G4 **Novovorontsovka** Ukr.
137 G4 **Novovoskresens'ke** Ukr.
121 I4 **Novovoznesenovka** Kyrg.
137 H3 **Novov"yazivs'ke** Ukr.
136 B3 **Novoyavorivs'ke** Ukr.
139 L5 **Novoye Dubovoye** Rus. Fed.
121 J2 **Novoyegor'yevskoye** Rus. Fed.
139 M3 **Novoye Leushino** Rus. Fed.
139 K3 **Novozavidovskiy** Rus. Fed.
136 E3 **Novozhyvotiv** Ukr.
139 H5 **Novozybkov** Rus. Fed.
188 F3 **Novska** Croatia
176 D1 **Nový Bor** Czech Rep.
176 E1 **Nový Bydžov** Czech Rep.
156 E3 **Novy-Chevrières** France
Novyj Cholmogory Rus. Fed. *see* **Arkhangel'sk**
Novyj Holmogory Rus. Fed. *see* **Arkhangel'sk**
177 G2 **Nový Jičín** Czech Rep.
176 G2 **Nový Malín** Czech Rep.
Novyy Afon Georgia *see* **Akhali Ap'oni**
134 K2 **Novyy Bor** Rus. Fed.
Novyy Bug Ukr. *see* **Novyy Buh**
137 G4 **Novyy Buh** Ukr.
137 F2 **Novyy Bykiv** Ukr.
Novyy Donbass Ukr. *see* **Dymytrov**
Novyye Aneny Moldova *see* **Anenii Noi**
Novyye Belokorovichi Ukr. *see* **Novi Bilokorovychi**
120 A1 **Novyye Burasy** Rus. Fed.
Novyye Petushki Rus. Fed. *see* **Petushki**
Novyy Kholmogory Rus. Fed. *see* **Arkhangel'sk**
Novyy Margelan Uzbek. *see* **Fergana**
137 H3 **Novyy Merchyk** Ukr.
139 L3 **Novyy Nekouz** Rus. Fed.
135 G6 **Novyy Oskol** Rus. Fed.
136 C3 **Novyy Rozdil** Ukr.
137 G3 **Novyystarodub** Ukr.
137 J4 **Novyy Svit** *Donets'ka Oblast'* Ukr.
137 H5 **Novyy Svit** *Respublika Krym* Ukr.
129 E2 **Novyy Terek** *r.* Rus. Fed.
134 J4 **Novyy Tor'yal** Rus. Fed.
130 I3 **Novyy Urengoy** Rus. Fed.
100 E2 **Novyy Urgal** Rus. Fed.
Novyy Uzen' Kazakh. *see* **Zhanaozen**
175 M5 **Novyy Vytkiv** Ukr.
175 M6 **Novyy Yarychiv** Ukr.
134 K5 **Novyy Zay** Rus. Fed.
176 G3 **Nový Život** Slovakia
175 H4 **Nowa Brzeźnica** Pol.
175 L2 **Nowa Chodorówka** Pol.
175 J5 **Nowa Dęba** Pol.
174 G1 **Nowa Karczma** Pol.
174 E5 **Nowa Ruda** Pol.
175 K5 **Nowa Sarzyna** Pol.
175 J5 **Nowa Słupia** Pol.
174 D4 **Nowa Sól** Pol.
237 E4 **Nowata** *OK* U.S.A.
175 K2 **Nowa Wieś Ełcka** Pol.
174 F1 **Nowa Wieś Lęborskie** Pol.
174 G3 **Nowa Wieś Wielka** Pol.
175 J4 **Nowa Wola Gołębiowska** Pol.
122 B2 **Nowdī** Iran
174 G2 **Nowe** Pol.
175 I5 **Nowe Brzesko** Pol.
174 D4 **Nowe Miasteczko** Pol.
175 I3 **Nowe Miasto** Pol.
175 H2 **Nowe Miasto Lubawskie** Pol.
175 I4 **Nowe Miasto nad Pilicą** Pol.
147 B5 **Nowen Hill** *hill* Rep. of Ireland
175 H3 **Nowe Ostrowy** Pol.
175 K3 **Nowe Piekuty** Pol.
174 F4 **Nowe Skalmierzyce** Pol.
174 C2 **Nowe Warpno** Pol.
Nowgong *Assam* India *see* **Nagaon**
116 D4 **Nowgong** *Madh. Prad.* India
175 K2 **Nowinka** Pol.
122 C2 **Now Kharegan** Iran
175 K4 **Nowodwór** Pol.
174 D2 **Nowogard** Pol.
175 J2 **Nowogród** Pol.
174 D4 **Nowogród Bobrzański** Pol.
174 D3 **Nowogródek Pomorski** Pol.
174 D4 **Nowogrodziec** Pol.
238 F2 **Nowood** *r.* *WY* U.S.A.
Noworadomsk Pol. *see* **Radomsko**
175 L3 **Nowosady** Pol.
175 K6 **Nowosielce** Pol.
175 K5 **Nowosielec** Pol.
175 H4 **Nowosolna** Pol.
83 G3 **Nowra** *N.S.W.* Austr.
122 B2 **Now Shahr** Iran
123 H3 **Nowshera** Pak.
175 K3 **Nowy Bartków** Pol.
175 H3 **Nowy Duninów** Pol.
174 F2 **Nowy Dwór** Pol.
175 L2 **Nowy Dwór** Pol.
143 H4 **Nowy Dwór Gdański** Pol.
175 I3 **Nowy Dwór Mazowiecki** Pol.
175 I5 **Nowy Korczyn** Pol.
175 L5 **Nowy Lubliniec** Pol.
175 I6 **Nowy Sącz** Pol.
143 H4 **Nowy Staw** Pol.
175 I6 **Nowy Targ** Pol.
174 E3 **Nowy Tomyśl** Pol.
175 J6 **Nowy Żmigród** Pol.
227 I5 **Noxen** *PA* U.S.A.
96 D3 **Noy, Xé** *r.* Laos
Noya *Cataluña* Spain *see* **L'Anoia**
Noya *Galicia* Spain *see* **Noia**
130 I3 **Noyabr'sk** Rus. Fed.
158 D4 **Noyal-Muzillac** France
158 D4 **Noyalo** France
158 D3 **Noyal-Pontivy** France
159 G4 **Noyant** France
159 F4 **Noyant-la-Plaine** France
161 D3 **Noyarey** France
129 D3 **Noyemberyan** Armenia
159 F4 **Noyen-sur-Sarthe** France
156 D5 **Noyers** France
159 H4 **Noyers-sur-Cher** France
161 D4 **Noyers-sur-Jabron** France
114 C4 **Noyil** *r.* India
156 C3 **Noyon** France
158 E4 **Nozay** France
175 K6 **Nozdrzec** Pol.
160 E2 **Nozeroy** France
129 E2 **Nozhay-Yurt** Rus. Fed.
215 E4 **Nozizwe** S. Africa
178 B5 **Nozza** *r.* Italy
210 B4 **Npitamaiong** *mt.* Kenya
215 H4 **Nqabeni** S. Africa
215 F5 **Nqamakwe** S. Africa
215 H3 **Nqutu** S. Africa
211 A8 **Nsalamu** Zambia
211 B8 **Nsanje** Malawi
206 E5 **Nsawam** Ghana
207 H6 **Nsoc** Equat. Guinea
209 F7 **Nsombo** Zambia
207 G5 **Nsukka** Nigeria
209 E8 **Ntambu** Zambia
208 C5 **Ntandembele** Dem. Rep. Congo
211 B8 **Ntcheu** Malawi
211 B8 **Ntchisi** Malawi
207 H6 **Ntem** *r.* Cameroon
215 F2 **Ntha** S. Africa
215 G2 **Nthorwane** S. Africa
215 G4 **Ntibane** S. Africa
208 A4 **Ntoum** Gabon
217 □3a **Ntsamouéni** *Njazidja* Comoros
217 □3a **Ntsoudjini** *Njazidja* Comoros
207 H5 **Ntui** Cameroon
211 A5 **Ntungamo** Uganda
212 E4 **Ntwetwe Pan** *salt pan* Botswana
215 G4 **Ntywenka** S. Africa
159 F4 **Nuaillé** France
162 B2 **Nuaillé-d'Aunis** France
Nuanetsi *r.* Zimbabwe *see* **Mwenezi**
234 C1 **Nuangola** *PA* U.S.A.
203 F4 **Nuba, Lake** *resr* Sudan
210 A2 **Nuba Mountains** Sudan
168 E1 **Nübbel** Ger.
245 F5 **Nube Flan, Cerro** *mt.* Mex.
168 E1 **Nübel** Ger.
203 G4 **Nubian Desert** Sudan
140 M1 **Nubivarri** *hill* Norway
260 A5 **Ñuble** *r.* Chile
182 E1 **Nubledo** Spain
197 F2 **Nucet** Romania
241 M2 **Nucla** *CO* U.S.A.
171 D4 **Nudersdorf** Ger.
169 F5 **Nüdlingen** Ger.
139 K3 **Nudol'** Rus. Fed.
175 M4 **Nudyzhe** Ukr.
237 D7 **Nueces** *r.* *TX* U.S.A.
159 F5 **Nueil-sur-Argent** France
223 L2 **Nueltin Lake** *Man./Nunavut* Can.
165 E3 **Nuenen** Neth.
186 C2 **Nueno** Spain
187 E6 **Nuestra Señora del Pilar** Spain
183 F1 **Nueva** Spain
259 D9 **Nueva, Isla** *i.* Chile
250 C6 **Nueva Alejandría** Peru
242 □H6 **Nueva Arcadia** Hond.
185 F3 **Nueva-Carteya** Spain
237 D7 **Nueva Ciudad Guerrero** Mex.
251 E2 **Nueva Esparta** *state* Venez.
253 F5 **Nueva Germania** Para.
246 B2 **Nueva Gerona** Cuba
261 I4 **Nueva Helvecia** Uru.
260 A6 **Nueva Imperial** Chile
244 C4 **Nueva Italia de Ruiz** Mex.
184 D4 **Nueva Jarilla** Spain
250 B4 **Nueva Loja** Ecuador
242 □H6 **Nueva Ocotepeque** Hond.
261 H3 **Nueva Palmira** Uru.
243 E3 **Nueva Rosita** Mex.
243 H6 **Nueva San Salvador** El Salvador
245 E1 **Nueva Villa de Padilla** Mex.
Nueve de Julio Arg. *see* **9 de Julio**
246 C2 **Nuevitas** Cuba
243 H4 **Nuevo, Cayo** *i.* Mex.
261 I3 **Nuevo Berlín** Uru.
242 D2 **Nuevo Casas Grandes** Mex.
242 D3 **Nuevo Ideal** Mex.
243 F3 **Nuevo Laredo** Mex.
241 J5 **Nuevo León** Mex.
244 E1 **Nuevo León** *state* Mex.
106 B1 **Nuga** Mongolia
210 F2 **Nugaal** *admin. reg.* Somalia
85 G5 **Nuga Nuga, Lake** *Qld* Austr.
81 B7 **Nugget Point** *South I.* N.Z.
192 B4 **Nughedu di San Nicolò** *Sardegna* Italy
139 K5 **Nugr'** *r.* Rus. Fed.
203 G3 **Nugrus, Gebel** *mt.* Egypt
114 C3 **Nugu** *r.* India
123 E5 **Nuh, Ras** *pt* Pak.
80 F3 **Nuhaka** *North I.* N.Z.
199 G2 **Nuhköy** Turkey
77 H2 **Nui** *i.* Tuvalu
Nui Con Voi *r.* Vietnam *see* **Hông, Sông**
159 F4 **Nuillé-sur-Vicoin** France
96 D4 **Nui Ti On** *mt.* Vietnam
156 E5 **Nuits** France
160 C1 **Nuits-St-Georges** France
108 A3 **Nu Jiang** *r.* China
Nu Jiang *r.* Myanmar *see* **Salween**
82 C3 **Nukey Bluff** *hill* *S.A.* Austr.
Nukha Azer. *see* **Şäki**
79 □2a **Nuku'alofa** *Tongatapu* Tonga
77 H2 **Nukufetau** *i.* Tuvalu
Nukuhiva *i.* Fr. Polynesia *see* **Nuku Hiva**
79 □3 **Nuku Hiva** *i.* Fr. Polynesia
77 H2 **Nukulaelae** *i.* Tuvalu
Nukulailai *i.* Tuvalu *see* **Nukulaelae**
Nukunau *i.* *Gilbert Is* Kiribati *see* **Nikunau**
Nukunono *atoll* Tokelau *see* **Nukunonu**
81 □1 **Nukunonu** *atoll* Tokelau
120 D4 **Nukus** Uzbek.
164 E3 **Nuland** Neth.
220 C3 **Nulato** *AK* U.S.A.
192 B4 **Nule** *Sardegna* Italy
187 C5 **Nules** Spain
86 D4 **Nullagine** *W.A.* Austr.
86 D4 **Nullagine** *r.* *W.A.* Austr.
82 B2 **Nullarbor** *S.A.* Austr.
82 B2 **Nullarbor Plain** *S.A.* Austr.
107 H3 **Nulu'erhu Shan** *mts* China
192 A4 **Nulvi** *Sardegna* Italy
83 F2 **Numalla, Lake** *salt flat* *Qld* Austr.
207 I4 **Numan** Nigeria
191 I5 **Numana** Italy
92 C4 **Numancia** Phil.
164 D3 **Numansdorp** Neth.
105 F2 **Numata** Japan
105 E3 **Numazu** Japan
215 H1 **Numbi Gate** S. Africa
84 C2 **Numbulwar** *N.T.* Austr.
142 C1 **Numedal** *val.* Norway
100 C3 **Numin** *r.* China
141 M3 **Nummi** Fin.
83 F4 **Numurkah** *Vic.* Austr.
221 N3 **Nunap Isua** *c.* Greenland
224 E1 **Nunavik** *reg.* Can.
223 L2 **Nunavut** *admin. div.* Can.
250 C3 **Nunchía** Col.
171 E4 **Nünchritz** Ger.
232 E3 **Nunda** *NY* U.S.A.
83 G2 **Nundle** *N.S.W.* Austr.
151 F2 **Nuneaton** *Warwickshire, England* U.K.
87 C6 **Nungarin** *W.A.* Austr.
107 H2 **Nungnain Sum** *Nei Mongol* China
213 H2 **Nungo** Moz.
220 B4 **Nunivak Island** *AK* U.S.A.
117 F5 **Nunkapasi** *Orissa* India
172 A2 **Nunkirchen** Ger.
116 D2 **Nunkun** *mt.* Jammu and Kashmir
131 T3 **Nunligran** Rus. Fed.
252 C3 **Nuñoa** Peru
182 D4 **Nuñomoral** Spain
171 E3 **Nunsdorf** Ger.
164 E2 **Nunspeet** Neth.
Nuojiang *Sichuan* China *see* **Tongjiang**
107 J1 **Nuomin** *r.* China
192 B4 **Nuoro** *Sardegna* Italy
192 B4 **Nuoro** *prov.* *Sardegna* Italy
78 □6 **Nupani** *i.* *Santa Cruz Is* Solomon Is
124 C2 **Nuqrah** Saudi Arabia
250 B3 **Nuquí** Col.
122 C2 **Nur** *r.* Iran
175 K3 **Nur** Pol.
121 G2 **Nura** *r.* Kazakh.
122 B4 **Nūrābād** Iran
192 B5 **Nuragus** *Sardegna* Italy
Nurakita *i.* Tuvalu *see* **Niulakita**
192 B5 **Nurallao** *Sardegna* Italy
192 B5 **Nuraminis** *Sardegna* Italy
120 F4 **Nurata** Uzbek.
121 F4 **Nuratau, Khrebet** *mts* Uzbek.
128 C1 **Nurdağı** Turkey
126 D3 **Nur Dağları** *mts* Turkey
190 E3 **Nure** *r.* Italy
192 A5 **Nureci** *Sardegna* Italy
Nurek Tajik. *see* **Norak**
Nurek Reservoir *l.* Tajik. *see* **Obanbori Norak**
Nurekskoye Vodokhranilishche *l.* Tajik. *see* **Obanbori Norak**
Nuremberg Ger. *see* **Nürnberg**
234 B2 **Nuremberg** *PA* U.S.A.
242 C2 **Nuri** Mex.
203 G5 **Nuri** Sudan
193 F2 **Nuria, Monte** *mt.* Italy
116 D2 **Nurla** Jammu and Kashmir
135 J5 **Nurlat** Rus. Fed.
134 J5 **Nurlaty** Rus. Fed.
140 O3 **Nurmes** Fin.
141 N3 **Nurmijärvi** Fin.
140 M3 **Nurmo** Fin.
173 F2 **Nürnberg** Ger.
148 C5 **Nurney** *Carlow* Rep. of Ireland
148 C4 **Nurney** *Kildare* Rep. of Ireland
Nurota Uzbek. *see* **Nurata**
123 G4 **Nurpur** Pak.
82 B2 **Nurrai Lakes** *salt flat* *S.A.* Austr.
192 B5 **Nurri** *Sardegna* Italy
83 F2 **Nurri, Mount** *hill* *N.S.W.* Austr.
140 K2 **Nursfjellet** *mt.* Norway
Nursia Italy *see* **Norcia**
172 D3 **Nürtingen** Ger.
175 K3 **Nurzec** *r.* Pol.
175 L3 **Nurzec-Stacja** Pol.
190 C3 **Nus** Italy
95 G5 **Nusa Tenggara Barat** *prov.* Indon.
93 B5 **Nusa Tenggara Timur** *prov.* Indon.
127 F3 **Nusaybin** Turkey
193 H4 **Nusco** Italy
93 D3 **Nusela, Kepulauan** *is* *Irian Jaya* Indon.
197 F2 **Nuşfalău** Romania
108 A3 **Nu Shan** *mts* China
123 F4 **Nushki** Pak.
172 C3 **Nusplingen** Ger.
179 F3 **Nußbach** Austria
173 G4 **Nußdorf** Ger.
173 G4 **Nußdorf am Inn** Ger.
178 D4 **Nußdorf-Debant** Austria
168 F2 **Nusse** Ger.
225 I1 **Nutak** *Nfld.* Can.
165 E4 **Nuth** Neth.
171 E3 **Nuthe** *r.* Ger.
151 G3 **Nuthurst** *West Sussex, England* U.K.
235 D2 **Nutley** *NJ* U.S.A.
241 M5 **Nutrioso** *AZ* U.S.A.
147 E2 **Nutt's Corner** *Northern Ireland* U.K.
84 C2 **Nutwood Downs** *N.T.* Austr.
221 M3 **Nuuk** Greenland
221 M2 **Nuussuaq** *pen.* Greenland
125 F2 **Nuway** Oman
214 B4 **Nuwerus** S. Africa
214 C5 **Nuweveldberge** *mts* S. Africa
192 A5 **Nuxis** *Sardegna* Italy
175 M4 **Nuyno** Ukr.
87 C7 **Nuyts, Point** *W.A.* Austr.
82 C3 **Nuyts Archipelago** *is* *S.A.* Austr.
178 A3 **Nüziders** Austria
114 D2 **Nuzvid** *Andhra Prad.* India
207 H5 **Nwa** Cameroon
212 E3 **Nxai Pan National Park** Botswana
95 F2 **Nyaän, Bukit** *hill* Indon.
87 C7 **Nyabing** *W.A.* Austr.
233 G4 **Nyack** *NY* U.S.A.
130 H3 **Nyagan'** Rus. Fed.
Nyagquka *Sichuan* China *see* **Yajiang**
Nyagrong *Sichuan* China *see* **Xinlong**
83 E3 **Nyah West** *Vic.* Austr.
111 E6 **Nyainqêntanglha Feng** *mt.* *Xizang* China
111 E6 **Nyainqêntanglha Shan** *mts* *Xizang* China
111 F5 **Nyainrong** *Xizang* China
215 F2 **Nyakallong** S. Africa
140 L3 **Nyåker** Sweden
Nyakh Rus. Fed. *see* **Nyagan'**
206 E5 **Nyakrom** Ghana
202 E6 **Nyala** Sudan
111 D6 **Nyalam** *Xizang* China
213 F3 **Nyamandhiovu** Zimbabwe
211 C7 **Nyamtumbo** Tanz.
Nyande Zimbabwe *see* **Masvingo**
134 H3 **Nyandoma** Rus. Fed.
134 G3 **Nyandomskiy Vozvyshennost'** *hills* Rus. Fed.
208 A5 **Nyanga** Congo
209 A5 **Nyanga** *prov.* Gabon
213 G3 **Nyanga** Zimbabwe
111 E6 **Nyang Qu** *r.* China
111 F6 **Nyang Qu** *r.* China
206 E4 **Nyankpala** Ghana
211 A5 **Nyanza** Rwanda
211 A6 **Nyanza-Lac** Burundi
95 G2 **Nyapa, Gunung** *mt.* Indon.
116 D3 **Nyar** *r.* India
176 G4 **Nyárád** Hungary
222 H2 **Nyarling** *r.* *N.W.T.* Can.
177 I5 **Nyárlőrinc** Hungary
177 I4 **Nyársapát** Hungary
211 A5 **Nyarugumba** Rwanda
211 B7 **Nyasa, Lake** Africa
Nyasaland *country* Africa *see* **Malawi**
138 F5 **Nyasvizh** Belarus
213 F3 **Nyathi** Zimbabwe
96 B3 **Nyaunglebin** Myanmar
96 A2 **Nyaungu** Myanmar
134 M3 **Nyays** *r.* Rus. Fed.
213 G3 **Nyazura** Zimbabwe
142 D4 **Nyborg** Denmark
140 O1 **Nyborg** Norway
140 M2 **Nyborg** Sweden
143 F3 **Nybro** Sweden
177 H2 **Nýdek** Czech Rep.
221 M1 **Nyeboe Land** *reg.* Greenland
138 F5 **Nyeharelaye** Belarus
111 E6 **Nyêmo** *Xizang* China
Nyenchen Tanglha Range *mts* *Xizang* China *see* **Nyainqêntanglha Shan**
210 C5 **Nyeri** Kenya
140 □ **Ny-Friesland** *reg.* Svalbard
143 F1 **Nyhammar** Sweden
111 D6 **Nyima** *Xizang* China
211 A8 **Nyimba** Zambia
111 F6 **Nyingchi** *Xizang* China
Nyinma *Gansu* China *see* **Maqu**
177 L4 **Nyírábrány** Hungary
177 K4 **Nyíracsád** Hungary
176 G4 **Nyirád** Hungary
177 K4 **Nyíradony** Hungary
177 L4 **Nyírbátor** Hungary
177 L4 **Nyírbéltek** Hungary
177 L4 **Nyírbogát** Hungary
177 K3 **Nyírbogdány** Hungary
177 L4 **Nyírcsászári** Hungary
177 K4 **Nyíregyháza** Hungary
177 K4 **Nyírgelse** Hungary
211 C5 **Nyiri Desert** Kenya
177 L4 **Nyírlugos** Hungary
177 K4 **Nyírmártonfalva** Hungary
177 K4 **Nyírmihályd** Hungary
177 K3 **Nyírtelek** Hungary
177 K3 **Nyírtét** Hungary
177 K3 **Nyírtura** Hungary
210 C4 **Nyiru, Mount** Kenya
177 L4 **Nyírvasvári** Hungary
140 M3 **Nykarleby** Fin.
142 D4 **Nykøbing** Denmark
142 C3 **Nykøbing Mors** Denmark
142 D4 **Nykøbing Sjælland** Denmark
143 G2 **Nyköping** Sweden
143 F2 **Nykroppa** Sweden
143 G2 **Nykvarn** Sweden
134 B3 **Nyland** Sweden
213 F5 **Nylstroom** S. Africa
83 F3 **Nymagee** *N.S.W.* Austr.
83 H2 **Nymboida** *N.S.W.* Austr.
176 E1 **Nymburk** Czech Rep.
142 C4 **Nymindegab** Denmark
143 G2 **Nynäshamn** Sweden
83 F2 **Nyngan** *N.S.W.* Austr.
105 F2 **Nyohō-san** *mt.* Japan
159 F4 **Nyoiseau** France
215 G5 **Nyokana** S. Africa
138 D5 **Nyoman** *r.* Belarus/Lith.
138 E5 **Nyomanskaya Nizina** *lowland* Belarus
190 B2 **Nyon** Switz.
207 H6 **Nyong** *r.* Cameroon
161 D4 **Nyons** France
170 C1 **Nyråd** Denmark
176 C2 **Nýřany** Czech Rep.
134 L3 **Nyrob** Rus. Fed.
176 C2 **Nýrsko** Czech Rep.
174 F5 **Nysa** Pol.
174 F5 **Nysa Kłodzka** *r.* Pol.
Nysa Łużycka *r.* Ger./Pol. *see* **Neiße**
142 E2 **Nysäter** Sweden
140 K3 **Nysätern** Sweden
238 C3 **Nyssa** *OR* U.S.A.
Nystad Fin. *see* **Uusikaupunki**
142 D4 **Nysted** Denmark
105 E3 **Nyūgasa-yama** *mt.* Japan
134 I3 **Nyuksenitsa** Rus. Fed.
177 G4 **Nyúl** Hungary
209 F6 **Nyunzu** Dem. Rep. Congo
131 M3 **Nyurba** Rus. Fed.
129 E4 **Nyuvadi** Armenia
134 J3 **Nyuvchim** Rus. Fed.
131 M3 **Nyuya** Rus. Fed.
131 M3 **Nyuya** *r.* Rus. Fed.
175 M5 **Nyvytsi** Ukr.
136 B3 **Nyzhankovychi** Ukr.
137 H4 **Nyzhni Sirohozy** Ukr.
137 H4 **Nyzhni Torhayi** Ukr.
136 B3 **Nyzhni Vorota** Ukr.
136 B3 **Nyzhniy Bystryy** Ukr.
137 J3 **Nyzhniy Nahol'chyk** Ukr.
137 H5 **Nyzhn'ohirs'kyy** Ukr.
137 J3 **Nyzhnya Dubanka** Ukr.
137 H2 **Nyzhnya Syrovatka** Ukr.
137 H3 **Nyzhnya Tersa** *r.* Ukr.
177 M2 **Nyzhnya Vysots'ke** Ukr.
177 L2 **Nyzhnya Yablun'ka** Ukr.
137 H2 **Nyzy** Ukr.
209 A5 **Nzambi** Congo
208 F3 **Nzara** Sudan
206 C4 **Nzébéla** Guinea
211 B6 **Nzega** Tanz.
206 C5 **Nzérékoré** Guinea
209 B6 **N'zeto** Angola
206 D5 **Nzi** *r.* Côte d'Ivoire
206 D5 **Nzo** *r.* Côte d'Ivoire
210 B4 **Nzoia** *r.* Kenya
208 F4 **Nzoro** *r.* Dem. Rep. Congo
217 □3 **Nzwani** *i.* Comoros

O

236 D3 **Oacoma** *SD* U.S.A.
151 F2 **Oadby** *Leicestershire, England* U.K.
236 C2 **Oahe, Lake** *SD* U.S.A.
240 □ **Oahu** *i.* *HI* U.S.A.
Oaitupu *i.* Tuvalu *see* **Vaitupu**
82 E3 **Oakbank** *S.A.* Austr.
233 H4 **Oak Bluffs** *MA* U.S.A.
241 K2 **Oak City** *UT* U.S.A.
226 D4 **Oak Creek** *WI* U.S.A.
240 G3 **Oakdale** *CA* U.S.A.
235 F1 **Oakdale** *CT* U.S.A.
237 E6 **Oakdale** *LA* U.S.A.
235 E2 **Oakdale** *NY* U.S.A.
150 E2 **Oakengates** *Telford and Wrekin, England* U.K.
236 D2 **Oakes** *ND* U.S.A.
85 G5 **Oakey** *Qld* Austr.

Oakfield to Omagh
343

232 D3 Oakfield NY U.S.A.
234 D2 Oakford PA U.S.A.
237 F5 Oak Grove LA U.S.A.
226 E3 Oak Grove MI U.S.A.
151 G2 Oakham Rutland, England U.K.
232 B4 Oak Harbor OH U.S.A.
238 B1 Oak Harbor WA U.S.A.
232 B5 Oak Hill OH U.S.A.
232 C6 Oak Hill WV U.S.A.
240 H3 Oakhurst CA U.S.A.
235 D2 Oakhurst NJ U.S.A.
240 G4 Oak Knolls CA U.S.A.
240 F3 Oakland CA U.S.A.
232 D5 Oakland MD U.S.A.
233 □I2 Oakland ME U.S.A.
236 D3 Oakland NE U.S.A.
235 D1 Oakland NJ U.S.A.
238 B3 Oakland OR U.S.A.
240 F3 Oakland airport CA U.S.A.
230 C4 Oakland City IN U.S.A.
83 F3 Oaklands N.S.W. Austr.
226 D5 Oak Lawn IL U.S.A.
151 G2 Oakley Bedfordshire, England U.K.
151 F3 Oakley Buckinghamshire, England U.K.
146 E5 Oakley Fife, Scotland U.K.
151 F3 Oakley Hampshire, England U.K.
236 C4 Oakley KS U.S.A.
227 E4 Oakley MI U.S.A.
232 D4 Oakmont PA U.S.A.
86 D4 Oakover r. W.A. Austr.
226 D5 Oak Park IL U.S.A.
235 D1 Oak Ridge NJ U.S.A.
238 B3 Oakridge OR U.S.A.
231 C4 Oak Ridge TN U.S.A.
234 C2 Oaks PA U.S.A.
234 D3 Oak Shade NJ U.S.A.
80 D3 Oakura North I. N.Z.
82 E3 Oakvale S.A. Austr.
240 H4 Oak View CA U.S.A.
224 E5 Oakville Ont. Can.
235 E1 Oakville CT U.S.A.
232 A4 Oakwood OH U.S.A.
232 A5 Oakwood OH U.S.A.
234 C3 Oakwood Beach NJ U.S.A.
81 C6 Oamaru South I. N.Z.
80 D3 Oaonui North I. N.Z.
81 D5 Oaro South I. N.Z.
105 F2 Ōashi-gawa r. Japan
240 I3 Oasis CA U.S.A.
238 D3 Oasis NV U.S.A.
197 F1 Oaşului, Munţii mts Romania
Oates Coast reg. Antarctica see Oates Land
263 K2 Oates Land reg. Antarctica
83 F5 Oatlands Tas. Austr.
214 E5 Oatlands S. Africa
245 F5 Oaxaca Mex.
245 F5 Oaxaca state Mex.
121 J1 Ob' r. Rus. Fed.
Ob, Gulf of sea chan. Rus. Fed. see Obskaya Guba
224 C3 Oba Ont. Can.
Oba i. Vanuatu see Aoba
Obaghan r. Kazakh. see Ubagan
104 B4 Obako-dake mt. Japan
128 A1 Obaköy Turkey
138 G4 Obal' Belarus
207 H5 Obala Cameroon
104 B3 Obama Japan
207 H5 Oban Nigeria
146 C5 Oban Argyll and Bute, Scotland U.K.
102 J4 Obanazawa Japan
123 G2 Obanbori Norak l. Tajik.
123 G1 Obanbori Qayroqqum resr Tajik.
207 H5 Oban Hills mt. Nigeria
182 D2 O Barco Spain
183 G2 Obarenes, Montes mts Spain
197 H2 Obârşeni, Dealul hill Romania
Obbia Somalia see Hobyo
140 M3 Obbola Sweden
197 G2 Obcina Feredeului ridge Romania
197 G2 Obcina Mare ridge Romania
197 G2 Obcina Mestecănişului ridge Romania
179 F3 Obdach Austria
164 D2 Obdam Neth.
Obdorsk Rus. Fed. see Salekhard
176 C2 Obecnice Czech Rep.
Óbecse Vojvodina, Srbija Yugo. see Bečej
222 G4 Obed Alta Can.
185 F2 Obejo Spain
129 A3 Öbektaş Turkey
138 E4 Obeliai Lith.
81 B6 Obelisk mt. South I. N.Z.
258 G2 Oberá Arg.
179 G3 Oberaich Austria
178 E3 Oberalm Austria
190 D2 Oberalpstock mt. Switz.
173 F4 Oberammergau Ger.
173 E2 Oberasbach Ger.
173 F4 Oberau Ger.
173 G4 Oberaudorf Ger.
169 E5 Oberaula Ger.
173 F4 Oberbayern admin. reg. Bayern Ger.
172 C2 Oberderdingen Ger.
173 F3 Oberding Ger.
169 F4 Oberdorla Ger.
178 D4 Oberdrauburg Austria
190 E1 Oberegg Switz.
169 F5 Oberelsbach Ger.
190 D1 Oberentfelden Switz.
172 D4 Oberessendorf Ger.
169 C5 Oberfell Ger.
171 C5 Oberfranken admin. reg. Bayern Ger.
169 F3 Oberg (Lahstedt) Ger.
190 C1 Obergösgen Switz.
179 G2 Ober-Grafendorf Austria
173 F3 Obergriesbach Ger.
173 E4 Obergünzburg Ger.
171 F4 Obergurig Ger.
179 G4 Oberhaag Austria
173 F3 Oberhaching Ger.
173 E2 Oberhaid Ger.
172 C3 Oberharmersbach Ger.
173 F3 Oberhausen Bayern Ger.
169 B4 Oberhausen Nordrhein-Westfalen Ger.
169 F5 Oberhof Ger.
190 C2 Oberhofen Switz.
178 C3 Oberhofen im Inntal Austria
157 H4 Oberhoffen-sur-Moder France
172 C3 Oberkirch Ger.
173 E3 Oberkochen Ger.
171 C5 Oberkotzau Ger.
168 C3 Oberlangen Ger.
171 F4 Oberlichtenau Ger.
178 D4 Oberlienz Austria
236 C4 Oberlin KS U.S.A.
237 E6 Oberlin LA U.S.A.
232 B4 Oberlin OH U.S.A.
172 D3 Obermarchtal Ger.
169 F5 Obermaßfeld-Grimmenthal Ger.
172 B2 Obermoschel Ger.
157 H4 Obernai France
179 E2 Obernberg am Inn Austria
172 D2 Obernburg am Main Ger.
173 E3 Oberndorf am Lech Ger.
172 C3 Oberndorf am Neckar Ger.
179 G2 Oberndorf an der Melk Austria
178 D3 Oberndorf bei Salzburg Austria
179 F2 Oberneukirchen Austria
169 F4 Obernfeld Ger.
172 C3 Obernheim Ger.
172 B2 Obernheim-Kirchenarnbach Ger.
169 E3 Obernkirchen Ger.
173 H3 Obernzell Ger.
173 E2 Obernzenn Ger.
171 F5 Oberoderwitz Ger.
172 C2 Ober-Olm Ger.
83 G3 Oberon N.S.W. Austr.
173 E4 Oberostendorf Ger.
179 E2 Oberösterreich land Austria
173 F2 Oberpfalz admin. reg. Bayern Ger.
173 G2 Oberpfälzer Wald mts Ger.
173 F3 Oberpframmern Ger.
179 H3 Oberpullendorf Austria
172 C2 Ober-Ramstadt Ger.
172 D4 Oberreute Ger.
172 B4 Oberried Ger.
173 E3 Oberrieden Ger.
190 E1 Oberriet Switz.
171 C4 Oberröblingen Ger.
172 C2 Ober-Roden Ger.
171 C4 Oberroßla Ger.
172 D2 Oberrot Ger.
172 B3 Oberrotweil Ger.
173 F3 Oberschleißheim Ger.
173 G3 Oberschneiding Ger.
171 E5 Oberschöna Ger.
179 H3 Oberschützen Austria
179 H2 Obersiebenbrunn Austria
190 D1 Obersiggenthal Switz.
169 E5 Obersinn Ger.
172 D2 Obersontheim Ger.
169 F4 Oberspier Ger.
172 D3 Oberstadion Ger.
173 E4 Oberstaufen Ger.
173 E4 Oberstdorf Ger.
172 D2 Oberstenfeld Ger.
173 G3 Obertaufkirchen Ger.
172 D4 Oberteuringen Ger.
172 B2 Oberthal Ger.
169 E5 Oberthulba Ger.
173 G3 Obertraubling Ger.
173 F2 Obertrubach Ger.
178 E3 Obertrum am See Austria
169 D5 Obertshausen Ger.
136 C3 Obertyn Ukr.
170 E2 Oberueckersee l. Ger.
169 D5 Oberursel (Taunus) Ger.
178 E4 Obervellach Austria
173 G2 Oberviechtach Ger.
190 D2 Oberwald Switz.
169 E4 Oberwälder Land reg. Ger.
179 H3 Oberwaltersdorf Austria
179 H3 Oberwart Austria
169 C5 Oberwesel Ger.
179 G2 Oberwölbling Austria
172 C3 Oberwolfach Ger.
179 F3 Oberwölz Austria
137 H2 Obesta r. Rus. Fed.
171 C4 Obhausen Ger.
93 C3 Obi i. Maluku Indon.
207 H4 Obi Nigeria
93 C3 Obi, Kepulauan is Maluku Indon.
251 H5 Óbidos Brazil
184 A1 Óbidos Port.
123 G2 Obigarm Tajik.
102 K2 Obihiro Japan
196 E4 Obilić Kosovo, Srbija Yugo.
135 I7 Obil'noye Rus. Fed.
173 G3 Obing Ger.
237 F4 Obion r. TN U.S.A.
250 D2 Obispos Venez.
261 F2 Obispo Trejo Arg.
105 F3 Obitsu-gawa r. Japan
162 D3 Objat France
174 F1 Objazda Pol.
175 M4 Oblapy Ukr.
179 E3 Öblarn Austria
135 H6 Oblivskaya Rus. Fed.
100 D2 Obluch'ye Rus. Fed.
139 K4 Obninsk Rus. Fed.
208 E3 Obo C.A.R.
214 C2 Obobogorap S. Africa
210 D2 Obock Djibouti
136 E3 Obodivka Ukr.
207 G5 Obolo Nigeria
182 C2 O Bolo Spain
137 G3 Obolon' Ukr.
186 C4 Obón Spain
95 F1 Obong, Gunung mt. Sarawak Malaysia
174 E3 Oborniki Pol.
174 E4 Oborniki Śląskie Pol.
135 G6 Oboyan' Rus. Fed.
134 H3 Obozerskiy Rus. Fed.
117 E4 Obra Uttar Prad. India
174 D3 Obra r. Pol.
196 E3 Obrenovac Srbija Yugo.
238 B3 O'Brien OR U.S.A.
172 D2 Obrigheim Ger.
172 C2 Obrigheim (Pfalz) Ger.
Obringa r. Switz. see Aare
176 C1 Obrnice Czech Rep.
197 I4 Obrochishte Bulg.
174 G3 Obrowo Pol.
126 D3 Obruk Turkey
175 J3 Obryte Pol.
174 E3 Obrzycko Pol.
82 C2 Observatory Hill hill S.A. Austr.
139 I4 Obsha r. Rus. Fed.
120 B2 Obshchiy Syrt hills Rus. Fed.
130 I3 Obskaya Guba sea chan. Rus. Fed.
175 K5 Obsza Pol.
137 G2 Obtove Ukr.
104 C3 Ōbu Japan
206 E5 Obuasi Ghana
207 H5 Obubra Nigeria
188 G3 Obudovac Bos.-Herz.
207 H5 Obudu Nigeria
136 F2 Obukhiv Ukr.
Obukhov Ukr. see Obukhiv
139 L4 Obukhovo Rus. Fed.
134 K4 Obva r. Rus. Fed.
190 D2 Obwalden canton Switz.
134 J3 Ob"yachevo Rus. Fed.
182 C1 O Cádabo Spain
231 D6 Ocala FL U.S.A.
242 E3 Ocampo Coahuila Mex.
244 D3 Ocampo Guanajuato Mex.
245 E2 Ocampo Tamaulipas Mex.
250 C2 Ocaña Col.
192 A3 Ocana Corse France
183 G5 Ocaña Spain
182 B2 O Castelo Spain
182 B2 O Castro Spain
191 G4 Occhiobello Italy
193 G3 Occhito, Lago di l. Italy
252 C4 Occidental, Cordillera mts Chile
250 B4 Occidental, Cordillera mts Col.
252 C4 Occidental, Cordillera mts Peru
190 D3 Occimiano Italy
232 E5 Occoquan VA U.S.A.
232 C6 Oceana WV U.S.A.
235 E2 Ocean Beach NY U.S.A.
233 F5 Ocean City MD U.S.A.
234 D3 Ocean City NJ U.S.A.
235 D3 Ocean County county NJ U.S.A.
222 E4 Ocean Falls B.C. Can.
235 D3 Ocean Gate NJ U.S.A.
235 D2 Ocean Grove NJ U.S.A.
Ocean Island Kiribati see Banaba
Ocean Island atoll HI U.S.A. see Kure Atoll
240 G4 Oceano CA U.S.A.
246 C1 Oceans Cay i. Bahamas
240 I5 Oceanside CA U.S.A.
237 F6 Ocean Springs MS U.S.A.
234 D3 Ocean View NJ U.S.A.
235 D3 Oceanville NJ U.S.A.
183 G3 Ocejón mt. Spain
78 □4a Ocha i. Chuuk Micronesia
186 B2 Ochagavía Spain
137 F4 Ochakiv Ukr.
129 B2 Och'amch'ire Georgia
134 K4 Ocher Rus. Fed.
136 E3 Ocheretnya Ukr.
137 H4 Ocheretuvate Ukr.
157 F4 Ochey France
146 E5 Ochil Hills Scotland U.K.
146 D6 Ochiltree East Ayrshire, Scotland U.K.
231 C6 Ochlockonee r. GA U.S.A.
175 H3 Ochnia r. Pol.
168 C2 Ocholt Ger.
246 □ Ocho Rios Jamaica
Ochrida, Lake Albania/Macedonia see Ohrid, Lake
173 E2 Ochsenfurt Ger.
172 D3 Ochsenhausen Ger.
169 C5 Ochtendung Ger.
198 D2 Ochthonia Greece
171 C3 Ochtmersleben Ger.
169 C3 Ochtrup Ger.
231 D6 Ocilla GA U.S.A.
141 L3 Ockelbo Sweden
168 D1 Ockholm Ger.
146 C5 Ockle Highland, Scotland U.K.
197 G2 Ocland Romania
231 D6 Ocmulgee r. GA U.S.A.
197 F2 Ocna Mureş Romania
197 G3 Ocna Sibiului Romania
136 D3 Ocniţa Moldova
197 G2 Ocolaşul Mare, Vârful mt. Romania
252 B4 Ocoña Peru
85 E4 O'Connell Creek r. Qld Austr.
226 C4 Oconomowoc WI U.S.A.
226 D3 Oconto WI U.S.A.
226 C3 Oconto Falls WI U.S.A.
182 B2 O Convento Spain
182 C2 O Corgo Spain
243 G6 Ocos Guat.
243 G5 Ocosingo Mex.
242 □I6 Ocotal Nic.
244 C3 Ocotlán Mex.
177 I3 Očová Slovakia
243 G5 Ocozocoautla Mex.
182 C5 Ocreza r. Port.
177 I4 Ócsa Hungary
177 H5 Ócsény Hungary
177 J5 Öcsöd Hungary
158 E2 Octeville France
159 G2 Octeville-sur-Mer France
October Revolution Island Severnaya Zemlya Rus. Fed. see Oktyabr'skoy Revolyutsii, Ostrov
234 B3 Octoraro Creek r. MD U.S.A.
242 □J8 Ocú Panama
213 H2 Ocua Moz.
245 E4 Ocuilan de Arteaga Mex.
252 D4 Ocurí Bol.
174 G2 Ocypel Pol.
206 E5 Oda Ghana
103 F6 Ōda Japan
203 H4 Oda, Jebel mt. Sudan
128 C1 Odabaşı Turkey
140 □C2 Ódáðahraun lava field Iceland
101 D4 Ŏdaejin N. Korea
104 C4 Ōdaigahara-zan mt. Japan
226 B2 Odanah WI U.S.A.
102 J3 Ōdate Japan
105 F3 Odawara Japan
142 B1 Odda Norway
142 D4 Odder Denmark
146 □H1 Oddsta Shetland, Scotland U.K.
184 C2 Odearce r. Port.
184 B3 Odeceixe Port.
223 L3 Odei r. Man. Can.
184 C3 Odeleite Port.
184 C3 Odeleite r. Port.
226 C5 Odell IL U.S.A.
184 B3 Odelouca r. Port.
173 F3 Odelzhausen Ger.
237 D7 Odem TX U.S.A.
184 B3 Odemira Port.
199 E2 Ödemiş Turkey
186 E3 Odena Spain
Ödenburg Hungary see Sopron
215 F2 Odendaalsrus S. Africa
143 F2 Odensbacken Sweden
142 D4 Odense Denmark
234 B3 Odenton MD U.S.A.
172 C2 Odenwald reg. Ger.
174 G6 Oder r. Ger. alt. Odra (Poland)
169 E4 Oder r. Ger./Pol.
170 F3 Oderberg Ger.
170 F1 Oderbucht b. Ger.
170 F2 Oderhaff b. Ger.
171 E3 Oderin Ger.
172 B2 Odernheim am Glan Ger.
191 H3 Oderzo Italy
136 F4 Odesa Ukr.
143 F2 Ödeshog Sweden
136 E4 Odes'ka Oblast' admin. div. Ukr.
Odessa Ukr. see Odesa
234 C3 Odessa DE U.S.A.
237 C6 Odessa TX U.S.A.
238 C2 Odessa WA U.S.A.
Odessa Oblast admin. div. Ukr. see Odes'ka Oblast'
Odesskaya Oblast' admin. div. Ukr. see Odes'ka Oblast'
121 H1 Odesskoye Rus. Fed.
Odessus Bulg. see Varna
158 B4 Odet r. France
184 B3 Odiáxere Port.
184 D3 Odiel r. Spain
206 D4 Odienné Côte d'Ivoire
151 G3 Odiham Hampshire, England U.K.
164 E2 Odijk Neth.
139 K4 Odintsovo Rus. Fed.
184 B2 Odivelas Beja Port.
184 A2 Odivelas Lisboa Port.
184 B2 Odivelas r. Port.
197 H3 Odobeşti Romania
197 H3 Odobeştilor, Măgura hill Romania
174 F4 Odolanów Pol.
171 F5 Odolena Voda Czech Rep.
159 F2 Odon r. France
183 I4 Odón Spain
164 F2 Odoorn Neth.
197 G2 Odorheiu Secuiesc Romania
139 K5 Odoyev Rus. Fed.
174 G6 Odra r. Pol. alt. Oder (Germany)
183 F2 Odra r. Spain
137 H4 Odradivka Ukr.
177 G2 Odry Czech Rep.
175 I4 Odrzywół Pol.
196 D3 Odžaci Vojvodina, Srbija Yugo.
213 G3 Odzi r. Zimbabwe
Oea Libya see Tripoli
169 F3 Oebisfelde Ger.
169 E4 Oedelsheim (Oberweser) Ger.
171 E5 Oederan Ger.
168 E2 Oederquart Ger.
163 A5 Œeyreluy France
164 E3 Oeffelt Neth.
164 D2 Oegstgeest Neth.
254 E3 Oeiras Brazil
184 A2 Oeiras Port.
184 C3 Oeiras r. Port.
169 D4 Oelde Ger.
168 E2 Oelixdorf Ger.
236 C3 Oelrichs SD U.S.A.
171 D5 Oelsnitz Sachsen Ger.
171 D5 Oelsnitz Sachsen Ger.
236 F3 Oelwein IA U.S.A.
164 F2 Oene Neth.
84 C2 Oenpelli N.T. Austr.
190 C1 Oensingen Switz.
168 E2 Oerel Ger.
168 F2 Oering Ger.
169 F5 Oerlenbach Ger.
169 D4 Oerlinghausen Ger.
Oesel i. Estonia see Hiiumaa
165 E5 Oesling hills Lux.
165 D3 Oesterdam barrage Neth.
171 C5 Oettersdorf Ger.
173 E3 Oettingen in Bayern Ger.
178 B3 Oetz Austria
168 F2 Oetzen Ger.
168 E1 Oeversee Ger.
104 B3 Ōe-yama hill Japan
127 F2 Of Turkey
238 F2 O'Fallon r. MT U.S.A.
193 I3 Ofanto r. Italy
193 F2 Ofena Italy
207 G4 Offa Nigeria
147 D3 Offaly county Rep. of Ireland
190 E3 Offanengo Italy
157 G5 Offemont France
169 D5 Offenbach am Main Ger.
172 C2 Offenbach an der Queich Ger.
173 G3 Offenberg Ger.
172 B3 Offenburg Ger.
140 K3 Offerdal Sweden
193 F2 Offida Italy
173 E3 Offingen Ger.
156 B3 Offranville France
140 L1 Ofotfjorden sea chan. Norway
172 D3 Ofterdingen Ger.
78 □2 Ofu i. American Samoa
102 J4 Ōfunato Japan
95 F2 Oga r. Indon.
102 I4 Oga Japan
105 F1 Oga-dake mt. Japan
210 E3 Ogadēn reg. Eth.
104 C3 Ōgaki Japan
236 C3 Ogallala NE U.S.A.
94 D3 Ogan r. Indon.
103 □3 Ogasawara-shotō is N. Pacific Ocean
105 E2 Ōga-tō mt. Japan
105 F2 Ogawa Japan
102 J3 Ogawara-ko l. Japan
Ogbomosho Nigeria see Ogbomoso
207 G4 Ogbomoso Nigeria
236 E3 Ogden IA U.S.A.
238 E3 Ogden UT U.S.A.
222 C3 Ogden, Mount B.C. Can.
234 D1 Ogdensburg NJ U.S.A.
233 F2 Ogdensburg NY U.S.A.
231 D6 Ogeechee r. GA U.S.A.
226 B3 Ogema WI U.S.A.
168 C2 Ogenbargen Ger.
156 E4 Oger France
163 B5 Ogeu-les-Bains France
157 G4 Ogéviller France
190 E3 Oggiono Italy
78 □6 Ogho Choiseul Solomon Is
224 C4 Ogidaki Ont. Can.
220 E3 Ogilvie r. Y.T. Can.
220 D3 Ogilvie Mountains Y.T. Can.
129 C4 Oğlaksuyu Turkey
122 C2 Oglanly Turkm.
192 B2 Ogliastro Corse France
190 F3 Oglio r. Italy
85 G4 Ogmore Qld Austr.
150 D3 Ogmore Vale of Glamorgan, Wales U.K.
150 D3 Ogmore Vale Bridgend, Wales U.K.
160 D1 Ognon r. France
Oğnut Turkey see Göynük
93 B2 Ogoamas, Gunung mt. Indon.
207 H5 Ogoja Nigeria
224 C3 Ogoki r. Ont. Can.
224 C3 Ogoki Lake Ont. Can.
208 A5 Ogooué r. Gabon
208 B5 Ogooué-Ivindo prov. Gabon
208 B5 Ogooué-Lolo prov. Gabon
208 A5 Ogooué-Maritime prov. Gabon
197 F4 Ogosta r. Bulg.
207 F5 Ogou r. Togo
87 C6 O'Grady, Lake salt flat W.A. Austr.
197 F5 Ogražden mts Bulg./Macedonia
Ograzhden mts Bulg./Macedonia see Ogražden
138 E3 Ogre Latvia
138 E3 Ogre r. Latvia
175 J3 Ogrodniki Pol.
175 H5 Ogrodzieniec Pol.
171 F4 Ogrosen Ger.
182 B2 O Grove Spain
139 L3 Ogudnevo Rus. Fed.
188 E3 Ogulin Croatia
207 F5 Ogun state Nigeria
233 □H3 Ogunquit ME U.S.A.
129 E3 Oğuz Azer.
177 K6 Ohaba Lungă Romania
207 G5 Ohafia Nigeria
81 A6 Ohai South I. N.Z.
80 E3 Ohakune North I. N.Z.
185 H3 Ohanes Spain
212 C3 Ohangwena admin. reg. Namibia
226 D5 O'Hare airport IL U.S.A.
80 E4 Ohau North I. N.Z.
81 C6 Ohau r. South I. N.Z.
80 E2 Ohaupo North I. N.Z.
Ohcejohka Fin. see Utsjoki
168 C2 Ohe r. Ger.
173 H3 Ohe r. Ger.
Ohétéroah i. Îs Australes Fr. Polynesia see Rurutu
165 E4 Ohey Belgium
260 B4 O'Higgins admin. reg. Chile
259 B8 O'Higgins, Lago l. Chile
80 E2 Ohinewai North I. N.Z.
226 C5 Ohio IL U.S.A.
236 F4 Ohio r. Ohio/West Virginia U.S.A.
232 B4 Ohio state U.S.A.
232 A4 Ohio City OH U.S.A.
262 Q1 Ohio Range mts Antarctica
235 D1 Ohioville NY U.S.A.
105 E3 Ōhito Japan
137 H3 Ohiyivka Ukr.
172 B3 Ohlsbach Ger.
179 E3 Ohlsdorf Austria
173 F4 Ohlstadt Ger.
169 D5 Ohm r. Ger.
138 F2 Õhne r. Estonia
169 C3 Ohne Ger.
172 C4 Öhningen Ger.
79 □2 'Ohonua Tonga
80 F2 Ohope North I. N.Z.
177 G3 Ohrady Slovakia
169 F5 Ohrdruf Ger.
176 D1 Ohře r. Czech Rep.
171 C3 Ohre r. Ger.
196 E5 Ohrid Macedonia
196 E5 Ohrid, Lake Albania/Macedonia
Ohridsko Ezero l. Albania/Macedonia see Ohrid, Lake
213 F5 Ohrigstad S. Africa
172 D2 Öhringen Ger.
Ohrit, Liqeni i l. Albania/Macedonia see Ohrid, Lake
169 F3 Ohrum Ger.
80 E3 Ohura North I. N.Z.
182 B4 Oiã Port.
251 I4 Oiapoque Brazil
251 I3 Oiapoque r. Brazil/Fr. Guiana
186 B1 Oiartzun Spain
146 D4 Oich r. Scotland U.K.
113 □1 Oidhuni i. S. Male Maldives
104 B3 Ōi-gawa r. Japan
105 E4 Ōi-gawa r. Japan
156 C2 Oignies France
160 D2 Oignin r. France
164 E3 Oijen Neth.
Oik Kazakh. see Uyuk
232 D4 Oil City PA U.S.A.
240 H4 Oildale CA U.S.A.
147 E4 Oilgate Rep. of Ireland
147 C2 Oily r. Rep. of Ireland
182 C3 Oímbra Spain
108 A2 Oi Qu r. Xizang China
102 J3 Oirase-gawa r. Japan
159 F5 Oiron France
164 E3 Oirschot Neth.
156 C3 Oise dept Picardie France
156 C4 Oise r. France
160 D1 Oiselay-et-Grachaux France
156 B3 Oisemont France
159 F3 Oisseau France
156 B3 Oissel France
164 E3 Oisterwijk Neth.
103 E7 Ōita Japan
103 E7 Ōita pref. Japan
182 B2 Oitavén r. Spain
198 C2 Oiti mt. Greece
197 H2 Oituz r. Romania
159 I4 Oizon France
104 C2 Oizuruga-dake mt. Japan
240 H4 Ojai CA U.S.A.
185 G2 Ojailén r. Spain
Ojalava i. Samoa see Upolu
138 F2 Ojamaa r. Estonia
141 K3 Öje Sweden
185 F4 Ojén Spain
104 B4 Ōji Japan
242 D2 Ojinaga Mex.
245 F4 Ojitlán Mex.
105 E1 Ojiya Japan
207 G5 Ojobo Nigeria
244 C2 Ojocaliente Mex.
239 F4 Ojo Caliente NM U.S.A.
258 C2 Ojos del Salado, Nevado mt. Arg./Chile
183 I4 Ojos Negros Spain
175 I3 Ojrzeń Pol.
207 H5 Oju Nigeria
141 K3 Öjung Sweden
207 G5 Oka Nigeria
139 M4 Oka r. Rus. Fed.
212 C4 Okahandja Namibia
Okahu b. South I. N.Z. see Jackson Bay
80 E3 Okahukura North I. N.Z.
80 D1 Okaihau North I. N.Z.
81 D5 Okains Bay Canterbury N.Z.
207 F4 Okaka Nigeria
212 C4 Okakarara Namibia
225 I1 Okak Islands Nfld. Can.
175 H2 Okalewo Pol.
222 G5 Okanagan Falls B.C. Can.
222 G5 Okanagan Lake B.C. Can.
238 C1 Okanogan WA U.S.A.
238 C1 Okanogan r. WA U.S.A.
177 K5 Okány Hungary
123 H4 Okara Pak.
80 D3 Okato North I. N.Z.
212 D3 Okavango r. Botswana/Namibia
212 C3 Okavango admin. reg. Namibia
212 D3 Okavango Delta swamp Botswana
103 E7 Ōkawa Japan
105 E2 Okaya Japan
103 F6 Okayama Japan
103 F6 Okayama pref. Japan
104 D4 Okazaki Japan
129 B3 Okçular Dağı mt. Turkey
231 D7 Okeechobee FL U.S.A.
231 D7 Okeechobee, Lake FL U.S.A.
237 D4 Okeene OK U.S.A.
105 F2 Okegawa Japan
150 C4 Okehampton Devon, England U.K.
207 F4 Oke-Iho Nigeria
237 D5 Okemah OK U.S.A.
150 C4 Okement r. England U.K.
207 G5 Okene Nigeria
169 F3 Oker r. Ger.
116 B5 Okha Gujarat India
100 G1 Okha Sakhalin Rus. Fed.
Okhadunga Nepal see Okhaldhunga
117 F4 Okhaldhunga Nepal
134 K4 Okhansk Rus. Fed.
131 P4 Okhotka r. Rus. Fed.
131 P4 Okhotsk Rus. Fed.
102 L1 Okhotsk, Sea of Japan/Rus. Fed.
Okhotskoye More sea Japan/Rus. Fed. see Okhotsk, Sea of
137 H4 Okhrimivka Ukr.
Okhthoniá Greece see Ochthonia
137 H2 Okhtyrka Ukr.
139 I3 Okhvat Rus. Fed.
214 A3 Okiep S. Africa
102 □2 Okinawa Japan
102 □2 Okinawa i. Japan
102 □1 Okinawa pref. Japan
Okinawa-guntō is Japan see Okinawa-shotō
102 □1 Okinawa-shotō is Japan
102 □1 Okinoerabu-jima i. Japan
103 F5 Oki-shotō is Japan
207 G5 Okitipupa Nigeria
96 A3 Okkan Myanmar
237 D5 Oklahoma state U.S.A.
237 D5 Oklahoma City OK U.S.A.
231 D6 Oklawaha r. FL U.S.A.
237 D5 Okmulgee OK U.S.A.
177 L3 Okna r. Slovakia
Oknitsa Moldova see Ocniţa
177 G4 Okoč Slovakia
207 H5 Okola Cameroon
237 F5 Okolona MS U.S.A.
232 A4 Okolona OH U.S.A.
208 B5 Okondja Gabon
174 E2 Okonek Pol.
175 L4 Okopy Pol.
177 G6 Okor r. Hungary
222 H5 Okotoks Alta Can.
139 I4 Okovskiy Les for. Rus. Fed.
208 B5 Okoyo Congo
121 J3 Okpety, Gora mt. Kazakh.
176 E2 Okříšky Czech Rep.
176 E2 Okrouhlice Czech Rep.
175 K4 Okrzeja Pol.
175 I5 Oksa Pol.
142 C4 Oksbøl Denmark
140 M1 Øksfjord Norway
134 G3 Oksovskiy Rus. Fed.
140 K2 Oksskolten mt. Norway
123 H2 Oksu r. Tajik.
Oktemberyan Armenia see Hoktemberyan
96 B3 Oktwin Myanmar
Oktyabr' Kazakh. see Kandyagash
121 I4 Oktyabr' Kazakh.
139 K3 Oktyabr' Rus. Fed.
Oktyabr'sk Kazakh. see Kandyagash
120 B1 Oktyabr'sk Rus. Fed.
Oktyabr'skaya Belarus see Aktsyabrskaya
137 J4 Oktyabr'skaya Rus. Fed.
Oktyabr'skiy Homyel'skaya Voblasts' Belarus see Aktsyabrski
Oktyabr'skiy Vitsyebskaya Voblasts' Belarus see Aktsyabrski
120 E1 Oktyabr'skiy Kazakh.
100 D1 Oktyabr'skiy Rus. Fed.
134 H3 Oktyabr'skiy Rus. Fed.
137 I2 Oktyabr'skiy Rus. Fed.
139 M3 Oktyabr'skiy Rus. Fed.
131 Q4 Oktyabr'skiy Rus. Fed.
137 J5 Oktyabr'skiy Rus. Fed.
Oktyabr'skiy Rus. Fed. see Takhtamukay
135 K5 Oktyabr'skiy Rus. Fed.
137 J4 Oktyabr'skiy Rus. Fed.
139 L4 Oktyabr'skiy Rus. Fed.
139 L5 Oktyabr'skiy Rus. Fed.
134 L4 Oktyabr'skiy Rus. Fed.
135 H7 Oktyabr'skiy Rus. Fed.
120 F1 Oktyabr'skoye Kazakh.
120 E1 Oktyabr'skoye Rus. Fed.
130 H3 Oktyabr'skoye Khanty-Mansiyskiy Avtonomnyy Okrug Rus. Fed.
139 L5 Oktyabr'skoye Rus. Fed.
120 C1 Oktyabr'skoye Rus. Fed.
129 D2 Oktyabr'skoye Rus. Fed.
131 K2 Oktyabr'skoy Revolyutsii, Ostrov i. Severnaya Zemlya Rus. Fed.
122 D1 Oktyah'sk Turkm.
188 F3 Okučani Croatia
103 E7 Ōkuchi Japan
139 I2 Okulovka Rus. Fed.
129 B2 Ok'umi Georgia
Okureshi Georgia see Oqureshi
81 B5 Okuru South I. N.Z.
104 D3 Oku-sangai-dake mt. Japan
102 I2 Okushiri-tō i. Japan
207 F4 Okuta Nigeria
131 Q4 Ola Rus. Fed.
237 E5 Ola AR U.S.A.
140 □B2 Ólafsvík Iceland
186 B2 Olague Spain
113 □1 Olahali i. N. Male Maldives
138 D3 Olaine Latvia
114 C3 Olakkur Tamil Nadu India
182 B5 Olalhas Port.
161 E4 Olan, Pic d' mt. France
240 H3 Olancha CA U.S.A.
240 H3 Olancha Peak CA U.S.A.
242 □I6 Olanchito Hond.
143 G3 Öland i. Sweden
161 A5 Olargues France
177 K5 Olari Romania
82 E3 Olary S.A. Austr.
177 K3 Olaszliszka Hungary
236 E4 Olathe KS U.S.A.
114 C4 Olavakod Kerala India
261 G5 Olavarría Arg.
183 I2 Olave Spain
140 □ Olav V Land reg. Svalbard
174 F5 Oława Pol.
183 H2 Olazagutía Spain
187 C4 Olba Spain
179 H3 Olbendorf Austria
171 E5 Olbernhau Ger.
171 F5 Olbersdorf Ger.
171 C4 Olbersleben Ger.
192 B4 Olbia Sardegna Italy
175 K5 Olbięcin Pol.
176 D2 Olbramovice Czech Rep.
177 K5 Olcea Romania
129 C3 Ölçek Turkey
173 F3 Olching Ger.
232 D3 Olcott NY U.S.A.
129 C3 Ölçülü Turkey
246 C2 Old Bahama Channel Bahamas/Cuba
151 F3 Old Basing Hampshire, England U.K.
114 D2 Old Bastar Madh. Prad. India
235 D2 Old Bridge NJ U.S.A.
150 E2 Oldbury West Midlands, England U.K.
147 D3 Oldcastle Rep. of Ireland
86 E3 Old Cherrabun W.A. Austr.
150 D1 Old Colwyn Conwy, Wales U.K.
85 E4 Old Cork Qld Austr.
220 E3 Old Crow Y.T. Can.
146 D6 Old Dailly South Ayrshire, Scotland U.K.
164 F2 Oldeberkoop Neth.
164 E1 Oldeboorn Neth.
164 E2 Oldebroek Neth.
164 F1 Oldehove Neth.
164 E2 Oldemarkt Neth.
168 D2 Oldenbrok Ger.
168 D2 Oldenburg Ger.
168 F1 Oldenburg in Holstein Ger.
168 E2 Oldendorf Ger.
168 F2 Oldendorf (Luhe) Ger.
168 D1 Oldenswort Ger.
164 F2 Oldenzaal Neth.
140 M1 Olderdalen Norway
151 I3 Old Felixstowe Suffolk, England U.K.
87 D7 Oldfield r. W.A. Austr.
233 F3 Old Forge NY U.S.A.
234 C1 Old Forge PA U.S.A.
232 B4 Old Fort OH U.S.A.
87 C5 Old Gidgee W.A. Austr.
149 G4 Oldham Greater Manchester, England U.K.
246 □ Old Harbour Jamaica
246 □ Old Harbour Bay Jamaica
147 C5 Old Head of Kinsale hd Rep. of Ireland
171 C4 Oldisleben Ger.
150 E3 Oldland South Gloucestershire, England U.K.
149 J4 Old Leake Lincolnshire, England U.K.
235 F1 Old Lyme CT U.S.A.
220 G5 Oldman r. Alta Can.
234 C3 Oldman's Creek r. NJ U.S.A.
146 F4 Oldmeldrum Aberdeenshire, Scotland U.K.
209 F8 Old Mkushi Zambia
215 G4 Old Morley S. Africa
235 G1 Old Mystic CT U.S.A.
233 □H3 Old Orchard Beach ME U.S.A.
225 K4 Old Perlican Nfld. Can.
240 H4 Old River CA U.S.A.
147 E4 Old Ross Rep. of Ireland
222 H5 Olds Alta Can.
235 F1 Old Saybrook CT U.S.A.
233 □H2 Old Speck Mountain ME U.S.A.
168 D1 Oldsum Ger.
147 E3 Oldtown Rep. of Ireland
149 G3 Old Town Cumbria, England U.K.
232 B5 Oldtown KY U.S.A.
233 □I2 Old Town ME U.S.A.
211 B5 Olduvai Gorge tourist site Tanz.
232 C4 Old Washington OH U.S.A.
234 D2 Oldwick NJ U.S.A.
241 J4 Old Woman Mountains CA U.S.A.
106 D1 Öldziyt Mongolia
232 D3 Olean NY U.S.A.
175 K1 Olecko Pol.
182 C5 Oledo Port.
190 D3 Oleggio Italy
182 C5 Oleiros Port.
131 N3 Olekma r. Rus. Fed.
131 N3 Olekminsk Rus. Fed.
137 G2 Oleksandrivka Chernihivs'ka Oblast' Ukr.
137 I3 Oleksandrivka Donets'ka Oblast' Ukr.
137 G3 Oleksandrivka Kirovohrads'ka Oblast' Ukr.
137 F4 Oleksandrivka Mykolayivs'ka Oblast' Ukr.
137 H4 Oleksandrivka Zaporiz'ka Oblast' Ukr.
Oleksandrivs'k Ukr. see Zaporizhzhya
137 G3 Oleksandriya Kirovohrads'ka Oblast' Ukr.
136 D2 Oleksandriya Rivnens'ka Oblast' Ukr.
137 I3 Oleksiyevo-Druzhkivka Ukr.
137 J3 Oleksiyivka Ukr.
165 D3 Olen Belgium
142 A2 Ølen Norway
134 F1 Olenegorsk Rus. Fed.
131 M3 Olenek Rus. Fed.
131 M2 Olenek r. Rus. Fed.
Ölengti r. Kazakh. see Olenti
139 I3 Olenino Rus. Fed.
137 I4 Olenivka Ukr.
Olenivs'ki Kar"yery Ukr. see Dokuchayevs'k
120 C2 Olenti r. Kazakh.
121 H1 Olenti r. Kazakh.
107 G1 Olentuy Rus. Fed.
Olenya Rus. Fed. see Olenegorsk
162 A3 Oléron, Île d' i. France
186 E3 Olesa de Montserrat Spain
Oleshky Ukr. see Tsyurupyns'k
137 F2 Oleshnya Chernihivs'ka Oblast' Ukr.
137 H2 Oleshnya Sums'ka Oblast' Ukr.
136 C3 Oles'ko Ukr.
174 F4 Oleśnica Pol.
175 J5 Oleśnica Pol.
175 I5 Olesno Małopolskie Pol.
174 G5 Olesno Opolskie Pol.
175 L5 Oleszyce Pol.
192 B2 Oletta Corse France
163 E6 Olette France
95 G5 Olet Tongo mt. Sumbawa Indon.
136 D2 Olevs'k Ukr.
234 C2 Oley PA U.S.A.
169 C4 Olfen Ger.
140 K2 Ølfjellet mt. Norway
100 E4 Ol'ga Rus. Fed.
224 E3 Olga, Lac l. Que. Can.
84 B5 Olga, Mount N.T. Austr.
140 □ Olgastretet str. Svalbard
190 E3 Olginate Italy
137 J5 Ol'ginskaya Rus. Fed.
137 J4 Ol'ginskaya Rus. Fed.
Olginskoye Rus. Fed. see Kochubeyevskoye
106 A1 Ölgiy Mongolia
146 E3 Olgrinmore Highland, Scotland U.K.
184 A1 Olhalvo Port.
184 C3 Olhão Port.
184 A1 Olho Marinho Port.
113 □1 Olhuveli i. S. Male Maldives
84 B5 Olia Chain mts N.T. Austr.
186 E2 Oliana Spain
183 G5 Olías del Rey Spain
188 E3 Olib i. Croatia
192 B4 Oliena Sardegna Italy
192 B4 Oliena r. Sardegna Italy
186 C3 Oliete Spain
212 C5 Olifants watercourse Namibia
214 B4 Olifants r. W. Cape S. Africa
214 C5 Olifants r. W. Cape S. Africa
213 F4 Olifants r. S. Africa
214 D2 Olifantshoek S. Africa
214 B5 Olifantsrivierberge mts S. Africa
193 G4 Oligastro Marina Italy
91 K5 Olimarao atoll Micronesia
Olimbos hill Cyprus see Olympos
Olimbos mt. Greece see Olympos
256 C4 Olímpia Brazil
245 E5 Olinalá Mex.
85 F1 Olinda Entrance sea chan. Qld Austr.
213 H3 Olinga Moz.
141 K3 Olingsjövallen Sweden
85 E4 Olio Qld Austr.
186 E3 Oliola Spain
Öli Qoltyq Sory dry lake Kazakh. see Sor Mertvyy Kultuk
Olisipo Port. see Lisboa
183 I2 Olite Spain
261 F3 Oliva Arg.
193 I5 Oliva r. Italy
187 C6 Oliva Spain
184 D2 Oliva hill Spain
258 C3 Oliva, Cordillera de mts Arg./Chile
184 D2 Oliva de la Frontera Spain
184 D2 Oliva de Mérida Spain
182 B3 Olival Port.
260 C2 Olivares, Cerro de mt. Arg./Chile
183 H5 Olivares de Júcar Spain
232 B5 Olive Hill KY U.S.A.
240 G2 Olivehurst CA U.S.A.
257 E4 Oliveira Brazil
182 B4 Oliveira de Azeméis Port.
182 B4 Oliveira de Frades Port.
182 B4 Oliveira do Bairro Port.
182 C4 Oliveira do Conde Port.
182 B3 Oliveira do Douro Port.
182 C4 Oliveira do Hospital Port.
254 E5 Oliveira dos Brejinhos Brazil
Olivença Moz. see Lupilichi
Olivença-a-Nova Angola see Capunda Cavilongo
193 H3 Olivento r. Italy
184 C2 Olivenza r. Port./Spain
184 C2 Olivenza Spain
222 G5 Oliver B.C. Can.
195 E4 Oliveri Sicilia Italy
261 G3 Oliveros Arg.
156 B5 Olivet France
226 E4 Olivet MI U.S.A.
236 D3 Olivet SD U.S.A.
193 H4 Oliveto Citra Italy
193 I4 Oliveto Lucano Italy
236 E2 Olivia MN U.S.A.
81 B6 Olivine Range mts South I. N.Z.
190 D2 Olivone Switz.
136 C3 Oliyiv Ukr.
177 K3 Olka r. Slovakia
210 C5 Ol Kalou Kenya
Ölkeyek r. Kazakh. see Ul'kayak
135 G6 Ol'khovatka Rus. Fed.
135 I6 Ol'khovka Rus. Fed.
175 H5 Olkusz Pol.
146 □G1 Ollaberry Shetland, Scotland U.K.
252 C3 Ollachea Peru
192 B5 Olla stu r. Sardegna Italy
149 H4 Ollerton Nottinghamshire, England U.K.
160 B3 Olliergues France
161 D5 Ollioules France
260 B2 Ollita, Cordillera de mts Arg./Chile
260 B2 Ollitas mt. Arg.
183 I2 Ollo Spain
192 B4 Ollolai Sardegna Italy
208 B5 Ollombo Congo
190 B2 Ollon Switz.
Olmaliq Uzbek. see Almalyk
183 G3 Olmedilla de Roa Spain
192 A4 Olmedo Sardegna Italy
183 F3 Olmedo Spain
192 B2 Olmeta-di-Tuda Corse France
192 A3 Olmeto Corse France
250 B6 Olmos Peru
183 F2 Olmos de Ojeda Spain
Olmütz Czech Rep. see Olomouc
151 G2 Olney Milton Keynes, England U.K.
236 F4 Olney IL U.S.A.
234 A3 Olney MD U.S.A.
237 D5 Olney TX U.S.A.
187 C5 Olocau Spain
186 C4 Olocau del Rey Spain
100 A2 Olochi Rus. Fed.
143 F3 Olofström Sweden
121 F1 Ol'oinka Kazakh.
225 I3 Olomane r. Que. Can.
176 G2 Olomouc Czech Rep.
176 G2 Olomoucký kraj admin. reg. Czech Rep.
190 E3 Olona r. Italy
139 I1 Olonets Rus. Fed.
139 I1 Olonetskaya Vozvyshennost' hills Rus. Fed.
92 B3 Olongapo Phil.
139 I1 Olonka r. Rus. Fed.
162 A2 Olonne-sur-Mer France
161 A5 Olonzac France
163 B5 Oloron-Ste-Marie France
78 □2 Olosega i. American Samoa
Olosenga i. American Samoa see Swains Island
186 F2 Olot Spain
Olot Uzbek. see Alat
171 D5 Oloví Czech Rep.
188 G3 Olovo Bos.-Herz.
107 G1 Olovyannaya Rus. Fed.
240 □C8 Olowalu HI U.S.A.
Oloy, Qatorkŭhi mts Asia see Alai Range
116 C5 Olpad Gujarat India
169 C4 Olpe Ger.
178 C3 Olperer mt. Austria
138 G5 Ol'sa r. Belarus
176 F2 Olšany Czech Rep.
176 G2 Olšany u Prostějova Czech Rep.
142 E2 Olsätter Sweden
177 G2 Olšava r. Czech Rep.
177 K3 Olšava r. Slovakia
169 D4 Olsberg Ger.
177 H2 Olše r. Czech Rep.
137 I2 Ol'shanka Rus. Fed.
137 F4 Ol'shans'ke Ukr.
164 F2 Olst Neth.
175 K3 Olszanka Mazowieckie Pol.
174 F5 Olszanka Opolskie Pol.
175 K6 Olszany Pol.
175 J2 Olszewka Pol.
175 J2 Olszewo-Borki Pol.
174 G3 Olszówka Pol.
175 H5 Olsztyn Śląskie Pol.
175 I2 Olsztyn Warmińsko-Mazurskie Pol.
175 I2 Olsztynek Pol.
175 L3 Olszyn Pol.
174 D4 Olszyna Pol.
197 G4 Olt r. Romania
260 D2 Olta Arg.
259 C6 Olte, Sierra de mts Arg.
190 C1 Olten Switz.
197 H3 Olteniţa Romania
197 G3 Olteţ r. Romania
197 H3 Oltina Romania
Oltinkŭl Uzbek. see Altynkul'
123 G1 Oltintopkan Tajik.
127 F2 Oltu Turkey
129 B3 Oltu r. Turkey
113 □1 Olugiri i. N. Male Maldives
129 C3 Oluklu Turkey
185 H3 Olula del Río Spain
129 C3 Olur Turkey
183 I3 Ólvega Spain
186 D2 Olvena Spain
185 E4 Olvera Spain
150 E3 Olveston South Gloucestershire, England U.K.
Ol'viopol' Ukr. see Pervomays'k
136 C2 Olyka Ukr.
139 L5 Olym r. Rus. Fed.
Olymbos hill Cyprus see Olympos
198 B3 Olympia tourist site Greece
238 B2 Olympia WA U.S.A.
128 A2 Olympos hill Cyprus
198 C1 Olympos mt. Greece
199 G3 Olympos tourist site Turkey
Olympus, Mount Greece see Olympos
238 B2 Olympus, Mount WA U.S.A.
137 J2 Olymskiy Rus. Fed.
234 C1 Olyphant PA U.S.A.
137 F2 Olyshivka Ukr.
131 R3 Olyutorskiy Rus. Fed.
131 R4 Olyutorskiy Zaliv b. Rus. Fed.
192 B4 Olzai Sardegna Italy
Olzheras Kemerovskaya Oblast' Rus. Fed. see Mezhdurechensk
111 C5 Oma Xizang China
134 I2 Oma r. Rus. Fed.
105 D2 Ōmachi Japan
102 J4 Ōmagari Japan
147 D2 Omagh Northern Ireland U.K.

Ōta to Panabá 345

105 F2 Ōta Japan
184 B1 Ota Port.
184 B1 Ota r. Port.
81 B6 Otago admin. reg. South I. N.Z.
81 C6 Otago Peninsula South I. N.Z.
Otahiti i. Fr. Polynesia see Tahiti
80 E3 Otairi North I. N.Z.
102 □1 O-take vol. Nansei-shotō Japan
102 □1 O-take vol. Nansei-shotō Japan
105 F3 Ōtake-san mt. Japan
80 E4 Otaki North I. N.Z.
81 B6 Otama South I. N.Z.
80 F3 Otamauri North I. N.Z.
121 H4 Otar Kazakh.
102 J2 Otaru Japan
176 G2 Otaslavice Czech Rep.
81 B7 Otatara South I. N.Z.
245 F4 Otatitlán Mex.
81 A7 Otautau South I. N.Z.
176 D2 Otava r. Czech Rep.
141 N3 Otava Fin.
250 B4 Otavalo Ecuador
212 C3 Otavi Namibia
105 G2 Ōtawara Japan
209 B9 Otchinjau Angola
Otdia atoll Marshall Is see Wotje
183 I2 Oteiza Spain
81 C6 Otekaieke South I. N.Z.
197 F3 Oțelu Roșu Romania
81 C6 Otematata South I. N.Z.
128 C1 Ötençay Turkey
138 F2 Otepää Estonia
138 F2 Otepää kõrgustik hills Estonia
140 L1 Oteren Norway
182 D3 Otero de Bodas Spain
183 F4 Otero de Herreros Spain
239 E7 Oteros r. Mex.
198 B1 Oteševo Macedonia
175 I5 Otfinów Pol.
151 H3 Otford Kent, England U.K.
106 C2 Otgon Tenger Uul mt. Mongolia
157 F3 Othain r. France
156 D4 Othe, Forêt d' for. France
238 C2 Othello WA U.S.A.
207 F4 Oti r. Ghana/Togo
177 G2 Otice Czech Rep.
172 C3 Ötigheim Ger.
215 H3 Otimati S. Africa
244 B1 Otinapa Mex.
81 C5 Otira South I. N.Z.
236 C3 Otis CO U.S.A.
172 C3 Ötisheim Ger.
234 D1 Otisville NY U.S.A.
185 G4 Otívar Spain
212 C4 Otjiwarongo Namibia
212 C4 Otjozondjupa admin. reg. Namibia
151 I2 Otley Suffolk, England U.K.
149 H4 Otley West Yorkshire, England U.K.
129 A4 Otlukbelı Erzincan Turkey
129 A4 Otlukbeli Dağları mts Turkey
174 F5 Otmuchów Pol.
179 H1 Otnice Czech Rep.
102 J2 Otobe-dake mt. Japan
188 E3 Otočac Croatia
Otog Qi Nei Mongol China see Ulan
188 G3 Otok Croatia
188 F3 Otoka Bos.-Herz.
80 F3 Otoko North I. N.Z.
207 F4 Otola Benin
80 E1 Otonga North I. N.Z.
210 A2 Otoro, Jebel mt. Sudan
80 E3 Otorohanga North I. N.Z.
174 E3 Otorowo Pol.
224 B3 Otoskwin r. Ont. Can.
103 □3 Otōto-jima i. Japan
120 B3 Otpan, Gora hill Kazakh.
Otpor Rus. Fed. see Zabaykal'sk
142 C2 Otra r. Norway
139 K5 Otradinskiy Rus. Fed.
129 B1 Otradnaya Rus. Fed.
139 H2 Otradnoye Leningradskaya Oblast' Rus. Fed.
Otradnoye Samarskaya Oblast' Rus. Fed. see Otradnyy
120 B1 Otradnyy Samarskaya Oblast' Rus. Fed.
195 H2 Otranto Italy
195 H2 Otranto, Strait of Albania/Italy
193 E2 Otricoli Italy
Otrogovo Saratovskaya Oblast' Rus. Fed. see Stepnoye
177 G2 Otrokovice Czech Rep.
131 S3 Otrozhnyy Rus. Fed.
226 E4 Otsego MI U.S.A.
104 B3 Ōtsu Japan
105 E3 Ōtsuki Japan
141 J3 Otta Norway
192 B4 Ottana Sardegna Italy
157 G3 Ottange France
224 F4 Ottawa Ont. Can.
224 F4 Ottawa r. Ont./Que. Can. alt. Outaouais, Rivière des
226 C5 Ottawa IL U.S.A.
236 E4 Ottawa KS U.S.A.
232 A4 Ottawa OH U.S.A.
224 D1 Ottawa Islands Nunavut Can.
171 E4 Ottendorf-Okrilla Ger.
172 B3 Ottenheim Ger.
172 C3 Ottenhöfen im Schwarzwald Ger.
179 G2 Ottenschlag Austria
179 F2 Ottensheim Austria
169 E4 Ottenstein Ger.
168 E2 Otter Ger.
150 D4 Otter r. England U.K.
172 B2 Otterbach Ger.
172 B2 Otterberg Ger.
149 G2 Otterburn Northumberland, England U.K.
146 C5 Otter Ferry Argyll and Bute, Scotland U.K.
173 F4 Otterfing Ger.
164 E2 Otterlo Neth.
168 D2 Otterndorf Ger.
224 D3 Otter Rapids Ont. Can.
168 E2 Ottersberg Ger.
142 E2 Otterstad Sweden
172 C3 Ottersweier Ger.
146 □G1 Otterswick Shetland, Scotland U.K.
142 D4 Otterup Denmark
171 D4 Otterwisch Ger.
150 C4 Ottery r. England U.K.
150 D4 Ottery St Mary Devon, England U.K.
177 G4 Öttevény Hungary
165 D4 Ottignies Belgium
157 H5 Ottmarsheim France
179 E2 Ottnang am Hausruck Austria
173 E4 Ottobeuren Ger.
173 F3 Ottobrunn Ger.
177 I5 Öttömös Hungary
190 E4 Ottone Italy
215 E2 Ottosdal S. Africa
215 E1 Ottoshoop S. Africa
169 E5 Ottrau Ger.
236 E3 Ottumwa IA U.S.A.
172 B2 Ottweiler Ger.
207 G5 Otukpa Nigeria
207 H5 Otukpo Nigeria
245 E4 Otumba Mex.
250 B6 Otuzco Peru
Otvazhniy Rus. Fed. see Zhigulevsk
232 B5 Otway OH U.S.A.
83 E4 Otway, Cape Vic. Austr.
83 E4 Otway Range mts Vic. Austr.
175 J3 Otwock Pol.
183 H1 Otxandio Spain
174 D4 Otyń Pol.
136 C3 Otyniya Ukr.
173 G3 Otzing Ger.
178 B4 Ötztaler Alpen mts Austria
96 C2 Ou, Nam r. Laos
207 H3 Ouacha Niger
237 F6 Ouachita r. AR U.S.A.
237 E5 Ouachita Mountains Arkansas/Oklahoma U.S.A.
228 H4 Ouachita Mountains AR/OK U.S.A.
208 D2 Ouadda C.A.R.
202 D6 Ouaddaï pref. Chad
206 B2 Ouâd Nâga Maur.
206 E3 Ouagadougou Burkina
206 E3 Ouahigouya Burkina
Ouahran Alg. see Oran
208 D3 Ouaka pref. C.A.R.
208 C3 Ouaka r. C.A.R.
206 D2 Oualâta Maur.
207 F4 Oualé r. Burkina
206 C3 Oualia Mali
207 F3 Ouallam Niger
251 I3 Ouanary Fr. Guiana
208 D2 Ouanda-Djailé C.A.R.
208 D3 Ouango C.A.R.
206 D4 Ouangolodougou Côte d'Ivoire
160 B1 Ouanne France
156 C5 Ouanne r. France
251 H4 Ouaqui Fr. Guiana
208 E3 Ouara r. C.A.R.
207 F4 Ouargaye Burkina
205 G3 Ouargla Alg.
204 C3 Ouarkziz, Jbel ridge Alg./Morocco
Ouarogou Burkina see Ouargaye
156 B4 Ouarville France
204 D3 Ouarzazate Morocco
207 F3 Ouatagouna Mali
Oubangui r. C.A.R./Dem. Rep. Congo see Ubangi
182 B4 Ouca Port.
160 D1 Ouche r. France
156 B5 Oucques France
164 D3 Oud-Beijerland Neth.
164 C3 Ouddorp Neth.
164 F1 Oudega Neth.
164 E2 Oudehaske Neth.
164 E2 Oudemirdum Neth.
165 C4 Oudenaarde Belgium
164 D3 Oudenbosch Neth.
165 C3 Oudenburg Belgium
164 G1 Oude Pekela Neth.
164 D2 Oude Rijn r. Neth.
164 D2 Ouderkerk aan de Amstel Neth.
164 D1 Oudeschild Neth.
164 D3 Oude-Tonge Neth.
164 D2 Oudewater Neth.
164 D3 Oud-Gastel Neth.
158 E4 Oudon France
159 F4 Oudon r. France
214 D5 Oudtshoorn S. Africa
165 D3 Oud-Turnhout Belgium
165 C3 Oudzele Belgium
204 D2 Oued Zem Morocco
78 □5 Ouégoa New Caledonia
206 D4 Ouéléssébougou Mali
207 F3 Ouella Niger
207 F5 Ouémé r. Benin
206 E4 Ouessa Burkina
158 A3 Ouessant, Île d' i. France
207 F4 Ouèssè Benin
208 C4 Ouésso Congo
207 H5 Ouest prov. Cameroon
204 D2 Ouezzane Morocco
165 E4 Ouffet Belgium
147 B3 Oughterard Rep. of Ireland
160 D1 Ougney France
104 A4 Ougo-gawa r. Japan
184 C1 Ouguela Port.
105 E2 Ougura-yama mt. Japan
208 C3 Ouham pref. C.A.R.
208 C2 Ouham r. C.A.R./Chad
208 C3 Ouham Pendé pref. C.A.R.
207 F5 Ouidah Benin
242 C3 Ouiriego Mex.
159 F2 Ouistreham France
204 E2 Oujda Morocco
206 B2 Oujeft Maur.
204 C3 Oulad Teïma Morocco
140 N2 Oulainen Fin.
156 D3 Oulchy-le-Château France
165 F4 Oulder Belgium
206 C3 Ould Yenjé Maur.
205 G2 Ouled Djellal Alg.
205 F2 Ouled Naïl, Monts des mts Alg.
160 C3 Oullins France
204 D2 Oulmès Morocco
151 I2 Oulton Suffolk, England U.K.
140 N2 Oulu Fin.
140 N2 Oulu prov. Fin.
140 N2 Oulujärvi l. Fin.
140 N2 Oulujoki r. Fin.
140 N2 Oulunsalo Fin.
190 B3 Oulx Italy
206 D5 Oumé Côte d'Ivoire
205 G2 Oum el Bouaghi Alg.
202 C6 Oum-Hadjer Chad
205 G4 Ounane, Djebel mt. Alg.
204 C3 Ounara Morocco
140 N2 Ounasjoki r. Fin.
151 G2 Oundle Northamptonshire, England U.K.
223 K5 Oungre Sask. Can.
165 E4 Oupeye Belgium
165 F5 Our r. Lux.
239 F4 Ouray CO U.S.A.
241 M1 Ouray UT U.S.A.
156 E4 Ource r. France
156 D3 Ourcq r. France
206 C4 Ouré Kaba Guinea
254 D2 Ourém Brazil
182 C2 Ourense Spain
182 C2 Ourense prov. Galicia Spain
254 E3 Ouricurí Brazil
256 C5 Ourinhos Brazil
184 B3 Ourique Port.
254 D4 Ouro r. Brazil
182 C1 Ouro r. Spain
257 F4 Ouro Branco Brazil
256 D5 Ouro Fino Brazil
182 C1 Ourol Spain
257 F4 Ouro Preto Brazil
160 B1 Ouroux-en-Morvan France
160 C2 Ouroux-sur-Saône France
165 E4 Ourthe r. Belgium
159 G2 Ourville-en-Caux France
151 H4 Ouse r. East Sussex, England U.K.
149 I4 Ouse r. England U.K.
163 D6 Oust France
158 D4 Oust r. France
184 B2 Outão Port.
224 F4 Outaouais, Rivière des r. Ont./Que. Can. alt. Ottawa
225 G3 Outardes r. Que. Can.
156 C4 Outarville France
204 E2 Outat Oulad el Haj Morocco
182 D3 Outeiro Bragança Port.
182 B3 Outeiro Viana do Castelo Port.
182 C1 Outeiro de Rei Spain
182 C3 Outeiro Seco Port.
214 D5 Outeniekwaberge mts S. Africa
146 A4 Outer Hebrides is Scotland U.K.
Outer Mongolia country Asia see Mongolia
240 H5 Outer Santa Barbara Channel CA U.S.A.
212 C4 Outjo Namibia
223 J5 Outlook Sask. Can.
134 E3 Outokumpu Fin.
182 C2 Outomuro Spain
81 C6 Outram South I. N.Z.
156 B2 Outreau France
146 □H1 Out Skerries is Scotland U.K.
151 H2 Outwell Norfolk, England U.K.
78 □5 Ouvéa i. Î. Loyauté New Caledonia
161 A5 Ouveillan France
161 C4 Ouvèze r. France
83 E3 Ouyen Vic. Austr.
151 G2 Ouzel r. England U.K.
156 B5 Ouzouer-le-Marché France
156 C5 Ouzouer-sur-Loire France
199 E1 Ova r. Turkey
192 B3 Ovace, Punta d' mt. Corse France
126 D3 Ovacık Turkey
126 E3 Ovacık Turkey
199 G3 Ovacık Dağı mt. Turkey
190 D4 Ovada Italy
199 E3 Ovaeymiri Turkey
199 F2 Ovakent İzmir Turkey
129 C4 Ovakışla Turkey
199 E3 Ovakışlacık Muğla Turkey
199 F3 Ovaköy Antalya Turkey
234 A1 Oval PA U.S.A.
79 □1a Ovalau i. Fiji
260 B2 Ovalle Chile
212 B3 Ovamboland reg. Namibia
208 B4 Ovan Gabon
182 B4 Ovar Port.
191 H2 Ovaro Italy
78 □6 Ovau i. Solomon Is
260 E3 Oveja mt. Arg.
168 D2 Ovelgönne Ger.
83 F4 Ovens r. Vic. Austr.
147 C5 Ovens Rep. of Ireland
169 C5 Overath Ger.
146 F2 Overbister Orkney, Scotland U.K.
164 G2 Overdinkel Neth.
140 J2 Overhalla Norway
165 D4 Overijse Belgium
164 F2 Overijssel prov. Neth.
140 M2 Överkalix Sweden
87 B5 Overlander Roadhouse W.A. Austr.
236 E4 Overland Park KS U.S.A.
234 B3 Overlea MD U.S.A.
164 E3 Overloon Neth.
260 B4 Overo, Volcán vol. Arg.
165 E3 Overpelt Belgium
151 F2 Overseal Derbyshire, England U.K.
151 F3 Overton Hampshire, England U.K.
150 E2 Overton Wrexham, Wales U.K.
241 J3 Overton NV U.S.A.
237 E5 Overton TX U.S.A.
140 M2 Övertorneå Sweden
146 E6 Overtown North Lanarkshire, Scotland U.K.
143 G3 Överum Sweden
140 K2 Överuman l. Sweden
164 D2 Overveen Neth.
151 F3 Over Wallop Hampshire, England U.K.
190 D2 Ovesca r. Italy
165 C3 Ovezande Neth.
236 C3 Ovid CO U.S.A.
226 E4 Ovid MI U.S.A.
232 E3 Ovid NY U.S.A.
136 F4 Ovidiopol' Ukr.
197 I3 Ovidiu Romania
182 E1 Oviedo Spain
182 D1 Oviedo prov. Asturias Spain
190 D4 Oviglio Italy
193 F2 Ovindoli Italy
139 K2 Ovinishchenskaya Vozvyshennost' hills Rus. Fed.
192 B4 Ovodda Sardegna Italy
Ovolau i. Fiji see Ovalau
107 G2 Ovoot Mongolia
106 D2 Övörhangay prov. Mongolia
141 I3 Øvre Årdal Norway
141 J3 Øvre Rendal Norway
140 M1 Övre Soppero Sweden
136 E2 Ovruch Ukr.
106 D2 Övt Mongolia
80 F4 Owahanga North I. N.Z.
81 B7 Owaka South I. N.Z.
226 B1 Owakonze Ont. Can.
208 B5 Owando Congo
Owa Rafa i. Solomon Is see Santa Ana
Owa Riki i. Solomon Is see Santa Catalina
104 C4 Owase Japan
237 E4 Owasso OK U.S.A.
236 E2 Owatonna MN U.S.A.
123 E3 Owbeh Afgh.
175 J4 Owczarnia Pol.
233 E3 Owego NY U.S.A.
147 D3 Owel, Lough l. Rep. of Ireland
172 D3 Owen Ger.
81 D4 Owen, Mount South I. N.Z.
207 G5 Owena Nigeria
147 C2 Owenbeg Rep. of Ireland
214 D3 Owendale S. Africa
147 B2 Owenduff r. Rep. of Ireland
210 B4 Owen Falls Dam Uganda
147 B2 Oweniny r. Rep. of Ireland
147 B2 Owenmore r. Rep. of Ireland
147 D2 Owenreagh r. Northern Ireland U.K.
81 D4 Owen River South I. N.Z.
240 I3 Owens r. CA U.S.A.
230 C4 Owensboro KY U.S.A.
224 D4 Owen Sound Ont. Can.
84 C4 Owen Springs N.T. Austr.
91 K8 Owen Stanley Range mts P.N.G.
236 F4 Owensville MO U.S.A.
232 A5 Owensville OH U.S.A.
230 C4 Owenton KY U.S.A.
207 G5 Owerri Nigeria
80 E3 Owhango North I. N.Z.
172 D4 Owingen Ger.
232 E5 Owings MD U.S.A.
234 B3 Owings Mills MD U.S.A.
232 B5 Owingsville KY U.S.A.
223 M3 Owl r. Man. Can.
238 E3 Owl Creek r. WY U.S.A.
233 □I2 Owls Head ME U.S.A.
Owminzatow Toghi hills Uzbek. see Auminzatau, Gory
207 G5 Owo Nigeria
227 E4 Owosso MI U.S.A.
168 E1 Owschlag Ger.
238 C3 Owyhee NV U.S.A.
238 C3 Owyhee r. OR U.S.A.
238 C3 Owyhee Mountains ID U.S.A.
238 C3 Owyhee North Fork r. ID U.S.A.
238 C3 Owyhee South Fork r. ID U.S.A.
252 B2 Oxapampa Peru
140 □C2 Öxarfjörður b. Iceland
223 K5 Oxbow Sask. Can.
236 C1 Ox Creek r. ND U.S.A.
143 G2 Oxelösund Sweden
149 H4 Oxenhope West Yorkshire, England U.K.
81 D5 Oxford South I. N.Z.
151 F3 Oxford Oxfordshire, England U.K.
235 E1 Oxford CT U.S.A.
233 H3 Oxford MA U.S.A.
233 □H2 Oxford ME U.S.A.
227 F4 Oxford MI U.S.A.
237 F5 Oxford MS U.S.A.
231 E4 Oxford NC U.S.A.
234 D2 Oxford NJ U.S.A.
233 F3 Oxford NY U.S.A.
232 A5 Oxford OH U.S.A.
234 C3 Oxford PA U.S.A.
226 C4 Oxford WI U.S.A.
85 G4 Oxford Downs Qld Austr.
223 M4 Oxford House Man. Can.
151 F3 Oxfordshire admin. div. England U.K.
142 E4 Oxie Sweden
243 H4 Oxkutzcab Mex.
83 F3 Oxley N.S.W. Austr.
83 G2 Oxleys Peak N.S.W. Austr.
Ox Mountains hills Rep. of Ireland see Slieve Gamph
240 H4 Oxnard CA U.S.A.
151 G3 Oxshott Surrey, England U.K.
151 H3 Oxted Surrey, England U.K.
146 F6 Oxton Scottish Borders, Scotland U.K.
227 H3 Oxtongue Lake Ont. Can.
Oxus r. Asia see Amudar'ya
198 D2 Oxylithos Greece
95 E2 Oya r. Sarawak Malaysia
140 K2 Øya Norway
104 C2 Oyabe Japan
104 D2 Oyabe-gawa r. Japan
105 F2 Oyama Japan
105 F3 Ō-yama mt. Japan
105 F4 Ō-yama vol. Japan
251 I3 Oyapock r. Brazil/Fr. Guiana
208 A4 Oyem Gabon
223 I5 Oyen Alta Can.
156 C2 Oye-Plage France
106 C1 Oygon Mongolia
146 D4 Oykel r. Scotland U.K.
146 D4 Oykel Bridge Highland, Scotland U.K.
173 E4 Oy-Mittelberg Ger.
208 B5 Oyo Congo
207 F5 Oyo Nigeria
207 F4 Oyo state Nigeria
252 A2 Oyón Peru
183 H2 Oyón Spain
160 D2 Oyonnax France
Oyoqquduq Uzbek. see Ayakkuduk
Oysangur Rus. Fed. see Oyskhara
129 E2 Oyskhara Rus. Fed.
214 E6 Oyster Bay S. Africa
235 E2 Oyster Bay NY U.S.A.
235 D3 Oyster Creek NJ U.S.A.
121 H4 Oytal Kazakh.
168 E2 Oyten Ger.
128 A1 Oyukludağı mt. Turkey
Oyyl Kazakh. see Uil
Oyyq Kazakh. see Uyuk
182 B1 Oza Spain
Ozaeta Spain see Ozeta
127 G3 Özalp Turkey
92 B4 Ozamiz Phil.
156 B4 Ozanne r. France
231 C6 Ozark AL U.S.A.
237 E5 Ozark AR U.S.A.
237 E4 Ozark MO U.S.A.
237 E4 Ozark Plateau MO U.S.A.
236 E4 Ozarks, Lake of the MO U.S.A.
175 J5 Ożarów Pol.
175 H5 Ożarowice Pol.
175 I3 Ożarów Mazowiecki Pol.
199 E3 Özbaşı Turkey
Ozbekiston country Asia see Uzbekistan
177 J3 Ózd Hungary
177 I3 Ožďany Slovakia
199 E3 Özdere Turkey
129 B4 Özdilek Turkey
Özen Kazakh. see Kyzylsay
139 J2 Ozerevo Rus. Fed.
136 E5 Ozerne Odes'ka Oblast' Ukr.
136 C2 Ozerne Volyns'ka Oblast' Ukr.
136 E2 Ozerne Zhytomyrs'ka Oblast' Ukr.
139 K4 Ozerninskoye Vodokhranilishche resr Rus. Fed.
131 Q4 Ozernovskiy Rus. Fed.
120 E1 Ozernoye Kustanayskaya Oblast' Kazakh.
120 B2 Ozernoye Rus. Fed.
Ozernyy Karagandinskaya Oblast' Kazakh. see Shashubay
Ozernyy Kustanayskaya Oblast' Kazakh. see Ozernoye
139 M3 Ozernyy Ivanovskaya Oblast' Rus. Fed.
120 E2 Ozernyy Orenburgskaya Oblast' Rus. Fed.
139 I4 Ozernyy Smolenskaya Oblast' Rus. Fed.
198 B2 Ozeros, Limni l. Greece
138 D4 Ozersk Rus. Fed.
100 G3 Ozerskiy Sakhalin Rus. Fed.
139 L4 Ozery Rus. Fed.
100 D2 Ozeryane Rus. Fed.
137 G2 Ozeryany Ukr.
183 H2 Ozeta Spain
121 H4 Özgön Kyrg.
139 L4 Ozherel'ye Rus. Fed.
131 Q3 Ozhogina r. Rus. Fed.
192 B4 Ozieri Sardegna Italy
174 G5 Ozimek Pol.
120 B2 Ozinki Rus. Fed.
156 C4 Ozoir-la-Ferrière France
138 D3 Ozolnieki Latvia
237 C6 Ozona TX U.S.A.
177 H5 Ozora Hungary
175 H4 Ozorków Pol.
207 G5 Ozoro Nigeria
103 F7 Ōzu Japan
245 E4 Ozumba de Alzate Mex.
129 C3 Ozurget'i Georgia
128 A1 Özyurt Dağı mts Turkey
175 M5 Ozyutychi Ukr.
191 G4 Ozzano dell'Emilia Italy
190 D3 Ozzano Monferrato Italy

P

206 E4 Pâ Burkina
165 E3 Paal Belgium
78 □5 Paama i. Vanuatu
221 N3 Paamiut Greenland
96 B3 Pa-an Myanmar
Paanopa i. Kiribati see Banaba
214 B5 Paarl S. Africa
78 □4a Paata i. Chuuk Micronesia
Paatsjoki r. Europe see Patsoyoki
240 □D8 Paauilo HI U.S.A.
Pabaigh i. Western Isles, Scotland U.K. see Pabbay
146 B3 Pabail Iarach Western Isles, Scotland U.K.
214 C3 Paballelo S. Africa
101 D4 P'abal-li N. Korea
146 A4 Pabbay i. Western Isles, Scotland U.K.
146 A5 Pabbay i. Western Isles, Scotland U.K.
244 C2 Pabellón de Arteaga Mex.
175 H4 Pabianice Pol.
Pabianitz Pol. see Pabianice
192 A5 Pabillonis Sardegna Italy
245 E1 Pablillo r. Mex.
117 G4 Pabna Bangl.
179 F2 Pabneukirchen Austria
138 E4 Pabradė Lith.
123 F5 Pab Range mts Pak.
158 C3 Pabu France
252 D2 Pacaás, Serra dos hills Brazil
256 B4 Pacaembu Brazil
252 D2 Pacahuaras r. Bol.
254 F3 Pacajus Brazil
214 D6 Pacaltsdorp S. Africa
175 J5 Pacanów Pol.
Pacaraimã, Serra mts S. America see Pakaraima Mountains
250 B6 Pacasmayo Peru
254 F2 Pacatuba Brazil
250 C6 Pacaya r. Peru
243 H6 Pacaya, Volcán de vol. Guat.
158 E3 Pacé France
194 B5 Paceco Sicilia Italy
242 C2 Pacheco Mex.
135 H5 Pachelma Rus. Fed.
195 E6 Pachino Sicilia Italy
252 B2 Pachitea r. Peru
252 A1 Pachiza Peru
116 D5 Pachmarhi Madh. Prad. India
198 D1 Pachni Greece
116 D5 Pachor Madh. Prad. India
116 C5 Pachora Mahar. India
116 C4 Pachpadra Rajasthan India
245 E3 Pachuca Mex.
192 E1 Paciano Italy
240 F3 Pacifica CA U.S.A.
267 I9 Pacific-Antarctic Ridge sea feature Pacific Ocean
240 G3 Pacific Grove CA U.S.A.
266 Pacific Ocean
177 K3 Pácin Hungary
196 D3 Pačir Vojvodina, Srbija Yugo.
95 E5 Pacitan Jawa Timur Indon.
83 E2 Packsaddle N.S.W. Austr.
182 B3 Pacos de Ferreira Port.
176 E2 Pacov Czech Rep.
176 G5 Pacsa Hungary
257 E2 Pacuí r. Brazil
177 K2 Pacutová hill Slovakia
175 H3 Pacyna Pol.
156 B3 Pacy-sur-Eure France
174 F5 Paczków Pol.
92 C5 Padada Phil.
Padali Rus. Fed. see Amursk
116 C3 Padampur Rajasthan India
94 C3 Padang Sumatera Indon.
94 C3 Padangpanjang Sumatera Indon.
94 B2 Padangsidimpuan Sumatera Indon.
134 F3 Padany Rus. Fed.
95 F1 Padas r. Sabah Malaysia
141 N3 Padasjoki Fin.
122 B3 Padatha, Kūh-e mt. Iran
251 E5 Padauiri r. Brazil
168 E1 Padborg Denmark
151 G3 Padbury Buckinghamshire, England U.K.
252 D5 Padcaya Bol.
83 F3 Paddington N.S.W. Austr.
215 H4 Paddock S. Africa
151 H3 Paddock Wood Kent, England U.K.
177 J6 Padej Vojvodina, Srbija Yugo.
232 C5 Paden City WV U.S.A.
169 D4 Paderborn Ger.
184 B3 Paderne Faro Port.
182 B2 Paderne Viana do Castelo Port.
182 C2 Paderne de Allariz Spain
197 F3 Padeșu, Vârful mt. Romania
175 J5 Padew Narodowa Pol.
149 G4 Padiham Lancashire,England U.K.
252 D4 Padilla Bol.
197 H3 Padina Romania
196 E3 Padina Vojvodina, Srbija Yugo.
196 E3 Padinska Skela Srbija Yugo.
163 D4 Padirac France
Padma r. Bangl. see Ganges
114 C4 Padmanabhapuram Tamil Nadu India
116 E5 Padmapur Mahar. India
157 G4 Padoux France
191 G3 Padova Italy
191 G3 Padova prov. Veneto Italy
116 C5 Padra Gujarat India
117 F4 Padrauna Uttar Prad. India
184 D3 Padre Caro hill Spain
257 G2 Padre Paraíso Brazil
192 A4 Padria Sardegna Italy
192 A2 Padro, Monte mt. Corse France
182 B2 Padrón Spain
192 B4 Padru Sardegna Italy
150 C4 Padstow Cornwall, England U.K.
138 F4 Padsvillye Belarus
82 E4 Padthaway S.A. Austr.
115 D2 Padua Orissa India
Padua Italy see Padova
237 F4 Paducah KY U.S.A.
237 C5 Paducah TX U.S.A.
185 G3 Padul Spain
193 H4 Padula Italy
193 G3 Paduli Italy
116 D2 Padum Jammu and Kashmir
197 F2 Pădurea Craiului, Munții mts Romania
81 E4 Paekakariki North I. N.Z.
101 D4 Paekdu-san mt. China/N. Korea
81 B6 Paerau South I. N.Z.
80 E2 Paeroa North I. N.Z.
80 F3 Paeroa hill North I. N.Z.
190 C4 Paesana Italy
191 H3 Paese Italy
195 D2 Paestum tourist site Italy
92 B3 Paete Phil.
128 A2 Pafos Cyprus
128 A2 Pafos airport Cyprus
188 E3 Pag Croatia
188 E3 Pag i. Croatia
134 M2 Paga r. Rus. Fed.
95 D4 Pagadenbaru Jawa Barat Indon.
92 B5 Pagadian Phil.
Pagalu i. Equat. Guinea see Annobón
91 K3 Pagan i. N. Mariana Is
191 G2 Paganella mt. Italy
193 F2 Paganica Italy
192 D2 Paganico Italy
94 C3 Pagaralam Sumatera Indon.
198 C2 Pagasitikos Kolpos b. Greece
95 F3 Pagatan Kalimantan Selatan Indon.
241 L3 Page AZ U.S.A.
86 E3 Page, Mount hill W.A. Austr.
138 C4 Pagėgiai Lith.
259 □ Paget, Mount S. Georgia
85 H3 Paget Cay rf Coral Sea Is Terr. Austr.
151 G4 Pagham West Sussex, England U.K.
138 E4 Pagiriai Kėdainiai Lith.
138 E4 Pagiriai Vilnius Lith.
192 E2 Paglia r. Italy
193 G2 Paglieta Italy
157 G4 Pagny-sur-Moselle France
Pagon i. N. Mariana Is see Pagan
78 □2 Pago Pago American Samoa
239 F4 Pagosa Springs CO U.S.A.
207 F4 Pagouda Togo
Paggên Qinghai China see Gadê
224 C3 Pagwachuan r. Ont. Can.
224 C3 Pagwa River Ont. Can.
240 □D9 Pahala HI U.S.A.
94 C2 Pahang r. Malaysia
94 C2 Pahang state Malaysia
117 G4 Paharpur tourist site Bangl.
123 G3 Paharpur Pak.
80 E4 Pahiatua North I. N.Z.
173 F4 Pähl Ger.
168 E1 Pahlen Ger.
116 C2 Pahlgam Jammu and Kashmir
240 □D9 Pahoa HI U.S.A.
231 D7 Pahokee FL U.S.A.
241 J3 Pahranagat Range mts NV U.S.A.
138 D5 Pahranichny Belarus
241 J3 Pahrump NV U.S.A.
116 D4 Pahuj r. India
240 I3 Pahute Mesa plat. NV U.S.A.
240 □C8 Paia HI U.S.A.
182 B4 Paião Port.
240 G3 Paicines CA U.S.A.
138 E2 Paide Estonia
150 D4 Paignton Torbay, England U.K.
80 E1 Paihia North I. N.Z.
250 B6 Paiján Peru
141 N3 Päijänne l. Fin.
207 G4 Paiko Nigeria
252 D4 Paila r. Bol.
260 A6 Pailahueque Chile
163 D5 Pailhès France
Pailing Zhejiang China see Chun'an
259 B6 Paillaco Chile
240 □C8 Pailolo Channel HI U.S.A.
158 D4 Paimbœuf France
141 M3 Paimio Fin.
158 C3 Paimpol France
158 D3 Paimpont France
94 C3 Painan Sumatera Indon.
114 C4 Painavu Kerala India
260 B3 Paine Chile
259 B8 Paine, Cerro mt. Chile
257 E3 Paineiras Brazil
226 C2 Painesdale MI U.S.A.
232 C4 Painesville OH U.S.A.
257 E4 Pains Brazil
150 E3 Painswick Gloucestershire, England U.K.
241 L3 Painted Desert AZ U.S.A.
173 F3 Painten Ger.
Paint Hills Que. Can. see Wemindji
237 D6 Paint Rock TX U.S.A.
232 B6 Paintsville KY U.S.A.
250 C3 Paipa Col.
116 E5 Pairi r. India
227 G3 Paisley Ont. Can.
146 D6 Paisley Renfrewshire, Scotland U.K.
183 H1 País Vasco aut. comm. Spain
78 □5 Païta New Caledonia
250 A6 Paita Peru
114 B2 Paithan Mahar. India
109 G2 Paitou Zhejiang China
182 B3 Paiva r. Port.
Paiva Couceiro Angola see Quipungo
109 E2 Paizhou Hubei China
140 M2 Pajala Sweden
250 A5 Pajan Ecuador
216 □3b Pájara Fuerteventura Canary Is
183 I5 Pajarón Spain
183 I5 Pajaroncillo Spain
174 G4 Pajęczno Pol.
176 F5 Páka Hungary
114 C3 Pakala Andhra Prad. India
Pakanbaru Sumatera Indon. see Pekanbaru
251 F4 Pakaraima Mountains S. America
117 F4 Pakaur Bihar India
80 D4 Pakawau South I. N.Z.
101 C5 Pakch'ŏn N. Korea
224 D4 Pakesley Ont. Can.
131 R3 Pakhachi Rus. Fed.
120 D2 Pakhar' Kazakh.
Pákhni Greece see Pachni
Pakhoi Guangxi China see Beihai
139 K4 Pakhomovo Rus. Fed.
121 H4 Pakhtaabad Uzbek.
123 F4 Pakistan country Asia
Paknampho Thai. see Nakhon Sawan
176 G5 Pakod Hungary
96 A2 Pakokku Myanmar
174 G3 Pakość Pol.
174 F4 Pakosław Pol.
188 E4 Pakoštane Croatia
80 D1 Pakotai North I. N.Z.
177 H4 Pákozd Hungary
123 H4 Pakpattan Pak.
97 C5 Pak Phanang Thai.
97 C6 Pak Phayun Thai.
188 F3 Pakra r. Croatia
188 F3 Pakrac Croatia
138 D4 Pakruojis Lith.
177 H5 Paks Hungary
Pakse Laos see Pakxé
109 □ Pak Tam Chung H.K. China
97 C4 Pak Thong Chai Thai.
123 G3 Paktīā prov. Afgh.
123 GH3 Paktīkā prov. Afgh.
95 F2 Paku r. Sarawak Malaysia
93 B3 Pakue Indon.
136 F2 Pakul' Ukr.
96 D4 Pakxé Laos
Pal Senegal see Mpal
208 B2 Pala Chad
94 D4 Palabuhanratu Jawa Barat Indon.
183 F3 Palacios de Goda Spain
183 G3 Palacios de la Sierra Spain
182 D2 Palacios del Sil Spain
182 D2 Palacios de Sanabria Spain
178 C4 Pala di San Martino mt. Italy
161 D3 Paladru, Lac de l. France
Palaestinia reg. Asia see Palestine
186 G3 Palafrugell Spain
195 F2 Palagianello Italy
195 G2 Palagiano Italy
194 D5 Palagonia Sicilia Italy
191 F5 Palaia Italy
198 C3 Palaia Fokaia Greece
198 C4 Palaiochora Kriti Greece
198 B2 Palairos Greece
156 C4 Palaiseau France
Palakkat Kerala India see Palghat
198 C2 Palamas Greece
186 G3 Palamós Spain
116 D2 Palam Pur Hima. Prad. India
116 C4 Palana Rajasthan India
131 Q4 Palana Rus. Fed.
92 B2 Palanan Phil.
187 C5 Palancia r. Spain
129 B4 Palandöken Dağları mts Turkey
116 E5 Palandur Mahar. India
138 C4 Palanga Lith.
122 E4 Palangān, Kūh-e mts Iran
161 A4 Palanges, Montagne des mts France
95 F3 Palangkaraya Kalimantan Tengah Indon.
114 C4 Palani Tamil Nadu India
116 C4 Palanpur Gujarat India
190 F4 Palanzano Italy
92 C3 Palapag Phil.
213 E4 Palapye Botswana
114 D3 Palar r. India
117 G4 Palasbari Assam India
182 C2 Palas de Rei Spain
138 G4 Palata r. Belarus
193 G3 Palata Italy
131 Q3 Palatka Rus. Fed.
231 D6 Palatka FL U.S.A.
192 B3 Palau Sardegna Italy
92 □ Palau country N. Pacific Ocean
92 A3 Palauig Phil.
91 H5 Palau Islands Palau
266 D5 Palau Trench sea feature N. Pacific Ocean
161 B5 Palavas-les-Flots France
97 B4 Palaw Myanmar
92 A4 Palawan i. Phil.
92 A4 Palawan Passage str. Phil.
266 C5 Palawan Trough sea feature N. Pacific Ocean
92 B3 Palayan Phil.
114 C4 Palayankottai Tamil Nadu India
183 F4 Palazuelos de Eresma Spain
194 C5 Palazzo Adriano Sicilia Italy
194 D5 Palazzolo Acreide Sicilia Italy
190 E3 Palazzolo sull'Oglio Italy
193 I4 Palazzo San Gervasio Italy
179 G4 Paldau Austria
138 E2 Paldiski Estonia
188 G4 Pale Bos.-Herz.
134 H4 Palekh Rus. Fed.
94 D3 Palembang Sumatera Indon.
259 C6 Palena Chile
193 G3 Palena Italy
183 F2 Palencia Spain
183 F2 Palencia prov. Castilla y León Spain
185 F3 Palenciana Spain
243 G5 Palenque Mex.
183 F2 Palenzuela Spain
194 C4 Palermo Sicilia Italy
194 C5 Palermo prov. Sicilia Italy
194 C4 Palermo, Golfo di b. Sicilia Italy
189 D6 Palermo Punta Raisi airport Sicilia Italy
128 B3 Palestine reg. Asia
237 E6 Palestine TX U.S.A.
193 E3 Palestrina Italy
177 H5 Pálfa Hungary
114 B2 Palghar Mahar. India
114 C4 Palghat Kerala India
87 B4 Palgrave, Mount hill W.A. Austr.
182 B4 Palhaça Port.
177 K3 Pálháza Hungary
255 C8 Palhoca Brazil
116 E5 Pali Madh. Prad. India
114 B2 Pali Mahar. India
116 C4 Pali Rajasthan India
193 F3 Paliano Italy
177 I5 Palić Vojvodina, Srbija Yugo.
78 □4b Palikir Pohnpei Micronesia
92 C5 Palimbang Phil.
160 C2 Palinges France
193 H4 Palinuro Italy
156 D4 Palis France
239 E4 Palisade CO U.S.A.
165 E5 Paliseul Belgium
116 B5 Palitana Gujarat India
138 D2 Palivere Estonia
195 F5 Palizzi Italy
140 L2 Palja hill Sweden
140 O2 Paljakka hill Fin.
141 N3 Pälkäne Fin.
114 C4 Palk Bay Sri Lanka
138 G3 Palkino Rus. Fed.
115 D2 Palkohda Andhra Prad. India
114 C3 Palkonda Range mts India
117 F5 Palkot Bihar India
177 H2 Palkovice Czech Rep.
114 C4 Palk Strait India/Sri Lanka
Palla Bianca mt. Austria/Italy see Weißkugel
114 C4 Palladani Tamil Nadu India
195 F3 Pallagorio Italy
252 B3 Pallapalla mt. Peru
184 D2 Pallarés Spain
186 E2 Pallaresa r. Spain
147 C4 Pallas Green Rep. of Ireland
147 C4 Pallaskenry Rep. of Ireland
120 A2 Pallasovka Rus. Fed.
114 D3 Pallavaram Tamil Nadu India
114 D2 Palleru r. India
173 G3 Palling Ger.
87 C7 Pallinup r. W.A. Austr.
210 B4 Pallisa Uganda
81 E4 Palliser, Cape North I. N.Z.
79 □3 Palliser, Îles is Arch. des Tuamotu Fr. Polynesia
81 E4 Palliser Bay North I. N.Z.
116 C3 Pallu Rajasthan India
158 E5 Palluau France
159 H5 Palluau-sur-Indre France
254 D5 Palma r. Brazil
211 D7 Palma Moz.
184 B2 Palma Port.
193 G4 Palma Campania Italy
185 E3 Palma del Río Spain
187 F5 Palma de Mallorca Spain
194 C5 Palma di Montechiaro Sicilia Italy
192 A4 Palmadula Sardegna Italy
114 C3 Palmaner Andhra Prad. India
191 I3 Palmanova Italy
187 F5 Palma Nova Spain
244 D2 Palma Pegada Mex.
244 D4 Palmar Chico Mex.
254 G4 Palmares Brazil
255 C9 Palmares do Sul Brazil
227 H1 Palmarolle Que. Can.
242 □J7 Palmar Sur Costa Rica
255 C8 Palmas Paraná Brazil
254 C4 Palmas Tocantins Brazil
246 D2 Palma Soriano Cuba
182 B4 Palmaz Port.
231 D7 Palm Bay FL U.S.A.
231 D6 Palm Coast FL U.S.A.
240 H4 Palmdale CA U.S.A.
241 I5 Palm Desert CA U.S.A.
256 C6 Palmeira Brazil
182 B3 Palmeira Port.
255 B8 Palmeira das Missões Brazil
254 F4 Palmeira dos Índios Brazil
254 E3 Palmeirais Brazil
254 D5 Palmeiras r. Brazil
256 C2 Palmeiras de Goiás Brazil
184 B2 Palmela Port.
262 T2 Palmer research stn Antarctica
85 E3 Palmer r. Qld Austr.
220 D3 Palmer AK U.S.A.
262 T2 Palmer Land reg. Antarctica
234 B4 Palmer Park MD U.S.A.
Palmerston N.T. Austr. see Darwin
84 B2 Palmerston N.T. Austr.
227 G4 Palmerston Ont. Can.
81 □2 Palmerston atoll Cook Is
81 C6 Palmerston South I. N.Z.
147 E3 Palmerston Rep. of Ireland
85 G4 Palmerston, Cape Qld Austr.
80 E4 Palmerston North North I. N.Z.
234 C2 Palmerton PA U.S.A.
85 F2 Palmerville Qld Austr.
231 D7 Palmetto FL U.S.A.
195 E4 Palmi Italy
245 E2 Palmillas Mex.
260 C3 Palmira Arg.
250 B4 Palmira Col.
246 B2 Palmira Cuba
256 A6 Palmital Paraná Brazil
256 B5 Palmital São Paulo Brazil
261 I3 Palmitas Uru.
Palmnicken Rus. Fed. see Yantarnyy
184 E4 Palmones r. Spain
177 I5 Pálmonostora Hungary
240 I5 Palm Springs CA U.S.A.
85 G5 Palm Tree Creek r. Qld Austr.
Palmyra Syria see Tadmur
236 F4 Palmyra MO U.S.A.
234 C2 Palmyra NJ U.S.A.
232 E3 Palmyra NY U.S.A.
227 I5 Palmyra PA U.S.A.
232 D6 Palmyra VA U.S.A.
75 I3 Palmyra Atoll N. Pacific Ocean
117 F5 Palmyras Point India
146 E7 Palnackie Dumfries and Galloway, Scotland U.K.
192 B3 Palneca Corse France
114 C4 Palni Hills India
92 C4 Palo Phil.
244 C3 Palo Alto Mex.
240 F3 Palo Alto CA U.S.A.
250 B3 Palo de las Letras Col.
195 F1 Palo del Colle Italy
252 C3 Palomani mt. Peru
186 C4 Palomar de Arroyos Spain
245 G5 Palomares Mex.
184 D3 Palomares del Río Spain
240 I5 Palomar Mountain CA U.S.A.
184 D2 Palomas Spain
193 G2 Palombaro Italy
194 E6 Palombieri r. Sicilia Italy
183 H4 Palomera Spain
186 B4 Palomera, Sierra mts Spain
183 H5 Palomeras del Campo Spain
184 D2 Palomilas r. Spain
193 H4 Palomonte Italy
191 G3 Palòn, Cima mt. Italy
114 D2 Paloncha Andhra Prad. India
237 D5 Palo Pinto TX U.S.A.
93 B3 Palopo Sulawesi Selatan Indon.
187 C7 Palos, Cabo de c. Spain
258 F2 Palo Santo Arg.
184 D3 Palos de la Frontera Spain
238 C2 Palouse r. WA U.S.A.
241 J5 Palo Verde CA U.S.A.
85 E5 Palparara Qld Austr.
186 G3 Pals Spain
116 C5 Palsana Gujarat India
140 N2 Paltamo Fin.
139 J5 Pal'tso Rus. Fed.
93 A3 Palu Sulawesi Tengah Indon.
93 A3 Palu r. Indon.
127 E3 Palu Turkey
92 B3 Paluan Phil.
195 F3 Paludi Italy
163 A5 Palue r. France
159 G2 Paluel France
191 I2 Paluzza Italy
123 F2 Pal'vart Turkm.
116 D3 Palwal Haryana India
Palwancha Andhra Prad. India see Paloncha
131 S3 Palyavaam r. Rus. Fed.
Palyeskaya Nizina marsh Belarus/Ukr. see Pripet Marshes
172 A2 Palzem Ger.
179 I2 Pama Austria
207 F4 Pama Burkina
208 C3 Pama r. C.A.R.
83 E3 Pamamaroo Lake N.S.W. Austr.
217 □3b Pamandzi Mayotte
95 D4 Pamanukan Jawa Barat Indon.
250 D5 Pamar Col.
129 D3 P'ambaki Lerrnashght'a mts Armenia
213 G4 Pambarra Moz.
83 G4 Pambula N.S.W. Austr.
179 G4 Pameče Slovenia
95 F4 Pamekasan Jawa Timur Indon.
95 D4 Pameungpeuk Jawa Barat Indon.
199 E2 Pamfylla Voreio Aigaio Greece
179 H3 Pamhagen Austria
174 E3 Pamiątkowo Pol.
114 C3 Pamidi Andhra Prad. India
163 D5 Pamiers France
123 H2 Pamir r. Afgh./Tajik.
121 H5 Pamir mts Asia
231 E5 Pamlico r. NC U.S.A.
231 E5 Pamlico Sound sea chan. NC U.S.A.
237 C5 Pampa TX U.S.A.
252 B3 Pampachiri Peru
258 E2 Pampa de Infierno Arg.
252 D4 Pampa Grande Bol.
93 B4 Pampanua Sulawesi Selatan Indon.
190 C4 Pamparato Italy
261 E5 Pampas reg. Arg.
252 B3 Pampas Peru
252 B3 Pampas r. Peru
163 E4 Pampelonne France
Pampeluna Spain see Pamplona
214 E2 Pampierstad S. Africa
182 B4 Pampilhosa Port.
182 C4 Pampilhosa da Serra Port.
183 G2 Pampliega Spain
232 D6 Pamplin VA U.S.A.
250 C3 Pamplona Col.
92 B4 Pamplona Phil.
183 I2 Pamplona Spain
170 C2 Pampow Ger.
162 B2 Pamproux France
199 E2 Pamukçu Turkey
199 G1 Pamukova Turkey
232 E6 Pamunkey r. VA U.S.A.
208 B5 Pana Gabon
236 F4 Pana IL U.S.A.
243 H4 Panabá Mex.

92 C5 Panabo Phil.
241 J3 Panaca NV U.S.A.
197 G2 Panaci Romania
116 E5 Panagar Madh. Prad. India
114 C2 Panagiri Andhra Prad. India
197 G4 Panagyurishte Bulg.
198 B2 Panaitolio Greece
114 B3 Panaji Goa India
246 B5 Panama country
          Central America
242 □K7 Panamá Panama
242 □K7 Panamá, Bahía de b. Panama
242 □K8 Panamá, Golfo de g. Panama
          Panama, Gulf of Panama see
          Panamá, Golfo de
242 □K7 Panama Canal Panama
          Panama City Panama see
231 C6 Panama City FL U.S.A.
240 I3 Panamint Range mts
          CA U.S.A.
240 I3 Panamint Valley CA U.S.A.
252 A2 Panao Peru
117 G4 Panar r. India
195 E4 Panarea, Isola i.
          Isole Lipari Italy
191 G4 Panaro r. Italy
95 F4 Panarukan Jawa Timur Indon.
163 C5 Panassac France
92 B4 Panay i. Phil.
92 B4 Panay Gulf Phil.
162 D3 Panazol France
215 H2 Panbult S. Africa
241 J2 Pancake Range mts NV U.S.A.
190 C4 Pancalieri Italy
257 G3 Pancas Brazil
196 E3 Pančevo Vojvodina, Srbija Yugo.
117 G4 Panchagarh Bangl.
137 F3 Panchève Ukr.
109 G3 Panch'iao Taiwan
95 F2 Pancingapan, Bukit mt. Indon.
197 H3 Panciu Romania
183 G2 Pancorbo Spain
197 E2 Pâncota Romania
186 B4 Pancrudo Spain
186 B4 Pancrudo r. Spain
          Pancsova Vojvodina, Srbija
          Yugo. see Pančevo
92 B4 Pandan Panay Phil.
92 C3 Pandan Phil.
116 E5 Pandaria Madh. Prad. India
114 D3 Pandavapura Karnataka India
04 D4 Pandeglang Jawa Barat Indon.
255 D5 Pandeiros r. Brazil
138 E3 Pandėlys Lith.
116 D5 Pandhana Madh. Prad. India
114 C2 Pandharpur Mahar. India
116 D5 Pandhurna Madh. Prad. India
82 D1 Pandie Pandie S.A. Austr.
190 E3 Pandino Italy
252 D2 Pando dept Bol.
261 J4 Pando Uru.
          Pandokrátor hill Ionioi Nisoi
          Greece see Pantokratoras
232 B4 Pandora OH U.S.A.
85 F1 Pandora Entrance sea chan.
          Qld Austr.
142 C3 Panduf Denmark
150 E3 Pandy Monmouthshire,
          Wales U.K.
177 H4 Pándzsa r. Hungary
          Paneas Syria see Bāniyās
194 E5 Panebianco r. Sicilia Italy
253 E2 Panelas Brazil
183 F1 Panes Spain
138 E4 Panevėžys Lith.
          Panfilov Kazakh. see Zharkent
135 H4 Panfilovo Rus. Fed.
137 F2 Panfyly Ukr.
100 C1 Pang r. China
96 B2 Pang, Nam r. Myanmar
79 □² Pangai Tonga
114 C2 Pangal Andhra Prad. India
114 C2 Pangal Andhra Prad. India
95 E4 Pangandaran Jawa Barat
          Indon.
211 C6 Pangani Tanz.
211 C6 Pangani r. Tanz.
92 C3 Pangaibanan Phil.
207 I5 Pangar r. Cameroon
151 F3 Pangbourne West Berkshire,
          England U.K.
157 G3 Pange France
78 □⁶ Panggoe Choiseul Solomon Is
123 H3 Pangi Range mts Pak.
93 A4 Pangkajene Sulawesi Selatan
          Indon.
95 E3 Pangkalanbuun
          Kalimantan Tengah Indon.
94 B1 Pangkalansusu
          Sumatera Indon.
94 C1 Pangkal Kalong Malaysia
94 D3 Pangkalpinang Indon.
223 J5 Pangman Sask. Can.
221 L3 Pangnirtung Nunavut Can.
209 B7 Pangong Africa Angola
130 I3 Pangody Rus. Fed.
94 D4 Pangrango vol. Indon.
259 B5 Panguipulli Chile
241 K3 Panguitch UT U.S.A.
78 □⁶ Panguna P.N.G.
80 D1 Panguru North I. N.Z.
92 B5 Pangutaran Group is Phil.
237 C5 Panhandle TX U.S.A.
260 B4 Paniahue Chile
209 F6 Pania-Mwanga
          Dem. Rep. Congo
192 E1 Panicale Italy
78 □⁶ Panie, Mont mt.
          New Caledonia
260 B4 Panimávida Chile
114 C3 Panj Mines Gujarat India
135 H6 Panino Rus. Fed.
116 D3 Panipat Haryana India
160 C3 Panissières France
92 A4 Panitan Phil.
186 B3 Paniza Spain
139 H4 Panizovye Belarus
123 G2 Panj Tajik.
          Panj r. Afgh./Tajik. see Pyandzh
123 F2 Panjakent Tajik.
          Panjang i. Cocos Is see
          West Island
94 D4 Panjang Sumatera Indon.
163 B5 Panjas France
123 F5 Panjgur Pak.
116 C5 Panjhra r. India
          Panjim Goa India see Panaji
107 I3 Panjin Liaoning China
123 G3 Panjkora r. Pak.
123 G4 Panjnad r. Pak.
140 U3 Pankakoski Fin.
158 F1 Panker Ger.
174 G5 Pankl Pol.
139 H2 Pankovka Rus. Fed.
207 H4 Pankshin Nigeria
          Panlian Sichuan China see Miyi
          Panlong Henan China see
          Queshan
98 D7 Panna Madh. Prad. India
86 C4 Pannawonica W.A. Austr.
156 C4 Pannes France
193 H3 Panni Italy
165 E3 Panningen Neth.
177 H4 Pannonhalma Hungary
123 G5 Pano Aqil Pak.
184 B3 Panóias Port.
          Panóplis Egypt see Akhmīm
256 D4 Panorama Brazil
          Panormus Sicilia Italy see
          Palermo
114 C4 Panruti Tamil Nadu India
171 F4 Panschwitz-Kuckau Ger.
          Panshan Liaoning China see
          Panjin
100 C4 Panshui Guizhou China see
          Pu'an
151 H3 Pant r. England U.K.
94 C3 Pantai Cermin, Gunung mt.
          Indon.
253 F4 Pantanal de São Lourenço
          marsh Brazil
253 F4 Pantanal do Taquarí
          marsh Brazil
241 L6 Pantano AZ U.S.A.
93 C5 Pantar i. Indon.
137 G3 Pantayivka Ukr.
          Pantelaria Sicilia Italy see
          Pantelleria
137 I3 Panteleymonivka Ukr.

194 A6 Pantelleria Sicilia Italy
194 B6 Pantelleria, Isola di i.
          Sicilia Italy
245 F3 Pantepec r. Mex.
186 C2 Panticosa Spain
163 G4 Pantoja Spain
198 A2 Pantokratoras hill Ionioi Nisoi
          Greece
86 F3 Panton r. W.A. Austr.
186 D3 Pantorrillas hill Spain
92 C5 Pantukan Phil.
150 D2 Pant-y-dwr Powys, Wales U.K.
245 E2 Pánuco Mex.
245 F2 Pánuco r. Mex.
114 B2 Panvel Mahar. India
116 D4 Panwari Uttar Prad. India
108 C3 Panxian Guizhou China
109 E4 Panyu Guangdong China
137 I3 Panyutyne Ukr.
108 B3 Panzhihua Sichuan China
209 C6 Panzi Dem. Rep. Congo
243 H6 Panzos Guat.
251 E2 Pao r. Venez.
254 F4 Pão de Açúcar Brazil
193 I5 Paola Italy
236 E4 Paola KS U.S.A.
230 C4 Paoli IN U.S.A.
234 C2 Paoli PA U.S.A.
192 B3 Paoloni, Serra hill Sardegna
          Italy
239 F4 Paonia CO U.S.A.
208 C3 Paoua C.A.R.
121 G4 Pap Uzbek.
176 G4 Pápa Hungary
240 □D9 Pāpa I. HI U.S.A.
193 H4 Papa, Monte del mt. Italy
240 □D9 Papa'aloa HI U.S.A.
198 C3 Papadianika Greece
          Papademos N. Korea see
          Saudiiunu
257 E3 Papagaios Brazil
245 F2 Papagayo r. Mex.
114 C3 Papagni r. India
191 J2 Papagorno Col.
80 E2 Papakura North I. N.Z.
245 G1 Papakura, Serra hill Brazil
245 G6 Papauari r. Brazil
129 E2 Papaularroen r. Rus. Fed.
256 B2 Papaúna Brazil
160 C2 Paray-le-Monial France
116 D4 Parbati r. India
          Parbatipur Bangl.
114 C2 Parbhani Mahar. India
149 G4 Parbold Lancashire,
          England U.K.
247 □¹ Parcelas Martorell
          Puerto Rico
187 C6 Parcent Spain
159 F4 Parcé-sur-Sarthe France
171 F2 Parchim Ger.
170 C2 Parchim Ger.
226 F4 Parchment MI U.S.A.
174 G3 Parchovany Slovakia
174 F1 Parchowo Pol.
175 J2 Parciaki Pol.
162 C3 Parcoul France
175 K4 Parczew Pol.
226 C4 Pardeeville WI U.S.A.
163 B5 Pardies France
182 B4 Pardilhó Port.
197 H3 Pardina Romania
256 A4 Pardo r. Mato Grosso do Sul
          Brazil
255 F5 Pardo r. Bahia Brazil
255 D5 Pardo r. Minas Gerais Brazil
256 C4 Pardo r. São Paulo Brazil
256 C6 Pardo r. São Paulo Brazil
176 F1 Pardubice Czech Rep.
176 F2 Pardubický kraj admin. reg.
          Czech Rep.
95 F4 Pare Jawa Timur Indon.
138 E5 Parechcha Belarus
111 B5 Pare Chu r. China
253 F3 Parecis r. Brazil
253 E2 Parecis, Serra dos hills Brazil
182 B3 Paredes Port.
182 B3 Paredes de Coura Port.
182 D2 Paredes de Nava Spain
260 B4 Paredones Chile
183 H4 Pareja Spain
161 K4 Pareloup, Lac de l. France
78 □ª Parem i. Chuuk Micronesia
81 E4 Paremata North I. N.Z.
162 B4 Parempuyre France
114 B2 Parenda Mahar. India
224 F4 Parent Que. Can.
195 F3 Parenti Italy
195 I4 Parentis-en-Born France
81 C6 Parenora South I. N.Z.
93 A4 Parepare Sulawesi Selatan
          Indon.
260 E4 Parera Arg.
186 E3 Parets del Vallès Spain
171 D3 Parey Ger.
134 H4 Par'evo Rus. Fed.
139 H3 Parfino Rus. Fed.
198 B2 Parga Greece
141 M3 Pargas Fin.
129 E1 Parghelia Italy
114 C2 Pargi Andhra Prad. India
157 E4 Pargny-sur-Saulx France
139 I1 Pargolovo Rus. Fed.
183 I5 Parham Antigua and Barbuda
251 G3 Pariá r. Brazil
241 J3 Paria r. AZ/UT U.S.A.
247 □⁷ Paria, Gulf of
          Trin. and Tob./Venez.
251 F2 Paria, Gulf of
          pen. Venez.
94 □ Pariaman Sumatera Indon.
241 H3 Paria Plateau AZ U.S.A.
244 C4 Paricutín, Volcán vol. Mex.
159 G4 Parigné-l'Évêque France
177 H5 Párí-hegy hill Hungary
141 D3 Parikkala Fin.
          Parima r. Brazil see Uatatás
251 E4 Parima, Serra mts Brazil
250 C6 Parinari Peru
250 A6 Pariñas, Punta pt Peru
82 E3 Paringa r. S.A. Austr.
178 A5 Parino r. Italy
251 G5 Parintins Brazil
227 O4 Paris Ont. Can.
156 C4 Paris France
237 E5 Paris AR U.S.A.
230 C4 Paris ID U.S.A.
232 A5 Paris KY U.S.A.
233 I2 Paris ME U.S.A.
225 F5 Paris MO U.S.A.
175 H5 Paris TN U.S.A.
237 E5 Paris TX U.S.A.
          Paris area map France
233 F3 Parish NY U.S.A.
163 H4 Parisot Midi-Pyrénées France
163 D5 Parisot Midi-Pyrénées France
171 F5 Parish Rus. Fed.
236 D1 Park r. ND U.S.A.
140 M2 Parkajoki Sweden
114 A2 Parkal Andhra Prad. India
141 M3 Parkano Fin.
237 G5 Parker AZ U.S.A.
236 D3 Parker CO U.S.A.
180 A4 Parker SD U.S.A.
87 C7 Parker Range hills W.A. Austr.
175 H2 Parkersburg PA U.S.A.
234 C4 Parkesburg PA U.S.A.
227 O4 Park Falls WI U.S.A.
226 D5 Park Forest IL U.S.A.
227 O5 Parkhill Ont. Can.
87 F4 Parkhomivka Ukr.
232 C5 Parkman WV U.S.A.
147 D3 Parknasilla Rep. of Ireland
236 E4 Park Rapids MN U.S.A.
236 G3 Parkton NY U.S.A.
222 G4 Parksville B.C. Can.
233 G2 Parkston Jammu and Kashmir
251 H3 Park Valley UT U.S.A.
232 D3 Parkville MD U.S.A.
183 I5 Parla Spain
          Parlakhemundi Orissa India
          Parlakimedi Orissa India see
          Parla Kimedi Orissa India

182 D2 Páramo del Sil Spain
252 A2 Paramonga Peru
182 B4 Paramos Port.
235 D2 Paramus NJ U.S.A.
131 Q4 Paramushir, Ostrov i.
          Kuril'skiye O-va Rus. Fed.
198 B2 Paramythia Greece
261 G2 Paraná Arg.
254 D5 Paraná Brazil
254 C5 Paraná r. Brazil
254 D5 Paraná state Brazil
261 H4 Paraná r. S. America
261 H4 Paraná, Delta del Arg.
254 D4 Paraguá Brazil
254 E2 Paraíba Brazil
254 E2 Paraíba r. Brazil
254 E2 Paraibinha r. Brazil
198 C2 Paraisópolis mt. Greece
81 D5 Parnassus South I. N.Z.
82 D3 Pardnana S.A. Austr.
138 E2 Pärnu Estonia
138 F2 Pärnu r. Estonia
138 E2 Pärnu-Jaagupi Estonia
117 G4 Paro Bhutan
81 C5 Paroa South I. N.Z.
138 E1 Parola Fin.
156 D4 Paron France
250 A6 Parona Turkey see Fındık
93 A3 Paroreang, Bukit mt. Indon.
198 D3 Paros i. Greece
214 B5 Parow S. Africa
241 H3 Parowan UT U.S.A.
161 H5 Parpaillon mts France
82 E3 Parparie S.A. Austr.
260 B5 Parral Chile
237 B7 Parral r. Mex.
83 G3 Parramatta N.S.W. Austr.
242 E3 Parras Mex.
150 D3 Parrett r. England U.K.
184 E4 Parrillas Spain
226 C3 Parrish WI U.S.A.
242 □I7 Parrita Costa Rica
225 H4 Parrsboro N.S. Can.
221 G2 Parry, Cape Nunavut Can.
86 D4 Parry Islands Nunavut Can.
224 D4 Parry Sound Ont. Can.
220 H2 Parryville PA U.S.A.
129 E4 Pars prov. Iran see Fārs
          Parsa Bihar India
          Parsa prov. Iran see Fārs
117 F4 Parsabad Iran
129 E4 Pārsābād Iran
168 F2 Parsberg Ger.
172 F2 Parsberg Ger.
178 B3 Parseierspitze mt. Austria
174 D1 Parsęta r. Pol.
236 C2 Parshall ND U.S.A.
129 D2 Parsipany NJ U.S.A.
241 J2 Parsnip Peak NV U.S.A.
237 E4 Parsons KS U.S.A.
232 C5 Parsons WV U.S.A.
170 F3 Parstein Ger.
170 E3 Parsteiner See l. Ger.
114 D2 Partabgarh Mahar. India
114 D2 Partapgarh Madh. Prad. India
116 E5 Partapur Madh. Prad. India
181 E5 Partaloa Spain
194 B5 Partanna Sicilia Italy
160 E2 Parte mt. Sweden
168 E5 Partenstein Ger.
162 B2 Parthenay France
192 A2 Parthenope Corse France
149 G4 Partington Greater Manchester,
          England U.K.
194 C4 Partinico Sicilia Italy
100 E4 Partizansk Rus. Fed.
177 I2 Partizánske Slovakia
177 H3 Partizánska Ľupča Slovakia
83 J4 Partney Lincolnshire,
          England U.K.
149 F4 Parton Cumbria, England U.K.
224 D3 Partridge r. Ont. Can.
147 B3 Partry Rep. of Ireland
129 C2 P'art's'khanaqanevi Georgia
137 H4 Partyzany Ukr.
251 E3 Paru, Serranía mts Venez.
251 G5 Paru de Oeste r. Brazil
114 C4 Parur Kerala India
137 F4 Parutyne Ukr.
123 J3 Parvān r. Afgh.
122 D3 Parvārah Iran
115 D2 Parvatipuram
          Andhra Prad. India
          Parvatsar Rajasthan India
111 D4 Parvatsar Xizang China
199 F3 Parychy Belarus
199 E3 Parýs Sweden
175 J4 Parysów Pol.
215 F2 Parys S. Africa
175 H4 Parzęczew Pol.
240 H4 Pasadena MD U.S.A.
237 E6 Pasadena TX U.S.A.
186 B1 Pasai Donibane Spain
250 B5 Pasaje Ecuador
97 C4 Pa Sak, Mae Nam r. Thai.
129 C3 Paşalı Turkey
116 C5 Pasan Madh. Prad. India
129 D2 P'asanauri Georgia
121 I5 Pascagarda tourist site Iran
231 F6 Pascagoula r. MS U.S.A.
231 F6 Pascagoula MS U.S.A.
260 D2 Pasco Arg.
198 B2 Patqoia r. Arg.

163 E4 Parlan France
114 C2 Parli Vaijnath Mahar. India
108 A2 Parlung Zangbo r. China
190 F4 Parma Italy
190 F4 Parma prov. Emilia-Romagna
          Italy
190 F4 Parma r. Italy
134 L2 Parma Rus. Fed.
238 C3 Parma ID U.S.A.
226 E4 Parma MI U.S.A.
232 C4 Parma OH U.S.A.
254 D4 Parnaguá Brazil
254 E2 Parnaíba Brazil
254 E2 Parnaíba r. Brazil
198 C2 Parnassos mt. Greece
81 D5 Parnassus South I. N.Z.
82 D3 Parndana S.A. Austr.
138 E2 Pärnu Estonia
138 F2 Pärnu r. Estonia
198 C3 Parnon mts Greece
138 E2 Pärnu Estonia
138 E2 Pärnu-Jaagupi Estonia
117 G4 Paro Bhutan
81 C5 Paroa South I. N.Z.
138 E1 Parola Fin.
156 D4 Paron France
250 A6 Parona Turkey see Fındık
93 A3 Paroreang, Bukit mt. Indon.
198 D3 Paros i. Greece
214 B5 Parow S. Africa
241 H3 Parowan UT U.S.A.
161 H5 Parpaillon mts France
82 E3 Parparie S.A. Austr.

159 F3 Passais France
217 □3b Passamaïnti Mayotte
257 E5 Passa Quatro Brazil
253 G2 Passa Tempo Brazil
173 H3 Passau Ger.
157 G5 Passavant-la-Rochère France
92 A4 Passi Phil.
192 E1 Passignano sul Trasimeno
          Italy
191 G2 Passírio r. Italy
255 B9 Passo Fundo Brazil
255 B9 Passo Real, Barragem resr
          Brazil
256 D4 Passos Brazil
170 F2 Passow Ger.
160 B2 Passy France
138 F4 Pastavy Belarus
250 B5 Pastaza prov. Ecuador
81 D5 Parnassus South I. N.Z.

177 H4 Páty Hungary
244 D4 Pátzcuaro Mex.
244 D4 Pátzcuaro, Laguna de l. Mex.
163 B5 Pau France
          Pau airport France
92 A4 Pau Phil.
192 E1 Passi WI U.S.A.
191 G2 Passírio r. Italy

127 F2 Pazar Turkey
126 E3 Pazarcık Turkey
127 G4 Pazardzhik Bulg.
199 G2 Pazarköy Turkey
199 F2 Pazaryeri Turkey
129 B3 Pazaryolu Turkey
250 C3 Paz de Río Col.
188 D3 Pazin Croatia
163 E6 Paziols France
183 C1 Pazo de Irixoa Spain
182 C3 Pazos Spain
139 H2 Pchevzha r. Rus. Fed.
175 H6 Pčim Pol.
197 K3 Pčinja r. Macedonia
182 B1 Peabira Brazil
236 D4 Peabody KS U.S.A.
233 H3 Peabody MA U.S.A.
221 D7 Peace r. FL U.S.A.
231 D7 Peace r. FL U.S.A.
151 J4 Peacehaven East Sussex,
          England U.K.
223 H3 Peace Point Alta Can.
222 G3 Peace River Alta Can.
222 C6 Peach Creek WV U.S.A.
222 G5 Peachland B.C. Can.
241 K4 Peach Springs AZ U.S.A.
87 D7 Peak Charles hill W.A. Austr.
149 H4 Peak District National Park
          England U.K.
233 □I1 Peaked Mountain hill ME
          U.S.A.
83 G3 Peak Hill N.S.W. Austr.
87 C5 Peak Hill W.A. Austr.
240 H4 Peak Mountain CA U.S.A.
85 G4 Peak Range hills Qld Austr.
185 G3 Peal de Becerro Spain
241 M2 Peale, Mount UT U.S.A.
241 M6 Pearce AZ U.S.A.
84 B2 Pearce Point N.T. Austr.
232 C6 Pearisburg VA U.S.A.
226 C1 Pearl r. Ont. Can.
237 F6 Pearl r. MS U.S.A.
75 H1 Pearl and Hermes Atoll HI
          U.S.A.
240 □ Pearl City HI U.S.A.
          Pearl River r. China see
          Zhu Jiang
235 D1 Pearl River NY U.S.A.
237 D6 Pearsall TX U.S.A.
231 D6 Pearson GA U.S.A.
226 C3 Pearson WI U.S.A.
82 C3 Pearson Islands S.A. Austr.
215 E5 Pearston S. Africa
221 I2 Peary Channel Nunavut Can.
221 N1 Peary Land reg. Greenland
237 D5 Pease r. TX U.S.A.
150 E3 Peasedown St John Bath and
          North East Somerset,
          England U.K.
158 B4 Peault France
86 C4 Peawah r. W.A. Austr.
224 C2 Peawanuck Ont. Can.
213 H3 Pebane Moz.
250 D5 Pebas Peru
161 B3 Pébrac France
          Peć Kosovo, Srbija Yugo.
237 D6 Pecan Bayou r. TX U.S.A.
257 F3 Peçanha Brazil
237 E6 Pecan Island LA U.S.A.
257 C6 Peças, Ilha das i. Brazil
190 D2 Peccia Switz.
191 F5 Peccioli Italy
177 I4 Pécel Hungary
135 J5 Pecha r. Rus. Fed.
140 O1 Pechenga r. Rus. Fed.
137 I3 Pechenihy Rus. Fed.
          Pechenizhyn Ukr.
          Vodoskhovyshche resr Ukr.
139 L4 Pecherniki Rus. Fed.
135 J4 Pechersk Rus. Fed.
134 L2 Pechina Spain
134 L2 Pechora Rus. Fed.
134 L2 Pechora r. Rus. Fed.
          Pechora Sea Rus. Fed. see
134 K1 Pechorskoye More sea
          Rus. Fed.
          Pechorskaya Guba b.
          Rus. Fed.
134 K1 Pechorskoye More sea
          Rus. Fed.
138 F3 Pechory Rus. Fed.
197 I2 Pecineaga Romania
227 F4 Peck MI U.S.A.
234 C1 Pecks Pond PA U.S.A.
176 F1 Pečky Czech Rep.
174 E4 Pęcław Pol.
237 C6 Pecos r. TX U.S.A.
237 C6 Pecos r.
          New Mexico/Texas U.S.A.
165 C4 Pecq Belgium
176 E5 Pécs Hungary
176 E5 Pécsvárad Hungary
176 F5 Pecznier Pol.
193 F1 Pedaso Italy
114 C2 Peddavagu r. India
114 C2 Peddie S. Africa
215 F6 Peddie S. Africa
138 F3 Pededze r. Latvia
250 A4 Pedernales Ecuador
246 C5 Pedernales Haiti
237 D6 Pedernales r. TX U.S.A.
251 F2 Pedernales Venez.
191 G3 Pederobba Italy
140 M3 Pedersöre Fin.
163 C6 Pedja r. Estonia
237 G1 Pedra Azul Brazil
206 □ Pedra Badejo São Tiago
          Cape Verde
182 B3 Pedrada mt. Port.
182 B3 Pedralba de Cebreiro Spain
182 B3 Pedralba de la Pradería Spain
254 C5 Pedra Preta, Serra da mts
          Brazil
251 F5 Pedras r. Amazonas Brazil
254 D5 Pedras r. Bahia Brazil
182 D2 Pedregal Venez.
187 C5 Pedreguer Spain
254 D5 Pedreguilho Brazil
254 D3 Pedreiras Maranhão Brazil
256 D2 Pedreiras São Paulo Brazil
252 B4 Pedrera Spain
186 D3 Pedres hill Spain
242 F3 Pedriceña Mex.
185 F3 Pedrick town U.S.A.
183 G3 Pedro r. Spain
185 F3 Pedro Abad Spain
246 B2 Pedro Afonso Brazil
246 D5 Pedro Avelino Brazil
246 B2 Pedro Bank sea feature
          Jamaica
256 D6 Pedro Barros Brazil
256 C2 Pedro Cays is Jamaica
185 F2 Pedroche Spain
255 D5 Pedro Chico Col.
254 □ Pedro de Valdivia Chile
254 □ Pedro Escobedo Mex.
114 C4 Pedrógão Port.
187 C5 Pedrógão Port.
255 D2 Pedrógão Grande Port.
236 E4 Pedrógão Pequeno Port.
255 D6 Pedro Gomes Brazil
184 E3 Pedro Juan Caballero Brazil
182 B2 Pedro II, Ilha reg. Brazil/Venez.
254 E4 Pedro Leopoldo Brazil
183 G3 Pedrola Spain
181 G3 Pedro-Martínez Spain
246 B3 Pedro Muñoz Spain
258 E2 Pedro Osório Brazil
236 C2 Pedrosa del Príncipe Spain
182 B2 Pedrosillo de los Aires Spain
183 C1 Pedroso Port.
256 D6 Pedro Toledo Brazil
237 C7 Pedrous, Pic mt. France
182 B2 Pedrouzos Spain

Phnom Penh Cambodia see Phnum Pénh
97 D5 Phnum Pénh Cambodia
233 F3 Phoenicia NY U.S.A.
241 K5 Phoenix AZ U.S.A.
233 E3 Phoenix NY U.S.A.
Phoenix Island Phoenix Is Kiribati see Rawaki
77 I2 Phoenix Islands Kiribati
234 C2 Phoenixville PA U.S.A.
215 G2 Phola S. Africa
215 F2 Phomolong S. Africa
96 C4 Phon Thai.
96 D3 Phong Nha Vietnam
96 C2 Phôngsali Laos
Phong Saly Laos see Phôngsali
83 E4 Phoques Bay Tas. Austr.
84 E4 Phosphate Hill Qld Austr.
96 C3 Phou San mt. Laos
96 C3 Phrae Thai.
Phra Nakhon Si Ayutthaya Thai. see Ayutthaya
96 B3 Phrao Thai.
97 B5 Phra Saeng Thai.
Phu Cuong Vietnam see Thu Dâu Môt
96 D2 Phuc Yên Vietnam
117 G4 Phuentsholing Bhutan
97 B6 Phuket Thai.
97 B6 Phuket, Ko i. Thai.
117 F5 Phulabani Orissa India
116 E4 Phulpur Uttar Prad. India
96 D2 Phu Ly Vietnam
97 D5 Phumĭ Chhuk Cambodia
97 D4 Phumĭ Kâmpóng Trâlach Cambodia
97 D4 Phumĭ Mlu Prey Cambodia
97 C4 Phumĭ Prâmaôy Cambodia
97 C4 Phumĭ Sâmraông Cambodia
Phuntsholing Bhutan see Phuentsholing
96 C2 Phu Phac Mo mt. Vietnam
97 C5 Phu Quôc, Đao i. Vietnam
215 G3 Phuthaditjhaba S. Africa
96 D2 Phư Tho Vietnam
Phu Vinh Vietnam see Tra Vinh
163 E6 Pia France
95 F2 Piabung, Gunung mt. Indon.
256 B4 Piacatu Brazil
190 E3 Piacenza Italy
190 E4 Piacenza prov. Emilia-Romagna Italy
190 F3 Piadena Italy
224 E2 Piagochioui r. Que. Can.
261 G3 Piamonte Arg.
83 G2 Pian r. N.S.W. Austr.
192 A2 Piana Corse France
190 D4 Piana Crixia Italy
194 C5 Piana degli Albanesi Sicilia Italy
194 D5 Piana di Catania plain Sicilia Italy
192 D2 Piancastagnaio Italy
191 H5 Piandimeleto Italy
192 B4 Pianedda, M. sa hill Sardegna Italy
193 G2 Pianella Italy
190 E4 Pianello Val Tidone Italy
83 E3 Piangil Vic. Austr.
107 F4 Pianguan Shanxi China
191 G4 Piano del Voglio Italy
191 G4 Pianoro Italy
192 C2 Pianosa Italy
192 B3 Pianotolli-Caldarello Corse France
192 D2 Piansano Italy
184 C2 Pias Port.
175 J3 Piaseczno Pol.
175 K4 Piaski Lubelskie Pol.
174 F4 Piaski Wielkopolskie Pol.
254 F4 Piassabussu Brazil
175 I3 Piastów Pol.
254 E5 Piatã Brazil
175 H3 Piątek Pol.
175 K2 Piątnica Poduchowna Pol.
197 G4 Piatra Romania
197 H2 Piatra Neamţ Romania
197 G3 Piatra Olt Romania
197 H2 Piatra Şoimului Romania
163 C6 Piau-Engaly France
254 E3 Piauí r. Brazil
254 E3 Piauí state Brazil
254 E4 Piauí, Serra de hills Brazil
191 H3 Piave r. Italy
244 A2 Piaxtla r. Mex.
190 F4 Piazza al Serchio Italy
194 D5 Piazza Armerina Sicilia Italy
190 E3 Piazza Brembana Italy
190 E3 Piazzatorre Italy
190 F2 Piazzi, Cima de' mt. Italy
191 G3 Piazzola sul Brenta Italy
210 B2 Pibor r. Sudan
163 D5 Pibrac France
224 C3 Pic r. Ont. Can.
252 C5 Pica Chile
241 L5 Picacho AZ U.S.A.
242 B2 Picachos, Cerro dos mt. Mex.
187 B5 Picaracho mt. Spain
156 C3 Picardie admin. reg. France
156 B3 Picardie reg. France
Picardy reg. France see Picardie
187 C5 Picassent Spain
158 E2 Picauville France
237 F6 Picayune MS U.S.A.
191 G2 Picco della Croce mt. Italy
258 D1 Pichanal Arg.
170 C2 Picher Ger.
260 A4 Pichilemu Chile
242 C3 Pichilingue Mex.
250 B5 Pichincha prov. Ecuador
179 E2 Pichl bei Wels Austria
116 D4 Pichor Madh. Prad. India
243 G5 Pichucalco Mex.
232 C5 Pickens WV U.S.A.
227 H4 Pickering Ont. Can.
149 I3 Pickering North Yorkshire, England U.K.
149 I3 Pickering, Vale of val. England U.K.
227 E2 Pickford MI U.S.A.
224 B3 Pickle Lake Ont. Can.
216 □1c Pico i. Azores
216 □1c Pico mt. Pico Azores
193 F3 Pico Italy
192 B5 Picocca r. Sardegna Italy
216 □1c Pico Gorda vol. Faial Azores
185 F1 Picón Spain
254 E3 Picos Brazil
250 B6 Picota Peru
259 D7 Pico Truncado Arg.
156 C3 Picquigny France
226 D1 Pic River Ont. Can.
83 G3 Picton N.S.W. Austr.
224 E5 Picton Ont. Can.
81 E4 Picton South I. N.Z.
83 F5 Picton, Mount Tas. Austr.
225 I4 Pictou N.S. Can.
222 H5 Picture Butte Alta Can.
234 B1 Picture Rocks PA U.S.A.
254 F3 Picuí Brazil
260 C6 Picún Leufú r. Arg.
175 M5 Pidberezzya Ukr.
175 L6 Pidbuzh Ukr.
Piddle r. England U.K. see Trent
150 E4 Piddletrenthide Dorset, England U.K.
136 C3 Pidhaytsi Ukr.
136 F3 Pidhorodna Ukr.
137 H3 Pidhorodne Ukr.
175 L6 Pidhorodtsi Ukr.
173 G4 Piding Ger.
217 □3a Pidjani Njazidja Comoros
136 C3 Pidkamin' Ukr.
137 G3 Pidlisne Ukr.
114 D5 Pidurutalagala mt. Sri Lanka
136 D3 Pidvolochys'k Ukr.
136 F3 Pidvysoke Ukr.
174 G3 Piechcin Pol.
174 D5 Piechowice Pol.
175 J2 Piecki Pol.
216 □1c Piedade Pico Azores
256 D5 Piedade Brazil
184 B3 Piedade, Ponta da pt Port.
192 B2 Piedicorte-di-Gaggio Corse France
192 B2 Piedicroce Corse France
195 E5 Piedimonte Etneo Sicilia Italy
193 G3 Piedimonte Matese Italy
190 D2 Piedimulera Italy
Piedmont admin. reg. Italy see Piemonte
231 C5 Piedmont AL U.S.A.
237 F4 Piedmont MO U.S.A.
232 C4 Piedmont OH U.S.A.
183 I3 Piedra r. Spain
185 F1 Piedrabuena Spain
259 C6 Piedra de Aguila Arg.
245 F5 Piedra de Olla, Cerro mt. Mex.
Piedrafita Spain see Pedrafita do Cebreiro
182 D2 Piedrafita de Babia Spain
183 E4 Piedrahita Spain
183 F4 Piedralaves Spain
182 D5 Piedras Albas Spain
182 E1 Piedras Blancas Spain
240 G4 Piedras Blancas Point CA U.S.A.
243 H5 Piedras Negras Guat.
243 E2 Piedras Negras Coahuila Mex.
245 F4 Piedras Negras Veracruz Mex.
192 E2 Piegaro Italy
162 C3 Piégut-Pluviers France
174 G5 Piekary Śląskie Pol.
170 E1 Piekberg hill Ger.
175 I5 Piekoszów Pol.
140 N3 Pieksämäki Fin.
207 E3 Piéla Burkina
179 G2 Pielach r. Austria
140 N3 Pielavesi Fin.
174 D4 Pielgrzymka Pol.
140 O3 Pielinen l. Fin.
190 C4 Piemonte admin. reg. Italy
215 G1 Pienaarsrivier S. Africa
143 I4 Pieniężno Pol.
157 F3 Piennes France
174 D4 Pieńsk Pol.
192 D1 Pienza Italy
186 E3 Piera Spain
236 D3 Pierce NE U.S.A.
223 I4 Pierceland Sask. Can.
226 E5 Pierceton IN U.S.A.
198 C1 Pieria mts Greece
146 F2 Pierowall Orkney, Scotland U.K.
236 C2 Pierre SD U.S.A.
237 F6 Pierre, Bayou r. MS U.S.A.
237 E6 Pierre Bayou r. LA U.S.A.
162 D3 Pierre-Buffière France
161 D4 Pierre-Châtel France
160 D2 Pierre-de-Bresse France
161 E5 Pierrefeu-du-Var France
163 B6 Pierrefitte-Nestalas France
157 F4 Pierrefitte-sur-Aire France
160 B2 Pierrefitte-sur-Loire France
156 C3 Pierrefonds France
160 E1 Pierrefontaine-les-Varans France
161 A4 Pierrefort France
161 C4 Pierrelatte France
157 F3 Pierrepont France
156 B4 Pierres France
160 B3 Pierre-sur-Haute mt. France
161 D5 Pierrevert France
247 □7 Pierreville Trin. and Tob.
156 D3 Pierry France
164 D3 Piershil Neth.
175 I5 Pierzchnica Pol.
171 C5 Piesau Ger.
178 D3 Piesendorf Austria
172 A2 Piesport Ger.
177 G3 Piešťany Slovakia
175 I1 Pieszkowo Pol.
174 E5 Pieszyce Pol.
215 H3 Pietermaritzburg S. Africa
Pietersaari Fin. see Jakobstad
213 F4 Pietersburg S. Africa
214 E2 Piet Plessis S. Africa
193 G3 Pietrabbondante Italy
193 G3 Pietracatella Italy
192 B2 Pietracorbara Corse France
192 B2 Pietra-di-Verde Corse France
193 H4 Pietragalla Italy
192 B2 Pietralba Corse France
190 D4 Pietra Ligure Italy
191 H5 Pietralunga Italy
193 G3 Pietramelara Italy
193 H3 Pietramontecorvino Italy
194 D5 Pietraperzia Sicilia Italy
190 C4 Pietraporzio Italy
190 F5 Pietrasanta Italy
193 G4 Pietrastornina Italy
193 G3 Pietravairano Italy
193 G3 Pietrelcina Italy
215 H2 Piet Retief S. Africa
177 L5 Pietroasa Bihor Romania
177 L6 Pietroasa Timiș Romania
192 A3 Pietrosella Corse France
197 G2 Pietrosu, Vârful mt. Romania
197 G2 Pietrosu, Vârful mt. Romania
174 G5 Pietrowice Wielkie Pol.
191 H2 Pieve d'Alpago Italy
190 D3 Pieve del Cairo Italy
178 B5 Pieve di Bono Italy
191 H2 Pieve di Cadore Italy
191 G4 Pieve di Cento Italy
191 H3 Pieve di Soligo Italy
190 C4 Pieve di Teco Italy
191 F4 Pievepelago Italy
191 H5 Pieve Santo Stefano Italy
193 F1 Pieve Torina Italy
190 D2 Pieve Vergonte Italy
156 D4 Piffonds France
224 B3 Pigeon r. Can./U.S.A.
227 F4 Pigeon MI U.S.A.
226 C1 Pigeon River MN U.S.A.
232 D6 Pigg r. VA U.S.A.
237 F4 Piggott AR U.S.A.
215 H1 Pigg's Peak Swaziland
193 F3 Piglio Italy
190 C5 Pigna Italy
161 B5 Pignan France
161 E5 Pignans France
193 F3 Pignataro Interamna Italy
194 D1 Pignataro Maggiore Italy
193 H4 Pignola Italy
198 B2 Pigon, Limni l. Greece
261 F5 Pigüé Arg.
245 E3 Piguicas mt. Mex.
80 E2 Piha North I. N.Z.
80 D3 Pihama North I. N.Z.
116 E4 Pihani Uttar Prad. India
109 F1 Pi He r. China
Pihkva järv l. Estonia/Rus. Fed. see Pskov, Lake
141 O3 Pihlajavesi l. Fin.
141 M3 Pihlava Fin.
140 N3 Pihtipudas Fin.
244 C4 Pihuamo Mex.
138 D1 Piikkiö Fin.
140 N2 Piippola Fin.
78 □4a Piis-Panewu i. Chuuk Micronesia
Piji Sichuan China see Puge
243 G6 Pijijiapan Mex.
164 D2 Pijnacker Neth.
139 J2 Pikalevo Rus. Fed.
232 D3 Pike NY U.S.A.
232 C5 Pike WV U.S.A.
227 G3 Pike Bay Ont. Can.
234 C1 Pike County county PA U.S.A.
91 K5 Pikelot i. Micronesia
239 F4 Pikes Peak CO U.S.A.
234 B3 Pikesville MD U.S.A.
214 B5 Piketberg S. Africa
232 B5 Piketon OH U.S.A.
232 B6 Pikeville KY U.S.A.
231 C5 Pikeville TN U.S.A.
Pikirakatahi mt. South I. N.Z. see Earnslaw, Mount
107 I4 Pikou Liaoning China
208 C4 Pikounda Congo
261 H5 Pila Arg.
191 H4 Pila Italy
174 E2 Piła Pol.
187 B6 Pila mt. Spain
258 F2 Pilagá r. Arg.
116 C3 Pilani Rajasthan India
261 H4 Pilar Buenos Aires Arg.
261 F2 Pilar Córdoba Arg.
261 G2 Pilar Santa Fé Arg.
253 F6 Pilar Para.
92 C4 Pilar Phil.
254 C5 Pilar de Goiás Brazil
187 C7 Pilar de la Horadada Spain
256 D5 Pilar do Sul Brazil
184 D3 Pilas Spain
161 C3 Pilat, Mont mt. France
190 D2 Pilatus mt. Switz.
175 J4 Pilawa Pol.
174 E2 Piława r. Pol.
174 E5 Piława Górna Pol.
252 D5 Pilaya r. Bol.
253 F6 Pilcomayo r. Bol./Para.
Pilenkovo Georgia see Gant'iadi
114 C3 Piler Andhra Prad. India
187 C6 Piles Spain
Píli Notio Aigaio Greece see Pyli
92 B3 Pili Phil.
252 D5 Pili, Cerro mt. Chile
138 E4 Piliakalnis hill Lith.
116 C3 Pilibangan Rajasthan India
116 D3 Pilibhit Uttar Prad. India
175 H5 Pilica Pol.
175 J4 Pilica r. Pol.
Pilipinas country Asia see Philippines
177 I4 Pilis Hungary
177 H4 Pilis hill Hungary
177 H4 Piliscsév Hungary
177 H4 Pilisszentiván Hungary
177 H4 Pilisszentkereszt Hungary
177 H4 Pilisvörösvár Hungary
149 F3 Pillar hill England U.K.
Pillau Rus. Fed. see Baltiysk
83 G2 Pilliga N.S.W. Austr.
149 G4 Pilling Lancashire, England U.K.
261 G3 Pillo, Isla del i. Arg.
234 B2 Pillow PA U.S.A.
134 I5 Pil'na Rus. Fed.
137 I2 Pil'na r. Ukr.
150 E3 Pilning South Gloucestershire, England U.K.
256 D2 Pilões, Serra dos mts Brazil
246 C3 Pilón Cuba
183 E1 Piloña r. Spain
Pílos Greece see Pylos
Piloto Juan Fernández i. S. Pacific Ocean see Alejandro Selkirk, Isla
240 I2 Pilot Peak NV U.S.A.
220 C4 Pilot Point AK U.S.A.
238 C2 Pilot Rock OR U.S.A.
220 B3 Pilot Station AK U.S.A.
237 F6 Pilottown LA U.S.A.
173 F2 Pilsach Ger.
Pilsen Czech Rep. see Plzeň
226 D3 Pilsen WI U.S.A.
175 H6 Pilsko mt. Pol.
173 G3 Pilsting Ger.
138 C3 Piltene Latvia
177 K5 Pilu Romania
96 B3 Pilu, Nam r. Myanmar
138 D4 Pilvė r. Lith.
138 D4 Pilviškiai Lith.
175 J6 Pilzno Pol.
241 M5 Pima AZ U.S.A.
253 E2 Pimenta Bueno Brazil
192 B5 Pimentel Sardegna Italy
116 C5 Pimpalner Mahar. India
150 E4 Pimperne Dorset, England U.K.
116 C5 Pimpri Gujarat India
116 D2 Pin r. India
96 A2 Pin r. Myanmar
136 D1 Pina r. Belarus
186 C3 Pina Spain
187 C4 Pina mt. Spain
241 K6 Pinacate, Cerro del mt. Mex.
183 F3 Piña de Esgueva Spain
116 D4 Pinahat Uttar Prad. India
241 L5 Pinaleno Mountains AZ U.S.A.
92 B3 Pinamalayan Phil.
261 I5 Pinamar Arg.
Pinang Malaysia see George Town
94 C1 Pinang i. Malaysia
94 C1 Pinang state Malaysia
185 E4 Pinar mt. Spain
187 G5 Pinar, Cap des c. Spain
126 E3 Pınarbaşı Turkey
246 B2 Pinar del Río Cuba
126 B2 Pinarhisar Turkey
129 A4 Pınarlar Turkey
129 C4 Pınarlı Turkey
250 B5 Piñas Ecuador
190 C4 Pinasca Italy
90 F3 Pinatubo, Mt vol. Phil.
177 H5 Pincehely Hungary
151 G2 Pinchbeck Lincolnshire, England U.K.
222 H5 Pincher Creek Alta Can.
236 F4 Pinckneyville IL U.S.A.
159 F3 Pinçon, Mont hill France
227 F4 Pinconning MI U.S.A.
Pîncota Romania see Pâncota
175 I5 Pińczów Pol.
257 E5 Pindamonhangaba Brazil
87 B6 Pindar W.A. Austr.
116 D3 Pindar r. India
254 D2 Pindaré r. Brazil
254 D2 Pindaré Mirim Brazil
123 H3 Pind Dadan Khay Pak.
Píndhos Óros mts Greece see Pindos
123 H4 Pindi Batiau Pak.
123 H3 Pindi Gheb Pak.
198 B2 Pindos mts Greece
Pindus Mountains Greece see Pindos
116 C4 Pindwara Rajasthan India
226 E3 Pine r. MI U.S.A.
226 E4 Pine r. MI U.S.A.
226 B4 Pine r. WI U.S.A.
226 C3 Pine r. WI U.S.A.
237 E5 Pine Bluff AR U.S.A.
238 F3 Pine Bluffs WY U.S.A.
235 D1 Pine Bush NY U.S.A.
226 A3 Pine City MN U.S.A.
84 B2 Pine Creek N.T. Austr.
232 E4 Pine Creek r. PA U.S.A.
240 G2 Pinecrest CA U.S.A.
183 H4 Pineda de Cigüela Spain
183 G2 Pineda de la Sierra Spain
186 F3 Pineda de Mar Spain
238 E3 Pinedale WY U.S.A.
223 L5 Pine Dock Man. Can.
223 L5 Pine Falls Man. Can.
134 H2 Pinega Rus. Fed.
134 H2 Pinega r. Rus. Fed.
87 B5 Pinegrove W.A. Austr.
232 A5 Pine Grove KY U.S.A.
227 I5 Pine Grove PA U.S.A.
232 C5 Pine Grove WV U.S.A.
84 C4 Pine Hill N.T. Austr.
234 D3 Pine Hill NJ U.S.A.
240 I4 Pine Hills CA U.S.A.
231 D6 Pine Hills FL U.S.A.
223 J4 Pinehouse Lake Sask. Can.
234 B3 Pinehurst MD U.S.A.
224 B2 Pineimuta r. Ont. Can.
198 C2 Pineios r. Greece
226 A3 Pine Island MN U.S.A.
235 D1 Pine Island NY U.S.A.
262 R1 Pine Island Glacier Antarctica
182 D3 Pinela Port.
237 E6 Pineland TX U.S.A.
183 F3 Piñel de Abajo Spain
81 B6 Pinelheugh mt. South I. N.Z.
231 D7 Pinellas Park FL U.S.A.
240 G4 Pine Mountain CA U.S.A.
241 K4 Pine Peak AZ U.S.A.
222 H2 Pine Point N.W.T. Can.
240 H3 Pineridge CA U.S.A.
236 C3 Pine Ridge SD U.S.A.
190 C4 Pinerolo Italy
Pines, Isle of i. Cuba see La Juventud, Isla de
Pines, Isle of i. New Caledonia see Pins, Île des
193 G2 Pineto Italy
241 M4 Pinetop AZ U.S.A.
215 H3 Pinetown S. Africa
163 C4 Pineuilh France
227 I4 Pine Valley NY U.S.A.
232 B6 Pineville KY U.S.A.
237 E6 Pineville LA U.S.A.
234 C2 Pineville PA U.S.A.
232 C6 Pineville WV U.S.A.
156 E4 Piney France
96 C4 Ping, Mae Nam r. Thai.
116 C1 Pingal Jammu and Kashmir
106 D4 Ping'an Qinghai China
Ping'anyi Qinghai China see Ping'an
87 C7 Pingaring W.A. Austr.
108 C3 Pingba Guizhou China
108 B4 Pingbian Yunnan China
108 C2 Pingchang Sichuan China
107 G4 Pingding Shanxi China
Pingdingbu Hebei China see Guyuan
109 E1 Pingdingshan Henan China
Pingdong Taiwan see P'ingtung
Pingdu Jiangxi China see Anfu
107 H4 Pingdu Shandong China
87 C7 Pingelly W.A. Austr.
179 H3 Pinggau Austria
107 H3 Pinggu Beijing China
108 C4 Pingguo Guangxi China
109 E4 Pinghai Guangdong China
109 F3 Pinghe Fujian China
Pinghu Guizhou China see Pingtang
109 G2 Pinghu Zhejiang China
109 E2 Pingjiang Hunan China
108 D3 Pingle Guangxi China
108 D1 Pingli Shaanxi China
106 E5 Pingliang Gansu China
107 F5 Pinglu Shanxi China
106 E4 Pingluo Ningxia China
Pingma Guangxi China see Tiandong
109 F3 Pingnan Fujian China
108 D4 Pingnan Guangxi China
107 H3 Pingquan Hebei China
87 C7 Pingrup W.A. Austr.
Pingshan Guangdong China see Huidong
107 G4 Pingshan Hebei China
108 C2 Pingshan Sichuan China
Pingshan Yunnan China see Luquan
109 E3 Pingshi Guangdong China
Pingshu Hebei China see Daicheng
109 F3 Pingtan Fujian China
108 C3 Pingtang Guizhou China
109 G4 P'ingtung Taiwan
108 C1 Pingwu Sichuan China
Pingxi Guizhou China see Yuping
Pingxiang Gansu China see Tongwei
108 C4 Pingxiang Guangxi China
109 E3 Pingxiang Jiangxi China
107 J1 Pingyang Heilong. China
109 G3 Pingyang Zhejiang China
107 G4 Pingyao Shanxi China
107 H5 Pingyi Shandong China
107 H4 Pingyin Shandong China
109 E1 Pingyu Henan China
109 E3 Pingyuan Guangdong China
107 H4 Pingyuan Shandong China
Pingyuan Yunnan China see Yingjiang
108 B4 Pingyuanjie Yunnan China
108 D3 Pingzhai Guizhou China
256 D5 Pinhal Brazil
184 B2 Pinhal Novo Port.
182 C3 Pinhão Port.
254 D2 Pinheiro Brazil
182 B3 Pinheiro Porto Port.
184 B2 Pinheiro Setúbal Port.
258 G3 Pinheiro Machado Brazil
257 G3 Pinheiros Brazil
182 C4 Pinhel Port.
150 D4 Pinhoe Devon, England U.K.
251 E6 Pinhuã r. Brazil
185 H2 Pinilla r. Spain
183 I4 Pinilla de Molina Spain
183 E3 Pinilla de Toro Spain
Piniós r. Greece see Pineios
87 B7 Pinjarra W.A. Austr.
87 D6 Pinjin W.A. Austr.
179 H3 Pinkafeld Austria
84 B2 Pinkerton Range hills N.T. Austr.
222 F3 Pink Mountain B.C. Can.
81 D4 Pinnacle mt. South I. N.Z.
232 D5 Pinnacle hill VA/WV U.S.A.
82 E3 Pinnaroo S.A. Austr.
168 E2 Pinnau r. Ger.
168 E2 Pinneberg Ger.
171 F4 Pinnow Ger.
192 B2 Pino Corse France
182 D3 Pino Spain
183 F2 Pino del Río Spain
182 D4 Pinofranqueado Spain
95 E3 Pinoh r. Indon.
161 B3 Pinols France
182 B2 Piñor Spain
244 D2 Pinos Mex.
186 E3 Pinós hill Spain
Pinos, Isla de i. Cuba see La Juventud, Isla de
240 H4 Pinos, Mount CA U.S.A.
187 B6 Pinoso Spain
183 H4 Pinoso mt. Spain
185 G3 Pinos-Puente Spain
245 E5 Pinotepa Nacional Mex.
93 A3 Pinrang Sulawesi Selatan Indon.
78 □5 Pins, Île des i. New Caledonia
163 D4 Pinsac France
179 E3 Pinsdorf Austria
136 D1 Pinsk Belarus
183 I2 Pinsoro Spain
250 □ Pinta, Isla i. Islas Galápagos Ecuador
241 K5 Pinta, Sierra hill AZ U.S.A.
186 B2 Pintano Spain
183 G4 Pinto Spain
241 K3 Pintura UT U.S.A.
192 B4 Pinu, Monte hill Sardegna Italy
146 D6 Pinwherry South Ayrshire, Scotland U.K.
191 H2 Pinzano al Tagliamento Italy
182 C4 Pinzio Port.
191 F2 Pinzolo Italy
191 H5 Piobbico Italy
241 J3 Pioche NV U.S.A.
78 □6 Pio Island Solomon Is
254 E3 Pio IX Brazil
161 C4 Piolenc France
190 E3 Pioltello Italy
193 G2 Piomba r. Italy
192 C2 Piombino Italy
191 G3 Piombino Dese Italy
232 A4 Pioneer OH U.S.A.
138 C4 Pionerskiy Kaliningradskaya Oblast' Rus. Fed.
130 H3 Pionerskiy Khanty-Mansiyskiy Avtonomnyy Okrug Rus. Fed.
175 J4 Pionki Pol.
160 A2 Pionsat France
80 E3 Piopio North I. N.Z.
Piopiotahi inlet South I. N.Z. see Milford Sound
193 E1 Pioraco Italy
251 F5 Piorini r. Brazil
251 F5 Piorini, Lago l. Brazil
190 C4 Piossasco Italy
174 G3 Piotrków Kujawski Pol.
175 H4 Piotrków Trybunalski Pol.
191 H3 Piove di Sacco Italy
191 G3 Piovene Rocchette Italy
190 E2 Pioverna r. Italy
122 E5 Pīp Iran
100 D4 Pipa Dingzi mt. China
116 C4 Pipar Rajasthan India
116 C4 Pipar Road Rajasthan India
240 I3 Piper Peak NV U.S.A.
234 C2 Pipersville PA U.S.A.
223 K5 Pipestone Man. Can.
224 B2 Pipestone r. Ont. Can.
236 D3 Pipestone MN U.S.A.
197 H2 Pipirig Romania
80 E3 Pipiriki North I. N.Z.
116 C3 Pipli Haryana India
225 G3 Pipmuacan, Réservoir resr Que. Can.
158 E4 Pipriac France
Piqan Xinjiang China see Shanshan
110 C3 Piqanlik Xinjiang China
232 A4 Piqua OH U.S.A.
163 C5 Pique r. France
254 F3 Piquet Carneiro Brazil
257 E5 Piquete Brazil
253 G4 Piquiri r. Mato Grosso do Sul Brazil
256 A6 Piquiri r. Paraná Brazil
177 L4 Pir Romania
256 D5 Piracaia Brazil
256 C2 Piracanjuba Brazil
256 C3 Piracanjuba r. Brazil
256 D5 Piracicaba Brazil
257 F3 Piracicaba r. Minas Gerais Brazil
256 C5 Piracicaba r. São Paulo Brazil
256 D4 Piraçununga Brazil
254 E2 Piracuruca Brazil
Piraeus Greece see Peiraias
256 C6 Piraí do Sul Brazil
Piráievs Greece see Peiraias
194 D4 Piraino Sicilia Italy
256 C5 Piraju Brazil
256 C3 Pirajuba Brazil
256 C4 Pirajuí Brazil
129 G3 Pirallahı Adası Azer.
191 I3 Piran Slovenia
258 F2 Pirané Arg.
257 F4 Piranga Brazil
257 F4 Piranga r. Brazil
257 E5 Piranguinho Brazil
254 F4 Piranhas Alagoas Brazil
256 B2 Piranhas Goiás Brazil
256 B2 Piranhas r. Goiás Brazil
254 F3 Piranhas r. Rio Grande do Norte Brazil
254 D2 Pirapemas Brazil
257 F4 Pirapetinga Brazil
256 A5 Pirapó r. Brazil
257 E2 Pirapora Brazil
256 B5 Pirapozinho Brazil
256 C6 Piraquara Brazil
258 G3 Piratini Brazil
256 C5 Piratininga Brazil
116 D4 Pirawa Rajasthan India
151 G3 Pirbright Surrey, England U.K.
Pirchevan Azer. see Zängilan
256 C1 Pirenópolis Brazil
256 C2 Pires do Rio Brazil
117 G4 Pirganj Bangl.
Pírgos Greece see Pyrgos
197 G4 Pirgovo Bulg.
158 D4 Piriac-sur-Mer France
80 E3 Piriaka North I. N.Z.
258 G4 Piriápolis Uru.
177 L4 Piricse Hungary
197 F5 Pirin mts Bulg.
Pirineos mts Europe see Pyrenees
254 E3 Piripiri Brazil
138 E2 Pirita r. Estonia
250 D2 Píritu Venez.
179 G3 Pirka Austria
141 M3 Pirkkala Fin.
Pirlerkondu Turkey see Taşkent
172 B2 Pirmasens Ger.
114 C4 Pirmed Kerala India
171 E5 Pirna Ger.
146 C6 Pirnmill North Ayrshire, Scotland U.K.
117 G5 Pirojpur Bangl.
183 F3 Pirón r. Spain
80 E2 Pirongia North I. N.Z.
80 E2 Pirongia vol. North I. N.Z.
139 I2 Piros, Ozero l. Rus. Fed.
197 F4 Pirot Srbija Yugo.
261 G5 Pirovano Arg.
117 F4 Pirpainti Bihar India
116 C2 Pir Panjal Range mts India/Pak.
127 F3 Pirrasit Dağ hill Turkey
129 F4 Pirsaat Azer.
129 F3 Pirsaatçay r. Azer.
177 I5 Pirtó Hungary
140 L2 Pirttivuopio Sweden
123 G2 Pir'yakh, Gora mt. Tajik.
Piryatin Ukr. see Pyryatyn
Piryetós Greece see Pyrgetos
Piryíon Voreio Aigaio Greece see Pyrgi
190 F5 Pisa Italy
191 F5 Pisa prov. Toscana Italy
175 J2 Pisa r. Pol.
252 C3 Pisac Peru
Pisae Italy see Pisa
78 □4a Pisamwe i. Chuuk Micronesia
162 B3 Pisany France
78 □4a Pisar i. Chuuk Micronesia
81 B6 Pisa Range mts South I. N.Z.
Pisaurum Italy see Pesaro
235 D2 Piscataway NJ U.S.A.
179 G3 Pischelsdorf in der Steiermark Austria
177 K6 Pişchia Romania
193 H4 Pisciotta Italy
252 A3 Pisco Peru
252 A3 Pisco r. Peru
177 L4 Pişcolt Romania
176 D2 Písek Czech Rep.
81 A6 Pisgah, Mount South I. N.Z.
81 C6 Pisgah, Mount South I. N.Z.
Pisha Sichuan China see Ningnan
111 B4 Pishan Xinjiang China
136 B2 Pishcha Ukr.
136 E3 Pishchana Ukr.
137 F3 Pishchane Ukr.
136 E3 Pishchanka Ukr.
123 E5 Pīshīn Iran
123 F4 Pishin Pak.
123 F4 Pishin Lora r. Pak.
Pishpek Kyrg. see Bishkek
175 I3 Pisia r. Pol.
241 K5 Pisinimo AZ U.S.A.
78 □4a Pisininin i. Chuuk Micronesia
Piskent Uzbek. see Pskent
136 E2 Piskivka Ukr.
137 I3 Pisky Kharkivs'ka Oblast' Ukr.
137 J3 Pisky Luhans'ka Oblast' Ukr.
240 G4 Pismo Beach CA U.S.A.
253 E3 Piso Firme Bol.
190 F3 Pisogne Italy
138 C4 Pissa r. Rus. Fed.
258 C2 Pissis, Cerro mt. Arg.
163 B4 Pissos France
140 O2 Pista r. Rus. Fed.
243 H4 Pisté Mex.
195 F2 Pisticci Italy
191 F5 Pistoia Italy
191 F5 Pistoia prov. Toscana Italy
Pistoriae Italy see Pistoia
139 M3 Pistsovo Rus. Fed.
183 F3 Pisuerga r. Spain
175 J2 Pisz Pol.
175 L4 Piszczac Pol.
238 B3 Pit r. CA U.S.A.
206 B4 Pita Guinea
225 H2 Pitaga Nfld. Can.
243 H5 Pital Mex.
250 B4 Pitalito Col.
256 B6 Pitanga Brazil
256 C4 Pitangueiras Brazil
257 E3 Pitangui Brazil
83 E3 Pitarpunga Lake imp. l. N.S.W. Austr.
186 C4 Pitarque Spain
267 K7 Pitcairn Island S. Pacific Ocean
206 B3 Pitche Guinea-Bissau
140 M2 Piteå Sweden
140 M2 Piteälven r. Sweden
191 F4 Piteglio Italy
135 H5 Pitelino Rus. Fed.
120 A2 Piterka Rus. Fed.
197 G3 Piteşti Romania
87 C6 Pithara W.A. Austr.
156 C4 Pithiviers France
116 E3 Pithoragarh Uttar Prad. India
192 D2 Pitigliano Italy
183 I2 Pitillas Spain
242 B2 Pitiquito Mex.
134 E3 Pitkyaranta Rus. Fed.
146 E5 Pitlochry Perth and Kinross, Scotland U.K.
234 C3 Pitman NJ U.S.A.
146 F4 Pitmedden Aberdeenshire, Scotland U.K.
150 D4 Pitminster Somerset, England U.K.
207 I4 Pitoa Cameroon
188 F3 Pitomača Croatia
217 □1c Piton de la Fournaise vol. Réunion
217 □1c Piton des Neiges mt. Réunion
Pitong Sichuan China see Pixian
156 B3 Pîtres France
185 G4 Pitres Spain
260 A6 Pitrufquén Chile
179 G4 Pitschgau Austria
151 G3 Pitstone Buckinghamshire, England U.K.
Pitsunda Georgia see Bichvint'a
151 F3 Pitt Hampshire, England U.K.
165 C4 Pittem Belgium
179 H3 Pitten Austria
146 D4 Pittentrail Highland, Scotland U.K.
146 F5 Pittenweem Fife, Scotland U.K.
222 D4 Pitt Island B.C. Can.
80 □ Pitt Island Chatham Is S. Pacific Ocean
Pitt Islands Solomon Is see Vanikoro Islands
237 F5 Pittsboro MS U.S.A.
231 E5 Pittsboro NC U.S.A.
240 G2 Pittsburg CA U.S.A.
237 E4 Pittsburg KS U.S.A.
233 H2 Pittsburg NH U.S.A.
237 E5 Pittsburg TX U.S.A.
232 D4 Pittsburgh PA U.S.A.
236 F4 Pittsfield IL U.S.A.
233 G3 Pittsfield MA U.S.A.
233 □I2 Pittsfield ME U.S.A.
233 H3 Pittsfield NH U.S.A.
233 G3 Pittsfield VT U.S.A.
234 C1 Pittston PA U.S.A.
233 □I2 Pittston Farm ME U.S.A.
226 B3 Pittsville WI U.S.A.
85 G5 Pittsworth Qld Austr.
177 J5 Pitvaros Hungary
254 C4 Pium Brazil
257 E4 Piumhí Brazil
250 A6 Piura Peru
250 A6 Piura dept Peru
138 F3 Piusa r. Estonia
241 J4 Piute Mountains CA U.S.A.
240 H4 Piute Peak CA U.S.A.
224 D3 Pivabiska r. Ont. Can.
136 F4 Pivdennyy Buh r. Ukr.
250 C2 Pivijay Col.
188 E3 Pivka Slovenia
191 J3 Pivka r. Slovenia
175 I6 Piwniczna Pol.
Pixariá mt. Greece see Pyxaria
108 B2 Pixian Sichuan China
240 H4 Pixley CA U.S.A.
243 H5 Pixoyal Mex.
252 C4 Pizacoma Peru
185 F4 Pizarra Spain
190 E2 Piz Bernina mt. Italy/Switz.
178 C4 Piz Boè mt. Italy
178 B4 Piz Buin mt. Austria/Switz.
190 E2 Piz d'Anarosa mt. Switz.
190 E2 Piz Duan mt. Switz.
190 E2 Piz Ela mt. Switz.
134 J4 Pizhanka Rus. Fed.
207 G4 Pizhi Nigeria
134 I4 Pizhma Rus. Fed.
134 J4 Pizhma r. Rus. Fed.
134 K2 Pizhma r. Rus. Fed.
107 H5 Pizhou Jiangsu China
190 E2 Piz Kesch mt. Switz.
190 D2 Piz Medel mt. Switz.
190 E2 Pizol mt. Switz.
190 F2 Piz Pisoc mt. Switz.
190 E2 Piz Platta mt. Switz.
190 E2 Piz Varuna mt. Italy/Switz.
190 E3 Pizzighettone Italy
195 F4 Pizzo Italy
190 E3 Pizzo Arera mt. Italy
194 C5 Pizzo Cangialoso mt. Sicilia Italy
194 D5 Pizzo Carbonara mt. Sicilia Italy
190 F3 Pizzo della Presolana mt. Italy
190 F2 Pizzo di Coca mt. Italy
193 G3 Pizzoferrato Italy
193 F2 Pizzoli Italy
190 D2 Pizzo Rotondo mt. Switz.
194 C5 Pizzo Telegrafo hill Sicilia Italy
193 E2 Pizzuto, Monte mt. Italy
170 D2 Plaaz Ger.
158 B3 Plabennec France
225 K4 Placentia Nfld. Can.
Placentia Italy see Piacenza
225 K4 Placentia Bay Nfld. Can.
92 B4 Placer Masbate Phil.
92 C4 Placer Mindanao Phil.
240 G2 Placerville CA U.S.A.
239 E4 Placerville CO U.S.A.
246 C2 Placetas Cuba
252 D2 Plácido de Castro Brazil
260 B3 Placilla Chile
190 C2 Plaffeien Switz.
169 C5 Plaidt Ger.
159 I4 Plaimpied-Givaudins France
237 E5 Plain Dealing LA U.S.A.
157 H4 Plainfaing France
235 G1 Plainfield CT U.S.A.
230 C4 Plainfield IN U.S.A.
235 D2 Plainfield NJ U.S.A.
233 G2 Plainfield VT U.S.A.
226 C3 Plainfield WI U.S.A.
237 C4 Plains KS U.S.A.
237 C5 Plains TX U.S.A.
234 D2 Plainsboro NJ U.S.A.
158 D3 Plaintel France
226 A3 Plainview MN U.S.A.
236 D3 Plainview NE U.S.A.
235 E2 Plainview NY U.S.A.
237 C5 Plainview TX U.S.A.
235 F1 Plainville CT U.S.A.
236 D4 Plainville KS U.S.A.
226 E4 Plainwell MI U.S.A.
163 C5 Plaisance France
246 D3 Plaisance Haiti
163 D5 Plaisance-du-Touch France
156 B4 Plaisir France
233 H3 Plaistow NH U.S.A.
94 D3 Plaju Sumatera Indon.
95 G5 Plampang Sumbawa Indon.
176 B2 Planá Czech Rep.
246 D2 Plana Cays is Bahamas
240 G3 Planada CA U.S.A.
256 D1 Planaltina Brazil
171 G5 Plaňany Czech Rep.
157 G5 Plancher-Bas France
157 G5 Plancher-les-Mines France
158 D3 Plancoët France
156 D4 Plancy-l'Abbaye France
244 D3 Plan de Ayala Mex.
161 D4 Plan-de-Baux France
161 D5 Plan-de-Cuques France
161 E5 Plan-de-la-Tour France
196 E3 Plandište Vojvodina, Srbija Yugo.
161 C5 Plan-d'Orgon France
171 D3 Plane r. Ger.
173 F3 Planegg Ger.
163 E6 Planès France
176 C2 Plánice Czech Rep.
191 J3 Planik mt. Croatia
173 F2 Plankenfels Ger.
236 D3 Plankinton SD U.S.A.
226 C5 Plano IL U.S.A.
237 D5 Plano TX U.S.A.
261 I1 Plano Alto Brazil
178 B3 Plansee l. Austria
163 D5 Plantaurel, Montagnes du hills France
231 D7 Plant City FL U.S.A.
235 F1 Plantsville CT U.S.A.
256 C4 Planura Brazil
237 F6 Plaquemine LA U.S.A.
182 D4 Plasencia Spain
186 C2 Plasencia del Monte Spain
175 L2 Płaska Pol.
188 E3 Plaški Croatia
196 E5 Plasnica Macedonia
120 E1 Plast Rus. Fed.
241 J5 Plaster City CA U.S.A.
225 H4 Plaster Rock N.B. Can.
215 H1 Plaston S. Africa
177 H3 Plášťovce Slovakia
100 F3 Plastun Rus. Fed.
129 A2 Plastunka Rus. Fed.
137 J5 Plastunovskaya Rus. Fed.
176 C2 Plasy Czech Rep.
192 A4 Platamona Lido Sardegna Italy
198 C2 Platamonas Greece
194 C5 Platani r. Sicilia Italy
195 F3 Platania Italy
198 B3 Platanos Greece
214 B4 Platbakkies S. Africa
215 G3 Platberg mt. S. Africa
170 C2 Plate Ger.
207 G4 Plateau state Nigeria
208 B5 Plateaux admin. reg. Congo
168 F3 Platendorf (Sassenburg) Ger.
214 C5 Plathuis S. Africa
195 F4 Platì Italy
196 D3 Platičevo Vojvodina, Srbija Yugo.
Platíkambos Greece see Platykampos
240 F1 Platina CA U.S.A.
220 B4 Platinum AK U.S.A.
137 J5 Platnirovskaya Rus. Fed.
250 C2 Plato Col.
215 G2 Platrand S. Africa
236 E4 Platte r. MO U.S.A.
236 E3 Platte r. NE U.S.A.
236 E4 Platte City MO U.S.A.
217 □2 Platte Island Seychelles
235 D1 Plattekill NY U.S.A.
179 F2 Plattenberg hill Austria
238 F3 Platteville CO U.S.A.
236 F3 Platteville WI U.S.A.
173 G3 Plattling Ger.
233 G2 Plattsburgh NY U.S.A.
236 E3 Plattsmouth NE U.S.A.
198 C1 Platy Greece
198 C2 Platykampos Greece
170 D2 Plau Ger.
169 F5 Plaue Ger.
171 D5 Plauen Ger.
170 D2 Plauer See l. Ger.
136 D2 Plav r. Ukr.
196 D4 Plav Crna Gora Yugo.
139 K5 Plava r. Rus. Fed.
179 I2 Plavecký Štvrtok Slovakia
138 E3 Pļaviņas Latvia
137 K1 Plavitsa r. Rus. Fed.
139 K5 Plavsk Rus. Fed.
216 □3c Playa Blanca Lanzarote Canary Is
184 D3 Playa de Castilla coastal area Spain
247 □1 Playa de Fajardo Puerto Rico
216 □3a Playa de las Americas Tenerife Canary Is
181 □ Playa del Inglés Gran Canaria Canary Is
261 I4 Playa Pascaul Uru.
250 A5 Playas Ecuador
245 H5 Playas r. Mex.
245 G5 Playa Vicente Mex.
97 E4 Plây Cu Vietnam
242 C3 Playón Mex.
162 D3 Plazac France
185 F2 Plaza del Judío mt. Spain
260 C6 Plaza Huincul Arg.
175 L5 Płazów Pol.
233 □J2 Pleasant, Mount hill N.B. Can.
234 C2 Pleasant Corners PA U.S.A.
235 D2 Pleasant Grove NJ U.S.A.
241 L1 Pleasant Grove UT U.S.A.
240 F3 Pleasant Hill CA U.S.A.
232 A4 Pleasant Hill OH U.S.A.
240 G3 Pleasanton CA U.S.A.
237 D6 Pleasanton TX U.S.A.
81 C6 Pleasant Point South I. N.Z.
235 E1 Pleasant Valley NY U.S.A.
234 C3 Pleasantville DE U.S.A.
234 D3 Pleasantville NJ U.S.A.
235 E1 Pleasantville NY U.S.A.
234 B3 Pleaseant Hill PA U.S.A.
149 H4 Pleasley Derbyshire, England U.K.
235 F1 Pleasure Beach CT U.S.A.
234 B3 Pleasureville PA U.S.A.
162 E3 Pleaux France
173 F2 Plech Ger.
176 C3 Plechý mt. Czech Rep.
175 H3 Plecka Dąbrowa Pol.
158 D3 Plédran France
158 C3 Pléhédel France
158 E3 Pleine-Fougères France
173 E2 Pleinfeld Ger.
173 G3 Pleiskirchen Ger.
171 D5 Pleiße Ger.
171 D4 Pleiße r. Ger.
137 J1 Plekhanovo Rus. Fed.
158 D3 Plélan-le-Grand France
158 D3 Plélan-le-Petit France
158 D3 Plélo France
158 D3 Plémet France
158 D3 Plénée-Jugon France
158 D3 Pléneuf-Val-André France
80 F2 Plenty, Bay of g. North I. N.Z.
238 F1 Plentywood MT U.S.A.
183 H1 Plentzia Spain
158 D3 Plérin France
139 M3 Ples Rus. Fed.
179 G3 Pleschkogel mt. Austria
158 D4 Plescop France
177 L5 Pleşcuţa Romania
134 H3 Plesetsk Rus. Fed.
120 C1 Pleshanovo Rus. Fed.
Pleshchentsy Belarus see Plyeshchanitsy
139 L3 Pleshcheyevo, Ozero l. Rus. Fed.
177 J3 Plešivec Slovakia
179 F4 Plešivec mt. Slovenia
158 D3 Pleslin-Trigavou France
176 B1 Plesná Czech Rep.
169 F5 Pleß hill Ger.
171 E4 Plessa Ger.
158 E4 Plessé France
158 C3 Plestin-les-Grèves France
174 F4 Pleszew Pol.
137 F3 Pletenyy Tashlyk Ukr.
188 F3 Pleternica Croatia
169 C4 Plettenberg Ger.
214 D6 Plettenberg Bay S. Africa
179 F3 Pletzen mt. Austria
158 C3 Pleubian France
158 E3 Pleudihen-sur-Rance France
159 G5 Pleumartin France
158 C3 Pleumeur-Bodou France
156 D4 Pleurs France
158 D3 Pleurtuit France
158 B4 Pleuven France
197 G4 Pleven Bulg.
Plevna Bulg. see Pleven
177 H2 Plevník-Drienové Slovakia
158 C3 Pleyben France
158 C3 Pleyber-Christ France
173 G2 Pleystein Ger.
187 B7 Pliego Spain
173 F3 Pliening Ger.
95 F2 Plieran r. Sarawak Malaysia
177 I3 Pliešovce Slovakia
163 C5 Plieux France
191 F2 Plima r. Italy
174 C3 Pliszka r. Pol.
188 E3 Plješevica mts Croatia
196 D4 Pljevlja Crna Gora Yugo.
192 A4 Ploaghe Sardegna Italy
158 B4 Plobannalec France
157 H4 Plobsheim France
188 F4 Ploče Croatia
172 D3 Plochingen Ger.
175 K1 Płociczno Pol.
175 H3 Płock Pol.
146 C4 Plockton Highland, Scotland U.K.
188 F4 Pločno mt. Bos.-Herz.
139 H1 Plodovoye Rus. Fed.
158 C4 Ploemeur France
158 D4 Ploeren France
158 D4 Ploërmel France
Ploeşti Romania see Ploieşti
158 D3 Plœuc-sur-Lié France
158 B4 Plogastel-St-Germain France
158 B3 Plogonnec France
170 E1 Plogshagen Ger.
197 H3 Ploieşti Romania
199 E2 Plomari Voreio Aigaio Greece
161 A3 Plomb du Cantal mt. France
157 G5 Plombières-les-Bains France
158 B4 Plomelin France
158 B4 Plomeur France
158 B3 Plomodiern France
168 F1 Plön Ger.
158 B4 Plonéour-Lanvern France
158 C3 Plonévez-du-Faou France
158 B3 Plonevez-Porzay France
174 C2 Płonia r. Pol.
175 I3 Płonka r. Pol.
175 I3 Płońsk Pol.
197 F2 Plopiş Romania
175 H1 Płoskinia Pol.
139 H3 Ploskosh' Rus. Fed.
Ploskoye Rus. Fed. see Stanovoye
175 I2 Płośnica Pol.
173 G2 Plößberg Ger.
174 D2 Płoty Pol.
171 D3 Plötzin Ger.
171 C3 Plötzky Ger.
158 D3 Plouagat France
158 C3 Plouaret France
158 B3 Plouarzel France
158 C4 Plouay France
158 D3 Ploubalay France

158 C3 Ploubazlanec France
158 C3 Ploubezre France
176 D1 Ploučnice r. Czech Rep.
158 B3 Ploudalmézeau France
158 B3 Ploudaniel France
158 B3 Ploudiry France
158 C3 Plouénan France
158 B3 Plouescat France
158 D3 Plouézec France
158 B3 Ploufragan France
158 C3 Plougasnou France
158 B3 Plougastel-Daoulas France
158 C3 Plougonvelin France
158 C3 Plougonver France
158 C3 Plougrescant France
158 C3 Plouguenast France
158 C3 Plouguerneau France
158 B3 Plouguiel France
158 B3 Plouguin France
158 B3 Plouha France
158 B3 Plouharnel France
158 B3 Plouhinec Bretagne France
158 C3 Plouhinec Bretagne France
158 C3 Plouigneau France
158 B3 Ploumagoar France
158 B3 Ploumilliau France
158 B3 Plounévez-Lochrist France
158 C3 Plounévez-Moëdec France
158 C3 Plounévez-Quintin France
158 B3 Plouray France
158 B3 Plourin-lès-Morlaix France
158 B3 Plouvien France
158 B3 Plouyé France
158 B3 Plouzané France
158 B3 Plouzévédé France
197 G4 Plovdiv Bulg.
226 C3 Plover W.I. U.S.A.
226 C3 Plover r. WI U.S.A.
158 B4 Plozévet France
          Plozk Pol. see Płock
147 D2 Pluck Rep. of Ireland
234 C2 Pluckemin NJ U.S.A.
213 E4 Plumtree Zimbabwe
138 C4 Plungė Lith.
175 K1 Pluszkiejmy Pol.
239 E6 Plutarco Elías Calles, Presa resr Mex.
158 C4 Pluvigner France
196 D4 Plužine Crna Gora Yugo.
174 G2 Plužnica Pol.
158 C3 Pluzunet France
138 F4 Plyeshchanitsy Belarus
96 B3 Ply Huey Wati, Khao mt. Myanmar/Thai.
150 C4 Plym r. England U.K.
247 □2 Plymouth Montserrat
150 C4 Plymouth Plymouth, England U.K.
150 C4 Plymouth admin. div. England U.K.
240 G2 Plymouth CA U.S.A.
235 E1 Plymouth CT U.S.A.
228 B5 Plymouth IL U.S.A.
230 C3 Plymouth IN U.S.A.
233 H4 Plymouth MA U.S.A.
231 E5 Plymouth NC U.S.A.
233 H3 Plymouth NH U.S.A.
234 C1 Plymouth PA U.S.A.
150 C4 Plympton Plymouth, England U.K.
150 C4 Plymstock Plymouth, England U.K.
150 D2 Plynlimon hill Wales U.K.
136 E3 Plyskiv Ukr.
137 G2 Plysky Ukr.
138 G2 Plyussa Rus. Fed.
138 G2 Plyussa r. Rus. Fed.
176 C2 Plzeň Czech Rep.
176 C2 Plzeňský kraj admin. reg. Czech Rep.
175 J3 Pniewo Pol.
175 I4 Pniewy Mazowieckie Pol.
174 F3 Pniewy Wielkopolskie Pol.
46 B4 Pô Burkina
191 H3 Po r. Italy
242 □1? Poás, Volcán vol. Costa Rica
207 F5 Pobè Benin
131 P3 Pobeda, Gora mt. Rus. Fed.
          Pobeda Peak China/Kyrg. see
          Pobedim Slovakia
177 G3 Pobedino Rus. Fed. see Zarechnyy
          Pobedinskiy Rus. Fed. see
          Pobedy, Pik mt. China/Kyrg. see Jengish Chokusu
176 B2 Poběžovice Czech Rep.
174 F3 Pobiedziska Pol.
175 K3 Pobikry Pol.
260 B4 Población Chile
182 E2 Población del Valle Spain
188 G2 Poblete Spain
174 F1 Pobłocie Pol.
186 D3 Pobleda Spain
136 F3 Pobuz'ke Ukr.
232 C5 Poca WV U.S.A.
237 F4 Pocahontas AR U.S.A.
236 C3 Pocahontas IA U.S.A.
232 C5 Pocatalico r. WV U.S.A.
238 D3 Pocatello ID U.S.A.
176 E2 Počátky Czech Rep.
184 B2 Poceirão Port.
136 C2 Pochayiv Ukr.
139 I5 Pochep Rus. Fed.
135 I5 Pochinki Rus. Fed.
139 I4 Pochinok Rus. Fed.
179 Q2 Pöchlarn Austria
185 F6 Pocho, Sierra de mts Arg.
245 F6 Pochutla Mex.
260 A5 Pocillas Chile
95 G1 Pock, Gunung hill Sabah Malaysia
171 E5 Pockau Bayern Ger.
173 I4 Pocking Bayern Ger.
149 I4 Pocklington East Riding of Yorkshire, England U.K.
254 E5 Poções Brazil
257 E4 Poço Fundo Brazil
177 L5 Pocola Romania
135 I5 Pocola Rus. Fed.
131 G2 Pocomoke City MD U.S.A.
MD/VA U.S.A.
252 D4 Pocona Bol.
253 D4 Poconé Brazil
234 C1 Pocono Mountains hills PA U.S.A.
234 C1 Pocono Pines PA U.S.A.
234 C1 Pocono Summit PA U.S.A.
93 B5 Poco Ranakah vol. Flores Indon.
256 D4 Poços de Caldas Brazil
257 G3 Pocrane Brazil
177 K4 Pócsaj Hungary
175 H5 Poczesna Pol.
177 I2 Podbiel Slovakia
176 D1 Poděbrady Czech Rep.
143 L3 Podcher'ye r. Rus. Fed.
176 E1 Podebřady Czech Rep.
139 H3 Pod 'or'yan Rus. Fed.
176 E1 Poděbrady Czech Rep.
175 I6 Podegrodzie Pol.
163 B4 Podensac France
250 E4 Podensano Brazil
190 E1 Poderzana Italy
179 I3 Podersdorf am See Austria
197 K4 Podgorac Srbija Yugo.
196 C6 Podgorica Crna Gora Yugo.
130 J1 Podgornoye Rus. Fed.
131 Q4 Podgornoye Rus. Fed.

114 C3 Podile Andhra Prad. India
191 H3 Po di Levante r. Italy
179 H2 Podivín Czech Rep.
131 K3 Podkamennaya Tunguska Rus. Fed.
131 K3 Podkamennaya Tunguska r. Rus. Fed.
175 K6 Podkarpackie prov. Pol.
139 L4 Podkhozheye Rus. Fed.
197 G5 Podkova Bulg.
175 I3 Podkowa Leśna Pol.
129 C1 Podkumok r. Rus. Fed.
175 K2 Podlaskie prov. Pol.
197 H2 Podlehnik Slovenia
179 H1 Podolí Czech Rep.
139 K4 Podol'sk Rus. Fed.
206 B2 Podor Senegal
175 M6 Podorozhnye Ukr.
139 M3 Podzerskiy Rus. Fed.
139 J1 Podporozh'ye Rus. Fed.
176 G5 Podravska Slatina Croatia
179 H3 Podturen Croatia
211 C6 Podujevo Kosovo, Srbija Yugo.
175 H6 Podwilk Pol.
134 H3 Poduyga Rus. Fed.
170 C1 Poel i. Ger.
164 D2 Poeldijk Neth.
          Poetovio Slovenia see Ptuj
214 B3 Pofadder S. Africa
193 F3 Pofi Italy
227 G2 Pogamasing Ont. Can.
239 I5 Pogar Rus. Fed.
170 E1 Poggendorf Austria
179 F4 Poggersdorf Austria
195 H2 Poggiardo Italy
191 G5 Poggibonsi Italy
192 C2 Poggio Ballone hill Italy
193 E2 Poggio Bustone Italy
192 D2 Poggio del Leccio hill Italy
192 D1 Poggio di Montieri mt. Italy
192 E2 Poggiodomo Italy
193 H3 Poggio Imperiale Italy
192 F2 Poggio Lecci hill Italy
192 B2 Poggio-Mezzana Corse France
193 F2 Poggio Mirteto Italy
193 E2 Poggio Moiano Italy
192 C2 Poggio Peroni hill Italy
193 F2 Poggio Picenze Italy
194 C5 Poggioreale Sicilia Italy
191 G4 Poggio Renatico Italy
193 I4 Poggio Rusco Italy
179 G2 Pöggstall Austria
196 E4 Pogled mt. Yugo.
156 E4 Pogny France
139 J3 Pogoreloye-Gorodishche Rus. Fed.
175 H6 Pogorzela Pol.
174 F1 Pogorzelice Pol.
137 I2 Pogozheye Rus. Fed.
196 E5 Pogradec Albania
          Pogrebishche Ukr. see Pohrebyshche
175 H1 Pogrodzie Pol.
253 G4 Poguba r. Brazil
          Po Hai g. China see Bo Hai
101 D5 P'ohang S. Korea
141 M3 Pohja Fin.
169 E3 Pohle Ger.
78 □1a Pohnpei atoll Micronesia
177 J3 Pohořelá Slovakia
176 F3 Pohořelice Czech Rep.
176 F3 Pohorje mts Slovenia
177 H3 Pohranice Slovakia
136 F2 Pohreby Kyivs'ka Oblast' Ukr.
137 G3 Pohreby Poltavs'ka Oblast' Ukr.
136 E3 Pohrebyshche Ukr.
116 D4 Pohri Madh. Prad. India
177 H3 Pohronská pahorkatina mts Slovakia
190 F2 Poia r. Italy
197 K4 Poiana Mare Romania
197 J3 Poiana Ruscă, Munţii mts Romania
197 G2 Poiana Stampei Romania
177 L5 Poiana Vadului Romania
197 H2 Poieneşti Romania
197 G2 Poienile de Sub Munte Romania
197 F2 Poienita, Vârful mt. Romania
156 C5 Poilly-lez-Gien France
135 H5 Poim Rus. Fed.
156 E5 Poinçon-lès-Larrey France
232 A5 Poindexter KY U.S.A.
77 G4 Poindimié New Caledonia
173 F3 Poing Ger.
263 H2 Poinsett, Cape Antarctica
240 F2 Point Arena CA U.S.A.
222 C3 Point Baker AK U.S.A.
227 J2 Point-Comfort Que. Can.
237 F6 Pointe à la Hache LA U.S.A.
247 □2 Pointe-à-Pitre Guadeloupe
227 G3 Pointe au Baril Station Can.
226 E3 Pointe Aux Pins MI U.S.A.
247 □2 Pointe Michel Dominica
206 A4 Pointe-Noire Congo
247 □2 Pointe Noire Guadeloupe
160 E3 Pointe Percée mt. France
247 □1? Point Fortin Trin. and Tob.
220 B3 Point Hope AK U.S.A.
220 E3 Pointis-Inard France
82 C3 Point Kenny S.A. Austr.
222 H1 Point Lake N.W.T. Can.
232 D5 Point Marion PA U.S.A.
232 E5 Point of Rocks MD U.S.A.
233 F4 Point of Rocks WY U.S.A.
85 F1 Point Pleasant NJ U.S.A.
232 B5 Point Pleasant WV U.S.A.
235 D2 Point Pleasant Beach NJ U.S.A.
76 B4 Point Samson W.A. Austr.
190 C4 Poirino Italy
160 B1 Poiseux France
134 K5 Poisevo Rus. Fed.
86 C3 Poissonnier Point W.A. Austr.
137 I2 Poissons France
156 C4 Poissy France
160 E3 Poisy France
162 C2 Poitiers France
162 B2 Poitou, Plaines et Seuil du plain France
162 B2 Poitou-Charentes admin. reg. France
217 □2 Poivre Atoll Seychelles
156 B3 Poix-de-Picardie France
156 B4 Poix-Terron France
179 G5 Pojatno Croatia
252 D4 Pojo Bol.
254 F5 Pojuca Brazil
116 C4 Pokaran Rajasthan India
176 F5 Pokaszepetk Hungary
83 G2 Pokataroo N.S.W. Austr.
139 H5 Pokati r. Belarus
80 E2 Pokeno North I. N.Z.
117 E3 Pokhara Nepal
139 I3 Pokhvistnevo Rus. Fed.
197 G3 Pokhvistnevo Romania
150 C4 Pokkorro Cornwall, England U.K.
139 J2 Pokrovka Azer.
121 G2 Pokrovka Kazakh.
121 G3 Pokrovka Kyrg.
          Pokrovka Ysyk-Köl Kyrg. see Kyzyl-Suu
100 D2 Pokrovka Primorskiy Kray Rus. Fed.
139 G3 Pokrovka Yevreyskaya Avtonomnaya Oblast' Rus. Fed. see Priamurskiy
131 N3 Pokrovsk Respublika Sakha (Yakutiya) Rus. Fed.
100 D3 Pokrovsk Saratovskaya Oblast' Rus. Fed.
137 I4 Pokrovs'ke Ukr.
137 J3 Pokrovs'ke Ukr.
137 K5 Pokrovs'ke Ukr.
          Pokrovskoye Oltovskaya Oblast' Rus. Fed.
135 G7 Pokrovskoye Rostovskaya Oblast' Rus. Fed.
134 L3 Pokrovsk-Ural'skiy Rus. Fed.
139 M4 Poksha r. Rus. Fed.
139 M4 Pol' i r. Rus. Fed.
196 C3 Pola Croatia see Pula

92 B3 Pola Phil.
139 H3 Pola r. Rus. Fed.
241 L4 Polacca AZ U.S.A.
241 L4 Polacca Wash watercourse AZ U.S.A.
182 D1 Pola de Allande Spain
182 E1 Pola de Laviana Spain
182 E1 Pola de Lena Spain
182 E1 Pola de Siero Spain
182 D1 Pola de Somiedo Spain
157 G5 Polaincourt-et-Clairefontaine France
174 E3 Polajewko Pol.
123 E5 Polān Iran
183 F5 Polán Spain
177 I3 Poľana mt. Slovakia
177 I3 Poľana mt. Slovakia
175 H3 Poland country Europe
233 F3 Poland NY U.S.A.
232 C4 Poland OH U.S.A.
174 E5 Polanica-Zdrój Pol.
175 J5 Polaniec Pol.
174 E1 Polanów Pol.
262 V1 Polar Plateau Antarctica
          Polathane Turkey see Akçaabat
126 D3 Polatlı Turkey
138 G4 Polatsk Belarus
138 G4 Polatskaya Nizina lowland Belarus
114 D2 Polavaram Andhra Prad. India
134 L4 Polazna Rus. Fed.
169 C5 Polch Ger.
260 B5 Polcura Chile
174 G1 Połczyn Zdrój Pol.
114 I3 Poldarsa Rus. Fed.
142 A2 Pol Dasht Iran
151 H4 Polegate East Sussex, England U.K.
257 F4 Polegate East Sussex, England U.K.
254 F3 Pombal Brazil
182 C3 Pombal Bragança Port.
184 A1 Pombal Leiria Port.
251 F6 Pombas r. Brazil
206 □ Pombas Cape Verde
213 G4 Pomene Moz.
183 I3 Pomer Spain
215 H3 Pomeroy S. Africa
147 E2 Pomeroy Northern Ireland U.K.
232 B5 Pomeroy OH U.S.A.
232 S5 Pomeroy PA U.S.A.
238 C2 Pomeroy WA U.S.A.
177 L5 Pomezeu Romania
176 F2 Pomězí Czech Rep.
193 E3 Pomezia Italy
214 D1 Pomfret S. Africa
137 F3 Pomichna Ukr.
175 I3 Pomiechówek Pol.
160 C1 Pommard France
158 C3 Pommerit-Jaudy France
174 D2 Pommersfelden Ger.
140 N2 Pomokaira reg. Fin.
85 H5 Pomona Qld Austr.
240 I4 Pomona CA U.S.A.
234 D3 Pomona NJ U.S.A.
197 H4 Pomorie Bulg.
174 C1 Pomorska, Zatoka b. Pol.
174 F1 Pomorskie prov. Pol.
134 F2 Pomorskiy Bereg coastal area Rus. Fed.
131 M2 Pomorskiy Proliv sea chan. Rus. Fed.
162 B2 Pompaire France
193 G4 Pompei Italy
256 B5 Pompéia Brazil
257 E3 Pompéu Brazil
257 G4 Pompéu Brazil
161 H5 Pompignan France
159 H3 Pomponne France
235 D2 Pompton Lakes NJ U.S.A.
174 F1 Pomysk Mały Pol.
134 I4 Ponazyrevo Rus. Fed.
236 D3 Ponca NE U.S.A.
237 D4 Ponca City OK U.S.A.
247 □1 Ponce Puerto Rico
239 F4 Poncha Springs CO U.S.A.
160 D2 Poncin France
86 E2 Pond, Cape W.A. Austr.
114 B3 Ponda Goa India
237 D4 Pond Creek OK U.S.A.
234 E2 Pond Eddy NY U.S.A.
151 G2 Pondersbridge Cambridgeshire, England U.K.
114 C4 Pondicherry India
114 C4 Pondicherry union terr. India
114 C4 Pondicherry Pondicherry India see Puducherry
221 K2 Pond Inlet Nunavut Can.
215 G4 Pondoland reg. S. Africa
179 E2 Pöndorf Austria
          Ponds Bay Nunavut Can. see Pond Inlet
242 □1 Poneloya Nic.
190 C5 Ponente, Riviera di coastal area Italy
          Pones i. Chuuk Micronesia see
137 J5 Ponezhukay Rus. Fed.
182 D2 Ponferrada Spain
80 F4 Pongakawa North I. N.Z.
179 E3 Pongau val. Austria
215 H2 Pongai S. Africa
215 I2 Pongola r. S. Africa
206 E4 Pong Tamale Ghana
175 H2 Poniatowa Pol.
175 H2 Poniatowo Pol.
174 E4 Poniec Pol.
93 B2 Poniki, Gunung mt. Indon.
177 I3 Poniky Slovakia
175 D5 Ponitz Ger.
114 C4 Ponnaivar r. India
114 B4 Ponnampet Karnataka India
114 B3 Ponnani r. India
114 B3 Ponnani r. India
114 D3 Ponneri Tamil Nadu India
96 A2 Ponnyadaung Range mts Myanmar
222 H4 Ponoka Alta Can.
137 G2 Ponomarevka Rus. Fed.
137 G2 Ponornytsya Ukr.
160 E4 Ponoroga Java Timur Indon.
206 E4 Ponorogo, Isole is Italy
225 G1 Pons r. Que. Can.
183 H4 Pons Spain
          Pons France see Ponts
191 F5 Ponsacco Italy
182 C5 Ponsul r. Port.
165 D6 Pont-à-Celles Belgium
149 H4 Pontaq West Yorkshire, England U.K.
216 □1b Ponta Delgada São Miguel Azores
254 □ Ponta Delgada Madeira
254 C2 Ponta de Pedras Brazil
184 □ Ponta do Pargo Madeira
206 □ Ponta do Sol Cape Verde
184 □ Ponta do Sol Madeira
216 □1b Ponta Garça São Miguel Azores
256 B6 Ponta Grossa Brazil
160 D1 Pontailler-sur-Saône France
83 F5 Pontaix France
85 B5 Pontal Brazil
252 D4 Pontal do Norte Brazil
150 □3 Pontardawe Neath Port Talbot, Wales U.K.
250 B4 Pontarddulais Swansea, Wales U.K.
150 □3 Pontardulais Swansea, Wales U.K.
235 D5 Ponteareas Spain
232 E5 Ponte Ceso Spain
131 C1 Pontenagu Fr.
214 C6 Ponte Nova Brazil
217 □1b Pont'antonio Italy
191 G2 Pontassieve Italy
159 G2 Pont-Audemer France
159 E4 Pontaubault France
235 F4 Pont-Aven France
185 G2 Pontax r. Que. Can.
224 E3 Pont-Canavese Italy
161 G3 Pontcharra France
237 F6 Pontchartrain, Lake LA U.S.A.
158 C3 Pontchâteau France
158 B3 Pont-Croix France
160 D2 Pont-d'Ain France

114 C3 Polur Tamil Nadu India
176 D3 Poluška Hill Czech Rep.
138 F2 Põlva Estonia
239 F5 Polvadera NM U.S.A.
191 I5 Polverigi Italy
140 O3 Polvijärvi Fin.
146 F6 Polwarth Scottish Borders, Scotland U.K.
121 G2 Polyaigos i. Greece
136 B3 Polyana Ukr.
          Polyanovgrad Bulg. see Karnobat
133 S3 Polyarnyy Chukotskiy Autonomnyy Okrug Rus. Fed.
140 P1 Polyarnyy Murmanskaya Oblast' Rus. Fed.
134 P2 Polyarnyye Zori Rus. Fed.
198 C2 Polydroso Greece
198 D2 Polygyros Greece
198 C1 Polykastro Greece
266 H6 Polynesia is Oceania
          Polynésie Française terr. S. Pacific Ocean see French Polynesia
179 G4 Polzela Slovenia
171 F2 Pölzig Ger.
81 B7 Pomahaka r. South I. N.Z.
183 G1 Pomaluengo Spain
258 D3 Pomán Arg.
191 F5 Pomarance Italy
184 C3 Pomarão Port.
163 B5 Pomarez France
195 F2 Pomarico Italy
141 M3 Pomarkku Fin.
177 I4 Pomáz Hungary
257 F4 Pomba r. Brazil
254 F3 Pombal Brazil
182 C3 Pombal Bragança Port.
184 A1 Pombal Leiria Port.
251 F6 Pombas r. Brazil
206 □ Pombas Cape Verde
213 G4 Pomene Moz.
183 I3 Pomer Spain
215 H3 Pomeroy S. Africa
147 E2 Pomeroy Northern Ireland U.K.
232 B5 Pomeroy OH U.S.A.
232 S5 Pomeroy PA U.S.A.
238 C2 Pomeroy WA U.S.A.
177 L5 Pomezeu Romania
176 F2 Pomězí Czech Rep.
193 E3 Pomezia Italy
214 D1 Pomfret S. Africa
137 F3 Pomichna Ukr.
175 I3 Pomiechówek Pol.
160 C1 Pommard France
158 C3 Pommerit-Jaudy France
174 D2 Pommersfelden Ger.
140 N2 Pomokaira reg. Fin.
85 H5 Pomona Qld Austr.
240 I4 Pomona CA U.S.A.
234 D3 Pomona NJ U.S.A.
197 H4 Pomorie Bulg.
174 C1 Pomorska, Zatoka b. Pol.
174 F1 Pomorskie prov. Pol.
134 F2 Pomorskiy Bereg coastal area Rus. Fed.
131 M2 Pomorskiy Proliv sea chan. Rus. Fed.
162 B2 Pompaire France
193 G4 Pompei Italy
256 B5 Pompéia Brazil
257 E3 Pompéu Brazil
235 D2 Pompton Lakes NJ U.S.A.
174 F1 Pomysk Mały Pol.
226 C5 Ponask Lake Ont. Can.
227 F4 Ponce Cay. Italy
95 E3 Pontianak Kalimantan Barat Indon.
156 D5 Pontigny France
156 D5 Pontigny France
193 F3 Pontinia Italy
156 D5 Pontine Islands is Italy see Ponziane, Isole
190 C5 Pontivy France
193 F3 Ponton Man. Can.
193 E3 Pontmain France
223 L4 Pontóy France
223 L4 Ponton r. Man. Can.
143 J3 Pontone Italy
159 G4 Pont-Péan France
150 D2 Pontrhydfendigaid Ceredigion, Wales U.K.
158 C3 Pontrieux France
156 D4 Pontrilas Herefordshire, England U.K.
160 B2 Ponts Spain
158 C3 Pont-Ste-Marie France
156 C3 Pont-Ste-Maxence France
161 C3 Pont-St-Esprit France
159 E3 Pont-St-Martin Italy
156 C3 Pont-Scorff France
152 C3 Pontsticill Reservoir Wales U.K.
150 D2 Pont-sur-Seine France
162 C2 Pont-sur-Yonne France
159 G4 Pontvallain France
150 C3 Pontyberem Carmarthenshire, Wales U.K.
150 C3 Pontyclun Rhondda Cynon Taff, Wales U.K.
150 C3 Pontypool Torfaen, Wales U.K.
150 D3 Pontypridd Rhondda Cynon Taff, Wales U.K.
137 J5 Ponza Rus. Fed.
193 E4 Ponza Italy
193 E4 Ponza, Isola di i. Italy
193 E4 Ponziane, Isole is Italy
190 D2 Ponzone Italy
158 C3 Ponzone r. Italy
236 D2 Pochera S.A. Austr.
209 B5 Pool admin. reg. Congo
149 H4 Pool West Yorkshire, England U.K.
151 F4 Poole Poole, England U.K.
151 F4 Poole admin. div. England U.K.
146 □ Poole Bay England U.K.
146 C6 Poolewe Highland, Scotland U.K.
149 □ Pooley Bridge Cumbria, England U.K.
82 D1 Poolowanna Lake salt flat S.A. Austr.
83 B5 Poona Mahar. India see Pune
83 C5 Poonarrie N.S.W. Austr.
258 B6 Poonaarrie, Mount hill W.A. Austr.
83 F2 Poopelloe Lake N.S.W. Austr.
252 D4 Poopó Bol.
252 D4 Poopó, Lago de l. Bol.
96 A2 Popa Mountain Myanmar
148 D3 Popasna Ukr.
140 P3 Popasnaya Ukr. see Popasna
250 B4 Popayán Col.

158 B3 Pont-de-Buis-lès-Quimerch France
160 D3 Pont-de-Chéruy France
163 E5 Pont-de-l'Arn France
165 D4 Pont-de-l'Isère France
160 D2 Pont-de-Loup Belgium
160 D2 Pont-de-Poitte France
160 E1 Pont-de-Roide France
160 E1 Pont-de-Salars France
186 A4 Pont de Suert Spain
160 C2 Pont-de-Veyle France
160 C2 Pont-du-Château France
161 B4 Pont-d'Hérault France
159 F3 Pont-d'Ouilly France
163 C4 Pont-du-Casse France
160 D2 Pont-du-Château France
160 D2 Pont-du-Navoy France
193 G3 Ponte Italy
182 B3 Ponte Port.
254 D4 Ponte Alta do Norte Brazil
182 C1 Ponte-Aranga Spain
182 B2 Ponteareas Spain
191 I2 Pontebba Italy
256 A2 Ponte Branca Brazil
182 B2 Ponte Caldelas Spain
182 B1 Ponte-Ceso Spain
190 C3 Pontechianale Italy
190 D2 Pontecorvo Italy
190 C4 Pontecurone Italy
182 B3 Ponte da Barca Port.
190 D5 Ponte dell'Olio Italy
191 F5 Pontedera Italy
184 B1 Ponte de Sor Port.
182 B1 Pontedeume Spain
182 B4 Ponte de Vagos Port.
191 H3 Ponte di Legno Italy
191 H3 Ponte di Piave Italy
184 A1 Ponte do Rol Port.
149 H4 Pontefract West Yorkshire, England U.K.
191 G2 Ponte Gardena Italy
223 J5 Pontejx Sask. Can.
149 H2 Ponteland Northumberland, England U.K.
193 G3 Pontelandolfo Italy
192 B2 Ponte-Leccia Corse France
191 H3 Pontelongo Italy
190 D3 Ponte Nossa Italy
257 F4 Ponte Nova Brazil
191 G2 Ponte Nova Brazil
161 D3 Pont-en-Royans France
160 D3 Pontenure Italy
163 A4 Pontenx-les-Forges France
182 B1 Pontepedra Spain
150 D2 Ponterwyd Ceredigion, Wales U.K.
191 G3 Pontes Port.
191 G3 Ponte San Nicolò Italy
190 E3 Ponte San Pietro Italy
150 E2 Pontesbury Shropshire, England U.K.
253 F3 Pontes-e-Lacerda Brazil
182 B2 Ponte Valga Spain
182 B2 Pontevedra Spain
182 B2 Pontevedra prov. Galicia Spain
184 B1 Pontével Port.
160 C3 Pont-Évêque France
190 F3 Pontevico Italy
159 E3 Pont-Farcy France
156 E3 Pontfaverger-Moronvilliers France
159 E3 Pont-Hébert France
159 E2 Ponthierville Dem. Rep. Congo see Ubundu
226 C5 Pontiac IL U.S.A.
227 F4 Pontiac MI U.S.A.
95 E3 Pontianak Kalimantan Barat Indon.
156 D5 Pontigny France
193 F3 Pontinia Italy
156 D5 Pontine Islands is Italy see Ponziane, Isole
190 C5 Pontivy France
193 F3 Ponton Man. Can.
223 L4 Ponton r. Man. Can.
193 E3 Pontmain France
159 G4 Pont-Péan France
150 D2 Pontrhydfendigaid Ceredigion, Wales U.K.
158 C3 Pontrieux France
156 D4 Pontrilas Herefordshire, England U.K.
160 B2 Ponts Spain
158 C3 Pont-Ste-Marie France
156 C3 Pont-Ste-Maxence France
161 C3 Pont-St-Esprit France
159 E3 Pont-St-Martin Italy
156 C3 Pont-Scorff France
152 C3 Pontsticill Reservoir Wales U.K.
150 D2 Pont-sur-Seine France
162 C2 Pont-sur-Yonne France
159 G4 Pontvallain France
150 C3 Pontyberem Carmarthenshire, Wales U.K.
150 C3 Pontyclun Rhondda Cynon Taff, Wales U.K.
150 C3 Pontypool Torfaen, Wales U.K.
150 D3 Pontypridd Rhondda Cynon Taff, Wales U.K.
137 J5 Ponza Rus. Fed.
193 E4 Ponza Italy
193 E4 Ponza, Isola di i. Italy
193 E4 Ponziane, Isole is Italy
190 D2 Ponzone Italy
236 D2 Pochera S.A. Austr.
209 B5 Pool admin. reg. Congo
187 D5 Pool West Yorkshire, England U.K.
187 E5 Portals Vells Spain
246 □ Poole Bay England U.K.
149 H4 Poolewe Highland, Scotland U.K.
198 C3 Pooley Bridge Cumbria, England U.K.
147 D2 Poolowanna Lake salt flat S.A. Austr.
83 F5 Poona Mahar. India see Pune
83 C5 Poonarrie N.S.W. Austr.
86 C5 Poonaarrie, Mount hill W.A. Austr.
83 F2 Poopelloe Lake N.S.W. Austr.
252 D4 Poopó Bol.
252 D4 Poopó, Lago de l. Bol.
96 A2 Popa Mountain Myanmar
148 D3 Popasna Ukr.
250 B4 Popayán Col.

245 E4 Popocatépetl, Volcán vol. Mex.
209 C6 Popokabaka Dem. Rep. Congo
193 F2 Popoli Italy
78 □6 Popomanaseu, Mount Guadalcanal Solomon Is
91 K8 Popondetta P.N.G.
188 F3 Popova Croatia
          Popovichskaya Rus. Fed. see Kalininskaya
139 K2 Popovka Rus. Fed.
197 H4 Popovo Bulg.
188 F4 Popovo Polje plain Bos.-Herz.
159 F3 Popovska Reka r. Bulg.
175 H3 Popów Pol.
175 G4 Popów Pol.
173 F2 Poppberg hill Ger.
169 F4 Poppenburg hill Ger.
169 F5 Poppenhausen Ger.
169 E5 Poppenhausen (Wasserkuppe) Ger.
173 F2 Poppenricht Ger.
191 G5 Poppi Italy
175 H6 Poprad r. Pol.
177 J2 Poprad Slovakia
177 J3 Poproč Slovakia
243 H5 Poptún Guat.
226 D3 Porcupine Italy
222 A2 Porangatu Brazil
254 C5 Porangatu Brazil
252 A2 Porangaba Belarus
116 B5 Porbandar Gujarat India
191 H5 Porcari Italy
191 H3 Porcia Italy
257 F4 Porciúncula Brazil
252 D4 Porco Bol.
161 B3 Porcuna Spain
171 F4 Porcsalma Hungary
185 F3 Porcuna Spain
220 B3 Porcupine r. Can./U.S.A.
220 D3 Porcupine r. Can./U.S.A.
264 H2 Porcupine Abyssal Plain sea feature N. Atlantic Ocean
85 F4 Porcupine Creek r. Qld Austr.
238 F1 Porcupine Creek r. MT U.S.A.
223 K4 Porcupine Hills Man./Sask. Can.
226 C2 Porcupine Mountains MI U.S.A.
191 H3 Porcupine Plain Sask. Can.
191 H2 Pordenone Italy
191 H2 Pordenone prov. Friuli - Venezia Giulia Italy
184 B2 Pontes Port.
191 G3 Pordic France
197 G4 Pordim Bulg.
250 D3 Pore Col.
188 D3 Poreč Croatia
139 K2 Porecatu Brazil
139 K2 Porech'ye r. Rus. Fed.
139 K2 Porech'ye-Rybnoye Rus. Fed.
135 I5 Poretskoye Rus. Fed.
192 B2 Poretta airport Corse France
139 E1 Porezen mt. Slovenia
207 F4 Porga Benin
141 M3 Pori Fin.
177 F5 Poříčany Czech Rep.
81 E4 Porirua North I. N.Z.
140 L2 Porjus Sweden
135 H3 Porkhov Rus. Fed.
251 F2 Porlamar Venez.
150 D2 Porlezza Italy
185 C6 Porlock Somerset, England U.K.
193 E2 Porma r. Spain
85 E2 Pormpuraaw Qld Austr.
141 N3 Pornainen Fin.
190 C3 Pornassio Italy
191 C3 Pornbach Ger.
158 C3 Pornic France
195 H4 Pornocskodás Italy
158 C3 Pornocskodás Italy
150 B4 Poroshiri-dake mt. Japan
150 B4 Porosozero Rus. Fed.
190 F1 Pörtschach am Wörther See Austria
184 E1 Poroszló Hungary
199 G2 Porsangen sea chan. Norway
140 N1 Porsangerhalvoya pen. Norway
140 N1 Porsgrunn Norway
142 C2 Porsgrunn Norway
190 G2 Porspoder France
147 F5 Port r. Turkey
146 □ Port of Ireland
181 G1 Porrentruy Switz.
194 F2 Porretta Terme Italy
191 G2 Porriño Spain
140 N2 Porsà r. Norway
140 N1 Porsanger sea chan. Norway
190 N1 Porsangerhalvøya pen. Norway

209 C6 Popokabaka Dem. Rep. Congo
222 C4 Port Clements B.C. Can.
232 B4 Port Clinton OH U.S.A.
234 B4 Port Clinton PA U.S.A.
233 □3 Port Clyde ME U.S.A.
224 E5 Port Colborne Ont. Can.
234 D2 Port Colden NJ U.S.A.
227 H4 Port Credit Ont. Can.
186 □ Port d'Addia Spain
186 □ Port d'Alcúdia Spain
84 B2 Port Darwin b. N.T. Austr.
83 F5 Port Davey b. Tas. Austr.
161 C5 Port-de-Bouc France
162 B3 Port-d'Envaux France
246 D3 Port-de-Paix Haiti
186 □ Port des Morts lake channel WI U.S.A.
180 D4 Port Edward B.C. Can.
215 H4 Port Edward S. Africa
226 C3 Port Edwards WI U.S.A.
257 F1 Porteirinha Brazil
251 I5 Portel Brazil
184 C2 Portel Port.
184 □ Portelândia Brazil
161 A5 Portel-des-Corbières France
225 H4 Port Elgin N.B. Can.
224 D4 Port Elgin Ont. Can.
215 F7 Port Elizabeth S. Africa
146 B5 Port Ellen Argyll and Bute, Scotland U.K.
261 F2 Portena Arg.
159 F2 Port-en-Bessin-Huppain France
148 L3 Port Erin Isle of Man
222 D3 Porter Landing B.C. Can.
234 C1 Porters Lake PA U.S.A.
214 B5 Porterville S. Africa
240 H3 Porterville CA U.S.A.
151 □ Portesham Dorset, England U.K.
161 C4 Portes-lès-Valence France
246 □ Port Esquivel Jamaica
          Port Étienne Maur. see Nouâdhibou
82 D3 Port Everglades FL U.S.A. see Fort Lauderdale
150 C3 Port Eynon Swansea, Wales U.K.
83 E4 Port Fairy Vic. Austr.
80 E2 Port Fitzroy North I. N.Z.
          Port Francqui Dem. Rep. Congo see Ilebo
208 A5 Port-Gentil Gabon
82 C3 Port Germein S.A. Austr.
237 F6 Port Gibson MS U.S.A.
146 D6 Port Glasgow Inverclyde, Scotland U.K.
147 E2 Portglenone Northern Ireland U.K.
161 E5 Port Grimaud France
215 G4 Port Grosvenor S. Africa
150 D3 Porth Rhondda Cynon Taff, Wales U.K.
          Porthaethwy see Menai Bridge
150 C3 Porth Tywyn Wales U.K. see Burry Port
207 G5 Port Harcourt Nigeria
222 E5 Port Hardy B.C. Can.
          Port Harrison Que. Can. see Inukjuak
225 I4 Port Hawkesbury N.S. Can.
150 D3 Porthcawl Bridgend, Wales U.K.
86 C4 Port Hedland W.A. Austr.
146 C4 Port Henderson Highland, Scotland U.K.
233 G2 Port Henry NY U.S.A.
          Port Herald Malawi see Nsanje
150 B4 Porthleven Cornwall, England U.K.
150 C2 Porthmadog Gwynedd, Wales U.K.
198 B3 Porthmos Zakynthou sea chan. Greece
227 H4 Port Hope Ont. Can.
233 I2 Port Hope MI U.S.A.
226 E4 Port Huron MI U.S.A.
184 B3 Portimão Port.
187 F4 Portinatx Spain
157 F4 Portieux France
129 H2 Portiqaux Azer.
183 D3 Portilla de la Reina Spain
183 D3 Portillo Cuba
183 G1 Portillo de la Sía mt. Spain
183 F2 Portillo de Toledo Spain
184 □ Portimão Port.
257 E5 Portinho Brazil
187 F5 Portinatx Spain
151 F2 Portishead North Somerset, England U.K.
          Port Isaac Bay England U.K.
146 □ Portknockie Moray, Scotland U.K.
          Port Láirge Rep. of Ireland see Waterford
83 G3 Portland N.S.W. Austr.
83 C4 Portland Vic. Austr.
246 □ Portland parish Jamaica
80 E1 Portland North I. N.Z.
235 I1 Portland CT U.S.A.
230 C3 Portland IN U.S.A.
233 □3 Portland ME U.S.A.
226 E4 Portland MI U.S.A.
238 C3 Portland OR U.S.A.
150 E4 Portland, Isle of pen. England U.K.
150 E4 Portland Bill Vic. Austr.
          Portland Bill hd England U.K. see Bill of Portland
246 □ Portland Point Jamaica
147 D4 Portland Roads Qld Austr.
147 D3 Port-la-Nouvelle France
147 D4 Portlaoise Rep. of Ireland
237 D6 Port Lavaca TX U.S.A.
147 D4 Portlaw Rep. of Ireland
163 F6 Port-Leucate France
147 E1 Port Lincoln S.A. Austr.
206 B4 Port Loko Sierra Leone
          Port-Louis France
247 □2 Port Louis Guadeloupe
217 □1b Port Louis Mauritius
          Port-Lyautrey Morocco see Kénitra
82 C3 Port MacDonnell S.A. Austr.
83 H2 Port Macquarie N.S.W. Austr.
150 C2 Portmadoc Gwynedd, Wales U.K. see Porthmadog
147 A5 Portmagee Rep. of Ireland
234 C2 Port Mahon S. Africa
158 C3 Portman France
158 C3 Port-Manec'h France
246 □ Port Maria Jamaica
147 E3 Portmarnock Rep. of Ireland
84 D2 Port McArthur b. N.T. Austr.

231 D7 Port Charlotte FL U.S.A.
151 F4 Portchester Hampshire, England U.K.
235 E1 Port Chester NY U.S.A.

Port McNeill to Przytyk

350

222 E5 Port McNeill B.C. Can.
225 H3 Port-Menier Que. Can.
246 □ Port Morant Jamaica
246 □ Portmore Jamaica
91 K8 Port Moresby P.N.G.
156 B3 Port-Mort France
147 F2 Portmuck Northern Ireland U.K.
85 E1 Port Musgrave b. Qld Austr.
146 C5 Portnacroish Argyll and Bute, Scotland U.K.
146 B3 Portnaguran Western Isles, Scotland U.K.
146 B6 Portnahaven Argyll and Bute, Scotland U.K.
146 B4 Portnalong Highland, Scotland U.K.
Port nan Giúran Western Isles, Scotland U.K. see Portnaguran
146 A4 Port nan Long Western Isles, Scotland U.K.
158 D4 Port-Navalo France
237 E6 Port Neches TX U.S.A.
82 D3 Port Neill S.A. Austr.
246 D2 Port Nelson Rum Cay Bahamas
225 G3 Portneuf r. Que. Can.
238 D3 Portneuf r. ID U.S.A.
146 B3 Port Nis Western Isles, Scotland U.K.
82 D3 Port Noarlunga S.A. Austr.
214 A3 Port Nolloth S. Africa
147 C2 Portnoo Rep. of Ireland
234 C3 Port Norris NJ U.S.A.
Port-Nouveau-Québec Que. Can. see Kangiqsualujjuaq
254 E2 Porto Brazil
192 A2 Porto Corse France
182 B3 Porto Port.
182 B3 Porto admin. dist. Port.
182 D2 Porto Spain
255 C9 Porto Alegre Brazil
Porto Alexandre Angola see Tombua
184 B2 Porto Alto Port.
209 B7 Porto Amboim Angola
Porto Amélia Moz. see Pemba
192 C2 Porto Azzurro Italy
81 C6 Portobello South I. N.Z.
255 C8 Porto Belo Brazil
192 A5 Porto Botte Sardegna Italy
182 B2 Portobravo Spain
254 G4 Porto Cavlo Brazil
192 B3 Porto Cervo Sardegna Italy
195 G2 Porto Cesareo Italy
187 G5 Porto Colom Spain
184 B3 Porto Covo da Bandeira Port.
187 G5 Porto Cristo Spain
184 □ Porto da Cruz Madeira
254 F4 Porto da Fôlha Brazil
182 B5 Porto de Mós Port.
251 H5 Porto de Moz Brazil
182 C1 Porto do Barqueiro Spain
253 F2 Porto dos Gaúchos Óbidos Brazil
182 A2 Porto do Son Spain
194 C5 Porto Empedocle Sicilia Italy
192 D2 Porto Ercole Italy
253 F3 Porto Esperidião Brazil
256 D5 Porto Feliz Brazil
192 C2 Portoferraio Italy
256 D4 Porto Ferreira Brazil
190 E4 Portofino Italy
257 F4 Porto Firme Brazil
146 D5 Port of Menteith Stirling, Scotland U.K.
254 D3 Porto Franco Brazil
247 □7 Port of Spain Trin. and Tob.
191 H4 Porto Garibaldi Italy
191 H3 Portogruaro Italy
206 □ Porto Inglês Cape Verde
216 □1a Porto Judeu Terceira Azores
240 G2 Portola CA U.S.A.
194 D4 Porto Levante Isole Lipari Italy
191 H3 Porto Levante Veneto Italy
255 B8 Porto Luceno Brazil
191 G4 Portomaggiore Italy
182 C2 Portomarín Spain
184 □ Porto Moniz Madeira
253 F5 Porto Murtinho Brazil
254 C4 Porto Nacional Brazil
207 F5 Porto-Novo Benin
206 □ Porto Novo Cape Verde
Porto Novo Tamil Nadu India see Parangipettai
194 B5 Porto Palo Sicilia Italy
189 E7 Portopalo di Capo Passero Sicilia Italy
192 A6 Porto Pino Sardegna Italy
256 A4 Porto Primavera, Represa resr Brazil
231 D6 Port Orange FL U.S.A.
238 B2 Port Orchard WA U.S.A.
191 I5 Porto Recanati Italy
238 A3 Port Orford OR U.S.A.
209 B6 Porto Rico Angola
192 B3 Porto Rotondo Sardegna Italy
191 I3 Portorož Slovenia
191 I5 Porto San Giorgio Italy
192 B4 Porto San Paolo Sardegna Italy
251 I5 Porto Santana Brazil
191 I5 Porto Sant'Elpidio Italy
184 □ Porto Santo Madeira
184 □ Porto Santo, Ilha de i. Madeira
192 D2 Porto Santo Stefano Italy
192 A5 Portoscuso Sardegna Italy
257 H2 Porto Seguro Brazil
191 H4 Porto Tolle Italy
192 A4 Porto Torres Sardegna Italy
255 C8 Porto União Brazil
192 B3 Porto-Vecchio Corse France
252 E2 Porto Velho Brazil
190 E4 Portovenere Italy
250 A5 Portoviejo Ecuador
146 C7 Portpatrick Dumfries and Galloway, Scotland U.K.
234 C3 Port Penn DE U.S.A.
227 H3 Port Perry Ont. Can.
83 F4 Port Phillip Bay Vic. Austr.
82 D3 Port Pirie S.A. Austr.
Port Radium N.W.T. Can. see Echo Bay
147 E3 Portrane Rep. of Ireland
150 B4 Portreath Cornwall, England U.K.
146 B4 Portree Highland, Scotland U.K.
222 E5 Port Renfrew B.C. Can.
225 K3 Port Rexton Nfld. Can.
147 C4 Portroe Rep. of Ireland
84 C2 Port Roper b. N.T. Austr.
227 G4 Port Rowan Ont. Can.
246 □ Port Royal Jamaica
232 E5 Port Royal VA U.S.A.
147 E1 Portrush Northern Ireland U.K.
Port Said Egypt see Bûr Sa'îd
163 C4 Port-Ste-Foy-et-Ponchapt France
163 C4 Port-Ste-Marie France
231 C6 Port St Joe FL U.S.A.
215 G4 Port St Johns S. Africa
161 C5 Port-St-Louis-du-Rhône France
231 D7 Port Saint Lucie City FL U.S.A.
148 E3 Port St Mary Isle of Man
158 E4 Port-St-Père France
158 B3 Portsall France
147 D1 Portsalon Rep. of Ireland
227 F4 Port Sanilac MI U.S.A.
179 F4 Pörtschach am Wörther See Austria
186 D4 Ports de Beseit mts Spain
227 H3 Port Severn Ont. Can.
215 H4 Port Shepstone S. Africa
Port Simpson B.C. Can. see Lax Kw'alaams
247 □2 Portsmouth Dominica
151 F4 Portsmouth Portsmouth, England U.K.
151 F4 Portsmouth admin. div. England U.K.
233 □H3 Portsmouth NH U.S.A.
232 B5 Portsmouth OH U.S.A.
233 E6 Portsmouth VA U.S.A.
146 F4 Portsoy Aberdeenshire, Scotland U.K.
Port Stanley Falkland Is see Stanley
83 H3 Port Stephens b. N.S.W. Austr.
147 E1 Portstewart Northern Ireland U.K.
203 H5 Port Sudan Sudan
237 F6 Port Sulphur LA U.S.A.
157 G5 Port-sur-Saône France
Port Swettenham Malaysia see Pelabuhan Kelang
150 D3 Port Talbot Neath Port Talbot, Wales U.K.
238 B1 Port Townsend WA U.S.A.
234 B2 Port Trevorton PA U.S.A.
180 C3 Portugal country Europe
183 G1 Portugalete Spain
Portugália Angola see Chitato
250 D2 Portuguesa state Venez.
Portuguese East Africa country Africa see Mozambique
Portuguese Guinea country Africa see Guinea-Bissau
Portuguese Timor terr. Asia see East Timor
Portuguese West Africa country Africa see Angola
147 C3 Portumna Rep. of Ireland
Portus Herculis Monoeci country Europe see Monaco
182 B3 Portuzelo Port.
163 F6 Port-Vendres France
82 D3 Port Victoria S.A. Austr.
78 □5 Port Vila Vanuatu
232 D3 Portville NY U.S.A.
82 D3 Port Vincent S.A. Austr.
140 P1 Port Vladimir Rus. Fed.
80 E2 Port Waikato North I. N.Z.
82 D3 Port Wakefield S.A. Austr.
86 E2 Port Warrender W.A. Austr.
235 E2 Port Washington NY U.S.A.
226 D4 Port Washington WI U.S.A.
146 D7 Port William Dumfries and Galloway, Scotland U.K.
226 B2 Port Wing WI U.S.A.
114 C3 Porumamilla Andhra Prad. India
246 □ Porus Jamaica
139 H3 Porus'ya r. Rus. Fed.
252 C2 Porvenir Pando Bol.
253 E3 Porvenir Santa Cruz Bol.
259 C9 Porvenir Chile
141 N3 Porvoo Fin.
138 E1 Porvoonjoki r. Fin.
101 C5 Poryŏng S. Korea
175 J3 Porządzie Pol.
185 F1 Porzuna Spain
192 B4 Posada Sardegna Italy
192 B4 Posada r. Sardegna Italy
182 E1 Posada de Llanera Spain
183 F1 Posada de Valdeón Spain
258 G2 Posadas Arg.
185 E3 Posadas Spain
137 G4 Posad-Pokrovs'ke Ukr.
190 F2 Poschiavo Switz.
Poseidonia tourist site Italy see Paestum
Posen Pol. see Poznań
227 F3 Posen MI U.S.A.
170 E1 Poseritz Ger.
186 D2 Posets mt. Spain
134 G4 Poshekhon'ye Rus. Fed.
Poshekon'ye-Volodarsk Rus. Fed. see Poshekhon'ye
122 D4 Poshteh-ye Chaqvīr hill Iran
122 A3 Posht-e Kūh mts Iran
122 B2 Posht Kūh hill Iran
137 G5 Poshtove Ukr.
178 C5 Posina r. Italy
173 G2 Pösing Ger.
140 O2 Posio Fin.
193 G4 Positano Italy
Poskam Xinjiang China see Zepu
235 F1 Posnet CT U.S.A.
93 B3 Poso Sulawesi Tengah Indon.
93 B3 Poso r. Indon.
127 F2 Posof Turkey
129 C3 Posof r. Turkey
250 A5 Posorja Ecuador
121 J1 Pospelikha Rus. Fed.
178 C5 Possagno Italy
254 D5 Posse Brazil
171 E5 Possendorf Ger.
157 E4 Possesse France
263 L2 Possession Islands Antarctica
171 C5 Pößneck Ger.
237 C5 Post TX U.S.A.
193 F2 Posta Italy
197 H3 Poşta Câlnău Romania
Poşta Cîlnău Romania see Poşta Câlnău
191 G2 Postal Italy
193 H3 Posta Piana Italy
173 G3 Postau Ger.
Postavy Belarus see Pastavy
173 F2 Postbauer-Heng Ger.
215 E5 Post Chalmers S. Africa
Poste-de-la-Baleine Que. Can. see Kuujjuarapik
165 F3 Posterholt Neth.
214 D3 Postmasburg S. Africa
173 G3 Postmünster Ger.
188 E3 Postojna Slovenia
175 J3 Postoliska Pol.
176 C1 Postoloprty Czech Rep.
174 C3 Postomia r. Pol.
174 E1 Postomino Pol.
241 J4 Poston AZ U.S.A.
225 J2 Postville Nfld. Can.
226 B4 Postville IA U.S.A.
Postysheve Ukr. see Krasnoarmiys'k
188 F4 Posušje Bos.-Herz.
175 I4 Poświętne Pol.
175 J3 Poświétne Pol.
175 K3 Poświętne Pol.
100 D4 Pos'yet Rus. Fed.
236 C3 Potato Creek SD U.S.A.
215 F2 Potchefstroom S. Africa
197 G3 Potcoava Romania
257 G2 Poté Brazil
237 E5 Poteau OK U.S.A.
114 D2 Potegaon Mahar. India
174 F1 Potęgowo Pol.
Potentia Italy see Potenza
193 H4 Potenza Italy
193 H4 Potenza prov. Basilicata Italy
191 I5 Potenza r. Italy
191 I5 Potenza Picena Italy
81 A7 Poteriteri, Lake South I. N.Z.
183 F1 Potes Spain
214 E4 Potfontein S. Africa
213 F5 Potgietersrus S. Africa
254 E3 Poti r. Brazil
129 B2 P'ot'i Georgia
159 F3 Potigny France
114 D2 Potikal Madh. Prad. India
255 F5 Potiraguá Brazil
207 H4 Potiskum Nigeria
136 E2 Potiyivka Ukr.
238 C2 Potlatch ID U.S.A.
175 K5 Potok Górny Pol.
175 H5 Potok Złoty Pol.
232 E5 Potomac MD U.S.A.
232 E5 Potomac r. MD/VA U.S.A.
232 D5 Potomac, South Branch r. WV U.S.A.
232 D5 Potomac, South Fork South Branch r. WV U.S.A.
93 C5 Potomana, Gunung mt. Indon.
206 C5 Potoru Sierra Leone
252 D4 Potosí Bol.
252 D5 Potosí dept Bol.
230 B4 Potosi MO U.S.A.
241 J4 Potosi Mountain NV U.S.A.
92 B4 Pototan Phil.
258 C2 Potrerillos Chile
242 □I6 Potrerillos Hond.
245 F3 Potrero del Llano Mex.
250 B6 Potro r. Peru
171 E3 Potsdam Ger.
233 F2 Potsdam NY U.S.A.
177 G2 Potštát Czech Rep.
78 □5 Pott, Île i. New Caledonia
115 D2 Pottangi Orissa India
179 H3 Pottendorf Austria
179 H3 Pottenstein Austria
173 F2 Pottenstein Ger.
236 C3 Potter NE U.S.A.
150 E3 Potterne Wiltshire, England U.K.
151 G3 Potters Bar Hertfordshire, England U.K.
240 F2 Potter Valley CA U.S.A.
232 A3 Potterville MI U.S.A.
173 F3 Pöttmes Ger.
151 G2 Potton Bedfordshire, England U.K.
179 H3 Pöttsching Austria
234 B1 Potts Grove PA U.S.A.
234 C2 Pottstown PA U.S.A.
234 B2 Pottsville PA U.S.A.
137 J2 Potudan' r. Rus. Fed.
175 I4 Potworów Pol.
172 B2 Potzberg hill Ger.
158 E4 Pouancé France
222 F4 Pouce Coupe B.C. Can.
225 K4 Pouch Cove Nfld. Can.
233 G4 Poughkeepsie NY U.S.A.
235 E1 Poughquag NY U.S.A.
160 B1 Pougny France
160 B1 Pougues-les-Eaux France
156 E4 Pougy France
160 D1 Pouilley-les-Vignes France
163 B5 Pouillon France
160 C1 Pouilly-en-Auxois France
160 C2 Pouilly-sous-Charlieu France
160 A1 Pouilly-sur-Loire France
160 D1 Pouilly-sur-Saône France
159 H4 Poulaines France
158 B4 Pouldreuzic France
160 C2 Poule-les-Écharmeaux France
147 B5 Poulgorm Bridge Rep. of Ireland
159 H5 Pouligny-St-Pierre France
158 C3 Poullaouen France
147 D4 Poulnamucky Rep. of Ireland
233 G3 Poultney VT U.S.A.
149 G4 Poulton-le-Fylde Lancashire, England U.K.
207 H6 Pouma Cameroon
232 B6 Pound VA U.S.A.
214 E4 Poupan S. Africa
163 C5 Poupas France
160 D2 Poupet, Mont hill France
161 D5 Pourcieux France
80 F4 Pourerere North I. N.Z.
156 D5 Pourrain France
160 E3 Pourri, Mont mt. France
161 D5 Pourrières France
182 C4 Pousada Port.
182 B3 Pousadela Port.
257 E5 Pouso Alegre Brazil
182 B5 Pousos Port.
161 B5 Poussan France
157 G4 Poussay France
97 C4 Poŭthĭsăt Cambodia
80 E2 Pouto North I. N.Z.
157 G4 Pouxeux France
96 C3 Pouy, Nam r. Laos
163 C5 Pouyastruc France
163 B5 Pouydesseaux France
163 D5 Pouy-de-Touges France
162 B2 Pouzauges France
159 G4 Pouzay France
139 K3 Povarovo Rus. Fed.
177 H2 Považská Bystrica Slovakia
177 G3 Považský Inovec mts Slovakia
139 J3 Poved' r. Rus. Fed.
185 H2 Povedilla Spain
134 F3 Povenets Rus. Fed.
80 F3 Poverty Bay North I. N.Z.
191 F4 Poviglio Italy
196 D3 Povlen mt. Yugo.
216 □1b Povoação São Miguel Azores
182 B3 Póvoa de Lanhoso Port.
184 C2 Póvoa de São Miguel Port.
182 B3 Póvoa de Varzim Port.
182 C4 Póvoa do Concelho Port.
191 I2 Povoletto Italy
135 H6 Povorino Rus. Fed.
136 C2 Povors'k Ukr.
171 F5 Povrly Czech Rep.
240 I5 Poway CA U.S.A.
149 H2 Powburn Northumberland, England U.K.
238 F2 Powder r. MT U.S.A.
238 C2 Powder r. OR U.S.A.
238 F3 Powder, South Fork r. WY U.S.A.
238 F3 Powder River WY U.S.A.
234 B1 Powell PA U.S.A.
238 E2 Powell WY U.S.A.
232 B6 Powell r. TN/VA U.S.A.
241 L3 Powell, Lake resr UT U.S.A.
240 H2 Powell Mountain NV U.S.A.
222 E5 Powell River B.C. Can.
226 D3 Powers MI U.S.A.
147 C3 Power's Cross Rep. of Ireland
237 F4 Powhatan AR U.S.A.
232 E6 Powhatan VA U.S.A.
232 C5 Powhatan Point OH U.S.A.
150 E2 Powick Worcestershire, England U.K.
174 F3 Powidz Pol.
146 E5 Powmill Perth and Kinross, Scotland U.K.
108 A1 Powo Sichuan China
Pöwrize Turkm. see Firyuza
150 D2 Powys admin. div. Wales U.K.
255 B5 Poxoréu Brazil
78 □5 Poya New Caledonia
183 E4 Poyales del Hoyo Spain
Poyang Jiangxi China see Boyang
109 F2 Poyang Hu l. China
100 D2 Poyarkovo Rus. Fed.
183 H4 Poyatos Spain
226 C4 Poynette WI U.S.A.
149 G4 Poynton Cheshire, England U.K.
147 E2 Poyntz Pass Northern Ireland U.K.
185 H3 Poyo, Cerro mt. Spain
199 E2 Poyrazcık İzmir Turkey
179 H2 Poysdorf Austria
141 M3 Pöytyä Fin.
183 G2 Poza de la Sal Spain
183 F3 Pozaldez Spain
126 D3 Pozantı Turkey
196 E3 Požarevac Srbija Yugo.
245 F3 Poza Rica Mex.
177 K3 Pozdišovce Slovakia
188 F3 Požega Croatia
196 E4 Požega Srbija Yugo.
175 J1 Pozezdrze Pol.
139 H3 Pozhnya Rus. Fed.
134 L4 Pozhva Rus. Fed.
177 G2 Pozlovice Czech Rep.
174 E3 Poznań Pol.
185 H3 Pozo Alcón Spain
183 E3 Pozoantiguo Spain
185 F2 Pozoblanco Spain
185 I2 Pozo Cañada Spain
253 F5 Pozo Colorado Para.
183 G4 Pozo de Guadalajara Spain
258 E2 Pozo del Tigre Arg.
258 D2 Pozo Hondo Arg.
185 I2 Pozohondo Spain
185 I1 Pozo-Lorente Spain
183 I4 Pozondón Spain
179 H1 Pozořice Czech Rep.
183 H5 Pozorrubio Spain
Pozsony Slovakia see Bratislava
185 H2 Pozuelo Spain
183 G4 Pozuelo de Alarcón Spain
183 I3 Pozuelo de Aragón Spain
182 E2 Pozuelo del Páramo Spain
183 G4 Pozuelo del Rey Spain
182 D4 Pozuelo de Zarzón Spain
185 F2 Pozuelos de Calatrava Spain
252 B2 Pozuzo Peru
191 G2 Pozza di Fasso Italy
194 D6 Pozzallo Sicilia Italy
190 D4 Pozzolo Formigaro Italy
192 A4 Pozzomaggiore Sardegna Italy
193 G4 Pozzuoli Italy
178 E5 Pozzuolo del Friuli Italy
206 E5 Pra r. Ghana
139 M4 Pra r. Rus. Fed.
94 D3 Prabumulih Sumatera Indon.
175 H2 Prabuty Pol.
176 D2 Prachatice Czech Rep.
115 E2 Prachi r. India
97 C4 Prachin Buri Thai.
169 C5 Pracht Ger.
97 B5 Prachuap Khiri Khan Thai.
173 G2 Prackenbach Ger.
182 C1 Pradairo mt. Spain
183 F2 Prádanos de Ojeda Spain
176 G1 Praděd mt. Czech Rep.
183 H2 Pradejón Spain
161 B4 Pradelles France
163 E5 Pradelles-en-Val France
183 G3 Prádena Spain
250 B4 Pradera Col.
163 E6 Prades Languedoc-Roussillon France
163 D6 Prades Midi-Pyrénées France
161 A4 Prades-d'Aubrac France
183 H2 Pradillo Spain
163 D4 Pradines France
257 H2 Prado Brazil
182 B3 Prado Port.
183 E2 Prado de la Guzpeña Spain
184 E4 Prado del Rey Spain
183 G2 Pradoluengo Spain
161 E4 Prads-Haute-Bléone France
Praeneste Italy see Palestrina
142 E4 Præstø Denmark
190 B3 Pragelato Italy
179 G4 Pragersko Slovenia
178 D3 Prägraten Austria
Prague Czech Rep. see Praha
176 D1 Praha Czech Rep.
176 D1 Praha admin. reg. Czech Rep.
176 C2 Praha hill Czech Rep.
162 B2 Prahecq France
197 H3 Prahova r. Romania
216 □1c Praia Graciosa Azores
206 □ Praia São Tiago Cape Verde
193 H5 Praia a Mare Italy
182 B4 Praia da Barra Port.
184 B3 Praia da Rocha Port.
182 B4 Praia da Tocha Port.
182 B4 Praia de Esmoriz Port.
182 B4 Praia de Mira Port.
216 □1c Praia do Almoxarife Faial Azores
216 □1c Praia do Norte Faial Azores
256 D6 Praia Grande Brazil
194 D2 Praiano Italy
184 B2 Praias do Sado Port.
216 □1c Prainha Pico Azores
251 H5 Prainha Brazil
85 F4 Prairie Qld Austr.
226 A2 Prairie r. MN U.S.A.
238 C2 Prairie City OR U.S.A.
237 C5 Prairie Dog Town Fork r. TX U.S.A.
226 B4 Prairie du Chien WI U.S.A.
223 K4 Prairie River Sask. Can.
97 C4 Prakhon Chai Thai.
177 J3 Prakovce Slovakia
161 E3 Pralognan-la-Vanoise France
161 E4 Pra-Loup France
179 E2 Pram r. Austria
198 B2 Pramanta Greece
179 E2 Prambachkirchen Austria
207 F5 Prampram Ghana
97 C4 Pran r. Thai.
97 B4 Pran Buri Thai.
206 E5 Prang Ghana
114 C2 Pranhita r. India
179 F3 Prankerhöhe mt. Austria
94 B2 Prapat Sumatera Indon.
177 H3 Prašice Slovakia
129 D1 Praskoveya Rus. Fed.
176 G2 Přáslavice Czech Rep.
157 F5 Praslay France
217 □2a Praslin i. Inner Islands Seychelles
247 □3 Praslin Bay St Lucia
174 G4 Praszka Pol.
256 C3 Prata Brazil
256 A3 Prata r. Goiás Brazil
256 C3 Prata r. Minas Gerais Brazil
256 D2 Prata r. Minas Gerais Brazil
191 H3 Prata di Pordenone Italy
116 C4 Pratapgarh Rajasthan India
171 D4 Pratau Ger.
186 D4 Prat de Comte Spain
Prat de Llobregat Spain see El Prat de Llobregat
186 D3 Pratdip Spain
193 G3 Pratella Italy
Prathes Thai country Asia see Thailand
256 D3 Pratinha Brazil
191 G5 Prato Italy
191 G5 Prato prov. Toscana Italy
191 F2 Prato allo Stelvio Italy
193 F2 Pratola Peligna Italy
194 D2 Pratola Serra Italy
191 G5 Pratovecchio Italy
186 F2 Prats de Lluçanes Spain
163 E6 Prats-de-Mollo-la-Preste France
237 D4 Pratt KS U.S.A.
190 C1 Pratteln Switz.
231 C5 Prattville AL U.S.A.
157 F5 Prauthoy France
114 B2 Pravara r. India
197 H4 Pravda Bulg.
138 C4 Pravdinsk Rus. Fed.
137 G4 Pravdyne Ukr.
182 D1 Pravia Spain
95 G5 Praya Lombok Indon.
163 D4 Prayssac France
163 C4 Prayssas France
160 E3 Praz-sur-Arly France
97 D4 Preah, Prêk r. Cambodia
97 D4 Preăh Vihear Cambodia
233 E3 Preble NY U.S.A.
179 G4 Prebold Slovenia
163 B4 Préchac France
163 B5 Préchacq-les-Bains France
139 I4 Prechistoye Smolenskaya Oblast' Rus. Fed.
134 H4 Prechistoye Yaroslavskaya Oblast' Rus. Fed.
193 F2 Preci Italy
159 F4 Précigné France
177 H2 Prečín Slovakia
160 C1 Précy-sous-Thil France
191 G4 Predappio Italy
191 G2 Predazzo Italy
197 G3 Predeal Romania
179 G4 Preding Austria
179 E3 Predlitz Austria
190 D4 Predosa Italy
223 K5 Preeceville Sask. Can.
159 F3 Pré-en-Pail France
150 E2 Prees Shropshire, England U.K.
149 G4 Preesall Lancashire, England U.K.
168 F1 Preetz Ger.
158 D4 Préfailles France
191 H3 Preganziòl Italy
179 F2 Pregarten Austria
138 C4 Pregolya r. Rus. Fed.
179 G4 Pregrada Croatia
129 B2 Pregradnaya Rus. Fed.
163 B4 Preignac France
163 C5 Preignan France
138 F3 Preiļi Latvia
179 F4 Preitenegg Austria
163 E5 Preixan France
196 D4 Prekornica mts Yugo.
223 I5 Prelate Sask. Can.
179 H2 Prellenkirchen Austria
179 H4 Prelog Croatia
176 E1 Přelouč Czech Rep.
83 G2 Premer N.S.W. Austr.
160 B1 Prémery France
190 D2 Premia Italy
186 F3 Premià de Mar Spain
191 G5 Premilcuore Italy
160 A2 Prémilhat France
170 D3 Premnitz Ger.
156 D3 Prémontré France
190 D2 Premosello Chiovenda Italy
136 E4 Prenistrului, Dealurile hills Moldova
188 F4 Prenj mts Bos.-Herz.
226 B3 Prentice WI U.S.A.
237 F6 Prentiss MS U.S.A.
170 E2 Prenzlau Ger.
100 E4 Preobrazheniye Rus. Fed.
137 H4 Preobrazhenka Ukr.
129 C1 Preobrazhenskoye Rus. Fed.
97 A4 Preparis Island Cocos Is
96 A4 Preparis North Channel Cocos Is
97 A4 Preparis South Channel Cocos Is
160 B2 Préporché France
176 G2 Přerov Czech Rep.
182 B5 Presa Port.
161 C4 Présailles France
160 E3 Pre-St-Didier Italy
191 F2 Presanella, Cima mt. Italy
Prescelly Mts hills Wales U.K. see Preseli, Mynydd
149 G4 Prescot Merseyside, England U.K.
224 F4 Prescott Ont. Can.
237 E5 Prescott AR U.S.A.
241 K4 Prescott AZ U.S.A.
226 A3 Prescott WI U.S.A.
241 K4 Prescott Valley AZ U.S.A.
150 C3 Preseli, Mynydd hills Wales U.K.
197 E4 Preševo Srbija Yugo.
236 C3 Presho SD U.S.A.
195 H3 Presicce Italy
258 F2 Presidencia Roca Arg.
258 E2 Presidencia Roque Sáenz Peña Arg.
256 C5 Presidente Alves Brazil
256 B5 Presidente Bernardes Brazil
258 F2 Presidente de la Plaza Arg.
254 D3 Presidente Dutra Brazil
262 U2 Presidente Eduardo Frei research stn Antarctica
256 A4 Presidente Epitácio Brazil
Presidente Juan Perón prov. Arg. see Chaco
257 E3 Presidente Juscelino Brazil
256 D3 Presidente Olegário Brazil
256 B5 Presidente Prudente Brazil
256 B4 Presidente Venceslau Brazil
244 A2 Presidio r. Mex.
239 F6 Presidio TX U.S.A.
Preslav Bulg. see Veliki Preslav
121 F1 Presnovka Kazakh.
177 K3 Prešov Slovakia
177 K2 Prešovský Kraj admin. reg. Slovakia
198 B1 Prespa, Lake Europe
Prespansko Ezero l. Europe see Prespa, Lake
Prespës, Liqeni i l. Europe see Prespa, Lake
233 □I1 Presque Isle ME U.S.A.
227 F3 Presque Isle MI U.S.A.
226 C2 Presque Isle WI U.S.A.
162 C2 Pressac France
173 F2 Pressath Ger.
179 H2 Pressbaum Austria
Pressburg Slovakia see Bratislava
171 C5 Presseck Ger.
171 D4 Pressel Ger.
171 C5 Pressig Ger.
150 D1 Prestatyn Denbighshire, Wales U.K.
149 G4 Prestbury Cheshire, England U.K.
150 E3 Prestbury Gloucestershire, England U.K.
206 E5 Prestea Ghana
150 D2 Presteigne Powys, Wales U.K.
176 C2 Přeštice Czech Rep.
150 E4 Preston Dorset, England U.K.
149 I4 Preston East Riding of Yorkshire, England U.K.
149 G4 Preston Lancashire, England U.K.
146 F6 Preston Scottish Borders, Scotland U.K.
231 C5 Preston GA U.S.A.
238 E3 Preston ID U.S.A.
233 F5 Preston MD U.S.A.
226 A4 Preston MN U.S.A.
237 E4 Preston MO U.S.A.
86 C4 Preston, Cape W.A. Austr.
149 G2 Prestonpans East Lothian, Scotland U.K.
232 B6 Prestonsburg KY U.S.A.
149 G4 Prestwich Greater Manchester, England U.K.
146 D6 Prestwick South Ayrshire, Scotland U.K.
251 E5 Preto r. Amazonas Brazil
251 F5 Preto r. Amazonas Brazil
254 E4 Preto r. Bahia Brazil
256 B3 Preto r. Goiás Brazil
256 D2 Preto r. Minas Gerais Brazil
253 E2 Preto r. Rondônia Brazil
256 C4 Preto r. São Paulo Brazil
215 G1 Pretoria S. Africa
Pretoria-Witwatersrand-Vereeniging prov. S. Africa see Gauteng
171 D4 Prettin Ger.
173 F2 Pretzfeld Ger.
170 C3 Pretzier Ger.
171 D4 Pretzsch Ger.
171 E5 Pretzschendorf Ger.
159 G5 Preuilly-sur-Claise France
Preussisch-Eylau Rus. Fed. see Bagrationovsk
169 D3 Preußisch Oldendorf Ger.
Preußisch Stargard Pol. see Starogard Gdański
179 F4 Prevalje Slovenia
161 B4 Prévenchères France
162 E2 Préveranges France
198 B2 Preveza Greece
97 D5 Prey Vêng Cambodia
157 F4 Prez-sous-Lafauche France
178 C5 Priaforà, Monte mt. Italy
100 E2 Priamurskiy Yevreyskaya Avtonomnaya Oblast' Rus. Fed.
120 E3 Priaral'skiye Karakumy, Peski des. Kazakh.
182 D2 Priaranza del Bierzo Spain
107 H1 Priargunsk Rus. Fed.
137 J5 Priazovskaya Rus. Fed.
137 H4 Priazovskaya Vozvyshennost' hills Ukr.
177 H4 Pribeta Slovakia
176 F3 Přibice Czech Rep.
220 A4 Pribilof Islands AK U.S.A.
188 F3 Pribinić Bos.-Herz.
179 H4 Pribislavec Croatia
196 D4 Priboj Srbija Yugo.
177 H2 Příbor Czech Rep.
170 D2 Priborn Ger.
176 D2 Příbram Czech Rep.
175 I1 Pribrezhnoye Rus. Fed.
176 E2 Přibyslav Czech Rep.
84 B2 Price r. N.T. Austr.
225 G3 Price Que. Can.
232 D6 Price NC U.S.A.
241 L2 Price UT U.S.A.
241 L2 Price r. UT U.S.A.
237 F6 Prichard AL U.S.A.
232 B5 Prichard WV U.S.A.
137 G4 Prichernomorskaya Nizmennost' lowland Ukr.
173 E2 Prichsenstadt Ger.
183 H4 Priego Spain
185 F3 Priego de Córdoba Spain
138 C3 Priekule Latvia
138 C4 Priekulė Lith.
138 E3 Priekuļi Latvia
138 D4 Prienai Lith.
173 G4 Prien am Chiemsee Ger.
171 E3 Prieros Ger.
214 D3 Prieska S. Africa
171 D4 Prießnitz Ger.
171 C4 Prießnitz Ger.
171 E4 Priestewitz Ger.
246 □ Priestman's River Jamaica
185 F4 Prieta, Sierra mt. Spain
185 G2 Prieto hill Spain
177 H3 Prievidza Slovakia
188 F3 Prijedor Bos.-Herz.
196 D4 Prijepolje Srbija Yugo.
120 A3 Prikaspiyskaya Nizmennost' lowland Kazakh./Rus. Fed.
206 E5 Prikro Côte d'Ivoire
137 J5 Prikubanskaya Nizmennost' lowland Rus. Fed.
197 E5 Prilep Macedonia
Priluki Ukr. see Pryluky
176 B2 Přimda Czech Rep.
254 E2 Primeira Cruz Brazil
261 F2 Primero r. Arg.
246 C2 Primero de Enero Cuba
236 E3 Primghar IA U.S.A.
191 G3 Primolano Italy
175 I1 Primorsk Kaliningradskaya Oblast' Rus. Fed.
138 G1 Primorsk Leningradskaya Oblast' Rus. Fed.
135 I6 Primorsk Volgogradskaya Oblast' Rus. Fed.
Primorsk Ukr. see Prymors'k
100 D4 Primorskiy Rus. Fed.
100 E3 Primorskiy Kray admin. div. Rus. Fed.
135 G7 Primorsko-Akhtarsk Rus. Fed.
Primorskoye Ukr. see Prymors'ke
222 B2 Primrose r. Y.T. Can.
172 A2 Prims r. Ger.
223 J4 Prince Albert Sask. Can.
214 D5 Prince Albert S. Africa
263 K1 Prince Albert Mountains Antarctica
220 G2 Prince Albert Peninsula N.W.T. Can.
214 C5 Prince Albert Road S. Africa
220 G2 Prince Albert Sound sea chan. N.W.T. Can.
214 B5 Prince Alfred Hamlet S. Africa
221 K3 Prince Charles Island Nunavut Can.
263 E2 Prince Charles Mountains Antarctica
225 I4 Prince Edward Island prov. Can.
265 G8 Prince Edward Islands Indian Ocean
232 E5 Prince Frederick MD U.S.A.
86 E2 Prince Frederick Harbour W.A. Austr.
222 F4 Prince George B.C. Can.
234 B4 Prince George's County county MD U.S.A.
221 H2 Prince Gustaf Adolf Sea Nunavut Can.
263 C2 Prince Harald Coast Antarctica
85 E1 Prince of Wales Island Qld Austr.
221 I2 Prince of Wales Island Nunavut Can.
220 E4 Prince of Wales Island AK U.S.A.
220 G2 Prince of Wales Strait N.W.T. Can.
220 G2 Prince Patrick Island N.W.T. Can.
86 E2 Prince Regent r. W.A. Austr.
221 I2 Prince Regent Inlet sea chan. Nunavut Can.
222 D4 Prince Rupert B.C. Can.
151 G3 Princes Risborough Buckinghamshire, England U.K.
233 F5 Princess Anne MD U.S.A.
263 A2 Princess Astrid Coast Antarctica
85 E2 Princess Charlotte Bay Qld Austr.
263 F2 Princess Elizabeth Land reg. Antarctica
86 E2 Princess May Range hills W.A. Austr.
81 A6 Princess Mountains South I. N.Z.
263 B2 Princess Ragnhild Coast Antarctica
87 D5 Princess Range hills W.A. Austr.
222 D4 Princess Royal Island B.C. Can.
247 □7 Prince's Town Trin. and Tob.
151 F2 Princethorpe Warwickshire, England U.K.
222 F5 Princeton B.C. Can.
240 F2 Princeton CA U.S.A.
226 C5 Princeton IL U.S.A.
230 C4 Princeton IN U.S.A.
230 C4 Princeton KY U.S.A.
233 □J2 Princeton ME U.S.A.
236 E3 Princeton MO U.S.A.
234 D2 Princeton NJ U.S.A.
226 C4 Princeton WI U.S.A.
232 C6 Princeton WV U.S.A.
234 D2 Princeton Junction NJ U.S.A.
150 D4 Princetown Devon, England U.K.
233 □J2 Prince William N.B. Can.
220 D3 Prince William Sound b. AK U.S.A.
207 G6 Príncipe i. São Tomé and Príncipe
238 B2 Prineville OR U.S.A.
164 D3 Prinsenbeek Neth.
Prins Harald Kyst coastal area Antarctica see Prince Harald Coast
140 □ Prins Karls Forland i. Svalbard
242 □J6 Prinzapolca Nic.
168 D3 Prinzhöfte Ger.
195 E5 Priolo Gargallo Sicilia Italy
183 F2 Prioro Spain
Priozernyy Kazakh. see Tugyl
139 H1 Priozersk Rus. Fed.
Priozyorsk Rus. Fed. see Priozersk
136 F2 Pripet r. Belarus/Ukr. alt. Pryp"yat' (Ukraine), alt. Prypyats' (Belarus)
136 C2 Pripet Marshes Belarus/Ukr.
134 L2 Pripolyarnyy Ural mts Rus. Fed.
197 H2 Priponeşti Romania
197 H2 Prisăcani Romania
188 F3 Priseka hill Croatia
176 E1 Příšovice Czech Rep.
162 D2 Prissac France
160 C2 Prissé France
Pristan' Przheval'sk Kyrg. see Przheval'sk Pristany
137 I2 Pristen' Rus. Fed.
196 E4 Priština Kosovo, Srbija Yugo.
116 D4 Prithvipur Madh. Prad. India
173 E3 Prittriching Ger.
171 D3 Pritzerbe Ger.
170 C2 Pritzier Ger.
170 D2 Pritzwalk Ger.
161 C4 Privas France
193 F3 Priverno Italy
188 E3 Privlaka Croatia
139 J4 Privokzal'nyy Rus. Fed.
137 J4 Privol'naya Rus. Fed.
139 M3 Privolzhsk Rus. Fed.
135 I6 Privolzhskaya Vozvyshennost' hills Rus. Fed.
135 I6 Privolzhskiy Rus. Fed.
120 B1 Privolzh'ye Rus. Fed.
135 H7 Priyutnoye Rus. Fed.
196 E4 Prizren Kosovo, Srbija Yugo.
194 C5 Prizzi Sicilia Italy
188 F3 Prnjavor Bos.-Herz.
182 D1 Proaza Spain
182 D2 Proba Spain
197 F4 Probištip Macedonia
95 F4 Probolinggo Jawa Timur Indon.
168 F1 Probsteierhagen Ger.
171 C5 Probstzella Ger.
150 C4 Probus Cornwall, England U.K.
192 D2 Proceno Italy
174 E4 Prochowice Pol.
193 G4 Procida Italy
226 A2 Proctor MN U.S.A.
233 G3 Proctor VT U.S.A.
232 B5 Proctorville OH U.S.A.
114 C3 Proddatur Andhra Prad. India
182 C5 Proença-a-Nova Port.
182 C4 Proença-a-Velha Port.
171 D4 Profen Ger.
251 H3 Professor van Blommestein Meer resr Suriname
165 D4 Profondeville Belgium
191 F3 Progno r. Italy
261 G2 Progreso Arg.
242 □I6 Progreso Hond.
243 E3 Progreso Coahuila Mex.
245 E3 Progreso Hidalgo Mex.
243 H4 Progreso Yucatán Mex.
244 C2 Progreso Zacatecas Mex.
100 D2 Progress Rus. Fed.
170 E1 Prohn Ger.
238 B3 Project City CA U.S.A.
175 I1 Prokhladnaya r. Rus. Fed.
129 D2 Prokhladnyy Rus. Fed.
137 I2 Prokhorovka Rus. Fed.
137 G2 Prokhory Ukr.
196 D4 Prokletije mts Albania/Yugo.
198 C2 Prokopi Sterea Ellas Greece
130 J4 Prokop'yevsk Rus. Fed.
197 E4 Prokuplje Srbija Yugo.
139 H2 Proletariy Rus. Fed.
135 H7 Proletarsk Rus. Fed.
Proletarskaya Rus. Fed. see Proletarsk
137 H2 Proletarskiy Rus. Fed.
Prome Myanmar see Pyè
256 C4 Promissão Brazil
256 C4 Promissão, Represa resr Brazil
175 I4 Promna Pol.
193 H3 Promontorio del Gargano plat. Italy
234 C1 Prompton PA U.S.A.
134 H4 Pronino Rus. Fed.
169 B5 Pronsfeld Ger.
139 L4 Pronsk Rus. Fed.
168 F2 Pronstorf Ger.
139 H5 Pronya r. Belarus
222 F3 Prophet r. B.C. Can.
222 F3 Prophet River B.C. Can.
226 C5 Prophetstown IL U.S.A.
254 F4 Propriá Brazil
192 A3 Propriano Corse France
129 E1 Prorva r. Rus. Fed.
120 F1 Proryvnoye Rus. Fed.
176 F2 Proseč Czech Rep.
171 E4 Prösen Ger.
146 F5 Prosen Water r. Scotland U.K.
85 G4 Proserpine Qld Austr.
Proskurov Ukr. see Khmel'nyts'kyy
199 D1 Proskynites Anatoliki Makedonia kai Thraki Greece
174 F3 Prosna r. Pol.
198 C1 Prosotsani Greece
235 F1 Prospect CT U.S.A.
233 F3 Prospect NY U.S.A.
232 B4 Prospect OH U.S.A.
238 B3 Prospect OR U.S.A.
232 C4 Prospect PA U.S.A.
235 D2 Prospect Plains NJ U.S.A.
92 C4 Prosperidad Phil.
148 C4 Prosperous Rep. of Ireland
238 C2 Prosser WA U.S.A.
176 G2 Prostějov Czech Rep.
175 K2 Prostki Pol.
85 G5 Proston Qld Austr.
137 H3 Prosyane Ukr.
174 F5 Prószków Pol.
175 I5 Proszowice Pol.
175 I5 Proszówki Pol.
214 C6 Protem S. Africa
176 F2 Protivanov Czech Rep.
176 D2 Protivín Czech Rep.
137 I5 Protoka r. Rus. Fed.
137 I3 Protopopivka Ukr.
136 F2 Protsiv Ukr.
139 K4 Protva Rus. Fed.
139 K4 Protva r. Rus. Fed.
139 K4 Protvino Rus. Fed.
170 E3 Prötzel Ger.
197 H4 Provadiya Bulg.
184 B3 Provença Port.
161 D5 Provence airport France
161 E5 Provence-Alpes-Côte-d'Azur admin. reg. France
157 H4 Provenchères-sur-Fave France
Providence MD U.S.A. see Annapolis
233 H4 Providence RI U.S.A.
81 A7 Providence, Cape South I. N.Z.
217 □2 Providence Atoll Seychelles
227 F3 Providence Bay Ont. Can.
246 B4 Providencia, Isla de i. Caribbean Sea
253 E2 Providência, Serra de hills Brazil
246 D2 Providenciales Island Turks and Caicos Is
131 T3 Provideniya Rus. Fed.
85 E2 Providential Channel Qld Austr.
233 H3 Provincetown MA U.S.A.
156 D4 Provins France
241 L1 Provo UT U.S.A.
223 I4 Provost Alta Can.
188 F4 Prozor Bos.-Herz.
139 K2 Prozorovo Rus. Fed.
196 E5 Prrenjas Albania
206 E4 Pru r. Ghana
134 K3 Prub r. Rus. Fed.
175 K6 Pruchnik Pol.
256 B6 Prudentópolis Brazil
149 H3 Prudhoe Northumberland, England U.K.
220 D2 Prudhoe Bay AK U.S.A.
85 G4 Prudhoe Island Qld Austr.
174 F5 Prudnik Pol.
137 I2 Prudyanka Ukr.
177 K3 Prügy Hungary
171 F5 Průhonice Czech Rep.
169 B5 Prüm Ger.
169 B6 Prüm r. Ger.
185 E4 Pruna Spain
197 G3 Prundeni Romania
197 H3 Prundu Romania
197 G2 Prundu Bârgăului Romania
Prundu Bîrgăului Romania see Prundu Bârgăului
192 B2 Prunelli-di-Fiumorbo Corse France
163 E4 Prunet France
161 E4 Prunières France
159 H4 Pruniers-en-Sologne France
232 C5 Pruntytown WV U.S.A.
Prusa Turkey see Bursa
179 H2 Prušánky Czech Rep.
Prushkov Pol. see Pruszków
174 E4 Prusice Pol.
177 G2 Prusinovice Czech Rep.
174 G2 Pruszcz Pol.
143 H4 Pruszcz Gdański Pol.
175 I3 Pruszków Pol.
136 E5 Prut r. Europe
173 G4 Prutting Ger.
178 B3 Prutz Austria
138 E5 Pruzhany Belarus
177 H2 Pružina Slovakia
179 E5 Prvačina Slovenia
188 E3 Prvić i. Croatia
137 H2 Pryamitsyno Rus. Fed.
137 H4 Pryazovs'ke Ukr.
137 I2 Prykolotne Ukr.
137 G2 Pryluky Ukr.
137 I4 Prymors'k Ukr.
Prymors'ke Ukr. see Sartana
137 G4 Prymors'ke Ukr.
136 E5 Prymors'ke Ukr.
137 H4 Prymors'ke Ukr.
137 H5 Prymors'kyy Ukr.
237 E4 Pryor OK U.S.A.
136 F2 Pryp"yat' Ukr.
136 F2 Pryp"yat' r. Ukr. alt. Prypyats' (Belarus), conv. Pripet
136 E2 Prypyats' r. Belarus alt. Pryp"yat' (Ukraine), conv. Pripet
137 J3 Pryvillya Ukr.
137 G4 Pryvil'ne Ukr.
136 C2 Pryvitne Ukr.
137 G3 Pryyutivka Ukr.
175 I2 Przasnysz Pol.
174 F2 Przechlewo Pol.
175 H5 Przeciszów Pol.
175 J5 Przecław Pol.
175 H4 Przedbórz Pol.
174 G3 Przedecz Pol.
174 D2 Przelewice Pol.
174 D4 Przemków Pol.
177 I1 Przemsza r. Pol.
175 K6 Przemyśl Pol.
175 K1 Przerośl Pol.
175 K3 Przesmyki Pol.
175 L5 Przewale Pol.
175 L4 Przewłoka Pol.
174 F5 Przeworno Pol.
175 K5 Przeworsk Pol.
174 C4 Przewóz Pol.
175 K3 Przeździatka Pol.
175 I2 Przezdzięk Wielki Pol.
175 H2 Przezmark Pol.
Przheval'sk Kyrg. see Karakol
139 H4 Przheval'skoye Smolenskaya Oblast' Rus. Fed.
121 I4 Przheval'sk Pristany Kyrg.
174 G1 Przodkowo Pol.
174 C2 Przybiernów Pol.
175 I3 Przyborowice Pol.
174 G3 Przybranowo Pol.
174 F4 Przygodzice Pol.
174 G4 Przykona Pol.
175 H5 Przyrów Pol.
175 J5 Przyrwa r. Pol.
174 G5 Przystajń Pol.
175 I4 Przysucha Pol.
174 D3 Przytoczna Pol.
175 K4 Przytoczno Pol.
175 K2 Przytuły Pol.
175 I4 Przytyk Pol.

Przywidz to **Qovlar**
351

174 G1 **Przywidz** Pol.
198 C2 **Psachna** Greece
Psakhná Greece *see* **Psachna**
199 D2 **Psara** *i.* Greece
129 B1 **Psebay** Rus. Fed.
129 D2 **Psedakh** Rus. Fed.
129 A1 **Psekups** *r.* Rus. Fed.
Psel *r.* Rus. Fed./Ukr. *see* **Ps'ol**
137 I2 **Pselets** Rus. Fed.
199 E3 **Pserimos** *i.* Greece
137 J5 **Pshada** Rus. Fed.
129 A1 **Pshekha** *r.* Rus. Fed.
129 A1 **Pshish** *r.* Rus. Fed.
121 G4 **Pskent** Uzbek.
138 G3 **Pskov** Rus. Fed.
138 F2 **Pskov, Lake** Estonia/Rus. Fed.
138 G3 **Pskova** *r.* Rus. Fed.
Pskov Oblast *admin. div.* Rus. Fed. *see* Pskovskaya Oblast'
138 G3 **Pskovskaya Oblast'** *admin. div.* Rus. Fed.
Pskovskoye Ozero *l.* Estonia/Rus. Fed. *see* **Pskov, Lake**
137 H2 **Ps'ol** *r.* Rus. Fed./Ukr.
188 F3 **Psunj** *mts* Croatia
174 D3 **Pszczew** Pol.
174 G1 **Pszczółki** Pol.
174 G6 **Pszczyna** Pol.
139 L5 **Ptan'** *r.* Rus. Fed.
198 C2 **Pteleos** *Thessalia* Greece
198 B1 **Ptolemaïda** Greece
Ptolemais Israel *see* **'Akko**
138 G5 **Ptsich** *r.* Belarus
188 E2 **Ptuj** Slovenia
179 G4 **Ptujsko jezero** *l.* Slovenia
136 C2 **Ptycha** Ukr.
107 E5 **Pu** *r.* China
94 C3 **Pu** *r.* Indon.
240 □D9 **Puako** *HI* U.S.A.
261 F5 **Puán** Arg.
108 C3 **Pu'an** *Guizhou* China
Pu'an *Sichuan* China *see* Jiange
96 E2 **Pubei** *Guangxi* China
160 E2 **Publier** France
250 B6 **Pucacaca** Peru
250 C5 **Pucacuro** *r.* Peru
252 B2 **Pucallpa** Peru
252 C3 **Pucara** Peru
252 C4 **Pucarani** Bol.
Pucarevo Bos.-Herz. *see* Novi Travnik
250 D5 **Puca Urco** Peru
178 E3 **Puch bei Hallein** Austria
179 G3 **Puchberg am Schneeberg** Austria
109 F3 **Pucheng** *Fujian* China
107 F5 **Pucheng** *Shaanxi* China
134 H4 **Puchezh** Rus. Fed.
173 F3 **Puchheim** Ger.
101 C5 **Puch'ŏn** S. Korea
177 H2 **Púchov** Slovakia
197 G3 **Pucioasa** Romania
143 H4 **Puck** Pol.
143 H4 **Pucka, Zatoka** *b.* Pol.
147 C4 **Puckaun** Rep. of Ireland
87 C5 **Puckford, Mount** *hill* *W.A.* Austr.
187 C5 **Puçol** Spain
260 B6 **Pucón** Chile
122 C3 **Pūdanū** Iran
140 N2 **Pudasjärvi** Fin.
150 E4 **Puddletown** *Dorset, England* U.K.
169 C5 **Puderbach** Ger.
215 E2 **Pudimoe** S. Africa
108 C3 **Puding** *Guizhou* China
109 G2 **Pudong** *airport* China
134 G3 **Pudozh** Rus. Fed.
149 H4 **Pudsey** *West Yorkshire, England* U.K.
Puduchcheri *Pondicherry* India *see* **Pondicherry**
114 C4 **Pudukkottai** *Tamil Nadu* India
245 F3 **Puebillo** Mex.
241 J5 **Puebla** *Baja California Norte* Mex.
245 E4 **Puebla** *Puebla* Mex.
245 E4 **Puebla** *state* Mex.
186 C3 **Puebla de Albortón** Spain
185 E2 **Puebla de Alcocer** Spain
186 C3 **Puebla de Alfindén** Spain
183 H5 **Puebla de Almenara** Spain
183 G4 **Puebla de Beleña** Spain
186 D4 **Puebla de Benifasar** Spain
182 C2 **Puebla de Brollón** Spain
185 H3 **Puebla de Don Fadrique** Spain
185 F1 **Puebla de Don Rodrigo** Spain
184 C3 **Puebla de Guzmán** Spain
184 D2 **Puebla de la Calzada** Spain
184 D2 **Puebla de la Reina** Spain
182 B2 **Puebla del Caramiñal** Spain
183 E1 **Puebla de Lillo** Spain
184 D2 **Puebla del Maestre** Spain
185 H2 **Puebla del Príncipe** Spain
184 D2 **Puebla del Prior** Spain
184 D1 **Puebla de Obando** Spain
182 D2 **Puebla de Sanabria** Spain
184 D2 **Puebla de Sancho Pérez** Spain
Puebla de San Julián Spain *see* **Puebla de San Xulián**
187 B4 **Puebla de San Miguel** Spain
182 C2 **Puebla de San Xulián** Spain
182 C2 **Puebla de Trives** Spain
182 D4 **Puebla de Yeltes** Spain
Puebla de Zaragoza *Puebla* Mex. *see* **Puebla**
239 F4 **Pueblo** *CO* U.S.A.
261 H2 **Pueblo Arrúa** Arg.
261 F3 **Pueblo Italiano** Arg.
242 □I6 **Pueblo Nuevo** Nic.
245 F2 **Pueblo Viejo, Laguna de** *lag.* Mex.
242 C3 **Pueblo Yaqui** Mex.
161 A4 **Puech del Pal** *mt.* France
163 E4 **Puech de Rouet** *hill* France
260 B3 **Puente Alto** Chile
Puenteareas Spain *see* Ponteareas
Puente Caldelas Spain *see* Ponte Caldelas
182 D2 **Puente de Domingo Flórez** Spain
185 H2 **Puente de Génave** Spain
245 E4 **Puente de Ixtla** Mex.
182 E4 **Puente del Congosto** Spain
186 D2 **Puente de Montañana** Spain
183 F1 **Puente de San Miguel** Spain
185 F3 **Puente-Genil** Spain
183 I2 **Puente la Reina** Spain
183 F1 **Puentenansa** Spain
Puentes de García Rodríguez Spain *see* **As Pontes de García Rodríguez**
250 D2 **Puente Torres** Venez.
183 G1 **Puente Viesgo** Spain
108 B4 **Pu'er** *Yunnan* China
252 C3 **Puerto Acosta** Bol.
259 B7 **Puerto Aisén** Chile
253 E3 **Puerto Alegre** Bol.
250 B6 **Puerto America** Peru
243 F6 **Puerto Ángel** Mex.
245 F6 **Puerto Angel** Mex.
253 F6 **Puerto Antequera** Para.
245 H6 **Puerto Arista** Mex.
242 □J7 **Puerto Armuelles** Panama
250 B4 **Puerto Asís** Col.
250 E3 **Puerto Ayacucho** Venez.
250 □ **Puerto Baquerizo Moreno** *Islas Galápagos* Ecuador
242 □H6 **Puerto Barrios** Guat.
258 F2 **Puerto Bermejo** Arg.
250 C3 **Puerto Berrío** Col.
250 D2 **Puerto Cabello** Venez.
242 □J6 **Puerto Cabezas** Nic.
242 □J6 **Puerto Cabo Gracias á Dios** Nic.
250 E3 **Puerto Carreño** Col.
253 F5 **Puerto Casado** Para.
250 B6 **Puerto Chicama** Peru
259 B7 **Puerto Cisnes** Chile
250 D5 **Puerto Córdoba** Col.
242 □I6 **Puerto Cortés** Hond.
242 C3 **Puerto Cortés** Mex.
250 D2 **Puerto Cumarebo** Venez.
182 E4 **Puerto de Béjar** Spain
Puerto de Cabras *Fuerteventura* Canary Is *see* **Puerto del Rosario**
216 □3a **Puerto de la Cruz** *Tenerife* Canary Is
Puerto de la Selva Spain *see* El Port de la Selva
216 □3b **Puerto del Rosario** *Fuerteventura* Canary Is
Puerto del Son Spain *see* Porto do Son
187 B7 **Puerto de Mazarrón** Spain
243 I4 **Puerto de Morelos** Mex.
Puerto de Pollensa Spain *see* Port de Pollença
185 E1 **Puerto de San Vicente** Spain
Puerto de Sóller Spain *see* Port de Sóller
245 F6 **Puerto Escondido** Mex.
250 B5 **Puerto Francisco de Orellana** Ecuador
253 E3 **Puerto Frey** Bol.
252 D4 **Puerto Grether** Bol.
252 B2 **Puerto Inca** Peru
250 E4 **Puerto Inírida** Col.
253 F4 **Puerto Isabel** Bol.
242 □I7 **Puerto Jesus** Costa Rica
243 I4 **Puerto Juáres** Mex.
247 F5 **Puerto La Cruz** Venez.
185 G1 **Puerto Lápice** Spain
186 D2 **Puértolas** Spain
242 □J6 **Puerto Lempira** Hond.
185 F2 **Puertollano** Spain
250 C3 **Puerto Lopéz** Col.
185 I3 **Puerto Lumbreras** Spain
243 G6 **Puerto Madero** Mex.
259 D6 **Puerto Madryn** Arg.
252 C3 **Puerto Maldonado** Peru
252 D4 **Puerto Mamoré** Bol.
246 C2 **Puerto Manatí** Cuba
250 A6 **Puerto Máncora** Peru
253 F5 **Puerto María Auxiliadora** Para.
Puertomarín Spain *see* Portomarín
Puerto México Mex. *see* Coatzacoalcos
253 F5 **Puerto Mihanovich** Para.
187 C4 **Puertomingalvo** Spain
250 E3 **Puerto Miranda** Venez.
259 B6 **Puerto Montt** Chile
242 □I6 **Puerto Morazán** Nic.
250 B7 **Puerto Morín** Peru
259 B8 **Puerto Natáles** Chile
250 D3 **Puerto Nuevo** Col.
246 C2 **Puerto Padre** Cuba
250 E3 **Puerto Páez** Venez.
252 D3 **Puerto Pando** Bol.
242 B2 **Puerto Peñasco** Mex.
253 F5 **Puerto Pinasco** Para.
251 E2 **Puerto Píritu** Venez.
246 E3 **Puerto Plata** Dom. Rep.
252 B2 **Puerto Portillo** Peru
252 B2 **Puerto Prado** Peru
Puerto Presidente Stroessner Para. *see* **Ciudad del Este**
92 A4 **Puerto Princesa** Phil.
242 □I7 **Puerto Quepos** Costa Rica
184 D4 **Puerto Real** Spain
258 G2 **Puerto Rico** Arg.
252 D2 **Puerto Rico** Bol.
247 □1 **Puerto Rico** *terr.* West Indies
264 E4 **Puerto Rico Trench** *sea feature* Caribbean Sea
259 B5 **Puerto Saavedra** Chile
Puerto Sama Cuba *see* **Samá**
242 □I6 **Puerto Sandino** Nic.
259 C8 **Puerto Santa Cruz** Arg.
253 F5 **Puerto Sastre** Para.
253 E3 **Puerto Saucedo** Bol.
Puertos de Beceite *mts* Spain *see* **Ports de Beseit**
182 D4 **Puerto Seguro** Spain
184 E4 **Puerto Serrano** Spain
250 D5 **Puerto Socorro** Peru
Puerto Somoza Nic. *see* Puerto Sandino
253 F4 **Puerto Suárez** Bol.
252 A2 **Puerto Supe** Peru
252 C3 **Puerto Tahuantisuyo** Peru
250 B4 **Puerto Tejado** Col.
250 B5 **Puerto Tunigrama** Peru
244 B3 **Puerto Vallarta** Mex.
259 B6 **Puerto Varas** Chile
252 B2 **Puerto Victoria** Peru
253 E3 **Puerto Villazon** Bol.
183 I2 **Pueyo** Spain
120 B1 **Pugachev** Rus. Fed.
134 K4 **Pugachevo** Rus. Fed.
116 C3 **Pugal** *Rajasthan* India
108 B3 **Puge** *Sichuan* China
161 E5 **Puget-sur-Argens** France
161 E5 **Puget-Théniers** France
161 E5 **Puget-Ville** France
234 C2 **Pughtown** *PA* U.S.A.
193 H3 **Puglia** *admin. reg.* Italy
193 E2 **Puglia** *r.* Italy
162 B3 **Pugnac** France
193 I3 **Pugnochiuso** Italy
225 I4 **Pugwash** *N.S.* Can.
80 F3 **Puha** *North I.* N.Z.
122 C5 **Pūhāl-e Khamīr, Kūh-e** *mts* Iran
Puhiwaero *c.* *Stewart I.* N.Z. *see* **South West Cape**
138 F2 **Puhja** Estonia
197 F3 **Pui** Romania
161 A5 **Puichéric** France
197 H3 **Puieşti** Romania
187 C5 **Puig** Spain
186 E2 **Puigcerdà** Spain
186 F3 **Puig d'Arques** *hill* Spain
181 H1 **Puig de Comanegra** *mt.* Spain
186 E2 **Puig de les Morreres** *mt.* Spain
187 G5 **Puig de Sant Salvador** *hill* Spain
187 F5 **Puig des Galatzó** *mt.* Spain
187 F5 **Puig Major** *mt.* Spain
186 F2 **Puigmal** *mt.* France/Spain
186 E2 **Puig Pedrós** *mt.* Spain
186 E3 **Puig-reig** Spain
186 D3 **Puigverd de Lleida** Spain
161 E5 **Puimoisson** France
156 C4 **Puiseaux** France
156 C2 **Puisieux** France
163 B4 **Puisseguin** France
161 B5 **Puisserguier** France
156 E4 **Puits** *r.* France
163 E6 **Puivert** France
161 C4 **Pujaut** France
206 C5 **Pujehun** Sierra Leone
Puji *Shaanxi* China *see* **Wugong**
109 F2 **Pujiang** *Zhejiang* China
163 C5 **Pujo** France
163 B4 **Pujols** *Aquitaine* France
163 C4 **Pujols** *Aquitaine* France
81 C6 **Pukaki, Lake** *South I.* N.Z.
177 H3 **Pukanec** Slovakia
81 □2 **Pukapuka** *atoll* Cook Is
79 □3 **Pukapuka** *i.* *Arch. des Tuamotu* Fr. Polynesia
79 □3 **Pukarua** *atoll* *Arch. des Tuamotu* Fr. Polynesia
226 E1 **Pukaskwa** *r.* *Ont.* Can.
223 K4 **Pukatawagan** *Man.* Can.
101 C4 **Pukchin** N. Korea
101 D4 **Pukch'ŏng** N. Korea
196 D4 **Pukë** Albania
80 G2 **Pukeamaru** *hill* *North I.* N.Z.
80 E3 **Pukearuhe** *North I.* N.Z.
80 F3 **Pukehoi** *North I.* N.Z.
80 E2 **Pukekohe** *North I.* N.Z.
80 D1 **Pukenui** *North I.* N.Z.
80 E3 **Pukeokahu** *North I.* N.Z.
81 C6 **Pukerangi** *South I.* N.Z.
81 B7 **Pukerau** *South I.* N.Z.
80 E3 **Pukeroa** *North I.* N.Z.
81 E4 **Pukerua Bay** *North I.* N.Z.
81 D5 **Puketeraki Range** *mts* *South I.* N.Z.
80 F3 **Puketitiri** *North I.* N.Z.
80 F2 **Puketoetoe** *mt.* *North I.* N.Z.
80 F4 **Puketoi Range** *hills* *North I.* N.Z.
80 E3 **Puketutu** *North I.* N.Z.
81 C6 **Pukeuri Junction** *South I.* N.Z.
141 N3 **Pukkila** Fin.
134 H3 **Puksoozero** Rus. Fed.
101 C4 **Puksubaek-san** *mt.* N. Korea
Pula *Xizang* China *see* **Nyingchi**
188 D3 **Pula** Croatia
191 I4 **Pula** *airport* Croatia
192 B5 **Pula** *Sardegna* Italy
252 D5 **Pulacayo** Bol.
107 I4 **Pulandian** *Liaoning* China
92 C5 **Pulangi** *r.* Phil.
91 K5 **Pulap** *atoll* Micronesia
252 C6 **Pular, Cerro** *mt.* Chile
233 E3 **Pulaski** *NY* U.S.A.
231 C5 **Pulaski** *TN* U.S.A.
232 C6 **Pulaski** *VA* U.S.A.
226 C3 **Pulaski** *WI* U.S.A.
91 I8 **Pulau** *r.* Indon.
Pulau Pinang *state* Malaysia *see* **Pinang**
175 J4 **Puławy** Pol.
151 G4 **Pulborough** *West Sussex, England* U.K.
191 I2 **Pulfero** Italy
183 F5 **Pulgar** Spain
169 B4 **Pulheim** Ger.
114 D3 **Pulicat** *Tamil Nadu* India
114 D3 **Pulicat Lake** *inlet* India
160 C2 **Puligny-Montrachet** France
114 C3 **Pulivendla** *Andhra Prad.* India
179 G2 **Pulkau** Austria
179 H2 **Pulkau** *r.* Austria
140 N2 **Pulkkila** Fin.
173 F3 **Pullach in Isartal** Ger.
238 C2 **Pullman** *WA* U.S.A.
91 H6 **Pulo Anna** *i.* Palau
92 B2 **Pulog, Mount** *Luzon* Phil.
140 P1 **Pulozero** Rus. Fed.
185 I3 **Pulpí** Spain
195 G2 **Pulsano** Italy
171 E4 **Pulsen** Ger.
171 F4 **Pulsnitz** Ger.
171 E4 **Pulsnitz** *r.* Ger.
175 J3 **Pułtusk** Pol.
86 □2 **Pulu Capelok** *i.* Cocos Is
127 E3 **Pülümür** Turkey
86 □2 **Pulu Pandang** *i.* Cocos Is
91 K5 **Pulusuk** *atoll* Micronesia
91 K5 **Puluwat** *atoll* Micronesia
157 H5 **Pulversheim** France
211 B6 **Puma** Tanz.
260 B4 **Pumanque** Chile
Pumiao *Guangxi* China *see* Yongning
238 F2 **Pumpkin Creek** *r.* *MT* U.S.A.
150 D2 **Pumsaint** *Carmarthenshire, Wales* U.K.
250 A5 **Puná, Isla** *i.* Ecuador
258 D2 **Puna de Atacama** *plat.* Arg.
81 C5 **Punakaiki** *South I.* N.Z.
117 G4 **Punakha** Bhutan
240 □D9 **Punaluu** *HI* U.S.A.
79 □3a **Punaruu** *r.* *Tahiti* Fr. Polynesia
191 J3 **Punat** Croatia
252 D4 **Punata** Bol.
123 H3 **Punch** Pak.
222 F4 **Punchaw** *B.C.* Can.
213 F4 **Punda Maria** S. Africa
116 D3 **Pundri** *Haryana* India
114 B2 **Pune** *Mahar.* India
114 C3 **Punganuru** *Andhra Prad.* India
209 B7 **Pungo Andango** Angola
101 D4 **P'ungsan** N. Korea
213 G3 **Púnguè** *r.* Moz.
191 F2 **Puni** *r.* Italy
208 E5 **Punia** Dem. Rep. Congo
109 F4 **Puning** *Guangdong* China
260 B2 **Punitaqui** Chile
116 C3 **Punjab** *state* India
123 G4 **Punjab** *prov.* Pak.
141 O3 **Punkaharju** Fin.
252 C3 **Puno** Peru
252 C3 **Puno** *dept* Peru
117 F4 **Punpun** *r.* India
175 L1 **Puńsk** Pol.
247 □1 **Punta, Cerro de** *mt.* Puerto Rico
192 C2 **Punta Ala** Italy
261 F6 **Punta Alta** Arg.
259 C9 **Punta Arenas** Chile
192 B4 **Punta Balestrieri** *mt.* *Sardegna* Italy
252 C4 **Punta de Bombón** Peru
242 □H5 **Punta Gorda** Belize
216 □3d **Puntagorda** *La Palma* Canary Is
231 D7 **Punta Gorda** *FL* U.S.A.
191 J4 **Punta Križa** Croatia
216 □3d **Puntallana** *La Palma* Canary Is
192 A5 **Punta Mumullonis** *hill* *Sardegna* Italy
242 □I7 **Puntarenas** Costa Rica
191 H3 **Punta Sabbioni** Italy
247 □1 **Punta Santiago** Puerto Rico
252 D5 **Puntas Negras, Cerro** *mt.* Chile
184 D3 **Punta Umbría** Spain
250 D2 **Punto Fijo** Venez.
186 C2 **Puntón de Guara** *mt.* Spain
232 D4 **Punxsutawney** *PA* U.S.A.
140 N2 **Puolanka** Fin.
140 M2 **Puoltikasvaara** Sweden
109 E2 **Puqi** *Hubei* China
252 B3 **Puquio** Peru
130 I3 **Pur** *r.* Rus. Fed.
116 E3 **Puranpur** *Uttar Prad.* India
91 J8 **Purari** *r.* P.N.G.
179 H3 **Purbach am Neusiedler See** Austria
95 E4 **Purbalingga** *Jawa Tengah* Indon.
150 E4 **Purbeck, Isle of** *pen.* *England* U.K.
237 D5 **Purcell** *OK* U.S.A.
222 G5 **Purcell Mountains** *B.C.* Can.
232 E5 **Purcellville** *VA* U.S.A.
185 H3 **Purchena** Spain
185 G3 **Purchil** Spain
258 B5 **Purén** Chile
244 C4 **Purépero** Mex.
151 H3 **Purfleet** *Thurrock, England* U.K.
237 C4 **Purgatoire** *r.* *CO* U.S.A.
173 E3 **Pürgen** Ger.
179 G2 **Purgstall an der Erlauf** Austria
209 B6 **Puri** Angola
115 E2 **Puri** *Orissa* India
244 B4 **Purificación** Mex.
245 E2 **Purificación** *r.* Mex.
150 E3 **Puriton** *Somerset, England* U.K.
179 H2 **Purkersdorf** Austria
151 G3 **Purley** *Greater London, England* U.K.
151 F3 **Purley on Thames** *West Berkshire, England* U.K.
164 D2 **Purmerend** Neth.
114 C2 **Purna** *Mahar.* India
114 C2 **Purna** *r.* *Mahar.* India
116 D5 **Purna** *r.* *Mahar.* India
117 G4 **Purnabhaba** *r.* India
82 B1 **Purndu Saltpan** *salt flat* *S.A.* Austr.
Purnea *Bihar* India *see* **Purnia**
117 F4 **Purnia** *Bihar* India
259 B6 **Purranque** Chile
Pursat Cambodia *see* Poŭthĭsăt
151 F3 **Purton** *Wiltshire, England* U.K.
221 K3 **Purtuniq** *Que.* Can.
244 D3 **Puruandíro** Mex.
244 D4 **Puruarán** Mex.
250 D5 **Puruê** *r.* Brazil
183 I3 **Purujosa** Spain
117 F5 **Puruliya** *W. Bengal* India
185 G3 **Purullena** Spain
251 F5 **Purus** *r.* Peru
141 O3 **Puruvesi** *l.* Fin.
237 F6 **Purvis** *MS* U.S.A.
197 G4 **Pŭrvomay** Bulg.
116 E4 **Purwa** *Uttar Prad.* India
94 D4 **Purwakarta** *Jawa Barat* Indon.
95 E4 **Purwareja** *Jawa Tengah* Indon.
95 E4 **Purwodadi** *Jawa Tengah* Indon.
95 E4 **Purwokerto** *Jawa Tengah* Indon.
101 D4 **Puryŏng** N. Korea
114 C2 **Pus** *r.* India
183 F5 **Pusa** *r.* Spain
114 C2 **Pusad** *Mahar.* India
101 D6 **Pusan** S. Korea
173 E2 **Puschendorf** Ger.
171 F4 **Puschwitz** Ger.
136 F2 **Pushcha-Vodytsya** Ukr.
139 K4 **Pushchino** Rus. Fed.
134 I3 **Pushemskiy** Rus. Fed.
116 C4 **Pushkar** *Rajasthan* India
139 H2 **Pushkin** Rus. Fed.
Pushkino Azer. *see* **Biläsuvar**
120 A2 **Pushkino** Rus. Fed.
100 G3 **Pushkinskaya, Gora** *mt.* *Sakhalin* Rus. Fed.
138 G3 **Pushkinskiye Gory** Rus. Fed.
186 C2 **Pusilibro** *mt.* Spain
177 K4 **Püspökladány** Hungary
138 F2 **Püssi** Estonia
177 H2 **Pustá Polom** Czech Rep.
191 G2 **Pusteria, Val** *val.* Italy
177 G3 **Pusté Úľany** Slovakia
196 D4 **Pusti Lisac** *mt.* Yugo.
176 G2 **Pustiměř** Czech Rep.
136 B3 **Pustomyty** Ukr.
138 G3 **Pustoshka** Rus. Fed.
136 F3 **Pustovity** Ukr.
138 D1 **Pusula** Fin.
117 G5 **Pusur** *r.* Bangl.
175 L2 **Puszcza Augustowska** *for.* Pol.
175 I4 **Puszcza Mariańska** Pol.
174 D3 **Puszcza Natecka** *for.* Pol.
174 E3 **Puszczykowo** Pol.
177 G5 **Pusztakovácsi** Hungary
177 I5 **Pusztamérges** Hungary
177 I4 **Pusztamonostor** Hungary
177 I5 **Pusztaszer** Hungary
177 I4 **Pusztavacs** Hungary
177 H4 **Pusztavám** Hungary
260 B3 **Putaendo** Chile
159 F3 **Putanges-Pont-Écrepin** France
80 E3 **Putaruru** *North I.* N.Z.
170 E1 **Putbus** Ger.
Puteoli Italy *see* **Pozzuoli**
80 F3 **Putere** *North I.* N.Z.
134 L2 **Puteyets** Rus. Fed.
Puthein Myanmar *see* **Bassein**
109 F3 **Putian** *Fujian* China
192 A4 **Putifigari** *Sardegna* Italy
195 G2 **Putignano** Italy
134 I4 **Putilovo** Rus. Fed.
252 C3 **Putina** Peru
Puting *Jiangxi* China *see* **De'an**
245 F5 **Putla** Mex.
170 D2 **Putlitz** Ger.
197 H3 **Putna** *r.* Romania
233 H4 **Putnam** *CT* U.S.A.
235 E1 **Putnam County** *county* *NY* U.S.A.
235 E1 **Putnam Valley** *NY* U.S.A.
233 G3 **Putney** *VT* U.S.A.
177 J3 **Putnok** Hungary
131 K3 **Putorana, Gory** *mts* Rus. Fed.
94 C2 **Putrajaya** Malaysia
252 C4 **Putre** Chile
214 C3 **Putsonderwater** S. Africa
114 C4 **Puttalam** Sri Lanka
114 C4 **Puttalam Lagoon** Sri Lanka
165 D3 **Putte** Belgium
165 D3 **Putte** Neth.
157 G3 **Puttelange-aux-Lacs** France
164 E2 **Putten** Neth.
170 C1 **Puttgarden** Ger.
172 A2 **Püttlingen** Ger.
114 B3 **Puttur** *Karnataka* India
260 A4 **Putú** Chile
250 C4 **Putumayo** *dept* Col.
250 D5 **Putumayo** *r.* Col.
101 B7 **Putuo** *Zhejiang* China
126 E3 **Pütürge** Turkey
95 F2 **Putusibau** *Kalimantan Barat* Indon.
135 H5 **Putyatino** Rus. Fed.
136 C4 **Putyla** Ukr.
136 E2 **Putylovychi** Ukr.
137 G2 **Putyvl'** Ukr.
170 E2 **Putzar** Ger.
171 F4 **Putzkau** Ger.
240 □D9 **Puuanahulu** *HI* U.S.A.
240 □C8 **Puukolii** *HI* U.S.A.
141 N3 **Puula** *l.* Fin.
141 O3 **Puumala** Fin.
165 D3 **Puurs** Belgium
240 □A8 **Puuwai** *HI* U.S.A.
221 K3 **Puvurnituq** *Que.* Can.
107 F4 **Puxian** *Shanxi* China
238 B2 **Puyallup** *WA* U.S.A.
107 G5 **Puyang** *Henan* China
Puyang *Zhejiang* China *see* Pujiang
163 D4 **Puybrun** France
163 C5 **Puycasquier** France
159 F5 **Puy Crapaud** *hill* France
160 B3 **Puy-de-Dôme** *dept* *Auvergne* France
160 A3 **Puy de Dôme** *mt.* France
163 D5 **Puy de Faucher** *hill* France
161 D4 **Puy de la Gagère** *mt.* France
160 B3 **Puy de Montoncel** *mt.* France
160 A3 **Puy de Sancy** *mt.* France
162 D2 **Puy des Trois-Cornes** *hill* France
163 E5 **Puygouzon** France
161 A3 **Puy Griou** *mt.* France
161 E3 **Puy Gris** *mt.* France
160 B3 **Puy-Guillaume** France
163 D4 **Puylaroque** France
163 E5 **Puylaurens** France
163 D4 **Puy-l'Évêque** France
161 A3 **Puy Mary** *mt.* France
163 C5 **Puymaurin** France
163 C4 **Puymirol** France
162 C3 **Puymoyen** France
250 B5 **Puyo** Ecuador
163 B5 **Puyôo** France
161 E4 **Puy-St-Vincent** France
Puzol Spain *see* **Puçol**
177 H4 **Puztaszabolcs** Hungary
211 C6 **Pwani** *admin. reg.* Tanz.
209 F7 **Pweto** Dem. Rep. Congo
150 C2 **Pwllheli** *Gwynedd, Wales* U.K.
134 F3 **Pyal'ma** Rus. Fed.
96 A4 **Pyamalaw** *r.* Myanmar
123 G2 **Pyandzh** *r.* Afgh./Tajik.
Pyandzh *Khatlon* Tajik. *see* **Dusti**
Pyandzh *Khatlon* Tajik. *see* **Panj**
Pyanskiy Perevoz Rus. Fed. *see* **Perevoz**
140 O2 **Pyaozero, Ozero** *l.* Rus. Fed.
140 O2 **Pyaozerskiy** Rus. Fed.
96 A3 **Pyapon** Myanmar
130 J2 **Pyasina** *r.* Rus. Fed.
197 G4 **Pyasŭchnik** *r.* Bulg.
129 C1 **Pyatigorsk** Rus. Fed.
Pyatikhatka Ukr. *see* **P"yatykhatka**
Pyatikhatki Ukr. *see* **P"yatykhatky**
Pyatimar Kazakh. *see* **Pyatimarskoye**
120 B2 **Pyatimarskoye** Kazakh.
136 E2 **P"yatka** Ukr.
137 I2 **Pyatnitskoye** Rus. Fed.
139 K4 **Pyatovskiy** Rus. Fed.
137 H5 **P"yatykhatka** Ukr.
137 G3 **P"yatykhatky** Ukr.
96 B3 **Pyaunglaung** *r.* Myanmar
96 B2 **Pyawbwe** Myanmar
139 J1 **Pyazhelka** Rus. Fed.
134 K4 **Pychas** Rus. Fed.
96 A3 **Pyè** Myanmar
81 B7 **Pye, Mount** *hill* *South I.* N.Z.
138 E5 **Pyershamayski** Belarus
80 F2 **Pyes Pa** *North I.* N.Z.
136 E1 **Pyetrykaw** Belarus
140 N2 **Pyhäjoki** Fin.
140 N2 **Pyhäjoki** *r.* Fin.
140 N2 **Pyhäntä** Fin.
141 M3 **Pyhäranta** Fin.
140 N3 **Pyhäsalmi** Fin.
140 O3 **Pyhäselkä** Fin.
140 O3 **Pyhäselkä** *l.* Fin.
179 G2 **Pyhra** Austria
141 N3 **Pyhtää** Fin.
Pyin Myanmar *see* **Pyè**
96 B3 **Pyinmana** Myanmar
163 A4 **Pyla-sur-Mer** France
150 D3 **Pyle** *Bridgend, Wales* U.K.
199 E3 **Pyli** *Notio Aigaio* Greece
198 B2 **Pyli** *Thessalia* Greece
140 N3 **Pylkönmäki** Fin.
198 B3 **Pylos** Greece
136 D2 **Pylypovychi** Ukr.
101 C5 **Pyŏksŏng** N. Korea
101 C4 **Pyŏktong** N. Korea
101 C5 **P'yŏnggang** N. Korea
101 C5 **P'yŏngsong** N. Korea
101 C5 **P'yŏngt'aek** S. Korea
101 C5 **P'yŏngyang** N. Korea
178 D3 **Pyramidenspitze** *mt.* Austria
83 F4 **Pyramid Hill** *Vic.* Austr.
87 D7 **Pyramid Lake** *salt flat* *W.A.* Austr.
240 H1 **Pyramid Lake** *NV* U.S.A.
240 H2 **Pyramid Range** *mts* *NV* U.S.A.
173 F2 **Pyrbaum** Ger.
Pyrénées *mts* Europe *see* Pyrenees
186 F2 **Pyrenees** *mts* Europe
163 B5 **Pyrénées** *airport* France
163 B5 **Pyrénées-Atlantiques** *dept* *Aquitaine* France
163 E6 **Pyrénées-Orientales** *dept* *Languedoc-Roussillon* France
198 C2 **Pyrgetos** Greece
199 D2 **Pyrgi** *Voreio Aigaio* Greece
198 B3 **Pyrgos** Greece
136 E2 **Pyrizhky** Ukr.
137 G3 **Pyrohy** Ukr.
86 C4 **Pyrton, Mount** *hill* *W.A.* Austr.
137 G2 **Pyryatyn** Ukr.
174 C2 **Pyrzyce** Pol.
134 I4 **Pyshchug** Rus. Fed.
174 G5 **Pyskowice** Pol.
137 H3 **Pys'menne** Ukr.
174 G4 **Pyszna** *r.* Pol.
175 K5 **Pysznica** Pol.
138 F3 **Pytalovo** Rus. Fed.
96 B3 **Pyu** Myanmar
198 C2 **Pyxaria** *mt.* Greece

Q

126 E4 **Qaa** Lebanon
129 E3 **Qäbälä** Azer.
Qabanbay Kazakh. *see* Kabanbay
128 B3 **Qabātiya** West Bank
125 F3 **Qābil** Oman
129 E3 **Qabırrı** *r.* Azer.
Qabka *Xizang* China *see* Xaitongmoin
Qabqa *Qinghai* China *see* Gonghe
125 E4 **Qabr Hūd** Oman
Qabyrgha *r.* Kazakh. *see* Kabyrga
Qacentina Alg. *see* Constantine
129 D3 **Qach'aghani** Georgia
215 G4 **Qacha's Nek** Lesotho
129 F3 **Qäçräş** Azer.
122 D2 **Qadamgāli** Iran
124 B3 **Qaḍīmah** Saudi Arabia
127 G4 **Qādir Karam** Iraq
125 F5 **Qādub** *Suquṭrā* Yemen
122 B4 **Qā'emiyeh** Iran
198 B1 **Qafzez** *Kolonjë* Albania
107 H1 **Qagan** *Nei Mongol* China
107 G3 **Qagan Nur** *Nei Mongol* China
107 G3 **Qagan Nur** *Nei Mongol* China
107 G3 **Qagan Teg** *Nei Mongol* China
Qagan Us *Qinghai* China *see* Dulan
106 C4 **Qagan Us He** *r.* China
108 A1 **Qagca** *Sichuan* China
Qagchêng *Sichuan* China *see* Xiangcheng
Qahar Youyi Houqi *Nei Mongol* China *see* **Bayan Qagan**
Qahar Youyi Qianqi *Nei Mongol* China *see* **Togrog Ul**
Qahar Youyi Zhongqi *Nei Mongol* China *see* **Hobor**
124 D4 **Qahr, Jibāl al** *hills* Saudi Arabia
129 E4 **Qährämanlı** Azer.
Qahremānshahr Iran *see* Kermānshāh
106 C4 **Qaidam He** *r.* China
111 F4 **Qaidam Pendi** *basin* China
123 F2 **Qaisar** *r.* Afgh.
123 F3 **Qaisar, Koh-i-** *mt.* Afgh.
195 □ **Qala** *Gozo* Malta
215 G2 **Qalabotjha** S. Africa
203 G6 **Qala'en Nahl** Sudan
123 G2 **Qal'aikhum** Tajik.
Qalamshia Georgia *see* Gant'iadi
125 F5 **Qalansīyah** *Suquṭrā* Yemen
123 F3 **Qalāt** Afgh.
128 C2 **Qal'at al Ḥiṣn** *tourist site* Syria
128 B2 **Qal'at al Marqab** *tourist site* Syria
124 B2 **Qal'at al Mu'aẓẓam** Saudi Arabia
124 C3 **Qal'at Bīshah** Saudi Arabia
128 D2 **Qal'at Muqaybirah, Jabal** *mt.* Syria
127 G5 **Qal'at Ṣāliḥ** Iraq
Qalbī Zhotasy *mts* Kazakh. *see* **Kalbinskiy Khrebet**
122 A2 **Qal'eh Dāgh** *mt.* Iran
123 E3 **Qal 'eh-ye Now** Afgh.
125 G3 **Qalhāt** Oman
128 B3 **Qalqīlya** West Bank
Qalqutan Kazakh. *see* **Koluton**
203 F2 **Qalyûb** *Qalyûbîya* Egypt
126 C5 **Qalyûbîya** *governorate* Egypt
Qamanittuaq *Nunavut* Can. *see* Baker Lake
125 F4 **Qamar, Ghubbat al** *b.* Yemen
125 F4 **Qamar, Jabal al** *mts* Oman
129 E3 **Qämärvan** Azer.
Qamashi Uzbek. *see* **Kamashi**
108 A2 **Qamdo** *Xizang* China
79 □1 **Qamea** *i.* Fiji
202 C2 **Qamīnis** Libya
122 B3 **Qamṣar** Iran
Qamystybas Kazakh. *see* Kamyshlybash
Qandahar Afgh. *see* **Kandahār**
210 F2 **Qandala** Somalia
122 A2 **Qandaranbashi** *mt.* Iran
Qandyaghash Kazakh. *see* Kandyagash
Qapal Kazakh. *see* **Kapal**
122 C2 **Qapan** Iran
110 C3 **Qapqal** *Xinjiang* China
Qapshagay Kazakh. *see* Kapchagay
Qapshagay Bögeni *resr* Kazakh. *see* **Kapchagayskoye Vodokhranilishche**
221 N3 **Qaqortoq** Greenland
125 F4 **Qarā', Jabal al** *mts* Oman
Qara Āghach *r.* Iran *see* **Mand, Rūd-e**
128 B3 **Qaraaoun** Lebanon
129 E3 **Qarabağ Silsiläsi** *hills* Azer.
129 D4 **Qarabağ Yaylası** *plat.* Armenia/Azer.
Qarabas Kazakh. *see* **Karabas**
Qarabulaq *Almatinskaya Oblast'* Kazakh. *see* **Karabulak**
Qarabutaq Kazakh. *see* **Karabutak**
129 F4 **Qaraçala** Azer.
Qara Ertis *r.* China/Kazakh. *see* **Ertix He**
Qaraghandy Kazakh. *see* Karaganda
Qaraghandy Oblysy *admin. div.* Kazakh. *see* **Karagandinskaya Oblast'**
Qaraghayly Kazakh. *see* Karagayly
124 D4 **Qārah, Jabal al** *hill* Saudi Arabia
Qaraköl Kazakh. *see* **Karakol'**
129 F3 **Qaramäryam** Azer.
122 A2 **Qaranqu** *r.* Iran
Qaraoy *Almatinskaya Oblast'* Kazakh. *see* **Karaoy**
Qara Özek Uzbek. *see* Karauzyak
Qaraqalpaqstan Respublikasy *aut. rep.* Uzbek. *see* **Karakalpakistan, Respublika**
Qaraqum *des.* Kazakh. *see* **Karakum, Peski**
Qaraqum *des.* Turkm. *see* **Karakumy, Peski**
Qarasor Köli *l.* Kazakh. *see* **Karasor, Ozero**
129 F3 **Qarasu** Azer.
129 E3 **Qarasu** *r.* Azer.
129 E4 **Qarasu** *r.* Azer.
Qarasū *Kustanayskaya Oblast'* Kazakh. *see* **Karasu**
Qara Şū Chāy *r.* Syria/Turkey *see* **Karasu**
123 F3 **Qara Tarai** *mt.* Afgh.
Qarataū Kazakh. *see* **Karatau**
Qarataū Zhotasy *mts* Kazakh. *see* **Karatau, Khrebet**
Qaratöbe Kazakh. *see* Karatobe
Qaratoghay Kazakh. *see* Karatogay
Qaraton Kazakh. *see* **Karaton**
Qaraūyl *Vostochnyy Kazakhstan* Kazakh. *see* **Karaul**
129 E3 **Qarayeri** Azer.
Qarazhal Kazakh. *see* **Karazhal**
210 F2 **Qardho** Somalia
122 B3 **Qareh Chāy** *r.* Iran
122 A2 **Qareh Dāgh** *mt.* Iran
122 A2 **Qareh Dāsh, Kūh-e** *mt.* Iran
122 A2 **Qareh Sū** *r.* Iran
129 D4 **Qareh Ẕīā' od Dīn** Iran
106 B4 **Qarhan** *Qinghai* China
Qarkilik *Xinjiang* China *see* Ruoqiang
124 C3 **Qarnayṭ, Jabal** *hill* Saudi Arabia
203 G2 **Qarn el Kabsh, Gebel** *mt.* Egypt
123 H2 **Qarokŭl** *l.* Tajik.
Qarqan *Xinjiang* China *see* Qiemo
110 D4 **Qarqan He** *r.* China
Qarqaraly Kazakh. *see* Karkaralinsk
129 E4 **Qarqarçay** *r.* Azer.
110 D3 **Qarqi** *Xinjiang* China
120 C5 **Qārqi** Iran
123 F2 **Qarqīn** Afgh.
Qarsaqbay Kazakh. *see* Karsakpay
Qarshi Uzbek. *see* **Karshi**
Qarshi Chŭli *plain* Uzbek. *see* **Karshinskaya Step'**
128 B2 **Qartaba** Lebanon
127 H5 **Qārūh, Jazīrat** *i.* Kuwait
125 D2 **Qaryat al Ulyā** Saudi Arabia
122 C2 **Qāsam, Kūh-e** *mt.* Iran
122 D3 **Qasamī** Iran
123 E3 **Qasa Murg** *mts* Afgh.
117 F4 **Qasba** *Bihar* India
Qashqadaryo *r.* Uzbek. *see* Kashkadar'ya
Qashqadaryo Wiloyati *admin. div.* Uzbek. *see* **Kashkadar'inskaya Oblast'**
221 M3 **Qasigiannguit** Greenland
Qaskelen Kazakh. *see* Kaskelen
107 F3 **Qasq** *Nei Mongol* China
128 B4 **Qaṣr ad Dayr, Jabal** *mt.* Jordan
128 C2 **Qaṣr al Ḥayr** *tourist site* Syria
128 C4 **Qaṣr 'Amrah** *tourist site* Jordan
127 H5 **Qaṣr aṣ Ṣabīyah** Kuwait
128 C3 **Qaṣr Burqu'** *tourist site* Jordan
122 E5 **Qaṣr-e-Qand** Iran
202 E3 **Qasr Farafra** Egypt
124 D3 **Qaṣr Ḥimām** Saudi Arabia
124 D5 **Qa'ṭabah** Yemen
128 C3 **Qaṭanā** Syria
125 E2 **Qatar** *country* Asia
119 H5 **Qatār, Jabal** *hill* Oman
122 D2 **Qatlish** Iran
202 E2 **Qattâra, Râs** *esc.* Egypt
202 E2 **Qattâra Depression** Egypt
Qaṭṭārah, Munkhafaḍ al *depr.* Egypt *see* **Qattâra Depression**
129 E3 **Qax** Azer.
122 D3 **Qāyen** Iran
Qayghy Kazakh. *see* **Kayga**
Qaynar Kazakh. *see* **Kaynar**
Qayraqty Kazakh. *see* **Kayrakty**
123 G1 **Qayroqqum** Tajik.
129 E3 **Qaysa** Georgia
128 C4 **Qaysīyah, Qa' al** *imp. l.* Jordan
127 F4 **Qayyārah** Iraq
Qazaly Kazakh. *see* **Kazalinsk**
129 E4 **Qazangödağ** *mt.* Armenia/Azer.
Qazaq Shyghanaghy *b.* Kazakh. *see* **Kazakhskiy Zaliv**
Qazaqstan *country* Asia *see* Kazakhstan
129 D3 **Qazax** Azer.
129 D2 **Qazbegi** Georgia
123 G5 **Qazi Ahmad** Pak.
129 F3 **Qazımämmäd** Azer.
122 B2 **Qazvīn** Iran
122 B2 **Qazvīn** *prov.* Iran
Qazyqurt *Yuzhnyy Kazakhstan* Kazakh. *see* **Kazygurt**
106 D3 **Qeh** *Nei Mongol* China
79 □1 **Qelelevu** *i.* Fiji
198 B1 **Qelqëzës, Mali i** *mt.* Albania
203 G3 **Qena** Egypt
124 A2 **Qena** *governorate* Egypt
221 M3 **Qeqertarsuaq** Greenland
221 M3 **Qeqertarsuaq** *i.* Greenland
221 M3 **Qeqertarsuup Tunua** *b.* Greenland
122 D5 **Qeshm** Iran
122 D5 **Qeshm** *i.* Iran
122 B2 **Qeydār** Iran
122 C5 **Qeys** *i.* Iran
122 B2 **Qezel Owzan, Rūdkhāneh-ye** *r.* Iran
129 D4 **Qezel Qeshlāq** Iran
107 G5 **Qi** *r.* China
107 E5 **Qian** *r.* China
107 H4 **Qian'an** *Hebei* China
107 J2 **Qian'an** *Jilin* China
108 D3 **Qiancheng** *Hunan* China
107 H5 **Qiang** *r.* China
Qian Gorlos *Jilin* China *see* Qianguozhen
100 C3 **Qianguozhen** *Jilin* China
108 D2 **Qianjiang** *Chongqing* China
109 E2 **Qianjiang** *Hubei* China
100 E3 **Qianjin** *Heilong.* China
108 B2 **Qianning** *Sichuan* China
109 F2 **Qianshan** *Anhui* China
107 I3 **Qian Shan** *mts* China
264 R4 **Qiansuo** *Zhejiang* China
108 B2 **Qianwei** *Sichuan* China
108 C3 **Qianxi** *Guizhou* China
107 H3 **Qianxi** *Hebei* China
107 F5 **Qianxian** *Shaanxi* China
108 D3 **Qianyang** *Hunan* China
107 E5 **Qianyang** *Shaanxi* China
109 F2 **Qianyang** *Zhejiang* China
Qianyou *Shaanxi* China *see* Zhashui
108 B3 **Qiaojia** *Yunnan* China
Qiaoshan *Shaanxi* China *see* Huangling
Qiaotou *Qinghai* China *see* Datong
108 B3 **Qiaotou** *Yunnan* China
Qiaowa *Sichuan* China *see* **Muli**
106 C3 **Qiaowan** *Gansu* China
Qiaozhuang *Sichuan* China *see* Qingchuan
124 D2 **Qibā'** Saudi Arabia
215 F3 **Qibing** S. Africa
Qibray Uzbek. *see* **Kibray**
109 E2 **Qichun** *Hubei* China
109 E3 **Qidong** *Hunan* China
109 G2 **Qidong** *Jiangsu* China
111 D4 **Qiemo** *Xinjiang* China
107 H4 **Qihe** *Shandong* China
108 C2 **Qijiang** *Chongqing* China
221 L3 **Qikiqtarjuaq** *Nunavut* Can.
Qili *Anhui* China *see* **Shitai**
106 D4 **Qilian** *Qinghai* China
106 C4 **Qilian Shan** *mts* China
106 C4 **Qilian Shan** *mts* China
Qīma Kazakh. *see* **Kiyma**
111 E4 **Qimantag** *mts* China
109 F2 **Qimen** *Anhui* China
221 L2 **Qimusseriarsuaq** *b.* Greenland
107 G5 **Qin** *r.* China
Qinā Egypt *see* **Qena**
125 E4 **Qināb, Wādī** *r.* Yemen
106 E5 **Qin'an** *Gansu* China
Qincheng *Jiangxi* China *see* Nanfeng
100 B4 **Qing** *r.* China
100 C3 **Qing'an** *Heilong.* China
Qingcheng *Gansu* China *see* Qingyang
101 B4 **Qingchengzi** *Liaoning* China
108 C1 **Qingchuan** *Sichuan* China
107 I4 **Qingdao** *Shandong* China
100 C3 **Qinggang** *Heilong.* China
Qinggil *Xinjiang* China *see* Qinghe
108 D2 **Qingguandu** *Hunan* China
106 C4 **Qinghai** *prov.* China
106 D4 **Qinghai Hu** *salt l.* *Qinghai* China
106 C4 **Qinghai Nanshan** *mts* China
107 G4 **Qinghe** *Hebei* China
106 A2 **Qinghe** *Xinjiang* China
Qinghua *Henan* China *see* **Bo'ai**
107 F4 **Qingjian** *Shaanxi* China
Qingjiang *Jiangsu* China *see* Huaiyin
Qingjiang *Jiangxi* China *see* Zhangshu
108 D2 **Qing Jiang** *r.* China
Qingkou *Jiangsu* China *see* Ganyu
109 F3 **Qingliu** *Fujian* China
108 C3 **Qinglong** *Guizhou* China
107 H3 **Qinglong** *Hebei* China
107 H4 **Qinglong** *r.* China
109 G2 **Qingpu** *Shanghai* China
Qingquan *Hubei* China *see* Xishui
Qingshan *Heilong.* China *see* Dedu
108 B2 **Qingshen** *Sichuan* China
106 D4 **Qingshizui** *Qinghai* China
106 E5 **Qingshui** *Gansu* China
107 F4 **Qingshuihe** *Nei Mongol* China
108 A1 **Qingshuihe** *Qinghai* China
109 G2 **Qingtian** *Zhejiang* China
106 E4 **Qingtongxia** *Ningxia* China
107 H4 **Qingxian** *Hebei* China
107 G4 **Qingxu** *Shanxi* China
109 F2 **Qingyang** *Anhui* China
107 E4 **Qingyang** *Gansu* China
Qingyang *Jiangsu* China *see* Sihong
Qingyuan *Gansu* China *see* Weiyuan
109 E4 **Qingyuan** *Guangdong* China
Qingyuan *Guangxi* China *see* Yizhou
100 C4 **Qingyuan** *Liaoning* China
Qingyuan *Shanxi* China *see* Qingxu
109 F3 **Qingyuan** *Zhejiang* China
107 H4 **Qingyun** *Shandong* China
111 D5 **Qing Zang Gaoyuan** *plat.* *Xizang* China
108 C3 **Qingzhen** *Guizhou* China
Qingzhou *Hebei* China *see* Qingxian
109 D2 **Qingzhou** *Hubei* China
107 H4 **Qingzhou** *Shandong* China
107 H4 **Qinhuangdao** *Hebei* China
Qinjiang *Jiangxi* China *see* Shicheng
108 C1 **Qin Ling** *mts* China
107 G5 **Qinshui** *Shanxi* China
Qinting *Jiangxi* China *see* Lianhua
107 G4 **Qinxian** *Shanxi* China
107 G5 **Qinyang** *Henan* China
107 G4 **Qinyuan** *Shanxi* China
108 D4 **Qinzhou** *Guangxi* China
108 D5 **Qionghai** *Hainan* China
Qiongjiexue *Xizang* China *see* Qonggyai
108 B2 **Qionglai** *Sichuan* China
108 B2 **Qionglai Shan** *mts* *Sichuan* China
108 D5 **Qiongshan** *Hainan* China
Qiongxi *Sichuan* China *see* Hongyuan
108 D5 **Qiongzhong** *Hainan* China
108 D5 **Qiongzhou Haixia** *str.* China
107 I2 **Qiqihar** *Heilong.* China
122 C4 **Qīr** Iran
111 C4 **Qira** *Xinjiang* China
129 E4 **Qırmızı Bazar** Azer.
129 F4 **Qırmızkänd** Azer.
128 B4 **Qiryat Gat** Israel
128 B3 **Qiryat Shemona** Israel
Qishan *Anhui* China *see* Qimen
107 E5 **Qishan** *Shaanxi* China
125 E5 **Qishn** Yemen
128 B3 **Qishon** *r.* Israel
124 C3 **Qishrān Island** Saudi Arabia
126 E5 **Qitab ash Shāmah** *vol. crater* Saudi Arabia
110 E3 **Qitai** *Xinjiang* China
100 D3 **Qitaihe** *Heilong.* China
125 F4 **Qitbīt, Wādī** *r.* Oman
108 C3 **Qiubei** *Yunnan* China
109 E2 **Qiujin** *Jiangxi* China
107 I4 **Qixia** *Shandong* China
107 G5 **Qixian** *Henan* China
107 G5 **Qixian** *Henan* China
107 G4 **Qixian** *Shanxi* China
100 E3 **Qixing** *r.* China
109 D3 **Qiyang** *Hunan* China
129 F4 **Qızılağac Körfäzi** *b.* Azer.
129 F3 **Qızıldaş** Azer.
Qizqetkan Uzbek. *see* Kyzketken
215 G5 **Qoboqobo** S. Africa
129 F3 **Qobustan** Azer.
Qoghaly Kazakh. *see* **Kugaly**
Qogir Feng *mt.* China/Jammu and Kashmir *see* **K2**
122 A2 **Qojūr** Iran
215 G5 **Qolora Mouth** S. Africa
122 B3 **Qom** Iran
122 B3 **Qom** *prov.* Iran
Qomdo *Xizang* China *see* Qumdo
122 B3 **Qomishēh** Iran
Qomolangma Feng *mt.* China/Nepal *see* **Everest, Mount**
129 F3 **Qonaqkänd** Azer.
111 E6 **Qonggyai** *Xizang* China
107 F3 **Qongj** *Nei Mongol* China
Qongrat Uzbek. *see* **Kungrad**
Qongyrat *Karagandinskaya Oblast'* Kazakh. *see* Kounradskiy
Qongyrat *Karagandinskaya Oblast'* Kazakh. *see* **Konyrat**
Qongyröleng Kazakh. *see* Konyrolen
Qonystanū Kazakh. *see* Konystanu
Qoqek *Xinjiang* China *see* Tacheng
215 F4 **Qoqodala** S. Africa
Qoradaryo *r.* Kyrg. *see* Kara-Darya
Qoraghaty Kazakh. *see* Kuragaty
Qoraqalpoghiston Uzbek. *see* Karakalpakiya
Qoraqalpoghiston Respublikasi *aut. rep.* Uzbek. *see* **Karakalpakistan, Respublika**
Qoraūzak Uzbek. *see* Karauzyak
Qorday Kazakh. *see* **Kurday**
Qorghalzhyn Kazakh. *see* **Kurgal'dzhinskiy**
128 C2 **Qornet es Saouda** *mt.* Lebanon
129 C2 **Qornisi** Georgia
Qorowulbozor Uzbek. *see* Karaulbazar
122 A3 **Qorveh** Iran
127 F3 **Qosh Tepe** Iraq
129 E3 **Qoşqarçay** *r.* Azer.
Qosshaghyl Kazakh. *see* Koschagyl
Qostanay Kazakh. *see* Kostanay
Qostanay Oblysy *admin. div.* Kazakh. *see* **Kustanayskaya Oblast'**
122 D5 **Qoṭbābād** Iran
122 A2 **Qoṭūr** Iran
128 C2 **Qoubaiyat** Lebanon
129 D3 **Qovlar** Azer.

Rooaun to Saalfelden am Steinernen Meer
355

147 C3 Rooaun Rep. of Ireland
215 G2 Roodebank S. Africa
164 F1 Roodeschool Neth.
215 G3 Rooiberg mt. Free State S. Africa
214 C5 Rooiberg mt. W. Cape S. Africa
215 G1 Rooikraal S. Africa
215 F2 Rooiwal S. Africa
147 B3 Roonah Quay Rep. of Ireland
164 E1 Roordahuizum Neth.
116 D3 Roorkee Uttar Prad. India
215 G3 Roosboom S. Africa
164 D3 Roosendaal Neth.
241 L5 Roosevelt AZ U.S.A.
235 D2 Roosevelt NJ U.S.A.
241 M1 Roosevelt UT U.S.A.
222 E3 Roosevelt, Mount B.C. Can.
235 D3 Roosevelt City NJ U.S.A.
262 N1 Roosevelt Island Antarctica
147 D3 Roosky Leitrim Rep. of Ireland
147 C3 Roosky Mayo Rep. of Ireland
215 G1 Roossenekal S. Africa
222 F2 Root r. N.W.T. Can.
226 B4 Root r. MN U.S.A.
175 J6 Ropa Pol.
175 J6 Ropa r. Pol.
138 E3 Ropaži Latvia
175 J5 Ropczyce Pol.
84 C2 Roper r. N.T. Austr.
84 C2 Roper Bar N.T. Austr.
85 G4 Roper Creek r. Qld Austr.
182 E2 Roperuelos del Páramo Spain
84 C2 Roper Valley N.T. Austr.
175 K6 Ropienka Pol.
178 B3 Roppen Austria
161 F4 Roquebillière France
161 B5 Roquebrun France
161 F5 Roquebrune-Cap-Martin France
161 E5 Roquebrune-sur-Argens France
163 C4 Roquecor France
163 E5 Roquecourbe France
216 □3d Roque de los Muchachos vol. La Palma Canary Is
163 B4 Roquefort France
161 A5 Roquefort-sur-Soulzon France
161 C4 Roquemaure France
261 H4 Roque Pérez Arg.
161 F5 Roquesteron France
186 D4 Roquetas Spain
185 H4 Roquetas de Mar Spain
161 D5 Roquevaire France
251 F4 Roraima state Brazil
251 F3 Roraima, Mount Guyana
116 C3 Rori Punjab India
140 J3 Røros Norway
190 E1 Rorschach Switz.
142 D4 Rørvig Denmark
140 J2 Rørvik Norway
175 M2 Ros' Belarus
138 E5 Ros' r. Belarus
136 F3 Ros' r. Ukr.
191 G3 Rosà Italy
190 C3 Rosa, Monte mt. Italy/Switz.
190 C2 Rosablanche mt. Switz.
216 □1c Rosais São Jorge Azores
184 C3 Rosal de la Frontera Spain
238 C2 Rosalia WA U.S.A.
246 B3 Rosalind Bank sea feature Caribbean Sea
240 H4 Rosamond CA U.S.A.
256 A5 Rosana Brazil
178 B3 Rosanna r. Austria
161 D4 Rosans France
147 D1 Rosapenna Rep. of Ireland
261 G3 Rosario Arg.
254 D2 Rosário Brazil
242 B2 Rosario Baja California Norte Mex.
244 B2 Rosario Sinaloa Mex.
242 C3 Rosario Sonora Mex.
253 F6 Rosario Para.
92 B2 Rosario Luzon Phil.
92 B3 Rosario Luzon Phil.
184 B3 Rosário Port.
261 I4 Rosario Uru.
250 C2 Rosario Venez.
258 D2 Rosario de la Frontera Arg.
258 D2 Rosario de Lerma Arg.
261 H3 Rosario del Tala Arg.
255 B9 Rosário do Sul Brazil
253 F3 Rosário Oeste Brazil
242 A1 Rosarito Baja California Norte Mex.
242 B2 Rosarito Baja California Norte Mex.
242 C3 Rosarito Baja California Sur Mex.
195 E4 Rosarno Italy
Rosas Spain see Roses
Rosas, Golfo de b. Spain see Roses, Golf de
137 F3 Rosava r. Ukr.
250 B4 Rosa Zárate Ecuador
169 D5 Rosbach vor der Höhe Ger.
147 C2 Rosbeg Rep. of Ireland
147 E4 Rosbercon Rep. of Ireland
158 B3 Roscanvel France
168 F3 Rosche Ger.
179 G2 Röschitz Austria
175 H3 Rościszewo Pol.
226 C4 Roscoe IL U.S.A.
158 C3 Roscoff France
147 C3 Roscommon Rep. of Ireland
147 C3 Roscommon county Rep. of Ireland
226 E3 Roscommon MI U.S.A.
147 D4 Roscrea Rep. of Ireland
169 E4 Rosdorf Ger.
84 C2 Rose r. N.T. Austr.
193 I5 Rose Italy
240 H2 Rose, Mount NV U.S.A.
247 □2 Roseau Dominica
236 E1 Roseau MN U.S.A.
236 D1 Roseau r. MN U.S.A.
149 H3 Roseberry Topping hill England U.K.
84 D5 Roseberth Qld Austr.
83 F5 Rosebery Tas. Austr.
225 J4 Rose Blanche Nfld. Can.
222 H5 Rosebud r. Alta Can.
238 F2 Rosebud MT U.S.A.
238 F2 Rosebud Creek r. MT U.S.A.
238 B3 Roseburg OR U.S.A.
227 E3 Rose City MI U.S.A.
226 A4 Rose Creek MN U.S.A.
85 G5 Rosedale Qld Austr.
83 F4 Rosedale Vic. Austr.
234 B3 Rosedale MD U.S.A.
237 F5 Rosedale MS U.S.A.
149 I3 Rosedale Abbey North Yorkshire, England U.K.
214 D5 Rosedene S. Africa
165 D4 Rosée Belgium
179 F4 Rosegg Austria
246 □ Rose Hall Jamaica
146 D4 Rosehall Highland, Scotland U.K.
146 F4 Rosehearty Aberdeenshire, Scotland U.K.
210 B2 Roseires Reservoir Sudan
75 H4 Rose Island American Samoa
231 □2 Rose Island Bahamas
186 D4 Rosell Spain
235 D2 Roselle NJ U.S.A.
146 D4 Rosemarkie Highland, Scotland U.K.
86 C4 Rosemary Island W.A. Austr.
147 D3 Rosenallis Rep. of Ireland
237 E6 Rosenberg TX U.S.A.
142 B2 Rosendal Norway
215 F3 Rosendal S. Africa
226 C4 Rosendale WI U.S.A.
172 C3 Rosenfeld Ger.
168 E2 Rosengarten Ger.
234 C3 Rosenhayn NJ U.S.A.
173 G4 Rosenheim Ger.
179 E4 Rosennock mt. Austria
170 E2 Rosenow Ger.
179 F4 Rosental val. Austria
169 D5 Rosenthal Ger.
241 M5 Rose Peak AZ U.S.A.
143 G2 Roserberg Sweden
186 G2 Roses Spain
186 G2 Roses, Golf de b. Spain
234 C2 Roseto PA U.S.A.
195 F3 Roseto Capo Spulico Italy
193 G2 Roseto degli Abruzzi Italy
193 H3 Roseto Valfortore Italy
223 J5 Rosetown Sask. Can.
Rosetta Egypt see Rashîd
85 F4 Rosetta Creek r. Qld Austr.
223 K4 Rose Valley Sask. Can.
240 G2 Roseville CA U.S.A.
236 F3 Roseville IL U.S.A.
227 F4 Roseville MI U.S.A.
232 B5 Roseville OH U.S.A.
146 E6 Rosewell Midlothian, Scotland U.K.
85 H5 Rosewood Qld Austr.
232 B4 Rosewood OH U.S.A.
139 L4 Roshal' Rus. Fed.
138 G1 Roshchino Rus. Fed.
157 H4 Rosheim France
226 C3 Rosholt WI U.S.A.
212 C5 Rosh Pinah Namibia
146 C5 Roshven Highland, Scotland U.K.
177 L5 Roșia Romania
176 F2 Rosice Czech Rep.
161 B3 Rosières France
156 C3 Rosières-en-Santerre France
156 E4 Rosières-près-Troyes France
190 F5 Rosignano Marittimo Italy
86 B4 Rosily Island W.A. Austr.
177 H2 Rosina Slovakia
197 H3 Roșiori Romania
197 G3 Roșiori de Vede Romania
197 H4 Rositsa Bulg.
197 G4 Rositsa r. Bulg.
171 D4 Rositz Ger.
146 B4 Roskhill Highland, Scotland U.K.
142 E4 Roskilde Denmark
142 E4 Roskilde county Denmark
174 E3 Rosko Pol.
198 A1 Roskovec Albania
171 D3 Roskow Ger.
241 L5 Roskruge Mountains AZ U.S.A.
171 C5 Röslau Ger.
171 D5 Röslau r. Ger.
139 I5 Roslavl' Rus. Fed.
146 E6 Roslin Midlothian, Scotland U.K.
140 P1 Roslyakovo Rus. Fed.
134 I4 Roslyatino Rus. Fed.
164 E3 Rosmalen Neth.
182 C5 Rosmaninhal Port.
215 E4 Rosmead S. Africa
147 B3 Rosmuck Rep. of Ireland
174 E1 Rosnowo Pol.
191 H3 Rosolina Italy
191 H3 Rosolina Mare Italy
194 D6 Rosolini Sicilia Italy
197 E5 Rosoman Macedonia
156 D4 Rosoy France
178 D3 Röspitze mt. Austria/Italy
158 C4 Rosporden France
169 C5 Rösrath Ger.
83 F5 Ross Tas. Austr.
222 C2 Ross r. Y.T. Can.
81 C5 Ross South I. N.Z.
81 E4 Ross, Mount hill North I. N.Z.
195 F3 Rossano Italy
191 G3 Rossano Veneto Italy
182 B3 Rossas Port.
147 B3 Rossaveel Rep. of Ireland
173 G3 Roßbach Ger.
171 C4 Roßbach Ger.
225 H2 Ross Bay Junction Nfld. Can.
147 B5 Rossbrin Rep. of Ireland
147 B3 Rosscahill Rep. of Ireland
147 B5 Ross Carbery Rep. of Ireland
147 C2 Rosscor Northern Ireland U.K.
262 N2 Ross Dependency Antarctica
172 C2 Roßdorf Ger.
186 D3 Rosselló Spain
191 F4 Rossenno r. Italy
147 C1 Rosses Bay Rep. of Ireland
147 C2 Rosses Point Rep. of Ireland
150 E1 Rossett Wrexham, Wales U.K.
173 E4 Roßhaupten Ger.
263 M1 Ross Ice Shelf Antarctica
190 D4 Rossiglione Italy
165 E5 Rossignol Belgium
169 E3 Rössing (Nordstemmen) Ger.
149 H4 Rossington South Yorkshire, England U.K.
147 C2 Rossinver Rep. of Ireland
184 B1 Rossio ao Sul do Tejo Port.
263 L1 Ross Island Antarctica
87 D7 Rossiter Bay W.A. Austr.
Rossiyskaya Sovetskaya Federativnaya Sotsialisticheskaya Respublika country Asia/Europe see Russian Federation
171 C4 Roßla Ger.
222 G5 Rossland B.C. Can.
147 E4 Rosslare Rep. of Ireland
147 E4 Rosslare Harbour Rep. of Ireland
147 E4 Rosslare Point Rep. of Ireland
171 D4 Roßlau Ger.
147 D2 Rosslea Northern Ireland U.K.
171 C4 Roßleben Ger.
179 F3 Roßleithen Austria
227 I3 Rossmore Ont. Can.
147 C2 Rossnowlagh Rep. of Ireland
206 B2 Rosso Maur.
140 L3 Rossön Sweden
150 E3 Ross-on-Wye Herefordshire, England U.K.
Rossony Belarus see Rasony
135 G6 Rossosh' Rus. Fed.
175 L4 Rossosz Pol.
174 G4 Rossoszyca Pol.
215 F4 Rossouw S. Africa
170 D2 Rossow Ger.
226 D1 Rossport Ont. Can.
84 C4 Ross River N.T. Austr.
222 C2 Ross River Y.T. Can.
263 L1 Ross Sea Antarctica
173 E2 Roßtal Ger.
164 E3 Rossum Neth.
140 K2 Røssvatnet l. Norway
226 B4 Rossville IA U.S.A.
226 D5 Rossville IL U.S.A.
226 D5 Rossville IN U.S.A.
234 B2 Rossville PA U.S.A.
171 E4 Roßwein Ger.
222 D4 Rosswood B.C. Can.
127 G3 Rōst Iraq
140 K2 Røst Norway
136 F3 Rostabytsya r. Ukr.
123 G2 Rostāq Afgh.
122 C4 Rostāq Iran
174 E3 Rostarzewo Pol.
140 K2 Røsthavet sea chan. Norway
223 J4 Rosthern Sask. Can.
170 D1 Rostock Ger.
140 M1 Rostonsölkä ridge Sweden
139 L3 Rostov Rus. Fed.
135 G7 Rostov-na-Donu Rus. Fed.
Rostov Oblast admin. div. Rus. Fed. see Rostovskaya Oblast'
Rostov-on-Don Rus. Fed. see Rostov-na-Donu
135 H7 Rostovskaya Oblast' admin. div. Rus. Fed.
215 E2 Rostrataville S. Africa
158 C3 Rostrenen France
147 E2 Rostrevor Northern Ireland U.K.
147 B3 Rosturk Rep. of Ireland
140 K2 Røsvik Norway
140 M2 Rosvik Sweden
231 C5 Roswell GA U.S.A.
239 F5 Roswell NM U.S.A.
177 J5 Röszke Hungary
172 D3 Rot r. Ger.
91 K4 Rota i. N. Mariana Is
184 D4 Rota Spain
172 D4 Rotach r. Ger.
193 I5 Rota Greca Italy
173 E2 Rot am See Ger.
173 E3 Rot an der Rot Ger.
171 D5 Rotava Czech Rep.
Rotch Island Gilbert Is Kiribati see Tamana
93 B5 Rote i. Indon.
193 G3 Rotello Italy
168 E2 Rotenburg (Wümme) Ger.
169 E4 Rotenburg an der Fulda Ger.
171 C5 Roter Main r. Ger.
178 A3 Rote Wand mt. Austria
Rot-Front Ukr. see Dobropillya
173 F2 Roth Ger.
173 E3 Roth r. Ger.
173 F2 Roth r. Ger.
171 D4 Rötha Ger.
169 D5 Rothaargebirge hills Ger.
149 H2 Rothbury Northumberland, England U.K.
149 H2 Rothbury Forest England U.K.
173 F2 Röthenbach an der Pegnitz Ger.
172 C2 Rothenberg Ger.
172 D2 Rothenbuch Ger.
171 C4 Rothenburg Ger.
171 F4 Rothenburg (Oberlausitz) Ger.
173 E2 Rothenburg ob der Tauber Ger.
158 E3 Rothéneuf France
172 D2 Rothenfels Ger.
171 C5 Rothenstein Ger.
151 G4 Rother r. England U.K.
262 T2 Rothera research stn Antarctica
151 H3 Rotherfield East Sussex, England U.K.
81 D5 Rotherham South I. N.Z.
149 H4 Rotherham South Yorkshire, England U.K.
146 E4 Rothes Moray, Scotland U.K.
146 C6 Rothesay Argyll and Bute, Scotland U.K.
165 E4 Rotheux-Rimière Belgium
146 F2 Rothiesholm Orkney, Scotland U.K.
173 E2 Röthlein Ger.
172 B4 Rothrist Switz.
226 C3 Rothschild WI U.S.A.
262 T2 Rothschild Island Antarctica
234 B2 Rothsville PA U.S.A.
151 G2 Rothwell Northamptonshire, England U.K.
149 H4 Rothwell West Yorkshire, England U.K.
169 E4 Rothwesten (Fuldatal) Ger.
Roti i. Indon. see Rote
83 F3 Roto N.S.W. Austr.
80 F3 Rotoiti, Lake North I. N.Z.
81 D4 Rotoiti, Lake South I. N.Z.
Rotomagus France see Rouen
81 C5 Rotomanu South I. N.Z.
193 I5 Rotonda Italy
195 F2 Rotondella Italy
192 B2 Rotondo, Monte mt. Corse France
81 D4 Rotoroa, Lake South I. N.Z.
80 F3 Rotorua North I. N.Z.
80 F3 Rotorua, Lake North I. N.Z.
165 D4 Rotselaar Belgium
178 D4 Rotsteinberg mt. Austria
173 E4 Rott Ger.
173 H3 Rott r. Ger.
171 D4 Rotta Ger.
173 F4 Rottach-Egern Ger.
173 G4 Rott am Inn Ger.
157 G4 Rotte r. France
172 D3 Rottenacker Ger.
173 E2 Röttenbach Bayern Ger.
173 F2 Röttenbach Bayern Ger.
171 C5 Rottenbach Thüringen Ger.
173 E4 Rottenbuch Ger.
172 C3 Rottenburg am Neckar Ger.
173 G3 Rottenburg an der Laaber Ger.
173 E2 Rottendorf Ger.
179 F3 Rottenmann Austria
164 D3 Rotterdam Neth.
233 G3 Rotterdam NY U.S.A.
164 F1 Rottevalle Neth.
173 H3 Rotthalmünster Ger.
151 G4 Rottingdean Brighton and Hove, England U.K.
172 D2 Röttingham Ger.
169 F4 Rottleberode Ger.
142 E2 Rottnan r. Sweden
87 B7 Rottnest Island W.A. Austr.
190 E3 Rottofreno Italy
172 C3 Rottweil Ger.
77 H3 Rotuma i. Fiji
197 G4 Rotunda Romania
140 K3 Rötviken Sweden
173 F4 Rotwand mt. Ger.
173 G2 Rötz Ger.
158 E4 Rouans France
156 D2 Roubaix France
161 C4 Roubion r. France
186 E2 Rouch, Mont mt. France/Spain
176 F2 Rouchovany Czech Rep.
176 D1 Roudnice nad Labem Czech Rep.
156 B3 Rouen France
157 H5 Rouffach France
162 E3 Rouffiac France
162 C3 Rouffignac France
158 E4 Rougé France
160 E1 Rougemont France
157 G5 Rougemont-le-Château France
81 B6 Rough Ridge South I. N.Z.
151 I2 Roughton Norfolk, England U.K.
147 B5 Roughty r. Rep. of Ireland
162 C3 Rougnac France
162 B3 Rouillac France
162 C2 Rouillé France
161 B5 Roujan France
160 E1 Roulans France
Roulers Belgium see Roeselare
232 D4 Roulette PA U.S.A.
Roumania country Europe see Romania
162 C3 Roumazières-Loubert France
161 E5 Roumoules France
232 B4 Roundhead OH U.S.A.
149 H3 Round Hill hill England U.K.
83 H2 Round Mountain mt. N.S.W. Austr.
240 I2 Round Mountain NV U.S.A.
241 M3 Round Rock AZ U.S.A.
237 D6 Round Rock TX U.S.A.
147 B3 Roundstone Rep. of Ireland
234 B2 Round Top hill PA U.S.A.
238 E2 Roundup MT U.S.A.
151 F3 Roundway Wiltshire, England U.K.
148 C4 Roundwood Rep. of Ireland
251 H3 Roura Fr. Guiana
190 C3 Roure Italy
146 E2 Rousay i. Scotland U.K.
233 G2 Rouses Point NY U.S.A.
176 F2 Rousínov Czech Rep.
148 B3 Rousky Northern Ireland U.K.
161 D5 Rousset France
161 D5 Roussillon Provence-Alpes-Côte-d'Azur France
155 G4 Roussillon Rhône-Alpes France
161 C4 Rousson France
159 G2 Routot France
164 F2 Rouveen Neth.
159 F3 Rouvre r. France
156 C2 Rouvroy France
156 E3 Rouvroy-sur-Audry France
215 F4 Rouxville S. Africa
160 B1 Rouy France
224 E3 Rouyn Que. Can.
Rouyuan Gansu China see Huachi
Rouyuanchengzi Gansu China see Huachi
140 N2 Rovaniemi Fin.
190 D3 Rovasenda r. Italy
190 F3 Rovato Italy
190 E4 Rovegno Italy
135 G6 Roven'ki Rus. Fed.
Rovenki Ukr. see Roven'ky
137 J3 Roven'ky Ukr.
Rovenskaya Oblast' admin. div. Ukr. see Rivnens'ka Oblast'
191 F3 Roverbella Italy
190 E2 Roveredo Switz.
191 G3 Rovereto Italy
170 D1 Rövershagen Ger.
193 E2 Roviano Italy
191 G3 Rovigo Italy
191 G3 Rovigo prov. Veneto Italy
197 F3 Rovinari Romania
188 D3 Rovinj Croatia
176 G3 Rovinka Slovakia
179 H5 Rovišće Croatia
Rovno Rivnens'ka Oblast' Ukr. see Rivne
Rovno Oblast admin. div. Ukr. see Rivnens'ka Oblast'
120 A2 Rovnoye Rus. Fed.
150 E3 Rowde Wiltshire, England U.K.
83 G2 Rowena N.S.W. Austr.
234 D1 Rowland PA U.S.A.
232 D5 Rowlesburg WV U.S.A.
86 C3 Rowley Shoals sea feature W.A. Austr.
Równe Rivnens'ka Oblast' Ukr. see Rivne
174 E4 Rów Polski r. Pol.
232 B4 Rowsburg OH U.S.A.
92 B2 Roxas Luzon Phil.
92 B4 Roxas Mindanao Phil.
92 B3 Roxas Mindoro Phil.
92 A4 Roxas Palawan Phil.
92 B4 Roxas Panay Phil.
231 E4 Roxboro NC U.S.A.
84 D4 Roxborough Downs Qld Austr.
81 B6 Roxburgh South I. N.Z.
Roxburgh Island Cook Is see Rarotonga
235 E1 Roxbury CT U.S.A.
235 E1 Roxbury Falls CT U.S.A.
82 D2 Roxby Downs S.A. Austr.
184 B3 Roxo r. Port.
184 B3 Roxo, Barragem do resr Port.
151 G2 Roxton Bedfordshire, England U.K.
146 D5 Roy r. Scotland U.K.
238 E2 Roy MT U.S.A.
239 F4 Roy NM U.S.A.
161 F5 Roya r. France/Italy
226 D5 Royal Center IN U.S.A.
117 F4 Royal Chitwan National Park Nepal
226 C1 Royale, Isle i. MI U.S.A.
227 F4 Royal Oak MI U.S.A.
263 K1 Royal Society Range mts Antarctica
234 B2 Royalton PA U.S.A.
226 C3 Royalton WI U.S.A.
162 A3 Royan France
160 B3 Royat France
161 D3 Roybon France
151 H2 Roydon Norfolk, England U.K.
151 I2 Roydon Norfolk, England U.K.
156 C3 Roye France
162 D3 Royère-de-Vassivière France
234 C2 Royersford PA U.S.A.
86 C4 Roy Hill W.A. Austr.
137 F2 Royishche Ukr.
151 G2 Royston Hertfordshire, England U.K.
149 H4 Royston South Yorkshire, England U.K.
149 G4 Royton Greater Manchester, England U.K.
183 I4 Royuela Spain
196 E4 Rožaje Crna Gora Yugo.
183 H5 Rozalén del Monte Spain
175 J3 Różan Pol.
196 D3 Rožanj hill Yugo.
156 C4 Rozay-en-Brie France
176 E1 Rožďalovice Czech Rep.
175 M6 Rozdil Ukr.
136 F4 Rozdil'na Ukr.
137 G5 Rozdol'ne Ukr.
137 H3 Rozdory Ukr.
174 F4 Rozdrażew Pol.
164 D3 Rozenburg Neth.
164 E2 Rozendaal Neth.
121 G2 Rozhdestvenka Kazakh.
139 K3 Rozhdestveno Tverskaya Oblast' Rus. Fed.
139 K3 Rozhdestveno Yaroslavskaya Oblast' Rus. Fed.
134 I4 Rozhdestvenskoye Rus. Fed.
139 I3 Rozhdestvo Rus. Fed.
137 G2 Rozhnivka Ukr.
136 F2 Rozhny Ukr.
136 C3 Rozhnyativ Ukr.
136 C2 Rozhyshche Ukr.
197 G4 Rozino Bulg.
137 I4 Rozivka Ukr.
176 C2 Rožmitál pod Třemšínem Czech Rep.
177 J3 Rožňava Slovakia
174 G3 Rożniatów Pol.
177 H2 Rožnov pod Radhoštěm Czech Rep.
175 I6 Rożnów Pol.
174 E3 Roznowo Pol.
175 J2 Rozoga r. Pol.
175 J2 Rozogi Pol.
156 E3 Rozoy-sur-Serre France
175 H4 Rozprza Pol.
175 I6 Roztoka Wielka Pol.
171 E5 Roztoky Středočeský kraj Czech Rep.
171 F5 Roztoky Středočeský kraj Czech Rep.
190 E3 Rozzano Italy
196 D5 Rrëshen Albania
196 D5 Rrogozhinë Albania
135 H5 Rtishchevo Rus. Fed.
182 B1 Ru Spain
182 C4 Rua Port.
150 D2 Ruabon Wrexham, Wales U.K.
211 B6 Ruaha National Park Tanz.
80 F4 Ruahine Range mts North I. N.Z.
80 E1 Ruakaka North I. N.Z.
147 C4 Ruan Rep. of Ireland
Ruanda country Africa see Rwanda
80 E3 Ruapehu, Mount vol. North I. N.Z.
81 B7 Ruapuke Island South I. N.Z.
150 E3 Ruardean Gloucestershire, England U.K.
80 E1 Ruatangata North I. N.Z.
81 C5 Ruatapu South I. N.Z.
80 G2 Ruatoria North I. N.Z.
159 G4 Ruaudin France
139 H4 Ruba Belarus
124 D4 Rub' al Khālī des. Saudi Arabia
177 H4 Rúbaň Slovakia
148 D3 Rubane Northern Ireland U.K.
137 H4 Rubanivka Ukr.
191 G3 Rubano Italy
125 E2 Rubaydā reg. Saudi Arabia
183 G1 Rubayo Spain
211 C6 Rubeho Mountains Tanz.
169 F4 Rübeland Ger.
257 F2 Rubelita Brazil
183 G2 Rubena Spain
171 E5 Rübenau Ger.
Rubezhnoye Ukr. see Rubizhne
Rubha an t-Siumpain hd Scotland U.K. see Tiumpan Head
Rubha Robhanais hd Scotland U.K. see Butt of Lewis
208 E4 Rubi r. Dem. Rep. Congo
186 F3 Rubí Spain
182 D2 Rubiá Spain
256 B4 Rubiácea Brazil
240 G2 Rubicon r. CA U.S.A.
191 H4 Rubicone r. Italy
183 F3 Rubí de Bracamonte Spain
186 B4 Rubielos de la Cérida Spain
187 C4 Rubielos de Mora Spain
191 F4 Rubiera Italy
257 G2 Rubim Brazil
183 G3 Rubio mt. Spain
137 J3 Rubizhne Ukr.
170 E2 Rubkow Ger.
183 G2 Rublacedo de Abajo Spain
211 A5 Rubondo National Park Tanz.
137 I3 Rubtsi Ukr.
121 J2 Rubtsovsk Rus. Fed.
124 C4 Rubūţ, Jabal ar hill Saudi Arabia
220 C3 Ruby AK U.S.A.
81 D4 Ruby Bay South I. N.Z.
238 D3 Ruby Dome mt. NV U.S.A.
136 D2 Rubyel' Belarus
241 J1 Ruby Mountains NV U.S.A.
241 K3 Rubys Inn UT U.S.A.
85 F4 Rubyvale Qld Austr.
241 J1 Ruby Valley NV U.S.A.
197 G3 Rucăr Romania
Rucheng Guangdong China see Ruyuan
109 E3 Rucheng Hunan China
137 G2 Ruchky Ukr.
175 J2 Ruciane-Nida Pol.
171 E4 Rückersdorf Ger.
232 D5 Ruckersville VA U.S.A.
164 D3 Rucphen Neth.
174 G4 Ruda Pol.
177 J3 Rudabánya Hungary
175 L4 Ruda-Huta Pol.
175 I4 Ruda Maleniecka Pol.
175 L5 Ruda Różaniecka Pol.
117 E4 Rudarpur Uttar Prad. India
174 G5 Ruda Śląska Pol.
116 E4 Rudauli Uttar Prad. India
122 B2 Rūdbār Iran
165 C3 Ruddervoorde Belgium
151 F2 Ruddington Nottinghamshire, England U.K.
173 F3 Rudelzhausen Ger.
179 F4 Ruden Austria
172 D3 Rudersberg Ger.
179 H3 Rudersdorf Austria
171 E3 Rüdersdorf Berlin Ger.
169 F4 Rüdershausen Ger.
173 H3 Ruderting Ger.
136 E3 Rude Selo Ukr.
172 B2 Rüdesheim Ger.
172 B2 Rüdesheim am Rhein Ger.
151 G3 Rudgwick West Sussex, England U.K.
138 E4 Rūdiškės Lith.
169 F5 Rudisleben Ger.
137 G2 Rudivka Ukr.
175 K3 Rudka Pol.
175 L4 Rudka r. Pol.
142 D4 Rudkøbing Denmark
175 L6 Rudky Ukr.
171 F5 Rudná Czech Rep.
174 E4 Rudna Pol.
197 F3 Rudna Glava Srbija Yugo.
174 E4 Rudna Wielka Pol.
100 E3 Rudnaya Pristan' Rus. Fed.
100 E4 Rudnaya Pristan' Rus. Fed.
136 B3 Rudne Ukr.
121 I3 Rudnichnyy Kazakh.
134 K4 Rudnichnyy Rus. Fed.
175 K5 Rudnik Podkarpackie Pol.
174 G5 Rudnik Śląskie Pol.
174 G4 Rudniki Pol.
Rudnik Ingichka Uzbek. see Ingichka
170 E3 Rüdnitz Ger.
139 H4 Rudnya Smolenskaya Oblast' Rus. Fed.
135 I6 Rudnya Volgogradskaya Oblast' Rus. Fed.
136 D2 Rudnya-Ivanivs'ka Ukr.
175 L6 Rudnyky Ukr.
136 E3 Rudnytsya Ukr.
120 E1 Rudnyy Kazakh.
100 E3 Rudnyy Rus. Fed.
Rudolf, Lake salt l. Eth./Kenya see Turkana, Lake
179 F2 Rudolfov Czech Rep.
171 C5 Rudolstadt Ger.
109 G1 Rudong Jiangsu China
197 G5 Rudozem Bulg.
122 B2 Rūdsar Iran
149 I3 Rudston East Riding of Yorkshire, England U.K.
226 E2 Rudyard MI U.S.A.
174 F5 Rudziczka Pol.
138 F5 Rudzyensk Belarus
156 B2 Rue France
184 E1 Ruecas r. Spain
183 F3 Rueda Spain
156 C4 Rueil-Malmaison France
227 G2 Ruel Ont. Can.
Ruen mt. Macedonia see Rujen
183 F1 Ruente Spain
213 G3 Ruenya r. Zimbabwe
178 C3 Ruetz r. Austria
203 G6 Rufa'a Sudan
195 H3 Ruffano Italy
159 H5 Ruffec Centre France
162 C2 Ruffec Poitou-Charentes France
160 D1 Ruffey-lès-Echirey France
160 D2 Ruffey-sur-Seille France
158 D4 Ruffiac France
160 D2 Ruffieu France
160 D3 Ruffieux France
149 G4 Rufford Lancashire, England U.K.
211 C7 Rufiji r. Tanz.
191 G5 Rufina Italy
261 F4 Rufino Arg.
206 A3 Rufisque Senegal
209 F8 Rufunsa Zambia
109 G1 Rugao Jiangsu China
170 C2 Rugberg hill Ger.
151 F2 Rugby Warwickshire, England U.K.
236 C1 Rugby ND U.S.A.
151 F2 Rugeley Staffordshire, England U.K.
170 E1 Rügen i. Ger.
222 E5 Rugged Mountain B.C. Can.
173 E2 Rügland Ger.
159 G3 Rugles France
169 F3 Rühen Ger.
211 A5 Ruhengeri Rwanda
169 F5 Ruhla Ger.
171 E4 Ruhland Ger.
173 G3 Ruhmannsfelden Ger.
170 C2 Rühn Ger.
173 G4 Ruhpolding Ger.
169 B4 Ruhr r. Ger.
173 H3 Ruhstorf an der Rott Ger.
211 B7 Ruhudji r. Tanz.
109 G3 Rui'an Zhejiang China
109 E2 Ruichang Jiangxi China
185 H2 Ruidera Spain
239 F6 Ruidosa TX U.S.A.
239 F5 Ruidoso NM U.S.A.
109 E3 Ruijin Jiangxi China
108 A3 Ruili Yunnan China
192 A5 Ruinas Sardegna Italy
164 F2 Ruinen Neth.
164 F2 Ruinerwold Neth.
211 C7 Ruipa Tanz.
165 C3 Ruiselede Belgium
182 B3 Ruivães Port.
184 □ Ruivo, Pico mt. Madeira
244 B3 Ruiz Mex.
197 F4 Ruj mt. Bulg.
138 E3 Rūja r. Latvia
174 E4 Ruja Pol.
128 C3 Rujaylah, Ḩarrat ar lava field Jordan
197 F4 Rujen mt. Macedonia
138 E3 Rūjiena Latvia
Ruk is Micronesia see Chuuk
129 F2 Rukel' Rus. Fed.
129 B2 Rukhi Georgia
208 C4 Ruki r. Dem. Rep. Congo
210 A5 Rukungiri Uganda
211 A6 Rukwa admin. reg. Tanz.
211 B7 Rukwa, Lake Tanz.
141 K3 Rulbo Sweden
125 G2 Rūl Ḑadnah U.A.E.
237 F5 Ruleville MS U.S.A.
86 E2 Rulhieres, Cape W.A. Austr.
Rulin Hunan China see Chengbu
169 D3 Rulle (Wallenhorst) Ger.
168 F2 Rullstorf Ger.
160 C2 Rully France
Rulong Sichuan China see Xinlong
172 C2 Rülzheim Ger.
178 C3 Rum Austria
176 F4 Rum Hungary
122 D3 Rūm Iran
146 B5 Rum i. Scotland U.K.
236 E2 Rum r. MN U.S.A.
Rum, Jebel mts Jordan see Ramm, Jabal
146 B5 Rum, Sound of sea chan. Scotland U.K.
207 G3 Ruma Nigeria
196 D3 Ruma Vojvodina, Srbija Yugo.
125 D2 Rumāh Saudi Arabia
210 B5 Ruma National Park Kenya
Rumania country Europe see Romania
208 F3 Rumbek Sudan
185 G2 Rumblar r. Spain
176 D1 Rumburk Czech Rep.
246 D2 Rum Cay i. Bahamas
165 F5 Rumelange Lux.
165 C4 Rumes Belgium
233 □H2 Rumford ME U.S.A.
143 H4 Rumia Pol.
156 E3 Rumigny France
160 D3 Rumilly France
84 B2 Rum Jungle N.T. Austr.
124 C2 Rummān, Jabal ar mts Saudi Arabia
128 D3 Rummānā hill Syria
150 D3 Rumney Cardiff, Wales U.K.
102 J2 Rumoi Japan
211 A5 Rumonge Burundi
157 F4 Rumont France
211 B7 Rumphi Malawi
235 E2 Rumson NJ U.S.A.
165 D3 Rumst Belgium
85 F3 Rumula Qld Austr.
184 A1 Runa Port.
109 E1 Runan Henan China
81 C5 Runanga South I. N.Z.
80 F2 Runaway, Cape North I. N.Z.
246 □ Runaway Bay Jamaica
149 G4 Runcorn Halton, England U.K.
197 F3 Runcu Romania
177 L6 Runcu r. Romania
213 G4 Runde r. Zimbabwe
212 C3 Rundu Namibia
140 L3 Rundvik Sweden
97 C5 Rŭng, Kaôh i. Cambodia
95 F3 Rungan r. Indon.
208 E4 Rungu Dem. Rep. Congo
211 B6 Rungwa Tanz.
211 A6 Rungwa r. Tanz.
109 F1 Runheji Anhui China
Runing Henan China see Runan
169 D5 Runkel Ger.
240 I4 Running Springs CA U.S.A.
87 D4 Runton Range hills W.A. Austr.
151 H3 Runwell Essex, England U.K.
78 □4a Ruo i. Chuuk Micronesia
141 O3 Ruokolahti Fin.
161 C4 Ruoms France
110 E4 Ruoqiang Xinjiang China
110 E4 Ruoqiang He r. China
193 H4 Ruoti Italy
141 N3 Ruotsinpyhtää Fin.
141 N3 Ruovesi Fin.
117 H4 Rupa Arun. Prad. India
94 C2 Rupat i. Indon.
197 G2 Rupea Romania
224 E3 Rupert r. Que. Can.
238 D3 Rupert ID U.S.A.
232 C6 Rupert WV U.S.A.
262 O1 Rupert Coast Antarctica
85 E4 Rupert Creek r. Qld Austr.
116 C4 Rupnagar Rajasthan India
170 D3 Ruppiner See l. Ger.
179 G2 Ruprechtshofen Austria
157 G5 Rupt-sur-Moselle France
232 C6 Rural Retreat VA U.S.A.
252 D3 Rurrenabaque Bol.
79 □3 Rurutu i. Îs Australes Fr. Polynesia
197 F2 Rus Romania
185 G2 Rus Spain
185 H1 Rus r. Spain
Rusaddir N. Africa see Melilla
137 G2 Rusanivka Ukr.
213 G3 Rusape Zimbabwe
197 F3 Rusca Montană Romania
Ruschuk Bulg. see Ruse
197 G2 Ruscova Romania
197 G4 Ruse Bulg.
179 G4 Ruše Slovenia
117 F4 Rusera Bihar India
197 H3 Rușețu Romania
147 E3 Rush Rep. of Ireland
151 F2 Rushall West Midlands, England U.K.
107 I4 Rushan Shandong China
Rushan Tajik. see Rushon
236 C4 Rush Creek r. CO U.S.A.
151 G2 Rushden Northamptonshire, England U.K.
226 B4 Rushford MN U.S.A.
213 G3 Rushinga Zimbabwe
232 E6 Rushmere VA U.S.A.
151 I2 Rushmere St Andrew Suffolk, England U.K.
123 G2 Rushon Tajik.
106 E5 Rushui r. China
236 F3 Rushville IL U.S.A.
230 C4 Rushville IN U.S.A.
236 C3 Rushville NE U.S.A.
232 B5 Rushville OH U.S.A.
83 F4 Rushworth Vic. Austr.
174 G4 Rusiec Pol.
175 I4 Rusinów Pol.
237 E6 Rusk TX U.S.A.
140 L2 Ruskele Sweden
196 D3 Ruski Krstur Vojvodina, Srbija Yugo.
231 D7 Ruskin FL U.S.A.
149 I4 Ruskington Lincolnshire, England U.K.
137 I2 Rus'ki Tyshky Ukr.
177 J6 Rusko Selo Vojvodina, Srbija Yugo.
177 K3 Ruskov Slovakia
138 C4 Rusnė Lith.
197 H4 Rusokastro Bulg.
136 E3 Rusova r. Ukr.
150 E3 Ruspidge Gloucestershire, England U.K.
254 F3 Russas Brazil
223 K5 Russell Man. Can.
233 F2 Russell Ont. Can.
80 E1 Russell North I. N.Z.
236 D4 Russell KS U.S.A.
232 D4 Russell PA U.S.A.
78 □6 Russell Islands Solomon Is
231 C5 Russellville AL U.S.A.
237 E5 Russellville AR U.S.A.
230 C4 Russellville KY U.S.A.
232 B5 Russellville OH U.S.A.
234 C3 Russellville PA U.S.A.
172 C1 Rüsselsheim Ger.
191 H4 Russi Italy
Russia country Asia/Europe see Russian Federation
130 F4 Russian Federation country Asia/Europe
Russian Soviet Federal Socialist Republic country Asia/Europe see Russian Federation
121 H1 Russkaya-Polyana Rus. Fed.
135 H6 Russkaya Zhuravka Rus. Fed.
139 K5 Russkiy Brod Rus. Fed.
120 A1 Russkiy Kameshkir Rus. Fed.
179 H3 Rust Austria
129 D3 Rüstäm Äliyev Azer.
129 D3 Rust'avi Georgia
232 D6 Rustburg VA U.S.A.
215 G1 Rust de Winter S. Africa
129 C4 Rüstemgedik Turkey
215 F1 Rustenburg S. Africa
142 B2 Rustfjellheii mt. Norway
215 F2 Rustig S. Africa
151 G4 Rustington West Sussex, England U.K.
237 E5 Ruston LA U.S.A.
161 D5 Rustrel France
190 D1 Ruswil Switz.
174 D4 Ruszów Pol.
139 K4 Rut' r. Rus. Fed.
192 B2 Rutali Corse France
211 A5 Rutana Burundi
Rutanzige, Lake Dem. Rep. Congo/Uganda see Edward, Lake
185 F3 Rute Spain
172 C3 Rutesheim Ger.
241 J2 Ruth NV U.S.A.
169 D4 Rüthen Ger.
Ruthenia admin. div. Ukr. see Zakarpats'ka Oblast'
235 D2 Rutherford NJ U.S.A.
231 D5 Rutherfordton NC U.S.A.
83 F4 Rutherglen Vic. Austr.
227 H2 Rutherglen Ont. Can.
146 D6 Rutherglen South Lanarkshire, Scotland U.K.
232 E6 Ruther Glen VA U.S.A.
150 D1 Ruthin Denbighshire, Wales U.K.
190 D1 Rüti Switz.
195 G1 Rutigliano Italy
193 H4 Rutino Italy
134 I4 Rutka r. Rus. Fed.
175 K1 Rutka-Tartak Pol.
175 K2 Rutki-Kossaki Pol.
151 G2 Rutland admin. div. England U.K.
233 G3 Rutland VT U.S.A.
85 E2 Rutland Plains Qld Austr.
151 G2 Rutland Water resr England U.K.
232 B6 Rutledge TN U.S.A.
111 B5 Rutog Xizang China
164 E2 Rutten Neth.
227 G2 Rutter Ont. Can.
129 E3 Rutul Rus. Fed.
140 N2 Ruukki Fin.
164 F2 Ruurlo Neth.
193 H4 Ruvo del Monte Italy
193 I3 Ruvo di Puglia Italy
Ruvu Tanz. see Pangani
211 D7 Ruvuma r. Moz./Tanz.
211 C7 Ruvuma admin. reg. Tanz.
125 F2 Ruweis U.A.E.
208 F5 Ruwenzori mts Dem. Rep. Congo/Uganda
160 D3 Ruy France
213 G3 Ruya r. Zimbabwe
211 A5 Ruyigi Burundi
161 B3 Ruynes-en-Margeride France
150 E2 Ruyton-XI-Towns Shropshire, England U.K.
109 E3 Ruyuan Guangdong China
139 K4 Ruza Rus. Fed.
121 F1 Ruzayevka Kazakh.
135 I5 Ruzayevka Rus. Fed.
138 E5 Ruzhany Belarus
107 G5 Ruzhou Henan China
136 E3 Ruzhyn Ukr.
177 I2 Ružomberok Slovakia
177 I5 Ruzsa Hungary
211 A5 Rwanda country Africa
142 C3 Ry Denmark
142 C3 Ryå r. Denmark
122 C2 Ryābād Iran
137 H2 Ryabyna Ukr.
81 B7 Ryal Bush South I. N.Z.
81 C5 Ryall, Mount South I. N.Z.
146 C6 Ryan, Loch b. Scotland U.K.
137 H3 Ryas'ke Ukr.
137 F4 Ryasnopil' Ukr.
139 L4 Ryazan' Rus. Fed.
Ryazan Oblast admin. div. Rus. Fed. see Ryazanskaya Oblast'
139 L4 Ryazanovskiy Rus. Fed.
137 J5 Ryazanskaya Rus. Fed.
139 M4 Ryazanskaya Oblast' admin. div. Rus. Fed.
139 L3 Ryazantsevo Rus. Fed.
139 M5 Ryazhsk Rus. Fed.
121 J3 Rybache Kazakh.
140 P1 Rybachiy, Poluostrov pen. Rus. Fed.
Rybach'ye Kyrg. see Balykchy
177 H3 Rybany Slovakia
139 L2 Rybinsk Rus. Fed.
139 L2 Rybinskoye Vodokhranilishche resr Rus. Fed.
176 E1 Rybitví Czech Rep.
174 G5 Rybnik Pol.
Rybnitsa Moldova see Rîbnița
175 I3 Rybno Mazowieckie Pol.
175 H2 Rybno Warmińsko-Mazurskie Pol.
175 J2 Rybno Warmińsko-Mazurskie Pol.
139 L4 Rybnoye Rus. Fed.
175 L3 Ryboły Pol.
134 F3 Rybreka Rus. Fed.
175 H2 Rychliki Pol.
176 F1 Rychnov nad Kněžnou Czech Rep.
171 G5 Rychnov u Jablonce nad Nisou Czech Rep.
175 I2 Rychnowo Pol.
174 F4 Rychtal Pol.
174 G3 Rychwał Pol.
170 E1 Ryck r. Ger.
222 G4 Rycroft Alta Can.
175 J4 Ryczywół Pol.
174 E3 Ryczywół Pol.
143 F3 Ryd Sweden
262 S2 Rydberg Peninsula Antarctica
151 F4 Ryde Isle of Wight, England U.K.
136 C3 Rydomyl' Ukr.
174 G5 Rydułtowy Pol.
174 E4 Rydzyna Pol.
151 H4 Rye East Sussex, England U.K.
149 I3 Rye r. England U.K.
235 E2 Rye NY U.S.A.
151 H4 Rye Bay England U.K.
233 □H3 Rye Beach NH U.S.A.
238 E2 Ryegate MT U.S.A.
240 H1 Rye Patch Reservoir NV U.S.A.
159 F2 Ryes France
175 J6 Ryglice Pol.
151 G2 Ryhall Rutland, England U.K.
174 G2 Ryjewo Pol.
136 D2 Rykhal's'ke Ukr.
175 J4 Ryki Pol.
Rykovo Ukr. see Yenakiyeve
175 M5 Rykovychi Ukr.
135 F6 Ryl'sk Rus. Fed.
83 G3 Rylstone N.S.W. Austr.
175 J6 Rymanów Pol.
176 G2 Rýmařov Czech Rep.
141 M3 Rymättylä Fin.
143 I4 Ryn Pol.
174 F2 Rynarzewo Pol.
120 B3 Ryn-Peski des. Kazakh.
174 G2 Ryńsk Pol.
105 E2 Ryōgami-san mt. Japan
104 C3 Ryōhaku-sanchi mts Japan
Ryojun Liaoning China see Lushunkou
102 I4 Ryōtsu Japan
104 C3 Ryōzen-zan mt. Japan
175 H2 Rypin Pol.
Ryshkany Moldova see Rîșcani
168 C2 Rysum (Krummhörn) Ger.
177 J2 Rysy mt. Pol.
174 F2 Rytel Pol.
143 F4 Rytterknægten hill Bornholm Denmark
138 E1 Ryttylä Fin.
175 J5 Rytwiany Pol.
104 C3 Ryūga-dake mt. Japan
105 G3 Ryūgasaki Japan
Ryukyu Islands Japan see Nansei-shotō
Ryūkyū-rettō is Japan see Nansei-shotō
266 D4 Ryukyu Trench sea feature N. Pacific Ocean
105 E3 Ryūsō-san mt. Japan
139 H4 Ryzhikovo Rus. Fed.
136 F3 Ryzyne Ukr.
175 J3 Rządza r. Pol.
175 H4 Rząśnia Pol.
175 J3 Rząśnik Pol.
188 G4 Rzav r. Bos.-Herz.
174 F2 Rzeczenica Pol.
174 G4 Rzeczyca Łódzkie Pol.
175 I4 Rzeczyca Łódzkie Pol.
175 I2 Rzęgnowo Pol.
175 H4 Rzejowice Pol.
175 J2 Rzekuń Pol.
175 J6 Rzepiennik Strzyżewski Pol.
174 C3 Rzepin Pol.
175 H5 Rzerzęczyce Pol.
175 K5 Rzeszów Pol.
175 H4 Rzgów Pol.
174 G3 Rzgów Pierwszy Pol.
135 H5 Rzhaksa Rus. Fed.
139 I5 Rzhanitsa Rus. Fed.
139 H5 Rzhawka r. Belarus
139 J3 Rzhev Rus. Fed.
137 F3 Rzhyshchiv Ukr.
175 I4 Rzuców Pol.

S

122 D3 Sa'ābād Iran
122 C4 Sa'ādatābād Iran
214 C4 Saaifontein S. Africa
170 D1 Saal Ger.
173 H4 Saalach r. Ger.
173 F3 Saal an der Donau Ger.
169 F5 Saal an der Saale Ger.
172 C2 Saalbach r. Ger.
178 D3 Saalbach-Hinterglemm Austria
171 C5 Saalburg Ger.
173 G4 Saaldorf Ger.
171 C4 Saale r. Ger.
157 H4 Saales France
171 C5 Saalfeld Ger.
178 D3 Saalfelden am Steinernen Meer Austria

Saâne to St-Lary-Soulan

356

156 A3 Saâne r. France
190 C2 Saane r. Switz.
190 C2 Saanen Switz.
222 F5 Saanich B.C. Can.
Saar land Ger. see Saarland
172 A2 Saar r. Ger.
172 A2 Saarbrücken Ger.
172 A2 Saarburg Ger.
138 D2 Saaremaa i. Estonia
140 N2 Saarenkylä Fin.
141 O3 Saari Fin.
140 N3 Saarijärvi Fin.
172 A2 Saarland land Ger.
172 A2 Saarlouis Ger.
172 A2 Saarwellingen Ger.
190 E2 Saas Switz.
190 C2 Saas Fee Switz.
190 C2 Saas Grund Switz.
190 C2 Saastal val. Switz.
129 F4 Saatlı Azer.
Saatly Azer. see Saatlı
261 F5 Saavedra Arg.
247 G3 Saba i. Neth. Antilles
128 C3 Sab' Ābār Syria
169 E4 Sababurg Ger.
196 D3 Šabac Srbija Yugo.
186 F3 Sabadell Spain
206 C4 Sabadou Baranama Guinea
104 C3 Sabae Japan
95 G1 Sabah state Malaysia
211 D5 Sabaki r. Kenya
93 A4 Sabalana, Kepulauan is Indon.
116 D4 Sabalgarh Madh. Prad. India
242 □I6 Sabamagrande Hond.
246 B2 Sabana, Archipiélago de is Cuba
247 E3 Sabana de la Mar Dom. Rep.
247 □1 Sabana Grande Puerto Rico
250 C2 Sabanalarga Col.
246 E3 Sabaneta Dom. Rep.
94 A1 Sabang Indon.
126 D2 Şabanözü Turkey
197 H2 Săbăoani Romania
257 F3 Sabará Brazil
163 D5 Sabarat France
114 D2 Sabari r. India
116 C5 Sabarmati r. Gujarat India
128 B3 Sabastiya West Bank
193 G3 Sabato r. Italy
193 F3 Sabaudia Italy
252 C4 Sabaya Bol.
129 B2 Sabazho Georgia
190 F4 Sabbionetta Italy
214 D4 Sabelo S. Africa
210 C4 Sabena Desert Kenya
183 E2 Sabero Spain
202 B3 Sabhā Libya
116 B5 Sabhrai Gujarat India
116 D3 Sabi r. India
Sabi r. Moz./Zimbabwe see Save
215 I1 Sabie r. Moz./S. Africa
213 F5 Sabie S. Africa
138 D3 Sabile Latvia
232 B5 Sabina OH U.S.A.
186 C2 Sabiñánigo Spain
185 H4 Sabinar, Punta del mt. Spain
243 E3 Sabinas Mex.
237 C7 Sabinas r. Coahuila Mex.
237 D7 Sabinas r. Nuevo León Mex.
243 E3 Sabinas Hidalgo Mex.
237 E6 Sabine r. Louisiana/Texas U.S.A.
140 □ Sabine Land reg. Svalbard
237 E6 Sabine Pass TX U.S.A.
193 E2 Sabini, Monti mts Italy
257 F3 Sabinópolis Brazil
177 K2 Sabinov Slovakia
185 G2 Sabiote Spain
129 F3 Sabir Azer.
129 F3 Sabirabad Azer.
92 B3 Sablayan Phil.
225 H5 Sable, Cape N.S. Can.
231 D7 Sable, Cape FL U.S.A.
78 □5 Sable, Île de i. New Caledonia
225 G2 Sable, Rivière du r. Que. Can.
225 J5 Sable Island N.S. Can.
227 F2 Sables, River aux r. Ont. Can.
158 D3 Sables-d'Or-les-Pins France
159 F4 Sablé-sur-Sarthe France
161 D4 Sablet France
161 C4 Sablières France
129 C1 Sablinskoye Rus. Fed.
161 C3 Sablons France
254 F3 Saboeiro Brazil
184 B3 Sabóia Port.
207 H3 Sabon Kafi Niger
182 C3 Sabor r. Port.
206 E3 Sabou Burkina
163 B4 Sabres France
263 H2 Sabrina Coast Antarctica
182 C3 Sabrosa Port.
129 D2 Sabue Georgia
182 C4 Sabugal Port.
184 B2 Sabugueiro Évora Port.
182 C4 Sabugueiro Guarda Port.
129 F3 Sabunçu Azer.
199 G2 Sabuncu Kütahya Turkey
105 E2 Saburyū-yama mt. Japan
124 C4 Şabyā Saudi Arabia
Sabzawar Afgh. see Shīndand
122 D2 Sabzevār Iran
Sabzvārān Iran see Jīroft
197 G2 Saca, Vârful mt. Romania
187 F5 Sa Cabaneta Spain
252 D4 Sacaca Bol.
177 L4 Săcădat Romania
177 K6 Săcălaz Romania
233 F3 Sacandaga r. NY U.S.A.
187 C5 Sacañet Spain
261 F2 Sacanta Arg.
177 L4 Săcășeni Romania
241 L5 Sacaton AZ U.S.A.
184 A2 Sacavém Port.
190 C4 Saccarel, Mont mt. France/Italy
236 E3 Sac City IA U.S.A.
193 F3 Sacco r. Italy
183 H4 Sacecorbo Spain
183 H4 Sacedón Spain
197 G3 Săcele Romania
197 I3 Săcele Romania
197 G3 Săceni Romania
185 F2 Saceruela Spain
223 N4 Sachigo r. Ont. Can.
116 C5 Sachin Gujarat India
129 C2 Sach'khere Georgia
101 D6 Sach'on S. Korea
190 D2 Sachseln Switz.
171 E4 Sachsen land Ger.
171 C3 Sachsen-Anhalt land Ger.
173 E2 Sachsen bei Ansbach Ger.
169 D4 Sachsenberg (Lichtenfels) Ger.
169 F5 Sachsenbrunn Ger.
179 E4 Sachsenburg Austria
169 E3 Sachsenhagen Ger.
169 E4 Sachsenhausen (Waldeck) Ger.
172 D3 Sachsenheim Ger.
220 F2 Sachs Harbour N.W.T. Can.
191 H3 Sacile Italy
Sacirsuyu r. Syria/Turkey see Sājūr, Nahr
233 E3 Sackets Harbor NY U.S.A.
169 D5 Sackpfeife hill Ger.
225 H4 Sackville N.B. Can.
233 □H3 Saco ME U.S.A.
238 F1 Saco MT U.S.A.
177 K6 Sacoșu Turcesc Romania
160 D1 Sacquenay France
183 G3 Sacramenia Spain
256 D3 Sacramento Brazil
240 G2 Sacramento CA U.S.A.
240 G2 Sacramento r. CA U.S.A.
252 A1 Sacramento, Pampa del plain Peru
239 F5 Sacramento Mountains NM U.S.A.
240 F1 Sacramento Valley CA U.S.A.
253 F3 Sacre r. Brazil
149 H3 Sacriston Durham, England U.K.
193 E2 Sacrofano Italy
197 F2 Săcueni Romania
177 L5 Săcuieu Romania
253 F3 Sacuriuiná r. Brazil
217 □3b Sada Mayotte
215 F5 Sada S. Africa
182 B1 Sada Spain
183 I2 Sádaba Spain
116 D4 Sadabad Uttar Prad. India
122 B4 Sa'dābād Iran
Sá da Bandeira Angola see Lubango
163 A6 Sada de Sangüesa Spain
124 C4 Şa'dah Yemen
124 C4 Şa'dah governorate Yemen
192 B5 Sadali Sardegna Italy
93 A3 Sadang r. Indon.
211 C6 Sadani Tanz.
97 C6 Sadao Thai.
125 E5 Şadārah Yemen
129 D4 Sädäräk Azer.
114 C2 Sadaseopet Andhra Prad. India
146 C6 Saddell Argyll and Bute, Scotland U.K.
Saddleback hill England U.K. see Blencathra
237 C5 Saddleback Mesa mt. NM U.S.A.
85 F2 Saddle Hill hill Qld Austr.
81 D4 Saddle Hill mt. South I. N.Z.
Saddle Island Vanuatu see Mota Lava
115 G3 Saddle Peak hill Andaman & Nicobar Is India
97 D5 Sa Đec Vietnam
125 F4 Sadḩ Oman
116 D3 Sadhaura Haryana India
123 G4 Sadiqabad Pak.
129 D3 Sadıqlı Azer.
127 G4 Sa'dīyah, Hawr as imp. l. Iraq
213 □K2 Sadjoavato Madag.
122 D2 Sad-Kharv Iran
174 F2 Sadki Pol.
175 I4 Sadkowice Pol.
174 G2 Sadlinki Pol.
184 B2 Sado r. Port.
102 I5 Sadoga-shima i. Japan
127 G2 Sadon Rus. Fed.
95 E2 Sadong r. Sarawak Malaysia
192 B4 Sa Donna, Pico mt. Sardegna Italy
137 H5 Sadove Ukr.
135 I7 Sadovoye Respublika Kalmykiya - Khalm'g-Tangch Rus. Fed.
137 K2 Sadovoye Voronezhskaya Oblast' Rus. Fed.
175 J5 Sadowie Pol.
175 J3 Sadowne Pol.
187 F5 Sa Dragonera i. Spain
116 C4 Sadri Rajasthan India
234 C3 Sadsburyville PA U.S.A.
171 F5 Sadská Czech Rep.
116 C3 Sadulshahar Rajasthan India
124 D2 Sādūs Saudi Arabia
142 D3 Sæby Denmark
168 D1 Sæd Denmark
232 C4 Saegertown PA U.S.A.
183 H5 Saelices Spain
183 H4 Saelices de la Sal Spain
183 E2 Saelices del Rio Spain
183 E2 Saelices de Mayorga Spain
Saena Julia Italy see Siena
169 C3 Saerbeck Ger.
165 E5 Saeul Lux.
Safad Israel see Ẕefat
206 E3 Safané Burkina
184 C2 Safara Port.
Šafárikovo Slovakia see Tornaľa
123 G2 Safed Khirs mts Afgh.
123 F3 Safed Koh mts Afgh.
142 E2 Säffle Sweden
241 M5 Safford AZ U.S.A.
158 E4 Saffré France
151 H2 Saffron Walden Essex, England U.K.
Safi Jordan see Aş Şāfī
204 C2 Safi Morocco
122 D2 Safiabad Iran
122 B2 Safīd r. Iran
122 E4 Safidabeh Iran
122 C4 Safīdār, Kūh-e mt. Iran
122 B3 Safid Dasht Iran
Safid Kūh mts Afgh. see Paropamisus
257 G3 Safiras, Serra das mts Brazil
128 C2 Şāfītā Syria
134 F1 Safonovo Murmanskaya Oblast' Rus. Fed.
139 I4 Safonovo Smolenskaya Oblast' Rus. Fed.
124 C2 Safrā' al Asyāḩ esc. Saudi Arabia
124 D2 Safrā' as Sark esc. Saudi Arabia
126 D2 Safranbolu Turkey
127 G5 Safwān Iraq
177 L4 Sâg Romania
196 E3 Şag Romania
111 D6 Saga Xizang China
103 E7 Saga Japan
103 E7 Saga pref. Japan
120 F2 Saga Kazakh.
102 J4 Sagae Japan
96 A2 Sagaing Myanmar
96 A2 Sagaing admin. div. Myanmar
192 A4 Sagama Sardegna Italy
105 F3 Sagamihara Japan
105 F4 Sagami-nada g. Japan
105 F3 Sagami-wan b. Japan
232 D4 Sagamore PA U.S.A.
207 F5 Sagamu Nigeria
97 B4 Saganthit Kyun i. Myanmar
114 B3 Sagar Karnataka India
114 C2 Sagar Karnataka India
116 D5 Sagar Madh. Prad. India
170 E1 Sagard Ger.
Sagaredzho Georgia see Sagarejo
129 D3 Sagarejo Georgia
117 G5 Sagaria Bangl.
117 G5 Sagar Island India
Sagarmatha mt. China/Nepal see Everest, Mount
117 F4 Sagarmatha National Park Nepal
117 F4 Sagauli Bihar India
220 D2 Sagavanirktok r. AK U.S.A.
168 D3 Sage Ger.
238 E3 Sage WY U.S.A.
238 E1 Sage Creek r. MT U.S.A.
143 F1 Sågen Sweden
147 E3 Saggart Rep. of Ireland
128 B4 Saggi, Har mt. Israel
235 F2 Sag Harbor NY U.S.A.
Saghyz Kazakh. see Sagiz
114 C3 Sagileru r. India
227 F4 Saginaw MI U.S.A.
226 A2 Saginaw MN U.S.A.
227 F4 Saginaw Bay MI U.S.A.
199 F2 Sağırlar Turkey
193 F2 Sagittario r. Italy
120 C2 Sagiz Kazakh.
Sagiz r. Kazakh. see Sagyz
199 E1 Sağlamtaş Turkey
129 F4 Şağlasär Azer.
206 C5 Sagleipie Liberia
Saglouc Que. Can. see Salluit
192 A2 Sagone Corse France
185 H3 Sagra mt. Spain
260 B4 Sagrada Familia Chile
184 B3 Sagres Port.
184 B4 Sagres, Ponta de pt Port.
96 A2 Sagu Myanmar
177 K5 Şagu Romania
239 F4 Saguache CO U.S.A.
239 F4 Saguache Creek r. CO U.S.A.
246 D2 Sagua de Tánamo Cuba
246 B2 Sagua la Grande Cuba
225 G3 Saguenay r. Que. Can.
Sagunt Spain see Sagunto
187 C5 Sagunto Spain
Saguntum Spain see Sagunto
137 J2 Saguny Rus. Fed.
142 A2 Sagvåg Norway
116 C5 Sagwara Rajasthan India
160 D2 Sagy France
120 C3 Sagyz r. Kazakh.
128 C4 Saḩāb Jordan
116 D3 Sahabab Uttar Prad. India
122 B2 Şahağac Azer.
245 E4 Sahagún Mex.
183 E2 Sahagún Spain
141 N3 Sahalahti Fin.
151 H2 Saham Toney Norfolk, England U.K.
122 A2 Sahand, Kūh-e mt. Iran
129 C3 Sahandöken Turkey
204 G6 Sahara des. Africa
203 F3 Şaḩara el Gharbîya des. Egypt
203 G3 Şaḩara el Sharqîya des. Egypt
Saharan Atlas mts Alg. see Atlas Saharien
116 D3 Saharanpur Uttar Prad. India
86 D4 Sahara Well W.A. Austr.
117 F4 Saharsa Bihar India
116 D3 Sahaswan Uttar Prad. India
122 C3 Sahat, Kūh-e hill Iran
117 F4 Sahatwar Uttar Prad. India
213 □K4 Sahavato Madag.
129 D4 Şahbuz Azer.
129 D3 Şahdağ Silsiläsi hills Armenia/Azer.
124 B4 Sahel prov. Eritrea
117 F4 Sahibganj Bihar India
123 H4 Sahiwal Punjab Pak.
123 H4 Sahiwal Punjab Pak.
122 D3 Sahlābād Iran
124 C3 Sahl Rakbah plain Saudi Arabia
125 G2 Şaḩm Oman
122 A3 Şaḩneh Iran
127 G5 Şaḩrā al Ḩijārah reg. Iraq
Sahu Qinghai China see Zadoi
242 C2 Sahuaripa Mex.
241 L6 Sahuarita AZ U.S.A.
244 C3 Sahuayo Mex.
186 D2 Sahún Spain
161 D4 Sahune France
137 G3 Sahunivka Ukr.
129 B4 Şahvelet Dağları mts Turkey
177 H3 Šahy Slovakia
Sahyadri mts India see Western Ghats
116 C5 Sahyadriparvat Range hills India
128 C2 Şahyūn tourist site Syria
116 E4 Sai r. India
97 C6 Sai Buri Thai.
97 C6 Sai Buri r. Thai.
205 F2 Saïda Alg.
128 B3 Saïda Lebanon
97 C4 Sai Dao Tai, Khao mt. Thai.
181 E5 Saïdia Morocco
117 G4 Saidpur Bangl.
117 E4 Saidpur Uttar Prad. India
123 H3 Saidu Pak.
104 C2 Sai-gawa r. Japan
105 E2 Sai-gawa r. Japan
146 A4 Saighdinis Western Isles, Scotland U.K.
162 E3 Saignes France
161 D5 Saignon France
Saigon Vietnam see Hô Chi Minh
117 H5 Saiha Mizoram India
107 G3 Saihan Tal Nei Mongol China
106 D3 Saihan Toroi Nei Mongol China
103 F7 Saijō Japan
103 E7 Saiki Japan
116 C5 Sailana Madh. Prad. India
163 E6 Saillagouse-Llo France
161 D4 Saillans France
162 C3 Saillat-sur-Vienne France
160 B3 Sail-sous-Couzan France
141 O3 Saimaa l. Fin.
141 O3 Saimaankanava r. Fin.
126 E3 Saimbeyli Turkey
244 C2 Sain Alto Mex.
160 B2 Saincaize-Meauce France
122 A2 Sa'indezh Iran
Sa'īn Qal'eh Iran see Sa'īndezh
156 D3 Sains-Richaumont France
236 F4 Saint r. MN U.S.A.
146 F6 St Abbs Scottish Borders, Scotland U.K.
146 F6 St Abb's Head hd Scotland U.K.
156 C2 St-Acheul France
161 A5 St-Affrique France
161 A4 St-Affrique, Causse de plat. France
160 B2 St-Agnan France
160 C1 St-Agnan France
161 D4 St-Agnan-en-Vercors France
162 B3 St-Agnant France
162 D2 St-Agnant-de-Versillat France
150 B4 St Agnes Cornwall, England U.K.
150 □ St Agnes i. England U.K.
161 C3 St-Agrève France
162 D1 St-Aignan France
159 E4 St-Aignan-sur-Roë France
162 B3 St-Aigulin France
160 C2 St-Albain France
158 D3 St-Alban France
161 C3 St-Alban-d'Ay France
160 D3 St-Alban-Leysse France
225 K4 St Alban's Nfld. Can.
151 G3 St Albans Hertfordshire, England U.K.
233 G2 St Albans VT U.S.A.
232 C5 St Albans WV U.S.A.
150 E4 St Alban's Head hd England U.K.
161 B4 St-Alban-sur-Limagnole France
222 H4 St Albert Alta Can.
St Aldhelm's Head hd England U.K. see St Alban's Head
159 F2 St-Amand France
160 B1 St-Amand-en-Puisaye France
156 D2 St-Amand-les-Eaux France
159 H4 St-Amand-Longpré France
160 A2 St-Amand-Montrond France
156 E4 St-Amand-sur-Fion France
161 B4 St-Amans France
161 A4 St-Amans-des-Cots France
163 E5 St-Amans-Soult France
162 C3 St-Amant-de-Boixe France
160 B3 St-Amant-Roche-Savine France
160 B3 St-Amant-Tallende France
157 H5 St-Amarin France
225 G3 St-Ambroise Que. Can.
161 C4 St-Ambroix France
160 D2 St-Amour France
161 C5 St-Andiol France
163 E6 St-André France
161 F5 St-André France
St-André, Cap pt Madag. see Vilanandro, Tanjona
160 C3 St-André-de-Corcy France
161 C4 St-André-de-Cruzières France
162 B4 St-André-de-Cubzac France
156 B4 St-André-de-l'Eure France
161 E4 St-André-d'Embrun France
161 B5 St-André-de-Sangonis France
163 A5 St-André-de-Seignanx France
161 B4 St-André-de-Valborgne France
160 B1 St-André-en-Morvan France
160 D3 St-André-le-Gaz France
161 E5 St-André-les-Alpes France
156 E4 St-André-les-Vergers France
246 □ St Andrew parish Jamaica
233 □J2 St Andrews N.B. Can.
81 C6 St Andrews South I. N.Z.
146 F5 St Andrews Fife, Scotland U.K.
162 E3 St-Angel France
246 □ St Ann parish Jamaica
158 D2 St Anne Channel Is
226 D5 Saint Anne IL U.S.A.
246 □ St Ann's Bay Jamaica
150 B3 St Ann's Head hd Wales U.K.
226 A4 St Ansgar IA U.S.A.
160 B3 St-Anthème France
225 K3 St Anthony Nfld. Can.
238 E3 Saint Anthony ID U.S.A.
163 D4 St-Antonin-Noble-Val France
159 H5 St-Août France
160 D1 St-Apollinaire France
161 B3 St-Arcons-d'Allier France
83 E4 St Arnaud Vic. Austr.
81 D4 St Arnaud South I. N.Z.
81 D5 St Arnaud Range mts South I. N.Z.
156 B4 St-Arnoult-en-Yvelines France
150 D1 St Asaph Denbighshire, Wales U.K.
84 B1 St Asaph Bay N.T. Austr.
162 C3 St-Astier France
163 C4 St-Astier France
150 D3 St Athan Vale of Glamorgan, Wales U.K.
161 E5 St-Auban France
161 D4 St-Auban-sur-l'Ouvèze France
160 D1 St-Aubin France
156 D5 St-Aubin-Château-Neuf France
158 E3 St-Aubin-d'Aubigné France
158 D3 St-Aubin-du-Cormier France
156 B3 St-Aubin-lès-Elbeuf France
159 F2 St-Aubin-sur-Mer France
225 J3 St-Augustin Que. Can.
225 J3 St Augustin r. Newfoundland/Québec Can.
231 D6 St Augustine FL U.S.A.
162 C3 St-Aulaye France
150 C4 St Austell Cornwall, England U.K.
150 C4 St Austell Bay England U.K.
158 D4 St-Avé France
159 G4 St-Avertin France
157 G3 St-Avold France
156 B5 St-Ay France
161 E5 St-Aygulf France
160 D3 St-Baldoph France
225 J3 St Barbe Nfld. Can.
225 F4 St-Barthélémi Que. Can.
247 G3 St Barthélemy i. West Indies
163 D6 St-Barthélemy, Pic de mt. France
163 C4 St-Barthélemy-d'Agenais France
159 F4 St-Barthélemy-d'Anjou France
162 C3 St-Barthélemy-de-Bellegarde France
161 C3 St-Barthélemy-de-Vals France
81 B6 St Bathans South I. N.Z.
81 B6 St Bathans, Mount South I. N.Z.
161 B5 St-Bauzille-de-Putois France
163 C6 St-Béat France
161 A4 St-Beauzély France
149 F3 St Bees Cumbria, England U.K.
149 F3 St Bees Head hd England U.K.
160 B1 St-Benin-d'Azy France
163 E5 St-Benoît France
162 D2 St-Benoît France
217 □1c St-Benoît Réunion
163 E4 St-Benoît-de-Carmaux France
162 D2 St-Benoît-du-Sault France
156 C5 St-Benoît-sur-Loire France
81 D5 St Bernard mt. South I. N.Z.
160 D3 St-Béron France
159 F3 St-Berthevin France
163 C5 St-Bertrand-de-Comminges France
190 B1 St-Blaise Switz.
157 H4 St-Blaise-la-Roche France
157 F4 St-Blin-Semilly France
160 C2 St-Boil France
162 C2 St-Bonnet-de-Bellac France
160 C2 St-Bonnet-de-Joux France
160 C2 St-Bonnet-des-Bruyères France
161 E4 St-Bonnet-en-Champsaur France
161 C3 St-Bonnet-le-Château France
160 C3 St-Bonnet-le-Froid France
162 B3 St-Bonnet-sur-Gironde France
160 E2 St-Brancher France
159 G4 St-Branchs France
158 D2 St Brelade Channel Is
158 D4 St-Brevin-les-Pins France
158 D3 St-Briac-sur-Mer France
150 E3 St Briavels Gloucestershire, England U.K.
156 E3 St-Brice-Courcelles France
158 E3 St-Brice-en-Coglès France
150 B3 St Brides Pembrokeshire, Wales U.K.
150 B3 St Bride's Bay Wales U.K.
150 D3 St Brides Major Vale of Glamorgan, Wales U.K.
158 D3 St-Brieuc France
158 D3 St-Brieuc, Baie de b. France
156 E3 St-Bris-le-Vineux France
160 C1 St-Brisson France
157 E5 St-Broing-les-Moines France
158 E3 St-Broladre France
150 □ St Buryan Cornwall, England U.K.
159 G4 St-Calais France
161 D5 St-Cannat France
158 D3 St-Cast-le-Guildo France
224 E5 St Catharines Ont. Can.
246 □ St Catherine parish Jamaica
247 □6 St Catherine, Mount hill Grenada
225 K4 St Catherine's Nfld. Can.
151 F4 St Catherine's Point England U.K.
163 D4 St-Céré France
190 B2 St-Cergue Switz.
160 E2 St-Cergues France
162 E3 St-Cernin France
233 G2 St-Césaire Que. Can.
161 E4 St-Chaffrey France
163 D4 St-Chamarand France
161 D5 St-Chamas France
161 C3 St-Chamond France
161 C5 St-Chaptes France
227 G2 St Charles Ont. Can.
238 E3 Saint Charles ID U.S.A.
232 E5 St Charles MD U.S.A.
227 E4 Saint Charles MI U.S.A.
226 A4 St Charles MN U.S.A.
236 F4 St Charles MO U.S.A.
160 D3 St-Chef France
161 B4 St-Chély-d'Apcher France
161 A4 St-Chély-d'Aubrac France
161 A5 St-Chinian France
161 D4 St-Christol France
161 C4 St-Christol-lès-Alès France
162 B3 St-Christoly-de-Blaye France
162 B3 St-Christoly-Médoc France
160 F3 St-Christophe Italy
158 E5 St-Christophe-du-Ligneron France
159 H4 St-Christophe-en-Bazelle France
160 C2 St-Christophe-en-Brionnais France
St Christopher i. St Kitts and Nevis see St Kitts
St Christopher and Nevis country West Indies see St Kitts and Nevis
162 B3 St-Ciers-sur-Gironde France
163 B5 St-Circq-Chalosse France
161 C4 St-Cirgues-en-Montagne France
163 D4 St-Cirq-Lapopie France
224 D5 St Clair r. Can./U.S.A.
227 F4 St Clair MI U.S.A.
234 B2 St Clair PA U.S.A.
227 F4 St Clair, Lake Can./U.S.A.
161 C3 St-Clair-du-Rhône France
156 B3 St-Clair-sur-Epte France
159 E2 St-Clair-sur-l'Elle France
232 C4 St Clairsville OH U.S.A.
163 C5 St-Clar France
162 C3 St-Claud France
160 D2 St-Claude France
150 C3 St Clears Carmarthenshire, Wales U.K.
158 D2 St Clement Channel Is
156 D4 St-Clément France
162 D3 St-Clément France
157 G4 St-Clément France
161 B5 St-Clément de-Rivière France
231 D6 Saint Cloud FL U.S.A.
236 E2 St Cloud MN U.S.A.
225 G3 St-Coeur-de-Marie Que. Can.
150 C4 St Columb Major Cornwall, England U.K.
146 G4 St Combs Aberdeenshire, Scotland U.K.
163 E4 St-Constant France
159 G3 St-Cosme-en-Vairais France
162 C3 St-Crépin-de-Richemont France
221 L5 St Croix r. Can./U.S.A.
226 A3 St Croix r. WI U.S.A.
226 A3 St Croix Falls WI U.S.A.
247 F3 St Croix Island Virgin Is (U.S.A.)
163 D4 St-Cyprien France
163 F6 St-Cyprien France
163 D4 St-Cyprien France
156 C4 St-Cyr-l'École France
162 C1 St-Cyr-sur-Loire France
161 D5 St-Cyr-sur-Mer France
156 D4 St-Cyr-sur-Morin France
161 E4 St-Dalmas-le-Selvage France
225 G4 St-Damien-de-Buckland Que. Can.
241 L6 St David AZ U.S.A.
226 B5 St David IL U.S.A.
150 B3 St David's Pembrokeshire, Wales U.K.
150 B3 St David's Head hd Wales U.K.
150 B4 St Day Cornwall, England U.K.
156 C4 St-Denis France
163 E5 St-Denis France
217 □1c St-Denis Réunion
159 F4 St-Denis-d'Anjou France
159 F3 St-Denis-de-Gastines France
162 D2 St-Denis-de-Jouhet France
162 A2 St-Denis-d'Oléron France
159 F3 St-Denis-d'Orques France
St-Denis-du-Sig Alg. see Sig
160 D3 St-Denis-en-Bugey France
160 D2 St-Denis-lès-Bourg France
150 C4 St Dennis Cornwall, England U.K.
158 D3 St-Denoual France
160 C2 St-Désert France
161 C3 St-Didier-en-Velay France
160 C2 St-Didier-sur-Chalaronne France
160 B3 St-Didier-sur-Rochefort France
157 G4 St-Dié France
160 B3 St-Dier-d'Auvergne France
157 E4 St-Dizier France
162 D2 St-Dizier-Leyrenne France
150 C2 St Dogmaels Pembrokeshire, Wales U.K.
158 D4 St-Dolay France
158 E3 St-Domineuc France
St-Domingue country West Indies see Haiti
161 C3 St-Donat-sur-l'Herbasse France
159 I4 St-Doulchard France
159 G2 Ste-Adresse France
162 C4 Ste-Alvère France
223 L5 Sainte Anne Man. Can.
247 □2 Ste-Anne Guadeloupe
158 D4 Ste-Anne-d'Auray France
225 G4 Ste-Anne-de-Beaupré Que. Can.
233 □I1 Ste-Anne-de-Madawaska N.B. Can.
225 G3 Ste-Anne-de-Portneuf Que. Can.
225 H3 Ste-Anne-des-Monts Que. Can.
227 J2 Ste-Anne-du-Lac Que. Can.
163 C4 Ste-Bazeille France
233 □H1 Ste-Camille-de-Lellis Que. Can.
161 C4 Ste-Cécile-les-Vignes France
160 D2 Ste-Croix France
190 B2 Ste-Croix Switz.
161 E5 Ste-Croix, Lac de l. France
163 D5 Ste-Croix-Volvestre France
224 F4 Ste-Émélie-de-l'Énergie Que. Can.
163 B5 Ste-Engrâce France
161 B4 Ste-Énimie France
161 A4 Ste-Eulalie d'Olt France
163 A4 Ste-Eulalie-en-Born France
162 D2 Ste-Feyre France
161 B3 Ste-Florine France
162 D3 Ste-Fortunade France
163 D5 Ste-Foy-de-Peyrolières France
163 C4 Ste-Foy-la-Grande France
160 C3 Ste-Foy-l'Argentière France
161 D3 Ste-Foy-lès-Lyon France
160 E3 Ste-Foy-Tarentaise France
159 G3 Ste-Gauburge-Ste-Colombe France
162 A2 Ste-Gemme-la-Plaine France
156 G3 Ste-Geneviève France
236 F4 Sainte Genevieve MO U.S.A.
161 A4 Ste-Geneviève-sur-Argence France
161 D3 St-Égrève France
162 B4 Ste-Hélène France
162 A2 Ste-Hermine France
233 □H1 Ste-Justine Que. Can.
233 □I1 St-Éleuthère Que. Can.
222 A2 St Elias Mountains Y.T. Can.
251 H3 St Élie Fr. Guiana
163 C4 Ste-Livrade-sur-Lot France
163 D5 St-Élix-le-Château France
163 C5 St-Élix-Theux France
246 □ St Elizabeth parish Jamaica
159 I4 Ste-Lizaigne France
160 A2 St-Éloy-les-Mines France
192 B3 Ste-Lucie-de-Tallano Corse France
225 H3 Sainte Marguerite r. Que. Can.
157 G4 Ste-Marguerite France
225 G4 Ste-Marie Que. Can.
161 A4 Ste-Marie France
163 F6 Ste-Marie France
247 □3 Ste-Marie Martinique
Ste-Marie, Cap c. Madag. see Vohimena, Tanjona
Sainte-Marie, Île i. Madag. see Boraha, Nosy
157 H4 Ste-Marie-aux-Mines France
163 C4 Ste-Maure-de-Peyriac France
162 C1 Ste-Maure-de-Touraine France
161 E5 Ste-Maxime France
157 E3 Ste-Menehould France
158 E2 Ste-Mère-Église France
160 D2 St-Émiland France
163 B4 St-Émilion France
150 C4 St Endellion Cornwall, England U.K.
150 C4 St Enoder Cornwall, England U.K.
162 D3 Ste-Orse France
158 E4 Ste-Pazanne France
159 F5 Ste-Radegonde France
156 D3 St Erme-Outre-et-Ramecourt France
247 □2 Ste-Rose Guadeloupe
Ste-Rose-du-Dégelé Que. Can. see Dégelis
223 L5 Sainte Rose du Lac Man. Can.
150 B4 St Erth Cornwall, England U.K.
162 B3 Saintes France
247 □2 Saintes, Îles des is Guadeloupe
160 C1 Ste-Sabine France
156 E4 Ste-Savine France
Ste-Scholastique Que. Can. see Mirabel
162 E2 Ste-Sévère-sur-Indre France
161 C3 Ste-Sigolène France
163 A5 St-Esteben France
162 B3 St-Estèphe France
163 E6 St-Estève France
159 F3 Ste-Suzanne France
233 G2 Ste-Thérèse Que. Can.
161 C3 St-Étienne France
162 E4 St-Étienne-Cantalès France
163 A5 St-Étienne-de-Baïgorry France
161 D3 St-Étienne-de-Crossey France
161 C4 St-Étienne-de-Fontbellon France
162 D2 St-Étienne-de-Fursac France
161 B4 St-Étienne-de-Lugdarès France
158 E4 St-Étienne-de-Montluc France
161 D3 St-Étienne-de-St-Geoirs France
161 E4 St-Étienne-de-Tinée France
163 D4 St-Étienne-de-Tulmont France
160 D2 St-Étienne-du-Bois France
156 B3 St-Étienne-du-Rouvray France
161 D4 St-Étienne-en-Dévoluy France
161 D4 St-Étienne-les-Orgues France
157 G4 St-Étienne-lès-Remiremont France
161 B4 St-Étienne-Vallée-Française France
161 D5 Ste-Tulle France
233 F2 St Eugene Ont. Can.
233 □I1 St-Eusèbe Que. Can.
233 G2 St-Eustache Que. Can.
247 □2 St Eustatius i. Neth. Antilles
158 B4 St-Évarzec France
156 D5 Ste-Vertu France
161 D5 Ste-Victoire, Montagne mt. France
225 G3 St-Fabien Que. Can.
215 H4 St Faith's S. Africa
160 B1 St-Fargeau France
225 F3 St-Félicien Que. Can.
161 C3 St-Félicien France
227 H1 St-Félix-de-Dalquier Que. Can.
163 D5 St-Félix-Lauragais France
146 G4 St Fergus Aberdeenshire, Scotland U.K.
163 C4 St-Ferme France
147 F2 Saintfield Northern Ireland U.K.
146 D5 St Fillans Perth and Kinross, Scotland U.K.
157 G4 St-Firmin France
161 E4 St-Firmin France
156 D4 St-Flavy France
192 B2 St-Florent Corse France
162 A2 St-Florent-des-Bois France
156 D4 St-Florentin France
159 E4 St-Florent-le-Vieil France
162 E2 St-Florent-sur-Cher France
161 B3 St-Flour France
159 H5 St-Flovier France
160 C3 St-Fons France
162 B3 St-Fort-sur-Gironde France
163 C5 St-Frajou France
237 F6 St Francesville LA U.S.A.
233 □I1 St Francis r. Can./U.S.A.
236 C4 Saint Francis KS U.S.A.
233 □I1 St Francis ME U.S.A.
237 F5 St Francis r. Arkansas/Missouri U.S.A.
215 E6 St Francis Bay S. Africa
82 C3 St Francis Isles S.A. Austr.
225 F4 St-François r. Que. Can.
247 □2 St-François Guadeloupe
217 □2 St François i. Seychelles
161 E3 St-François-Longchamp France
161 C4 St-Front France
162 C3 St-Front-de-Pradoux France
159 E5 St-Fulgent France
160 C3 St-Galmier France
159 G2 St-Gatien-des-Bois France
163 C5 St-Gaudens France
162 D2 St-Gaultier France
233 □H2 St-Gédéon Que. Can.
163 B5 St-Gein France
161 B5 St-Gély-du-Fesc France
165 D4 St-Genesius-Rode Belgium
161 D3 St-Genest-Malifaux France
160 C2 St-Gengoux-le-National France
161 C5 St-Geniès-de-Malgoirès France
161 E4 St-Geniez France
161 A4 St-Geniez-d'Olt France
162 B3 St-Genis-de-Saintonge France
163 E6 St-Génis-des-Fontaines France
160 C3 St-Genis-Laval France
160 E2 St-Genis-Pouilly France
160 D3 St-Genix-sur-Guiers France
150 C4 St Gennys Cornwall, England U.K.
159 H5 St-Genou France
161 D3 St-Geoire-en-Valdaine France
83 G2 St George Qld Austr.
85 F3 St George r. Qld Austr.
225 H4 St George N.B. Can.
220 B4 St George AK U.S.A.
231 D5 St George SC U.S.A.
241 I3 St George UT U.S.A.
83 G3 St George Head hd A.C.T. Austr.
86 E3 St George Range hills W.A. Austr.
225 J3 St George's Nfld. Can.
225 G4 St-Georges Que. Can.
251 I4 St Georges Fr. Guiana
247 □6 St George's Grenada
234 C3 St Georges DE U.S.A.
225 J3 St George's Bay Nfld. Can.
225 I4 St George's Bay N.S. Can.
159 F3 St-Georges-Buttavent France
147 E5 St George's Channel Rep. of Ireland/U.K.
161 B3 St-Georges-d'Aurac France
161 D3 St-Georges-de-Commiers France
162 B3 St-Georges-de-Didonne France
161 A4 St-Georges-de-Luzençon France
160 A3 St-Georges-de-Mons France
158 E5 St-Georges-de-Montaigu France
160 C2 St-Georges-de-Reneins France
159 F3 St-Georges-des-Groseillers France
160 D3 St-Georges-d'Espéranche France
162 A3 St-Georges-d'Oléron France
159 G2 St-Georges-du-Vièvre France
160 B3 St-Georges-en-Couzan France
159 G5 St-Georges-lès-Baillargeaux France
156 D5 St-Georges-sur-Baulche France
159 H4 St-Georges-sur-Cher France
156 B4 St-Georges-sur-Eure France
159 F4 St-Georges-sur-Loire France
163 A5 St-Geours-de-Maremne France
160 B2 St-Gérand-le-Puy France
226 C3 St Germain WI U.S.A.
160 B2 St-Germain-Chassenay France
161 B4 St-Germain-de-Calberte France
159 G3 St-Germain-de-la-Coudre France
160 B2 St-Germain-des-Fossés France
162 B3 St-Germain-d'Esteuil France
163 D3 St-Germain-du-Bel-Air France
160 D2 St-Germain-du-Bois France
159 G3 St-Germain-du-Corbéis France
160 C2 St-Germain-du-Plain France
162 E1 St-Germain-du-Puy France
161 B4 St-Germain-du-Teil France
156 C4 St-Germain-en-Laye France
160 C3 St-Germain-Laval France
161 B3 St-Germain-Lembron France
162 D3 St-Germain-les-Belles France
160 B2 St-Germain-Lespinasse France
162 D3 St-Germain-les-Vergnes France
161 B3 St-Germain-l'Herm France
150 C4 St Germans Cornwall, England U.K.
163 B5 St-Germé France
156 B3 St-Germer-de-Fly France
158 D5 St-Gervais France
161 D3 St-Gervais France
160 A2 St-Gervais-d'Auvergne France
159 H4 St-Gervais-la-Forêt France
160 E3 St-Gervais-les-Bains France
159 G5 St-Gervais-les-Trois-Clochers France
161 B5 St-Gervais-sur-Mare France
163 D4 St-Géry France
165 C4 St-Ghislain Belgium
158 D4 St-Gildas-de-Rhuys France
158 D4 St-Gildas-des-Bois France
161 C5 St-Gilles France
158 E5 St-Gilles-Croix-de-Vie France
160 E2 St-Gingolph France
163 D6 St-Girons France
163 A5 St-Girons-Plage France
156 D3 St-Gobain France
St Gotthard Pass pass Switz. see San Gottardo, Passo del
158 E3 St-Grégoire France
158 B4 St-Guénolé France
161 B5 St-Guilhem-le-Désert France
160 B2 St-Haon-le-Châtel France
160 C3 St-Héand France
226 E3 St Helen MI U.S.A.
216 □2b St Helena terr. S. Atlantic Ocean
240 F2 St Helena CA U.S.A.
214 B5 St Helena Bay S. Africa
83 G5 St Helens Tas. Austr.
149 G4 St Helens Merseyside, England U.K.
238 B2 St Helens OR U.S.A.
238 B2 St Helens, Mount vol. WA U.S.A.
83 G5 St Helens Point Tas. Austr.
158 D2 St Helier Channel Is
158 E4 St-Herblain France
163 E5 St-Hilaire France
156 E3 St-Hilaire-au-Temple France
161 C4 St-Hilaire-de-Brethmas France
158 E4 St-Hilaire-de-Loulay France
163 C4 St-Hilaire-de-Lusignan France
158 E5 St-Hilaire-de-Riez France
162 B2 St-Hilaire-des-Loges France
162 B3 St-Hilaire-de-Villefranche France
159 E3 St-Hilaire-du-Harcouët France
161 D3 St-Hilaire-du-Rosier France
160 B2 St-Hilaire-Fontaine France
156 E3 St-Hilaire-le-Grand France
159 F4 St-Hilaire-St-Florent France
157 H4 St-Hippolyte France
160 E1 St-Hippolyte France
161 B5 St-Hippolyte-du-Fort France
117 F5 Sainthiya W. Bengal India
161 E4 St-Honorat, Mont mt. France
160 B2 St-Honoré-les-Bains France
161 C3 St-Hostien France
165 E5 St-Hubert Belgium
225 F4 St-Hyacinthe Que. Can.
226 E3 St Ignace MI U.S.A.
190 B1 St-Imier Switz.
150 C3 St Ishmael Carmarthenshire, Wales U.K.
161 D3 St-Ismier France
150 C4 St Ive Cornwall, England U.K.
151 G2 St Ives Cambridgeshire, England U.K.
150 □ St Ives Cornwall, England U.K.
161 A5 St-Izaire France
233 □I1 St-Jacques N.B. Can.
St Jacques, Cap Vietnam see Vung Tau
224 E3 St-Jacques-de-Dupuy Que. Can.
158 E3 St-Jacques-de-la-Lande France
158 D3 St-Jacut-de-la-Mer France
158 E3 St-James France
246 □ St James parish Jamaica
226 E3 St James MI U.S.A.
236 E3 St James MN U.S.A.
236 F4 St James MO U.S.A.
235 E2 St James NY U.S.A.
225 H3 St-Jean r. Que. Can.
225 H3 St-Jean r. Que. Can.
163 D5 St-Jean France
251 H3 St-Jean Fr. Guiana
225 F3 St-Jean, Lac l. Que. Can.
158 D4 St-Jean-Brévelay France
161 F5 St-Jean-Cap-Ferrat France
St-Jean-d'Acre Israel see 'Akko
162 B3 St-Jean-d'Angély France
159 G3 St-Jean-d'Assé France
160 D3 St-Jean-de-Bournay France
156 B5 St-Jean-de-Braye France
159 E2 St-Jean-de-Daye France
156 B5 St-Jean-de-la-Ruelle France
160 D1 St-Jean-de-Losne France
163 A5 St-Jean-de-Luz France
161 C4 St-Jean-de-Maruéjols-et-Avéjan France
161 E3 St-Jean-de-Maurienne France
158 D5 St-Jean-de-Monts France
161 C3 St-Jean-de-Muzols France
225 G4 St-Jean-de-Port-Joli Que. Can.
159 G5 St-Jean-de-Sauves France
160 E3 St-Jean-de-Sixt France
161 B5 St-Jean-de-Védas France
163 B4 St-Jean-d'Illac France
161 B4 St-Jean-du-Bruel France
163 D5 St-Jean-du-Falga France
161 B4 St-Jean-du-Gard France
161 D3 St-Jean-en-Royans France
163 A5 St-Jean-Pied-de-Port France
163 C5 St-Jean-Poutge France
160 C3 St-Jean-Soleymieux France
159 F3 St-Jean-sur-Erve France
160 D2 St-Jean-sur-Reyssouze France
225 F4 St-Jean-sur-Richelieu Que. Can.
160 E2 St-Jeoire France
224 F4 St-Jérôme Que. Can.
161 C3 St-Jeure-d'Ay France
161 C3 St-Jeures France
158 D4 St-Joachim France
238 C2 St Joe r. ID U.S.A.
225 H4 Saint John N.B. Can.
158 D2 St John Channel Is
206 C5 St John r. Liberia
236 D4 St John KS U.S.A.
233 □J2 St John r. ME U.S.A.
247 F3 St John Island Virgin Is (U.S.A.)
247 □2 St John's Antigua and Barbuda
225 K4 St John's Nfld. Can.
241 M4 St Johns AZ U.S.A.
226 E4 St Johns MI U.S.A.
232 A4 St Johns OH U.S.A.
231 D6 St Johns r. FL U.S.A.
233 G2 St Johnsbury VT U.S.A.
148 B3 St Johnstown Rep. of Ireland
146 D6 St John's Town of Dalry Dumfries and Galloway, Scotland U.K.
233 F3 St Johnsville NY U.S.A.
158 E2 St-Jores France
160 E3 St-Jorioz France
165 C3 St-Joris Belgium
163 D5 St-Jory France
162 D3 St-Jory-de-Chalais France
247 □3 St-Joseph Martinique
237 F6 St Joseph LA U.S.A.
226 D4 St Joseph MI U.S.A.
236 E4 St Joseph MO U.S.A.
226 D4 St Joseph r. MI U.S.A.
226 E5 St Joseph r. MI U.S.A.
224 B3 St Joseph, Lake Ont. Can.
St-Joseph-d'Alma Que. Can. see Alma
158 E3 St-Jouan-des-Guérets France
159 G2 St-Jouin-Bruneval France
159 F5 St-Jouin-de-Marnes France
224 F4 St Jovité Que. Can.
163 E5 St-Juéry France
St Julian's Malta see San Giljan
160 D2 St-Julien France
163 D5 St-Julien France
162 B3 St-Julien-Beychevelle France
161 C4 St-Julien-Boutières France
160 C2 St-Julien-de-Civry France
158 E4 St-Julien-de-Concelles France
158 E4 St-Julien-de-Vouvantes France
156 D4 St-Julien-du-Sault France
161 E5 St-Julien-du-Verdon France
161 D4 St-Julien-en-Beauchêne France
163 A4 St-Julien-en-Born France
160 E2 St-Julien-en-Genevois France
161 D4 St-Julien-en-Quint France
162 C2 St-Julien-l'Ars France
161 C4 St-Julien-les-Rosiers France
157 E4 St-Julien-les-Villas France
160 D2 St-Julien-sur-Reyssouze France
162 C3 St-Junien France
161 C4 St-Just France
150 □ St Just Cornwall, England U.K.
156 C3 St-Just-en-Chaussée France
160 B3 St-Just-en-Chevalet France
163 A5 St-Just-Ibarre France
163 E5 St-Justin France
150 B4 St Just in Roseland Cornwall, England U.K.
160 C3 St-Just-la-Pendue France
162 A3 St-Just-Luzac France
156 D4 St-Just-Sauvage France
160 C3 St-Just-St-Rambert France
150 C4 St Keverne Cornwall, England U.K.
146 □ St Kilda i. Scotland U.K.
247 □2 St Kitts i. St Kitts and Nevis
247 □2 St Kitts and Nevis country West Indies
159 F4 St-Lambert-des-Levées France
159 F4 St-Lambert-du-Lattay France
163 C5 St-Lary France
163 C6 St-Lary-Soulan France

St-Laurent, Golfe du to Samkhret' Oset'i
357

St-Laurent, Golfe du g. Que. Can. see St Lawrence, Gulf of
156 C2 St-Laurent-Blangy France
163 B5 St-Laurent-Bretagne France
161 C5 St-Laurent-d'Aigouze France
161 C4 St-Laurent-de-Carnols France
186 F2 St-Laurent-de-Cerdans France
160 C3 St-Laurent-de-Chamousset France
161 A5 St-Laurent-de-la-Cabrerisse France
163 E6 St-Laurent-de-la-Salanque France
163 C5 St-Laurent-de-Neste France
251 H3 St-Laurent-du-Maroni Fr. Guiana
161 D3 St-Laurent-du-Pont France
161 F5 St-Laurent-du-Var France
161 E4 St-Laurent-du-Verdon France
159 G2 St-Laurent-en-Caux France
160 D2 St-Laurent-en-Grandvaux France
161 B4 St-Laurent-les-Bains France
162 B3 St-Laurent-Médoc France
156 B5 St-Laurent-Nouan France
162 C3 St-Laurent-sur-Gorre France
157 F3 St-Laurent-sur-Othain France
159 F5 St-Laurent-sur-Sèvre France
85 G4 St Lawrence Qld Austr.
225 K4 St Lawrence Nfld. Can.
225 G3 St Lawrence inlet Que. Can.
234 C2 St Lawrence PA U.S.A.
225 I3 St Lawrence, Gulf of Que. Can.
220 B3 St Lawrence Island AK U.S.A.
224 F4 St Lawrence Seaway sea chan. Can./U.S.A.
223 K5 St Lazare Man. Can.
165 E5 St-Léger Belgium
160 B1 St-Léger-de-Fougeret France
160 B2 St-Léger-des-Vignes France
156 B4 St-Léger-en-Yvelines France
160 C2 St-Léger-sous-Beuvray France
160 C2 St-Léger-sur-Dheune France
225 H4 St-Léonard N.B. Can.
225 F4 St-Léonard Que. Can.
157 G4 St-Léonard France
232 E5 St Leonard MD U.S.A.
162 D3 St-Léonard-de-Noblat France
151 F4 St Leonards Dorset, England U.K.
162 C3 St-Léon-sur-l'Isle France
156 C3 St-Leu-d'Esserent France
225 K2 St Lewis Nfld. Can.
225 J2 St Lewis r. Nfld. Can.
163 D5 St-Lizier France
159 E2 St-Lô France
163 A5 St-Lon-les-Mines France
160 D2 St-Lothian France
163 B4 St-Loubès France
160 F1 St-Louis France
247 □2 St-Louis Guadeloupe
206 A2 St-Louis Senegal
226 E4 St Louis MI U.S.A.
236 F4 St Louis MO U.S.A.
226 A2 St Louis r. MN U.S.A.
246 D3 St-Louis du Nord Haiti
157 H4 St-Louis-lès-Bitche France
161 B5 St-Loup, Pic hill France
160 C2 St-Loup-de-la-Salle France
156 D4 St-Loup-de-Naud France
159 F5 St-Loup-Lamairé France
157 G5 St-Loup-sur-Semouse France
156 B4 St-Lubin-des-Joncherets France
158 E4 St-Luce-sur-Loire France
247 □3 St Lucia country West Indies
215 I3 St Lucia, Lake S. Africa
215 I3 St Lucia Estuary S. Africa
St Luke's Island Myanmar see Zadetkale Kyun
158 D3 St-Lunaire France
160 D2 St-Lupicin France
156 E4 St-Lyé France
163 D5 St-Lys France
163 B4 St-Macaire France
162 B1 St-Macaire-en-Mauges France
163 B4 St-Magne France
163 B4 St-Magne-de-Castillon France
146 □G1 St Magnus Bay Scotland U.K.
161 D5 St-Maime France
162 B2 St-Maixent-l'École France
158 D3 St-Malo France
158 D3 St-Malo, Golfe de g. France
158 E2 St-Malo-de-la-Lande France
161 C5 St-Mamert-du-Gard France
163 E4 St-Mamet-la-Salvetat France
161 D5 St-Mandrier-sur-Mer France
246 D3 St Marc Haiti
160 C2 St-Marcel France
162 D2 St-Marcel France
156 B3 St-Marcel France
161 C4 St-Marcel-d'Ardèche France
161 C3 St-Marcel-lès-Annonay France
161 C4 St-Marcel-lès-Sauzet France
161 C4 St-Marcel-lès-Valence France
161 D3 St-Marcellin France
163 C5 St-Marcet France
156 E5 St-Marc-sur-Seine France
156 D4 St-Mards-en-Othe France
151 I3 St Margaret's at Cliffe Kent, England U.K.
146 F3 St Margaret's Hope Orkney, Scotland U.K.
238 C2 Saint Maries ID U.S.A.
St Mark's S. Africa see Cofimvaba
215 F5 St Marks E. Cape S. Africa
163 E6 St-Marsal France
159 G4 St-Mars-d'Outillé France
158 E4 St-Mars-du-Désert France
159 G3 St-Mars-la-Brière France
158 E4 St-Mars-la-Jaille France
161 B4 St-Martial France
163 D4 St-Martial-de-Nabirat France
162 C3 St-Martial-de-Valette France
158 D2 St Martin Channel Is
158 D2 St Martin Channel Is
161 D5 St-Martin France
247 G3 St Martin i. West Indies
156 B2 St-Martin-Boulogne France
156 D3 St-Martin-d'Ablois France
163 A5 St-Martin-d'Arrossa France
159 I4 St-Martin-d'Auxigny France
161 E3 St-Martin-de-Belleville France
161 D5 St-Martin-de-Castillon France
161 C5 St-Martin-de-Crau France
161 B4 St-Martin-de-Fugères France
158 E3 St-Martin-de-Landelles France
161 B5 St-Martin-de-Londres France
161 E4 St-Martin-d'Entraunes France
162 A2 St-Martin-de-Ré France
159 F2 St-Martin-des-Besaces France
158 E3 St-Martin-des-Champs France
158 C3 St-Martin-des-Champs France
163 A5 St-Martin-de-Seignanx France
161 C4 St-Martin-de-Valamas France
161 C4 St-Martin-de-Valgalgues France
161 D3 St-Martin-d'Hères France
163 B5 St-Martin-d'Oney France
160 D2 St-Martin-du-Frêne France
160 D2 St-Martin-du-Mont France
161 F5 St-Martin-du-Var France
160 D2 St-Martin-en-Bresse France
160 C3 St-Martin-en-Haut France
160 C3 St-Martin-la-Plaine France
159 G4 St-Martin-le-Beau France
150 D2 St Martin's Shropshire, England U.K.
150 □ St Martin's i. England U.K.
156 D5 St-Martin-sur-Ouanne France
162 E3 St-Martin-Valmeroux France
161 F4 St-Martin-Vésubie France
163 C5 St-Martory France
222 H5 St Mary r. B.C. Can.
246 □ St Mary parish Jamaica
81 B6 St Mary, Mount South I. N.Z.
151 F3 St Mary Bourne Hampshire, England U.K.
151 H3 St Mary in the Marsh Kent, England U.K.
82 D2 St Mary Peak S.A. Austr.
83 G5 St Marys Tas. Austr.
227 G4 St Mary's Ont. Can.
146 F3 St Mary's Orkney, Scotland U.K.
150 □ St Mary's i. England U.K.
236 D4 Saint Marys KS U.S.A.
232 A4 St Marys OH U.S.A.
232 D4 St Marys PA U.S.A.
232 C5 St Marys WV U.S.A.
236 G3 St Marys r. OH U.S.A.
225 K4 St Mary's Bay b. Nfld. Can.
151 H3 St Mary's Bay Kent, England U.K.
232 E5 St Marys City MD U.S.A.
227 H1 St-Mathieu Que. Can.
162 C3 St-Mathieu France
158 B3 St-Mathieu, Pointe de pt France
162 A2 St-Mathurin France
220 A3 St Matthew Island AK U.S.A.
231 D5 Saint Matthews SC U.S.A.
159 H5 St-Maur France
156 C4 St-Maur-des-Fossés France
224 F4 St Maurice r. Que. Can.
190 B2 St-Maurice Switz.
160 C3 St-Maurice-de-Beynost France
161 C3 St-Maurice-de-Lignon France
162 C3 St-Maurice-des-Lions France
162 D2 St-Maurice-la-Souterraine France
161 C3 St-Maurice-l'Exil France
161 B5 St-Maurice-Navacelles France
163 C4 St-Maurin France
150 B4 St Mawes Cornwall, England U.K.
157 G4 St-Max France
156 B2 St-Maxent France
156 C3 St-Maximin France
161 D5 St-Maximin-la-Ste-Baume France
162 C3 St-Méard-de-Drône France
162 B3 St-Médard-de-Guizières France
163 B4 St-Médard-en-Jalles France
158 D3 St-Méen-le-Grand France
158 E3 St-Méloir-des-Ondes France
162 B3 St-Même-les-Carrières France
156 E4 St-Memmie France
157 E3 St-Menges France
160 B2 St-Menoux France
150 C4 St Merryn Cornwall, England U.K.
162 D3 St-Mesmin France
156 D4 St-Mesmin France
159 F5 St-Mesmin France
163 C4 St-Mézard France
233 E5 St Michaels MD U.S.A.
150 □ St Michael's Mount tourist site England U.K.
163 C5 St-Michel France
156 E3 St-Michel France
162 C3 St-Michel France
158 C3 St-Michel, Montagne hill France
158 D4 St-Michel-Chef-Chef France
163 B4 St-Michel-de-Castelnau France
161 E3 St-Michel-de-Maurienne France
224 F4 St-Michel-des-Saints Que. Can.
158 C3 St-Michel-en-Grève France
162 A2 St-Michel-en-l'Herm France
159 F5 St-Michel-Mont-Mercure France
157 G4 St-Michel-sur-Meurthe France
157 F4 St-Mihiel France
146 F5 St Monans Fife, Scotland U.K.
163 B5 St-Mont France
161 C4 St-Montant France
157 G4 St-Nabord France
163 D5 St-Nauphary France
158 D4 St-Nazaire France
St-Nazaire, Étang de lag. France see Canet, Étang de
161 D3 St-Nazaire-en-Royans France
161 D4 St-Nazaire-le-Désert France
160 A3 St-Nectaire France
151 G2 St Neots Cambridgeshire, England U.K.
St Nicolas Belgium see Sint Niklaas
156 C2 St-Nicolas France
165 F5 St-Nicolas, Mont hill Lux.
156 B3 St-Nicolas-d'Aliermont France
163 D4 St-Nicolas-de-la-Grave France
157 G4 St-Nicolas-de-Port France
158 D4 St-Nicolas-de-Redon France
158 C3 St-Nicolas-du-Pélem France
190 C2 St Niklaus Switz.
146 □G2 St Ninian's Isle i. Scotland U.K.
158 D4 St-Nolff France
164 E3 St-Oedenrode Neth.
156 C2 St-Omer France
163 D5 St-Orens-de-Gameville France
163 C5 St-Ost France
151 I3 St Osyth Essex, England U.K.
158 D2 St Ouen Channel Is
156 B5 St-Ouen France
156 C2 St-Ouen France
159 F3 St-Ouen-des-Toits France
156 E4 St-Ouen-Domprot France
150 E3 St Owen's Cross Herefordshire, England U.K.
225 G4 St-Pacôme Que. Can.
158 E3 St-Pair-sur-Mer France
163 A5 St-Palais France
162 A3 St-Palais-sur-Mer France
161 B3 St-Pal-de-Chalancon France
161 C3 St-Pal-de-Mons France
233 □I1 St-Pamphile Que. Can.
160 C2 St-Pantaléon France
163 D4 St-Pantaléon France
162 D3 St-Pantaléon-de-Larche France
163 E5 St-Papoul France
162 D2 St-Pardoux, Lac de l. France
163 C4 St-Pardoux-Isaac France
162 C3 St-Pardoux-la-Rivière France
232 B4 St Paris OH U.S.A.
160 B2 St-Parize-le-Châtel France
156 E4 St-Parres-lès-Vaudes France
225 G4 St Pascal Que. Can.
159 G3 St-Paterne France
159 G4 St-Paterne-Racan France
223 I4 St Paul Alta Can.
225 J3 St Paul r. Newfoundland/Québec Can.
161 E4 St-Paul France
St Paul atoll Arch. des Tuamotu Fr. Polynesia see Hérèhérètué
206 C5 St Paul r. Liberia
217 □1c St Paul Réunion
226 A3 St Paul MN U.S.A.
236 D3 St Paul NE U.S.A.
232 B6 St Paul VA U.S.A.
265 J7 St Paul, Île i. Indian Ocean
163 D5 St-Paul-Cap-de-Joux France
163 E6 St-Paul-de-Fenouillet France
163 D6 St-Paul-de-Jarrat France
162 E4 St-Paul-des-Landes France
163 C4 St-Paul-d'Espis France
163 A4 St-Paul-en-Born France
161 E5 St-Paul-en-Forêt France
161 B5 St-Paul-et-Valmalle France
161 B3 St-Paulien France
161 C4 St-Paul-le-Jeune France
163 A5 St-Paul-lès-Dax France
161 D5 St-Paul-lès-Durance France
161 D3 St-Paul-lès-Romans France
161 C4 St-Paul-Trois-Châteaux France
163 B5 St-Pé-de-Bigorre France
163 A5 St-Pée-sur-Nivelle France
161 C4 St-Péray France
160 B1 St-Père France
158 D4 St-Père-en-Retz France
236 E2 St Peter MN U.S.A.
St Peter and St Paul Rocks is N. Atlantic Ocean see São Pedro e São Paulo
158 D2 St Peter in the Wood Channel Is
158 D2 St Peter Port Channel Is
225 I4 St Peter's N.S. Can.
225 I4 St Peters P.E.I. Can.
151 I3 St Peter's Kent, England U.K.
231 D7 St Petersburg FL U.S.A.
156 D4 St-Phal France
158 E5 St-Philbert-de-Bouaine France
158 E4 St-Philbert-de-Grand-Lieu France
161 D5 St-Pierre mt. France
160 F3 St-Pierre Italy
247 □3 St-Pierre Martinique
217 □1c St-Pierre Réunion
217 □2 St Pierre i. Seychelles
225 K4 St-Pierre St Pierre and Miquelon
225 J4 St Pierre and Miquelon terr. N. America
160 E3 St-Pierre-d'Albigny France
161 E3 St-Pierre-d'Allevard France
163 B4 St-Pierre-d'Aurillac France
161 D3 St-Pierre-de-Chartreuse France
162 C3 St-Pierre-de-Chignac France
162 C3 St-Pierre-de-Côle France
161 B5 St-Pierre-de-la-Fage France
159 G5 St-Pierre-de-Maillé France
158 E3 St-Pierre-de-Plesguen France
162 C1 St-Pierre-des-Corps France
159 F4 St-Pierre-des-Échaubrognes France
159 E3 St-Pierre-des-Landes France
159 F3 St-Pierre-des-Nids France
163 E5 St-Pierre-de-Trivisy France
163 A5 St-Pierre-d'Irube France
162 A3 St-Pierre-d'Oléron France
159 F5 St-Pierre-du-Chemin France
163 B5 St-Pierre-du-Mont France
158 E2 St-Pierre-Église France
160 E2 St-Pierre-en-Faucigny France
159 G2 St-Pierre-en-Port France
159 E3 St-Pierre-la-Cour France
160 B2 St-Pierre-le-Moûtier France
156 B3 St-Pierre-lès-Elbeuf France
156 C4 St-Pierre-lès-Nemours France
158 C4 St-Pierre-Quiberon France
159 F2 St-Pierre-sur-Dives France
161 C4 St-Pierreville France
163 C5 St-Plancard France
159 E3 St-Pois France
159 E4 St-Poix France
158 C3 St-Pol-de-Léon France
156 C1 St-Pol-sur-Mer France
156 C2 St-Pol-sur-Ternoise France
163 D4 St-Pompont France
161 E4 St-Pons France
161 A5 St-Pons-de-Thomières France
162 B3 St-Porchaire France
163 D4 St-Porquier France
160 B2 St-Pourçain-sur-Sioule France
190 B2 St-Prex Switz.
160 C3 St-Priest France
160 A3 St-Priest-de-Champs France
160 B3 St-Priest-Laprugne France
162 D3 St-Priest-Taurion France
162 E3 St-Privat France
161 B4 St-Privat-d'Allier France
161 C4 St-Privat-des-Vieux France
160 B2 St-Prix France
161 C4 St-Prix France
163 D4 St-Projet France
233 □H1 St-Prosper Que. Can.
163 C5 St-Puy France
225 H4 St Quentin N.B. Can.
156 D3 St-Quentin France
161 C4 St-Quentin-la-Poterie France
161 D3 St-Quentin-sur-Isère France
157 H4 St-Quirin France
161 C3 St-Rambert-d'Albon France
160 D3 St-Rambert-en-Bugey France
161 E5 St-Raphaël France
238 D2 Saint Regis MT U.S.A.
233 F2 St Regis r. NY U.S.A.
233 F2 St Regis Falls NY U.S.A.
161 C4 St-Remèze France
233 G2 St-Rémi Que. Can.
160 C2 St-Rémy France
161 C5 St-Rémy-de-Provence France
156 E4 St-Remy-en-Bouzemont-St-Genest-et-Isson France
156 B4 St-Rémy-sur-Avre France
160 B3 St-Rémy-sur-Durolle France
158 B3 St-Renan France
160 B1 St-Révérien France
190 C3 St-Rhemy Italy
160 C2 St-Rigaud, Mont mt. France
156 B2 St-Riquier France
159 G2 St-Romain-de-Colbosc France
160 D3 St-Romain-de-Jalionas France
160 C3 St-Romain-en-Gal France
160 C3 St-Romain-le-Puy France
160 C2 St-Romain-sous-Versigny France
159 H4 St-Romain-sur-Cher France
161 D3 St-Romans France
161 A4 St-Rome-de-Cernon France
161 A4 St-Rome-de-Tarn France
156 B3 St-Saëns France
158 D2 St Sampson Channel Is
163 E4 St-Santin France
162 E2 St-Saturnin France
161 D5 St-Saturnin-lès-Apt France
162 C3 St-Saud-Lacoussière France
160 B1 St-Saulge France
160 A3 St-Sauves-d'Auvergne France
158 B3 St-Sauveur France
157 G5 St-Sauveur France
161 C4 St-Sauveur-de-Montagut France
224 F4 St-Sauveur-des-Monts Que. Can.
160 B1 St-Sauveur-en-Puisaye France
161 D4 St-Sauveur-Gouvernet France
158 E2 St-Sauveur-Lendelin France
158 E2 St-Sauveur-le-Vicomte France
161 F4 St-Sauveur-sur-Tinée France
163 C5 St-Sauvy France
162 B3 St-Savin France
162 C2 St-Savin France
162 B3 St-Savinien France
158 D2 St Saviour Channel Is
233 □H2 St-Sébastien Que. Can.
156 B3 St-Sébastien-de-Morsent France
158 E4 St-Sébastien-sur-Loire France
160 C1 St-Seine-l'Abbaye France
163 B4 St-Selve France
161 C4 St-Semin France
161 A5 St-Sernin-sur-Rance France
156 D4 St-Sérotin France
163 B5 St-Sever France
159 E3 St-Sever-Calvados France
225 G4 St Siméon Que. Can.
161 D3 St-Siméon-de-Bressieux France
162 E4 St-Simon France
156 D3 St-Simon France
160 E2 St-Sorlin, Mont de mt. France
161 E3 St-Sorlin-d'Arves France
156 C3 St-Soupplets France
233 □J2 St Stephen N.B. Can.
150 C4 St Stephen Cornwall, England U.K.
231 E5 St Stephen SC U.S.A.
163 D5 St-Sulpice France
162 A3 St-Sulpice-de-Royan France
158 E4 St-Sulpice-des-Landes France
162 D2 St-Sulpice-Laurière France
162 D2 St-Sulpice-le-Guérétois France
162 E3 St-Sulpice-les-Champs France
162 D2 St-Sulpice-les-Feuilles France
163 D5 St-Sulpice-sur-Lèze France
159 G3 St-Sulpice-sur-Risle France
159 F2 St-Sylvain France
159 F4 St-Sylvain-d'Anjou France
163 C4 St-Sylvestre-sur-Lot France
163 B4 St-Symphorien France
160 C3 St-Symphorien-de-Lay France
160 C3 St-Symphorien-d'Ozon France
160 C3 St-Symphorien-sur-Coise France
150 C4 St Teath Cornwall, England U.K.
222 C3 St Terese AK U.S.A.
158 C3 St-Thégonnec France
233 □H2 St-Théophile Que. Can.
223 M4 St Theresa Point Man. Can.
161 B5 St-Thibéry France
157 F4 St-Thiébault France
224 D5 St Thomas Ont. Can.
246 □ St Thomas parish Jamaica
247 F3 St Thomas Island Virgin Is (U.S.A.)
158 C4 St-Thurien France
225 G4 St-Tite-des-Caps Que. Can.
160 D2 St-Trivier-de-Courtes France
160 C2 St-Trivier-sur-Moignans France
162 A3 St-Trojan-les-Bains France
St Trond Belgium see Sint Truiden
161 E5 St-Tropez France
163 D5 St-Urcisse France
161 B4 St-Urcize France
161 C3 St-Uze France
158 E2 St-Vaast-la-Hougue France
156 D4 St-Valérien France
159 G2 St-Valery-en-Caux France
156 B2 St-Valery-sur-Somme France
160 C2 St-Vallier France
161 C3 St-Vallier France
161 E5 St-Vallier-de-Thiey France
159 F5 St-Varent France
162 D2 St-Vaury France
161 E4 St-Véran France
161 C3 St-Victor France
161 D5 St-Victoret France
161 C4 St-Victor-la-Coste France
159 F2 St-Vigor-le-Grand France
190 C3 St-Vincent Italy
236 D1 St Vincent MN U.S.A.
247 □3 St Vincent i. West Indies
St-Vincent, Cap pt Madag. see Ankaboa, Tanjona
83 F5 St Vincent, Cape Tas. Austr.
St Vincent, Cape Port. see São Vicente, Cabo de
82 D3 St Vincent, Gulf S.A. Austr.
247 □3 St Vincent and the Grenadines i. West Indies
162 C3 St-Vincent-de-Connezac France
163 B5 St-Vincent-de-Paul France
163 A5 St-Vincent-de-Tyrosse France
231 C6 St Vincent Island FL U.S.A.
161 E4 St-Vincent-les-Forts France
247 □3 St Vincent Passage St Lucia/St Vincent
160 D1 St-Vit France
163 C4 St-Vite France
162 A3 St-Vivien-de-Médoc France
223 I4 St Walburg Sask. Can.
227 G4 St Williams Ont. Can.
162 A2 St-Xandre France
160 C2 St-Yan France
163 D5 St-Ybars France
160 B2 St-Yorre France
162 D3 St-Yrieix-la-Perche France
162 C3 St-Yrieix-sur-Charente France
158 C4 St-Yvy France
161 D5 St-Zacharie France
156 B4 Sainville France
116 E3 Saipal mt. Nepal
91 K3 Saipan i. N. Mariana Is
158 E2 Saire r. France
163 B5 Saison r. France
163 E5 Saissac France
105 E3 Saitama pref. Japan
Saiteli Turkey see Kadınhanı
103 E7 Saito Japan
140 M1 Saivomuotka Sweden
163 E5 Saïx France
252 C4 Sajama, Nevado mt. Bol.
197 F4 Šajince Srbija Yugo.
124 D2 Sājir Saudi Arabia
175 J1 Sajna r. Pol.
177 J4 Sajó r. Hungary
177 J3 Sajóhidvég Hungary
177 J3 Sajókaza Hungary
177 J3 Sajópetri Hungary
177 J3 Sajószentpéter Hungary
177 K4 Sajószöged Hungary
177 J3 Sajóvámos Hungary
128 D1 Sājūr, Nahr r. Syria/Turkey
210 C2 Saka Eth.
105 F3 Sakado Japan
105 F2 Sakai Gumma Japan
104 B4 Sakai Ōsaka Japan
103 F6 Sakaide Japan
103 F6 Sakaiminato Japan
127 F5 Sakākah Saudi Arabia
236 C2 Sakakawea, Lake ND U.S.A.
224 F2 Sakami Que. Can.
224 E2 Sakami r. Que. Can.
105 F3 Sakami-gawa r. Japan
224 E2 Sakami Lake Que. Can.
209 F8 Sakania Dem. Rep. Congo
197 H5 Sakar mts Bulg.
123 E2 Sakar Turkm.
213 □J4 Sakaraha Madag.
123 E2 Sakar-Chaga Turkm.
Sakartvelo country Asia see Georgia
199 G1 Sakarya Turkey
199 G1 Sakarya prov. Turkey
199 G1 Sakarya r. Turkey
206 D5 Sakassou Côte d'Ivoire
102 I4 Sakata Japan
101 C4 Sakchu N. Korea
121 H2 Saken Seyfullin Kazakh.
97 C4 Sa Keo r. Thai.
207 F5 Sakété Benin
100 G2 Sakhalin i. Rus. Fed.
Sakhalin Oblast admin. div. Rus. Fed. see Sakhalinskaya Oblast'
100 G2 Sakhalinskaya Oblast' admin. div. Rus. Fed.
100 G1 Sakhalinskiy Zaliv b. Sakhalin Rus. Fed.
139 K3 Sakharovo Rus. Fed.
215 H1 Sakhelwe S. Africa
215 G2 Sakhile S. Africa
136 D3 Sakhnivtsi Ukr.
137 H3 Sakhnovshchyna Ukr.
122 D2 Sakhra Turkm.
122 B2 Sakht-Sar Iran
129 E3 Şäki Azer.
207 F4 Şaki Nigeria
Saki Ukr. see Saky
138 D4 Šakiai Lith.
189 B7 Sakiet Sidi Youssef Tunisia
123 F4 Sakir mt. Pak.
102 □1 Sakishima-shotō is Japan
114 B3 Sakleshpur Karnataka India
120 C2 Sakmara Rus. Fed.
116 D5 Sakoli Mahar. India
96 D3 Sakon Nakhon Thai.
233 H4 Sakonnet r. RI U.S.A.
123 G5 Sakrand Pak.
214 C4 Sakrivier S. Africa
120 E3 Saksaul'skiy Kazakh.
Saksaul'skoye Kazakh. see Saksaul'skiy
140 J3 Sakshaug Norway
170 C1 Sakskøbing Denmark
117 E5 Sakti Madh. Prad. India
138 E2 Saku Estonia
105 E2 Saku Japan
105 G3 Sakura Japan
105 G2 Sakura-gawa r. Japan
104 B4 Sakurai Japan
103 E8 Sakura-jima vol. Japan
137 G5 Saky Ukr.
141 M3 Säkylä Fin.
206 □ Sal i. Cape Verde
135 H7 Sal r. Rus. Fed.
138 E3 Sala Latvia
177 G3 Šaľa Slovakia
143 G2 Sala Sweden
93 B3 Salabangka, Kepulauan is Indon.
224 F4 Salaberry-de-Valleyfield Que. Can.
138 E3 Salaca r. Latvia
197 F2 Sălacea Romania
138 E3 Salacgrīva Latvia
193 H4 Sala Consilina Italy
186 E2 Salada r. Spain
258 C2 Salada, Bahía b. Chile
242 B1 Salada, Laguna salt l. Mex.
258 F3 Saladas Arg.
261 H4 Saladillo Arg.
261 H4 Saladillo r. Buenos Aires Arg.
261 F3 Saladillo r. Córdoba Arg.
261 G2 Saladillo r. Santa Fé Arg.
258 E3 Saladillo r. Santiago del Estero Arg.
260 D5 Salado r. Arg.
261 I4 Salado r. Buenos Aires Arg.
258 F2 Salado r. Formosa Arg.
258 C3 Salado r. La Rioja Arg.
259 D6 Salado r. Río Negro Arg.
261 G3 Salado r. Santa Fé Arg.
246 C2 Salado r. Cuba
245 E3 Salado r. Hidalgo/México Mex.
245 F5 Salado r. Oaxaca/Puebla Mex.
243 F3 Salado r. Mex.
184 D4 Salado r. Andalucía Spain
184 E4 Salado r. Andalucía Spain
185 F3 Salado r. Andalucía Spain
185 F3 Salado r. Andalucía Spain
206 C4 Saladou Guinea
206 E4 Salaga Ghana
162 D3 Salagnac France
161 B5 Salagou, Lac du l. France
128 D3 Şalāḩ, Tall hill Jordan
127 F4 Şalāḩ ad Dīn governorate Iraq
127 G3 Salahuddin Iraq
161 C3 Salaise-sur-Sanne France
177 M4 Sălaj county Romania
212 E4 Salajwe Botswana
125 G3 Salakh, Jabal mt. Oman
202 C6 Salal Chad
125 F4 Şalālah Oman
243 H6 Salamá Guat.
242 □I6 Salamá Hond.
260 B2 Salamanca Chile
244 D3 Salamanca Mex.
182 E4 Salamanca Spain
182 D4 Salamanca prov. Castilla y León Spain
232 D3 Salamanca NY U.S.A.
Salamantica Spain see Salamanca
208 D2 Salamat pref. Chad
208 C2 Salamat, Bahr r. Chad
122 A3 Salāmatābād Iran
198 C3 Salamina Greece
198 C3 Salamina i. Greece
128 A2 Salamis tourist site Cyprus
Salamís i. Greece see Salamina
128 C2 Salamīyah Syria
226 E5 Salamonie r. IN U.S.A.
117 F5 Salandi r. India
193 I4 Salandra Italy
138 C3 Salantai Lith.
216 □1c Salão Faial Azores
194 B5 Salaparuta Sicilia Italy
107 F3 Salaqi Nei Mongol China
185 F3 Salar Spain
197 F2 Sălard Romania
186 D2 Salardu Spain
250 B6 Salas Peru
182 D1 Salas Spain
197 F3 Salaš Srbija Yugo.
183 G2 Salas de los Infantes Spain
138 E3 Salaspils Latvia
163 C5 Salat r. France
95 E4 Salatiga Jawa Tengah Indon.
162 B4 Salaunes France
134 K4 Salaush Rus. Fed.
197 G2 Sălăuța r. Romania
120 C1 Salavat Rus. Fed.
252 A2 Salaverry Peru
93 D3 Salawati i. Irian Jaya Indon.
92 C4 Salay Phil.
116 B5 Salaya Gujarat India
93 B4 Salayar i. Indon.
267 L7 Sala y Gómez, Isla i. S. Pacific Ocean
Salazar Angola see N'dalatando
261 F5 Salazar Arg.
186 B2 Salazar r. Spain
190 B3 Salbertrand Italy
162 E1 Salbris France
252 B3 Salccantay, Cerro mt. Peru
246 E3 Salcedo Dom. Rep.
173 G3 Salching Ger.
138 E4 Šalčia r. Lith.
197 H3 Sălciile Romania
138 E4 Šalčininkai Lith.
197 H3 Sălcioara Romania
150 D4 Salcombe Devon, England U.K.
Saldae Alg. see Bejaïa
183 F2 Saldaña Spain
214 A5 Saldanha S. Africa
173 H3 Saldenburg Ger.
183 I4 Saldón Spain
183 H3 Salduero Spain
261 G6 Saldungaray Arg.
191 F2 Saldura r. Italy
138 D3 Saldus Latvia
83 F4 Sale Vic. Austr.
86 E3 Sale r. W.A. Austr.
190 D4 Sale Italy
96 A2 Sale Myanmar
149 G4 Sale Greater Manchester, England U.K.
163 C6 Saléchan France
95 G5 Saleh, Teluk b. Sumbawa Indon.
122 B3 Şāleḩābād Iran
122 A3 Şāleḩābād Iran
151 H4 Salehurst East Sussex, England U.K.
130 H3 Salekhard Rus. Fed.
172 D4 Salem Baden-Württemberg Ger.
168 F2 Salem Schleswig-Holstein Ger.
114 C4 Salem Tamil Nadu India
215 F5 Salem S. Africa
237 F4 Salem AR U.S.A.
236 F4 Salem IL U.S.A.
230 C4 Salem IN U.S.A.
233 H3 Salem MA U.S.A.
237 F4 Salem MO U.S.A.
234 C3 Salem NJ U.S.A.
233 G3 Salem NY U.S.A.
232 C4 Salem OH U.S.A.
238 B2 Salem OR U.S.A.
236 D3 Salem SD U.S.A.
241 L1 Salem UT U.S.A.
232 C6 Salem VA U.S.A.
232 C5 Salem WV U.S.A.
234 C3 Salem r. NJ U.S.A.
234 C3 Salem County county NJ U.S.A.
194 B5 Salemi Sicilia Italy
141 K3 Sälen Sweden
146 C5 Salen Argyll and Bute, Scotland U.K.
146 C5 Salen Highland, Scotland U.K.
161 E5 Salernes France
193 G4 Salerno Italy
193 H4 Salerno prov. Campania Italy
193 G4 Salerno, Golfo di g. Italy
Salernum Italy see Salerno
162 E3 Salers France
256 D4 Sales Oliveira Brazil
257 E5 Salesópolis Brazil
161 B4 Salettes France
156 C3 Saleux France
149 G4 Salford Greater Manchester, England U.K.
151 G3 Salfords Surrey, England U.K.
254 F4 Salgado Brazil
254 F3 Salgado r. Brazil
177 I3 Salgótarján Hungary
254 F4 Salgueiro Brazil
182 C5 Salgueiro Port.
182 C3 Salgueiros Port.
151 I2 Salhouse Norfolk, England U.K.
142 A1 Salhus Norway
137 H5 Salhyr r. Ukr.
195 G2 Salice Salentino Italy
190 D4 Saliceto Italy
194 D5 Salici, Monte mt. Sicilia Italy
239 F4 Salida CO U.S.A.
138 D3 Saliena Latvia
163 B5 Salies-de-Béarn France
163 C5 Salies-du-Salat France
162 D4 Salignac-Eyvignes France
199 F2 Salihli Turkey
138 F5 Salihorsk Belarus
206 B3 Salikénié Senegal
186 B3 Salillas de Jalón Spain
211 B8 Salima Malawi
236 D4 Salina KS U.S.A.
241 L2 Salina UT U.S.A.
194 D4 Salina, Isola i. Isole Lipari Italy
245 G5 Salina Cruz Mex.
257 F2 Salinas Brazil
250 A5 Salinas Ecuador
244 D2 Salinas Mex.
237 D7 Salinas r. Mex.
247 □1 Salinas Puerto Rico
182 E1 Salinas Asturias Spain
187 C6 Salinas Valencia Spain
240 G3 Salinas CA U.S.A.
240 G3 Salinas r. CA U.S.A.
183 H2 Salinas de Añana Spain
252 D4 Salinas de Garci Mendoza Bol.
183 I4 Salinas del Manzano Spain
183 I2 Salinas de Pamplona Spain
183 F2 Salinas de Pisuerga Spain
186 D2 Salinas de Sín Spain
239 F5 Salinas Peak NM U.S.A.
161 C5 Salin-de-Giraud France
161 C4 Salindres France
193 G2 Saline r. Italy
149 F1 Saline Fife, Scotland U.K.
227 F4 Saline MI U.S.A.
237 E5 Saline r. AR U.S.A.
236 D4 Saline r. KS U.S.A.
191 F5 Saline di Volterra Italy
193 F2 Salinello r. Italy
240 I3 Saline Valley depr. CA U.S.A.
232 C4 Salineville OH U.S.A.
96 A2 Salingyi Myanmar
254 D2 Salinópolis Brazil
162 E3 Salins France
160 D2 Salins-les-Bains France
184 B3 Salir Port.
151 F3 Salisbury Wiltshire, England U.K.
233 F5 Salisbury MD U.S.A.
231 D5 Salisbury NC U.S.A.
232 D5 Salisbury PA U.S.A.
Salisbury Zimbabwe see Harare
235 D1 Salisbury Mills NY U.S.A.
151 E3 Salisbury Plain England U.K.
197 F3 Săliște Romania
197 G2 Săliștea de Sus Romania
194 C5 Salito r. Sicilia Italy
244 C2 Salitral de Carrera Mex.
254 E4 Salitre r. Brazil
177 H4 Salka Slovakia
128 C3 Şalkhad Syria
117 F5 Salki r. India
128 C1 Salkım Turkey
136 E3 Sal'kove Ukr.
140 O2 Salla Fin.
234 A1 Salladasburg PA U.S.A.
160 E3 Sallanches France
186 E3 Sallent Spain
186 C2 Sallent de Gállego Spain
163 B4 Salles France
161 A4 Salles-Curan France
162 B3 Salles-d'Angles France
161 B5 Salles-d'Aude France
163 E4 Salles-la-Source France
163 D5 Salles-sur-l'Hers France
171 E4 Sallgast Ger.
179 G2 Sallingberg Austria
147 E3 Sallins Rep. of Ireland
261 F5 Salliqueló Arg.
237 E5 Sallisaw OK U.S.A.
221 K3 Salluit Que. Can.
116 E3 Sallyana Nepal
147 C4 Sallypark Rep. of Ireland
165 E4 Salm r. Belgium
128 C2 Salmá Syria
122 A2 Salmās Iran
183 H4 Salmerón Spain
183 H4 Salmeroncillos de Abajo Spain
134 E3 Salmi Rus. Fed.
222 G5 Salmo B.C. Can.
238 D2 Salmon ID U.S.A.
235 F1 Salmon r. CT U.S.A.
238 C2 Salmon r. ID U.S.A.
238 D2 Salmon, Middle Fork r. ID U.S.A.
222 G5 Salmon Arm B.C. Can.
238 D3 Salmon Falls Creek r. Idaho/Nevada U.S.A.
87 D7 Salmon Gums W.A. Austr.
Salmonhurst N.B. Can. see New Denmark
238 D2 Salmon River Mountains ID U.S.A.
183 E4 Salmoral Spain
172 A2 Salmtal Ger.
141 M3 Salo Fin.
191 F3 Salò Italy
185 H2 Salobre Spain
185 G4 Salobreña Spain
140 N2 Saloinen Fin.
241 K5 Salome AZ U.S.A.
156 E4 Salon France
160 D1 Salon r. France
116 E4 Salon Uttar Prad. India
161 D5 Salon-de-Provence France
208 D5 Salonga r. Dem. Rep. Congo
Salonica Greece see Thessaloniki
Salonika Greece see Thessaloniki
197 E2 Salonta Romania
Salop admin. div. England U.K. see Shropshire
182 C5 Salor r. Spain
186 E2 Salòria, Pic de mt. Spain
184 C1 Salorino Spain
160 C2 Salornay-sur-Guye France
191 G2 Salorno Italy
186 E3 Salou Spain
186 E3 Salou, Cap de c. Spain
156 C3 Salouël France
141 N3 Salpausselkä reg. Fin.
128 C1 Salqīn Syria
147 B3 Salruck Rep. of Ireland
260 E2 Salsacate Arg.
186 D4 Salsadella Spain
163 E6 Salses-le-Château France
135 H7 Sal'sk Rus. Fed.
194 C5 Salso r. Sicilia Italy
194 D5 Salso r. Sicilia Italy
193 H3 Salsola r. Italy
190 E4 Salsomaggiore Terme Italy
Salt Jordan see As Salţ
186 F3 Salt Spain
241 K5 Salt r. AZ U.S.A.
236 F4 Salt r. MO U.S.A.
238 E3 Salt r. WY U.S.A.
258 D2 Salta Arg.
258 D2 Salta prov. Arg.
235 E2 Saltaire NY U.S.A.
191 H5 Saltara Italy
150 C4 Saltash Cornwall, England U.K.
149 I3 Saltburn-by-the-Sea Redcar and Cleveland, England U.K.
146 D6 Saltcoats North Ayrshire, Scotland U.K.
232 B5 Salt Creek r. OH U.S.A.
151 G4 Saltdean Brighton and Hove, England U.K.
147 E4 Saltee Islands Rep. of Ireland
184 D3 Salteras Spain
222 E5 Saltery Bay B.C. Can.
140 K2 Saltfjorden sea chan. Norway
239 F6 Salt Flat TX U.S.A.
150 E3 Saltford Bath and North East Somerset, England U.K.
237 D4 Salt Fork r. KS U.S.A.
237 D4 Salt Fork Arkansas r. KS U.S.A.
237 C5 Salt Fork Brazos r. TX U.S.A.
237 D5 Salt Fork Red r. OK U.S.A.
147 B3 Salthill Rep. of Ireland
243 E3 Saltillo Mex.
Salt Island Vanuatu see Loh
214 E3 Salt Lake S. Africa
238 E3 Salt Lake City UT U.S.A.
232 B5 Salt Lick KY U.S.A.
150 E1 Saltney Flintshire, Wales U.K.
261 G4 Salto Arg.
256 D5 Salto Brazil
193 E2 Salto r. Italy
182 C3 Salto Port.
261 I2 Salto Uru.
261 I2 Salto dept Uru.
257 H2 Salto da Divisa Brazil
243 G5 Salto de Agua Mex.
253 G6 Salto del Guaíra Para.
261 G3 Salto Grande Arg.
256 C5 Salto Grande Brazil
241 I5 Salton City CA U.S.A.
241 J5 Salton Sea salt l. CA U.S.A.
206 E5 Saltpond Ghana
223 H2 Salt River N.W.T. Can.
Saltrou Haiti see Belle-Anse
143 H2 Saltsjöbaden Sweden
141 M3 Saltvik Åland Fin.
232 C6 Saltville VA U.S.A.
231 D5 Saluda SC U.S.A.
232 E6 Saluda VA U.S.A.
231 D5 Saluda r. SC U.S.A.
191 H5 Saludecio Italy
190 D3 Saluggia Italy
202 E2 Salûm, Gulf of Egypt
116 C4 Salumbar Rajasthan India
122 D2 Saluq, Kūh-e mt. Iran
115 D2 Salur Andhra Prad. India
190 D3 Salussola Italy
190 C4 Saluzzo Italy
183 I4 Salvacañete Spain
184 C3 Salvada Port.
254 F5 Salvador Brazil
Salvador country Central America see El Salvador
182 C4 Salvador Port.
258 E1 Salvador Mazza Arg.
163 D5 Salvagnac France
184 D2 Salvaleón Spain
254 C2 Salvaterra Brazil
184 B1 Salvaterra de Magos Port.
182 D5 Salvaterra do Extremo Port.
244 D3 Salvatierra Mex.
183 H2 Salvatierra Spain
184 D2 Salvatierra de los Barros Spain
184 D1 Salvatierra de Santiago Spain
241 L2 Salvation Creek r. UT U.S.A.
195 H3 Salve Italy
163 D4 Salviac France
125 E2 Salwah Saudi Arabia
125 E2 Salwah, Dawḩat b. Qatar/Saudi Arabia
Salween r. China see Nu Jiang
96 B3 Salween r. Myanmar
129 C4 Salyamaç Turkey
129 F4 Salyan Azer.
Sal'yany Azer. see Salyan
232 B6 Salyersville KY U.S.A.
179 F3 Salza r. Austria
178 D2 Salzach r. Austria/Ger.
179 E3 Salza-Stausee resr Austria
169 C3 Salzbergen Ger.
178 E3 Salzburg Austria
178 E3 Salzburg land Austria
169 F3 Salzgitter Ger.
168 F2 Salzhausen Ger.
169 E3 Salzhemmendorf Ger.
169 D4 Salzkotten Ger.
171 C4 Salzmünde Ger.
170 C3 Salzwedel Ger.
173 H3 Salzweg Ger.
116 B4 Sam Rajasthan India
96 D3 Sam, Nam r. Laos/Vietnam
246 D2 Samá Cuba
174 E3 Sama r. Pol.
Šamac Bos.-Herz. see Bosanski Šamac
125 G3 Şamad Oman
163 B5 Samadet France
106 B1 Samagaltay Rus. Fed.
252 E4 Samaipata Bol.
242 D2 Samalayuca Mex.
92 B5 Samales Group is Phil.
114 D2 Samalkot Andhra Prad. India
203 F2 Samâlût Egypt
247 E3 Samaná Dom. Rep.
116 D3 Samana Punjab India
246 D2 Samana Cay i. Bahamas
Samanala mt. Sri Lanka see Sri Pada
126 D3 Samandağı Turkey
123 F2 Samangān prov. Afgh.
250 B4 Samaniego Col.
199 F1 Samanlı Dağları mts Turkey
203 F2 Samannûd Egypt
225 F3 Samaqua r. Que. Can.
Samar Kazakh. see Samarskoye
92 C4 Samar i. Phil.
120 B1 Samara Samarskaya Oblast' Rus. Fed.
120 B1 Samara r. Rus. Fed.
137 H3 Samara r. Ukr.
Samarahan Sarawak Malaysia see Sri Aman
Samara Oblast admin. div. Rus. Fed. see Samarskaya Oblast'
190 D3 Samarate Italy
100 F3 Samarga Rus. Fed.
95 G3 Samarinda Kalimantan Timur Indon.
100 E3 Samarka Rus. Fed.
121 F5 Samarkand Uzbek.
123 G2 Samarkand, Pik mt. Tajik.
Samarkand Oblast admin. div. Uzbek. see Samarkandskaya Oblast'
121 F5 Samarkandskaya Oblast' admin. div. Uzbek.
Samarobriva France see Amiens
Samarqand Uzbek. see Samarkand
Samarqand, Qullai mt. Tajik. see Samarkand, Pik
Samarqand Wiloyati admin. div. Uzbek. see Samarkandskaya Oblast'
127 F4 Sāmarrā' Iraq
92 C4 Samar Sea g. Phil.
120 B1 Samarskaya Oblast' admin. div. Rus. Fed.
121 J2 Samarskoye Kazakh.
137 J4 Samarskoye Rus. Fed.
136 C2 Samary Ukr.
123 G4 Samasata Pak.
192 A5 Samassi Sardegna Italy
117 F4 Samastipur Bihar India
163 C5 Samatan France
192 B5 Samatzai Sardegna Italy
129 F3 Şamaxı Azer.
209 E6 Šamba Dem. Rep. Congo
95 F3 Samba r. Indon.
116 C2 Samba Jammu and Kashmir
209 B7 Samba Cajú Angola
182 D3 Sambade Port.
254 D3 Sambaiba Brazil
206 B3 Sambaïlo Guinea
95 G2 Sambaliung mts Indon.
117 E5 Sambalpur Orissa India
95 E2 Sambas Kalimantan Barat Indon.
Sambat Ukr. see Kyiv
177 L5 Sâmbăta Romania
213 □K2 Sambava Madag.
137 J4 Sambek Rostovskaya Oblast' Rus. Fed.
137 J4 Sambek Rostovskaya Oblast' Rus. Fed.
Sambe-san vol. Japan see Sanbe-san
116 D3 Sambhal Uttar Prad. India
116 C4 Sambhar Rajasthan India
193 I6 Sambiase Italy
136 B3 Sambir Ukr.
93 A3 Sambo Sulawesi Selatan Indon.
183 F3 Samboal Spain
95 G3 Samboja Kalimantan Timur Indon.
Sambor Ukr. see Sambir
261 I4 Samborombón r. Arg.
261 I4 Samborombón, Bahía b. Arg.
175 J5 Samborzec Pol.
165 D4 Sambre r. Belgium/France
194 C5 Sambuca di Sicilia Sicilia Italy
191 G4 Sambuca Pistoiese Italy
161 F4 Sambuco Italy
194 D5 Sambughetti, Monte mt. Sicilia Italy
101 D5 Samch'ŏk S. Korea
Samch'ŏnp'o S. Korea see Sach'on
118 E2 Samdi Dag mt. Turkey
190 E2 Samedan Switz.
182 C4 Sameiro Port.
156 B2 Samer France
169 C3 Samern Ger.
129 C2 Samerts'khle, Mt'a Georgia
183 E1 Sames Spain
139 M3 Samet' Rus. Fed.
209 F7 Samfya Zambia
136 E3 Samhorodok Kyivs'ka Oblast' Ukr.
136 E3 Samhorodok Vinnyts'ka Oblast' Ukr.
116 B5 Sami Gujarat India
182 D3 Samil Port.
124 C2 Samīrah Saudi Arabia
182 D3 Samir de los Caños Spain
250 C6 Samiria r. Peru
Samirum Iran see Yazd-e Khvāst
129 D2 Samkhret' Oset'i aut. reg. Georgia

Şămkir to Sânpetru Mare
358

129 E3 Şămkir Azer.
129 E3 Şămkirçay r. Azer.
128 C1 Şamköy Turkey
199 E2 Şamlı Turkey
195 F2 Sammichele di Bari Italy
190 F2 Samnaun Switz.
Samneua Laos see Xam Hua
182 B2 Samo r. Spain
78 □2 Samoa country S. Pacific Ocean
266 H7 Samoa Basin sea feature Pacific Ocean
Samoa i Sisifo country S. Pacific Ocean see Samoa
188 E3 Samobor Croatia
179 G5 Samoborska Gora hills Croatia
134 H3 Samoded Rus. Fed.
160 E2 Samoëns France
191 G4 Samoggia r. Italy
197 F4 Samokov Bulg.
190 E2 Samolaco Italy
130 C3 Samoluskivtsi Ukr.
184 B2 Samora Correia Port.
176 G3 Šamorín Slovakia
199 E3 Samos Voreio Aigaio Greece
199 E3 Samos i. Greece
182 C2 Samos Spain
Samothrace i. Greece see Samothraki
199 D1 Samothraki i. Greece
197 G4 Samovodene Bulg.
135 H6 Samoylovka Rus. Fed.
206 E5 Sampa Côte d'Ivoire
260 E3 Sampacho Arg.
95 F4 Sampang Jawa Timur Indon.
186 C3 Samper de Calanda Spain
190 C4 Sampeyre Italy
194 D6 Sampieri Sicilia Italy
157 F4 Sampigny France
95 F3 Sampit Kalimantan Tengah Indon.
95 F3 Sampit r. Indon.
95 F3 Sampit, Teluk b. Indon.
135 H5 Sampur Rus. Fed.
209 E7 Sampwe Dem. Rep. Congo
237 E6 Sam Rayburn Reservoir TX U.S.A.
206 E5 Samreboe Ghana
138 G2 Samro, Ozero l. Rus. Fed.
Samrong Cambodia see Phumi Sâmraông
111 C6 Samsang Xizang China
96 C2 Sam Sao, Phou mts Laos/Vietnam
142 D4 Samsø i. Denmark
142 D4 Samsø Bælt sea chan. Denmark
96 D3 Sâm Sơn Vietnam
177 L4 Şamşud Romania
126 E2 Samsun Turkey
171 C3 Samswegen Ger.
121 I4 Samsy Kazakh.
170 E1 Samtens Ger.
116 D4 Samthar Uttar Prad. India
129 C2 Samtredia Georgia
84 C3 Samuel, Mount hill N.T. Austr.
192 A5 Samugheo Sardegna Italy
95 C5 Samui, Ko i. Thai.
105 F3 Samukawa Japan
123 H4 Samundri Pak.
129 F3 Samur Azer.
129 F3 Samur r. Azer./Rus. Fed.
Samutlu Turkey see Temelli
97 C4 Samut Prakan Thai.
97 C4 Samut Sakhon Thai.
97 C4 Samut Songkhram Thai.
206 D3 San Mali
175 J5 San r. Pol.
97 D4 San, Tônlé r. Cambodia
188 F3 Sana r. Bos.-Herz.
124 D5 Şan'ā' Yemen
124 C5 Şan'ā' governorate Yemen
210 E2 Sanaag admin. reg. Somalia
183 I2 San Adrián Spain
262 X2 Sanae research stn Antarctica
207 H6 Sanaga r. Cameroon
San Agostín FL U.S.A. see St Augustine
260 E2 San Agustín Arg.
250 B4 San Agustín Col.
92 C5 San Agustin, Cape Phil.
183 G4 San Agustín de Guadalix Spain
146 B6 Sanaigmore Argyll and Bute, Scotland U.K.
124 D3 Sanām Saudi Arabia
182 B2 San Amaro Spain
252 A6 San Ambrosio i. S. Pacific Ocean
122 A3 Sanandaj Iran
206 D3 Sanando Mali
240 G2 San Andreas CA U.S.A.
177 K6 Sânandrei Romania
252 D3 San Andrés Bol.
250 C3 San Andrés Col.
92 C3 San Andres Phil.
246 B4 San Andrés, Isla de i. Caribbean Sea
261 H4 San Andrés de Giles Arg.
182 E2 San Andrés del Rabanedo Spain
244 C4 San Andrés Ixtlán Mex.
239 F5 San Andres Mountains NM U.S.A.
245 G4 San Andrés Tuxtla Mex.
237 C6 San Angelo TX U.S.A.
206 D3 Sanankoroba Mali
240 F3 San Anselmo CA U.S.A.
182 D1 San Antolín de Ibias Spain
182 B2 San Antoniño Spain
258 D3 San Antonio Arg.
242 □H5 San Antonio Belize
252 D3 San Antonio Bol.
260 B3 San Antonio Chile
92 B3 San Antonio Phil.
187 B5 San Antonio Spain
239 F5 San Antonio NM U.S.A.
237 D6 San Antonio TX U.S.A.
240 G4 San Antonio r. CA U.S.A.
237 D6 San Antonio r. TX U.S.A.
240 I4 San Antonio, Mount CA U.S.A.
187 E6 San Antonio Abad Spain
261 H4 San Antonio de Areco Arg.
258 D2 San Antonio de los Cobres Arg.
242 □I6 San Antonio de Oriente Hond.
207 G7 San Antonio de Palé Equat. Guinea
259 D6 San Antonio Oeste Arg.
161 D5 Sanary-sur-Mer France
183 H2 San Asensio Spain
78 □4a Sanat i. Chuuk Micronesia
234 C2 Sanatoga PA U.S.A.
260 D2 San Augustín de Valle Fértil Arg.
237 E6 San Augustine TX U.S.A.
116 D5 Sanawad Madh. Prad. India
244 D2 San Bartolo Mex.
216 □3c San Bartolomé Lanzarote Canary Is
183 F5 San Bartolomé de las Abiertas Spain
184 C3 San Bartolomé de la Torre Spain
183 F4 San Bartolomé de Pinares Spain
216 □3f San Bartolomé de Tirajana Gran Canaria Canary Is
193 H3 San Bartolomeo in Galdo Italy
245 E4 San Bartolo Morelos Mex.
245 E3 San Bartolo Tutotepec Mex.
260 E3 San Basilio Arg.
192 B5 San Basilio Sardegna Italy
San Baudillo de Llobregat Spain see Sant Boi de Llobregat
193 F2 San Benedetto del Tronto Italy
191 F3 San Benedetto Po Italy
243 H5 San Benito Guat.
185 F2 San Benito Spain
237 D7 San Benito TX U.S.A.
240 G3 San Benito r. CA U.S.A.
184 C2 San Benito de la Contienda Spain
240 G3 San Benito Mountain CA U.S.A.
240 I4 San Bernardino CA U.S.A.
190 E2 San Bernardino, Passo di pass Switz.
241 I4 San Bernardino Mountains CA U.S.A.
260 B3 San Bernardo Chile
242 D3 San Bernardo Mex.
103 F6 Sanbe-san vol. Japan
191 H3 San Biagio di Callalta Italy
194 C5 San Biagio Platani Sicilia Italy
244 B3 San Blas Nayarit Mex.
242 C3 San Blas Sinaloa Mex.
242 □K7 San Blas, Archipiélago de is Panama
242 □K7 San Blas, Cordillera de mts Panama
191 G3 San Bonifacio Italy
252 D3 San Borja Bol.
236 E3 Sanborn IA U.S.A.
233 □H3 Sanbornville NH U.S.A.
243 E3 San Buenaventura Mex.
213 G3 Sança Moz.
191 H2 San Candido Italy
186 C3 San Caprasio hill Spain
260 C3 San Carlos Mendoza Arg.
258 D2 San Carlos Salta Arg.
260 B5 San Carlos Chile
San Carlos Equat. Guinea see Luba
243 E2 San Carlos Coahuila Mex.
245 E1 San Carlos Tamaulipas Mex.
242 □I7 San Carlos Nic.
253 F5 San Carlos Para.
253 F5 San Carlos r. Para.
92 B3 San Carlos Luzon Phil.
92 B4 San Carlos Negros Phil.
258 G4 San Carlos Uru.
241 L5 San Carlos AZ U.S.A.
250 E3 San Carlos Apure Venez.
250 D2 San Carlos Cojedes Venez.
261 G2 San Carlos Centro Arg.
259 C6 San Carlos de Bariloche Arg.
261 G5 San Carlos de Bolívar Arg.
San Carlos de la Rápita Spain see Sant Carles de la Ràpita
185 G2 San Carlos del Valle Spain
250 D2 San Carlos del Zulia Venez.
261 G2 San Carlos Sur Arg.
192 D2 San Casciano dei Bagni Italy
191 G5 San Casciano in Val di Pesa Italy
195 H2 San Cataldo Puglia Italy
194 C5 San Cataldo Sicilia Italy
261 H6 San Cayetano Arg.
182 E3 San Cebrián de Castro Spain
187 F5 Sancellas Spain
San Celoni Spain see Sant Celoni
160 A1 Sancergues France
160 A1 Sancerre France
160 A1 Sancerrois, Collines du hills France
195 H2 San Cesario di Lecce Italy
160 E1 Sancey-le-Grand France
Sanchahe Jilin China see Fuyu
108 C3 Sancha He r. Guizhou China
156 B4 Sancheville France
245 H4 Sánchez Magallanes Mex.
116 D5 Sanchi Madh. Prad. India
183 F4 Sanchidrián Spain
96 D2 San Chien Pau mt. Laos
193 I4 San Chirico Nuovo Italy
193 I4 San Chirico Raparo Italy
116 B4 Sanchor Rajasthan India
107 F4 Sanchuan r. China
134 I4 Sanchursk Rus. Fed.
182 C2 San Cibrao das Viñas Spain
194 C5 San Cipirello Sicilia Italy
193 G4 San Cipriano d'Aversa Italy
245 E3 San Ciro de Acosta Mex.
260 B4 San Clemente Chile
185 H3 San Clemente Spain
240 I5 San Clemente CA U.S.A.
261 I5 San Clemente del Tuyú Arg.
240 H5 San Clemente Island CA U.S.A.
182 C2 San Clodio Spain
160 A2 Sancoins France
258 F2 San Cosme Arg.
182 C1 San Cosme Spain
193 I4 San Costantino Albanese Italy
191 I5 San Costanzo Italy
261 G2 San Cristóbal Arg.
252 D5 San Cristóbal Bol.
253 E3 San Cristóbal Bol.
182 E3 San Cristóbal Dom. Rep.
78 □6 San Cristobal i. Solomon Is
250 C3 San Cristóbal Venez.
250 □ San Cristóbal, Isla i. Islas Galápagos Ecuador
242 □I6 San Cristóbal, Volcán vol. Nic.
San Cristóbal de Cea Galicia Spain see Cea
182 E2 San Cristóbal de Entreviñas Spain
216 □3a San Cristóbal de la Laguna Tenerife Canary Is
243 G5 San Cristóbal de las Casas Mex.
183 F3 San Cristóbal de la Vega Spain
193 H4 San Croce, Monte mt. Italy
261 F3 Sancti Spíritu Arg.
246 C2 Sancti Spíritus Cuba
246 C2 Sancti Spíritus prov. Cuba
182 D4 Sancti-Spíritus Spain
185 E2 Sancti-Spíritus Spain
157 F3 Sancy France
142 B2 Sand Norway
215 F3 Sand r. Free State S. Africa
213 F4 Sand r. Northern S. Africa
104 B4 Sanda Japan
146 C6 Sanda Island Scotland U.K.
95 G1 Sandakan Sabah Malaysia
117 G4 Sandakphu Peak Sikkim India
190 C4 San Damiano d'Asti Italy
190 D4 San Damiano Macra Italy
169 F6 Sand am Main Ger.
141 I3 Sandane Norway
178 E4 San Daniele del Friuli Italy
191 F3 San Daniele Po Italy
197 F5 Sandanski Bulg.
Sandaohezi Xinjiang China see Shawan
206 C3 Sandaré Mali
170 D3 Sandau Ger.
146 F2 Sanday i. Scotland U.K.
146 F2 Sanday Sound sea chan. Scotland U.K.
172 D2 Sandbach r. Ger.
149 G4 Sandbach Cheshire, England U.K.
169 F5 Sandberg Ger.
214 B5 Sandberg S. Africa
168 G1 Sandby Denmark
140 K2 Sanddøla r. Norway
168 D2 Sande Ger.
141 I3 Sande Sogn og Fjordane Norway
142 D2 Sande Vestfold Norway
182 B3 Sande Port.
142 D2 Sandefjord Norway
142 D2 Sandefjord (Torp) airport Norway
142 A2 Sandeid Norway
195 F3 San Demetrio Corone Italy
193 F2 San Demetrio ne Vestini Italy
263 D2 Sandercock Nunataks nunataks Antarctica
241 M4 Sanders AZ U.S.A.
171 D4 Sandersdorf Ger.
169 E4 Sandershausen (Niestetal) Ger.
171 C4 Sandersleben Ger.
237 C6 Sanderson TX U.S.A.
231 D5 Sandersville GA U.S.A.
168 F2 Sandesneben Ger.
86 D3 Sandfire Roadhouse W.A. Austr.
142 B2 Sandfloeggi mt. Norway
232 C5 Sand Fork WV U.S.A.
146 F2 Sandgarth Orkney, Scotland U.K.
172 C2 Sandhausen Ger.
146 D7 Sandhead Dumfries and Galloway, Scotland U.K.
236 D2 Sand Hill r. MN U.S.A.
236 C3 Sand Hills NE U.S.A.
140 K2 Sandhornøy i. Norway
151 G3 Sandhurst Bracknell Forest, England U.K.
116 E4 Sandi Uttar Prad. India
252 C3 Sandia Peru
182 C2 Sandiás Spain
240 D3 San Diego Mex.
240 I5 San Diego CA U.S.A.
237 D7 San Diego TX U.S.A.
242 C2 San Diego, Sierra mts Mex.
199 G2 Sandıklı Turkey
116 E4 Sandila Uttar Prad. India
156 C5 Sandillon France
87 B5 Sandiman, Mount hill W.A. Austr.
134 L2 Sandivey r. Rus. Fed.
170 E3 Sandkrug Ger.
179 F2 Sandl Austria
224 C4 Sand Lake Ont. Can.
142 A2 Sandnes Norway
146 □G1 Sandness Shetland, Scotland U.K.
140 K2 Sandnessjøen Norway
Sandoi i. Faroe Is see Sandoy
182 D4 Sando Spain
209 D7 Sandoa Dem. Rep. Congo
175 J5 Sandomierz Pol.
197 G2 Sândominic Romania
250 B4 Sandoná Col.
195 G2 San Donaci Italy
191 H3 San Donà di Piave Italy
195 H2 San Donato di Lecce Italy
193 I5 San Donato di Ninea Italy
190 E3 San Donato Milanese Italy
193 F3 San Donato Val di Comino Italy
177 J5 Sándorfalva Hungary
139 K2 Sandovo Rus. Fed.
263 G2 Sandow, Mount Antarctica
96 A3 Sandoway Myanmar
151 F4 Sandown Isle of Wight, England U.K.
144 D1 Sandoy i. Faroe Is
140 I3 Sandøy Norway
150 C4 Sandplace Cornwall, England U.K.
238 C1 Sandpoint ID U.S.A.
146 A5 Sandray i. Scotland U.K.
151 G3 Sandridge Hertfordshire, England U.K.
84 D5 Sandringham Qld Austr.
215 H2 Sand River Reservoir Swaziland
140 L2 Sandsele Sweden
149 I3 Sandsend North Yorkshire, England U.K.
222 D4 Sandspit B.C. Can.
237 D4 Sand Springs OK U.S.A.
215 F2 Sandspruit r. S. Africa
168 D2 Sandstedt Ger.
232 E6 Sandston VA U.S.A.
87 C5 Sandstone W.A. Austr.
236 E2 Sandstone MN U.S.A.
241 K5 Sand Tank Mountains AZ U.S.A.
215 G2 Sandton S. Africa
234 C2 Sandts Eddy PA U.S.A.
108 C3 Sandu Guizhou China
109 E3 Sandu Hunan China
114 C3 Sandur Karnataka India
227 F4 Sandusky MI U.S.A.
232 B4 Sandusky OH U.S.A.
142 D2 Sandvika Norway
143 G1 Sandviken Sweden
214 E5 Sandvlakte S. Africa
151 I3 Sandwich Kent, England U.K.
233 H4 Sandwich MA U.S.A.
Sandwich Island Vanuatu see Éfaté
Sandwich Islands N. Pacific Ocean see Hawaiian Islands
117 G5 Sandwip Bangl.
151 G2 Sandy Bedfordshire, England U.K.
238 E3 Sandy UT U.S.A.
233 □I2 Sandy r. ME U.S.A.
223 K4 Sandy Bay Sask. Can.
246 □ Sandy Bay Jamaica
87 D7 Sandy Bight b. W.A. Austr.
85 H5 Sandy Cape Qld Austr.
83 F5 Sandy Cape Tas. Austr.
84 D3 Sandy Creek r. Qld Austr.
235 E1 Sandy Hook CT U.S.A.
232 B5 Sandy Hook KY U.S.A.
86 D2 Sandy Island W.A. Austr.
123 E2 Sandykachi Turkm.
Sandykly Gumy des. Turkm. see Sundukli, Peski
222 H4 Sandy Lake Alta Can.
223 M4 Sandy Lake Ont. Can.
231 C5 Sandy Springs GA U.S.A.
232 C5 Sandyville WV U.S.A.
182 D2 Sâne r. France
165 E5 Sanem Lux.
182 E2 San Emiliano Spain
253 F6 San Estanislao Para.
245 F4 San Esteban Cuautempan Mex.
183 G3 San Esteban de Gormaz Spain
182 E4 San Esteban de la Sierra Spain
260 B5 San Fabián de Alico Chile
193 H4 San Fele Italy
193 G3 San Felice a Cancello Italy
193 F3 San Felice Circeo Italy
182 D4 San Felices de los Gallegos Spain
191 G4 San Felice sul Panaro Italy
260 B3 San Felipe Chile
242 B2 San Felipe Baja California Norte Mex.
242 D3 San Felipe Chihuahua Mex.
244 D3 San Felipe Guanajuato Mex.
183 I4 San Felipe mt. Spain
250 D2 San Felipe Venez.
San Feliú de Guixols Spain see Sant Feliu de Guíxols
San Feliú de Pallarols Spain see Sant Feliu de Pallerols
San Feliú Sasserra Spain see Sant Feliu Sasserra
252 A6 San Félix, Isla i. S. Pacific Ocean
195 E4 San Ferdinando Italy
193 I3 San Ferdinando di Puglia Italy
261 H4 San Fernando Arg.
260 B4 San Fernando Chile
242 B2 San Fernando Baja California Norte Mex.
243 F3 San Fernando Tamaulipas Mex.
92 B2 San Fernando Luzon Phil.
92 B3 San Fernando Luzon Phil.
184 D4 San Fernando Spain
247 □7 San Fernando Trin. and Tob.
240 H4 San Fernando CA U.S.A.
250 E3 San Fernando de Apure Venez.
250 E3 San Fernando de Atabapo Venez.
183 G4 San Fernando de Henares Spain
193 I5 San Fili Italy
195 E4 San Filippo del Mela Sicilia Italy
182 C3 Sanfins do Douro Port.
87 B5 Sanford r. W.A. Austr.
231 D6 Sanford FL U.S.A.
233 □H3 Sanford ME U.S.A.
226 E4 Sanford MI U.S.A.
231 E5 Sanford NC U.S.A.
261 F2 San Francisco Arg.
252 D2 San Francisco Bol.
245 E1 San Francisco Mex.
250 B4 San Francisco Peru
240 F3 San Francisco CA U.S.A.
239 E5 San Francisco r. NM U.S.A.
240 F3 San Francisco Bay inlet CA U.S.A.
245 F6 San Francisco Cozoaltepec Mex.
258 E3 San Francisco del Chañar Arg.
260 D3 San Francisco del Monte de Oro Arg.
242 D3 San Francisco del Oro Mex.
244 D3 San Francisco del Rincón Mex.
246 E3 San Francisco de Macorís Dom. Rep.
260 B3 San Francisco de Mostazal Chile
259 D8 San Francisco de Paula, Cabo c. Arg.
242 □H6 San Francisco Gotera El Salvador
187 E6 San Francisco Javier Spain
194 D4 San Fratello Sicilia Italy
190 C4 Sanfront Italy
250 B4 San Gabriel Ecuador
245 F4 San Gabriel Chilac Mex.
240 H4 San Gabriel Mountains CA U.S.A.
Sangachaly Azer. see Sanqaçal
94 D3 Sangaigerong Sumatera Indon.
108 A2 Sa'ngain Xizang China
187 B4 Sangalhos Port.
252 A3 San Gallan, Isla i. Peru
114 E3 Sangam Andhra Prad. India
114 B2 Sangameshwar Mahar. India
114 B2 Sangamner Mahar. India
236 F3 Sangamon r. IL U.S.A.
123 F3 Sangan, Koh-i- mt. Afgh.
123 G4 Sangar r. Pak.
131 N3 Sangar Rus. Fed.
183 F4 Sangarcía Spain
206 B4 Sangaréa Guinea
114 C2 Sangareddi Andhra Prad. India
206 B4 Sangarédi Guinea
116 C3 Sangaria Rajasthan India
95 G3 Sangasanga Kalimantan Timur Indon.
Sangasso Mali see Zangasso
156 B2 Sangatte France
192 A5 San Gavino Monreale Sardegna Italy
250 B5 Sangay, Volcán vol. Ecuador
141 K3 Sångbäcken Sweden
122 D3 Sang Bast Iran
92 B5 Sangboy Islands Phil.
93 A5 Sangeang i. Indon.
106 E3 Sangejing Nei Mongol China
193 E2 San Gemini Italy
261 G3 San Genaro Arg.
Sangenjo Spain see Sanxenxo
197 G2 Sângeorgiu de Pădure Romania
197 G2 Sângeorz-Băi Romania
197 G2 Sânger Romania
240 H3 Sanger CA U.S.A.
Sângera Moldova see Sîngera
Sângerei Moldova see Sîngerei
233 F3 Sangerfield NY U.S.A.
171 C4 Sangerhausen Ger.
247 □1 San Germán Puerto Rico
161 F4 San Germano Chisone Italy
107 G3 Sanggan r. China
108 B1 Sanggarmai Sichuan China
95 E2 Sanggau Kalimantan Barat Indon.
207 F4 Sangha Burkina
208 B4 Sangha admin. reg. Congo
208 C5 Sangha r. Congo
208 C4 Sangha-Mbaéré pref. C.A.R.
123 G5 Sanghar Pak.
191 G2 San Giacomo, Cima mt. Italy
250 C3 San Gil Col.
106 B1 Sangilen, Nagor'ye mts Rus. Fed.
195 □ San Giljan Malta
191 G5 San Gimignano Italy
183 I4 San Ginés mt. Spain
193 F1 San Ginesio Italy
193 F3 San Giorgio a Liri Italy
191 H2 San Giorgio della Richinvelda Italy
191 I3 San Giorgio di Nogaro Italy
191 G4 San Giorgio di Piano Italy
195 G2 San Giorgio Ionico Italy
193 G3 San Giorgio la Molara Italy
195 F2 San Giorgio Lucano Italy
193 H4 San Giovanni a Piro Italy
190 E3 San Giovanni Bianco Italy
192 D1 San Giovanni d'Asso Italy
194 C5 San Giovanni Gemini Sicilia Italy
193 F3 San Giovanni Incarico Italy
190 E3 San Giovanni in Croce Italy
195 F3 San Giovanni in Fiore Italy
191 G4 San Giovanni in Persiceto Italy
191 G3 San Giovanni Lupatoto Italy
193 H3 San Giovanni Rotondo Italy
192 A5 San Giovanni Suegiu Sardegna Italy
193 G2 San Giovanni Teatino Italy
191 G5 San Giovanni Valdarno Italy
116 C5 Sangir Mahar. India
93 C2 Sangir i. Indon.
93 C2 Sangir, Kepulauan is Indon.
190 F5 San Giuliano Terme Italy
194 C5 San Giuseppe Jato Sicilia Italy
194 C5 San Giuseppe Vesuviano Italy
191 H5 San Giustino Italy
106 E2 Sangiyn Dalay Mongolia
101 D5 Sangju S. Korea
93 A4 Sangkarang, Kepulauan is Indon.
97 C4 Sângke, Stœng r. Cambodia
95 G2 Sangkulirang Kalimantan Timur Indon.
123 H4 Sangla Pak.
114 B2 Sangli Mahar. India
207 H6 Sangmélima Cameroon
116 D4 Sangod Rajasthan India
191 G5 San Godenzo Italy
114 B2 Sangole Mahar. India
187 B7 Sangonera r. Spain
240 I4 San Gorgonio Mountain CA U.S.A.
190 D2 San Gottardo, Passo del pass Switz.
Sangpi Sichuan China see Xiangcheng
108 A2 Sang Qu r. Xizang China
239 F4 Sangre de Cristo Range mts CO U.S.A.
261 F4 San Gregorio Arg.
260 B5 San Gregorio Chile
258 G4 San Gregorio de Polanca Uru.
193 H4 San Gregorio Magno Italy
193 G3 San Gregorio Matese Italy
247 □7 Sangre Grande Trin. and Tob.
183 F5 Sangrera r. Spain
111 F6 Sangri Xizang China
193 G2 Sangro r. Italy
116 C3 Sangrur Punjab India
111 D6 Sangsang Xizang China
117 G5 Sangu r. Bangl.
222 H4 Sangudo Alta Can.
252 C4 Sangue r. Brazil
183 I2 Sangüesa Spain
190 E3 San Guiliano Milanese Italy
186 E3 San Guim de Freixenet Spain
163 A4 Sanguinet France
191 G3 Sanguinetto Italy
Sanguan Hebei China see Wuqiao
108 D2 Sangzhi Hunan China
206 D4 Sanhala Côte d'Ivoire
Sanhe Guizhou China see Sandu
107 I1 Sanhe Nei Mongol China
109 F2 Sanhezhen Anhui China
San Hilario Sacalm Spain see Sant Hilari Sacalm
203 F2 Sanhûr Egypt
243 H5 San Ignacio Belize
252 D3 San Ignacio Beni Bol.
252 E4 San Ignacio Santa Cruz Bol.
253 E4 San Ignacio Santa Cruz Bol.
253 F6 San Ignacio Para.
250 B6 San Ignacio Peru
224 E1 Sanikiluaq Nunavut Can.
183 G4 San Ildefonso Spain
197 F2 Sanislău Romania
170 D1 Sanitz Ger.
252 D2 San Jacinto Col.
92 B3 San Jacinto Phil.
240 I5 San Jacinto CA U.S.A.
240 I5 San Jacinto Peak CA U.S.A.
117 F5 Sanjai r. Bihar India
261 H2 San Jaime Arg.
261 H2 San Javier Arg.
252 D3 San Javier Beni Bol.
253 E4 San Javier Santa Cruz Bol.
187 C7 San Javier Spain
261 H3 San Javier Uru.
260 B4 San Javier de Loncomilla Chile
123 G4 Sanjawi Pak.
244 D5 San Jerónimo Mex.
Sanjiang Guangdong China see Liannan
108 D3 Sanjiang Guangxi China
Sanjiang Guizhou China see Jinping
Sanjiaocheng Qinghai China see Haiyan
108 D2 Sanjiaoping Hunan China
109 G2 Sanjie Zhejiang China
103 I5 Sanjō Japan
252 D3 San Joaquín Bol.
253 F6 San Joaquín Para.
240 G3 San Joaquin CA U.S.A.
240 G2 San Joaquin r. CA U.S.A.
240 G3 San Joaquin Valley CA U.S.A.
237 C5 San Jon NM U.S.A.
261 G2 San Jorge Arg.
78 □6 San Jorge i. Solomon Is
186 D4 San Jorge Spain
259 D7 San Jorge, Golfo de g. Arg.
San Jorge, Golfo de g. Spain see Sant Jordi, Golf de
184 C2 San Jorge de Alor Spain
242 □I7 San José Costa Rica
183 H6 San José Guat.
92 B3 San Jose Luzon Phil.
92 B3 San Jose Mindoro Phil.
92 B3 San Jose Mindoro Phil.
185 H4 San José Spain
187 E6 San José Spain
261 I4 San José dept Uru.
261 I4 San José r. Uru.
240 G3 San Jose CA U.S.A.
239 F5 San Jose NM U.S.A.
261 I2 San José, Cuchilla de hills Uru.
260 C3 San José, Volcán vol. Chile
242 D2 San José de Bavicora Mex.
92 B4 San Jose de Buenavista Phil.
253 E4 San José de Chiquitos Bol.
242 C3 San José de Comondú Mex.
261 H2 San José de Feliciano Arg.
244 C2 San José de Gracia Aguascalientes Mex.
242 B3 San José de Gracia Mex.
244 C4 San José de Gracia Mex.
242 C3 San José de Gracia Mex.
247 F5 San José de Guaribe Venez.
260 C2 San José de Jáchal Arg.
242 C3 San Josede la Brecha Mex.
261 F3 San José de la Dormida Arg.
259 B5 San José de la Mariquina Chile
242 C4 San José del Cabo Mex.
250 C4 San José del Guaviare Col.
245 F5 San José del Progreso Mex.
184 E4 San José del Valle Spain
260 B3 San José de Maipó Chile
261 I4 San José de Mayo Uru.
246 E3 San José de Ocoa Dom. Rep.
250 D3 San José de Ocuné Col.
239 E6 San José de Primas Mex.
244 D1 San José de Raíces Mex.
244 D3 San José Iturbide Mex.
260 C2 San Juan Arg.
260 C2 San Juan prov. Arg.
250 B3 San Juan r. Col.
242 □J7 San Juan r. Costa Rica/Nic.
246 B2 San Juan mt. Cuba
246 E3 San Juan Dom. Rep.
242 D3 San Juan Mex.
244 C3 San Juan r. Jalisco Mex.
245 E1 San Juan r. Veracruz Mex.
252 B3 San Juan Peru
92 C4 San Juan Leyte Phil.
92 C4 San Juan Mindanao Phil.
247 □1 San Juan Puerto Rico
184 D2 San Juan r. Spain
240 H4 San Juan r. CA U.S.A.
241 L3 San Juan r. UT U.S.A.
253 F6 San Juan Bautista Para.
252 □ San Juan Bautista S. Pacific Ocean
187 E5 San Juan Bautista Spain
240 G3 San Juan Bautista CA U.S.A.
245 F4 San Juan Bautista Tuxtepec Mex.
240 I5 San Juan Capistrano CA U.S.A.
242 □I6 San Juancito Hond.
187 C6 San Juan de Alicante Spain
184 D3 San Juan de Aznalfarache Spain
244 C1 San Juan de Guadalupe Mex.
259 B6 San Juan de la Costa Chile
245 E4 San Juan de las Huertas Mex.
242 □J7 San Juan del Norte Nic.
242 □J7 San Juan del Norte, Bahía de b. Nic.
244 C3 San Juan de los Lagos Mex.
250 E2 San Juan de los Morros Venez.
184 D3 San Juan del Puerto Spain
242 D3 San Juan del Río Mex.
245 E3 San Juan del Río Mex.
242 □I7 San Juan del Sur Nic.
244 D3 San Juan Evangelista Mex.
245 F4 San Juan Ixcaquixtla Mex.
239 F4 San Juan Mountains CO U.S.A.
246 B2 San Juan y Martínez Cuba
259 D8 San Julián Arg.
252 B4 San Julián Mex.
183 F3 San Just mt. Spain
186 C4 San Just mt. Spain
261 G2 San Justo Arg.
182 D2 San Justo de la Vega Spain
206 C4 Sankanbiaiwa mt. Sierra Leone
206 C4 Sankarani r. Côte d'Ivoire/Guinea
114 C4 Sankarankovil Tamil Nadu India
114 B2 Sankeshwar Karnataka India
117 F5 Sankh r. Bihar India
122 D2 Sankhāş Iran
Sankosh r. Bhutan see Sunkosh Chhu
116 E5 Sankra Madh. Prad. India
116 B4 Sankra Rajasthan India
179 G3 Sankt Aegyd am Neuwalde Austria
179 F4 Sankt Andrä Austria
179 H3 Sankt Andrä im Zicksee Austria
169 F4 Sankt Andreasberg Ger.
179 G4 Sankt Anna am Aigen Austria
178 B3 Sankt Anton am Arlberg Austria
179 G3 Sankt Anton an der Jeßnitz Austria
169 C5 Sankt Augustin Ger.
172 C4 Sankt Blasien Ger.
171 D5 Sankt Egidien Ger.
179 F3 Sankt Gallen Austria
190 E1 Sankt Gallen Switz.
190 E1 Sankt Gallen canton Switz.
178 A3 Sankt Gallenkirch Austria
171 C5 Sankt Gangloff Ger.
179 F4 Sankt Georgen am Längsee Austria
179 F2 Sankt Georgen am Walde Austria
179 F2 Sankt Georgen an der Gusen Austria
179 E3 Sankt Georgen im Attergau Austria
179 F4 Sankt Georgen im Lavanttal Austria
172 C3 Sankt Georgen im Schwarzwald Ger.
179 E3 Sankt Gilgen Austria
169 C5 Sankt Goar Ger.
169 C5 Sankt Goarshausen Ger.
Sankt Gotthard Hungary see Szentgotthárd
172 B2 Sankt Ingbert Ger.
179 F4 Sankt Jakob im Rosental Austria
179 G3 Sankt Jakob im Walde Austria
178 D4 Sankt Jakob in Defereggen Austria
178 E3 Sankt Johann im Pongau Austria
179 G4 Sankt Johann im Saggautal Austria
178 D3 Sankt Johann in Tirol Austria
172 B2 Sankt Julian Ger.
179 F4 Sankt Kanzian am Klopeiner See Austria
179 F3 Sankt Lambrecht Austria
179 G2 Sankt Leonhard am Forst Austria
179 G2 Sankt Leonhard am Hornerwald Austria
178 B3 Sankt Leonhard im Pitztal Austria
179 E3 Sankt Lorenz Austria
179 G3 Sankt Lorenzen im Mürztal Austria
179 F3 Sankt Lorenzen ob Murau Austria
179 G3 Sankt Marein im Mürztal Austria
179 F4 Sankt Margareten im Rosental Austria
168 E2 Sankt Margarethen Ger.
179 G3 Sankt Margarethen an der Raab Austria
179 F3 Sankt Margarethen bei Knittelfeld Austria
179 H3 Sankt Margarethen im Burgenland Austria
172 C3 Sankt Märgen Ger.
179 F2 Sankt Marien Austria
179 E2 Sankt Marienkirchen an der Polsenz Austria
179 F2 Sankt Martin Niederösterreich Austria
179 E3 Sankt Martin Salzburg Austria
179 H4 Sankt Martin an der Raab Austria
179 F2 Sankt Martin im Mühlkreis Austria
179 G4 Sankt Martin im Sulmtal Austria
179 H3 Sankt Michael im Burgenland Austria
179 G3 Sankt Michael im Lungau Austria
179 G3 Sankt Michael in Obersteiermark Austria
168 E2 Sankt Michaelisdonn Ger.
190 E2 Sankt Moritz Switz.
179 G4 Sankt Nikolai im Sausal Austria
179 F2 Sankt Oswald bei Freistadt Austria
173 H3 Sankt Oswald-Riedlhütte Ger.
178 D2 Sankt Pantaleon Austria
179 F4 Sankt Paul im Lavanttal Austria
172 C3 Sankt Peter Ger.
178 E2 Sankt Peter am Hart Austria
179 F3 Sankt Peter am Kammersberg Austria
179 G4 Sankt Peter am Ottersbach Austria
139 H2 Sankt-Peterburg Rus. Fed.
179 G3 Sankt Peter-Freienstein Austria
179 G4 Sankt Peter im Sulmtal Austria
179 F2 Sankt Peter in der Au Austria
168 D1 Sankt Peter-Ording Ger.
Sankt Petersburg Rus. Fed. see Sankt-Peterburg
179 G2 Sankt Pölten Austria
179 G3 Sankt Ruprecht an der Raab Austria
179 F4 Sankt Stefan Austria
179 E4 Sankt Stefan im Gailtal Austria
179 G4 Sankt Stefan im Rosental Austria
179 F3 Sankt Stefan ob Leoben Austria
179 G4 Sankt Stefan ob Stainz Austria
178 D3 Sankt Ulrich am Pillersee Austria
179 F2 Sankt Ulrich bei Steyr Austria
179 F4 Sankt Urban Austria
179 F2 Sankt Valentin Austria
179 G4 Sankt Veit am Vogau Austria
179 F4 Sankt Veit an der Glan Austria
179 G2 Sankt Veit an der Gölsen Austria
178 E3 Sankt Veit im Pongau Austria
172 B2 Sankt Wendel Ger.
173 G3 Sankt Wolfgang Ger.
179 E3 Sankt Wolfgang im Salzkammergut Austria
209 D6 Sankuru r. Dem. Rep. Congo
253 F5 San Lázaro Para.
191 G4 San Lazzaro di Savena Italy
240 F3 San Leandro CA U.S.A.
191 I5 San Leo Italy
194 C5 San Leonardo r. Sicilia Italy
183 G3 San Leonardo de Yagüe Spain
191 G2 San Leonardo in Passiria Italy
126 E3 Şanlıurfa Turkey
128 D1 Şanlıurfa prov. Turkey
258 F3 San Lorenzo Corrientes Arg.
261 G3 San Lorenzo Santa Fé Arg.
252 D3 San Lorenzo Beni Bol.
252 D5 San Lorenzo Tarija Bol.
250 B4 San Lorenzo Ecuador
195 E5 San Lorenzo Italy
242 D2 San Lorenzo Mex.
252 C2 San Lorenzo Peru
183 H2 San Lorenzo mt. Spain
259 B7 San Lorenzo, Cerro mt. Arg./Chile
252 A3 San Lorenzo, Isla i. Peru
190 C5 San Lorenzo al Mare Italy
193 I5 San Lorenzo Bellizzi Italy
185 G2 San Lorenzo de Calatrava Spain
183 F4 San Lorenzo de El Escorial Spain
183 H5 San Lorenzo de la Parrilla Spain
San Lorenzo de Morunys Spain see Sant Llorenç de Morunys
191 G2 San Lorenzo di Sebato Italy
191 H5 San Lorenzo in Campo Italy
192 D2 San Lorenzo Nuovo Italy
195 F4 San Luca Italy
184 C3 Sanlúcar de Barrameda Spain
184 C3 Sanlúcar de Guadiana Spain
184 D3 Sanlúcar la Mayor Spain
252 D5 San Lucas Bol.
242 C4 San Lucas Mex.
250 C3 San Lucas, Serranía de mts Col.
193 I5 San Lucido Italy
260 D3 San Luis Arg.
260 D3 San Luis prov. Arg.
246 D2 San Luis Cuba
243 H5 San Luis Guat.
244 D5 San Luis Mex.
186 □ San Luis Spain
241 J5 San Luis AZ U.S.A.
241 L5 San Luis AZ U.S.A.
239 F4 San Luis CO U.S.A.
241 J5 San Luis, Sierra de mts Arg.
244 D3 San Luis de la Paz Mex.
258 F2 San Luis del Palmar Arg.
240 G4 San Luis Obispo CA U.S.A.
240 G4 San Luis Obispo Bay CA U.S.A.
242 □H6 San Luis Pajón Hond.
244 D2 San Luis Potosí Mex.
244 D2 San Luis Potosí state Mex.
242 B1 San Luis Río Colorado Mex.
192 A5 Sanluri Sardegna Italy
191 H2 San Maddalena Vallalta Italy
182 C2 San Mamede, Serra do mts Spain
183 F2 San Mamés de Campos Spain
193 I5 San Mango d'Aquino Italy
261 H5 San Manuel Arg.
241 L5 San Manuel AZ U.S.A.
191 I5 San Marcello Italy
191 F4 San Marcello Pistoiese Italy
193 I5 San Marco Argentano Italy
194 D4 San Marco d'Alunzio Sicilia Italy
193 G3 San Marco dei Cavoti Italy
193 H3 San Marco in Lamis Italy
250 C2 San Marcos Col.
243 H6 San Marcos Guat.
242 □I6 San Marcos Hond.
245 E5 San Marcos Mex.
252 A1 San Marcos Peru
182 B1 San Marcos Spain
240 I5 San Marcos CA U.S.A.
237 D6 San Marcos TX U.S.A.
237 D6 San Marcos r. TX U.S.A.
191 H5 San Marino country Europe
191 H5 San Marino San Marino
262 T2 San Martín research stn Antarctica
260 C3 San Martín Arg.
253 E3 San Martín r. Bol.
252 A1 San Martín dept Peru
177 K4 Sânmartin Romania
186 A1 San Martín Spain
259 B8 San Martín, Lago l. Arg./Chile
245 G4 San Martín, Volcán vol. Mex.
183 G4 San Martín de la Vega Spain
183 E4 San Martín de la Vega del Alberche Spain
259 C6 San Martín de los Andes Arg.
183 E4 San Martin del Pimpollar Spain
183 F5 San Martín de Montalbán Spain
183 F5 San Martín de Pusa Spain
183 I2 San Martin de Unx Spain
183 F4 San Martín de Valdeiglesias Spain
191 G3 San Martino Buon Albergo Italy
191 G2 San Martino di Castrozza Italy
192 B2 San-Martino-di-Lota Corse France
191 G3 San Martino di Lupari Italy
191 G3 San Martino di Venezze Italy
191 G2 San Martino in Badia Italy
191 G2 San Martino in Passiria Italy
193 H3 San Martino in Pensilis Italy
San Mateo Spain see Sant Mateu
240 F3 San Mateo CA U.S.A.
186 C3 San Mateo de Gállego Spain
243 H6 San Mateo Ixtatán Guat.
253 F4 San Matías Bol.
259 D6 San Matías, Golfo g. Arg.
194 D5 San Mauro Castelverde Sicilia Italy
193 I4 San Mauro Forte Italy
191 H4 San Mauro Pascoli Italy
190 C3 San Mauro Torinese Italy
109 G2 Sanmen Zhejiang China
193 H3 San Menaio Italy
109 G2 Sanmen Wan b. China
107 F5 Sanmenxia Henan China
191 H3 San Michele al Tagliamento Italy
190 C4 San Michele Mondovì Italy
195 G2 San Michele Salentino Italy
258 F3 San Miguel Arg.
253 E4 San Miguel Bol.
252 E3 San Miguel r. Bol.
250 C4 San Miguel r. Col.
242 □H6 San Miguel El Salvador
244 B2 San Miguel Mex.
252 B3 San Miguel Peru
92 B3 San Miguel Phil.
San Miguel Spain see Sant Miquel
187 D4 San Miguel r. Spain
240 G4 San Miguel CA U.S.A.
239 E4 San Miguel r. CO U.S.A.
216 □3a San Miguel de Abona Tenerife Canary Is
244 D3 San Miguel de Allende Mex.
183 F3 San Miguel de Arroyo Spain
183 G3 San Miguel de Bernuy Spain
244 B1 San Miguel de Cruces Mex.
242 C2 San Miguel de Horcasitas r. Mex.
252 D3 San Miguel de Huachi Bol.
261 H4 San Miguel del Monte Arg.
187 C7 San Miguel de Salinas Spain
258 D2 San Miguel de Tucumán Arg.
254 C5 San Miguel do Araguaia Brazil
244 C3 San Miguel el Alto Mex.
240 G4 San Miguel Island CA U.S.A.
92 A5 San Miguel Islands Phil.
242 □K7 San Miguelito Panama
244 D3 San Miguel Octopan Mex.
245 F5 San Miguel Sola de Vega Mex.
183 G2 San Millán mt. Spain
183 H2 San Millán de la Cogolla Spain
109 F3 Sanming Fujian China
191 F5 San Miniato Italy
175 J5 Sanna r. Pol.
92 B3 San Narciso Phil.
215 F3 Sannaspos S. Africa
190 D3 Sannazzaro de'Burgondi Italy
114 B3 Sanndatti Karnataka India
Sanndraigh i. Scotland U.K. see Sandray
195 F2 Sannicandro di Bari Italy
193 H3 Sannicandro Garganico Italy
195 H2 Sannicola Italy
195 F3 San Nicola dell'Alto Italy
192 B2 San-Nicolao Corse France
260 A5 San Nicolás Chile
244 B4 San Nicolás r. Mex.
92 B2 San Nicolas Phil.
244 D3 San Nicolás de los Agustinos Mex.
261 G3 San Nicolás de los Arroyos Arg.
184 E2 San Nicolás del Puerto Spain
216 □3f San Nicolás de Tolentino Gran Canaria Canary Is
239 C5 San Nicolas Island CA U.S.A.
196 E2 Sânnicolau Mare Romania
191 G4 San Nicolò Italy
192 A5 San Nicolò d'Arcidano Sardegna Italy
192 B5 San Nicolò Gerrei Sardegna Italy
215 E2 Sannieshof S. Africa
175 H3 Sanniki Pol.
193 G3 Sannio, Monti del mts Italy
206 C5 Sanniquellie Liberia
105 F2 Sano Japan
258 D3 Sañogasta, Sierra de mts Arg.
175 K6 Sanok Pol.
250 C2 San Onofre Col.
252 D5 San Pablo Potosí Bol.
253 E3 San Pablo Santa Cruz Bol.
253 E3 San Pablo r. Bol.
245 E3 San Pablo Mex.
92 B3 San Pablo Phil.
240 F3 San Pablo CA U.S.A.
183 F5 San Pablo de los Montes Spain
San Pablo de Manta Ecuador see Manta
191 G2 San Pancrazio Italy
195 G2 San Pancrazio Salentino Italy
193 H3 San Paolo di Civitate Italy
261 H3 San Pedro Buenos Aires Arg.
258 D2 San Pedro Catamarca Arg.
260 E2 San Pedro Córdoba Arg.
258 D2 San Pedro Jujuy Arg.
258 G2 San Pedro Misiones Arg.
243 I5 San Pedro Belize
252 D3 San Pedro Beni Bol.
253 E4 San Pedro Santa Cruz Bol.
252 D4 San Pedro r. Bol.
260 B3 San Pedro Santiago Chile
260 B3 San Pedro Valparaíso Chile
206 D5 San-Pédro Côte d'Ivoire
246 C2 San Pedro r. Cuba
242 C4 San Pedro Mex.
239 F6 San Pedro r. Chihuahua Mex.
244 B3 San Pedro r. Nayarit Mex.
253 F6 San Pedro Para.
92 B3 San Pedro Phil.
185 H2 San Pedro Spain
241 L5 San Pedro watercourse AZ U.S.A.
184 C1 San Pedro, Sierra de mts Spain
244 D3 San Pedro Almoloyan Mex.
245 F5 San Pedro Apóstol Mex.
243 H6 San Pedro Carchá Guat.
240 H5 San Pedro Channel CA U.S.A.
185 F4 San Pedro de Alcántara Spain
250 D3 San Pedro de Arimena Col.
252 C5 San Pedro de Atacama Chile
182 D2 San Pedro de Ceque Spain
239 E6 San Pedro de la Cueva Mex.
183 F4 San Pedro del Arroyo Spain
242 E3 San Pedro de las Colonias Mex.
183 E3 San Pedro de Latarce Spain
250 B6 San Pedro de Lloc Peru
253 F6 San Pedro del Paraná Para.
187 C7 San Pedro del Pinatar Spain
183 G1 San Pedro del Romeral Spain
247 E3 San Pedro de Macoris Dom. Rep.
182 E4 San Pedro de Rozados Spain
242 C2 San Pedro el Saucito Mex.
183 H2 San Pedro Manrique Spain
242 □H6 San Pedro Sula Hond.
177 J5 Sânpetru Mare Romania

Seaman Range to Shafter 361

241 J3 **Seaman Range** mts NV U.S.A.
149 I3 **Seamer** North Yorkshire, England U.K.
148 E2 **Seamill** North Ayrshire, Scotland U.K.
182 B3 **Seara** Port.
241 J4 **Searchlight** NV U.S.A.
237 F5 **Searcy** AR U.S.A.
233 □I2 **Searsport** ME U.S.A.
149 F3 **Seascale** Cumbria, England U.K.
240 G3 **Seaside** CA U.S.A.
238 B2 **Seaside** OR U.S.A.
235 D3 **Seaside Park** NJ U.S.A.
149 F3 **Seaton** Cumbria, England U.K.
150 D4 **Seaton** Devon, England U.K.
149 H2 **Seaton Delaval** Northumberland, England U.K.
149 H2 **Seaton Sluice** Northumberland, England U.K.
238 B2 **Seattle** WA U.S.A.
222 B2 **Seattle, Mount** Can./U.S.A.
215 E6 **Sea View** S. Africa
151 F4 **Seaview** Isle of Wight, England U.K.
85 F3 **Seaview Range** mts Qld Austr.
234 D3 **Seaville** NJ U.S.A.
81 D5 **Seaward Kaikoura Range** mts South I. N.Z.
242 □I6 **Sebaco** Nic.
182 B4 **Sebal** Port.
Sebastea Turkey see **Sivas**
231 D7 **Sebastian** FL U.S.A.
261 F2 **Sebastián Elcano** Arg.
242 B2 **Sebastián Vizcaíno, Bahía** b. Mex.
233 □I2 **Sebasticook** r. ME U.S.A.
Sebastopol Ukr. see Sevastopol'
240 F2 **Sebastopol** CA U.S.A.
95 G1 **Sebatik** i. Indon.
95 E3 **Sebayan, Bukit** mt. Indon.
161 A4 **Sébazac-Concourès** France
207 F3 **Sebba** Burkina
142 C3 **Sebbersund** Denmark
205 E2 **Sebdou** Alg.
206 C3 **Sébékoro** Mali
126 C2 **Seben** Turkey
Sebenico Croatia see **Šibenik**
Sebennytos Egypt see Samannûd
197 F3 **Sebeș** Romania
197 F2 **Sebeș** r. Romania
177 J5 **Sebes-Körös** r. Hungary
227 F4 **Sebewaing** MI U.S.A.
138 G3 **Sebezh** Rus. Fed.
126 E2 **Şebinkarahisar** Turkey
197 F2 **Sebiș** Romania
139 K2 **Sebla** r. Rus. Fed.
94 C3 **Seblat, Gunung** mt. Indon.
171 F5 **Sebnitz** Ger.
233 □I2 **Seboeis** ME U.S.A.
232 E6 **Sebrell** VA U.S.A.
231 D7 **Sebring** FL U.S.A.
135 H6 **Sebrovo** Rus. Fed.
95 G3 **Sebuku** i. Indon.
95 G1 **Sebuku** r. Indon.
260 D5 **Seca, Pampa** plain Arg.
196 E3 **Sečanj** Vojvodina, Srbija Yugo.
182 B4 **Secarias** Port.
177 K6 **Secaș** Romania
197 F2 **Secaș** r. Romania
242 □J8 **Secas, Islas** is Panama
191 G3 **Secchia** r. Italy
175 H5 **Secemin** Pol.
222 F5 **Sechelt** B.C. Can.
135 I5 **Sechenovo** Rus. Fed.
250 A6 **Sechura** Peru
250 A6 **Sechura, Bahía de** b. Peru
172 D2 **Seckach** Ger.
179 F3 **Seckau** Austria
156 D2 **Seclin** France
186 D4 **Seco** r. Spain
203 F4 **Second Cataract** rapids Sudan
162 B2 **Secondigny** France
241 L4 **Second Mesa** AZ U.S.A.
234 B2 **Second Mountain** ridge PA U.S.A.
85 E2 **Second Three Mile Opening** sea chan. Qld Austr.
206 □ **Secos, Ilhéus** is Cape Verde
177 K3 **Sečovce** Slovakia
81 A6 **Secretary Island** South I. N.Z.
215 G2 **Secunda** S. Africa
114 C2 **Secunderabad** Andhra Prad. India
252 D3 **Sécure** r. Bol.
177 J5 **Secusigiu** Romania
138 E3 **Seda** Latvia
138 E3 **Seda** r. Latvia
138 D3 **Seda** Lith.
184 C1 **Seda** Port.
184 B2 **Seda** r. Port.
236 E4 **Sedalia** MO U.S.A.
114 C2 **Sedam** Karnataka India
82 D3 **Sedan** S.A. Austr.
157 E3 **Sedan** France
237 D4 **Sedan** KS U.S.A.
85 E3 **Sedan Dip** Qld Austr.
183 G2 **Sedano** Spain
149 G3 **Sedbergh** Cumbria, England U.K.
81 E4 **Seddon** South I. N.Z.
81 C4 **Seddonville** South I. N.Z.
122 C4 **Sedeh** Fārs Iran
122 D3 **Sedeh** Khorāsan Iran
161 D4 **Séderon** France
149 H3 **Sedgefield** Durham, England U.K.
223 I4 **Sedgewick** Alta Can.
150 E2 **Sedgley** West Midlands, England U.K.
233 □I2 **Sedgwick** ME U.S.A.
206 B3 **Sédhiou** Senegal
191 H2 **Sedico** Italy
192 A4 **Sedilo** Sardegna Italy
192 A4 **Sedini** Sardegna Italy
176 G6 **Sedlarica** Croatia
176 D2 **Sedlčany** Czech Rep.
176 D2 **Sedlec Prčice** Czech Rep.
Sedlets Pol. see **Siedlce**
177 K3 **Sedlice** Slovakia
171 F4 **Sedlitz** Ger.
171 F5 **Sedlo** hill Czech Rep.
136 C2 **Sedlyshche** Ukr.
241 L4 **Sedona** AZ U.S.A.
Sedovo Ukr. see **Syedove**
205 G1 **Sédrata** Alg.
190 E3 **Sedrina** Italy
138 D4 **Šeduva** Lith.
175 H4 **Sędziejowice** Pol.
174 G3 **Sędzin** Pol.
175 I5 **Sędziszów** Pol.
175 J5 **Sędziszów Małopolski** Pol.
178 B3 **See** Austria
159 E3 **Sée** r. France
172 C3 **Seebach** Baden-Württemberg Ger.
169 F5 **Seebach** Thüringen Ger.
170 F2 **Seebad Ahlbeck** Ger.
170 F2 **Seebad Bansin** Ger.
170 F2 **Seebad Heringsdorf** Ger.
169 F5 **Seebergen** Ger.
179 E4 **Seeboden** Austria
173 G4 **Seebruck** Ger.
169 F4 **Seeburg** Ger.
168 F1 **Seedorf** Schleswig-Holstein Ger.
168 F2 **Seedorf** Schleswig-Holstein Ger.
173 F3 **Seefeld** Bayern Ger.
170 E3 **Seefeld** Brandenburg Ger.
168 D2 **Seefeld (Stadland)** Ger.
178 C3 **Seefeld in Tirol** Austria
147 D4 **Seefin** hill Rep. of Ireland
173 E4 **Seeg** Ger.
171 D4 **Seegrehna** Ger.
170 E2 **Seehausen** Brandenburg Ger.
171 C3 **Seehausen** Sachsen-Anhalt Ger.
170 C3 **Seehausen (Altmark)** Ger.
173 F4 **Seehausen am Staffelsee** Ger.
172 C2 **Seeheim-Jugenheim** Ger.
178 E3 **Seekirchen am Wallersee** Austria
214 D5 **Seekoegat** S. Africa
215 E4 **Seekoei** r. S. Africa
172 B3 **Seelbach** Ger.
241 J5 **Seeley** CA U.S.A.
262 R1 **Seelig, Mount** Antarctica
171 D5 **Seelingstädt** Ger.
170 F3 **Seelow** Ger.
169 E3 **Seelze** Ger.
Seenu Atoll Maldives see **Addu Atoll**
173 G4 **Seeon** Ger.
190 D1 **Seerücken** val. Switz.
159 G3 **Sées** France
169 F4 **Seesen** Ger.
173 F4 **Seeshaupt** Ger.
168 F2 **Seevetal** Ger.
179 E3 **Seewalchen am Attersee** Austria
160 E3 **Séez** France
206 C4 **Sefadu** Sierra Leone
199 E2 **Seferihisar** Turkey
206 C3 **Séféto** Mali
122 B3 **Sefīd, Kūh-e** mt. Iran
213 E4 **Sefophe** Botswana
204 D2 **Sefrou** Morocco
81 C5 **Sefton, Mount** South I. N.Z.
206 C3 **Ségala** Mali
141 J3 **Segalstad** Norway
95 G1 **Segama** r. Sabah Malaysia
94 C2 **Segamat** Malaysia
180 E5 **Segangane** Morocco
197 F3 **Şegarcea** Romania
207 F4 **Ségbana** Benin
176 G5 **Segesd** Hungary
134 F3 **Segezha** Rus. Fed.
192 D2 **Seggiano** Italy
158 C3 **Séglien** France
193 F3 **Segni** Italy
Segontia Gwynedd, Wales U.K. see **Caernarfon**
Segontium Gwynedd, Wales U.K. see **Caernarfon**
162 B3 **Segonzac** France
187 C5 **Segorbe** Spain
206 D3 **Ségou** Mali
206 D3 **Ségou** admin. reg. Mali
250 C3 **Segovia** Col.
Segovia r. Hond./Nic. see **Coco**
183 F4 **Segovia** Spain
183 F3 **Segovia** prov. Castilla y León Spain
134 F3 **Segozerskoye, Ozero** resr Rus. Fed.
159 F4 **Segré** France
186 D3 **Segre** r. Spain
159 G3 **Ségrie** France
206 D5 **Séguéla** Côte d'Ivoire
206 D4 **Séguélon** Côte d'Ivoire
206 E3 **Séguénéga** Burkina
261 G3 **Seguí** Arg.
237 D6 **Seguin** TX U.S.A.
261 F2 **Segundo** r. Arg.
161 A4 **Ségur** France
182 D5 **Segura** Port.
185 I2 **Segura** r. Spain
185 H3 **Segura, Sierra de** mts Spain
185 H2 **Segura de la Sierra** Spain
184 D2 **Segura de León** Spain
186 C4 **Segura de los Baños** Spain
183 F4 **Segurilla** Spain
212 D4 **Sehithwa** Botswana
169 F3 **Sehlde** Ger.
169 E3 **Sehnde** Ger.
116 D5 **Sehore** Madh. Prad. India
123 F5 **Sehwan** Pak.
182 C4 **Seia** Port.
236 C4 **Seibert** CO U.S.A.
158 E4 **Seiche** r. France
159 F4 **Seiches-sur-le-Loir** France
179 G3 **Seiersberg** Austria
140 J2 **Seierstad** Norway
171 F5 **Seifhennersdorf** Ger.
150 E2 **Seighford** Staffordshire, England U.K.
161 A4 **Seigne, Mont** mt. France
225 G3 **Seignelay** r. Que. Can.
156 D5 **Seignelay** France
190 B1 **Seignelégier** Switz.
163 A5 **Seignosse** France
96 A2 **Seikpyu** Myanmar
146 C5 **Seil** i. Scotland U.K.
140 M1 **Seiland** i. Norway
162 D3 **Seilhac** France
237 D4 **Seiling** OK U.S.A.
161 E5 **Seillans** France
160 C2 **Seille** r. France
157 G3 **Seille** r. France
165 E4 **Seilles** Belgium
138 D4 **Šeimena** r. Lith.
140 M3 **Seinäjoki** Fin.
224 B3 **Seine** r. Ont. Can.
156 A3 **Seine** r. France
159 F2 **Seine, Baie de** b. France
160 C1 **Seine, Sources de la** tourist site France
156 D4 **Seine, Val de** val. France
156 D4 **Seine-et-Marne** dept Île-de-France France
Seine-Inférieure dept Haute-Normandie France see **Seine-Maritime**
156 A3 **Seine-Maritime** dept Haute-Normandie France
159 I3 **Seine-St-Denis** dept France
197 F2 **Seini** Romania
173 E2 **Seinsheim** Ger.
186 D2 **Seira** Spain
163 C5 **Seissan** France
179 F2 **Seitenstetten** Austria
177 J5 **Şeitin** Romania
163 D6 **Seix** France
184 □ **Seixal** Madeira
184 A2 **Seixal** Port.
182 B3 **Seixas** Port.
184 B3 **Seixe** r. Port.
182 C4 **Seixo da Beira** Port.
142 D4 **Sejerby** Denmark
142 D4 **Sejerø** i. Denmark
142 D4 **Sejerø Bugt** b. Denmark
175 L1 **Sejny** Pol.
94 C3 **Sekayu** Sumatera Indon.
177 K3 **Sekčov** r. Slovakia
Seke Sichuan China see **Sêrtar**
209 B6 **Seke-Banza** Dem. Rep. Congo
104 C3 **Seki** Japan
199 F3 **Seki** Turkey
199 F3 **Seki** r. Turkey
102 □1 **Sekibi-sho** i. Japan
94 D4 **Sekicau, Gunung** vol. Indon.
104 C2 **Sekidō-san** hill Japan
206 E5 **Sekondi** Ghana
210 C1 **Sek'ot'a** Eth.
175 J6 **Sękowa** Pol.
Sekseüil Kazakh. see Saksaul'skiy
123 E4 **Sekūheh** Iran
Şela Rus. Fed. see **Shali**
94 C3 **Selagan** r. Indon.
238 B2 **Selah** WA U.S.A.
94 C2 **Selangor** state Malaysia
192 B5 **Selargius** Sardegna Italy
94 C2 **Selatpanjang** Sumatera Indon.
150 D2 **Selattyn** Shropshire, England U.K.
220 B3 **Selawik** AK U.S.A.
183 G1 **Selaya** Spain
171 D5 **Selb** Ger.
178 D3 **Selbhorn** mt. Austria
171 C5 **Selbitz** Ger.
140 J3 **Selbu** Norway
149 H4 **Selby** North Yorkshire, England U.K.
236 C2 **Selby** SD U.S.A.
233 F5 **Selbyville** DE U.S.A.
191 J3 **Selce** Croatia
199 E3 **Selçuk** Turkey
236 C4 **Selden** KS U.S.A.
220 C4 **Seldovia** AK U.S.A.
193 G4 **Sele** r. Italy
213 E4 **Selebi-Phikwe** Botswana
Selebi-Pikwe Botswana see Selebi-Phikwe
197 E5 **Selečka Planina** mts Macedonia
192 B5 **Selegas** Sardegna Italy
192 B4 **S'Elema** r. Sardegna Italy
100 D1 **Selemdzha** r. Rus. Fed.
199 F2 **Selendi** Turkey
106 E1 **Selenduma** Rus. Fed.
106 E1 **Selenga** r. Rus. Fed.
106 E1 **Selenge** prov. Mongolia
106 E1 **Selenge Mörön** r. Mongolia
198 A1 **Selenicë** Albania
168 F1 **Selent** Ger.
168 F1 **Selenter See** l. Ger.
157 H4 **Sélestat** France
121 H1 **Seletinskoye** Kazakh.
Selety r. Kazakh. see **Sileti**
Seletyteniz, Oz. salt l. Kazakh. see **Siletiteniz, Ozero**
Seleucia Turkey see **Silifke**
Seleucia Pieria Turkey see Samandağı
177 K5 **Seleuș** Romania
138 G1 **Seleznevo** Rus. Fed.
140 □B3 **Selfoss** Iceland
236 C2 **Selfridge** ND U.S.A.
206 B3 **Sélibabi** Maur.
Selidovo Ukr. see **Selydove**
169 D5 **Seligenstadt** Ger.
139 I3 **Seliger, Ozero** l. Rus. Fed.
241 K4 **Seligman** AZ U.S.A.
129 C3 **Selim** Turkey
203 F4 **Selîma Oasis** Sudan
199 E3 **Selimiye** Turkey
206 C4 **Sélingué, Lac de** l. Mali
206 C3 **Selinnkegni** Mali
198 C2 **Selinous** r. Greece
234 B2 **Selinsgrove** PA U.S.A.
139 I3 **Selishche** Rus. Fed.
135 H5 **Selishchi** Rus. Fed.
120 A3 **Selitrennoye** Rus. Fed.
139 I3 **Selizharovo** Rus. Fed.
141 I3 **Selje** Norway
142 C2 **Seljord** Norway
171 C4 **Selke** r. Ger.
223 L5 **Selkirk** Man. Can.
146 F6 **Selkirk** Scottish Borders, Scotland U.K.
222 G4 **Selkirk Mountains** B.C. Can.
Şelkovski Rus. Fed. see **Shelkovskaya**
187 C6 **Sella** Spain
183 E1 **Sella** r. Spain
149 F3 **Sellafield** Cumbria, England U.K.
146 □G1 **Sellafirth** Shetland, Scotland U.K.
193 E2 **Sellano** Italy
234 C2 **Sellersville** PA U.S.A.
162 D1 **Selles-St-Denis** France
159 H4 **Selles-sur-Cher** France
85 F4 **Sellheim** r. Qld Austr.
195 F4 **Sellia Marina** Italy
160 D2 **Sellières** France
151 H3 **Sellindge** Kent, England U.K.
164 G2 **Sellingen** Neth.
Sellore Island Myanmar see **Saganthit Kyun**
178 C3 **Sellrain** Austria
241 L6 **Sells** AZ U.S.A.
177 G6 **Sellye** Hungary
169 C4 **Selm** Ger.
231 C5 **Selma** AL U.S.A.
240 H3 **Selma** CA U.S.A.
237 F5 **Selmer** TN U.S.A.
184 C2 **Selmes** Port.
182 D2 **Selmo** r. Spain
168 F2 **Selmsdorf** Ger.
156 B5 **Selommes** France
95 G5 **Selong** Lombok Indon.
160 D1 **Selongey** France
161 E4 **Selonnet** France
215 G1 **Selonsrivier** S. Africa
206 C4 **Sélouma** Guinea
222 C2 **Selous, Mount** Y.T. Can.
170 C2 **Selow** Ger.
122 E4 **Selseleh-ye Pīr Shūrān** mts Iran
151 G4 **Selsey** West Sussex, England U.K.
151 G4 **Selsey Bill** hd England U.K.
168 E2 **Selsingen** Ger.
169 C5 **Selters (Westerwald)** Ger.
139 J5 **Sel'tso** Rus. Fed.
134 K4 **Selty** Rus. Fed.
157 I4 **Seltz** France
Selukwe Zimbabwe see Shurugwi
159 E3 **Sélune** r. France
195 G2 **Selva** Italy
187 F5 **Selva** Spain
186 B2 **Selva** mt. Spain
191 G2 **Selva dei Molini** Italy
191 G3 **Selva di Progno** Italy
178 C4 **Selva di Val Gardena** Italy
204 B3 **Selvagens, Ilhas** is Madeira
127 G3 **Selvānā** Iran
260 A6 **Selva Obscura** Chile
250 D6 **Selvas** reg. Brazil
191 G3 **Selvazzano Dentro** Italy
190 E3 **Selvino** Italy
238 D2 **Selway** r. ID U.S.A.
223 J2 **Selwyn Lake** N.W.T./Sask. Can.
222 D1 **Selwyn Mountains** N.W.T./Y.T. Can.
84 D4 **Selwyn Range** hills Qld Austr.
136 C4 **Selyatyn** Ukr.
137 I3 **Selydove** Ukr.
172 C2 **Selz** r. Ger.
179 F3 **Selzthal** Austria
163 E5 **Sémalens** France
198 A1 **Seman** r. Albania
95 E4 **Semarang** Jawa Tengah Indon.
161 B3 **Sembadel** France
95 G2 **Sembakung** r. Indon.
208 B4 **Sembé** Congo
159 G4 **Semblançay** France
190 C2 **Sembrancher** Switz.
127 G3 **Şemdinli** Turkey
163 C5 **Séméac** France
160 B2 **Sémelay** France
Semendire Srbija Yugo. see Smederevo
197 F3 **Semenic, Vârful** mt. Romania
137 G1 **Semenivka** Chernihivs'ka Oblast' Ukr.
137 I3 **Semenivka** Kharkivs'ka Oblast' Ukr.
137 F2 **Semenivka** Kyivs'ka Oblast' Ukr.
137 G3 **Semenivka** Poltavs'ka Oblast' Ukr.
120 C1 **Semenkino** Rus. Fed.
137 K2 **Semeno-Aleksandrovka** Rus. Fed.
134 I4 **Semenov** Rus. Fed.
Semenovka Chernihivs'ka Oblast' Ukr. see **Semenivka**
94 F5 **Semeru, Gunung** vol. Indon.
Semey Kazakh. see Semipalatinsk
124 B5 **Semhar** prov. Eritrea
137 J4 **Semibalki** Rus. Fed.
139 L3 **Semibratovo** Rus. Fed.
182 B4 **Semide** Port.
137 J2 **Semidesyatnoye** Rus. Fed.
134 H4 **Semigorodnyaya** Rus. Fed.
135 H7 **Semikarakorsk** Rus. Fed.
135 G6 **Semiluki** Rus. Fed.
176 E1 **Semily** Czech Rep.
195 E4 **Seminara** Italy
160 D2 **Semine** r. France
237 C5 **Seminole** TX U.S.A.
121 K2 **Seminskiy Khrebet** mts Rus. Fed.
120 F1 **Semiozernoye** Kazakh.
121 J2 **Semipalatinsk** Kazakh.
121 F1 **Semipolka** Kazakh.
92 B4 **Semirara Islands** Phil.
95 E2 **Semitau** Kalimantan Barat Indon.
121 I2 **Semiyarka** Kazakh.
121 H2 **Semizbuga** Kazakh.
Semizbughy Kazakh. see Semizbuga
139 L3 **Semkhoz** Rus. Fed.
Sem Kolodezey Respublika Krym Ukr. see **Lenine**
196 E2 **Semlac** Romania
139 I4 **Semlevo** Rus. Fed.
208 F4 **Semliki** r. Dem. Rep. Congo/Uganda
170 D1 **Semlow** Ger.
169 F3 **Semmenstedt** Ger.
122 C3 **Semnān** Iran
122 B3 **Semnān** prov. Iran
106 D4 **Sêmnyi** Qinghai China
165 D5 **Semois** r. Belgium
165 D5 **Semois, Vallée de la** val. Belgium/France
157 F4 **Semoutiers-Montsaon** France
190 D1 **Sempach** Switz.
179 E5 **Šempeter** Slovenia
192 D2 **Semproniano** Italy
173 F3 **Sempt** r. Ger.
179 G3 **Semriach** Austria
139 I5 **Semtsy** Rus. Fed.
160 C1 **Semur-en-Auxois** France
160 C2 **Semur-en-Brionnais** France
162 B3 **Semussac** France
Semyonovskoye Arkhangel'skaya Oblast' Rus. Fed. see **Bereznik**
Semyonovskoye Kostromskaya Oblast' Rus. Fed. see Ostrovskoye
97 D4 **Sên, Stœng** r. Cambodia
252 D2 **Sena** Bol.
177 K3 **Seňa** Slovakia
186 C3 **Sena** Spain
256 C2 **Senador Canedo** Brazil
254 F3 **Senador Pompeu** Brazil
203 H6 **Senafe** Eritrea
191 G2 **Senaiga** r. Italy
129 C2 **Senaki** Georgia
191 F2 **Senales** Italy
192 B4 **Senalonga, Punta** mt. Sardegna Italy
252 C2 **Sena Madureira** Brazil
209 D9 **Senanga** Zambia
156 B3 **Senarpont** France
161 D5 **Sénas** France
237 F5 **Senatobia** MS U.S.A.
Sencelles Spain see **Sancellas**
137 G2 **Sencha** Ukr.
179 F4 **Šenčur** Slovenia
103 E8 **Sendai** Kagoshima Japan
102 J4 **Sendai** Miyagi Japan
103 E8 **Sendai-gawa** r. Japan
215 F2 **Sendelingsfontein** S. Africa
173 E3 **Senden** Bayern Ger.
169 C4 **Senden** Nordrhein-Westfalen Ger.
169 C4 **Sendenhorst** Ger.
182 D3 **Sendim** Bragança Port.
182 B3 **Sendim** Porto Port.
Sêndo Xizang China see **Chido**
197 H3 **Şendreni** Romania
158 D4 **Séné** France
206 E5 **Sene** r. Ghana
176 G3 **Senec** Slovakia
226 C5 **Seneca** IL U.S.A.
236 D4 **Seneca** KS U.S.A.
238 C2 **Seneca** OR U.S.A.
232 D4 **Seneca** PA U.S.A.
232 D5 **Seneca Rocks** WV U.S.A.
165 D4 **Seneffe** Belgium
206 B3 **Senegal** country Africa
206 A2 **Sénégal** r. Maur./Senegal
192 A4 **Seneghe** Sardegna Italy
215 F3 **Senekal** S. Africa
185 H3 **Senes** Spain
192 B4 **Senes, Monte** hill Sardegna Italy
226 E2 **Seney** MI U.S.A.
161 E5 **Senez** France
179 G2 **Senftenberg** Austria
171 F4 **Senftenberg** Ger.
211 B8 **Senga** Malawi
116 D4 **Sengar** r. India
173 F2 **Sengenthal** Ger.
211 B5 **Sengerema** Tanz.
256 C6 **Sengés** Brazil
135 J5 **Sengiley** Rus. Fed.
Sengirli, Mys pt Kazakh. see **Syngyrli, Mys**
163 C6 **Sengouagnet** France
259 C7 **Senguerr** r. Arg.
213 F3 **Sengwa** r. Zimbabwe
124 B5 **Senhit** prov. Eritrea
184 C1 **Senhora do Rosário** Port.
254 E4 **Senhor do Bonfim** Brazil
176 G3 **Senica** Slovakia
176 G2 **Senice na Hané** Czech Rep.
191 I5 **Senigallia** Italy
191 H4 **Senio** r. Italy
199 G2 **Senirkent** Turkey
192 A5 **Senis** Sardegna Italy
193 I4 **Senise** Italy
188 E3 **Senj** Croatia
140 L1 **Senja** i. Norway
104 B4 **Senjōga-dake** mt. Japan
105 E3 **Senjōga-dake** mt. Japan
127 F2 **Şenkaya** Turkey
206 C4 **Šenko** Guinea
209 E9 **Senkobo** Zambia
137 I3 **Sen'kove** Ukr.
128 C1 **Şenköy** Turkey
116 D2 **Šenku** Jammu and Kashmir
214 D1 **Senlac** S. Africa
100 D4 **Senlin Shan** mt. Jilin China
156 C3 **Senlis** France
97 D4 **Senmonorom** Cambodia
104 B4 **Sennan** Japan
203 G6 **Sennar** Sudan
203 G6 **Sennar** state Sudan
192 A4 **Sennariolo** Sardegna Italy
160 C2 **Sennecey-le-Grand** France
160 D1 **Sennecey-lès-Dijon** France
150 □ **Sennen** Cornwall, England U.K.
224 E3 **Senneterre** Que. Can.
171 C4 **Sennewitz** Ger.
Senno Belarus see **Syanno**
105 E2 **Sennokura-yama** mt. Japan
192 A4 **Sennori** Sardegna Italy
190 E1 **Sennwald** Switz.
150 D3 **Sennybridge** Powys, Wales U.K.
156 B4 **Senonches** France
157 G4 **Senones** France
192 B5 **Senorbì** Sardegna Italy
163 D5 **Senouillac** France
161 B3 **Senouire** r. France
179 G4 **Senovo** Slovenia
215 F4 **Senqu** r. Lesotho
156 D4 **Sens** France
158 E3 **Sens-de-Bretagne** France
156 D2 **Sensée** r. France
242 □H6 **Sensuntepeque** El Salvador
196 E3 **Senta** Vojvodina, Srbija Yugo.
163 C6 **Sentein** France
163 D6 **Sentenac-d'Oust** France
186 D2 **Senterada** Spain
179 G4 **Šentilj** Slovenia
241 K5 **Sentinel** AZ U.S.A.
193 G3 **Sentinella, Colle della** hill Italy
222 F4 **Sentinel Peak** B.C. Can.
262 S1 **Sentinel Range** mts Antarctica
Sentinum Italy see Sassoferrato
179 G5 **Šentjernej** Slovenia
179 G4 **Šentjur pri Celju** Slovenia
94 □ **Sentosa** i. Sing.
157 E3 **Senuc** France
177 K4 **Sényő** Hungary
129 B3 **Senyurt** Erzurum Turkey
127 F3 **Şenyurt** Turkey
171 E3 **Senzig** Ger.
Seo de Urgell Spain see **Le Seu d'Urgell**
190 D1 **Seon** Switz.
116 E5 **Seonath** r. India
116 D4 **Seondha** Madh. Prad. India
116 D5 **Seoni** Madh. Prad. India
116 D5 **Seoni Chhapara** Madh. Prad. India
116 D5 **Seoni-Malwa** Madh. Prad. India
Seoul S. Korea see **Sŏul**
163 C4 **Séoune** r. France
86 D4 **Separation Well** W.A. Austr.
122 A3 **Separ Shāhābād** Iran
252 D1 **Sepatini** r. Brazil
257 E5 **Sepetiba, Baía de** b. Brazil
91 J7 **Sepik** r. P.N.G.
95 F2 **Seping** r. Sarawak Malaysia
193 G3 **Sepino** Italy
101 C5 **Sep'o** N. Korea
174 F2 **Sępólno Krajeńskie** Pol.
117 H4 **Sepon** Assam India
253 F3 **Sepotuba** r. Brazil
117 H4 **Seppa** Arun. Prad. India
160 F1 **Seppois-le-Bas** France
197 E2 **Şepreuș** Romania
161 D5 **Septèmes-les-Vallons** France
156 B4 **Septeuil** France
163 D4 **Septfonds** France
225 H3 **Sept-Îles** Que. Can.
160 D2 **Septmoncel** France
182 D4 **Sepulcro-Hilario** Spain
183 G3 **Sepúlveda** Spain
94 D4 **Seputih** r. Indon.
191 H2 **Sequals** Italy
231 C5 **Sequatchie** r. TN U.S.A.
182 D4 **Sequeros** Spain
183 E3 **Sequillo** r. Spain
124 B5 **Serae** prov. Eritrea
129 B4 **Şerafettin Dağları** mts Turkey
135 H6 **Serafimovich** Rus. Fed.
156 E3 **Seraincourt** France
165 E4 **Seraing** Belgium
Sêraitang Qinghai China see Baima
93 D3 **Seram** i. Maluku Indon.
93 D3 **Seram Sea** Indon.
160 D3 **Séran** r. France
94 D4 **Serang** Jawa Barat Indon.
161 E5 **Séranon** France
95 E2 **Serasan, Selat** sea chan. Indon.
190 F5 **Seravezza** Italy
128 A5 **Serbâl, Gebel** mt. Egypt
Serbia aut. rep. Yugo. see Srbija
136 D3 **Serbynivtsi** Ukr.
111 F6 **Sêrca** Xizang China
191 F5 **Serchio** r. Italy
192 B5 **Serdiana** Sardegna Italy
Serdica Bulg. see **Sofiya**
135 I5 **Serdoba** r. Rus. Fed.
135 I5 **Serdobsk** Rus. Fed.
121 J2 **Serebryansk** Kazakh.
139 L4 **Serebryanyye Prudy** Rus. Fed.
177 G3 **Sereď** Slovakia
139 M3 **Sereda** Rus. Fed.
139 J4 **Seredeyskiy** Rus. Fed.
138 G2 **Seredka** Rus. Fed.
136 F4 **Seredniy Kuyal'nyk** r. Ukr.
206 C4 **Sérédou** Guinea
137 H1 **Seredyna-Buda** Rus. Fed.
136 B3 **Seredyne** Ukr.
126 D3 **Şereflikoçhisar** Turkey
177 H4 **Seregélyes** Hungary
190 E3 **Seregno** Italy
162 D3 **Séreilhac** France
156 D5 **Serein** r. France
94 C2 **Seremban** Malaysia
211 B5 **Serengeti National Park** Tanz.
211 B5 **Serengeti Plain** Tanz.
209 F8 **Serenje** Zambia
158 D4 **Sérent** France
210 B4 **Serere** Uganda
136 C3 **Seret** r. Ukr.
134 H5 **Serezha** r. Rus. Fed.
139 H3 **Serezha** r. Rus. Fed.
178 B3 **Serfaus** Austria
134 L4 **Ser'ga** Rus. Fed.
134 I5 **Sergach** Rus. Fed.
107 F2 **Sergelen** Mongolia
197 H5 **Sergen** Turkey
121 G2 **Sergeyevka** Akmolinskaya Oblast' Kazakh.
121 F1 **Sergeyevka** Severnyy Kazakhstan Kazakh.
137 J2 **Sergeyevka** Rus. Fed.
156 D4 **Sergines** France
130 H3 **Sergino** Rus. Fed.
254 F4 **Sergipe** state Brazil
139 L3 **Sergiyev Posad** Rus. Fed.
135 J5 **Sergiyevsk** Rus. Fed.
Sergiyevskiy Rus. Fed. see **Fakel**
190 E3 **Sergnano** Italy
Sergo Ukr. see **Stakhanov**
129 E2 **Sergokala** Rus. Fed.
137 G2 **Serhiyivka** Chernihivs'ka Oblast' Ukr.
137 H4 **Serhiyivka** Khersons'ka Oblast' Ukr.
136 F4 **Serhiyivka** Odes'ka Oblast' Ukr.
95 F1 **Seria** Brunei
190 E3 **Seriate** Italy
156 B3 **Sérifontaine** France
198 D3 **Serifos** i. Greece
161 B5 **Sérignan** France
161 C4 **Sérignan-du-Comtat** France
225 G2 **Sérigny** r. Que. Can.
199 G3 **Serik** Turkey
190 E3 **Serina** Italy
213 □J3 **Sèrinama** Madag.
251 I6 **Seringa, Serra da** hills Brazil
86 D2 **Seringapatam Reef** W.A. Austr.
199 F3 **Serinhisar** Turkey
129 B4 **Serinova** Turkey
128 C1 **Serinyol** Turkey
190 E3 **Serio** r. Italy
Sêrkang Xizang China see Nyainrong
136 C2 **Serkhiv** Ukr.
205 G5 **Serkout** mt. Alg.
Serle atoll Arch. des Tuamotu Fr. Polynesia see **Pukarua**
156 C4 **Sermaises** France
157 E4 **Sermaize-les-Bains** France
192 B2 **Sermano** Corse France
197 F5 **Sermenin** Macedonia
191 G4 **Sermide** Italy
160 B2 **Sermoise-sur-Loire** France
193 F3 **Sermoneta** Italy
160 C2 **Sermoyer** France
182 C4 **Sernancelhe** Port.
177 L3 **Serne** r. Ukr.
175 K4 **Serniki** Pol.
171 D4 **Serno** Ger.
135 J5 **Sernovodsk** Rus. Fed.
134 J4 **Sernur** Rus. Fed.
136 D2 **Sernyky** Ukr.
174 G2 **Serock** Kujawsko-Pomorskie Pol.
175 J3 **Serock** Mazowieckie Pol.
261 G3 **Serodino** Arg.
185 H3 **Serón** Spain
183 H3 **Serón de Nájima** Spain
164 C3 **Serooskerke** Neth.
186 D3 **Seròs** Spain
130 H4 **Serov** Rus. Fed.
212 E4 **Serowe** Botswana
184 C3 **Serpa** Port.
Serpa Pinto Angola see Menongue
225 G3 **Serpent** r. Que. Can.
87 B7 **Serpentine** r. W.A. Austr.
82 B2 **Serpentine Lakes** salt flat S.A. Austr.
247 G5 **Serpent's Mouth** sea chan. Trin. and Tob./Venez.
182 B4 **Serpins** Port.
187 C6 **Serpis** r. Spain
136 E4 **Serpneve** Ukr.
139 K4 **Serpukhov** Rus. Fed.
157 F5 **Serqueux** France
159 G2 **Serquigny** France
257 G4 **Serra** Brazil
192 A4 **Serra** r. Sardegna Italy
187 C5 **Serra** Spain
193 H3 **Serracapriola** Italy
183 F3 **Serrada** Spain
191 I5 **Serra de'Conti** Italy
182 B2 **Serra de Outes** Spain
216 □1a **Serra de Santa Barbara** vol. Terceira Azores
194 C5 **Serradifalco** Sicilia Italy
192 A3 **Serra-di-Ferro** Corse France
182 D5 **Serradilla** Spain
182 D4 **Serradilla del Arroyo** Spain
257 G2 **Serra dos Aimorés** Brazil
256 D3 **Serra do Salitre** Brazil
Sérrai Greece see **Serres**
192 A5 **Serramanna** Sardegna Italy
191 F4 **Serramazzoni** Italy
256 D4 **Serrana** Brazil
246 C4 **Serranilla Bank** sea feature Caribbean Sea
183 F4 **Serranillos** Spain
256 A3 **Serranópolis** Brazil
190 D4 **Serra Riccò** Italy
195 F4 **Serra San Bruno** Italy
191 I5 **Serra San Quirico** Italy
254 F3 **Serra Talhada** Brazil
191 H5 **Serravalle** San Marino
193 E1 **Serravalle di Chienti** Italy
190 D4 **Serravalle Scrivia** Italy
156 D3 **Serre** r. France
193 H4 **Serre** Italy
161 E4 **Serre-Chevalier** France
182 E5 **Serrejón** Spain
192 A5 **Serrenti** Sardegna Italy
Serrera, Pic de la mt. Andorra see **Serrère, Pic de**
186 E2 **Serrère, Pic de** mt. Andorra
161 D4 **Serres** France
198 C1 **Serres** Greece
163 B5 **Serres-Castet** France
216 □1a **Serreta** Terceira Azores
192 B5 **Serri** Sardegna Italy
192 A2 **Serriera** Corse France
160 D3 **Serrière-de-Briord** France
161 C3 **Serrières** France
172 A2 **Serrig** Ger.
254 F4 **Serrinha** Brazil
254 F3 **Serrita** Brazil
257 F3 **Sêrro** Brazil
183 E4 **Serrota** mt. Spain
162 C3 **Sers** France
195 F3 **Sersale** Italy
182 B5 **Sertã** Port.
254 F4 **Sertânia** Brazil
256 B5 **Sertanópolis** Brazil
256 A3 **Sertão de Camapuã** reg. Brazil
256 D4 **Sertãozinho** Brazil
108 B1 **Sêrtar** Sichuan China
139 H1 **Sertolovo** Rus. Fed.
93 D4 **Serua** vol. Maluku Indon.
213 E4 **Serule** Botswana
95 F3 **Seruyan** r. Indon.
138 F4 **Servach** r. Belarus
157 G5 **Servance** France
161 B4 **Serverette** France
198 C1 **Servia** Greece
161 B5 **Servian** France
193 F1 **Servigliano** Italy
186 D4 **Servol** r. Spain
158 E3 **Servon-sur-Vilaine** France
160 E3 **Servoz** France
108 A1 **Sêrxu** Sichuan China
156 E3 **Sery** France
186 C3 **Sesa** Spain
95 G2 **Sesayap** r. Indon.
227 G1 **Sesekinika** Ont. Can.
Sesel country Indian Ocean see Seychelles
183 G4 **Seseña** Spain
212 B3 **Sesfontein** Namibia
114 C3 **Seshachalam Hills** India
209 E9 **Sesheke** Zambia
190 D3 **Sesia** r. Italy
184 A2 **Sesimbra** Port.
183 H2 **Sesma** Spain
209 D8 **Sessa** Angola
193 F3 **Sessa Aurunca** Italy
193 H4 **Sessa Cilento** Italy
187 G5 **Ses Salines** Spain
190 D3 **Sessera** r. Italy
169 F5 **Seßlach** Ger.
190 E4 **Sesta Godano** Italy
183 H1 **Sestao** Spain
191 H5 **Sestino** Italy
191 H2 **Sesto** Italy
191 H3 **Sesto al Reghena** Italy
190 D3 **Sesto Calende** Italy
193 G3 **Sesto Campano** Italy
191 G5 **Sesto Fiorentino** Italy
191 F4 **Sestola** Italy
190 E3 **Sesto San Giovanni** Italy
139 K3 **Sestra** r. Rus. Fed.
190 B4 **Sestriere** Italy
190 E4 **Sestri Levante** Italy
138 G1 **Sestroretsk** Rus. Fed.
188 E3 **Sestrunj** i. Croatia
192 B5 **Sestu** Sardegna Italy
138 D4 **Šešupė** r. Lith./Rus. Fed.
188 F3 **Sesvete** Croatia
186 D3 **Set** r. Spain
96 D4 **Set, Phou** mt. Laos
235 E2 **Setauket** NY U.S.A.
161 B5 **Sète** France
256 D6 **Sete Barras** Brazil
138 E4 **Šetekšna** r. Lith.
257 E3 **Sete Lagoas** Brazil
185 E4 **Setenil** Spain
140 L1 **Setermoen** Norway
142 B2 **Setesdal** val. Norway
102 □1 **Seteuchi** Japan
168 F2 **Seth** Ger.
Seti Georgia see **Mestia**
116 E3 **Seti** r. Nepal
117 F4 **Seti** r. Nepal
Setia Italy see **Sezze**
205 G1 **Sétif** Alg.
183 I4 **Setiles** Spain
203 G6 **Setit** r. Africa
104 D3 **Seto** Japan
103 F7 **Seto-naikai** sea Japan
191 G4 **Setta** r. Italy
204 D2 **Settat** Morocco
208 A5 **Setté Cama** Gabon
192 B5 **Sette Fratelli, Monte dei** mt. Sardegna Italy
190 D4 **Settepani, Monte** mt. Italy
190 C3 **Settimo Torinese** Italy
190 C3 **Settimo Vittone** Italy
149 G3 **Settle** North Yorkshire, England U.K.
84 D3 **Settlement Creek** r. Qld Austr.
216 □2c **Settlement of Edinburgh** Tristan da Cunha S. Atlantic Ocean
257 F2 **Setúbal** r. Brazil
184 B2 **Setúbal** Port.
184 B2 **Setúbal** admin. dist. Port.
184 A2 **Setúbal, Baía de** b. Port.
257 F2 **Setubinha** Brazil
Seu i. Vanuatu see **Hiu**
173 F2 **Seubersdorf in der Oberpfalz** Ger.
162 B3 **Seudre** r. France
162 B3 **Seugne** r. France
192 B5 **Seui** Sardegna Italy
157 F4 **Seuil-d'Argonne** France
223 M5 **Seul, Lac** l. Ont. Can.
169 F4 **Seulingen** Ger.
159 F2 **Seulles** r. France
192 B5 **Seulo** Sardegna Italy
160 D1 **Seurre** France
137 H1 **Sev** r. Rus. Fed.
186 F3 **Seva** Spain
129 D3 **Sevan** Armenia
Sevan, Lake Armenia see Sevana Lich
Sevan, Ozero l. Armenia see Sevana Lich
129 D3 **Sevana Lich** l. Armenia
137 G5 **Sevastopol'** Ukr.
149 I3 **Seven** r. England U.K.
Seven Islands Que. Can. see Sept-Îles
87 C4 **Seven Mile Creek** r. W.A. Austr.
215 H3 **Sevenoaks** S. Africa
151 H3 **Sevenoaks** Kent, England U.K.
150 D3 **Seven Sisters** Neath Port Talbot, Wales U.K.
85 G5 **Seventeen Seventy** Qld Austr.
Seventy Mile House B.C. Can. see **70 Mile House**
165 F3 **Sevenum** Neth.
234 B3 **Seven Valleys** PA U.S.A.
182 C3 **Sever** Port.
161 B4 **Sévérac-le-Château** France
182 B4 **Sever do Vouga** Port.
139 L4 **Severka** r. Rus. Fed.
83 G2 **Severn** r. N.S.W. Austr.
224 C2 **Severn** r. Ont. Can.
81 D5 **Severn** mt. South I. N.Z.
214 D2 **Severn** S. Africa
150 E3 **Severn** r. England/Wales U.K.
234 B3 **Severn** MD U.S.A.
232 E6 **Severn** NC U.S.A.
234 B4 **Severn** r. MD U.S.A.
234 B3 **Severna Park** MD U.S.A.
134 H2 **Severnaya Dvina** r. Rus. Fed.
134 L3 **Severnaya Mylva** r. Rus. Fed.
129 D2 **Severnaya Osetiya, Respublika** aut. rep. Rus. Fed.
130 H3 **Severnaya Sos'va** r. Rus. Fed.
131 L1 **Severnaya Zemlya** is Rus. Fed.
150 E3 **Severn Beach** South Gloucestershire, England U.K.
135 K5 **Severnoye** Rus. Fed.
137 I2 **Severnyy** Belgorodskaya Oblast' Rus. Fed.
139 K3 **Severnyy** Moskovskaya Oblast' Rus. Fed.
134 N2 **Severnyy** Respublika Komi Rus. Fed.
175 H1 **Severnyy, Mys** pt Rus. Fed.
131 S3 **Severnyy Anyuyskiy Khrebet** mts Rus. Fed.
120 D3 **Severnyy Chink Ustyurta** esc. Kazakh.
121 G1 **Severnyy Kazakhstan** admin. div. Kazakh.
134 K4 **Severnyy Kommunar** Rus. Fed.
Severnyy Suchan Rus. Fed. see **Uglekamensk**
134 L3 **Severnyy Ural** mts Rus. Fed.
99 I1 **Severobaykal'sk** Rus. Fed.
131 M4 **Severo-Baykalskoye Nagor'ye** mts Rus. Fed.
110 D1 **Severo-Chuyskiy Khrebet** mts Rus. Fed.
Severodonetsk Ukr. see Syeverodonets'k
134 G2 **Severodvinsk** Arkhangel'skaya Oblast' Rus. Fed.
Severo-Kazakhstanskaya Oblast' admin. div. Kazakh. see **Severnyy Kazakhstan**
131 Q4 **Severo-Kuril'sk** Kuril'skiye O-va Rus. Fed.
140 P1 **Severomorsk** Rus. Fed.
134 G3 **Severoonezhsk** Rus. Fed.
Severo-Osetinskaya A.S.S.R. aut. rep. Rus. Fed. see **Severnaya Osetiya, Respublika**
131 L2 **Severo-Sibirskaya Nizmennost'** lowland Rus. Fed.
134 L3 **Severoural'sk** Rus. Fed.
131 K3 **Severo-Yeniseyskiy** Rus. Fed.
139 L4 **Severo-Zadonsk** Rus. Fed.
Seversk Ukr. see **Sivers'k**
135 G7 **Severskaya** Rus. Fed.
135 H7 **Severskiy Donets** r. Rus. Fed.
Severskiy Donets r. Ukr. see Sivers'kyy Donets'
158 E2 **Sèves** r. France
155 I4 **Seveso** Italy
190 E3 **Seveso** r. Italy
179 F1 **Ševětín** Czech Rep.
241 K2 **Sevier** UT U.S.A.
241 K2 **Sevier** r. UT U.S.A.
231 D5 **Sevierville** TN U.S.A.
158 D3 **Sévignac** France
163 B5 **Sévignacq** France
156 E3 **Sévigny-Waleppe** France
250 C3 **Sevilla** Col.
184 E3 **Sevilla** Spain
184 E3 **Sevilla** prov. Andalucía Spain
183 F4 **Sevilla la Nueva** Spain
Seville Spain see **Sevilla**
183 F5 **Sevilleja de la Jara** Spain
197 G4 **Sevlievo** Bulg.
Sevlyush Ukr. see **Vynohradiv**
188 E2 **Sevnica** Slovenia
196 D4 **Sevojno** Srbija Yugo.
162 A1 **Sèvre Nantaise** r. France
162 A2 **Sèvre Niortaise** r. France
160 E3 **Sévrier** France
160 D2 **Sevron** r. France
137 H1 **Sevsk** Rus. Fed.
114 B2 **Sewand** r. India
116 C3 **Sewani** Haryana India
220 D3 **Seward** AK U.S.A.
226 C4 **Seward** IL U.S.A.
236 D3 **Seward** NE U.S.A.
232 D4 **Seward** PA U.S.A.
262 T2 **Seward Mountains** Antarctica
220 B3 **Seward Peninsula** AK U.S.A.
260 B4 **Sewell** Chile
234 C3 **Sewell** NJ U.S.A.
222 C4 **Sewell Inlet** B.C. Can.
172 B3 **Sexau** Ger.
Sexi Spain see **Almuñécar**
222 G4 **Sexsmith** Alta Can.
242 D3 **Sextín** r. Mex.
123 E3 **Seyah Band Koh** mts Afgh.
243 H5 **Seybaplaya** Mex.
217 □2 **Seychelles** country Indian Ocean
163 C4 **Seyches** France
171 D4 **Seyda** Ger.
199 G2 **Seydi** r. Turkey
123 E2 **Seydi** Turkm.
126 C3 **Seydişehir** Turkey
158 E2 **Seye** r. France
Seyhan Turkey see **Adana**
126 D3 **Seyhan** r. Turkey
199 G2 **Seyitgazi** Turkey
199 F2 **Seyitömer** Turkey
137 I2 **Seym** Rus. Fed.
137 H2 **Seym** r. Rus. Fed./Ukr.
131 Q3 **Seymchan** Rus. Fed.
199 F1 **Seymen** Turkey
83 F4 **Seymour** Vic. Austr.
215 F5 **Seymour** S. Africa
235 E1 **Seymour** CT U.S.A.
230 C4 **Seymour** IN U.S.A.
237 D5 **Seymour** TX U.S.A.
84 C5 **Seymour Range** mts N.T. Austr.
161 E4 **Seyne** France
161 C4 **Seynes** France
160 E3 **Seynod** France
Seypan i. N. Mariana Is see Saipan
160 D3 **Seyssel** France
163 D5 **Seysses** France
160 C3 **Seysseuel** France
161 D3 **Seyssins** France
197 H5 **Seytan** r. Turkey
188 D3 **Sežana** Slovenia
156 D4 **Sézanne** France
215 H4 **Sezela** S. Africa
139 J4 **Sezha** r. Rus. Fed.
176 D2 **Sezimovo Ústí** Czech Rep.
193 F3 **Sezze** Italy
197 G3 **Sfântu Gheorghe** Romania
197 I3 **Sfântu Gheorghe** Romania
205 H2 **Sfax** Tunisia
198 C1 **Sfendami** Greece
198 C1 **Sfikia, Limni** resr Greece
Sfîntu Gheorghe Romania see Sfântu Gheorghe
Sgiersch Pol. see **Zgierz**
146 B3 **Sgiogarstaigh** Western Isles, Scotland U.K.
146 C4 **Sgorr Ruadh** hill Scotland U.K.
164 D3 **'s-Gravendeel** Neth.
164 D2 **'s-Gravenhage** Neth.
165 C3 **'s-Gravenpolder** Neth.
165 E4 **'s-Gravenvoeren** Belgium
164 D3 **'s-Gravenzande** Neth.
193 F3 **Sgurgola** Italy
146 C4 **Sgurr a'Chaorachain** mt. Scotland U.K.
146 D4 **Sgurr a'Choire Ghlais** mt. Scotland U.K.
146 B4 **Sgurr Alasdair** hill Scotland U.K.
146 D4 **Sgurr a'Mhuilinn** hill Scotland U.K.
146 C5 **Sgurr Dhomhnuill** hill Scotland U.K.
146 C4 **Sgurr Fhuaran** mt. Scotland U.K.
146 C4 **Sgurr Mor** mt. Scotland U.K.
146 C4 **Sgurr na Ciche** mt. Scotland U.K.
107 G4 **Sha** r. China
107 F5 **Shaanxi** prov. China
Shaartuz Tajik. see **Shahrtuz**
Shaba admin. reg. Dem. Rep. Congo see **Katanga**
Shabani Zimbabwe see Zvishavane
Shabbaz Uzbek. see **Beruni**
210 E4 **Shabeellaha Dhexe** admin. reg. Somalia
210 D4 **Shabeellaha Hoose** admin. reg. Somalia
135 G7 **Shabel'sk** Rus. Fed.
122 A2 **Shabestar** Iran
197 I4 **Shabla** Bulg.
139 J5 **Shablykino** Rus. Fed.
208 E5 **Shabunda** Dem. Rep. Congo
124 D5 **Shabwah** Yemen
124 D5 **Shabwah** governorate Yemen
110 B4 **Shache** Xinjiang China
Shacheng Hebei China see **Huailai**
263 L1 **Shackleton Coast** Antarctica
262 V1 **Shackleton Range** mts Antarctica
123 F5 **Shadadkot** Pak.
108 D2 **Shadaogou** Hubei China
232 B5 **Shade** OH U.S.A.
122 B4 **Shādegān** Iran
234 C1 **Shades Glen** PA U.S.A.
130 H4 **Shadrinsk** Rus. Fed.
232 D5 **Shadwell** VA U.S.A.
238 B3 **Shady Grove** OR U.S.A.
234 B4 **Shady Side** MD U.S.A.
232 C6 **Shady Spring** WV U.S.A.
263 K2 **Shafer Peak** Antarctica
122 D2 **Shafi'abad** Iran
120 F4 **Shafirkan** Uzbek.
120 C1 **Shafranovo** Rus. Fed.
Shafrikan Uzbek. see Shafirkan
240 H4 **Shafter** CA U.S.A.

150 E3	**Shaftesbury** *Dorset, England* U.K.
81 C6	**Shag** *r. South I.* N.Z.
224 C2	**Shagamu** *r. Ont.* Can.
	Shagamu Nigeria see Sagamu
107 F4	**Shagedu** *Nei Mongol* China
220 C3	**Shageluk** *AK* U.S.A.
	Shaghan *Vostochnyy Kazakhstan* Kazakh. see Chagan
	Shaghray Üstirti *plat.* Kazakh. see Shagyray, Plato
121 G1	**Shaglyteniz, Ozero** *l.* Kazakh.
249 G7	**Shag Rocks** *is S.* Georgia
249 G7	**Shagyray, Plato** *plat.* Kazakh.
114 C2	**Shahabad** *Andhra Prad.* India
116 D3	**Shahabad** *Haryana* India
114 C2	**Shahabad** *Karnataka* India
116 D4	**Shahabad** *Rajasthan* India
116 E4	**Shahabad** *Uttar Prad.* India
	Shāhābād Iran see Showt
	Shāhābād Iran see Eslāmābād-e Gharb
116 C5	**Shahada** *Mahar.* India
94 C2	**Shah Alam** Malaysia
114 B3	**Shahapur** *Karnataka* India
114 B2	**Shahapur** *Mahar.* India
128 C3	**Shahbā'** Syria
122 D4	**Shahdād** Iran
123 G5	**Shahdadpur** Pak.
116 E5	**Shahdol** *Madh. Prad.* India
	Shahejie *Gansu* China see Jiuquan
	Shahepu *Gansu* China see Linze
	Shahezhen *Gansu* China see Linze
	Shahezhen *Gansu* China see Jiuquan
123 F3	**Shah Fuladi** *mt.* Afgh.
117 E4	**Shahganj** *Uttar Prad.* India
116 D4	**Shahgarh** *Madh. Prad.* India
116 B4	**Shahgarh** *Rajasthan* India
202 D1	**Shaḩḩāt** Libya
	Shāhīn Dezh Iran see Sa'indezh
116 D4	**Shahjahanpur** *Rajasthan* India
116 D4	**Shahjahanpur** *Uttar Prad.* India
122 D2	**Shāh Jehān, Kūh-e** *mts* Iran
122 D4	**Shāh Kūh** *mt.* Iran
127 I4	**Shahmīrzād** Iran
114 C2	**Shahpur** *Karnataka* India
116 C5	**Shahpur** *Madh. Prad.* India
116 D5	**Shahpur** *Madh. Prad.* India
116 D5	**Shahpur** *Madh. Prad.* India
	Shāhpūr Iran see Salmās
123 G4	**Shahpur** *Balochistan* Pak.
123 H3	**Shahpur** *Punjab* Pak.
123 G5	**Shahpur** *Sindh* Pak.
116 E5	**Shahpura** *Madh. Prad.* India
116 C4	**Shahpura** *Rajasthan* India
122 C4	**Shahr-e Bābak** Iran
122 B3	**Shahr-e Kord** Iran
	Shahrezā Iran see Qomishēh
	Shahrisabz Uzbek. see Shakhrisabz
123 J3	**Shahriston** Tajik.
122 B3	**Shahr Rey** Iran
123 G4	**Shahr Sultan** Pak.
123 G2	**Shahrtuz** Tajik.
	Shāhrūd Iran see Emāmrūd
122 B2	**Shāhrūd, Rūdkhāneh-ye** *r.* Iran
122 D4	**Shāh Savārān, Kūh-e** *mts* Iran
121 F4	**Shaidara, Step'** *plain* Kazakh.
123 F4	**Shaikh Husain** *mt.* Pak.
128 B5	**Sha'īra, Gebel** *mt.* Egypt
125 E2	**Shā'ir, Jabal** *hill* Saudi Arabia
116 D5	**Shajapur** *Madh. Prad.* India
104 B4	**Shakaga-dake** *mt.* Japan
215 H3	**Shakaskraal** S. Africa
215 H3	**Shakaville** S. Africa
212 D3	**Shakawe** Botswana
123 G2	**Shakh Khatlon** Tajik.
	Shakhbuz Azer. see Şahbuz
	Shakhagach Azer. see Şahağac
	Shakhbuz Azer. see Şahbuz
139 J3	**Shakhovskaya** Rus. Fed.
121 H4	**Shakhrikhan** Uzbek.
121 F5	**Shakhrisabz** Uzbek.
	Shahriston
137 J3	**Shakhtars'k** Ukr.
	Shakhtersk Ukr. see
	Shakhtars'k
	Shakhterskoye Ukr. see Pershotravens'k
121 H2	**Shakhtinsk** Kazakh.
	Shakhty *Respublika Buryatiya* Rus. Fed. see Gusinoozersk
135 H7	**Shakhty** *Rostovskaya Oblast'* Rus. Fed.
	Shakhtyorsk Ukr. see Shakhtars'k
	Shakhtyorskoye Ukr. see Pershotravens'k
134 I4	**Shakhun'ya** Rus. Fed.
	Shaki Nigeria see Saki
236 E2	**Shakopee** *MN* U.S.A.
102 J2	**Shakotan-hantō** *pen.* Japan
109 E3	**Shakou** *Guangdong* China
210 C3	**Shala Hāyk'** *l.* Eth.
134 H3	**Shalakusha** Rus. Fed.
122 B3	**Shālamzār** Iran
129 E3	**Shalbuzdag, Gora** *mt.* Rus. Fed.
121 I2	**Shalday** Kazakh.
151 F4	**Shalfleet** *Isle of Wight, England* U.K.
151 G3	**Shalford** *Surrey, England* U.K.
121 G3	**Shalginskiy** Kazakh.
	Shalgiya Kazakh. see Shalginskiy
129 D2	**Shali** Rus. Fed.
125 F4	**Shalim** Oman
	Shaliuhe *Qinghai* China see Gangca
120 D2	**Shalkar, Ozero** *salt l.* Kazakh.
	Shalqar Kazakh. see Chelkar
	Shalqar Köli *salt l.* Kazakh. see Shalkar, Ozero
	Shalqīnskīy
108 A2	**Shaluli Shan** *mts Sichuan* China
117 I3	**Shaluni** *mt. Arun. Prad.* India
134 L4	**Shalya** Rus. Fed.
137 H2	**Shalyhyne** Ukr.
119 H5	**Shām, Jabal** *mt.* Oman
211 B6	**Shama** *r.* Tanz.
128 A4	**Shamāl Sīnā'** *governorate* Egypt
134 L4	**Shamary** Rus. Fed.
124 C1	**Shāmat al Akbad** *des.* Saudi Arabia
223 M3	**Shamattawa** Man. Can.
224 C2	**Shamattawa** *r.* Ont. Can.
122 B3	**Shambār** Iran
210 C2	**Shambu** Eth.
116 C4	**Shamgarh** *Madh. Prad.* India
	Shamgong Bhutan see Zhemgang
129 D2	**Shamil'kala** *Respublika Dagestan* Rus. Fed.
129 E2	**Shamkhal** Rus. Fed.
	Shamkhor Azer. see Şämkir
234 B2	**Shamokin** *PA* U.S.A.
234 B2	**Shamokin Dam** *PA* U.S.A.
136 E3	**Shamrayivka** Ukr.
237 C5	**Shamrock** *TX* U.S.A.
213 F3	**Shamva** Zimbabwe
96 B2	**Shan** *state* Myanmar
	Shancheng *Fujian* China see Nanjing
	Shancheng *Shandong* China see Minhe
106 D4	**Shandan** *Gansu* China
107 H3	**Shandian** *r.* China
122 D2	**Shandīz** Iran
107 H4	**Shandong** *prov.* China
107 I3	**Shandong Bandao** *pen.* China
127 G4	**Shandrūkh** Iraq
234 C2	**Shanesville** *PA* U.S.A.
213 E3	**Shangani** *r.* Zimbabwe
109 E1	**Shangcai** *Henan* China
111 E6	**Shangchuan Dao** *i.* China
	Shangchuankou *Qinghai* China see Minhe

107 H3	**Shangdu** *Nei Mongol* China
100 D3	**Shangganling** Heilong. China
109 E2	**Shanggao** *Jiangxi* China
111 E3	**Shanghai** *Shanghai* China
111 E3	**Shanghai** *mun.* China
109 F3	**Shanghang** *Fujian* China
	Shanghe *Shandong* China
101 C4	**Shanghekou** *Liaoning* China
	Shangji *Henan* China see Xichuan
	Shangjie *Yunnan* China see Yangbi
108 D1	**Shangluo** *Shaanxi* China
108 I1	**Shangkuli** *Nei Mongol* China
108 D1	**Shangnan** *Shaanxi* China
	Shangpai *Anhui* China see Feixi
	Shangpai *Yunnan* China see Fugong
	Shangpaihe *Anhui* China see Feixi
107 G5	**Shangqiu** *Henan* China
107 G5	**Shangqiu** *Henan* China
109 E2	**Shangrao** *Jiangxi* China
109 E1	**Shangshui** *Henan* China
108 D4	**Shangsi** *Guangxi* China
	Shangtang *Zhejiang* China see Yongjia
109 E3	**Shangyou** *Jiangxi* China
109 G2	**Shangyu** *Zhejiang* China
100 C3	**Shangzhi** Heilong. China
107 H3	**Shanhaiguan** *Hebei* China
	Shanhe *Gansu* China see Zhengning
100 C3	**Shanhetun** Heilong. China
207 I4	**Shani** Nigeria
129 D2	**Shani, Mt'a** Georgia/Rus. Fed.
151 F4	**Shanklin** *Isle of Wight, England* U.K.
106 B3	**Shankou** *Xinjiang* China
80 E4	**Shannon** *North I.* N.Z.
147 C4	**Shannon** *airport* Rep. of Ireland
147 C4	**Shannon** *est.* Rep. of Ireland
215 F3	**Shannon** S. Africa
226 C4	**Shannon** *IL* U.S.A.
147 B4	**Shannon, Mouth of the** Rep. of Ireland
221 Q2	**Shannon Ø.** *i.* Greenland
96 B2	**Shan Plateau** Myanmar
106 A3	**Shanshan** *Xinjiang* China
106 A3	**Shanshanzhan** *Xinjiang* China
	Shansi *prov.* China see Shanxi
131 O4	**Shantarskiye Ostrova** *is* Rus. Fed.
	Shan Teng *hill* H.K. China see Victoria Peak
117 G5	**Shantipur** W. Bengal India
148 C3	**Shantonagh** Rep. of Ireland
109 F4	**Shantou** *Guangdong* China
	Shantung *prov.* China see Shandong
147 D4	**Shanvus** Rep. of Ireland
109 E4	**Shanwei** *Guangdong* China
107 G4	**Shanxi** *prov.* China
107 H5	**Shanxian** *Shandong* China
139 J4	**Shanya** *r.* Rus. Fed.
108 D1	**Shanyang** *Shaanxi* China
107 H3	**Shanyin** *Shanxi* China
109 D3	**Shaodong** *Hunan* China
109 E3	**Shaoguan** *Guangdong* China
109 F3	**Shaoshan** *Hunan* China
109 D3	**Shaowu** *Fujian* China
109 G2	**Shaoxing** *Zhejiang* China
109 D3	**Shaoyang** *Hunan* China
109 D3	**Shaoyang** *Hunan* China
149 G3	**Shap** *Cumbria, England* U.K.
	Shapa *Guangdong* China see Ebian
146 F2	**Shapinsay** *i.* Scotland U.K.
	Shapinsay Sound *sea chan.* Scotland U.K.
134 K2	**Shapkina** *r.* Rus. Fed.
121 J2	**Shapoval'ska** Ukr.
147 B5	**Shappa Mountains** *hills* Rep. of Ireland
	Sheikh, Jebel esh *mt.* Lebanon/Syria see Hermon, Mount
124 C3	**Shaqrā'** Saudi Arabia
124 A2	**Shar, Jabal** *mt.* Saudi Arabia
128 B4	**Sharāh, Jibāl ash** *mts* Jordan
107 I1	**Shiraidary** Rus. Fed.
134 K5	**Sharan** Rus. Fed.
134 I4	**Sharanga** Rus. Fed.
138 E5	**Sharashova** Belarus
147 D3	**Sharavogue** Rep. of Ireland
	Sharbaqty Kazakh. see Sharbakty
121 J1	**Sharchino** Rus. Fed.
121 F4	**Shardara** Kazakh.
	Shardara Bögeni *resr* Kazakh./Uzbek. see Chardarinskoye Vodokhranilishche
123 H3	**Shardi** Pak.
106 C1	**Sharga** *Govĭ-Altay* Mongolia
	Sharga *Övörhangay* Mongolia see Sharhorod
121 F5	**Shargun'** Uzbek.
136 E3	**Sharhorod** Ukr.
106 E2	**Sharhulsan** Mongolia
102 L2	**Shari** *r.* Cameroon/Chad see Chari
137 H2	**Sharivka** Ukr.
134 K4	**Sharkan** Rus. Fed.
138 F4	**Sharkawshchyna** Belarus
87 B5	**Shark Bay** W.A. Austr.
125 E5	**Sharkhāt** Yemen
85 F2	**Shark Reef** Coral Sea Is Terr. Austr.
235 D2	**Shark River Hills** *NJ* U.S.A.
120 C1	**Sharlyk** Rus. Fed.
203 G3	**Sharm el Sheikh** Egypt
129 D2	**Sharo-Argun** *r.* Rus. Fed.
220 C4	**Shelikof Strait** *AK* U.S.A.
129 C2	**Sharoiskaya** Rus. Fed.
232 C4	**Sharon** *PA* U.S.A.
128 B3	**Sharon, Plain of** Israel
236 C4	**Sharon Springs** *KS* U.S.A.
232 A5	**Sharonville** *OH* U.S.A.
87 D7	**Sharpe, Lake** *salt flat* W.A. Austr.
150 C2	**Sharpness** *Gloucestershire, England* U.K.
232 E5	**Sharpsburg** *MD* U.S.A.
232 C5	**Sharpsburg** *PA* U.S.A.
	Sharqat Iraq see Ash Sharqāt
128 B2	**Sharqi, Jabal ash** *mts* Lebanon/Syria
126 C5	**Sharqīya** *governorate* Egypt
123 H4	**Sharqpur** Pak.
234 B2	**Sharqtesville** *PA* U.S.A.
	Sharur Azer. see Şärur
134 I4	**Shar'ya** Rus. Fed.
106 C1	**Shar Us Gol** *r.* Mongolia
134 I4	**Shar'ya** Rus. Fed.
139 I2	**Shar'ya** Rus. Fed.
207 G5	**Shasha** Nigeria
213 E4	**Shashe** Botswana
213 E4	**Shashe** *r.* Botswana/Zimbabwe
210 C3	**Shashemenē** Eth.
	Shashi *Hubei* China see Jingsha
121 H3	**Shashubay** *Karagandinskaya Oblast'* Kazakh.
238 B3	**Shasta, Mount** *vol.* CA U.S.A.
238 B3	**Shasta Lake** *resr* CA U.S.A.
139 I4	**Shatalovo** Rus. Fed.
	Shatibi Belarus see Syetlahorsk
127 G2	**Shatoy** Rus. Fed.
135 H5	**Shatsk** Rus. Fed.
136 B2	**Shats'k** Ukr.
122 B4	**Shaṭṭ al 'Arab** *r.* Iran/Iraq
127 G4	**Shaṭṭ al Gharrāf** *r.* Iraq
203 G5	**Shau** Sudan
	Shending Shan *hill* Heilong. China
110 B3	**Shengel'di** Kazakh.
196 D5	**Shëngjin** Albania
109 E2	**Shengli Feng** *mt.* China/Kyrg. see Pobeda Peak
109 G2	**Shengsi** Zhejiang China
109 G2	**Shengsi Liedao** *is* China

129 D2	**Shavi Klde, Mt'a** Georgia/Rus. Fed.
196 D5	**Shënkoll** Albania
134 H3	**Shavkunk** Rus. Fed.
149 G4	**Shavington** *Cheshire, England* U.K.
86 C4	**Shaw** *r.* W.A. Austr.
149 G4	**Shaw** *Greater Manchester, England* U.K.
	Shawangunk Kill *r.* NY U.S.A.
110 D2	**Shawan** MD U.S.A.
234 B3	**Shawan** MD U.S.A.
235 D1	**Shawangunk Mountains** *hills* NY U.S.A.
226 C3	**Shawan** WI U.S.A.
232 A5	**Shawnee** KY U.S.A.
237 D5	**Shawnee** *OK* U.S.A.
238 F3	**Shawnee** WY U.S.A.
232 C6	**Shawsville** VA U.S.A.
109 F3	**Sha Xi** *r.* China
109 F3	**Shaxian** *Fujian* China
121 G4	**Shayan** Kazakh.
109 E2	**Shayang** *Hubei* China
131 R3	**Shayboveyem** *r.* Rus. Fed.
86 D4	**Shay Gap** W.A. Austr.
127 G4	**Shaykh Jūwī** Iraq
127 G4	**Shaykh Sa'd** Iraq
137 I4	**Shayanka** *r.* Ukr.
110 F4	**Shazaoyuan** *Gansu* China
124 C2	**Shaʼgā, Jabal** *mt.*
138 E5	**Shchara** *r.* Belarus
137 J3	**Shchastya** Ukr.
137 H5	**Shchebetovka** Ukr.
139 K4	**Shchekino** Rus. Fed.
134 H4	**Shchekyn** Ukr.
139 L4	**Shchelkovo** Rus. Fed.
134 K2	**Shchel'yayur** Rus. Fed.
	Shcherbakov Rus. Fed. see Rybinsk
121 I1	**Shcherbakty** Kazakh.
137 H4	**Shcherbani** Ukr.
	Shcherbinovka Ukr. see Dzerzhyns'k
134 G4	**Shchetinskoye** Rus. Fed.
135 G6	**Shchigry** Rus. Fed.
137 H5	**Shcholkine** Ukr.
137 F2	**Shchors** Ukr.
136 C4	**Shchors'k** Ukr.
147 B4	**Shchuchin** Belarus
	Shchuchin Belarus see Shchuchyn
121 G1	**Shchuchinsk** Kazakh.
138 F5	**Shchuch'ye** Rus. Fed.
138 E5	**Shchuchyn** Belarus
134 L2	**Shchugor** *r.* Rus. Fed.
136 B3	**Shchyrets'** Ukr.
121 K2	**Shebalino** Rus. Fed.
135 J5	**Shebekino** Rus. Fed.
123 F2	**Sheberghān** Afgh.
226 C4	**Sheboygan** WI U.S.A.
123 F3	**Shebsh** *r.* Rus. Fed.
207 H4	**Shebshi Mountains** Nigeria
100 G3	**Shebunino** Sakhalin Rus. Fed.
225 H4	**Shediac** N.B. Can.
222 D4	**Shedin Peak** B.C. Can.
129 D1	**Shedok** Rus. Fed.
147 D3	**Sheelin, Lough** *l.* Rep. of Ireland
215 H2	**Sheepmoor** S. Africa
241 J3	**Sheep Peak** NV U.S.A.
164 F3	**'s-Heerenberg** Neth.
151 I3	**Sheering** *Essex, England* U.K.
151 I4	**Sheerness** *Kent, England* U.K.
80 I5	**Sheet Harbour** N.S. Can.
149 H4	**Sheffer'am** Israel
	Sheffield *South I.* N.Z.
231 C5	**Sheffield** AL U.S.A.
226 C5	**Sheffield** IL U.S.A.
232 E4	**Sheffield** PA U.S.A.
237 C6	**Sheffield** TX U.S.A.
151 G2	**Shefford** *Bedfordshire, England* U.K.
116 D5	**Shegaon** *Mahar.* India
227 G3	**Shegouianbah** Ont. Can.
108 C2	**Shehong** *Sichuan* China
147 B5	**Shehy Mountains** *hills* Rep. of Ireland
215 H2	**Sheikh, Jebel esh** *mt.* Lebanon/Syria see Hermon, Mount
224 C3	**Sheikh Othman** Yemen see Ash Shaykh 'Uthman
137 K1	**Shekhman'** Rus. Fed.
123 H4	**Shekhupura** Pak.
	Sheki Azer. see Şäki
134 G4	**Sheksna** Rus. Fed.
	Sheksninskoye Vodokhranilishche *resr* Rus. Fed.
121 J1	**Shelabolikha** Rus. Fed.
232 B6	**Shelbiana** KY U.S.A.
226 D3	**Shelburn** MO U.S.A.
230 C4	**Shelburn** IN U.S.A.
225 H5	**Shelburne** N.S. Can.
231 C4	**Shelburne** Ont. Can.
80 E1	**Shelburne Bay** Qld Austr.
234 B3	**Shelburne Falls** MA U.S.A.
226 C2	**Shelby** MI U.S.A.
237 F5	**Shelby** MS U.S.A.
238 E2	**Shelby** MT U.S.A.
231 D5	**Shelby** NC U.S.A.
232 B4	**Shelby** OH U.S.A.
226 C5	**Shelbyville** IL U.S.A.
230 C4	**Shelbyville** IN U.S.A.
230 C4	**Shelbyville** KY U.S.A.
231 C5	**Shelbyville** TN U.S.A.
215 H5	**Sheldon** S. Africa
225 F3	**Sheldon** IA U.S.A.
226 C5	**Sheldon** IL U.S.A.
226 B3	**Sheldon** WI U.S.A.
233 G2	**Sheldon Springs** VT U.S.A.
225 H3	**Sheldrake** Que. Can.
	Shelek Kazakh. see Chilik
136 B4	**Shelekhove** Ukr.
235 I2	**Shelikhova, Zaliv** *g.* Rus. Fed.
102 L5	**Shell** WY U.S.A.
148 B3	**Shell Lake** *inlet* Scotland U.K.
223 J4	**Shellbrook** Sask. Can.
238 D3	**Shelley** ID U.S.A.
83 G3	**Shellharbour** N.S.W. Austr.
223 J4	**Shell Lake** Sask. Can.
226 B3	**Shell Lake** WI U.S.A.
87 E6	**Shell Lakes** *salt flat* W.A. Austr.
138 H2	**Shell Mountain** CA U.S.A.
225 F1	**Shelter Bay** Que. Can. see Port-Cartier
235 F1	**Shelter Island** NY U.S.A.
	Shelter Island Heights NY U.S.A.
235 C1	**Shelton** CT U.S.A.
238 B2	**Shelton** WA U.S.A.
134 F3	**Sheltozero** Rus. Fed.
	Shelyakino Rus. Fed. see Sovetskoye
207 H4	**Shemankar** *r.* Nigeria
134 J4	**Shemok'medi** Georgia
134 J4	**Shemordan** Rus. Fed.
134 J5	**Shemursha** Rus. Fed.
149 F2	**Shenandoah** *PA* U.S.A.
236 E3	**Shenandoah** IA U.S.A.
232 D5	**Shenandoah** PA U.S.A.
232 D5	**Shenandoah** VA U.S.A.
232 D5	**Shenandoah Mountains** VA/WV U.S.A.
207 G4	**Shendi** Sudan
200 B4	**Shendam** Nigeria
203 G5	**Shendi** Sudan
135 I5	**Shengel'di** Kazakh.
100 C2	**Shengjin** Albania
196 E2	**Shengjin** Hubei China
107 F3	**Shengli Feng** *mt.* China/Kyrg.

	Shengxian *Zhejiang* China see Shengzhou
107 G4	**Shijiazhuang** *Hebei* China
	Shijiusuo *Shandong* China see Rizhao
109 G2	**Shengzhou** *Zhejiang* China
196 D5	**Shënkoll** Albania
134 H3	**Shenkursk** Rus. Fed.
107 F4	**Shenmu** *Shaanxi* China
108 D2	**Shennongjia** Hubei China
109 E1	**Shenqiu** *Henan* China
109 E1	**Shenshu** Heilong. China
	Shensi *prov.* China see Shaanxi
151 F2	**Shenstone** Staffordshire, England U.K.
135 J5	**Shentala** Rus. Fed.
87 D6	**Shenton, Mount** *hill* W.A. Austr.
	Shenxian *Hebei* China see Shenzhou
	Shenzhen *Guangdong* China
107 G4	**Shenxian** *Shandong* China
109 E4	**Shenzhen** *Guangdong* China
107 G4	**Shenzhou** *Hebei* China
116 C4	**Sheoganj** *Rajasthan* India
116 D4	**Sheopur** *Madh. Prad.* India
262 P2	**Shepard Island** Antarctica
136 D2	**Shepetivka** Ukr.
	Shepetovka Ukr. see Shepetivka
232 A3	**Shepherd** MI U.S.A.
78 D5	**Shepherd Islands** Vanuatu
83 F4	**Shepparton** Vic. Austr.
151 G3	**Shepperton** Surrey, England U.K.
234 C2	**Sheppton** PA U.S.A.
151 F2	**Shepshed** Leicestershire, England U.K.
125 G3	**Sheptaky** Ukr.
150 E3	**Shepton Mallet** Somerset, England U.K.
137 H2	**Sheptukhovka** Rus. Fed.
109 E1	**Sheqi** Henan China
121 F5	**Sherabad** Uzbek.
215 E4	**Sherborne** S. Africa
150 E4	**Sherborne** Dorset, England U.K.
151 F3	**Sherborne St John** Hampshire, England U.K.
206 B5	**Sherbro Island** Sierra Leone
225 I4	**Sherbrooke** N.S. Can.
225 G4	**Sherbrooke** Que. Can.
149 I3	**Sherburn** Durham, England U.K.
233 F3	**Sherburne** NY U.S.A.
149 H4	**Sherburn in Elmet** North Yorkshire, England U.K.
147 E3	**Shercock** Rep. of Ireland
121 J2	**Sherdoyak** Kazakh.
151 G3	**Shere** Surrey, England U.K.
116 C4	**Shergarh** Rajasthan India
117 F4	**Shergarh** Bihar India
237 E5	**Sheridan** AR U.S.A.
238 F2	**Sheridan** WY U.S.A.
149 I3	**Sheriff Hutton** North Yorkshire, England U.K.
82 C3	**Sheringa** S.A. Austr.
151 I2	**Sheringham** Norfolk, England U.K.
130 I3	**Sherkaly** Rus. Fed.
147 B5	**Sherkin Island** Rep. of Ireland
86 C4	**Sherlock** *r.* W.A. Austr.
107 H1	**Sherlovaya Gora** Rus. Fed.
237 E5	**Sherman** TX U.S.A.
233 G1	**Sherman** NY U.S.A.
234 B3	**Sherman Mills** ME U.S.A.
233 □12	**Sherman** TX U.S.A.
241 J1	**Sherman Mountain** NV U.S.A.
	Sherobod Uzbek. see Sherabad
139 H4	**Sherovichi** Rus. Fed.
226 D2	**Shingleton** MI U.S.A.
121 J3	**Sherpur** Dhaka Bangl.
117 G4	**Sherpur** Rajshahi Bangl.
223 K4	**Sherridon** Man. Can.
150 E3	**Sherston** Wiltshire, England U.K.
114 C4	**Shertally** Kerala India
164 E3	**'s-Hertogenbosch** Neth.
232 A4	**Sherwood** OH U.S.A.
81 C5	**Sherwood Downs** South I. N.Z.
149 H4	**Sherwood Forest** reg. England U.K.
100 D2	**Sheryshevo** Rus. Fed.
227 F3	**Sheshegwaning** Ont. Can.
222 D3	**Sheslay** *r.* B.C. Can.
134 J4	**Sheslakovo** Kirovskaya Oblast' Rus. Fed.
137 K2	**Sheslakovo** Voronezhskaya Oblast' Rus. Fed.
139 I3	**Shestikhino** Rus. Fed.
137 G4	**Shestirnya** Ukr.
146 □H1	**Shetland** admin. div. Scotland U.K.
144 G1	**Shetland** *is* Scotland U.K.
120 C3	**Shetpe** Kazakh.
235 F1	**Shetucket** *r.* CT U.S.A.
137 □	**Shevchenko** Kazakh. see Aktau
137 F3	**Shevchenkivka** Ukr.
	Shevchenko Kazakh. see Aktau
137 G2	**Shevchenkove** Cherkas'ka Oblast' Ukr.
137 I3	**Shevchenkove** Kharkivs'ka Oblast' Ukr.
	Shevchenkovo Ukr. see Dolyns'ka
114 B2	**Shevgaon** Mahar. India
100 E1	**Shevli** *r.* Rus. Fed.
210 B3	**Shewa Gimira** Eth.
109 F2	**Shexian** Anhui China
107 G4	**Shexian** Hebei China
109 G1	**Sheyang** Jiangsu China
	Sheyanzhen Jiangsu China see Sheyang
236 D2	**Sheyenne** N.D U.S.A.
236 D2	**Sheyenne** *r.* N.D U.S.A.
125 E5	**Sheykh Sho'eyb** *i.* Iran
146 B4	**Shiant, Sound of** *str.* Scotland U.K.
146 B4	**Shiant Islands** Scotland U.K.
227 F4	**Shiawassee** *r.* MI U.S.A.
108 D1	**Shiquanhe** Xizang China see Gar
102 I5	**Shibata** Japan
100 C1	**Shibata** Japan
102 K1	**Shibetsu** Hokkaidō Japan
102 J3	**Shibetsu** Hokkaidō Japan
128 C6	**Shibīn al Kawm** Egypt
100 D3	**Shibing** Guizhou China
105 F2	**Shibukawa** Japan
83 B3	**Shieldhaig** N.S.W. Austr.
223 J4	**Shell Lakes** Kazakh.
125 F2	**Shibutsu-san** *mt.* Japan
104 D3	**Shichigahama** Japan
104 C3	**Shichiri-mihama** *mt.* Japan
105 E2	**Shichuan** *r.* China
104 E3	**Shida** Shandong China
108 H1	**Shidian** Yunnan China
107 H4	**Shidongsi** Gansu China see Gaolan
146 C5	**Shiel, Loch** *l.* Scotland U.K.
146 C4	**Shiel Bridge** Highland, Scotland U.K.
150 D3	**Shirenewton** Monmouthshire, Wales U.K.
108 D2	**Shichao-hantō** *pen.* Japan
123 F2	**Shirin** Uzbek.
135 I5	**Shifnal** Derbyshire, England U.K.
150 E2	**Shieldaig** Falkirk, U.K.
	Shieli Kazakh. see Chiili
124 A1	**Shifa, Jabal** *mts* Saudi Arabia
150 F1	**Shifnal** Shropshire, England U.K.
105 F2	**Shiono** Japan
104 B3	**Shiga** *pref.* Japan
104 D4	**Shenchi** Shanxi China
104 C4	**Shenchuan** Nigeria
203 G5	**Shigatse** Xizang China see Xigazê
207 G4	**Shiro** Nigeria
104 D4	**Shirten Hōloy** des. China
122 E2	**Shirvan** Iran
	Shirvanskaya Step' plain Azer.
207 G4	**Shirgjal** Nei Mongol China
100 C2	**Shisanzhan** Xinjiang China
100 C2	**Shishaldin Volcano** AK U.S.A.
110 D2	**Shisha Pangma** *mt.* Xizang China see Xixabangma Feng
196 D5	**Shijak** Albania

107 G4	**Shijiao** *Guangdong* China see Fogang
123 E4	**Shikar** *r.* Pak.
116 C4	**Shikar** Karnataka India
123 G5	**Shikarpur** Pak.
109 E3	**Shikengkong** *mt.* Guangdong China
120 A1	**Shikhany** Rus. Fed.
105 F3	**Shikine-jima** *i.* Japan
116 D4	**Shikohabad** Uttar Prad. India
103 F7	**Shikoku** *i.* Japan
241 K3	**Shivwits Plateau** AZ U.S.A.
96 D2	**Shiwan Dashan** *mts* China
241 A7	**Shiwa Ngandu** Zambia
109 C3	**Shixing** Guangdong China
100 D1	**Shiyan** Hubei China
108 D2	**Shizhu** Chongqing China
	Shiziu Chongqing China see Junan
109 E3	**Shizong** Yunnan China
106 B3	**Shizuishan** Ningxia China
106 E4	**Shizuoka** Japan
105 E4	**Shizuoka** *pref.* Japan
196 E4	**Shkodër** Albania
	Shkodrës, Liqeni i *l.* Albania/Yugo. see Scutari, Lake
117 F4	**Shkumbin** *r.* Albania
137 J4	**Shkurinskaya** Rus. Fed.
139 J3	**Shlina** *r.* Rus. Fed.
139 I3	**Shlino, Ozero** *l.* Rus. Fed.
139 H2	**Shlisel'burg** Rus. Fed.
139 I3	**Shlüisberg** Rus. Fed. see Shlisel'burg
100 C3	**Shmakovo** Rus. Fed.
83 G3	**Shoalhaven** *r. N.S.W.* Austr.
223 K5	**Shoal Lake** Man. Can.
223 K4	**Shoal Lake** Sask. Can.
230 C4	**Shoals** IN U.S.A.
85 G4	**Shoalwater Bay** Qld Austr.
103 F6	**Shōbara** Japan
151 H3	**Shoeburyness** Southend, England U.K.
104 D2	**Shō-gawa** *r.* Japan
234 D1	**Shohola** PA U.S.A.
102 J2	**Shokotsu-gawa** *r.* Japan
107 H3	**Shokpar** Kazakh. see Chokpar
139 K1	**Shola** *r.* Rus. Fed.
120 F2	**Sholapur** Mahar. India see Solapur
	Sholaqorgan Kazakh. see Shollakorgan
	Sholaqsay Kazakh. see Sholaksay
121 G4	**Shollakorgan** Kazakh.
86 B4	**Sholl Island** W.A. Austr.
110 A4	**Shoma** *r.* Rus. Fed.
103 F6	**Shōmyō-gawa** *r.* Japan
146 C5	**Shona, Eilean** *i.* Scotland U.K.
264 J9	**Shona Ridge** *sea feature* S. Atlantic Ocean
	Shonzha Kazakh. see Chundzha
139 L3	**Shopsha** Rus. Fed.
148 C3	**Shoptown** Northern Ireland U.K.
	Shopqar Kazakh. see Chokpar
114 C4	**Shoranur** Karnataka India
114 B2	**Shorapur** Karnataka India
120 D4	**Shor Barsa-Kel'mes** *salt marsh* Uzbek.
235 D2	**Shore Acres** NJ U.S.A.
151 H5	**Shoreham-by-Sea** West Sussex, England U.K.
	Shorghun Uzbek. see Shargun'
123 H4	**Shorkot** Pak.
121 G2	**Shortandy** Kazakh.
78 □6	**Shortland Island** Solomon Is
78 □6	**Shortland Islands** Solomon Is
232 E3	**Shortsville** PA U.S.A.
139 K3	**Shosha** *r.* Rus. Fed.
232 D6	**Shoshone** ID U.S.A.
238 D3	**Shoshone** *r.* WY U.S.A.
240 I2	**Shoshone** CA U.S.A.
241 I3	**Shoshone Mountains** NV U.S.A.
212 E4	**Shoshong** Botswana
238 E3	**Shoshoni** WY U.S.A.
137 G2	**Shostka** Ukr.
151 I3	**Shotley Gate** Suffolk, England U.K.
149 C5	**Shotton** Flintshire, Wales U.K.
146 E5	**Shotts** North Lanarkshire, Scotland U.K.
107 H4	**Shouguang** Shandong China
109 F1	**Shouxian** Anhui China
107 G4	**Shouyang** Shanxi China
109 D1	**Shouyang Shan** *mt.* China
241 L4	**Show Low** AZ U.S.A.
129 D4	**Showt** Iran
137 H3	**Shpola** Ukr.
137 F2	**Shpykiv** Ukr.
136 E2	**Shpyli** Ukr.
	Shqipërisë, Republika e country Europe see Albania
137 G2	**Shramkivka** Ukr.
237 E5	**Shreveport** LA U.S.A.
150 E2	**Shrewsbury** Shropshire, England U.K.
235 D2	**Shrewsbury** NJ U.S.A.
232 E5	**Shrewsbury** PA U.S.A.
151 F3	**Shrewton** Wiltshire, England U.K.
148 D3	**Shrigley** Northern Ireland U.K.
114 B2	**Shrigonda** Mahar. India
	Shri Lanka country Asia see Sri Lanka
116 D4	**Shri Mohangarh** Rajasthan India
114 C3	**Shrirampur** W. Bengal India
151 F3	**Shrivenham** Oxfordshire, England U.K.
150 E2	**Shropshire** admin. div. England U.K.
235 I2	**Shrub Oak** NY U.S.A.
	Shtefan-Vodă Moldova see Ştefan Vodă
196 E4	**Shtiqën** Albania
107 H5	**Shu** *r.* China
127 G5	**Shu'aiba** Iraq
137 G3	**Shuakhevi** Georgia
109 E3	**Shuangcheng** Fujian China
123 H3	**Shirin** Uzbek.
108 D3	**Shuangbai** Yunnan China
107 I3	**Shuangcheng** Fujian China
109 E2	**Shuanghe** Hubei China
100 C3	**Shuanghedagang** Heilong. China
	Shuanghuyu Shaanxi China see Zizhou
107 I3	**Shuangjiang** Guizhou China see Jiangkou
108 D4	**Shuangjiang** Hunan China see Tongdao
108 A4	**Shuangjiang** Yunnan China
107 H3	**Shuangliao** Jilin China
100 C3	**Shuangyang** Jilin China
100 C3	**Shuangyashan** Heilong. China

120 D2	**Shubarkuduk** Kazakh.
120 D2	**Shubarshi** Kazakh.
118 C3	**Shubrā el Kheima** Egypt
109 F2	**Shucheng** Anhui China
110 A4	**Shufu** Xinjiang China
117 H4	**Shuganu** Manipur India
139 J2	**Shugozero** Rus. Fed.
	Shuicheng Guizhou China see Lupanshui
	Shuiding Xinjiang China see Huocheng
	Shuidong Guangdong China see Dianbai
	Shuihu Anhui China see Changfeng
109 F3	**Shuiji** Fujian China
	Shuiji Shandong China see Laixi
108 C1	**Shuijing** Sichuan China
109 E4	**Shuikou** Guangdong China
109 D3	**Shuikou** Hunan China
109 E3	**Shuikoushan** Hunan China
109 E3	**Shuiluocheng** Gansu China see Zhuanglang
108 C1	**Shuituo He** *r.* Sichuan China
	Shuizhai Guangdong China see Wuhua
123 G4	**Shujaabad** Pak.
110 C3	**Shule** Jilin China
110 B4	**Shule** Xinjiang China
110 B4	**Shule He** *r.* China
106 C4	**Shule Nanshan** *mts* China
137 K1	**Shul'gino** Rus. Fed.
137 J3	**Shul'hynka** Ukr.
107 F3	**Shulinzhao** Nei Mongol China
	Shul'mak Tajik. see Novobod
	Shulu Hebei China see Xinji
139 H2	**Shum** Rus. Fed.
128 B4	**Shumagin Islands** AK U.S.A.
109 E4	**Shumakov** Rus. Fed.
137 I2	**Shumanay** Uzbek.
102 K1	**Shumarinai-ko** *l.* Japan
197 H4	**Shumen** Bulg.
134 I5	**Shumerlya** Rus. Fed.
130 H4	**Shumikha** Rus. Fed.
138 D4	**Shumilina** Belarus
136 D2	**Shums'k** Ukr.
139 I5	**Shumyachi** Rus. Fed.
121 H3	**Shunak, Gora** *mt.* Kazakh.
128 B4	**Shūnat Nimrin** Jordan
109 E4	**Shunde** Guangdong China
139 M3	**Shunga** Rus. Fed.
220 C3	**Shungnak** AK U.S.A.
234 B1	**Shunk** PA U.S.A.
108 C2	**Shunuodag, Gora** *mt.* Rus. Fed.
107 H3	**Shunyi** Beijing China
108 C2	**Shuolong** Guangxi China
	Shuoxian Shanxi China see Shuozhou
107 G4	**Shuozhou**
124 D4	**Shuqqat Najrān** depr. Saudi Arabia
122 C4	**Shūr** *r.* Iran
122 D3	**Shūr** *r.* Iran
122 E3	**Shūr** *r.* Iran
122 B3	**Shūr** *watercourse* Iran
122 E4	**Shūr Āb** Iran
122 B3	**Shūr Āb** Iran
122 E3	**Shūrāb** Iran
121 F5	**Shurab** Tajik. see Shŭrob
122 D4	**Shūr Gaz** Iran
134 J4	**Shurma** Rus. Fed.
121 G5	**Shŭrob** Tajik.
122 C4	**Shūrū** Iran
122 E3	**Shūrū** Iran
213 F3	**Shurugwi** Zimbabwe
121 F5	**Shurupuak** tourist site Iraq
122 E4	**Shusf** Iran
122 B3	**Shūsh** Iran
	Shusha Azer. see Şuşa
198 A1	**Shushicë** *r.* Albania
122 B3	**Shūshtar** Iran
222 F5	**Shuswap Lake** B.C. Can.
128 C4	**Shuwaysh, Tall ash** *hill* Jordan
139 M3	**Shuya** Ivanovskaya Oblast' Rus. Fed.
134 G3	**Shuya** Respublika Kareliya Rus. Fed.
107 H5	**Shuyang** Jiangsu China
	Shuyskoye Rus. Fed.
139 K4	**Shvartsevskiy** Rus. Fed.
96 A2	**Shwebo** Myanmar
96 B3	**Shwedaung** Myanmar
96 B3	**Shwegyin** Myanmar
96 A3	**Shweli** *r.* Myanmar
96 B2	**Shwedaung** *mt.* Myanmar
116 D3	**Shyena** Ukr.
	Shyghanaq Kazakh. see Chiganak
	Shyghys Qazaqstan Oblysy admin. div. Kazakh. see Vostochnyy Kazakhstan
	Shyghys-Konyrat Kazakh.
121 G4	**Shygys Konyrat** Kazakh.
110 A4	**Shymkent** Kazakh.
116 D2	**Shyok** Jammu and Kashmir
137 I3	**Shypuvate** Ukr.
137 H3	**Shyroke** Dnipropetrovs'ka Oblast' Ukr.
137 H3	**Shyroke** Zaporiz'ka Oblast' Ukr.
137 H3	**Shyrokolanivka** Ukr.
137 H3	**Shyryayeve** Ukr.
146 □	**Shetland** Western Isles, Scotland U.K.
161 E5	**Siagne** *r.* France
251 E4	**Siahan Range** *mts* Pak.
122 A2	**Siah Chashmeh** Iran
123 F3	**Siah Koh** *mts* Afgh.
94 C2	**Siak** *r.* Indon.
143 G4	**Siapa** *r.* Venez.
251 E4	**Siargao** *i.* Phil.
233 I4	**Siasconset** MA U.S.A.
92 B5	**Siasi** Phil.
198 B1	**Siatista** Greece
138 D4	**Siaton** Phil.
209 F3	**Siavonga** Zambia
	Siazan' Azer. see Siyäzän
125 G3	**Sib** Oman
246 C2	**Sibanicú** Cuba
246 C2	**Sibay** *i.* Phil.
197 H2	**Sibay** Rus. Fed.
	Sibati Xinjiang China see Xibet
215 I2	**Sibayi, Lake** S. Africa
188 B2	**Šibenik** Croatia
188 B2	**Sibbald, Cape** Antarctica
141 N3	**Sibbo** Fin.
71 G2	**Šibenik** reg. Croatia
135 I3	**Siberut** *i.* Indon.
94 B3	**Siberut, Selat** sea chan. Indon.
123 H4	**Sibi** Pak.
210 C4	**Sibiloi National Park** Kenya
	Sibir' reg. Rus. Fed. see Siberia
100 E3	**Sibirtsevo** Rus. Fed.
	Sibiryakova, Ostrov *i.* Rus. Fed.
209 B4	**Sibiti** Congo
197 G3	**Sibiu** Romania
151 H3	**Sible Hedingham** Essex, England U.K.
236 E3	**Sibley** IA U.S.A.
94 B2	**Sibolga** Sumatera Indon.
94 B2	**Siborongborong** Sumatera Indon.
215 H2	**Sibowe** *r.* Swaziland
117 H4	**Sibsagar** Assam India

Sibsey to Slavgorod
363

149 J4 Sibsey Lincolnshire, England U.K.
95 E2 Sibu Sarawak Malaysia
92 B5 Sibuco Phil.
92 B5 Sibuguey r. Phil.
92 B5 Sibuguey Bay Phil.
208 C3 Sibut C.A.R.
92 B3 Sibuyan i. Phil.
197 F2 Sic Romania
222 G5 Sicamous B.C. Can.
92 B2 Sicapoo mt. Luzon Phil.
252 D4 Sicasica Bol.
92 B4 Sicayac Phil.
Sicca Veneria Tunisia see Le Kef
Sicheng Guangxi China see Lingyun
97 B5 Sichon Thai.
108 B2 Sichuan prov. China
108 C2 Sichuan Pendi basin Sichuan China
194 D5 Sicilia admin. reg. Italy
194 D4 Sicilia i. Italy
194 B5 Sicilian Channel Italy/Tunisia
Sicily i. Italy see Sicilia
174 E4 Siciny Pol.
234 D3 Sicklerville NJ U.S.A.
169 F3 Sickte Ger.
252 C3 Sicuani Peru
177 K5 Şicula Romania
194 C5 Şiculiana Sicilia Italy
177 I3 Šíd Slovakia
196 D3 Šid Vojvodina, Srbija Yugo.
150 D4 Sidbury Devon, England U.K.
164 F1 Siddeburen Neth.
116 C5 Siddhapur Gujarat India
Siddharthanagar Nepal see Bhairawa
114 C2 Siddipet Andhra Prad. India
140 L3 Sidensjö Sweden
206 D4 Sidéradougou Burkina
195 F4 Siderno Italy
214 D5 Sidesaviwa S. Africa
150 D4 Sidford Devon, England U.K.
116 E4 Sidhauli Uttar Prad. India
116 E4 Sidhi Madh. Prad. India
Sidhirókastron Greece see Sidirokastro
Sidhpur Gujarat India see Siddhapur
205 F2 Sidi Aïssa Alg.
202 E2 Sidi Barrani Egypt
205 E2 Sidi Bel Abbès Alg.
204 C2 Sidi Bennour Morocco
Sidi Bou Sa'id Tunisia see Sidi Bouzid
205 H2 Sidi Bouzid Tunisia
204 C3 Sidi Ifni Morocco
204 D2 Sidi Kacem Morocco
94 B2 Sidikalang Sumatera Indon.
205 G2 Sidi Khaled Alg.
204 B5 Sidi Mhamed well Western Sahara
205 G2 Sidi Okba Alg.
198 C1 Sidirokastro Greece
204 C2 Sidi-Smaïl Morocco
146 E5 Sidlaw Hills Scotland U.K.
151 H4 Sidley East Sussex, England U.K.
262 P1 Sidley, Mount Antarctica
150 D4 Sidmouth Devon, England U.K.
85 E2 Sidmouth, Cape Qld Austr.
226 C2 Sidnaw MI U.S.A.
222 F5 Sidney B.C. Can.
236 E3 Sidney IA U.S.A.
238 F2 Sidney MT U.S.A.
236 C3 Sidney NE U.S.A.
233 F3 Sidney NY U.S.A.
232 A4 Sidney OH U.S.A.
231 D5 Sidney Lanier, Lake GA U.S.A.
214 E3 Sidney-on-Vaal S. Africa
206 D4 Sido Mali
95 F4 Sidoarjo Jawa Timur Indon.
163 E5 Sidobre reg. France
Sidon Lebanon see Saïda
134 H4 Sidorovo Rus. Fed.
175 L2 Sidra r. Pol.
255 B7 Sidrolândia Brazil
215 H2 Sidvokodvo Swaziland
215 G4 Sidwadweni S. Africa
121 G4 Sidzhak Uzbek.
174 F5 Sidzina Pol.
140 M1 Siebejokka r. Norway
164 F3 Siebengewald Neth.
171 E4 Siebenlehn Ger.
174 D4 Siecieborzyce Pol.
175 J4 Sieciechów Pol.
168 D3 Siedenburg Ger.
175 J5 Siedlanka Pol.
175 K3 Siedlce Pol.
174 E3 Siedlec Pol.
174 D4 Siedlisko Lubuskie Pol.
174 E3 Siedlisko Wielkopolskie Pol.
175 L4 Siedliszcze Lubelskie Pol.
175 L4 Siedliszcze Lubelskie Pol.
169 C5 Sieg r. Ger.
169 C5 Siegburg Ger.
169 D5 Siegen Ger.
173 F3 Siegenburg Ger.
179 H3 Siegendorf im Burgenland Austria
179 H3 Sieggraben Austria
179 H2 Sieghartskirchen Austria
173 G4 Siegsdorf Ger.
168 F2 Siek Ger.
171 G4 Siekierczyn Pol.
175 L4 Sielec Pol.
177 I3 Sielnica Slovakia
171 F4 Sielow Ger.
175 L3 Siemianówka Pol.
175 L3 Siemianówka, Jezioro l. Pol.
175 K3 Siemiatycze Pol.
175 K4 Siemień Pol.
174 G4 Siemkowice Pol.
97 C4 Siĕmréab Cambodia
Siem Reap Cambodia see Siĕmréab
174 D1 Siemyśl Pol.
Si'en Guangxi China see Huanjiang
191 G5 Siena Italy
191 G5 Siena prov. Toscana Italy
175 K5 Sieniawa Pol.
158 E2 Sienne r. France
175 J3 Siennica Pol.
175 J4 Sienno Pol.
175 H6 Siepraw Pol.
174 G4 Sieradz Pol.
174 G5 Sieraków Pol.
174 E3 Sieraków Pol.
175 H3 Sierakówek Pol.
174 F1 Sierakowice Pol.
157 G3 Sierck-les-Bains France
157 H5 Sierentz France
168 F1 Sierksdorf Ger.
179 H2 Sierndorf Austria
179 F2 Sierning Austria
174 F4 Sieroszewice Pol.
175 H3 Sierpc Pol.
175 H3 Sierpienica r. Pol.
239 F6 Sierra Blanca TX U.S.A.
261 G5 Sierra Chica Arg.
184 D1 Sierra de Fuentes Spain
Sierra del Gistral mts Spain see Xistral, Serra do
186 C2 Sierra de Luna Spain
185 F3 Sierra de Yeguas Spain
187 D4 Sierra Engarcerán Spain
259 D6 Sierra Grande Arg.
206 C4 Sierra Leone country Africa
264 H5 Sierra Leone Basin sea feature N. Atlantic Ocean
264 H5 Sierra Leone Rise sea feature N. Atlantic Ocean
240 G4 Sierra Madre Mountains CA U.S.A.
242 E3 Sierra Mojada Mex.
240 G2 Sierraville CA U.S.A.
241 L6 Sierra Vista AZ U.S.A.
190 C2 Sierre Switz.
185 H3 Sierro Spain
185 H3 Sierro r. Spain
171 C4 Siersleben Ger.
138 D4 Siesartis r. Lith.
138 E4 Siesartis r. Lith.
187 C5 Siete Aguas Spain
183 E3 Siete Iglesias de Trabancos Spain
170 D2 Sietow Ger.
197 G2 Şieu Romania
197 G2 Şieu r. Romania
191 G5 Sieve r. Italy
170 D3 Sieversdorf Ger.
168 E1 Sieverstedt Ger.
140 N3 Sievi Fin.
175 H5 Siewierz Pol.
108 C4 Sifang Ling mts China
206 D5 Sifié Côte d'Ivoire
198 D3 Sifnos i. Greece
205 E2 Sig Alg.
139 I3 Sig, Ozero l. Rus. Fed.
79 □1a Sigatoka Viti Levu Fiji
77 I3 Sigave Wallis and Futuna Is
161 A5 Sigean France
170 C2 Siggelkow Ger.
149 I4 Sigglesthorne East Riding of Yorkshire, England U.K.
221 M2 Sigguup Nunaa pen. Greenland
197 F2 Sighetu Marmaţiei Romania
197 G2 Sighişoara Romania
191 H5 Sigillo Italy
114 D5 Sigiriya Sri Lanka
129 F3 Sığırlı Azer.
94 A1 Sigli Sumatera Indon.
140 □C2 Siglufjörður Iceland
92 B4 Sigma Phil.
172 D3 Sigmaringen Ger.
172 D3 Sigmaringendorf Ger.
179 G2 Sigmundsherberg Austria
191 G5 Signa Italy
173 G2 Signalberg hill Ger.
165 F4 Signal de Botrange hill Belgium
161 D5 Signal de la Ste-Baume mt. France
161 B4 Signal de Mailhebiau mt. France
161 B4 Signal de Randon mt. France
160 C3 Signal de St-André hill France
162 D2 Signal de Sauvagnac hill France
162 D3 Signal du Pic hill France
159 F3 Signal du Viviers hill France
241 J5 Signal Peak AZ U.S.A.
190 C2 Signau Switz.
161 D5 Signes France
156 E3 Signy-l'Abbaye France
156 E3 Signy-le-Petit France
215 G4 Sigoga S. Africa
162 B3 Sigogne France
163 C4 Sigoulès France
236 E3 Sigourney IA U.S.A.
264 C4 Sigsbee Deep sea feature G. of Mexico
143 G2 Sigtuna Sweden
243 I6 Siguatepeque Hond.
182 B2 Sigüeiro Spain
183 H3 Sigüenza Spain
163 D6 Siguer r. France
186 B2 Sigües Spain
206 C4 Siguiri Guinea
138 E3 Sigulda Latvia
241 L2 Sigurd UT U.S.A.
97 C5 Sihanoukville Cambodia
116 E5 Sihawa Madh. Prad. India
177 I2 Sihelné Slovakia
109 F1 Sihong Jiangsu China
116 E5 Sihora Madh. Prad. India
116 D5 Sihora Mahar. India
Sihou Shandong China see Changdao
252 A2 Sihuas Peru
109 E4 Sihui Guangdong China
141 M3 Siikainen Fin.
140 N2 Siikajoki Fin.
140 N2 Siikajoki r. Fin.
140 N3 Siilinjärvi Fin.
127 F3 Siirt Turkey
78 □4a Siis i. Chuuk Micronesia
Sijjak Uzbek. see Sidzhak
165 C3 Sijsele Belgium
94 C3 Sijunjung Sumatera Indon.
116 B5 Sika Gujarat India
Sikaka Saudi Arabia see Sakākah
116 D4 Sikandra Rao Uttar Prad. India
222 F3 Sikanni Chief B.C. Can.
222 F3 Sikanni Chief r. B.C. Can.
116 C4 Sikar Rajasthan India
123 G3 Sikaram mt. Afgh.
206 D4 Sikasso Mali
206 D4 Sikasso admin. reg. Mali
198 C1 Sikea Kentriki Makedonia Greece
Sikéa Greece see Sykea
177 H4 Sikenica r. Slovakia
237 F4 Sikeston MO U.S.A.
177 H5 Sik-hegy hill Hungary
100 E4 Sikhote-Alin' mts Rus. Fed.
198 D3 Sikinos i. Greece
188 G3 Sikirevci Croatia
117 G4 Sikkim state India
177 H6 Siklós Hungary
175 H3 Sikórz Pol.
140 L2 Siksjö Sweden
117 F4 Sikta Bihar India
Sikuaishi Liaoning China see Changhai
182 C2 Sil r. Spain
92 C4 Silago Phil.
138 D4 Šilalė Lith.
191 F2 Silandro Italy
192 A4 Silanus Sardegna Italy
244 D3 Silao Mex.
237 F6 Silas AL U.S.A.
94 A1 Silawaih Agam vol. Indon.
92 B4 Silay Phil.
188 E3 Silba i. Croatia
168 E2 Silberberg hill Ger.
168 E1 Silberstedt Ger.
117 H4 Silchar Assam India
191 H3 Sile r. Italy
199 F1 Şile Turkey
151 F2 Sileby Leicestershire, England U.K.
149 F3 Silecroft Cumbria, England U.K.
138 F4 Silene Latvia
190 D2 Silenen Switz.
165 D4 Silenrieux Belgium
231 E5 Siler City NC U.S.A.
114 D2 Sileru r. India
185 H2 Siles Spain
174 E4 Silesia reg. Europe
Sileti Kazakh. see Seletinskoye
121 H1 Sileti r. Kazakh.
121 H1 Siletiteniz, Ozero salt l. Kazakh.
158 C3 Silfiac France
Silgadi Nepal see Silgarhi
116 E3 Silgarhi Nepal
117 H4 Silghat Assam India
217 □2a Silhouette i. Inner Islands Seychelles
205 H1 Siliana Tunisia
189 B8 Siliana admin. div. Tunisia
126 D3 Silifke Turkey
192 A4 Siligo Sardegna Italy
Siliguri W. Bengal India see Shiliguri
177 K5 Şilindia Romania
111 E6 Siling Co salt l. China
116 D4 Silipur Madh. Prad. India
192 A5 Siliqua Sardegna Italy
192 A4 Silis r. Sardegna Italy
78 □2 Silisili, Mount Samoa
Silistat Turkey see Bozkır
197 G3 Siliştea Romania
197 G3 Siliştea Nouă Romania
197 H3 Silistra Bulg.
Silistria Bulg. see Silistra
199 F1 Silivri Turkey
142 C2 Siljan Norway
141 K3 Siljan l. Sweden
143 F1 Siljansnäs Sweden
142 C3 Silkeborg Denmark
85 F3 Silkwood Qld Austr.
234 B1 Silkworth PA U.S.A.
178 C3 Sill r. Austria
187 C5 Silla Spain
138 F2 Sillamäe Estonia
190 F4 Sillano Italy
161 E5 Sillans-la-Cascade France
191 G4 Sillaro r. Italy
126 D3 Sille Turkey
182 B2 Silleda Spain
159 F3 Sillé-le-Guillaume France
156 E3 Sillery France
117 F5 Silli Bihar India
178 D4 Sillian Austria
116 C5 Sillod Mahar. India
149 F3 Silloth Cumbria, England U.K.
237 E4 Siloam Springs AR U.S.A.
215 H2 Silobela S. Africa
184 D3 Silos de Calañas Spain
134 M2 Silovayakha r. Rus. Fed.
186 F3 Sils Spain
190 E2 Sils Switz.
237 E6 Silsbee TX U.S.A.
149 H4 Silsden West Yorkshire, England U.K.
169 F4 Silstedt Ger.
138 F1 Siltakylä Fin.
123 E5 Sīlūp r. Iran
138 C4 Šilutė Lith.
215 H3 Silutshana S. Africa
257 F5 Silva Jardim Brazil
127 F3 Silvan Turkey
256 C2 Silvânia Brazil
190 E2 Silvaplana Switz.
182 B3 Silvares Braga Port.
182 C4 Silvares Castelo Branco Port.
116 C5 Silvassa Dadra India
184 B2 Silveiras Port.
143 G3 Silverån r. Sweden
247 E2 Silver Bank sea feature Turks and Caicos Is
246 E2 Silver Bank Passage Turks and Caicos Is
226 B2 Silver Bay MN U.S.A.
222 B2 Silver City Y.T. Can.
239 E5 Silver City NM U.S.A.
240 H2 Silver City NV U.S.A.
232 D3 Silver Creek NY U.S.A.
241 L4 Silver Creek r. AZ U.S.A.
80 E2 Silverdale North I. N.Z.
149 G3 Silverdale Lancashire, England U.K.
234 C2 Silverdale PA U.S.A.
151 H3 Silver End Essex, England U.K.
80 E3 Silverhope North I. N.Z.
226 C1 Silver Islet Ont. Can.
238 B3 Silver Lake OR U.S.A.
226 C3 Silver Lake WI U.S.A.
147 C4 Silvermine Mountains hills Rep. of Ireland
147 C4 Silvermines Rep. of Ireland
240 I3 Silver Peak Range mts NV U.S.A.
234 B4 Silver Spring MD U.S.A.
240 H2 Silver Springs NV U.S.A.
151 F2 Silverstone Northamptonshire, England U.K.
214 D3 Silver Streams S. Africa
222 E5 Silverthrone Mountain B.C. Can.
238 B1 Silvertip Mountain B.C. Can.
82 E2 Silverton N.S.W. Austr.
222 G5 Silverton B.C. Can.
150 D4 Silverton Devon, England U.K.
239 F4 Silverton CO U.S.A.
235 D2 Silverton NJ U.S.A.
237 C5 Silverton TX U.S.A.
227 F3 Silver Water Ont. Can.
251 G5 Silves Brazil
184 B3 Silves Port.
193 G2 Silvi Italy
250 B4 Silvia Col.
238 C3 Silvies r. OR U.S.A.
243 H5 Silvituc Mex.
190 F2 Silvretta Gruppe mts Switz.
178 B4 Silvrettahorn mt. Austria
129 F3 Şilyan Azer.
178 B3 Silz Austria
134 L5 Sim Rus. Fed.
134 L5 Sim r. Rus. Fed.
217 □3 Sima Comoros
139 L3 Sima Rus. Fed.
192 A5 Simala Sardegna Italy
183 F3 Simancas Spain
177 K5 Şimand Romania
160 C2 Simandre France
136 E2 Simanichy Belarus
198 C1 Simantra Greece
108 B4 Simao Yunnan China
254 F4 Simão Dias Brazil
127 G4 Şīmareh, Rūdkhāneh-ye r. Iran
117 F4 Simaria Bihar India
116 E4 Simaria Madh. Prad. India
187 C5 Simat de la Valdigna Spain
199 F2 Simav Turkey
199 F2 Simav Dağları mts Turkey
192 A5 Simaxis Sardegna Italy
173 G3 Simbach Ger.
173 H3 Simbach am Inn Ger.
195 F4 Simbario Italy
Simbirsk Rus. Fed. see Ul'yanovsk
78 □6 Simbo i. New Georgia Is Solomon Is
193 F3 Simbruini, Monti mts Italy
224 D5 Simcoe Ont. Can.
224 E4 Simcoe, Lake Ont. Can.
117 F5 Simdega Bihar India
141 L3 Simeå Sweden
203 H6 Simēn Mountains Eth.
197 G4 Simeonovgrad Bulg.
195 F4 Simeri r. Italy
197 F3 Simeria Romania
195 F4 Simeri-Crichi Italy
194 E5 Simeto r. Sicilia Italy
94 B2 Simeuluë i. Indon.
137 H5 Simferopol' Ukr.
Sími i. Greece see Symi
177 L4 Şimian Romania
161 D5 Simiane-la-Rotonde France
178 B4 Similaun mt. Austria/Italy
177 J2 Siminy mt. Slovakia
197 F5 Simitli Bulg.
240 H4 Simi Valley CA U.S.A.
Simla Hima. Prad. India see Shimla
239 F4 Simla CO U.S.A.
142 E3 Simlångsdalen Sweden
197 F2 Şimleu Silvaniei Romania
190 C2 Simme r. Switz.
173 F2 Simmelsdorf Ger.
169 B5 Simmerath Ger.
172 B2 Simmern (Hunsrück) Ger.
237 F6 Simmesport LA U.S.A.
246 D2 Simm's Long I. Bahamas
238 E2 Simms MT U.S.A.
138 D4 Simnas Lith.
140 N2 Simo Fin.
222 G4 Simonette r. Alta Can.
223 K4 Simonhouse Man. Can.
177 K3 Šimonka mt. Slovakia
232 C4 Simons OH U.S.A.
150 D3 Simonsbath Somerset, England U.K.
168 D1 Simonsberg Ger.
214 B6 Simon's Town S. Africa
164 F1 Simonszand i. Neth.
177 H5 Simontornya Hungary
222 E5 Simoom Sound B.C. Can.
Simoon Sound B.C. Can. see Simoom Sound
163 C5 Simorre France
94 D3 Simpang Sumatera Indon.
165 E4 Simpelveld Neth.
254 E3 Simplício Mendes Brazil
190 D2 Simplon Switz.
190 D2 Simplon Pass Switz.
223 J5 Simpson Sask. Can.
238 E1 Simpson MT U.S.A.
234 C1 Simpson PA U.S.A.
84 D5 Simpson Desert N.T. Austr.
87 E5 Simpson Hill hill W.A. Austr.
240 I2 Simpson Park Mountains NV U.S.A.
234 B3 Simpsonville MD U.S.A.
231 D5 Simpsonville SC U.S.A.
143 F4 Simrishamn Sweden
131 Q5 Simushir, Ostrov i. Kuril'skiye O-va Rus. Fed.
114 B2 Sina r. India
Sīnā', Shibh Jazīrat pen. Egypt see Sinai
94 B2 Sinabang Indon.
179 G3 Sinabelkirchen Austria
94 B2 Sinabung vol. Indon.
203 G2 Sinai pen. Egypt
156 E3 Sinai, Mont hill France
197 G3 Sinaia Romania
Sinai al Janûbîya governorate Egypt see Janūb Sīnā'
Sinai ash Shamâlîya governorate Egypt see Shamāl Sīnā'
97 B4 Si Nakarin Reservoir Thai.
244 A2 Sinaloa state Mex.
191 G5 Sinalunga Italy
Sinancha Rus. Fed. see Cheremshany
101 C5 Sinanju N. Korea
198 A2 Sinarades Ionioi Nisoi Greece
187 B5 Sinarcas Spain
209 E9 Sinazongwe Zambia
96 A3 Sinbaungwe Myanmar
96 A2 Sinbyugyun Myanmar
126 E3 Sincan Turkey
199 G2 Sincanlı Turkey
250 C2 Sincé Col.
250 C2 Sincelejo Col.
156 D3 Sinceny France
Sinchu Taiwan see T'aoyüan
222 F4 Sinclair Mills B.C. Can.
146 E3 Sinclair's Bay Scotland U.K.
254 E5 Sincora, Serra do hills Brazil
116 D4 Sind r. India
Sind prov. Pak. see Sindh
100 F2 Sinda Rus. Fed.
142 D3 Sindal Denmark
92 B4 Sindañgan Phil.
94 D4 Sindangbarang Jawa Barat Indon.
208 A5 Sindara Gabon
116 B4 Sindari Rajasthan India
172 C3 Sindelfingen Ger.
114 C2 Sindgi Karnataka India
123 G5 Sindh prov. Pak.
114 C3 Sindhnur Karnataka India
Síndhos Greece see Sindos
117 F4 Sindhuli Garhi Nepal
Sindhulimadi Nepal see Sindhuli Garhi
138 E2 Sindi Estonia
116 D5 Sindi Mahar. India
192 A4 Sindia Sardegna Italy
199 F2 Sındırgı Turkey
114 C2 Sindkhed Mahar. India
116 C5 Sindkheda Mahar. India
Sîndominic Romania see Sândominic
134 J3 Sindor Rus. Fed.
198 C1 Sindos Greece
206 D4 Sindou Burkina
114 C2 Sindphana r. India
117 F5 Sindri Bihar India
123 G4 Sind Sagar Doab lowland Pak.
134 J4 Sinegor'ye Rus. Fed.
199 E1 Sinekçi Turkey
193 G2 Sinello r. Italy
Sinel'nikovo Ukr. see Synel'nykove
207 F4 Sinendé Benin
184 B3 Sines Port.
184 B3 Sines, Cabo de c. Port.
187 G5 Sineu Spain
139 J5 Sinezerki Rus. Fed.
206 D5 Sinfra Côte d'Ivoire
203 G6 Singa Sudan
116 E3 Singahi Uttar Prad. India
217 □3a Singani Njazidja Comoros
94 D2 Singapore country Asia
94 □ Singapore Sing.
94 □ Singapore, Strait of Indon./Sing.
Singapura country Asia see Singapore
Singapura Sing. see Singapore
95 F5 Singaraja Bali Indon.
114 D2 Singareni Andhra Prad. India
Singatoka Viti Levu Fiji see Sigatoka
Singave Wallis and Futuna Is see Sigave
97 C4 Sing Buri Thai.
172 C4 Singen (Hohentwiel) Ger.
Sîngeorgiu de Pădure Romania see Sângeorgiu de Pădure
Sîngeorz-Băi Romania see Sângeorz-Băi
136 E4 Sîngera Moldova
136 E4 Sîngerei Moldova
110 E3 Singgimtay Xinjiang China
227 G3 Singhampton Ont. Can.
169 C5 Singhofen Ger.
211 B6 Singida Tanz.
211 B6 Singida admin. reg. Tanz.
Singidunum Srbija Yugo. see Beograd
Singim Xinjiang China see Singgimtay
93 B4 Singkang Sulawesi Selatan Indon.
95 E2 Singkawang Kalimantan Barat Indon.
94 D3 Singkep i. Indon.
94 B2 Singkil Sumatera Indon.
83 G3 Singleton N.S.W. Austr.
84 C4 Singleton N.T. Austr.
84 B4 Singleton, Mount hill N.T. Austr.
87 C6 Singleton, Mount hill W.A. Austr.
116 C4 Singoli Madh. Prad. India
Singora Thai. see Songkhla
Sin'gosan N. Korea see Kosan
117 G4 Singra Assam India
96 A2 Singu Myanmar
245 E4 Singuilucan Mex.
197 G3 Singureni Romania
101 C5 Sin'gye N. Korea
124 D4 Sinḩ, Jabal hill Saudi Arabia
Sinhala country Asia see Sri Lanka
101 C4 Sinhŭng N. Korea
192 A5 Sini Sardegna Italy
178 C4 Sinigo r. Italy
92 B3 Siniloan Phil.
Sining Qinghai China see Xining
93 A3 Sinio, Gunung mt. Indon.
192 B4 Siniscola Sardegna Italy
197 G5 Sini Vrŭkh mt. Bulg.
137 J2 Siniye Lipyagi Rus. Fed.
120 E2 Siniy-Shikhan Rus. Fed.
188 F4 Sinj Croatia
93 B4 Sinjai Sulawesi Selatan Indon.
127 F3 Sinjār Iraq
127 F3 Sinjār, Jabal mt. Iraq
203 H5 Sinkat Sudan
Sinkiang aut. reg. China see Xinjiang Uygur Zizhiqu
Sinkiang Uighur Autonomous Region aut. reg. China see Xinjiang Uygur Zizhiqu
147 C3 Sinking r. Rep. of Ireland
232 B5 Sinking Spring OH U.S.A.
136 D1 Sinkyevichy Belarus
183 F3 Sinlabajos Spain
156 D2 Sin-le-Noble France
Sînmartin Romania see Sânmartin
169 D5 Sinn Ger.
169 E5 Sinn r. Ger.
192 B5 Sinnai Sardegna Italy
251 H3 Sinnamary Fr. Guiana
114 B2 Sinnar Mahar. India
128 A5 Sinn Bishr, Gebel hill Egypt
137 H2 Sinne Ukr.
Sinneh Iran see Sanandaj
232 D4 Sinnemahoning PA U.S.A.
193 I4 Sinni r. Italy
Sînnicolau Mare Romania see Sânnicolau Mare
Sinoia Zimbabwe see Chinhoyi
197 I3 Sinoie, Lacul lag. Romania
253 G2 Sinop Brazil
126 D2 Sinop Turkey
Sinope Turkey see Sinop
195 E4 Sinopoli Italy
101 C4 Sinp'a N. Korea
Sînpetru Mare Romania see Sânpetru Mare
101 D4 Sinp'o N. Korea
101 C5 Sinp'yŏng N. Korea
172 C4 Sins Switz.
101 C5 Sinsang N. Korea
172 C2 Sinsheim Ger.
95 E2 Sintang Kalimantan Barat Indon.
164 D3 Sint Annaland Neth.
164 E1 Sint Annaparochie Neth.
164 E3 Sint Anthonis Neth.
247 □10 Sint Christoffelberg hill Curaçao Neth. Antilles
177 K5 Sintea Mare Romania
177 L4 Şinteu Romania
165 D3 Sint Gillis-Waas Belgium
165 E3 Sint Huibrechts-Lille Belgium
164 E1 Sint Jacobiparochie Neth.
165 D3 Sint Jansteen Neth.
165 D3 Sint Katelijne-Waver Belgium
165 C3 Sint Laureins Belgium
165 D3 Sint Lenaarts Belgium
247 G3 Sint Maarten i. Neth. Antilles
164 D3 Sint Maartensdijk Neth.
165 C3 Sint Margriete Belgium
165 C4 Sint Maria-Lierde Belgium
165 C3 Sint Martens-Latem Belgium
247 □9 Sint Nicolaas Aruba
164 E2 Sint Nicolaasga Neth.
165 D3 Sint Niklaas Belgium
237 D6 Sinton TX U.S.A.
164 D2 Sint Pancras Neth.
164 D3 Sint Philipsland Neth.
165 D4 Sint Pieters-Leeuw Belgium
184 A2 Sintra Port.
191 G4 Sintria r. Italy
139 K3 Sintsovo Rus. Fed.
165 E4 Sint Truiden Belgium
165 F4 Sint Vith Belgium
250 C2 Sinú r. Col.
101 C4 Sinŭiju N. Korea
138 G3 Sinyaya r. Rus. Fed.
172 C3 Sinzheim Ger.
169 C5 Sinzig Ger.
173 G3 Sinzing Ger.
177 H5 Sió r. Romania
186 D3 Sió r. Spain
177 H5 Sióagárd Hungary
92 B5 Siocon Phil.
177 H5 Siófok Hungary
209 D9 Sioma Zambia
190 C2 Sion Switz.
146 C3 Sionascaig, Loch l. Scotland U.K.
147 D2 Sion Mills Northern Ireland U.K.
160 B2 Sioule r. France
236 D3 Sioux Center IA U.S.A.
236 D3 Sioux City IA U.S.A.
236 D3 Sioux Falls SD U.S.A.
224 B3 Sioux Lookout Ont. Can.
243 H6 Sipacate Guat.
92 B4 Sipalay Phil.
247 □7 Siparia Trin. and Tob.
Siphaqeni S. Africa see Flagstaff
100 C4 Siping Jilin China
223 L4 Sipiwesk Man. Can.
262 P2 Siple, Mount Antarctica
262 N1 Siple Coast Antarctica
262 P2 Siple Island Antarctica
Sipolilo Zimbabwe see Guruve
197 H2 Şipote Romania
188 F3 Šipovo Bos.-Herz.
172 D4 Sipplingen Ger.
237 F5 Sipsey r. AL U.S.A.
125 F5 Siqirah Suquṭrā Yemen
256 C5 Siqueira Campos Brazil
242 □I6 Siquia r. Nic.
92 B4 Siquijor Phil.
92 B4 Siquijor i. Phil.
123 G6 Sir r. Pak.
114 C3 Sira Karnataka India
142 B2 Sira r. Norway
161 E4 Sirac mt. France
97 C4 Si Racha Thai.
195 E5 Siracusa Sicilia Italy
195 E5 Siracusa prov. Sicilia Italy
117 G4 Sirajganj Bangl.
222 F4 Sir Alexander, Mount B.C. Can.
162 E4 Siran France
126 E2 Şiran Turkey
116 E4 Sirathu Uttar Prad. India
207 F3 Sirba r. Burkina/Niger
Sircilla Andhra Prad. India see Sirsilla
Sirdaryo r. Asia see Syrdar'ya
Sirdaryo Uzbek. see Syrdar'ya
Sirdaryo Wiloyati admin. div. Uzbek. see Syrdar'inskaya Oblast'
Sirdingka Xizang China see Lhari
210 C2 Sīrē Oromia Eth.
210 C2 Sīrē Oromia Eth.
84 D2 Sir Edward Pellew Group is N.T. Austr.
226 A3 Siren WI U.S.A.
193 F2 Sirente, Monte mt. Italy
197 H2 Siret Romania
197 I3 Siret r. Romania
Siret r. Ukr. see Seret
86 E2 Sir Graham Moore Islands W.A. Austr.
128 C4 Sirḩān, Wādī as watercourse Jordan/Saudi Arabia
116 D3 Sirhind Punjab India
197 E2 Şiria Romania
122 D5 Sīrīk Iran
142 C2 Sirikjerka hill Norway
Sirína i. Greece see Syrna
123 G4 Siritoi r. Pak.
222 E2 Sir James MacBrien, Mount N.W.T. Can.
122 C4 Sīrjān Kermān Iran
122 C4 Sīrjān salt flat Iran
116 D3 Sirmaur Hima. Prad. India
191 F3 Sirmione Italy
Sirmium Vojvodina, Srbija Yugo. see Sremska Mitrovica
116 E4 Sirmour Madh. Prad. India
Sirmur Hima. Prad. India see Sirmaur
190 E1 Sirnach Switz.
127 F3 Şırnak Turkey
179 F4 Sirnitz Austria
160 E2 Sirod France
116 C4 Sirohi Rajasthan India
177 J4 Sirok Hungary
177 J2 Široké Slovakia
191 I5 Sirolo Italy
114 D2 Sironcha Mahar. India
116 D4 Sironj Madh. Prad. India
191 G2 Siròr Italy
Síros i. Greece see Syros
204 D3 Siroua, Jbel mt. Morocco
114 C2 Sirpur Andhra Prad. India
240 H4 Sirretta Peak CA U.S.A.
122 C5 Sīrrī, Jazīreh-ye i. Iran
116 C3 Sirsa Haryana India
222 G5 Sir Sandford, Mount B.C. Can.
114 B3 Sirsi Karnataka India
116 D3 Sirsi Uttar Prad. India
114 C2 Sirsilla Andhra Prad. India
Sirte Libya see Surt
Sirte, Gulf of Libya see Surt, Khalīj
82 B1 Sir Thomas, Mount hill S.A. Austr.
185 E2 Siruela Spain
114 C3 Siruguppa Karnataka India
239 E6 Sirupa r. Mex.
114 B2 Sirur Karnataka India
114 B2 Sirur Mahar. India
127 F3 Şirvan Turkey
129 E3 Şirvan Düzü lowland Azer.
129 F3 Şirvanovka Azer.
114 C3 Sirvel Andhra Prad. India
175 K1 Širvinta r. Lith.
138 E4 Širvintos Lith.
127 G4 Sīrwān r. Iraq
222 G4 Sir Wilfrid Laurier, Mount B.C. Can.
85 E2 Sir William Thompson Range hills Qld Austr.
122 D3 Siryan Iran
Sis Turkey see Kozan
188 F3 Sisak Croatia
96 D4 Sisaket Thai.
243 H4 Sisal Mex.
185 H1 Sisante Spain
Siscia Croatia see Sisak
192 B2 Sisco Corse France
214 D2 Sishen S. Africa
129 E4 Sisian Armenia
206 E4 Sisili r. Burkina/Ghana
221 M3 Sisimiut Greenland
97 C4 Sisŏphŏn Cambodia
240 G4 Sisquoc r. CA U.S.A.
190 C1 Sissach Switz.
236 D2 Sisseton SD U.S.A.
206 E4 Sissili r. Burkina
156 D3 Sissonne France
232 C5 Sissonville WV U.S.A.
177 K5 Şiştarovăţ Romania
226 D3 Sister Bay WI U.S.A.
161 D4 Sisteron France
238 B2 Sisters OR U.S.A.
232 C5 Sistersville WV U.S.A.
193 F3 Sisto r. Italy
178 C3 Sistrans Austria
139 K2 Sit' r. Rus. Fed.
117 F4 Sitamarhi Bihar India
116 C5 Sitamau Madh. Prad. India
175 L5 Sitaniec Pol.
116 E4 Sitapur Uttar Prad. India
176 F2 Šitbořice Czech Rep.
199 E4 Siteia Kriti Greece
215 H2 Siteki Swaziland
186 E3 Sitges Spain
198 C1 Sithonia pen. Greece
Sitía Kriti Greece see Siteia
106 B3 Sitian Xinjiang China
108 C3 Siting Guizhou China
254 D5 Sítio da Abadia Brazil
254 E5 Sítio do Mato Brazil
111 D7 Sitka Bihar India
220 E4 Sitka AK U.S.A.
175 I5 Sitkówka-Nowiny Pol.
196 E4 Sitnica r. Yugo.
177 H3 Sitno mt. Slovakia
138 G3 Sitnya r. Rus. Fed.
202 E2 Sitra oasis Egypt
96 B3 Sittang r. Myanmar
165 E4 Sittard Neth.
Sittaung r. Myanmar see Sittang
168 E2 Sittensen Ger.
172 D4 Sitter r. Ger.
179 F4 Sittersdorf Austria
215 F5 Sittingbourne S. Africa
151 H3 Sittingbourne Kent, England U.K.
Sittoung r. Myanmar see Sittang
96 A2 Sittwe Myanmar
95 F4 Situbondo Jawa Timur Indon.
171 C5 Sitzendorf Ger.
179 G2 Sitzendorf an der Schmida Austria
171 D4 Sitzenroda Ger.
242 □I6 Siuna Nic.
141 N3 Siuntio Fin.
192 B5 Siurgus Donigala Sardegna Italy
117 F5 Siuri W. Bengal India
134 K4 Siva Rus. Fed.
177 I6 Sivac Vojvodina, Srbija Yugo.
114 C4 Sivaganga Tamil Nadu India
114 C4 Sivakasi Tamil Nadu India
100 C1 Sivaki Rus. Fed.
122 C4 Sivand Iran
126 E3 Sivas Turkey
199 F2 Sivaslı Turkey
206 B3 Sivé Maur.
126 E3 Siverek Turkey
137 J3 Sivers'k Ukr.
139 H2 Siverskiy Rus. Fed.
Sivers'kyy Donets' r. Rus. Fed. see Severskiy Donets
137 J3 Sivers'kyy Donets' r. Ukr.
175 M6 Sivka-Voynylivs'ka Ukr.
134 M2 Sivomaskinskiy Rus. Fed.
126 E3 Sivrice Turkey
126 C3 Sivrihisar Turkey
165 D4 Sivry Belgium
157 F3 Sivry-sur-Meuse France
215 G2 Sivukile S. Africa
202 E2 Siwa Egypt
116 D3 Siwalik Range mts India/Nepal
117 F4 Siwan Bihar India
116 C4 Siwana Rajasthan India
202 E2 Siwa Oasis Egypt
129 E3 Şıxarx Azer.
161 D5 Six-Fours-les-Plages France
109 F1 Sixian Anhui China
226 E4 Six Lakes MI U.S.A.
147 C4 Sixmilebridge Rep. of Ireland
147 D2 Sixmilecross Northern Ireland U.K.
160 E2 Sixt-Fer-à-Cheval France
215 G1 Siyabuswa S. Africa
Siyang Guangxi China see Shangsi
109 F1 Siyang Jiangsu China
215 G2 Siyathemba S. Africa
215 H1 Siyathuthuka S. Africa
129 F3 Siyäzän Azer.
107 F3 Siyitang Nei Mongol China
184 A1 Sizandro r. Port.
Siziwang Qi Nei Mongol China see Ulan Hua
158 B3 Sizun France
134 K2 Sizyabsk Rus. Fed.
142 D4 Sjælland i. Denmark
196 E4 Sjenica Srbija Yugo.
143 E4 Sjöbo Sweden
140 I3 Sjøholt Norway
140 K2 Sjona sea chan. Norway
140 K2 Sjoutnäset Sweden
140 L1 Sjøvegan Norway
140 M2 Sjulsmark Sweden
140 □ Sjuøyane is Svalbard
140 K3 Skäckerfjällen mts Sweden
137 G4 Skadovs'k Ukr.
142 D4 Skælsør Denmark
142 C4 Skærbæk Denmark
221 Q2 Skærfjorden inlet Greenland
140 □C3 Skaftárós r. mouth Iceland
140 □C2 Skagafjörður inlet Iceland
140 □B2 Skagaheiði reg. Iceland
142 D3 Skagen Denmark
143 F2 Skagern l. Sweden
142 C3 Skagerrak str. Denmark/Norway
238 B1 Skagit r. WA U.S.A.
222 F5 Skagit Mountain B.C. Can.
220 E4 Skagway AK U.S.A.
138 E4 Skaidiškės Lith.
146 E2 Skaill Orkney, Scotland U.K.
146 F3 Skaill Orkney, Scotland U.K.
199 E3 Skala Notio Aigaio Greece
198 C3 Skala Peloponnisos Greece
175 H5 Skała Pol.
140 L1 Skaland Norway
136 D3 Skala-Podil's'ka Ukr.
171 F5 Skalice Czech Rep.
129 B1 Skalistyy Khrebet reg. Rus. Fed.
177 H2 Skalité Slovakia
140 K2 Skalmodal Sweden
176 B1 Skalná Czech Rep.
142 C3 Skals r. Denmark
142 C3 Skanderborg Denmark
142 E4 Skåne county Sweden
232 E3 Skaneateles NY U.S.A.
140 L2 Skansholm Sweden
174 D3 Skąpe Pol.
142 E2 Skara Sweden
146 E2 Skara Brae tourist site Scotland U.K.
Skardarsko Jezero l. Albania/Yugo. see Scutari, Lake
85 E1 Skardon r. Qld Austr.
116 C2 Skardu Jammu and Kashmir
142 B2 Skåreheia mt. Norway
142 D3 Skärhamn Sweden
142 D1 Skarnes Norway
143 G1 Skärplinge Sweden
141 K3 Skärsjövålen Sweden
141 J3 Skarstind mt. Norway
174 G1 Skarszewy Pol.
141 J3 Skarvedalseggen mt. Norway
140 L2 Skarvsjöby Sweden
175 J4 Skaryszew Pol.
136 D3 Skarzhyntsi Ukr.
175 I4 Skarżysko-Kamienna Pol.
142 E1 Skasberget hill Norway
138 D4 Skaudvilė Lith.
140 M2 Skaulo Sweden
142 C3 Skave Denmark
146 □H1 Skaw Shetland, Scotland U.K.
175 H5 Skawa r. Pol.
175 H6 Skawina Pol.
143 H2 Skebobruk Sweden
143 F2 Skeda udde Sweden
222 D4 Skeena r. B.C. Can.
222 D3 Skeena Mountains B.C. Can.
149 J4 Skegness Lincolnshire, England U.K.
140 □C3 Skeiðarársandur sand area Iceland
146 □G1 Skeld Shetland, Scotland U.K.
168 E1 Skelde Denmark
140 M2 Skellefteå Sweden
140 M2 Skellefteälven r. Sweden
140 M2 Skelleftebukten b. Sweden
140 M2 Skelleftehamn Sweden
149 G4 Skelmersdale Lancashire, England U.K.
146 D6 Skelmorlie North Ayrshire, Scotland U.K.
149 I3 Skelton Redcar and Cleveland, England U.K.
150 E3 Skenfrith Monmouthshire, Wales U.K.
175 H3 Skępe Pol.
141 L3 Skeppshamn Sweden
214 D3 Skerpioenpunt S. Africa
146 D3 Skerray Highland, Scotland U.K.
147 E3 Skerries Rep. of Ireland
150 D3 Sketty Swansea, Wales U.K.
136 B3 Skhidni Beskydy mts Pol./Ukr.
136 B3 Skhidni Karpaty mts Ukr.
175 L6 Skhidnytsya Ukr.
Skhimatárion Greece see Schimatari
142 D2 Ski Norway
198 C2 Skiathos Greece
198 C2 Skiathos i. Greece
147 B5 Skibbereen Rep. of Ireland
138 E5 Skidal' Belarus
149 F3 Skiddaw hill England U.K.
222 D4 Skidegate Mission B.C. Can.
Skidel' Belarus see Skidal'
234 B3 Skidmore MD U.S.A.
142 C2 Skien Norway
175 L5 Skierbieszów Pol.
175 I4 Skierniewice Pol.
205 G1 Skikda Alg.
143 F2 Skinnskatteberg Sweden
116 D2 Skio Jammu and Kashmir
146 C6 Skipness Argyll and Bute, Scotland U.K.
234 C2 Skippack PA U.S.A.
149 I4 Skipsea East Riding of Yorkshire, England U.K.
214 C6 Skipskop S. Africa
83 E4 Skipton Vic. Austr.
149 G4 Skipton North Yorkshire, England U.K.
234 B4 Skipton MD U.S.A.
Skíros i. Greece see Skyros
142 C3 Skive Denmark
175 K3 Skiwy Duże Pol.
140 □C2 Skjálfandafljót r. Iceland
140 □C2 Skjálfandi b. Iceland
140 K2 Skjelatinden mt. Norway
142 D1 Skjellinhovde hill Norway
142 B1 Skjemmene mt. Norway
142 B2 Skjerkeknuten hill Norway
142 C4 Skjern Denmark
142 C4 Skjern r. Denmark
140 M1 Skjervøy Norway
Skobelev Uzbek. see Fergana
121 H5 Skobeleva, Pik mt. Kyrg.
179 E5 Skocjanske Jame tourist site Slovenia
174 G6 Skoczów Pol.
215 E6 Skoenmakerskop S. Africa
188 E2 Škofja Loka Slovenia
179 F5 Škofljica Slovenia
141 L3 Skog Sweden
143 F3 Skoghult Sweden
150 B3 Skokholm Island Wales U.K.
174 F3 Skoki Pol.
226 D4 Skokie IL U.S.A.
136 B3 Skole Ukr.
143 F2 Sköllersta Sweden
175 J6 Skołyszyn Pol.
150 B3 Skomer Island Wales U.K.
174 G4 Skomlin Pol.
215 F2 Skoonspruit r. S. Africa
198 C2 Skopelos Greece
198 C2 Skopelos i. Greece
198 D2 Skopia hill Voreio Aigaio Greece
139 L5 Skopin Rus. Fed.
196 E5 Skopje Macedonia
Skoplje Macedonia see Skopje
174 G2 Skórcz Pol.
135 G6 Skorodnoye Rus. Fed.
174 F5 Skorogoszcz Pol.
174 F5 Skoroszyce Pol.
144 J1 Skorpa i. Norway
142 C3 Skørping Denmark
175 K3 Skórzec Pol.
198 C1 Skotoussa Greece
142 E2 Skotterud Norway
198 C1 Skoutari Greece
199 E2 Skoutaros Voreio Aigaio Greece
143 E2 Skövde Sweden
100 B1 Skovorodino Rus. Fed.
233 □I2 Skowhegan ME U.S.A.
142 C2 Skrimfjell hill Norway
138 E3 Skrīveri Latvia
188 D2 Škrlatica mt. Slovenia
175 J2 Skroda r. Pol.
140 M2 Skröven Sweden
138 D3 Skrunda Latvia
175 H3 Skrwa r. Pol.
175 H2 Skrwilno Pol.
174 E2 Skrzatusz Pol.
175 G6 Skrzyczne mt. Pol.
175 I4 Skrzyńsko Pol.
175 J6 Skrzyszów Pol.
142 A2 Skudeneshavn Norway
144 D1 Skúgvoy i. Faroe Is
215 F1 Skuinsdrif S. Africa
222 C2 Skukum, Mount Y.T. Can.
213 F5 Skukuza S. Africa
241 I3 Skull Peak NV U.S.A.
241 K4 Skull Valley AZ U.S.A.
174 G3 Skulsk Pol.
143 G2 Skultuna Sweden
236 F3 Skunk r. IA U.S.A.
138 C3 Skuodas Lith.
139 K4 Skuratovskiy Rus. Fed.
142 E4 Skurup Sweden
197 F4 Skŭt r. Bulg.
143 G1 Skutskär Sweden
175 M6 Skvaryava Ukr.
136 E3 Skvyra Ukr.
174 D3 Skwierzyna Pol.
177 H3 Skýcov Slovakia
198 C1 Skydra Kentriki Makedonia Greece
146 B4 Skye i. Scotland U.K.
142 B2 Skykula hill Norway
198 D2 Skyros Sterea Ellas Greece
198 D2 Skyros i. Greece
234 C1 Skytop PA U.S.A.
262 S1 Skytrain Ice Rise Antarctica
175 I5 Słaboszów Pol.
234 B2 Slabtown PA U.S.A.
234 D2 Slack Woods NJ U.S.A.
Sládečkovce Slovakia see Močenok
144 D1 Slættaratindur hill Faroe Is
142 D4 Slagelse Denmark
164 F2 Slagharen Neth.
140 L2 Slagnäs Sweden
149 G4 Slaidburn Lancashire, England U.K.
146 E6 Slamannan Falkirk, Scotland U.K.
95 E4 Slamet, Gunung vol. Indon.
177 J3 Slaná r. Slovakia
147 E3 Slane Rep. of Ireland
177 K3 Slanec Slovakia
147 E4 Slaney r. Rep. of Ireland
197 G3 Slănic Romania
197 H3 Slănic r. Romania
197 H2 Slănic Moldova Romania
177 K3 Slanské Vrchy mts Slovakia
138 G2 Slantsy Rus. Fed.
176 D1 Slaný Czech Rep.
176 F2 Šlapanice Czech Rep.
85 F3 Slashers Reefs Qld Austr.
Śląsk reg. Europe see Silesia
175 G5 Śląska, Wyżyna hills Pol.
174 G5 Śląskie prov. Pol.
234 C2 Slateford PA U.S.A.
235 D1 Slate Hill NY U.S.A.
188 F3 Slatina Croatia
197 G3 Slatina Romania
177 I3 Slatina r. Slovakia
197 F3 Slatina-Timiş Romania
234 C2 Slatington PA U.S.A.
176 G2 Slatinice Czech Rep.
232 C5 Slaty Fork WV U.S.A.
137 I2 Slatyne Ukr.
222 H2 Slave r. Alta/N.W.T. Can.
207 F5 Slave Coast Africa
222 H4 Slave Lake Alta Can.
Slavgorod Belarus see Slawharad
121 I1 Slavgorod Rus. Fed.
Slavgorod Dnipropetrovs'ka Oblast' Ukr. see Slavhorod

Slavhorod to Soufrière

364

137 H3 **Slavhorod** *Dnipropetrovs'ka Oblast'* Ukr.
137 H2 **Slavhorod** *Sums'ka Oblast'* Ukr.
177 G2 **Slavičín** Czech Rep.
197 F4 **Slavinja** *Srbija* Yugo.
138 G3 **Slavkovichi** Rus. Fed.
176 B1 **Slavkovský Les** *hill* Czech Rep.
176 F2 **Slavkov u Brna** Czech Rep.
191 I3 **Slavnik** *mt.* Slovenia
176 E3 **Slavonice** Czech Rep.
Slavonska Požega Croatia *see* **Požega**
188 G3 **Slavonski Brod** Croatia
177 J3 **Slavošovce** Slovakia
138 C4 **Slavsk** Rus. Fed.
136 D2 **Slavuta** Ukr.
136 F2 **Slavutych** Ukr.
Slavyanka Kazakh. *see* **Myrzakent**
100 D4 **Slavyanka** Rus. Fed.
197 G4 **Slavyanovo** Bulg.
Slavyansk Ukr. *see* **Slov"yans'k**
Slavyanskaya Rus. Fed. *see* **Slavyansk-na-Kubani**
135 G7 **Slavyansk-na-Kubani** Rus. Fed.
174 E4 **Sława** Pol.
175 L4 **Sławatycze** Pol.
174 F2 **Sławęcin** Pol.
139 H5 **Slawharad** Belarus
143 G4 **Sławno** Pol.
174 D2 **Sławoborze** Pol.
236 E3 **Slayton** *MN* U.S.A.
149 I4 **Slea** *r. England* U.K.
149 I4 **Sleaford** *Lincolnshire, England* U.K.
82 C3 **Sleaford Bay** *S.A.* Austr.
146 C4 **Sleat** *pen. Scotland* U.K.
146 C4 **Sleat, Sound of** *sea chan. Scotland* U.K.
149 I3 **Sledmere** *East Riding of Yorkshire, England* U.K.
164 F2 **Sleen** Neth.
164 D3 **Sleeuwijk** Neth.
149 I3 **Sleights** *North Yorkshire, England* U.K.
95 E4 **Sleman** Indon.
175 H6 **Ślemień** Pol.
129 D2 **Sleptsovskaya** Rus. Fed.
174 G3 **Ślesin** Pol.
174 E5 **Ślęża** *hill* Pol.
174 E4 **Ślęża** *r.* Pol.
Slezsko *reg.* Europe *see* **Silesia**
177 I3 **Sliač** Slovakia
241 M2 **Slick Rock** *CO* U.S.A.
237 F6 **Slidell** *LA* U.S.A.
233 F4 **Slide Mountain** *NY* U.S.A.
141 J3 **Slidre** Norway
164 D3 **Sliedrecht** Neth.
195 □ **Sliema** Malta
147 A4 **Slievanea** *hill* Rep. of Ireland
147 D2 **Slieve Anierin** *hill* Rep. of Ireland
147 D4 **Slieveardagh Hills** Rep. of Ireland
147 C3 **Slieve Aughty Mountains** *hills* Rep. of Ireland
147 D2 **Slieve Beagh** *hill* Rep. of Ireland/U.K.
147 C4 **Slieve Bernagh** *hills* Rep. of Ireland
147 D4 **Slieve Bloom Mountains** *hills* Rep. of Ireland
147 B4 **Slievecallan** *hill* Rep. of Ireland
147 B2 **Slieve Car** *hill* Rep. of Ireland
147 F2 **Slieve Donard** *hill Northern Ireland* U.K.
147 C4 **Slievefelim Mountains** *hills* Rep. of Ireland
148 C3 **Slieve Gallion** *hill Northern Ireland* U.K.
147 B3 **Slieve Gamph** *hills* Rep. of Ireland
147 C4 **Slievekimalta** *hill* Rep. of Ireland
147 D2 **Slievekirk** *hill Northern Ireland* U.K.
147 A4 **Slieve Mish Mountains** *hills* Rep. of Ireland
147 A5 **Slieve Miskish Mountains** *hills* Rep. of Ireland
147 D2 **Slievenakilla** *hill* Rep. of Ireland
147 D4 **Slievenamon** *hill* Rep. of Ireland
148 B3 **Slieve Rushen** *hill Northern Ireland* U.K.
147 C2 **Slieve Snaght** *hill Donegal* Rep. of Ireland
147 D1 **Slieve Snaght** *hill Donegal* Rep. of Ireland
146 B4 **Sligachan** *Highland, Scotland* U.K.
Sligeach Rep. of Ireland *see* **Sligo**
147 C2 **Sligo** Rep. of Ireland
147 C2 **Sligo** *county* Rep. of Ireland
232 D4 **Sligo** *PA* U.S.A.
147 C2 **Sligo Bay** Rep. of Ireland
175 K2 **Ślina** *r.* Pol.
151 G3 **Slinfold** *West Sussex, England* U.K.
164 F2 **Slinge** *r.* Neth.
146 C4 **Slioch** *hill Scotland* U.K.
137 G3 **Sliporid** *r.* Ukr.
232 C4 **Slippery Rock** *PA* U.S.A.
143 H3 **Slite** *Gotland* Sweden
197 H4 **Sliven** Bulg.
197 F4 **Slivnitsa** Bulg.
197 H4 **Slivo Pole** Bulg.
174 G2 **Śliwice** Pol.
188 E3 **Sljeme** *mt.* Croatia
241 J4 **Sloan** *NV* U.S.A.
240 G2 **Sloat** *CA* U.S.A.
235 D1 **Sloatsburg** *NY* U.S.A.
136 E4 **Slobidka** Ukr.
Sloboda *Respublika Komi* Rus. Fed. *see* **Ezhva**
Sloboda *Smolenskaya Oblast'* Rus. Fed. *see* **Przheval'skoye**
135 H6 **Sloboda** *Voronezhskaya Oblast'* Rus. Fed.
137 G2 **Sloboda** Ukr.
134 J4 **Slobodskoy** Rus. Fed.
Slobodzeya Moldova *see* **Slobozia**
136 E4 **Slobozia** Moldova
197 H3 **Slobozia** Romania
197 H3 **Slobozia Bradului** Romania
222 G5 **Slocan** *B.C.* Can.
164 F1 **Slochteren** Neth.
175 I5 **Słomniki** Pol.
138 E5 **Slonim** Belarus
137 I2 **Slonovka** Rus. Fed.
174 C3 **Słońsk** Pol.
164 D2 **Slootdorp** Neth.
164 E2 **Sloten** Neth.
151 G3 **Slough** *Slough, England* U.K.
151 G3 **Slough** *admin. div. England* U.K.
176 F2 **Sloupnice** Czech Rep.
177 I3 **Slovakia** *country* Europe
136 E2 **Slovechna** *r.* Ukr.
136 E2 **Slovechne** Ukr.
188 E2 **Slovenia** *country* Europe
Slovenija *country* Europe *see* **Slovenia**
188 E2 **Slovenj Gradec** Slovenia
188 E2 **Slovenska Bistrica** Slovenia
177 J2 **Slovenská Ves** Slovakia
188 E2 **Slovenske Gorice** *hills* Slovenia
179 G4 **Slovenske Konjice** Slovenia
177 K3 **Slovenské Nové Mesto** Slovakia
177 I3 **Slovenské Rudohorie** *mts* Slovakia
Slovensko *country* Europe *see* **Slovakia**
177 J3 **Slovenský kras** *mts* Slovakia
177 J3 **Slovinky** Slovakia
175 M6 **Slovita** Ukr.
137 I3 **Slov"yanka** Ukr.
137 I3 **Slov"yanohirs'k** Ukr.
137 J3 **Slov"yanoserbs'k** Ukr.
137 I3 **Slov"yans'k** Ukr.
136 E2 **Slovyechna** *r.* Belarus
175 H4 **Słowik** Pol.
174 C3 **Słubice** Pol.
175 H3 **Słubice** Pol.
138 F5 **Sluch** *r.* Belarus
136 D2 **Sluch** *r.* Ukr.
191 F2 **Sluderno** Italy
134 J4 **Sludka** Rus. Fed.
165 C3 **Sluis** Neth.
165 C3 **Sluiskil** Neth.
176 D1 **Šluknov** Czech Rep.
176 G2 **Slunečná** *hill* Czech Rep.
188 E3 **Slunj** Croatia
174 F3 **Słupca** Pol.
175 J5 **Słupcza** Pol.
175 H4 **Słupia** Pol.
175 H5 **Słupia** Pol.
175 I4 **Słupia** Pol.
143 G4 **Słupia** *r.* Pol.
175 H3 **Słupno** Pol.
143 G4 **Słupsk** Pol.
140 L2 **Slussfors** Sweden
174 G4 **Słuszków** Pol.
138 F5 **Slutsk** Belarus
138 D4 **Šlyna** *r.* Lith.
98 H1 **Slyudyanka** Rus. Fed.
237 E5 **Smackover** *AR* U.S.A.
162 A2 **Smagne** *r.* France
146 F6 **Smailholm** *Scottish Borders, Scotland* U.K.
143 F3 **Småland** *reg.* Sweden
142 D4 **Smålandsfarvandet** *sea chan.* Denmark
142 E3 **Smålandsstenar** Sweden
151 F2 **Smalley** *Derbyshire, England* U.K.
225 H2 **Smallwood Reservoir** *Nfld.* Can.
138 G4 **Smalyavichy** Belarus
175 I4 **Smardzewice** Pol.
138 F4 **Smarhon'** Belarus
179 G4 **Šmarje pri Jelšah** Slovenia
179 G4 **Šmartno** Slovenia
162 C2 **Smarves** France
223 J4 **Smeaton** *Sask.* Can.
171 F5 **Smečno** Czech Rep.
176 D1 **Smědá** *r.* Czech Rep.
143 G3 **Smedby** Sweden
196 E3 **Smederevo** *Srbija* Yugo.
196 E3 **Smederevska Palanka** *Srbija* Yugo.
197 H3 **Smeeni** Romania
151 H3 **Smeeth** *Kent, England* U.K.
Smela Ukr. *see* **Smila**
232 D4 **Smethport** *PA* U.S.A.
151 F2 **Smethwick** *West Midlands, England* U.K.
174 G2 **Smętowo Graniczne** Pol.
176 E1 **Smidary** Czech Rep.
175 M4 **Smidyn** Ukr.
174 E3 **Śmigiel** Pol.
137 F3 **Smila** Ukr.
138 G5 **Smilavichy** Belarus
164 F2 **Smilde** Neth.
137 G2 **Smile** Ukr.
136 D2 **Smilka** *r.* Ukr.
138 E3 **Smiltene** Latvia
138 D3 **Smiltiņu kalns** *hill* Latvia
176 E1 **Smiřice** Czech Rep.
121 G1 **Smirnovo** Kazakh.
Smirnovskiy Kazakh. *see* **Smirnovo**
100 G2 **Smirnykh** *Sakhalin* Rus. Fed.
222 H4 **Smith** *Alta* Can.
238 E2 **Smith** *r. MT* U.S.A.
232 D6 **Smith** *r. VA* U.S.A.
220 F3 **Smith Arm** *b. N.W.T.* Can.
147 D2 **Smithborough** Rep. of Ireland
236 D4 **Smith Center** *KS* U.S.A.
222 E4 **Smithers** *B.C.* Can.
222 E4 **Smithers Landing** *B.C.* Can.
215 F4 **Smithfield** S. Africa
231 E5 **Smithfield** *NC* U.S.A.
238 E3 **Smithfield** *UT* U.S.A.
232 E6 **Smithfield** *VA* U.S.A.
262 Q1 **Smith Glacier** Antarctica
262 T2 **Smith Island** Antarctica
237 F4 **Smithland** *KY* U.S.A.
84 B1 **Smith Point** *N.T.* Austr.
222 E3 **Smith River** *B.C.* Can.
232 E5 **Smithsburg** *MD* U.S.A.
224 E4 **Smiths Falls** *Ont.* Can.
83 F5 **Smithton** *Tas.* Austr.
83 H2 **Smithtown** *N.S.W.* Austr.
235 E2 **Smithtown** *NY* U.S.A.
235 D3 **Smithville** *NJ* U.S.A.
237 E5 **Smithville** *OK* U.S.A.
231 C5 **Smithville** *TN* U.S.A.
232 C5 **Smithville** *WV* U.S.A.
214 E5 **Smitskraal** S. Africa
177 J3 **Smižany** Slovakia
140 □D2 **Smjörfjöll** *mts* Iceland
240 H1 **Smoke Creek Desert** *NV* U.S.A.
222 G3 **Smoky** *r. Alta* Can.
82 C3 **Smoky Bay** *S.A.* Austr.
82 C3 **Smoky Bay** *b. S.A.* Austr.
83 H2 **Smoky Cape** *N.S.W.* Austr.
224 D3 **Smoky Falls** *Ont.* Can.
236 D4 **Smoky Hill** *r. KS* U.S.A.
236 C4 **Smoky Hill, North Fork** *r. KS* U.S.A.
228 G3 **Smoky Hills** *KS* U.S.A.
223 H4 **Smoky Lake** *Alta* Can.
140 I3 **Smøla** *i.* Norway
174 F1 **Smołdzino** Pol.
120 B2 **Smolenka** Rus. Fed.
139 I4 **Smolensk** Rus. Fed.
139 I4 **Smolenskaya Oblast'** *admin. div.* Rus. Fed.
Smolensk Oblast *admin. div.* Rus. Fed. *see* **Smolenskaya Oblast'**
139 I4 **Smolensko-Moskovskaya Vozvyshennost'** *hills* Rus. Fed.
121 K1 **Smolenskoye** Rus. Fed.
Smolevichi Belarus *see* **Smalyavichy**
174 F4 **Smolice** Pol.
198 B1 **Smolikas** *mt.* Greece
137 F3 **Smoline** Ukr.
142 E2 **Smolmark** Sweden
177 J3 **Smolník** Slovakia
197 G5 **Smolyan** Bulg.
100 E4 **Smolyoninovo** Rus. Fed.
224 D3 **Smooth Rock Falls** *Ont.* Can.
Smorgon' Belarus *see* **Smarhon'**
139 I5 **Smotrova Buda** Rus. Fed.
136 D3 **Smotrych** Ukr.
176 G1 **Smrk** *mt.* Czech Rep.
171 G5 **Smrk** *mt.* Czech Rep.
137 F2 **Smyach** Ukr.
197 H4 **Smyadovo** Bulg.
142 E4 **Smygehamn** Sweden
136 C2 **Smyha** Ukr.
175 I4 **Smyków** Pol.
262 S2 **Smyley Island** Antarctica
Smyrna Turkey *see* **İzmir**
234 C3 **Smyrna** *DE* U.S.A.
231 C5 **Smyrna** *GA* U.S.A.
231 C5 **Smyrna** *TN* U.S.A.
234 C3 **Smyrna** *r. DE* U.S.A.
233 □I1 **Smyrna Mills** *ME* U.S.A.
Smyth Island *atoll* Marshall Is *see* **Majuro**
140 □D2 **Snæfell** *mt.* Iceland
148 E3 **Snaefell** *hill* Isle of Man
140 □B2 **Snæfellsjökull** *ice cap* Iceland
140 □B2 **Snæfellsnes** *pen.* Iceland
222 A2 **Snag** *Y.T.* Can.
149 I3 **Snainton** *North Yorkshire, England* U.K.
149 H4 **Snaith** *East Riding of Yorkshire, England* U.K.
236 C3 **Snake** *r. NE* U.S.A.
238 C2 **Snake** *r.* U.S.A.
84 B2 **Snake Creek** *r. N.T.* Austr.
241 J2 **Snake Range** *mts NV* U.S.A.
222 F3 **Snake River** *B.C.* Can.
238 D3 **Snake River Plain** *ID* U.S.A.
222 G2 **Snare** *r. N.W.T.* Can.
Snare Lakes *N.W.T.* Can. *see* **Wekwetì**
77 G6 **Snares Islands** N.Z.
140 K2 **Snåsa** Norway
232 B6 **Sneedville** *TN* U.S.A.
164 E1 **Sneek** Neth.
147 B5 **Sneem** Rep. of Ireland
214 B5 **Sneeuberg** *mt.* S. Africa
214 E4 **Sneeuberge** *mts* S. Africa
Snegurovka Ukr. *see* **Tetiyiv**
240 G3 **Snelling** *CA* U.S.A.
151 H2 **Snettisham** *Norfolk, England* U.K.
139 K5 **Snezhed'** *r.* Rus. Fed.
130 J3 **Snezhnogorsk** Rus. Fed.
Snezhnoye Ukr. *see* **Snizhne**
176 E1 **Sněžka** *mt.* Czech Rep.
188 E3 **Snežnik** *mt.* Slovenia
175 J2 **Śniadowo** Pol.
175 J2 **Śniardwy, Jezioro** *l.* Pol.
Sniečkus Lith. *see* **Visaginas**
Snieżka *mt.* Czech Rep. *see* **Sněžka**
174 E5 **Śnieżnik** *mt.* Pol.
137 G4 **Snihurivka** Ukr.
177 L3 **Snina** Slovakia
151 F2 **Snitterfield** *Warwickshire, England* U.K.
137 G2 **Snityn** Ukr.
137 J3 **Snizhne** Ukr.
146 B4 **Snizort, Loch** *b. Scotland* U.K.
141 J3 **Snøhetta** *mt.* Norway
238 B2 **Snohomish** *WA* U.S.A.
142 B2 **Snønuten** *mt.* Norway
139 I5 **Snopot'** *r.* Rus. Fed.
137 F2 **Snov** *r.* Ukr.
137 I2 **Snova** *r.* Rus. Fed.
139 L5 **Snova** *r.* Rus. Fed.
Snovsk Ukr. *see* **Shchors**
138 F5 **Snow** Belarus
222 G5 **Snowcrest Mountain** *B.C.* Can.
81 B6 **Snowdon** *mt. South I.* N.Z.
150 C1 **Snowdon** *mt. Wales* U.K.
150 D2 **Snowdonia National Park** *Wales* U.K.
Snowdrift *N.W.T.* Can. *see* **Łutselk'e**
223 I2 **Snowdrift** *r. N.W.T.* Can.
241 L4 **Snowflake** *AZ* U.S.A.
233 F5 **Snow Hill** *MD* U.S.A.
231 E5 **Snow Hill** *NC* U.S.A.
223 K4 **Snow Lake** *Man.* Can.
82 D3 **Snowtown** *S.A.* Austr.
238 D3 **Snowville** *UT* U.S.A.
83 G4 **Snowy** *r. N.S.W./Vic.* Austr.
233 F3 **Snowy Mountain** *NY* U.S.A.
83 F4 **Snowy Mountains** *N.S.W.* Austr.
246 D2 **Snug Corner** *Acklins I.* Bahamas
225 K2 **Snug Harbour** *Nfld.* Can.
227 G3 **Snug Harbour** *Ont.* Can.
136 C3 **Snyatyn** Ukr.
237 D5 **Snyder** *OK* U.S.A.
237 C5 **Snyder** *TX* U.S.A.
234 A2 **Snyder County** *county PA* U.S.A.
234 C2 **Snyders** *PA* U.S.A.
136 E3 **Snyvoda** *r.* Ukr.
Soaigh *i. Western Isles, Scotland* U.K. *see* **Soay**
182 B3 **Soajo** Port.
81 A6 **Soaker, Mount** *South I.* N.Z.
213 □J3 **Soalala** Madag.
182 B3 **Soalhães** Port.
182 C4 **Soalheira** Port.
213 □J4 **Soamanonga** Madag.
190 C3 **Soana** *r.* Italy
213 □K3 **Soanierana-Ivongo** Madag.
191 H5 **Soara** *r.* Italy
191 G3 **Soave** Italy
213 □J3 **Soavinandriana** Madag.
146 B4 **Soay** *i. Highland, Scotland* U.K.
146 □ **Soay** *i. Western Isles, Scotland* U.K.
136 E3 **Sob** *r.* Ukr.
207 H4 **Soba** Nigeria
101 C6 **Sobaek-sanmaek** *mts* S. Korea
210 A2 **Sobat** *r.* Sudan
105 E3 **Sobatsubu-yama** *mt.* Japan
182 C2 **Sober** Spain
172 B2 **Sobernheim** Ger.
176 D2 **Soběslav** Czech Rep.
91 J7 **Sobger** *r.* Indon.
139 M4 **Sobinka** Rus. Fed.
139 L4 **Sobolevo** Rus. Fed.
175 J4 **Sobolew** Pol.
103 E7 **Sobo-san** *mt.* Japan
175 H3 **Sobota** Pol.
176 G1 **Sobotín** Czech Rep.
176 G3 **Sobotište** Slovakia
176 E1 **Sobotka** Czech Rep.
174 E5 **Sobótka** Pol.
175 J5 **Sobótka** Pol.
174 F4 **Sobótka** Pol.
174 G1 **Sobowidz** Pol.
182 D2 **Sobradelo** Spain
256 D1 **Sobradinho** Brazil
182 B1 **Sobrado** *Galicia* Spain
182 B2 **Sobrado** *Galicia* Spain
254 E2 **Sobral** Brazil
182 B4 **Sobral** Port.
184 C2 **Sobral da Adiça** Port.
184 A1 **Sobral de Monte Agraço** Port.
182 C4 **Sobral do Campo** Port.
177 L3 **Sobrance** Slovakia
182 B3 **Sobreira** Port.
182 C5 **Sobreira Formosa** Port.
168 F1 **Søby** Denmark
137 G2 **Sobych** Ukr.
Soča *r.* Italy *see* **Isonzo**
188 D3 **Soča** *r.* Slovenia
191 H2 **Socchieve** Italy
175 I3 **Sochaczew** Pol.
129 A2 **Sochi** Rus. Fed.
175 I3 **Sochocin** Pol.
101 C5 **Sŏch'ŏn** S. Korea
198 C1 **Sochos** Greece
Society Islands Fr. Polynesia *see* **La Société, Archipel de**
177 K5 **Socodor** Romania
196 E3 **Socol** Romania
177 L4 **Socond** Romania
Soconusco, Sierra de *mts* Mex. *see* **Madre, Sierra**
256 D5 **Socorro** Brazil
250 C3 **Socorro** Col.
239 F5 **Socorro** *NM* U.S.A.
228 D7 **Socorro, Isla** *i.* Mex.
250 B6 **Socota** Peru
Socotra *i.* Yemen *see* **Suquṭrā**
185 I2 **Socovos** Spain
97 D5 **Soc Trăng** Vietnam
185 H1 **Socuéllamos** Spain
140 N2 **Sodankylä** Fin.
111 B5 **Soda Plains** Aksai Chin
238 E3 **Soda Springs** *ID* U.S.A.
105 F3 **Sodegaura** Japan
143 G3 **Söderåkra** Sweden
143 F1 **Söderbärke** Sweden
143 H1 **Söderboda** Sweden
143 G1 **Söderfors** Sweden
141 L3 **Söderhamn** Sweden
143 G2 **Söderköping** Sweden
143 G2 **Södermanland** *county* Sweden
168 F2 **Soderstorf** Ger.
143 G2 **Södertälje** Sweden
203 F6 **Sodiri** Sudan
214 D4 **Sodium** S. Africa
210 C3 **Sodo** Eth.
140 M3 **Södra Gloppet** *b.* Fin.
141 L3 **Södra Kvarken** *str.* Fin./Sweden
143 F3 **Södra Vi** Sweden
232 E3 **Sodus** *NY* U.S.A.
214 A4 **Soebatsfontein** S. Africa
213 F4 **Soekmekaar** S. Africa
Soerabaia *Jawa Timur* Indon. *see* **Surabaya**
165 E3 **Soerendonk** Neth.
169 D4 **Soest** Ger.
164 E2 **Soest** Neth.
168 C2 **Soeste** *r.* Ger.
198 C2 **Sofades** Greece
83 G3 **Sofala** *N.S.W.* Austr.
213 G4 **Sofala** Moz.
213 G3 **Sofala** *prov.* Moz.
Sofia Bulg. *see* **Sofiya**
213 □J2 **Sofia** *r.* Madag.
198 C3 **Sofiko** Greece
197 F4 **Sofiya** Bulg.
Sofiyevka Ukr. *see* **Vil'nyans'k**
137 G3 **Sofiyivka** Ukr.
100 E1 **Sofiysk** *Khabarovskiy Kray* Rus. Fed.
100 F2 **Sofiysk** *Khabarovskiy Kray* Rus. Fed.
139 K3 **Sofrino** Rus. Fed.
177 K5 **Şofronea** Romania
128 A1 **Softa Kalesi** *tourist site* Turkey
103 J9 **Sōfu-gan** *i.* Japan
111 F6 **Sog** *Xizang* China
250 C3 **Sogamoso** Col.
129 A3 **Soğanlı Dağları** *mts* Turkey
110 D3 **Sogat** *Xinjiang* China
100 E2 **Sogda** Rus. Fed.
168 C3 **Sögel** Ger.
142 B2 **Søgne** Norway
141 I3 **Sognefjorden** *inlet* Norway
141 I3 **Sogn og Fjordane** *county* Norway
92 C4 **Sogod** Phil.
129 D4 **Soğuksu** Turkey
199 G1 **Söğüt** Turkey
199 F3 **Söğüt Dağı** *mts* Turkey
129 B4 **Söğütlü** Turkey
101 C6 **Sŏgwip'o** S. Korea
203 F3 **Sohâg** Egypt
116 D5 **Sohagpur** *Madh. Prad.* India
151 H2 **Soham** *Cambridgeshire, England* U.K.
123 G3 **Sohan** *r.* Pak.
Sohar Oman *see* **Şuḥār**
165 E4 **Soheit-Tinlot** Belgium
117 E5 **Sohela** *Orissa* India
171 F4 **Sohland am Rotstein** Ger.
169 F3 **Söhlde** Ger.
116 D3 **Sohna** *Haryana* India
97 B4 **Sohng Gwe, Khao** *hill* Myanmar/Thai.
172 B2 **Sohren** Ger.
156 E2 **Soignes, Forêt de** *for.* Belgium
165 D4 **Soignies** Belgium
108 A2 **Soila** *Xizang* China
177 L5 **Şoimi** Romania
160 D1 **Soing** France
159 H4 **Soings-en-Sologne** France
140 N3 **Soini** Fin.
157 E2 **Soire-le-Château** France
169 E5 **Soisberg** *hill* Ger.
156 D3 **Soissons** France
156 D4 **Soizy-aux-Bois** France
103 F6 **Sōja** Japan
116 C4 **Sojat** *Rajasthan* India
116 C4 **Sojat Road** *Rajasthan* India
175 K5 **Sójkowa** Pol.
179 H4 **Söjtör** Hungary
135 J5 **Sok** *r.* Rus. Fed.
105 F3 **Sōka** Japan
136 C2 **Sokal'** Ukr.
101 D5 **Sokch'o** S. Korea
199 E3 **Söke** Turkey
209 E7 **Sokele** Dem. Rep. Congo
107 F1 **Sokhondo, Gora** *mt.* Rus. Fed.
106 E1 **Sokhor, Gora** *mt.* Rus. Fed.
Sokhós Greece *see* **Sochos**
129 B2 **Sokhumi** Georgia
129 B2 **Sokhumi-Babushara** *airport* Georgia
Sokiryany Ukr. *see* **Sokyryany**
103 D6 **Sŏkkuram Grotto** *tourist site* S. Korea
197 E4 **Sokobanja** *Srbija* Yugo.
207 F4 **Sokodé** Togo
100 G3 **Sokol** *Sakhalin* Rus. Fed.
134 H4 **Sokol** *Vologod. Obl.* Rus. Fed.
188 G4 **Sokolac** Bos.-Herz.
175 L2 **Sokolany** Pol.
136 F3 **Sokolivka** *Cherkas'ka Oblast'* Ukr.
175 M5 **Sokolivka** *L'vivs'ka Oblast'* Ukr.
175 L2 **Sokółka** Pol.
175 K1 **Sokółki** Pol.
179 H1 **Sokolnice** Czech Rep.
139 L4 **Sokol'niki** Rus. Fed.
139 J3 **Sokol'niki** Rus. Fed.
206 D3 **Sokolo** Mali
137 H4 **Sokolohirne** Ukr.
176 B1 **Sokolov** Czech Rep.
137 H3 **Sokolova Balka** Ukr.
179 H4 **Sokolovac** Croatia
121 G1 **Sokolovka** Kazakh.
121 K1 **Sokolovo** Rus. Fed.
137 J4 **Sokolovo-Kundryuchenskiy** Rus. Fed.
175 K5 **Sokołów Małopolski** Pol.
175 K3 **Sokołow Podlaski** Pol.
134 H4 **Sokol'skoye** Rus. Fed.
175 K3 **Sokoły** Pol.
206 A3 **Sokone** Senegal
177 G4 **Sokorópátka** Hungary
140 O1 **Sokosti** *hill* Fin.
207 G3 **Sokoto** Nigeria
207 G4 **Sokoto** *r.* Nigeria
207 G3 **Sokoto** *state* Nigeria
206 C4 **Sokourala** Guinea
136 D3 **Sokyryany** Ukr.
175 K5 **Sól** Pol.
246 C2 **Sola** Cuba
175 H6 **Soła** *r.* Pol.
Sola *i.* Tonga *see* **Ata**
116 D3 **Solan** *Hima. Prad.* India
240 I5 **Solana Beach** *CA* U.S.A.
184 D2 **Solana de los Barros** Spain
185 F2 **Solana del Pino** Spain
183 F4 **Solana de Rioalmar** Spain
142 C1 **Sølandsfjellet** *mt.* Norway
92 B2 **Solano** Phil.
114 B2 **Solapur** *Mahar.* India
195 E5 **Solarino** *Sicilia* Italy
192 B3 **Solaro** *Corse* France
192 A5 **Solarussa** *Sardegna* Italy
146 A4 **Solas** *Western Isles, Scotland* U.K.
140 L3 **Solberg** Sweden
143 F3 **Solberga** Sweden
197 G2 **Solca** Romania
177 H3 **Solčany** Slovakia
191 F2 **Solda** Italy
191 F2 **Solda** *r.* Italy
136 E4 **Şoldăneşti** Moldova
129 C1 **Soldato-Aleksandrovskoye** Rus. Fed.
129 C2 **Soldatskaya** Rus. Fed.
178 C4 **Sölden** Austria
186 E2 **Soldeu** Andorra
233 □I1 **Soldier Pond** *ME* U.S.A.
220 C3 **Soldotna** *AK* U.S.A.
174 G2 **Solec Kujawski** Pol.
175 I5 **Solec-Zdrój** Pol.
246 D5 **Soledad** Col.
240 G3 **Soledad** *CA* U.S.A.
245 F4 **Soledad de Doblado** Mex.
244 D2 **Soledad Diez Gutierrez** Mex.
255 B9 **Soledade** Brazil
137 J3 **Soledar** Ukr.
192 B5 **Soleminis** *Sardegna* Italy
141 J3 **Sølen** *mt.* Norway
135 H7 **Solenoye** Rus. Fed.
192 B3 **Solenzara** *Corse* France
206 D3 **Solenzo** Burkina
191 G3 **Solesino** Italy
156 D2 **Solesmes** *Nord - Pas-de-Calais* France
159 F4 **Solesmes** *Pays de la Loire* France
195 H2 **Soleto** Italy
163 B4 **Solférino** France
191 F3 **Solferino** Italy
140 K2 **Solfjellsjøen** Norway
134 H3 **Solginskiy** Rus. Fed.
127 F3 **Solhan** Turkey
191 F4 **Soliera** Italy
134 H4 **Soligalich** Rus. Fed.
162 D3 **Solignac** France
190 E4 **Solignano** Italy
191 H3 **Soligo** *r.* Italy
Soligorsk Belarus *see* **Salihorsk**
151 F2 **Solihull** *West Midlands, England* U.K.
134 L4 **Solikamsk** Rus. Fed.
120 C2 **Sol'-Iletsk** Rus. Fed.
189 C7 **Soliman** Tunisia
175 K6 **Solina** Pol.
169 C4 **Solingen** Ger.
175 K6 **Solinka** *r.* Pol.
175 K6 **Solińskie, Jezioro** *l.* Pol.
250 C4 **Solita** Col.
81 A6 **Solitary, Mount** *South I.* N.Z.
186 E3 **Solivella** Spain
Sol-Karmala Rus. Fed. *see* **Severnoye**
178 D3 **Söll** Austria
192 A3 **Sollacaro** *Corse* France
142 E2 **Sollebrunn** Sweden
140 L3 **Sollefteå** Sweden
179 H3 **Sollenau** Austria
143 G2 **Sollentuna** Sweden
187 F5 **Sóller** Spain
141 K3 **Sollerön** Sweden
168 G1 **Søllested** Denmark
171 D4 **Söllichau** Ger.
161 E5 **Solliès-Pont** France
161 E5 **Solliès-Ville** France
169 E4 **Solling** *hills* Ger.
169 F3 **Söllingen** Ger.
169 F4 **Sollstedt** Ger.
169 D5 **Solms** Ger.
139 K3 **Solnechnogorsk** Rus. Fed.
100 F2 **Solnechnyy** *Khabarovskiy Kray* Rus. Fed.
Solnechnyy *Khabarovskiy Kray* Rus. Fed. *see* **Gornyy**
176 F1 **Solnice** Czech Rep.
137 I2 **Solntsevo** Rus. Fed.
93 B3 **Solo** *r.* Indon.
95 F4 **Solo** *r.* Indon.
136 D3 **Solobkivtsi** Ukr.
193 G4 **Solofra** Italy
94 C3 **Solok** *Sumatera* Indon.
136 C2 **Solokiya** *r.* Ukr.
243 H6 **Sololá** Guat.
129 D1 **Solomenskoye** Rus. Fed.
163 C5 **Solomiac** France
136 D3 **Solomna** Ukr.
241 M5 **Solomon** *AZ* U.S.A.
236 D4 **Solomon** *r. KS* U.S.A.
236 D4 **Solomon, North Fork** *r. KS* U.S.A.
236 D4 **Solomon, South Fork** *r. KS* U.S.A.
78 □6 **Solomon Islands** *country* S. Pacific Ocean
91 L8 **Solomon Sea** P.N.G./Solomon Is
107 I2 **Solon** *Nei Mongol* China
233 □I2 **Solon** *ME* U.S.A.
137 H4 **Solona** *r.* Ukr.
137 I3 **Solona** *r.* Ukr.
137 H3 **Solone** Ukr.
121 K2 **Soloneshnoye** Rus. Fed.
226 B2 **Solon Springs** *WI* U.S.A.
194 D1 **Solopaca** Italy
93 B5 **Solor, Kepulauan** *is* Indon.
183 G1 **Solórzano** Spain
183 F4 **Solosancho** Spain
139 L4 **Solotcha** Rus. Fed.
190 C1 **Solothurn** Switz.
190 C1 **Solothurn** *canton* Switz.
136 C3 **Solotvyn** Ukr.
134 F2 **Solovetskiy** Rus. Fed.
134 F2 **Solovetskiye Ostrova** *is* Rus. Fed.
134 I4 **Solovetskoye** Rus. Fed.
136 E2 **Soloviyivka** Ukr.
107 G1 **Solov'yevsk** Mongolia
100 C1 **Solov'yevsk** Rus. Fed.
186 E3 **Solsona** Spain
177 I5 **Solt** Hungary
188 F4 **Šolta** *i.* Croatia
122 D2 **Soltānābād** Iran
122 B3 **Soltānābād** Iran
129 E4 **Soltanlı** Azer.
168 E3 **Soltau** Ger.
168 F3 **Soltendieck** Ger.
121 K1 **Solton** Rus. Fed.
139 H2 **Sol'tsy** Rus. Fed.
Soltüstik Qazaqstan Oblysy *admin. div.* Kazakh. *see* **Severnyy Kazakhstan**
177 I5 **Soltvadkert** Hungary
177 I5 **Soltzentimre** Hungary
196 E5 **Solunska Glava** *mt.* Macedonia
160 C2 **Solutré-Pouilly** France
150 B3 **Solva** *Pembrokeshire, Wales* U.K.
150 B3 **Solva** *r. Wales* U.K.
240 G4 **Solvang** *CA* U.S.A.
233 E3 **Solvay** *NY* U.S.A.
143 F3 **Sölvesborg** Sweden
134 I3 **Sol'vychegodsk** Rus. Fed.
146 E7 **Solway Firth** *est. Scotland* U.K.
209 E8 **Solwezi** Zambia
102 J5 **Sōma** Japan
199 E2 **Soma** Turkey
156 D2 **Somain** France
210 D3 **Somali** *admin. reg.* Eth.
210 E4 **Somalia** *country* Africa
265 H5 **Somali Basin** *sea feature* Indian Ocean
Somali Republic *country* Africa *see* **Somalia**
207 E5 **Somanya** Ghana
95 G2 **Sombang, Gunung** *mt.* Indon.
177 H5 **Somberek** Hungary
160 C1 **Sombernon** France
209 D7 **Sombo** Angola
196 D3 **Sombor** *Vojvodina, Srbija* Yugo.
169 E5 **Somborn** Ger.
165 D4 **Sombreffe** Belgium
244 C2 **Sombrerete** Mex.
259 C9 **Sombrero** Chile
115 G5 **Sombrero Channel** *Andaman & Nicobar Is* India
197 F2 **Şomcuţa Mare** Romania
116 C4 **Somdari** *Rajasthan* India
234 C3 **Somerdale** *NJ* U.S.A.
165 E3 **Someren** Neth.
141 M3 **Somero** Fin.
150 E3 **Somerset** *admin. div. England* U.K.
230 C4 **Somerset** *KY* U.S.A.
233 H4 **Somerset** *MA* U.S.A.
226 E4 **Somerset** *MI* U.S.A.
232 B5 **Somerset** *OH* U.S.A.
232 D5 **Somerset** *PA* U.S.A.
234 D2 **Somerset County** *county NJ* U.S.A.
215 E5 **Somerset East** S. Africa
221 I2 **Somerset Island** *Nunavut* Can.
214 B6 **Somerset West** S. Africa
151 H2 **Somersham** *Cambridgeshire, England* U.K.
234 D3 **Somers Point** *NJ* U.S.A.
233 □H3 **Somersworth** *NH* U.S.A.
150 E3 **Somerton** *Somerset, England* U.K.
241 J5 **Somerton** *AZ* U.S.A.
138 F2 **Sõmeru** Estonia
234 D2 **Somerville** *NJ* U.S.A.
237 F5 **Somerville** *TN* U.S.A.
197 F2 **Someş** *r.* Romania
197 F2 **Someşan, Podişul** *plat.* Romania
197 F2 **Someşu Cald** *r.* Romania
197 F2 **Someşul Mare** *r.* Romania
197 F2 **Someşului, Câmpia** *plain* Romania
197 F2 **Someşu Mic** *r.* Romania
233 □I2 **Somesville** *ME* U.S.A.
175 J3 **Somianka** Pol.
139 J2 **Somino** Rus. Fed.
215 I3 **Somkele** S. Africa
176 G4 **Somlóvásárhely** Hungary
191 F3 **Sommacampagna** Italy
190 D3 **Somma Lombardo** Italy
190 C4 **Sommariva del Bosco** Italy
194 C5 **Sommatino** *Sicilia* Italy
156 C3 **Somme** *dept Picardie* France
160 B2 **Somme** *r.* France
165 A4 **Somme** *r.* France
157 F3 **Sommedieue** France
165 E4 **Somme-Leuze** Belgium
143 F2 **Sommen** Sweden
143 F2 **Sommen** *l.* Sweden
156 E3 **Sommepy-Tahure** France
171 C4 **Sömmerda** Ger.
170 E3 **Sommerfeld** Ger.
171 C3 **Sommersdorf** Ger.
156 E3 **Somme-Soude** *r.* France
156 E4 **Sommesous** France
156 E3 **Somme-Suippe** France
157 E4 **Sommevoire** France
161 C5 **Sommières** France
162 C2 **Sommières-du-Clain** France
116 B5 **Somnath** *Gujarat* India
176 G5 **Somogy** *county* Hungary
177 G5 **Somogyapáti** Hungary
177 G5 **Somogyjád** Hungary
177 G5 **Somogysárd** Hungary
176 G5 **Somogyszentpál** Hungary
176 G5 **Somogyszob** Hungary
226 C5 **Somonauk** *IL* U.S.A.
174 G1 **Somonino** Pol.
185 H3 **Somontín** Spain
79 □1 **Somosomo** *Taveuni* Fiji
242 □I6 **Somotillo** Nic.
242 □I6 **Somoto** Nic.
137 J2 **Somovo** Rus. Fed.
115 E2 **Sompeta** *Andhra Prad.* India
174 G3 **Sompolno** Pol.
151 G4 **Sompting** *West Sussex, England* U.K.
156 E4 **Sompuis** France
197 E3 **Šomrda** *hill* Yugo.
259 D6 **Somuncurá, Mesa Volcánica de** *plat.* Arg.
114 B3 **Somvarpet** *Karnataka* India
165 D4 **Somzée** Belgium
117 F4 **Son** *r.* India
164 E3 **Son** Neth.
142 D2 **Son** Norway
191 F3 **Sona** Italy
242 □J8 **Soná** Panama
175 I3 **Sona** *r.* Pol.
Sonag *Qinghai* China *see* **Zêkog**
117 H4 **Sonai** *r.* India
117 H4 **Sonai** *r.* India
117 E5 **Sonakhan** *Madh. Prad.* India
116 D5 **Sonala** *Mahar.* India
121 G2 **Sonaly** Kazakh.
117 F5 **Sonamukhi** *W. Bengal* India
117 E5 **Sonapur** *Orissa* India
117 H4 **Sonari** *Assam* India
190 C1 **Sonceboz** Switz.
101 C5 **Sŏnch'ŏn** N. Korea
183 G2 **Soncillo** Spain
190 E3 **Soncino** Italy
190 F2 **Sondalo** Italy
142 C4 **Sønderå** *r.* Denmark
142 C4 **Sønderborg** Denmark
142 C4 **Sønderjylland** *county* Denmark
142 C4 **Sønder Omme** Denmark
169 F4 **Sondershausen** Ger.
142 D4 **Søndersø** Denmark
142 C3 **Sønderup** Denmark
Søndre Strømfjord Greenland *see* **Kangerlussuaq**
190 E2 **Sondrio** Italy
190 E2 **Sondrio** *prov. Lombardia* Italy
187 C5 **Soneja** Spain
114 C2 **Sonepet** *Mahar.* India
234 B1 **Sonestown** *PA* U.S.A.
207 I4 **Song** Nigeria
116 B5 **Songad** *Gujarat* India
Songbai *Hubei* China *see* **Shennongjia**
109 E2 **Songbu** *Hubei* China
97 E4 **Sông Cau** Vietnam
Songcheng *Fujian* China *see* **Xiapu**
97 D5 **Sông Co Chiên** *r. mouth* Vietnam
211 B7 **Songea** Tanz.
156 B3 **Songeons** France
101 C4 **Sŏnggan** N. Korea
97 D5 **Sông Ham Luông** *r. mouth* Vietnam
100 E3 **Songhua Jiang** *r.* China
Songjiachuan *Shaanxi* China *see* **Wubu**
100 D4 **Songjiang** *Jilin* China
109 G2 **Songjiang** *Shanghai* China
101 C4 **Songjianghe** *Jilin* China
Sŏngjin N. Korea *see* **Kimch'aek**
108 C2 **Songkan** *Guizhou* China
97 C6 **Songkhla** Thai.
96 D3 **Song Khram, Mae Nam** *r.* Thai.
121 H4 **Songköl** *l.* Kyrg.
107 I2 **Songling** *Nei Mongol* China
107 H3 **Song Ling** *mts* China
Songmai *Sichuan* China *see* **Dêrong**
108 B3 **Songming** *Yunnan* China
101 C5 **Sŏngnam** S. Korea
101 C5 **Songnim** N. Korea
209 B6 **Songo** Angola
213 G2 **Songo** Moz.
Songololo Dem. Rep. Congo *see* **Mbanza-Ngungu**
209 B6 **Songololo** Dem. Rep. Congo
108 B1 **Songpan** *Sichuan* China
117 G4 **Songsak** *Meghalaya* India
101 C6 **Sŏngsan** S. Korea
Songshan *Guizhou* China *see* **Ziyun**
107 G5 **Song Shan** *mt. Henan* China
108 D2 **Songtao** *Guizhou* China
109 F3 **Songxi** *Fujian* China
107 G5 **Songxian** *Henan* China
Songyang *Yunnan* China *see* **Songming**
Songyuan *Fujian* China *see* **Songxi**
100 C3 **Songyuan** *Jilin* China
109 D2 **Songzi** *Hubei* China
117 E5 **Sonhat** *Madh. Prad.* India
Sonid Youqi *Nei Mongol* China *see* **Saihan Tal**
Sonid Zuoqi *Nei Mongol* China *see* **Mandalt**
182 C3 **Sonim** Port.
116 D3 **Sonipat** *Haryana* India
116 D5 **Sonkach** *Madh. Prad.* India
134 D3 **Sonkajärvi** Fin.
Sonkël', Ozero *l.* Kyrg. *see* **Songköl**
139 K3 **Sonkovo** Rus. Fed.
96 C2 **Sơn La** Vietnam
123 F5 **Sonmiani Bay** Pak.
178 D3 **Sonnblick** *mt.* Austria
171 C5 **Sonneberg** Ger.
169 F5 **Sonneborn** Ger.
171 C5 **Sonnefeld** Ger.
178 D3 **Sonnenjoch** *mt.* Austria
171 E4 **Sonnewalde** Ger.
151 G3 **Sonning Common** *Oxfordshire, England* U.K.
193 F3 **Sonnino** Italy
179 F3 **Sonntagberg** Austria
257 E2 **Sono** *r. Minas Gerais* Brazil
254 C4 **Sono** *r. Tocantins* Brazil
241 L6 **Sonoita** *AZ* U.S.A.
240 F2 **Sonoma** *CA* U.S.A.
215 F1 **Sonop** S. Africa
242 C2 **Sonora** *r.* Mex.
242 C2 **Sonora** *state* Mex.
240 G3 **Sonora** *CA* U.S.A.
237 C6 **Sonora** *TX* U.S.A.
240 H2 **Sonora Peak** *CA* U.S.A.
122 A3 **Sonqor** Iran
183 G5 **Sonseca** Spain
187 G5 **Son Servera** Spain
175 I3 **Sońsk** Pol.
250 C3 **Sonsón** Col.
243 H6 **Sonsonate** El Salvador
91 H5 **Sonsorol Islands** Palau
214 D2 **Sonstraal** S. Africa
96 D2 **Sơn Tây** Vietnam
173 E3 **Sontheim** Ger.
173 E3 **Sontheim an der Brenz** Ger.
173 E4 **Sonthofen** Ger.
169 E4 **Sontra** Ger.
215 G4 **Sonwabile** S. Africa
Soochow *Jiangsu* China *see* **Suzhou**
138 E2 **Soodla** *r.* Estonia
Soomaaliya *country* Africa *see* **Somalia**
163 A5 **Soorts-Hossegor** France
261 I2 **Sopas** *r.* Uru.
186 D2 **Sopeira** Spain
231 D5 **Soperton** *GA* U.S.A.
161 F5 **Sophia-Antipolis** France
196 E5 **Sopište** Macedonia
197 G4 **Sopot** Bulg.
143 H4 **Sopot** Pol.
196 E3 **Sopot** *Srbija* Yugo.
108 A5 **Sop Prap** Thai.
176 F4 **Sopron** Hungary
176 F4 **Sopronkövesd** Hungary
183 G1 **Sopuerta** Spain
116 C2 **Sopur** Jammu and Kashmir
93 C2 **Soputan, Gunung** *vol.* Indon.
78 □4a **Sopweru** *i. Chuuk* Micronesia
111 F5 **Soq Qu** *r. Xizang* China
163 E5 **Sor** *r.* France
184 B2 **Sôr** *r.* Port.
182 C1 **Sor** *r.* Spain
193 F3 **Sora** Italy
179 F4 **Sora** *r.* Slovenia
114 B3 **Sorab** *Karnataka* India
191 G2 **Soraga** Italy
190 F4 **Soragna** Italy
141 L3 **Söråker** Sweden
101 D5 **Sŏrak-san** *mt.* S. Korea
192 D2 **Sorano** Italy
191 H2 **Sorapis** *mt.* Italy
252 C3 **Sorata** Bol.
142 B2 **Sør-Audnedal** Norway
185 H3 **Sorbas** Spain
183 G4 **Sorbe** *r.* Spain
146 D7 **Sorbie** *Dumfries and Galloway, Scotland* U.K.
190 F4 **Sorbolo** Italy
157 F4 **Sorcy-St-Martin** France
163 A5 **Sorde-l'Abbaye** France
163 B4 **Sore** France
163 E6 **Sorède** France
221 K5 **Sorel** *Que.* Can.
83 F5 **Sorell** *Tas.* Austr.
128 B4 **Soreq** *r.* Israel
190 E3 **Soresina** Italy
163 E5 **Sorèze** France
169 F4 **Sorge** Ger.
168 E1 **Sorge** *r.* Ger.
162 C3 **Sorges** France
192 B4 **Sorgono** *Sardegna* Italy
161 C4 **Sorgues** France
161 A5 **Sorgues** *r.* France
128 B1 **Sorgun** *İçel* Turkey
126 D3 **Sorgun** *Yozgat* Turkey
128 B1 **Sorgun** *r.* Turkey
183 H3 **Soria** Spain
183 H3 **Soria** *prov. Castilla y León* Spain
261 H3 **Soriano** Uru.
261 I3 **Soriano** *dept* Uru.
195 F4 **Soriano Calabro** Italy
193 E2 **Soriano nel Cimino** Italy
182 E4 **Sorihuela** Spain
185 G2 **Sorihuela del Gaudalimar** Spain
94 B2 **Sorikmarapi** *vol.* Indon.
146 B5 **Sorisdale** *Argyll and Bute, Scotland* U.K.
140 □ **Sørkapp Land** *reg.* Svalbard
120 C3 **Sor Kaydak** *dry lake* Kazakh.
122 C3 **Sorkh, Kūh-e** *mts* Iran
122 C3 **Sorkheh** Iran
128 A1 **Sorkun** Turkey
175 J2 **Sorkwity** Pol.
140 K2 **Sørland** Norway
120 C3 **Sor Mertvyy Kultuk** *dry lake* Kazakh.
140 M3 **Sörmjöle** Sweden
156 E3 **Sormonne** *r.* France
148 E2 **Sorn** *East Ayrshire, Scotland* U.K.
162 E3 **Sornac** France
172 B4 **Sorne** *r.* Switz.
142 D4 **Sorø** Denmark
117 F5 **Soro** *Orissa* India
194 D5 **Soro, Monte** *mt. Sicilia* Italy
136 E3 **Soroca** Moldova
256 D5 **Sorocaba** Brazil
120 C1 **Sorochinsk** Rus. Fed.
Soroki Moldova *see* **Soroca**
121 K1 **Sorokino** Rus. Fed.
Sorokino *Luhans'ka Oblast'* Ukr. *see* **Krasnodon**
91 J5 **Sorol** *atoll* Micronesia
93 D3 **Sorong** *Irian Jaya* Indon.
138 G3 **Sorot'** *r.* Rus. Fed.
210 B4 **Soroti** Uganda
140 M1 **Sørøya** *i.* Norway
140 M1 **Sørøysundet** *sea chan.* Norway
Sorp Turkey *see* **Reşadıye**
192 A4 **Sorradile** *Sardegna* Italy
184 B1 **Sorraia** *r.* Port.
140 L1 **Sørreisa** Norway
193 G4 **Sorrento** Italy
140 N3 **Sorsakoski** Fin.
140 O2 **Sorsatunturi** *hill* Fin.
140 L2 **Sorsele** Sweden
192 A4 **Sorso** *Sardegna* Italy
92 C3 **Sorsogon** Phil.
186 E2 **Sort** Spain
141 O3 **Sortavala** Rus. Fed.
182 C4 **Sortelha** Port.
195 E5 **Sortino** *Sicilia* Italy
140 K1 **Sortland** Norway
140 J3 **Sør-Trøndelag** *county* Norway
143 G2 **Sorunda** Sweden
168 E1 **Sörup** Ger.
Sõrve väin *sea chan.* Estonia/Latvia *see* **Irbe Strait**
185 G4 **Sorvilán** Spain
163 C4 **Sos** France
101 C5 **Sŏsan** S. Korea
143 E3 **Sösdala** Sweden
186 B2 **Sos del Rey Católico** Spain
139 J4 **Sosenskiy** Rus. Fed.
186 D3 **Soses** Spain
215 G1 **Soshanguve** S. Africa
175 M4 **Soshychne** Ukr.
194 C5 **Sosio** *r. Sicilia* Italy
139 J5 **Soskovo** Rus. Fed.
177 H4 **Sóskút** Hungary
139 L5 **Sosna** *r.* Rus. Fed.
260 C4 **Sosneado** *mt.* Arg.
174 F4 **Sośnie** Pol.
136 C2 **Sosnivka** *L'vivs'ka Oblast'* Ukr.
137 G2 **Sosnivka** *Sums'ka Oblast'* Ukr.
136 C2 **Sosnivka** *Ternopils'ka Oblast'* Ukr.
174 F2 **Sośno** Pol.
134 K3 **Sosnogorsk** *Respublika Komi* Rus. Fed.
136 D2 **Sosnove** Ukr.
121 I2 **Sosnovka** Kazakh.
134 I3 **Sosnovka** *Arkhangel'skaya Oblast'* Rus. Fed.
135 H5 **Sosnovka** *Tambovskaya Oblast'* Rus. Fed.
139 K2 **Sosnovka** *Vologod. Obl.* Rus. Fed.
139 H1 **Sosnovo** Rus. Fed.
135 I5 **Sosnovoborsk** Rus. Fed.
99 J1 **Sosnovo-Ozerskoye** Rus. Fed.
134 F2 **Sosnovyy** Rus. Fed.
Sosnovyy Bor Belarus *see* **Sasnovy Bor**
138 G2 **Sosnovyy Bor** Rus. Fed.
175 L4 **Sosnowica** Pol.
175 H5 **Sosnowiec** Pol.
Sosnowitz Pol. *see* **Sosnowiec**
175 L4 **Sosnówka** Pol.
137 G2 **Sosnytsya** Ukr.
161 F5 **Sospel** France
163 C6 **Sost** France
179 G4 **Šoštanj** Slovenia
130 H4 **Sos'va** Rus. Fed.
137 J4 **Sosyka** *r.* Rus. Fed.
207 F4 **Sota** *r.* Benin
260 B2 **Sotaquí** Chile
252 D2 **Sotério** *r.* Brazil
184 D3 **Sotiel Coronada** Spain
184 E2 **Sotillo** *r.* Spain
183 F4 **Sotillo de la Adrada** Spain
183 H3 **Sotillo del Rincón** Spain
140 O2 **Sotkamo** Fin.
260 E2 **Soto** Arg.
182 D1 **Soto** Spain
182 E2 **Soto de la Vega** Spain
183 G4 **Soto del Real** Spain
182 E1 **Soto de Ribera** Spain
245 E2 **Soto la Marina** Mex.
245 F2 **Soto La Marina** *r.* Mex.
183 G2 **Sotopalacios** Spain
183 H4 **Sotos** Spain
182 D4 **Sotoserrano** Spain
207 F4 **Sotouboua** Togo
182 E2 **Soto y Amio** Spain
183 F1 **Sotres** Spain
183 F2 **Sotresgudo** Spain
182 E1 **Sotrondio** Spain
Sotsgorodok *Donets'ka Oblast'* Ukr. *see* **Hirnyk**
192 B3 **Sotta** *Corse* France
156 B3 **Sotteville-lès-Rouen** France
194 D5 **Sotto di Troina** *r. Sicilia* Italy
191 H3 **Sottomarina** Italy
168 E2 **Sottrum** Ger.
141 M3 **Sottunga** *Åland* Fin.
185 H1 **Sotuélamos** Spain
243 H4 **Sotuta** Mex.
156 E3 **Souain-Perthes-lès-Hurlus** France
163 E5 **Soual** France
208 B4 **Souanké** Congo
161 B5 **Soubès** France
206 D5 **Soubré** Côte d'Ivoire
156 D4 **Soucy** France
198 D4 **Souda** *Kriti* Greece
84 D4 **Soudan** *N.T.* Austr.
158 E4 **Soudan** France
234 C2 **Souderton** *PA* U.S.A.
Soúdha *Kriti* Greece *see* **Souda**
163 C5 **Soueich** France
163 D6 **Soueix** France
159 I4 **Souesmes** France
157 H4 **Soufflenheim** France
199 E1 **Soufli** Greece
247 □2 **Soufrière** *vol.* Guadeloupe
247 □3 **Soufrière** St Lucia

Soufrière to Stawell
365

247 □3 Soufrière vol. St Vincent
247 □2 Soufrière Hills Montserrat
206 B4 Souguéta Guinea
163 D4 Souillac France
157 F3 Souilly France
205 G1 Souk Ahras Alg.
189 A7 Souk Ahras prov. Alg.
204 D2 Souk el Arbaâ du Rharb Morocco
180 D5 Souk el Had el Rharbia Morocco
180 C5 Souk Khemis du Sahel Morocco
180 D5 Souk Tleta Taghramet Morocco
180 D5 Souk-Tnine-de-Sidi-el-Yamani Morocco
101 C5 Sŏul S. Korea
162 A3 Soulac-sur-Mer France
156 E4 Soulaines-Dhuys France
163 D6 Soulan France
163 E6 Soulatgé France
159 F3 Soulgé-sur-Ouette France
158 E5 Soullans France
158 E2 Soulles r. France
157 H4 Soultz-sous-Forêts France
165 E4 Soumagne Belgium
163 B5 Soumoulou France
235 F2 Sound Beach NY U.S.A.
223 I4 Sounding Creek r. Alta Can.
156 C4 Souppes-sur-Loing France
163 B5 Souprosse France
128 B3 Soûr Lebanon
159 F3 Sourdeval France
254 C2 Soure Brazil
182 B4 Soure Port.
223 K5 Souris Man. Can.
225 I4 Souris P.E.I. Can.
223 L5 Souris r. Sask. Can.
Souriya country Asia see Syria
163 E6 Sournia France
182 C4 Souro Pires Port.
198 C2 Sourpi Greece
156 B4 Sours France
162 C3 Sourzac France
254 F3 Sousa Brazil
182 B3 Sousa r. Port.
Sousa Lara Angola see Bocoio
163 E4 Sousceyrac France
184 C2 Sousel Port.
182 B4 Souselas Port.
79 □3 Sous le Vent, Îles is Arch. de la Société Fr. Polynesia
205 H2 Sousse Tunisia
163 A5 Soustons France
214 B4 Sout r. S. Africa
234 B4 South r. MD U.S.A.
South Africa country Africa see South Africa, Republic of
212 E6 South Africa, Republic of country Africa
84 C2 South Alligator r. N.T. Austr.
151 F2 Southam Warwickshire, England U.K.
235 D2 South Amboy NJ U.S.A.
248 South America continent
224 D4 Southampton Ont. Can.
151 F4 Southampton Southampton, England U.K.
151 F4 Southampton admin. div. England U.K.
233 G4 Southampton NY U.S.A.
223 O1 Southampton Island Nunavut Can.
151 F4 Southampton Water est. England U.K.
115 G4 South Andaman i. Andaman & Nicobar Is India
232 E6 South Anna r. VA U.S.A.
149 H4 South Anston South Yorkshire, England U.K.
235 D2 Southard NJ U.S.A.
82 C2 South Australia state Austr.
265 L7 South Australian Basin sea feature Indian Ocean
237 F5 Southaven MS U.S.A.
146 D6 South Ayrshire admin. div. Scotland U.K.
239 F5 South Baldy mt. NM U.S.A.
149 H3 South Bank Redcar and Cleveland, England U.K.
231 D7 South Bay FL U.S.A.
224 D4 South Baymouth Ont. Can.
230 C3 South Bend IN U.S.A.
238 B2 South Bend WA U.S.A.
151 H3 South Benfleet Essex, England U.K.
151 H3 Southborough Kent, England U.K.
232 D6 South Boston VA U.S.A.
150 D4 South Brent Devon, England U.K.
81 D5 Southbridge South I. N.Z.
233 G3 Southbridge MA U.S.A.
225 J3 South Brook Nfld. Can.
215 H5 Southbroom S. Africa
233 G2 South Burlington VT U.S.A.
81 C6 Southburn South I. N.Z.
235 E1 Southbury CT U.S.A.
234 C1 South Canaan PA U.S.A.
231 D5 South Carolina state U.S.A.
149 I4 South Cave East Riding of Yorkshire, England U.K.
151 F3 South Cerney Gloucestershire, England U.K.
150 E4 South Chard Somerset, England U.K.
232 B5 South Charleston OH U.S.A.
232 C5 South Charleston WV U.S.A.
90 E4 South China Sea N. Pacific Ocean
South Coast Town Qld Austr. see Gold Coast
236 C2 South Dakota state U.S.A.
146 F6 Southdean Scottish Borders, Scotland U.K.
233 G3 South Deerfield MA U.S.A.
234 D3 South Dennis NJ U.S.A.
151 G4 South Downs hills England U.K.
83 F5 South East Cape Tas. Austr.
265 J7 Southeast Indian Ridge sea feature Indian Ocean
87 D7 South East Isles W.A. Austr.
267 L10 Southeast Pacific Basin sea feature S. Pacific Ocean
234 D3 South Egg Harbor NJ U.S.A.
223 K3 Southend Sask. Can.
146 C6 Southend Argyll and Bute, Scotland U.K.
151 H3 Southend admin. div. England U.K.
151 H3 Southend-on-Sea Southend, England U.K.
210 C3 Southern admin. reg. Eth.
211 B8 Southern admin. reg. Malawi
206 B5 Southern prov. Sierra Leone
209 E9 Southern prov. Zambia
Southern Aegean admin. reg. Greece see Notio Aigaio
81 C5 Southern Alps mts South I. N.Z.
81 □2 Southern Cook Islands Cook Is
87 C6 Southern Cross W.A. Austr.
208 E2 Southern Darfur state Sudan
223 L3 Southern Indian Lake Man. Can.
208 F2 Southern Kordofan state Sudan
77 I3 Southern Lau Group is Fiji
262 R3 Southern Ocean OCEAN
231 E5 Southern Pines NC U.S.A.
Southern Rhodesia country Africa see Zimbabwe
146 D6 Southern Uplands hills Scotland U.K.
Southern Urals mts Rus. Fed. see Yuzhnyy Ural
151 H2 Southery Norfolk, England U.K.
146 F5 South Esk r. Angus, Scotland U.K.
86 E3 South Esk Tableland reg. W.A. Austr.
223 J5 Southey Sask. Can.
215 F4 Southeyville S. Africa
236 F4 South Fabius r. MO U.S.A.
232 B3 Southfield MI U.S.A.
235 D1 Southfields NY U.S.A.
266 G7 South Fiji Basin sea feature S. Pacific Ocean
151 I3 South Foreland pt England U.K.
240 F1 South Fork CA U.S.A.
239 F4 South Fork CO U.S.A.
234 D2 South Fork PA U.S.A.
222 E5 Southgate r. B.C. Can.
151 G3 Southgate Greater London, England U.K.
263 H1 South Geomagnetic Pole (1995) Antarctica
264 G9 South Georgia terr. S. Atlantic Ocean
249 G7 South Georgia and South Sandwich Islands terr. S. Atlantic Ocean
234 C1 South Gibson PA U.S.A.
226 C1 South Gillies Ont. Can.
235 F1 South Glastonbury CT U.S.A.
150 E3 South Gloucestershire admin. div. England U.K.
236 E4 South Grand r. MO U.S.A.
151 G4 South Harting West Sussex, England U.K.
226 D4 South Haven MI U.S.A.
80 E2 South Head North I. N.Z.
233 G2 South Hero VT U.S.A.
149 H3 South Hetton Durham, England U.K.
232 D6 South Hill VA U.S.A.
266 E3 South Honshu Ridge sea feature N. Pacific Ocean
223 L3 South Indian Lake Man. Can.
235 F1 Southington CT U.S.A.
86 □2 South Island Cocos Is
81 D6 South Island N.Z.
210 C4 South Island National Park Kenya
223 M5 South Junction Man. Can.
South Kazakhstan Oblast admin. div. Kazakh. see Yuzhnyy Kazakhstan
149 I4 South Kelsey Lincolnshire, England U.K.
149 H4 South Kirkby West Yorkshire, England U.K.
117 F5 South Koel r. Bihar India
240 G2 South Lake Tahoe CA U.S.A.
146 E6 South Lanarkshire admin. div. Scotland U.K.
81 A6 Southland admin. reg. South I. N.Z.
151 H2 South Lopham Norfolk, England U.K.
236 D3 South Loup r. NE U.S.A.
235 F1 South Lyme CT U.S.A.
222 C2 South Macmillan r. Y.T. Can.
263 J2 South Magnetic Pole (1995) Antarctica
113 □1 South Male Atoll Maldives
151 H3 Southminster Essex, England U.K.
150 D3 South Molton Devon, England U.K.
234 A3 South Mountains hills PA U.S.A.
86 B4 South Muiron Island W.A. Austr.
222 D1 South Nahanni r. N.W.T. Can.
146 □G3 South Nesting Bay Scotland U.K.
233 F3 South New Berlin NY U.S.A.
151 H3 South Ockendon Thurrock, England U.K.
235 F1 Southold NY U.S.A.
264 G10 South Orkney Islands S. Atlantic Ocean
South Ossetia aut. reg. Georgia see Samkhret' Oset'i
151 G3 South Oxhey Hertfordshire, England U.K.
233 □H2 South Paris ME U.S.A.
87 B5 South Passage W.A. Austr.
231 D6 South Patrick Shores FL U.S.A.
150 E4 South Petherton Somerset, England U.K.
235 D2 South Plainfield NJ U.S.A.
236 C3 South Platte r. CO U.S.A.
262 T1 South Pole Antarctica
224 D3 South Porcupine Ont. Can.
85 H5 Southport Qld Austr.
83 F5 Southport Tas. Austr.
149 F4 Southport Merseyside, England U.K.
235 E1 Southport CT U.S.A.
231 E5 Southport NC U.S.A.
227 I4 Southport NY U.S.A.
233 □H3 South Portland ME U.S.A.
149 F2 South Queensferry Edinburgh, Scotland U.K.
227 H3 South River Ont. Can.
South Rona i. Highland, Scotland U.K. see Rona
146 F3 South Ronaldsay i. Scotland U.K.
233 G3 South Royalton VT U.S.A.
226 A3 South Saint Paul MN U.S.A.
264 H9 South Sandwich Islands S. Atlantic Ocean
264 H9 South Sandwich Trench sea feature S. Atlantic Ocean
240 F3 South San Francisco CA U.S.A.
223 J4 South Saskatchewan r. Alberta/Saskatchewan Can.
223 L3 South Seal r. Man. Can.
262 U2 South Shetland Islands Antarctica
264 E10 South Shetland Trough sea feature S. Atlantic Ocean
149 H2 South Shields Tyne and Wear, England U.K.
South Sinai governorate Egypt see Janûb Sînâ'
149 I4 South Skirlaugh East Riding of Yorkshire, England U.K.
236 E3 South Skunk r. IA U.S.A.
266 F6 South Solomon Trench sea feature Pacific Ocean
234 C1 South Sterling PA U.S.A.
234 C2 South Tamaqua PA U.S.A.
80 E3 South Taranaki Bight b. North I. N.Z.
265 N8 South Tasman Rise sea feature Southern Ocean
241 L2 South Tent mt. UT U.S.A.
235 D3 South Toms River NJ U.S.A.
116 E4 South Tons r. India
241 L5 South Tucson AZ U.S.A.
149 G3 South Tyne r. England U.K.
South Tyrol prov. Trentino - Alto Adige Italy see Bolzano
146 A4 South Uist i. Scotland U.K.
238 B3 South Umpqua r. OR U.S.A.
146 E3 South Walls pen. Scotland U.K.
151 G3 Southwater West Sussex, England U.K.
149 I4 Southwell Nottinghamshire, England U.K.
84 D3 South Wellesley Islands Qld Austr.
South-West Africa country Africa see Namibia
83 F5 South West Cape Tas. Austr.
81 A7 South West Cape Stewart I. N.Z.
85 H4 South West Cay rf Coral Sea Is Terr. Austr.
233 □I2 Southwest Harbor ME U.S.A.
265 G7 Southwest Indian Ridge sea feature Indian Ocean
85 G3 South West Island Coral Sea Is Terr. Austr.
267 I8 Southwest Pacific Basin sea feature S. Pacific Ocean
Southwest Peru Ridge sea feature S. Pacific Ocean see Nazca Ridge
83 H2 South West Rocks N.S.W. Austr.
226 E5 South Whitley IN U.S.A.
237 D5 South Wichita r. TX U.S.A.
150 E3 Southwick Wiltshire, England U.K.
232 B6 South Williamson KY U.S.A.
227 I5 South Williamsport PA U.S.A.
233 □H3 South Windham ME U.S.A.
151 I2 Southwold Suffolk, England U.K.
151 H3 South Woodham Ferrers Essex, England U.K.
151 H2 South Wootton Norfolk, England U.K.
149 H4 South Yorkshire admin. div. England U.K.
232 B5 South Zanesville OH U.S.A.
182 D4 Souto Guarda Port.
182 B5 Souto Santarém Port.
182 C2 Souto Spain
182 C4 Souto da Casa Port.
215 F3 Soutpan S. Africa
213 F4 Soutpansberg mts S. Africa
204 B5 Souttouf, Adrar mts Western Sahara
160 B2 Souvigny France
142 B1 Sovarnuten mt. Norway
197 G2 Sovata Romania
197 H2 Soveja Romania
195 F4 Soverato Italy
192 B2 Soveria Corse France
195 F3 Soveria Mannelli Italy
123 G2 Sovet Tajik.
Sovetabad Uzbek. see Khanabad
Sovetashen Armenia see Zangakatun
138 C4 Sovetsk Kaliningradskaya Oblast' Rus. Fed.
134 J4 Sovetsk Kirovskaya Oblast' Rus. Fed.
139 K5 Sovetsk Tul'skaya Oblast' Rus. Fed.
129 B1 Sovetskaya Krasnodarskiy Kray Rus. Fed.
129 D1 Sovetskaya Stavropol'skiy Kray Rus. Fed.
100 G2 Sovetskaya Gavan' Rus. Fed.
130 H3 Sovetskiy Khanty-Mansiyskiy Avtonomnyy Okrug Rus. Fed.
138 G1 Sovetskiy Leningradskaya Oblast' Rus. Fed.
134 N2 Sovetskiy Respublika Komi Rus. Fed.
134 J4 Sovetskiy Respublika Mariy El Rus. Fed.
Sovetskiy Tajik. see Sovet
137 J2 Sovetskoye Belgorodskaya Oblast' Rus. Fed.
Sovetskoye Chechenskaya Respublika Rus. Fed. see Shatoy
Sovetskoye Kabardino-Balkarskaya Respublika Rus. Fed. see Kashkhatau
Sovetskoye Respublika Dagestan Rus. Fed. see Khebda
120 A2 Sovetskoye Saratovskaya Oblast' Rus. Fed.
Sovetskoye Stavropol'skiy Kray Rus. Fed. see Zelenokumsk
188 F4 Sovići Bos.-Herz.
191 G5 Sovicille Italy
137 H5 Sovyets'kyy Ukr.
212 E4 Sowa Botswana
108 A2 Sowa Sichuan China
212 E4 Sowa Pan salt pan Botswana
149 H3 Sowerby North Yorkshire, England U.K.
149 H4 Sowerby Bridge West Yorkshire, England U.K.
215 F2 Soweto S. Africa
Sōya-kaikyō str. Japan/Rus. Fed. see La Pérouse Strait
243 G5 Soyaló Mex.
134 H2 Soyana r. Rus. Fed.
162 C3 Soyaux France
160 E1 Soye France
173 G3 Soyen Ger.
Soylan Armenia see Vayk'
134 J2 Soyma r. Rus. Fed.
209 B6 Soyo Angola
161 C4 Soyons France
Sozaq Kazakh. see Suzak
139 H5 Sozh r. Europe
134 K4 Sozimskiy Rus. Fed.
197 H4 Sozopol Bulg.
165 E4 Spa Belgium
262 T2 Spaatz Island Antarctica
172 B2 Spabrücken Ger.
195 E4 Spadafora Sicilia Italy
168 C3 Spahnharrenstätte Ger.
172 C3 Spaichingen Ger.
180 E2 Spain country Europe
Spalato Croatia see Split
Spalatum Croatia see Split
82 D3 Spalding S.A. Austr.
151 G2 Spalding Lincolnshire, England U.K.
176 C2 Spálené Poříčí Czech Rep.
173 E2 Spalt Ger.
169 E4 Spangenberg Ger.
150 D3 Span Head hill England U.K.
225 K4 Spaniard's Bay Nfld. Can.
224 D4 Spanish Ont. Can.
224 D4 Spanish r. Ont. Can.
241 L1 Spanish Fork UT U.S.A.
Spanish Guinea country Africa see Equatorial Guinea
Spanish Netherlands country Europe see Belgium
145 C5 Spanish Point Rep. of Ireland
Spanish Sahara terr. Africa see Western Sahara
246 □ Spanish Town Jamaica
246 C1 Spanish Wells Eleuthera Bahamas
170 E2 Spantekow Ger.
194 B4 Sparagio, Monte mt. Sicilia Italy
193 G3 Sparanise Italy
240 H2 Sparks NV U.S.A.
232 B3 Sparlingville MI U.S.A.
234 D1 Sparrow Bush NY U.S.A.
Sparta Greece see Sparti
195 E4 Spartà Sicilia Italy
231 D5 Sparta GA U.S.A.
226 E4 Sparta MI U.S.A.
232 C6 Sparta NC U.S.A.
234 D1 Sparta NJ U.S.A.
231 C5 Sparta TN U.S.A.
226 B4 Sparta WI U.S.A.
231 D5 Spartanburg SC U.S.A.
232 D4 Spartansburg PA U.S.A.
198 C3 Sparti Greece
195 F5 Spartivento, Capo c. Italy
222 H5 Sparwood B.C. Can.
139 J4 Spas-Demensk Rus. Fed.
137 H3 Spas'ke Ukr.
139 M4 Spas-Klepiki Rus. Fed.
137 I3 Spas'ko-Mykhaylivka Ukr.
137 G3 Spasove Ukr.
100 E3 Spassk-Dal'niy Rus. Fed.
139 M4 Spassk-Ryazanskiy Rus. Fed.
169 C5 Spay Ger.
146 D5 Spean Bridge Highland, Scotland U.K.
236 C2 Spearfish SD U.S.A.
237 C4 Spearman TX U.S.A.
195 H3 Specchia Italy
233 F3 Speculator NY U.S.A.
151 F3 Speen West Berkshire, England U.K.
190 E1 Speer mt. Switz.
223 J4 Speers Sask. Can.
172 A2 Speicher Ger.
173 F2 Speichersdorf Ger.
247 □4 Speightstown Barbados
179 G3 Speikkogel mt. Austria
211 B5 Speke Gulf Tanz.
169 C3 Spelle Ger.
193 E2 Spello Italy
146 C5 Spelve, Loch inlet Scotland U.K.
Spence Bay Nunavut Can. see Taloyoak
236 E3 Spencer IA U.S.A.
238 D2 Spencer ID U.S.A.
230 C4 Spencer IN U.S.A.
233 H3 Spencer MA U.S.A.
236 D3 Spencer NE U.S.A.
227 I4 Spencer NY U.S.A.
232 C6 Spencer VA U.S.A.
232 C5 Spencer WV U.S.A.
82 D3 Spencer, Cape S.A. Austr.
212 B5 Spencer Bay Namibia
82 D3 Spencer Gulf est. S.A. Austr.
84 B2 Spencer Range hills N.T. Austr.
222 F5 Spences Bridge B.C. Can.
169 D3 Spenge Ger.
149 H3 Spennymoor Durham, England U.K.
81 D5 Spenser Mountains South I. N.Z.
198 C2 Spercheios r. Greece
171 E3 Sperenberg Ger.
Sperkhiós r. Greece see Spercheios
194 D5 Sperlinga Sicilia Italy
193 F3 Sperlonga Italy
197 G2 Spermezeu Romania
147 D2 Sperrin Mountains hills Northern Ireland U.K.
232 D5 Sperryville VA U.S.A.
169 E6 Spessart reg. Ger.
Spétsai i. Greece see Spetses
198 C3 Spetses Greece
198 C3 Spetses i. Greece
146 E4 Spey r. Scotland U.K.
146 E4 Spey Bay Moray, Scotland U.K.
172 C2 Speyer Ger.
158 C3 Spézet France
193 I5 Spezzano Albanese Italy
Spice Islands Indon. see Maluku
175 K4 Spiczyn Pol.
147 B3 Spiddal Rep. of Ireland
173 H3 Spiegelau Ger.
168 C2 Spiekeroog Ger.
168 C2 Spiekeroog i. Ger.
179 F3 Spielberg bei Knittelfeld Austria
179 G4 Spielfeld Austria
172 B2 Spiesen-Elversberg Ger.
190 C2 Spiez Switz.
190 D4 Spigno Monferrato Italy
193 G3 Spigno Saturnia Italy
164 F1 Spijk Neth.
164 D3 Spijkenisse Neth.
191 G4 Spilamberto Italy
191 H2 Spilimbergo Italy
195 F5 Spilinga Italy
149 J4 Spilsby Lincolnshire, England U.K.
193 I4 Spinazzola Italy
157 F3 Spincourt France
191 H3 Spinea Italy
193 F2 Spinetoli Italy
234 C2 Spinnerstown PA U.S.A.
193 H4 Spinoso Italy
177 L4 Spinuș Romania
236 E3 Spirit Lake IA U.S.A.
238 C1 Spirit Lake ID U.S.A.
223 J4 Spiritwood Sask. Can.
139 J3 Spirovo Rus. Fed.
176 G6 Špišić-Bukovica Croatia
177 J2 Spišská Belá Slovakia
177 J3 Spišská Nová Ves Slovakia
177 J2 Spišská Stará Ves Slovakia
177 J3 Spišské Podhradie Slovakia
177 J3 Spišské Vlachy Slovakia
177 J2 Spišský Štvrtok Slovakia
129 D3 Spitak Armenia
179 F3 Spital am Pyhrn Austria
179 G3 Spital am Semmering Austria
116 D3 Spiti r. India
86 C4 Spit Point W.A. Austr.
140 □ Spitsbergen i. Svalbard
214 D5 Spitskop mt. S. Africa
215 F4 Spitskopvlei S. Africa
179 E4 Spittal an der Drau Austria
146 E5 Spittal of Glenshee Perth and Kinross, Scotland U.K.
179 G2 Spitz Austria
Spitzbergen i. Svalbard see Spitsbergen
178 D4 Spitzkofel mt. Austria
190 E1 Spitzmeilen mt. Switz.
137 J3 Spivakivka Ukr.
151 I2 Spixworth Norfolk, England U.K.
142 C3 Spjald Denmark
188 F4 Split Croatia
223 L3 Split Lake Man. Can.
190 E2 Splügen Switz.
136 E3 Spodakhy Ukr.
179 F4 Spodnja Idrija Slovenia
179 G4 Spodnje Hoče Slovenia
168 F1 Spodsbjerg Denmark
149 H3 Spofforth North Yorkshire, England U.K.
238 C2 Spokane WA U.S.A.
238 C2 Spokane r. WA U.S.A.
129 B1 Spokoynaya Rus. Fed.
190 F2 Spöl r. Italy
Spoletium Italy see Spoleto
193 E2 Spoleto Italy
193 G2 Spoltore Italy
191 F2 Spondigna Italy
165 E4 Spontin Belgium
226 B5 Spoon r. IL U.S.A.
226 B3 Spooner WI U.S.A.
171 D4 Spora Ger.
170 C2 Spornitz Ger.
234 B2 Sporting Hill PA U.S.A.
190 D4 Spotorno Italy
235 D2 Spotswood NJ U.S.A.
232 E5 Spotsylvania VA U.S.A.
238 F2 Spotted Horse WY U.S.A.
227 F2 Spragge Ont. Can.
238 B3 Sprague r. OR U.S.A.
172 D3 Spraitbach Ger.
168 F3 Sprakensehl Ger.
222 F4 Spranger, Mount B.C. Can.
90 D5 Spratly Island S. China Sea
90 D5 Spratly Islands S. China Sea
238 C2 Spray OR U.S.A.
226 C3 Spread Eagle WI U.S.A.
188 G3 Spreča r. Bos.-Herz.
171 E3 Spree r. Ger.
171 E3 Spreenhagen Ger.
172 C4 Spreitenbach Switz.
171 F4 Spremberg Ger.
172 B2 Sprendlingen Ger.
191 H3 Spresiano Italy
190 E2 Spriana Italy
165 E4 Sprimont Belgium
237 E4 Spring r. MO U.S.A.
227 F3 Spring Bay Ont. Can.
214 A3 Springbok S. Africa
234 C2 Spring City PA U.S.A.
241 L2 Spring City UT U.S.A.
84 D3 Spring Creek r. N.T. Austr.
236 C3 Spring Creek r. NE U.S.A.
225 K3 Springdale Nfld. Can.
237 E4 Springdale AR U.S.A.
169 E3 Springe Ger.
239 F4 Springer NM U.S.A.
241 M4 Springerville AZ U.S.A.
81 C5 Springfield South I. N.Z.
147 D2 Springfield Northern Ireland U.K.
237 C4 Springfield CO U.S.A.
231 D5 Springfield GA U.S.A.
238 D3 Springfield ID U.S.A.
236 F4 Springfield IL U.S.A.
230 C4 Springfield KY U.S.A.
233 G3 Springfield MA U.S.A.
233 □I2 Springfield ME U.S.A.
236 E2 Springfield MN U.S.A.
237 E4 Springfield MO U.S.A.
232 B5 Springfield OH U.S.A.
238 B2 Springfield OR U.S.A.
234 C3 Springfield PA U.S.A.
231 C4 Springfield TN U.S.A.
233 G3 Springfield VT U.S.A.
232 D5 Springfield WV U.S.A.
215 E4 Springfontein S. Africa
251 G3 Spring Garden Guyana
235 D1 Spring Glen NY U.S.A.
234 B2 Spring Glen PA U.S.A.
241 L2 Spring Glen UT U.S.A.
226 B4 Spring Green WI U.S.A.
226 B4 Spring Grove MN U.S.A.
234 B3 Spring Grove PA U.S.A.
232 D6 Spring Grove VA U.S.A.
225 H4 Springhill N.S. Can.
231 D6 Spring Hill FL U.S.A.
146 E6 Springholm Dumfries and Galloway, Scotland U.K.
222 F5 Springhouse B.C. Can.
226 D4 Spring Lake MI U.S.A.
235 D2 Spring Lake Heights NJ U.S.A.
241 J3 Spring Mountains NV U.S.A.
226 E4 Springport MI U.S.A.
215 G2 Springs S. Africa
235 F1 Springs NY U.S.A.
81 B5 Springs Junction South I. N.Z.
85 G5 Springsure Qld Austr.
85 E4 Springvale Qld Austr.
215 F5 Spring Valley S. Africa
240 I5 Spring Valley CA U.S.A.
226 A4 Spring Valley MN U.S.A.
235 D1 Spring Valley NY U.S.A.
226 A3 Spring Valley WI U.S.A.
236 D3 Springview NE U.S.A.
240 H3 Springville CA U.S.A.
232 D3 Springville NY U.S.A.
234 C1 Springville PA U.S.A.
241 L1 Springville UT U.S.A.
232 E3 Springwater NY U.S.A.
149 I4 Sproatley East Riding of Yorkshire, England U.K.
169 C4 Sprockhövel Ger.
151 I2 Sprowston Norfolk, England U.K.
222 H4 Spruce Grove Alta Can.
232 D5 Spruce Knob mt. WV U.S.A.
241 M2 Spruce Mountain CO U.S.A.
241 J1 Spruce Mountain NV U.S.A.
164 D3 Sprundel Neth.
234 B3 Spry PA U.S.A.
149 J4 Spurn Head hd England U.K.
220 C5 Spurr, Mount vol. AK U.S.A.
222 F5 Spuzzum B.C. Can.
175 J2 Spychowo Pol.
222 F5 Squamish B.C. Can.
222 F5 Squamish r. B.C. Can.
191 G3 Squaranto r. Italy
195 F4 Squillace Italy
195 F4 Squillace, Golfo di g. Italy
195 H2 Squinzano Italy
232 C6 Squire WV U.S.A.
87 E5 Squires, Mount hill W.A. Austr.
95 E4 Sragen Jawa Tengah Indon.
196 E4 Srbica Kosovo, Srbija Yugo.
196 E4 Srbija aut. rep. Yugo.
Srbinje Bos.-Herz. see Foča
Srbobran Bos.-Herz. see Donji Vakuf
196 D3 Srbobran Vojvodina, Srbija Yugo.
197 H3 Srebărna tourist site Bulg.
188 G3 Srebrenica Bos.-Herz.
197 H4 Sredets Burgas Bulg.
Sredets Grad Sofiya Bulg. see Sofiya
197 H4 Sredetska Reka r. Bulg.
131 Q4 Sredinnyy Khrebet mts Rus. Fed.
179 H4 Središče Slovenia
197 H4 Sredishte Bulg.
197 F4 Sredna Gora mts Bulg.
100 C2 Srednebelaya Rus. Fed.
131 Q3 Srednekolymsk Rus. Fed.
139 K4 Sredne-Russkaya Vozvyshennost' hills Rus. Fed.
131 M3 Sredne-Sibirskoye Ploskogor'ye plat. Rus. Fed.
137 J2 Sredniy Ikorets Rus. Fed.
197 G4 Srednogorie Bulg.
135 I6 Srednyaya Akhtuba Rus. Fed.
174 F3 Śrem Pol.
196 D3 Sremska Mitrovica Vojvodina, Srbija Yugo.
97 D4 Srêpok, Tônlé r. Cambodia
99 K1 Sretensk Rus. Fed.
95 E2 Sri Aman Sarawak Malaysia
137 G2 Sribne Ukr.
114 D3 Sriharikota Island India
114 C5 Sri Jayewardenepura Kotte Sri Lanka
115 E2 Srikakulam Andhra Prad. India
114 C3 Sri Kalahasti Andhra Prad. India
114 D5 Sri Lanka country Asia
116 C4 Sri Madhopur Rajasthan India
117 G4 Srimangal Bangl.
116 D3 Srinagar Uttar Prad. India
116 C2 Srinagar Jammu and Kashmir India
114 B3 Sringeri Karnataka India
114 D5 Sri Pada mt. Sri Lanka
114 C4 Srirangam Tamil Nadu India
114 C4 Srisailam Andhra Prad. India
114 C4 Srivaikuntam Tamil Nadu India
114 B2 Srivardhan Mahar. India
114 C4 Srivilliputtur Tamil Nadu India
188 F3 Srnetica mts Bos.-Herz.
188 G3 Srnice Bos.-Herz.
175 J1 Srockowo Pol.
174 E4 Środa Śląska Pol.
174 F3 Środa Wielkopolska Pol.
146 D4 Sron a' Choire Ghairbh hill Scotland U.K.
121 K1 Srostki Rus. Fed.
196 E3 Srpska Crnja Vojvodina, Srbija Yugo.
Srpska Kostajnica Bos.-Herz. see Bosanska Kostajnica
Srpski Brod Bos.-Herz. see Bosanski Brod
196 E3 Srpski Itebej Vojvodina, Srbija Yugo.
115 D2 Srungavarapukota Andhra Prad. India
139 L5 Sselki Rus. Fed.
214 C2 Staansaam S. Africa
85 E3 Staaten r. Qld Austr.
179 H2 Staatz Austria
165 D3 Stabroek Belgium
Stabroek Guyana see Georgetown
176 C2 Stachy Czech Rep.
146 C3 Stac Pollaidh hill Scotland U.K.
Stac Polly hill Scotland U.K. see Stac Pollaidh
226 A3 Stacy MN U.S.A.
226 A4 Stacyville IA U.S.A.
168 E2 Stade Ger.
173 G4 Stadelhorn mt. Ger.
165 C4 Staden Belgium
168 F3 Stadensen Ger.
151 F3 Stadhampton Oxfordshire, England U.K.
146 A4 Stadhlaigearraidh Western Isles, Scotland U.K.
179 E2 Stadl-Paura Austria
164 F2 Stadskanaal Neth.
169 E5 Stadtallendorf Ger.
173 E3 Stadtbergen Ger.
169 E3 Stadthagen Ger.
171 C5 Stadtilm Ger.
169 B5 Stadtkyll Ger.
169 F5 Stadtlauringen Ger.
169 F5 Stadtlengsfeld Ger.
169 B4 Stadtlohn Ger.
169 E4 Stadtoldendorf Ger.
172 D2 Stadtprozelten Ger.
171 C5 Stadtroda Ger.
179 H3 Stadtschlaining Austria
171 C5 Stadtsteinach Ger.
168 E1 Stadum Ger.
190 D1 Stäfa Switz.
146 B5 Staffa i. Scotland U.K.
171 C5 Staffelberg hill Ger.
157 H5 Staffelfelden France
169 F5 Staffelstein Ger.
168 D3 Staffhorst Ger.
146 B4 Staffin Highland, Scotland U.K.
191 I5 Staffolo Italy
190 E3 Staffora r. Italy
150 E2 Stafford Staffordshire, England U.K.
232 E5 Stafford VA U.S.A.
246 C1 Stafford Creek Andros Bahamas
150 E2 Staffordshire admin. div. England U.K.
215 G4 Stafford's Post S. Africa
233 G4 Stafford Springs CT U.S.A.
173 H2 Štåhlavy Czech Rep.
232 D4 Stahlstown PA U.S.A.
171 E3 Stahnsdorf Ger.
138 E3 Staicele Latvia
172 D3 Staig Ger.
193 H3 Staina r. Italy
179 F3 Stainach Austria
149 H3 Staindrop Durham, England U.K.
151 G3 Staines Surrey, England U.K.
149 G3 Stainforth North Yorkshire, England U.K.
149 H4 Stainforth South Yorkshire, England U.K.
149 I3 Staintondale North Yorkshire, England U.K.
157 F4 Stainville France
179 G4 Stainz Austria
195 F5 Staìti Italy
177 L3 Stakčín Slovakia
146 D6 Stake, Hill of hill Scotland U.K.
137 J3 Stakhanov Ukr.
Stakhanovo Rus. Fed. see Zhukovskiy
150 E4 Stalbridge Dorset, England U.K.
190 C2 Stalden Switz.
151 I2 Stalham Norfolk, England U.K.
Stalin Bulg. see Varna
222 E3 Stalin, Mount B.C. Can.
Stalinabad Tajik. see Dushanbe
Stalingrad Rus. Fed. see Volgograd
Stalingradskaya Oblast' admin. div. Rus. Fed. see Volgogradskaya Oblast'
Staliniri Georgia see Ts'khinvali
Stalino Ukr. see Donets'k
Stalino Uzbek. see Shakhrikhan
Stalinogorsk Rus. Fed. see Novomoskovsk
Stalinogród Pol. see Katowice
Stalinsk Rus. Fed. see Novokuznetsk
178 E4 Stall Austria
143 G2 Stallarholmen Sweden
179 G3 Stallhofen Austria
149 G3 Stalling Busk North Yorkshire, England U.K.
173 G2 Stallwang Ger.
175 K5 Stalowa Wola Pol.
197 H3 Stâlpu Romania
149 G4 Stalybridge Greater Manchester, England U.K.
197 G4 Stamboliyski Bulg.
85 E4 Stamford Qld Austr.
151 G2 Stamford Lincolnshire, England U.K.
233 G4 Stamford CT U.S.A.
233 F3 Stamford NY U.S.A.
237 D5 Stamford TX U.S.A.
149 I4 Stamford Bridge East Riding of Yorkshire, England U.K.
149 H2 Stamfordham Northumberland, England U.K.
171 C5 Stammbach Ger.
173 F3 Stammham Ger.
Stampalia i. Greece see Astypalaia
212 C5 Stampriet Namibia
178 B3 Stams Austria
173 G2 Stamsried Ger.
140 K1 Stamsund Norway
147 E3 Stamullen Rep. of Ireland
232 D5 Stanardsville VA U.S.A.
236 E3 Stanberry MO U.S.A.
222 H5 Standard Alta Can.
164 D3 Standdaarbuiten Neth.
215 G2 Standerton S. Africa
149 G4 Standish Greater Manchester, England U.K.
227 F4 Standish MI U.S.A.
151 H3 Standon Hertfordshire, England U.K.
148 F2 Stane North Lanarkshire, Scotland U.K.
197 G3 Stănești Romania
241 L5 Stanfield AZ U.S.A.
214 B6 Stanford S. Africa
230 C4 Stanford KY U.S.A.
238 E2 Stanford MT U.S.A.
151 H3 Stanford-le-Hope Thurrock, England U.K.
143 H3 Stånga Gotland Sweden
143 G3 Stångån r. Sweden
193 H4 St'Angelo a Fasanella Italy
193 H4 St'Angelo dei Lombardi Italy
140 O1 Stangenestind hill Norway
215 H3 Stanger S. Africa
151 H2 Stanhoe Norfolk, England U.K.
149 G3 Stanhope Durham, England U.K.
234 D2 Stanhope NJ U.S.A.
197 I2 Stănilești Romania
175 K4 Stanin Pol.
196 D3 Stanišić Vojvodina, Srbija Yugo.
Stanislav Ivano-Frankivs'ka Oblast' Ukr. see Ivano-Frankivs'k
137 G4 Stanislav Khersons'ka Oblast' Ukr.
175 M5 Stanislavchyk Ukr.
175 J3 Stanisławów Pol.
197 G2 Stânișoarei, Munții mts Romania
Stanke Dimitrov Bulg. see Dupnitsa
176 C2 Staňkov Czech Rep.
83 F5 Stanley Tas. Austr.
233 □J1 Stanley N.B. Can.
109 □ Stanley H.K. China
259 F8 Stanley Falkland Is
149 H3 Stanley Durham, England U.K.
146 E5 Stanley Perth and Kinross, Scotland U.K.
238 D2 Stanley ID U.S.A.
236 C1 Stanley ND U.S.A.
232 D5 Stanley VA U.S.A.
226 B3 Stanley WI U.S.A.
84 B4 Stanley, Mount hill N.T. Austr.
83 F5 Stanley, Mount hill Tas. Austr.
Stanley, Mount Dem. Rep. Congo/Uganda see Margherita Peak
Stanleyville Dem. Rep. Congo see Kisangani
Stann Creek Belize see Dangriga
149 H2 Stannington Northumberland, England U.K.
198 B2 Stanos Greece
139 L5 Stanovaya Ryasa r. Rus. Fed.
139 L5 Stanovoye Rus. Fed.
131 M4 Stanovoye Nagor'ye mts Rus. Fed.
131 N4 Stanovoy Khrebet mts Rus. Fed.
139 K5 Stanovoy Kolodez' Rus. Fed.
178 C3 Stans Austria
190 D2 Stans Switz.
82 D3 Stansbury S.A. Austr.
86 F4 Stansmore Range hills W.A. Austr.
151 H3 Stansted airport England U.K.
151 H3 Stansted Mountfitchet Essex, England U.K.
83 G2 Stanthorpe Qld Austr.
151 H2 Stanton Suffolk, England U.K.
234 C3 Stanton DE U.S.A.
232 B6 Stanton KY U.S.A.
226 E4 Stanton MI U.S.A.
236 C2 Stanton ND U.S.A.
236 D3 Stanton NE U.S.A.
237 C5 Stanton TX U.S.A.
139 K5 Stantsiya Skuratovo Rus. Fed.
Stantsiya-Yakkabag Uzbek. see Yakkabag
151 H3 Stanway Essex, England U.K.
137 J3 Stanychno-Luhans'ke Ukr.
179 G3 Stanz im Mürztal Austria
168 F2 Stapel Ger.
169 F4 Stapelburg Ger.
168 F2 Stapelfeld Ger.
164 F2 Staphorst Neth.
151 F2 Stapleford Nottinghamshire, England U.K.
151 H3 Staplehurst Kent, England U.K.
236 E2 Staples MN U.S.A.
236 C3 Stapleton NE U.S.A.
175 I4 Stąporków Pol.
85 F3 Star r. Qld Austr.
139 J5 Star' Rus. Fed.
137 F2 Stara Basan' Ukr.
177 H2 Stará Bystrica Slovakia
136 D2 Stara Chortoryya Ukr.
175 J4 Starachowice Pol.
176 D2 Stará Huť Czech Rep.
174 G2 Stara Kiszewa Pol.
175 K3 Stara Kornica Pol.
136 E2 Stara Kotel'nya Ukr.
174 E2 Stara Łubianka Pol.
177 J2 Stará Ľubovňa Slovakia
177 I6 Stara Moravica Vojvodina, Srbija Yugo.
176 E1 Stará Paka Czech Rep.
196 E3 Stara Pazova Vojvodina, Srbija Yugo.
197 F4 Stara Planina mts Bulg./Yugo.
179 H5 Stara Plošćica Croatia
175 K6 Stara Sil' Ukr.
177 G3 Stará Turá Slovakia
136 D3 Stara Ushytsya Ukr.
136 C2 Stara Vyzhivka Ukr.
175 K5 Stara Wieś Pol.
Staraya Barda Altayskiy Kray Rus. Fed. see Krasnogorskoye
137 K2 Staraya Chigla Rus. Fed.
137 J2 Staraya Kalitva Rus. Fed.
120 A1 Staraya Kulatka Rus. Fed.
120 A2 Staraya Poltavka Rus. Fed.
139 H3 Staraya Russa Rus. Fed.
139 H3 Staraya Toropa Rus. Fed.
135 J5 Staraya Tumba Rus. Fed.
197 G4 Stara Zagora Bulg.
136 C3 Stara Zhadova Ukr.
267 I6 Starbuck Island Kiribati
137 I4 Starchenkove Ukr.
197 H3 Starchiojd Romania
237 F5 Star City AR U.S.A.
226 D5 Star City IN U.S.A.
150 D4 Starcross Devon, England U.K.
174 G5 Stare Budkowice Pol.
179 G1 Stařeč Czech Rep.
174 C2 Stare Czarnowo Pol.
174 D2 Stare Dąbrowa Pol.
175 K2 Stare Dolistowo Pol.
175 K3 Stare Hołowczyce Pol.
171 F5 Staré Křečany Czech Rep.
174 D3 Stare Kurowo Pol.
176 F1 Staré Město Czech Rep.
174 G3 Stare Miasto Pol.
175 H1 Stare Pole Pol.
136 C3 Stare Selo Ukr.
174 E4 Stare Strącze Pol.
Stargard in Pommern Pol. see Stargard Szczeciński
174 D2 Stargard Szczeciński Pol.
175 M4 Stari Koshary Ukr.
136 F2 Stari Petrivtsi Ukr.
196 E4 Stari Ras and Sopoćani tourist site Yugo.
139 J3 Staritsa Rus. Fed.
231 D6 Starke FL U.S.A.
171 D5 Starkenberg Ger.
232 D6 Starkey VA U.S.A.
237 F5 Starkville MS U.S.A.
233 F2 Star Lake NY U.S.A.
173 F4 Starnberg Ger.
173 F4 Starnberger See l. Ger.
110 C1 Staroaleyskoye Rus. Fed.
Starobel'sk Ukr. see Starobil's'k
137 J4 Starobesheve Ukr.
137 J3 Starobil's'k Ukr.
137 H4 Starobohdanivka Ukr.
138 F5 Starobyn Belarus
137 J4 Staroderevyankovskaya Rus. Fed.
139 I5 Starodub Rus. Fed.
174 G2 Starogard Gdański Pol.
Starokonstantinov Ukr. see Starokostyantyniv
136 D3 Starokostyantyniv Ukr.
136 E4 Starokozache Ukr.
137 J5 Staroleushkovskaya Rus. Fed.
135 G7 Starominskaya Rus. Fed.
137 I4 Staromlynivka Ukr.
137 J5 Staronizhestebliyevskaya Rus. Fed.
197 H4 Staro Oryakhovo Bulg.
137 I2 Starooskol'skoye Vodokhranilishche resr Rus. Fed.
197 G4 Starosel Bulg.
197 H4 Staro Selo Bulg.
139 M5 Staroseslavino Rus. Fed.
135 G7 Staroshcherbinovskaya Rus. Fed.
120 D1 Starosubkhangulovo Rus. Fed.
137 I5 Starotitarovskaya Rus. Fed.
137 H3 Starovirivka Ukr.
175 H4 Starowa Góra Pol.
134 H4 Staroye Rus. Fed.
135 I5 Staroye Drozhzhanoye Rus. Fed.
139 K3 Staroye Melkovo Rus. Fed.
135 H5 Staroyur'yevo Rus. Fed.
139 L4 Starozhilovo Rus. Fed.
175 H3 Staroźreby Pol.
240 H1 Star Peak NV U.S.A.
193 H4 St'Arsenio Italy
150 D4 Start Bay England U.K.
149 H3 Startforth Durham, England U.K.
Starve Island Kiribati see Starbuck Island
175 H2 Stary Dzierzgoń Pol.
177 L1 Stary Dzików Pol.
177 G2 Starý Jičín Czech Rep.
174 D4 Stary Kisielin Pol.
175 H3 Stary Kobrzyniec Pol.
175 K5 Stary Majdan Pol.
176 C2 Starý Plzenec Czech Rep.
175 I6 Stary Sącz Pol.
177 J2 Starý Smokovec Slovakia
175 J3 Stary Szelków Pol.
175 H2 Stary Targ Pol.
177 H3 Starý Tekov Slovakia
137 I2 Starytsya Ukr.
175 K4 Stary Uścimów Pol.
138 G5 Staryya Darohi Belarus
136 C2 Staryy Chortoryys'k Ukr.
Staryye Dorogi Belarus see Staryya Darohi
137 I4 Staryy Krym Donets'ka Oblast' Ukr.
137 H5 Staryy Krym Respublika Krym Ukr.
129 C2 Staryy Lesken Rus. Fed.
130 I3 Staryy Nadym Rus. Fed.
136 C3 Staryy Oleksynets' Ukr.
135 G6 Staryy Oskol Rus. Fed.
136 D3 Staryy Ostropil' Ukr.
Staryy Salavan Rus. Fed. see Novocheremshansk
137 I2 Staryy Saltiv Ukr.
136 B3 Staryy Sambir Ukr.
Staryy Sambor Ukr. see Staryy Sambir
129 E2 Staryy Terek r. Rus. Fed.
129 D2 Staryy Urukh Rus. Fed.
174 G1 Starzyno Pol.
171 C4 Staßfurt Ger.
175 J5 Staszów Pol.
232 E4 State College PA U.S.A.
237 F6 State Line MS U.S.A.
Staten Island Arg. see Los Estados, Isla de
235 D2 Staten Island NY U.S.A.
231 D6 Statenville GA U.S.A.
231 D5 Statesboro GA U.S.A.
231 D5 Statesville NC U.S.A.
142 C2 Stathelle Norway
235 D2 Statue of Liberty tourist site NJ U.S.A.
179 G2 Statzberg hill Austria
179 G2 Statzendorf Austria
136 E4 Stăuceni Moldova
171 E4 Stauchitz Ger.
172 B4 Staufen im Breisgau Ger.
173 E3 Staufersberg hill Ger.
150 E3 Staunton Gloucestershire, England U.K.
232 D5 Staunton VA U.S.A.
171 E4 Staupitz Ger.
142 A2 Stavanger Norway
81 C5 Staveley South I. N.Z.
149 H4 Staveley Derbyshire, England U.K.
165 E4 Stavelot Belgium
164 D3 Stavenisse Neth.
142 D2 Stavern Norway
197 G4 Stavertsi Bulg.
136 F4 Stavkove Ukr.
177 L3 Stavne Ukr.
164 E2 Stavoren Neth.
135 H7 Stavropol' Rus. Fed.
Stavropol Kray admin. div. Rus. Fed. see Stavropol'skiy Kray
Stavropol'-na-Volge Rus. Fed. see Tol'yatti
135 H7 Stavropol'skaya Vozvyshennost' hills Rus. Fed.
129 C1 Stavropol'skiy Kray admin. div. Rus. Fed.
198 C1 Stavros Kentriki Makedonia Greece
198 C1 Stavros Kentriki Makedonia Greece
198 D1 Stavroupoli Anatoliki Makedonia kai Thraki Greece
83 E4 Stawell Vic. Austr.

Stawell to **Sukumo**

366

85 E4 **Stawell** *r. Qld* Austr.
175 I2 **Stawiguda** Pol.
175 K2 **Stawiski** Pol.
174 G4 **Stawiszyn** Pol.
149 I3 **Staxton** *North Yorkshire, England* U.K.
136 F2 **Stayky** Ukr.
227 G3 **Stayner** *Ont.* Can.
238 B2 **Stayton** *OR* U.S.A.
215 G3 **Steadville** S. Africa
240 H2 **Steamboat** *NV* U.S.A.
238 F3 **Steamboat Springs** *CO* U.S.A.
175 I2 **Stębark** Pol.
220 B3 **Stebbins** *AK* U.S.A.
137 F3 **Stebliv** Ukr.
175 L6 **Stebnyk** Ukr.
195 F4 **Steccato** Italy
176 D2 **Štěchovice** Czech Rep.
170 D3 **Stechow** Ger.
190 D1 **Steckborn** Switz.
168 C2 **Stedesdorf** Ger.
171 C4 **Stedten** Ger.
164 F1 **Stedum** Neth.
214 E2 **Steekdorings** S. Africa
224 C3 **Steel** *r. Ont.* Can.
236 D2 **Steele** *ND* U.S.A.
262 T2 **Steele Island** Antarctica
234 B2 **Steelton** *PA* U.S.A.
236 F4 **Steelville** *MO* U.S.A.
222 G3 **Steen** *r. Alta* Can.
164 D3 **Steenbergen** Neth.
164 F2 **Steenderen** Neth.
215 H1 **Steenkampsberge** *mts* S. Africa
222 G3 **Steen River** *Alta* Can.
238 C3 **Steens Mountain** *OR* U.S.A.
156 C2 **Steenvoorde** France
164 F2 **Steenwijk** Neth.
149 J4 **Steeping** *r. England* U.K.
151 G3 **Steeple Claydon** *Buckinghamshire, England* U.K.
87 B5 **Steep Point** *W.A.* Austr.
149 H4 **Steeton** *West Yorkshire, England* U.K.
176 G3 **Štefanov** Slovakia
198 C2 **Stefanoviki** Greece
221 H2 **Stefansson Island** *Nunavut* Can.
136 E4 **Ștefan Vodă** Moldova
197 H3 **Ștefan Vodă** Romania
190 C2 **Steffisburg** Switz.
139 L5 **Stegalovka** Rus. Fed.
173 E2 **Stegaurath** Ger.
142 E4 **Stege** Denmark
171 C3 **Stegelitz** Ger.
179 H3 **Stegersbach** Austria
164 F2 **Steggerda** Neth.
Stegi Swaziland *see* **Siteki**
175 H1 **Stegny** Pol.
197 F2 **Ștei** Romania
179 G3 **Steiermark** *land* Austria
173 E2 **Steigerwald** *mts* Ger.
215 H2 **Steilrand** S. Africa
168 E3 **Steimbke** Ger.
173 F2 **Stein** Ger.
165 E4 **Stein** Neth.
172 B4 **Stein** Switz.
172 C4 **Steina** *r.* Ger.
172 C3 **Steinach** *Baden-Württemberg* Ger.
173 G3 **Steinach** *Bayern* Ger.
171 C5 **Steinach** *Thüringen* Ger.
178 C3 **Steinach am Brenner** Austria
179 G2 **Steinakirchen am Forst** Austria
190 D1 **Stein am Rhein** Switz.
168 D2 **Steinau** Ger.
169 E5 **Steinau an der Straße** Ger.
223 L5 **Steinbach** *Man.* Can.
171 E5 **Steinbach** Ger.
169 D5 **Steinbach (Taunus)** Ger.
179 E3 **Steinbach am Attersee** Austria
171 C5 **Steinbach am Wald** Ger.
179 F3 **Steinbach an der Steyr** Austria
173 G2 **Steinberg** *Bayern* Ger.
168 E1 **Steinberg** *Schleswig-Holstein* Ger.
168 E1 **Steinbergkirche** Ger.
168 F2 **Steinburg** Ger.
179 F4 **Steindorf am Ossiacher See** Austria
172 B4 **Steinen** Ger.
178 E4 **Steinfeld** Austria
172 D2 **Steinfeld** *Bayern* Ger.
172 C2 **Steinfeld** *Rheinland-Pfalz* Ger.
168 D3 **Steinfeld (Oldenburg)** Ger.
165 E5 **Steinfort** Lux.
169 C3 **Steinfurt** Ger.
173 E4 **Steingaden** Ger.
170 D1 **Steinhagen** *Mecklenburg-Vorpommern* Ger.
169 D3 **Steinhagen** *Nordrhein-Westfalen* Ger.
171 C5 **Steinheid** Ger.
169 E4 **Steinheim** Ger.
173 E3 **Steinheim am Albuch** Ger.
172 D3 **Steinheim an der Murr** Ger.
171 F3 **Steinhöfel** Ger.
173 G3 **Steinhöring** Ger.
168 F3 **Steinhorst** *Niedersachsen* Ger.
168 F2 **Steinhorst** *Schleswig-Holstein* Ger.
171 F4 **Steinigtwolmsdorf** Ger.
168 E2 **Steinkirchen** Ger.
140 J2 **Steinkjer** Norway
169 D5 **Steinkopf** *hill* Ger.
214 A3 **Steinkopf** S. Africa
171 F3 **Steinsdorf** Ger.
173 E2 **Steinsfeld** Ger.
142 A1 **Steinsland** Norway
172 B2 **Steinwenden** Ger.
171 C5 **Steinwiesen** Ger.
172 C4 **Steißlingen** Ger.
214 D4 **Stekaar** S. Africa
165 D3 **Stekene** Belgium
191 G5 **Stella** *r.* Italy
191 I3 **Stella** *r.* Italy
215 E2 **Stella** S. Africa
168 F2 **Stelle** Ger.
214 B5 **Stellenbosch** S. Africa
164 D3 **Stellendam** Neth.
192 B2 **Stello, Monte** *mt. Corse* France
168 E2 **Stemmen** Ger.
169 D3 **Stemshorn** Ger.
174 E5 **Stěnava** *r.* Pol.
157 F3 **Stenay** France
143 G3 **Stenbo** Sweden
170 C3 **Stendal** Ger.
138 D3 **Stende** Latvia
143 G2 **Stenhamra** Sweden
146 E5 **Stenhousemuir** *Falkirk, Scotland* U.K.
191 F2 **Stenico** Italy
142 E4 **Stenløse** Denmark
146 □G1 **Stenness** *Shetland, Scotland* U.K.
146 E2 **Stenness, Loch of** *l. Scotland* U.K.
173 H2 **Štěnovice** Czech Rep.
142 E4 **Stensved** Denmark
146 F6 **Stenton** *East Lothian, Scotland* U.K.
140 L2 **Stenudden** Sweden
142 D2 **Stenungsund** Sweden
175 M5 **Stenyatyn** Ukr.
136 C2 **Stenzharychi** Ukr.
Steornabhagh *Western Isles, Scotland* U.K. *see* **Stornoway**
136 D2 **Stepan'** Ukr.
Stepanakert Azer. *see* **Xankändi**
129 D3 **Step'anavan** Armenia
136 D2 **Stepanivka** *Khmel'nyts'ka Oblast'* Ukr.
137 H2 **Stepanivka** *Sums'ka Oblast'* Ukr.
137 H4 **Stepanivka Persha** Ukr.
120 D2 **Stepanovka** Kazakh.
147 E3 **Stepaside** Rep. of Ireland
168 F2 **Stepenitz** *r.* Ger.
173 G4 **Stephanskirchen** Ger.
173 G3 **Stephansposching** Ger.
236 D1 **Stephen** *MN* U.S.A.
80 D4 **Stephens, Cape** *South I.* N.Z.
234 D2 **Stephensburg** *NJ* U.S.A.
232 D5 **Stephens City** *VA* U.S.A.
83 E2 **Stephens Creek** *N.S.W.* Austr.
226 D3 **Stephenson** *MI* U.S.A.
262 T2 **Stephenson, Mount** Antarctica
225 J3 **Stephenville** *Nfld.* Can.
237 D5 **Stephenville** *TX* U.S.A.
137 J5 **Stepnaya** Rus. Fed.
137 G1 **Stepne** Ukr.
235 E1 **Stepney** *CT* U.S.A.
174 C2 **Stepnica** Pol.
121 H1 **Stepnogorsk** Kazakh.
137 H4 **Stepnohirs'k** Ukr.
Stepnoy Rus. Fed. *see* **Elista**
120 E1 **Stepnoye** *Chelyabinskaya Oblast'* Rus. Fed.
120 A2 **Stepnoye** *Saratovskaya Oblast'* Rus. Fed.
129 D1 **Stepnoye** *Stavropol'skiy Kray* Rus. Fed.
121 G1 **Stepnyak** Kazakh.
196 E3 **Stepojevac** *Srbija* Yugo.
175 K3 **Sterdyń** Pol.
198 C2 **Sterea Ellas** *admin. reg.* Greece
215 F4 **Sterkspruit** S. Africa
215 F4 **Sterkstroom** S. Africa
175 J1 **Sterławki-Wielkie** Pol.
120 C1 **Sterlibashevo** Rus. Fed.
214 C4 **Sterling** S. Africa
236 C3 **Sterling** *CO* U.S.A.
235 G1 **Sterling** *CT* U.S.A.
226 C5 **Sterling** *IL* U.S.A.
236 D4 **Sterling** *KS* U.S.A.
227 E3 **Sterling** *MI* U.S.A.
236 C2 **Sterling** *ND* U.S.A.
241 L2 **Sterling** *UT* U.S.A.
237 C6 **Sterling City** *TX* U.S.A.
227 F4 **Sterling Heights** *MI* U.S.A.
120 C1 **Sterlitamak** Rus. Fed.
170 C2 **Sternberg** Ger.
176 G2 **Šternberk** Czech Rep.
168 E1 **Sterup** Ger.
157 F5 **Stes-Geosmes** France
161 C5 **Stes Maries, Golfe des** *b.* France
161 C5 **Stes-Maries-de-la-Mer** France
174 E3 **Stęszew** Pol.
176 D1 **Štětí** Czech Rep.
137 G3 **Stetsivka** Ukr.
137 H2 **Stets'kivka** Ukr.
172 D3 **Stetten am kalten Markt** Ger.
Stettin Pol. *see* **Szczecin**
Stettiner Haff *b.* Ger. *see* **Oderhaff**
238 D1 **Stettler** *Alta* Can.
232 C4 **Steubenville** *OH* U.S.A.
179 F4 **Steuerberg** Austria
171 D4 **Steutz** Ger.
151 G3 **Stevenage** *Hertfordshire, England* U.K.
80 D4 **Stevens, Mount** *South I.* N.Z.
238 B2 **Stevenson** *WA* U.S.A.
226 C3 **Stevens Point** *WI* U.S.A.
146 D6 **Stevenston** *North Ayrshire, Scotland* U.K.
220 D3 **Stevens Village** *AK* U.S.A.
234 B4 **Stevensville** *MD* U.S.A.
226 D4 **Stevensville** *MI* U.S.A.
227 I5 **Stevensville** *PA* U.S.A.
262 O1 **Steventon Island** Antarctica
85 E2 **Stewart** *r. Qld* Austr.
222 D4 **Stewart** *B.C.* Can.
222 B2 **Stewart** *r. Y.T.* Can.
240 L5 **Stewart** *NV* U.S.A.
84 C1 **Stewart, Cape** *N.T.* Austr.
259 C9 **Stewart, Isla** *i.* Chile
222 B2 **Stewart Crossing** *Y.T.* Can.
81 A7 **Stewart Island** N.Z.
78 □6 **Stewart Islands** Solomon Is
146 D6 **Stewarton** *East Ayrshire, Scotland* U.K.
240 F2 **Stewarts Point** *CA* U.S.A.
147 E2 **Stewartstown** *Northern Ireland* U.K.
234 B3 **Stewartstown** *PA* U.S.A.
246 □ **Stewart Town** Jamaica
223 J5 **Stewart Valley** *Sask.* Can.
226 A4 **Stewartville** *MN* U.S.A.
225 I4 **Stewiacke** *N.S.* Can.
168 E3 **Steyerberg** Ger.
151 G4 **Steyning** *West Sussex, England* U.K.
215 F2 **Steynrus** S. Africa
215 E4 **Steynsburg** S. Africa
179 F2 **Steyr** Austria
179 F3 **Steyr** *r.* Austria
179 F2 **Steyregg** Austria
214 E5 **Steytlerville** S. Africa
175 J4 **Stężyca** Pol.
174 F1 **Stężyca** Pol.
191 G5 **Stia** Italy
177 H3 **Štiavnické Vrchy** *mts* Slovakia
177 H2 **Štiavnik** Slovakia
150 C4 **Stibb Cross** *Devon, England* U.K.
149 G2 **Stichill** *Scottish Borders, Scotland* U.K.
149 J4 **Stickney** *Lincolnshire, England* U.K.
169 F4 **Stiege** Ger.
164 E1 **Stiens** Neth.
191 G4 **Stienta** Italy
Stif Alg. *see* **Sétif**
237 E5 **Stigler** *OK* U.S.A.
193 I4 **Stigliano** Italy
195 F4 **Stignano** Italy
143 G2 **Stigtomta** Sweden
222 C3 **Stikine** *r. B.C.* Can.
222 D3 **Stikine Plateau** *B.C.* Can.
142 D2 **Stikkvasskollen** *hill* Norway
214 C6 **Stilbaai** S. Africa
226 C3 **Stiles** *WI* U.S.A.
215 F2 **Stilfontein** S. Africa
Stilís Greece *see* **Stylida**
149 H3 **Stillington** *North Yorkshire, England* U.K.
234 B3 **Still Pond** *MD* U.S.A.
226 A3 **Stillwater** *MN* U.S.A.
237 D4 **Stillwater** *OK* U.S.A.
238 E2 **Stillwater** *r. MT* U.S.A.
240 H2 **Stillwater Range** *mts NV* U.S.A.
195 F4 **Stilo** Italy
195 F4 **Stilo, Punta** *pt* Italy
188 F4 **Štilt** *mt.* Bos.-Herz.
151 G2 **Stilton** *Cambridgeshire, England* U.K.
237 E5 **Stilwell** *OK* U.S.A.
196 E4 **Štimlje** *Kosovo, Srbija* Yugo.
173 E2 **Stimpfach** Ger.
263 E2 **Stinear, Mount** Antarctica
237 C5 **Stinnett** *TX* U.S.A.
192 A4 **Stintino** *Sardegna* Italy
193 H4 **Stio** Italy
197 F5 **Štip** Macedonia
188 E3 **Stipanov Grič** *mt.* Croatia
157 G3 **Stiring-Wendel** France
84 C4 **Stirling** *N.T.* Austr.
227 I3 **Stirling** *Ont.* Can.
146 E5 **Stirling** *Stirling, Scotland* U.K.
146 D5 **Stirling** *admin. div. Scotland* U.K.
235 D2 **Stirling** *NJ* U.S.A.
87 C6 **Stirling, Mount** *hill W.A.* Austr.
84 B3 **Stirling Creek** *r. N.T.* Austr.
82 D3 **Stirling North** *S.A.* Austr.
87 C7 **Stirling Range** *mts W.A.* Austr.
190 F4 **Stirone** *r.* Italy
232 B6 **Stirrat** *WV* U.S.A.
150 B4 **Stithians** *Cornwall, England* U.K.
177 J3 **Štítnik** Slovakia
227 J3 **Stittsville** *Ont.* Can.
176 F2 **Štíty** Czech Rep.
191 G3 **Stizzon** *r.* Italy
140 M1 **Stjernøya** *i.* Norway
140 J3 **Stjørdalshalsen** Norway
146 D5 **Stob Choire Claurigh** *mt. Scotland* U.K.
146 D5 **Stob Ghabhar** *mt. Scotland* U.K.
175 J6 **Stobnica** *r.* Pol.
174 F5 **Stobrawa** *r.* Pol.
176 C1 **Stochov** Czech Rep.
151 H3 **Stock** *Essex, England* U.K.
157 G4 **Stock, Étang du** *l.* France
172 D4 **Stockach** Ger.
151 F3 **Stockbridge** *Hampshire, England* U.K.
227 E4 **Stockbridge** *MI* U.S.A.
168 F2 **Stockelsdorf** Ger.
179 E4 **Stockenboi** Austria
179 H2 **Stockerau** Austria
234 C2 **Stockertown** *PA* U.S.A.
171 C5 **Stockheim** Ger.
143 H2 **Stockholm** Sweden
143 G2 **Stockholm** *county* Sweden
233 □I1 **Stockholm** *ME* U.S.A.
235 D1 **Stockholm** *NJ* U.S.A.
190 C2 **Stockhorn** *mt.* Switz.
83 F3 **Stockinbingal** *N.S.W.* Austr.
179 G4 **Stocking** Austria
149 G4 **Stockport** *Greater Manchester, England* U.K.
149 H4 **Stocksbridge** *South Yorkshire, England* U.K.
168 E3 **Stöckse** Ger.
149 H3 **Stocksfield** *Northumberland, England* U.K.
264 G6 **Stocks Seamount** *sea feature* S. Atlantic Ocean
172 D2 **Stockstadt am Main** Ger.
172 C2 **Stockstadt am Rhein** Ger.
240 G3 **Stockton** *CA* U.S.A.
226 B4 **Stockton** *IL* U.S.A.
236 D4 **Stockton** *KS* U.S.A.
237 E4 **Stockton** *MO* U.S.A.
234 D2 **Stockton** *NJ* U.S.A.
241 K1 **Stockton** *UT* U.S.A.
149 G4 **Stockton Heath** *Warrington, England* U.K.
149 H3 **Stockton-on-Tees** *Stockton-on-Tees, England* U.K.
149 H3 **Stockton-on-Tees** *admin. div. England* U.K.
237 C6 **Stockton Plateau** *TX* U.S.A.
233 □I2 **Stockton Springs** *ME* U.S.A.
236 C3 **Stockville** *NE* U.S.A.
175 J4 **Stoczek Łukowski** Pol.
175 J3 **Stoczek-Osada** Pol.
176 C2 **Stod** Czech Rep.
141 L3 **Stöde** Sweden
139 I4 **Stodolishche** Rus. Fed.
97 D4 **Stœng Trêng** Cambodia
146 C3 **Stoer** *Highland, Scotland* U.K.
215 G1 **Stoffberg** S. Africa
196 E5 **Stogovo Planina** *mts* Macedonia
150 D3 **Stogursey** *Somerset, England* U.K.
151 G2 **Stoke Albany** *Northamptonshire, England* U.K.
151 I2 **Stoke Ash** *Suffolk, England* U.K.
151 H3 **Stoke-by-Nayland** *Suffolk, England* U.K.
151 I2 **Stoke Holy Cross** *Norfolk, England* U.K.
151 G3 **Stoke Mandeville** *Buckinghamshire, England* U.K.
151 G3 **Stokenchurch** *Buckinghamshire, England* U.K.
150 D4 **Stokenham** *Devon, England* U.K.
149 G4 **Stoke-on-Trent** *Stoke-on-Trent, England* U.K.
149 G4 **Stoke-on-Trent** *admin. div. England* U.K.
151 G3 **Stoke Poges** *Buckinghamshire, England* U.K.
150 E2 **Stoke Prior** *Worcestershire, England* U.K.
81 E4 **Stokes, Mount** *South I.* N.Z.
150 E2 **Stokesay** *Shropshire, England* U.K.
87 D7 **Stokes Inlet** *W.A.* Austr.
149 H3 **Stokesley** *North Yorkshire, England* U.K.
83 E5 **Stokes Point** *Tas.* Austr.
84 B3 **Stokes Range** *hills N.T.* Austr.
150 D4 **Stoke St Mary** *Somerset, England* U.K.
150 E4 **Stoke sub Hamdon** *Somerset, England* U.K.
81 E4 **Stokes Valley** *North I.* N.Z.
136 C2 **Stokhid** *r.* Ukr.
168 G1 **Stokkemarke** Denmark
140 K1 **Stokmarknes** Norway
176 E2 **Štoky** Czech Rep.
179 E4 **Stol** *mt.* Slovenia
197 F3 **Stol** *mt.* Yugo.
188 F4 **Stolac** Bos.-Herz.
169 F4 **Stolberg (Harz) Kurort** Ger.
169 B5 **Stolberg (Rheinland)** Ger.
121 K2 **Stolboukha** Kazakh.
Stolbtsy Belarus *see* **Stowbtsy**
174 F2 **Stołczno** Pol.
177 J3 **Stolica** *mt.* Slovakia
188 G3 **Stolice** *hill* Bos.-Herz.
136 D2 **Stolin** Belarus
171 D5 **Stollberg** Ger.
168 D2 **Stollhamm (Butjadingen)** Ger.
174 G2 **Stolno** Pol.
Stolp Pol. *see* **Słupsk**
170 F3 **Stolpe** *Brandenburg* Ger.
168 F1 **Stolpe** *Schleswig-Holstein* Ger.
171 F4 **Stolpen** Ger.
164 D3 **Stolwijk** Neth.
169 E3 **Stolzenau** Ger.
214 A5 **Stompneusbaai** S. Africa
150 E3 **Stone** *Gloucestershire, England* U.K.
151 H3 **Stone** *Kent, England* U.K.
150 E2 **Stone** *Staffordshire, England* U.K.
232 C4 **Stoneboro** *PA* U.S.A.
224 E4 **Stonecliffe** *Ont.* Can.
236 C3 **Stoneham** *CO* U.S.A.
234 D3 **Stone Harbor** *NJ* U.S.A.
146 F5 **Stonehaven** *Aberdeenshire, Scotland* U.K.
85 E5 **Stonehenge** *Qld* Austr.
151 F3 **Stonehenge** *tourist site England* U.K.
150 E3 **Stonehouse** *Gloucestershire, England* U.K.
146 E6 **Stonehouse** *South Lanarkshire, Scotland* U.K.
226 B3 **Stone Lake** *WI* U.S.A.
233 F4 **Stone Ridge** *NY* U.S.A.
232 D6 **Stoneville** *NC* U.S.A.
223 L5 **Stonewall** *Man.* Can.
237 D5 **Stonewall** *OK* U.S.A.
227 H4 **Stoney Creek** *Ont.* Can.
234 C2 **Stoney Creek Mills** *PA* U.S.A.
147 D4 **Stoneyford** Rep. of Ireland
146 D7 **Stoneykirk** *Dumfries and Galloway, Scotland* U.K.
227 F4 **Stoney Point** *Ont.* Can.
215 G4 **Stoneyride** S. Africa
235 G1 **Stonington** *CT* U.S.A.
233 □I2 **Stonington** *ME* U.S.A.
146 □G2 **Stonybreck** *Shetland, Scotland* U.K.
235 E2 **Stony Brook** *NY* U.S.A.
234 B3 **Stony Brook** *PA* U.S.A.
235 F1 **Stony Creek** *CT* U.S.A.
232 E6 **Stony Creek** *VA* U.S.A.
222 H4 **Stony Plain** *Alta* Can.
223 J3 **Stony Rapids** *Sask.* Can.
151 G2 **Stony Stratford** *Milton Keynes, England* U.K.
179 H3 **Stoob** Austria
224 D2 **Stooping** *r. Ont.* Can.
175 J1 **Stopki** Pol.
175 I5 **Stopnica** Pol.
168 E2 **Stör** *r.* Ger.
142 C3 **Stora** *r.* Denmark
143 F2 **Storå** Sweden
143 G3 **Stora Alvaret** *i.* Sweden
141 K3 **Storbäcken** Sweden
141 J3 **Storbekkfjellet** *mt.* Norway
141 K3 **Storbo** Sweden
142 A2 **Stord** *i.* Norway
140 I3 **Stordal** Norway
141 J3 **Store** *mt.* Norway
179 G4 **Štore** Slovenia
142 D4 **Store Bælt** *sea chan.* Denmark
142 A1 **Storebø** Norway
170 D1 **Store Damme** Denmark
142 E4 **Store Heddinge** Denmark
141 J3 **Store Jukleeggi** *mt.* Norway
140 M1 **Store Lenangstind** *mt.* Norway
140 J3 **Støren** Norway
142 B2 **Store Nup** *mt.* Norway
168 F1 **Store Rise** Denmark
142 A1 **Store Sotra** *i.* Norway
140 □ **Storfjorden** *sea chan.* Svalbard
143 F2 **Storfors** Sweden
140 K2 **Storforshei** Norway
140 K2 **Storjola** Sweden
142 B2 **Storkarshei** *hill* Norway
221 H2 **Storkerson Peninsula** *Nunavut* Can.
171 E3 **Storkow** Ger.
83 F5 **Storm Bay** *Tas.* Austr.
215 F4 **Stormberg** S. Africa
215 F4 **Stormberg** *mt.* S. Africa
215 F4 **Stormberg** *r.* S. Africa
215 F4 **Stormberge** *mts* S. Africa
236 E3 **Storm Lake** *IA* U.S.A.
214 D5 **Stormsrivier** S. Africa
193 H3 **Stornara** Italy
193 H3 **Stornarella** Italy
146 B3 **Stornoway** *Western Isles, Scotland* U.K.
191 F3 **Storo** Italy
140 □ **Storøya** *i.* Svalbard
134 K3 **Storozhevsk** Rus. Fed.
136 C3 **Storozhynets'** Ukr.
151 G4 **Storrington** *West Sussex, England* U.K.
142 C2 **Stor-Roan** *mt.* Norway
233 G4 **Storrs** *CT* U.S.A.
140 L2 **Storseleby** Sweden
143 G1 **Storsjön** *l.* Sweden
143 G2 **Storsjön** *l.* Sweden
140 K3 **Storsjön** *l.* Sweden
140 J3 **Storskarhø** *mt.* Norway
140 K2 **Storskog** Sweden
140 M1 **Storslett** Norway
142 D4 **Storstrøm** *county* Denmark
140 M2 **Storsund** Sweden
151 H3 **Stort** *r. England* U.K.
164 E1 **Stortemelk** *sea chan.* Neth.
140 L2 **Storuman** Sweden
140 L2 **Storuman** *l.* Sweden
140 K3 **Storvigelen** *mt.* Norway
143 G1 **Storvik** Sweden
142 D3 **Storvorde** Denmark
143 G2 **Storvreta** Sweden
238 F2 **Story** *WY* U.S.A.
259 B8 **Stosch, Isla** *i.* Chile
171 C4 **Stößen** Ger.
151 G2 **Stotfold** *Bedfordshire, England* U.K.
173 E4 **Stötten am Auerberg** Ger.
171 C4 **Stotternheim** Ger.
234 B2 **Stouchsburg** *PA* U.S.A.
223 K5 **Stoughton** *Sask.* Can.
165 E4 **Stoumont** Belgium
97 D4 **Stoŭng, Stœ̆ng** *r.* Cambodia
150 F4 **Stour** *r. Dorset, England* U.K.
151 I3 **Stour** *r. Essex/Suffolk, England* U.K.
151 I3 **Stour** *r. Kent, England* U.K.
151 F2 **Stour** *r. Oxfordshire/Warwickshire, England* U.K.
150 E2 **Stourbridge** *West Midlands, England* U.K.
150 E2 **Stourport-on-Severn** *Worcestershire, England* U.K.
146 F6 **Stow** *Scottish Borders, Scotland* U.K.
138 F5 **Stowbtsy** Belarus
234 C2 **Stowe** *PA* U.S.A.
174 F1 **Stowięcino** Pol.
151 H2 **Stowmarket** *Suffolk, England* U.K.
151 F3 **Stow-on-the-Wold** *Gloucestershire, England* U.K.
136 C2 **Stoyaniv** Ukr.
100 D1 **Stoyba** Rus. Fed.
175 K1 **Stożne** Pol.
191 H3 **Stra** Italy
171 D4 **Straach** Ger.
215 F1 **Straatsdrif** S. Africa
147 D2 **Strabane** *Northern Ireland* U.K.
175 L3 **Strabla** Pol.
146 F4 **Strachan** *Aberdeenshire, Scotland* U.K.
146 C5 **Strachur** *Argyll and Bute, Scotland* U.K.
168 C2 **Strackholt (Großefehn)** Ger.
147 D3 **Stradbally** Rep. of Ireland
151 I2 **Stradbroke** *Suffolk, England* U.K.
190 E3 **Stradella** Italy
179 G4 **Straden** Austria
151 H2 **Stradishall** *Suffolk, England* U.K.
147 D3 **Stradone** Rep. of Ireland
151 H2 **Stradsett** *Norfolk, England* U.K.
169 B4 **Straelen** Ger.
83 F5 **Strahan** *Tas.* Austr.
241 L3 **Straight Cliffs** *ridge UT* U.S.A.
165 E5 **Straimont** Belgium
176 C2 **Strakonice** Czech Rep.
197 H4 **Straldzha** Bulg.
179 G3 **Strallegg** Austria
146 E5 **Straloch** *Perth and Kinross, Scotland* U.K.
170 E1 **Stralsund** Ger.
190 C3 **Strambino** Italy
165 E3 **Stramproy** Neth.
214 B6 **Strand** S. Africa
140 I3 **Stranda** Norway
168 F1 **Strande** Ger.
147 C2 **Strandhill** Rep. of Ireland
231 E7 **Strangers Cay** *i.* Bahamas
147 F2 **Strangford** *Northern Ireland* U.K.
147 F2 **Strangford Lough** *inlet Northern Ireland* U.K.
143 G2 **Strängnäs** Sweden
193 F3 **Strangolagalli** Italy
84 C2 **Strangways** *r. N.T.* Austr.
84 C4 **Strangways Range** *mts N.T.* Austr.
177 G3 **Strání** Czech Rep.
147 E1 **Stranocum** *Northern Ireland* U.K.
147 D2 **Stranorlar** Rep. of Ireland
146 C7 **Stranraer** *Dumfries and Galloway, Scotland* U.K.
194 B5 **Strasatti** *Sicilia* Italy
157 H4 **Strasbourg** France
170 E2 **Strasburg** Ger.
232 C4 **Strasburg** *OH* U.S.A.
234 B3 **Strasburg** *PA* U.S.A.
232 D5 **Strasburg** *VA* U.S.A.
136 E4 **Strășeni** Moldova
Strasheny Moldova *see* **Strășeni**
173 H2 **Strašice** Czech Rep.
172 D3 **Straßberg** Ger.
171 C4 **Straßberg** Ger.
179 F4 **Straßburg** Austria
Strassburg France *see* **Strasbourg**
165 F5 **Strassen** Lux.
179 G3 **Straßengel** Austria
169 C5 **Straßenhaus** Ger.
179 H2 **Strasshof an der Norbahn** Austria
173 G3 **Straßkirchen** Ger.
178 E3 **Straßwalchen** Austria
151 F3 **Stratfield Mortimer** *West Berkshire, England* U.K.
224 D5 **Stratford** *Ont.* Can.
80 E3 **Stratford** *North I.* N.Z.
147 E4 **Stratford** Rep. of Ireland
240 H3 **Stratford** *CA* U.S.A.
235 E1 **Stratford** *CT* U.S.A.
237 C4 **Stratford** *TX* U.S.A.
226 B3 **Stratford** *WI* U.S.A.
151 F2 **Stratford-upon-Avon** *Warwickshire, England* U.K.
82 D3 **Strathalbyn** *S.A.* Austr.
146 D6 **Strathaven** *South Lanarkshire, Scotland* U.K.
148 E2 **Strathblane** *Stirling, Scotland* U.K.
146 F4 **Strathbogie** *reg. Scotland* U.K.
146 D4 **Strathcarron** *val. Scotland* U.K.
263 G2 **Strathcona, Mount** Antarctica
146 D4 **Strathconon** *val. Scotland* U.K.
146 D4 **Strath Dearn** *val. Scotland* U.K.
146 E4 **Strathdon** *Aberdeenshire, Scotland* U.K.
146 D5 **Strath Earn** *val. Scotland* U.K.
146 D3 **Strath Fleet** *val. Scotland* U.K.
146 D4 **Strathglass** *val. Scotland* U.K.
83 F5 **Strathgordon** *Tas.* Austr.
146 E3 **Strath Halladale** *val. Scotland* U.K.
222 H5 **Strathmore** *Alta* Can.
146 D3 **Strathmore** *r. Scotland* U.K.
240 H3 **Strathmore** *CA* U.S.A.
222 F4 **Strathnaver** *B.C.* Can.
146 D3 **Strathnaver** *val. Scotland* U.K.
146 E3 **Strath of Kildonan** *val. Scotland* U.K.
146 D4 **Strathpeffer** *Highland, Scotland* U.K.
227 G4 **Strathroy** *Ont.* Can.
146 E4 **Strathspey** *val. Scotland* U.K.
146 E5 **Strath Tay** *val. Scotland* U.K.
146 E3 **Strathy** *Highland, Scotland* U.K.
146 D3 **Strathy Point** *Scotland* U.K.
146 D5 **Strathyre** *Stirling, Scotland* U.K.
198 C1 **Stratoni** *Kentriki Makedonia* Greece
199 F3 **Stratonikeia** *tourist site* Turkey
198 B2 **Stratos** *Dytiki Ellas* Greece
150 C4 **Stratton** *Cornwall, England* U.K.
233 □H2 **Stratton** *ME* U.S.A.
233 G3 **Stratton Mountain** *VT* U.S.A.
151 F3 **Stratton St Margaret** *Swindon, England* U.K.
173 G3 **Straubing** Ger.
140 K1 **Straume** Norway
140 □B2 **Straumnes** *pt* Iceland
171 F4 **Straupitz** Ger.
170 E3 **Strausberg** Ger.
169 F4 **Straußfurt** Ger.
234 B2 **Strausstown** *PA* U.S.A.
241 L4 **Strawberry** *AZ* U.S.A.
238 C2 **Strawberry Mountain** *OR* U.S.A.
175 I5 **Strawczyn** Pol.
226 C5 **Strawn** *IL* U.S.A.
197 F4 **Straža** *mt.* Macedonia
197 G4 **Strazhitsa** Bulg.
176 D2 **Stráž nad Nežárkou** Czech Rep.
171 G5 **Stráž nad Nisou** Czech Rep.
179 E2 **Strážný** Czech Rep.
176 C2 **Strážov** Czech Rep.
177 H3 **Strážov** *mt.* Slovakia
171 F5 **Stráž pod Ralskem** Czech Rep.
177 K3 **Strážske** Slovakia
82 C3 **Streaky Bay** *S.A.* Austr.
82 C3 **Streaky Bay** *b. S.A.* Austr.
147 D3 **Streamstown** Rep. of Ireland
151 F3 **Streatley** *West Berkshire, England* U.K.
226 C5 **Streator** *IL* U.S.A.
176 D2 **Středočeský Kraj** *admin. reg.* Czech Rep.
168 D2 **Streek** Ger.
150 E3 **Street** *Somerset, England* U.K.
197 F3 **Strehaia** Romania
171 E4 **Strehla** Ger.
197 F3 **Strei** *r.* Romania
87 D6 **Streich Mound** *hill W.A.* Austr.
177 H4 **Strekov** Slovakia
176 C2 **Střela** *r.* Czech Rep.
197 G4 **Strelcha** Bulg.
137 I2 **Streletskoye** Rus. Fed.
176 F2 **Střelice** Czech Rep.
137 J2 **Strelitsa** Rus. Fed.
86 C4 **Strelley** *W.A.* Austr.
86 C4 **Strelley** *r. W.A.* Austr.
134 G2 **Strel'na** *r.* Rus. Fed.
179 H3 **Strem** Austria
191 F2 **Strembo** Italy
171 D3 **Stremme** *r.* Ger.
136 E2 **Stremyhorod** Ukr.
138 E3 **Strenči** Latvia
179 F2 **Strengberg** Austria
178 B3 **Strengen** Austria
149 H3 **Strensall** *York, England* U.K.
175 M5 **Streptiv** Ukr.
190 D3 **Stresa** Italy
149 G4 **Stretford** *Greater Manchester, England* U.K.
151 H2 **Stretham** *Cambridgeshire, England* U.K.
151 F2 **Stretton** *Staffordshire, England* U.K.
169 F5 **Streu** *r.* Ger.
169 F5 **Streufdorf** Ger.
144 D1 **Streymoy** *i.* Faroe Is
130 I3 **Strezhevoy** Rus. Fed.
176 B2 **Stříbro** Czech Rep.
146 F4 **Strichen** *Aberdeenshire, Scotland* U.K.
91 J8 **Strickland** *r.* P.N.G.
191 G2 **Strigno** Italy
179 H4 **Štrigova** Croatia
164 D3 **Strijen** Neth.
176 E2 **Strimilov** Czech Rep.
198 C1 **Strimonas** *r.* Greece
Strimonikón Greece *see* **Strymoniko**
148 D2 **Striven, Loch** *inlet Scotland* U.K.
188 G3 **Strizivojna** Croatia
179 G5 **Strmec** Croatia
169 F4 **Ströbeck** Ger.
179 E3 **Strobl** Austria
259 E6 **Stroeder** Arg.
173 F3 **Strogen** *r.* Ger.
137 G4 **Strohanivka** Ukr.
168 D3 **Ströhen** Ger.
136 E4 **Stroiești** Moldova
137 I2 **Stroitel'** Rus. Fed.
147 C3 **Strokestown** Rep. of Ireland
170 E2 **Strom** *r.* Ger.
146 E3 **Stroma, Island of** *Scotland* U.K.
141 L3 **Strömbacka** Sweden
172 B2 **Stromberg** Ger.
195 E4 **Stromboli, Isola** *i. Isole Lipari* Italy
146 C4 **Stromeferry** *Highland, Scotland* U.K.
259 □ **Stromness** S. Georgia
146 E3 **Stromness** *Orkney, Scotland* U.K.
141 L3 **Strömsbruk** Sweden
236 D3 **Stromsburg** *NE* U.S.A.
142 D2 **Strömstad** Sweden
140 K3 **Strömsund** Sweden
193 E2 **Stroncone** Italy
190 F3 **Strone** *r.* Italy
146 D6 **Strone** *Argyll and Bute, Scotland* U.K.
237 E5 **Strong** *AR* U.S.A.
195 G3 **Strongoli** Italy
232 C4 **Strongsville** *OH* U.S.A.
174 E5 **Stronie Śląskie** Pol.
146 F2 **Stronsay** *i. Scotland* U.K.
146 F2 **Stronsay Firth** *sea chan. Scotland* U.K.
179 H2 **Stronsdorf** Austria
146 C5 **Strontian** *Highland, Scotland* U.K.
177 K2 **Stropkov** Slovakia
176 D3 **Stropnice** *r.* Czech Rep.
190 D3 **Stroppiana** Italy
190 C4 **Stroppo** Italy
150 E3 **Stroud** *Gloucestershire, England* U.K.
83 G3 **Stroud Road** *N.S.W.* Austr.
234 C2 **Stroudsburg** *PA* U.S.A.
Stroyentsy Moldova *see* **Stroiești**
175 H6 **Stróża** Pol.
168 C2 **Strücklingen (Saterland)** Ger.
142 C3 **Struer** Denmark
196 E5 **Struga** Macedonia
174 F3 **Struga** *r.* Pol.
138 G2 **Strugi-Krasnyye** Rus. Fed.
214 C6 **Struis Bay** S. Africa
147 D2 **Strule** *r. Northern Ireland* U.K.
173 E2 **Strullendorf** Ger.
197 F5 **Struma** *r.* Bulg.
150 B2 **Strumble Head** *hd Wales* U.K.
198 C1 **Strumeshnitsa** *r.* Bulg.
197 F5 **Strumica** Macedonia
197 F5 **Strumica** *r.* Macedonia
174 G6 **Strumień** Pol.
177 L3 **Strumkivka** Ukr.
139 L3 **Strunino** Rus. Fed.
179 F1 **Strunkovice nad Blanicí** Czech Rep.
169 F4 **Struth** Ger.
232 C4 **Struthers** *OH* U.S.A.
197 G4 **Stryama** *r.* Bulg.
214 D3 **Strydenburg** S. Africa
215 E2 **Strydpoort** S. Africa
175 H4 **Stryków** Pol.
198 C1 **Strymoniko** Greece
141 I3 **Stryn** Norway
136 C3 **Strypa** *r.* Ukr.
136 F4 **Stryukove** Ukr.
136 B3 **Stryy** Ukr.
136 C3 **Stryy** *r.* Ukr.
136 E3 **Stryzhavka** Ukr.
174 F3 **Strzałkowo** Pol.
174 G5 **Strzebień** Pol.
175 I3 **Strzegocin** Pol.
174 E5 **Strzegom** Pol.
174 E5 **Strzegomka** *r.* Pol.
175 I3 **Strzegowo-Osada** Pol.
175 H3 **Strzelce** Pol.
174 D3 **Strzelce Krajeńskie** Pol.
174 G5 **Strzelce Opolskie** Pol.
175 H4 **Strzelce Wielkie** Pol.
84 C4 **Strzelecki, Mount** *hill N.T.* Austr.
174 F5 **Strzeleczki** Pol.
174 F5 **Strzelin** Pol.
174 G3 **Strzelno** Pol.
174 G1 **Strzepcz** Pol.
175 J6 **Strzyżów** Pol.
136 D1 **Stsvina** *r.* Belarus
85 G5 **Stuart** *r. Qld* Austr.
231 D7 **Stuart** *FL* U.S.A.
236 E3 **Stuart** *IA* U.S.A.
236 D3 **Stuart** *NE* U.S.A.
232 C6 **Stuart** *VA* U.S.A.
84 C4 **Stuart Bluff Range** *mts N.T.* Austr.
146 F4 **Stuartfield** *Aberdeenshire, Scotland* U.K.
81 A6 **Stuart Mountains** *South I.* N.Z.
82 C2 **Stuart Range** *hills S.A.* Austr.
232 D5 **Stuarts Draft** *VA* U.S.A.
178 C3 **Stubaier Alpen** *mts* Austria
168 E1 **Stubbæk** Denmark
170 D1 **Stubbekøbing** Denmark
168 D2 **Stubben** Ger.
151 F4 **Stubbington** *Hampshire, England* U.K.
179 G3 **Stubenberg** Austria
196 E4 **Stubica** *Srbija* Yugo.
196 E3 **Stubline** *Srbija* Yugo.
175 K6 **Stubno** Pol.
Stuchka Latvia *see* **Aizkraukle**
Stučka Latvia *see* **Aizkraukle**
176 E2 **Studená** Czech Rep.
136 E3 **Studena** Ukr.
179 E2 **Studená Vltava** *r.* Czech Rep.
196 E4 **Studenica** *tourist site* Yugo.
170 D3 **Stüdenitz** Ger.
177 H2 **Studénka** Czech Rep.
136 D2 **Studenytsya** *r.* Ukr.
151 G3 **Studham** *Bedfordshire, England* U.K.
81 C6 **Studholme Junction** *South I.* N.Z.
176 G3 **Studienka** Slovakia
214 E5 **Studis** S. Africa
151 F4 **Studland** *Dorset, England* U.K.
151 F2 **Studley** *Warwickshire, England* U.K.
143 G2 **Studsvik** Sweden
134 B3 **Studsviken** Sweden
237 C6 **Study Butte** *TX* U.S.A.
174 F1 **Studzienice** Pol.
140 K3 **Stugun** Sweden
178 D3 **Stuhlfelden** Austria
172 C4 **Stühlingen** Ger.
136 F2 **Stuhna** *r.* Ukr.
168 D2 **Stuhr** Ger.
171 E3 **Stülpe** Ger.
197 G2 **Stulpicani** Romania
178 C3 **Stumm** Austria
Stung Treng Cambodia *see* **Stœ̆ng Trêng**
223 M4 **Stupart** *r. Man.* Can.
176 G3 **Stupava** Slovakia
139 L4 **Stupino** Rus. Fed.
175 I2 **Stupsk** Pol.
190 D3 **Stura** *r.* Italy
190 C3 **Stura di Ala** *r.* Italy
190 C4 **Stura di Demonte** *r.* Italy
161 F3 **Stura di Val Grande** *r.* Italy
190 C3 **Stura di Viù** *r.* Italy
263 K2 **Sturge Island** Antarctica
224 E4 **Sturgeon** *r. Ont.* Can.
223 J4 **Sturgeon** *r. Sask.* Can.
226 D3 **Sturgeon** *r. MI* U.S.A.
226 D3 **Sturgeon Bay** *WI* U.S.A.
226 E3 **Sturgeon Bay** *b. MI* U.S.A.
224 E4 **Sturgeon Falls** *Ont.* Can.
230 C4 **Sturgis** *KY* U.S.A.
226 E5 **Sturgis** *MI* U.S.A.
236 C2 **Sturgis** *SD* U.S.A.
190 E4 **Sturla** *r.* Italy
188 E3 **Šturlić** Bos.-Herz.
150 E4 **Sturminster Newton** *Dorset, England* U.K.
177 H4 **Štúrovo** Slovakia
151 I3 **Sturry** *Kent, England* U.K.
83 E2 **Sturt, Mount** *hill N.S.W.* Austr.
82 D3 **Sturt Bay** *S.A.* Austr.
86 F3 **Sturt Creek** *W.A.* Austr.
226 D4 **Sturtevant** *WI* U.S.A.
84 C3 **Sturt Plain** *N.T.* Austr.
82 E2 **Sturt Stony Desert** *Qld* Austr.
157 H3 **Sturzelbronn** France
215 F5 **Stutterheim** S. Africa
172 D3 **Stuttgart** Ger.
172 D2 **Stuttgart** *admin. reg. Baden-Württemberg* Ger.
237 F5 **Stuttgart** *AR* U.S.A.
Stutthof Pol. *see* **Sztutowo**
169 F5 **Stützerbach** Ger.
136 D2 **Stvyha** *r.* Ukr.
140 □B2 **Stykkishólmur** Iceland
137 I4 **Styla** Ukr.
198 C2 **Stylida** Greece
136 D1 **Styr** *r.* Belarus/Ukr.
Styria *land* Austria *see* **Steiermark**
257 G3 **Suaçuí Grande** *r.* Brazil
203 H5 **Suakin** Sudan
203 H5 **Suakin Archipelago** *is* Sudan
164 F1 **Suameer** Neth.
183 F1 **Suances** Spain
109 G3 **Suao** Taiwan
242 C2 **Suaqui Grande** Mex.
203 H5 **Suara, Mount** Eritrea
138 E4 **Subačius** Lith.
95 D4 **Subang** *Jawa Barat* Indon.
111 F7 **Subansiri** *r.* India
117 F5 **Subarnarekha** *r. W. Bengal* India
199 F1 **Subaşı** Turkey
199 E2 **Subaşı** Turkey
193 E1 **Subasio, Monte** *mt.* Italy
138 E3 **Subate** Latvia
191 G5 **Subbiano** Italy
197 G2 **Subcetate** Romania
110 F4 **Subei** *Gansu* China
Subeita *tourist site* Israel *see* **Shivta**
179 E2 **Suben** Austria
193 F3 **Subiaco** Italy
174 G1 **Subkowy** Pol.
237 C4 **Sublette** *KS* U.S.A.
196 D2 **Subotica** *Vojvodina, Srbija* Yugo.
203 I6 **Subucle** *mt.* Eritrea
177 H2 **Sučany** Slovakia
162 D3 **Suc-au-May** *hill* France
234 D2 **Succasunna** *NJ* U.S.A.
190 F4 **Succiso, Alpi di** *mts* Italy
197 H2 **Suceava** Romania
197 G2 **Suceava** *r.* Romania
158 E4 **Sucé-sur-Erdre** France
175 H6 **Sucha Beskidzka** Pol.
175 H1 **Suchacz** Pol.
177 G3 **Suchá Loz** Czech Rep.
174 D2 **Suchań** Pol.
Suchan Rus. Fed. *see* **Partizansk**
100 E4 **Suchan** *r.* Rus. Fed.
176 E2 **Suchdol** Czech Rep.
176 D3 **Suchdol nad Lužnicí** Czech Rep.
175 I4 **Suchedniów** Pol.
190 B2 **Suchet, Mont** *mt.* Switz.
244 C2 **Suchil** Mex.
175 L2 **Suchowola** Pol.
175 K3 **Suchożebry** Pol.
187 C7 **Sucina** Spain
250 B3 **Sucio** *r.* Col.
197 G2 **Suciu de Sus** Romania
147 C3 **Suck** *r.* Rep. of Ireland
227 G2 **Sucker Creek Landing** *Ont.* Can.
170 C2 **Suckow** Ger.
252 D4 **Sucre** Bol.
250 C2 **Sucre** *dept* Col.
251 F2 **Sucre** *state* Venez.
250 B5 **Sucumbíos** *prov.* Ecuador
251 G6 **Sucunduri** *r.* Brazil
256 B4 **Sucuriú** *r.* Brazil
Suczawa Romania *see* **Suceava**
207 H6 **Sud** *prov.* Cameroon
233 G2 **Sud, Rivière du** *r. Que.* Can.
139 K2 **Suda** Rus. Fed.
139 K2 **Suda** *r.* Rus. Fed.
137 H5 **Sudak** Ukr.
203 F6 **Sudan** *country* Africa
134 H4 **Suday** Rus. Fed.
120 C1 **Sud'bodarovka** Rus. Fed.
224 D4 **Sudbury** *Ont.* Can.
151 F2 **Sudbury** *Derbyshire, England* U.K.
151 H2 **Sudbury** *Suffolk, England* U.K.
210 A3 **Sudd** *swamp* Sudan
169 C3 **Suddendorf** Ger.
251 G3 **Suddie** Guyana
168 F2 **Sude** *r.* Ger.
168 D1 **Süden** Ger.
168 E1 **Süderbrarup** Ger.
168 F3 **Suderburg** Ger.
168 F2 **Südergellersen** Ger.
168 E1 **Süderhastedt** Ger.
168 D1 **Süderlügum** Ger.
168 D1 **Süderoogsand** *i.* Ger.
168 E1 **Süderstapel** Ger.
Sudetenland *mts* Czech Rep./Pol. *see* **Sudety**
174 D5 **Sudety** *mts* Czech Rep./Pol.
139 J5 **Sudimir** Rus. Fed.
139 M3 **Sudislavl'** Rus. Fed.
209 F5 **Sud-Kivu** *admin. reg.* Dem. Rep. Congo
234 C3 **Sudlersville** *MD* U.S.A.
169 B4 **Südlohn** Ger.
139 M4 **Sudogda** Rus. Fed.
139 M3 **Sudogda** *r.* Rus. Fed.
176 G3 **Sudoměřice** Czech Rep.
138 G3 **Sudomskiye Vysoty** *hills* Rus. Fed.
139 I5 **Sudost'** *r.* Rus. Fed.
207 H5 **Sud-Ouest** *prov.* Cameroon
136 B3 **Sudova Vyshnya** Ukr.
203 G2 **Sudr** Egypt
Südtirol *prov. Trentino - Alto Adige* Italy *see* **Bolzano**
140 □B2 **Suðurland** *constituency* Iceland
130 A3 **Suðuroy** *i.* Faroe Is
144 D1 **Suðuroy** *i.* Faroe Is
168 D3 **Sudwalde** Ger.
137 H2 **Sudzha** Rus. Fed.
137 H2 **Sudzha** *r.* Rus. Fed.
187 C5 **Sueca** Spain
197 G4 **Sŭedinenie** Bulg.
192 B5 **Suelli** *Sardegna* Italy
156 B5 **Suèvres** France
Suez Egypt *see* **El Suweis**
203 G2 **Suez, Gulf of** Egypt
203 G2 **Suez Canal** Egypt
124 C3 **Şufaynah** Saudi Arabia
235 D1 **Suffern** *NY* U.S.A.
151 H2 **Suffolk** *admin. div. England* U.K.
232 E6 **Suffolk** *VA* U.S.A.
235 F2 **Suffolk County** *county NY* U.S.A.
122 A2 **Sūfiān** Iran
129 C2 **Sugan, Gora** *mt.* Rus. Fed.
226 C4 **Sugar** *r. WI* U.S.A.
226 C3 **Sugarbush Hill** *hill WI* U.S.A.
232 B5 **Sugar Grove** *OH* U.S.A.
235 D1 **Sugar Loaf** *NY* U.S.A.
147 B5 **Sugarloaf Mountain** *hill* Rep. of Ireland
233 □H2 **Sugarloaf Mountain** *ME* U.S.A.
83 H3 **Sugarloaf Point** *N.S.W.* Austr.
234 C1 **Sugar Notch** *PA* U.S.A.
234 B1 **Sugar Run** *PA* U.S.A.
173 E2 **Sugenheim** Ger.
Süget *Xinjiang* China *see* **Sogat**
95 G1 **Sugut** *r. Sabah* Malaysia
197 G4 **Suhaia** Romania
106 E4 **Suhait** *Nei Mongol* China
Sūhāj Egypt *see* **Sohâg**
125 G2 **Şuḩār** Oman
197 H1 **Suharău** Romania
106 E1 **Sühbaatar** Mongolia
107 G2 **Sühbaatar** *prov.* Mongolia
179 F5 **Suhi vrh** *mt.* Slovenia
169 F5 **Suhl** Ger.
168 F3 **Suhlendorf** Ger.
188 F3 **Suhopolje** Croatia
172 C4 **Suhr** Switz.
125 F3 **Suhūl al Kidan** *plain* Saudi Arabia
206 E5 **Suhum** Ghana
199 G2 **Şuhut** Turkey
254 B4 **Suiá Missur** *r.* Brazil
Sui'an *Fujian* China *see* **Zhangpu**
100 D3 **Suibin** *Heilong.* China
109 F2 **Suichang** *Zhejiang* China
Suicheng *Fujian* China *see* **Jianning**
Suicheng *Guangdong* China *see* **Suixi**
109 E3 **Suichuan** *Jiangxi* China
Suid-Afrika *country* Africa *see* **South Africa, Republic of**
107 F4 **Suide** *Shaanxi* China
182 B2 **Suido, Serra do** *mts* Spain
100 D4 **Suifen** *r.* China
100 D3 **Suifenhe** *Heilong.* China
116 B4 **Suigam** *Gujarat* India
100 C3 **Suihua** *Heilong.* China
108 B2 **Suijiang** *Yunnan* China
100 C3 **Suileng** *Heilong.* China
160 B1 **Suilly-la-Tour** France
146 C3 **Suilven** *hill Scotland* U.K.
108 D3 **Suining** *Hunan* China
109 F1 **Suining** *Jiangsu* China
108 C2 **Suining** *Sichuan* China
252 D5 **Suipacha** Bol.
109 E1 **Suiping** *Henan* China
156 D3 **Suippe** *r.* France
156 E3 **Suippes** France
147 D4 **Suir** *r.* Rep. of Ireland
Suisse *country* Europe *see* **Switzerland**
104 B4 **Suita** Japan
234 B4 **Suitland** *MD* U.S.A.
109 F1 **Suixi** *Anhui* China
108 D4 **Suixi** *Guangdong* China
107 G5 **Suixian** *Henan* China
Suixian *Hubei* China *see* **Suizhou**
108 C3 **Suiyang** *Guizhou* China
Suizhai *Henan* China *see* **Xiancheng**
107 I3 **Suizhong** *Liaoning* China
109 E2 **Suizhou** *Hubei* China
116 C4 **Sujangarh** *Rajasthan* India
123 G5 **Sujawal** Pak.
Suk *atoll* Micronesia *see* **Pulusuk**
94 D4 **Sukabumi** *Jawa Barat* Indon.
95 E3 **Sukadana** *Kalimantan Barat* Indon.
94 D4 **Sukadana** *Sumatera* Indon.
105 G1 **Sukagawa** Japan
Sukarnapura *Irian Jaya* Indon. *see* **Jayapura**
Sukarno, Puntjak *mt.* Indon. *see* **Jaya, Puncak**
116 D4 **Suket** *Rajasthan* India
140 N3 **Sukeva** Fin.
139 J4 **Sukhinichi** Rus. Fed.
137 I4 **Sukhi Yaly** *r.* Ukr.
175 M6 **Sukhodil** Ukr.
139 L5 **Sukhodol'skiy** Rus. Fed.
139 J4 **Sukhodrev** *r.* Rus. Fed.
Sukhoivanovka Ukr. *see* **Stepnohirs'k**
134 I3 **Sukhona** *r.* Rus. Fed.
96 B3 **Sukhothai** Thai.
139 J3 **Sukhoverkovo** Rus. Fed.
Sukhumi Georgia *see* **Sokhumi**
Sukhum-Kale Georgia *see* **Sokhumi**
137 I3 **Sukhyy Torets'** *r.* Ukr.
137 F4 **Sukhyy Yelanets'** Ukr.
Sukkertoppen Greenland *see* **Maniitsoq**
134 F3 **Sukkozero** Rus. Fed.
123 G5 **Sukkur** Pak.
114 D2 **Sukma** *Madh. Prad.* India
177 H5 **Sükösd** Hungary
170 C2 **Sukow** Ger.
100 F3 **Sukpay** *r.* Rus. Fed.
116 C4 **Sukri** *r.* India
116 C4 **Sukri** *r.* India
139 K3 **Sukromny** Rus. Fed.
134 L4 **Suksun** Rus. Fed.
117 E5 **Suktel** *r.* India
103 F7 **Sukumo** Japan

Şükürbäyli to Tadmur 367

29 E4 Şükürbäyli Azer.
57 F4 Şul, Pico do mt. Brazil
44 J1 Sula i. Norway
34 J2 Sula r. Rus. Fed.
37 G3 Sula r. Ukr.
93 C3 Sula, Kepulauan is Indon.
23 G4 Sulaiman Ranges mts Pak.
29 E2 Sulak Rus. Fed.
29 E2 Sulak r. Rus. Fed.
94 C3 Sulasih, Gunung vol. Indon.
92 C4 Sulat Phil.
93 B3 Sulawesi i. Indon.
93 A3 Sulawesi Selatan prov. Indon.
93 B3 Sulawesi Tengah prov. Indon.
93 B4 Sulawesi Tenggara prov. Indon.
93 C2 Sulawesi Utara prov. Indon.
27 G4 Sulaymān Beg Iraq
24 D3 Sulayyimah Saudi Arabia
Sulci Sardegna Italy see Sant'Antioco
Sulcis Sardegna Italy see Sant'Antioco
92 A5 Sulcis reg. Sardegna Italy
74 D3 Sulechów Pol.
74 D3 Sulęcin Pol.
74 F3 Sulęcinek Pol.
74 F1 Sulęczyno Pol.
22 B2 Suledeh Iran
07 G4 Suleja Nigeria
75 H4 Sulejów Pol.
75 J3 Sulejówek Pol.
75 H4 Sulejowskie, Jezioro l. Pol.
95 G2 Suleman, Teluk b. Indon.
92 B4 Su Lernu r. Sardegna Italy
26 E3 Süleymanlı Turkey
99 E2 Süleymanlı Manisa Turkey
74 D4 Sulików Pol.
06 C5 Sulima Sierra Leone
97 I3 Sulina Romania
68 D3 Sulingen Ger.
40 L2 Suliskongen mt. Norway
40 L2 Sulitjelma Norway
41 O3 Sulkava Fin.
75 H6 Sułkowice Pol.
29 E2 Sulla-Chubutla r. Rus. Fed.
50 A6 Sullana Peru
47 C5 Sullane r. Rep. of Ireland
99 F2 Süller Turkey
51 G4 Sullington West Sussex, England U.K.
236 F4 Sullivan IL U.S.A.
230 C4 Sullivan IN U.S.A.
236 F4 Sullivan MO U.S.A.
222 E5 Sullivan Bay B.C. Can.
234 D1 Sullivan County county NY U.S.A.
234 B1 Sullivan County county PA U.S.A.
Sullivan Island Myanmar see Lanbi Kyun
146 □G1 Sullom Voe inlet Scotland U.K.
233 □I1 Sully Que. Can.
160 C1 Sully France
150 D3 Sully Vale of Glamorgan, Wales U.K.
156 C5 Sully-sur-Loire France
179 G4 Sulm r. Austria
175 H4 Sulmierzyce Łódzkie Pol.
174 F4 Sulmierzyce Wielkopolskie Pol.
Sulmo Italy see Sulmona
193 F2 Sulmona Italy
158 D4 Sulniac France
197 H5 Süloğlu Turkey
175 H5 Sułoszowa Pol.
174 F4 Sułów Pol.
175 K5 Sułów Pol.
237 E6 Sulphur LA U.S.A.
237 D5 Sulphur OK U.S.A.
237 E5 Sulphur r. TX U.S.A.
237 E5 Sulphur Springs TX U.S.A.
224 D4 Sultan Ont. Can.
123 E4 Sultan, Koh-i- mts Pak.
Sultanabad Andhra Prad. India see Osmannagar
Sultanabad Iran see Arāk
199 F1 Sultanbeyli Turkey
199 G2 Sultandağı Turkey
126 D3 Sultanhanı Turkey
199 F3 Sultanhisar Turkey
199 E1 Sultaniça Turkey
Sultanıye Turkey see Karapınar
116 E4 Sultanpur Uttar Prad. India
129 C1 Sultanskoye Rus. Fed.
92 B5 Sulu Archipelago is Phil.
126 D3 Sülüklü Turkey
121 G5 Sülüktü Kyrg.
202 D1 Suluntah Libya
202 D2 Sulūq Libya
114 D3 Suluru Andhra Prad. India
266 C5 Sulu Sea N. Pacific Ocean
137 F2 Sulymivka Ukr.
Sulyukta Kyrg. see Sülüktü
178 A3 Sulz Austria
173 F2 Sulz r. Ger.
173 E2 Sulzach r. Ger.
172 C3 Sulz am Neckar Ger.
173 H3 Sulzbach r. Ger.
172 D2 Sulzbach am Main Ger.
172 D2 Sulzbach an der Murr Ger.
172 D3 Sulzbach-Laufen Ger.
173 F2 Sulzbach-Rosenberg Ger.
172 B2 Sulzbach/Saar Ger.
178 A3 Sulzberg Austria
173 E4 Sulzberg Ger.
172 B4 Sulzburg Ger.
169 F5 Sulzdorf an der Lederhecke Ger.
173 F3 Sulzemoos Ger.
172 C2 Sulzfeld Baden-Württemberg Ger.
169 F5 Sulzfeld Bayern Ger.
173 E2 Sulzheim Ger.
169 F5 Sulzthal Ger.
250 B5 Sumaco, Volcán vol. Ecuador
125 G3 Sumāil Oman
94 B2 Sumatera i. Indon.
94 C3 Sumatera Barat prov. Indon.
94 C3 Sumatera Selatan prov. Indon.
94 B2 Sumatera Utara prov. Indon.
Sumatra i. Indon. see Sumatera
176 C2 Šumava mts Czech Rep.
93 B5 Sumba i. Indon.
93 A5 Sumba, Selat sea chan. Indon.
122 C2 Sumbar r. Turkm.
93 A5 Sumbawa i. Indon.
95 G5 Sumbawabesar Sumbawa Indon.
211 A6 Sumbawanga Tanz.
252 C3 Sumbay Peru
209 B7 Sumbe Angola
186 B1 Sumbilla Spain
94 C3 Sumbing, Gunung vol. Indon.
146 □G2 Sumburgh Shetland, Scotland U.K.
146 □G2 Sumburgh Head hd Scotland U.K.
206 C5 Sumbuya Sierra Leone
108 B2 Sumdo Sichuan China
222 C3 Sumdum AK U.S.A.
222 C3 Sumdum, Mount AK U.S.A.
254 F3 Sumé Brazil
95 D4 Sumedang Jawa Barat Indon.
122 B2 Sume'eh Sarā Iran
176 G5 Sümeg Hungary
161 B5 Sumène France
95 F4 Sumenep Jawa Timur Indon.
116 C4 Sumerpur Rajasthan India
Sumgait Azer. see Sumqayıt
177 J3 Šumiac Slovakia
190 C1 Sumiswald Switz.
102 □1 Sumiyō Japan
127 F3 Summēl Iraq
224 B2 Summer Beaver Ont. Can.
149 H3 Summer Bridge North Yorkshire, England U.K.
225 K3 Summerford Nfld. Can.
147 E3 Summerhill Rep. of Ireland
146 C3 Summer Isles Scotland U.K.
222 G5 Summerland B.C. Can.
225 I4 Summerside P.E.I. Can.
232 C5 Summersville WV U.S.A.
231 C5 Summerville GA U.S.A.
231 D5 Summerville SC U.S.A.
80 F4 Summit hill North I. N.Z.
235 D2 Summit NJ U.S.A.
236 D2 Summit SD U.S.A.
234 C2 Summit Hill PA U.S.A.
222 E3 Summit Lake B.C. Can.
222 F4 Summit Lake B.C. Can.
241 I2 Summit Mountain NV U.S.A.
239 F4 Summit Peak CO U.S.A.
234 B2 Summit Station PA U.S.A.
81 D5 Sumner South I. N.Z.
237 F5 Sumner MS U.S.A.
81 D5 Sumner, Lake South I. N.Z.
103 I5 Sumon-dake mt. Japan
104 A4 Sumoto Japan
93 A4 Sumpangbinangae Sulawesi Selatan Indon.
176 F2 Šumperk Czech Rep.
Sumpu Japan see Shizuoka
129 F3 Sumqayıt Azer.
129 F3 Sumqayıt r. Azer.
121 G4 Sumsar Kyrg.
137 G2 Sums'ka Oblast' admin. div. Ukr.
Sumskaya Oblast' admin. div. Ukr. see Sums'ka Oblast'
134 F2 Sumskiy Posad Rus. Fed.
168 F2 Sumte Ger.
231 D5 Sumter SC U.S.A.
116 D2 Sumur Jammu and Kashmir
176 G2 Šumvald Czech Rep.
190 D2 Sumvitg Switz.
137 H2 Sumy Ukr.
Sumy Oblast admin. div. Ukr. see Sums'ka Oblast'
238 E2 Sun r. MT U.S.A.
134 J4 Suna Rus. Fed.
102 J2 Sunagawa Japan
116 C3 Sunam Punjab India
117 G4 Sunamganj Bangl.
106 C4 Sunan Gansu China
101 C5 Sunan N. Korea
146 C5 Sunart, Loch inlet Scotland U.K.
177 J2 Šuňava Slovakia
125 F3 Şunaynah Oman
238 E1 Sunburst MT U.S.A.
83 F4 Sunbury Vic. Austr.
151 G3 Sunbury Surrey, England U.K.
232 B4 Sunbury OH U.S.A.
227 I5 Sunbury PA U.S.A.
261 G2 Sunchales Arg.
173 G3 Sünching Ger.
253 E6 Suncho Corral Arg.
101 C5 Sunch'ŏn N. Korea
101 C6 Sunch'ŏn S. Korea
215 F1 Sun City S. Africa
241 K5 Sun City AZ U.S.A.
240 I5 Sun City CA U.S.A.
233 H3 Suncook NH U.S.A.
177 L5 Suncuiuş Romania
138 C1 Sund Åland Fin.
94 D4 Sunda, Selat str. Indon.
Sunda Kalapa Indon. see Jakarta
238 F2 Sundance WY U.S.A.
117 G5 Sundarbans reg. Bangl./India
117 F5 Sundargarh Orissa India
116 D3 Sundarnagar Hima. Prad. India
265 L4 Sunda Shelf sea feature Indian Ocean
Sunda Strait Indon. see Sunda, Selat
Sunda Trench sea feature Indian Ocean see Java Trench
214 E5 Sundays r. E. Cape S. Africa
215 H3 Sundays r. Kwazulu-Natal S. Africa
86 D3 Sunday Strait W.A. Austr.
142 A2 Sunde Norway
149 H3 Sunderland Tyne and Wear, England U.K.
169 D4 Sundern (Sauerland) Ger.
169 F4 Sundhausen Ger.
199 G2 Sündiken Dağları mts Turkey
222 H5 Sundre Alta Can.
224 E4 Sundridge Ont. Can.
142 C3 Sunds Denmark
141 L3 Sundsvall Sweden
129 F3 Sündü Azer.
123 E2 Sundukli, Peski des. Turkm.
215 H3 Sundumbili S. Africa
116 D4 Sunel Rajasthan India
211 C6 Sunga Tanz.
94 D3 Sungailiat Sumatera Indon.
94 C3 Sungaipenuh Sumatera Indon.
Sungari r. China see Songhua Jiang
94 C1 Sungei Petani Malaysia
93 A4 Sungguminasa Sulawesi Selatan Indon.
Sungkiang Shanghai China see Songjiang
213 G3 Sungo Moz.
Sungqu Sichuan China see Songpan
129 C3 Süngülü Turkey
197 H4 Sungurlare Bulg.
126 D2 Sungurlu Turkey
192 A4 Suni Sardegna Italy
188 F3 Sunja Croatia
121 H3 Sunkar, Gora mt. Kazakh.
117 G4 Sunkosh Chhu r. Bhutan
117F4 Sun Kosi r. Nepal
137 G3 Sunky Ukr.
169 F5 Sünna Ger.
140 J3 Sunndalsøra Norway
142 E2 Sunne Sweden
141 I3 Sunnfjord reg. Norway
151 G3 Sunninghill Windsor and Maidenhead, England U.K.
241 L2 Sunnyside UT U.S.A.
238 C2 Sunnyside WA U.S.A.
240 F3 Sunnyvale CA U.S.A.
226 C4 Sun Prairie WI U.S.A.
253 F4 Sunsas, Sierra de hills Bol.
240 □ Sunset Beach HI U.S.A.
222 G4 Sunset House Alta Can.
131 M3 Suntar Rus. Fed.
210 C2 Suntu Eth.
238 D3 Sun Valley ID U.S.A.
100 C2 Sunwu Heilong. China
206 E5 Sunyani Ghana
129 E2 Sunzha r. Rus. Fed.
140 N3 Suolahti Fin.
141 N3 Suomenniemi Fin.
226 C1 Suomi Ont. Can.
Suomi country Europe see Finland
138 D1 Suomusjärvi Fin.
140 O2 Suomussalmi Fin.
103 E7 Suō-nada b. Japan
140 N3 Suonenjoki Fin.
97 D5 Suŏng Cambodia
96 C3 Suong r. Laos
134 F3 Suoyarvi Rus. Fed.
Suozhen Shandong China see Huantai
114 B3 Supa Karnataka India
241 K3 Supai AZ U.S.A.
117 F4 Supaul Bihar India
163 C6 Superbagnères France
156 D4 Superbe r. France
160 A3 Superbesse France
161 D4 Superdévoluy France
121 F5 Superfosfatnyy Uzbek.
241 L5 Superior AZ U.S.A.
238 D2 Superior MT U.S.A.
236 D3 Superior NE U.S.A.
226 A2 Superior WI U.S.A.
245 G5 Superior, Laguna lag. Mex.
226 D2 Superior, Lake Can./U.S.A.
161 A3 Superlioran France
191 J4 Supertarska Draga Croatia
188 F4 Supetar Croatia
97 C4 Suphan Buri Thai.
127 F3 Süphan Dağı mt. Turkey
193 F3 Supino Italy
91 I7 Supiori i. Indon.
137 F3 Supiy r. Ukr.
177 L4 Suplacu de Barcău Romania
139 J5 Suponevo Rus. Fed.
169 F3 Süpplingen Ger.
175 L2 Supraśl Pol.
175 L2 Supraśl r. Pol.
129 B2 Sup'sa r. Georgia
101 C4 Supung N. Korea
177 L4 Supur Romania
124 D4 Sūq al Inān Yemen
127 G5 Sūq ash Shuyūkh Iraq
109 F1 Suqian Jiangsu China
124 B2 Sūq Suwayq Saudi Arabia
125 F5 Suquṭrā i. Yemen
173 G4 Sur r. Ger.
206 E4 Sur r. Ghana
177 H4 Súr Hungary
125 G3 Şūr Oman
240 G3 Sur, Point CA U.S.A.
135 I5 Sura Rus. Fed.
120 A1 Sura r. Rus. Fed.
129 F3 Şuraabad Azer.
95 F4 Surabaya Jawa Timur Indon.
117 E5 Surajpur Madh. Prad. India
95 E4 Surakarta Jawa Tengah Indon.
197 G3 Şura Mare Romania
160 D2 Suran r. France
123 E5 Sūran Iran
128 C2 Şūrān Syria
177 H3 Šurany Slovakia
85 G5 Surat Qld Austr.
116 C5 Surat Gujarat India
116 C3 Suratgarh Rajasthan India
97 B5 Surat Thani Thai.
175 K3 Suraż Pol.
139 H4 Surazh Belarus
139 I5 Surazh Rus. Fed.
173 G4 Surberg Ger.
85 F4 Surbiton Qld Austr.
195 H2 Surbo Italy
127 G4 Sūrdāsh Iraq
197 H3 Surdila-Greci Romania
197 F2 Surduc Romania
197 F4 Surdulica Srbija Yugo.
172 A2 Sûre r. Ger./Lux.
116 B5 Surendranagar Gujarat India
240 G4 Surf CA U.S.A.
235 D3 Surf City NJ U.S.A.
151 G2 Surfleet Lincolnshire, England U.K.
116 C5 Surgana Mahar. India
162 B2 Surgères France
246 B2 Surgidero de Batabanó Cuba
130 I3 Surgut Rus. Fed.
164 F1 Surhuizum Neth.
Suri W. Bengal India see Siuri
186 E3 Súria Spain
114 C2 Suriapet Andhra Prad. India
190 C3 Surier Italy
92 C4 Surigao Phil.
92 C4 Surigao Strait Phil.
97 C4 Surin Thai.
Surinam country S. America see Suriname
251 G3 Suriname country S. America
251 H3 Suriname r. Suriname
122 C4 Suriyān Iran
127 I4 Surkhābād Iran
121 F5 Surkhandar'inskaya Oblast' admin. div. Uzbek.
121 F5 Surkhandar'ya r. Uzbek.
Surkhandarya Oblast admin. div. Uzbek. see Surkhandar'inskaya Oblast'
116 E3 Surkhet Nepal
123 G2 Surkhob r. Tajik.
Surkhondaryo r. Uzbek. see Surkhandar'ya
Surkhondaryo Wiloyati admin. div. Uzbek. see Surkhandar'inskaya Oblast'
156 D3 Surmelin r. France
127 F2 Sürmene Turkey
140 J3 Surnadalsøra Norway
197 G4 Sŭrnevo Bulg.
135 H6 Surovikino Rus. Fed.
222 C3 Surprise B.C. Can.
184 C1 Surrazala r. Port.
222 F5 Surrey B.C. Can.
151 G3 Surrey admin. div. England U.K.
190 D1 Sursee Switz.
137 H3 Surs'ko-Mykhaylivka Ukr.
135 I5 Surskoye Rus. Fed.
202 C2 Surt Libya
202 C2 Surt, Khalīj g. Libya
140 □B3 Surtsey i. Iceland
197 G3 Suru, Vârful mt. Romania
254 C2 Surubiú r. Brazil
126 E3 Sürüç Turkey
Surud Ad mt. Somalia see Shimbiris
105 E4 Suruga-wan b. Japan
94 C3 Surulangun Sumatera Indon.
251 F4 Surumú r. Brazil
92 C5 Surup Phil.
156 C3 Survilliers France
168 C3 Surwold Ger.
Suryapet Andhra Prad. India see Suriapet
160 C3 Sury-le-Comtal France
158 D4 Surzur France
129 E4 Şuşa Azer.
142 D4 Suså r. Denmark
190 C3 Susa Italy
190 B3 Susa, Valle di val. Italy
Susah Tunisia see Sousse
103 F7 Susaki Japan
Susamyr Kyrg. see Suusamyr
233 E6 Susan VA U.S.A.
122 B4 Sūsangerd Iran
134 H4 Susanino Rus. Fed.
240 G1 Susanville CA U.S.A.
190 F2 Susch Switz.
136 D2 Suschany Ukr.
191 H3 Susegana Italy
126 E2 Suşehri Turkey
168 F1 Süsel Ger.
197 G4 Sushitsa Bulg.
107 F5 Sushui r. China
176 C2 Sušice Czech Rep.
175 L5 Susiec Pol.
116 D5 Susner Madh. Prad. India
105 E2 Susobana-gawa r. Japan
109 F2 Susong Anhui China
105 E3 Susono Japan
233 F4 Susquehanna PA U.S.A.
227 I5 Susquehanna r. PA U.S.A.
232 E4 Susquehanna, West Branch r. PA U.S.A.
172 D3 Süßen Ger.
225 H4 Sussex N.B. Can.
234 D1 Sussex NJ U.S.A.
232 E6 Sussex VA U.S.A.
234 D1 Sussex County county NJ U.S.A.
168 D3 Süstedt Ger.
165 E3 Susteren Neth.
191 G3 Sustinente Italy
168 C3 Sustrum Ger.
78 □6 Susubona Sta Isabel Solomon Is
78 □6 Susuka Choiseul Solomon Is
131 P3 Susuman Rus. Fed.
199 F2 Susurluk Turkey
129 C3 Susuz Turkey
138 D4 Šušvė r. Lith.
211 B5 Suswa, Mount Kenya
175 H2 Susz Pol.
106 B2 Sutay Uul mt. Mongolia
199 G3 Sütçüler Turkey
194 C5 Sutera Sicilia Italy
83 G3 Sutherland N.S.W. Austr.
214 C5 Sutherland S. Africa
146 D3 Sutherland reg. Scotland U.K.
236 C3 Sutherland NE U.S.A.
232 E6 Sutherland VA U.S.A.
87 E5 Sutherland Range hills W.A. Austr.
116 B3 Sutlej r. India/Pak.
128 A1 Sütlüce Turkey
197 H5 Sütlüce Turkey
192 E2 Sutri Italy
240 G2 Sutter CA U.S.A.
240 G2 Sutter Creek CA U.S.A.
151 G2 Sutterton Lincolnshire, England U.K.
233 G2 Sutton Que. Can.
224 D2 Sutton r. Ont. Can.
81 C6 Sutton South I. N.Z.
151 H2 Sutton Cambridgeshire, England U.K.
236 D3 Sutton NE U.S.A.
232 C5 Sutton WV U.S.A.
151 H2 Sutton Bridge Lincolnshire, England U.K.
151 F2 Sutton Coldfield West Midlands, England U.K.
151 F3 Sutton Courtenay Oxfordshire, England U.K.
149 H4 Sutton in Ashfield Nottinghamshire, England U.K.
149 H3 Sutton-on-the-Forest North Yorkshire, England U.K.
149 I4 Sutton on Trent Nottinghamshire, England U.K.
151 H3 Sutton Valence Kent, England U.K.
85 F4 Suttor r. Qld Austr.
100 E2 Sutyr' r. Rus. Fed.
136 E3 Sutysky Ukr.
107 E2 Suugant Mongolia
215 E4 Suurberg mt. S. Africa
215 E5 Suurberg mts S. Africa
214 C6 Suurbraak S. Africa
138 E2 Suure-Jaani Estonia
121 H4 Suusamyr Kyrg.
79 □1a Suva Viti Levu Fiji
Suvalki Pol. see Suwałki
196 E4 Suva Reka Kosovo, Srbija Yugo.
129 D4 Suveren Turkey
192 C1 Suvereto Italy
Suvorov atoll Cook Is see Suwarrow
136 E5 Suvorov Moldova
139 K4 Suvorov Rus. Fed.
137 G4 Suvorove Dnipropetrovs'ka Oblast' Ukr.
136 E5 Suvorove Odes'ka Oblast' Ukr.
197 H4 Suvorovo Bulg.
Suvorovo Moldova see Ştefan Vodă
129 C1 Suvorovskaya Rus. Fed.
105 E2 Suwa Japan
175 K1 Suwałki Pol.
96 C4 Suwannaphum Thai.
231 D6 Suwannee r. FL U.S.A.
102 □1 Suwanose-jima i. Japan
95 G2 Suwaran, Gunung mt. Indon.
81 □2 Suwarrow atoll Cook Is
128 B3 Suwaylih Jordan
127 G4 Suwayqīyah, Hawr as imp. l. Iraq
Suways, Khalīj as g. Egypt see Suez, Gulf of
Suweilih Jordan see Suwaylih
Suweis, Khalîg el g. Egypt see Suez, Gulf of
Suweis, Qanâ el canal Egypt see Suez Canal
101 C5 Suwŏn S. Korea
108 D4 Suxu Guangxi China
121 J2 Suykbulak Kazakh.
250 A6 Suyo Peru
Sūyqbulaq Kazakh. see Suykbulak
122 D5 Sūzā Iran
121 G3 Suzak Kazakh.
105 E2 Suzaka Japan
139 M3 Suzdal' Rus. Fed.
161 C4 Suze-la-Rousse France
137 H1 Suzemka Rus. Fed.
109 F1 Suzhou Anhui China
Suzhou Gansu China see Jiuquan
109 G2 Suzhou Jiangsu China
101 C4 Suzi r. China
103 H5 Suzu Japan
104 C4 Suzuka Japan
104 C4 Suzuka-gawa r. Japan
104 C4 Suzuka-sanmyaku mts Japan
191 F4 Suzzara Italy
141 K3 Svabensverk Sweden
140 N1 Sværholthalvøya pen. Norway
140 □ Svalbard terr. Arctic Ocean
197 H4 Svalenik Bulg.
142 D4 Svallerup Denmark
136 B3 Svalyava Ukr.
143 H2 Svanberga Sweden
129 C2 Svanet'is K'edi hills Georgia
143 F3 Svängsta Sweden
140 M2 Svanstein Sweden
137 H2 Svapa r. Rus. Fed.
140 M2 Svappavaara Sweden
143 F1 Svärdsjö Sweden
142 C2 Svarstad Norway
138 E1 Svarta r. Fin.
143 F2 Svartå Sweden
143 F2 Svartälven r. Sweden
143 E1 Svartån r. Sweden
143 G2 Svartån r. Sweden
140 M2 Svartbyn Sweden
Svartenhuk Halvø pen. Greenland see Sigguup Nunaa
140 M2 Svartlä Sweden
136 D2 Svarytsevychi Ukr.
171 D5 Svatava Czech Rep.
144 J1 Svatjell hill Norway
179 I2 Svatobořice-Mistřín Czech Rep.
137 J3 Svatove Ukr.
176 G3 Svätý Jur Slovakia
177 H4 Svätý Peter Slovakia
97 D5 Svay Riĕng Cambodia
134 I4 Svecha Rus. Fed.
138 E4 Svėdasai Lith.
141 K3 Sveg Sweden
142 A2 Sveio Norway
138 C4 Švėkšna Lith.
141 I3 Svelgen Norway
140 J3 Svellingen Norway
137 H1 Sven' Rus. Fed.
138 E4 Švenčionėliai Lith.
138 F4 Švenčionys Lith.
142 D4 Svendborg Denmark
142 E3 Svenljunga Sweden
140 □ Svenskøya i. Svalbard
140 K3 Svenstavik Sweden
138 E4 Šventoji r. Lith.
Sverdlovsk Rus. Fed. see Yekaterinburg
137 J3 Sverdlovs'k Ukr.
120 F5 Sverdlovsk Uzbek.
134 M4 Sverdlovskaya Oblast' admin. div. Rus. Fed.
Sverdlovsk Oblast admin. div. Rus. Fed. see Sverdlovskaya Oblast'
221 I2 Sverdrup Islands Nunavut Can.
Sverige country Europe see Sweden
Švermovo Slovakia see Telgárt
137 G2 Svesa Ukr.
179 H4 Sveta Marija Croatia
138 D3 Švėtė r. Lith.
Sveti Ivan Zelina Croatia see Zelina
188 F4 Sveti Jure mt. Croatia
197 E5 Sveti Nikole Macedonia
176 G1 Světlá Hora Czech Rep.
176 E2 Světlá nad Sázavou Czech Rep.
100 F3 Svetlaya Rus. Fed.
100 G2 Svetlodarskoye Sakhalin Rus. Fed.
Svetlogorsk Belarus see Svyetlahorsk
138 C4 Svetlogorsk Kaliningradskaya Oblast' Rus. Fed.
130 J3 Svetlogorsk Krasnoyarskiy Kray Rus. Fed.
135 H7 Svetlograd Stavropol'skiy Kray Rus. Fed.
134 K4 Svetlopolyansk Rus. Fed.
Svetlovodsk Ukr. see Svitlovods'k
138 C4 Svetlyy Kaliningradskaya Oblast' Rus. Fed.
120 E2 Svetlyy Orenburgskaya Oblast' Rus. Fed.
135 I6 Svetlyy Yar Rus. Fed.
138 G1 Svetogorsk Leningradskaya Oblast' Rus. Fed.
Svetogorsk Respublika Dagestan Rus. Fed. see Shamil'kala
Svetozarevo Srbija Yugo. see Jagodina
196 D3 Svetozar Miletić Vojvodina, Srbija Yugo.
138 E3 Svētupe r. Latvia
140 □C2 Svíahnúkar vol. Iceland
136 C3 Svicha r. Ukr.
177 K2 Svidník Slovakia
176 C2 Švihov Czech Rep.
188 F4 Svilaja mts Croatia
196 E3 Svilajnac Srbija Yugo.
197 H5 Svilengrad Bulg.
197 F3 Svinecea Mare, Vârful mt. Romania
177 K2 Svinia Slovakia
177 H3 Svinná Slovakia
142 D4 Svinninge Denmark
138 F4 Svir Belarus
139 J1 Svir' r. Rus. Fed.
139 I1 Svirskaya Guba b. Rus. Fed.
139 I1 Svir'stroy Rus. Fed.
175 M6 Svirzh r. Ukr.
197 G4 Svishtov Bulg.
138 E5 Svislach Hrodzyenskaya Voblasts' Belarus
138 F5 Svislach Minskaya Voblasts' Belarus
175 M2 Svislach r. Belarus
138 D5 Svislach r. Belarus
138 G5 Svislach r. Belarus
Svisloch r. Belarus see Svislach
Svisloch r. Belarus see Svislach
Svisloch r. Belarus see Svislach
177 J2 Svit Slovakia
176 F3 Svitava r. Czech Rep.
176 F2 Svitavy Czech Rep.
137 J3 Svitlodars'k Ukr.
137 H3 Svitlohirs'ke Ukr.
137 G3 Svitlovods'k Ukr.
175 L4 Svityaz' Ukr.
Svizzera country Europe see Switzerland
137 I2 Svoboda Rus. Fed.
176 E1 Svoboda nad Úpou Czech Rep.
100 D2 Svobodnyy Rus. Fed.
129 C1 Svobody Rus. Fed.
197 F4 Svoge Bulg.
138 G4 Svol'nya r. Belarus
140 K1 Svolvær Norway
176 F2 Svratka Czech Rep.
176 F2 Svratka r. Czech Rep.
177 H2 Svrčinovec Slovakia
197 F4 Svrljig Srbija Yugo.
197 F4 Svrljiške Planine mts Yugo.
Svyatogorovskiy Rudnik Ukr. see Dobropillya
139 M4 Svyatoye, Ozero l. Rus. Fed.
138 G5 Svyetlahorsk Belarus
137 G1 Svyha r. Ukr.
136 C2 Svynya r. Ukr.
136 D2 Svyten'ka r. Ukr.
123 H3 Swabi Pak.
151 F2 Swadlincote Derbyshire, England U.K.
215 E5 Swaershoek S. Africa
151 H2 Swaffham Norfolk, England U.K.
85 H4 Swain Reefs Qld Austr.
231 D5 Swainsboro GA U.S.A.
77 I3 Swains Island American Samoa
212 B4 Swakopmund Namibia
149 H3 Swale r. England U.K.
78 □6 Swallow Islands Santa Cruz Is Solomon Is
165 F3 Swalmen Neth.
225 G1 Swampy r. Que. Can.
87 B6 Swan r. W.A. Austr.
223 K4 Swan r. Man./Sask. Can.
224 D2 Swan r. Ont. Can.
148 B5 Swan Rep. of Ireland
151 F4 Swanage Dorset, England U.K.
232 C5 Swandale WV U.S.A.
214 D5 Swanepoelspoort mt. S. Africa
83 E3 Swan Hill Vic. Austr.
222 H4 Swan Hills Alta Can.
246 B3 Swan Islands is Caribbean Sea
234 D1 Swan Lake NY U.S.A.
151 H3 Swanley Kent, England U.K.
147 D2 Swanlinbar Rep. of Ireland
81 D5 Swannanoa South I. N.Z.
231 E5 Swanquarter NC U.S.A.
82 D3 Swan Reach S.A. Austr.
223 K4 Swan River Man. Can.
226 A2 Swan River MN U.S.A.
148 C3 Swan's Cross Roads Rep. of Ireland
83 G5 Swansea Tas. Austr.
150 D3 Swansea Swansea, Wales U.K.
150 D3 Swansea admin. div. Wales U.K.
150 D3 Swansea Bay Wales U.K.
240 F3 Swanton CA U.S.A.
233 G2 Swanton VT U.S.A.
151 H2 Swanton Morley Norfolk, England U.K.
174 G1 Swarożyn Pol.
215 G4 Swartberg S. Africa
214 B6 Swartberg mt. S. Africa
214 A4 Swartdoorn r. S. Africa
234 C3 Swarthmore PA U.S.A.
215 F5 Swart Kei r. S. Africa
215 E5 Swartkops S. Africa
215 E5 Swartkops r. S. Africa
Swart Nossob watercourse Namibia see Black Nossob
215 F2 Swartplaas S. Africa
214 D3 Swartputs S. Africa
215 F1 Swartruggens S. Africa
234 D1 Swartswood NJ U.S.A.
215 H2 Swart Umfolozi S. Africa
227 F4 Swartz Creek MI U.S.A.
174 F3 Swarzędz Pol.
241 K2 Swasey Peak UT U.S.A.
227 G1 Swastika Ont. Can.
123 G3 Swat r. Pak.
234 B2 Swatara Creek r. PA U.S.A.
Swatow Guangdong China see Shantou
148 C3 Swatragh Northern Ireland U.K.
151 F4 Sway Hampshire, England U.K.
215 H2 Swaziland country Africa
141 K3 Sweden country Europe
234 C3 Swedesboro NJ U.S.A.
84 D3 Sweers Island Qld Austr.
232 D6 Sweet Briar VA U.S.A.
238 B2 Sweet Home OR U.S.A.
232 C6 Sweet Springs WV U.S.A.
234 B1 Sweet Valley PA U.S.A.
237 C5 Sweetwater TX U.S.A.
238 F3 Sweetwater r. WY U.S.A.
238 E3 Sweetwater Station WY U.S.A.
214 C6 Swellendam S. Africa
215 F4 Swempoort S. Africa
175 I2 Świątki Pol.
174 G1 Świbno Pol.
175 J3 Świder r. Pol.
174 E5 Świdnica Pol.
174 D4 Świdnica Pol.
175 K4 Świdnik Pol.
174 D2 Świdwin Pol.
174 E5 Świebodzice Pol.
174 D3 Świebodzin Pol.
174 G2 Świecie Pol.
174 E4 Święciechowa Pol.
175 H2 Świecie nad Osą Pol.
175 H2 Świedziebnia Pol.
174 G2 Świekatowo Pol.
174 D5 Świeradów-Zdrój Pol.
175 I3 Świercze Pol.
174 F5 Świerczów Pol.
174 G5 Świerklaniec Pol.
174 D4 Świerzawa Pol.
174 C2 Świerzno Pol.
174 E1 Świeszyno Pol.
175 J2 Świętajno Pol.
175 K1 Świętajno Pol.
175 I5 Świętokrzyskie prov. Pol.
175 I5 Świętokrzyskie, Góry hills Pol.
233 □H2 Swift r. ME U.S.A.
223 J5 Swift Current Sask. Can.
223 J5 Swiftcurrent Creek r. Sask. Can.
164 E2 Swifterbant Neth.
234 C1 Swiftwater PA U.S.A.
148 B3 Swilly r. Rep. of Ireland
147 D1 Swilly, Lough inlet Rep. of Ireland
151 F3 Swindon Swindon, England U.K.
151 F3 Swindon admin. div. England U.K.
149 I4 Swinefleet East Riding of Yorkshire, England U.K.
151 G2 Swineshead Lincolnshire, England U.K.
147 C3 Swinford Rep. of Ireland
174 G3 Świnice Warckie Pol.
175 H6 Świnna Pol.
174 C2 Świnoujście Pol.
146 F6 Swinton Scottish Borders, Scotland U.K.
149 H4 Swinton South Yorkshire, England U.K.
Swiss Confederation country Europe see Switzerland
Świstocz r. Belarus see Svislach
190 D2 Switzerland country Europe
147 E3 Swords Rep. of Ireland
85 E4 Swords Range hills Qld Austr.
174 F2 Swornegacie Pol.
234 C1 Swoyerville PA U.S.A.
134 F3 Syamozero, Ozero l. Rus. Fed.
134 H3 Syamzha Rus. Fed.
138 G4 Syanno Belarus
138 E5 Syarednenemanskaya Nizina lowland Belarus/Lith.
138 F5 Syarhyeyevichy Belarus
139 I1 Syas' r. Rus. Fed.
139 I1 Syas'troy Rus. Fed.
134 I4 Syava Rus. Fed.
215 G1 Sybrandskraal S. Africa
226 C5 Sycamore IL U.S.A.
139 J4 Sychevka Rus. Fed.
139 K4 Sychevo Rus. Fed.
174 F4 Syców Pol.
Sydenham atoll Gilbert Is Kiribati see Nonouti
83 G3 Sydney N.S.W. Austr.
225 I4 Sydney N.S. Can.
84 D3 Sydney Island Qld Austr.
Sydney Island Phoenix Is Kiribati see Manra
225 I4 Sydney Mines N.S. Can.
Sydzhak Uzbek. see Sidzhak
137 J4 Syedove Ukr.
128 A1 Syedra tourist site Turkey
137 J3 Syeverne Ukr.
137 J3 Syeverodonets'k Ukr.
168 D3 Syke Ger.
198 C3 Sykea Greece
234 B3 Sykesville MD U.S.A.
232 D4 Sykesville PA U.S.A.
140 I3 Sykkylven Norway
134 J3 Syktyvkar Rus. Fed.
231 C5 Sylacauga AL U.S.A.
117 G4 Sylhet Bangl.
117 G4 Sylhet admin. div. Bangl.
168 D1 Sylt i. Ger.
168 D1 Sylt-Ost Ger.
134 L4 Sylva r. Rus. Fed.
231 D5 Sylva NC U.S.A.
87 C4 Sylvania W.A. Austr.
231 D5 Sylvania GA U.S.A.
232 B4 Sylvania OH U.S.A.
222 H4 Sylvan Lake Alta Can.
231 D6 Sylvester GA U.S.A.
84 C3 Sylvester, Lake salt flat N.T. Austr.
222 E3 Sylvia, Mount B.C. Can.
199 E3 Symi Greece
199 E3 Symi i. Greece
146 E6 Symington South Lanarkshire, Scotland U.K.
92 B3 Syndicate Phil.
137 H3 Synel'nykove Ukr.
127 I2 Syngyrli, Mys pt Kazakh.
137 H2 Synivka Ukr.
131 N4 Synnagyn, Khrebet mts Rus. Fed.
141 J3 Synnfjell mt. Norway
86 E3 Synnott, Mount hill W.A. Austr.
86 E3 Synnott Range hills W.A. Austr.
150 C2 Synod Inn Ceredigion, Wales U.K.
134 L2 Synya Rus. Fed.
134 N2 Synya r. Rus. Fed.
136 F3 Synytsya r. Ukr.
136 F3 Synyukha r. Ukr.
Synzhera Moldova see Sîngerei
Synzherey Moldova see Sîngerei
235 E2 Syosset NY U.S.A.
263 C2 Syowa research stn Antarctica
175 J2 Sypniewo Pol.
Syracusae Sicilia Italy see Siracusa
Syracuse Sicilia Italy see Siracusa
236 C4 Syracuse KS U.S.A.
233 E3 Syracuse NY U.S.A.
171 D5 Syrau Ger.
121 G4 Syrdar'inskaya Oblast' admin. div. Uzbek.
121 E3 Syrdar'ya r. Asia
121 G4 Syrdar'ya Uzbek.
Syrdarya Oblast admin. div. Uzbek. see Syrdar'inskaya Oblast'
Syrdaryinskiy Uzbek. see Syrdar'ya
173 E3 Syrgenstein Ger.
126 E4 Syria country Asia
96 B3 Syriam Myanmar
Syrian Desert Asia see Bādiyat ash Shām
199 E3 Syrna i. Greece
198 D3 Syros i. Greece
139 L5 Syrskiy Rus. Fed.
141 N3 Sysmä Fin.
134 J3 Sysola r. Rus. Fed.
151 F2 Syston Leicestershire, England U.K.
136 E3 Sytkivtsi Ukr.
134 J4 Syumsi Rus. Fed.
134 K5 Syun r. Rus. Fed.
100 G2 Syurkum Rus. Fed.
137 H5 Syvash, Zatoka lag. Ukr.
137 H4 Syvas'ke Ukr.
137 G5 Syzivka Ukr.
120 B1 Syzran' Rus. Fed.
177 H4 Szabadbattyán Hungary
177 H4 Szabadegyháza Hungary
Szabadka Vojvodina, Srbija Yugo. see Subotica
177 K5 Szabadkígyós Hungary
177 I5 Szabadszállás Hungary
177 L3 Szabolcs-Szatmár-Bereg county Hungary
174 G4 Szadek Pol.
175 I6 Szaflary Pol.
177 J4 Szajol Hungary
177 H5 Szakes Hungary
177 I5 Szakmár Hungary
177 H4 Szákszend Hungary
177 K3 Szalaszend Hungary
177 I5 Szalkszentmárton Hungary
177 J3 Szalonna Hungary
174 F2 Szamocin Pol.
177 L3 Szamos r. Hungary
177 L3 Szamosszeg Hungary
174 E3 Szamotuły Pol.
177 I5 Szank Hungary
176 G4 Szany Hungary
177 H4 Szár Hungary
177 J5 Szarvas Hungary
177 J4 Szászberek Hungary
177 H5 Szászvár Hungary
177 L3 Szatmárcseke Hungary
177 J5 Szatymaz Hungary
177 H4 Százhalombatta Hungary
174 D3 Szczaniec Pol.
175 K6 Szczawne Pol.
175 I6 Szczawnica Pol.
174 E5 Szczawno-Zdrój Pol.
175 K5 Szczebrzeszyn Pol.
174 C2 Szczecin Pol.
174 E2 Szczecinek Pol.
175 H5 Szczekociny Pol.
175 J2 Szczepankowo Pol.
175 H4 Szczerców Pol.
175 J5 Szczucin Pol.
175 K2 Szczuczyn Pol.
175 I1 Szczurkowo Pol.
175 I5 Szczurowa Pol.
175 H6 Szczyrk Pol.
174 E5 Szczytna Pol.
174 G4 Szczytniki Pol.
175 I2 Szczytno Pol.
Szechwan prov. China see Sichuan
177 I3 Szécsény Hungary
177 H5 Szederkény Hungary
177 H5 Szedres Hungary
177 J5 Szeged Hungary
177 K4 Szeghalom Hungary
177 J5 Szegvár Hungary
177 H4 Székesfehérvár Hungary
177 J5 Székkutas Hungary
177 H5 Szekszárd Hungary
174 G1 Szemud Pol.
177 I4 Szendehely Hungary
177 J3 Szendrő Hungary
177 J3 Szendrőlád Hungary
177 I4 Szentendre Hungary
177 J5 Szentes Hungary
176 F5 Szentgotthárd Hungary
177 J4 Szentistván Hungary
177 I5 Szentkirály Hungary
177 G5 Szentlászló Hungary
177 I4 Szentlőrinckáta Hungary
177 I4 Szentmártonkáta Hungary
177 G5 Szentőrinc Hungary
176 F4 Szentpéterfa Hungary
177 K4 Szentpéterszeg Hungary
176 F5 Szepetnek Hungary
175 K3 Szepietowo Pol.
177 H5 Szeremle Hungary
177 K3 Szerencs Hungary
177 K4 Szerep Hungary
175 J6 Szerzyny Pol.
175 K1 Szeska Góra hill Pol.
175 J2 Szestno Pol.
177 H4 Szigetbecse Hungary
177 H4 Szigethalom Hungary
177 I4 Szigetszentmiklós Hungary
177 H4 Szigetújfalu Hungary
177 G5 Szigetvár Hungary
176 G5 Szigliget Hungary
177 J4 Szihalom Hungary
177 J3 Szikszó Hungary
176 G4 Szil Hungary
177 J3 Szilvásvárad Hungary
174 F4 Szkaradowo Pol.
174 D5 Szklarska Poręba Pol.
174 E4 Szklary Górne Pol.
175 K6 Szkło r. Pol.
175 J2 Szkwa r. Pol.
174 E4 Szlichtyngowa Pol.
177 H4 Szob Hungary
177 J3 Szögliget Hungary
177 J4 Szolnok Hungary
177 G5 Szőlősgyörök Hungary
176 F4 Szombathely Hungary
177 J4 Szomolya Hungary
175 K5 Szówsko Pol.
174 D4 Szprotawa Pol.
174 D4 Szprotawa r. Pol.
175 I5 Szreniawa r. Pol.
176 E1 Szrenica mt. Czech Rep.
175 I2 Szreńsk Pol.
175 H2 Szropy Pol.
175 L2 Sztabin Pol.
Sztálinváros Hungary see Dunaújváros
175 H2 Sztum Pol.
175 H1 Sztutowo Pol.
174 F2 Szubin Pol.
177 I4 Szűcsi Hungary
175 L2 Szudziałowo Pol.
177 I3 Szügy Hungary
177 J3 Szuhogy Hungary
175 K3 Szulborze Wielkie Pol.
175 K3 Szumowa Pol.
177 I4 Szurdokpüspöki Hungary
175 I4 Szydłowiec Pol.
175 I2 Szydłowo Pol.
174 E2 Szydłowo Pol.
175 J2 Szymonka Pol.
174 F4 Szymonków Pol.
174 G4 Szynkielów Pol.
175 L1 Szypliszki Pol.

T

210 D2 Taagga Duudka reg. Somalia
81 □3 Taakoka i. Rarotonga Cook Is
177 H5 Tab Hungary
92 B3 Tabaco Phil.
124 C2 Tābah Saudi Arabia
177 H4 Tabajd Hungary
95 F5 Tabanan Bali Indon.
183 F2 Tabanera de Cerrato Spain
95 F2 Tabang r. Indon.
215 G4 Tabankulu S. Africa
Ţabaqah Syria see Madīnat ath Thawrah
247 □7 Tabaquite Trin. and Tob.
182 E3 Tábara Spain
169 F5 Tabarz Ger.
122 D3 Ţabas Khorāsan Iran
122 E3 Ţabas Khorāsan Iran
138 E2 Tabasalu Estonia
245 H4 Tabasco state Mex.
122 D4 Tabāsin Iran
122 B4 Tābask, Kūh-e mt. Iran
250 D6 Tabatinga Amazonas Brazil
256 C4 Tabatinga São Paulo Brazil
254 D4 Tabatinga, Serra da hills Brazil
92 B2 Tabayoo, Mount Luzon Phil.
177 I5 Tabdi Hungary
204 E3 Tabelbala Alg.
223 H5 Taber Alta Can.
205 G2 Taberdga Alg.
143 F3 Taberg hill Sweden
185 H3 Tabernas Spain
Tabernes de Valldigna Spain see Tavernes de la Valldigna
185 H3 Taberno Spain
96 B1 Tabet, Nam r. Myanmar
78 □3a Tabik i. Kwajalein Marshall Is
94 C3 Tabir r. Indon.
77 H2 Tabiteuea atoll Gilbert Is Kiribati
138 F2 Tabivere Estonia
92 B3 Tablas i. Phil.
92 B3 Tablas Strait Phil.
214 B5 Table Mountain hill S. Africa
207 F5 Tabligbo Togo
185 F2 Tablillas r. Spain
182 C2 Taboada Spain
251 F6 Tabocal r. Brazil
253 G4 Tabocó r. Brazil
176 D2 Tábor Czech Rep.
211 B6 Tabora Tanz.
211 B6 Tabora admin. reg. Tanz.
177 I4 Táborfalva Hungary
123 G1 Taboshar Tajik.
261 H2 Tabossi Arg.
146 B3 Tabost Western Isles, Scotland U.K.
206 D5 Tabou Côte d'Ivoire
122 A2 Tabrīz Iran
182 B4 Tábua Port.
182 C3 Tabuaço Port.
267 I5 Tabuaeran i. Kiribati
183 I3 Tabuenca Spain
124 B1 Tabūk Saudi Arabia
124 B1 Tabūk prov. Saudi Arabia
83 H2 Tabulam N.S.W. Austr.
121 I1 Tabuny Rus. Fed.
193 G3 Taburno, Monte mt. Italy
78 □5 Tabwémasana, Mount Vanuatu
143 H2 Täby Sweden
177 H4 Tác Hungary
251 H5 Tacaipu, Serra hills Brazil
244 D4 Tacámbaro Mex.
243 G6 Tacaná, Volcán de vol. Mex.
242 □K7 Tacarcuna, Cerro mt. Panama
179 F4 Tacen Slovenia
110 C2 Tacheng Xinjiang China
173 G3 Tacherting Ger.
222 E4 Tachie B.C. Can.
105 F3 Tachikawa Tōkyō Japan
102 I4 Tachikawa Yamagata Japan
250 C2 Táchira state Venez.
176 B2 Tachov Czech Rep.
195 F4 Tacina r. Italy
92 C4 Tacloban Phil.
252 C4 Tacna Peru
252 C4 Tacna dept Peru
241 K5 Tacna AZ U.S.A.
238 B2 Tacoma WA U.S.A.
226 B2 Taconite Harbor MN U.S.A.
258 E2 Taco Pozo Arg.
216 □3a Tacoronte Tenerife Canary Is
258 G3 Tacuarembó Uru.
261 J3 Tacuarembó dept Uru.
242 C2 Tacupeto Mex.
174 F4 Taczanów Drugi Pol.
103 I5 Tadami-gawa r. Japan
192 A4 Tadasuni Sardegna Italy
149 H4 Tadcaster North Yorkshire, England U.K.
205 F3 Tademaït, Plateau du Alg.
78 □5 Tadine Î. Loyauté New Caledonia
205 H4 Tadjentourt hill Alg.
Tadjikistan country Asia see Tajikistan
210 D2 Tadjoura Djibouti
210 D2 Tadjoura, Golfe de g. Djibouti
151 F3 Tadley Hampshire, England U.K.
128 D2 Tadmur Syria

250 B3 Tadó Col.
225 G3 Tadoussac Que. Can.
114 C3 Tadpatri Andhra Prad. India
205 H4 Tadrart hills Alg.
202 A3 Tadrart Acacus tourist site Libya
114 C2 Tadvale Mahar. India
Tadzhikskaya S.S.R. country Asia see Tajikistan
138 D2 Taebla Estonia
Taech'ŏn S. Korea see Poryŏng
101 C5 Taedong-gang r. N. Korea
101 D6 Taegu S. Korea
101 C6 Taejŏn S. Korea
101 C5 Taejŏng S. Korea
101 D5 T'aepaek S. Korea
150 C3 Taf r. Wales U.K.
77 I3 Tafahi i. Tonga
183 I2 Tafalla Spain
215 E4 Tafelberg S. Africa
214 C3 Tafelberg mt. S. Africa
251 G4 Tafelberg mt. Suriname
190 C2 Tafers Switz.
150 D3 Taffs Well Cardiff, Wales U.K.
Tafila Jordan see Aṭ Ṭafīlah
206 D4 Tafiré Côte d'Ivoire
258 D2 Tafí Viejo Arg.
204 C3 Tafraoute Morocco
122 B3 Tafresh Iran
240 H4 Taft CA U.S.A.
123 E4 Taftān, Kūh-e mt. Iran
128 C2 Taftanāz Syria
234 C1 Tafton PA U.S.A.
186 F2 Taga mt. Spain
102 J4 Tagajō Japan
135 G7 Taganak i. Phil.
137 J4 Taganrog, Gulf of Rus. Fed./Ukr.
Taganrogskiy Zaliv b. Rus. Fed./Ukr. see Taganrog, Gulf of
206 C2 Tagant admin. reg. Maur.
122 D2 Tagarev, Gora mt. Iran/Turkm.
103 E7 Tagawa Japan
135 I5 Tagay Rus. Fed.
92 B4 Tagbilaran Phil.
111 C5 Tagchagpu Ri mt. Xizang China
Tagdempt Alg. see Tiaret
190 C5 Taggia Italy
206 E3 Taghin-Dassouri Burkina
Tăghira Moldova see Țighira
222 C2 Tagish Y.T. Can.
193 F2 Tagliacozzo Italy
191 I3 Tagliamento r. Italy
192 B2 Taglio-Isolaccio Corse France
156 E3 Tagnon France
92 C4 Tagoloan r. Phil.
122 D1 Tagta Turkm.
123 E3 Tagtabazar Turkm.
256 C1 Taguatinga Minas Gerais Brazil
254 D5 Taguatinga Tocantins Brazil
92 B2 Tagudin Phil.
77 F3 Tagula Island P.N.G.
92 C5 Tagum Phil.
184 B1 Tagus r. Port./Spain
alt. Tejo (Spain),
alt. Tejo (Portugal)
107 J2 Taha Heilong. China
222 G5 Tahaetkun Mountain B.C. Can.
185 H3 Tahal Spain
94 C1 Tahan, Gunung mt. Malaysia
204 D3 Tahanaoute Morocco
79 ☐3 Tahanea atoll
Arch. des Tuamotu Fr. Polynesia
Tahanroz'ka Zatoka b. Rus. Fed./Ukr. see Taganrog, Gulf of
205 G5 Tahat, Mont mt. Alg.
Tahaurawe i. HI U.S.A. see Kahoolawe
100 C1 Tahe Heilong. China
80 D1 Taheke North I. N.Z.
147 B5 Tahilla Rep. of Ireland
106 C2 Tahilt Mongolia
79 ☐3a Tahiti i. Fr. Polynesia
177 I4 Tahitótfalu Hungary
123 E4 Tahlāb r. Iran/Pak.
123 E4 Tahlāb, Dasht-i plain Pak.
237 E5 Tahlequah OK U.S.A.
222 D3 Tahltan B.C. Can.
240 G2 Tahoe City CA U.S.A.
240 G2 Tahoe Vista CA U.S.A.
237 C5 Tahoka TX U.S.A.
80 E3 Tahora North I. N.Z.
80 F3 Tahorakuri North I. N.Z.
207 G3 Tahoua Niger
207 G3 Tahoua dept Niger
122 D4 Tahrūd Iran
122 C4 Tahrūd r. Iran
222 E5 Tahsis B.C. Can.
203 F3 Tahta Egypt
199 G2 Tahtaköprü Bursa Turkey
199 G3 Tahtali Dağ mt. Turkey
222 E4 Tahtsa Peak B.C. Can.
252 D2 Tahuamanú Bol.
252 C2 Tahuamanú Peru
79 ☐3 Tahuata i. Fr. Polynesia
93 C2 Tahuna Sulawesi Utara Indon.
206 D5 Taï Côte d'Ivoire
107 I3 Tai'an Liaoning China
107 H4 Tai'an Shandong China
107 E5 Taibai Shaanxi China
108 C1 Taibai Shaanxi China
Taibei Taiwan see T'aipei
185 H2 Taibilla r. Spain
191 H2 Taibón Agordino Italy
Taibus Qi Nei Mongol China see Baochang
109 G3 T'aichung Taiwan
Taidong Taiwan see T'aitung
81 C7 Taieri r. South I. N.Z.
81 C6 Taieri Ridge South I. N.Z.
205 E5 Taïfa Niger
107 G4 Taigu Shanxi China
107 G4 Taihang Shan mts China
107 G4 Taihang Shan mts China
80 E3 Taihape North I. N.Z.
109 E1 Taihe Anhui China
109 E3 Taihe Jiangxi China
Taihe Sichuan China see Shehong
Taihezhen Sichuan China see Shehong
109 F2 Taihu Anhui China
108 D3 Taijiang Guizhou China
107 J2 Taikang Henan China
107 G5 Taikang Henan China
96 A3 Taikkyi Myanmar
104 B3 Taiko-yama hill Japan
107 I2 Tailai Heilong. China
82 D3 Tailem Bend S.A. Austr.
Tailuge Taiwan see T'ailuko
109 G3 T'ailuko Taiwan
206 E4 Tain r. Ghana
146 E1 Tain Highland, Scotland U.K.
109 G4 T'ainan Taiwan
160 B1 Taingy France
161 C3 Tain-l'Hermitage France
157 G2 Taintrux France
100 ☐1 Taio r. H.K. China
109 ☐1 Tai Po H.K. China
254 G3 Taipu Brazil
102 ☐1 Taipu i. Japan

179 E2 Taiskirchen im Innkreis Austria
156 E3 Taissy France
81 D5 Taitanu South I. N.Z.
259 B7 Taitao, Península de pen. Chile
210 B4 Taiti mt. Kenya
109 G4 T'aitung Taiwan
140 O2 Taivalkoski Fin.
141 N1 Taivassalo Fin.
141 M3 Taivassalo Fin.
109 G4 Taiwan country Asia
Taiwan Haixia str. China/Taiwan see Taiwan Strait
Taiwan Shan mts Taiwan see Chungyang Shanmo
109 F4 Taiwan Strait China/Taiwan
Taixian Jiangsu China see Jiangyan
109 G1 Taïyetos Óros mts Greece see Tavgetos
107 G4 Taiyuan Shanxi China
107 F4 Taiyue Shan mts China
111 F6 Taize France
111 F6 Taizhao Xizang China
109 F1 Taizhou Jiangsu China
109 G3 Taizhou Jiangsu China
109 F2 Taizhou Wan b. China
101 C4 Taizi r. China
124 C5 Ta'izz Yemen
124 C5 Ta'izz governorate Yemen
93 D3 Tajem, Gunung hill Indon.
205 H2 Tajerouine Tunisia
123 G2 Tajikistan country Asia
104 D3 Tajimi Japan
116 D4 Taj Mahal tourist site Uttar Prad. India
180 C3 Tajo r. Spain
alt. Tejo (Portugal),
conv. Tagus
127 H4 Tajrish Iran
252 D5 Tajsara, Cordillera de mts Bol.
183 G4 Tajuña r. Spain
96 B3 Tak Thai.
122 A2 Taka'Bonerate, Kepulauan atolls Indon.
93 B4 Takabba Kenya
176 G4 Takácsi Hungary
105 G2 Takahagi Japan
104 D2 Takahama Japan
103 F6 Takahashi Japan
262 Q1 Takahe, Mount Antarctica
104 C3 Takaishi Japan
116 D5 Takal Madh. Prad. India
103 G6 Takamatsu Japan
104 D2 Takamori Japan
104 D2 Takaoka Japan
80 F4 Takapau North I. N.Z.
80 G3 Takapau North I. N.Z.
80 E2 Takapuna North I. N.Z.
102 ☐1 Takara-jima i. Japan
104 A4 Takasago Japan
105 F2 Takasaki Japan
104 C2 Takashōzu-yama mt. Japan
105 G2 Takasu-yama hill Indon.
105 G2 Takasuna-san hill Ibaraki Japan
104 C2 Takatokuwara Botswana
104 B4 Takatsuki Japan
103 F7 Takatsuki-yama mt. Japan
251 G4 Takatu r. Brazil/Guyana
104 D2 Takayama Japan
105 G3 Tak Bai Thai.
104 C3 Takefu Japan
103 F6 Takehara Japan
151 H3 Takeley Essex, England U.K.
94 B1 Takengon Sumatera Indon.
Takeo Cambodia see Takêv
103 E7 Take-shima i. N. Pacific Ocean see Liancourt Rocks
122 B2 Takestan Iran
103 E7 Taketa Japan
104 C4 Taketoyo Japan
97 D5 Takêv Cambodia
123 G2 Takhar prov. Afgh.
116 E5 Takhatpur Madh. Prad. India
181 G5 Takhemaret Alg.
Takhiatash Uzbek. see Gulable
222 C2 Takhini r. Y.T. Can.
222 C2 Takhini Hotspring Y.T. Can.
96 C4 Ta Khli Thai.
97 D5 Ta Khmau Cambodia
135 H7 Takhta Rus. Fed.
Takhta Rus. Fed. see Tagta
Takhta-Bazar Turkm. see Tagtabazar
197 M3 Takhtabrod Kazakh.
120 F1 Takhtakupyr Uzbek.
137 J5 Takhtamukay Rus. Fed. see Takhtamukay
122 B3 Takht Apān, Kūh-e mt. Iran
127 I5 Takht-e Jamshid tourist site Iran
123 G4 Takht-i-Sulaiman mt. Pak.
122 B2 Takht-i-Sulaiman mt. Iran
207 H3 Takijuq Lake Nunavut Can. see Napaktulik Lake
102 J2 Takikawa Japan
181 A6 Takitimu Mountains South I. N.Z.
129 F4 Täklä Azer.
222 E4 Takla Landing B.C. Can.
Takla Makan des. China see Taklimakan Shamo
Taklamakan Shamo des. China see Taklimakan Shamo
122 B3 Takob Tajik.
111 F6 Takpa Shiri mt. Xizang China
177 I4 Taksony Hungary
177 K4 Takta r. Hungary
177 I4 Taktaharkány Hungary
222 C3 Taku B.C. Can.
220 D4 Taku r. Can./U.S.A.
103 E7 Taku Japan
207 H5 Takum Nigeria
81 ☐2 Takutea i. Cook Is
78 ☐6 Takwa Malaita Solomon Is
105 F3 Tama Japan
183 F1 Tama Spain
95 ☐ Tama Abu, Banjaran mts Sarawak Malaysia see Tama Abu, Banjaran
105 F3 Tama-gawa r. Japan
206 D4 Tamale Ghana
182 D4 Talamanca Spain
177 J4 Tamana i. Gilbert Is Kiribati
204 D2 Tamanar Morocco
206 D3 Tamani Mali
103 F6 Tamano Japan
205 G5 Tamanrasset Alg.
205 G5 Tamanrasset, Oued watercourse Alg.
117 G5 Tamar r. Bihar India
150 C4 Tamar r. England U.K.
186 D3 Tamarite de Litera Spain
258 C1 Tamarugal, Pampa de plain Chile
177 H5 Tamási Hungary
197 H2 Tamási Romania
213 ☐I4 Tamatave Madag. see Toamasina
192 B4 Tamatea state Mex.
117 G5 Tambaga Sri Lanka
244 C4 Tamazula Mex.
242 ☐J7 Tamazunchale Mex.
210 B4 Tambach Kenya
169 F5 Tambach-Dietharz Ger.

128 B4 Tal'at al Jamā'ah, Rujm mt. Jordan
207 G3 Talata-Mafara Nigeria
128 C2 Tal 'at Mūsá mt. Lebanon/Syria
93 C1 Talaud, Kepulauan is Indon.
182 D5 Talavera de la Reina Spain
184 D2 Talavera la Real Spain
84 E3 Talawanta Qld Austr.
131 G3 Talaya Rus. Fed.
92 C5 Talayan Phil.
187 B7 Talayón hill Spain
182 E5 Talayuela Spain
187 B5 Talayuelas Spain
185 H5 Talayuelo mt. Spain
116 D4 Talbehat Uttar Prad. India
87 E5 Talbot, Mount hill W.A. Austr.
234 B2 Talbot County county MD U.S.A.
231 C5 Talbotton GA U.S.A.
258 B5 Talbragar r. N.S.W. Austr.
258 B4 Talca Chile
118 D5 Talcahuano Chile
117 F5 Talcher Orissa India
100 C1 Taldan Rus. Fed.
139 K3 Taldom Rus. Fed.
121 I3 Taldy-Kurgan Kazakh. see Taldykorgan
Taldykorgan
Taldykorgan Kazakh. see Taldykorgan
Taldysu Kyrg. see Taldy-Suu
121 I4 Talegaon Mahar. India
114 C1 Talegaon Mahar. India
123 E3 Taleh Zang Iran
116 D5 Taleh Madh. Prad. India
215 G5 Teleni S. Africa
158 E3 Talensac France
187 C5 Tales Spain
122 B2 Tälesh Gīlān Iran
Talesh Gīlān Iran see Hashtpar
139 K2 Talets, Ozero i. Rus. Fed.
86 C4 Talga r. W.A. Austr.
121 I4 Talgar Kazakh.
121 I4 Talgar, Pik mt. Kazakh.
150 C2 Talgarreg Ceredigion, Wales U.K.
150 D3 Talgarth Powys, Wales U.K.
116 C5 Talikota Karnataka India
245 F3 Talihina Mex.
245 F3 Taliahua, Laguna de lag. Mex.
94 B1 Taliabu i. Indon.
161 E4 Tali Nadu state India
234 C1 Taliment PA U.S.A.
234 C1 Tamins Switz.
106 D2 Tamirin Gol r. Mongolia
196 E3 Tamiš r. Yugo.
124 C5 Tamitatoala r. Brazil
203 F2 Ṭāmiyah Egypt
204 E2 Tamiyah, Jabal hill Saudi Arabia
204 E2 Tamlett, Plaine de plain Morocco
117 F5 Tamluk r. W. Bengal India
172 D3 Tamm Ger.
193 M3 Tammarvi r. Nunavut Can.
223 K1 Tammela Fin.
168 D1 Tammensiel Ger.
Tammfors Fin. see Tampere
Tammisaari Fin. see Ekenäs
196 B1 Tamnava r. Yugo.
182 C1 Támoga r. Spain
231 D7 Tampa FL U.S.A.
231 D7 Tampa Bay FL U.S.A.
141 M3 Tampere Fin.
245 F2 Tampico Mex.
117 H4 Tamu r. Nepal
185 F2 Tamurejo Spain
83 G2 Tamworth N.S.W. Austr.
149 I5 Tamworth Staffordshire, England U.K.
210 B4 Tana r. Fin./Norway see Tenojoki
210 B4 Tana r. Kenya
256 C4 Tana Madag. see Antananarivo
Tana i. Vanuatu see Tanna
Tana, Lake Eth. see T'ana Häyk'
103 C3 Tanabe Japan
256 C4 Tanabi Brazil
140 O1 Tana Bru Norway
140 O1 Tanafjorden inlet Norway
192 B4 Tanaga Island AK U.S.A.
193 G2 Tanagro r. Italy
95 G3 Tanahgrogot Kalimantan Timur Indon.
94 B3 Tanahjampea i. Indon.
116 E3 Tanakpur Uttar Prad. India
93 A3 Tanambung Sulawesi Selatan Indon.
241 N.T. Austr.
84 B3 Tanami N.T. Austr.
97 D5 Tân An Vietnam
220 C3 Tanana AK U.S.A.
Tananarive Madag. see Antananarivo
213 ☐I4 Tananarive Madag.
190 D3 Tanaro r. Italy
207 H3 Tanout Niger
245 G4 Tanquian Mex.
192 A3 Tanaro r. Corse France
129 B3 Tansilla Burkina
149 H4 Tansley Derbyshire, England U.K.
107 G4 Tancheng Shandong China
101 D4 Tanchon N. Korea
244 C4 Tancitario, Cerro de mt. Mex.
245 E5 Tancoco Mex.
206 C4 Tancoco Côte d'Ivoire
116 D3 Tanda Uttar Prad. India
117 E4 Tanda Uttar Prad. India
141 K3 Tandådalen Sweden
128 B3 Tandara Israel
114 C2 Tanuku Andhra Prad. India
117 H4 Tandil Arg.
261 H5 Tandil Arg.
261 I5 Tandil, Sierra del hills Arg.
206 D4 Tandjilé pref. Chad
222 D3 Tanzilla r. B.C. Can.
211 B6 Tanzania country Africa
222 D3 Tanzilla r. B.C. Can.

78 ☐6 Tangarare Guadalcanal Solomon Is
245 G3 Tapanatepec Mex.
114 C4 Tangasseri Kerala India
108 B3 Tangdan Yunnan China
Tangdukou Hunan China see Shaoyang
122 C2 Tangeli Iran
263 D2 Tange Promontory hd Antarctica
204 D2 Tanger Morocco
180 D5 Tanger prov. Morocco
94 C4 Tangerang Jawa Barat Indon.
170 D3 Tangermünde Ger.
108 B1 Tanggor Sichuan China
170 C3 Tangermünde Ger.
107 H4 Tanggu Tianjin China
111 E5 Tanggula Shan mt. China
Qinghai China
111 E5 Tanggula Shan mts
Xizang China
111 E5 Tanggula Shan mt.
Qinghai China
94 C4 Tangguo Jawa Barat Indon.
96 A1 Tangla Assam India
108 A1 Tangla Qinghai China
111 F6 Tanglag Qinghai China
85 F4 Tangorin Qld Austr.
111 D6 Tangra Yumco salt l. China
96 B2 Tangte mt. Myanmar
92 B4 Tangub Mindanao Phil.
92 B4 Tangub Phil.
108 B3 Tangwanghe China
207 F4 Tanguieta Benin
94 D4 Tangwan Hunan China
207 G2 Tangwang Hebei China
100 D2 Tangwanghe Heilong. China
107 G4 Tangyan Hebei China
107 G5 Tangyan He r. China
96 B2 Tangyan r. Myanmar
109 F1 Tangyin Henan China
100 D2 Tangyuan Heilong. China
254 E5 Tanhaçu Brazil
108 A2 Taniantaweng Shan mts Xizang China
105 G2 Tanigawa-dake mt. Japan
160 E2 Tanimena France
160 E2 Taninthari Myanmar see Tenasserim
Tanintharyi r. Myanmar see Tenasserim
Tanintharyi admin. div. Myanmar see Tenasserim
Tanintharyi Myanmar see Tenasserim
92 B4 Tanjah Morocco see Tanger
256 B5 Tanjori r. Brazil
252 D4 Tanjore Tamil Nadu India see Thanjavur
95 F3 Tanjung Kalimantan Selatan Indon.
136 E5 Taniungbalai Sumatera Indon.
80 F3 Tanjung Indon.
94 D4 Tanjungkarang-Telukbetung Sumatera Indon.
95 D3 Tanjungpandan Indon.
94 D4 Tanjungpinang Indon.
94 D2 Tanjungraja Sumatera Indon.
83 G3 Tanjungredeb Kalimantan Timur Indon.
102 ☐1 Tanjungselor Kalimantan Timur Indon.
95 G2 Tank Pak.
123 G3 Tankara Gujarat India
116 C5 Tankhala Gujarat India
106 C1 Tankhoi Rus. Fed.
117 F4 Tankuhi Uttar Prad. India
214 B3 Tankwa r. S. Africa
156 C5 Tanlay France
114 C4 Tanmay France
173 B2 Tann (Rhön) Ger.
169 F5 Tann Ger.
78 ☐5 Tanna i. Vanuatu
141 K3 Tännäs Sweden
160 B1 Tannay Bourgogne France
157 F3 Tannay Champagne-Ardenne France
169 F4 Tanne Ger.
159 Tannenberg Pol. see Stębark
222 G5 Tanner, Mount B.C. Can.
161 G5 Tanneron France
234 B1 Tannersville PA U.S.A.
173 B3 Tannhein Ger.
173 B4 Tannheim Ger.
161 G5 Tarascon France
163 D6 Tarascon-sur-Ariège France
158 C2 Tarashany Ukr.
163 B5 Taraskula Ukr.
190 A3 Tanne r. Italy
116 B3 Tannu Bugt b. Denmark
85 A6 Tannum Sands Qld Austr.
106 A1 Tannu-Ola, Khrebet mts Rus. Fed.
Tannu Tuva aut. rep. Rus. Fed. see Tyva, Respublika
92 B4 Tañon Strait Phil.
207 H3 Tanout Niger
245 G3 Tanquian Mex.
192 A3 Tanaro r. Corse France
129 B3 Tansilla Burkina
149 H4 Tansley Derbyshire, England U.K.
203 F2 Tanta Egypt
207 G3 Tan-Tan Morocco
244 D3 Tantoyuca Mex.
157 G4 Tantonville France
170 F2 Tantow Ger.
116 D4 Tantpur Uttar Prad. India
107 I2 Tantu Jilin China
102 J4 Tanuma Japan
128 B3 Tantura Israel
114 C2 Tanuku Andhra Prad. India
146 E2 Tanumafili II. N.T. Austr.
141 J4 Tanumshede Sweden
176 E1 Tanvald Czech Rep.
137 J3 Tanyushivka Ukr.
211 B6 Tanzania country Africa
222 B6 Tanzilla r. B.C. Can.

251 H3 Tapanahoni r. Suriname
245 G3 Tapanatepec Mex.
251 E6 Tapauá Brazil
259 B9 Tapera Brazil
254 B5 Tapera Brazil
255 C9 Tapes Brazil
206 C5 Tapeta Liberia
173 E3 Tapfheim Ger.
182 D1 Tapia de Casariego Spain
170 C3 Tapiau Rus. Fed. see Gvardeysk
250 C6 Tapiche r. Peru
152 F1 Tapio Hungary
177 I4 Tápiógyörgye Hungary
177 I4 Tápióság Hungary
177 I4 Tápiószecsö Hungary
177 I4 Tápiószele Hungary
177 I4 Tápiószölös Hungary
256 D3 Tapira Minas Gerais Brazil
256 A5 Tapira Paraná Brazil
256 D5 Tapiraí Brazil
253 H2 Tapirapé r. Brazil
251 E4 Tapirapecó, Sierra mts Brazil/Venez.
94 C1 Tapis, mt. Malaysia
176 F4 Táplánszentkereszt Hungary
176 G5 Tapolca Hungary
176 G4 Tapolcafő Hungary
232 E6 Tappahannock VA U.S.A.
172 E1 Tappan Ger.
235 E1 Tappan NY U.S.A.
96 B1 Tappeh, Kūh-e hill Iran
129 E3 Tap Qaraqoyunlu Azer.
207 F4 Taprobane country India see Sri Lanka
176 G5 Tapsony Hungary
109 F4 Tapuaenuku mt. South I. N.Z.
92 B5 Tapul Phil.
92 B5 Tapul Group is Phil.
108 D2 Tapulonanjing mt. Indon.
94 C2 Tapung r. Indon.
124 C5 Tapurucuara Brazil
255 C9 Taquara Brazil
253 F4 Taquaral, Serra do hills Brazil
256 A2 Taquari r. Brazil
256 A4 Taquarituba Brazil
256 A2 Taquaruçu r. Brazil
197 G2 Târnăveni Romania
147 I4 Tar r. Rep. of Ireland
85 G5 Tara Qld Austr.
196 D4 Tara r. Bos.-Herz./Yugo.
147 E3 Tara, Hill of Hill Rep. of Ireland
207 H4 Taraba state Nigeria
256 B5 Tarabaí Brazil
252 D4 Tarabuco Bol.
Tarabulus Libya see Tripoli
136 E5 Taracena Spain
80 F3 Taradale Indon.
161 E5 Taradeau France
161 E5 Taradeau France
199 H5 Tarakçı Turkey
Tarakliya Moldova see Taraclia
83 G3 Tarlaga N.S.W. Austr.
102 ☐1 Tarama-jima i. Japan
182 C1 Taramundi Spain
116 D5 Tarana Madh. Prad. India
83 G3 Tarana N.S.W. Austr.
122 D3 Taranagar Rajasthan India
80 D3 Taranaki admin. reg. North I. N.Z.
80 E3 Taranaki, Mount vol. North I. N.Z.
183 G4 Tarancón Spain
114 C4 Tarangambadi Tamil Nadu India
211 C6 Tarangire National Park Tanz.
Tarankol', Ozero
I. Kazakh. see Tarankol', Ozero
146 A1 Tarannay i. Scotland U.K.
193 I5 Tarano Italy
195 C7 Taranto Italy
195 G2 Taranto prov. Puglia Italy
195 G2 Taranto, Golfo di g. Italy
176 G5 Tarany Hungary
246 C2 Tarapacá admin. reg. Chile
252 C1 Tarapacá Chile
160 D4 Tarapoto Peru
160 D2 Tararas r. Italy
261 I4 Tararua Range mts North I. N.Z.
182 D4 Tarasaigh i. Scotland U.K. see Taransay
161 G5 Tarascon France
163 D6 Tarascon-sur-Ariège France
136 D5 Tarashany Ukr.
137 F3 Tarashcha Ukr.
137 G4 Tarasivka Ukr.
Tarasivka Kherson'ska Oblast' Ukr.
137 J3 Tarasivka Luhans'ka Oblast' Ukr.
135 H6 Tarasovskiy Rus. Fed.
205 H6 Tarat Alg.
252 C4 Tarata Bol.
252 C2 Tarauacá Brazil
250 D5 Tarauacá r. Brazil
160 D3 Tarare France
77 A1 Tarawa atoll Kiribati
80 F3 Tarawera North I. N.Z.
80 F3 Tarawera, Lake North I. N.Z.
80 F3 Tarawera, Mount North I. N.Z.
121 G4 Taraz Zhambylskaya Oblast' Kazakh.
183 I3 Tarazona Spain
185 I1 Tarazona de la Mancha Spain
121 I3 Tarbagatay Kazakh.
107 I1 Tarbagatay Rus. Fed.
191 H3 Tarbagatay, Khrebet mts Kazakh.
187 D6 Tárbena Spain
147 B4 Tarbert Rep. of Ireland
146 C5 Tarbert Argyll and Bute, Scotland U.K.
146 B3 Tarbert Western Isles, Scotland U.K.
146 B3 Tarbert Western Isles, Scotland U.K.
146 B6 Tarbert, Loch inlet Scotland U.K.
146 C5 Tarbert Argyll and Bute, Scotland U.K.
80 E1 Tarbolton South Ayrshire, Scotland U.K.
163 C5 Tarbes France
204 C2 Tarcaou Morocco
88 C4 Tarcoola S.A. Austr.
83 B2 Tarcoon N.S.W. Austr.
197 F3 Tarculești, Munţii mts Romania
175 I4 Tarczyn Pol.
158 I3 Tardets-Sorholus France
163 B5 Tardienta Spain
161 C3 Tardoire r. France
204 E2 Tarfaya Morocco
162 D2 Tarfá, Wādī aţ watercourse Egypt
255 E3 Tarfside Angus, Scotland U.K.
115 E5 Tárg Spain

197 H3 Târgu Bujor Romania
197 H3 Târgu Cărbuneşti Romania
204 D2 Targuist Morocco
197 F3 Târgu Jiu Romania
197 I2 Târgu Lăpuş Romania
197 G2 Târgu Mureş Romania
197 H2 Târgu Neamţ Romania
197 H2 Târgu Ocna Romania
197 H2 Târgu Secuiesc Romania
121 J2 Targyn Kazakh.
122 A3 Tarhān Iran
177 K5 Târhos Hungary
202 B1 Tarhūnah Libya
125 F2 Tārīf U.A.E.
184 E4 Tarifa Spain
125 E2 Tarīf Bol.
252 D5 Tarija Bol.
114 B3 Tarikere Karnataka India
91 I7 Tariku r. Indon.
125 I3 Tarim Yemen
Tarim Basin China see Tarim Pendi
211 B5 Tarime Tanz.
110 D3 Tarim He r. China
110 D3 Tarim Liuchang Xinjiang China
244 D3 Tarimoro Mex.
111 I4 Tarim Pendi basin China
123 F3 Tārīn Kowt Afgh.
91 I7 Taritatu r. Indon.
177 H4 Tárján Hungary
215 K3 Tarka r. S. Africa
129 E2 Tärkä Rus. Fed.
154 MO U.S.A.
206 E5 Tarkwa Ghana
92 B3 Tarlac Phil.
92 B2 Tarlac r. Phil.
149 G4 Tarleton Lancashire, England U.K.
232 B5 Tarlton OH U.S.A.
141 Tarm Denmark
252 B2 Tarma Peru
168 D5 Tarmstedt Ger.
163 E5 Tarn dept Midi-Pyrénées France
161 A4 Tarn r. France
163 D5 Tarn r. France
177 I4 Tarna r. Hungary
140 K2 Tärnaby Sweden
177 I4 Tarnalelesz Hungary
177 J3 Tarnaméra Hungary
177 I4 Tarnaörs Hungary
177 J4 Tarnaszentmiklós Hungary
175 M4 Tárnava Mare r. Romania
197 G2 Tarnaveni Romania
175 K5 Tarnawa Duża Pol.
175 L5 Tarnawatka Pol.
175 J6 Tarnawka Pol.
141 Tarnobrzeg Pol.
175 K5 Tarnogski Gorodok Rus. Fed.
177 H4 Tarnok Hungary
175 A5 Tarnopol Pol. see Ternopil'
197 K5 Tarnoszyn Pol.
197 I3 Tarnova Romania
177 K5 Tárnova Romania
252 E5 Tarnów Pol.
175 J6 Tarnowiec ☐1 Pol. see Tarnowiec
Tarnowskie Góry
174 G4 Tarnowo Podgórne Pol.
174 G5 Tarnów Opolski Pol.
174 G4 Tarnowskie Góry Pol.
190 F4 Taro r. Italy
137 I4 Taroms'ke Ukr.
163 B5 Taron-Sadirac-Viellenave France
85 G5 Taroom Qld Austr.
105 F2 Tarō-san mt. Japan
204 C2 Taroudant Morocco
192 D2 Tarquinia Lido Italy
177 L3 Tarpa Hungary
117 G5 Tarpau Brazil
84 D3 Tarpaulin Swamp N.T. Austr.
195 E4 Tarquinia Italy
192 D2 Tarquinia Lido Italy
Tarquinii Italy see Tarquinia
84 C2 Tarrabool Lake salt flat N.T. Austr.
Tarracina Italy see Terracina
Tarraco Spain see Tarragona
186 E3 Tarragona Spain
186 E3 Tarragona prov. Cataluña Spain
83 F5 Tarraleah Tas. Austr.
83 F1 Tarran Hills hill N.S.W. Austr.
186 E3 Tarrasa Spain see Terrassa
147 E4 Tarrega Spain
147 E4 Tarrsa Spain
147 E4 Tarrin r. France
178 D3 Tarrin r.
182 B2 Tarrenz Austria
186 E3 Tàrrega Spain
186 E3 Tarroja de Segarra Spain
252 C2 Tarrouge Xizang China see Nyêmo
235 H6 Tarrytown NY U.S.A.
193 I5 Tarsia Italy
241 A3 Tarso Ahon mt. Chad
202 C4 Tarso Emissi mt. Chad
202 C4 Tarso Kobour mt. Chad
126 D3 Tarsus Turkey
258 C1 Tarsus r. Turkey
258 C2 Tartagal Salta Arg.
258 F2 Tartagal Santa Fé Arg.
129 E3 Tärtär r. Azer.
129 E3 Tärtär r. Azer.
129 E3 Tärtär Azer.
191 H3 Tartas France
163 F5 Tartas France
138 F3 Tartu Estonia
128 C2 Tarțūs Syria
104 C4 Tarțūs governorate Syria
104 E4 Tarui Japan
Tarumae-san vol. Japan see Shikotsu
257 G3 Tarumirim Brazil
103 G6 Tarumizu Japan
135 H6 Tarumovka Rus. Fed.
96 B1 Tarung Hka r. Myanmar
139 V4 Tarusa r. Rus. Fed.
94 B2 Tarutung Sumatera Indon.
146 F2 Tarutyne Ukr.
146 F4 Tarves Aberdeenshire, Scotland U.K.
149 I3 Tarvin Cheshire, England U.K.
191 J2 Tarvisio Italy
Tarvisium Italy see Treviso
195 Tarxien Malta
252 Tarz Iran
115 F2 Tasbuget Kazakh.
224 C1 Taschereau Que. Can.
137 K3 Taseko Mountain B.C. Can.
122 B3 Tashan' r. China
Dashkhovuz
Tashauzskaya Oblast'
admin. div. Turkm. see
Dashkhovuzskaya Oblast'
83 H2 Tashi Chho Bhutan see Thimphu
101 Tashigang Bhutan see Trashigang
Tashino Rus. Fed. see Pervomaysk
244 D4 Tashir Armenia
124 C4 Tashk, Daryācheh-ye l. Iran
129 G4 Tashkent Uzbek. see Tashkent
Tashkent Oblast
admin. div. Uzbek. see
Tashkentskaya Oblast'
121 G4 Tashkentskaya Oblast'
admin. div. Uzbek.

Tlacolula to Trasubbie
371

245 F5 Tlacolula Mex.
245 G4 Tlacotalpán Mex.
245 E4 Tlacotenco Mex.
244 D5 Tlacotepec, Cerro mt. Mex.
245 E4 Tlahuapan Mex.
244 C3 Tlajomulco Mex.
245 F4 Tlalchichuca Mex.
245 F4 Tlalixcoyan Mex.
245 E4 Tlalmanalco Mex.
245 E4 Tlalnepantla Mex.
245 E4 Tlálpan Mex.
244 D4 Tlalpujahua Mex.
244 C3 Tlaltenango de Sánchez Román Mex.
245 E5 Tlapa Mex.
245 F4 Tlapacoyan Mex.
245 E4 Tlapaneco r. Mex.
244 D4 Tlapehuala Mex.
244 C3 Tlaquepaque Mex.
245 E4 Tlaxcala Mex.
245 E4 Tlaxcala state Mex.
245 E4 Tlaxco Mex.
245 F5 Tlaxiaco Mex.
222 D4 Tlell B.C. Can.
205 E2 Tlemcen Alg.
174 G2 Tleń Pol.
180 D5 Tleta Rissana Morocco
215 F2 Tlhabologang S. Africa
214 D3 Tlhakalatlou S. Africa
214 E2 Tlhakgameng S. Africa
215 G3 Tlholong S. Africa
177 H3 Tlmače Slovakia
212 E5 Tlokweng Botswana
175 H3 Tłuchowo Pol.
173 H2 Tlučná Czech Rep.
136 C3 Tlumach Ukr.
174 F6 Tlumačov Czech Rep.
175 J3 Tłuszcz Pol.
129 E2 Tlyarata Rus. Fed.
137 J5 Tlyustenkhabl' Rus. Fed.
139 J3 T'ma r. Rus. Fed.
204 B5 Tmeïmîchât Maur.
97 D5 Tnaôt, Prêk r. Cambodia
136 D2 Tnya r. Ukr.
96 B3 To r. Myanmar
246 D2 Toa r. Cuba
247 □1 Toa Alta Puerto Rico
146 □G2 Toab Shetland, Scotland U.K.
247 □1 Toa Baja Puerto Rico
222 E3 Toad r. B.C. Can.
222 E3 Toad River B.C. Can.
177 I4 Tóalmás Hungary
213 □K3 Toamasina Madag.
213 □K3 Toamasina prov. Madag.
147 C5 Toames Rep. of Ireland
241 J1 Toana mts NV U.S.A.
191 F4 Toano Italy
232 E6 Toano VA U.S.A.
232 C6 Toast NC U.S.A.
80 F3 Toatoa North I. N.Z.
260 E5 Toay Arg.
108 A2 Toba Xizang China
169 F4 Toba Ger.
104 C4 Toba Japan
94 B2 Toba, Danau l. Indon.
Toba, Lake Indon. see Toba, Danau
123 F4 Toba and Kakar Ranges mts Pak.
247 □5 Tobago i. Trin. and Tob.
213 F4 Tobane Botswana
185 I2 Tobarra Spain
123 H4 Toba Tek Singh Pak.
179 G4 Tobelbad Austria
147 E2 Tobermore Northern Ireland U.K.
84 D4 Tobermorey N.T. Austr.
85 E5 Tobermory Qld Austr.
224 D4 Tobermory Ont. Can.
146 B5 Tobermory Argyll and Bute, Scotland U.K.
146 C5 Toberonochy Argyll and Bute, Scotland U.K.
91 H6 Tobi i. Palau
254 F4 Tobias Barreto Brazil
86 E4 Tobin, Lake salt flat W.A. Austr.
240 I1 Tobin, Mount NV U.S.A.
225 H4 Tobique r. N.B. Can.
94 D3 Toboali Indon.
120 E1 Tobol Kazakh.
120 F1 Tobol r. Kazakh./Rus. Fed.
130 H4 Tobol'sk Rus. Fed.
78 □6 Tobona Island Solomon Is
92 B4 Toboso Phil.
Tobruk Libya see Tubruq
234 C1 Tobyhanna PA U.S.A.
Tobyl Kazakh. see Tobol
Tobyl r. Kazakh./Rus. Fed. see Tobol
134 J2 Tobysh r. Rus. Fed.
252 A2 Tocache Nuevo Peru
162 C3 Tocane-St-Apre France
254 D3 Tocantinópolis Brazil
251 G6 Tocantins r. Pará Brazil
251 I5 Tocantins r. Brazil
254 C4 Tocantins state Brazil
231 D5 Toccoa GA U.S.A.
193 F2 Tocco da Casauria Italy
190 D3 Toce r. Italy
182 B4 Tocha Port.
123 G3 Tochi r. Pak.
105 F2 Tochigi Japan
105 F2 Tochigi pref. Japan
103 I5 Tochio Japan
142 D2 Töcksfors Sweden
185 G3 Tocón Spain
252 C5 Tocopilla Chile
252 D5 Tocorpuri, Cerros de mts Bol./Chile
83 F3 Tocumwal N.S.W. Austr.
175 K3 Toczna r. Pol.
203 G3 Tôd Egypt
222 G5 Tod, Mount B.C. Can.
105 F3 Toda Japan
116 D4 Toda Bhim Rajasthan India
116 C4 Toda Rai Singh Rajasthan India
261 G4 Todd Arg.
151 G3 Toddington Bedfordshire, England U.K.
151 F3 Toddington Gloucestershire, England U.K.
233 □J1 Todd Mountain hill N.B. Can.
87 E5 Todd Range hills W.A. Austr.
235 E1 Toddville NY U.S.A.
168 F2 Todesfelde Ger.
193 E2 Todi Italy
190 D2 Todi mt. Switz.
149 G4 Todmorden West Yorkshire, England U.K.
257 G2 Todos os Santos r. Brazil
252 D4 Todos Santos Bol.
242 C4 Todos Santos Mex.
172 B4 Todtmoos Ger.
172 B4 Todtnau Ger.
146 A4 Toe Head hd Scotland U.K.
96 B4 Toe Jaga, Khao hill Thai.
182 C2 Toén Spain
206 E3 Toéni Burkina
81 B7 Toetoes Bay South I. N.Z.
222 H4 Tofield Alta Can.
222 E5 Tofino B.C. Can.
146 □G1 Toft Shetland, Scotland U.K.
226 B2 Tofte MN U.S.A.
142 C4 Toftlund Denmark
79 □2 Tofua i. Tonga
232 D6 Toga VA U.S.A.
78 □5 Toga i. Vanuatu
105 G3 Tōgane Japan
210 E2 Togdheer admin. reg. Somalia
147 B5 Togher Cork Rep. of Ireland
147 E3 Togher Louth Rep. of Ireland
147 D3 Togher Offaly Rep. of Ireland
220 B4 Togiak AK U.S.A.
93 B3 Togian, Kepulauan is Indon.
173 G3 Töging am Inn Ger.
Togliatti Rus. Fed. see Tol'yatti
207 F4 Togo country Africa
226 A2 Togo MN U.S.A.
111 E4 Tograsay He r. China
106 B2 Tögrög Mongolia
107 G3 Togrog Ul Nei Mongol China
149 H2 Togston Northumberland, England U.K.
107 F3 Togtoh Nei Mongol China
130 J4 Toguchin Rus. Fed.
116 C3 Tohana Haryana India
241 M4 Tohatchi NM U.S.A.
95 F2 Tohenbatu mt. Sarawak Malaysia
140 O3 Tohmajärvi Fin.
140 N3 Toholampi Fin.
106 E3 Tohom Nei Mongol China
107 F2 Töhöm Mongolia
207 F5 Tohoun Togo
111 E6 Toiba Xizang China
141 M3 Toijala Fin.
190 D4 Toirano Italy
141 N3 Toivakka Fin.
240 I2 Toiyabe Range mts NV U.S.A.
Tojikiston country Asia see Tajikistan
120 C1 Tok r. Rus. Fed.
220 D3 Tok AK U.S.A.
102 K2 Tokachi-gawa r. Japan
104 C3 Tōkai Japan
177 K3 Tokaj Hungary
93 B3 Tokala, Gunung mt. Indon.
105 E1 Tōkamachi Japan
81 B7 Tokanui South I. N.Z.
203 H5 Tokar Sudan
81 C6 Tokarahi South I. N.Z.
102 □1 Tokara-rettō is Japan
121 H2 Tokarevka Kazakh.
135 H6 Tokarevka Rus. Fed.
175 I5 Tokarnia Pol.
102 □1 Tokasiki-jima i. Japan
126 E2 Tokat Turkey
80 D2 Tokatoka North I. N.Z.
137 K2 Tokay r. Rus. Fed.
101 C5 Tŏkch'ŏn N. Korea
Tokdo i. N. Pacific Ocean see Liancourt Rocks
81 □1 Tokelau terr. S. Pacific Ocean
T'okhluja Armenia see Drakhtik
Tokhtamysh Tajik. see Tŭkhtamish
104 D3 Toki Japan
104 C3 Toki-gawa r. Japan
Tokkuztara Xinjiang China see Gongliu
137 H4 Tokmachka r. Ukr.
121 H4 Tokmak Kyrg.
137 H4 Tokmak Ukr.
Tokmok Kyrg. see Tokmak
177 H4 Tokod Hungary
80 G3 Tokomaru Bay North I. N.Z.
104 C4 Tokoname Japan
80 E3 Tokoroa North I. N.Z.
102 L1 Tokoro-gawa r. Japan
105 F3 Tokorozawa Japan
206 C4 Tokounou Guinea
215 G2 Tokoza S. Africa
Toksu Xinjiang China see Xinhe
110 E3 Toksun Xinjiang China
Tok-tō i. N. Pacific Ocean see Liancourt Rocks
121 H4 Toktogul Kyrg.
Toktogul'skoye Vodokhranilishche resr Kyrg. see Toktogul Suu Saktagychy
121 H4 Toktogul Suu Saktagychy resr Kyrg.
Tokto-ri i. N. Pacific Ocean see Liancourt Rocks
77 I3 Tokû i. Tonga
102 □1 Tokunoshima Japan
102 □1 Toku-no-shima i. Japan
100 E1 Tokur Rus. Fed.
104 A4 Tokushima Japan
103 G7 Tokushima pref. Japan
103 E6 Tokuyama Japan
Tokwe r. Zimbabwe see Tugwi
105 F3 Tōkyō Japan
105 F3 Tōkyō mun. Japan
105 F3 Tōkyō-wan b. Japan
78 □4a Tol i. Chuuk Micronesia
80 G3 Tolaga Bay North I. N.Z.
213 □J5 Tôlañaro Madag.
258 D2 Tolar, Cerro mt. Arg.
146 B3 Tolastadh Úr Western Isles, Scotland U.K.
183 F4 Tolbaños Spain
120 C1 Tolbazy Rus. Fed.
164 F1 Tolbert Neth.
106 A1 Tolbo Mongolia
Tolbukhin Bulg. see Dobrich
139 M3 Tolbukhino Rus. Fed.
262 T1 Tolchin, Mount Antarctica
177 K3 Tolcsva Hungary
121 H4 Tole Bi Kazakh.
255 B8 Toledo Brazil
183 F5 Toledo Spain
183 F5 Toledo prov. Castilla - La Mancha Spain
236 E3 Toledo IA U.S.A.
236 F4 Toledo IL U.S.A.
232 B4 Toledo OH U.S.A.
238 B2 Toledo OR U.S.A.
183 F5 Toledo, Montes de mts Spain
237 E6 Toledo Bend Reservoir Louisiana/Texas U.S.A.
191 I5 Tolentino Italy
Toletum Spain see Toledo
192 D2 Tolfa Italy
85 F3 Tolga Qld Austr.
141 J3 Tolga Norway
110 C2 Toli Xinjiang China
213 □I4 Toliara Madag.
213 □J4 Toliara prov. Madag.
250 C4 Tolima dept Col.
Toling Xizang China see Zanda
93 B2 Tolitoli Sulawesi Tengah Indon.
168 E1 Tolk Ger.
143 H4 Tolkmicko Pol.
164 E2 Tollebeek Neth.
170 E2 Tollense r. Ger.
170 E2 Tollensesee l. Ger.
151 H3 Tollesbury Essex, England U.K.
151 H3 Tolleshunt D'Arcy Essex, England U.K.
241 K5 Tolleson AZ U.S.A.
Tollimarjon Uzbek. see Talimardzhan
193 G2 Tollo Italy
142 D4 Tølløse Denmark
138 G2 Tolmachevo Rus. Fed.
191 I2 Tolmezzo Italy
188 D2 Tolmin Slovenia
177 H5 Tolna Hungary
177 H5 Tolna county Hungary
177 H5 Tolnai-hegyhát hills Hungary
177 H5 Tolnanémedi Hungary
242 □I6 Toloa Creek Hond.
Tolochin Belarus see Talachyn
Tolosa France see Toulouse
184 C1 Tolosa Port.
186 A1 Tolosa Spain
185 F4 Tolox Spain
227 F3 Tolsmaville Ont. Can.
146 B3 Tolsta Head hd Scotland U.K.
259 B5 Toltén Chile
250 C2 Tolú Col.
245 E4 Toluca Mex.
186 D2 Tolva Spain
193 I4 Tolve Italy
193 I4 Tolve r. Italy
135 J5 Tol'yatti Rus. Fed.
120 E2 Tolybay Kazakh.
163 C4 Tolzac r. France
100 C2 Tom' r. Rus. Fed.
206 E3 Toma Burkina
226 B4 Tomah WI U.S.A.
226 C3 Tomahawk WI U.S.A.
137 H4 Tomakivka r. Ukr.
102 J2 Tomakomai Japan
240 F2 Tomales CA U.S.A.
79 □1a Tomanivi mt. Viti Levu Fiji
182 B5 Tomar Port.
100 G3 Tomari Sakhalin Rus. Fed.
129 C3 Tomarlı Turkey
198 B2 Tomaros mt. Greece
137 I2 Tomarovka Rus. Fed.
126 D3 Tomarza Turkey
252 D4 Tomás Barron Bol.
261 I2 Tomás Gomensoro Uru.
136 D2 Tomashhorod Rivnens'ka Oblast' Ukr.
136 D2 Tomashhorod Rivnens'ka Oblast' Ukr.
136 E3 Tomashpil' Ukr.
176 G3 Tomášov Slovakia
177 I3 Tomášovce Slovakia
175 L5 Tomaszów Lubelski Pol.
175 I4 Tomaszów Mazowiecki Pol.
146 E4 Tomatin Highland, Scotland U.K.
244 B4 Tomatlán Mex.
252 D5 Tomave Bol.
256 C5 Tomazina Brazil
254 E4 Tombador, Serra do hills Bahia Brazil
253 F3 Tombador, Serra do hills Mato Grosso Brazil
163 C4 Tombebœf France
231 C6 Tombigbee r. AL U.S.A.
215 G4 Tombo S. Africa
209 B6 Tomboco Angola
257 F4 Tombos Brazil
206 E2 Tombouctou Mali
206 E2 Tombouctou admin. reg. Mali
241 L6 Tombstone AZ U.S.A.
209 A8 Tombua Angola
213 E4 Tom Burke S. Africa
Tomdibuloq Uzbek. see Tamdybulak
Tomditow Toghi hills Uzbek. see Tamdytau, Gory
258 B5 Tomé Chile
143 E4 Tomelilla Sweden
185 G1 Tomelloso Spain
121 F4 Tomenaryk Kazakh.
177 L5 Tomeşti Romania
177 L6 Tomeşti Romania
Tomi Romania see Constanța
175 H6 Tomice Pol.
102 □2 Tomigusuku Japan
227 H2 Tomiko Ont. Can.
252 D4 Tomina Bol.
206 B3 Tominé r. Guinea
83 G3 Tomingley N.S.W. Austr.
93 B3 Tomini, Teluk g. Indon.
206 D3 Tominian Mali
146 E4 Tomintoul Moray, Scotland U.K.
105 E2 Tomioka Japan
188 F4 Tomislavgrad Bos.-Herz.
235 E1 Tomkins Cove NY U.S.A.
82 B1 Tomkinson Ranges mts S.A. Austr.
131 N4 Tommot Rus. Fed.
146 E4 Tomnavoulin Moray, Scotland U.K.
250 E3 Tomo r. Col.
198 B1 Tomorit, Maja e mt. Albania
111 E4 Tomorlog Qinghai China
107 G3 Tomortei Nei Mongol China
177 I5 Tompa Hungary
86 C4 Tom Price W.A. Austr.
235 D3 Toms r. NJ U.S.A.
130 J4 Tomsk Rus. Fed.
233 F5 Toms River NJ U.S.A.
143 F3 Tomtabacken hill Sweden
131 P3 Tomtor Rus. Fed.
128 B1 Tömük Turkey
102 K2 Tomuraushi-yama mt. Japan
Tomur Feng mt. China/Kyrg. see Jengish Chokusu
129 D1 Tomuzlovka r. Rus. Fed.
220 D3 Tom White, Mount AK U.S.A.
186 F3 Tona Spain
102 □1 Tonaki-jima i. Japan
245 H5 Tonalá Mex.
244 C3 Tonala Jalisco Mex.
104 C2 Tonami Japan
250 E5 Tonantins Brazil
192 B4 Tonara Sardegna Italy
238 C1 Tonasket WA U.S.A.
251 H3 Tonate Fr. Guiana
232 D3 Tonawanda NY U.S.A.
244 C4 Tonaya Mex.
Tonb-e Bozorg, Jazīreh-ye i. The Gulf see Greater Tunb
Tonb-e Küchek, Jazīreh-ye i. The Gulf see Lesser Tunb
151 H3 Tonbridge Kent, England U.K.
182 B4 Tonda Port.
104 B4 Tondabayashi Japan
93 C2 Tondano Sulawesi Utara Indon.
182 B4 Tondela Port.
142 C4 Tønder Denmark
114 C4 Tondi Tamil Nadu India
150 E3 Tone r. England U.K.
105 G3 Tone-gawa r. Japan
262 Q1 Toney Mount Antarctica
191 G3 Tonezza del Cimone Italy
207 H5 Tonga Cameroon
79 □2 Tonga country S. Pacific Ocean
215 H3 Tongaat S. Africa
109 F3 Tong'an Fujian China
80 E3 Tongaporutu North I. N.Z.
Tongareva atoll Cook Is see Penrhyn
80 E3 Tongariro vol. North I. N.Z.
79 □2a Tongatapu i. Tonga
79 □2a Tongatapu Group is Tonga
266 H7 Tonga Trench sea feature S. Pacific Ocean
109 E1 Tongbai Henan China
109 E1 Tongbai Shan mts China
109 F2 Tongcheng Anhui China
109 E2 Tongcheng Hubei China
Tongcheng Shandong China see Dong'e
101 C5 T'ongch'ŏn N. Korea
107 F5 Tongchuan Shaanxi China
Tongchuan Sichuan China see Santai
108 D3 Tongdao Hunan China
106 D5 Tongde Qinghai China
101 C5 Tongduch'ŏn S. Korea
165 E4 Tongeren Belgium
109 E2 Tonggu Jiangxi China
107 F5 Tongguan Shaanxi China
101 D5 Tonghae S. Korea
108 B3 Tonghai Yunnan China
100 D3 Tonghe Heilong. China
101 C4 Tonghua Jilin China
101 C4 Tonghua Jilin China
Tongi Bangl. see Tungi
100 E3 Tongjiang Heilong. China
108 C2 Tongjiang Sichuan China
100 C3 Tongken r. China
96 E2 Tongking, Gulf of China/Vietnam
146 D7 Tongland Dumfries and Galloway, Scotland U.K.
Tongle Guangxi China see Leye
107 I3 Tongliao Nei Mongol China
109 F2 Tongling Anhui China
109 F2 Tongling Anhui China
109 F2 Tonglu Zhejiang China
103 D6 Tongnae S. Korea
83 E2 Tongo N.S.W. Austr.
78 □5 Tongoa i. Vanuatu
213 □J4 Tongobory Madag.
260 B2 Tongoi, Bahía b. Chile
83 E2 Tongo Lake salt flat N.S.W. Austr.
260 B2 Tongoy Chile
Tongquan Yunnan China see Malong
108 D3 Tongren Guizhou China
106 D5 Tongren Qinghai China
Tongres Belgium see Tongeren
Tongsa Bhutan see Trongsa
Tongshan Jiangsu China see Xuzhou
108 D5 Tongshi Hainan China
108 A1 Tongtian He r. China alt. Chang Jiang, alt. Jinsha Jiang, alt. Zhi Qu, conv. Yangtze, long Yangtze Kiang
146 D3 Tongue Highland, Scotland U.K.
238 F2 Tongue r. MT U.S.A.
Tongue of Arabat spit Ukr. see Arabats'ka Strilka, Kosa
246 C1 Tongue of the Ocean sea chan. Bahamas
106 E5 Tongwei Gansu China
107 H4 Tongxian Beijing China
109 G2 Tongxiang Zhejiang China
106 E4 Tongxin Ningxia China
101 D6 T'ongyŏng S. Korea
107 I2 Tongyu Jilin China
Tongzhou Beijing China see Tongxian
108 C2 Tongzi Guizhou China
Tonhil Mongolia see Dzüyl
226 C5 Tonica IL U.S.A.
244 C4 Tonila Mex.
208 F3 Tonj Sudan
116 C4 Tonk Rajasthan India
122 B2 Tonkābon Iran
237 D4 Tonkawa OK U.S.A.
134 I4 Tonkino Rus. Fed.
97 D4 Tônle Repou r. Laos
97 C4 Tônlé Sab l. Cambodia
Tonle Sap l. Cambodia see Tônlé Sab
150 D3 Tonna Neath Port Talbot, Wales U.K.
162 B3 Tonnay-Boutonne France
162 B3 Tonnay-Charente France
163 C4 Tonneins France
156 D5 Tonnerre France
168 D1 Tönning Ger.
102 J4 Tōno Japan
78 □4a Tonoas i. Chuuk Micronesia
241 K5 Tonopah AZ U.S.A.
240 I2 Tonopah NV U.S.A.
111 B6 Tons r. India
142 D2 Tønsberg Norway
139 K2 Tonshalovo Rus. Fed.
142 B2 Tonstad Norway
260 C2 Tontal, Sierra mts Arg.
214 C4 Tontelbos S. Africa
245 F4 Tonto r. Mex.
241 L5 Tonto Basin AZ U.S.A.
150 D3 Tonyrefail Rhondda Cynon Taff, Wales U.K.
83 G2 Toobeah Qld Austr.
206 C5 Toobli Liberia
87 C6 Toodyay W.A. Austr.
241 K1 Tooele UT U.S.A.
85 H5 Toogoolawah Qld Austr.
83 E3 Tooleybuc N.S.W. Austr.
82 C3 Tooligie S.A. Austr.
83 G4 Tooma r. N.S.W. Austr.
147 E2 Toomebridge Northern Ireland U.K.
85 F5 Toompine Qld Austr.
83 F4 Toora Vic. Austr.
83 G2 Tooraweenah N.S.W. Austr.
214 E5 Toorberg mt. S. Africa
147 B5 Toormore Rep. of Ireland
85 G5 Toowoomba Qld Austr.
210 F2 Tooxin Somalia
139 K2 Topalki Rus. Fed.
197 G3 Topana Romania
185 H3 Topares Spain
121 J1 Topchikha Rus. Fed.
171 E3 Töpchin Ger.
137 H3 Topchyne Ukr.
149 H3 Topcliffe North Yorkshire, England U.K.
129 B4 Topçu Dağı mt. Turkey
129 C4 Top Dağı mt. Turkey
236 E4 Topeka KS U.S.A.
171 C5 Töpen Ger.
242 D3 Topia Mex.
193 E2 Topino r. Italy
130 J4 Topki Rus. Fed.
177 K3 Topľa r. Slovakia
93 D3 Toplana, Gunung mt. Seram Indon.
222 E4 Topley B.C. Can.
222 E4 Topley Landing B.C. Can.
196 E4 Toplica r. Yugo.
197 G2 Toplița Romania
177 L6 Toplița Romania
171 D3 Töplitz Ger.
216 □1c Topo São Jorge Azores
241 J4 Topock AZ U.S.A.
177 H3 Topoľčany Slovakia
177 H3 Topoľčianky Slovakia
174 G3 Topólka Pol.
177 G2 Topolná Czech Rep.
197 G4 Topolnitsa r. Bulg.
242 C3 Topolobampo Mex.
197 I3 Topolog Romania
197 G3 Topolog r. Romania
177 K6 Topolovățu Mare Romania
197 G3 Topoloveni Romania
197 H4 Topolovgrad Bulg.
179 G4 Topolšica Slovenia
177 J2 Toporec Slovakia
136 D2 Topory Ukr.
136 E2 Toporyshche Ukr.
134 F2 Topozero, Ozero l. Rus. Fed.
238 B2 Toppenish WA U.S.A.
197 I3 Topraisar Romania
129 C4 Toprakkale Ağrı Turkey
128 C1 Toprakkale Osmaniye Turkey
233 □J2 Topsfield ME U.S.A.
150 D4 Topsham Devon, England U.K.
129 B4 Toptepe Turkey
234 C2 Topton PA U.S.A.
80 E2 Topuni North I. N.Z.
252 C4 Toquepala Peru
186 E3 Torá de Riubreós Spain
129 F3 Torağay Dağı hill Azer.
182 E2 Toral de los Guzmanes Spain
182 D2 Toral de los Vados Spain
Toraman Turkey see Halilçavuş
193 I5 Torano Castello Italy
252 C4 Torata Peru
123 F4 Tor Baldak mt. Afgh.
199 E2 Torbalı Turkey
122 D3 Torbat-e Heydarīyeh Iran
122 E3 Torbat-e Jām Iran
150 D4 Torbay admin. div. England U.K.
87 C7 Torbay Bay W.A. Austr.
135 H5 Torbeyevo Rus. Fed.
223 K4 Torch r. Sask. Can.
193 H4 Torchiara Italy
195 H2 Torchiarolo Italy
139 M3 Torchino Rus. Fed.
136 C2 Torchyn Ukr.
183 F5 Torcón r. Spain
160 C2 Torcy France
156 B3 Torcy-le-Petit France
177 H4 Tordas Hungary
183 E3 Tordehumos Spain
186 F3 Tordera Spain
183 F3 Tordesillas Spain
183 I4 Tordesilos Spain
193 F2 Tordino r. Italy
140 M2 Töre Sweden
146 D4 Tore Highland, Scotland U.K.
143 F2 Töreboda Sweden
170 C1 Toreby Denmark
142 E3 Torekov Sweden
193 G3 Torella del Sannio Italy
187 C6 Torellano Spain
140 □ Torell Land reg. Svalbard
186 F2 Torelló Spain
164 E2 Torenberg hill Neth.
182 D2 Toreno Spain
80 F2 Torere North I. N.Z.
106 E1 Torey Rus. Fed.
137 J3 Torez Ukr.
150 D3 Torfaen admin. div. Wales U.K.
Torga i. Vanuatu see Toga
171 D4 Torgau Ger.
170 F2 Torgelow Ger.
Torghay Kustanayskaya Oblast' Kazakh. see Turgay
193 E1 Torgiano Italy
120 A2 Torgun r. Rus. Fed.
143 F3 Torhamn Sweden
165 C3 Torhout Belgium
136 C2 Torhovytsya Ukr.
117 F5 Tori Bihar India
210 A3 Tori r. Sudan
105 G3 Toride Japan
159 F2 Torigni-sur-Vire France
183 G4 Torija Spain
105 E2 Torikabuto-yama mt. Japan
190 C3 Torino Italy
190 C3 Torino prov. Piemonte Italy
193 G2 Torino di Sangro Italy
103 J8 Tori-shima i. Japan
210 B3 Torit Sudan
195 F2 Toritto Italy
256 A2 Torixoreu Brazil
122 A2 Torkamān Iran
139 H2 Torkovichi Rus. Fed.
186 C2 Torla Spain
86 D3 Torment, Point W.A. Austr.
182 D3 Tormes r. Spain
187 B4 Tormón Spain
146 C6 Tormore North Ayrshire, Scotland U.K.
183 F4 Tornadizos de Ávila Spain
222 H5 Tornado Mountain Alta/B.C. Can.
185 H3 Tornajuelos mt. Spain
177 J3 Tornaľa Slovakia
182 E4 Tornavacas Spain
149 I4 Torne r. England U.K.
Torneå Fin. see Tornio
140 N2 Torneälven r. Sweden
168 E2 Tornesch Ger.
140 L1 Torneträsk Sweden
140 L1 Torneträsk l. Sweden
Torngat, Monts mts Newfoundland/Québec Can. see Torngat Mountains
225 H1 Torngat Mountains Newfoundland/Québec Can.
196 D4 Tornik mt. Yugo.
140 N2 Tornio Fin.
177 I6 Tornjoš Vojvodina, Srbija Yugo.
190 E3 Torno Italy
183 I4 Tornos Spain
170 E2 Tornow Ger.
261 F6 Tornquist Arg.
177 L3 Tornyospálca Hungary
207 H4 Toro Nigeria
183 E3 Toro Spain
244 D1 Toro, Pico del mt. Mex.
207 F3 Torodi Niger
177 H4 Törökbálint Hungary
177 J4 Törökszentmiklós Hungary
224 E5 Toronto Ont. Can.
232 C4 Toronto OH U.S.A.
179 H3 Torony Hungary
139 H3 Toropatsa Rus. Fed.
241 I5 Toro Peak CA U.S.A.
139 H3 Toropets Rus. Fed.
210 B4 Tororo Uganda
126 D3 Toros Dağları mts Turkey
192 B4 Torpè Sardegna Italy
146 F4 Torphins Aberdeenshire, Scotland U.K.
150 C4 Torpoint Cornwall, England U.K.
83 F4 Torquay Vic. Austr.
150 D4 Torquay Torbay, England U.K.
183 F2 Torquemada Spain
147 E1 Torr Northern Ireland U.K.
185 G1 Torralba de Calatrava Spain
192 A4 Torralba Sardegna Italy
183 H4 Torralba Spain
186 C3 Torralba de Aragón Spain
183 H3 Torralba de El Burgo Spain
183 E5 Torralba de Oropesa Spain
183 I4 Torralba de Sisones Spain
240 H5 Torrance CA U.S.A.
184 B2 Torrão Port.
182 C4 Torre mt. Port.
193 G4 Torre Annunziata Italy
187 B4 Torrebaja Spain
183 H3 Torreblacos Spain
187 D4 Torreblanca Spain
242 B1 Torre Blanco, Cerro mt. Mex.
185 G3 Torreblascopedro Spain
193 G3 Torrebruna Italy
183 F4 Torrecaballeros Spain
185 F2 Torrecampo Spain
195 G2 Torre Canne Italy
185 G3 Torre-Cardela Spain
185 F4 Torrecilla mt. Spain
183 F5 Torrecilla de la Jara Spain
183 E3 Torrecilla de la Orden Spain
186 B4 Torrecilla del Rebollar Spain
183 H2 Torrecilla en Cameros Spain
182 E5 Torrecillas de la Tiesa Spain
193 G3 Torrecuso Italy
184 B2 Torre da Gadanha Port.
184 C1 Torre das Vargens Port.
186 E2 Torre de Cadí mt. Spain
182 C3 Torre de Dona Chama Port.
182 B4 Torredeita Port.
185 G2 Torre de Juan Abad Spain
182 D2 Torre del Bierzo Spain
183 G4 Torre del Burgo Spain
185 G3 Torre del Campo Spain
193 G4 Torre del Greco Italy
185 F4 Torre del Mar Spain
186 E3 Torredembarra Spain
184 D2 Torre de Miguel Sesmero Spain
182 C3 Torre de Moncorvo Port.
193 F2 Torre de'Passeri Italy
185 G3 Torredonjimeno Spain
182 C4 Torre do Terrenho Port.
182 D3 Torregamones Spain
186 D3 Torregrossa Spain
183 F3 Torreiglesias Spain
182 B4 Torreira Port.
182 D5 Torrejoncillo Spain
183 H4 Torrejoncillo del Rey Spain
183 G4 Torrejón de Ardoz Spain
183 G4 Torrejón del Rey Spain
182 E5 Torrejón el Rubio Spain
186 B4 Torrelacarcel Spain
183 G4 Torrelaguna Spain
183 I3 Torrelapaja Spain
183 F1 Torrelavega Spain
183 I3 Torrellas Spain
186 E3 Torrelles de Foix Spain
183 E3 Torrelobatón Spain
183 G4 Torrelodones Spain
193 H3 Torremaggiore Italy
187 C6 Torremanzanas Spain
184 D2 Torremayor Spain
184 D2 Torremegía Spain
193 H3 Torre Mileto Italy
184 D1 Torremocha Spain
185 F4 Torremolinos Spain
187 D4 Torrenostra Spain
82 D2 Torrens, Lake salt flat S.A. Austr.
85 F4 Torrens Creek Qld Austr.
187 C5 Torrent Spain
Torrente Spain see Torrent
186 D3 Torrente de Cinca Spain
185 G2 Torrenueva Spain
190 E5 Torre Nuovo Scalo Italy
242 E3 Torreón Mex.
184 D1 Torreorgaz Spain
193 H4 Torre Orsaia Italy
187 C7 Torre-Pacheco Spain
185 F3 Torreparedones hill Spain
190 C4 Torre Pellice Italy
185 G2 Torreperogil Spain
255 C9 Torres Brazil
185 G3 Torres Spain
185 G3 Torres r. Spain
183 G3 Torresandino Spain
195 H3 Torre San Giovanni Italy
195 G2 Torre Santa Susanna Italy
185 H2 Torres de Albánchez Spain
186 B3 Torres de Berrellén Spain
183 G4 Torres de la Alameda Spain
182 E3 Torres del Carrizal Spain
186 D3 Torres de Segre Spain
78 □5 Torres Islands Vanuatu
182 E3 Torresmenudas Spain
184 B1 Torres Novas Port.
76 E2 Torres Strait Qld Austr.
184 A1 Torres Vedras Port.
187 E5 Torreta, Sierra hill Spain
193 H4 Torretta, Monte mt. Italy
186 C4 Torrevelilla Spain
187 C7 Torrevieja Spain
241 L2 Torrey UT U.S.A.
193 F3 Torrice Italy
195 G2 Torricella Italy
193 E2 Torricella in Sabina Italy
193 G2 Torricella Peligna Italy
193 F2 Torricella Sicura Italy
190 D2 Torricella Taverne Switz.
183 E5 Torrico Spain
184 D1 Torrico de San Pedro hill Spain
191 F3 Torri del Benaco Italy
150 C4 Torridge r. England U.K.
146 C4 Torridon Highland, Scotland U.K.
146 C4 Torridon, Loch b. Scotland U.K.
190 E4 Torriglia Italy
193 E2 Torri in Sabina Italy
187 C4 Torrijas Spain
183 I3 Torrijo Spain
183 F5 Torrijos Spain
146 B4 Torrin Highland, Scotland U.K.
233 G4 Torrington CT U.S.A.
238 F3 Torrington WY U.S.A.
256 C5 Torrinha Brazil
192 D1 Torrita di Siena Italy
184 B2 Torroal Port.
186 G2 Torroella de Montgrí Spain
140 K3 Torrön l. Sweden
185 G4 Torrox Spain
183 H5 Torrubia del Campo Spain
183 H3 Torrubia de Soria Spain
117 G4 Torsa Chhu r. Bhutan
142 D1 Torsæterkampen hill Norway
168 E1 Tørsbøl Denmark
142 E1 Torsby Sweden
143 G2 Torshälla Sweden
144 D1 Tórshavn Faroe Is
177 I4 Törtel Hungary
241 L5 Tortilla Flat AZ U.S.A.
Törtköl Uzbek. see Turtkul'
194 C5 Torto r. Sicilia Italy
247 F3 Tortola i. Virgin Is (U.K.)
183 G4 Tórtola de Henares Spain
183 F3 Tórtoles de Esgueva Spain
192 B5 Tortolì Sardegna Italy
197 I3 Tortomanu Romania
190 D4 Tortona Italy
193 H5 Tortora Italy
193 F2 Tortoreto Italy
194 D4 Tortorici Sicilia Italy
186 D4 Tortosa Spain
182 C4 Tortozendo Port.
183 I4 Tortuera Spain
245 E2 Tortuga, Laguna l. Mex.
261 G3 Tortugas Arg.
127 F2 Tortum Turkey
122 C3 Ţorūd Iran
126 E2 Torul Turkey
174 G2 Toruń Pol.
138 E2 Tõrva Estonia
193 E3 Tor Vaianica Italy
149 F3 Torver Cumbria, England U.K.
185 G4 Torvizcón Spain
141 I3 Torvløysa mt. Norway
140 L2 Torvsjö Sweden
147 C1 Tory Island Rep. of Ireland
177 J2 Torysa Slovakia
177 K3 Torysa r. Slovakia
147 C1 Tory Sound sea chan. Rep. of Ireland
139 J3 Torzhok Rus. Fed.
174 D3 Torzym Pol.
103 F7 Tosa Japan
191 F2 Tosa, Cima mt. Italy
103 F7 Tosashimizu Japan
103 F7 Tosa-wan b. Japan
214 D1 Tosca S. Africa
146 C4 Toscaig Highland, Scotland U.K.
191 G5 Toscana admin. reg. Italy
192 B1 Toscano, Arcipelago is Italy
191 F3 Toscolano-Maderno Italy
102 J3 Tōshima-yama mt. Japan
Toshkent Uzbek. see Tashkent
Toshkent Wiloyati admin. div. Uzbek. see Tashkentskaya Oblast'
139 H2 Tosno Rus. Fed.
106 C1 Tosontsengel Mongolia
190 D1 Töss r. Switz.
186 F3 Tossa Spain
186 E3 Tossal de la Baltasana mt. Spain
186 E2 Tossal de l'Orri mt. Spain
163 A5 Tosse France
193 F2 Tossicia Italy
149 G3 Tosside Lancashire, England U.K.
258 E3 Tostado Arg.
168 E2 Tostedt Ger.
103 E7 Tosu Japan
126 D2 Tosya Turkey
177 J4 Tószeg Hungary
174 G5 Toszek Pol.
187 B7 Totana Spain
114 D5 Totapola mt. Sri Lanka
81 C6 Totara South I. N.Z.
80 D4 Totaranui South I. N.Z.
172 B3 Totenkopf hill Ger.
156 B3 Tôtes France
78 □4a Totiw i. Chuuk Micronesia
151 F4 Totland Isle of Wight, England U.K.
134 H4 Tot'ma Rus. Fed.
150 D4 Totnes Devon, England U.K.
251 G3 Totness Suriname
134 H4 Totomitsa Rus. Fed.
243 H6 Totonicapán Guat.
261 G3 Totoras Arg.
206 C5 Totota Liberia
244 C3 Tototlán Mex.
79 □1 Totoya i. Fiji
120 C1 Totskoye Rus. Fed.
104 B5 Totsu-kawa r. Japan
176 F5 Tótszentmárton Hungary
176 F5 Tótszerdahely Hungary
151 F4 Totton Hampshire, England U.K.
103 G6 Tottori Japan
103 F6 Tottori pref. Japan
177 G4 Tótvázsony Hungary
206 D4 Touba Côte d'Ivoire
206 B3 Touba Senegal
204 D3 Toubkal, Jbel mt. Morocco
207 I5 Touboro Cameroon
182 C3 Touça Port.
163 D5 Touch r. France
238 C2 Touchet r. WA U.S.A.
156 D5 Toucy France
106 E4 Toudaohu Nei Mongol China
163 D4 Touffailles France
206 E3 Tougan Burkina
163 C5 Touget France
205 G2 Touggourt Alg.
206 E3 Tougouri Burkina
206 C4 Tougué Guinea
78 □5 Touho New Caledonia
206 C3 Touil Maur.
206 C3 Toukoto Mali
207 F4 Toukountouna Benin
157 F4 Toul France
206 C5 Toulépleu Côte d'Ivoire
206 E3 Toulfé Burkina
109 G4 Touliu Taiwan
225 G3 Toulnustouc r. Que. Can.
161 D5 Toulon France
226 C5 Toulon IL U.S.A.
160 B2 Toulon-sur-Allier France
160 C2 Toulon-sur-Arroux France
163 E6 Toulouges France
163 D5 Toulouse France
206 D5 Toumodi Côte d'Ivoire
206 D4 Touna Mali
207 I4 Toungo Nigeria
96 B3 Toungoo Myanmar
108 D3 Toupai Guangxi China
159 G2 Touques France
159 G2 Touques r. France
206 D5 Toura, Monts mt. Côte d'Ivoire
159 G4 Touraine, Val de val. France
182 B2 Toural Spain
Tourane Vietnam see Đa Năng
158 C3 Tourch France
156 D2 Tourcoing France
161 F5 Tourette-sur-Loup France
182 A1 Touriñán, Cabo c. Spain
158 E2 Tourlaville France
147 B3 Tourmakeady Rep. of Ireland
160 C3 Tour Matagrin hill France
165 C4 Tournai Belgium
161 F4 Tournairet, Mont mt. France
156 C4 Tournan-en-Brie France
252 B2 Tournavista Peru
163 C5 Tournay France
163 C5 Tournecoupe France
163 D5 Tournefeuille France
163 C4 Tournon-d'Agenais France
159 G5 Tournon-St-Martin France
161 C3 Tournon-sur-Rhône France
160 C2 Tournus France
156 B3 Tourny France
182 C4 Touro Port.
254 G3 Touros Brazil
159 G3 Tourouvre France
161 F5 Tourrette-Levens France
162 C1 Tours France
156 E3 Tourteron France
162 D3 Tourtoirac France
161 D5 Tourves France
156 B4 Toury France
206 D4 Toussiana Burkina
202 C4 Toussidé, Pic mt. Chad
208 D2 Toussoro, Mont mt. C.A.R.
100 C3 Toutai Heilong. China
184 C2 Toutalga r. Port.
158 E5 Touvois France
214 C5 Touws r. S. Africa
214 C5 Touwsrivier S. Africa
176 B1 Toužim Czech Rep.
106 E2 Töv prov. Mongolia
176 G2 Tovačov Czech Rep.
250 D2 Tovar Venez.
139 J4 Tovarkovo Rus. Fed.
139 L5 Tovarkovskiy Rus. Fed.
177 K3 Tovarné Slovakia
188 G3 Tovarnik Croatia
151 G2 Tove r. England U.K.
136 C3 Tovste Ukr.
129 D3 Tovuz Azer.
Tovuzçay r. Armenia see Tavush
235 D2 Towaco NJ U.S.A.
102 J3 Towada Japan
102 J3 Towada-ko l. Japan
80 E1 Towai North I. N.Z.
131 U3 Towak Mountain hill AK U.S.A.
227 I5 Towanda PA U.S.A.
234 B1 Towanda Creek r. PA U.S.A.
241 M3 Towaoc CO U.S.A.
151 G2 Towcester Northamptonshire, England U.K.
147 C5 Tower Rep. of Ireland
226 A2 Tower MN U.S.A.
234 B2 Tower City PA U.S.A.
Tower Island Islas Galápagos Ecuador see Genovesa, Isla
81 A7 Tower Peak South I. N.Z.
149 H3 Tow Law Durham, England U.K.
234 D4 Town Bank NJ U.S.A.
236 C1 Towner ND U.S.A.
146 E7 Townhead of Greenlaw Dumfries and Galloway, Scotland U.K.
146 E5 Townhill Fife, Scotland U.K.
84 C2 Towns r. N.T. Austr.
234 C3 Townsend DE U.S.A.
233 H3 Townsend MA U.S.A.
238 E2 Townsend MT U.S.A.
85 G4 Townshend Island Qld Austr.
85 F3 Townsville Qld Austr.
93 B3 Towori, Teluk b. Indon.
234 B3 Towson MD U.S.A.
150 D1 Towyn Conwy, Wales U.K.
Towyn Gwynedd, Wales U.K. see Tywyn
110 C3 Toxkan He r. China
240 H1 Toy NV U.S.A.
237 C6 Toyah TX U.S.A.
104 D2 Toyama Japan
104 D2 Toyama pref. Japan
104 D2 Toyama-wan b. Japan
136 C2 Toykut Ukr.
103 F7 Tōyo Japan
104 D3 Toyoake Japan
104 D4 Toyohashi Japan
104 D4 Toyokawa Japan
104 D4 Toyo-kawa r. Japan
104 B4 Toyonaka Japan
104 A3 Toyooka Japan
102 I5 Toyosaka Japan
105 D2 Toyoshina Japan
104 D3 Toyota Japan
140 M3 Töysä Fin.
121 G4 Toytepa Uzbek.
Tozal del Orri mt. Spain see Tossal de l'Orri
Tozanlı Turkey see Almus
111 C5 Tozê Kangri mt. Xizang China
205 H2 Tozeur Tunisia
129 E3 Tpig Rus. Fed.
129 C2 Tqibuli Georgia
129 B2 Tqvarch'eli Georgia
182 C1 Trabada Spain
182 D3 Trabanca Spain
182 D3 Trabazos Spain
194 C5 Trabia Sicilia Italy
174 G1 Trąbki Wielkie Pol.
128 B2 Trâblous Lebanon
179 F3 Traboch Austria
197 F5 Trabotivište Macedonia
127 E2 Trabzon Turkey
129 A3 Trabzon prov. Turkey
194 B6 Tracino Sicilia Italy
233 □J2 Tracy N.B. Can.
240 G3 Tracy CA U.S.A.
236 E2 Tracy MN U.S.A.
160 A1 Tracy-sur-Loire France
190 D3 Tradate Italy
169 D4 Traddelkopf hill Ger.
226 A3 Trade Lake WI U.S.A.
237 F4 Tradewater r. KY U.S.A.
224 B3 Trading r. Ont. Can.
140 K2 Trænfjorden sea chan. Norway
236 E3 Traer IA U.S.A.
184 D4 Trafalgar, Cabo c. Spain
222 D2 Traffic Mountain Y.T. Can.
183 I4 Tragacete Spain
185 H2 Tragoncillo mt. Spain
179 F2 Tragwein Austria
197 G4 Traian Romania
177 L6 Traian Vuia Romania
183 I4 Traid Spain
260 A6 Traiguén Chile
186 D4 Traiguera Spain
222 G5 Trail B.C. Can.
237 D5 Trail OK U.S.A.
173 F3 Train Ger.
156 D4 Traînel France
234 C3 Trainer PA U.S.A.
156 C5 Traînou France
254 F4 Traipu Brazil
250 D5 Traíra r. Brazil
256 D2 Trairas r. Brazil
254 F2 Trairi Brazil
179 G2 Traisen Austria
179 G2 Traisen r. Austria
179 H2 Traiskirchen Austria
179 G2 Traismauer Austria
173 G2 Traitsching Ger.
257 F5 Trajano de Morais Brazil
Trajectum Neth. see Utrecht
214 D5 Traka r. S. Africa
138 E4 Trakai Lith.
134 J3 Trakt Rus. Fed.
147 B4 Tralee Rep. of Ireland
147 B4 Tralee Bay Rep. of Ireland
Trá Li Rep. of Ireland see Tralee
183 I4 Tramacastilla Spain
192 A4 Tramariglio Sardegna Italy
187 B4 Tramascastiel Spain
192 A4 Tramatza Sardegna Italy
191 G4 Tramazzo r. Italy
172 B4 Tramelan Switz.
163 C6 Tramezaïgues France
Trá Mhór Rep. of Ireland see Tramore
232 B6 Trammel VA U.S.A.
191 H2 Tramonti di Sopra Italy
178 D4 Tramonti di Sotto Italy
147 D4 Tramore Rep. of Ireland
187 F5 Tramuntana, Serra de mts Spain
193 H4 Tramutola Italy
143 F2 Tranås Sweden
142 D3 Tranbjerg Denmark
182 C4 Trancoso Port.
142 D4 Tranebjerg Denmark
142 E3 Tranemo Sweden
146 F6 Tranent East Lothian, Scotland U.K.
97 B6 Trang Thai.
91 H8 Trangan i. Indon.
83 F3 Trangie N.S.W. Austr.
193 I3 Trani Italy
156 E4 Trannes France
258 G3 Tranqueras Uru.
260 B3 Tranquilla Chile
158 E3 Trans France
263 K2 Transantarctic Mountains Antarctica
223 H5 Trans Canada Highway Can.
Transcarpathian Oblast admin. div. Ukr. see Zakarpats'ka Oblast'
223 L5 Transcona Man. Can.
161 E5 Trans-en-Provence France
245 E4 Transfiguracion Mex.
197 G2 Transilvaniei, Podişul plat. Romania
141 K3 Transtrand Sweden
Transylvanian Alps mts Romania see Carpaţii Meridionali
Transylvanian Basin plat. Romania see Transilvaniei, Podişul
146 E3 Trantlemore Highland, Scotland U.K.
194 B4 Trapani Sicilia Italy
194 B5 Trapani prov. Sicilia Italy
Trapezus Turkey see Trabzon
234 C2 Trappe PA U.S.A.
168 F1 Trappenkamp Ger.
238 D2 Trapper Peak MT U.S.A.
156 C4 Trappes France
255 B9 Trapua r. Brazil
83 F4 Traralgon Vic. Austr.
172 B2 Trarbach Ger.
143 E3 Traryd Sweden
206 B2 Trarza admin. reg. Maur.
193 F3 Trasacco Italy
197 F2 Trascăului, Munţii mts Romania
117 G4 Trashigang Bhutan
192 E1 Trasimeno, Lago l. Italy
182 C2 Trasmiras Spain
192 D2 Trasubbie r. Italy

Trat to Turégano

372

97 C4 Trat Thai.
192 A5 Tratalias Sardegna Italy
179 F2 Traun Austria
179 F2 Traun r. Austria
173 G3 Traun r. Ger.
173 G4 Traunreut Ger.
179 E3 Traunsee l. Austria
179 G2 Traunstein Austria
173 G4 Traunstein Ger.
179 H2 Trautmannsdorf an der Leitha Austria
190 F3 Travagliato Italy
182 B4 Travanca do Mondego Port.
182 B4 Travassô Port.
182 C4 Travassós de Cima Port.
168 F2 Trave r. Ger.
83 E3 Travellers Lake imp. l. N.S.W. Austr.
168 F2 Travemünde Ger.
168 F2 Travenbrück Ger.
190 B2 Travers Switz.
81 D5 Travers, Mount South I. N.Z.
226 E3 Traverse City MI U.S.A.
190 F4 Traversetolo Italy
260 D4 Travesia Puntana des. Arg.
260 D3 Travesia Tunuyán des. Arg.
191 G2 Travignolo r. Italy
97 D5 Tra Vinh Vietnam
188 F3 Travnik Bos.-Herz.
192 B3 Travo r. Corse France
190 E4 Travo Italy
150 D2 Trawsfynydd Gwynedd, Wales U.K.
87 C6 Trayning W.A. Austr.
188 E2 Trbovlje Slovenia
147 B3 Trean Rep. of Ireland
246 □ Treasure Beach Jamaica
78 □6 Treasury Islands Solomon Is
177 G3 Trebatice Slovakia
171 F3 Trebatsch Ger.
190 E3 Trebbia r. Italy
171 E3 Trebbin Ger.
170 C3 Trebel Ger.
170 E2 Trebel r. Ger.
171 D4 Treben Ger.
176 C1 Třebenice Czech Rep.
170 E2 Trebenow Ger.
163 E5 Trèbes France
179 E4 Trebesing Austria
158 C3 Trébeurden France
176 E2 Třebíč Czech Rep.
188 G4 Trebinje Bos.-Herz.
195 F3 Trebisacce Italy
188 F4 Trebišnjica r. Bos.-Herz.
177 K3 Trebišov Slovakia
171 D4 Trebitz Ger.
188 F4 Trebižat r. Bos.-Herz.
Trebizond Turkey see Trabzon
188 E3 Trebnje Slovenia
182 C2 Trebolle Spain
176 D2 Třeboň Czech Rep.
85 F3 Trebonne Qld Austr.
158 B3 Tréboul France
171 D4 Trebsen Ger.
184 D4 Trebujena Spain
172 C2 Trebur Ger.
150 D3 Trecastle Powys, Wales U.K.
190 D3 Trecate Italy
193 H4 Trecchina Italy
191 G3 Trecenta Italy
150 D3 Tredegar Blaenau Gwent, Wales U.K.
151 F2 Tredington Warwickshire, England U.K.
191 G4 Tredozio Italy
148 B3 Treehoo Rep. of Ireland
168 E1 Treene r. Ger.
Trefaldwyn Powys, Wales U.K. see Montgomery
150 D2 Trefeglwys Powys, Wales U.K.
179 E4 Treffen Austria
158 B4 Treffiagat France
160 D2 Treffort-Cuisiat France
169 F4 Treffurt Ger.
Treffynnon Flintshire, Wales U.K. see Holywell
150 D1 Trefriw Conwy, Wales U.K.
Trefynwy Monmouthshire, Wales U.K. see Monmouth
150 D2 Tregaron Ceredigion, Wales U.K.
158 C3 Trégastel France
191 G3 Tregnago Italy
226 B3 Trego WI U.S.A.
150 C4 Tregony Cornwall, England U.K.
85 G3 Tregosse Islets and Reefs Coral Sea Is Terr. Austr.
260 A5 Treguaco Chile
158 D3 Trégueux France
158 C3 Tréguier France
158 C4 Trégunc France
150 D2 Tregynon Powys, Wales U.K.
140 L3 Trehörningsjö Sweden
168 E1 Treia Ger.
191 I5 Treia Italy
146 D5 Treig, Loch l. Scotland U.K.
162 D3 Treignac France
160 B1 Treigny France
Treinta de Agosto Arg. see 30 de Agosto
258 G4 Treinta y Tres Uru.
169 C5 Treis Ger.
246 □ Trelawney parish Jamaica
159 F4 Trélazé France
150 C3 Trelech Carmarthenshire, Wales U.K.
259 D6 Trelew Arg.
162 C3 Trélissac France
158 D3 Trélivan France
142 E4 Trelleborg Sweden
156 E2 Trélon France
197 F4 Trem mt. Yugo.
150 C2 Tremadog Gwynedd, Wales U.K.
150 C2 Tremadog Bay Wales U.K.
224 F4 Tremblant, Mont hill Que. Can.
158 E3 Tremblay France
156 B4 Tremblay-les-Villages France
182 D3 Tremedal de Tormes Spain
165 D4 Tremelo Belgium
159 F4 Trémentines France
184 B1 Tremês Port.
158 C4 Tréméven France
190 E3 Tremezzo Italy
193 H2 Tremiti, Isole is Italy
138 G5 Tremlya r. Belarus
163 C4 Trémolat France
227 I5 Tremont PA U.S.A.
238 D3 Tremonton UT U.S.A.
176 C2 Třemošná Czech Rep.
176 E2 Třemošnice Czech Rep.
161 A4 Trémouilles France
186 D2 Tremp Spain
226 B3 Trempealeau r. WI U.S.A.
168 F2 Tremsbüttel Ger.
150 B4 Trenance Cornwall, England U.K.
226 D2 Trenary MI U.S.A.
225 F4 Trenche r. Que. Can.
177 H3 Trenčianska Turná Slovakia
177 G3 Trenčianske Stankovce Slovakia
177 H3 Trenčianske Teplice Slovakia
177 H3 Trenčiansky Kraj admin. reg. Slovakia
177 H3 Trenčín Slovakia
169 E4 Trendelburg Ger.
261 E4 Trenel Arg.
95 E5 Trenggalek Jawa Timur Indon.
Trengganu state Malaysia see Terengganu
261 F4 Trenque Lauquén Arg.
163 B4 Trensacq France
170 E1 Trent Ger.
Trent Italy see Trento
149 I4 Trent r. Dorset, England U.K.
150 E4 Trent r. England U.K.
163 C4 Trentels France
191 G2 Trentino - Alto Adige admin. reg. Italy
191 G2 Trento Italy
191 G2 Trento prov. Trentino - Alto Adige Italy
193 G4 Trentola-Ducenta Italy
224 E4 Trenton Ont. Can.
231 D6 Trenton FL U.S.A.
231 C5 Trenton GA U.S.A.
236 E3 Trenton MO U.S.A.
231 E5 Trenton NC U.S.A.
236 C3 Trenton NE U.S.A.
234 D2 Trenton NJ U.S.A.
237 F5 Trenton TN U.S.A.
156 B4 Tréon France
150 D3 Treorchy Rhondda Cynon Taff, Wales U.K.
84 B1 Trepang Bay N.T. Austr.
225 K4 Trepassey Nfld. Can.
171 F3 Treppeln Ger.
160 D3 Trept France
195 H2 Trepuzzi Italy
192 D1 Trequanda Italy
190 D2 Tresa r. Italy
261 F4 Tres Algarrobas Arg.
190 E4 Tresana Italy
261 G6 Tres Arroyos Arg.
256 B6 Três Bicos Brazil
234 C2 Tresckow PA U.S.A.
161 D4 Trescléoux France
150 □ Tresco i. England U.K.
257 E4 Três Corações Brazil
190 E3 Trescore Balneario Italy
190 F2 Tresenda Italy
250 C4 Tres Esquinas Col.
Tres Forcas, Cabo c. Morocco see Trois Fourches, Cap des
146 B5 Treshnish Isles Scotland U.K.
191 G4 Tresigallo Italy
190 F2 Tre Signori, Corno dei mt. Italy
256 B4 Três Irmãos, Represa resr Brazil
258 E2 Tres Isletas Arg.
196 E4 Treska r. Macedonia
256 B4 Três Lagoas Brazil
261 F5 Tres Lomas Arg.
183 F1 Tres Mares, Pico mt. Spain
257 E3 Três Marias Brazil
257 E3 Três Marias, Represa resr Brazil
259 B7 Tres Montes, Península pen. Chile
192 A4 Tresnuraghes Sardegna Italy
183 G2 Trespaderne Spain
245 E5 Tres Palos Mex.
239 F6 Tres Picachos, Sierra mts Mex.
259 C6 Tres Picos mt. Arg.
243 G6 Tres Picos Mex.
261 G6 Tres Picos, Cerro mt. Arg.
245 H5 Tres Picos, Cerro mt. Mex.
239 F4 Tres Piedras NM U.S.A.
240 G3 Tres Pinos CA U.S.A.
257 E4 Três Pontas Brazil
256 C6 Tres Pontões, Pico mt. Brazil
260 C3 Tres Porteñas Arg.
256 D3 Três Ranchos Brazil
257 F5 Três Rios Brazil
146 E5 Tressait Perth and Kinross, Scotland U.K.
160 D3 Tresserve France
176 E2 Třešť Czech Rep.
193 G3 Treste r. Italy
245 F4 Tres Valles Mex.
245 G4 Tres Zapotes tourist site Mex.
150 D3 Tretower Powys, Wales U.K.
161 D5 Trets France
173 E3 Treuchtlingen Ger.
171 D5 Treuen Ger.
171 D3 Treuenbrietzen Ger.
142 C2 Treungen Norway
158 D3 Trévé France
185 G4 Trevélez Spain
185 G4 Trevélez r. Spain
259 C6 Trevelín Arg.
157 F4 Tréveray France
161 B4 Trèves France
Treves Ger. see Trier
193 E2 Trevi Italy
183 G2 Treviana Spain
159 F2 Trévières France
190 E3 Treviglio Italy
192 E2 Trevignano Romano Italy
160 E1 Trévillers France
183 H2 Treviño Spain
191 H3 Treviso Italy
191 H3 Treviso airport Italy
191 H3 Treviso prov. Veneto Italy
182 C3 Trevões Port.
234 B2 Trevorton PA U.S.A.
234 D2 Trevose PA U.S.A.
150 B4 Trevose Head hd England U.K.
160 C3 Trévoux France
234 C2 Trexlertown PA U.S.A.
160 B2 Trézelles France
197 F4 Trgovište Srbija Yugo.
176 D3 Trhové Sviny Czech Rep.
177 K3 Trhovište Slovakia
83 F5 Triabunna Tas. Austr.
182 C2 Triacastela Spain
162 A2 Triaize France
84 D2 Trial Bay N.T. Austr.
129 D3 T'rialet'i Georgia
129 C3 T'rialet'is K'edi hills Georgia
Triánda Notio Aigaio Greece see Trianta
232 E5 Triangle VA U.S.A.
199 F3 Trianta Notio Aigaio Greece
123 G3 Tribal Areas admin. div. Pak.
177 H3 Tribeč mts Slovakia
158 E2 Tribehou France
172 C3 Triberg im Schwarzwald Ger.
100 G1 Tri Brata, Gora hill Sakhalin Rus. Fed.
170 D1 Tribsees Ger.
85 F3 Tribulation, Cape Qld Austr.
236 C4 Tribune KS U.S.A.
193 I4 Tricarico Italy
195 H3 Tricase Italy
191 I2 Tricesimo Italy
191 H2 Trichiana Italy
Trichinopoly Tamil Nadu India see Tiruchchirappalli
198 B2 Trichonida, Limni l. Greece
114 C4 Trichur Kerala India
156 C3 Tricot France
83 F3 Trida N.S.W. Austr.
Tridentum Italy see Trento
171 D5 Triebel r. Ger.
179 F3 Trieben Austria
171 D5 Triebes Ger.
156 B3 Trie-Château France
192 B4 Triei Sardegna Italy
172 C4 Triengen Switz.
172 A2 Trier Ger.
169 B5 Trier admin. reg. Rheinland-Pfalz Ger.
172 A2 Trierweiler Ger.
191 I3 Trieste Italy
191 I3 Trieste prov. Friuli - Venezia Giulia Italy
Trieste, Golfo di g. Europe see Trieste, Gulf of
188 D3 Trieste, Gulf of Europe
191 I3 Trieste-Ronchi dei Legionari airport Italy
163 C5 Trie-sur-Baïse France
157 F3 Trieux France
158 C3 Trieux r. France
173 H3 Triftern Ger.
184 C2 Trigaches Port.
161 E5 Trigance France
195 F1 Triggiano Italy
179 E4 Triglav mt. Slovenia
170 D2 Triglitz Ger.
158 D4 Trignac France
193 G2 Trigno r. Italy
216 □1c Trigo, Monte hill São Jorge Azores
156 C5 Triguères France
184 D3 Trigueros Spain
183 F3 Trigueros del Valle Spain
198 B2 Trikala Greece
Tríkkala Greece see Trikala
91 I7 Trikora, Puncak mt. Indon.
198 C2 Trikorfa mt. Greece
188 F4 Trilj Croatia
147 D2 Trillick Northern Ireland U.K.
183 H4 Trillo Spain
156 C4 Trilport France
147 E3 Trim Rep. of Ireland
149 H3 Trimdon Durham, England U.K.
151 I3 Trimley St Mary Suffolk, England U.K.
190 E2 Trimmis Switz.
86 B4 Trimouille Island W.A. Austr.
150 C3 Trimsaran Carmarthenshire, Wales U.K.
114 D4 Trincomalee Sri Lanka
256 C2 Trindade Brazil
184 C3 Trindade Beja Port.
182 C3 Trindade Bragança Port.
264 H7 Trindade, Ilha da i. S. Atlantic Ocean
177 H2 Třinec Czech Rep.
151 G3 Tring Hertfordshire, England U.K.
198 B2 Tringia mt. Greece
252 D3 Trinidad Bol.
246 C2 Trinidad Cuba
245 G5 Trinidad r. Mex.
247 □7 Trinidad i. Trin. and Tob.
261 I3 Trinidad Uru.
239 F4 Trinidad CO U.S.A.
261 G6 Trinidad, Isla i. Arg.
247 G5 Trinidad and Tobago country West Indies
192 A4 Trinità d'Agultu Sardegna Italy
193 I3 Trinitapoli Italy
237 E6 Trinity TX U.S.A.
238 B3 Trinity r. CA U.S.A.
237 E6 Trinity r. TX U.S.A.
237 D5 Trinity, West Fork r. OK U.S.A.
85 F3 Trinity Bay Qld Austr.
225 K4 Trinity Bay Nfld. Can.
240 H1 Trinity Range mts NV U.S.A.
190 D3 Trino Italy
178 C3 Trins Austria
182 C4 Trinta Port.
232 B4 Trinway OH U.S.A.
170 D1 Trinwillershagen Ger.
183 F2 Triollo Spain
193 H3 Triolo r. Italy
195 F3 Trionto r. Italy
190 C5 Triora Italy
94 B2 Tripa r. Indon.
170 C2 Tripkau Ger.
198 C3 Tripoli Greece
Tripoli Lebanon see Trâblous
202 B1 Tripoli Libya
Trípolis Greece see Tripoli
Tripolis Lebanon see Trâblous
202 B2 Tripolitania reg. Libya
172 B2 Trippstadt Ger.
171 C5 Triptis Ger.
114 C4 Tripunittura Kerala India
117 G5 Tripura state India
178 B3 Trisanna r. Austria
178 D4 Tristach Austria
216 □2c Tristan da Cunha i. S. Atlantic Ocean
206 B4 Tristao, Îles is Guinea
178 E4 Tristenspitze mt. Austria
116 D3 Trisul mt. Uttar Prad. India
225 K3 Triton Nfld. Can.
168 F2 Trittau Ger.
172 A2 Trittenheim Ger.
254 F3 Triunfo Brazil
114 C4 Trivandrum Kerala India
193 G3 Trivento Italy
190 D3 Trivero Italy
190 D4 Triversa r. Italy
193 H4 Trivigno Italy
161 A3 Trizac France
177 G2 Trnava Czech Rep.
177 G3 Trnava Slovakia
177 H3 Trnavá Hora Slovakia
177 G3 Trnavský Kraj admin. reg. Slovakia
179 H4 Trnovec Bartolovečki Croatia
179 E5 Trnovski gozd mts Slovenia
159 F2 Troarn France
171 E4 Tröbitz Ger.
172 D3 Trochtelfingen Ger.
222 H5 Trochu Alta Can.
141 L3 Trödje Sweden
182 B3 Trofa Port.
179 G3 Trofaiach Austria
140 K2 Trofors Norway
188 F4 Trogir Croatia
178 E4 Trogkofel mt. Austria/Italy
188 F4 Troglav mt. Croatia
142 D2 Trøgstad Norway
193 H3 Troia Italy
184 B2 Tróia Port.
194 D5 Troina Sicilia Italy
194 D5 Troina r. Sicilia Italy
169 C5 Troisdorf Ger.
157 H4 Troisfontaines France
204 E2 Trois Fourches, Cap des c. Morocco
225 G3 Trois-Pistoles Que. Can.
165 E4 Trois-Ponts Belgium
225 F4 Trois-Rivières Que. Can.
247 □2 Trois-Rivières Guadeloupe
163 D6 Trois Seigneurs, Pic des mt. France
156 C3 Troissereux France
160 B2 Trois-Vèvres France
165 F4 Troisvierges Lux.
139 M4 Troitsa Rus. Fed.
120 E1 Troitsk Chelyabinskaya Oblast' Rus. Fed.
139 K4 Troitsk Moskovskaya Oblast' Rus. Fed.
137 I2 Troitskiy Belgorodskaya Oblast' Rus. Fed.
Troitskiy Moskovskaya Oblast' Rus. Fed. see Troitsk
134 L3 Troitsko-Pechorsk Rus. Fed.
121 K1 Troitskoye Altayskiy Kray Rus. Fed.
100 F2 Troitskoye Khabarovskiy Kray Rus. Fed.
120 C1 Troitskoye Orenburgskaya Oblast' Rus. Fed.
120 D1 Troitskoye Respublika Bashkortostan Rus. Fed.
135 I7 Troitskoye Respublika Kalmykiya - Khalm'g-Tangch Rus. Fed.
246 □ Troja Jamaica
174 G5 Troja r. Pol.
142 E2 Trollhättan Sweden
251 G5 Trombetas r. Brazil
217 □1 Tromelin, Île i. Indian Ocean
Tromelin Island Micronesia see Fais
190 D3 Tromello Italy
260 B5 Tromen, Volcán vol. Arg.
146 D4 Tromie r. Scotland U.K.
215 E4 Trompsburg S. Africa
140 L1 Troms county Norway
140 L1 Tromsø Norway
240 I4 Trona CA U.S.A.
259 C6 Tronador, Monte mt. Arg.
160 A2 Tronçais, Forêt de for. France
182 C3 Tronco Port.
244 C2 Troncoso Mex.
140 J3 Trondheim Norway
140 J3 Trondheimsfjorden sea chan. Norway
150 D4 Troney r. England U.K.
117 G4 Trongsa Bhutan
117 G4 Trongsa Chhu r. Bhutan
193 F2 Tronto r. Italy
157 F4 Tronville-en-Barrois France
190 D3 Tronzano Vercellese Italy
159 G4 Troo France
128 A2 Troödos, Mount Cyprus
128 A2 Troödos Mountains Cyprus
146 D6 Troon South Ayrshire, Scotland U.K.
198 B3 Tropaia Greece
251 G6 Tropas r. Brazil
195 E4 Tropea Italy
254 D5 Tropeiros, Serra dos hills Brazil
241 K3 Tropic UT U.S.A.
147 D2 Trory Northern Ireland U.K.
139 J5 Trosna Rus. Fed.
171 D4 Trossin Ger.
172 C3 Trossingen Ger.
139 I5 Trostan' Rus. Fed.
147 E1 Trostan hill Northern Ireland U.K.
173 F1 Tröstau Ger.
173 G3 Trostberg Ger.
137 H2 Trostyanets' Ukr.
136 E3 Trostyanets' Ukr.
136 C2 Trostyanets' Ukr.
146 B4 Trotternish hills Scotland U.K.
197 H2 Trotuș r. Romania
222 E3 Trout r. B.C. Can.
222 G2 Trout r. N.W.T. Can.
149 G3 Troutbeck Cumbria, England U.K.
227 H3 Trout Creek Ont. Can.
226 C2 Trout Creek MI U.S.A.
232 C6 Trout Dale VA U.S.A.
222 H3 Trout Lake Alta Can.
222 F2 Trout Lake N.W.T. Can.
222 F2 Trout Lake l. N.W.T. Can.
223 M5 Trout Lake l. Ont. Can.
226 E2 Trout Lake MI U.S.A.
225 J3 Trout River Nfld. Can.
227 I5 Trout Run PA U.S.A.
232 D6 Troutville VA U.S.A.
159 G2 Trouville-sur-Mer France
159 I4 Trouy France
182 B5 Troviscal Port.
150 E3 Trowbridge Wiltshire, England U.K.
83 F5 Trowutta Tas. Austr.
Troy tourist site Turkey see Truva
231 C6 Troy AL U.S.A.
236 E4 Troy KS U.S.A.
227 F4 Troy MI U.S.A.
236 F4 Troy MO U.S.A.
238 D1 Troy MT U.S.A.
231 E5 Troy NC U.S.A.
233 G3 Troy NH U.S.A.
233 G3 Troy NY U.S.A.
232 A4 Troy OH U.S.A.
227 I5 Troy PA U.S.A.
197 G4 Troyan Bulg.
136 E2 Troyaniv Ukr.
136 F3 Troyanka Ukr.
139 L5 Troyekurovo Lipetskaya Oblast' Rus. Fed.
139 L5 Troyekurovo Lipetskaya Oblast' Rus. Fed.
156 E4 Troyes France
137 J3 Troyits'ke Ukr.
136 F4 Troyits'ke Ukr.
137 G4 Troyits'ko-Safonove Ukr.
157 F3 Troyon France
241 J2 Troy Peak NV U.S.A.
176 G2 Tršice Czech Rep.
179 E5 Trstelj hill Slovenia
177 I2 Trstená Slovakia
196 E4 Trstenik Srbija Yugo.
177 G3 Trstice Slovakia
176 G3 Trstín Slovakia
84 D1 Truant Island N.T. Austr.
139 I5 Trubchevsk Rus. Fed.
139 L5 Trubetchino Rus. Fed.
182 E1 Trubia Spain
182 E1 Trubia r. Spain
137 F2 Trubizh r. Ukr.
161 B4 Truc de la Garde mt. France
Truc Giang Vietnam see Bên Tre
182 D2 Truchas Spain
157 H4 Truchtersheim France
Trucial Coast country Asia see United Arab Emirates
Trucial States country Asia see United Arab Emirates
240 G2 Truckee CA U.S.A.
120 A3 Trudfront Rus. Fed.
Trudovoy Kazakh. see Kuybyshevskiy
Trudovoy Rus. Fed. see Yusta
100 E4 Trudovoye Rus. Fed.
139 K5 Trudy r. Rus. Fed.
84 B4 Truer Range hills N.T. Austr.
184 D2 Trujillanos Spain
242 □I6 Trujillo Hond.
252 A2 Trujillo Peru
184 E1 Trujillo Spain
250 D2 Trujillo Venez.
250 D2 Trujillo state Venez.
Trujillo, Monte mt. Dom. Rep. see Duarte, Pico
247 □1 Trujillo Alto Puerto Rico
Truk is Micronesia see Chuuk
172 B2 Trulben Ger.
150 D4 Trull Somerset, England U.K.
237 F5 Trumann AR U.S.A.
232 E3 Trumansburg NY U.S.A.
235 E1 Trumbull CT U.S.A.
241 K3 Trumbull, Mount AZ U.S.A.
151 H2 Trumpington Cambridgeshire, England U.K.
197 F4 Trŭn Bulg.
159 G3 Trun France
190 D2 Trun Switz.
197 F4 Trŭna mt. Bulg.
83 F3 Trundle N.S.W. Austr.
Truong Sa is S. China Sea see Spratly Islands
225 I4 Truro N.S. Can.
150 B4 Truro Cornwall, England U.K.
95 F1 Trusan r. Sarawak Malaysia
197 H2 Trușești Romania
169 F5 Trusetal Ger.
196 D5 Trush Albania
137 G3 Trushivtsi Ukr.
136 B3 Truskavets' Ukr.
147 C2 Truskmore hill Rep. of Ireland
95 G1 Trus Madi, Gunung mt. Sabah Malaysia
197 G4 Trŭstenik Bulg.
222 F3 Trutch B.C. Can.
222 F3 Trutch Creek r. B.C. Can.
239 F5 Truth or Consequences NM U.S.A.
176 E1 Trutnov Czech Rep.
199 E2 Truva tourist site Turkey
161 A4 Truyère r. France
139 J2 Truzhenik Rus. Fed.
197 G4 Tryavna Bulg.
198 B2 Tryfos Dytiki Ellas Greece
168 F1 Tryggelev Denmark
175 K5 Tryńcza Pol.
236 C3 Tryon NE U.S.A.
141 K3 Trysil Norway
141 K3 Trysilelva r. Norway
141 K3 Trysilfjellet mt. Norway
138 D3 Tryškiai Lith.
188 E3 Tržac Bos.-Herz.
175 J3 Trzcianka Mazowieckie Pol.
174 E2 Trzcianka Wielkopolskie Pol.
175 K2 Trzcianne Pol.
174 D3 Trzciel Pol.
174 G4 Trzcinica Pol.
174 D1 Trzebiatów Pol.
174 C4 Trzebiel Pol.
174 F1 Trzebielino Pol.
175 K4 Trzebieszów Pol.
174 C2 Trzebież Pol.
175 H5 Trzebinia Pol.
174 F4 Trzebnica Pol.
175 K5 Trzebośnica r. Pol.
174 F3 Trzemeszno Pol.
175 L3 Trześcianka Pol.
175 J6 Trześniów Pol.
175 J5 Trześniówka r. Pol.
175 L5 Trzeszczany Pierwsze Pol.
188 E2 Tržič Slovenia
179 F4 Trzin Slovenia
174 C3 Trzrcińsko-Zdrój Pol.
175 H5 Trzyciąż Pol.
175 K5 Trzydnik Duży Pol.
106 A1 Tsagaannuur Bayan-Ölgiy Mongolia
107 H2 Tsagaannuur Dornod Mongolia
106 B2 Tsagaan Nuur salt l. Mongolia
Tsagaan-Uul Hövsgöl Mongolia see Sharga
135 I7 Tsagan Aman Rus. Fed.
135 I7 Tsagan-Nur Rus. Fed.
129 C2 Ts'ageri Georgia
Tsaidam Basin China see Qaidam Pendi
140 M1 Tsåktso mt. Sweden
129 C2 Tsalenjikha Georgia
140 K2 Tsangatjåkkå mt. Sweden
213 □J3 Tsaramandroso Madag.
213 □J3 Tsaratanana Madag.
213 □K2 Tsaratanana, Massif du mts Madag.
197 H4 Tsarevo Bulg.
Tsaribrod Srbija Yugo. see Dimitrovgrad
197 G4 Tsarimir Bulg.
Tsaritsyn Rus. Fed. see Volgograd
137 H3 Tsarychanka Ukr.
215 G4 Tsatsana mt. S. Africa
211 C5 Tsavo East National Park Kenya
211 C5 Tsavo West National Park Kenya
215 F4 Tsazo S. Africa
178 A3 Tschagguns Austria
171 F4 Tschernitz Ger.
106 B2 Tseel Mongolia
Tsefat Israel see Ẕefat
135 H7 Tselina Rus. Fed.
121 K1 Tselinnoye Rus. Fed.
120 E2 Tselinnyy Rus. Fed.
Tselinograd Kazakh. see Astana
Tselinogradskaya Oblast' admin. div. Kazakh. see Akmolinskaya Oblast'
Tsementnyy Rus. Fed. see Fokino
106 D1 Tsengel Mongolia
134 J4 Tsentral'nyy Rus. Fed.
Tsentral'nyy Rus. Fed. see Radovitskiy
139 L5 Tsentral'nyy Rus. Fed.
197 F4 Tserovo Bulg.
106 B2 Tsetsegnuur Mongolia
106 D2 Tsetserleg Arhangay Mongolia
Tsetserleg Hövsgöl Mongolia see Halban
207 F5 Tsévié Togo
212 D5 Tshabong Botswana
Tshad country Africa see Chad
209 B6 Tshela Dem. Rep. Congo
213 E4 Tshesebe Botswana
209 D6 Tshibala Dem. Rep. Congo
209 D6 Tshikapa Dem. Rep. Congo
209 D6 Tshikapa r. Dem. Rep. Congo
209 D6 Tshilenge Dem. Rep. Congo
209 D6 Tshimbulu Dem. Rep. Congo
215 F2 Tshing S. Africa
213 F4 Tshipise S. Africa
209 D6 Tshiumbe r. Angola/Dem. Rep. Congo
209 E6 Tshofa Dem. Rep. Congo
213 F5 Tshokwane S. Africa
213 E3 Tsholotsho Zimbabwe
212 D4 Tshootsha Botswana
208 D5 Tshuapa r. Dem. Rep. Congo
213 □J3 Tsiazonano mt. Madag.
197 F4 Tsibritsa r. Bulg.
220 E3 Tsiigehtchic N.W.T. Can.
134 J2 Tsil'ma r. Rus. Fed.
135 H7 Tsimlyansk Rus. Fed.
135 H7 Tsimlyanskoye Vodokhranilishche resr Rus. Fed.
Tsinan Shandong China see Jinan
214 D2 Tsineng S. Africa
Tsinghai prov. China see Qinghai
217 □3b Tsingoni Mayotte
Tsingtao Shandong China see Qingdao
Tsining Nei Mongol China see Jining
213 □J3 Tsinjomay mt. Madag.
213 □J5 Tsiombe Madag.
213 □J3 Tsiroanomandidy Madag.
Tsiteli Tskaro Georgia see Dedop'listsqaro
Tsitsihar Heilong. China see Qiqihar
222 E4 Tsitsutl Peak B.C. Can.
129 B2 Ts'ivi r. Georgia
129 D3 Ts'ivi, Mt'a Georgia
134 I5 Tsivil'sk Rus. Fed.
Tskhakaia Georgia see Senaki
Tskhaltubo Georgia see Tsqaltubo
129 C2 Ts'khinvali Georgia
129 D3 Ts'khneti Georgia
138 F5 Tsna r. Belarus
135 H5 Tsna r. Rus. Fed.
139 J3 Tsna r. Rus. Fed.
139 L4 Tsna r. Rus. Fed.
129 D3 Tsnori Georgia
212 D3 Tsodilo Hills Botswana
116 D2 Tsokr Chumo l. Jammu and Kashmir
215 G4 Tsolo S. Africa
215 F5 Tsomo S. Africa
215 F5 Tsomo r. S. Africa
116 D2 Tso Morari Lake Jammu and Kashmir
139 K5 Tson r. Rus. Fed.
Tsona Xizang China see Cona
199 D1 Tsopan hill Greece
198 B1 Tsotili Dytiki Makedonia Greece
129 D3 Tsovinar Armenia
129 C2 Tsqaltubo Georgia
104 C4 Tsu Japan
103 I5 Tsubame Japan
105 G2 Tsuchiura Japan
109 □ Tsuen Wan H.K. China
102 J3 Tsugarū-kaikyō str. Japan
Tsugaru Strait Japan see Tsugarū-kaikyō
105 G2 Tsukuba Japan
103 E7 Tsukumi Japan
106 E2 Tsul-Ulaan Mongolia
136 C2 Tsuman' Ukr.
212 C3 Tsumeb Namibia
212 D3 Tsumkwe Namibia
129 E2 Tsurib Rus. Fed.
105 E3 Tsuru Japan
104 C3 Tsuruga Japan
104 D2 Tsurugi-dake mt. Japan
103 G7 Tsurugi-san mt. Japan
Tsurukhaytuy Rus. Fed. see Priargunsk
102 I4 Tsuruoka Japan
104 C3 Tsushima Japan
Tsushima-kaikyō str. Japan/S. Korea see Korea Strait
103 G6 Tsuyama Japan
197 F5 Tsvetino Bulg.
137 F3 Tsvitkove Ukr.
137 G3 Tsvitne Ukr.
215 E3 Tswaraganang S. Africa
215 E2 Tswelelang S. Africa
136 E3 Tsybuliv Ukr.
138 E5 Tsyelyakhany Belarus
137 F1 Tsyerakhowka Belarus
Tsygira Moldova see Țîghira
175 N4 Tsyr r. Ukr.
137 G4 Tsyurupyns'k Ukr.
Tthenaagoo N.W.T. Can. see Nahanni Butte
182 C3 Tua r. Port.
80 E2 Tuakau North I. N.Z.
147 C3 Tuam Rep. of Ireland
81 D4 Tuamarina South I. N.Z.
147 C4 Tuamgraney Rep. of Ireland
79 □3 Tuamotu, Archipel des is Fr. Polynesia
Tuamotu Islands Fr. Polynesia see Tuamotu, Archipel des
81 B7 Tuapeka Mouth South I. N.Z.
129 A1 Tuapse Rus. Fed.
94 □ Tuas Sing.
81 A7 Tuatapere South I. N.Z.
146 B5 Tuath, Loch sea chan. Scotland U.K.
Tuath, Loch a' b. Scotland U.K. see Broad Bay
241 L3 Tuba City AZ U.S.A.
95 F4 Tuban Jawa Timur Indon.
255 C9 Tubarão Brazil
128 B3 Ţūbās West Bank
92 A4 Tubbataha Reefs Phil.
147 C2 Tubbercurry Rep. of Ireland
164 F2 Tubbergen Neth.
148 B5 Tubbrid Rep. of Ireland
183 G2 Tubilla del Agua Spain
172 D3 Tübingen Ger.
172 D3 Tübingen admin. reg. Baden-Württemberg Ger.
120 D1 Tubinskiy Rus. Fed.
165 D4 Tubize Belgium
206 C5 Tubmanburg Liberia
207 G4 Tubo r. Nigeria
92 B4 Tubod Phil.
190 F2 Tubre Italy
202 D1 Tubruq Libya
95 G2 Tubu r. Indon.
79 □3 Tubuai i. Îs Australes Fr. Polynesia
242 C2 Tubutama Mex.
238 C2 Tucannon r. WA U.S.A.
254 F4 Tucano Brazil
260 B5 Tucapel Chile
253 F4 Tucavaca Bol.
253 F4 Tucavaca r. Bol.
163 C6 Tuc de les Carants mt. Spain
163 E6 Tuchan France
170 D2 Tüchen Ger.
171 D3 Tuchheim Ger.
222 D2 Tuchitua Y.T. Can.
139 K4 Tuchkovo Rus. Fed.
171 E5 Tuchlovice Czech Rep.
222 F3 Tuchodi r. B.C. Can.
174 F2 Tuchola Pol.
174 F1 Tuchomie Pol.
175 J6 Tuchów Pol.
175 K4 Tuchowicz Pol.
136 D2 Tuchyn Ukr.
234 D3 Tuckahoe NJ U.S.A.
235 F2 Tuckahoe NY U.S.A.
234 D3 Tuckahoe r. NJ U.S.A.
234 C4 Tuckahoe Creek r. MD U.S.A.
87 C5 Tuckanarra W.A. Austr.
235 D3 Tuckerton NJ U.S.A.
234 C2 Tuckerton PA U.S.A.
Tucopia i. Solomon Is see Tikopia
157 F3 Tucquegnieux France
241 L5 Tucson AZ U.S.A.
241 L5 Tucson Mountains AZ U.S.A.
225 H1 Tuctuc r. Que. Can.
Tucumán Arg. see San Miguel de Tucumán
258 D2 Tucumán prov. Arg.
237 C5 Tucumcari NM U.S.A.
251 F2 Tucupita Venez.
251 I5 Tucuruí Brazil
251 I6 Tucuruí, Represa resr Brazil
175 L4 Tuczna Pol.
174 E2 Tuczno Pol.
142 D4 Tudeå r. Denmark
183 I2 Tudela Spain
183 F3 Tudela de Duero Spain
Tuder Italy see Todi
197 H2 Tudora Romania
197 H3 Tudor Vladimirescu Romania
139 I3 Tudovka r. Rus. Fed.
150 C2 Tudweiliog Gwynedd, Wales U.K.
187 B5 Tuejar Spain
182 C3 Tuela r. Port.
109 □ Tuen Mun H.K. China
191 G2 Tuenno Italy
117 H4 Tuensang Nagaland India
251 I5 Tueré r. Brazil
182 E2 Tuerto r. Spain
125 E2 Ţufayḩ Saudi Arabia
159 G3 Tuffé France
267 J2 Tufts Abyssal Plain sea feature N. Pacific Ocean
Tuga i. Vanuatu see Tégua
215 H3 Tugela r. S. Africa
215 H3 Tugela Ferry S. Africa
Tūghyl Kazakh. see Tugyl
108 B3 Tuguancun Yunnan China
92 B2 Tuguegarao Phil.
213 F4 Tugwi r. Zimbabwe
121 K3 Tugyl Kazakh.
107 H4 Tuhai r. China
182 B2 Tui Spain
252 D3 Tuichi r. Bol.
192 A5 Tuili Sardegna Italy
117 H5 Tuilianpui r. Bangl./India
216 □3b Tuineje Fuerteventura Canary Is
Tujiabu Jiangxi China see Yongxiu
120 D1 Tukan Rus. Fed.
93 B4 Tukangbesi, Kepulauan is Indon.
136 B3 Tukhol'ka Ukr.
123 H2 Tŭkhtamish Tajik.
80 F3 Tukituki r. North I. N.Z.
202 D1 Tūkrah Libya
220 E3 Tuktoyaktuk N.W.T. Can.
138 D3 Tukums Latvia
95 E3 Tukung, Bukit mt. Indon.
100 C1 Tukuringra, Khrebet mts Rus. Fed.
129 D1 Tukuy-Mekteb Rus. Fed.
211 B7 Tukuyu Tanz.
192 A4 Tula Sardegna Italy
245 E3 Tula Hidalgo Mex.
245 E2 Tula Tamaulipas Mex.
245 E3 Tula r. Mex.
139 K4 Tula Rus. Fed.
Tulach Mhór Rep. of Ireland see Tullamore
78 □6 Tulaghi Solomon Is
111 F4 Tulagt Ar Gol r. China
106 C4 Tulai Qinghai China
106 C4 Tulai Nanshan mts China
106 C4 Tulai Shan mts China
263 D2 Tula Mountains Antarctica
245 E3 Tulancingo Mex.
94 D4 Tulangbawang r. Indon.
Tula Oblast admin. div. Rus. Fed. see Tul'skaya Oblast'
240 H3 Tulare CA U.S.A.
239 F5 Tularosa NM U.S.A.
114 D2 Tulasi mt. Madh. Prad./Orissa India
168 F3 Tülau Ger.
175 I2 Tuławki Pol.
214 B5 Tulbagh S. Africa
179 H2 Tulbing Austria
177 K5 Tulca Romania
250 B4 Tulcán Ecuador
174 F3 Tulce Pol.
197 I3 Tulcea Romania
Tul'chin Ukr. see Tul'chyn
136 E3 Tul'chyn Ukr.
240 H3 Tule r. CA U.S.A.
Tuléar Madag. see Toliara
238 B3 Tulelake CA U.S.A.
161 C4 Tulette France
176 F5 Tulfás r. Hungary
178 C3 Tulfes Austria
197 G2 Tulgheș Romania
237 C5 Tulia TX U.S.A.
107 I1 Tulihe Nei Mongol China
174 G3 Tuliszków Pol.
222 E1 Tulít'a N.W.T. Can.
114 C2 Tuljapur Mahar. India
128 B3 Ţūlkarm West Bank
147 C4 Tulla Rep. of Ireland
147 C2 Tullaghan Rep. of Ireland
231 C5 Tullahoma TN U.S.A.
83 F3 Tullamore N.S.W. Austr.
147 D3 Tullamore Rep. of Ireland
148 B5 Tullaroan Rep. of Ireland
162 D3 Tulle France
83 F3 Tullibigeal N.S.W. Austr.
161 D3 Tullins France
179 H2 Tulln Austria
237 E6 Tullos LA U.S.A.
147 E4 Tullow Rep. of Ireland
85 F3 Tully Qld Austr.
147 D2 Tully Northern Ireland U.K.
147 D2 Tully Northern Ireland U.K.
147 E3 Tullyallen Rep. of Ireland
147 D2 Tullybrack hill Northern Ireland U.K.
147 E4 Tullycanna Rep. of Ireland
147 E2 Tullyhogue Northern Ireland U.K.
234 D2 Tullytown PA U.S.A.
147 D2 Tullyvin Rep. of Ireland
147 C2 Tullyvoos Rep. of Ireland
197 H3 Tulnici Romania
140 P1 Tuloma r. Rus. Fed.
175 I3 Tułowice Pol.
174 F5 Tułowice Pol.
237 E4 Tulsa OK U.S.A.
222 C3 Tulsequah B.C. Can.
116 E3 Tulsipur Nepal
147 C3 Tulsk Rep. of Ireland
139 K5 Tul'skaya Oblast' admin. div. Rus. Fed.
129 B1 Tul'skiy Rus. Fed.
121 H1 Tul'skoye Kazakh.
250 B3 Tuluá Col.
197 I3 Tulucești Romania
220 B3 Tuluksak AK U.S.A.
128 C3 Tulūl al Ashāqif hills Jordan
243 I4 Tulum tourist site Mex.
260 C2 Tulum, Valle de val. Arg.
98 H1 Tulun Rus. Fed.
95 E5 Tulungagung Jawa Timur Indon.
Tulusdu N. Male Maldives see Thulusdhu
251 F4 Tulu-Tuloi, Serra hills Brazil
210 B2 Tulu Welel mt. Eth.
134 K4 Tulva r. Rus. Fed.
137 G2 Tulyholove Ukr.
242 □I6 Tuma r. Nic.
139 M4 Tuma Rus. Fed.
250 B4 Tumaco Col.
215 F2 Tumahole S. Africa
111 E5 Tumain Xizang China
120 B3 Tumak Rus. Fed.
Tuman-gang r. Asia see Tumen Jiang
Tumannaya r. Asia see Tumen Jiang
134 F1 Tumannyy Rus. Fed.
139 J4 Tumanovo Rus. Fed.
131 S3 Tumanskiy Rus. Fed.
Tumasik Sing. see Singapore
251 G3 Tumatumari Guyana
143 G2 Tumba Sweden
92 C5 Tumbao Phil.
83 G3 Tumbarumba N.S.W. Austr.
250 A5 Tumbes Peru
250 A5 Tumbes dept Peru
222 F4 Tumbler Ridge B.C. Can.
82 D3 Tumby Bay S.A. Austr.
140 O2 Tumcha r. Fin./Rus. Fed.
Tumd Youqi Nei Mongol China see Salaqi
Tumd Zuoqi Nei Mongol China see Qasq
100 D4 Tumen Jilin China
108 D1 Tumen Shaanxi China
100 D4 Tumen Jiang r. Asia
251 F3 Tumereng Guyana
257 G3 Tumiritinga Brazil
114 C3 Tumkur Karnataka India
146 E5 Tummel, Loch l. Scotland U.K.
146 D5 Tummel Bridge Perth and Kinross, Scotland U.K.
202 B4 Tummo, Mountains of Libya/Niger
100 G2 Tumnin r. Rus. Fed.
97 C4 Tumpôr, Phnum mt. Cambodia
93 B3 Tumpu, Gunung mt. Indon.
93 B3 Tumputiga, Gunung mt. Indon.
116 D5 Tumsar Mahar. India
206 E4 Tumu Ghana
251 G4 Tumucumaque, Serra hills Brazil
115 D2 Tumudibandh Orissa India
182 D5 Tumuja r. Spain
252 D3 Tumupasa Bol.
121 G4 Tumur Yuzhnyy Kazakhstan Kazakh.
252 D5 Tumusla Bol.
83 G3 Tumut N.S.W. Austr.
134 K5 Tumutuk Rus. Fed.
110 C3 Tumxuk Xinjiang China
206 E4 Tuna Ghana
247 □1 Tuna, Punta pt Puerto Rico
143 F1 Tuna-Hästberg Sweden
247 □7 Tunapuna Trin. and Tob.
246 C2 Tunas de Zaza Cuba
Ţunb al Kubrá i. The Gulf see Greater Tunb
Ţunb aş Şughrá i. The Gulf see Lesser Tunb
151 H3 Tunbridge Wells, Royal Kent, England U.K.
199 F2 Tunçbilek Turkey
126 E3 Tunceli Turkey
129 A4 Tunceli prov. Turkey
108 D5 Tunchang Hainan China
129 C3 Tunçoluk Turkey
83 H3 Tuncurry N.S.W. Austr.
111 B7 Tundla Uttar Prad. India
211 B7 Tunduma Tanz.
207 H4 Tundun-Wada Nigeria
211 C7 Tunduru Tanz.
197 H5 Tundzha r. Bulg.
142 E4 Tune Denmark
Tunes Tunisia see Tunis
207 H4 Tunga Nigeria
146 B3 Tunga Western Isles, Scotland U.K.
114 C3 Tungabhadra r. India
92 B5 Tungawan Phil.
Tungdor Xizang China see Mainling
117 G5 Tungi Bangl.
140 □C2 Tungnaá r. Iceland
100 G1 Tungor Sakhalin Rus. Fed.
222 D2 Tungsten N.W.T. Can.
95 F2 Tungun, Bukit mt. Indon.
115 D2 Tuni Andhra Prad. India
237 F5 Tunica MS U.S.A.
172 C3 Tuningen Ger.
227 G1 Tunis Ont. Can.
205 H1 Tunis Tunisia
205 H1 Tunis, Golfe de g. Tunisia
205 H2 Tunisia country Africa
250 C3 Tunja Col.
234 C1 Tunkhannock PA U.S.A.
107 G4 Tunliu Shanxi China
226 B3 Tunnel City WI U.S.A.
232 D5 Tunnelton WV U.S.A.
139 M3 Tunoshna Rus. Fed.
151 I2 Tunstall Suffolk, England U.K.
173 G4 Tuntenhausen Ger.
225 H1 Tunulic r. Que. Can.
220 B3 Tununak AK U.S.A.
260 C3 Tunuyán Arg.
260 D4 Tunuyán r. Arg.
Tunxi Anhui China see Huangshan
177 L4 Tunyogmatolcs Hungary
Tuodian Yunnan China see Shuangbai
109 F1 Tuo He r. China
Tuojiang Hunan China see Fenghuang
Tuojiang Hunan China see Shuikou
108 C2 Tuo Jiang r. Sichuan China
240 G3 Tuolumne CA U.S.A.
240 G3 Tuolumne r. CA U.S.A.
240 H3 Tuolumne Meadows CA U.S.A.
192 D1 Tuoma r. Italy
108 C3 Tuoniang Jiang r. Guangxi China
Tuoputiereke Xinjiang China see Jeminay (Topterek)
191 H5 Tuoro sul Trasimeno Italy
111 F5 Tuotuo He r. China
106 B5 Tuotuoheyan Qinghai China
121 I4 Tüp Kyrg.
256 B4 Tupã Brazil
256 C3 Tupaciguara Brazil
Tupai i. Fr. Polynesia see Motu Iti
255 B9 Tupanciretã Brazil
237 F5 Tupelo MS U.S.A.
176 G2 Tupesy Czech Rep.
251 G5 Tupinambarama, Ilha i. Brazil
256 B4 Tupi Paulista Brazil
252 D5 Tupiza Bol.
174 C4 Tuplice Pol.
222 F4 Tupper B.C. Can.
233 F2 Tupper Lake NY U.S.A.
Tüpqaraghan Tübegi pen. Kazakh. see Mangyshlak, Poluostrov
260 C3 Tupungato Arg.
260 C3 Tupungato, Cerro mt. Arg./Chile
107 I2 Tuquan Nei Mongol China
250 B4 Túquerres Col.
197 F1 Tur r. Romania
111 D4 Tura Xinjiang China
177 I4 Tura Hungary
117 G4 Tura Meghalaya India
131 L3 Tura Rus. Fed.
124 C3 Turabah Saudi Arabia
251 E3 Turagua, Serranía mt. Venez.
80 E4 Turakina North I. N.Z.
80 E4 Turakina r. North I. N.Z.
100 D2 Turana, Khrebet mts Rus. Fed.
80 E3 Turangi North I. N.Z.
120 D5 Turan Lowland Asia
193 E2 Turano r. Italy
Turanskaya Nizmennost' lowland Asia see Turan Lowland
121 G4 Tura-Ryskulova Kazakh.
136 D1 Turaw Belarus
138 E2 Turba Estonia
250 C2 Turbaco Col.
175 I6 Turbacz mt. Pol.
123 E5 Turbat Pak.
190 D1 Turbenthal Switz.
244 D3 Turbio r. Mex.
136 E3 Turbiv Ukr.
250 B2 Turbo Col.
234 B1 Turbotville PA U.S.A.
178 E3 Türchlwand mt. Austria
182 E2 Turcia Spain
177 H3 Turčianske Teplice Slovakia
157 H4 Turckheim France
197 F2 Turda Romania
160 C3 Turdine r. France
87 C4 Turee Creek r. W.A. Austr.
183 F3 Turégano Spain

Turek to Unterdietfurt 373

174 G3 **Turek** Pol.
138 E1 **Turenki** Fin.
174 E3 **Turew** Pol.
Turfan Xinjiang China see Turpan
Turfan Depression China see Turpan Pendi
121 H2 **Turgay** Akmolinskaya Oblast' Kazakh.
120 E2 **Turgay** Kustanayskaya Oblast' Kazakh.
120 E3 **Turgay** r. Kazakh.
120 E2 **Turgayskaya Dolina** val. Kazakh.
120 E2 **Turgayskaya Stolovaya Strana** reg. Kazakh.
106 A1 **Türgen Uul** mt. Mongolia
106 A1 **Türgen Uul** mt. Mongolia
224 E3 **Turgeon** r. Ont./Que. Can.
197 H4 **Tŭrgovishte** Bulg.
126 C3 **Turgut** Konya Turkey
199 F3 **Turgut** Muğla Turkey
199 E2 **Turgutalp** Turkey
199 E2 **Turgutlu** Turkey
199 E3 **Turgutreis** Turkey
126 E2 **Turhal** Turkey
138 E2 **Türi** Estonia
195 G2 **Turi** Italy
187 C5 **Turia** r. Spain
254 D2 **Turiaçu** Brazil
254 D2 **Turiaçu** r. Brazil
177 H2 **Turie** Slovakia
177 H3 **Turiec** r. Slovakia
223 H5 **Turin** Alta Can.
Turin Italy see **Torino**
130 H4 **Turinsk** Rus. Fed.
187 C5 **Turís** Spain
136 C2 **Turiya** r. Ukr.
136 C2 **Turiys'k** Ukr.
176 G5 **Türje** Hungary
99 I1 **Turka** Rus. Fed.
136 B3 **Turka** Ukr.
210 B4 **Turkana, Lake** salt l. Eth./Kenya
199 E1 **Türkeli** Turkey
173 F3 **Türkenfeld** Ger.
121 G4 **Turkestan** Kazakh.
123 F2 **Turkestan Range** mts Asia
177 J4 **Túrkeve** Hungary
126 D3 **Turkey** country Asia
232 B6 **Turkey** KY U.S.A.
236 F3 **Turkey** r. IA U.S.A.
86 F3 **Turkey Creek** W.A. Austr.
173 E3 **Türkheim** Ger.
135 H6 **Turki** Rus. Fed.
Türkistan Kazakh. see Turkestan
122 C1 **Turkmenbashi** Turkm.
199 G2 **Türkmen Dağı** mt. Turkey
123 E2 **Turkmengala** Turkm.
122 D1 **Turkmenistan** country Asia
Turkmeniya country Asia see Turkmenistan
Turkmen-Kala Turkm. see Turkmengala
Türkmenostan country Asia see **Turkmenistan**
Turkmenskaya S.S.R. country Asia see **Turkmenistan**
126 E3 **Türkoğlu** Turkey
246 E2 **Turks and Caicos Islands** terr. West Indies
246 E2 **Turks Island Passage** Turks and Caicos Is
246 E2 **Turks Islands** Turks and Caicos Is
141 M3 **Turku** Fin.
183 G5 **Turleque** Spain
240 G3 **Turlock** CA U.S.A.
147 B3 **Turlough** Clare Rep. of Ireland
147 B3 **Turlough** Mayo Rep. of Ireland
257 F2 **Turmalina** Brazil
222 E3 **Turnagain** r. B.C. Can.
80 F4 **Turnagain, Cape** North I. N.Z.
129 A3 **Turnalı** Turkey
177 J3 **Turňa nad Bodvou** Slovakia
179 G3 **Turnau** Austria
146 D6 **Turnberry** South Ayrshire, Scotland U.K.
81 B6 **Turnbull, Mount** South I. N.Z.
241 L5 **Turnbull, Mount** AZ U.S.A.
86 C4 **Turner** r. W.A. Austr.
227 F3 **Turner** MI U.S.A.
86 F3 **Turner River** W.A. Austr.
151 G3 **Turners Hill** West Sussex, England U.K.
206 B5 **Turner's Peninsula** Sierra Leone
222 H5 **Turner Valley** Alta Can.
165 D3 **Turnhout** Belgium
179 H4 **Turnišče** Slovenia
179 G3 **Türnitz** Austria
223 I3 **Turnor Lake** Sask. Can.
176 E1 **Turnov** Czech Rep.
Tŭrnovo Bulg. see **Veliko Tŭrnovo**
197 G4 **Turnu Măgurele** Romania
Turnu Severin Romania see **Drobeta - Turnu Severin**
175 K5 **Turobin** Pol.
83 G3 **Turon** r. N.S.W. Austr.
185 F4 **Turón** r. Spain
Turones France see **Tours**
188 E3 **Turopolje** plain Croatia
175 J2 **Turośl** Pol.
175 J2 **Turośl** Pol.
134 H4 **Turovets** Rus. Fed.
175 K4 **Turów** Pol.
110 E3 **Turpan** Xinjiang China
110 E3 **Turpan Pendi** depr. China
110 E3 **Turpan Zhan** Xinjiang China
184 B1 **Turquel** Port.
185 I3 **Turre** Spain
242 □J7 **Turrialba** Costa Rica
161 E4 **Turriers** France
146 F4 **Turriff** Aberdeenshire, Scotland U.K.
Turris Libisonis Sardegna Italy see **Porto Torres**
195 F2 **Tursi** Italy
197 F2 **Turț** Romania
120 E4 **Turtkul'** Uzbek.
223 I4 **Turtleford** Sask. Can.
85 G3 **Turtle Island** Coral Sea Is Terr. Austr.
Turtle Island Fiji see **Vatoa**
92 A5 **Turtle Islands** Phil.
206 B5 **Turtle Islands** Sierra Leone
226 A3 **Turtle Lake** WI U.S.A.
130 J3 **Turukhansk** Rus. Fed.
177 M4 **Turulung** Romania
251 G4 **Turuna** r. Brazil
136 F4 **Turunchuk** r. Ukr.
128 B1 **Turunçlu** Turkey
199 G3 **Turunçova** Turkey
114 C3 **Turuvanur** Karnataka India
256 B2 **Turvelândia** Brazil
255 C9 **Turvo** Brazil
256 B2 **Turvo** r. Goiás Brazil
256 C3 **Turvo** r. São Paulo Brazil
256 C5 **Turvo** r. São Paulo Brazil
177 L3 **Tur"ya** r. Ukr.
177 L3 **Tur"ya-Bystra** Ukr.
129 E3 **Türyançay** Azer.
129 E3 **Türyançay** r. Azer.
177 L3 **Tur"ya-Polyana** Ukr.
136 B3 **Tur"ye** Ukr.
177 L3 **Tur"yi Remety** Ukr.
136 C2 **Turynka** Ukr.
175 I2 **Turza Wielka** Pol.
177 H2 **Turzovka** Slovakia
122 D2 **Ţūs** Iran
185 H2 **Tús** r. Spain
194 D5 **Tusa** Sicilia Italy
194 D4 **Tusa** r. Sicilia Italy
241 K4 **Tusayan** AZ U.S.A.
231 C5 **Tuscaloosa** AL U.S.A.
192 D2 **Tuscania** Italy
Tuscany admin. reg. Italy see Toscana
232 C4 **Tuscarawas** r. OH U.S.A.
234 B2 **Tuscarora** PA U.S.A.
232 E4 **Tuscarora Mountains** hills PA U.S.A.
236 F4 **Tuscola** IL U.S.A.
237 D5 **Tuscola** TX U.S.A.
231 C5 **Tuscumbia** AL U.S.A.
236 E4 **Tuscumbia** MO U.S.A.
137 I2 **Tuskar'** r. Rus. Fed.
231 C5 **Tuskegee** AL U.S.A.
173 E3 **Tussenhausen** Ger.
232 D4 **Tussey Mountains** hills PA U.S.A.
173 G3 **Tüßling** Ger.
226 E3 **Tustin** MI U.S.A.
175 J5 **Tuszów Narodowy** Pol.
175 J5 **Tuszyma** Pol.
175 H4 **Tuszyn** Pol.
127 F3 **Tutak** Turkey
139 L3 **Tutayev** Rus. Fed.
151 F2 **Tutbury** Staffordshire, England U.K.
Tutera Spain see **Tudela**
114 C4 **Tuticorin** Tamil Nadu India
95 F2 **Tutoh** r. Sarawak Malaysia
95 F1 **Tutong** Brunei
197 H2 **Tutova** r. Romania
170 E2 **Tutow** Ger.
197 H3 **Tutrakan** Bulg.
150 E3 **Tutshill** Gloucestershire, England U.K.
234 D1 **Tuttles Corner** NJ U.S.A.
172 C4 **Tuttlingen** Ger.
221 P2 **Tuttut Nunaat** reg. Greenland
211 B6 **Tutubu** Tanz.
78 □2 **Tutuila** i. American Samoa
80 E1 **Tutukaka** North I. N.Z.
213 E4 **Tutume** Botswana
252 C4 **Tutupaca, Volcán** vol. Peru
81 E4 **Tuturumuri** North I. N.Z.
245 F5 **Tututepec** Mex.
173 F4 **Tutzing** Ger.
170 E2 **Tützpatz** Ger.
106 E1 **Tuul Gol** r. Mongolia
138 E1 **Tuulos** Fin.
101 C4 **Tuun-bong** mt. N. Korea
140 O3 **Tuupovaara** Fin.
140 O3 **Tuusniemi** Fin.
141 N3 **Tuusula** Fin.
Tuva aut. rep. Rus. Fed. see **Tyva, Respublika**
77 H2 **Tuvalu** country S. Pacific Ocean
77 I4 **Tuvana-i-Colo** i. Fiji
77 I4 **Tuvana-i-Ra** i. Fiji
Tuvana-i-Tholo i. Fiji see **Tuvana-i-Colo**
142 D3 **Tuve** Sweden
262 S2 **Tuve, Mount** Antarctica
Tuvinskaya A.S.S.R. aut. rep. Rus. Fed. see **Tyva, Respublika**
121 I4 **Tuvuk** Kazakh.
95 G2 **Tuwau** r. Indon.
124 D2 **Tuwayq, Jabal** hills Saudi Arabia
124 D3 **Tuwayq, Jabal** mts Saudi Arabia
128 B5 **Ţuwayyil al Ḩājj** mt. Jordan
128 C4 **Ţuwayyil ash Shihāq** mt. Jordan
124 B3 **Tuwwal** Saudi Arabia
235 D1 **Tuxedo Park** NY U.S.A.
178 C3 **Tuxer Gebirge** mts Austria
149 I4 **Tuxford** Nottinghamshire, England U.K.
244 C4 **Tuxpan** Jalisco Mex.
244 B3 **Tuxpan** Nayarit Mex.
245 F3 **Tuxpan** Veracruz Mex.
243 G5 **Tuxtla Gutiérrez** Mex.
Túy Spain see **Tui**
247 F5 **Tuy** r. Venez.
96 D2 **Tuyên Quang** Vietnam
97 E4 **Tuy Hoa** Vietnam
135 K5 **Tuymazy** Rus. Fed.
122 B3 **Tūysarkān** Iran
Tŭytepa Uzbek. see **Toytepa**
Tuz, Lake salt l. Turkey see **Tuz Gölü**
244 D4 **Tuzantla** r. Mex.
126 D3 **Tuz Gölü** salt l. Turkey
197 G4 **Tŭzha** Bulg.
134 I4 **Tuzha** Rus. Fed.
196 D4 **Tuzi** Crna Gora Yugo.
127 G4 **Tuz Khurmātū** Iraq
188 G3 **Tuzla** Bos.-Herz.
197 I3 **Tuzla** Romania
126 D3 **Tuzla** Turkey
127 F3 **Tuzla** r. Turkey
135 H7 **Tuzlov** r. Rus. Fed.
129 C3 **Tuzluca** Turkey
179 H4 **Tužno** Croatia
96 A1 **Tuzu** r. Myanmar
142 E3 **Tvååker** Sweden
140 L2 **Tvärålund** Sweden
176 F2 **Tvarožná** Czech Rep.
142 C2 **Tvedestrand** Norway
142 A1 **Tveitakvitingen** mt. Norway
139 J3 **Tver'** Rus. Fed.
Tver Oblast admin. div. Rus. Fed. see **Tverskaya Oblast'**
129 A1 **Tverskaya** Rus. Fed.
139 J3 **Tverskaya Oblast'** admin. div. Rus. Fed.
139 J3 **Tvertsa** r. Rus. Fed.
144 D1 **Tvøroyri** Faroe Is
179 H2 **Tvrdonice** Czech Rep.
177 I2 **Tvrdošín** Slovakia
197 G4 **Tvŭrditsa** Bulg.
240 G2 **Twain Harte** CA U.S.A.
174 F4 **Twardogóra** Pol.
146 E2 **Twatt** Orkney, Scotland U.K.
227 I3 **Tweed** Ont. Can.
149 G2 **Tweed** r. England/Scotland U.K.
146 E6 **Tweeddale** val. Scotland U.K.
164 F2 **Tweede Exloërmond** Neth.
83 H2 **Tweed Heads** N.S.W. Austr.
223 I4 **Tweedie** Alta Can.
149 G2 **Tweedmouth** Northumberland, England U.K.
146 E6 **Tweedsmuir** Scottish Borders, Scotland U.K.
214 B5 **Tweefontein** S. Africa
215 G2 **Tweeling** S. Africa
215 F3 **Tweespruit** S. Africa
164 F2 **Twello** Neth.
241 I4 **Twentynine Palms** CA U.S.A.
225 K3 **Twillingate** Nfld. Can.
240 G2 **Twin Bridges** CA U.S.A.
238 D2 **Twin Bridges** MT U.S.A.
225 H2 **Twin Falls** Nfld. Can.
238 D3 **Twin Falls** ID U.S.A.
86 E4 **Twin Heads** hill W.A. Austr.
234 D1 **Twin Lakes** PA U.S.A.
233 H2 **Twin Mountain** NH U.S.A.
240 G2 **Twin Peak** CA U.S.A.
87 C7 **Twin Peaks** hill W.A. Austr.
232 C4 **Twinsburg** OH U.S.A.
238 B1 **Twisp** WA U.S.A.
168 C3 **Twist** Ger.
169 D4 **Twiste (Twistetal)** Ger.
168 D3 **Twistringen** Ger.
222 D1 **Twitya** r. N.W.T. Can.
81 C6 **Twizel** South I. N.Z.
237 C4 **Two Butte Creek** r. CO U.S.A.
226 B2 **Two Harbors** MN U.S.A.
223 I4 **Two Hills** Alta Can.
148 B5 **Twomileborris** Rep. of Ireland
147 D3 **Two Mile Bridge** Rep. of Ireland
226 D3 **Two Rivers** WI U.S.A.
174 G5 **Tworóg** Pol.
151 F3 **Twyford** Hampshire, England U.K.
151 G3 **Twyford** Wokingham, England U.K.
146 D7 **Twynholm** Dumfries and Galloway, Scotland U.K.
Tyachev Ukr. see **Tyachiv**
136 B3 **Tyachiv** Ukr.
137 G4 **Tyahynka** Ukr.
Tyan' Shan' mts China/Kyrg. see **Tien Shan**
Tyanshanskaya Oblast' admin. div. Kyrg. see **Naryn**
96 A2 **Tyao** r. India/Myanmar
137 G3 **Tyasmyn** r. Ukr.
102 M1 **Tyatya, Vulkan** vol. Rus. Fed.
174 E2 **Tychowo** Pol.
174 G5 **Tychy** Pol.
175 K6 **Tyczyn** Pol.
140 J3 **Tydal** Norway
148 B3 **Tydavnet** Rep. of Ireland
Tyddewi Pembrokeshire, Wales U.K. see **St David's**
232 D5 **Tygart Valley** WV U.S.A.
100 C1 **Tygda** Rus. Fed.
100 C1 **Tygda** r. Rus. Fed.
147 E2 **Tyholland** Rep. of Ireland
199 E1 **Tykhero** Greece
137 G2 **Tykhonovychi** Ukr.
175 K2 **Tykocin** Pol.
175 J6 **Tylawa** Pol.
237 E5 **Tyler** TX U.S.A.
237 F6 **Tylertown** MS U.S.A.
136 F4 **Tylihul** r. Ukr.
100 G2 **Tym'** r. Sakhalin Rus. Fed.
175 I6 **Tymbark** Pol.
137 G3 **Tymchenky** Ukr.
137 J3 **Tymonove** Ukr.
137 H4 **Tymoshivka** Ukr.
100 G2 **Tymovskoye** Sakhalin Rus. Fed.
198 D4 **Tympaki** Kriti Greece
164 F1 **Tynaarlo** Neth.
148 C3 **Tynan** Northern Ireland U.K.
131 N4 **Tynda** Rus. Fed.
236 D3 **Tyndall** SD U.S.A.
Tyndinskiy Rus. Fed. see Tynda
146 D5 **Tyndrum** Stirling, Scotland U.K.
146 F5 **Tyne** r. Scotland U.K.
149 H3 **Tyne and Wear** admin. div. England U.K.
176 E1 **Týnec nad Labem** Czech Rep.
176 D2 **Týnec nad Sázavou** Czech Rep.
149 H2 **Tynemouth** Tyne and Wear, England U.K.
233 H3 **Tyngsboro** MA U.S.A.
143 E1 **Tyngsjö** Sweden
176 F1 **Týniště nad Orlicí** Czech Rep.
136 F3 **Tynivka** Ukr.
176 D2 **Týn nad Vltavou** Czech Rep.
136 D2 **Tynne** Ukr.
141 J3 **Tynset** Norway
Tyr Lebanon see **Soûr**
Tyras Ukr. see **Bilhorod-Dnistrovs'kyy**
175 K6 **Tyrawa Wołoska** Pol.
Tyre Lebanon see **Soûr**
262 S1 **Tyree, Mount** Antarctica
148 D3 **Tyrella** Northern Ireland U.K.
143 H2 **Tyresö** Sweden
173 G3 **Tyrlaching** Ger.
100 E2 **Tyrma** Rus. Fed.
100 D2 **Tyrma** r. Rus. Fed.
140 N2 **Tyrnävä** Fin.
198 C2 **Tyrnavos** Greece
129 C2 **Tyrnyauz** Rus. Fed.
Tyrol land Austria see **Tirol**
147 D2 **Tyrone** county Northern Ireland U.K.
239 E5 **Tyrone** NM U.S.A.
232 D4 **Tyrone** PA U.S.A.
83 E3 **Tyrrell** r. Vic. Austr.
83 E3 **Tyrrell, Lake** dry lake Vic. Austr.
147 D3 **Tyrrellspass** Rep. of Ireland
189 C5 **Tyrrhenian Sea** France/Italy
Tyrus Lebanon see **Soûr**
136 B3 **Tysa** r. Ukr. alt. **Tisa (Yugoslavia)**, alt. **Tisza (Hungary)**
136 C3 **Tysmenytsya** Ukr.
142 A2 **Tysnesøy** i. Norway
142 A1 **Tysse** Norway
142 B1 **Tyssedal** Norway
175 L5 **Tyszowce** Pol.
150 D3 **Tythegston** Bridgend, Wales U.K.
138 D4 **Tytuvėnai** Lith.
129 E2 **Tyube** Rus. Fed.
129 G1 **Tyub-Karagan, Poluostrov** pen. Kazakh.
130 I4 **Tyukalinsk** Rus. Fed.
120 B3 **Tyulen'i, Ostrova** is Kazakh.
129 E1 **Tyuleniy, Ostrov** i. Rus. Fed.
120 D1 **Tyul'gan** Rus. Fed.
134 L4 **Tyul'kino** Rus. Fed.
130 H4 **Tyumen'** Rus. Fed.
Tyumen'-Aryk Kazakh. see Tomenaryk
121 J1 **Tyumentsevo** Rus. Fed.
131 N3 **Tyung** r. Rus. Fed.
Tyup Kyrg. see **Tüp**
106 C1 **Tyva, Respublika** aut. rep. Rus. Fed.
136 E3 **Tyvriv** Ukr.
174 C2 **Tywa** r. Pol.
150 C4 **Tywardreath** Cornwall, England U.K.
150 C3 **Tywi** r. Wales U.K.
150 C2 **Tywyn** Gwynedd, Wales U.K.
213 F4 **Tzaneen** S. Africa
243 H4 **Tzucacab** Mex.
164 E1 **Tzummarum** Neth.

U

Uaco Congo Angola see Waku-Kungo
79 □3 **Ua Huka** i. Fr. Polynesia
250 D4 **Uainambi** Brazil
Ualan atoll Micronesia see Kosrae
Ūālīkhanov Kazakh. see Valikhanovo
79 □3 **Ua Pou** i. Fr. Polynesia
Ua Pu i. Fr. Polynesia see Ua Pou
251 E5 **Uarini** Brazil
87 B4 **Uaroo** W.A. Austr.
251 E3 **Uasadi-jidi, Sierra** mts Venez.
251 F4 **Uatatás** r. Brazil
251 G5 **Uatumã** r. Brazil
254 F4 **Uauá** Brazil
250 E5 **Uaupés** Brazil
250 E4 **Uaupés** r. Brazil
243 H5 **Uaxactún** Guat.
196 E3 **Ub** Srbija Yugo.
257 F4 **Ubá** Brazil
121 J2 **Uba** r. Kazakh.
169 B5 **Übach-Palenberg** Ger.
120 F1 **Ubagan** r. Kazakh.
257 E2 **Ubaí** Brazil
254 F5 **Ubaitaba** Brazil
124 C5 **'Ubāl** Yemen
120 C4 **Ubal Karabaur** hills Uzbek.
120 C4 **Ubal Muzbel'** hills Kazakh.
208 C5 **Ubangi** r. C.A.R./Dem. Rep. Congo
Ubangi-Shari country Africa see **Central African Republic**
257 F3 **Ubaporanga** Brazil
136 E1 **Ubarts** r. Belarus
250 C3 **Ubate** Col.
257 E5 **Ubatuba** Brazil
123 G4 **Ubauro** Pak.
161 E4 **Ubaye** r. France
103 E7 **Ube** Japan
185 G2 **Úbeda** Spain
256 D3 **Uberaba** Brazil
256 C4 **Uberaba** r. Brazil
172 A2 **Überherrn** Ger.
256 C3 **Uberlândia** Brazil
172 D4 **Überlingen** Ger.
173 G4 **Übersee** Ger.
183 H1 **Ubidea** Spain
256 A6 **Ubiratã** Brazil
227 F4 **Ubly** MI U.S.A.
137 I2 **Ublya** r. Rus. Fed.
96 C3 **Ubolratna Reservoir** Thai.
215 I2 **Ubombo** S. Africa
96 D4 **Ubon Ratchathani** Thai.
136 D2 **Ubort'** r. Ukr.
161 E5 **Ubraye** France
185 E4 **Ubrique** Spain
172 C2 **Ubstadt-Weiher** Ger.
208 E5 **Ubundu** Dem. Rep. Congo
261 F3 **Ucacha** Arg.
129 E3 **Ucar** Azer.
252 B2 **Ucayali** dept Peru
250 C6 **Ucayali** r. Peru
192 A2 **Ucciani** Corse France
165 D4 **Uccle** Belgium
183 G4 **Uceda** Spain
161 C4 **Ucel** France
183 G3 **Ucero** Spain
183 G3 **Ucero** r. Spain
123 G4 **Uch** Pak.
182 B3 **Ucha** Port.
123 E2 **Uch-Adzhi** Turkm.
Üchajy Turkm. see **Uch-Adzhi**
122 B2 **Ūchān** Iran
121 J3 **Ucharal** Kazakh.
161 C4 **Uchaux** France
105 E2 **Uchimura-gawa** r. Japan
104 C2 **Uchinada** Japan
102 J2 **Uchiura-wan** b. Japan
252 A2 **Uchiza** Peru
160 C2 **Uchizy** France
129 C2 **Uchkeken** Rus. Fed.
120 E4 **Uchkuduk** Uzbek.
121 F5 **Uchkyay** Uzbek.
Uchquduq Uzbek. see Uchkuduk
120 D4 **Uchsay** Uzbek.
Uchsoy Uzbek. see **Uchsay**
169 D3 **Uchte** Ger.
170 C3 **Uchte** r. Ger.
169 F5 **Üchtelhausen** Ger.
123 F5 **Uchto** r. Pak.
170 C3 **Uchtspringe** Ger.
131 O4 **Uchur** r. Rus. Fed.
183 F2 **Ucieza** r. Spain
157 G3 **Uckange** France
170 F1 **Ückeritz** Ger.
151 H4 **Uckfield** East Sussex, England U.K.
121 F4 **Uckkulach** Uzbek.
171 E4 **Uckro** Ger.
183 H5 **Uclés** Spain
222 E5 **Ucluelet** B.C. Can.
128 A1 **Üçpınar** Turkey
238 F2 **Ucross** WY U.S.A.
100 E1 **Uda** r. Rus. Fed.
137 I3 **Uda** r. Ukr.
129 D3 **Udabno, Mt'a** hill Georgia
135 I7 **Udachnoye** Rus. Fed.
131 M3 **Udachnyy** Rus. Fed.
114 C4 **Udagamandalam** Tamil Nadu India
116 C4 **Udaipur** Rajasthan India
116 C4 **Udaipur** Rajasthan India
117 G5 **Udaipur** Tripura India
116 D5 **Udaipura** Madh. Prad. India
175 L4 **Udal** r. Pol.
117 H4 **Udalguri** Assam India
174 E4 **Udanin** Pol.
117 E5 **Udanti** r. India/Myanmar
129 C1 **Udarnyy** Rus. Fed.
177 K3 **Udava** r. Slovakia
177 K3 **Udavské** Slovakia
137 G2 **Uday** r. Ukr.
114 C3 **Udayagiri** Andhra Prad. India
143 E1 **Uddeholm** Sweden
164 E2 **Uddel** Neth.
142 D2 **Uddevalla** Sweden
148 E2 **Uddingston** South Lanarkshire, Scotland U.K.
146 E6 **Uddington** South Lanarkshire, Scotland U.K.
140 L2 **Uddjaure** l. Sweden
129 C3 **Ude** Georgia
164 E3 **Uden** Neth.
164 E3 **Udenhout** Neth.
169 F4 **Uder** Ger.
178 C3 **Uderns** Austria
169 B5 **Üdersdorf** Ger.
114 C2 **Udgir** Mahar. India
Udhagamandalam Tamil Nadu India see **Udagamandalam**
116 C2 **Udhampur** Jammu and Kashmir
177 H2 **Udiča** Slovakia
134 I3 **Udimskiy** Rus. Fed.
191 I2 **Udine** Italy
191 H2 **Udine** prov. Friuli - Venezia Giulia Italy
Udmalaippettai Tamil Nadu India see **Udumalaippettai**
Udmurtia aut. rep. Rus. Fed. see **Udmurtskaya Respublika**
Udmurtskaya A.S.S.R. aut. rep. Rus. Fed. see **Udmurtskaya Respublika**
134 K4 **Udmurtskaya Respublika** aut. rep. Rus. Fed.
129 B1 **Udobnaya** Rus. Fed.
131 M4 **Udokan, Khrebet** mts Rus. Fed.
139 J3 **Udomlya** Rus. Fed.
96 C3 **Udon Thani** Thai.
174 F1 **Udorpie** Pol.
78 □4a **Udot** i. Chuuk Micronesia
175 L5 **Udrycze** Pol.
114 C4 **Udumalaippettai** Tamil Nadu India
114 B3 **Udupi** Karnataka India
137 I2 **Udy** Ukr.
Udzharma Georgia see **Ujarma**
Udzhary Azer. see **Ucar**
Uéa i. Î. Loyauté New Caledonia see **Ouvéa**
171 E4 **Uebigau** Ger.
170 F2 **Uecker** r. Ger.
170 F2 **Ueckermünde** Ger.
105 E2 **Ueda** Japan
173 E2 **Uehlfeld** Ger.
169 F3 **Uehrde** Ger.
93 B3 **Uekuli** Sulawesi Tengah Indon.
208 D3 **Uele** r. Dem. Rep. Congo
131 U3 **Uelen** Rus. Fed.
131 T3 **Uel'kal'** Rus. Fed.
169 B3 **Uelsen** Ger.
168 F3 **Uelzen** Ger.
104 C4 **Ueno** Japan
208 E4 **Uere** r. Dem. Rep. Congo
190 C2 **Uetendorf** Switz.
168 E2 **Uetersen** Ger.
172 D2 **Uettingen** Ger.
169 F3 **Uetze** Ger.
134 K5 **Ufa** Rus. Fed.
134 L5 **Ufa** r. Rus. Fed.
150 D4 **Uffculme** Devon, England U.K.
173 E2 **Uffenheim** Ger.
173 F4 **Uffing am Staffelsee** Ger.
193 H3 **Ufita** r. Italy
169 F4 **Uftrungen** Ger.
134 I3 **Uftyuga** r. Rus. Fed.
138 D3 **Ugāle** Latvia
211 A6 **Ugalla** r. Tanz.
210 B4 **Uganda** country Africa
188 F3 **Ugar** r. Bos.-Herz.
183 H1 **Ugarana** Spain
150 D4 **Ugborough** Devon, England U.K.
168 E1 **Uge** Denmark
195 H3 **Ugento** Italy
142 A1 **Uggdal** Norway
142 D3 **Uggerby** r. Denmark
195 H2 **Uggiano la Chiesa** Italy
207 G5 **Ughelli** Nigeria
215 G4 **Ugie** S. Africa
Ugi Island Solomon Is see **Uki Island**
185 G4 **Ugíjar** Spain
160 E3 **Ugine** France
100 G2 **Uglegorsk** Sakhalin Rus. Fed.
100 E4 **Uglekamensk** Rus. Fed.
134 L4 **Ugleural'skiy** Rus. Fed.
139 L3 **Uglich** Rus. Fed.
188 E3 **Ugljan** i. Croatia
139 I2 **Uglovka** Rus. Fed.
100 D2 **Uglovoye** Amurskaya Oblast' Rus. Fed.
100 E4 **Uglovoye** Primorskiy Kray Rus. Fed.
121 J2 **Uglovskoye** Rus. Fed.
177 G4 **Ugod** Hungary
Ugodskiy Zavod Rus. Fed. see **Zhukovo**
131 P3 **Ugol'noye** Rus. Fed.
Ugolnyy Chukotskiy Avtonomnyy Okrug Rus. Fed. see **Beringovskiy**
129 C2 **Ugol'nyy** Rus. Fed.
131 S3 **Ugol'nyye Kopi** Rus. Fed.
139 J4 **Ugra** Rus. Fed.
139 K4 **Ugra** r. Rus. Fed.
197 G4 **Ugŭrchin** Bulg.
130 I3 **Ugut** Rus. Fed.
177 K3 **Uh** r. Slovakia
Uharte-Arakil Spain see **Huarte-Araquil**
179 H2 **Uherčice** Czech Rep.
175 L4 **Uherka** r. Pol.
176 G2 **Uherské Hradiště** Czech Rep.
177 G2 **Uherský Brod** Czech Rep.
172 D3 **Uhingen** Ger.
176 C2 **Úhlava** r. Czech Rep.
172 D4 **Uhldingen** Ger.
176 E2 **Uhlířské Janovice** Czech Rep.
171 C5 **Uhlstädt** Ger.
136 B2 **Uhniv** Ukr.
232 C4 **Uhrichsville** OH U.S.A.
177 H3 **Uhrovec** Slovakia
137 H2 **Uhroyidy** Ukr.
171 C3 **Uhrsleben** Ger.
171 F4 **Uhyst** Ger.
254 E4 **Uibaí** Brazil
Uibhist a' Deas i. Scotland U.K. see **South Uist**
Uibhist a' Tuath i. Scotland U.K. see **North Uist**
171 C4 **Uichteritz** Ger.
146 B4 **Uig** Highland, Scotland U.K.
209 B6 **Uíge** Angola
209 B6 **Uíge** prov. Angola
101 C5 **Ŭijŏngbu** S. Korea
101 C4 **Ŭiju** N. Korea
120 C2 **Uil** Kazakh.
120 C2 **Uil** r. Kazakh.
129 C2 **Uilpata, Gora** mt. Rus. Fed.
140 O3 **Uimaharju** Fin.
241 K3 **Uinkaret Plateau** AZ U.S.A.
134 L4 **Uinskoye** Rus. Fed.
238 E3 **Uinta** r. CO U.S.A.
238 E3 **Uinta Mountains** UT U.S.A.
215 E5 **Uitenhage** S. Africa
164 D2 **Uitgeest** Neth.
164 D2 **Uithoorn** Neth.
164 F1 **Uithuizen** Neth.
164 F1 **Uithuizermeeden** Neth.
214 B3 **Uitkyk** S. Africa
214 C2 **Uitsakpan** salt pan S. Africa
214 B5 **Uitspankraal** S. Africa
177 J6 **Uivar** Romania
129 D3 **Ujarma** Georgia
175 H4 **Ujazd** Łódzkie Pol.
174 G5 **Ujazd** Opolskie Pol.
177 G2 **Újezd** Czech Rep.
176 F2 **Újezd u Brna** Czech Rep.
177 K4 **Újfehértó** Hungary
116 D4 **Ujhani** Uttar Prad. India
177 I4 **Újhartyán** Hungary
104 B4 **Uji** Japan
104 B4 **Uji-gawa** r. Japan
Ujiyamada Japan see **Ise**
116 C5 **Ujjain** Madh. Prad. India
177 L3 **Újkenéz** Hungary
176 F4 **Újkér** Hungary
177 K5 **Újkígyós** Hungary
177 K4 **Újléta** Hungary
177 H6 **Újpetre** Hungary
174 E2 **Ujście** Pol.
175 H6 **Ujsoły** Pol.
177 K5 **Újszalonta** Hungary
177 J4 **Újszász** Hungary
177 J5 **Újszentiván** Hungary
177 K4 **Újszentmargita** Hungary
177 I4 **Újszilvás** Hungary
177 K4 **Újtikos** Hungary
176 F5 **Újudvar** Hungary
93 A4 **Ujung Pandang** Sulawesi Selatan Indon.
Újvidék Vojvodina, Srbija Yugo. see **Novi Sad**
207 G4 **Ukata** Nigeria
102 □1 **Uke-jima** i. Japan
127 F4 **Ukhaydir** tourist site Iraq
124 D4 **Ukhdūd** tourist site Saudi Arabia
135 H5 **Ukholovo** Rus. Fed.
175 M4 **Ukhovets'k** Ukr.
117 H4 **Ukhrul** Manipur India
Ukhta Respublika Kareliya Rus. Fed. see **Kalevala**
134 K3 **Ukhta** Respublika Komi Rus. Fed.
134 K3 **Ukhta** r. Rus. Fed.
83 H2 **Uki** N.S.W. Austr.
240 F2 **Ukiah** CA U.S.A.
238 C2 **Ukiah** OR U.S.A.
78 □6 **Uki Island** Solomon Is
174 D2 **Ukleja** r. Pol.
138 E4 **Ukmergė** Lith.
136 F3 **Ukraine** country Europe
121 J2 **Ukrainka** Vostochnyy Kazakhstan Kazakh.
121 J2 **Ukrainka** Vostochnyy Kazakhstan Kazakh.
Ukrainka Ukr. see **Ukrayinka**
Ukrainskaya S.S.R. country Europe see **Ukraine**
Ukrainskoye Ukr. see **Ukrayins'ke**
Ukrayina country Europe see **Ukraine**
136 F2 **Ukrayinka** Ukr.
137 G2 **Ukrayins'ke** Ukr.
188 F3 **Ukrina** r. Bos.-Herz.
209 B7 **Uku** Angola
209 B8 **Ukuma** Angola
111 B6 **Ul** r. India
138 G4 **Ula** Belarus
138 G4 **Ula** r. Belarus
175 M1 **Ūla** r. Lith.
199 F3 **Ula** Turkey
106 E2 **Ulaanbaatar** Mongolia
106 E2 **Ulaanbaatar** mun. Mongolia
107 F2 **Ulaan-Ereg** Mongolia
106 B1 **Ulaangom** Mongolia
106 E2 **Ulaanhudag** Mongolia
106 D2 **Ulaan-Uul** Mongolia
107 F2 **Ulaan-Uul** Mongolia
83 G3 **Ulan** N.S.W. Austr.
107 F4 **Ulan** Nei Mongol China
106 C4 **Ulan** Qinghai China
Ulan Bator Mongolia see **Ulaanbaatar**
121 G3 **Ulanbel'** Kazakh.
135 I7 **Ulan Erge** Respublika Kalmykiya - Khalm'g-Tangch Rus. Fed.
Ulanhad Nei Mongol China see **Chifeng**
107 I2 **Ulanhot** Nei Mongol China
107 F3 **Ulan Hua** Nei Mongol China
136 E3 **Ulaniv** Ukr.
135 I7 **Ulan-Khol** Rus. Fed.
175 K4 **Ulan-Majorat** Pol.
137 H2 **Ulanove** Ukr.
175 K5 **Ulanów** Pol.
106 D3 **Ulan Tohoi** Nei Mongol China
98 I1 **Ulan-Ude** Rus. Fed.
260 D2 **Ulapes** Arg.
126 E3 **Ulaş** Turkey
199 E1 **Ulaş** Turkey
192 B5 **Ulassai** Sardegna Italy
78 □6 **Ulawa Island** Solomon Is
121 J2 **Ul'ba** Kazakh.
Ülbi Kazakh. see **Ul'ba**
138 E3 **Ulbroka** Latvia
146 E3 **Ulbster** Highland, Scotland U.K.
149 I4 **Ulceby** North Lincolnshire, England U.K.
101 D5 **Ulchin** S. Korea
196 D5 **Ulcinj** Crna Gora Yugo.
214 E3 **Ulco** S. Africa
142 C4 **Uldum** Denmark
107 F1 **Uldz** Mongolia
107 G1 **Uldz** r. Mongolia
Uleåborg Fin. see **Oulu**
142 C2 **Ulefoss** Norway
185 H3 **Uleila del Campo** Spain
138 F2 **Ülenurme** Estonia
107 G1 **Ulety** Rus. Fed.
175 K4 **Ułęż** Pol.
142 C3 **Ulfborg** Denmark
Ulflingen Lux. see **Troisvierges**
164 F3 **Ulft** Neth.
107 H2 **Ulgain Gol** r. China
149 H2 **Ulgham** Northumberland, England U.K.
114 B2 **Ulhasnagar** Mahar. India
175 L5 **Ulhówek** Pol.
107 H2 **Uliastai** Nei Mongol China
106 C2 **Uliastay** Mongolia
Uliatea i. Arch. de la Société Fr. Polynesia see **Raiatea**
177 L3 **Ulič** Slovakia
165 D3 **Ulicoten** Neth.
Ulie atoll Micronesia see **Woleai**
78 □3b **Uliga** i. Majuro Marshall Is
208 E5 **Ulindi** r. Dem. Rep. Congo
134 F1 **Ulita** r. Rus. Fed.
91 I4 **Ulithi** atoll Micronesia
Uljanovsk Rus. Fed. see **Ul'yanovsk**
120 E2 **Ul'kayak** r. Kazakh.
Ülkenözen r. Kazakh./Rus. Fed. see **Bol'shoy Uzen'**
121 H4 **Ul'ken Sulutar** Kazakh.
Ülken Vladīmīrovka Kazakh. see **Bol'shaya Vladimirovka**
182 B2 **Ulla** r. Spain
83 G3 **Ulladulla** N.S.W. Austr.
146 C4 **Ullapool** Highland, Scotland U.K.
142 E3 **Ullared** Sweden
140 M2 **Ullatti** Sweden
186 D4 **Ulldecona** Spain
186 D3 **Ulldemolins** Spain
142 D4 **Ullerslev** Denmark
177 I5 **Üllés** Hungary
149 H4 **Ulleskelf** North Yorkshire, England U.K.
262 S1 **Ullmer, Mount** Antarctica
252 C4 **Ulloma** Bol.
140 L1 **Ullsfjorden** sea chan. Norway
129 F2 **Ulluchay** r. Rus. Fed.
101 D5 **Ullŭng-do** i. S. Korea
172 D3 **Ulm** Ger.
100 D2 **Ul'ma** r. Rus. Fed.
169 E5 **Ulmbach** Ger.
184 B1 **Ulme** r. Port.
169 B5 **Ulmen** Ger.
197 H3 **Ulmeni** Călărași Romania
197 F2 **Ulmeni** Maramureș Romania
188 G4 **Ulog** Bos.-Herz.
213 G2 **Ulongue** Moz.
82 D1 **Uloowaranie, Lake** salt flat S.A. Austr.
149 F3 **Ulpha** Cumbria, England U.K.
142 E3 **Ulricehamn** Sweden
179 E2 **Ulrichsberg** Austria
169 E5 **Ulrichstein** Ger.
164 F1 **Ulrum** Neth.
101 D6 **Ulsan** S. Korea
146 □G1 **Ulsta** Shetland, Scotland U.K.
142 D3 **Ulsted** Denmark
140 I3 **Ulsteinvik** Norway
147 D2 **Ulster** reg. Rep. of Ireland/U.K.
227 I5 **Ulster** PA U.S.A.
235 D1 **Ulster County** county NY U.S.A.
83 E3 **Ultima** Vic. Austr.
252 B1 **Ultraoriental, Cordillera** mts Peru
242 □I6 **Ulua** r. Hond.
129 B3 **Ulubağ** Turkey
199 F2 **Ulubey** Turkey
199 G2 **Uluborlu** Turkey
199 F1 **Uludağ** mt. Turkey
94 C2 **Ulu Kali, Gunung** mt. Malaysia
126 D3 **Ulukışla** Turkey
199 G2 **Uluköy** Turkey
215 H3 **Ulundi** S. Africa
110 D2 **Ulungur He** r. China
110 D2 **Ulungur Hu** l. China
240 □C8 **Ulupalakua** HI U.S.A.
Uluqsaqtuuq N.W.T. Can. see Holman
84 B5 **Uluru** hill N.T. Austr.
199 F2 **Ulus Dağı** mt. Turkey
Ulutau Kazakh. see **Ulytau**
121 F3 **Ulutau, Gory** mts Kazakh.
146 B5 **Ulva** i. Scotland U.K.
Ulvéah i. Vanuatu see **Lopévi**
142 A2 **Ulvenåso** mt. Norway
164 D3 **Ulvenhout** Neth.
149 F3 **Ulverston** Cumbria, England U.K.
83 F5 **Ulverstone** Tas. Austr.
142 B1 **Ulvik** Norway
141 L3 **Ulvsjön** Sweden
139 K2 **Ul'yanikha** Rus. Fed.
137 F4 **Ulyanivka** Mykolayivs'ka Oblast' Ukr.
137 H2 **Ulyanivka** Sums'ka Oblast' Ukr.
Ūl'yanov Kazakh. see Ul'yanovskiy
139 H2 **Ul'yanovka** Rus. Fed.
136 F3 **Ul'yanovka** Ukr.
139 J5 **Ul'yanovo** Rus. Fed.
121 G4 **Ul'yanovo** Uzbek.
135 J5 **Ul'yanovsk** Rus. Fed.
135 I5 **Ul'yanovskaya Oblast'** admin. div. Rus. Fed.
121 H2 **Ul'yanovskiy** Kazakh.
Ulyanovsk Oblast admin. div. Rus. Fed. see **Ul'yanovskaya Oblast'**
Ul'yanovskoye Kazakh. see **Ul'yanovskiy**
107 H1 **Ulyatuy** Rus. Fed.
237 C4 **Ulysses** KS U.S.A.
232 B6 **Ulysses** KY U.S.A.
121 F2 **Ulytau** Kazakh.
120 E2 **Uly-Zhylanshyk** r. Kazakh.
183 I2 **Ulzama** r. Spain
100 B1 **Uma** Rus. Fed.
188 D3 **Umag** Croatia
252 D4 **Umala** Bol.
'Umān country Asia see **Oman**
243 H4 **Umán** Mex.
78 □4a **Uman** i. Chuuk Micronesia
136 F3 **Uman'** Ukr.
258 C3 **Umango, Cerro** mt. Arg.
116 E5 **Umaria** Madh. Prad. India
114 C2 **Umarkhed** Mahar. India
114 D2 **Umarkot** Orissa India
123 G5 **Umarkot** Pak.
82 D1 **Umaroona, Lake** salt flat S.A. Austr.
116 C5 **Umarpada** Gujarat India
238 C2 **Umatilla** OR U.S.A.
92 C4 **Umayan** r. Phil.
134 F2 **Umba** Murmanskaya Oblast' Rus. Fed.
84 D2 **Umbakumba** N.T. Austr.
84 C5 **Umbeara** N.T. Austr.
150 D4 **Umberleigh** Devon, England U.K.
191 H5 **Umbertide** Italy
81 B6 **Umbrella Mountains** South I. N.Z.
191 H5 **Umbria** admin. reg. Italy
195 F3 **Umbriatico** Italy
215 H3 **Umdloti Beach** S. Africa
213 F3 **Ume** r. Zimbabwe
140 M3 **Umeå** Sweden
140 M3 **Umeälven** r. Sweden
135 H5 **Umet** Rus. Fed.
215 I3 **Umfolozi** r. S. Africa
140 K2 **Umfors** Sweden
Umfuli r. Zimbabwe see **Mupfure**
215 H4 **Umgababa** S. Africa
215 H3 **Umgeni** r. S. Africa
125 D1 **Umgharah** Kuwait
215 H3 **Umhali** S. Africa
178 B3 **Umhausen** Austria
215 H3 **Umhlanga** S. Africa
182 B2 **Umia** r. Spain
105 D1 **Umi-gawa** r. Japan
240 □D9 **Umikoa** HI U.S.A.
220 H3 **Umingmaktok** Nunavut Can.
120 B4 **Umirzak** Kazakh.
224 E1 **Umiujaq** Que. Can.
172 B3 **Umkirch** Ger.
215 H4 **Umkomaas** S. Africa
215 H4 **Umkomaas** r. S. Africa
215 H3 **Umlazi** S. Africa
127 G5 **Umma** tourist site Iraq
128 B3 **Umm ad Daraj, Jabal** mt. Jordan
124 B3 **Umm al Birak** Saudi Arabia
128 B5 **Umm al Hashīm, Jabal** mt. Jordan
Umm al Qaywayn U.A.E. see **Umm al Qaiwain**
125 F2 **Umm al Qaiwain** U.A.E.
125 F3 **Umm as Samīm** salt flat Oman
125 E2 **Umm Bāb** Qatar
172 D3 **Ummendorf** Ger.
124 B2 **Umm Lajj** Saudi Arabia
128 B5 **Umm Mafrûd, Gebel** mt. Egypt
124 B3 **Umm Mukhbār, Jabal** hill Saudi Arabia
128 D5 **Umm Nukhaylah** hill Saudi Arabia
203 F6 **Umm Ruwaba** Sudan
202 E2 **Umm Sa'ad** Libya
125 E2 **Umm Sa'id** Qatar
128 B5 **Umm Saysabān, Jabal** mt. Jordan
128 A5 **Umm Shomar, Gebel** mt. Egypt
128 A5 **Umm Tināṣṣib, Gebel** mt. Egypt
128 D4 **Umm Wa'āl** hill Saudi Arabia
128 A5 **Umm Zanatir** mt. Egypt
220 B4 **Umnak Island** AK U.S.A.
238 A3 **Umpqua** r. OR U.S.A.
199 G2 **Umraniye** Turkey
116 D5 **Umred** Mahar. India
114 B1 **Umreth** Gujarat India
Umtali Zimbabwe see **Mutare**
215 H4 **Umtamvuna** r. S. Africa
215 G4 **Umtata** S. Africa
215 G4 **Umtata** r. S. Africa
215 H4 **Umtentweni** S. Africa
207 G5 **Umuahia** Nigeria
256 A5 **Umuarama** Brazil
129 E3 **Umudlu** Azer.
129 B3 **Umudum** Turkey
199 E1 **Umurbey** Turkey
199 F2 **Umurlar** Turkey
80 E4 **Umutoi** North I. N.Z.
215 H3 **Umvoti** r. S. Africa
Umvuma Zimbabwe see Mvuma
215 G4 **Umzimhlava** r. S. Africa
215 G4 **Umzimkulu** S. Africa
215 H4 **Umzimkulu** r. S. Africa
215 G4 **Umzimvubu** r. S. Africa
Umzingwani r. Zimbabwe see **Mzingwani**
215 H4 **Umzinto** S. Africa
215 H4 **Umzumbe** S. Africa
188 F3 **Una** r. Bos.-Herz./Croatia
255 F5 **Una** Brazil
254 G4 **Una** r. Brazil
116 D3 **Una** Hima. Prad. India
183 I4 **Uña** Spain
81 D5 **Una, Mount** South I. N.Z.
128 C5 **'Unāb, Jabal al** hill Jordan
188 F3 **Unac** r. Bos.-Herz.
182 D2 **Uña de Quintana** Spain
233 F3 **Unadilla** NY U.S.A.
233 F3 **Unadilla** r. NY U.S.A.
256 D2 **Unaí** Brazil
220 B3 **Unalakleet** AK U.S.A.
220 B4 **Unalaska** AK U.S.A.
220 B4 **Unalaska Island** AK U.S.A.
211 B8 **Unango** Moz.
176 F3 **Únanov** Czech Rep.
146 C3 **Unapool** Highland, Scotland U.K.
136 F2 **Unava** r. Ukr.
124 C2 **'Unayzah** Saudi Arabia
126 E4 **'Unayzah, Jabal** hill Iraq
186 B2 **Uncastillo** Spain
116 E4 **Unchahra** Madh. Prad. India
241 M2 **Uncompahgre Plateau** CO U.S.A.
215 G3 **Underberg** S. Africa
83 E3 **Underbool** Vic. Austr.
140 K3 **Undersåker** Sweden
236 C2 **Underwood** ND U.S.A.
172 D3 **Undingen** Ger.
135 J5 **Undory** Rus. Fed.
163 A6 **Undués de Lerda** Spain
150 E3 **Undy** Monmouthshire, Wales U.K.
139 I5 **Unecha** Rus. Fed.
139 H5 **Unecha** r. Rus. Fed.
251 E5 **Uneiuxi** r. Brazil
83 F3 **Ungarie** N.S.W. Austr.
82 D3 **Ungarra** S.A. Austr.
Ungava, Baie d' b. Que. Can. see **Ungava Bay**
221 K3 **Ungava, Péninsule d'** pen. Que. Can.
225 H1 **Ungava Bay** Que. Can.
Ungava Peninsula Que. Can. see **Ungava, Péninsule d'**
Ungeny Moldova see **Ungheni**
173 E3 **Ungerhausen** Ger.
100 D4 **Unggi** N. Korea
136 D4 **Ungheni** Moldova
197 G2 **Ungheni** Romania
Unguja North admin. reg. Tanz. see **Zanzibar North**
Unguja South admin. reg. Tanz. see **Zanzibar South**
Unguja West admin. reg. Tanz. see **Zanzibar West**
197 G2 **Ungurași** Romania
122 D2 **Unguz, Solonchakovyye Vpadiny** salt flat Turkm.
Üngüz Angyrsyndaky Garagum des. Turkm. see **Zaunguzskiye Karakumy**
Ungvár Ukr. see **Uzhhorod**
211 D5 **Ungwana Bay** Kenya
182 C4 **Unhais da Serra** Port.
182 C4 **Unhais-o-Velho** Port.
171 F5 **Unhošť** Czech Rep.
134 J4 **Uni** Rus. Fed.
254 E3 **União** Brazil
255 C8 **União da Vitória** Brazil
254 G4 **União dos Palmares** Brazil
116 D4 **Uniara** Rajasthan India
176 G2 **Uničov** Czech Rep.
174 G4 **Uniejów** Pol.
161 C3 **Unieux** France
188 E3 **Unije** i. Croatia
220 B4 **Unimak Island** AK U.S.A.
176 G3 **Unín** Slovakia
251 F5 **Unini** r. Brazil
252 B2 **Unini** Peru
260 E4 **Unión** Arg.
253 F6 **Unión** Para.
233 □I2 **Union** ME U.S.A.
236 F4 **Union** MO U.S.A.
235 D2 **Union** NJ U.S.A.
238 C2 **Union** OR U.S.A.
231 D5 **Union** SC U.S.A.
232 C6 **Union** WV U.S.A.
259 E5 **Unión, Bahía** b. Arg.
241 K4 **Union, Mount** AZ U.S.A.
235 D2 **Union Beach** NJ U.S.A.
234 A3 **Union Bridge** MD U.S.A.
232 A4 **Union City** OH U.S.A.
232 D4 **Union City** PA U.S.A.
237 F4 **Union City** TN U.S.A.
235 D2 **Union County** county NJ U.S.A.
234 A2 **Union County** county PA U.S.A.
214 D5 **Uniondale** S. Africa
234 C1 **Union Dale** PA U.S.A.
246 B2 **Unión de Reyes** Cuba
244 B4 **Unión de Tula** Mex.
147 B5 **Unionhall** Rep. of Ireland
245 G5 **Unión Hidalgo** Mex.
247 □3 **Union Island** St Vincent
231 C5 **Union Springs** AL U.S.A.
232 E3 **Union Springs** NY U.S.A.
231 C5 **Uniontown** AL U.S.A.
232 D5 **Uniontown** PA U.S.A.
235 F1 **Unionville** CT U.S.A.
227 F4 **Unionville** MI U.S.A.
236 E3 **Unionville** MO U.S.A.
240 H1 **Unionville** NV U.S.A.
234 D1 **Unionville** NY U.S.A.
234 C3 **Unionville** PA U.S.A.
232 E5 **Unionville** VA U.S.A.
174 G2 **Unisław** Pol.
125 F3 **United Arab Emirates** country Asia
United Arab Republic country Africa see **Egypt**
145 G4 **United Kingdom** country Europe
United Provinces state India see **Uttar Pradesh**
228 G3 **United States of America** country N. America
221 L1 **United States Range** mts Nunavut Can.
191 H4 **Uniti** r. Italy
223 I4 **Unity** Sask. Can.
238 C2 **Unity** OR U.S.A.
234 B1 **Unityville** PA U.S.A.
116 C5 **Unjha** Gujarat India
169 C5 **Unkel** Ger.
178 D3 **Unken** Austria
172 D3 **Unlingen** Ger.
169 C4 **Unna** Ger.
116 E4 **Unnao** Uttar Prad. India
169 C5 **Unnau** Ger.
101 C5 **Ŭnp'a** N. Korea
261 E2 **Unquillo** Arg.
101 C4 **Unsan** P'yŏngan-bukto N. Korea
101 C5 **Ŭnsan** P'yŏngan-namdo N. Korea
129 C4 **Ünseli** Turkey
146 □H1 **Unst** i. Scotland U.K.
149 H4 **Unstone** Derbyshire, England U.K.
171 C4 **Unstrut** r. Ger.
117 E4 **Untari** Bihar India
197 H2 **Unțeni** Romania
190 D1 **Unterägeri** Switz.
173 F4 **Unterammergau** Ger.
169 E5 **Unterbreizbach** Ger.
173 E4 **Unterdießen** Ger.
173 G3 **Unterdietfurt** Ger.

Unterfranken to Vanavara

374

169 E5 Unterfranken admin. reg. Bayern Ger.
173 H3 Untergriesbach Ger.
173 F3 Unterhaching Ger.
178 C3 Unter Inn Thal val. Austria
190 D1 Unterkulm Switz.
179 H4 Unterlamm Austria
168 F3 Unterlüß Ger.
169 F5 Untermaßfeld Ger.
173 E3 Untermeitingen Ger.
169 F5 Untermerzbach Ger.
172 D2 Untermünkheim Ger.
173 G3 Unterneukirchen Ger.
173 E2 Unterpleichfeld Ger.
173 G3 Unterreit Ger.
190 D2 Unterschächen Switz.
173 F3 Unterschleißheim Ger.
173 E3 Unterschneidheim Ger.
169 F5 Untersiemau Ger.
171 C5 Untersteinach Ger.
173 E4 Unterthingau Ger.
170 E2 Unterueckersee l. Ger.
179 F2 Unterweißenbach Austria
171 C5 Unterwellenborn Ger.
173 G4 Unterwössen Ger.
129 E2 Untsukul' Rus. Fed.
251 E4 Unturán, Sierra de mts Venez.
222 D3 Unuk r. Can./U.S.A.
106 A5 Unuli Horog Qinghai China
155 B4 Unverre France
134 L3 Un'ya r. Rus. Fed.
134 I4 Unzha Rus. Fed.
183 I2 Unzue Spain
102 □1 Uoturi-shima i. Japan
104 D2 Uozu Japan
176 E1 Úpa r. Czech Rep.
139 K4 Upa r. Rus. Fed.
241 L1 Upalco UT U.S.A.
117 F5 Upar Ghat reg. Madh. Prad. India
151 F3 Upavon Wiltshire, England U.K.
221 M2 Upernavik Greenland
168 C2 Upgant-Schott Ger.
92 C5 Upi Phil.
250 C3 Upía r. Col.
176 F1 Úpice Czech Rep.
214 C3 Upington S. Africa
141 N3 Upinniemi Fin.
240 I4 Upland CA U.S.A.
116 B5 Upleta Gujarat India
156 E4 Uplyme Devon, England U.K.
80 E3 Upokongaro North I. N.Z.
78 □2 Upolu i. Samoa
129 B1 Upornaya Rus. Fed.
232 B4 Upper Arlington OH U.S.A.
222 G5 Upper Arrow Lake B.C. Can.
Upper Austria land Austria see Oberösterreich
234 C2 Upper Black Eddy PA U.S.A.
146 E3 Upper Camster Highland, Scotland U.K.
150 D2 Upper Chapel Powys, Wales U.K.
Upper Chindwin Myanmar see Mawlaik
151 F3 Upper Clatford Hampshire, England U.K.
234 B3 Upper Crossroads MD U.S.A.
234 C3 Upper Darby PA U.S.A.
206 E4 Upper East admin. reg. Ghana
222 F4 Upper Fraser B.C. Can.
151 F3 Upper Heyford Oxfordshire, England U.K.
81 E4 Upper Hutt North I. N.Z.
226 B4 Upper Iowa r. IA U.S.A.
233 □J1 Upper Kent N.B. Can.
238 B3 Upper Klamath Lake OR U.S.A.
146 E4 Upper Knockando Moray, Scotland U.K.
147 E2 Upperlands Northern Ireland U.K.
222 D2 Upper Liard Y.T. Can.
147 D2 Upper Lough Erne l. Northern Ireland U.K.
234 B4 Upper Marlboro MD U.S.A.
210 B2 Upper Nile state Sudan
235 E1 Upper Nyack NY U.S.A.
232 B4 Upper Sandusky OH U.S.A.
Upper Seal Lake Que. Can. see Iberville, Lac d'
81 D4 Upper Takaka South I. N.Z.
151 F2 Upper Tean Staffordshire, England U.K.
Upper Tunguska r. Rus. Fed. see Angara
Upper Volta country Africa see Burkina
114 B3 Uppinangadi Karnataka India
151 G2 Uppingham Rutland, England U.K.
143 G2 Uppland reg. Sweden
143 G1 Upplanda Sweden
143 G2 Upplands-Väsby Sweden
143 G2 Uppsala Sweden
143 G1 Uppsala county Sweden
224 B3 Upsala Ont. Can.
116 D2 Upshi Jammu and Kashmir
226 B2 Upson WI U.S.A.
85 F3 Upstart Bay Qld Austr.
150 E4 Upton Dorset, England U.K.
233 H3 Upton MA U.S.A.
150 E3 Upton St Leonards Gloucestershire, England U.K.
150 E2 Upton upon Severn Worcestershire, England U.K.
80 E1 Upua North I. N.Z.
128 C2 'Uqayribāt Syria
124 C2 'Uqlat aş Şuqūr Saudi Arabia
Uqturpan Xinjiang China see Wushi
127 G5 Ur tourist site Iraq
Urad Qianqi Nei Mongol China see Xishanzui
107 F3 Urad Zhongqi Nei Mongol China
146 □G1 Urafirth Shetland, Scotland U.K.
190 E3 Urago d'Oglio Italy
140 P1 Ura-Guba Rus. Fed.
256 B5 Uraí Brazil
176 F4 Uraiújfalu Hungary
114 C4 Urakam Kerala India
83 F3 Ural hill N.S.W. Austr.
120 B3 Ural r. Kazakh./Rus. Fed.
83 G2 Uralla N.S.W. Austr.
Ural Mountains Rus. Fed. see Ural'skiy Khrebet
120 B2 Ural'sk Kazakh.
Ural'skaya Oblast' admin. div. Kazakh. see Zapadnyy Kazakhstan
Ural'skiye Gory mts Rus. Fed. see Ural'skiy Khrebet
134 L2 Ural'skiy Khrebet mts Rus. Fed.
211 B6 Urambo Tanz.
114 B2 Uran Mahar. India
83 F3 Urana N.S.W. Austr.
83 F3 Urana, Lake N.S.W. Austr.
84 D4 Urandangi Qld Austr.
255 E4 Urandi Brazil
223 I3 Uranium City Sask. Can.
83 F3 Uranquity N.S.W. Austr.
82 C2 Urapunga N.T. Austr.
84 C4 Urapuntja N.T. Austr.
251 F4 Uraricoera r. Brazil
Urartu country Asia see Armenia
192 A5 Uras Sardegna Italy
Ura-Tyube Tajik. see Üroteppa
114 C3 Uravakonda Andhra Prad. India
241 M2 Uravan CO U.S.A.
105 F3 Urawa Japan
130 H3 Uray Rus. Fed.
105 F3 Urayasu Japan
125 E2 Uray'irah Saudi Arabia
124 D2 'Urayq ad Duḥūl des. Saudi Arabia
124 D2 'Urayq Sāqān des. Saudi Arabia
174 E4 Uraz Pol.
135 I5 Urazovka Rus. Fed.
135 G6 Urazovo Rus. Fed.
169 C5 Urbach Ger.
230 C4 Urbana IL U.S.A.
226 E5 Urbana IN U.S.A.
232 B4 Urbana OH U.S.A.
191 H5 Urbania Italy
254 E2 Urbano Santos Brazil
169 C5 Urbar Ger.
190 D4 Urbe Italy
183 G2 Urbel r. Spain
83 H2 Urbenville N.S.W. Austr.
172 C2 Urberach Ger.
191 H5 Urbino Italy
Urbinum Italy see Urbino
183 H2 Urbión mt. Spain
191 I5 Urbisaglia Italy
160 B2 Urbise France
Urbs Vetus Italy see Orvieto
176 G2 Určice Czech Rep.
252 C3 Urcos Peru
163 A5 Urcuit France
185 G1 Urda Spain
261 G5 Urdampolleta Arg.
186 B1 Urdax Spain
Ur'devarri hill Fin./Norway see Urtivaara
261 H3 Urdinarrain Arg.
134 J2 Urdoma Rus. Fed.
172 C4 Urdorf Switz.
163 B6 Urdos France
110 D2 Urd Tamir Gol r. Mongolia
183 H1 Urduliz Spain
120 D3 Urdzhar Kazakh.
149 H3 Ure r. England U.K.
138 F5 Urechcha Belarus
197 H2 Urechești Romania
134 I4 Uren' Rus. Fed.
130 I3 Urengoy Rus. Fed.
142 B2 Urenosi mt. Norway
80 E3 Urenui North I. N.Z.
78 □5 Ureparapara i. Vanuatu
163 A5 Urepel France
164 F1 Ureterp Neth.
Urfa Turkey see Şanlıurfa
169 B5 Urft r. Ger.
Urga Mongolia see Ulaanbaatar
100 E2 Urgal r. Rus. Fed.
Urganch Uzbek. see Urgench
199 E2 Urganlı Turkey
120 E4 Urgench Uzbek.
126 D3 Ürgüp Turkey
121 F5 Urgut Uzbek.
108 E2 Urho Xinjiang China
192 A4 Uri Sardegna Italy
116 C2 Uri Jammu and Kashmir
190 D2 Uri canton Switz.
81 C5 Uriah, Mount South I. N.Z.
250 C2 Uribia Col.
146 F4 Urie r. Scotland U.K.
157 G4 Uriménil France
244 C4 Uripitijuata, Cerro mt. Mex.
239 F7 Urique r. Mex.
190 D2 Uri-Rotstock mt. Switz.
83 E2 Urisino N.S.W. Austr.
120 F1 Uritskiy Kazakh.
137 J1 Uritskoye Rus. Fed.
210 C1 Urī Wenz r. Eth.
141 M3 Urjala Fin.
164 E2 Urk Neth.
101 C1 Urkan Rus. Fed.
101 C1 Urkan r. Rus. Fed.
129 E2 Urkarakh Rus. Fed.
177 G4 Úrkút Hungary
199 E2 Urla Turkey
197 H3 Urlați Romania
147 D4 Urlingford Rep. of Ireland
197 G4 Urlui r. Romania
107 E1 Urluk Rus. Fed.
134 I5 Urmary Rus. Fed.
123 G2 Urmetan Tajik.
100 E2 Urmi r. Rus. Fed.
Urmia Iran see Orūmīyeh
Urmia, Lake salt l. Iran see Orūmīyeh, Daryācheh-ye
157 H2 Urmitz Ger.
149 G4 Urmston Greater Manchester, England U.K.
190 E1 Urnäsch Switz.
186 A1 Urola r. Spain
207 G5 Uromi Nigeria
196 E4 Uroševac Kosovo, Srbija Yugo.
123 G2 Üroteppa Tajik.
137 H5 Urozhane Ukr.
129 D2 Urozhaynoye Rus. Fed.
183 H2 Urquilla, Sierra de mts Spain
184 C1 Urra Port.
186 C3 Urrea de Gaén Spain
186 B3 Urrea de Jalón Spain
163 A6 Urriés Spain
182 C3 Urros Port.
183 I2 Urroz Spain
162 B2 Urrugne France
Ursat'yevskaya Uzbek. see Khavast
173 E3 Ursberg Ger.
173 F2 Ursensollen Ger.
135 M4 Urshel'skiy Rus. Fed.
245 E1 Ursulo Galván Mex.
245 F4 Úrsulo Galván Mex.
163 A5 Ursuya, Mont hill France
175 L4 Urszulin Pol.
163 A5 Urt France
172 C5 Urtenen Switz.
140 M1 Urtivaara hill Fin./Norway
242 C3 Uruáchic Mex.
254 C5 Uruaçu Brazil
253 H3 Uruana Brazil
239 C6 Uruapan Baja California Norte Mex.
244 C4 Uruapan Michoacán Mex.
252 B3 Urubamba Peru
251 E5 Urubaxi r. Brazil
251 G5 Urubu r. Brazil
256 B4 Urubupungá, Salto do waterfall Brazil
251 G5 Urucara Brazil
251 F6 Urucu r. Brazil
254 D3 Uruçuí Brazil
254 D3 Uruçuí, Serra do hills Brazil
257 E2 Urucuia r. Brazil
254 D3 Uruçuí Preto r. Brazil
251 G5 Urucurituba Brazil
183 E3 Urueña Spain
258 F3 Uruguai r. Brazil alt. Uruguay (Arg./Uru.)
258 F3 Uruguaiana Brazil
261 H3 Uruguay r. Arg./Uru. alt. Uruguai (Brazil)
258 G4 Uruguay country S. America
Uruk tourist site Iraq see Erech
129 D2 Urukh r. Rus. Fed.
92 □ Urukthapel i. Palau
Urumchi Xinjiang China see Ürümqi
110 D3 Ürümqi Xinjiang China
Urundi country Africa see Burundi
83 H2 Urunga N.S.W. Austr.
129 B2 Urup Rus. Fed.
129 B2 Urup r. Rus. Fed.
131 Q5 Urup, Ostrov i. Kuril'skiye O-va Rus. Fed.
253 E2 Urupá r. Brazil
256 C4 Urupês Brazil
Urupskaya Krasnodarskiy Kray Rus. Fed. see Sovetskaya
124 D4 'Urūq al Awārik des. Saudi Arabia
125 F5 'Urūq ash Shaybah des. Saudi Arabia
193 H3 Ururi Italy
100 B1 Urusha Rus. Fed.
100 B1 Urusha r. Rus. Fed.
129 D2 Urus-Martan Rus. Fed.
135 K5 Urussu Rus. Fed.
256 C2 Urutaí Brazil
80 E3 Uruti North I. N.Z.
211 A6 Uruwira Tanz.
129 C2 Urvan' Rus. Fed.
158 E2 Urville Nacqueville France
121 F1 Uryl' Kazakh.
102 J2 Uryū-gawa r. Japan
100 E1 Uryumkan r. Rus. Fed.
135 H6 Uryupinsk Rus. Fed.
184 B3 Urza hill Port.
175 K5 Urzędów Pol.
216 □1c Urzelina São Jorge Azores
Urzhar Kazakh. see Urdzhar
134 J4 Urzhum Rus. Fed.
197 H3 Urziceni Ialomița Romania
177 L4 Urziceni Satu Mare Romania
137 I4 Urzuf Ukr.
192 B4 Urzulei Sardegna Italy
160 B1 Urzy France
138 G5 Usa r. Belarus
104 B3 Usa Japan
120 B1 Usa r. Rus. Fed.
134 L2 Usa r. Rus. Fed.
184 D2 Usagre Spain
199 F2 Uşak Turkey
199 F2 Uşak prov. Turkey
212 B4 Usakos Namibia
211 C6 Usambara Mountains Tanz.
263 K2 Usarp Mountains Antarctica
259 F8 Usborne, Mount hill Falkland Is
196 E4 Ušće Srbija Yugo.
169 E4 Uschlag (Staufenberg) Ger.
175 J6 Uście Gorlickie Pol.
175 I5 Uście Solne Pol.
190 E4 Uscio Italy
170 E2 Usedom Ger.
170 F2 Usedom i. Ger.
87 B5 Useless Loop W.A. Austr.
192 A5 Usellus Sardegna Italy
124 B3 Usfān Saudi Arabia
138 E5 Usha r. Belarus
138 G5 Usha r. Belarus
Ushachi Belarus see Ushachy
138 G4 Ushachy Belarus
121 J2 Ushanovo Kazakh.
Ushant i. France see Ouessant, Île d'
Usharal Kazakh. see Ucharal
121 G4 Usharal Zhambylskaya Oblast' Kazakh.
149 H3 Ushaw Moor Durham, England U.K.
124 D2 Ushayqir Saudi Arabia
124 C3 'Ushayrah Saudi Arabia
129 C2 Ushba, Mt'a Georgia
124 G3 Ushcha r. Rus. Fed.
139 H5 Ushcherp'ye Rus. Fed.
103 E7 Ushibuka Japan
105 G2 Ushiku Japan
104 B5 Ushimawashi-yama mt. Japan
121 I3 Ushtobe Kazakh.
Ush-Tyube Kazakh. see Ushtobe
259 C9 Ushuaia Arg.
136 D3 Ushytsya r. Ukr.
169 D5 Usingen Ger.
192 A4 Usini Sardegna Italy
134 L2 Usinsk Rus. Fed.
150 E3 Usk Monmouthshire, Wales U.K.
150 E3 Usk r. Wales U.K.
117 E4 Uska Uttar Prad. India
138 F5 Uskhodni Belarus
Uskoplje Bos.-Herz. see Gornji Vakuf
199 F1 Üsküdar Turkey
197 H5 Üsküp Turkey
169 E4 Uslar Ger.
176 G2 Úslava r. Czech Rep.
139 L5 Usman' Rus. Fed.
139 L5 Usman' r. Rus. Fed.
121 F5 Usmat Uzbek.
Usmet Uzbek. see Usmat
183 E5 Uso r. Spain
134 J3 Usogorsk Rus. Fed.
211 B6 Usoke Tanz.
134 L4 Usol'ye Rus. Fed.
98 H1 Usol'ye-Sibirskoye Rus. Fed.
188 G3 Usora r. Bos.-Herz.
176 G2 Úsov Czech Rep.
137 H1 Usozha r. Rus. Fed.
137 H1 Usozha r. Rus. Fed.
260 C3 Uspallata Arg.
137 I4 Uspenivka Ukr.
121 I1 Uspenka Kazakh.
137 G3 Uspenka Kirovohrads'ka Oblast' Ukr.
137 G2 Uspenka Sums'ka Oblast' Ukr.
121 H2 Uspenskiy Kazakh.
132 H2 Uspenskoye Rus. Fed.
134 H4 Uspen'ye Rus. Fed.
164 F1 Usquert Neth.
192 B5 Ussana Sardegna Italy
192 B5 Ussassai Sardegna Italy
193 G3 Usseglio Italy
161 A3 Ussel Auvergne France
162 E3 Ussel Limousin France
160 D3 Usses r. France
162 C2 Usson-du-Poitou France
161 B3 Usson-en-Forez France
100 E2 Ussuri r. China/Rus. Fed.
100 D4 Ussuriysk Rus. Fed.
134 I4 Usta r. Rus. Fed.
Ust'-Abakanskoye Rus. Fed. see Abakan
134 I3 Ust'-Alekseyevo Rus. Fed.
123 G4 Usta Muhammad Pak.
163 A5 Ustaritz France
Ust'-Balyk Rus. Fed. see Nefteyugansk
99 I1 Ust'-Barguzin Rus. Fed.
135 H7 Ust'-Donetskiy Rus. Fed.
129 B1 Ust'-Dzheguta Rus. Fed.
Ust'-Dzhegutinskaya Rus. Fed. see Ust'-Dzheguta
176 C1 Ústecký kraj admin. reg. Czech Rep.
176 D1 Úštěk Czech Rep.
190 D1 Uster Switz.
194 C4 Ustica Sicilia Italy
194 C4 Ustica, Isola di i. Sicilia Italy
131 L4 Ust'-Ilimsk Rus. Fed.
131 L4 Ust'-Ilimskiy Vodokhranilishche resr Rus. Fed.
107 G1 Ust'-Ilya Rus. Fed.
176 D1 Ústí nad Labem Czech Rep.
176 F1 Ústí nad Orlicí Czech Rep.
Ustinov Rus. Fed. see Izhevsk
Ustirt plat. Kazakh./Uzbek. see Ustyurt Plateau
143 G4 Ustka Pol.
121 J1 Ust'-Kalmanka Rus. Fed.
131 R4 Ust'-Kamchatsk Rus. Fed.
121 J2 Ust'-Kamenogorsk Kazakh.
110 D1 Ust'-Kan Rus. Fed.
110 D1 Ust'-Karsk Rus. Fed.
110 D1 Ust'-Koksa Rus. Fed.
134 K3 Ust'-Kulom Rus. Fed.
131 L4 Ust'-Kut Rus. Fed.
131 Q3 Ust'-Kuyga Rus. Fed.
135 G7 Ust'-Labinsk Rus. Fed.
Ust'-Labinskaya Rus. Fed. see Ust'-Labinsk
131 O3 Ust'-Maya Rus. Fed.
Ust'-Mongunay Rus. Fed. see Primorskiy
131 P3 Ust'-Nera Rus. Fed.
131 M2 Ust'-Olenek Rus. Fed.
131 P3 Ust'-Omchug Rus. Fed.
98 H1 Ust'-Ordynskiy Rus. Fed.
98 H1 Ust'-Ordynskiy Buryatskiy Avtonomnyy Okrug admin. div. Rus. Fed.
163 D6 Ustou France
197 H4 Ustrem Bulg.
174 G6 Ustroń Pol.
174 D1 Ustronie Morskie Pol.
175 K6 Ustrzyki Dolne Pol.
134 H3 Ust'-Shonosha Rus. Fed.
134 K2 Ust'-Tsil'ma Rus. Fed.
110 D1 Ust'-Ulagan Rus. Fed.
100 E2 Ust'-Umalta Rus. Fed.
134 L2 Ust'-Usa Rus. Fed.
120 E1 Ust'-Uyskoye Kazakh.
134 H3 Ust'-Vayen'ga Rus. Fed.
134 H3 Ust'ya r. Rus. Fed.
134 G4 Ust'ye Rus. Fed.
134 H4 Ust'ye Rus. Fed.
139 L3 Ust'ye r. Rus. Fed.
139 J2 Ust'ye-Kirovskoye Rus. Fed.
136 C2 Ustyluh Ukr.
137 G4 Ustynivka Ukr.
Ustyurt, Plato plat. Kazakh./Uzbek. see Ustyurt Plateau
120 D4 Ustyurt Plateau Kazakh./Uzbek.
Ustyurt Platosi plat. Kazakh./Uzbek. see Ustyurt Plateau
139 J2 Ustyutskoye Rus. Fed.
139 K2 Ustyuzhna Rus. Fed.
110 D2 Usu Xinjiang China
103 E7 Usuki Japan
242 □H6 Usulután El Salvador
243 G5 Usumacinta r. Guat./Mex.
Usumbura Burundi see Bujumbura
95 F2 Usun Apau, Dataran Tinggi plat. Sarawak Malaysia
186 A1 Usurbil Spain
175 H6 Ušust mt. Pol.
215 I2 Usutu r. Africa
134 L4 Us'va Rus. Fed.
139 H4 Usvyaty Rus. Fed.
138 G4 Usvyeyka r. Belarus
175 I6 Uszew Pol.
177 H5 Uszód Hungary
175 I5 Uszwica r. Pol.
192 A5 Uta Sardegna Italy
241 L2 Utah state U.S.A.
241 L1 Utah Lake UT U.S.A.
140 N2 Utajärvi Fin.
168 C2 Utarp Ger.
Utashinai Kuril'skiye O-va Rus. Fed. see Yuzhno-Kuril'sk
125 E2 Utayyiq Saudi Arabia
186 C3 Utebo Spain
237 C5 Ute Creek r. NM U.S.A.
161 F5 Utelle France
209 D9 Utembo r. Angola
138 E4 Utena Lith.
168 D1 Utersum Ger.
211 C7 Utete Tanz.
96 C4 Uthai Thani Thai.
123 F5 Uthal Pak.
169 F4 Uthleben Ger.
168 D2 Uthlede Ger.
227 F4 Utica MI U.S.A.
237 F5 Utica MS U.S.A.
233 F3 Utica NY U.S.A.
232 B4 Utica OH U.S.A.
187 B5 Utiel Spain
242 □I5 Utila Hond.
254 E5 Utinga r. Brazil
215 E2 Utlwanang S. Africa
103 E7 Uto Japan
84 C4 Utopia N.T. Austr.
175 I3 Utrata r. Pol.
116 E4 Utraula Uttar Prad. India
164 E2 Utrecht Neth.
164 E2 Utrecht prov. Neth.
215 H2 Utrecht S. Africa
184 E3 Utrera Spain
186 C4 Utrillas Spain
177 I6 Utrine Vojvodina, Srbija Yugo.
138 G3 Utroya r. Rus. Fed.
142 A2 Utsira Norway
140 N1 Utsjoki Fin.
105 D3 Utsugi-dake mt. Japan
105 F2 Utsunomiya Japan
135 I7 Utta Rus. Fed.
96 C3 Uttaradit Thai.
116 D3 Uttarkashi Uttar Prad. India
116 D4 Uttar Pradesh state India
178 E2 Uttendorf Oberösterreich Austria
178 D3 Uttendorf Salzburg Austria
173 F2 Uttenreuth Ger.
172 D3 Uttenweiler Ger.
168 G1 Utterslev Denmark
173 F3 Utting am Ammersee Ger.
151 F2 Uttoxeter Staffordshire, England U.K.
Utu Xinjiang China see Miao'ergou
247 □1 Utuado Puerto Rico
110 D2 Utubulak Xinjiang China
78 □6 Utupua i. Solomon Is
120 C2 Utva r. Kazakh.
170 E2 Utzedel Ger.
221 M2 Uummannaq Greenland
Uummannarsuaq c. Greenland see Nunap Isua
140 N3 Uurainen Fin.
106 D1 Üür Gol r. Mongolia
Uusikaarlepyy Fin. see Nykarleby
141 M3 Uusikaupunki Fin.
212 B3 Uutapi Namibia
250 D4 Uva r. Col.
134 K4 Uva Rus. Fed.
196 D4 Uvac r. Bos.-Herz./Yugo.
237 D6 Uvalde TX U.S.A.
176 D1 Úvaly Czech Rep.
139 H5 Uvarovichi Belarus
139 J4 Uvarovka Rus. Fed.
135 H6 Uvarovo Rus. Fed.
Uvéa i. Îles Loyauté New Caledonia see Ouvéa
120 E1 Uvel'ka r. Rus. Fed.
139 J2 Uver' r. Rus. Fed.
161 E4 Uvernet-Fours France
211 A6 Uvinza Tanz.
209 F5 Uvira Dem. Rep. Congo
139 M3 Uvod' r. Rus. Fed.
215 H4 Uvongo S. Africa
106 B1 Uvs prov. Mongolia
106 B1 Uvs Nuur salt l. Mongolia
103 F7 Uwajima Japan
124 B2 'Uwayriḍ, Ḥarrat al lava field Saudi Arabia
202 E4 Uweinat, Jebel mt. Sudan
227 H3 Uxbridge Ont. Can.
151 G3 Uxbridge Greater London, England U.K.
160 C2 Uxeau France
169 B5 Üxheim Ger.
107 F4 Uxin Ju Nei Mongol China
Uxin Qi Nei Mongol China see Dabqig
243 H4 Uxmal tourist site Mex.
245 G5 Uxpanapa r. Mex.
110 D3 Uxxaktal Xinjiang China
120 E1 Uy r. Rus. Fed.
131 K4 Uyar Rus. Fed.
106 E2 Üydzin Mongolia
146 □H1 Uyea i. Scotland U.K.
146 □H1 Uyeasound Shetland, Scotland U.K.
207 G5 Uyo Nigeria
106 B2 Üyönch Mongolia
106 A2 Üyönch Gol r. China
120 E1 Uyskoye Rus. Fed.
96 A1 Uyu Chaung r. Myanmar
121 G4 Uyuk Kazakh.
125 E2 Uyun Saudi Arabia
252 D5 Uyuni, Salar de salt flat Bol.
163 A4 Uza France
120 A1 Uza r. Rus. Fed.
127 G4 'Uzaym, Nahr al r. Iraq
120 E4 Uzbekistan country Asia
Ŭzbekiston country Asia see Uzbekistan
Uzbekskaya S.S.R. country Asia see Uzbekistan
Uzbek S.S.R. country Asia see Uzbekistan
138 F5 Uzda Belarus
158 D3 Uzel France
Uzen' Kazakh. see Kyzylsay
121 I4 Uzengyu-Kuush, Gora mt. China/Kyrg.
161 C4 Uzer France
162 D3 Uzerche France
161 C4 Uzès France
Uzgen Kyrg. see Özgön
136 B3 Uzh r. Ukr.
136 F2 Uzh r. Ukr.
139 I4 Uzha r. Rus. Fed.
Uzhgorod Ukr. see Uzhhorod
136 B3 Uzhhorod Ukr.
136 B3 Uzhok Ukr.
Užhorod Ukr. see Uzhhorod
196 D4 Užice Srbija Yugo.
139 L5 Uzlovaya Rus. Fed.
134 H4 Uzola r. Rus. Fed.
129 A4 Üzümlü Turkey
199 F3 Üzümlü Turkey
121 G5 Uzun Uzbek.
121 I4 Uzunagach Almatinskaya Oblast' Kazakh.
121 I4 Uzunagach Almatinskaya Oblast' Kazakh.
110 D2 Uzunbulak Xinjiang China
128 A1 Uzuncaburç Turkey
129 B3 Uzundere Turkey
129 B3 Uzungöl Turkey
199 E1 Uzunköprü Turkey
129 F4 Uzuntäpä Azer.
138 D4 Užventis Lith.
136 F3 Uzyn Ukr.
Uzynaghash Almatinskaya Oblast' Kazakh. see Uzunagach
120 E3 Uzynkair Kazakh.

V

113 □1 Vaadhu i. S. Male Maldives
113 □1 Vaagali i. S. Male Maldives
134 D3 Vaajakoski Fin.
215 D3 Vaal r. S. Africa
140 N2 Vaala Fin.
215 G2 Vaal Dam S. Africa
168 E2 Vaale Ger.
215 G1 Vaalplaas S. Africa
165 F4 Vaals Neth.
165 F4 Vaalserberg hill Neth.
213 F5 Vaalwater S. Africa
159 G4 Vaas France
140 M3 Vaasa Fin.
164 E2 Vaassen Neth.
113 □1 Vaataru i. N. Male Maldives
138 E4 Vabalninkas Lith.
138 G5 Vabich r. Belarus
120 F4 Vabkent Uzbek.
139 I5 Vablya r. Rus. Fed.
163 E5 Vabre France
161 A5 Vabres-l'Abbaye France
177 I4 Vác Hungary
195 F4 Vacale r. Italy
257 E4 Vacaré r. Brazil
255 C9 Vacaria Brazil
255 F2 Vacaria r. Minas Gerais Brazil
255 B7 Vacaria r. Mato Grosso do Sul Brazil
240 C2 Vacaville CA U.S.A.
161 C5 Vaccarès, Étang de lag. France
195 F3 Vaccarizzo Albanese Italy
169 F5 Vacha Ger.
134 H5 Vacha Rus. Fed.
177 I4 Váchartyán Hungary
160 E2 Vacherresse France
177 E2 Vachi Rus. Fed.
143 F3 Väckelsång Sweden
176 H2 Vacov Czech Rep.
161 C4 Vacqueyras France
197 H2 Văculești Romania
134 I5 Vad Rus. Fed.
135 H5 Vad r. Rus. Fed.
114 B2 Vada Mahar. India
138 D3 Vadakste r. Latvia/Lith.
197 G4 Vădăstrița Romania
142 D1 Vadehavet sea chan. Denmark
197 H3 Vădeni Romania
136 E4 Vădeni, Dealul hill Moldova
114 B3 Vadi Mahar. India
135 H5 Vadinsk Rus. Fed.
183 G3 Vadocondes Spain
116 C5 Vadodara Gujarat India
190 D4 Vado Ligure Italy
140 O1 Vadsø Norway
143 F3 Vadstena Sweden
197 F2 Vadu Crișului Romania
172 D4 Vaduz Liechtenstein
142 E1 Væggerløse Denmark
140 C1 Værøy i. Norway
134 K3 Vaga r. Rus. Fed.
141 J3 Vågåmo Norway
188 E3 Vaganski Vrh mt. Croatia
144 D1 Vágar i. Faroe Is
114 D2 Vagavaram Andhra Prad. India
143 F3 Vaggeryd Sweden
78 □6 Vaghena i. Solomon Is
198 C2 Vagia Sterea Ellas Greece
191 G5 Vaglia Italy
193 H4 Vaglio Basilicata Italy
190 F4 Vagli Sotto Italy
157 G4 Vagney France
143 G2 Vagnhärad Sweden
182 B4 Vagos Port.
140 L2 Vägsele Sweden
142 B1 Vågsfjorden sea chan. Norway
177 H5 Váh r. Slovakia
140 M3 Vähäkyrö Fin.
169 E4 Vahlbruch Ger.
259 □ Vahsel, Cape S. Georgia
141 M3 Vahto Fin.
77 H2 Vaiaku Tuvalu
184 C1 Vaiamonte Port.
191 G5 Vaiano Italy
138 E2 Vaida Estonia
237 F5 Vaiden MS U.S.A.
114 C4 Vaigai r. India
159 F3 Vaiges France
172 C3 Vaihingen an der Enz Ger.
114 B2 Vaijapur Mahar. India
114 C4 Vaikam Kerala India
138 F2 Väike Emajõgi r. Estonia
138 F2 Väike-Maarja Estonia
140 L2 Vaikijaur Sweden
236 B4 Vail CO U.S.A.
146 □G1 Vaila i. Scotland U.K.
156 D3 Vailly-sur-Aisne France
160 A1 Vailly-sur-Sauldre France
235 D1 Vails Gate NY U.S.A.
138 F3 Väimela Estonia
138 C3 Vaiņode Latvia
114 C4 Vaippar r. India
157 F4 Vair r. France
193 G3 Vairano Patenora Italy
193 G3 Vairano Scalo Italy
161 E5 Vaire r. France
116 C3 Vairowal Punjab India
182 B4 Vais Port.
161 D4 Vaison-la-Romaine France
163 D4 Vaïssac France
77 H2 Vaitupu i. Tuvalu
160 E1 Vaivre-et-Montoille France
177 L4 Vaja Hungary
Vajrakarur Andhra Prad. India see Kanur
177 G6 Vajszló Hungary
177 H5 Vajta Hungary
208 D2 Vakaga pref. C.A.R.
208 D2 Vakaga r. C.A.R.
137 J3 Vakhrusheve Ukr.
123 G2 Vakhsh Tajik.
123 G2 Vakhsh r. Tajik.
Vakhstroy Tajik. see Vakhsh
134 I4 Vakhtan Rus. Fed.
142 A1 Vaksdal Norway
197 E4 Vaksince Macedonia
177 H4 Vál Hungary
140 K3 Vålådalen Sweden
182 B2 Valadares Port.
182 C1 Valadouro mts Spain
190 C2 Valais canton Switz.
177 K3 Valaliky Slovakia
134 K4 Valamaz Rus. Fed.
197 F5 Valandovo Macedonia
159 F4 Valanjou France
183 I2 Valareña Spain
177 I3 Valaská Slovakia
177 G2 Valašská Polanka Czech Rep.
177 H2 Valašské Klobouky Czech Rep.
177 G2 Valašské Meziříčí Czech Rep.
227 J2 Val-Barrette Que. Can.
161 E4 Valberg France
143 G1 Valbo Sweden
187 C4 Valbona Spain
190 F2 Valbondione Italy
161 D4 Valbonnais France
161 F5 Valbonne France
183 F3 Valbuena de Duero Spain
177 H2 Valča Slovakia
197 G3 Vâlcănești Romania
197 F3 Vâlcanului, Munții mts Romania
177 L4 Valcău de Jos Romania
161 E3 Val-Cenis France
259 D6 Valcheta Arg.
186 D3 Valcuerna r. Spain
191 G3 Valdagno Italy
160 E1 Valdahon France
Valdai Hills Rus. Fed. see Valdayskaya Vozvyshennost'
191 H2 Valdaora Italy
183 F2 Valdavia r. Spain
139 I3 Valday Rus. Fed.
139 I3 Valdayskaya Vozvyshennost' hills Rus. Fed.
139 I2 Valdayskoye, Ozero l. Rus. Fed.
186 C3 Valdealgorfa Spain
185 F2 Valdeazogues r. Spain
161 F4 Valdeblore France
185 E1 Valdecaballeros Spain
182 E5 Valdecañas, Embalse de resr Spain
182 E5 Valdecañas de Tajo Spain
183 E4 Valdecarros Spain
183 F2 Valdecebollas mt. Spain
183 G1 Valdecilla Spain
183 I4 Valdecuenca Spain
184 D1 Valdefuentes Spain
185 I1 Valdeganga Spain
183 F2 Valdeginate r. Spain
182 E4 Valdelacasa Spain
185 E1 Valdelacasa de Tajo Spain
184 D3 Valdelamusa Spain
186 C4 Valdelinares Spain
183 I4 Valdellosa mt. Spain
185 F2 Valdemanco del Esteras Spain
159 I3 Val-de-Marne dept France
138 D3 Valdemārpils Latvia
143 G2 Valdemarsvik Sweden
183 I4 Valdemeca Spain
184 D2 Valdemedé r. Spain
183 I5 Valdemembra r. Spain
157 F4 Val-de-Meuse France
183 F4 Valdemorillo Spain
183 G4 Valdemoro Spain
183 I4 Valdemoro-Sierra Spain
183 F3 Valdenoches Spain
261 I4 Valdense Uru.
182 D4 Valdeobispo Spain
183 G4 Valdepeñas Spain
185 G3 Valdepeñas de Jaén Spain
183 F2 Valdepiélago Spain
183 E2 Valderaduey r. Spain
183 E3 Valderas Spain
156 B3 Val-de-Reuil France
194 B4 Valderice Sicilia Italy
163 E4 Valderiès France
183 F3 Valderrobres Spain
183 F2 Valderrueda Spain
226 D3 Valders WI U.S.A.
261 G4 Valdés Arg.
259 E6 Valdés, Península pen. Arg.
183 F4 Val de Santo Domingo Spain
227 J3 Val-des-Bois Que. Can.
183 F3 Valdestillas Spain
183 F3 Valdetormo Spain
184 D2 Valdetorres Spain
183 E5 Valdeverdeja Spain
183 F4 Valdevimbre Spain
250 B4 Valdez Ecuador
220 D3 Valdez AK U.S.A.
Valdgeym Ukr. see Dobropillya
190 F2 Valdidentro Italy
183 F4 Valdilinaho mt. Spain
183 G4 Valdilecha Spain
161 E3 Val-d'Isère France
190 F2 Valdisotto Italy
259 B5 Valdivia Chile
250 C3 Valdivia Col.
156 C3 Valdivienne France
158 E3 Val-d'Izé France
191 G3 Valdobbiadene Italy
157 G5 Valdoie France
156 C3 Val-d'Oise dept Île-de-France France
224 E3 Val-d'Or Que. Can.
183 G3 Valdosa mt. Spain
231 D6 Valdosta GA U.S.A.
141 J3 Valdres val. Norway
161 D4 Valdrôme France
183 D2 Valdunquillo Spain
Vale Channel Is
129 C3 Vale Georgia
238 C2 Vale OR U.S.A.
197 F2 Valea lui Mihai Romania
197 G2 Valea Lungă Romania
197 G3 Valea Lungă Romania
184 C3 Vale da Rosa Port.
184 B1 Vale das Mós Port.
184 C3 Vale de Açor Port.
184 C1 Vale de Açor Port.
182 E4 Vale de Cambra Port.
184 B1 Vale de Cavalos Port.
182 D4 Vale de Espinho Port.
182 C4 Vale de Estrela Port.
184 B1 Vale de Figueira Port.
182 D4 Vale de Guiso Port.
182 C4 Vale de Prazeres Port.
184 B2 Vale de Reis Port.
182 C3 Vale de Salgueiro Port.
184 B1 Vale de Santarém Port.
184 C3 Vale de Vargo Port.
184 D2 Vale do Pereiro Port.
184 C1 Vale do Peso Port.
182 B4 Válega Port.
191 F3 Valeggio sul Mincio Italy
222 G4 Valemount B.C. Can.
254 F5 Valença Brazil
182 B2 Valença Port.
254 E3 Valença do Piauí Brazil
162 D1 Valençay France
163 C4 Valence Midi-Pyrénées France
161 C4 Valence Rhône-Alpes France
163 C4 Valence-d'Albigeois France
163 C5 Valence-sur-Baïse France
187 C5 Valencia aut. comm. Spain
187 C5 Valencia prov. Valencia Spain
250 E2 Valencia Venez.
187 D5 Valencia, Golfo de g. Spain
184 C1 Valencia de Alcántara Spain
182 E2 Valencia de Don Juan Spain
184 D2 Valencia de las Torres Spain
184 C2 Valencia del Mombuey Spain
184 D2 Valencia del Ventoso Spain
147 A5 Valencia Island Rep. of Ireland
Valenciana, Comunidad aut. comm. Spain see Valencia
156 D2 Valenciennes France
197 H3 Vălenii de Munte Romania
161 D5 Valensole France
161 E5 Valensole, Plateau de France
192 D2 Valentano Italy
245 F4 Valente Díaz y La Loma Mex.
Valentia Spain see Valencia
160 E1 Valentigney France
100 E4 Valentin Rus. Fed.
163 C5 Valentine France
236 C3 Valentine NE U.S.A.
239 F6 Valentine TX U.S.A.
190 D3 Valenza Italy
195 F1 Valenzano Italy
92 B3 Valenzuela Phil.
185 F3 Valenzuela Spain
185 G2 Valenzuela de Calatrava Spain
150 D3 Vale of Glamorgan admin. div. Wales U.K.
142 D1 Våler Norway
250 D2 Valera Venez.
183 H5 Valera de Arriba Spain
161 D4 Valernes France
184 C3 Vales Mortos Port.
193 E1 Valfabbrica Italy
186 C3 Valfarta Spain
157 G4 Valfroicourt France
190 F2 Valfurva Italy
138 F3 Valga Estonia
Valga Spain see Ponte Valga
138 E2 Valgejõgi r. Estonia
161 C4 Valgorge France
190 C3 Valgrisenche Italy
194 D5 Valguarnera Caropepe Sicilia Italy
235 E1 Valhalla NY U.S.A.
182 C4 Valhelhas Port.
183 I4 Valhermoso Spain
163 D6 Valier, Mont mt. France
121 G1 Valikhanovo Kazakh.
256 D5 Valinhos Brazil
186 E2 Valira r. Andorra/Spain
196 D3 Valjevo Srbija Yugo.
186 D4 Valjunquera Spain
138 F3 Valka Latvia
141 N3 Valkeakoski Fin.
165 E4 Valkenburg Limburg Neth.
164 D2 Valkenburg Zuid-Holland Neth.
165 E3 Valkenswaard Neth.
138 F1 Valko Fin.
177 I4 Valkó Hungary
Valkoni Fin. see Valko
137 H3 Valky Ukr.
263 C1 Valkyrie Dome ice feature Antarctica
116 B5 Vallabhipur Gujarat India
161 C5 Vallabrègues France
187 C6 Vallada Spain
243 H4 Valladolid Mex.
183 F3 Valladolid Spain
183 F3 Valladolid prov. Castilla y León Spain
187 B7 Valladolises Spain
177 L4 Vállaj Hungary
161 F5 Vallauris France
146 A4 Vallay i. Scotland U.K.
140 I3 Valldal Norway
187 C4 Vall d'Alba Spain
187 F5 Valldemossa Spain
187 C5 Vall de Uxó Spain
250 B4 Valle dept Col.
142 B2 Valle Norway
183 F1 Valle Spain
193 F2 Valle Castellana Italy
190 C3 Valle d'Aosta admin. reg. Italy
185 F4 Valle de Abdalajís Spain
244 D4 Valle de Bravo Mex.
184 E2 Valle de la Serena Spain
184 D2 Valle de Matamoros Spain
184 D2 Valle de Santa Ana Spain
244 D3 Valle de Santiago Mex.
191 H2 Valle di Cadore Italy
194 C5 Valledolmo Sicilia Italy
192 A4 Valledoria Sardegna Italy
250 C2 Valledupar Col.
217 □2a Vallée de Mai tourist site Seychelles
225 G4 Vallée-Jonction Que. Can.
260 C2 Valle Fértil, Sierra de mts Arg.
252 D4 Valle Grande Bol.
216 □3a Vallehermoso La Gomera Canary Is
243 F3 Valle Hermoso Mex.
160 D2 Valleiry France
240 F2 Vallejo CA U.S.A.
194 C5 Vallelunga Pratameno Sicilia Italy
190 C3 Valle Mosso Italy
140 J3 Vallen Sweden
245 F5 Valle Nacional Mex.
258 C3 Vallenar Chile
187 B4 Vallenca Spain
169 C5 Vallendar Ger.
156 E4 Vallentigny France
143 H2 Vallentuna Sweden
161 B4 Valleraugue France
192 A5 Vallermosa Sardegna Italy
193 F4 Vallerotonda Italy
216 □3f Valleseco Gran Canaria Canary Is
158 E4 Vallet France
195 □ Valletta Malta
223 L5 Valley r. Man. Can.
173 F4 Valley Ger.
150 C1 Valley Isle of Anglesey, Wales U.K.
240 I5 Valley Center CA U.S.A.
236 D2 Valley City ND U.S.A.
238 B3 Valley Falls OR U.S.A.
234 C2 Valley Forge PA U.S.A.
232 C5 Valley Head WV U.S.A.
147 E3 Valleymount Rep. of Ireland
203 G3 Valley of The Kings tourist site Egypt
240 G2 Valley Springs CA U.S.A.
230 C4 Valley Station KY U.S.A.
235 E2 Valley Stream NY U.S.A.
222 G4 Valleyview Alta Can.
234 B2 Valley View PA U.S.A.
186 E3 Vallfogona de Riucorb Spain
162 E3 Vallières France
186 E3 Vallmoll Spain
193 H4 Vallo della Lucania Italy
161 E3 Valloire France
160 A2 Vallon-en-Sully France
161 C4 Vallon-Pont-d'Arc France
190 B2 Vallorbe Switz.
160 E2 Vallorcine France
161 E4 Vallouise France
186 E3 Valls Spain
141 L3 Vallsta Sweden
190 E3 Valmadrera Italy
186 C3 Valmadrid Spain
223 J5 Val Marie Sask. Can.
Valmaseda Spain see Balmaseda
185 F2 Valmayor r. Spain
138 E3 Valmiera Latvia
183 F4 Valmojado Spain
159 G2 Valmont France
193 E3 Valmontone Italy
161 E3 Valmorel France
156 E3 Valmy France
183 G1 Valnera mt. Spain
158 E2 Valognes France
Valona Albania see Vlorë
184 C1 Valongo Portalegre Port.
182 B3 Valongo Porto Port.
185 G4 Válor Spain
183 F3 Valoria la Buena Spain
138 F4 Valozhyn Belarus
182 C3 Valpaços Port.
186 C2 Valpalmas Spain
224 E1 Val-Paradis Que. Can.
114 C4 Valparai Tamil Nadu India
256 B4 Valparaíso Brazil
260 B3 Valparaíso Chile
260 B3 Valparaíso admin. reg. Chile
244 C2 Valparaíso Mex.
243 I2 Valparaiso FL U.S.A.
230 C3 Valparaiso IN U.S.A.
160 F3 Valpelline Italy
190 C3 Valpelline val. Italy
190 C3 Valperga Italy
114 B3 Valpoi Goa India
188 G3 Valpovo Croatia
161 B5 Valras-Plage France
161 C4 Valréas France
185 F1 Valronquillo hill Spain
161 B5 Valros France
215 F2 Vals r. S. Africa
190 E2 Vals Switz.
116 C5 Valsad Gujarat India
190 C3 Valsavarenche Italy
170 C1 Vålse Denmark
183 F3 Valseca Spain
216 □3f Valsequillo Gran Canaria Canary Is
185 E2 Valsequillo Spain
160 D2 Valserine r. France
195 F2 Valsinni Italy
140 K2 Valsjöbyn Sweden
161 C4 Vals-les-Bains France
215 E2 Valspan S. Africa
215 G3 Valsrivier S. Africa
191 G3 Valstagna Italy
191 G2 Valsura r. Italy
160 C1 Val-Suzon France
161 E3 Val-Thorens France
176 F3 Valtice Czech Rep.
183 G3 Valtiendas Spain
183 I2 Valtierra Spain
140 O3 Valtimo Fin.
193 E1 Valtopina Italy
198 B2 Valtou mts Greece
190 C3 Valtournenche Italy
Valua i. Vanuatu see Mota Lava
161 A3 Valuéjols France
137 J2 Valuy r. Rus. Fed.
135 H7 Valuyevka Rus. Fed.
135 G6 Valuyki Rus. Fed.
129 F3 Välväläçay r. Azer.
216 □3e Valverde El Hierro Canary Is
Valverde Dom. Rep. see Mao
184 D2 Valverde de Burguillos Spain
183 H5 Valverde de Júcar Spain
184 D3 Valverde del Camino Spain
184 D2 Valverde de Leganés Spain
182 D4 Valverde del Fresno Spain
184 E2 Valverde de Llerena Spain
183 G3 Valverde de los Arroyos Spain
184 D2 Valverde de Mérida Spain
197 F2 Vama Satu Mare Romania
197 G2 Vama Suceava Romania
176 F1 Vamberk Czech Rep.
97 D5 Vam Co Dông r. Vietnam
97 D5 Vam Co Tay r. Vietnam
142 C4 Vamdrup Denmark
141 M3 Vammala Fin.
177 I4 Vámosgyörk Hungary
177 H4 Vámosmikola Hungary
177 K4 Vámospércs Hungary
177 K3 Vámosújfalu Hungary
141 M3 Vampula Fin.
115 E2 Vamsadhara r. India
127 F3 Van Turkey
129 C4 Van prov. Turkey
Van, Lake salt l. Turkey see Van Gölü
129 D3 Vanadzor Armenia
141 K3 Vanån r. Sweden
197 I3 Vânători Romania
197 G2 Vânători Romania
156 E4 Vanault-les-Dames France
131 L3 Vanavara Rus. Fed.

Van Buren to Vetlanda
375

237 E5 Van Buren AR U.S.A.
226 E5 Van Buren IN U.S.A.
233 □J1 Van Buren ME U.S.A.
237 F4 Van Buren MO U.S.A.
Van Buren OH U.S.A. see Kettering
233 □J2 Vanceboro ME U.S.A.
232 B5 Vanceburg KY U.S.A.
Vanch Tajik. see Vanj
Vanchskiy Khrebet mts Tajik. see Vanj, Qatorkŭhi
232 B6 Vancleve KY U.S.A.
235 E1 Van Cortlandtville NY U.S.A.
222 F5 Vancouver B.C. Can.
238 B2 Vancouver WA U.S.A.
87 C7 Vancouver, Cape W.A. Austr.
222 B2 Vancouver, Mount Can./U.S.A.
222 E5 Vancouver Island B.C. Can.
177 K4 Váncsod Hungary
Vanda Fin. see Vantaa
236 F4 Vandalia IL U.S.A.
232 A5 Vandalia OH U.S.A.
129 E3 Vandam Azer.
178 A3 Vandans Austria
114 C3 Vandavasi Tamil Nadu India
186 D3 Vandellós Spain
160 B2 Vandenesse France
160 C1 Vandenesse-en-Auxois France
215 F2 Vanderbijlpark S. Africa
226 E3 Vanderbilt MI U.S.A.
232 D4 Vandergrift PA U.S.A.
222 E4 Vanderhoof B.C. Can.
84 D2 Vanderlin Island N.T. Austr.
84 B1 Van Diemen, Cape N.T. Austr.
84 D3 Van Diemen, Cape Qld Austr.
84 C1 Van Diemen Gulf N.T. Austr.
Van Diemen's Land state Austr. see Tasmania
234 C1 Vandling PA U.S.A.
157 G4 Vandœuvre-lès-Nancy France
191 G2 Vandoies Italy
138 E2 Vändra Estonia
193 G3 Vandra r. Italy
215 G2 Vandyksdrif S. Africa
Väner, Lake Sweden see Vänern
142 E2 Vänern l. Sweden
142 E2 Vänersborg Sweden
183 F2 Vañes Spain
262 T2 Vang, Mount Antarctica
211 C6 Vanga Kenya
213 □J4 Vangaindrano Madag.
138 E3 Vangaži Latvia
129 E3 Vängli Azer.
127 F3 Van Gölü salt l. Turkey
140 L1 Vangsvik Norway
223 J5 Vanguard Sask. Can.
78 □6 Vangunu i. New Georgia Is Solomon Is
78 □6 Vangunu, Mount New Georgia Is Solomon Is
239 F6 Van Horn TX U.S.A.
129 C2 Vani Georgia
224 F4 Vanier Ont. Can.
78 □6 Vanikoro Islands Solomon Is
190 C2 Vanil Noir mt. Switz.
91 J7 Vanimo P.N.G.
100 G2 Vanino Rus. Fed.
114 C3 Vaniyambadi Tamil Nadu India
123 G2 Vanj Tajik.
123 G2 Vanj, Qatorkŭhi mts Tajik.
140 L2 Vänjaurträsk Sweden
197 F3 Vânju Mare Romania
131 T3 Vankarem Rus. Fed.
233 F2 Vankleek Hill Ont. Can.
232 B4 Vanlue OH U.S.A.
140 □ Van Mijenfjorden inlet Svalbard
140 L1 Vanna i. Norway
140 L3 Vännäs Sweden
156 D4 Vanne r. France
158 D4 Vannes France
Vannovka Kazakh. see Tura-Ryskulova
140 L1 Vanntindan mt. Norway
191 G3 Vanoi r. Italy
215 G3 Van Reenen S. Africa
91 I7 Van Rees, Pegunungan mts Indon.
214 B4 Vanrhynsdorp S. Africa
85 E3 Vanrook Qld Austr.
85 E3 Vanrook Creek r. Qld Austr.
116 C5 Vansada Gujarat India
232 B6 Vansant VA U.S.A.
143 F1 Vansbro Sweden
142 B2 Vanse Norway
86 E2 Vansittart Bay W.A. Austr.
215 F3 Vanstadensrus S. Africa
141 N3 Vantaa Fin.
138 E1 Vantaa r. Fin.
87 D5 Van Truer Tableland reg. W.A. Austr.
215 H3 Vant's Drift S. Africa
77 I3 Vanua Balavu i. Fiji
78 □5 Vanua Lava i. Vanuatu
79 □1 Vanua Levu i. Fiji
Vanua Mbalavu i. Fiji see Vanua Balavu
78 □5 Vanuatu country S. Pacific Ocean
Vanua Valavo i. Fiji see Vanua Balavu
156 E5 Vanvey France
236 G3 Van Wert OH U.S.A.
214 C5 Van Wyksdorp S. Africa
214 C4 Vanwyksvlei S. Africa
177 I4 Vanyarc Hungary
190 D3 Vanzone Italy
214 D2 Van Zylsrus S. Africa
78 □5 Vao New Caledonia
163 D4 Vaour France
176 G1 Vápenná Czech Rep.
136 E3 Vapnyarka Ukr.
184 C3 Vaqueiros Port.
161 E5 Var dept Provence-Alpes-Côte-d'Azur France
161 F5 Var r. France
190 E4 Vara r. Italy
142 E2 Vara Sweden
114 C3 Varada r. India
185 H1 Vara del Rey Spain
246 B2 Varadero Cuba
159 E4 Varades France
177 L5 Vărădia de Mureş Romania
161 D5 Varages France
116 B5 Varahi Gujarat India
163 D4 Varaire France
190 C4 Varaita r. Italy
138 F3 Varakļāni Latvia
177 H5 Varalja Hungary
190 D3 Varallo Italy
122 B3 Varāmīn Iran
117 E4 Varanasi Uttar Prad. India
134 L1 Varandey Rus. Fed.
140 O1 Varangerfjorden sea chan. Norway
140 O1 Varangerhalvøya pen. Norway
193 H3 Varano, Lago di lag. Italy
190 E4 Varano de'Melegari Italy
138 F4 Varapayeva Belarus
185 F2 Varas r. Spain
188 F2 Varaždin Croatia
179 H4 Varaždinske Toplice Croatia
190 D4 Varazze Italy
142 E3 Varberg Sweden
177 J3 Varbó Hungary
161 D3 Varces France
177 L5 Vârciorog Romania
198 B2 Varda Greece
123 G3 Vardak prov. Afgh.
114 C2 Vardannapet Andhra Prad. India
196 F5 Vardar r. Macedonia
142 C4 Varde Denmark
142 C4 Varde r. Denmark
129 D3 Vardenis Armenia
129 D3 Vardenisi Lerr mt. Armenia
129 D4 Vardenisi Lerrnashght'a mts Armenia
129 D3 Vardisubani Georgia
141 M3 Vårdö Åland Fin.
140 O1 Vardø Norway
177 H5 Várdomb Hungary
138 D3 Varduva r. Lith.
139 L3 Varegovo Rus. Fed.
168 D2 Varel Ger.
206 A3 Varela Guinea-Bissau
138 E4 Varėna Lith.
138 E4 Varėnė r. Lith.
156 A3 Varengeville-sur-Mer France
137 I5 Varenikovskaya Rus. Fed.
156 B3 Varenne r. France
156 C5 Varennes-Changy France
157 F3 Varennes-en-Argonne France
160 D2 Varennes-St-Sauveur France
160 B2 Varennes-sur-Allier France
160 B1 Varennes-Vauzelles France
137 J4 Varenovka Rus. Fed.
188 G3 Vareš Bos.-Herz.
190 D3 Varese Italy
190 D3 Varese prov. Lombardia Italy
190 E4 Varese Ligure Italy
162 D3 Varetz France
100 E3 Varfolomeyevka Rus. Fed.
177 L5 Vârfuraşu, Vârful mt. Romania
177 L5 Vârfurile Romania
142 E2 Vårgårda Sweden
254 F4 Vargem r. Brazil
257 G4 Vargem Alta Brazil
254 E2 Vargem Grande Brazil
256 D4 Vargem Grande do Sul Brazil
257 E4 Varginha Brazil
142 A2 Varhaug Norway
177 J5 Variaş Romania
163 D5 Varilhes France
177 H2 Varín Slovakia
Varkana Iran see Gorgān
140 N3 Varkaus Fin.
169 E4 Varlosen (Niemetal) Ger.
142 E2 Värmland county Sweden
142 E2 Värmland reg. Sweden
197 H4 Varna Bulg.
114 B2 Varna r. India
191 G2 Varna Italy
120 E1 Varna Rus. Fed.
143 F3 Värnamo Sweden
142 E1 Värnäs Sweden
134 I4 Varnavino Rus. Fed.
138 D4 Varniai Lith.
Várnjárg pen. Norway see Varangerhalvøya
176 D1 Varnsdorf Czech Rep.
231 D5 Varnville SC U.S.A.
177 I5 Városföld Hungary
Varosha Cyprus see Varosia
128 A2 Varosia Cyprus
188 F3 Varoška Rijeka Bos.-Herz.
177 G4 Városlőd Hungary
140 N3 Varpaisjärvi Fin.
177 H4 Várpalota Hungary
168 D3 Varrel Ger.
162 C3 Vars Poitou-Charentes France
161 E4 Vars Provence-Alpes-Côte-d'Azur France
197 G2 Vârşag Romania
199 G3 Varsak Turkey
196 E2 Vărşand Romania
177 I3 Varsány Hungary
190 E4 Varsi Italy
164 F3 Varsseveld Neth.
143 G2 Vårsta Sweden
Vartashen Azer. see Oğuz
142 D2 Varteig Norway
198 B3 Vartholomio Greece
127 F3 Varto Turkey
197 F3 Vârtop Romania
129 C2 Varts'ikhe Georgia
140 O3 Värtsilä Fin.
137 G2 Varva Ukr.
137 I2 Varvarivka Kharkivs'ka Oblast' Ukr.
136 D2 Varvarivka Khmel'nyts'ka Oblast' Ukr.
137 J2 Varvarovka Rus. Fed.
177 L3 Vary Ukr.
136 C2 Varyazh Ukr.
254 F3 Várzea Alegre Brazil
257 E2 Várzea da Palma Brazil
254 E3 Várzea Grande Brazil
190 E4 Varzi Italy
190 D2 Varzo Italy
160 B1 Varzy France
176 F4 Vas county Hungary
Vasa Fin. see Vaasa
254 F4 Vasa Barris r. Brazil
177 I4 Vasad Hungary
114 B2 Vasai Mahar. India
138 E2 Vasalemma Estonia
138 E2 Vasalemma r. Estonia
193 E2 Vasanello Italy
177 H5 Vásárosdombó Hungary
177 L3 Vásárosnamény Hungary
184 C3 Vascão r. Port.
197 F2 Vaşcău Romania
134 I2 Vashka r. Rus. Fed.
136 C3 Vashkivtsi Ukr.
Vasht Iran see Khāsh
198 C1 Vasilika Greece
Vasilkov Ukr. see Vasyl'kiv
Vasilkovka Ukr. see Vasyl'kivka
134 I4 Vasil'sursk Rus. Fed.
136 E1 Vasilyevichy Belarus
135 H6 Vasil'yevka Rus. Fed.
139 J3 Vasil'yevskiy Mokh Rus. Fed.
136 E2 Vas'kovychi Ukr.
177 H5 Vaskút Hungary
162 B2 Vasles France
197 H2 Vaslui Romania
177 K3 Vasmegyer Hungary
227 F4 Vassar MI U.S.A.
141 K3 Vassbo Sweden
161 D4 Vassieux-en-Vercors France
162 D3 Vassivière, Lac de l. France
176 F4 Vas-Soproni-síkság hills Hungary
257 F5 Vassouras Brazil
159 F3 Vassy France
176 F4 Vasszécseny Hungary
Vastan Turkey see Gevaş
140 L3 Västana Sweden
138 D1 Västanfjärd Fin.
140 L2 Västansjö Sweden
143 G2 Västerås Sweden
140 K2 Västerbotten county Sweden
141 K3 Västerdalälven r. Sweden
140 L2 Västerfjäll Sweden
143 H2 Västerhaninge Sweden
140 L3 Västernorrland county Sweden
143 G3 Västervik Sweden
143 F2 Västmanland county Sweden
193 G2 Vasto Italy
168 F2 Vastorf Ger.
142 E2 Västra Ämtervik Sweden
142 E2 Västra Götaland county Sweden
140 M3 Västra Kvarken sea chan. Sweden
140 L2 Västra Ormsjö Sweden
176 F4 Vasvár Hungary
137 G3 Vasylivka Kirovohrads'ka Oblast' Ukr.
137 H2 Vasylivka Sums'ka Oblast' Ukr.
137 H4 Vasylivka Zaporiz'ka Oblast' Ukr.
136 F2 Vasyl'kiv Ukr.
137 I3 Vasyl'kivka Ukr.
175 M6 Vasyuchyn Ukr.
137 G3 Vasyutyntsi Ukr.
177 G4 Vaszar Hungary
177 L5 Vaţa de Jos Romania
162 D1 Vatan France
143 H3 Väte Gotland Sweden
Vaté i. Vanuatu see Éfaté
146 B4 Vaternish Point Scotland U.K.
146 A5 Vatersay i. Scotland U.K.
173 F3 Vaterstetten Ger.
Vathi Ionioi Nisoi Greece see Ithaki
Vathí Greece see Vathy
199 E3 Vathy Greece
193 E3 Vatican City Europe
195 E4 Vaticano, Capo c. Italy
Vaticano, Città del Europe see Vatican City
78 □6 Vatilau i. Solomon Is
Vatiu i. Cook Is see Atiu
140 □C2 Vatnajökull ice cap Iceland
140 I3 Vatne Norway
77 I3 Vatoa i. Fiji
213 □K3 Vatomandry Madag.
197 G2 Vatra Dornei Romania
177 J4 Vatta Hungary
Vätter, Lake Sweden see Vättern
143 F2 Vättern l. Sweden
143 G1 Vattholma Sweden
141 L3 Vattrång Sweden
79 □1a Vatukoula Viti Levu Fiji
79 □1 Vatulele i. Fiji
159 F2 Vaubadon France
157 F4 Vaubecourt France
156 D4 Vauchassis France
160 B1 Vauclaix France
161 D4 Vaucluse dept Provence-Alpes-Côte-d'Azur France
161 D5 Vaucluse, Monts de mts France
160 D1 Vauconcourt-Nervezain France
157 F4 Vaucouleurs France
190 B2 Vaud canton Switz.
157 G4 Vaudémont France
156 D4 Vaudeurs France
84 B4 Vaughan Springs N.T. Austr.
239 F5 Vaughn NM U.S.A.
160 C3 Vaugneray France
160 B1 Vault-de-Lugny France
160 C3 Vaulx-en-Velin France
160 D3 Vaulx-Milieu France
250 D4 Vaupés dept Col.
250 D4 Vaupés r. Col.
224 E2 Vauquelin r. Que. Can.
161 D5 Vauvenargues France
161 C5 Vauvert France
157 G5 Vauvillers France
157 F3 Vaux-devant-Damloup France
223 H5 Vauxhall Alta Can.
156 C4 Vaux-le-Pénil France
162 A3 Vaux-sur-Mer France
165 E5 Vaux-sur-Sûre Belgium
116 B4 Vav Gujarat India
213 □K3 Vavatenina Madag.
77 I3 Vava'u i. Tonga
79 □2 Vava'u Group is Tonga
157 F4 Vavincourt France
Vavitao i. Îs Australes Fr. Polynesia see Raivavae
206 D5 Vavoua Côte d'Ivoire
134 J4 Vavozh Rus. Fed.
114 D4 Vavuniya Sri Lanka
138 E5 Vawkavysk Belarus
138 E5 Vawkavyskaye Wzvyshsha hills Belarus
143 H2 Vaxholm Sweden
143 F3 Växjö Sweden
114 C3 Vayalpad Andhra Prad. India
Vayenga Rus. Fed. see Severomorsk
130 G2 Vaygach, Ostrov i. Rus. Fed.
114 C4 Vayittiri Kerala India
129 D4 Vayk' Armenia
162 D4 Vayrac France
162 C3 Vayres France
256 D2 Vazante Brazil
Vazáš Sweden see Vittangi
129 D3 Vazashen Armenia
177 I2 Važec Slovakia
139 J1 Vazhinka r. Rus. Fed.
129 D3 Vaziani Georgia
213 □J3 Vazobe mt. Madag.
139 J4 Vazuza r. Rus. Fed.
139 J4 Vazuzskoye Vodokhranilishche resr Rus. Fed.
176 D3 Včelná Czech Rep.
Veaikevárri Sweden see Svappavaara
160 C3 Veauche France
142 E4 Veberöd Sweden
140 M2 Vebomark Sweden
161 B4 Vebron France
190 F5 Vecchiano Italy
177 K3 Vechec Slovakia
169 F3 Vechelde Ger.
164 F2 Vecht r. Neth. alt. Vechte (Germany)
168 D3 Vechta Ger.
169 B3 Vechte r. Ger. alt. Vecht (Neth.)
182 E4 Vecinos Spain
169 F4 Veckenstedt Ger.
169 E4 Veckerhagen (Reinhardshagen) Ger.
177 I4 Vecsés Hungary
176 E2 Vectec hill Czech Rep.
138 E3 Vecumnieki Latvia
Vedana Rus. Fed. see Vedeno
114 C4 Vedaranniyam Tamil Nadu India
114 C4 Vedasandur Tamil Nadu India
142 E3 Veddige Sweden
197 G3 Vedea Argeş Romania
197 G4 Vedea Giurgiu Romania
197 G4 Vedea r. Romania
191 H3 Vedelago Italy
161 C5 Vedène France
129 E2 Vedeno Rus. Fed.
143 F2 Vedevåg Sweden
129 D4 Vedi Armenia
261 G4 Vedia Arg.
134 F3 Vedlozero Rus. Fed.
137 J3 Vedmezha r. Ukr.
182 B2 Vedra Spain
161 B3 Védrines-St-Loup France
136 F1 Vedrych r. Belarus
137 J2 Veduga r. Rus. Fed.
164 F1 Veendam Neth.
164 E2 Veenendaal Neth.
164 F1 Veenhuizen Neth.
168 C2 Veenhusen Ger.
164 F2 Veenoord Neth.
164 E1 Veenwouden Neth.
164 C3 Veere Neth.
168 E2 Veerse r. Ger.
140 K2 Vefsnfjord sea chan. Norway
140 J2 Vega i. Norway
237 C5 Vega TX U.S.A.
247 □1 Vega Alta Puerto Rico
247 □1 Vega Baja Puerto Rico
182 E2 Vegacervera Spain
182 D2 Vega de Espinareda Spain
182 C1 Vegadeo Spain
183 G1 Vega de Pas Spain
216 □3f Vega de San Mateo Gran Canaria Canary Is
182 E3 Vega de Tirados Spain
182 D2 Vega de Valcarce Spain
183 E3 Vega de Valdetronco Spain
183 G3 Veganzones Spain
182 D2 Vegarienza Spain
142 C2 Vegarshei Norway
183 E2 Vegas del Condado Spain
183 F4 Vegas de Matute Spain
164 E3 Veghel Neth.
195 G2 Veglie Italy
198 B1 Vegoritis, Limni l. Greece
159 F4 Vègre r. France
223 H4 Vegreville Alta Can.
252 A2 Végueta Peru
138 F1 Vehkalahti Fin.
170 D2 Vehlow Ger.
141 M3 Vehmaa Fin.
123 G4 Vehoa r. Pak.
159 G4 Veigné France
160 E2 Veigy-Foncenex France
169 F5 Veilsdorf Ger.
Veinticinco de Mayo Buenos Aires Arg. see 25 de Mayo
Veinticinco de Mayo La Pampa Arg. see 25 de Mayo
Veinticinco de Mayo Mendoza Arg. see 25 de Mayo
Veinticinco de Mayo Uru. see 25 de Mayo
184 C2 Veiros Port.
138 D4 Veisiejis Lith.
173 E2 Veitsbronn Ger.
179 G3 Veitsch Austria
179 G3 Veitsch mt. Austria
172 D2 Veitshöchheim Ger.
140 N2 Veitsiluoto Fin.
138 C4 Veiviržas r. Lith.
192 E2 Vejano Italy
142 C4 Vejen Denmark
184 E4 Vejer de la Frontera Spain
142 C4 Vejle Denmark
142 C4 Vejle county Denmark
173 H2 Vejprnice Czech Rep.
176 C1 Vejprty Czech Rep.
120 E5 Vekil'bazar Turkm.
116 C5 Velachha Gujarat India
183 F5 Velada Spain
188 F4 Vela Luka Croatia
183 H3 Velamazán Spain
216 □1c Velas São Jorge Azores
258 D3 Velasco, Sierra de mts Arg.
113 □1 Velassary i. S. Male Maldives
161 D5 Velaux France
258 G4 Velázquez Uru.
169 C4 Velbert Ger.
173 F2 Velburg Ger.
214 B5 Velddrif S. Africa
165 C3 Veldegem Belgium
173 F2 Velden Bayern Ger.
173 G3 Velden Bayern Ger.
165 F3 Velden Neth.
179 F4 Velden am Wörther See Austria
165 E3 Veldhoven Neth.
114 C3 Veldurti Andhra Prad. India
188 E3 Velebit mts Croatia
188 E3 Velebitski Kanal sea chan. Croatia
185 H3 Velefique Spain
197 H4 Veleka r. Bulg.
169 B4 Velen Ger.
177 H4 Velence Hungary
188 E2 Velenje Slovenia
197 E5 Veles Macedonia
196 D5 Velës, Mali i mt. Albania
176 D3 Velešín Czech Rep.
185 G3 Veleta, Pico mt. Spain
188 F4 Velež mts Bos.-Herz.
250 C3 Vélez Col.
185 H3 Vélez-Blanco Spain
185 G4 Vélez de Benaudalla Spain
185 F4 Vélez-Málaga Spain
185 H3 Vélez-Rubio Spain
170 D1 Velgast Ger.
256 D3 Velhas r. Minas Gerais Brazil
257 E2 Velhas r. Minas Gerais Brazil
Velibaba Turkey see Aras
135 I7 Velichayevskoye Rus. Fed.
136 C3 Velika Berezovytsya Ukr.
196 E4 Velika Drenova Srbija Yugo.
188 F3 Velika Gorica Croatia
136 C2 Velika Hlusha Ukr.
188 E3 Velika Kapela mts Croatia
188 E3 Velika Kladuša Bos.-Herz.
188 F3 Velika Mlaka Croatia
176 G6 Velika Pisanica Croatia
196 E3 Velika Plana Srbija Yugo.
179 F4 Velika Rogatec mt. Slovenia
134 J4 Velikaya Rus. Fed.
134 J4 Velikaya r. Rus. Fed.
131 S3 Velikaya r. Rus. Fed.
138 G3 Velikaya r. Rus. Fed.
134 F3 Velikaya Guba Rus. Fed.
100 F3 Velikaya Kema Rus. Fed.
Velikaya Novoselka Ukr. see Velyka Novosilka
188 F4 Veliki Drvenik i. Croatia
176 G6 Veliki Grđevac Croatia
196 E4 Veliki Jastrebac mts Yugo.
136 C3 Veliki Kunynets' Ukr.
197 H4 Veliki Preslav Bulg.
188 E3 Veliki Risnjak mt. Croatia
197 E4 Veliki Šiljegovac Srbija Yugo.
197 F4 Veliki Strešer mt. Yugo.
196 E3 Veliki Šturac mt. Yugo.
139 H3 Velikiye Luki Rus. Fed.
137 F2 Velikiy Lystven Ukr.
136 B3 Velikiy Lyubin' Ukr.
139 H2 Velikiy Novgorod Rus. Fed.
134 I3 Velikiy Ustyug Rus. Fed.
137 K2 Velikoarkhangel'skoye Rus. Fed.
139 M4 Velikodvorskiy Rus. Fed.
137 I2 Velikomikhaylovka Rus. Fed.
114 C3 Velikonda Range hills India
139 I3 Velikooktyabr'skiy Rus. Fed.
176 F6 Veliko Trojstvo Croatia
197 G4 Veliko Tŭrnovo Bulg.
129 C3 Veliköy Turkey
139 K2 Velikoye Vologod. Obl. Rus. Fed.
139 L3 Velikoye Yaroslavskaya Oblast' Rus. Fed.
139 M4 Velikoye, Ozero l. Rus. Fed.
186 D3 Velilla de Cinca Spain
186 C3 Velilla de Ebro Spain
Velilla de Guardo Spain see Velilla del Río Carrión
183 F2 Velilla del Río Carrión Spain
185 G3 Velillas r. Spain
188 E3 Veli Lošinj Croatia
196 D4 Velimlje Crna Gora Yugo.
163 C4 Vélines France
206 B3 Vélingara Senegal
197 G4 Velingrad Bulg.
193 E2 Velino r. Italy
193 F2 Velino, Monte mt. Italy
139 H4 Velizh Rus. Fed.
176 F2 Velká Bíteš Czech Rep.
176 D1 Velká Dobrá Czech Rep.
177 K2 Veľká Domaša, Vodná nádrž resr Slovakia
177 H3 Veľká Fatra mts Slovakia
176 G2 Velká Haná r. Czech Rep.
173 G2 Velká Hleďsebe Czech Rep.
177 G3 Velká Javořina hill Czech Rep./Slovakia
177 K2 Veľká Javořina mt. Slovakia
177 H3 Veľká Lehota Slovakia
177 H2 Veľká Lúka mt. Slovakia
177 H2 Veľká Polom Czech Rep.
Veľká Rača mt. Pol./Slovakia see Wielka Racza
176 F3 Velké Bílovice Czech Rep.
171 F5 Velké Březno Czech Rep.
177 L3 Veľké Kapušany Slovakia
177 H2 Velké Karlovice Czech Rep.
179 I2 Veľké Leváre Slovakia
176 G1 Velké Losiny Czech Rep.
177 H3 Veľké Lovce Slovakia
177 H4 Veľké Ludince Slovakia
176 F2 Velké Meziříčí Czech Rep.
176 F3 Velké Němčice Czech Rep.
176 F3 Velké Pavlovice Czech Rep.
177 G3 Veľké Rípňany Slovakia
177 L3 Veľké Trakany Slovakia
177 H3 Veľké Uherce Slovakia
138 C1 Velkua Fin.
177 J3 Veľký Blh Slovakia
177 H3 Veľký Ďur Slovakia
177 H2 Veľký Javorník mt. Slovakia
177 I2 Veľký Kriváň mt. Slovakia
177 I3 Veľký Krtíš Slovakia
177 H3 Veľký Kýr Slovakia
177 G3 Veľký Lopeník hill Czech Rep.
177 G4 Veľký Meder Slovakia
177 K2 Veľký Šariš Slovakia
177 H3 Veľký Tribeč hill Slovakia
176 G2 Velký Týnec Czech Rep.
176 B2 Velký Zvon hill Czech Rep.
179 F4 Vellach r. Austria
168 F2 Vellahn Ger.
78 □6 Vella Lavella i. New Georgia Is Solomon Is
114 C4 Vellar r. India
172 D2 Vellberg Ger.
193 E3 Velletri Italy
160 E1 Vellevans France
160 D1 Vellexon-Queutrey-et-Vaudey France
142 E4 Vellinge Sweden
183 H4 Vellisca Spain
169 E4 Vellmar Ger.
114 C3 Vellore Tamil Nadu India
186 D2 Vellos r. Spain
131 K3 Vel'mo r. Rus. Fed.
198 C3 Velo Peloponnisos Greece
157 F3 Velosnes France
165 E4 Velp r. Belgium
164 E3 Velp Neth.
169 F3 Velpke Ger.
134 H3 Vel'sk Rus. Fed.
Velsuna Italy see Orvieto
170 E3 Velten Ger.
169 F3 Veltheim (Ohe) Ger.
176 D1 Veltrusy Czech Rep.
191 G2 Velturno Italy
164 E2 Veluwemeer l. Neth.
236 C1 Velva ND U.S.A.
176 D1 Velvary Czech Rep.
198 C1 Velvendos Greece
139 I3 Vel'ye, Ozero l. Rus. Fed.
137 G3 Velyka Andrusivka Ukr.
137 I3 Velyka Babka Ukr.
137 G3 Velyka Bahachka Ukr.
137 H4 Velyka Bilozerka Ukr.
137 H4 Velyka Bilozerka r. Ukr.
137 G3 Velyka Burimka Ukr.
136 F2 Velyka Dymerka Ukr.
175 L6 Velyka Horozhanna Ukr.
136 E3 Velyka Kisnytsya Ukr.
137 I3 Velyka Komyshuvakha Ukr.
177 M3 Velyka Kopanya Ukr.
137 F4 Velyka Korenykha Ukr.
137 G4 Velyka Kostromka Ukr.
137 G4 Velyka Lepetykha Ukr.
136 E4 Velyka Mykhaylivka Ukr.
137 I4 Velyka Novosilka Ukr.
137 G4 Velyka Oleksandrivka Ukr.
137 H2 Velyka Pysarivka Ukr.
137 H3 Velyka Rublivka Ukr.
136 D2 Velyka Tsvilya Ukr.
137 F3 Velyka Vys' r. Ukr.
137 F3 Velyka Vyska Ukr.
137 H4 Velyka Znam"yanka Ukr.
177 L3 Velyki Kom"yaty Ukr.
137 G4 Velyki Kopani Ukr.
136 E3 Velyki Korovyntsi Ukr.
137 G3 Velyki Krynky Ukr.
177 L3 Velyki Luchky Ukr.
136 C2 Velyki Mosty Ukr.
137 G2 Velyki Sorochyntsi Ukr.
137 G3 Velykiy Khutir Ukr.
136 F4 Velykiy Kuyal'nyk r. Ukr.
137 G2 Velykiy Sambir Ukr.
136 F4 Velykodolyns'ke Ukr.
137 I4 Velykomykhaylivka Ukr.
137 H3 Velykooleksandrivka Ukr.
137 F4 Velykoserbulivka Ukr.
136 B3 Velykyy Bereznyy Ukr.
137 I2 Velykyy Burluk Ukr.
136 C4 Velykyy Bychkiv Ukr.
Velykyy Tokmak Ukr. see Tokmak
134 K3 Vel'yu r. Rus. Fed.
114 C2 Vemalwada Andhra Prad. India
264 J8 Vema Seamount sea feature S. Atlantic Ocean
265 I5 Vema Trench sea feature Indian Ocean
177 H5 Véménd Hungary
100 G3 Vemor'ye Sakhalin Rus. Fed.
114 C3 Vempalle Andhra Prad. India
192 B2 Venaco Corse France
245 E3 Venados r. Mex.
261 G3 Venado Tuerto Arg.
193 G3 Venafro Italy
251 F3 Venamo r. Guyana/Venez.
251 F3 Venamo, Cerro mt. Venez.
158 E5 Venansault France
160 C1 Venarey-les-Laumes France
190 C3 Venaria Italy
193 F2 Venarotta Italy
161 F4 Venasca Italy
161 F5 Vence France
256 C5 Venceslau Bráz Brazil
138 E4 Venciūnai Lith.
191 G3 Venda, Monte hill Italy
184 A2 Venda do Pinheiro Port.
257 G4 Venda Nova Brazil
182 C3 Venda Nova, Barragem de resr Port.
161 B5 Vendargues France
184 B2 Vendas de Azeitão Port.
184 B2 Vendas Novas Port.
160 B2 Vendat France
162 A3 Vendays-Montalivet France
158 E5 Vendée dept Pays de la Loire France
162 B2 Vendée r. France
157 H4 Vendenheim France
159 G5 Vendeuvre-du-Poitou France
156 E4 Vendeuvre-sur-Barse France
184 C2 Vendinha Port.
159 H5 Vendœuvres France
156 B5 Vendôme France
184 D2 Vendoval r. Spain
Vendrell Spain see El Vendrell
136 D3 Vendychany Ukr.
244 D2 Venegas Mex.
161 D5 Venelles France
163 E5 Vénès France
191 H3 Veneta, Laguna lag. Italy
Venetia Italy see Venezia
191 G3 Veneto admin. reg. Italy
139 L4 Venev Rus. Fed.
191 H3 Venezia Italy
191 H3 Venezia prov. Veneto Italy
Venezia, Golfo di g. Europe see Venice, Gulf of
251 E3 Venezuela country S. America
250 D2 Venezuela, Golfo de g. Venez.
264 E4 Venezuelan Basin sea feature S. Atlantic Ocean
114 B3 Vengurla Mahar. India
164 E2 Venhuizen Neth.
182 E3 Venialbo Spain
220 C4 Veniaminof Volcano AK U.S.A.
Venice Italy see Venezia
231 D7 Venice FL U.S.A.
237 F6 Venice LA U.S.A.
188 D3 Venice, Gulf of Europe
190 E2 Venina r. Italy
160 C3 Vénissieux France
156 D3 Venizel France
141 K3 Venjan Sweden
114 C3 Venkatagiri Andhra Prad. India
114 D2 Venkatapuram Andhra Prad. India
165 F3 Venlo Neth.
142 B2 Vennesla Norway
193 H4 Venosa Italy
193 H3 Venosa r. Italy
191 F2 Venosta, Val val. Italy
156 D5 Venoy France
164 E3 Venray Neth.
79 □3 Vent, Îles du is Arch. de la Société Fr. Polynesia
138 D3 Venta r. Latvia/Lith.
138 D3 Venta Lith.
161 D5 Ventabren France
161 F5 Ventabren, Mont mt. France
183 F3 Venta de Baños Spain
182 E1 Venta de las Ranas Spain
185 F2 Venta del Charco Spain
187 B5 Venta del Moro Spain
185 G2 Venta de los Santos Spain
182 D1 Venta Nueva Spain
185 G3 Ventas de Huelma Spain
185 F4 Ventas de Zafarraya Spain
161 D4 Ventavon France
215 F3 Ventersburg S. Africa
215 F2 Ventersdorp S. Africa
215 F2 Venterskroon S. Africa
215 E4 Venterstad S. Africa
161 B4 Venteuges France
190 C5 Ventimiglia Italy
192 B3 Ventiseri Corse France
259 C6 Ventisquero mt. Arg.
151 F4 Ventnor Isle of Wight, England U.K.
235 D3 Ventnor City NJ U.S.A.
193 F4 Ventotene, Isola i. Italy
161 D4 Ventoux, Mont mt. France
170 C2 Ventschow Ger.
138 C3 Ventspils Latvia
251 E3 Ventuari r. Venez.
240 H4 Ventura CA U.S.A.
83 F4 Venus Bay Vic. Austr.
Venusia Italy see Venosa
244 C4 Venustiano Mex.
245 F3 Venustiano Carranza Puebla Mex.
243 E3 Venustiano Carranza, Presa resr Mex.
192 B2 Venzolasca Corse France
191 I2 Venzone Italy
176 F4 Vép Hungary
137 H2 Vepryk Ukr.
139 J1 Vepsovskaya Vozvyshennost' hills Rus. Fed.
258 E3 Vera Arg.
185 I3 Vera Spain
256 C5 Vera Cruz Brazil
245 F4 Veracruz Mex.
Vera Cruz Mex. see Veracruz
245 F3 Veracruz state Mex.
184 C2 Vera Cruz Port.
234 C2 Vera Cruz PA U.S.A.
186 B1 Vera de Bidasoa Spain
186 C2 Veral r. Spain
255 C9 Veranópolis Brazil
116 B5 Veraval Gujarat India
136 C2 Verba Rivnens'ka Oblast' Ukr.
136 C2 Verba Volyns'ka Oblast' Ukr.
190 D3 Verbania Italy
235 E1 Verbank NY U.S.A.
190 D2 Verbano-Cusio-Ossola prov. Piemonte Italy
156 C3 Verberie France
193 H5 Verbicaro Italy
190 C2 Verbier Switz.
139 K3 Verbilki Rus. Fed.
137 G3 Verblyuzhka Ukr.
137 H4 Verbove Ukr.
136 C3 Verbovets' Ukr.
135 H5 Verbovskiy Rus. Fed.
190 E2 Verceia Italy
190 D3 Vercelli Italy
190 D3 Vercelli prov. Piemonte Italy
160 E1 Vercel-Villedieu-le-Camp France
170 D2 Verchen Ger.
161 D4 Vercors reg. France
Vercovicium tourist site England U.K. see Housesteads
179 F5 Verd Slovenia
139 M5 Verda r. Rus. Fed.
161 E4 Verdaches France
140 J3 Verdalsøra Norway
259 D6 Verde r. Arg.
256 B3 Verde r. Goiás Brazil
256 D3 Verde r. Goiás/Minas Gerais Brazil
256 B4 Verde r. Mato Grosso do Sul Brazil
256 B3 Verde r. Minas Gerais Brazil
256 C3 Verde r. Minas Gerais Brazil
257 E4 Verde r. Minas Gerais Brazil
254 E4 Verde r. Bahia Brazil
253 F3 Verde r. Mato Grosso Brazil
253 G2 Verde r. Mato Grosso Brazil
244 C3 Verde r. Aguascalientes/Jalisco Mex.
242 D3 Verde r. Chihuahua/Durango Mex.
245 E5 Verde r. Guerrero/Oaxaca Mex.
245 F6 Verde r. Oaxaca Mex.
245 E3 Verde r. San Luis Potosí Mex.
253 F5 Verde r. Para.
185 G3 Verde r. Spain
185 G4 Verde r. Spain
241 L5 Verde r. AZ U.S.A.
Verde, Cabo c. Senegal see Vert, Cap
261 F6 Verde, Península pen. Arg.
257 F1 Verde Grande r. Brazil
168 E3 Verden (Aller) Ger.
254 E5 Verde Pequeno r. Brazil
240 H2 Verdi NV U.S.A.
237 E5 Verdigris r. KS U.S.A.
198 B2 Verdikoussa Greece
256 B2 Verdinho r. Brazil
256 B3 Verdinho, Serra do mts Brazil
161 D5 Verdon r. France
182 B2 Verdugo r. Spain
157 F3 Verdun France
163 D5 Verdun-sur-Garonne France
160 D2 Verdun-sur-le-Doubs France
194 C5 Verdura r. Sicilia Italy
215 F2 Vereeniging S. Africa
137 G3 Veremiyivka Ukr.
215 G1 Verena S. Africa
177 I4 Veresegyház Hungary
134 K4 Vereshchagino Rus. Fed.
137 F2 Veresoch Ukr.
139 K3 Verestovo, Ozero l. Rus. Fed.
139 K4 Vereya Rus. Fed.
163 D4 Verfeil Midi-Pyrénées France
163 D5 Verfeil Midi-Pyrénées France
Vergara Spain see Bergara
258 G4 Vergara Uru.
191 G4 Vergato Italy
157 G4 Vergaville France
187 D6 Vergel Spain
214 E1 Vergeleë S. Africa
233 G2 Vergennes VT U.S.A.
186 G2 Verges Spain
161 C5 Vergèze France
191 H5 Verghereto Italy
156 D5 Vergigny France
198 C1 Vergina Greece
161 B3 Vergongheon France
162 C3 Vergt France
137 G3 Verhuny Cherkas'ka Oblast' Ukr.
137 G3 Verhuny Poltavs'ka Oblast' Ukr.
Véria Greece see Veroia
182 C3 Verín Spain
172 D3 Veringenstadt Ger.
Verin T'alin Armenia see T'alin
256 C3 Veríssimo Brazil
Veríssimo Sarmento Angola see Camissombo
215 F3 Verkeerdevlei S. Africa
137 H3 Verkhivtseve Ukr.
120 D1 Verkhne-Avzyan Rus. Fed.
137 I5 Verkhnebakanskiy Rus. Fed.
121 J2 Verkhne-berezovskiy Kazakh.
Verkhnedneprovsk Ukr. see Verkhn'odniprovs'k
139 I4 Verkhnedneprovskiy Rus. Fed.
130 J3 Verkhneimbatsk Rus. Fed.
134 L2 Verkhnekolvinsk Rus. Fed.
139 J4 Verkhneruzskoye Vodokhranilishche resr Rus. Fed.
134 I4 Verkhnespasskoye Rus. Fed.
140 O1 Verkhnetulomskiy Rus. Fed.
140 O1 Verkhnetulomskoye Vodokhranilishche resr Rus. Fed.
137 J2 Verkhneturovo Rus. Fed.
120 D1 Verkhneural'sk Rus. Fed.
131 N3 Verkhnevilyuysk Rus. Fed.
139 I3 Verkhnevolzhskoye Vodokhranilishche resr Rus. Fed.
134 K5 Verkhneyarkeyevo Rus. Fed.
131 Q3 Verkhniy At-Uryakh Rus. Fed.
135 I6 Verkhniy Baskunchak Rus. Fed.
137 I3 Verkhniy Byshkyn Ukr.
129 D2 Verkhniye Achaluki Rus. Fed.
Verkhniye Kholokhory Moldova see Halahora de Sus
129 D2 Verkhniy Fiagdon Rus. Fed.
Verkhniy Karabulag Georgia see Zemo Qarabulakhi
139 L5 Verkhniy Lomovets Rus. Fed.
135 H6 Verkhniy Mamon Rus. Fed.
Verkhniy Naur Rus. Fed. see Lakkha-Nevre
137 H4 Verkhniy Rohachyk Ukr.
107 F1 Verkhniy Shergol'dzhin Rus. Fed.
134 K4 Verkhniy Tatyshly Rus. Fed.
137 I4 Verkhniytokmak Ukr.
137 H3 Verkhn'odniprovs'k Ukr.
136 F3 Verkhnyachka Ukr.
175 M6 Verkhnya Lypytsya Ukr.
137 H2 Verkhnya Syrovatka Ukr.
137 H3 Verkhnya Tersa r. Ukr.
136 B3 Verkhnya Vysots'ke Ukr.
177 L3 Verkhnya Vyznytsya Ukr.
129 C2 Verkhnyaya Balkariya Rus. Fed.
177 L2 Verkhnya Yablun'ka Ukr.
137 I2 Verkhnyaya Grayvoronka Rus. Fed.
134 M2 Verkhnyaya Inta Rus. Fed.
135 G6 Verkhnyaya Khava Rus. Fed.
129 C2 Verkhnyaya Mara Rus. Fed.
131 K2 Verkhnyaya Taymyra r. Rus. Fed.
129 B2 Verkhnyaya Teberda Rus. Fed.
137 K2 Verkhnyaya Tishanka Rus. Fed.
137 K2 Verkhnyaya Toyda Rus. Fed.
134 I3 Verkhnyaya Toyma Rus. Fed.
139 K3 Verkhnyaya Troitsa Rus. Fed.
Verkhnyaya Tunguska r. Rus. Fed. see Angara
136 B3 Verkhnye Syn'ovydne Ukr.
134 J4 Verkhoshizhem'ye Rus. Fed.
139 N1 Verkhovazh'ye Rus. Fed.
Verkhovina Ukr. see Verkhovyna
139 K5 Verkhov'ye Rus. Fed.
136 C3 Verkhovyna Ukr.
131 N2 Verkhoyanskiy Khrebet mts Rus. Fed.
121 J2 Verkhuba Kazakh.
138 E4 Verknė r. Lith.
215 G2 Verkykerskop S. Africa
169 D4 Verl Ger.
165 E4 Verlaine Belgium
214 C6 Vermaaklikheid S. Africa
156 D3 Vermand France
256 B5 Vermelha, Serra hills Brazil
253 H3 Vermelho r. Mato Grosso Brazil
254 C3 Vermelho r. Pará Brazil
254 D3 Vermelho r. Tocantins Brazil
156 D5 Vermenton France
197 E3 Vermeş Romania
191 F2 Vermiglio Italy
223 I4 Vermilion Alta Can.
232 B4 Vermilion OH U.S.A.
226 C5 Vermilion r. IL U.S.A.
241 K3 Vermilion Cliffs esc. AZ U.S.A.
241 K3 Vermilion Cliffs esc. UT U.S.A.
226 A2 Vermilion Range hills MN U.S.A.
236 D3 Vermillion SD U.S.A.
236 D3 Vermillion r. SD U.S.A.
236 D3 Vermillion, East Fork r. SD U.S.A.
223 M5 Vermillion Bay Ont. Can.
230 F2 Vermillon r. Que. Can.
182 D4 Vermiosa Port.
182 B5 Vermoil Port.
233 G2 Vermont state U.S.A.
262 T2 Vernadsky research stn Antarctica
163 D6 Vernajoul France
238 E3 Vernal UT U.S.A.
190 C4 Vernante Italy
159 G4 Vernantes France
190 C2 Vernayaz Switz.
159 F4 Vern-d'Anjou France
224 D4 Verner Ont. Can.
176 D1 Verneřice Czech Rep.
163 D5 Vernet France
163 E6 Vernet-les-Bains France
159 G3 Verneuil-sur-Avre France
162 D3 Verneuil-sur-Vienne France
214 C3 Verneuk Pan salt pan S. Africa
190 B2 Vernier Switz.
191 G4 Vernio Italy
163 D5 Verniolle France
195 H2 Vernole Italy
222 G5 Vernon B.C. Can.
156 B3 Vernon France
237 F5 Vernon AL U.S.A.
230 C4 Vernon IN U.S.A.
235 D1 Vernon NJ U.S.A.
237 D5 Vernon TX U.S.A.
241 K1 Vernon UT U.S.A.
87 C5 Vernon, Mount hill W.A. Austr.
84 B2 Vernon Islands N.T. Austr.
156 B4 Vernouillet France
161 C4 Vernoux-en-Vivarais France
234 D2 Vernoy NJ U.S.A.
100 D2 Vernoye Rus. Fed.
158 E3 Vern-sur-Seiche France
157 G3 Verny France
Vernyy Kazakh. see Almaty
192 A2 Vero Corse France
186 D3 Vero r. Spain
231 D7 Vero Beach FL U.S.A.
177 I4 Verőcemaros Hungary
198 C1 Veroia Greece
190 F3 Verolanuova Italy
193 F3 Veroli Italy
156 D4 Véron France
191 F3 Verona Italy
191 G3 Verona prov. Veneto Italy
232 D5 Verona VA U.S.A.
226 C4 Verona WI U.S.A.
261 I4 Verónica Arg.
160 C2 Verosvres France
177 J4 Verpelét Hungary
235 E1 Verplanck NY U.S.A.
82 D3 Verran S.A. Austr.
190 C3 Verres Italy
162 C2 Verrières France
193 G3 Verrino r. Italy
190 D4 Versa r. Italy
190 E3 Versa r. Italy
191 I3 Versa r. Italy
156 C4 Versailles France
230 C4 Versailles IN U.S.A.
230 C4 Versailles KY U.S.A.
236 E4 Versailles MO U.S.A.
232 A4 Versailles OH U.S.A.
252 E3 Versalles Bol.
Versec Vojvodina, Srbija Yugo. see Vršac
138 E4 Verseka r. Lith.
160 D2 Vers-en-Montage France
169 D3 Versmold Ger.
190 B2 Versoix Switz.
161 A5 Versols-et-Lapeyre France
159 F2 Verson France
161 C5 Vers-Pont-du-Gard France
163 B4 Vert France
163 D4 Vert r. France
206 A3 Vert, Cap c. Senegal
160 B3 Vertaizon France
162 C3 Verteillac France
254 C4 Vertentes r. Brazil
177 H4 Vértesacsa Hungary
177 H4 Vértesboglár Hungary
163 C4 Verteuil-d'Agenais France
162 C3 Verteuil-sur-Charente France
162 B3 Vertheuil France
246 C2 Vertientes Cuba
137 F2 Vertiyivka Ukr.
156 B2 Verton France
191 F2 Vertona, Cima mt. Italy
158 E4 Vertou France
156 E4 Vertus France
191 H5 Verucchio Italy
215 H3 Verulam S. Africa
Verulamium Hertfordshire, England U.K. see St Albans
165 E4 Verviers Belgium
156 D3 Vervins France
Verwoerdburg S. Africa see Centurion
223 J5 Verwood Sask. Can.
151 F4 Verwood Dorset, England U.K.
Veryína Greece see Vergina
159 F4 Verzée r. France
156 E3 Verzenay France
195 F3 Verzino Italy
190 C4 Verzuolo Italy
156 E3 Verzy France
140 N3 Vesanto Fin.
192 B2 Vescovato Corse France
190 F3 Vescovato Italy
165 E4 Vesdre r. Belgium
176 G5 Vése Hungary
137 H4 Vesele Ukr.
197 G4 Veselina r. Bulg.
176 D2 Veselí nad Lužnicí Czech Rep.
176 G3 Veselí nad Moravou Czech Rep.
136 E2 Veselivka Ukr.
137 J4 Veselo-Voznesenka Rus. Fed.
121 J2 Veseloyarsk Rus. Fed.
137 J2 Veseloye Rus. Fed.
137 F2 Veselynivka Ukr.
137 F4 Veselynove Ukr.
135 H7 Veselyy Rus. Fed.
120 F1 Veselyy Podol Kazakh.
156 B4 Vesgre r. France
135 H6 Veshenskaya Rus. Fed.
190 D4 Vesime Italy
156 D3 Vesle r. France
134 K3 Veslyana r. Rus. Fed.
Vesontio France see Besançon
160 E1 Vesoul France
190 D3 Vespolate Italy
165 E3 Vessem Neth.
142 B2 Vest-Agder county Norway
140 K1 Vesterålen is Norway
140 K1 Vesterålsfjorden sea chan. Norway
168 G1 Vesterby Denmark
168 E1 Vester Sottrup Denmark
140 □B2 Vestfirðir constituency Iceland
142 C2 Vestfjorddalen val. Norway
140 K2 Vestfjorden sea chan. Norway
142 D2 Vestfold county Norway
263 F2 Vestfold Hills Antarctica
140 □ Vestfonna ice cap Svalbard
144 D1 Vestmanna Faroe Is
140 □B3 Vestmannaeyjar is Iceland
140 I3 Vestnes Norway
190 F3 Vestone Italy
142 D4 Vestsjælland county Denmark
140 □B2 Vesturland constituency Iceland
140 K1 Vestvågøy i. Norway
161 F5 Vésubie r. France
193 G4 Vesuvio vol. Italy
Vesuvius vol. Italy see Vesuvio
139 K2 Ves'yegonsk Rus. Fed.
176 G4 Veszkény Hungary
177 G4 Veszprém Hungary
176 G4 Veszprém county Hungary
177 G4 Veszprémvarsány Hungary
177 K5 Vésztő Hungary
215 E2 Vet r. S. Africa
79 □1 Vetauua i. Fiji
140 M3 Veteli Fin.
223 I4 Veteran Alta Can.
196 D3 Veternik Vojvodina, Srbija Yugo.
156 B3 Vétheuil France
177 L4 Vetiş Romania
143 F3 Vetlanda Sweden

Vinné to Wajima
377

177 K3 Vinné Slovakia
138 F2 Vinni Estonia
172 B2 Vinningen Ger.
Vinnitsa Ukr. see Vinnytsya
Vinnitsa Oblast admin. div. Ukr. see Vinnyts'ka Oblast'
Vinnitskaya Oblast' admin. div. Ukr. see Vinnyts'ka Oblast'
139 J1 Vinnitsy Rus. Fed.
136 D3 Vinnyts'ka Oblast' admin. div. Ukr.
136 E3 Vinnytsya Ukr.
Vinnytsya Oblast admin. div. Ukr. see Vinnyts'ka Oblast'
177 H3 Vinodol Slovakia
Vinogradov Ukr. see Vynohradiv
177 G3 Vinohrady nad Váhom Slovakia
161 D5 Vinon-sur-Verdon France
161 D4 Vinsobres France
262 S1 Vinson Massif mt. Antarctica
141 J3 Vinstra Norway
92 B2 Vintar Phil.
236 E3 Vinton IA U.S.A.
183 G4 Viñuelas Spain
183 H3 Vinuesa Spain
114 C2 Vinukonda Andhra Prad. India
209 B5 Vinza Congo
170 C3 Vinzelberg Ger.
168 E1 Viöl Ger.
160 C3 Violay France
161 C4 Violès France
Violeta Cuba see Primero de Enero
161 B5 Viols-le-Fort France
214 A3 Vioolsdrif S. Africa
156 C3 Viosne r. France
179 E5 Vipava Slovenia
179 E5 Vipava r. Slovenia
211 B8 Viphya Mountains Malawi
191 G2 Vipiteno Italy
170 D2 Vipperow Ger.
188 E3 Vir i. Croatia
179 F4 Vir Slovenia
92 C3 Virac Phil.
256 C4 Viradouro Brazil
116 C5 Viramgam Gujarat India
127 E3 Viranşehir Turkey
114 B3 Virarajendrapet Karnataka India
163 C4 Virazeil France
138 D3 Vircava r. Latvia/Lith.
86 C4 Virchow, Mount hill W.A. Austr.
223 K5 Virden Man. Can.
159 F3 Vire France
159 E2 Vire r. France
209 B8 Virei Angola
156 E2 Vireux-Molhain France
156 E2 Vireux-Wallerand France
156 E4 Virey-sous-Bar France
197 E2 Vîrful Highiş hill Romania
257 F2 Virgem da Lapa Brazil
178 D3 Virgen Austria
232 D6 Virgilina VA U.S.A.
241 J3 Virgin r. AZ U.S.A.
227 H1 Virginatown Ont. Can.
247 F3 Virgin Gorda i. Virgin Is (U.K.)
147 D3 Virginia Rep. of Ireland
215 F3 Virginia S. Africa
226 A2 Virginia MN U.S.A.
232 D6 Virginia state U.S.A.
233 F6 Virginia Beach VA U.S.A.
238 E2 Virginia City MT U.S.A.
240 H2 Virginia City NV U.S.A.
151 G3 Virginia Water Surrey, England U.K.
247 F3 Virgin Islands (U.K.) terr. West Indies
247 F3 Virgin Islands (U.S.A.) terr. West Indies
241 J3 Virgin Mountains AZ U.S.A.
257 F3 Virginópolis Brazil
160 D2 Viriat France
160 D3 Virieu France
160 D3 Virieu-le-Grand France
160 C3 Virigneux France
160 D3 Virignin France
161 D3 Viriville France
188 F2 Virje Croatia
138 E1 Virkkala Fin.
97 D4 Virôchey Cambodia
165 D4 Viroin r. Belgium
141 N3 Virolahti Fin.
226 B4 Viroqua WI U.S.A.
188 F3 Virovitica Croatia
141 M3 Virrat Fin.
143 F3 Virserum Sweden
165 E5 Virton Belgium
252 A2 Virú Peru
114 C4 Virudunagar Tamil Nadu India
138 D3 Virvytė r. Lith.
160 D2 Viry Franche-Comté France
160 E2 Viry Rhône-Alpes France
156 D3 Viry-Noureuil France
188 F4 Vis Croatia
188 F4 Vis i. Croatia
138 F4 Visaginas Lith.
Visakhapatnam Andhra Prad. India see Vishakhapatnam
240 H3 Visalia CA U.S.A.
161 C4 Visan France
197 H3 Vişani Romania
114 B2 Visapur Mahar. India
116 B5 Visavadar Gujarat India
92 B4 Visayan Sea Phil.
168 D3 Visbek Ger.
168 D1 Visby Denmark
143 H3 Visby Gotland Sweden
257 F4 Visconde do Rio Branco Brazil
221 G2 Viscount Melville Sound sea chan. N.W.T./Nunavut Can.
165 E4 Visé Belgium
188 G4 Višegrad Bos.-Herz.
191 H4 Viserba Italy
254 D2 Viseu Brazil
182 C4 Viseu Port.
182 C4 Viseu admin. dist. Port.
197 G2 Vişeu r. Romania
197 G2 Vişeu de Sus Romania
191 J3 Viševica mt. Croatia
115 D2 Vishakhapatnam Andhra Prad. India
197 H5 Vishegrad hill Bulg.
134 K3 Vishera r. Rus. Fed.
134 L4 Vishera r. Rus. Fed.
139 H2 Vishera r. Rus. Fed.
121 H2 Vishnevka Kazakh.
135 H5 Vishnevoye Rus. Fed.
Vishnevoye Dnipropetrovs'ka Oblast' Ukr. see Vyshneve
186 B4 Visiedo Spain
197 G3 Vişina Romania
143 F2 Visingsö i. Sweden
142 E3 Viskan r. Sweden
138 F3 Višķi Latvia
188 F4 Viški Kanal sea chan. Croatia
143 F3 Vislanda Sweden
116 C5 Visnagar Gujarat India
171 G5 Višňová Czech Rep.
176 F3 Višňové Czech Rep.
177 H2 Višňové Slovakia
190 C4 Viso, Monte mt. Italy
185 G2 Viso del Marqués Spain
188 G4 Visoko Bos.-Herz.
190 D4 Visone Italy
177 J4 Visonta Hungary
190 C2 Visp Switz.
215 E4 Visrivier S. Africa
161 B3 Vissac-Auteyrac France
114 D2 Vissannapeta Andhra Prad. India
143 F3 Visselfjärda Sweden
168 E3 Visselhövede Ger.
193 F2 Visso Italy
190 C2 Vissoie Switz.
240 I5 Vista CA U.S.A.
235 E1 Vista NY U.S.A.
187 C4 Vistabella del Maestrazgo Spain
260 C3 Vista Flores Arg.
Vistula r. Pol. see Wisła
137 G4 Visun' r. Ukr.
177 J4 Visznek Hungary
197 G4 Vit r. Bulg.
250 E3 Vita r. Col.
194 B5 Vita Sicilia Italy
196 D4 Vitao mt. Yugo.
177 J3 Vítaz Slovakia
Vitebsk Belarus see Vitsyebsk
Vitebskaya Oblast' admin. div. Belarus see Vitsyebskaya Voblasts'
Vitebsk Oblast admin. div. Belarus see Vitsyebskaya Voblasts'
192 E2 Viterbo Italy
192 D2 Viterbo prov. Lazio Italy
157 G4 Viterne France
188 F3 Vitez Bos.-Herz.
252 D5 Vitichi Bol.
182 D3 Vitigudino Spain
79 □1a Viti Levu i. Fiji
99 K1 Vitim r. Rus. Fed.
99 J1 Vitimskoye Ploskogor'ye plat. Rus. Fed.
196 E4 Vitina Kosovo, Srbija Yugo.
179 G2 Vitis Austria
177 G2 Vítkov Czech Rep.
179 H3 Vitnyéd Hungary
197 E5 Vitolište Macedonia
196 E4 Vitomirica Kosovo, Srbija Yugo.
252 C4 Vitor Peru
252 B4 Vitor r. Peru
192 E2 Vitorchiano Italy
257 G4 Vitória Brazil
Vitoria Spain see Vitoria-Gasteiz
183 H2 Vitoria airport Spain
255 E5 Vitória da Conquista Brazil
183 H2 Vitoria-Gasteiz Spain
264 G7 Vitória Seamount sea feature S. Atlantic Ocean
195 G3 Vitravo r. Italy
158 E3 Vitré France
157 F5 Vitrey-sur-Mance France
161 D5 Vitrolles France
156 C2 Vitry-en-Artois France
156 E4 Vitry-en-Perthois France
156 E4 Vitry-la-Ville France
156 E4 Vitry-le-François France
160 B2 Vitry-sur-Loire France
156 C4 Vitry-sur-Seine France
136 E2 Vits' r. Belarus
139 H4 Vitsyebsk Belarus
138 G4 Vitsyebskaya Voblasts' admin. div. Belarus
140 M2 Vittangi Sweden
160 C1 Vitteaux France
157 F4 Vittel France
194 D6 Vittoria Sicilia Italy
191 H3 Vittorio Veneto Italy
193 G3 Vitulazio Italy
137 I5 Vityazevo Rus. Fed.
171 C4 Vitzenburg Ger.
187 C5 Viuda r. Spain
160 E2 Viuz-en-Sallaz France
161 C4 Vivarais, Monts du mts France
192 B2 Vivario Corse France
137 J3 Vivcharove Ukr.
182 C1 Viveiro Spain
186 C4 Vivel del Río Martín Spain
187 C5 Viver Spain
Vivero Spain see Viveiro
161 B3 Viverols France
185 H2 Viveros Spain
237 E5 Vivian LA U.S.A.
157 E3 Vivier-au-Court France
161 C4 Viviers France
163 E4 Viviez France
161 C5 Viv-le-Fesq France
213 F4 Vivo S. Africa
179 F4 Vivodnik mt. Slovenia
162 C2 Vivonne France
156 E5 Vix Bourgogne France
162 B2 Vix Pays de la Loire France
137 H3 Viys'kove Ukr.
136 D3 Viytivtsi Ukr.
Vizagapatam Andhra Prad. India see Vishakhapatnam
242 B3 Vizcaíno, Desierto de des. Mex.
242 B3 Vizcaíno, Sierra mts Mex.
183 H1 Vizcaya prov. País Vasco Spain
126 B2 Vize Turkey
160 C3 Vizézy r. France
134 I2 Vizhas r. Rus. Fed.
175 L6 Vizhomlya Ukr.
115 D2 Vizianagaram Andhra Prad. India
161 D3 Vizille France
134 J3 Vizinga Rus. Fed.
197 H3 Viziru Romania
177 G2 Vizovice Czech Rep.
177 I3 Vizslás Hungary
177 K3 Vizsoly Hungary
194 D5 Vizzini Sicilia Italy
198 A1 Vjosë r. Albania
165 D4 Vlaams Brabant prov. Belgium
164 D3 Vlaardingen Neth.
179 E1 Vlachovo Březí Czech Rep.
177 L5 Vlădeasa, Munţii mts Romania
197 F2 Vlădeasa, Vârful mt. Romania
197 F4 Vladičin Han Srbija Yugo.
129 D2 Vladikavkaz Rus. Fed.
139 M3 Vladimir Rus. Fed.
177 K5 Vladimirescu Romania
100 E4 Vladimiro-Aleksandrovskoye Rus. Fed.
Vladimir Oblast admin. div. Rus. Fed. see Vladimirskaya Oblast'
120 F1 Vladimirovka Kazakh.
129 D1 Vladimirovka Rus. Fed.
197 F4 Vladimirovo Bulg.
Vladimirovskiy Kazakh. see Vladimirovka
139 M4 Vladimirskaya Oblast' admin. div. Rus. Fed.
Vladimir-Volynskiy Ukr. see Volodymyr-Volyns'kyy
176 E2 Vladislav Czech Rep.
100 D4 Vladivostok Rus. Fed.
134 G4 Vladychnoye Rus. Fed.
164 G1 Vlagtwedde Neth.
197 G2 Vlăhiţa Romania
197 E4 Vlajna mt. Yugo.
188 G3 Vlasenica Bos.-Herz.
196 D3 Vlašić Planina mts Yugo.
176 D2 Vlašim Czech Rep.
137 G3 Vlasivka Ukr.
197 F4 Vlasotince Srbija Yugo.
Vlasova-Ayuta Rus. Fed. see Ayutinskiy
139 L4 Vlasovo Rus. Fed.
177 G3 Vlčany Slovakia
164 F2 Vledder Neth.
214 C5 Vleiland S. Africa
164 E2 Vleuten Neth.
164 D1 Vlieland i. Neth.
164 E3 Vlijmen Neth.
165 C3 Vlissingen Neth.
198 A1 Vlorë Albania
198 A1 Vlorës, Gjiri i b. Albania
169 D3 Vlotho Ger.
Vlotslavsk Pol. see Włocławek
176 D1 Vltava r. Czech Rep.
179 F4 Vnanje Gorice Slovenia
139 K2 Vnina r. Rus. Fed.
171 D4 Vockerode Ger.
179 E2 Vöcklabruck Austria
179 E2 Vöcklamarkt Austria
177 G3 Voderady Slovakia
191 J3 Vodice Istra Croatia
188 E4 Vodice Šibenik Croatia
134 G3 Vodlozero, Ozero l. Rus. Fed.
176 D2 Vodňany Czech Rep.
188 D3 Vodnjan Croatia
Vodopyanovo Lipetskaya Oblast' Rus. Fed. see Donskoye
146 □G1 Voe Shetland, Scotland U.K.
215 E5 Voël r. S. Africa
169 B4 Voerde (Niederrhein) Ger.
165 E4 Voerendaal Neth.
142 D3 Voersă Denmark
207 F5 Vogan Togo
164 D2 Vogelenzang Neth.
157 H4 Vogelgrun France
Vogelkop Peninsula Indon. see Doberai, Jazirah
207 H4 Vogel Peak Nigeria
170 E2 Vogelsang Ger.
169 D5 Vogelsberg hills Ger.
171 E3 Vogelsdorf Ger.
157 H4 Vogelsheim France
172 B2 Vogelweh Ger.
190 E4 Voghera Italy
191 G4 Voghiera Italy
129 E4 Voghji r. Armenia
188 G4 Vogošća Bos.-Herz.
172 D4 Vogt Ger.
173 G4 Vogtareuth Ger.
161 C4 Vogüé France
78 □5 Voh New Caledonia
173 F3 Vohburg an der Donau Ger.
Vohémar Madag. see Iharaña
173 G2 Vohenstrauß Ger.
Vohibinany Madag. see Ampasimanolotra
213 □J4 Vohilava Fianarantsoa Madag.
213 □K4 Vohilava Fianarantsoa Madag.
Vohimarina Madag. see Iharaña
213 □J5 Vohimena, Tanjona c. Madag.
213 □J4 Vohipeno Madag.
213 □K4 Vohitrandriana Madag.
169 D4 Vöhl Ger.
138 E2 Võhma Estonia
172 C3 Vöhrenbach Ger.
172 C3 Vöhringen Ger.
173 E3 Vöhringen Ger.
211 C5 Voi Kenya
157 F4 Void-Vacon France
171 C4 Voigtstedt Ger.
157 E4 Voillecomte France
197 F3 Voineasa Romania
197 H2 Voineşti Romania
206 C4 Voinjama Liberia
161 D3 Voiron France
156 B4 Voise r. France
160 D2 Voiteur France
179 G3 Voitsberg Austria
177 K3 Vojčice Slovakia
142 C4 Vojens Denmark
Vojnice Slovakia see Bátorove Kosihy
179 G4 Vojnik Slovenia
196 D3 Vojvodina prov. Yugo.
138 F2 Voka Estonia
177 H6 Vokány Hungary
134 I4 Vokhma Rus. Fed.
207 I4 Voko Cameroon
134 K3 Vol' r. Rus. Fed.
176 C3 Volary Czech Rep.
Volaterrae Italy see Volterra
238 F2 Volborg MT U.S.A.
258 D1 Volcán Arg.
252 D5 Volcán, Cerro vol. Bol.
260 B2 Volcán, Cerro del vol. Chile
261 H5 Volcán, Sierra del hills Arg.
Volcano Bay Japan see Uchiura-wan
240 □D9 Volcano House HI U.S.A.
Volcano Islands N. Pacific Ocean see Kazan-rettō
Volchansk Ukr. see Vovchans'k
139 H5 Volchas r. Belarus
121 J1 Volchikha Rus. Fed.
139 J3 Volchina r. Rus. Fed.
141 I3 Volda Norway
173 H2 Volduchy Czech Rep.
164 E2 Volendam Neth.
232 D6 Volens VA U.S.A.
139 L3 Volga Rus. Fed.
139 L3 Volga r. Rus. Fed.
Volga Upland hills Rus. Fed. see Privolzhskaya Vozvyshennost'
135 H7 Volgodonsk Rus. Fed.
135 I6 Volgograd Rus. Fed.
Volgograd Oblast admin. div. Rus. Fed. see Volgogradskaya Oblast'
135 I6 Volgogradskaya Oblast' admin. div. Rus. Fed.
135 I6 Volgogradskoye Vodokhranilishche resr Rus. Fed.
139 M3 Volgorechensk Rus. Fed.
Volhynia admin. div. Ukr. see Volyns'ka Oblast'
136 E4 Volintiri Moldova
173 E2 Volkach Ger.
173 E2 Volkach r. Ger.
179 F4 Völkermarkt Austria
172 C4 Volkertshausen Ger.
190 D1 Volketswil Switz.
139 I2 Volkhov Rus. Fed.
139 I1 Volkhov r. Rus. Fed.
139 I1 Volkhovskaya Guba b. Rus. Fed.
139 H2 Volkhovskiy Rus. Fed.
172 A2 Völklingen Ger.
169 E4 Volkmarsen Ger.
Volkovysk Belarus see Vawkavysk
Volkovyskiye Vysoty hills Belarus see Vawkavyskaye Wzvyshsha
215 G2 Volksrust S. Africa
171 C4 Volkstedt Ger.
168 C2 Völlen Ger.
164 E2 Vollenhove Neth.
168 D2 Vollersode Ger.
160 B3 Vollore-Montagne France
157 H3 Volmunster France
160 C1 Volnay France
Vol'nogorsk Ukr. see Vil'nohirs'k
100 D4 Vol'no-Nadezhdinskoye Rus. Fed.
137 I4 Volnovakha Ukr.
121 G1 Vol'noye Rus. Fed.
Vol'nyansk Ukr. see Vil'nyans'k
100 E2 Volochayevka-Vtoraya Rus. Fed.
Volochisk Ukr. see Volochys'k
136 D3 Volochys'k Ukr.
136 E3 Volodarka Ukr.
137 I4 Volodars'ke Ukr.
120 B3 Volodarskiy Rus. Fed.
Volodarskoye Kazakh. see Saumalkol'
136 E2 Volodars'k-Volyns'kyy Ukr.
136 D2 Volodymyrets' Ukr.
137 G4 Volodymyrivka Ukr.
136 C2 Volodymyr-Volyns'kyy Ukr.
134 G4 Vologda Rus. Fed.
Vologda Oblast admin. div. Rus. Fed. see Vologodskaya Oblast'
157 G4 Vologne r. France
139 M2 Vologodskaya Oblast' admin. div. Rus. Fed.
137 I3 Volokhiv Yar Ukr.
139 J3 Volokolamsk Rus. Fed.
135 G6 Volokonovka Rus. Fed.
161 E4 Volonne France
214 D3 Volop S. Africa
198 C2 Volos Greece
175 L6 Voloshcha Ukr.
137 J3 Voloshino Rus. Fed.
134 H3 Voloshka Rus. Fed.
137 I3 Volos'ka Balakliya Ukr.
137 I3 Volos'ka Balakliyka r. Ukr.
138 G2 Volosovo Rus. Fed.
177 L3 Volosyanka Ukr.
139 H3 Volot Rus. Fed.
137 J2 Volotovo Rus. Fed.
136 B3 Volovets' Ukr.
135 G5 Volovo Lipetskaya Oblast' Rus. Fed.
139 L5 Volovo Tul'skaya Oblast' Rus. Fed.
177 J3 Volovské vrchy mts Slovakia
Volozhin Belarus see Valozhyn
178 D5 Volpago del Mòntello Italy
190 D4 Volpedo Italy
190 C3 Volpiano Italy
171 C3 Völpke Ger.
178 C3 Völs Austria
170 E2 Völschow Ger.
192 D2 Volsini, Monti mts Italy
Volsinii Italy see Orvieto
120 A1 Vol'sk Rus. Fed.
214 D5 Volstruisleegte S. Africa
207 F5 Volta admin. reg. Ghana
207 F5 Volta r. Ghana
207 F5 Volta, Lake resr Ghana
Volta Blanche r. Africa see White Volta
86 E2 Voltaire, Cape W.A. Austr.
Volta Noire r. Africa see Black Volta
257 E5 Volta Redonda Brazil
Volta Rouge r. Burkina/Ghana see Nazinon
191 F5 Volterra Italy
169 C3 Voltlage Ger.
183 F3 Voltoya r. Spain
193 H3 Volturara Appula Italy
194 D2 Volturara Irpina Italy
193 H3 Volturino Italy
193 H4 Volturino, Monte mt. Italy
193 F3 Volturno r. Italy
204 D2 Volubilis tourist site Morocco
197 H3 Voluntari Romania
235 G1 Voluntown CT U.S.A.
198 C1 Volvi, Limni l. Greece
160 B3 Volvic France
161 D5 Volx France
137 J2 Volya Rus. Fed.
134 M3 Vol'ya r. Rus. Fed.
175 L6 Volya Arlamivs'ka Ukr.
176 C2 Volyně Czech Rep.
176 C2 Volyňka r. Czech Rep.
137 G2 Volynka Ukr.
Volyn Oblast admin. div. Ukr. see Volyns'ka Oblast'
136 C2 Volyns'ka Oblast' admin. div. Ukr.
Volynskaya Oblast' admin. div. Ukr. see Volyns'ka Oblast'
136 D3 Volytsya Ukr.
136 D3 Volytsya Druha Ukr.
134 J5 Volzhsk Rus. Fed.
120 B1 Volzhskiy Samarskaya Oblast' Rus. Fed.
135 I6 Volzhskiy Volgogradskaya Oblast' Rus. Fed.
193 G2 Vomano r. Italy
178 C3 Vomp Austria
78 □6 Vonavona i. New Georgia Is Solomon Is
223 J4 Vonda Sask. Can.
134 I4 Vondanka Rus. Fed.
213 □J4 Vondrozo Madag.
160 D1 Vonges France
198 B2 Vonitsa Greece
160 C2 Vonnas France
114 C3 Vontimitta Andhra Prad. India
176 G5 Vonyarcvashegy Hungary
164 D2 Voorburg Neth.
233 G3 Voorheesville NY U.S.A.
164 D2 Voorschoten Neth.
164 F2 Voorst Neth.
164 E2 Voorthuizen Neth.
138 D2 Voosi kurk sea chan. Estonia
139 I4 Vop' r. Rus. Fed.
140 □D2 Vopnafjörður b. Iceland
140 M3 Vörå Fin.
179 F3 Voralm mt. Austria
138 E4 Voranava Belarus
178 A3 Vorarlberg land Austria
179 E2 Vorchdorf Austria
164 F2 Vorden Neth.
179 F3 Vordernberg Austria
190 E1 Vorderrhein r. Switz.
142 D4 Vordingborg Denmark
169 F3 Vordorf Ger.
196 D5 Vorë Albania
198 B1 Voreia Pindos mts Greece
199 D2 Voreio Aigaio admin. reg. Greece
198 C2 Voreioi Sporades is Greece
198 C2 Voreios Evvoïkos Kolpos sea chan. Greece
161 D3 Voreppe France
161 B3 Vorey France
139 I5 Vorga Rus. Fed.
134 M2 Vorgashor Rus. Fed.
Vorίai Sporádhes is Greece see Voreioi Sporades
Voría Píndhos mts Greece see Voreia Pindos
264 J1 Voring Plateau sea feature N. Atlantic Ocean
117 H3 Vorjing mt. Arun. Prad. India
134 N2 Vorkuta Rus. Fed.
142 D1 Vorma r. Norway
138 D2 Vormsi i. Estonia
139 L5 Vorob'yevka Rus. Fed.
135 H6 Vorob'yevka Rus. Fed.
130 J3 Vorogovo Rus. Fed.
136 C3 Vorokhta Ukr.
197 H2 Vorona Romania
135 H6 Vorona r. Rus. Fed.
135 G6 Voronezh Rus. Fed.
139 L5 Voronezh r. Rus. Fed.
Voronezh Oblast admin. div. Rus. Fed. see Voronezhskaya Oblast'
135 H6 Voronezhskaya Oblast' admin. div. Rus. Fed.
137 G2 Voronizh Ukr.
137 G2 Voron'ky Ukr.
136 D2 Voronky Rivnens'ka Oblast' Ukr.
139 I1 Voronov, Mys pt Rus. Fed.
139 K4 Voronovo Rus. Fed.
136 E3 Voronovytsya Ukr.
121 J2 Vorontsovka Kazakh.
135 H6 Vorontsovka Rus. Fed.
Vorontsovo-Aleksandrovskoye Stavropol'skiy Kray Rus. Fed. see Zelenokumsk
136 C3 Voronyaky hills Ukr.
134 H4 Voron'ye Rus. Fed.
Voroshilov Rus. Fed. see Ussuriysk
Voroshilovgrad Ukr. see Luhans'k
Voroshilovsk Rus. Fed. see Stavropol'
Voroshilovsk Ukr. see Alchevs'k
129 E4 Vorotan r. Iran
134 I4 Vorotynets Rus. Fed.
139 K4 Vorotynsk Rus. Fed.
129 C1 Vorovskolesskaya Rus. Fed.
137 H2 Vorozhba Sums'ka Oblast' Ukr.
137 H2 Vorozhba Sums'ka Oblast' Ukr.
263 B2 Vorposten Peak Antarctica
173 F2 Vorra Ger.
179 G3 Vorsau Austria
165 D3 Vorselaar Belgium
135 F6 Vorskla r. Rus. Fed.
137 H2 Vorsklitsa r. Rus. Fed./Ukr.
165 E3 Vorst Belgium
214 D1 Vorstershoop S. Africa
177 L5 Vorţa Romania
263 B2 Vørterkaka Nunatak mt. Antarctica
138 E2 Võrtsjärv l. Estonia
138 F3 Võru Estonia
168 E2 Vorwerk Ger.
139 J4 Vorya r. Rus. Fed.
136 F2 Vorzel' Ukr.
214 D4 Vosburg S. Africa
123 G2 Vose Tajik.
179 H2 Vösendorf Austria
157 G4 Vosges dept Lorraine France
157 G5 Vosges mts France
139 L3 Voshchazhnikovo Rus. Fed.
129 D3 Voskevan Armenia
139 L4 Voskresensk Rus. Fed.
137 G4 Voskresens'ke Ukr.
139 L5 Voskresenskoye Lipetskaya Oblast' Rus. Fed.
134 I4 Voskresenskoye Nizhegorodskaya Oblast' Rus. Fed.
120 D1 Voskresenskoye Respublika Bashkortostan Rus. Fed.
139 K4 Voskresenskoye Tul'skaya Oblast' Rus. Fed.
139 K2 Voskresenskoye Vologod. Obl. Rus. Fed.
160 C1 Vosne-Romanée France
141 I3 Voss Norway
165 D3 Vosselaar Belgium
Vostochno-Kazakhstanskaya Oblast' admin. div. Kazakh. see Vostochnyy Kazakhstan
Vostochno-Kounradskiy Kazakh. see Shygys Konyrat
100 G2 Vostochno-Sakhalinskiy Gory mts Sakhalin Rus. Fed.
134 K4 Vostochnyy Rus. Fed.
120 D4 Vostochnyy Chink Ustyurta esc. Uzbek.
121 K2 Vostochnyy Kazakhstan admin. div. Kazakh.
98 F1 Vostochnyy Sayan mts Rus. Fed.
100 E3 Vostok Primorskiy Kray Rus. Fed.
Vostok Sakhalin Rus. Fed. see Neftegorsk
176 D2 Votice Czech Rep.
134 K4 Votkinsk Rus. Fed.
134 K4 Votkinskoye Vodokhranilishche resr Rus. Fed.
142 C1 Votna r. Norway
256 D5 Votorantim Brazil
139 I4 Votrya r. Rus. Fed.
256 C4 Votuporanga Brazil
162 E2 Voueize r. France
Vouga Angola see Cunhinga
182 B4 Vouga r. Port.
160 C1 Vougeot France
162 B2 Vouillé France
162 C2 Vouillé France
198 C3 Voula Greece
156 E5 Voulaines-les-Templiers France
156 C4 Voulx France
162 C2 Vouneuil-sous-Biard France
159 G5 Vouneuil-sur-Vienne France
198 B1 Vourinos mt. Greece
160 B1 Voutenay-sur-Cure France
162 D3 Voutezac France
162 B2 Vouvant France
159 G4 Vouvray France
190 B2 Vouvry Switz.
182 B4 Vouzela Port.
156 E3 Vouziers France
156 C5 Vouzon France
137 H3 Vovcha r. Ukr.
137 I2 Vovcha r. Ukr.
137 I2 Vovchans'k Ukr.
137 G2 Vovchyk Ukr.
156 B4 Voves France
136 D3 Vovk r. Ukr.
136 D2 Vovkoshiv Ukr.
136 D3 Vovkovyntsi Ukr.
208 E3 Vovodo r. C.A.R.
141 K3 Voxna Sweden
141 L3 Voxnan r. Sweden
134 J4 Voya r. Rus. Fed.
137 F3 Voyevods'ke Ukr.
175 M6 Voynyliv Ukr.
Vöyri Fin. see Vörå
134 K3 Voyvozh Rus. Fed.
78 □6 Voza Choiseul Solomon Is
139 K3 Vozdvizhenskoye Rus. Fed.
139 L4 Vozha r. Rus. Fed.
134 G3 Vozhe, Ozero l. Rus. Fed.
134 H3 Vozhega Rus. Fed.
183 I3 Vozmediano Spain
121 G1 Voznesenka Kazakh.
137 F4 Voznesens'k Ukr.
129 D2 Voznesenskaya Ingushskaya Respublika Rus. Fed.
129 B1 Voznesenskaya Krasnodarskiy Kray Rus. Fed.
137 F4 Voznesens'ke Ukr.
135 H5 Voznesenskoye Rus. Fed.
139 M3 Voznesen'ye Rus. Fed.
139 J1 Voznesen'ye Rus. Fed.
137 G4 Vozsiyats'ke Ukr.
121 G1 Vozvyshenka Kazakh.
Vozvyshenskiy Kazakh. see Vozvyshenka
100 D2 Vozzhayevka Rus. Fed.
142 C3 Vrå Denmark
197 G4 Vrabevo Bulg.
177 H3 Vráble Slovakia
198 B3 Vrachionas hill Ionioi Nisoi Greece
198 B2 Vrachnaiika Greece
142 C2 Vrådal Norway
136 F4 Vradiyivka Ukr.
Vrakhiónas Óros hill Ionioi Nisoi Greece see Vrachionas
Vrakhnaíika Greece see Vrachnaiika
188 F4 Vran mt. Bos.-Herz.
197 H4 Vrana r. Bulg.
100 E4 Vrangel' Rus. Fed.
100 F1 Vrangelya, Mys pt Rus. Fed.
131 T2 Vrangelya, Ostrov i. Rus. Fed.
188 G3 Vranjak Bos.-Herz.
197 E4 Vranje Srbija Yugo.
197 F4 Vranjska Banja Srbija Yugo.
179 H2 Vranovice Czech Rep.
177 K3 Vranov nad Topľou Slovakia
196 E5 Vrapčište Macedonia
197 F4 Vratarnica Srbija Yugo.
197 F4 Vratsa Bulg.
188 F3 Vrbanja r. Bos.-Herz.
188 F3 Vrbas r. Bos.-Herz.
196 D3 Vrbas Vojvodina, Srbija Yugo.
176 G1 Vrbno pod Pradědem Czech Rep.
177 J2 Vrbov Slovakia
176 G3 Vrbovce Slovakia
177 G3 Vrbové Slovakia
188 F3 Vrbovec Croatia
188 E3 Vrbovsko Croatia
176 E1 Vrchlabí Czech Rep.
157 F4 Vrécourt France
215 G2 Vrede S. Africa
215 F2 Vredefort S. Africa
169 B3 Vreden Ger.
214 A5 Vredenburg S. Africa
214 B4 Vredendal S. Africa
251 G3 Vreed-en-Hoop Guyana
164 E2 Vreeland Neth.
168 C3 Vrees Ger.
182 C3 Vreia de Jales Port.
196 E4 Vrela Kosovo, Srbija Yugo.
179 F5 Vremščica mt. Slovenia
165 D5 Vresse Belgium
188 E3 Vrhnika Slovenia
114 C4 Vriddhachalam Tamil Nadu India
164 F1 Vries Neth.
164 F2 Vriezenveen Neth.
143 F3 Vrigstad Sweden
160 A1 Vrille r. France
111 B7 Vrindavan Uttar Prad. India
156 E3 Vrizy France
196 E4 Vrnjačka Banja Srbija Yugo.
156 B2 Vron France
164 F2 Vroomshoop Neth.
176 C1 Vroutek Czech Rep.
164 C3 Vrouwenpolder Neth.
196 D5 Vrrin Albania
196 E3 Vršac Vojvodina, Srbija Yugo.
191 I3 Vrsar Croatia
179 E5 Vrtojba Slovenia
215 E2 Vryburg S. Africa
215 H2 Vryheid S. Africa
173 H2 Všeruby Czech Rep.
171 F5 Všetaty Czech Rep.
177 G2 Vsetín Czech Rep.
139 H1 Vsevolozhsk Rus. Fed.
137 H3 Vshyva r. Ukr.
177 H3 Vtáčnik mt. Slovakia
177 H3 Vtáčnik mts Slovakia
160 D2 Vuache, Montagne de mt. France
79 □1 Vuaqava i. Fiji
197 G5 Vŭcha r. Bulg.
188 G3 Vučica r. Croatia
196 E4 Vučitrn Kosovo, Srbija Yugo.
197 E4 Vučje Srbija Yugo.
164 E3 Vught Neth.
137 I4 Vuhledar Ukr.
137 J3 Vuhlehirs'k Ukr.
188 G3 Vuka r. Croatia
188 G3 Vukovar Croatia
134 L3 Vuktyl' Rus. Fed.
215 G2 Vukuzakhe S. Africa
222 H5 Vulcan Alta Can.
197 F3 Vulcan Romania
136 E5 Vulcăneşti Moldova
194 D4 Vulcano, Isola i. Isole Lipari Italy
197 F4 Vŭlchedrŭm Bulg.
197 H4 Vŭlchidol Bulg.
193 H3 Vulgano r. Italy
Vulkaneshty Moldova see Vulcăneşti
193 H4 Vulture, Monte mt. Italy
241 K5 Vulture Mountains AZ U.S.A.
97 D5 Vung Tau Vietnam
138 F1 Vuohijärvi Fin.
140 O2 Vuokatti Fin.
138 H1 Vuoksa r. Rus. Fed.
138 G1 Vuoksi r. Fin.
140 N2 Vuolijoki Fin.
140 M2 Vuollerim Sweden
197 H4 Vŭrbitsa Bulg.
197 G3 Vurpăr Romania
197 F4 Vŭrshets Bulg.
197 H2 Vutcani Romania
114 D2 Vuyyuru Andhra Prad. India
179 G4 Vuzenica Slovenia
136 C2 Vuzlove L'vivs'ka Oblast' Ukr.
136 B3 Vuzlove Zakarpats'ka Oblast' Ukr.
138 F4 Vuzlyanka r. Belarus
120 E1 Vvedenka Kazakh.
139 M3 Vveden'ye Rus. Fed.
211 B7 Vwawa Tanz.
175 M2 Vyalikaya Byerastavitsa Belarus
139 H2 Vyal'ye, Ozero l. Rus. Fed.
116 C5 Vyara Gujarat India
Vyarkhowye Belarus see Ruba
Vyatka Kirovskaya Oblast' Rus. Fed. see Kirov
134 J5 Vyatka r. Rus. Fed.
134 J4 Vyatskiye Polyany Rus. Fed.
100 E3 Vyazemskiy Rus. Fed.
139 J4 Vyaz'ma Rus. Fed.
139 I4 Vyaz'ma r. Rus. Fed.
134 H4 Vyazniki Rus. Fed.
120 A1 Vyazovka Saratovskaya Oblast' Rus. Fed.
135 H6 Vyazovka Volgogradskaya Oblast' Rus. Fed.
137 I2 Vyazovoye Rus. Fed.
138 G1 Vyborg Rus. Fed.
138 G1 Vyborgskiy Zaliv b. Rus. Fed.
134 I3 Vychegda r. Rus. Fed.
134 I3 Vychegodskiy Rus. Fed.
177 I2 Východná Slovakia
175 N4 Vyderta Ukr.
175 M4 Vydranytsya Ukr.
106 E1 Vydrino Rus. Fed.
175 M4 Vydrychi Ukr.
138 F4 Vyerkhnyadzvinsk Belarus
139 H5 Vyetka Belarus
138 G4 Vyetryna Belarus
139 J5 Vygonichi Rus. Fed.
134 F3 Vygozero, Ozero l. Rus. Fed.
177 H3 Vyhne Slovakia
135 H5 Vyksa Rus. Fed.
160 E1 Vy-lès-Lure France
136 E5 Vylkove Ukr.
136 B3 Vylok Ukr.
134 J3 Vym' r. Rus. Fed.
136 C3 Vynnyky Ukr.
136 B3 Vynohradiv Ukr.
137 F4 Vynohradne Ukr.
137 G4 Vynohradove Khersons'ka Oblast' Ukr.
137 G5 Vynohradove Respublika Krym Ukr.
139 I3 Vypolzovo Rus. Fed.
137 G2 Vyrishal'ne Ukr.
139 H2 Vyritsa Rus. Fed.
137 H2 Vyry Ukr.
135 G7 Vyselki Rus. Fed.
136 F2 Vyshcha Dubechnya Ukr.
137 I3 Vyshche Solone Ukr.
137 H4 Vyshchetarasivka Ukr.
139 M4 Vyshgorod Rus. Fed.
136 F2 Vyshhorod Ukr.
136 B3 Vyshka Ukr.
139 H5 Vyshkov Rus. Fed.
136 B3 Vyshkove Ukr.
137 G3 Vyshneve Dnipropetrovs'ka Oblast' Ukr.
136 F2 Vyshneve Kyivs'ka Oblast' Ukr.
139 J3 Vyshnevolotskaya Gryada ridge Rus. Fed.
139 J3 Vyshnevolotskoye Vodokhranilishche resr Rus. Fed.
137 I1 Vyshneye-Ol'shanoye Rus. Fed.
175 M4 Vyshniv Ukr.
136 C3 Vyshnivets' Ukr.
139 J3 Vyshniy-Volochek Rus. Fed.
136 B3 Vyshnya r. Ukr.
137 G3 Vyshnyaky Ukr.
176 G2 Vyškov Czech Rep.
176 D3 Vysoká mt. Czech Rep.
176 G3 Vysoká hill Slovakia
136 E2 Vysoka Pich Ukr.
176 F3 Vysoká pri Morave Slovakia
138 D5 Vysokaye Belarus
176 F2 Vysoké Mýto Czech Rep.
139 K4 Vysokinichi Rus. Fed.
137 H3 Vysokopillya Kharkivs'ka Oblast' Ukr.
137 G4 Vysokopillya Khersons'ka Oblast' Ukr.
139 K3 Vysokovsk Rus. Fed.
Vysokoye Belarus see Vysokaye
139 J3 Vysokoye Rus. Fed.
138 G1 Vysotsk Rus. Fed.
136 D2 Vysots'k Ukr.
179 F2 Vyšší Brod Czech Rep.
136 E2 Vystupovychi Ukr.
139 K1 Vytegra Rus. Fed.
134 I3 Vyya r. Rus. Fed.
136 C2 Vyzhivka r. Ukr.
136 C3 Vyzhnytsya Ukr.
138 E4 Vyžuona r. Lith.
175 I1 Vzmor'ye Rus. Fed.

W

206 E4 Wa Ghana
168 E1 Waabs Ger.
210 D4 Waajid Somalia
169 F4 Waake Ger.
173 F4 Waakirchen Ger.
173 E4 Waal Ger.
164 D3 Waal r. Neth.
165 E3 Waalre Neth.
164 E3 Waalwijk Neth.
164 D2 Waarland Neth.
165 C3 Waarschoot Belgium
165 D3 Waasmunster Belgium
91 J8 Wabag P.N.G.
224 B3 Wabakimi Lake Ont. Can.
222 H4 Wabamun Alta Can.
222 H3 Wabasca r. Alta Can.
222 H4 Wabasca-Desmarais Alta Can.
230 C3 Wabash IN U.S.A.
232 A4 Wabash OH U.S.A.
236 F4 Wabash r. IN U.S.A.
226 A3 Wabasha MN U.S.A.
224 C3 Wabassi r. Ont. Can.
210 D3 Wabē Gestro r. Eth.
210 D3 Wabē Mena r. Eth.
226 C3 Wabeno WI U.S.A.
169 E4 Wabern Ger.
210 E3 Wabē Shebelē Wenz r. Eth.
223 L4 Wabowden Man. Can.
174 G2 Wąbrzeźno Pol.
109 F1 Wabu Anhui China
225 H2 Wabush Nfld. Can.
231 E5 Waccamaw r. SC U.S.A.
233 F6 Wachapreague VA U.S.A.
172 C2 Wachenheim an der Weinstraße Ger.
170 D3 Wachow Ger.
165 C3 Wachtebeke Belgium
169 E5 Wächtersbach Ger.
168 E1 Wacken Ger.
173 G2 Wackersdorf Ger.
225 H3 Waco Que. Can.
237 D6 Waco TX U.S.A.
226 A3 Wacouta MN U.S.A.
202 E6 Wad Banda Sudan
202 B2 Waddān, Jabal hills Libya
164 D1 Waddeneilanden is Neth.
Wadden Islands Neth. see Waddeneilanden
164 D2 Waddenzee sea chan. Neth.
151 G3 Waddesdon Buckinghamshire, England U.K.
168 F2 Waddeweitz Ger.
82 D3 Waddikee S.A. Austr.
149 I4 Waddington Lincolnshire, England U.K.
222 E5 Waddington, Mount B.C. Can.
147 E4 Waddingtown Rep. of Ireland
164 D2 Waddinxveen Neth.
85 H5 Waddy Point Qld Austr.
150 C4 Wadebridge Cornwall, England U.K.
223 K5 Wadena Sask. Can.
236 E2 Wadena MN U.S.A.
190 D1 Wädenswil Switz.
172 A2 Wadern Ger.
169 D4 Wadersloh Ger.
231 D5 Wadesboro NC U.S.A.
84 B2 Wadeye N.T. Austr.
114 B2 Wadgaon Mahar. India
116 D5 Wadgaon Mahar. India
172 A2 Wadgassen Ger.
151 H3 Wadhurst East Sussex, England U.K.
116 B5 Wadhwan Gujarat India
Wadhwan Gujarat India see Surendranagar
114 C2 Wadi Karnataka India
109 E1 Wadian Henan China
128 B4 Wādī as Sīr Jordan
203 F4 Wadi Halfa Sudan
128 B4 Wādī Mūsá Jordan
234 D3 Wading r. NJ U.S.A.
235 F2 Wading River NY U.S.A.
175 H4 Wadlew Pol.
203 G6 Wad Medani Sudan
102 □1 Wadomari Japan
175 H6 Wadowice Pol.
175 J5 Wadowice Górne Pol.
240 H2 Wadsworth NV U.S.A.
232 C4 Wadsworth OH U.S.A.
Wadu i. S. Male Maldives see Vaadhu
214 C6 Waenhuiskrans S. Africa
262 P1 Waesche, Mount Antarctica
107 I4 Wafangdian Liaoning China
102 J4 Waga-gawa r. Japan
116 C3 Wagah Punjab India
174 G3 Waganiec Pol.
168 D3 Wagenfeld Ger.
168 F3 Wagenhoff Ger.
164 E3 Wageningen Neth.
251 G3 Wageningen Suriname
221 J3 Wager Bay Nunavut Can.
83 F3 Wagga Wagga N.S.W. Austr.
172 C2 Waghäusel Ger.
87 C7 Wagin W.A. Austr.
173 G4 Waging am See Ger.
173 G4 Waginger See l. Ger.
222 D4 Waglisla B.C. Can.
254 E5 Wagner Brazil
236 D3 Wagner SD U.S.A.
237 E4 Wagoner OK U.S.A.
239 F4 Wagon Mound NM U.S.A.
178 E3 Wagrain Austria
174 F3 Wągrowiec Pol.
123 H3 Wah Pak.
207 F5 Wahala Togo
208 F2 Wahda state Sudan
240 □ Wahiawa HI U.S.A.
169 E4 Wahlhausen Ger.
171 E4 Wahlsdorf Ger.
168 F2 Wahlstedt Ger.
236 D3 Wahoo NE U.S.A.
236 D2 Wahpeton ND U.S.A.
Wahran Alg. see Oran
168 F3 Wahrenholz Ger.
241 K2 Wah Wah Mountains UT U.S.A.
114 B2 Wai Mahar. India
240 □C8 Waiakoa HI U.S.A.
240 □B8 Waialeale, Mount HI U.S.A.
240 □ Waialee HI U.S.A.
240 □ Waialua HI U.S.A.
240 □ Waianae HI U.S.A.
80 G2 Waiapu r. North I. N.Z.
80 F4 Waiaruhe North I. N.Z.
81 D5 Waiau South I. N.Z.
80 F3 Waiau r. North I. N.Z.
81 A7 Waiau r. South I. N.Z.
81 D5 Waiau r. South I. N.Z.
172 D3 Waiblingen Ger.
172 C2 Waibstadt Ger.
173 G2 Waidhaus Ger.
173 F3 Waidhofen Ger.
179 G2 Waidhofen an der Thaya Austria
179 F3 Waidhofen an der Ybbs Austria
93 D3 Waigeo i. Irian Jaya Indon.
173 E2 Waigolshausen Ger.
81 C6 Waihao Downs South I. N.Z.
80 D1 Waiharara North I. N.Z.
80 E2 Waiharoa North I. N.Z.
80 E2 Waiheke Island North I. N.Z.
80 E2 Waihi North I. N.Z.
80 E2 Waihi Beach North I. N.Z.
80 E2 Waihou r. North I. N.Z.
80 F3 Waihua North I. N.Z.
81 B6 Waikaia South I. N.Z.
81 B6 Waikaia r. South I. N.Z.
81 B6 Waikaka South I. N.Z.
81 E4 Waikanae North I. N.Z.
240 □ Waikane HI U.S.A.
240 □C8 Waikapu HI U.S.A.
80 E2 Waikare, Lake North I. N.Z.
80 F3 Waikaremoana, Lake North I. N.Z.
80 E2 Waikaretu North I. N.Z.
81 D5 Waikari South I. N.Z.
80 E2 Waikato admin. reg. North I. N.Z.
80 E2 Waikato r. North I. N.Z.
81 B7 Waikawa South I. N.Z.
80 E3 Waikeria North I. N.Z.
82 D3 Waikerie S.A. Austr.
240 □D9 Waikii HI U.S.A.
80 F3 Waikirikiri North I. N.Z.
81 B7 Waikoikoi South I. N.Z.
80 F3 Waikokopa North I. N.Z.
81 C6 Waikouaiti South I. N.Z.
240 □B7 Wailua HI U.S.A.
240 □C8 Wailua HI U.S.A.
240 □C8 Wailuku HI U.S.A.
81 B7 Waimahake South I. N.Z.
81 D5 Waimakariri r. South I. N.Z.
80 F3 Waimana North I. N.Z.
240 □ Waimanalo HI U.S.A.
81 C4 Waimangaroa South I. N.Z.
80 F3 Waimarama North I. N.Z.
81 C4 Waimarie South I. N.Z.
81 C6 Waimate South I. N.Z.
80 D1 Waimatenui North I. N.Z.
80 E2 Waimauku North I. N.Z.
240 □B8 Waimea HI U.S.A.
240 □D8 Waimea HI U.S.A.
240 □ Waimea HI U.S.A.
165 F4 Waimes Belgium
173 E3 Wain Ger.
232 D3 Wainfleet Ont. Can.
149 J4 Wainfleet All Saints Lincolnshire, England U.K.
114 C2 Wainganga r. India
81 E4 Waingawa North I. N.Z.
150 C4 Wainhouse Corner Cornwall, England U.K.
223 I4 Wainwright Alta Can.
220 C2 Wainwright AK U.S.A.
80 F3 Waioeka r. North I. N.Z.
80 E1 Waiotira North I. N.Z.
80 E3 Waiouru North I. N.Z.
80 E2 Waipa r. North I. N.Z.
81 B7 Waipahi South I. N.Z.
240 □ Waipahu HI U.S.A.
80 F3 Waipaoa r. North I. N.Z.
81 D5 Waipara South I. N.Z.
80 F3 Waipawa North I. N.Z.
80 E2 Waipipi North I. N.Z.
80 E1 Waipu North I. N.Z.
80 F3 Waipukurau North I. N.Z.
80 F3 Wairakei North I. N.Z.
81 E4 Wairarapa, Lake North I. N.Z.
81 E4 Wairau r. South I. N.Z.
81 D4 Wairau Valley South I. N.Z.
80 F3 Wairoa North I. N.Z.
80 E2 Wairoa r. North I. N.Z.
80 F3 Wairoa r. North I. N.Z.
173 F2 Waischenfeld Ger.
109 F2 Waishe Zhejiang China
80 F3 Waitahanui North I. N.Z.
81 B6 Waitahuna South I. N.Z.
80 E2 Waitakaruru North I. N.Z.
81 C6 Waitaki South I. N.Z.
81 C6 Waitaki r. South I. N.Z.
80 □ Waitangi Chatham Is S. Pacific Ocean
81 C5 Waitangitaona r. South I. N.Z.
80 E3 Waitara North I. N.Z.
81 C6 Waitati South I. N.Z.
84 C4 Waite River N.T. Austr.
80 E2 Waitoa North I. N.Z.
80 E3 Waitomo Caves North I. N.Z.
80 E3 Waitotara North I. N.Z.
80 E3 Waitotari r. North I. N.Z.
238 C2 Waitsburg WA U.S.A.
80 E2 Waiuku North I. N.Z.
81 B7 Waiwera South South I. N.Z.
109 F3 Waiyang Fujian China
79 □1 Waiyevu Taveuni Fiji
179 E2 Waizenkirchen Austria
103 H5 Wajima Japan

210 D4 Wajir Kenya
81 D4 Wakapuaka South I. N.Z.
104 B3 Wakasa-wan b. Japan
81 B6 Wakatipu, Lake South I. N.Z.
223 J4 Wakaw Sask. Can.
79 □1 Wakaya i. Fiji
104 B4 Wakayama Japan
104 B5 Wakayama pref. Japan
75 F2 Wake Atoll N. Pacific Ocean
236 D4 WaKeeney KS U.S.A.
227 J3 Wakefield Que. Can.
246 □ Wakefield Jamaica
81 D4 Wakefield South I. N.Z.
149 H4 Wakefield West Yorkshire, England U.K.
226 C2 Wakefield MI U.S.A.
232 B5 Wakefield OH U.S.A.
234 B3 Wakefield PA U.S.A.
233 H4 Wakefield RI U.S.A.
232 E6 Wakefield VA U.S.A.
Wakeham Que. Can. see Kangiqsujuaq
240 F3 Wake Island N. Pacific Ocean see Wake Atoll
96 A3 Wakema Myanmar
102 J1 Wakanai Japan
215 H2 Wakkerstroom S. Africa
83 F3 Wakool N.S.W. Austr.
83 E3 Wakool r. N.S.W. Austr.
209 B7 Waku-Kungo Angola
224 D3 Wakwayowkastic r. Ont. Can.
114 C3 Walajapet Tamil Nadu India
171 C3 Walbeck Ger.
151 I2 Walberswick Suffolk, England U.K.
174 E5 Walbrzych Pol.
169 E4 Walburg Ger.
83 G2 Walcha N.S.W. Austr.
173 F4 Walchensee I. Ger.
178 D3 Walchsee Austria
173 J4 Walchum Ger.
238 F3 Walcott WY U.S.A.
165 D4 Walcourt Belgium
174 E2 Wałcz Pol.
172 D4 Wald Baden-Württemberg Ger.
173 G2 Wald Bayern Ger.
172 G4 Wald Switz.
172 C3 Waldachtal Ger.
179 F2 Waldaist r. Austria
172 B2 Waldböckelheim Ger.
169 C5 Waldbreitbach Ger.
169 C5 Waldbröl Ger.
172 D2 Waldbrunn Ger.
169 D5 Waldbrunn-Lahr Ger.
87 C5 Waldburg Range mts W.A. Austr.
171 E4 Walddrehna Ger.
169 E4 Waldeck Ger.
179 H3 Waldegg Austria
235 D1 Walden NY U.S.A.
226 D5 Walden IN U.S.A.
172 D2 Waldenbuch Ger.
172 D2 Waldenburg Baden-Württemberg Ger.
171 D5 Waldenburg Sachsen Ger.
Waldenburg Pol. see Walbrzych
190 C1 Waldenburg Switz.
173 G2 Waldenbach Ger.
173 G2 Waldershof Ger.
151 H3 Walderslade Medway, England U.K.
172 B2 Waldfischbach-Burgalben Ger.
179 G2 Waldhausen Austria
179 F2 Waldhausen im Strudengau Austria
171 E4 Waldheim Ger.
179 F2 Walding Austria
169 E4 Waldkappel Ger.
179 F3 Waldkirch Ger.
173 H3 Waldkirchen Ger.
173 J3 Waldkraiburg Ger.
172 C2 Wald-Michelbach Ger.
173 G2 Waldmünchen Ger.
231 D6 Waldo FL U.S.A.
226 D4 Waldo WI U.S.A.
233 □12 Waldoboro ME U.S.A.
149 □ Waldon r. England U.K.
232 E5 Waldorf MD U.S.A.
174 G2 Wałdowo-Szlacheckie Pol.
238 A2 Waldport OR U.S.A.
172 A2 Waldrach Ger.
237 E5 Waldron AR U.S.A.
226 E5 Waldron MI U.S.A.
263 H2 Waldron, Cape Antarctica
171 D5 Waldsassen Ger.
190 E1 Waldstatt Switz.
172 D3 Waldstetten Baden-Württemberg Ger.
173 E3 Waldstetten Bayern Ger.
173 G2 Waldthurn Ger.
87 C6 Walebing W.A. Austr.
108 B2 Waleg Sichuan China
190 E1 Walenstadt Switz.
151 H2 Wales admin. div. U.K.
206 E4 Walewale Ghana
165 F5 Walferdange Lux.
83 G2 Walgett N.S.W. Austr.
262 Q1 Walgreen Coast Antarctica
226 D4 Walhalla MI U.S.A.
226 D1 Walhalla ND U.S.A.
231 D5 Walhalla SC U.S.A.
87 B6 Walkaway W.A. Austr.
170 D2 Walkendorf Ger.
169 F4 Walkenried Ger.
84 C2 Walker r. N.T. Austr.
226 E4 Walker MI U.S.A.
236 E2 Walker MN U.S.A.
240 H2 Walker r. NV U.S.A.
169 E4 Walker Cay i. Bahamas
85 E3 Walker Creek r. Qld Austr.
240 H2 Walker Lake NV U.S.A.
262 R2 Walker Mountains Antarctica
232 E5 Walkersville MD U.S.A.
232 C5 Walkersville WV U.S.A.
227 G3 Walkerton Ont. Can.
226 D5 Walkerton IN U.S.A.
235 D1 Walker Valley NY U.S.A.
236 C2 Wall SD U.S.A.
87 C4 Wall, Mount hill W.A. Austr.
87 B6 Wallal Group i. W.A. Austr.
85 E2 Wallaby Island Qld Austr.
238 C2 Wallace ID U.S.A.
231 E5 Wallace NC U.S.A.
236 C3 Wallace NE U.S.A.
232 D6 Wallace VA U.S.A.
224 D5 Wallaceburg Ont. Can.
81 B7 Wallacetown South I. N.Z.
86 D3 Wallal Downs W.A. Austr.
87 C6 Wallambin, Lake salt flat W.A. Austr.
83 G2 Wallangarra Qld Austr.
82 D3 Wallaroo S.A. Austr.
149 F4 Wallasey Merseyside, England U.K.
85 G5 Wallaville Qld Austr.
238 C2 Walla Walla WA U.S.A.
172 C2 Walldorf Baden-Württemberg Ger.
172 C1 Walldorf Hessen Ger.
169 F5 Walldorf Thüringen Ger.
172 D1 Walldürn Ger.
214 A4 Walkraal S. Africa
83 G3 Wallendbeen N.S.W. Austr.
190 E1 Wallensee I. Switz.
179 H3 Wallerfing Ger.
179 H3 Wallern im Burgenland Austria
173 G3 Wallersdorf Ger.
178 E3 Wallersee I. Austria
173 E3 Wallerstein Ger.
173 F4 Wallgau Ger.
172 B2 Wallhausen Baden-Württemberg Ger.
172 B2 Wallhausen Rheinland-Pfalz Ger.
80 F1 Wallingford North I. N.Z.
151 F3 Wallingford Oxfordshire, England U.K.
235 F1 Wallingford CT U.S.A.
233 G3 Wallingford VT U.S.A.
Wallis canton Switz. see Valais
77 □1 Wallis, Îles is Wallis and Futuna Is
173 I3 Wallis and Futuna Islands terr. S. Pacific Ocean
172 C4 Wallisellen Switz.

Wallis et Futuna, Îles terr. S. Pacific Ocean see Wallis and Futuna Islands
Wallis and Futuna Islands see Wallis and Futuna Is
Wallis, Îles see Wallis, Îles
235 D1 Wallkill NY U.S.A.
235 E1 Wallkill r. NY U.S.A.
238 C2 Wallowa OR U.S.A.
238 C2 Wallowa Mountains OR U.S.A.
146 □G1 Walls Shetland, Scotland U.K.
168 E1 Wallsbüll Ger.
169 B4 Wallstawe Ger.
170 C3 Wallstawe Ger.
169 D5 Walluf Ger.
238 C2 Wallula WA U.S.A.
85 G5 Wallumbilla Qld Austr.
151 I3 Walmer Kent, England U.K.
149 F3 Walney, Isle of i. England U.K.
226 C5 Walnut IL U.S.A.
232 E4 Walnut Bottom PA U.S.A.
240 F3 Walnut Creek CA U.S.A.
236 D4 Walnut Creek r. KS U.S.A.
240 G2 Walnut Grove CA U.S.A.
234 C2 Walnutport PA U.S.A.
237 F4 Walnut Ridge AR U.S.A.
173 F3 Walpertskirchen Ger.
87 C7 Walpole W.A. Austr.
233 G3 Walpole NH U.S.A.
78 □5 Walpole, Île i. New Caledonia
175 J2 Walpusza r. Pol.
178 D3 Wals Austria
151 F4 Walsall West Midlands, England U.K.
173 E2 Walsdorf Ger.
239 H4 Walsenburg CO U.S.A.
85 E3 Walsh r. Qld Austr.
237 C4 Walsh CO U.S.A.
170 D3 Walsleben Ger.
151 H2 Walsoken Cambridgeshire, England U.K.
168 E3 Walsrode Ger.
175 H1 Walsza r. Pol.
115 D2 Waltair Andhra Prad. India
168 E3 Waltenhofen Ger.
231 D5 Walterboro SC U.S.A.
237 D5 Walters OK U.S.A.
169 F5 Waltershausen Ger.
83 F2 Walter's Range hills Qld Austr.
237 F5 Walthall MS U.S.A.
227 I3 Waltham Que. Can.
149 I4 Waltham North East Lincolnshire, England U.K.
233 H3 Waltham MA U.S.A.
233 □12 Waltham ME U.S.A.
164 E1 Waltham Abbey Essex, England U.K.
151 G2 Waltham on the Wolds Leicestershire, England U.K.
173 F3 Walting Ger.
173 F3 Walton NY U.S.A.
233 F3 Walton r. NY U.S.A.
232 C5 Walton WV U.S.A.
149 G4 Walton-le-Dale Lancashire, England U.K.
151 G3 Walton-on-Thames Surrey, England U.K.
151 I3 Walton-on-the-Naze Essex, England U.K.
Walvisbaai Namibia see Walvis Bay
212 B4 Walvis Bay Namibia
212 B4 Walvis Bay b. Namibia
264 I8 Walvis Ridge sea feature S. Atlantic Ocean
87 C6 Walyahmoing hill W.A. Austr.
208 E4 Wamba Dem. Rep. Congo
209 C5 Wamba r. Dem. Rep. Congo
207 H4 Wamba Nigeria
183 F3 Wamba Spain
236 D4 Wamego KS U.S.A.
211 C6 Wami r. Tanz.
238 F3 Wamsutter WY U.S.A.
83 F2 Wanaaring N.S.W. Austr.
81 B6 Wanaka South I. N.Z.
81 B6 Wanaka, Lake South I. N.Z.
235 D2 Wanamassa NJ U.S.A.
234 B1 Wanamie PA U.S.A.
109 E3 Wan'an Jiangxi China
235 D1 Wanaque NJ U.S.A.
82 E3 Wanbi S.A. Austr.
108 B3 Wanbi Yunnan China
231 F5 Wanchese NC U.S.A.
258 G2 Wanda Arg.
108 D3 Wanda Shan mts China
223 H4 Wandering River Alta Can.
169 F5 Wandersleben Ger.
168 E1 Wanderup Ger.
108 A3 Wanding Yunnan China
Wandingzhen Yunnan China see Wanding
Wandiwash Tamil Nadu India see Vandavasi
81 D5 Wandle Downs South I. N.Z.
170 E3 Wanditz Ger.
85 G5 Wandoan Qld Austr.
151 G3 Wandsworth Greater London, England U.K.
179 G2 Wang Austria
96 B3 Wang, Mae Nam r. Thai.
80 E3 Wanganui r. North I. N.Z.
80 E3 Wanganui North I. N.Z.
81 C5 Wanganui r. South I. N.Z.
83 F4 Wangaratta Vic. Austr.
82 C3 Wangary S.A. Austr.
108 C1 Wangcang Sichuan China
109 E2 Wangcheng Hunan China
Wangda Xizang China see Zogang
107 G4 Wangdu Hebei China
117 G4 Wangdue Phodrang Bhutan
169 E4 Wangen Ger.
168 F1 Wangels Ger.
190 C1 Wangen Switz.
172 D4 Wangen im Allgäu Ger.
168 C2 Wangerooge Ger.
168 C2 Wangerooge i. Ger.
93 B5 Wanggamet, Gunung mt. Sumba Indon.
106 C4 Wanggezhuang Shandong China see Jiaonan
190 D1 Wangi Switz.
109 F2 Wangjiang Anhui China
100 C3 Wangkui Heilong. China
Wang Mai Khon Thai. see Sawankhalok
108 D4 Wangmo Guangxi China
108 D3 Wangmo Guizhou China
Wangolodougou Côte d'Ivoire see Ouangolodougou
100 D4 Wangqing Jilin China
Wangying Jiangsu China see Huaiyin
108 C1 Wangziguan Gansu China
222 C4 Wanham Alta Can.
251 H3 Wanhatti Suriname
208 E4 Wanie-Rukula Dem. Rep. Congo
116 B5 Wankaner Gujarat India
168 F1 Wankendorf Ger.
Wankie Zimbabwe see Hwange
210 E4 Wanlaweyn Somalia
168 D2 Wanna Ger.
87 F6 Wanna Lakes salt flat W.A. Austr.
81 B6 Wannoroo W.A. Austr.
109 C6 Wanning Hainan China
164 E3 Wanroij Neth.
179 G2 Wannonga Shanxi China
170 D3 Wansdorf Ger.
171 C4 Wansleben am See Ger.
80 F4 Wanstead North I. N.Z.
151 F3 Wantage Oxfordshire, England U.K.
235 D2 Wantagh NY U.S.A.
227 G2 Wanup Ont. Can.
108 D2 Wanxian Chongqing China
108 D1 Wanxian Chongqing China
108 C1 Wanyuan Sichuan China
109 E2 Wanzai Jiangxi China
165 D4 Wanze Belgium
Wanzhi Anhui China see Wuhu
226 B5 Wapakoneta OH U.S.A.
222 A2 Wapato WA U.S.A.
224 B3 Wapawekka Lake Sask. Can.
169 F5 Wapenveld Neth.
174 F3 Wapno Pol.
108 A3 Waping? China

235 E1 Wappinger Creek r. NY U.S.A.
235 E1 Wappingers Falls NY U.S.A.
236 F3 Waspaiminicon r. IA U.S.A.
108 B1 Waqên Sichuan China
232 C6 War WV U.S.A.
208 F2 Warab Sudan
208 F2 Warab state Sudan
105 F3 Warabi Japan
123 F5 Warah Pak.
114 C2 Warangal Andhra Prad. India
116 E5 Waraseoni Madh. Prad. India
83 F5 Waratah Tas. Austr.
83 F4 Warboy Ger.
151 G2 Warboys Cambridgeshire, England U.K.
85 G5 Warbreccan Qld Austr.
222 H4 Warburg Alta Can.
169 E4 Warburg Ger.
83 F4 Warburton Vic. Austr.
87 E5 Warburton W.A. Austr.
87 E5 Warburton watercourse S.A. Austr.
165 C4 Warche r. Belgium
149 G3 Warcop Cumbria, England U.K.
173 F3 Warcq France
81 E4 Ward South I. N.Z.
262 T2 Ward, Mount Antarctica
81 A6 Ward, Mount South I. N.Z.
81 B5 Ward, Mount South I. N.Z.
82 D3 Wardang Island S.A. Austr.
215 G2 Warden S. Africa
168 D2 Wardenburg Ger.
116 D5 Wardha Mahar. India
114 C2 Wardha r. India
146 I3 Ward Hill hill Scotland U.K.
151 F2 Wardington Oxfordshire, England U.K.
146 □G1 Ward of Bressay hill Scotland U.K.
170 D2 Wardow Ger.
146 I3 Ward's Stone hill England U.K.
222 E3 Ware B.C. Can.
151 G3 Ware Hertfordshire, England U.K.
233 G3 Ware MA U.S.A.
165 C4 Waregem Belgium
151 H6 Wareham Dorset, England U.K.
233 H4 Wareham MA U.S.A.
165 E4 Waremme Belgium
170 D2 Waren Ger.
169 C4 Warendorf Ger.
164 E1 Warffum Neth.
Wargla Alg. see Ouargla
164 E1 Warga Neth.
Wargiil i. S. Male Maldives see Vaagali
85 G4 Warginburra Peninsula Qld Austr.
Wargla Alg. see Ouargla
151 G3 Wargrave Wokingham, England U.K.
83 G2 Warialda N.S.W. Austr.
170 C2 Warin Ger.
96 D4 Warin Chamrap Thai.
147 E2 Waringstown Northern Ireland U.K.
149 G2 Wark Northumberland, England U.K.
175 J4 Warka Pol.
80 E2 Warkworth North I. N.Z.
149 H2 Warkworth Northumberland, England U.K.
Warli Sichuan China see Walêg
151 G3 Warlingham Surrey, England U.K.
156 C2 Warloy-Baillon France
174 G2 Warlubie Pol.
223 J4 Warman Sask. Can.
212 C6 Warmbad Namibia
164 C2 Warmenhuizen Neth.
156 E3 Warmeriville France
174 E2 Warmia reg. Pol.
151 F2 Warmington Warwickshire, England U.K.
175 I2 Warmińsko-Mazurskie prov. Pol.
150 E3 Warminster Wiltshire, England U.K.
234 C2 Warminster PA U.S.A.
164 D2 Warmond Neth.
169 D3 Warmsen Ger.
241 I2 Warm Springs NV U.S.A.
232 D5 Warm Springs VA U.S.A.
214 C5 Warmwaterberg S. Africa
170 D1 Warnemünde Ger.
223 H5 Warner Alta Can.
233 H3 Warner NH U.S.A.
238 B4 Warner Mountains CA U.S.A.
231 D5 Warner Robins GA U.S.A.
240 I5 Warner Springs CA U.S.A.
253 E4 Warnes Bol.
165 B4 Warneton Belgium
173 H4 Warngau Ger.
151 I3 Warnham West Sussex, England U.K.
174 C2 Warnow r. Ger.
170 C2 Warnow r. Ger.
170 D1 Warnow r. Ger.
169 E4 Warnsveld Neth.
114 C2 Waronda Mahar. India
116 D5 Warora Mahar. India
168 E3 Warpe Ger.
85 G5 Warra Qld Austr.
83 E4 Warracknabeal Vic. Austr.
83 G3 Warragamba Reservoir N.S.W. Austr.
83 F4 Warragul Vic. Austr.
82 D2 Warrakalanna, Lake salt flat S.A. Austr.
82 C3 Warrambool S.A. Austr.
87 E6 Warramboo hill W.A. Austr.
83 F4 Warrambool Vic. Austr.
82 D1 Warrandirinna, Lake salt flat S.A. Austr.
83 F4 Warrandyte Vic. Austr.
86 D4 Warrawagine W.A. Austr.
83 F2 Warrego r. N.S.W./Qld Austr.
85 F5 Warrego Range hills Qld Austr.
83 F2 Warren r. N.S.W./Qld Austr.
87 B7 Warren r. W.A. Austr.
234 C4 Warren AR U.S.A.
226 C4 Warren IN U.S.A.
226 E5 Warren MI U.S.A.
236 E1 Warren MN U.S.A.
234 B2 Warren OH U.S.A.
234 B2 Warren PA U.S.A.
231 D5 Warren County county GA U.S.A.
235 D3 Warren Grove NJ U.S.A.
Warren Hastings Island Palau see Merir
147 E2 Warrenpoint Northern Ireland U.K.
226 B3 Warrens WI U.S.A.
235 G3 Warrensburg MO U.S.A.
235 E1 Warrensburg NY U.S.A.
234 A4 Warrensville WV U.S.A.
215 G4 Warrenton S. Africa
231 D5 Warrenton GA U.S.A.
236 H4 Warrenton MO U.S.A.
231 E4 Warrenton NC U.S.A.
238 A2 Warrenton OR U.S.A.
232 E5 Warrenton VA U.S.A.
207 G5 Warri Nigeria
87 C6 Warriedar hill W.A. Austr.
81 C6 Warrington South I. N.Z.
149 G4 Warrington Warrington, England U.K.
149 G4 Warrington admin. div. England U.K.
231 C6 Warrington FL U.S.A.
83 E4 Warrnambool Vic. Austr.
236 E1 Warroad MN U.S.A.
83 F2 Warroo N.S.W. Austr.
213 H3 Warsingsfehn Somalia
147 D2 Warrenpoint Northern Ireland U.K.
226 C5 Warsaw IL U.S.A.
230 C3 Warsaw IN U.S.A.
232 C4 Warsaw KY U.S.A.
236 H4 Warsaw MO U.S.A.
235 F1 Warsaw NY U.S.A.
232 C4 Warsaw OH U.S.A.
232 E6 Warsaw VA U.S.A.
179 F3 Warscheneck mt. Austria
168 D2 Warsingsfehn Ger.
210 E4 Warshiikh Somalia
170 D1 Warsow Ger.
149 H4 Warsop Nottinghamshire, England U.K.

169 D4 Warstein Ger.
175 J3 Warszawa Pol.
174 D3 Warta Pol.
174 A4 Warta r. Pol.
174 D4 Warta Bolesławiecka Pol.
179 F3 Wartberg an der Krems Austria
231 C4 Wartburg TN U.S.A.
171 B5 Wartburg Schloß tourist site Thüringen Ger.
237 C4 Wartburg City ND U.S.A.
223 K3 Wartbaman r. Sask. Can.
222 D4 Watheroo W.A. Austr.
169 E5 Wartenberg Ger.
171 E6 Wartenberg Ger.
170 F2 Wartin Ger.
175 H4 Wartkowice Pol.
169 E5 Wartmannsroth Ger.
149 G3 Warton Lancashire, England U.K.
116 D5 Warud Mahar. India
83 H2 Warwick Qld Austr.
151 F2 Warwick Warwickshire, England U.K.
84 D2 Warwick Channel N.T. Austr.
235 I3 Warwick NY U.S.A.
233 I4 Warwick RI U.S.A.
151 F2 Warwickshire admin. div. England U.K.
108 B2 Warzhong Sichuan China
222 H5 Wasa B.C. Can.
222 H5 Wasa B.C. Can.
227 G3 Wasaga Beach Ont. Can.
241 L2 Wasatch Range mts UT U.S.A.
215 H3 Wasbank S. Africa
168 E1 Wasbek Ger.
146 E2 Wasbister Orkney, Scotland U.K.
169 F3 Wasbüttel Ger.
223 J5 Wascana Creek r. Sask. Can.
172 D2 Wäschenbeuren Ger.
240 H4 Wasco CA U.S.A.
238 B3 Wasco OR U.S.A.
236 E2 Waseca MN U.S.A.
175 H3 Wąsewo Pol.
225 C6 Washburn IL U.S.A.
233 □I1 Washburn ME U.S.A.
236 C1 Washburn ND U.S.A.
226 B2 Washburn WI U.S.A.
104 C3 Washiga-take mt. Japan
116 D5 Washim Mahar. India
225 F3 Washimeska r. Que. Can.
149 H3 Washington Tyne and Wear, England U.K.
235 E1 Washington CT U.S.A.
234 A4 Washington DC U.S.A.
231 D5 Washington GA U.S.A.
236 F3 Washington IA U.S.A.
226 C5 Washington IL U.S.A.
226 C4 Washington IN U.S.A.
236 D4 Washington KS U.S.A.
232 B5 Washington KY U.S.A.
231 E5 Washington NC U.S.A.
233 H3 Washington NH U.S.A.
235 G2 Washington NJ U.S.A.
234 C2 Washington PA U.S.A.
241 N3 Washington UT U.S.A.
232 D4 Washington VA U.S.A.
238 B2 Washington state U.S.A.
263 L2 Washington, Cape Antarctica
233 H2 Washington, Mount NH U.S.A.
234 D2 Washington Court House OH U.S.A.
234 D2 Washington Crossing NJ U.S.A.
235 E1 Washington Depot CT U.S.A.
234 A3 Washington Grove MD U.S.A.
232 D5 Washington Island WI U.S.A.
221 L2 Washington Land reg. Greenland
235 D1 Washingtonville NY U.S.A.
235 D1 Washingtonville PA U.S.A.
237 D5 Washita r. OK U.S.A.
238 C2 Washtucna WA U.S.A.
156 C2 Wasigny France
175 L2 Wasiółkow Pol.
127 G4 Wāsit governorate Iraq
127 G4 Wasit tourist site Iraq
222 H4 Waskaganish r. Alta Can.
174 F4 Wasko Sask. Can.
175 K4 Wasoso Pol.
174 F5 Wasosz Pol.
174 E3 Wasowo Pol.
242 □I6 Waspán Nic.
164 D3 Waspik Neth.
149 H3 Wass North Yorkshire, England U.K.
206 B3 Wassadou Senegal
165 E3 Wasseiges Belgium
157 H4 Wasselonne France
190 D2 Wassen Switz.
164 D2 Wassenaar Neth.
172 B2 Wasserbillig Lux.
173 G3 Wasserburg am Inn Ger.
169 C4 Wasserkuppe hill Ger.
169 E5 Wasserleben Ger.
169 F5 Wasserlosen Ger.
173 E2 Wassertrüdingen Ger.
156 D2 Wassigny France
206 B4 Wassou Guinea
240 H2 Wassuk Range mts NV U.S.A.
157 F4 Wassy France
93 A4 Watampone Sulawesi Selatan Indon.
Watansoppeng Sulawesi Selatan Indon.
207 I4 Waza Cameroon
156 D2 Waziers France
123 H3 Wazirabad Pak.
174 G2 Wda r. Pol.
Wdig Pembrokeshire, Wales U.K. see Goodwick
78 □1 We i. Loyauté New Caledonia
149 H3 Wear r. England U.K.
233 H3 Weare NH U.S.A.
85 F2 Weary Bay Qld Austr.
231 D5 Weatherford OK U.S.A.
237 D5 Weatherford TX U.S.A.
234 C2 Weatherly PA U.S.A.
149 G4 Weaverham Cheshire, England U.K.
238 B3 Weaverville CA U.S.A.
86 F4 Webb, Mount hill N.T. Austr.
224 D4 Webbwood Ont. Can.
224 C2 Webequie Ont. Can.
80 F4 Weber North I. N.Z.
222 D4 Weber r. B.C. Can.
86 M5 Weber, Mount B.C. Can.
210 D3 Webi Shabeelle r. Somalia
233 H3 Webster MA U.S.A.
236 C2 Webster SD U.S.A.
232 A5 Webster Groves MO U.S.A.
236 F2 Webster City IA U.S.A.
232 C5 Webster Springs WV U.S.A.
165 D3 Wechelderzande Belgium
Wechmar Ger. see Günthersleben-Wechmar
122 H2 Wecho r. N.W.T. Can.
171 H4 Wechselburg Ger.
168 F2 Wedde Neth.
262 V2 Weddell Abyssal Plain sea feature Southern Ocean
259 E8 Weddell Island Falkland Is
83 E4 Wedderburn Vic. Austr.
81 B7 Wedderburn South I. N.Z.
168 E2 Weddingstedt Ger.
168 E2 Wedel (Holstein) Ger.
140 □ Wedel Jarlsberg Land reg. Svalbard
232 F5 Wedge Mountain B.C. Can.
179 G3 Weiz Sichuan China
150 E2 Wedmore Somerset, England U.K.
151 E4 Wednesbury West Midlands, England U.K.
143 H4 Wednesfield West Midlands, England U.K.
151 F2 Weedon Bec Northamptonshire, England U.K.
232 E4 Weedville PA U.S.A.
165 D4 Weelde Belgium
82 D2 Weemelah N.S.W. Austr.

147 A5 Waterville Rep. of Ireland
233 □I2 Waterville ME U.S.A.
232 B4 Waterville OH U.S.A.
235 D3 Waterville PA U.S.A.
233 D3 Waterville VT U.S.A.
95 E4 Wates Indon.
227 G4 Watford Ont. Can.
151 G3 Watford Hertfordshire, England U.K.
236 C1 Watford City ND U.S.A.
223 K4 Wathaman r. Sask. Can.
87 C6 Watheroo W.A. Austr.
222 G4 Watino Alta Can.
232 E3 Watkins Glen NY U.S.A.
231 D5 Watkinsville GA U.S.A.
Watling Island Bahamas see San Salvador
151 F3 Watlington Oxfordshire, England U.K.
237 D5 Watonga OK U.S.A.
93 D2 Watowato, Bukit mt. Halmahera Indon.
223 J5 Watrous Sask. Can.
239 F5 Watrous NM U.S.A.
208 F4 Watsa Dem. Rep. Congo
226 C5 Watseka IL U.S.A.
223 J4 Watson r. Sask. Can.
224 H4 Watson Sask. Can.
262 P1 Watson Escarpment Antarctica
222 C2 Watson Lake Y.T. Can.
234 B1 Watsontown PA U.S.A.
240 G3 Watsonville CA U.S.A.
87 E5 Watt, Mount hill W.A. Austr.
156 C2 Watten France
146 I3 Watten Highland, Scotland U.K.
168 E1 Wattenbek Ger.
168 F1 Wattenbek Ger.
190 C2 Wattenwil Switz.
178 C3 Wattens Austria
149 I2 Wattignies-la-Victoire France
147 D2 Wattlebridge Northern Ireland U.K.
170 D2 Wattmannshagen Ger.
151 H2 Watton Norfolk, England U.K.
151 G3 Watton-at-Stone Hertfordshire, England U.K.
156 D2 Wattrelos France
231 C5 Watts Bar Lake resr TN U.S.A.
232 D3 Wattsburg PA U.S.A.
190 E1 Wattwil Switz.
93 B3 Watubela, Kepulauan is Indon.
169 D5 Watzenborn-Steinberg Ger.
208 □ Wau Sudan
83 H2 Wauchope N.S.W. Austr.
84 C4 Wauchope N.T. Austr.
231 D7 Wauchula FL U.S.A.
93 A3 Waukara, Gunung mt. Indon.
86 D4 Waukarlycarly, Lake salt flat W.A. Austr.
226 C4 Waukegan IL U.S.A.
226 C4 Waukesha WI U.S.A.
226 A4 Waukon IA U.S.A.
226 C4 Waunakee WI U.S.A.
226 A4 Wauneta NE U.S.A.
226 A4 Waupaca WI U.S.A.
226 C4 Waupun WI U.S.A.
235 G1 Wauregan CT U.S.A.
237 E5 Waurika OK U.S.A.
226 C3 Wausau WI U.S.A.
226 C3 Wausaukee WI U.S.A.
226 C4 Wauseon OH U.S.A.
226 C3 Wautoma WI U.S.A.
226 C4 Wauwatosa WI U.S.A.
84 B3 Wave Hill N.T. Austr.
151 I2 Waveney r. England U.K.
80 E3 Waverley North I. N.Z.
226 A3 Waverly IA U.S.A.
232 B5 Waverly KY U.S.A.
232 B5 Waverly OH U.S.A.
231 C4 Waverly TN U.S.A.
232 E6 Waverly VA U.S.A.
165 D4 Wavre Belgium
207 H4 Wawa Nigeria
224 D4 Wawa Ont. Can.
207 G4 Wawa Nigeria
224 D4 Wawagosic r. Que. Can.
235 D1 Wawarsing NY U.S.A.
174 F5 Wawelno Pol.
91 J8 Wawoi r. P.N.G.
175 K4 Wawolnica Pol.
175 I3 Wawrów Pol.
175 I5 Wawrzeńczyce Pol.
237 D5 Waxahachie TX U.S.A.
169 B5 Waxweiler Ger.
110 D4 Waxxari Xinjiang China
79 □1a Waya i. Fiji
107 I3 Wayaobu Shaanxi China see Zichang
231 D6 Waycross GA U.S.A.
232 B6 Wayland KY U.S.A.
226 E4 Wayland MI U.S.A.
236 D3 Wayne NE U.S.A.
234 C2 Wayne PA U.S.A.
232 B5 Wayne WV U.S.A.
234 C1 Wayne County county PA U.S.A.
231 D6 Waynesboro GA U.S.A.
237 F6 Waynesboro MS U.S.A.
231 C5 Waynesboro TN U.S.A.
232 E4 Waynesboro PA U.S.A.
232 D5 Waynesboro VA U.S.A.
232 C5 Waynesburg PA U.S.A.
231 D5 Waynesville NC U.S.A.
236 H4 Waynesville MO U.S.A.
237 D4 Waynoka OK U.S.A.
123 H3 Wazirabad Pak.
174 F5 Wdzydze, Jezioro l. Pol.

215 H3 Weenen S. Africa
168 C2 Weener Ger.
179 G2 Weener Austria
164 F2 Weerselo Neth.
165 E3 Weert Neth.
168 E1 Wees Ger.
190 E1 Weesen Switz.
164 E2 Weesp Neth.
169 B4 Weeze Ger.
171 F2 Weferlingen Ger.
169 B4 Wegberg Ger.
215 H3 Wegdraai S. Africa
171 C4 Wegeleben Ger.
174 C4 Wegenstedt Ger.
174 C3 Wegliniec Pol.
175 I1 Węgorzewo Pol.
175 K3 Węgorzyno Pol.
175 K3 Węgrów Pol.
179 K3 Wegscheid Ger.
151 G2 Wehdel Ger.
83 G3 Wehe-den Hoorn Neth.
164 F1 Wehl Neth.
172 B4 Wehr Ger.
168 D3 Wehrbleck Ger.
169 D5 Wehrheim Ger.
169 C5 Wehringen Ger.
168 E1 Wei r. Henan China
107 F5 Wei r. Shaanxi China
107 H4 Wei r. Shandong China
169 D2 Weibern Ger.
172 D2 Weiberbrunn Ger.
107 H3 Weichang Hebei China
173 F3 Weichering Ger.
171 D5 Weichs Ger.
171 D5 Weida Ger.
171 D5 Weida r. Ger.
173 F2 Weidenbach Ger.
173 G2 Weiden in der Oberpfalz Ger.
172 B2 Weidenstetten Ger.
172 D3 Weidenthal Ger.
173 G2 Weiding Ger.
173 G2 Weidingen Ger.
156 D2 Weidongmen Heilong. China see Qianjin
212 F4 Weiersbach Ger.
107 H4 Weifang Shandong China
171 F4 Weigersdorf Ger.
234 B3 Weigelstown PA U.S.A.
107 I4 Weihai Shandong China
173 G3 Weihenzell Ger.
169 E4 Weihermühl Ger.
173 G3 Weihmichl Ger.
107 H2 Weihnoof Austria
172 D2 Weikersheim Ger.
173 G2 Weil Ger.
172 A4 Weil am Rhein Ger.
172 B2 Weilbach Ger.
172 C3 Weil der Stadt Ger.
143 A3 Weiler Austria
172 A2 Weiler Ger.
172 B2 Weilerbach Ger.
172 B2 Weilerswist Ger.
172 D3 Weilheim an der Teck Ger.
172 D3 Weilheim in Oberbayern Ger.
83 F2 Weilmoringle N.S.W. Austr.
171 D5 Weimar (Annstal) Ger.
169 C4 Weimar Thüringen Ger.
107 F5 Weinan Shaanxi China
169 D3 Weinbach Ger.
169 D5 Weinböhla Ger.
190 E1 Weinfelden Switz.
172 C2 Weingarten (Baden) Ger.
172 D2 Weingarten Ger.
108 D3 Weining Guizhou China
172 D2 Weinsberg Ger.
172 D3 Weinstadt Ger.
169 D5 Weinsheim Rheinland-Pfalz Ger.
169 B5 Weinsheim Rheinland-Pfalz Ger.
172 D3 Weinstadt Ger.
85 E2 Weipa Qld Austr.
Weiqu Shaanxi China see Chang'an
87 C5 Weir r. Qld Austr.
223 M3 Weir River Man. Can.
232 C4 Weirton WV U.S.A.
171 D5 Weischlitz Ger.
146 □G1 Weisdale Shetland, Scotland U.K.
172 D3 Weisen Ger.
173 E2 Weisendorf Ger.
238 C2 Weiser ID U.S.A.
238 C2 Weiser r. ID U.S.A.
108 B3 Weishan Yunnan China
107 G5 Weishi Henan China
172 A2 Weiße Elster r. Ger.
172 B2 Weiße Laber r. Ger.
171 B8 Weißenbach am Lech Austria
169 F4 Weißenborn Ger.
169 E5 Weißenborn-Lüderode Ger.
171 C4 Weißenbrunn Ger.
171 G4 Weißenburg in Bayern Ger.
171 C4 Weißenfels Ger.
173 G3 Weißenhorn Ger.
171 C4 Weißensberg Ger.
171 C4 Weißensee Ger.
171 C4 Weißenstein Austria
179 B3 Weißkirchen in Steiermark Austria
171 F4 Weißkeissel Ger.
178 B3 Weißkugel mt. Austria/Italy
190 D2 Weissmies mt. Switz.
212 C5 Weissrand Mountains Namibia
171 F4 Weißwasser Ger.
172 B2 Weistrach Austria
169 G2 Weiswil Switz.
173 B3 Weitenfeld Austria
179 G2 Weitendorf Ger.
178 G1 Weitenhagen Ger.
179 C2 Weitensfeld Austria
172 C2 Weiterstadt Ger.
164 E2 Weiteveen Neth.
173 H4 Weitnau Ger.
169 G5 Weitramsdorf Ger.
171 F4 Weixdorf Ger.
108 A3 Weixi Yunnan China
108 C3 Weixin Yunnan China see Mengzi
108 D3 Weixin Yunnan China
110 D2 Weiya Xinjiang China
108 C1 Weiyuan Gansu China
108 B2 Weiyuan Qinghai China see Huzhu
108 B2 Weiyuan Sichuan China
108 C3 Weiyuan Jiang r. Yunnan China
179 G2 Weiz Austria
107 H4 Weizhou Sichuan China see Wenchuan
107 I3 Weizi Liaoning China
175 I1 Wejherowo Pol.
223 H4 Wekusko Man. Can.
175 H4 Wekweti N.W.T. Can.
174 G2 Wel r. Pol.
82 C1 Welbourn Hill S.A. Austr.
232 F5 Welch WV U.S.A.
87 D6 Weld, Mount hill W.A. Austr.
83 G2 Welden N.S.W. Austr.
210 C2 Weldiya Eth.
110 C3 Weldon Xinjiang China

151 G2 Weldon Northamptonshire, England U.K.
87 C5 Weld Range hills W.A. Austr.
165 E4 Welkenraedt Belgium
210 C2 Welk'īt'ē Eth.
215 F2 Welkom S. Africa
164 F3 Well Neth.
172 E4 Welland Ger.
151 G2 Welland r. England U.K.
227 H4 Welland Canal Ont. Can.
171 H4 Wellaune Ger.
168 E2 Welle Ger.
165 E4 Wellen Belgium
172 C2 Wellendingen Ger.
151 F2 Wellesbourne Warwickshire, England U.K.
227 G4 Wellesley Ont. Can.
84 D3 Wellesley Islands Qld Austr.
233 H4 Wellfleet MA U.S.A.
173 F3 Wellheim Ger.
165 E4 Wellin Belgium
169 C5 Welling Ger.
151 G2 Wellingborough Northamptonshire, England U.K.
83 G3 Wellington N.S.W. Austr.
82 D3 Wellington S.A. Austr.
81 E4 Wellington North I. N.Z.
81 E4 Wellington admin. reg. North I. N.Z.
214 B5 Wellington S. Africa
150 D4 Wellington Somerset, England U.K.
151 E2 Wellington Telford and Wrekin, England U.K.
238 F3 Wellington CO U.S.A.
237 D4 Wellington KS U.S.A.
240 H2 Wellington NV U.S.A.
232 B4 Wellington OH U.S.A.
237 C5 Wellington TX U.S.A.
241 L2 Wellington UT U.S.A.
259 B8 Wellington, Isla i. Chile
179 F2 Wellington Bridge Rep. of Ireland
84 C2 Wellington Range hills N.T. Austr.
87 D5 Wellington Range hills W.A. Austr.
150 C5 Wells B.C. Can.
222 F4 Wells B.C. Can.
150 E3 Wells Somerset, England U.K.
238 D3 Wells NV U.S.A.
87 D5 Wells, Lake salt flat W.A. Austr.
232 E3 Wells NY U.S.A.
80 E2 Wellsford North I. N.Z.
151 H2 Wells-next-the-Sea Norfolk, England U.K.
226 E3 Wellston MI U.S.A.
232 E3 Wellsville NY U.S.A.
232 C4 Wellsville OH U.S.A.
234 B2 Wellsville PA U.S.A.
241 J5 Wellton AZ U.S.A.
174 E3 Wełna r. Pol.
151 H2 Welney Norfolk, England U.K.
175 I4 Wełnianka r. Pol.
179 F2 Wels Austria
170 A2 Welse r. Ger.
150 D2 Welshpool Powys, Wales U.K.
171 C4 Welsickendorf Ger.
171 C4 Welsleben Ger.
149 I4 Welton Lincolnshire, England U.K.
169 C4 Welver Ger.
Welwitschia Namibia see Khorixas
151 G3 Welwyn Hertfordshire, England U.K.
151 G3 Welwyn Garden City Hertfordshire, England U.K.
172 D3 Welzheim Ger.
171 F4 Welzow Ger.
94 Wem Shropshire, England U.K.
150 D2 Wembdon Somerset, England U.K.
211 B6 Wembere r. Tanz.
215 G3 Wembesi S. Africa
222 G4 Wembley Alta Can.
173 E3 Wemding Ger.
164 D3 Wemeldinge Neth.
210 D3 Wemel Shet' r. Eth.
224 E2 Wemindji Que. Can.
146 D6 Wemyss Bay Inverclyde, Scotland U.K.
146 G1 Wemyss Bight Eleuthera Bahamas
107 H5 Wen r. China
251 F3 Wenamu r. Guyana/Venez.
238 B2 Wenatchee WA U.S.A.
238 B2 Wenatchee Mountains WA U.S.A.
108 D5 Wenchang Hainan China
Wenchang Sichuan China see Zitong
109 E3 Wencheng Zhejiang China
206 E5 Wenchi Ghana
210 C2 Wench'ît Shet' r. Eth.
109 E3 Wencheng Zhejiang China see Wenzhou
108 B2 Wenchuan Sichuan China
169 F3 Wendeburg Ger.
172 C2 Wendelsheim Ger.
173 F2 Wendelstein Ger.
169 G4 Wendelstein mt. Ger.
241 K5 Wenden AZ U.S.A.
110 C4 Wendeng Shandong China
151 H2 Wendens Ambo Essex, England U.K.
168 F2 Wenden Latvia see Cēsis
168 E2 Wennden Ger.
170 C2 Wendisch Evern Ger.
171 F4 Wendisch Priborn Ger.
171 F1 Wendisch Rietz Ger.
172 D3 Wendlingen am Neckar Ger.
210 C3 Wendo Eth.
206 B4 Wéndou Mbôrou Guinea
151 G3 Wendover Buckinghamshire, England U.K.
241 J1 Wendover UT U.S.A.
150 B4 Wendron Cornwall, England U.K.
165 C3 Wenduine Belgium
109 E3 Wenfeng Jiangxi China see Yongfeng
190 C2 Wengen Switz.
169 C3 Wengsel (Isterberg) Ger.
109 A2 Wengshui Yunnan China
109 E3 Wenguan Guangdong China
Wenhua Yunnan China see Weishan
109 E3 Wenjiashi Jiangxi China
Wenlan Sichuan China see Mengzi
Wenlin Sichuan China see Renshou
109 G2 Wenling Zhejiang China
150 E2 Wenlock Edge ridge England U.K.
250 □ Wenman, Isla i. Islas Galápagos Ecuador
169 D4 Wenner r. Ger.
169 E3 Wennigsen (Deister) Ger.
169 G2 Wennington r. England U.K.
179 B3 Wenns Austria
168 E2 Wennsee Ger.
78 □4a Weno i. Chuuk Micronesia
226 C5 Wenona IL U.S.A.
233 F5 Wenona MD U.S.A.
Wenping Yunnan China see Ludian
108 D2 Wenquan Chongqing China
108 D2 Wenquan Guizhou China
110 B3 Wenquan Qinghai China
116 D1 Wenquan Xizang China
110 C2 Wenquan Xinjiang China
108 C4 Wenshan Yunnan China
108 C3 Wenshan Yunnan China
149 H3 Wensley North Yorkshire, England U.K.
149 H3 Wensleydale val. England U.K.
110 C3 Wensu Xinjiang China

Wensum to Windischgarsten
379

151 I2 Wensum r. England U.K.
149 I4 Went r. England U.K.
168 F2 Wentorf Ger.
168 F2 Wentorf bei Hamburg Ger.
83 E3 Wentworth N.S.W. Austr.
231 E4 Wentworth NC U.S.A.
233 H3 Wentworth NH U.S.A.
226 B2 Wentworth WI U.S.A.
107 F5 Wenxi Shanxi China
108 C1 Wenxian Gansu China
107 F4 Wenyu r. China
173 G2 Wenzenbach Ger.
109 G3 Wenzhou Zhejiang China
171 D3 Wenzlow Ger.
150 E2 Weobley Herefordshire, England U.K.
215 F3 Wepener S. Africa
165 D4 Wépion Belgium
116 D4 Wer Rajasthan India
172 D2 Werbach Ger.
170 E3 Werbellin Ger.
171 F4 Werben Ger.
170 C3 Werben (Elbe) Ger.
171 E4 Werbig Ger.
175 L5 Werbkowice Pol.
165 E4 Werbomont Belgium
212 D5 Werda Botswana
171 D5 Werdau Ger.
210 E3 Werdēr Eth.
171 D3 Werder Brandenburg Ger.
170 E2 Werder Mecklenburg-Vorpommern Ger.
169 C4 Werdohl Ger.
168 C2 Werdum Ger.
151 H2 Wereham Norfolk, England U.K.
178 E3 Werfen Austria
169 C4 Werl Ger.
168 C3 Werlte Ger.
169 C4 Wermelskirchen Ger.
171 D4 Wermsdorf Ger.
169 E5 Wern r. Ger.
172 D3 Wernau Ger.
179 E4 Wernberg Austria
173 G2 Wernberg-Köblitz Ger.
179 G4 Werndorf Austria
169 C4 Werne Ger.
171 B5 Werneck Ger.
170 E3 Werneuchen Ger.
169 F4 Wernigerode Ger.
169 F5 Wernshausen Ger.
168 C3 Werpeloh Ger.
169 E4 Werra r. Ger.
169 D3 Werre r. Ger.
82 E3 Werrimull Vic. Austr.
83 G2 Werris Creek N.S.W. Austr.
173 E4 Wertach Ger.
173 E3 Wertach r. Ger.
172 D2 Wertheim Ger.
172 C4 Werthenstein Switz.
169 F4 Werther Ger.
169 D3 Werther (Westfalen) Ger.
173 E3 Wertingen Ger.
164 E2 Wervershoof Neth.
165 C4 Wervik Belgium
169 B4 Wesel Ger.
170 D2 Wesenberg Ger.
168 F3 Wesendorf Ger.
164 F2 Wesepe Neth.
169 D2 Weser r. Ger.
168 D2 Weser sea chan. Ger.
168 C3 Weser-Ems admin. reg. Niedersachsen Ger.
169 D3 Wesergebirge hills Ger.
236 C4 Weskan KS U.S.A.
237 D7 Weslaco TX U.S.A.
215 F5 Wesley S. Africa
233 □J2 Wesley ME U.S.A.
225 K3 Wesleyville Nfld. Can.
232 C3 Wesleyville PA U.S.A.
175 J3 Wesoła Pol.
84 D1 Wessel, Cape N.T. Austr.
168 D1 Wesselburen Ger.
169 B5 Wesseling Ger.
84 D1 Wessel Islands N.T. Austr.
168 E1 Wesseln Ger.
215 F2 Wesselsbron S. Africa
214 D2 Wesselsvlei S. Africa
215 G2 Wesselton S. Africa
165 E3 Wessem Neth.
236 D2 Wessington Springs SD U.S.A.
173 F3 Weßling Ger.
173 F4 Wessobrunn Ger.
234 B4 West r. MD U.S.A.
82 C3 Westall, Point S.A. Austr.
84 C2 West Alligator r. N.T. Austr.
226 C4 West Allis WI U.S.A.
262 P1 West Antarctica reg. Antarctica
235 D3 West Atlantic City NJ U.S.A.
149 H3 West Auckland Durham, England U.K.
265 K6 West Australian Basin sea feature Indian Ocean
235 E2 West Babylon NY U.S.A.
84 B2 West Baines r. N.T. Austr.
116 B5 West Banas r. India
128 B4 West Bank terr. Asia
225 J2 West Bay Nfld. Can.
246 B3 West Bay Cayman Is
226 C4 West Bend WI U.S.A.
117 F5 West Bengal state India
151 H3 West Bergholt Essex, England U.K.
151 F3 West Berkshire admin. div. England U.K.
234 D3 West Berlin NJ U.S.A.
232 B5 Westboro OH U.S.A.
227 E3 West Branch MI U.S.A.
151 F2 West Bridgford Nottinghamshire, England U.K.
151 F2 West Bromwich West Midlands, England U.K.
235 F1 Westbrook CT U.S.A.
233 □H3 Westbrook ME U.S.A.
234 D1 Westbrookville NY U.S.A.
233 H2 West Burke VT U.S.A.
83 F5 Westbury Tas. Austr.
150 E3 Westbury Wiltshire, England U.K.
226 B4 Westby WI U.S.A.
246 D2 West Caicos i. Turks and Caicos Is
146 E6 West Calder West Lothian, Scotland U.K.
234 B2 West Cameron PA U.S.A.
81 A6 West Cape South I. N.Z.
87 C7 West Cape Howe W.A. Austr.
234 D4 West Cape May NJ U.S.A.
266 E5 West Caroline Basin sea feature N. Pacific Ocean
234 C3 West Chester PA U.S.A.
235 E1 Westchester County county NY U.S.A.
239 F4 Westcliffe CO U.S.A.
81 C5 West Coast admin. reg. South I. N.Z.
150 E4 West Coker Somerset, England U.K.
226 A3 West Concord MN U.S.A.
151 G3 Westcott Surrey, England U.K.
235 D3 West Creek NJ U.S.A.
81 B6 West Dome mt. South I. N.Z.
165 C3 Westdorpe Neth.
227 F3 West Duck Island Ont. Can.
146 D6 West Dunbartonshire admin. div. Scotland U.K.
231 E7 West End Bahamas
233 F3 West End NY U.S.A.
165 B3 Westende Belgium
178 D3 Westendorf Austria
164 F2 Westenholte Neth.
168 E1 Westensee Ger.
168 F3 Westerbeck (Sassenburg) Ger.
214 D3 Westerberg S. Africa
164 F2 Westerbork Neth.
169 C5 Westerburg Ger.
146 E3 Westerdale Highland, Scotland U.K.
171 C4 Westeregeln Ger.
168 C2 Westerende-Kirchloog (Ihlow) Ger.
81 C5 Westerfield South I. N.Z.
151 G4 Westergate West Sussex, England U.K.
168 F2 Westergellersen Ger.
164 F2 Westerhaar Neth.
151 H3 Westerham Kent, England U.K.
171 C4 Westerhausen Ger.
172 D3 Westerheim Baden-Württemberg Ger.
173 E3 Westerheim Bayern Ger.
168 C2 Westerholt Ger.
168 E2 Westerhorn Ger.
165 E3 Westerhoven Neth.
168 D1 Westerland Ger.
165 D3 Westerlo Belgium
235 G1 Westerly RI U.S.A.
206 E5 Western admin. reg. Ghana
209 D8 Western prov. Zambia
206 B4 Western Area admin. div. Sierra Leone
87 D5 Western Australia state Austr.
208 E3 Western Bahr el Ghazal state Sudan
214 C5 Western Cape prov. S. Africa
202 D6 Western Darfur state Sudan
Western Dvina r. Europe see Zapadnaya Dvina
208 F3 Western Equatoria state Sudan
114 B3 Western Ghats mts India
146 B3 Western Isles admin. div. Scotland U.K.
208 F2 Western Kordofan state Sudan
Western Lesser Sunda Islands prov. Indon. see Nusa Tenggara Barat
83 F4 Western Port b. Vic. Austr.
Western Province prov. Zambia see Copperbelt
204 D3 Western Sahara terr. Africa
Western Samoa country S. Pacific Ocean see Samoa
Western Sayan Mountains reg. Rus. Fed. see Zapadnyy Sayan
168 E1 Wester-Ohrstedt Ger.
146 E6 Wester Parkgate Dumfries and Galloway, Scotland U.K.
146 C4 Wester Ross reg. Scotland U.K.
165 C3 Westerschelde est. Neth.
168 C2 Westerstede Ger.
172 D3 Westerstetten Ger.
232 B4 Westerville OH U.S.A.
164 E3 Westervoort Neth.
169 C5 Westerwald hills Ger.
171 E4 Westewitz Ger.
259 E8 West Falkland i. Falkland Is
236 D2 West Fargo ND U.S.A.
91 K5 West Fayu atoll Micronesia
149 I4 West Fen reg. Lincolnshire, England U.K.
151 H4 Westfield East Sussex, England U.K.
233 G3 Westfield MA U.S.A.
233 □J1 Westfield ME U.S.A.
235 D2 Westfield NJ U.S.A.
232 D3 Westfield NY U.S.A.
232 E4 Westfield PA U.S.A.
226 C4 Westfield WI U.S.A.
West Flanders prov. Belgium see West-Vlaanderen
233 □I2 West Forks ME U.S.A.
235 D2 West Freehold NJ U.S.A.
West Frisian Islands Neth. see Waddeneilanden
164 F1 Westgat sea chan. Neth.
85 F5 Westgate Qld Austr.
149 G3 Westgate Durham, England U.K.
238 D1 West Glacier MT U.S.A.
151 G4 West Grinstead West Sussex, England U.K.
234 C3 West Grove PA U.S.A.
151 F2 West Haddon Northamptonshire, England U.K.
232 B5 West Hamlin WV U.S.A.
235 F2 Westhampton NY U.S.A.
150 E3 West Harptree Bath and North East Somerset, England U.K.
235 F1 West Hartford CT U.S.A.
173 E3 Westhausen Ger.
235 F1 West Haven CT U.S.A.
235 E1 West Haverstraw NY U.S.A.
234 C2 West Hazleton PA U.S.A.
146 F4 Westhill Aberdeenshire, Scotland U.K.
172 C2 Westhofen Ger.
157 H4 Westhoffen France
236 C1 Westhope ND U.S.A.
263 F2 West Ice Shelf Antarctica
247 F2 West Indies N. America
146 □H1 Westing Shetland, Scotland U.K.
West Irian prov. Indon. see Irian Jaya
84 D2 West Island N.T. Austr.
86 □2 West Island Cocos Is
235 E2 West Islip NY U.S.A.
232 B5 West Jefferson OH U.S.A.
164 C3 Westkapelle Neth.
West Kazakhstan Oblast admin. div. Kazakh. see Zapadnyy Kazakhstan
146 D6 West Kilbride North Ayrshire, Scotland U.K.
233 H4 West Kingston RI U.S.A.
149 F4 West Kirby Merseyside, England U.K.
149 I3 West Knapton North Yorkshire, England U.K.
230 C3 West Lafayette IN U.S.A.
85 E4 Westland Qld Austr.
232 B3 Westland MI U.S.A.
78 □3b West Landing i. Majuro Marshall Is
151 F3 West Lavington Wiltshire, England U.K.
234 C2 West Lawn PA U.S.A.
215 F2 Westleigh S. Africa
151 I2 Westleton Suffolk, England U.K.
232 B6 West Liberty KY U.S.A.
232 B4 West Liberty OH U.S.A.
146 E6 West Linton Scottish Borders, Scotland U.K.
146 C6 West Loch Tarbert inlet Scotland U.K.
222 H4 Westlock Alta Can.
150 C4 West Looe Cornwall, England U.K.
224 D5 West Lorne Ont. Can.
146 E6 West Lothian admin. div. Scotland U.K.
150 E4 West Lulworth Dorset, England U.K.
209 E8 West Lunga r. Zambia
West Malaysia pen. Malaysia see Malaysia, Semenanjung
165 D3 Westmalle Belgium
151 H3 West Malling Kent, England U.K.
Westman Islands Iceland see Vestmannaeyjar
85 G5 Westmar Qld Austr.
266 E4 West Mariana Basin sea feature Pacific Ocean
147 D3 Westmeath county Rep. of Ireland
237 F5 West Memphis AR U.S.A.
151 F3 West Meon Hampshire, England U.K.
80 E3 Westmere North I. N.Z.
151 H3 West Mersea Essex, England U.K.
151 F2 West Midlands admin. div. England U.K.
235 D1 West Milford NJ U.S.A.
227 F5 West Millgrove OH U.S.A.
232 A5 West Milton OH U.S.A.
234 B1 West Milton PA U.S.A.
234 B3 Westminster MD U.S.A.
150 D3 West Monkton Somerset, England U.K.
237 E5 West Monroe LA U.S.A.
151 F4 West Moors Dorset, England U.K.
84 D3 Westmoreland Qld Austr.
236 D4 Westmoreland KS U.S.A.
246 □ Westmorland Jamaica
241 J5 Westmorland CA U.S.A.
234 B1 West Nanticoke PA U.S.A.
146 E2 Westness Orkney, Scotland U.K.
149 F3 Westnewton Cumbria, England U.K.
213 F4 West Nicholson Zimbabwe
237 D6 West Nueces r. TX U.S.A.
235 E1 West Nyack NY U.S.A.
81 C6 Weston South I. N.Z.
150 E4 Weston Dorset, England U.K.
150 E2 Weston Staffordshire, England U.K.
235 E1 Weston CT U.S.A.
232 B4 Weston OH U.S.A.
232 C5 Weston WV U.S.A.
215 F2 Westonaria S. Africa
150 E3 Weston-super-Mare North Somerset, England U.K.
150 E3 Westonzoyland Somerset, England U.K.
233 F5 Westover MD U.S.A.
231 D7 West Palm Beach FL U.S.A.
West Papua prov. Indon. see Irian Jaya
237 F4 West Plains MO U.S.A.
83 F5 West Point pt. Tas. Austr.
240 G2 West Point CA U.S.A.
226 D5 Westpoint IN U.S.A.
237 F5 West Point MS U.S.A.
236 D3 West Point NE U.S.A.
233 G4 West Point NY U.S.A.
232 C4 West Point OH U.S.A.
232 E6 West Point VA U.S.A.
231 C5 West Point Lake resr Alabama/Georgia U.S.A.
227 I3 Westport Ont. Can.
81 C4 Westport South I. N.Z.
147 B3 Westport Rep. of Ireland
240 F2 Westport CA U.S.A.
235 E1 Westport CT U.S.A.
233 G2 Westport NY U.S.A.
147 B3 Westport Quay Rep. of Ireland
149 H3 West Rainton Durham, England U.K.
223 K4 Westray Man. Can.
146 E2 Westray i. Scotland U.K.
146 E2 Westray Firth sea chan. Scotland U.K.
235 E1 West Redding CT U.S.A.
224 D4 Westree Ont. Can.
222 F4 West Road r. B.C. Can.
146 F6 Westruther Scottish Borders, Scotland U.K.
233 G3 West Rutland VT U.S.A.
240 G2 West Sacramento CA U.S.A.
232 B4 West Salem OH U.S.A.
227 H4 West Seneca NY U.S.A.
West Siberian Plain Rus. Fed. see Zapadno-Sibirskaya Ravnina
83 F4 West Sister Island Tas. Austr.
151 I2 West Somerton Norfolk, England U.K.
233 H2 West Stewartstown NH U.S.A.
151 G3 West Sussex admin. div. England U.K.
164 E1 West-Terschelling Neth.
233 G2 West Topsham VT U.S.A.
151 G4 West Town Hampshire, England U.K.
234 D1 Westtown NY U.S.A.
226 B4 West Union IA U.S.A.
232 B5 West Union OH U.S.A.
232 C5 West Union WV U.S.A.
238 E3 West Valley City UT U.S.A.
226 D5 Westville IN U.S.A.
237 E5 Westville OK U.S.A.
232 C5 West Virginia state U.S.A.
165 B4 West-Vlaanderen prov. Belgium
240 H2 West Walker r. NV U.S.A.
150 C3 Westward Ho! Devon, England U.K.
151 F4 West Wellow Hampshire, England U.K.
146 E5 West Wemyss Fife, Scotland U.K.
149 J5 West Winch Norfolk, England U.K.
85 G4 Westwood Qld Austr.
240 G1 Westwood CA U.S.A.
235 D2 Westwood NJ U.S.A.
83 F3 West Wyalong N.S.W. Austr.
151 G3 West Wycombe Buckinghamshire, England U.K.
146 □G1 West Yell Shetland, Scotland U.K.
238 E2 West Yellowstone MT U.S.A.
234 B3 West York PA U.S.A.
149 G4 West Yorkshire admin. div. England U.K.
164 D2 Westzaan Neth.
93 C4 Wetar i. Maluku Indon.
93 C5 Wetar, Selat sea chan. Indon.
222 H4 Wetaskiwin Alta Can.
211 C6 Wete Tanz.
171 C4 Wethau Ger.
149 G3 Wetheral Cumbria, England U.K.
149 H4 Wetherby West Yorkshire, England U.K.
235 F1 Wethersfield CT U.S.A.
175 K6 Wetlina Pol.
226 D2 Wetmore MI U.S.A.
168 D3 Wetschen Ger.
169 D5 Wetter r. Ger.
169 D5 Wetter (Hessen) Ger.
169 C4 Wetter (Ruhr) Ger.
165 C3 Wetteren Belgium
171 D4 Wetterzeube Ger.
171 C4 Wettin Ger.
190 D1 Wettingen Switz.
169 C3 Wettringen Ger.
168 C3 Wettrup Ger.
173 F3 Wettstetten Ger.
231 C5 Wetumpka AL U.S.A.
190 D1 Wetzikon Switz.
169 D5 Wetzlar Ger.
165 C4 Wevelgem Belgium
231 C6 Wewahitchka FL U.S.A.
91 J7 Wewak P.N.G.
168 E2 Wewelsfleth Ger.
237 D5 Wewoka OK U.S.A.
147 E4 Wexford Rep. of Ireland
147 E4 Wexford county Rep. of Ireland
147 E4 Wexford Bay Rep. of Ireland
223 J4 Weyakwin Sask. Can.
173 F4 Weyarn Ger.
226 C3 Weyauwega WI U.S.A.
151 G3 Weybridge Surrey, England U.K.
223 K5 Weyburn Sask. Can.
169 C5 Weyerbusch Ger.
179 F3 Weyer Markt Austria
157 H4 Weyersheim France
169 F3 Weyhausen Ger.
168 D3 Weyhe Ger.
225 H4 Weymouth N.S. Can.
150 E4 Weymouth Dorset, England U.K.
233 H3 Weymouth MA U.S.A.
234 D3 Weymouth NJ U.S.A.
85 E2 Weymouth, Cape Qld Austr.
164 F2 Wezep Neth.
80 F3 Whakaki North I. N.Z.
80 E3 Whakamaru North I. N.Z.
80 F3 Whakapunake hill North I. N.Z.
Whakaraupō inlet South I. N.Z. see Lyttelton Harbour
80 F2 Whakatane North I. N.Z.
Whakatipu Kā Tuka r. South I. N.Z. see Hollyford
83 G2 Whalan Creek r. N.S.W. Austr.
Whale r. Que. Can. see La Baleine, Rivière à
222 C3 Whale Bay AK U.S.A.
246 C1 Whale Cay i. Bahamas
223 M2 Whale Cove Nunavut Can.
222 C3 Whale Pass AK U.S.A.
149 H4 Whaley Bridge Derbyshire, England U.K.
232 E6 Whaleyville VA U.S.A.
146 □H1 Whalsay i. Scotland U.K.
149 H2 Whalton Northumberland, England U.K.
80 E4 Whangaehu r. North I. N.Z.
80 E2 Whangamata North I. N.Z.
81 D4 Whangamoa South I. N.Z.
80 E3 Whangamomona North I. N.Z.
80 E2 Whangaparaoa North I. N.Z.
80 G3 Whangara North I. N.Z.
80 E1 Whangarei North I. N.Z.
151 G2 Whaplode Lincolnshire, England U.K.
224 E2 Whapmagoostui Que. Can.
81 E4 Wharanui South I. N.Z.
81 F4 Whareama North I. N.Z.
149 H4 Wharfe r. England U.K.
227 F2 Wharncliffe Ont. Can.
232 C6 Wharncliffe WV U.S.A.
234 D2 Wharton NJ U.S.A.
237 D6 Wharton TX U.S.A.
81 C5 Whataroa South I. N.Z.
222 G2 Wha Ti N.W.T. Can.
146 D7 Whauphill Dumfries and Galloway, Scotland U.K.
240 G2 Wheatland CA U.S.A.
238 F3 Wheatland WY U.S.A.
227 F4 Wheatley Ont. Can.
226 C5 Wheaton IL U.S.A.
236 D2 Wheaton MN U.S.A.
150 E2 Wheaton Aston Staffordshire, England U.K.
234 A3 Wheaton-Glenmont MD U.S.A.
150 D3 Wheddon Cross Somerset, England U.K.
237 C5 Wheeler TX U.S.A.
226 B3 Wheeler WI U.S.A.
231 C5 Wheeler Lake resr AL U.S.A.
239 F4 Wheeler Peak NM U.S.A.
241 J2 Wheeler Peak NV U.S.A.
232 B5 Wheelersburg OH U.S.A.
240 H4 Wheeler Springs CA U.S.A.
232 C4 Wheeling WV U.S.A.
261 G3 Wheelwright Arg.
149 G3 Whernside hill England U.K.
151 F3 Wherwell Hampshire, England U.K.
149 H3 Whickham Tyne and Wear, England U.K.
150 D4 Whiddon Down Devon, England U.K.
147 B5 Whiddy Island Rep. of Ireland
86 C4 Whim Creek W.A. Austr.
150 D4 Whimple Devon, England U.K.
82 B1 Whinham, Mount S.A. Austr.
235 D2 Whippany NJ U.S.A.
240 F2 Whispering Pines CA U.S.A.
222 F5 Whistler B.C. Can.
225 K4 Whitbourne Nfld. Can.
146 E6 Whitburn West Lothian, Scotland U.K.
227 H4 Whitby Ont. Can.
149 I3 Whitby North Yorkshire, England U.K.
151 G3 Whitchurch Buckinghamshire, England U.K.
150 D3 Whitchurch Cardiff, Wales U.K.
151 F3 Whitchurch Hampshire, England U.K.
150 E2 Whitchurch Shropshire, England U.K.
227 H4 Whitchurch-Stouffville Ont. Can.
81 C5 Whitcombe, Mount South I. N.Z.
224 C3 White r. Ont. Can.
222 B2 White r. Can./U.S.A.
229 H4 White r. AR U.S.A.
237 F5 White r. AR U.S.A.
241 M1 White r. CO U.S.A.
230 C4 White r. IN U.S.A.
226 D4 White r. MI U.S.A.
241 J3 White r. NV U.S.A.
236 D3 White r. SD U.S.A.
233 G3 White r. VT U.S.A.
226 B2 White r. WI U.S.A.
230 C4 White, East Fork r. IN U.S.A.
84 B4 White, Lake salt flat N.T. Austr.
237 E4 White, North Fork r. MO U.S.A.
149 G2 Whiteadder Water r. Scotland U.K.
225 J3 White Bay Nfld. Can.
236 C2 White Butte mt. ND U.S.A.
241 L3 White Canyon UT U.S.A.
147 C5 Whitechurch Cork Rep. of Ireland
147 D4 Whitechurch Waterford Rep. of Ireland
83 E2 White Cliffs N.S.W. Austr.
226 E4 White Cloud MI U.S.A.
81 B6 Whitecoomb mt. South I. N.Z.
146 E6 White Coomb hill Scotland U.K.
222 H4 Whitecourt Alta Can.
146 E6 Whitecraig East Lothian, Scotland U.K.
147 E2 Whitecross Northern Ireland U.K.
234 B1 White Deer PA U.S.A.
233 G2 Whiteface Mountain NY U.S.A.
233 H2 Whitefield NH U.S.A.
227 G2 Whitefish Ont. Can.
222 E1 Whitefish r. N.W.T. Can.
238 D1 Whitefish MT U.S.A.
226 D3 Whitefish r. MI U.S.A.
226 D3 Whitefish Bay WI U.S.A.
223 J2 Whitefish Lake N.W.T. Can.
234 B3 Whiteford MD U.S.A.
147 C4 Whitegate Clare Rep. of Ireland
147 C5 Whitegate Cork Rep. of Ireland
147 B5 White Hall Rep. of Ireland
147 D4 Whitehall Rep. of Ireland
146 F2 Whitehall Orkney, Scotland U.K.
236 F4 White Hall IL U.S.A.
234 B3 White Hall MD U.S.A.
226 D4 Whitehall MI U.S.A.
238 D2 Whitehall MT U.S.A.
233 G3 Whitehall NY U.S.A.
232 B5 Whitehall OH U.S.A.
234 B1 White Hall PA U.S.A.
234 C2 Whitehall PA U.S.A.
226 B3 Whitehall WI U.S.A.
149 F3 Whitehaven Cumbria, England U.K.
234 C1 White Haven PA U.S.A.
147 F2 Whitehead Northern Ireland U.K.
225 I4 White Hill hill N.S. Can.
151 G3 Whitehill Hampshire, England U.K.
146 F4 Whitehills Aberdeenshire, Scotland U.K.
222 C2 Whitehorse Y.T. Can.
234 D2 White Horse NJ U.S.A.
151 F3 White Horse, Vale of val. England U.K.
234 D2 Whitehouse NJ U.S.A.
234 D2 White House Station NJ U.S.A.
263 D2 White Island Antarctica
215 F5 White Kei r. S. Africa
87 D5 White Lake salt flat W.A. Austr.
234 D1 White Lake NY U.S.A.
83 G5 Whitemark Tas. Austr.
234 C1 White Mills PA U.S.A.
240 H3 White Mountain Peak CA U.S.A.
233 H2 White Mountains NH U.S.A.
228 G1 Whitemouth r. Man. Can.
222 G3 Whitemud r. Alta Can.
203 G6 White Nile state Sudan
203 G6 White Nile r. Sudan/Uganda alt. Abiad, Bahr el, alt. Jebel, Bahr el
203 G6 White Nile Dam Sudan
212 C4 White Nossob watercourse Namibia
232 B6 White Oak KY U.S.A.
226 E5 White Pigeon MI U.S.A.
226 C2 White Pine MI U.S.A.
241 J2 White Pine Range mts NV U.S.A.
235 E1 White Plains NY U.S.A.
146 F4 Whiterashes Aberdeenshire, Scotland U.K.
224 C3 White River Ont. Can.
241 M5 Whiteriver AZ U.S.A.
236 C3 White River SD U.S.A.
233 G3 White River Junction VT U.S.A.
241 J2 White River Valley NV U.S.A.
241 J2 White Rock Peak NV U.S.A.
White Russia country Europe see Belarus
238 B2 White Salmon WA U.S.A.
222 H2 Whitesand r. Alta/N.W.T. Can.
223 K5 Whitesand r. Sask. Can.
234 D3 Whitesboro NJ U.S.A.
233 F3 Whitesboro NY U.S.A.
232 B6 Whitesburg KY U.S.A.
White Sea Rus. Fed. see Beloye More
233 E6 White Stone VA U.S.A.
238 E2 White Sulphur Springs MT U.S.A.
232 C6 White Sulphur Springs WV U.S.A.
234 C1 Whites Valley PA U.S.A.
232 C6 Whitesville WV U.S.A.
215 H3 White Umfolozi r. S. Africa
231 E5 Whiteville NC U.S.A.
206 E4 White Volta watercourse Burkina/Ghana alt. Nakambé, alt. Nakanbe, alt. Volta Blanche
206 E4 White Volta r. Ghana
240 I5 White Water CA U.S.A.
241 M2 Whitewater CO U.S.A.
226 C4 Whitewater WI U.S.A.
239 E5 Whitewater Baldy mt. NM U.S.A.
82 B2 White Well S.A. Austr.
236 C4 White Woman Creek r. KS U.S.A.
85 E4 Whitewood Qld Austr.
223 K5 Whitewood Sask. Can.
83 F4 Whitfield Vic. Austr.
151 I3 Whitfield Kent, England U.K.
150 D1 Whitford Flintshire, Wales U.K.
146 D7 Whithorn Dumfries and Galloway, Scotland U.K.
80 E2 Whitianga North I. N.Z.
233 □J2 Whiting ME U.S.A.
235 D3 Whiting NJ U.S.A.
226 C3 Whiting WI U.S.A.
146 C6 Whiting Bay North Ayrshire, Scotland U.K.
150 C3 Whitland Carmarthenshire, Wales U.K.
149 H2 Whitley Bay Tyne and Wear, England U.K.
231 C4 Whitley City KY U.S.A.
234 C3 Whitman Square NJ U.S.A.
231 D5 Whitmire SC U.S.A.
215 G4 Whitmore S. Africa
262 Q1 Whitmore Mountains Antarctica
151 F2 Whitnash Warwickshire, England U.K.
227 H3 Whitney Ont. Can.
240 H3 Whitney, Mount CA U.S.A.
233 F3 Whitney Point NY U.S.A.
150 C4 Whitsand Bay England U.K.
151 I3 Whitstable Kent, England U.K.
85 G4 Whitsunday Group is Qld Austr.
85 G4 Whitsunday Island Qld Austr.
85 G4 Whitsunday Passage Qld Austr.
Whitsun Island Vanuatu see Pentecost Island
227 F3 Whittemore MI U.S.A.
240 H5 Whittier CA U.S.A.
149 H2 Whittingham Northumberland, England U.K.
150 D2 Whittington Shropshire, England U.K.
83 F4 Whittlesea Vic. Austr.
215 F5 Whittlesea S. Africa
151 G2 Whittlesey Cambridgeshire, England U.K.
226 B3 Whittlesey WI U.S.A.
226 B2 Whittlesey, Mount hill WI U.S.A.
83 F3 Whitton N.S.W. Austr.
149 G4 Whitworth Lancashire, England U.K.
223 J2 Wholdaia Lake N.W.T. Can.
241 K5 Why AZ U.S.A.
82 D3 Whyalla S.A. Austr.
Whydah Benin see Ouidah
96 B3 Wiang Pa Pao Thai.
96 C3 Wiang Sa Thai.
175 K6 Wiar r. Pol.
175 J2 Wiartel Pol.
224 D4 Wiarton Ont. Can.
206 E4 Wiasi Ghana
174 F3 Wiatrowo Pol.
206 E5 Wiawso Ghana
146 A4 Wiay i. Scotland U.K.
174 F5 Wiązów Pol.
238 F2 Wibaux MT U.S.A.
165 C3 Wichelen Belgium
237 D4 Wichita KS U.S.A.
237 D5 Wichita r. TX U.S.A.
237 D5 Wichita Falls TX U.S.A.
237 D5 Wichita Mountains OK U.S.A.
146 E3 Wick Highland, Scotland U.K.
150 E3 Wick South Gloucestershire, England U.K.
150 D3 Wick Vale of Glamorgan, Wales U.K.
151 G4 Wick West Sussex, England U.K.
146 E3 Wick r. Scotland U.K.
169 C4 Wickede airport Ger.
169 C4 Wickede (Ruhr) Ger.
241 K5 Wickenburg AZ U.S.A.
87 C7 Wickepin W.A. Austr.
237 E5 Wickes AR U.S.A.
151 H3 Wickford Essex, England U.K.
86 C4 Wickham W.A. Austr.
84 B3 Wickham r. N.T. Austr.
151 F4 Wickham Hampshire, England U.K.
83 E4 Wickham, Cape Tas. Austr.
84 B3 Wickham, Mount hill N.T. Austr.
151 I2 Wickham Market Suffolk, England U.K.
237 F4 Wickliffe KY U.S.A.
147 E4 Wicklow Rep. of Ireland
147 E3 Wicklow county Rep. of Ireland
147 F4 Wicklow Head hd Rep. of Ireland
147 E4 Wicklow Mountains Rep. of Ireland
174 F1 Wicko Pol.
150 E3 Wickwar South Gloucestershire, England U.K.
234 B2 Wiconisco PA U.S.A.
234 B2 Wiconisco Creek r. PA U.S.A.
174 G4 Widawa Pol.
174 F4 Widawa r. Pol.
175 G4 Widawka r. Pol.
85 H5 Wide Bay Qld Austr.
150 D4 Widecombe in the Moor Devon, England U.K.
146 E2 Wide Firth sea chan. Scotland U.K.
263 B2 Widerøe, Mount Antarctica
151 H3 Widford Hertfordshire, England U.K.
87 D6 Widgiemooltha W.A. Austr.
93 D3 Widi, Kepulauan is Maluku Indon.
190 E1 Widnau Switz.
149 G4 Widnes Halton, England U.K.
174 C2 Widuchowa Pol.
174 F2 Więcbork Pol.
170 D1 Wieck am Darß Ger.
175 I2 Wieczfnia Kościelna Pol.
169 C5 Wied r. Ger.
169 F4 Wieda Ger.
171 D5 Wiederau Ger.
171 D4 Wiederitzsch Ger.
171 F4 Wiednitz Ger.
168 D2 Wiefelstede Ger.
171 C4 Wiehe Ger.
169 D3 Wiehengebirge hills Ger.
169 C5 Wiehl Ger.
170 E1 Wiek Ger.
174 G5 Większyce Pol.
175 I2 Wielbark Pol.
174 E3 Wieleń Pol.
173 F4 Wielenbach Ger.
175 H3 Wielgie Pol.
174 E3 Wielichowo Pol.
175 I6 Wieliczka Pol.
175 K2 Wieliczki Pol.
174 G2 Wielka Nieszawka Pol.
177 H2 Wielka Racza mt. Pol./Slovakia
175 K6 Wielka Rawka mt. Pol.
174 E5 Wielka Sowa mt. Pol.
175 L5 Wielkie Oczy Pol.
174 G1 Wielki Klincz Pol.
174 F3 Wielkopolskie prov. Pol.
175 J6 Wielopole Skrzyńskie Pol.
174 G5 Wielowieś Pol.
165 C4 Wielsbeke Belgium
174 G4 Wieluń Pol.
168 E2 Wiemersdorf Ger.
179 H2 Wien Austria
179 H2 Wien land Austria
179 H2 Wiener Neudorf Austria
179 H3 Wiener Neustadt Austria
168 F3 Wienhausen Ger.
175 I4 Wieniawa Pol.
174 G3 Wieniec Pol.
179 G2 Wiensberg mt. Austria
170 C3 Wiepke Ger.
175 H6 Wieprz Pol.
175 J4 Wieprz r. Pol.
143 G4 Wieprza r. Pol.
175 K3 Wiercień Duży Pol.
164 F2 Wierden Neth.
168 F3 Wieren Ger.
164 D2 Wieringermeer Polder Neth.
164 E2 Wieringerwerf Neth.
172 C3 Wiernsheim Ger.
174 G4 Wieruszów Pol.
175 L4 Wierzbica Lubelskie Pol.
175 J4 Wierzbica Mazowieckie Pol.
174 F4 Wierzbica Górna Pol.
174 G3 Wierzbinek Pol.
174 F5 Wierzbnik Pol.
175 L2 Wierzchlesie Pol.
174 G3 Wierzchosławice Pol.
175 I5 Wierzchosławice Pol.
174 E2 Wierzchowo Pol.
174 G1 Wierzchucino Pol.
174 G2 Wierzyca r. Pol.
179 G4 Wies Austria
173 E4 Wies Ger.
171 D5 Wiesa Ger.
173 G2 Wiesau Ger.
169 D5 Wiesbaden Ger.
172 B4 Wiese r. Ger.
179 G2 Wieselburg Austria
179 H3 Wiesen Austria
169 E5 Wiesen Ger.
190 E2 Wiesen Switz.
171 F3 Wiesenau Ger.
171 D3 Wiesenburg Ger.
173 G2 Wiesenfelden Ger.
172 D3 Wiesensteig Ger.
173 G2 Wiesent Ger.
173 F2 Wiesent r. Ger.
173 F2 Wiesenthau Ger.
173 E2 Wiesentheid Ger.
173 F2 Wiesenttal Ger.
178 C3 Wiesing Austria
168 E2 Wiesle r. Ger.
172 C2 Wiesloch Ger.
179 H3 Wiesmath Austria
168 C2 Wiesmoor Ger.
234 C2 Wiessport PA U.S.A.
168 C3 Wietmarschen Ger.
175 I5 Wietrzychowice Pol.
168 E3 Wietze Ger.
169 E3 Wietze r. Ger.
168 E3 Wietzen Ger.
168 E3 Wietzendorf Ger.
143 H4 Wieżyca hill Pol.
149 G4 Wigan Greater Manchester, England U.K.
173 E4 Wiggensbach Ger.
237 F6 Wiggins MS U.S.A.
145 G6 Wight, Isle of i. England U.K.
150 E2 Wigmore Herefordshire, England U.K.
151 F2 Wigston Leicestershire, England U.K.
149 F3 Wigton Cumbria, England U.K.
146 D7 Wigtown Dumfries and Galloway, Scotland U.K.
146 D7 Wigtown Bay Scotland U.K.
164 E3 Wijchen Neth.
140 □ Wijdefjorden inlet Svalbard
174 E4 Wijewo Pol.
164 F2 Wijhe Neth.
164 D2 Wijk aan Zee Neth.
164 E3 Wijk bij Duurstede Neth.
164 E3 Wijk en Aalburg Neth.
165 D3 Wijnegem Belgium
164 F1 Wijnjewoude Neth.
241 K4 Wikieup AZ U.S.A.
210 C1 Wik'ro Eth.
227 G3 Wikwemikong Ont. Can.
190 E1 Wil Switz.
175 H6 Wilamowice Pol.
236 D3 Wilber NE U.S.A.
81 C5 Wilberforce r. South I. N.Z.
84 D1 Wilberforce, Cape N.T. Austr.
238 C2 Wilbur WA U.S.A.
173 E2 Wilburgstetten Ger.
237 E5 Wilburton OK U.S.A.
83 E2 Wilcannia N.S.W. Austr.
232 D4 Wilcox PA U.S.A.
Wilczek Land i. Zemlya Frantsa-Iosifa Rus. Fed. see Zemlya Vil'cheka
175 H1 Wilczęta Pol.
174 G3 Wilczogóra Pol.
174 G3 Wilczyn Pol.
171 E3 Wildau Ger.
172 C3 Wildbad im Schwarzwald Ger.
172 C3 Wildberg Baden-Württemberg Ger.
170 D3 Wildberg Brandenburg Ger.
170 E2 Wildberg Mecklenburg-Vorpommern Ger.
240 I2 Wildcat Peak NV U.S.A.
215 G4 Wild Coast S. Africa
169 F5 Wildeck-Obersuhl Ger.
169 F5 Wildeck-Richelsdorf Ger.
169 F4 Wildemann Ger.
179 H2 Wildendürnbach Austria
171 D5 Wildenfels Ger.
214 D5 Wilderness S. Africa
232 E5 Wilderness VA U.S.A.
168 D3 Wildeshausen Ger.
169 E5 Wildflecken Ger.
226 C1 Wild Goose Ont. Can.
222 G4 Wildhay r. Alta Can.
190 C2 Wildhorn mt. Switz.
239 F6 Wild Horse Draw r. TX U.S.A.
236 C3 Wild Horse Hill mt. NE U.S.A.
179 G4 Wildon Austria
173 E4 Wildpoldsried Ger.
236 D2 Wild Rice r. MN U.S.A.
236 D2 Wild Rice r. ND U.S.A.
178 D3 Wildseeloder mt. Austria
178 D2 Wildshut Austria
178 B4 Wildspitze mt. Austria
222 H4 Wildwood Alta Can.
231 D6 Wildwood FL U.S.A.
234 D4 Wildwood NJ U.S.A.
234 D4 Wildwood Crest NJ U.S.A.
236 C4 Wiley CO U.S.A.
232 D5 Wiley Ford WV U.S.A.
175 J4 Wilga Pol.
175 J4 Wilga r. Pol.
215 G2 Wilge r. Free State S. Africa
215 G1 Wilge r. Gauteng/Mpumalanga S. Africa
82 C2 Wilgena S.A. Austr.
91 J8 Wilhelm, Mount P.N.G.
251 G4 Wilhelmina Gebergte mts Suriname
140 □ Wilhelmøya i. Svalbard
Wilhelm-Pieck-Stadt Ger. see Guben
179 G2 Wilhelmsburg Austria
170 E2 Wilhelmsburg Ger.
172 D4 Wilhelmsdorf Ger.
168 D2 Wilhelmshaven Ger.
171 C5 Wilhelmsthal Ger.
179 F2 Wilhering Austria
173 E2 Wilhermsdorf Ger.
113 □2 Wilingili i. Addu Atoll Maldives
171 D5 Wilkau-Haßlau Ger.
234 C1 Wilkes-Barre PA U.S.A.
231 D4 Wilkesboro NC U.S.A.
263 I2 Wilkes Coast Antarctica
263 I2 Wilkes Land reg. Antarctica
223 I4 Wilkie Sask. Can.
232 D4 Wilkinsburg PA U.S.A.
262 T2 Wilkins Coast Antarctica
82 C2 Wilkinson Lakes salt flat S.A. Austr.
147 E3 Wilkinstown Rep. of Ireland
175 K4 Wilkołaz Pierwszy Pol.
175 J4 Wilków Pol.
174 F4 Wilków Pol.
222 D3 Will, Mount B.C. Can.
238 B2 Willamette r. OR U.S.A.
150 D4 Willand Devon, England U.K.
239 F5 Willard NM U.S.A.
232 B4 Willard OH U.S.A.
233 F5 Willards MD U.S.A.
149 F4 Willaston Cheshire, England U.K.
241 M5 Willcox AZ U.S.A.
169 E4 Willebadessen Ger.
165 D3 Willebroek Belgium
164 D3 Willemstad Neth.
247 □10 Willemstad Curaçao Neth. Antilles
84 B2 Willeroo N.T. Austr.
223 I3 William r. Sask. Can.
83 E4 William, Mount Vic. Austr.
87 B4 Williambury W.A. Austr.
82 D2 William Creek S.A. Austr.
87 C7 Williams W.A. Austr.
85 E4 Williams r. Qld Austr.
87 C7 Williams r. W.A. Austr.
241 K4 Williams AZ U.S.A.
240 F2 Williams CA U.S.A.
236 E3 Williamsburg IA U.S.A.
232 A6 Williamsburg KY U.S.A.
226 E3 Williamsburg MI U.S.A.
232 A5 Williamsburg OH U.S.A.
232 D4 Williamsburg PA U.S.A.
232 E6 Williamsburg VA U.S.A.
246 C1 Williams Island Bahamas
222 F4 Williams Lake B.C. Can.
232 E3 Williamson NY U.S.A.
232 B6 Williamson WV U.S.A.
230 C3 Williamsport IN U.S.A.
232 B5 Williamsport OH U.S.A.
227 I5 Williamsport PA U.S.A.
227 E4 Williamston MI U.S.A.
231 E5 Williamston NC U.S.A.
233 G3 Williamstown MA U.S.A.
234 D3 Williamstown NJ U.S.A.
233 F3 Williamstown NY U.S.A.
234 B2 Williamstown PA U.S.A.
232 C5 Williamstown WV U.S.A.
169 B4 Willich Ger.
233 G4 Willimantic CT U.S.A.
235 F1 Willimantic r. CT U.S.A.
234 D2 Willingboro NJ U.S.A.
151 H4 Willingdon East Sussex, England U.K.
169 D4 Willingen (Upland) Ger.
151 H2 Willingham Cambridgeshire, England U.K.
Willingili i. N. Male Maldives see Villingli
Willingili i. N. Male Maldives see Vilingli
169 E5 Willingshausen Ger.
151 F2 Willington Derbyshire, England U.K.
190 D1 Willisau Switz.
85 G3 Willis Group atolls Coral Sea Is Terr. Austr.
259 □ Willis Islands S. Georgia
214 C4 Williston S. Africa
231 D6 Williston FL U.S.A.
236 C1 Williston ND U.S.A.
231 D5 Williston SC U.S.A.
222 F4 Williston Lake B.C. Can.
150 D3 Williton Somerset, England U.K.
240 F2 Willits CA U.S.A.
236 E2 Willmar MN U.S.A.
149 J4 Willoughby Lincolnshire, England U.K.
232 C4 Willoughby OH U.S.A.
233 G2 Willoughby, Lake VT U.S.A.
222 F4 Willow r. B.C. Can.
241 J4 Willow Beach AZ U.S.A.
223 J5 Willow Bunch Sask. Can.
222 H5 Willow Creek r. Alta Can.
238 B3 Willow Creek CA U.S.A.
238 B2 Willow Creek r. OR U.S.A.
241 M1 Willow Creek r. UT U.S.A.
234 C3 Willow Grove DE U.S.A.
234 C2 Willow Grove PA U.S.A.
232 E4 Willow Hill PA U.S.A.
222 F2 Willowlake r. N.W.T. Can.
214 D5 Willowmore S. Africa
84 C4 Willowra N.T. Austr.
240 F2 Willows CA U.S.A.
237 F4 Willow Springs MO U.S.A.
234 B3 Willow Street PA U.S.A.
215 G5 Willowvale S. Africa
86 F4 Wills, Lake salt flat W.A. Austr.
172 B3 Willstätt Ger.
82 D3 Willunga S.A. Austr.
231 C6 Wilma FL U.S.A.
170 E2 Wilmersdorf Brandenburg Ger.
171 F4 Wilmersdorf Brandenburg Ger.
82 D3 Wilmington S.A. Austr.
234 C3 Wilmington DE U.S.A.
231 E5 Wilmington NC U.S.A.
232 B5 Wilmington OH U.S.A.
233 G3 Wilmington VT U.S.A.
231 D5 Wilmington Island GA U.S.A.
149 G4 Wilmslow Cheshire, England U.K.
164 D2 Wilnis Neth.
Wilno Lith. see Vilnius
169 D5 Wilnsdorf Ger.
164 F2 Wilp Neth.
171 E4 Wilsdruff Ger.
168 E2 Wilseder Berg hill Ger.
170 E2 Wilsickow Ger.
86 F3 Wilson r. W.A. Austr.
Wilson atoll Micronesia see Ifalik
236 D4 Wilson KS U.S.A.
226 B4 Wilson MN U.S.A.
231 E5 Wilson NC U.S.A.
232 D3 Wilson NY U.S.A.
234 C2 Wilson PA U.S.A.
239 F4 Wilson, Mount CO U.S.A.
241 J2 Wilson, Mount NV U.S.A.
238 B2 Wilson, Mount OR U.S.A.
263 K2 Wilson Hills Antarctica
240 H3 Wilsonia CA U.S.A.
232 E6 Wilsons VA U.S.A.
83 F4 Wilson's Promontory pen. Vic. Austr.
168 E2 Wilstedt Ger.
168 E2 Wilster Ger.
168 B3 Wilsum Ger.
179 H2 Wiltersdorf Austria
171 F4 Wilthen Ger.
172 A2 Wiltingen Ger.
84 C2 Wilton r. N.T. Austr.
151 F3 Wilton Wiltshire, England U.K.
235 E1 Wilton CT U.S.A.
233 □H2 Wilton ME U.S.A.
236 C2 Wilton ND U.S.A.
233 H3 Wilton NH U.S.A.
150 F3 Wiltshire admin. div. England U.K.
165 E5 Wiltz Lux.
87 D5 Wiluna W.A. Austr.
80 F4 Wimbledon North I. N.Z.
151 H2 Wimblington Cambridgeshire, England U.K.
151 F4 Wimborne Minster Dorset, England U.K.
156 B2 Wimereux France
171 C4 Wimmelburg Ger.
83 E4 Wimmera r. Vic. Austr.
190 C2 Wimmis Switz.
179 H3 Wimpassing Austria
Wina r. Cameroon see Vina
230 C3 Winamac IN U.S.A.
215 F3 Winburg S. Africa
214 D2 Wincanton S. Africa
150 E3 Wincanton Somerset, England U.K.
151 F3 Winchcombe Gloucestershire, England U.K.
151 H4 Winchelsea East Sussex, England U.K.
233 G3 Winchendon MA U.S.A.
172 A2 Wincheringen Ger.
233 F2 Winchester Ont. Can.
81 C6 Winchester South I. N.Z.
151 F3 Winchester Hampshire, England U.K.
236 F4 Winchester IL U.S.A.
230 C3 Winchester IN U.S.A.
232 A6 Winchester KY U.S.A.
233 G3 Winchester NH U.S.A.
231 C5 Winchester TN U.S.A.
232 D5 Winchester VA U.S.A.
165 E4 Wincrange Lux.
220 E3 Wind r. Y.T. Can.
238 E3 Wind r. WY U.S.A.
175 J1 Winda Pol.
82 D2 Windabout, Lake salt flat S.A. Austr.
173 F3 Windach Ger.
Windau Latvia see Ventspils
232 D4 Windber PA U.S.A.
168 E1 Windeby Ger.
231 D5 Winder GA U.S.A.
149 G3 Windermere Cumbria, England U.K.
149 G3 Windermere l. England U.K.
172 B2 Windesheim Ger.
234 C2 Windgap PA U.S.A.
169 C5 Windhagen Ger.
222 C3 Windham AK U.S.A.
235 F1 Windham CT U.S.A.
232 C4 Windham OH U.S.A.
169 F4 Windhausen Ger.
212 C4 Windhoek Namibia
221 I4 Windigo r. Ont. Can.
179 G2 Windigsteig Austria
173 G2 Windischeschenbach Ger.
179 F3 Windischgarsten Austria

Windlestraw Law to Xinhua

380

146 F6 **Windlestraw Law** hill Scotland U.K.
148 C4 **Windmill** Rep. of Ireland
239 F5 **Wind Mountain** NM U.S.A.
236 E3 **Windom** MN U.S.A.
85 E5 **Windorah** Qld Austr.
173 H3 **Windorf** Ger.
241 M4 **Window Rock** AZ U.S.A.
232 C5 **Wind Ridge** PA U.S.A.
238 E3 **Wind River Range** mts WY U.S.A.
151 F3 **Windrush** r. England U.K.
173 E2 **Windsbach** Ger.
83 G3 **Windsor** N.S.W. Austr.
225 K3 **Windsor** Nfld. Can.
225 H4 **Windsor** N.S. Can.
224 D5 **Windsor** Ont. Can.
225 F4 **Windsor** Que. Can.
151 G3 **Windsor** Windsor and Maidenhead, England U.K.
233 G4 **Windsor** CT U.S.A.
231 E4 **Windsor** NC U.S.A.
234 D2 **Windsor** NJ U.S.A.
233 F3 **Windsor** NY U.S.A.
234 B3 **Windsor** PA U.S.A.
232 E6 **Windsor** VA U.S.A.
233 G3 **Windsor** VT U.S.A.
151 G3 **Windsor and Maidenhead** admin. div. England U.K.
233 G4 **Windsor Locks** CT U.S.A.
214 E3 **Windsorton** S. Africa
247 G4 **Windward Islands** Caribbean Sea
Windward Islands Arch. de la Société Fr. Polynesia see **Vent, Îles du**
246 D3 **Windward Passage** Cuba/Haiti
87 B7 **Windy Harbour** W.A. Austr.
231 C5 **Winfield** AL U.S.A.
237 D4 **Winfield** KS U.S.A.
232 C5 **Winfield** WV U.S.A.
150 E3 **Winford** North Somerset, England U.K.
151 G3 **Wing** Buckinghamshire, England U.K.
149 H3 **Wingate** Durham, England U.K.
84 B2 **Wingate Mountains** hills N.T. Austr.
235 E1 **Wingdale** NY U.S.A.
83 G2 **Wingen** N.S.W. Austr.
165 C3 **Wingene** Belgium
157 H4 **Wingen-sur-Moder** France
169 F4 **Wingerode** Ger.
83 H2 **Wingham** N.S.W. Austr.
224 D5 **Wingham** Ont. Can.
151 I3 **Wingham** Kent, England U.K.
156 C2 **Wingles** France
168 E2 **Wingst** Ger.
173 G3 **Winhöring** Ger.
86 D4 **Winifred, Lake** salt flat W.A. Austr.
261 E5 **Winifreda** Arg.
224 C2 **Winisk** Ont. Can.
224 C2 **Winisk** r. Ont. Can.
214 B5 **Winkelhaaks** r. S. Africa
173 F2 **Winkelhaid** Ger.
241 L5 **Winkelman** AZ U.S.A.
215 F2 **Winkelpos** S. Africa
168 D3 **Winkelsett** Ger.
151 G3 **Winkfield** Bracknell Forest, England U.K.
173 G2 **Winklarn** Ger.
150 D4 **Winkleigh** Devon, England U.K.
223 L5 **Winkler** Man. Can.
178 D4 **Winklern** Austria
179 F3 **Winklern bei Oberwölz** Austria
238 B2 **Winlock** WA U.S.A.
84 B5 **Winnalls Ridge** N.T. Austr.
206 E5 **Winneba** Ghana
236 E3 **Winnebago** MN U.S.A.
226 C3 **Winneconne** WI U.S.A.
238 C3 **Winnemucca** NV U.S.A.
172 D3 **Winnenden** Ger.
236 C3 **Winner** SD U.S.A.
151 G3 **Winnersh** Wokingham, England U.K.
168 E1 **Winnert** Ger.
238 E2 **Winnett** MT U.S.A.
237 E6 **Winnfield** LA U.S.A.
175 I3 **Winnica** Pol.
237 E6 **Winnie** TX U.S.A.
87 B4 **Winning** W.A. Austr.
169 C5 **Winningen** Rheinland-Pfalz Ger.
171 C4 **Winningen** Sachsen-Anhalt Ger.
223 L5 **Winnipeg** Man. Can.
223 L5 **Winnipeg** r. Man./Ont. Can.
223 L5 **Winnipeg, Lake** Man. Can.
223 L5 **Winnipegosis** Man. Can.
223 K4 **Winnipegosis, Lake** Man. Can.
237 F5 **Winnsboro** LA U.S.A.
231 D5 **Winnsboro** SC U.S.A.
237 E5 **Winnsboro** TX U.S.A.
172 B2 **Winnweiler** Ger.
241 L4 **Winona** AZ U.S.A.
226 C2 **Winona** MI U.S.A.
226 B3 **Winona** MN U.S.A.
237 F4 **Winona** MO U.S.A.
237 F5 **Winona** MS U.S.A.
233 G2 **Winooski** VT U.S.A.
233 G2 **Winooski** r. VT U.S.A.
164 G1 **Winschoten** Neth.
150 E3 **Winscombe** North Somerset, England U.K.
168 E3 **Winsen (Aller)** Ger.
168 F2 **Winsen (Luhe)** Ger.
149 G4 **Winsford** Cheshire, England U.K.
174 E4 **Wińsko** Pol.
150 E3 **Winsley** Wiltshire, England U.K.
151 G3 **Winslow** Buckinghamshire, England U.K.
241 L4 **Winslow** AZ U.S.A.
233 □I2 **Winslow** ME U.S.A.
234 D3 **Winslow** NJ U.S.A.
233 G4 **Winsted** CT U.S.A.
149 H3 **Winston** Durham, England U.K.
231 D4 **Winston-Salem** NC U.S.A.
164 E1 **Winsum** Friesland Neth.
164 F1 **Winsum** Groningen Neth.
226 B3 **Winter** WI U.S.A.
169 D4 **Winterberg** Ger.
215 F5 **Winterberg** mts S. Africa
150 E3 **Winterbourne** South Gloucestershire, England U.K.
150 E4 **Winterbourne Abbas** Dorset, England U.K.
170 C3 **Winterfeld** Ger.
233 □I2 **Winter Harbor** ME U.S.A.
231 D6 **Winter Haven** FL U.S.A.
172 D3 **Winterlingen** Ger.
231 D6 **Winter Park** FL U.S.A.
233 □I2 **Winterport** ME U.S.A.
240 G2 **Winters** CA U.S.A.
237 D6 **Winters** TX U.S.A.
171 D4 **Wintersdorf** Ger.
236 E3 **Winterset** IA U.S.A.
234 B3 **Winters Run** r. MD U.S.A.
234 B3 **Winterstown** PA U.S.A.
164 F3 **Winterswijk** Neth.
190 D1 **Winterthur** Switz.
215 G3 **Winterton** S. Africa
149 I4 **Winterton** North Lincolnshire, England U.K.
215 G1 **Winterveld** S. Africa
233 □I1 **Winterville** ME U.S.A.
235 F1 **Winthrop** CT U.S.A.
233 □I2 **Winthrop** ME U.S.A.
85 E4 **Winton** Qld Austr.
81 B7 **Winton** South I. N.Z.
149 G3 **Winton** Cumbria, England U.K.
231 E4 **Winton** NC U.S.A.
172 A2 **Wintrich** Ger.
157 H4 **Wintzenheim** France
151 G2 **Winwick** Cambridgeshire, England U.K.
169 E4 **Winzenburg** Ger.
179 H3 **Winzendorf** Austria
173 H3 **Winzer** Ger.
171 C4 **Wipper** r. Ger.
169 F4 **Wipperdorf** Ger.
169 C4 **Wipperfürth** Ger.
168 C3 **Wippingen** Ger.
171 C4 **Wippra Kurort** Ger.
168 C2 **Wirdumer (Wirdum)** Ger.
169 C5 **Wirges** Ger.
149 H4 **Wirksworth** Derbyshire, England U.K.
82 D3 **Wirrabara** S.A. Austr.
149 F4 **Wirral** pen. England U.K.
82 D2 **Wirraminna** S.A. Austr.
82 E4 **Wirrega** S.A. Austr.
82 C2 **Wirrida, Lake** salt flat S.A. Austr.
82 C3 **Wirrulla** S.A. Austr.
171 C5 **Wirsberg** Ger.
78 □4a **Wisas** i. Chuuk Micronesia
151 H2 **Wisbech** Cambridgeshire, England U.K.
233 □I2 **Wiscasset** ME U.S.A.
168 E2 **Wischhafen** Ger.
226 B4 **Wisconsin** r. WI U.S.A.
236 F2 **Wisconsin** state U.S.A.
226 C4 **Wisconsin, Lake** WI U.S.A.
226 C4 **Wisconsin Dells** WI U.S.A.
226 C3 **Wisconsin Rapids** WI U.S.A.
232 B6 **Wise** VA U.S.A.
146 E6 **Wishaw** North Lanarkshire, Scotland U.K.
236 D2 **Wisher** ND U.S.A.
210 F3 **Wisil Dabarow** Somalia
149 H3 **Wiske** r. England U.K.
175 I3 **Wiskitki** Pol.
174 G6 **Wisła** Pol.
143 H4 **Wisła** r. Pol.
175 I5 **Wiślica** Pol.
175 K5 **Wisłok** r. Pol.
175 J5 **Wisłoka** r. Pol.
170 C2 **Wismar** Ger.
237 F6 **Wisner** LA U.S.A.
175 K3 **Wiśniew** Pol.
175 I2 **Wiśniewo** Pol.
175 I6 **Wiśniowa** Pol.
156 B2 **Wissant** France
157 H3 **Wissembourg** France
169 C5 **Wissen** Ger.
150 E2 **Wistanstow** Shropshire, England U.K.
222 E4 **Wistaria** B.C. Can.
149 G4 **Wistaston** Cheshire, England U.K.
168 E2 **Wistedt** Ger.
175 K6 **Wisznia** r. Pol.
174 F4 **Wisznia Mała** Pol.
175 L4 **Wisznice** Pol.
215 G1 **Witbank** S. Africa
214 C2 **Witdraai** S. Africa
151 H3 **Witham** Essex, England U.K.
151 H2 **Witham** r. England U.K.
233 G2 **Witherbee** NY U.S.A.
150 D4 **Witheridge** Devon, England U.K.
149 J4 **Withernsea** East Riding of Yorkshire, England U.K.
231 D6 **Withlacoochee** r. FL U.S.A.
231 D6 **Withlacoochee** r. FL U.S.A.
215 G2 **Witkoppies** mt. S. Africa
174 F3 **Witkowo** Wielkopolskie Pol.
174 D2 **Witkowo** Zachodniopomorskie Pol.
151 G3 **Witley** Surrey, England U.K.
164 E1 **Witmarsum** Neth.
215 E5 **Witmos** S. Africa
215 G1 **Witnek** S. Africa
151 F3 **Witney** Oxfordshire, England U.K.
174 C3 **Witnica** Pol.
175 H3 **Witonia** Pol.
174 F2 **Witosław** Pol.
214 E3 **Witput** S. Africa
215 H1 **Witrivier** S. Africa
156 E3 **Witry-lès-Reims** France
168 D1 **Wittdün** Ger.
214 D5 **Witteberg** mt. E. Cape S. Africa
215 G3 **Witteberg** mt. Free State S. Africa
214 C5 **Witteberge** mts S. Africa
157 H5 **Wittelsheim** France
169 C4 **Witten** Ger.
172 D4 **Wittenbach** Switz.
Wittenberg Ger. see **Lutherstadt Wittenberg**
226 C3 **Wittenberg** WI U.S.A.
170 C3 **Wittenberge** Ger.
170 C2 **Wittenburg** Ger.
170 C2 **Wittenförden** Ger.
170 E1 **Wittenhagen** Ger.
157 H5 **Wittenheim** France
86 C4 **Wittenoom** W.A. Austr.
Wittenoom Gorge W.A. Austr. see **Wittenoom**
151 G2 **Wittering** Peterborough, England U.K.
171 D5 **Wittgensdorf** Ger.
95 G1 **Witti, Banjaran** mts Sabah Malaysia
173 G3 **Wittibreut** Ger.
171 F4 **Wittichenau** Ger.
172 D2 **Wittighausen** Ger.
168 F3 **Wittingen** Ger.
173 E3 **Wittislingen** Ger.
172 A2 **Wittlich** Ger.
234 B4 **Wittman** MD U.S.A.
169 F3 **Wittmar** Ger.
168 C2 **Wittmund** Ger.
149 H3 **Witton Gilbert** Durham, England U.K.
170 E1 **Wittow** pen. Ger.
170 D2 **Wittstock** Ger.
212 C4 **Witvlei** Namibia
215 F2 **Witwatersberg** mts S. Africa
215 F2 **Witwatersrand** mts S. Africa
169 E4 **Witzenhausen** Ger.
168 F2 **Witzhave** Ger.
170 C2 **Witzin** Ger.
168 D1 **Witzwort** Ger.
150 D3 **Wiveliscombe** Somerset, England U.K.
151 H3 **Wivenhoe** Essex, England U.K.
175 K1 **Wiżajny** Pol.
156 C2 **Wizernes** France
175 K2 **Wizna** Pol.
175 I3 **Wkra** r. Pol.
174 G3 **Władysławów** Pol.
143 H4 **Władysławowo** Pol.
174 D4 **Wleń** Pol.
175 H3 **Włocławek** Pol.
175 L4 **Włodawa** Pol.
175 L4 **Włodawka** r. Pol.
175 H5 **Włodowice** Pol.
174 F5 **Włodzienin** Pol.
175 H4 **Włodzimierzów** Pol.
174 E4 **Włoszakowice** Pol.
175 H5 **Włoszczowa** Pol.
170 C2 **Wöbbelin** Ger.
Wobkent Uzbek. see **Vabkent**
233 □H2 **Woburn** Que. Can.
151 G3 **Woburn** Bedfordshire, England U.K.
151 G2 **Woburn Sands** Milton Keynes, England U.K.
83 F4 **Wodonga** Vic. Austr.
175 J3 **Wodynie** Pol.
175 H4 **Wodzierady** Pol.
175 I5 **Wodzisław** Pol.
174 G5 **Wodzisław Śląski** Pol.
164 D2 **Woerden** Neth.
157 H4 **Wœrth** France
157 F3 **Wœvre, Forêt de** for. France
164 E2 **Wognum** Neth.
190 D1 **Wohlen** Aargau Switz.
190 C2 **Wohlen** Bern Switz.
171 C4 **Wohlmirstedt** Ger.
263 A2 **Wohlthat Mountains** Antarctica
168 F2 **Wohltorf** Ger.
169 D5 **Wohra** r. Ger.
168 E1 **Wöhrden** Ger.
175 K4 **Wohyń** Pol.
157 G3 **Woippy** France
175 J6 **Wojaszówka** Pol.
175 J5 **Wojciechowice** Pol.
175 K4 **Wojcieszków** Pol.
174 D5 **Wojcieszów** Pol.
174 G3 **Wójcin** Pol.
78 □3b **Woje Majuro** i. Majuro Marshall Is
Wōjjā atoll Marshall Is see **Wotje**
175 H5 **Wojkowice** Pol.
175 I6 **Wojnicz** Pol.
174 F2 **Wojnowo** Pol.
175 L5 **Wojsławice** Pol.
175 L5 **Wojsławka** r. Pol.
91 H8 **Wokam** i. Indon.
100 D3 **Woken** r. China
117 H4 **Wokha** Nagaland India
151 G3 **Woking** Surrey, England U.K.
151 G3 **Wokingham** Wokingham, England U.K.
151 G3 **Wokingham** admin. div. England U.K.
170 E2 **Wokuhl** Ger.
175 H3 **Wola** Pol.
175 J4 **Wola Mysłowska** Pol.
175 I4 **Wolanów** Pol.
175 L4 **Wola Uhruska** Pol.
175 I3 **Wola Wierzbowska** Pol.
175 H4 **Wolbórz** Pol.
175 H5 **Wolbrom** Pol.
235 F1 **Wolcott** CT U.S.A.
226 D5 **Wolcott** IN U.S.A.
232 E3 **Wolcott** NY U.S.A.
233 G2 **Wolcott** VT U.S.A.
226 E5 **Wolcottville** IN U.S.A.
174 G4 **Wołczyn** Pol.
170 E2 **Woldegk** Ger.
164 G1 **Woldendorp** Neth.
149 I3 **Wold Newton** East Riding of Yorkshire, England U.K.
Wolea atoll Micronesia see **Woleai**
91 J5 **Woleai** atoll Micronesia
208 A4 **Woleu-Ntem** prov. Gabon
222 C2 **Wolf** r. Y.T. Can.
237 F5 **Wolf** r. TN U.S.A.
226 C3 **Wolf** r. WI U.S.A.
250 □ **Wolf, Volcán** vol. Islas Galápagos Ecuador
172 C3 **Wolfach** Ger.
238 D2 **Wolf Creek** MT U.S.A.
238 B3 **Wolf Creek** OR U.S.A.
237 D4 **Wolf Creek** r. OK U.S.A.
233 □H3 **Wolfeboro** NH U.S.A.
172 D4 **Wolfegg** Ger.
171 D4 **Wolfen** Ger.
169 F3 **Wolfenbüttel** Ger.
169 D5 **Wölfersheim** Ger.
179 E3 **Wolfgangsee** l. Austria
169 E4 **Wolfhagen** Ger.
169 F5 **Wölfis** Ger.
Wolf Island Islas Galápagos Ecuador see **Wenman, Isla**
226 D4 **Wolf Lake** MI U.S.A.
179 G2 **Wolfpassing** Austria
238 F1 **Wolf Point** MT U.S.A.
173 E2 **Wolframs-Eschenbach** Ger.
173 F4 **Wolfratshausen** Ger.
179 F4 **Wolfsberg** Austria
169 F3 **Wolfsburg** Ger.
172 B2 **Wolfstein** Ger.
225 H4 **Wolfville** N.S. Can.
170 E1 **Wolgast** Ger.
190 D1 **Wolhusen** Switz.
175 L5 **Wolica** r. Pol.
174 C2 **Wolin** Pol.
174 C2 **Wolin** i. Pol.
175 H3 **Wólka** Pol.
175 K4 **Wólka** Pol.
175 L3 **Wólka Dobryńska** Pol.
171 E5 **Wolkenstein** Ger.
179 H2 **Wolkersdorf** Austria
169 F4 **Wolkramshausen** Ger.
151 G2 **Wollaston** Northamptonshire, England U.K.
259 D9 **Wollaston, Islas** is Chile
223 K3 **Wollaston Lake** Sask. Can.
223 K3 **Wollaston Lake** l. Sask. Can.
220 G3 **Wollaston Peninsula** N.W.T./Nunavut Can.
190 D1 **Wollerau** Switz.
83 G3 **Wollongong** N.S.W. Austr.
215 E2 **Wolmaransstad** S. Africa
171 C4 **Wolmirsleben** Ger.
171 C3 **Wolmirstedt** Ger.
173 F3 **Wolnzach** Ger.
175 J3 **Wołomin** Pol.
174 E4 **Wołów** Pol.
172 D2 **Wolpertshausen** Ger.
172 D4 **Wolpertswende** Ger.
169 E3 **Wölpinghausen** Ger.
169 F3 **Wolsdorf** Ger.
82 E4 **Wolseley** S.A. Austr.
214 B5 **Wolseley** S. Africa
236 D2 **Wolsey** SD U.S.A.
149 H3 **Wolsingham** Durham, England U.K.
151 F2 **Wolston** Warwickshire, England U.K.
174 E3 **Wolsztyn** Pol.
171 E3 **Woltersdorf** Brandenburg Ger.
171 E3 **Woltersdorf** Brandenburg Ger.
170 C3 **Woltersdorf** Niedersachsen Ger.
169 E4 **Woltershausen** Ger.
164 F2 **Wolvega** Neth.
150 E2 **Wolverhampton** West Midlands, England U.K.
226 E3 **Wolverine** MI U.S.A.
215 E5 **Wolwefontein** S. Africa
215 E3 **Wolwespruit** S. Africa
94 A1 **Wolya** r. Indon.
150 E2 **Wombourne** Staffordshire, England U.K.
149 H4 **Wombwell** South Yorkshire, England U.K.
234 B2 **Womelsdorf** PA U.S.A.
164 E1 **Wommels** Neth.
172 B2 **Womrather Höhe** hill Ger.
84 D3 **Wonarah** N.T. Austr.
85 G5 **Wondai** Qld Austr.
165 C3 **Wondelgem** Belgium
215 G1 **Wonderfontein** S. Africa
215 F2 **Wonderkop** S. Africa
215 F3 **Wonderkop** mt. S. Africa
215 F1 **Wondermere** S. Africa
173 G1 **Wondreb** r. Ger.
83 F2 **Wongalarroo Lake** salt l. N.S.W. Austr.
87 C6 **Wongan Hills** W.A. Austr.
117 G4 **Wong Chhu** r. Bhutan
109 □ **Wong Chuk Hang** H.K. China
109 □ **Wong Leng** hill H.K. China
101 C5 **Wŏnju** S. Korea
95 E4 **Wonogiri** Jawa Tengah Indon.
95 E4 **Wonosari** Indon.
95 E4 **Wonosobo** Jawa Tengah Indon.
222 F3 **Wonowon** B.C. Can.
101 C5 **Wŏnsan** N. Korea
173 F2 **Wonsees** Ger.
151 F3 **Wonston** Hampshire, England U.K.
83 F4 **Wonthaggi** Vic. Austr.
87 C5 **Wonyulgunna, Mount** hill W.A. Austr.
151 G3 **Wooburn** Buckinghamshire, England U.K.
82 D2 **Woocalla** S.A. Austr.
222 A2 **Wood, Mount** Y.T. Can.
84 D2 **Woodah, Isle** i. N.T. Austr.
231 D6 **Woodbine** GA U.S.A.
234 A3 **Woodbine** MD U.S.A.
234 D3 **Woodbine** NJ U.S.A.
226 C3 **Woodboro** WI U.S.A.
81 D4 **Woodbourne** South I. N.Z.
234 D1 **Woodbourne** NY U.S.A.
151 I2 **Woodbridge** Suffolk, England U.K.
235 E1 **Woodbridge** CT U.S.A.
235 D2 **Woodbridge** NJ U.S.A.
232 E5 **Woodbridge** VA U.S.A.
83 H2 **Woodburn** N.S.W. Austr.
226 E5 **Woodburn** IN U.S.A.
238 B2 **Woodburn** OR U.S.A.
235 E1 **Woodbury** CT U.S.A.
226 E4 **Woodbury** MI U.S.A.
234 C3 **Woodbury** NJ U.S.A.
234 C3 **Woodbury Heights** NJ U.S.A.
84 C3 **Woodcock, Mount** hill N.T. Austr.
151 F3 **Woodcote** Oxfordshire, England U.K.
83 H2 **Woodenbong** N.S.W. Austr.
147 E4 **Woodenbridge** Rep. of Ireland
83 F4 **Woodend** Vic. Austr.
81 B7 **Woodend** South I. N.Z.
81 D5 **Woodend** South I. N.Z.
147 C3 **Woodford** Rep. of Ireland
240 H2 **Woodfords** CA U.S.A.
149 I4 **Woodhall Spa** Lincolnshire, England U.K.
151 G4 **Woodingdean** Brighton and Hove, England U.K.
240 H3 **Woodlake** CA U.S.A.
240 G2 **Woodland** CA U.S.A.
233 □J2 **Woodland** ME U.S.A.
238 B2 **Woodland** WA U.S.A.
234 B4 **Woodland Beach** MD U.S.A.
239 F4 **Woodland Park** CO U.S.A.
94 □ **Woodlands** Sing.
91 L8 **Woodlark Island** P.N.G.
234 B3 **Woodlawn** MD U.S.A.
151 G3 **Woodley** Wokingham, England U.K.
234 C3 **Woodlyn** PA U.S.A.
149 I4 **Woodmansey** East Riding of Yorkshire, England U.K.
149 G4 **Woodplumpton** Lancashire, England U.K.
223 L5 **Woodridge** Man. Can.
234 D1 **Woodridge** NY U.S.A.
82 B1 **Woodroffe, Mount** S.A. Austr.
238 E3 **Woodruff** UT U.S.A.
226 C3 **Woodruff** WI U.S.A.
84 C3 **Woods, Lake** salt flat N.T. Austr.
228 H1 **Woods, Lake of the** Can./U.S.A.
232 C5 **Woodsfield** OH U.S.A.
233 H4 **Woods Hole** MA U.S.A.
83 F4 **Woodside** Vic. Austr.
234 C3 **Woodside** DE U.S.A.
83 G3 **Woodstock** N.S.W. Austr.
85 F3 **Woodstock** Qld Austr.
225 H4 **Woodstock** N.B. Can.
224 D5 **Woodstock** Ont. Can.
151 F3 **Woodstock** Oxfordshire, England U.K.
226 C4 **Woodstock** IL U.S.A.
232 D5 **Woodstock** VA U.S.A.
233 G3 **Woodstock** VT U.S.A.
147 D4 **Woodstown** Rep. of Ireland
234 C3 **Woodstown** NJ U.S.A.
233 G2 **Woodsville** NH U.S.A.
151 I2 **Woodton** Norfolk, England U.K.
147 E3 **Woodtown** Rep. of Ireland
227 H3 **Woodville** Ont. Can.
80 E4 **Woodville** North I. N.Z.
237 F6 **Woodville** MS U.S.A.
232 B4 **Woodville** OH U.S.A.
237 E6 **Woodville** TX U.S.A.
237 D4 **Woodward** OK U.S.A.
240 H4 **Woody** CA U.S.A.
150 E2 **Woofferton** Shropshire, England U.K.
150 E4 **Wool** Dorset, England U.K.
150 C3 **Woolacombe** Devon, England U.K.
84 C2 **Woolen** r. N.T. Austr.
149 G2 **Wooler** Northumberland, England U.K.
85 E4 **Woolgar** r. Qld Austr.
83 H2 **Woolgoolga** N.S.W. Austr.
83 H2 **Wooli** N.S.W. Austr.
84 C4 **Woolla Downs** N.T. Austr.
262 W1 **Woollard, Mount** Antarctica
82 D2 **Wooltana** S.A. Austr.
232 C6 **Woolwine** VA U.S.A.
87 D7 **Woolyeenyer Hill** hill W.A. Austr.
82 D2 **Woomera** S.A. Austr.
233 H3 **Woonsocket** RI U.S.A.
236 D2 **Woonsocket** SD U.S.A.
85 G5 **Woorabinda** Qld Austr.
87 B5 **Wooramel** r. W.A. Austr.
232 C4 **Wooster** OH U.S.A.
151 G2 **Wootton** Bedfordshire, England U.K.
151 F3 **Wootton Bassett** Wiltshire, England U.K.
210 D2 **Woqooyi Galbeed** admin. reg. Somalia
190 C2 **Worb** Switz.
85 E2 **Worbody Point** Qld Austr.
214 B5 **Worcester** S. Africa
150 E2 **Worcester** Worcestershire, England U.K.
233 H3 **Worcester** MA U.S.A.
233 F3 **Worcester** NY U.S.A.
150 E2 **Worcestershire** admin. div. England U.K.
179 H2 **Wördern** Austria
150 E2 **Worfield** Shropshire, England U.K.
178 D3 **Wörgl** Austria
173 E4 **Woringen** Ger.
149 F3 **Workington** Cumbria, England U.K.
149 H4 **Worksop** Nottinghamshire, England U.K.
164 E2 **Workum** Neth.
238 F2 **Worland** WY U.S.A.
171 D4 **Wörlitz** Ger.
165 F5 **Wormeldange** Lux.
164 D2 **Wormer** Neth.
156 C2 **Wormhout** France
146 F5 **Wormit** Fife, Scotland U.K.
172 C2 **Worms** Ger.
173 E3 **Wörnitz** r. Ger.
206 D4 **Worofla** Côte d'Ivoire
151 G3 **Worplesdon** Surrey, England U.K.
168 D2 **Worpswede** Ger.
172 C2 **Wörrstadt** Ger.
179 F3 **Wörschach** Austria
165 D3 **Wortel** Belgium
173 F3 **Wörth** Ger.
151 G3 **Worth** West Sussex, England U.K.
172 D2 **Wörth am Main** Ger.
172 C2 **Wörth am Rhein** Ger.
173 G2 **Wörth an der Donau** Ger.
173 G3 **Wörth an der Isar** Ger.
151 G4 **Worthing** West Sussex, England U.K.
236 E3 **Worthington** MN U.S.A.
232 B4 **Worthington** OH U.S.A.
234 B3 **Worton** MD U.S.A.
266 G6 **Wotje** atoll Marshall Is
150 E3 **Wotton-under-Edge** Gloucestershire, England U.K.
93 B3 **Wotu** Sulawesi Selatan Indon.
164 E2 **Woudenberg** Neth.
164 D3 **Woudrichem** Neth.
164 E2 **Woudsend** Neth.
151 G2 **Woughton on the Green** Milton Keynes, England U.K.
236 C3 **Wounded Knee** SD U.S.A.
207 H5 **Wouri** r. Cameroon
157 H3 **Woustviller** France
164 D3 **Wouw** Neth.
85 G4 **Wowan** Qld Austr.
93 B4 **Wowoni** i. Indon.
175 H5 **Woźniki** Pol.
149 I4 **Wragby** Lincolnshire, England U.K.
Wrangel Island Rus. Fed. see **Vrangelya, Ostrov**
220 E4 **Wrangell** AK U.S.A.
220 C4 **Wrangell Mountains** AK U.S.A.
149 J4 **Wrangle** Lincolnshire, England U.K.
146 C3 **Wrath, Cape** Scotland U.K.
236 C3 **Wray** CO U.S.A.
151 F2 **Wreake** r. England U.K.
Wrecsam Wrexham, Wales U.K. see **Wrexham**
174 G5 **Wręczyca Wielka** Pol.
170 D2 **Wredenhagen** Ger.
149 I3 **Wrelton** North Yorkshire, England U.K.
168 D2 **Wremen** Ger.
231 D5 **Wrens** GA U.S.A.
168 F3 **Wrestedt** Ger.
169 D4 **Wrexen (Diemelstadt)** Ger.
150 E1 **Wrexham** Wrexham, Wales U.K.
150 E1 **Wrexham** admin. div. Wales U.K.
81 B7 **Wreys Bush** South I. N.Z.
168 F2 **Wriedel** Ger.
170 F3 **Wriezen** Ger.
92 C4 **Wright** Phil.
238 F3 **Wright** WY U.S.A.
241 L6 **Wrightson, Mount** AZ U.S.A.
234 D2 **Wrightstown** PA U.S.A.
226 C3 **Wrightstown** WI U.S.A.
231 D5 **Wrightsville** GA U.S.A.
234 B2 **Wrightsville** PA U.S.A.
240 I4 **Wrightwood** CA U.S.A.
222 F2 **Wrigley** N.W.T. Can.
232 B5 **Wrigley** KY U.S.A.
150 E3 **Wrington** North Somerset, England U.K.
168 E2 **Wrist** Ger.
151 H3 **Writtle** Essex, England U.K.
174 G4 **Wróblew** Pol.
174 F4 **Wrocław** Pol.
168 E1 **Wrohm** Ger.
175 K1 **Wronki** Warmińsko-Mazurskie Pol.
174 E3 **Wronki** Wielkopolskie Pol.
175 K3 **Wrotnów** Pol.
151 F3 **Wroughton** Swindon, England U.K.
174 G3 **Wrząielka** Pol.
175 J4 **Wrzelowiec** Pol.
174 F1 **Wrzeście** Pol.
174 F3 **Września** Pol.
174 F3 **Wrześnica** r. Pol.
175 J5 **Wschodnia** r. Pol.
174 E4 **Wschowa** Pol.
Wu'an Fujian China see **Changtai**
107 G4 **Wu'an** Hebei China
87 C6 **Wubin** W.A. Austr.
107 F4 **Wubu** Shaanxi China
107 I2 **Wuchagou** Nei Mongol China
100 C3 **Wuchang** Heilong. China
109 E2 **Wuchang** Hubei China
109 F2 **Wucheng** Anhui China
Wuchow Guangxi China see **Wuzhou**
108 D4 **Wuchuan** Guangdong China
108 C2 **Wuchuan** Guizhou China
107 F3 **Wuchuan** Nei Mongol China
106 E4 **Wuda** Nei Mongol China
107 H3 **Wudan** Nei Mongol China
107 I4 **Wudao** Liaoning China
107 H4 **Wudi** Shandong China
207 H4 **Wudil** Nigeria
108 B3 **Wuding** Yunnan China
107 F4 **Wuding** r. China
82 C3 **Wudinna** S.A. Austr.
108 C1 **Wudu** Gansu China
108 D2 **Wufeng** Hubei China
Wufeng Yunnan China see **Zhenxiong**
108 D3 **Wugang** Hunan China
107 F5 **Wugong** Shaanxi China
106 E4 **Wuhai** Nei Mongol China
109 E2 **Wuhan** Hubei China
109 F1 **Wuhe** Anhui China
109 F2 **Wuhu** Anhui China
109 F2 **Wuhu** Anhui China
109 E4 **Wuhua** Guangdong China
109 G2 **Wujiang** Jiangsu China
108 C2 **Wu Jiang** r. China
Wujin Jiangsu China see **Changzhou**
Wujin Sichuan China see **Xinjin**
207 H5 **Wukari** Nigeria
171 C4 **Wulfen** Ger.
170 D2 **Wulfersdorf** Ger.
169 F5 **Wülfershausen an der Saale** Ger.
168 F2 **Wulfsen** Ger.
169 F4 **Wulften** Ger.
108 B2 **Wulian Feng** mts Yunnan China
108 B3 **Wuliang Shan** mts Yunnan China
108 D4 **Wuli Jiang** r. China
108 D2 **Wuling Shan** mts China
170 D3 **Wulkau** Ger.
179 H2 **Wullersdorf** Austria
108 C2 **Wulong** Chongqing China
107 I4 **Wulong** r. China
Wulongji Henan China see **Huaibin**
168 D2 **Wulsbüttel** Ger.
207 H5 **Wum** Cameroon
108 B3 **Wumeng Shan** mts Yunnan China
108 D4 **Wuming** Guangxi China
168 D2 **Wümme** r. Ger.
108 B2 **Wungda** Sichuan China
109 E2 **Wuning** Jiangxi China
169 D4 **Wünnenberg** Ger.
171 D5 **Wünschendorf** Ger.
171 E3 **Wünsdorf** Ger.
171 D5 **Wunsiedel** Ger.
169 E3 **Wunstorf** Ger.
96 A2 **Wuntho** Myanmar
109 F3 **Wuping** Fujian China
169 C4 **Wuppertal** Ger.
214 B5 **Wuppertal** S. Africa
107 F4 **Wuqi** Shaanxi China
107 G4 **Wuqiang** Hebei China
107 H4 **Wuqiao** Hebei China
107 H4 **Wuqing** Tianjin China
Wuquan Henan China see **Wuyang**
87 C6 **Wuranga** W.A. Austr.
173 F3 **Würm** r. Ger.
173 G3 **Wurmannsquick** Ger.
172 C3 **Wurmlingen** Ger.
207 G3 **Wurno** Nigeria
169 B5 **Würselen** Ger.
235 D1 **Wurtsboro** NY U.S.A.
171 C5 **Wurzbach** Ger.
172 D2 **Würzburg** Ger.
171 D4 **Wurzen** Ger.
108 D2 **Wushan** Chongqing China
106 E5 **Wushan** Gansu China
108 C2 **Wusheng** Sichuan China
109 F2 **Wusheng** Zhejiang China
110 B3 **Wushi** Xinjiang China
170 D3 **Wust** Ger.
169 E4 **Wüstegarten** hill Ger.
172 D2 **Wüstenrot** Ger.
170 D3 **Wusterhausen** Ger.
170 E1 **Wusterhusen** Ger.
170 D3 **Wustermark** Ger.
171 D3 **Wusterwitz** Ger.
169 F4 **Wüstheuterode** Ger.
170 D3 **Wustrau-Altfriesack** Ger.
170 D2 **Wustrow** Mecklenburg-Vorpommern Ger.
170 C3 **Wustrow** Niedersachsen Ger.
Wusuli Jiang r. Rus. Fed. see **Ussuri**
172 C4 **Wutach** r. Ger.
107 G4 **Wutai** Shanxi China
169 F5 **Wutha** Ger.
100 D3 **Wutong** r. China
110 E3 **Wutonggou** Xinjiang China
165 D3 **Wuustwezel** Belgium
109 F2 **Wuwei** Anhui China
106 D4 **Wuwei** Gansu China
108 D2 **Wuxi** Chongqing China
Wuxi Hunan China see **Luxi**
109 G2 **Wuxi** Jiangsu China
Wuxia Chongqing China see **Wushan**
107 G4 **Wuxiang** Shanxi China
Wuxing Zhejiang China see **Huzhou**
108 D4 **Wuxu** Guangxi China
108 D4 **Wuxuan** Guangxi China
109 E2 **Wuxue** Hubei China
Wuyang Guizhou China see **Zhenyuan**
109 E1 **Wuyang** Henan China
109 F2 **Wuyi** Zhejiang China
100 D2 **Wuyiling** Heilong. China
109 F3 **Wuyishan** Fujian China
109 F3 **Wuyi Shan** mts China
109 F3 **Wuyi Shan** tourist site Fujian China
109 F2 **Wuyuan** Jiangxi China
107 F3 **Wuyuan** Nei Mongol China
Wuyuan Zhejiang China see **Haiyan**
Wuyun Zhejiang China see **Jinyun**
107 F4 **Wuzhai** Shanxi China
109 D2 **Wuzhen** Hubei China
107 G5 **Wuzhi** Henan China
106 E4 **Wuzhong** Ningxia China
109 D4 **Wuzhou** Guangxi China
85 E3 **Wyaaba Creek** r. Qld Austr.
226 B5 **Wyaconda** r. MO U.S.A.
87 C6 **Wyalkatchem** W.A. Austr.
227 I5 **Wyalusing** PA U.S.A.
227 F4 **Wyandotte** MI U.S.A.
85 F5 **Wyandra** Qld Austr.
226 C5 **Wyanet** IL U.S.A.
83 F2 **Wyara, Lake** salt flat Qld Austr.
151 G2 **Wyberton** Lincolnshire, England U.K.
83 E4 **Wycheproof** Vic. Austr.
235 D1 **Wyckoff** NJ U.S.A.
175 K2 **Wydminy** Pol.
151 H3 **Wye** Kent, England U.K.
149 H4 **Wye** r. Derbyshire, England U.K.
150 E3 **Wye** r. England/Wales U.K.
87 C6 **Wyemandoo** hill W.A. Austr.
234 B4 **Wye Mills** MD U.S.A.
226 B3 **Wyeville** WI U.S.A.
177 I1 **Wygoda** Pol.
172 B3 **Wyhl** Ger.
171 D4 **Wyhra** r. Ger.
168 D1 **Wyk auf Föhr** Ger.
174 F3 **Wylatowo** Pol.
232 D6 **Wylliesburg** VA U.S.A.
87 C4 **Wyloo** W.A. Austr.
151 F3 **Wylye** Wiltshire, England U.K.
151 F3 **Wylye** r. England U.K.
168 C2 **Wymeer** Ger.
171 G4 **Wymiarki** Pol.
151 I2 **Wymondham** Norfolk, England U.K.
236 D3 **Wymore** NE U.S.A.
82 C2 **Wynbring** S.A. Austr.
86 F2 **Wyndham** W.A. Austr.
81 B7 **Wyndham** South I. N.Z.
83 F4 **Wyndham-Werribee** Vic. Austr.
237 F5 **Wynne** AR U.S.A.
83 F5 **Wynyard** Tas. Austr.
223 J5 **Wynyard** Sask. Can.
226 C4 **Wyocena** WI U.S.A.
82 B2 **Wyola Lake** salt flat S.A. Austr.
234 C3 **Wyoming** DE U.S.A.
226 C5 **Wyoming** IL U.S.A.
226 E4 **Wyoming** MI U.S.A.
238 F3 **Wyoming** state U.S.A.
234 B1 **Wyoming County** county PA U.S.A.
238 E3 **Wyoming Peak** WY U.S.A.
238 E3 **Wyoming Range** mts WY U.S.A.
234 C2 **Wyomissing** PA U.S.A.
83 G3 **Wyong** N.S.W. Austr.
84 D2 **Wyonga** r. N.T. Austr.
146 F2 **Wyre** i. Scotland U.K.
149 G4 **Wyre** r. England U.K.
175 L4 **Wyryki-Połód** Pol.
174 F2 **Wyrzysk** Pol.
175 I4 **Wyśmierzyce** Pol.
175 J6 **Wysoka** Podkarpackie Pol.
174 F2 **Wysoka** Wielkopolskie Pol.
174 D5 **Wysoka Kopa** mt. Pol.
175 K5 **Wysokie** Lubelskie Pol.
175 K2 **Wysokie** Warmińsko-Mazurskie Pol.
175 K3 **Wysokie Mazowieckie** Pol.
175 J6 **Wysowa** Pol.
227 I5 **Wysox** PA U.S.A.
175 K3 **Wyszki** Pol.
175 J3 **Wyszków** Pol.
175 I3 **Wyszogród** Pol.
151 F2 **Wythall** Worcestershire, England U.K.
232 C6 **Wytheville** VA U.S.A.
175 L4 **Wytyczno** Pol.
175 J4 **Wyżnica** r. Pol.

X

210 F2 **Xaafun, Raas** pt Somalia
210 F2 **Xaafuun** Somalia
129 E3 **Xaçınçay** r. Azer.
129 F3 **Xaçmaz** Azer.
195 □ **Xagħra** Gozo Malta
111 F6 **Xagquka** Xizang China
111 E6 **Xainza** Xizang China
111 E6 **Xaitongmoin** Xizang China
213 G5 **Xai-Xai** Moz.
243 H4 **Xal, Cerro de** hill Mex.
Xalapa Mex. see **Jalapa Enríquez**
182 A2 **Xallas** r. Spain
209 D9 **Xamavera** Angola
107 E3 **Xamba** Nei Mongol China
254 C3 **Xambioá** Brazil
256 A5 **Xambrê** Brazil
96 D2 **Xam Hua** Laos
209 C7 **Xá-Muteba** Angola
96 C3 **Xan** r. Laos
97 D4 **Xan, Xé** r. Vietnam
182 B1 **Xanceda** Spain
Xangda Qinghai China see **Nangqên**
209 B9 **Xangongo** Angola
96 D3 **Xangxoy, Xé** r. Laos
129 E4 **Xankändi** Azer.
129 E3 **Xanlar** Azer.
169 B4 **Xanten** Ger.
198 D1 **Xanthi** Greece
255 B8 **Xanxerê** Brazil
252 C2 **Xapuri** Brazil
252 C2 **Xapuri** r. Brazil
210 E3 **Xarardheere** Somalia
Xar Burd Nei Mongol China see **Bayan Nuru**
182 C2 **Xares** r. Spain
107 F3 **Xar Moron** r. China
107 I3 **Xar Moron** r. China
184 B2 **Xarrama** r. Port.
198 B2 **Xarrë** Albania
Xarsingma Xizang China see **Yadong**
209 C7 **Xassengue** Angola
129 D3 **Xatınlı** Azer.
187 C6 **Xátiva** Spain
212 E4 **Xau, Lake** Botswana
256 C5 **Xavantes, Represa de** resr Brazil
254 C5 **Xavantes, Serra dos** hills Brazil
97 D5 **Xa Vo Đat** Vietnam
110 C3 **Xayar** Xinjiang China
243 I4 **X-Can** Mex.
232 B5 **Xenia** OH U.S.A.
187 C5 **Xeraco** Spain
187 C5 **Xeresa** Spain
251 F5 **Xeriuini** r. Brazil
182 C1 **Xermade** Spain
Xero Potamos r. Cyprus see **Xeros**
128 A2 **Xeros** r. Cyprus
186 D4 **Xerta** Spain
157 G4 **Xertigny** France
195 □ **Xewkija** Gozo Malta
Xhora S. Africa see **Elliotdale**
212 E4 **Xhumo** Botswana
107 I3 **Xi** r. Liaoning China
107 H3 **Xiabancheng** Hebei China
100 C2 **Xiabole Shan** mt. China
100 D3 **Xiachengzi** Heilong. China
Xiacun Shandong China see **Rushan**
Xiaguan Yunnan China see **Dali**
106 D5 **Xiahe** Gansu China
109 E3 **Xiajiang** Jiangxi China
Xiajiang Xizang China see **Qusum**
107 H4 **Xiajin** Shandong China
109 F3 **Xiamen** Fujian China
107 F5 **Xi'an** Shaanxi China
109 E1 **Xiancheng** Henan China
108 D2 **Xianfeng** Hubei China
109 E1 **Xiangcheng** Henan China
108 A2 **Xiangcheng** Sichuan China
Xiangcheng Yunnan China see **Xiangyun**
109 E1 **Xiangfan** Hubei China
107 F5 **Xiangfen** Shanxi China
Xiangfeng Hubei China see **Laifeng**
Xianggang H.K. China see **Hong Kong**
Xianggang Tebie Xingzhengqu special admin. reg. China see **Hong Kong**
Xianghuang Qi Nei Mongol China see **Xin Bulag**
Xiangjiang Jiangxi China see **Huichang**
109 E2 **Xiang Jiang** r. China
96 C3 **Xiangkhoang** Laos
Xiangkou Chongqing China see **Wulong**
107 F5 **Xiangning** Shanxi China
111 B6 **Xiangquan He** r. China
106 C5 **Xiangride** Qinghai China
Xiangshan Yunnan China see **Menghai**
109 G2 **Xiangshan** Zhejiang China
107 H5 **Xiangshui** Jiangsu China
108 D3 **Xiangshuiba** Hunan China
109 E3 **Xiangtan** Hunan China
109 E3 **Xiangxiang** Hunan China
Xiangyang Hubei China see **Xiangfan**
109 E2 **Xiangyin** Hunan China
108 B3 **Xiangyun** Yunnan China
109 G2 **Xianju** Zhejiang China
109 E2 **Xianning** Hubei China
Xiannümiao Jiangsu China see **Jiangdu**
Xianshui Sichuan China see **Dawu**
108 B2 **Xianshui He** r. Sichuan China
109 E2 **Xiantao** Hubei China
109 F3 **Xianxia Ling** mts China
107 H4 **Xianxian** Hebei China
107 F5 **Xianyang** Shaanxi China
109 F3 **Xianyou** Fujian China
Xiaoba Ningxia China see **Qingtongxia**
109 E2 **Xiaochang** Hubei China
108 D4 **Xiaodong** Guangxi China
107 I1 **Xiao'ergou** Nei Mongol China
Xiaofan Hebei China see **Wuqiang**
109 E2 **Xiaogan** Hubei China
100 C2 **Xiao Hinggan Ling** mts China
108 B2 **Xiaojin** Sichuan China
109 F3 **Xiaomei** Zhejiang China
106 B5 **Xiaonanchuan** Qinghai China
111 F4 **Xiao Qaidam** Qinghai China
107 H4 **Xiaoqing** r. China
109 E3 **Xiaosanjiang** Guangdong China
109 G2 **Xiaoshan** Zhejiang China
108 A1 **Xiao Surmang** Qinghai China
109 F3 **Xiaotao** Fujian China
107 G4 **Xiaowutai Shan** mt. Hebei China
Xiaoxi Fujian China see **Pinghe**
107 H5 **Xiaoxian** Anhui China
108 B2 **Xiaoxiang Ling** mts Sichuan China
Xiaoyi Henan China see **Gongyi**
107 F4 **Xiaoyi** Shanxi China
109 G3 **Xiapu** Fujian China
Xiaqiong Sichuan China see **Batang**
107 F5 **Xiaxian** Shanxi China
Xiayanjing Xizang China see **Yanjing**
Xiayingpan Guizhou China see **Lupanshui**
Xiayingpan Guizhou China see **Luzhi**
Xiazhen Shandong China see **Weishan**
Xiazhuang Shandong China see **Linshu**
108 A2 **Xibdê** Sichuan China
110 E2 **Xibet** Xinjiang China
109 F3 **Xibing** Fujian China
Xibu Fujian China see **Dongshan**
108 B3 **Xichang** Sichuan China
Xicheng Hebei China see **Yangyuan**
108 C4 **Xichou** Yunnan China
109 D1 **Xichuan** Henan China
245 F4 **Xico** Mex.
245 E2 **Xicohténcatl** Mex.
245 F3 **Xicotepec de Juárez** Mex.
108 B2 **Xide** Sichuan China
Xidu Hunan China see **Hengyang**
250 E4 **Xié** r. Brazil
Xiejiaji Shandong China see **Qingyun**
109 D2 **Xiemahe'** Hubei China
Xieng Khouang Laos see **Xiangkhoang**
109 F1 **Xifei He** r. China
107 E5 **Xifeng** Gansu China
108 C3 **Xifeng** Guizhou China
100 C4 **Xifeng** Liaoning China
Xifengzhen Gansu China see **Xifeng**
111 E6 **Xigazê** Xizang China
108 C1 **Xihan Shui** r. Gansu China
108 C1 **Xihe** Gansu China
108 C2 **Xi He** r. Sichuan China
109 E1 **Xihua** Henan China
Xihuachi Gansu China see **Heshui**
106 E5 **Xiji** Ningxia China
109 E4 **Xi Jiang** r. Guangdong China
108 D4 **Xijin** Guangxi China
100 B1 **Xikouzi** Nei Mongol China
107 G3 **Xil** Nei Mongol China
Xilaganí Greece see **Xylagani**
107 I2 **Xilaotou Shan** mt. Nei Mongol China
107 I3 **Xiliao** r. China
Xiligou Qinghai China see **Ulan**
108 C3 **Xilin** Guangxi China
107 H3 **Xilinhot** Nei Mongol China
Xilinji Heilong. China see **Mohe**
129 F4 **Xıllı** Azer.
129 F3 **Xilmilli** Azer.
Xilókastron Greece see **Xylokastro**
Xilópolis Greece see **Xylopoli**
106 D3 **Ximiao** Nei Mongol China
107 F4 **Xin** Nei Mongol China
129 F3 **Xınalıq** Azer.
Xin'an Anhui China see **Lai'an**
Xin'an Hebei China see **Anxin**
107 G5 **Xin'an** Henan China
Xin Barag Youqi Nei Mongol China see **Altan Emel**
Xin Barag Zuoqi Nei Mongol China see **Amgalang**
101 C4 **Xinbin** Liaoning China
131 M5 **Xin Bulag** Nei Mongol China
109 E1 **Xincai** Henan China
Xinchang Jiangxi China see **Yifeng**
109 G2 **Xinchang** Zhejiang China
Xincheng Fujian China see **Gutian**
Xincheng Guangdong China see **Xinxing**
108 D3 **Xincheng** Guangxi China
106 E4 **Xincheng** Ningxia China
Xincheng Shanxi China see **Yuanqu**
Xincheng Sichuan China see **Zhaojue**
107 F4 **Xinchengbu** Shaanxi China
Xincun Yunnan China see **Dongchuan**
109 D4 **Xindi** Guangxi China
Xindi Hubei China see **Honghu**
109 D4 **Xindu** Guangxi China
Xindu Sichuan China see **Luhuo**
108 C2 **Xindu** Sichuan China
108 B2 **Xinduqiao** Sichuan China
109 E3 **Xinfeng** Guangdong China
109 E3 **Xinfeng** Jiangxi China
108 D3 **Xing'an** Guangxi China
109 E3 **Xingan** Jiangxi China
Xingba Xizang China see **Lhünzê**
Xingcheng Hebei China see **Qianxi**
107 I3 **Xingcheng** Liaoning China
Xingguo Gansu China see **Qin'an**
109 E3 **Xingguo** Jiangxi China
106 C5 **Xinghai** Qinghai China
109 F1 **Xinghua** Jiangsu China
100 E3 **Xingkai** Heilong. China
107 H3 **Xinglong** Hebei China
100 C2 **Xinglong** Heilong. China
100 C3 **Xinglongzhen** Heilong. China
109 E3 **Xingning** Guangdong China
109 E2 **Xingou** Hubei China
107 F5 **Xingping** Shaanxi China
108 C3 **Xingren** Guizhou China
Xingshan Guizhou China see **Majiang**
108 D2 **Xingshan** Hubei China
107 G4 **Xingtai** Hebei China
107 G4 **Xingtang** Hebei China
251 H5 **Xingu** r. Brazil
254 C3 **Xinguara** Brazil
108 C2 **Xingwen** Sichuan China
107 F4 **Xingxian** Shanxi China
106 B3 **Xingxingxia** Xinjiang China
107 G5 **Xingyang** Henan China
108 C3 **Xingyi** Guizhou China
109 F2 **Xingzi** Jiangxi China
107 G4 **Xinhe** Hebei China
110 C3 **Xinhe** Xinjiang China
107 G3 **Xin Hot** Nei Mongol China
Xinhua Guangdong China see **Huadu**
109 D3 **Xinhua** Hunan China
Xinhua Yunnan China see **Qiaojia**

Xinhua to Yongding 381

Xinhua Yunnan China see Funing
106 D4 Xinhuacun Gansu China
108 D3 Xinhuang Hunan China
107 H3 Xinhui Nei Mongol China
106 D4 Xining Qinghai China
107 G4 Xinji Hebei China
Xinji Henan China see Xinxian
109 E2 Xinjian Jiangxi China
107 F5 Xinjiang Shanxi China
Xinjiang aut. reg. China see Xinjiang Uygur Zizhiqu
109 F2 Xin Jiang r. China
Xinjiangkou Hubei China see Songzi
106 A3 Xinjiang Uygur Zizhiqu aut. reg. China
Xinjie Yunnan China see Yuanyang
Xinjin Liaoning China see Pulandian
108 B2 Xinjin Sichuan China
Xinjing Guangxi China see Jingxi
107 I3 Xinkai r. China
Xinling Hubei China see Badong
108 B2 Xinlong Sichuan China
107 G5 Xinmi Henan China
Xinmian Sichuan China see Shimian
107 I3 Xinmin Liaoning China
Xinning Gansu China see Ningxian
Xinning Guangxi China see Fusui
108 D3 Xinning Hunan China
Xinning Jiangxi China see Wuning
Xinning Sichuan China see Kaijiang
108 B3 Xinping Yunnan China
100 D2 Xinqing Heilong. China
109 F3 Xinquan Fujian China
Xinshan Jiangxi China see Anyuan
109 D3 Xinshao Hunan China
Xinshi Hubei China see Jingshan
Xinshiba Sichuan China see Ganluo
107 H5 Xintai Shandong China
109 E2 Xintanpu Hubei China
109 E3 Xintian Hunan China
109 E2 Xinxian Henan China
107 G5 Xinxiang Henan China
109 E4 Xinxing Guangdong China
109 E1 Xinyang Henan China
109 G1 Xinyang Gang r. China
109 E1 Xinye Henan China
107 H5 Xinye r. China
109 D4 Xinyi Guangdong China
107 H5 Xinyi Jiangsu China
Xinying Taiwan see Hsinying
109 E3 Xinyu Jiangxi China
Xinyuan Qinghai China see Tianjun
110 C3 Xinyuan Xinjiang China
107 I1 Xinzhangfang Nei Mongol China
107 G5 Xinzheng Henan China
Xinzhou Guangxi China see Longlin
Xinzhou Guizhou China see Huangping
109 E2 Xinzhou Hubei China
107 G4 Xinzhou Shanxi China
Xinzhu Taiwan see Hsinchu
182 C2 Xinzo de Limia Spain
Xiongshan Fujian China see Zhenghe
Xiongzhou Guangdong China see Nanxiong
252 D2 Xipamanu r. Bol./Brazil
109 D1 Xiping Henan China
109 E1 Xiping Henan China
106 D5 Xiqing Shan mts China
254 E4 Xique Xique Brazil
129 F3 Xırdalan Azer.
187 C5 Xirivella Spain
198 C2 Xiro hill Greece
199 E3 Xirokampo Greece
250 E6 Xiruá r. Brazil
Xisa Yunnan China see Xichou
107 F3 Xishanzui Nei Mongol China
Xisha Qundao is S. China Sea see Paracel Islands
108 C2 Xishui Guizhou China
109 E2 Xishui Hubei China
182 C1 Xistral, Serra do mts Spain
206 B4 Xitole Guinea-Bissau
Xiucaiwan Chongqing China see Fengdu
Xiugu Jiangxi China see Jinxi
Xi Ujimqin Qi Nei Mongol China see Bayan Ul Hot
109 F2 Xiuning Anhui China
108 D2 Xiushan Chongqing China
Xiushan Yunnan China see Tonghai
109 E2 Xiushui Jiangxi China
109 E2 Xiu Shui r. China
108 C3 Xiuwen Guizhou China
107 G5 Xiuwu Henan China
107 I3 Xiuyan Liaoning China
Xiuyan Shaanxi China see Qingjian
108 D4 Xiuying Hainan China
Xiwanzi Hebei China see Chongli
108 A1 Xiwu Qinghai China
111 D6 Xixabangma Feng mt. Xizang China
109 D1 Xixia Henan China
109 E1 Xixian Henan China
107 F4 Xixian Shanxi China
108 C1 Xixiang Shaanxi China
Xixón Spain see Gijón
107 G4 Xiyang Shanxi China
108 C3 Xiyang Jiang r. Yunnan China
Xizang aut. reg. China see Xizang Zizhiqu
Xizang Gaoyuan plat. Xizang China see Qing Zang Gaoyuan
108 A2 Xizang Zizhiqu aut. reg. China
129 F3 Xızı Azer.
210 E2 Xjis Somalia
129 E4 Xocalı Azer.
129 E4 Xocavänd Azer.
245 E3 Xochiatiapan Mex.
245 E4 Xochicalco tourist site Mex.
245 E4 Xochimilco Mex.
245 E5 Xochistlahuaca Mex.
Xoi Xizang China see Qüxü
215 F5 Xolobe S. Africa
129 F4 Xol Qarabucaq Azer.
97 D5 Xom An Lôc Vietnam
97 D5 Xom Dưc Hanh Vietnam
245 E4 Xonacatlán Mex.
Xonrupt France see Xonrupt-Longemer
157 G4 Xonrupt-Longemer France
110 E4 Xorkol Xinjiang China
129 E3 Xosrov Azer.
182 C1 Xove Spain
Xuancheng Anhui China see Xuanzhou
108 D2 Xuan'en Hubei China
108 C2 Xuanhan Sichuan China
107 G3 Xuanhua Hebei China
97 D5 Xuân Lôc Vietnam
108 C3 Xuanwei Yunnan China
109 F2 Xuanzhou Anhui China
182 B2 Xubín Spain
109 E1 Xuchang Henan China
99 J5 Xuchang Henan China
Xucheng Guangdong China see Xuwen
129 F3 Xudat Azer.
210 D3 Xuddur Somalia
Xueba Xizang China see Sangri
Xuefeng Fujian China see Mingxi
108 D3 Xuefeng Shan mts China
107 F5 Xuehua Shan hill Shanxi China
108 A3 Xue Shan mts Yunnan China
107 H5 Xugou Jiangsu China
Xuguit Qi Nei Mongol China see Yakeshi
Xujiang Jiangxi China see Guangchang
Xulun Hobot Qagan Qi Nei Mongol China see Qagan Nur
Xulun Hoh Qi Nei Mongol China see Dund Hot
100 D2 Xun r. China
108 B3 Xundian Yunnan China
111 F6 Xung Qu r. Xizang China
111 D6 Xungru Xizang China
100 C2 Xunhe Heilong. China
108 D1 Xun He r. China
106 D5 Xunhua Qinghai China
108 D4 Xun Jiang r. China
100 D2 Xunke Heilong. China
182 C2 Xunqueira de Ambía Spain
109 E3 Xunwu Jiangxi China
107 G5 Xunxian Henan China
108 D1 Xunyang Shaanxi China
107 F5 Xunyi Shaanxi China
108 D3 Xupu Hunan China
107 G4 Xushui Hebei China
108 D4 Xuwen Guangdong China
Xuyang Sichuan China see Rongxian
109 F1 Xuyi Jiangsu China
108 C2 Xuyong Sichuan China
107 H5 Xuzhou Jiangsu China
199 D1 Xylagani Greece
198 C2 Xylokastro Greece
198 C1 Xylopoli Greece

Y

85 G4 Yaamba Qld Austr.
108 B2 Ya'an Sichuan China
83 E3 Yaapeet Vic. Austr.
Yabanabat Turkey see Kızılcahamam
207 H5 Yabassi Cameroon
78 □3a Yabbenohr i. Kwajalein Marshall Is
210 C3 Yabēlo Eth.
197 G4 Yablanitsa Bulg.
197 H4 Yablanovo Bulg.
137 J2 Yablochnoye Rus. Fed.
137 K1 Yablonovets Rus. Fed.
137 J5 Yablonovskiy Rus. Fed.
107 F1 Yablonovyy Khrebet mts Rus. Fed.
136 C3 Yabluniv Ukr.
137 F3 Yablunivka Ukr.
207 G3 Yabo Nigeria
106 D4 Yabrai Shan mts China
106 D4 Yabrai Yanchang Nei Mongol China
128 C3 Yabrūd Syria
247 □1 Yabucoa Puerto Rico
100 D3 Yabuli Heilong. China
136 E2 Yabunets' Ukr.
Yacha Hainan China see Baisha
108 D5 Yacheng Hainan China
108 C3 Yachi He r. China
105 G3 Yachiyo Chiba Japan
105 F2 Yachiyo Ibaraki Japan
83 F4 Yackandandah Vic. Austr.
252 E5 Yacuiba Bol.
114 C2 Yadgir Karnataka India
114 C3 Yadiki Andhra Prad. India
231 D5 Yadkin r. NC U.S.A.
231 D4 Yadkinville NC U.S.A.
111 E7 Yadong Xizang China
134 I5 Yadrin Rus. Fed.
79 □1 Yadua i. Fiji
Yafa Israel see Tel Aviv-Yafo
202 B1 Yafran Libya
206 E4 Yagaba Ghana
Yagaing state Myanmar see Arakan
199 E2 Yağcılı Turkey
Yağda Turkey see Erdemli
264 E9 Yaghan Basin sea feature S. Atlantic Ocean
128 B1 Yağızlar Turkey
129 C3 Yağlıca Dağı mt. Turkey
122 C2 Yagman Turkm.
129 C4 Yağmurlu r. Turkey
139 K2 Yagnitsa Rus. Fed.
197 G4 Yagoda Bulg.
120 A2 Yagodnaya Polyana Rus. Fed.
131 P3 Yagodnoye Rus. Fed.
Yagotin Ukr. see Yahotyn
207 I4 Yagoua Cameroon
111 C6 Yagra Xizang China
106 B5 Yagradagzê Shan mt. Qinghai China
246 C2 Yaguajay Cuba
Yaguarón r. Brazil/Uru. see Jaguarão
250 D5 Yaguas r. Peru
97 C6 Yaha Thai.
104 C4 Yahagi-gawa r. Japan
222 G5 Yahk B.C. Can.
136 E4 Yahorlyk r. Ukr.
137 F2 Yahotyn Ukr.
244 C3 Yahualica Mex.
118 D2 Yahyalı Turkey
97 B4 Yai, Khao hill Thai.
105 F2 Yaita Japan
216 □3c Yaiza Lanzarote Canary Is
105 E4 Yaizu Japan
108 B2 Yajiang Sichuan China
128 C1 Yakacık Turkey
128 B1 Yakapınar Turkey
104 D2 Yake-dake vol. Japan
107 I1 Yakeshi Nei Mongol China
136 D3 Yakhivtsi Ukr.
137 G2 Yakhnyky Ukr.
139 K3 Yakhroma Rus. Fed.
238 B2 Yakima WA U.S.A.
238 C2 Yakima r. WA U.S.A.
121 F5 Yakkabag Uzbek.
206 E3 Yako Burkina
197 F4 Yakoruda Bulg.
137 I3 Yakovenkove Ukr.
100 E3 Yakovlevka Rus. Fed.
137 I2 Yakovlevo Rus. Fed.
134 K4 Yakshur-Bod'ya Rus. Fed.
102 □1 Yaku-shima i. Japan
220 E4 Yakutat AK U.S.A.
131 N3 Yakutsk Rus. Fed.
137 H4 Yakymivka Ukr.
97 C6 Yala Thai.
199 F1 Yalakdere Turkey
129 F3 Yalama Azer.
128 A1 Yalan Dünya Mağarası tourist site Turkey
81 D5 Yaldhurst South I. N.Z.
222 F5 Yale B.C. Can.
227 F4 Yale MI U.S.A.
206 E3 Yalgo Burkina
87 C6 Yalgoo W.A. Austr.
199 E3 Yalıkavak Turkey
197 I5 Yalıköy Turkey
208 D3 Yalinga C.A.R.
138 G5 Yalizava Belarus
246 □1 Yallahs Jamaica
85 F5 Yalleroi Qld Austr.
87 B7 Yallingup W.A. Austr.
83 F4 Yallourn Vic. Austr.
129 C3 Yalnızçam Dağları mts Turkey
237 F5 Yalobusha r. MS U.S.A.
Yalogo Burkina see Yalgo
208 C3 Yaloké C.A.R.
108 B3 Yalong Jiang r. Sichuan China
199 F1 Yalova Turkey
197 I5 Yalova prov. Turkey
Yaloven' Moldova see Ialoveni
136 E5 Yalpuh, Ozero l. Ukr.
Yalpukh r. Moldova see Ialpug
137 I4 Yalta Donets'ka Oblast' Ukr.
137 H5 Yalta Respublika Krym Ukr.
136 D3 Yaltushkiv Ukr.
107 I2 Yalu Jiang r. China
101 C4 Yalu Jiang r. China/N. Korea
130 H4 Yalutorovsk Rus. Fed.
199 G2 Yalvaç Turkey
Yama Ukr. see Sivers'k
103 E7 Yamaga Japan
102 J3 Yamagata Iwate Japan
102 J4 Yamagata Yamagata Japan
102 I4 Yamagata pref. Japan
103 E6 Yamaguchi Japan
103 E6 Yamaguchi pref. Japan
105 F3 Yamakita Japan
130 H2 Yamal, Poluostrov pen. Rus. Fed.
Yamal Peninsula Rus. Fed. see Yamal, Poluostrov
104 C2 Yamanaka Japan
105 E3 Yamanashi Japan
105 E3 Yamanashi pref. Japan
Yamankhalinka Kazakh. see Makhambet
105 E2 Yamanouchi Japan
107 F1 Yamarovka Rus. Fed.
105 F3 Yamato Kanagawa Japan
102 □1 Yamato Nansei-shotō Japan
104 B4 Yamato-kōriyama Japan
104 B4 Yamatotakada Japan
83 H2 Yamba N.S.W. Austr.
83 E4 Yambacoona Tas. Austr.
84 B2 Yambarran Range hills N.T. Austr.
208 B2 Yamba Tchangsou Chad
206 B4 Yambéring Guinea
250 D4 Yambi, Mesa de hills Col.
208 F3 Yambio Sudan
197 H4 Yambol Bulg.
250 B6 Yambrasbamba Peru
91 H8 Yamdena i. Indon.
103 E7 Yame Japan
96 B2 Yamethin Myanmar
105 G2 Yamizo-san mt. Japan
114 B2 Yamkanmardi Karnataka India
Yamkhad Syria see Ḥalab
138 G2 Yamm Rus. Fed.
85 E5 Yamma Yamma, Lake salt flat Qld Austr.
137 H2 Yamne Ukr.
206 D5 Yamoussoukro Côte d'Ivoire
137 F3 Yampil' Cherkas'ka Oblast' Ukr.
136 D3 Yampil' Khmel'nyts'ka Oblast' Ukr.
137 G2 Yampil' Sums'ka Oblast' Ukr.
136 E3 Yampil' Vinnyts'ka Oblast' Ukr.
Yampol' Cherkas'ka Oblast' Ukr. see Yampil'
Yampol' Khmel'nyts'ka Oblast' Ukr. see Yampil'
Yampol' Sums'ka Oblast' Ukr. see Yampil'
Yampol' Vinnyts'ka Oblast' Ukr. see Yampil'
116 E4 Yamuna r. India
116 D3 Yamunanagar Haryana India
111 E6 Yamzho Yumco l. China
107 F4 Yan r. China
207 H4 Yana Nigeria
131 O2 Yana r. Rus. Fed.
82 E4 Yanac Vic. Austr.
103 F7 Yanadani Japan
103 F7 Yanai Japan
114 D2 Yanam Andhra Prad. India
107 F4 Yan'an Shaanxi China
252 C3 Yanaoca Peru
Yanaon Andhra Prad. India see Yanam
134 K4 Yanaul Rus. Fed.
139 H4 Yanavichy Belarus
108 B3 Yanbian Sichuan China
124 B2 Yanbu' al Baḥr Saudi Arabia
124 B2 Yanbu' an Nakhl reg. Saudi Arabia
231 E4 Yanceyville NC U.S.A.
107 F4 Yanchang Shaanxi China
109 G1 Yancheng Jiangsu China
Yancheng Shandong China see Qihe
Yancheng Sichuan China see Jingyan
87 B6 Yanchep W.A. Austr.
107 E4 Yanchi Ningxia China
107 F4 Yanchuan Shaanxi China
137 I4 Yanchur r. Ukr.
83 F3 Yanco N.S.W. Austr.
83 F3 Yanco Creek r. N.S.W. Austr.
83 E2 Yanco Glen N.S.W. Austr.
Yandao Sichuan China see Yingjing
110 E4 Yandaxkak Xinjiang China
87 C5 Yandil W.A. Austr.
85 H5 Yandina Qld Austr.
96 A3 Yandoon Myanmar
Yandua i. Fiji see Yadua
106 B3 Yandun Xinjiang China
139 I1 Yanega Rus. Fed.
206 C4 Yanfolila Mali
107 G3 Yang r. China
208 E4 Yangambi Dem. Rep. Congo
111 F6 Ya'ngamdo Xizang China
111 F6 Ya'ngamdo Xizang China
206 D3 Yangasso Mali
111 E6 Yangbajain Xizang China
108 A3 Yangbi Yunnan China
Yangcheng Guangdong China see Yangshan
107 G5 Yangcheng Shanxi China
Yangchuan Guizhou China see Suiyang
109 D4 Yangchun Guangdong China
109 E4 Yangcun Guangdong China
Yangcun Tianjin China see Wuqing
101 C5 Yangdok N. Korea
107 G3 Yanggao Shanxi China
107 G4 Yanggu Shandong China
Yanghe Ningxia China see Yongning
120 E4 Yangiaryk Uzbek.
121 F4 Yangikishlak Uzbek.
120 F5 Yangi-Nishan Uzbek.
123 G2 Yangi Qal'eh Afgh.
120 F4 Yangirabad Uzbek.
121 G4 Yangiyul' Uzbek.
109 D4 Yangjiang Guangdong China
96 B3 Yangôn Myanmar
115 H2 Yangôn admin. div. Myanmar
109 D2 Yangping Hubei China
107 G4 Yangquan Shanxi China
109 E3 Yangshan Guangdong China
108 D3 Yangshuo Guangxi China
96 C3 Yang Talat Thai.
108 B3 Yangtouyan Yunnan China
108 A1 Yangtze r. China
alt. Chang Jiang,
alt. Jinsha Jiang,
alt. Tongtian He,
alt. Zhi Qu,
long Yangtze Kiang
Yangtze, Mouth of the China see Changjiang Kou
Yangtze Kiang r. China see Yangtze
183 H2 Yanguas Spain
109 D4 Yangxi Guangdong China
108 C1 Yangxian Shaanxi China
101 D5 Yangyang S. Korea
107 G3 Yangyuan Hebei China
109 F1 Yangzhou Jiangsu China
108 D2 Yanhe Guizhou China
82 C3 Yaninee, Lake salt flat S.A. Austr.
134 F3 Yanishpole Rus. Fed.
100 D4 Yanji Jilin China
107 G5 Yanjin Henan China
108 C2 Yanjin Yunnan China
Yanjing Sichuan China see Yanyuan
108 A2 Yanjing Xizang China
Yanjing Yunnan China see Yanjin
Yankou Sichuan China see Wusheng
236 D3 Yankton SD U.S.A.
129 C1 Yankul' Rus. Fed.
129 C1 Yankul' r. Rus. Fed.
107 G5 Yanling Henan China
109 E3 Yanling Hunan China
Yannina Greece see Ioannina
131 P2 Yano-Indigirskaya Nizmennost' lowland Rus. Fed.
114 D4 Yan Oya r. Sri Lanka
110 D3 Yanqi Xinjiang China
107 G3 Yanqing Beijing China
125 G3 Yanqul Oman
87 B4 Yanrey r. W.A. Austr.
107 H4 Yanshan Hebei China
109 F2 Yanshan Jiangxi China
108 C4 Yanshan Yunnan China
107 H3 Yan Shan mts China
107 G5 Yanshi Henan China
111 F5 Yanshiping Qinghai China
100 D3 Yanshou Heilong. China
131 O2 Yanskiy Zaliv g. Rus. Fed.
83 F2 Yantabulla N.S.W. Austr.
122 B2 Yantagh Iran
107 I4 Yantai Shandong China
259 B6 Yántales, Cerro mt. Chile
138 B4 Yantarnyy Rus. Fed.
235 F1 Yantic r. CT U.S.A.
108 C2 Yanting Sichuan China
100 C4 Yantongshan Jilin China
109 G2 Yantou Zhejiang China
197 G4 Yantra r. Bulg.
124 C3 Yanūfī, Jabal al hill Saudi Arabia
Yany-Kurgan Kazakh. see Zhanakorgan
108 B3 Yanyuan Sichuan China
107 H5 Yanzhou Shandong China
104 B4 Yao Japan
108 B3 Yao'an Yunnan China
Yaodu Anhui China see Dongzhi
109 F2 Yaoli Jiangxi China
207 H6 Yaoundé Cameroon
107 F5 Yaoxian Shaanxi China
107 F4 Yaozhen Shaanxi China
91 I5 Yap i. Micronesia
252 D3 Yapacani r. Bol.
258 F3 Yapeyú Arg.
235 F2 Yaphank NY U.S.A.
85 E3 Yappar r. Qld Austr.
151 G4 Yapton West Sussex, England U.K.
266 E5 Yap Trench sea feature N. Pacific Ocean
251 G4 Yapukarri Guyana
242 C3 Yaqui r. Mex.
134 K4 Yar Rus. Fed.
246 C2 Yara Cuba
250 D2 Yaracuy state Venez.
85 F5 Yaraka Qld Austr.
Yarangüme Turkey see Tavas
134 I4 Yaransk Rus. Fed.
82 C3 Yardea S.A. Austr.
129 F4 Yardımlı Azer.
234 D2 Yardley PA U.S.A.
234 D2 Yardville NJ U.S.A.
Yardymly Azer. see Yardımlı
151 I2 Yare r. England U.K.
134 K3 Yarega Rus. Fed.
136 C3 Yaremcha Ukr.
77 G2 Yaren Nauru
134 J3 Yarenga r. Rus. Fed.
134 J3 Yarensk Rus. Fed.
137 G3 Yares'ky Ukr.
Yargara Moldova see Iargara
250 C5 Yari r. Col.
104 D2 Yariga-take mt. Japan
124 D5 Yarīm Yemen
Yarımca Turkey see Körfez
247 E5 Yaritagua Venez.
Yarkand Xinjiang China see Shache
Yarkant Xinjiang China see Shache
111 B4 Yarkant He r. China
227 I3 Yarker Ont. Can.
123 H2 Yarkhun r. Pak.
87 F6 Yarle Lakes salt flat S.A. Austr.
197 F4 Yarlovo Bulg.
111 E7 Yarlung Zangbo r. China
alt. Dihang (India),
conv. Brahmaputra
149 H3 Yarm Stockton-on-Tees, England U.K.
136 D3 Yarmolyntsi Ukr.
225 H5 Yarmouth N.S. Can.
151 F4 Yarmouth Isle of Wight, England U.K.
Yarmouth Norfolk, England U.K. see Great Yarmouth
233 □H3 Yarmouth ME U.S.A.
128 B3 Yarmūk r. Asia
241 K4 Yarnell AZ U.S.A.
151 F3 Yarnton Oxfordshire, England U.K.
137 G2 Yaroshivka Ukr.
137 G2 Yaroslavets' Ukr.
139 L3 Yaroslavl' Rus. Fed.
Yaroslavl Oblast admin. div. Rus. Fed. see Yaroslavskaya Oblast'
129 B1 Yaroslavskaya Rus. Fed.
139 L3 Yaroslavskaya Oblast' admin. div. Rus. Fed.
100 E3 Yaroslavskiy Rus. Fed.
128 B3 Yarqon r. Israel
85 E2 Yarraden Qld Austr.
83 F4 Yarra Junction Vic. Austr.
86 B4 Yarraloola W.A. Austr.
83 F4 Yarram Vic. Austr.
85 G5 Yarraman Qld Austr.
83 F4 Yarrawonga Vic. Austr.
87 B6 Yarra Yarra Lakes salt flat W.A. Austr.
86 D4 Yarrie W.A. Austr.
85 F5 Yarronvale Qld Austr.
85 F4 Yarrowmere Qld Austr.
139 I4 Yartsevo Rus. Fed.
111 D6 Yaru r. China
250 C3 Yarumal Col.
108 A2 Yarwa Sichuan China
108 A2 Yarzhong Xizang China
Yaş Romania see Iaşi
115 E1 Yasai r. W. Bengal India
79 □1 Yasawa i. Fiji
79 □1 Yasawa Group is Fiji
136 C3 Yasen' Ukr.
137 J4 Yaseni r. Rus. Fed.
197 H4 Yasenkovo Bulg.
135 G7 Yasenskaya Rus. Fed.
135 H7 Yashalta Rus. Fed.
207 G3 Yashi Nigeria
207 F4 Yashikera Nigeria
135 K5 Yashkino Rus. Fed.
135 I7 Yashkul' Rus. Fed.
116 C1 Yasin Jammu and Kashmir
Yasinovataya Ukr. see Yasynuvata
136 C3 Yasinya Ukr.
197 H4 Yasna Polyana Bulg.
139 K4 Yasnogorsk Rus. Fed.
137 I3 Yasnohirka Ukr.
136 F2 Yasnohorodka Ukr.
120 D2 Yasnyy Rus. Fed.
96 D4 Yasothon Thai.
83 G3 Yass N.S.W. Austr.
83 G3 Yass r. N.S.W. Austr.
199 F3 Yassıhüyük Denizli Turkey
137 H2 Yastrubyne Ukr.
104 C3 Yasu Japan
103 F6 Yasugi Japan
122 B4 Yāsūj Iran
77 G3 Yasur vol. Vanuatu
136 D1 Yasyel'da r. Belarus
137 I3 Yasynuvata Ukr.
252 D2 Yata r. Bol.
208 D2 Yata r. C.A.R.
199 F3 Yatağan Turkey
211 C5 Yata Plateau Kenya
78 □5 Yaté New Caledonia
150 E3 Yate South Gloucestershire, England U.K.
151 G3 Yateley Hampshire, England U.K.
222 H2 Yates r. Alta/N.W.T. Can.
237 E4 Yates Center KS U.S.A.
Yatou Shandong China see Rongcheng
187 C5 Yatova Spain
136 F3 Yatran' r. Ukr.
105 E3 Yatsuga-take vol. Japan
103 E7 Yatsushiro Japan
103 E7 Yatsushiro-kai b. Japan
128 B4 Yaṭṭa West Bank
150 E3 Yatton North Somerset, England U.K.
252 B3 Yauca Peru
252 B3 Yauca r. Peru
247 □1 Yauco Puerto Rico
252 A2 Yauli Peru
250 D5 Yauna Maloca Col.
252 C3 Yauri Peru
245 E4 Yautepec Mex.
252 B3 Yauyos Peru
Yavan Tajik. see Yovon
250 D6 Yavari r. Brazil/Peru
alt. Javari
242 C3 Yávaros Mex.
116 D5 Yavatmal Mahar. India
252 B3 Yavero r. Peru
251 E3 Yaví, Cerro mt. Venez.
137 G4 Yavkyne Ukr.
121 G1 Yavlenka Kazakh.
175 L6 Yavora Ukr.
136 C3 Yavoriv Ivano-Frankivs'ka Oblast' Ukr.
136 B3 Yavoriv L'vivs'ka Oblast' Ukr.
140 O1 Yavr r. Fin./Rus. Fed.
128 C1 Yavuzlu Turkey
104 B4 Yawata Japan
103 F7 Yawatahama Japan
111 C4 Yawatongguz He r. China
111 C4 Yawatongguzlangar Xinjiang China
96 A2 Yaw Chaung r. Myanmar
243 H5 Yaxchilan tourist site Guat.
Yaxian Hainan China see Sanya
151 G2 Yaxley Cambridgeshire, England U.K.
129 B4 Yaygın Turkey
129 A4 Yaylabaşı Turkey
128 C2 Yayladağı Hatay Turkey
129 B4 Yayladere Turkey
129 C4 Yayladüzü Turkey
134 L4 Yayva Rus. Fed.
96 A2 Yazagyo Myanmar
122 C4 Yazd Iran
122 C4 Yazd prov. Iran
122 C4 Yazd-e Khvāst Iran
Yazgulemskiy Khrebet mts Tajik. see Yazgulom, Qatorkŭhi
123 G2 Yazgulom, Qatorkŭhi mts Tajik.
139 I2 Yazhelbitsy Rus. Fed.
126 E3 Yazıhan Malatya Turkey
199 F3 Yazıkent Turkey
199 G3 Yazır Turkey
237 F5 Yazoo r. MS U.S.A.
237 F5 Yazoo City MS U.S.A.
134 L3 Yaz'va r. Rus. Fed.
Y Bala Gwynedd, Wales U.K. see Bala
179 G2 Ybbs r. Austria
179 G2 Ybbs an der Donau Austria
179 F3 Ybbsitz Austria
253 F6 Ybycui Para.
163 B4 Ychoux France
162 E3 Ydes France
142 C4 Yding Skovhøj hill Denmark
198 C3 Ydra Greece
198 C3 Ydra i. Greece
Y Drenewydd Powys, Wales U.K. see Newtown
96 B4 Ye Myanmar
96 B4 Ye r. Myanmar
149 H4 Yeadon West Yorkshire, England U.K.
150 D4 Yealmpton Devon, England U.K.
Yebaishou Liaoning China see Jianping
121 G4 Yebekshi Kazakh.
183 H4 Yebra Spain
186 C2 Yebra de Basa Spain
111 B4 Yecheng Xinjiang China
187 B6 Yecla Spain
182 D4 Yecla de Yeltes Spain
242 C2 Yécora Mex.
114 C3 Yedatore Karnataka India
Yedintsy Moldova see Edineţ
129 B4 Yedisu Turkey
128 B2 Yeditepe Turkey
139 I3 Yedrovo Rus. Fed.
86 D3 Yeeda River W.A. Austr.
231 D7 Yeehaw Junction FL U.S.A.
82 C3 Yeelanna S.A. Austr.
139 J2 Yefimovskiy Rus. Fed.
139 L5 Yefremov Rus. Fed.
Yêgainnyin Qinghai China see Henan
129 D4 Yeghegis r. Armenia
129 D4 Yeghegnadzor Armenia
129 D3 Yeghvard Armenia
121 I2 Yegindybulak Kazakh.
135 H7 Yegorlyk r. Rus. Fed.
135 H7 Yegorlykskaya Rus. Fed.
139 L4 Yegor'yevsk Rus. Fed.
185 F2 Yeguas r. Spain
207 F4 Yégué Togo
210 A3 Yei r. Sudan
109 E2 Yeji Anhui China
206 E4 Yeji Ghana
Yejiaji Anhui China see Yeji
130 H4 Yekaterinburg Rus. Fed.
Yekaterinodar Rus. Fed. see Krasnodar
Yekaterinoslav Ukr. see Dnipropetrovs'k
100 D2 Yekaterinoslavka Rus. Fed.
137 J4 Yekaterinovka Rostovskaya Oblast' Rus. Fed.
135 I5 Yekaterinovka Saratovskaya Oblast' Rus. Fed.
Yekaterinovskaya Krasnodarskiy Kray Rus. Fed. see Krylovskaya
129 D2 Yekatorinogradskaya Rus. Fed.
Yekhegnadzor Armenia see Yeghegnadzor
139 I4 Yekimovichi Rus. Fed.
208 D4 Yekokora r. Dem. Rep. Congo
100 E2 Yelabuga Khabarovskiy Kray Rus. Fed.
134 J5 Yelabuga Respublika Tatarstan Rus. Fed.
135 H6 Yelan' Rus. Fed.
135 H6 Yelan' r. Rus. Fed.
135 H6 Yelan' r. Rus. Fed.
137 F4 Yelanets' Ukr.
83 G2 Yelarbon Qld Austr.
135 H5 Yelat'ma Rus. Fed.
199 F2 Yeleğen Turkey
Yelenovka Ukr. see Zoryns'k
Yelenovskiye Kar'yery Ukr. see Dokuchayevs'k
139 J5 Yelenskiy Rus. Fed.
139 L5 Yelets Rus. Fed.
134 N2 Yeletskiy Rus. Fed.
139 I2 Yeligovo Rus. Fed.
206 C3 Yélimané Mali
139 L4 Yelino Rus. Fed.
Yelizavetgrad Kirovohrads'ka Oblast' Ukr. see Kirovohrad
137 J4 Yelizavetovka Rostovskaya Oblast' Rus. Fed.
137 K2 Yelizavetovka Voronezhskaya Oblast' Rus. Fed.
131 Q4 Yelizovo Rus. Fed.
135 J5 Yelkhovka Rus. Fed.
146 □G1 Yell i. Scotland U.K.
114 D2 Yellandu Andhra Prad. India
114 B3 Yellapur Karnataka India
114 C2 Yellareddi Andhra Prad. India
226 B4 Yellow r. WI U.S.A.
87 C6 Yellowdine W.A. Austr.
234 D2 Yellow Frame NJ U.S.A.
234 C2 Yellow House PA U.S.A.
222 H2 Yellowknife N.W.T. Can.
222 H2 Yellowknife r. N.W.T. Can.
83 F3 Yellow Mountain hill N.S.W. Austr.
Yellow River r. China see Huang He
266 D3 Yellow Sea N. Pacific Ocean
232 B5 Yellow Springs OH U.S.A.
236 C2 Yellowstone r. MT U.S.A.
146 □G1 Yell Sound str. Scotland U.K.
237 E4 Yellville AR U.S.A.
238 B2 Yelm WA U.S.A.
185 H2 Yelmo mt. Spain
135 H5 Yel'niki Rus. Fed.
139 I4 Yel'nya Rus. Fed.
123 E2 Yeloten Turkm.
134 K4 Yelovo Rus. Fed.
129 D4 Yelp'in Armenia
136 E2 Yel'sk Belarus
182 D4 Yeltes r. Spain
242 □I6 Yelucá mt. Nic.
134 J3 Yelva r. Rus. Fed.
137 I4 Yelyseyivka Ukr.
137 G3 Yelyzavethradka Ukr.
106 C4 Yematan Qinghai China
183 I5 Yémeda Spain
124 D5 Yemen country Asia
136 D2 Yemil'chyne Ukr.
Yemişenbükü Turkey see Taşova
Yemmiganur Andhra Prad. India see Emmiganuru
134 H3 Yemtsa Rus. Fed.
134 J3 Yemva Respublika Komi Rus. Fed.
207 G5 Yenagoa Nigeria
137 J3 Yenakiyeve Ukr.
Yenakiyevo Ukr. see Yenakiyeve
96 A2 Yenangyaung Myanmar
96 D2 Yên Bai Vietnam
83 F3 Yenda N.S.W. Austr.
207 E4 Yendi Ghana
Yêndum Xizang China see Zhag'yab
208 D5 Yenge r. Dem. Rep. Congo
206 C4 Yengema Sierra Leone
110 B4 Yengisar Xinjiang China
110 D3 Yengisar Xinjiang China
129 B4 Yenibaşlar Turkey
135 F8 Yeniçağa Turkey
199 E2 Yenice anakkale Turkey
128 B1 Yenice İel Turkey
199 F1 Yeniceköy Bursa Turkey
126 D3 Yeniceoba Turkey
199 E1 Yeniçiftlik anakkale Turkey
199 E1 Yeniçiftlik Turkey
129 B4 Yenidal Turkey
199 F3 Yenidere r. Turkey
199 E2 Yenifoça Turkey
Yenıhan Turkey see Yıldızeli
199 E3 Yenihisar Turkey
Yenije-i-Vardar Greece see Giannitsa
129 F3 Yenikänd Azer.
199 E2 Yeniköy İzmir Turkey
199 F2 Yeniköy Turkey
199 F2 Yeniköy Turkey
199 E1 Yenimuhacirköy Edirne Turkey
199 F3 Yenipazar Aydın Turkey
199 G1 Yenipazar Bilecik Turkey
199 E2 Yenişakran Turkey
Yeniséa Greece see Genisea
Yenişehir Greece see Larisa
199 F1 Yenişehir Turkey
98 Yenisey r. Rus. Fed.
131 K4 Yeniseysk Rus. Fed.
131 K4 Yeniseyskiy Kryazh ridge Rus. Fed.
106 C5 Yeniugou Qinghai China
Yeniyol Turkey see Borçka
160 D3 Yenne France
135 I7 Yenotayevka Rus. Fed.
150 D4 Yeo r. England U.K.
116 C5 Yeola Mahar. India
87 E5 Yeo Lake salt flat W.A. Austr.
Yeotmal Mahar. India see Yavatmal
83 G3 Yeoval N.S.W. Austr.
150 E4 Yeovil Somerset, England U.K.
150 E3 Yeovilton Somerset, England U.K.
Yeo Yeo r. N.S.W. Austr. see Bland
183 G5 Yepes Spain
139 L5 Yepifan' Rus. Fed.
85 G4 Yeppoon Qld Austr.
Yerakaroú Greece see Gerakarou
135 H5 Yerakhtur Rus. Fed.
Yerákion Greece see Geraki
Yeraliyev Kazakh. see Kuryk
131 L3 Yerbogachen Rus. Fed.
114 C4 Yercaud Tamil Nadu India
121 H2 Yerementau, Gory hills Kazakh.
129 D3 Yerevan Armenia
121 H2 Yereymentau Kazakh.
114 C2 Yergara Karnataka India
135 I7 Yergeni hills Rus. Fed.
Yergoğu Romania see Giurgiu
Yeriḥo West Bank see Jericho
87 D6 Yerilla W.A. Austr.
240 H2 Yerington NV U.S.A.
199 F3 Yerkesik Muğla Turkey
128 A1 Yerköprü Mağarası tourist site Turkey
126 D3 Yerköy Turkey
114 B2 Yerla r. India
Yermak Pavlodarskaya Oblast' Kazakh. see Aksu
Yermentau Kazakh. see Yereymentau
135 H5 Yermish' Rus. Fed.
242 D3 Yermo Mex.
240 I4 Yermo CA U.S.A.
139 M3 Yermolino Rus. Fed.
100 B1 Yerofey Pavlovich Rus. Fed.
128 B4 Yeroham Israel
Yeropótamos r. Kriti Greece see Geropotamos
156 B4 Yerre r. France
156 C4 Yerres r. France
134 K2 Yersa r. Rus. Fed.
164 D3 Yerseke Neth.
139 I5 Yershichi Rus. Fed.
120 B2 Yershov Rus. Fed.
139 M1 Yertsevo Rus. Fed.
252 A2 Yerupaja mt. Peru
Yerushalayim Israel/West Bank see Jerusalem
120 A2 Yeruslan r. Rus. Fed.
159 G2 Yerville France
137 K2 Yeryshevka Rus. Fed.
Yerzhar Uzbek. see Gagarin
186 B2 Yesa Spain
Yeshera Georgia see Eshera
121 F2 Yesil' Kazakh.
128 C1 Yeşil Turkey
199 F3 Yeşildere Turkey
128 C1 Yeşildere Turkey
128 A1 Yeşildere Turkey
126 D3 Yeşilhisar Turkey
126 E2 Yeşilırmak r. Turkey
128 C1 Yeşilkent Turkey
199 F2 Yeşilköy Kütahya Turkey
199 F3 Yeşilova Turkey
Yeşilova Yozgat Turkey see Sorgun
199 G3 Yeşilyayla Turkey
199 F2 Yeşilyurt Manisa Turkey
199 F3 Yeşilyuva Turkey
146 E2 Yesnaby Orkney, Scotland U.K.
260 B4 Yeso, Cerro mt. Chile
129 C1 Yessentuki Rus. Fed.
129 C1 Yessentukskaya Rus. Fed.
131 L3 Yessey Rus. Fed.
185 H2 Yeste Spain
150 C4 Yes Tor hill England U.K.
185 H2 Yetas de Abajo Spain
Yêtatang Xizang China see Baqên
83 G2 Yetman N.S.W. Austr.
96 A2 Yeu Myanmar
158 D5 Yeu, Île d' i. France
Yevdokimovskoye Stavropol'skiy Kray Rus. Fed. see Krasnogvardeyskoye
Yevlakh Azer. see Yevlax
129 E3 Yevlax Azer.
137 G5 Yevpatoriya Ukr.
160 A1 Yèvre r. France
100 E2 Yevreyskaya Avtonomnaya Oblast' admin. div. Rus. Fed.
137 J3 Yevsuh r. Ukr.
109 E1 Yexian Henan China
Yexian Shandong China see Laizhou
121 I4 Yeygen'yevka Kazakh.
135 G7 Yeysk Rus. Fed.
137 J4 Yeyskoye Ukreplenie Rus. Fed.
110 D3 Yeyungou Xinjiang China
Yezhou Hubei China see Jianshi
134 I2 Yezhuga r. Rus. Fed.
Yezo i. Japan see Hokkaidō
138 G4 Yezyaryshcha Belarus
Y Fenni Monmouthshire, Wales U.K. see Abergavenny
158 D3 Yffiniac France
Y Fflint Flintshire, Wales U.K. see Flint
163 B5 Ygos-St-Saturnin France
160 A2 Ygrande France
107 G5 Yi r. Henan China
107 H5 Yi r. Shandong China
261 I3 Yí r. Uru.
Yialí i. Greece see Gyali
128 A4 Yi'allaq, Gebel mt. Egypt
Yialousa Cyprus see Aigialousa
100 C3 Yi'an Heilong. China
Yiannitsá Greece see Giannitsa
108 C2 Yibin Sichuan China
108 C2 Yibin Sichuan China
109 D2 Yichang Hubei China
109 E2 Yicheng Hubei China
107 F5 Yicheng Shanxi China
107 G5 Yichuan Henan China
107 F5 Yichuan Shaanxi China
100 D3 Yichun Heilong. China
109 E3 Yichun Jiangxi China
Yidu Shandong China see Qingzhou
108 A2 Yidun Sichuan China
109 E2 Yifeng Jiangxi China
Yiggêtang Qinghai China see Qumarlêb
199 G1 Yığılca Turkey
128 C1 Yiğityolu Turkey
109 F3 Yihuang Jiangxi China
Yijiang Jiangxi China see Yiyang
107 F5 Yijun Shaanxi China
107 J1 Yilaha Heilong. China
100 D3 Yilan Heilong. China
Yilan Taiwan see Ilan
129 B3 Yıldırım Turkey
126 B2 Yıldız Dağları mts Turkey
126 E3 Yıldızeli Turkey
108 B3 Yiliang Yunnan China
108 C3 Yiliang Yunnan China
87 C7 Yilliminning W.A. Austr.
100 C3 Yilong Heilong. China
108 C2 Yilong Sichuan China
Yilong Yunnan China see Shiping
107 H3 Yimatu r. China
96 C1 Yimen Yunnan China
100 D3 Yimianpo Heilong. China
107 H1 Yimin r. China
107 H5 Yinan Shandong China
Yincheng Jiangxi China see Dexing
106 E4 Yinchuan Ningxia China
87 D6 Yindarlgooda, Lake salt flat W.A. Austr.
109 E2 Yingcheng Hubei China
109 E3 Yingde Guangdong China
Yinggen Hainan China see Qiongzhong
109 F1 Ying He r. China
108 A3 Yingjiang Yunnan China
108 B2 Yingjing Sichuan China
Yingkou Liaoning China see Dashiqiao
107 I3 Yingkou Liaoning China
109 E2 Yingshan Hubei China
108 C2 Yingshan Sichuan China
109 F1 Yingshang Anhui China
109 F2 Yingtan Jiangxi China
Yingtaoyuan Henan China see Fanxian
207 H5 Yingui Cameroon
107 G4 Yingxian Shanxi China
Yining Jiangxi China see Xiushui
110 C3 Yining Xinjiang China
108 D3 Yinjiang Guizhou China
109 E3 Yinkeng Jiangxi China
100 C3 Yinma r. China
96 A2 Yinmabin Myanmar
107 F3 Yin Shan mts China
Yinxian Zhejiang China see Ningbo
Yiófiros r. Kriti Greece see Giofyros
111 F6 Yi'ong Zangbo r. Xizang China
Yioúra i. Greece see Gioura
108 B3 Yipinglang Yunnan China
199 G2 Yıprak Turkey
Yiquan Guizhou China see Meitan
257 E5 Yira Chapeu, Monte mt. Brazil
210 C3 Yirga Alem Eth.
210 C3 Yirga Ch'efē Eth.
84 D2 Yirrkala N.T. Austr.
Yirshi Nei Mongol China see Yirxie
107 H2 Yirxie Nei Mongol China
Yisa Yunnan China see Honghe
Yishan Guangxi China see Yizhou
Yishan Jiangsu China see Guanyun
107 H4 Yi Shan mt. Shandong China
107 H5 Yishui Shandong China
Yíthion Greece see Gytheio
Yitiaoshan Gansu China see Jingtai
100 C4 Yitong Jilin China
100 C3 Yitong r. China
96 B2 Yi Tu, Nam r. Myanmar
107 I1 Yitulihe Nei Mongol China
106 B3 Yiwanquan Xinjiang China
106 B3 Yiwu Xinjiang China
109 F2 Yixian Anhui China
107 G4 Yixian Hebei China
107 I3 Yixian Liaoning China
109 F2 Yixing Jiangsu China
107 H3 Yixun r. China
109 E2 Yiyang Hunan China
109 F2 Yiyang Jiangxi China
107 H4 Yiyuan Shandong China
109 E3 Yizhang Hunan China
109 F1 Yizheng Jiangsu China
108 D3 Yizhou Guangxi China
Yizhou Hebei China see Yixian
Yizhou Liaoning China see Yixian
Yizra'el country Asia see Israel
141 O3 Ylämaa Fin.
141 M3 Yläne Fin.
140 M3 Ylihärmä Fin.
140 N2 Yli-Ii Fin.
140 N2 Ylikiiminki Fin.
140 M3 Ylistaro Fin.
140 M2 Ylitornio Fin.
140 N2 Ylivieska Fin.
140 N2 Ylläs hill Fin.
150 D2 Y Llethr hill Wales U.K.
141 M3 Ylöjärvi Fin.
221 P2 Ymer Nunatak Greenland
156 B4 Ymonville France
131 O3 Ynykchanskiy Rus. Fed.
Ynys Môn i. Wales U.K. see Anglesey
237 D6 Yoakum TX U.S.A.
207 H4 Yobe state Nigeria
102 J2 Yobetsu-dake vol. Japan
104 B4 Yodo-gawa r. Japan
234 B3 Yoe PA U.S.A.
259 C9 Yogan, Cerro mt. Chile
95 E4 Yogyakarta Indon.
95 E5 Yogyakarta admin. dist. Indon.
102 J2 Yoichi-dake mt. Japan
242 □I6 Yojoa, Lago de l. Hond.
101 C5 Yŏju S. Korea
207 I6 Yokadouma Cameroon
104 C3 Yōkaichi Japan
105 G3 Yōkaichiba Japan
102 □1 Yokate-jima i. Japan
104 C4 Yokkaichi Japan
207 I5 Yoko Cameroon
105 F3 Yokohama Japan
105 F3 Yokosuka Japan
102 J4 Yokote Japan
102 J3 Yokotsu-dake mt. Japan
207 I4 Yola Nigeria
240 G2 Yolo CA U.S.A.
Yolöten Turkm. see Yeloten
96 C4 Yom, Mae Nam r. Thai.
105 G1 Yomogida-dake hill Fukushima Japan
206 C5 Yomou Guinea
129 A3 Yomra Turkey
162 A2 Yon r. France
103 F6 Yonago Japan
102 □1 Yonaguni-jima i. Japan
101 C5 Yŏnan N. Korea
102 J3 Yoneshiro-gawa r. Japan
105 E1 Yone-yama hill Japan
102 J5 Yonezawa Japan
82 D3 Yongala S.A. Austr.
101 C6 Yŏng-am S. Korea
Yong'an Chongqing China see Fengjie
109 F3 Yong'an Fujian China
Yongbei Yunnan China see Yongsheng
106 D4 Yongchang Gansu China
109 F1 Yongcheng Henan China
101 D6 Yŏngch'ŏn S. Korea
108 C2 Yongchuan Chongqing China
109 F3 Yongchun Fujian China
108 A3 Yongde Yunnan China
106 D4 Yongdeng Gansu China
109 F3 Yongding Fujian China
Yongding Yunnan China see Fumin

Yongding to Zezë, Maja e
382

Yongding Yunnan China see Yongren
107 H4 Yongding r. China
109 E3 Yongfeng Jiangxi China
Yongfeng Jiangxi China see Guangfeng
108 D3 Yongfu Guangxi China
101 C6 Yŏnggwang S. Korea
107 F4 Yonghe Shanxi China
101 C5 Yŏnghŭng N. Korea
100 C4 Yongji Jilin China
109 G2 Yongjia Zhejiang China
106 D5 Yongjing Gansu China
Yongjing Guizhou China see Xifeng
Yongjing Liaoning China see Xifeng
101 D5 Yŏngju S. Korea
109 G2 Yongkang Zhejiang China
Yongle Shaanxi China see Zhen'an
Yongle Sichuan China see Nanping
101 C4 Yongling Liaoning China
107 G4 Yongnian Hebei China
108 D4 Yongning Guangxi China
Yongning Jiangxi China see Tonggu
106 E4 Yongning Ningxia China
Yongning Sichuan China see Xuyong
108 A3 Yongping Yunnan China
Yongqing Gansu China see Qingshui
108 B3 Yongren Yunnan China
101 C6 Yŏngsan-gang r. S. Korea
108 B2 Yongshan Yunnan China
108 B3 Yongsheng Yunnan China
107 F5 Yongshou Shaanxi China
108 D2 Yongshun Hunan China
109 F3 Yongtai Fujian China
101 D5 Yŏngwol S. Korea
Yongxi Guizhou China see Nayong
109 E3 Yongxing Hunan China
109 E3 Yongxing Jiangxi China
109 E2 Yongxiu Jiangxi China
109 D3 Yongzhou Hunan China
233 G4 Yonkers NY U.S.A.
156 D5 Yonne dept Bourgogne France
156 C4 Yonne r. France
250 C3 Yopal Col.
110 B4 Yopurga Xinjiang China
116 C2 Yordu Jammu and Kashmir
87 C6 York W.A. Austr.
227 H4 York Ont. Can.
223 M4 York r. Man. Can.
149 H4 York York, England U.K.
149 H4 York admin. div. England U.K.
237 F5 York AL U.S.A.
236 D3 York NE U.S.A.
234 B3 York PA U.S.A.
231 D5 York SC U.S.A.
85 E1 York, Cape Qld Austr.
149 H3 York, Vale of val. England U.K.
234 B3 York County county PA U.S.A.
85 E2 York Downs Qld Austr.
82 D3 Yorke Peninsula S.A. Austr.
82 D3 Yorketown S.A. Austr.
234 B2 York Haven PA U.S.A.
149 G3 Yorkshire Dales National Park England U.K.
149 I4 Yorkshire Wolds hills England U.K.
234 A2 York Springs PA U.S.A.
223 K5 Yorkton Sask. Can.
232 E6 Yorktown VA U.S.A.
235 E1 Yorktown Heights NY U.S.A.
242 □I6 Yoro Hond.
104 C3 Yōrō Japan
102 □1 Yoro-jima i. Japan
102 □1 Yoron-tō i. Japan
106 E1 Yöröö Gol r. Mongolia
206 D3 Yorosso Mali
240 H3 Yosemite Village CA U.S.A.
105 E4 Yoshida Japan
103 G6 Yoshii-gawa r. Japan
104 B4 Yoshino-gawa r. Japan
103 G6 Yoshino-gawa r. Japan
134 I4 Yoshkar-Ola Rus. Fed.
253 E4 Yotau Bol.
102 J2 Yōtei-zan mt. Japan
105 G3 Yotsukaidō Japan
222 E5 Youbou B.C. Can.
111 E4 Youdunzi Qinghai China
147 D5 Youghal Rep. of Ireland
147 C5 Youghal Bay Rep. of Ireland
108 D4 You Jiang r. China
149 H4 Youlgreave Derbyshire, England U.K.
83 G3 Young N.S.W. Austr.
87 D7 Young r. W.A. Austr.
261 I3 Young Uru.
241 L4 Young AZ U.S.A.
82 D2 Younghusband, Lake salt flat S.A. Austr.
82 D3 Younghusband Peninsula S.A. Austr.
263 K2 Young Island Antarctica
81 B6 Young Range mts South I. N.Z.
223 I5 Youngstown Alta Can.
232 C4 Youngstown OH U.S.A.
232 D4 Youngsville PA U.S.A.
240 F2 Yountville CA U.S.A.
111 E4 Youshashan Qinghai China
108 D2 You Shui r. China
204 C2 Youssoufia Morocco
206 D3 Youvarou Mali
109 F3 Youxi Fujian China
109 E3 Youxian Hunan China
108 D2 Youyang Chongqing China
100 D3 Youyi Heilong. China
110 D1 Youyi Feng mt. China/Rus. Fed.
107 G4 Youyu Shanxi China
123 G2 Yovon Tajik.
87 C5 Yowereena Hill hill W.A. Austr.
151 F2 Yoxall Staffordshire, England U.K.
151 I2 Yoxford Suffolk, England U.K.
126 D3 Yozgat Turkey
253 G5 Ypé-Jhú Para.
159 G2 Yport France
Ypres Belgium see Ieper
227 F4 Ypsilanti MI U.S.A.
238 B3 Yreka CA U.S.A.
Yrghyz Kazakh. see Irgiz
Yr Wyddfa mt. Wales U.K. see Snowdon
Yr Wyddgrug Flintshire, Wales U.K. see Mold
150 D2 Ysbyty Ystwyth Ceredigion, Wales U.K.
156 C2 Yser r. France
alt. IJzer (Belgium)
164 E3 Ysselsteyn Neth.
161 C3 Yssingeaux France
143 E4 Ystad Sweden
150 D3 Ystalyfera Neath Port Talbot, Wales U.K.
150 D1 Ystrad r. Wales U.K.
150 D3 Ystradgynlais Powys, Wales U.K.
150 C2 Ystwyth r. Wales U.K.
Ysyk-Köl Kyrg. see Balykchy
121 I4 Ysyk-Köl admin. div. Kyrg.
121 I4 Ysyk-Köl salt l. Kyrg.
146 F4 Ythan r. Scotland U.K.
Y Trallwng Powys, Wales U.K. see Welshpool
Ytre Vinje Norway see Åmot
131 O3 Ytyk-Kyuyel' Rus. Fed.
107 G4 Yu r. China
109 D2 Yuan'an Hubei China
108 D3 Yuanbao Shan mt. Guangxi China
109 E2 Yuanjiang Hunan China
108 B4 Yuanjiang Yunnan China
108 D2 Yuan Jiang r. Hunan China
108 B4 Yuan Jiang r. Yunnan China
Yuanjiazhuang Shaanxi China see Foping
109 G3 Yüanli Taiwan
107 I1 Yuanlin Nei Mongol China
108 D2 Yuanling Hunan China
Yuanma Yunnan China see Yuanmou
108 B3 Yuanmou Yunnan China
107 G4 Yuanping Shanxi China
107 F5 Yuanqu Shanxi China
Yuanquan Gansu China see Anxi
Yuanshan Guangdong China see Lianping
106 C4 Yuanshanzi Gansu China
108 B4 Yuanyang Yunnan China
240 G2 Yuba City CA U.S.A.
102 J2 Yūbari Japan
102 K2 Yūbari-dake mt. Japan
102 K2 Yūbari-sanchi mts Japan
108 C2 Yubei Chongqing China
102 K1 Yūbetsu-gawa r. Japan
121 J2 Yubileynyy Kazakh.
240 I4 Yucaipa CA U.S.A.
243 H5 Yucatán pen. Mex.
243 H4 Yucatán state Mex.
243 I4 Yucatan Channel Cuba/Mex.
241 J4 Yucca AZ U.S.A.
241 I3 Yucca Lake NV U.S.A.
241 I4 Yucca Valley CA U.S.A.
129 B4 Yücetepe Turkey
Yucheng Guangdong China see Yunan
107 G5 Yucheng Henan China
107 H4 Yucheng Shandong China
107 G4 Yuci Shanxi China
134 J5 Yudino Respublika Tatarstan Rus. Fed.
134 G4 Yudino Yaroslavskaya Oblast' Rus. Fed.
100 B1 Yudi Shan mt. China
131 O4 Yudoma r. Rus. Fed.
109 E3 Yudu Jiangxi China
Yuecheng Sichuan China see Yuexi
108 C2 Yuechi Sichuan China
Yuelai Heilong. China see Huachuan
84 B4 Yuendumu N.T. Austr.
109 □ Yuen Long H.K. China
109 G2 Yueqing Zhejiang China
109 F2 Yuexi Anhui China
108 B2 Yuexi Sichuan China
109 E2 Yueyang Hunan China
109 E2 Yueyang Hunan China
Yueyang Sichuan China see Anyue
134 L4 Yug Rus. Fed.
134 I3 Yug r. Rus. Fed.
109 F2 Yugan Jiangxi China
128 A1 Yuğluk Dağı mts Turkey
134 K4 Yugo-Kamskiy Rus. Fed.
Yugo-Osetinskaya Avtonomnaya Oblast' aut. reg. Georgia see Samkhret' Oset'i
130 H3 Yugorsk Rus. Fed.
134 M1 Yugorskiy Poluostrov pen. Rus. Fed.
196 E3 Yugoslavia country Europe
109 G2 Yuhang Zhejiang China
Yuhu Yunnan China see Eryuan
109 G2 Yuhuan Zhejiang China
107 H4 Yuhuang Ding mt. Shandong China
105 E3 Yui Japan
87 C5 Yuin W.A. Austr.
109 F2 Yujiang Jiangxi China
108 D4 Yu Jiang r. China
Yujin Sichuan China see Qianwei
131 Q3 Yukagirskoye Ploskogor'ye plat. Rus. Fed.
134 K4 Yukamenskoye Rus. Fed.
199 E2 Yukarıbey Turkey
129 C3 Yukarıgündeş Turkey
129 C3 Yukarıkaragüney Turkey
199 G2 Yukarı Sakarya Ovaları plain Turkey
129 C3 Yukarısarıkamış Turkey
126 D3 Yukarısarıkaya Turkey
135 J5 Yukhmachi Rus. Fed.
139 J4 Yukhnov Rus. Fed.
209 C5 Yuki Dem. Rep. Congo
105 F2 Yūki Japan
220 B3 Yukon r. Can./U.S.A.
222 B2 Yukon Crossing Y.T. Can.
222 C2 Yukon Territory admin. div. Can.
127 G3 Yüksekova Turkey
103 E7 Yukuhashi Japan
84 B5 Yulara N.T. Austr.
120 D1 Yuldybayevo Rus. Fed.
86 C4 Yule r. W.A. Austr.
85 G5 Yuleba Qld Austr.
231 D6 Yulee FL U.S.A.
110 D3 Yuli Xinjiang China
109 G4 Yüli Taiwan
108 D4 Yulin Guangxi China
107 F4 Yulin Shaanxi China
108 B3 Yulongxue Shan mt. Yunnan China
241 J5 Yuma AZ U.S.A.
236 C3 Yuma CO U.S.A.
241 J5 Yuma Desert AZ U.S.A.
120 D1 Yumaguzino Rus. Fed.
260 A5 Yumbel Chile
250 B4 Yumbo Col.
106 C4 Yumen Gansu China
106 C3 Yumenzhen Gansu China
110 C2 Yumin Xinjiang China
106 C2 Yumt Uul mt. Mongolia
128 B1 Yumurtalık Turkey
87 B6 Yuna W.A. Austr.
246 E3 Yuna r. Dom. Rep.
126 C3 Yunak Turkey
137 H2 Yunakivka Ukr.
109 D4 Yunan Guangdong China
107 G5 Yuncheng Shandong China
107 F5 Yuncheng Shanxi China
87 D6 Yundamindera W.A. Austr.
109 E4 Yunfu Guangdong China
252 D4 Yungas reg. Bol.
252 C4 Yungayo Peru
108 B3 Yun Gui Gaoyuan plat. Yunnan China
Yunhe Jiangsu China see Pizhou
Yunhe Yunnan China see Heqing
109 F2 Yunhe Zhejiang China
Yunjinghong Yunnan China see Jinghong
108 D4 Yunkai Dashan mts China
Yunling Fujian China see Yunxiao
108 A3 Yun Ling mts Yunnan China
108 A3 Yunlong Yunnan China
109 E2 Yunmeng Hubei China
109 E3 Yunmenling Jiangxi China
108 B3 Yunnan prov. China
137 J3 Yunokomunarivs'k Ukr.
185 F4 Yunquera Spain
183 G4 Yunquera de Henares Spain
109 E2 Yun Shui r. China
82 D3 Yunta S.A. Austr.
128 A1 Yunt Dağı mt. Turkey
199 F2 Yunuslar Turkey
108 D1 Yunxi Hubei China
Yunxi Sichuan China see Yanting
108 D1 Yunxian Hubei China
108 B3 Yunxian Yunnan China
109 F4 Yunxiao Fujian China
134 M2 Yun'yakha r. Rus. Fed.
108 D2 Yunyang Chongqing China
109 E1 Yunyang Henan China
Yupin Yunnan China see Pingbian
Yuping Guizhou China see Libo
108 D3 Yuping Guizhou China
108 C3 Yuqing Guizhou China
252 D5 Yura Bol.
252 D5 Yura r. Bol.
250 B6 Yuracyacu Peru
104 B3 Yura-gawa r. Japan
102 J2 Yūrappu-dake mt. Japan
138 E4 Yuratsishki Belarus
137 I3 Yurchenkove Ukr.
128 B1 Yürekli Turkey
130 J4 Yurga Rus. Fed.
250 B6 Yurimaguas Peru
134 I4 Yurino Rus. Fed.
244 D3 Yuriria Mex.
244 D3 Yuriria, Laguna l. Mex.
129 E1 Yurkovka Rus. Fed.
134 K4 Yurla Rus. Fed.
137 I5 Yurovka Rus. Fed.
199 E1 Yürük Turkey
111 C4 Yurungkax He r. China
134 J4 Yur'ya Rus. Fed.
134 K2 Yur'yakha r. Rus. Fed.
Yuryev Estonia see Tartu
134 H4 Yur'yevets Rus. Fed.
139 M3 Yur'yevets Rus. Fed.
139 L3 Yur'yev-Pol'skiy Rus. Fed.
137 I3 Yur"yivka Ukr.
137 I4 Yur"yivka Ukr.
242 □I6 Yuscarán Hond.
109 F3 Yushan Fujian China
109 F2 Yushan Jiangxi China
109 G4 Yü Shan mt. Taiwan
107 G4 Yushe Shanxi China
134 F2 Yushkozero Rus. Fed.
100 C3 Yushu Jilin China
108 A1 Yushu Qinghai China
110 D3 Yushugou Xinjiang China
134 J4 Yushut r. Rus. Fed.
Yushuwan Hunan China see Huaihua
135 I7 Yusta Rus. Fed.
127 F2 Yusufeli Turkey
134 K4 Yus'va Rus. Fed.
Yuta West Bank see Yaṭṭa
107 H5 Yutai Shandong China
135 K5 Yutaza Rus. Fed.
107 H4 Yutian Hebei China
111 C4 Yutian Xinjiang China
253 F6 Yuty Para.
157 G3 Yutz France
199 F3 Yuva Turkey
102 □1 Yuwan-dake mt. Nansei-shotō Japan
106 E4 Yuwang Ningxia China
129 D3 Yuxarı Salahlı Azer.
129 E3 Yuxarı Tala Azer.
Yuxi Guizhou China see Daozhen
109 D2 Yuxi Hubei China
108 B3 Yuxi Yunnan China
108 D2 Yuxiakou Hubei China
107 G4 Yuxian Hebei China
107 G4 Yuxian Shanxi China
109 F2 Yuxikou Anhui China
109 D2 Yuyangguan Hubei China
109 G2 Yuyao Zhejiang China
Yuyue Hubei China see Jiayu
102 J4 Yuzawa Japan
129 D3 Yüzbaşılar Turkey
134 H4 Yuzha Rus. Fed.
137 F4 Yuzhne Ukr.
Yuzhno-Kazakhstanskaya Oblast' admin. div. Kazakh. see Yuzhnyy Kazakhstan
99 Q3 Yuzhno-Kuril'sk Kuril'skiye O-va Rus. Fed.
131 M4 Yuzhno-Muyskiy Khrebet mts Rus. Fed.
100 G3 Yuzhno-Sakhalinsk Sakhalin Rus. Fed.
129 D1 Yuzhno-Sukhokumsk Rus. Fed.
135 E7 Yuzhnoukrayinsk Ukr.
120 E1 Yuzhnoural'sk Rus. Fed.
121 J1 Yuzhnyy Altayskiy Kray Rus. Fed.
Yuzhnyy Respublika Kalmykiya - Khalm'g-Tangch Rus. Fed. see Adyk
135 H7 Yuzhnyy Rostovskaya Oblast' Rus. Fed.
121 K2 Yuzhnyy Altay, Khrebet mts Kazakh.
Yuzhnyy Bug r. Ukr. see Pivdennyy Buh
121 G4 Yuzhnyy Kazakhstan admin. div. Kazakh.
120 D1 Yuzhnyy Ural mts Rus. Fed.
106 E5 Yuzhong Gansu China
Yuzhou Hebei China see Yuxian
107 G5 Yuzhou Henan China
Yuzovka Ukr. see Donets'k
104 A4 Yuzuruha-yama hill Japan
158 D3 Yvel r. France
156 B4 Yvelines dept Île-de-France France
190 B2 Yverdon Switz.
159 G2 Yvetot France
158 D3 Yvignac France
165 D4 Yvoir Belgium
160 E2 Yvoire France
190 B2 Yvonand Switz.
122 D1 Yylanly Turkm.
214 B5 Yzerfontein S. Africa
160 B2 Yzeure France
159 G5 Yzeures-sur-Creuse France

Z

204 E2 Za, Oued r. Morocco
245 F5 Zaachila Mex.
214 D5 Zaaimansdal S. Africa
121 G5 Zaamin Uzbek.
165 C3 Zaamslag Neth.
164 D2 Zaandam Neth.
164 D2 Zaandijk Neth.
197 H3 Zăbala r. Romania
196 E3 Žabalj Vojvodina, Srbija Yugo.
127 F3 Zāb al Kabīr, Nahr az r. Iraq
127 F4 Zāb aş Şaghīr, Nahr az r. Iraq
107 H1 Zabaykal'sk Rus. Fed.
195 □ Żabbar Malta
176 F2 Žabčice Czech Rep.
122 A3 Zab-e Kuchek r. Iran
171 E4 Zabeltitz-Treugeböhla Ger.
175 I3 Żabia Wola Pol.
124 C5 Zabīd Yemen
175 J2 Zabiele Pol.
175 J3 Ząbki Pol.
174 E5 Ząbkowice Śląskie Pol.
175 L4 Zabłocie Pol.
175 L2 Zabłudów Pol.
179 H5 Žabno Croatia
175 I5 Żabno Pol.
188 E2 Zabok Croatia
177 H2 Žabokreky Slovakia
123 F3 Zābol prov. Afgh.
123 E4 Zābol Iran
123 E5 Zābolī Iran
136 C3 Zabolotiv Ukr.
136 C2 Zabolottya Ukr.
139 J2 Zabor'ye Rus. Fed.
170 F2 Żabów Pol.
111 D6 Zabqung Xizang China
197 E2 Zăbrani Romania
129 F3 Zabrat Azer.
206 E4 Zabré Burkina
176 F2 Zábřeh Czech Rep.
174 G5 Zabrze Pol.
136 E2 Zabuyannya Ukr.
136 B2 Zabuzhzhya Ukr.
207 F4 Zabzugu Ghana
243 H6 Zacapa Guat.
245 F4 Zacapoaxtla Mex.
244 D4 Zacapu Mex.
254 C4 Zacarias r. Brazil
244 C2 Zacatecas Mex.
244 C2 Zacatecas state Mex.
242 □H6 Zacatecoluca El Salvador
245 E4 Zacatepec Morelos Mex.
245 F5 Zacatepec Oaxaca Mex.
245 F4 Zacatlán Mex.
120 B2 Zachagansk Kazakh.
198 B3 Zacharo Greece
174 F2 Zacharzyn Pol.
173 H3 Zachenberg Ger.
137 H3 Zachepylivka Ukr.
174 D2 Zachodniopomorskie prov. Pol.
244 C3 Zacoalco Mex.
244 B3 Zacualpan Mex.
Zacynthus i. Greece see Zakynthos
188 E3 Zadar Croatia
188 E3 Zadarski Kanal sea chan. Croatia
97 B5 Zadetkale Kyun i. Myanmar
111 F5 Zadoi Qinghai China
139 L5 Zadonsk Rus. Fed.
183 H2 Zadorra r. Spain
177 G2 Zádveřice Czech Rep.
203 G2 Za'farâna Egypt
185 F4 Zafarraya Spain
123 H3 Zafarwal Pak.
195 E5 Zafferana Etnea Sicilia Italy
184 D2 Zafra Spain
183 H5 Zafra de Záncara Spain
183 I4 Zafrilla Spain
204 C3 Zag Morocco
174 D4 Żagań Pol.
138 D3 Žagarė Lith.
193 E3 Zagarolo Italy
203 F2 Zagazig Egypt
129 D3 Zages Georgia
122 B3 Zāgheh Iran
205 H1 Zaghouan Tunisia
189 C7 Zaghouan admin. div. Tunisia
175 I5 Zagnańsk Pol.
197 H3 Zagon Romania
198 C2 Zagora Greece
204 D3 Zagora Morocco
188 E2 Zagorje ob Savi Slovenia
174 F3 Zagórów Pol.
Zagorsk Rus. Fed. see Sergiyev Posad
175 K6 Zagórz Pol.
185 F3 Zagra Spain
197 G5 Zagrazhden Bulg.
188 E3 Zagreb Croatia
174 D4 Zagrodno Pol.
122 A3 Zagros, Kūhhā-ye mts Iran
Zagros Mountains Iran see Zagros, Kūhhā-ye
197 E3 Žagubica Srbija Yugo.
Zagunao Sichuan China see Lixian
111 E6 Za'gya Zangbo r. Xizang China
177 J4 Zagyva r. Hungary
177 J4 Zagyvarékas Hungary
136 E2 Zahal'tsi Ukr.
185 E4 Zahara Spain
184 E4 Zahara de los Atunes Spain
125 E4 Zahawn, Wādī r. Yemen
122 E4 Zāhedān Iran
122 C4 Zāhedān Iran
184 D2 Zahinos Spain
128 B3 Zahlé Lebanon
Zähmet Turkm. see Zakhmet
171 D4 Zahna Ger.
177 L3 Záhony Hungary
177 G2 Záhorovice Czech Rep.
176 F3 Záhorská Ves Slovakia
124 C4 Zahrān Saudi Arabia
186 D3 Zaidín Spain
124 D3 Zā'in, Jabal hill Saudi Arabia
122 C3 Zaindeh r. Iran
Zainlha Sichuan China see Xiaojin
Zaire country Africa see Congo, Democratic Republic of
209 B6 Zaire prov. Angola
Zaïre r. Congo/Dem. Rep. Congo see Congo
196 E5 Zajas Macedonia
197 F4 Zaječar Srbija Yugo.
173 H2 Zaječov Czech Rep.
213 F4 Zaka Zimbabwe
106 D1 Zakamensk Rus. Fed.
176 F5 Zákány Hungary
177 I5 Zákányszek Hungary
136 B3 Zakarpats'ka Oblast' admin. div. Ukr.
Zakarpatskaya Oblast' admin. div. Ukr. see Zakarpats'ka Oblast'
Zakataly Azer. see Zaqatala
Zakháro Greece see Zacharo
139 L4 Zakharovo Rus. Fed.
136 C2 Zakhidnyy Buh r. Ukr.
123 E2 Zakhmet Turkm.
127 F3 Zākhō Iraq
Zakhodnyaya Dzvina r. Europe see Zapadnaya Dvina
122 A2 Zakī, Kūh-e mt. Iran
Zákinthos i. Greece see Zakynthos
175 I6 Zakliczyn Pol.
175 K5 Zaklików Pol.
175 H6 Zakopane Pol.
175 K5 Zakrzew Lubelskie Pol.
175 J4 Zakrzew Mazowieckie Pol.
174 G3 Zakrzewo Kujawsko-Pomorskie Pol.
174 F2 Zakrzewo Wielkopolskie Pol.
175 K5 Zakrzówek-Osada Pol.
176 D1 Zákupy Czech Rep.
222 F5 Zakwaski, Mount B.C. Can.
198 B3 Zakynthos Ionioi Nisoi Greece
198 B3 Zakynthos i. Greece
209 B6 Zala Angola
176 F5 Zala county Hungary
196 C2 Zala r. Romania
176 G5 Zalaapáti Hungary
176 F5 Zalaegerszeg Hungary
176 F5 Zalai-domsag hills Hungary
176 G5 Zalakaros Hungary
176 G5 Zalakomár Hungary
176 F5 Zalalövő Hungary
184 E2 Zalamea de la Serena Spain
184 D3 Zalamea la Real Spain
207 H4 Zalanga Nigeria
107 I2 Zalantun Nei Mongol China
176 G5 Zalaszántó Hungary
176 F5 Zalaszentbalázs Hungary
176 G5 Zalaszentgrót Hungary
176 F5 Zalaszentiván Hungary
176 F5 Zalaszentmihály Hungary
197 F2 Zalău Romania
177 L4 Zalău r. Romania
176 G5 Zalavár Hungary
175 J4 Załazy Pol.
188 E2 Žalec Slovenia
139 K5 Zalegoshch' Rus. Fed.
174 F3 Zalesie Kujawsko-Pomorskie Pol.
175 L3 Zalesie Lubelskie Pol.
232 B5 Zaleski OH U.S.A.
139 K2 Zales'ye Rus. Fed.
175 H2 Zalewo Pol.
174 C2 Zalew Szczeciński b. Pol.
143 H4 Zalew Wiślany b. Pol.
124 C3 Zalim Saudi Arabia
136 C3 Zalishchyky Ukr.
136 C3 Zalissya Ukr.
137 I4 Zaliznychne Ukr.
137 G4 Zaliznyy Port Ukr.
136 C3 Zaliztsi Ukr.
183 G1 Zalla Spain
124 B2 Zalmā, Jabal az mt. Saudi Arabia
174 F2 Zalno Pol.
164 E3 Zaltbommel Neth.
139 H3 Zaluch'ye Rus. Fed.
129 C2 Zalukokoazhe Rus. Fed.
175 M2 Zal'vyanka r. Belarus
177 L5 Zam Romania
105 F3 Zama Japan
222 G3 Zama City Alta Can.
125 D4 Zamakh Saudi Arabia
215 G2 Zamani S. Africa
126 D3 Zamanti r. Turkey
177 G5 Zamárdi Hungary
174 F2 Zamarte Pol.
92 B3 Zambales Mountains Phil.
176 F1 Žamberk Czech Rep.
209 D7 Zambeze r. Angola
alt. Zambezi
209 D8 Zambezi r. Africa
alt. Zambeze (Angola)
209 D8 Zambezi Zambia
213 H3 Zambézia prov. Moz.
209 E8 Zambia country Africa
92 B5 Zamboanga Phil.
92 B5 Zamboanga Peninsula Phil.
92 B4 Zamboanguita Phil.
183 H2 Zambrana Spain
175 K3 Zambrów Pol.
184 A2 Zambujal de Cima Port.
184 B3 Zambujeira do Mar Port.
207 G3 Zamfara state Nigeria
204 B4 Zamlat Amagraj hills Western Sahara
177 H4 Zámoly Hungary
250 B6 Zamora Ecuador
250 B5 Zamora r. Ecuador
182 E3 Zamora Spain
182 E3 Zamora prov. Castilla y León Spain
244 C4 Zamora de Hidalgo Mex.
175 L5 Zamość Pol.
175 J2 Zamość Pol.
Zamost'ye Pol. see Zamość
129 C3 Zamp Dağı mt. Turkey
178 B3 Zams Austria
108 B1 Zamtang Sichuan China
251 F3 Zamuro, Sierra del mts Venez.
208 B5 Zanaga Congo
245 G5 Zanatepec Mex.
183 G5 Záncara r. Spain
Zancle Sicilia Italy see Messina
111 B6 Zanda Xizang China
251 H3 Zanderij Suriname
165 D3 Zandhoven Belgium
171 F5 Žandov Czech Rep.
165 D3 Zandvliet Belgium
164 D2 Zandvoort Neth.
232 B5 Zanesville OH U.S.A.
129 D4 Zangakutan Armenia
206 D3 Zangasso Mali
Zangelan Azer. see Zängilan
129 D4 Zangezuri Lerrnashght'a mts Armenia/Azer.
129 E4 Zängilan Azer.
116 D2 Zangla Jammu and Kashmir
111 D5 Zangsêr Kangri mt. Xizang China
107 G4 Zanhuang Hebei China
174 F3 Zaniemyśl Pol.
122 B2 Zanjān Iran
122 B2 Zanjān prov. Iran
127 G3 Zanjān Rūd r. Iran
125 F2 Zannah, Jabal az hill U.A.E.
87 D6 Zanthus W.A. Austr.
206 D4 Zantiébougou Mali
211 C6 Zanzibar Tanz.
211 C6 Zanzibar Channel Tanz.
211 C6 Zanzibar Island Tanz.
211 C6 Zanzibar North admin. reg. Tanz.
211 C6 Zanzibar South admin. reg. Tanz.
211 C6 Zanzibar West admin. reg. Tanz.
139 K4 Zaokskiy Rus. Fed.
189 C7 Zaonia Mornag Tunisia
183 H4 Zaorejas Spain
109 E2 Zaoshi Hubei China
109 E3 Zaoshi Hunan China
109 E1 Zaoyang Hubei China
109 E1 Zaoyangzhan Hubei China
102 J4 Zaō-zan vol. Japan
137 G5 Zaozerne Ukr.
131 K4 Zaozernyy Rus. Fed.
139 L3 Zaozer'ye Rus. Fed.
107 H5 Zaozhuang Shandong China
127 F3 Zap r. Turkey
196 E4 Zapadna Morava r. Yugo.
139 H4 Zapadnaya Dvina r. Europe
alt. Daugava (Latvia),
alt. Zakhodnyaya Dzvina,
conv. Western Dvina
139 I3 Zapadnaya Dvina Rus. Fed.
197 F5 Zapadni Rodopi mts Bulg.
Zapadno-Kazakhstanskaya Oblast' admin. div. Kazakh. see Zapadnyy Kazakhstan
100 G2 Zapadno-Sakhalinskiy Khrebet mts Rus. Fed.
Zapadno-Sibirskaya Nizmennost' plain Rus. Fed. see Zapadno-Sibirskaya Ravnina
130 J3 Zapadno-Sibirskaya Ravnina plain Rus. Fed.
121 H4 Zapadnyy Alamedin, Pik mt. Kyrg.
120 C4 Zapadnyy Chink Ustyurta esc. Kazakh.
120 B2 Zapadnyy Kazakhstan admin. div. Kazakh.
98 E1 Zapadnyy Sayan reg. Rus. Fed.
136 D3 Zapadyntsi Ukr.
260 B6 Zapala Arg.
260 B3 Zapallar Chile
175 K5 Zapałów Pol.
183 E3 Zapardiel r. Spain
237 D7 Zapata TX U.S.A.
246 B2 Zapata, Península de pen. Cuba
250 C3 Zapatoca Col.
184 D2 Zapatón r. Spain
169 F5 Zapfendorf Ger.
138 G2 Zaplyus'ye Rus. Fed.
197 H2 Zăpodeni Romania
174 G4 Zapolice Pol.
140 O1 Zapolyarnyy Murmanskaya Oblast' Rus. Fed.
134 M2 Zapolyarnyy Respublika Komi Rus. Fed.
139 K2 Zapol'ye Rus. Fed.
244 C3 Zapopan Mex.
137 H4 Zaporizhzhya Ukr.
Zaporizhzhya Oblast admin. div. Ukr. see Zaporiz'ka Oblast'
137 H4 Zaporiz'ka Oblast' admin. div. Ukr.
Zaporozhskaya Oblast' admin. div. Ukr. see Zaporiz'ka Oblast'
Zaporozh'ye Ukr. see Zaporizhzhya
Zaporozhye Oblast admin. div. Ukr. see Zaporiz'ka Oblast'
244 C4 Zapotiltic Mex.
244 C3 Zapotlanejo Mex.
171 C4 Zappendorf Ger.
193 H3 Zapponeta Italy
188 E3 Zaprešić Croatia
139 K3 Zaprudnya Rus. Fed.
175 M6 Zapytiv Ukr.
129 E3 Zaqatala Azer.
111 F5 Zaqên Qinghai China
108 A2 Za Qu r. Qinghai China
111 E5 Zaqungngomar mt. Xizang China
Zara Croatia see Zadar
126 E3 Zara Turkey
120 F4 Zarafshan Uzbek.
123 G2 Zarafshon Tajik.
123 G2 Zarafshon r. Tajik.
Zarafshon Uzbek. see Zarafshan
Zarafshon r. Uzbek. see Zeravshan
123 F2 Zarafshon, Qatorkŭhi mts Tajik.
250 C3 Zaragoza Col.
243 E2 Zaragoza Coahuila Mex.
245 F4 Zaragoza Puebla Mex.
186 C3 Zaragoza Spain
183 I3 Zaragoza prov. Aragón Spain
186 C4 Zaragozana mt. Spain
122 D4 Zarand Kermān Iran
122 B3 Zarand Markazī Iran
177 K5 Zărand Romania
197 F2 Zarandului, Munții hills Romania
123 E4 Zaranj Afgh.
138 F4 Zarasai Lith.
183 H1 Zaratamo Spain
183 F3 Zaratán Spain
261 H4 Zárate Arg.
186 A1 Zarautz Spain
139 L4 Zaraysk Rus. Fed.
251 E2 Zaraza Venez.
121 G4 Zarbdar Uzbek.
185 I3 Zarcilla de Ramos Spain
129 E3 Zärdab Azer.
175 J2 Zaręby Pol.
175 K3 Zaręby-Kościelne Pol.
134 E2 Zarechensk Rus. Fed.
139 L5 Zarechnyy Rus. Fed.
123 F4 Zargun mt. Pak.
207 G4 Zaria Nigeria
Zariaspa Afgh. see Balkh
177 L3 Zaricheve Ukr.
136 D2 Zarichne Ukr.
122 A2 Zarīneh Rūd r. Iran
175 H5 Żarki Pol.
197 G3 Zărnești Romania
177 H3 Žarnovica Slovakia
175 I4 Żarnów Pol.
175 H5 Żarnowiec Pol.
174 E5 Żarów Pol.
168 F2 Zarpen Ger.
Zarqā' Jordan see Az Zarqā'
128 B3 Zarqā', Nahr az r. Jordan
122 C4 Zarqān Iran
129 F3 Zärqava Azer.
165 B3 Zarren Belgium
168 F2 Zarrentin Ger.
175 K6 Zarszyn Pol.
139 I2 Zarubino Novgorodskaya Oblast' Rus. Fed.
100 D4 Zarubino Primorskiy Kray Rus. Fed.
105 E3 Zaruga-dake mt. Japan
174 D4 Żary Pol.
185 E2 Zarza Capilla Spain
184 D2 Zarza de Alange Spain
182 D4 Zarza de Granadilla Spain
183 G4 Zarza de Tajo Spain
185 I3 Zarzadilla de Totana Spain
250 B3 Zarzal Col.
182 D5 Zarza la Mayor Spain
175 K6 Zarzecze Pol.
205 H2 Zarzis Tunisia
183 F4 Zarzuela del Monte Spain
183 F3 Zarzuela del Pinar Spain
182 B1 Zas Spain
121 J2 Zashchita Kazakh.
116 D2 Zaskar r. India
116 D2 Zaskar Mountains India
177 I2 Žaškov Slovakia
138 F4 Zaslawye Belarus
176 E2 Zásmuky Czech Rep.
137 J2 Zasosna Rus. Fed.
175 J5 Zasów Pol.
129 B1 Zassovskaya Rus. Fed.
136 C3 Zastavna Ukr.
215 F4 Zastron S. Africa
176 C1 Žatec Czech Rep.
129 D1 Zaterechnyy Rus. Fed.
120 E1 Zatobol'sk Kazakh.
136 F4 Zatoka Ukr.
177 G1 Zátor Czech Rep.
175 H6 Zator Pol.
175 J3 Zatory Pol.
136 C2 Zaturtsi Ukr.
136 E4 Zatyshshya Ukr.
122 D1 Zaunguzskiye Karakumy des. Turkm.
245 F4 Zautla Mex.
177 M2 Zavadka Ukr.
177 I3 Závadka nad Hronom Slovakia
263 F2 Zavadovskiy Island Antarctica
261 G3 Zavalla Arg.
237 E6 Zavalla TX U.S.A.
136 F3 Zavallya Ukr.
122 C3 Zavareh Iran
190 E4 Zavattarello Italy
165 D4 Zaventem Belgium
135 H7 Zavetnoye Rus. Fed.
100 G2 Zavety Il'icha Rus. Fed.
188 G3 Zavidoviči Bos.-Herz.
Zavitaya Rus. Fed. see Zavitinsk
100 D2 Zavitinsk Rus. Fed.
176 G3 Závod Slovakia
175 M5 Zavods'ke Ukr.
136 C3 Zavods'ke Ukr.
121 K1 Zavodskoy Altayskiy Kray Rus. Fed.
Zavodskoy Respublika Mordoviya Rus. Fed. see Komsomol'skiy
129 D2 Zavodskoy Respublika Severnaya Osetiya Rus. Fed.
134 H4 Zavolzhsk Rus. Fed.
Zavolzh'ye Rus. Fed. see Zavolzhsk
137 F2 Zavorychi Ukr.
121 J1 Zav'yalovo Rus. Fed.
175 L6 Zavydovychi Ukr.
106 D4 Zawa Qinghai China
175 H4 Zawada Łódzkie Pol.
175 L5 Zawada Lubelskie Pol.
174 D4 Zawada Lubuskie Pol.
174 F5 Zawada Opolskie Pol.
175 H5 Zawada Śląskie Pol.
175 K2 Zawady Pol.
174 G5 Zawadzkie Pol.
96 B2 Zawgyi r. Myanmar
175 J5 Zawichost Pol.
174 D4 Zawidów Pol.
175 H3 Zawidz Kościelny Pol.
175 H5 Zawiercie Pol.
128 C2 Zāwīyah, Jabal az hills Syria
125 F3 Zawlīyah, Jiddat az plain Oman
175 H6 Zawoja Pol.
174 F4 Zawonia Pol.
134 J5 Zay r. Rus. Fed.
179 H2 Zaya r. Austria
129 D3 Zäyäm Azer.
129 D3 Zäyämçay r. Azer.
121 K3 Zaysan Kazakh.
Zaysan, Lake Kazakh. see Zaysan, Ozero
121 J2 Zaysan, Ozero l. Kazakh.
137 J3 Zaytseve Ukr.
108 A2 Zayü Xizang China
108 A2 Zayü Xizang China
129 C2 Zayukovo Rus. Fed.
108 A2 Zayü Qu r. China/India
177 I2 Zázrivá Slovakia
136 C3 Zbarazh Ukr.
174 D3 Zbąszyn Pol.
174 D3 Zbąszynek Pol.
175 H2 Zbiczno Pol.
174 G4 Zbiersk Pol.
173 H2 Zbiroh Czech Rep.
174 G2 Zblewo Pol.
175 I5 Zbludowice Pol.
175 J2 Zbójna Pol.
175 H2 Zbójno Pol.
196 D4 Zborište mt. Yugo.
136 C3 Zboriv Ukr.
177 K2 Zborov Slovakia
174 F6 Zborovice Czech Rep.
179 H1 Zbraslav Czech Rep.
176 E2 Zbraslavice Czech Rep.
136 D3 Zbruch r. Ukr.
176 C2 Zbůch Czech Rep.
175 K3 Zbuczyn Poduchowny Pol.
179 H1 Zbýšov Czech Rep.
176 G5 Ždala Croatia
179 I1 Ždánice Czech Rep.
176 F2 Ždánický Les for. Czech Rep.
171 G5 Ždár Czech Rep.
176 E2 Žďar nad Sázavou Czech Rep.
176 E2 Žďárské Vrchy hills Czech Rep.
177 J2 Ždiar Slovakia
176 C2 Zdíkov Czech Rep.
176 E2 Ždírec nad Doubravou Czech Rep.
136 D2 Zdolbuniv Ukr.
Zdolbunov Ukr. see Zdolbuniv
176 G2 Zdounky Czech Rep.
174 G4 Zduńska Wola Pol.
175 H3 Zduny Łódzkie Pol.
174 F4 Zduny Wielkopolskie Pol.
136 F2 Zdvyzh r. Ukr.
175 J6 Zdynia Pol.
174 G4 Zdziechowice Opolskie Pol.
175 K5 Zdziechowice Podkarpackie Pol.
174 G5 Zdzieszowice Pol.
175 K5 Zdziłowice Pol.
Zealand i. Denmark see Sjælland
259 C7 Zeballos mt. Arg.
222 E5 Zeballos B.C. Can.
127 G3 Zēbār Iraq
195 □ Żebbuġ Gozo Malta
195 □ Żebbuġ Malta
174 G5 Zębowice Pol.
173 H2 Žebrák Czech Rep.
182 C5 Zebreira Port.
174 D4 Zebrzydowa Pol.
174 G6 Zebrzydowice Dolne Pol.
231 C5 Zebulon GA U.S.A.
232 B6 Zebulon KY U.S.A.
231 E5 Zebulon NC U.S.A.
170 D2 Zechlin Dorf Ger.
170 D2 Zechlinerhütte Ger.
164 F3 Zeddam Neth.
192 A5 Zeddiani Sardegna Italy
165 C3 Zedelgem Belgium
179 E3 Zederhaus Austria
177 I6 Žednik Vojvodina, Srbija Yugo.
165 C3 Zeebrugge Belgium
83 F5 Zeehan Tas. Austr.
164 E3 Zeeland Neth.
164 C3 Zeeland prov. Neth.
226 D4 Zeeland MI U.S.A.
215 F1 Zeerust S. Africa
171 E3 Zeesen Ger.
164 E2 Zeewolde Neth.
128 B3 Zefat Israel
186 A2 Zegama Spain
175 I6 Żegiestów Pol.
175 I6 Żegocina Pol.
175 J3 Zegrzyńskie, Jezioro l. Pol.
170 E3 Zehdenick Ger.
170 D2 Zehna Ger.
171 E4 Zehren Ger.
84 C4 Zeil, Mount N.T. Austr.
169 F5 Zeil am Main Ger.
173 G3 Zeilarn Ger.
138 E3 Žeimelis Lith.
179 H2 Zeiselmauer Austria
164 E2 Zeist Neth.
171 E4 Zeithain Ger.
173 G2 Zeitlarn Ger.
169 E5 Zeitlofs Ger.
171 D4 Zeitz Ger.
195 □ Żejtun Malta
106 D5 Zêkog Qinghai China
Zela Turkey see Zile
174 G4 Żelazków Pol.
165 D3 Zele Belgium
175 I4 Żelechlinek Pol.
175 J4 Żelechów Pol.
136 D3 Zelena Chernivets'ka Oblast' Ukr.
136 C3 Zelena Ivano-Frankivs'ka Oblast' Ukr.
136 C3 Zelena Ivano-Frankivs'ka Oblast' Ukr.
188 F4 Zelena Gora mt. Bos.-Herz.
176 G2 Zelená Hora tourist site Czech Rep.
121 H1 Zelenaya Roshcha Kazakh.
129 B2 Zelenchukskaya Rus. Fed.
171 F5 Zeleneč Czech Rep.
177 G3 Zeleneč Slovakia
188 G4 Zelengora mts Bos.-Herz.
137 G4 Zelenivka Ukr.
134 I3 Zelennik Rus. Fed.
140 P2 Zelenoborskiy Rus. Fed.
134 J5 Zelenodol'sk Rus. Fed.
137 G4 Zelenodol's'k Ukr.
138 G1 Zelenogorsk Rus. Fed.
139 K3 Zelenograd Rus. Fed.
138 C4 Zelenogradsk Rus. Fed.
136 F4 Zelenohirs'ke Ukr.
129 C1 Zelenokumsk Stavropol'skiy Kray Rus. Fed.
134 I4 Zelentsovo Rus. Fed.
121 G2 Zelenyy Gay Kazakh.
179 H1 Želešice Czech Rep.
176 E2 Želetava Czech Rep.
176 C2 Železná Ruda Czech Rep.
176 E2 Železné Hory hills Czech Rep.
179 F4 Železniki Slovenia
176 E1 Železný Brod Czech Rep.
164 F2 Zelhem Neth.
232 C4 Zelienople PA U.S.A.
177 H3 Želiezovce Slovakia
188 F3 Zelina Croatia
106 C4 Zelinggou Qinghai China
196 E5 Želino Macedonia
176 E2 Želivka r. Czech Rep.
196 E4 Željin mt. Yugo.
175 K3 Żelków-Kolonia Pol.
171 C5 Zell Ger.
169 C5 Zell (Mosel) Ger.
169 F5 Zella-Mehlis Ger.
172 C3 Zell am Harmersbach Ger.
178 D3 Zell am See Austria
178 C3 Zell am Ziller Austria
179 E2 Zell an der Pram Austria
179 G2 Zellerndorf Austria
172 D4 Zellersee l. Ger.
172 B4 Zell im Wiesental Ger.
172 D2 Zellingen Ger.
177 I3 Želovce Slovakia
175 H4 Zelów Pol.
172 B2 Zeltingen-Rachtig Ger.
179 F3 Zeltweg Austria
138 E5 Zel'va Belarus
165 C3 Zelzate Belgium
138 C4 Žemaičių Naumiestis Lith.
177 H3 Žemberovce Slovakia
198 B1 Zemblak Korçë Albania
175 K3 Zembrów Pol.
175 H6 Zembrzyce Pol.
108 B1 Zêmdasam Sichuan China
197 F4 Zemen Bulg.
197 H2 Zemeş Romania
135 H5 Zemetchino Rus. Fed.
177 G4 Zemianska Oľča Slovakia
208 E3 Zémio C.A.R.
170 E2 Zemitz Ger.
130 F1 Zemlya Aleksandry i. Zemlya Frantsa-Iosifa Rus. Fed.
130 G2 Zemlya Frantsa-Iosifa is Rus. Fed.
130 F1 Zemlya Georga i. Zemlya Frantsa-Iosifa Rus. Fed.
137 J2 Zemlyansk Rus. Fed.
130 H1 Zemlya Vil'cheka i. Zemlya Frantsa-Iosifa Rus. Fed.
172 A2 Zemmer Ger.
129 B2 Zemo Barghebi Georgia
129 C3 Zemo Khveduret'i Georgia
129 D3 Zemo Qarabulakhi Georgia
177 L3 Zemplénagárd Hungary
177 K3 Zempléni-hegység hills Hungary
177 L3 Zemplínska šírava l. Slovakia
177 K3 Zemplínska Teplica Slovakia
177 L3 Zemplínske Hámre Slovakia
245 E4 Zempoala Hidalgo Mex.
245 F4 Zempoala Veracruz Mex.
245 G5 Zempoaltépetl, Nudo de mt. Mex.
165 D4 Zemst Belgium
139 I3 Zemtsy Rus. Fed.
196 E3 Zemun Srbija Yugo.
108 A1 Zênda Sichuan China
109 E4 Zengcheng Guangdong China
100 D4 Zengfeng Shan mt. China
177 H5 Zengő hill Hungary
188 F3 Zenica Bos.-Herz.
173 E2 Zenn r. Ger.
150 □ Zennor Cornwall, England U.K.
Zenta Vojvodina, Srbija Yugo. see Senta
103 F6 Zentsūji Japan
205 F2 Zenzach Alg.
188 G3 Žepče Bos.-Herz.
170 E3 Zepernick Ger.
240 H2 Zephyr Cove NV U.S.A.
231 D6 Zephyrhills FL U.S.A.
111 B4 Zepu Xinjiang China
210 A2 Zeraf, Bahr el r. Sudan
Zeravshan Tajik. see Zarafshon
Zeravshan r. Tajik. see Zarafshon
121 E5 Zeravshan r. Uzbek.
Zeravshanskiy Khrebet mts Tajik. see Zarafshon, Qatorkŭhi
171 D4 Zerbst Ger.
121 G1 Zerenda Kazakh.
172 A2 Zerf Ger.
205 G2 Zeribet el Oued Alg.
177 K5 Zerind Romania
174 F3 Żerków Pol.
190 C2 Zermatt Switz.
190 F2 Zernez Switz.
168 F2 Zernien Ger.
170 D3 Zernitz Ger.
135 H7 Zernograd Rus. Fed.
Zernovoy Rus. Fed. see Zernograd
191 H3 Zero r. Italy
170 E3 Zerpenschleuse Ger.
170 F2 Zerrenthin Ger.
Zestafoni Georgia see Zestap'oni
129 C2 Zestap'oni Georgia
186 A1 Zestoa Spain
196 D4 Zeta r. Yugo.
111 E6 Zêtang Xizang China
197 G2 Zetea Romania
168 C2 Zetel Ger.
171 C5 Zeulenroda Ger.
171 E3 Zeuthen Ger.
168 E2 Zeven Ger.
164 F3 Zevenaar Neth.
164 D3 Zevenbergen Neth.
164 F1 Zevenhuizen Neth.
198 C3 Zevgolatio Greece
191 G3 Zevio Italy
100 C1 Zeya Rus. Fed.
100 C2 Zeya r. Rus. Fed.
122 C4 Zeydābād Iran
122 D2 Zeydar Iran
122 D4 Zeynalābād Iran
100 D2 Zeysko-Bureinskaya Vpadina depr. Rus. Fed.
100 C1 Zeyskoye Vodokhranilishche resr Rus. Fed.
199 E2 Zeytindağ Turkey
198 B1 Zezë, Maja e mt. Albania

ACKNOWLEDGEMENTS

MAPS AND DATA

Maps designed and created by
HarperCollins Cartographic, Glasgow

Additional work by:
Alan Collinson Design, Llandudno, UK
Cosmographics, Watford,
Dave Edwards Cartography, North Berwick
Lovell Johns Ltd, Long Hanborough, UK

Design: One O'Clock Gun Design Consultants Ltd,
Edinburgh

Data acknowledgements
Plate 121: Antarctic Digital Database (versions 1 and 2),
© Scientific Committee on Antarctic Research (SCAR),
Cambridge (1993, 1998)
Bathymetric data: The GEBCO Digital Atlas published
by the British Oceanographic Data Centre on behalf of
IOC and IHO, 1994

The mapping in this atlas is available in digital form
from Bartholomew Mapping Services. For details and
information visit
www.bartholomewmaps.com
or contact
Bartholomew Mapping Services
Tel: +44 (01) 141 306 3344
Fax: +44 (01) 141 306 3104
E-mail:bartholomew@harpercollins.co.uk

The publishers would like to thank all National
Survey Departments, Road, Rail and National
Park authorities, Statistical Offices and national
place name committees throughout the World
for their valuable assistance, and in particular the
following:

Antarctic Place-Names Committee, FCO,
London, UK

Australian Surveying & Land Information Group,
Belconnen, Australia

Automobile Association of South Africa,
Johannesburg, Republic of South Africa

British Antarctic Survey, Cambridge, UK

BP Amoco PLC, London, UK

British Geological Survey, Keyworth,
Nottingham, UK

Chief Directorate: Surveys and Mapping, Mowbray,
Republic of South Africa

Commission de toponymie du Québec,
Québec, Canada

Defence Geographic and Imagery Intelligence Agency,
Geographic Information Group, Tolworth, UK

Federal Survey Division, Lagos, Nigeria

Food and Agriculture Organization of the United
Nations, Rome, Italy

Foreign and Commonwealth Office, London, UK

Mr P J M Geelan, London, UK

General Directorate of Highways, Ankara, Turkey

Hydrographic Office, Ministry of Defence,
Taunton, UK

Institut Géographique National, Brussels, Belgium

Institut Géographique National, Paris, France

Instituto Brasileiro de Geografia e Estatistica,
Rio de Janeiro, Brazil

Instituto Geográfico Nacional, Lima, Peru

Instituto Geográfico Nacional, Madrid, Spain

Instituto Português de Cartografia e Cadastro,
Lisbon, Portugal

International Atomic Energy Agency, Vienna, Austria

International Boundary Research Unit,
University of Durham, UK

International Hydrographic Organization, Monaco

International Union for the Conservation of Nature,
Gland, Switzerland and Cambridge, UK

Kort- og Matrikelstyrelsen, Copenhagen, Denmark

Land Information New Zealand, Wellington,
New Zealand

Lands and Surveys Department, Kampala, Uganda

H A G Lewis OBE

National Geographic Society, Washington DC, USA

National Library of Scotland, Edinburgh, UK

National Mapping and Resources Information Authority
(NAMRIA), Manila, Philippines

National Oceanic and Atmospheric Administration, USA

Permanent Committee on Geographical Names,
London, UK

Royal Geographical Society, London, UK

Royal Scottish Geographical Society, Glasgow, UK

Scientific Committee on Antarctic Research,
Cambridge, UK

Scott Polar Research Institute, Cambridge, UK

Scottish Office Development Department,
Edinburgh, UK

SNCF French Railways, London, UK

Statens Kartverket, Hønefoss, Norway

Survey Department, Singapore

Survey of India, Dehra Dun, India

Survey of Israel, Tel Aviv, Israel

Survey of Kenya, Nairobi, Kenya

Surveyor General, Harare, Zimbabwe

Surveyor General, Ministry of Lands and Natural
Resources, Lusaka, Zambia

Surveys and Mapping Branch, Natural Resources,
Ottawa, Canada

Surveys and Mapping Division, Dar-es-Salaam,
Tanzania

Terralink New Zealand Ltd, Wellington,
New Zealand

The Meteorological Office, Bracknell, Berkshire, UK

The National Imagery and Mapping Agency (NIMA),
Bethesda, Maryland, USA

The Stationery Office, London, UK

The United States Board on Geographic Names,
Washington DC, USA

The United States Department of State,
Washington DC, USA

The United States Geological Survey,
Earth Science Information Center, Reston, Virginia, USA

United Nations, specialized agencies, New York, USA

Marcel Vârlan, University 'Al. I. Cuza', Iaşi, Romania

IMAGES AND PHOTOS

pages 8–19
Remote Sensing Applications Consultants Ltd,
4 Mansfield Park, Medstead, Alton, Hants,
GU34 5PZ, UK

pages 20–21
NRSC Ltd/Science Photo Library

pages 22–23
The Sun: Jisas/Lockheed/Science Photo Library
Mercury: NASA/Science Photo Library
Venus: NASA/Science Photo Library
Earth: Photo Library International/Science Photo
Library
Mars: US Geological Survey/Science Photo Library
Jupiter: NASA/Science Photo Library
Saturn: Space Telescope ScienceInstitute/NASA/
Science Photo Library
Uranus: NASA/Science Photo Library
Neptune: NASA/Science Photo Library
Pluto and Charon: Space Telescope Science Institute/
NASA/Science Photo Library

pages 24–25
Kobe earthquake: Axiom Photographic Agency Ltd
Kilauea volcano: Soames Summerhays/Science Photo
Library

pages 26–27
1: WHF Smith, US National Oceanic and Atmospheric
Administration (NOAA), USA
2: A McDonald and C Wunsch, USA
4: NASA/JPL, USA
5: L Talley, USA

pages 28–29
Hurricane Floyd: National Climatic Data Centre
(NCDC), National Oceanic and Atmospheric
Administration (NOAA), USA

pages 30–31
2: Earth Satellite Corporation/Science Photo
Library
3: CNES 1989 Distribution SPOT Image/Science
Photo Library

page 41
TeleGeography Inc, Washington D.C., USA
www.telegeography.com

pages 42–43
1: © British Museum, London, UK
2: The British Library, London, UK
3: Hereford Cathedral/Bridgeman Art Library
4: E T Archive/Bibliothèque National, Paris
5: E T Archive/The British Library
6: The British Library, London, UK
7 and 8: Reproduced by permission of the Trustees of
the National Library of Scotland, Edinburgh, UK
9: Derived from data collected in Parry, R.B. and
Perkins, C.R. (2000) World Mapping Today.
Edition 2. London:Bowker Saur

pages 44–45
1, 2, and 3: National Maritime Museum, Greenwich,
London, UK
4: CNES, 1994 Distribution SPOT Image/Science
Photo Library
6: Alan Collinson Design, Llandudno, UK

pages 46–47
Elbrus: Giles Pittman
Kilimanjaro and Mt McKinley: Tony Stone Images Ltd
Vinson Massif: B. Storey/British Antarctic Survey
Puncak Jaya: Alpine Ascents International Inc.
Everest: Simon Fraser/Science Photo Library
Cerro Aconcagua: Andes Press Agency
Continental images: Mountain High Maps™
Copyright © 1993 Digital Wisdom Inc

pages 48–49
Volga: CNES, 1996 Distribution SPOT Image/Science
Photo Library
Nile: Earth Satellite Corporation/Science Photo
Library
Chang Jiang (Yangtze): Earth Satellite Corporation/
Science Photo Library
Mississippi-Missouri: NASA/Science Photo Library
Amazon (Amazonas): Earth Satellite Corporation/
Science Photo Library

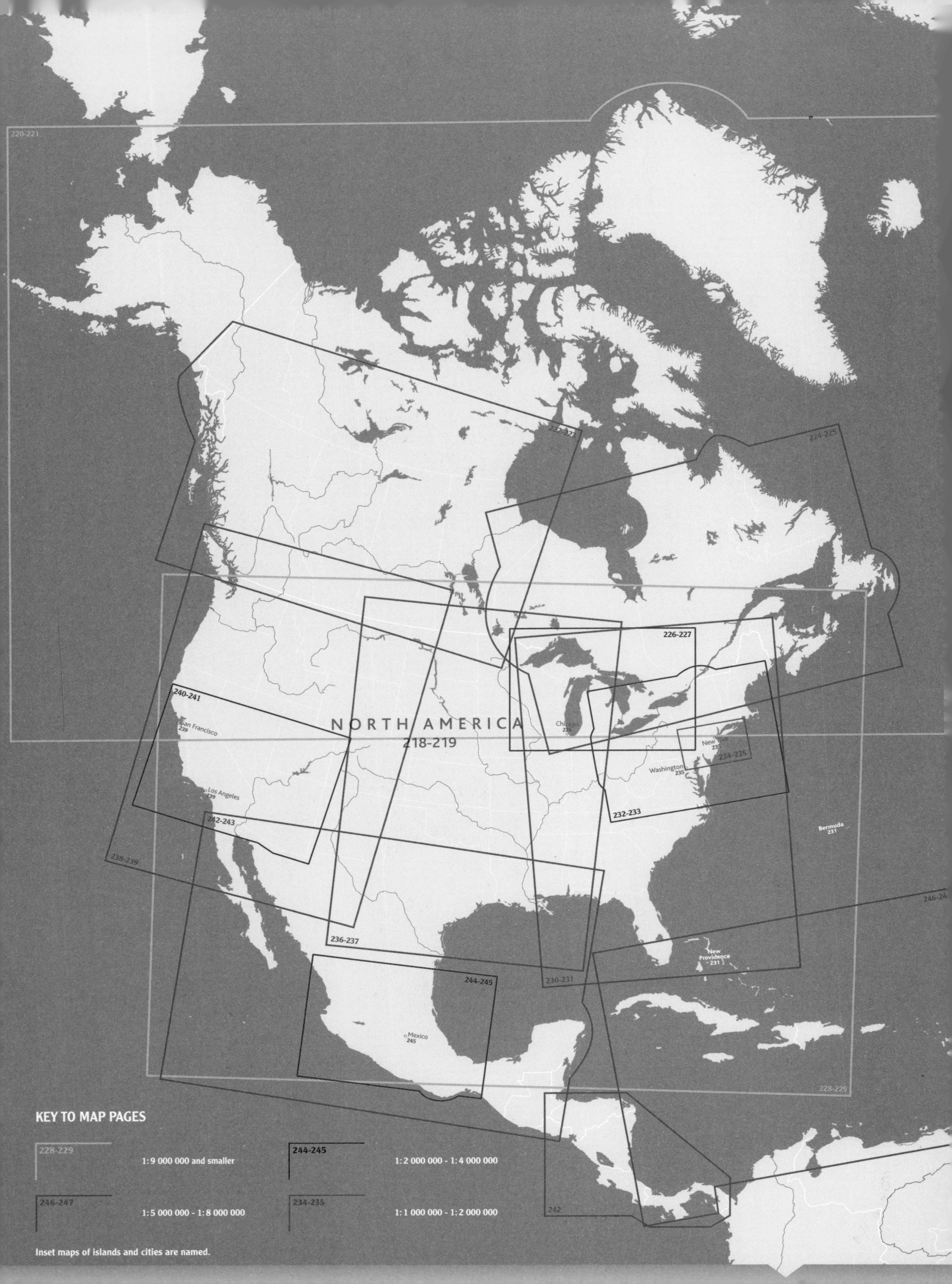

NORTH AMERICA
218-219

220-221

222-223

274-225

226-227

240-241

San Francisco
239

Los Angeles
239

238-239

242-243

236-237

244-245

Mexico
245

New York
235

Washington
235

234-235

232-233

Bermuda
231

New Providence
231

246-247

230-231

228-229

242

KEY TO MAP PAGES

228-229
    1:9 000 000 and smaller

244-245
    1:2 000 000 - 1:4 000 000

246-247
    1:5 000 000 - 1:8 000 000

234-235
    1:1 000 000 - 1:2 000 000

Inset maps of islands and cities are named.